Praise for *The Moody Handbook of Messianic Prophecy*

Here's a comprehensive and compelling resource exploring the messianic promise of the Old Testament. Powerfully and persuasively, these esteemed authors build a clear case for the Hebrew Scriptures foretelling the coming Savior of Israel and the world. All serious students of the Bible need this volume in their library!

Lee Strobel
Bestselling author of *The Case for Christ* and *The Case for Faith*

The arrival of Jesus of Nazareth as Savior and King was no surprise . . . throughout the Old Testament there were both hints of a redeemer as well as bold proclamations of the assured hope that a deliverer messiah would be coming. This prophetic stream of headlines and descriptive detail was the basis of hope and confidence for Israel even in the most challenging of times. For those of us who navigate our lives as followers of this Messiah, reflecting on the reliability of the prophetic announcements gives us hope and confidence as well that the God who kept His promise of a Messiah is true to His Word and that we too can have hope and confidence in the promise of the return of this risen Messiah as our conquering King. Well beyond information, you'll find this collection to be an inspiration as well . . . a great resource for both scholar and student!

Joe Stowell
President, Cornerstone University, Grand Rapids, MI

Ever wonder what the Lord Jesus shared about Old Testament messianic prophecies as He walked with two of His disciples on the road to Emmaus? This book is probably as close as we'll ever get to that conversation. I've heard a great deal about the need to find Messiah everywhere in the Old Testament, but *The Moody Handbook of Messianic Prophecy* actually explains how to understand the prophecies about the Messiah within the context of Old Testament literature and New Testament fulfillment.

This volume is comprehensive, thoroughly biblical, and brings us a deeper appreciation of Jesus the Messiah. I only regret that it was not available when I began preaching so many years ago. In these pages you'll find insight for the mind, resources for the biblical student, and food for the soul—a valuable reference book for decades to come.

Erwin W. Lutzer
Pastor Emeritus, The Moody Church, Chicago

Too often we approach the Scriptures with a microscope mentality, only reading passages through the lens of our particular theology , devotions, or personal challenges. Thank you Drs. Rydelnik and Blum for this comprehensive work that reminds us from the garden of beginnings to the city that will come God's story is about the Messiah, our King, our Savior, our Priest, and Friend. I highly recommend it!

Chip Ingram
Teaching Pastor, Living on the Edge
Author of *The Real God: How He Longs for You to See Him*

When preaching about Jesus in Acts 7, Stephen declared that the Old Testament prophets "announced beforehand the coming of the Righteous One" (v. 52). This was the enthusiastic claim of first-century preaching and must continue to be the zealous appeal of our preaching in the twenty-first century. We cannot afford to be fuzzy on the predictive prophecies regarding the Christ. In our skeptical age, trifold pamphlets at Christmas aren't going to cut it when it comes to Old Testament texts regarding the Messiah. This book is the treasure-trove of scholarly insight that we need to deepen our convictions and strengthen our assertions that "the Scripture had to be fulfilled, which the Holy Spirit spoke beforehand by the mouth" of God's Old Testament prophets (Acts 1:16 ESV). Get a copy of this book and start reading it today.

Mike Fabarez
Pastor, Compass Bible Church, Aliso Viejo, CA
Host, Focal Point Radio

We are grateful to Michael Rydelnik and Edwin Blum for this superb *Handbook of Messianic Prophecy*. Our messianic hope is central to our understanding of the message of the Bible. This scholarly volume will give each reader a new passion for studying the many Bible passages about Messiah's first coming and His future, second coming.

George Sweeting
Sixth president of Moody Bible Institute

What an expansive and helpful work! Not only are the full range of messianic prophecies covered with great depth, but the volume also addresses many of the hermeneutical, critical, and interpretational issues related to these prophecies of the Messiah and Messianic Age. The array of highly qualified and thoughtfully chosen authors reflect a breadth of evangelical theological positions. The contributors also include a significant number of Messianic Jews, like Dr. Rydelnik, who bring a significant authenticity to the book since these prophecies brought most of them to faith in the Messiah Jesus. Moreover, messianic prophecy has been their primary tool in helping their fellow Jewish people understand the Messiah through the lens of Old Testament prophecy. Every pastor, missionary, Christian worker, and informed layman will find this long-needed resource to be eminently useful.

Mitch Glaser
President, Chosen People Ministries

What did Jesus teach when He revealed the Messiah from the Hebrew Bible while on the road to Emmaus (Lk 24:26-27)? We get a glimpse of the answer to that question with the *Moody Handbook of Messianic Prophecy*. Using a broad group of biblical scholars, including several Messianic Jews, this volume gives an exhaustive explanation of the Messiah in the Old Testament. Every person who wants to understand messianic prophecy needs this book.

Joel C. Rosenberg
New York Times bestselling author and Bible teacher

THE MOODY HANDBOOK OF MESSIANIC PROPHECY

Studies and Expositions of the MESSIAH *in the* OLD TESTAMENT

Michael Rydelnik
and Edwin Blum | GENERAL EDITORS

MOODY PUBLISHERS
CHICAGO

All emphasis in Scripture has been added.

Managing Editor: Allan Sholes
Cover and interior design: Erik M. Peterson

Library of Congress Control Number: 2019028846
ISBN: 978-0-8024-0963-8

Moody Publishers
820 N. LaSalle Boulevard
Chicago, IL 60610

1 3 5 7 9 10 8 6 4 2

Printed in the United States of America

This book is affectionately dedicated to
John H. Sailhamer, PhD,
brilliant student of Ed Blum, beloved professor of Michael Rydelnik,
and faithful friend to us both.
John's deep insight and teaching skill opened
the minds of countless students
to the Messiah of the Old Testament.
Although John is absent from the body,
he is now present with the Lord Jesus the Messiah,
but his many writings will continue to enlighten readers
about the promised Messiah Jesus for generations to come.

Contents

Foreword . . . 11
Contributors . . . 15
Acknowledgments . . . 21
List of Abbreviations . . . 22
Introduction . . . 25
The Messiah and His Titles . . . 29
Messiah and the Hebrew Bible . . . 41
Textual Criticism and Messianic Prophecy . . . 61
Interpretive Approaches to Messianic Prophecy . . . 73
The Old Testament in the Old Testament . . . 93
The Old Testament in the New Testament . . . 103
Canonical Perspectives on Messianic Prophecy . . . 119
Messiah: Prophet, Priest, and King . . . 135
The Deity of Messiah in the Old Testament . . . 147
Typology in the Old Testament . . . 161
Sacrifice in the Old Testament . . . 177
Messiah in Intertestamental Literature . . . 191
Messiah in Rabbinic Literature . . . 201
Targums, the New Testament, and Biblical Theology of the Messiah . . . 213
Messiah in Medieval Jewish Literature . . . 227
Genesis 3:15: The Promised Seed . . . 239
Genesis 9:25-27: The Promise through Noah . . . 251
Genesis 12:1-3; 22:16-18: The Covenant with Abraham . . . 259
Genesis 49:8-12: The Lion of Judah . . . 271
Numbers 24:5-9, 15-19: The Distant Star . . . 285
Deuteronomy 17:14-20: The Foundations of Messianic Kingship . . . 309
Deuteronomy 18:15-19: The Prophet Like Moses . . . 325
Messianism in Ruth . . . 343
1 Samuel 2:1-10, 35: Hannah's Song of the Messianic King . . . 361
1 Samuel 17: David: A Messianic Prototype . . . 373
2 Samuel 7: The Davidic Covenant (I) . . . 385

2 Samuel 23:1-7: David's Last Words 399
Messianism in 1 & 2 Kings 411
1 Chronicles 17: The Davidic Covenant (II). 425
Job 19:23-27: A Living Redeemer 437
Compositional Unity in the Five Books of the Psalms: A Canonical Approach. . 451
Messianism in the Psalms 457
Psalms 1-2: The Divine Son of God 477
Psalm 3: The Victory of the Messiah 491
Psalm 8: The Messianic Son of Adam 503
Psalm 16: The Resurrected Messiah 513
Psalm 22: The Suffering of the Messianic King 529
Psalm 23: The Lord Is Messiah's Shepherd 543
Psalm 40: A Body Prepared for Death 559
Psalm 45: The Messiah as Bridegroom 573
Psalm 69: The Lament of the Messiah 591
Psalm 72: The Messiah as Ideal King 605
Psalms 86-88: The Suffering, Death, and Resurrection of the Messianic King . . 617
Psalm 89: God's Faithful Promise of Messiah 631
Psalm 90: The Fulfillment of the Davidic Covenant 645
Psalm 109: The Betrayal of the Messiah 663
Psalm 110: The Messiah as Eternal King Priest 673
Psalm 118: The Rejected Stone 693
Psalm 132: The Messianic Restoration of the Davidic Throne 701
Messianism in the Psalms of Ascent 711
Messianism in Proverbs. 727
Proverbs 8: The Messiah: Personification of Divine Wisdom 739
Proverbs 30:4: The Riddle of the Son 747
Messianism in Ecclesiastes 757
Messianism in Song of Songs 769
Isaiah 2:1-4/Micah 4:1-5: The Restoration of Israel in the Messianic Age 785
Isaiah 4:2: The Branch of the Lord in the Messianic Age 803
Isaiah 7:1-16: The Virgin Birth in Prophecy 815
Isaiah 9:1-7: The Deity of Messiah 831
Isaiah 11:1-16: The Reign of the Righteous Messianic King 845
Isaiah 16:5: The Context of the Promise. 859
Isaiah 24:21-23: The Victory and Rule of the Messianic King 865
Isaiah 28:16: The Messianic Cornerstone. 873
Isaiah 30:19-26: The Messianic Teacher King: 885
Isaiah 32:1-8; 33:17-24: The Righteous and Majestic King 897

Isaiah 35:1-10: The Messianic Era 907
The Message of the Servant Songs 921
Isaiah 42:1-9: The Commission of the Servant of the Lord 931
Isaiah 49:1-13: The Ministry of the Servant of the Lord. 941
Isaiah 50:4-11: The Mission of the Servant in a Darkened World. 953
Isaiah 52:13–53:12: The Substitution of the Servant of the Lord 961
Isaiah 55:3-5: The Fulfillment of the Davidic Promise. 975
Isaiah 61:1-6: The Spirit-Anointed Messiah and His Promise of Restoration . . . 983
Isaiah 63:1-6: The Messianic Warrior-Judge 997
Jeremiah 23:5-6: The Divine Branch of the Lord 1011
Jeremiah 30:1-24: The Messiah: Israel's Deliverer and King 1021
Jeremiah 31:31-34: The New Covenant 1035
Jeremiah 33:14-26: The Branch and the Abrahamic Promises 1049
Ezekiel 17:22-24: Ezekiel's Tender Sprig and the Messiah 1063
Ezekiel 21:25-27: The Hope of Israel 1073
Ezekiel 34:20-31: The Shepherd of Israel 1083
Ezekiel 37:15-28: The Restoration of Israel under the One Shepherd 1097
Daniel 2:29-45: The Times of the Gentiles and the Messianic Kingdom 1115
Daniel 7:13-27: The Glorious Son of Man 1127
Daniel 9:24-27: When Will Messiah Come? 1139
Hosea 3:4-5: Israel's Present Estrangement and Future Restoration 1153
Joel 2:23: The Teacher of Righteousness 1167
Joel 2:28-32: The Messianic Outpouring of the Spirit. 1177
Amos 9:11-15: The Messiah and the Restoration of the House of David. 1187
Micah 2:12-13: Messiah, the Breaker and the Deliverance of Israel 1195
Micah 5:2-5a: Bethlehem: Birthplace of the Messianic King. 1207
Haggai 2:6-9, 21-23: The Messiah: The Chosen Signet Ring of God 1219
Zechariah 3:1-10: The Messiah and His Restoration of Israel 1235
Zechariah 6:9-15: The Royal Priesthood of Messiah 1247
Zechariah 9:9-10: Rejoice, Your King Is Coming 1261
Zechariah 11:4-14: The Rejected Shepherd 1271
Zechariah 12:10–13:1: The Pierced Messiah 1285
Zechariah 13:7-9: The Striking of the Shepherd King 1301
Zechariah 14:1-11: The Return of the Messiah 1315
Malachi 3:1; 4:1-5: The Messiah as Messenger of the Lord 1327
Scripture Index 1339
Subject Index. 1395

Foreword

It is impossible to read the Bible without being aware of its numerous predictions of the coming of the Messiah found in both Testaments. This prophetic message was first given to Israel, and then subsequently it was shared with the whole world. The reception of this message, the messianic hope of the Hebrew Bible, by the literate public prior to the 18th and early 19th centuries was one of acceptance and joy. It is no wonder that messianic prediction has been so highly regarded, for the Messiah forms the central theme of Scripture, and the message concerning Him is pivotal to understanding the rest of the message of the Bible.

One example of such a warm reception of this teaching about messianic prophecy appears in the literary work by Alfred Edersheim (1825–1889). Interesting enough, Edersheim was born into a Jewish family, where he received both a classical and Jewish education. But while he was teaching in Pest, Hungary, he became a follower of the Messiah Jesus under the tutelage of a Scottish chaplain and friend named John Duncan. He later returned to England with his tutor Duncan to study in Edinburgh and then at Berlin. This was followed by a period during which he served in Scotland in a number of Presbyterian pastorates. In 1883, he published two impressive volumes entitled *The Life and Times of Jesus the Messiah,* in which he declared there were some 456 OT passages that referred to the Messiah's comings or to the messianic times. However, not all of these 456 texts could be shown to be truly messianic based on a sound exegesis and understanding of the text of Scripture. The reason is that he at times appealed not only to OT contexts, but he also occasionally used some dubious rabbinical interpretive methods. This valuable work, however, remains in print to this day—a real testimony to its importance and its continued usefulness in the main!

However, beginning in the 18th century, when the scholarly world began to be taken up with the false and heretical view of deism, they started to openly question the legitimacy of the OT predictions about the coming of Messiah.[1] The accusing finger of history tended to point to Anthony Collins (1676–1729) as one of the key initiators of this new detracting interpretation, who published in 1724 two volumes with the title of *Discourses on the Grounds and Reasons of the Christian Religion* along with a sequel in 1727 entitled *The Scheme of Literal Prophecy Considered.*[2] The shocking conclusion to which Collins came was this: the literal meaning of the biblical text cannot support the messianic interpretations placed on these OT texts, both by the OT itself and by the NT.

Nonetheless, in a most remarkable way, fewer than 20 years after Collins's first volume had appeared, George F. Handel's monumental oratorio, entitled *Messiah*, had its first performance in 1742. Its libretto was filled entirely with scores of passages from the very same disputed texts in the Old and New Testaments about which Collins had shown his doubts. This oratorio has endured as a classic ever since, especially throughout the Western world, and it continues to this very day to delight audiences globally and to give glory to God and to praise Him for all these Scriptures announcing God's Messiah and His works!

This initial wave of demeaning and denying the OT's messianic predictions was a whole new departure for the Christian faith. In fact, in more recent times the late evangelical professor John Sailhamer has taken precisely the direct opposite point of view: He has asserted that all the canonical books of the OT are indeed, in one way or another, truly messianic; for our Lord offered just such a challenging assertion, especially to his Jewish audience, when He said: "Your accuser is Moses, on whom you have set your [Jewish] hope. For if you [had] believed Moses, you would believe Me, because he wrote about Me" (Jn 5:45b-46).[3] Sailhamer put it this way:

> I believe the messianic thrust of the OT was the *whole* reason the books of the Hebrew Bible were written. In other words, the Hebrew Bible was not written as the national literature of Israel. . . . It was written, in my opinion, as the expression of the deep-seated messianic hope of a small group of faithful prophets and their followers.[4]

Sailhamer observed that there was a discernible messianic strategy in the structure of the OT, which was preserved in two "canonical seams" within the canon. The first seam (coming in Dt 34:9-12 and Jos 1:1-9), united the Pentateuch and the earlier prophetic sections (Joshua, Judges, Samuel, and Kings) of the OT. That then set forth a pattern for the second canonical seam in the Hebrew Bible (coming in Mal 3:22-24 and Ps 1), which united the later prophetic section (Isaiah, Jeremiah, Ezekiel, Daniel, and the twelve Minor Prophets) with the Writings (Psalms, Proverbs, Ecclesiastes, and Song of Solomon) of the OT. Because no prophet like Moses had ever since arisen in Israel—for he was a prophet "whom the Lord knew face to face" (Dt 34:10, alluding to Dt 18:15-19)—this meant that Messiah was still to be revealed in the future, as a number of predictions in this will show. Thus, the seam between the Prophets and the Writings sections, according to Sailhamer, was similar to the one between the Pentateuch and the Prophets. Both were messianic and eschatological in their outlook, while the correlation exhibited in the seams of Jos 1:1-9 and Ps 1 presented the ideal wise man who meditated on the law of God.

Who then was this Messiah? How did this term develop, and why is it so central to biblical teaching?

Apparently, the way this term gained its technical status took place after Saul was rejected as Israel's first king, for God sought to replace him with "a man after his own heart" (1Sm 13:14 NKJV). As a result, David, a shepherd boy and the son of Jesse from Bethlehem, was anointed as king over Judah (2Sm 2:4) for seven and a half years in Hebron, but later he became king over all Israel for another 33 years in Jerusalem (2Sm 5:3). King Saul had previously been called to be the "the LORD's anointed" (1Sm 24:6,10; 26:9,11,16,23; 2Sm 1:14,16), so the title became a technical term for the anointed king. However, the day David was anointed by Samuel, the Spirit came on him mightily (1Sm 16:13), as he was anointed to the office of king. Ultimately, the OT uses the term ("Anointed") at least nine times in a technical sense of the Messiah, the future son of David. And David was given the gift of leadership by the Spirit of God, a gift he would share with no one less than God's own Son, our Lord Jesus the Messiah.

The messianic promise is pervasive throughout the Hebrew Bible. Different biblical authors used other titles for the Messiah, such as the Servant, the Branch, or the Holy One (and others as well). Nevertheless, as Luke related the words of the apostle Peter, "all the prophets who have spoken, from Samuel and those after him, have also announced these days" (Ac 3:24). It is therefore with joy and anticipation that I welcome this volume that addresses many of the issues of the promise of Messiah and provides exposition for so many key passages of Scripture.

May our Lord graciously restore back to us, His people, a whole new zeal for studying the numerous passages about Messiah—both in His first coming at Christmas and His still future second coming.

WALTER C. KAISER JR.
President Emeritus
Gordon-Conwell Theological Seminary
Hamilton, MA

---

1. This was the conclusion of Ronald E. Clements, "Messianic Prophecy or Messianic History," 1 (1979): 87.

2. For a larger discussion on this movement, see Walter C. Kaiser, Jr., "Introduction: The Study of Messianism," (Grand Rapids: Zondervan, 1995), 13–35.

3. Some evangelical scholars unfortunately deem messianism a rather marginal topic in the OT as argued by Gordon D. Fee and Douglas Stuart, (Grand Rapids: Zondervan, 2003), 182. They see messianic prophecy of the OT as occupying less than 2 percent of the text! But on this they were decidedly mistaken!

4. John H. Sailhamer, "The Messiah and the Hebrew Bible," *Journal of the Evangelical Theological Society* 44, no.1 (2001): 23.

Contributors

T. Desmond Alexander | *Senior Lecturer in Biblical Studies and Director of Postgraduate Studies, Union Theological College, Belfast*
BA, Queen's University of Belfast; PhD, Queen's University Belfast

James E. Allman | *Professor of Bible Exposition and Old Testament Studies, Dallas Theological Seminary*
BA, University of Oklahoma; ThM, ThD, Dallas Theological Seminary

Charles P. Baylis | *Professor of Bible Exposition, Dallas Theological Seminary; President, Biblical Story, Inc. (www.BiblicalStory.org)*
BSE(EE) University of Michigan; MBA Eastern Michigan University; ThM Dallas Theological Seminary; ThD Dallas Theological Seminary

Daniel I. Block | *Gunther H. Knoedler Professor Emeritus of Old Testament, Wheaton College*
Diploma, Bethany Bible Institute; BEd, BA, University of Saskatchewan; MA, Trinity Evangelical Divinity School; DPhil, University of Liverpool.

Edwin A. Blum | *General Editor of the HCSB*
ThM, ThD, Dallas Theological Seminary; DTheol, University of Basel, Switzerland

Michael L. Brown | *Founder and President, FIRE School of Ministry*
BA, Queens College; MA, PhD, New York University

Robert B. Chisholm Jr. | *Chair and Senior Professor of Old Testament Studies, Dallas Theological Seminary*
BA, Syracuse University; MDiv, Grace Theological Seminary; ThM, Grace Theological Seminary; ThD, Dallas Theological Seminary

Abner Chou | *John F. MacArthur Endowed Fellow, The Master's University and Seminary*
BA, MDiv, ThM, ThD, The Master's University and Seminary

E. Ray Clendenen | *Senior Editor of Bible and Reference Publishing, LifeWay Christian Resources*
BA, Rice University; ThM, Dallas Theological Seminary; MA, Dropsie University; PhD, University of Texas at Arlington

James F. Coakley | *Professor of Bible, Moody Bible Institute*
BA, Calvary Bible College; MDiv, ThM, Grace Theological Seminary; DMin, Covenant Theological Seminary

Robert L. Cole | *Former Professor, Southeastern Baptist Theological Seminary*
MDiv, ThM, Trinity Evangelical Divinity School; MA, PhD, University of California, Los Angeles

Ryan J. Cook | *Assistant Professor of Bible, Moody Theological Seminary*
BA, Moody Bible Institute; MA, Grand Rapids Theological Seminary; PhD, Asbury Theological Seminary

Leon D. Engman | *Senior Pastor, Evangelical Covenant Church, Woodstock, CT*
BS, Western Washington University; MS, Air Force Institute of Technology; MDiv, DMin, Trinity Evangelical Divinity School

Craig A. Evans | *John Bisagno Distinguished Professor of Christian Origins, Houston Baptist University*
BA, Claremont McKenna College; MDiv, Western Seminary; MA, PhD, Claremont Graduate University; DHabil, Karoli Gaspar University

Larry S. Feldman | *Messianic Rabbi, Shuvah Yisrael Messianic Jewish Congregation; Southwest Regional Director, Chosen People Ministries; West Coast Regional Director, Messianic Jewish Alliance of America*
BA, Temple University; ASP Certificate, Special Studies, Moody Bible Institute; ThM, Dallas Theological Seminary

David B. Finkbeiner | *Professor of Theology, Moody Bible Institute*
BA, Bob Jones University; MA, MDiv, Biblical Theological Seminary; PhD, Trinity Evangelical Divinity School

Michael Gabizon | *PhD student in the Biblical Field (Early Judaism) at McMaster University*
BA, Moody Bible Institute; ThM, Dallas Theological Seminary; PhD (ABD) McMaster University

Daniel D. Green | *Adjunct Professor of Preaching and Applied Theology, Moody Theological Seminary*
BA, Michigan State University; ThM, Dallas Theological Seminary; DMin, Trinity Evangelical Divinity School

James M. Hamilton Jr. | *Professor of Biblical Theology, The Southern Baptist Theological Seminary*
BA, University of Arkansas; ThM, Dallas Theological Seminary; PhD, The Southern Baptist Theological Seminary

Edward E. Hindson | *Dean of the Rawlings School of Divinity and Distinguished Professor of Religion, Liberty University*
BA, William Tyndale College; ThM, Grace Theological Seminary; ThD, Trinity Graduate School; DMin, Westminster Theological Seminary; DLitt et Phil, University of South Africa

John A. Jelinek | *Professor of Theology, Moody Theological Seminary*
BRE, William Tyndale College; ThM, Dallas Theological Seminary; ThD, Grace Theological Seminary

Elliott E. Johnson | *Professor of Bible Exposition, Dallas Theological Seminary*
BS, Northwestern University; ThM, ThD, Dallas Theological Seminary

Walter C. Kaiser Jr. | *President Emeritus, Gordon-Conwell Theological Seminary*
BA, Wheaton College; BD, Wheaton Graduate School of Theology; MA, PhD, Brandeis University

Glenn R. Kreider | *Professor of Theological Studies, Dallas Theological Seminary*
BS, Lancaster Bible College; ThM, PhD, Dallas Theological Seminary

Barry R. Leventhal | *Distinguished Senior Professor Southern Evangelical Seminary*
BS, UCLA; ThM, Dallas Theological Seminary; PhD, Dallas Theological Seminary

Josh Mathews | *Assistant Professor of Biblical Studies, Western Seminary*
BA, Multnomah University; MA, MA, Wheaton College Graduate School; PhD, Golden Gate Baptist Theological Seminary

EUGENE H. MERRILL | *Distinguished Professor of Old Testament Studies (Emeritus), Dallas Theological Seminary*
BA, Bob Jones University; MA, Bob Jones University; PhD, Bob Jones University; MA, New York University; PhD, Columbia University

RANDALL L. MCKINION | *Associate Professor of Old Testament, Cedarville University*
BS, University of South Alabama; MDiv, The Master's Seminary; PhD, Southeastern Baptist Theological Seminary

NICHOLAS PERRIN | *President, Trinity International University*
BA, Johns Hopkins University; MDiv, Covenant Theological Seminary; PhD, Marquette University

SETH D. POSTELL | *Academic Dean, Israel College of the Bible*
BA, Moody Bible Institute; MDiv/ABS, Southeastern Baptist Theological Seminary; PhD, Gateway Seminary (formerly Golden Gate Baptist Theological Seminary)

J. RANDALL PRICE | *Distinguished Research Professor of Biblical and Judaic Studies, Liberty University*
ThM, Dallas Theological Seminary; PhD, The University of Texas (Austin); Postgraduate work: The Hebrew University (Jerusalem)

MICHAEL A. RYDELNIK | *Professor of Jewish Studies, Moody Bible Institute*
Diploma, Moody Bible Institute; BA, Azusa Pacific University; ThM, Dallas Theological Seminary; DMiss, Trinity Evangelical Divinity School

EVA RYDELNIK | *Adjunct Professor, Moody Bible Institute.*
Diploma, Moody Bible Institute; BA, Azusa Pacific University; MA, Wheaton College Graduate School

JOHN SAILHAMER | *Noted Old Testament Professor and Author (deceased)*
BA, California State University; ThM, Dallas Theological Seminary; MA, PhD, University of California, Los Angeles

MICHAEL B. SHEPHERD | *Associate Professor of Biblical Studies, Cedarville University*
Diploma, Interlochen Arts Academy; BFA, The New School University; MDiv, Southeastern Baptist Theological Seminary; PhD, Southeastern Baptist Theological Seminary

Jim R. Sibley | *Professor of Biblical Studies, Israel College of the Bible*
BA, Baylor University; MDiv, Southwestern Baptist Theological Seminary; STM, Dallas Theological Seminary; PhD, Southwestern Baptist Theological Seminary

Michael K. Snearly | *Pastor, Red Hill Church, San Anselmo, CA*
BA, Southwest Baptist University; MDiv, The Southern Baptist Theological Seminary; PhD, Golden Gate Baptist Theological Seminary

James Spencer | *Adjunct Instructor, Moody Bible Institute*
BS, University of Illinois at Chicago; MDiv, Moody Theological Seminary; MA, Wheaton College; PhD, Trinity Evangelical Divinity School

Mike Stallard | *Director of International Ministry, The Friends of Israel Gospel Ministry*
BS, University of Alabama in Huntsville; MDiv, Liberty Baptist Seminary; STM, Dallas Theological Seminary; PhD, Dallas Theological Seminary

Dan Stuart | *Apologetics Instructor, The King's Academy*
BS, MDiv, Liberty University

J. Paul Tanner | *Middle East Director, BEE World*
BSc, Texas Tech University; ThM, Dallas Theological Seminary; PhD, The University of Texas at Austin

William C. Varner | *Professor of Biblical Studies, Chairman MA in Biblical Studies, The Master's University*
BA, Bob Jones University; MDiv, ThM, Biblical Theological Seminary; MA, Dropsie College; EdD, Temple University

Michael J. Vlach | *Professor of Theology, The Master's Seminary*
BS, University of Nebraska-Lincoln; MDiv, The Master's Seminary; PhD, Southeastern Baptist Theological Seminary

Michael Vowell | *Senior Messianic Rabbi, Beth El Shalom Messianic Congregation, Houston, TX*
Diploma, Bradford School of Accounting; BA, Moody Bible Institute; ThM, Dallas Theological Seminary

Larry J. Waters | *Former Associate Professor of Biblical Exposition, Former Lead Editor of Bibliotheca Sacra (deceased)*
BA, East Texas Baptist University; MDiv, Asian Theological Seminary; ThM, Asian Graduate School of Theology; PhD, Dallas Theological Seminary

Andrew M. Woods | *Pastor, Sugar Land Bible Church; President, Chafer Theological Seminary*
BA, University of Redlands; JD, Whittier College; ThM, PhD, Dallas Theological Seminary

Kevin D. Zuber | *Associate Professor of Theology, The Master's Seminary*
BA, Grace College; MDiv, ThM, Grace Theological Seminary; PhD, Trinity Evangelical Divinity School

Acknowledgments

Any project as ambitious as *The Moody Handbook of Messianic Prophecy* requires the talents and efforts of many people to bring it to print. As general editors, we are greatly indebted to each and every one of the 46 contributors to this book. These fine scholars combined deep biblical knowledge, strong research, and excellent writing skills to produce superb articles on the messianic ideas and predictions of the Hebrew Bible. It is an honor and privilege for us to serve the Lord Jesus together with them and to have co-labored with them to provide this resource for God's people.

Also, we are indebted to Greg Thornton, Senior Vice President of Media at Moody Bible Institute, whose vision for this project helped make it possible. Thanks also go to Paul Santhouse, Vice President of Publishing at Moody Publishers, who encouraged and supported this venture from start to finish. Also, we are grateful to Randall Payleitner, Associate Publisher of Moody Publishers, whose encouragement, patience, cheerleading, and guidance helped make this *Handbook* not just a dream but a reality. We are beyond thankful for Allan Sholes, MA, Project Editor, for his extraordinary editorial skill and his careful diligence with all the details of bringing this work to publication. Additionally, we are grateful for Connor Sterchi, Moody Publishers Managing Editor, for bringing this book to the finish line. Our thanks also go to Erik Peterson, Creative Director, for the outstanding cover design and to Ryan Lloyd, Production Director at Moody Publishers, for his oversight of the typesetting and printing. We also want to recognize Karen Waddles, Assistant to the Publisher, for her terrific administrative skill in handling the intricate details associated with a book containing the work of so many contributors. Words cannot fully express our unfailing gratitude to our wives, Eva and Ann, who consistently supported our efforts in bringing this book to print and always did so with kindness, grace, and encouragement.

Finally, and most importantly, we give our greatest thanks to God our Father who, according to the promises of His Word, sent the Lord Jesus to fulfill the messianic hope, and to the Lord Jesus Himself, who opened our eyes to understand the promises of Messiah (Luke 24:45), and to His Spirit, who enabled all of us to complete this book.

Blessed are you, O Lord our God, King of the Universe, who has granted us life, sustained us, and allowed us to reach this day. Amen.

List of Abbreviations

SCRIPTURE ABBREVIATIONS

Old Testament

Gn	Genesis
Ex	Exodus
Lv	Leviticus
Nm	Numbers
Dt	Deuteronomy
Jos	Joshua
Jdg	Judges
Ru	Ruth
1Sm	1 Samuel
2Sm	2 Samuel
1Kg	1 Kings
2Kg	2 Kings
1Chr	1 Chronicles
2Chr	2 Chronicles
Ezr	Ezra
Neh	Nehemiah
Est	Esther
Job	Job
Ps(s)	Psalms
Prv	Proverbs
Ecc	Ecclesiastes
Sg	Song of Songs
Isa	Isaiah
Jer	Jeremiah
Lam	Lamentations
Ezk	Ezekiel
Dan	Daniel
Hos	Hosea
Jl	Joel
Am	Amos
Ob	Obadiah
Jon	Jonah
Mic	Micah
Nah	Nahum
Hab	Habakkuk
Zph	Zephaniah
Hag	Haggai
Zch	Zechariah
Mal	Malachi

New Testament

Mt	Matthew
Mk	Mark
Lk	Luke
Jn	John
Ac	Acts
Rom	Romans
1Co	1 Corinthians
2Co	2 Corinthians
Gal	Galatians
Eph	Ephesians
Phl	Philippians
Col	Colossians
1Th	1 Thessalonians
2Th	2 Thessalonians
1Tm	1 Timothy
2Tm	2 Timothy
Ti	Titus
Phm	Philemon
Heb	Hebrews
Jms	James
1Pt	1 Peter
2Pt	2 Peter
1Jn	1 John
2Jn	2 John
3Jn	3 John
Jd	Jude
Rev	Revelation

Abbreviations of Bible Translations

ESV	English Standard Version
HCSB	Holman Christian Standard Bible
KJV	King James Version
NASB	New American Standard Bible
NET	New English Translation
NIV	New International Version
NKJV	New King James Version
NLT	New Living Translation
RSV	Revised Standard Version

General Abbreviations

1 En	*1 Enoch*
1 Macc	1 Maccabees
AD	in the year of our Lord
ANE	ancient Near Eastern
Aram.	Aramaic
b. Ketub	Babylonian Ketubbot (Talmud)
Bar	Baruch
b. Sanh.	Babylonian Sanhedrin (Talmud)
BC	before Christ
c.	circa
cf.	compare or consult
chap(s).	chapter or chapters
DSS	Dead Sea Scrolls
e.g.,	for example
Eng.	English
esp.	especially
ET	English translation
et al.	and others
etc.	and so forth
Gk.	Greek
Hb.	Hebrew
i.e.,	that is
Lat.	Latin
lit.,	literally
LXX	Septuagint
MT	Masoretic Text
ms(s)	manuscript(s)
NT	New Testament
OT	Old Testament
par.	parallel
p(p).	page(s)
pl.	plural
Pss Sol	*Psalms of Solomon*
1QIsa[a]	Isaiah[a]
1QS	Rule of the Community
sg.	singular
Sir	Sirach/Ecclesiasticus
Tg	Targum
v(v).	verse(s)
Vg	Vulgate
viz.	namely
vol(s).	volume(s)

Introduction

When the Lord Jesus met Cleopas and his companion on the road to Emmaus, He spoke of His own sufferings and glory: "beginning with Moses and with all the Prophets, He interpreted for them the things concerning Himself in all the Scriptures" (Lk 24:27). Commenting on this nearly a century ago, A. T. Robertson remarked, "Jesus found himself in the Old Testament, a thing that some modern scholars do not seem to be able to do."[1] Robertson was jabbing the critical scholars of his own day, whose anti-supernaturalism kept them from recognizing any direct predictions of the Messiah in the Hebrew Bible (the Old Testament). However, today even among evangelicals, interpretive presuppositions have shifted to reflect a similar rejection of predictive messianic prophecy. Although some evangelical scholars may recognize direct messianic prophecies in the OT, it is becoming increasingly popular for many to assert that there are virtually no Hebrew Scripture predictions of the Messiah at all. Some evangelical scholars even insist that not one passage in the Hebrew Bible should be understood as directly predicting the Messiah.

This shift in thought is no minor issue. How messianic prophecy is viewed will ultimately affect the evangelical understanding of the inspiration and interpretation of the Scriptures, the defense of the gospel, and the identification of Jesus as the promised Messiah. Walter Kaiser captured the critical importance of recognizing the messianic hope of the Hebrew Bible: "This issue of the interpretation of the Messiah in the OT could be a defining moment for evangelical scholarship and ultimately for the Church's view of the way we regard Scripture." He adds the reason messianic prophecy is so pivotal: "But if it is not in the OT text, who cares how ingenious later writers are in their ability to reload the OT text with truths that it never claimed or revealed in the first place? The issue is more than hermeneutics; it is the authority and content of revelation itself!"[2]

The need to reclaim and explain messianic prophecy is the reason for *The Moody Handbook of Messianic Prophecy.* It is vital to the health of the church, sound biblical exegesis, and the defense of the gospel to have a book that enables believers to understand the messianic nature of the Hebrew Bible.

Contributors to this volume come from varied doctrinal perspectives and different denominational backgrounds. Nevertheless, they all share the following essential views about the Hebrew Bible's revelation of the Messiah.

1. **The Bible is the inspired and authoritative Word of God (2Tm 3:16).** As such, the Scriptures are inerrant in their original manuscripts and trustworthy in all that they affirm and teach. Also, we all believe that the human authors of Scripture were superintended by the Holy Spirit (2Pt 1:21) and therefore their writings could include predictive prophecy. In the book of Isaiah, God revealed that He alone could predict the future. He says, "I declare the end from the beginning, and from long ago what is not yet done, saying: My plan will take place, and I will do all My will" (Isa 46:10). Foundational to understanding messianic prophecy is that God could and did supernaturally reveal the coming Messiah to His ancient prophets.
2. **All of the Hebrew Bible reveals the Messiah.** In a resurrection appearance in the upper room, the Lord Jesus gave His disciples a seminar on messianic prophecy. Just as He did with those on the Emmaus Road, He taught His disciples that the whole OT reveals the Messiah, saying, "These are My words that I spoke to you while I was still with you—that everything written about Me in the Law of Moses, the Prophets, and the Psalms must be fulfilled" (Lk 24:44). The Lord's point was not that there is one verse in each section of the Hebrew Bible that points to the Messiah. Rather, Jesus was saying that the whole Hebrew Bible, down to the DNA level, was messianic. The Messiah was to be found in the overall message of the Hebrew Bible, not just in some selected proof-texts. This perspective is similar to the famous rabbinic dictum of Rabbi Johanan, "Every prophet prophesied only of the days of Messiah" (b. Ber. 34b) and also underlies the apostle Peter's statement, "All the prophets who have spoken, from Samuel and those after him, have also announced these days" (Ac 3:24). It appears that both ancient Judaism and early Christianity also understood the Hebrew Bible to be messianic.
3. **The Hebrew Prophets understood they were writing about the Messiah.** The gospel of John records a dispute between the first-century Jewish leadership and the Lord Jesus about His identity as the Messiah. He challenged them based on their allegiance to the Torah and Moses, saying, "Do not think that I will accuse you to the Father. Your accuser is Moses, on whom you have set your hope. For if you believed Moses, you would believe Me, because he wrote about Me. But if you don't believe his writings, how will you believe My words?" (Jn 5:45-47). Jesus' point was that anyone who actually believed in Moses' writings would also believe in Him as the Messiah. Some have wondered that perhaps Jesus only meant that Moses wrote of Him unknowingly,

> not that Moses understood that he was writing about the Messiah. This does not make sense since the Lord was saying this in light of what would happen at the final judgment. How could Moses be the one to accuse them if he himself did not understand his own words? For Jesus' words to have any force, Moses needed not only to write about the Messiah but also to *understand* that he was writing about the Messiah.

These three principles guided the general editors as well as all the authors of the various articles in this book. Whether dealing with interpretive issues or expositions of numerous passages, Jesus' perspective on the messianic nature of the inspired Word of God steered all of our work. As you read these articles, we hope you will be guided by the same perspectives. Moreover, once you have read the articles, it is our keen desire that they give you greater confidence in the inspiration of Scripture, a deeper understanding of the Hebrew Bible, and a growing faith and love for Jesus, the Messiah of Israel and the world.

As you look at the book, note that the first chapters deal with interpretive and theological issues related to messianic prophecy. The second, much longer part of the book has extended expositions of many messianic passages in the Hebrew Bible. Some will be familiar to you, dealing with texts that have long been recognized as messianic. Other texts may not be as well known, but they remain significant nonetheless in revealing the Messiah of the Hebrew Bible. Regardless, we hope you will be like the Jewish people in the synagogue in Berea, long ago, "welcom[ing] the message with eagerness and examin[ing] the Scriptures daily to see if these things were so" (Ac 17:11).

Michael A. Rydelnik
Edwin A. Blum
General Editors

1. A. T. Robertson, *Word Pictures in the New Testament* (Nashville: Broadman, 1930), 2:294.
2. Walter C. Kaiser, "The Lord's Anointed: Interpretation of Old Testament Messianic Texts," *Journal of the Evangelical Theological Society* 4, no. 21 (1999): 102.

The Messiah and His Titles

MICHAEL A. RYDELNIK

This is a book about the Messiah in the Old Testament. Although it has become accepted in critical scholarship that the term "Messiah" has no technical usages in the OT and that the concept of a messianic deliverer did not develop until the second century BC,[1] this book has taken a decidedly different direction. It affirms, along with many outstanding biblical scholars, that there indeed was a clearly intended messianic message in the Hebrew Bible.[2]

But where should this study of OT messianism begin? It seems necessary, before addressing any other subject or passage, to be clear about the subject—to understand what is meant about the Messiah. Therefore, this article will address two foundational elements of this entire study. First, it will seek to develop a biblical, theological definition of the word "Messiah." Then, it will examine some (though not all) of the other titles the OT uses for this individual.

THE MEANING OF THE MESSIAH

At the outset, it is imperative to define the term "Messiah" as it is used throughout this entire book. So this section will examine a number of biblical ideas and passages that describe the Messiah, and then it will articulate a biblical, theological definition derived from that examination.

A Biblical Description of the Messiah

The Messiah is described in the Bible beginning with the word "Messiah" or "Anointed One," and then in a variety of other ways. All of the following provide a portrait of the future messianic figure.

A Consecrated Person. The Hebrew root of the word "Messiah" is the verb *mashach*, meaning "to rub or smear." For example, it is used of rubbing oil on a shield (Isa 21:5) or smearing paint on a wall (Jer 22:14). The verb is also used of smearing oil or anointing objects used in worship such as an altar (Gn 31:13), the tent of meeting (Ex 30:26), and the tabernacle and all that is in it (Ex 40:9-11). These texts indicate that the purpose of this anointing was to consecrate or set apart these items for use in worshiping God. The adjectival noun form of the word is used 39 times in the OT and exclusively with living beings. The noun and verb are both used of people, such as the anointed priest (Lv 4:3), anointing a king (2Sm 2:4; 5:3), or anointing a prophet (1Kg 19:16). It indicates that all these were consecrated to serve God. Even a pagan king (Cyrus) is called "anointed" because, in His providence, God consecrated (set apart) Cyrus to serve in bringing the people of Israel and Judah back from captivity (Isa 45:1).

With regard to the technical use of the term "Messiah" or "Anointed One" to refer to an eschatological Deliverer, it is commonly understood to be somewhat rare in the OT. Most will acknowledge that Dan 9:25-26 ("until *Messiah* the Prince;" "The *Messiah* will be cut off") and Ps 2:2 ("the LORD and His *Anointed One*") use the term "*Mashiach*" to refer to this end-of-days Redeemer. W. C. Kaiser, Jr. indicates six additional OT uses of the technical sense of Messiah (1Sm 2:10,35; Ps 20:6; 28:8; 84:9; Hab 3:13).[3] Some additional technical usages are 2Sm 22:51; 23:1; and Ps 89:51. Thus, in the narrow sense, the word "Messiah" is referring to an individual, uniquely consecrated to the service of God. However, since other passages of the OT reveal more about this figure, the definition of the term must go beyond this narrow definition.

A King from the Line of David. In addition to being consecrated to God's service, the Messiah is viewed as a royal figure. This first becomes apparent in Gn 49:10, where the scepter and the ruler's staff are promised to the royal descendant of Judah, "He whose right it is."[4] This is developed further in the Davidic covenant, where David is promised a seed or offspring, a royal heir of his house, who would have an eternal house, kingdom, and throne (2Sm 7:12-16). Isaiah also promised a divine child who would rule over a vast dominion and "reign on the throne of David and over his kingdom" (Isa 9:6-7 [5-6]). According to Isaiah, this King will be established "in the tent of David" (Isa 16:5). Amos anticipated the fall of the Davidic house and foresaw this King coming when God restores "the fallen booth of David" (Am 9:11-12). These passages, and in particular the Davidic covenant, reveal that the future Redeemer will be a royal figure, a King from the line of David.

The Servant of the Lord. Although the Scriptures present the future Redeemer as a King, the prophet Isaiah also depicts Him as the Servant of the Lord. This is His title in the Servant Songs of Isaiah (Isa 42:1-13; 49:1-7; 50:4-11; 52:13–53:12). As God's unique Servant, "He will bring justice to the nations" (42:1) and restore Israel to

righteousness. Therefore, when speaking of OT messianic prophecy, it is this King that the Hebrew Bible foretells, through both prophetic prediction and pattern.

THE TITLES OF THE MESSIAH

Beyond the above description and definition of the Messiah, there are numerous titles used throughout the OT for this eschatological King. Many of them will be highlighted in the articles in this book. Nevertheless, what follows is a brief summary of some of the most important titles, beyond the word "Messiah" itself. However, this is by no means to be taken as a comprehensive list.[8]

The Son of God

In Ps 2, David uses two words for the Lord's Son, *ben* (2:7) and *bar* (2:12). The Lord says of the Anointed One (Messiah, 2:2), "You are My Son; today I have become Your Father" (2:7). The last phrase is literally translated, "Today I have begotten You." The term "begotten" refers to coronation. It is describing the day the King is declared the Son of God and thus begotten. Even those who understand the psalm to refer to David, and not the Messiah, realize that David was a grown man when he was declared the son and begotten. Therefore, they conclude that begotten must refer not to his birth but to his coronation as king, or his enthronement. When spoken of the Messiah, it is describing the eternal Son taking His throne and does not imply that He is a created being. Allen Ross writes, "This is also a figure of speech (an implied comparison), assuming a comparison between the coronation of the king and the idea of begetting a son. Since 'today' the king is designated God's son, today is also his begetting, his coronation. He was already grown, even if a youth, but was being crowned as king, that is, the 'today' on which he is 'being begotten.' . . . The psalm in its context of a coronation decree is therefore used properly for the exaltation and coronation of Jesus."[9] Therefore, the title "Son of God" indicates the deity of the Messiah and the term "begotten" refers to His exaltation and coronation.

The Son of Man

The title "Son of Man" is Jesus' favorite self-identification and is commonly understood to refer to His full humanity. However, in the interpretation of this title from its OT background, it is more likely an expression of deity. It appears in Dan 7:13-14 in the midst of the vision of the Ancient of Days. In this scene, "thrones were set in place" (7:9) with one obviously for the Ancient of Days. But for whom was the second throne? None other than the other figure present, "One like a son of man" (7:13). This One also is deity, but He appears to be fully human ("like a son of man").[10]

As the Divine Son of Man, He is granted all power and authority: "He was given authority to rule, and glory, and a kingdom; so that those of every people, nation, and language should serve Him. His dominion is an everlasting dominion that will not pass away, and His kingdom is one that will not be destroyed" (7:14). Therefore, when the High Priest asked Jesus to state plainly if He was "the Messiah, the Son of God" and Jesus responded by citing Dan 7:13-14 in Matthew's Gospel, "'But I tell you, in the future you will see the Son of Man seated at the right hand of the Power and coming on the clouds of heaven'" (Mt 26:64), this was taken as Jesus affirming His full deity. The High Priest tore his garments and declared Jesus guilty of blasphemy (26:65). He clearly understood the title "Son of Man" to mean full deity and not mere humanity. The title "Son of Man" is an OT expression for the divine Messiah.

The Son of David

The Messiah was understood to be one who would come from the line of David. It is because of the Davidic covenant that the future King was called the son of David. There God states, "I will raise up after you your descendant (lit. "seed"), who will come from your body, and I will establish his kingdom" (2Sm 7:12). The Latter Prophets keep reminding their hearers of this promise. Isaiah called the Messiah "a shoot . . . from the stump of Jesse" (David's father, Isa 11:1), and Jeremiah identified Him as "a righteous Branch of David" (Jer 23:5; 33:15). Jeremiah and other prophets, when depicting the King Messiah's reign, merely called Him "David," although they actually were referring to David's greatest Son (Jer 30:9; Ezk 34:23-24; Hos 3:4-5). According to P. J. and E. Achaemenes, the coming of the son of David is the only hope of Israel at the end of the books of 1 and 2 Kings, when Israel is in captivity: "The authors of this history are telling a defeated and exiled Israel that a descendant of David still lives. God yet preserves alive the bearer of the promise of David, and thus there is still hope that the expected Messiah will come. As long as the seed of David is preserved, Israel has a hope for the future." The son of David is the true hope of Israel.

The Teacher

The Messiah is called "the Teacher of Righteousness" (Jl 2:23a) in some translations and the Teacher who will guide Israel, saying, "This is the way, walk in it" (Isa 30:20-21). In both passages, the Messianic Teacher will not only guide to truth but also provide for Israel, giving them rain and crops (Jl 2:23b; Isa 30:23).[11]

The Servant of the Lord

In Isaiah, Israel is depicted as a failed servant, spiritually deaf and blind (Isa 42:19). Regardless, the nation remains a chosen servant, just incapable of fulfilling its commission (43:10; 44:1). God promises never to forget His servant Israel (44:21), but what will He do to restore the nation? In His kindness, God promises the mysterious Servant of the Lord, who will be successful (in contrast to Israel's failure). He "will act wisely" (52:13), a metonymy for "He will succeed." God's ideal and perfect Servant "will bring Jacob back to Him" (49:5) and restore "the protected ones of Israel" (49:6). The Servant of the Lord will achieve this by being "cut off from the land of the living . . . because of my people's [Israel's] rebellion" (53:8). But the Lord declares it is insufficient for the messianic Servant of the Lord to merely restore Israel. Therefore, God promises, "I will also make you a light for the nations, to be my salvation to the ends of the earth" (49:6). Israel was called to be a nation of priests (Ex 19:6), mediating the truth of the one true God to the nations. Although the servant nation failed, the messianic Servant of the Lord will succeed.

The Prophet Like Moses

God promised that He would one day raise up for Israel a Prophet like Moses (Dt 18:15-19). Although all the prophets were like Moses in that they spoke for God, the Torah itself indicates what was unique about Moses' prophetic office—He spoke to God directly (lit. mouth to mouth; Nm 12:6-8). Therefore, the expectation was that one day, God would send the Prophet like Moses who would also speak directly with God. Many years later, at the time of the close of the canon of Scripture,[12] when the epilogue was placed at the end of the Pentateuch, the inspired addendum reminded Israel that after all these years, "No prophet [had] arisen again in Israel like Moses, whom the Lord knew face to face" (Dt 34:10). So the key message at the time when the canon of the OT was closing was to keep looking for the Messiah, the Prophet like Moses.

Immanuel

In Isaiah 7:14, Isaiah predicts the virgin birth of the Messiah.[13] The passage says that the virgin mother of the Messiah will give Him the title, "Immanuel." This indicates that God would be with the nation of Judah in a special way through the birth of this boy. Moreover, the title suggests that this boy will be deity, "God with us." In Isa 8:8, Isaiah confirms that he intended this as a divine title, saying that the Assyrian army will conquer Judah "and its spreading streams will fill your entire land, Immanuel!" Here the child Immanuel is identified as deity because the land of Israel is seen as actually belonging to Him. Additionally, in the next great vision of the King Messiah, Isaiah uses a variety of divine titles to describe Him (see below).

Wonderful Counselor

In Isa 9:6, the King Messiah is given four glorious dual throne titles, each reflecting His deity.[14] In the first one, the word "Wonder" stands in epexegetical construct to Counselor; Hence, the child is "a wonder of a counselor" or more simply, "Wonderful Counselor." The term "wonder" is used exclusively of the acts of God on behalf of His people and the judgment of their enemies (Cf. Ex 3:20; 15:11; 34:10; Jos 3:5; Neh 9:17; 1Ch 16:12; Ps 40:5 [MT 40:6]; Isa 25:1; 29:14). This wondrous nature of God is especially evident in Jdg 13:15-21, where the name of the Angel of the Lord is "wonderful" (13:18) meaning beyond comprehension. Then the Angel does a "wonderful thing" (13:19) and ascends in the flame of Manoah's sacrifice. Additionally, the word Counselor reflects a uniquely divine attribute. For example, God needs no counselor (Isa 40:13), and the Messiah has the Spirit of counsel upon Him (Isa 11:2). Ultimately, Isaiah uses both of these titles together to describe the Lord, indicating that God alone is wonderful in counsel (Isa 28:29).

Mighty God

Some have tried to assert that this phrase in Isa 9:6, commonly translated "Mighty God" (*'el Gibbor*) should be understood as "mighty warrior." However, the title is used consistently of deity (Dt 10:17; Ps 24:8; Jer 32:18; Neh 9:32). In fact, in the nearest context it is used of God (Isa 10:21). Although *gibbor* can mean "hero," and *'el* can mean "great," whenever these two words are used together, they refer to deity. Thus, the born child and the given son, is no less than God Himself.

Father of Eternity

This title in Isa 9:6, commonly translated "eternal Father," indicates the divine eternality of the Messiah. The word translated "eternity" does not merely mean a long time, but rather it refers to "forever." This is supported by the very next verse that speaks of His reign never ending. Some have misunderstood this name as a declaration that the child is God the Father. Rather, it is stating that He is the Father of forever, a phrase that means He is the Creator of time or Author of eternity. Thus, the child is identified with the divine Creator whose first act was to create time.

Prince of Peace

The word "prince" used in Isa 9:6 does not necessarily mean "the son of the king." Rather it means "ruler" or "leader" (Isa 3:14). Here it indicates one who will be the Ruler of Peace. According to Isaiah, Messiah will establish peace between humanity and God (Isa 53:5), and His reign will institute universal peace (Isa 2:4; 11:6-9) for all humanity.

The Branch of the Lord

The title "the Branch" is used for the Messiah repeatedly in the OT (Isa 4:2; Jer 23:5; 33:15; Zch 3:8; 6:12). The root word means sprout, growth, or branch. A Phoenician inscription (third century BC) uses the phrase "Tsemach Tsedek" for the rightful heir to the throne. When used this way it refers to a son or scion of a king.[15] David used the verb (*tsamach*) in his last words when reflecting on his hope for the Messiah based on the Davidic covenant: "He has not (yet) made it *grow*?" (2Sm 23:5, author's translation).[16] Isaiah 4:2 states that the Branch of the Lord will be glorious in His kingdom. This statement views the Messiah as the Son of Yahweh, and the verses that follow describe the cleansing of Israel, similarly described in Zch 3:8-10, a passage that also uses the messianic title "the Branch." In Jer 23:5-6 and 33:15-16, "the Branch" is the righteous son of David who will save Judah and Israel and execute justice. His deity is recognized by His other title "The LORD [Yahweh] Our Righteousness." Jeremiah 33:19-26 goes on to assure readers of the coming of the Branch because of God's faithfulness to His covenants. In Zch 6:12, "the Branch" is the rightful king who unites the priesthood and the monarchy.

The Lord (Yahweh) our Righteousness

Having already called the Messiah the "Righteous Branch" (Jer 23:5), Jeremiah also uses another messianic title, "Yahweh Our Righteousness" (Jer 23:6). It is most likely that the thought here is not to be construed as a divine epithet because the same title is used of the city of Jerusalem in Jer 33:16. Thus, it should be understood to mean "Yahweh is Our Righteousness." However, it should not be considered a mere theophoric title without divine significance because theophoric titles generally use the shortened form of God's name, "Yah." This is seen in the names like Jeremiah (Yah Exalts) or Elijah (My God is Yah). Only messianic titles use the full name of God, "Yahweh." This indicates that in some unique way, like the Angel of Yahweh (Ex 3:1-6; Jdg 13:1-23), the Messiah is identified as God Himself.

The One Shepherd

In Ps 80:1, God Himself is called the Shepherd of Israel. This makes the messianic title "One Shepherd" even more significant. In Ezk 34, after rebuking the false shepherds of Israel, God promises to restore the nation at the end of days. At that time, God will regather the people from all the lands in which they have been scattered (Ezk 34:13). Then, God will appoint "a single shepherd" (lit. "One Shepherd") over them, called "My servant David" (Ezk 34:23). Under the care of the One Shepherd, "Yahweh will be their [Israel's] God" (Ezk 34:24). Ezekiel repeats the same promise in 37:24, looking at the day when Israel is restored to their land and to their God, under the care of the One Shepherd.[17]

While the above references refer to the One Shepherd when He will establish the messianic kingdom, Zechariah uses the term "Shepherd" to describe a much different situation. In speaking of the death of the Messiah, He writes, "Sword, awake against My shepherd . . . Strike the shepherd and the sheep will be scattered" (Zch 13:7). Seemingly before the Messiah ever begins to shepherd the people of Israel, He must be struck and Israel will be scattered. Then God will one day regather them under that Shepherd, and they will know the Lord.

The Light to the Nations

In the Servant Songs, God promises that the Servant will restore Israel to their God (Isa 49:5-6). But these same songs indicate that the Servant's ministry will go beyond Israel to the whole world. Thus, He will establish justice on earth, and the islands will wait for His instruction (Isa 42:4). Not only will the Servant be a new covenant mediator for the people of Israel, but He will also be "a light for the nations." In Isa 49:6, God tells His Servant that the task of restoring Israel is insufficient for One so great as He, promising "I will also make you a light for the nations, to be My salvation to the ends of the earth." The Servant of the Lord is not just the Messiah of Israel but also the Messiah of the whole world.

CONCLUSION

Much more could be written about the Messiah's OT titles, and much more has been written in the other articles in this *Handbook*. The purpose of this article has been to explain what the word "Messiah" means. The understanding of this OT figure should not be limited just to those passages that use the specific word "Messiah." Therefore, to develop and present a comprehensive biblical, theological definition of the term Messiah, the other key attributes of this biblical person were examined. Then, some of the other titles used for Him were surveyed. Based on this description, definition, and other titles, this *Handbook* uses an expansive approach to the issue of messianic prophecy. Under the heading of messianic, virtually all the predictions about this glorious individual, whatever the title, are examined—to make it possible for readers to see, as Jesus said, that everything written about [Him] in the Law of Moses, the Prophets, and the Psalms must be fulfilled" (Lk 24:44).

---

1. J. Becker influenced many with his view that no messianic figure from the Davidic house is discernible in Jewish thought until the second century BC (*Messianic Expectation in the Old Testament*, trans. D. E. Green [Philadelphia: Fortress Press, 1977], 79).

2. See W. C. Kaiser, Jr. *The Messiah in the Old Testament* (Grand Rapids: Zondervan, 1995); also, J. H. Sailhamer, *Introduction to Old Testament Theology* (Grand Rapids: Zondervan, 1995), 153–54; W. Horbury, *Jewish Messianism and the Cult of Christ* (London: SCM Press, 1998), 1–35.

3. Kaiser, *The Messiah in the Old Testament.*
4. The MT takes this as a proper noun, Shiloh.
5. J. A. Motyer, *The Prophecy of Isaiah: An Introduction and Commentary* (Downers Grove, IL: InterVarsity Press, 1993), 13.
6. Many translations understand these verbs in Ps 72 as if they have a jussive force and so translate them as if they are a prayer or request (e.g. "may He rule"). It is better to understand them as a simple imperfect (as the NET Bible does), anticipating the Messiah and His kingdom.
7. The HCSB renders *shalom* (peace) as "prosperity."
8. Approximately 65 titles have been identified as messianic.
9. Allen Ross, *A Commentary on the Psalms: Volume I* (Grand Rapids: Kregel Academic, 2011), 208.
10. Of course, the Messiah Jesus is indeed fully God and fully man, a fact foretold in Isa 9:6 and affirmed in the NT, especially Phl 2:6-9. Yet this text is describing Him as deity who looks like humanity.
11. For this alternative translation of Jl 2:23 and the linkage of these two passages, see the article "The Teacher of Righteousness" in this *Handbook.*
12. For a defense of seeing Dt 33–34 being added to the Pentateuch near the end of the canonical period by a biblical writer from the time of Ezra, or even Ezra himself, see Michael Rydelnik, *The Messianic Hope: Is the Hebrew Bible Really Messianic?* (Nashville: B&H Publishers, 2010), 60–65. There it demonstrates that the passage is clearly post-Mosaic since it includes Moses' death and burial. It uses postexilic terms like "man of God" to speak of Moses (Dt 33:1), does not remember where Moses was buried, and assumes it has been a long time since Moses' ministry, long past the time of Joshua.
13. For a defense of interpreting Isa 7:14 as a direct messianic prophecy, see the article "The Virgin Birth in Prophecy" in this *Handbook.*
14. Some have maintained that these are merely theophoric names, a long title that contains the name of God but which does not indicate that the bearer of the name is deity. They often will compare these titles in Isa 9:6 grammatically to the long title in 8:3, "Maher-shalal-hash-baz" ("Swift is the booty, fast is the prey"). Then the title is translated "A Wonderful Counselor is the Mighty God, The Eternal Father is the Prince of Peace." In response, the name in 8:3 ("Maher-shalal-hash-baz") is dependent on the same words being used in 8:1. Second, the title in 8:3 is not parallel syntactically to 9:6 because all the words in 9:6 are substantives that do not have subjects and predicates. Moreover, titles such as used in 9:6 frequently reflect the nature of the person who is named (e.g. 2Sm 12:24-25; Isa 1:26; Hos 1:10).
15. W. C. Kaiser, Jr., "Tsemach" in *Theological Wordbook of the Old Testament*, ed. R. Laird Harris, Gleason L. Archer, Jr., Bruce K. Waltke (Chicago: Moody Publishers, 1980), 769.
16. See the article "David's Last Words" in this *Handbook.*
17. Ecclesiastes 12:11 also uses the term "One Shepherd" as the One who was the source of the divinely inspired wisdom of Ecclesiastes. See the article "Messianism in Ecclesiastes" in this Handbook.

Messiah and the Hebrew Bible[1]

JOHN H. SAILHAMER

In a book review for the *Journal of the Evangelical Theological Society*, Walt Kaiser has made a strong plea for the importance of the question concerning the Messiah and the Hebrew Bible. The question, says Kaiser, "could be a defining moment for evangelical scholarship and ultimately for the Church's view of the way we regard Scripture."[2] According to Kaiser, the question ultimately comes down to whether the NT interpretation of an OT text is, in fact, the meaning intended by the OT author. Kaiser states, "if it is not in the OT text, who cares how ingenious later writers are in their ability to reload the OT text with truths that it never claimed or revealed in the first place? The issue is more than hermeneutics," says Kaiser. The issue is that of "the authority and content of revelation itself!"[3]

Another evangelical OT scholar, Gordon McConville, has also stressed the importance of the Messiah in the OT. McConville says, "If the Old Testament is *the* problem of Christian theology . . . [then] the Messiah is at the heart of that problem."[4] McConville goes on to say that "the validity of a Christian understanding of the Old Testament must depend in the last analysis on [the] cogency of the argument that the Old Testament is messianic."[5]

These are strong statements. And they come from two respected biblical scholars. I believe they accurately reflect the current state of mind of evangelical scholarship. If liberalism once defined itself as a quest for the *historical* Jesus, evangelicalism may well be in the process of defining itself as a quest for the *biblical* Jesus. I believe this question lies at the heart of much of the current evangelical discussion about biblical theology.

EVANGELICAL VIEWS OF THE MESSIAH AND THE HEBREW BIBLE

Evangelical views of messianic prophecy can be traced to the work of two early 19th century OT scholars, Ernst Wilhelm Hengstenberg (1802–1869) and Johann Christian Konrad von Hofmann (1810–1877). The views of these two men still set the agenda for much of evangelical biblical scholarship. In many respects, their views were similar. Both were influenced greatly by the Berlin revivals in the early 19th century. For both, the last word on the meaning of messianic prophecy in the OT was that of Jesus and the NT. Both believed fulfilled prophecy offered essential support for the truth of the gospel. Both also believed that in giving us messianic prophecy, God had intervened in a real way in human history. He had made known His will and purpose. Messianic prophecy was thus not a product of a human yearning for a better life, but the result of a "supernatural" revelation.

In spite of these basic similarities, each man offered a fundamentally different set of answers to essential questions.

Hengstenberg. Hengstenberg's understanding of messianic prophecy was shaped by two primary concerns: (1) his own experience of conversion, which was sudden and undeniable; and (2) his desire to use his spiritual experience as a basis for the defense of the Bible. For Hengstenberg, God's work in the world was accomplished by means of specific divine interventions. These were miraculous events within the arena of ordinary history. The incarnation was a prime example. It marked a new beginning for God's relationship with the world. In the incarnation, the Word had become part of the world. Israel's history was a record of the many and diverse instances of that intervention. Although Israel's history was a part of ordinary human history, it was also, like his own conversion, punctuated with miraculous exceptions.

That a prophet could foresee the exact name of the future Persian king Cyrus (e.g. Isa 45:1) was an exception to ordinary history, but such an exception was to be expected given the divine origin of the prophetic Word. When God stepped into the flow of human history, His actions were direct and clear to anyone who witnessed them. They were, in fact, so self-evident that they could be used as proof of the truth of the gospel.

As Hengstenberg saw it, God's acts in history had an immediate but short-range effect on the rest of history. As miracles, they did not become part of the rest of history. They were historical, but not part of history. They were, in fact, exceptions to history and as such were clear signs of God's activity. God's acts in history were like our stepping into the current of a river. Our feet may make a splash, but there are no ripples made in the river. The ripples are lost in the flow of the river. Hengstenberg's own conversion was a divine splash whose ripples were quickly dissolved by the flow of time. There was nothing left for the historian to fix upon and to draw conclusions from. It was a "super"-natural (miraculous) event lost within the course of ordinary history.

For Hengstenberg, the divine revelation of messianic prophecy consisted of similar kinds of miraculous events. In this way, his entire understanding of messianic prophecy came to be shaped by his own conversion experience. As Hengstenberg understood it, the prophets of old were given sudden, miraculous, panoramic visions of the whole of the messianic future. Those visions were like flashes of supernatural light and insight. Often, they came so suddenly and faded so quickly the prophet could record only a small portion of the vision. One is reminded of flashbulbs from the 1950s which left one momentarily stunned and unable to see anything but a large blue dot that faded slowly from one's eyes. The prophet hurriedly recorded the vision as it faded from his sight.

Hengstenberg believed the prophetic visions came so quickly that in some cases, new visions would appear to the prophet in the midst of other visions. The prophet would have to stop recording one vision to pick up his description of another. What the prophet was ultimately able to record were only bits and pieces of the visions he had seen. Hence, for Hengstenberg, to discover Messiah in the OT meant gathering all the bits and pieces of the one grand vision and piecing them back together. It was as if the prophetic books were large scrapbooks containing scattered fragments of once-whole Rembrandts and Michelangelos. A single verse in the Bible might contain fragmented pieces of several visions. Only the trained eye could spot a piece of both a Rembrandt and a Michelangelo and in the same verse. Only one who knew the whole vision could piece the fragments together.

In finding and piecing together such splintered visions, the NT was indispensable. It was like the picture on the cover of a jigsaw puzzle. For Hengstenberg, little or nothing was left to the prophet. He merely recorded the visionary fragments from which the student of prophecy must piece together the whole.

Given these assumptions about the nature of prophecy (which were novel and unusual in Hengstenberg's day), it is not hard to understand the approach he took to the Messiah in the OT. Following Hengstenberg through the Hebrew Bible is like following a trained geologist through the Black Hills. We watch him pick up a stone here and a rock there and tell us they were once part of a great prehistoric mountain range. Hengstenberg can point to a fragment here and a text there and reconstruct for us the great messianic mountain range that once inhabited the prophet's mind. Without knowing the whole scope of messianic prophecy as Hengstenberg, we have to follow him and take his word about the messianic parts of a verse.

Though few evangelicals today openly adopt Hengstenberg's approach, his legacy continues to influence the contemporary discussion. That legacy, as I understand it, consists of three commonly held assumptions:

—*Assumption 1*: The meaning of any one messianic prophecy is not immediately transparent. There is a need for some kind of translation of what is *said* in the OT into what is *seen* in the NT. For Hengstenberg it meant a "spiritual" interpretation—looking to the NT for clues to the OT's meaning. Another word for this is typology. In any event, for Hengstenberg, the NT held the key to the meaning of the OT.

—*Assumption 2*: The messianic meaning of the OT consists of the predictive nature of its prophecy. To be messianic, the OT must accurately *predict* the historical events in the life of Jesus. We thus judge the messianic intent of the OT by indexing it to the picture of Jesus in the Gospels. Once again, the NT holds the key to the meaning of the OT.

—*Assumption 3*: The value of the messianic prophecies in the OT is largely apologetic. To the extent that an OT passage proves to be messianic and thus predictive of the life of Jesus, it shows that Christianity, or the gospel, is true. This is the argument from prophecy. In actual fact, this legacy goes back to the apologists in the early church. It is to Hengstenberg, however, that the credit must go for reviving this concern. In saying this is one of the legacies of Hengstenberg, I am not saying it remains, at present, a productive use of messianic prophecy. Hengstenberg did not convince many, even among his own evangelical colleagues.[6]

von Hofmann. Whereas Hengstenberg had focused his attention on piecing together the messianic prophecies in the text of Scripture, von Hofmann looked beyond the text to the historical events they recorded. According to von Hofmann, it was not the text of Scripture that was messianic; it was history itself that was messianic. It was not Israel's historical writings that were messianic, but the history that Israel itself experienced. That history was a "living picture" of the coming Messiah. It was a *vaticinium reale*,[7] a "material prophecy" consisting of the actual events. Von Hofmann believed the events of Israel's history were an "inspired" messianic picture—just as he believed the Bible was an "inspired text."

To be sure, the Hebrew Bible functions as our primary means of "seeing" the picture in history, but the *messianic* picture itself and the means of "seeing" that picture were found by looking beyond the Scriptures to Israel's history as *history*. The full messianic picture can only be seen as one observes Israel's history unfold itself into the first century and the life of Christ. The history becomes clearer, and the picture more focused, as it moves closer to the coming of the Redeemer. Because it was truly God at work in this history, Israel's history was unlike any other. It was a "holy history." God Himself had caused it. God was not merely working *in* history, history *was God at work*. Von Hofmann believed that just as God can be seen by a botanist in every leaf of a tree, so God can be seen by the historian in every moment of Israel's history. For von Hofmann, in fact, there was not a moment in all of world history in which something divine does not dwell.[8] History is God working out His will in the world. In Israel's history, God was, as it were, submerging Himself into history, making it increasingly more sacred and increasingly more messianic. Ultimately Israel's sacred history culminated in God's final act stepping into history, that is, the incarnation.

For von Hofmann, God did not momentarily step in and out of history, as Hengstenberg had envisioned. In Israel's history, God was increasingly immersing Himself in the world. The incarnation of Christ was thus not a unique and new beginning, but a final stage in a long process of God's becoming a part of the world. The boundaries of world history had already been permanently breached by a real divine presence with Israel. God, in effect, had carved out a "sacred history" (*Heilsgeschichte*) in the midst of His work in the world (*Weltgeschichte*).

With such a view of the Bible and history it is not hard to see how everything in the Hebrew Bible could ultimately be about the Messiah. It does not initially have to look messianic for it to be an early stage of a developing prophecy. To quote von Hofmann: "It is a long way between the death of an animal whose skin covered [man's] nakedness, and the death of the Son of God whose righteousness covers [man's] sin. Yet these are like the beginning and the end of the same journey."[9]

It is thus also not hard to see how, in von Hofmann's approach, everything in the Bible could be understood in strictly historical terms. Only the one who understands history as moving toward Christ can understand the messianic element in the Hebrew Bible. The meaning of Israel's history is messianic only when one sees God's messianic intentions behind the actual events of that history. The task of understanding the OT as messianic lies in recognizing the divine patterns in these early events and pointing to how they replay themselves throughout the remainder of Israel's history. History's meaning thus becomes typological and finds its ultimate meaning only with the coming of the antitype. The mere historical similarity between the exodus and our Lord's sojourn to Egypt in Mt 2 constitutes for von Hoffman a "material prophecy" of the coming Messiah. Once again, in such an approach, the NT holds the key to the meaning of the OT.

In such a context, the meaning of biblical words and terms, such as "the anointed one" or "the king," spoken at a certain moment in Israel's history, transcended the meaning of those words when understood solely within the context of the rest of history. Behind *all* events in Israel's "holy history" lay the mind of God and His will. Every word spoken within Israel's history had thus a horizontal (historical) range of meaning as well as a vertical (messianic) one. Within Israel's salvation history, not only were biblical words fraught with divine intentionality, but so were the historical events that constituted that history. God was the author of both. His will and intention lay behind both. While David might have referred to *himself* as "the anointed one" in Ps 18, the real event that lay behind Ps 18 carried with it the potential of being understood by the historian as part of a prophetic history. Proof of this comes when the historian views Ps 18 from the perspective of its NT fulfillment.

To appreciate the legacy of von Hofmann, one must know something of how evangelicals viewed "history" before his time. Before von Hofmann there was a fundamental distinction between how evangelicals viewed biblical history and how it was viewed by biblical critics. Biblical history, as critical scholarship had come to view it, was an understanding of the history of Israel within the context of what we might call "ancient analogies." By that I mean that Israel's history was not viewed on its own terms but as part of the history of other ancient peoples. The Bible played an increasingly minor role in reconstructing its own history.

For evangelicals before von Hofmann, biblical history meant simply that history which could be read off the pages of the Bible. Before von Hoffman, evangelical biblical scholars had a largely *realistic* historical understanding of the Bible. What they read in the Bible was what they understood to have happened. If the Bible said the Nile turned to blood, they took that to mean the Nile River turned to "*real* blood." Von Hofmann marks the turning point of evangelical biblical scholarship away from such a realistic view of history. Even C. F. Keil, the most conservative evangelical OT scholar of his day, was willing to concede that "the changing of the water into blood is to be interpreted . . . not as a chemical change into real blood, but as a change in the colour, which caused it to assume the appearance of blood."[10] Note that von Hofmann did not alter the newly developing critical attitude toward Israel's history. He accepted it as such, though he practiced it conservatively and was even willing to render it the status of divine revelation. Nevertheless, with von Hofmann, the holy history that progressively revealed the coming Messiah was no longer merely the history we read in the Bible. Revelatory prophetic history (*Heilsgeschichte*) must be reconstructed and augmented from our knowledge of the ancient world.

A second, and important, legacy of von Hofmann is that OT messianic prophecy could no longer be viewed apologetically. Having assigned the meaning of the OT to a history that finds its meaning in the events of the NT, one could no longer speak of fulfillment in terms of verification or validation. It was the fulfillment that validated the earlier history, not the other way around. Von Hofmann was thus quick to jettison the notion that OT messianic prophecy could be used in any way to defend the truth of Christianity. With von Hofmann it was *history* that validated Christianity, not the *miracle* of fulfilled prophecy.

Von Hofmann's legacy among modern evangelical approaches to the OT is felt at many levels. Nowhere is it more tangible than in the study of messianic prophecy. My purpose is not to critique modern evangelical approaches for their dependence on von Hofmann. I have tried to do this elsewhere.[11] My purpose now, as I stated earlier, is to seek an alternative to the approaches of both von Hofmann and Hengstenberg.

Before moving on to that part of the article, let me briefly summarize what, I think, these two evangelical views have in common. Though quite different in detail, both Hengstenberg and von Hofmann share important evangelical assumptions about the Messiah in the OT. Here I have listed three:

—*Assumption 1*: Both men (Hengstenberg and von Hofmann) understood messianic prophecy as a genuine (supernatural) "vision" of the future. Prophecy was a "history of the future."

—*Assumption 2*: Both men saw the NT as the primary guide for understanding OT messianic prophecy. Without a NT picture of Jesus, we could not truly understand the OT. The NT serves as a kind of searchlight cast back over the OT. Without that light from the NT, the OT messianic vision is at best hazy and uncertain.

—*Assumption 3*: For both Hengstenberg and von Hofmann, the messianic vision of the OT is not presented in a straightforward, holistic manner. The messianic picture is scattered in bits and pieces throughout the OT.

As stated above, Hengstenberg explained this as a function of the rapidity of the visions. The visions came so quickly, the prophets simply could not record them fast enough. The prophetic books were like large scrapbooks containing scattered fragments. To be sure, the prophets saw the whole picture, but they recorded only a small portion of what they had seen. Only one who knew the whole vision (from the NT) could piece the fragments together.

A RESPONSE TO HENGSTENBERG AND VON HOFFMAN

I want to make it clear that I believe there is much truth in these three assumptions. Nevertheless, I still believe there is room for more work in each of these areas. As a summary of what lies ahead in this paper, I would like to add my own response to each of these three points.

—*Response 1*: Prophecy is not just a "history *of* the future." It is also a "history *for* the future." It is not merely a description of the destination of Israel's history, it is also a road map that explains how to get there.

—*Response 2*: The NT is not so much a *guide* to understanding the OT as it is the *goal* of understanding the OT. Unless we understand the OT picture of the Messiah, we will not understand the NT picture of Jesus. The OT, not the NT, is the messianic searchlight.

—*Response 3*: For Hengstenberg (and von Hofmann) viewing the messianic vision in the OT was like looking into a huge mirror that had been shattered into a thousand pieces. Hengstenberg believed that to see the Messiah in the OT, we must look at the NT picture of Jesus as it is reflected through the pieces of this shattered mirror. What remains of the OT messianic picture is now only small bits and pieces scattered throughout the OT.

Now, I think most of us would agree with Hengstenberg on this point— at least in part. That is certainly the impression one gets from reading the OT prophets. I would like to suggest, however, that these bits and pieces (of the messianic vision) are not *randomly* scattered, as Hengstenberg believed. There is a recognizable pattern. They follow an order. A good number of them, for example, fall along what we might call the "compositional seams" of the OT books, the transitional comments the biblical authors use to tie their texts together.

Some of these bits and pieces of prophetic visions also fall along the "seams" of the OT as a whole, what is called the Tanakh.[12] What I am suggesting is that the shape of the Hebrew Bible as a whole is a meaningful context for viewing the scattered bits and pieces of prophetic visions. Rather than a shattered mirror, I think a better image of the OT is a stained-glass window. To be sure, it is made of fragmented pieces of glass, but like a stained-glass window, each piece belongs with the others and plays a crucial part in the picture of the whole.

If these initial observations are valid, I believe they suggest new possibilities for viewing the Messiah in the OT. If there is an order and pattern to the distribution of messianic texts, then we should ask: what is the meaning that lies behind the order?

Let me briefly outline what taking such an approach might entail. There are many ways to look at the messianic stained-glass window in the Hebrew Bible. The approach I have in mind begins by looking at the Hebrew Bible in the shape we find it just at the threshold of the coming of Christ. It looks at the OT's last word about itself, at how the OT was understood by those who gave it its final shape. Here I have in mind the Tanakh: the Law, the Prophets, and the Writings. To be sure, there were and are other shapes to the Hebrew Bible, but judging from texts such as Lk 24:44, the Tanakh is the form of the OT with which Jesus and the NT authors were most familiar.

Viewed from this perspective, the OT has all the appearance of being a single work with a single purpose. It is connected by literary seams linking Dt 34 and Jos 1 and similar seams linking Mal 3 and Ps 1. These passages fall together in the order of books in the Tanakh. There are also clear links within these individual parts and a distinct compositional strategy that goes from the first word in the Hebrew Bible (*bereshit*) to the last (*veyāʿal*). If we follow along the lines of these compositional seams, I believe, we will find the Tanakh to be motivated primarily by a hope in the soon coming of the promised messiah. It is that perspective on the OT that, I believe, gives us the best view of what the OT authors believed about the Messiah. It is also that perspective that shows most clearly the literary and theological dependency of the NT on the OT.

A PROPOSAL FOR UNDERSTANDING THE MESSIAH IN THE HEBREW BIBLE

In the remainder of this article, I would like to describe what I think is a possible approach to understanding the Messiah in the Hebrew Bible. I can only describe it in outline. I am not going to try to argue a case for it.[13] I am not going to try to convince you of it. My goal is simply to explain to you what I think is a plausible approach for understanding Jesus in light of the teaching of the Hebrew Scriptures. I will attempt to describe this approach with the help of three basic propositions: (1) the nature of OT messianic prophecy consists of both prediction and identification; (2) the OT messianic vision is a fragmented vision that becomes increasingly more cohesive as one moves toward the final stages of the formation of the Hebrew Bible; and (3) the Hebrew Bible is both text and commentary.

Proposition #1: Prophecy as Prediction and Identification

The central element of the approach I have in mind lies in an attempt to clarify the question of predictive messianic prophecy. There is, of course, prophetic prediction in the OT. Prediction is a major apologetic theme, for example, in passages such as Isa 41. There are also other important features to the notion of prophetic fulfillment. To highlight those features, I would suggest that alongside terms such as "fulfillment" we also use the terms "identification" and "exposition." The OT not only *predicts* the coming of a Messiah; it also *describes* and *identifies* that Messiah.

Here is an important difference from Hengstenberg and von Hofmann's idea of prophecy as a "history of the future." As we said above, messianic visions in the OT are not only visions *of* the future, they are also visions *for* the future. They *explain* the future as well as *reveal* it. The amazing thing about OT prophecy is not only that the prophets foresaw what would happen. That, as Hengstenberg rightly held, was miraculous. But equally amazing was that, when it came, the future the prophets foresaw (and here I have in mind the NT) actually followed the plan the prophets had laid out for it. When the future came at a specific time and place, there were people waiting for it. There were those, like Simeon and Anna, who understood it in terms of the OT prophetic vision. In other words, the prophet's vision was such that it preserved and carried with it a people who both understood the prophets and were there waiting for the fulfillment of their vision. By falling in line with that vision, the NT writers show that they accepted the OT as pre-interpreted, and they also were in fundamental agreement with its interpretation. That interpretation, we can see, began long before the time of its fulfillment. Already within the OT itself we can discover clear signs of an ongoing process of inter-biblical, or (I would prefer to say) intertextual interpretation.

In the Pentateuch, for example, the Messiah is a prophetic priest-king like Moses, who will reign over God's kingdom, bring salvation to Israel and the nations, and fulfill God's covenants. As I understand it, this messianic vision is part of the compositional strategy of the whole of the Pentateuch. In the Prophets and Writings, we find a full and detailed *exposition* of the Pentateuch's messianism. It is in that exposition that the OT messianic hope is extended and deepened to the very point at which we find it in the NT. Thus, the last word in the Hebrew Bible is as messianic as any passage in the NT. I have in mind, of course, texts such as the vision of the Son of Man in Dan 7. That vision, and the book of Daniel as a whole, is equal to any messianic Christology in the NT.

To be clear, what I am describing is often viewed in terms of a process of "re-interpretation." Earlier, nonmessianic sections of the OT are re-interpreted by later authors and subsequently understood as messianic. That is very far from what I have in mind. What I have in mind is that when the OT reads and interprets itself, as is happening in Dan 7, it does so by drawing on the real, historical intent of the other OT authors. There is no need to speak of a re-interpretation of texts. I think, for example, it is possible to show that the Pentateuch is already thoroughly messianic and that the rest of the OT understands this and expands on it by way of textual commentary and exposition.

There is a direct link, in other words, between the beginning of the OT and the end of the OT, as well as the end of the OT and the beginning of the NT. From a literary perspective, there is no intertestamental gap between the Testaments. The last word in the Hebrew Bible can also be understood as the first word in the NT. It is a verb without a subject (*veyā'al*, 2Chr 36:23, lit., "let him go up"). Its subject could very well be taken from the first chapter of Matthew in the NT. It is a call for the coming of that one "whose God is with him," and who is to build the Temple in Jerusalem. In Chronicles (and the postexilic prophets) this one is the messianic (priestly) son of David. Matthew's Gospel, which follows immediately after this last word, begins like Chronicles, with a genealogy identifying Jesus as the Christ (Messiah), the son of David, who is Immanuel, "God with us."

So what I am suggesting is that the Hebrew Bible, when viewed in its final historical context (on the eve of the Christian era), is already messianic in a NT sense. When the NT says that the OT is fulfilled in Jesus, it means that we can identify Jesus as the Messiah because He fits the picture of the Messiah in the OT. The *proof* that the Gospel is true (and I believe there is a proof here) lies not only in an accurate *prediction*, but also in an accurate *identification* of Jesus with the one promised by the Law and the Prophets. To say it another way, it is only when we have identified Jesus as the OT Messiah that we can speak of verification of OT prophecy by prediction. Thus, the messianic thrust of the NT is not merely an argument that the OT is true prophecy. It also includes the argument that Jesus is the true Messiah.

Let me return for a moment to the metaphor of the NT as a "messianic searchlight." Here, I believe, a shift in focus is necessary. As I would see it, it is not the NT, but the OT, that is the "messianic searchlight."[14] It is only when the OT casts its light onto the pages of the NT that we see the meaning of the life of Jesus.[15] In such an approach, the OT (without the NT) is *not* understood as "inadequate and incomplete," as Eichrodt once described it.[16] The messianism of the OT is fully developed and is the context from which we must *identify* Jesus as the promised Messiah.

Proposition #2: The OT Messianic Vision Moving toward Greater Cohesiveness

The OT messianic vision is a fragmented vision that becomes increasingly more cohesive as one moves toward the final stages of the formation of the Hebrew Bible. The second point I want to make is taken from Hengstenberg's notion of a shattered vision. No one who has read the prophets will want to disagree with Hengstenberg that the messianic vision of these books lies before us in bits and pieces. As Calvin once said, "Those who have carefully . . . perused the Prophets will agree with me in thinking that their discourses have not always been arranged in a regular order."[17]

Hengstenberg proposed to piece this fractured vision together by looking at the picture that emerges from the NT. I propose reading the fragmented prophetic visions, not in light of the NT, but in light of the picture that emerges from within the OT itself. There is, I believe, a coherent picture behind the composition of the prophetic books and the Pentateuch. The pieces fit into that picture. I also believe it can be shown that if we follow the order of the Hebrew Bible—the Law, the Prophets, and the Writings (Tanakh)—the messianic picture becomes increasingly more transparent. That is because later biblical texts focus on and provide interpretation for earlier biblical texts. By "later" I do not mean chronologically late. I mean, rather, the stage at which the biblical author is at work making a book. As far as we can tell, most biblical authors, such as the authors of Kings and Chronicles, worked with existing written texts. They organized and presented those texts so that their narratives gave meaning and sense to the events they recorded. The question of *how* they did this leads to my next proposition—the Hebrew Bible as text and commentary.

Proposition #3: The Hebrew Bible as Both Text and Commentary

If we ask what possible intertextual relationship lies between the compositional shape of the Pentateuch, the Prophets, and the Writings of the Hebrew Bible, I would suggest it is akin to that of text and commentary. The Prophets and the Writings are not intent on giving us a *new* vision for the future. Their aim is to help us understand the messianic vision that has already been laid down in the Pentateuch and repeated in their own writings. God told the prophet Habakkuk, for example, to "write the vision" and also "to explain it" (Hab 2:2, author's translation, cf. Dt 1:5). Like Habakkuk, the prophets wrote their vision along with its explanation. As Abraham Joshua Heschel put it, the interpretation of prophecy is already "an exegesis of an exegesis."[18] Our task is not to explain the prophetic vision, but to explain the prophets' own explanation of their vision. The aim of the authors of the Prophets and the Writings was to provide a full and detailed textual commentary on the messianic vision that begins in the Pentateuch and is carried along through the rest of the Bible.

Like a stained-glass window, the Prophets and the Writings give us the important bits and pieces of the prophets' vision. I have in mind something like the way Isa 63:1-6 draws a glimmer of light from the poem in Gn 3:15 and passes it on to Dan 7 through the prism of Gn 49. From there on it passes through the NT on its way to the vision of the "rider on the white horse" in Rev 19. Isaiah takes as his starting point the picture of the king who, in Gn 49, "washes his clothes in the blood of grapes." He then builds that picture into one of a mighty warrior treading in the wine presses of divine wrath. In doing so, Isaiah consciously links Gn 49 to the first messianic poem in the Pentateuch, Gn 3:15. Isaiah has thus linked two strategically important *poems* in the Pentateuch (Gn 3 and Gn 49). In doing so, he shows that he is reading the Pentateuch along its compositional seams. As in a stained-glass window, the light he draws from the Pentateuch is given color and texture as it passes through the remainder of the OT. But also like a stained-glass window, these points of light converge into the larger picture.

Here, let me reiterate the point I made earlier. The line of thought reflected in Isaiah and Daniel and the book of Revelation is, I believe, the same as the historical intention of the Pentateuch itself.

When Ps 72 says of the Davidic king, "All the nations will be blessed in him,"[19] it draws directly from the eschatology of the Pentateuch in Gn 12:3. When the same psalm says of the king's enemies, may they "lick the dust" (Ps 72:9b), it holds its vision up to a piece of light coming from Gn 3.[20]

In the same way, when speaking of the eschatological future, Hosea says, "Out of Egypt I called My son." In doing so, Hosea draws directly from the poetic vision of Balaam in the Pentateuch (Nm 24). Also, by focusing on the poetic texts, Hosea shows he is reading the Pentateuch along its compositional seams.[21] In the Numbers passage, Israel's messianic future (in Nm 24) is viewed in terms of their glorious past, that is, the exodus (in Nm 23).[22] The compositional strategy *within the Pentateuch itself* has thus linked the exodus with the messianic future. Hosea draws his own messianic hope from just those passages. Both Hosea and the Pentateuch see the fulfillment of their visions in terms of the same eschatological future, that is, "the last days" (*be'acharit hayyāmiym,* Hos 3:5; Nm 24:14). Hosea's messianic vision is thus cast as a commentary on the Pentateuch's own messianic eschatology. Matthew's application of the Hosea passage to Jesus suggests he has properly read both the Pentateuch and its commentary in Hosea.

Here we can take another example from the Immanuel prophecy in Isa 7:14. It is an all-too-common practice to look *beyond* the book of Isaiah and *beyond* the words of Isa 7 to the historically reconstructed social location of those words. When we do that, it becomes very difficult to see the kind of prophecy of a virgin birth that Matthew saw. But, if we look at the passage within the compositional unity of the book of Isaiah, quite another view emerges. According to v. 15, for example, when Immanuel is born, "he shall eat curds and honey until he knows to reject the evil and choose the good" (author's translation).

As the author of the book of Isaiah saw it, v. 15 is as much a part of the sign given to Ahaz as v. 14. The sign is not only that the virgin is pregnant with a son, but also that when the son is born, he (and thus Israel as a whole) will be eating "curds and honey." According to the description of the destruction of Judah in the following verses (Isa 7:17-25), they will be eating "curds and honey," because the land will have been ruined first by the Assyrians (v.17), then by the Babylonians (chap. 39), and finally by others after that (chaps. 41–66). Within the whole of the book of Isaiah, the birth of the young Immanuel is located long *after* the ruin of the northern and southern kingdoms.

The 19th-century critic Bernhard Duhm was so struck by the implications of v. 15 that he could only image it was a late "messianic gloss"[23] to vv. 14 and 16. Though I believe Duhm rightly understood the sense of v. 15, his notion that it was a late gloss is rendered unlikely by the presence of the verse in the Qumran Isaiah manuscript. No one here would dispute that the ultimate focus of the book of Isaiah is far beyond the exile, that is, long after the time of Isaiah and Ahaz. According to v. 15, the sign is for that distant future. Isaiah, of course, had a message for Ahaz, but that message was about something that was to happen in the "last days." Among other things, the rest of the book of Isaiah is intended as an exegesis of the prophet's tersely recorded vision in 7:14-15. Here we must understand not only the vision, but also the prophet's exegesis of that vision as it plays out in the remainder of the book.

Summary

I hope by now I have made clear enough a general idea of one possible approach to the Messiah and the Hebrew Bible. There are many questions raised by this approach. One important question has to do with the notion of the "final shape" of the Bible. This is largely uncharted waters for most of us evangelicals. It is, of course, an idea that has been around in OT studies since the time of Wellhausen and earlier. Let me be clear that I am not suggesting we abandon the long-established evangelical concern for the meaning of the "original authors." Far from it.

What I am suggesting is that by not paying close attention to the whole of the Hebrew Bible as we now have it, we are neglecting some important "original authors." Who was it, for example, who wrote of the death of Moses and tells us that a prophet like Moses never arose again in Israel? He was an inspired biblical author of the same stature and importance as any other. His contribution to the meaning of the Pentateuch cannot be overestimated. His brief comments at the close of the book tell us in no uncertain terms that the prophet that Moses spoke of in Dt 18 was not any of the later prophets of Israel. There was still a prophet yet to come. In other words, the author who gave us the "final" ending of the Pentateuch understands the words of Moses in Dt 18 exactly as they were understood by the NT authors. That prophet, like Moses, was the expected Messiah—and He had not yet come. I am suggesting we pay just as close attention to that biblical author, and his colleagues, as we do to the better-known OT authors. Is an inspired author any less important because we do not know his name?

A Test Case: Is the Pentateuch Messianic?

So, is the Pentateuch messianic? If so, how? In what follows, I want to lay out the main lines of argument which, I believe, support the view that the Pentateuch was written primarily as a presentation of a future messianic hope centered in the tribe of Judah and grounded both in creation and covenant.[24]

a. *The Pentateuch is a single book with a single purpose.* First, the whole of the Pentateuch (from Genesis to Deuteronomy) was intended to be read as a single book with a distinct purpose, focus, and message. That is to say, the Pentateuch had an author, and its author had a purpose in writing this great literary work. The Pentateuch is about something. What this means is that the whole of the Pentateuch has a definite shape and structure. It is not haphazardly thrown together. It is not merely a diary of events. It is not a hodgepodge of early documents. To me this has been the most beguiling feature of the Documentary Hypothesis—its complete disregard of and disdain for the text as we now have it. The Pentateuch is surely going somewhere, and its author has taken great pains to guide us along that route. There is a single literary strategy that runs through the whole of the Pentateuch.

Several lines of argument, I believe, show us that the Pentateuch is a unity and has a single, intentional structure.

(1) The Pentateuch recounts a single story that begins with the creation of the world and the preparation of the land, and ends with the postponement of the possession of that land. A central theme of the Pentateuch is the land.

(2) The large blocks of narrative (primeval history, patriarchs, exodus, wilderness, conquest) are linked by a single theme—that is, faith. Someone, namely its author, has linked all the events in Israel's early history to the theme of faith.[25]

(3) The arrangement of major, homogeneous poetic texts in Gn 49, Nm 24, and Dt 32 suggests the Pentateuch's narratives are linked by the single messianic theme that recurs in these poems. In this regard, the Pentateuch is like a Hollywood musical. As in a musical, the story is both interrupted and developed by the songs (poems). Also, like in a musical, the songs (poems) are not randomly thrown into the story. The songs (poems) carry the central theme of the story. They are the primary means for developing what the narratives are about. A careful attention to the songs (poems) enables us to see what the Pentateuch is about.[26]

(4) A fourth element in the shaping of the Pentateuch is the way the various collections of laws have been purposefully arranged within the narratives. What Wellhausen and others maintained were remnants of earlier law codes, I believe, can be shown to follow a carefully laid-out textual strategy. At its center lies the account of the golden calf. That story shows that something has gone fundamentally wrong. It is only near the end of the book, in Dt 30, that we come to the author's answer—that is, the circumcised heart and the promise of a new covenant.[27] The message of the Pentateuch lies not in its textual *strata* but in its textual *strategy*.

b. *The message of the Pentateuch.* Having established that the Pentateuch has a shape and a central message, I want to develop briefly what I believe that central message to be. My point is to show how the central message is linked to the actual textual strategies of its composition. It is not enough to point to broad themes and ideas. There is no end to that. What must be shown is *how those broad themes and ideas are specifically tied to the compositional shape of the Pentateuch.*

Here I want to list what I take to be the central components of the compositional themes of the Pentateuch. I want also to discuss briefly how those themes are tied to the compositional strategy of the Pentateuch.

(1) *Component #1: The prophetic critique of Israel's faith.* As we mentioned

earlier, the single story of the Pentateuch takes us from God's creation and preparation of the land to Israel's failure in the wilderness and postponed possession of the land. Neither Moses (Nm 20:12) nor the people (Nm 14:11) have the faith that would bring them into the land. The overall strategy reflected in the Pentateuch, in other words, is anything but optimistic about Israel's immediate future. They have at best a rocky future. In one of the final compositional seams linking the poems to the Pentateuch (Dt 31:29), Moses on his death bed tells Israel, "I know that after my death you will become completely corrupt and turn from the path I have commanded you." One can already hear in these words the distant voice of the prophets.[28] Exile is on the way. The future is at risk. There is at this time little room for hope among God's people.

Nevertheless, as in the prophetic books, there is also a message of hope to be found in the Pentateuch. As in the prophets, it is a message centered on a coming king. It is that king who is the center of focus of the poems in the Pentateuch. Each major (and minor) poem in the Pentateuch centers on His coming. He is the king who will arise from the house of Judah. He will rule over the nations, and He will restore God's good land to all of humanity. The Pentateuch leaves little doubt about when this king will come. He will come "in the last days" (*be'acharit hayyāmiym*).

The prophetic critique of Israel's lack of faith leads to the second element of the message of the Pentateuch.

(2) *Component #2: The centrality of faith as the way that is pleasing to God.* The unified "faith theme" in the Pentateuch stresses the role of faith and obedience from the heart that lies at the center of the prophetic notion of the new covenant (Jer 31; Ezk 36). According to the logic of the Pentateuch's own narrative, Israel failed to obey their covenant with God at Sinai (Ex 32). Nevertheless, a future blessing still awaits them. That blessing is tied to Israel's faith, not their obedience to the law. How else can you explain Gn 26:5 which tells us, very clearly, I believe, that Abraham's *faith* amounted to (not resulted in, but amounted to) his keeping God's statues, commandments, and laws? Abraham could not have kept the Sinai Law, which had not been given until the time of Moses. Abraham lived a life of faith and that *was* his keeping the law. This emphasis on the role of faith, so clearly NT in its outlook, is not found randomly throughout the Pentateuch. It lies along the compositional seams that tie together the whole of the book.

(3) *Component #3: The promise of a coming eschatological king.* As we have suggested above, the central theme of each of the major poems in the Pentateuch is the promise of a coming "king." As an introduction to each of those poems we find the phrase "in the last days." This is terminology that is paralleled closely in the messianic eschatology of the prophets. It can hardly be accidental that each of these poems that stress the coming of the king is set in the context of "the last days."

In the Masoretic Text, this king is said to conquer and rule over the kingdom of Agag (Nm 24:7). That has led to the identification of this king (in the MT) with David, who conquered Agag.[29] Rashi, for example, says of this king "this is David" (*zeh Dāviyd*). But that is only in the MT. In all other ancient texts *and* versions,[30] this king is said to conquer and rule over the kingdom of Gog. This can only be the Gog of Ezk 38, the only other Scriptural reference to this Gog.[31] Ezekiel himself acknowledges he knows of Gog from earlier Scripture (Ezk 38:17).[32] According to Nm 24:24, this king will come after the defeat of Assyria and Babylon, and the rise of the Kittim. This can hardly be David. There is, thus, in the textual history of the Pentateuch a running debate over the identity of this king. The MT sees the historical David as the focus of these prophecies. The earlier and more widely represented texts (including Ezekiel's own copy of the Pentateuch) identify the king with an eschatological Redeemer who will defeat Gog.

c. *The Pentateuch and the prophets.* What is most striking when looking at these features of the composition of the Pentateuch is how similar its themes are to the central themes of Israel's later prophetic literature. By that I mean its messianic focus on a future new covenant in which God will give a new heart to those who trust in His Word. At the center of that focus is the coming king who will defeat Israel's enemies and establish a perfect kingdom.

To be sure, the Pentateuch is about the Mosaic covenant and the law given at Sinai. But what it tells us about the law is much the same as what Paul says in Gal 3. The law did not produce a living faith in Israel's heart. There was nothing inherently wrong with the law, nevertheless, Israel failed to keep it. God thus gave Israel a hope for the future and laws to hold them until that future should come. The Pentateuch is therefore a commentary on the laws of Sinai Covenant. It, like the prophetic books, looks for something better. That "something better" is a "new covenant" that includes both Jews and Gentiles and has as its centerpiece a royal, that is, messianic, Redeemer.

The Messiah in the Details

The ultimate task is, of course, to show the messianic intent in all the many details of the narratives and poetry of the Pentateuch—even in the arrangement and composition of the laws themselves. Here one has to ask, What is the relationship of the details in the Pentateuch to the overall themes we have briefly outlined? This, I believe, is just why the prophets (and psalmists) have given us their inspired "commentaries" on the Pentateuch. Their commentaries are in many ways similar to the stained-glass window we mentioned earlier. By means of fragmentary bits and pieces of their vision, they capture the light cast by the Pentateuch and focus it not only on the needs of their own day, but also on their hope for the future.

CONCLUSION

In summary, first, as evangelicals, our approach to the question of the Messiah in the OT has generally been to read the NT back into the Old. I am suggesting we can also move in the other direction. The OT sheds a lot of light on the events of the NT. Our primary objective should be to read the NT in light of the Old, rather than the OT in light of the New.

Second, as evangelicals, we have spent a good deal of our time looking at the earliest stages of the biblical history for the answer to the meaning of the OT. We have paid a good deal of attention to how Eve may have understood Gn 3:15. As important as that is, I am suggesting we also ask how Moses and the inspired biblical authors understood Gn 3:15. There is little to go on to discover how Eve might have understood God's first promise. There is, however, much to go on if we read Gn 3:15 from the perspective of Moses and onto the final shape of the Pentateuch, that is, the last eight verses in Deuteronomy that take us far beyond the death of Moses.

Third, the more closely we examine the final shape of the Hebrew Bible (Tanakh), the clearer it becomes that its shape and structure are not accidental. There are clear signs of intelligent life behind its formation. If that is so, we should be asking, What is the theological message behind this shape? My answer to that question is that it is strongly messianic. I do not mean by that that the earlier forms of the Bible are not also messianic. What I mean is that in the later stages of the formation of the Hebrew Bible its authors were primarily concerned with making more explicit the messianic hope that was already explicit in the earliest texts. This is what I call "text and commentary." In other words, the later stages in the formation of the Hebrew Bible treat the earlier stages much as the NT treats the OT. They build on and develop the messianic vision that is already present in the earlier texts.

I heard someone recently describe the lens of an old lighthouse along the New England coastline. It was a lighthouse used long before the discovery of electricity. Its light source was a single candle. The lens of its light consisted of thousands of triangular surfaces. Each surface focused and refracted a small portion of the original candlelight. The result was a beam of light that was cast 20 miles out to sea. The original light was just a small candle. As it passed through the lens it became a bright beacon of light. This is not unlike the Hebrew Bible. As the original messianic candlelight passes through, first the Pentateuch, and then the rest of the Tanakh, it becomes a bright light that shines on the NT. Unfortunately, we have become accustomed to holding only the candle (Gn 3:15) up to the NT—instead of reading the NT in the light cast by the lens of the whole of the Tanakh.

Several years ago, I taught a course which I entitled "The Use of the OT in the

OT." It was a course on how later biblical authors (like Ezra and Nehemiah, or the prophets) understood the Pentateuch. Every time I offered the course, the registrar would change the title in the class schedule to "The Use of the OT in the NT." This happened every time I taught the course. You could see that the registrar always assumed I had made a typo. The phrase "Use of the OT in the OT" was meaningless to him. Nowadays, however, it is not meaningless. This question is being asked by many today. It is the question I have been trying to clarify in this article. How do the OT writers understand the early messianism of OT books like the Pentateuch?

In the end, I believe Walt Kaiser is right. The question of the Messiah and the Hebrew Bible "could be a defining moment for evangelical scholarship and ultimately for the Church's view of the way we regard Scripture." Dr. Kaiser, I believe, is also right in insisting that the question is ultimately whether the NT interpretation of an OT text is in fact the meaning intended by the OT author.

I also believe Gordon McConville is right: "The validity of a Christian understanding of the Old Testament must depend in the last analysis on [the] cogency of the argument that the Old Testament *is* messianic." Whether or not you are convinced of the cogency of the argument I have outlined, I hope I have at least provided a sense of what possibilities lie open to us today.

Let me conclude with a bold, but sincere, claim: What I have tried to suggest is that it can be argued that the books of the OT are messianic in the full NT sense of the word. The OT is the *light* that points the way to the NT. The NT is not only to cast its light back on the Old, but more important, the light of the OT is to be cast on the New. The books of the OT were written as the embodiment of a real, messianic hope—a hope in a future miraculous work of God in sending a promised Redeemer. This was not an afterthought in the Hebrew Bible. This was not the work of final redactors.

I believe the messianic thrust of the OT was the *whole* reason the books of the Hebrew Bible were written. In other words, the Hebrew Bible was not written as the national literature of Israel. It probably also was not written to the nation of Israel as such. Rather, it was written, in my opinion, as the expression of the deep-seated messianic hope of a small group of faithful prophets and their followers.

---

1. This article is adapted from John H. Sailhamer "The Messiah and the Hebrew Bible" *Journal of the Evangelical Theological Society* 44 (2001), 5–23.

2. *Journal of the Evangelical Theological Society* 42/1 (1999), 99–102.

3. Ibid., 101.

4. *The Lord's Anointed: Interpretation of the Old Testament Messianic Texts* (Grand Rapids: Baker, 1995), 2.

5. Ibid., 17.

6. His popularity among evangelicals in English translation was probably primarily due to his strong stand on Reformed orthodoxy and his sustained attack on biblical criticism.

7. Franz Delitzsch, *Die Biblisch Prophetische Theologie* (Leipzig: Gebauersche Buchhandlung, 1845), 175.

8. J. Chr. K. von Hofmann, *Weissagung und Erfullung im Alten und im Neuen Testamente*, vol. 1 (Nordlingen C H Beck'sche Buchhandlung, 1841), 7.

9. Idem, *Interpreting the Bible* (Minneapolis: Augsburg, 1959), 137.

10. C. F. Keil, Biblical Commentary on the Old Testament, Vol. 1 (Grand Rapids: Eerdmans, 1971), 478.

11. John H. Sailhamer, *Introduction to Old Testament Theology* (Grand Rapids: Zondervan, 1995), 36–85.

12. The Tanakh is the name given to the Hebrew Bible within Judaism. It is an abbreviation of the three parts of Scripture: the "*Torah*," the "*Nevi'im*," and the "*Ketubim*." The Hebrew Bible has a different shape from our English OT. The individual books are the same, but the order is different.

13. I have attempted this in the following articles: "Biblical Theology and the Composition of the Hebrew Bible," Papers from the Wheaton College Theology Conference (Downers Grove, IL: InterVarsity, forthcoming); *Introduction to Old Testament Theology*, 197–252; *The Pentateuch As Narrative* (Grand Rapids: Zondervan, 1992), 1–79; *The NIV Compact Bible Commentary* (Grand Rapids: Zondervan, 1994); *How We Got the Bible* (Grand Rapids: Zondervan, 1998), 38–42; "Creation, Genesis 1–11, and the Canon," *Bulletin for Biblical Research* 10 (2000), 89–106; "A Wisdom Composition of the Pentateuch?" *The Way of Wisdom*, ed. J. I. Packer and Sven K. Soderlund (Grand Rapids: Zondervan, 2000), 15–35; "Hosea 11:1 and Matthew 2:1," *Westminster Theological Journal* 63 (2001), 87–96.

14. Cf. 2Pt 1:19—the "prophetic word" is "a lamp shining in a dismal place."

15. As is said in the Gospel of John, "Jesus performed many other signs in the presence of His disciples that are not written in this book. But these are written that you may believe Jesus is the Messiah, the Son of God" (Jn 20:30-31). The signs Jesus performed are like road signs that reflect in the headlights of the OT.

16. Walter Eichrodt, *Old Testament Theology* (Philadelphia: Westminster, 1967), 26.

17. John Calvin, *Commentary on the Book of Isaiah* (Grand Rapids: Baker, reprint 1979), xxxii.

18. Abraham Heschel, *The Prophets: An Introduction* (New York: Harper & Row, 1962), xiv.

19. Ps 72:17.

20. Just as in Isa 65:25b, "the serpent's food will be dust!"

21. Sailhamer, "Creation, Genesis 1–11, and the Canon," 89–106; idem, "A Wisdom Composition of the Pentateuch?" 15–35.

22. Idem, "Hosea 11:1 and Matthew 2:15."

23. Bernhard Duhm, *Das Buch Jesaia ubersetzt und erklart* (HKAT; Gottingen: Vandenhoeck & Ruprecht, 1892), 54.

24. Let me quickly add that I am not raising the question of whether the Pentateuch "points to" Jesus and the NT. To say the Pentateuch is about the Messiah is not yet to say it is about Jesus. Those are two separate and equally important questions. We must first ask whether the Pentateuch is about the Messiah and then ask whether Jesus is the Messiah. The Pentateuch (and the rest of the Hebrew Bible) tells us there will be a Messiah. The NT tells us that Jesus is the Messiah spoken of in the Hebrew Bible. It does so by identifying Jesus as the one about whom the Hebrew Bible speaks. This means that, in my opinion, there is an important apologetic value to the identity of Jesus as the OT Messiah. By identifying Jesus as the OT Messiah, the NT claims that Jesus is the true Messiah.

25. Sailhamer, "The Mosaic Law and the Theology of the Pentateuch," *Westminister Theological Journal* 53 (1991), 241–261; Hans-Christoph Schmitt, "Redaktion des Pentateuch im Geiste der Prophetie," *Vetus Testamentum* 32 (1982), 170–189.

26. Sailhamer, *The Pentateuch as Narrative*, 35–37.

27. Ibid., 46–59.

28. This, to me, is the major weakness of the approach of double or multiple fulfillment. The Torah itself does not see the immediate events in the life of Israel as a positive fulfillment (cf. Dt 31:29).

29. Cf. 1Sm 15:8; 2Sm 1:1.

30. Cf. *Biblia Hebraica Stuttgartensia*, Samaritan Pentateuch, LXX, Aquila, Symmachus, and Theodotion.

31. The Gog in 1Chr 5:4 is one of the sons of Reuben.

32. "This is what the Lord God says: Are you the one I spoke about in former times through My servants, the prophets of Israel, who for years prophesied in those times that I would bring you against them?"

Textual Criticism and Messianic Prophecy[1]

MICHAEL A. RYDELNIK

Jesus taught that the Law, the Prophets, and the Psalms all spoke of Him (Lk 24:44). Nevertheless, for the last three centuries, interpreters have struggled with discovering precisely in what sense the Hebrew Bible spoke of the Messiah (See the article "Interpretive Approaches to Messianic Prophecy" in this *Handbook*). Although direct messianic prediction is one method offered as a possible explanation, it is certainly not the view most scholars accept now, even among evangelicals. The focus of this article is a look at the contribution of textual criticism (the study of determining the actual words of the original manuscripts of the Bible)[2] in reading the Hebrew Bible as a directly predictive messianic work.

There are three reasons textual criticism of the Hebrew Bible must be considered. First, it is a crucial area of discussion because the Masoretic Text is frequently treated as a received text rather than as a version of the biblical text. Yet the MT, although generally sound and truly the best OT text available, is a somewhat late version of the Hebrew Bible. Therefore, other versions, such as the Samaritan Pentateuch, and ancient translations, such as the Septuagint, should be consulted to determine the best possible readings of the OT. Clearly, the first task in exegesis is to establish the original text of any given passage. This is just as true when studying the OT as it is for the NT.

Second, textual criticism is especially significant for studying messianic prophecy because a considerable number of textual variants appear in OT passages commonly understood to be messianic. The critical apparatus (the critical notes about the text of the Hebrew Bible, identifying the variant readings included at the bottom of each page) of the Hebrew Bible (*Biblia Hebraica Stuttgartensia*) frequently is larger in those passages that have been thought to be messianic.

Third, the MT may at times interpret some messianic passages as referring merely to historical figures. On the other hand, other earlier versions may reflect a more eschatological/messianic reading. Therefore, what follows is a discussion of the role of the MT and textual criticism as it applies to messianic prophecy.

THE MASORETIC TEXT AND OTHER VERSIONS

John H. Sailhamer clarifies the way interpreters should view the MT by warning, "Evangelicals, in the desire to stress the verbal inspiration of the OT text, should be careful not to identify the 'original' Hebrew text with the Masoretic Text."[3] Eminent textual criticism scholar Emmanuel Tov concurs, writing that "the Masoretic Text does *not* (italics his) reflect the 'original text' of the biblical books in many details."[4] He further states that "it should not be postulated that 𝔐 [i.e., the MT] reflects the original text of the biblical books better than other texts."[5] In light of this, the MT should not be accorded a status comparable to a *textus receptus*. Although the MT is generally accurate and OT exegesis would be near to impossible without it, it would be unwise to consider it as fully valid as the autographa. In fact, as Sailhamer says, "The history of the Masoretic Text is of vital importance . . . because it is the starting point of textual criticism, not because it is the final destination."[6] How is this so?

The MT reflects a consonantal text that was not clearly consolidated until the second century AD.[7] Furthermore, the pointings and accents were not formulated until the ninth and tenth centuries AD.[8] With so many centuries between the consonantal text and the addition of vowels and accents, Wurthwein wisely cautions: "The pointing does not possess the same authority as the consonantal text."[9] Therefore, it is best *not* to view the MT as the received text of the OT, regardless of its strength and importance. Rather, it should be seen as the top layer of a distinct postbiblical exegetical tradition. Although the MT seeks to identify the original intent of the biblical autographs in a consistent fashion, and often does, it also has an interpretive tradition embedded in it. As Jewish scribes, the Masoretes faithfully transmitted the textual traditions that they had received from rabbinic Judaism. Thus, there is significant rabbinic theology embedded in the MT's standardization of the consonantal text and its addition of accents and vowels.[10]

In light of this, the theological importance of other ancient versions becomes readily apparent. For example, the Septuagint is a Greek translation of the OT derived from a text nearly 1,000 years older than the MT.[11] The point here is not that the MT always, or even frequently, has an inferior reading. Rather, the point is that the Septuagint and other ancient versions provide "a viable alternative witness to the meaning of the text of Scripture, and thus the potential for an alternative biblical theology."[12] Furthermore, the NT authors' frequent use of the Septuagint when quoting the OT lends further importance to this version.[13]

THE MASORETIC TEXT AND MESSIANIC PROPHECY

So what does all this about the MT have to do with messianic prophecy? It is significant to messianic prophecy because it has been shown that the MT is a post-Christian, Jewish version of the OT. As such, it reflects the theological perspective of post-Christian, rabbinic Judaism. Thus, there are several significant examples of the MT interpreting OT messianic texts in a distinctly nonmessianic (or historical) fashion, whereas other ancient versions interpret the same texts as referring to the Messiah. This is not to say that the MT is the product of some conspiracy to excise the Messiah from the OT, as some medieval polemicists claimed.[14] If that were so, the MT would not have retained as much about the Messiah as it did. However, it can be argued that in some places the MT reflects a less messianic view than other ancient texts and versions. What follows will highlight several of these examples.[15]

Judges 18:30

This first example serves to demonstrate that rabbinic thought is embedded in the MT but does not address the interpretation of a messianic text specifically. The theological perspective of the MT is evident in the suspended *nun* in Jdg 18:30, which reads, "The Danites set up the carved image for themselves. Jonathan son of Gershom, son of Moses, and his sons were priests for the Danite tribe until the time of the exile from the land."

This verse records the establishment of the first pagan priesthood in Israel. The consonantal text's original reading indicated that *Mosheh* (or Moses) was the grandfather of Jonathan, the founder of this pagan priesthood. The Masoretes inserted the raised letter נ (*n* or *nun*), making the word read *Me**n**asheh* (or Menassah).[16] According to Tov, the suspended *nun* was a correction of "an earlier reading which ascribed the erecting of the idol in Dan to one of the descendants of Moses. . . . The addition can therefore be understood as a deliberate change of content."[17]

The motive for the change is critical. Keil and Delitzsch cite R. Tanchum, who said that the written "Moses" reading ought to be corrected with a suspended *nun*, so that it would read "Manasseh."[18] Keil and Delitzsch also quote Rabba bar bar Channa who argued for the "Manasseh" reading "because it would have been ignominious to Moses to have an ungodly son."[19] Therefore, the *nun* was suspended to protect the honor of Moses. It was unthinkable for the exalted lawgiver and prophet of Judaism to have been the grandfather of the founder of a pagan priesthood.[20] Although, this example does not pertain directly to messianic prophecy, it is significant because it demonstrates that the MT can reflect a later theological perspective.[21]

NUMBERS 24:7

The MT of Nm 24:7 presents a prophecy that would find its fulfillment in Israel's history. However, the alternate versions of this verse look forward to an eschatological, messianic fulfillment. The MT of Nm 24:7 literally reads:

> Water will flow from his buckets, and his seed will be in the many waters,
> His king will be higher *than Agag* and his kingdom will be exalted.[22]

According to the Masoretic reading, the verse predicts that a king would arise from Jacob who was to be higher than Agag. This is a prediction alluding to the king whom Saul failed to kill (1Sm 15:8-9). Thus, according to the Masoretic reading, the high king that Balaam foresaw would come is linked to the days of Saul's rejection and David's elevation. Based on the Masoretic reading, most interpreters understand the coming king to be a prediction of King David.[23]

However, the variant reading substitutes Gog for Agag. This reading has wide support, being found in the Septuagint, the Samaritan Pentateuch, Aquila, Symmachus, and Theodotion. According to this reading, Balaam foresees a king from Jacob who would be exalted over Gog, the end-time enemy of Israel (Ezk 38:3). Thus, the passage links this prophecy with Messiah's day, when He will have victory over the eschatological foes of Israel.

The Gog reading is supported by the context, in which Balaam says he is speaking of "the end of days" (Nm 24:14).[24] Further, the context identifies the king as the messianic royal figure of Gn 49 when it says of Him, "He crouches, he lies down like a lion" (Nm 24:9) in a deliberate innertextual allusion to Gn 49:9. The prophecy also promises that this future king's "kingdom will be exalted" (Nm 24:7), using more glorious terminology than what would be used of David or one of his nonmessianic descendants. Additionally, Ezk 38:17 includes a recognition that Gog is known from earlier Scripture. There the Lord addresses Gog and asks, "Are you the one I spoke about in former times?" This is an obvious reference to the variant reading in Nm 24:7.

Curiously, Timothy Ashley, after recognizing the antiquity of the Septuagintal messianic reading and noting that the MT on this verse is "difficult and obscure (and possibly corrupt)," still prefers the MT reading. He dismisses the messianic rendering of the Septuagint as a mere reflection of the intense messianic speculations of the second century BC and not as an authentic reading that would yield a messianic prophecy.[25]

Ashley's approach, although common, seems ill advised. In light of broad witness to the "Gog" reading, the internal evidence, and the weaknesses of the MT, it is better in this instance, as Albright suggested, to take the Septuagint as the original reading.[26] Thus, in an obscure verse in the Torah, it appears that the variant readings point to a future, glorious Messiah with an exalted kingdom, not merely to King David.

Second Samuel 23:1

Second Samuel 23:1 provides another example of the MT exhibiting a historical reading rather than the more messianic variant reading of the versions. In this verse, the MT contains a seeming self-description of David, when it reads:

> These are the last words of David:
> the declaration of David son of Jesse,
> the declaration of the man raised on high,
> the one anointed by the God of Jacob,
> the favorite singer of Israel.

In the MT reading, the passage contains five synonymous identifications of the author of these words. They come from David, who is the "son of Jesse," who is "the man raised on high," who is "anointed by the God of Jacob," who is "the favorite singer [lit. "the delightful one of the songs"] of Israel." This translation and interpretation hinges on the MT reading *'āl*, "on high." However, the Septuagint translates this as *epi* ("concerning"), apparently reading the same Hebrew consonants with the Hebrew vowel *patach* (*'al*) and not with a *qamets* ('āl). This slight difference in pointing results in a substantial difference in translation:

> These are the last words of David:
> The declaration of David son of Jesse,
> And the declaration of the man raised up *concerning*
> The Messiah [Anointed One] of the God of Jacob,
> And the Delightful One of the songs of Israel.

Sailhamer aptly explains the significance of the different readings when he writes, "The effect of the difference in the length of the vowel is such that the title 'anointed one' in the MT refers to King David, whereas in other, non-Masoretic versions of the text, David's words are taken as a reference to the Messiah (cf. 2 Sa 22:51)."[27]

The internal evidence is against the interpretation that David was writing about himself. In 2Sm 23:3-4, David proceeds to describe the righteous reign of the king as "the one who rules the people with justice" (2Sm 23:3-4). In v. 5, David makes a declarative statement (lit.): "For not so is my house with God" (author translation of *kiy lo ken beti 'im 'el;* 2Sm 23:5). Most translations recognize the internal contradiction. In v. 1, David seems to be saying it is all about him, and then in v. 5, he plainly states it is not. Therefore, most English versions translate v. 5 as a question to avoid this internal contradiction with the first verse in the paragraph: "Is it not true my house is with God?" (HCSB), "Truly is not my house so with God?" (NASB), "For does not my house stand so with God?" (ESV), "Is not my house right with God?" (NIV 1984), or "Is it not my family God has chosen?" (NLT). However, the problem with taking 2Sm 23:5 as a question is that there is no interrogative particle (prefixed ה), the Hebrew form normally found in yes/no questions.[28] Hence, it is unlikely that the phrase should be understood as a question.

It makes far more sense to understand that, in his last words, David has said that the future Messiah was his favorite subject to write about in the Psalms (2Sm 23:1 LXX), that David knew about the Messiah because the Spirit of God spoke to him (2Sm 23:2), that the Messiah would be a righteous ruler (2Sm 23:3-4), that readers ought not to confuse David with that future righteous ruler because "his house is not so with God"; and finally, that David had assurance that the Messiah would come because God had "established an everlasting covenant" with him (2Sm 23:5), namely, the Davidic covenant.

If the alternate, non-Masoretic reading is correct (and it must be remembered that the vocalization of the consonantal text occurred in the ninth through tenth century AD), then 2Sm 23:1 gives a crucial interpretive clue to reading Davidic Psalms. By David the psalmist's own admission, he frequently wrote about the Messiah, the Delightful One of the songs of Israel, indicating that the Psalms should be understood to have an eschatological, messianic focus rather than merely a historical one.

Psalm 72:5

Psalm 72:5 is another example of a significant difference between the MT and the Septuagint.[29] The MT reads, "*They will* [or "May they"] *fear you* while the sun endures, and as long as the moon throughout all generations." On the other hand, the Septuagint reads, "*May he continue* while the sun endures, and as long as the moon, throughout all generations." The difference in the two versions is in the MT *yira'uka*, "they will [may they] fear you," and the Septuagintal reading *kai sumparamenei*, which is a translation of the Hebrew *weya'arik*, "he will continue/endure."[30] The resulting meanings are quite different. The MT refers to a righteous king who would have such a significant impact on the nation that the people would fear God and submit to Him forever. The Septuagint's meaning reflects the messianic interpretation inherent in the psalm, asking for the Messianic King's life and reign to endure forever.

There are several reasons to prefer the Septuagintal reading over the MT in Ps 72:5. First, there is no clear reason for the MT to change pronominal subjects from the surrounding verses, which use the third person singular ("he will judge" in v. 2 and "may he vindicate" in v. 4), obviously describing the king/king's son introduced in v. 1, to a third person plural subject ("they") and a second person address to the Lord ("you"), resulting in the phrase "*they* will fear *you*." The second person pronoun cannot properly refer to the king (who is described in the third person singular), but would have to refer to God. Yet a second person address to God in v. 5 would be clearly out of place, especially since the next verse returns to the third person singular pronoun reference to the king ("may he be like rain").[31]

Second, the subject of *yirāʼukā* ("they will fear you") has no clear antecedent.[32] It would have to be "the people" (which is singular) from vv. 2-4, but the action of "fear" on the part of the king's people would be out of place here (the king's enemies kneel before him in vv. 9-11).[33]

Third, the verb *weya'arik* ("continue") fits better with the temporal allusions in vv. 5-7. There it speaks of the permanence of the sun, the moon continuing through all generations, and abundant peace "until the moon is no more." The context refers to time, not the fear of God.[34]

It might be argued that the MT is the harder reading and therefore original. However, it would be necessary to demonstrate that there is a literary basis for the MT reading somewhere in the context. Yet, a careful study of the psalm reveals no clear explanation.

Knut Heim has argued against the messianic rendering because the psalm is preexilic and "at this early stage in Israel's history a developed messianism or expectation of 'eternal life' is highly unlikely."[35] Nevertheless, this is nothing more than circular logic as he himself admits: "This argument could of course be accused of circular reasoning."[36] It is the same kind of logic that caused Duhm, who accepted the Septuagintal reading, to date the psalm as postexilic. He believed the messianic meaning could not have been present in the preexilic period.[37] Both of these writers seem to deny the possibility of supernatural revelation, which would allow the author to write of the Messiah prior to the exile. In light of all of the above evidence, it seems best to accept the Septuagintal reading for this verse, with all its messianic implications.

Isaiah 9:5(6)

In this central messianic verse, the MT's accentuation can produce a significantly different interpretation from what the Hebrew words alone might express. The verse is commonly read as, "He will be named Wonderful Counselor, Mighty God, Eternal Father, Prince of Peace." In this rendering, the title "Mighty God" is applied to the child who is to be born as Davidic king, seemingly indicating the deity of the king (cf. Isa 10:21).

However, the MT inserts accents that divide the titles, resulting in this translation: "The Wonderful Counselor, the Mighty God, calls his name eternal father, prince of peace."[38] According to this translation, the first two couplets are names that refer to God Himself, and the second two refer to the child that was born. The point of this reading appears to be to negate any thought of a child being considered as deity. Additionally, the MT reading is decidedly different from the NT rendering in Lk 1:32-33.[39]

Hebrew scholar Franz Delitzsch objects to the Masoretic accents and their attendant translation for a number of reasons.[40] First, he contends that it is unlikely that there are two sets of names here, one for God and one for the child. Second, he finds it "impossible to conceive for what precise reason such a periphrastic description of God should be employed" when naming the child.[41] Third, he argues that a dual-name construction, as the Masoretic accents indicate, is not found elsewhere in Isaiah. Fourth, he conjectures that the first two titles would have been written with definite articles (*The* Wonderful Counselor and *the* Mighty God) had the author intended to distinguish God from the child. Thus, he concludes regarding the Masoretic accentuation: "We must necessarily reject it, as resting upon a misunderstanding and misinterpretation."[42] Once more, it appears to be an example of the MT exhibiting an interpretive bias, advancing the perspective that a born child could not be the "Mighty God."

PSALM 22:16

Psalm 22:16 (v. 17 Hb.) is one of the most controversial verses in the OT and the source of much contention. A multitude of variants exist, but here are the basic differences: The MT reads *kā'ariy* ("as a lion"), and the Septuagint reads *oruxan*, from the verb *orusso*, "to dig/excavate" or "to perforate/pierce,"[43] apparently a translation of the Hebrew *k'ru* ("they pierced").[44] Thus, the verse in the MT reads, "For dogs have surrounded me; a gang of evildoers has closed in on me; *as a lion* . . . my hands and my feet." However, the LXX, Syriac, and the Vulgate read, "For dogs have surrounded me; a gang of evildoers has closed in on me; *they pierced* my hands and my feet."

Plainly, the MT rendering avoids the Christological implications of predicting the crucifixion, thereby taking the less messianic rendering and making it more acceptable to Judaism.[45] The primary arguments for taking the MT as the correct reading is that preference should always be given to the MT and to the harder reading. The absence of the verb, making the phrase elliptical, yields not only the harder reading but a virtually unintelligible one. On the other hand, the Septuagintal reading has the older support and makes grammatical sense within the literary context.[46]

In the final analysis, it seems that the Septuagintal reading should be preferred for several reasons. First, although the MT has the harder reading, there is a difference between a harder reading and an impossible one. One would have to assume incoherence on the part of the author, which is far more than the principle of taking the harder reading requires. As Peter Craigie has noted, the MT reading "presents numerous problems and can scarcely be correct."[47] Second, defining the harder reading depends on the audience reading it. For a Masorete, "they pierced my hands and my feet," a seeming prediction of the Messiah's crucifixion, would certainly have been the harder reading. Third, the LXX reading fits the literary context, makes grammatical sense, and is supported by the other versions (and even some Masoretic traditions). Perhaps most important, in 1997, the translation of a textual discovery from Nahal Hever in the Judean Wilderness brought strong support to the Septuagintal reading.

The discovery of a fragment of the book of Psalms, dated between AD 50 to 68,[48] contains Ps 22:16 and reads, *k'ru* ("they pierced").[49] It might be objected that this was a Christian interpolation or contamination. But a Christian interpolation is unlikely because it would have been far too early in Christian history for a Christian corruption to make its way into this text. Moreover, it has strong support from the earlier Septuagintal reading.[50] Thus, the oldest extant Hebrew manuscript of Ps 22:16 (v. 17 Hb.) reinforces the Septuagintal, Syriac, and Vulgate readings, supporting the translation, "They pierced my hands and my feet." In this case, it is better to take the more messianic variant readings than the nonmessianic rendering of the MT.

CONCLUSION

The above examples have shown the occasional tendency of the MT to offer readings that find their fulfillment in historical figures rather than in eschatological times or a personal Messiah. The passages discussed are not unusual or unique. Even though there are others, these serve to demonstrate the tendency of the Masoretic tradition. As valuable as the MT is, it should be viewed as the topmost strata of the interpretive layers of the Hebrew Bible. The careful interpreter of messianic prophecy should be aware of text-critical issues because these predictions may be buried in the Hebrew Bible's critical apparatus rather than in the MT itself. Nevertheless, there is much in the MT that reveals the Messiah. A careful, innerbiblical examination of the Scriptures themselves will reveal that the Hebrew Bible reads itself in a messianic way (see the article in this *Handbook* by Seth Postell titled, "The Old Testament in the Old Testament").

---

1. This article is adapted from a chapter in Michael Rydelnik, *The Messianic Hope: Is the Hebrew Bible Really Messianic?* NAC Studies in Bible and Theology, ed. E. Ray Clendenen (Nashville: B&H Publishers, 2010), 34–46. Used with permission.
2. The original manuscripts of the Bible no longer exist, but many copies of the biblical books remain, having been produced from ancient times until today. Textual criticism is used to discover which readings are original.
3. J. H. Sailhamer, *Introduction to Old Testament Theology* (Grand Rapids: Zondervan, 1995), 224.
4. E. Tov, *Textual Criticism of the Hebrew Bible* (Minneapolis: Fortress, 1992), 11.
5. Ibid. "𝔐" is the *Biblia Hebraica Stuttgartensia* symbol for the MT.
6. Sailhamer, *Introduction to Old Testament Theology*, 224.
7. E. Wurthwein, *The Text of the Old Testament*, trans. E. F. Rhodes (Grand Rapids: Eerdmans, 1979), 26.
8. Ibid.
9. Ibid., 27.
10. For a more in-depth discussion of rabbinic influence, see Sailhamer, *Introduction to Old Testament Theology*, 204–5, 218–21.
11. Tov, *Textual Criticism of the Hebrew Bible*, 136–37.
12. Sailhamer, *Introduction to Old Testament Theology*, 205.
13. Ibid. See the chapter, "The Old Testament in the New."
14. This was maintained by medieval disputants with Judaism, such as P. Christiani and R. Martini. For a more thorough historical discussion of their claims, see J. Cohen, *The Friars and the Jews* (Ithaca and London: Cornell, 1982), 148–52.
15. Sailhamer (*Introduction to Old Testament Theology*, 204–05, 220–21) discusses a number of these passages, and I am indebted to him for pointing me in this direction. I will include some of the passages he cites, as well as several others.
16. These two forms are also reflected in Septuagintal variants, with codex Alexandrinus (A) reading "Moses" and codex Vaticanus (B) reading "Manasseh" demonstrating that this variant is extremely ancient.
17. Tov, *Textual Criticism of the Hebrew Bible*, 57.
18. So, according to Rabbi Tanchum, this should be viewed as a Ketib Qere, "Moses" being written and "Manasseh" being read.
19. C. F. Keil and F. Delitzsch, "Joshua, Judges, Ruth," in *Commentary on the Old Testament in Ten Volumes*, trans. J. Martin (repr., Grand Rapids: Eerdmans, 1980), 2:438.
20. Sailhamer, *Introduction to Old Testament Theology*, 220.
21. Another example of embedded rabbinic theology in the MT is Hos 14:3 (Eng. 14:2), which adjusts the place of the word division between the two last words. This shift changes the meaning of the words from offering praise as "the fruit of our lips" to offering "our lips as bulls." The slight change makes a world of difference. In the LXX, praise is the result of being forgiven for sin. In the MT, prayers become a substitution for animal sacrifice, an important element in the restructuring of Judaism at Yavneh after the destruction of the temple in AD 70 (cf. *Avot of Rabbi Nathan*, 4). Hosea 14:3 is also cited in the daily prayer book as justification for the end of sacrifice as follows: "But thou hast said, that the prayers of our lips shall be accepted as the offering of steers." A. Th. Philips, *Daily Prayers with English Translation*, rev. ed. (New York: Hebrew Publishing, n.d.), 40–41.
22. Author's translation.

23. This is expressed well by M. Pickup, who cites several commentators holding to David or Davidic kingship as the future king envisioned here, including R. K. Harrison, *Numbers*, Wycliffe Exegetical Commentary (Chicago: Moody, 1990), 323; R. Allen, "The Theology of the Balaam Oracles," in *Tradition and Testament*, ed. J. Feinberg and P. Feinberg (Chicago: Moody, 1981), 118; R. D. Cole, *Numbers*, New American Commentary (Nashville: Broadman & Holman, 2000), 420. Pickup writes: "The word 'king' in Num 24:7 (cf. v. 17) probably refers to the *state* of kingship in Israel's future history, yet David seems to be the primary referent due to his subjugation of Moab, Edom, and Amalek" (M. Pickup, "New Testament Interpretation of the Old Testament: The Theological Rationale of Midrashic Exegesis," *Journal of the Evangelical Theological Society* 51 [2008]: 375–76).

24. The HCSB translates the Hebrew *b'acharit hayyamim* as "in the future," but the literal "in the end of days" is preferable.

25. T. R. Ashley, *The Book of Numbers*, New International Commentary on the Old Testament (Grand Rapids: Eerdmans, 1993), 491.

26. W. F. Albright, *Yahweh and the Gods of Canaan* (Garden City, NY: Doubleday, 1968), 16. See also Sailhamer, *Introduction to Old Testament Theology*, 220–21.

27. Ibid., 221.

28. GKC §150.2 states, "As a rule, however, the simple question is introduced by *He interrogative*" (*Gesenius' Hebrew Grammar*, 2nd ed. Edited by E. Kautzsch, translated by A. E. Cowley. Oxford, 1910). This does not include factual or Wh- questions (Who? What? Why? etc.), for which there are other particles or interrogative pronouns. See C. H. J. van der Merwe, J. A. Naudé, and J. H. Kroeze, *A Biblical Hebrew Reference Grammar* (Sheffield: Sheffield Academic Press, 1999), §43.

29. Note that 72:17 has a similar difficulty between the MT and the LXX. The MT reads "may his name sprout forth before the sun shines," while the LXX reads, "his name shall remain continually before the sun." See R. E. Murphy, *A Study of Psalm 72* (Washington, DC: The Catholic University of America, 1948), 42–43.

30. The MT reads a third-person plural qal imperfect of *yr'*, "fear," with a second-person masculine singular accusative pronoun. The LXX reading reflects a third-person singular hiphil imperfect/jussive of *'rkh*, "continue."

31. C. C. Broyles notes this shift in pronouns and the odd verb choice in the MT reading, concluding "The LXX probably points us to the original." See "The Redeeming King: Psalm 72's Contribution to the Messianic Ideal," in *Eschatology, Messianism, and the Dead Sea Scrolls*, ed. C. A. Evans and P. W. Flint (Grand Rapids: Eerdmans, 1997), 27n11.

32. See M. E. Tate, *Psalms 51–100*, WBC 20 (Dallas: Word, 1990), 220. Tate further explains that the MT reading "changes the focus of the psalm" from "the king and his subjects and other kings" to the people and God. Yet the LXX reading "fits easily into the context of the psalm."

33. C. C. Broyles notes this shift in pronouns and the odd verb choice in the MT reading, concluding "The LXX probably points us to the original." See "The Redeeming King: Psalm 72's Contribution to the Messianic Ideal," in *Eschatology, Messianism, and the Dead Sea Scrolls*, ed. C. A. Evans and P. W. Flint (Grand Rapids: Eerdmans, 1997), 27n11.

34. Murphy, *A Study of Psalm 72*, 21.

35. K. Heim, "The Perfect King of Psalm 72: An Intertextual Enquiry," in *The Lord's Anointed: Interpretation of Old Testament Messianic Texts*, ed. P. E. Satterthwaite, R. S. Hess and G. J. Wenham (Grand Rapids: Baker, 1995), 241.

36. Ibid.

37. Duhm is cited by Heim, "The Perfect King of Psalm 72," 239.

38. F. Delitzsch, "Isaiah," in *Commentary on the Old Testament in Ten Volumes*, trans. J. Martin (repr., Grand Rapids: Eerdmans, 1980), 7:249. Delitzsch addresses this rendering but does not affirm it.

39. Sailhamer, *Introduction to Old Testament Theology*, 221.

40. Delitzsch, "Isaiah," 249–50.

41. Ibid., 249.

42. Ibid., 250.

43. T. Muraoka, *A Greek-English Lexicon of the Septuagint* (Leuven: Peeters, 2009), 507.

44. It is uncertain whether the verb rendered by the LXX was *k'r* or kur, both of which occur in a few Masoretic mss. R. L. Harris took it from *kur*, giving the meaning as "bore, dig, hew (meaning dubious)." He explains that it "occurs only in Ps 22:16 [H 17]," and "may be an hapax *kā'ar*. The meaning 'dig, wound, pierce' would derive from the context and LXX" (R. L. Harris, "*kur*," *Theological Wordbook of the Old Testament*, ed. R. Laird Harris, Gleason L. Archer, Jr., Bruce K. Waltke [Chicago: Moody, 1980], 435).

45. The MT reading is also supported by the editors of the NET Bible. Although they recognize that the reading is "grammatically awkward" and characterized by "broken syntax," their apparent commitment to the MT above all,

motivates them to retain the Masoretic reading and to argue that "it is better not to interpret this particular verse as referring to Jesus' crucifixion in a specific or direct way." *The NET Bible* (Richardson, TX: Biblical Studies Press, 1997), 924n20.

46. For a thorough analysis of the text-critical problem and a compelling argument for the LXX reading, see C. R. Gren, "Piercing the Ambiguities of Psalm 22:16 and the Messiah's Mission," *Journal of the Evangelical Theological Society* 48 (2005): 284–99.

47. P. C. Craigie, *Psalms 1–50*, WBC (Waco, TX: Word, 1983), 196.

48. P. Flint, "Biblical Scrolls from Nah Hever and 'Wadi Seiyal': Introduction," in *Miscellaneous Texts from the Judaean Desert,* ed. J. Charlesworth, N. Cohen, H. Cotton, and E. Eshel, DJD 38 (Oxford: Clarendon, 2000), 143.

49. M. Abegg Jr., P. Flint, E. Ulrich, *The Dead Sea Scrolls Bible* (New York: Harper Collins, 1999), 519.

50. Gren, "Piercing the Ambiguities of Psalm 22:16 and the Messiah's Mission," 297.

Interpretive Approaches to Messianic Prophecy[1]

MICHAEL A. RYDELNIK

A vast amount of literature exists on messianic prophecy. Since New Testament times, those who have believed that Jesus is the Messiah have affirmed that He fulfilled the messianic expectations of the Hebrew Scriptures in some way. As a result, much has been written on messianic prophecy through the centuries. The purpose of this article is to survey the scholarly literature written in the modern period on messianic prophecy. Then this chapter will summarize the various approaches to interpreting messianic prophecy and fulfillment.

THE SURVEY OF LITERATURE

From the NT period until the modern period, the church spoke unanimously that in some way Jesus of Nazareth fulfilled OT messianic prophecies. However, a shift began to occur in the modern period. The traditional view was first challenged by Anthony Collins in his *Discourse of the Grounds and Reasons of the Christian Religion* (1724) and then in his *The Scheme of Literal Prophecy Considered*.[2] Both works deal with the use of messianic proof texts from the OT. Collins argued that the literal meaning of the texts could not support the messianic interpretations given them by the NT. In a sense, Collins's approach stripped classical apologetics of one of its major features, namely, the argument from prophecy. Moreover, Collins's view that the OT should only be understood to refer to historical figures "became the dominant view not only in the universities but also in the Protestant Christian Church, right across the theological spectrum."[3]

As a rebuttal to the criticisms that Collins raised, Thomas Sherlock wrote *The*

Use and Intent of Prophecy (1732). Sherlock argued for a dual fulfillment of prophecy. First, there was the original meaning, which was determined from the text, context, and historical circumstances. Second, there was a later or fuller meaning, which was the typical or spiritual understanding, upholding a broader messianic interpretation.[4] Although this approach became and remains popular, as Kaiser states, it forfeited "most of the predictive value of the anticipations of the Messiah in their Old Testament context."[5]

By the end of the 18th century, with the emergence of the two giants of the critical approach to the OT, J. G. von Herder (1744–1803) and J. G. Eichhorn (1752–1827), the shift away from any concept of messianic predictions became pronounced. Herder maintained that it was a mistake to believe that the Hebrew prophets foretold the distant future. Eichhorn was even more decisive in his rejection of all messianic predictions. He saw this is as a dogmatic and theological imposition on the biblical text. Eichhorn asserted that the meaning of the text could only be discerned from the time and circumstances of the biblical authors. This changed the focus of interpretation away from the study of the text to the study of the individual prophets and their historical circumstances. As a result, Eichhorn rejected the approach that interpreted the prophetic text as revealing a long series of messianic predictions. In 1793, he boasted, "The last three decades have erased the Messiah from the Old Testament."[6] Herder's and Eichhorn's works caused the traditional understanding of messianic prophecy—as a series of predictions fulfilled at a remote later period by a particular individual—to be almost entirely repudiated.

In an attempt to reaffirm the messianic predictions and arrest the critical attacks on predictive prophecy, E. W. von Hengstenberg produced his massive *Christology of the Old Testament and Commentary on the Messianic Predictions* (1835).[7] Hengstenberg's interpretation allowed the NT to be the final arbiter of the OT prophecies. This was essentially a confessional/dogmatic approach which paid scant attention to the historical setting or context of the given messianic predictions. It was decidedly antirationalist in tone and content. Despite the impressive work of Hengstenberg, it did not put an end to the critical approach to messianic prophecy.

In 1879, Paton J. Gloag published *Messianic Prophecies*, which was also a rejection of the rationalist approach.[8] At the outset, he "proposed to direct attention to Jesus as the Christ or the Messiah of ancient prophecy."[9] In general, this work was an attack on the critical and antisupernatural approaches to prophecy taking hold in the 19th century. He affirmed the approach of Hengstenberg, stating, "This work must always occupy a high position in theology, as being perhaps the most complete investigation of the subject."[10] Gloag takes an evidentialist approach and makes a polemical argument for supernatural, predictive messianic prophecy.

From 1880 through 1884, Alfred Edersheim delivered the Warburton Lectures in the chapel of Lincoln's Inn. These lectures were published as *Prophecy and History in Relation to the Messiah* (1901, reprinted 1955 and 1980).[11] Following the method of Hengstenberg, Edersheim asserts, "To say that Jesus is the Christ means that He is the Messiah promised and predicted in the Old Testament."[12] In addition to contending for the messianic nature of the OT, Edersheim also attempted to show the weaknesses of the rationalistic approaches to prophecy and to the OT as a whole.

In 1900, G. S. Goodspeed published *Israel's Messianic Hope to the Time of Jesus*, which affirmed so broad a view of messianic prophecy that it was hardly recognizable compared to the traditional view.[13] Goodspeed accepted the extreme literary and historical criticism of Wellhausen, Graf, and Keunen and as a result rejected any confidence in a supernaturally inspired text. He adopted "the historical method" of investigation.[14] Hence, his study of messianic prophecy shifted away from examining the prophecies of the person and work of the future redeemer of Israel to studying the progress of moral insight in the history of Israel. The messianic hope was no longer viewed as the outcome of various predictions of a future person but the logical outcome of Israel's history.[15] Jesus was the natural fulfillment of Israel's history, not the supernatural fulfillment of Israelite prophecy.

Several writers sought to bridge the gap between the historical and the confessional/dogmatic approaches to messianic prophecy. They did so by taking a developmental view of prophecy. First, Edward Riehm published *Messianic Prophecy: Its Origin, Historical Growth, and Relation to New Testament Fulfillment* (1884 and revised in 1891).[16] Riehm argued that the OT must be understood in light of the prophet's immediate knowledge, which did not include direct prophecies of the Messiah. However, all the prophets did speak of the saving purpose of God that found its ultimate fulfillment in Christ. This fulfillment transcended their previous conception.[17] Thus, the prophets had an immediate fulfillment in view, whereas God's view included an ultimate fulfillment in the Messiah.

A second scholar, Franz Delitzsch, published *Messianic Prophecies in Historical Succession* (1891).[18] This book affirmed that the prophets' words only had a single sense and that there were no dual prophecies. He also argued that the prophecies should be understood according to their historical and literary context, but he did allow for the supernatural element of prophecy.[19] He maintained that the prophecies pertained to redemption, and as such they did not speak clearly to messianic fulfillment. However, they did indeed point to the Messiah who would ultimately fulfill them by providing redemption. He states:

> Since the idea of the God-man is first announced in single rays of light, the Mediator of salvation, in general, does not yet stand in the centre of Old Testament faith, but the completion of the kingdom of God appears mostly as the work of the God of salvation Himself with the recession of human mediation. But we also classify these prophecies under the general conception of Messianic, because indeed in the history of fulfillment it is God in Christ who from Israel works out and secures for mankind the highest spiritual blessings. . . . Therefore, from a historical point of view, we regard the prophecies concerning the ultimate salvation, which are even silent concerning the Messiah, as Christological.[20]

Walter Kaiser's assessment is correct when he writes of Delitzsch's developmental view: "This allowed Delitzsch to have the Old Testament say *less* than its fulfillment in Jesus required, but to provide for the Old Testament to say *more* when the original prophecy was filled out by later doctrine and Christian experience."[21] Nevertheless, Delitzsch did allow for specific predictions about the coming Redeemer, specifically fulfilled by Jesus. He says, "These passages of Scripture are, indeed, like isolated points without connecting lines."[22] Additionally, he describes the Christological development of the OT messianic predictions as "rays of light proceeding from single points of light."[23] Thus, Delitzsch viewed messianic fulfillment as the outcome of the progress of redemption while allowing for individual messianic predictions.

Charles A. Briggs was a third OT scholar to adopt a developmental view. In his work, *Messianic Prophecy: The Prediction of the Fulfillment of Redemption through the Messiah* (1896), Briggs argues for a single sense of prophetic writings and that they pertain to the messianic ideal.[24] However, he believed that history provided foreshadowings of the coming Messiah. Here is his explanation of prophecy and fulfillment:

> History constantly approximates to the Messianic ideal. It seems to fulfil the prediction as it advances, and to give ground for the theory of a double sense or a progressive fulfillment. But this is only the preparation of history for the real fulfillment which awaits it at the end of the course in the Messiah of history, the suffering, reigning, and glorified Redeemer.[25]

Thus, according to Briggs, the apparent historical fulfillments of prophecy were merely historical preparation for their ultimate and actual fulfillment in the promised Messiah.

In 1905, Willis J. Beecher published *The Prophets and the Promise*, which argued for a view of prophecy that distinguished between *promise* and *prediction*.[26] In his view, the prophets' message pertained to the promise made to Abraham that would ultimately culminate in the Messiah. Yet Beecher did not isolate individual predictions. He affirmed that the promise had but one meaning which included a progression of historical fulfillments, culminating in the Messiah. Beecher argued for an eternally operative promise that must necessarily imply a cumulative fulfillment. Hence, throughout history God fulfilled His promise through a long line of fulfillments that could vary in different ages and that found their ultimate fulfillment in Jesus.

Beecher maintained that "the idea of a long line of fulfillment is not a hypothesis offered for the solution of difficulties, but a part of the primary conception of a promise that is for eternity."[27] Thus, Beecher asserted that the promise had but one meaning. However, that single meaning included a series of mini-fulfillments culminating in the ultimate fulfillment in the Messiah.

The developmental views of Riehm, Delitzsch, Briggs, and Beecher found followers among some of the more conservative biblical interpreters. Nevertheless, for the most part this approach failed to resolve the tension of prophecy and fulfillment as it pertains to the Messiah.

Still the critical, historical view prevailed. It did allow for some messianic hope, but it was a far cry from the traditional understanding of prediction and fulfillment. For example, W. Robertson Smith in *The Prophets of Israel and Their Place in History* (1882) and A. F. Kirkpatrick in *The Doctrine of the Prophets* (1901) reduced the messianic hope to a vague hope in the love of God and an assurance of the future.[28] Essentially, Jesus was viewed as the fulfillment of the prophets' moral goal but not of their predictions.

In 1908, W. O. E. Oesterley wrote *The Evolution of the Messianic Idea: A Study in Comparative Religion*, which presented a new way of looking at the messianic idea.[29] Oesterley argued that the OT borrowed from ancient Near Eastern pagan literature and even preserved fragments of this literature in the biblical text. This called for the coming of a future divine savior figure to appear as a herald of the kingdom of God. H. Gressmann developed much the same view in his work *Der Messias* (1929).[30]

B. B. Warfield challenged Oesterley's evolutionary approach in 1916, publishing "The Divine Messiah of the Old Testament."[31] In this extended article he argued for an OT expectation of a Messiah who would be God. Citing numerous texts to support his view, Warfield bluntly affirmed direct messianic prediction. He agreed with Hengstenberg's approach, calling him "one of the most searching expounders of the Scriptures that God has as yet given His church."[32] He disputed the idea that the OT prophets borrowed from pagan literature, stating the OT savior ideal bore no relationship to ancient Near Eastern pagan literature.[33]

Despite Warfield's rejection of the idea that Israel's prophets borrowed from pagan literature, the view continued to gain adherents among critical scholars for the decades that followed. The rise of several Scandinavian scholars who held to a divine kingship view derived from pagan sources led to new discussions of messianic expectation.

Ivan Engnell in his *Studies of Divine Kingship in the Near East* (1943) argued that Israel's prophets borrowed a divine-royal formula from pagan mythology.[34] He studied ancient Egyptian, Sumerian, Akkadian, Hittite, and Canaanite literature, in which the reigning king was considered divine, functioning as a god on earth. Israel borrowed such ideas, developed them into sacral kingship (the king as priest), and ultimately developed an eschatological kingship idea.

Helmer Ringgren held a similar view in his *The Messiah in the Old Testament* (1956).[35] He maintained that Pss 2 and 110 fit the divine kingship model, concluding that "this picture of Israelite kingship agrees in an astonishing way with ancient Mesopotamian kingship ideology. The Babylonian and Assyrian king, too, is a son of a god, he is the god's messenger and rules with divine authority."[36] Ringgren asserted that there was a gradual evolution from king to Messiah but that it was impossible to date exactly when the transition took place. Thus, he states, "the divine kingship of ancient Israel is part of the preparations that were necessary for the realization of God's plan of salvation."[37] In essence, Ringgren's view is that there was a natural evolution from the ancient Near Eastern pagan divine king to the plan of salvation that included the belief in Christ as the Messiah.

Aage Bentzen held a similar view in *King and Messiah* (1955).[38] Bentzen's position was that just as ancient Mesopotamians viewed their king as the son of god by adoption, so ancient Israelites came to regard their kings in the same way. He states that "the king of Israel has been invested with the same divine qualities as elsewhere in the ancient East."[39] In his view, the king of Israel was not an eschatological figure but the anointed messenger of God who guaranteed Israel's happiness through the New Year ritual. After the fall of the two Israelite kingdoms, Bentzen asserted, kingship took on an eschatological interpretation. The king was no longer present—he was the Coming King.[40] Thus, the king messiah of Ps 2, for example, is not to be considered the eschatological Messiah. Rather he was regarded as the king of Israel who served as a prefiguration (a type) of the eschatological Messiah.[41]

Sigmund Mowinckel developed this theme in his work entitled *He That Cometh* (1959).[42] He argued that Israel borrowed a divine kingship concept from pagan Canaanite neighbors. Then Israel expressed the divine kingship motif through enthronement festivals and rituals. The king was extolled in the Psalms as superhuman and divine, but this never became a historical reality. Eventually, the divine king of ancient Israel became the ideal for the future, eschatological, messianic king.

These Scandinavian scholars, all operating with the presupposition of critical views of the Bible, failed to recognize that the prophets of Israel would have roundly condemned any ascription of deity to the king. Even so, as Van Groningen says, "Most twentieth-century OT scholars who have paid attention to the messianic concept have followed the divine-royal formula."[43]

European scholar, Joachim Becker influenced much of contemporary scholarship's view of the Messiah and messianic hope with his publication of *Messianic Expectation in the Old Testament* (1977).[44] His argument was that the figure of a savior of the Davidic house, which is essential to messianism, is indiscernible until the second century BC.[45] Thus, the OT "messianic prophecies cannot be considered visionary predictions of a New Testament fulfillment."[46] He asserted that the NT's use of fulfillment should be understood as a first-century Jewish hermeneutic known as "pesher."[47] Pesher is an arbitrary reading of the text that identifies fulfillment with current events. The Christ event, according to Becker, was the fulfillment of sacral history, not OT prophecy.[48]

Richard Longenecker argued for a view similar to Becker in his *Biblical Exegesis in the Apostolic Period* (1975), although without adopting Becker's critical approach to Scripture.[49] Longenecker maintained that the NT used "midrash" or "pesher" to identify Jesus as the promised Messiah. According to him, it was valid for Jesus and the apostles to use this method, but not for modern interpreters.[50] The latter are to interpret the OT only according to historico-grammatical exegesis.[51]

The "midrash" or "pesher" argument for messianic fulfillment was also advocated by Donald Juel, in his book *Messianic Exegesis* (1988).[52] According to Juel, the OT had no clear messianic hope. However, by NT times, the Messiah was conceived as an eschatological king. Since Jesus was presented as a crucified and risen Messiah, the apostles had to use "creative exegesis" to substantiate His messianic claim.[53]

While the "midrash" or "pesher" approach may possibly fit first-century Jewish hermeneutics, it does not genuinely trace the growth of the messianic hope in the OT. R. E. Clements, in an article entitled "The Messianic Hope in the OT" (1989), has proposed "relecture" (reading an earlier saying or prophecy in a new way) as a method for understanding messianic prophecy and fulfillment.[54] According to Clements, some biblical texts were considered by later editors to be messianic, and thus they reread them as messianic expectations. In his words, "new wine was being poured into old bottles."[55] Clements's method was applied by his student, Paul D. Wegner, in his *An Examination of Kingship and Messianic Expectation in Isaiah 1–35* (1992). However, by Clements's own admission, in the relecture method "some of the important features of the older belief in a 'dual meaning' in certain prophecies has come to re-assert itself."[56] While the method does not adhere to the presuppositions of Thomas Sherlock, much of the outcome is the same.

Attempting to restore the traditional view, J. Barton Payne in his *Encyclopedia of Biblical Prophecy* (1973) maintained the single sense of Scripture as well as the predictive nature of prophecy.[57] He asserted that the OT has a variety of ways in which it predicts the Messiah, from direct prediction to type. Still he cited 103 direct messianic prophecies,[58] leading Waltke to classify Payne with Hengstenberg as "non-critical." According to Waltke, "non-critical scholars by their prooftexting actually discredit the claims of Jesus in the eyes of literary and historical critics."[59]

Along the same lines as Payne, Gerard Van Groningen wrote *Messianic Revelation in the Old Testament* (1990). This work is massive, thoroughly evangelical, and reflective of the state of OT studies up to the time it was written. Van Groningen allows for a dual meaning in some cases, such as Ps 16, where he alleges that the divine author had a deeper meaning than the human author's.[60] Van Groningen is eclectic in his understanding of messianic prophecy, affirming direct fulfillment, dual fulfillment, and typological fulfillment.

Chris Wright in his *Knowing Jesus through the Old Testament* (1992) views the OT more as a book of promise than prediction.[61] In his view, unlike prediction, promises can be fulfilled in ways that people alive at the time of the promise may never have imagined. Thus, the promises of the OT have a "transformable quality" that allows them to be fulfilled in ways different from those in which they were originally understood.[62]

In 1993, James E. Smith published *What the Bible Teaches about the Promised Messiah*, which takes the old prooftexting method and presents little in the way of new ideas or approaches. It is essentially a chronological look at 73 messianic prophecies, with little regard for historical or literary context.

Walter C. Kaiser Jr. in his *The Messiah in the Old Testament* (1995) presents a reworking of Beecher's *The Prophets and the Promise*. Arguing for the single meaning of Scripture, Kaiser maintained that the biblical prophecies had an epigenetic meaning.[63] Kaiser applied this biological concept to prophetic literature:

> The fixed core of ideas connected with the promise-plan of God and the representative of that promise remained constant. But as time went on, the content of that given word of blessing, promise, or judgment grew in accordance with seed thoughts that were contained within its earliest statements, much as a seed is uniquely related to the plant that it will become if it has life at all.[64]

Thus, according to Kaiser, the promise had a single meaning that could find expression in multiple lesser fulfillments, ultimately culminating in the Messiah.[65] This approach, which is basically a form of progressive fulfillment, was significantly influenced by the previous work of Beecher.

In 1997 Antti Laato, Professor at the Abo Academy in Turku, Finland, published *A Star is Rising: The Historical Development of the Old Testament Royal Ideology and the Rise of the Jewish Messianic Expectations*.[66] His stated purpose was "to examine how certain historical circumstances have provided the impulse for the birth and the development of the Old Testament royal ideology and how this ideology generated different messianic expectations in Judaism(s) of late antiquity."[67] Laato takes a historical-redactional approach, spending more time using the Bible to recreate the history of Israel. Nevertheless, he maintains that messianic ideology arose in the tenth century BC with the Davidic covenant (2Sm 7) rather than as a result of the Babylonian exile or the disillusionment with the Hasmonean dynasty in the intertestamental period.[68] Taking a maximalist approach, Laato sees the prophets progressively developing the royal messianic ideal Nathan gave to David. While affirming messianic hope, Laato's historical-rather-than-textual approach weakened his book. In using this historical method, Laato sees each prophet speaking independently of each other. A literary approach would recognize that these are works that interact with and build upon each other. Moreover, in the final canonical redaction, there are literary glosses to link messianic passages with those that came before and those that follow.

In recent years, John Sailhamer proposed understanding the OT as a holistic book with one overriding purpose, namely, to reveal the hope of the coming Messiah. He affirms direct messianic prediction but with a fresh approach, eschewing the old prooftexting methods. His view is found in his *Introduction to Old Testament Theology* (1995), a work that discusses messianic prophecy but is not solely about that subject.[69] Using a compositional/canonical approach to the OT,[70] Sailhamer's basic premise is that study of the text of Scripture itself (and not the historical events behind it), at both the compositional and canonical levels, will yield a messianic meaning.[71]

Sailhamer's understanding of messianic prophecy has two significant elements. First, Sailhamer asserts that the Masoretic Text should be viewed *not* as the original Hebrew text but as its final stage.[72] As such, the Masoretic Text is a consolidation of the Hebrew text and reflects postbiblical interpretation. In a variety of places, the Masoretic Text reveals a historical interpretation of texts that are messianic in other ancient versions.[73] Hence, the first task of the interpreter of the Hebrew Bible, particularly in messianic passages, is to establish the text through textual criticism.

Second, Sailhamer builds on the well-established fact that the medieval Jewish "peshat" (simple) interpretations of the text were designed as an answer to the Christian messianic interpretation of the Tanakh. Through the rise and influence of Christian Hebraism,[74] Jewish nonmessianic interpretations slipped into the Protestant understanding of the OT. As a result, Protestant interpretation either denied messianic prophecy altogether or adopted alternative interpretations, such as dual, typological, and progressive fulfillment.[75]

Sailhamer concludes his discussion of messianic prophecy by suggesting that the Tanakh does indeed point directly to the Messiah. He contends that the NT's use of the Old does reflect the OT author's intent. He states:

> We strongly urge the consideration of a return to the notion that the literal meaning of the Old Testament may, in fact, be linked to the messianic hope of the pre-Christian, Israelite prophets. By paying careful attention to the compositional strategies of the biblical books themselves, we believe in them can be found many essential clues to the meaning intended by their authors—clues that point beyond their immediate historical referent to a future, messianic age. By looking at the works of the scriptural authors, rather than at the events that lie behind their accounts of them, we can find appropriate textual clues to the meaning of these biblical books. Those clues, we also suggest, point to an essentially messianic and eschatological focus of the biblical texts.[76]

Sailhamer summarized his view of messianic prophecy in his article "The Messiah and the Hebrew Bible." There he argued that the shape of the Hebrew Bible and its compositional strategies were "motivated primarily by a hope in the soon coming of the promised Messiah."[77] Thus Sailhamer makes the case that "the OT does not only *predict* the coming of a Messiah. It also *describes* and *identifies* that Messiah." Furthermore, the NT writers accepted the OT's preinterpretation and "were in fundamental agreement with its interpretation."[78]

Shortly after the publication of Sailhamer's *Introduction to Old Testament Theology*, William Horbury offered a similar understanding of messianic hope in his *Jewish Messianism and the Cult of Christ*.[79] He maintained that the messianic hope of the preexilic prophets was clarified in the editing and collecting of the OT books, thus explaining the presence of the messianic idea in the intertestamental period, the NT, and in the rabbinic writings. Responding to much of contemporary critical scholarship on messianism, which argues that the messianic idea did not develop until the intertestamental period,[80] Horbury states:

> Messianism grew up in Old Testament times; the Old Testament books, especially in their edited and collected form, offered what were understood in the post-exilic age and later as a series of messianic prophecies; and this series formed the heart of a coherent set of expectations, which profoundly influenced ancient Judaism and early Christianity.[81]

Old Testament scholarship is now divided: The majority takes a more historical approach to the OT, resulting in a minimalist view of the Messiah in the Hebrew Bible. The minority embraces a more holistic reading of the OT in its final form, resulting in an affirmation that messianism is present in the Hebrew Scriptures. As a reflection of this divide, a group of OT scholars released a collection of essays on the interpretation of OT messianic texts, *The Lord's Anointed* (1995).[82] This compendium of interpretations of messianic texts reflects the varied perspectives of the different authors. A few fully embrace messianic prediction in the OT, while most see little messianic expectation there. This book is a reflection of where OT scholarship on messianic prophecy stands at the present time, with a minority of scholars maintaining a messianic hope but the majority taking minimalist, nonmessianic interpretation of the Hebrew Bible.[83]

Kaiser finds the book's inconsistency and frequently minimalist messianic interpretations to be "disturbing." Although recognizing that a number of the chapters present a strong emphasis on messianic prediction, still Kaiser objects that "a number of the essays take a much too cautious and minimalistic approach to the question as to whether the messiah was predicted in the portion they wrote on or not. This muting of the messianic presence in the OT began with Anthony Collins' two volumes published in 1724 and 1727 and has continued to the present moment."[84]

THE SUMMARY OF POSITIONS

In surveying all these works on messianic prophecy, it is evident that they present a maze of approaches to the OT and messianic hope. In order to clarify the differing interpretations just enumerated, it is helpful to summarize them systematically. So, what follows is a summary of the basic approaches.

Figure 1

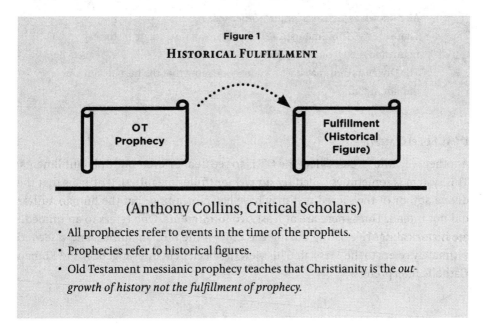

HISTORICAL FULFILLMENT

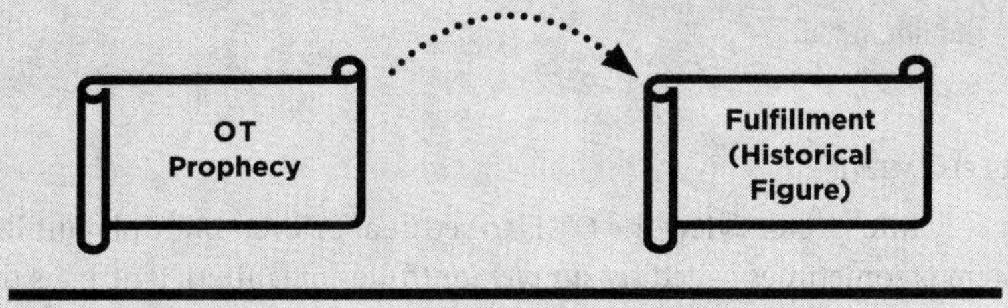

(Anthony Collins, Critical Scholars)

- All prophecies refer to events in the time of the prophets.
- Prophecies refer to historical figures.
- Old Testament messianic prophecy teaches that Christianity is the *outgrowth of history not the fulfillment of prophecy.*

HISTORICAL FULFILLMENT

One of the ways of dealing with the OT and the messianic hope is to deny that the Tanakh has any such hope. This approach understands the Scriptures to be referring to events in the time of the writers. Therefore, it refers all the biblical author's words to historical figures. For example, in Psalms, passages that interpreters have traditionally understood as messianic are thought to refer to David or to other Davidic kings. This view is generally held by those who approach the Scriptures from a critical viewpoint, as well as by many medieval and modern Jewish interpreters. Liberal Christian interpreters who adopt this view see Christianity not as a fulfillment of prophecy but as the natural outgrowth of history.

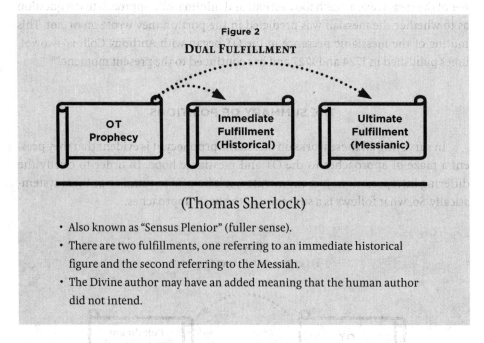

Figure 2

DUAL FULFILLMENT

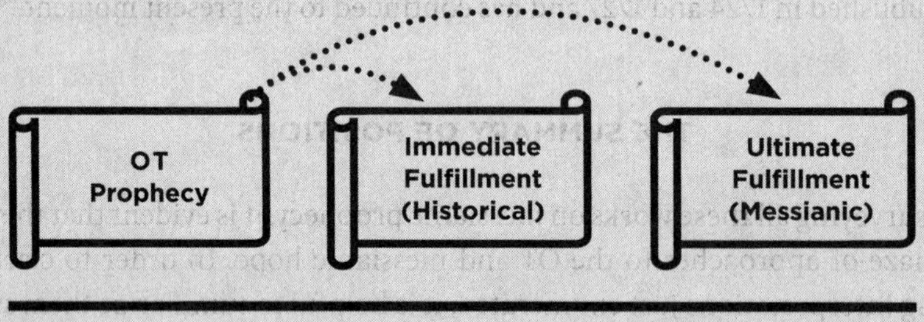

(Thomas Sherlock)

- Also known as "Sensus Plenior" (fuller sense).
- There are two fulfillments, one referring to an immediate historical figure and the second referring to the Messiah.
- The Divine author may have an added meaning that the human author did not intend.

DUAL FULFILLMENT

Another way interpreters view the OT is to see dual or even multiple fulfillments. This system is sometimes called *sensus plenior* (fuller meaning). It affirms that the divine author of the sacred text may have had a meaning that the human author did not intend. Thus, there are at least two fulfillments. One refers to an immediate historical figure existing during the time of the human author, and a second ultimately refers to the Messiah. This view has been held by evangelical and Roman Catholic interpreters.

Figure 3

Typical Fulfillment

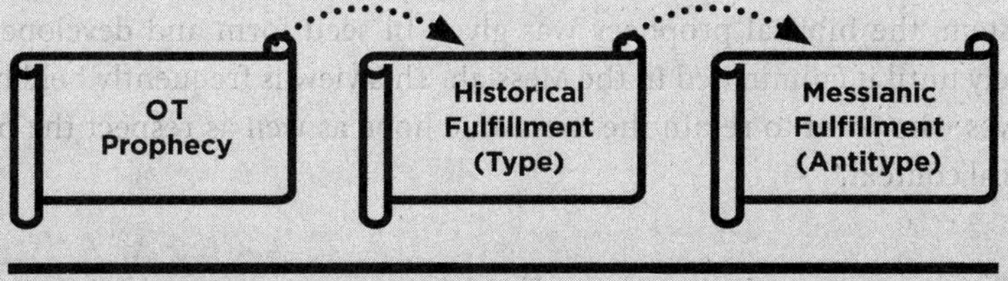

(Aage Bentzen)

- The literal meaning refers to a historical figure.
- The historical figure is a type of the Messiah (or something related to his life).
- The type/antitype is the messianic sense of the Hebrew Bible seen in the New Testament.

Typical Fulfillment

Some interpreters understand OT messianic fulfillment by means of types. In this approach, the literal sense of a given OT passage is taken to refer to a historical person. This person then becomes a type for the future Messiah who is the antitype. For example, in the Psalms, it is commonly asserted that David or a Davidic descendant was the literal subject. However, he formed a type of the future son of David, the Messiah. This view is also commonly held by those who want to respect the historical context of a passage and do justice to the NT contention that Jesus fulfilled OT prophecies.

Figure 4

Progressive (Epigenetic) Fulfillment

(Willis Beecher, Walter Kaiser)

- There is but one, single meaning of the passage and it is the meaning the author intended.
- The prophecy is given in seed form and grows progressively, with various historical figures, into the ultimate intended Messianic fulfillment.

Progressive (Epigenetic) Fulfillment

An alternative approach to the question of OT messianic fulfillment views the prophecies as predictions that grow to their ultimate fulfillment. According to this system, the biblical prophecy was given in seed form and developed progressively until it culminated in the Messiah. This view is frequently held by conservatives who want to retain the messianic hope as well as respect the biblical historical context.

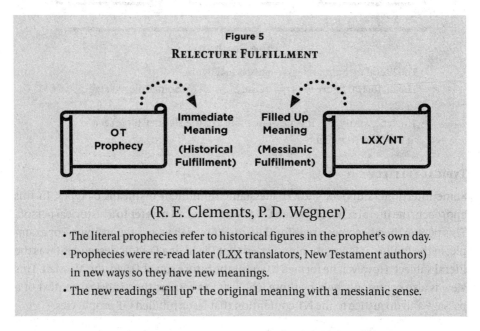

Figure 5

Relecture Fulfillment

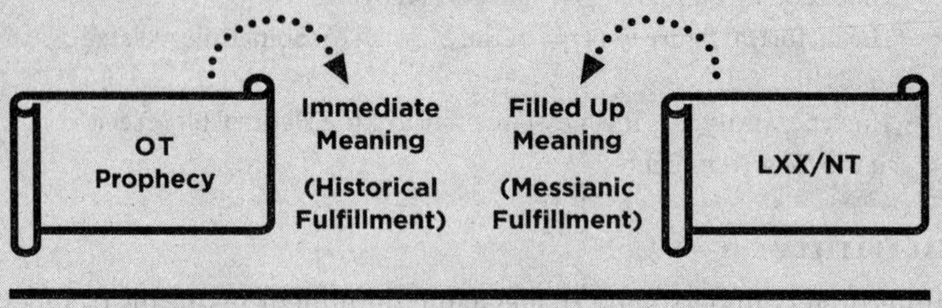

(R. E. Clements, P. D. Wegner)

- The literal prophecies refer to historical figures in the prophet's own day.
- Prophecies were re-read later (LXX translators, New Testament authors) in new ways so they have new meanings.
- The new readings "fill up" the original meaning with a messianic sense.

Relecture Fulfillment

Yet another method of interpreting messianic prophecy and fulfillment is relecture or rereading. According to this view, earlier prophecies were read in new ways so that they were filled with new meanings. This view has been adopted mainly by those who hold to critical views of the Bible, although some evangelicals have espoused it as well.

Figure 6

MIDRASH OR PESHER FULFILLMENT

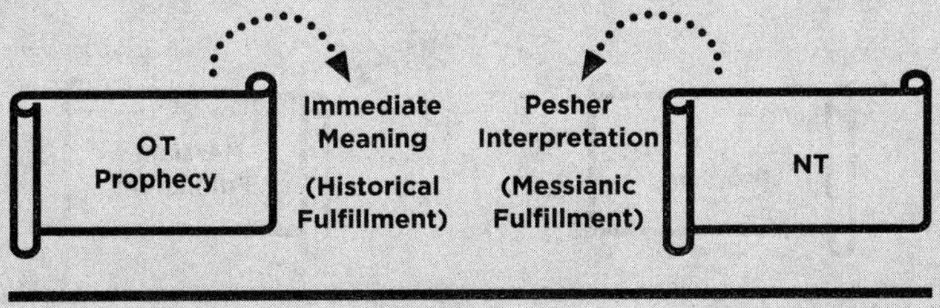

(R. L. Longnecker, Donald Juel)

- The literal prophecies refer to historical figures in the prophet's own day.
- Prophecies were interpreted according to the intertestamental Jewish method called Midrash or Pesher.
- Midrash or Pesher interprets ancient passages in a creative way to show their fulfillment in contemporary events.
- New Testament writers can do this under the inspiration of the Holy Spirit.

MIDRASH OR PESHER FULFILLMENT

A hermeneutic that is growing in popularity is the midrash or pesher approach, which asserts that the NT understood the OT messianic hope using the interpretive methods of early Judaism. According to this view, the OT prophecies commonly referred to historical figures present in the prophets' own days. Then, the NT interpreted these passages according to the intertestamental Jewish method called midrash or pesher. The NT cited these ancient passages in creative ways to show their fulfillment in contemporary events. Adherents of this view hold that this method of interpretation should be rejected by modern exegetes. They believe that NT writers could use it because they wrote under the inspiration of the Holy Spirit. This approach has been adopted by critical as well as evangelical scholars.

Figure 7

DIRECT FULFILLMENT

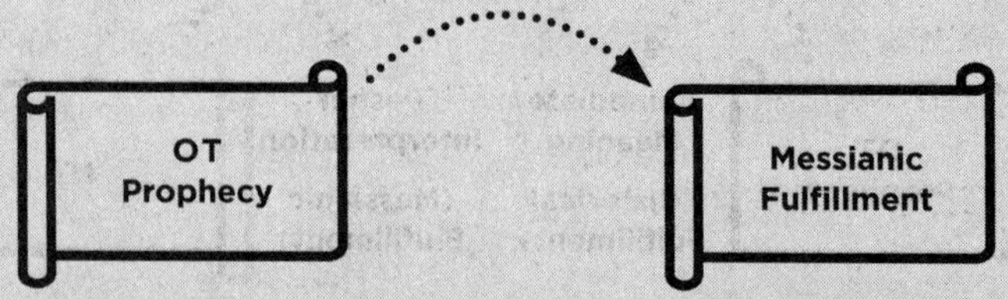

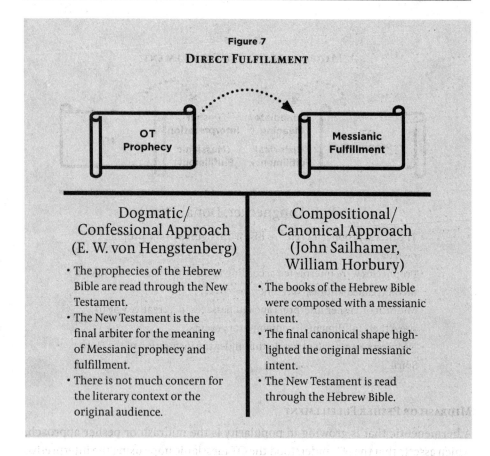

Dogmatic/ Confessional Approach (E. W. von Hengstenberg)	Compositional/ Canonical Approach (John Sailhamer, William Horbury)
• The prophecies of the Hebrew Bible are read through the New Testament. • The New Testament is the final arbiter for the meaning of Messianic prophecy and fulfillment. • There is not much concern for the literary context or the original audience.	• The books of the Hebrew Bible were composed with a messianic intent. • The final canonical shape highlighted the original messianic intent. • The New Testament is read through the Hebrew Bible.

DIRECT FULFILLMENT

The most traditional approach to messianic prophecy is to view it as predictions that refer directly to the Messiah. That is not to say that all OT messianic prophecy must refer directly and exclusively to the Messiah.[85] The traditional approach simply affirms that much of messianic prophecy is direct. There are two basic systems to this approach.

The first is the confessional/dogmatic approach, which Hengstenberg defended. This method allows the NT to be the final arbiter as to the meaning of messianic prophecy and fulfillment and does not show much concern for the original audience or literary context.

The second is the compositional/canonical approach, which Sailhamer has proposed. This view maintains that when the OT books were composed the authors had a messianic intention. Further, it observes a canonical shaping that recognizes the messianic nature of the text. This view asserts that, when the Hebrew text is established through textual criticism, a close reading of that Hebrew text in its canonical context will result in a messianic interpretation.

CONCLUSION

The relationship between OT prophecy and messianic fulfillment is essential to a theological defense of the messiahship of Jesus of Nazareth. It is so central to understanding the OT's relationship to the New that it has produced a vast literature proposing various interpretive schemes. Despite the variety of approaches, this *Handbook* maintains that the OT according to its literary strategies and canonical shape will yield a clear messianic intent, with far more direct messianic prediction than is commonly held.

---

1. This article is adapted from a chapter in Michael Rydelnik, *The Messianic Hope: Is the Hebrew Bible Really Messianic?* NAC Studies in Bible and Theology, ed. E. Ray Clendenen (Nashville: B&H Publishers, 2010), 13–33. Used with permission.
2. R. E. Clements, "Messianic Prophecy or Messianic History?" *Horizons in Biblical Theology* 1 (1979): 87. (I am indebted to Ronald E. Clements for his excellent survey of messianic interpretation, particularly for his discussion of Collins.)
3. I. W. Provan, "The Messiah in the Book of Kings" in *The Lord's Anointed: Interpretation of Old Testament Messianic Texts*, ed. P. E. Satterthwaite, R. S. Hess and G. J. Wenham, (Grand Rapids: Baker, 1995), 68.
4. Clements, "Messianic Prophecy or Messianic History?" 88.
5. W. C. Kaiser Jr., *Messiah in the Old Testament* (Grand Rapids: Zondervan, 1995), 19. (Kaiser, 34, acknowledges the legitimacy of types, including messianic ones, in the OT.) The NT, on occasion, authorizes some typological interpretation as demonstrated by L. Goppelt in *Typos*, trans. D. H. Madvig (Grand Rapids: Eerdmans, 1982). Moreover, the OT often intends its readers to understand its narrative as a form of typology. See J. Sailhamer's discussion of narrative typology in *The Pentateuch as Narrative* (Grand Rapids: Zondervan, 1992), 37–44.
6. As quoted in Clements, "Messianic Prophecy or Messianic History?" 88–89.
7. It was published in three volumes in 1835 and then a revised edition with four volumes was published in 1858. It was republished in 1970 in an abridged edition. E. W. Hengstenberg, *Christology of the Old Testament*, trans. Reuel Keith (London: Francis and John Rivington, 1847; repr., Grand Rapids: Kregel, 1970).
8. P. J. Gloag, *Messianic Prophecies* (Edinburgh: T&T Clark, 1879).
9. Ibid., 1.
10. Ibid., 34.
11. A. Edersheim, *Prophecy and History in Relation to the Messiah* (London: Longmans, 1901).
12. Ibid., x.
13. G. S. Goodspeed, *Israel's Messianic Hope to the Time of Jesus* (New York: MacMillan, 1900).
14. Ibid., 4–5.
15. Ibid., 8–9.
16. E. Riehm, *Messianic Prophecy: Its Origin, Historical Growth, and Relation to New Testament Fulfilment*, trans. L. A. Muirhead, 2nd ed. (Edinburgh: T&T Clark, 1891).
17. Ibid., 322.
18. F. Delitzsch, *Messianic Prophecies in Historical Succession*, trans. S. I. Curtiss. (Edinburgh: T&T Clark, 1891).

19. Ibid., 12.
20. Ibid., 21.
21. Kaiser, *Messiah in the Old Testament*, 21.
22. Delitzsch, *Messianic Prophecies in Historical Succession*, 10.
23. Ibid., 11.
24. C. A. Briggs, *Messianic Prophecy: The Prediction of the Fulfillment of Redemption through the Messiah* (New York: Scribner, 1886).
25. Ibid., 63.
26. W. J. Beecher, *The Prophets and the Promise* (New York: Crowell, 1905).
27. Ibid., 376–77.
28. Clements, "Messianic Prophecy or Messianic History?" 89.
29. W. O. E. Oesterley, *The Evolution of the Messianic Idea: A Study in Comparative Religion* (London: Pitman, 1908).
30. H. Gressmann, *Der Messias* (Gottingen: Vandenhoeck & Ruprecht, 1929).
31. This was originally published in *Princeton Theological Review* (1916) and reprinted in the collection of Warfield writings entitled *Christology and Criticism* (New York: Oxford, 1921).
32. B. B. Warfield, "The Divine Messiah of the Old Testament," in *Christology and Criticism* (New York: Oxford, 1921), 7.
33. Ibid., 20.
34. I. Engnell, *Studies in Divine Kingship in the Near East* (Oxford: Blackwell, 1943).
35. H. Ringgren, *The Messiah in the Old Testament* (Chicago: Allenson, 1956).
36. Ibid., 20.
37. Ibid., 24.
38. A. Bentzen, *King and Messiah* (London: Lutterworth, 1955). This was originally published in German in 1948 and then translated by the author himself in 1955.
39. Ibid., 19.
40. Ibid., 73.
41. Ibid., 75–76.
42. S. Mowinckel, *He That Cometh*, trans. G. W. Anderson (Oxford: Blackwell, 1959). This was originally published in Norwegian in 1954.
43. G. Van Groningen, *Messianic Revelation in the Old Testament* (Grand Rapids: Baker, 1990), 88.
44. J. Becker, *Messianic Expectation in the Old Testament*, trans. D. E. Green. (Philadelphia: Fortress, 1977).
45. Ibid., 79.
46. Ibid., 93.
47. Ibid., 94.
48. Ibid., 96.
49. R. N. Longenecker, *Biblical Exegesis in the Apostolic Period* (Grand Rapids: Eerdmans, 1975).
50. Ibid., 74.
51. Ibid., 219.
52. D. Juel, *Messianic Exegesis: Christological Interpretation of the Old Testament in Early Christianity* (Philadelphia: Fortress, 1988).
53. Ibid., 13.
54. R. E. Clements, "The Messianic Hope in the Old Testament," *Journal for the Study of the Old Testament* 43 (1989): 3–19.
55. Ibid., 14.
56. Clements, "Messianic Prophecy or Messianic History?" 96.
57. J. B. Payne, *Encyclopedia of Biblical Prophecy* (Grand Rapids: Baker, 1973).
58. Ibid., 665–68.

59. B. K Waltke, "A Canonical Process Approach to the Psalms," in *Tradition and Testament*, ed. J. Feinberg and P. Feinberg (Chicago: Moody, 1981), 5.

60. Van Groningen, *Messianic Revelation in the Old Testament*, 347–48.

61. Chris Wright, *Knowing Jesus through the Old Testament* (London: Marshall Pickering, 1992)

62. Ibid., 70–77.

63. This is a term borrowed from biology, meaning "the theory that an individual is developed by successive differentiation of an unstructured egg rather than by a simple enlarging of a preformed entity." *American Heritage Dictionary of the English Language*, 3rd ed., s. v. "epigenesis."

64. Kaiser, *Messiah in the Old Testament*, 27.

65. Ibid., 24–25.

66. A. Laato, *A Star is Rising: The Historical Development of the Old Testament Royal Ideology and the Rise of the Jewish Messianic Expectations* (Atlanta: Scholars Press, 1997).

67. Ibid., 1.

68. Ibid., 33–47.

69. J. Sailhamer, *Introduction to Old Testament Theology: A Canonical Approach* (Grand Rapids: Zondervan, 1995).

70. Sailhamer is careful to distinguish his method from B. Childs's canon criticism when he states, "Our use of the word *canonical* should not be understood in light of the particular focus of *canon criticism.* Though there are surface similarities between canon criticism and the canonical theology of the Old Testament that we are proposing here, there are, as well, fundamental differences. Chief among those differences are the understanding of the historicity of the biblical narratives and the nature of the composition of the biblical books." Ibid., 198.

71. Ibid.,154.

72. Ibid., 224.

73. Ibid., 220–221.

74. The post-Reformation movement of Christian scholars studying Hebrew and Rabbinics.

75. Sailhamer, *Introduction to Old Testament Theology: A Canonical Approach*, 132 54.

76. Ibid., 154.

77. J. H. Sailhamer, "The Messiah and the Hebrew Bible," *Journal of the Evangelical Theological Society* 44 (2001): 12.

78. Ibid., 12–13.

79. W. Horbury, *Jewish Messianism and the Cult of Christ* (London: SCM, 1998).

80. Horbury cites J. Becker as a representative of current critical scholarship that finds a "messianological vacuum" in the OT. He says, "What may be called a 'no hope list'—a list of books wherein it is thought that no messianic hope can be found—has long been a standard item in writings on messianism." Ibid., 5.

81. Ibid., 6.

82. P. E. Satterthwaite, R. S. Hess and G. J. Wenham, eds. *The Lord's Anointed: Interpretation of Old Testament Messianic Texts* (Grand Rapids: Baker, 1995).

83. Two other compilations that reflect the same inconsistent approach, predominated by messianic minimalists are R. S. Hess and M. Daniel Carroll R., eds., *Israel's Messiah in the Bible and the Dead Sea Scrolls* (Grand Rapids: Baker, 2003); and S. E. Porter, ed., *The Messiah in the Old and New Testaments* (Grand Rapids: Eerdmans, 2007).

84. W. C. Kaiser Jr., review of P. E. Satterthwaite, R. S. Hess, and G. J. Wenham, eds., *The Lord's Anointed: Interpretation of Old Testament Messianic Texts, Journal of the Evangelical Theological Society* 42 (1999): 101–2.

85. There are clearly several other forms of messianic prophecy in the OT. In addition to (1) direct fulfillment, at least three more categories should be recognized. I would add (2) typical fulfillment, which identifies the authorially intended patterns of certain OT persons, events, or objects and finds corresponding fulfillment in the NT; (3) applicational fulfillment, which seeks to demonstrate the practical contemporary relevance of an OT principle in a NT setting; and (4) summary fulfillment, which summarizes the teaching of several OT passages while not directly quoting any of them. See the article "The Old Testament in the New Testament" by Michael A. Rydelnik in this *Handbook*. For another inventory of OT fulfillment types, including typical, typico-messianic, eschatologico-messianic, divine parousia, messianic by extension, messianic by way of preparation, see R. D. Culver, "The Old Testament as Messianic Prophecy" *Journal of the Evangelical Theological Society* 7 (1964): 91–97.

The Old Testament in the Old Testament[1]

SETH D. POSTELL

Commentaries, handbooks, monographs, and countless journal articles have been devoted to explaining the New Testament's use of the Old Testament.[2] This plethora of scholarly resources and seemingly never-ending discussion begs the question: Why all the bother? Jonathan Lunde offers a poignant answer:

> [W]hen we examine the NT authors' use of the OT closely, rather than sharing the wonder that filled Jesus' companions on the road to Emmaus, it is sometimes difficult to avoid the impression that the NT application of OT texts is arbitrary and forced.[3]

The bottom line: though all followers of Jesus believe He is the "Promised" Messiah, many disagree about the sense in which He was actually promised. Scholars tend to be uncomfortable with the traditional "single meaning" approach to messianic prophecy, whereby a list of OT prophecies and their NT fulfillments are provided in two columns as proof-texts for the messiahship of Jesus.[4] Missing from this approach is an awareness of the larger context from which these OT verses have been taken. All too often, single meaning adherents lack the ability to demonstrate convincingly from the OT itself that their historical authors intended these verses to be messianic prophecies.

Ironically, this modern struggle[5] over the NT's use of the OT and the "literal sense" of the OT itself presents a rather uncomfortable position historically and theologically speaking. While wholeheartedly affirming the apostolic testimony that Jesus is the Promised Messiah, there is an uncomfortable agreement with the synagogue, which for 2,000 years has argued that the original intent of several key OT passages cited in the NT have nothing to do with Jesus.[6] It is like the words of Tevya's wise friend in *Fiddler on the Roof*, "He's right? And he's right? They can't both be right!" To which Tevya responds, "You're right too!" Tevya's response, comical as it may be, has no theological or apologetic value. As evangelicals, therefore, the ability to explain and defend the NT's use of the OT, particularly to unbelieving Israel, is essential to our affirmation that Jesus is truly the Messiah.[7]

The purpose of this article is to offer a paradigm for understanding and defending the NT's interpretation of the OT and its identification of Jesus as "the One Moses wrote about in the Law (and so did the prophets)" (Jn 1:45). To achieve that, it is necessary to consider the OT's use of the OT itself. The argument presented here is as follows: understanding of the NT's use of the OT will grow in proportion to understanding the OT's use of the OT itself.[8] To demonstrate this thesis, three examples will be examined: one from the Torah, one from the Prophets, and one from the Writings, in honor of the pattern laid down by our Master Teacher on the Road to Emmaus (Lk 24:44).

THE MEANING OF THE OT'S USE OF THE OT

Before delving into three specific examples of the OT's use of the OT, it is necessary to say a few words about the concept itself. Most have heard the old adage, "The best commentary on Scripture is Scripture." For many, however, this statement is merely a truism with little exegetical payload. While growing well accustomed to the notion of the NT's use of the OT,[9] the thought of the OT's use of the OT may at first sound quite strange.

What is meant by "the OT's use of the OT"? Stated quite simply, later OT prophets diligently studied and applied the inspired writings of earlier OT prophets for the making of their own books.[10] The apostle Peter clearly shares this perspective in 1Pt 1:10-11:

> Concerning this salvation, the prophets who prophesied about the grace that would come to you searched and carefully investigated. They inquired into what time or what circumstances the Spirit of Christ within them was indicating when He testified in advance to the messianic sufferings and the glories that would follow.

Peter makes it clear the OT prophets "searched and carefully investigated." Though he does not explicitly state the obvious, these prophets were searching and investigating the writings of prophets who preceded them. Proof for this "OT use of the OT" is provided by an expansive web of inner-biblical OT commentary on the OT—itself inspired—that sheds invaluable light on the intentionality of the earlier prophetic writings.[11] Frequently, this web of inner-biblical commentary is not only messianic in nature but also remarkably similar to the interpretations we find in the NT itself.

THE TORAH'S USE OF THE TORAH FOR UNDERSTANDING THE NEW TESTAMENT

This study begins by looking first at the Torah's use of the Torah.[12] Jesus states unabashedly in Jn 5:46: "For if you believed Moses, you would believe Me, because he wrote about Me."[13] Certainly "already persuaded" believers accept Jesus' statement as authoritative truth. A stalwart commitment to the authority of the NT, however, is no substitute for *Berean* efforts to "examine the Scriptures daily to see if these things were so" (see Ac 17:11).

For the purpose here, it is essential to observe what John Sailhamer called "the poetic seams of the Torah."[14] At specific points in the macro-structure of the Torah's narrative, Moses inserted large poetic discourses that focus on the coming of a king from the tribe of Judah in "the last days" (see Gn 49:1,8-12; Nm 24:14,17-24; Dt 31:28-29; 33:5,7). The repetition of this key feature within the macro-structure of the Torah suggests the Torah was written intentionally to engender faith in the coming Messiah.

Now, the discourses of Balaam (Nm 23–24) reveal the ways inner-biblical commentary on Israel's exodus (OT use of the OT) directly leads to Matthew's description of Jesus' early years as a fulfillment of prophecy (Nm 23:22; 24:8; Mt 2:15).[15] According to context, these discourses are tied to the larger theme of "the last days" and the coming Messiah (Nm 24:14,17ff.). Also, the Balaam narrative (Nm 22–24), at the conclusion of the wilderness wanderings, is literarily linked to the beginning of Israel's Egyptian sojourn (Ex 1–2).[16] In both texts, a foreign king (Pharaoh/Balak) sees the numerical prosperity of the people of Israel (the blessings of the Abrahamic covenant, e.g. Gn 15:5), then fears, and attempts to thwart, its fulfillment three times.[17]

In the third attempt to impede the covenantal blessings, the author draws our attention to the ascendancy of Israel's redeemer (Moses, Ex 2:1ff; the Messiah, Nm 24:7-9,17-24). Moreover, the author highlights the significance of Balaam's third discourse (Nm 24:1-9), not only by contrasting it with the other oracles,[18] but also by means of literary parallels to the narrative account of Balaam's encounter with the "Angel of the LORD" (Nm 22). In both cases, Balaam attempts to circumvent in vain divine barriers (the "Angel of the LORD," 22:28,32-33; the Abrahamic covenant, 24:10), and on his third attempt God opens Balaam's eyes (22:31; 24:3-4) to see Israel's mighty deliverer (the "Angel of the LORD," 22:31; the Messiah, 24:7-9).

Not only does the context strongly suggest that Balaam's third discourse points to Israel's future king-redeemer, but the citation in Nm 24:9 of Gn 49:9—a messianic prophecy about the coming king from the tribe of Judah—reinforces the likelihood that Nm 24:7-9 is messianic (see chart).

COMPARISON OF JACOB'S AND BALAAM'S PROPHECIES

He crouches; he lies down like a lion or a lioness—who dares to rouse him? (Gn 49:9)	He crouches, he lies down like a lion or a lioness—who dares to rouse him? (Nm 24:9)

Note also the remarkable prophecy about this king in Nm 24:8: "God brought him out of Egypt."

In order to appreciate this "out of Egypt" prediction in Balaam's third discourse, first consider its relationship to a virtually identical statement in Balaam's second discourse (Nm 23:18-24). According to Nm 23:22, Balaam's gaze is cast upon the people of Israel as a totality and states, "God brings *them* out of Egypt, He is for *them* like the horns of the wild ox" (NASB, emphasis added). There is little doubt this refers to Israel's exodus from Egypt.

In Nm 24:8, this verse is cited in a nearly verbatim manner, with one key difference: "God brings *him* out of Egypt, He is for *him* like the horns of the wild ox" (NASB, emphasis added). The pronoun is singular, and the referent is no longer the people of Israel as a totality, but Israel's individual king. Just as God brought Israel out of Egypt in former days, so God will bring the Messiah-king out of Egypt in "the last days."

A theological precedent is thereby established by Moses to interpret Israel's exodus as a foreshadowing of eschatological and messianic realities.[19] In light of this prior inner-biblical precedent, it is not difficult to see how Matthew's retelling of the Messiah's escape from the Pharaoh-like Herod and His exodus from Egypt (Mt 2:15) is thoroughly grounded in the eschatological portraiture of the Hebrew Bible. In this case, the Torah's use of the Torah provides a firm foundation for defending Matthew's understanding of Israel's exodus and draws a direct line from the expectations of the Torah to the person of Jesus.

Matthew's hermeneutic can be trusted not just because it falls within the bounds of the accepted rabbinic hermeneutical norms of his day, but because

Moses himself validated a messianic understanding of Israel's exodus.[20] This inspired OT commentary serves as the basis for Matthew's interpretation of the OT.

THE PROPHETS' USE OF THE OLD TESTAMENT FOR UNDERSTANDING THE NEW TESTAMENT

Given the literary relationship of the Prophets and the Writings to the Torah, it appears that the completion of the Mosaic Pentateuch catalyzed a flurry of prophetic activity and writings with respect to the certainties of Israel's failure under the Sinai covenant and Moses' promises of a future work of grace in "the last days." The prophets meditated on the Torah day and night, and this resulted in a Hebrew Bible fixated on a future glorious hope despite Israel's continual covenantal failures. In this light, a second OT use of the OT can be examined—Jeremiah's reflections and commentary on the theology of the Pentateuch.

It may come as a surprise to hear that Jeremiah's prophecy of the new covenant was not a sudden burst of new developments in the course of progressive revelation. In other words, Jeremiah's "new" covenant was not an entirely new concept. Rather, several citations and allusions to the Torah suggest that Jeremiah's message was simply a reiteration (albeit a divinely inspired reiteration and commentary) of Moses' prophecy in Dt 30 (and of other eschatological passages from the Torah).

Scholars have long noted Jeremiah's dependency on Deuteronomy. Charles Feinberg, for instance, writes, "Some sixty-six passages from Deuteronomy find an echo in Jeremiah's eighty-six references to the book."[21] Chapters 1–28 of Jeremiah primarily focus on the coming destruction of Jerusalem because of covenant disobedience. Chapters 29–33 unexpectedly turn to the theme of redemption in "the last days" (30:24) that also includes the promise of the new covenant (31:31-34) and the coming Messiah (30:9).[22] Jeremiah 29–33 (the new covenant section) is full of allusions to and citations of Dt 30 as well as other eschatological texts from the Torah.[23] J. G. McConville is quite clear about this when he writes,

> Deut. xxx 1-10, first of all, has clear connexions with passages from the prophetic literature, notably Jer. xxx-xxxiii; Ezek. xxxvi. The affinities are greater with Jeremiah. Once again, linguistic usage signals the link. Jeremiah knows both a circumcising of the heart (Jer. iv 4; cf. Deut. xxx 6–with x 16) and a "restoration of fortunes" (*šûb šebût*: Jer xxix 10, xxx 3, 18, xxxi 23, xxxii 44, xxxiii 7, 11, 26). The later motif clearly clusters round the so-called Book of Consolation. Its association with Deut. xxx 1-10 is strengthened by its occurrence twice in collocation with the verb *rḥm*, where Yahweh is the subject and said to have compassion on his people (xxx 18, xxxiii 26). The Book of Consolation also develops the idea connoted both in Deut. xxx 6 and Jer. iv 4 by "circumcising

> the heart." The essence of that idea is Yahweh's initiative in producing Israel's repentance, present in Jeremiah in the New Covenant theology of xxxi 31-4 and xxxii 39-40, and in Ezek. xxxvi 26-7, where it is also in collocation with the idea of a return to the land, *v.* 28. This feature of Deut. xxx 1-10 is quite as important a factor in the novelty and individuality of that passage as its introduction of the hope of restoration to the land.[24]

There are two noteworthy points for consideration. First, Jeremiah's allusions to Dt 30 strongly indicate that he seemingly understood that text as the promise of a new covenant (see Jer 31:31-34). Thus, Jeremiah's book provides an inspired vantage point for looking at the Torah's theology (the punch line of its message) as essentially a *new covenant theology*. Second, Jeremiah's reading of Deuteronomy sheds invaluable light on Paul's interpretation of Dt 30:12-14 in Rom 10:6-8. In the context, Paul contrasts Lv 18:5 (a righteousness based on law) with Dt 30:12-14 (a righteousness based on faith). It appears that Paul understands Lv 18 and Dt 30 as two different covenants within the Torah itself, the Sinai and the new covenants, respectively. And while many commentators are hard pressed to find promises of the Messiah and the new covenant in Dt 30,[25] Jeremiah's pre-Christian interpretation opens wide the path leading from Dt 30 directly to Rom 10, and to Jesus the Messiah. Thus, the Prophets' use of the Torah (OT use of the OT) provides a vital link from the OT to Jesus as the promised Messiah.

THE WRITINGS' USE OF THE OLD TESTAMENT FOR UNDERSTANDING THE NEW TESTAMENT

Jeremiah wrote a letter to those inhabitants of Judea exiled by Nebuchadnezzar (Jer 29:1-3). As Dan 1:1-6 clearly shows, Daniel was among those taken to Babylon in the third year of Jehoiakim's reign, and thus was a recipient of the Weeping Prophet's letter.[26] This information proves crucial for our understanding of Dan 9. There Daniel was studying and responsively praying over[27] the very letters (*seferim*)[28] referred to in Jer 29—letters that determine the duration of a 70-year period of time[29] until the fulfillment of God's promises regarding "the last days" (compare Dt 4:29; 30:3; 29:10-14). Jeremiah 29 reveals Jeremiah's own understanding of Dt 30 (and other key texts of the Torah) as the promised new covenant and coming of the Messiah in "the last days" (compare Jer 29:13-14 with Dt 4:29; 30:3). Jeremiah's use of the OT,[30] in this case, clarifies what Jeremiah means by the "good word" ("end" and "hope") promised to Israel in Jer 29:10-11. Clearly, the goal (in the fullest sense) of Jeremiah's 70-year prophecy was not, and could not be, the anticlimactic events described in the book of Ezra-Nehemiah.[31]

With this in mind, it is necessary to discuss the relationship between the first and second parts of Dan 9,[32] namely, Daniel's *initial understanding* of Jeremiah's 70-year prophecy (v. 2) and Gabriel's task of *bringing understanding* of Jeremiah's 70-year prophecy to Daniel (vv. 20-23,25). If Daniel already understood Jeremiah's words (v. 2), why was it necessary for Gabriel to come and impart understanding to Daniel?

Although some scholars perceive an irreconcilable tension here, this tension is solved by considering the timing of Daniel's prayer. Apparently, from Dan 1:1 and 9:1, Daniel uttered this prayer approximately 68 years after his own exile.[33] As far as Daniel was concerned, the timing of the fulfillment of Jeremiah's 70-year prophecy should have been imminent. Gabriel's task, therefore, was to provide Daniel with a clearer understanding of Jeremiah's prophecy and the timing of its fulfillment. Gabriel symbolically interpreted Jeremiah's 70 years: 70 years become 70 weeks of years.[34] This is not to deny the connection between Jeremiah's 70 years and the historical return of the Babylonian exiles after a 70-year period. Rather, it is an argument that Jeremiah's 70-year prophecy in chap. 29 is inseparably linked to the promise of the new covenant in chaps. 30–33. In that sense, the return described in the book of Ezra-Nehemiah is not the FULL-fillment of Jeremiah's prophecy. Daniel 9, therefore, provides the necessary biblical background for evaluating the events described in Ezra-Nehemiah and also explains the reasons for the delay in the timing of Jeremiah's eschatological prophecies. To be clear, there is an indissoluble link between Jeremiah's prophecy of 70 years and Daniel's prophecy of 70 weeks: they are both descriptions of one and the same vision. Daniel 9:24-27 is simply an inspired inner-biblical OT interpretation of Jeremiah's prophecy, a shining example of the OT's use of the OT.[35]

Based on the paradigm of the OT's use of the OT, it seems fairly certain that Dan 9:24-27 is messianic[36] because of its inner-biblical relationship to other overtly eschatological passages elsewhere in the Hebrew Bible. In fact, "the last days" is a key phrase in the compositional strategy of Daniel that unites the Aramaic and Hebrew portions of the book (2:28; 10:14)[37]—a phrase no doubt borrowed from the Torah (Gn 49:1; Nm 24:14; Dt 4:30; 31:29) and incorporated by the Prophets (e.g. Isa 2:2; Jer 23:20; 30:24; 48:47; 49:39; Ezk 38:16; Hos 3:5; Mic 4:1).

Daniel's interpretation of Jeremiah (and the Torah) contributes to a more nuanced understanding of the new covenant, one that unites the removal of Israel's sin (Jer 31:34) with the death of the Messiah (Dan 9:26). Given the web of inner-biblical links from the eschatology of the Torah to Dan 9 via Jeremiah, Jesus' allusion to Jer 31:31 on the eve of His Passover death (Lk 22:20) makes perfect sense. The inner-biblical prophetic tapestry necessarily includes the death of the Messiah. Once again, the OT's use of the OT provides a significant defense of a messianic interpretation of the OT that clarifies the NT's use of the OT—and, more important, leads directly to Jesus of Nazareth as the promised Messiah.

CONCLUSION

The OT already comes to its readers with a thorough network of inner-biblical interpretation. The goal here was not to interpret the raw data of the OT in a vacuum, rather, to be sensitive to the interpretations already laid out within the Tanakh itself. The remarkable congruence between the OT interpretations of the OT on the one hand and the NT interpretation of the OT on the other can be seen according to the paradigm for reading and interpreting the OT presented here. This paradigm offers extraordinary explanatory and apologetic possibilities for defending the NT's interpretation of the OT. Perhaps another commentary should be written as a companion guide to the *Commentary on the New Testament's Use of the Old Testament*. It could be called the *Commentary on the Old Testament's Use of the Old Testament as a Prologue to the New Testament's Use of the Old Testament.*

---

1. Adapted from Seth Postell, "The Old Testament's use of the Old Testament for Messianic Jewish Apologetics," *Mishkan* 63 (2010): 30–40 with permission.

2. See for example, J. Daniel Hays, "The Persecuted Prophet and Judgment on Jerusalem: The Use of LXX Jeremiah in the Gospel of Luke," *Bulletin for Biblical Research* 25, no. 4 (2015): 453–75; Paul Han, *Swimming in the Sea of Scripture: Paul's Use of the Old Testament in 2 Corinthians 4.7-13.13* (New York: T&T Clark, 2014); G. K. Beale, *Handbook on the New Testament Use of the Old Testament: Exegesis and Interpretation* (Grand Rapids: Baker Academic, 2012); Gregory K. Beale, "The Use of Hosea 11:1 in Matthew 2:15: One More Time," *Journal of the Evangelical Theological Society* 55, no. 4 (2012): 697–715; David Starling, "Meditations on a Slippery Citation: Paul's Use of Psalm 112:9 in 2 Corinthians 9:9," *Journal of Theological Interpretation* 6, no. 2 (2012): 241–55; Stephen L. Young, "Romans 1.1-5 and Paul's Christological Use of Hab. 2.4 in Rom. 1.17: An Underutilized Consideration in the Debate," *Journal for the Study of the New Testament* 34, no. 3 (2012): 277–85; Jonathan Lunde and John Anthony Dunne, "Paul's Creative and Contextual Use of Isaiah in Ephesians 5:14," *Journal of the Evangelical Theological Society* 55, no. 1 (2012): 87–110; Brian J. Abasciano, *Paul's Use of the Old Testament in Romans 9.10-18: An Intertextual and Theological Exegesis*, The Library of New Testament Studies (London: T & T Clark, 2011); Steve Moyise, *Jesus and Scripture* (London: SPCK, 2010); *Paul and Scripture* (London: SPCK, 2010); G. K. Beale and D. A. Carson, *Commentary on the New Testament Use of the Old Testament* (Grand Rapids: Baker Academic, 2007); Kenneth Berding and Jonathan Lunde, *Three Views on the New Testament Use of the Old Testament*, Counterpoints Series Bible & Theology (Grand Rapids: Zondervan, 2007).

3. Jonathan Lunde, "An Introduction to the Central Issues in the New Testament Use of the Old Testament," in *Three Views on the New Testament Use of the Old Testament*, ed. Kenneth Berding and Jonathan Lunde (Grand Rapids: Zondervan, 2008), 9.

4. One good example of the classic approach (known as the single-meaning position) is Josh McDowell's *More Than a Carpenter* (Wheaton, IL: Tyndale, 2004); for a helpful discussion of the issues involved in the relationship of the Testaments and the various critical and evangelical approaches to these issues, see Gerhard Hasel, *Old Testament Theology: Basic Issues in the Current Debate*, 3rd ed. (Grand Rapids: Eerdmans, 1984), 145–67. Regarding the single-meaning approach, Roger Nicole, "The Old Testament in the New Testament," in vol. 1 of *Expositor's Bible Commentary*, ed. Frank E. Gaebelein (Grand Rapids: Zondervan, 1979), 623, states the following: "Its advocates are, however, faced with the difficult task of showing how the meaning ascribed by NT writers to a number of OT quotations was already in the purview of the prophets who originally wrote the statements." Jonathan Lunde, *Three*

Views on the New Testament Use of the Old Testament, 8, further notes, "[S]ome of the OT passages that are 'fulfilled' in the NT don't look at all like predictions in their original context."

5. Michael Rydelnik, in an article in this *Handbook* ("Interpretive Approaches to Messianic Prophecy," p. 73), 13, traces this struggle back to the 18th century with the publication of *Discourse of the Grounds and Reasons of the Christian Religion* by Anthony Collins.

6. Yisroel Blumenthal, "Answering Dr. Brown's Objections to Judaism," https://judaismresources.net/contra-brown/, accessed July 6, 2019, a well-known anti-missionary, drives this point home when he writes, "The Christian accepts Jesus on the basis of the Christian understanding that Jesus fulfilled the Messianic prophecies of the Jewish Bible. The Jew cannot accept Jesus based on the Jewish understanding of the same Bible."

7. Michael Rydelnik, in an article in this *Handbook* ("Interpretive Approaches to Messianic Prophecy," pp. 83–89), offers a helpful list of seven approaches to the NT's use of the OT and their major proponents.

8. The concept of the OT's use of the OT was first introduced to me by my doctoral mentor, Dr. John Sailhamer.

9. Moisés Silva, "The New Testament's Use of the Old Testament: Text Form and Authority," in *Scripture and Truth*, ed. D. A. Carson and John D. Woodbridge, 147–65 (Grand Rapids: Baker, 1992); Roger Nicole, "The Old Testament in the New Testament," in vol. 1, *Expositor's Bible Commentary*, ed. Frank E. Gaebelein, 617–28 (Grand Rapids: Zondervan, 1979). Stanley N. Gundry, Kenneth Berding, Jonathan Lunde, eds., *Three Views on the New Testament Use of the Old Testament*. See G. K. Beale and D. A. Carson, eds., *Commentary on the New Testament Use of the Old Testament* (Grand Rapids: Baker; Nottingham: Apollos, 2007).

10. For a thorough defense of this position from a critical perspective, see Benjamin D. Sommer, *A Prophet Reads Scripture: Allusion in Isaiah 40–66*, Contraversions: Jews and Other Differences (Stanford, CA: Stanford University Press, 1998).

11. For a classic text on the subject, see Michael A. Fishbane, *Biblical Interpretation in Ancient Israel* (Oxford: Oxford University Press, 1985); Odil Hannes Steck, *The Prophetic Books and Their Theological Witness*, trans. James D. Nogalski (St. Louis: Chalice Press, 2000), 130, though referring to the development of individual prophetic books, captures this notion well when he writes, "If a literarily existing prophetic writing is constantly received and interpreted productively by these redactions, then we already encounter prophetic exegesis in the literary growth of the prophetic books themselves." Elsewhere (p. 118), he writes, "Seen from the perspective of their development, prophetic books are exegesis of the prophets. In fact, if one adds elaboration to prophecy as tradition, then prophetic books are prophetic exegesis of the prophets."

12. I am using "Torah" and "Pentateuch" synonymously here.

13. All Scriptures are taken from the Holman Christian Standard Bible unless noted otherwise.

14. See John H. Sailhamer, *The Pentateuch as Narrative* (Grand Rapids: Zondervan, 1992), 35–37.

15. For an in-depth treatment of the messianism of the Balaam narrative, see also Seth D. Postell, "The Messiah in the Balaam Narrative" in this *Moody Handbook of Messianic Prophecy*.

16. Ibid., 41–44.

17. In Exodus, Pharaoh (1) enslaves the people, (2) commands the midwives to kill the male babies, and (3) drowns the baby boys in the Nile River. In Numbers, Balak hires Balaam, who in turn tries to curse the Israelites three times (see Nm 24:10).

18. The text says that Balaam's third oracle was (1) not done by means of omens (24:1), (2) empowered by the Spirit of God (24:2), (3) a prophetic oracle (24:3-4), and (4) spoken with eyes completely open (24:3-4).

19. See for example Isa 11:10-16 and Zch 14:4-5.

20. For a survey of first-century Jewish hermeneutics, see Longenecker, 6–35.

21. Charles L. Feinberg, *Jeremiah*, vol. 6 of Expositor's Bible Commentary, ed. Frank E. Gaebelein (Grand Rapids: Zondervan, 1986), 368.

22. Chapter 29 narrates the contents of Jeremiah's letter of instruction to the exiles. Chapters 30–33 are known as the Book of Consolation.

23. For example, compare Jer 29:13-14 to Dt 30:3 and Dt 4:29 (both texts from Dt are themselves inner-textually linked; compare Dt 4:30 and Dt 30:2a, 3a). The key phrase, "restore the fortunes" (Jer 29:14; 30:3,18; 31:23; 32:44; 33:7,11,26), is taken directly from Dt 30:3. Also compare Jer 30:3 and Dt 30:5; Jer 32:37 and Dt 30:3-4; Jer 29:18 and Dt 28:25; for possible allusions, compare Jer 31:33 and Dt 30:3; Jer 32:41 and Dt 30:9; Jer 29:17 and Dt 28:48.

24. J. G. McConville, "1 Kings VIII 46–53 and the Deuteronomic Hope," *Vetus Testamentum* 42, no. 1 (1992): 77.

25. Richard Hays, *Echoes of Scripture in the Letters of Paul* (New Haven, CT & London: Yale University Press, 1989), 1, refers to Paul's use of Dt here as a tour de force that "must have startled his first audience." Darrell L. Bock, "Single Meaning, Multiple Contexts and Referents," in *Three Views on the New Testament Use of the Old Testament*, eds.

Stanley N. Gundry, Kenneth Berding, and Jonathan Lunde (Grand Rapids: Zondervan, 2008), 132, identifies Rom 10 as an "exegetical minefield."

26. A letter (*sefer*) written to the exiles on the eve of Jerusalem's desolation (see Jer 29:1-3). Daniel would have been part of those identified by Jeremiah as the "good figs," namely, those through whom God would fulfill His eschatological promises (Jer 25:1-7).

27. Gerald H. Wilson, "The Prayer of Daniel 9: Reflection on Jeremiah 29," *Journal for the Study of the Old Testament* 48 (1990): 97, writes, "The prayer is best understood as an attempt to have Daniel fulfill the conditions for restoration set out in Jer 29:12-14."

28. Ibid., 93. Wilson accounts for the plural reference to "letters/books" in Dan 9:2 on the basis of the structure of Jer 29, where he argues there is evidence of at least two letters written by Jeremiah to the exiles (vv. 10-14 and 29:24-32).

29. Ibid. According to Wilson, chaps. 27–29 of Jeremiah deal with the prophet's attempt to counter false prophecies of a swift return from exile (ibid., 93).

30. E.g., Deuteronomy; also compare Daniel 9 with Leviticus 26.

31. Paul L. Redditt, "Daniel 9: Its Structure and Meaning," *Catholic Biblical Quarterly* 62, vol. 2 (2000): 237, writing from a critical-historical perspective, states the following: "Whatever others may have thought of the restoration described in Ezra-Nehemiah, the author of Daniel was not prepared to accept the conditions of 165 BC (or 539 BC either) as a fulfillment of God's promise through Jeremiah."

32. Daniel's meditation on Jeremiah and his prayer in vv. 1-19 and Gabriel's words of clarification in vv. 20-27.

33. Wilson, 97. Daniel was exiled in 606 BC. His prayer was uttered in 538 BC.

34. See Redditt, 236; Michael Fishbane, *Biblical Interpretation in Ancient Israel* (Oxford: Clarendon, 1988), 482. My purpose here is not to explain the precise chronological nuances of the 70 weeks. Much depends on the identification of the decree in v. 25. Conservative evangelicals have argued for at least three possibilities: (1) Cyrus's decree (Ezr 1:1-4), c. 539 BC (e.g., Michael B. Shepherd, *Daniel in the Context of the Hebrew Bible*, Studies in Biblical Literature 123, ed. Hemchand Gossai [New York: Peter Lang, 2009]); (2) Artaxerxes' decree to Ezra (Ezr 7:11-26), c. 458–457 BC (e.g., Gleason Archer, *Daniel*, vol. 7 of Expositor's Bible Commentary, ed. Frank E. Gaebelein [Grand Rapids: Zondervan, 1985]; and (3) Artaxerxes' decree to Nehemiah (Neh 2:1-9), c. 444 BC [e.g., Harold W. Hoehner, *Chronological Aspects of the Life of Christ* [Grand Rapids: Zondervan, 1981, 115–39]).

35. Based on the presence of several innerbiblical citations and allusions, Fishbane, 489, argues that all of Daniel 9 is "a skillful exegetical ensemble."

36. J. Paul Tanner, "Is Daniel's Seventy-Weeks Prophecy Messianic? Part 1," *Bibliotheca Sacra* 166 (April–June 2009): 181, calls attention to the pervasive tendency among critical and Jewish scholars to regard this passage as nonmessianic. "[S]ome writers see no reference to Messiah in this passage. This includes most critical scholars, who typically favor a Maccabean fulfillment (i.e., in the second century BC), and Jewish exegetes, who—although differing about various details—tend to see the fulfillment of this passage with the destruction of the Temple in AD 70 and/or its aftermath." The tendency of historical-critical scholars is, first, to adduce a late dating for the book of Daniel (the Maccabean period), and second, to interpret Daniel's message in light of the historical events of that period. The paradigm I am suggesting (the OT's use of the OT) seeks to interpret Daniel's message as an integral part of the ongoing inner-biblical prophetic discussion regarding the meaning of the Torah and its eschatology. Daniel 9, moreover, must be understood within the compositional strategy of the book as a whole, a strategy whose primary concern is the events of "the last days" (Dan 2:28; 10:14).

37. Shepherd, *Daniel*, 73.

The Old Testament in the New Testament[1]

MICHAEL A. RYDELNIK

"In their attempt to show that the Messiah and many of the events in the first-century church had indeed been anticipated by the Old Testament writers, have the New Testament writers fairly cited the Old Testament quotations, according to their real truth-intention and original writer's meaning?" Walter C. Kaiser has asked.[2]

His question brings into sharp focus the core issue at stake in all discussions concerning the NT's use of the OT. Plainly, the NT consistently interprets the OT as messianic. However, how the NT came to this interpretive conclusion has become a controversial subject.[3] Did the NT writers use the OT fairly, or did they read their own meanings into the texts they cited?

One common explanation is that the NT authors interpreted OT texts according to rabbinic midrashic method. G. F. Moore's defines midrashic method as

> an atomistic exegesis, which interprets sentences, clauses, phrases, and even single words, independently of the context or the historical occasion, as divine oracles; combines them with other similarly detached utterances; and makes large use of analogy of expressions, often by purely verbal association.[4]

According to this view, like the midrashim, the NT cites the Old atomistically, arbitrarily, and therefore, inaccurately, without any regard for the intentions of the OT authors. This view is based on the idea that the NT authors used OT texts much in the same way that their Jewish contemporaries did, namely, without concern for context or authorial intent.[5] Nevertheless, frequently those who hold this view also maintain that the NT's interpretations can be accepted because the writers were "guided by the exalted Christ, through immediate direction of the Holy Spirit."[6]

However, these interpreters would also assert that present-day interpreters should in no way mimic or use apostolic exegetical methods. Longenecker states, "I do not, however, think it my business to try to reproduce the exegetical procedures and practices of the NT writers, particularly when they engage in what I define as 'midrash,' 'pesher,' or 'allegorical' exegesis."[7]

Moisés Silva has objected to Longenecker's thesis, stating, "If we refuse to pattern our exegesis after that of the apostles, we are in practice denying the authoritative character of their scriptural interpretation."[8] Silva's position about the understandability of NT citations from the OT is mine as well.[9] The NT's exegesis of OT texts is both discernable and reproducible. This article will attempt to demonstrate how the NT writers interpret the Hebrew Bible by examining the four OT quotations in Mt 2. The second chapter of Matthew contains four categories of OT quotations that are identifiable throughout the NT.[10] They are not mysterious, creative, or incomprehensible but intelligible and reproducible. After examining the four categories in Mt 2, it will become evident that the NT usage of the Old is accurate, comprehensible, and still usable by current interpreters of the Bible.

The narrative purpose of Mt 2 is to show the world's reception of the Messiah, with Jewish leadership being essentially apathetic to His arrival but the Gentile magi more responsive. These events foreshadow the Messiah's reception in the rest of the gospel.[11] Nevertheless, Mt 2 has a secondary purpose, that is, to reveal that Jesus fulfilled the messianic hope of the Hebrew Bible. Thus, Matthew's second chapter sets forth four OT predictions that find their fulfillment in the life of Jesus of Nazareth.[12] The literary link of all four of these OT citations is that each has a geographical element: the first speaks of Bethlehem, the second of Egypt, the third of Ramah, and the last of Nazareth. Each of these OT citations demonstrates a different kind of fulfillment, providing a paradigm for the four ways the NT uses the Old.

DIRECT FULFILLMENT: MATTHEW 2:5-6 / MICAH 5:2

The first kind of prophecy and fulfillment motif is literal prediction and direct fulfillment, as seen in Matthew's quotation of Mic 5:2.[13] After the birth narrative (Mt 1:18-25), Matthew wrote that wise men from the East arrived at the court of King Herod, asking, "Where is He who has been born King of the Jews?" (Mt 2:2). In response, Herod gathered chief priests and scribes to repeat the wise men's question to them. The Jewish scholars in turn cited Mic 5:2 [Hb. 5:1]:

> And you, Bethlehem, in the land of Judah, are by no means least among the leaders of Judah: because out of you will come a leader who will shepherd My people Israel. (Mt 2:5-6)

The quotation appears to be a loose, paraphrastic translation of the Masoretic version of Mic 5:2 [1]:[14]

> Bethlehem Ephrathah, you are small among the clans of Judah; / One will come from you to be ruler over Israel for Me. / His origin is from antiquity, from eternity [lit. "from days of eternity"].

The literary strategy of Micah follows the common pattern of the prophets, alternating between prophecies of judgment and prophecies of hope. In contrast to the previous paragraph, in which the gathering of the nations to judge Jerusalem is predicted (4:9–5:1), Micah turned to a prediction of hope and restoration in 5:24. There, Micah foretold the coming of a future ruler of Israel who would one day shepherd the flock of Israel. Micah also prophesied that when this king's greatness would extend to the ends of the earth, then Israel would also live securely in their land. This is clearly a messianic prediction, which conflates the two comings of the Messiah.

Micah's prophecy in 5:2 speaks of the origins of the king. It foretold that this future ruler of Israel would come forth from Bethlehem. Although this is plainly an allusion to the restoration of the Davidic house, it is also foretelling that once again a king of Israel will be born in Bethlehem. It is not only saying that Messiah would come from the Davidic line but also that he would actually come from the town of Bethlehem.[15]

Additionally, Micah predicted that this king's origins would be from eternity past. The two Hebrew temporal nouns used can speak of eternity when they stand alone, although this is not always the case. Used chronologically, *qedem*, "antiquity," can refer to ancient times as in "long ago," to the earliest imaginable times as when the mountains first came to be (Dt 33:15), or to the "eternal" God and His eternal dwelling place (Dt 33:27; Hab 1:12, Pss 55:19; 68:33). The second term, *olam*, "eternity," usually refers to the distant or unending future (although sometimes within the context of one's lifetime). But it is also used of ancient times in the past (Ps 24:7) or of the beginning of creation (Ps 25:6; Jl 2:2) or before. According to Ps 93:2, God's "throne has been established from the beginning [lit. "from then"] / You are from eternity." And Ps 90:2 declares, "Before the mountains were born, / before You gave birth to the earth and the world, / from eternity to eternity, You are God." When *qedem* and *olam* are used together, however, as in Prv 8:22-23, they always denote eternity past (cf. Dt 33:27). In Mic 5:2, these words are placed together to emphasize the ruler's true origin, being far earlier than his arrival in Bethlehem or even antiquity. Rather, he comes from eternity past.[16] Kaiser accurately describes this juxtaposition of the temporal and eternal origin of Messiah as follows:

> According to his human heritage, he will descend from the family of David who lived in Bethlehem and will be born in that same town, even though he has a divine line of descent that takes him clear back to eternity. He will be both human and divine. What a mystery![17]

Thus, according to Matthew's record, when Herod asked the priests and scribes where Messiah would be born, the Jewish scholars answered correctly. They chose the correct verse (Mic 5:2) and interpreted it literally. This is a classic example of a literal prediction fulfilled directly. Micah 5:2 and its citation in Mt 2:56 are, in the words of Craig Blomberg, "a very straightforward scheme of prediction and fulfillment. . . . Micah prophesied that the Messiah would be born in Bethlehem, and now it has happened."[18]

This kind of literal prediction and direct fulfillment is to be expected in the NT,[19] but it is clearly not the only way the NT cites the Old. In fact, the next quotation of the OT in Mt 2 demonstrates a second category OT citation, that of typical fulfillment.

TYPICAL FULFILLMENT: MATTHEW 2:15 / HOSEA 11:1

The second OT citation in Mt 2 is generally understood to be "a classic example of pure typology"[20] or typical fulfillment.[21] R. T. France provides a traditional definition of typology as "the recognition of a correspondence between New and Old Testaments, based on a conviction of the unchanging character of the principles of God's working."[22] This section will explore whether Matthew's citation of Hos 11:1 as a type is valid.

After the narrative of the angel telling Joseph to flee to Egypt to save the child from Herod's soldiers, Matthew recounted that the family stayed in Egypt until Herod's death. According to Matthew, these events took place to fulfill "what was spoken by the Lord through the prophet . . . 'Out of Egypt I called My Son.'" Although Matthew's quotation is brief, and there is little to which to compare it, the rendering is distinct from the Septuagint's translation of Hos 11:1. In fact, Matthew's translation is taken from the Masoretic version and is far more literal and accurate than the Septuagint's rendering.[23] This is evident in that the Septuagint uses the word *tekna* (children) as opposed to the more literal *huios* (son) that Matthew uses.

The citation from Hos 11:1 has been found problematic through the years because Hosea was plainly speaking of Israel's departure from Egypt at the exodus and not about the Messiah. The synonymous parallelism in Hos 11:1 shows this beyond a shadow of a doubt: "When Israel was a child, I loved him, and out of Egypt I called my son." "Israel" in the first strophe is parallel to the "son" spoken of in the second strophe. Hosea undoubtedly had Ex 4:22-23 in mind, where God calls Israel, "My firstborn son." Hence the same parallelism is evident in Hosea.[24]

So why does Matthew take a verse that clearly refers to Israel and then maintain that Jesus' return from Egypt is its fulfillment? According to W. S. LaSor this is a case of *sensus plenior*, meaning that while Hosea only had Israel in mind, God had the fuller messianic sense in His mind.[25] As Carson points out,

> So blunt an appeal to what God has absolutely hidden seems a strange background for Matthew's insisting that Jesus' exodus from Egypt in any sense fulfills the Hosea passage. This observation is not trivial; Matthew is reasoning with Jews who could say, "You are not playing fair with the text!"[26]

Blomberg states that the OT author need not have intended the future Messiah when he wrote but rather that "for believing Jews, merely to discern striking parallels between God's actions in history, especially in decisive moments of revelation and redemption, could convince them of divinely intended 'coincidence.'"[27] While an improvement on LaSor's *sensus plenior*, is it really a sufficient explanation for Matthew's typological interpretation? Carson's objection appears to be just as valid in response to Blomberg as it was to LaSor—it does not appear to be fair to the OT text. Although this is indeed an example of typical fulfillment, there should be, and there is, a more plausible explanation for Matthew's use of Hos 11:1 as a type than merely noting striking parallels.

The basis of Matthew's use of Israel as a type of the Messiah is from Nm 23 and 24, which present Israel as a general type of the Messiah. Moreover, that type specifically identifies coming out of Egypt as a point of correspondence between Israel and the future Messiah.[28] This becomes apparent by examining the second and third Balaam oracles (Nm 23:22-24; 24:7-9).

The second Balaam oracle (Nm 23:22-24) describes God's care for the nation of Israel. Singular pronominal suffixes are used of Israel in 23:21, treating the people of Israel as a collective singular. But in 23:22, there is a deliberate shift to a plural pronoun to clarify that it is the whole people of Israel in view. Thus, Nm 23:22a (*'el motsiyam mimmitsrayim*) literally reads, "God brings *them* out of Egypt." The phrase *hen 'am* in Nm 23:24 (lit., "Behold, a people") makes it plain that Balaam's second oracle is about the whole people of Israel. In summary, the oracle states that God brings Israel out of Egypt (23:22a), that He is for Israel like the horns of a wild ox (23:22b), and that Israel will be as powerful as a lion (23:24).

The third Balaam oracle (Nm 24:5-9) begins by describing the fruitfulness of Israel (24:5-6). Then, in Nm 24:7, it predicts a future "seed" or descendant of Jacob (literally, "And his seed [i.e., Jacob's seed] is in the many waters"). Furthermore, this "seed" will also be a king with an exalted kingdom (24:7). In the Masoretic Text, the

King is said to be higher than Agag, but other ancient versions read, "He shall be higher than Gog," the end-time enemy of Israel.[29] The combination of His exalted kingdom and His superiority to Gog, no doubt, was the foundation for the ancient Targum's correct interpretation of the third Balaam oracle as a reference to the future Messiah.

Especially significant is that the third oracle, juxtaposed to the second, deliberately uses similar descriptions of its subject (24:8-9). However, just as deliberately, there is a difference, namely, a shift to the singular pronoun. While in the second oracle "God brings *them* [Israel] out of Egypt," in the third, lit. "God brings *him* [the future king] out of Egypt" (*'el motsiy'o mimmitsrayim*).[30] Further, the third oracle, in a fashion similar to the second, states that God is for Him (the King) like the horns of a wild ox and that the King will be as powerful as a lion.[31]

The author of the Pentateuch is using a significant compositional strategy in placing these two oracles next to each other. The following chart shows the deliberate repetition of phrases.

The Typology of the Balaam Oracles

Israel's past experience prefigures the King's future experience.

ISRAEL Numbers 23:18-24	KING Numbers 24:7-9
God brings **them** out of Egypt	God brings **Him** out of Egypt
God is for **them** like the horns of an ox	God is for **Him** like the horns of an ox
Israel is like a lion	The **King** is like a lion

The oracles are intentionally similar (same phrases) and intentionally different (singular versus plural pronouns). The writer's strategy was to establish a pattern or a type: what God will do for Israel, He will also do for the future King of Israel. Sailhamer makes this point when he writes,

> The writer's purpose appears to be to view the reign of the future king in terms taken from God's great acts of salvation in the past. The future is going to be like the past. What God did for Israel in the past is seen as a type of what he will do for them in the future when he sends his promised king.[32]

By placing the two oracles side by side, the author of the Pentateuch deliberately establishes one of the foundational types found in the Bible—Israel as a type of the future King Messiah. Beyond this general typology, these two Balaam oracles provide a specific similarity between the people of Israel and the future King of Israel—God will bring them both out of Egypt.

Understanding this typology lays the foundation for Matthew's typical use of Hos 11:1. While others have noted that perhaps Matthew had Nm 24:8 in mind[33] and some have even suggested that the verse Matthew may have been citing was Nm 24:8,[34] they both miss the point. Matthew understood that the Pentateuch had established Israel as a type of the future King Messiah. Furthermore, he understood that the Torah had established a specific parallel between Israel and the future king, namely, that God would bring them both out of Egypt. Hence, based on this established typology, Matthew saw it as perfectly sound, when narrating God's deliverance of Messiah from Egypt, to cite Hos 11:1, which speaks of God bringing Israel out of Egypt.

The question remains, "Why not just cite Nm 24:8?" The answer is that Matthew was not just describing the journey from Egypt—he wanted to emphasize the Messiah's relationship to His Father as Son. The Hosea passage states that "Out of Egypt I called My son." This was so important to Matthew that he rejected the Septuagint translation of Hos 11:1 ("Out of Egypt I called my children") and made his own, more accurate translation of the Hebrew text, using the word "son."[35]

The purpose of this discussion has been to demonstrate that Matthew did not indiscriminately flip through his Hebrew Bible and pull a verse out of context to "fulfill" a nonexistent prediction of the Messiah. Nor did he arbitrarily and without biblical justification create a far-fetched typical interpretation. Matthew's case of typical fulfillment exemplifies deep knowledge of the Scriptures, using a valid type that is well established in the Torah.[36]

The point here is to show that even when the NT uses the OT typologically, it is doing so in a reasonable way. Matthew's typical citation of Hos 11:1 makes perfect sense in light of the type established by Moses in the Pentateuch. However, what is Matthew's meaning in the next OT quotation? That, too, will be seen as a logical and fair use of the OT.

APPLICATIONAL FULFILLMENT: MATTHEW 2:16-18 / JEREMIAH 31:15

The third OT citation in Mt 2 is an example of applicational fulfillment.[37] In this section, Matthew recorded Herod's response to being outwitted by the magi. In relating the events of the Slaughter of the Innocents, when every male child under age two in Bethlehem was slaughtered,[38] Matthew states, "Then what was spoken by Jeremiah the prophet was fulfilled," and cites Jer 31:15:

> A voice was heard in Ramah,
> a lament with bitter weeping—
> Rachel weeping for her children,
> refusing to be comforted for her children
> because they are no more.

Matthew's quotation appears to be closer to the Masoretic Text than the Septuagint but does show some dependency on the LXX.[39] The context of the quote from Jeremiah is essentially an eschatological declaration of hope. The chapter revolves around an expectation of the end-time deliverance of Israel. Yet tucked into the middle of Jer 31 is the reason that Judah needed to be reminded of her future deliverance—the death and exile of Jewish youth at the hands of the Babylonians.

Jeremiah 31:15 speaks of Ramah as the place of weeping because it was there the Babylonians gathered the captive young men of Judah before sending them into exile (Jer 40:1-2). There Rachel was said to weep for her children. Obviously, the matriarch Rachel had been long dead when Jeremiah wrote. So Jeremiah did not use her name literally (i.e., weeping from her grave) but rather symbolically, representing all of Jewish mothers.[40] Thus, Jeremiah states that Jewish mothers were weeping for their sons who had died in the war with Babylon and for the young men who were being taken to a distant land as captives. Jeremiah was referring to the deep pain of Jewish mothers at the loss of their young men to Nebuchadnezzar and the Babylonians. So the question is, since Jer 31:15 refers to the Babylonian exile, how could Matthew cite the Slaughter of the Innocents as fulfilling this text?

According to France, "This is one of Matthew's most elusive OT quotations, and few claim with any confidence to have fathomed just what he intended." France goes on to speak of Matthew's "creativity" in formula quotations.[41] Some might consider Matthew's quotation of Jer 31:15 to be midrashic interpretation.[42] Longenecker maintains that the NT frequently quotes the Old without concern for its literary context, even as ancient rabbis did in their midrashic interpretations.

Therefore, according to this midrashic view, Matthew's quotation is merely an atomistic quotation offered without any regard for Jeremiah's intention, the literary context, or the original meaning of the verse. Matthew could quote Jeremiah in this way because he was operating under the inspiration of the Holy Spirit, but modern interpreters must never reproduce this sort of atomistic exegesis.[43]

One problem with citing midrashic background as the explanation of the NT's exegesis of the Old is that this is historically anachronistic. It is based on rabbinic exegesis of a later time but substantially misunderstands how pre-AD 70

Jewish interpreters used biblical texts. David Instone-Brewer has examined all the instances of pre-AD 70 protorabbinic exegesis. He concludes that unlike later rabbinic methods, Jewish exegesis in the prerabbinic period before the destruction of the Temple was concerned with using Scripture in context. He writes, "Every single scribal exegesis examined could be quoted as an example to show that Scripture was interpreted according to its context."[44] Moreover, at that time, protorabbinic exegetes would have posited that "Scripture does not have a secondary meaning," and they would have indeed been concerned with discovering "the primary or plain sense of the text."[45] Klyne Snodgrass summarizes this distinction when he writes, "In the earlier rabbinic material, midrashic interpretation is fairly straightforward, but later rabbinic practices often focused more on individual words and even letters. The result is a 'creative' exegesis in which the original concern of the text is often lost."[46] So if the NT writers were truly using a Jewish hermeneutic from the first century, their citations should have been concerned with context and the true meaning of the text.

A second flaw in taking NT citations of the Old as creative exegesis in the form of midrash is that it misunderstands the true purpose of midrash. The point of midrash is not to pull texts out of context. Rather, a more correct understanding of midrash is that it was to show the continuing relevance of Scripture to contemporary life. Even Longenecker recognizes this when he writes that the purpose of midrash was "to contemporize the revelation of God given earlier for the people of God living later in a different situation."[47] The focus of midrash was on the application of ancient texts in later circumstances.[48] This should not be surprising since the midrashim are homiletic in nature and application is the priority of preaching.

Applicational fulfillment, the third category of OT citation, did indeed use Scripture midrashically in conformity with early protorabbinic methods. This was not an arbitrary (or even creative) form of interpretation that showed no regard for context or original meaning. So, in Mt 2:16-18, Matthew was citing an OT text, deriving a principle found in that text, and showing its relevance to his own day and time. Matthew was *applying* Scripture, not twisting it.

A question might be, why did the NT authors not specify what principle they were applying? The answer is that they expected the principle to be so obvious to their readers that it did not require further explication. Moving from exegesis to biblical principle to contemporary application is so intuitive that the writers expected their readers to discern the bridging principle even as they read it.

Contemporary readers of Scripture apply God's Word in much the same way, moving from an exegetical idea to contemporary relevance without explaining the process but still doing so accurately. For example, a number of years ago, my family faced a serious medical problem. To encourage me, many of my friends would assure me that all would be fine because "we had the best doctors and the best hospital." I would always respond with Ps 20:7: "Some trust in chariots and some in horses, but we trust in the name of the Lord our God" (NIV). I never explained that this text actually was not about how to face a medical emergency but what Israel's attitude should have been when going to war. Nor did I say the principle of this text is that we are to trust not in human might but in God's protective care. And I did not state that although we may have excellent medical care, the application for me was that we were to trust God in dealing with serious illness, not physicians or hospitals. I did not explain all this because it was intuitive—I expected my hearers to comprehend what I was saying without explication, and they did.

The reason for Matthew's citation of Jer 31:15 was to show that Scripture had a continuing relevance. As David L. Cooper wrote, "Matthew simply applies the language of this prophecy to a similar situation of his day."[49] Just as Rachel represented Jewish mothers who wept at the death and exile of their sons, so Jewish mothers once again mourned when wicked Herod murdered their children. And Rachel has continued to lament and has refused to be consoled for her children as they have been murdered by Crusaders, Nazis, and terrorists. Sadly, this is a Scripture that has had continuing relevance for centuries.

To summarize, the third category of NT citation of the OT is applicational fulfillment. It uses the text in a way that protorabbinic writers did before AD 70, seeking to apply ancient biblical texts to their contemporary situation. Applicational fulfillment recognizes that ancient texts have continuing relevance. By quoting these texts, the writers understood a principle in a biblical passage and then applied it to their contemporary situation.[50] Thus, Matthew recognized that Jeremiah wrote of the suffering of Rachel, the personification of Jewish mothers, at the exile. He, in turn, applied the principle that the Jewish mothers of Bethlehem still wept because of the suffering of their children at the hands of wicked Herod.

SUMMARY FULFILLMENT: MATTHEW 2:19-23

The fourth prophecy and fulfillment category in Mt 2 is summary fulfillment.[51] The Matthew narrative relates the events for the Messiah's family after the death of Herod. The Lord appeared to Joseph in a dream and told him it was safe to return Mary and the toddler Jesus to the land of Israel. However, when Joseph found Archelaus ruling over Judea, he was afraid to return there[52] and instead went to his hometown of Nazareth.[53] According to Matthew, this was to "to fulfill what was spoken through the prophets, that He will be called a Nazarene" (Mt 2:23).[54]

Of course, the long-recognized difficulty with Matthew's fulfillment formula here is that in no place does the Hebrew Bible predict that "He will be called a Nazarene." As a result, a number of possible explanations have been proposed.

The most popular is to take Matthew's citation as a play on words derived from the Hebrew word *netser* used of the "branch" in Isa 11:1. There it speaks of Messiah, the Branch, who will spring forth from the obscurity of Jesse's household.[55] The difficulty with this view is that the wordplay is entirely absent in Greek, the language of Matthew's Gospel, and makes no sense of the fulfillment.

A second option has been to view Jesus as a "Nazarite."[56] Some even cite the phrase "the boy will be a Nazarite" (Jdg 13:7) in support of this interpretation. However, the word Nazarite has an entirely different root and spelling from Nazareth in Hebrew (*nazir* vs. *natsaret*) and is no way related to being a Nazarene. Moreover, the verse in Judges is a prediction of the birth of Samson, not the Messiah. Above all, Jesus was not a Nazarite, nor does an upbringing in Nazareth connect Him to the Hebrew word for Nazarite.

The best interpretation is to view this as a summary fulfillment, meaning that the phrase "He will be called a Nazarene" summarizes a teaching from the prophets about the Messiah.[57] This is supported from within the text because here alone Matthew states that this fulfills the words of the "prophets" (plural), referring to many prophecies, not just an individual one. Moreover, the conjunction *hoti*, which indicates an indirect statement, shows that Matthew was not referring to a specific quotation but a general idea—a paraphrase of Mt 2:23 would be that Jesus grew up in Nazareth "to fulfill the general teaching of the prophets that the Messiah would be a Nazarene."

Matthew is not unique in using this sort of citation to summarize a biblical lesson. For example, there is an OT example of just such a citation. Ezra 9:10-12 states,

> Now, our God, what can we say in light of this? For we have abandoned the commands You gave through Your servants the prophets, saying: "The land you are entering to possess is an impure land. The surrounding peoples have filled it from end to end with their uncleanness by their impurity and detestable practices. So do not give your daughters to their sons in marriage or take their daughters for your sons. Never seek their peace or prosperity, so that you will be strong, eat the good things of the land, and leave it as an inheritance to your sons forever."

Ezra's quotation cannot be found anywhere in the Hebrew Bible. Rather, he was summarizing the teachings found in Dt 11:8-9, Isa 1:19, and Ezk 37:25.[58]

But what theme is Matthew summarizing by calling Jesus a Nazarene? He is using "Nazarene" as a term of derision and is summarizing the OT teaching that the Messiah was to be despised. That "Nazarene" was itself a disparaging term in the first century is evident from Nathanael's reaction to hearing of a Messiah from

Nazareth, objecting, "Can anything good come out of Nazareth?" (see also Jn 7:41-42,52). Moreover, in the only other place Matthew uses "Nazarene," it is used in a derogatory way (Mt 26:71).[59] Thus, according to Matthew, the prophets taught that Messiah would be despised. Moreover, Matthew maintained that the negative reaction to Messiah's coming from the poor, despised village of Nazareth would epitomize the derisive attitude of Israel to her King.

Although Judaism tended to emphasize the glorious Messiah, the Hebrew Bible repeatedly presents the Messiah as a despised figure. For example, see the psalms of the rejected and suffering Messiah (Pss 22 and 69). Zechariah speaks of Israel esteeming her future messianic king with the value of a dead slave (Zch 11:4-14 referring to Ex 21:32). Isaiah predicts most clearly that the Messiah would be "One who is despised" and "abhorred by people" (49:7); that He would suffer "scorn and spitting" (50:6); that He would arise from obscurity, "like a root out of dry ground" (53:2), and that He would be "despised and rejected by men" (53:3). Thus, Matthew, using summary fulfillment, encapsulates all that the prophets wrote of the Messiah being despised and scorned with the terse phrase "He shall be called a Nazarene."[60]

CONCLUSION

S. L. Johnson, Jr. has asked,

> Can we reproduce the exegesis of the New Testament? Unhesitatingly, the reply is yes, although we are not allowed to claim for our results the infallibility of the Lord and His apostles. They are reliable teachers of biblical doctrine and they are reliable teachers of hermeneutics and exegesis. We not only *can* reproduce their exegetical methodology, we *must* if we are to be taught their understanding of Holy Scripture. Their principles, probably taught them by the Lord in His post-resurrection ministry, are not abstruse and difficult. They are simple, plain, and logical. The things they find in the OT are really there.[61]

Johnson has answered his question correctly. The point of this article has been to show that the NT writers did not interpret the Hebrew Bible in a creative, atomistic, or noncontextual way. Rather, their hermeneutics were contextual and reflective of the intent of the OT passages. Although NT authors commonly cited direct fulfillments of OT messianic prophecies, they also noted typical, applicational, and summary fulfillments. Too often it is present-day interpreters who fail to see the true meaning of OT texts by limiting themselves to their historical rather than their literary sense. Therefore, it is contemporary readers who need to adjust their lenses to see the Hebrew Bible as the NT authors did, as a messianic book written with a messianic intention.

1. This article is adapted from a chapter in Michael Rydelnik, *The Messianic Hope: Is the Hebrew Bible Really Messianic?* NAC Studies in Bible and Theology, ed. E. Ray Clendenen (Nashville: B&H Publishers, 2010), 95–111. Used with permission.

2. W. C. Kaiser, *The Uses of the Old Testament in the New* (Chicago: Moody, 1985), x–xi.

3. For a collection of essays on this issue, reflecting different viewpoints, see G. K. Beale, ed., *The Right Doctrine from the Wrong Texts?* (Grand Rapids: Baker, 1994).

4. G. F. Moore, *Judaism in the First Centuries of the Christian Era* (New York: Schocken, 1975), 1:248, as cited by R. N. Longenecker, "'Who Is the Prophet Talking About?' Some Reflections on the New Testament's Use of the Old," in Beale, *The Right Doctrine from the Wrong Texts*, 381.

5. Longenecker, "'Who is the Prophet Talking About?' Some Reflections on the New Testament's Use of the Old," 379–84.

6. Ibid., 384.

7. R. N. Longenecker, *Biblical Exegesis in the Apostolic Period*, 2nd ed. (Grand Rapids: Eerdmans, 1999), xxxviii.

8. M. Silva, "The New Testament Use of the Old Testament: Text Form and Authority," in *Scripture and Truth*, ed. D. A. Carson and J. D. Woodbridge (Grand Rapids: Zondervan, 1983), 164. See also S. L. Johnson Jr., *The Old Testament in the New: An Argument for Biblical Inspiration* (Grand Rapids: Zondervan, 1980), 93–94.

9. See also G. Beale's argument that the NT uses legitimate hermeneutical methods to interpret the Hebrew Bible ("Did Jesus and His Followers Preach the Right Doctrine from the Wrong Texts?" *Them* 14 [1989], 89–96).

10. Thanks to A. G. Fruchtenbaum, who drew my attention to an older work by D. L. Cooper. Cooper identified four broad classifications of OT quotations in the NT in his examination of Mt 2. These became the launching pad for the basic ideas in this article (D. L. Cooper, *Messiah: His Historical Appearance* [Los Angeles: Biblical Research Society, 1958], 174–78).

11. S. D. Toussaint, *Behold the King* (Portland: Multnomah, 1980), 47.

12. Ibid.

13. This is the classification that Cooper labels "literal prophecy" (Cooper, *Messiah: His Historical Appearance*, 174).

14. G. L. Archer and G. C. Chirichigno, *Old Testament Quotations in the New Testament: A Complete Survey* (Chicago: Moody, 1983), 157.

15. Even traditional Jewish sources see Bethlehem as the birthplace of Messiah. The *Targum Pseudo-Jonathan* on Gn 35:21, using the name Migdal Edar for Bethlehem, states that it is "the place from whence the Messiah shall be revealed in the last days." In the Jerusalem Talmud, *Ber.* 5a states, "The King Messiah . . . from where does he come forth? From the royal city of Bethlehem in Judah."

16. This is possibly the source of the Talmudic idea of a preexistent Messiah. See S. Goldman, "Micah," in *The Twelve Prophets*, Soncino Books of the Bible (London: Soncino, 1957), 175. However, while the Talmud recognizes the Messiah as preexistent, it does not see Him as eternal.

17. W. C. Kaiser, *The Messiah in the Old Testament* (Grand Rapids: Zondervan, 1994), 154.

18. C. L. Blomberg, "Matthew," in *Commentary on the New Testament Use of the Old Testament*, ed. G. K. Beale and D. A. Carson (Grand Rapids: Baker, 2007), 7.

19. Direct fulfillments form the vast majority of prediction/fulfillments in Matthew. Other examples of direct fulfillments in Matthew are 1:23/Isa 7:14; 4:15-16/Isa 9:1-2; 8:17/Isa 53:4; 11:10/Mal 3:1; 12:17-21/Isa 42:1-4; 21:5/Zch 9:9; 21:42/Ps 118:22-23; 22:44/Ps 110:1; 26:31/Zch 13:7; 27:9-10/Zch 11:12-13; 27:46/Ps 22:1.

20. Sailhamer objects to this: "When Matthew quoted Hos 11:1 as fulfilled in the life of Christ, he was not resorting to a typological interpretation. Rather, he was drawing the *sensus literalis* from the book of Hosea and it, in turn, was drawn from Hosea's exegesis of the *sensus literalis* of the Pentateuch" ("Hosea 11:1 and Matthew 2:15" *Westminster Theological Journal* 63 [2001]: 91). Although there is much to commend in this interpretation, particularly Sailhamer's demonstration of Hosea's dependence on Nm 24, still it does fall short. It seems to me that Hosea was looking back to Israel's exodus from Egypt literally, not using it as a metaphor for the Messiah's future redemption as Sailhamer contends. However, Sailhamer's understanding of Hosea's dependence on Numbers does indeed, as will be seen, make Matthew's typical interpretation not farfetched but entirely defensible.

21. Ibid. Cooper categorizes this example in Mt 2:15 as a "literal prophecy with typical import." (*Messiah: His Historical Appearance*, 175).

22. R. T. France, *The Gospel according to Matthew*, Tyndale New Testament Commentaries (Grand Rapids: Eerdmans, 1985), 40.

23. Archer and Chirichigno, *Old Testament Quotations in the New Testament: A Complete Survey*, 147.

24. Cooper, *Messiah: His Historical Appearance*, 175.

25. W. L. LaSor, "Prophecy, Inspiration, and *Sensus Plenior*," *Tyndale Bulletin* 29 (1978): 49–60.

26. D. A. Carson, "Matthew," *Expositor's Bible Commentary*, 8:92.

27. Blomberg, "Matthew," in Beale and Carson, *Commentary on the New Testament Use of the Old Testament*, 8.

28. Note also the vine imagery applied to Israel in the OT (Ps 80:8 ["You uprooted a vine from Egypt"]; Isa 5:1-7; 27:2-6; Jer 2:21; 12:10; Ezk 15:1-8; 19:10-14; Hos 10:1), which Jesus applied to Himself in Jn 15:1.

29. The variant reading is preferable. It has wide support being found in the Septuagint, the Samaritan Pentateuch, Aquila, Symmachus, and Theodotion. It is also supported by the context, in which Balaam says he is speaking of "the end of days" (24:14, lit.). For a more in-depth discussion, see Michael Rydelnik, *The Messianic Hope: Is the Hebrew Bible Really Messianic?* (Nashville: B&H Publishers, 2010), 38–39.

30. Sailhamer, "Hosea 11:1 and Matthew 2:15," 94–95.

31. "He crouches, he lies down like a lion or a lioness—who dares to rouse him?" (24:9). This is an almost literal repetition of the messianic prophecy in Gn 49:9. The use of an innertextual reference gives further confirmation that Nm 24:7-9 is referring to the messianic king.

32. J. H. Sailhamer, *The Pentateuch as Narrative* (Grand Rapids: Zondervan, 1992), 408.

33. R. H. Gundry, *Matthew: A Commentary on His Literary and Theological Art* (Grand Rapids: Eerdmans, 1982), 34.

34. According to W. D. Davies and D. C. Allison, "For those familiar with the LXX, Matthew's quotation would have seemed closer to Nm 24:8 than to Hos 11:1. This explains the scribal note in the margin of א, which ascribes the text to Numbers." (*A Critical and Exegetical Commentary on the Gospel according to Saint Matthew*, International Critical Commentary [Edinburgh: T&T Clark, 1988], 1:262n8).

35. Gundry, *Matthew: A Commentary on His Literary and Theological Art*, 33. Also Davies and Allison, *A Critical and Exegetical Commentary on the Gospel according to Saint Matthew*, 1:262–64.

36. Typology is less common than what some expect, but it is still present in the NT. One example is in Acts 13:47, where Paul quotes Isa 49:6. The Isaiah passage refers directly to the Messiah, who establishes a pattern or type for His followers. In this fashion, they are appointed as lights for the Gentiles. Another example is the typology of Melchizedek found in Heb 7. The basis of this type is the linkage between the Messiah and Melchizedek in Ps 110:4.

37. D. L. Cooper calls this "literal prophecy plus an application" (*Messiah: His Historical Appearance*, 175).

38. The historicity of this account is frequently denied. Yet it is entirely in keeping with what is known of Herod's character and actions. Moreover, since Bethlehem was so small, the deaths, though grievous in that community, would have numbered in the dozens, not the thousands. Therefore, it is no surprise that there is no extrabiblical record of this event. See R. T. France, *The Gospel of Matthew*, New International Commentary on the New Testament (Grand Rapids: Eerdmans, 2007), 84–85.

39. Archer and Chirichigno, *Old Testament Quotations in the New Testament: A Complete Survey*, 136–37.

40. *Bereshit Rabbah* 71:2, commenting on Gn 29:31, identifies the matriarch Rachel as the principal or chief mother of Israel and cites Jer 31:15 in support of this idea.

41. R. T. France, *The Gospel of Matthew*, 88.

42. "*Midrash* derives from a Hebrew word meaning 'to seek' and refers to interpretive exposition." Klyne Snodgrass, "The Use of the Old Testament in the New" in Beale, *The Right Doctrine from the Wrong Texts?* (Grand Rapids: Baker, 1994), 42.

43. Ibid., 384–85.

44. David Instone-Brewer, *Techniques and Assumptions in Jewish Exegesis before 70 CE* (Tubingen: J. C. B. Mohr, 1992), 167.

45. Ibid., 169.

46. Snodgrass, "The Old Testament in the New," 42.

47. Richard N. Longenecker, "'Who is the Prophet Talking About?' Some Reflections on the New Testament's Use of the Old" in *The Right Doctrine from the Wrong Texts?* 381.

48. Snodgrass, "The Old Testament in the New," 42.

49. Cooper, *Messiah: His Historical Appearance*, 177.

50. Some other examples of applicational fulfillment in Matthew are 4:6/Ps 91:11-12; 13:14-15/Isa 6:9-10; 13:35/Ps 78:2; 15:8-9/Isa 29:13.

51. Cooper calls this "literal prophecy plus a summation" (*Messiah: His Historical Appearance*, 175).

52. The text implies but leaves unstated what is known from Josephus—that Herod Archelaus was brutal in his

treatment of his subjects, including the murder of 3,000 Judeans celebrating Passover upon his ascension to the throne (*Antiquities* 17.342).

53. Although Matthew fails to mention that this was Joseph's hometown.

54. Against many other translations, the HCSB, ESV, and NIV translate this correctly, taking the Greek word *hoti* not as introducing a direct quotation but rather an indirect statement. As R. T. France explains (*The Gospel of Matthew*, 91), "The quotation-formula [in 2:23] differs from all Matthew's other formulae in two respects: instead of a single prophet (named or anonymous) he speaks here of 'the prophets,' and the participle *legontos* ('who said') which leads into all the other quotations is here missing; in its place is *hoti* ('that'), which sometimes functions as the equivalent of our quotation marks, but can also indicate not so much a direct quotation as a paraphrase or summary of what was said. These two distinctive features together suggest strongly that what Matthew is here providing is not a quotation of a specific passage but rather a theme of prophecy (as in 26:56, where again plural 'prophets' are mentioned and no particular passage is cited)."

55. According to France, this is the view "mentioned in most commentaries" (*The Gospel of Matthew*, 92n10).

56. Multiple authors have adopted this interpretation, including McNeile, Schaeder, Schweizer, Sanders, Zuckschwerdt, Soares, Prabhu, Brown, and Allan. See Davies and Allison for citations (*Matthew*, 1:276).

57. This view is ably supported by both France, *The Gospel of Matthew*, 94–95, and Carson, "Matthew," 8:97.

58. Davies and Allison (*The Gospel of Matthew*, 1:275) suggest that there is a rabbinic example of a summary quotation in *b. Ketub.* 111a, but I cannot identify it in my reading of that text.

59. France adds that the phrase "He shall be called" is referring specifically to "derogatory name calling" (*The Gospel of Matthew*, 94).

60. Some might object that summary fulfillment is unique to Mt 2:23, so it should not even be considered a category of prophetic fulfillment. This is not the case. Although rare, it is also in Mt 26:56, Acts 3:18-24, and Rom 1:2.

61. Italics his. Johnson, *The Old Testament in the New: An Argument for Biblical Inspiration*, 93–94.

Canonical Perspectives on Messianic Prophecy[1]

MICHAEL A. RYDELNIK

The term "canon" refers to those books that have been accepted as authoritative Scripture. The books of the Hebrew canon (the Old Testament) are divided into three sections: The Law (**T**orah), Prophets (**N**evi'im), and Writings (**K**etuvim). The Hebrew Bible is called the Tanakh, which is an acronym derived from the Hebrew names of these three sections of the Hebrew Bible ("t" from the Hebrew letter *tav* [ת], the first letter of the word *Torah;* "n" for the Hebrew letter *nun* [נ], the first letter of the word *Nevi'im*; "k" for the Hebrew letter *kaf* [כ], the first letter of the word *Ketuvim* but softened to "kh" since it is at the end of a syllable). It is virtually without dispute that this threefold division was fixed sometime during the intertestamental period, although it is unknown who exactly was responsible for it. Nevertheless, it appears that the individual or community that shaped the Tanakh in this way understood and sought to reflect the messianic message of the Hebrew Bible. This observation corroborates that the Hebrew Bible should indeed be read messianically. This article will examine the canonical evidence supporting this messianic perspective. First, it will do so by examining how the redactional shape of the Hebrew Bible sustains a messianic reading of these texts. Second, it will consider how a book's messianic message was an essential element for its inclusion in the OT canon.

SHAPING OF THE HEBREW CANON

On what basis was the OT canon structured as Law, Prophets, and Writings? The conventional view, advocated by Herbert Edward Ryle,[2] was that each section was recognized as a complete whole in three different eras. He maintained that there was "a gradual development in the formation of the canon through three successive stages."[3] First, the Torah was canonized (by the fifth century BC), then the Prophets (by the third century BC), and finally the Writings (by AD 90). Basing the canonization process purely on the historical emergence of scriptural books, Ryle concluded that there was no discernible rhyme or reason for the division of books into the Prophets or the Writings.

Beckwith has challenged this view and has argued the canon of the Hebrew Bible was closed in the form of the Tanakh no later than the second century BC.[4] Moreover, he has demonstrated that "a rational principle is discernible in the distribution of books between the Prophets and the Hagiographa."[5] First, he notes that the narrative books in all three sections generally cover successive historical periods: The Law covers the period from creation to the death of Moses; The Prophets covers the period from the Conquest to the Exile; The Writings (Hagiographa) covers the period from the Exile to the Return.[6]

Beckwith also identifies a second discernible principle:

> It is clear that the order of the non-narrative books in the Prophets and the Hagiographa is not chronological, and they are in fact arranged in descending order of size, with the single and trivial exception that the Song of Songs is put before Lamentations, so as to keep the three books associated with Solomon together.[7]

As seen above, the threefold structure of the Hebrew canon is not the result of random development but rather a consequence of editorial shaping and design. However, there is further evidence of an editorial configuration, namely, that the Tanakh was given its final redactional shape to give an eschatological/messianic hope. If that is so, then it would be safe to say that those who shaped the canon read it, and expected others to read it, as a messianic primer.

Sailhamer has suggested that this discernible messianic strategy in the canonical redaction of the Tanakh is found in the two "canonical seams," the first seam uniting the Law and the Prophets, and the second uniting the Prophets and the Writings. He has observed that the last paragraph of the Pentateuch (Dt 34:9-12) and the first in the Prophets (Jos 1:1-9) have a pattern that is reproduced in the last paragraph of the Prophets (Mal 4:4-6) and the first in the Writings (Ps 1).[8]

The Torah's last paragraph (Dt 34:9-12) is essentially eschatological and messianic. It states that at the time when prophecy ceased, the "prophet like Moses" had not come ("no prophet has arisen again like Moses, whom the Lord knew face to face" v. 10), implying that Israel is to continue to look for him. Immediately after this, the opening paragraph of the Prophets (Jos 1:1-9) calls upon Joshua to exercise a new form of leadership, that of the wise scholar. He is to keep the law and "recite it day and night" (Jos 1:7-8). Thus, the narrative presents Joshua as the ideal wise man who models godly behavior until the eschatological prophet (the Messiah) comes.

The seam between the Prophets and the Writings is similar. The concluding paragraph of the Prophets (Mal 4:4-6) is similar to the end of the Torah. It is eschatological and messianic in its outlook, pointing to the day when Elijah will come before the Day of the Lord. When viewed canonically, it is plain that Elijah is being distinguished from the eschatological "Prophet like Moses." Elijah is to come to prepare the people for the arrival of the prophet like Moses (Mal 4:5). Following immediately after this section, the Writings begin with "Psalm 1, which presents the ideal of the wise man who meditates day and night on the Torah (Ps 1:2-3)."[9]

The textual and verbal links in the canonical seams are transparent: Dt 34:9-12 and Mal 4:4-6 both point to the eschatological prophet, the Messiah. Joshua 1:1-9 and Ps 1 both present the ideal wise man who prospers as he meditates on the Torah (See Figure 1). It becomes obvious that the final shape of the Tanakh was not the result of historical chance but the deliberate attempt to communicate the messianic message of the Hebrew Bible. In Sailhamer's words,

> The more closely we examine the final shape of the Hebrew Bible (TaNaK), the clearer it becomes that its shape and structure are not accidental. There are clear signs of intelligent life behind its formation. . . . In the later stages of the formation of the Hebrew Bible its authors were primarily concerned with making more explicit the messianic hope that was already explicit in the earliest texts.[10]

Figure 1

THE CANONICAL SHAPING OF THE TANAK POINTS TO MESSIANIC HOPE

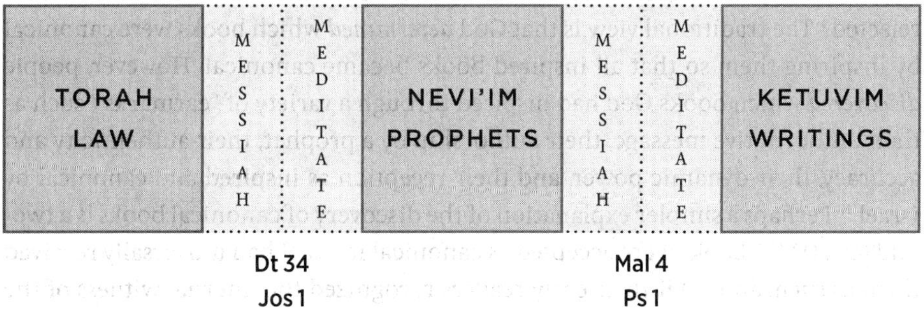

Based on a chart by John H. Sailhamer, *Introduction to Old Testament Theology* (Grand Rapids: Zondervan, 1995): 240.

Some might object to seeing intentionality in this framework, but I am reminded of a family vacation some time ago. We rented a cabin in Pennsylvania and were amazed at the perfect symmetry of the forest behind our cabin. Never before had I seen a forest in which each tree lined up to each other with the same distance in both directions, from side to side and front to back. Upon paying the bill for our stay, I commented on this phenomenon to the owner of the cabin. He replied that it was not so phenomenal—the property had previously been a Christmas tree farm. Obviously the lay of the trees was not random but intentional. This is the same conclusion that must be derived from the shaping of the Tanakh. The seams of the Hebrew Bible, connecting the Law, the Prophets, and the Writings, were deliberately shaped in order to communicate an essential message of the OT—that of the Messiah and His presence in the text of the Scriptures. The wise man, meditating on the Word of God, will discover the future Messiah in the words of Scripture.

The significance of the canonical redaction of the Tanakh is apparent. It was designed to teach its readers to be faithful to the Torah until the Messiah comes. Hence, it is safe to say that the actual shaping of the Tanakh was fashioned to present the messianic hope. In this way, the canonical redaction of the text reflects the viewpoint of the prophets, who interpreted previous revelation as messianic.[11] Just as the prophets read the Torah messianically, so those who shaped the canon read the Tanakh in the same way. This is reflected not only in the canonical redaction of the Tanakh, as seen above, but also in what follows regarding the inclusion of the individual books in the Tanakh.

INCLUSION IN AND DISCOVERY OF THE HEBREW CANON

Why were certain books accepted as canonical in the OT while others were rejected? The traditional view is that God *determined* which books were canonical by inspiring them so that all inspired books became canonical. However, people *discovered* which books God had inspired through a variety of "earmarks," such as their authoritative message, their authorship by a prophet, their authenticity and accuracy, their dynamic power, and their reception as inspired and canonical by Israel.[12] Perhaps a simpler explanation of the discovery of canonical books is a two-fold test: (1) OT books were accepted as canonical if Israel had universally received them as such, and (2) if their early readers recognized the internal witness of the Holy Spirit confirming their canonical nature.[13]

There appears to be one more element that was used to discover canonicity: namely, that any canonical OT book had to have a messianic hope as part of its message. The reason is that the OT in its entirety is in some way messianic. That is not to say that all ancient books with a messianic hope were necessarily canonical but rather that all canonical books are indeed messianic.

Sailhamer writes,

> I believe the messianic thrust of the OT was the *whole* reason the books of the Hebrew Bible were written. In other words, the Hebrew Bible was not written as the national literature of Israel. It probably also was not written to the nation of Israel as such. It was rather written in my opinion, as the expression of the deep-seated messianic hope of a small group of faithful prophets and their followers.[14]

This is also the view of James Hamilton, who writes, "The OT is a messianic document, written from a messianic perspective, to sustain a messianic hope."[15] In rabbinic literature, there is Rabbi Johanan's famous dictum, "Every prophet prophesied only of the days of the Messiah" (*b. Ber.* 34b). The apostle Peter also seems to advocate this view when he declares that "all the prophets who have spoken, from Samuel and those after him, have also announced these days" (Ac 3:24).

If messianic hope is the central thrust of the Hebrew Bible, then it is likely that this messianic theme was also one of the essential earmarks for recognizing the canonicity of OT books. Is it possible to find a messianic theme in all the books of the Hebrew canon? That is what must be examined now.

THE MESSIANIC THEME OF THE CANON

The messianic "earmark" becomes even more apparent when actually looking at the sections of the Tanakh and discovering that they all do reveal the Messiah. From the Law to the Prophets to the Writings, it is plain that the central message of each of the books is the future king who will rule the nations, namely, the Messiah.

MESSIAH IN THE TORAH

Starting in the Pentateuch, the author makes messianic expectation central to the overall structure of the Torah. This becomes clear by observing that the overall structure of the Pentateuch follows a consistent pattern: narrative, poem, epilogue (see Figure 2). So, for example, the Torah begins with an extended narrative of the primeval and patriarchal world (Gn 1–48), followed by a poetic section containing Jacob's oracle concerning his sons (Gn 49), and then the epilogue concerning the deaths of Jacob and Joseph (Gn 50).[16] This structure continues throughout the Pentateuch with the poetic sections in Ex 15, Nm 23–24, and Dt 32–33.

It becomes evident that much like the songs in a Broadway musical, the poetic passages carry the main theme of the story. All the poems (except for the one in Ex 15) indicate that the fulfillment of these passages will take place at "the end of days" (Gn 49:1; Nm 24:14; Dt 31:29; author's translation).[17] Additionally, these passages speak of a coming king, one who will ultimately receive the obedience of all people (Gn 49:8-11) and will rule over an exalted kingdom including the kingdom of Gog (Nm 24:7), the end-time enemy of Israel (Ezk 38-39).[18] The structure itself points to a future Messianic King.

Figure 2

The structure of the Torah points to Messiah in the Torah

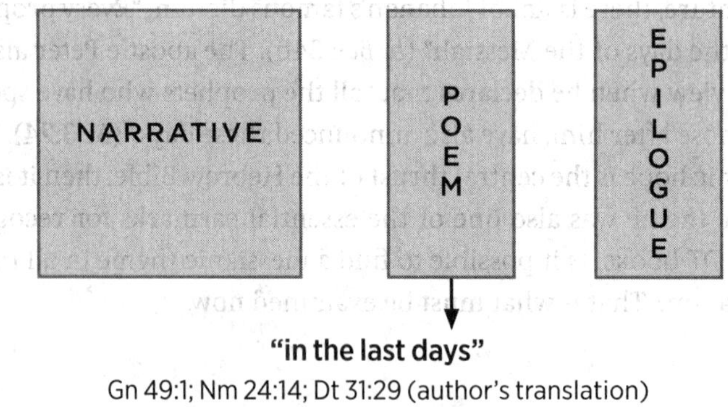

Not only the structure, but also the skeleton of the Pentateuchal story follows a particular individual. This is evident in tracing the family line, or "the seed," in the Torah.[19] He is the "seed" who will descend from Eve (Gn 3:15), the future king who will descend from Abraham (Gn 17:6), the seed who will bless all nations (Gn 22:17b-19).[20] Additionally, He is the lion of the tribe of Judah, the king who will rule over all people (Gn 49:8-12), and the seed who will be a king with an exalted end-time kingdom (Nm 24:7-9).[21]

Ultimately, the conclusion of the Torah (Dt 34) calls the reader to look for a prophet like Moses yet to come. The author already predicted that there would be a future prophet like Moses (Dt 18:15-19). Moses' unique quality as a prophet was that he spoke to God face-to-face (Nm 12:6-8), a characteristic not found in any other prophets. Thus, none of the later prophets of Israel fulfilled the prediction of being the prophet like Moses. So, the final words of the Torah, written near the end of the canonical period, indicate that the prophet like Moses, who spoke directly to God, had not come (Dt 34:10-12). The logical conclusion is that the epilogue ends the book by directing the reader to continue looking for that prophet, the Messiah.[22] Therefore, it is plain that the Torah, taken as a whole, has as its major theme the future Messiah.

MESSIAH IN THE PROPHETS

The Former Prophets

The essential message of the Prophets is also the messianic hope, expanding and clarifying the message of the Torah. The Former Prophets, beginning with Joshua and Judges, are designed to make Israel look for a future Messianic King. While the book of Joshua paints a positive picture of the initial conquest of the land, the circumstances rapidly turn negative in the book of Judges as Israel goes through a cycle of disobedience to God, discipline by God, and then deliverance by God through a chosen judge. As events spiral out of control, the author adds an appendix to the book of Judges, which begins and ends with the repeated refrain, "In those days there was no king in Israel; everyone did whatever he wanted" (Jdg 17:6; 21:25).

T. Desmond Alexander correctly explains the role this refrain plays in the narrative: it identifies Israel's difficulties as stemming from the lack of a king. The author thereby points the reader to the anticipation of Saul and David and the establishment of kingship in Israel. The book of Judges also concludes with the horrific behavior of the tribe of Benjamin, who rape and kill a young woman from Judah. Alexander points out that "by focusing on the fate of the Benjamites and two individuals from 'Bethlehem in Judah', these chapters anticipate developments in 1 Samuel concerning the first two kings of Israel: Saul from the tribe of Benjamin and David from Bethlehem in Judah."[23] Thus, the narrative draws attention to "the tribe of Judah and the special part which it will play in establishing a monarch through whom the nations of the earth will be blessed."[24]

Although Alexander is correct in showing how the narrative uses history to point to the future Lion of Judah, there is even more to the messianic message. The book of Judges appears to have been written (or undergone final editing) not during the time of the events in the book but sometime after the fall of the Davidic dynasty and the captivity. This is evident from the time notation in Jdg 18:30. There it says that the pagan priesthood begun by Moses' grandson Jonathan continued "until the time of the exile from the land." Thus, the recurring phrase "In those days there was no king in Israel; everyone did whatever he wanted" reminds the reader that the circumstances prior to the monarchy have returned. Yet the solution is not to look back to David but forward, to the future restoration of kingship by the Davidic Messiah (cf. Am 9:11-14).

The continuing narrative of Former Prophets 1Sm through 2Kg makes the focal point the Davidic house. Saul's kingship is presented as a foil for David—Saul fails to do the will of God and his house will end. Instead, David, the man after God's own heart, the one chosen by God, is presented as the dynasty through which the Messiah will come. Central to this presentation is the Davidic covenant (2Sm

7:12-16), in which God's promise of seed, previously given to Abraham (Gn 22:17-18), was further expanded. This covenant is foundational for the messianic hope of the Hebrew Bible and the basis of the NT expectation of a future kingdom. When David wanted to build a house for God (a Temple), instead God promised David that He would build a house for David (2Sm 7:11). God affirmed that He would give David an eternal dynasty and kingdom with an eternal ruler to sit on David's throne (2Sm 7:16). That ruler was to be one of David's sons (his seed), who would also have a father-son relationship with God (2Sm 7:12-16).

In the course of the historical narrative of 1Kg, it appears that this promise would be fulfilled through Solomon. In fact, since Solomon believed that he was the potential fulfillment, he built the Temple. But the Lord warned Solomon that the promise would be fulfilled through him only if he would "walk in My statutes, observe My ordinances, and keep all My commands" (1Kg 6:12). The author of 1Kg quickly points out how miserably Solomon failed to obey God with his marriages to foreign women, who turned his heart away from God (1Kg 11:1-4). After Solomon failed, the promise was transferred to the next Davidic king. As a result, "beginning with the time when the oracle of Nathan fixed the hope of Israel on the dynasty of David (2 Sam 7:12-16), each king issuing from him became the actual 'Messiah' by whom God wished to fulfill His plan with regard to His people."[25] But, in fact, in the subsequent narrative, no Davidic king succeeded in obeying God completely. Instead, all of them, even the good kings, ended with failure. Hence, the book of 2 Kings ends with Israel in captivity and the Davidic covenant unfulfilled. Clearly, the author's intention was to maintain the hope and expectation that God would one day send an eternal ruler who would build the true temple of God and sit on the throne of David. Thus, the Former Prophets make the messianic hope the central message of the narrative from Joshua to 2 Kings.

The Latter Prophets

The Latter Prophets (Isaiah, Jeremiah, Ezekiel, and the Twelve Minor Prophets) also continue to explicate the promise of Messiah previously revealed in the Torah. Although some might argue that they see the fulfillment of their words in events in their own day, in reality their focus is on the end of days and messianic fulfillment.

The book of Isaiah addresses ancient issues with a messianic perspective. While Judah will indeed be oppressed by Assyria and taken captive by Babylon, redemption will not come in those days. Rather, the hope of Israel is in the future Davidic king (Isa 9:6; 11:1-10) who will be born Immanuel (Isa 7:14). He will come as a Servant-King (Isa 42:1-9; 49:1-13; 50:4-11) who will provide a sacrificial atonement for Israel and the world (Isa 52:13–53:12). The remnant of Israel, to whom the book is addressed, is to find their comfort and hope not in Cyrus (Isa 45:1) but in the future Messianic King (Isa 61:1-4).

The book of Jeremiah predicts that Babylon will be God's instrument of righteous wrath on His sinning people, Israel. Nevertheless, it also points to hope of restoration in the "righteous Branch of David" who "will reign wisely as king and administer justice and righteousness in the land. In His days Judah will be saved and Israel will dwell securely. This is what He will be named: The LORD Is Our Righteousness" (Jer 23:5-6). This king will ultimately deliver Israel from a time of trouble more severe than the Babylonian exile (Jer 30:1-9) and establish a new covenant with Israel and Judah (Jer 31:31-34), just as Moses had foretold in the Torah (Dt 30:4-6).

The book of Ezekiel is a first-person account of the prophecies God gave through Ezekiel during the Babylonian exile. It reveals that hope is not to be found in the words of false prophets but instead in the far distant future, in the coming of the messianic son of David, the true Shepherd of Israel (Ezk 34:23-24). In those days, God will restore the house of David under the son of David, who will return the people of Israel to their land and give the people a new heart (Ezk 36:1-38). This too is the new covenant spoken of by Moses (Dt 30:4-6) and Jeremiah (Jer 31:31-34).

The Twelve Minor Prophets also reveal that hope is to be found in a future son of David. For example, Hosea predicts that in the last days, "the people of Israel will return and seek the Lord their God and David their king" (Hos 3:4-5). Other prophets among those Twelve promise that God "will restore the fallen booth of David" (Am 9:11-12) and provide a king from the house of David to shepherd His people (Mic 5:1-4). Ultimately, the house of David and the people of Jerusalem will repent, turn to the Lord, call upon this king who had been previously pierced (Zch 12:10), and experience a fountain of cleansing "from sin and impurity" (Zch 13:1). The Twelve concludes the Prophets with the hope of the return of Elijah to announce the Day of the Lord and the coming the Messiah (Mal 4:4-5).

Horbury summarizes the messianic perspective of the Prophets when he writes,

> There is thus a genuine thematic link between the Pentateuch and the Prophets. So Isaiah ends with a great eschatological scene of the exaltation of Jerusalem and divine judgment, which came to be associated with specifically messianic hope. Ezekiel ends with the oracles which have shaped later articulation of the eschatological events: from chapter 36 onward the book successively mentions the outpouring of the spirit, the revival of the dry bones, the new kingdom of David, the wars of Gog of the land of Magog, and the building of the new Jerusalem. Among the minor prophets, Hosea has an eschatological ending, Amos a Davidic ending, and Zechariah a conclusion which, for all its obscurity, is plainly and in succession messianic, royal, Davidic, Zion-centered and eschatological. The whole Book of the Twelve ends at the close of Malachi with announcement of the

> day of the Lord and sending of Elijah the prophet. Once again, just as in the case of the Pentateuch noted already, it is natural to read the specifically messianic prophecies, like those in Ezekiel, Amos and Zechariah, in the context of the more general prophecies of the future among which they are interspersed.[26]

So just as the Messiah is central to the message of the Torah, He is also crucial to the substantial theme of both the Former and Latter Prophets.

MESSIAH IN THE WRITINGS

In addition to the Law and Prophets, the Messiah also is the theme of the Writings. Beginning with the Psalms, the messianic hope is the central message. It is common for contemporary interpreters to view the Psalms as individual texts gathered with little regard for structure or theme. However, in recent years, trends have begun to shift. There is a movement to see the book of Psalms as the product of a purposeful redaction in the postexilic period with an identifiable theme.[27]

If indeed the Psalms were a postexilic redaction, as seems likely, it is most probable that the theme looks forward to the restoration of the Davidic dynasty in fulfillment of the Davidic covenant.[28] As Brevard Childs says of the royal psalms, "Indeed, at the time of the final redaction, when the institution of kingship had long since been destroyed, what earthly king would have come to mind other than God's Messiah?"[29]

This postexilic messianic expectation is plainly seen, for example, in Ps 89. The first half of the psalm celebrates the eternal Davidic covenant (vv. 1-37), the second part shifts to sorrow because postexilic conditions prevail, namely, the Davidic crown has been cast to the ground (v. 39), the walls of Jerusalem have been destroyed (v. 40), and the throne of David has been overturned (v. 44). Psalm 89 concludes with a plea for the Lord to restore the Davidic throne as promised in the Davidic covenant (vv. 49-51) because His enemies have mocked "every step of Your anointed [or Messiah]" (v. 51).

By recognizing the Psalms as a coherent collection of the postexilic period, the message of the entire book, not just individual songs, should be read as referring to the future king, namely, the Messiah.[30] Mitchell accurately states, "the messianic theme is central to the purpose of the collection."[31]

Other parts of the Writings also present a messianic message. In the book of Job, Job's hope of vindication is found in a "Redeemer," a living person who will stand on the earth at the end of days (Job 19:25). Although the messianic interpretation of this passage is frequently disputed, it is hard to dismiss this as a messianic hope of redemption, particularly when read innertextually. Job desperately longs for an arbitrator or "judge" to vindicate him (Job 9:33). He has confidence in his "advocate in the heights" (Job 16:19-21). At the end of the book, Elihu speaks of a "mediator" who is above thousands of angels (Job 33:23-28) or, as Delitzsch translated it, one who "soars above the thousands, and has not his equal among them."[32] The message of the book of Job is that righteous sufferers should not demand answers of the Lord but accept His sovereign decisions in all things, even suffering. Nonetheless, there is also an encouragement for them, derived from the hope of a Redeemer who will mediate for righteous sufferers and vindicate them.[33]

Other wisdom literature in the Writings also has a messianic emphasis. This is evident in that the underlying source for the wisdom taught in these books, namely, the wise sage, the Messiah, is the basis of its message. In the book of Proverbs, there is the enigmatic Woman Wisdom (Prv 8:22-36), whom most interpreters consider merely a personification of an attribute of God. Yet Hartmut Gese effectively argues for viewing her as a symbol of the future Messiah. Woman Wisdom, as an eternal being and the agent of creation, becomes the OT source of the NT depiction of the Messiah as wisdom (Col 2:3).[34] According to Nicholas Perrin, because of the exalted description of Woman Wisdom, "more than one scholar has noticed the presence of messianic terms in the portrayal of this female figure."[35]

Building on this concept of Wisdom as Messiah, Perrin argues for a messianic reading of the book of Ecclesiastes.[36] First, he maintains that the phrase "son of David" (Ecc 1:1), when used without Solomon's name, would be an early use of a messianic title. And even if Solomon were intended, it would be as a "prototypical Messiah." Second, Perrin makes a stronger argument for a messianic reading by citing the words "one Shepherd" in the epilogue (Ecc 12:11). He shows definitively that the title "one Shepherd" is only used in Scripture as a messianic appellation (Ezk 34:23-24; 37:24-25).[37] The point of the epilogue would be to demonstrate that the source of wisdom for the Preacher is the Shepherd (Messiah).

The relationship of the "one Shepherd" to the Preacher is similar to the call of Woman Wisdom in Proverbs to her sons to "listen to instruction . . . for the one who finds me finds life" (Prv 8:33,35), followed by the proverbs of Solomon (Prv 10:1). In Perrin's words,

> While Solomon is the personage who gives historic and human expression to the Proverbs, it is Woman Wisdom who introduces and hence authorizes and inspires the Solomonic text. Thus, Proverbs in its final form presents an economy of authorship that, much like prophetic utterance, was at once human and divine.[38]

In an analogous way, the Preacher's words are not merely human but are given force and authority because they are given by the "one Shepherd." This Shepherd, as Perrin writes, "is the transcendent messiah. It is this latter assurance that substantiates the divine origin and authority of the wisdom contained within the rest of the book."[39]

The Church has long viewed the Song of Solomon as an allegorical work about the Messiah and His love for the Church, much as Judaism has viewed it as an allegory for the God of Israel's love for the people of Israel. With the contemporary rejection of allegorical interpretation, it has become far more common to view the book as a romantic song between human lovers. Nevertheless, Roland Murphy has concluded that "the eventual canonization of the work . . . can best be explained if the poetry originated as religious rather than secular literature."[40] Therefore, James Hamilton has recently posited that "the Song of Songs is in the canon because it was written from a messianic perspective in order to nourish a messianic hope."[41] Is it possible that this love song was written with the authorial intent to advance and explain the messianic hope?

One approach, proposed by Sailhamer, is to view the Song as an allegory not of Messiah's love for the Church but as Messiah's love for divine wisdom. He defends this position by citing, "I awakened you under the apricot tree. There your mother conceived you; there she conceived and gave you birth" (Sg 8:5b) and proposing an intertextual reference to the prologue of the book of Proverbs and the account of the fall in Genesis 3.[42] In his view, the author of the Song intended "the beloved" to be understood as "wisdom" and "the lover" as Solomon, who represents the promised seed first mentioned in Gn 3:15.[43]

While this is plausible when read innerbiblically, an alternative view proposed by Hamilton is more likely. He posits a non-allegorical but symbolic interpretation in which King Solomon, as the son of David, "represents the ultimate expression of David's royal seed . . . the Davidic king, with all the messianic connotations that status carries."[44] Furthermore, Hamilton also sees the Song's innertextual allusions to Gn 3, but maintains that the theme of the Song "seems to be the recovery of intimacy after alienation, and this appears to match the hope engendered by Gen 3:15 for a seed of the woman who would come as the royal Messiah to restore the gladness of Eden."[45]

After demonstrating the development of this theme of intimacy recovered throughout the Song, Hamilton concludes by pointing out that Sg 7:10 functions as a climax to the poem.[46] There it states, "I belong to my love and his *desire* is for me," using the very word for "desire" that appears in Gn 3:16 in the curse on the woman ("Your *desire* will be for your husband and he will dominate you"). The word for desire (*teshukah*) is used only three times in the Hebrew Bible (Gn 3:16; 4:7; Sg 7:10), the first two times referring to the alienation of the fall. The author of the Song appears to be making a direct allusion to the alienation found in the curse of Gn 3:16. In Sg 7:10 he seems to be saying that the Messianic King will ultimately reverse the curse on the woman.[47] As Hamilton writes, "This messianic interpretation of the Song . . . explains the Song's presence in the canon and sheds light on how it exposits the Pentateuch's messianism."[48]

All the Writings contain a messianic theme. Ruth ends with a Davidic genealogy, to help establish the Davidic line of the future Messiah. Lamentations, although sorrowful, has a strong element of hope, emphasizing God's ultimate restoration through the fulfillment of the Davidic covenant. Thus, it ends with "LORD, restore us to Yourself, so we may return; renew our days as in former times" (Lam 5:21).

Esther is the story of God's providential preservation of Israel. It emphasizes providence in that God's name is excluded from the book. Although the Jewish people seem to have forgotten God, nevertheless He is working behind the scenes to save them. In this way, God not only preserves the people but also assures the fulfillment of His promise to send the messianic Redeemer to His people. Daniel presents Messiah as the hope of the Jewish people in the times of the Gentiles. In doing so, the book presents two major predictions: (1) Dan 7 reveals the Son of Man who will inherit God's kingdom (Dan 7:13-14), and (2) Dan 9 predicts God's program for Israel and the nations, indicating precisely when Messiah will come (Dan 9:24-27).

Ezra-Nehemiah, which the ancient Jewish canon takes as one book, views the return from captivity as a promise of an even greater return. Ezra presents the return from the exile as a fulfillment of prophecy (Ezr 1:1-4), but the conclusion to Nehemiah shows how Israel had still not kept the Mosaic covenant. So, although the return from exile was part of God's kindness to Israel, it did not tell the entire story. Rather, it pointed to an eschatological day of fulfillment, when Messiah would fulfill all the promises God made to His people.

The two books of Chronicles retell the history of the Davidic dynasty. But they were not written merely to glorify the past. Rather, they were composed to remind the returning exiles of the promise God had made to David (1Ch 17) and cause them to look with hope and faith in a coming messianic king.[49] As Sailhamer indicates, the conclusion of the book contains the call of the Persian king Cyrus to rebuild the Temple. By focusing on the Temple and the Messianic King who would rebuild it, the last words of the book (lit. "let him go up") "become a call for the return of the Messiah . . . thus provid[ing] a fitting bridge to the coming of the Messiah in the New Testament."[50] What has just been discussed is the messianic theme of the Writings. But this entire section has maintained that the point of the whole Tanakh is to reveal Messiah, from the promise of a seed who will crush the head of the serpent (Gn 3:15) to the call for the Messianic King to rebuild the holy Temple (2Ch 36:23). From the beginning to the end, from Genesis to 2 Chronicles, the entire Hebrew Bible is messianic.

CONCLUSION

As a child, I watched a good deal of television—probably more than was good for me. Back then, a large food company sponsored special television programs and used the commercial time to present recipes using the company's food products, particularly their cheeses. Even as a child, I was always amazed by how much cheese each of these recipes required. At the end of the program, viewers could send away for the cookbook with all the recipes from the commercials. As I grew older and began to understand advertising, I realized that it was not the tastiness of the food or the healthfulness of these meals that led to their inclusion in the cookbook. Rather, they all had one essential requirement—they had to sell cheese. In much the same way, for books to be accepted into the OT canon, they all required an essential characteristic—they had to reveal the Messiah.

The point of this article has been to show that messianic hope influenced the canonical redaction of the Hebrew Bible.[51] The messianic theme influenced the shaping of the Hebrew canon and became a prominent feature used to help discover which books would be included in the canon. It is not surprising, therefore, that the NT reads the Hebrew Bible as a messianic document.[52] It is because the messianic theme is rooted in the Hebrew canon itself.

---

1. This article is adapted from a chapter in Michael Rydelnik, *The Messianic Hope: Is the Hebrew Bible Really Messianic?* NAC Studies in Bible and Theology, ed. E. Ray Clendenen (Nashville: B&H Publishers, 2010), 65–82. Used with permission.
2. H. E. Ryle, *The Canon of the Old Testament*, 2nd ed. (London: Macmillan, 1914).
3. Ibid., 10–11.
4. R. T. Beckwith, "Formation of the Hebrew Bible," in *Mikra: Text, Translation, Reading and Interpretation of the Hebrew Bible in Ancient Judaism and Early Christianity*, ed. M. J. Muldur, (Minneapolis: Fortress, 1990), 39–86.
5. Ibid., 56.
6. Ibid., 57–58.
7. Ibid., 58.
8. J. H. Sailhamer, *Introduction to Old Testament Theology* (Grand Rapids: Zondervan, 1995), 239–52.
9. Ibid., 249.
10. J. H. Sailhamer, "The Messiah and the Hebrew Bible" *Journal of the Evangelical Theological Society* 44 (2001): 22. This is also the view of Horbury: "The collection of the books, therefore, and the editing of the individual books, produces a series of what can be properly called messianic prophecies, envisaging the future—sometimes evidently the immediate future." W. Horbury, *Jewish Messianism and the Cult of Christ* (London: SCM, 1998), 29.
11. See S. Postell, "The Old Testament's Use of the Old Testament" in this *Handbook*.
12. N. L. Geisler and W. E. Nix, *A General Introduction to the Bible* (Chicago: Moody, 1968), 130–47.
13. J. H. Sailhamer, *How We Got the Bible* (Grand Rapids: Zondervan, 1998), 11.
14. Sailhamer, "The Messiah and the Hebrew Bible," 23.

15. J. Hamilton, "The Skull Crushing Seed of the Woman: Inner-Biblical Interpretation of Genesis 3:15," *Southern Baptist Journal of Theology* 10, no. 2 (2006): 30.

16. J. H. Sailhamer, *The Pentateuch as Narrative* (Grand Rapids: Zondervan, 1992), 35–37.

17. W. Horbury, *Jewish Messianism and the Cult of Christ* (London: SCM, 1998), 27.

18. Note also that the Masoretic Text most likely sees this passage as referring to David, who will be higher than Agag. However, all other versions take this as one who will be higher than Gog. See M. Rydelnik, "Textual Criticism and Messianic Prophecy" in this *Handbook* for further discussion of this text-critical issue. Also see J. Sailhamer, "The Messiah in the Hebrew Bible," in this *Handbook* as well.

19. T. D. Alexander, "Messianic Ideology in Genesis," in *The Lord's Anointed: Interpretation of Old Testament Messianic Texts*, ed. P. E. Satterthwaite, R. S. Hess, and G. J. Wenham (Grand Rapids: Baker, 1995), 23–32.

20. T. D. Alexander, "Further Observations on the Term 'Seed' in Genesis," *Tyndale Bulletin* 48 (1997): 363–67.

21. Note the deliberate authorial linking of this passage with Gn 49:9: "He crouches; he lies down like a lion or a lioness—who dares to rouse him?"

22. See J. Sibley "Deuteronomy 18:15-19" in this *Handbook* for a lengthier discussion of the prophet like Moses.

23. T. D. Alexander, *The Servant King* (Vancouver, BC: Regent College, 1998), 47.

24. Ibid., 48.

25. P. E. Bonnard and P. Grelot, "Messiah," in *Dictionary of Biblical Theology*, ed. X. Leon-Dulfour, trans. P. J. Cahill (London: Geoffrey Chapman, 1967), 312.

26. Horbury, *Jewish Messianism and the Cult of Christ*, 28–29.

27. G. H. Wilson has effectively made the case for viewing the Psalms as having a purposeful postexilic redaction with an identifiable theme (*The Editing of the Hebrew Psalter* [Chico, CA: Scholars Press, 1985], 9–10, 182–99). However, according to Wilson, that theme looks backward historically, focusing on the failure of the Davidic dynasty. In his view, the Psalms do not look forward to a restored Davidic dynasty under the Messiah but rather a return to the pre-monarchic days, when the Lord alone was Israel's king (214–15).

28. D. C. Mitchell has persuasively argued for interpreting the Psalms as a coherent postexilic redaction with an eschatological/messianic theme (*The Message of the Psalter: An Eschatological Programme in the Book of Psalms*, Journal for the Study of the Old Testament Supplement 252 [Sheffield, England: Sheffield Academic Press, 1997]).

29. B. S. Childs, *Introduction to the Old Testament as Scripture* (Philadelphia: Fortress, 1979), 516.

30. See S. Postell, "Messiah in the Psalms" in this *Handbook*. Also B. K. Waltke, "A Canonical Process Approach to the Psalms," in *Tradition and Testament*, ed. J. Feinberg and P. Feinberg (Chicago: Moody, 1981), 3–18.

31. Mitchell, *The Message of the Psalter*, 87.

32. F. Delitzsch, *Biblical Commentary on the Book of Job* (Grand Rapids: Eerdmans, 1949), 230.

33. W. C. Kaiser Jr., *The Messiah in the Old Testament* (Grand Rapids: Zondervan, 1995), 61–64.

34. H. Gese, "Wisdom, Son of Man, and the Origins of Christology: The Consistent Development of Biblical Theology," *Horizons in Biblical Theology* 3 (1981): 23–57.

35. N. Perrin, "Messianism in the Narrative Frame of Ecclesiastes," *Revue Biblique* 1 (2001): 58.

36. Also, see N. Perrin's article "The Messianic Message in Ecclesiastes" in this *Handbook*.

37. N. Perrin, "Messianism in the Narrative Frame of Ecclesiastes," *Revue Biblique* 1 (2001): 53–54.

38. Ibid., 59.

39. Ibid.

40. R. E. Murphy, *The Song of Songs* (Minneapolis: Fortress, 1990), 94–95.

41. J. M. Hamilton Jr., "The Messianic Music of the Song of Songs: A Non-Allegorical Interpretation," *Westminster Theological Journal* 68 (2006): 331.

42. J. H. Sailhamer, *NIV Compact Bible Commentary* (Grand Rapids: Zondervan, 1994), 359–60.

43. Ibid., 360.

44. Hamilton, "The Messianic Music of the Song of Songs: A Non-Allegorical Interpretation," 337.

45. Ibid., 339–40.

46. Ibid., 340–42.

47. Ibid., 344.

48. Ibid.

49. See Horbury, *Jewish Messianism and the Cult of Christ*, 45–46.

50. J. H. Sailhamer, *The Books of the Bible* (Grand Rapids: Zondervan, 1998), 31.

51. As Horbury has written, "The Old Testament books were so edited that they emerge collectively as a messianic document. Within the Pentateuch and the books of Joshua and Chronicles, royal and messianic themes were developed especially in the portraits of Moses, Joshua, David, Solomon and the righteous kings. Messianic hope was prominent in the prophetic books of Haggai and Zechariah. These messianic elements in the composition and interpretation of the biblical books were then reflected and developed at the end of the Persian period, not long after Alexander the Great, in the messianism of the Septuagint Pentateuch." *Jewish Messianism and the Cult of Christ*, 37.

52. M. B. Shepherd has posited that the messianic theme of the Hebrew Bible later influenced both the rabbinic Targumim and the NT's understanding of the Hebrew Bible. He states, "The Targums and the NT exegete Scripture messianically. . . . These messianic readings are rooted in the text of the Hebrew Bible itself." "Targums, New Testament, and Biblical Theology of the Messiah" *Journal of the Evangelical Theological Society* 51 (2008): 46.

Messiah: Prophet, Priest, and King

GLENN R. KREIDER

The perspective that the Messiah fulfills the three offices of prophet, priest, and king has a long legacy in the history of biblical interpretation.[1] The London Baptist Confession (1689), for instance, puts it this way: "This office of mediator between God and man is proper only to Christ, who is the prophet, priest, and king of the church of God; and may not be either in whole, or any part thereof, transferred from him to any other."[2] John Calvin is often credited with popularizing this view, although he was not the first to observe it.[3] Berkhof observes, "While some of the early church fathers already speak of the different offices of Christ, Calvin was the first to recognize the importance of distinguishing the three offices of the Mediator and to call attention to it in a separate chapter of his *Institutes*."[4] Here is Calvin's claim: "Therefore, that faith may find a firm basis of salvation in Christ, and thus rest in him, this principle must be laid down: the office enjoined upon Christ by the Father consists of three parts. For he was given to be prophet, king, and priest."[5]

These three functions figure prominently in the biblical story, from the OT through the NT books.[6] Both the functions and people who hold the office can be seen as types of the Messiah. Other texts predict a messianic prophet, priest, or king. This essay will argue that although there are many prophets, priests, and kings in the Scriptures, several characters in the OT are particularly significant as types of the Messiah.[7] Each of these explicitly and implicitly points forward to the fulfillment in the perfect antitype, Jesus the Christ. Berkhof concludes, "Hence it was necessary that Christ, as our Mediator, should be prophet, priest, and king. As Prophet He represents God with man; as Priest He represents man in the presence of God; and as King He exercises dominion and restores the original dominion of man."[8]

FUNCTIONS OF THE OFFICES

Prophet. A prophet speaks for God. Primarily, the prophet speaks to God's people, but he or she often speaks to nonbelievers and even to the creation. The first person designated as a prophet in the Scriptures is Abraham (Gn 20:7), but "OT prophecy received its normative form in the life and person of Moses, who constituted a standard of comparison for all future prophets."[9]

A clear description of the prophetic function appears in Ex 7: "The LORD answered Moses, 'See, I have made you like God to Pharaoh, and Aaron your brother will be your prophet. You must say whatever I command you; then Aaron your brother must declare it to Pharaoh so that he will let the Israelites go from his land'" (vv. 1-2). Moses will speak God's words, and Aaron, who is to be Moses' prophet, must declare those words to Pharaoh. Aaron will speak for Moses. Then, in Dt 18, the prophetic function is emphasized when the Lord declares that He will raise up another prophet, "I will raise up for them a prophet like you from among their brothers. I will put My words in his mouth, and he will tell them everything I command him" (Dt 18:18). A prophet, thus, speaks for God. When the prophet speaks, God speaks. This "prophet like Moses" is the Messiah, but between Moses and Jesus there is a line of prophets.[10] They brought messages from God to the people. Sometimes these prophets predicted the future, but their function was not limited to foretelling. Sometimes the prophets spoke to people of faith, and other times they spoke to unbelievers. Prophets delivered messages of encouragement and comfort, as well as oracles of doom and judgment. When the prophet spoke, the words were to be received as the words of God because the prophet spoke not his own words, but as the mouthpiece of God.

Priest. A priest primarily mediates between God and people, and this mediation extends in both directions.[11] Thielman explains, "Some kind of mediation between God and humanity is necessary simply because God is separate from all he has created and, yet, graciously extends his fellowship to his creatures. Mediation takes on a particularly important role, however, in light of humanity's rebellion against the Creator. The situation of hostility that resulted from Adam's fall could only be remedied through the mediation of a third party."[12] Priests also mediated God's blessing to creation, especially the land occupied by the Israelites. For example, the Lord promised to bless not merely His people but also the animals and the land itself (Dt 28:1-14). The blessings of God mediated to Israel by the priests would be mediated to creation as well.

The first human priest identified in the biblical story is Melchizedek, whose priesthood predates the establishment of the Levitical priesthood by several generations. In God's grace, He established the Levitical priesthood to mediate blessing to the people of Israel. According to the law of Moses, "The LORD set apart the tribe of Levi to carry the ark of the LORD's covenant, to stand before Yahweh to serve Him, and to pronounce blessings in His name, as it is today" (Dt 10:8). Only males from this tribe qualified to serve as priests.

King. A king rules or reigns over people and territory. Although there were kings before him, the first righteous king in the biblical story was Melchizedek (Gn 14:18), and the first king of Israel was Saul (1Sm 10:1). But there was no king like David, to whom God promised an eternal kingdom (2Sm 7:16). Walter C. Kaiser Jr. observes that in nine of the uses of "messiah" in the OT, "the reference is to some 'anointed one' who would be coming in the future, usually in the line of David, and who would be Yahweh's king: 1 Samuel 2:10,35; Psalms 2:2; 20:6; 28:8; 84:9; Habakkuk 3:13; Daniel 9:25,26."[13] God's reign over His creation, and His provision of blessing for it, is mediated through human kings, and ultimately through the Messiah (Rom 1:3).

TYPES OF PROPHET, PRIEST, AND KING

The Hebrew term (*mashiach*) is used in the OT to designate someone or something that has been anointed, set apart in some relationship to God, whether prophet, priest, or king.[14] All of these messianic expectations are fulfilled in the Messiah, the Anointed One, the divine King who is also Prophet and Priest.

From the beginning of the biblical story, God provided types of the Messiah as prophet, priest, and king. There are many individuals who fulfill one or more of these functions. Increasingly, this expectation becomes more and more explicit and clear, and this messianic expectation in types, foreshadowing, implicit prophecies, and explicit predictions becomes more and more well defined. Of particular interest are those characters that foreshadow the Messiah by fulfilling all three functions in one person.

Adam. When God created humanity, He created them male and female (Gn 1:27; cf. 5:1-2) and gave the two of them a simple command: "Be fruitful, multiply, fill the earth, and subdue it" (Gn 1:28a).[15] That "subdue" is a ruling function is clear when God continued: "Rule the fish of the sea, the birds of the sky, and every creature that crawls on the earth" (Gn 1:28b). To rule over creation apparently includes the responsibility to mediate blessing to these creatures, for prior to creating humans and blessing them, God had blessed the creatures that live in the water and the sky: "So God blessed them, 'Be fruitful, multiply, and fill the waters of the seas, and let the birds multiply on the earth'" (Gn 1:22). Particularly in a pre-fall world, to rule over such creatures would be to care for them, to bless them, and to provide good for them. Since the fall had not yet occurred, there would be no need to exercise force, or the threat of force, to control animals or to protect some from others.

In the expanded account of the sixth day of creation, the narrator gives further details: "The LORD God took the man and placed him in the garden of Eden to work it and watch over it" (Gn 2:15). Then "the LORD God formed out of the ground every wild animal and every bird of the sky, and brought each to the man to see what he would call it. And whatever the man called a living creature, that was its name" (Gn 2:19). In so doing, the man functioned as a prophet (he spoke for God), a priest (mediating blessing to these creatures), and a king (naming them exercised rule over them). Eugene Merrill writes, "When Yahweh brought the animals to Adam 'to see what he would name them,' He was in effect transferring from Himself to Adam the dominion for which man was created."[16] Naming the creatures, which had already been blessed by God, would thus fulfill all three functions.

The Creator gave Adam dominion over creation, which he exercised when he named the animals, spoke as an agent of the Creator (as the *imago Dei*), and mediated blessing to them by caring for them. Sadly, he failed to carry out those tasks; instead of mediating life and blessing to creation, he was the cause of its curse. He failed to produce innocent offspring; his children all share his condemnation and guilt. He failed to speak for God; instead, he silently accepted the serpent's lie (Gn 2:1-6). He failed to rule over creation; instead, he was the cause of creation's curse and would struggle with it until he would die and return to the dust (Gn 3:19).

Another Adam came and accomplished perfectly what the first Adam was created to be and do (1Co 15:21-22,45-49; Rom 5:12-21). Merrill summarizes succinctly: "Jesus fulfilled in His life the potentialities of unfallen Adam, just as by His death He restored all mankind to those potentialities."[17] Berkhof makes the connection between the first and last Adam when he observes, "The fact that Christ was anointed to a threefold office finds its explanation in the fact that man was originally intended for this threefold office and work. As created by God, he was prophet, priest, and king, and as such was endowed with knowledge and understanding, with righteousness and holiness, and with dominion over the lower creation."[18] Wayne Grudem similarly concludes, "If we look back at the situation of Adam before the fall and forward to our future status with Christ in heaven for eternity, we can see that these roles of prophet, priest, and king had parallels in the experience that God originally intended for man, and will be fulfilled in our lives in heaven."[19]

Melchizedek. In Gn 14, Moses tells the story of the capture of Abram's nephew Lot by a confederation of four kings (Gn 14:8-12).[20] Abram mustered an army and delivered his nephew from his captors. As Abram and his troops returned home he met a visitor in the Valley of Shaveh: "Melchizedek, king of Salem, brought out bread and wine; he was a priest to God Most High" (Gn 14:18). Melchizedek is identified as both a king and a priest, but he was also a prophet. He spoke to Abram and blessed him in the name of "God Most High," "Creator of heaven and earth" (Gn 14:19-20). Melchizedek spoke to Abram on behalf of Abram's God; this is the function of a prophet.

In addition to the first righteous king, "Melchizedek is the first priest mentioned in Scripture."[21] Since Genesis was written to the Israelites in the context of the exodus and the giving of the law, they would have understood the role of a priest, and they should have recognized that their Levitical priesthood was not the first priesthood established by the God of Abraham, Isaac, and Jacob.

The significance of Melchizedek can hardly be overemphasized. In Ps 110, David, the prophet, quoted the Lord, "This is the declaration of the Lord to my Lord" (Ps 110:1). He then asserted that his Lord, the Messiah, would be a priest forever, "like Melchizedek" (Ps 110:4).[22] In short, the Messiah will be an eternal priest, in the pattern or type of Melchizedek. Since the king would come from the tribe of Judah (Gn 49:10), specifically in the line of David (2Sm 7:12-16), and priests from the line of Levi (Dt 18:1-5), no Israelite could be both king and priest. Since the Messiah will be both, His right to the throne is through the line of David but His priesthood is through Melchizedek. The Messiah's priesthood is not based in heredity but in a type or pattern. That seems to be the point, as explained by the writer of Hebrews: Melchizedek "without father, mother, or genealogy, having neither beginning of days nor end of life, but resembling the Son of God—remains a priest forever" (Heb 7:3). Some have misunderstood this phrase as asserting that Melchizedek had no parents because he was the pre-incarnate Christ Himself. But that would destroy the typology. David Peterson's explanation is superior:

> It is also noted that, unlike other significant figures in Genesis, Melchizedek is introduced without genealogy and without reference to his birth or death (7:3). Since the legitimacy of a man's priesthood in the ancient world depended on such factors, the silence of Scripture at this point is remarkable. The implication is that Melchizedek did not obtain his priesthood because of hereditary rights.[23]

Similarly, the Messiah's priesthood is not based upon heredity. Melchizedek's blessing of Abram is also significant, according to the book of Hebrews, because it reveals his superiority to Abram. Abram, the father of the people of Israel and of all people of faith, is inferior to this Canaanite prophet, priest, and king. Two things evidence this. First, Abram was blessed by Melchizedek and "without a doubt, the inferior is blessed by the superior" (Heb 7:7). Further, Abraham paid tithes to Melchizedek. By Abraham's doing so, even Levi, who as a priest was the recipient of Israel's tithes, paid tithes to Melchizedek (Heb 7:8-10).

Moses. Moses was a prophet, the greatest of a long line of prophets. As a prophet, Moses spoke for God. In Dt 18, God states the job description for a prophet when He promises to send another prophet, a prophet like Moses: "I will raise up for them a prophet like you from among their brothers. I will put My words in his mouth, and he will tell them everything I command him" (Dt 18:18).[24] Since there were many prophets between Moses and Jesus, this is the promise of both a succession of prophets (as there was promised a succession of priests and would be promised a succession of kings) and the promise of a great prophet who would come. Jesus is the ultimate fulfillment of this promise.[25]

A prophet must speak for God and not presumptuously: "I will hold accountable whoever does not listen to My words that he speaks in My name. But the prophet who dares to speak a message in My name that I have not commanded him to speak, or who speaks in the name of other gods—that prophet must die" (Dt 18:19-20).[26] The Messiah spoke only what His Father told Him to say (Jn 12:49-50); there was no presumption in Him.

Moses and Aaron, the first high priest of Israel, were descendants of Levi (Ex 6:16-20). Moses served as a priest (Ps 99:6). As the mediator between God and the people of Israel, he represented God to the people and the people to God, which was their request when God appeared to them on Mt. Sinai (Ex 20:19).[27] Moses set up a tent in which he communicated with God face-to-face, representing God to the people and taking their concerns to God (Ex 33:7-11). Originally, he attempted to fulfill this role by himself; his father-in-law recommended a better method, delegating this responsibility to others (Ex 18:17-23). Moses adopted this approach; those he appointed "judged the people at all times; they would bring the hard cases to Moses, but they would judge every minor case themselves" (Ex 18:26). Moses' mediatorial function foreshadowed the Messiah's, as the unique mediator between God and humanity, the God-man, Jesus (1Tm 2:5).

Moses is never called the king of Israel. Israel's first king was Saul. But Moses functioned as the ruler, the leader, and the judge of the Israelites. In short, as the mediator between God and the people, Moses performed the role that a king would have fulfilled. He had God-given authority as the ruler. The Lord declared that He had made Moses like God (Ex 7:1), which surely indicated his rule over the people.

Moses' functions of prophet, priest, and king came together clearly in the aftermath of the golden calf incident (Ex 32–34). While Moses was on the mountain with the Lord, the people asked Aaron to make a god for them. Aaron agreed, formed a golden calf, and called for a festival celebrating the Lord who delivered them out of Egypt. This rebellion made God angry. When God threatened to destroy the people because of their sin, Moses pleaded with God to forgive them (Ex 32:11-13). Moses represented the people to their God; he mediated with God on their behalf. In doing so, he functioned as their priest but also their leader. Moses spoke to God for the people, as their priest, but he also spoke to the people for God, as a prophet. He pleaded with God to deliver His people. In a similar way, Jesus, while being unjustly executed for the sins of the whole world, will ask God to forgive His murderers, "because they do not know what they are doing" (Lk 23:34).

David. David also functioned as prophet, priest, and king. David spoke for God. He wrote many psalms, nearly half of the psalter.[28] His psalms are widely quoted in the NT and many in messianic texts. David wrote Ps 110, the most often quoted psalm by the NT writers.[29] Ross observes, "The expressions are those of a prophet who had received a revelation from God."[30] David claimed to be quoting the Lord, thus speaking for Him, when he wrote, "This is the declaration of the Lord to my Lord: 'Sit at My right hand until I make Your enemies Your footstool'" (Ps 110:1). Jesus quoted from the psalm, attributing it to David, to defend that the Messiah would be the son of David (Mt 22:41-45).

David was a king, but he was more than a king; he was the father of a line of kings in a kingdom that would never end. God made a covenant with David, promising him an eternal dynasty (2Sm 7; Ps 89). Rather than a succession of sons of David reigning as king, the greater son of David, Jesus of Nazareth, will fulfill this promise eternally (Rom 1:3; Col 1:11-20). Strauss explains, "David is the prototype of the ideal coming king—the Messiah. God's promise to David of a perpetual line (2Sm 7) becomes in the royal psalms and the prophets the expectation of an ideal king from David's line."[31]

David functioned as a priest. He served as a mediator between Saul and God. Although Saul wanted him dead, David refused to respond in kind. Instead, although he had many opportunities to kill his enemy, he refused. In so doing, he mediated grace to Saul, not judgment. David also offered sacrifices, a function of the priesthood, several times. For example, David recaptured the ark of the covenant and was transporting it from Baale-judah (2Sm 6:2). When the oxen pulling the cart stumbled, Uzzah reached out to steady the ark, and he died (2Sm 6:7).

Eventually the ark was returned to Jerusalem, and "set it in its place inside the tent David had set up for it. Then David offered burnt offerings and fellowship offerings in the Lord's presence" (2Sm 6:17). Lest there be any misunderstanding, the narrator repeats: "When David had finished offering the burnt offering and the fellowship offerings, he blessed the people in the name of Yahweh of Hosts" (2Sm 6:18). Thus, David offered sacrifices and blessed the people. David functioned as a priest.[32] Merrill observes, "David was not a descendant of Aaron, and could not therefore ordinarily qualify to be a priest. He was, however, the anointed of the Lord, the founder of that messianic line that would be fulfilled in the King who would also embrace the offices of priest and prophet (7:12-16; 1 Sam. 2:35; Deut. 18:15-19)."[33]

Later, the Lord was angry with Israel and David was enticed to number the people (2Sm 24:1). David realized his mistake and confessed his sin to the Lord (2Sm 24:10). As a consequence, the Lord offered David three choices: "Do you want three years of famine to come on your land, to flee from your foes three months while they pursue you, or to have a plague in your land three days?" (2Sm 24:13). David's choice was to trust the mercy of God: "Let us fall into the LORD's hands because His mercies are great, but don't let me fall into human hands" (2Sm 24:14). In a plague, 70,000 people died (2Sm 24:15). The prophet Gad instructed David to set up an altar; David complied (2Sm 24:18-19). He purchased a threshing floor and oxen, and then "built an altar to the LORD there and offered burnt offerings and fellowship offerings" (2Sm 24:25; cf. 1Chr 21:28).[34] David was not a priest in the line of Levi, but again he offered sacrifices and prayer, which the Lord accepted: "Then the LORD answered prayer on behalf of the land, and the plague on Israel ended" (2Sm 24:25).

Of course, that David offered sacrifices does not establish precedent; it does not prove that any king could presume to function as a priest.[35] Rather, this is evidence of God's grace, and it seems particularly significant that David, like Adam, Melchizedek, and Moses before him, was functioning as a type of the Messiah by fulfilling the offices of prophet, priest, and king.

JESUS AS PROPHET, PRIEST, AND KING

In His first advent, Jesus filled the offices of prophet, priest, and king. He fulfilled the expectations set for those offices. In the eschaton, He will fulfill them perfectly and eternally; there is no succession of prophets, priests, or kings following Him. According to Thomas Oden, "The Son of God became incarnate to do the threefold work of messianic prophet, priest, and king. His work consisted in the fulfillment and consummation of the prophetic office, the priestly office, and the kingly office, to which servants of God in the Old Testament were anointed."[36]

When the angel appeared to Mary and announced the birth of the Messiah, he promised that the Son of God would fulfill the promise made to David. According to Gabriel, "He will be great and will be called the Son of the Most High, and the Lord God will give Him the throne of His father David. He will reign over the house of Jacob forever, and His kingdom will have no end" (Lk 1:32-33). After the angel made a similar announcement to Joseph, Matthew explains, "Now all this took place to fulfill what was spoken by the Lord through the prophet: 'See, the virgin will become pregnant and give birth to a son, and they will name Him Immanuel,' which is translated 'God is with us'" (Mt 1:23). This child is the Son of God, God with us, and the fulfillment of the promise of prophet, priest, and king. Defending this claim seems to have been the author's purpose in the book of Hebrews.

Hebrews begins with the assertion that the Son of God is the superior and final Word of God: "Long ago God spoke to the fathers by the prophets at different times and in different ways. In these last days, He has spoken to us by His Son" (Heb 1:1-2). The Son is divine; He is the Creator and "the radiance of God's glory and the exact expression of His nature, sustaining all things by His powerful word. After making purification for sins, He sat down at the right hand of the Majesty on high" (Heb 1:3). The three functions of prophet, priest, and king come together in this prologue. David Allen summarizes, "It was marvelous enough that God should speak through the prophets, but now comes an extraordinary truth: God has spoken to us in one who is by his very character and nature a Son."[37] He also notes that these verses articulate "the two major themes of Hebrews: high priestly sacrifice of the Son and kingly exaltation of the Son. This theme of Christ exalted to the right hand of God permeates the Christology of the epistle."[38]

Jesus is greater than angels (Heb 1:5-14) and greater than Moses, the great prophet (Nm 12:6-8; Heb 3:6). He is also a great high priest, "One who has been tested in every way as we are, yet without sin" (Heb 4:15). He functioned as a priest when "He became the source of eternal salvation for all who obey Him, and He was declared by God a high priest in the order of Melchizedek" (Heb 5:9-10). He was greater than Melchizedek because He is the Son of God (Heb 5:5; cf. 7:1-22). His covenant is better than the old covenant (Heb 7:22) and as perfect high priest His priesthood is superior (Heb 7:23–8:12). His sacrifice is superior to the sacrifices under the old covenant, since "the law has only a shadow of the good things to come, and not the actual form of those realities" (Heb 10:1). The sacrifice of the Son is perfect and has made His people perfect: "By this will of God, we have been sanctified through the offering of the body of Jesus Christ once and for all. Every priest stands day after day ministering and offering the same sacrifices time after time, which can never take away sins. But this man, after offering one sacrifice for sins forever, sat down at the right hand of God" (Heb 10:10-12).

Jesus' work of redemption is not yet complete. He will one day reign over an eternal kingdom: "He is now waiting until His enemies are made His footstool"

(Heb 10:13). Jesus is "the source and perfecter of our faith" (Heb 12:2) and has promised that "we are receiving a kingdom that cannot be shaken" (Heb 12:28).

The benediction to the book of Hebrews praises the work God accomplished through this prophet, priest, and king: "Now may the God of peace, who brought up from the dead our Lord Jesus—the great Shepherd of the sheep—with the blood of the everlasting covenant, equip you with all that is good to do His will, working in us what is pleasing in His sight, through Jesus Christ. Glory belongs to Him forever and ever. Amen" (Heb 13:20-21).

CONCLUSION

The Messiah came to fulfill perfectly the offices and functions of prophet, priest, and king. The Scriptures foreshadow Him through a line of prophets, beginning with Abraham and particularly in Moses; priests, particularly Melchizedek and the Levites; and kings, David and his sons. Although there are many prophets, priests, and kings, a handful of biblical heroes combine the three functions in one person, foreshadowing the Messiah who will fulfill all three perfectly and permanently. In these biblical types of the Messiah, Adam, Melchizedek, Moses, and David, the Scriptures point forward to the coming Immanuel who will be the final Adam, the priest like Melchizedek, a prophet like Moses, and the son of David because He is the Son of Man and the Son of God. These men are types, foreshadowing the one who would fulfill all three functions perfectly and completely, when God took on flesh.[39] Walvoord correctly observed: "The offices of Christ are one of the major themes of the Old Testament as they relate to Christ."[40] He concluded, "Taken together, the three offices of Christ as Prophet, Priest and King are the key to the purpose of the incarnation. His prophetic office was concerned with the revelation of the truth of God; the priestly office was related to His work as Savior and Mediator; His kingly office had in view His right to reign over Israel and over the entire earth. In Christ, the supreme dignity of these offices is reached."[41]

---

1. Joel Beeke, "Jesus' Threefold Office as Prophet, Priest, and King," Ligonier Ministries, 8 April 2016, http://www.ligonier.org/blog/jesus-threefold-office-prophet-priest-and-king/, "He is your Prophet to teach you; your Priest to sacrifice for, intercede for, and bless you; and your King to rule and guide you."

2. "The London Confession of Faith," 8.9, accessed July 25, 2016, http://www.reformedreader.org/ccc/1689lbc/english/Chapter08.htm. "This number and order of offices is necessary; for in respect of our ignorance, we stand in need of his prophetical office; and in respect of our alienation from God, and imperfection of the best of our services, we need his priestly office to reconcile us and present us acceptable unto God; and in respect to our

averseness and utter inability to return to God, and for our rescue and security from our spiritual adversaries, we need his kingly office to convince, subdue, draw, uphold, deliver, and preserve us to his heavenly kingdom" (8.10).

3. Eusebius seems to be the first to have observed this: "And a proof of this is that no one of those who were of old symbolically anointed, whether priests, or kings, or prophets, possessed so great a power of inspired virtue as was exhibited by our Saviour and Lord Jesus, the true and only Christ." Eusebius, *Church History,* 1.3.7–9, accessed July 7, 2016, http://www.ccel.org/ccel/schaff/npnf201.iii.vi.iii.html.

4. Louis Berkhof, *Systematic Theology* (Grand Rapids: Eerdmans, 1938), 356.

5. John Calvin, *Institutes of the Christian Religion* 2.15.1, Library of Christian Classics, vol. 20, ed. John T. McNeill, trans. Ford Lewis Battles (Philadelphia: Westminster Press, 1960), 494. Calvin continues, "The title 'Christ' pertains to these three offices: for we know that under the law prophets as well as priests and kings were anointed with holy oil. . . . I recognize that Christ was called Messiah especially with respect to, and by virtue of his kingship. Yet his anointings as prophet and as priest have their place and must not be overlooked by us" (2.15.2).

6. Gerry Breashears, "The Body of Christ: Prophet, Priest, or King?" *Journal of the Evangelical Theological Society,* 37 (March 1994): 5, muses: "Traditionally, theologians follow Calvin in speaking of the work of Christ in terms of three OT offices that relate to God and man . . . One wonders why other offices are not considered: Judge, warrior, shepherd, and sage are all possibilities." Perhaps the best explanation is that the other offices are each within the semantic fields of these three.

7. John F. Walvoord, *Jesus Christ Our Lord* (Chicago: Moody Press, 1969), 62, writes, "Latent in the Old Testament is a rich treasury of Christological truth in the form of biblical types."

8. Berkhof, *Systematic Theology,* 357.

9. J. P. Baker, "Prophecy, Prophets," in *New Bible Dictionary,* 2nd ed., ed. J. D. Douglas et al. (Wheaton, IL: Tyndale House, 1982), 975. Baker goes on to describe the function of a prophet as combining proclamation of a message from God and prediction of the future.

10. Many of them are named; Elijah, Elisha, Isaiah, Jeremiah, etc., and others are not named. There were many spokespeople for God throughout the history of Israel.

11. Henry W. Holloman, "Priest, Priesthood," in *Kregel Dictionary of the Bible and Theology* (Grand Rapids: Kregel, 2005), 419. Holloman adds this responsibility, "to perform certain religious acts that have been passed along from generation to generation."

12. Frank Thielman, "Mediator, Mediation," in *Evangelical Dictionary of Biblical Theology,* ed. Walter A. Elwell (Grand Rapids: Baker, 1996), 517.

13. Walter C. Kaiser Jr., *The Messiah in the Old Testament,* Studies in Old Testament Biblical Theology (Grand Rapids: Zondervan, 1995), 16.

14. Randall Price, "The Concept of the Messiah in the Old Testament," accessed July 8, 2016, http://www.worldofthebible.com/resources.htm.

15. That the name "Adam" is given to the two of them and the two, male and female, are referenced with the singular pronoun, does not deny that God created a man and woman. Moses, in Gn 1, is emphasizing the unity of the two, the common Adamic nature of the man and woman.

16. Eugene H. Merrill, "A Theology of the Pentateuch," in *A Biblical Theology of the Old Testament,* ed. Roy B. Zuck (Chicago: Moody Press, 1991), 15.

17. Merrill, "Theology of the Penteteuch," 17.

18. Berkhof, *Systematic Theology,* 357.

19. Wayne Grudem, *Systematic Theology: An Introduction to Biblical Doctrine* (Grand Rapids: Zondervan, 1994), 629.

20. Lot's vulnerability to capture happened because he was no longer under the protection of his uncle Abram (cf. Gn 13). Had Abram and Lot found a way to coexist in the land, Lot would not have been captured, and Abram would not have met Melchizedek. God's grace is often seen in the context of human sin.

21. D. G. Peterson, "Melchizedek," in *New Dictionary of Biblical Imagery: Exploring the Unity and Diversity of Scripture,* ed. T. Desmond Alexander, et al. (Downers Grove, IL: InterVarsity, 2000), 659. Peterson also observes that "although Israelite kings sometimes exercised priestly functions, the distinction between the offices was much more definite in Israel than in neighboring cultures. Psalm 110 therefore appears to be prophetic of a new situation in proclaiming that a Davidic king will be 'a priest forever according to the order of Melchizedek' (v. 4)."

22. The NET Bible translates this verse: "You are an eternal priest after the pattern of Melchizedek." The "likeness" is a "pattern" or "type."

23. D. G. Peterson, "Melchizedek," 660.

24. The people of Israel were familiar with Moses and his prophetic role. This "job description" was a reminder of what they already understood.

25. This is the view of Walter C. Kaiser in *The Messiah in the Old Testament*, 57–61. Michael Rydelnik has argued "the prophet like Moses" refers exclusively to the Messiah (see *The Messianic Hope: Is the Hebrew Bible Really Messianic?* [Nashville: B&H, 2010], 57–64.)

26. The test of a false or presumptuous prophet is that what he proclaims does not come true (Dt 18:22). The God of truth speaks only truth and thus one who speaks for God speaks truth. A similar test of a false prophet appears in Dt 13:1–5. There are no tests of a true prophet, only for a false or presumptuous one.

27. Moses was also the mediator between God and the nations, especially Egypt. God spoke to Pharaoh through Moses, brought judgment on them through him, and thus mediated His sovereign rule over Egypt through Moses.

28. Allen Ross, "Psalms," in *Bible Knowledge Commentary: Old Testament*, ed. John F. Walvoord and Roy B. Zuck (Wheaton, IL: Victor Books, 1985), 783, attributes 73 of the 150 to David.

29. L. Michael Morales, "Jesus and the Psalms," accessed July 6, 2016, http://www.ligonier.org/learn/articles/jesus-and-psalms/.

30. Ross, "Psalms," 873.

31. M. L. Strauss, "David," in *New Dictionary of Biblical Imagery: Exploring the Unity and Diversity of Scripture*, ed. T. Desmond Alexander, et al. (Downers Grove, IL: InterVarsity, 2000), 435.

32. Winfred O. Neely objects: "Saying that David sacrificed does not mean that David acted as a priest, but rather that he gave the animals which were then offered through the mediation of a Levitical priest." See "2 Samuel" in *The Moody Bible Commentary*, Michael Rydelnik and Michael Vanlaningham, eds. (Chicago: Moody Publishers, 2014), 453.

33. Eugene H. Merrill, E. H. (1985), "2 Samuel," in *Bible Knowledge Commentary: Old Testament*, ed. John F. Walvoord and Roy B. Zuck (Wheaton, IL: Victor Books, 1985), 463.

34. According to Merrill, "This was where Abraham had offered Isaac (Gen. 22:2). And on this same spot Solomon later constructed his magnificent temple (1 Chron. 22:1; 2 Chron. 3:1)" (Merrill, "2 Samuel," 482).

35. Saul had offered a burnt offering and was rebuked by Samuel: "You have been foolish. You have not kept the command which the LORD your God gave you. It was at this time that the LORD would have permanently established your reign over Israel, but now your reign will not endure. The LORD has found a man loyal to him, and the LORD appointed him as ruler over His people, because you have not done what the LORD commanded" (1Sm 13:13-14).

36. Thomas C. Oden, *The Word of Life*, vol. 2 of *Systematic Theology* (San Francisco: Harper Collins, 1989), 280.

37. David L. Allen, *Hebrews*, New American Commentary (Nashville: B&H, 2010), 103.

38. Allen, *Hebrews*, 128.

39. See Gavin Ortland, "Resurrected as Messiah: The Risen Christ as Prophet, Priest, and King," *Journal of the Evangelical Theological Society* 54 (2011): 749–66.

40. John F. Walvoord, *Jesus Christ Our Lord* (Chicago: Moody Press, 1969), 209.

41. Walvoord, *Jesus Christ Our Lord*, 137.

The Deity of the Messiah in the Old Testament

GLENN R. KREIDER

The Hebrew term (*mashiach*), usually translated "anointed," is used 39 times in the Hebrew Bible, generally as a compound noun, such as "the anointed priest."[1] The overwhelming significance of the term and the fulfillment of all of the messianic expectations is in a coming ruler, an eschatological king, as Wallace explains, "The primary sense of the title is 'king,' as the anointed man of God, but it also suggests election, i.e., the king was chosen, elect, and therefore honored. It could scarcely be otherwise . . . the entire evidence of later Judaism points to a Messiah not only as king but as eschatological king, a ruler who would appear at the end of time."[2] All the messianic expectations culminate in one person, as Rydelnik summarizes: "To put it plainly, it appears that the best way of understanding the Bible as a whole is to see the Old Testament as predicting the coming of the Messiah and the New Testament revealing him to be Jesus of Nazareth."[3]

Jesus is fully human and fully divine. His humanity was accepted by all who met Him (e.g., Jn 10:35) and His deity is widely attested in the NT (e.g., Jn 1:1-18; 20:28). His deity is also affirmed in the messianic expectations of the OT. B. B. Warfield concludes: "The salient fact regarding [the deity of the Messiah] is that it is an essential element in the eschatological system of the Old Testament and is inseparably imbedded in the hope of the coming of God to His kingdom, which formed the heart of Israelitish religion from its origin."[4]

From the beginning of the predictions of His eschatological rule, the coming Messiah is understood to be divine. Of course, the clarity of this conviction grows with progressive revelation, not a change from belief in human messianic figures to a divine one, but an increasing clarity of the revelation that the Messiah is a single figure and that He is God Himself. Two key factors support this conviction. First, if the messianic expectation is to be understood correctly, it must be revealed clearly. The Messiah was and is "God with us" and thus must have been revealed as such.[5] J. Gresham Machen put it this way, "The Messiah, according to the Old Testament, is clearly to be a supernatural person, and he is clearly possessed of attributes that are truly divine."[6] Second, Jesus' own words seem to indicate that, properly interpreted, the OT reveals that the Messiah would be a divine person.

CHRISTOLOGICAL HERMENEUTICS

In Jn 5, Jesus healed a lame man on the Sabbath. The Jewish leaders objected (Jn 5:10) and even persecuted Jesus for His kindness to the man who had been sick for 38 years (Jn 5:5). In response, Jesus linked Himself to the Father, "My Father is still working, and I am working also" (Jn 5:17). This led His opponents to try to kill Him; it was bad enough that He worked on the Sabbath, but now "He was even calling God His own Father, making Himself equal with God" (Jn 5:18).

What follows is a profoundly pointed rebuke of the biblical scholarship of these opponents. Jesus again claimed to be doing the works of the Father, including giving life in the resurrection of the dead and functioning as the Judge on the day of judgment (Jn 5:21-29). He claimed that John the Baptist and the Father testified to who He is (Jn 5:31-37). Further testimony comes from the Scriptures: "The Father who sent Me has Himself testified about Me. . . . You don't have His word living in you, because you don't believe the One He sent. You pore over the Scriptures because you think you have eternal life in them, yet they testify about Me" (Jn 5:37-39). To these experts in the Scriptures, Jesus delivered a devastating critique of their hermeneutical method. They thought the Scriptures were in themselves the words of life; they were wrong. Jesus is the life and the Scriptures testify to Him. To read the Scriptures and fail to see the Messiah in them is to fail to read the Scriptures correctly. Therefore, on the day of judgment, God will not be their accuser but rather Moses. "For if you believed Moses, you would believe Me, because he wrote about Me. But if you don't believe his writings, how will you believe My words?" (Jn 5:46-47).

This declaration from the mouth of the Messiah should be enough to establish the point that the OT reveals that the Messiah will be divine, yet it is not the only time Jesus made such a claim. After His resurrection, in a conversation with two disciples on the road to Emmaus, Jesus rebuked their lack of faith when He asserted, "How unwise and slow you are to believe in your hearts all that the prophets have spoken! Didn't the Messiah have to suffer these things and enter into His glory?" (Lk 24:25-26). "Then," Luke declares, "beginning with Moses and all the Prophets, He interpreted for them the things concerning Himself in all the Scriptures" (Lk 24:27). Later, when He joined these and the rest of His disciples back in Jerusalem, Jesus spoke to the group: "These are My words that I spoke to you while I was still with you—that everything written about Me in the Law of Moses, the Prophets, and the Psalms must be fulfilled." Luke concludes, "Then He opened their minds to understand the Scriptures" (Lk 24:44-45). In short, like the teachers of the law (Jn 5), Jesus' disciples apparently lacked the ability to see what the Scriptures taught. The entire Scriptures reveal Him.

Surely Jesus does not mean that every word in every verse in the Scripture must be interpreted as an explicit reference to the Messiah, but that every text must be understood in light of Him.[7] Those who have the Spirit have the mind of Christ and thus are able to understand the Scriptures correctly (cf. 1Co 2:11-16). Augustine put it this way: "Everything in those Scriptures speaks of Christ, but only to him who has ears."[8] So the deity of the Messiah need not be defended through a handful of proof texts, but rather through the proper, Christological reading of the entire Scriptures. If all of the Scriptures are Christological, then the entirety of the Scriptures is messianic. Yet some texts more directly and specifically address the Messiah's deity, and it is to those texts that we turn.

DEITY OF THE MESSIAH IN THE LAW

The Protevangelium

The hope of a divine deliverer is found in each of the three sections of the Hebrew Scriptures. Rose observes: "From the earliest traditions of Jewish and Christian exegesis onward, students of the Pentateuch had found references to the Messiah in the first five books of the OT."[9]

After two accounts of the creative work of God in bringing into existence a good world, Moses told the tragic tale of the introduction of sin and death into this world through the fall of Adam and Eve (Gn 3). Although God had given them many trees from which to eat, He told them not to eat from one tree, the tree of the knowledge of good and evil, or they would die (Gn 2:17). They listened to the lie of the serpent, who told them, "You will not die" (Gn 3:4), and immediately experienced consequences of their sin. This is a catastrophic story of rebellion, betrayal, and infidelity. God's words of condemnation and judgment are painful to read. Yet, in the midst of an oracle of judgment, there is some good news, a *protevangelium* (Gn 3:15).[10]

In pronouncing judgment on the rebellion in the garden, God spoke to the serpent first, and then to the woman and man. To the woman, He promised increased labor pains and an unrequited desire for her husband's affection (Gn 3:16).[11] When He turned to Adam, God cursed the ground, promising painful labor (Gn 3:17) "until you return to the ground, since you were taken from it. For you are dust, and you will return to dust" (Gn 3:19). Clearly, this judgment applies equally to both men and women, since both sexes struggle to produce crops from a cursed earth and both die. There is hardly any good news in any of this. But the first words God had spoken were to the serpent: "Because you have done this, you are cursed more than any livestock and more than any wild animal. You will move on your belly and eat dust all the days of your life. I will put hostility between you and the woman, and between your seed and her seed. He will strike your head, and you will strike his heel" (Gn 3:14-15). A great deal of speculation surrounds the meaning of this text.[12]

Irenaeus of Lyons (AD 135–202) provides an early Christological interpretation of these words to the serpent:

> For this end did He put enmity between the serpent and the woman and her seed, they keeping it up mutually: He, the sole of whose foot should be bitten, having power also to tread upon the enemy's head; but the other biting, killing, and impeding the steps of man, until the seed did come appointed to tread down his head—which was born of Mary.[13]

The imagery of the seed of the serpent striking the heel of the seed of the woman, and the seed of the woman striking the head of the serpent, is stunning when read through the lens of the crucifixion of Christ. Charles Hodge explained,

> Immediately after the apostasy of our first parents it was announced that the seed of the woman should bruise the serpent's head. The meaning of this promise and prediction is to be determined by subsequent revelations. When interpreted in the light of the Scriptures themselves, it is manifest that the seed of the woman means the Redeemer, and that bruising the serpent's head means his final triumph over the powers of darkness. In this protevangelium, as it has ever been called, we have the dawning revelation of the humanity and divinity of the great deliverer.[14]

At a minimum, there is a hint that the seed of the serpent will be destroyed, and that is good news. But the hope of a divine deliverer seems more explicit, as Rydelnik observed,

> Not only the structure but the skeleton of the Pentateuchal story follows a particular individual. This is evident in tracing the family line, or "the seed," in the Torah. He is the "seed" that will descend from Eve (Gn 3:15), the future king

> who will descend from Abraham (Gn 17:6), the seed who will bless all nations (Gn 22:17b-19). Additionally, He is the lion of the tribe of Judah, the king who will rule over all people (Gn 49:8-12), and the seed who will be a king with an exalted end-time kingdom (Nm 24:7-9).[15]

Ray Pritchard claims, "Everything else in the Bible flows from these words in Genesis 3:15."[16] Further, in Romans, the apostle Paul appears to echo Gn 3:15 as he anticipated this hope and expressed his confidence, "The God of peace will soon crush Satan under your feet" (Rom 16:20).

What is beyond controversy is that the fall did not bring the immediate consequences of death. The threat was clear: "You must not eat from the tree of the knowledge of good and evil, for on the day you eat from it, you will certainly die" (Gn 2:17). Even the reference to the seed of the woman is a statement of mercy (Gn 3:15); these rebels will not die immediately, but will live long enough to produce offspring. Rather than experiencing the death they deserved, Adam and his wife were driven from the garden, lest they "reach out, take from the tree of life, eat, and live forever" (Gn 3:22). Adam lived 930 years, and then he died (Gn 5:5), and this is the fate of his offspring.[17] Further, atonement through animal sacrifice, foreshadowing "the Lamb of God, who takes away the sin of the world!" (Jn 1:29), was introduced when God killed an animal to make garments of skin for the rebellious humans (Gn 3:21). God Himself acted to provide for them what they were probably not even aware they needed.

If the rebellion in the garden was at the instigation of a usurper, the serpent, redemption could only come through someone who has the right to the garden, who could only be the Creator. The only other option would be a human, one created in the image of God, but image bearers of God had forfeited their place. Yet redemption will come through the One who is both the image of God and also God Himself (Gn 1:26-28; Col 1:15; Heb 1:3).

The Angel of the Lord

The incarnation of the second person of the Trinity was not the first time that God came into the world He created.[18] God walked in the garden of Eden (Gn 3:8). Enoch (Gn 5:22) and Noah (Gn 6:9) walked with God. God appeared to Abraham and had lunch and an extended conversation with him (Gn 18). There are many more examples. A particularly intriguing category is those stories in which a figure, identified as the Angel of the Lord, appears on earth and engages with a human.[19] Who is this figure? Is He merely an angelic messenger or is He God Himself?[20]

The first appearance of the Angel is in Genesis 16.[21] Although God had promised Abram that he would have many descendants (Gn 15:5), Abram and Sarai remained childless. In an attempt to build a family through her Egyptian slave, Sarai offered

Hagar to Abram (Gn 16:2). Abram took Hagar as his second wife, slept with her, and she became pregnant (Gn 16:3-4). Not surprisingly, this resulted in no small conflict between the two wives. Sarai mistreated Hagar, with Abram's permission, and the pregnant Hagar fled (Gn 16:6).

This likely would have been the end of the story, but for the intervention of the God of Abram. The Angel of the Lord found the pregnant Hagar by a spring of water in the wilderness (Gn 16:7).[22] The Angel asked Hagar to identify herself and then sent her back to her mistress (Gn 16:8-10).[23] The Angel spoke words of promise and protection to her: "You have conceived and will have a son. You will name him Ishmael, for the LORD has heard your cry of affliction. This man will be like a wild donkey. His hand will be against everyone, and everyone's hand will be against him; he will live at odds with all his brothers" (Gn 16:11-12). This is a message from the Lord, the God of Abram. The narrator, Moses, then wrote, "So she called the LORD who spoke to her: The God Who Sees [*El Roi*], for she said, 'In this place, have I actually seen the One who sees me?'" (Gn 16:13). She also "named the spring, 'A Well of the Living One Who Sees Me' [*Beer-lahai-roi*]" (Gn 16:14). This shift from "Angel of the LORD" to "LORD" indicates that this Angel was not merely a divine messenger but was the Lord Himself. Further indication appears in Abram's response: When Hagar returned to him with the message that she had received from the Lord, Abram apparently believed her, because Hagar remained with Abram, and when his son was born Abram gave him the name Ishmael (Gn 16:15-16).[24]

Similarly, the Angel of God appeared to Hagar and her son Ishmael in Gn 21. Here, too, He is identified as an Angel/Messenger in v. 17; He delivered the divine declaration that "God has heard the voice of the boy from the place where he is." The Angel further declared, "I will make him a great nation" (Gn 21:18). The Angel spoke for Himself and called Himself God.

In Gn 31 the Angel of the Lord identified Himself as God.[25] When the Angel of the Lord appeared to Jacob in a dream and gave him instructions to leave the household of Laban, He called Himself "the God of Bethel, where you poured oil on the stone marker and made a solemn vow to Me" (Gn 31:13). This is a reference to when Jacob fled from his brother and met Yahweh at Bethel in a dream in which he saw a stairway between heaven and earth with angels ascending and descending (Gn 28:10-12). Yahweh said to him there, "I am Yahweh, the God of your father Abraham and the God of Isaac. I will give you and your offspring the land that you are now sleeping on" (Gn 28:13). Thus, the Angel claimed to be Yahweh.

That the Angel is identified as a messenger of the Lord might merely mean that He speaks for the Lord, as His ambassador. But the language attributing the divine name to Him seems to indicate that He is both a messenger and the Lord Himself. But is He the second person of the Godhead, the preincarnate Messiah?

Goldberg surely overstates the case when he asserts: "The connection between the angel of the Lord and the preincarnate appearance of the Messiah cannot be denied."[26] Many have, in fact, denied such a connection. But the testimony of the early church is compelling. Norwood explains: "The Fathers exhibit a consensus that Yahweh is manifested through all of the Old Testament theophanies (Angel of Yahweh, burning bush, cloud and fire, Son of Man, and others) by the preincarnate Word, just as God is made visible in the New Testament through the incarnate Word (Jn 1:1, 14)."[27] For example, Justin Martyr insisted, "Neither Abraham, nor Isaac, nor Jacob, nor any other man, saw the Father and ineffable Lord of all, and also of Christ, but [saw] Him who was according to His will His Son, being God, and the Angel because He ministered to His will; whom also it pleased Him to be born man by the Virgin."[28]

The Angel of the Lord is called "wonderful" in Jdg 13:18, the same designation the Messiah receives in Isa 9:6.[29] Further, the Angel and the Messiah are linked in Zch 12:8: "On that day the LORD will defend the inhabitants of Jerusalem, so that on that day the one who is weakest among them will be like David on that day, and the house of David will be like God, like the Angel of the LORD, before them."[30] Two verses later, the speaker is identified, "Then I will pour out a spirit of grace and prayer on the house of David and the residents of Jerusalem, and they will look at Me whom they pierced" (Zch 12:10). Only the Messiah, the second person of the Trinity, could be in view here.

The Angel of the Lord is a Messenger who has come from the Lord who is the Lord Himself. The differentiation between the Lord and the Angel implies plurality in the Godhead, early evidence of the Trinity. That the Angel is the second person is further indicated when Jesus the Messiah explicitly identified Himself as one sent from the Father (Jn 13:20; 17:18; 20:21). The Lord sent the Angel; the Lord sent Jesus.

DEITY OF THE MESSIAH IN THE PROPHETS

Multiple texts in the canon of prophetic books could be examined for evidence of the deity of the Messiah. Several selected texts will have to suffice.

In Isa 7, the prophet brought a message of deliverance to King Ahaz, when Jerusalem was under siege by her enemies. The Lord promised that the threats of destruction would not come to pass; rather, these enemies would be shattered (Isa 7:8). The Lord offered Ahaz a sign, "Ask for a sign from the LORD your God—from the depths of Sheol to the heights of heaven" (Isa 7:11).[31] When Ahaz refused the offer, the Lord rebuked the king and declared,

> Therefore, the Lord Himself will give you a sign: The virgin will conceive, have a son, and name him Immanuel. By the time he learns to reject what is bad and choose what is good, he will be eating butter and honey. For before the boy knows to reject what is bad and choose what is good, the land of the two kings you dread will be abandoned. The LORD will bring on you, your people, and the house of your father, such a time as has never been since Ephraim separated from Judah—the king of Assyria is coming. (Isa 7:14-17)[32]

There seems to be some contemporary significance of the sign for Ahaz's day. Note that Ephraim would be shattered within 65 years (Isa 7:8). Before the child could choose good and evil, the land of these enemies would be abandoned (Isa 7:15-16), and the king of Assyria would come (Isa 7:17). Yet the language of Isa 7:14 transcends this historical situation. The claim, "The virgin will conceive," points to a miraculous birth, and the child's name seems more than a metaphorical sign.[33] When the Messiah came, He was God in the flesh. His was both a miraculous birth, and He was a unique and supernatural sign.

In Isa 9, the prophet describes a future day of light, life, deliverance, peace, and prosperity through a child, a Son (Isa 9:1-6). Of this Son, on whose shoulder will rest government, Isaiah declares, "He will be named Wonderful Counselor, Mighty God, Eternal Father, Prince of Peace" (Isa 9:6). His kingdom will never end and "He will reign on the throne of David" (Isa 9:7; a clear reference to the promise of an eternal kingdom promised to David in 2Sm 7; cf. Ps 89). Since only God is eternal, this could only be a reference to the Messiah, God with us. The names are divine names, including the explicit designation "Mighty God." L. S. Chafer observes, "Incomparable titles are here ascribed to that unique Person who is never duplicated in heaven or on earth, who combines both humanity as a child born and deity as a Son given. He is here said to be Wonderful, Counselor, the Mighty God, the Father of eternity, and the Prince of Peace."[34]

In chap. 44, the prophet Isaiah quotes "The LORD, the King of Israel and its Redeemer, the LORD of Hosts" (Isa 44:6). The Lord and the Redeemer of Israel declares:

> I am the first and I am the last. There is no God but Me. Who, like Me, can announce the future? Let him say so and make a case before Me, since I have established an ancient people. Let these gods declare the coming things, and what will take place. Do not be startled or afraid. Have I not told you and declared it long ago? You are my witnesses! Is there any God but Me? There is no other Rock; I do not know any. (Isa 44:6-8)

Both the Lord and Israel's promised Redeemer, who is also called "the LORD of Hosts," are identified as God. The Redeemer of Israel is the Messiah.

The prophet Isaiah later quoted one sent from the Lord: "Approach Me and listen to this. From the beginning I have not spoken in secret; from the time anything existed, I was there. And now the Lord GOD has sent me and His Spirit" (Isa 48:16). Martin explains that this is "probably the Messiah, God's Servant, ... because of His association (as in 42:1; also note 11:1-2) with the Spirit. Just as Cyrus would not fail in his mission (48:15), so the Messiah-Servant, sent by God with the Holy Spirit on Him, will not fail in His mission."[35] Further, only a divine person could be said to have existed before creation. Similar language appears in Isa 61:1-3, quoted by Jesus and applied to Himself in Lk 4:18-19.

The prophet Jeremiah refers to the coming Messiah as the "Branch" in chap. 23. He explains that the Lord promises to raise up "a Righteous Branch of David. He will reign wisely as king and administer justice and righteousness in the land" (Jer 23:5). This is an obvious reference to the Davidic covenant. As he continues, Jeremiah quotes the Lord as naming this Davidic king, "Yahweh Our Righteousness" (Jer 23:6). The Branch is not merely named Yahweh, but He shares the Righteousness of Yahweh, an apparent indication of plurality in the Godhead. Similarly, Jer 33:15 names the coming Davidic king "a Righteous Branch" and names Jerusalem "Yahweh Our Righteousness" (Jer 33:16), presumably a metonymy for the One who reigns from that city.

In Mic 5, the prophet promises his audience, identified as "daughter who is under attack" (Mic 5:1), that deliverance is coming. This deliverer will be born in "Bethlehem Ephrathah, you who are small among the clans of Judah" (Mic 5:2; cf. Mt 2:1-7). This one, identified as "ruler over Israel for Me" (Mic 5:2), is not a mere human ruler. Rather, "His origin is from antiquity, from eternity" (Mic 5:2). In short, this ruler is a divine king.[36] Since only God is eternal, only God could come from eternity.

Micah's contemporary, Hosea, prophesied similarly. Hosea's daughter, named by the Lord's command, was a sign to the house of Israel. The Lord said to Hosea, "Name her No Compassion, for I will no longer have compassion on the house of Israel. I will certainly take them away. But I will have compassion on the house of Judah, and will deliver them by the LORD their God" (Hos 1:6-7). Judah's deliverer will not be a mere human, "I will not deliver them by bow, sword, or war, or by horses and cavalry" (Hos 1:7), rather, deliverance will come by the Lord Himself. The deliverer, the Messiah, will be Yahweh.

Zechariah promises a day in which the Lord Himself will dwell in the midst of His people, in Jerusalem: "'Daughter Zion, shout for joy and be glad, for I am coming to dwell among you'—this is the LORD's declaration" (Zch 2:10). The promise continues, "Many nations will join themselves to the LORD on that day and become My people. I will dwell among you, and you will know that the LORD of Hosts has sent Me to you" (Zch 2:11). When this happens, when the Lord Himself comes to earth and lives among His people, that people will include not only Israel and Judah, but people of all nations, thus fulfilling the promise made to Abraham that all peoples will be blessed through his Seed, the Messiah (Gn 12:3; cf. Gal 3:8).

DEITY OF THE MESSIAH IN THE WRITINGS

In Ps 2, David (cf. Ac 4:24-26) describes the Lord's response to the opposition from the kings of the earth toward Himself and His Messiah: "The One enthroned in heaven laughs; the Lord ridicules them" (Ps 2:4). In v. 7, David identifies the Messiah as God's unique Son.[37] God promised to break them and to shatter them (Ps 2:9) and to establish His Son as King and to give Him "the ends of the earth [as His] possession" (Ps 2:8). The psalm concludes with a call to worship the Son, a clear declaration of His deity (Ps 2:11-12).

In Ps 45, the sons of Korah explicitly call the Messiah "God." The psalm praises the King for His conquest of His enemies; He is a Mighty Warrior (Ps 45:1-5). Then, the psalmist continues, "Your throne, God, is forever and ever; the scepter of Your kingdom is a scepter of justice" (Ps 45:6). The King reigns over an eternal kingdom, which would require an eternal king. And it is a kingdom of righteousness. Who is this King? According to v. 7, He is the Anointed One, the Messiah: "Therefore God, your God, has anointed you with the oil of joy more than your companions" (Ps 45:7).

In Ps 110, David begins, "This is the declaration of the LORD to my Lord: 'Sit at My right hand until I make Your enemies Your footstool'" (Ps 110:1). The Lord sits at the right hand of the Lord. Reymond concludes, "Some angels are privileged to stand before God (Lk 1:19), but none are ever said to sit before him, much less sit upon his throne. The One who sits *with* God must surely share in the divine reign as being himself divine."[38] This divine King reigns with the Lord. David also connects His reign as king with His priesthood, in the order of Melchizedek (Ps 110:4).

The prophet Daniel describes the coming reign of the Messiah in several visions. In chap. 2, King Nebuchadnezzar sees a dream of a statue representing four kingdoms, beginning with his own (Dan 2:38). These four are followed by an eternal kingdom, which is represented by a stone that destroys the four previous kingdoms and grows into a mountain that fills the whole earth (Dan 2:31-35). According to Daniel's interpretation, this kingdom will be established by the God of heaven and "will never be destroyed. . . . but will itself endure forever" (Dan 2:44). This kingdom is the one promised to David (2Sm 7:12-16).

In the seventh chapter, Daniel relates his dream. He saw four kingdoms represented by four beasts. As in Dan 2, a fifth kingdom would follow these four (Dan 7:1-8). But then Daniel sees the throne of God, and "the Ancient of Days took His seat. His clothing was white like snow, and the hair of His head like whitest wool. His throne was flaming fire; its wheels were blazing fire" (Dan 7:9). Daniel has seen the God of heaven, the Creator of heaven and earth. As he continued to watch, Daniel saw "One like a son of man coming with the clouds of heaven. He approached the Ancient of Days and was escorted before Him" (Dan 7:13). As Reymond explains, the phrase "coming with the clouds" is "employed as descriptive metaphor only of deity."[39] The Son of Man is the Messiah, the Davidic King, which is made plain when He "was given authority to rule, and glory, and a kingdom; so that those of every people, nation, and language should serve Him. His dominion is an everlasting dominion that will not pass away, and His kingdom is one that will not be destroyed" (Dan 7:14). Further, "The holy ones of the Most High will receive the kingdom and possess it forever, yes, forever and ever" (Dan 7:18).[40]

CONCLUSION

From the "Seed of the woman" to an eternal kingdom promised to David to the "Son of Man" in Daniel's vision, the Hebrew Scriptures look forward to the reign of God over the earth through a Messianic King. This King will be literally and eternally God with us. When, in Jesus, the Word became flesh, these expectations were realized partially. His eternal kingdom is yet in the future, and fulfillment of so many of those expectations in His first advent establishes the hope of that future fulfillment.

---

1. Michael Rydelnik, *The Messianic Hope: Is the Hebrew Bible Really Messianic?* (Nashville: B&H Publishing, 2010), 2.

2. D. H. Wallace, "Messiah," *Evangelical Dictionary of Theology*, ed. Walter A. Elwell (Grand Rapids: Baker, 1984), 710. R. T. France, "Messiah," in *New Bible Dictionary*, 2nd ed. (Wheaton, IL: Tyndale House, 1982), 764, argues from the designation applied to Cyrus (Isa 45:1), for five features of a messianic figure: chosen by God, appointed to a redemptive purpose for God's people and judgment of their enemies, given dominion over the nations, and an agent of Yahweh Himself; "These five points are pre-eminently true of the Lord Jesus Christ."

3. Rydelnik, *The Messianic Hope*, 8.

4. B. B. Warfield, "Christology and Criticism," in *The Works of Benjamin B. Warfield: Christology and Criticism* (New York: Oxford University Press, 1927), 3:47–48. Warfield also observes: "There is no reason why, in the delivery of doctrine, the Deity of the Messiah might not be taught before the multiplicity in the unity of the Godhead had been revealed. In the history of Christian doctrine the conviction of the Deity of Christ was the condition, not the result, of the formulation of the doctrine of the Trinity" (Ibid., 3–4).

5. Lewis Sperry Chafer, *Systematic Theology* (Dallas: Dallas Seminary Press, 1948), 5:43.

6. J. Gresham Machen, "Does the Bible Teach the Deity of Christ?" accessed June 6, 2016, http://www.the-highway.com/deity2_Machen.html, continues, "It is true, the Old Testament does not set forth the doctrine of the deity of Christ with any fullness. I do not suppose that either the prophets or their hearers knew in any clear fashion that the coming Messiah was to be one of the persons in the Godhead. Yet there are wonderful intimations of the doctrine of the deity of Christ even in the Old Testament."

7. See "Article I—The Scriptures," Dallas Theological Seminary Doctrinal Statement, accessed June 6, 2016, http://www.dts.edu/about/doctrinalstatement/: "We believe that all the Scriptures center about the Lord Jesus Christ in His person and work in His first and second coming, and hence that no portion, even of the Old Testament, is properly read, or understood, until it leads to Him."

8. Augustine, Homily 2.1, *Ancient Christian Commentary on Scripture*, Ancient Christian Commentary, 27 vols., ed. Thomas C. Oden (Downers Grove, IL: InterVarsity, 1998–2009), 4A:15.

9. W. H. Rose, "Messiah," in *Dictionary of the Old Testament: Pentateuch*, ed. T. Desmond Alexander and David W. Barker (Downers Grove, IL: InterVarsity, 2003), 565. He cites the conflict between the woman and the serpent (Gn 3:15), the scepter promised to Judah (Gn 49:8-12), the star and scepter coming from Judah (Nm 24:17-19), and the prophet like Moses (Dt 18:18-19). W. Berry Norwood, "The Church Fathers and the Deity of Christ," *American Theological Inquiry* 3 (2010): 17, observes: "The Fathers make it clear that Christ's deity is revealed by specific Old Testament material, by Christ's identification as a member of the Trinity, and by Christ's role and attributes as the Logos or Word."

10. For an excellent survey of the interpretive options, the history of interpretation, and a defense of the messianic interpretation, see David Pettus, "Reading a Protoevangelium in the Context of Genesis," *Eruditio Ardescens* 1 (2014): 1-18.

11. Gordon Wenham states, "Under the curse, those who were created to be one flesh will find themselves tearing each other apart." *Genesis 1–15*, vol. 1, *Word Biblical Commentary* (Dallas: Word, 1998), 89.

12. Not everyone sees a promise of the Messiah in this text. For example, Andrew Perriman claims: "There appears to be no basis in scripture for interpreting Genesis 3:15 in the traditional messianic sense as referring to a future saviour of mankind who would crush the head of Satan." He calls this a "misreading of the text." "Does the Gospel First Appear in Genesis 3:15?" accessed June 9, 2016, http://www.postost.net/2015/11/does-gospel-first-appear-genesis-315.

13. Irenaeus, *Against Heresies* 3.23.7, accessed June 9, 2016, http://www.newadvent.org/fathers/0103323.htm.

14. Charles Hodge, *Systematic Theology* (reprint; Grand Rapids: Eerdmans, 1986), 1:483-84.

15. Rydelnik, *The Messianic Hope*, 71.

16. Ray Pritchard, "What Is the Protoevangelium?" accessed July 6, 2016, http://www.jesus.org/is-jesus-god/old-testament-prophecies/what-is-the-protoevangelium-protoevangelion.html.

17. The only exceptions are those who have not yet died, Enoch (Gn 5:24), and Elijah (2Kgs 2:11).

18. See Glenn R. Kreider, *God with Us: Exploring God's Personal Interactions with His People Throughout the Bible* (Phillipsburg, NJ: P&R, 2014) for a biblical/theological examination of this theme.

19. See, for example, Gn 16:7-14; 21:17-18; 22:9-16; 31:11-3; 32:24-30; Ex 3:1-5; Jdg 2:1-4; 5:23; 6:11-24; 2Sm 14:16; Zch 1:12; 3:1; 12:8. This list is from Charles C. Ryrie, *Basic Theology* (Wheaton, IL: Victor Books, 1986), 239. Daniel Finestone, "Is the Angel of Jehovah in the Old Testament the Lord Jesus Christ?" *Bibliotheca Sacra* 97 (1940): 373, explains, "It will be observed that without exception the appearances of the Angel of Jehovah are always in connection with Israel's destiny."

20. For an excellent and accessible treatment of the "Angel," see Tom Brewer, "Who Is the Messenger?" accessed July 5, 2016, http://jewsforjesus.org/publications/issues/v14-n06/messenger.

21. See discussion in Kreider, *God with Us*, 30–33.

22. There are significant echoes of this story in the account of Jesus' conversation with the Samaritan woman (Jn 4). See Glenn Kreider, "God's Humility: Reflections on an Unappreciated Attribute of the Father, Son, and Holy Spirit," *Criswell Theological Review* n.s. 9 (Fall 2011): 33-57.

23. This story must never be used to justify sending an abused spouse back to her abuser. The Angel sent Hagar back with the implied assurance that He would care for her.

24. Abram was 86 years old when Ishmael was born (Gn 16:16). When the Lord appeared to Abram next, he was 99 (Gn 17:1).

25. Millard J. Erickson, *Christian Theology*, 3rd ed. (Grand Rapids: Baker, 2013), 413.

26. Louis Goldberg, "Angel of the Lord," in *Evangelical Dictionary of Biblical Theology*, ed. Walter A. Elwell (Grand Rapids: Baker, 1996), 23. Much more nuanced is Henry H. Holloman, "Angel of the Lord," in *Kregel Dictionary of*

the Bible and Theology (Grand Rapids: Kregel, 2005), 20: "There is evidence in these descriptions to conclude that the visitations are *theophanies* or divine appearances by the second person of the Trinity (i.e., *Christophanies*)."

27. Norwood, "The Church Fathers and the Deity of Christ," 31.

28. Justin Martyr, *Dialogue with Trypho*, 127, accessed June 9, 2016, http://www.ccel.org/ccel/schaff/anf01.viii.iv.cxxvii.html#.

29. Holloman, "Angel of the Lord," 21.

30. Daniel Finestone, "Is the Angel of Jehovah in the Old Testament the Lord Jesus Christ?" *Bibliotheca Sacra* 97 (1940): 376.

31. This language implies a miraculous sign.

32. There is a great deal of literature dealing with the interpretation of this text, particularly v. 14 and its use in the NT in Mt 2:15. A good treatment, taking a relecture approach, is found in Paul D. Wegner, "How Many Virgin Births Are in the Bible?: A Prophetic Pattern Approach, *Journal of the Evangelical Theological Society* 54 (2011): 467–84. Michael Rydelnik, in his chap. on Isa 7:14 in this *Handbook*, pp. 815–27, provides a different approach, treating the passage as a direct messianic prediction. For a defense of "virgin" in Isa 7:14, see Richard Niessen, "The Virginity of the 'almah in Isaiah 7:14," *Bibliotheca Sacra* 137 (1980): 133–50.

33. It is true that God's deliverance of His people would be evidence of "God with us," but this language seems to point beyond that.

34. Chafer, *Systematic Theology*, 5:29.

35. John A. Martin, "Isaiah," in *The Bible Knowledge Commentary: An Exposition of the Scriptures*, ed. John F. Walvoord and Roy B. Zuck (Wheaton, IL: Victor Books, 1985), 1:1102–3.

36. A similar phrase ("from eternity to eternity") is used in Ps 90:2 for Yahweh. Robert L. Reymond, *A New Systematic Theology of the Christian Faith* (Nashville: Thomas Nelson, 1998), 213.

37. Reymond, *New Systematic Theology*, 212.

38. Reymond, *New Systematic Theology*, 213.

39. Reymond, *New Systematic Theology*, 213. He cites Nah 1:3 as an example.

40. In Dan 9, this king is called "the Messiah" (v. 26).

Typology in the Old Testament

SETH D. POSTELL

INTRODUCTION

Have NT authors shoehorned the Jesus event back onto the pages of the OT, or were they right to make the typological links replete in their writings? In what follows, evidence will be examined to show that Adam, Moses, Israel, and the Tabernacle were already interpreted typologically in the OT long before the time of Christ. The OT's design was to prepare its readers for the future through careful meditation on the past. The NT interpretation of these passages and concepts is not only an appropriate continuation but demonstrates highly sensitive treatment of the OT texts revealing many similar typological interpretations.[1] Ancient rabbis were also comfortable discussing the typological patterns and projections they saw in the Jewish Scriptures alone, as seen in this segment from Ecclesiastes Rabbah:

> That which was will be . . . Rabbi Berekiah said in the name of Rabbi Isaac. "As the first redeemer was, so will be the last redeemer. What was said of the first redeemer? (Exodus 4). 'And Moses took his wife and his sons and placed them upon the donkey' (Ex 4:20). Thus it shall be with the last redeemer, as it is said, 'Humble and riding upon a donkey' (Zch 9:9). What upon the first redeemer? He brought down the manna, as it is said, 'Behold I will cause manna to rain upon you from the heavens' (Ex 16:4). Even so the last redeemer will bring down the manna, as it is written, 'Let there be an abundance of grain in the land' (Ps 72:16). What about the first redeemer? He brought up the well. Even so the last redeemer will bring the water, as it is written, 'And a well from the house of the Lord will go forth and water the river valley of the acacias' (Jl 4:18 [EVV 3:18])."[2]

This quotation of Rabbi Berekiah in the name of Rabbi Isaac offers typological interpretations of the story of Moses that are in many ways identical to the kinds of interpretations found in the NT.[3] For example, Rabbi Isaac cites the story of Moses returning to Egypt with his wife and children upon the donkey in Ex 4:20. The apostle Matthew likewise alludes to the same verses to show his readers that Jesus is the "Prophet like Moses" and "last redeemer."[4] Followers of Jesus are reminded of the corresponding verses in the NT that point to Jesus as the "last redeemer." Jesus entered Jerusalem upon a donkey (Mt 21:1-7). Jesus was the perfect manna from heaven (Jn 6:51-58). Jesus provided living water to those who believed in Him (Jn 4:10; 7:37-38). Significantly, all these references cited for a typological interpretation of Moses are taken from within the OT. Though it is open to debate whether Joel, Zechariah, and the psalmist intended to portray the "Last Redeemer" as the antitype of the first redeemer in these verses, this article will contend that it is essential to consider typological interpretations *within* the OT as a framework in order to appreciate typological interpretations in the NT.

To show how the NT authors were continuing a pattern that had already been established in the OT, three typological interpretations will be examined: (1) Paul's typological interpretation of Adam, (2) Matthew's typological reading of the Moses and Israel stories, and (3) Hebrews' typological understanding of the Tabernacle as a shadow of better things. It will become clear that the NT's interpretations are a natural and expected extension of the typological interpretations of Adam, Moses, and Israel, and the Tabernacle already present in the OT.

EXAMPLE 1: THE NEW ADAM AND ADAM TYPOLOGY IN THE OT

The apostle Paul looked to the first Adam as a type of Christ: "The last Adam" (1Co 15:45).[5] In Rom 5:14, Paul explicitly calls Adam a type of the coming one. Like Adam's, Jesus' actions had universal implications for all humanity, since both men stand as representatives of all humanity in the physical creation as well as in the new creation (see Rom 5:12-21; 1Co 15:20-22,44-49). In Eph 5:31-32, Paul interprets Adam's union with Eve with reference to the profound mystery of Messiah and the Church.

Paul was not the originator of Adam typology, for it was evident in the Hebrew Bible itself. The creation mandate embodies God's purpose for all humanity. "God blessed them, and God said to them, 'Be fruitful, multiply, fill the earth, and subdue it'" (Gn 1:28). This creation mandate can be summarized in three words: blessing, seed, and land.[6] Adam's failure in the garden represents the antithesis of this threefold purpose. God desired to bless humanity; Adam's sin resulted in curses

(Gn 3:14,17; 4:11; 5:29; 9:25). God desired humanity's seed to multiply and fill the land, Adam's sin resulted in difficulties in childbearing along with marital conflict (Gn 3:16). Multiplication after the curse would be further hindered by death (Gn 3:19), murder (Gn 4:8), heavenly rebellion (Gn 6:1-2), and divine judgment (Gn 6:7).

God desired humanity to subdue (in Hebrew, conquer) the land and rule over it.[7] Adam's failure to conquer the garden by ruling over the serpent resulted in exile from the special land God prepared for Adam and his family (Gn 3:23-24). God's response to Adam's sin is a promise. He said to the serpent: "I will put hostility between you and the woman, and between your seed and her seed. He will strike your head, and you will strike his heel" (Gn 3:15). This promise embodies the hope that God's threefold purpose for humanity would be restored through the seed of the woman, a future "Adam." Henceforth, biblical authors intentionally describe key figures in the story of redemption with hues and tones that remind of the "first Adam." Through Adam typology it is possible to understand God's purposes for choosing Noah, Abram, Israel, Israel's king, and the Messiah.

Adam and Noah

Noah's story shares a number of lexical and thematic links, indicating that Noah must be understood as another Adam; an example of OT typology within the OT.[8]

1. God's wind over the waters in the Noah story (Gn 8:1) hearkens back to God's Spirit[9] over the waters in the Adam story (Gn 1:2).
2. Animals coming to Noah (Gn 7:6-9) remind of the animals brought to Adam (Gn 2:18-20).
3. God's mandate to Noah (Gn 9:1-9) includes blessing, seed, land, dietary provisions, and a covenant, clearly parallel to God's mandate to Adam (Gn 1:28–2:2), containing blessing, seed, land, dietary provisions, and the Sabbath.
4. Noah's fall parallels Adam's fall in remarkable detail: in both stories, someone plants a garden/vineyard (2:8-9; 9:2), someone takes of the fruit/fruit of the vine (3:6; 9:21), someone is naked and then covered (3:7,21; 9:23), someone is cursed (3:14; 9:25), and a certain seed becomes the key to God's redemptive program (3:15; 9:26-27).

These numerous parallels make it clear that Noah is a type of Adam, or that Adam foreshadows Noah.

Adam and Abram

Adam typology continues to play a key role as the Torah story continues. Just as God speaks to Adam regarding *blessing, seed,* and *land* (Gn 1:28), so God's promise to Abram involves *blessing, seed,* and *land* (Gn 12:1-3; 28:3-4). Abram, like Noah before him, is cast as another "Adam" through whom God would restore His creation purposes.

ADAM AND ISRAEL

Likewise, God's purposes for Israel as a whole become clear in light of Adam's story.

1. Adam's mandate of blessing, seed, and the conquering of a land is echoed in God's purposes for Israel. God's desire for Israel is to bring blessings to and through them (Gn 12:3; Dt 33:1). God promises to make Israel fruitful (compare Gn 1:28; Ex 1:7). God calls Israel to "conquer the land," the exact phrase found in the creation mandate (compare Gn 1:28; Nm 32:22,29; Jos 18:1).
2. Adam's rule over creation (Gn 1:28) and his intimacy with God in the garden (2:10-15; 3:8) foreshadow Israel's call to be a royal priesthood (Ex 19:6). Israel is to rule over the land and to enjoy God's special presence among them in the Tabernacle, and later the Temple.
3. Adam's disobedience and exile from the garden foreshadow Israel's disobedience and exile from the promised land. The core elements of Adam's story literally become the story line of the Former Prophets,[10] as can be seen in the chart below.

GENESIS 1-11	JOSHUA-2 KINGS
God's Mandate to Adam (Gn 1:28)	God's Promise to Israel (Gn 12:1-3, et al)
God brings Adam into the garden (Gn 2:15)	God brings Israel into the promised land (Jos 1:1-9)
Adam is tempted by the Serpent (Gn 3:1, 14)	Israel is tempted by the Canaanites (Jos 9:4,23)
Adam disobeys God's commandments (Gn 3:6)	Israel disobeys God's commandments (Jdg)
God promises to bless the world through the seed of the woman (Gn 3:15)	God promises to bless the world through the seed of David (2Sm 7:11-14)
Adam is exiled to the east, and his descendants find themselves in Babylon (Gn 3:23-24; 11:1-9)	Israel is exiled to the east, to the land of Babylon (2Kg 25)

Israel is described as another Adam, and Adam foreshadows Israel. Israel's failure, like Adam's, means that the reader should expect another Adam, the seed of the woman, who will restore God's creation purposes.

Adam and Israel's King

The king of Israel, from the tribe of Judah, of the seed of David embodies and represents Israel's national calling. It is no surprise, therefore, to see that Solomon also is depicted as another Adam.

1. Solomon's rule over the kingdoms of the earth is described with the same terms used for Adam's creation mandate (compare 1Kg 4:21 [5:1 MT], 24 [5:4 MT]).
2. Solomon's great knowledge of trees, animals, birds, reptiles, and fish (1Kg 4:33 [1Kg 5:13 MT]) is described with words elsewhere only used to describe Adam's rule over creation (Gn 1:26,28-30; 2:19).
3. Solomon's request to discern between good and evil (1Kg 3:9) has an ominous tone in light of Adam's newly acquired capacity to know good and evil after the fall (Gn 3:22).
4. Solomon's construction of the Temple has numerous allusions to the original creation and the garden of Eden (compare Gn 2:2 with 1Kg 7:40; Gn 2:12 with 1Kg 6:22; 7:9; Gn 3:24 with 1Kg 6:23-28; Gn 2:2 with 1Kg 6:38; 7:14; 8:12-13; Gn 2:3 with 1Kg 8:14,55; Gn 2:2-3 with 1Kg 8:56; Gn 2:3 with 1Kg 8:64).
5. Solomon's cleaving to foreign women and subsequent fall is depicted with expressions taken from the story of Adam and Eve (Gn 2:22–3:1,6; 1Kg 11:1-6).
6. Solomon, like Noah, Abram, and Israel, is depicted as another Adam. Adam foreshadows King Solomon. Once again, Solomon's failure kindles an expectation for the coming of a future son of David from the tribe of Judah (Gn 49:8-12) who will be the truest and final antitype of the "first Adam."

Adam and Messiah

The trail of Adam typology within the OT ultimately leads to a future king, a son of David, who will bring the knowledge of God over the face of the earth. Remarkably, Isa 11:5-9 describes the reign of this future king using images taken right from the garden of Eden.

> Righteousness will be a belt around His loins; faithfulness will be a belt around His waist. The wolf will live with the lamb, and the leopard will lie down with the goat. The calf, the young lion, and the fatling will be together, and a child will lead them. The cow and the bear will graze, their young ones will lie down together, and the lion will eat straw like the ox. An infant will play beside the cobra's pit,

> and a toddler will put his hand into a snake's den. None will harm or destroy another on my entire holy mountain, for the land will be as full of the knowledge of the LORD as the sea is filled with water. (Isa 11:5-9)

This future Messiah and "last Adam" will lift the curse so that the earth will once again become like the garden of Eden.

Paul's use of Adam-Jesus typology is neither unique nor creative exegesis. Rather, it is the anticipated goal of the multiple typological interpretations of the "first Adam" found throughout the OT.

EXAMPLE 2: THE "PROPHET LIKE MOSES" AND THE TRUEST ISRAELITE

Matthew's presentation of Jesus relies extensively on typological readings of the OT. Matthew's Gospel places particular emphasis on two overlapping OT figures in the Pentateuch: Moses and Israel. A glance at the structure of Matthew reveals a systematic presentation of Jesus as the Prophet like Moses and as Israel's greatest representative.[11] Matthew's purpose in beginning his Gospel with a genealogy is to trace the line of the promised seed to the person of Jesus.[12] Likewise, a primary function of the book of Genesis in the Torah is to blaze a trail leading from the seed of the woman in Gn 3:15 to the coming Messiah in Gn 49:8-12 (see also Nm 24:17-19).[13] In Mt 2, there are numerous allusions to the story of the exodus. Jesus' parents rescued baby Jesus from the hands of Herod just as Moses' parents rescued the baby Moses from the hands of Pharaoh (v. 13). Jesus was brought out of Egypt just as Israel was (v. 14). Jesus' return to Israel to "save them from their sins" (Mt 1:21) is described using wording borrowed from the Septuagint describing Moses' return to Egypt to rescue Israel from their bondage.

After Herod died, an angel of the Lord suddenly appeared in a dream to Joseph in Egypt, saying, "Get up! Take the child and His mother and go to the land of Israel, because those who sought the child's life are dead." So he got up, took the child and His mother, and entered the land of Israel. (Mt 2:20-21)	Now after those many days, the king of Egypt died. And the Lord said to Moses in Midian. "Go! Depart to Egypt, because those who sought your life are dead." So Moses took his wife and children and placed them on the donkeys and returned to Egypt. (Ex 4:19-20a)[14]

Jesus' exodus from Egypt is quickly followed by the story of His immersion in the waters of the Jordan (Mt 3:13) and His temptation in the desert (Mt 4:1-11). The juxtaposition of these events makes it difficult not to see a repetition of key events in the stories of Moses and Israel. Jesus' immersion is a typological interpretation of the parting of the sea, and His temptation in the desert recalls both Israel's 40-year journey in the wilderness as well as Moses' 40 days and 40 nights without food and water (Ex 34:28). Having chosen disciples at the end of chap. 4 (vv. 18-22), Jesus brought His disciples up a mount to give His Torah.[15] Matthew roots his depiction of Jesus deeply in the narratives of the Torah to reveal that Jesus is the Prophet like Moses as well as Israel's victorious representative.[16]

OT Typological Interpretations of Moses and Israel

Matthew's Gospel interprets the story of Moses typologically. Events in the life of Jesus only make sense with reference to the story of Moses. Moses typology is not only a frequent feature in the Gospels, it is quite prominent in the OT, most likely resulting from the promise in Dt 18:15: "The Lord your God will raise up for you a prophet like me from among your own brothers. You must listen to him."[17] Dale Allison offers convincing textual evidence in favor of Moses typology in the depictions of Joshua, Gideon, Samuel, David, Elijah, and Josiah, among others.[18] For instance, Joshua's story shares many lexical and thematic parallels with the Moses narratives:

1. Moses spoke of a prophet to whom Israel must listen (Dt 18:15). According to Dt 34:9, Joshua was filled with the spirit of wisdom and the Israelites "obeyed him" (in Hebrew, "listened to him"). In Jos 1:17, this phrase is picked up yet again: "We will obey you ["listen to you"], just as we obeyed Moses in everything. And may the Lord your God be with you, as He was with Moses."
2. Joshua 3:16-17 and 4:18,22 describe the crossing of the Jordan with language borrowed from the crossing of the Reed Sea (Ex 14:16,21,29; 15:8). Joshua, as did Moses before him, brought his people through the waters on their journey to the promised land.
3. Joshua and Moses both sent spies to the promised land (Nm 13:2-3; Jos 2:1).
4. Joshua and Moses both met a divine figure and were told to remove their shoes. The Hebrew in both cases is virtually identical. "'Do not come closer,' He said. 'Remove the sandals from your feet, for the place where you are standing is holy ground'" (Ex 3:5). "The commander of the Lord's army said to Joshua, 'Remove the sandals from your feet, for the place where you are standing is holy'" (Jos 5:15).
5. In both the Moses and the Joshua narratives, people were saved from destruction through a red element in the doorway or window of their homes (Ex 12:7; Jos 2:18).

6. When Moses and Joshua lifted their arms, the armies of Israel defeated their enemies (Ex 17:11-13; Jos 8:18-19,25).
7. Moses and Joshua offered parting words to the people of Israel, and in both cases spoke with prophetic certainty about Israel's future apostasy (Dt 31:16-21; Jos 24:14-20).

The numerous parallels make it clear that the biblical author intentionally portrays Joshua as a prophet who is quite similar to Moses. And though it might be tempting to think Joshua fulfills the promise of *the* prophet like Moses in Dt 18:15, the Torah's concluding words in Dt 34:9-10 exclude this possibility.

> Joshua son of Nun was filled with the spirit of wisdom because Moses had laid his hands on him. So the Israelites obeyed him and did as the LORD had commanded Moses. No prophet has arisen again in Israel like Moses, whom the LORD knew face to face.

Though the Israelites "listen to Joshua" (an allusion to the promise in Dt 18:15), no prophet rose again in Israel like Moses (another allusion to Dt 18:15). Similarity does not mean fulfillment. It does mean, however, the biblical authors described Israel's prophets and heroes using lexical and thematic parallels to the greatest of all the prophets in the OT.

The identity of the servant in Isaiah's four "Servant Songs" (Isa 42:1-4; 49:1-6; 50:4-9; 52:12-13) has been subject to fierce debate and this, in large part, because of the stakes involved with the interpretation of the 53rd chapter. Earlier on, the Church interpreted Isaiah 53 as a messianic prophecy pointing to Jesus (Ac 8:35). In response, the Jewish interpreters, starting with Rashi in the Middle Ages, argued that Isaiah 53, along with the other Servant Songs, referred to the people of Israel.[19] Rashi's identification of the servant of Isa 52:13 as the people of Israel comes in large part from several other verses within the immediate context of the Servant Songs that identify Israel as the servant.[20]

Although a thorough analysis of the Servant Songs is not within the purview of this article, Hugenberger convincingly demonstrates that the exegetical challenges are resolved by identifying the servant of the Servant Songs as the prophet like Moses.[21] Such an identification stems from seeing the Servant Songs in the context of the second of three macro-structural units in the book of Isaiah.[22] The "second exodus" is a prominent and repeated theme in Isaiah 40–55.[23] For example, Isa 43:16-19 makes an explicit link between the first and the second exodus.

> This is what the LORD says—who makes a way in the sea, and a path through surging waters, who brings out the chariot and horse, the army and the mighty one together (they lie down, they do not rise again; they are extinguished,

> quenched like a wick)—"Do not remember the past events, pay no attention to things of old. Look, I am about to do something new; even now it is coming. Do you not see it? Indeed, I will make a way in the wilderness, rivers in the desert." (Isa 43:16-19)

Here, the promise of the second exodus is grounded in the reality of the first exodus (see Isa 51:9-10).[24]

Hugenberger also points to "second exodus" allusions located in the immediate literary context of each of the four Servant Songs.[25] Key aspects of the servant's ministry to redeem Israel are remarkably similar to Moses'. According to Isa 42:7, the servant will bring prisoners out of the house of confinement.[26] Like Moses, the servant is called from his mother's womb (Isa 49:1), hidden (49:2), frustrated with his people (49:4), and will gather the tribes of Israel (49:5-6; see Dt 33:5).[27] The servant of Isaiah 53, like Moses, has prophetic, priestly, and royal features.[28] As a prophet, he faces rejection (Isa 53:3; see Ex 2:14; Nm 16:1-2). As a priestly figure, he makes atonement for his people (Isa 53:4-5,10; Lv 8:14-15) and intercedes on their behalf (Isa 53:12; 32:11). As a royal figure, the servant is highly exalted (Isa 52:13; Ex 18; Nm 27:16-17). In fact, "servant" is the most frequent title used for Moses in the Hebrew Bible.[29] Even the use of the term "servant" to apply both to corporate Israel and an individual can be explained in light of the Moses motif.[30] Many of the motifs in Moses' life are repeated by the people of Israel, such that Moses' life foreshadows the story of Israel.

1. Moses was rescued from water in the reeds (Ex 2:1-10). Israel was also rescued from the Sea of Reeds (Ex 15:4).
2. Moses fled from Egypt (Ex 2:15). Likewise, Israel fled from Egypt (Ex 14:5).
3. Moses spent 40 years in the wilderness (Ex 2:15). Israel also spent 40 years in the wilderness (Nm 14:33).
4. Moses met God at Mount Sinai (Ex 3:2). Israel met God at Mount Sinai (Ex 19:1).

Moses, like Jesus, was Israel's truest representative (Ex 20:18-19), so it is not surprising to find close parallels between Moses and Israel. Likewise in the NT, the Israel-Jesus parallels are there to show that events in Jesus' life uniquely prepared Him to be Israel's perfect representative.

In summary, Isaiah's presentation of the second exodus was a typological reading of Israel's first exodus. Given the central role of Moses in Israel's first exodus, one would expect another Moses-like figure in Isaiah's foretelling of the second exodus. Once again, OT typological interpretation prepares the way for

NT typological interpretation. Centuries before Matthew's new Moses appeared, Isaiah's new Moses prepared the Jewish people to expect His coming.

EXAMPLE 3: THE TABERNACLE AND THE BETTER THINGS

The Epistle to the Hebrews interprets the Tabernacle, as well as the entire worship system of the Sinai Covenant, as shadows of better things to come (Heb 8:5; 9:9; 10:1). The author cites from Ex 25:40 as evidence of his interpretation in Heb 8:5, which reads: "These serve as a copy and shadow of the heavenly things, as Moses was warned when he was about to complete the Tabernacle. For God said, 'be careful that you make everything according to the pattern that was shown to you on the mountain.'" The author goes on to describe in detail the manner in which the Tabernacle and its worship system with all its imperfections and limitations functioned as a shadow of the better realities in Christ.

Typological Interpretations of the Tabernacle

It should come as no surprise by now that the author of Hebrews was not the first to regard the Tabernacle as a shadow of better things to come. Numerous parallels between the Tabernacle and the garden of Eden suggest that the author of Hebrews has properly understood the divinely intended function of the Tabernacle.

Commentators have long noted that the Tabernacle shares lexical and thematic parallels with the creation account in Gn 1:1–2:3 and the garden of Eden narrative in Gn 2:4–4:26. For instance, Rashi connects a verse about the Tabernacle back to the garden of Eden when commenting on the clause in Lv 26:12, "I will walk among you" (a phrase used only one other time in the Torah in Gn 3:8): "'And I will walk among you'—I will walk with you [plural] in the garden of Eden as one from among you [plural], and you will not be frightened." Is Rashi's identification of the Tabernacle with the garden of Eden, based on one shared word, creative interpretation or solid exegesis? The answer will become evident by examining the creation account and the garden of Eden narrative separately and then making some observations.[31]

Parallels between the Tabernacle and the creation narrative include these:

1. The Spirit of God was vital for the construction of the Tabernacle as well as in creation (Ex 31:3; 35:31; Gn 1:2).
2. The seven divine instructions for the construction of the Tabernacle, with the seventh focused on the Sabbath (Ex 25:1; 30:11,17,22,34; 31:1,12), correspond to the seven days of creation culminating in the Sabbath (Gn 1:5,8,13, 19,23,31; 2:1-3).[32]

3. The consummation of the construction of the Tabernacle includes a statement of completion with terms specifically used to describe the consummation of creation (Ex 40:33b; see 39:32; Gn 2:2).
4. Moses' inspection of the completed Tabernacle is described with terms specifically used to describe God's inspection of creation (Ex 39:43a; Gn 1:31a).
5. Moses blessed the completed Tabernacle just as God blessed the completed creation (Ex 39:43b; Gn 1:22,28; 2:3).
6. The Sabbath day of the Tabernacle narrative is followed by a fall narrative (the Golden Calf) just as the Sabbath day of creation is followed by a fall narrative (Ex 31:12-18; Ex 32; Gn 2:1-4).
7. Numerous lexical parallels exist between the description of the Tabernacle and the creation account: "to separate" (Ex 26:33; Gn 1:4,7); "to hammer out/expanse" (Ex 39:3; Gn 1:6-8); "I will meet/appointed times" (Ex 25:22; Gn 1:14); "light" (Ex 25:6; 27:20; 35:8; Gn 1:14-16); "to sanctify" (Ex 28:3,41; Gn 2:3).

Moving on to the garden of Eden narrative, Gordon Wenham argues that the garden of Eden is portrayed as an archetypal sanctuary and prototype for the Tabernacle.[33] Wenham offers several obvious parallels between the Tabernacle and Eden.[34]

1. The specific form of the word "walk" (*hiṯhalēḵ*) describing God's presence in the Tabernacle is used elsewhere in the Torah only to describe God's walking in the garden (Lv 26:12; Dt 23:14; Gn 3:8).
2. Cherubim are prominent in the design of the Tabernacle and stand guard over the ark. Likewise, cherubim stand guard at the entrance to the garden. Both the Tabernacle and Eden are entered from the east (Ex 25:18-22; 26:31; Gn 3:24).
3. The menorah is designed in the pattern of a fruit tree, suggestive of the fruit trees in Eden (Ex 25:32-36; Gn 2:9).
4. The Levites' role in the Tabernacle is described using the same two verbs describing Adam's role in the garden: "work and keep" (Nm 3:7-8; 8:26; 18:5-6; Gn 2:15).
5. The priests are clothed with tunics, the same word used to describe the garments prepared by God to cover Adam's nakedness (Ex 20:26; 29:5,8; 40:14; Lv 8:7,13; 16:4; Gn 3:21).
6. The precious materials used in the construction of the Tabernacle (e.g., gold, onyx, and bdellium) are present in the Eden narrative (Ex 25:7; 28:9-14,20; Nm 11:7; Gn 2:12).

Why does the Torah depict the Tabernacle as a copy of Eden and how do the parallels affect the interpretation of the Tabernacle narrative? When looking at the creation account and Eden narrative through a wider lens, a threefold structure of creation emerges. Genesis 1, the outer perimeter of God's creation, focuses on the earth. Genesis 2 narrows in to focus on a land called Eden, and then zooms in further to a specific garden within Eden where God walks with His people (Gn 2:8; 3:8). This foreshadows Mount Sinai's three-tiered holiness. Sinai is divided into three tiers: The bottom of the mountain represents the outer tier and corresponds to creation in Gn 1, where all the people of Israel meet God (Ex 24:3). At the middle of the mountain, the second tier, only select representatives from among the people of Israel are permitted to enter, corresponding to the land of Eden (Ex 24:1, 9-11; see Gn 4:16). At the top of the mountain where God's cloud-covered presence appears, the first tier, only Moses is permitted to enter (Ex 24:14-18). This top tier corresponds to the garden within Eden. The three-tiered structure also corresponds to the outer court, the Holy Place, and the Holy of Holies of the Tabernacle and Israel's Temple.

These parallels suggest that the world was created for worship. God wants to be present with His people. The original creation and the garden of Eden represent the perfect conditions of a pre-fallen world, a world without the curse. The Tabernacle, on the other hand, though clearly a copy of the pre-fallen world, takes into account the realities of a world defiled with sin. The Tabernacle is designed to deal with the defilement of sin by means of priestly mediators and various offerings for sin. The Tabernacle was not designed to remove the curse. Rather, it was intended to deal with the contaminations of the curse. As long as the Tabernacle and, later, the Temple stood, the copy of God's perfect creation and the garden of Eden stood as a reminder of what was once lost and what would eventually be restored when God lifted the curse (see Isa 11:1-9; Ezk 47–48; Zch 14:8-21). The typological interpretations of the Tabernacle within the OT prepare NT readers well for the "better things" to which the Tabernacle was intended to point.

CONCLUSION

The purpose of this article was to explain the phenomenon of NT typological interpretation of the OT in light of the typological interpretations manifest among the stories within the OT itself. It began by looking at typological interpretations of Adam, Moses, Israel, and the Tabernacle in the NT. It also attempted to demonstrate from the OT that similar interpretations were already a vital aspect of the eschatology of the OT. Israel's ancient prophets expected the coming of the "last

Adam," the "Prophet like Moses," Israel's perfect representative, and a perfect Tabernacle where God's presence would be mediated without the restrictions of the curse. Though many frequently try to understand the OT through the lens of the NT, this study in OT typology has shown that the OT illuminates the NT and provides a fuller and more meaningful context for identifying Jesus as the One of whom Moses in the Law and the Prophets did indeed write (Jn 1:45).

---

1. It is commonly argued that typological interpretation is not exegetical. For example, David L. Baker, "Typology and the Christian Use of the Old Testament," in *The Right Doctrine from the Wrong Texts*, ed. G. K. Beale (Grand Rapids: Baker, 1994), 324, argues, "Typology is not an exegesis or interpretation of a text but the study of relationships between events, persons and institutions recorded in the biblical texts." See also John VanMaaren, "The Adam-Christ Typology in Paul and Its Development in the Early Church Fathers," *Tyndale Bulletin* 64, vol. 2 (2013): 277, who writes, "Typology is also not a form of exegesis because it seeks to do more than understand the text in its original context and therefore cannot be systematized." While typological interpretation finds real historical correspondences between the OT and the person of Christ, these correspondences are "secretly placed in history by God only to be revealed in Christ" (VanMaaren, 277). I will offer evidence from the OT that NT typological interpretation does in fact represent an exegesis of the OT through the grid of inner-biblical OT interpretation, and, as such, represents an accurate exposition of the grammatical-historical meaning of the OT.
2. Eccl. R. 1.28 (translation from Hebrew my own); see also David Mitchell, *The Message of the Psalter: An Eschatological Programme in the Book of Psalms*, Journal for the Study of Old Testament Supplement Series 252 (Sheffield, England: SAP, 1997), 84–85. The composition of Ecclesiastes Rabbah is dated between the sixth and eighth centuries, though it is obviously quoting sources from a much earlier period.
3. According to *The Pocket Dictionary of Theological Terms*, eds. Stanley J. Grenz, David Guretzki, and Cherith Fee Nordling (Downers Grove, IL: InterVarsity, 1999), typological interpretation "deals with the parallels between actual, historical (usually OT) figures or events in salvation history and their later, analogous fulfillment."
4. The wording of Mt 2:19-21 in the original Greek is nearly identical to Ex 4:19-20 in the Greek Old Testament.

"After Herod died, an angel of the Lord suddenly appeared in a dream to Joseph in Egypt, saying, 'Get up! Take the child and His mother and go to the land of Israel, because those who sought the child's life are dead.' So he got up, took the child and His mother, and entered the land of Israel." (Mt 2:19-21)	"Now after those many days, the king of Egypt died. And the Lord said to Moses in Midian. 'Go! Depart to Egypt, because those who sought your life are dead.' So Moses took his wife and children and placed them on the donkeys and returned to Egypt." (Ex 4:19-20a; Old Greek; author's translation)

5. See VanMaaren, "The Adam-Christ Typology," 278–81.
6. English translations blur the fact that "earth" in Gn 1:28 frequently means "land" in the Hebrew Bible. The same word, for example, is used in Gn 12:1: "The Lord said to Abram: Go out from your *land*... to the *land* that I will show you."
7. The word for "land" and "earth" are the same in Hebrew.
8. Many scholars recognize commonly accepted criteria for identifying literary parallels and analogies. See Moshe Garsiel, *The First Book of Samuel: A Literary Study of Comparative Structures, Analogies and Parallels* (Ramat Gan, Israel: Revivim 1985), 25; Yonatan Grossman, "Dynamic Analogies," in the Book of Esther, *Vetus Testamentum* 59 (2009), 396; Richard Hays, *Echoes of Scripture in the Letters of Paul* (London: Yale University Press, 1989), 29–32; Jeffrey M. Leonard, "Identifying Inner-Biblical Allusions: Psalm 78 as a Test Case," *Journal of Biblical Literature* 127 (2008): 241–65; Yohanan (Ian) Stanfield, "The Song 'Ha'azinu' and its Presence in Isaiah 1–39" (Ph.D. diss., Hebrew University of Jerusalem, 2012 [Hebrew]), 15–16. I propose the presence of an intentional literary analogy when both stories share unique and/or rare words and phrases as well as corresponding themes and motifs.
9. The words for "wind" and "Spirit" are the same in Hebrew.

10. The Former Prophets in the Hebrew Bible include the books of Joshua, Judges, 1–2 Samuel, and 1–2 Kings. The book of Ruth is located with the four other "scrolls" in the Writings (Ruth, Song of Songs, Ecclesiastes, Lamentations, and Esther).

11. Though Jesus is frequently referred to as the "true Israel," this term is misleading. Does this mean Israel loses its significance as a people now that Jesus has come? According to Leonhard Goppelt, *Typology: The Typological Interpretation of the Old Testament in the New* (Grand Rapids: Eerdmans, 1982), 177, typology is a "prefiguration in a different stage of redemptive history that indicates the outline or essential features of the future reality *and that loses its own significance when that reality appears*" (emphasis added). I believe a more faithful reading of the Jesus-Israel typology is to see Jesus as the "truest Israelite" who does not remove the significance of the nation of Israel now that He has appeared. Instead, Jesus came to represent Israel perfectly, thereby imputing all His victories to them, just as is the case in David's victory over Goliath on behalf of Israel.

12. Matthew opens his Gospel with a Greek phrase, "the book of the genealogy" (HCSB footnote), found elsewhere in biblical literature only in the introduction to Genesis in the Greek OT (compare Mt 1:1; Gn 2:4; 5:1). In Donald Hagner's words, *Matthew 1–13*, Word Biblical Commentary 33A (Grand Rapids: Zondervan, 1993), 10, "βίβλος γενέσεως, lit 'book of the origin' or 'genealogical scroll,' is deliberately an allusion to the formulaic title used in the LXX (Gn 2:4; 5:1; the Hebrew word underlying γενέσεως is *tôlĕdôt*, 'generations'), which can be used to introduce both genealogies and historical narratives"; so also Michael J. Wilkins, *Matthew*, The NIV Application Commentary, ed. Terry C. Muck (Grand Rapids: Zondervan, 2004), 55; D. A. Carson, *Matthew*, Expositor's Bible, Commentary vol. 8, ed. Frank E. Gaebelein, J. D. Douglas (Grand Rapids: Zondervan, 1984), 61; W. D. Davies and Dale C. Allison Jr., *A Critical and Exegetical Commentary on the Gospel according to Saint Matthew*, International Critical Commentary, vol. 1 (Edinburgh: T&T Clark, 1988), 153.

13. See Gn 5:1; 6:9; 10:1; 11:10,27; 25:19; 37:2.

14. Translation of the Greek Old Testament (Septuagint) my own.

15. The Sermon on the Mount is the first installment of five discourses in Matthew, the first of which likely draws on the association of Moses with the fivefold book called the Torah. Jesus' five discourses in Matthew are as follows: (1) the Sermon on the Mount Discourse (Mt 5–7); (2) the Mission Discourse (Mt 10); (3) the Parables of the Kingdom Discourse (Mt 13); (4) the Church Discourse (Mt 18); and (5) the Olivet Discourse (Mt 24–25). Like Moses', Jesus' first Torah (instruction) was given on a mountain (Mt 5:1; Ex 19:1), and his last Torah describes things that will take place in the last days (Mt 24; Dt 4:30; 31:29).

16. Time and space do not permit me to discuss other Moses-Israel analogies in Matthew's Gospel. Suffice it to say, the macro-structure of the Gospel as well as its parts are driven by strategic allusions to the Torah story. For more on Moses typology in Matthew's Gospel, see Dale C. Allison Jr., *The New Moses: A Matthean Typology* (Minneapolis: Fortress, 1993).

17. Though commentators like Rashi and Ibn Ezra have tried to argue that this verse refers to a chain of prophets, rather than to a single eschatological prophet, Dt 34:10 makes it quite clear that just because an OT prophet is similar to Moses does not mean that the prophet is THE prophet like Moses. "No prophet has arisen again in Israel like Moses, whom the Lord knew face to face." Moses' uniqueness as a prophet is described as speaking to God face-to-face (Nm 12:6-8). Deuteronomy 34:10 anticipates an eschatological prophet like Moses, who will also speak to God face-to-face.

18. Dale Allison, *The New Moses*, 11–95.

19. Commenting on Isa 52:13, Rashi writes: "'Behold my servant will act wisely.' Behold in the last days my servant Jacob will prosper—the righteous who are among them" (translation of the Hebrew my own).

20. For example: "But you, Israel, My servant, Jacob, whom I have chosen, descendant of Abraham, My friend—I brought you from the ends of the earth and called you from its farthest corners. I said to you: You are My servant; I have chosen you and not rejected you" (Isa 41:8-9).

21. G. P. Hugenberger, "The Servant of the Lord in the 'Servant Songs' of Isaiah: A Second Moses Figure," in *The Lord's Anointed: Interpretation of Old Testament Messianic Texts*, eds. Philip E. Satterthwaite, Richard S. Hess, and Gordon J. Wenham (Grand Rapids: Baker, 1995), 119.

22. The book of Isaiah has three major divisions: chapters 1–39, 40–55, and 56–66.

23. The second section of Isaiah opens and closes with an allusion to the second exodus (Isa 40:1-11; 55:12-13). Hugenberger notes ten texts with explicit second exodus imagery (40:3-5; 41:17-20; 42:14-16; 43:1-3; 43:14-21; 48:20-21; 49:8-12; 51:9-10; 52:11-12; 55:12-13) and offers several other passages with implicit references to the second exodus (41:4,9; 44:2,7; 46:3; 48:8; 52:4), 122–128.

24. Hugenberger, "Servant of the Lord," 123.

25. Isaiah 42:1-4 (cf. Isa 41:17-20 with Ex 15:27; 17:1-7; cf. Isa 42:13-16 with Ex 13:21-22; 14:16-29; 15:3); Isa 49:1-6 (cf. Isa 48:20-22 with Ex 6:6; 11:8; 12:31; 14:5; cf. Isa 49:8-12 with Ex 15:27; 16:4; 17:6); Isa 50:4-9 (cf. Isa 50:2 with Ex 14:21; 7:18,21; Nm 11:23); Is 52:13–53:12 (cf. Isa 52:2-4,10-12 with Ex 6:6; 12:11; 13:21; 14:19-20; 15:6; Dt 1:30-33; 4:34; 16:3).

26. See Ex 13:3,14; 20:2; Dt 5:6; 6:12; 7:8; 8:14; 13:5,10.

27. Hugenberger, "Servant of the Lord," 129–138.

28. Ibid., 116–19, 129–30.

29. Moses is called "the servant of the Lord" (Dt 34:5; Jos 1:1,13,15; 8:31,33; 11:12; 12:6; 13:8; 14:7; 18:7; 22:2,4-5; 2Kg 18:12; 2Chr 1:3; 24:6), "the servant of God" (1Chr 6:49; 2Chr 24:9; Neh 10:29; Dan 9:11), "His servant" (Ex 14:31; Jos 9:24; 11:15; 1Kg 8:56; Ps 105:26); "My servant" (Nm 12:7-8; Jos 1:2,7; 2Kg 21:8; Mal 4:4 [3:22 MT]), "Your servant" (Ex 4:10; Nm 11:11; 1Kg 8:53; Neh 1:7-8; 9:14).

30. Hugenberger, "Servant of the Lord," 119.

31. For more on these parallels, see Seth D. Postell, *Adam as Israel* (Eugene, OR: Pickwick, 2011), 110–14.

32. Peter J. Kearny, "Creation and Liturgy: The P Redaction of Ex 25–40," *Zeitschrift für die Alttestamentliche Wissenschaft* [*Journal of Old Testament Scholarship*] 89 (1977): 375.

33. Gordon J. Wenham, "Sanctuary Symbolism in the Garden of Eden Story," in *I Studied Inscriptions before the Flood*, eds. Richard Hess and David Toshio Tsumura, Sources for Biblical and Theological Study 4 (Winona Lake, IN: Eisenbrauns, 1994), 399–404.

34. Note that later prophets make the link between the garden of Eden and Israel's future sanctuary explicit (see Ezk 28:13-16; Ezk 47; Zch 14:8).

Sacrifice in the Old Testament

JAMES E. ALLMAN

For 15 centuries (1446 BC to AD 70), God taught Israel what sacrifice was, how it functioned, and what its results were. He gave them a system that focused on five sacrifices that formed the basis of the whole tabernacle, and later temple, ministry. Leviticus gave detailed guidelines for the types of animals to be used and the process of preparing them for the altar, though one was entirely of grain. Each sacrifice met specific purposes and accomplished specific results. Some were for worship; others were to address particular sins.

However, sacrifice began much before Sinai. Apparently, God gave mankind instructions about sacrifice very early. The patriarchs were already sacrificing centuries before Moses (Gn 12:7-8; 13:4,18; 22:9; 26:25; 31:54; 33:20; 35:1,3,7; 46:1). Noah built an altar and made sacrifices after the flood (Gn 8:20), and Cain and Abel offered grain and animal sacrifices (Gn 4:3-5). Sacrifice is embedded into the life of the human race.

Why is there such emphasis on sacrifice? Overt reference to our subject begins after Gn 3, humanity's fall into sin. And that passage contains the key verse, v. 15, the protevangelium. From the beginning of human sin (indeed from eternity past, Rev 13:8, "the Lamb who was slain from the creation of the world" NIV), God has planned to send the Redeemer through whose sacrifice people will find deliverance from all the penalty of death and restoration to the blessing of God. So in the first century AD, God sent Jesus "to give His life—a ransom for many" (Mk 10:45).

This article seeks to lay out the essential concepts of sacrifice in the Old Testament and trace their impact on our understanding of Jesus. This requires addressing several subjects: the language of sacrifice; the purposes of sacrifice; the major passages on sacrifice (Lv 1–7; 16) and other sacrificial issues (Passover, firstfruits, the firstborn, priestly ordination, and accompanying sacrifices); indications of dissatisfaction with sacrifice in the OT; and the New Testament's application of these ideas to Jesus.

THE LANGUAGE OF SACRIFICE

The language of sacrifice is far larger than one can cover in an article such as this. However, we will take up five major terms that appear throughout the biblical teaching.

Sacrifice (Hb. *zevach*, Gk. *thusia*). These are the foundational words for the whole subject. Both of them refer primarily to slaughtering animals in the worship or service of deity, though each can stand for general preparation of animals for eating. This may have added significance since a debate still continues about whether the Hebrew term *'ishsheh* means "food" or "offering by fire." The major lexical resources[1] all opt for the latter. However, Ross and Wenham[2] both opt for the former translation. If this is the right view, then the choice of the two terms is apt since the terms, outside their use in sacrifice, have to do with preparing food (see Dt 12:15,21; Lk 15:23,27,30).

Unclean (Hb. *tame'*, Gk. *koinos*) *and clean* (Hb. *tahor*, Gk. *katharos*). These terms do not refer so much to sacrifice itself as to the purposes of sacrifice. The clean person is one who may at any time enter the worshiping community and engage in the service of the Lord. It is important to see that being clean is not primarily a moral issue. It is first a ritual issue, as becomes evident by considering uncleanness. In some cases, one who is unclean has violated restrictions that God placed on foods, animals, or conditions of life. In other circumstances, a person may be unclean through no fault of their own (see especially Lv 10–16, with special reference to the condition of the new mother, Lv 12, and the person afflicted by "a disease on the skin of his body," Lv 13:2). These violations and circumstances render the Israelite unfit to enter the worshiping community. Only by sacrifice that removes the ritual defilement can one reenter the community. Douglas rightly proposes to interpret these terms as "normal" and "non-normal."[3] What comes into God's presence must be as near as possible as God created it. The special ritual element that removes the non-normality (defilement) is, usually, sprinkled blood.

Sprinkle (Hb. *hizzah*, *zaraq*, Gk. *hrantizo*). While the terms do not always appear in sacrificial contexts, they so frequently do that they are virtually technical terms for the application of blood (or water) in cleansing ceremonies (cf. Lv 14:7; Nm 19:13,18-21). So serious is this issue, as the reference to Nm 19 makes clear, that the person who fails to seek cleansing "will be cut off from the assembly because he has defiled the sanctuary of the Lord" (v. 20). Sprinkling rites occur with the burnt offering (Lv 1:5), the peace offering (Lv 3:2,8,13), the sin offering (Lv 4:6,17), and the guilt offering (Lv 7:2,14). At times, the blood is smeared on the horns of the altar (Lv 4:25). But the sprinkling of sacrificial blood removed the defilement, reinstating the one who caused the uncleanness to the community and the possibility of serving and worshiping God. An example comes in Ex 24:8 where Moses sprinkled the blood "on the people." This is an external cleansing, leaving the inner person untouched.

Atone (Hb. *kaphar*, Gk. *hilaskomai*). These word groups represent what English Bibles translate in the OT as "make atonement" (Lv 1:4). The English word derives from an earlier form[4] "at" and "onement" expressing reconciliation. The Greek word frequently translates the Hebrew word. The verb *kaphar* appears in various senses: to appease (Gn 32:20), to make amends (2Sm 21:3). In various contexts it can result in exemption from punishment (2Chr 30:18), thus forgiveness. The atoning sacrifice related to cleansing, since frequently the estrangement came about through defilement. Thus, *hilaskomai* and its related terms appear in the OT representing the reconciliation accomplished by cleansing defilement so that God removes His wrath.[5] This atonement, though, was never a blanket atonement releasing the sinner from all sin. It was an atonement that dealt only with sins committed. Even after atonement for a sin, when the sin was committed again, the law required a repeated atonement.

Forgiveness (Hb. *salach, nasa'* [*'awon*], Gk. *aphiemi*). In the Bible, forgiveness means the cancellation of merited punishment. Where forgiveness occurs in the ritual of sacrifice, the just penalty against the sin has fallen on the sinner's substitute. Therefore, God releases the sinner from the necessity of bearing the law's penalty. Once again, though, there is in the sacrificial system no universal forgiveness. The forgiven who sins in the same way again must make the same sacrifice again.

THE PURPOSES OF SACRIFICE

In the OT, the Lord established a sacrificial system that aimed to protect His reputation against Israel's sins, to provide a means of restoration to right standing under the law, and to qualify otherwise sinful people to participate in the worship and service of God.

To protect God's reputation. An element of sacrificial practice that seems odd to moderns is the sprinkling of blood. We know that sprinkling removes defilement. The implication is that whatever one sprinkles has been polluted by sin. In Lv 4 this observation raises interesting issues, for there, the sin of the anointed priest (vv. 3-12) or of the whole community requires sprinkling in the tabernacle before the veil (vv. 6,17) and application of the blood to the altar of incense (vv. 7,18). One way to account for this practice is to understand God's history with Israel. Only on rare occasions did God judge sin, either the individual's or the nation's, immediately and exactly. This raises the question of God's justice (see Ps 50:16-21, especially v. 21). The repeated process of sprinkling blood surely would have left stains on the veil. The action of sprinkling and the stains on the veil would be permanent evidence that God does judge sin, though He judges it in the substitute. God's highest motive is the protection of His great name. Sacrifice accomplishes this.

To provide a means of restoration. The transgressor falls under the wrath of God. Sacrifice gives options for restoration. Leviticus 5 identifies situations where the sinner becomes aware of a violation and gives the "guilt" offering as a means of addressing guilt. The sinner jeopardizes his relationship to God. Law demands death for the offense, but God offered the alternative of animal sacrifice. The completed sacrifice restores the offender to a righteous status under the law. It is not that the wrongdoer has not sinned, but that the wrongdoer has rectified his condition by adopting God's means of reconciliation.

To qualify sinful people for worship and service. Though it is difficult to work out all of the chronological issues in Exodus and Leviticus, it is clear that God chose flawed people to serve Him as priests. Aaron, the first high priest, made a golden calf (Ex 32). How could he stand as intermediary between God and man? The ordination ritual for the priesthood (Ex 29; Lv 8–9) provides the answer. Three animals stand as sin offering, burnt offering, and ordination offering for the priests. Only thus may such people mediate between God and man.

What is required for the priesthood is significant also for the laity. Contact with a dead body, for example, disqualifies one from participating in the worshiping community. Application of the proper sacrificial ritual (the ashes of the red heifer, Nm 19; see also the regulations in Lv 11–15) requalifies the defiled to participate in the life of the community and the service of God.

MAJOR PASSAGES ON SACRIFICE

The OT gives prominence to five major sacrifices, dividing them into two groups: those that serve a primary purpose of worship and celebration and those that serve the purpose of penalty for sins. The first group was voluntary. When coming to the Lord's sanctuary, one had to bring a sacrifice, but one might choose any of the three. The second group, those that expressed penalty for sin, was mandatory. On the occasion of any such sin, one had to bring the appropriate sacrifice. There are other sacrifices: for Passover, firstfruits, offerings for the firstborn, and accompanying sacrifices (grain offerings and libations).

The order of their presentation in Leviticus is significant. Some hold that the order reflects the frequency with which they were offered. Others see them following a God-to-man order: full consecration (burnt offering) to dealing with everyday sins (guilt offering). Other arrangements of the sacrifices appear in the text, as for example in Lv 6–7 where the peace offering appears last (as being the only offering that lay people had access to for food).

The major offerings appear in Lv 1–7, listed twice. The first part of the passage, 1:1–6:13, is often called the layman's handbook for sacrifice. The passage explains the kinds of animals to offer for each purpose. That is followed by 6:14–7:38, the priest's manual, explaining the responsibilities and prerogatives given to the priests in each offering.

WORSHIP AND CELEBRATION OFFERINGS

The burnt offering (Lv 1; 6:8-13). The first sacrifice is the burnt offering, fully consumed. Hence, the Bible calls it the *kalil,* the entire burnt offering. The whole animal was to be burned, with the exception of the hide, which was given to the priest. Since those offering the sacrifice identified it as their substitute by the laying on of hands (cf. Lv 16:21-22), the sacrifice signified worshipers' entire offering of themselves to God.

The animals that God authorized included both large and small cattle, as well as birds. Everyone in Israel was permitted to make a burnt offering, and the offerings needed to be as nearly perfect as possible, with no physical blemishes (cf. Lv 22:18-25; Mal 1:6-13). This means that the cattle offerings particularly would be costly for a herdsman, for they were the breeding stock on which his wealth depended. To make such a sacrifice implied faith that God would provide for the future. God always honors such trust.

The burnt offering is the most basic offering in the Levitical system. The high priest makes it every day of the year, morning and evening, and on special days, two or even three times morning and evening. The priest would lay any other sacrifice that one might offer on top of the burnt offering, making the burnt offering the foundation. Since the burnt offering was always to be on the altar, one of its Hebrew names is the *tamid,* the continual burnt offering.

The grain offering (Lv 2; 6:14-18). The proper meaning of the name of the sacrifice (*minchah*) is debated. Some hold that it means primarily "gift." Others hold rightly that the term refers to a tribute offering, one offered to an overlord demonstrating the offerer's submission (see Jdg 3:15). Since it is from the grain, the tribute offering acknowledges that God is the true owner of all that the Israelite has and that He has granted the harvest as a gift to His faithful servants. Normally the sacrifice included olive oil and salt (Lv 2:13), as "the salt of the covenant with your God" (see also Nm 18:19 and 2Chr 13:5). The priest burned only a handful (the *'azkarah*, the memorial portion) of the sacrifice. The rest the officiating priest had to eat. As I once heard a professor tell his class, "A fat priest was a sign of a spiritual Israel!"

The peace offering (Lv 3; 7:11-27). Once again, scholars debate the exact meaning of the name (Hb. *zevach hashelamim*) for the sacrifice of *shelamim*. The connection with "shalom" is evident, but it is not clear what exactly is meant. Some prefer the name "fellowship" offering, while others prefer the name "well-being" offering. Since its ritual includes a large, shared meal, "fellowship" may be best. It celebrates restoration of fellowship between God and man, and also man and man. Hence one finds the sacrifice referred to when people made covenants (cf. Gn 31; Ex 24).

The circumstances of the offering implied that no inexpensive fellowship offering was acceptable. Those who made the fellowship offering were people who had experienced God's blessing. Thus only food appropriate to a celebration was fit. And depending on the purpose of the sacrifice, God limited the time for eating. If the sacrifice was a freewill offering or a fulfillment of a vow, the worshipers might eat it for two days, but they had to destroy anything left to the third day. On the other hand, if it was a thanksgiving offering (in which offerers made a public declaration of how God had delivered them; cf. Pss 30; 22:22-31), they had to eat all of the meat overnight. If anything remained until morning, the sacrifice was invalid. This means that the sacrifice occasioned a communal meal.

One must think of the tabernacle, and later temple, as a royal palace with the holy of holies as the throne room. The priests were the royal officials with the high priest as God's prime minister. Malachi 1:7,12 refer to the altar as the Lord's Table. When people made fellowship offerings, they were "sharing table fellowship" with the Lord, for His priests participated in the meal (they ate part of most sacrifices) and part of the animal was consumed on the altar, given to God as His portion of the celebration (the parts placed on the altar are also significant; reference to the major commentaries will guide in thinking about their significance).

OFFERINGS THAT SERVE AS PENALTY OR REMEDY FOR SIN

The "sin" offering (Lv 4:1–5:13; 6:24-30). Several major commentaries on Leviticus offer the name "purification" offering for this sacrifice. Since the core event of the ritual is the manipulation of the blood, it is right to see its main purpose as cleansing. All humanity lives in a world of sin and defilement. This was more so true of ancient humanity, and even more so of Israel. Death was on every side. Disease stalked at every turn. A major concern of Leviticus is with these defilements (chaps. 11–15) and their remedy (the great remedy, the Day of Atonement, Lv 16). The sin or purification offering (in Gk. *peri hamartias*) aimed directly at solving the pollutions caused by sin, disease, and death for a people among whom God dwells. More specifically, the sin or purification offering addressed the sanctuary's defilement by Israel's sin. R. T. Beckwith notes that the only place where anyone offered the sacrifice apart from the sanctuary is Nm 19:19-20, where, however, its purpose was to fit people for participation at the sanctuary. He proposes that when atonement was necessary away from the tabernacle/temple, the burnt offering was the appropriate sacrifice.[6]

The passage that addresses the sacrifice falls into four major portions. Leviticus 4:1-21 deals with pollution of the sanctuary; 4:22-35 deals with pollution of the bronze altar; 5:1-4 gives sample sins that incur the need for the sacrifice; and 5:5-13 deals with the purification offering of the very poor (cf. Heb 9:22). Since all may transgress, and all face the ravages of death and disease, all must have access to purification.

Of special interest in the first two portions of the passage (4:1-21; 22-35) is the ritual with the blood. The blood from the sacrifice for the priest and for the congregation was sprinkled before the veil inside the sanctuary (note that on the Day of Atonement, the priest sprinkled it inside the most holy place). But the priest applied the blood offered by the leader of the congregation and by the common Israelite only to the bronze altar outside the sanctuary. In light of the discussion above, it appears that the blood went only as far as the sinner could go into the presence of God. In the person of the high priest, the congregation could go into the sanctuary, even into the most holy place, so the blood had to go that far. But lay Israelites could approach only as far as the bronze altar. The blood for their defilement went only so far, as well. The blood shed, sprinkled, and poured was a sign that God had poured out His wrath against the substitute. The blood was the sign that cleansing occurred; the sinner would live. (For the very poor, God provided a purification offering of grain, Lv 5:11-13. This did not negate the need for a blood sacrifice. Rather, the poor added their grain to the animal sacrifice already present on the altar, thereby mingling the grain with a blood sacrifice. Thus, even those without the means for a blood sacrifice received the benefit of one.[7] Everyone, even the poor, needs purification from time to time. And it is available to all.)

The sins for which the purification offering was offered fit into a scale of sin that ranges from "inadvertent sin" on the one hand to defiant sin on the other. In Nm 15:30, Moses is clear that defiant sin (sin committed "with a high hand," *beyad ramah*) had no sacrifice. Inadvertent sin (*bishegagah*, something one "strays" into; cf. Ezk 34:6; Lv 4:13) is more difficult to categorize. The sins listed at the beginning of Lv 5 seem to be deliberate. But one must acknowledge a difference between even deliberate sin and defiant sin. One may do evil without realizing the significance or the ramifications of one's actions. Therefore, we must think of sin as falling on a continuum from ignorant or inadvertent sin to deliberate sin and ultimately to defiant sin, one done with one's fist in God's face (e.g., adultery, premeditated murder, or blasphemy).[8] Sacrifice was possible for the one; God prohibited it for the other.

For our culture the disturbing element of this sacrifice is that it is mandated for women who are affected by elements of childbearing, so a new mother must make one of these sacrifices (e.g., Lv 12). Is she sinful for having a child, and more sinful for having a female child? On this we reiterate what we dealt with above: what is "clean" is normal, the condition of life as created. What is "unclean" is non-normal, a non-standard condition. Women who have given birth, like men who have bodily discharges (Lv 15:1-18) are in a non-standard condition. Childbirth brings fluids from the body that under normal conditions remain in the body. And giving birth to a female child initiates the same cycle for the child. Thus, the purification sacrifice returns the non-standard to a standard condition and reintegrates her (and her husband when he is leaving his non-standard condition) into the worshiping community. She is not sinful or dirty. She is non-standard and returning to her standard condition.

Finally, with the exception of the burnt offering, the officiating priest normally had to eat part of every sacrifice that he offered. This was a way of showing to worshipers that God had accepted their sacrifices (as well as providing food for the priests). Nonetheless, limitations existed. In both the tribute offering and the purification offering, the law prohibited priests from eating food from sacrifices made for priests.

The "guilt" offering (Lv 5:14–6:7; 7:1-10). The term guilt offering both aids and detracts from understanding the sacrifice. On the one hand, the Hebrew term *'asham* can mean "to be aware of guilt" (so probably Lv 5:3-4). On the other hand, when one has sinned, one is guilty even without awareness. The word in this case means to be guilty, liable to penalty (Lv 5:2). Additionally, the sins associated with this sacrifice (Lv 5:14-19; 6:2-5) have caused loss, either to the Lord or to another human. The penalty (again the word *'asham*) for the sin includes both the sacrifice and the restitution of the loss (with a penalty of 20 percent). The order of the acts varies. If the loss is to the Lord, the sacrifice precedes the restitution; if to another human, the restitution comes first.

The unusual element in the sacrifice is its prescription for the healed "leper" (Lv 14:10-20 NASB; this is not Hansen's disease but some sort of skin disease)[9] and the completion of the Nazirite vow (Nm 6:12). In the first case, the sacrifice is the indemnity imposed because during the time of the disease, a major defilement, the afflicted was not able to serve God. For the Nazirite, the sacrifice was prescribed when, during the time of the vow, the person accidentally came into contact with death. The time of the Nazirite's vow was a time of service to God that the death interrupted. The sacrifice redeemed the loss of service to God.

Failure to serve the Lord, or even defrauding Him of service, intentionally or unintentionally, subjects the sinner to penalty, the penalty of death. The shocking element of all of this is that no mere human being has ever served God properly, loving Him with no mixed allegiances, from the beginning of life on. So no restitution that we can make will ever be adequate (see Ps 49:5-9). The good news is that the restitution offering recurs in the last of the Suffering Servant passages in Isaiah. Israel, in its sin, had gone astray, pursuing its own interests. But the Lord laid on the Servant their iniquity! Indeed, the Lord made Him *a restitution offering* (Isa 53:10).

The Day of Atonement (Lv 16). The Day of Atonement climaxes Israel's sacrificial year. The Feast of Booths follows it with elaborate sacrifices (Nm 29:12-38), but they are primarily for worship and celebration, though God required one sin offering daily. But the Day of Atonement is the high point of dealing with sin. The major ritual revolved around the purification offerings, whose goal was to "purify the most holy place in this way for all their sins because of the Israelites' impurities and rebellious acts. . . . Atonement will be made for you on this day to cleanse you, and you will be clean from all your sins before the LORD" (Lv 16:16,30). But this was only for sins already committed. The Day of Atonement was needed every year.

Other sacrifices. God's requirements included a host of other sacrifices. In addition to the daily burnt offerings, each Sabbath and New Moon required special offerings, as did Passover and the Feasts of Unleavened Bread, Weeks, and Trumpets (Nm 28–29). The birth of a firstborn son or animal required special sacrifice. The sacrifice for the firstborn also calls to mind the firstfruit offerings that were required in the spring at the Feast of Firstfruits (immediately following Passover) and the firstfruits offering made when inaugurating the use of a vineyard or orchard. Since every animal offered provided food for the priests, the offerer also brought the necessities of a meal, bread, and wine to accompany the meat (also detailed in Nm 28–29). This listing omits the tithe and offering system that God instituted, but these were part of the offerings that Israel made, too.

INDICATIONS OF DISSATISFACTION WITH SACRIFICE IN THE OT

Throughout our treatment to this point we have seen evidence that the sacrificial system had its limitations. There were sins for which no sacrifice could be made. Also, the sacrifices, even when made, did not deal with all sin, only with past sin.

Repeated sin required repeated sacrifice. Once cleansed from pollution, new defilement required new cleansing. The sacrifices, a great gift from God to enable Israel to survive in their relationship with Him, did not address some of the deepest problems of sin. Cleansing was for the flesh. Forgiveness was for the past. But what of the future? How efficacious were the sacrifices?

As to their efficacy, we have intimated some answers. To make proper sacrifice was costly. To do it repeatedly could jeopardize a family's future. Most evaluations of wealth were in terms of flocks and herds. And most sacrifices required animals with no blemish, the breeding stock. Continuing to offer sacrifice, whether for worship or for dealing with personal sin, would decimate the breeding stock for the future of the family. So continuing to offer proper sacrifice was a noteworthy act of faith. God always honors faith. So God always honored the faith of worshipers who risked their own future to serve Him properly. It was not so much that the sacrifices were efficacious as that God responded to the faith that offered them. Now the sacrifices did bring deliverance from the temporal consequences of sin. But faith addressed the spiritual issues involved in sin and sacrifice. Through faith came true forgiveness, hope for the future, and fellowship with God.

As to their permanent usefulness, even the OT begins to raise questions. Because it was possible to make a sacrifice the way we pay speeding tickets, as a matter of duty but with no vital repentance, the OT points out the flaw in the sacrificial system. Accordingly, the prophets gave oracles from God critiquing Israel's sacrifices. Key passages include 1Sm 15:22; Isa 1:11-17; Jer 7:21-22; Hos 6:6; Am 5:21-24; Mal 1:6-13; Pss 40:6-8 and 51:16-19. Scholars have used these to suggest that the prophets rejected all sacrifice,[10] setting the prophets in antagonism to the Torah. Yet a careful reading indicates that the prophets aimed to confront Israel with a disingenuous worship. Indeed, the passage in Isaiah immediately precedes a call to repentance. And yet Psalms begins to offer an alternative: spiritual sacrifices in which God finds more pleasure (Pss 50:8-14; 51:16-17; 69:30-31; 141:2). Most significant here is Ps 40, where the psalmist, very likely the king,[11] thinks of himself, his own body, as a sacrifice: "You do not delight in sacrifice and offering; You open my ears to listen. You do not ask for a whole burnt offering or a sin offering. Then I said, 'See, I have come; it is written about me in the volume of the scroll. I delight to do Your will, my God; Your instruction lives within me.'" (See the article "Psalm 40" by Daniel Green in this *Handbook*.) The point here is that the OT seemed to anticipate a more perfect sacrifice, one that would deal with sin permanently and more effectively. For this reason, Isaiah indicates that the coming Servant's death and resurrection would be that sacrifice (Isa 52:13–53:12).

NEW TESTAMENT'S APPLICATION OF THESE IDEAS TO JESUS

These ideas supply the foundation for the NT's evaluation of the sacrifices. The approach that the NT takes goes in two directions: critique of the OT sacrifices, and transfer of their functions (heightened) to Jesus and His sacrifice.

Critique of the OT sacrifices. God created the human race for blessing (Gn 1:26-28). Sin made blessing impossible because blessing could come only through relationship with God who is life. This set in motion God's plans to reestablish the race in blessing, but also to show that only His grace could enable fallen humanity to return to Him. Thus in successive ages of history He offered to us what would have seemed to be adequate ways of relationship, what some have called dispensations: of conscience, human government, promise, law, the church, and subsequently the messianic kingdom. Each, including the messianic kingdom, ends in apparent failure, proving that God's grace alone can give mankind what we have always sought: a full and meaningful life, i.e., the blessing of God. Levitical sacrifice is part of God's demonstration. Yet, as we have seen, even in OT times the insufficiency of the sacrifices, and indeed of the covenant that they helped to mediate, became obvious. When Jesus came the stage was set to prove climactically the inadequacy of the sacrifices. Yet for all that, the sacrifices play an important role, setting up for us what is necessary in relating to God, who plans to deal with sin and remedy all the ills that sin has inflicted on human history.

The major critique of the function of OT sacrifice comes in Heb 9:1–10:18.[12] The book of Hebrews presents the old covenant sacrifices as God commanded, but insufficient to achieve all the purposes that God had for humanity. Hebrews makes nine points about the inadequacy of the OT sacrifices. First, it was only in an earthly tabernacle, a pattern of the real, that the sacrifices were made (9:1-10). Second, they granted no access to God (9:6-9), for the veil remained in place. Third, the sacrifices could not perfect[13] (9:9) the consciences of those who offered them. Fourth, they dealt only with ceremonial defilement (9:10), hence not with the conscience. Fifth, in that respect then, they were fleshly ordinances (9:10). Sixth, they were temporary (9:10), established only "until the time of restoration." Seventh, they provided only the blood of animals (9:12-13). In the larger context (cf. 10:5-7, the quotation of Ps 40:6-8), it is the blood of animals who could not volitionally be sacrifices. What was needed was One whose will would be perfectly attuned to the Father's desire—who would become a sacrifice for sin by virtue of doing God's will (10:9). Eighth, the sacrifices had, by their nature, to be constantly repeated (10:1) since they did not solve the sin problem; they only ameliorated it. And ninth, they constituted a reminder of sins yearly (10:3), since "it is impossible for the blood of bulls and goats to take away sins."

Application of their functions to Jesus. We have seen that the OT leaves us with an incomplete sacrificial system. It does what was intended, and does it well, but it does not have the ability to restore the human race to the full blessing of God. The unaccomplished purpose and the incomplete system lead us to anticipate a fuller work of God that will provide this full restoration, and that work comes in Jesus. He accomplished what the burnt offering promised, expiation/propitiation (*hilaskomai,* Heb 2:17; 1Jn 2:2; 4:10). So "God publicly displayed him at his death as the mercy seat [*hilasterion*] accessible through faith" (Rom 3:25 NET). He has ransomed us from death since He accomplished eternal redemption (cf. Hb. *kaphar* meaning ransom, Ps 49:8; Mt 20:28; Ti 2:14; Heb 9:12; 1Pt 1:18). He has brought forgiveness for all our transgressions, not merely those of the past (Col 2:13). He has cleansed (Heb 10:22) and continues to cleanse us (Eph 5:26) in order to present us to Himself. He is our sin offering (*peri hamartias,* 2Co 5:21). And all of this He did by one sacrifice, offered only once, never to be repeated (Heb 9:26-28). What the OT sacrifices provided temporally,[14] Jesus provides eternally. God's purposes now suffer no hindrance from human sin and pollution. Jesus paid it all.

---

1. Ludwig Koehler, Walter Baumgartner, M. E. J. Richardson, and Johann Jakob Stamm, *The Hebrew and Aramaic Lexicon of the Old Testament* (Leiden, Netherlands: E. J. Brill, 1994–2000), s.v., "אִשֶּׁה," 93–94; Francis Brown, Samuel Rolles Driver, and Charles Augustus Briggs, *Enhanced Brown-Driver-Briggs Hebrew and English Lexicon* (repr., Oxford: Clarendon Press, 1977), s.v., "אִשֶּׁה," 77–78; Clines, David J. A., ed., *The Dictionary of Classical Hebrew* (Sheffield, England: Sheffield Academic Press; Sheffield Phoenix Press, 1993–2011), s.v., "אִשֶּׁה," 1:411–12; Willem VanGemeren, ed., *New International Dictionary of Old Testament Theology and Exegesis* (Grand Rapids: Zondervan, 1997), s.v., "אִשֶּׁה," 1:540–49.

2. Allen P. Ross, *Holiness to the Lord: A Guide to the Exposition of the Book of Leviticus* (Grand Rapids: Baker Academic, 2002), 118; Gordon J. Wenham, *The Book of Leviticus,* New International Commentary on the Old Testament (Grand Rapids: Eerdmans, 1979), 48.

3. Mary Douglas, *Purity and Danger* (London: Routledge and Kegan Paul, 1966).

4. R. W. Burchfield, *The Compact Edition of the Oxford English Dictionary: Complete Text Reproduced Micrographically* (Oxford; New York: Clarendon Press Oxford University Press, 1987), s.v., "atonement," 1:539.

5. James E. Allman, "ἱλάσκεσθαι: To Propitiate or to Expiate?" *Bibliotheca Sacra* 172 (2015): 335–55.

6. R. T. Beckwith, "Sacrifice," in *New Dictionary of Biblical Theology,* ed. T. Desmond Alexander and Brian S. Rosner (Downers Grove, IL: InterVarsity, 2000), 756–67.

7. Milgrom comments: "Because the token portion is burned on the altar, it is the equivalent to the suet of the purification-offering animal (4:8–10, 19, 26, 31, 35; *Keter Torah*) and, hence, the ingredient that effects the purgation (v 13)." Jacob Milgrom, *Leviticus 1–16: A New Translation with Introduction and Commentary,* vol. 3 of Anchor Yale Bible (New Haven; London: Yale University Press, 2008), 306.

8. Examples of deliberate but not defiant sins (5:1,4) include the failure to give testimony in a court case or contact with uncleanness. "It is possible that the social standing and living conditions of the poor made them more hesitant to come forward as witnesses, more frequently in contact with a carcass or uncleanness, or more forgetful to keep their word. When they became aware of the violation, they were required to make the purification offering—but at their level of ability." Allen P. Ross, *Holiness to the Lord: A Guide to the Exposition of the Book of Leviticus* (Grand Rapids: Baker Academic, 2002), 143.

9. R. K. Harrison, *Introduction to the Old Testament* (Grand Rapids: Eerdmans), 136–39.

10. Roy E. Gane, "Sacrifice and Atonement," in *Dictionary of the Old Testament: Prophets* (Downers Grove, IL: InterVarsity, 2012), 685.

11. On this see John H. Eaton, *Kingship and the Psalms,* vol. 32 of Studies in Biblical Theology, second series, (London: SCM Press, 1976); and Bruce K. Waltke, *An Old Testament Theology* (Grand Rapids: Zondervan, 2007), 872–92, who agrees with Eaton and argues strongly for the originality of the psalms' so-called headings.

12. William L. Lane, *Hebrews 9–13*, vol. 47B of Word Biblical Commentary (Dallas: Word, 1998), 213–71.

13. This may be a reference to "fitting" or "ordaining" people to serve God. The verb is *teleioo,* a word used in the Gk. translation of the OT for the ordination of priests (see Ex 29:26-27,29,31,33-35; Lv 8:22,28-29,31,33).

14. The sacrifices did release the offerer from the law's penalty for the sin committed.

Messiah in Intertestamental Literature

CRAIG A. EVANS

The messianic ideas and hopes that arose in the intertestamental period (that is, from the end of the Persian Empire to the beginnings of the Roman Empire) were inspired by the success of King David, founder of Israel's ancient dynasty and kingdom and informed by the messianism of the Hebrew Scriptures. These important antecedents gave rise to various speculations and expectations that came to expression in Jewish literature of the intertestamental period and beyond. Acquaintance with this literature is prerequisite for an informed understanding of the messianic ideas in circulation in the time of Jesus and the early Church. In short, the messianism of the intertestamental period centered on the hopes for the revival of the glory days of King David.

OLD TESTAMENT ANTECEDENTS

The messianism of the intertestamental period is rooted in the kingship of David (10th century BC). But the language of "messiah," or "anointed" (Hebrew: *meshiach*), reaches back to the anointing of high priests, as in Ex 30:30, where God commands: "Anoint Aaron and his sons and consecrate them to serve Me as priests." When the people of Israel clamor for a king, the priest Samuel anoints Saul (1Sm 9:16; 10:1 "Hasn't the Lord anointed you ruler"). However, it is in David, who reigns for decades over a united kingdom of Israel, that messianism has its roots.

David's reign seems to be adumbrated in Hannah's song of thanks (1Sm 2:1-10):

"The LORD will judge the ends of the earth. He will give power to His king; He will lift up the horn of His anointed" (v. 10b). (In later Jewish interpretation, including the Targum, Hannah's song is understood as eschatological and messianic.) But it is Nathan's oracle, in response to David's stated intention to build a house for God, that lays the foundation of Israel's royal messianism: "When your time comes and you rest with your fathers, I will raise up after you your descendant, who will come from your body, and I will establish his kingdom. He will build a house for My name, and I will establish the throne of his kingdom forever. I will be a father to him, and he will be a son to me . . . Your house and kingdom will endure before Me forever, and your throne will be established forever" (2Sm 7:12-14a,16). From this oracle, the messianic "paradigm" will emerge: The Davidic descendant is expected to build God's House, He will be established on the throne of His kingdom, and God will be His Father, while He will be God's Son.

Some of the royal psalms allude to this covenant. Best known among them are Pss 2 and 89. The first asks why the heathen plot against the Lord and His anointed (2:1) and then affirms the divine decree: "You are My son; today I have become Your Father. Ask of Me, and I will make the nations Your inheritance and the ends of the earth Your possession" (2:7-8). The second has the anointed affirm: "You are my Father, my God, and the rock of my salvation" (89:26), with God responding: "I will also make him My firstborn, greatest of the kings of the earth. I will always preserve My faithful love for him, and My covenant with him will endure. I will establish his line forever, his throne as long as heaven lasts" (89:27-29).

The idealization of the Davidic covenant and dynasty is enhanced in prophetic oracles. The appearance of the Davidic covenant in the prophetic tradition proved to be an important step toward infusing royal idealism with eschatological expectations. This combination—royal ideology and eschatological hopes—provides the matrix out of which subsequent messianism would grow.

The prophet Hosea expresses the hope and confidence that "in the last days" the estranged northern tribes of Israel will repent and seek out God and "David their king" (Hos 3:4-5). Micah anticipates that Bethlehem will someday once again provide Israel with a Davidic king: "Bethlehem Ephrathah, you are small among the clans of Judah; One will come from you to be ruler over Israel for Me. His origin is from antiquity, from eternity" (Mic 5:2).

The mysterious quality of the awaited Davidic king is augmented in Isaiah's famous oracle (Isa 9:1-7), part of which reads: "For a child will be born for us, a son will be given to us, and the government will be on his shoulders. He will be named Wonderful Counselor, Mighty God, Eternal Father, Prince of Peace. The dominion will be vast, and its prosperity will never end. He will reign on the throne of David and over his kingdom, to establish and sustain it with justice and righteousness from now on and forever" (vv. 6-7). The Davidic covenant is clearly echoed in the promise that the "throne of David" will be "over his kingdom, to establish . . . it . . . forever." The intriguing language in v. 6 has occasioned a great deal of scholarly discussion. Whatever its original meaning and application, it is not hard to see how it contributed new ideas to royal ideology, ideas that would fuel later emerging messianism.

Another Isaianic oracle reflects royal ideology near the end of, or shortly after the end of, the dynasty: "Then a shoot will grow from the stump of Jesse, and a branch from his roots will bear fruit. The Spirit of the LORD will rest on Him" (Isa 11:1-2). The Davidic dimension is brought to mind immediately in the reference to the "stump of Jesse," that is, David's father. The "Spirit of the LORD" will rest upon this royal Davidic descendant, just as it came upon David (e.g., 1Sm 16:13). But the qualities of David's descendant are expressed in terms that seem to surpass his great ancestor. This oracle also contributed significantly to the emerging messianic expectation (e.g., 1QSb 5:22,25,26; 4Q161 7 iii 15-29; 4Q285 5 i 3; *Pss Sol* 17:24,29,36-37). The wise, ideal king is mentioned elsewhere in Isaiah: "Indeed, a king will reign righteously, and rulers will rule justly" (Isa 32:1).

Hopes for a renewed Davidic dynasty are expressed in the exilic period, notably by Jeremiah and Ezekiel. The former assures Judah: "On that day. . . . They will serve the LORD their God and I will raise up David their king for them" (Jer 30:8-9). The latter expresses a similar hope: "I will appoint over them a single shepherd, My servant David, and he will shepherd them. He will tend them himself and will be their shepherd. I, Yahweh, will be their God, and My servant David will be a prince among them" (Ezk 34:23-24a; cf. 37:24-25).

Jeremiah promises that for Judah God will raise up "David their king." An eschatological figure, possibly endowed with extraordinary powers, is not envisioned here. The prophet looks for an idealized Davidic scion, through whom the dynasty and the nation will be restored.

Ezekiel longs for a new David, a "shepherd," "king," and "prince" who will faithfully lead God's people. The epithet "shepherd," of course, recalls the Mosaic prayer that God provide a shepherd for His people (Nm 27:17: "who will go out before them and come back in before them, who will bring them out and bring them in, so that the LORD's community won't be like sheep without a shepherd"), while the epithet "prince" probably implies a subordination of Judah's monarch, a subordination to God, who is the true King.

The prophecies of the Second Temple and exilic periods anticipated the coming of a king who would fulfill the Davidic ideal—a king who would obey Torah, reestablish and defend in Jerusalem true worship, and bring about an everlasting and unprecedented era of peace and prosperity. These hopes would ultimately prove to be a foundation for the messianism of the intertestamental period.

A few prophets envisioned what may be described as diarchic messianism, that is, rule over Israel by two anointed personages, one a priest and the other a king. We find this expectation in Haggai (1:12-14; 2:2-4,20-23) and in Zechariah (3:6-10; 4:2-5,11-14). The latter speaks of the "two sons of oil" (4:14, literally translated). This distinctive phrase appears in 4Q254, a Qumran scroll that offers commentary on Gn 49. The diarchy of Haggai, Zechariah, and 4Q254 is consistent with the eschatology of the men of Qumran who anticipate the appearance of the "Anointed of Aaron and of Israel" (1QS 9:11). Diarchy is also attested in the *Testaments of the Twelve Patriarchs*, a pseudepigraphal work that appeared in the intertestamental period.

EXPRESSIONS OF MESSIANISM IN INTERTESTAMENTAL LITERATURE

It is during the intertestamental period that messianic expectation flourishes. What may be regarded as fully articulated "messianism" emerges with the expectation of the coming of a divinely anointed and empowered figure who inaugurates a reign that is dramatically new, even exceeding the idealized reigns of David and his son Solomon. When this anointed king comes, no successor is expected. Everything will forever be changed. Some traditions envision judgment taking place at this time (as in Dan 12), with history as we have known it coming to an end. Other traditions envision history ending after the reign of Israel's Messiah (as in *4 Ezra*).

The transition to messianism, of course, did not take place everywhere at the same time and in the same way. The hope for a restored Davidic dynasty did not die out in the intertestamental period and likely continued until well into the Common Era. But in the late intertestamental period, hopes of royal restoration began taking on new characteristics—characteristics, which through hindsight now seem to represent important steps in the development of "messianism." One might say that "Davidism," the hope of a restored Davidic dynasty, evolved into "messianism," as idealism began to yield to apocalyptic surrealism. With this surrealism came a diversity of expectations.

There are traces of Davidism, perhaps even messianism, in the Greek translation of Hebrew Scripture (i.e., the LXX). One immediately thinks of Ezk 34:25, which in the Hebrew reads: "I will make with them a covenant of peace," but in the Greek reads: "I will make with David a covenant of peace." The expectation that the eschatological "David" will (re)build the Temple may be attested in 2Sm 7:11, where the Hebrew reads: "the Lord announces to you that the Lord will make a house for you," but in the Greek, it reads: "the Lord announces to you that you will build a house for him." If these elements are indeed adumbrations of messianism, then they may be the oldest elements.

In *Pss Sol* 17–18 we have perhaps the earliest explicit expression of messianism in the intertestamental period. Passages of major importance include the following:

> Lord, you chose David to be king over Israel, and swore to him about his descendants forever, that his kingdom should not fail before you (v. 4).
>
> See, Lord, and raise up for them their king, the son of David, to rule over your servant Israel in the time known to you, O God (v. 21).
>
> He will gather a holy people whom he will lead in righteousness; and he will judge the tribes of the people that have been made holy by the Lord their God (v. 26).
>
> He will distribute them upon the land according to their tribes . . . (v. 28).
>
> And he will purge Jerusalem (and make it) holy as it was even from the beginning (v. 30b).
>
> And he will be a righteous king over them, taught by God. There will be no unrighteousness among them in his days, for all shall be holy, and their king shall be the Lord Messiah (v. 32).
>
> And he himself (will be) free from sin, (in order) to rule a great people. He will expose officials and drive out sinners by the strength of his word. And he will not weaken in his days, (relying) upon his God, for God made him powerful in the Holy Spirit and wise in the counsel of understanding, with strength and righteousness (vv. 36-37).
>
> Faithfully and righteously shepherding the Lord's flock, he will not let any of them stumble in their pasture (v. 40b).
>
> This is the beauty of the king of Israel which God knew, to raise him over the house of Israel to discipline it (v. 42).

These passages, and others not cited, allude to 2Sm 7, Isa 11, Isaiah's Servant hymns, and the promise of a righteous king in Jer 23:5. In *Pss Sol* 17:31 we are told that the nations will come "from the ends of the earth to see his glory." The passage alludes to Isa 55:5 (and perhaps 56:6-7) and reminds us of Solomon's fame (a tradition in circulation, as attested by Jesus in Mt 12:42 = Lk 11:31). The allusion to Jer 23:5 is qualified by a further allusion to Isa 54:13, when it says that the expected Messiah will be "taught by the LORD." His fidelity to Torah is underscored elsewhere in *Pss Sol* 17. This theme will become greatly embellished in the later rabbinic writings, where in some traditions the Messiah is portrayed as a great Scripture scholar.

Perhaps the most intriguing feature of all is *Pss Sol* 17's reference to Israel's awaited king as "the Lord Messiah." The Greek manuscripts read *basileus auton christos kyrios*, though modern editions are frequently emended to read *basileus auton christos kyriou* ("their king is the Lord's Messiah"). But there really is no compelling reason to emend the text in this way, for the reading "the Lord Messiah" is found in all Greek and Syriac manuscripts. Moreover, the appearance of *christos kyrios* in Lk 2:11 demonstrates the messianic function of this epithet, while references to Herod the Great and Herod Agrippa as *basileus kyrios* ("the lord king") demonstrate that "lord" can function in a purely honorific manner. The assumption that *christos kyrios* ("Lord Messiah") cannot have been spoken or written by a devout Jew is to interpret *christos* ("Messiah") as Christians themselves eventually did. Thus, calling the expected Davidic king the "Lord Messiah" confers great honor, but not divinity on this figure.

Other pseudepigrapha portray messianic figures in a variety of ways. In the *Testaments of the Twelve Patriarchs*, whose dating and history of composition are quite complex, priestly and royal figures are exalted, perhaps reflecting the diarchic messianism of Haggai and Zechariah. According to *T. Issachar* 5:7-8:

> And Levi and Judah were glorified by the Lord among the sons of Jacob. For the Lord made choice among them: and to one he gave the priesthood, and to the other the kingship. Therefore, obey them.

Whereas this passage looks to Israel's past, *T. Naphtali* 8:2 looks to the future:

> Accordingly, command your children to unite with Levi and Judah, for through Judah salvation will arise for Israel and in him Jacob will be blessed.

Diarchy seems quite clear in *T. Simeon* 7:1-2:

> And now, my children, obey Levi and by Judah you will be redeemed. And do not exalt yourselves over these two tribes, because from them will arise for you the salvation of God. For the Lord will raise up from Levi someone as High Priest and from Judah someone as King.

Hopes of diarchic restoration seem clear enough, but messianic elements, if any, are vague.

In *4 Ezra*, a late first-century AD text, there are two important references to the Messiah (Latin: *unctus*). Other passages that refer to the "Servant" (in Semitic texts, though, probably secondarily, *filius meus* in the Latin) include 13:32,37,52 and 14:9; *4 Ezra* 7:27-30 and 12:32-34 read:

> And every one who has been delivered from the evils that I have foretold shall see my wonders. For my son the Messiah shall be revealed with those who are with him, and those who remain shall rejoice four hundred years. And after these years my son the Messiah shall die, and all who draw human breath. And the

> world shall be turned back to primeval silence for seven days, as it was at the first beginnings; so that no one shall be left.
>
> This is the Messiah whom the Most High has kept until the end of days, who will arise from the posterity of David, and will come and speak to them; he will denounce them for their ungodliness and for their wickedness, and will cast up before them their contemptuous dealings. For first he will set them living before his judgment seat, and when he has reproved them, then he will destroy them. But he will deliver in mercy the remnant of my people, those who have been saved throughout my borders, and he will make them joyful until the end comes, the day of judgment, of which I spoke to you at the beginning.

In the first passage the Messiah reigns 400 years, thus concluding human history, as we know it. It is interesting that human history does not end with his appearance, but ends *after his reign*. In the second passage the Messiah is explicitly identified as arising "from the posterity of David." In a manner reminiscent of *Pss Sol* 17, this Davidic Messiah will denounce and eliminate ungodliness. Consistent with the first passage, the messianic reign will bring joy "until the end comes, the day of judgment."

In the *Similitudes of Enoch*, there are several references to the "son of man," the "chosen one," and even two references to "Messiah" (48:10; 52:4). The son of man references are clearly based on the vision of Dan 7 (cf. *1 En* 46:1-6). The son of man becomes the "chosen one" (48:6) and probably should be identified with the "Messiah." The Messiah will sit on a throne and judge the kings of the earth.

Most of the terms used in reference to messianic figures in Second Temple Judaism are attested in the Dead Sea Scrolls. The obvious terms include mashiach ("anointed"), *nasi'* ("prince"), *tsemach david* ("branch of David"), and *shevit* ("staff" or "rod"). Less certain, often disputed, epithets include *ben* ("son") and its many variations: "Son of the great God," "Son of God," "Son of the Most High," "first-born Son," and "Elect One of God." The messianism of the Scrolls has been extensively discussed by scholars, and with the recent release of all remaining texts, mostly from Qumran's fourth cave, we can expect the discussion to continue unabated.

The messianic texts of Qumran fall into two basic groupings: the sectarian texts that evidently reveal what the men of the new covenant anticipated, and the other texts, which are nonsectarian, or at least non-Qumranian in origin, that probably tell us about the views of other Jews and Jewish groups from various parts of Palestine. Some of the more sensational texts belong to this second group. Three will be briefly considered.

The text 4Q521 speaks of a "Messiah, whom heaven and earth will obey." The text goes on to describe things expected to take place: God's "Spirit will hover over the poor, and he will renew the faithful with his strength." He will free prisoners, restore the sight of the blind, heal the wounded, make alive the dead, and proclaim good news to the poor. The parallels to Jesus' reply to the imprisoned John the Baptist have been pointed out (Mt 11:5 = Lk 7:22). Jesus' reply, like 4Q521, is derived from words and phrases found in Ps 146:6-8; Isa 26:19; 35:5-6; and 61:1-2. The Isaianic parallels suggest at the very least that Jesus' reply would have been understood as an implicit claim to a messianic role (though whether principally in a royal or prophetic capacity remains an open question).

But 4Q521's parallels with Ps 146 seem to imply a divine identity, or at least a divine authority. The words "heaven and earth . . . and everything in them" are taken from Ps 146:6. The promises of justice for the oppressed, "setting prisoners free," "lifting up those bowed down," and "opening the eyes of the blind" are all derived from Ps 146:7-8, though the last phrase also parallels the language of Isaiah. What is remarkable here is that according to Ps 146, these are the deeds of Yahweh. Yet in 4Q521 they are the deeds of the Lord's anointed one, or Messiah. The author of 4Q521 almost certainly knew that he was drawing upon Ps 146 and surely would have known that it was Yahweh who is the subject of vv. 6-8.

The anticipation that heaven and earth will obey the Lord's Messiah may well be illustrated in the life and ministry of Jesus of Nazareth. The account of the stilling the storm (Mk 4:35-41 and par.), walking upon the water (Mk 6:47-52 and par.), the miraculous catch of fish (Lk 5:1-11; cf. v. 8: "Go away from me, because I'm a sinful man, Lord!"), and perhaps also the destruction of the fig tree (Mk 11:12-14,20-21), seem to be examples of how heaven and earth—the very natural world—will indeed obey the Messiah.

In 4Q246 we may have another example of exalted messianism. In this Aramaic text, in which a seer evidently interprets a vision, or dream, to a king, we hear of a coming royal son described in divine terms. Although it is disputed, many think that the "son of God" and "son of the Most High" personage, whose "kingdom will be an eternal kingdom," is a messianic figure. Again, the parallels with the NT are suggestive. This time, however, the parallels help with the interpretation of the Qumran text.

The angelic announcement in Lk 1:31-35 offers several striking parallels to the 4Q246 text: "you will bear a son . . . he will be called the Son of the Most High . . . of his kingdom there will be no end . . . the child to be born will be called holy, the Son of God." We have here four very close parallels. Because the angel's epithets are obviously intended to convey messianic import in the context of the Gospel of Luke, it is reasonable to assume that the epithets of 4Q246 do also. Thus, although the anticipated actions of the figures envisioned in Luke and 4Q246 are significantly different, the common language suggests that both writings are speaking of the Messiah.

There is yet another text from Qumran that seems to envision a redemptive personage who is either divine or possesses divine authority. The Melchizedek figure in 11Q13 in at least one place seems to be identified with Yahweh Himself. The author of this fragmentary text foresees an eschatological jubilee (Lv 25:13), at which time the prophecy of Isa 61:1-2 will be fulfilled. But part of the passage is paraphrased in a remarkable way: "this is the time decreed for 'the year of Melchizedek's favor'" (11Q13 2:9; cf. Isa 61:2). Instead of "Yahweh's favor," as Isaiah actually reads, it is "Melchizedek's favor." Clarification, if not justification, for this surprising reading is found in Pss 82:1 and 7:7-8, which are cited and briefly interpreted. The author of 11Q13 believes that Melchizedek is a heavenly or god-like being, superior to the angels, yet distinct from Yahweh.

The heavenly Melchizedek's superiority to the angels is seen in his ability to defeat Satan (or Belial) and his evil host, forgive Israel her sins, and fulfill the prophecy of Isa 52:7, in which the good news of God's rule will be announced. The mysterious Melchizedek here in 11Q13 is probably not the Messiah. But the expectation of a figure who is neither an angel nor Yahweh Himself opens up the possibility that the Messiah figure of 4Q521, whom heaven and earth obey and who does the very deeds of Yahweh, and the "son of God" figure of 4Q246 could be super-mundane in some sense, or perhaps divine.

The portrait of the Messiah in the sectarian writings is consistent and makes use of terminology such as "Messiah" (CD 12:23–13:1; 14:19 [= 4Q266 18 iii 12]; 1QS 9:11; 1QSa 2:11-15, 20-21; 4Q252 1 v 3-4), "branch of David" (4Q161 7-10 iii 22; 4Q174 1-3 i 11; 4Q252 1 v 3-4; 4Q285 5 3-4), and "Prince" or "Prince of (all) the congregation" (CD 7:19-20 [= 4Q266 3 iv 9]; 1QSb 5:20; 1QM 5:1; 4Q161 2-6 ii 19; 4Q285 4 2, 4 6; 5 4; 6 2; 4Q376 1 iii 1). In the *Damascus* and *Community Rule* documents the coming of the Messiah is linked with the coming of the High Priest (i.e., the "anointed one of Aaron"). His cooperation with the High Priest is strongly implied in 1QSa and 1QSb. His bellicosity is made clear in 4Q285, where evidently he meets on the field of battle and slays the leader of the Kittim, who may have been understood to refer to the Roman Emperor. It is thought by some that 4Q285 is part of the *War* document (1QM), a document that envisions a great eschatological war between good and evil.

The Messiah of the Dead Sea Scrolls is similar at points to the Messiah of *Pss Sol* 17 and *4 Ezra*. However, the former portrayal is less exalted and is more closely linked to the High Priest and the legal, priestly interests of the community of the new covenant. In the latter portrayals, nothing is said about the role of the High Priest.

Perhaps the most distinctive feature of Qumran's Messiah is his association with the restored priesthood. He cooperates with the high priest, perhaps is even subordinate to him, and plays on the whole a relatively minor role (at least so far as the extant materials seem to indicate). He is so closely linked with the high priest that the two are frequently referred to as the "anointed of Aaron and of Israel" (as seen especially in the *Damascus* document). In most of these passages "anointed" is in the singular, though in one the word is plural (1QS 9:11). It is from these passages that a great deal of excitement arose in the early years following the discovery of the Scrolls. Many thought it surprising that the people of Qumran expected two Messiahs. But there is nothing strange here at all; Qumran's diarchic messianism simply reflected what they believed was contained in Israel's scriptures and history. Following the model of David the king and Zadok the priest, it was expected that God would someday raise up an anointed High Priest and an anointed Prince. At that time prophecy will be fulfilled, Israel restored, and the wicked empire destroyed.

SUMMING UP

The messianic expectations of the intertestamental period were not uniform. Not all Jews expected a messiah, and those who did expect a messiah did not necessarily expect the same type of messiah. Some apparently expected a militant messiah who, like David of old, would defeat the Roman army and other Gentile forces and regain Israel's political freedom (as seems to be envisioned in 4Q285). Others expected a figure who possessed a heavenly power, perhaps even a divine identity, that would exceed that of David (as Jesus apparently presupposed in Mk 12:35-37 and par.).

The messianic expectations of the intertestamental period provide a rich and diverse background, against which the teaching of Jesus and the faith of the early Church should be studied. This background sheds light on the messianism of Jesus, but His messianic self-understanding is not necessarily limited to this background.

Messiah in Rabbinic Literature

MICHAEL L. BROWN

Although the subject of the Messiah and the Messianic Era plays an important role in rabbinic literature, it does not play a central role, as do more legally related subjects such as the observance of the Sabbath, dietary laws, or laws concerning marriage and divorce. Accordingly, there are only two references to the Messiah in the entire Mishnah (m. Ber 1:5; m. Sot 9:15), while the fullest Talmudic discussion of the Messiah son of David is limited to less than five folio pages, front and back (b. Sanhedrin 96b–99a). Also, in keeping with the nature of rabbinic literature, there is no systematic or definitive treatment of the identity of the Messiah(s) and his (or, their) role (for the subject of Messiah son of Joseph, a secondary messianic figure, see below, The Messiah in the Talmuds). Nonetheless, there are hundreds of references to the Messiah found throughout the rabbinic writings, and rabbinic interpretation of Scripture sees the Messiah in the widest imaginable range of biblical texts (see below, Scriptural References Interpreted with Reference to the Messiah in Early Rabbinic Literature).

THE MESSIAH IN THE TARGUMS[1]

C. Evans points out that, "compared to the targums to the Prophets and the Writings, the Pentateuch Targums are relatively conservative in finding messianic implications in the text."[2] Onkelos renders only Gn 49:10-12 and Nm 24:17-24 messianically; to these, Neofiti adds Gn 3:15; Ex 12:42; Nm 11:26; 24:7 (cf., similarly, the fragmentary Targum); Pseudo-Jonathan has Gn 3:15; 35:21; 49:1,10-12; Ex 17:16; 40:9-11; Nm 23:21; 24:17-24; Dt 30:4-9. Among verses treated messianically by the Targums to the Prophets, Evans lists: 1Sm 2:7-10,35 (and note the reference at 2:35

to the priest who will serve with the Messiah); 2Sm 2:28-32; 23:1-5; 1Kg 5:13; Isa 4:1-6; 9:5-6; 10:24-27; 11:1-16; 14:29-30; 16:1-5; 28:5-6; 42:1-9;[3] 43:10; 52:13–53:12 (note, however, that the Targum completely rewrites the text so that the messianic servant triumphs without suffering); Jer 23:1-8; 30:8-11,21; 33:12-26; Ezk 17:22-24; 34:20-31; 37:21-28; Hos 2:2; 3:3-5; 14:5-8; Mic 4:8; 5:1-3 (2-4); Hab 3:17-18; Zch 3:8; 4:7; 6:12-13; 10:4; 12:10 (in the Reuchlinianus ms).[4] In the Targums to the Writings, Evans lists: Pss 18:28-32 (27-31); 21:1-8; 45:7-18 (6-17); 61:7-9 (6-8); 72:1-20; 80:15-18 (14-17); 132:10-18; Sg 1:8,17; 4:5; 7:4; 8:1-4; Ru 1:1; 3:15; Lam 2:22; 4:22; Ecc 1:11; 7:24; Est 1:1; 1Chr 3:24.[5] With regard to dating, Evans writes, "Several of these texts in all probability reflect traditions dating to the first century CE or earlier. A few others may also derive from the first century, but the evidence is too meager to be certain."[6] Where there is comparative evidence, a good case can be made for the early dating of the Jewish traditions behind the messianic interpretation of Gn 3:15; 49:10-12; Nm 24:17-24; 1Sm 2:1-10; Isa 9:5-6 (6-7); 11:1-16; 52:13–53:12; Jer 23:5; 33:15;[7] Mic 5:1 (2); Pss 45:8 (7);[8] 72:1 (cf. the giving of gifts by the magi in Mt 2:10-11).[9] In contrast, the Targums to books like Ruth and Song of Songs are of much later date and therefore preserve material not reflected in earlier texts.

Treating the documents as a whole, the Messiah of the Targums reflects the general description found in other rabbinic texts. He will be a royal descendant of David who will establish God's triumphant kingdom with Israel at the center, ruling over the nations. He will rebuild the Temple and restore Israel's sovereignty, as the nation lives in obedience to the Torah. As for a suffering Messiah (specifically, the son of Joseph), he does not figure prominently, if at all (see above, n. 5). And so, while Isa 52:13–53:12 is interpreted messianically, the Messiah of the Targum does not suffer. Instead, he is wholly triumphant (beginning in 52:13), interceding for his people Israel who suffer in exile and who are forgiven for his sake, ultimately bringing judgment on the nations.[10]

THE MESSIAH IN THE MISHNAH

In. b. Berakhot 1:5 (cf. t. Berakhot 1:12), reference is made to the Messianic Age (lit., the days of the Messiah), but it is in the context of the recitation of prayers in accordance with Dt 16:3, so the text is not discussing the Messiah himself. The lengthy passage in m. Sotah 9:15 (see also b. Sot 49b; y. Sot 9:16; b. Sanh 97a) deals with the perilous conditions that will occur "in the footprints of the Messiah" (meaning, when he comes):

> With the footprints of the Messiah: presumption increases, and dearth increases. The vine gives its fruit and wine at great cost. And the government turns to heresy.

> And there is no reproof. The gathering place will be for prostitution. And Galilee will be laid waste. And the Gablan [a beautiful region] will be made desolate. And the men of the frontier will go about from town to town, and none will take pity on them. And the wisdom of scribes will putrefy. And those who fear sin will be rejected. And the truth will be locked away. Children will shame elders, and elders will stand up before children. *For the son dishonors the father and the daughter rises up against her mother, the daughter-in-law against her mother-in-law; a man's enemies are the men of his own house* (Mic 7:6). The face of the generation is the face of a dog. A son is not ashamed before his father. Upon whom shall we depend? Upon our Father in heaven.[11]

The above discussion is in keeping with a theme found frequently in rabbinic literature, namely, that the end of this age will be one of conflict, apostasy, and upheaval (this is fleshed out in more detail in the Talmuds, midrashim, and later rabbinic traditions). In the NT, see, e.g., Mt 24:4-13, and note that Jesus quotes Mic 7:6 in Mt 10:34-36, pointing to the apparent widespread use of this passage with reference to conflicts of allegiance with the advent of the Messiah. As summarized by E. Schürer (and his subsequent editors), the expected events at the end of this age are: "1. The Final Ordeal and Confusion; 2. Elijah as Precursor;[12] 3. The Coming of the Messiah; 4. The Last Assault of the Hostile Powers; 5. Destruction of Hostile Powers; 6. The Renewal of Jerusalem; 7. The Gathering of the Dispersed; 8. The Kingdom of Glory in the Holy Land; 9. The Renewal of the World; 10. A General Resurrection; 11. The Last Judgment. Eternal Bliss and Damnation."[13]

As to why there are so few references to the Messiah in the Mishnah, some scholars point to the plan and purpose of the Mishnah, having to do with the sanctifying of daily Jewish life by keeping the commandments, thus making rabbinic speculation about the future not suitable for this work. Others suggest that there is a distinct reaction against the politicizing of the messianic hope, which contributed to two devastatingly bloody wars against Rome, the first (AD 66–70) resulting in the destruction of the Temple and the deaths of hundreds of thousands of Jews (Josephus claims there were one million Jewish casualties); the second (AD 132–135) resulting in the banishing of Jews from Jerusalem and their exile to many points worldwide, along with countless thousands of additional casualties.

This second Jewish revolt was led by the violent general Bar Kochba, hailed as King Messiah by none other than Rabbi Akiva,[14] although at least one of his contemporaries rebuked him for making that claim (see y. Taan 4:5; Lam Rab 2:4; in the words of R. Yohanan ben Toreta, "Aqiva! Grass will grow on your cheeks, and the Messiah will not yet have come!"; see also b. Sanh 93, which states that when the rabbis saw that Bar Kochba was unable to judge, as the Messiah was expected to do, according to Isa 11:3, they put him to death).[15]

THE MESSIAH IN THE TALMUDS

There is one extended and wide-ranging discussion of the Messiah in the Talmuds, b. Sanh 96b-99a, focused primarily on the time of the Messiah's coming and the final upheaval that will signal that event, with little said about the Messiah himself or the Messianic Age (aside from the projected length of that age).

In 97a-b, it is stated on Tannaitic authority (among several different traditions) that the world will last for six thousand years, two thousand years of desolation (normally understood to be from Adam to Abraham), two thousand years of Torah (from Abraham, to whom both the Oral and Written Torah were allegedly revealed, to the Messiah),[16] and two thousand years of Torah (from the Messiah until the end of the age), "but on account of our numerous sins what has been lost [of those years, in which the Messiah should have come but has not come] has been lost."[17] Nonetheless, with all the rabbinic speculation as to when the Messiah would come, based on various traditions and/or calculations derived from biblical texts, a curse is invoked on anyone who would try to calculate the exact time of the end, since people might say, "Since the end has come and he has not come, he will not come" (b. Sanh 97b).

Other opinions focus on Israel's responsibilities to usher in the Messianic Age: "Said Rab, 'All of the ends have passed, and the matter now depends only on repentance and good deeds.' . . . R. Eliezer says, 'If the Israelites repent, they will be redeemed, and if not, they will not be redeemed.' And said R. Yohanan, 'The son of David will come to a generation that is either entirely righteous or entirely wicked. A generation that is entirely righteous, as it is written, "Your people also shall be all righteous, they shall inherit the land forever" (Isa 60:21), or a generation that is entirely wicked, as it is written, "And he saw that there was no man and wondered that there was no intercessor" (Isa 59:16), and it is written, "For my own sake, even for my own sake I will do it" (Isa 60:22 [cf. Isa 48:11, KJV])'" (b. Sanh 97b). Further speculation regarding the world becoming entirely wicked includes the whole world turning to heresy (presumably Christianity) and scholars in Israel being few, part of the apostasy of the nation (following m. Sot 9:15).

The Talmudic discussion continues: "Said R. Alexandri, 'R. Joshua b. Levi contrasted verses as follows: "It is written; 'in its time [will the Messiah come],' and it is also written; 'I [the Lord] will hasten it.' [What is the meaning of the contrast?] If [the Israelites] have merit, I will hasten it, if they do not, [the messiah] will come in due course. It is written, 'And behold, one like the son of man came with the clouds of heaven' (Dn 7:13, and it is written, 'Behold your king comes to you . . . lowly and riding upon an ass' (Zch 9:7). [What is the meaning of the contrast?] If [the

Israelites] have merit, it will be 'with the clouds of heaven' (Dn 7:13), and if they do not have merit, it will be 'lowly and riding upon an ass' (Zch. 9:7)" (b. Sanh. 98b).[18]

It is this discussion that leads to an oft-quoted account: "R. Joshua b. Levi found Elijah standing at the door of the burial vault of R. Simeon b. Yohai. He said to him, 'Am I going to come to the world to come?' He said to him, 'If this master wants.' Said R. Joshua b. Levi, 'Two did I see, but a third voice did I hear.' He said to him, 'When is the Messiah coming?' He said to him, 'Go and ask him.' 'And where is he sitting?' 'At the gate of the city.' 'And what are the marks that indicate who he is?' 'He is sitting among the poor who suffer illness, and all of them untie and tie their bandages all together, but he unties them and ties them one by one. He is thinking, "Perhaps I may be wanted, and I do not want to be held up."' He went to him, saying to him, 'Peace be unto you, my master and teacher.' He said to him, 'Peace be unto you, son of Levi.' He said to him, 'When is the master coming?' He said to him, 'Today.' He went back to Elijah, who said to him, 'What did he tell you?' He said to him, 'Peace be unto you, son of Levi.' He said to him, 'He [thereby] promised you and your father the world to come.' He said to him, 'But he lied to me. For he said to me, "I am coming today," but he did not come.' He said to him, 'This is what he said to you, "Today, if you will obey his voice" (Ps 95:7)'" (b. Sanh 98b).

Accordingly, b. Yoma states that repentance has the power to bring the final redemption near; y. Taan 64a states that if Israel repented for a single day or observed just one Sabbath, the son of David would come immediately; and b. Shab 118b states that redemption would come if Israel would observe two Sabbaths in accordance with the Torah.

Elsewhere in the Talmuds, references to the Messiah are scattered throughout numerous tractates, including: when he will come (e.g., b. Sanh 93b; b. R.H. 11b; b. Chul 63a; b. A.Z. 9a–b); descriptions of the Messianic Era (e.g., b. Sanh 91b; b. Ber 34b; b. Shab 30b; 63a; 151b; b. Pes 68b; b. Taan 14b–15a; b. Ket 112b);[19] the name(s) of the Messiah (e.g., b. B.B. 75b); his preexistence (or, the preexistence of his name; e.g., b. Pes. 54a; b. Ned. 39a),[20] his association with David (e.g., b. Sanh 98b; he is frequently called "the son of David"; and note y. Ber 2:4: "The rabbis said, 'If this Messiah-king comes from among the living, David will be his name; if he comes from among the dead, it will be David himself.'"),[21] and his suffering (e.g., b. Sanh 98b). In the Jerusalem Talmud, it is stated that the Messiah was born the day the Second Temple was destroyed (see y. Ber. 2:4, with ref. to Isa 11:1). This would agree with b. Sanh 98b, cited above, where the leprous Messiah sits at the gates of Rome changing his bandages;[22] cf. also Targ. Jon. to Mic 4:8, where the Messiah, apparently here on earth, is hidden because of our sins.

Both y. Kil 9:3 and y. Ket 12:3 speak of the resurrection of the dead in the Messianic Age; and y. Hag 2:2 states that the Torah is not going to be restored to its place until the son of David comes. It is unclear, however, if Talmudic (and midrashic) references to the world to come refer to the Messianic Era or the era following, and there are differences of opinion as to what to expect during the Messianic Era. See, in particular, b. Sanh 99a: "Said R. Hiyya bar Abba said R. Yohanan, 'All of the prophets prophesied only concerning the days of the Messiah.'[23] But as to the world to come [thereafter]: 'Eye has not seen, O Lord, beside you, what he has prepared for him who waits for him' (Isa 64:3). That statement differs from the view of Samuel. For said Samuel, 'There is no difference between this world and the days of the Messiah except for [Israel's] subjugation to the rule of the empires alone.'"[24] This, in turn, can be contrasted with some of the midrashic descriptions of the Messianic Age, which abound with the miraculous (see the section below, The Messiah in the Early Midrashim).[25] What is universally expected, however, is that Israel will be exalted in the earth, with the nations subjected to them, and that the twelve tribes will be regathered and reestablished in the land.

As for the Messiah son of Joseph, he is mentioned only in b. Suk 52a-b (there are three separate references to him there; cf. also y. Suk 5:2), although without explanation, meaning his identity was taken for granted. The first reference (b. Suk 52a) is connected to Zch 12:12, where the house of David is in great mourning at the end of the age. According to one interpretation, they are mourning because of the evil inclination (meaning, they were grieved that it was so easy to overcome it yet they failed to). According to another interpretation, they are mourning over the slaying of Messiah son of Joseph, which is then explained by Zch 12:10, "They shall look upon me, whom they have pierced, and they shall mourn for him" [KJV]. The next reference to Messiah ben Joseph then follows (also b. Suk 52a), stating that Messiah son of David will raise him from the dead (citing Ps 21:4-5). The final reference (b. Suk 52b) explains the four craftsmen of Zch 2:3 to be Messiah son of David, Messiah son of Joseph, Elijah, and the righteous priest (for parallel references, see below, to S. of S. Rab 2:33). In post-Talmudic literature, along with the midrashic writings, the figure of Messiah son of Joseph becomes much more prominent and is developed in depth. See immediately below, and, more fully, the article "The Messiah in Medieval Rabbinic Literature" in this book.

THE MESSIAH IN THE EARLY MIDRASHIM[26]

The earliest midrashic writings are legal in character and based on a legal reading of the biblical text (midrash halakha as opposed to midrash aggada), covering the books of Exodus to Deuteronomy, respectively, the Mekhilta of R. Ishmael, Sifra, and Sifre Numbers and Deuteronomy. There are hardly any references to the

Messiah or the Messianic Era in these documents, which mirrors the situation in the Mishnah.

In the Mekhilta (Lauterbach ed., 2:120), R. Eliezer of Modiin taught that if Israel kept the Sabbath, it would receive "six good portions," including the future world, the new world, and the kingdom of David. According to R. Eliezer, "If you succeed in keeping the Sabbath you will escape the three visitations: The day of God, the suffering preceding the advent of the Messiah, and the Great Judgment Day."[27] This parallels some of the Talmudic teaching (see above), while the idea that an obedient Israel would be spared some of the end-time calamities is repeated by Sa'adiah Gaon in the ninth century (see the article "The Messiah in Medieval Rabbinic Literature" in this book). There are no Messianic references in Sifra or Sifre Numbers, while in Sifre Deuteronomy, Neusner observes that "the references point mostly to 'the age of the Messiah' in contrast to 'this age.'" Significantly, "when the exegetes represented in Sifre Deuteronomy come to the Song of Moses, Dt 32:1-43 . . . they fail to introduce a single reference to the Messiah as an active figure or even to the history of Israel in their own day."[28]

In contrast, the aggadic midrashim are replete with messianic references, and thus "King Messiah" occurs more than 150 times in these writings, whereas the phrase is not found once in the halakhic midrashim. In keeping with the homiletical, midrashic method, some of the scriptural allusions seem to be quite obscure (see, e.g., Gn Rab 23:5; 51:8, citing Eve's words on the birth of Seth in Gn 4:25: "[She hinted at] that seed which would arise from another source, viz. the king Messiah"; Lv Rab 15:1; Ecc Rab 1:12, that the King Messiah will not come until all the souls have been created that God intended to bring into the world, citing Gn 5:1; or Nm Rab 13:2, which interprets Isa 41:25 with reference to the Messiah).

Elsewhere, the midrash states: "When you see the Powers fighting each other, look for the coming [lit. 'feet'] of the King Messiah" (Gn Rab 42:4, citing Gn 14); it is King Messiah who asks God for the nations (Gn Rab 44:8, citing Ps 2:8); God appoints King Messiah to be His firstborn (Ex Rab 19:7, citing Ps 89:28); all the nations will bring gifts to King Messiah in the millennial kingdom (Ex Rab 35:5, citing Ps 68:29); that King Messiah will reign supreme on land and sea is derived from Ps 72:8 (Nm Rab 13:14); King Messiah will hold in his hand Aaron's staff, which every previous Israelite king had also held (Nm Rab 18:23, citing Ps 110:2); his name will be YHWH (Lam Rab 1:51, citing Jer 23:6; cf. b. B. B. 75b); his name will be David (Lam Rab 1:51, citing Ps 18:51; in Gn Rab 1:4, his name was contemplated before the creation of the world).

There are also detailed descriptions of the coming age, although there is debate among scholars as to whether "the age to come" and the Messianic Era are synonymous. According to Ex Rab 15:21 (commenting on the "new things" prophesied in Isa 42:9, and with apparent reference to the Messianic Era here, based on the verses cited), there are "ten things which the Holy One, blessed be He, will renew in the Time to Come." They are: (1) God Himself will illumine the whole world (Isa 60:19; 30:26); (2) "He will bring out living water from Jerusalem and heal therewith all those who have a disease" (Ezk 47:9); (3) "He will make trees yield their fruit each month, and when a man eats of them he will be healed" (Ezk 47:12); (4) all the waste cities will be rebuilt, including Sodom and Gomorrah (Ezk 16:55); (5) God will rebuild Jerusalem with sapphire stones (Isa 54:11-12); (6) the cow and bear will feed together (Isa 11:7); (7) God will make a covenant with all the wild animals (Hos 2:20); (8) there will be no more weeping and wailing in the world (Isa 65:19); (9) there will be no more death in the world (Isa 25:9); (10) "there will no longer be any sighing, wailing or anguish, but that all will be rejoicing" (Isa 35:10).[29]

In Sg Rab 2:33, the "War Messiah"[30] refers to Messiah ben Joseph (he is listed there with Elijah, the Messiah—meaning ben David—and Melchizedek, with reference to the four craftsmen of Zch 2:3; see above, to b. Suk 52a-b); cf. also Gn Rab 75:6; 99:2; Nm Rab 14:1; Tanch 11:3; Yalk. Shim. § 570 (to Zch 4:3, which explains that there are "two Messiahs, one anointed for war and one anointed King over Israel").

SCRIPTURAL REFERENCES INTERPRETED WITH REFERENCE TO THE MESSIAH IN EARLY RABBINIC LITERATURE

The Hebrew Christian scholar Alfred Edersheim (1825–1889) compiled a list of 456 verses "applied to the Messiah or to Messianic times in the most ancient Jewish writings. They amount in all to 456, thus distributed: 75 from the Pentateuch, 243 from the Prophets, and 138 from the Hagiographa, and supported by more than 558 separate quotations from Rabbinic writings."[31] This list, however, reflects rabbinic interpretation of Scripture, which is often atomistic and homiletical, rather than reflecting a unified exegetical statement, and so, for the most part, the list represents disparate comments about the Messiah being connected to the biblical texts rather than a description of the Messiah being derived from those texts. In other words, through Scripture and tradition the ancient rabbis developed a concept of the Messiah, which was then linked back to various verses in the Tanakh.

In some instances, the biblical text lays the foundation for the messianic interpretation; in other cases, the messianic interpretation is superimposed on the biblical text.[32] For examples of the latter practice, in the opening verses of Genesis, at Gn 1:2, the Spirit of God hovering over the waters is said to be "the spirit of the Messianic king" (Lv. Rab. 14:1); at Gn 1:3, the light God commands is associated with the future light of the Messianic Era (Gn Rab. 2:5, with reference to Isa 60:1); and at Gn 1:4, although the Messianic Era is not explicitly mentioned, the light that God divides from the darkness is reserved "for the righteous in the time to come," which means in the messianic kingdom (b. Hag. 12a). Elsewhere, however, recognized messianic passages are interpreted messianically in the rabbinic writings. See, for example, Gn 49:10 (cf. the Targums; b. Sanh. 98b; Gn Rab. 98:8; Yalkut Shimoni, to Gn 49:10); Nm 24:17 (cf. Targum Onkelos; Targum Pseudo-Jonathan; y. Taan. 4:8; see also Dt Rab 1:20, without specifically mentioning "the Messiah"); Isa 11 (see Targum Jonathan to 11:1, 6; cf. also b. Sanh. 93b; y. Ber. 5a; cf. also various midrashim, including Gn Rab. 85:9). With regard to Ps 2, Edersheim notes, "Ps. 2, as might be expected, is treated as full of messianic references. To begin with, Ps. 2:1 is applied to the wars of Gog and Magog in the Talmud (Berach. 7 *b*, and Abhod. Zarah 3 *b*), and also in the Midrash on Ps. 2."[33]

As far as assessing the rabbinic interpretation of these biblical texts, more can be learned about ancient rabbinic expectations of the Messiah and the Messianic Age from the larger picture painted in their writings than from their hermeneutical method. In contrast, among the rabbinic Bible commentators of the medieval period (see the article "The Messiah in Medieval Rabbinic Literature" in this book), the scriptural verses are exegeted more consistently and closely, thus providing insight into rabbinic views of the Messiah as tied more closely to the biblical text.[34]

---

1. It is misleading to speak of the Targums as a unitary set of documents, since they were composed by different authors over a period of almost one thousand years. But since some targumic traditions date back to NT times (and before), and because they are unified within the totality of rabbinic Jewish thought, they are included together here. See further Samson H. Levey, *The Messiah: An Aramaic Interpretation* (Cincinnati: Hebrew Union College – Jewish Institute of Religion, 1974); Jacob Neusner, *Messiah in Context: Israel's History and Destiny in Formative Judaism* (Philadelphia: Fortress Press, 1984), 239–47.

2. Craig A. Evans, *Jesus and His Contemporaries: Comparative Studies* (Arbeiten Zur Geschichte Des Antiken Judentums Und Des Urchristentums, 25; Leiden, Netherlands: E. J. Brill, 1997), 155.

3. But not explicitly in all mss.

4. Evans, *Jesus and His Contemporaries*, 155. According to Kevin J. Cathcart and Robert P. Gordon, *The Targum of the Minor Prophets: Translated, with a Critical Introduction, Apparatus, and Notes* (The Aramaic Bible, vol. 14; Collegeville, MN: The Liturgical Press, 1989), 7, "The Reuchlinianus variant at Zech 12:10 belongs to a small number of texts which, probably because of the dashed hopes of messianic pretenders like Bar Kochba, know of a Messiah son of Ephraim who is mortally wounded in a confrontation with Gog at the gate of Jerusalem." For a rejection of any connection between the failed revolt of Bar Kochba and the suffering Messiah son of Joseph, see David C. Mitchell, *Messiah ben Joseph* (Newton Mearns, Scotland: Campbell Publications, 2016), 129–32. See ibid., 100–105 for a detailed treatment of the "Targumic Tosefta" to Zch 12:10, which parallels b. Suk 52a. For other explicit references to Messiah son of Joseph (or, Ephraim) in the Targums, Mitchell cites Targum Yerushalmi to Ex 40:9-11, Targum to Song of Songs 4:5 and 7:4, and Targum to Lam 4:21-22 (see ibid., 105–10). For the Targum to Mic 4:8, see the section above in this article, "The Messiah in the Talmuds."

5. Evans, *Jesus and His Contemporaries*, 155.

6. Ibid. See further, ibid., 155–81, and cf. Gerbern S. Oegema, *The Anointed and His People: Messianic Expectations from the Maccabees to Bar Kochba* (Journal for the Study of the Pseudepigrapha Supplement Series 27; Sheffield: Sheffield Academic Press, 1998), 262–74.

7. Less certain are Zch 3:8; 6:12, which Evans lists as well, albeit tentatively. These verses, along with Jer 23:5; 33:15 are connected by the use of the messianic title "the Branch."

8. Evans adds Ps 45:3.

9. Evans also adds Ex 12:42; Nm 11:26; Ps 89:51-52.

10. As summarized by Bruce D. Chilton, *The Isaiah Targum: Introduction, Translation, Apparatus and Notes* (The Aramaic Bible: Collegeville, MN: The Liturgical Press, 1990), note to Isa 53:12, "The chapter is developed to refer to the Messiah and the '*righteous*' (v. 2) who depend on him, but in no sense can the Messiah (or the 'servant,' cf. 52:13) be said to suffer. Indeed, the point of the interpretation is to emphasize the triumph of the Messiah (cf. 52:13–15) at the expense of '*all the kingdoms*' (v. 3a; cf. vv. 7,11,12). The enemies are to be put in the position of Israel when the Shekhinah was removed (v. 3b). But the sufferings of Israel are to be relieved because the Messiah will pray effectively (vv. 4,6,7,12), and even '*build the sanctuary*' again (v. 5a). Adherence to the Messiah's '*words*' (v. 5), which teach the law (vv. 10–12), is to be the engine of Israel's new prosperity (v. 10). The actual rebuilding of the Temple was a reward promised to Israel along with the Messiah and the defeat of Rome during the Tannaitic period (cf. Pesaḥim 5a). The present interpretation would seem to fit easily within such a period. . . . Although there is no reference to anything like the suffering of the Messiah, imagery which was applied to Jesus in the course of Christian mission . . . , neither is there any attempt to claim the Messiah did not '*hand[ed] over* his soul to the death' (v. 12). Such an attempt would probably have been made if the purpose of the interpretation was to deny that the Messiah should die, as Jesus had. It would appear that such Christian claims were not in mind. Rather, the point of the phrase is probably that the Messiah risked his very life for the sake of his ministry; that appears to be the sense in which Isa 53:12 is applied to the hero Phinehas (cf. Numbers 25:13) in *Sifre* (∮131). As in the case of the Messiah of the *Psalms of Solomon* (cf. 17:27–29 and Tg Isaiah 11 in the Notes), the Targumic Messiah is a zealous victor, a guardian of the righteous (vv. 8,9)."

11. Based on the translation of Jacob Neusner, *The Mishnah: A New Translation* (New Haven, CT: Yale University Press, 1988), 465–66.

12. For Elijah and the Messiah in the Mishnah, see Karin Hedner-Zetterholm, "Elijah and the Messiah as Spokesmen of Rabbinic Ideology," in Magnus Zetterholm, ed., *The Messiah in Early Judaism and Christianity* (Minneapolis: Fortress Press, 2007), 57–58 (most specifically, 65–67).

13. Emil Schurer, *The History of the Jewish People in the Age of Jesus Christ (175 BC–AD 135)*, vol. 11, New English Version, rev. and ed. Geza Vermes, Fergus Millar, and Matthew Black (Edinburgh: T&T Clark, 1979), 514–46.

14. As to the historicity of this account, see Evans, *Jesus and His Contemporaries*, 183–212.

15. For further discussion of Jewish beliefs about the Messiah in the Tannaitic period, see Neusner, *Messiah in Context*; William Horbury, *Jewish Messianism and the Cult of Christ* (London: SCM Press, 2012). Note that Horbury sees the importance of messianism in the first two centuries of CE as underscored by the Bar Kochba revolt, Jewish prayers for redemption like the Amidah, as well as references to the Messiah found in the Targums.

16. Others understand this to mean from creation to Sinai, despite shortening the period of Adam to Sinai to just 2,000 years.

17. All citations from the Babylonian Talmud are adapted from Jacob Neusner, *The Babylonian Talmud: A Translation and Commentary* (Peabody, MA: Hendrickson Publishers, 2011).

18. Rashi interprets this to mean swiftly or slowly.

19. There is debate concerning the Messianic Era and the world to come. Are they synonymous, or does the world to come follow the Messianic Era? See further, below, to Ex Rab 15:21.

20. Summarizing rabbinic interpretation of Mic 5:1 (2 in most Eng. versions), Rabbi Yitzchok Stavsky, *Trei Asar: The Twelve Prophets: Micah, Nahum, Habakkuk, Zephaniah, Haggai, Zechariah, Malachi*, ArtScroll Tanach Series, vol. 2 (Brooklyn: Mesorah Publications, 2009), 37, notes that, "the Talmud explains that the name of the Messiah was one of the seven things that God created before He created the world (*Rashi; Mahari Kara* from *Pesachim* 54a). [See also *Pirkei D'Rabbi Eliezer* chap. 3.] *Ran* (*Nedarim* 39b) explains that the existence of the world depends on these seven things. God therefore created them before He created the world. *Malbim* adds that the entire purpose of creation is the perfection of the human race, which will not occur until Messianic times." According to Joseph Klausner, *The Messianic Idea in Israel* (New York: MacMillan, 1955), 460–61, when the Talmud speaks of the preexistence of the Messiah's name it means "the *idea* of the Messiah, or, more exactly, *the idea of redemption through the Messiah*. This idea did precede Creation. Before Creation, Israel was predestined to produce from itself a Messiah, to be redeemed by him, and through him to redeem all mankind from evil in the world" (emphasis his). Cf. 1 Pet 1:19-20; Rev 13:8b.

21. For two interesting references to the Messiah and King Hezekiah, see b. Sanh 98b; b. Ber 28b.

22. According to the Schottenstein Talmud (*Sanhedrin*, vol. 8, 98a5), "They [namely, those sitting with Messiah] were afflicted with *tzaraas*—a disease whose symptoms include discolored patches on the skin (see *Leviticus* ch. 13). The Messiah himself is likewise afflicted, as stated in *Isaiah* (53:4): . . . *Indeed, it was our diseases that he bore and our*

pains that he endured, whereas we considered him plagued (i.e. suffering *tzaraas* [see 98b, note 39] *smitten by God, and afflicted*. This verse teaches that the diseases that the people ought to have suffered because of their sins are borne instead by the Messiah" (their emphasis).

23. Meaning, they prophesied only of the messianic kingdom, not the world to come.

24. Maimonides espouses this latter view, for which see the article "The Messiah in Medieval Rabbinic Literature" in this book.

25. It is not clear if miraculous descriptions of the world to come refer to the Messianic Era or to the following era in b. Ket 111b or y. Taan 64a (among others).

26. The primary midrashim treated here are Mekhilta deRabbi Ishmael; Sifra; Sifre Numbers; Sifre Deuteronomy; and Midrash Rabbah (Five Books of Moses and the Five Scrolls). Treated in the article "The Messiah in Medieval Rabbinic Literature" in this book are Pesikta de Rav Kahana, Pesikta Rabbati, and Midrash Tanchuma among others. There is, however, chronological overlap among these different texts, especially in collections like Yalkut Shimoni, which cites both early and late midrashim.

27. Cf. Neusner, *Messiah in Context*, 134.

28. Ibid., 137.

29. The Soncino translation was used here.

30. Note that "Messiah" is spelled *mšwḥ* rather than *mšyḥ*.

31. Alfred Edersheim, *The Life and Times of Jesus the Messiah* (New York: Longmans, Green, and Co., 1896), 2:710.

32. See Robert H. Gundry, *The Use of the Old Testament in St. Matthew's Gospel, with Special Reference to the Messianic Hope* (Supplements to Novum Testamentum 18; Leiden, Netherlands: Brill, 1967), who compares ancient rabbinic interpretation of Scripture to the use of the Tanakh in the Dead Sea Scrolls and in Matthew's Gospel.

33. Edersheim, *Life and Times of Jesus the Messiah*, 716; see ibid., 710–41, for further references.

34. For a collection of relevant studies to the Messiah in ancient rabbinic literature, see Leo Landman, ed., *Messianism in the Talmudic Era* (New York: Ktav Publishing House, 1979).

Targums, the New Testament, and Biblical Theology of the Messiah[1]

MICHAEL B. SHEPHERD

Renewed interest in the Targums, the ancient Rabbinic paraphrases of the Hebrew Bible into Aramaic, and their relationship to the New Testament was ignited by three events during the mid-20th century: Paul Kahle's publication of fragments from the Cairo Geniza, the discovery of Targums at Qumran, and Alejandro Díez Macho's discovery of *Targum Neofiti*.[2] Parallel to these developments in biblical studies was the research on the supposed Aramaic substratum of the NT.[3] Initially there was a great deal of excitement over the possible pre-Christian dating of the Palestinian Targums. But eventually the smoke cleared, and the last 30 years have now seen a substantial amount of reevaluation of the evidence.

Regardless of the dates of the extant Targums, it is universally recognized that targumic tradition goes back to a very early period and that the Targums display similar methods of exegesis to those of the NT.[4] Of course, this does not mean that the NT authors were necessarily dependent upon the Targums,[5] but there does seem to be what Martin McNamara has called "convergence of evidence" when the conceptual frameworks and readings of biblical texts are compared. Much work has been done on the shared thought world of the Targums and the NT.[6] But perhaps the more fruitful research problem is still that of what can be tied down to specific texts. The Targumists and NT authors were not textual critics seeking to establish original readings, but they were interpreters of Scripture, and it is in this regard that they both show remarkable insight into the Hebrew Bible.

The thesis here is that the Targums and the NT exegete Scripture messianically.[7]

That is, they both tend to "disambiguate" messianic texts. The Targums most often do this through the use of the title "the Messiah" (*mashiyakha'*). The NT, on the other hand, is unique in its application of messianic texts to Jesus. These messianic readings are rooted in the text of the Hebrew Bible itself. The messianic link between the Targums and the NT is of special importance for biblical theology—a discipline that has historically been concerned, among other things, with the NT's messianic use of Scripture.

The present article falls into three main sections. The first section provides a brief discussion of the dating of the Targums to expose any otherwise unstated assumptions about directionality in their relationship to the NT. The second section examines the synagogue tradition common both to the Targums and the NT. The third and final section works through specific examples of similar exegetical practice as applied to messianic texts. It is believed that this course of study deepens understanding not only of the Targums and the NT, but also of the composition of the Hebrew Bible.

DATING THE TARGUMS

Over against Gustaf Dalman and E. Y. Kutscher, Paul Kahle argued that *Targum Onkelos* (Pentateuch) had little to do with the spoken Aramaic of first-century Palestine—being instead a literary production of Babylonia that was introduced to Palestine only in the medieval period.[8] On the other hand, Kahle believed that *Targum Jonathan* (Prophets) contained old midrashic elements, even though it also received its known form in Babylonia.[9] Of greater interest to Kahle, however, were what he thought to be representatives more or less of Palestinian Aramaic: the Cairo Geniza fragments, the *Fragmentary Targum*, *Targum Pseudo-Jonathan*, and *Targum Neofiti*—all pentateuchal.[10] The Kahle School has often been chided for speaking of a single Palestinian Targum instead of a multiplicity of Palestinian Targums, but Kahle himself admitted that the Palestinian Targum was never official or uniform; "there were always different texts in existence."[11] Kahle held that the pre-mishnaic features of the Palestinian Targum as represented by *Targum Neofiti* indicated that they were in circulation by the second century BC in essentially the same form as the manuscript discovered by Macho.[12] Kahle pulled no punches in his statement of the significance of this:

> In the Palestinian Targum of the Pentateuch we have in the main material coming from pre-Christian times which must be studied by everyone who wishes to understand the state of Judaism at the time of the birth of Christianity. And we possess this material in a language of which we can say that it is very similar to

> that spoken by the earliest Christians. It is material the importance of which can scarcely be exaggerated.[13]

Others were not so sure about Kahle's conclusions, although everyone appreciated the value of the new discoveries. Macho dated the text reproduced by the 16th-century copy of *Targum Neofiti*, which he found miscataloged in the Vatican library as *Targum Onkelos*, to only the second century AD—a date still too early for McNamara.[14] Nevertheless, McNamara believed that the later additions and recensional emendations were "the exception and do not invalidate the arguments in favour of an early date for the bulk of the material."[15] For McNamara, this early date was maintained by the relationship of the Targums to the NT.

The Cairo Geniza fragments are also relatively late, dating to about the eighth or ninth century AD. According to Matthew Black, however, "the comparatively late date of the manuscripts has nothing to do with the date of the translation."[16] For example, the agreement between the Cairo Geniza fragments and *Targum Neofiti* on the *halakha* of Ex 22:5-6 over against the Jewish authorities demonstrates the preservation of a non-official reading over at least eight centuries.[17] This is, of course, not unprecedented. The discovery of the second Isaiah scroll in Qumran Cave 1 illustrates a remarkable ability to preserve not only oral, but also written tradition, since the manuscript essentially agrees with the medieval Masoretic tradition.[18] Indeed, the discovery of Targums to Leviticus and Job at Qumran necessitates the consideration of not only oral, but also written targumic renderings that are pre-Christian.

It might be asked at this point what criteria can be used to isolate pre-Christian renderings when dealing with late manuscripts. For the purposes of this article, the unlikely mass production of new messianic renderings in the wake of Jewish-Christian polemics is certainly relevant. This is not to say that the Jewish community abandoned its messianic hopes after the first century. It is only to say that there is considerable evidence for a Jewish consolidation against a messianic Tanakh as employed by the Christians.[19] This article is primarily interested in adducing parallels between the Targums and the NT. Whether or not there is dependence between the two on a given messianic rendering, the fact remains that a messianic theology of the Hebrew Scriptures is shared by two markedly different sources.

In conclusion, one of the most balanced approaches to the dating of the Targums has been provided by A. D. York.[20] Against Kahle, York argues that anti-mishnaic does not necessarily mean pre-mishnaic.[21] Moreover, York points out that *Targum Neofiti*, *Targum Onkelos*, and *Targum Jonathan* all have messianic renderings (e.g., Nm 24:17; Mic 5:2); so why is *Targum Neofiti* alone considered early on this basis?[22] Why not speak of a proto-Palestinian Targum and a proto-*Onkelos*?[23] There is no need to dichotomize the Palestinian and Babylonian traditions. Both contain old material and evidence of early written Targums.[24] Stephen Kaufman has built on York's work to say that "the language of the Palestinian Targum [though no earlier than the third century AD] is still our best guide to the spoken dialect of first century Galilee" (the literary language reflects an earlier colloquial language, contra McNamara who argued that the Palestinian Targum was colloquial itself).[25] For Kaufman, the best picture of written Aramaic antecedents of the NT can be gained from the literary dialects of Qumran and *Onkelos-Jonathan*.[26] Thus, even though most of the known Targums in their final forms are later than the first century AD, many of them have something to say about the exegesis and Aramaic of pre-Christian times.

THE SYNAGOGUE TRADITION

The early church shared the synagogue tradition of the centrality of Scripture exposition in public worship (e.g., 1Tm 4:13).[27] This tradition can be traced at least as far back as Neh 8:8 where it is said that the Levites read the book, the Torah of God, "translating" it for the people. The reading was then accompanied by "giving the meaning so that the people could understand." In this case, the reading was not followed by translation, but by interpretation. The types of interpretations that were later worked into the Aramaic translations have been well documented,[28] but *derashic* techniques can also be located in the composition of the Bible itself.[29] For example, the relationship between the 318 men of Gn 14:14 and the man Eliezer in Gn 15:2 is forged by *gematria* (Eliezer = 318). The identification of Sheshak with Babylon in Jer 51:41 is made known through *atbash*,[30] and so on.

As for the Targums themselves, there is some debate over the reason for the use of Aramaic. A common view is that Hebrew was no longer spoken, necessitating a translation in the vernacular of the people. Others, such as James Barr, have contended that some form of Hebrew was still spoken when the targumic tradition began.[31] According to C. Rabin, the rabbinic literature never limits the reading of Aramaic to those who do not know Hebrew, as it does with the reading of Greek.[32] Rabin believes there is another explanation for the Aramaic:

> In the synagogue, explanations had to be brief and clear, and closely linked to each verse; they also had to be complete, as no dialogue between teacher and taught was possible. A paraphrase into Hebrew was impossible, because the uninstructed could easily take the paraphrase as part of the sacred text. The difference between the mixed language and pure biblical Hebrew was hardly such that it would assure the clear distinction, at speaking speed, between the two kinds of text. It was therefore an almost ideal way out of the difficulty to provide

> the explanations in a literary language, transitional Aramaic, which was no doubt widely understood, resembling both spoken mishnaic Hebrew and spoken Aramaic, but almost word for word clearly set off from its Hebrew equivalents.[33]

The transposed Hebrew words, Hebraisms, and midrashic expansions within the Targums all presuppose knowledge of the Hebrew original.[34] Therefore, a Targum has more value as an ancient commentary on the Hebrew text—"a guide to the correct understanding of a Hebrew text for those who already understood the words"—than as a translation.[35] Rabin has not been alone with this perspective,[36] yet he is confronted with at least one difficulty: the explanation of the Scripture reading was already set apart by the fact that it was given by someone other than the reader—a *meturgeman*.[37] Furthermore, the *meturgeman* was not allowed to read the explanation from a written text, making the separation from the canonical text even more evident.[38] Thus, the change from Hebrew to Aramaic would have only enhanced an already clear distinction, if in fact this was the purpose for the Aramaic. Nevertheless, Rabin's view on the whole is most probably correct. It is certainly difficult to disprove the existence of spoken Hebrew in the postexilic period. Moreover, that the Targums go well beyond mere translation is recognized by all.[39] In this regard, the Targums have much in common with the NT. The NT authors are much more interested in the explanation of Scripture than they are in word-for-word translation or "text-critical" establishment of the original text.[40]

The synagogue and the targumic tradition helped to solidify the shift from Temple to text in the postexilic Jewish community. By the first century AD, the average Jewish person was more familiar with rabbinic teachings and targumic renderings than with apocalyptic literature or the sectarian literature of Qumran.[41] The synagogue made the Targums part of the weekly life of the Jewish people. In Ac 15:21 it is said, "For since ancient times, Moses has had those who proclaim him in every city, and every Sabbath day he is read aloud in the synagogues." The Targums were perhaps in a position to influence the NT authors more than any other literature. It has even been suggested that the Syriac Peshitta was originally a kind of Targum for Jews that was later taken over by the Christian Church.[42]

The NT itself contains a number of accounts connected to a synagogue. Luke's unique and programmatic account of Jesus' reading of Isa 61 is among these (Lk 4:16-30). The passage does not indicate whether or not Jesus was prompted, it only says that He "stood up to read" (Lk 4:16). An Isaiah scroll was handed to Him, and Jesus Himself found His text (Lk 4:17). Presumably a reading from the Pentateuch preceded Jesus' reading. Regardless, Jesus' own reading met the requirements for reading the Prophets to an interpreter:

> He who reads in the Law may not read less than three verses. He may not read to the interpreter more than one verse at a time, or, in the Prophets, not more than three verses. But if these three are three separate paragraphs, he must read them out one by one. They may leave out verses in the Prophets, but not in the Law.[43]

The *meturgeman* is never mentioned in Luke's account, yet the insertion of Isa 58:6 in Lk 4:18 (Isa 61:1) would not have been the prerogative of the reader. It is possible that Luke himself has become the Targumist at this point. Moreover, it is easy to see why the *meturgeman* never had a chance to interpret Jesus' reading. Jesus closed the scroll, returned it "to the attendant, and sat down" (Lk 4:20). Then He said, "Today as you listen, this Scripture has been fulfilled" (Lk 4:21). It is interesting that Jesus refers to Himself as an unwelcome prophet in Lk 4:24. *Targum Jonathan* begins Isa 61:1 in the following way: "The prophet says, 'The spirit of prophecy from before the LORD God is upon me.'" Apparently, it was this self-designation that drove the entire scene from the synagogue to the cliff (Lk 4:29).

Another synagogue scene worthy of mention appears in Ac 13:13-41. Paul and Barnabas enter a synagogue at Pisidian Antioch on a Sabbath day (Ac 13:14). After the reading of both the Law and the Prophets (cf. Lk 4:17), Paul and Barnabas, not the *meturgeman*, are invited to offer a "word of exhortation" (Ac 13:15 NASB; cf. Heb 13:22). Paul's subsequent sermon is reminiscent of Stephen's speech in Ac 7:2-53, and both are reminiscent of Neh 9:5-37—a passage that also follows a reading of the Law (Neh 8:8). All three of these texts provide targumic interpretations of what is largely a pentateuchal history. They all apply Scripture to the current situation (Neh 9:32-37; Ac 7:51-53; 13:38-41).

EXAMPLES OF EXEGESIS

1. *Genesis 1:1. Targum Neofiti* reads, "In the beginning, with wisdom, the Son of Yahweh created the heavens and the earth." The Targum is not alone in its indication of wisdom as the means by which God created. Jeremiah 10:12; 51:15 says that He established the world (*tevel*) by His wisdom (*bechakhmato*). In Ps 104:24 the psalmist says, "How countless are Your works, LORD! In wisdom [*bechakhma*] You have made them all." Proverbs 8:22-31 says that wisdom was at the Lord's side as a "skilled craftsman" (*'amon*) when the heavens were established.

The Targum also finds support within the book of Proverbs for its understanding of the Son's role in creation. Proverbs 30:4 reveals that the one who established all the ends of the earth has a Son. It is difficult to say what the relationship of the Targum to Prv 30:4 is, but what does seem certain is that the Targum is engaged in a fascinating exegesis of the word *bara'*. In the Hebrew text of Gn 1:1, *bara'* clearly means "he created." But in Aramaic *bara'* can also be *bar* ("son") plus the suffixed definite article *'* ("the"). The Targum features this Aramaic option and adds *shkll* for "he created" (or "he finished/decorated").

New Testament Christology picks up the thread of the above-mentioned texts. For instance, 1Co 1:30 says Christ "became God-given wisdom for us." First Corinthians 8:6 speaks of Christ as the one "by whom are all things" [NASB]. Colossians 1:15 calls the Son of God "the firstborn over all creation." Just as wisdom in Prv 8:22 says, "The LORD begot me at the beginning [*re'shiyt*, HCSB footnote]," so Col 1:18 refers to the Son as "the beginning" (*arche*). Hebrews 1:2 says that God made the world through His Son.

But perhaps more than any of these NT texts, it is the opening of John's prologue that best passes as an actual reference to Gn 1:1.[44] John 1:1 signals this with the phrase "in the beginning" (*en arche*). The phrase is repeated in Jn 1:2 where the Word is again said to have been with God in the beginning (cf. Prv 8:22-31). McNamara has made a study of the conceptual influence of the Targums on John's prologue with particular regard to the way the Targums use the terms "Word" (*Memra*), "Dwelling" (*Shekinta*), and "Glory" (*Yeqara*) as substitutes for "the LORD."[45] McNamara comments:

> Present-day scholars tend to reject the targumic Memra as a background to, or contributing factor towards, John's doctrine of the *Logos*. This they prefer to see prepared in the prophetic word (*dabar*) and in the Wisdom literature. This neglect of targumic evidence is unfortunate. Granted that the *Memra* of God and the Lord is but another way of saying 'God' or 'the Lord', it by no means follows that John was not influenced by targumic usage in his choice of Logos as a designation for Christ. For John, too, 'the Word was God' (Jn 1:1). John got his doctrine on the nature of the Logos from the New Testament revelation. The question at issue for us is the sources from which he drew the concepts and terms in which he expressed it.[46]

For John, the Word is also the Son of God (Jn 1:14; 3:16). Thus, both *Targum Neofiti* of Gn 1:1 and Jn 1:1-3 identify the Son as the agent of creation in Gn 1:1.

2. *Genesis 3:15.* The *Fragmentary Targum*, *Targum Pseudo-Jonathan*, and *Targum Neofiti* all cast Gn 3:15 as an opposition between the descendants of the woman and the descendants of the serpent, in which the woman's descendants strike the serpent's head in keeping the commandments of the law, and in which failure to keep the commandments is identified with the woman's descendants being bit in the heel.[47] There is no cure for the serpent, but there is a cure for the heel "in the day of King Messiah." It is noteworthy that this Palestinian tradition does not identify the seed as an individual in accordance with the Hebrew Bible (Gn 12:1-7; 27:29; 49:8; Nm 24:9). Nevertheless, it does read Gn 3:15 messianically.

The Hebrew text of Gn 3:15 employs the verb "to bruise" (*shuf*, NKJV), which only occurs in two other passages (Ps 139:11 NASB footnote; Job 9:17 NASB). The verb *shuf* is more common in Aramaic in either the sense "to blow" or the sense "to rub off."[48] It is no surprise then that the Targums find another word, but it is remarkable that the word chosen does not mean "to bruise." It is rather "to strike" (*mchy*). The source of this choice is not difficult to trace. The ancient poem of Gn 3:14-19 shares a common theme with other relatively ancient poems in the Hebrew Bible—that of striking the head of the enemy. Numbers 24:17 says that the star from Jacob, the scepter from Israel, will strike (*machats*, HCSB "smash") the forehead of Moab. Judges 5:26 says that Jael crushed (*machats*) the head of Sisera and pierced the temple of his head. Habakkuk 3:13 says that the Lord goes "out to save" His people with His Messiah and strikes (*machats*, HCSB "crush") the head of the house of the wicked. In Ps 68:22, God crushes (*machats*) the head of His enemies (cf. Ps 110:6).

Paul picks up this theme in Rom 16:20 where he says, "The God of peace will soon crush [*suntribo*] Satan under your feet." According to Hatch and Redpath, the verb *suntribo* never translates *machats* in the Septuagint. Nevertheless, Paul's allusion to Gn 3:15 is unmistakable. The ending of Romans is riddled with textual difficulties, but the evidence appears to favor the inclusion of "The grace of our Lord Jesus be with you" in Rom 16:20. This comes across as somewhat of a premature conclusion to the epistle, but it fits well with the targumic understanding of Gn 3:15. Both Paul and the Palestinian Targum tradition associate the defeat of the enemy and the deliverance of God's people with the time of the Messiah. For Paul, the Messiah is none other than the Lord Jesus.

3. *Genesis 49:1, 8-12.* McNamara has drawn attention to two passages of the Palestinian Targum tradition (Gn 49:1; Nm 24:3,15) in which it is said that something about the Messiah has been withheld.[49] *Targum Pseudo-Jonathan* indicates that "the definite time of the future in which King Messiah is to come was hidden from him [Jacob]." This perspective on the time of the Messiah is shared by 1Pt 1:10-11: "Of this salvation the prophets have inquired and searched carefully, who prophesied of the grace that would come to you, searching what, or what manner of time, the Spirit of Christ who was in them was indicating when He testified beforehand the sufferings of Christ and the glories that would follow" (NKJV). The Palestinian Targums of Nm 24:3,15 seem to be saying that the vision of the Messiah in Nm 24:17 was given to Balaam, but not to the prophets. Likewise, Jesus says that many prophets and righteous men desired to see and hear what was happening in His time, but did not (Mt 13:17; Lk 10:24).

Genesis 49:10 has the enigmatic phrase *'ad kiy yavo shiyloh.* If *shiyloh* is understood as a proper noun, then it is, "until Shiloh comes." If *shiyloh* is understood as the relative particle (*sh*) plus preposition and pronoun (*loh*), then it is, "until the one to whom it belongs comes." *Targum Onkelos* removes the ambiguity and renders, "until the Messiah to whom the kingdom belongs comes."[50] The imagery of this passage—specifically Gn 49:11—is picked up later in Isa 63:2 and again in Rev 19:13,15. John says that the individual is the called "the Word of God" (Rev 19:13), "King of kings," and "Lord of lords" (Rev 19:16 ESV).

4. *Numbers 24:17.* Numbers 24 contains a number of links to Gn 49 and Dt 33, not the least of which are the phrase "at the end of the days" (*be'achariyt hayamiym*) and the expression "he [the king] lies down like a lion or like a lioness—who dares to rouse him?" (see Gn 49:9; Nm 24:9,14; 33:20).[51] The Hebrew text of Nm 24:17b can be translated, "A star treads from Jacob,[52] and a scepter rises from Israel;[53] and he strikes the forehead of Moab, and he tears down all the sons of Sheth."[54] *Targum Onkelos* removes any ambiguity occasioned by the mention of a star from Jacob: "The King will rise from Jacob, and the Messiah will be exalted from Israel; and he will slay the nobles of Moab, and he will rule over all the children of humanity." It has been suggested that the replacement of "Sheth" with "the children of humanity" (*beney 'enosh'* is dependent on Gn 4:25-26, where Sheth's son is called Enosh or "human"). *Targum Pseudo-Jonathan* reads, "A mighty King will rule from the house of Jacob, and the Messiah will be exalted, a mighty scepter from Israel; and he will slay the nobles of the Moabites, and he will empty all the children of Sheth. . . ."[55]

In Mt 2:2, the wise men ask, "Where is the one born King of the Jews? For we have seen his star in the east, and we have come to worship him" (author's translation). The account comes in the midst of Matthew's barrage of fulfillment quotations by means of which he demonstrates that Jesus is the Messiah of the Scriptures. The star is unique to Matthew, and he directly associates it with the King of the Jews, just as the Targums substitute "King" for "star" in Nm 24:17. *Testimonia* from Cave 4 (4Q175), which was current in Matthew's day, brings Nm 24:15-17 together with Dt 5:28-29; 18:18-19; 33:8-11; and Jos 6:26.

In Rev 22:16, Jesus says, "I, Jesus, have sent My angel to testify these things to you for the churches. I am the Root and the Offspring of David, the Bright Morning Star." Jesus' identification of Himself as "the root and progeny of David" hearkens back to Isa 11:1,10. He is the King of the targumic Nm 24:17 and of Mt 2:2. Unlike Mt 2:2, however, Jesus does not simply *have* a star in Rev 22:16; He *is* the star. Earlier in Rev 2:26-28, Jesus promises to give the authority of Ps 2:8-9 and the morning star to the one who overcomes. Thus, messianic texts that are normally applied to Jesus are here applied to believers.[56] The Messiah will reign, but the saints will reign with Him (Rev 5:10). This is the same picture of the future kingdom portrayed in Dan 7:14,27. The Targums and the NT agree. The star of Nm 24:17 is the King, the Messiah. The NT goes two steps further and applies the text to Jesus and His saints.

5. *Isaiah 52:13–53:12.* That the fourth servant song of Isaiah is applied to Jesus

by the NT authors is certainly not news to anyone. But the individual, messianic interpretation of this text was often overshadowed in pre-Christian interpretation by a corporate/national understanding of the servant of the Lord. The one outstanding exception to this is the Targum of Isaiah. Donald Gowan comments:

> In Judaism he [the Messiah] is not expected to suffer and die an atoning death, for atonement is made in other ways. One of these later texts is revealing enough to be worth noting; it is the Targum of Isaiah which, unlike earlier Jewish literature, does identify the Servant as the Messiah. But, having done so, it must then make drastic changes in the meaning of the text, for the Messiah does not suffer; he triumphs. In place of, "He was despised and rejected by men," the Targum reads, "Then shall the glory of all the kingdoms be despised and come to an end," and rather than being described as "like a lamb that is led to slaughter," it is said of him: "The mighty ones of the peoples shall he deliver up like a lamb to the slaughter" (Isa 53:3, 7).[57]

Whenever the Targum speaks of exaltation, the individual Messiah is in view (e.g., Isa 52:13). Whenever the Targum speaks of suffering, a nation is in view. For example, the disfigured appearance in Isa 52:14 is that of the house of Israel, not that of the Messiah. On the other hand, the appearance of the Messiah in Isa 53:2 is not that of an ordinary man, but a holy countenance. The individual servant who suffers as a substitute for the people (e.g. Isa 53:4-5,11) is replaced by an individual who builds up the house of an afflicted, yet holy people.

What is remarkable about all of this is the tension sustained between the meaning of the Hebrew text and the prevailing messianic tradition. The Targumist could not avoid the fact that the Hebrew text spoke of an individual servant who would act on behalf of the people. But according to tradition this individual was not to suffer vicariously. Instead of choosing one over the other, the Targumist attempts to accommodate both.

Like the Targum of Isaiah, Jesus and the NT authors identify the servant of Isa 52:13–53:12 as an individual messianic figure. But unlike the Targum, the NT views this figure as a suffering servant. Quoting Isa 53:12 Jesus says, "For I tell you that this which is written must be fulfilled in Me, 'and he was numbered with transgressors'; for that which refers to Me has its fulfillment" (Lk 22:37 NASB). Here Jesus interprets the servant of Isa 52:13–53:12 to be an individual, suffering servant; and He identifies Himself as that servant. When Philip encounters the Ethiopian eunuch reading Isa 53:7-8 (Ac 8:27-39), he does not give the targumic interpretation that says the Messiah will deliver up the mighty ones of the peoples to be slaughtered like a lamb. No, he begins from this Scripture and proclaims Jesus to him (Ac 8:35).

There can be no doubt where Peter stood on the possibility of a suffering

Messiah. Faced with the plain meaning of Isa 52:13–53:12, the reality of the cross, and the coming of the Spirit, Peter speaks of the sinlessness of Christ from Isa 53:9 (1Pt 2:22) and of His death for "our sins" from Isa 53:5 (1Pt 2:24). For Peter (unlike the Targum), the people are not merely afflicted victims. They are wandering sheep (Isa 53:6) in need of a shepherd (1Pt 2:25). Thus, the NT and the Targum agree that Isa 52:13–53:12 speaks of an individual, but they do not agree that the passage speaks of a suffering individual.

6. *Micah 5:2*. The Hebrew text of Mic 5:2 can be translated: "As for you, Bethlehem Ephrathah, too little to be among the tribes of Judah, from you for me he will go out to be a ruler in Israel; and his goings forth are from aforetime, from days of antiquity" (author's translation). The identity of the ruler is of immediate interest; namely, the subject of the verb "he will go out" (*yatsa '*). The ruler is said to be "from" Bethlehem, so the possibility of Bethlehem being in some sense a ruler over Israel is excluded. Although the ruler is further described in Mic 5:3-5a, there is no explicit referent given for him in the immediate context.

Targum Jonathan renders Mic 5:2 as follows: "As for you, Bethlehem Ephrath, you were too little to be numbered among the tribes of the house of Judah. From you before me the Messiah will go out to be a servant, a ruler (or "a servant of rulership") over Israel, whose name has been spoken from the beginning, from days of antiquity." Besides the insertion of "the Messiah," there appears to be a reference to the servant of Isaiah and a reference to *Targum Neofiti's* "from the beginning" of Gn 1:1. Is there any warrant for identifying the ruler here as the Messiah? One possibility is that the Targumist has taken "Bethlehem" as a link to Ru 4:11 and the Davidic genealogy in Ru 4:17-22. The author of Micah has already expressed interest in a coming king (Mic 2:12-13), an interest that is aligned with the hope of a Davidic king within the Book of the Twelve (the Minor Prophets) as a whole (Hos 3:4-5). Moreover, the language of Mic 5:3-5a is that of the Messiah and messianic kingdom found elsewhere. For example, the ruler's reign is said to be "to the ends of the earth" in both Mic 5:4b and Zch 9:10b. Also, the association of "peace" with the messianic kingdom is found in many passages such as Isa 9:6; Mic 5:5a; and Zch 9:10a.

Matthew 2:4-6 takes Mic 5:2 to be a prophecy about the birthplace of the Messiah. But Matthew's text is very much different from the extant Hebrew, Aramaic, and Greek texts of Mic 5:2. Matthew does not say that Bethlehem is "too little," but that Bethlehem is "by no means the littlest/least." Matthew has thus removed the irony of the passage in order to focus on Bethlehem's significance as the birthplace of the Messiah. Matthew has also forged a wordplay between "among the rulers of Judah" (*en tois egemosin Iouda*) and "a ruler will go out" (*exeleusetai hegoumenos*). Finally, Matthew has moved the description of the ruler in Mic 5:4 to the position of Mic 5:2b in the form of 2Sm 5:2; 1Chr 11:2. However these textual issues are resolved, what is clear is that both *Targum Jonathan* and Matthew, two texts with very different purposes, have located the Messiah in Mic 5:2. In more ways than one, the text of Mic 5:2-5a has invited this messianic exegesis.

CONCLUSION

As stated in the opening paragraphs of this article, the Targums and the NT exegete Scripture messianically. In other words, the Targums and the NT both have a biblical theology of the Messiah. It is highly unlikely that Judaism after the first century AD produced such a rash of messianic renderings that coincided with the very texts that formed the heart of Christian exegesis. Perhaps the NT authors were influenced in some way by targumic renderings, but some measure of independence has to be allowed. The solution probably lies somewhere between these two options. In any case, the exegetical work of these separate corpora highlights the messianic theology of the Hebrew Bible itself.

It is difficult to overstate the significance of the synagogue tradition shared by the Targums and the early church. The postexilic Jewish community and the early Christian community were characterized by gatherings around the teaching of Scripture (Ac 2:42) during which messianic theology was expounded. This is not to say, of course, that there is no difference between the Targums and the NT. It is equally difficult to overstate the significance of the NT's application of messianic texts to Jesus. This is clearly where the Targums and the NT part ways. Nevertheless, the Targums are in a position to inform scholars not only text-critically, but also in regard to the history of interpretation preceding the NT. Clearly, the Targums and the NT both reflect the ancient Jewish understanding of the Hebrew Bible as a messianic text.

---

1. This article is adapted from "Targums, the New Testament and Biblical Theology of the Messiah" *Journal of the Evangelical Theological Society* 51.1 (March 2008): 45–58. Used with permission.

2. Roger Le Déaut, "The Current State of Targumic Studies," *Biblical Theological Bulletin* 4 (1974): 3–32.

3. E.g., Matthew Black, *An Aramaic Approach to the Gospels and Acts*, 3rd ed. (Oxford: Clarendon, 1967); Joseph A. Fitzmyer, *A Wandering Aramean: Collected Aramaic Essays*, Society for Biblical Literature Monograph Series 25 (Missoula, MT: Scholars Press, 1979); Bruce Chilton, *Targumic Approaches to the Gospels: Essays in the Mutual Definition of Judaism and Christianity* (Lanham, MD: University Press of America, 1986); Max Wilcox, "The Aramaic Background of the New Testament," in *The Aramaic Bible: Targums in Their Historical Context*, ed. D. R. G. Beattie and M. J. McNamara, *Journal for the Study of the Old Testament, Supplement Series* 166 (Sheffield, England: JSOT, 1994), 362–78.

4. Richard N. Longenecker, *Biblical Exegesis in the Apostolic Period*, 2nd ed. (Grand Rapids: Eerdmans, 1999), 8–9.

5. According to G. Vermes, the NT is simply a dated segment in relation to undated material (i.e. the Targums) within a developing tradition (*Jesus and the World of Judaism* [Philadelphia: Fortress, 1983], 85–87).

6. E.g., Roger Le Déaut, *The Message of the New Testament and the Aramaic Bible (Targum)*, trans. Stephen Miletic, Subsidia biblica 5 (Rome: Biblical Institute Press, 1982), 37–43.

7. According to Josep Ribera, *Targum Jonathan* presents the prophet as a teacher of the Torah who announces the coming of the Messiah and the eschatological era ("Prophecy according to Targum Jonathan to the Prophets and the Palestinian Targum to the Pentateuch," trans. Fiona Ritchie in *Targum Studies*, vol. 1, *Textual and Contextual Studies in the Pentateuchal Targums*, ed. Paul V. M. Flesher, South Florida Studies in the History of Judaism 55 [Atlanta: Scholars Press, 1992], 66).

8. Paul Kahle, *The Cairo Geniza*, 2nd ed. (New York: Praeger, 1960), 191–95.

9. Ibid., 195–98.

10. Ibid., 200–208.

11. Ibid., 202.

12. Ibid., 207–8.

13. Ibid., 208.

14. Martin McNamara, *The New Testament and the Palestinian Targum to the Pentateuch*, Analecta Biblica 27 (Rome: Pontifical Biblical Institute, 1966), 45.

15. Ibid., 65–66.

16. Black, *An Aramaic Approach*, 22–23.

17. Ibid., 38–39.

18. Ernst Würthwein, *The Text of the Old Testament*, 2nd ed., trans. Erroll F. Rhodes (Grand Rapids: Eerdmans, 1995), 14.

19. See John H. Sailhamer, "Biblical Theology and the Composition of the Hebrew Bible," in *Biblical Theology: Retrospect and Prospect*, ed. Scott J. Hafemann (Downers Grove, IL: InterVarsity, 2002), 25–37.

20. A. D. York, "The Dating of Targumic Literature," *Journal for the Study of Judaism* 5 (1974), 49–62.

21. Ibid., 52–53.

22. Ibid., 55.

23. Ibid., 56.

24. Ibid., 60–61.

25. Stephen A. Kaufman, "On Methodology in the Study of the Targums and their Chronology," *Journal for the Study of the New Testament* 23 (1985), 123.

26. Ibid.

27. David S. Dockery, *Christian Scripture: An Evangelical Perspective on Inspiration, Authority, and Interpretation* (Nashville: Broadman & Holman, 1995), 152–54.

28. See Philip S. Alexander, "Jewish Aramaic Translations of Hebrew Scriptures," in *Mikra: Text, Translation, Reading and Interpretation of the Hebrew Bible in Ancient Judaism and Early Christianity*, vol. 1, ed. M. J. Mulder, CRINT 2 (Philadelphia: Fortress, 1988), 225–28.

29. See Michael Fishbane, *Biblical Interpretation in Ancient Israel* (Oxford: Oxford University Press, 1985).

30. *Atbash* is a Hebrew code or cypher, which replaces the first letter of the Hebrew alphabet with the last letter; the second letter is replaced with the next-to-last letter; etc. Thus, Sheshak is substituted for Babel (Babylon).

31. James Barr, *Comparative Philology and the Text of the Old Testament* (Oxford: Oxford University Press, 1968; repr. with additions and corrections, Winona Lake, IN: Eisenbrauns, 1987), 38–43.

32. C. Rabin, "Hebrew and Aramaic in the First Century," in *The Jewish People in the First Century*, vol. 2, ed. S. Safrai and M. Stern, CRINT 1 (Philadelphia: Fortress, 1976), 1030.

33. Ibid.

34. Ibid., 1031–32.

35. Ibid., 1032; "The fact that its language differed greatly from the spoken Aramaic of those whom it served, that it was artificial and bristled with semantic difficulties, did therefore not matter" (ibid.).

36. E.g., Ernest G. Clarke, "Jacob's Dream at Bethel as Interpreted in the Targums and the New Testament," *Studies in Religion* 4 (1974–75), 369; Michael G. Steinhauser, "The Targums and the New Testament," *Toronto Journal of Theology* 2 (1986), 264.

37. A religious official who translated the Hebrew Bible into the vernacular as it was being read in Hebrew.

38. E. Lévine, "The Biography of the Aramaic Bible," *Zeitschrift für die alttestamentliche Wissenschaft* 94 (1982), 374.

39. "The Targums, like LXX, followed the Hebrew text verse by verse, but they incorporated in the representation of the text a great deal of explanation and interpretation. Thus, the text and its interpretation were woven together, and the interpretation often extended and amplified the text greatly" (John Bowker, *The Targums and Rabbinic Literature: An Introduction to Jewish Interpretations of Scripture* [London: Cambridge University Press, 1969], 8).

40. Contra those who view the quotations in the NT as the text-critical work of the Holy Spirit, the textual critic par excellence; the presence of different citations of the same verse is enough to dispel this view (e.g., Rom 1:17; Gal 3:6; Heb 10:38).

41. Martin McNamara, *Targum and Testament, Aramaic Paraphrases of the Hebrew Bible: A Light on the New Testament* (Grand Rapids: Eerdmans, 1972), 19.

42. Kahle, *The Cairo Geniza* 266, 272–73.

43. *Mishnah Megillah* 4:4.

44. See Peder Borgen, "Observations on the Targumic Character of the Prologue of John," *New Testament Studies* 16 (1969–70), 288–95.

45. McNamara, *Targum and Testament* 98–106; all three terms occur together in John 1:14: "And the Word became flesh and dwelt among us, and we beheld his glory. . . ."

46. Ibid. 102–3; see also Craig A. Evans, *Word and Glory: On the Exegetical and Theological Background of John's Prologue, Journal for the Study of the New Testament, Supplement Series* 89 (Sheffield, England: JSNT, 1993).

47. McNamara sees a parallel here with Rev 12:17 (*The New Testament and the Palestinian Targum*, 221–22).

48. Marcus Jastrow, *Dictionary of the Targumim, Talmud Babli, Yerushalmi and Midrashic Literature* (New York: Judaica, 1903) 1538–39.

49. McNamara, *The New Testament and the Palestinian Targum*, 242–45.

50. The Palestinian tradition has, "until the time of King Messiah to whom the kingdom belongs comes."

51. See John H. Sailhamer, *The Pentateuch as Narrative* (Grand Rapids: Zondervan, 1992) 35–37.

52. The Septuagint, Syriac, and Vulgate all have, "A star shines from Jacob."

53. Cf. Gn 49:10.

54. On the basis of the Samaritan Pentateuch and Jer 48:45, it has been suggested that *qarqar* ("he tears down") should be read *qarqor* ("crown of head").

55. The verb behind "he will empty" (*yrokn*) is graphically related to the verb behind "he tears down" (*qarqar*); *Targum Pseudo-Jonathan* goes on to speak of Gog (cf. Nm 24:7; Ezk 38:2) and the corpses that will fall before the Messiah in the future.

56. The same phenomenon appears to occur with the use of Isa 42:6 in Ac 13:47.

57. Donald E. Gowan, *Bridge between the Testaments: A Reappraisal of Judaism from the Exile to the Birth of Christianity* (Pittsburgh: Pickwick, 1976), 501–2; the Messiah is also identified in the Targum of Isa 42:1.

Messiah in Medieval Jewish Literature

MICHAEL L. BROWN

Medieval Jewish literature builds upon the foundation rabbinic literature provided regarding Judaism's view of the Messiah. In doing so, three distinct developments emerged. The first was the systematic commentary on the sacred texts (note in particular Rashi, Ibn Ezra, and Radak on the Tanakh, and Rashi and Tosafot on the Talmud, all in the 11th to 13th centuries). A second was the codification of rabbinic law (beginning with Maimonides' *Mishneh Torah* in the 12th century, and culminating in Yoseph Karo's *Shulchan Aruch* in the 16th century). Third was the writing of philosophical treatises (beginning with Sa'adiah Gaon's *Emunot veDe'ot* [*Beliefs and Opinions*] in the ninth century, representing the transitional time between the final editing of the Talmud and the emergence of medieval Jewish literature, and including Maimonides' *Moreh Nebukhim* [*Guide for the Perplexed*] and Judah HaLevi's *The Kuzari* in the 12th century).[1]

Of these three, the first two are of particular importance with regard to rabbinic views of the Messiah because the systematic interpretation of the sacred texts, in particular Scripture, clarified the Jewish view of Messiah (or, Messiahs). This perspective was based more on consensus, while the law code of Maimonides directly treated the subject of the Messiah son of David. It is Maimonides' description that has dominated traditional Jewish theology from the 12th century until today.[2] Yet the philosophical treatises also address the question of Messiah. Moreover, during the medieval period the figure of Messiah son of Joseph, mentioned only once in the Talmud (b. Sukkah 52a)[3], comes into greater focus.

As to the importance of the Messiah to these medieval Jewish thinkers,

J. Sarachek writes, "The intense hold which the expectation of the Messiah had on medieval Jewry is evidenced by the fact that its intellectual and spiritual leaders introduced it into their philosophic works, their Halakic codes, their Bible commentaries, their poetry, and their abundant apologetic literature."[4]

MESSIAH SON OF JOSEPH AND MESSIAH SON OF DAVID

According to many rabbinic writings, this age will end with a final conflict between the hostile, Gentile world and the people of Israel (see the article "The Messiah in Rabbinic Literature" in this book). A champion will arise for Israel, the Messiah son of Joseph, and he will fight for Israel with great success before he himself is cut down in the last great war. Afterward, the Messiah son of David, the Messiah *par excellence* in the rabbinic writings, will raise him from the dead, along with others who have died, firmly establishing the messianic kingdom on the earth with Jerusalem as its center.[5] As explained by G. Scholem, "The coming of the Messiah was supposed to shake the foundations of the world. In the view of the prophets and Aggadists, redemption would only follow upon a universal revolutionary disturbance, unparalleled disasters in which history would be dislodged and destroyed."[6]

This picture, however, was not presented with sufficient detail, clarity, or harmony in the Talmud or midrashim, mainly because the Talmud is neither a law code nor a theological textbook. Therefore, in the centuries following the completion of the Babylonian Talmud, Jewish communities wrote to their spiritual leaders looking for clarification. At that time, they not only asked for halachic (legal) clarification; they also requested an explanation of what to expect and believe regarding the Messiah. Therefore, Sa'adiah Gaon addressed the role of the Messiah in his *Beliefs and Opinions*. He explained that if the Jewish people did not repent, then the events concerning the final wars would result in much suffering despite the prowess of Messiah son of Joseph. If they did repent, however, then "Messiah son of David will appear to us suddenly," meaning, without the calamitous suffering and without Messiah son of Joseph (see *Beliefs and Opinions*, Book 8, chaps. 4–5).[7] Hai Gaon (939–1038), the last of the geonim (referring to the leaders of Babylonian Jewry), echoed Sa'adiah's teaching in a responsum. Nevertheless, his need to respond to this question again indicates the lack of clarity in the Talmudic (and related) texts concerning the advent of the era.[8]

There can be no question, however, that the idea of a suffering Messiah was firmly entrenched in Jewish thought, with the Messiah son of Joseph (often identified with Ephraim, the grandson of the patriarch Joseph and the eponymous ancestor of the tribe of Ephraim) playing an important role. Even so, in some texts, it is the Messiah son of David who suffers (see, e.g., b. Sanh 98b). As summarized by R. Patai,

> Despised and afflicted with unhealing wounds, he sits in the gates of Great Rome and winds and unwinds the bandages of his festering sores [with reference to b. Sanh 98b]; as a Midrash expresses it, "pains have adopted him." According to one of the most moving, and at the same time psychologically most meaningful, of all Messiah legends, God, when He created the Messiah, gave him the choice of whether or not to accept the sufferings for the sins of Israel. And the Messiah answered: "I accept it with joy, so that not a single soul of Israel should perish."... In the later, Zoharic formulation of this legend, the Messiah himself summons all the diseases, pains, and sufferings of Israel to come upon him, in order thus to ease the anguish of Israel, which otherwise would be unbearable.[9]

Patai, moreover, believes that there is a conceptual tie between the sufferings of Israel as a people and the sufferings of the Messiah: "There can be little doubt that psychologically the Suffering Messiah is but a projection and personification of Suffering Israel.... And it is undoubtedly true in the psychological sense that, as the Zohar states, the acceptance of Israel's sufferings by the Messiah (read: their projection onto the Messiah) eases that suffering which otherwise could not be endured."[10]

The most extensive picture of the suffering Messiah is found in the ninth-century midrashic work Pesikta Rabbati, chaps. 33–37.[11] There, the Messiah is depicted as preexistent (born when the world was created and mounting "into God's thoughts before the world was made") and is sometimes referred to as Ephraim (or, in full, "Ephraim, My Righteous Messiah"). He suffers in heaven to alleviate Israel's suffering on earth, with verses from Ps 22, an important psalm from the perspective of the NT writers, put on the lips of this suffering Messiah. The Messiah's sufferings will culminate here on earth during the calamitous years at the end of this age:

> The Fathers of the World [Abraham, Isaac, and Jacob] will in the future rise up in the month of Nissan and will speak to him: "Ephraim, our True Messiah! Even though we are your fathers, you are greater than we, for you suffered because of the sins of our children, and cruel punishments have come upon you the like of which have not come upon the early and the later generations, and you were put to ridicule and held in contempt by the nations of the world because of Israel, and you sat in darkness and blackness and your eyes saw no light, and your skin cleft to your bones, and your body dried out was like wood, and your eyes grew dim from fasting, and your strength became like a potsherd. All this because of the sins of our children. Do you want that our children should enjoy the happiness that the Holy One, blessed be He, allotted to Israel, or perhaps, because of the great sufferings that have come upon you on their account, and because they imprisoned you in the jailhouse, your mind is not reconciled with them?" And the Messiah answers them: "Fathers of the World! Everything I did, I did

> only for you and for your children, and for your honor and for the honor of your children, so that they should enjoy this happiness the Holy One, blessed be He, has allotted to Israel."[12]

Pesikta Rabbati also repeats the tradition of two Messiahs, one anointed for war and one anointed King over Israel (Pes. Rab. 8.4; see the article "The Messiah in Ancient Rabbinic Literature" in this book for additional rabbinic references), a tradition reflected in Pesitka d'Rav Kahane 5.9, which speaks of "the priest anointed for war." But Pesitka d'Rav Kahane does not focus on a suffering Messiah. Instead, as Neusner explains, the midrashic collection "brings us into a new and amazing world. Here eschatology forms a prevailing and dominant motif of discourse.... In Pesiqta deR. Kahana, the formulative canonical literature reaches a climax in messianic fervor. Established themes recur, but... a wholly new mood comes to expression, a powerful yearning for the fall of Edom (Rome) and for the coming of the Messiah."[13] And so pervasive is the Messiah's redemptive work that "even where the Messiah in particular plays no role, the larger eschatological framework will now demand his presence and take it for granted."[14]

MAIMONIDES ON THE MESSIAH

Strikingly, there is no mention of a suffering Messiah, let alone a Messiah son of Joseph, in the Law Code of Maimonides. Even so, it is his formulation, reflecting his rationalism, that is most widely cited in terms of traditional Jewish expectations of the Messiah. It was also Maimonides who established belief in the Messiah as one of the 13 principles of Jewish faith. As stated in the poetic, *Ani Ma'amin* ("I believe") formulation, "I believe with complete faith in the coming of the Messiah, and even though he may delay, nevertheless I anticipate every day that he will come."[15]

At the same time, the details of the Messiah's coming were nonessentials of the faith: "Regardless of the debate concerning these questions, neither the order of the occurrence of these events or their precise detail are among the fundamental principles of the faith. A person should not occupy himself with the *Aggadot* and homiletics concerning these and similar matters, nor should he consider them as essentials, for study of them will neither bring fear or love of God" (*Mishneh Torah, Hilkhot Melachim and Milchamotehem* [Laws of Kings and Their Wars], 12:2).[16]

Maimonides, however, did present a broad outline of what could be expected with the Messiah's advent. Writing in the 11th chapter of *Hilkhot Melachim and Milchamotehem*, Maimonides explains:

> In the future, the Messianic king will arise and renew the Davidic dynasty, restoring it to its initial sovereignty. He will build the Temple and gather the dispersed of Israel.
>
> Then, in his days, the observance of all the statutes will return to their previous state. We will offer sacrifices, observe the Sabbatical and Jubilee years according to all their particulars as described by the Torah.
>
> Anyone who does not believe in him or does not await his coming, denies not only the statements of the other prophets, but those of the Torah and Moses, our teacher.

In support of a final regathering, Maimonides cites Dt 30:3-5, and he points to Nm 24:17-18 as referring to David (near) and the Messiah (far), also citing Zch 9:10 and Ob 1:21 with reference to the Messianic Era (cf. also Dt 19:8-9 regarding the promised expansion of Israel's borders). Then, in what appears to be a direct polemic against Christianity, Maimonides states that the Messiah need not work miracles or raise the dead, which is why a sage as great as Rabbi Akiva believed that the warring general Bar Kochba was the Messiah, while other sages never asked him to perform signs and wonders. Once he died, however, they recognized that he was not the Messiah.

As to how the Messiah will be recognized, Maimonides writes (11:4), "If a king will arise from the House of David who diligently contemplates the Torah and observes its mitzvot as prescribed by the Written Law and the Oral Law as David, his ancestor, will compel all of Israel to walk in (the way of the Torah) and rectify the breaches in its observance, and fight the wars of God, we may, with assurance, consider him Mashiach. If he succeeds in the above, builds the Temple in its place, and gathers the dispersed of Israel, he is definitely the Mashiach."

As for Jesus of Nazareth, he "aspired to be the Mashiach and was executed by the court as was also alluded to in Daniel's prophecies as [Dan] 11:14 states: 'The vulgar among your people shall exalt themselves in an attempt to fulfill the vision, but they shall stumble.'" Indeed, Maimonides asks, "Can there be a greater stumbling block than Christianity? All the prophets spoke of Mashiach as the redeemer of Israel and their savior who would gather their dispersed and strengthen their observance of the mitzvot. In contrast, Christianity caused the Jews to be slain by the sword, their remnants to be scattered and humbled, the Torah to be altered, and the majority of the world to err and serve a god other than the Lord." Despite this harsh judgment, Maimonides sees a redemptive purpose in both Christianity and Islam, since these two religions have helped advance the ideas of Messiah and Torah and commandments. Thus, "When the true Messianic king will arise and prove successful, his position becoming exalted and uplifted, they will all return and realize that their ancestors endowed them with a false heritage and their prophets and ancestors caused them to err."

As for the nature of the Messianic Age (see ch. 12), Maimonides writes, "Do not presume that in the Messianic Age any facet of the world's nature will change or there will be innovations in the work of creation. Rather, the world will continue according to its pattern." He then interprets verses like Isa 11:6-7, which depict the wolf lying down with the lamb and the lion eating straw like an ox, in metaphorical (rather than supernatural) terms.[17] Regarding the sequence of events that usher in the Messianic Age, it appears "that the war of Gog and Magog will take place at the beginning of the Messianic age. Before the war of Gog and Magog, a prophet will arise to inspire Israel to be upright and prepare their hearts, as Mal 3:22 [Mal 4:5 in the English versions] states: 'Behold, I am sending you Elijah.'" Nonetheless, while some believe Elijah will come before the Messiah, one cannot be dogmatic, since the prophets do not state these things clearly. "Regardless," then, "of the debate concerning these questions, neither the order of the occurrence of these events or their precise details are among the fundamental principles of the faith. A person should not occupy himself with the *Aggadot* and homiletics concerning these and similar matters, nor should he consider them as essentials, for study of them will neither bring fear or love of God."

The same ambivalence applies to trying to determine the appointed time of the Messiah's arrival, concerning which the sages declared: "'May the spirits of those who attempt to determine the time of Mashiach's coming expire!' Rather, one should await and believe in the general conception of the matter as explained." Once his messianic reign is established, the Messiah will determine the "entire nation's line of [tribal] descent," beginning with the Levites.

As to why the sages yearned for the Messianic Era, it was not in order to exercise dominion over the nations or "to be exalted by the nations, or to eat, drink, and celebrate. Rather, they desired to be free to involve themselves in Torah and wisdom without any pressures or disturbances, so that they would merit the world to come." Thus, in this beatific setting without famine or war, "The occupation of the entire world will be solely to know God. Therefore, the Jews will be great sages and know the hidden matters, grasping the knowledge of their Creator according to the full extent of human potential, as Isaiah 11:9 states: 'The world will be filled with the knowledge of God as the waters cover the ocean bed.'"

This, then, becomes the classic description of the Messiah and the Messianic Era: He will be a great teacher (of both written and oral Torah) rather than a miracle worker, bringing the nation into Torah observance and fighting the wars of the Lord. (When he has done these things, he is the presumptive Messiah.) He will then build the Temple and gather the exiles, at which point he is definitely to be recognized as the Messiah.

THE MESSIAH IN THE BIBLICAL COMMENTARIES

The most prominent commentators of this period include Rashi, Ibn Ezra, Radak, Nachmanides, Abravanel, and Sforno. Generally speaking, the main lines of messianic interpretation are confirmed, based on passages such as Gn 49:10; Nm 24:17-19; Isa 11:1ff.; and Mic 5:1(2). There is, of course, deviation among the interpreters, with Rashi rejecting the messianic interpretation of Isa 9:5-6(6-7), Ps 2 (despite b. Ber 7b, which Rashi cites), and Zch 6:12-15 (he understands the Branch to be Zerubbabel). Rashi does read Dan 2:44 with reference to the messianic kingdom and sees an allusion to the Messiah in more surprising passages such as Ps 43:3 (where God's light and truth refer to the Messiah and Elijah).

According to Ibn Ezra, Nm 24:17 speaks of David, Ps 2 speaks of David and the Messiah, Isa 11:1 speaks of either Hezekiah or the Messiah, and Zch 9:9 speaks of Judah Maccabee. He understands Gn 49:10; Isa 59:20; Hos 3:5; Mic 4:1,3 to be messianic (among others). The commentaries of Radak at times are more polemical, perhaps in the spirit of his father Joseph, who penned the anti-Christian book *Sepher HaBrit* (Book of the Covenant); see, e.g., Radak's commentary to Pss 2 and 110. He gives a messianic interpretation to Isa 11:1; Mic 5:1; Jer 23:5-6, among other passages, but sees Isa 9:5-6 as referring to Hezekiah and Zch 6:12-15 as referring to Zerubbabel. Note, however, that he interprets the servant of Isa 42:1ff. as the Messiah.

All of the major commentaries, however, agree that Isa 53 refers to Israel (or, the righteous remnant) rather than to the Messiah, further galvanizing this viewpoint in traditional Judaism, although at least one later commentator found this surprising.[18] The role of Messiah son of Joseph is also recognized, but not in a prominent way (see, e.g., Rashi to Isa 11:13, which he interprets to mean there will be no more envy between Messiah ben Joseph and Messiah ben David; Rashi to Isa 24:18, speaking of the sword of Messiah ben Joseph and Messiah ben David; according to Ibn Ezra, Zch 13:7 speaks of the war that will take place in the days of Messiah ben Joseph, while Mal 3:1 "my messenger" may refer to him).

There is dispute regarding whether Zch 12:10 should be applied to Messiah ben Joseph, despite the Talmudic tradition in b. Suk 52a. Note, however, that the prominent darshan Moshe al-Sheikh (16th c.) explicitly applied Zch 12:10 to Messiah ben Joseph, explaining that it "shall be accounted as if Israel had pierced him, for on account of their sin he has died; and, therefore, in order that it may be reckoned to them as a perfect atonement they will repent and look to the blessed One, saying that there is none beside him to forgive those that mourn on account of him who died for their sin: this is the meaning of 'They shall look upon me.'"

As for detailed views of the Messianic Era, according to Abravanel (and following earlier midrashic traditions), the Messiah will make a sudden appearance after living in obscurity for years,[19] emancipating and regathering his people, destroying the nations that oppressed Israel, and restoring the earth "to what previous generations had forfeited through Adam's fatal sin; heavenly radiance, strength of life, stature, plentiful harvests and the pristine brightness of the luminaries. He will renew prophecy, which has been discontinued since the dispersion."[20]

In contrast with Maimonides, who felt it unwise to speculate too much concerning the chronology of the end of days, the more mystical Nachmanides wrote with greater assurance. For now, Paradise and Gehinnom exist (where the righteous go after death); next will be the Messianic Age, lasting for one thousand years; this will be followed by Judgment Day, "for eternal reward and punishment"; then Resurrection, at which time there will be "reward for body and soul"; and finally, the Future World, "where the bodies will become spiritualized and the souls will attain the highest degree of divine knowledge."[21]

THE MESSIAH IN JEWISH MYSTICISM

According to Scholem, "The *Zohar* follows talmudic Aggadah in seeing redemption not as the product of inward progress in the historical world, but as a supernatural miracle involving the gradual illumination of the world by the light of the Messiah. It begins with an initial gleam and ends with full revelation: the light of the Messiah."[22] In this regard, "redemption becomes a spiritual revolution which will uncover the mystic meaning, the 'true interpretation,' of the Torah. Thus, a mystic utopia takes the place of the national and secular utopia of the earlier writers."[23]

Scholem sees a shift of attitude in the aftermath of the Jewish expulsion from Spain in 1492, culminating in the work of Isaac Luria of Safed (1534–72; this theory is rejected by M. Idel).[24] In this later conception, the Jewish exile reflected "the condition of the universe as a whole, even of the deity. . . . In other words, all being is in Galut [exile]."[25] Redemption from this fallen, broken state would come about by the joint efforts of the people of Israel as they observe the Torah and keep the commandments, thereby repairing the world and restoring God's light, thus paving the way for the Messianic Era. "This conception," Scholem writes, "is no longer catastrophic: when duty has been fulfilled the son of David, the Messiah, will come of himself, for his appearance at the End of Days is only a symbol for the completion of a process, a testimony that the world has in fact been amended. . . . We are all involved in one Messianic venture, and we all are called up to do our part."[26] And so, even though there will be final upheaval and revolution, it will not resemble the darkly apocalyptic descriptions found elsewhere in rabbinic literature and known as the "travails of the Messiah."

Additionally, Lurianic Kabbalah places little emphasis on the person and work of the Messiah, since he himself does not bring about the redemption. In contrast, M. Idel speaks of "a profound relationship between mysticism and messianism" as well as of "the traditional apocalypse presided over by the omnipotent figure of the Messiah."[27] He is also skeptical of the degree to which the Lurianic Kabbalah marked a turning point in mystical messianic expectations noting, more broadly, that, "Messianic Kabbalists did not share one particular spiritual physiognomy."[28]

In short, just as Jewish mysticism is complex and esoteric, so also messianic mysticism is complex and esoteric, embracing the extant Jewish traditions about the Messiah (primarily focusing on the future Davidic king) and interpreting them through the lens of mysticism. The same principle applies to mystical treatments of the suffering Messiah son of Joseph, who is mentioned several dozen times in the Zohar. Zechariah 9:9 is said to speak of him and, in one extended passage, Isa 53 is interpreted with reference to this suffering Messiah, as He enters the temple of the sons of sickness in the garden of Eden to take upon Himself the sufferings and pain of Israel in exile, without which Israel could not endure.[29]

CONCLUSION

Medieval Jewish literature advances the Jewish understanding of the Messiah considerably. Although it did not present the final and complete interpretation of the Messiah (as if this were even possible in Judaism), nevertheless, it went far in fleshing out the skeletal presentation of earlier rabbinic literature.

---

1. There was also the further development of the Responsa Literature (Questions and Answers), which focused primarily on providing answers to practical questions of daily living, in particular, wanting to understand how to apply the teachings of Torah and tradition to specific legal controversies.

2. Note that neither the *Shulchan Aruch*, nor its predecessor the *Arba'ah Turim*, focus on the future work of the Messiah, since that subject is outside the purview of these codes, which concentrate on laws for daily living. This remains true for subsequent adaptations of these earlier law codes, such as the 19th century *Aruch HaShulchan*. As for the philosophical works, while some do interact with messianic questions, their contribution is less important than that of the biblical commentaries and the *Mishneh Torah*.

3. For further discussion, see the article "The Messiah in Ancient Rabbinic Literature" and its section "The Messiah in the Mishnah" in this book, with reference to m. Sot 9:15.

4. Joseph Sarachek, *The Doctrine of the Messiah in Medieval Jewish Literature* (New York: Hermon Press, n.d.), 1.

5. See the convenient summary in Raphael Patai, *The Messiah Texts* (Detroit: Wayne State University Press, 1988), 104. For a comprehensive collection of all traditional Jewish texts on the Messiah ben Joseph, see David C. Mitchell, *Messiah ben Joseph* (Newton Mearns, Scotland: Campbell Publications, 2016).

6. Gershom Scholem, *The Messianic Idea in Judaism: And Other Essays on Jewish Spirituality* (New York: Schocken Books, 1971).

7. This mirrors b. Sanhedrin 96b-97a (and 98a). For an English translation of the relevant portions of Sa'adiah's book, see Mitchell, *Messiah ben Joseph*, 200–06.

8. Hai Gaon is also known as Sherira Gaon; for the full text of his responsum in translation, see Mitchell, ibid., 211–17.

9. *Messiah Texts*, 104.

10. Ibid., 105.

11. Some scholars date this collection as early as the fifth to sixth centuries; others, while accepting a later date, recognize that the text contains some material that is much earlier. See William G. Braude, ed. and trans., *Pesikta Rabbati: Homiletical Discourses for Festal Days and Special Sabbaths 1 & 2* (Yale Judaica Series; New Haven: Yale Univ. Press, 1988). Note that earlier midrashim are treated in the article "The Messiah in Ancient Rabbinic Literature" in this book (in particular, the halakhic midrashim to the Torah—Mekhilta d'Rab. Ishmahel, Sifra, Sifre Numbers and Sifre Deuteronomy, and the Rabbah midrashim to the Torah and the Five Scrolls). For a popular summary of Talmudic and midrashic statements about the Messiah, see Abraham Cohen, *Everyman's Talmud: The Major Teachings of the Rabbinic Sages* (New York: Schocken Books, 1949), 346–56. For reflections on these traditions through the lens of Reform Judaism, see Rabbi Elaine Rose Glickman, *The Messiah and the Jews: Three Thousand Years of Tradition, Belief, and Hope* (Woodstock, NY: Jewish Lights Publishing, 2013).

12. Excerpted from chap. 36, as rendered by Patai. Other descriptions of the Messiah's sufferings are found in Sefer Zerubbabel, dating to the seventh century but not as widely known in traditional Judaism as Pesikta Rabbati. As to whether the Messiah son of David also suffers in Sefer Zerubbabel, see Martha Himmelfarb, *Jewish Messiahs in a Christian Empire: A History of the Book of Zerubbabel* (Cambridge, MA and London, England: Harvard University Press, 2017). Himmelfarb also disputes some of the interpretations of Mitchell, *Messiah ben Joseph*, while at the same time confirming the importance of the suffering Messiah traditions. She points as well to the image of the suffering Messiah, based on Isa 53, that is found in the Yom Kippur poetic prayer (piyyut) called *az milifnei vreisheet* (ibid., 79–89).

13. Jacob Neusner, *Messiah in Context: Israel's History and Destiny in Formative Judaism* (Philadelphia: Fortress Press, 1984), 154–57.

14. Ibid., 158.

15. See Louis Jacobs, *Principles of Jewish Faith: An Analytical Study* (Portland, OR: Valentine Mitchell, 1964).

16. All translations taken from https://www.chabad.org/library/article_cdo/aid/1188357/jewish/Melachim-uMilchamot-Chapter-12.htm. For further discussion and concise commentary, see Rabbi Eliyahu Touger, *Maimonides, Mishneh Torah: Hilchot Melachim U'Milchamoteihem The Laws of Kings and Their Wars* (Brooklyn: Maznaim, 1987).

17. The rationalist, Maimonidean vision of the Messianic Era and world to come stands in stark contrast with the description offered by Sa'adiah Gaon, which follows many of the midrashic descriptions and is markedly supernatural. See Sarachek, *The Doctrine of the Messiah*, 27–50, 126–61.

18. Napthali ben Asher Altschuler (d. after 1607): "I am surprised that Rashi and Radak have not, with the Targums, applied it to the Messiah likewise. . . ." See Mitchell, *Messiah ben Joseph*, 232. Note that Targum Jonathan does interpret the passage messianically, but with a total reworking of the text, whereby the Messiah does not suffer (see the chapter "The Messiah in Rabbinic Literature" in this book). The famous midrash interpreting Isa 52:13 to the Messiah (Yalk. Shim. 2:571) is limited to that verse, although logic would say that the interpretation should carry over to the rest of the passage, through 53:12, since it is clearly the same subject throughout.

19. If, in fact, the Messiah was born on the day the Temple was destroyed, as per y. Ber. 2:4, "he was transferred to Paradise to await the propitious hour because of the unworthiness of the generation to receive him."

20. Sarachek, *The Doctrine of the Messiah*, 270.

21. Ibid., 187–91; all quotes are his (188).

22. *The Messianic Idea in Judaism*, 39.

23. Ibid., 40. Scholem was speaking here in particular with reference to the latest sections of the Zohar.

24. See Moshe Idel, *Kabbalah: New Perspectives* (New Haven: Yale Univ. Press, 1989).

25. *The Messianic Idea in Judaism.*, 43, 45.

26. Ibid., 47–48.

27. *Messianic Mystics* (New Haven: Yale University Press, 1998), 213, 283.

28. Ibid., 260. See also Shmuel Boteach, *The Wolf Shall Lie with the Lamb: The Messiah in Hasidic Thought* (Northvale, NJ: Jason Aronson, 1993).

29. See Mitchell, *Messiah ben Joseph*, 227–30. The Isa 53 tradition mirrors Pesikta Rabbati 36, where Israel could not endure had the Messiah not borne its pains.

Genesis 3:15

The Promised Seed

SETH D. POSTELL

> "I will put hostility between you and the woman,
> and between your seed and her seed.
> He will strike your head, and you will strike his heel." (Gn 3:15)

Is this curse in Gn 3:15 about snakes or Satan? Is the seed of the woman about humanity or the ultimate human—the Messiah? Recently scorn has been poured on the idea that this verse points to the Messiah, but careful study of the verse in the context of the wider story of Genesis, and the Pentateuch as a whole, leads to the inevitable conclusion that it is indeed messianic. Far from being a human struggle with snakes or even an ongoing battle between good and evil, this verse is intrinsic to the overarching Torah story of messianic victory to come.

The messianic interpretation of Gn 3:15 since the time of the Reformation has fallen on hard times. John Calvin, though not denying the prophetic trajectory of this verse, clearly rejects the messianic interpretation of this verse. In his words,

> I interpret this simply to mean that there should always be the hostile strife between the human race and serpents, which is now apparent; for, by a secret feeling of nature, man abhors them.[1]

Similarly, John Walton argues against the messianic interpretation when he writes,

> Throughout the history of the church, this has been read as the first foreshadowing of Christ's defeat of Satan.... Given the repetition of the verb and the potentially mortal nature of both attacks, it becomes difficult to understand the verse as suggesting an eventual outcome to the struggle. Instead, both sides are exchanging potentially mortal blows of equal threat to the part of the body most vulnerable to their attack. The verse is depicting a continual, unresolved conflict between humans and the representatives of evil.[2]

Perhaps the first seeds of doubt were planted in the Church when Rashi, the famous medieval Jewish commentator, challenged the common notion that the serpent suffers the more fatal blow, and consequently, assumes the triumph of the seed of the woman over the serpent. Given the fact, however, that snakes are often poisonous, and since snakes crawl on the ground, it is a natural phenomenon that snakes kill people by striking them on the heel. In Rashi's words, "You shall not have height, so that you will bite him on his heel, but even from there you will kill him."[3] Rashi's understanding of equally mortal blows even appears to be confirmed within the book of Genesis itself: "He will be a snake by the road, a viper beside the path, that bites the horses' heels so that its rider falls backward" (Gn 49:17). This simple, yet devastating (to the traditional understanding of the verse) observation, led many to the conclusion that Gn 3:15 is no more than an etiological[4] explanation for a natural phenomenon: the endless hatred between humans and snakes.[5]

The purpose of this article is to defend the messianic interpretation of this verse, showing that it does indeed speak of the Messiah to come, by means of a careful reading of Gn 3:15 within its immediate and larger literary context. Though the rejection of the messianic interpretation was done in the name of the grammatical-historical method, the etiological and other nonmessianic interpretations[6] of this verse suffer from a failure to appreciate the significance of this verse within its larger literary context. In what follows, we will look at Gn 3:15 within progressively wider literary contexts in order to demonstrate that the messianic interpretation has very strong textual support and leaves theories limited to the origins of ophidiophobia in the dust. Three junctions in the Genesis story will receive our concentrated attention: The fall narrative in Gn 3 will be analyzed in comparison to Gn 4 (the story of Cain), then to Gn 9 (Noah), and finally to Gn 49 (Jacob blessing his sons). This analysis will show that an appreciation of the wider story told throughout Genesis can only lead to one conclusion: the literary trail of Gn 3:15 *within the book of Genesis* leads to the Messiah.

GENESIS 3:15 IN ITS LITERARY CONTEXT

Context is king. This axiom expresses a foundational rule in biblical interpretation. This axiom is crucial for interpreting a verse that has all the appearance of being programmatic for the ensuing plot of the book as a whole. John Sailhamer calls attention to both the enigmatic and programmatic nature of this verse when he writes,

> In light of the fact that similar programmatic discourses are strategically placed throughout the remainder of the book, it seems probable that the author intended these words also to be read as programmatic and foundational to the plot and characterization of the book as a whole. . . . Verse 15 thus contains a puzzling yet centrally important question: Who is the "seed" of the woman? The purpose of this verse is not to answer that question but to raise it. The remainder of the book of Genesis and the Pentateuch gives the author's answer.[7]

The verse anticipates hostility between the serpent and the woman, and between his seed and her seed. It is little wonder, therefore, that "seed"[8] becomes a key word in the book of Genesis, and an ensuing conflict (at times mortal) between a chosen and rejected seed becomes its plot.[9] It makes good exegetical sense, therefore, to allow the book to shine interpretive light on the literal sense of this challenging verse.

GENESIS 1–11 AS A PLOT SETTER

In order to grasp the programmatic nature of Gn 3:15 it is essential to understand how Gn 1–11 functions as the introduction to the Torah.[10] Genesis 1–11 introduces all the key themes in the remainder of the Torah story, and serves as the needed background for understanding God's election of Abram and, in him, the nation of Israel. Genesis 1:28 contains all the essential elements of God's promise and purposes for the patriarchs: blessing, seed, and land.

> God blessed them, and God said to them, "Be fruitful, multiply, fill the earth, and subdue it. Rule the fish of the sea, the birds of the sky, and every creature that crawls on the earth." (Gn 1:28)

God blessed them, and henceforth desires to bless all the families of the earth (Gn 12:3). God commanded them to be fruitful, a command that anticipated God's promise to multiply Abraham's seed (Gn 17:2,6). God also commanded the first couple to "subdue the earth." The word "earth" in Hebrew is the same word used for "land" (cf. Gn 2:11,13; 4:16) and "subdue" in other contexts means "to conquer" (Nm 32:22,29; Jos 18:1), an obvious allusion to Israel's mission to conquer the promised land.

When we look more broadly, we see other themes and patterns in Gn 1–11 that are programmatic for Israel's story as told in the Torah as well as the Former Prophets.[11] God prepares a special place (land) for the first man, and graciously brings him into it (Gn 2:7-16). Life in this special place is contingent on his obedience to God's commandments (Gn 2:16-17). Although Adam and Eve were commanded to subdue the land and rule over its creatures, they fell prey to the serpent's temptations and disobeyed God's commandments.

Disobedience brought curses (Gn 3:14,17; 4:11; 5:29; 9:25), exile from the garden in Eden (Gn 3:23-24; cf. 2:8), as well as the land of Eden (Gn 4:16), and death (Gn 2:17; 3:19; 5:5,8,11,14,17,20,27,31; 7:22; 9:29; 11:28,32). Adam's posterity eventually found themselves in Babylon (Gn 11:1-9) from whence God chose and called Abram back to a specially prepared land.

All the key themes of Israel's story are present in this story: blessing (Gn 49; Dt 33), a special land (Gn 15:18), seed, commandments (Ex 20:1-17), temptations to forsake the Lord's commandments by those who share this special land (Dt 7:1-4), disobedience and curses (Dt 28:16-19), exile (Lv 26:33; Dt 4:26-28; 30:1; 2Kg 25), and death. Adam and Eve's disobedience in Gn 3 became the catalyst of a plot embracing all humanity, a plot that ultimately found resolution through the victory of a particular seed (collective and singular) from Adam's line (Gn 3:15; 4:25; 9:26-27; 11:10) over hostile enemies (Gn 9:25; 12:3; 22:17; 24:60; 49:8; Nm 24:17-19).[12]

In light of the relationship of Gn 1–11 to the rest of the Torah story, it seems to be a rather impoverished interpretation to suggest that Gn 3:15 is there to simply tell a "just-so story" of why the snake crawls or a never-ending "ying-yang" struggle between people and snakes or the forces of evil. Genesis 3:15 must be grasped as the acorn out of which the entire story grows, a story whose outcome is the final triumph of Adam's seed, through Abraham, Isaac, Jacob, and Judah, over the forces of evil.

LOOK FOR THE FAMILY RESEMBLANCE

To understand the way in which the author connects the various characters and stories together into a single narrative, it is essential to note how the "deeds of the fathers are a sign to the sons," or as Alexander states,

> [T]he members of the family line often resemble each other. This is in keeping with the observation, made above, that the concept of "seed" implies a resemblance between the progenitor and the progeny.[13]

The author not only presents Adam, Eve, and the serpent as historical figures, he also presents them as representative figures, carefully and systematically noting ways in which subsequent characters find their meaning and their destiny in the former. Who is the serpent? Who is/are the seed of the serpent? Who is/are the seed of the woman? What meaning do each of these figures have in the larger story? Literary parallels in Gn 1–11 are crucial for answering these questions and for discerning the grammatical-historical meaning of Gn 3:15.

COMPARING THE FALL NARRATIVE WITH THE STORY OF CAIN

Let us begin by looking closely at the tragic story of Adam and Eve's children in Gn 4. Although Cain's birth at first evokes words of praise (Gn 4:1), his animosity toward his younger brother results in the first murder. This story has several thematic and lexical (words) parallels with Gn 2–3. In both stories:

God gives clear instructions that must be obeyed.	"But you must not eat from the tree of the knowledge of good and evil, for on the day you eat from it, you will certainly die." (Gn 2:17)	"If you do what is right, won't you be accepted? But if you do not do what is right, sin is crouching at the door." (Gn 4:7a)
God warns the main characters not to give in to their desires.	"He said to the woman: 'I will intensify your labor pains; you will bear children in anguish. *Your desire will be for your husband, yet he will rule over you.*'" (Gn 3:16)	"*Its desire is for you, but you must rule over it.*" (Gn 4:7b)
The main characters brazenly disobey God's instructions.	"Then the woman saw that the tree was good for food and delightful to look at, and that it was desirable for obtaining wisdom. So she took some of its fruit and ate it; she also gave some to her husband, who was with her, and he ate it." (Gn 3:6)	"Cain said to his brother Abel, 'Let's go out to the field.' And while they were in the field, Cain attacked his brother Abel and killed him." (Gn 4:8)

God interrogates the main characters seeking to know "where" and "why."	"Then the man and his wife heard the sound of the LORD God walking in the garden at the time of the evening breeze, and they hid themselves from the LORD God among the trees of the garden. So the LORD God called out to the man and said to him, *"Where are you?"* . . . So the LORD God asked the woman, *"What is this you have done?"* (Gn 3:8-9,13a)	"Then the LORD said to Cain, *'Where is your brother Abel?'* 'I don't know,' he replied. 'Am I my brother's guardian?' Then He said, *'What have you done?* Your brother's blood cries out to Me from the ground!'" (Gn 4:9-10)
Characters are cursed by God.	"Then the LORD God said to the serpent: 'Because you have *done* this, *you are cursed more* than any livestock and more than any wild animal. You will move on your belly and eat dust all the days of your life.'" (Gn 3:14)	"Then He said, 'What have you *done*? Your brother's blood cries out to Me from the ground! So now *you are cursed*, alienated, *from* the ground that opened its mouth to receive your brother's blood you have shed.'" (Gn 4:10-11)
Characters are banished from Eden.	"So the LORD God sent him away from the garden of Eden to work the ground from which he was taken. *He drove man out* [*banished*] and stationed the cherubim and the flaming, whirling sword *east of the garden of Eden* to guard the way to the tree of life." (Gn 3:23-24)	"'*Since You are banishing me today from the soil*, and I must hide myself from Your presence and become a restless wanderer on the earth, whoever finds me will kill me.' . . . Then Cain went out from the LORD's presence and lived in the land of Nod, *east of Eden*." (Gn 4:14,16)
A "seed" of the woman is highlighted in contradistinction from an evil "seed."	"*I will put* hostility between you and the *woman*, and between your *seed* and her *seed*. He will strike your head, and you will strike his heel." (Gn 3:15)	"Cain was intimate with his wife, and she conceived and gave birth to Enoch. . . . Adam was intimate with his wife [*woman*] again, and she gave birth to a son and named him *Seth*, for she said, 'God *has given* [*has put*] me another *child* [*seed*] in place of Abel, since Cain killed him.'" (Gn 4:17,25)

When we allow Gn 4 to shed light on the meaning of Gn 3, several interpretive insights follow. First, though Cain's actions of disobedience and subsequent expulsion from Eden mirror Adam and Eve's story, God's curse on Cain ("cursed are you") marks him and his children as the seed of the serpent ("cursed are you"). Second, a number of key words in Gn 4:25 (woman, to put, seed) appear in only one other place in the entire Hebrew Bible, Gn 3:15. This means we must look to Gn 4:25 to gain further insight into the meaning of Gn 3:15. Eve interprets the seed of the woman in Gn 3:15 as an individual son, i.e., "God has given me another seed." The precise wording of her comments also suggests that she understands the hostilities between Cain and Abel in light of Gn 3:15, in which this conflict was already anticipated.

In light of Gn 4, it becomes clear that the "seed of the serpent" is not referring to literal snakes (contra the etiological interpretation of Gn 3:15). Rather, the close parallels between the fates of the serpent and Cain, followed by Cain's genealogy in chap. 4, suggests that the author of Genesis wants us to understand the serpent's "seed" metaphorically. The serpent's seed are not to be identified by physical progeny since Cain is also a child of Eve. Rather, the serpent's seed must be identified by its actions, in this case, murder. The identification of Seth as a seed appointed by God in Gn 4:25 further suggests that divine election is crucial for identifying the "seed of the woman." In this we also find a clue as to the identity of the serpent. The serpent stands as the parent-creature in a metaphorical line of evildoers who oppose God's purposes for humanity and who war against a divinely appointed seed.

Already in chap. 4, the author provides vital clues for understanding Gn 3:15 as far more significant than a description of a natural phenomenon. Rather, it is the plot of the entire story in a nutshell. As Gn 1–11 continues to unfold, it becomes clear that its story line does not allow for interpreting the equal blows in Gn 3:15 as a vicious, never-ending cycle of good versus evil. The story's plot brings us to a very different conclusion, namely, the triumph of God's elected seed (collective and individual) to restore divine blessing to all humanity.

COMPARING THE FALL NARRATIVE WITH THE STORY OF NOAH

Seth's line leads us to Noah (Gn 5:1), and Noah's election once again points us back to the fall in Gn 3 and God's remedial plan. "And he named him Noah, saying, 'This one will bring us relief from the agonizing labor of our hands, caused by the ground the Lord has cursed'" (Gn 5:29). Not only is the allusion to Gn 3:17-19 transparent,[14] God's purposes for the "seed of the woman" are made explicit by means of this allusion. The "seed of the woman" will bring relief from the curse, presumably by triumphing over the serpent and its "children."

It comes as no surprise that parallels between Noah's moral failure and Adam's sin provide more insights into the grammatical-historical meaning of Gn 3:15.[15] Noah was clearly chosen to "fulfill" God's mandate to Adam. God's blessing on Noah and His command to be fruitful and multiply and to fill the earth point to Noah's role as another "Adam," a "seed of the woman" through whom God will restore creation (compare Gn 1:28-31; 9:1-9). Noah, however, like Adam before him, slips into a moral failure that intentionally mirrors Adam's fall. More important, Noah's failure and the cursing and blessing of his progeny continues to fill in important blanks on the meaning of Gn 3:15. Let us look at the parallels and then make some observations.

Both fall narratives are introduced by the planting of a garden/vineyard.	"The Lord *God planted a garden in Eden*, in the east, and there He placed the man He had formed. The Lord God caused to grow out of the ground every tree pleasing in appearance and good for food, including the tree of life in the middle of the garden, as well as the tree of the knowledge of good and evil." (Gn 2:8-9)	*"Noah, a man of the soil, was the first to plant a vineyard."* (Gn 9:20)
Both fall narratives include an inappropriate use of its produce by the main characters.	"Then the woman saw that the tree was good for food and delightful to look at, and that it was desirable for obtaining wisdom. *So she took some of its fruit and ate it*; she also gave some to her husband, who was with her, and *he ate it*." (Gn 3:6)	*"He drank some of the wine*, became drunk . . ." (Gn 9:21a)
Both fall narratives refer to the nakedness of the main characters.	"Then the eyes of both of them were opened, and they knew they were *naked* . . ." (Gn 3:7a)	". . . and *uncovered* himself inside his tent. Ham, the father of Canaan, saw his father *naked* and told his two brothers outside." (Gn 9:21b-22)

Both fall narratives necessitate the covering of nakedness.	"... so they sewed fig leaves together and made loincloths for themselves." (Gn 3:7b)	"Then Shem and Japheth took a cloak and placed it over both their shoulders, and walking backward, they covered their father's nakedness. Their faces were turned away, and they did not see their father naked." (Gn 9:23)
Both fall narratives conclude with a focus on two different "seeds," one seed is cursed to subjugation and the other given promises of triumph.	"I will put hostility between you and the woman, and between your seed and her seed. He will strike your head, and you will strike his heel." (Gn 3:15)	"He said: 'Canaan will be cursed. He will be the lowest of slaves to his brothers.' He also said: 'Praise the LORD, the God of Shem; Canaan will be his slave. God will extend Japheth; he will dwell in the tents of Shem; Canaan will be his slave.'" (Gn 9:25-27)

The parallels between the two fall narratives are obvious, the import of which cannot be overemphasized. First, it is quite clear that Canaan, like Cain before him, inherits the curse of the serpent. By highlighting the curse of Canaan and his line, the author identifies Canaan, like Cain, as the hostile seed of the serpent in Gn 3:15. Canaan's subjugation as a slave clearly parallels the serpent's humiliation, i.e., to "eat dust all the days of [his] life" (Gn 3:14). Here we also see a clear link between the serpent, whose temptation led to Adam's exile from the garden, and the Canaanites, who likewise will be a stumbling block to the people of Israel in the promised land. Second, the parallels between Shem with the seed of the woman are also unmistakable. Shem is blessed, and receives a promise that he will one day triumph over the Canaanites, i.e., the seed of the serpent. Here we see an inner-biblical interpretation of Gn 3:15 that completely undermines not only the etiological interpretation, but also shows that the author does not regard the "striking of the heel" and the "striking of the head" as mutually self-defeating. The blessing of Shem and the curse on Canaan in Gn 9:26-27 make it clear that the "seed of the woman" will ultimately triumph over the forces of evil in the redemptive plan of God.

COMPARING THE FALL NARRATIVE AND JACOB'S BLESSINGS

The story line of Genesis leads us from the seed of the woman through Isaac and Jacob, to Jacob's 12 sons, and all along the way anticipates a future victory over Israel's enemies through a particular seed (Gn 3:15; 4:25; 9:26; 12:3; 22:17; 24:60; 27:29). The patriarchal narratives conclude with a large poetic blessing in Gn 49, where we find that the acorn of the story of redemption in Gn 3:15 blossomed into a final eschatological victory. Jacob gathered his 12 sons and declared to them what will happen in "the days to come" (Gn 49:1).[16] John Sailhamer notes the significance of Jacob's "last day" blessing within its larger literary context when he writes,

> At three macrostructural junctures in the Pentateuch, the author has spliced a major poetic discourse onto the end of a large unit of narrative (Ge 49; Nu 24; Dt 31). A close look at the material lying between and connecting the narrative and poetic sections reveals the presence of a homogeneous compositional stratum. It is most noticeably marked by the recurrence of the same terminology and narrative motifs. In each of the three segments, the central figure (Jacob, Balaam, Moses) calls an audience together (imperative: Ge 49:1; Nu 24:14; Dt 31:28) and proclaims (cohortative: Ge 49:1; Nu 24:14; Dt 31:28) what will happen (Ge 49:1; Nu 24:14; Dt 31:29) in "the end of days" (Ge 49:1; Nu 24:14; Dt 31:29).[17]

In the context of this end-time blessing, Jacob prophesied the coming of a king from the tribe of Judah who will triumph over Israel's enemies and restore the paradisiacal blessing to all nations (Gn 49:8-12). The later OT prophets identify this king in Jacob's blessing as the Messiah.[18]

CONCLUSION

This article began by noting the tendency of recent scholarship to reject the messianic interpretation of Gn 3:15 in favor of an etiological explanation. The purpose of Gn 3:15, it is claimed, is to explain why people and snakes hate each other. Others have opted for a more symbolic explanation, wherein Gn 3:15 explains the never-ending conflict between the forces of good and evil. The messianic interpretation, it is further claimed, is more allegorical than exegetical. NET notes on Gn 3:15 are quite explicit on this point when they write:

> Many Christian theologians (going back to Irenaeus) understand v. 15 as the so-called protevangelium, supposedly prophesying Christ's victory over Satan. . . . In this allegorical approach, the woman's offspring is initially Cain, then the whole human race, and ultimately Jesus Christ, the offspring (Heb "seed") of the woman (see Gal 4:4). The offspring of the serpent includes the evil powers and

> demons of the spirit world, as well as those humans who are in the kingdom of darkness (see Jn 8:44). According to this view, the passage gives the first hint of the gospel. Satan delivers a crippling blow to the Seed of the woman (Jesus), who in turn delivers a fatal blow to the Serpent (first defeating him through the death and resurrection [1Co 15:55-57] and then destroying him in the judgment [Rev 12:7-9; 20:7-10]). However, the grammatical structure of Gn 3:15b does not suggest this view.[19]

We have demonstrated that the messianic interpretation of Gn 3:15 is not allegorical as the critics claim, but rather based on a close reading of the text. The nonmessianic interpretation of this verse, on the other hand, is far more difficult to defend and suffers from an atomistic focus on a verse completely alienated from its literary context. Once we notice the network of strategic parallels and allusions to Gn 3:15 in Gn 1–11, we see that the serpent is identified as the parent of all evil, its seed as those who are hostile to the redemptive purposes of God, and the seed of the woman as a divinely chosen line, the culmination of which is a king from the tribe of Judah who will come in the last days. Though the text in Genesis does not explicitly identify the serpent as the devil, its literary trajectory clearly leads to the interpretation we find in Rev 12[20] where that identification is made. Therefore, we completely agree with Michael Rydelnik when he writes,

> A more likely explanation is that the author of the Torah offered a hint of a coming redeemer in Gn 3:15 and then used the rest of the Pentateuch to identify Him as the future Messiah. Later Old Testament writers also recognized the seed as the future deliverer and referred to Gn 3:15 as a messianic text.[21]

---

1. John Calvin, *Commentaries on the Book of Genesis*, vol. 1, trans. John King (Grand Rapids: Eerdmans, 1948), 167.
2. John Walton, *Genesis*, NIV Application Commentary (Grand Rapids: Zondervan, 2001), 226.
3. Rashi on Gn 3:15 (translation from Hebrew my own).
4. Todd J. Murphy, *Pocket Dictionary for the Study of Biblical Hebrew* (Downers Grove, IL: InterVarsity, 2003), 69, defines an etiology as "[t]he disciplined study of origins or causation of a particular phenomenon."
5. See, for example, John Skinner, *Genesis*, The International Critical Commentary (New York: Charles Scribner's Sons, 1910), 81; Claus Westermann, *Genesis 1–11*, A Continental Commentary, trans. John J. Scullion S. J. (Minneapolis: Fortress, 1994), 259; Nahum M. Sarna, *Genesis*, The JPS Torah Commentary (Philadelphia; New York; Jerusalem: The Jewish Publication Society, 1989), 27; for a more nuanced view, see Gordon J. Wenham, *Genesis 1–15*, Word Biblical Commentary, vol. 1, ed. David A. Hubbard and Glenn W. Barker (Waco, TX: Word Books, 1987), 80–81.
6. Michael Rydelnik, *The Messianic Hope*, (Nashville: Broadman & Holman, 2010), 131–34, helpfully classifies the nonmessianic interpretations of Gn 3:15 as follows: (1) The naturalistic view, i.e., the etiological explanation; (2) the symbolic view, which sees this verse as a depiction of continual, unresolved conflict between humans and the forces of evil; and (3) the *Sensus Plenior* view, a view granting the Messianic interpretation of this verse, not because of the historical sense, but only because of subsequent progressive revelation (i.e., a "fuller meaning" than what the original author intended).

7. John H. Sailhamer, *Genesis*, The Expositor's Bible Commentary, rev. ed., vol. 1 Genesis–Leviticus, ed. Tremper Longman III and David E. Garland (Grand Rapids: Zondervan, 2008), 91.

8. Seed can have a singular (one individual; cf. Gn 4:25) or a collective sense (a group of people; cf. Gn 15:13) depending on the context. According to Jack Collins, "A Syntactical Note on Genesis 3:15: Is the Woman's Seed Singular or Plural?" *Tyndale Bulletin* 48 (1997): 141–48, the individual sense can be distinguished from the collective sense primarily by the pronouns and adjectives modifying the seed. For example, when seed refers to a group, though it can have singular verb inflections, the pronouns and adjectives will be plural: "Then the LORD said to Abram, 'Know this for certain: Your offspring [seed] will be foreigners in a land that does not belong to them [plural pronoun]'" (Gn 15:13; words in brackets provided). On the other hand, if the pronouns and adjective are singular, seed refers to a single individual: "God has given me another [singular adjective] child [seed] in place of Abel, since Cain killed him" (Gn 4:25; words in brackets provided). "But I will also make a nation of the slave's son because he [singular pronoun] is your offspring [seed]" (Gn 21:13). Collins's findings have been challenged on the basis of Gn 22:17, where some argue that the collective seed ("offspring [seed] as numerous as the stars of the sky . . .") is modified with a singular pronoun ("possess the gate of his enemies," KJV). In response, some defend Collins's findings by arguing that the second reference to seed in Gn 22:17 must be singular since the verb form of the second clause is an imperfect with a non-converting *waw* rather than a *waw*-consecutive (see T. Desmond Alexander, "Further Observations on the Term 'Seed' in Genesis," *Tyndale Bulletin* 48 (1997): 363–67; J. Hamilton, "The Skull Crushing Seed of the Woman: Inner-Biblical Interpretation of Genesis 3:15," *Southern Baptist Journal of Theology* 10, no. 2 [2006]: 32). Granting the possibility of circular reasoning, and given the programmatic and enigmatic nature of this verse, I believe it is prudent to view the author's use of seed in Gn 3:15 as intentionally ambiguous. The ambiguity in no way undermines the messianic interpretation; rather, it provides the room for the plot to lead us from the group to the individual.

9. T. Desmond Alexander, "Messianic Ideology in Genesis," in *The Lord's Anointed: Interpretation of Old Testament Messianic Texts*, ed. P. E. Satterthwaite, R. S. Hess and G. J. Wenham (Grand Rapids: Baker, 1995), 22.

10. For a thorough treatment of Genesis 1–11 as the introduction to the Torah, see Seth D. Postell, *Adam as Israel* (Eugene, OR: Pickwick, 2011).

11. The Former Prophets are those books that function as the continuation of Israel's story after Moses' death: Joshua, Judges, 1–2 Samuel, 1–2 Kings. Ruth always appears in the third section in the tripartite structure of the Hebrew Bible, the Writings.

12. Alexander, "Messianic Ideology in Genesis," 22–23, writes, "Taken together these features focus attention on a unique lineage which begins with Adam and concludes with the sons of Israel. This family line forms the backbone of the book."

13. Ibid., 24.

14. "And He said to Adam, 'Because you listened to your wife's voice and ate from the tree about which I commanded you, "Do not eat from it": The ground is cursed because of you. You will eat from it by means of painful labor all the days of your life. It will produce thorns and thistles for you, and you will eat the plants of the field. You will eat bread by the sweat of your brow until you return to the ground, since you were taken from it. For you are dust, and you will return to dust'" (Gn 3:17-19).

15. See John H. Sailhamer, *The Pentateuch as Narrative* (Grand Rapids: Zondervan, 1992), 129–30.

16. The HCSB translates the phrase "in the days to come."

17. Sailhamer, *The Pentateuch as Narrative*, 36.

18. Compare Nm 24:7-9 with Gn 49:9; Zch 9:9 with Gn 49:10-11; Isa 63:1-3 with Gn 49:11; Ezk 21:27 [MT 32] with Gn 49:10. Concerning the messianic interpretation of Gn 49:8-12, Alexander, "Messianic Ideology in Genesis," writes, "Whether we interpret 49:8-12 as anticipating the time of the united monarchy or some future 'messianic' period, it is clear that this passage forms an integral part of the overall picture being presented by the writer of Genesis. The king who will arise in the future from the tribe of Judah is clearly linked to the line of 'seed' that is traced throughout the book of Genesis" (36).

19. W. Hall Harris, ed., The NET Bible Notes, 1st Accordance electronic edition, version 4.1 (Richardson, TX: Biblical Studies Press, 2005).

20. "So the great dragon was thrown out—the ancient serpent, who is called the Devil and Satan, the one who deceives the whole world. He was thrown to earth, and his angels with him. . . . When the dragon saw that he had been thrown to earth, he persecuted the woman who gave birth to the male child" (Rev 12:9,13).

21. Rydelnik, *The Messianic Hope*, 135.

Genesis 9:25-27

The Promise through Noah

WILLIAM C. VARNER

The ark had been parked. With the deluge past, it was now time for Noah and his family to enter into the postdiluvian *renewed world* that lay before them. Noah's first act after debarkation was to build an altar and offer sacrifices to the Lord. This act elicited God's promise that He would not smite every living thing again as He had done (Gn 8:20-22). The Lord then established a "covenant" with Noah and his descendants (9:9). Since we all are his descendants, the regulations of this covenant apply to all of mankind.

Jewish tradition states that the Noahic covenant, embodying what are called the "Noahide Laws," illustrates what God expects of all people, not just the Jewish people. The provisions of the Noahic covenant regarding the spread of life, the source of life, and the sanctity of life are given in Gn 9:1-7. God pledged His faithfulness to these promises by the token of a "bow in the clouds" (Gn 9:12-17). A warrior or hunter hangs up his bow after using it; the Lord placed His bow in the sky after He shot it at the earth with the flood. By this sign, He promised that He would not again send that same specific act of a flood judgment!

Noah's three sons—Shem, Ham, and Japheth—became the progenitors of new life on an earth that had been wrecked by the flood but also purified from its ungodly inhabitants (cf. Gn 6:7). As the sons are mentioned in the text, Gn 9:18 records a tiny piece of information that is important in understanding the rest of the account: "Ham was the father of Canaan." The following verses (9:20-27) record a sad event in the life of Noah, the man of whom it had been said, "Noah was a righteous man, blameless among his contemporaries; Noah walked with God" (Gn 6:9).

These verses describe the temporary fall of a good man. "Noah, a man of the soil, was the first to plant a vineyard. He drank some of the wine, became drunk, and uncovered himself in his tent" (Gn 9:20-21). Scripture records both the victories and the defeats of God's people. That fact is an all-too-often overlooked proof of the Bible's truthfulness, since authors often tend to play down the faults of their "heroes." Here is Noah with all his warts and blemishes.

Those who have been touched by the evil of drunkenness in the family can most fully appreciate the terrible shame for the family that results from a parent's overindulgence. "Wine is a mocker, strong drink a brawler, and whoever is led astray by it is not wise" (Prv 20:1 ESV). In this instance, the fairest flower that humanity had thus far yielded suddenly wilted. However, Noah's disgrace was only increased by his younger son's subsequent action. "Ham, the father of Canaan, saw his father naked and told his two brothers outside" (Gn 9:22). The exact nature of Ham's deed has caused much discussion among commentators. An accidental glance at his father's nakedness would not seem to merit the harsh judgment on a group of Ham's descendants that later follows.

Leviticus 18 may provide help in this regard. That chapter warns the Israelites against some of the abominable sexual practices of the Canaanites. The particular sexual sin condemned is that of unlawful relations between near relatives (i.e., incest). The phrase that is used to describe the act is "to uncover the nakedness" (Lv 18:6-18 ESV; HCSB "have sexual intercourse"). Therefore, there are many who see Ham's sin as sexual abuse of Noah while his father was in a drunken stupor. Then to make matters even worse, Ham went out and declared (Hebrew word *nagad*) the fact to his brothers in a boastful and arrogant spirit.

Ham's brothers, however, did not share his disgraceful glee. "Then Shem and Japheth took a cloak and placed it over both their shoulders, and walking backwards, they covered their father's nakedness. Their faces were turned away, and they did not see their father naked" (Gn 9:23). Shem and Japheth continued to honor their father (Ex 20:12), even when he was in a state of dishonor. Their approach was characterized by sensitivity and not sensuality.

"Noah awoke from his drinking and learned what his youngest son had done to him" (Gn 9:24). When his head cleared and Noah realized what had happened, he uttered what could be described as "the most far-reaching prophecy in the entire Bible." Genesis 9:25-27 records a series of simple yet profound prophetic utterances consisting of one curse and two blessings. These prophecies extend far beyond Noah's immediate offspring to the yet-unborn generations that would issue from his sons. In effect, the future history of the human race is revealed in its broadest outlines in these verses.

Before considering the messianic implications of this utterance, notice how messianic prophecies are not isolated statements, separated from the overall narrative of the Hebrew Bible. One could actually describe the individual messianic prophecies as the numerous tips of a rather large iceberg! That huge "iceberg" is the story that moves progressively through the Hebrew Bible until its consummation in the new covenant Scriptures. This article is not the place to trace that entire narrative, but it is necessary to show the connection of this passage to the previous passage about the Messiah in Gn 3 and leave the rest of the chapters to trace how this promise continues.[1]

Just as in the account of creation when God planted (2:8) a garden for the man and woman to enjoy, so in this account Noah plants (9:20) an orchard. The outcome is similar to that of the story in the garden of Eden when both ate from their garden/orchard and became aware of their nakedness (3:7; 9:21-22,24). Human enjoyment of God's gifts in both passages could not be sustained. Like Adam, Noah sinned, and the effects of that sin were felt in the generations to follow. "When read in the context of the events of the Garden of Eden, the allusive details of Noah's drunkenness become quite transparent. In a subtle parody of humanity's original state ('They were both naked and not ashamed,' 2:25), Noah in his drunkenness 'uncovered himself in his tent.'"[2]

With the connection between Gn 9 and Gn 2–3 observed, it is necessary to examine Gn 9:25-27 and consider the far-reaching implications of the curse/blessing on Noah's sons.

CANAAN, SON OF HAM

By divine inspiration, the Torah records Noah's first prophecy about Canaan and his descendants: he said, "Canaan will be cursed. He will be the lowest of slaves to his brothers" (Gn 9:25). The observant reader at this point may ask, *If Ham committed the act, why is his son Canaan cursed?* This important question is not directly answered in the immediate context. No reason is clearly stated why a son of Ham is cursed and not Ham himself. Perhaps the reason is that as Noah was dishonored by one of his sons, so Ham will be dishonored by one of his sons. Or, perhaps Noah prophetically saw that Canaan and his descendants would reproduce the sensuous character of their father Ham more than Noah's other descendants. Biblical history and archaeology do inform us that the Canaanites became notoriously ungodly and sensuous (see Gn 15:16; Lv 18). Or, perhaps it is that because Gn 9:1 states that God had already blessed Noah and his sons (including Ham), it would be impossible for Ham himself to then be cursed (see Nm 23:20).

Whatever the reason God through Noah prophetically cursed Canaan, notice that not all of Ham's descendants were placed under a curse of servitude and bondage (the phrase "lowest of slaves" describes the most severe slavery imaginable!). Additionally, the next passage in Genesis is what is called the Table of Nations (Gn 10), a chapter that is actually out of chronological order within Genesis. It describes the location where the nations descended from Shem, Ham, and Japheth settled after their scattering occasioned by the Tower of Babel incident (Gn 11). This out-of-order placement is to show where the descendants of the sons in Gn 9:25-27—Shem, Ham, and Japheth—would eventually settle.

The section that describes Ham's descendants (10:6-20) shows that Ham had three other sons: Cush, Egypt, and Put (10:6). In Gn 10:7-14 their sons are listed along with the places they eventually settled. Cush refers to Ethiopia, and Put refers to North Africa/Libya. Thus, three of Ham's sons and their descendants eventually settled in what came to be called Africa. Their brother Canaan's descendants, however, did not settle in Africa, but in the land to which they gave their father's name—the land of Canaan—in the eastern Mediterranean, not in Africa. It was this land that Yahweh later promised to Abraham, a descendant of Shem (Gn 11:10-26; 12:5-7; 15:18-21). Joshua eventually conquered this land and placed the Canaanites under forced slave labor (Jos 9:23), and even later, Solomon followed the same practice by enslaving the surviving Canaanites in his day (1Kg 9:20-21). Thus, the prophetic curse of slavery was literally fulfilled on the Canaanites. The curse, therefore, applies to no ethnic group in existence today. Even though the myth that Ham's African descendants were cursed has been used to justify racism, it is absolutely false. The so-called "curse on Ham" is the "curse that never was."

Returning again to the parallels with the events in the garden of Eden, Ham did not follow the lead of Shem and Japheth who, like Adam and Eve and God Himself, did not look upon human nakedness but covered it with coats of skin (3:21). The sons of Noah thus belong to "two groups of humankind, those who like Adam and Eve hide the shame of their nakedness and those who like Ham, or rather the Canaanites, have no sense of their shame before God. The Canaanites can only be cursed; the line of Shem will be blessed (9:26)."[3]

SHEM

This of course leads to a consideration of the different response of God to the act of Shem and Japheth. "He also said: Praise the LORD, the God of Shem; Canaan will be his slave" (Gn 9:26). Leaving the prophetic curse, Noah began to issue two "blessings"—a spiritual blessing on Shem and a temporal blessing on Japheth. Actually, it was not Shem himself who was blessed, but He who would eventually be the God of Shem (i.e., "the LORD"). Our English versions indicate by the four capital letters "LORD" that the word used for God's name is the sacred personal name originally translated by William Tyndale as "Jehovah," but probably more accurately pronounced as "Yahweh." It is God's covenant name, indicating His eternal existence and His personal relationship to His covenant people. It is "the LORD" (i.e., Yahweh) who would be the God of Shem and his descendants.[4]

Ethnically, Shem became the ancestor of the "Shemites" (i.e., Semites), the vast group of the great Middle Eastern peoples, including those who would later be called Arabs and Jews. What this prophecy indicates, therefore, is that God would establish a personal covenant relationship with people in the line of Shem. The family descendants of Shem are also listed as part of the "Table of Nations" in Gn 10:21-31. Most important, however, is that from Gn 11:10 through the book of Revelation, the biblical account deals almost exclusively with Shem's descendants. Genesis 11:27 introduces us to Abram, a descendant of Shem, and it is with him that God made a special covenant, forming the basis for all of His later dealings in salvation history.

Notice, however, both what the passage says, and what it does not say. Some may hesitate to classify this passage as messianic because an individual Messiah is not mentioned—only a great blessing on the Shemites. This shortsightedness on the part of readers, however, will lead to them missing what is actually a necessary chapter in the messianic narrative of the Bible, i.e., His ancestral lineage. Noah's long-range prophecy actually has its fulfillment in later biblical history.

To lay out the context, here is a brief summary of the chronological and genealogical development of Genesis. In Gn 3:15, the promise was given that the ultimate deliverance from Satan would come through the seed of a woman, i.e., the deliverer will come not from the angels nor from an interplanetary visitor, but from the human race, a descendant of Eve. Here, in Gn 9:26, the promise was narrowed to one branch of mankind—namely the line of Shem. We should expect, therefore, that the descendants of Shem will be the branch of mankind through whom the messianic promise will be channeled. The Table of Nations in Gn 10:21 calls attention to the relationship of Shem and Japheth ("Shem, Japheth's, older brother . . . the father of all the children of Eber"). The reference to Shem and Japheth together recalls Noah's blessing on these two here in 9:26-27. The "sons of Eber" anticipate the genealogy that lies ahead, which leads to the birth of Abram, a descendant of the blessed Shem (11:10-26).

Unsurprisingly, therefore, soon afterward in Gn 12:1-3, the promise of a Messiah-King is further narrowed to one of Shem's descendants, Abram. While the drama of Abram/Abraham and his sons is too long to be recounted here, predictably the promised blessing was eventually channeled through Abraham's son Isaac

(Gn 21:12) and later through his grandson Jacob (Gn 28:13-15). Finally, the family tree, at least in Genesis, is traced through Jacob's son, Judah, and his descendants (49:10). Years after that, the promise was narrowed to one individual within that tribe of Judah named David (2Sm 7:4-17).

The OT narrative gives many more characteristics of this promised one, but these and many other prophecies find their remarkable fulfillment in one individual—Jesus of Nazareth, a descendant of David, Judah, Abraham, Shem, Noah, and Eve. Note how Luke is careful to mention Shem in the Messiah's genealogy in Lk 3:23,36. Again, Noah's prophecy proved to be far reaching and provides another link in the unbroken chain of redemption centering in the Messiah—the hope of Israel and the Savior of the world. In this amazing manner, this passage is quite messianic, even though an individual Messiah is not mentioned.

JAPHETH

Immediately following the blessing on Shem, Noah, with a clear head, turns to the other brother in his prophecy, stating "God will extend Japheth; he will dwell in the tents of Shem; Canaan will be his slave" (Gn 9:27). The last of Noah's prophecies thus concerns the blessing on Japheth and his descendants. According to the Table of Nations again (Gn 10:2-5), Japheth's sons included Gomer, Magog, Javan, and Meshech—names familiar to Bible readers as describing those tribes which settled in areas that would later be called Eastern Europe and Russia. "From these the coastland peoples of the Gentiles were separated into their lands, everyone according to his language, according to their families, into their nations" (Gn 10:5 NKJV). An anthropologist would refer to Japheth's descendants as the Indo-European peoples. What was the prophetic blessing for these *goyim* or "nations"? According to Gn 9:27, they would be extended. This must refer to territorial and temporal enlargement—exactly what took place in the later history of the Indo-European peoples and their culture. It is not disrespectful of the achievements of all peoples to note that much of the world's exploration, as well as creative culture, appeared among Japheth's descendants.[5]

But it is not only the temporal blessing of territory and influence that fulfills the promise to Japheth. Note the second line in Noah's prophecy about his descendants: "and he will dwell in the tents of Shem" (Gn 9:27b). The phrase "dwell in the tents" does not mean a military conquest or a displacement but must be understood in the language of its Middle Eastern context. To dwell in someone's tent means to share in the belongings of your host who owns the tent (cf. Ps 84:10). This image was brought home to me in a graphic way when I visited with a Bedouin man in his tent in the spring of 1980. His hospitality (for which the Bedouin are famous) knew no limits as he invited me to share what he owned. Although I only asked for and received a cup of strong Bedouin coffee, I will never forget his hospitality and how I learned firsthand the meaning of this phrase as I "dwelt in his tent" by sharing what was his.

According to Gn 9:27, therefore, someday the Gentile peoples will dwell in the tents of the Shemites.[6] In other words, Japheth will partake of Shem's unique privilege—a special relationship to the one true God, as was mentioned above through Abraham, Isaac, Jacob, and Judah. In this regard, see the reference to Abram's seed blessing the nations (12:3) and the descendant of Judah being the One to whom the "peoples" (*amim*) shall someday gather (49:10). Although the descendants of Japheth will not displace Shem, they will someday come to share in what was promised to Shem, i.e., a special relationship with God. An understanding of the cultural meaning of "dwelling in another's tents" helps to clarify the role of Japheth, not as a displacer, but as a sharer.

Generations of Torah readers, especially the Jewish people, must have wondered and speculated about how this prophecy from Noah would find its fulfillment. Not until the appearance of Shem's greatest Son did the prophecy begin to "flesh out" its full significance—a blessing for Shem's descendants, but also for Japheth's and even for Ham's descendants. Jesus the Messiah declared that He was initially sent to the lost sheep of Israel, but He also indicated that His work would be extended beyond the realms of the Jewish people by His declaration in Jn 10:16, "But I have other sheep that are not of this fold; I must bring them also, and they will listen to my voice. Then there will be one flock, one shepherd." It was not until after His resurrection, ascension, and granting of the Holy Spirit to the young church that the tent door was finally opened wide to the Japhetites. He commissioned His Jewish apostles to disciple all "nations" (Mt 28:19), as they would go "to the ends of the earth" (Ac 1:8). Despite these commissions, those early Jewish believers were hesitant to go to those supposedly "unclean" Gentiles. Finally, God showed Peter that the Gentiles were to be granted the same opportunity that the Jews had received. In Joppa, where an earlier reluctant Jonah had fled to avoid a commission to the Gentiles, an initially reluctant Peter received a vision to go to the Gentiles. And so, Cornelius, a descendant of Japheth, eventually came to dwell by faith in the tents of Shem (Ac 10). And the great apostle Paul came to be known as the "apostle to the Gentiles" (Gal 2:8 NIV; see also Rm 15:16; 1Tm 2:7).

The way the gospel relates to each of Noah's three branches of mankind is evident in the narrative of Ac 8–10. Acts 8 records the conversion of the Ethiopian eunuch, a descendant of Ham. The Hamites thus are not omitted. Note even that Canaan is not omitted from the blessings of the gospel, despite the curse. Jesus Himself lovingly blessed a Canaanite woman in Syro-Phoenicia (Mt 15:21-28). Acts 9 then records the conversion of Saul, who was a Benjamite descendant of Shem (Phl 3:5). And as just mentioned, Ac 10 records the conversion of Cornelius, who was a descendant of Japheth. While the chapter divisions were not the work of Luke, it appears that he had a purpose in mind to exemplify the universal application of the Gospel to all the branches of mankind by recording these three separate conversions in a row!

This is God's marvelous plan of redemption of all mankind, both Jew and Greek, barbarian, Scythian, slave, and free (Col 3:11; Gal 3:28)! Whatever their ethnic or racial ancestry, individuals among the many and varied people groups of this world can find their salvation through the promised Messiah, a descendant Himself of Shem. It is He who brings life, peace, and hope to any individual from any nation who trusts Him as Savior (Rev 5:9). He who is the true Messiah of Israel is also the true Savior of the World!

---

1. Also, see the article in this Handbook on Gn 3:15 by Seth Postell.
2. John Sailhamer, *The Pentateuch as Narrative* (Grand Rapids: Zondervan, 1992) 129.
3. Ibid., 130.
4. There also may be an indirect reference in the son's name, Shem, to the two great lines of humanity that come from Noah in the account of the Tower of Babel and its aftermath. Two lines of humanity diverge from the midst of the sons of Noah at Babel. Those who seek to make a "name" (*shem*, 11:4) for themselves by refusing to obey the command to spread abroad and by building Babylon comprise one group. The other group are those who descend from Abram for whom the Lord will also make a "name" (*shem*, 12:2).
5. It is simply not clear from which son of Noah the great peoples of the Far East descended. Some believe they were also Japhetic, but it is simply unknown from which of Noah's sons the people of *Sinim* descended (Isa 49:12).
6. I am aware that not all interpreters have concluded that this is a prophecy of Japheth dwelling in the tents of Shem. Some argue that God is the proper subject of the verb "dwell," and the prophecy thus refers to God's special covenant relationship to the descendants of Shem, which of course includes the Israelite/Jewish people. Among scholars advocating that God will dwell in Shem's tents are Charles Briggs (*Messianic Prophecy*, Peabody, MA: Hendrickson Publishers, 1988), 82; Walter Kaiser (*The Messiah in the Old Testament*, Grand Rapids: Zondervan, 1995), 45; and James Smith (*The Promised Messiah*, Nashville: Thomas Nelson, 1993), 45. Arguments for Japheth dwelling in Shem's tents can be found in E. W. Hengstenberg (*Christology of the Old Testament*, Grand Rapids: Kregel, 1970), 41; Gerard Van Groningen (*Messianic Revelation in the Old Testament*, Eugene, OR: Wipf and Stock, 1997), 129; and William Varner (*The Messiah: Revealed, Rejected, Received*, Bloomington, IN: AuthorHouse, 2004), 27–28. Briggs adds that Jewish interpreters such as Targum Onkelos, Philo, Maimonides, Rashi, and Ibn Ezra take God as the subject, while "ancient Fathers and Reformers and the great body of modern interpreters regard Japhet as the subject" (82fn). While I believe that Japheth is the correct subject, the ultimate Messianic interpretation of this text is still clear, whichever view one adopts as to the identity of the "dweller in Shem's tents."

Genesis 12:1-3; 22:16-18

The Covenant with Abraham

T. DESMOND ALEXANDER

The origins of messianic thinking in the OT may be traced back to the book of Genesis, even though the text makes no direct reference to the Messiah or "Anointed One" (Hb. *māšîaḥ*), and the only reference to anointing involves a stone pillar (Gn 31:13).[1] While the vocabulary normally associated with the concept of a messiah is absent from Genesis, the idea of a future, unique King, who will bring God's blessing to other people, emerges from the plot of the entire book. This idea rests not on a few isolated verses, scattered here and there, but on the central plot that binds together the diverse episodes comprising Genesis. Different elements contribute to this plot, creating an expectation that God will bring to fulfillment His redemptive plan through a royal descendant of Abraham. The divine speeches recorded in Gn 12:1-3 and 22:16-18, which frame the core of the Abraham narrative, play a significant part within the broader Genesis story. Neither of these speeches is normally regarded as "messianic," but they both contribute much to a messianic reading of Genesis as a whole.

Of the two divine speeches, Gn 12:1-3 is better known, coming near the beginning of the narrative block associated with Abram/Abraham[2] that extends from Gn 11:27 to 25:11. The boundaries of this major narrative section are marked by distinctive headings in Gn 11:27 and 25:12.[3] Placed after assorted details in 11:27-32 that set the background scene (including the fact that Sarai/Sarah[4] is childless, v. 30), Gn 12:1-3 records God's summons to Abraham to separate from his immediate family in order to relocate to a new country. Setting the agenda for everything recorded in Gn 12–25 and beyond, this short divine speech holds a significance that should not be underestimated.[5]

If Gn 12:1-3 introduces a train of events that will center on Abraham, the divine speech in Gn 22:16-18 marks the climax of God's dealings with Abraham. As is generally recognized, Gn 11:27–22:19 forms the core of the Abraham story, with Gn 22:20–25:11 functioning as an appendix that focuses on the deaths of Sarah (23:1-20) and Abraham (25:1-11), and Isaac's marriage to Rebekah (24:1-67), an event anticipated by a brief reference to Rebekah in 22:23.[6]

As the last recorded words of God to Abraham, Gn 22:16-18 brings the narrative in chaps. 12–22 to an important climax. The significance of this short speech is underlined by its taking the form of a solemn oath, in which God swears by Himself; such divine oaths are exceptionally rare.[7] The contents of this final divine speech are closely related to the initial call of Abraham in Gn 12:1-3, but some variation does occur. When comparing the two speeches, consideration must be given to where each is placed within the Abraham narrative: certain differences between these speeches result from their occurrence at the beginning and end of the Abraham story. Intentionally, the two speeches form an important frame or inclusio around the main part of the Abraham narrative.[8]

Before exploring in detail these divine speeches, it may be helpful to consider the broader literary context within which the Abraham narrative is set. The story of Abraham's life forms part of a larger narrative that traces the progress of a particular human lineage, beginning with Adam and ending with the children and grandchildren of Jacob/Israel.[9] This family line includes Adam, Noah, Abraham, Isaac, Jacob, and Joseph, all of whom occupy center stage at different times in the Genesis story. The literary structure of Genesis is designed to help the reader follow the progress of this unique family line as narrative blocks are interspersed with genealogies. In chaps. 5 and 11 two linear genealogies swiftly trace this continuous family line through multiple generations, with minimal information being recorded about those named. Elsewhere, longer narrative sections recount carefully selected information that contributes to a fuller understanding of the significance of this family for the overall plot of Genesis. The narrator of Genesis is especially interested in this distinctive lineage because of its role in God's plan to reverse the consequences of Adam and Eve's betrayal of the Lord God in the garden of Eden.

A number of connected features underscore the importance of the unique lineage that forms the backbone of Genesis. At the outset, this family line is linked to the Lord God's pronouncement upon the serpent in Gn 3:14-15, which states that the "seed" (HCSB) or "offspring" (NIV) (Hb. *zera'*) of the woman will "strike" the serpent's head.[10] This promise, which has long been viewed as the first announcement of the gospel, is sometimes designated the protevangelium. Traditionally, the offspring of the woman mentioned in v. 15 has been viewed as an individual, but modern scholarship, especially influenced by form-criticism, has preferred to understand the offspring as denoting humanity in general.[11] This latter interpretation, however, requires Gn 3 to be wrested from its present literary context, for the book of Genesis as a whole offers its own explanation of the woman's offspring.

Genesis 4 begins by implying that the offspring of the woman may possibly be linked to Abel, but his untimely death at the hand of Cain creates uncertainty. Cain's evil action excludes him from being the one who will overcome the serpent, and the genealogical information concerning Cain's descendants in Gn 4:17-24 offers little prospect of hope, concluding in the seventh generation with Lamech, a polygamist. When he vengefully kills a young man for striking him, Lamech boasts that he is greater than Cain.

After tracing the line of Cain for seven generations, the narrative jumps back in time to record that Eve gave birth to another son, Seth. Importantly, Eve declares that God has granted her another "child" (HCSB) or "offspring" (ESV) (Hb. *zera'*) "in place of Abel" (Gn 4:25). The mantel of hope regarding the woman's offspring, who will overcome the serpent, is now placed on Seth. This possibility is underlined by the immediately following comment that "at that time people began to call on the name of Yahweh" (Gn 4:26).

The subsequent genealogy in Gn 5 traces a particular line of Adam's descendants through Seth, coming eventually to Noah. The genealogy is largely formulaic in style, but a subtle comparison with Cain's family takes place. By contrasting seventh-generation Enoch with Lamech, the genealogy gives the impression that Seth's descendants are righteous, and it concludes with a hopeful prediction that Noah will bring relief for humanity as it struggles under God's curse (Gn 5:29).[12]

Noah's role within the Genesis story is significant. Humanity's violence defiles the earth and causes God to decide to eradicate every person, apart from Noah and his close family (Gn 6:11-21). Their survival is a testimony to Noah's obedience and trust in God. Moreover, Noah is associated with a divine covenant that offers hope to people estranged from God (Gn 9:8-17).

A second linear genealogy in Gn 11 lists ten generations, moving from Shem, Noah's son, to Terah, the father of Abraham. This leads into the Abraham narrative, which is the first of three major narrative sections (Gn 11:27–25:11; 25:19–35:29; 37:2–50:26), separated by segmented genealogies (Gn 25:12-18; 36:1–37:1). These longer narrative sections focus attention mainly on Abraham, Jacob, and Joseph, respectively, representing different generations of the same family, although other individuals have significant parts to play in this story (e.g. Sarah, Lot, Ishmael, Isaac, Rebekah, Esau, Laban, Rachel, Leah, and Judah).

Beginning with Abraham, the patriarchal narratives are dominated by the idea that humanity will experience God's blessing through those who are at the center of this unique family line. As will become apparent in more detail below, the hope of divine blessing is highlighted when God summons Abraham to be a blessing for the benefit of the families of the earth (Gn 12:1-3). Blessing is later associated with Abraham's son Isaac, his grandson Jacob, and his great-grandson Joseph.

The Jacob narrative (Gn 25:19–35:29) highlights an important link between blessing and the birthright normally associated with the eldest son. This connection between blessing and birthright surfaces in the turbulent relationship that exists between the twin boys Esau and Jacob, and involves a subtle wordplay in the Hebrew text where the terms for birthright and blessing are *bĕrākâ* and *bĕkōrâ*, respectively.[13] Whereas Jacob, the younger of the twins, yearns to possess the birthright, his older brother Esau considers it of little value.

A short incident illustrates this: Exhausted and hungry from hunting game, Esau is easily persuaded by Jacob to sell his birthright to his younger brother for a bowl of stew (Gn 25:29-34). Tellingly, the narrator remarks, "So Esau despised his birthright" (Gn 25:34).

In the subsequent narrative, the significance of this birthright is conveyed through the content of the blessing that the elderly Isaac pronounces upon Jacob. Jacob, who has been encouraged by his mother to disguise himself as Esau, deceives his father into thinking that he is his firstborn son. Isaac says to Jacob, "Ah, the smell of my son is like the smell of a field that the Lord has blessed. May God give to you—from the dew of the sky and from the richness of the land—an abundance of grain and new wine. May peoples serve you and nations bow down to you. Be master over your brothers; may your mother's sons bow down to you. Those who curse you will be cursed, and those who bless you will be blessed" (Gn 27:27-29). The expectations articulated by Isaac for his son are extraordinary, given that Isaac is a seminomadic herdsman/farmer, living as a foreigner in Canaan. Importantly, Isaac's blessing of Jacob echoes in part the call of Abraham in Gn 12:1-3, implying that the divine promises, covenanted by God to Abraham,[14] now pass to Jacob. Additionally, the prospect that peoples will serve and nations will bow down to Jacob reinforces the expectation that the family line will produce a unique king. Previously, God informed Abraham and Sarah that kings would be among their descendants (Gn 17:6,16).

The motif of kingship comes to the fore at the start of the final major narrative section in Genesis.[15] Focusing on Jacob's sons, chaps. 37–50 begin by giving prominence to Joseph, observing how he was set apart from his brothers in a variety of ways. Various factors associate Joseph with royalty.[16] In spite of Joseph's having 10 older brothers, Jacob privileged him above his brothers, giving him a special robe that possibly indicated his father's wish to treat him as his "firstborn."[17] Later tradition, as revealed in 1Chr 5:1-2, confirms that Joseph replaced Rueben as firstborn,[18] and this accords with Joseph, through his two sons, Ephraim and Manasseh, receiving a double portion of the land of Canaan allocated to the 12 tribes descended from Jacob.[19] In addition to being privileged by his father, Joseph had two dreams that portrayed him as a king before whom his whole family, including parents and siblings, would bow in submission (Gn 37:5-10). As his brothers stated, "Are you really going to rule us?" (Gn 37:8).

Viewed in light of the family tradition that began with Abraham, this picture of Joseph as a king took on added significance. The expectation was created that through Joseph's lineage God's blessing would come to all the nations of the earth. Moreover, the remarkable account of Joseph's journey from prized son to imprisoned slave to prime minister reveals at every stage how Joseph, by God's help, brought blessing to others.[20] Ultimately, as Joseph himself recognized, what his brothers meant for harm, God used for good (Gn 50:20). Through saving many people from famine, Joseph's actions anticipated an even greater salvation that would come through a future royal descendant of Abraham.

While Joseph was clearly identified as the one through whom the unique family line would continue, Gn 48 reveals that this line would subsequently be traced through Joseph's younger son Ephraim. Once again, an older brother was passed over in favor of a younger brother. This pattern, seen in the lives of Isaac, Jacob, and Joseph, underlines that the continuity of the potential royal line would not be determined merely by order of birth, but in some measure by other factors that brought into consideration the character of those chosen.

Although Joseph was undoubtedly the one to whom the divine promise of blessing passed, the Genesis narrative introduces an unexpected complication in chap. 38. After Joseph's departure to Egypt, the narrative turns to consider how Judah's family line develops. Some scholars have considered chap. 38 a digression from the main plot of the Joseph story. Yet the motifs in this chapter, in light of their wider significance, suggest that chap. 38 is an integral part of the overall Genesis story. It is hardly a coincidence that the chapter begins by focusing on Judah's "firstborn" son, Er, and certain troublesome family issues associated with the continuity of his line of "seed" or "offspring" (*zera'*). Moreover, the chapter concludes by recording a birthing episode in which the apparent "firstborn" son was pushed aside by a younger brother.[21] Because the family line of Judah, through Perez, eventually led to King David (see Ru 4:18-22), this interruption to the Joseph story cannot be dismissed as insignificant.

Moreover, although Joseph is the preeminent son in chaps. 37–50, Judah rose to prominence within Jacob's family in Joseph's absence. Accompanying this rise,

Judah underwent a remarkable transformation in character as a result of his dealings with Tamar.[22] Whereas in chap. 37, he is the instigator of the plot to sell Joseph into slavery in Egypt, later Judah was willing to become a slave in Egypt so that Benjamin, Joseph's younger brother, might go free (Gn 44:18-34, esp. v. 33). Later, in chap. 49, Jacob pronounces a blessing on Judah on a par with that given to Joseph.[23] Surprisingly, perhaps, in light of Joseph's status, Jacob appears to associate future kingship with Judah. While the wording of Gn 49:10 is somewhat cryptic, it fits well with the idea recorded in Ps 78:67-72 that God rejected the "tent of Joseph" in the time of Samuel and chose David from the tribe of Judah to shepherd His people.[24] Although future kingship was initially linked to the tribe of Ephraim, it later passed to the tribe of Judah.

In Genesis as a whole, there are solid grounds for believing that the entire book associates the promised offspring of the woman in Gn 3:15 with the Davidic dynasty. This link comes primarily through the unique family line traced throughout Genesis and beyond. Importantly, the continuation of this unique family line would depend on God's intervention, as He enabled the barren matriarchs, Sarah, Rebekah, and Rachel, to bear children.[25] Moreover, God committed Himself to bring blessing to the nations of the earth through this distinctive lineage. This commitment is especially evident in the divine speeches in Gn 12:1-3 and 22:16-18.

With regard to the divine call of Abraham in Gn 12:1-3, the majority of English translations render the Hebrew text in a similar way. The HCSB translation is typical: "The LORD said to Abram: Go out from your land, your relatives, and your father's house to the land that I will show you. I will make you into a great nation, I will bless you, I will make your name great, and you will be a blessing. I will bless those who bless you, I will curse those who treat you with contempt, and all the peoples on earth will be blessed through you." While most English versions express something similar, at several points the precise meaning of the Hebrew text is open to debate. This is reflected in the HCSB footnotes for vv. 2-3. The first of these concerns the second half of v. 2, which may alternatively be translated: "I will make your name great. Be a blessing" (cf. JPS)! This wording draws attention more clearly to the presence of a second imperative in the speech, the first occurring at the very beginning ("Go . . ."). If both imperatives are given equal weight, the Lord's instruction to Abraham required him to fulfill two distinctive commands, each resulting in different outcomes. As regards "going," God indicated that the purpose or consequence of this would involve Abraham becoming a great nation, being blessed by God, and becoming famous (lit. having his name made great).[26] Consequently, the first half of the speech emphasizes how Abraham's descendants would become a great nation. As regards the second imperative ("Be a blessing . . ."), if Abraham did this, then God promised to bless those who blessed Abraham, but curse those who disdained him. Here Abraham's role in healing humanity's broken relationship with God is stressed. Unlike the first half of the speech, the second half takes on a more universal dimension, involving other nations.

The second translation issue concerns the final part of v. 3, where the HCSB footnote offers the alternative rendering, "will bless themselves by you" (cf. RSV; NET; TNK). This variant translation changes significantly the meaning of the final part of the verse, for it lessens the idea that Abraham himself had a key role to play in bringing God's blessing to others. This alternative wording implies that others would desire to be blessed as Abraham has been blessed. On balance, however, the weight of evidence supports the translation, "All the clans/families on earth will be blessed by/through you."[27] This statement brings to a climax God's speech to Abraham.[28] By being a blessing, Abraham would impact the whole of humanity. However, this was not a guarantee of divine blessing for everyone, for, as the first half of v. 3 makes clear, those who disdained Abraham would exclude themselves from experiencing God's favor.

The realization of the divine promises given to Abraham in Gn 12:1-3 depended upon the patriarch's obedience. God's speech presented Abraham with a significant challenge, for he had to abandon the security of his own family and territory in order to travel elsewhere. Moreover, Sarah's inability to have children, mentioned briefly in Gn 11:30, was a major barrier to Abraham becoming a great nation. For Abraham to believe God's promises and to act accordingly would require considerable faith. Thus, only after Abraham obediently followed God's charge to "go" did the promised blessings become unconditional.

If the call of Abraham in Gn 12:1-3 sets the direction for the story that follows, God's speech to Abraham in Gn 22:16-18 is a fitting conclusion to the main events of Abraham's life, but it also anticipates future developments. Genesis 12:1-3 introduces divine promises conditioned upon Abraham's future obedience; Gn 22:16-18 is a solemn divine oath responding to what Abraham had already done. Whereas Gn 12:1-3 includes two imperatives that challenge Abraham to obey, God's oath in Gn 22:16-18 begins and ends by acknowledging Abraham's obedience to a prior command. The test set by God at the start of Gn 22 involved sacrificing Isaac as a whole-burnt offering. Tellingly, this test placed in jeopardy the fulfillment of the divine promises previously given to Abraham.

Because Abraham obeyed God, God promised unconditionally to fulfill certain obligations. According to Gn 22:15, the "Angel of the LORD" spoke to Abraham from heaven, stating: "'By Myself I have sworn,' this is the LORD's declaration: 'Because you have done this thing and have not withheld your only son, I will indeed bless you and make your offspring as numerous as the stars of the sky and the sand on the seashore. Your offspring will possess the gates of their enemies. And all the nations of the earth will be blessed by your offspring because you have obeyed My command'" (Gn 22:16-18).

A comparison of the HCSB translation with other English versions reveals an alternative understanding of the second half of the speech. Whereas HCSB refers to "your offspring" possessing "the gates of their enemies," the ESV reads, "And your offspring shall possess the gate of his enemies" (cf. JPS; KJV). The ESV translation understands "offspring" to denote a single individual. This alternative reading has important implications for the process by which blessing will be mediated to "all the nations of the earth"; blessing will come to the "nations of the earth" through an individual rather than through all of Abraham's descendants.

The task of deciding between these alternative readings is not easy because the Hebrew word for "offspring" (*zera'*) does not change form between singular and plural (like the English word "sheep"). The first half of v. 17 speaks of Abraham's offspring becoming numerous. In light of this, it could easily be assumed that the rest of v. 17 refers to how these offspring will overcome their enemies. Against this reading, however, the verb associated with "offspring" in v. 17b is singular, as is the pronoun conjoined to "enemies." These grammatical features point toward a singular understanding of "offspring" (a similar argument may be applied to the use of "offspring" in Gn 3:15).[29] Moreover, when viewed within the context of Genesis as a whole, a strong case can be made for associating the concept of blessing with a single descendant of Abraham, rather than with all of his descendants (see below).

As with Gn 12:3, some translations of 22:18 interpret the expression involving blessing to mean either "will bless themselves" or "will find blessing" (Gn 12:3 HCSB footnote). On balance, however, it is more likely that God swears here that blessing will come to others through a single offspring of Abraham (a reality illustrated clearly later in Genesis in the lives of both Jacob and Joseph). Although Gn 22:18 recalls God's words to Abraham in 12:3, subtle variations in wording occur, drawing attention to the blessing in 22:18 being linked to Abraham's offspring rather than to Abraham himself.[30]

Within the Abraham narrative, there is undoubtedly a progression from the initial call of Abraham to the giving of the divine oath on Mount Moriah. In the first speech, the promise is conditional on Abraham's obedience to the command to go, but in the second speech the promise is in the form of an oath that guarantees unconditionally the fulfillment of what is promised. Between these two events a variety of incidents involving Abraham are recorded. Initially, attention is focused on identifying the specific territory where Abraham's descendants will become a great nation. Genesis 12–15 comes to a climax with the making of a covenant that reassures Abraham that his descendants will, after a period of time, occupy the land of Canaan (Gn 15:18-21; cf. Gn 12:7; 14:19-20).

Some years after the birth of Ishmael (Gn 16:1-16), God appeared to Abraham and, in a series of speeches, introduced what appears to be a second covenant that centers on Abraham becoming the father of many nations (Gn 17:1-27). The relationship of this covenant to the one described in Gn 15 has been the subject of debate. The covenants described in the two chapters are sufficiently different to suggest that they should be viewed as independent covenants, although there is some element of overlap.[31]

Whereas the covenant in Gn 15 guarantees that Abraham's descendants will occupy territory inhabited by various peoples, the covenant in Gn 17 focuses on Abraham's role as the spiritual father of many nations.[32] To emphasize this outcome, God changed Abram's name to Abraham. In keeping with this, the benefits of the covenant extended to those not biologically related to Abraham; this was shown through the circumcision of all the males within Abraham's household, including those bought from foreigners. Circumcision is clearly not viewed here as a sign of consanguinity. More likely, given its association with the male reproductive organ, circumcision as a covenant sign points toward the significance of the promised offspring. In light of this, God emphasized that the covenant would be established with Isaac, but not Ishmael. This distinction suggests that all males who are circumcised may experience the benefits of the covenant, but the covenant itself centered on those descendants of Abraham who comprised the unique family lineage. Centuries later an expansion of this covenant with Abraham would be established with David and his offspring (cf. Ps 89:3-4,19-37), leading eventually to Jesus Christ.

As already observed, the divine speeches in Gn 12:1-3 and 22:16-18 are integral to the book of Genesis as a whole, and Genesis itself is the first in a series of interrelated books that narrate a coherent story—beginning with creation and ending with the fall of Jerusalem to the Babylonians. In the context of this broader story the divine promises in Gn 12:1-3 and 22:16-18 help create the expectation that God's blessing will come to the nations of the earth through a future Davidic King. According to Acts 3:25-26, Peter highlighted this hope when he addressed fellow Jews in Jerusalem: "You are the sons of the prophets and of the covenant that God made with your ancestors, saying to Abraham, And all the families of the earth will be blessed through your offspring. God raised up His Servant and sent Him first to you to bless you by turning each of you from your evil ways." For Peter, Jesus Christ's coming fulfilled that aspect of God's covenant with Abraham that promised a particular "offspring" who would bless the world. A similar understanding underpins Paul's argument in Gal 3, when he contended that God's blessing comes to Gentiles through this particular offspring of Abraham, whom Paul identified as Jesus Christ (Gal 3:16).[33] Drawing on the Genesis account of Abraham and its placement chronologically prior to the Exodus account of the ratification of the covenant at Mount Sinai, Paul argued that the divine promises given to Abraham take precedence over the covenant between God and the Israelites sealed at Mount Sinai. With good reason, the divine promises given to Abraham are central to Paul's understanding of Jesus as the One who brings to fulfillment the messianic expectations associated with the Davidic dynasty.[34]

---

1. The noun "messiah" is derived from the Hebrew word *māšîaḥ*, which means "anointed one." The Greek equivalent of *māšîaḥ* is *christos*, from which comes the English word "Christ."
2. The name Abraham will be used consistently in this essay, although it is only introduced in Gn 17:5, when God changes Abram's name to Abraham.
3. Cf. M. H. Wouldstra, "The Toledot of the Book of Genesis and Their Redemptive-Historical Significance," *Calvin Theological Journal* 5 (1970): 184–89; M. A. Thomas, *These Are the Generations: Identity, Covenant, and the Toledot Formula*, The Library of Hebrew Bible/Old Testament Studies, 551 (London: T&T Clark, 2011).
4. The name Sarai is only changed to Sarah in Gn 17:15.
5. Cf. H. W. Wolff, "The Kerygma of the Yahwist," *Interpretation* 20 (1966): 131–58.
6. Genealogies are frequently used in Genesis to separate narrative sections. Although 22:20-24 is short and does not follow the pattern of the main genealogies in Genesis, its contents are genealogical in nature; cf. T. D. Alexander, *Abraham in the Negev: A Source-Critical Investigation of* Genesis *20:1-22:19* (Carlisle, PA: Paternoster, 1997), 102–103.
7. See K. A. Mathews, *Genesis 11:27–50:26*, New American Commentary 1B (Nashville: Broadman & Holman, 2005), 297–98. The use of an oath here may suggest that the events of chap. 22 are linked to the covenant introduced in chap. 17. See T. D. Alexander, "Genesis 22 and the Covenant of Circumcision," *Journal for the Study of the Old Testament* 25 (1983): 17–22; P. R. Williamson, *Abraham, Israel and the Nations: The Patriarchal Promise and Its Covenantal Development in Genesis*, Journal for the Study of the Old Testament, Supplement Series, 315 (Sheffield, UK: Sheffield Academic Press, 2000), 234–59.
8. R. W. L. Moberly, "The Earliest Commentary on the Akedah," *Vetus Testamentum* 38 (1988): 322–23; R. W. L. Moberly, *From Eden to Golgotha: Essays in Biblical Theology*, South Florida Studies in the History of Judaism (Atlanta: Scholars Press, 1992), 73.
9. Jacob is also named Israel by God in Gn 32:28.
10. T. D. Alexander, "Messianic Ideology in the Book of Genesis," in *The Lord's Anointed: Interpretation of Old Testament Messianic Texts*, ed. P. E. Satterthwaite, R. S. Hess, and G. J. Wenham (Grand Rapids/Carlisle: Baker/Paternoster, 1995), 19–39; J. Hamilton, "The Skull Crushing Seed of the Woman: Inner-Biblical Interpretation of Genesis 3:15," *Southern Baptist Journal of Theology* 10, no. 2 (2006): 30–54.
11. S. Mowinckel, *He That Cometh* (New York/Nashville: Abingdon, 1956), 11; cf. C. Westermann, *Genesis 1–11: A Commentary*, trans. J. J. Scullion (London: SPCK, 1984), 259–60. For a strong defense of Gn 3:15 as the protevangelium, see M. A. Rydelnik, *The Messianic Hope: Is the Hebrew Bible Really Messianic?*, ed. E. R. Clendenen, NAC Studies in Bible and Theology (Nashville: B&H, 2010), 129–45; cf. W. C. Kaiser, *The Messiah in the Old Testament*, Studies in Old Testament Biblical Theology (Carlisle, PA: Paternoster Press, 1997), 37–42. While the evidence for linking the "offspring of the woman" to Jesus Christ is compelling, some evangelical scholars are reluctant to designate Gn 3:15 as messianic (e.g. H. W. Bateman, D. L. Bock, and G. H. Johnston, *Jesus the Messiah: Tracing the Promises, Expectations, and Coming of Israel's King* (Grand Rapids: Kregel, 2010), 459–72.
12. Drawing on R. S. Hess, *Studies in the Personal Names of Genesis 1-11*, Alter Orient und Altes Testament 234 (Kevelaer, Germany: Butzon & Bercker, 1993), 111–62, P. E. Satterthwaite, "Genealogy in the Old Testament," in *New International Dictionary of Old Testament Theology and Exegesis* (1996), 660–61, comments, "The names in Cain's line (4:17-24), for example, seem to be related to words that suggest urban culture (Irad), religion (Mehujael, Methusael), art and music (Adah, Zillah, Naamah), and religious processions (Jabal, Jubal, Tubal-Cain). But none of this culture and religion can prevent the murderous passion of Cain recurring in a yet more lethal form in Lamech, seven generations later (4:23-24). By contrast, the line of Adam through Seth (Gn 5:1-32) contains names

that suggest the thoughts of substitution (Seth; cf. 4:25), the renewal and reestablishment of humankind (Enosh, Kenan), praise (Mahalalel), prayer for God to come down and aid (Jared), and rest from labor (Noah)."

13. M. A. Fishbane, "Composition and Structure in the Jacob Cycle (Gn 25:19–35:22)," *Journal of Jewish Studies* 26 (1975): 15–38.

14. The divine promises mentioned in Gn 12:1-3 are linked to covenants recorded in Gn 15 and 17.

15. By stating that there were kings ruling in Edom before any Israelite king reigned, Gn 36:31 raises the expectation that kingship will be established in Israel.

16. G. Van Groningen, *Messianic Revelation in the Old Testament* (Grand Rapids: Baker, 1990), 150–67.

17. On the significance of the robe, see T. D. Alexander, "The Regal Dimension of the בקעי־תולדת: Recovering the Literary Context of Genesis 37–50," in *Reading the Law: Studies in Honour of Gordon J. Wenham*, ed. J. G. McConville and K. Möller, The Library of Hebrew Bible/Old Testament Studies, (Edinburgh: T&T Clark, 2007), 202. V. P. Hamilton, *The Book of Genesis: Chapters 18–50*, New International Commentary on the Old Testament (Grand Rapids: Eerdmans, 1995), 406, observes that the syntax of 37:2 may imply that Joseph was a shepherd to his brothers, and E. I. Lowenthal, *The Joseph Narrative in Genesis: An Interpretation* (New York: Ktav, 1973), 167, fn. 7, suggests that the Hebrew expression *ben-zĕqunîm* in Gn 37:3, which HCSB translates "a son born to him in his old age," should be interpreted as meaning "born leader."

18. First Chronicles 5:1-2 records: "These were the sons of Reuben the firstborn of Israel. He was the firstborn, but his birthright was given to the sons of Joseph son of Israel, because Reuben defiled his father's bed. He is not listed in the genealogy according to birthright. Although Judah became strong among his brothers and a ruler came from him, the birthright was given to Joseph." The reference to Reuben defiling his father's bed alludes to Gn 35:22, which states, "While Israel was living in that region, Reuben went in and slept with his father's concubine Bilhah, and Israel heard about it." This action is later mentioned by Jacob in Gn 49:4: "Turbulent as water, you will no longer excel, because you got into your father's bed and you defiled it—he got into my bed." By seeking to usurp his father's place, Reuben forfeited his privileged status as firstborn.

19. See Jos 16:1-18.

20. See, in particular, Gn 39:5.

21. The midwife tied the scarlet thread to the wrist of Zerah to be able to identify him as the one born first.

22. Judah's acknowledgement in Gn 38:26 that Tamar was more righteous than he himself was appears to mark the point at which Judah underwent some kind of personal transformation. His character after this is portrayed much more positively in the Genesis account.

23. Of the different blessings pronounced by the aged Jacob upon his sons, those given to Judah (Gn 49:8-12) and Joseph (Gn 49:22-26) are the longest and most positive in content.

24. The books of Joshua and Judges provide an interesting account of how, after the time of Joshua, the tribe of Ephraim became more and more morally corrupt. In contrast, the tribe of Judah is presented in a more favorable light. See Alexander, "The Regal Dimension of the בקעי־תולדת: Recovering the Literary Context of Genesis 37–50," 207–10.

25. The barrenness of these women is mentioned in Gn 11:30; 25:21; 29:31. When children are born to them, God's role is acknowledged (Gn 21:1-2; 25:21; 30:22-24).

26. The syntax of the verbs in Gn 12:1-3 involves the sequence imperative followed by several cohortatives. According to B. K. Waltke and M. O'Connor, *An Introduction to Biblical Hebrew Syntax* (Winona Lake, IN: Eisenbrauns, 1990), 577, the cohortative verbs in this arrangement signify purpose or result.

27. There are three possible readings of the verb *nibrĕkû*: (a) a passive ("they will be blessed"), (b) a middle ("they will find blessing"), or (c) a reflexive ("they will bless themselves"). The earliest versions (LXX, Targum Onkelos, Vg; cf. Ac 3:25; Gal 3:8) reflect the passive sense; cf. O. T. Allis, "The Blessing of Abraham," *Princeton Theological Review,* 25 (1927): 263–98; V. P. Hamilton, *The Book of Genesis: Chapters 1–17*, New International Commentary on the Old Testament (Grand Rapids: Eerdmans, 1990), 374–76. A strong case for the passive reading is made by B. J. Noonan, "Abraham, Blessing, and the Nations: A Reexamination of the Niphal and Hitpael of ברך in the Patriarchal Narratives," *Hebrew Studies,* 51 (2010): 73–93; cf. W. Yarchin, "Imperative and Promise in Genesis 12:1-3," *Studia Biblica and Theologica* 10 (1980): 164–78; Williamson, *Abraham, Israel and the Nations: The Patriarchal Promise and Its Covenantal Development in Genesis*, 220–34; P. R. Williamson, *Sealed with an Oath: Covenant in God's Unfolding Purpose*, New Studies in Biblical Theology 23 (Downers Grove, IL; Leicester, England: IVP/Apollos, 2007), 80–81.

28. G. J. Wenham, *Genesis 1–15*, Word Biblical Commentary 1 (Waco, TX: Word, 1987), 278, comments, "This clause brings the passage to a triumphant and universal conclusion."

29. Cf. C. J. Collins, "A Syntactical Note (Genesis 3:15): Is the Woman's Seed Singular or Plural?" *Tyndale Bulletin* 48 (1997): 139–48; T. D. Alexander, "Further Observations of the Term 'Seed' in Genesis," *Tyndale Bulletin* 48 (1997): 363–67.

30. Williamson, *Abraham, Israel and the Nations*, 223–28; 250–51.

31. Williamson, *Abraham, Israel and the Nations*; Williamson, *Sealed with an Oath*, 84–91; T. D. Alexander, "Abraham Re-Assessed Theologically: The Abraham Narrative and the New Testament Understanding of Justification by Faith," in *He Swore an Oath: Biblical Themes from Genesis*, ed. R. S. Hess, P. E. Satterthwaite, and G. J. Wenham (Grand Rapids/Carlisle: Baker/Paternoster, 1994), 7–28; T. D. Alexander, *From Paradise to the Promised Land: An Introduction to the Pentateuch*, 3rd ed. (Grand Rapids: Baker, 2012), 173–79. For a brief critique of this approach, see P. J. Gentry and S. J. Wellum, *Kingdom through Covenant: A Biblical-Theological Understanding of the Covenants* (Wheaton, IL: Crossway, 2012), 275–80.

32. God promises that Abraham will be the "father of many nations" (Gn 17:4-5). The OT says little about Abraham becoming the biological ancestor of different nations, though the term "father" is sometimes "used of a variety of social roles that carried authority or exercised a protective or caring function. It could be used of a prophet (2Kg 6:21), priest (Jdg 18:19), king (1Sm 24:11), or governor (Isa 22:20-21)" (C. J. H. Wright, "אב (*'ab*)," in *New International Dictionary of Old Testament Theology and Exegesis* [1996], 221). Abraham becomes the "father of many nations" by being a channel of divine blessing. As N. M. Sarna, *Genesis*, JPS Torah Commentary (New York: Jewish Publication Society, 1989), 124, observes, the phrase "father of many nations" "has a more universal application in that a large segment of humanity looks upon Abraham as its spiritual father." This understanding of "father" is also reflected in the remark that Joseph "was father to Pharaoh" (Gn 45:8).

33. Cf. C. J. Collins, "Galatians 3:16: What Kind of an Exegete Was Paul?" *Tyndale Bulletin* 54 (2003): 75–86; J. M. Hamilton, "The Seed of the Woman and the Blessing of Abraham," *Tyndale Bulletin* 58 (2007): 271–73; J. S. DeRouchie and J. C. Meyer, "Christ or Family as the 'Seed' of Promise? An Evaluation of N. T. Wright on Galatians 3:16," *Southern Baptist Journal of Theology* 14 (2010): 36–48.

34. A similar understanding probably explains why Matthew begins his genealogy of Jesus with Abraham and not David (see Mt 1:1-17).

Genesis 49:8-12

The Lion of Judah

EUGENE H. MERRILL

One of the earliest, most cited, and most important of the messianic texts of the OT is Gn 49:8-12, embedded in the blessing of Jacob on his death-bed to his 12 sons (49:1-27). The sons are listed in order of birth, with Judah being fourth, but in terms of space allotted to the respective blessings, Judah is second to Joseph only. However, when Joseph's blessing is halved between Ephraim and Manasseh, Judah's total is greatest of all (some 9 lines of Hebrew text compared to 11 for Joseph's two tribes together)[1] But it is the content of the blessing that was important, not its length. References to key terms such as "praise," "scepter," "ruler's staff," "Shiloh," "foal," "colt," "wine," and "blood"—all are redolent of eschatological and messianic import. The following résumé of interpretations of the text covering more than 3,500 years shows beyond doubt its significance in both Judaism and Christianity.

HISTORY OF INTERPRETATION OF GENESIS 49:10

Old Testament Innertextual Use

First, among many other points to be made here is the truth that God does not work only through "perfect" people but also through those whom He has graciously set aside for His redemptive purposes. This is so despite Israel's and Judah's sin against God in the past. Although His people forsook Him, He has not forsaken them (Jer 51:5). In the Judah-David connection to the Abrahamic covenant of land and people

(Gn 12:1-3; 15:17-21; 17:6,15-16) has been added that of nationhood and monarchy, major tenets of the Davidic covenant (2Sm 7:8-17). David himself celebrated his divine appointment in many of the psalms attributed to him, including Pss 60:7 and 108:8. In these identical texts, David celebrates Yahweh's gracious dealings with the tribes of Israel, and of Judah he says, "Judah is My scepter (*mechoqeqiy*)," the same term used in Gn 49:10 (translated as "staff"; cf. Dt 33:21; Jdg 5:15; 2Sm 7:7). The sense in these references is "governing rod." To say Judah is the rod is a figure of speech (metonymy) in which the object (Judah) becomes the subject. The rod also served as a cudgel to beat the nonsubmissive, should they fail to keep their place. In fact, Isaiah says of the messianic figure that "he shall smite the earth with the rod of his mouth" (Isa 11:4). Similarly, Ps 45:6 reads: "Your throne, God, is forever and ever; the scepter of Your kingdom is a scepter of equity."[2] Asaph and others also contributed greatly to the messianic nature of the Davidic kingship. Psalm 76:1-2 explains that "God is known in Judah; His name is great in Israel. His tent is in Salem, His dwelling place in Zion." In this manner the elevation of Judah, and subsequently Jerusalem, indirectly elevates David as king as well, as is echoed in Ps 78:68-70:

> He [Yahweh] chose instead the tribe of Judah,
> Mount Zion, which He loved.
> He built His sanctuary like the heights,
> like the earth that He established forever.
> He chose David His servant,
> and took him from the sheepfolds.

The poet who composed Ps 114 declared of Yahweh that "Judah became His sanctuary, Israel, His dominion" (v. 2), thus once more underscoring the special status of David's tribe. In addition to the political aspect of its status, Judah was not only the home of the king but also of Yahweh Himself, who dwelt between the cherubim in the Most Holy Place (Ps 74:2; cf. 1Sm 4:4; Pss 80:1; 99:1; Isa 37:16).

More obliquely, Isaiah looks to the day when out of Judah shall come "heirs to My mountains from Judah; My chosen ones will possess it" (Isa 65:9, author's translation). Jeremiah spoke of a time when a "Righteous Branch"[3] will grow up to David, and he will execute justice and righteousness in the land. "In those days," he continued, Jerusalem "will be named: Yahweh Our Righteousness," and "David will never fail[4] to have a man sitting on the throne of the house of Israel" (Jer 33:15-17). Ezekiel tells of Zedekiah's woeful end as king, that his crown "will be no more until He comes whose right it is,[5] and I will give it to Him" (Ezk 21:27 [Heb 32] NASB). Joel adds to this: "Judah will be inhabited forever, and Jerusalem from generation to generation. I will pardon their bloodguilt, which I have not pardoned, for the LORD dwells in Zion" (Jl 3:20-21). Micah focuses on Bethlehem, of which he says that it is "small among the clans of Judah," and yet, "One will come from you to be ruler over Israel for Me. His origin is from antiquity, from eternity" (Mic 5:2). Such a one will bring peace (v. 5).

The postexilic prophet Zechariah has the most to say on the future of Judah and Jerusalem as a messianic motif. "The LORD will take possession of Judah as His portion," he says, "and He will once again choose Jerusalem" (2:12). Judah will yet "be a blessing" (8:13) and will be the recipient of good things from the Lord (v. 15). Speaking of the just and lowly king who will bring salvation (9:9), that one will also be a chieftain in Judah (v. 7). The Lord Himself will provide to Judah a cornerstone, a nail (tent peg, HCSB), and a warrior's bow to enable His people to be successful in battle, all as an act of His mercy (10:4-6).

SECOND TEMPLE JEWISH INTERPRETATION LXX (CA. 250 BC)

The LXX of Gn 49:10 reads, "A ruler from Judah will not come to an end nor hegemony[6] from (between) his legs until that one who is set apart [thus, 'Shiloh'] comes; and (in) him will be the expectation of the nations."[7]

In this instance "scepter" again stands for "ruler," "hegemony" is the definition of "staff," "the one who is set apart" is the translation of Shiloh, and the "nations" are the ill-defined "peoples."

QUMRAN (DEAD SEA SCROLLS, CA. 100 BC)

4Q252-254a: Col 5

Though technically not an exposition, the text is in fact a running commentary in which "scepter" is "a ruler," "ruler's staff" is the "covenant," "Shiloh" is the "Branch of David," and "obedience of the people" is the "assembly" of certain men.[8]

"A ruler shall [not] depart from the tribe of Judah when Israel has dominion. [And] the one who sits on the throne of David [shall never] be cut off, because the 'ruler's staff' is the covenant of the kingdom, [and the thous]ands of Israel are 'the feet,' until the Righteous Messiah, the Branch of David, has come. For to Him and to His seed the covenant of the kingdom of His people has been given for the eternal generations, because He has kept [. . .] the Law with men of the *Yahad*. For [. . .] the 'obedience of the people is the assembly of the men of [. . .] he gave.'"[9]

TARGUMS (CA. 50 BC)[10]

Targum Onkelos (or Aquila): "He who exercises dominion shall not pass away from the house of Judah, nor the *safra* (Aram, "scribe") from his children's children forever, until the Meshsiha; whose is the kingdom, and unto him shall be the obedience of the nations (or, whom the peoples shall obey)."

Targum Jonathan (or Yerushalmi): "Kings shall not cease, nor rulers from the house of Judah, nor *sopherim* teaching the law from his seed, till the time that King Messiah shall come, who will arise from Judah."

Fragmentary Targum on Gn 49:10: "Kings shall not cease from the house of Judah, nor scribes who teach the Torah from his children's children forever, until the time of the coming of the King Messiah, to whom belongs the Kingdom, and to whom all dominions of the earth shall become subservient."

On Gn 49:12 the *Fragmentary Targum*[11] reads: "How beautiful to behold are they, the eyes of the King Messiah, more so than pure wine, not looking upon incest and the shedding of innocent blood. His feet are pure, according to the Halakah, refraining from partaking of that which is taken by violence or robbery. His mountains shall be red with wine. His hills shall be white with abundance of his grain and flocks of his sheep."

Clearly, these three most important of the *targumim* are in complete agreement in their interpretation of (1) the notion that the coming king will be a Judahite; (2) the dynasty will not end until he comes; (3) the view that the *mechoqeq* is a scribe or scribes; and (4) that "Shiloh" is a cipher for his messianic character and mission. They differ substantially in that Onkelos reads the last clause quite literally and with MT, "to him will the obedience of the people be." Targum Jonathan or Yerushalmi appears to possess a different text tradition, understanding the same phrase as "who will arise from Judah." Most likely, it is an interpretive rendition, as is frequently the case with this Targum. The Fragment, though associated with Jonathan, more clearly understands *shiloh to* mean "that belongs to him."

New Testament Interpretation of Genesis 49:10

The NT everywhere attests to David *redivivus* (reborn) in Jesus Christ (Mt 1:1; 21:9; 22:42-45; Lk 20:41-42; Rom 1:3) but not specifically or clearly with reference to Gn 49:10, with the possible exception of Rev 5:5; 22:16.

Mishnayot Interpretation (c. 150 BC onward)

The term *Mishnah* evokes the sense of interpretation or clarification. The Hebrew lexeme *mishnah* refers to the idea of "second" or even "copy," thus leading to the idea of what might be called subsidiary versions of a text (*Hebrew and Aramaic Lexicon of the Old Testament*, 650). The Aramaic *mishnah* (the feminine form) signifies "repetition," so the *Mishnah* refers to the the written expression of a long oral tradition.[12]

Midrashim[13]

The Hebrew *Midrash Rabbah*[14] *Genesis*: "Judah is a lion's whelp. R. Hama b. R. Hanina said: 'This alludes to Messiah the son of David.'"

Midrash Rabbah Genesis: "Until Shiloh come. This indicates that all the nations of the world will bring a gift to Messiah the son of David."

Midrash Rabbah Genesis: "'The scepter shall not depart from Judah.' This refers to the throne of kingship. The throne given of God is for ever and ever; a scepter of equity is the scepter of thy kingdom. When will that be? 'Nor the ruler's staff from between his feet:' When he comes of whom it is written, 'The crown of pride of the drunkards of Ephraim shall be trodden under foot.'"

Midrash Rabbah Genesis on Gn 49:11: "'Binding his foal unto the vine.' R. Judah, R. Nehemiah, and the rabbis discuss this verse. R. Judah explained it: 'When a vine has a poor yield, an ass is tied to it,' [and this too is the meaning of] 'and his ass's colt unto the choice vine and *beni athono* unto the choice vine means: [morally] strong sons (*banim ethanim*) will spring from him.' The Rabbis interpreted: 'I,' [said God], 'am bound to the vine and the choice vine [Israel].' 'His foal and his colt' intimate: when he will come of whom it is written, 'lowly, and riding upon an ass, even upon a colt the foal of an ass' (Zech. 9:9)."

Babylonian and Jerusalem Talmuds

B(abylonian)T(almud) San(hedrin) 98b: "Rab said, 'The world was created only for the sake of David'; but Samuel said, 'For the sake of Moses'; but R. Yohannan said, 'For the sake of the Messiah.' 'What is his name?—the School of R. Shila said: His name is Shiloh, for it is written, until Shiloh come.'" Clearly there were some authorities of the time who saw obvious messianic overtones to the term "Shiloh."

BT San 41a: "A little more than forty years before the destruction of the Temple [in AD 70], the power of pronouncing capital sentences was taken away from the Jews."

Ante-Nicene Church Fathers

This describes the history of the Church from the time of the apostles to the Council of Nicaea in 325. The following are only a few of the major Christian leaders and thinkers who lived and ministered in that period. Each of them had something to say regarding the interpretation of Jacob's blessing of Judah.

Ignatius of Antioch (AD 35–108), in his "Epistle to the Philadelphians," rendered Gn 49:10 as follows: "Until He comes for whom it is reserved . . . [our Lord saying], 'go ye and teach all nations.'"

Justin Martyr of Samaria (ca. 100–165) wrote a number of "Apologies" in defense of the Christian faith and in the first, addressed to the Church at large, he spoke about Shiloh of Gn 49:10: "After He appeared, you began to rule the Jews, and gained possession of their territory" (xxxii; cf. liv). He made the same argument in his famous "Dialogue with Trypho" (cii).

The great Alexandrian scholar Origen (185–254), also referring to Shiloh (Jesus), wrote, "manifestly He is the only one among those who preceded . . . and among those also who followed Him, that was the expectation of the Gentiles."

Post-Nicene Church Fathers

Athanasius of Alexandria (296–373), who championed the cause for a proper Christology at Nicaea, clearly understood the mysterious Shiloh to be referring to Christ in his treatise on "The Incarnation of the Word": "A ruler shall not fail from Judah nor a prince from his loins until the things laid up for him [Shiloh] shall come and the Expectation of the nations himself."[15] Further, "that is why the Saviour Himself was always proclaiming, 'The law and the prophets prophesied until John.'"

Ambrose of Milan (339–397) observed in Jacob's words that "Juda [*sic*] receives the preference by his father's blessing, and rightly so, when it is said to him, 'The sons of your father shall bow down to you. A lion's whelp is Juda, and he is the expectation of nations.' Surely this is appropriate to Christ alone."[16]

John Chrysostom (ca. 345–407), also of the Eastern Church, in his commentary "The Gospel of St. Matthew," Homily II, maintained of Shiloh that "[Gn 49:10] doth indeed make it clear that He was of the tribe of Judah, but not [*sic*] also that he was of the family of David."[17]

Jerome (345–420) also comes into consideration. His belief in the reality of predictive prophecy comes to the fore in his unambiguous comment on the identity of Shiloh in Gn 49:10. Addressing a skeptic by name, he wrote in "Letter to Eustochium," "You will charge Jacob with sin, whose vision became so dim that he could not see Ephraim and Manasseh, although with the inner eye and the prophetic spirit he could foresee the distant future and the Christ that was to come out of [Judah's] royal line" (cviii.10).

Finally, the towering figure of Augustine of Hippo (354–430) added his own authoritative word on the passage in his *City of God*, Book XVIII: "Jacob died in Egypt a hundred and forty-seven years old, after he had, when dying, blessed his sons and grandsons by Joseph, and prophesied most plainly of Christ, saying in the blessing of Judah, 'A prince shall not fail out of Judah, nor a leader from his thighs, until those things come which are laid up for him; and He is the expectation of the nations.'"[18]

Medieval Jewish and Christian Interpretations

The eminent Medieval rabbi Rashi of Troyes, France (1040–1105), whose name is an acronym of ***Ra****bbi* ***Sh****lomo* ***Y****itzchaki*, wrote on the matter of the term "Shiloh": *ki yabo Shiloh [means until]* the King Messiah [will come], whose the kingdom will be. And so does Onkelos translate it [i.e., Shiloh is taken to mean "She'lo"—to whom the power belongs]. A midrashic explanation [says that "Shiloh" is two words, "Shai-lo"]—'to him' [i.e., the Anointed One, they will bring presents, as it is said [Psalms 76:12] 'they bring presents [*shai*] to him that ought to be feared.'"[19]

Rashi's later Christian counterpart, Nicholas de Lyra of Normandy (1270–1340), offered in his major work a quite different take on the passage, as one might suppose. In his *Postilla litteralis super totum Bibliam,* he comments on Shiloh: "*Until he come.* . . . That is, Christ, who was sent by God the Father for the salvation of mankind" (ibid.).

Interestingly (and strangely), neither tradition sees a reference to David except, in Rashi's case, where he speaks of the rod not departing from Judah as the time when "the house of David ceases to rule." However, de Lyra makes a point about the scepter and ruler not departing and the one to come that is most relevant to the times of the Chronicler and to his theology:

> Because after the royal rule had ceased and king Zedekiah [had been] slain in the Babylonian exile, the Jewish people [were] from that time ruled by those who were of the tribe of Judah; because Zerubbabel was the leader of those returning from the said exile, Zech. and Haggai. And afterward the priests ruled the people, as is evident in the time of the Maccabees, who also were of the tribe of Judah, because the priestly and royal tribes were related to each other as is evident in Kings, where it is said that Jehoshaba, the sister of King Ahaziah, king of Judah, took Joash and he was with her "six years in the house of the Lord"—because she was the wife of Jehoiada, the high priest. And their rule lasted up to the time of Herod . . . under whose rule Christ was born. (ibid.)

Protestant Reformation Scholars

Martin Luther (1483–1546): After considerable linguistic deliberation, Luther settled on the idea advocated by the Jewish scholar Bernard Ziegler that *shiloh is* a variation of *shilyāh* (by a reversal and repointing of the vowels), "womb" or "afterbirth." Though surely wrong on this count, he redeemed himself at the end by affirming that "thanks to the blessing of God, we enjoy the completely clear light of the Gospel by which the word *shiloh* is cleared up and explained as meaning the Son of a virgin and of God at the same time. This grammar pleases me, and in it I acquiesce with the greatest confidence."[20]

Jean (John) Calvin (1509–1564): Perhaps the most erudite of the great reformers, Calvin nonetheless had to wrestle vigorously over the etymology and meaning of Shiloh as had his predecessors, Jewish and Christian alike. After an extended discussion of the matter (some seven pages in the source cited here), he concluded (falsely, it seems) that the term should be viewed as *shil* with final *h* taking the place of the pronominal suffix *vav.*[21] As with Luther, though Calvin's linguistic gymnastics may lack some precision, his conclusion most assuredly does not: "To us . . . it is not less useful, for the confirmation of our faith, to know that Christ had been not only promised, but that his origin had been pointed out, as with a finger, two thousand years before he appeared."[22]

POST-ENLIGHTENMENT AND MODERN SCHOLARS

Franz Delitzsch (1813–1890): "The prophecy has Christ as the goal of its [Gn 49:10] fulfilment; it is Messianic without our needing to understand [*shiyloh*] personally."[23] However, his eminent friend and co-author C. F. Keil (1807–1878) disagrees, asserting that "[Ezk 21:27] not only confirms the correctness of the personal and Messianic explanation of the word *Shiloh,* but shows that Jacob's prophecy of the scepter not passing from Judah until Shiloh came, did not preclude the punishment of the sins of the elect, and yet, notwithstanding that punishment, assuredly and completely attains to their ultimate fulfilment. And thus did the kingdom of Judah arise from its temporary overthrow to a new and imperishable glory in Jesus Christ."[24]

John Skinner (1910): A stark contrast to this uplifting point of view is expressed by Skinner, a Wellhausian mindset common to the turn of the 20th century: "justice is done to the terms and the tenor of the oracle if we regard it as a prophecy of David and his dynasty,—a *vaticinium ex eventu,* like all the other oracles in the chapter."[25]

Hermann Gunkel (1910): "V10b is, as is almost universally acknowledged today, 'Messianic,' that is, to be understood in relation to the ruler of the end time. Only 'an ideal date' can be portrayed here, and וְלוֹ demonstrates that the foregoing discusses a specific personality. This alone clearly indicates that this coming one is only alluded to from afar. . . . In this passage we have [Messianism's] earliest attestation. עַד־כִּי [*'ad kiy*] does not mean that Judah's dominion ceases with the Messiah, but that it is only then truly secured."[26]

Claus Westermann (1986):[27] "שִׁילֹה [*shiyloh*] . . . is the one who wins the obedience of the nations. This can only mean a ruler." Yet, even as a Christian, Westermann cannot bring himself to see, ultimately, that Jesus is the mysterious "Shiloh." Continuing, he avers, "It is not a messianic prophecy in the sense that it promises a king of salvation at the end time" (p. 232).

This aversion to predictive prophecy continues to the present day as illustrated by Brevard Childs (1993): "such prophecies as Gen 49.8-12 and Num 24.15-24 are usually judged [and by Childs] to be later projections back into the pre-Davidic period."[28]

German evangelical scholarship includes the illustrious theologian and commentator Walther Eichrodt (1961): "it cannot have been possible to speak of the rule of Judah over his brethren before [David's reign], [but] there can nevertheless [be] no objection to using it to illustrate the expectations of pre-monarchical times, since the whole character of the language presupposes that the Coming One is already a well-known figure."[29]

The tentativeness of the "British school" of evangelicals is represented by

Gordon Wenham, who seems to view the messianic interpretation as somewhat of a fallback position. Gordon J. Wenham (1994): "On this understanding [of Shiloh as "to him"], we have at least a reference to the Davidic dynasty if not to a king superior to that dynasty, i. e., the messiah."[30]

The best of American conservative evangelicalism is seen in Kenneth A. Mathews in his monumental commentary on Genesis (2005): "The Christian interpreter, who identifies the king of our passage explicitly as Jesus of Nazareth, therefore can agree with the historian that the Davidic monarchy must be initially in view and also can agree with ancient Jewish interpretation that our text requires a messianic fulfillment."[31]

AN EXEGETICAL, LITERARY, AND THEOLOGICAL STUDY

The brief analysis that follows addresses (1) a development of the poem's *Sitz im Leben,* (2) a fresh translation, (3) a literary analysis, and (4) a theological overview.

Introduction to the Passage: Authorship, Date, and Setting

Ancient Jewish and Christian tradition held unanimously to the Mosaic authorship of the Pentateuch and thus of its first book, Genesis.[32] The biblical chronology itself locates Moses and his penning of the treatise at c. 1400 BC and in the Plains of Moab, just across the Jordan River, 15 miles east of Jericho.[33] The occasion was Moses' impending death and the conquest and occupation of Canaan as the promised land, thus provoking an urgent need for Moses to record the history of his people—from their germinal form in Abraham, 700 years in the past, through their semi-nomadic life in Canaan for two centuries, then their 350-year sojourn in semi-bondage in Egypt, and finally their deliverance by their God who parted the waters of the Red Sea just 40 years earlier and in other ways in the desert demonstrated His great mercy and power to save.

They had been called to be His special people, an act of pure grace cemented by a series of covenant promises, first with Abraham and then reaffirmed to Isaac and Jacob.[34] The covenant relationship with a single man and his son and grandson had now blossomed into a covenant with a descendant people at Mount Sinai. This people was to be "My kingdom of priests and My holy nation" (Ex 19:4-6) in the midst of all the nations of the earth who would be blessed or cursed, depending on their attitude and behavior toward God's chosen ones. This rather loose federation of tribes would eventually become a nation in the true sense, with a monarchy and all. This latter feature was hinted at as early as the times of the patriarchs, demanded by an impetuous, impatient, and rebellious tribal federation in the days of the judges, and finally brought to fruition, first in the untimely and disastrous reign of Saul and then in the divinely selected dynasty of King David.

David's eponymous ancestor Jacob (Israel) had spoken in his last will and testament about this line of monarchs, centering his attention on Judah, the inauspicious fourth son of Leah, the daughter of Laban foisted on Jacob as his first and not favorite wife by his unscrupulous father-in-law (Gn 29:35). Nothing in subsequent narratives suggests how or why Judah would come to be the messianic channel. It is true he persuaded his brothers not to abandon Joseph in the pit, but at the same time he was mercenary enough to sell him as a slave to the passing Ishmaelites (Gn 37:25-28). Genesis 38 is a tawdry tale of Judah's marriage to a Canaanite woman by whom he fathered three sons: Er, Onan, and Shelah. All three died and finally Judah's wife died (vv. 1-11). Judah then committed adultery with his own daughter-in-law Tamar in order that his name should not cease. Worse still, the sexual act was done when Tamar had disguised herself as a prostitute, thus tarring Judah's reputation all the more (vv. 12-26). Yet, from this illicit rendezvous issued twin sons of Judah and Tamar, namely, Perez and Zerah. Perez would go on to further the line of Judah that would eventuate ten generations later in King David.

> 8 Judah, as for you, your brothers will praise[35] you;
> Your powerful hand[36] will grasp your enemies' necks.
> Your fathers' sons will lie prostrate before you.
> 9 Judah, you are a lion's[37] cub;
> You rise up from the prey, my son,
> Like a lion (that) takes its rest, lying down
> Like a lioness: Who is willing to arouse it?
> 10 The scepter[38] will never leave Judah
> nor [his] insignia, the ruler's staff, from between his feet,[39]
> Until the one comes to whom it belongs[40];
> He will become the ruler of the nations,
> 11 One who ties a she-ass to a vine,
> And to a grape-plant his young donkey;
> He will wash his clothing in wine,
> And in grape-juice his garments.
> 12 (His) eyes (will be) sparkling from wine,
> his teeth whiter than milk.[41] (author's translation)

Preliminary Glance at the Passage

The poem is unique among the blessings of the tribes in that it intimates at once the primacy of Judah despite his birth position as the fourth son of Leah, the secondary wife of Jacob, at least in terms of his affections.[42] Ironically, she named him *Yehudah*, "he praises," though Jacob later prophesied of him that his brothers would praise him (*yoducha*). The second line of the couplet suggests by poetic parallelism that his brothers would become his enemies but that he would nonetheless prevail over them, the image for which is his hand placed firmly and victoriously on their necks as a yoke of bondage.[43]

Literary Analysis of the Passage

- Judah's primacy (vv. 8-9)
  - His power (v. 8)
  - His character (v. 9)
- Judah's regency (v. 10)
  - His historical permanency (v. 10a)
  - His eschatological identity (v. 10b)
- Judah's *shalom* (vv. 11-12)
  - His conquest (v. 11)
  - His bountifulness (v. 12)

The text of Genesis reveals an anticipation of a royal seed descending from the patriarchs. For example, God promised Abraham He would make "kings come from you" (Gn 17:6) and then reiterated the same promise to Jacob, saying "kings will descend from you" (Gn 35:11). T. Desmond Alexander rightly recognizes "that the entire book of Genesis is structured around a unique line of 'seed' which will eventually become a royal dynasty."[44]

Within the narrative, the royal line promised seems to focus on Judah and his descendants. Judah's story begins with his ignoble behavior. First, he revealed his pragmatic attitude about the mistreatment of his brother ("What do we gain if we kill our brother . . . ? Come, let's sell him to the Ishmaelites," Gn 37:26-27) and later his callous approach toward raising up an heir for his own line, refusing to give his son Shelah to Tamar as a husband ("He might die too, like his brothers," Gn 38:11). However, after these events, the story begins to elevate Judah above his brothers. For example, Jacob ignored Reuben's request to return to Egypt for more food (42:37-38) but listened to Judah when he asked (43:8-11). Also, the narrator begins to recognize Judah as the leader of Jacob's sons ("When Judah and his brothers reached Joseph's house," 44:14). Ultimately, Judah's behavior appears transformed from the greedy and callous outlook displayed earlier, to a compassionate and sacrificial attitude, begging Joseph to punish him rather than Benjamin, lest it break his father Jacob's heart (Gn 44:24-28). This transformation prepares the way for Judah's elevation as the progenitor of the future King Messiah in Jacob's oracle (Gn 49:8-12).

Jacob begins his oracle by declaring that he will reveal what will happen "in the days to come." This Hebrew phrase, *b'acharit hayamim*, is better translated "in the end of days," giving the passage a decidedly eschatological perspective.

This is repeated in the Balaam oracles, when Balaam reveals that he will declare what will happen to Israel "in the future" (Nm 24:14), repeating the phrase *b'acharit hayamim* (lit. "in the end of days"), giving these oracles an eschatological perspective as well. Thus, in the third Balaam oracle (Nm 24:3-9), which promises a great eschatological king[45] with an exalted kingdom, it describes him using the same terms Jacob used: "He crouches, he lies down like a lion or a lioness—who dares to rouse him?" (Nm 24:9; Gn 49:9).

Thus, the oracle of Jacob promises an eschatological, royal figure from the line of Judah, who will be the ultimate rightful king ("to whom it belongs," Gn 49:10 NIV). This view is supported intertexually by Ezk 21:24-27 [Hb. 29-32]). There the fall of the Davidic house is predicted, with Zedekiah, the last Davidic king, being told, "Remove the turban, take off the crown," signifying the end of his kingship. With an emphatic threefold repetition ("A ruin, a ruin, I will make it a ruin!" Ezk 21:27), the Lord declares the destruction of the Davidic house but includes the promise that this devastation is only temporary. It will last only "until He comes whose right it is" (21:27 NASB),[46] a direct allusion to Gn 49:10.[47] The promise is that Davidic kingship will fall until the promised eschatological King from the line of Judah comes, and He will restore the Davidic dynasty. Not only does Gn 49:10 indicate a messianic royal figure who will fulfill this passage, but also Ezekiel, nearly a thousand years after Genesis, read it as a promise of the restoration of the house of David by the future Davidic Messiah.

Theology of the Passage

The metanarrative of the OT is the account of God's person and purposes as displayed in creation, redemption, and restoration. This passage embraces the second and third phases in that it describes the vehicle of salvation and the eventual eschatological outcome of God's merciful "new beginning." The framework of the "mini-narrative" exemplified in this text is covenant, the proactive extension by Yahweh of promises—both unconditional and conditional—that constitute a bridging between Himself and His broken image, namely, humankind.

The process of reconciliation began virtually as early as Eden with the pledge by Yahweh that the head of Evil would be crushed at the cost of the bruising of the heel of Righteousness (Gn 3:15). It later took the form of the selection of Shem as the progenitor of a people who would be custodians of the promise, the most prominent individual of whom was Abraham (Gn 11:10-32). The historical narrowing and sifting of the covenant development passed through Isaac, Jacob, and here, in our text, culminated in Judah. However, Judah was just a stopping-place, as it were, as both an individual and a subsequent tribe. The resumption of the messianic trajectory climaxed in David, king of Judah and all Israel (2Sm 2:4; 5:3). To him and through him coursed the stream of redemptive hope, a stream that both poets and prophets predictively proclaimed to be finally and perfectly a stream of "living water" embodied in and announced by Jesus Christ, "son of David" and Son of God, and the Shiloh of Jacob's blessing.

---

1. A helpful comparison can be found in Moses' blessing of the tribes in Dt 33. There Reuben comes first again, but in a greatly truncated form as though to pass over him quickly to get to Judah, who is listed next. Reuben had forfeited his blessing of the firstborn by committing the egregious sin of having sex with his father's concubine Bilhah (Gn 35:22; cf. 49:4; 1Chr 5:1-2).
2. The literal "scepter of your kingdom" should be understood to mean "your royal scepter," that is, the king who bears the scepter as a symbol of power and authority, that same scepter spoken of in Gn 49:10.
3. The phrase צֶמַח צְדָקָה [*tzemach ts'dakah*] should better be rendered "righteous branch," a clear messianic epithet. Cf. Zch 3:8: "I will bring forth my servant the branch."
4. Literally "never be cut off" (Ni impf). That is, the Davidic line will exist forever.
5. Here *asher lo hammishpat* ("whose right it is") a seeming expansion of the *shelo* (LXX, "to whom it belongs"), contrary to the MT *Shiloh* Gn 49:10. Thus also Yalk. Is. 288 with reference to Gn 49:10.
6. The Targums, Samar, (Ven): a leader in peace and war (Jud 5:15).
7. Author's translation.
8. The Targum of 49:10 reads the interpretive *Mashiach* (Messiah) for *Shiloh*, "[which] points to a clear messianic understanding as the tradition-historical context." Gerbern S. Oegma, "'The Coming of the Righteous One' in 1 Enoch, Qumran, and the New Testament," *The Bible and the Dead Sea Scrolls*, vol. 3, ed. James H. Charlesworth (Waco, TX: Baylor University Press, 2006), 390. For 'Righteous One' as messianic in other contexts, see Ascension of Isaiah 3:13; 1 Clement 17:1; Polycarp to the Philippians 6:3; Acts of Philip 78.
9. *The Dead Sea Scrolls: A New Translation*, trans. Michael Wise, Martin Abegg Jr., and Edward Cook (San Francisco: HarperCollins, 1996), 277.
10. J. W. Etheridge, *The Targums of Onkelos and Jonathan ben Uzziel on the Pentateuch; with the Fragments of the Jerusalem Targum: From the Chaldee* (London: Longman, Green, Longman, and Roberts, 1862). The Targums of Onkelos and Jonathan (or Palestinian or Yerushalmi) were both produced c. 50 BC. Onkelos covers the entire Bible except Daniel, and Jonathan addresses the Pentateuch and Former and Latter Prophets. Onkelos is thought to be a Babylonian corruption of the name Aquila, a translator of the OT into Greek, and Jonathan the same as Theodotion, also a translator, both as early as the second century BC. They gave their names to these later targumic works as indicators of their styles, Onkelos being much more literal than Jonathan.
11. This is a fragmentary collection that appears to be essentially the same as Jonathan.
12. Marcus Jastrow, *A Dictionary of the Targumim, the Talmud Babli and Yerushalmi, and the Midrashic Literature* (repr. Peabody, MA: Hendrickson, 2005), 857.
13. The Hebrew (and Aramaic) root of this term is דָרַשׁ [*darash*], "to seek, look for," and thus מִדְרָשׁ [*midrash*] "research" or "investigation" (*Hebrew and Aramaic Lexicon of the Old Testament*, 550; Jastrow, 735). One might use the term "commentary" also to fill out the meaning. They are divided into two categories, the *halachic* and the *aggadic*. The former concerns doctrine or instigation to obedience, whereas the latter has to do with practical ways of living out one's life. Both achieved written status by the mid-second century AD. The distinction between Mishnah and Midrash may be crystallized as follows: The Mishnah is the body of sacred text and the Midrash the exegesis or interpretation of the text. They overlap in some respects since both can be viewed as collections of texts as well as their exposition.
14. The "Rabbah" Midrashim were a collection of ten commentaries on the Bible, five on Torah and five on Ketubim, composed c. AD 550. Genesis Rabbah is one of the most important, and certainly for expositions of Genesis.
15. St. Athanasius, *The Incarnation of the Word of God* (Yonkers, NY: St. Vladimir's Seminary Press, 2012), 4.40.
16. St. Ambrose, *Saint Ambrose: Seven Exegetical Works*, The Fathers of the Church, vol. 60 (Washington, DC: The Catholic University of America Press, 1971), 195.
17. There is virtual unanimity that the "not" is a scribal error in the original text of the document.
18. St. Augustine, *The City of God Books XVII–XXII* (Washington, DC: The Catholic University of America Press, 2008), 5.

19. Eugene H. Merrill, "Rashi, Nicholas de Lyra, and Christian Exegesis," *Westminster Theological Journal* 38/1 (1975): 66–79.
20. Jaroslav Pelikan, ed. *Luther's Works*, vol. 8, Lectures on Genesis Chapters 45–50 (Saint Louis: Concordia, 1966), 243.
21. John Calvin, *Commentaries on the First Book of Moses Called Genesis,* vol. 1, trans. John King (repr. Grand Rapids: Baker, 1989), 454.
22. Ibid.
23. Franz Delitzsch, *A New Commentary on Genesis,* vol. II, trans. Sophia Taylor (Edinburgh: T&T Clark, 1888; repr. Minneapolis: Klock & Klock, 1978), 384.
24. C. F. Keil, *The Pentateuch,* vol. I of Commentary on the Old Testament, trans. James Martin (Edinburgh: T. & T. Clark, 1864–1865; repr., Grand Rapids: Eerdmans, n.d.), 400–401.
25. John Skinner, *A Critical and Exegetical Commentary on Genesis,* International Critical Commentary (New York: Charles Scribner's Sons, 1910), 524.
26. Hermann Gunkel, *Genesis*, trans. Mark E. Biddle (Macon, GA: Mercer University Press, 1997), 524; Calvin, *Genesis*, 456.
27. Claus Westermann, *Genesis 37–50: A Commentary*, trans. John J. Scullion (Minneapolis: Augsburg, 1986).
28. Brevard S. Childs, *Biblical Theology of the Old and New Testaments* (Minneapolis: Fortress, 1992), 453.
29. Walther Eichrodt, *Theology of the Old Testament,* vol. 1, trans. J. A. Baker (Philadelphia: Westminster, 1961), 473, n. 4.
30. Gordon J. Wenham, *Genesis 16–50*, vol. 2 of Word Biblical Commentary (Dallas: Word, 1994), 477.
31. Kenneth A. Mathews, *Genesis 11:27–50:26*, vol. 1B of New American Commentary (Nashville: Broadman & Holman, 2005), 896.
32. Since the so-called Enlightenment of the 17th and 18th centuries, Mosaic authorship of the Pentateuch has been largely abandoned except by conservative Evangelical scholars. For a history of this movement and a critique of it, see Eugene H. Merrill, Mark F. Rooker, and Michael S. Grisanti, *The World and the Word: An Introduction to the Old Testament* (Nashville: B&H), 2013).
33. See Eugene H. Merrill, *Kingdom of Priests: A History of Old Testament Israel,* 2nd ed. (Grand Rapids: Baker, 2008), 83–96.
34. See Gn 12:1-3; 15:1-21; 17:1-21; 26:1-5; 28:13-16; 48:3-4.
35. The verb "praise" (*yadah*) is, of course, cognate to the name of the tribe Judah (*yehudah*).
36. Assonance follows in this clause with "your hand" (*yadkha*).
37. For the lion as a messianic symbol of Judah, see Hos 5:14; Rev 5:5.
38. This term *shevet* is a figure of speech (metonymy) in which the thing held stands for him who holds it; i. e., a king.
39. "Between his feet" may be clarified by Jdg 5:27, "between her [Jael's] feet he [Sisera] fell." The concept is that of total capitulation, even to the point of death. Shiloh will have such judgmental and punishing power.
40. The Septuagint in both Lucian's and Origen's versions, as well as various others, read, "to whom it is reserved," leading to the proposed Hebrew reading *shelloh* or *shello* (cf. commentaries above). The Hebrew word would be derived from the particle *sh* ("which") + the archaic relative pronoun *lo* ("to him"), meaning "that which [belongs to] him." This appears to be a contraction as follows *sh*, the shortened form of the relative particle *asher* ("which, whose"), *le* (belonging to"), and the suffix *oh* or *o* for ("him").
41. For the rest of the messianic imagery, see Zch 9:9; Mt 21:5; Rev 7:14; 14:10; 16:19.
42. Exceptions to the "natural" listings of the sons (tribes), the leadership of Judah, and Judah's position as the favored son and/or tribe are in Nm 2:1-3; 10:14-16; Jos 15:1-63; Jdg 1:1-20; 20:18; 1Chr 5:2; 28:4; Pss 60:7; 78:68; 108:8.
43. For this image elsewhere, see Gn 27:40; Dt 28:48; 2Sm 22:41; Job 16:12; Isa 10:27; 52:2; Jer 27:2,12; 28:14.
44. T. Desmond Alexander, "Messianic Ideology in the Book of Genesis" in *The Lord's Anointed: Interpretation of Old Testament Messianic Texts*, ed. Philip E. Satterthwaite, Richard S. Hess, and Gordon J. Wenham (Grand Rapids: Baker, 1995), 27.
45. Michael Rydelnik makes the case that "the king greater than Agag" should actually be read based on the variant readings, making him an eschatological king, "greater than Gog," the end-time enemy of Israel. See *The Messianic Hope: Is the Hebrew Bible Really Messianic?* (Nashville: B&H, 2010), 38–39.
46. Ezekiel 21:27 uses the same phrase as Gn 49:10, however it is the full expression of the phrase, not the contracted word used in Genesis.
47. Ralph Alexander writes that Ezk 21:27 is "a definite reference to Genesis 49:10." According to him, Ezekiel used this phrase to show that "kingship . . . would be removed in judgment but returned ultimately in the Messiah's coming in accord with Genesis 49:10." "Ezekiel," vol. 6 of *The Expositor's Commentary*, ed. Frank E. Gabelein, (Grand Rapids: Zondervan, 1986), 845.

Numbers 24:5-9, 15-19

The Distant Star

SETH D. POSTELL

Please come and put a curse on these people for me because they are more powerful than I am. I may be able to defeat them and drive them out of the land, for I know that those you bless are blessed and those you curse are cursed.
(Nm 22:6)

He crouches, he lies down like a lion or a lioness—who dares to rouse him? Those who bless you will be blessed, and those who curse you will be cursed. (Nm 24:9)

The story of Balaam (Nm 22:2–24:25) is a theologically loaded passage, at times perplexing, and contains one of the strangest stories in the Old Testament: the story of a talking donkey. Was Balaam a good man and true prophet, determined to speak God's word (Nm 22:18; 24:13), or a villainous sorcerer, deserving to be despised (Mic 6:3-5; Jos 24:9-10; Dt 23:4-7; Neh 13:2; Nm 31:16; 2Pt 2:15-16; Jd 11; Rev 2:14)? Since Balaam was responsible for leading Israel astray (Nm 31:16; Jd 11), why consider his oracles about a star from Jacob (Nm 24:17) trustworthy, and how, for that matter, can Balaam's seven discourses be Scripture (Nm 23:7,18; 24:3,15,20-21,23)?[1]

Two of Balaam's seven discourses, the third (Nm 24:5-9) and the fourth (Nm 24:17-19), are particularly significant passages in the history of interpretation, and have long been interpreted messianically.[2] Though some scholars continue to espouse messianic interpretations of Nm 24:7-9 and 24:17-19,[3] the nonmessianic interpretation of these passages has become far more common.[4] However, this article will maintain that a close reading of Balaam's third and fourth discourses in their immediate and more extended literary contexts reveals that Balaam's third and fourth oracles refer to the Messiah and not to one of Israel's historical kings (e.g., Saul or David). It will do so, first, by showing the place of the Balaam narrative in its literary context and, second, by carefully examining the third and fourth discourses themselves.

THE BALAAM NARRATIVE IN ITS LITERARY CONTEXT

Blessings, Curses, and the Abrahamic Covenant

The theme of blessing is the heart of the Balaam narrative. The verb "to bless" appears 14 times in this brief narrative (Nm 22:6,12; 23:11,20,25; 24:1,9-10). Conversely, the verb "to curse" is used a total of 17 times, 10 times with the Hebrew verb *qḇḇ* (Nm 22:11,17; 23:8,11,13,25,27; 24:10),[5] and 7 times with the Hebrew verb 'rr (Nm 22:6,12; 23:7; 24:9). The verbs *ḇrḵ* ("to bless") and 'rr ("to curse") are used together in the same verse only five times in the Torah (Gn 12:3; 27:29; Nm 22:6,12; 24:9),[6] and the similarities between God's promises to Abraham and the references in the Balaam narrative are unmistakable. Though Balak may not have knowingly cited (and distorted) God's promises to Abraham, the nearly verbatim allusion to God's earlier promise is obvious.

"I will make you into a great nation, I will bless you, I will make your name great, and you will be a blessing. I will bless those who bless you, I will curse those who treat you with contempt, and all the peoples on earth will be blessed through you." (Gn 12:2-3)	"Please come and put a curse on these people for me because they are more powerful than I am. I may be able to defeat them and drive them out of the land, for *I know that those you bless are blessed and those you curse are cursed.*" (Nm 22:6)[7]

In the third of Balaam's seven discourses, there is another clear allusion to Isaac's prophetic blessing on Jacob. (All italics in Scripture quotations added.)

"May peoples serve you and nations bow down to you. Be master over your brothers; may your mother's sons bow down to you. *Those who curse you will be cursed, and those who bless you will be blessed.*" (Gn 27:29)	"He crouches, he lies down like a lion or a lioness—who dares to rouse him? *Those who bless you will be blessed, and those who curse you will be cursed.*" (Nm 24:9)

Central to the Balaam narrative is the outworking of God's plan to bless the nations through Abraham and his seed—a plan that was already set in motion in the creation mandate, with its threefold theme of blessing, seed, and land (Gn 1:28).

Pharaoh and Balak

The Balaam narrative shares many thematic and verbal parallels with the first chapter of Exodus, with its story of a Gentile king who sets his heart on thwarting God's purposes for Abraham's seed.[8] In both cases, a Gentile king is threatened by Israel's great numbers (Ex 1:12; Nm 22:3).[9] In both stories, a Gentile king makes three attempts to thwart Israel's numerical prosperity (in essence, to undermine God's promise to bless Abraham's seed) but each attempt only results in more blessing for the people of Israel.[10] On the parallel third attempt to stop God's program of blessing, both narratives focus on the coming of Israel's redeemers: Moses (in the case of Pharaoh, Ex 2) and a future king (in the case of Balak, Nm 24:7-9,17-19).[11]

The Poems of the Torah

Balaam's poetic blessing in Nm 23–24, located at the end of Israel's 40-year period of wandering in the wilderness, is one of three key poems in the story line of the Pentateuch.[12] The other two poems are located at the end of Genesis and Deuteronomy, where a central figure (Jacob and Moses) blesses the tribes of Israel. All three poems share unique common language and themes[13] and are clearly and strategically related one to the other in the macrostructure of the Pentateuch. In each poem, a central figure blesses the tribes of Israel (Gn 49:28; Nm 24:3-9; Dt 33:1), and they each refer to a royal figure/king (Gn 49:10; Nm 24:7,17; Dt 33:5[14]). Strikingly, references and allusions to Jacob's prophecy concerning Judah (Gn 49:8-12) are apparent in both Balaam's and Moses' blessings.

JACOB'S BLESSING	BALAAM'S BLESSING	MOSES' BLESSING
"Judah is a young lion—my son, you return from the kill. He crouches; he lies down like a lion or a lioness—who dares to rouse him?" (Gn 49:9)	"A people rise up like a lioness; They rouse themselves like a lion. They will not lie down until they devour the prey and drink the blood of the slain." (Nm 23:24) "He crouches, he lies down like a lion or a lioness—who dares to rouse him?" (Nm 24:9)	"He said about Gad: The one who enlarges Gad's territory will be blessed. He lies down like a lion and tears off an arm or even a head." (Dt 33:20)

"The scepter will not depart from Judah or the staff [*ûmᵉḥōqēq*] from between his feet until He whose right it is comes [*kî-yāḇōʾ*] and the obedience of the peoples belongs to Him." (Gn 49:10)	"a scepter will arise from Israel." (Nm 24:17)	"He said this about Judah: Lord, hear Judah's cry and bring him [*tᵉḇîʾennû*] to his people . . ." (Dt 33:7) "He chose the best part for himself, because a ruler's [*mᵉḥōqēq*] portion was assigned there for him . . ." (Dt 33:21)

While all of the three poetic blessings are remarkably similar, Balaam's "blessing" is obviously distinctive. Unlike Jacob and Moses, Balaam is a Gentile who was hired to curse Israel. As noted earlier, God's promises to Abraham are clearly in focus in the Balaam narrative. The Balaam narrative takes up the theme of blessing from the perspective of the Gentiles.[15] How shall the nations receive and/or spurn God's plan of blessing through Abraham? The answer to this question is found in the allusions to Jacob's promise of a coming king from the tribe of Judah, located in Balaam's third (Nm 24:7-9) and fourth discourses (24:17-19). The Balaam narrative traces the divine plan to bless the Gentiles through the people of Israel, the pinnacle of Jacob's prediction of the king who would come in the last days (Gn 49:1,8-12; Nm 24:7-9,17-19).[16] With such striking parallels and reverberations between these three poems, it is reasonable to place Balaam's poem alongside the other two as similarly messianic in nature.

THE LITERARY STRUCTURE OF THE BALAAM NARRATIVES

A Two-Part, Threefold Structure

To discover the keys to unlock some of the mystery in the Balaam narrative, it is necessary to examine and analyze the structure of the story carefully, yielding some literary insights. Understanding the relationship of the various pericopes in the literary structure of the Balaam narrative is crucial for interpretation, particularly with respect to the third and fourth discourses.

The Balaam narrative is divided into two major sections, both of which divide into three pericopes.[17] In the first section, Nm 22:2-35, Balaam makes three attempts to go and curse Israel at Balak's behest. In Balaam's first attempt to go, God denies him permission (Nm 22:2-14). In his second attempt, God seemingly grants permission to go (Nm 22:15-21).[18] In Balaam's third attempt, God speaks to Balaam, first, through his donkey, and then by means of the Angel of the Lord, solemnly warning him to speak only what God tells him to say (Nm 22:22-35). In the pericope of Balaam's third attempt to go and curse Israel (the story of Balaam and his donkey; vv. 22-35), there are also three parts. Balaam tries to force his donkey to circumvent the Angel of the Lord three times (vv. 22-23,24-25,26-35), and on the third time, God miraculously opens the donkey's mouth as well as Balaam's eyes (vv. 28, 31).

In the second section of the Balaam narrative (Nm 22:36–24:25), there are also three parts; in each, Balak makes three attempts to persuade Balaam to curse Israel (22:26–23:12; 23:13-26; 23:27–24:25). This pattern of three is particularly clear in Nm 24:10, where Balak proclaims with exasperation, "I summoned you to put a curse on my enemies, but instead, you have blessed them these three times." As in the corresponding pericope in section one (i.e., Nm 22:2-35), the third pericope in the Balaam narrative also divides into several more parts, namely, Balaam's third discourse along with an additional four discourses (Nm 24:3,15,20-21,23). As will be seen, the structural parallels between sections one and two cast important light on the significance of Balaam's third discourse (Nm 23:27–24:13, with emphasis on 24:5-9). Furthermore, the structure reveals the significance of the talking donkey!

Literary Structure

SECTION ONE (NM 22:2-35)	SECTION TWO (NM 22:36–24:25)
Balaam's first attempt to go to curse Israel (Nm 22:2-14)	Balaam's first attempt to curse Israel (22:26–23:12)
Balaam's second attempt to go to curse Israel (Nm 22:15-21)	Balaam's second attempt to curse Israel (23:13-26)
Balaam's third attempt to go to curse Israel (Nm 22:22-35) First attempt to go around the Angel of the Lord (22-23) Second attempt to go around the Angel of the Lord (24-25) Third attempt to go around the Angel of the Lord (26-35)	Balaam's third attempt to curse Israel (23:27–24:25) Third Discourse (23:27–24:13) Fourth Discourse (24:14-19) Fifth Discourse (24:20) Sixth Discourse (24:21-22) Seventh Discourse (24:23-25)

Balaam's Talking Donkey is the Punchline

Though the story of the donkey is one of the strangest narratives in the Hebrew Bible, its importance for the interpretation of Balaam's discourses cannot be overstated.[19] Intentional parallels between the third pericopes (Nm 22:22-35 and

23:27–24:25) in each of the two major sections of the Balaam narrative prompt the reader to accept Balaam's discourses as the word of God even though he is identified as a negative figure elsewhere in the OT (Nm 31:8,16; Dt 23:5-6; Jos 13:22; 24:9-10; Mic 6:5; Neh 13:2). Additionally, the parallels serve to highlight the revelatory significance of Balaam's third discourse (Nm 24:5-9). In other words, the donkey story leads to the theological punchline of the entire Balaam narrative: Gentiles will find themselves blessed or cursed with respect to their posture toward the seed of Abraham (Nm 24:9).

Balaam is Just a Donkey

One major hurdle in relating to Balaam's third and fourth discourses as a prophetic word about the Messiah is the character of Balaam himself. Though the Balaam narrative seemingly gives a picture of an individual committed to speaking God's word at all cost (Nm 22:18; 24:13), other passages make it clear that Balaam was put to death for his wickedness (Nm 31:8). The apostle Peter states in no uncertain terms that Balaam "loved the wages of unrighteousness" (2Pt 2:15; see Jd 11; Rev 2:14). How then can the discourses of Balaam be God's word?

The story of Balaam's donkey resolves this issue by casting the Balaam-donkey incident as a precursor to the Balak-Balaam story. In the donkey narrative, Balaam blindly tries to force his donkey to go around the Angel of the Lord (Nm 22:22-35). The donkey clearly has the spiritual upper hand, and sees spiritual realities for what they are. Balaam, on the other hand, does not. After trying to force the donkey to go around the Angel of the Lord for the third time, God miraculously opens its mouth:

> Then the Lord opened the donkey's mouth, and she asked Balaam, "What have I done to you that you have beaten me these three times?" Balaam answered the donkey, "You made me look like a fool. If I had a sword in my hand, I'd kill you now!" But the donkey said, "Am I not the donkey you've ridden all your life until today? Have I ever treated you this way before?" "No," he replied.[20]

Typically, a donkey is not reliable for spiritual guidance nor would its words be dependable even if it could speak. But if God opens the donkey's mouth, its words are trustworthy regardless of the mouthpiece.

Similarly, when Balaam finally arrives to do Balak's bidding, Balak tries to force Balaam to curse Israel three times, just as Balaam had tried to force the donkey to go around the angel three times. In spite of Balak's pleas, Balaam blesses them (22:41–23:12; 23:13-26; 23:27–24:9). In his exasperation, Balak's words to Balaam echo Balaam's earlier frustration with his donkey.

"Then Balak became furious with Balaam, struck his hands together, and said to him, 'I summoned you to put a curse on my enemies, but instead, you have blessed them these three times.'" (Nm 24:10)	"Then the Lord opened the donkey's mouth, and she asked Balaam, 'What have I done to you that you have beaten me these three times?' Balaam answered the donkey, 'You made me look like a fool. If I had a sword in my hand, I'd kill you now!'" (Nm 22:28-29)

The parallels between the two stories suggest that Balak, like Balaam in the earlier narrative, blindly and perilously attempted to go against the Lord. And Balaam, like the donkey in the earlier narrative, supernaturally spoke the words God put in his mouth (Nm 22:28; 23:5,16). Typically, the discourses of a wicked pagan enchanter are unreliable, but if God puts words in his mouth, those words are trustworthy regardless of the mouthpiece. Balaam is God's donkey!

The Literary Significance of the Third Discourse

In addition to providing much needed guidance with respect to the reliability of Balaam's discourses, the parallels also highlight the revelatory significance of Balaam's third discourse. On Balaam's third attempt to circumvent the Angel of the Lord, God not only opened the donkey's mouth, He also opened Balaam's eyes to see Israel's heavenly warrior (Nm 22:31). The author clearly did not want the reader to miss the point that this "eye opening" takes place on Balaam's third attempt to go around the Angel of the Lord, for the text repeats on three occasions that he tried three times (Nm 22:28,32-33). Just as God opened Balaam's eyes on his third attempt to go around the Angel of the Lord in Nm 22, so God opened Balaam's eyes on his third attempt to curse Israel. While delivering his third discourse (Nm 24:4; see 24:16), Balaam saw Israel's royal warrior (Nm 24:7-9,17-19).

Parallels in Balaam's Two Third Attempts

Balaam's eyes are opened:	"Then the Lord opened Balaam's eyes [*wayᵉg̱al yhwh 'eṯ-'ênê ḇil'ām*]..." (Nm 22:31a)	"The oracle of one who hears the sayings of God, who sees a vision from the Almighty, who falls into a trance with his eyes uncovered [*opened: ûg̱ᵉlûy 'ênāyim*]" (Nm 24:4)

Balaam sees a warrior:	"and he saw the Angel of the LORD standing in the path with a drawn sword in His hand." (Nm 22:31b)	"His king will be greater than Agag, and his kingdom will be exalted. God brought him out of Egypt; He is like the horns of a wild ox for them. He will feed on enemy nations and gnaw their bones; he will strike them with his arrows. He crouches, he lies down like a lion or a lioness—who dares to rouse him?" (Nm 24:7b-9a)
Balaam's spiritual insight is given after three attempts:	"The Angel of the LORD asked him, 'Why have you beaten your donkey *these three times*? Look, I came out to oppose you, because what you are doing is evil in My sight. The donkey saw Me and turned away from Me *these three times*. If she had not turned away from Me, I would have killed you by now and let her live.'" (Nm 22:32-33)	"Then Balak became furious with Balaam, struck his hands together, and said to him, 'I summoned you to put a curse on my enemies, but instead, you have blessed them *these three times*.'" (Nm 24:10)

The parallels between the two stories highlight the special nature of Balaam's third discourse, and invite the reader to pay more careful attention to it. Several other textual clues serve to call attention to the third discourse, pointing to its unique revelatory significance. First, the text relates that Balaam did not use omens as he had in the previous two discourses (Nm 24:1). Second, in the third discourse Balaam saw all of Israel "encamped tribe by tribe" (Nm 24:2), whereas in the previous two discourses he saw only a portion of the people (Nm 22:41; 23:13). Third, Balaam uttered his third discourse when the "Spirit of God" came upon him (Nm 24:2), making plain the prophetic nature of the third discourse in no uncertain terms. The author emphasizes the prophetic significance of the third discourse by referring to it as an "oracle" (Nm 24:4), a word used almost exclusively to refer to the utterances of the OT prophets.[21] The text also describes Balaam's oracle as a vision (Nm 24:4).[22] In short, Balaam's third discourse is heavily marked as a prophetic word spoken through the Spirit of God.

BALAAM'S THIRD DISCOURSE (NM 23:27–24:13)

Out of Egypt: Israel or Israel's King?

There are two pressing interpretive questions to ask in order to understand the meaning of Balaam's third discourse. First, who is the "king" mentioned in Nm 24:7: "Water will flow from his buckets, and his seed will be by abundant water. His king will be greater than Agag, and his kingdom will be exalted." Typically, this king is identified as King Saul, Israel's first king who defeated Agag, the king of the Amalekites in 1Sm 15 (see vv. 8,9,20,32-33).[23] The second question is: Who is the antecedent of the pronoun "him" in Nm 24:8: "God brought him out of Egypt"? Does "him" refer to Israel collectively (i.e., God brought Israel [him = them] out of Israel) or to Israel's king?[24] Support for the collective interpretation comes from Nm 23:22, a verse that is nearly identical with Nm 24:8, with the exception of the plural pronoun "them": "God brought them out of Egypt." Another possibility, however, is that "him" refers to the king who is mentioned in the previous verse (i.e., God brings the king with the exalted kingdom out of Egypt).

Who is the "Him" in Nm 24:8?

ISRAEL	THE KING
"Water will flow from his [*Israel's*] buckets, and his [*Israel's*] seed will be by abundant water. His [*Israel's*] king will be greater than Agag, and his [*Israel's*] kingdom will be exalted. God brought him [*Israel*] out of Egypt." (Nm 24:7-8a)	"Water will flow from his [*Israel's*] buckets, and his seed will be by abundant water. His [*Israel's*] king will be greater than Agag, and his [*the king's*] kingdom will be exalted. God brought him [*the king*] out of Egypt." (Nm 24:7-8a)

In what follows, the messianic interpretation of vv. 7-9 will be supported, specifically by showing the reasons the "king" in v. 7 and the singular pronoun "him" in v. 8 should be understood as references to the Messiah-King.

Textual Support for Messianic Interpretation: Focus on an Individual King

To identify the king in v. 7, it is important first to answer the syntactical question in 24:8. Is "him" a collective reference to Israel, or a singular reference to the king of v. 7? As the old adage goes, the best commentary on Scripture is Scripture. In this particular case, it is essential to note the close relationship between Balaam's second (23:18-24) and third (24:5-9) discourses. There are many similarities between the second and third discourses, and the similarities also draw attention to key differences between the two. Both discourses refer to Israel and to a king, both discourses refer to an exodus from Egypt, and both discourses allude to Jacob's prophecy in Gn 49:8-12, specifically Gn 49:9.[25] For clarification and explanation, brackets in the following chart indicate when the HCSB translates singular pronouns and verbs as collective plural references to Israel.

Comparison of the Second and Third Discourses

	SECOND DISCOURSE	THIRD DISCOURSE
Israel and the king	"He considers no disaster for Jacob; He sees no trouble for Israel. The LORD their [*his*] God is with them [*him*], and there is rejoicing over the King among them [*him*]." (Nm 23:21)	"How beautiful are your tents, Jacob, your dwellings, Israel. . . . Water will flow from his buckets, and his seed will be by abundant water. His king will be greater than Agag, and his kingdom will be exalted." (Nm 24:5,7)
Exodus from Egypt	"God brought them out of Egypt; He is like the horns of a wild ox for them [*him*]."[26] (Nm 23:22)	"God brought him out of Egypt; He is like the horns of a wild ox for them. He will feed on enemy nations and gnaw their bones; he will strike them with his arrows." (Nm 24:8)
Allusion to Gn 49:9	"A people rise up like a lioness; They [*he*] rouse[*s*] themselves [*himself*] like a lion. They [*He*] will not lie down until they [*he*] devour[*s*] the prey and drink[*s*] the blood of the slain." (Nm 23:24)	"He crouches, he lies down like a lion or a lioness—who dares to rouse him? Those who bless you will be blessed, and those who curse you will be cursed." (Nm 24:9)

Though the similarities between the second and third discourses are quite obvious, in order to understand the third discourse, careful attention must be paid to the differences between the two. In 23:21, the pronouns used to refer to Israel are all singular even though the HCSB correctly interprets them as references to the people of Israel as a whole. A literal translation of the verse will be helpful: "He considers no disaster for Jacob; he sees no trouble for Israel; the Lord his God is with him, and the shout of a king is in him." The words "Jacob" and "Israel" are singular nouns in the Hebrew, but clearly refer to a collective group of people. Though the singular pronoun is used ("his God," "with him," "in him"), it obviously modifies the words Jacob and Israel. The HCSB, therefore, accurately conveys its meaning: "his God" = "Israel's God"; "with him" = "with Israel"; "in him" = "in Israel." In the following verse, 23:22, however, the author uses a plural pronoun to refer to Israel ("God brought *them* out of Egypt") even though the pronoun continues to refer to the singular nouns Jacob and Israel (see v. 23). In 23:24, the author also uses singular verbs, the referent of which is "people," a singular noun that refers collectively to Israel as a whole.

Why does Balaam suddenly use a plural pronoun "them" in v. 22 to refer to the singular nouns in v. 21, particularly since he also uses singular pronouns to refer to Israel in v. 21 as well? The answer is quite simple. The author uses the plural pronoun in v. 22 to distinguish between Israel and the king who are mentioned side by side in v. 21, both of which are singular nouns. A literal translation of 23:21-22 makes this clear: "The Lord his [Israel's] God is with him [Israel], and a shout of a king is in him [Israel]. God brings *them* [i.e., Israel, not the king] out of Egypt." Even though Balaam mentions Israel's king in v. 21, the people as a whole are the focus of the second discourse. A more literal translation of v. 24 makes this national focus clear: "Behold a people [singular collective noun] arises [singular verb referring to a collective group] like a lioness, and like a lion rouses itself up." The allusion to Jacob's prophecy in Gn 49:9 is obvious, yet the addition of the word "people" makes it clear that Gn 49:9 is viewed through the lens of Israel's current collective victory over their enemies. In short, Balaam's second discourse focuses on Israel's historical exodus out of Egypt.

In Balaam's third discourse, however, the author uses a singular pronoun rather than a plural pronoun: "God brought *him* out of Egypt" (Nm 24:8). Why? The author uses the singular pronoun in the third discourse in order to make it clear he is now referring to Israel's king, and not to Israel collectively. Again, a literal translation of 24:7-8 makes this quite clear:

> Water will flow from his [Israel's] buckets; and his [Israel's] seed upon the many waters; let his [Israel's] king be exalted over Agag, and his [the king's] kingdom be exalted. God brings him [i.e., the king, not Israel collectively] out of Egypt . . .

The singular pronoun in the third discourse reflects a focus not on Israel collectively, but rather on the victories of Israel's king. This becomes particularly clear in Nm 24:9, another obvious allusion to Gn 49:9:

COMPARISON OF NUMBERS 24:9 WITH NUMBERS 23:24

"He crouches, he lies down like a lion or a lioness—who dares to rouse him? Those who bless you will be blessed, and those who curse you will be cursed." (Nm 24:9)	"A *people*[27] rise up like a lioness; they rouse themselves like a lion. They will not lie down until they devour the prey and drink the blood of the slain." (Nm 23:24)

Numbers 24:9 lacks a reference to "people," making clear that the focus of the third discourse is on an individual king rather than on the people of Israel as a whole.

TEXTUAL SUPPORT FOR MESSIANIC INTERPRETATION: PROPHETIC EMPHASIS OF THIRD DISCOURSE

A focus on the coming of a future king makes much more sense textually in light of the places of the third discourse in the literary structure and the special emphases placed on the third discourse. As noted earlier, Balaam's third discourse stands apart from the earlier discourses, and the author goes to great lengths to present Balaam's third discourse as a prophecy spoken under the inspiration of the Spirit of God. According to 24:2-4, Balaam's third discourse is an "oracle," a word most associated with the prophetical literature. Moreover, Balaam speaks this oracle with "open eyes" during his third attempt to curse Israel (23:27-29). As already noted, in the parallel text, God opened Balaam's eyes to see a mighty warrior on his third attempt to circumvent the Angel of the Lord (22:31). Given that he saw Israel in the previous discourse, it would be expected for Balaam to see something different being that his eyes were supernaturally opened in the third oracle. In the second discourse, he saw Israel. In the third discourse, he saw a prophetic vision of a future king. As to the identity of this king, several factors in the text suggest that this king is none other than the future Messiah.

TEXTUAL SUPPORT FOR MESSIANIC INTERPRETATION: THIRD DISCOURSE AND JACOB'S BLESSING

Perhaps one of the strongest reasons for identifying the king in Balaam's third discourse as the Messiah is the nearly verbatim repetition of Jacob's prophecy in Gn 49:9:[28]

"*He crouches, he lies down like a lion or a lioness—who dares to rouse him?* Those who bless you will be blessed, and those who curse you will be cursed." (Nm 24:9)	"Judah is a young lion— my son, you return from the kill. *He crouches; he lies down like a lion or a lioness—who dares to rouse him?* The scepter will not depart from Judah or the staff from between his feet until He whose right it is comes and the obedience of the peoples belongs to Him." (Gn 49:9-10)

The importance of Balaam's poetic discourses within the broader context of the large poems in the Torah was previously noted. John Sailhamer helpfully identifies the significance of the poems about "the last days" in the Pentateuch. It is worth quoting Sailhamer at length:

> At three macrostructural junctures in the Pentateuch, the author has spliced a major poetic discourse onto the end of a large unit of narrative (Ge 49; Nu 24; Dt 31). A close look at the material lying between and connecting the narrative and poetic sections reveals the presence of a homogeneous compositional stratum. It is most noticeably marked by the recurrence of the same terminology and narrative motifs. In each of the three segments, the central narrative figure (Jacob, Balaam, Moses) calls an audience together (imperative: Ge 49:1; Nu 24:14; Dt 31:28) and proclaims (cohortative: Ge 49:1; Nu 24:14; Dt 31:28) what will happen (Ge 49:1; Nu 24:14; Dt 31:29) in "the end of days" (Ge 49:1; Nu 24:14; Dt 31:29).[29]

Although the phrase "the last days" is used with reference to Balaam's fourth discourse (Nm 24:14-19), the clear allusion to Jacob's prediction in Nm 24:9 makes it quite likely that Balaam was referring to the same king, particularly when the prophetic genre of Balaam's third discourse is considered.

Although Balaam's fourth discourse (Nm 24:14-19) will be discussed below, it is important to first discuss the meaning of "the end of days" as it is used in the three larger poems of the Pentateuch, particularly since it sheds light on the identity of the king in Balaam's third discourse. Though the phrase *b*^{e}*ʾaḥ*^{a}*rîṯ hayyāmîm* is typically translated as a general reference to a future time in the English translations,[30] it is literally translated "the end of days" or "the last days." An eschatological sense of each of the four appearances (Gn 49:1; Nm 24:14; Dt 4:30; 31:29) is highly likely for a number of reasons. First, "the end of days" in Dt 4:25-31 is clearly referring to a time period after God has scattered Israel among the nations for breaking the Sinai covenant, long after king Saul and the ruling Davidic dynasty (see esp. v. 27). This is the exact sense in which Israel's later prophets refer to an eschatological work of God sometime after Israel's exile (Isa 2:2; Jer 23:20; 30:24; 48:47; 49:39;

Ezk 38:16; Hos 3:5; Mic 4:1; Dan 10:14). Second, there are strong literary and thematic parallels linking Moses' prophecy in Dt 4:25-31 with Dt 30:1-10 and 32:1-43, strongly suggesting that the meaning of "the end of days" in Dt 31:29 is the same as in Dt 4:30. In other words, at least one of three of the macrostructural junctures in the Pentateuch is referring to God's eschatological work. Third, given the literary relationship of the other two "end day" poems (i.e., Gn 49; Nm 24) with Dt 32, one would expect the sense of "the end of days" in Gn 49:1 and Nm 24:14 to be the same as it is in Deuteronomy, namely, the eschatological future. When Jacob and Balaam speak of a king who will come "in the end of days" (Gn 49:1,8-12; Nm 24:14-19), i.e., after Israel's exile, the messianic interpretation is practically assured.

Regarding the king in Balaam's third discourse, Balaam's allusion to Jacob's prophecy in the context of a prophetic oracle strongly suggests that Balaam is referring to the same royal figure of whom Jacob prophesied previously, in Gn 49:8-12. This king will "crouch/lie down like a lion" (Gn 49:9; Nm 24:9), he will defeat Israel's enemies (Gn 49:8; Nm 24:8), and he will bring blessings to the nations who bless him, and curses to the nations who curse him (Gn 49:9-10; Nm 24:9; cf. Ps 72).

Jacob and Balaam's King

Crouching Lion-King	"He crouches; he lies down like a lion or a lioness—who dares to rouse him?" (Gn 49:9)	"He crouches, he lies down like a lion or a lioness—who dares to rouse him?" (Nm 24:9)
Victor over Israel's Enemies	"Your hand will be on the necks of your enemies" (Gn 49:8)	"He will feed on enemy nations and gnaw their bones; he will strike them with his arrows." (Nm 24:8)
Channel of Blessing to the Nations	"and the obedience of the peoples belongs to Him." (Gn 49:10)	"Those who bless you will be blessed, and those who curse you will be cursed." (Nm 24:9)

Textual Support for Messianic Interpretation: Agag and the Third Oracle

One of the reasons the king of the third oracle is typically identified as King Saul is the reference to Agag in Nm 24:7: "His king will be greater than Agag, and his kingdom will be exalted." Since Agag, the Amalekite king, is mentioned only in the story of Saul, it is argued, this verse must be referring to the episode in 1Sm 15

(vv. 8-9,20,32-33). However, there are strong reasons to question the originality of the word "Agag" in the Masoretic Text (MT). But for the sake of argument, consideration should be given to the implications of "Agag" being the original reading. Numbers 24:7 predicts the coming of an Israelite king who will be greater than Agag. However, quite contrary to the positive expectations, Saul's failure to put Agag, the Amalekite, to death does not result in the establishment of an exalted kingdom (see Nm 24:7), but rather to God's rejection of Saul and his lineage (1Sm 15:23). If anything, the description of Saul's disobedience in 1Sm 15 casts doubt that Saul could possibly be the king of whom Balaam prophesied in Nm 24:7-9.

Saul's failure to destroy the Amalekites and their king resulted in unfinished business (Ex 17:16). It comes as no surprise that this unfinished business resurfaced long after the throne of David had failed. The book of Esther tells the story of a renewed battle between a descendent of Kish from the tribe of Benjamin (Est 2:5; cf. 1Sm 9:1) and the archenemy of the Jewish people, an Agagite named Haman (Est 3:1,10; 8:3,5; 9:24). For this reason, Hans-Christoph Schmitt argues that the name Agag in Nm 24:7 is used as an image or representative of an eschatological enemy, an enemy that Israel's first king failed to defeat.[31] If Agag is original, therefore, the effective overthrow of Saul's kingdom by Agag leaves open the need for a decisive triumph over Agag to be accomplished by a future king.

In all likelihood, however, the use of "Agag" in the MT is not original. In several of the key witnesses to the original Hebrew text, "Gog" is used rather than "Agag."[32] The name "Gog" is found in the Septuagint, the Samaritan Pentateuch, the Dead Sea Scrolls,[33] Aquila, Symmachus, and Theodotion. Moreover, Aquila, Symmachus, and Theodotion were all Greek translations the Jewish community produced to replace the Septuagint, a translation rejected by the Jewish community because of its use by the Christians. The presence of Gog in these Greek translations provides strong evidence in favor of "Gog" as the original reading. The strongest evidence in favor of Gog, however, does not come from the ancient witnesses, but from the OT itself.[34] The only other reference to Gog in the OT is found in Ezk 38–39 (Ezk 38:2-3,14,16,18; 39:1,11,15), in a context that is clearly eschatological. According to Ezk. 38, God commanded Ezekiel to prophesy against Gog, chief prince of Meshech and Tubal (Ezk 38:3), a future enemy from the north who will come against Israel in the end of years/days (Ezk 38:8,16). According to Ezk 38:17, God had already spoken through the prophets about the coming of Gog in "the last days":

> This is what the Lord God says: Are you the one I spoke about in former times through My servants, the prophets of Israel, who for years prophesied in those times that I would bring you against them?

This verse, however, makes no sense in the MT if there are no other references to a king called Gog in the Hebrew Bible other than those in Ezk 38–39. Ezekiel 38:16, however, does make sense if the original reading of Nm 24:7 is Gog—a representative of an eschatological enemy of Israel.

Conclusion on Balaam's Third Discourse

To summarize the above findings, several reasons favor the messianic interpretation of Balaam's third discourse.

1. Balaam's poem finds strong parallels with the two other poems of the Torah, fitting into the macrostructural narrative pointing toward Abraham's seed: The Messiah.
2. Examination of the structure of the Balaam narratives unlocks the mystery of the talking donkey and the character of Balaam: God can (and will) use anyone, man or beast, as His mouthpiece. Balaam brings a word from God, just like the donkey. There is something unique and highly significant about Balaam's third discourse; it is identified as a prophetic oracle spoken when God supernaturally opened Balaam's eyes.
3. The parallels and differences between Balaam's second and third discourses point to a focus on an individual king, rather than on collective Israel.
4. The nearly verbatim citation of Jacob's prophecy about the coming of a king from the tribe of Judah leads to identifying the king in Balaam's third discourse as the same king in Jacob's prophecy: the Messiah from the tribe of Judah who will come in the end of days.
5. There is strong text-critical evidence in favor of Gog. Balaam's third discourse prophesies the defeat of Gog, Israel's eschatological enemy, at the hands of Israel's future king.

One final factor that favors the messianic interpretation of Balaam's third discourse is the close lexical and thematic parallels with Balaam's fourth discourse (Nm 24:17-19), strongly suggesting that these are intended to provide additional commentary on the third discourse. This king will come in the end of days (Nm 24:14, third discourse) as the star and scepter who will crush the heads of Israel's enemies (Nm 24:17, fourth discourse). In the following section, this close relationship between the two oracles will be examined, along with the implications for interpretation.

BALAAM'S FOURTH DISCOURSE (NM 24:17-19)

David or Messiah?

Balaam's fourth oracle, Nm 24:17-19, has an ancient history of being interpreted messianically.[35] It is interpreted messianically by the Septuagint, Testament of Levi, Testament of Judah, Targum Onkelos, Pseudo-Jonathan, the Fragmentary Targum, Ramban, *Midrash Eikha*, etc. In John Calvin's words, "The coming forth of the Star and the Sceptre, therefore, of which Balaam speaks explicitly, refers to Christ."[36] Rashi, on the other hand, identified the star who crushes the heads of Moab in v. 17 as King David since it was David who defeated the Moabites and made them lie face down to the ground (2Sm 8:2).[37] Other scholars have followed Rashi's line of reasoning,[38] arguing that Balaam's star is a short-term prophecy pointing to David, though they do not deny the possibility of an eschatological trajectory.[39] There is strong evidence in support of the ancient interpretation that considers the literal sense of the passage to be messianic.

The Last Days in the Pentateuch

The previous section discussed the significance of Balaam's discourses in the larger matrix of the Pentateuch's poetry. Any attempts to identify the star/scepter in Nm 24:17 must consider the other large poems in the Pentateuch, particularly Gn 49. Jacob's blessing and Balaam's fourth discourse both focus on things that will take place in the end of days.

"Then Jacob called his sons and said, 'Gather around, and I will tell you what will happen to you in the days to come [*the end of days*].'" (Gn 49:1)	"Now I am going back to my people, but first, let me warn you what these people will do to your people in the future [*the end of days*]." (Nm 24:14)

Given the tight connection between the Pentateuch's poems about the last days, as well as the description of "the later days" as a period sometime after Israel's exile from the land of Canaan in the book of Deuteronomy (4:30), the long-term messianic interpretation fits better than the idea that it was limited to King David. Not only did David live long before the time period identified as the end of days in the Pentateuch, but also his victory over the Moabites was partial and short-lived (cf. 2Sm 8:2; 2Kg 3:4-27).[40]

The Fourth Oracle in Light of the Third Oracle

A close relationship exists between Balaam's third and fourth discourses. Of all the seven discourses of Balaam, only the third and the fourth are described as "oracles."

In fact, both discourses are described as oracles three times (Nm 24:3-4,15-16) and as prophetic visions (Nm 23:4,16). They both are proclaimed through "open eyes" (Nm 24:3-4,15-16) and both anticipate the "smashing" (*mḥṣ*) of Israel's enemies (Nm 24:8,17). Both discourses also allude to Jacob's prophecy of the coming Messiah in Gn 49:8-12, with Nm 24:9 repeating, nearly verbatim, Jacob's prophecy of a crouching lion-king (cf. Gn 49:9) and Nm 24:17 predicting the coming of a "scepter" (king) from the people of Israel. There are only two places in the entire Hebrew Bible that speak of the coming of a scepter in the end of days: Jacob's blessing and Balaam's fourth discourse.

Comparison of Balaam's Third and Fourth Discourses

	Balaam's Third Discourse (Nm 23:27–24:13)	Balaam's Fourth Discourse (Nm 24:14-19)
Prophetic Oracle	"and he proclaimed his poem: The *oracle* of Balaam son of Beor, the *oracle* of the man whose eyes are opened, the *oracle* of one who hears the sayings of God." (Nm 24:3-4)	"Then he proclaimed his poem: The *oracle* of Balaam son of Beor, the *oracle* of the man whose eyes are opened; the *oracle* of one who hears the sayings of God." (Nm 24:15-16)
Prophetic Vision	"who sees a vision from the Almighty" (Nm 24:4)	"who sees a vision from the Almighty" (Nm 24:16)
Open Eyes	"the oracle of the man whose eyes are opened" (Nm 24:3) "who falls into a trance with his eyes uncovered" (Nm 24:4)	"the oracle of the man whose eyes are opened" (Nm 24:15) "who falls into a trance with his eyes uncovered" (Nm 24:16)
Smashing (*mḥṣ*) Israel's Enemies	"he will strike [*smash*: *mḥṣ*] them with his arrows" (Nm 24:8)	"He will smash [*mḥṣ*] the forehead of Moab" (Nm 24:17)

Allusion to Jacob's Prophecy in Gn 49	"He crouches, he lies down like a lion or a lioness—who dares to rouse him?" (Nm 24:9; cf. Gn 49:9)	"Now I am going back to my people, but first, let me warn you what these people will do to your people in the future [in the end of days]." (Nm 24:14; cf. Gn 49:1) "and a scepter will arise from Israel." (Nm 24:17; cf. Gn 49:10)

The close relationship between the third and fourth discourses makes it likely that both are focused on the same king. Moreover, this relationship is essential for identifying the antecedent of the two third-person singular pronouns ("him") in Nm 24:17: "I see *him*, but not now; I perceive *him*, but not near." The reason Balaam does not see the "him" of v. 17 "now/close" is provided in v. 14: the "him" is coming in the end of days. What is not immediately clear, however, is the identity of this "him." In Balaam's first discourse (23:7-10), he used similar language to describe his visual perception of Israel.

"I see them [*him; 'er'ennû*] from the top of rocky cliffs, and I watch them [him; *'ᵃšûrennû*] from the hills. There is a people living alone; it does not consider itself among the nations." (Nm 23:9)	"I see him [*'er'ennû*], but not now; I perceive [watch: *'ᵃšûrennû*] him, but not near. A star will come from Jacob, and a scepter will arise from Israel. He will smash the forehead of Moab and strike down all the Shethites." (Nm 24:17)

The similarities of perception verbs are crucial for clarifying the referent of the fourth discourse. Since Balaam sees/watches the people of Israel in the first discourse as a present reality, he must be seeing something different in the fourth discourse, something only seen when God supernaturally opens his eyes. This returns discussion to the individual king in Balaam's third discourse. Whom does Balaam see in the distant future, i.e., in the last days? He sees the same king of whom he spoke in the third discourse. This king will crush Israel's enemies (Nm 24:8,17) and rule over Israel and the nations (Nm 24:7,19).

Intertextuality in the Fourth Discourse

Another feature of Balaam's fourth discourse is the way it, as in Balaam's third discourse, relates to earlier poetic blessings and promises in the Pentateuch. As previously noted, the threefold strand of blessing, seed, and land as expressed in the creation mandate (Gn 1:28) sets the stage for God's redemptive drama through Abraham. The Balaam narrative is strategically aligned with this threefold strand and ultimately sees its fulfillment through an individual king who will rise up from the people of Israel in the last days. "Smash[ing] the forehead of Moab" in Nm 24:17 is thematically tied to the poetic anticipation of the skull crushing seed of the woman in Gn 3:15.[41] The verb used to describe the dominion of this future king ("to rule;" *rād h*) in Nm 24:19 is also used to describe Adam's dominion over creation (Gn 1:26,28), and is later used of Solomon's reign over the promised land (1Kg 4:24 [5:4 MT]). It is not surprising that this verb is used twice outside the Torah to describe the Messiah's dominion (Pss 72:8; 110:2).

"God blessed them, and God said to them, 'Be fruitful, multiply, fill the earth, and subdue it. *Rule* the fish of the sea, the birds of the sky, and every creature that crawls on the earth.'" (Gn 1:28)	"One who comes from Jacob will *rule*; he will destroy the city's survivors." (Nm 24:19)	"May he *rule* from sea to sea and from the Euphrates to the ends of the earth." (Ps 72:8)	"The LORD will extend Your mighty scepter from Zion. *Rule* over Your surrounding enemies." (Ps 110:2)

The reference to "the last days" in Nm 24:14 and the "scepter" in 24:17 are unmistakable allusions to Jacob's messianic prophecy in Gn 49:1,8. The king's triumph over his enemies in Nm 24:18 picks up a number of key words and themes in God's promises to Abraham's seed in Gn 22:17 and 24:60:

"Your offspring will possess [*yiras*] the gates [*ša ar*] of their (literally, his) enemies." (Gn 22:17)	". . . May your offspring possess the gates of their (literally, his) enemies." (Gn 24:60)	"Edom will become a possession [*yᵉrēšāh*]; Seir [*śē ʿîr*][42] will become a possession [*yᵉrēšāh*] of its enemies [*ʾōyᵉḇāyw*] . . ." (Nm 24:18)

The king's end-time victories over Israel's enemies in Nm 24:18 are fully aligned with, and part of, the trajectory of God's promises to Abraham. This trajectory began with the first prophetic anticipation of hostility between the seed of the woman, the serpent, and its seed in Gn 3:15, and continues to the ultimate crushing of that enemy. The numerous allusions to God's promise-plan of blessing through Abraham's seed are not random. Rather, the Balaam narrative with its discourses provides the interpretive key for connecting the dots between the creation mandate, God's promises to Abraham, and the coming Messianic King. God's plan for humanity through Adam, and through Abraham, will be fully and completely realized through the Messiah's rule in the last days. Those who bless this coming king will themselves be blessed. Those who curse this king will themselves be cursed. "He crouches, he lies down like a lion or a lioness—who dares to rouse him? Those who bless you will be blessed, and those who curse you will be cursed" (Nm 24:9).

CONCLUSION

This analysis of Balaam's fourth discourse began by asking the question: Is Balaam's fourth discourse a reference to King David or to King Messiah? A number of reasons have been advanced to show that the nonmessianic interpretation falls far short of the grandeur of Balaam's prophetic oracles. Balaam's fourth discourse is placed in the prophetic context of "the last days"—a period of time that is defined elsewhere in the Torah as a period long after the rule of David. Also noted was the literary relationship of the third and fourth discourses, a relationship that makes explicitly clear that the rising star of the fourth discourse is the coming king of the third discourse, the Messiah King of whom Jacob prophesied in Gn 49:1,8-12. Finally, the numerous allusions to earlier promises in the Pentateuch suggest that the fourth discourse, like the third, provides the climactic expression of God's promises to Abraham and his seed. God's purposes for Adam, His prophecy in Gn 3:15, and His promises to Abraham would all be fulfilled in the coming Messiah. In a very real sense, Paul's interpretation of God's promises to the seed of Abraham in Gal 3:16 is neither novel, nor creative, but well-rooted in the promises' literal, grammatical-historical meaning.[43]

---

1. See Shubert Spero, "'Moses Wrote His Book and the Portion of Balaam': (Tb Bava Batra 14b)," *Jewish Bible Quarterly* 41, no. 3 (2013): 193–94, who writes, "But perhaps the most interesting question of all centers around the character and personality of Balaam who, the Rabbis decided, was a *rasha*—'wicked' and dissolute. How can an individual who is a practitioner of magic and sorcery suddenly turn into a *navi* upon whom the *spirit of God* rests? (Num. 24:22)." See *Or HeChaim Berayshi* 27.29; *Or HeChaim Bemidbar* 23.25; *M. Berakhot* 7; 55; *M. Ta'anit* 20; *M. Sanhedrin* 105; 106; *M. Zebachim* 116; *M. Nida* 31; *Jer. M. Sanhedrin* 51; *M. Avoth* 5.19; *M. Avoth Divrei Natan* 1.4; 2.5; *M. Khalah Rabati* 7; *Gen.Rab.* 19.11; 99.7; *Exod.Rab.* 20.5; 27.6; *Num.Rab.* 20.6, 11, 20; *Dt.Rab.* 3.4; *Esth.Rab.* 7.13; *Song.Rab.* 6.23;

Eccl.Rab. 2.19; 7.12; *Exod.Rab.Margalioth* 4.3; *Dt.Rab.Margalioth* 1.5; *Midrash Gen.* 19.16; 103.15; *Midrash Prov.* 19.5; *Otzar HaMidrashim HaYekholoth* 46; *Otzar HaMidrashim Chofat Eliyahu* 4; *Otzar HaMidrashim Mashiach* 8; *Otzar HaMidrashim Shimon Ben Yochai* 4; *2 Batei Midrashoth* 6.20; *Debei Eliyahuh Rabba* 19.3; *Midrash Abba Gorion* 3.16; *2 Pesikta DeRav Khana* 1.4, 12; *1 Pesikta Rabetai* 20.2; *Pirke DeRab Eliezer* 46; *Aggadath Berayshit* 82; *Tanchuma* 96.1 *(Warsaw; Buber)*; *Tanchuma Balak* 14 *(Warsaw)*; *Tanchuma Devarim 3 (Warsaw; Buber)*; *Tanchuma Bemidbar 11 (Buber)*; *Tanchuma Balak* 8; 23 *(Buber)*; *Melkhita Jethro B'Chadash* 1; 5; *Sha'ar Otioth Emek Beracha* 2(22); *M. Pesachim Derush Shishi* (28); *Zohar Tikunei HaZohar* 51.71; et al.

2. Numbers 24:7-9 is interpreted messianically in the Septuagint; Targum Neofiti; Targum Psuedo Jonathan; Gen. Rab. Seder Wahei 98; Yoel Ba'al HaRemezim 98; Ba'al HaTorim (Yaakov Ben Asher); Numbers 24:17-19 is interpreted messianically by the Septuagint; Targum Onkelos, Pseudo-Jonathan, Neofiti; Josephus (Antiq. 4.125); the Dead Sea Scrolls (CD 7:19-20=4Q266 frag 3, 3:20; 1QM 11:6-7, and 4Q175.9-13; and is alluded to in 1Q28b 5:27; see Matthew E. Gordley, "Seeing Stars at Qumran: The Interpretation of Balaam and His Oracle in the Damascus Document and Other Qumran Texts," *Proceedings: Eastern Great Lakes and Midwest Biblical Societies* 25 (2005): 107; Testament of Levi 18:3; Testament of Judah 2:1. Rabbi Akiba understood this as a reference to Simon bar Kosiba (see Jerusalem Talmud *Ta'anit* 24).

3. John H. Sailhamer, *The Pentateuch as Narrative: A Biblical-Theological Commentary* (Grand Rapids: Zondervan, 1992); William Horbury, *Jewish Messianism and the Cult of Christ* (London: SCM Press, 1998); Hans-Christoph Schmitt, "Der Heidnische Mantiker Als Eschatologischer Jahweprophet. Zum Verständnis Bileams in der Endgestalt von Num 22-24," in *Theologie in Prophetie und Pentateuch: Gesammelte Schriften*, Beihefte zur Zeitschrift für die Alttestamentliche Wissenschaft (Berlin: W. de Gruyter, 2001); Michael Rydelnik, *The Messianic Hope: Is the Hebrew Bible Really Messianic?* NAC Studies in Bible & Theology (Nashville: B&H Academic, 2010).

4. This is particularly clear in the case of Nm 24:8-9, where some modern translations interpret the masculine singular pronoun as a collective reference to Israel (see NET; NJPS; NIV). Philip J. Budd, *Numbers*, Word Biblical Commentary 5 (Nashville: Thomas Nelson, 1984), 269–70, identifies the king in Nm 24:7 as Saul, and the scepter in 24:17 as a reference to David; so also Timothy R. Ashley, *The Book of Numbers*, ed. R. K. Harrison and Robert L. Hubbard Jr., The New International Commentary on the Old Testament (Grand Rapids: Eerdmans, 1993), 493, 500–501; John Calvin, *Commentaries on the Last Books of Moses*, vol. IV (Edinburgh: Calvin Translation Society, 1855), 222; R. Dennis Cole, *Numbers*, New American Commentary 3B, ed. E. Ray Clendenen (Nashville: B&H, 2000), 421; Roy Gane, *Leviticus, Numbers*, NIV Application Commentary (Grand Rapids: Zondervan, 2004), 709–10; Ronald B. Allen, "Numbers," *Expositor's Bible Commentary*, ed. Frank E. Gaebelein and J. D. Douglas (Grand Rapids: Zondervan, 1990), 2:906.

5. Used elsewhere, only in Nm 24:10; Job 3:8; 5:3; Prv 11:26; 24:24.

6. This combination of verbs appears in three other verses outside the Torah (Jer 20:14; Mal 2:2; Prv 3:33).

7. Emphasis added.

8. For a detailed literary analysis of the parallels between Exodus 1 and the Balaam narrative, see Sailhamer, *The Pentateuch as Narrative*, 405–09.

9. Given the shared language (lexical parallels), there is a strong likelihood Nm 22:3 is an intentional allusion to Ex 1:12. The shared language also draws the readers' focus to the thematic parallels for comparison and contrast of both stories in the larger matrix of the Torah story.

10. Pharaoh enslaved the people of Israel (1:7-14); commanded the midwives to kill the Hebrew boys (1:15-21); and commanded his people to drown the Hebrew boys in the Nile River (Ex 1:22). Balak sent Balaam to curse Israel three times (see Nm 24:10).

11. This analysis will show that the literary structure of the Balaam narrative hangs on two major sections that are divided into three pericopes. The third pericopes in both sections are not only distinguished from the two preceding pericopes, they also parallel one another with shared language and shared themes.

12. See Sailhamer, *The Pentateuch as Narrative*, 36; Terje Stordalen, *Echoes of Eden: Genesis 2–3 and Symbolism of the Eden Garden in Biblical Hebrew Literature*, Contributions to Biblical Exegesis and Theology (Leuven, Belgium: Peeters, 2000), 442, n. 179; Gilmore Henry Guyot, "The Prophecy of Balaam," *The Catholic Biblical Quarterly* 2, no. 4 (1940): 339–40.

13. All three poems use the word *rē'šîṯ*("beginning"; Gn 49:3; Nm 24:20; Dt 33:21); two of the three poems use the exact same wording for the blessing of Joseph (Gn 49:26; Dt 33:16; see also Nm 24:17); two of the three poems refer to God as *šaḏay* (Gn 49:25; Nm 24:4,16); two of the three poems repeat the word *'êṯān* ("enduring"; Gn 49:24; Nm 24:21); two of the three poems pair the verbs *ṭrp*_("to tear") and *'ḵl* ("to eat/devour") together (Gn 49:27; Nm 23:24); two of the three poems refer to God as a helper (Gn 49:25; Dt 33:7,26,29); two of the three poems refer to the "eastern/ancient mountains" (Nm 23:7; Dt 33:15); two of the three poems refer to the "eternal hills" and "head" (Gn 49:26; Dt 33:15); two of the three poems refer to a wild ox (Nm 23:22; 24:8; Dt 33:17); and two of the three poems specifically mention "the last days" (Gn 49:1; Nm 24:14; see Dt 31:29).

14. The Septuagint and Targum Neofiti both translate Dt 33:5 with reference to a future king ("a king will arise"). Since the translator of the Septuagint was working in the second century BC with an unpointed Hebrew text (meaning that the Hebrew text of the Bible did not have vowel pointings or accents until the 8th–10th centuries), it is easy to see how he would understand the verb in 33:5 as a *waw* + jussive (*wîhî*; see 33:6b) rather than a *wayyiqtol* (*wayᵉhî*). Neofiti's translation may point to the origins of this Targum to before the Masoretic pointing was added.

15. Ulrike Sals, "The Hybrid Story of Balaam (Numbers 22-24): Theology for the Diaspora in the Torah," *Biblical Interpretation* 16, no. 4 (2008): 317.

16. See Guyot, "The Prophecy of Balaam," 339.

17. Schmitt, "Der heidnische Mantiker als eschatologischer Jahweprophet. Zum Verständnis Bileams in der Endgestalt von Num 22-24," 240–41; for more on the significance of the pattern of three for the interpretation of the Balaam narrative, see Robert Alter, *The Art of Biblical Narrative* (New York: Basic Books, 1981), 95–96, 105–06.

18. According to Clinton J. Moyer, "Who Is the Prophet, and Who the Ass?: Role-Reversing Interludes and the Unity of the Balaam Narrative (Numbers 22–24)," *Journal for the Study of the Old Testament* 37, no. 2 (2012): 173, the point of Nm 22:20 is not to give Balaam permission to go, but to remind him through a rhetorical "if" that he has already been given clear instructions (Nm 22:12) not to go. God's anger in v. 22 comes in response to Balaam's decision not to follow God's instructions.

19. I could not agree more with Michael L. Barré, "The Portrait of Balaam in Numbers 22–24," *Interpretation* 51, no. 3 (1997): 255, who writes, "Far from being merely an amusing anecdote, this little tale contains important clues for interpreting the story as a whole."

20. Nm 22:28-30.

21. See "נְאֻם," *Hebrew and Aramaic Lexicon of the Old Testament*, 2:657. Of its 376 occurrences in the OT, "oracle" appears 356 times in Isaiah–Malachi. Remarkably, "oracle" is only used eight times in the Pentateuch, and six times in Nm 24 (Gn 22:16; Nm 14:28; 24:3-4,15-16).

22. Remarkably, four of the seven references to the root "to see [a vision]" in the Pentateuch appear in Nm 24 (4,16).

23. See, for example, Rashi; Ramban; Calvin; Budd, *Numbers*, Word Biblical Commentary, 269; Cole, *Numbers*, New American Commentary, 420.

24. The New Jewish Publication Society translation clearly understands the singular pronoun as a collective reference to Israel: "God who freed them from Egypt Is for them like the horns of the wild ox. They shall devour enemy nations, Crush their bones, And smash their arrows" (see also Targum Onkelos; Targum Neofiti; NLT; NIV).

25. "Judah is a young lion—my son, you return from the kill. He crouches; he lies down like a lion or a lioness—who dares to rouse him?"

26. The singular pronoun "him" is likely not a reference to Israel, i.e., "He is like the horns of a wild ox for them." Rather, the singular pronoun is probably a reference to God, i.e., God brings Israel out of Egypt, defending her and leading her like a powerful wild ox with powerful horns. See Robert Alter, *The Five Books of Moses: A Translation with Commentary*, 1st ed. (New York: W. W. Norton & Co., 2004), 808 (note on v. 22).

27. Emphasis added.

28. John H. Sailhamer, "Creation, Genesis 1–11, and the Canon," *Bulletin for Biblical Research* 10, no. 1 (2000): 93, writes:

> Balaam's words about a future king in Num 24:9a, for example, are virtually identical to Jacob's words about the king of Judah in Gen 49:9b: "He crouches, he lies down like a lion. Like a lion, who will arouse him?" Again, Balaam repeats Isaac's words of blessing to Jacob in Gen 27:29, "Those who bless you will be blessed and those who curse you will be cursed" (Num 24:9b). Such close verbal parallels are not likely accidental. By means of such parallels and others that we will discuss below, the poetry of Numbers 24 is closely linked to the poetic texts in Gen 49:8-12; 27:29; 12:3; 9:25-27; and 3:15. Their themes are not only connected and intertwined but also extended and linked to the larger themes of the Pentateuch.

29. Sailhamer, *The Pentateuch as Narrative*, 36.

30. In the HCSB: "in the days to come" (Gn 49:1); "in the future" (Nm 24:14); "in later days" (Dt 4:30); "In the future" (Dt 31:29).

31. Schmitt, "Der heidnische Mantiker als eschatologischer Jahweprophet," 244–45; see also C. F. Keil and F. Delitzsch, *Commentary on the Old Testament*, vol. 1 (Peabody: Hendrickson Publishers, 1996), 189.

32. A word about textual criticism in the OT is essential at this point. The most reliable text of the Hebrew Bible is the Masoretic Text, the fact of which OT scholars are in agreement. That being stated, there are a few instances in which the English versions of the OT prefer readings not represented in the MT. For instance, many English versions choose the reading "pierced" in Ps 22:16 [17 MT], even though the MT reads "like a lion" (e.g., HCSB; NASB; ESV; KJV). The reason for this choice is strong ancient textual evidence in favor of this reading.

33. 4Q27 f24ii.

34. I am indebted to John Sailhamer who pointed out Ezekiel's use of Gog during a class lecture.

35. Gordley, "Seeing Stars at Qumran," 113.

36. John Calvin, *Commentaries on the Last Books of Moses*, 228.

37. Rashi does, however, identify the ruler in v. 19 as the Messiah, based on the shared use of the verb "to rule" (rād_h) in another passage that describes the Messiah's rule (Ps 72:8).

38. Guyot, "The Prophecy of Balaam," 335.

39. According to W. Hall Harris, ed., The NET Bible Notes, 1st Accordance electronic ed. (Richardson: Biblical Studies Press, 2005), paragraph 12440, "The immediate reference of the prophecy seems to be to David, but the eschatological theme goes beyond him."

40. Guyot, "The Prophecy of Balaam," 337.

41. Sailhamer, "Creation," 93; James Hamilton, "The Skull Crushing Seed of the Woman: Inner-Biblical Interpretation of Genesis 3:15," *Southern Baptist Journal of Theology* 10, no. 2 (2006).

42. "Seir its enemies" [*śēʿîr ʾōyeḇāyw*] is likely a play on the phrase "gates of his enemies" [*šaʿar ʾōyeḇāyw*] used in Gn 22:17.

43. "Now the promises were spoken to Abraham and to his seed. He does not say 'and to seeds,' as though referring to many, but referring to one, and to your seed, who is Christ" (Gal 3:16). Paul's messianic interpretation of the promise is not only found in the Balaam narratives, but also in Ps 72:17.

Deuteronomy 17:14-20

The Foundations of Messianic Kingship

DANIEL I. BLOCK

Some hold that the book of Deuteronomy contains no explicit references to the Messiah. Although many interpret the promise that YHWH will raise up a prophet like Moses in 18:15 messianically,[1] in the context of vv. 9-22 Moses' concern is first, to assure Israel that after his own departure YHWH will continue to speak to His people through commissioned prophets (v. 18), and second, to challenge the people to listen to the prophet when he comes, or face extremely dire consequences (v. 19). As an addendum, He adds that the sentence of death hangs over any prophet who poses as an authorized prophet of YHWH, even though YHWH has never sent him (vv. 20-22; cf. Jer 23:16-22).[2] Both Peter (Ac 3:14-26) and Stephen (7:35-39,51-53) condemn their audiences for rejecting Jesus, because in rejecting Him they have rejected Moses and the train of prophets like Moses who spoke of Him, the Messiah (3:21), the Servant of God (3:26), and "the Righteous One" (7:52).

Even if Dt 18:15 is not considered as a messianic text, does Deuteronomy help us understand the role and mission of the Messiah? The answer comes in a brief text, located at the heart of Moses' third address (Dt 12–26, 28), namely in 17:14-20. Although concerned with the third of four provisions of leadership in the Israelite community (judges [Dt 16:18]; Levitical priests [Dt 17:8-13; 18:1-8]; the king [Dt 17:14-20]; prophets [Dt 18:9-22]), it occurs within the context of injunctions for the people, whose watchword is "Pursue justice and justice alone" (16:20). Moses' instructions concerning the four public offices in 16:18–18:22 were not intended primarily for the officeholders, but for public consumption, that lay people might understand the roles their leaders played in the corporate pursuit of righteousness and justice. Accordingly, the people should know that judges are to be agents and administrators of righteousness, Levitical priests were to be guardians of and instructors in the way of righteousness, prophets would represent the conscience of righteousness, and kings would serve as paradigms of righteousness.

THE MOSAIC PARADIGM OF KINGSHIP

The Request for a King (v. 14)

Deuteronomy 17:14-20 is logically constructed, beginning with a hypothetical wish expressed by an interlocutor who represents Israel as a nation after they have established themselves in the land that YHWH had promised to the ancestors and had now delivered into their hands: "I would like to set a king over me like all the nations around me" (author's translation). Remarkably, as was the case in 12:20, speaking for YHWH, Moses grants the people's request—even though the request is based on a non-Israelite model of kingship ("like all the nations around me"). This ready granting of permission must be understood in the light of earlier anticipations of kings among Abraham's descendants (Gn 17:6,16; 35:11), Jacob's divinely inspired promise to Judah, that "the scepter will not depart from Judah, or the staff from between his feet, until He whose right it is comes and the obedience of the peoples belongs to Him" (Gn 49:10), and Balaam's prediction not only of a generally exalted king and kingdom, but also of his specific foresight:

> I see him, but not now;
> I perceive him, but not near.
> A star will come from Jacob,
> and a scepter will arise from Israel.
> He will smash the forehead of Moab
> and strike down all the Shethites. (Nm 24:17)

While the history of the monarchy in Israel would prove disastrous in many respects, no Israelite prophet and no biblical author rejected the monarchy in principle.

The Qualifications of the King (v. 15)

Having granted the Israelites permission to install a king over themselves, Moses set the parameters of kingship in Israel. First, he narrowed the field of candidates (v. 15), by declaring that the king must be an Israelite chosen by YHWH. The concept of divine election surfaces often in Deuteronomy. Elsewhere the verb *bāḥar*, "to choose," with YHWH as subject applies to the election of Israel out of all the peoples on earth (4:37; 7:6,7; 10:15; 14:2), of a place to establish his name (12:5,14, etc.), and of the Levites as priests out of all the tribes (18:5; 21:5). The notion of divinity choosing a person to serve as his royal representative is widely attested in the ancient Near East, from as early as the 18th century BC to beyond the OT period.

Moses is even more emphatic about the second qualification—the king must be an Israelite, "from the midst of your brothers," and then excluding any outsider "who is not your brother."[3] Unlike the Egyptians, who were ruled by the Asiatic Hyksos from Avaris for more than a century (1650–1530 BC),[4] the people of YHWH were to be ruled by a viceroy of YHWH chosen from their own ranks, not a strongman brought in from outside.

The Conduct of the King (vv. 16-20)

The remainder of this literary unit is taken up with instructions regarding the king's performance of his royal duties. The text continues in third person, reminding hearers that the purpose of this paragraph is not to provide the king with a manual for leadership, but to create in the minds of the Israelites an image of responsible leadership. In contrast to the office of judge, which the Israelites are to institute (16:18-20; 17:9), the office of priest, which YHWH had already instituted (17:9; 18:1-8), and the office of prophet, which YHWH will institute in the future (18:9-22), the office of king is presented as optional, subject to the desire of the people. To highlight the contrast with prevailing approaches to kingship in biblical times, Moses began with a triad of proscriptions designed to curb royal, self-interested abuse of power, the office that arises out of greed and ambition (vv. 16-17), and ended by prescribing an extraordinary spiritual and ethical standard for the king (vv. 18-20).

Moses' Negative Commands (vv. 16-17). Although Moses' proscriptions consist of four main statements, they actually involve three prohibitions: excessive accumulation of horses, women, and precious metals, respectively. Since in the ancient Near East horses were used primarily for pulling chariots, the proscription on horses was intended to stifle militaristic impulses (cf. Dt 20:1; Jos 17:16-18; Jdg 1:19). The intent of the prohibition on multiplying women in the court extended far beyond limiting the opportunities for the king to satisfy his sexual cravings with the most beautiful women in the kingdom.[5] Since marriages were often arranged to strengthen alliances with other states (cf. 1Kg 9:15-16; 16:31), the institution of the harem enabled a king to be allied simultaneously with many outside rulers (cf. 1Kg 11:1). Moreover, along with good-looking male courtiers (cf. Dan 1:3-4), these women served as decoration for the court to impress foreign visitors with the glory of the king when they visited his court. But these are not Moses' primary concerns; he viewed the harem as a threat to spiritual fidelity to YHWH: The women would turn the king's heart away. The warning concerns defection into idolatry (cf. Dt

7:3-4), though in light of what follows, it may involve defection from the Torah generally and the Supreme Command (Dt 6:5) in particular. The reference to "his heart" suggests such defection is not viewed primarily as an external act, but as a fundamental aspect of one's being (cf. 6:5). Like wine and strong drink, pursuing pleasure and status could be intoxicating and inhibit the proper exercise of the king's responsibilities (cf. Prv 31:3-9).[6]

In the prohibition of excessive accumulation of silver and gold, these precious metals function as shorthand for wealth and opulence in general. In the ancient Near Eastern political world, this wealth was generally amassed at the expense of the people by taxing the citizens and demanding tribute from subject states.

Together these prohibitions of common royal behavior address three major temptations facing ancient rulers: lust for power, lust for status, and lust for wealth. The text does not prohibit the purchase of horses, or marriage, or the accumulation of some silver and gold. The threefold repetition of "for himself" (*lô*) reflects the propensity of kings to exploit their office for personal gain.

Moses' Positive Commands (vv. 18-20). Moses' positive instructions for the king are even more remarkable than the prohibitions. This "standard for kingship"[7] involves three commands relating to the Torah, followed by a fourfold declaration of the rationale underlying the commands. First, Moses commanded that the king was to copy the Torah for himself. While scholars debate the significance of "this Torah" or "instruction" (*hattôrâ hazzōʾt*, v. 18), given the way this and related expressions are used in the book, it seems best to understand "this Torah" minimally as Moses' second and third addresses (Dt 5–11; 12–26; 28), and maximally as the collection of all the utterances preserved in Deuteronomy that he delivered as his farewell to his people, including the first address (1:6–4:40), the fourth address (29:2 [Hb. 29:1]–30:20), Israel's "national anthem" (32:1-43), and Moses' final benediction of the tribes (33:2-29). Deuteronomy 31:9-13 notes that Moses wrote down "this Torah" ("this law," HCSB) and instructed the Levitical priests to place it beside the ark of the covenant, in recognition of its immediate authority as Scripture. For the king, copying the Torah was a covenantal act performed in the presence of priests. This bound the king himself to all that these words promised and demanded. He hereby affirmed his spiritual subordination to the priests as guardians of the Torah and his subordination to the Torah itself as a symbol of the covenant that bound YHWH and Israel.

Second, the king was to "wear the Torah" (v. 19a). The two-word sentence (in Hebrew), "It is to remain with him," declares that the king was not to treat the Torah, a concrete expression of YHWH's covenant with Israel, as a museum piece or as a good luck charm (cf. Jer 8:8). Instead it was to accompany him constantly, providing a written reminder of his personal vassal status before YHWH and his primary role as a model of covenant righteousness (cf. Prv 3:1-9).

Third, the king was to read the Torah all the days of his life (Dt 17:19b). The directive is simple, but its importance is highlighted by four infinitive purpose clauses arranged in a chiastic ABBA pattern, with the first and last beginning with "in order that [X happens]" *(lĕmaʿan)* + imperfect verb and the middle two beginning with "in order that X does not happen *(lĕbiltî)* + infinitive construct. Whereas the first three identify specific responses that are dependent on the reading, the last announces the long-range reward for the king and his successors. Even so, all four statements echo earlier injunctions to the people that now become the spiritual and ethical foundations for Israel's monarchy.

First, faithful reading of the Torah is the key to a proper disposition toward YHWH, the divine suzerain. The king is to read it "that he may learn to fear YHWH his God." As is often the case in Deuteronomy and elsewhere, the fear of which he speaks is not terror, but trusting awe that inspires keeping "all the words of this Torah and these ordinances by doing them" *(laʿăśôtām)*. The Torah of Moses provides repeated reminders of the gracious and trustworthy God who has fulfilled His promises to the ancestors by delivering His people from bondage, calling them to covenant relationship with Himself, revealing to them His will, and delivering the land of the Canaanites into their hands (cf. 6:20-25).

Second, faithful reading of the Torah is the key to a proper disposition toward one's fellow members of the covenant community. The king is to read the Torah to keep his heart from rising above his brothers. With this warning that includes a strong biblical idiom for pride, Moses responded explicitly to prevailing Near Eastern patterns of kings elevating themselves high above their people and acting as if they were the center of the universe. In the first clause of v. 20, Moses asserted that the king is not even the greatest among equals—he is one with his brothers. And in here lies the paradox: he may have been chosen by YHWH and installed by the people as king over them, but he must resist every temptation to consider himself as essentially superior or of a different genre of humanity.

Third, faithful reading of the Torah is the key to the king's staying on course in his devotion to YHWH. The clause, "[that he not] turn aside from *the command (hammitzvâ)* to the right or to the left,"[8] echoes 5:31-32. As elsewhere the singular "the command" refers to the Supreme Command (see 6:5); like the people, the king must demonstrate total covenant commitment to YHWH.

Fourth, faithful reading of the Torah is the key to a secure future, described here as lengthened days over his kingdom. Although the statement echoes earlier statements involving the people of Israel,[9] it anticipates a dynastic monarchy and applies to the king's household the principle enunciated in the Decalogue: people's actions determine both their own well-being and the well-being of their households (cf. 5:9).

THE HISTORICAL SIGNIFICANCE OF THE MOSAIC PARADIGM OF KINGSHIP

Within its ancient Near Eastern context, the Mosaic vision of kingship is revolutionary in many respects.

(1) Although the kings of other nations often gained power by force and at the expense of their rivals and their subjects, the Israelite kingship would be established in response to a democratic impulse and with the blessing of YHWH.

(2) Although foreigners, either usurpers from the outside or imperial overlords, often governed other states, the Israelites were to be governed by one of their own under the imperial reign of YHWH.

(3) Although elsewhere in the ancient world monarchs assumed responsibility for three primary administrative duties—defending their people against external threats by leading in battle, defending them against internal threats by administering justice, and defending them against threats from the gods by maintaining the national cult and building temples for the deities—in Israel the king had one primary role: to embody covenant righteousness as spelled out in the Torah, and in so doing act as the exemplary Israelite (cf. 1Kg 10:9; 2Chr 9:8).

(4) Although kings of other nations regularly used their office to satisfy their own lust for power, status, and wealth, Israelite kings were always to act as servants of YHWH and in the interests of their people.

(5) Although other kings codified laws to protect their own interests and to regulate the conduct of subjects rather than themselves,[10] the Israelite laws were codified by YHWH, interpreted by His spokesman who had no vested interests in the kingship, and then required of the king himself.

(6) Although the kings of other nations used epithets like "son of God" and "image of Bel/Shamash"[11] to elevate themselves above their subjects, Deuteronomy applies the former title to the people of Israel (14:1; 32:6,18; cf. 1:31),[12] and the latter is missing altogether. Apart from "king" (*melek*), the only epithet Israel's monarch may claim was "brother" (*ʾāḥ*) of his people.

The paradigm of kingship spelled out in Dt 17:14-20 should have secured the place of Israel's kings as the appointed rulers over God's people. There are occasional echoes of this passage in later texts. Although Joshua did not technically fit this royal paradigm—he was not a king *(melek)* chosen by YHWH in response to the people's request and then installed by the people, as Moses' successor at the head of the Israelites—in

Jos 1:8 YHWH required of him what this text demanded of the king (note the singular). Psalm 1 opens the Psalter by characterizing the blessed man as one who delights in the Torah and meditates on it day and night (v. 2). If the Psalter is indeed a fundamentally royal document, as some have argued,[13] this psalm serves particularly as a guide for the king on how to read the Torah (specifically Deuteronomy).[14]

Deuteronomy 17:14-20 is important for understanding Israel's political history. Several centuries later, when the elders demanded that Samuel install a king over them, their appeal echoed Dt 17:14: "We must have a king over us. Then we'll be like all the other nations" (1Sm 8:19-20). Samuel seems to have composed his prior "pronouncement concerning the king" *(mišpaṭ hammelek)* in 1Sm 8:11-17 against the backdrop of Dt 17:16-17. He warned the people that the king they demanded would use his office for selfish ends and run roughshod over their interests. YHWH answered this request by giving them Saul, from the tribe of Benjamin, who had proved by deed and disposition to be like the lowest of the nations (Jdg 19-21; cf. Gn 19). But Saul's rule was doomed from the outset, and he ultimately served primarily as a foil for the one YHWH had in mind from the beginning (1Sm 13:14).[15] And when David prepared to pass the royal mantle to his son Solomon, he appealed to him to keep the charge of YHWH his God, "by walking in his ways, by keeping his ordinances, his commands, and his judgments [concerning covenant righteousness], and his testimonies, as it is written in the Torah of Moses," that he might prosper in all his activities (1Kg 2:3, author's translation).

The paradigm of kingship established in Dt 17:14-20 provides the lens used by Israel's historians and prophets to evaluate their kings. This is most evident in the portrayal of Solomon. Although he famously constructed the temple for YHWH (David's project), he multiplied horses (1Kg 4:26-28 [Hb. 5:6-8]; 10:26-29) and wives (11:1-13), and amassed vast riches for the crown (10:23). To be fair, the historian did not condemn Solomon explicitly for multiplying wealth or horses, but he denounced him sharply for marrying foreign women (11:1-13), forcefully ruling over his countrymen (5:13-18), and breaking the covenant (11:9-13,33). Ultimately, responsibility for Israel's exile in 586 BC rested on the shoulders of kings who abused the people and led the nation in apostasy (2Kg 24:3-4).[16]

THE MESSIANIC SIGNIFICANCE OF THE MOSAIC PARADIGM OF KINGSHIP

Based on the history of the northern kingdom of Israel recounted in 1Kg 12–17, it is evident that the Torah of Moses generally and his vision of kingship specifically had no influence on that nation's kings. Their apostate spirit and political state are reflected in the ubiquitous assessment by the narrator: "They did the evil (*hāraʿ*) in the eyes of YHWH."[17] In this expression the article "the evil" is significant; it always refers primarily to violating the Supreme Command, that is, betraying YHWH and going after other gods (Dt 5:7; cf. 6:13; 10:20; 13:5 [Hb. 4]). Although David exhibited significant character flaws (acknowledged in 1Kg 15:5), the historian's overall assessment of his performance vis-à-vis the Mosaic law was remarkable. Solomon recognized that David walked before YHWH "in faithfulness, righteousness, and integrity" with him (1Kg 3:6); YHWH Himself acknowledged that David "walked [before me] . . . with integrity of heart and uprightness, doing according to all that I have commanded you, [and by keeping] my ordinances and my judgments" (1Kg 9:4; cf. 3:14, author's translation). As for the narrator's own assessment, unlike Solomon, whose foreign wives turned his heart away to other gods, David's heart was "wholly true" with YHWH his God (1Kg 11:4; cf. 15:3; 2Ch 17:3) and was full after YHWH (11:6),[18] a fidelity that was demonstrated generally in "doing the right thing in the eyes of YHWH" (15:3; 2Ch 17:3, author's translation) and specifically in obedience to the revealed will of YHWH (11:34,38; 14:8; 15:5; 16:2; 2Ch 7:17; 28:1; 29:2; 34:2).

When Solomon had completed all his construction projects (including the temple), YHWH appeared to him a second time at Gibeon and reminded him of David's paradigmatic faithfulness (1Kg 9:2-9), and the importance of following this model if he and his successors hoped to be secure on the throne. However, he also added a strong note of the kings' representative role before the people:

> If you or your sons turn away from following Me and do not keep My commands—My statutes that I have set before you—and if you go and serve other gods and worship them, I will cut off Israel from the land I gave them, and I will reject the temple I have sanctified for My name. Israel will become an object of scorn and ridicule among all the peoples. Though this temple is *now* exalted, every passerby will be appalled and will mock. They will say: Why did the LORD do this to this land and this temple? Then they will say: Because they abandoned the LORD their God who brought their ancestors out of the land of Egypt. They clung to other gods and worshiped and served them. Because of this, the LORD brought all this ruin on them.

Samuel warned Israel of the apparently inevitable administrative style of the kind of king they demanded, though without explicit reference to the kings' obligations to the Torah (1Sm 8:11-18). This contrasts with YHWH's warning to Solomon in this text. Remarkably he said nothing about how well the kings administered justice in the land, or how successful they were in military conflicts with outsiders; his only declared concern was their fidelity to YHWH and to His covenant with Israel. On these counts David set the royal standard for both the northern kingdom of Israel[19] and the southern kingdom of Judah (1Kg 9:4; 11:30-39; 2Ch 7:17). With regard to the kings of Judah, where comparisons are drawn, some results are negative,[20] some are qualified,[21] and a handful are positive: Asa (1Kg 15:11), Jehoshaphat (2Chr 17:3), Hezekiah (2Kg 18:3), Josiah (2Kg 22:2).

Solomon and Josiah present particularly interesting cases. Although Solomon began with deep covenant commitment (i.e., "love," Hb. *ʾāhab*) for YHWH, demonstrated in imitating David ethically (1Kg 3:3), his extraordinary wisdom (1Kg 3:4-28; 4:29-34 [Hb. 5:9-14]; 10:1-25), and piety, and his faithful completion of David's temple project (note his dedication prayer in 1Kg 8), by the end of his life everything had changed. Preoccupied with private construction projects (1Kg 9:17-19,24), and driven by the lure of wealth (9:26-28), he exploited and abused his own subjects (9:15,20-22), leading to both human and divine resistance that resulted ultimately in the disintegration of the kingdom (11:9-43). While the narrator notes other features of his reign, his closing critique is scathing, noting particularly his violation of the three prohibitions in Dt 17:16-17: his excessive militarism, symbolized by the multiplication of horses (1Kg 10:26,28-29; cf. Dt 17:16), his excessive multiplication of wives, who did indeed lead his heart astray (1Kg 11:1-8; cf. Dt 17:17a), and his accumulation of wealth (1Kg 9:26-28; 10:11-23). The opening image of Solomon is impressive; he began as a humble son of David, awed by his new role as heir to the Davidic throne and kingdom and pleading with YHWH for a special gift of wisdom to rule well (3:3-9)—a prayer that YHWH answered immediately in superlative degree in the form of a dream (3:10-15). The concluding image is pathetic; Solomon ended as the consummate fool, driven by lust of every sort and setting the nation on a downward spiritual spiral from which it would never recover. Although the apostasy is characterized as personal and domestic, resulting in the disintegration of the Davidic hold on the throne (11:11-43), ultimately, as the king went, so went the kingdom. In 11:32-33 the narrator intentionally generalizes the resulting spiritual problem with plural forms, whose antecedent is "all the tribes of Israel" (11:32):

> For they [the tribes of Israel] have abandoned Me; they have bowed the knee to Ashtoreth, the goddess of the Sidonians, to Chemosh, the god of Moab, and to Milcom, the god of the Ammonites. They have not walked in My ways to do what is right in My eyes and to carry out My statutes and My judgments as his father David did.

Josiah represents the opposite kind of paradigm. The narrator's assessments of the man are thoroughly deuteronomic from beginning to end:

> He did what was right in the LORD's sight and walked in all the ways of his ancestor David; he did not turn to the right or the left. (2Kg 22:2)

> Before him there was no king like him, who turned to YHWH with all his heart/mind *(lēb)*, and with all his being *(nepeš)*, and with all his resources *(mĕʾōd)*, according to all the Torah of Moses, nor did any like him arise after him (2Kg 23:25, author's translation).[22]

As if to highlight the link between the narrative and Dt 17:14-20, the entire account (2 Kg 22:1–23:30) is driven by the narrator's (and Josiah's) interest in the Torah document—the scroll of Deuteronomy—his workers found in the temple. Although Josiah's life was headed in a positive direction even before the discovery of the scroll in the Temple (22:1-8), the discovery gave added impetus to his personal spiritual commitments and focus to his administration. With exemplary humility, upon hearing the Torah read, Josiah recognized the desperate spiritual state of his nation and immediately sought further guidance from YHWH regarding an appropriate response to the crisis (vv. 12-13). YHWH's answer was twofold: (1) Because of their history of apostasy, the doom of what remained of the nation of Israel had been irrevocably decreed (vv. 15-17). (2) Because Josiah's own heart was tender *(rak)* and he humbled himself before YHWH, his own future was guaranteed—he would die in peace and would be spared the sight of the horrors to come. Unlike Solomon, who in the end embodied all that was wrong with his people, Josiah stood out as a paragon of righteousness in contrast to a thoroughly corrupted people. Almost as an Enoch figure, because he was spiritually out of step with his generation and more at home with God than with his countrymen, YHWH removed him before the disaster struck.

For Josiah, knowledge of his personal destiny did not result in a diminished deuteronomic fervor. On the contrary, not satisfied with refurbishing the Temple after generations of neglect and abuse sponsored by his predecessors, he arranged for a public covenant renewal ritual in Jerusalem (23:1-3) and oversaw the observance with unprecedented fervor of the foundational national celebration, the Festival of Passover (vv. 21-23). He purged Jerusalem and Judah of all vestiges of pagan worship (23:24-25), and then extended the purge to the territories of what used to be the northern kingdom of Israel, even though at the time it was an Assyrian province (23:4-20). The only non-spiritual act reported by the narrator resulted in his death. With striking irony, while trying at Megiddo to intercept the Egyptian army, which was headed north to join the Assyrians in battle against the rising Babylonians, the man who had been promised a peaceful demise died a violent death, a victim of a deadly arrow (23:28-30; cf. 2Chr 35:20-27). Ironically, as an act of divine mercy, contrary to the promise of Dt 17:20, the life of the occupant of the Davidic throne who most fully embodied the Mosaic vision of royal righteousness while occupying the throne of David was cut short, rather than extended. Apparently Jerusalem's appointment with destiny in 586 BC had been written irrevocably on her calendar; not even the efforts of a righteous Josiah could halt fulfillment of the curses of Deuteronomy in all their divine fury.[23]

With Josiah's demise, it was only a matter of time before the nation would fall. The narrator characterized all of his successors as he had so many of the northern kings: "They committed *the evil* (*hāraʿ*) in the eyes of YHWH according to all that their father/fathers had done."[24] If the northern kingdom fell to the Assyrians because of the people's persistent rebellion against YHWH (note the deuteronomic flavor of the narrator's interpretation in 2Kg 17:7-18), the narrator repeatedly blames the kings for having led them down this course.[25] Although, of the Judean kings, the narrator explicitly holds only Manasseh responsible for leading the people down this sinful path (2Kg 21:11,16-17), with few exceptions they were equally guilty of sponsoring state and regional apostasy (cf. 2Kg 24:3-4). However, the demise of the nation and the Davidic dynasty in 586 BC left the people wondering not only about the veracity of YHWH's promise of an eternal Davidic dynasty (2Sm 7:13,16,29; 1Kg 2:33,45; 9:5; 1Chr 17:12,14; 22:10; 28:4; Pss 89:29,36 [Hb. 30, 37]; 132:12), but also about the relevance of Dt 17:14-20.

The ending to the books of Kings is auspicious: after the death of Zedekiah, and with him the Davidic dynasty, all hope seemed lost (Ps 89:46-51 [Hb. 47-52])—except that, mysteriously, the king of Babylon released a 55-year-old Judean from prison, who happened to be the surviving link to the original house of David, and elevated him to a prominent position in the Babylonian court (2 Kg 25:27-30). With Jehoiachin's release the royal hope was reignited, albeit as only a glimmering coal. However, the question remained: given the history of the monarchy in Israel, even if the Davidic dynasty would be restored, what would prevent it from going down the same path once again?

Enter the prophetic messianic hope. Like Dt 17:14-20, earlier psalmists had linked the Davidic throne with the pursuit of righteousness (Pss 45:1-7 [Hb. 2-8]; 89:30-37), but it was left to the prophets to develop this theme. The eighth-century BC prophet Isaiah looked forward to the birth of a child who would bear the throne names of "Wonderful Counselor, Mighty God, Eternal Father, Prince of Peace," and who would secure David's throne forever by pursuing "justice and righteousness" (*mišpāṭ ûṣĕdāqâ*; Isa 9:6-7 [Hb. 8-9]; cf. 1Kg 10:9). This "branch" (*nēṣer*) from the stem/roots of Jesse would be girded with the belt of righteousness and faithfulness (*ʾēzôr ṣedeq weʾĕmûnâ*), and through his righteous administration of justice, peace will come not only to Israel, but also to the entire cosmos (Dt 11:1-10).[26] Later in Isaiah, the four Servant Songs (Isa 42:1-9; 49:1-6; 50:4-9; 52:13–53:12) characterize the Servant of YHWH (*ʿebed YHWH*), clearly a Davidic figure,[27] as the vassal of YHWH *par excellence*.

It is extremely significant that the word for "righteous"/"righteousness" (*ṣedeq*/

ṣĕdāqāh), so significant in Dt 16:20, occurs in the first and last of these Servant Songs. Isaiah 42:6 portrays the call of the Servant as an act of divine righteousness (*ṣedeq*); He always acts in accord with His covenant commitments. Indeed, He has appointed him as "a covenant for the people" (*bĕrît ʿam*) and "a light to the nations" (*ʾôr gôyim).* In the last Servant Song YHWH acknowledges that He is the embodiment of righteousness, identifying Him as "the Righteous One, My Servant" (*ṣaddîq ʿabdî*, 53:11), who declares many righteous (*yaṣdîq*) by offering Himself as a "restitution offering" (*ʾāšām*, v. 10), and bearing their iniquities (*ʿăwônōtām hûʾ yisbōl*, v. 11). Far from His heart being lifted up above his countrymen (cf. Dt 17:20), He is portrayed in this Song as the good shepherd, who gives up His life for the sheep (Jn 10:15).

Jeremiah had less to say about the Messiah than Isaiah, but what little he says is directly related to the Mosaic vision of kingship in Dt 17:14-29. Speaking for YHWH, in Jer 23:1-6 he pronounced doom on the Davidic kings who, instead of caring for the sheep, had cared only for themselves, and in so doing had driven the flock away (he held them accountable for the exile, vv. 1-2). But he promised that YHWH would one day regather the sheep (Israel) and cause them to flourish again, and appoint over them shepherds who would actually care for *(rāʿâ)* the flock and secure their well-being (vv. 3-4). This short oracle reaches its climax with YHWH's announcement that He will raise up for David "a Righteous Branch" (*ṣemaḥ ṣaddîq*), who will reign as king by acting justly and righteously" (*wĕʿāśâ mišpāṭ ûṣĕdāqâ*). His effectiveness (*hiškîl*) will be demonstrated by Judah's salvation (*yšʿ*) and Israel's security (*beṭaḥ*). The Torah righteousness that He will embody and that He will secure for His people will be reflected in His title: "Yahweh Our Righteousness" (*yhwh ṣidkēnû*, vv. 5-6).

Although Ezekiel does not use the word "righteous" or "righteousness," it is obvious in Ezk 34 that the exiles' prophet had access to Jeremiah's prophecy and intentionally developed it further.[28] After pronouncing doom on the dynasty of David for having misused their role and abused their people (Ezk 34:1-10), YHWH promised to regather the scattered flock, bring them back to their homeland, and personally care for them, including ensuring that the sheep do not abuse each other (vv. 11-22). The oracle reaches its climax in vv. 23-24, where YHWH announced that He would set over His people "a single shepherd, My servant David," who will exercise his princely role by feeding and caring for the sheep. This would confirm YHWH's "covenant of peace" (*bĕrît šālôm*), which will secure for them eternal well-being and security in the land (vv. 25-31). As David recognized in 2Sm 7:18-26, the appointment of the Davidic king confirmed YHWH's commitment to Israel as His covenant people (cf. Ezk 34:24a,31).

One more echo of these notions appears in Mic 5:2-5a [Hb. 2:1-4a]. The prophet

Micah foresaw the coming of a ruler from humble Bethlehem who would rise and shepherd His people, His "brothers" (*ʾeḥāyw*, the same expression used in Dt 17:20; "countrymen," HCSB) in the strength and name of YHWH (Mic 5:2-5a [Hb. 2:1-4a]). Although He would shepherd His own people, His greatness would be acknowledged to the ends of the earth. Indeed, He will secure universal well-being (*šālôm*).

In the NT, it becomes clear that the Mosaic vision of kingship was ultimately fulfilled by Jesus the Messiah, the son of David. This is especially evident in the portrayal of Jesus as the suffering servant of Isaiah 53, echoes of which occur throughout the NT. [29] But it also appears in Jesus' own statement when, at the time of His baptism, He was introduced as the Messiah: He needed to be baptized "to fulfill all righteousness" (*plērōsai pasan dikaiosunēn*, Mt 3:15). Immediately thereafter the voice from heaven proclaimed the significance of this event: "This is My beloved Son. I take delight in Him!" This is not only a declaration of Jesus' membership within the Trinity, but also an announcement of His Davidic messianic status. All three expressions have messianic significance. "My Son" (i.e., "son of God") is used of the Davidic king in Ps 2:6-8 [Hb. 27-28]).[30] "Beloved" (*agapētos*) has its roots in the Hebrew verb, *ʾāhab*, "to love," and probably alludes to YHWH's covenant commitment to the Davidic house. The verb is never used of David, but is used of Solomon with YHWH as subject in 2Sm 12:24 and Neh 13:26.[31] "Take delight in" (*eudokeō*) speaks of the special favor Jesus enjoyed with the Father, as in 1Chr 29:23, "And Solomon sat on YHWH's throne as king in place of his father David, and he was favored/taken delight in" (LXX).[32] In short, Jesus is the Davidic king whom YHWH had in mind from the beginning (cf. Dt 17:15; 1Sm 13:14). In fulfilling all righteousness, Jesus embodied perfectly the ideals of covenant relationship as represented in the Torah. He was the climax of the royal metanarrative underlying the entire OT, and His kingdom is secure.

Moreover, Jesus' declaration that He came not to abolish the Law and the Prophets, but to fulfill [them] (Mt 5:17) ought to be viewed in relation to Dt 17:14-20. Based on the broader context this cannot mean that He came to terminate the authority or relevance of the OT Scriptures for His followers (cf. vv. 18-19). Although here the expression, *ho nomos* ("the law") designates the entire Pentateuch—in keeping with custom by NT times—in Dt 17:18 and in most occurrences in the OT (e.g., Jos 1:8; 1Kg 2:3; 2Kg 22:8-16; 23:25; Ezr 7:6; Neh 8:1-18; Ps 1:2; Jer 8:8; Dn 9:11,13) *hattôrâ* (consistently rendered in LXX as *ho nomos*) refers primarily to the written version of the Torah that the king was to copy for himself in Dt 17:18, which is largely our book of Deuteronomy. For Jesus, the Messianic descendant of David, this book had special authority. In the context of the Sermon on the Mount, for Him "to fulfill" the Torah meant in part to recover for His followers the spirit of Moses as declared in the latter's addresses in Deuteronomy and encapsulated especially in Dt 10:12–11:1. That Jesus quoted from and alluded to Deuteronomy more frequently than to any other book of the OT reinforces this conclusion.

At its heart the Torah is not merely about keeping the commands as a duty to God. Rather, keeping the Torah is essentially and primarily a matter of the heart—with awe and gratitude saying, "Not My will, but Yours be done" (Lk 22:42). In the words of Moses, for God's people it means to fear YHWH, to walk in all His ways, to demonstrate covenant love for Him, to serve Him with all of one's being, and last, to keep His commands (Dt 10:12-13), in response to the favors He has lavished on them (Dt 10:14–11:1). This was the essence of the surpassing righteousness of which Jesus spoke in Mt 5:20, in contrast to the righteousness of the scribes and Pharisees, who were supercilious with their tithe, but had neglected the weightier matters of Torah: practicing justice, mercy, and faithfulness.[33] As the Messiah, Jesus' mission was not only to recover the essence of the Torah and to teach it to His followers, but also to embody and model it perfectly. When, at the time of His crucifixion the crowd in Jerusalem screamed, "We have no king but Caesar!" (Jn 19:15), tragically they flushed away a thousand years of Messianic hope. Nevertheless, one day, Israel will welcome her King, as Jesus foretold Matthew (Mt 23:37-39), saying "He who comes in the name of the Lord is the blessed One." Then Israel will finally experience the rule of the righteous King anticipated in Dt 17:14-20.

---

1. The article on Dt 18:15-19 in this *Handbook* makes the case for a messianic interpretation of this passage.
2. For further discussion, see Daniel I. Block, "My Servant David: Ancient Israel's Vision of the Messiah," in *Israel's Messiah in the Bible and the Dead Sea Scrolls*, ed. R. S. Hess and M. D. Carroll R. (Grand Rapids: Baker, 2003), 26–32; also *Deuteronomy*, NIV Application Commentary (Grand Rapids: Zondervan, 2012), 438–46.
3. On *nokrî*, see above on 14:21 and 15:3 (cf. also 23:21 and 29:21 [ET 20]). On the status of the *nokrÐ* see Daniel I. Block, "Sojourner; Alien; Stranger," *International Standard Bible Encyclopedia*, rev. ed., 4.562.
4. Cf. Donald B. Redford, "Hyksos," *ABD* 3.341–44.
5. Since in our world "wives" connotes a marital relationship, *nāšîm* is better rendered generically as "women," the reference being to the harem of a typical oriental king.
6. Cf. the warning of Lemuel's mother in Prv 31:3-9.
7. Translating *mišpaṭ hammelek*, literally "the judgment/standard of the king," in 1Sm 8:11, but representing a positive model in contrast to the image Samuel presents.
8. This is equivalent to "walking in his ways" (i.e., "the ways of YHWH"; Dt 8:6; 10:12; 11:22; 19:9; 26:17; 28:9; 30:16; 32:4).
9. For references to the Israelites lengthening their days, see Dt 4:26,40; 5:33; 11:9; 22:7; 30:18; 32:47. For references to their days lengthening, see 5:16; 6:2; 25:15.
10. See especially the prologue to the Law Code of Hammurabi in Martha T. Roth, *Law Collections from Mesopotamia and Asia Minor*, 2nd ed., Society of Biblical Literature Writings from the Ancient World 6 (Atlanta: Scholars Press, 1995), 76–81. This is not to deny extrabiblical evidence for comparable ideals for their kings. See "Advice to a Prince," in Wilfred G. Lambert, *Babylonian Wisdom Literature* (Oxford: Clarendon, 1960), 113–15; the Ugaritic epic

of *Kirta*, in Simon B. Parker, ed, *Ugaritic Narrative Poetry,* Society of Biblical Literature Writings from the Ancient World 9 (Atlanta: Scholars Press, 1997), 41, as well as Job 29:7-17 and Prv 31:1-9, which concern non-Israelite rulers.

11. See the characterization of Esarhaddon as "the father of the king, my lord, was the very image of Bel, and the king, my lord, is likewise the image of Bel." See Simo Parpola, *Letters from Assyrian and Babylonian Scholars,* State Archives of Syria 10 (Helsinki: Helsinki University Press, 1993), 181 (§228:18–20).

12. Though later texts refer to Israel's kings as "the son of God." See 2Sm 7:14; 89:27-28; 22:10. In these contexts, the "father-son" language functions as a metaphor for the suzerain-vassal relationship that existed between YHWH and the king (cf. 2 Kg 16:7). On "divine sonship" of kings in the ancient world see J. Fossum, "Son of God," *Dictionary of Deities and Demons in the Bible,* 2nd ed., Karel van der Toorn, Bob Becking, and Pieter W. van der Horst, eds. (Leiden, Netherlands: Brill, 1999), 788–89.

13. Bruce K. Waltke, *An Old Testament Theology: An Exegetical, Canonical, and Thematic Approach* (Grand Rapids: Zondervan, 2007), 871–84.

14. It may very well anticipate the royal messianic king, as maintained in the article on Ps 1–2 in this *Handbook.*

15. Cf. Block, "My Servant David," 39; Jason S. DeRouchie, "The Heart of YHWH and His Chosen One in 1 Samuel 13:14," *Bulletin for Biblical Research* 24 (2014): 467–89.

16. On Dt 17:14-20 and the later evaluation of Solomon, see G. N. Knoppers, "Rethinking the Relationship between Deuteronomy and the Deuteronomistic History: The Case of Kings," *Catholic Biblical Quarterly* 63 (2002): 393–415.

17. First Kings 15:34 (Baasha); 16:19,25 (Omri); 16:30; 21:20,25 (Ahab); 22:52 (Ahaziah); 2Kg 3:2 (Jehoram); 8:27 (Ahaziah); 13:2 (Jehoahaz); 13:11 (Jehoash); 14:24 (Jeroboam II); 15:9 (Zechariah); 15:18 (Menahem); 15:24 (Pekahiah); 15:28 (Pekah); 17:2 (Hoshea). Jeroboam I (son of Nebat) is identified as the paradigmatic apostate king (1Kg 15:34; 16:19; 22:52; 2Kg 13:2,11; 14:24; 15:9,18,24,28).

18. "To be full after YHWH" ("follow the Lord completely" HCSB) is an awkward idiom, used elsewhere only of Caleb, in contrast to the rest of the Israelites (Nm 32:11-12; Dt 1:36; Jos 14:8,9,14).

19. Compare Ahijah's detailed assessment of Jeroboam I in 1Kg 14:7-16, and the narrator's accusing Jeroboam of driving Israel away from YHWH and causing them to commit extreme sin (*wāheḥĕṭiy'ām ḥăṭā'â gĕdôlâ*) in 2Kg 17:21. Indeed, in contrast to David, the paradigmatic pursuer of righteousness (cf. Dt 16:2), Jeroboam is repeatedly identified as the paradigmatic pursuer of evil; those explicitly compared with Jeroboam include Baasha (1Kg 15:34; 16:2), Omri (16:19,26), Ahab (16:31), Ahaziah (22:52), Jehoram (2Kg 3:3), Jehu (10:31), Jehoahaz (13:2), Jehoash (13:11), Jeroboam II (14:24), Zechariah (15:9), Menahem (15:18), Pekahiah (15:24), Pekah (15:28).

20. Solomon (1Kg 11:4,6), Rehoboam (14:22), Abijam (15:3), Ahaz (2Kg 16:2; 2Chr 28:1).

21. Solomon (1Kg 3:3), Amaziah (2Kg 14:3-4).

22. Although the narrator changes the verb from *'āhab*, "to love," to *šûb 'el*, "to turn to," the triad of expressions, *bĕkol lĕbābô ûbĕkol napšô ûbĕkol mĕ'ōdô*, derives verbatim from the Shema' in Dt 6:4-5.

23. Cf. YHWH's rejection of Noah, Daniel, and Job as lightning rods to stave off His fury in Ezk 14:12-23.

24. The assessment for each is virtually identical, with slight variation in the identity of the models: Jehoahaz (2Kg 23:32, his fathers), Jehoiakim (23:37, his fathers), Jehoiachin (24:9, his father); Zedekiah (24:19, Jehoiakim).

25. With Jeroboam as the paradigmatic evil-doer who led Israel into sin: 1Kg 14:16; 15:26,30,34; 16:2,13,19,26; 21:22; 22:52; 2Kg 3:3; 10:29,31; 13:2,6,11; 14:24; 15:9,18,24,28; 23:15.

26. For fuller development of the Isaianic vision of the righteous messianic king, see Isa 32.

27. On the Servant of YHWH as a royal Davidic figure, see Block, "My Servant David," 49–55.

28. For discussion of the relationship between these two texts, see Daniel I. Block, *The Book of Ezekiel Chapters 25–48,* New International Commentary on the Old Testament (Grand Rapids: Eerdmans, 1998), 275–77.

29. Mt 8:17; Lk 22:37; Jn 6:45; 10:15; 12:38; Ac 8:32-33; 13:34; Rm 2:24; 10:15,16; 15:21; 2Co 6:17; 1Pt 2:22.

30. These texts are rooted in 2Sm 7:14-15, where YHWH declares of Solomon, "I will be a father to him and he will be a son to Me." This has long been acknowledged as an adaptation of the adoption formula. See Shalom Paul, "Adoption Formulae: A Study in Cuneiform and Biblical Legal Clauses," *Maarav* 2 (1978–80): 173–85, esp. 178. In Ps 89:27 [28] the Davidic king is also called YHWH's "firstborn" (*bĕkōr*).

31. When used of Abraham in Isa 41:8, *'ōhăbî*, usually translated "my friend," clearly refers to him as YHWH's vassal covenant partner (cf. vv. 9-10).

32. Here the passive form, *eudokēthē*, translates Hebrew *wayyaṣlaḥ*, "and he prospered/was effective."

33. Here Greek *krisis, eleos,* and *pistis* correspond to Deuteronomy's *mišpāṭ, ḥesed,* and *'ĕmûnâ*, respectively.

Deuteronomy 18:15-19

The Prophet Like Moses

JIM R. SIBLEY

Following a warning against "the detestable things" the Israelites would encounter when they engaged with the inhabitants of Canaan, and especially against the evil and unreliable practices of spiritism and necromancy, in Dt 18:15-19, Moses looked further into the future and offered an absolutely reliable source of truth:

> The LORD your God will raise up for you a prophet like me from among you, from your brothers. You must listen to him. This is what you requested from the LORD your God at Horeb on the day of the of the assembly when you said, "Let us not continue to hear the voice of the LORD our God or see this great fire any longer, so that we will not die!" Then the LORD said to me, "They have spoken well. I will raise up for them a prophet like you from among their brothers. I will put My words in his mouth, and he will tell them everything I command him. I will hold accountable whoever does not listen to My words that he speaks in My name."

THE PROPHECY IN JUDAISM AND ISLAM

The views of Judaism and of Islam must be noted in any survey of interpretations of this passage. Traditionally, the majority of Jewish interpretation, probably in reaction against early Jewish Christian claims, denies any messianic interpretation and holds instead that this passage in Deuteronomy is only teaching that there will be a succession of prophets following Moses. It does not generally admit a messianic interpretation. This is the case, even though the ancient midrash, *Qoheleth Rabbah*, says, "As the first redeemer was, so shall the latter redeemer be."[1] An exception to this consensus appears in R. Levi ben Gershon (1288–1344). Calling attention to "from among your own brothers" (see vv. 15,18), he comments, "So you will not need to go to some other country to know the future."[2] But when he comments on Dt 34:10, which he himself links to 18:15, he says:

> He is King Messiah . . . and he is the one about whom the prophet said, "and he will delight in the fear of the Lord, not by the sight of his eyes will he judge nor by the hearing of his ears will he rebuke" (Isaiah 11 verse 3, see also Sanhedrin 93 page B); but by his signs and his wonders HaShem will change [the languages of the nations] to a clear language to call everyone in the name of the Lord and to worship him with one intent (Zeph 3:9), just as HaShem took Israel to be raised up to His worship by tremendous signs and wonders which He showed them in Egypt and at the sea and in the desert. And here I would think that the most wondrous sign will be the resurrection from the dead, He will be revealed and He will be seen to the ends of the earth; and at this all the Gentiles will believe that the Lord is God and they will say that their fathers had inherited a lie and nothing that they had is of any value (Jer. 16:19).[3]

R. Levi ben Gershon is therefore significant, because: (1) Earlier in his comments, he links Dt 18:15-19 with 34:10; (2) He says that this prophet must have a ministry not just to Israel, but also to the nations; (3) He takes the prophecy as referring to the Messiah rather than to a succession of prophets, even citing Isa 11, a tremendously messianic passage, and his reference to the nations may be an allusion to Isa 11:10; (4) He says that the coming prophet must have greater signs and wonders than Moses, including possibly resurrection from the dead. His is the "minority report," and though rabbinic opinion is certainly not authoritative, it does provide interesting corroboration at these points.[4]

In mystical Judaism, v. 15 is considered especially significant, for it begins and ends with the same Hebrew letter, the *nun*. As such, it is one of only 11 other verses in the Hebrew Scriptures with this same characteristic (Lv 13:9; Nm 32:32; Jer 50:8; Pss 46:5; 71:21; 78:12; Prv 7:17; 20:27; Sg 4:11; and 1Chr 12:2). R. Chaim David Azulai (1724–1807) superstitiously affirms that saying these verses provides protection from the evil eye, evil speech (e.g., gossip), and witchcraft. These 11 verses are also thought to protect against Satan.

Briefly put, Islam teaches that Mohammed was the prophet like Moses (see suras 3.85 and 46.9-10). The views of Islam and of many Christians are therefore similar, in that they understand the passage as prophetic of a specific individual, whereas the view of traditional Judaism generally does not.

THE PROPHECY IN CONTEMPORARY SCHOLARSHIP

Many contemporary biblical scholars have lost confidence in a messianic reading of the Hebrew Scriptures. For example, Mark J. Boda says, "For an Old Testament scholar to venture into a study of Messiah is a daring act indeed."[5] So it comes as no surprise that no consensus exists among modern scholars regarding the correct interpretation of Dt 18:15-19. The positions can be categorized as (1) nonmessianic, (2) indirectly messianic, and (3) directly messianic.

Nonmessianic View

Daniel I. Block is one who denies that Dt 18:15-19 is speaking of the Messiah. For him, to speak of Jesus as a prophet like Moses is to put Jesus and Moses on the same level and is therefore "demeaning."[6] He points out that Heb 3:1-6 says that Jesus is greater than Moses. Nevertheless, he apparently has no problem speaking of Jesus as a King like David.[7] He objects to Jesus being called a prophet.[8] Jesus testified that John the Baptist was both a prophet and more than a prophet (Mt 11:9). If John the Baptist could be both a prophet, yet "more than a prophet," how much more could Jesus be both? Block also claims more broadly, "one doubts whether we may even speak of *an* Old Testament messianic vision, as if there were a single, universally accepted view of the messiah."[9] Tremper Longman III concurs by saying, "It is impossible to establish that any passage in its original literary and historical context must or even should be understood as portending a future messianic figure."[10]

From this perspective, some understand the referent of this prophecy to have been an individual other than Messiah. Joshua, Elijah, and Jeremiah are most often proposed.[11] Joshua was Moses' successor, so it is understandable that some would assume Moses was speaking of him. However, following a comprehensive review of Joshua in the context of the Torah, Yoon-Hee Kim concludes:

> In the significant prophetic succession narrative in Numbers, Joshua is by no means portrayed as the one who is "like Moses." Rather a conscious effort is made to present him as the one who is "unlike Moses in many ways (e.g., his subordination to Moses, his dependence on the priestly guidance)."[12]

Not only so, but Joshua is never regarded or referred to as a prophet. It might be argued that in assuming the role as Moses' successor, his identity as a prophet is implied. However, the most cogent evidence that Joshua was not to be considered the prophet like Moses comes from Dt 34:9-10, where Joshua is presented as Moses' agent and successor, and this is followed by the statement that "no prophet has risen in Israel like Moses, whom the Lord knew face to face."

Turning to Elijah, the parallels between him and Moses are remarkable.[13]

Writing from a critical perspective, Ellie Assis calls attention to Mal 3:22-24 (in most English Bibles, Mal 4:4-6) and seems convinced that Israel had lost hope in a messianic king and had transferred these hopes to a future prophet like Moses. Assis writes: "The first person to be both a prophet and leader was Moses. It is possible that Malachi saw the similarity between Moses and Elijah and he expected Elijah, who, it was believed, was not dead [for he was taken up to heaven without first dying (see 2Kgs 2:1-14)], to return in the role of prophet-messiah."[14] Yet, Assis' view seems to be overly speculative, idiosyncratic, and therefore, unconvincing. Indeed, the biblical text seems to move in the opposite direction. As Dale Allison notes, "the numerous parallels with Moses accentuate the surprising weaknesses of Elijah, who, with God on his side, and in the wake of victory, only feels sorry for himself."[15]

Considering Jeremiah, the similarity between his call in Jer 1 and the call of Moses in Ex 3 is striking. This has given rise to many texts, both ancient and modern, that point out the similarities, and some also argue that Jeremiah saw himself as the direct fulfillment of the prophecy of Dt 18:15-19. J. A. Thompson, like William Holladay before him, reaches this conclusion and says, "It is altogether likely that Jeremiah formed the conviction that he was himself the prophet like Moses."[16] Again, Allison summarizes the commonalities, and concludes that "it is more probable than not that Jeremiah considered himself . . . to be a prophet like Moses."[17]

But the similarities between Jeremiah and Moses are clearly not as marked as those between Elijah and Moses, and the contrasts between Jeremiah and Moses remain: Moses' ministry was one of deliverance, whereas the ministry of Jeremiah was characterized by proclamations of doom.[18] Even more significant is that Moses was actually involved in the institution of the Covenant of Sinai, whereas Jeremiah only prophesied regarding the future inauguration of a "new covenant" (Jer 31:31-34).[19] Holladay recognizes this as a problem, but claims Jeremiah saw the defects ("loopholes") in the law that would need to be corrected, but that task "would be left for another to accomplish."[20] According to this position, Jeremiah was a servant of Moses and the Torah who saw the deficiencies of the Covenant of Sinai and the need for a new one. Yet however distinguished the ministry of Jeremiah was, it was *within* the community of Israel. In contrast, Moses was instrumental in actually forming that community.

In the storyline of Torah, written by the hand of Moses, mankind's greatest problem is sin, which is universal and which alienates humanity from God. In the call of Abraham and in the covenant promises made to him and his son, Isaac, and grandson, Jacob, the answer for this universal dilemma would be addressed. With Moses, the Torah introduces a man whose work towers over the remainder of the Hebrew Scriptures. God used him to provide deliverance for Israel from bondage in Egypt, but the greater need is deliverance from sin. A provisional answer for this deliverance may be found in the sacrificial system (Lv 17:11), but it required the substitution of the life of a bull or a goat for that of a human, created in the image of God. This inequity meant that the sacrifices were provisional and pointed forward to an ultimate and perfect substitute, symbolized by the lamb of the first Passover. Although Passover would be observed for subsequent millennia, never again would the blood of a lamb bring deliverance from death.

Through Moses, God worked mighty signs and miracles. John Gill says that Manasseh Ben-Israel counted the miracles in the Scriptures and concluded that those of Moses exceeded those of all the subsequent prophets put together.[21] Furthermore, Moses' relationship to God was exceptionally close. This, in fact, is brought out clearly in Nm 12:6-8, following the rebellion of Aaron and Miriam:

> He [God] said, "Listen to what I say: If there is a prophet among you from the LORD, I make Myself known to him in a vision; I speak with him in a dream. Not so with My servant Moses; he is faithful in all My household. I speak with him directly, openly, and not in riddles; he sees the form of the LORD. So why were you not afraid to speak against My servant Moses?"

In this, God sets Moses apart from other prophets and accentuates the closeness of their communication. In this connection, note the "frame" of this passage. In v. 15, Moses says of the coming prophet, "You must listen to him." In v. 19, God says, "I will hold accountable whoever does not listen to My words that he speaks in My name." A central characteristic of this coming prophet is the authority with which he speaks. Michael Rydelnik says, "Whoever that prophet would be, he would be required to speak for God face to face."[22] Moses was to be the mouthpiece, the voice, of God among men. So, it must be asked, "Is Dt 18:15-19 messianic, or not?"

Since it has already been made clear that Moses would prefigure God's ultimate answer for the sin of man through his role as a deliverer, through his supernatural signs and wonders, and through his intimate relationship with God, to fail to recognize the messianic character of Dt 18:15-19 is thus to miss the whole point of Torah.[23] The prophet God promised to raise up in Dt 15:18 can be none other than the ultimate deliverer from sin, later to be known as the Messiah. He would be identified with even greater signs and wonders and would have an even closer relationship with God.

Indirectly Messianic View

This position is characterized by an understanding of the passage in Dt 18:15-19 as speaking of a succession of the prophets, or of a specific prophet, but culminating ultimately in the Messiah. The actual word for "prophet" in Dt 18:15-19 is in the singular form. Hebrew grammar recognizes that in the Scriptures sometimes singular words carry a collective meaning (thus the grammatical form is singular but refers to more than one). These are not words for which no plural form is used, such as "deer" or "fruit" in English, but singular forms that are pressed into the service of a plural meaning. Two readily available examples are the words "man" and "seed." Both words have plural forms in Scripture, but the singular forms of both are also used in a plural or collective sense.[24]

Taken in a straightforward and literal sense, Dt 18:15 is speaking of a singular individual who is to come. Many argue, however, that this would be to misread the text, for the word should be understood as a collective singular and refers both to the coming Messiah and also to one of the following: a succession of prophets who would follow Moses, the prophetic office, or one particular prophet.[25] All of these proposals require the understanding of "prophet" in Dt 18:15 to be collective. The question to be answered here is this: "Is the referent of Dt 18:15-19 an individual, or not?" To answer this question, consideration must be given to the context: first, of Dt 18, second, of the wider context of Dt 16–18, then of Torah, and finally of the Hebrew Scriptures as a whole.[26]

Deuteronomy 18:9-22. This portion is divided into three sections: A prohibition against pagan practices of divination (vv. 9-14), the prophecy of a prophet "like" Moses (vv. 15-19); and a warning against false prophets (vv. 20-22). Those who understand the true prophet spoken of here to be a reference to all true prophets point out that the first portion, against pagan divination, seems to contrast with the next section, in which the wrong order or manner of revelation is contrasted with the right order or manner. In other words, Israel should not seek a witch, a sorcerer, a magician, or a medium, but instead, God will raise up prophets. Since the first is a category or an order of people, so also the "prophet" that follows should be understood as a prophetic order. This position is further bolstered by the following section, which warns against false prophets—again, a category. Just as in vv. 15 and 18 (true prophets), so in verses 20 and 22 (false prophets), "prophet" is a collective singular.[27]

In response to this position, it can be said that rather than to conclude that the contrast between vv. 9-14 and the following section implies a contrast between two groups or classes of people, instead the contrast is between two sources of revelation: these false, pagan sources versus the great end-time Prophet, who would be the ultimate and perfect revelation of God. With regard to the following section about false prophets, Rydelnik says that it is also perfectly consistent with an individual prophet:

> This is seen in two ways. First, the particle *'akh* ["but"] in 18:20 is an adversative that is short of a full antithesis and can best be translated as *however*. . . . A close examination of the text demonstrates that what is being contrasted is that the

prophet like Moses will speak in God's name, whereas false prophets will only presume to do so.[28]

Another argument against the use of "prophet" in a collective sense is that when a collective is intended, it is usual to use both singular and plural forms (e.g., a singular noun with plural pronouns or pronominal suffixes). The use of the singular noun, "prophet," with singular pronouns ("like *me* [Moses]," v. 15; "*he* will tell . . . everything I command *him*," v. 18, emphases added) demonstrates an intention to refer to a specific individual, the Prophet like Moses, and not to a collective, i.e., an order of prophets.[29]

Deuteronomy 16–18. In the wider context, the argument is made that the offices of kings and of priests and Levites, which are discussed in 16:18–17:20 and 18:1-8 respectively, support taking 18:15-19 as referring to the office of prophet. This argument does not seem to be especially compelling, however, because the comparison could just as easily be between these offices of king, judge, priest, and Levite, on one hand, and the messianic Prophet on the other.

Torah. Kim makes the crucially significant observation that most of the arguments by modern scholars are based solely on Dt 18:15-19, but the evidence most often can be argued from either side, as discussed above. The same remains the case, even if the discussion involves Dt 16–18. Thus, the matter is really only resolved by considering evidence from the entirety of Torah. Kim argues that "it is important to take the whole Pentateuch into consideration to see the compositional strategy the author lays out with literary units belonging to it and the theological viewpoint that the author reflects behind that literary strategy."[30]

A study of the concept of a prophet in Torah, for example, reveals that Moses is not the first prophet. Prophets both preceded Moses and succeeded him. Yet Moses is distinguished as the prophet *par excellence* (see especially Nm 11–12). By considering the entirety of the Pentateuch, one can see that Moses' leadership was unique. John Sailhamer brings this out by pointing to the connection between the snake in Ex 4:3, leprosy ("white as snow") in 4:6 and in Nm 12:10, and snakes again in Nm 21:6-9.[31] In Ex 4, the issue was Moses' election, and in Nm 12 and 21, it was Moses' leadership. On both occasions, God vindicated Moses and set him apart from others in a dramatic and supernatural manner.[32]

MOSES' ELECTION VINDICATED		WILDERNESS NARRATIVES	MOSES' LEADERSHIP VINDICATED	
Snake	**Leprosy**		**Leprosy**	**Snakes**
Exodus 4:3	Exodus 4:6		Numbers 12:10	Numbers 21:6-9

Kim also notes that the parallel between Nm 11 and Ex 33:7-11 "communicates the fact that the Torah as the direct revelation of God's words is mediated only through Moses and that the prophets are subordinated to it."[33]

Likewise, Joshua is never presented in the text as being "like Moses," but instead he is a man distinctly different from Moses.[34] He is presented favorably, and as one the one to whom "the sons of Israel listened . . . and did as the Lord had commanded Moses" (Dt 34:9), but he is never referred to as the prophet like Moses. In the very next verse, it states that "no prophet has arisen like Moses" eliminating Joshua as the fulfillment of Dt 18. David Clines comments that with v. 10, "the text immediately turns its back upon Joshua in order to pronounce its final encomium upon Moses."[35] Kim reasons that "if it [i.e., the prophecy of Dt 18:15-19] refers to the collective sense of a 'succession of prophets,' then the very first candidate and also the natural one for this reference is eliminated by the larger context of Pentateuch."[36] Also, in connection with Dt 34, Sailhamer notes that v. 10 "does not say, 'the office of prophecy never arose'; it says, 'A prophet [singular] like Moses never arose.'"[37]

Another important theme is related to Moses and his prophecy. Both Moses and the prophets, who by serving God and calling for keeping of the Torah, were opposed by the majority of the people. David Turner writes, "The congregation's refusal at Kadesh to go into the land is clearly portrayed as rebellion against God, and by implication against his messenger Moses."[38] Moses, Joshua, and Caleb represent the remnant during the wilderness wanderings. Over and over again, Israel complains, murmurs, and threatens violence against Moses. This opposition would also characterize the ministries of the prophets—their messages often suffered outright rejection, while sometimes they even suffered physical persecution.[39] Though the majority of the people rejected the call to return to Torah faithfulness, the prophets succeeded in calling out a remnant, who were indeed faithful.

Whether parallels are noted between Moses and Joshua, Elijah, Jeremiah, Ezekiel, or another of the prophets, perhaps it is best to account for these similarities as pointing to the identities of these individuals as faithful servants of Torah and as *some* prophets, like Moses in certain respects, though not as *the* Prophet like Moses. Again, as Turner says, "Moses is viewed as the archetypal prophet, yet his successors are viewed as derivatives of his message and power."[40] They were faithful in calling Israel back to the Torah and to the God of Israel, but they were opposed by many in Israel, persecuted, and in many cases their messages went unheeded. As Allison says, "One of the outstanding features of the Pentateuch is the interminable opposition to Moses by those he unselfishly serves."[41] In all of this, the prophets to some extent—and Moses, to a greater extent—anticipated the ministry of Messiah.

DIRECTLY MESSIANIC VIEW

There is no need to repeat the arguments advanced above, except to say that it is clear that this view particularly emphasizes the singular form of "prophet" found in Dt 18, the uniqueness and authority of Moses who alone among God's prophets would speak to God face to face (e.g., Nm 12:6-8), and the unsuitability of Joshua (and thus of his successors) as the fulfillment of Dt 18 since they did not speak to God directly. It affirms the narrative strategy of the Torah, and the concluding verdict of Dt 34:10, added at the time of the closing of the Hebrew canon of Scripture, that "no prophet has arisen again in Israel like Moses, whom the LORD knew face to face."[42]

The evidence from Scripture would seem to indicate that the prophecy of the Prophet like Moses was intended to speak solely and directly of an individual, namely, the coming Deliverer—the Messiah, who would inaugurate a new covenant.

The only individual presented in the Hebrew Scriptures who can be said to be truly "like Moses" is the Servant of Isaiah.[43] G. P. Hugenberger, after evaluating other attempts to identify the Servant in these texts, says, "What is proposed here is that this dominant and unifying image is that of a second Moses figure. In other words, the servant is the 'prophet like Moses' promised in Deuteronomy 18:14ff. and 34:10ff."[44]

Hugenberger bases this proposal on the context of the Servant Songs in Isaiah, and particularly on chapters 40–55, in which he says, "the controlling and sustained theme of these chs. is that of a second exodus."[45] Second, exodus imagery appears in each of the Servant Songs, and the parallel is clear. God raised up Moses and the Servant to provide deliverance. Both Pharaoh and Cyrus also were raised up as pagan leaders to oppress Israel, but for the purpose of bringing the nations to see God's glory in providing ultimate deliverance for Israel. Furthermore, the tension between a corporate understanding of the servant and an individual interpretation is resolved if the servant is identified as the prophet like Moses. As Hugenberger says, "The servant is the representative of and model for his people: they share a common calling to be the servant of Yahweh, a light to the nations, etc."[46] One significant difference is that Jerusalem becomes the center of God's eschatological salvation in Isaiah. David Pao says, "Just as the Law of Moses came from Sinai, so now the [Torah] will go out from Zion."[47]

Both Moses and the Servant of Isa 40–55 are God's servants, so any opposition to them is opposition against the God whom they serve (Ex 16:8). Moses faced strong opposition (e.g., Ex 2:14; 4:1; 15:24; 16:2-3; 17:2-3; Nm 11–17), and so did the Servant (e.g., Isa 42:4; 50:6; 53:3,7,8). The people of Israel were close to stoning Moses (Ex 17:4), and the Servant is rejected by the people (Isa 53:3), scourged, and put to death (Isa 53:5). Israel was spiritually blinded during both the wilderness wanderings (Dt 29:1-4) and the ministry of Isaiah (Isa 6:9-10; 29:9-10; 42:18-20; 43:8; 44:18; 67:17). This spiritual blindness is explicitly connected to the suffering of the Servant in Isa 53:1 (see also the use of this verse in Jn 12:38; Rom 10:16). Both Moses and the Servant intercede for Israel (Ex 32:30-32; Isa 53:12). The Servant is like the prophet of Dt 18 also in his relationship with God. He is the one, God says, "in whom My soul delights" (Isa 42:1 NASB). Isaiah 50:4 indicates that the Servant listens directly to God daily so that he can communicate God's message effectively. F. Duane Lindsey says, "thus the Servant asserts claim to a disciple's ear in preparation for His exercise of a disciple's tongue."[48] Even as Moses was the mediator of the covenant at Sinai, Lindsey also makes a compelling argument, based on Isa 42:6c, that the Servant "is the mediator of the new covenant with Israel, elaborated in Jeremiah 31:31-34 and referred to in numerous other prophetic texts."[49]

Hugenberger says, "A felicitous consequence of the present approach to the servant songs is the substantial support it offers for the New Testament's messianic interpretation without presupposing that interpretation." Certainly, if the Servant is to be identified with the prophet like Moses, and if the Servant is to be identified as the Messiah, then Moses was directly prophesying the Messiah, whom God would raise up. As David Cooper says:

> The nation looked forward to a perfect sacrifice that would make complete and perfect satisfaction for all sins. The prophet Isaiah, therefore, foretold such an offering which would be made for the nation (Isa. 53). In the same way, Moses pointed forward to a lawgiver greater than himself (Dt. 18:15-18).[50]

As the Servant of the Lord, the Prophet like Moses would provide final atonement for sin. Sailhamer says, "The mediator Moses becomes one of the central narrative vehicles for depicting the messianic hope."[51] Here, Isaiah refers to God's Servant as a lamb (Isa 53:7), who would be the ultimate guilt offering (v. 10), bearing the guilt "of us all" (v. 6).

THE PROPHECY IN SECTARIAN INTERPRETATIONS OF THE FIRST CENTURY

The Dead Sea Scroll community of Qumran interpreted Dt 18:15-19 as speaking of an eschatological messiah, but one distinguished from both a Davidic messiah and a priestly messiah.[52] While there were undoubtedly questions regarding the coming messiah, the prophet like Moses was an individual whom they expected in the future.

There were also expectations of this prophet in the writings of the Samaritans.[53] The dominant eschatological figure during the early first century was the prophet like Moses.[54] This resulted in their theology that emphasizes a messianic concept they refer to as the *Taheb* ("restorer"), and this is based upon the passage in Dt 18. Kim says, "If one is to come who will prepare the way for God's judgment and restore everything for God, then that person must be either Moses *ridivivus* or one like him. Deuteronomy 18 provided the basis for this future messianic expectation of the Samaritans."[55]

THE PROPHECY IN THE NEW TESTAMENT

In the NT, Jesus is viewed as the direct fulfillment of the prophecy of Dt 18:15-19. To make this claim is not to "read the New Testament into the Old Testament," or post-resurrection revisionism,[56] but to read the Hebrew Scriptures correctly. If the apostles were slow to fully recognize Jesus' identity, or to understand exactly how the events of His life, death, and resurrection related to prophecy in the Scriptures, it is because their eyes "were prevented from recognizing Him" (Lk 24:16).

In identifying Jesus as the Messiah, the disciples were not rebuked for their ignorance or their mishandling of the sacred Scriptures, but instead, He rebuked the two on the road to Emmaus because they did not recognize Him from those very Scriptures. He said, "How unwise and slow you are to believe in your hearts all that the prophets have spoken!" (Lk 24:25). They must have taken His rebuke to heart. Once their eyes were opened, and especially when they were inspired by the Spirit to write the gospel accounts, they recognized how perfectly the Scriptures had been fulfilled and how the events of His life matched the prophecies of old.

In the gospels, there is no explicit quotation of the prophecy in Dt 18, nor is reference ever made to Jesus as "the prophet like Moses." Instead, references to Jesus as "a prophet" or as "the prophet" are salted throughout the gospel accounts. Even more striking, however, are the ways in which the events of His life point to His identity as the promised Prophet.

These are seen as early as the narratives of His birth and the beginning of His public ministry. Just as Pharaoh ordered the deaths of all male babies (Ex 1:10,16), so Herod ordered the deaths of all male babies under age two in Bethlehem (Mt 2:16-18). The parents of both Moses and Jesus ensured their son's safety through their actions and their reliance on the Lord. Years later, with John the Baptist's denial that he was either the Messiah or the Prophet like Moses (Jn 1:21), the implication is that the One for whom he was preparing the way was both. Following Jesus' baptism, He was "led by the Spirit in the wilderness for 40 days. . . . He ate nothing during those days" (Lk 4:1-2). Likewise, it was Moses who was with the Lord "40 days and 40 nights," during which time "he did not eat bread or drink water" (Ex

24:18; 34:28; Dt 9:9). Wayne Baxter says, "The first exodus, led by Moses and ending in failure, anticipated the final exodus accomplished by Jesus, who never fails."[57]

Water figures significantly in the lives of both. Even as Moses' first public miracle was turning water to blood in Egypt, so Jesus' first miracle was changing water to wine, recorded in Jn 2. While blood symbolized judgment and death, wine symbolized salvation and its accompanying joy. Similarly, Jesus was recognized as "prophet" by the woman at the well in Jn 4. Moses gave water to the people of Israel in the wilderness (Ex 15; 17; Nm 20-21), and, significantly, the place where the water was given in Nm 21:18 is called Mattanah, which means "gift." In Jn 4:10, Jesus told the woman, "If you knew the gift [Hb. *mattanah*] of God, and who is saying to you, 'Give Me a drink,' you would ask Him, and He would give you living water." Jesus presented Himself to this Samaritan woman as the Prophet like Moses.[58]

Likewise, mountains are significant to both. Regarding the Sermon on the Mount, Frederic Godet pronounced that "the mount where Jesus speaks is as the Sinai of the new covenant."[59] If so, Jesus is the Prophet like Moses. Allison concludes: "The point is simply this: the image of Moses sitting on Sinai . . . was firmly established in the imagination of pre-Christian Jews."[60] Allison also points out that even as the opening words of Mt 5 are similar to the biblical texts about Moses and Sinai, the same is true of 8:1, which concludes the Sermon on the Mount.[61] Here, Jesus is a teacher like Moses, delivering a new Torah. The implication, of course, is that Jesus is the Prophet like Moses.

The feeding of the 5,000 is the only miracle recorded by all four gospels.[62] All the accounts contain elements that point to Jesus' identity as the Prophet like Moses,[63] but none as clearly as John. In John's account of the feeding of the 5,000, the most explicit reference to Jesus as the Prophet like Moses is in the reaction of the crowd, following the miraculous provision of food: "This really is the Prophet who was to come into the world!" (Jn 6:14). The identification of Jesus with the Prophet is undoubtedly related to the miraculous provision of food, which was paralleled by Moses' provision of food in the wilderness. See also Jn 7:40 where many of the people at the festival said, "This really is the Prophet!" Similarly, all three synoptic Gospels record Jesus' transfiguration (Mt 17:1-8; Mk 9:2-8; and Lk 9:28-36). A. M. Ramsey writes, "Moses went up into the Mount . . . and when he came down to the people the skin of his face shone. Here, in contrast is the new and greater Moses, whose face shines not with a reflected glory but with the unborrowed glory as of the sun's own rays."[64]

In the Last Supper, Jesus is offered as the Prophet like Moses. All four gospels recount the Messiah's final Passover observance with His disciples (Mt 26:17-30; Mk 14:12-25; Lk 22:7-23; and Jn 13) and present Him as the antitype of the sacrifice at the original Passover. Moses instituted a divine covenant in which provisional atonement for sin was provided; Jesus inaugurated the promised New Covenant in which ultimate atonement was provided. Moses commanded the slaying of a lamb; Jesus offered Himself as the Lamb. No other prophet instituted a covenant.

About the Emmaus road story, Paul Frede Feiler notes "Luke summarizes Jesus' ministry in a way that shows that, in the broad outline of his ministry, Jesus is precisely like Moses: he comes as a prophet mighty in word and deed to proclaim deliverance to the oppressed, but he is rejected by the people."[65] As far as these disciples were concerned, Jesus was the Prophet like Moses, but they had not yet understood that He would have to suffer rejection and death. Then their eyes were opened.

The Gospel of Luke is a prequel to the book of Acts, so it should come as no surprise that Luke's "narrative about the events that have been fulfilled among us" (Lk 1:1) should set the stage for the events that followed. Feiler says of the Emmaus road account: "Luke . . . through Cleopas' summary of Jesus' earthly ministry, prepares the reader for the explicit identification of Jesus as the prophet like Moses in Ac 3:22-23."[66] Indeed, the only explicit citations of Dt 18:15 come from the book of Acts.

In the courts of the Temple, Peter proclaimed Jesus to be the Prophet like Moses (Ac 3:22-23). Here, it is not that Jesus and Moses are adversaries, but that Moses is actually a witness to the identity of Jesus—more than that, Moses is the prosecuting attorney, demanding obedience to Him and warning that the only alternative is destruction.[67] As Feiler says, "The quotation bases a soteriological imperative upon a Christological claim."[68] The Jewish people must listen to Jesus or suffer the discipline of God, even as their forefathers in the wilderness, since Jesus is the Prophet like Moses.

Then in Ac 7, Stephen quoted the prophecy from Dt 18 in his sermon prior to his martyrdom. He made the point that Jesus was the Prophet like Moses, and the leaders had not heeded the warning to listen to Him, but instead had offered Him up for crucifixion. In Ac 7:37, he said, "This is the Moses who said to the Israelites, God will raise up for you a Prophet like me from among your brothers." Understand that the Prophet like Moses does not *reject* Israel, but He has *divided* Israel. In the book of Acts, as Jacob Jervell says, "Israel has not rejected the gospel, but has become divided over the issue."[69]

In the Epistles, references to the prophecy of the Prophet like Moses are more oblique, yet this prophecy lies in the background of several texts. Passages have been suggested in Galatians, 2 Corinthians, and Hebrews that may express an understanding of Jesus as the Prophet like Moses.[70] Certainly there are Mosaic themes woven throughout the fabric of these materials. Hebrews may contain the majority of the Mosaic material in the Epistles, especially in 3:1-6, 11:23-27, and in the central section, 8:1–10:18. Since Jesus is the Prophet like Moses, one must submit to His Torah, especially in light of the warning of Dt 18:19.

CONCLUSION

The prophecy of the Prophet like Moses, found in Dt 18:15-19, is a messianic prophecy that speaks directly and solely of the coming Deliverer, later known as the Messiah. Isaiah's prophecies of the Servant of the Lord provide evidence of this. Moreover, as Paul says, "when the time came to completion, God sent His Son, born of a woman, born under the law, to redeem those under the law, so that we might receive adoption as sons" (Gal 4:4-5). Isaiah's prophecy of the coming messianic reign (Isa 2:1-4) looks to the time when the Lord will teach all the nations of His ways. Those who were the human instruments in the production of the books that comprise the Scriptures of the new covenant were not ignorant of the original intent of Torah, neither did they twist Scripture to conform to their faith in Jesus. When they saw fulfillment of this prophecy in Jesus, it was because they were reading Torah correctly.

Unlike the prognostications of the false prophets, this prophecy of Moses has come true! This is a witness, not only concerning Jesus' identity, but also Moses' validity as a true prophet of God. The unjustified abandonment of a messianic reading of this passage not only robs believers in Jesus of precious truth, but also concedes valuable ground to those who oppose the gospel altogether. To paraphrase a remark of Allison: I do acknowledge that in more than one recent work the directly messianic interpretation of the prophecy of the Prophet like Moses has in fact, for whatever reason, suffered interment. But the burial is premature.[71] It is to be hoped that a restored confidence in the directly messianic interpretation will revive the messianic hope that first animated the remnant of Israel—and later the early believers in Jesus.

---

1. Eccl. Rab. 1(א).
2. Michael Carasik, *Deuteronomy*, The Commentators' Bible; Accordance electronic ed. (Philadelphia: The Jewish Publication Society, 2015), paragraph 2479.
3. Translation is the author's.
4. Cf. Rachmiel Frydland, *What the Rabbis Know about the Messiah* (Worthington, OH: Messianic Publishing 1991), 21–22.
5. Mark J. Boda, "Figuring the Future: The Prophets and Messiah," in *The Messiah in the Old and New Testaments*, ed. Stanley E. Porter (Grand Rapids: Eerdmans, 2007), 35.
6. Matt Smethurst, "Slow Down! A Different Perspective on Christ in the Old Testament," *Bible & Theology*, The Gospel Coalition, (November 19, 2012) [blog on-line], https://www.thegospelcoalition.org/article/slow-down-a-different-perspective-on-christ-in-the-old-testament.
7. Ibid.

8. Daniel I. Block, "My Servant David: Ancient Israel's Vision of the Messiah," in *Israel's Messiah in the Bible and the Dead Sea Scrolls*, ed. Richard S. Hess and M. Daniel Carroll (Grand Rapids: Baker Academic, 2003), 26–27.

9. Ibid., 19 (emphasis in the original).

10. Tremper Longman III, "The Messiah: Explorations in the Law and Writings," in *The Messiah in the Old and New Testaments*, ed. Stanley E. Porter (Grand Rapids: Eerdmans, 2007), 13. For a contemporary Jewish polemicist who also takes a nonmessianic view of this text, see Samuel Levin, *You Take Jesus, I'll Take God: How to Refute Christian Missionaries* (Los Angeles, CA: Hamoreh Press, 1980), 36–37. Sometimes it is objected that the word, "Messiah," is not used at such an early date; however, while the word comes later, the concept of a deliverer from the consequences of sin can be traced back to Gn 3:15.

11. Abarbanel proposes Jeremiah, and the prophecy is applied to Joshua by Aben Ezra and Bechai. David L. Cooper interacts specifically with their arguments. See David L. Cooper, *Messiah: His Nature and Person*, Messianic Series Number Two (Los Angeles, CA: Biblical Research Society, 1933), 154–55. Dale Allison discusses the parallels between Moses and Joshua, Gideon, Samuel, David, Elijah, Josiah, Ezekiel, Jeremiah, Ezra, Baruch, the Suffering Servant of Isaiah 53, and Hillel. See Dale C. Allison, Jr., *The New Moses: A Matthean Typology* (Minneapolis, MN: Fortress Press, 1993), 23–73. Ezekiel's identity as the prophet like Moses is argued by H. McKeating, "Ezekiel the 'Prophet Like Moses'?" *Journal for the Study of the Old Testament* 61 (1994): 97–109, and Risa Levitt Kohn, "A Prophet Like Moses? Rethinking Ezekiel's Relationship to the Torah," *Zeitschrift für die alttestamentliche Wissenschaft* 114 (2002): 236–54.

12. Yoon-Hee Kim, "'The Prophet Like Moses': Deut 18:15–22 Reexamined within the Context of the Pentateuch and in Light of the Final Shape of the TaNaK" (PhD diss., Trinity Evangelical Divinity School, 1995), 206. For the full discussion, see 190–207.

13. Allison summarizes the parallels, 40–42.

14. Elie Assis, "Moses, Elijah and the Messianic Hope: A New Reading of Malachi 3,22-24," *Zeitschrift für die alttestamentliche Wissenschaft* 123 (2011): 220. See also Morris M. Faierstein, "Why Do the Scribes Say That Elijah Must Come First?" *Journal of Biblical Literature* 100 (1981): 75–86, and the review by Dale C. Allison, Jr. in *Journal of Biblical Literature* 103 (1984): 256–58.

15. Allison, *The New Moses*, 45.

16. William L. Holladay, "The Background of Jeremiah's Self-Understanding: Moses, Samuel, and Psalm 22," *Journal of Biblical Literature* 83 (1964): 153–64; J. A. Thompson, *A Book of Jeremiah*, The New International Commentary on the Old Testament (Grand Rapids: Eerdmans, 1980), 148. See also, Jack R. Lundbom, *Jeremiah: Prophet Like Moses* (Eugene, OR: Cascade, 2015); Christopher Seitz, "The Prophet Moses and the Canonical Shape of Jeremiah," *Zeitschrift für die alttestamentliche Wissenschaft* 101 (1989): 3–27.

17. Allison, *The New Moses*, 60.

18. See Michael Rydelnik, *The Messianic Hope: Is the Hebrew Bible Really Messianic?* New American Commentary Studies in Bible and Theology 9 (Nashville: B&H Academic, 2010), 56. See also, Alexander McCaul, *The Messiahship of Jesus: The Concluding Series of the Twelve Lectures on the Prophecies* (London: John W. Parker and Son, 1852), 146.

19. Allison notes other contrasts, as well. See Allison, *The New Moses*, 60–61.

20. Holladay, "Background of Jeremiah's Self-Understanding," 163–64.

21. According to John Gill, Manasseh Ben-Israel says the miracles of the Prophets number 74, while those of Moses number 76. John Gill, *The Prophecies of the Old Testament respecting the Messiah Consider'd and Prov'd to be literally Fulfill'd in Jesus* [etc.] (London: Printed for Aaron Ward, 1728), 135–36.

22. Rydelnik, *The Messianic Hope*, 61.

23. See Seth D. Postell, Eitan Bar, and Erez Soref, *The Torah's Goal* (Netanya, Israel: One for Israel Ministry, 2015).

24. "Man" is used this way in Gn 2:24; 6:7; 7:21; and 8:21 (and many other places as well). "Seed" is used in a collective sense many times (for example, see Gn 1:11; 3:15; 13:16; and 22:17).

25. Those who take this position, also take "God will raise up" (v. 15) and "I [God] will raise up" (v. 18), in a distributive sense. Allison, *The New Moses*, 74; cf., e.g., Peter C. Craigie, *The Book of Deuteronomy*, The New International Commentary on the Old Testament (Grand Rapids: Eerdmans, 1976), 262; Earl S. Kalland, "Deuteronomy" in *The Expositor's Bible Commentary*, vol. 3 (Grand Rapids: Zondervan, 1992), 121–22; C. F. Keil and F. Delitzsch, *Commentary on the Old Testament*, trans. James Martin, vol. 1 (Edinburgh: T.&T. Clark, 1885), 933–36; and Eugene H. Merrill, *Deuteronomy*, The New American Commentary (Nashville: Broadman & Holman, 1994), 273. Wayne Meeks believes the passage refers to a succession of prophetic rulers, such as Joshua, Samuel, Jeremiah, etc. See Wayne A. Meeks, *The Prophet King: Moses Traditions and the Johannine Christology* (Leiden, Netherlands: E. J. Brill, 1967).

26. See the excellent work by Kim, cited above.

27. See, for example, Carl F. Keil's commentary (in Keil and Delitzsch, 933–36). For the opposing view, see Franz Delitzsch, *Messianic Prophecies in Historical Succession*, trans. Samuel Ives Curtiss (Edinburgh: T.&T. Clark, 1891), 60–65.

28. Rydelnik, *The Messianic Hope*, 57–58.

29. Kim, "Prophet Like Moses," 88.

30. Ibid., 100.

31. In the diagram below, Kim has slightly altered the wording. See John Sailhamer, *The Pentateuch as Narrative: A Biblical-Theological Commentary* (Grand Rapids: Zondervan, 1992), 386–87, and Kim, "Prophet Like Moses," 177.

32. Sailhamer, *The Pentateuch as Narrative*, 386–87.

33. Kim, "Prophet Like Moses," 184. Glorious.

34. See the excellent survey of the evidence by Kim. Ibid., 190–207.

35. David Clines, *The Theme of the Pentateuch*, Journal for the Study of the Old Testament Supplement Series 10 (Sheffield, England: The University of Sheffield, 1994), 25. Indebtedness must be expressed to Kim for this reference.

36. Ibid., 206–07.

37. John H. Sailhamer, *The Meaning of the Pentateuch: Revelation, Composition and Interpretation* (Downers Grove, IL: IVP Academic, 2009), 18.

38. David L. Turner, *Israel's Last Prophet: Jesus and the Jewish Leaders in Matthew 23* (Minneapolis, MN: Fortress Press, 2015), 17.

39. See, e.g., 1Kg 13; 18:4,13; 19:10,14; 21:15,21,25; 2Kg 6; 9:7; Jer 18:20,22; and 38:1-16.

40. Turner, *Israel's Last Prophet*, 20–21.

41. Allison, *The New Moses*, 61.

42. Craigie translates it, "A prophet like Moses did not rise again in Israel" (Craigie, *Book of Deuteronomy*, 406). See also Sailhamer, *The Pentateuch as Narrative*, 456.

43. See Isa 42:1-4; 49:1-6; 50:4-9; 52:13–53:12; and, perhaps 61:1-3.

44. G. P. Hugenberger, "The Servant of the Lord in the 'Servant Songs' of Isaiah: A Second Moses Figure," in *The Lord's Anointed: Interpretations of Old Testament Messianic Texts*, ed. Philip E. Satterthwaite, Richard S. Hess, and Gordon J. Wenham (Grand Rapids: Baker, 1995), 119. Far from a novel view, it may be found in b. Sota 14a. Other evidence, both ancient and modern, of this view may be found in Hugenberger, 119–20. See also Allison, *The New Moses*, 142.

45. Hugenberger, "Servant of the Lord," 122. See also, David W. Pao, *Acts and the Isaianic New Exodus* (Grand Rapids: Baker Academic, 2000).

46. Hugenberger, "Servant of the Lord," 131.

47. Pao, *Acts*, 158.

48. F. Duane Lindsey, "The Commitment of the Servant in Isaiah 50:4-11" (Part 3 in the series: "Isaiah's Songs of the Servant"), *Bibliotheca Sacra* 139 (1982): 220.

49. Lindsey, "The Call of the Servant in Isaiah 42:1-9" (Part 1 in the series: "Isaiah's Songs of the Servant"), *Bibliotheca Sacra* 139 (1982): 25.

50. David L. Cooper, *Messiah: His Nature and Person*, Messianic Series Number Two (Los Angeles, CA: Biblical Research Society, 1933), 154.

51. Sailhamer, *The Pentateuch as Narrative*, 245.

52. 1QS 9:11 speaks of "the prophet and the anointed ones of Aaron and Israel." See Allison, *The New Moses*, 74–75 and Craigie, *Book of Deuteronomy*, 263, n. 20.

53. Meeks, *The Prophet King*, 246–50.

54. Paul Frede Feiler, "Jesus the Prophet: The Lukan Portrayal of Jesus as the Prophet Like Moses" (PhD diss., Princeton Theological Seminary, 1986), 37–38.

55. Kim, "Prophet Like Moses," 63.

56. For a representative example of this approach, see J. Severino Croatto, "Jesus, the Prophet like Elijah, and Prophet-Teacher like Moses in Luke-Acts," *Journal of Biblical Literature* 124 (2005): 451–65.

57. Wayne S. Baxter, "Mosaic Imagery in the Gospel of Matthew," *Trinity Journal* 20 (1999), 73.

58. Sukmin Cho, *Jesus as Prophet in the Fourth Gospel*, New Testament Monographs 15 (Sheffield, England: Sheffield

Phoenix Press, 2006), 2–3, 175. See also Marie-Emile Boismard, *Moses or Jesus: An Essay in Johannine Christology*, trans. B. T. Viviano (Minneapolis, MN: Fortress Press, 1993).

59. Frederic Godet, *Introduction to the New Testament: The Collection of the Four Gospels and the Gospel of St. Matthew* (Edinburgh: T&T Clark, 1899), 131.

60. Allison, *The New Moses*, 179.

61. Ibid., 179–80.

62. Mt 14:13-21; Mk 6:32-44; Lk 9:10-17; and Jn 6:1-15.

63. See Allison, *The New Moses*, 238–42.

64. Arthur Michael Ramsey, *The Glory of God and the Transfiguration of Christ* (London: Longmans, Green and Co., 1949), 120.

65. Feiler, "Jesus the Prophet," 189. But note Mt 21:9-11. For God's characterization of Moses' mighty deeds, see Ex 34:10.

66. Ibid., 188.

67. The warning here comes from Lv 23:29, but is consistent with the warning in Dt 18:19.

68. Feiler, "Jesus the Prophet," 47.

69. Jacob Jervell, "The Divided People of God," in *Luke and the People of God: A New Look at Luke-Acts* (Minneapolis, MN; Augsburg Publishing, 1972), 49.

70. Rodney Reeves, "The New Moses of the Law of Christ: Paul in Galatians," *Criswell Theological Review* n.s. 12 (2015): 71–82 (for 2Co, see 72–76), For Hebrews, see Mary Rose D'Angelo, *Moses in the Letter to the Hebrews*, SBL Dissertation Series 42 (Missoula, MT: Scholars Press, 1979).

71. Allison, *The New Moses*, 267.

Messianism in Ruth

CHARLES P. BAYLIS[1]

The story contained in the book of Ruth is one of the most well-known stories in the Bible. Yet while the overall plot of the Hebrew Scriptures leads to the Messiah, the book of Ruth is generally regarded as isolated from that storyline. The varying interpretations tend to be relational (e.g., a romantic short story[2]), or highly application oriented.[3] Often, when a messianic link is proposed, it is achieved by reading back into the Old Testament from the New Testament. The goal of this article is to demonstrate that the book of Ruth is inherently related to the whole of the OT narrative leading to the Messiah.[4]

FROM EMPTINESS TO FRUITFULNESS

The story opens as a Jewish family left their homeland to sojourn east to the land of Moab. A famine had occurred in the land of Israel where their God, YHWH, was the provider of food, but because of His seeming inactivity they sought food in Moab from the god Chemosh.[5]

Yet this trip was not without underlying concerns. Moabites were pagans, enemies of YHWH. From their inauspicious beginning as a product of incest between Lot and his daughter (Gn 19:30-38), they grew into a nation that worshiped other gods. Their king, Balak, had attempted to curse Israel when they paused at the Moabite border on the way to the promised land (Nm 22–24). It was at that time that Balaam had lured them into fornication and idol worship with the Midianites (Nm 25:1-18; 31:1-16). It was also there in the plains of Moab that YHWH instructed Israel never to seek Moab's peace or prosperity (Dt 23:3-6). Even during the days of the judges, when the events of this book took place, Israel was forced to pay tribute to Eglon, King of Moab (Jdg 3:12-30).

So, while this trip may have seemed a necessity, it was not justifiable to the God who gave the Torah (the Law). And so their foray for food in the land of another god resulted in the death of the patriarch, Elimelech, at the hand of YHWH.[6]

But that death did not alter the behavior of the remaining members. Desiring to preserve their heritage with children, the two sons, Mahlon and Chilion, intermarried with two local Moabite women, Ruth and Orpah. The Torah prohibited marriage to foreign women (Dt 7:1-3, see also 1Kg 11:1-8). So their pragmatic plans once again resulted in death as YHWH struck the sons as He had the father. Now, only five verses into the story, the family's wayward pursuit of happiness had ended in dire tragedy.

But Ru 1:6 states that YHWH had restored food to Israel, and Naomi turned her face westward toward her homeland. From that point the story turns from barrenness in the land of another god to provision of food and a child by YHWH in Israel. For soon after arriving in Bethlehem, Ruth met a righteous man, Boaz, who provided them with food and, finally, a child. In the last scene, as Naomi held the child in her lap, the story ends happily.

And that is the end of the story . . . or is it?

END GOAL, OR DENOUEMENT, FOR RUTH

One of the most important questions to ask when analyzing dramatic narrative is, "Where is it headed?" The obvious answer is, "to the end." Yet many interpreters of the Bible never go to the very end of the story to find the story's goal. This "end" goal of the plot in dramatic narrative is called the denouement.

For instance, God's goal in the whole of the biblical plot is determined by how it ends.[7] While the glorious return of Jesus Christ in victory and judgment in Rev 19 is the absolutely awesome, victorious "resolution" of the narrative, God's ultimate desire is found at the end, in Rev 20:1–22:5, when His Son will rule forever over the kingdom on earth.[8]

Yet regularly interpreters stop short of the denouement, breaking up the overall story into separate and independent pieces so as to find simple tenets for living, justify some personal doctrine, create autonomous applications, or bring forth other reader-desired outcomes. Few realize that every discourse and pericope in a dramatic plot is incomplete, with its only function to make its unique contribution and move the plot along to the next discourse or pericope, which in turn moves the plot along to the next, until it comes to its final resting place . . . *the end.*

Even in simple plots, as in the fairy tale "Cinderella," it is not the wedding to the prince (resolution) that is the ultimate goal, but the results (denouement) of that marriage . . . "they lived happily ever after." Every scene of the story, incomplete on its own, brings its unique contribution to transporting the heroine, Cinderella, to the "end" . . . "living happily ever after."

The goal of the book of Ruth is not found in the marriage of Boaz and Ruth, not in the birth of their baby, or even in the last scene when Naomi held the baby in her lap. The goal, the denouement, is found following those events, in the listing of a simple genealogy that begins with Perez and continues to David.[9]

At first glance, this matter-of-fact listing of a family's line appears to have little to do with the journey of a widowed, childless alien who traveled from Moab to Bethlehem, married, and bore a child. Because of this errant perception, this ending all too frequently becomes an "oh by the way," an interesting aside to what became of this marriage, that is, a great-grandchild, David, the King of Israel.[10] Yet dramatic plots do not end in an "oh by the way," but in the all-important *denouement* that dictates the goal of the totality of the preceding plot.

Yet this genealogy that leads to David is what connects the book of Ruth, inherently and inseparably, into the biblical plot that leads to Jesus, the Messiah.[11] Without that ending, the book would have no literary connection to the movement of the biblical plot and thus to the Messiah.

GENEALOGY OF THE MESSIANIC "SEED"

Since Ruth is part of the biblical story, it must move the plot along in terms of the contextual movement, that is, God's continuing purpose to bring forth His Messiah and Satan's continuing opposition to that purpose. Thus, the denouement in Ruth, and its preceding plot, must be understood in terms of the whole of the flow of the biblical story.

It was in the beginning (the setting) of the biblical story that God determined that humankind was to rule the created earth by representing God's desires (i.e., "image," Gn 1:26,28).

But the serpent (i.e., Satan[12]) soon deceived Eve. The whole creation, including the man and the woman, came under the rule of Satan (the conflict, Gn 3:1-6). God then came on the scene and promised (philosophy of the Hero) that a new Adam would come, called the seed of the woman (Gn 3:15). This new Adam would replace the condemned old Adam and restore the rule of God over the old earth, destroying Satan and his followers (the seed of the serpent), and then create a new earth.[13]

God subsequently began the long journey to His Son by providing a seed in each generation. The OT is the story of God moving unalterably (rising action), seed by seed, to form a foundational genealogy beginning with Adam, moving to David, and finally to the arrival of Jesus the Messiah in the Gospels.

The story, beginning in the book of Genesis, tracks this messianic genealogy through selected men: Adam to Noah (Gn 5), Shem to Abraham (Gn 11:10-32), Jacob (Gn 25:19-23; 28:13-14) to Judah (Gn 49:8,10). However, the genealogy goes one generation further than Judah, identifying that the seed would come from Judah's son Perez (Gn 38:27-30).[14]

Following Perez in Genesis, the messianic genealogy is seemingly absent from Exodus through Judges until 2Sm 7:16, where David was identified as the one from whom would come the Messiah, who would sit on the throne forever.

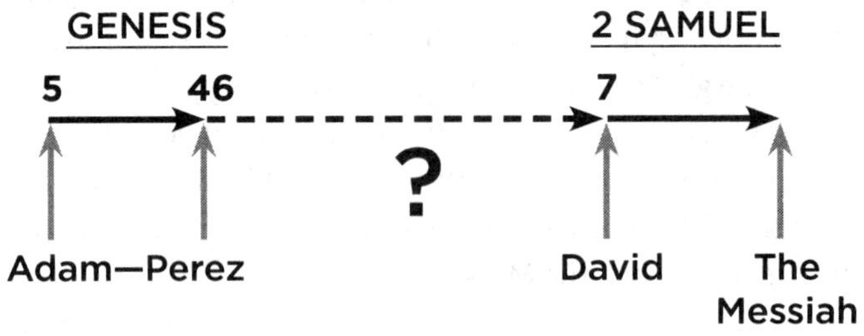

THE "SEED OF THE WOMAN"

Of course, this lineage is not missing, but it appears in the book of Ruth, where it exactly fills in the gap from Perez in Genesis to David in 2Sm 7:16. Thus this denouement of the book of Ruth fills in the genealogical seed movement of God to His Son, from Genesis (Perez) to 2 Samuel (David).

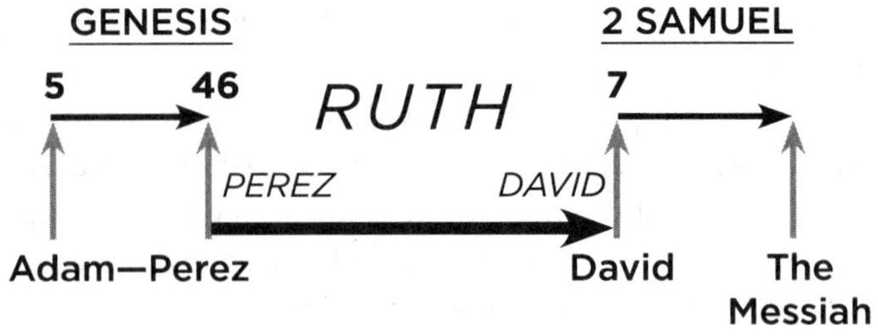

THE "SEED OF THE WOMAN"

PLOT OF THE BOOK OF RUTH

But the denouement of the book of Ruth is only the outcome of the message of the book. The unwinding plot that precedes it is the movement of "how" this end was brought to bear. The plot of the book is, therefore, the story of how God overcame the conflict (of Satan) to bring this seed-provider, Boaz, into the genealogy that leads to His Messiah.

The connection from the beginning of the plot to the ending, with Boaz and the genealogy, is Elimelech. In the beginning, he appears as a nondescript father in a family of four. But the narrator lets the reader look ahead as he quickly makes the connection to Boaz in 2:1; Elimelech is in the same family as Boaz.

Now Naomi had a relative[15] on her husband's side named Boaz. He was a prominent man of noble character from Elimelech's family (2:1).

Because of the importance of this family relationship to the plot, it is repeated in 2:3, acknowledged by Naomi in 2:20 and 3:2, cited by Ruth in 3:9, and agreed on by Boaz in 3:12. Elimelech was acknowledged as a "brother" by Boaz with the nearer kinsman in 4:3, and reconfirmed in 4:9-10.

But again, it is not until the denouement that it is revealed that this was not just any family, but the one family in the whole of Israel with the right to provide the seed of Messiah.

The plot traces the messianic seed-provider from Elimelech at the beginning to Boaz at the end. Elimelech had that right at the beginning and passed it to his eldest son, Mahlon. But when Elimelech and both sons died and there were no heirs, the right to provide the seed moved to Elimelech's family in Bethlehem. There the nearest kinsman, the eldest of the remaining brothers of Elimelech,[16] rejected that right. Thus, Boaz, the next in line, became the one who provided the seed, as he stated in 4:10:

> Boaz said to the elders and all the people, "You are witnesses today that I am buying (קָנִיתִי)[17] from Naomi everything that belonged to Elimelech, Chilion, and Mahlon. I will also acquire (קָנִיתִי) Ruth the Moabitess, Mahlon's widow, as my wife, to perpetuate the deceased man's name on his property, so that his name will not disappear among his relatives or from the gate of his home. You are witnesses today."

CONFLICT AND SERPENT'S DECEPTION

Yet plots do not simply follow a smooth positive movement from beginning to end, as the simple transfer of seed rights from Elimelech to the next of kin would appear. In dramatic plots, the hero must overcome opposition in order to achieve his goal at the end. In the biblical story, that opposition is provided by Satan, who would deceive and kill to stop the rule of God, the Hero of the Bible. That contextual opposition to God's Messiah and His followers continued from the beginning and will continue until Satan is thrown into the lake of fire in Rev 20:10.

Satan opposed God's plan from the beginning. He deceived Eve to take over the rule of the earth, and he continued to deceive the seed-providers to stop the new Adam from coming and recovering that rule for God. Satan had to stop this seed because this coming Messiah was to destroy Satan and his followers. Satan's plan was to deceive (so as to have them reject God and follow him), and if that failed, he would kill (so as to remove them from opposing his rule).[18]

And so Satan's antagonism continued. When Eve bore her firstborn, Cain, she hoped that he would be this seed.[19] Yet the serpent deceived Cain ("sin is crouching at the door. Its desire is for you . . . " Gn 4:7). And then Cain, acting on behalf of the serpent, killed his righteous brother, Abel.[20] But God overcame Cain's rejection of the seed and the killing of Abel by giving Eve a "substitute" son to whom God passed the right to provide the seed (Gn 4:25-26).

Later in Genesis, Esau was the firstborn with the right to the seed. Yet Satan deceived him into believing that the birthright (to provide the seed) was worthless and then selling it to Jacob for a bowl of stew (25:21-34). In Ex 1:15-16, Pharaoh, deceived by the serpent, tried to stop the seed from coming by drowning all the male babies in the Nile. Later, the serpent deceived David as he, like Eve, "saw" that she (Bathsheba) was exceedingly good to the sight and took her[21] (1Sm 11:1-4). Following David's deception, Satan continually deceived successive kings, beginning with Solomon, whom Satan lured to worship idols and intermarry with pagans (1Kg 11:1-10).

Because Ruth occurs in the progress of the plot of the biblical story, Satan's determination to destroy the coming Messiah must be essentially related to the plot of the book.

The first five verses of the story are the record of a family who was deceived by Satan. The man who had the right as messianic seed-provider, Elimelech, had journeyed away from the land of YHWH to the land of another god in a search for food. The sons had intermarried with women from among a pagan people who worshiped other gods. In response, God removed all of the males in this family. Only their childless widows remained.

But . . . and this is the crux of the book . . . because of the disobedience of the men in the family, Satan's plan to disrupt the seed from coming had brought the legal right to "bear" the seed of Messiah to . . . a Moabite!

EXCURSUS: "ONE FLESH" AND LEVIRATE MARRIAGE

This is the crux of the book. This issue needing resolution is the narrowest of problems that must be overcome for the goal (denouement) to come about. In the book of Ruth, this issue is centered in the woman, Ruth. The potential seed-provider *must* marry Ruth, and Ruth alone, to actually provide the seed and move into the genealogy of Messiah in the denouement.

Thus the actual story, the plot, is about God overcoming Satan's obstacles by bringing Ruth on a journey from Moab to Bethlehem to marry the seed-provider and become the messianic seed-bearer.

The nearer kinsman (the next in line with the rights as the seed-provider) could not simply ignore Ruth, find another Israelite woman, and bear a child. He would have to marry this woman, Ruth, in order to enter the messianic genealogy.

Boaz (next in line after the nearer kinsman) *only* entered the genealogy at the end because he married Ruth and provided the seed to her. So he, as well, must marry the one woman, Ruth, to provide the seed for Messiah.

That this Moabite named Ruth, located in Moab, is the key factor in the book has not escaped interpreters and readers through the centuries. And, not realizing the absolute necessity of her legal status, they have offered many and varied views.

The question to interpreters is, what was the *main* issue that prompted God to focus on this one woman in the whole world of Jews and Gentiles? Was it her Moabite status as a Gentile, since God does pursue Gentiles to bring them to Christ (Gn 12:3, Mt 28:19)?[22] Or did Ruth possess some other inherent characteristic (the romantic view)?[23]

But a simple reading of the text reveals it was not her Moabite heritage, nor any other personal or ethnic trait,[24] but strictly the legal covenant position, which was simply a result of her marriage to the holder of the seed right, Mahlon. And that legality required that she be the bearer, the mother, of the messianic seed. It is through this legal covenant that God not only honored but also pursued Ruth with His sacrificial love toward this hopeless alien. That legality that reflected God's character was fundamental in what was known as the "levirate marriage."

Most commentators recognize that the levirate marriage of Dt 25:5-10 is instrumental in this narrative. However, the levirate marriage was not some new requirement that God had originated and encoded into the law there on the plains of Moab. The basis for the levirate marriage was founded in the "one flesh" requirement of the husband and wife established in Gn 2:18-24 and later encoded into the law.

Genesis 2:18-24 was more than just a description of how marriage came to be; it developed the woman's essential role with respect to the man's seed as related to the following narrative of the biblical story. For while the man was the seed-provider because he inherited the actual seed from his parents by blood, the woman he married would possess the absolute legal right to bear that same seed.

So because Eve was taken out of Adam's side,[25] she was "one flesh," inseparable with regard to Adam's inheritance. Thus in Gn 2:24, God pronounced the means by which this was to be continued: "For this reason, a man shall leave his father and mother and shall cleave to his woman and they two shall become, with respect to flesh, one."[26]

That right establishes that the male heir will join with a female, someone apart from his own bloodline ("leave father and mother"), and move to make her an heiress ("cleave"). It is then that God will make them indissoluble ("one flesh") to provide and bear the seed.

Genesis 2:24 has often been misallocated to 21st-century psychological tenets, frequently advocating the separation of the new union from parental influence. But the actual meaning is that this son, with right of blood inheritance from his father and mother, will "leave" that line of inheritance (i.e., not a blood relative) to find a woman who has no right to the inheritance.

He then "cleaves" to this "woman." This is his one-way action (through a vow) that the potential husband makes to indicate his unchangeable commitment (i.e., sacrificial love) toward this one woman, not formerly a party to the blood inheritance of his family.

While the male cleaved to the female (the heir cleaved to the new heiress), it was God alone who then accomplished the bond, the "one flesh." While the man had the seed of his parents in him, he was helpless to have children without a "seed-bearer." Thus, this verse radically changed the legal position of this, formerly unassociated, woman to that seed. Since this couple was "one flesh," the man would never have the choice to separate (i.e., "un-cleave") her from himself and his inheritance. Even if he should die, her relationship to his inheritance, including his family, continued.

Jesus was asked exactly this question in Mk 10:2 ("Is it lawful for a man to divorce his wife?") as to whether a man could, in fact, separate (i.e., divorce) the "one flesh" wife from himself and his inheritance. Jesus quoted Gn 2:24 to show that the man could not separate out ("un-cleave") the "one flesh" woman (i.e., divorce her from himself and his inheritance) since God was the One who made them "one flesh."

> For this reason a man will leave his father and mother [and be joined to his wife], and the two will become one flesh. So they are no longer two, but one flesh. Therefore what God has joined together, man[27] must not separate. (Mk 10:7-9)

But, like all events and discourses within a narrative plot, this does not have enough information by itself, and can only be related to its function in the progressive unfolding of the story. The following events in the narrative of Genesis will show that the male could not choose to "un-cleave" and dissolve this "one flesh" inheritance, particularly with regard to the (messianic) seed, since that union had been made by God.

In Gn 12:10-20 when famine struck, Abram sought relief from Pharaoh. But when he felt threatened because of his beautiful "one flesh" wife, Abram tried to "un-cleave" her so Pharaoh would not kill him. Yet God would not dissolve the "one-flesh" relationship, and so cursed Pharaoh while returning her to Abram.[28]

Genesis 2:24 provides the foundation that allows one to understand the story of Judah and Tamar. Tamar had become "one flesh" with Er, Judah's eldest son, and thus held the right to bear his seed (in this case, the seed of Messiah). When God killed Er, Onan, the next eldest brother, was sent to impregnate her but refused, and was also killed by God. So Judah then refused to send the last son, Shelah, to Tamar since he was now afraid of losing his last heir. So he sent Tamar back to her father's house, seeking to "un-cleave" her from the "one flesh" right to bear the seed of the deceased eldest son.

But Tamar refused to abandon her God-given "one flesh" right and thus pursued and obtained the seed of Messiah, not from Shelah, but from Judah.

The levirate marriage (Dt 25:5-10) was the encoding of the "one flesh" requirement of Gn 2:24 (played out in Gn 38), but with specific regard to the seed of the deceased husband. If a man should die and leave his wife childless, the eldest brother in the same family would marry her and bring up seed to the deceased brother. In addition, she could not marry outside the family, as it was her legal responsibility to bear her deceased husband's seed through the eldest of the remaining brothers. But this duty was not an easy task, as it required a unique type of love, a great sacrifice on behalf of his brother for the benefit of his widow. That sacrificial mercy was called *chesed*.

CHESED, THE CHARACTER OF GOD

Chesed was revealed in the Torah as the self-sacrificing character of God (see Dt 10:17-20). God's *chesed* was seen in Gn 3:15, as He promised to give up His only Son for execution (sacrificially) so that His enemies (all those who rejected him in Adam) could be saved into the kingdom of His Son (mercy). It was in the Torah that the Israelite, as God's representative (i.e., "sons," Dt 14:1), could discover God's character and reflect it to others (i.e., the *Shema*, Dt 6:4-9). God's sacrificial love is so extreme He would even pursue His enemies to give mercy to them (Mt 5:44-47). Those who asked for mercy then received *chesed* and would in turn give it out on behalf of YHWH to those who were as hopeless as they.

> But love your enemies, do what is good, and lend, expecting nothing in return. Then your reward will be great, and you will be sons of the Most High. For He is gracious to the ungrateful and evil. (Lk 6:35)

Since marriage is to represent God's love (i.e., the "image," Gn 1:26), the man is obligated to love this woman as if she were his own body (i.e., "one flesh"), even to the point of giving his own life for her.[29] Paul referenced Gn 2:24 in Eph 5:25-30, comparing marriage to the ultimate "one flesh" union, Christ and the Church:

> Husbands, love your wives, just as Christ loved the church and gave Himself for her... In the same way, husbands are to love their wives as their own bodies. He who loves his wife loves himself. For no one ever hates his own flesh but provides and cares for it, just as Christ does for the church, since we are members of His body.

Unfortunately, interpreters, assuming today's common value system, have too often supposed that the levirate marriage must have brought some personal benefit to the brother of the deceased, else why would he accept such an arrangement? Yet this could not be further from the actual case as the motivation of the Torah (which reflected God's sacrificial love, *chesed*) was exactly the opposite of man's self-beneficial, natural desires.[30]

Contrary to today's self-centered desires (selfish lusts, Eph 4:17-19; and reciprocal love, Mt 5:46-47; Lk 6:32-34), the levirate marriage was a great sacrifice done solely for the benefit of the deceased and his (helpless[31]) widow. In other words, the levir would give up his own marital right to choose the woman of his own desires, and, instead, eagerly and joyfully accept the responsibility to marry, and provide seed for, his deceased brother's childless widow regardless of personal benefits or liabilities. He would do this solely based on God's provision for him and thus would act mercifully on behalf of God.

The connection of this "levirate marriage" and the "one flesh" requirement to Ruth was that she was a childless widow who had the legal, God-given right to bear her husband's seed. Thus, any rightful seed-provider must marry her, and her alone, regardless of any liabilities such as her Moabite heritage, financial condition, or other.

GOD RESOLVES SATAN'S ATTACK ON THE SEED

Satan's attack on the seed became a great problem that had to be solved by God for the messianic seed to come, particularly with regard to this Moabite widow.

• *Ruth was a Moabite, a worshiper of Chemosh.*[32] Ruth was a Moabite, and as such would have been a worshiper of Chemosh from her youth. Changing one's alliance to the God of an enemy was no small issue.

• *She would have to leave her own mother, father, and family in Moab, to go with the poor, old mother of her dead husband.* The natural blood bond to one's family was a solid link from birth. The corresponding link to Naomi, her mother by marriage, was an unseen, invisible bond made by the God of Israel through her deceased husband (i.e., "one flesh"). To go with this mother-in-law, as opposed to her own family, was a major decision to choose the invisible revelation of the God of Israel instead of a blood bond. In addition, going with her mother-in-law had no visible benefits, since Naomi was poor, past childbearing, with no husband and no children.

• *There appeared to be no qualified redeemer (Hb.* goel*).* Naomi had stated it clearly. The requirement of Dt 25:5-10 and the levirate marriage limited Ruth's marriage options to that of brothers in the immediate family. Mahlon's only brother was dead and Naomi was too old to have any more sons (1:11-13). Thus, Ruth's venture with Naomi held no visible hope of her ever marrying and having children. So Naomi urged her to return to Chemosh (1:15) who, unlike YHWH, had no such requirement that would prevent her from marrying and bearing children.

As God returned the food to Israel (1:6), Naomi also returned based on her natural instincts. Since it was food that had motivated her to leave Israel in the first place, it was food that caused her to return. Naomi, relying on her own ability to self-deliver instead of trust in YHWH, then tempted both Ruth and Orpah to share her reasoning. She told them that they should stay in Moab where, under the god Chemosh,[33] they could have husbands and children and cling to their natural family. In Israel, because of YHWH's restriction that they could only marry brothers, there would be no chance of having a husband or children. So Naomi urged them both to "un-cleave" from their "one flesh" bond with her family through their deceased husbands, and return to Moab to bond with Moabite men (1:9).

God's solution from Genesis to Revelation was, is, and always will be, to bring one to faith in YHWH and His coming Son. Ruth would trust in YHWH and honor the Gn 2:24 "one flesh" bond despite Naomi's insistence on an alternative solution. Thus Ruth, by faith in YHWH, overcame the temptation.

Because of Ruth's bond to Naomi through the "one flesh" bond with her son,

Mahlon, Ruth would not leave her mother-in-law. She claimed this in 1:14 and 16, alluding to Gn 2:24 (i.e., "leaves," "bonds").

> Again they wept loudly, and Orpah kissed her mother-in-law, but Ruth clung [lit. "cleaved"] to her (Ru 1:14).

> But Ruth replied, "Do not persuade me to *leave* you" (Ru 1:16).

Ruth's only visible inheritance was Naomi, and that inheritance was a poor, older widow requiring care. So Ruth responded with *chesed*, that is, she would honor the "one flesh" relationship and willingly sacrifice for Naomi at her own cost. And to reassure her commitment to the "one flesh" that had been established with Mahlon, she vowed (see Dt 23:21-23) regarding her continuing relationship to Naomi. Ruth would care for Naomi for the rest of her life, and when she died she would be buried with her.[34]

Ruth told Naomi: "For wherever you go, I will go, and wherever you live, I will live; your people will be my people, and your God will be my God. Where you die, I will die, and there I will be buried. May Yahweh punish me, and do so severely, if anything but death separates you and me" (Ru 1:16-17).

GOD MOVED RUTH TO MEET THE RIGHTEOUS *GOEL*

Having brought Ruth by faith to overcome the natural temptation and instead go to Bethlehem, God's unseen hand then moved her to the field of Boaz (2:3) to meet her future righteous *goel*, Boaz. The narrator established Boaz as a potential *goel* in 2:3, and then showed the reader that he was righteous and acted with *chesed* as he sacrificially provided food to Ruth and Naomi through the covenant provision of gleaning[35] (Lv 19:9-10; 23:22).

It's possible Naomi was still seeking an earthly solution and decided, like the people of her times who did what was right in their own eyes (Jdg 17:6; 21:25),[36] to lure[37] Boaz into providing seed for Ruth by appealing to his natural lusts. If this was the case, perhaps that is the reason she instructed Ruth to make herself alluring[38] and approach Boaz when he was well relaxed with food and drink. She was to approach him in the middle of the night on the threshing floor, instead of during the daylight hours at the city gate where legal transactions were to take place.

Of course, once again Naomi's plans would not succeed because Boaz was a righteous man, and he was not even the rightful heir—there was another before him who held the legal right. In obedience to the Torah, Boaz would not acquiesce to this sensual solution. Also, he recognized the Torah gave a prior right to the nearer kinsman that he could not disregard.

But faithful Ruth rejected this self-determined solution, and before Boaz could decide what to do, she confronted him with his *chesed* responsibility as a *goel* under the Torah.[39] According to Ruth (and the Torah), he was to marry her and provide a child for the sake of Naomi and for her deceased husband.[40] Boaz, a righteous man,[41] recognized the Torah requirement and assured her that she would have a *goel*. However, he informed her that there was a nearer *goel*, but if that man did not take her (i.e., rejected *chesed* responsibility), then Boaz would perform the legal duty (i.e., accept the *chesed* responsibility).

Boaz then presented the nearer kinsman with the legal requirement from the Torah. This *goel* had two options. First, he could exercise *chesed* and marry this childless widow. If he exercised his right, he would never be able to marry the woman of his own choice, and it would threaten his own inheritance as well.[42] Being unrighteous, he, like Naomi, Elimelech, and their sons, took the second option, the expedient, pragmatic solution, choosing to self-determine his future and reject his Torah duty as a *goel*.

As always, the solution was for God's people to walk by faith. Thus, God had His man in place, Boaz, who would make the Torah decision and exercise his legal privilege to show *chesed* to this woman by being her redeemer. The losses that deterred the nearer kinsman did not deter Boaz. Boaz recognized through the Torah that God had placed him in the right place and given him the ability to provide for the helpless widows of his deceased brother, Elimelech, and of his nephew, Mahlon. So he would act in trust.

THE DENOUEMENT: PEREZ TO BOAZ TO DAVID TO THE CHRIST

But that was not the end. That child was Obed, the grandfather of King David, from whom would come the Messiah (2Sm 7:16). Thus, the journey of the biblical story continued as God overcame the threat of the serpent, who tried once again to prevent the seed from coming.

Appropriately Boaz is remembered throughout future generations as one who trusted in YHWH and, through his act of *chesed*, provided the seed for Messiah. That name is recorded, not only in the denouement of the book of Ruth, but also in 1Chr 2:11-12, Mt 1:5, and Lk 3:32. By contrast, the nearer kinsman had his name removed forever from the annals of Scripture.[43] And, of course, Ruth is also remembered with Boaz, since she honored her faith in YHWH by clinging to the "one-flesh" inheritance given her. While others thought of temporal benefits, she bore the seed of the One who would not only deliver her, her husband, and her mother-in-law, but also would one day resurrect the believers of her nation and of the world into the ultimate denouement of the biblical story, the eternal earthly kingdom.

The book of Ruth demonstrates God's love for the coming seed, as He overcame Satan's deceit during the times of the judges to keep His promise to bring forth that seed through the righteous man, Boaz, with the righteous "one flesh" woman, Ruth. Thus, God's movement in the book of Ruth brought about the all-important messianic denouement that connects the book into the messianic movement from Adam to the Christ, who will reign on the throne of the universe.

APPLICATION: BELIEVE IN THE SON

Each reader is in this story—the story of God's movement to place His Son on the throne of the universe. The book of Ruth confirms that God was always successful in bringing forth His Son and, now that He has appeared, God will still be successful in bringing forth the ultimate reign of His Son. The application for the reader is, as it was for Ruth and Boaz, to trust in this Messiah who has now appeared. This single application pervades the whole Bible: trust in the One whom God loves, the Son. That trust and that faith alone will enable the believer to enjoy the ultimate denouement with His Son forever.

> The Father loves the Son and has given all things into His hands. The one who believes in the Son has eternal life, but the one who refuses to believe in the Son will not see life; instead, the wrath of God remains on him. (Jn 3:35-36)

---

1. The author's exposition of the book of Ruth and the biblical story appears at thebiblicalstory.org. Since this article cannot explain all the details necessary for understanding the exposition of Ruth, the reader is referred to the Ruth Commentary on that website for further information.

2. "Romance" here and throughout this discussion indicates a human reasoning type of romance, that is, one that draws two people together based on mutual attraction due to personal attributes. "Romance" is sometimes related to God's relationship with His people, but this "romance" is due to God's desire based on His sacrificial character toward one who has no beneficial traits (see Hos 2:14). Ray Stedman illustrates using the former (human romance) to relate to the latter (God's desire). In "Ruth: The Romance of Redemption" (http://www.raystedman.org/bible-overview/adventuring/ruth-the-romance-of-redemption, accessed May 27, 2016), he states, "Then we have this wonderful story of 'boy meets girl,' and it never gets old, does it?"

3. For instance, John Piper sees multiple purposes of the book. While he does mention one of the purposes is moving the genealogical line to David, he also sees additional purposes as practical applications for the reader: "It's a story for people who can't imagine that anything great could ever come of their ordinary lives of faith" ("Ruth: Sweet and Bitter Providence," message delivered on July 1, 1984, http://www.desiringgod.org/messages/ruth-sweet-and-bitter-providence).

4. This is the nature of dramatic narrative. Every event in the story contributes to the main plot. There are no separate meanings apart from that contribution.

5. The use of the phrase, "there was a famine in the land" occurs several other times in the OT besides this use in Ru 1:1. Genesis 12:10 was the motivation for Abram's (like Elimelech's) disobedient departure from the land to go to Egypt for food. Genesis 26:1-2 is similar in that it contained a warning by God to Isaac not to go to Egypt as Abram had done (12:10). See also the story of Elisha with the sons of the prophets and the deadly stew (2Kg 4:38-41).

6. For a discussion on the deaths of Elimelech and his sons as the judgment of God, refer to this author's article, "Naomi in the Book of Ruth in Light of the Mosaic Covenant," *Bibliotheca Sacra* 161 (October–December 2004): 413–431. Also reference Daniel I. Block's commentary on Ru 1:3-5 (*Judges, Ruth*, The New American Commentary [Nashville: Broadman & Holman, 1999], online version). Naomi, herself, implicated YHWH in their deaths in 1:13, "the LORD's hand has turned against me."

7. Of course, the ending to the biblical story has been known since the beginning when God revealed it in Gn 1:26 and 3:15, and further detailed it in Gn 12:1-3.

8. The denouement is related to, and completes, the beginning plans of the Hero, God. In the beginning, God desired man to rule over a physical universe. In the end, the Man, Jesus, will reign over the physical earth and skies, thus realizing God's achievement of that original goal.

9. That David was the king of Israel, the one to whom was promised that the Messiah would come from his genealogical line, is known only by following the story beyond the events of the book of Ruth, to the book of Samuel.

10. This typically takes the form of an author developing other, multiple, purposes for the book, one of which is to bring the messianic line to David. But bringing about the seed to Messiah is not just one of multiple purposes of the book. It is the single main purpose of the book. Any derivations from the narrative must be shown to be an integral part of this single main purpose.

11. Daniel Block identifies this book as performing a function to provide this segment to the biblical story. "This book and this genealogy demonstrate that in the dark days of the judges the chosen line is preserved not by heroic exploits by deliverers or kings but by the good hand of God" (Ru 4:18-22). (Daniel Block, *Judges, Ruth*, The New American Commentary, online version, accessed July 19, 2016).

12. The serpent was the antagonist to the Hero, God, introduced in Gn 3:1, since he is, by definition, diametrically opposed to the Protagonist. However, that he was more than a serpent is clear because he interacts with God's theology, something beyond the ability of a natural created being other than man. For more detail refer to this author's chapter "How is Christ Revealed in the Old Testament?," in *The Theory and Practice of Biblical Hermeneutics: Essays in Honor of Elliott E. Johnson* (Silverton, OR: Lampion Press, 2015), 134–35. While the name Satan is not attached to the antagonist until later in the biblical story, it will be used interchangeably with the title "the serpent" throughout this discussion to identify the continuing nature of the antagonism from its single original source in the beginning.

13. While the explanation of Gn 3:15 presented here is terse, for details, refer to this author's chapter "How Is Christ Revealed in the Old Testament?," in *The Theory and Practice of Biblical Hermeneutics: Essays in Honor of Elliott E. Johnson* (Silverton, OR: Lampion Press, 2015). Also, refer to the Commentary section at thebiblicalstory.org, Gn 3:15.

14. This can be noted by reading the end of the story of Tamar (Gn 38:27-30; see also 46:12), where again a genealogy appears that describes the struggle of her twins to determine the firstborn. The allusion is to the earlier birth of the twins, Jacob and Esau, and the struggle of the firstborn and the identity of the future seed-bearer by God. The narrator is noting this rare description of the birth of twins so as to identify which one will carry the "seed" of Messiah. This is reconfirmed in Gn 46:12, where of all the sons of Judah, only Perez's children are listed.

15. Generally, this is translated "kinsman," and is indicating a specific (close) relationship. Naomi repeated it in 3:2 when pointing out to Ruth the relationship of Boaz to both of them.

16. Boaz referenced himself and the nearer kinsman as "brothers" in 4:3. While by itself this might be taken as a general term, in the case of the levirate marriage, Dt 25:5-10 required that the levir must be one of the "brothers (of the deceased) who live together." Obviously, the point was that the levir must be a son of the same father and mother (i.e., immediate family), since to move outside of the immediate family would make duplicating the seed of the deceased brother impossible (not the same parents).

    Boaz and the nearer kinsman were brothers to Elimelech, the deceased husband of Noami. In the denouement, where the goal of the story is revealed, the women of Bethlehem conclude, "A child has been born to Naomi," indicating that the childless widow for whom these brothers were legal redeemers was Naomi. By marrying Ruth, the childless, widowed, daughter-in-law of Naomi, Boaz would be able to bring up a child to Naomi, and thus fulfill his duty as brother to Elimelech. Since Ruth was "one flesh" with Mahlon, the son of Naomi, she was considered to be of the same "inheritance," and as such would bear the child. Of course, this also managed to fulfill the need to perpetuate the line of the deceased Mahlon, through his widow, as well (see 4:10).

17. This word (הנק) is used in 4:4,5(3),8,9,10, and is translated "acquire" or "buy," and is used as the means of implementing the redemption both of Naomi's field and of Ruth as a wife.

18. For instance, when the Christ arrived, Satan first tried to deceive Him (Mt 4:1-11), and then, failing that, killed Him (Mt 27).

19. Eve voiced this expectation in Gn 4:1, when she stated (lit. trans. from the Hb. text), "I have born a man . . . YHWH." This comes from her hope in the promise of Gn 3:15. Refer to the discussion at http://thebiblicalstory.org, "Commentary," Gn 4:1.

20. Refer to John 8:44 where Jesus identified Satan as a murderer. Also see 1Jn 3:12 where Cain is referenced as "of the evil one and murdered his brother."

21. The Hebrew words for "saw," "good," and "took" occur only three times in the OT; here in 1Sm 11:2-4 when David was deceived by Satan, Gn 6:2 when the "sons of God" were deceived, and in Gn 3:1-6 when Eve was deceived.

22. God does pursue the Gentiles, as demonstrated in Gn 12:3 and throughout the OT (see the book of Jonah). However, His main purpose here is due to the relationship of Ruth through the "one flesh" covenant of Gn 2:24.

23. Some, like Stedman (op. cit.), then link human romance to parallel the romance of God with His people. Yet, God's romance of Israel (see Hos 2:14) is based on YHWH's sacrificial mercy toward the hopeless, while human romance is typically based on mutual attraction based on personal attributes.

24. However, her lack of status demonstrated God's character, which was that He would act beneficially to the hopeless.

25. Following Eve's arrival, Adam declared, she is "bone of my bone and flesh of my flesh." There he was expressing that she was identical to him with respect to his inheritance. She was, as he was, "one flesh." They were one, inseparable partners with respect to his inheritance. Peter expressed this to husbands regarding their wives in 1Pt 3:7, telling the husbands to show them "honor as coheirs of the grace of life."

26. This reflects a literal translation of the Hebrew text.

27. While this is generally held to be "man" as in "mankind" (i.e., the law of men), it likely references the husband. Thus having cleaved to his wife, he cannot ever go back.

28. Abraham repeated this attempt to "un-cleave" in Gn 20 by sending Sarah to Abimelech, and again God prevented the "un-cleaving" of Sarah. Isaac did the same with Rebekah in Gn 24, but God again prevented it.

29. In the Sermon on the Mount, God's love is defined by the love that He has for His enemy (Mt 5:44-48). This then is applied in 5:21-48 to one's love of brother, and the love of one's wife. Thus murder and divorce were prohibited since man was to love his brother and his wife even when they became his enemy.

30. God's *chesed* is not the same as men's thinking. That God would give His own Son for God's enemies is not reasonable to man's thinking (e.g., what human would do that? See Rm 5:1-11). Not infrequently the interpreter does not understand *chesed*, and inputs his own value system into the story to explain the motivation for a character's actions. Thus, instead of sacrificial love (i.e., *chesed*) for a hopeless widow, the interpreter errantly assumes she must have had some personal allure and Boaz must have had some self-beneficial romantic desires in mind.

31. It was not that this woman could not have had some physical, or even financial, benefit, but it did not enter into the consideration of *chesed*, and thus the levirate marriage.

32. This is only stating that originally she would have been a follower of Moabite gods. When YHWH brought her to faith is not known, although her confession of 1:16 established that it was at least at the time of her trip to Israel. But that He brought her to faith (1:16) so as to bear His seed is the important issue here.

33. That Naomi implored them to return to the god Chemosh is apparent in 1:15 where she tells Ruth to follow Orpah, who has returned to her people and her god.

34. See Kenneth Barker, "Problems in the Book of Ruth" (ThM thesis, Dallas Theological Seminary, 1960), 41.

35. Ru 2:14-18. The phrase "She ate and was satisfied and had some left over" (2:14) demonstrates covenant blessing by the God of Israel through a covenant implementer on behalf of YHWH. See also Ru 2:18 where the phrase is referenced again. Refer to Dt 6:11, 11:15, 14:29, 23:24, and 26:12 for its covenantal foundation. It is then used in the NT, after Jesus fed the 5,000 in Mt 14:20 and fed the 4,000 in 15:37, to show Jesus as the ultimate implementer of covenant blessing.

36. The events of Ruth are tied to the times of the book of Judges. See also a discussion on the "Bethlehem Trilogy," by Eugene H. Merrill, where Ruth is tied literarily to the last two episodes in the book of Judges: "The Book of Ruth: Narration and Shared Themes," *Bibliotheca Sacra* 142 (April–June 1985): 131–32.

37. Boaz's comment regarding Ruth's visit in the middle of the night demonstrated that her trip to the threshing floor could be perceived as immoral. Therefore, to protect Ruth's reputation, he sent her home under the cover of darkness, and instructed those with him to keep it a secret (3:14).

38. Naomi's language of 3:3, "Wash, put on perfumed oil, and wear your best clothes," indicated that Ruth had been wearing her widow's garments to demonstrate her legal standing within Israel. Naomi told her to appear, not as a mourning widow, but as a physically appealing woman. This story is to be compared to Tamar's in Gn 38:14,19, when Tamar, who had been wearing widow's clothes to establish her right to Shelah, changed them when she wanted to entice Judah. The woman of Tekoa was told by Joab not to change her widow's clothes and not to anoint herself with oil so as to appear to David as one who had been mourning for her only son for a long time (2Sm 14:2). Refer to Charles P. Baylis, "Naomi in the Book of Ruth in Light of the Mosaic Covenant," *Bibliotheca Sacra* 161 (October–December, 2004): 429–30.

39. Naomi was correct when she said there were no more legitimate levirs for Ruth since all her sons (i.e., "brothers" to Mahlon) were dead and she was not able to have any more. What Ruth was stating to Boaz on the threshing floor was that he was qualified as a goel, since he was a "brother" to Elimelech. Thus, he could be a goel to Naomi and bring up a child to her. Ruth was proposing that she, as a childless widow herself, would sacrificially marry Boaz and through her a child would be provided for Naomi. This would also provide a child for her deceased husband (see 4:9-10).

40. What Ruth suggests was *chesed*, for she was proposing that Boaz marry her for Naomi's sake, so that the childless widow, Naomi, would have a child (see the ending, the denouement) of the story which concluded that "a son has been born to Naomi"). Following Ruth's presentation on the threshing floor, Boaz responded that what she was doing was even greater than what she had done when she left her homeland to come and care for Naomi (see his prior assessment in the field in 2:11). Thus, his reaction on the threshing floor was that this was even greater *chesed*, as she was offering to marry a man of an older generation (i.e., brother of Elimelech) for Naomi's sake, so Naomi could have a child through her. That this was a sacrifice for Ruth was evident in their age differences alone. Edward Campbell, Jr. states that Ruth was likely in her later twenties, while Naomi was in her midforties (*Ruth*, Anchor Bible [Garden City, NY: Doubleday, 1975], 67).

41. Michael G. Wechsler comments on the sexual morality of Boaz and Ruth, as follows, "Although some have claimed that uncovering Boaz's feet was a sexual act, there was no hint of immorality here. Boaz greeted her in the name of **the Lord** (3:10), called her **a woman of excellence** (or "virtue," i.e., godly character; 3:11), protected her through the night (3:13), and guarded her reputation in the morning (3:14)" ("Ruth," in *The Moody Bible Commentary*, ed. Michael Rydelnik and Michael G. Vanlaningham [Chicago: Moody Publishers, 2014], 396).

42. Exactly how his inheritance would be threatened is debated. For a discussion on this, refer to Daniel Block, *Judges, Ruth*, comments on Ruth 4:6.

43. This was the requirement of Dt 25:5-10, that if a man rejected his duty as a levir, his name would fall into disrepute. "His family name in Israel will be called, 'The house of the man whose sandal was removed'" (Dt 25:10).

1 Samuel 2:1-10, 35

Hannah's Song of the Messianic King

JAMES F. COAKLEY

The song of Hannah (1Sm 2:1-10) is a significant passage in that it is the first biblical text in the Scriptures to use the term "Messiah" or "His anointed," in v. 10. Hannah was a barren woman and had prayed to the Lord for a son (1Sm 1:10-12). The Lord remembered her (1:19-20) by allowing her to give birth to Samuel. This song is a poetic expression of her joy and contributes to the progressive unveiling of messianic prophecy. This study will seek to delineate how this text advances messianic themes in the Bible.

INITIAL QUESTIONS AND CHALLENGES

Although this passage is often viewed as messianic prophecy, contemporary scholarship is not universally agreed. The main concern is whether the reference to "His anointed" in v. 10 refers only to David[1] or to Messiah or both. Many critical scholars doubt that Hannah could have written this text because of its more militaristic tone (why would a housewife use such terminology?) or that she wrote about a king before there was even kingship in Israel. These concerns will be addressed below. The following presuppositions undergird this study.

PRESUPPOSITIONS

Authorship: This study assumes that 1 and 2 Samuel together represent a unified work, that a single author/editor composed it, and that it was written down sometime after the death of David.[2] Although the identity of the human author cannot be ascertained, 1Sm 2:1-10 is clearly attributed to Hannah. The assumption here is that this song represents her actual words and not the words of a later editor attributing it to her.[3] However, the compiler of the books of Samuel intentionally placed her song in its setting to set the thematic tone for the entire composition. One of the criticisms often raised against Hannah's being the author of this song is that it contains such strong militaristic language, an unexpected characteristic of a woman. This is clearly a specious argument, as previous women in the Scriptures such as Miriam, Deborah, and Jael were well-versed in military language and were associated with songs extolling acts of the Lord's salvation/deliverance (Ex 15, Jdg 5). Even though Israel did not have a king at the time that Hannah composed this song, Hannah was almost certainly aware that military conflict would contribute to a king ascending a throne, so it would not be unexpected for her to include terms and metaphors of warfare.

Authorial intent: Some argue that the Song of Hannah was placed here secondarily because the prayer does not affect the plot of the surrounding narrative in any way. First Samuel 1:28 joins smoothly with 2:11, leaving no evidence of a gap, and, as the argument goes, it is hard for readers to detect the purpose of the song within the overall flow of the narrative.[4] However, the insertion of embedded poetry within narrative texts, as was the Song of Hannah, and the role that such poetic sections have on the surrounding narrative text, actually add to the messianic thrust of this passage.

Although it is popular to view the Song of Hannah as anachronistic, since Israel did not have a king when she composed it, nevertheless, the song of Hannah could have been written before kingship in Israel, and would thus be prophetic. Moreover, this text contains predictive prophecy not just about a future king but also regarding the Messiah. It appears that Hannah was well versed in the Torah regarding the future office of kingship (Dt 17:15), that both Abraham (Gn 17:6,16) and Jacob (Gn 35:11) were told that kings would come forth from them, and that there were already prophecies regarding the tribe of Judah and the messianic king (Gn 49:10; Nm 24:17-19).

Genre: First Samuel 2:1-10 is presented as a prayer, as v. 1 indicates, yet it is commonly labeled as the "Song of Hannah" because of its poetic qualities and similarities to other ancient OT hymns (e.g., the Song of the Sea, Ex 15:1-18, 21; the Song of Moses, Dt 32:1-43; and the Song of Deborah, Jdg 5). As such, this article will refer to this passage as the "Song of Hannah" rather than the "Prayer of Hannah." That it is lyrical speech and not just standard narrative adds to the heightened quality and importance of this passage within the wider context. Because the song does not advance the plot of the surrounding narrative, that indicates it was intentionally placed here for other reasons. This poetic genre helps to emphasize the theme of the book and may be another subtle reason for its messianic content.

STRUCTURAL AND CONTEXTUAL ANALYSIS

A careful contextual, exegetical study of 1Sm 2 will reveal its key role in the books of Samuel as well as its messianic overtones.

The Song of Hannah is significant structurally in several ways. As VanGemeren notes, the song

> provides the interpretive framework for the two books of Samuel. The books begin with the ministry of Samuel and climax with King David's expectations of God's fidelity to the covenant with him and his descendants. Hannah's song expresses (1) confidence in God, the Rock of Israel; (2) hope in the Lord's victory over Israel's enemies; (3) hope in the restoration of the fortunes of His people; (4) hope in the establishment of His kingdom on earth; and (5) an allusion to the anointed (messiah) of the Lord.[5]

The Song of Hannah plays a key role in developing the themes of the books of Samuel. Often, early on in a biblical book the author/compiler places a seminal text to introduce its major themes.[6] Threads of many of the leading themes of the books of Samuel, as well as events and key characters, are introduced in this song to process those themes, events, and characters in preparation for their appearance later in the work. This convention advances the author's didactic goals in composing the book, and also enhances the reader's understanding of it. Here are some examples of how the song proleptically prepares the reader for later content:

1. That *proud and arrogant boasts* (1Sm 2:3) should not come out of anyone's mouth anticipates Goliath's taunts (1Sm 17:43-44) before his downfall. The statement that "the Lord is a God of knowledge" (1Sm 2:3) is preparatory for Samuel selecting David over Eliab since "Man does not see what the Lord sees, for man sees what is visible, but the Lord sees the heart" (1Sm 16:7).
2. That the *bows of the warriors* in Hannah's song (2:4) are broken and useless anticipates David's lament of the bow in 2Sm 1:18. It is more than coincidental that the books of Samuel are framed by songs with similar themes at the beginning and end of the composition (1Sm 2:1-10 and 2Sm 22) and that David's "Song of the Bow" is placed in the center of the book in 2Sm 1:17-27.
3. *The barren woman* who gives birth to seven (2:5) anticipates Hanna's fertility after her barrenness (2:21).[7] On the flip side "the woman with many sons

pines away" (2:5) is pictured by a later event when women from Saul's household (Rizpah and Merab) lost seven sons as punishment for Saul's treatment of the Gibeonites (2Sm 21).

4. The *raising of the dead*, seen in the statement that the Lord "sends some down to Sheol, and he raises others up" (2:6) anticipates the unusual encounter between Saul and the medium at Endor (1Sm 28) where Samuel comes back from the grave in spirit form to chastise Saul.[8]

5. The Lord's *humbling and exalting* (2:7) could very well be the thematic center of the books of Samuel. He exalts Saul but then humbles him after he is unfaithful. He exalts faithful David but then humbles him after his sin with Bathsheba.

6. The reference to the Lord's "*thunder* in the heavens" (2:10) foreshadows several future accounts in the book when the Lord thundered loudly. First, He thundered (7:10) against the Philistine army, throwing them into confusion. Second, in 1Sm 12:16-18, the Lord sent thunder and rain as punishment for the evil of requesting a king for themselves. Third, the Song of David mentions that the "LORD thundered from heaven" (2Sm 22:14).

Two additional themes from the song that are crucial to the books of Samuel are the references to kingship and the Lord's anointed (2:10). These themes will be discussed in detail later in this study.

INTEXTUAL INTERPRETATION

This article will not provide a detailed exposition of each line of the Song of Hannah but will instead focus on the following portions of the passage that lay the groundwork for viewing this text as one containing messianic prophecy:

1. *Hannah's adoration of the Lord (2:1)*

Hannah's poetic prayer was personal: "my heart," "my horn," "my mouth." It is the only verse that contains first-person pronouns in the passage. Even though her baby Samuel was the answer to her prayer, it was the Lord who was the focal point of her adoration and praise. It was the Lord who delivered her from her enemies (presumably including Peninnah, the rival wife of her husband Elkanah who regularly and severely taunted her, 1:6-7). This use of heightened combative language ("enemies") and salvific terms ("salvation") reveals that Hannah was already beginning to project her own personal experience onto a grander, broader scheme beyond herself. That her words are composed in poetic style rather than straightforward narrative prose allows her highly emotive, metaphor-laden vocabulary to prepare the reader for its rich content. This opening verse lays the groundwork, and then the poem crescendos toward a messianic prophecy at its end.

2. *Hannah's acclamations about the Lord (2:2-8)*
Hannah moves from her personal emotive response in v. 1 to a majestic expositional description of the Lord's attributes. She begins by extolling the Lord's incomparable holiness (v. 2) but then invokes a metaphor that demonstrates deep engagement with the Torah by stating there is no "rock" like our God. This mirrors Moses' words in a similar poetic form in Dt 32:4,15,31, a passage also containing messianic themes. For example, 1Sm 2:6 says, "The Lord brings death and gives life, He sends some to Sheol, and He raises others up," seeming to invoke a "death and resurrection" theme into the song. There are a number of reversals in this passage (e.g., v. 5), but the notion of power resurrecting life from the grave gives a heightened example of the Lord's incomparable power and sovereignty. This passage uses the same "death and resurrection" theme from another poetic messianic passage in Dt 32 (vv. 26,39). Certainly in Hannah's experience her "dead" womb was brought to life with the conception and birth of Samuel. The "throne of honor" in v. 8 draws upon kingship imagery, which coupled with the notion of the Lord's power as a creator in the same verse, powerfully combines messianic overtones.

3. *Hannah's anticipation about the Lord (2:9-10)*
The climax of the poem is the second half of v. 10: "The Lord will judge the ends of the earth. He will give power to His king; He will lift up the horn of His anointed." Much scholarly discussion has centered on Hannah's use of the terms "king" and "anointed" (Hb. *melek* and *meshiach*) in her prayer. One exegetical question is whether or not this is synonymous parallelism where "His king" is totally equivalent to "His anointed" in the second line. This makes a difference if it is an example of pure synonymous parallelism (the two lines are referencing the same subject), so that it might be that "his anointed" (Hb. *meshiach*) might only be referring to David. One might contend that there is dual fulfillment here in that "king" and "His anointed" refer to both King David and Messiah, as has been maintained in the use of "anointed" in the Song of David (2Sm 22:51). However, Sailhamer has made a strong case that in 2Sm 22:51 "his anointed" does not refer to king David but to the Messiah—based on the evidence in the Septuagint and Vulgate and the internal secondary characteristics of the Masoretic text's reading.[9] If his argument is correct, it would mirror what is happening in in the Song of Hannah: The line "He will

give power to His king" would refer solely to David, and the second line "He will lift up the horn of His anointed" would refer to the Messiah and not to King David.

1 Samuel 2:35

Although 1Sm 2:35 is not a part of the Song of Hannah, it is helpful to discuss that text here in light of the messianic overtones of this chapter. It reads "Then I will raise up a faithful priest for Myself. He will do whatever is in My heart and mind. I will establish a lasting dynasty for him, and he will walk before My anointed one for all time." The promise of a faithful priest falls on the heels of God's judgment on three unfaithful priests (Eli, Hophni, and Phinehas) who would die on the same day (2:34; 4:11,18). So, based on context, to whom would the "faithful priest" refer? Samuel, although he functioned as a priest, did not have a lasting dynasty, ruling him out. Zadok is another option, since 1Kg 2:27 states that "Solomon banished Abiathar from being the Lord's priest" in fulfillment of what was prophesied to Eli at Shiloh—and in 1Kg 2:35 Solomon appointed Zadok.

The same pairing of a reference to the Lord's person and work along with judgment on evildoers, used in 1Sm 2:9-10, is also used in 1Sm 2:34-35. Earlier in the chapter, the focus was on kingship, but here it is on the priesthood. Both texts stress that the Lord would continue working to fulfill a messianic vision. Here it is done by the raising up of a faithful priest who would typify a messianic type high priest to come. Kaiser notes that the word "faithful" is "*ne'eman*—the same word (with a slight variation) used of David's dynasty in 2 Samuel 7:16, whose 'house and kingdom *will endure* . . . forever.' In 1 Samuel 25:28, the word is used again of David's dynasty, that it will be a '*lasting* dynasty.' Thus, the house of the coming priest will be secure, firmly established, and reliable."[10] While Zadok may have been the initial fulfillment of this prophecy of 1Sm 2:35, the author of Hebrews (2:17) uses the phrase "faithful high priest" in reference to the Messiah Jesus as the ultimate fulfilment.

INNERTEXTUAL INTERPRETATION

Many scholars have seen the connection between the Song of Hannah and the Song of David because there are many lexical and thematic links between the two, as can be seen in the chart below. There is hardly one word used in the Song of Hannah that is not repeated in the Song of David (2Sm 22).

Lexical Similarity between 1 Samuel 2:1-10 and 2 Samuel 22

	1Sm 2	2Sm 22
lifted *rwm*	1, 7, 10	28, 47, 49
Horn *qeren*	1, 10	3
Mouth *peh*	1	9
boasts *rhb*	1	20, 37
Enemy *oyeb*	1	4, 18, 38, 41, 49
Save *ys'*	1	3 (3x), 4, 28, 36, 42, 47, 51
Rock *sur*	2	2, 32, 47 (2x)
Boast/make great *rbh*	3	36
Come out *ys'*	3	20, 49
God 'el	3	31, 32, 33, 48
Bow *qeset*	4	35
Warriors/mighty *gibbor*	4	26
Clothed *'zr*	4	40
Strength *hayil*	4	33, 40
Death, kill *mwt*	6	5, 6
Life *hyh*	6	47
Bring down *yrd*	6	48
Sheol *se'ol*	6	6
raises up *'lh*	6	9
humbles *spl*	7	28
exalts *qwm*	7	39, 40, 49
Dust *'pr*	8	43
set *syt*	8	12
World *tebel*	8	16
Guard *smr*	9	22, 24, 44
Steps/foot *regel*	9	10, 34, 39
Faithful *hsd*	9	26 (2x), 51
Wicked *rs'*	9	22
Darkness *hosek*	9	12, 29
man *'ish*	9	49
oppose *rybw*	10	44
Heavens *shamayim*	10	8, 10, 14
Thunder *r'm*	10	14
Earth *eres*	10	8, 43
Gives *ntn*	10	14, 36, 41, 48
Power *'z*	10	18
His king *melek*	10	51
His anointed *masiah*	10	51

While there are many common elements between both texts[11] such as firm trust in the Lord, the ineffectual powers of man, and reward and justice in this world, what are often missed are the messianic overtones of both of these songs. Weitzman observes that the interpolation of the Song of Hannah and the Song of David was perhaps an attempt to restructure the narrative of Samuel in imitation of the Pentateuch, which also features songs at key points.[12]

I have argued elsewhere that the major poems of the Pentateuch insert key information about the coming Messiah within those songs and that Moses crafted the Pentateuch with these forward-looking poetic pieces to provide an emphasis on the future Messiah.[13] It is the same case here with the songs in the books of Samuel. This characteristic is proven by the thematic linkage between both of these songs in Samuel with Dt 32 (i.e. God as "Rock" Dt 32:4; 1Sm 2:2; 2Sm 22:2,47). The song of Hannah in tandem with the Song of David might play a similar role that the song of the Sea (Ex 15) has with the Song of Moses (Dt 32–33). The song of Miriam (another woman[14]) in Ex 15 works in tandem with the Song of Moses (Dt 32–33), with both containing praise for God's salvation over enemies (Ex 15:1-4; 1Sm 2:1). These are bracketed at the end of the composition with praise for the Lord from a key messianic type leader (Dt 31:30; 32:3; 33:26-29; 34:10; 2Sm 22:1,47-51), and both contain messianic themes and prophecy (Dt 32:10; 2Sm 22:51).[15] Just as Miriam's song is prophetic in its anticipation of Israel's entering the promised land and its notion that the Lord will "reign forever and ever" (Ex 15:18), Hannah's song is prophetic in that it anticipates a king for Israel and the Messiah ("his anointed" 1Sm 2:10).

INNERTEXTUAL THEMES

Besides the shared messianic themes of the Song of Hannah and the Song of David (1Sm 2:10; 2Sm 22:51) there are other themes in Hannah's song, developed in the larger corpus of the books of Samuel:

Horn: In one sense the entire Song of Hannah is about a raised horn, as this theme bookends the whole poetic inset (2:1;10). The raised horn of an animal represents its power and splendor (Dt 33:17). Not only was the horn a symbol of strength, but it also was typically used as the container to store the oil for anointing the king. Intriguingly Samuel used a horn (Hb. *qeren*) of oil to anoint David (1Sm 16:1,13) but used a flask (Hb. *pak*) to anoint Saul (1Sm 10:1). The development of the horn theme progresses from the Lord's power to lift up the lowly Hannah's humble horn by allowing her to bear a son and crescendos to the Lord's elevation of the king of Israel and the horn of His Anointed v. 10.

Rock: The term "rock" (1Sm 2:2) was repeatedly used by Moses earlier in his song (Dt 32:4,15,31) and thus became a common metaphor for God. Hannah and David (2Sm 22:2-4,32) both used this term in their songs. Since all three of these songs have messianic overtones, it is understandable that several NT writers attach this term to the Messiah (Mt 16:18; 1Co 10:4)

Kingship: Hannah's Song clearly predicts a king for Israel in the statement "He will give power to His king" (2:10) and in the mention of a "throne" (2:8). Of course, Hannah at this point does not know who this king will be, but the previous canonical book of Judges had prepared readers for a king with statements such as, "In those days there was no king in Israel" (Jdg 21:25). The connections of this song to the song of King David in 2Sm 22 have been discussed above. Both of these songs extol kingship and frame the entire corpus of the books of Samuel. Therefore, kingship is a strong theme not just for the Song of Hannah but for the entire book. Even Samuel's birth narrative (1Sm 1) can be seen as preparatory for the beginning of kingship in Israel and a subtle indication that kingship is a major thematic purpose for this book. Hannah's desire for a son (1Sm 1) is matched by Israel's desire for a king (1Sm 8), even if their motive is selfish. Hannah points the way by trusting in the Lord as a "God of knowledge" (2:3) and praying that He will exalt (2:7,10) the king. The king in Hannah's Song is certainly idealized in line with previous royal messianic prophecies, such as Gn 49:10, in which Jacob predicted that the scepter would not depart from Judah, and Nm 24:17, which prophesied that a "star will come from Jacob, and a scepter will arise from Israel" who would strike down the enemies of God's people. In the progressive development of this emerging messianic king, Hannah predicted the exaltation of another anointed Messiah.

INTERTEXTUAL INTERPRETATION

Many have noticed the similarity of the Song of Hannah to Mary's Magnificat (Lk 1:46-55). For instance, in Lk 1:48 Mary says "because He has looked with favor on the humble condition of His slave." The Greek word used for "humble condition" (*tapeinosis*) is the same lexeme used in the Septuagint version of 1Sm 1:11 when Hannah vowed: "if You will take notice of Your servant's affliction" (*tapeinosis*). Both songs are written by women who have been marginalized but who craft a song about the miraculous birth of their son. In both songs: (1) the mother names the child (Lk 1:31,60; 1Sm 1:20); (2) The child is brought to the tabernacle/temple to be blessed (Lk 2:22-35; 1Sm 1:24-25; 2:20;[16] (3) Each child is described by two statements about their maturation process using similar language (Lk 2:40,52; 1Sm 2:21,26).

The close lexical and thematic affinity between the Magnificat of Mary and the

Song of Hannah suggests that the writers of the NT considered Hannah's song to be predictive prophetic references to the Messiah Jesus and His person and work. In addition, the Song of Mary, which echoes the song of Hannah, becomes the source for Luke's portrayal of Jesus. Further, in similar fashion, it is placed "early on" in the composition to lay the foundation for several key themes to be expanded upon later.

CONCLUSION

The Song of Hannah and 1Sm 2:35 are strong messianic prophecies. This is the first time that the Hebrew term underlying the title Messiah ("His anointed" in 2:10) is used in a nominal manner in conjunction with Israel's kingship. Prior to this, the term "anointed" had been used only in connection with the priesthood (Lv 4:3,5,16; 6:22). Hannah's song is in the same stream of other key poetic messianic prophecies that precede it (Gn 49; Ex 15; Nm 23–24; Dt 32–34). It expands upon the theme of Dt 32, which concluded the Pentateuch noting the nation of Israel's rebellion and restoration using "death and resurrection" language (Dt 32:26,39) to establish the Lord's greatness and power. Hannah does the same in her song using the same "death and resurrection" language in the pivotal center of her poem (1Sm 2:6) to sing the Lord's praises after her "dead" womb was brought to life to bear the first kingmaker for the nation Israel. When Hannah predicted that the Lord would give strength to His king, David was the one she foretold. But the ultimate referent of "his anointed" in 1Sm 2:10 is the Messiah who will one day "judge the ends of the earth" and rule over a glorious kingdom forever (Lk 1:32-33,69). Neely sums up the importance of this text as it relates to messianic prophecy: "Hannah's words point prophetically not merely to the Davidic dynasty, but also to David's greatest son, the Lord Jesus the Messiah."[17]

---

1. For instance, Rose states "I find it difficult to consider the end of Hannah's song (1Sm 2:10) as belonging to the so-called messianic expectations . . . The two psalms in the last two chapters of 2 Samuel (2Sm 22:2-51; 23:1-7) refer back to Hannah's song in the beginning of 1 Samuel, and this is done in such a way that the writer makes it clear to his readers that David is the one who has fulfilled the expectations expressed in Hannah's song" ("Messianic Expectations in the Old Testament," *In die Skriflig* 35, no. 2 [2001]: 282).
2. There is a clue within the book of Samuel itself that it was compiled sometime after the split of the kingdom, for 1Sm 27:6 states, "That day Achish gave Ziklag to him, and it still belongs to the kings of Judah today." This could have been stated only after Solomon's death, unless the comment was inserted much later by an inspired editor.
3. There is honest debate over when Hannah crafted this poetic prayer. Did she write it soon after the birth of Samuel, or even earlier after her encounter with Eli at the tabernacle in Shiloh? Or did she compose it much later after she had more children, as the text states that she had three more sons and two daughters (1Sm 2:21)?

4. James W. Watts summarizes much of the evidence used to defend a secondary insertion, see Hannah's Song (1Sm 2:1-10), "*Psalm and Story: Inset Hymns in Hebrew Narrative*," ed. James W. Watts (Sheffield: Sheffield Academic Press, 1992), 32–33.

5. Willem VanGemeren, *The Progress of Redemption: The Story of Salvation from Creation to the New Jerusalem* (Grand Rapids: Zondervan, 1988), chap 15.

6. For instance, the Cain and Abel story in Gn 4 introduces the theme of sibling rivalry in Genesis, and Pss 1–2 are intentionally placed up front in the psalter to introduce the themes of "read the word" and "kiss the Son." Isaiah 1:1–2:4 introduces a number of key themes that are expanded on later in the book. I call this phenomenon "early on" in that biblical authors "early on" in their books introduce in seminal form themes that will be expanded and developed later. These have the effect of functioning as tables of contents or thesis statements do in our modern way of writing.

7. Regarding the discrepancy between seven children of 2:5 versus Hannah's six (2:21), Sternberg is correct in stating the genre differences between the two verses and noting that "divergences from the prose version find their coherence in the laws of the genre: formal constraints, poetic license, stylized expression, the language of symbols or morals. It makes no sense, therefore, to ask why Hannah sings of the barren woman bearing seven children while she herself bore only six" (M. Sternberg, *The Politics of Biblical Narrative* [Bloomington: Indiana University Press, 1987], 246–47).

8. Radday suggests that the Hebrew names Sheol, Saul, and Samuel may represent an intentional word play on the Hebrew root s'l (to ask) since that is a prominent word in the story of Samuel's birth in 1Sm 1:20, 27 (Yhuda T. Radday, "Chiasm in Samuel," *Liguistica Biblica* 9/10 [1973]: 28).

9. J. H. Sailhamer, *Introduction to Old Testament Theology: A Canonical Approach* (Grand Rapids: Zondervan, 1995) 221.

10. Walter Kaiser, *The Messiah in the Old Testament* (Grand Rapids: Zondervan, 1995), 74–75.

11. Radday states that their "difference in length is sufficiently warranted by the difference in social status of the speakers and in function: one is meant to be an anticipatory prologue, the other a recapitulative epilogue" (Radday, "Chiasm in Samuel," 31).

12. Steven Weitzman, *Song and Story in Biblical Narrative: The History of a Literary Convention in Ancient Israel* (Bloomington: Indiana University Press, 1997), 121.

13. James Coakley, "Deuteronomy" in *The Moody Bible Commentary*, ed. Michael Rydelnik and Michael G. Vanlaningham (Chicago: Moody Publishers, 2014), 308. The chart of the Pentateuch on p. 250 shows how all the major poems in the Pentateuch are strategically placed to foreground the coming Messiah.

14. Watts observes that "out of the nine psalms in narrative contexts in the Hebrew Bible, three are sung by women either in whole or in part: Ex 15, Jdg 5, 1Sm 2. All three are victory hymns. Of the six psalms in narrative contexts sung only by men, none are victory hymns, though some contain victory themes (e.g. 2Sm 22)," (Watts, "Hannah's Song," 29).

15. See note 9.

16. Intriguingly Jesus' parents meet "Anna," an aged prophetess who served God and did not leave the temple complex (Lk 2:36-38). Anna is the Greek form of the Hebrew Hannah. First Samuel 2:22 mentions women who served at the entrance to the tent of meeting, but it is sad that Eli's sons were sleeping with these women.

17. Winfred Neely, "1 Samuel," in *The Moody Bible Commentary*, 406.

1 Samuel 17

David: A Messianic Prototype

JAMES E. ALLMAN

Story is essential to Christianity. Without story we would have no faith, for our faith rests on the persons and deeds recorded in Scripture, preeminently in the person of Jesus Christ. But the story of Jesus comes in the middle of the times, 2,000 years after Abraham and 2,000 years prior to our own day. So a lot of story occurred before the days of Jesus. Nearly 50 percent of the OT is story (omitting the narratives in the prophets), and almost 60 percent of the NT is narrative. Our faith depends on story! These observations require Bible students to become connoisseurs of story. If we are to "humbly receive the implanted word, which is able to save" us (Jms 1:21), we must know how to discern the meaning of stories. Here we must say enough about studying story to lay a foundation for understanding the contribution of 1Sm 17 to our understanding of messianic prophecy.

HOW STORY WORKS

Stories ought to recount things that are important (as contrasted with the stories that five-year-olds tell). They recount the author's perception of reality, morality, or values. Reading a story properly allows the reader to comprehend the author's point of view. For works apart from the Bible, readers then face the necessity of choosing whether to adopt or reject the author's point of view. Readers face the same choice in reading the Bible's stories, but with a predicament. The Bible is the Word of God, not the word of man, which the reader is embracing or rejecting. It confronts, and demands a decision from, the reader.

But how shall we understand the message of the story? Authors signal the direction of the story by repetition—of themes, events, similar characters—so that attentive readers pick up clues throughout the story about what is coming, preparing for a sound understanding of the story. So as one reads, one should watch for earlier events reflected in later ones. The aim is not to reinterpret the earlier events by the later ones; it is to remember the story, assuming the author has chosen characters, events, and settings, and arranged them intentionally to assist the reader in making sense of the story. So a well-crafted narrative is full of patterns.

Writers use repetition to highlight what is most important in the story, either by reflection of previous events or by contrast. Thus, in the stories of King Saul and David, Saul's life is a foil for David's. As Saul degenerates, David becomes more and more powerful. But there are more explicit repetitions, for example, Saul's attempts to kill David (cf. 1Sm 18:10-11,12-19,20-29; 19; [20:28-34; 22:11-19;] 23:1-14,19-28; etc.), or David's opportunities (which he rejects) to kill Saul (24; 26). Another form of repetition is by repeating plots.

Stories speak with, not about, character, and they often reveal character by plot. Plot is the orderly arrangement of events that allows writers to communicate their view of reality, morality, or values. Furthermore, a story's plot often contains conflict. It can be a challenge to create compelling stories about happy times, so most stories are about difficulties that protagonists face and how they overcome them.[1] The conflict often represents a test for the protagonist, whose views of reality, morality, or values are questioned. The way the story ends is the writer's comment on the adequacy of the protagonist's philosophy of life, shown by the way the character confronts the problem. An example may be helpful.

STORY OF KING SAUL

King Saul began his reign so well. Though some despised him initially ("How can this guy save us?" 1Sm 10:27), he kept quiet. But Israel wanted a king to "judge us, go out before us, and fight our battles" (8:20). The opportunity came very quickly. In 1Sm 11, the Ammonites attacked Jabesh Gilead. Saul's victory there confirmed him as God's chosen king. So convincing was the victory that people wanted those who despised Saul executed. But in good kingly fashion, King Saul refused to execute people "for today the Lord has provided deliverance in Israel" (1Sm 11:13). All of this has been what narratologists call "exposition."[2]

The real conflict in Saul's story comes at two points, first in chap. 13, at Gilgal, and then in chap. 15, the war with Amalek. Is Saul the kind of king who can administer the reign of God on earth? The two events demonstrate Saul's philosophy of rule, and by it, his unfitness to be king. When taken together with Saul's treatment of Jonathan in chap. 20, Saul's approach to the kingship is clear. Realizing that Jonathan is protecting David, Saul said, "You son of a perverse and rebellious woman! Don't I know that you are siding with Jesse's son to your own shame and to the disgrace of your mother? Every day Jesse's son lives on earth you and your kingship are not secure. Now send for him and bring him to me—he deserves to die" (30-31). Saul's basic assumption was that the kingdom belonged to him and he would give it as he pleased, without reference to God's will. His madness did not cause this turn in his character. It revealed it.

Chapter 31 forms the resolution of the story.[3] After the climax at the house of the medium in Endor (chap. 28) and an interlude showing David's victory over the Amalekites (chap. 30[4]), the story resolves in the death of Saul and his sons. The author has now commented on the illegitimacy of Saul's philosophy of rule. It was wrong-headed and would lead to disaster. Saul's approach contrasts markedly with David's philosophy of life, and the disparity with David could not be more stark. David's life demonstrated that he believed the kingdom was God's and that he was God's servant. But by the end of David's life, his philosophy of life became similar to Saul's. Civil wars and the deaths of his most prominent sons form the end of his story in 2Sm.

Why should his story line end so tragically? Because, at one crucial period of his life he acted as if he thought he really was the king and not God's servant: "In the spring when kings march out to war, David sent Joab with his officers and all Israel" (2Sm 11:1).[5] Kings are war leaders. But David stayed in Jerusalem. The two plots reflect each other, but they also contrast. David was genuinely repentant: he pleaded for no mercy from God, accepting merely what God would require. Contrast Saul who pleaded for honor before his army.

PATTERNING IN STORIES—TYPOLOGY

A literary friend once objected that reality is rarely as neat as a well-crafted story. But it is the eye of the artist that finds the patterns and alerts us to the beauty in the subject. And it is the eye of the narrator that guides the reader to discern the patterns in events. More to the point, it is the ministry of the Holy Spirit that allowed the inspired writers of Scripture to perceive the patterns in what God had been doing to alert us as children of God to them. By seeing what God has done in the past, we come to understand how to respond to God in our present and future. The past is the key to the future because God is the preeminent artist. He implanted beauty in His world, not only in the marvel of the created order, but also in the spectacle of history.

Within Scripture itself we learn that God's actions in the past model for us what He will do in the future. But there is a caveat: He is too creative to do the same thing *the same way* twice. The models are themselves promises embedded in history and revealed by the Scripture writers. This approach represents a departure from an earlier attitude about typology. Some have held that we cannot even recognize a type until its antitype (the reality to which it points) comes into history. Our discussion to this point intimates that such a view overlooks the use of typology within the OT itself. The prophetic authors assume that their readers will understand the forward-pointing nature of the history and will read their accounts of Israel's past to enlighten themselves about the future and prepare to respond to God in faith. Faith is rooted in the past, but it is focused on the future. And while the historical books are rooted in the events of Israel's past, they are written for the future. The point here is that when the biblical writers wrote, they were instructing their readers about how to live for the future, following patterns of relationship to God that are revealed in their historical accounts.[6]

God has been building history since the beginning. His aim is to assist people in their faith, so He has embedded repeated patterns in history from creation. One pattern may suffice to understand this. On one occasion God had a people whom He wanted to have life and serve Him, but a great body of water opposed them. There they would have to die. So God parted the water and caused dry land to appear. The most obvious event that comes to mind is the crossing of the Red Sea. But this pattern actually started with the creation story. The pattern of God's work in the past provided a setting for Israel to see His plan and trust Him. But that was not the end of it. For they faced the same pattern again at the crossing of the Jordan,[7] and even that was not the end. Isaiah 41:17-20 begins the use of the exodus theme that continues in 42:14-16 as well as 43:1-4 and 16-21 (cf. Jer 16:14-15 and 23:7-8).[8] God taught Moses, and Moses taught the prophets, to think about the patterns of history as revealing His plans for the future.

THE BOOKS OF SAMUEL

The books of Samuel are messianic: they focus on three anointed figures: Eli, Saul, and David. Inasmuch as the Hebrew word for anointed is *mashiach*, in a sense these books teach about messiah, what a messiah is and how one should respond to a messiah. In turn, these establish the basis for the Messiah, the special anointed eschatological King of the house of David. Two poetic passages are essential to ground this claim, 1Sm 2 and 2Sm 22–23. It is a bit disconcerting for Western readers to read a book that purports to be history and immediately confront poetry, but the author of the books used the poetry to summarize the message.[9] The passages reveal that the story revolves around the term "messiah" ("anointed") (1Sm 2:10, cf. also v. 35; 2Sm 22:51; 23:1; the Hb. terms *mashach,* to anoint, and *mashiach* occur 31 times in these books). Saul serves as the negative example (see 1Sm 15:1,17) and David as the positive.

David serves positively in two ways: as the model king against whom all others are judged, but also as the model of how one should relate to God's messiah. David faced a dilemma that no other messiah in Israel's history ever faced: the presence of two messiahs among the people at the same time. But he passed the test, for he was careful about the sacrosanct character of God's king. He had Saul in his power in a cave at En-gedi, and his men said,

> "Look, this is the day the Lord told you about: 'I will hand your enemy over to you so you can do to him whatever you desire.' Then David got up and secretly cut off the corner of Saul's robe. Afterward, David's conscience bothered him because he had cut off the corner of Saul's robe. He said to his men, 'I swear before the Lord: I would never do such a thing to my lord, the Lord's anointed. I will never lift my hand against him, since he is the Lord's anointed'" (1Sm 24:4-6).

Even cutting off the corner of the messiah's robe was too much for him. As we have seen, what is negative in David's story comes when he comes nearest forgetting about his status as messiah. So both the successes and failures in the book of Samuel enlighten us about the nature of a messiah.

Furthermore, both Saul's and David's stories point beyond themselves to a future in which messiah will play a key role. Since Gn 49, it has been evident that God planned for a king: "The scepter will not depart from Judah or the staff from between his feet until He whose right it is comes and the obedience of the peoples belongs to Him" (49:10; cf. Nm 24:17). Second Samuel furthers this theme. In chap. 7 God grants to David a covenant, a house for the would-be house builder (2Sm 7:11-16):

> The Lord declares to you: The Lord Himself will make a house for you. When your time comes and you rest with your fathers, I will raise up after you your descendant, who will come from your body, and I will establish his kingdom. He will build a house for My name, and I will establish the throne of his kingdom forever. I will be a father to him, and he will be a son to Me. When he does wrong, I will discipline him with a human rod and with blows from others. But My faithful love will never leave him as I removed it from Saul; I removed him from your way. Your house and kingdom will endure before Me forever, and your throne will be established forever.

One of two possibilities must occur to fulfill this covenant promise. One option is that David must have an unending line of descendants, all of whom follow his example of covenant loyalty. The history of the line, even beginning with David, suggests that there is no hope in that direction. The other possibility is that David will eventually have an heir who can continue forever. Thus the very promise to David as an anointed one entails messianic prophecy and fulfillment. So we may conclude that the narrative patterning already established in the OT causes us to anticipate a messiah on the model of David (cf. 1Sm 2:35).

THE STORY OF DAVID AND GOLIATH

The immediate setting of 1Sm 17. With this background we may turn to the story of David and Goliath (1Sm 17). The main point that we are making in this study is that the very plot line of 1Sm 17 sets a pattern that the author intended to point to the future. For Israel and the ancient Near East, kings were war leaders; even more, war was essential to the economy. No one can create gold or silver, or land. Thus, if a king wished to maintain his status, he needed gifts to give his supporters, and war provided for that. So at least part of Israel's plea to Samuel to give them a king may have been the infrequency of war (and especially victory, in their recent past).

When God identified Saul as His response to their request, some doubted his ability (1Sm 10:27). But God proved the rightness of His choice in the very next chapter by giving Israel under Saul victory at Jabesh Gilead. Chapter 17, the story of David and Goliath, fills the same role in the book. David was the youngest son of Jesse, the one overlooked when Samuel came to Bethlehem to make sacrifice. It is possible that David did not hold a high place of esteem with the family. Certainly Eliab showed little respect for him (17:28). Perhaps even his parents did not value him highly (see Ps 27:10). His three oldest brothers all looked the part of a king in Samuel's eyes (but so had Saul). So it may have been a shock both to Samuel and to Jesse that God chose David ("Can any good thing come from . . .").

Are kings made of such stuff? Chapter 17 answers that question decisively. As Saul had proven his divine election to be king by bringing victory in battle, so will David. The chapter is therefore essential to the narrative. For Israel it is the first evidence that God has a new king. The story is not just good narrative. It is thematically at the core of the book of Samuel.

The plot structure of the story. Like any good story, 1Sm 17 has a plot structure, but it is complex.[10] The opening of the passage (vv. 1-3) introduces the setting in southwest Judah and the supporting cast, the armies of Israel and Philistia.

The first plot line (vv. 1-11). Verse 4 starts the inciting moment, the point in the story where the conflict begins. At this stage, the protagonist of the story is the army of Israel, but it is an Israel that is technologically weak (13:19-22). The Philistines had reserved for themselves a monopoly on iron working. So the story starts on a negative note straightaway.

But another obstacle arises: Goliath. The Bible rarely gives physical descriptions of its characters; it leaves their appearance to our imagination. But not so with Goliath. Youngblood,[11] referring to an article by Boogart, surmises that this may be the longest description of any character in the entire Bible. We do not even get this much for David. The time is well spent, however, for the description helps to increase the narrative tension. Whether we conclude with the Hebrew Bible that Goliath was 8 ft. 7 in. tall,[12] or with the Septuagint that he was 6 ft. 9 in,[13] he was an unusually powerful warrior armed with fierce and potent weapons. We must remember that Saul was taller, head and shoulders, than anyone in Israel, but Goliath would have been taller than Saul.

In the eighth verse, Goliath opens his challenge to Israel. If the Philistines were indeed from Crete, there would likely be a long tradition of offering single combat in place of the general carnage of war. Goliath offers single combat, but the very offer brought terror to the ranks. "When Saul and all Israel heard these words from the Philistine, they lost their courage and were terrified" (v. 11). The Hb. text may be slightly more specific. The verb at the beginning of the verse is singular: "And Saul heard, together with all Israel, and they trembled." It is not merely that they all trembled. It was that Saul himself did. The first conflict now takes on an even more ominous form. It is not a conflict between Israel and Philistia alone: it is a conflict between "the warrior" in Philistia and "the warrior" in Israel.[14] Critical to the meaning of this passage are the last two verbs of v. 11: "they lost their courage and were terrified" (*chatat* and *yare'*), verbs that virtually frame the book of Deuteronomy (Dt 1:21; 31:8) and express the converse of faith. They show that Israel does not trust the Lord to fight for them.

The second plot line (vv. 12-27). It is only with v. 12 that David enters the story, and he does not look like much of a solution to Israel's difficulties. However, his entry on the scene constitutes a new exposition that runs through v. 22. A conflict begins in v. 23: "suddenly the champion named Goliath, the Philistine from Gath, came forward from the Philistine battle line and shouted his usual words, which David heard." Since almost nothing has come to light about David's character, this passage becomes an important step in the development of the book. We will learn what kind of person will be the king of God's choice. We also note that the plot has no resolution; no "difference-maker"[15] has arisen. The first plot line also remains unresolved.

The third plot line (vv. 28-30). Matters develop quickly from this point. In v. 28

Eliab reacted as one would expect an older brother to do. Yet he surely knew what had happened when Samuel went to Bethlehem. But it may be that that event only increased Eliab's impatience with David. God passed by the eldest to select the youngest, who was not the most favored in the family. Moreover, Eliab's response may reflect the other brothers' reaction to David. David's "What have I done now?" may reveal long standing tension between the two.[16] But Eliab's irritation may grow out of his own fear of Goliath and his shame at failing to go out to fight.[17]

Additionally, there may be an undercurrent of social blame toward David suggested by this irritation. Verse 15 says, "David kept going back and forth from Saul to tend his father's flock in Bethlehem." This suggests that he periodically left Saul to return to the family. However Auld rightly questions this reading.[18] The Hebrew phrase is *holek washab*, a construction that appears regularly in a different sense, seen in 17:41, "came closer and closer."[19] If this reading is correct, then the point made in 17:15 is that David is turning more and more away from Saul (given Saul's growing madness?). In vv. 13 and 14 the text tells us three times (in the Hb. text) that David's brothers had gone with Saul to the war. Youngblood[20] wonders if Jesse's word to David is a mild rebuke for his failure to go.[21]

David's overarching motivation in pursuing the issue about fighting Goliath appears in v. 26: "What will be done for the man who kills that Philistine and removes this disgrace from Israel? Just who is this uncircumcised Philistine that he should defy the armies of the living God?" Whatever personal interest he might have in the reward, his great motive was to defend God's honor in the face of the Philistine's bluster.

The fourth plot line (vv. 31-39). Word finally got around to King Saul—possibly David's intention was to continue asking questions so that the king would hear of him. David's questions and implicit offer of himself as a champion may have piqued Saul's interest, giving him no little amusement. David was, after all, a *na'ar*, a youth (v. 33). Since the word is key to the interpretation of this whole passage, it is worth making a few comments on it. The word is broad in its usage. It is used for an infant (Ex 2:6), for an unweaned child (1Sm 1:22), or one just weaned (1Sm 1:24), but also for the spies who went into Canaan (Jos 6:23) and for a supervisor of workmen (Ru 2:5). The term does not of itself address specific age. De Vaux also shows[22] that as a military term, *na'ar* (lad) might have the sense of "cadet," as distinct from the standing army (cf. 1Kg 20:14-19). Perhaps the term would even be better translated "reservist" as compared to "regular" army. As such he would never have had or trained in the equipment Saul possessed. For these reasons Saul convinced himself that David would never be able to face Goliath. Yet David persisted, *giving his past experience* as evidence that God would fight for him. And all the more could he depend on God since God's reputation was at stake (vv. 34-37).

The outcome of this encounter with Saul was that the king sent him on his way. He even added the statement, "Go, and may the LORD be with you" (v. 37). Translations handle this differently. Most translations consulted treat it as a prayer/wish (including HCSB), which appears to be the right way of handling it. Still, one wonders about the sense in which Saul meant it. Was it a prayer offered with confidence that God would grant it? That does not seem reasonable. If that were Saul's thinking, he would have sent someone out earlier to face Goliath in the same confidence. Was it a wish that he hoped might come true, and that he thought perhaps would? Again, that does not seem reasonable. Saul by this time is a man of little faith. He has no real confidence that God will fight for him or for Israel. It appears to be a wish that expressed no confidence of ever seeing David again. It is in this sense that we may argue that Saul, sending David to fight, thought he was sending David to die. The divinely rejected king of Israel hands Israel's deliverer over to death.[23]

So far we have seen four plot lines developing in this story. Israel is in conflict with Philistia, heightened by Goliath's challenge. Then from v. 12 a second plot line begins, between David and Goliath. The third conflict (v. 28) arises between David and his brothers, and the fourth between David and Saul. Now back to the second plot line.

The second plot line resumes (vv. 40-51a). From this point David's whole focus was on Goliath. David equipped himself with a sling, five smooth stones, and his shepherd staff, and set out to meet Goliath. The story already prepared readers to expect more than Saul did. Surely by the time the books of Samuel were written, everyone knew the stories of David. So the rest is a hero story.[24] It holds up a hero who embodies the best of virtues of a society. In this sense, everything in 1Sm 17 to this point has been introduction, establishing the need for just such a man as David.

He went out to face the Philistine.[25] The Philistine immediately commenced his approach to David, walking as he talked and evaluated David. The narrator put the weight of the story on two aspects of the narrative: the dialogue and the death of the Philistine.

The dialogue. The Philistine mentioned deity only in malediction. A key term in the story has been "defy" (or "taunt"), which expresses his attitude toward Israel (vv. 10,25; he also despised David and cursed him by his gods, v. 43). David, though, saw in it his defiance not merely of Israel but of Israel's God (vv. 26,36,45). David's commitment to fight in the name of the Lord fit entirely with Dt 20, the law of warfare: Israel is not to fear in battle since it is the LORD who is fighting for them.

Thus, David's more lengthy reply comes in vv. 45 and 46:

> "You come against me with a dagger, spear, and sword, but I come against you in the name of Yahweh of Hosts, the God of Israel's armies—you have defied Him. Today, the Lord will hand you over to me. Today, I'll strike you down, cut your head off, and give the corpses of the Philistine camp to the birds of the sky and the creatures of the earth. Then all the world will know that Israel has a God, and this whole assembly will know that it is not by sword or by spear that the Lord saves, for the battle is the LORD's. He will hand you over to us."

He fights as God's servant to lead Israel to know their God and to reveal Him to the nations. He fights as a shepherd, using a shepherd's weapons, because the Lord is able to deliver, by many or by few, by the sword or by His word.

THE RESOLUTION

One of the characteristics that makes this story so great is that all four of its conflicts resolve at the same place (vv. 50-51): "David defeated the Philistine with a sling and a stone. Even though David had no sword, he struck down the Philistine and killed him. David ran and stood over him. He grabbed the Philistine's sword, pulled it from its sheath, and used it to kill him. Then he cut off his head. When the Philistines saw that their hero was dead, they ran." No more did Israel face the threat of Philistia. No more did they need to tremble at their tents. No more could anyone despise David. Now the king of Israel would need to reckon with another war leader, one who approached battles in faith-filled courage. He did not shun them. Now God had proven David's election as messiah, his future on Israel's throne. And, at least for the present, Israel was free from slavery and oppression.

CONCLUSION

So David proved the unlikely hero, hated by his brothers and turned over to death by the rejected king of Israel. But he went out to battle with his people's enemy and won a great victory, delivering them from slavery and oppression. This sounds remarkably like another story, one that would come centuries later: a story about another man from Bethlehem, an unlikely Hero (for He grew up in Nazareth); a Hero despised by His brothers; a Hero committed to death by a rejected ruler of Israel; a Hero who would fight His people's battle and free them from slavery and death; a Hero driven to act to defend and enhance the glory of God. This is the anticipated Messiah, the deliverer of Israel.

The reader will miss the essence of this study if one more facet is omitted from the conclusion. All of what has been said here about biblical narrative revolves around patterns intentionally embedded in the story that the human authors and the Divine Author expected even the original readers to recognize and understand. Moses and his successors knew that they were writing for the future. They knew that they were anticipating a future that they did not fully understand, but they knew that it was coming. "They inquired into what time or what circumstances the Spirit of Christ within them was indicating when He testified in advance to the messianic sufferings and the glories that would follow" (1Pt 1:11).

---

1. Leland Ryken, *How to Read the Bible as Literature . . . And Get More Out of It* (Grand Rapids: Academie Books, 1984), 33–73.

2. Shimeon Bar-Efrat, *Narrative Art in the Bible* (London; New York: T & T Clark International, 2004), 111: "The situation existing at the beginning of the action is presented in what is usually called the exposition. This serves as an introduction to the action described in the narrative, supplying the background information, introducing the characters, informing us of their names, traits, physical appearance, state in life and the relations obtaining among them, and providing the other details needed for understanding the story."

3. The resolution of a story comes when there can be no more story told. In children's books, we know that the story is over by the phrase, "And they lived happily ever after." The plot's conflict is over. No more of that story is available.

4. Note the repetition from chap. 15; but David exterminated the force he faced!

5. One of the key words in the beginning of this part of the story is "send." Initially David, or other powerful characters, "sent" people to do their will. This continued until the Lord "sent" Nathan to David.

6. According to David C. Mitchell, the ancient Jewish understanding of biblical historical events was that past events prefigure the future. According to him, "this became a fixed hermeneutical idea":

That which has been is that which shall be (Eccl. 1.9) . . . R. Berekiah said in the name of R. Isaac: As the first redeemer was, so shall the latter redeemer be. What is stated of the former redeemer? *And Moses took his wife and his sons, and set them upon an ass* (Exod. 4.20). Similarly will it be with the latter redeemer, as it is said, *Lowly and riding upon an ass* (Zech. 9.9). As the former redeemer caused manna to descend, as it is said, *Behold I will cause to rain bread from heaven for you* (Exod. 16.4), so will the latter redeemer cause manna to descend, as it is said, *May he be as a rich cornfield in the land* (Ps. 72.16). As the former redeemer made a well to rise, so will the latter redeemer bring up water, as it is said, *And a fountain shall come forth out of the house of the Lord, and shall water the valley of Shittim* (Joel 4.18). (*Eccl. R.* to 1.9)

See David C. Mitchell, *The Message of the Psalter: An Eschatological Programme in the Book of Psalms* (Sheffield, England: Sheffield Academic Press, 1997), 84–85.

7. An additional element of this pattern is that the crossing of the Red Sea was preceded by Passover, and the crossing of the Jordan was followed by Passover!

8. Rikki E. Watts has even published a book titled *Isaiah's New Exodus in Mark*, Biblical Studies Library (Grand Rapids: Baker, 2001).

9. William Dumbrell, *The Faith of Israel: Its Expression in the Books of the Old Testament* (Grand Rapids: Baker, 1988), 76.

10. See Robert B. Chisholm Jr., *1 & 2 Samuel*, Teach the Text Commentary Series, ed. Mark L. Strauss, John H. Walton, and Rosalie de Rosset (Grand Rapids: Baker Books, 2013) 116.

11. Ronald F. Youngblood, "1, 2 Samuel," in *1 Samuel–2 Kings* (rev. ed.), vol. 3 of The Expositors Bible Commentary, ed. Tremper Longman III and David E. Garland (Grand Rapids: Zondervan, 2009), 178.

12. Clyde E. Billington, "Goliath and the Exodus Giants: How Tall Were They?" Journal of the Evangelical Theological Society 50 (2007): 508: "It is nearly certain that he was not over 9 feet tall. But, it is likely that he was over 8 feet tall, and he may have been as tall as 8 feet 7 inches."

13. J. Daniel Hays, "The Height of Goliath: A Response to Clyde Billington," *Journal of the Evangelical Theological Society* 50, no. 3 (September 2007): 514.

14. Harry A. Hoffner Jr., *1 & 2 Samuel*, Evangelical Exegetical Commentary, ed. by H. Wayne House and William Barrick (Bellingham, WA: Lexham Press, 2015), intimates that Goliath's challenge in v. 8 may have been directed as an insult to King Saul. Later, though, Hoffner acknowledges, in a comment on v. 29, that it was equals who normally engaged in single combat.

15. Hoffner, *1 & 2 Samuel*, note on v. 21.

16. A. Graeme Auld, *I & II Samuel: A Commentary*, The Old Testament Library, 1st ed., ed. William P. Brown, Carol A. Newsom, and Brent A. Strawn (Louisville, KY: Westminster John Knox Press, 2012) 209; Hoffner, *1 & 2 Samuel*, note on v. 29.

17. Hoffner, *1 & 2 Samuel*, note on v. 29.

18. A. Graeme Auld, *I & II Samuel: A Commentary*, 199.

19. GKC §113u. This construction is a common one in the Hebrew Bible.

20. Youngblood, "1, 2 Samuel," 181.

21. This approach to vv. 13-15 ameliorates some of the historical problems of relating chap. 17 to chap. 16.

22. Roland de Vaux, *Ancient Israel: Its Life and Institutions*, trans. John McHugh (Grand Rapids: Eerdmans, 1997), 220–21.

23. In this respect, consider the tie to the story of Joseph, Israel's deliverer, whose brothers hand him over to death!

24. Ryken, *How to Read the Bible as Literature . . . And Get More Out of It*, 75–78.

25. Goliath is named only in some sections of the narrative but is merely called "the Philistine" in others.

2 Samuel 7

The Davidic Covenant (I)

WALTER C. KAISER JR.

Second Samuel 7 and 1 Chronicles 17 are two of the most pivotal chapters in all of the OT; in fact, they could be referred to as the real powerhouse chapters of Scripture. Both of these chapters build upon the Abrahamic promise made first in Gn 12:1-3 and 15:1-6, and then repeated to Isaac and Jacob. Three key promises were given to Abram (later to be called Abraham) to announce to all his descendants: he and they together were to receive a "land," a "seed" that had a male representative of the whole nation to come, and a "gospel," that all the nations of the earth would receive through Abram and his genealogical line spiritual blessing of enormous benefit.

But now in the promise made to David, our Lord adds three more major gifts besides those three already promised to Abraham: God would make a "house/dynasty out of David and his heirs, He would also gift them with a throne, and David's rule would become a kingdom that would last forever (2Sm 7:16; 1Chr 17:11-12). But that was not everything, for this promise to David would result in a "revelation" [custom or instruction] for all humanity" (7:19b; 17:17b), just as in the Abrahamic promise all the nations of the earth would be blessed by the Lord through Abraham and his seed. But even more significantly, at the heart of all these gifts was the central promise of a male scion who would be the Anointed One, Messiah the Lord.

To properly understand this Davidic covenant that led to the Messiah, it is best to examine these two texts themselves.

2 SAMUEL 7:1-3; 1 CHRONICLES 17:1-2

The narrative of both chapters begins by noting that David at this point "was settled into his palace" (2Sm 7:1; 1Chr 17:1), with the Samuel text adding that "the LORD had given him [David] rest from all his enemies round about." The prophet Nathan apparently was visiting King David at his open house for his newly completed palace. Nathan might have been among the last of the guests to leave that ceremony of the dedication of the new cedar palace when he got into a conversation with the king. This was a grand structure according to its description in Scripture, and this was indeed a memorable celebration of its opening, but something was bothering King David. So, King David confided his misgivings to his prophet and friend Nathan. He told him: "Look! I am living in a cedar house while the ark of the Lord's covenant is under tent curtains" (2Sm 7:2; 1Chr 17:1b). It was not enough for David that he had now brought the ark back to Jerusalem from the house of Obed-Edom after it had stayed with Abinadab in Kiriath-Jearim for some 20 years (1Sm 7:1-2; 2Sm 6). David had provided a tent for the ark of the covenant in Jerusalem for all this time. However, despite such royal efforts on behalf of the ark, this was not enough, for how could a mortal like himself dwell in a new cedar paneled palace while the ark of God, where Yahweh the Lord of lords, King of kings, was left to dwell in a tent? It was just plain disgraceful! Moreover, David knew that the Lord had affirmed that God would dwell in Zion "forever" (Ps 68:16). Nevertheless, Nathan knew exactly where David was going with this embarrassed comparison, so he told David, in effect, "Just do it! Go ahead and build a temple for Yahweh." But on this occasion Nathan did not speak as the messenger of God using the scriptural formula that usually was indicated by such words as: "The LORD declares to you." Instead he just gave David his own personal assessment. That was the wrong advice, according to the Lord!

2 SAMUEL 7:4-11; 1 CHRONICLES 17:3-9

It was the wrong advice because not everything a prophet said was always a word from God. Only those words that have their origin in God alone (as indicated by the introductory formula "The LORD declares") were authoritative and part of God's plan. Nathan at first had spoken on his own *before* he had received a communication from God. That night, therefore, the Lord appeared to Nathan and revealed that he was to tell David that he was *not* the person who was to build a house for God; instead God would make a "house/dynasty" out of David himself! (2Sm 7:5,11c; 1Chr 17:4b,10c). Clearly, David was not to be the active initiator of this building project (7:11c); instead he was to be a passive recipient of the work God would do for him and for this project through others. The Lord, therefore, would take the initiative for such a building.

The Lord also put an obvious spin on the word "house," which usually meant a home where someone lived, but in this case the Lord used that same word in a way that meant He would make David into a "family," or a "household," or in the case of royalty, He would form David and his descendants into a "dynasty." All of this would be the exact opposite of what was so common in the ancient Near East. In that ancient culture, a king would build or restore an idol's temple, and then the pagan god would proceed to reward that monarch for his diligence, or so it was thought. This worthless deity would promise this monarch a good reign with victories over his enemies and all types of gifts. The only problem was these idols did not exist! They were "nothings"!

To illustrate how this worked in the ancient Near East, contrary to the covenant Yahweh had just promised to King David, one needs to contrast that with what Pharaoh Thutmose III (c. 1490–1436 BC) claimed he heard from his idol god Amon-Re. When he was allegedly told by his god to build a house for the sun god Amon-Re, Amon-Re is supposed to have declared:

> Thou hast erected my dwelling place as the work of eternity, made longer and wider than that which had been before. . . . Thy monuments are greater than [those of] any king who has been. I commanded thee to make them, and I am satisfied with them. I have established thee upon the throne of Horus for millions of years, that thou mightest lead the living for eternity.[1]

Likewise, later on Pharaoh Amen-hotep III (c. 1413–1377 BC) also described elaborate building plans for the construction of a temple for the same sun god, Amon-Re. The stela, recording this extensive work of Pharaoh, is now in Cairo. In part the stela read:

> [Amen-hotep III] made as his monument for his father [the god] Amon, Lord of the Thrones of the Two Lands, the erecting for him of an august temple on the west side of Thebes, an everlasting fortress, a possessor of eternity, of fine sandstone, worked with gold throughout. Its pavement was washed with silver, all its doorways with fine gold.[2]

Later Amon-Re went on to express his gratitude to Amen-hotep III by promising him victory over all his enemies wherever he went. This sun god stressed the point of his reward for such work over and over again as he announced:

> When I turn my face to the south, I [will] work a wonder for thee: I [will] make the princes of the wretched Ethiopia [to] bestir themselves for thee. . . .
> When I turn my face to the north, I [will] work a wonder for thee: I [will] make the countries of the ends of Asia come to thee. . . .
> When I turn my face to the west, I [will] work a wonder for thee: I [will] let thee take Libya—they cannot escape. . . .
> When I turn my face to the orient, I [will] work a wonder for thee: I will make the countries of Punt come to thee, bearing all the sweet plants of their countries, to beg peace from [thee and to] breathe the breath of your giving.[3]

All that was a lot of talking from a deity that did not exist or could not talk! These monarchs must have been listening to themselves mumbling. However, this same pattern of a monarch feeling rewarded for building a temple for his god persisted throughout the ancient Near East. The ruler who had done for the idol what he promised would expect help and support to come from that deity in return for his deeds. This pattern went all the way back to the Sumerian culture in the third millennium BC. Yet, despite the slight number of similarities to the narrative with David contained in this ancient Near Eastern literature, what they reflected is nowhere near to what God had promised to David, nor to the fact that God had taken the initiative to bless David and his line even apart from his doing any kind of temple building.

As already noted above in 2Sm 7:4-11, Yahweh instructed the prophet Nathan to inform David that he was not to build a house for the Lord (2Sm 7:5; 1Chr 17:4b); instead, God would build a "dynasty-house" for David (2Sm 7:11; 1Chr 17:10c). Yahweh was not at all like the pagan gods who exchanged favors for a temple built in their honor. Instead, Yahweh is a God who enjoys lavishing His grace on undeserving persons just because He loves them, which in this case is evident in two promises immediately given to David: (1) God would make David's name great as He had promised to Abraham (Gn 12:2), similar to the names of the great mortals on earth (2Sm 7:9); and (2) God would give him rest from the pressures of all his enemies round about (7:11b).

Squeezed between these two divine promises was a pledge exclusively to the people of Israel: "I will establish a place for My people Israel and plant them, so that they may live there and not be disturbed again" (7:10). Our Lord strengthened that promise by further pledging that the wicked would no longer oppress them as a nation just as they had been doing from the beginning, and ever since God had appointed leaders over the people (7:10c-11a). In talking in this manner, God revealed that David's kingship was part of God's plan to "plant" Israel in her land (7:10a) and to provide the security and protection they would need. So, our Lord was determined that Israel should have a home in the land He had promised long ago to Abram (Gn 12:7). God would never abandon His passion to see that Israel had a homeland, which would be made safe and secure for all to enjoy. Revelation 21:25 says that it would be so safe in that final day that the gates of Jerusalem would be left wide open, for all enemies of Israel would have been vanquished by that time in the kingdom of God.

2 SAMUEL 7:11-16; 1 CHRONICLES 17:10-14

But the core of the Davidic covenant was expressed in 2Sm 7:11d-16 and in 1Chr 17:10-14. The Lord Himself began in 7:11d and 17:10c with the promise that God would establish a "house for [David]." Moreover, when it came time for David to pass on to his reward and receive his "rest with [his] fathers" (7:12a; 17:11a-b), God would graciously raise up David's "descendant" to succeed him, that is a person from his own flesh and blood, and the Lord Himself would "establish his kingdom" (7:12c; 17:11c) and the "throne of his kingdom" (7:13b; 17:12). Moreover, God would be a personal "father" to the Davidic scion, and that descendant would be God's own "son" (7:14a; 17:13). Even if that relative in David's line would practice what was evil and wrong in God's eyes, God would "discipline him with a human rod and with blows from others" (7:14b-c), but in no way would God remove His "love" from that erring Davidic leader, as He previously had to take that cloak of leadership away from King Saul (7:15). The Chronicler, however, omitted this discussion of the Davidic line committing sin and being chastised, apparently because the Samuel text dealt with the whole line of David, but Chronicles dealt only with Solomon himself for the moment, who in the beginning of his reign was seen in a favorable light.

David's "house," "his line," and his "kingdom" would "endure forever" before the Lord; indeed, his "throne [would] be established forever" (7:16; 17:14). In other words, God's promise would be marked with the superscript: "Indefectible!"[4] for David's throne, dynasty, and kingdom would endure every type of adversity and circumstance that would arise against it! As Dale David put it in his commentary: (1) "death would not annul it [7:12-13], sin could not destroy it [7:14-15], and time would not exhaust it [7:16; 17:14b-c]."[5] It indeed was indefectible.

PSALM 132 AND PSALM 89 AS PARALLELS

The great promise to David, therefore, was that the Lord would build him into a "house"—not his own personal home, nor the Temple of the Lord, but a family tree that would lead directly to Christ the Messiah, the Son of God. Both Ps 132 and Ps

89 can be cited as divine commentaries that further explain this promise about this dynasty for David in 2Sm 7:11c and 1Chr 17:10c. For example, Ps 132, one of the psalms of ascent, states:

> The LORD swore an oath to David,
> a promise He will not abandon:
> "I will set one of your descendants
> on your throne."
>
> For the LORD has chosen Zion;
> He has desired it for His home:
> "This is My resting place forever;
> I will make My home here
> because I have desired it."
>
> There I will make a horn grow for David;
> I have prepared a lamp for My anointed one.
> I will clothe his enemies with shame,
> But the crown he wears will be glorious." (Ps 132:11,13-14,17-18)

Psalm 132 belongs to the group of 15 psalms known as the pilgrim psalms, or the Psalms of Ascent, perhaps sung by the pilgrims on their way to Jerusalem to attend one of the three festivals. The psalm begins with a vow from David that he would not allow sleep to come to his eyes (a hyperbole) until he had built a house for Yahweh (132:1-5). The response of the people followed in vv. 6-7, and Solomon used the same words of vv. 8-10 when he dedicated the Temple. But in the second half of this psalm, David's requests are fulfilled, and three significant symbols for Messiah are described in vv. 17-18: He is called a "horn," a "lamp" and a "crown." The "lamp" (Hb. *nar*) had already pointed to the Davidic Messiah in 2Sm 21:17, just as the "horn" "sprouting/growing up" likewise as a word pointed to Messiah, for God would later use the word "horn" (Hb. *qeren*) as a symbol for a powerful king of a world empire in Dan 7:7-8,24. The word "to sprout" (Hb. *tsamach*) is the verbal form of the messianic title for the "Branch" (Hb. *tsemach*) who would "branch/sprout out" in the future (Jer 23:5; 33:15; Zch 3:8; 6:12). Also the word "crown" (Hb. *nezer*), as found here in Ps 132:18 and in Ps 89:39, marked one who was both a king and a priest—unmistakable evidence that this person was not simply one of earth's usually anointed mortal appointments, but that he had divine approval and appointment from on high as well.

Psalm 89 has a similar witness to the promise to David being fulfilled in Messiah Himself. It read in part:

> "Once and for all
> I have sworn an oath by My holiness;
> I will not lie to David.
> His offspring will continue forever,
> his throne like the sun before Me,
> like the moon, established forever,
> a faithful witness in the sky." (Ps 89:35-37)

David, of course, did not live "forever," but Messiah is a being who has lived for all eternity, and He will continue through all eternity in the future. David's line will not fail, for Messiah will be born in the line of David (as Mt 1:1-17 and Mic 5:2 demonstrate), and He will have a rule, a dynasty, and a kingdom that will go on without end into the eternal state. Messiah must be divine to carry these various credentials. Three times the promise that the Davidic Messiah would endure "forever" (Hb. *`ad `olam*) is emphasized (7:16 twice, and 7:13 once). Ralph Davis quoted a wonderful summary of this fact from James Oscar Boyd. Even though it was written in 1927, it still rings with the excitement similar to that when it was first heard. Boyd argued against the negative critics of his day:

> Do critics who assert vers. 13 contains nothing save what was in vers. 12 realize that this is the first time that David's ear caught the music of those wonderful words which are repeated twice in vers. 16 as the climax to the whole oracle, and which are echoed and re-echoed in David's prayer, and therefore in poets' psalms and prophets' visions down the centuries, until at last in the "Hallelujah Chorus of the Apocalypse" they break in waves of glory, "And he shall reign for ever and ever, for ever and ever, Hallelujah! Hallelujah!" Here—here in this wretchedly misunderstood and maltreated verse 13 of 2 Sam vii—we hear for the first time the determination of Almighty God, that as long as He shall have a human people for His own possession (and that too is "forever," see vers. 24), so long shall the seed of David be the covenanted bearer of a divinely conferred and divinely maintained sovereignty over it.[6]

So, let death, sin, and time do whatever they think they must do, but nothing in all creation is going to frustrate the arrival of the kingdom of God, nor His plan to bring the messianic rule and reign of God through David's dynasty-house; there was both a certainty and an inevitability to this plan.

What is more, the span of David's dynasty as compared to the unusually short reigns of the kings of the ancient Near East is likewise remarkable. As O. Palmer Robertson expressed it:

> From David's accession [to the throne from] somewhere around 1000 B.C. to the fall of Jerusalem, over 400 years had transpired. The average [ruler's] dynasty in Egypt and Mesopotamia during their days of greatest stability was something

> less than 100 years. David's successors even outlasted the long-lived eighteenth dynasty of Egypt, which endured for about 250 years.[7]

These 400 years, of course, fail to take into account the fact that the Davidic line continued, for as already noted, Mt 1:12-16 has this line surface in the times of the Christian era in "Jesus who is called the Messiah."

David attempted to comprehend all of this blessing being poured out on him, for he immediately recognized that much of what was promised to him was but a repeat of what God had centuries ago promised to Abraham, Isaac, and Jacob in the Abrahamic covenant. Yes, God promised a "seed," a "land," as well as the fact that the people of Israel would be a "blessing" to all the families and nations of the earth. Those three promises were now being reiterated to David with the addition of three more promises that included that he would be given a "throne," a "dynasty," and a "kingdom" that would likewise last forever. David could only marvel at the grace of God. Who was David? A nobody! Why had God brought him that far with all these numerous promises? (2Sm 7:18; 1Chr 17:16).

ADONAI YAHWEH'S UNIQUE NAME USED IN THE COVENANTS

Note that a very unusual name for God is used in both the Abrahamic covenant (Gn 15:2,8) and in the Davidic covenant (2Sm 7:19,20,22,28,29). It is Adonai Yahweh (Hb. *'adonay YHWH*), which seems to be a direct linking of these two covenants. Even though this combination of names does appear elsewhere, it is generally used sparingly.

TRANSLATIONS OF 2 SAMUEL 7:19B AND 1 CHRONICLES 17:17B

David had come not from cosmopolitan Jerusalem, but from rural Bethlehem, six miles south of that center of Jewish life and culture. And as if that were not enough, God went on to extend his promises to David in 2Sm 7:19b and 1Chr 17:17b even beyond what had been said up to that point! But the last clause in these verses has been poorly translated by almost every English version, which misses the point of the gospel the Hebrew text contains. Some of these mistranslations of 7:19b and 17:17b include:

> Is this your usual way of dealing with men? (NIV 1984)
> And this is the custom of man (NASB)
> Is this the manner of man? (NKJV)
> And hast shown me future generations (RSV, correcting the text)

Such . . . is the lot of a man embarked on a high career (NEB, correcting 1Chr 17:17)
And hast regarded me according to the estate of a man of high degree (1Chr 17:17b KJV)
You have looked on me as though I were the most exalted of men (1Chr 17:17b NIV 2011)
May this be instruction for the people (NRSV)
Is this the manner of man? (Harkavy Jewish Scriptures)
And this is instruction for mankind (ESV)
May that be the law for the people (NJPS)
Such is human destiny (NJB)

The literal translation of the Hebrew text of the last clause in 2Sm 7:19b (Hb. *wezo't torat ha'adam*) would be "And this is the torah/teaching of/for man/humanity." To be sure, this remark by David is concise, rather abrupt, and possibly puzzling for the moment, but it cannot be at all as difficult as these versions generally make it (at least the form in 2Sm 7:19b). Some think it is so difficult that, like the Jerusalem Bible, they just put an ellipsis in place of v. 19b with a footnote stating the Hebrew "here makes no sense." However, given David's sheer amazement and wonder, it is not in the form of a question; rather, it is in the form of an exclamation or interjection of amazement. Moreover, the word *torat* (Hb. construct form meaning "law" or "instruction"), does not refer to the legal connotation of this word, for that would not fit this context. Rather, a better translation would be "teaching," "instruction," or "direction" that comes from the Lord. Thus the word *torah/torat* deals with the *content*, but not the *manner* of the promise; it points to the *substance* of what is taught, not *how* it is taught!

When David began this clause with "And this" in 7:19b, he was referring back to the promise Yahweh had just given to him about a throne, a dynasty, and a kingdom that would belong to him and his descendants (7:12-16). And if "torat" refers to the divine teaching included in this promise, then the source of this teaching would not come from mortals like David and his kin, but from the living God. And the beneficiaries of that teaching would extend to all mankind. Thus, I render this otherwise poorly translated clause as "And this is the charter/instruction for all humanity" ["And this is a revelation for mankind" HCSB].

The parallel passage in 1Chr 17:17b is much more difficult to translate, for it appears in the Hebrew text as *ure'itani ketor ha'adam hama'alah*, "You showed me/regarded me as an outline (or it might suggest: "a teaching") for humanity of standing/high estate." It would appear that the Hebrew letter "heh" has been dropped by haplography from the copied text, because it appeared on the next word as the article on the word for "man/humanity" (*ha'adam*). If subsequent Hebrew scrolls should reveal this is accurate, then it was parallel to the 2Sm text: "You have shown me/caused me to see teaching for humanity of high standing!"

If David got overly enthusiastic and excited at this point over what he had just been told, we can easily forgive him, for Yahweh had just guaranteed David's dynasty and through this dynasty Yahweh would extend the instruction about the benefits of His plan, His throne, and His kingdom to stretch over all the human race.

> We call this *torah* a "charter" because it is the plan and prescription for God's kingdom whereby the whole world [could] be blessed. . . . It is a grant conferring powers, rights, and privileges to David and his seed for the benefit of all mankind.[8]

THE UNCONDITIONAL NATURE OF THE DAVIDIC COVENANT

Thus, the covenant that God made with David in 2Sm 7 and 1Chr 17 shows that God was interested in the teaching contained in this covenant, along with the continuation of what He had promised in the Abrahamic covenant—that it should give instruction that would be effective for all humanity in all ages. This plan of God was to be in effect as an unconditional word that would benefit Israel first of all, and then all the nations on the face of the earth in all territories and in all times. This divine word was to spell out Israel's future, which in part would be distinct from the promises made to the believing body of Gentiles, usually referred to as the Church. Importantly, neither the Abrahamic nor the Davidic covenants listed any conditions when they were ratified. They were unilateral, not bilateral, covenants, and therefore they were not subject to cancellation. The everlasting nature of these covenants was stressed repeatedly (Gn 13:15; 17:7-8; 2Sm 7:13-16; Ps 89:28-37).

Another reason for underscoring the unconditional nature of these covenants lies in the very concept of a covenantal relationship. For example, the most prominent gifts in these two covenants were the "land" and the "house/dynasty," exactly the same two prominent features included in the Hittite and Syro-Palestinian land grants. Thus, we read in a Hittite Suzerainty Treaty that Hattusilis III (aka Tudhaliyas) made with Ulmi-Teshup of Datasa:

> After you, your son, and grandson will possess it, nobody will take it from them. If one of your descendants sins, the king will prosecute him in his court. Then when he is found guilty . . . if he deserves death he will die. But nobody will take away from the descendants of Ulmi-Teshup either his house or his land in order to give it to a descendant of somebody else.[9]

The clear language used for both the Abrahamic and Davidic covenants depicts them as being unconditional: only God walked between the pieces (not Abram, Gn 15:1-6), taking a self-malediction upon Himself if He did not fulfill what He promised. Yet a possibility of a conditional covenant seems to be raised both in Scripture and by many believers today. For example, some point to 1Kg 2:2-4, which warns, in part:

> If your descendants watch how they live, and if they walk faithfully before me with all their heart and soul, you will never fail to have a successor on the throne of Israel. (NIV)

Likewise, at the dedication of the Temple, the Lord responded to Solomon with a similar warning:

> But if you or your descendants turn away from me and do not observe the commands and decrees I have given you and go off to serve other gods and worship them, then I will cut off Israel from the land I have given them and will reject this temple I have consecrated for my Name. Israel will then become a byword and an object of ridicule among all peoples. This temple will become a heap of rubble. All who pass by will be appalled and will scoff and say, "Why has the LORD done such a thing to this land and to this temple?" People will answer, "Because they have forsaken the LORD their God . . . that is why the LORD brought all this disaster on them." (1Kg 9:4-9 NIV)

While there are no conditions expressed in the Abrahamic or Davidic covenants, yet some believe that passages like those above, along with others in 1Kg 6:12; 8:25; Pss 89:28-37; 132:11-12, admit that it would be possible for Israel to forfeit the promise of the succession to the throne of David. Is this promise of succession to the throne at the heart and essence of the covenant, or is it merely one of the benefits, which if lost does not imperil the whole covenant?

The answer is that even though David's line may fail and therefore the expected and threatened judgment will apply, yet God will by no means remove His *hesed* from David's line (e.g., Ps 89:33). David's descendants are duty-bound to *transmit* the covenant to the next one in that line of descendants, even though that particular descendant may not *participate* in the joys and promises of the covenant.

Accordingly, even though some in the Davidic line may not obey the commands and decrees of *torah*, such deficiency of behavior will not make the *entire* covenant conditional and bilateral in its effect. Nothing mortals can do can damage the revelatory nature of God's everlasting promise. Yes, obedience is necessary if one is to enjoy the benefits of the covenant, but in no way does that obedience make the covenant conditional. In fact, the Hebrew phrase *berit 'olam*, "everlasting covenant," occurs 16 times in the OT. Thus, the "land" promise is said to be an "everlasting" promise (Ps 105:10; 1Chr 16:17), for the covenant made with David is said to be "everlasting" (2Sm 23:5; Isa 55:3). And the new covenant is just as "everlasting" as well (Isa 61:8; Jer 32:40; 50:5; Ezk 16:60; 37:26). Of course, *'olam* does not mean "eternity," "enduring," "endless in time" in every instance it is used in the OT, for it is used in connection with the covenants of circumcision (Gn 17:10,11,13,14), Sabbath (Ex 31:16), and showbread (Lv 24:8). But in the case of God's promise in the covenants, it is best to understand the meaning of "eternal" or "everlasting" as paralleled by the endurance of the sun, moon, and stars as an appropriate gauge for the longevity of the covenant (e.g., Jer 31:35-37). Moreover, God Himself is called the "Everlasting God" and "eternal" (Gn 21:33; Dt 33:27; Jer 10:10).

WHAT IS THE CONNECTION BETWEEN DAVID'S LINE AND MESSIAH?

But does this promise made to David and his descendants lead us to Jesus the Messiah? Is it too much to ask of these ancient prophets and writers of Scripture a messianic understanding of their prophecies in the OT? Some evangelicals are willing to grant that if we use an imposition of the NT over the OT text, we today may see what these ancients never came even close to understanding about the Messiah as they announced the text to those in that earlier day! But that method would involve the improper method of eisegesis, i.e., a "reading into" the text what was not there in the first place. This would be a false use of the NT and a demeaning of God's revelation in the OT. It would leave those listeners of the text in OT times without a word about Messiah in that word from God. Would this mean there is a hidden code in the Bible? Such a suggestion is totally out of the picture of Scripture, for it gives no hint of such a view.

Indeed, we are taught to think differently from Scripture. The Bible did not hide a sort of spiritual code that awaited a future day for its elucidation. For instance, Peter preached on the day of Pentecost that when David wrote Psalm 16, David knew that God would "seat one of his descendants on his throne" (Ac 2:30). Moreover, David saw what was to come, so "he spoke concerning the resurrection of the Messiah" (Ac 2:31). Therefore, David had an understanding that his line of descent would end up in the person of Christ and that this Christ would also be resurrected from the dead. Why do some today miss what David had seen and written about?

This is why the apostle Peter firmly announced that the prophets clearly taught about the awesome salvation we enjoy and share with Israel. Even though these prophets did not know the time or the circumstances surrounding the coming of

Messiah, they did know: (1) that they were talking about the Messiah Himself, (2) that He would suffer, (3) that His suffering would come before He was glorified, and finally (4) that they were not serving merely their own times and their own generation, but also believers in a much later era—like those who were scattered all over what is the present land of Turkey to whom Peter was writing a good number of years after the death, burial, and resurrection of Jesus (1Pt 1:1-12).

CONCLUSION

Second Samuel 7 and 1Chr 17 set forth the Davidic covenant that leads directly to Christ the Messiah. Just as God earlier had given His everlasting promise-plan to Abraham in Gn 12 and 15, God later further built into that ancient word additional promises He then gave to David. The ancient trilogy of the promise of a "land," a "seed," and a "gospel" in which all nations would be blessed (Gn 12:2-3) was now to be enhanced by another trilogy of promises in this same plan of God: a "throne," a "dynasty," and a "kingdom" (2Sm 7:16) that would endure forever. David's promise would conclude with Jesus the Messiah coming in His first advent to fulfill part of the divine plan, but Messiah would return a second time to bring the plan to completion.

---

1. John A. Wilson, trans., "Hymn of Victory of Thut-mose III," in *Ancient Near Eastern Texts Relating to the Old Testament,* 2nd ed., ed. James B. Pritchard (Princeton, NJ: Princeton University Press, 1955), 375.
2. Ibid.
3. Ibid., 376.
4. This was the word Dale Ralph Davis used in his *2 Samuel: Out of Every Adversity* (Ross-Shire, UK: Christian Focus, 1999), 77.
5. Ibid., 77.
6. James Oscar Boyd, "The Davidic Covenant: The Oracle," *The Princeton Theological Review* 25 (1927): 430, as cited by Dale Ralph Davis, *2 Samuel: Out of Every Adversity,* 79, n 13.
7. O. Palmer Robertson, *The Christ of the Covenants* (Phillipsburg, NJ: Presbyterian and Reformed, 1980), 239, as cited by Dale Ralph Davis, *2 Samuel: Out of Every Adversity,* 79, n. 13.
8. Walter C. Kaiser Jr., "The Blessing of David: The Charter for Humanity," in *The Law and the Prophets: Old Testament Studies Prepared in Honor of Oswald Thompson Allis,* ed. John H. Skilton (Nutley, NJ: Presbyterian & Reformed, 1974), 189.
9. M. Weinfeld, "The Covenant of Grant in the Old Testament and in the Ancient Near East," *Journal of the American Oriental Society,* 90 (1970): 189.

2 Samuel 23:1-7

David's Last Words

MICHAEL A. RYDELNIK

In recent years, some interpreters have once again begun to understand the Psalms as messianic, much as the New Testament does (Lk 24:44).[1] This is an outgrowth of two factors, the first being the recognition of the psalms as a postexilic collection, at a time when there was no Davidic king on Israel's throne. Consequently, the psalms should be read not as looking backwards to David or some other Davidic king but rather pointing forward to the eschatological son of David, who will one day fulfill the Davidic covenant.

Another factor supporting the messianic interpretation of the Psalms is reading them holistically and rejecting the form-critical approach that treats each psalm as if it stood alone and had no context. By appreciating the contextual relationships of each individual psalm to those that precede and follow it, it is possible to identify the lexical and thematic links that connect the psalms to each other and, thereby, point to a messianic king.[2]

For those who hold the canonical approach to the Psalms and therefore support a messianic interpretation, there does appear to be one significant challenge. It is evident in B. Waltke's "canonical process approach,"[3] which does not recognize the psalms as messianic when originally composed. According to Waltke, a historical king is the subject of the psalms when they were written. He affirms David as the author of 73 Psalms (LXX credits 84 to David), and therefore he identifies the Davidic psalms as referring to David and not the Messiah. Waltke writes, "In the original composition the king is the human subject of the psalms . . . we must bear in mind that the king is presented idealistically and prays to God and praises Him through the inspiration of God's Spirit."[4] It is only in the period of the postexilic redaction that Waltke understands the psalms as receiving a messianic interpretation. He writes,

> Thus, when the Old Testament canon closed, no son of David was sitting on Yahweh's throne, and no living scion of David's line was associated with that hope. Accordingly, we may safely conclude that the royal psalms in the final shape of the Old Testament canon must have been interpreted prophetically precisely as we found them interpreted in the New Testament. This prophetic interpretation of these old texts is *not a reinterpretation* [emphasis added] of them away from their original, authorial meaning; rather, it is a more precise interpretation of them in the light of the historical realities.[5]

Although Waltke states that the postexilic redaction "is not a reinterpretation" of the original sense of the psalm or the authorial intent, it is not clear how that can be. If David only meant himself in his psalms and then the meaning shifted to the more precise messianic interpretation when the book of psalms was redacted, how is that not a reinterpretation? Perhaps Waltke would respond that David was only writing of himself as an ideal king, and not really about himself as a real, historical figure.

Regardless, another approach besides the above would be to consider the possibility that David was not speaking of his own life in the royal psalms but rather prophesying of the future Messiah. That would require a different understanding of David's own authorial intent. The good news is that David does give his own perspective about the meaning of his writings in a passage identified as "David's Last Words" (2Sm 23:1-7). Therefore, this article will examine David's last words as the clue to discerning David's intentions in writing the Psalms and will seek to demonstrate that David's royal psalms were deliberately composed as prophetic predictions of the Messiah. As such, this passage of David's last words constitutes a significant messianic prophecy in and of itself. This will become evident through an exposition of 2Sm 23:1-7 followed by an examination of both OT and NT passages that confirm David's messianic intent.

THE EXPOSITION OF DAVID'S LAST WORDS (2 SAMUEL 23:1-7)

Introduction (2Sm 23:1a)

The poem is introduced as David's last words. These words are not to be construed as the last words David spoke before he took his final breath. Rather, they should be viewed as David's final and formal statement about his writings and kingship. His words are similar to an author interview in the *Paris Review*, a literary magazine in which authors frequently explain their writings. After close examination of David's poem, it will become evident that his authorial intent, both here and in his psalms, was to clarify his own expectation of the Messiah, the one promised to him in the Davidic covenant.

David's Favorite Subject (2Sm 23:1b)

This poem is called an oracle (*ne'um,* "declaration" in the HCSB), a technical term used of a prophetic oracle. Normally, the genitive that follows this noun is Yahweh, meaning "the declaration of Yahweh" or "the oracle of Yahweh." Here, David's last words are described as "the oracle of David" and "the oracle of the man raised on high." In only three other places in the Hebrew Bible is the Hebrew word *ne'um* linked to a man as it is here (Nm 24:3-4,15-16; Prv 30:1). Each of these is a prophetic oracle about the Messiah, as is 2Sm 23:1.

In the Masoretic Text of 2Sm 23:1, David gives a fourfold description of himself. Using synonymous parallelism, David describes himself as "David, the Son of Jesse," "the man raised on high," "the one anointed by the God of Jacob," and "the favorite singer of Israel." The last depiction of himself as "the favorite singer" is a possible but somewhat free translation. The literal translation seems more apropos: "the delightful one of the songs of Israel." Thus, in the MT, David is identifying himself as his favorite subject in the Psalms he wrote.

However, there is a small but noteworthy textual variant that, if correct, would identify David's favorite subject not as himself but as the Messiah. The issue concerns the translation of the Hebrew word translated "on high." In the MT, the Hebrew word *'āl* is understood with the vowel *qamets.* However, the Septuagint reads the Hebrew consonant as if it was a *pathah* (*'al*) and translates it with the Greek word *epi* ("concerning").[6] J. H. Sailhamer explains the significance of this different reading: "The effect of the difference in the length of the vowel is such that the title 'anointed one' in the Masoretic Text refers to King David, whereas in other, non-Masoretic versions of the text, David's words are taken as a reference to the Messiah (cf. 2 Sm 22:51)."[7] If the alternate reading is correct, then the verse would read:

> The oracle of David son of Jesse
> the oracle of the man raised up
> *concerning* the Anointed (Messiah) of the God of Jacob
> the Delightful One of the songs of Israel (author's translation).

According to this reading, David is declaring that his favorite subject in the Psalms is the Messiah.

So which is the correct reading? For several reasons, it appears that the variant ("concerning") is superior. First, note that the vowels were not included in the original Hebrew text of the Bible but only added to the Masoretic Text in the early Middle Ages. Therefore, an alternate reading based on a different understanding of original intended vowel is certainly possible.

Second, not only did the LXX and the Vulgate understand David to be writing about the Messiah, the ancient rabbinic Targum of Jonathan (Aramaic Paraphrase) also interpreted David's last words to be about "the Messiah by the *Memra* (Word) of the God of Jacob."[8] Third, the internal evidence of the poem supports the Septuagint's perspective that David was writing about the Messiah and not himself. The support for this is that after his declaration, David goes on to describe the characteristics of the righteous King (2Sm 23:3-4). Then, in the following verse, David declares, "For not so is my house with God" (lit., 2Sm 23:5), indicating that he himself is not the righteous king he just described. Most English translations recognize the difficulty of harmonizing this declarative statement with David's self-description in 23:1 (MT). Therefore, most versions, without grammatical support,[9] translate v. 5 as a question. The HCSB is typical of this unwarranted translation, reading 23:5 as "Is it not true my house is with God?"[10] If 2Sm 23:5 is translated accurately, it undermines the MT reading. For these reasons, it seems best to accept the variant reading and recognize that David himself, in a prophetic oracle, declares that he was writing about the Messiah, his favorite subject in the Psalms.

David's Prophetic Role (2Sm 23:2-3a)

It would only be expected for David to explain how it would be possible for him to have written about the future Messiah as his favorite subject. Therefore, in the next two verses (vv. 2-3a), he claims divine inspiration for his writings using four separate parallel expressions. In v. 2 he declares the first two, "The Spirit of the Lord spoke through me, His word was on my tongue." The verse literally says the Lord "spoke in me" (*diber be*), referring to God speaking into David.[11] This fits with his use of the word "*ne'um*" (prophetic oracle) in v. 1 and demonstrates that David viewed himself as a prophet.

David continues his claim of divine inspiration with two more parallel expressions: "The God of Israel spoke; the Rock of Israel said to me" (v. 3a). J. P. Lange indicates that David's prophetic inspiration referred to all of his psalms and to his prediction of the seed promised to him, "That is: 'The Spirit of the Lord has always spoken through me, His word has always been on my tongue in all my lays and songs, and especially the God of Israel has spoken through me the prophecy of the future Messiah.'"[12]

The fourfold statement of prophetic inspiration suggests that the prophecy that will follow is no ordinary prediction. Rather, it requires David's prophecy to be of an exalted nature. W. G. Blaikie states,

> So remarkable an introduction must be followed by no ordinary prophecy. If the prophecy should bear on nothing more remarkable than some earthly successor of David, all this preliminary glorification would be singularly out of place. It would be like a great procession of heralds and flourishing of trumpets in an earthly kingdom to announce some event of the most ordinary kind, the repeal of a tax or the appointment of an officer.[13]

David's claim of divine inspiration prepares the way for his prophecy of the exalted King, described in vv. 3b-4. This is none other than the glorious Messiah promised to David in the Davidic covenant (2Sm 7:12-16).

David's Righteous King (2Sm 23:3b-4)

Having proclaimed that his vision of the coming King was given to him by divine inspiration, David proceeds with a lyrical and glorious portrait of the righteous King. Keil and Delitzsch point out that the ruler David depicts is not himself, any other king, or his collective offspring, but rather, they concur with the Targum[14] and identify him as "the Messiah himself, the righteous Shoot who the Lord would raise up to David (Jer. xxiii. 5), and who would execute righteousness and judgment upon the earth (Jer. xxxiii. 15)."[15]

A literal translation of David's description is "One who rules over men righteously (shall arise),[16] who will rule in the fear of God" (v. 3b). Other Hebrew prophets also use the same words found in this verse to describe the Messianic King. To begin, David describes the future king as a *ruler* over men (v. 3), the identical word Micah used in his prediction that a King would come from Bethlehem "to be *ruler* over Israel" (Mic 5:2). David also calls this King "righteous" not to be understood in a relative sense, compared to other people, but in the absolute sense, of perfect righteousness. This is evident from His comparison to the sun rising "on a cloudless morning" (v. 4), thereby comparing the King to a perfect day. Other prophets also see the Messianic King as "righteous." For example, Isaiah promised that this King will reign in "righteousness" (9:7) and judge the poor "righteously" (Isa 11:4). Similarly, in Jer 23:5, He is called a "Righteous Branch" who reigns with "righteousness" (cf. Jer 33:15). Furthermore, Zechariah predicts a humble King coming to Jerusalem and calls Him "righteous" (Zch 9:9). Additionally, David indicates this King's righteousness stems from ruling in the "fear of God" (v. 3), just as Isaiah also characterized the King as being endowed with "the fear of the Lord" (Isa 11:2).

As mentioned above, David uses a simile to describe the King (v. 4), comparing Him to the morning light of the sun "on a cloudless morning." Out of darkness of night, this King will arise and provide glorious light. The prophet Malachi described the Messiah in similar fashion, stating that "the sun of righteousness will rise with healing in its wings" (Mal 4:2). Isaiah also presented the Messianic King as a light arising out of the darkness of distress (Isa 8:22–9:2), declaring that "the people walking in darkness have seen a great light; a light has dawned on those living in the land of darkness" (Isa 9:2).

According to David, the King's light will be like "the glisten of rain on sprouting grass." Keil and Delitzsch capture the sense of these words: "The green grass which springs up from the earth after the rain is an image of the blessings of the messianic salvation (Isa. xliv. 4, xlv.8)."[17] Other biblical authors also relate the rain and resulting fruitfulness of the land to the coming of the Messiah. For example, Solomon, likely influenced by his father's portrait of the Messiah, says, "May he be (or lit. He will be) like rain that falls on the cut grass, like spring showers that water the earth" (Ps 72:6). Other prophecies that relate the coming of the Messiah to rain and fruitfulness are Jl 2:23 and Isa 30:19-23 (esp. v. 23).

David uses his last words to provide a beautifully poetic picture of the future Messianic King. Significantly, the representation of the Messiah found here is similar to the echoes found in other biblical authors. These multiple innerbiblical associations to 2Sm 23:3b-4 demonstrate that David's last words are another part of the cumulative portrait of the Hebrew Bible's depiction of the glorious Messianic King.

David's Messianic Hope (2Sm 23:5)

Having described the Messianic King, David next seeks to express the basis of his confidence in the King's coming. In so doing, he makes three clear statements about his expectation.

(1) *First, David declares that he and his house are unrighteous, unlike the King he has just described.* This statement is found in the first sentence of v. 5. As noted previously, most English versions translate this as a question; for example, the HCSB reads, "Is it not true my house is with God?" and the NASB is, "Truly is not my house so with God?" (See also the ESV, NRSV, and NIV.) Alternatively, both the KJV and the NKJV translate it as a statement, "Although my house is not so with God" (NKJV), as does the Greek Septuagint ("For my house is not so . . .").

Translating this as an interrogative is an attempt to harmonize these words with 2Sm 23:1 in the Masoretic Text. There David appears to be saying that he was the subject of this and all his psalms. If that is so, why then does he say in v. 5 that his house is not like the righteous King just described? Thus, translating the sentence as a question synchronizes these words with v. 1.

However, the problem with translating this as a question is that the Hebrew lacks the necessary particle that would make this sentence an interrogative. *Gesenius' Hebrew Grammar*,[18] in §150.2 states, "As a rule, however, the simple question is introduced by *He interrogative*."[19] S. R. Driver argues that "the question is indicated by the tone." Yet he concedes that this is an extreme case and that it would be an improvement if the Hebrew actually had an interrogative *h*.[20]

But there is no need to translate this sentence as a question. If the variant reading found in v. 1 is accepted (for which this article has argued above), then David is saying in v. 1 that he is not writing about himself but about the Messiah. Therefore, this statement in v. 5 is in complete accord with that perspective. David is writing about the Anointed One and here makes clear, to all who might misinterpret his perspective, that he is not writing about himself at all. Therefore, the most literal translation from the Hebrew ("For not so is my house with God") makes perfect sense.

David, here in the first sentence of v. 5, is articulating the difficulty that he faced about the coming Messiah—he and his household were undeserving of Him. He has not ruled righteously, "in the fear of God" (v. 3). J. H. Sailhamer states that "the narratives that follow God's promise to the house of David in chap. 7 [the Davidic covenant] have focused on the failure of David and his house . . ."[21] This includes David's sin with Bathsheba (2Sm 12) and the later sin of counting the people (2Sm 24). By declaring that his house is unrighteous, David makes clear that the coming of the Messiah is not based on his own merit but on God's gracious promise.[22]

(2) This leads to David's second assertion in v. 5: *David's hope for the coming Messiah is derived from God's gracious covenant and not his own righteousness.* He declares, "For He has established an everlasting covenant with me"—an obvious reference to the Davidic covenant (2Sm 7:12-16; 1Chr 17:10-15). In that covenant, God assured David that one day he would have a descendant, the son of David, the Messiah, who would have an eternal house, kingdom, and throne. This promise to David is described as "ordered and secured in every detail." David understands that the Davidic covenant has certified God's faithfulness to His promises, including the coming of the Messiah despite David's own sins and the failures of his future descendants.

(3) Having demonstrated his own failures and his confidence in God's faithfulness to the covenant, David makes the third declaration of v. 5: *God's faithfulness to His promises guarantees David's own salvation, although the fulfillment has not yet come to pass.* Once again many of the English versions translate the next sentence as a question and not a statement. The HCSB is representative: "Will He not bring about my whole salvation and my every desire?" But as in the first sentence of the verse, the same problem exists: the lack of the interrogative *h*.[23] Thus, the translation should more likely be the literal Hebrew statement, "For all my salvation and all my desire but *He has not made it sprout*."[24]

The difficulty with translating the sentence as a statement is that it seems to contradict David's previous declaration of confident faith in God's promise.

However, the simple Hebrew negative used here (*lo'*) can carry the sense of "not yet" (for example, see Gn 15:16 and Jer 37:4). Thus, the sentence should be translated "For all my salvation and all my desire but He has not *yet* made it to sprout." Cooper recognizes this when he writes,

> The context shows clearly that, notwithstanding the indications of his day, the promise would spring forth and become fruitful. Hence, we might paraphrase the last statement: "Although he maketh it not to grow *now* [emphasis added], He will surely cause it to develop into most bountiful fruition."[25]

Therefore, the sentence is a statement of confidence—although God has not yet fulfilled His promise of the Messiah, David is certain that the ordered and secured Davidic covenant will bring about his longing and his salvation.

That David was thinking of the Messiah in this last sentence may be evident through the verb "sprout" (*yatsmiyakh*). It is from the same Hebrew root used for the messianic title "Branch" (*tsemakh*, Jer 23:5; 33:15). In effect, David is saying the Davidic covenant assures the coming of the King, but He has not yet "Branched forth" (sprouted).

David has expressed a clear messianic hope in v. 5. He recognized his own lack of merit but also affirmed his confidence in the ordered and secured Davidic covenant. Moreover, David was certain that the promise of Messiah would be fulfilled (for all his desire and salvation) despite having to yet wait for the King.

David's Ultimate Warning (2Sm 23:6-7)

In the final section of David's last words, he moves from a depiction of the Righteous Ruler to the judgment of the wicked. The word "wicked" means worthless (*beliya'al*) and they are characterized as "thorns" (v. 6) since they cause pain to others and are so quickly consumed in fire. As to their destiny, "they will be completely burned up" (v. 7). Likely David included this final, ultimate warning to motivate others to adopt his confident hope in the coming Messiah and avoid this dreadful end.

David's last words reveal much about the Messiah. He is David's favorite subject to write about, both here and in the psalms he wrote (v. 1). David could write of the future Messianic King because of being a prophet (vv. 2-3a). The future King of Israel is righteous and will rule in the fear of God (vv. 3b-4). Ultimately, David recognized his own failure to live up to God's standard of righteousness but still had confident hope in the coming Messiah because of God's firm promise made in the Davidic covenant (v. 5).

THE CONFIRMATION OF DAVID'S LAST WORDS

David's last words, even when read in isolation, clearly indicate that, as a prophet and as a result of the covenant God had given him, David looked with great expectation for the Messiah. Even so, the messianic nature of this prophecy is confirmed by examining other texts of Scripture.

Confirmation in the Hebrew Scriptures

When reading 2Sm 23:1-7 innertextually (within the same book), it is plain that David's last words are deliberately linked to the Davidic covenant (2Sm 7:12-16), a passage that promises an eternal son of David. When David declares his confidence that the Messiah will come despite his own failures, it is because God "has established an everlasting covenant with me" (2Sm 23:5).

David's last words also are confirmed by numerous intertextual references (other books and authors) who use language similar to his when speaking of the Messiah. David uses the same word for ruler (*moshel*; 2Sm 23:3) as Micah does in the prophecy of Messiah's birth in Bethlehem (Mic 5:2; [Hb. 5:1]). In David's prophecy, the future Messiah is a righteous King (*tsaddiq*; 2Sm 23:3), a word Isaiah uses to describe the Messiah as wearing "righteousness" as a belt (Isa 11:5). Jeremiah also called this King "a righteous Branch" (Jer 23:5; 33:15), and Zechariah said he would be humble and "righteous" (Zch 9:9). According to both David (2Sm 23:3) and Isaiah (Isa 11:2), the Messianic King would be endowed with the "fear of God." David and Isaiah also compare the King to "light" (2Sm 23:4) that will shine on God's people (Isa 9:2). David depicts the future King as the sun rising (2Sm 23:4) even as Malachi calls Him the sun of righteousness (Mal 4:2). David also anticipates a future day when the King will "branch forth" (*yatsmiyakh*; 2Sm 23:5), so Jeremiah calls Him the "Righteous Branch" (Jer 23:5; 33:15). The echoes of Scripture plainly identify the King Messiah as the one that David and the other prophets were revealing.

Confirmation in the New Testament

It is not only the First Testament that confirms David's messianic perspective; the NT does as well. Luke recorded Peter's first sermon, preached at Pentecost, in Ac 2:29-31. There Peter cites Ps 16:8-11 as a messianic prophecy of the resurrection. His point was that David, as a prophet, intended this passage to be read about the Messiah, not himself. Furthermore, the apostle also asserted that David could not have seen himself in Ps 16 because David had died and his body had decomposed. Peter asserts that David had confidence in God's promise (the Davidic covenant), so "seeing this in advance, he spoke concerning the resurrection of the Messiah" (Ac 2:31).

Plainly, Peter based his messianic hermeneutic of David's psalms on a close reading of David's last words. The following are parallels between David's own perception of himself and Peter's understanding of him. By saying that the Spirit of the Lord spoke through him (2Sm 23:2-3a), David was claiming prophetic status. Similarly, Peter said "he was a prophet" (Ac 2:30). David declared his confidence in the coming Messiah was rooted in the Davidic covenant (2Sm 23:5); Peter affirmed that David was looking forward to the Messiah because "God had sworn an oath to him" (Ac 2:30), a reference to that same covenant. David said his psalms concerned the Messiah (2Sm 23:1), and Peter declared that David prophesied directly "concerning the resurrection of the Messiah" (Ac 2:31). Having used David's last words as an interpretive guide to David's authorial intent, Peter then claimed that David intended the Messiah to be the subject of Ps 16:10. Certainly, Peter understood David's last words as referring to the Messiah and further, that they revealed David's understanding that he was writing about the Messiah in his psalms.

CONCLUSION

As others have noted, reading the Psalms as a postexilic book is compelling evidence that the composer of the book saw the future Messianic King as the dominant theme of the Psalter. Nevertheless, it is not only the postexilic redactor who intended that sort of reading. In David's last words, the ancient king of Israel revealed that he too was looking forward to that Righteous Ruler. The compiler of the book of Psalms understood David's songs in much the same way as David himself did. David understood himself to be a prophet who gave oracles "concerning the Messiah of the God of Jacob."

---

1. The eschatological and messianic view of the Psalms is ably supported by D. C. Mitchell in *The Message of the Psalter: An Eschatological Programme in the Book of Psalms, Journal for the Study of the Old Testament, Supplement Series* 252, ed. D. J. A. Clines and P. R. Davies (Sheffield: Sheffield Academic Press, 1997), a work that reflects the much earlier book by J. Forbes, *Studies on the Book of Psalms: The Structural Connection of the Book of Psalms, Both in Single Psalms and in the Psalter as an Organic Whole*, ed. J. Forrest (Edinburgh: T&T Clark, 1888).
2. This canonical approach, that recognizes the compositional unity of the book of Psalms and its messianic intent, is advocated in two articles in this *Handbook*, R. L. Cole's "Compositional Unity in the Five Books of the Psalms: A Canonical Approach" and S. D. Postell's "Messianism in the Psalms."
3. B. K. Waltke, "A Canonical Process Approach to the Psalms," *Tradition and Testament: Essays in Honor of Charles Lee Feinberg*, ed. J. S. and P. D. Feinberg (Chicago: Moody Press, 1981), 3–18.
4. Ibid., 12.
5. Ibid., 15.
6. The Vulgate follows the LXX reading as well.

7. J. H. Sailhamer, *Introduction to Old Testament Theology* (Grand Rapids: Zondervan, 1995), 221.

8. The full paraphrase of 2Sm 23:1 is, "And these are the words of the prophecy of David that he prophesied about the end of the world, about the days of the consolation that are about to come. David son of Jesse spoke, and the utterance of the man who was anointed for kingship; Messiah by the Memra of the God of Jacob." (2Sm 23:1 TARG-E) https://accordance.bible/link/read/TARG-E#2Sam._23:1

9. The sentence lacks the prefixed particle, the interrogative *h*. This will be discussed in greater detail later in this exposition.

10. The KJV and the NKJV are distinctive in translating 23:5 as a declarative sentence ("Although my house is not so with God," NKJV).

11. C. F. Keil and F. Delitzsch, "The Books of Samuel," *Commentary on the Old Testament*, vol. 2, trans. J. Martin (Grand Rapids: Eerdmans, 1980), 486.

12. J. P. Lange, *Samuel, Commentary on the Holy Scriptures: Critical, Doctrinal, and Homiletical*, vol. 5, trans. and ed. P. Schaff (Grand Rapids: Zondervan, 1960), 586.

13. W. G. Blaikie, *The Second Book of Samuel* (Minneapolis: Klock and Klock, 1978; reprint, A. C. Armstrong and Son, 1893), 366.

14. David said, "The God of Israel spoke to me, the Strong One of Israel who rules over mankind, judging in truth, has commanded to appoint for me the king, he is the Messiah who will arise and rule in the fear of the Lord." (2 Samuel 23:3 TARG-E) https://accordance.bible/link/read/TARG-E#2Sam._23:3

15. Keil and Delitzsch, "The Books of Samuel," *Commentary on the Old Testament*, vol. 2, 487.

16. For the implied phrase "shall" or "will arise" see Keil and Delitzsch, "The Books of Samuel," *Commentary on the Old Testament* vol. 2, 487, and D. L. Cooper, *Messiah: His Nature and Person* (Los Angeles: Biblical Research Society, 1933), 115.

17. Keil and Delitzsch, "The Books of Samuel," *Commentary on the Old Testament*, vol. 2, 488.

18. W. Gesenius, *Gesenius' Hebrew Grammar*, ed. E. Kautzsch and A. E. Cowley, 2nd English ed. (Oxford: Clarendon Press, 1982).

19. This does not include factual or "Wh" questions (Who? What? Why? etc.), for which there are other particles or interrogative pronouns. See C. H. J. van der Merwe, J. A. Naudé, and J. H. Kroeze, *A Biblical Hebrew Reference Grammar* (Sheffield: Sheffield Academic Press, 1999), §43.

20. S. R. Driver, *The Books of Samuel*, 2nd ed., rev. (Oxford: Oxford University Press, 1912; repr., Winona Lake, IN: Alpha Publications, 1984), 360.

21. J. H. Sailhamer, *The NIV Compact Bible Commentary* (Grand Rapids: Zondervan, 1994), 248.

22. Cooper comes to the same conclusion, seeing the sentence as a statement of David's failures and the recognition that "he was standing upon the basis of the pure grace of God." *Messiah: His Nature and Person*, 119.

23. Both Driver (p. 360) and GKC §150.2[a], without any basis, propose emending the text from the negative *lo'* to *halo'*, as if there was an interrogative *h*.

24. This is similar to the KJV and *Young's Literal translation*.

25. Cooper, *Messiah: His Nature and Person*, 120.

Messianism in 1 & 2 Kings

JAMES SPENCER

The messianic message of 1 and 2 Kings is, in one sense, quite straightforward: God will honor His covenant, and a Davidic king will reign over God's people. Unlike more direct messianic prophecies that foretell a coming king who will deliver Israel from sin and death, 1–2Kg narrate the succession of Judean and Israelite kings incapable of delivering God's people. The Davidic line from which the Messiah will ultimately arise provides a muddled legacy, with some kings seeking to serve the Lord and others seeking their own path apart from God.

God's covenant with David places obligations on the house of David to walk in the ways of the Lord. The kings who seek to rule by their own devices only serve to underscore the need for God to intervene in judgment. Even those kings who "did what was right in the LORD's sight and walked in all the ways of [their] ancestor David" (2Kg 22:2) were incapable of saving God's people from their sin and turning back God's judgment. As Robin Routledge rightly notes, "Some covenants, such as the Abrahamic and Davidic, contain unconditional elements; but those to whom the promises are addressed may still cut themselves off from the blessing through disobedience."[1] It seems clear that, no matter how righteous the ruler, how many reforms were made, how ornate and holy the temple, God's people will feel the consequences for their sins. Despite the ebbs and flows of Israelite and Judean leadership after the deportation of the kingdoms of Israel and Judah, the books of 1–2Kg present a clear messianic message rooted in God's faithfulness to His people and His commitment to His covenant through the preservation of the Davidic king.

STRUCTURE OF 1 AND 2 KINGS

The books of 1–2Kg convey this messianic message, this commitment to the preservation of the house of David through their structure and theology. The revival of the line of David is embedded in the broader plot and structure of 1–2Kg. No matter how bad things may seem, God preserves one of David's descendants. Perhaps the most prominent example of God's preservation of the Davidic line is Jehoiachin, who found favor while in exile in Babylon (2Kg 25:27-30). Commenting on this passage, Gerhard von Rad notes, "an occurrence is referred to which has immense significance for the Deuteronomist, since it provides a basis upon which Yahweh could build further if he so willed. At all events the reader must understand this passage to be an indication of the fact that the line of David has not come to an irrevocable end."[2]

Identifying the structure of 1–2Kg can be difficult, as interpreters have offered a variety of different suggestions for understanding the way in which 1–2Kg are organized. Some have divided the books based on the three broad historical eras of the united kingdom (1Kg 1–11), the divided kingdom (1Kg 12–2Kg 17), and Judah after the deportation of Israel (2Kg 18–25).[3]

G. Savran identifies a chiastic structure centered on the Omride dynasty and the "rise and fall of Baal cult in Israel and Judah."[4] He suggests that the central position of 1Kg 16:23–2Kg 12 "is a function of the section's presentation of a model for the victory of prophetic over monarchic forces."[5] Savran's chiastic structure highlights the prophetic actions related to the elimination of Baal worship in Israel and stands as a central feature of the books of 1–2Kg. As Savran notes, "By placing the idea of prophetic continuity at the very center of his work, the narrator emphasizes that as long as dynastic kingship continues, there will be a corresponding prophetic response."[6] This prophetic response serves the monarchy by ensuring that the voice of God is available to Judean and Israelite rulers. The prominence of the prophetic witness in 1–2Kg is a sign of God's continued commitment to the Davidic dynasty and to the covenant.

Richard D. Nelson offers a more thematic structure for 1–2Kg, suggesting that the books' unity "is not created by a single structure or scheme. Rather Kings offers a complicated network of overlapping patterns."[7] Nelson identifies five major sections: A Kingdom of Shalom (1Kg 1–10), Shalom is Broken (1 Kg 11–16), Israel under the Prophetic Word (1Kg 17:1–2Kg 8:15), Israel's Last Chance and the End (2Kg 8:16–17:41), and Judah: Paradox of Promise and Punishment (2Kg 18–25). He suggests a contrast between Solomon's reign and the failures of the kings that follow noting, "In a larger sense, the contrast between the peace and prosperity of Solomon in the early chapters and the apostasies, famines, defeats, and follies of the rest of the story, including the final undoing of all of Solomon's works, provides the overarching structure for the plot of the entire book."[8] While Nelson's observations are helpful, Solomon cannot be put on a pedestal. As Nelson recognizes, it is Solomon's folly that breaks "shalom" in 1Kg 11 and results in the division of the kingdom.

Nelson's structure ends with 2Kg 18–25, which he labels as "Judah: Paradox of Promise and Punishment" reflecting the favor Jehoiachin receives in Babylon. This final accounting of a Davidic king finding favor in exile demonstrates both the reality of God's judgment and the hope of God's ongoing commitment to His people. Nelson's structure highlights the broad strokes of God's interactions with His people, the inevitable progression toward judgment, and the final preservation of a Davidic king during exile, though it tends to gloss over the multiple instances in which God, in His grace, preserves a Davidic king. For instance, in 1Kg 11:13, which would fall within the section Nelson calls "Shalom is Broken," God rips the kingdom away from Solomon, but preserves one tribe to give to Solomon's heir, for David's sake.

Peter J. Leithart offers an alternative structural analysis derived from the manner in which the author contrasts David and Omri, presenting the Omride dynasty as "a photo negative of the Davidic [dynasty]." He captures these narrative tensions in what he refers to as "a blueprint for the architecture of the book as a whole," which he describes as a collection of interwoven narratives.[9] Leithart's structure highlights the aspect of "Davidic revival," demonstrating God's steadfastness to the covenant He made with David and making more explicit the messianic message of 1–2Kg. God remains with Israel despite the destruction of the Temple, and deportation of Israel and Judah. A king from the house of David will remain on the throne of Israel. Leithart sums this up well stating, "For all the parallels between the Omride and Davidic dynasties, and for all the similarities between the history of northern and southern kingdoms, the narrative structure of 1–2 Kings highlights their differences: while counterfeit Davids fall, never to rise, YHWH takes the true David from the ash heap and sets him in a place of honour, heir to an everlasting kingdom."[10]

Determining a book's overarching structure, as is suggested by the differences between interpreters in the case of 1–2Kg, is no easy task. While Savran's chiastic structure offers a clear outline of the book, it is largely arranged around specific dynasties or events and does not offer a transparent explanation of the theology of 1–2Kg. Nelson's more thematic approach offers a more cohesive theological schema, though it tends to overshadow some of the theological variation within a given section. Leithart's discussion of the structure of the book provides support for the messianic message of 1–2Kg suggested here, as well as identifying parallels between God's interactions with the various rulers of Israel and Judah. His observation concerning the recurring theme of Davidic revival points toward the covenantal background of 1–2Kg and that background's vital connection to the messianic message of 1–2Kg.

THEOLOGY OF 1 AND 2 KINGS

The Davidic Covenant: To grasp the message of 1–2Kg, it is important to recognize the significance of the Davidic covenant articulated in 2Sm 7. The covenant between God and David is strongly connected to the covenants that came before it. As Bruce K. Waltke notes, "The Davidic covenant also supplements the Abrahamic covenant. *I AM* promises unconditionally to both Abraham and David an eternal posterity: to Abraham an enduring nation; to David an enduring dynasty to rule that nation. Indeed, David's eternal dynasty mediates the kings whom *I AM* promised to give from Abraham and Sarah's own bodies."[11] With the Davidic covenant, God not only commits to giving His people the land, seed, and blessing (Gn 12:1-4), but also to establishing the house of David through which God would rule over His people. Through the Davidic covenant, God will raise up an Anointed (Messiah) from the house of David to deliver Israel.

The narrative of 1–2Kg, particularly 1Kg 1–11, demonstrates the significance of the Davidic covenant for understanding 1–2Kg. Solomon's establishment as king over Israel represents an initial step in the fulfilment of God's covenant with David. Paul R. House summarizes these connections well:

> Solomon's career, as depicted in 1 Kings 1–11, fulfills many of the nearest predictions. Perhaps the most significant aspects 2 Samuel 6–7 addresses are his temple building and his establishment of the Davidic dynasty. God places his name on the temple (1 Kg 9:3), which in turn establishes Jerusalem as a specially chosen city. Despite Solomon's idolatry (1 Kg 11:1-8), Yahweh does not end the dynasty because of the promises made to David (1 Kg 11:11-13). Solomon stands as the link to David's fidelity and the dynasty's later consistent covenant breaking.[12]

Despite the unfaithfulness of the kings who follow Solomon, and to some degree Solomon himself (1Kg 11:1-8), God is determined to keep His covenant "for the sake of David" (1Kg 11:12-13 ESV). The division of the kingdom and the subsequent giving over of Israel to Jeroboam are the consequences of Solomon's unfaithfulness. Despite God's promise to Jeroboam to "build [him] a sure house, as I built for David," [ESV] God makes clear that David's house will not be afflicted forever (1Kg 11:30-39).

In addition to its importance as a theological foundation for Davidic succession in 1–2Kg, the Davidic covenant also connects the house of David to messianic expectations. Andrew E. Steinmann addresses the messianic aspects of the Davidic covenant. He argues that while it seems most likely that Nathan's proclamation is identifying David's immediate successor, who turns out to be Solomon, rather than an individual Messiah to come, the prophecy also refers to a coming messianic kingdom.[13] As such, 1–2Kg recognizes the Davidic covenant and writes a history that demonstrates God's faithfulness to that covenant through the preservation of a Davidic king. Though the books of 1–2Kg deal with the apostasy of Israel and Judah and the infiltration of idolatrous religions, God is unwavering in His fidelity to His people and to the preservation of the house of David even as He dispenses justice and disciplines His people.

God in 1 and 2 Kings: The covenantal background and the rather complex dynamics between God and His people in the books of 1–2Kg raise questions concerning those books' portrayal of God. Clearly, God has been faithful to His covenant with David. It is also plain that He intends to discipline the people for their sins. God seeks to demonstrate His power by revealing His opposition to idolatrous practices and by preserving His people even in the most difficult circumstances—ranging from poverty (2Kg 4:1-7) to death (2Kg 4:18-37) and almost everything in between. The prophetic ministries of both Elijah and Elisha underscore that God rules over Israel and is capable of providing everything for those who are faithful to Him.

The roles of the prophets in 1–2Kg not only underscore the reality of God's reign, but also the manner in which God exercises His authority. As David makes clear to Solomon, success as a king requires faithfulness:

> Be strong, and show yourself a man, and keep the charge of the Lord your God, walking in his ways and keeping his statutes, his commandments, his rules, and his testimonies, as it is written in the Law of Moses, that you may prosper in all that you do and wherever you turn, that the Lord may establish his word that he spoke concerning me, saying, "If your sons pay close attention to their way, to walk before me in faithfulness with all their heart and with all their soul, you shall not lack a man on the throne of Israel." (1Kg 2:2-4)

Some among the kings of Israel and Judah followed the Lord while others pursued false gods and refused to acknowledge the Lord. The prophets reminded the kings of Judah and Israel, as well as the people of Israel more generally, that God alone decides the course of the nation. No other gods, no king, no political power could determine the fates of Israel and Judah. The prophets, as Waltke notes, "represent I AM's historic covenants, guaranteeing the fulfillment of his promises to Abraham and David, and at the same time bringing blessings and curses upon the nation according to the Mosaic covenant. The book of Kings shows beyond question that the prophetic word is mightier than the king's sword."[14] God's prophets make clear that the Lord shapes the events that shape the nations of Israel and Judah. God's people are not subject to the vicissitudes of history but are guided by the hand of the Lord.

THE ESTABLISHMENT OF SOLOMON AND THE MESSIANIC MESSAGE OF 1 AND 2 KINGS

The significance of the Davidic covenant along with a number of other factors have led some scholars to suggest that 1–2Kg continues the story of David begun in 1–2Sm.[15] Since the story begins as it does with the account of David's final days and the installation of Solomon as king (1Kg 1–2), such suggestions have merit. However, no matter how strongly 1–2Kg may be connected to the rest of the canon, these books also stand alone as theological works intended to convey a unique message to God's people. The story of Solomon's ascent to the throne and subsequent reign (1Kg 1–11) is not a historical account devoid of theological purpose. Instead, this first account underscores God's covenant faithfulness to the house of David even after Solomon turns away from the Lord and worships Chemosh and Molech (1Kg 11:7).

During David's final days, the king's failing health kept him secluded within his chambers, seemingly ignorant of the political maneuvering of his oldest surviving son Adonijah. Adonijah "exalted himself" and gathered some of David's strongest supporters, including Joab and Abiathar, to lay claim to his father's throne. He hosted a banquet to celebrate his self-proclaimed coronation and to unite those of influence in David's kingdom. Unfortunately for Adonijah, some key players, notably Zadok the priest, Benaiah the son of Jehoiada, Nathan the prophet, Shimei, Rei, and David's mighty men (1Kg 1:8), decided not to join him on his quest for the throne (1Kg 1:7-8) and were excluded from Adonijah's core group of supporters along with David's youngest heir Solomon.

Nathan recognized the rather precarious position he occupied by not supporting Adonijah and constructed a plan to gain audience with King David. Nathan instructed Bathsheba to go to David and remind him of his promise, which is not recorded elsewhere in the OT, that David would make Solomon king. Nathan would then confirm Bathsheba's words in David's presence, and they would convince the king to name Solomon his successor. Nathan's plan was successful and Solomon was anointed "ruler over Israel and Judah" (1Kg 1:35).

Once David anointed Solomon, he gave a series of instructions to Solomon, calling him to walk in all the ways of the Lord "so that you [Solomon] will have success in everything you do and wherever you turn, and, so that the Lord will carry out His promise that He made to me, saying, 'If your sons are careful to walk faithfully before Me in truth with their whole mind and heart, you will never fail to have a man on the throne of Israel'" (1Kg 2:3-4). He also called upon Solomon to deal with Joab and Shimei, both of whom had left stains on David's reign.

This narrative of Solomon's installation as co-regent, as well as the subsequent chapter in which David gives instructions to Solomon, introduce some of the theological themes that shape the messianic message of 1–2Kg. David's instructions to Solomon emphasize the importance of covenant fidelity. As Lissa Wray-Beal notes, "While that dynasty is confirmed, it is also now conditionalized. Each generation must do as David has just charged Solomon (2:3); they must 'guard their way' (2:4) with all their heart and soul (Deut. 4:29; 6:5; 26:16; 30:2,6). This conditionalization does not discharge the Davidic covenant, but emphasizes the obligations of its recipients (cf. 6:12-13; 8:25; 9:4, 6-7)."[16] David's successors cannot keep the covenant stipulations any more than David did. The Davidic dynasty will not stand on the obedience of kings, but on the forbearance and faithfulness of the Lord.

In addition, Solomon's dealings with Adonijah, Joab, and Shimei demonstrated the inevitable retribution that comes from opposing the Lord's anointed. Adonijah, who was formerly vying for the throne, afterward asked for Abishag the Shunammite. The request was likely another attempt by Adonijah to lay claim to the throne. Jerome T. Walsh notes, "The significance of this request can only be seen in its political context. One of the privileges of a monarch was to inherit his predecessor's harem. Any claim on the wife or concubine of a living monarch was tantamount to a claim on the throne."[17] Solomon vowed to have Adonijah put to death and thereby further solidified his own grip on the throne.

Joab's execution is described as an act of cleansing retribution. Solomon described the elimination of Joab as the means of removing the guilt from his father's house of the blood Joab had shed (1Kg 2:31). With Joab's death, the house of David was finally freed from any culpability in the deaths of Abner and Amasa so that "for David, his descendants, his dynasty, and his throne, there will be peace from the LORD forever" (1Kg 2:33). Solomon proclaimed David's innocence in the matters of Abner and Amasa, noting that Joab acted "without my father David's knowledge" (1Kg 2:32).

Shimei does not feature as prominently in the history of David as Joab. He initially appeared in 2Sm 16 after the death of Saul. There, he cursed David, accusing him of taking his kingship through force. David chose to spare Shimei in 2Sm 16:11-12, but called upon Solomon "not to let him go unpunished" (1Kg 2:9). Solomon initially gave Shimei quarter in Jerusalem, but if Shimei were to leave Jerusalem he would die and guilt for Shimei's death would be on his own head (1Kg 2:36-37). This agreement freed the house of David from guilt when Shimei broke his vow so that "King Solomon will be blessed, and David's throne will remain established before the Lord forever" (1Kg 2:45).

Solomon's dealings with Adonijah, Joab, and Shimei served at least two functions within the narrative that contribute to the messianic message of 1–2Kg. First, the elimination of Adonijah, who was portrayed as a usurper and threat to

Solomon, the Lord's anointed, solidified Solomon as David's true, God-ordained heir. While Adonijah was also of the house of David, Solomon had been established by the Lord (1Kg 2:24). Any attempt at usurpation represented an act of opposition to the Davidic covenant. Wray-Beal describes the dynamics between Solomon and Adonijah well: "His [Solomon's] oath before YHWH carefully blames Adonijah for his own death (v. 23), publicly absolving the king from bloodguilt and enabling him to claim adherence to Torah."[18] Adonijah himself, not David or Solomon, was responsible for Adonijah's death, thereby preserving Solomon's innocence as he took hold of the throne of Israel.

Second, the executions of Joab and Shimei represented the culmination of events that occurred during David's reign and could be interpreted as a shrewd political maneuver to ensure that Solomon retained his relatively tenuous grasp on the throne. While the elimination of Joab and Shimei certainly had a political upside, executing Joab and Shimei underscored the certainty of God's justice. Dealing with Joab and Shimei also underscored God's role in the establishment of the house of David. David and Solomon were not warlords who had taken control through bloodshed. The deaths of Abner and Amasa, regardless of the manner in which their deaths benefited David, fell squarely on the shoulders of Joab. Shimei's death appears to stand as a vindication of David and as evidence that God established the Davidic kingship. Shimei, who accused David of taking Saul's throne by force, was killed for "all the evil that you did to my father David" (1Kg 2:44).

THE OMRIDE DYNASTY AND THE MESSIANIC MESSAGE OF 1 AND 2 KINGS

This aspect of the messianic message is also evident in one of the more central narratives of 1–2Kg, which describe the Omride dynasty (1Kg 16:21–2Kg 12). This portion of 1–2Kg is perhaps best well known for the exploits of Elijah and Elisha and the manner in which the narrative demonstrates that the Lord is the only true God. The narrative also functions to underscore the messianic message of 1–2Kg.

Omri, the first ruler of the Omride dynasty, has been contrasted with David. Concerning Omri, Leithart notes, "he was a counterfeit David, a photo negative of his famed predecessor."[19] He goes on to argue that "If Omri is a new David, Ahab is a new Solomon."[20] Despite their failures, David and Solomon sought to honor the Lord and keep covenant. Perhaps more important, the Davidic covenant was made with the house of David, not with the Omride dynasty. Some of Omri's dynasty seem to have recognized the need for an affiliation with the line of David, infiltrating the house of David through intermarriage and swaying the Davidic line away from the Lord. This is made clear in the description of Ahaziah:

> In the twelfth year of Israel's King Joram son of Ahab, Ahaziah son of Jehoram became king of Judah. Ahaziah was 22 years old when he became king; he reigned one year in Jerusalem. His mother's name was Athaliah, granddaughter of Israel's King Omri. He walked in the way of the house of Ahab and did what was evil in the LORD's sight like the house of Ahab, for he was a son-in-law to Ahab's family. (2Kg 8:25-27)

Ahaziah, despite being from the house of David, had been heavily influenced by the Omride dynasty. It was at this point that Jehu was called upon to put an end to the house of Ahab. Ahaziah, who had sought an alliance of sorts with Joram in Israel, was killed at the hands of Jehu. Athaliah, Ahaziah's mother, having heard of Ahaziah's death, "proceeded to annihilate all the royal heirs" (2Kg 11:1) except for Joash who was hidden and raised by Jehosheba (2Kg 11:2). Athaliah, a member of the Omride dynasty, reigned in Judah for six years until Jehoiada the priest anointed Joash king and had Athaliah executed (2Kg 2:12-16).

As the Omrides threatened to overcome the house of David, God preserved one heir of David's line. The infiltration of the Omrides into the house of David represented a true threat to the messianic line. Even as God ended the Omride dynasty through Jehu, Athaliah almost succeeded in exterminating the Davidic line as well.

Ahab's reign over Israel is not simply portrayed as that of another king who "did what was evil in the LORD's sight, more than all who were before him" (1Kg 16:30) and "did more to provoke the LORD God of Israel than all the kings of Israel who were before him" (1Kg 16:33). Ahab, along with Jezebel, instituted a program to systematically eliminate God from the northern kingdom of Israel. In addition to establishing the Baal cult and building the Asherah (1Kg 16:32-33), Ahab was also associated with rebuilding Jericho, resulting in the fulfillment of the curse spoken in Jos 6:26 and the death of two of Hiel's sons. As Gina Hens-Piazza observes, "Not only does Ahab appear to provoke the Lord with his attention to the Baal, but he also dismisses the binding significance of the sacral past."[21]

Ahab's decision to trust in Baal over the Lord became a key factor during the rest of his reign, as the amazing acts of Elijah and Elisha highlighted the folly of placing the nation in the hands of a false fertility god incapable of bringing prosperity to the nation. Elijah's first word to Ahab made clear that the prosperity of Israel depended on the God of Israel, not Baal (1Kg 17:1). Commenting on Elijah's words, Hillel Millgram notes, "With these words Elijah flings down the gauntlet to Baal, 'The Rider of Clouds,' the bringer of rain. Swearing a mighty oath by the very life of the Lord, God of Israel, Elijah asserts that only his word will produce precipitation. Without it the heavens will yield not a drop. Baal is being challenged, on his own turf as it were, to counter God's edict. With these words, Elijah struck at the very heart of the pagan faith in Baal."[22] Ahab, whose wife Jezebel had "slaughtered the LORD's prophets" (1Kg 18:4), had been actively seeking to remove the Lord's presence from Israel.

Elijah and Elisha offered resistance to Ahab and Jezebel's program to eliminate the voice of God from the northern kingdom. The prophetic witness against Baal and the rulers of Israel is attributed rightly to the defense of monotheistic faith. As Ahab led Israel toward Baal, Elijah proclaimed that the Lord alone is God in Israel. John Goldingay expresses this well stating, "Mono-Yahwism is not a primitive stage of development on the way to monotheism. It is the sophisticated, radical affirmation needed in Elijah's context (and perhaps most others?) when an affirmation of monotheism would be a piece of irrelevant rationalism."[23] This emphasis on monotheism has tended to obscure the messianic significance of the confrontation between God and Baal. In defeating Baal and eliminating the Omride dynasty, God further affirmed and legitimized the Davidic dynasty, the dynasty of His choosing. God's elimination of the Omride dynasty and the removal of its idolatrous practices represented the removal of a threat to the Davidic dynasty and a reaffirmation of God's commitment to the Davidic line.

EXILE AND THE MESSIANIC MESSAGE OF 1 AND 2 KINGS

The deportations of Israel and Judah represent the consequences of disobedience. Despite the efforts of Josiah to reform Israel's practices, he was only able to delay the Lord's actions:

> In spite of all that, the LORD did not turn from the fierceness of His great wrath and anger, which burned against Judah because of all the provocations Manasseh had provoked Him with. For the LORD had said, "I will also remove Judah from My sight just as I have removed Israel. I will reject this city Jerusalem, that I have chosen, and the temple about which I said, 'My name will be there.'" (2Kg 23:26-27).

Once God's people had sinned, exile was inevitable. In 1Kg 8:46-53, Solomon anticipated the exile, calling upon God to have compassion on His people when they repented from exile and prayed that the nation that had taken God's people captive would also have compassion upon them (8:49-50). When Israel, and eventually Judah, were exiled, the Davidic dynasty needed God's deliverance once again. The Babylonians besieged Jerusalem, destroyed the temple, and took Judah into exile. Jehoiachin, the reigning king of Judah when Babylon attacked Judah, was imprisoned in Babylon. Everything depended on God's faithfulness to the covenant, and God's faithfulness never disappoints. In a turn of events that echoes Solomon's prayer for compassion upon God's people in exile, Evil-merodach freed Jehoiachin, the last of the Davidic line (1–2Kg), from prison and "he [Evil-merodach] spoke kindly to him [Jehoiachin] and set his throne over the thrones of the kings who were with him in Babylon" (2Kg 25:28).

The kind treatment of Jehoiachin in Babylon represents a final instance of God's preservation of David's house. Having established Solomon on the throne and delivered the house of David from the threat of the Omride dynasty, God next had compassion on Jehoiachin in Babylon. The Davidic dynasty, through which the Messiah would come, would be preserved and cared for even in exile. God's people had not been abandoned, nor did the exile signal God's failure. Instead, it demonstrated that the wisdom of Solomon, the Temple and its operations, or the revival of the law could not overcome Israel's sin. Neither the faithfulness of the kings, the institutions of Israel, nor attempts at religious reform were capable of restoring the nation and avoiding the consequences of sin. The people of God were left in a constant state of anticipation, hope, and dependency. Even as they longed for God's deliverance, their faith was bolstered by the ongoing faithfulness of the Lord and the covenants He made with Abraham and David.

With 2Kg ending with Judah and their king Jehoiachin in exile, plainly the Davidic covenant, with its promise of a descendant who would have an eternal house, kingdom, and throne, was not yet fulfilled. The intention of the author of 1–2Kg becomes plain. According to Michael Rydelnik, it "was to maintain the hope and expectation that God would one day send an eternal ruler who would build the true temple of God and sit on the throne of David."[24] The end of these books is designed to encourage the reader keep looking for the coming son of David, the Messianic King.

CONCLUSION

The books of 1–2Kg leave Israel with an astounding hope. While some commentators suggest that Jehoiachin's release from prison "is only a paltry mitigation of the deluge that has engulfed the chosen people," God showed compassion and strength even when Israel and Judah were in exile.[25] Ultimately, through the release of Jehoiachin, the end of 1–2Kg provided a glimmer of hope that God would restore a Davidic king to the throne. Moreover, the books of 1–2Kg also highlight the sobering truth that the kings of Judah and Israel were incapable of remaining faithful to the covenant. Idolatry, abuse of power, and pride plagued the rulers of Israel and

Judah. The reforms of imperfect kings who "did what was right in the eyes of the Lord" did not sustain the nation throughout its generations, nor did their efforts keep God from ultimately disciplining His people with exile.

The people of Israel would need a final resolution for sin. Jesus Christ, the Davidic Messiah, is that final resolution. The books of 1–2Kg do not flesh out this final resolution, and they do not point directly to the Messiah in the way that many other portions of the OT do. Instead, 1–2Kg offer a messianic message rooted in God's commitment to His people and to the house of David. The books of 1–2Kg remind God's people that the Lord reigns and has committed Himself to keeping covenant with Israel. The continuation of the Davidic line, even after the exile of Judah, demonstrates the steadfastness of God's commitment and reminds the people of God that a Davidic ruler will arise, through whom God will restore His people and bring blessing to Israel and the nations.

---

1. Robin Routledge, *Old Testament Theology: A Thematic Approach* (Downers Grove, IL: InterVarsity, 2008), 171.
2. Gerhard von Rad, *From Genesis to Chronicles: Explorations in Old Testament Theology* (Minneapolis: Fortress, 2005), 165.
3. Burke O. Long, *1 Kings and 2 Kings*, The Forms of Old Testament Literature 10 (Grand Rapids: Eerdmans, 1991), 3–4.
4. G. Savran, "1 and 2 Kings," in *The Literary Guide to the Bible*, ed. R. Alter and F. Kermode (Cambridge: Harvard University Press, 1987), 148.
5. Ibid., 149.
6. Ibid., 149.
7. Richard D. Nelson, *First and Second Kings*, Interpretation: A Bible Commentary (Louisville: John Knox, 1987), 9.
8. Ibid., 11.
9. Peter J. Leithart, *1 & 2 Kings*, Brazos Theological Commentary on the Bible (Grand Rapids: Brazos, 2006), 23. Leithart provides greater explanation of the structure in "Counterfeit Davids: Davidic Restoration and the Architecture of 1–2 Kings," *Tyndale Bulletin* 56.2 (2005), 19–33.
10. Leithart, "Counterfeit Davids," 33.
11. Bruce K. Waltke, *An Old Testament Theology: An Exegetical, Canonical, and Thematic Approach* (Grand Rapids: Zondervan, 2007), 693.
12. Paul R. House, *Old Testament Theology* (Downers Grove, IL: InterVarsity, 1998), 242.
13. Andrew E. Steinmann, "What Did David Understand about the Promises in the Davidic Covenant?" *Bibliotheca Sacra* 171 (2014), 21.
14. Bruce K. Waltke, *An Old Testament Theology*, 702.
15. Martin Noth offered one of the seminal treatments in this regard, arguing that Joshua, Judges, Samuel, and Kings were written by a single author influenced by the "Deuteronomic Law and the admonitory speeches which precede and follow the Law" (Martin Noth, *The Deuteronomistic History*, trans. D. Orton, Journal for the Study of the Old Testament Supplement Series 15 [Sheffield: Sheffield Academic Press, 1981], 4).
16. Lissa Wray Beal, *1 & 2 Kings*, Apollos Old Testament Commentary (Downers Grove, IL: InterVarsity, 2014), 75.
17. Jerome T. Walsh and David W. Colter, *1 Kings Berit Olam: Studies in Hebrew Narrative and Poetry* (Collegeville: Liturgical, 1996), 50.
18. Lissa Wray-Beal, *1 & 2 Kings*, 76–77.

19. Leithart, "Counterfeit Davids," 24.

20. Ibid., 24.

21. Gina Hens-Piazza, *1–2 Kings*, Abingdon Old Testament Commentaries (Nashville: Abingdon, 2006), 159.

22. Hillel I. Millgram, *The Elijah Enigma: The Prophet, King Ahab and the Rebirth of Monotheism in the Book of Kings* (North Carolina: McFarland & Company, 2014), 52–53.

23. John Goldingay, *Old Testament Theology: Israel's Gospel* (Downers Grove, IL: InterVarsity, 2003), 619.

24. Michael Rydelnik, *The Messianic Hope: Is the Hebrew Bible Really Messianic?* (Nashville: B&H, 2010), 74.

25. J. G. McConville, *God and Earthly Power: An Old Testament Political Theology* (New York: T&T Clark, 2007), 151.

1 Chronicles 17

The Davidic Covenant (II)

EUGENE H. MERRILL

First Chronicles 17:4-14 (along with 2 Samuel 7:5-16) embodies the so-called "Davidic covenant," the terminology of which is most apropos in light of the contents of the two texts. The passages' significance to OT Israel is apparent in that this text occurs in two of the canonical books, one composed prior to the return of the exiled Jews from Babylon, and the other at least 150 years later.[1] Clearly, the promises contained in the respective treatises were perceived as ongoing, despite the times and circumstances surrounding the traumatic events of the destruction of the Solomon Temple and Holy City, the 70 years of deportation to a pagan and distant land and back, and the struggles of the postexilic community of Yehud[2] to regain a new political, social, and religious footing.

Studies of the comparisons between Samuel–Kings and Chronicles in general abound,[3] but in this study comparison must be limited to the two passages containing the texts of the Davidic covenant. Part of the agenda for this essay is to determine how many, if any, deviations occur between the two versions, especially in theological progress or development. Examples of obvious textual differences are well known, and these are set out in the following table. However, the objective here is to point out ideological comparisons and how the historical and sociological environment of the composers of Samuel and Chronicles, respectively, affected the later account vis-à-vis the earlier.

TABLE 1: COMPOSITIONAL AND THEMATIC COMPARISONS

REFERENCES	2Sm 7:5-16	1Chr 17:4-14
2Sm 7:5/ 1 Ch 17:4	Are you the one to build me a house?	You are **not the one** to build me a house
7:6/17:5	I have not dwelt in a house	I have not dwelt in a house
7:7/17:6	Did I ever ask for a house?	Did I ever ask for a house?
7:8/17:7	I took you from the pasture to reign	I took you from the pasture to reign
7:9/17:8	I have been with you and will make you great	I have been with you and will make you great
7:10/17:9	I will give my people their own home where they can live safe from those who oppress them,	I will give my people their own home where they can live safe from those who oppress them,
7:11/17:10	as they have done since the days of the judges. Yahweh will *make* (ʻāsāh) you a house.	as they have done since **Yahweh gave them** judges. Yahweh will *build* (*bānāh*) you a house.
7:12a/17:11b	When your days are finished and you join your ancestors in death	After you have grown old and go to your fathers
7:12b/17:11b	I will raise up a descendant after you who will come *from your very body.*	I will establish your descendant after you who will come ***from among your own sons;***
7:12c/17:11c	and I will set up his rule/kingdom;	and I will set up his rule/kingdom;
7:13a/17:12a	He will build a house for me;	He will build a house for me;
7:13b/17:12b	I will establish his *throne*[4] forever	I will establish his *throne* forever;
7:14a-b/17:13a	I will be like a father to him, and he will be like a son to me,	I will be like a father to him, and he will be like a son to me.
7:14c/(lacking)	who, if he is iniquitous, I will strike with a common rod and ordinary whips.[5]	(lacking in Chronicles)
7:15/17:13b	However, my merciful grace will never abandon him as it did from *Saul,* whom I rejected in your[6] very presence.	I will not turn from him my merciful grace as I turned it away from ***that one***[7] **who preceded you.**
7:16/17:14	Your dynasty and kingship will never be at risk in my presence forever. Your throne will be established world without end.	Instead, **I will make him to stand in my house, even in my kingdom,** unto eternity; and ***his*** *throne* will endure forever.

These differences appear to be minor at first glance. However, deeper literary, rhetorical, and intentionally instructive features will emerge in full presentations of the respective texts, their translations, and attention to the pluses and minuses they exhibit in relation to each other. A more careful look at the respective texts will bring to the surface even more points of comparison.

LITERARY AND THEOLOGICAL COMPARISONS BETWEEN THE TWO DAVIDIC COVENANT TEXTS

The Historical Settings

In undertaking a comparison, it is important to consider the *Sitzen im Leben* of the two passages. First, the clues for such comparisons reside in the texts themselves unless one posits processes of redaction that were at work after—and perhaps long after—the main body of each reached essentially its present shape. Of such processes, no objective or direct evidence exists that they were ever undertaken, and attempts to see clues within the passages to support the hypotheses to this point have never proved satisfying. Rather, assumed redactions are in most cases reasons advanced by the critic to support some other historical and/or theological ideology. Begging the question in this way is, on its face, unacceptable.

The parameters for the investigation include (1) geographical environments, (2) historical settings, (3) religious and ideological contexts, and (4) literary idiosyncrasies. As noted previously, the last recorded event in the so-called "Deuteronomistic History (hereafter DH)" (Joshua through Kings) is the release of Jehoiachin from house arrest in Babylon following the death of Nebuchadnezzar II in 562 BC and the accession to the throne by Evil-merodach (2Kg 25:27-30).[8] One might argue that since the writer refers to "all the days of [Jehoichin's] life" it might be possible to date the end point somewhat later than 562, but there is no way to determine this one way or the other. This dismal note characterizes the last generations of Israel and Judah's national life from Hezekiah (729–686) onward with the exception—an important one—of the voices of the prophets, but their hope lay in an exclusively eschatological reversal of fortune.[9] Only the postexilic prophets—Haggai, Zechariah, and Malachi—approach the time and circumstances in which the book of Chronicles was compiled: Haggai and Zechariah ca. 520–516 BC and Malachi likely sometime a little earlier, ca. 570.[10]

The Babylonian exile occurred in three stages: (1) that in 605 as a result of a swift foray by Nebuchadnezzar into the southern Levant, including Jerusalem, upon learning of his father Nabo-Polassar's death that year (2Kg 24:1-7); (2) that of 598 in which Jerusalem was penetrated and Jehoiachin was taken prisoner (2Kg

24:8-17); and (3) that of 586 that resulted in the destruction of Jerusalem, the leveling of the Temple, and the capture of Judah's last king, Zedekiah (2Kg 25:1-22). One might say without exaggeration that the loss of the Temple was a sort of "Maginot Line" between the era of the DH historian (DH[11]) and that of the Chronicler. The world of the Jewish community had been shaken to its core in every way, especially, perhaps, in its assessment of the past that led to this calamitous turn of events.

Second Samuel speaks of the sins that condemned Judah to this fate, and 2 Kings offers some glimmer of messianic hope with the partial rehabilitation of Jehoiachin (2Kg 17:7-23; 25:27-30). The Chronicler views the matter from the perspective of one who has had 120 years or more to think upon these things, to interpret the factors that had brought them to pass, and more important, to conclude that all had not been lost.[12] Cyrus, redeemer of Jerusalem and patron of Judaism, was, to him, an undeniable "messiah-figure" who had accomplished the saving work of Yahweh (2Ch 36:22-23), a view explicitly stated by Isaiah in particular (Isa 44:24–45:7) and more implicitly hinted at in the postexilic prophets, most clearly Zechariah (12:7–13:1). Not only was the Davidic covenant still in place and operative in every way, but the future was as bright as the promises of God.

Note that the grand historical work at hand ends in a most peculiar manner in that it cites the biblical version of the Cyrus decree as though to say that it is a harbinger of something greater to come. The peculiarities are (1) its anachronistic position in the record; (2) its isolation from any compatible context; and (3) its startling and unexpected usage as a closure to the history as a whole.[13] This is in keeping with the previously stated point that Cyrus functioned as a "servant" of Yahweh, chosen by Him to deliver His people from their dire and despairing situation in the clutches of the enemies of God, the pagan empires of their world. The epithets applied to Cyrus prophetically by the great prophet Isaiah are redolent of his messianic character and function. First, the great emperor, the most celebrated up to his time, is addressed by Yahweh as His shepherd. This eponym was by no means a term of subordination since an honorific common in the ancient Near Eastern world to refer to kings was precisely the same. The Akkadian version of Cyrus's decree confirms this: "He (Marduk) called out his name: Cyrus . . . and he (Cyrus) shepherded with justice and righteousness."[14]

Considerations of the literary comparisons between DH and Chronicles as a whole cannot be done here, but the larger Davidic covenant contexts can and must be pursued.[15] The former embodies 2Sm 7:5-16 and the latter 1Chr 17:4-14.[16] Table 1 presents some technical details of a textual nature. Table 2 covers a broader swath in some respects but also considers more narrowly the technical language of the covenant renditions. Thus it attempts to discern what modifications or advancements, if any, the Chronicler brought to the Davidic covenant wording and emphasis that was introduced, or driven by, the "Maginot Line" described above.

TABLE 2: IDEOLOGICAL AND/OR THEOLOGICAL COMPARISONS

VERSE	2 Samuel 7:5-16		1 Chronicles 17:4-14
5	Will you build me a house?	4	**Do not** build a house
6	I dwelt in a tent in the desert	5	**I have not been in a house** but a tent
7	I never asked for a house	6	I never asked for a house since the time of the **judges**
8	David from sheep to sovereign	7	David from sheep to sovereign
9	I have been with you and will make you great	8	I have been with you and will make you great
10	I will find a place for my people	9	I will provide a place for my people to live in **peace**
11	As there was peace in the times of the **judges**, there will be peace in the future	10	As there has been peace since the **judges**, there will be peace in the future, and **I will build you a house**
12	A **seed** (sg.) of David will reign	11	**After you die**, I will appoint a **son** to succeed you
13	The **seed** will build a temple and will reign forever	12	**He** will build me a house and **I will build him one**
14	**If he sins, I will punish him**	13	**I will make a father-son relationship with him** and I will preserve my ***hesed***
15	My ***hesed*** will not leave him	14	My **house and kingdom** and **his throne will be eternal**
16	Your house, kingdom, and throne will be everlasting		

The following observations about these parallel texts simply demonstrate that changes in times, circumstances, and purposes of certain events or propositions are reflected in the texts that relate to and/or describe them. This, of course, is a key principle in the concept of biblical theology—that later revelation invariably adds to or reshapes earlier revelation. Such is the case here in the following respects:

1. It is striking that 2 Samuel records the clear statement that a messianic figure is promised who will build a house (the Temple) whereas in Chronicles he is

forbidden to do so. In light of the postexilic setting of Chronicles, with the Solomon Temple lying in ruins, the historian is much more attuned to the ultimate, eschatological period and the Temple building promised there by the prophets than in even the Second Temple, which was then standing, or any other possibility of a historical construction of such a building.

2. The substitution in 1 Chronicles with "son" for "seed" in 2 Samuel suggests a closer incarnational view of the messianic figure or, at least, a more clearly defined personality rather than the more generic "seed."
3. The Chronicler refrains from speaking of any punishment of the son who is to come whereas 2 Samuel is most graphic in describing the measures that will be taken should he fail in his duties and thus disobey Yahweh. It is likely the Chronicler already understands the nature of the son to be such that failure will be impossible and thus discipline is inappropriate. Second Samuel, on the other hand, is speaking of the whole line of Davidic descendants who, like David, sinned and were invariably punished for it.

Moreover, the idealistic way the Chronicler views David and his dynasty, one of perfect obedience to the sovereignty of God, precludes, in his view perhaps, any need to trot out David's terrible behavior in the past. David's sin with Bathsheba and its consequences are thus largely omitted in Chronicles.[17]

EARLY TEXTUAL READINGS AND INTERPRETATIONS

Apart from the simple comparisons and contrasts between the two canonical versions of the Davidic covenant just presented, subsequent translations, versions, and editions also weighed in on the matter and are briefly documented below.

Second Temple

LXX: Most notable is the omission in 1Chr 17 (as well as MT) of the plural, the shift of persons from "he" to "you," and the inclusion of daughters.

LXX: "If there be found unrighteousness in him, I will punish him with the devices ordinarily used." This is virtually a word-for-word rendition of 2Sm 7:13b.

Qumran: Thus far, 1Chr 17 is unattested in the Dead Sea Scrolls, but 2Sm 7 is found in abundance. Donald H. Juel observes with reference to this passage and to the Davidic covenant: "For the first time in Jewish literature prior to the New Testament we encounter a messianic reading of Nathan's Oracle in 2Sm 7 (in *Florilegium* [4Q174]), a passage quoted in the New Testament (Heb 1:5) that was of considerable importance in providing language with which to speak of Jesus as

God's 'Son.'"[18] Another text, "Words of the Luminaries" (4Q504), reads, "You chose the tribe of Judah, your covenant you established with David so that he would be like a shepherd, a prince over your people, and would sit on the throne of Israel in your presence forever" (frg.4.5-8).[19]

Apocrypha

Second Esdras 12:31-32 reads: "As for the lion you saw roused roaring out of the forest... he is the Anointed One, whom the Most High has kept until the end of the days who will spring from the posterity of David."

First Maccabees, in Mattathias's blessing of his sons (2:49-70), rehearsed the list of the names of the "hall of fame" of the fathers beginning with the adjuration, "be zealous for the Torah, and be ready to give your lives for the covenant of our fathers" (v. 50). Of David he said, "David for his piety received as his heritage a royal throne for ages" (v. 57).[20] Goldstein makes much of the plural "remote, lifetimes" (αἰῴνιος) as opposed to the singular (αἰῴν), "age, lifetime," but usually "forever," thus suggesting that the author's intent was not to supplant the Hasmonean Dynasty by any other, including David's.[21] However, he concedes that the plural can mean "forever" also as seen in Isa 26:4; 45:17; Dn 9:24; Pss 77:8; 145:13; 1QS 2:3–4:22; and 1QM.[22]

Maccabees is a little more veiled in its messianic witness, but the following reference to "covenant" and the Patriarchs certainly points in that direction: "A good peace may God make for you, and may He be good to you, and may He remember His covenant with His faithful servants Abraham, Isaac, and Jacob" (1:1-2). More substantial is the reference to Jer 33:2-26, and in particular, vv. 7-9, 15, and 17. The whole is triggered by the "good peace," a construction found here (2:9) and in Jer 33:9 (cf. Est 9:30) in close juxtaposition "for abundance of good and of peace."[23] In any case, there can be no doubt that the author of this early first-century BC historical account held to at least a "loose" Davidic messianic expectation.

The books of Tobit, Judith, Additions to Esther, and Wisdom of Solomon are virtually silent about the matter, as are the books of Baruch, the Letter of Jeremiah, the Story of Susanna, The Song of the Three Children, Bel and the Dragon, and The Prayer of Manasseh. The name of David at least appears in Sirach, in terms not of messiahship but almost of indifference. His deeds in war are celebrated (47:3 7) as is his faithfulness in the cultus (47:9-11). The closest hints of any eschatological end result of David's reign are the references to his dynastic succession (47:15,22). Most of his named descendants are evil, however, and thus not adding to the possibility of a beneficent and godly Davidic reign in the last days (cf. 47:9). The conclusion is that "a prince remained in the house of David. Some of them did what was right, and some of them sinned more and more" (48:15-16). In sum, "Except David and

Hezekiah and Josiah, they all sinned greatly, for they forsook the Law of the Most High" (49:4).

New Testament

The quotations and/or allusions to 2Sm 7:5-16 and 1Chr 17:4-14 in the NT are attested to in a few places as, indeed, one would expect.[24] The following are some of the clearest examples:

Example I

2Sm 7:14a: "I will be to him (as) a father and he will be to me (as) a son."

2Co 6:18: "I will be to you as a father and you (pl) will be to me as sons and daughters."

Heb 1:5: "I will be to him as a father and he will be to me as a son." The wording here is exactly the same as in LXX and in the Hebrew of MT; cf. also Rev 21:7.

Example II

2Sm 7:14b: "who, if he commits iniquity, I will punish with ordinary, customary rods." This is not found in NT quotations or allusions.

Medieval Judaism

Talmuds (Babylonian and Jerusalem)

Midrash

Pesiqta Rabbati (ca. AD 850)

"pesiqta" (verse) Ruah-ha-qodesh Homilies 36.2 (ca. AD 630):

"In the year when the Messiah reveals himself . . . the King of Persia will wage war against a king of Arabia, and this king of Arabia will go to Edom in order to consult with the Edomites."[25]

Wa-Yosha 15.8 (ca. AD 1075); "Armilos will slay the Messiah from Joseph but will himself be slain by the Messiah from Judah."[26]

Seder Eliyahu Rabbah (ca. AD 650): "700 years of Jewish servitude have passed because of their sins during which time Messiah's coming has been delayed."[27]

CONCLUSION

In line with the principal stated objective of this article, namely, to determine what evidence exists for a theological nuancing of the Davidic covenant text in 1Chr 17 as compared to that of 2Sm 7, the following are proposed:[28]

- In Samuel (hereafter S), Yahweh asks whether He had ever suggested to David that he build a house (Temple) for Yahweh. The Chronicler (hereafter C) reports that Yahweh said in no uncertain terms, 'You[29] will *not* build me a house.' S only hints at the matter when Yahweh asks, "Are you the one to build" (v. 5)? The point here seems to be that by the time the Solomon line of kingship had been re-established following the exile, it was certain to continue onward and to include the building of another temple in the future.[30]
- S brings to mind the exodus "from Egypt" but C says only "brought . . . out of" (6). The change may be explained by C's knowledge of and his being profoundly moved by the "second" exodus, that from Babylon inspired by Cyrus the Great, one anointed and chosen,[31] as was Moses, to be a messianic redeemer.[32]
- On most occasions, S refers to Israel as "the sons/people of Israel"[33] whereas C calls them merely "Israel," as if to say the looseness of a tribal federation in an earlier time had given way to a nation following the exile, albeit one under Persian dominion.
- Finally, the messianic name David occurs a mere 19 times in 2Kg as against about 70 in 2Chr, each of which covers the Solomon and divided monarchy, the former to the note about the release of Jehoiachin from house arrest in Babylon, and the latter through to the firm re-establishment of the state of Yehud under Ezra and Nehemiah after the return of the exiles from Babylon. The difference in density is astounding.[34] Clearly, the messianic hope had come nearly to extinction during the exile, but afterward had an explosive rekindling.

---

1. The books of Samuel are commonly identified as part of the larger corpus called the "Deuteronomic History" (Joshua–2 Kings). They are designated thus because of the assumption in historical-critical circles that they were composed in part and then in finality by the unknown author(s) or composer(s) of Deuteronomy. For the initial and exhaustive proponent of this hypothesis, see Martin Noth, *History of Pentateuchal Traditions,* trans. Bernhard W. Anderson (Englewood Cliffs, NJ: Prentice-Hall, 1972). Brian Peckham published a sympathetic but refined work on the matter in *The Composition of the Deuteronomistic History,* Harvard Semitic Studies 35 (Atlanta: Scholars Press, 1985), esp. 13–39. However, 2Kgs (the latest of the so-called Deuteronomic History accounts) sets its own dates by referring to the release of King Jehoiachin from house arrest by the Babylonian King Evil-merodach in the year 560 BC, the last event recorded in the book (2 Kgs 25:27-30). As for Chronicles, it was composed by an unknown scribe (or scribes) late in the First Temple period, perhaps as late as 375 BC. For support of this date and other introductory matters, see Eugene H. Merrill, Mark F. Rooker, and Michael A. Grisanti, *The World and the Word: An Introduction to the Old Testament,* (Nashville: B&H Academic, 2011), 336.
2. Yehud was a corruption of the name Judah given to the postexilic homeland of the Jews by their Persian overlords. It was part of a larger entity known as a satrapy (or province), in this case Abar Nahar ("across the river [Euphrates]").
3. See especially Diane Edelman, "The Deuteronomist's David and the Chronicler's David: Competing or Contrasting

Ideologies?" *The Future of the Deuteronomistic History*, ed. Thomas Romer (Leuven: University Press, 2000), 67–83; W. E. Lemke, "The Synoptic Problem in the Chronicler's History," Harvard Theological Review 58 (1965): 349–363; Steven L. McKenzie, *The Chronicler's Use of the Deuteronomistic History*, (Atlanta: Scholars Press, 1984); Eugene H. Merrill, "The Chronicler: What Kind of Historian Was He, Anyway? *Bibliotheca Sacra* 165 (2008): 397–412.

4. Literally, "throne of his kingdom" (כִּסֵּא מַמְלַכְתּוֹ).

5. This entire clause is lacking in Chronicles.

6. Read with the Septuagint, "from my presence" (ἐκ [Septuagint, Lucian Rescension ἀπὸ] προσώπου μου).

7. The Chronicler seems loath even to mention Saul's name and dynasty.

8. For the Babylonian evidence, see Babylon Text 28186, which speaks of "*Ia-ku-u-ki-nu*, the son of the king of *I-a-ku-du* (clearly a reference to Judah and its king Jehoiakim, father of Jehoiachin), the latter to receive as rations 10 sila (ca. 10 liters) of (olive) oil, perhaps daily. James B. Pritchard, ed. *Ancient Near Eastern Texts Relating to the Old Testament*, 2nd ed. (Princeton: Princeton University Press, 1955), 308. Speaking of King Evil-merodach of Babylon (clearly Em/wil-Marduk, "the man of Marduk" in Akkadian), the biblical historian notes that after 48 years of Jehoiachin's imprisonment (562 BC), he "pardoned King Jehoiachin of Judah and released him from prison. He spoke kindly to him and set his throne above the thrones of the kings who were with him in Babylon. So Jehoiachin changed his prison clothes, and he dined regularly in the presence of the king of Babylon for the rest of his life" (Jer 52:31-33).

9. See Hos 2:14-23; 14:4-7; Am 9:11-15; Isa 4:2-6; 7:10-17; 9:1-7; 11:1-16; 26:11-21; 27:12-13; 33:17-24; 35:1-10; 40:9-11; 41:8-16; 42:1-17; 43:1-21; 44:1-8,21-23; 45:1-7; 49:1-13,22-26; 51:9-16; 52:7-10,13-15; 53:1-12; 54:1-17; 59:20-21; 60:4-22; 61:1-11; 62:1-12; 65:8-25; 66:7-24; Mic 2:12-13; 4:1-8; 5:2-9; 7:7-20; Zph 3:8-20.

10. Eugene H. Merrill, *Haggai, Zechariah, Malachi: An Exegetical Commentary* (Chicago: Moody, 1994), 3–4, 373–378.

11. The term refers to the hypothesis that Joshua through Kings constitutes one massive work of historiography governed in its narrative perspective by the book of Deuteronomy, itself held to be a product of an unknown author or compiler of the early or mid-seventh century. See Martin Noth, *A History of Pentateuchal Traditions*, trans. Bernhard W. Anderson (Engelwood Cliffs, NJ: Prentice-Hall, 1972). The designation is used here only as a convenient and widely accepted code term for this segment of the OT, a position not held by this author.

12. One might, for example, think of World War II, the history of which told in 1945 would surely differ considerably from the history of that event in 2025. The one, right on the heels of the surrender of the Axis powers and the treaties made with each by the Allies, and the other from the perspective of the reconstruction of Germany and Japan and the forging of new, now peaceful, relations among the nations, might differ little on the details of that horrendous conflict. Yet the lenses through which historians looked at each would certainly render different appraisals concerning the reason for the war, its justness, its immediate after-effects, and the present state of affairs in both Europe and the rest of the world. Such was the situation in Judah/Yehud in the interval between 562 BC and 400.

13. Eugene H. Merrill, *A Commentary on 1 & 2 Chronicles* (Grand Rapids: Kregel, 2015), 611–613.

14. William W. Hallo and K. Lawson Younger, Jr, eds., *The Context of Scripture*, vol. 2 (Leiden, Netherlands: Brill, 2000), 314–315.

15. For a full discussion of these similarities and differences, see Merrill, *Commentary on 1 & 2 Chronicles*, 217–223.

16. The literary and form-critical parameters of the Samuel and Chronicles versions of the covenant text proper are spelled out respectively in A. A. Anderson, *2 Samuel*, Word Biblical Commentary 11 (Dallas: Word, 1989), 112–114; Simon J. De Vries, *1 and 2 Chronicles*. Forms of Old Testament Literature Series (Grand Rapids: Eerdmans, 1989), 151–159.

17. Merrill, *Commentary on 1 & 2 Chronicles*, 222–223.

18. Donald H. Juel, "The Future of a Religious Past: Qumran and the Palestinian Jesus Movement," *The Bible and the Dead Sea Scrolls*, vol. 3, ed. John H. Charlesworth (Waco, TX: Baylor University Press, 2006), 65. The pertinent passage "affirms the 'throne of his kingdom forever'" and "interprets the 'Son' of 2 Sm 7:14 as the 'Shoot of David, is to [arise] in Zi[on in the La]st Days.'" Peter W. Flint, "David," Lawrence H. Schiffman and James C. VanderKam, eds. *Encyclopedia of the Dead Sea Scrolls*, vol. 1 (Oxford: Oxford University Press, 2000), 180. See also CD (4Q269) 7:15-174; QpGen (=4Q252), 4Q246; 4Q269. Texts that identify the rulers of Israel as a "divine son" include 4Q174; 4Q369; 4Q254.

19. Peter W. Flint, "David," Ed. Lawrence H. Schiffman and James C. VanderKam (Oxford: Oxford University Press, 2000), 180.

20. Jonathan A. Goldstein, *I Maccabees*, Anchor Bible 41 (Garden City, NY: Doubleday, 1976), 238.

21. Ibid., 142.

22. Ibid., 240.

23. Very like the combination of "good" and "peace" should be understood as a hendiadys, i.e., the same as "good and peaceful" or "good peace."

24. Mt 1:1; Lk 1:32-33; Jn 7:42; Ac 2:30; 7:45-46; 13:33; Heb 1:5; 12:7; Rev 21:7.

25. H. L. Strack and G. Stemberger, *Introduction to the Talmud and Midrash*, trans. Markus Bockmuehl (Minneapolis: Fortress Press, 1992), 327.

26. Ibid., 368.

27. Ibid., 370.

28. S refers to the Samuel version of the covenant text and C that of the Chronicler. Second Kings serves as the base text to which Chronicles is compared with regard to the terminology being examined here. The reason is that the compilers write of what they hear and know by experience (no earlier than 562 BC). As we have argued above, Chronicles was composed late in the postexilic period, as late as 400–375. The perspective as well as the reality of politics, sociology and everyday descriptive language wrought changes of many kinds.

29. The use of the independent personal pronoun emphasizes it is *not* for David to build it, the reason being that he was a man of war who shed much blood (1Chr 22:6-10).

30. By "Solomon line" is meant the incontestable fact that by the time of the postexilic era, the focus was on the Solomon dynasty, issuing at last in Joseph, foster-father of the messianic king (1Chr 29:22b-25; 2Chr 6:8-9; 7:18; Mt 1:6,16).

31. Is 44:28; 45:1. Cyrus claimed to have been chosen by the Babylonian deity Marduk: "He [Marduk] scoured all the lands for a friend, seeking for the upright prince whom he would have to take his hand. He called King Cyrus of Anshan . . . [All the foreign peoples] . . . who had been brought into the land, I at the bidding of Marduk, the great lord, made to dwell in peace in their habitations." Bill T. Arnold and Bryan E. Beyer, eds., *Readings from the Ancient Near East* (Grand Rapids: Baker, 2002), 147–149.

32. 1Sm 16:1; 1Kg 8:16; Isa 41:8; 43:10; 44:1.

33. See the numerical data presented in Solomon Mandelkern, *Veteris Testamenti Concordantae Hebraicae atque Chaldaicae.* Lipsiae: Veit et Comp., 1896.

34. The book of 2 Kings occupies 55 pages of the MT, 2 Chronicles 61 pages, or a respective ratio of the number of occurrences of David's name in 2 Kings of 0.3 per page of text to 2 Chronicles at 16.4 times per page, 54 times as dense! One cannot deny the messianic fervor and hope that had been reborn upon the re-occupation of the Holy Land and the reconstruction of the Holy Temple. Messiah must be just around the corner!

Job 19:23–27

A Living Redeemer

LARRY J. WATERS

Written by an unknown author, and possibly the most ancient literary account in the Bible, the book of Job is a mixture of prose and poetry that both distresses and comforts the reader. Samuel E. Balentine observes, "Job is clearly part of Judaism's Scripture."[1] Most evangelical scholars see Job as a real historical character.[2] For instance, August H. Konkel states, "There is no reason to doubt that Job was a historical individual whose story was well known. The prophet Ezekiel (Ezk 4:14, [20]) refers to Noah, Daniel, and Job as three historical individuals."[3] James also recognizes Job as a historical person (Jms 5:11). Not only is Job a historical character, but also "a heroic figure in the mold of Noah and Adam . . . patriarchal, or better, prepatriarchal."[4]

The reader of the book of Job is immediately introduced to the integrity and virtue of the main character (chaps. 1–2). Job[5] is considered to be the greatest of "all the men of the east" by the writer of the book (1:3), and a man like no other "on earth" by God Himself (v. 8). Job was therefore a well-known individual, or at the least a key individual representative of the Lord, at this time in history. In chaps. 1 and 2, the author takes the reader into the throne room of God, "Now there was a day when the sons of God came to present themselves before the Lord, and Satan [ha-Satan, the Adversary][6] also came among them" (1:6 ESV). God introduced Job into the conversation with Satan. . . . God took the initiative[7] to move His redemptive purpose forward.[8] The writer was introducing concepts that are vital to God's redemptive message for humankind: God's covenant love and grace in the midst of human suffering.

The first two chapters not only introduce Job, but also highlight Satan's attack on God's redemptive message. "Does Job fear God for nothing? Haven't You placed a hedge around him, his household, and everything he owns?" (1:9-10).[9] Satan proposed that Job feared God, or worshiped God, because of what he was materially gaining from the relationship. More directly, Satan accused God of buying worshipers through material prosperity. This would be a serious charge since humanity's relationship with God must be based on grace, not works. God is not so impotent that He must purchase human worship through materialism. God should be worshiped because He is God, and true worship is not based on a *quid pro quo* system of theology, as in other ancient Near Eastern religions. God blesses humankind on the basis of grace, and Job's undeserved suffering is the field on which such beliefs are decided. Will Job reject God and lose all hope? There is ample evidence here, despite the unrelenting suffering endured by Job, that he will not give up on God and that he will retain hope, even if he dies.

BACKGROUND

Job knew nothing of the conversations between God and Satan in chaps. 1 and 2, nor did he know anything about the limitations God placed on Satan. Death was a real possibility in the mind of Job, even though the reader knows Satan was not allowed to take Job's life. Job's intense suffering would immediately lend itself to the conclusion that death was imminent. Satan attacked Job with a viciousness almost beyond comprehension: "While he was still speaking" (1:16,17 NASB) indicates that within minutes, several catastrophic things happened (vv. 13-21). A Sabean raiding party rustled all of Job's donkeys and oxen, and murdered all but one of the servants. Fire fell from heaven and consumed Job's sheep, and killed all but one of the servants. A Chaldean raiding party rustled all of Job's camels, killing all but one of the servants, and a windstorm caused the collapse of the oldest son's house killing all ten of Job's children. Furthermore, over the next few months Job's suffering increased (7:3; 29:2).

The seriousness and variety of Job's suffering during that period can be classified into four categories. First, Job suffered physical pain and disease that included: inflamed, ulcerous boils (2:7), itching (2:8), degenerative changes in facial skin (2:7,12), loss of appetite (3:24), insomnia (7:4), hardened skin, running sores, worms in the boils (7:5), loss of weight (16:8), eye difficulties (16:16), emaciation (17:7; 19:20), bad breath (19:17), trembling of the limbs (21:6), continual pain in the bones (30:17), restlessness (30:27), blackened, peeling skin (30:28,30), and fever (30:30).[10]

Second, he was socially alienated from family and friends and lost his high status within the community. Job's wife turned against him (2:9), and he was rejected, jeered, and mocked by friends (12:4; 16:10; 17:2,6), even by children (19:18).[11] Several derogatory terms were used, or implied, to describe Job: fool (5:2,3); sinful (4:7; 18:5-22; 22:5-11); arrogant (8:2; 11:4; 15:11-16; 18:3); evil (11:13,14; 15:20; 22:5); stupid (11:12); empty (15:2); unteachable (15:8-9); a "byword" (ESV) or object of scorn (17:6; 30:9); ugly (19:17-20); dishonest (20:19); a persecutor of widows and orphans (22:9).

Third, emotionally, Job was grief-stricken over the loss of his children (1:20-21), lacked a sense of inner tranquility (3:26), lost his desire to live (9:21), was depressed (3:24-25), experienced troubled thoughts (7:4,13-14), felt uncertain (9:20), was without joy (9:25; 30:31), and suffered from loneliness (19:13-19). Finally, Job was spiritually distressed over his conflict with a theology that could only conclude that God was, in John Hartley's words, "a capricious despot, who delights in afflicting his servant" (see 6:4; 7:17-19; 19:22). He was terrified by God's silence (23:8-9,15).[12]

The list of Job's sufferings established his suffering as allowed by God, and a reality in the "contest" or conflict with Satan—and it prompts a key question: Will suffering move Job to reject God, giving up all hope of vindication? If God allows suffering, and if it is part of the conflict with evil and the evil one, then it seems likely that God used suffering to deal with the lies of Satan and the assumptions connected with his lie. The proper response to suffering would then lead to triumphing over the enemy's accusations. Job 19:23-27 indicates that Job has hope in a Redeemer who will vindicate him and uphold his "innocence," regardless of the relentless attacks from Satan and Job's three "friends." The three, according to H. L. Ellison, "were not concerned so much with turning him to God as with getting him to acquiesce in their judgment. . . . The greatest wrong his friends did Job was resolutely to refuse to see that he was genuine in his efforts to come to terms with God."[13] Job's suffering was not commensurate with any wrong he had done.

There are some who hold that Job's struggle with God's justice means that he "characterizes God as his enemy,"[14] a "cruel opponent . . . quite illogical, inconsistent, and from Job's perspective, intolerable."[15] Hartley observes that Job "felt a full range of emotions. . . . The center of Job's test is that the anguish caused by God's apparently unreasoned anger threatens to break his moral resolve."[16] But does it? The author, through Job's life experience, was testing the traditional understanding that all suffering is caused by some personal act of sin.[17] It is true that pain and loss drove Job to despair and near blasphemy in his accusations against thc justice of God. However, in that pain, as he experienced the depths of anger and doubt, he also had heights of hope that transcended his suffering. It is not correct that his "repeated accusations against God show that Job's hope is not in God."[18] This exposition of 19:23-27 will demonstrate that in this example, Job moves, as Warren Wiersbe says, "from the depths of despair to the heights of faith, and then back into the depths again. *This is often the normal experience of people experiencing great suffering.*"[19] A person in pain is particularly capable of new insights, and deep reflection on death, eternity, and God. Hartley maintains that Job was actually "beseeching the God in whom he [had] faith to help him against the God who [was] punishing him. While this view seems irrational, this paradox lies at the core of Job's struggle. These two conflicting views of God are at war in his own mind."[20]

HISTORY OF THE PASSAGE

Scholars have labored over the meaning of the Hebrew terms and disagree on specific interpretations of Job 19:23-27. T. J. Meek even states, "so varied are the interpretations that no two of them are in agreement."[21] Generally the interpretations fall under one of two possibilities: *antemortem*[22] (redemption while yet alive), or *postmortem* (redemption after death).[23] Would Job live through the suffering and be eventually vindicated by his Redeemer, or would he be vindicated after death at the resurrection?[24] Generally the more recent commentators hold the first view, while earlier writers hold the latter. It might be well to recall C. S. Lewis's admonition about what he called "chronological snobbery," or "the uncritical acceptance of the intellectual climate common to our own age and the assumption that whatever has gone out of date is on that account discredited."[25] An older interpretation need not be discredited simply because it was held by earlier interpreters and is now held by their current followers.

It is said that George Frederick Handel composed his *Messiah* in 24 days. A servant interrupted him as he was writing the "Hallelujah Chorus," and found Handel weeping profusely. When asked the reason, Handel replied, "'I think I did see all heaven before me and the great God Himself.' Is it any wonder that the resurrection passage that immediately follows the 'Hallelujah Chorus' is opened with, 'I know that my Redeemer liveth?'"[26] Job may have had the same emotional response when he declared, "I will see Him myself; my eyes will look at Him, and not as a stranger. My heart longs [faints] within me" (Job 19:27).

This interpretation can be traced to the influence of the church fathers who saw in the passage a classical source for the doctrine of the resurrection.[27] Clement of Rome is generally recognized as the first of the postapostolic writers to see resurrection in this context. Origen adopted the same view and identified *gō'ēl* as a messianic title for Christ, as did Augustine and Jerome. [28] Later, John Chrysostom rejected this interpretation seeing it simply as a hope for physical recovery. Later, the Reformers generally held that Job 19:23-27 referred to a bodily resurrection and that the Redeemer pointed to Messiah.[29] Even though older Jewish and Christian scholars saw this passage referring to resurrection, Gordis states that this "view has been . . . surrendered by modern scholars."[30]

However, this article asserts that, as J. Gerald Janzen says, this "so-called modern consensus is mistaken and that the ancient view is substantially correct."[31] Chrysostom's objections can be answered by comparing chaps. 14 and 19 in context. Often those who reject the ancient interpretation see chap. 14 supporting a negative view of resurrection. The argument that Job's dialogues follow along unimaginative, clearly defined lines is defective. If this was true, why did Job "keep turning to any kind of hopeful affirmations after so many reiterated portrayals of hopelessness?"[32] Job "is affirming his faith that behind the God of violence, so tragically manifest in the world, stands the God of righteousness and love—and they are not two but one!"[33] The fault in Chrysostom's logic, and that of those who follow, can be exposed by a careful examination of chap. 14. It is almost universally agreed that 14:13-17 reflects the bodily resurrection or *postmortem* reading. "If so soon after the negative conclusion of vv. 7-12, Job in vv. 13-17 could imagine resurrection in such a poignant (if hypothetical) detail, there should be no difficulty in a resurrectionist reading of 19:25-27, if the details of the latter passage are seen to point in that direction."[34] Can this be established?

INTERPRETATION OF JOB 19:23-27

I wish that my words were written down, that they were recorded on a scroll or were inscribed in stone forever by an iron stylus and lead! (vv. 23-24)

A natural request of a person facing sure death would be to leave a legacy, a record of his life and words. Job's desire that his words be written down with an iron pen and lead, on a scroll or engraved in a rock forever was certainly fulfilled. We are reading his words today. Job was responding to Bildad's terse criticism in 18:17, "All memory of him [a wicked man—Job by implication] perishes from the earth." Job wanted his record to remain, so he began his "outcry of faith by requesting that his words of protestation be given permanence. . . . This memorial would allow future generations to judge the justice of his case."[35] Job was "Fearful that he might die before his honor [was] restored."[36] Stone inscriptions endure for centuries; long after the subject has passed away.[37] Art and writing are the materials of history.

But I know my living Redeemer (v. 25a)

Of even more importance to our interpretation is the identification of *gō'ēl*, "Redeemer."[38] The term *gō'ēl* can refer to one who marries a childless widow to raise and preserve the family name of the deceased (Gn 30:1; Ru 4:5-6); an avenger of blood (Jos 20:3-9); or one who buys back a property of a relative (Lv 25:25; Ru 4:2-4). In Job's case his defender needed to vindicate him in a court of law.[39] Some scholars hold that the identification is either a living person,[40] a divine being other than God,[41] or God.[42] Neither Job's family nor his friends proved to be redeemers or mediators, yet Job's faith in God held true. In a surge of faith, he declared, "I know my living Redeemer." The expression "I know," in "forensic contexts," means, "I have a strong conviction" or "I firmly believe" (Job 9:2,28; 10:13; 13:18).[43] Job described his Redeemer as one who would stand on the earth sometime in the future (Job 19:25), and that he would see Him after his death. The near referent is clearly stated to be God (v. 26).[44]

While admitting that the passage does not provide explicit Christological meaning to the word "Redeemer," or give a full description of the doctrines of immortality and personal bodily resurrection, there is sufficient reason to see in Job's words hope of a positive meeting with God after death. Andersen gives three reasons for this position.

> First, there is no need for Job to deposit a written testimony, if he expects to be vindicated before he dies. Secondly, the word translated *earth*, as used in Job, is constantly connected with Sheol, and the statement that the Redeemer *lives* is a direct answer to the fact that a man dies (14:10). The repetition of the word *after* (-wards) in the prominent position at the beginning of verses 25b and 26a suggests an interval, or even, with the meaning *at last*, something eschatological. Finally, the argument that Job does not expect personal reconstitution as a man, because this idea entered Judaism only towards the very end of the biblical period, can be dismissed in the light of much recent research that shows interest in the afterlife as an ancient concern for Israelite faith. . . . Job 14:13ff. . . . shows that the hope of resurrection lies at the very heart of Job's faith.[45]

Boorer states, "His [Job's] hope in relation to death and his hope in relation to vindication are distinct aspects of his hope and yet they interact and become intertwined in the ongoing movement of the text."[46]

The Redeemer is more than just an angelic or human arbiter, one other than God, who will defend Job before God. The "title *redeemer* had a special place in Israel's confessional theology."[47] Numerous passages in both the Old and New Testament distinctly point to the Lord (Yahweh) and Christ as the Redeemer or One who redeems.[48] In Isaiah, *gō'ēl* appears as a title of God nine times. Certainly, if the "author did not want to make this identification, he would have chosen another term that would have clearly meant an intermediary between God and man, for he has already used many: angel or holy one (5:1), umpire or arbiter (9:33-34), witness (16:19), and friend (16:20)."[49] The writer of Job also chose to refer to the Redeemer as "living" or "alive."[50] If Job dies, his Redeemer lives, surviving him and coming to his aid. In contrast to the "stone inscription," a living Redeemer is a much better witness, "vindicating Job's integrity and avenging Job's death, as Job implied in [19:]28-29."[51] Kaiser confidently affirms, "This 'Redeemer' will be a living person whom God will raise up 'in the end,' i.e., who will appear on the earth at the end of all things. At that time . . . as the final vindicator of the beaten-down Job and vindicate him."[52]

He will stand on the dust at last, v. 25b

The term for dust (earth or soil) occurs 26 times in Job and depicts human weakness leading to death, returning to dust (1:12; 4:19; 7:21; 10:9; 14:8,19; 16:15; 17:16). "In 19:2 Job has said that his friends pulverize him (or reduce him to fine dust) by their words. In 19:20 he portrays himself as already reduced to mere bones, a state which (as Ezk 37) is but one step removed from dust."[53] Rowley takes the Vulgate of "he will stand" as "I shall arise," thus "importing the idea of Job's resurrection," and "upon the earth" as "upon dust" as "upon my grave," and is an "explicit" statement of "vindication after death"[54] The term can mean "dust" or "earth" but refers to "grave" in 7:21; 17:16; 20:11; 21:26; Ps 22:29, and Isa 26:19. "Since the context is about Job's decaying body, it may be a specific reference to his grave."[55]

As noted above, Job 14:10-14 indicates that Job "believed in God's power to raise the dead and had a desire and hope that God would set a time and raise him. So here in chapter 19 we may see a similar resurrection in which Job would see God with his own eyes and as a friend."[56] Jones sees "He will stand" as the act of a witness in a court of law (16:8), or as a judge (31:4), declaring that this points to the "Christian expectation of being owned and vindicated at the Last Day."[57] Although possible, "at last" seems unlikely to refer to the end of the book, but rather to a time after Job's skin is peeled off and he is dead and resurrected (v. 26).

Even after my skin has been destroyed, yet I will see God in my flesh. I will see Him myself; my eyes will look at Him, and not as a stranger. My heart longs within me. (vv. 26-27)

It would seem best to see this as a continuation of v. 25. Some understand the translation of "destroyed" as the most difficult of the passage.[58] With Habel, Tur-Sinai posits that this emphasizes "Job's confidence that even after he died, his 'redeemer' would arise to testify in his behalf."[59] The discussion of "see" is interesting. It is true that 42:5 speaks of Job not only hearing about God, but also "seeing" Him. Rather than a fulfillment of this passage, the context and reading would seem to indicate Job's surprise rather than expectation. His expectation would be death and his surprise to see God before he dies. For some it would seem that a disembodied spirit has no ability to see.[60] However, NT Scripture supports the ability of those who have died and have yet to be resurrected to see the Lord and more (Mt 17:3; 22:32; Lk 16:22-23; 23:43; Ac 7:55-56,59; 2Co 5:1-8; 1Th 5:23; Heb 12:23; Rev 6:9-11). S. Lewis Johnson comments,

> First, there is an answer to Job's query, "If a man die, shall he live again?" (Job 14:14). Men have always sought to seize every hint and probability that nature might give to indicate that life survived the grave. . . . It is just possible that the incident tells us much more than that there is a life beyond the grave. It surely stresses the fact that the life beyond the grave is a conscious life. It may also point to the fact that the dead are conscious of the living. . . . Can we not posit something of the same for those who are with the Lord?[61]

It may not be clear in Job's own mind whether or not he was thinking of being disembodied or in a resurrection body, but it seems clear that Job expects to be vindicated and to see God with his own eyes. "[T]he Vindicator is God; this means that he will be aware of his vindication. That this vindication is not expected until after Job's death is likely . . . [for] this passage is a notable landmark in the progress toward . . . a belief" in life after death.[62] Calvin concludes:

> Those who would make a display of the acuteness of their intellect pretend that these words of Job are to be understood to mean the day when Job expected that God would deal more gently with him, and not the last resurrection. Granting that this is partly meant, we shall, however, compel them, whether they will or not, to admit that Job never could have attained to such fullness of hope if his thoughts had risen no higher than the earth. It must, therefore, be confessed that he who saw that the Redeemer would be present with him when lying in the grave must have raised his eyes to a future immortality. Those who think only of the present life, death is the extremity of despair; but it could not destroy the hope of Job.[63]

Summary

This passage has produced an enormous amount of literature, presenting variant readings and interpretations. The first obstacle addressed above was to see that Job's struggle with God's justice and seeming unfairness did not mean that he lost faith in the Sovereign God he loved. People who go through intense suffering often ask the same questions posited by Job, but also hold on to their faith in the God who seems to have abandoned them.[64] Suffering produces doubt, but it also produces heights of spiritual insight that would not come by any other means.

Second, there is the question of resurrection and the history surrounding this passage. Was Job expressing that he would see God before he died and that he would be vindicated and restored, as the last chapter seems to indicate? Or, was Job expressing a faith that even if he died, he would live again and that his Redeemer would stand beside him, vindicating him before his accusers at some future date? While both views have ardent support from interpreters, there is ample reason to agree with both ancient and current scholarship that Job was speaking of a *post-mortem* (after death) vindication. Though Job lived, and was eventually vindicated in chap. 42, that does not disprove Job's opinion that he was facing death and even if he died, he would be vindicated by his Redeemer.[65] Both the history and the context of the passage show this as a viable interpretation: (1) Job desired to leave a lasting record in stone, (2) the terms, "earth," "live," "afterward," and "at last" point to an eschatological time, and (3) current research sees chaps. 14 and 19 as pointing to Israel's belief in an afterlife and resurrection.

The third issue dealt with the Redeemer. Job makes a number of assertions about this One who will vindicate him. Job "knows" this Redeemer. Some see him as an angel, a friend, a human arbiter, or a human witness. However, the book and the context present God as the arbitrator, the Redeemer whom Job knows. This Redeemer is living, and One who will appear on earth at the end as the final vindicator of Job.

CONCLUSION AND APPLICATION

It is difficult to see this passage as less than eschatological. It has stood the test of time as the pinnacle of a poetic description of the resurrection of the believer from the grave. Even in the throes of intense suffering, Job was compelled to speak words that have become an eternal part of God's revelation. His faith was in a Redeemer who, when all others failed, would live forever and testify of Job's righteousness and hope in eternal life. If Job must die and his flesh must decompose, he will yet see God, in his glorified body or in a disembodied state. He will see God, "not as a stranger," not as an enemy, but as a friend and advocate standing by his side. "The lesson that suffering does not show that God is alienated is one of the most enduring themes in the book. . . . Job would learn that his God was not alienated or unconcerned but was both his Vindicator (*gōʼēl*) and his friend."[66] He feels this so intensely that his "heart longs within" him. It can be said with Mombert, "while I cannot admit that the passage proves the *Christian* doctrine of the Resurrection, it is certainly the proclamation of *a* resurrection, and even the most divergent renderings of the original—no matter how disguised, weakened, distorted, and perverted—bear their testimony to that."[67]

Hartley rightly states, "Although Job's confession as interpreted does not explicitly support the [full] doctrine of resurrection, it is built on the same logic that will lead to that doctrine becoming the cornerstone of NT faith."[68] The same hope that Job is expressing here is expressed by the writers of the NT. Job and the authors of Scripture hold that even when God permits terrible injustices and undeserved suffering in the lives of those He loves, He is still just and fair. "God, himself, identified with Job's sufferings in the sufferings of his Son, Jesus Christ, who suffered unto death even though he was innocent. Jesus overcame his ignominious death by rising from the grave. In his victory he, as God's Son and mankind's kinsman-redeemer, secured redemption for all who believe on him."[69] God the Son is the Redeemer of all who suffer in this life for His sake. Regardless of how one interprets these eternal words of Job, his "confidence in God as his Redeemer amidst excruciating suffering stands as a model for all Christians."[70] It is amazing that Job could have revealed so much, "knowing so little! What a rebuke to some of us, who know so much more of God than Job ever did, that we trust him so little."[71] Job's full understanding of God's plan for redemption through the death of Christ certainly was limited, but that does not repudiate the truth of the passage. "For Job and for every believer . . . there is a divine Redeemer. We know his name is Jesus, and at the last day he will stand up and defend us because he has bought us with his blood (Acts 20:28; Eph 1:7; 2:13; Col 1:20; 1Pt 1:18-19; Rev 1:5; 5:9)."[72] "Viewed through the larger canonical context, Job 19:25-27 is messianic in character. It anticipates the beatific vision of glory—and the resurrection of the body. It does have Christological and soteriological dimensions."[73]

"For even the Son of Man did not come to be served, but to serve, and to give His life —a ransom for many." (Mk 10:45)

"For there is one God and one mediator between God and humanity, Christ Jesus, Himself human." (1Tm 2:5)

---

1. Samuel E. Balentine, *Job*, Smyth & Helwys Bible Commentary (Macon, GA: Smyth & Helwys Publishing, 2006), 23.
2. See Balentine, *Job*, 3–24; William H. Green, *The Argument of the Book of Job Unfolded* (Minneapolis: Klock & Klock, 1979), 1–11; John E. Hartley, *The Book of Job*, New International Commentary on the Old Testament (Grand Rapids: Eerdmans, 1988), 3–50. Hartley assumes historicity for all the characters; Norman C. Habel, *The Book of Job: A Commentary*, Cambridge Bible Commentary (London: Cambridge University Press, 1975), 39; Gerald H. Wilson, *Job*, New International Biblical Commentary (Peabody, MA: Hendrickson Publishers, 2007), 1, 17; Francis I. Andersen, *Job*, Tyndale Old Testament Commentaries, ed. D. J. Wiseman (Downers Grove, IL: Tyndale, n.d.), 77–78; and more.
3. August H. Konkel, *Job*, Cornerstone Biblical Commentary (Carol Stream, IL: Tyndale House, 2006), 30.
4. Habel, *The Book of Job: A Commentary*, 39. Hartley, *The Book of Job*, 66, agrees, using the same phrase "prepatriarchal."

5. The Hebrew form אִיּוֹב (ʾiyyôb) probably signifies "where is my (divine) father?" and is an appeal to a deity for help. See David J. A. Clines, *Job 1–20*, vol. 17, Word Biblical Commentary (Dallas: Word, 2002), 11.

6. This term occurs 13 times in the first two chaps. Clines says, "In general, . . . 'the Satan' here is some kind of opponent or adversary; but that much is obvious from the narrative itself. Further precisions about his function can come only from the story. First, is he God's adversary or Job's? Later theological development of the figure of Satan preconditions the reader to say, 'God's'; but the story here makes it evident that the Satan is Yahweh's subordinate, presenting himself before him as one of his courtiers, responding to Yahweh's initiatives, and powerless to act without Yahweh's authorization. His only undelegated capacity is to 'allure, incite' Yahweh (2:3)." See Clines, *Job 1–20*, 20.

7. This is not to imply that God does not know what Satan has been doing or his intent on accusing Job. The term clearly indicates the one who is "the accuser." The question is asked in the narrative for the benefit of the reader.

8. See Larry J. Waters, "*Missio Dei* in the Book of Job," *Bibliotheca Sacra* 166 (January–March 2009): 19–35.

9. A helpful discussion on this passage is found in Susannah Ticciati, "Does Job Fear God for Naught?" *Modern Theology* 21:3 (July 2005): 353–66.

10. Roy B. Zuck, "A Theology of the Wisdom Books and Song of Songs," in *A Biblical Theology of the Old Testament*, ed. Roy B. Zuck (Chicago: Moody Press, 1991), 227.

11. Ibid.

12. Hartley, *The Book of Job*, 47–48. Hartley's six prominent themes include the "dimensions of human suffering" where he shows that Job's suffering involved "every dimension of his existence—physical, social, spiritual, and emotional." So with Zuck, "A Theology of the Wisdom Books," 227. Zuck calls this the "four dimensions of suffering": (a) physical, 1:13-20; 2:7-8, etc.; (b) social, 19:13-19 (alienated from family); 6:14-23 (disloyalty of friends); 16:10; 30:1-15 (taunt songs); (c) spiritual, 6:4; 7:17-19; 19:25; 23:8-9,15; and (d) emotional, 3:26; 7:4,11,13-14; 9:2,20,28; 10:1-3; 12:4; 19:13-19; 21:6; 27:2 (Roy B. Zuck, *Job*, Everyman's Bible Commentary [Chicago: Moody Press, 1978], 15–19). Zuck discusses the losses and suffering of Job in some detail, pointing to such skin conditions as leprosy, smallpox, psoriasis, pityriasis, keratosis, and pemphigus foliaceus (ibid.). Also see A. Rendle Short, *The Bible and Modern Medicine* (Chicago: Moody Press, 1953), 6–61; and C. Raimer Smith, *The Physician Examines the Bible* (New York: Philosophical Library, 1950), 60.

13. H. L. Ellison, *A Study of Job: from Tragedy to Triumph* (Grand Rapids: Zondervan, 1971), 68.

14. Brian P. Gault, "Job's Hope: Redeemer or Retribution," *Bibliotheca Sacra* 173 (April–June 2016): 156.

15. Habel, *Job*, 305.

16. Hartley, *Job*, 48.

17. Ibid., 48–49. Hartley gives an opening salvo against this false doctrine perpetrated by the three friends.

18. Gault, "Job's Hope: Redeemer or Retribution," 157. Gault argues against the idea that Job had periods of high spiritual revelation of God and great hope. He sees Job's statements in 19:23-27 as anger and continued frustration rather than as a moment of great hope and faith in the God he does not fully understand.

19. Warren W. Wiersbe, *Be Patient* (Wheaton, IL: Victor Books, 1991), 74 (italics his). As a sufferer from a debilitating illness, I can attest to this truth. Some of my most depressing and angry times with God were when the pain was the worst. However, I have also experienced some of the most wonderful moments with God's "sufficient grace" during such times. The highs and the lows are inevitable. See also Job 13:15 and chap. 28, as well as Job's responses to God in chaps. 40 and 42.

20. Hartley, *Job*, 295.

21. T. J. Meek, "Job 19:25-27," *Vetus Testamentum*, 6 (January, 1956): 100.

22. Those who hold to an *antemortem* interpretation of this passage include: Hartley, *Job*, 290–97 (yet with a caveat to be presented later); Gault, "Job's Hope: Redeemer or Retribution," 147–165; Marvin H. Pope, *Job*, The Anchor Bible (New York: Doubleday, 1965); David C. Deuel, "Job 19:25 and 23:10 Revisted: An Exegetical Note," *The Master's Seminary Journal* 5, no. 1: 97–99; Edwin M. Good, *In Turns of Tempest: A Reading of Job with a Translation* (Stanford, CA: Stanford University Press, 1990); Samuel Rolles Driver and George Buchanan Gray, *A Critical and Exegetical Commentary on the Book of Job* (Edinburgh: T&T Clark, 1971; E. Dhorme, *A Commentary on the Book of Job* (Nashville: Thomas Nelson Publishers, 1984); and C. F. Keil and F. Delitzsch, *Job*, vol. IV, Commentary on the Old Testament in Ten Volumes (Grand Rapids: Eerdmans, 1978).

23. Those who hold to the possibility of a *postmortem* interpretation of Job 19:23-27 include: N. H. Tur-Sinai, *The Book of Job a New Commentary* (Jerusalem: Kiryath Sepher, 1957); Mona P. Bias and Larry J. Waters, *Job*, Asia Bible Commentary Series, ed. Bruce J. Nicholls (Manila: Asia Theological Association, 2011); Daniel J. Simundson, *The Message of Job*, Augsburg Old Testament Studies (Minneapolis: Augsburg Publishing House, 1986), Simundson sees both as a possibility; Albert Barnes, "Job 19:25-29," in *Sitting with Job*, ed. Roy B. Zuck (Grand Rapids: Baker Book

House, 1992); Christopher Ash, *Job: The Wisdom of the Cross* (Wheaton, IL: Crossway, 2014), Ash gives a brief but useful history of the views, likewise, Manlio Simonetti and Marco Conti, *Job*, Ancient Christian Commentary on Scripture, ed. Thomas C. Oden (Downers Grove, IL: InterVarsity Press, 2006); Roy B. Zuck, *Job* (Chicago: Moody Press, 1978); J. Gerald Janzen, *Job*, Interpretation: A Bible Commentary for Teaching and Preaching (Atlanta: John Knox Press, 1985); H. L. Ellison, *A Study of Job from Tragedy to Triumph* (Grand Rapids: Zondervan, 1971); Elmer B. Smick, *Job*, The Expositor's Bible Commentary (Grand Rapids: Zondervan, 1988); Steven J. Lawson, *Job*, Holman Old Testament Commentary, ed. Max Anders (Nashville: Broadman & Holman, 2004); Norman C. Habel, *The Book of Job: A Commentary* (Philadelphia: The Westminster Press, 1985) who sees resurrection as possible; and Hartley, *Job*.

24. Hartley, *Job*, 295–97, offers the four most common interpretations of this passage: "(1) God will raise Job from the grave so that he will experience his vindication before his accusers. This view is dominant in the Christian community, going back to the early church fathers . . . except for Chrysostrom; (2) From the grave, Job, a bodiless spirit, will witness the occasion when God appears before the local assembly to verify Job's innocence. This goes back to early Jewish interpreters; (3) Job's thoughts in these verses are conditional: if he should see God, he would behold God's vindication of him; and (4) God will intervene before Job's death and restore him to his former status."

25. Alister McGrath, *C. S. Lewis, a Life: Eccentric Genius, Reluctant Prophet* (Carol Stream, IL: Tyndale, 2013), 102.

26. David McKenna, *Job*, Mastering the Old Testament, ed. Lloyd J. Ogilvie (Dallas: Word Publishing, 1986), 145–46.

27. James K. Zink, "Impatient Job: An Interpretation of Job 19:25-27, *Journal of Biblical Literature* 84, no. 2 (June 1965): 147–152.

28. Ibid.

29 Ibid. This was the view of Anselm, Aquinas, Luther, and Calvin.

30. Robert Gordis, *The Book of Job: Commentary, New Translation and Special Studies*. Moreset Series, vol. 2 (New York: Jewish Theological Seminary of America, 1978), 204.

31. Janzen, *Job*, 136.

32. Ibid.

33. Gordis, *Job*, 527.

34. Janzen, *Job*, 137.

35. Zuck, *Job*, 89.

36. Hartley, *Job*, 291.

37. Tur-Sinai, *Job*, 941, states that "permanency is the issue—inscribed forever," and so it is.

38. Those who hold the *postmortem* view generally agree that the Redeemer is the Lord, pointing to Christ or the Messiah.

39. Smick, "Job," 942.

40. Matthew Suriano, "Death, Disinheritance, and Job's Kinsman-Redeemer," *Journal of Biblical Literature* 129, no. 1 (Spring 2010): 60.

41. Sigmund Mowinckel, "Hiobs gō'ēl und Zeuge im Himmel," *Beihefte zur Zeitschrift für die alttestamentliche Wissenschaft* 41 (1925): 2017. Mowinckel is the first to suggest this view.

42. Hartley, *Job*, 292–94. This is the most common among commentators.

43. Habel, *Job*, 304.

44. Andersen, *Job*, 194. Anderson states, "verses 25–27 are so tightly knit that there should be no doubt that the *Redeemer is God*."

45. Ibid.

46. Suzanne Boorer, "Job's Hope: A Reading of the Book of Job from the Perspective of Hope," *Colloquium* 30, no. 2 (Nov 1998): 103.

47. Hartley, *Job*, 292–93. Hartley points out that the "term 'kinsman-redeemer' (*gō'ēl*) also functions as one of Yahweh's titles. It is rooted in the interpretation of Israel's deliverance from Egyptian bondage (e.g., Ex 6:6; 15:13; Pss 74:2; 77:16 [Eng. 15]. The theology of this title is that since Yahweh brought Israel into existence as a nation, he recognizes his obligation to deliver them from all hostile foes. Drawing on this extensive tradition, Isaiah frequently uses the title for Yahweh . . . (Isa 41:14; 43:1-7; 49:7-9,26)."

48. Cf. Ex 6:6; 15:13; Dt 7:8; 9:26; 13:5; 15:15; 21:8; 24:18; 2Sm 4:9; 7:23; 1Kg 1:29; 1Chr 17:21; Neh 1:10; Pss 19:14; 31:5; 34:22; 44:26; 49:15; 74:2; 77:15; 78:35; 103:4; 107:2; 119:134,154; Prv 23:11; Isa 29:22; 35:9-10; 41:14; 43:1,14; 44:6,23-24; 47:4; 48:17,20; 49:7,26; 51:3; 54:5,8; 59:20; 60:16; 62:12; 63:16; Jer 50:34; Lam 3:58; Mic 6:4; Zch 10:8; Lk 24:21; Gal 3:13; 4:5; Ti 2:14; 1Pt 1:18; Rev 5:9; 14:3-4.

49. Ibid., 293.

50. Hywel R. Jones, *A Study Commentary on Job* (Webster, NY: Evangelical Press, 2007), 159. Jones states, "The Hebrew word for 'living' that is used here is used elsewhere of God (Num 14:21,28; Deut 32:40; 1 Kings 17:1). Job's 'Redeemer' is therefore the living God who will never die (Deut 5:26; Job 16:19)."

51. Smick, *Job,* 942.

52. Walter Kaiser, Jr., *The Messiah in the Old Testament* (Grand Rapids: Zondervan, 1995), 63.

53. Janzen, *Job,* 141,144. Janzen sees this not as a reference to the earth or ground upon which a redeemer shall stand, but as a "graphic reference to Job-gone-to-dust." He also states on p. 144 that "The envisaged reversal (as in the imagery of Ezek. 37) surely includes re-embodiment, at least as the level of the imagery of renewal. . . . The language . . . portrays Job as seeing God from a newly embodied state."

54. H. H. Rowley, *Job,* New Century Bible Commentary, ed. R. E. Clements, 2nd ed. (London: Oliphants, 1976), 139. He notes that "wherever the word is used of Sheol or the tomb, the context leaves no room for ambiguity."

55. Tur-Sinai, *Job,* 943.

56. Ibid.

57. Jones, *Job,* 159.

58. Zuck, *Job,* 90. Also see, Tur-Sinai, *Job,* 943.

59. Tur-Sinai, *Job,* 943. He cautions however that "dogmatism should be avoided." Also see Habel, *Job,* 307–08. Wilson, *Job,* 209, says, "Job then 'sees' the redeemer in a post-death resurrection experience at the end of time. The reference in v. 26 to 'after my skin has been destroyed' is taken to indicate Job's death so the subsequent expectation to see God 'in my flesh' can only be in a resurrection body."

60. So with Jones, *Job,* 162, and Andersen, *Job,* 193.

61. S. Lewis Johnson, "The Transfiguration of Christ," *Bibliotheca Sacra* 124 (April–June 1969): 137–38.

62. Rowley, *Job,* 140.

63. Joseph A. Hill, *John Calvin: Suffering—Understanding the Love of God* (Webster, NY: Evangelical Press, 2005), 296–97. See also *Calvin's Institutes II* 10.19.

64. This is evidenced throughout the OT, profusely in the Psalms. Even our Lord expressed abandonment on the cross.

65. One is reminded of the three Hebrew men in Dan 3:17-18 facing the fiery furnace: *If the God we serve exists, then He can rescue us from the furnace of blazing fire, and He can rescue us from the power of you, the king. But even if He does not rescue us, we want you as king to know that we will not serve your gods or worship the gold statue you set up.* Job may be thinking, "If God redeems me now, fine, but if I have to wait for death and eventual resurrection, I'm okay with that too."

66. Tur-Sinai, *Job,* 943r.

67. Jacob Isidor Mombert, "On Job xix. 25–27," *Journal of the Society of Biblical Literature and Exegesis,* no. 2 (June–December 1882): 38–39. (Emphasis his).

68. Hartley, *Job,* 297.

69. Ibid.

70. Ibid.

71. David Atkinson, *The Message of Job: Suffering and Grace* (Downers Grove, IL: InterVarsity Press, 1991), 95.

72. Robert Alden, *Job,* The New American Commentary, vol. 11 (Nashville: Broadman & Holman, 1993), 207.

73. Jones, *Job,* 164.

Compositional Unity in the Five Books of the Psalms: A Canonical Approach

ROBERT L. COLE

The book of Psalms is an integrated literary work and exhibits compositional unity, both from individual psalm to psalm and throughout the whole book. It is divided into five books through similar concluding doxologies. Psalm 90 opens Book IV, which continues through Ps 106. Psalm 89 concludes Book III, as proven by its doxological conclusion.

Each of the five books exhibits its own unique focus, but at the same time the books are linked to each other at the seams by common themes and language. Psalm 90 not only opens Book IV (Pss 90–106) with its emphasis on the rule of the Lord, but also transitions coherently from the previous Book III (Pss 73–89). The latter is dominated by temporal questions such as, "How long?" or "Why . . . ?" directed to God for His continued delay in the implementation of previous promises (cf. Ps 74:1,10; 77:8; 79:5,10; 88:14; 89:46). Psalm 90 answers those temporal questions of Book III through a discourse on time as viewed from the divine infinite perspective. It also expresses again a temporal question in v. 13 of the same type seen in Book III previously, "How long?"

The last temporal question of Book III is expressed in Ps 89:46 regarding the Davidic covenant. The "How long?" of that verse is preceded by multiple references to the covenant made with David across Ps 89 and followed by another in v. 49. It asks pointedly, "Where are the former acts of Your faithful love that You swore to David?" Psalm 90 also questions how long (v. 13) before God returns and is "faithful" (v. 14, and six times across the previous Ps 89) to His word to "your servants"

(vv. 13,14, and Ps 89:50). The faithfulness (*chesed*) associated multiple times across Ps 89 in reference to the Davidic covenant is now repeated in Ps 90:14. That covenant is associated in the context of Ps 90:13-17 with the complete restoration and reversal of the conditions of ephemerality, toil, trouble, and death narrated in Ps 90:3-12. In other words, the psalmist expects the implementation of the Davidic covenant to usher in an entirely new era of endless life characterized by joy and glory for God's servants.

Consequently, the transition from Book III to IV is relatively smooth, and temporal questions of the like appear only once more (Ps 94:3), within a general atmosphere in Book IV of confidence and praise. Such temporal questions of protest essentially cease thereafter. Likewise, the interrogative "Why?" (*lamah*), so prominent in Book III (74:1,11; 79:10; 80:12; 88:14), and the previous two of the Psalter (cf. Pss 2:1; 10:1; 22:1; 43:2; 44:23; 49:5), ceases in Book IV, and then occurs once more only in Book V (Ps 115:2). Psalm 90 then, functions as a transition from the insistent questioning mood of Book III to a general atmosphere of joy and confidence in Book IV.

The "why?" of Book III is directed to God's anger against His people (Pss 74:1; 79:10; 88:14), which is spelled out in detail in Ps 90 as well (vv. 7,9,11). The requests concluding Ps 90 represent another appeal to God that He withdraw His anger, end the endless cycle of suffering, ephemerality, and death, and establish the eternal Davidic throne. In fact, Book III had complained incessantly with these questions since Book II had concluded (Ps 72) with a prophecy of an eternal and Edenic portrayal of life under the son of David. That promise was far from reality, and so the repeated temporal questions. However, the paucity of such questions in the rest of Book IV and practical disappearance in Book V, suggests confidence and assurance that the Davidic kingdom, which is actually the kingdom of God, will be established. Repetition of "the Lord reigns" across Book IV (Pss 93:1; 97:1; 99:1) represents that conviction. Note that the lofty position promised to the Davidic king in Ps 89:27 as the highest (*'elyon*—a term used for God Himself in Book IV, HCSB "Most High": Pss 91:1,9; 92:1; 97:9) of "the kings of the earth," matches the same "kings of the earth" in Ps 102:15 who fear God's name and glory.

The reality of the five book divisions is evident from compositionally induced doxologies at their conclusions: Pss 41:13; 72:18,19; 89:52; and 106:48. Book III ends with the doxology of Ps 89:52, similar to the others in which an eternal blessing is invoked upon God, followed by either a double or single "amen." The distribution across the Psalter of such similar content was not merely by chance but was a deliberate part of the book's composition. Superscriptions or titles and their distribution are consistent with the doxologies and consequently should not be jettisoned, or ignored, in the reading and interpretation of the Psalter.[1]

The place of Ps 90 at the head of Book IV following Ps 89 (and preceding Ps 91 as well), is calculated and significant. As will be shown here, there are abundant linguistic and literary parallels that obviate any random or insignificant pairing of the two. This evidence has been largely ignored, and instead foreign form-critical categories of one type or another are imposed upon the psalms, in place of the ancient and *original*[2] canonical order.[3] Language links in the particular case of Ps 90 and its neighboring psalms, as well as in the Psalter at large, are either ignored or even deliberately discounted.[4] The result is a wholly different reading of these two psalms from the one implied by their juxtaposition and unique linguistic links.

Serious consideration of the Psalter's sequence is not innovative by any means in the history of interpretation. The *Midrash on Psalms* quotes ancient rabbis debating this very issue in a discussion of Ps 3 and its position vis-à-vis Ps 2.[5] Although David Qimhi (RaDaQ) in the Middle Ages did not read Pss 1 and 2 together, he was familiar with the Jewish custom of doing so.[6] Commentaries on the Psalms from the 19th century regularly observed connections between psalms,[7] before the dominance of form criticism practically eliminated such discussions throughout the better part of the 20th century. As is well known, there have been a flurry of studies in the last two decades attempting to grapple with the abundant thematic and linguistic evidence that points to a unified Psalter.[8] Studies of specific books of the Psalter continue to appear, recognizing the connection of the books to each other and the way the psalms within them link to each other.[9]

Others have attempted to analyze the sequence while at the same time applying form-critical categories, two ultimately incompatible approaches.[10] Form criticism is based on the premise that the order is chaotic for the most part, while canonical approaches presume the opposite. The former seeks to understand the psalms through an imagined social or cultic setting, while the latter considers the literary context of the Psalter, as it is in its canonical form, as the proper lens through which to view each psalm. Choice of approach will predetermine the interpretive outcome. Form criticism's results inevitably mirror modern scholarly preconceived notions, and its outcomes are predictable. On the other hand, a serious grappling with the order and attendant lexical links reveals a purpose and message for the Psalter quite distinct from contemporary expectations. It is hard for scholarship, steeped as it is in its traditions and notions, to think outside the box and simply consider the possibility that there may be a reason for the canonical arrangement.

The linking of juxtaposed psalms of quite different "genre/type," as conceived by modern scholarship through distinctive vocabulary, points to a deliberate arrangement.[11] In order to understand the Psalter, one must carefully analyze its language (in the original Hebrew of course), not only within each individual psalm, but also between neighboring psalms, and then within the larger context of the entire book.

Note that the chaining of diverse texts or discrete discourses by parallel and distinct vocabulary is not limited to the Psalter. Writers of the Hebrew Bible practice it regularly.[12] For example, the Hebrew word "name" (*shem*) is a repeated term linking together Gn 9 (Noah's son), 11 (goal of Babel's builders), and 12 (promise to Abram). Other deliberate parallels among extensive examples throughout the Hebrew Bible are: "her children" (*yeladeiha*) in Ex 21:4,22, "afflict" (*'anah*) in Gn 15:13 and 16:6, "shield/handed over" between Gn 14:20 and 15:1, "living being" (*nephesh hayah*) in Gn 1:24 and 2:7, "walk with God" (*hithalekh 'et ha'elohim*) in Gn 5:22,24; 6:9; 17:1, "hear ye" (*shim'u*) in Isa 6:9; 7:13, all of which are explicit and compositionally induced pointers to an integrated reading of what appear on the surface to be separate and unconnected texts. A serious consideration of the juxtaposition of larger texts often results in the detection of these lexical links, which throw a whole new light on their meaning. The same deliberate and meaningful linking through verbal parallels can be seen between whole books. Joel 3:16 (Hb. 4:16) declares near the end of the book, "the Lord will roar from Zion and raise His voice from Jerusalem" (*vayhvh mitsiyon yish'ag umirushalayim yiten qolo*), while Am 1:2 opens the next book with the identical statement. The technique pervades the composition of the Hebrew Bible, including, of course, the Psalms.

Linking by common language of neighboring books also occurs in the case of the Psalter. In the Hebrew canon, the book of Psalms follows Malachi and precedes Job, a position supported by internal unique lexical and phrasal parallels,[13] which are by no means incidental. It reveals pointedly the ancient canonical editor's view of its message. Job is the righteous man who rejects "the counsel of the wicked" (*'atsat resh'aim*), a phrase that occurs in Job 21:16; 22:18; and then only again in Ps 1:1. Thus, according to the Hebrew arrangement of these two books, the impeccable men of Ps 1 and Job represent the same righteous sufferer who is restored. In either case, they provide a portrait and description of a future messianic figure who will suffer and eventually be restored. Thus, the canonical arrangements represent a deliberately given context, and signal how the texts are to be read and interpreted.[14] Malachi 4 ends with a warning to the wicked of their destruction as chaff (4:1, translated "stubble" in the HCSB), as well as a call to the Torah of the Lord (Mal 4:4), the same language used in Ps 1. Juxtaposition of these two at the divide between Prophets and Writings is thus accompanied by obvious verbal parallels and points to an eschatological reading of Ps 1.[15]

The order of books in the Greek tradition (LXX) represents an entirely different view of their meaning. Its divisions are according to perceived genre (Law, History, Poetry, Prophecy), within which there is an evident attempt to impose chronology.

This arrangement reveals a view of the books through the lens of Hellenistic conceptions of genre, in which they are simply a collection of ancient Israel's literature. The tripartite Hebrew order (Torah, Prophets, Writings) represents an eschatological and messianic reading of the material, and is supported by the NT (Lk 24:44; Mt 23:35). Ironically, the tripartite Hebrew order, the choice of rabbinic Judaism following the rise of Christianity as against the Septuagint, arranges the order of the material with a messianic and eschatological thrust.[16]

The Septuagint, on the other hand, exhibits an arrangement of the books that sees them as simply a record of Israel's past history and literature. So Psalms are regularly preceded by Job in the Greek tradition, as in most English Bibles today as well, surely for chronological reasons. Presumably Job lived in an ancient time previous to David, and so his book should precede Psalms.[17] In the Hebrew Bible, on the other hand, Psalms follows Malachi (part of the Book of the Twelve), and Job follows. Although this order appears to be anachronistic, it is supported by the content and unique language supporting it, and by further explicit verbal and phraseological links between Job and Proverbs. Furthermore, it points to a future, messianic interpretation. It does not ignore history, but rather uses it to communicate hope for, and prediction of, the future. Writers reflected on past events and then later narrated them with a meaning far beyond a simple rehearsal.[18] This principle of using the past to paint the future dominates the Hebrew Bible from beginning to end.[19]

---

1. Gerald Henry Wilson, *The Editing of the Hebrew Psalter*, Society of Biblical Literature Dissertation Series 76 (Chico, CA: Scholars Press, 1981), 155–67.

2. The antiquity of the present canonical order can be proven simply by the fact that it mystifies modern interpreters and many ancients as well. It almost certainly predates the Hellenistic period, because it represents a different view of the psalms. Qumran manuscripts reveal various arrangements besides the canonical order seen in the Masoretic Hebrew text, which is also represented at Qumran, and the earlier LXX (250 BC). The evidence reveals a failure of ancient interpreters, similar to contemporary ones, to recognize the cohesiveness and coherence of the ancient canonical order.

3. The father of form criticism was Hermann Gunkel, *An Introduction to the Psalms*, compl. Joachim Begrich, trans. James D. Nogalski (Macon, GA: Mercer University Press, 1998). He remains perhaps the dominant force in Psalms studies as shown by those who follow his program. The following examples could be multiplied extensively: Craig C. Broyles, *Psalms*, New International Biblical Commentary (Peabody, MA: Hendrickson, 1999); Erhard S. Gerstenberger, *Psalms*, Vols. XIV and XV Forms of the Old Testament Literature (Grand Rapids: Eerdmans, 1988, 2001); John Goldingay, *Psalms*, Vols. 1 and 2 Baker Commentary on the Old Testament (Grand Rapids: Baker, 2006); Hans-Joachim Kraus, *Psalms 60–150: A Commentary*, trans. Hilton C. Oswald (Minneapolis: Augsburg, 1989); Norman Whybray, *Reading the Psalms as a Book*, Journal for the Study of the Old Testament Supplement Series 222 (Sheffield: Sheffield Academic Press, 1996); Marvin E. Tate, *Psalms 51–100*, Vol. 20 Word Biblical Commentary (Dallas, TX: Word Books, 1990); Samuel Terrien, *The Psalms: Strophic Structure and Theological Commentary* (Grand Rapids: Eerdmans, 2003), refers on the one hand to the order of Psalms sometimes as "bizarre" (p. 44), due undoubtedly to a form critical disposition, while at the same time observing a "transitional link" (p. 23), between Pss 89 and 90; John D. Barry, et al., *Faithlife Study Bible* (Bellingham, WA: Lexham Press, 2016).

4. Willem Van Gemeren, *Psalms*, Vol. 5 The Expositor's Bible Commentary, ed. Frank E. Gaebelein (Grand Rapids:

Zondervan, 1991), points out rightly the dangers of the form critical enterprise (p. 14), but as in the case of Ps 90 (pp. 592–98), makes no mention of multiple lexical and formal parallels with the previous Ps 89 or following Ps 91. A recent work, David Willgren, *Like a Garden of Flowers: A Study of the Formation of the 'Book' of Psalms* (Lund, Sweden: Lund University, 2016), 397, explicitly ignores this most basic element of the book's composition: "features such as lexical and thematic links between adjacent psalms have not been considered in depth, except for in some cases . . . might have served as points of departure when juxtaposing psalms." Astonishingly, Willgren admits to deliberately ignoring the lexical evidence essential and critical to the entire question. The linguistic evidence which undermines his entire thesis is unabashedly jettisoned. Form criticism in general has been critiqued by minimal attention to the unique rhetorical features of individual psalms, and now as well to the linguistic evidence for their context in the Psalter. James Muilenburg pointed out this deficiency of form-critical practice for individual psalms decades ago in his seminal article, "Form Criticism and Beyond" *Journal of Biblical Literature* 88 (1969), 1–18.

5. *The Midrash on Psalms*, trans. William G. Braude (New Haven, CT: Yale University Press, 1958), 49–50.

6. Menahem Cohen, ed., *Miqra'ot Gedolot HeKeter: Psalms 1* (Ramat Gan, Israel: Bar-Ilan University Press, 2003), 5.

7. For example, Joseph A. Alexander, *Commentary on the Psalms* (Edinburgh: A. Elliott & J. Thin, 1864; repr., Grand Rapids: Kregel, 1991), John Forbes, *Studies on the Book of Psalms: The Structural Connection of the Book of Psalms, Both in Single Psalms and in the Psalter as an Organic Whole* (Edinburgh: T.&T. Clark, 1888).

8. For example, Gianni Barbiero, *Das erste Psalmenbuch als Einheit* (Frankfurt am Main: Peter Lang, 1999), charts verbal links across the entirety of Book I of the Psalter. He proceeds based on the working hypothesis, "that the final form of the Psalter forms a meaningful compositional unit" (p. 20—my translation of, "daβ der Endtext des Psalters . . . eine sinnvolle kompositorische Einheit bildet").

9. Michael G. McKelvey, *Moses, David and the High Kingship of Yahweh: A Canonical Study of Book IV of the Psalter* (Piscataway, NJ: Gorgias Press, 2014).

10. Frank-Lothar Hossfeld and Erich Zenger, *Psalms 2: A Commentary on Psalms 51–100*, trans. Linda M. Maloney (Minneapolis: Fortress Press, 2005).

11. Contra Gordon D. Fee and Douglas Stuart, *How to Read the Bible for All Its Worth* (Grand Rapids: Zondervan, 2003), 206–223. Note how in the analysis of Ps 3 its literary context is ignored, true to form-critical practice.

12. Umberto Cassutto, "The Sequence and Arrangement of the Biblical Sections," in *Biblical and Oriental Studies I: Bible*, trans. I. Abrahams (Jerusalem: Magnes Press, 1973), 1–6.

13. Compare as well the confession of Ps 113:2 and Job 1:21, "may the name of the Lord be blessed" (author's translation), which is found only in these two verses in the entire Hebrew Bible.

14. Carol Hupping, ed., *The Jewish Bible* (Philadelphia: The Jewish Publication Society, 2008), 2.

15. Gianni Barbiero, *Das erste Psalmenbuch als Einheit* (Frankfurt am Main: Lang, 1999), 33–34.

16. This is a common contemporary view of the Hebrew Bible, following the same Hellenistic approach of the LXX as against the Hebrew Bible; cf. Andreas Köstenberger and Richard Patterson, *Invitation to Biblical Interpretation* (Grand Rapids MI: Kregel, 2011), 238. The "game" played by the latter, and many others, is certainly not the game played by the writers of the Hebrew Bible, either at the level of individual books or the canonical composition at large. The game played by Hebrew writers is eminently literary/linguistic, and requires close attention to the original language in order to discern its rules and resulting meaning.

17. The Greek editor who was responsible for this arrangement failed to distinguish between two wholly different dates, the date of events described within the book and the date of its writing. The same is common today among those who speak of understanding the "historical context." Dating the final composition of books is a very subjective enterprise and can be conjectured only in very general terms, thus undermining the entire enterprise of dating the so-called "historical context."

18. Deliberate anachronisms in the order of the Hebrew Bible, such as Ezra/Nehemiah-Chronicles (note the surprise at this expressed by D. N. Freedman, *The Unity of the Hebrew Bible*, [Ann Arbor: University of Michigan, 1993], 76, "normal or expected chronological sequence. . . . odd") or Esther-Daniel, etc., are due to a compositional purpose beyond simply reciting past history. They reveal thematic pairing, supported by numerous lexical links, all for the purpose of providing hope in the ultimate restoration of God's people through His messianic king. Psalms 89–90 represent a deliberate anachronism within the book of Psalms with the same messianic and eschatological purpose.

19. Contra Fee and Stuart, *How to Read*, 92, "the purpose of the individual narratives is to tell what God did in the history of Israel." As noted by Michael Fishbane, *Biblical Interpretation in Ancient Israel* (Oxford: Clarendon Press, 1989), 350–79, typology in fact dominates Hebrew narrative, and points to a much larger purpose than description of past events. This fundamental aspect of the Hebrew Bible in general is overlooked by most works purporting to address "biblical hermeneutics," cf. Grant R. Osborne, *The Hermeneutical Spiral* (Downers Grove, IL: IVP Academic, 2006), 203—"The historical nature of the Bible leads one to treat the story as a window to the event behind the text." The latter represents a fundamental misunderstanding of the narratives of the *Hebrew* Bible.

Messianism in the Psalms

SETH D. POSTELL

"There are two faces to the psalms in the Psalter. Indeed, they are prayers. That is to say, the words of man to his God, but they are also words which were spoken by the Holy Spirit and written in the Holy Scriptures, and therefore, they are so to speak, words God speaks to man." So writes Amos Chakham.[1]

Many read the Psalms only as individual prayers or songs and fail to see that they have been carefully arranged to form a book: a prophetic book telling a story. Some might spot the prophetic hints within individual psalms that speak of the Messiah, but still fail to appreciate the landscape of the psalms that have been composed as a prophetic message when seen as a book. There are reasons for this, primarily a movement of 20th-century scholarship that sought the meaning of the individual psalms in isolation from their canonical context and saw the superscriptions and doxologies as unimportant, thus missing vital clues to the intended structure of the book of Psalms. This article will examine more recent scholarship challenging this atomistic approach, which much of contemporary scholarship has come to believe unquestioningly.

MISSING THE MESSAGE

The significant tension between the NT uses of the Psalms versus the view of most contemporary evangelical scholars is evident in what follows.

> For David says of Him: "I saw the Lord ever before me; because He is at my right hand, I will not be shaken. Therefore my heart was glad, and my tongue rejoiced. Moreover, my flesh will rest in hope, because You will not leave me in Hades or allow Your Holy One to see decay. You have revealed the paths of life to me; You will fill me with gladness in Your presence." Brothers, I can confidently speak to

> you about the patriarch David: He is both dead and buried, and his tomb is with us to this day. Since he was a prophet, he knew that God had sworn an oath to him to seat one of his descendants on his throne. *Seeing this in advance, he spoke concerning the resurrection of the Messiah.*[2]

> It is important to realize that psalms are not prophetic in the narrow sense. In some circles it is believed that a small number of very significant psalms have no Old Testament referent, but apply only to the coming Messiah. Examples include Psalms 2, 16, 22, 69, and 110. *Indeed these psalms are particularly important psalms if for no other reason than the New Testament writers quote them more than any other psalm. However, they too have an Old Testament context.*[3]

These quotations, one from the apostle Peter in Ac 2 and the other from a well-known evangelical introduction to the OT, both make confident assertions about the psalms. In the first quotation, Peter unequivocally claims that David is the author of the 16th Psalm and that he was a prophet who intentionally predicted the Messiah's resurrection in Ps 16. In the second quotation, the authors argue that the "psalms are not prophetic in the narrow sense," and therefore, David's intention when writing Ps 16 was not specifically to predict the Messiah's resurrection. Rather, the historical-grammatical meaning of Ps 16 must be established in its OT context, namely, its original function as part of the liturgy in the first and/or second temple.

Although many Christians would bristle at the apparently contradictory claims of the second quotation, they would also likely admit that they would never have guessed that Ps 16 prophesied the Messiah's resurrection had Peter not told us so in Ac 2. The interpretive challenge of finding the Messiah in the book of Psalms is not limited to Ps 16. Many of the NT's Messianic interpretations of the psalms appear to be quite arbitrary at face value.[4]

However, the problem of interpreting Psalms as messianic is located in modern critical assumptions about the book of Psalms. This article will argue that the NT's interpretation reflects a more careful reading of the psalms in their OT context, both in terms of the individual psalms as well as the book of Psalms as a whole.

TWO MODERN ASSUMPTIONS ABOUT THE BOOK OF PSALMS

These quotations express two modern critical assumptions about the psalms:

> When examined closely, however, the Psalter surprises us and we have difficulty understanding its message. . . . [T]he individual psalms seem to be without a context, either historical or literary, in a way that is virtually unique to the Old Testament.[5]

> A discussion of the theological message of the Psalter is difficult for two reasons. First, the book is composed of 150 individual compositions and, accordingly, does not present a systematically developed argument. Second, as will be more fully explored below, the psalms are prayers sung to God; thus they present us with the words of the congregation addressed to God, rather than the Word of God addressed to the people of Israel. How, then, is it possible to speak of the theological concerns of the Psalter?[6]

The first assumption found in the quotations is that the book of Psalms is not really a *book*. Whole books provide literary contexts to the individual chapters, and individual chapters find their places in the overall message of the book. However, these authors maintain that the book of Psalms is not really a book. According to their view, it would be a mistake to interpret Ps 3 in the context of Pss 2 and 4 or in the context of the book of Psalms as a whole, any more than trying to understand "Amazing Grace" in the context of "Blessed Assurance" and "It Is Well" in a hymnbook.[7]

The second assumption is that the individual psalms are not, technically speaking, God's prophetic word to His people. Whereas the prophetic literature is directly God's word to the community and frequently intended to be predictive, the psalms come to us as prayers *to* God rather than prophecies *from* God. To interpret Psalms as predictive prophecy, therefore, is to misunderstand its original function and purpose in the OT community. Let us deal with these common modern assumptions.

THE BOOK OF PSALMS REALLY IS A BOOK

Though evangelical scholarship tends to regard the hymnbook approach to the Psalter as conservative, its origins can be traced to the work of two critical scholars in 19th century: Hermann Gunkel and Sigmund Mowinkel.[8] First, these scholars discarded the canonical order of the 150 psalms in favor of a focus on the individual psalms.[9] Second, these scholars relegated the superscriptions[10] as late editorial and noncanonical labels even though the superscriptions are included in all ancient manuscripts and translations of the Hebrew Bible (Dead Sea Scrolls, the Septuagint, etc.), are included in the versification of the Hebrew Bible, and are treated as Scripture by Christian interpreters before the time of Gunkel (e.g., KJV).[11] Since the superscriptions were regarded as noncanonical (not inspired), they were also regarded as irrelevant for interpretation.[12] The abandonment of the canonical order and the superscriptions necessitated a new framework for interpreting the psalms. Form criticism provided this new framework. Gunkel identified certain patterns in each of the various kinds of psalms, and consequently classified, arranged, and interpreted the psalms according to their forms (form criticism). Each form was identified with various situations (*Sitz im Leben*) in the context of Israel's worship.[13]

One significant result of this hymnbook approach to the book of Psalms was a "rupture with the traditional Jewish-Christian understanding of the Psalter,"[14] and this for two reasons. First, once the psalms are loosed from their canonical context (i.e., within the context of their specific arrangement in the 150 psalms of the Psalter), the messianic interpretation of an individual psalm, in many cases, appears to be completely arbitrary. For instance, Peter used Ps 90:4 as a proof text for the delay of the second coming of the Lord (2Pt 3:4,8-9).[15] It is difficult to see how this verse in Ps 90 addresses that specific concern when it is not interpreted in light of the previous psalm, with its anguished question "How long, LORD?" (Ps 89:46), an enquiry directly tied to the timing of the fulfillment of the Davidic covenant (see Ps 89:33-45).

Second, once the superscriptions are considered irrelevant for interpretation, Jesus' and Peter's messianic interpretations of Pss 16 and 110 are suspect, since the logic of their argument depends on the superscriptions identifying David as the author (see Mt 22:41-45; Ac 2:25-31). Moreover, as will be discussed, a rejection of the canonicity of superscriptions also brings with it a rejection of the prophetic origins of the psalms themselves.[16]

Although the "hymnbook approach" has been seriously challenged in the past 40 years in academic circles (conservative and nonconservative),[17] this body of scholarly literature has not been popularized for nonscholarly consumption, so has had limited influence upon the way Christians read and interpret the psalms. In what follows, I hope to make the latest psalms research accessible and, in the process, show why the book of Psalms is really a book and should be interpreted in its canonical order (as a book, superscriptions included).

EVIDENCE THAT PSALMS WAS COMPOSED AS A BOOK

In Gerald Wilson's ground-breaking and highly influential work on Psalms research, he offered persuasive evidence in favor of the intentional and purposeful compositional[18] shaping of the Hebrew Psalter (book of Psalms) into a unified literary composition. The literary evidence presented in favor of understanding the book of Psalms as a single book is not only impressive, it also has literally changed the face of Psalms scholarship.

1. Fivefold Structure

First, he showed how the book of Psalms was intentionally arranged into a fivefold structure (Five Books) by means of doxologies marking the last verses of each of the five books of the Psalter.[19] Each of these doxologies shares unique language and themes found only in the doxologies themselves, strongly suggesting that these doxologies were strategically placed to mark the end of the Books, rather than to simply mark the end of the individual psalms themselves.

Book I: Psalms 3[20]–41	**Book II:** Psalms 42–72	**Book III:** Psalms 73–89	**Book IV:** Psalms 90–106	**Book V:** Psalms 107–145[21]
May Yahweh, the God of Israel, be praised from everlasting to everlasting. Amen and amen. (41:13)	May the LORD God, the God of Israel, who alone does wonders, be praised. May His glorious name be praised forever; the whole earth is filled with His glory. Amen and amen. (72:18-19)	May the LORD be praised forever. Amen and amen. (89:52)	May Yahweh, the God of Israel, be praised from everlasting to everlasting. Let all the people say, "Amen!" Hallelujah! (106:48)	My mouth will declare Yahweh's praise; let every living thing praise His holy name forever and ever. (145:21)

Thus, one can understand the macrostructure of the book of Psalms as follows:

Psalms 1–2: Introduction to the book of Psalms
Psalms 3–41: Book I
Psalms 42–72: Book II
Psalms 73–89: Book III
Psalms 90–106: Book IV
Psalms 107–145: Book V
Psalms 146–150: Conclusion to the book of Psalms[22]

A crucial aspect of identifying these doxologies at the ends of the five books means that the fivefold structure is, by implication, inspired, since their function is not to mark the end of each of the individual psalms, but rather to signal the ends of the five books.[23] These doxologies have a function and meaning beyond the individual psalms where they are located that extends to the composition of the entire book.

2. Superscriptions Are Strategic

Second, Wilson showed how the superscriptions strategically link groups of psalms together within each of the five books of the Psalter, soften the transitions between groups of psalms, and mark major transitions between each of the five books of the Psalter.[24] In other words, the superscriptions bind individual psalms into a larger literary framework and provide shape to the book as a whole. Each psalm finds its place within a larger matrix of psalms whose superscriptions share catchwords and phrases linking each together. That the Psalter was intentionally organized by means of doxologies and superscriptions further suggests the canonical arrangement of the Psalter must be factored into the interpretation of the individual psalms. Each psalm has an inspired literary context.

3. The Uniqueness of Psalms 1–2

Third, Wilson (and others) showed that Pss 1–2 stand apart from the body of Book I (Pss 3–42), given their lack of superscriptions, and as such, introduce the major themes of the Psalter as a whole.[25] According to David Howard Jr., the following themes are introduced in Pss 1–2 and may be traced throughout the Psalter.[26]

1. The way of the righteous vs. the way of the wicked
2. The importance of God's word
3. God as Sovereign King over all the nations
4. David as God's anointed king, his vice-regent

Crucial to note is the importance of the Davidic king with reference to God's purpose for Israel and the nations in the introduction to the Psalter. Though God's vice-regent sits in Zion (2:6), God intends this king's rule to extend to the ends of the earth (2:8).

In addition to Wilson's evidence in support of a unified and strategic arrangement of the Psalter (as outlined in the three points above), further substantiation comes in the presence of concatenation, inclusios, and observable patterns of key words.

4. Concatenation—Literary Linking Devices

Concatenation[27] by means of unique words and phrases is a common phenomenon throughout the Psalter.[28] Throughout the Psalter, juxtaposing psalms frequently share unique words and phrases, binding the psalms together. For example, David is introduced as the "servant of the Lord" for the first time in the Psalter in Ps 18. In Ps 19, the juxtaposing psalm, David calls himself servant two times (Ps 19:11,13). In Ps 1, the blessed man "meditates" (Hebrew verb *hagah*) in the Lord's instruction (v. 2), and in Ps 2:1, the peoples "plot (literally, meditate) in vain."[29] In Ps 3:5, David says he "will lie down and sleep." In Ps 4:8, David says he "will both lie down and sleep in peace." The verbs "lie down" and "sleep" are used together only these two times in the entire Psalter. Psalms 3:2 and 4:6 both share the phrase "many are saying," a phrase found only in these two places in the entire Bible.

Likewise, the juxtaposing psalms have been carefully situated within a matrix of questions and answers, intentions and fulfillments, etc. For example, Ps 106:47 ends with a request that "Yahweh our God . . . gather us from the nations, so that we may give thanks to Your holy name . . ." Psalm 107:1-3 fittingly begins with the psalmist "giv[ing] thanks to the LORD [Yahweh]" who "has gathered them from the lands." Psalm 7:17 ends with David's intention to "thank the Lord" and to "sing about the name of Yahweh the Most High." Psalm 8 is a song[30] dedicated to magnifying the name of Yahweh (see Ps 8:1). Psalm 89 ends Book III of the Psalter with an agonizing question about the timing of the fulfillment of the Davidic covenant (Ps 89:46). Fittingly, Book IV begins with a psalm all about time in the divine economy (Ps 90:4). More evidence can be multiplied exponentially, but for the purposes of this article, it is worth noting that the concatenation of juxtaposing psalms is extensive, and once again strongly suggests that meaning crosses the boundaries of individual psalms. The individual psalms do in fact have an inspired, canonical context that must be factored into interpretation.

5. Inclusios—Literary Framing Devices

Literary inclusios[31] are also used throughout the Psalter to bind groups of psalms together, at both the micro- as well as the macro-compositional level. For instance, the introduction of the first psalm and the end of the second are framed by the phrase "happy is/are." Both psalms also end with the phrase "perish" and "way" (Ps 1:6; 2:12). The framing of these two untitled psalms binds the two into a unified introduction to the Psalter. Psalm 1, at the beginning of Book I, opens with the word "happy." This word appears again as the first word of the last psalm of Book I (41:1). The verb form of "happy" (*ashar*—to call blessed or happy) appears only twice in the Psalter, once in the beginning of the final psalm in Book I (Heb. 41:3; Eng. 41:2) and again near the end of the final psalm in Book II just before the doxology (72:17, "call him blessed"). The author of the Psalter has arranged the first two books of the Psalter by means of "happy" inclusios. Fittingly, a verse at the end of Book II marks the special unity of Books I (1–41) and II (42–72): "The prayers of David son of Jesse are concluded" (Ps 72:20). Inclusios are also used to arrange Book IV (Pss 90–106). Book IV begins and ends with references to Moses (Pss 90:1; 106:16,23,32). Moses in fact is a key figure in Book IV of the Psalter, yet mentioned only one other time elsewhere in the Psalter (90:1; 99:6; 103:7; 105:26; 106:16,23,32; see 77:20). One other significant example will suffice. The Psalter begins and ends with a cluster of words and phrases that are found only in Pss 2 and 149.

Why do the *nations* rebel and the *peoples* plot in vain? . . . "Let us tear off their *chains* and free ourselves from their *restraints*." . . . ". . . You will break them with a rod of *iron*; You will shatter them like pottery. So now, *kings*, be wise; receive instruction, you *judges* of the earth. (Ps 2:1,3,9-10)	. . . inflicting vengeance on the *nations* and punishment on the *peoples*, *binding* their *kings* with *chains* and their dignitaries with *iron shackles*, carrying out the *judgment* decreed against them. This honor is for all His godly people. Hallelujah! (Ps 149:7-9)

This inclusio demonstrates the careful arrangement, not only of juxtaposing psalms, but also of the entire composition.

6. The Prominence and Absence of Key Words as an Indicator

Certain words that are prominent in some books are absent in others. For instance, "Selah," a word frequently used in Books I–III (67 times), is completely absent in Book IV, and used only four times in Book V (140:4,6,9; 143:6). "Hallelujah" is found almost exclusively in Book V. It appears 24 times in the Psalter, four times in Book IV (Pss 104:35; 105:45–106:1; 106:48) and 20 times in Book V (Pss 111:1; 112:1; 113:1,9; 115:18; 116:19; 117:2; 135:1,21; 146:1,10; 147:1; 147:20–148:1; 148:14–149:1; 149:9–150:1; 150:6).

Additionally, personal names are used to provide careful order to the Psalter. The name "David" is used extensively in Books I–III and V (89 times), yet appears only twice in the superscriptions of Book IV (Pss 101; 103). "Moses" is a key name in Book IV (7 times), yet found only one other time in the rest of the Psalter (Ps 77:20). Finally, the divine names are used quite consistently to organize each of the books. A search of every psalm that uses the name Yahweh and excludes the name Elohim (God), and conversely, every psalm that uses the name Elohim and excludes the name Yahweh reveals a remarkably consistent pattern across the Psalter. Only in Books I, IV, and V do whole psalms refer to Yahweh and not Elohim. Likewise, only in Books II and III do psalms refer to Elohim and not to Yahweh.

The evidence in favor of a careful arrangement of the Psalter is compelling. Doxologies, superscriptions, concatenation, inclusios, key words, and personal names have all been meticulously and strategically employed to bind the individual psalms into a single, carefully composed work of literature.[32] Contrary to the opinion that the canonical order and the superscriptions are irrelevant to interpretation of the individual psalms, the book of Psalms is not merely a collection but truly a book, and should be interpreted as such.

EVIDENCE FOR THE PROPHETIC NATURE OF THE PSALMS

Not only is the Psalter demonstrably a book rather than a random selection of songs, but it is a prophetic book with a message to convey.

1. The Authors Are Recognized Prophets

Previously, another common assumption about the problematic nature of the theological intentionality of individual psalms was raised. As the argument goes,

> [T]he psalms are prayers sung to God; thus they present us with the words of the congregation addressed to God, rather than the Word of God addressed to the people of Israel. How, then, is it possible to speak of the theological concerns of the Psalter?[33]

The problem with this assumption is that it completely ignores the OT's testimony about the individual authors who are mentioned in the Psalter's superscriptions. Several authors are named in the superscriptions of the Psalter including David, Moses, Asaph, the Sons of Korah, and Solomon. Several of the musicians accredited with prophecy in 1Chr 25:1-4 are referred to in the superscriptions of the psalms: Asaph (Pss 50, 73, 74, 75, 76, 77, 78, 79, 80, 81, 82, 83); Heman (Ps 88); Jeduthun (Pss 39, 62, 77). Second Chronicles 29:30 identifies Asaph as a seer (a prophet).[34] Moses, mentioned in the superscription of Ps 90, is certainly the greatest of all OT prophets (Nm 12:6-8; Dt 34:10). The superscriptions give the distinct impression that, beyond their importance for organizing the book of Psalms as a whole, they also serve to identify the contents of the psalms with the inspired words of the prophets. One unfortunate consequence of the critical rejection of the authenticity and canonicity of the superscriptions is a broken connection between the psalms and their prophetic authors.

2. Music Is a Recognized Partner to Prophecy

David, who is mentioned in the great majority of the superscriptions,[35] is noted in Scripture for his supernatural gifting as a musician, one whose music could even drive out evil spirits (1Sm 16:18,23). There is an important connection between music and prophecy in the OT. For instance, Elisha the prophet required the presence of a musician in order to prophecy to king Jehoshaphat (2Kg 3:15). Also, 1Sm 10:5 refers to a group of prophets who prophesy by the accompaniment of various musical instruments. It would be an error to think that because the Psalms are musical in nature that they are not prophetic. The opposite is true. Moreover, Scripture also testifies that David declared his psalms through the Spirit of the Lord (2Sm 23:1-2; see Ac 1:16; 2:30-31). In other words, David, the author of the majority of psalms in the Psalter, is identified as an inspired author with supernatural musical abilities (1Sm 16:23).

Moreover, Scripture also affirms that the Levites whom David appointed to praise the Lord in the temple were also musician-prophets.

> David and the officers of the army also set apart some of the sons of Asaph, Heman, and Jeduthun, who were to prophesy accompanied by lyres, harps, and cymbals. This is the list of the men who performed their service: From Asaph's sons: Zaccur, Joseph, Nethaniah, and Asarelah, sons of Asaph, under Asaph's authority, who prophesied under the authority of the king. From Jeduthun: Jeduthun's sons: Gedaliah, Zeri, Jeshaiah, Shimei, Hashabiah, and Mattithiah—six—under the authority of their father Jeduthun, prophesying to the accompaniment of lyres, giving thanks and praise to the LORD. . . . All these sons of Heman, the king's seer, were given by the promises of God to exalt him, for God had given Heman fourteen sons and three daughters.[36]

> Hezekiah stationed the Levites in the LORD's temple with cymbals, harps, and lyres according to the command of David, Gad the king's seer, and Nathan the prophet. For the command was from the LORD through His prophets. . . . Then King Hezekiah and the officials told the Levites to sing praise to the LORD in the words of David and of Asaph the seer. So they sang praises with rejoicing and bowed down and worshiped.[37]

> The singers, the descendants of Asaph, were at their stations according to the command of David, Asaph, Heman, and Jeduthun the king's seer. Also, the gatekeepers were at each gate. None of them left their tasks because their Levite brothers had made preparations for them.[38]

The OT itself, therefore, testifies of the relationship between the writers of the psalms and prophecy. Furthermore, the evidence suggests that the author of the canonical Psalter understood this relationship and regarded the psalms as the word of these prophets. The thoughtful, intentional arrangement of the psalms serves to highlight and expound their meaning, as is the case with all the other prophetic writings in the OT (e.g., Isaiah, Amos, etc.). To understand the prophetic witness of the psalms, therefore, interpreters must pay careful attention to the macro-structural arrangement of the Psalter, rather than treating the book of Psalms as a loose collection of prayers and hymns.

THE BOOK OF PSALMS HAS A STORY TO TELL

Few books of the Bible explicitly state their purpose. A noteworthy exception is the Gospel of John: "But these are written so that you may believe Jesus is the Messiah, the Son of God, and by believing you may have life in His name" (Jn 20:31). Rather, the books of the Bible have been composed with numerous literary clues. Wilson argues that the best place to look for the purpose of the book of Psalms is in those places where the fingerprints of the composer are most clearly evident, namely, in the seam psalms at the end of each of the books, as well as in the introduction to the book of Psalms as a whole.

Without a doubt, the Davidic covenant (Royal Psalms) stands out in all of the psalms at the seams in Books I–III.[39] In Wilson's words, "It has been suggested . . . that to discuss the editorial purpose behind the Psalter arrangement one must begin by looking at the Pss which mark the seams between the books. A brief glance at Pss 2, 41, 72, and 89 reveals an interesting progression in thought regarding kingship and the Davidic covenant."[40] Psalms 2 and 72 frame Books I–II with an expectation that God, in fulfillment of the Davidic covenant,[41] will raise up an exalted descendant of David whose reign will extend to the ends of the earth (Ps 2:8; 72:8). A comparison between Ps 72:8 and Zch 9:9-10 makes clear the identity of this exalted king.

May he rule from sea to sea and from the Euphrates to the ends of the earth. (Ps 72:8)	Rejoice greatly, Daughter Zion! Shout in triumph, Daughter Jerusalem! Look, your King is coming to you; He is righteous and victorious, humble and riding on a donkey, on a colt, the foal of a donkey. . . . He will proclaim peace to the nations. *His dominion will extend from sea to sea, from the Euphrates River to the ends of the earth.* (Zch 9:9-10)

Zechariah 9:10 is a nearly verbatim quotation of Ps 72:8, making clear that this king can be none other than King Messiah. Moreover, the final verse of Ps 72 before the doxology makes it clear that God's purpose through this exalted king is to fulfill His promises to Abraham: "May his name endure forever; as long as the sun shines,

may his fame increase. May all nations be blessed by him and call him blessed" (Ps 72:17; compare Gn 12:2-3; 22:18).

Moreover, the exaltation of the Davidic scion on Mount Zion at the seams of Book I–II stands in stark contrast to the numerous laments of the king (see, e.g., Pss 3–7). These laments, however, are already anticipated in the introduction of the Psalter. If "the wicked will not survive the judgment" and the "way of the wicked leads to ruin" (Ps 1:5-6), "why do the nations rebel and the peoples plot in vain? The kings of the earth take their stand and the rulers conspire together against the LORD and His Anointed One" (i.e., his Messiah; Ps 2:1-2). Yes, God will ultimately establish His Son upon Mount Zion (Ps 2:6), but this will not be without opposition. The lament psalms throughout the Psalter, therefore, may be heard as the cries of God's persecuted king.

Psalm 89, a seam-psalm marking the end of Book III, marks a significant psalm in the structure of the Psalter. Not only does this psalm explicitly mention God's faithfulness with respect to the Davidic covenant (Ps 89:4,29,35), it also laments its apparent failure (Ps 89:39-52). The sinful behavior of David and his sons (see for example, Ps 51) results in the destruction of the southern kingdom, and with it, the Davidic throne is overthrown (Ps 89:44). While David is mentioned 65 times in Books I–III, he practically disappears in Book IV (Ps 101:1; 103:1). Though Wilson argued that the purpose of Book IV is to provide an alternative to the failure of the Davidic covenant,[42] David Alexander Gundersen, in a recent dissertation, vigorously and persuasively argues that Book IV provides the resolution to the problem of the broken Davidic covenant by appealing to God's merciful dealings with sinful Israel in the wilderness through the mediation of Moses (the key figure in Book IV).[43] According to Gundersen, Pss 90 (a prayer of Moses) and 103 (the second of only two Davidic psalms in Book IV) have a crucial relationship to God's ongoing purposes through the house of David. It is worth quoting Gundersen at length:

> Psalm 103 also alludes to Exodus 32–34, so that Psalms 90 and 103 share a common allusion to the golden calf incident and Yahweh's subsequent self-revelation. In Psalm 90, Israel's blatant idolatry, Yahweh's burning anger, Moses' desperate intercession, and Yahweh's self-revelation are reimagined once again. Psalm 103, however, picks up only positive elements from the story, while Psalm 90 echoed only negative elements. Psalm 90 repeats themes of sin and iniquity, God's consuming anger, and Moses' pleas that Yahweh turn and relent. But Psalm 103 picks up themes of sin and iniquity being forgiven, Yahweh keeping his covenant, and God proclaiming his steadfast love afresh to his people.[44]
>
> Psalm 103 stands as a magnificent psalm on its own, anywhere in the Psalter, with Davidic titling or without. But its Davidic authorship, its celebration of individual

> and communal restoration by the mercies of God, and its placement at the height of the Davidic progression in 101–103 suggest that Psalm 103 upholds the hope for a king from David's line.[45]

Book IV encourages its readers to look back to a period, long before the establishment of the Davidic dynasty, to realize that God is still king (Pss 93:1; 95:3; 96:10; 97:1; 98:6; 99:1,4), and that, in spite of Israel's sin, God "revealed his ways to Moses," and He is "compassionate and gracious, slow to anger and rich in faithful love" (Ps 103:7-8; see Ex 34:6). And so Ps 106 takes us through Israel's ongoing history of disobedience, noting that in all this, God "remembered His covenant with them, and relented according to the riches of His faithful love" (Ps 106:45). The psalmist, therefore, can confidently conclude Book IV with a prayer of faith: "Save us, Yahweh our God, and gather us from the nations, so that we may give thanks to Your holy name and rejoice in Your praise" (Ps 106:47).

Book V rekindles this hope by noting that God, whose faithful love endures forever (Ps 107:1), "has gathered them from the lands—from the east and the west, from the north and the south" (Ps 107:3). Psalm 126 refers to the return of the remnant from the Babylonian exile, thereby providing confidence that God will indeed keep His promises to the house of David. And, as in the earlier books, David (and his Lord) returns once again as the hero of Book V.[46] In Ps 110, a Davidic descendant sits at God's hand, only to return yet again to take his seat on Mount Zion to rule and reign forever (Ps 132:11-18). David's dishonored crown (Ps 89:39) will once again be glorious (Ps 132:18). The mood of the Psalter, therefore, shifts from mourning (Books I–III) to a growing chorus of praise that embraces Israel and all nations (Pss 146–150).

Before concluding this article, it is essential to discuss the dating of the composition of the canonical Psalter. Given the reference to a return from exile in Pss 107:3 and 126:1, clearly the book of Psalms must have been composed sometime after the return from the Babylonian exile, during the Second Temple period. This being the case, the prominent position of the royal psalms in a book composed long after the house of David was in eclipse means that this exalted king, and the numerous references to David throughout the Psalter, reinforce the sole possibility that the book must be understood as messianic.[47] For what other reason would the Davidic covenant be celebrated during the Second Temple period? To quote Brevard Childs, "Indeed, at the time of the final redaction, when the institution of kingship had long since been destroyed, what earthly king would have come to mind other than God's Messiah?"[48]

Finally, it is essential to deal with one common objection to the claim that the psalms are directly messianic. As the argument goes, some psalms, such as Ps 69, cannot be directly messianic because of the confession of guilt and sin that is altogether inappropriate for the sinless Messiah.[49] David says in Ps 69:5 [MT 69:6], "God, You know my foolishness, and my guilty acts are not hidden from You." Yet the NT authors frequently allude to and cite Ps 69 as a Messianic prophecy that was fulfilled in Jesus (see Mt 27:34,38; Mk 15:36; Lk 23:36; Jn 2:17; 15:25; 19:28; Rom 15:3; see also Ac 1:20). Though the NT authors did not regard v. 5 as a disqualification of their messianic interpretation, it is necessary to provide an explanation of this verse, and others like it (see also Ps 40:12 [MT 13]), to defend the messianic message of the individual psalms as well as the book of Psalms as a whole.[50]

Accordingly, to reject the messianism of these psalms on the basis of the confessions of sinfulness on the part of the psalmist fails to consider other analogies of comparison between the biblical figures and the Messiah in the Hebrew Bible—and it also misses the purpose of these confessions in the plot of the book of Psalms as a whole.

First, consider another crucial Messianic analogy in the Pentateuch. In Dt 18:15, Moses predicts the coming of a prophet like him: "The Lord your God will raise up for you a prophet like me from among your own brothers . . ." (cf. 34:10; also cf. Nm 23:21-22 with 24:7-8). When Moses promises that God will raise up a prophet like him, he obviously does not mean in every way, since there are several examples of Moses' moral and spiritual failures in the Pentateuch (e.g., Nm 20:12). The promise of a prophet like Moses, rather, focuses specifically on Moses' unique role in God's redemptive program. Thus, in the context of Isaiah's "New Exodus" (Isa 40–55), there is the promise of a future redeemer who will be like Moses (Isa 42:1-4; 49:1-6; 50:4-9; 52:13–53:12), but obviously not with respect to Moses' sin.[51]

When considering God's promise to David in 2Sm 7:11-16 in light of the larger Davidic narrative in 1 and 2Sm, David is revealed as an ideal king, but an imperfect one at that. In one sense, the author presents David as an example of a man after God's own heart, and a mighty warrior on Israel's behalf. At the same time, David's moral failure with Bathsheba comes to signify the beginning of a long history of the failures of David and his royal line, failures ultimately leading to the Babylonian exile. Obviously, the author of 1 and 2Sm considers David as a figure or pattern of the coming Messiah, but not in every way. Moreover, God's promise to establish an eternal throne (2Sm 7:16) creates the need for a Davidic descendant who will not be like David. Rather, he must be someone far greater than David.

This tension between the ideal king (Pss 2; 72) and the historical David with all his failures (Pss 32; 51) is felt throughout the story line of the Psalter. In fact, Ps 89 represents the major crisis in the story line, wherein David's throne and crown are cast into the dust, leading the psalmist to struggle in anguish over the timing of God's faithful promises (Ps 89:5,29,34 [MT 5,30,35]) to a faithless line (Ps 89:46 [MT 47]). The problem of the sinfulness of David's house finally finds resolution in Book

IV (Ps 103:1-5), and with this resolution, there is a renewed focus on the coming of the ideal Messianic King in Book V of the Psalter (Pss 110; 132).

So, what to do with the verses describing David's confessions of guilt? In the book of Psalms, they are to be understood as a persistent reminder of the coming of a future King who will be like David, but not in every way since the author of the Psalter presents the real David, warts and all.[52] David's confessions reveal the guilt of a man who imperfectly symbolizes the coming King who will be far greater and without sin. In fact, this coming King is so great that David calls him Lord (Ps 110:1).

CONCLUSION: THE BOOK OF PSALMS HAS A MESSIANIC MESSAGE TO TELL

Many modern readers struggle to see the messianic message of the book of Psalms. This article has attempted to show that this struggle is rooted in the so-called higher criticism of the 20th century, a criticism that literally removed or minimized all the compositionally inspired stitches (superscriptions, doxologies) holding the Psalter together as a unified book with a unified message, as well as the canonical superscriptions identifying the authors as inspired prophets. Though modern proponents of the grammatical-historical method of interpretation tend to look down upon the pre-critical reading of the Psalter, and have found the NT's use of the Psalms creative and eisegetical, this study has shown the opposite. It is the modern critical reading of the Psalter that has been measured in the balance and been found wanting. The NT authors have correctly received the individual psalms and the book of Psalms as a whole as a witness to the sufferings of the Messiah and His glories to follow. David's laments, voiced through God's inspired prophets, predict Messiah's sufferings (e.g., Pss 22; 69). David's Lord sitting at the right hand of God (Ps 110) is also God's Son whom God will seat upon Mount Zion (Pss 2:6; 132:11-18). God will eventually bind the rebellious kings and dignitaries with iron shackles (Ps 149:6-9), and Israel and all nations will celebrate the victory, such that everything that has breath will join in the triumphal celebrations (Ps 150:6).

---

1. Amos Chakham, *The Book of Psalms*, Vol. 1, *Da'at Miqra* (Jerusalem: Mossad Harav Kook, 1989), 13 (Hebrew; translation of Hebrew by author).
2. Acts 2:25-31 (HCSB; emphasis added).
3. Raymond Dillard and Tremper Longman III, *An Introduction to the Old Testament* (Grand Rapids: Zondervan, 1994), 233 (emphasis added).
4. For example, the Gospel of John appeals to Ps 69:9 to explain Jesus' actions in the temple (Jn 2:17). John 15:25 states

that the hatred Jesus experienced was a fulfillment of the prophecy in Ps 69:4. Acts 1:16-20 also appeals to Ps 69:25 as a prediction of the Messiah's betrayal at the hands of Judas. While it is obvious the NT authors interpreted Ps 69 as messianic, it is not obvious how this psalm of individual lament is messianic.

5. Dillard and Longman, *Introduction to the OT*, 211.

6. Ibid., 227.

7. Gerald Wilson, *The Editing of the Hebrew Psalter*, Society of Biblical Literature, Dissertation Series 76 (Chico, CA: Scholars Press, 1985), 206, writes, "The Psalter has on occasion been styled 'the Hymn Book of the Second Temple.' This rather unfortunate designation has had the adverse effect of focusing a disproportionate amount of attention on the individual compositions contained within. A 'hymn book' collects hymns so that they may be readily available for individual use in worship. Emphasis is placed on the secondary use of the individual members of the collection rather than the collection itself. While some hymn books evidence a limited attempt to group their contents by theme, interest or liturgical function, there is seldom any sustained, organizational purpose at work in consecutive arrangement."

8. See ibid., 1; Dillard and Longman, *Introduction to the OT*, 217.

9. Wilson, *Editing*, 1, writes: "Current Psalm scholarship emphasizes the study of individual psalms (pss), or at the most, those earlier collections of pss which can be discerned embedded within the final form of the canonical Psalter. The roots of this current trend can be traced to the influential works of the early, major figures in the field, namely Hermann Gunkel and Sigmund Mowinkel. Both men have been largely concerned to focus on individual pss, loosed from their traditional moorings in the Psalter (MT 150) and rearranged according to other criteria in groups which (in effect) ignore the canonical order."

10. Psalm 3 contains the first superscription in the book of Psalms: "A psalm of David when he fled from his son Absalom." This particular superscription contains information about the genre (mizmor [psalm]), the author (David), and the historical content ("when he fled from his son Absalom") (Wilson, *Editing*, 155). All superscriptions are considered the first verse in the Hebrew Bible. Obviously, the Christian English translations (e.g., HCSB), do not attribute canonical status (inspiration) to the superscriptions, which are therefore excluded from the versification of the psalm itself and presented in a font that is distinguished from the psalm itself. Superscriptions contain information about the author, genre, instructions, and historical content. Genre categories include the following: *Shiggaion* (Book I: Ps 7); *Miktam* (Book I: Ps 16; Book II: Pss 56,57,58,59,60); prayer (Book I: Ps 17; Book III: Ps 86; Book IV: Pss 90,102); *Maskil* (Book I: Ps 32; Book II: Pss 42,44,45,52,53,54,55; Book III: Pss 74,78,88,89; Book V: Ps 142); praise (Book V: Ps 145); Hallelujah (Book V: Pss 111,112,113,135,146,147,148,149,150); psalm (Book I: Pss 3,4,5, 6,8,9,12,13,15,19,20,21,22,23,24,29,30,31,38,39,40,41; Book II: Pss 47,48,49,50,51,62,63,64,65,66,67,68; Book III: Pss 73,75,76,77,79,80,82,83,84,85,87,88; Book IV: Pss 92,98,100,101; Book V: Pss 108,109,110,139,140,141,143); and song (Book I: Ps 30; Book II: Pss 45,46,48,65,66,67,68; Book III: Pss 75,76,83,87,88; Book IV: Ps 92; Book V: Pss 108,120,121, 123,124,125,126,127,128,129,130,131,132,133,134) (Wilson, *Editing*, 158).

11. See Brevard Childs, *Introduction to the Old Testament as Scripture* (Philadelphia: Fortress, 1979), 509.

12. Dillard and Longman, *Introduction*, 216, make this point clear when they write, "Therefore, while the titles are not canonical, they may be reliable. Nonetheless, they are not important to the interpretation of individual psalms."

13. Form Criticism, or *Gattungsforschung*, treats each psalm independently and divorced from its canonical context, with special attention on the genre of the particular psalm (see Wilson, *Editing*, 1–2). Psalm types include hymns, lament psalms, royal psalms, thanksgiving psalms, and wisdom psalms.

14. Brevard Childs, *Introduction to the Old Testament as Scripture*, 509.

15. Examples of seemingly arbitrary messianic interpretations of the psalms isolated from their canonical context include Hebrews' use of Ps 8:4-6 (Heb 2:6-8); Acts' use of Ps 16:8-11 (Ac 2:25-28; 13:35); Hebrews' use of Ps 40:6-8 (Heb 10:5-7); Ephesians' use of Ps 68:18 (Eph 4:8); and John's use of Ps 69 (Jn 2:17; 15:25).

16. The importance of the superscriptions for the prophetic origins of the psalms will be discussed in the following section.

17. Brevard Childs, *Introduction to the Old Testament as Scripture*, 511–13; Wilson, *Editing*; David C. Mitchell, *The Message of the Psalter: An Eschatological Programme in the Book of Psalms*, Journal for the Study of Old Testament Supplement Series 252 (Sheffield: SAP, 1997); David M. Howard, *The Structure of Psalms 93–100* (Winona Lake, IN: Eisenbrauns, 1997); Robert L. Cole, *The Shape and Message of Book III (Psalms 73–89)*, Journal for the Study of Old Testament Supplement Series 307 (Sheffield: SAP, 2000); Michael K. Snearly, *The Return of the King: Messianic Expectation in Book V of the Psalter*, Library of Hebrew Bible/Old Testament Studies 624 (London: Bloomsbury T&T Clark, 2015); Clinton J. McCann, ed., *The Shape and Shaping of the Psalter* (Sheffield: SAP, 1993).

18. Wilson uses the word "editorial" rather than "compositional" (see Wilson, *Editing*, 155). I believe the word "editor" does not correctly convey the essence of the making of a biblical book, nor the significance of the maker of a biblical book (see John van Seters, *The Edited Bible* [Winona Lake, IN: Eisenbrauns, 2006]). An editor, at least in the

modern sense, is a person in charge of the final content of a text, but typically at the level of corrections and suggestions to the author. The individual responsible for the final form of the book of Psalms made a book (an author in his own right), and did so under the guidance and inspiration of the Holy Spirit. The word "editor," therefore, falls far short of a title fitting for an inspired maker of a biblical book.

19. Wilson, *Editing*, 182–90. More recently, Michael Snearly has argued that Ps 145:21 shares key terminology with the other doxologies and should also be understood as the doxology of Book V. Michael Snearly, *Return of the King*, 164–68.

20. Psalms 1–2 serve as the introduction to the Psalter (the book of Psalms) as a whole, as will be shown.

21. Psalms 146–150 serve as the conclusion to the Psalter as a whole, as will be shown.

22. See also, David M. Howard Jr., "Divine and Human Kingship as Organizing Motifs in the Psalter," in *The Psalms: Language for All Seasons of the Soul*, ed. Andrew J. Schmutzer and David M. Howard Jr. (Chicago: Moody Publishers, 2013), 199.

23. All ancient manuscripts and translations include the doxologies.

24. "For Books One through Three of the Psalter (Pss 3–89) the primary organizational concern is apparently authorship" (Wilson, *Editing*, 155). While authorship in the superscriptions links psalms together within the books of Psalms, there is a shift in authorship at the seams of the major divisions of the first four books of the Psalter (Books I–IV). From David at the end of Book I (Ps 41:1) to the sons of Korah at the beginning of Book II (42:1); from Solomon at the end of Book II (72:1) to Asaph at the beginning of Book III (73:1); from Ethan at the end of Book III (89:1) to Moses at the beginning of Book IV (90:1) (Wilson, *Editing*, 157).

25. Though Wilson explicitly treats Ps 1 as the introduction to the Psalter, he implicitly treats Ps 2 as part of the introduction when he notes the absence of its superscription in Books I–III (Wilson, *Editing*, 155, 173). For a thorough treatment of the function of Pss 1–2 in the Psalter, see Robert L. Cole, *Psalms 1–2: Gateway to the Psalter* (Sheffield: Phoenix Press, 2013).

26. David M. Howard Jr., "Divine and Human Kingship as Organizing Motifs in the Psalter," in *The Psalms: Language for All Seasons of the Soul*, eds. Andrew J. Schmutzer and David M. Howard Jr. (Chicago: Moody Publishers, 2013), 202–203; see also Robert L. Cole, *Gateway to the Psalter*, Hebrew Monographs 37, ed. David J. A. Clines, J. Cheryl Exum, and Keith W. Whitelam (Sheffield: Sheffield Phoenix Press, 2013).

27. Todd J. Murphy, *Pocket Dictionary for the Study of Biblical Hebrew* (Downers Grove, IL: InterVarsity, 2003), 47, defines concatenation as the "joining of a group of immediate constituents into a chain, such as a construct relationship . . ." See also Mark D. Futato, *Interpreting the Psalms: An Exegetical Handbook*, Handbooks for Old Testament Exegesis, ed. David M. Howard Jr. (Grand Rapids: Kregel, 2007), 231.

28. See Mitchell, *The Message of the Psalter*, 46. Chakham, *The Book of Psalms*, 36, "'There is no early and late' in the psalms of the book of Psalms. The sages already highlighted (in *M. Ber.* 10a) that 'a psalm of David when he fled from Absalom his son' (Ps 3) brings up an event that was later than the time of an event that is mentioned in 'For the choir director: "Do Not Destroy." A *Miktam* of David when he fled before Saul into the cave' (Ps 57). The conclusion from this observation is that the psalms of the Psalter are not arranged according to the chronological order of the events mentioned in them, but by allusions and common topics in the juxtaposing psalms" (author's translation of the Hebrew).

29. The word "plot" in the HCSB is the same word used for "meditate" in Ps 1:2. The same word does not appear again in the Psalter until Ps 35:28 where the HCSB translates it "proclaim."

30. The word used for "psalm" in the superscription of Ps 8 comes from the same Hebrew root of the word used for "sing" in Ps 7:17.

31. Murphy, *Pocket Dictionary for the Study of Biblical Hebrew*, 90, defines an inclusio as a "literary construction in which the discourse boundaries are marked off by a similar word, clause or phrase." See also Mark D. Futato, *Interpreting the Psalms*, 32, 232. For example, Ps 8 begins and ends with the same phrase, "Yahweh, our Lord, how magnificent is Your name throughout the earth! (8:1,9). An inclusio is used to mark literary boundaries for texts of various levels, from the smallest (i.e., for a single literary unity like Ps 8) to the largest (i.e., a literary frame around an entire book).

32. Another line of evidence in favor of a purposeful arrangement of the Psalter is its movement from lamentation to praise in the macrostructure of the book (see Claus Westermann, *Praise and Lament in the Psalms* [Atlanta: John Knox, 1981], 257–58; Futato, *Interpreting the Psalms*, 80).

33. Dillard and Longman, *Introduction to the OT*, 227. Peter C. Craigie, Psalms 1–50, Word Biblical Commentary 19 (Grand Rapids: Zondervan, 1983), 39, shares a similar perspective when he writes,

> Within the OT as a whole, the biblical literature may be divided loosely into two categories. First, there is that which purports to be God's direct revelation to mankind (specifically to Israel) through the medium of the

prophet; for example, much of the Law of Moses and the oracles of the prophets fall into this category. Second, there is that literature which purports to be primarily a human creation, though it is created in the religious context and pertains to the relationship between Israel and God, or in some cases to the relationship between Hebrew and Hebrew. The Psalms fall into this second category. With the exception of a few psalms which have a prophetic character, the Book of Psalms as a whole contains Israel's songs and prayers which constitute the response of the chosen people to their revelation from God. (The Book of Psalms is thus recognized as "revelation," or inspired, by virtue of its inclusion in the canon of Holy Scripture, rather than by any internal characteristics specifying God's direct self-revelation in word.)

34. See 2Sm 24:11; Am 7:12; 1Chr 21:9; 25:5; 29:29; 2Chr 9:29; 12:15; 19:2; 29:25,30; 33:18; 35:15.

35. Pss 3:1; 4:1; 5:1; 6:1; 7:1; 8:1; 9:1; 11:1; 12:1; 13:1; 14:1; 15:1; 16:1; 17:1; 18:1; 19:1; 20:1; 21:1; 22:1; 23:1; 24:1; 25:1; 26:1; 27:1; 28:1; 29:1; 30:1; 31:1; 32:1; 34:1; 35:1; 36:1; 37:1; 38:1; 39:1; 40:1; 41:1; 51:1; 52:1; 53:1; 54:1; 55:1; 56:1; 57:1; 58:1; 59:1; 60:1; 61:1; 62:1; 63:1; 64:1; 65:1; 68:1; 69:1; 70:1; 86:1; 101:1; 103:1; 108:1; 109:1; 110:1; 122:1; 124:1; 131:1; 133:1; 138:1; 139:1; 140:1; 141:1; 142:1; 143:1; 144:1; 145:1.

36. 1Chr 25:1-3,5.

37. 2Chr 29:25,30.

38. 2Chr 35:15.

39. Rolf Rendtorf, *The Old Testament: An Introduction*, trans. John Bowden (Philadelphia: Fortress, 1986), 249, writes, "[T]he emphatic position of the royal psalms is of great significance. They conclude subsidiary collections (72; 89) and provide a framework for the first collection (2; 110)." See also Childs, *Introduction*, 515–17.

40. Wilson, *Editing*, 209.

41. Compare Ps 2:7 with 2Sm 7:14; 1Chr 17:13; Isa 9:6-7.

42. Wilson, *Editing*, 215, writes, "In my opinion, Pss 90–106 function as the editorial 'center' of the final form of the Psalter. As such this grouping stands as the 'answer' to the problem posed in Ps 89 as to the apparent failure of the Davidic covenant with which Books One–Three are primarily concerned."

43. David Alexander Gundersen, "Davidic Hope in Book IV of the Psalter (Psalms 90–106)," Dissertation, Southern Baptist Theological Seminary, 2015; see also David C. Mitchell, "Lord, Remember David: G. H. Wilson and the Message of the Psalter," *Vetus Testamentum* 56, no. 4 (2006): 526–48; Jamie A. Grant, *The King as Exemplar: The Function of Deuteronomy's Kingship Law in the Shaping of the Book of Psalms*, SBL Academia Biblica 17 (Atlanta: Society of Biblical Literature, 2004); David M. Howard Jr., "The Case for Kingship in the Old Testament Narrative Books and the Psalms," *Trinity Journal* 9.1 (Mar. 1988): 19–35; ibid., "The Case for Kingship in Deuteronomy and the Former Prophets," *Westminster Theological Journal* 52.1 (Spring 1990): 101–15; ibid., "The Proto-MT Psalter, the King, and Psalms 1 and 2: A Response to Klaus Seybold," in S. Gillingham, ed., *Jewish and Christian Approaches to the Psalter: Conflict and Convergence* (Oxford: Oxford University Press, 2012), 182–89; Michael G. McKelvey, *Moses, David and the High Kingship of Yahweh: A Canonical Study of Book IV of the Psalter*, Gorgias Biblical Studies 55 (Piscataway, NJ: Gorgias, 2014); David C. Mitchell, *The Songs of Ascents: Psalms 120–134 in the Worship of Jerusalem's Temple* (Newton Mears, Scotland: Campbell Publications, 2015); David Willgren, *Like a Garden of Flowers: A Study of the Formation of the 'Book' of Psalms* (Lund: Lund University 2016); Michael K. Snearly, *The Return of the King*; Carissa M. Quinn Richards, "The King and the Kingdom: The Message of Psalms 15–24" (Ph.D., Golden Gate Baptist Theological Seminary, 2015); Mark D. Futato, *Interpreting the Psalms: An Exegetical Handbook*, Handbooks for Old Testament Exegesis (Grand Rapids: Kregel, 2007); Robert L. Cole, *Psalms 1-2: A Gateway to the Psalter*; Jerome L. Skinner, "The Historical Superscriptions of Davidic Psalms: An Exegetical, Intertextual, and Methodological Analysis" (Ph.D., Andrews University, Seventh-day Adventist Theological Seminary, 2016). I want to offer a special word of thanks to David Howard Jr. for calling my attention to many of the works referenced in this footnote.

44. Gundersen, "Davidic Hope," 235.

45. Ibid., 239.

46. Pss 108:1; 109:1; 110:1; 122:1,5; 124:1; 131:1; 132:1,10-11,17; 133:1; 138:1; 139:1; 140:1; 141:1; 142:1; 143:1; 144:1,10; 145:1.

47. Mitchell, "Lord, Remember David": 529; ibid., *The Message of the Psalter*, 82–83.

48. Childs, *Introduction*, 516.

49. See Tremper Longman III, Raymond B. Dillard, *An Introduction to the Old Testament*, 2nd ed. (Grand Rapids: Zondervan, 2006), 262.

50. Some have explained these confessions by identifying David as a type, one who did not understand that he was writing about the Messiah but is identified as a type in the NT (e.g. H. C. Leupold, *Exposition of the Psalms*, [Grand Rapids: Baker, 1969], 501). Others see the confessions in the Psalms as the vicarious confessions of the Messiah, taking the sins of others upon Himself (E. W. Hengstenberg, *Christology of the Old Testament*, [Grand Rapids: Kregel, 1970], 92. Bruce Waltke, who understands the final form of the book of Psalms as messianic, merely dismisses these

confessions as "the historical eggshells from the preexilic period when the psalms were used for Israel's less than ideal kings" (Bruce K. Waltke, "A Canonical Process Approach to the Psalms," *Tradition and Testament: Essays in Honor of Charles Lee Feinberg*, ed. John S. and Paul D. Feinberg [Chicago: Moody Press, 1981], 16).

51. On the relationship of Isaiah's Servant Songs with the prophet like Moses, see G. P. Hugenberger, "The Servant of the Lord in the 'Servant Songs' of Isaiah: A Second Moses Figure," in *The Lord's Anointed: Interpretation of Old Testament Messianic Texts*, ed. P. E. Satterthwaite, R. S. Hess, G. J. Wenham (Grand Rapids: Baker, 1995): 105–40.

52. *The Moody Bible Commentary*, ed. Michael Rydelnik and Michael Vanlaningham (Chicago: Moody Publishers, 2014), 816, calls these confessions "'symbolic realism' in which the real David becomes a symbol of the Messiah. Hence, David used his own flawed experiences as the symbol of the Messiah and therefore included his own confession of guilt."

Psalms 1–2

The Divine Son of God

ROBERT L. COLE

The Psalter has an introduction.[1] Its first two psalms together constitute a foreword to the topics and subject matter of the rest of the book. Readers both modern and ancient assume and expect with good reason that the opening of any book will contain an overture to its content. Indeed, the chapters immediately succeeding Ps 3, and all those following, continue in the same vein as the first two. This can be seen in the continued and repeated use of terminology and language from the introduction throughout. From the beginning of the book to the end, each psalm is linked to the next, through the use of common, often unique, and rare vocabulary.

At the other end of the book is an example of inclusion or enveloping, in which the introductory themes are explicitly mentioned again. Psalm 149 takes up vocabulary especially from the introductory Ps 2 in a reaffirmation and expansion of its message.[2] In other words, there is good evidence in the language of the book itself for reading the first two psalms as an integrated introduction.

Form criticism has conditioned many to read the book as a loose and disordered collection, meaning it is unlike any other book in the Hebrew Bible. However, the linguistic evidence belies this theory. Gunkel, the father of this approach to the Psalter, considered the first two psalms as unrelated and categorized them as "wisdom" (Ps 1) and "royal" (Ps 2).[3] This labeling according to "forms" constituted a replacement of the canonical order with another, with the former seen as accidental.[4] In other words, the order made no sense to him and so was jettisoned, ignoring the explicit linguistic evidence indicating otherwise. Much of scholarship across the theological and ideological spectrum has generally followed his lead in one way or another.[5] Overt evidence on the verbal level linking juxtaposed psalms is effectively eclipsed by the form critical method. The latter relegates them to a general category and from there deduces interpretive conclusions with little concern for their distinctive language and literary features.

Two scholars, Brevard Childs and his student Gerald Wilson, published studies more than three decades ago alerting the scholarly world to the Psalter's sequence exhibiting signs of purpose and meaning.[6] Since then, most have attempted to blend the two approaches, canonical and form critical. Such a procedure ignores the incompatibility of these two approaches. Gunkel's entire reason for producing form critical categories was that he found the canonical order meaningless and substituted it with another grouping based on form-critical categories of his own making.[7] The Psalter's composer did not organize the psalms following a form-critical classification. Instead he arranged the order in a cohesive and coherent manner, which expressed thematic and theological consistency from one psalm to another, from beginning to end.

Recognition of the introductory function of the first two psalms is not recent. Ancient commentators have recognized it going back two thousand years or more. For instance, the Septuagint supplies titles to every psalm except the first two.[8] The effect is to separate the first two as a unity at the beginning from what follows, and thereby imply their function as an introduction. The ancient Talmud likewise affirms the unity of Pss 1 and 2: "'Blessed' (Ps 1) and 'Why do they conspire' (Ps 2) are one unit."[9]

During the Middle Ages the commentator David Kimchi (aka RaDaK) was familiar with the tradition of counting the first two psalms as one.[10] Another medieval rabbinic commentator, the Karaite Japheth ben Eli, also recognized their interrelatedness.[11] According to Eissler, Japheth also read both Pss 1 and 2 eschatologically.[12]

Nineteenth century commentators likewise noticed the linguistic evidence linking the first two psalms—and with varying judgments on their meaning. Among them were Hitzig, Hengstenberg, Delitzsch, Alexander, and Forbes.[13] The twentieth century saw the dominance of form criticism, but despite this there were some such as Manatti and de Solms, Zimmerli, and Barth, who noticed the binding linguistic evidence and its implications.[14]

In summary, the relatively recent resurgence of interest in the introductory role of the first two psalms and in the book as an integrated whole is by no means innovative or without precedent. Clearly many interpreters in the past took seriously the overwhelming linguistic evidence supporting its unity and harmony.

The first signal to readers that Pss 1 and 2 are deliberately juxtaposed and integrated is the evidence of *inclusio* that enfolds the pair at either end.[15] Psalm 1 begins with the same term, "blessed is/are..." *('ashrey)*, that occurs at the end of Ps 2. Both psalms are effectively united as if one, in spite of exhibiting some characteristics supporting their distinctiveness.

Neither Ps 1 nor Ps 2 is prefaced by a superscription as is common throughout Books I to III. Only two psalms (Pss 10,33) in Book I are without a superscription, and in either case it is quite possible they were part and parcel of the previous psalms. Lack of a title for Ps 2 creates an uninterrupted transition to it from the previous Ps 1. Indeed the condemned wicked mentioned at the end of Ps 1 are specified as the rebellious nations at the outset of Ps 2 by the identically stated fate if they persist in rebellion.[16] A clever consonantal pun linking the terms "wicked" and "conspire," occurring precisely at the transition between both psalms, adds support to this identification of the wicked with the recalcitrant peoples (*resha'iym... rogshu goyim*—Ps 1:6b-2:1a).[17] This phonological feature creates an aura of seamlessness between the two psalms.

Parallels of a linguistic type between their content further supports their unity. The first verse of Ps 1 functions in a variety of ways. Its first word is repeated at the end of Ps 2 and so creates a unity around the first two psalms. Book I concludes with the same word "happy" or "blessed" *('ashrey)* at the outset of Ps 41, and so it functions twice as part of an *inclusio*.

The following is a complete list of verbal parallels between the first two psalms:

'ashrey 1:1	"blessed"	2:12 *'ashrey*
derekh 1:1,6 (2x)	"way"	2:12 *derekh*
yashab, moshab 1:1	"sit," "seat" / "one sitting"	2:4 *yosheb*
yehegeh 1:2	"meditate"	2:1 *yehegu*
yomam 1:2	"daily" / "today"	2:7 *hayom*
k- 1:3,4	"like"	2:9 *k-*
'l 1:3	"upon"	2:6 *'l*
yiten 1:3	"give"	2:8 *v'etnah*
b'itto 1:3	"in its time" / "and now"	2:10 *v'attah*
bmishpat 1:5	"in the judgment" / "judges"	2:10 *shaphtey*
vederekh...to'bed 1:6	"way destroyed" / "destroyed in way"	2:12 *vto'bdu edrekh*

Note that both psalms conclude (1:6; 2:12) with the same combination of "way destroyed." Also, the preposition "upon" is found in Ps 2:2 twice more, but in the sense of "against." The latter two function as a link to Ps 3, where the same preposition with the identical meaning "against" (the speaker) appears in vv. 1 and 6. Presumably the speaker of Ps 3 (David) gives voice to the words of the Messiah under attack in Ps 2. In other words, David's words in Ps 3 are prophetic of the future King Messiah described in Pss 1–2.

The second term of v. 1, *ha'iysh*, ("the man"), is repeated, not coincidentally, in the very next book of the Hebrew Bible—Job.[18] Job, like Psalms, opens with the portrayal of an impeccable man who is repeatedly called "my servant,"[19] and who suffers innocently before final restoration. In fact, the portrayal of the "servant of the Lord" in Job (1:8; 2:3; 42:7 [3x],8—a total of four times in two verses!) as one who suffers innocently, and yet who is restored in the end, is a perfect sequel to the "servant of the Lord" in Psalms (19:13; 27:9; 31:16; 86:2,4,16; 89:39; 116:16; 119:38,84,176; 132:10; 143:2,12, etc.).

Juxtaposition of the two books with the numerous accompanying parallels has the effect of casting "my servant Job" as a figure like the man of Psalms. As will be seen later in this article, the introductory Pss 1 and 2 emphatically identify him as the messianic king. It appears that the sequence Psalms-Job seeks to picture both as descriptions of the future servant.

Psalm 1:1 provides further confirmation of the deliberate juxtaposition and coherence with the following book of Job. The phrase "the advice of the wicked" occurs only in these two books of the Hebrew Bible (Ps 1:1; Job 10:3; 21:16; 22:18). Such a limited distribution of this term is by no means coincidental. In all three instances, Job, the impeccable servant of the Lord, separates himself from the counsel of the wicked, as does the faultless man of Ps 1.

The final clause of the first verse of the first psalm also creates overt and deliberate links to Ps 2 following. This man does not, or will not "sit" (*yashab*, HCSB footnote) in the "seat" (*moshab*) of mockers. Where then does he sit? Psalm 2:4 provides the answer by means of explicit lexical, semantic, and phonological parallels. The "one sitting" (*yosheb*, HCSB footnote) and laughing in heaven in Ps 2:4 constitutes a direct lexical and semantic contrast to the "seat" of laughing scorners in Ps 1:1. In addition, the place of their seating matches on the phonological level (*moshab* ...*shamayim*). This explicit link between Pss 1:1 and 2:4 supports the reality of similar parallels in the already semantically similar expressions, "seat of scoffers" and "scoffs at them" (NASB). Linguistic parallels between the two texts exist on practically every conceivable level, whether semantic, lexical, morphological, or phonological.

An obvious implication of the resonance on multiple levels between these two verses is that *the man* of Ps 1 is now identified as *divine*, being the Adonay of Ps 2:4. Indeed, the explicit anthropomorphic descriptions of sitting, laughing, and derision in 2:4 add support to the assertion.[20] Of a similar expression in the original Hebrew is Isa 6:1, which also describes God anthropomorphically as Adonay who is seated (*Adonay yoshev*). Both terms are identical to those of Ps 2:4. Likewise Ps 110:1 uses both terms, the divine epithet Adonay[21] and the same verbal root "to sit" (*shev*), to describe one who is distinct from "the Lord" (YHWH) who addresses Him. Both texts imply a plurality in the Godhead.

The second verse by itself of Ps 1 also contains an implicit reference to the deity of this impeccable and blessed man. A translation following the word order of the original would be: "Rather in the torah of the Lord is *his delight and in his torah* he meditates day and night." The highlighted text reveals that the immediate antecedent of "his (torah)" is "his (delight)," the latter referring to the man. As a result, the torah of the Lord could be read as the torah of the man, equating him with the deity. Rashi noticed this morpho-syntactic feature of the text, but concluded that the torah was now "owned" by the man because of his constant meditation on it.[22]

An additional supporting feature of this reading of the verse is the phonological parallel between the divine name and the verb "meditate" (YHWH . . . ***yehegeh***). Three out of the four consonants are identical and follow the same order. The effect is to link the act of human meditation with YHWH. Both the consonantal parallels and word order blur the lines of distinction between this man and deity. Likewise, as already demonstrated, multiple parallels between the first verse of Ps 1 and Ps 2:4 point to the same divine identification of this unequivocally impeccable man.

Verses 2 and 3 of this first psalm also demonstrate resonance with Jos 1:7-9. Joshua is promised success in all his ways if he meditates day and night on the book of the Torah. For Ps 1:2-3 it is not conditional but an accomplished fact. He does indeed meditate constantly, and his success is without qualification. Joshua is successful for the most part with a couple of exceptions: the initial battle with Ai and the deception by the Gibeonites.

Both Ps 1 and Jos 1 begin successive divisions of the Hebrew Bible—Prophets and Writings. There can be no doubt that this is intentional, as are the parallels between Dt 34 and Mal 4 at the end of the Torah and Prophets, thereby forming parallel seams.[23] Joshua's success is military as the ensuing narrative of the conquest of the land illustrates. Psalm 1 is also understood by the Psalter's composer as military, as shown by the additional information regarding this man in Ps 2. There he likewise smashes his enemies by the authority given to him by God. Indeed, both Jos 1 and Ps 2 contain the same verbal root *ntn* (give) expressing the divinely *given* authority over all the land or over all nations on the earth (Jos 1:3; Ps 2:8).[24]

Verse 3 opens with a verb common in references to the distant eschatological future (*hayah;* he will be, NASB).[25] Further, the expression, "whose leaf does not wither," also supports a future orientation. Ezekiel 47:12 repeats the identical clause in a description of the new Jerusalem.[26] Likewise Ezk 47:12 mentions the tree's fruit (*piryo*), which is precisely the term in Ps 1:3 and in Gn 1:11,29, and 2. The full clause is unique to both Ezk 47 and Ps 1 and indicates both are referring to the same restored paradise.

Ezekiel 47 sees the restored paradise as eschatological Jerusalem and the juxtaposition of Pss 1 and 2 also links the new Eden of the former with the Jerusalem or Zion of the latter. Both psalms speak of the placement of a man "upon" a temple locale. The messianic king of Ps 2 is established "on" (*'al*) Mt. Zion and the man of Ps 1:3 is transplanted "by" (*'al*) streams of water.

Sanctuary or temple language dominates Ps 1:3ab through arboreal and water imagery. Psalm 92:12 describes the righteous one as a palm tree or a cedar, transplanted and flourishing in the house of the Lord. The language describing a righteous man as "like a palm tree" (*katamar*) and "like a cedar" (*ke'erez*) in Ps 92 matches the perfect man, who is "like a tree" (*ke'ets*) in Ps 1. Furthermore, the verbal form "planted" in Ps 1:3 (*shatul*) is also repeated in Ps 92:13 (*shtulim*), which also refers to these temple dwellers. "Streams of water" (*palgey mayim*) of Ps 1:3 are also associated with the city and dwelling of God in Ps 46:4 (*pelagayv*).[27] Consequently, the man of Ps 1 is dwelling in a temple, and so playing a priestly role in this restored paradise.

Psalm 2:6 further describes him as a king established on Zion the holy mountain. However, the description of Ps 1:2-3 is that of a king as well. Verbal parallels between Ps 1, Jos 1, and Dt 17 point to a royal figure in each case. The description of him in Ps 1:2-3 as one who meditates day and night on the Torah with subsequent success is a direct reference to Jos 1. The command given there to Joshua is also that given to the future king of Dt 17. This can be proven by multiple verbal parallels common to both Dt 17:18-20 and Jos 1:7-8 such as "torah," "book," "all his days in order that," "to keep and to do," "right and left," "depart." The parallels are too numerous to be coincidental, and so it is safe to say that Joshua was given a royal command.[28] The portrayal of the man of Pss 1 and 2 thus constitutes one who is both priest and king in the new paradise temple. Note that the command to Joshua was conditional in nature, while Ps 1:3 states it as an accomplished fact. Joshua did not have success in every case as opposed to the flawless man of Ps 1 who never fails once.

This unique priest king is also described as a military conqueror by the Psalter's introduction. Joshua's promised success in Jos 1:8 was military, as the subsequent victories for the most part over Canaanite kings demonstrate. Psalm 1 has portrayed the blessed man using the language of Jos 1, and so presumably his success is likewise military in nature. Indeed, his continued description in Ps 2 as the king who smashes rebellious kings confirms this.

Further language parallels between Pss 1 and 2 support such a reading. Just as the tree "bears" (*yiten*, gives) its fruits in its season, so God declares in Ps 2:8 His expressed intent to "give" (NASB, *ve etnah*) His chosen messianic king the nations and ends of the earth. The "season" (*be'ito*) of the tree's harvest in Ps 1:3 is from a Hebrew root found again in Ps 2:10—"so now" (*ve'atah*). This ominous adverb is followed by a warning to the rebellious kings and judges of the earth to serve and submit to His chosen king to whom He has given them as His inheritance. Psalm 2 thus takes the metaphor of a tree giving its fruit at its appointed time as the time when the Son of God is given authority and power to forcefully bring the entire world into submission.

As demonstrated above, the tree and garden metaphor of Ps 1 portrays a future paradise. The parallels with Ps 2 indicate that there too the writer describes an eschatological triumph of God's kingdom through His king (the same man pictured as a tree in Ps 1) over all the earth. Both psalms together assure the ultimate fulfilment of God's promises given in various ways throughout the Pentateuch and Prophets in the Hebrew Bible.

The second half of Ps 1 in v. 4 opens with a reference to "the wicked" who have been contrasted directly since v. 1 with the blessed man. That contrast continues here through repetition of the definite article only in these two verses: "the man" versus "the wicked." They are compared to chaff in another deliberate contrast through sound with the man who is compared to a tree: (*ke'ets*; like a tree . . . *kamots;* like chaff). In the Hebrew, two out of three consonants are identical, as is their order. Chaff is by nature short-lived and unstable, while a healthy fruit-producing tree is firmly established and long lasting.

The contrast between the images of tree and chaff is further supported by the number of words used in each simile. There are 17 words describing the tree and for the chaff only nine. Ephemerality and permanency are thus contrasted through imagery, phonology, and length of description.

Verse 5 continues the contrast between the perfect man and the wicked by use of the negative particle, which was found three times in v. 1. We are told that the wicked and sinners will not (*l'o*) survive in the judgment. Verse 1 has told us where the blessed man did not walk, stand, or sit (*l'o*, 3x). What type of judgment is meant here?

As noted above, v. 3 opens with a verb ("He will be" *vehayah*) that references the ultimate and eschatological end of this blessed man in the restored paradise. By contrast, v. 4 describes the final destiny of the wicked, and so further comment on their end in v. 5 does likewise. They will not arise in the *final* judgment and will be ultimately and eternally separated from the congregation of the righteous.

Psalm 1 exhibits various parallels that point to a fourfold chiastic literary structure:

A. The blessed man contrasted with the wicked (vv. 1-2)
B. Simile of the blessed man as a fruit bearing tree (v. 3)
B'. Simile of the wicked as driven chaff (v. 4)
A'. The wicked contrasted with the righteous ones (vv. 5-6)

This outline is supported by numerous verbal parallels between vv. 1 and 5-6 and between vv. 3 and 4. Terms such as "the wicked," "sinners," the "way," the negative particle "not," open and close the psalm. A contrast by means of agricultural similes characterizes the two central strophes as well as the negative particle and relative pronoun. However, as is the case in Ps 2 as well, there are multiple linguistic parallels that cross these strophe boundaries. For instance, the contrasting particle "instead" in vv. 2 and 4 (*kiy 'im*) falls outside of this particular outline. In general, the psalm seeks to present a strong contrast between the impeccably righteous man and his ultimate fate, and that of the wicked.

That contrast is expressed poetically in the first verse by a deliberate use of "happy" (or literally "the happinesses of"), which in Hebrew is spelled, *'aleph* (a guttural consonant), *shin, resh* (*'shr*), and "(the) wicked," spelled *resh, shin, 'ayin* (a guttural consonant) (*rsh'nm*). Here the opposite order of identical or similar consonants highlights their absolute dissimilarity. The same is true of the contrasting and yet phonologically similar expressions in the original Hebrew of vv. 1 and 5, "advice of the wicked," and "community of the righteous." Two similes expressed through practically identical consonants, as mentioned above in vv. 3 and 4 ("like a tree... like chaff"), function in the same manner.

The assurance expressed at the conclusion of Ps 1, that the way of the wicked will perish (HCSB "leads to ruin"), is immediately brought into question by the opening of Ps 2. If they are doomed to destruction, then why are they in open revolt against God and His Anointed One? The answer appears at the end of Ps 2 through identical terms used in the initial promised assurance of Ps 1:6. Psalm 2:12 repeats the same noun and verb (*veto 'vedu derekh*, lit., "you perish in the way") found in Ps 1:6 (*vederekh... to 'ved*, lit., "the way of the wicked will perish") and thereby confirms the promise. In other words, the questioning of Ps 1:6 in Ps 2:1 is answered in Ps 2:12. This pattern of promise made, bringing it into question, and subsequent answer, is seen often in the Psalter. Examples are Pss 72 and 73, Pss 89 and 90, and many others. Psalm 72 promises a restored and universal kingdom of peace and justice, which Ps 73 immediately questions. However, Ps 73 concludes with renewed confidence in the promises of 72, and subsequent psalms throughout Book III will do the same.

Psalm 89 concludes with questions regarding the apparent nonfulfillment of the promises made to David, which the subsequent Ps 90 answers. Consequently, Pss 1 and 2 exhibit a pattern of composition that continues throughout the entire Psalter and has as its principal concern the Davidic covenant.

As noted previously, Ps 2:1 uses a verb (*rogshu*) that resembles phonologically the noun "wicked" (*resha'iym*), which indicates that the topics and characters in Ps 1 are continued in the second. Further linguistic and conceptual parallels between the two psalms will confirm that the wicked of Ps 1 appear in Ps 2 as rebellious rulers and nations and the individual man of Ps 1 as king and Messiah ("Anointed One") of Ps 2. The blessings enumerated of the impeccably successful man in Ps 1 are also reaffirmed and restated in Ps 2. His absolute universal authority and destructive military power over the entire earth (Ps 2:8-9) defines the success of Ps 1:3c. Indeed, the language of Ps 1:3 is precisely that of Jos 1:8-9,[29] which is clearly military.

Psalm 2 ends therefore with a reaffirmation of the ultimate destiny of the wicked stated previously at the conclusion of Ps 1. It also ends with a description and definition of the community of righteous ones first mentioned in Ps 1:5-6. They are those who trust "in him" (*bo*), a pronoun whose antecedent is the masculine singular subject of v. 12. He is the "Son" (*bar*) who is to be rendered homage at the outset of v. 12 and whose "anger" (*'po*) can be kindled quickly. The identical form *'po* appears in Ps 2:5, and there it is clearly referring to the anger of the "One" sitting in heaven of v. 4. This confirms, as argued above, the identity of the seated heavenly "One" of v. 4 as the King and Son of God of Ps 2, and the man of Ps 1.[30] His enthronement in heaven is declared emphatically in v. 6, presumably by His Father God, whose words to Him are quoted in vv. 7 and 8. The close Father/Son relationship clarifies how the rebellion of vv. 1 and 2 can be directed against both the Lord and His Messiah. It also explains how service to the Lord demanded in v. 11a ("serve the LORD," includes homage to the son, "pay homage to the Son"). Rebellion against the Son is rebellion against God and submission to Him is likewise submission to God.

Reference to "My Son" in Hebrew (*beniy*) of v. 7 continues now in v. 12 with an Aramaic loan word for "Son" (*bar*). Many interpreters, including the editor of *Biblia Hebraica Stuttgartensia* emend this reading, presumably rejecting an Aramaic form in what is otherwise a Hebrew poem. However, there are various examples within and without this psalm that support a deliberate use of the Aramaic loan word by the composer.

First of all, the same Aramaic term "Son" appears three times in Prv 31:2 in what is otherwise a Hebrew text (*beriy . . . bar . . . bar*). Proverbs 31:3 spells "kings" with the Aramaic masculine plural ending (*melakhiy**n***). The following v. 4 reverts (twice) to the Hebrew masculine plural ending (*melakhy**m***).

Second, the first verb of this psalm, they "rebel" (*ragshu*, lit. they conspire), is never found in verb form again except in the Aramaic of Dan 6:6,11,15. There, as noted previously, the Aramaic is used in order to resonate consonantally ("pun") with the term "(the) wicked" (*resha'iym*) in Ps 1:4. Its identification as an Aramaism is supported by the Syriac Peshitta translation (an eastern Aramaic dialect), which renders it with the identical Aramaic verb form.[31] Note that in Dan 6 there is a conspiracy to kill the successful man of God. In the immediately following Ps 2:2 the verb "they conspire (together against)" expresses the same desire to kill, as Ps 31:13 proves. This psalm thus opens with a murderous plot against the Lord's Messiah and king. Given His divine status and essence, it constitutes a scheme against the Lord Himself.

Finally, consonantal resonance or paronomasia (play on words, a pun) is also at work here between "Son" *(bar)* of Ps 2:12 and "iron" *(barzel)* of v. 9, as it was between the Aramaism of Ps 2:1 and its phonologically parallel noun in Ps 1:5,6. God had given His divine Son and King Messiah the authority to smash His enemies with a rod of iron. The literary effect is to draw together the warning, "pay homage to the Son," and the consequences of failing to heed it, which is to be smashed by a rod of "iron." A similar word play is found between the warning to "serve" (*'ivdu*) the Lord in v. 11 and the consequence of failing to do so, "you will perish" *(to'vdu),* in v. 12.

Another objection to the reading of *bar* as "son" is the lack of a definite article. However, Hebrew poetry is often characterized by the omission of the definite article, as well as the typical narrative verb form *wayyiqtol*, and the definite direct object marker. In v. 12 we find "way" HCSB "rebellion" (*derekh*), which literally means "in the way." As noted previously, this noun and its governing verb are a deliberate reiteration of the same in Ps 1:6, in which the noun is also anarthrous (*derekh*) and yet definite in sense.[32] Likewise "nations" of vv. 1 and 8, as well as "earth" in vv. 2, 8 and 10, are also anarthrous in their Hebrew form, but certainly definite in meaning.

Further support for the originality of *bar* in Ps 2:12 comes from the immediate context of vv. 11 and 12. A sequence of *bet resh* is evident across the first two clauses of v. 11 and the first clause of v. 12, binding closely together the three plural imperatives: *beyir'ah* (with reverential awe) . . . *beyirah* (with trembling) . . . *bar* (Son). The repetition serves to focus on the final example of the sequence, which means of course "Son."

From the first to the third command there is also a decrease in length so that the final command to pay homage to the son is emphatically concise: "Serve the Lord in fear, rejoice with trembling, kiss the son!" (author's translation). The sound parallels point to similarity in meaning as well. Service to the Lord and reverent rejoicing are accomplished by obedience and submission to the Son.

Psalm 2 opens with a murderous rebellion against the Lord and the divinely chosen Messiah. The conspiracy is international in scope but its target is also plural since both YHWH and His Messiah are objects of the subversion. Plural pronouns in v. 3 ("their chains . . . their restraints") confirm this. A combined international attack is followed in vv. 4-9 by a joint and unified response from God and His Son/Messiah/King. The latter response consists of a response from both the Lord and King (vv. 4-6) and the relationship between them (vv. 7-9). These verses are followed by a direct warning to the recalcitrant rulers in vv. 10-12, to submit to the Lord and His King or face the consequences. The resulting outline constitutes a typical chiasm seen commonly in Hebrew composition:

A. Kings of the earth speak rebellion against the Lord and His Messiah (vv. 1-3)
  B. The response of the Lord and His King (vv. 4-6)
  B'. The relationship of the Lord and His Son (vv. 7-9)
A'. Kings of the earth warned to submit to the Lord and His Son (vv. 10-12)

The two central strophes describe a heavenly scenario. In the first, the King Messiah is seated on a heavenly throne because God has established Him there, and in the second His status as God's Son and resulting universal domain and inheritance are delineated. Both central strophes represent the response in heaven to the earthly rebellion, while the final three verses constitute a direct warning to these earthly rulers. However, these divisions should not be applied absolutely since there exist deliberate lexical parallels between the first strophe of vv. 1-3 and v. 8 of the third. In other words, the heavenly dialogue between God and His Son includes reference to the "nations" and the "earth" in v. 8, seen also at the outset in vv. 1-2.

The final three vv. 10-12 contain numerous phonological parallels to the initial insurrection in vv. 1-3. In other words, the divine response to the earthly rebellion is resonant in kind. So, the two plural imperatives of v. 10, to "be wise" and "receive instruction" sound very much like the reference to "chains" and the cohortative (expressions of wish or desire in first person plural) "let us . . . free ourselves (literally, cast off)" of v. 3:

mosrotiymo vnsshliykhah (chains and free ourselves) 2:3
haskiylu hivvosru (be wise; receive instruction) 2:10

There is no doubt that the heavenly warning is pointed and forcefully expressed to the terrestrial uprising.

Two plural imperatives of warning in v. 10 are continued in v. 11 by the threefold commands as mentioned previously. Failure to heed them will cause the Son's wrath to ignite, which will then bring His destructive iron rod of v. 9 down upon them.

There is, however, blessing for those who submit to the Son of God and seek refuge in Him in the final words of the psalm. The specific term "happy" (blessed, *'ashrey*) in v. 12 matches that at the beginning of Ps 1:1 ("happy," blessed *'ashrey*), with which it creates an *inclusio* binding the two poems together. Repetition of this identical term from Ps 1:1 has a remarkable effect for interpretation. Since the same blessing of Ps 1 includes His place in the new Eden (Ps 1:3ab) and complete military victory over all His enemies (Ps 1:3c), it is safe to assume that those who trust in Him will enjoy the same.

Those blessings do not end in Ps 1, but also continue with the same impeccable man in Ps 2 who is God's Son and King. There He sits on a throne in heaven (Ps 2:4), inherits the entire world (Ps 2:8) and has the authority to destroy His enemies (Ps 2:9), all of which are also blessings and rights of those who trust in Him, according to Ps 2:12d. Paul the apostle apparently was reading these two psalms in this manner as well when he attributed to believers in Messiah Jesus His privileges of sonship, a seat in heaven, and a worldwide inheritance (Eph 1:3,5,10,11, 14,19-22; 2:6).

The foregoing analysis of Pss 1 and 2 supports their integration as a unified introduction to the book. Numerous linguistic factors sustain such a conclusion. Among them are the unique verbal parallels, the lack of a superscription for Ps 2, the *inclusio* at either end, and the consonantally similar terms occurring precisely at the transition between the two.

The Psalter's introductory two psalms also establish the principal topics for the rest of the book. Psalms 1 and 2 portray a divine King, Messiah, and Conqueror, who is opposed by the rulers and kings of the earth. Psalm 2:7 is clearly a reference to the Davidic covenant, and so He is of that royal house. The opposition consists of a plot to kill Him, and that rejection and suffering will be lamented in the ensuing psalms. He is nonetheless ultimately enthroned in heaven with power and authority to destroy His enemies, and becomes the source of blessing for those who trust in Him. Resurrection is obviously implied here, and the following psalms will confirm it. The immediately following Ps 3 will give further details of this victory over death, as will numerous others. Indeed, the Psalms/Psalter is a book accurately described by the Messiah Himself in Lk 24:26,27,44. He will undergo suffering and death but then arise and enter heavenly glory.

If *the man* of Ps 1 is indeed the divine Messiah, how then are these two Psalms to be applied? There is a textually based application of these two psalms as follows: Ps 2:12 calls on all to trust in Him—the Son of God—in order to receive the blessing of knowing Him. Thus, the final verse of the introduction of the Psalter (Psalms 1 and 2 together) gives the application. Since it is the same word (*ashrei*; how happy or how blessed) that opens the description of the man, the Messiah (Ps 1:1), it applies to all who trust in Him. The implication is that faithful ones will enjoy His blessings and inheritance as well. This is essentially the gospel and the reason Paul sees Christ followers seated in heavenly places with Him (Eph 1:3; 2:6), enjoying all His blessings.

---

1. The singular "Psalter" is preferred here since it reflects better the reality of an integrated whole. It is not a loose or random collection of poems or hymns, as "Psalms" can imply. For a detailed study of these two psalms see my *Psalms 1-2: Gateway to the Psalter* (Sheffield: Sheffield Phoenix Press, 2013).

2. Joseph P. Brennan, "Some Hidden Harmonies in the Fifth Book of Psalms," in *Essays in Honor of Joseph P. Brennan*, ed. R. F. McNamara (Rochester, NY: St. Bernard's Seminary, 1976), 25-26.

3. Hermann Gunkel, *An Introduction to the Psalms*, trans. James D. Nogalski (Macon, Georgia: Mercer University Press, 1998), 17, 67.

4. Gunkel, *Psalms*, 2-3.

5. Tremper Longman III and Raymond B. Dillard, *An Introduction to the Old Testament* (Grand Rapids: Zondervan, 2006), 255. Samuel Terrien, *The Psalms: Strophic Structure and Theological Commentary* (Grand Rapids: Eerdmans, 2003), 41-44. Craig C. Broyles, *Psalms*, New International Biblical Commentary (Peabody, MA: Hendrickson, 1999), 9. Carol Hupping, ed., *The Jewish Bible* (Philadelphia: The Jewish Publication Society, 2008), 202. Peter C. Craigie, *Psalms 1-50*, Word Biblical Commentary 19 (Nashville: Thomas Nelson, 2004), 47. Gerald H. Wilson, *Psalms Volume 1*, The NIV Application Commentary (Grand Rapids: Zondervan, 2002), 65. Bill T. Arnold and Brian E. Beyer, *Encountering the Old Testament* (Grand Rapids: Baker, 1998), 307.

6. Brevard S. Childs, *Introduction to the Old Testament as Scripture* (Philadelphia: Fortress Press, 1979), 518. Gerald H. Wilson, *The Editing of the Hebrew Psalter*, Society for Biblical Literature, Dissertation Series 76 (Chico: CA: Scholars Press, 1985). Rolf Rendtorff, *The Old Testament: An Introduction* (Philadelphia: Fortress Press, 1986), 246-250.

7. Gunkel, *Psalms*, 2-3.

8. David C. Mitchell, *The Message of the Psalter: An Eschatological Programme in the Book of Psalms*, Journal for the Study of the Old Testament, Supplement Series 252 (Sheffield: SAF, 1997), 17-18.

9. *b. Ber.* 9d, "'Blessed' and 'Why do the nations conspire?' are one chapter" (author's translation). Translations of the Hebrew text of commentaries or the biblical text are the author's.

10. Menahem Cohen, ed., *Miqra'ot Gedolot HaKeter: Psalms I* (Ramat Gan: Bar-Ilan University Press, 2003), 5.

11. Friedmann Eissler, *Könipsalmen und Karäische Mesiaserwartung: Jefet ben Elis Auslegung von Ps. 2.72.89.110.132 im Vergleich mit Saadja Gaons Deutung* (Tübingen: J. C. B. Mohr [Paul Siebeck], 2002), 33.

12. Eissler, *Königpsalmen*, 34.

13. Ferdinand Hitzig, *Die Psalmen* (Leipzig: C. F. Winter, 1863), 1-2; E.W. Hengstenberg, *Commentary on the Psalms*, trans. P. Fairbairn and J. Thomson (Edinburgh: T&T Clark, 3rd ed., 1851), 5-6; Franz Delitzsch, *Commentary on the Old Testament in Ten Volumes, V, Psalms*, trans. Francis Bolton (Grand Rapids: Kregel, 1991), 19-20, 82; Joseph A. Alexander, *Commentary on the Psalms* (Edinburgh: A. Elliott & J. Thin, 1864, reprint, Grand Rapids: Kregel, 1991), 12; John Forbes, *Studies on the Book of Psalms: The Structural Connection of the Book of Psalms, Both in Single Psalms and in the Psalter as an Organic Whole* (Edinburg: T&T Clark, 1888).

14. M. Manatti and E. de Solms, *Les Psaumes I* (Paris: Desclée de Brouwer, 1966), 17-8; Walther Zimmerli, "Zwillingpsalmen," in *Wort, Lied und Gottespruch: Beiträgre zu Psalmen und Prophete*, ed. Josef Schreiner (Würzburg: Echter Verlag, 1972), 105-113; Christoph Barth, "Concatenatio im ersten Buch des Psalters," in *Wort und Wirklichkeit*, ed. B. Benzing, O. Böcher and G. Mayer (Meisenheim am Glan: Verlag Anton Hain, 1976), 30-40.

15. An *inclusio* is a common literary phenomenon in the Hebrew Bible in which the same word or phrase is repeated at the beginning and end of a particular text, whether short or long. The repeated language between Ps 2 and Ps 149:7-9 creates an enveloping *inclusio* around the entire book.

16. As noted previously both 1:6 and 2:12 repeat the same phrase:

vederekh...to'ved 1:6

veto'vdu derekh 2:12

17. The term *rogshu* ("they have conspired") is an Aramaism, found only here in the entire Hebrew Bible, but three times in the Aramaic of Daniel 6:6,11,15.

Undoubtedly it was deliberately chosen to produce vocal resonance with the term "wicked" (*resha'iym*).

18. The text of Job 1:1 opens with *'iysh* ("a man") and then is followed by *h'iysh* ("the man") in the same opening verse. The latter matches the second word of Ps 1:1—*h'iysh*. Such similarities in language do not happen by chance.

19. "Servant" occurs seven times in Job, including twice in the first two chapters and twice in the last.

20. The evidence supporting this assertion is abundant, occurring at every conceivable linguistic level—phonological, morphological, lexical, semantic, and syntactic. One may disagree with the conclusions offered here, but must offer a cogent alternative explanation based on the linguistic evidence. The parallels cannot simply be ignored.

21. The medieval vocalization by the Masoretic scribes is inconsistent between Pss 2:4 and 110:1. In Ps 2:4 the vocalization is "*'adonay*" implying the deity, whereas in 110:1 the vocalization "*'adoni*" reveals their interpretation of it to be human. However, the parallel verb form in both texts and a similar context of warfare and victory support the reading of "*'adonay*" in both cases.

22. Rashi writes on Psalm 1:2: "In the beginning, it is called the law of the Lord, and after he has toiled to master it, it is called his own Torah."

23. The most significant parallel between Dt 34 and Mal 4 is that they both look forward to the Messiah. Deuteronomy 34 was attached later to the Pentateuch (after Moses' death) with the reminder that the Prophet like Moses (Dt 18:15-19) who spoke to God directly had not yet come (Dt 34:10; and with the implicit command to keep looking for Him). In Malachi, there is the anticipation of Elijah, as the forerunner of the Messiah, announcing the Day of the Lord.

24. The same verb is found in Gn 1:29 in the context of Adam's authority and gift of the entire earth. Its appearance at the outset of the Torah in Gn 1, the Prophets in Jos 1, and the Writings in Pss 1–2 is not fortuitous. It speaks to a deliberate organization and redaction of the canon in its tripartite order. Adam, Joshua, and the king of Pss 1–2 are deliberately paralleled.

25. Compare Isa 30:25 and Ezk 47:9,10, passages which display other verbal parallels with Pss 1–2.

26. *lo' yibol 'alehu*—Ezk 47:12, *v'alehu lo'-yibol*—Ps 1:3.

27. Compare the use of *qdosh* in both Pss 46:4 and 65:4 to prove the reference to the sanctuary.

28. This was also the interpretation of other biblical writers such as the author of Chronicles. The transition from David to Solomon in 1 Chronicles includes a command from father to son identical to that of God to Joshua (cf. 1Chr 28:20; Jos 1:6,7,9). Note as well the repetition of "a copy of the Torah" between Dt 17:18 and Jos 8:32, the only two occurrences of this phrase in the Hebrew Bible.

29. "you will prosper and succeed in whatever you do" (Jos 1:7-9); "whatever he does, prospers" (Ps 1:3).

30. Note, as previously mentioned, the heavenly seated one of Ps 2:4 is identified as *'adonay*, a divine title.

31. D. M. Walter, ed., *The Old Testament in Syriac According to the Peshitta Version: The Book of Psalms.* (Leiden, Netherlands: E. J. Brill, 1980), 1.

32. Note the anarthrous form *melekh* in Ps 21:1 with definite meaning as noted by Dominique Barthélemy, *Critique textuelle de l' Ancien Testament* (Fribourg: Academic Press, Götttingen: Vandenhoeck & Ruprecht, 2005), 4–5. It presumably refers to the same king of Ps 20:9, which is articular.

Psalm 3

The Victory of the Messiah

ROBERT L. COLE

Psalms 1 and 2, two chapters, constitute the introduction to the Psalter. One might reasonably expect that the immediately following Ps 3 would continue topics and subject matter presented in the introduction. Indeed, that is the case. The Psalter is not unlike the rest of the books of the Hebrew Bible, where the author/composer sets out the material in a logical and consistent manner.[1] Another reasonable expectation would be repetition of common vocabulary between Ps 3 and the previous two (as well as with the following Ps 4), as occurs between Pss 1 and 2. In other words, the same compositional practice established at the beginning could reasonably be anticipated in subsequent chapters. In fact, evidence of common subject matter and lexical links in the first two psalms is also present in the third. The result is a coherent and sensible reading between the introduction and this psalm.[2]

Psalm 3 can be divided into three major strophes based on the distribution of repeated terms and Hebrew roots:

Title: Prayer of the Messianic King Under Deadly Attack
I. Astonishment over number and words of attackers (vv. 2-3, Eng. 1-2)[3]
II. Answer to His cry (vv. 4-6, Eng. 3-5)
III. Confidence of vengeance on the attackers (vv. 7-9, Eng. 6-8)

Recurring vocabulary such as "multiplied/many," "arise," "against me," and "salvation" in the first and third strophes without any in the second serve to isolate the latter. This isolation highlights the central and most important part of the psalm—vv. 4-6. As will be seen, the death threatened in Ps 2:2-3 and assumed in vv. 2-3 does take place.[4] However, the speaker, who can be identified as the messianic king of Pss 1–2, is delivered out of that death in v. 6 (Eng. v. 5). In other words, this is a psalm of resurrection.[5]

In contrast to the introductory first two psalms, Ps 3 contains a superscription or title that places these words into a specific historical event in the life of David. No such title is evident either for the first or second psalm, but is common for most of the psalms in Book I. This supports their discreteness as an introduction to the book. David is the dominant figure of superscriptions throughout the first and second books of the Psalter and is present in at least one or more superscriptions in the third, fourth, and fifth as well.

The obvious strategy of keeping David before the reader in superscriptions, and in the content of many psalms as well, underscores the importance in this book of the covenant made with him in 2Sm 7:13. In that chapter, God promised to give David's descendant an eternal throne. A major concern of the Psalter is to answer the problem of this apparently delayed promise of an eternal throne and kingdom for David.[6] Psalm 2:7 mentions that covenant implicitly by use of the same language. It rehearses again the promise to David that one of his descendants will also be the unique and divine Son of God.

Psalm 3's superscription, however, recalls a very human David who sinned, and the result was the rebellion of his very own son. Consequently, this firstborn son, Absalom, hardly qualifies as the Son of God and of David from the previous Ps 2. God calls the righteous king in Ps 2:7 "My Son" (*bny*), while in Ps 3:1[MT][7] there is reference to David's ambitious and rebellious son (*bnw*). Absalom clearly does not fulfill the prophecy in 2Sm 7. Neither did Solomon, who eventually took the throne after David, ever attain the extent or timelessness of the promised future kingdom. Psalm 2 reveals that the son of David who will eventually take the universal and eternal throne is also the Son of God and will rule the entire world with absolute power and might. This could not be said of Solomon or the subsequent Davidic line down to its exile and demise.

The question remains then as to the meaning of words, which, according to the superscription, David spoke while fleeing from and battling his own son. Why would the Psalter's composer place these words of Ps 3 spoken during a sad time in David's life immediately following a description of the messianic king in Pss 1–2? It is because within the superscription itself, the phrase "when he fled" has the preposition "*b*" prefixed to the infinitive construct (*bbrchw*), meaning "*when/while* he fled" from Absalom. In other words, the words of the psalm are not "about" Absalom or even necessarily "about" David's flight from him, but simply identified as having been uttered *when* he fled.

The message of Ps 3 should be determined based on the words and message within, and its context in the Psalter. Its position following Ps 2 cannot be accidental, and indeed, the vocabulary common to both confirms its intentional placement. Psalm 2 opens with an expression of surprise at the revolt of the nations against God and His king. Psalm 3 opens with a similar expression, both in form and meaning. The "Why?" of Ps 2:1 (*lmh*) and the "How!" of Ps 3:2 (Eng. 3:1) (*mh*) are similar morphologically.[8] Both Hebrew terms express amazement at the opposition against either the speaker in Ps 3 or against the Lord and His Messianic King in Ps 2.

Many have doubted whether these words could be David's because of his attitude to his enemies in 3:8, unlike the expressed desire to save his son Absalom in 2Sm 18:5,32.[9] Furthermore, there is reference in v. 5 to the "holy mountain," an edifice not yet built in the lifetime of David. As a result, the superscription ascribing these words to King David has been labeled "midrash," meaning a secondary, later addition by scribes of little historical value.[10] Other commentators have responded and defended its historicity by noting points of similarity between the account in 2 Samuel and this psalm. Indeed, the Psalter's composer certainly considered David the author, but he also saw it as a perfect sequel to Pss 1 and 2.

The numerous verbal parallels between Ps 3 and the two previous Pss 1 and 2 point to its function and meaning within the book. Interpretation through identification of a supposed "genre," according to modern form-critical conceptions, works contrary to the composer's visible and expressed purpose as a continuation of the message of Pss 1–2.[11] According to modern "generic" categories the first three psalms are wholly different and thus should read separately and without regard to their particular literary context.[12] For the book's composer/author, they were perfectly coherent and consistent.

There may be various ways of understanding the significance of explicit verbal links, but ignoring them is not an option. Here they are listed:

PSALMS 1–2	PSALM 3
'l "against (the Lord and his messiah)" 2:2	*'ly* "against (me)" 3:2,7 (Eng. 3:1 "attack," 6)
'mr "He said" 2:7	*'mr* "(many) are saying" 3:3 (Eng. 3:2)
'th "You (ms)" 2:7	*w'th* "but You (ms)" 3:4 (Eng. 3:3)
w'ny "[but] I" 2:6	*'ny* "I" 3:6 (Eng. 3:5)
'l...hr qdshy "on My holy mountain" 2:6	*mhr qdshw* "from His holy mountain" 3:5 (Eng. 3:4)

bny "My Son" 2:7	*bnw* "his son" 3:1 (Eng. superscription)
byr'h "with fear" (HCSB reverential awe) 2:11	*'yr'h* "I will (not) fear" 3:7 (Eng. I am not afraid, 3:6)
rsh'ym "the wicked" 1:1,5,6	*rsh'ym* "the wicked" 3:8 (Eng. 3:7)
yqmw "will (not) arise" (HCSB survive) 1:5	*qmym . . .qwmh* "are arising . . . arise!" 3:2,8 (Eng. "attack me" 3:1; "rise up" 3:7)

While some parallels are common enough, others are unique, especially the two references to the holy mountain and to the wicked. The common vocabulary proves a deliberate juxtaposition of the two psalms by the book's composer and demands an explanation.

Most parallels are found between the adjacent Pss 2 and 3, as would be expected, not between Pss 3 and 1.[13] The wicked in Ps 3:8 represent one direct link to Ps 1, where they are mentioned three times (vv. 1,5,6). This term has no parallel in Ps 2. However, as seen in comments on Ps 2, common language and theme make it quite clear that the rebellious nations and their leaders described within are certainly the same group designated "the wicked" in Ps 1. Consequently, reference made to them again explicitly in Ps 3 constitutes continued focus on them in their lethal and conspiratorial role against the Messianic King.

The textual and linguistic evidence presented here has hermeneutical implications for reading the Psalter and the Hebrew Bible in general. By placing this psalm following the book's introduction, the composer was revealing his understanding of these words as prophetic of the future Messianic King in the previous introductory psalms. Attempts to understand them based on modern reconstructions of the historical situation of David apart from the textual evidence would be at odds with the authorial purpose. The historical event of David's prayer can only be understood properly through the interpretation given to it by the book's composer/author.

It bears mentioning as well that David's prophetic function and role is explicitly stated in 2Sm 23:1-2,[14] "The oracle (*n'm*) of David, the son of Jesse, and the oracle (*n'm*) of the man who was exalted, concerning (*'l*)[15] the Messiah of the God of Jacob, and of the delight of the songs of Israel. The spirit of the Lord spoke through me and his word was on my tongue"[16] (author's translation). These verses are especially relevant for interpretation of Psalms since the immediately preceding chap. 22 of 2 Samuel is identical for the most part with Ps 18. The preceding and following words of David (described as a song composer) in 2 Samuel are to be read prophetically. Thus, the wider canonical as well as the immediate literary context are both consistent and parallel in this oracular comprehension of David's words. This holds not only for Ps 3 but likewise the rest of the Psalter.

The literary context determines the meaning of the psalm, not a contrived interpretation based on the supposed "historical," "social," or "liturgical" context.[17] In fact, the "grammatical historical" approach so-called, as typically practiced today in the Psalter, is neither grammatical nor historical. It works at cross purposes with the explicit linguistic evidence linking individual psalms together and integrating the book into a coherent whole. It ignores the grammar of discourse and the historical fact of composition. Practice of the "grammatical historical" approach, so-called, guarantees a misapprehension of this psalm or of any other's meaning and purpose.

The two issues of hermeneutics and messianic prophecy are inextricably intertwined and merit discussion at this point. A chosen theory of interpretation will determine from the start a predictable outcome. In other words, "where you stand will determine where you land." The interpretive stance labeled "historical grammatical" can be traced back to medieval rabbinic interpreters, among whom the most influential was Rashi[18] (1040–1105).[19] It was labeled *peshat* and presumably represented the "literal," "plain," or "historical" meaning of a text.[20] A primary purpose of this "peshat" or "literal/historical" method by Rashi was to refute Christian claims of prophecy in the OT.[21] Rashi was worried the Jewish community of northern France where he lived would be swayed by Christian teachers. He was willing to abandon traditional rabbinic messianic interpretation of certain psalms for the express purpose of refuting the Christian messianic interpretation.[22] Rashi's opening statement in his commentary on Ps 2 is telling: "Our rabbis interpreted the meaning as being about the messianic king, but according to its meaning and for a response to the heretics (Christians), it is correct to interpret it of he himself concerning whom it is said, 'And the Philistines heard that Israel had anointed David over themselves as king.'"[23]

It was Nicholas de Lyra (1270–1349) who mediated Rashi's *peshat* to medieval and later Christian interpreters through his commentary *Postilla literralis super Bibliam*,[24] [Literal Commentary on the Epistle to the Hebrews] including Luther and Calvin, and eventually down to the present.[25] Remarkably, an anti-messianic, historical hermeneutic used to safeguard the Jewish community in northern France from Christian arguments for a messianic reading of the OT has become the standard evangelical Christian method of reading Scripture.[26] This approach, which claims to be "literal," is in fact not at all so. The "literal" meaning of a text is also its "literary" meaning, expressed by the writer through linguistic signals. To ignore the latter is to distort and misapprehend its message.

Psalm 3 is a prime example of a text whose meaning and message clearly reach far beyond the historical moment. Its words and content are quite unlike the stated sentiments of David toward his rebellious son Absalom, e.g., (2Sm 14:24; 15:9; 18:5, 31-33). This incongruity simply highlights the compositional understanding of it as prophecy reaching far beyond the lifetime of David to the time of his royal messianic and eschatological descendant described in Pss 1–2. The literary and linguistic signals all point in this direction, as does its placement immediately following the introductory psalms. Position in the Psalter is as crucial to meaning as is the position of any text in any book of the Hebrew Bible. To ignore the compositional arrangement of the discourse of biblical texts is as inappropriate as ignoring the arrangement of words in a sentence or clause. "Syntext" of larger texts is as indispensable to interpretation as clausal or sentence "syntax."

Psalm 3 opens with an attack against the speaker with intent to kill: "(many) are arising against me" (*qmym ʿly*). The same language in Ps 86:14 ("Oh God, arrogant ones have risen up against me (*qmw ʿly*) . . . they seek my life," [author's translation]) clearly refers to murderous intent and is in fact directed to the same messianic king.[27] Just as Ps 2 opens with a plot against the life of the God's king, so likewise Ps 3. Both psalms also follow with a direct quote of the words of the attackers (Ps 2:3; 3:3, Eng. 3:2). They differ only in that Ps 2 refers to the Messiah King in third person, while the first-person quotation in Ps 3 indicates He Himself is speaking. Psalm 2 does not explain how the Messianic King went from being the subject of a death plot in Ps 2:2-3 to being crowned and seated in heaven (vv. 4-6). Psalm 3 provides that information, including the opposition to Him and His death and resurrection.

As the prepositional phrase of v. 2 (Eng. v. 1) indicates, this opposition and attack is intensely personal and focused, "against me" (*ʿly*). Furthermore, the attackers are numerous as the threefold repetition of the root *rbb* ("to multiply, become numerous") between vv. 2 and 3 (Eng. vv. 1 and 2) indicates. The same root is found in v. 7[6] in the noun "thousands" (*rbbwt*) to describe the enormous opposition against him. Verse 7 also repeats the same prepositional phrase "against me" of v. 2 (*ʿly*) to highlight through repetition the focused, personal attack against Him. In fact, vv. 2 and 7 describe the same situation but with one difference. Verse 2 expresses surprise or astonishment, "How!" (*mh*), while v. 7 expresses confidence in the face of the attack, "I do not fear" (*lʾ ʾyrʾ*).

The statement of confidence in v. 7[6] is followed by a request for vengeance on His enemies in v. 8[7]. He asks God to arise (*qwmh*) and to save Him (*hwshyʿny*), which terms are also found in the initial attack against Him in vv. 2 and 3. There His enemies have arisen (*qmym*) against Him and precluded any divine intervention and salvation (*yshwʿth*) on His behalf. Verse 8 turns the tables on them by making request of God using the same terminology. It continues then with stated assurance (*ky* = "indeed"), that God will destroy them violently, just as they have mounted a deadly effort against Him.

In v. 4, the King has already expressed faith in God as His defender ("shield"), as opposed to those attacking Him, who are certain God will not save Him (v. 3). The opening words, "But You, LORD" (*w'th yhwh*), express the confident contrast between their assurance of His abandonment and his trust in God's help. Verse 3 also quotes their confident assertion that there is no chance that God will save His life (*lnphshy*), which is explicitly contradicted through sound parallels by the following v. 4:

v. 3[2] *'mrym lnfshy* ("they are saying of my life"; HCSB "many say about me")
v. 4[3] *wmrym r'shy* ("and the one who lifts my head")

While His enemies declare that he has been abandoned by God to death, He asserts with full certainty that God is in fact the one who "lifts his head."

Verse 3 also exhibits a contrast between God's words to Him in Ps 2:7, "He said to me, 'You are My son'" (*'mr 'ly*), and the words of his foes doubting any divine help for him, "[many] are saying of my life" (*'mrym lnphshy*). There is astonishment on the King's behalf that so many are saying God has abandoned Him, when God Himself has declared Him to be His son. Verse 4, however, explicitly confesses His faith in God who will rescue Him, although not necessarily before He dies. His eventual demise is hinted in the phrase, "the One who lifts my head." Verse 6 confirms that He had lain down and arisen because of divine help, which is a further reference to His rising mentioned in v. 4.

Parallels between Pss 2 and 3 are also of a structural nature. It is not coincidence that the two pronouns "You" (*'th*) and "I" (*'ny*) are repeated in the two psalms within a dialogue between God and the King. They appear in Ps 2:6-7 and in Ps 3:4-6 but in reverse order. The first instance in each case of these pronouns (*w'ny* – "But I" Ps 2:6, *w'th* "But you" Ps 3:4) expresses through the *vav*, a strong contrast and reaction to the previous attack against the King (*'l mshychw*—Ps 2:2; *'ly* 3:2).

The clustering of pronouns in Ps 2:6-7 ("But I . . . You are My son, I today . . ." [author's translation]) is unmistakable and so their repetition in Ps 3:4,6 ("But You . . . I") is certainly not by chance. Note that neither one is found in the initial Ps 1.[28] Furthermore, they are concentrated more in Pss 2–6 than elsewhere in the rest of the book.[29] Implied is a personal and intimate dialogue between Father and Son that begin in Ps 2 and continues through Book I especially, where 31 instances of "you" appear and 26 of "I."

Immediately following these two personal independent pronouns is reference to "My/His holy mountain" (*hr qdshy* Ps 2:6; *hr qdshw* Ps 3:5). In Ps 2 it is God's holy abode, the place the King is established after the attack. By contrast it is the place from which help is sent during the attack in Ps 3. His prayer in Ps 3 is answered from God's holy mountain, where He will eventually be reigning as King, as stated previously in Ps 2. Implied by this repetition of the same phrase is that Ps 3 will supply the gap of information between the murderous attack in Ps 2:1-3 and immediately following enthronement in Ps 2:6.

As stated above, the parallel use of personal, independent pronouns between Pss 2 and 3 highlights the intimate, personal relationship between the King and God His Father. Another parallel on the phonological level occurs within Ps 3:4[3] between "(a shield) around me," and "my glory" (*b'dy kbdy*). The prepositional phrase indicating complete protection and enclosure around him is connected by a term that essentially means "my life," as proven by its use in Ps 7:6[5]. There "my glory" (HCSB "my honor") is directly parallel to the terms "my soul" and "my life." The King in Ps 3 is asserting that God Himself is His life, which is defined immediately following by "the One who lifts my head." He, God, who is literally His life and the author of life, lifts Him out of death. Notable is the repeated first-person possessive pronoun linking all three: "about *me, my* glory . . . *my* head" (*-iy, -iy . . . - iy*). He is not only His protector as expressed in the shield metaphor but also His *very* life.

Verse 5 again highlights the close relationship between the royal Son and His Father. He cries to Him because of the attack, and God answers Him from His heavenly and holy mountain. The particular collocation "I called and He answered" is repeated with the same verbal roots in Ps 4:2, "when I call He answered" (or "answer me!") (author's translation). This deliberate double parallel in Ps 4 indicates that it will continue describing the distress of Ps 3. The two psalms are again linked to one another deliberately. In fact, Ps 4:7 repeats the first two words of Ps 3:3 verbatim, and Ps 4:9 repeats the two verbs, "lie down" and "sleep" of Ps 3:6. Clearly, the two were deliberately juxtaposed because they were considered to have common complementary subject matter.

Psalm 3:6[30] represents the decisive and central statement of the chapter. A simple word count reveals that 30 words precede it (vv. 2-5) and 27 follow (vv. 7-9). As noted in the outline, vv. 2-3 and 7-9 are filled with lexical parallels not found in the middle strophe of vv. 4-6. Verse 6 represents the final and decisive statement of this central panel. Previously in vv. 3 and 4 the implicit reference to death and resurrection had been made. His enemies considered His death an accomplished fact (v. 3), while the following raising of His head (v. 4) implied victory over death. Now He lies down (*shkvty*), sleeps (*w'yshnh*), and awakes (*hqytswty*) because of the Lord's continual support. Why would anyone lie down in normal sleep and then awake, while under a deadly attack? Furthermore, there is no record of David sleeping through a peaceful night in the Absalom narrative. The statement is wholly out of character for one whose life is at risk if it refers simply to normal sleep and waking. There is, however, a much more cogent and logical explanation of this verse.

Only once more in the Hebrew Bible is this same triad of verbs in 3:6 found. In a discourse on the brevity of life and the certainty and finality of death, Job 14:12 states: "A man lies down and does not arise until there are no heavens, he does not awake from his sleep" (author's translation). There is no doubt then that these terms can refer to death and resurrection.

Other passages also reveal that lying down and sleeping were common metaphors for death. Second Samuel 7:12 describes David's own future death as lying down: "and you will lie down with your fathers" (author's translation, *wshkvt 't 'vtyk*). Within the Psalter itself, Pss 41:8 (*shkv*) and 88:5 (*shkvy*) describe death as lying down. Throughout Chronicles and Kings, the writers characterize the deaths of monarchs in the same manner.[31] For instance, David "lies down" (HCSB "rested") in death (1Kg 2:10), and Nathan the prophet described it previously with the same idiom (1:21). Solomon sleeps (*wyshkv*) with his fathers in 2Chr 9:31. The book of Job refers to death as "lying down" six times (7:21; 11:18; 14:12; 20:11; 21:26; 27:19).

Psalm 13 is directly relevant to Ps 3 because of its similar language and content. The speaker is under attack from his enemy(ies) in vv. 3[2] and 5[4] (*'yby . . . tsry*), who are identical to the enemies in Ps 3:2[1] and 8[7] (*tsry . . .'yvy*). The attack is similarly "against me" (*'ly*) in both Pss 13:3 and 3:2,7. Both psalms refer to God's "salvation" (*yshw'th*) in identical terms (3:3; 13:6) as the speaker's "life" (*nphshy*, 3:3; 13:3). In the same Ps 13 the speaker explicitly refers to death as "sleep" (*'yshn*), as he did in Ps 3:6 (*w'yshnh*). Note that both are first person *yiqtol* verb forms. Not only does Ps 13 confirm the death reference of Ps 3, it also indicates further exposition of the suffering death introduced in Pss 2–3.

The verb "wake" (*hqytswty*) in Ps 3:6 is also used repeatedly to describe resurrection. For example, both Jer 51:39 and 57 refer to death as "asleep forever" (*wyshnw shnt 'wlm*), from which they "never wake up" (*wl' hqytsw*). In a more well-known reference to death and resurrection, Dan 12:2 states that many "of those who sleep" (*myshny*) in the dust "will awake" (*yqytsw*). The latter two instances of the verb "to awake" (*hqyts*), in the sense of resurrection, are found following the verb "to sleep" (*yshn*), of which both are found in Ps 3:6[5]. Isaiah 26:19 also references resurrection of "your dead" (*mtyk*), by means of the term "awake," in parallel with the two verbs "rise" (*yqwmwn*) and "live" (*ychyw*).

As noted earlier, two allusions to death plots exist in Ps 2:2 and Ps 3:2[1]. Such a context is consistent with the more explicit reference to death in Ps 3:6[5]. Furthermore, if God answered His prayer in such a scenario, assuming the plot succeeded, resurrection would be the only option.

The final verb of v. 6[5], "(the LORD) sustains me" also communicates the sense of resurrection. In Ps 119:116 the speaker requests that God "sustain" Him so that He may "live" (*smkny . . . w'chyh*). In Ps 145:14 the Lord "sustains" ("helps") all those who "fall" (*swmk . . . hnphlym*). Given the numerous parallels already cited with Ps 2 on various levels, it appears that this verb is used to create deliberate resonance with Ps 2:6 through consonance: *nskty/ysmkny* ("I have established [consecrated]/ He sustains me"). They are both preceded in the same verse by the pronoun "I" (*'ny*–2:6, 3:6). In Ps 2 the speaker is God Himself establishing the King in the eschatological Zion, and in Ps 3 the King attributes His resurrection to divine support. As a result, the King's coronation in Zion of Ps 2:6 is further explained as His resurrection from the dead. This represents another example of how Ps 3 provides further clarification of the change from personal and deadly attack against Him in Ps 2:1-3, to messianic rule in Ps 2:4-6. He in fact passed through death prior to His ultimate enthronement.

Psalm 3 finally concludes on a note following the patterns of the two previous psalms. The picture of the defeated and smashed wicked in Ps 3:8[7] matches the same in Ps 1:6 and Ps 2:9,12. The concluding verses of Pss 1:6 and 2:12 (cf. HCSB endnote) are linked explicitly by identical references to the "way" (*drk*) and "destruction" (*'bd*). They are named specifically in Ps 1:1,5,6 as the "wicked" (*rsh'ym*) and so by implication are also the rebels of Ps 2:12. Now they are named again directly in Ps 3:8[7] (*rsh'ym*). Nonetheless, the righteous of Ps 1:5-6, who by implication and parallel are the faithful, trusting ones of Ps 2:12, are now found also in Ps 3:9[8]. They are God's own people (*'mk*) and recipients of His "blessing" (*brktyk*).

In the final verb of v. 6[5] the speaker attributes His awakening to the fact that "(the LORD) sustains me" (*smkny*). Psalm 145:14 states that the Lord "raises up" the fallen and oppressed by means of the same verb (*swmk*). Similarly, Ps 119:116 requests God's support (*smkny*) so that the speaker can live.

Each of the first three psalms opens with a description of the Messianic King followed by a description of His enemies but concludes with their destruction. Those who do not rebel against God and His King receive blessing.

---

1. Contra Tremper Longman III and Raymond B. Dillard, *An Introduction to the Old Testament* (Grand Rapids: 2006), 252–56, who consider it "obvious that most psalms do not have a normal literary context" and that it is "incontestably true that the psalms are prayers, not oracles" (pp. 255–56). Both assertions can be refuted through the ubiquity of *dislegomena* between neighboring psalms. Also, contra Gleason Archer Jr., who judges form-critical categorization by Gunkel to be "a much more valid and appropriate way" and lists the five main types apparently with approval, *A Survey of Old Testament Introduction* (Chicago: Moody, 2007), 420–22. He asserts with confidence that the Psalter "accumulated by stages over a long period of time" (p. 420). There is in fact good textual and linguistic evidence that the Psalter is an integrated whole that was composed at a single point in time and with a specific purpose. Implicit and explicit evidence from ancient interpreters, as well as from the more recent modern period,

reveals recognition of its unitary evidence; see my *The Shape and Message of Book III: (Psalms 73–89)* (Sheffield: Sheffield Academic Press, 2000), 2–45, 151–64.

2. Contra Hermann Gunkel, *An Introduction to the Psalms*, trans. James D. Nogalski (Macon, GA: Mercer University Press, 1998), 2–3, 19, 334, and his successors. However, there have been ancient as well as more modern interpreters who have recognized in some form or other the deliberate juxtaposition of Pss 2 and 3, such as Rabbis Aha and Jacob in *The Midrash on Psalms*, trans. William G. Braude (New Haven: Yale University Press, 1959), 50; Amos Hacham, *Sefer Tehillim* (Jerusalem: Mossad haRav Kook, 1979), 13; Jean-Marie Auwers, *La Composition littéraire du Psautier: Un Etat de la question* (Paris: J. Gabalda, 2000), 11, who also notes discussions on the order in the patristic era. In the 19th century John Forbes, *Studies on the Book of Psalms: The Structural Connection of the Book of Psalms, Both in Single Psalms and in the Psalter as an Organic Whole* (Edinburgh: T&T Clark, 1888), 201–202; and Joseph Alexander, *Commentary on Psalms* (Edinburgh: A. Elliott and J. Thin, 1864; repr. Grand Rapids: Kregel, 1991), 27, are examples of the same. A recent useful study on Book I, which lists all lexical links between its psalms, including Pss 2 and 3, is Gianni Barbiero, *Das erste Psalmenbuch als Einheit* (Frankfurt am Main: Peter Lang, 1999), 65–69.

3. Versification in this article is according to the Hebrew text, with the superscription or title constituting verse 1. Psalm 3 has the superscription "A psalm of David when he fled from his son Absalom," which in the Hebrew text is v. 1. Psalms 1 and 2 do not have superscriptions and so follow the numbering of English language Bibles. Psalm 4 has a superscription, and in this article, as in Ps 3, will follow the numbering of the Hebrew Bible. English version numbering in this article will be followed by "Eng." or enclosed in brackets immediately after Hebrew verse numbers.

4. See the article on Psalms 1 and 2, "The Divine Son of God" by Robert L. Cole in this *Handbook*.

5. Both Augustine and Justin Martyr see v. 6 as a prophecy of Christ's death and resurrection: Alexander Roberts and James Donaldson, eds., *The Anti-Nicene Fathers*, Vol. I, (Grand Rapids: Eerdmans, 1967), 175; John E. Rotelle, ed., Maria Boulding, trans., *The Works of Saint Augustine: A Translation for the 21st Century, Exposition of the Psalms 1–32*, III/15 (Hyde Park, New York: New City Press, 2000), 76; and Luis Alonso Schökel and Cecilia Carniti, *Salmos I (Salmos 1–72)* (Navarra, Spain: Editorial Verbo Divino, 2002), 169. While their arguments are not explicitly based on parallels between Pss 2 and 3, as argued here, they are undoubtedly heirs to a tradition of interpretation that recognized their mutual coherence.

6. Cole, *The Shape and Message*, passim.

7. Psalm 3:1 in the numbering of the Hebrew Bible represents the superscription, which in English Bible versions does not have a verse number.

8. Here the versification follows the practice in Hebrew editions of numbering the superscription as verse 1. The result is that verses in modern language versions are one less than those in the Hebrew versions. Thus Ps 3:2 in Hebrew versions is Ps 3:1 in most English versions. Since Ps 2 lacks a superscription, the numbering there is identical between the Hebrew edition and modern language versions.

9. Hans-Joachim Kraus, *Psalms 1–59: A Continental Commentary*, trans. Hilton C. Oswald (Minneapolis: Fortress Press, 1993), 139.

10. Brevard S. Childs, "Psalm Titles and Midrashic Exegesis," *Journal of Semitic Studies* 16 (1971): 137–50.

11. Contra Willem A. VanGemeren, *Psalms*, The Expositor's Bible Commentary, Vol. 5 (Grand Rapids: Zondervan, 1991), 72; Gerald H. Wilson, *Psalms Volume 1*, The NIV Application Commentary (Grand Rapids: Zondervan, 2002), 127–148; Craig C. Broyles, *Psalms*, New International Bible Commentary (Peabody, MA: Hendrickson Publishers, Inc., 1999), 49–51; Erhard S. Gerstenberger, *Psalms Part I, With An Introduction to Cultic Poetry*, Forms of the Old Testment Literature Volume XIV (Grand Rapids: Eerdmans, 1988), 50–54; Norman Whybray, *Reading the Psalms as a Book* (Sheffield: Sheffield Academic Press, 1996), etc., being simply a few representatives of the many studies and commentaries on the Psalms that presume a priori the validity of form criticism, as against the literary context.

12. Gunkel, *Introduction*, 17, 67, 19, identifies the first three psalms as "wisdom" (Ps 1), "royal" (Ps 2), and "complaint song of the individual" (Ps 3).

13. Incidentally, this provides further proof of their intentional collocation.

14. See the article "2 Samuel 23:1-7" by Michael A. Rydelnik in this *Handbook*.

15. Reading this preposition *'l* with *patach*, not *qamats*, as in Isa 1:1, 2:1, 1Kg 22:8, etc.

16. The editors of *Biblia Hebraica Stuttgartensia* have laid out v. 1 as a pair of bicola, missing the obvious threefold consonance of *n'm . . . n'm . . . n'ym*, which supports a tricolon.

17. Contra Grant R. Osborne, *The Hermeneutical Spiral* (Downers Grove, IL: IVP Academic, 2007), and Andreas J. Köstenberger and Richard Patterson, *Invitation to Biblical Interpretation: Exploring the Hermeneutical Triad of History, Literature, and Theology* (Grand Rapids: Kregel, 2011).

18. An acronym for Rabi Shlomoh Yitzchaqi.

19. Abraham Grossman, "The School of Literal Jewish Exegesis in Northern France," in *Hebrew Bible Old Testament: The History of Its Interpretation: I/2: The Middle Ages*, ed. Magne Saebo (Göttingen: Vandenhoeck & Ruprecht, 2000), 323.

20. Deeana Copeland Klepper, *The Insight of Unbelievers* (Philadelphia: University of Pennsylvania Press, 2007), 6, 10, 12, 106, 133.

21. Grossman, "School of Literal," 325–26.

22. See Michael Rydelnik, *The Messianic Hope: Is the Hebrew Bible Really Messianic?* specifically chap. 8, "Rashi's Influence on Messianic Prophecy" (Nashville: B&H Publishers, 2010), 112–28.

23. My own translation of Menahem Cohen, ed., *Miqr'aot Gedolot HaKeter* (Ramat Gan, Israel: Bar Ilan University, 2003), 4.

24. Klepper, *Insight of Unbelievers*, 10.

25. Grossman, "School of Literal," 344; Kleppert, *Insight of Unbelievers*, 125.

26. It is for this reason that numerous published attempts by evangelicals to explain the use of the OT in the NT are so unconvincing. When the historical approach to the OT (that in its origin and later permutations is designed to refute the NT's Christology) is taken as a given, there is little chance, and in fact no chance, of a solution to this perennial problem. It will continue to be a problem until scholars take seriously the literary expression and composition of the OT, which the NT writers clearly understood.

27. Cf. also Ps 124:2–3, Jdg 9:18,43, etc.

28. Hebrew pronouns are not usually necessary because indicative verbs indicate person, number, and gender through prefixes and suffixes. That is why the appearance of independent personal pronouns can be considered deliberate and emphatic.

29. *'th* ("you") – Pss 2:7; 3:4[3]; 4:9[8]; 5:5[4]; 13[12], *'ny* ("I") – Pss 2:6-7; 3:6; 5:8[7]; 6:3[2]. They are highly concentrated in the one lengthy Ps 119, which itself is an expanded exposition of the description of the man of Ps 1 who meditates day and night in God's instruction. The concentration across Pss 2–6 is of adjacent psalms one after another and is thus unique.

30. Note that all of the verse numbering for Psalm 3 in this article follows that of the Hebrew Bible.

31. Thirty-eight times across both books.

Psalm 8

The Messianic Son of Adam

JOSH MATHEWS

Psalm 8 offers a simple yet intense expression of praise to Yahweh for His majesty in creation, and for the special place He has granted to humanity within His creation. It marvels at the magnificent Creator who would pay attention to the humans He created. New Testament writers attach Christological significance to the psalm (1Co 15:27; Eph 1:22; Heb 2:6-8). Identifying the son of man in Ps 8:4 as a prophetic reference to Christ, the writers see a meaning within the psalm that goes beyond praise for the special role of humanity.

Throughout the history of this psalm's interpretation, many have taken this Christological interpretation to be either an illegitimate interpretive move by the apostles, or a theological development that is appropriate only from the vantage point of the NT looking back through the lens of Christ. In both instances, the common commitment is to an interpretation of the psalm itself, in its historical meaning, that does not include an eschatological, messianic element. The psalm's original intent, by its author (David presumably), was simply to praise the Creator God and to celebrate the special place for humanity in creation.

Hans-Joachim Kraus may be taken as representative of this common view. He mentions the way the NT writers appropriate the psalm and then says he recognizes "not even a trace of this eschatological-messianic message of the NT." The psalmist, says Kraus, is purely focused on the present, visible realities of his experience, not on any kind of future fulfillment of the psalm's vision of humanity in relation to Yahweh.[1]

Others allow some room for messianic application of the psalm, while maintaining its original nonmessianic meaning. Calvin, for instance, interpreted it as a psalm about humanity, but gave some latitude to transfer the sense to Christ indirectly. He saw the NT Christological use of the psalm not as an interpretation in line with what David meant, but still theologically appropriate. What the psalm says of humankind can legitimately be transferred to the ultimate representative of humankind, Christ. Only by this step of transference or application did Calvin allow for the psalm to point indirectly ahead to Christ as the one who restores the *imago Dei*.[2]

In contrast to the above perspectives, in this article I will seek to demonstrate that Ps 8 is inherently messianic. That is to say, the anticipation of a future, messianic fulfillment was intended within the psalm itself, particularly when considered in the context of the rest of the Psalter and the Tanakh as a whole. The psalmist *does* wonder at the exalted role for humanity in God's creation, but his marveling also goes beyond this. He also intentionally and demonstrably, though subtly, envisions a royal individual with godlike characteristics. This messianic portrait is rooted in the textual world of Gn 1–3, and it is presented poetically in such a way that it can be fulfilled only by a messianic Second Adam.

MAGNIFICENT GOD, GLORIOUS MAN

Psalm 8 begins and ends with the same statement of praise: "LORD, our Lord, how magnificent is Your name throughout the earth!" (Ps 8:1,9). This declaration not only frames the psalm itself, but also connects it to its surrounding context in the Psalter. Psalm 7 ended with the announcement, "I will thank the LORD (Yahweh) for His righteousness; I will sing about the name of the LORD, the Most High" (Ps 7:17). The mention of Yahweh and His name *(shem)* links this last verse in Ps 7 with the opening lines of Ps 8.[3] Then the closing line of Ps 8, repeating v. 1, links to the beginning of Ps 9 and the line, "I will thank the LORD [Yahweh] with all my heart... I will sing about Your name *(shem)*, Most high" (Ps 9:1-2).[4] The psalm is meant to be read within its context in the Psalter. The significance of this will be shown below, considering further links to surrounding psalms and the interpretive implications of those contextual connections.

The last part of v. 1 parallels the initial expression of magnificence. Just as the Lord's name is magnificent throughout all the earth, so also His majesty covers the heavens. This pairing of heaven and earth conveys the totality of God's creation, and it recalls Gn 1 and the creation account. Psalm 8 may be considered a hymnic commentary on the first few chapters of Genesis. The opening verse establishes this canonical context from the outset.

In v. 3 the psalm continues its reflection on the beginning of Genesis, but the focus then shifts to the astounding reality of God's care for and exaltation of humanity. He looks up at the heavens, at the moon and the stars in the night sky, and wonders, "What is man that You remember him, the son of man that You look after him?" (v. 4). Then the psalm reviews the exalted role that has been given to the son of man. He has been made a little less than God,[5] been crowned with glory and honor, and made lord over creation and its creatures (vv. 5-8). As almost all commentators recognize, these lines have in mind Gn 1:26,28 and God's creation mandate for Adam to rule the animals that roam the earth, sea, and sky.

The psalm concludes by returning again to the refrain of v. 1 and its exclamation of the magnificence of the name of the Lord in all the earth. This is more than simply a restatement of that sentiment, however. Now the intervening theme of humankind's place in God's creation is a further basis for praise. The exclamatory question in vv. 1 and 9 ("how magnificent . . ." *mah-'adiyr*) frames the similarly stated question ("what is man . . ." *mah-'enosh*) at the heart of the psalm in v. 4.[6] In this way, then, the concluding refrain carries a nuanced emphasis. Whereas God's magnificence as Creator was the basis for praise in v. 1, in v. 9 the basis for praise is the exalted role of humanity.[7]

But is the psalmist simply reveling in the elevated role of humanity, or is there more to the psalm's anthropological statement of wonder? Several elements throughout the psalm indicate that the psalmist intended a more profound meaning. The psalmist's point is that the kind of idealized humanity portrayed in Ps 8 is such that he expects his readers to recognize it can only be realized in an *ideal individual* with both divine and royal qualities and status.

THE ROYAL, DIVINE SON OF MAN

Verses 5-6 are at the heart of the psalm, and its messianic meaning rests upon these verses. Setting up these profound statements is the rhetorical question posed in v. 4, which is a neatly arranged set of two parallel lines. "Man" (*'enosh*) in the first line corresponds with "son of man" (*ben-'adam*) in the second line, and "You remember him" parallels "You look after him." In OT parlance, the phrase "son of man," or "son of Adam," is a common designation for a generic human (e.g., Job 16:21; Ps 146:3). It is one of many details in the psalm recalling the early chapters of Genesis. Whatever the psalmist has to say about humankind in general or a future representative of humanity in particular, it is to be understood with reference to the first man, Adam.

"Son of man" occurs most frequently in Ezekiel, where the prophet is addressed by this title over 90 times (e.g., Ezk 2:1; also cf. Dan 8:17). In almost every occurrence of the phrase outside of Ezekiel, it is paired with "man" (either *'enosh* or *'ish*), as it is in Ps 8. For example, in Nm 23:19, Balaam says, "God is not a man (*'ish*) who lies, or a son of man who changes His mind" (also see e.g., Isa 56:2 and Job 35:8 in NASB). The title typically designates humanity in general, or a generic representative thereof.[8]

Verse 5 continues and elaborates on the astonished rhetorical question of v. 4. As the psalmist gazes at the night sky, he is amazed that the Creator of the heavens and the earth, who set the moon and the stars into place, would even remember him. But He has not only remembered him, He has "made him little less than God." The term translated "little less" *(me'at)* in v. 5 could also refer to duration instead of degree (e.g., Jer 51:33; Hos 1:4; Job 10:20; 24:24; Ru 2:7). The LXX uses *brachu*, which can also indicate either a short time or a small amount/degree (e.g., 1Sm 14:29,43; 2Sm 16:1). The author of Hebrews in Heb 2:6-9 is not, therefore, making a careless interpretive leap to draw temporal significance out of the term ("for a short time," Heb 2:9). Another way of saying this is that the LXX does not require a temporal, incarnational reading, but leaves open more room for that than the Hebrew text does. It is appropriate for Hebrews to make the interpretive move to the incarnational/temporal meaning based on the other messianic themes and theology evident within the psalm itself, which will become apparent in this article.

These verses continue with the amazing idea that the Lord does not simply care for humankind, but also has elevated the son of man to a place above the rest of creation, yet less than God. As noted above, the translation "God" for *elohim* is preferable to "angels." Given that the psalm actually envisions a messianic Son of Man, this is not to imply that the Messiah is less than God or that the Son is less than the Father in Trinitarian terms. The statement in v. 5 is not a matter of essence. Rather, if *elohim* does refer to God and not angels, then it anticipates the incarnation and is comparable to the self-emptying of Phl 2. Nevertheless, the emphasis in the psalm is on the elevated status of humanity in the son-of-man representative. It is the messianic son of man who elevates humanity to the level that causes the psalmist to marvel at humanity's status. Once this association is understood, once Jesus is identified as the Messiah, and once the Christological implications of that identification are elaborated upon in the NT, then the slightly lowered (for a time) condescension of God in Christ incarnate becomes clear. This is the way the author of Hebrews also reads Ps 8; he uses the LXX to draw out an appropriate messianic interpretation, making the same point as the intrinsically messianic psalm, though with a different emphasis.

Again, keeping in mind the creation motif repeatedly drawn upon in the psalm, the picture here is of all humanity made in the image of God. Human beings are creatures, distinct from the Creator, yet also distinct from the rest of creation.

This latter difference is what the psalm is highlighting. Humankind is elevated to an almost-divine level, in a category different from the rest of creation. The emphasis is on the closeness of the son of man to God, and the rest of vv. 5-6 accentuates this closeness even more.

In the second line of v. 5, the statement that the Lord has "crowned him with glory and honor" moves the psalm another step forward in praising the Lord for the special status of humankind, and it is here that the messianic implications of the psalm rise to the surface. This is an even more striking statement of the son of man's exaltation. First, he is given royal status, crowned (*'asar*) as a king. This elicits thoughts of kingship themes in the story of the OT and throughout the psalms, particularly keeping in mind the Davidic designation of Ps 8.

In Ps 2 Yahweh's Anointed One (*meshicho*) is opposed by the kings and rulers of the earth (Ps 2:2). The Lord responds, speaking in His anger that He has consecrated His King on His holy mountain, Zion (Ps 2:4-6). These references to an Anointed King are explicitly and literally messianic designations. Moreover, Ps 2 adds another designation to this anointed figure who rules as God's king. In v. 7 Yahweh declares to him, "You are my Son; today I have become Your Father," and later the psalmist addresses the kings of the earth and instructs them to serve Yahweh and pay homage to the Son (Ps 2:10-12).

Through several connections, Ps 2 provides some important background to Ps 8. Psalm 2 describes rebellious nations and kings of the earth conspiring against Yahweh and His Anointed One. These come to mind when Ps 8 speaks of the Lord's adversaries and the enemy who is silenced by the mouth of children and infants (Ps 8:2). Similarly, the one who is "crowned" with glory and honor in Ps 8 calls to mind the Lord's Anointed King from Ps 2. Perhaps the same individual is in mind. The son of man in Ps 8 is in fact Yahweh's Son of Ps 2.

The second striking feature from the second line of Ps 8:5 has to do with the content or substance with which the son of man has been crowned. The two terms "glory" (*kabod*) and "honor" (*hadar*) are synonymous with the terms used to praise Yahweh in v. 1; "magnificent" (*'adir*) and "majesty" (*hod*). These four terms are used in various combinations throughout the OT, usually referring to God (e.g., Pss 45:3-4; 96:3-8 [1Ch 16:24-29]; Pss 104:1,31; 145:5,11-12). When they occur together, the two terms in v. 5 refer exclusively to Yahweh,[9] with one notable exception. Psalm 21:5, referring to the king, says, "His glory (*kabod*) is great through Your victory; You confer majesty (*hod*) and splendor (*hadar*) on him." Not only does this psalm employ three of the four synonyms of Ps 8, but it has other links as well. This psalm is framed with the theme of Yahweh's strength (*'oz*, vv. 1,13; cf. Ps 8:2), and this strength is displayed in the defeat of His enemies (vv. 8-12). The focus of this Davidic psalm is on the king whom the Lord has crowned with a crown (*'asarah*, cf. Ps 8:5) of gold (Ps 21:1-3). Like Ps 2, Ps 21 closely associates Yahweh with His king, and part of that close link is reflected in Ps 8 as well. When the psalmist says that the son of man is crowned with glory and honor, it appears he is intentionally investing him with royal qualities that elsewhere in Scripture are attributed only to God Himself or to His Messianic King.

Especially in Psalms, and also throughout the OT, glory and honor are qualities primarily reserved for God himself. What is more, the emphasis throughout Scripture is that God has a unique claim on these qualities. In Isa 42:8 for instance, The Lord says, "I am Yahweh, that is My name; I will not give My glory to another."[10] The qualities this son of man enjoys are God-like qualities. At the very least, the psalmist is expressing a status for humanity that is given by God Himself. Yet this status, these qualities, even if they are derivative, have their limits. This psalm presses and then bursts through those limits. The son of man pictured here cannot be simply a generic man representing humankind.

As the psalm progresses, it continues to exceed those limits in its description of the son of man. Verse 6 reads, "You made him lord over the works of Your hands; You put everything under his feet." The term translated "You made him lord" (*mashal*) would perhaps be better rendered "You made him ruler" (so CSB; cf. NIV, NET). This term, and the related noun, *memshalah* (rule), carry kingly connotation. One particularly relevant example is in Ps 145:13. There, expressing high praise of Yahweh, His "rule" (*memshalah*) parallels His "kingdom" (*malkut*). Psalm 145 is also connected to Ps 8 by its grouping of the terms already discussed. The psalmist uses "glory" (*kabod*), "splendor"/ "honor" (*hadar*), and "majesty" (*hod*) to describe God and His kingdom (145:5,11-12). One more detail repeated in Ps 145 further aids understanding of Ps 8. Yahweh's works (*ma'aseh*) are also praised repeatedly in Ps 145 (vv. 4,9-10,17; cf. 8:3,6). God's glorious works and kingdom are features that distinguish Him as God.

The phrase "the works of Your hands" in Ps 8:6 is reminiscent of the "work of Your fingers" in v. 3. Thus, the psalmist again connects the second half of the psalm with the first and associates the realm of the son of man's rule with the works of Yahweh's creation. The next two verses (vv. 7-8) focus on earthly creatures under the man's rule, unmistakably and intentionally recalling God's commission for Adam to "rule the fish of the sea, the birds of the sky, the livestock, all the earth, and the creatures that crawl on the earth" (Gn 1:26,28). Nevertheless, this phrase "the works of Your hands" linked with the heavenly "works of Your fingers" at least hints at a realm of the son of man's rule that includes the heavens as well.[11] If this psalm merely depicts the exalted status of a generic man, standing for humankind, this extension of his realm to the heavens is unprecedented. The psalm's vision of humanity has risen to a level that includes both royal and divine features, and the rule over God's creation—earthly, at least with hints of the heavenly as well.

The psalm urges us to consider whether humankind actually does enjoy this status. Peter Craigie is another representative of the position that the NT writers add a new, messianic meaning to the psalm's original meaning. Commenting on this verse, he acknowledges that the NT picture of Jesus' dominion "is a natural development of the thought of the psalm, for the dominion of which the psalmist spoke may have had theological reality, yet it did not always appear to have historical reality in the developing history of the human race."[12] However, is this not quite an understatement from the perspective of the biblical context of the Psalter and the rest of the Tanakh, not to mention the world as we observe it around us today? The biblical picture of the human race from Gn 3 onward is such that humankind's dominion does not only "not always appear to have historical reality." Rather, the son of man's ruling status imagined in Ps 8 is quite conspicuously contrary to the historical reality of humanity since Adam.

Adam failed to succeed in the task of earthly rule. Instead of subduing the earth (Gn 1:28), he was subdued by a created being, the serpent. And as a result, the ground itself would resist his rule (Gn 3:17-19). The reality of human experience in the world directly contradicts the portrait of the son of man in Ps 8.[13] Adam and all the sons and daughters descended from him have failed to achieve the rule with which he was commissioned by God. The movement of the psalm appears to insist on the expectation of another son of Adam to fulfill what Adam and his offspring did not and could not achieve.

From the perspective of the NT, the second half of v. 6 is the psalm's most significant line, carrying the weight of its prophetic, messianic meaning.[14] The Lord has put everything under the feet of the son of man. As is typical of Hebrew parallelism, this second line reiterates the message of the first line, while also elaborating on it in some significant way: The son of man rules the works of God's hands, and what is more, He has put everything under his feet.[15] In the language of the Hebrew Bible, having someone under one's feet is to have authority over him. It also carries connotations of victorious rule over an enemy, resulting from a decisive defeat (see Jos 10:24; 2Sm 22:39/Ps 18:38; 1Kg 5:3; Ps 47:3; Lam 3:34; Mal 4:3).

In Ps 110:1, Yahweh addresses the one designated "my Lord," the Messianic Priest-King in this eschatological psalm. He says to Him, "Sit at My right hand until I make Your enemies Your footstool." The picture is one of defeating and subduing the enemy, and that is what Ps 8 envisions as well. A few verses prior to this line, the psalmist declared that the Lord had established a stronghold, by the mouth of infants, because of his adversaries,[16] and had silenced the enemy and avenger (v. 2).

This enemy motif further connects Ps 8 to the surrounding grouping of lament psalms. In Ps 7 the psalmist implored Yahweh to rise up against the fury of His adversaries (vv. 4-6), and in Ps 9 the psalmist anticipates his enemy's retreat to eternal ruin before the righteous judgment of the Lord (vv. 3-6). Completing the acrostic of Ps 9, Ps 10 develops the enemy theme more fully, describing in detail the enemy's apparent prosperity in spite of their blatant rebellion and denial of God (Ps 10:1-11).[17]

It is evident from this context surrounding Ps 8 that humankind does not currently experience defeat of and dominion over our enemies. Just as creation is not subdued under man's rule, so neither are his enemies. In fact, quite the contrary. Victory over the enemies of God, of His king, and of His people is not a present reality; it is a future hope. This fits with the eschatological, messianic perspective of Pss 2, 110, and many other psalms, and it goes back as far as Gn 3:15 and the enmity between the seed of the woman and the seed of the serpent.[18]

Finally, in the surrounding collection of psalms,[19] several details contrast the portrait of the Son of Man in Ps 8 with that of humanity more generally, further solidifying the prophetic viewpoint of the psalm. In Ps 9 the psalmist requests the Lord to arise and not let man (*'enosh*) prevail, and that the nations would be judged and know they are only men (*'enosh*, vv. 19-20). Psalm 12 begins with a cry for salvation from Yahweh because the faithful and loyal "have disappeared from the human race" (v. 1). The phrase translated "human race" here is *beney 'adam*, which recalls *ben-'adam* (son of man/Adam) in Ps 8:4. Psalm 14 begins with a similar statement, though with a more extensive denial of the goodness of humanity. As the Lord looks down from heaven on "the human race" (*beney-'adam*), He sees that all have turned away and become corrupt. "There is no one who does good, not even one" (Ps 14:1-3).

This picture of humanity is a dark one indeed. Men and the sons of man in these passages in the near context of Ps 8 designate humankind in general, and they are characterized in entirely opposite ways to the exalted picture of the Son of Man we see in Ps 8. The psalm must not simply refer to a generic man, representing humankind in general. Rather, the psalm's idealized vision points ahead to a future reality, and to an ideal representative of humanity, a Son of Man *par excellence*.

CONCLUSION

Psalm 8 is a praise psalm, proclaiming the magnificence of Yahweh for His wonderful works and creation. This praise turns its focus to humanity and the special, exalted role they have been given. And yet, the psalmist keeps pressing the question forward: What is man? How can this be? It is an astounding thing that the Lord remembers humankind. It is almost too much to grasp that He would grant him a status almost as high as God Himself. And it is utterly beyond comprehension that He would crown humankind with glory, make Him ruler of His creation, and subdue all under his feet.

This image of humanity evoked in the psalm cannot refer to a generic son of man, standing for the human race as a whole. The psalm urges its readers to imagine a Son of Adam who is different from Adam and every descendant after him. In Ps 8, particularly in vv. 5-6, there is a depiction of humanity that Adam did not sustain, his descendants did not achieve, and that intentionally points ahead to its future fulfillment in a divine, royal Son of Adam. This Son of Man would realize the role of humankind perfectly in His rule over God's creation and His defeat of the enemies of God and God's people. This One would fit the psalm's description in a way no one else could. The psalm points to a fulfillment that can only be realized by Jesus, the last Adam, the messianic Son of Man.

When the NT writers identify Jesus as the fulfillment of this psalm, they are not introducing a messianic viewpoint extrinsic to the psalm. The messianic meaning is intrinsic to the psalm itself, and it is recognizable within the psalm as the reader follows its poetic and logical development and considers it within the context of the Psalter and the rest of the Tanakh. The NT extrapolates Christological application from the psalm related to Jesus' incarnation, life, death, resurrection, and ascension, but the intentional prophetic meaning, which points ahead to the future Messiah, is present in the psalm itself. Psalm 8 is indeed prophetic and messianic.

---

1. Hans-Joachim Kraus, *Psalms 1–59*, trans. Hilton C. Oswald, Continental Commentaries (Minneapolis: Fortress, 1993), 186.

2. John Calvin, *Commentary on the Book of Joshua and Psalms 1–35*, trans. Henry Beveridge, vol. IV of *Calvin's Commentaries* (Grand Rapids: Baker, 1998), 103–4. See also Willem J. van Asselt, "'Quid Est Homo Quod Memor Es Ipsius?': Calvin and Cocceius (1603–1669) on Psalm 8," *Church History and Religious Culture* 91.1–2 (2011): 139–40.

3. "I will sing" *(wa'azmerah)* in Ps 7:17, from the Hebrew root *zmr*, also connects to the superscript of Ps 8. *mizmor*, translated "psalm" of David, which is from *zmr* also.

4. The term for "sing" is *'azamerah*, again from the root *zmr*. See Bruce K. Waltke, James M. Houston, and Erika Moore, *The Psalms as Christian Worship: A Historical Commentary* (Grand Rapids: Eerdmans, 2010), 256.

5. Some translations follow the LXX and translate *elohim* at the end of v. 5a using "the heavenly beings" (ESV) or "the angels" (NIV). While I do not take either of these options to be preferable, they may be possible. The point the psalmist is making is that the ideal son of man has been given a status that is godlike and divine. Calvin says, "I explain the words of David as meaning the same thing as if he had said that the condition of men is nothing less than a divine and celestial state" (Calvin, *Psalms*, 102–3).

6. Retief argues for a messianic reading of the psalm on the basis of this connection between the refrain in vv. 1,9 and the rhetorical question in v. 4, proposing the following translation of the refrain: "O Lord, our Lord, what is the magnificent one of your name . . ." (C. Wynand Retief, "A Messianic Reading of Psalm 8," *Old Testament Essays* 27.3 (2014): 992–1008) While this is an intriguing suggestion, and the literary observation of the similarly stated questions in vv. 1,4, and 9 is helpful, I do not find the proposed translation for vv. 1 and 9 to be tenable.

7. See Gerald H. Wilson, *Psalms, Volume 1*, NIV Application Commentary (Grand Rapids: Zondervan, 2002), 209.

8. Psalm 80:17 might suggest a more nuanced association, with "the son of man" parallel with "the man at Your right hand." This verse is an expansion of v. 15 and, while on its surface the title is another designation for God's people, the vine the Lord has planted, it also moves beyond that to envision an individual representative. And in the psalms, a man at Yahweh's right hand evokes messianic connotations (cf. Ps 110:1,5). Daniel 7:13 also may contribute to messianic associations with the title. There Daniel sees a vision of "One like a son of man." The Aramaic phrase is *kebar 'enash*, and the eschatological implications of this apocalyptic passage are obvious.

9. In addition to Ps 8:5, the combination of *kabod* and *hadar* occurs in Isa 35:2; Ps 21:5; 29:2; 145:5,12; and 1Chr 16:29. In Isa 35:2 each term is used twice. At first, they refer to Lebanon and Carmel and Sharon, but the next lines clarify that the glory and splendor are the Lord's.

10. McConville remarks on Ps 8 that the movement from v. 4 to the exalted view of humanity in v. 5 "is unexpected and astonishing. . . . This ascription of 'glory' to the human is especially remarkable when one bears in mind the OT's strong critique of human pretensions to the glory that belongs properly to God, notably in the book of Isaiah, where such aspirations are shown to be self-deceiving and doomed (e.g., Isa. 2; 10:12-19, 37-38)" (J. Gordon McConville, *Being Human in God's World: An Old Testament Theology of Humanity* [Grand Rapids: Baker Academic, 2016], 174).

11. Also see Ps 19:1; 102:25, both of which associate the work of God's hands with the heavens.

12. Peter C. Craigie, *Psalms 1–50*, 2nd ed., vol. 19 of *Word Biblical Commentary* (Nashville: Thomas Nelson, 2004), 110.

13. Commenting on verse 6, C. S. Lewis remarks that the writer of Hebrews "observes that, in the actual state of the universe, this is not strictly true. Man is often killed, and still more often defeated, by beasts, poisonous vegetables, weather, earthquakes, etc." He goes on to say that this kind of thought process could lead the writer of Hebrews, and us, to think of Christ who ascended to heaven and to whom, "in due time," all things will be subjected. "It is He who, having been made (for a while) 'lower than the angels', will become the conqueror and ruler of all things, including death and (death's patron) the devil" (C. S. Lewis, *Reflections on the Psalms* [London: Fount, 1958], 115).

14. First Corinthians 15:27-28 and Eph 1:22 both quote Ps 8:6b, and Heb 2:8 includes the line in a quotation of Ps 8:4-6. Also see Mt 28:18 (and cross references); Jn 5:27; 1Pt 3:22.

15. See James L. Kugel, *The Idea of Biblical Poetry: Parallelism and Its History* (New Haven, CT: Yale University Press, 1981), 58. Kugel argued against neatly categorizing Hebrew parallel lines into just a few groups. His famous statement in response to Robert Lowth was, "Biblical parallelism is of one sort, 'A, and what's more, B,' or a hundred sorts; but it is not three."

16. The term translated "stronghold" in the HCSB is *'oz*, the most basic meaning of which is strength (so ESV) or might. The LXX renders it *ainon* (praise) and the NT follows the LXX. This interpretive step by the LXX and NT is not without justification, for the strength is coming from the mouths of babies. Kidner refers to it as an "audible bulwark" (Derek Kidner, *Psalms 1–72: An Introduction and Commentary*, vol. 15 of Tyndale Old Testament Commentaries [Downers Grove, IL: IVP Academic, 1973], 83, n. 15). Also see Øystein Lund, "From the Mouth of Babes and Infants You Have Established Strength," *Scandinavian Journal of the Old Testament* 11.1 (1997): 78–99.

17. Note here additional details that contrast the picture of Ps 8. For example, the enemy's mouth curses and deceives instead of rendering strength/praise (10:7; cf 8:2). He says God has forgotten instead of remembering man and the son of man (10:11; cf 8:4).

18. Genesis 3:15 is likely in mind with the hopeful note of praise on which Ps 7 ends, setting the stage for Ps 8. The fall of the wicked is anticipated, where his trouble and violence come falling back onto his own head (Ps 7:16).

19. Craigie observes not only the connections between Ps 8 and the surrounding laments of Pss 7 and 9–10, but also says that "Ps 8 is the central psalm of the whole complex of Pss 3–14" (Craigie, *Psalms 1–50*, 463).

Psalm 16

The Resurrected Messiah

SETH D. POSTELL

The NT use of OT Scripture has often perplexed Christian readers. The apostles and authors sometimes seem to take passages completely out of context and use them in a way that might appear to violate the original meaning. However, a growing body of research is finding quite the opposite to be the case. The original meaning of NT quotes from the Psalms, as will be discussed here, points directly to the Messiah in a manner that may be obscured when individual psalms are not understood in the context of the Psalter as a whole. Examples of literary discoveries demonstrating the significance of the canon of the Psalter will be reviewed, followed by a focus on Psalm 16 in particular.

> Seeing this in advance, he spoke concerning the resurrection of the Messiah: "He was not left in Hades, and His flesh did not experience decay." (Ac 2:31).

> For David, after serving his own generation in God's plan, fell asleep, was buried with his fathers, and decayed. But the One God raised up did not decay. (Ac 13:36-37)

There is little doubt the early Jewish followers of Jesus read Ps 16 as a messianic psalm. According to the Greek, David "saw in advance" (*prooraō*) the resurrection of the Messiah (Ps 15:8 LXX; Ac 2:31).[1] Both Peter and Paul clearly regarded Ps 16 as a key psalm in their messianic apologetic since they both refer to it in their debut sermons to the Jewish people.

The amount of discussion generated by Peter's and Paul's use of this psalm as a proof text for the resurrection of the Messiah points to the widening gap between the NT's messianic interpretation of this psalm on the one hand and the modern grammatical-historical interpretation on the other.[2] Many scholarly attempts to explain the NT's use of Ps 16 have been offered.[3] Little attention, however, has been placed on the function and importance of the larger literary context of Ps 16 in Book I of the Psalter (Pss 1–41) and in the book of Psalms as a whole (Pss 1–150). Peter's and Paul's citations of Ps 16 appear in a broader matrix of other allusions and citations of other psalms in the Psalter that are also considered messianic. Carl R. Holladay notes how Peter alludes to at least three other OT passages in Ac 2:30, including 2Sm 7:12-13, Pss 89:4-5, and 132:11.[4] There are other allusions to the book of Psalms in the immediate context of Peter's sermon as well. Acts 2:24 appears to be an allusion to Ps 18:6 (see 2Sm 22:6), and in Ac 2:33-35, Peter first alludes to and then cites Ps 110:1. Acts 2:37 appears to be an allusion to the Greek translation of Ps 109:16 (LXX). Likewise, Paul cites Ps 2:7 in Ac 13:33, and his reference to Ps 16:10 (Ac 13:36) appears in a matrix of other citations and allusions to the book of Psalms.

In contrast to the NT's contextual and intertextual reading of Ps 16, the modern grammatical-historical reading of Ps 16, which is strongly influenced by form-criticism,[5] interprets the individual psalms in isolation from the immediately surrounding psalms and in isolation of the book of Psalms as a whole. The form-critical reading of Ps 16 asks how this individual psalm functioned within the First and Second Temple periods, rather than how this psalm functions in its literary context, i.e., as a part of the book of Psalms. According to the form-critical classification, Ps 16 is a psalm of confidence or thanksgiving,[6] in which the author thanks God for keeping him from death, rather than a messianic psalm that foretells God's resurrection of the Messiah from death. From this perspective, the location of Ps 16 within the book of Psalms (i.e., literary context) has no relevance for understanding the authorial intent of the psalm itself.

However, the NT's messianic interpretation of Ps 16, with its incorporation of other messianic psalms, is supported by an ever-growing amount of textual evidence demonstrating that the book of Psalms is truly a book with a well-planned compositional structure and a theological message.[7] This body of evidence weighs heavily in favor of understanding Ps 16 as the authors of the NT did—as a messianic psalm.

The next section of this article will attempt to locate Ps 16 in its broader literary context (Book I of Psalms) as well as in its immediate literary context (Pss 15–24). By paying attention to this inspired literary (canonical) context, the reader, it is hoped, can see how the overtly royal psalms in Book I of the Psalms (Pss 2, 8, 18, 20–21) are intended to guide, inform, and influence one's reading of Ps 16. The final section of this article will look specifically at Ps 16 and argue that David is not thanking God for rescuing him from the dangers of death, but rather prophesying how God will raise the Messiah-King from the dead, the resurrection.

PSALM 16 IN ITS LITERARY CONTEXT

Psalm 16 in the Context of Book I:

The growing body of biblical research points to a carefully designed literary structure for the book of Psalms as a whole.[8] Crucial to the overall structure are:

1. The introduction and conclusion to the book of Psalms (Pss 1–2, 146–150)
2. The fivefold divisions of the book (Pss 3–41, 42–72, 73–89, 90–106, 107–145)
3. The carefully arranged groupings of the individual psalms by means of key words in the superscriptions
4. The pervasive use of literary links and inclusios (literary framing devices) in the adjacent psalms and groupings of psalms.

This literary design begs the question of the author's theological concern for the message of the Psalter as a book. The careful placement of psalms that envision the rule of a Davidic messianic king in the literary seams between and introducing the five books (Pss 2, 45, 72, 89, 107–110), as well as in the seams of the individual books (e.g. the Royal Psalms in Book I: Pss 2, 8, 18, 20–21), supports a growing consensus that the book of Psalms reflects a unified composition about God's promises to the house of David, namely, the coming Davidic Messiah. In what follows, I will outline the literary structure of Book I and argue that this structure is consistent with the overall theme of this messianic hope.

In his monograph on the Psalms, Gianni Barbiero puts forth a cogent argument that Book I of the Psalms (Pss 1–41) has a carefully designed literary structure.[9] According to Barbiero, the structure of Book I is as follows: Pss 1–14 (2 x 7 = 14 psalms); Pss 15–24 (10 psalms); Pss 25–34 (10 psalms); and Pss 35–41 (7 psalms).[10] Using form-critical categories, Barbiero argues for a symmetrical structure of the whole of Book I, which is patterned after the content of the first 14 psalms:[11]

Psalms 3–7	A	Lament	Psalms 3–14
Psalm 8	B	Praise	Psalms 15–24
Psalm 9	B`	Thanksgiving	Psalms 25–34
Psalms 10–14	A`	Lament	Psalms 35–41

Though Barbiero's form-critical analysis appears to be forced at times, several literary features do in fact support his thesis regarding the careful arrangement of Book I. First, the introduction and the conclusion of Book I share key terms and phrases, pointing to an intentional introduction and conclusion to the First Book (i.e., literary inclusio). Psalms 1–7[12] share numerous literary links with the last set of seven psalms in Book I (Pss 35–41). To name just a few:

1. Psalms 1 and 2 begin and end with the same word, "blessed" (HCSB "happy," *ašre*; Ps 1:1; 2:12), which also opens the final psalm of Book I (Ps 41:1).
2. Only in Pss 1:4 and 35:5 does the phrase "chaff in the wind" appear.
3. Psalms 1:2 and 2:1 record the meditations (using the Hebrew verb "*hagah*" for "meditates" and "plots") of the righteous man and the wicked. Likewise, Pss 35:28, 37:30, 38:12 use the same Hebrew verb (translated "proclaim," "utters" and "plot") to record the meditations of the righteous and the wicked.
4. The "Lord mocks/laughs" in Pss 2:4 and 37:13.
5. The phrase "upon their beds" only appears in Pss 4:4, 36:4 (sections from the introduction and conclusion of Book I), and Ps 149:5 (part of the conclusion of the book of Psalms).
6. The phrase "my groaning" is found only in Pss 5:1 (NASB) and 32:3.

Of interest, Ps 3 begins with a historical superscription that tells of a rebellion against David by Absalom, his son (Ps 3:1 MT). Psalm 41:9 (HCSB footnote) tells of a "man of my peace" (both Absalom and "man of my peace" share the noun "*shalom*," peace) who has lifted up his heel against King David.[13]

As for the specific groupings of psalms within Book I, many have argued quite persuasively that Psalms 15–24 (the immediate literary context of Psalm 16) is a carefully arranged group of psalms with a chiastic structure. (The next section will look more closely at this group).[14] Psalms 15 and 24 are clearly parallel both in content and in theme: Who can ascend into the presence of the Lord in His temple? Only one who lives according to the Torah's morals. As for the following group of psalms (Pss 25–34), the first and the last psalms in this group, Pss 25 and 34, are both alphabetic acrostics. Remarkably, both psalms end with an extra verse not included in the acrostic pattern, and both of these verses begin with the Hebrew letter *peh*. These verses, outside the scope of the acrostic, are remarkably similar in lexical and thematic content (compare Pss 25:22; 34:22 MT).

Finally, Pss 35–41, the closing group of psalms in Book I, bear all the markings of a carefully connected group as well.

1. The Hebrew root for the verb "repay" and the noun "peace" appears 18 times in Book I, 10 times in this last grouping of psalms (Pss 35:12, 20, 27; 37:11, HCSB "prosperity, 21, 37; 38:4, 20; 41:10-11).
2. David is repaid evil for good in Ps 35:12; in 38:20; and in Ps 41:10, a "man of his peace" comes against him. After God graciously raises up David, he repays David's enemies (41:11).
3. There are only three references to the phrase "exalt over me" (*hig dil a ālay*) in the Hebrew Bible (Ezk 35:13, Pss 35:26, 41:9, two of which appear in the opening and closing of the final group of psalms (35–41).
4. In Ps 41:3, there is a reference to "bed" (*mišk āb*), a word referenced only in the seams of groupings of psalms in Book I, and in the second-to-last psalm (Pss 4:4; 36:4; 149:5).
5. Psalms 35 and 41 refer to "my haters" (Pss 35:19; 38:19; 41:7). There are only three references to "those who think evil" in the Hebrew Bible, two of which are in this final grouping of psalms in Book I (Pss 35:4; 41:7; 140:2). Psalms 35 and 41 are clearly related.
6. "Lie down" (*šk b*) appears on the borders of Book I (Pss 3:5; 4:4, 8; 36:4; 41:3, 8).
7. The phrase "Aha Aha" appears three times in the Hebrew Bible, two times in this final grouping of Psalms (Pss 35:21; 40:15; 70:3).
8. Finally, the phrase "poor and needy" (*āni w eb yôn*) appears eight times in the Psalter, three times in this final group of psalms (Pss 35:10; 37:14; 40:18).

Returning to Pss 1–14, there are also some obvious literary and structural patterns. For instance, Psalm 1 presents an ideal man who meditates on the Torah day and night. Robert Cole and others have argued persuasively that this man is none other than the king of Psalm 2.[15] Psalm 2 begins with a rebellion against the Lord and Hs messianic viceroy (Ps 2:1-2), a rebellion that is subsequently squelched when the Messiah is given rule over the entire earth (Ps 2:8-9). In a dramatic turn of events, the next cluster of psalms (Pss 3–7) is framed with historical superscriptions, the first of which refers to the beginning of Absalom's rebellion (Ps 3), and the final psalm referring to the end of Absalom's rebellion (Ps 7). Psalm 3:1 specifically mentions Absalom's rebellion against David, and Ps 7:1 refers to the words of Cush. The reference to Cush in the superscription in light of the earlier reference to Absalom in Ps 3:1 suggests that Cush is the "Cushite" who told David that Absalom, as well as those who "rise up against" (a key phrase that opens up this group of psalms—Ps 3:1), are dead (see 2Sm 18:31-32). This suggests that Pss 3–7 offer a figural reading of Pss 1–2: Absalom's rebellion against David in Pss 3–7 is intended to give us a prophetic picture of the rebellion against the Messiah.[16] God's deliverance of David from the hand of Absalom and his armies is meant to assure, as well as prophetically illustrate, God's deliverance of the Messiah and His final victory. It does not appear to be coincidental that once this rebellion against the king is squelched in Ps 7,[17] Ps 8 depicts the universal rule of the Son of Man, the future Davidic King, over all creation.

> What is man that You remember him, the son of man that You look after him? You made him little less than God and crowned him with glory and honor. You made him lord over the works of Your hands; You put everything under his feet. (Ps 8:4-6; see Heb 2:5-8)

The placement of Pss 3–7 with their historical superscriptions about David within a messianic framework, i.e., Pss 2 and 8, suggests that the author of the Psalter wants the readers to interpret these psalms about this historical David both figuratively and prophetically: as in the life of David, so it will be with the future Messiah.

David commits to praising the name of God at the end of Psalm 7 (Ps 7:17), the very thing he does in Pss 8–9, before the next cluster of lament psalms (Pss 11–14) is introduced. The words of the superscription of Ps 7 remind readers that the rebellion is over and the enemy is defeated. It comes as no surprise, therefore, that Ps 8 once again takes up the same themes of Ps 2: The Davidic king is given rule over the entire creation. Psalms 10–14 return again to the theme of rebellion against the Davidic king. In light of this rebellion, Ps 14 ends with a longing for messianic salvation to come forth out of Zion. This longing begins with the Hebrew interrogative, "who" (*mi*; translated "Oh" in the HCSB and in most English translations; 14:7), a question that not only frames the next grouping of psalms in Book I, Pss 15–24, but also points us to the Davidic king through whom this redemption will come:

> "LORD, who (*mi*) can dwell in Your tent? Who (*mi*) can live on Your holy mountain?" (Ps 15:1 MT) . . . "Who (*mi*) may ascend the mountain of the LORD? Who may stand in His holy place?" (Ps 24:3)

In summary, evidence suggests carefully structured groupings of psalms in Book I of the Psalter, of which Ps 16 plays an important role. Next follows a look at Ps 16 in the context of Pss 15–24.

PSALM 16 IN THE CONTEXT OF PSALMS 15–24

A number of scholars have demonstrated the literary cohesion of Pss 15–24 as a carefully structured group of psalms, such that these psalms move concentrically (or chiastically) from the outward psalms framing the group toward the central psalm, namely Ps 19, a psalm celebrating the centrality of the Torah for the prosperity of the Messianic King (so also Pss 1 [Torah] and 2 [Messianic King]). Philip Sumpter offers the following helpful chiastic structure:[18]

A Psalm 15: Entrance Liturgy
  B Psalm 16: Song of Trust
    C Psalm 17: Prayer for Help
      D Psalm 18: Royal Psalm
        E Psalm 19: Creation/Torah Psalm
      D` Psalms 20–21: Royal Psalms
    C` Psalm 22: Prayer for Help
  B` Psalm 23: Song of Trust
A` Psalm 24: Entrance Liturgy

The shared language and common themes in these concentric psalms point to their intentional arrangement, i.e., the work of the composer of the Psalter.

Psalms 15, 24: Entrance Liturgy (A/A`)	LORD, who can dwell in Your tent? Who can live on Your holy mountain? The one who lives honestly, practices righteousness, and acknowledges the truth in his heart—who does not slander with his tongue, who does not harm his friend or discredit his neighbor, who despises the one rejected by the LORD but honors those who fear the LORD, who keeps his word whatever the cost, who does not lend his money at interest or take a bribe against the innocent—the one who does these things will never be moved. (Ps 15:1-5)	Who may ascend the mountain of the LORD? Who may stand in His holy place? The one who has clean hands and a pure heart, who has not set his mind on what is false, and who has not sworn deceitfully. He will receive blessing from the LORD, and righteousness from the God of his salvation. (Ps 24:3-5)

Psalms 16, 23: Song of Trust (B/B`)	"I have nothing **good** besides You." (Ps 16:2)	"Only **goodness** and faithful love will pursue me all the days of my life" (Ps 23:6)
	"LORD, You are my portion and **my cup** of blessing; You hold my future." (Ps 16:5)	"You anoint my head with oil; **my cup** overflows."[19] (Ps 23:5)
	"in Your presence is abundant joy; in Your right hand are eternal pleasures." (Ps 16:11)	"and I will dwell in the house of the LORD as long as I live." (Ps 23:6)
Psalms 17, 22: Prayer for Help (C/C`)	"from the wicked who treat me violently, my deadly enemies **who surround me.**" (Ps 17:9)	"For dogs have surrounded me; a gang of evildoers has **closed in on me;**[20] they pierced my hands and my feet." (Ps 22:16)
	"They advance against me; now they **surround me** [*sᵉḇāḇûnyy*]." (Ps 17:11)	"Many bulls surround me [*sᵉḇāḇûnyy*]." (Ps 22:12) "For dogs have surrounded me" [*sᵉḇāḇûnyy*]. (Ps 22:16)
	"They are like a **lion** eager to **tear**." (Ps 17:12)	"**lions, mauling**[21] and roaring." (Ps 22:13) "Save me from the mouth of the **lion**!" (Ps 22:21)
	"With Your sword, **save** [*plṭ*] me from the wicked." (Ps 17:13)	"You **rescued** [*plṭ*] them." (Ps 22:4) "Let Him **rescue** [*plt*] him." (Ps 22:8)
	"But I will see Your face in righteousness; when I awake, I will be satisfied with Your presence." (Ps 17:15)	"I will proclaim Your name to my brothers; I will praise You in the congregation." (Ps 22:22)[22]
Psalms 18, 20-21: Royal Psalms (D/D`)	"The LORD is . . . my **fortress** [*miśgab*]." (Ps 18:2).	"may the name of Jacob's God **protect** [*yᵉśaggeḇ*] you." (Ps 20:2)
	"Your right hand **upholds me** [*ṯis'āḏeni*]." (Ps 18:35)	"and **sustain you** [*yîs'āḏeḵo*] from Zion." (Ps 20:2)

"**He gives great victories to His king**; He shows loyalty to His anointed, to David and his descendants forever." (Ps 18:50)	Now I know that **the LORD gives victory to His anointed**; He will answer him from His holy heaven with mighty victories from His right hand. . . . **LORD, give victory to the king**!" (Ps 20:6,9)
"**Your right hand** upholds me." (Ps 18:35)	"with mighty victories from **His right hand**." (Ps 20:6) "**your right hand** will seize those who hate you." (Ps 21:8)

The numerous lexical and thematic links between these concentric psalms, with the royal (messianic) psalms (Pss 18; 20–21) strategically placed around the central psalm, Ps 19, suggests that the figure in Ps 16 must be identified as the messianic King (Pss 2; 18; 20–1). This King is devoted to the Torah (Pss 1; 15; 19; 24), unlike the flawed Davidic kings before him, and will ultimately triumph over his enemies (Pss 18; 22) to enjoy eternal life in God's presence (Pss 16, 23). Now follows a look at the details of Psalm 16.

PSALM 16 AND THE HOPE OF RESURRECTION

Psalm 15 describes Israel's ideal king, one who lives a pious life, and who, therefore, qualifies to dwell in the Lord's holy mountain (Ps 15:1-5a). David assures us that this ideal king will "never be moved," *lōʾ yîmmôṭ lᵉʿôlām* (Ps 15:5b). The following psalm takes up this confident hope: "I keep the LORD in mind always. Because He is at my right hand, I will not be shaken [moved]," *bal-ʾemmôṭ* (Ps 16:8; see 17:5). This confidence leads to assurance of the king's eternal pleasures at God's right hand (Ps 16:11), which was defined in the preceding psalm as the Lord's tent and holy mountain (Ps 15:1). In order to ascend to the mount of the Lord (Ps 15:1), the king must first descend into the grave and conquer death (Ps 16:10-11).

Psalm 16 is not easy to outline, and a number of structural outlines have been proposed. I would like to propose an outline based on the grammatical and syntactical features of the psalm, which fits nicely with the flow of thought.

I. The King's Confident Request for Preservation: Ps 16:1[23] (*šāmreni*: imperative)
II. The King's Confidence in the Lord's Goodness in the Land of the Living: Ps 16:2-7[24]
III. The King's Confidence in the Lord's Presence in Sheol: Ps 16:8-11[25]

Perhaps the most crucial question regarding the meaning of this psalm, particularly with respect to the NT's usage, has to do with the interpretation of Ps 16:8-10: Does this psalm foretell the king's resurrection from the grave, or simply express thanks for keeping him from death?

> I keep the Lord in mind always. Because He is at my right hand, I will not be shaken. Therefore my heart is glad and my spirit rejoices; my body also rests securely. For You will not abandon me to Sheol; You will not allow Your Faithful One to see decay. (Ps 16:8-10)

The crux of the debate revolves around the meaning of the Hebrew word translated "decay" (*šāḥaṯ*) in Ps 16:10. Though many translations, ancient and modern, interpret this word with reference to the corruption of decay of death (LXX, HCSB, NASB, KJV, NIV), other translations interpret this word as "pit" (JPS, NRSV, NET). If the meaning of the word is "pit," then the king is rescued from dying rather than being rescued out of death (resurrection). The debate revolves around a grammatical question: Is the Hebrew word *šāḥaṯ* a feminine noun, which derives from the verbal root *šwḥ*, "to sink down, grave," and hence "pit," or a masculine noun that derives from the verbal root *šḥṯ*, "to ruin, do harm," and therefore "decay, corruption"?

To answer this question, one must first consider those passages in this group of psalms (Pss 15–24) that explicitly mention the death of the ideal king of Psalm 15, later identified as the Messiah in Psalm 18:50 and 20:6 ("anointed" in Hebrew is *mashiach* or Messiah). Already noted in the structure of Pss 15–24 is the close literary and thematic relationship between Pss 17 and 22. The king's enemies have surrounded him (*nqp hiphil* in Pss 17:9; 22:16; *sᵉḇāḇûnyy* in Pss 17:11; 22:13,17) and seek to devour him like a lion (Pss 17:12; 22:13, 21). Of interest, Ps 17 ends with the king's confident proclamation that he will be satisfied (*śbʿ*) with the Lord's likeness when he *awakes* (v. 15), the same satisfaction (*śḇaʿ*) in the Lord's eternal presence that the speaker expressed at the end of Ps 16 (v. 11). The word "awake" in Ps 17:15 (*hāqiṣ*) is commonly used for resurrection/being raised from the dead/come to life elsewhere in the Hebrew Bible (2Kg 4:31; Isa 26:19; Jer 51:39, 57; Hab 2:19; Job 14:12; Dan 12:2).[26] Given the general context of vicious assault in Psalm 17, and its counterpart in Psalm 22, it is difficult to understand why the speaker would express hope in simply waking up from a good night's sleep to see God's presence, particularly when his enemies are bent on killing him and dividing his garments. Rather, Psalm 17:15 expresses a confidence in seeing God's presence in spite of death, i.e., at the resurrection.

A closer look at Psalm 22, moreover, makes it clear that David and the composer of the Psalter knew that the Messiah would in fact die. Psalm 22:15 states that the king is put "into the dust of death." "Dust" is used later in the same psalm to refer to those who have died (Ps 22:29). Granted the huge text-critical debate of Ps 22:16 ("like a lion" vs. "they pierced"), it is clear the enemy divides the speaker's garments in Ps 22:18, the clear intent of which is that the speaker no longer needed his clothing because of death (see also Ps 22:29). More references to the death of the king in the immediately surrounding psalms (Ps 18:4-5) and confidence to overcome it (Ps 23:4, 6) cast further contextual light on our interpretation of Psalm 16. It is clear from the psalms in the immediate context that David knew the Messiah would die.

Returning now to the specific interpretation of the word *šāḥaṯ* in Ps 16:10 in light of the certainties of the Messiah's death in the surrounding psalms, there are strong reasons to interprete *šāḥaṯ* as "decay/corruption." First, this is how the word was understood by the Greek translators of the OT before the time of Christ (*diaphthora*; LXX).

Second, Psalm 16 is identified as a *miḵtām* psalm in the superscription. Though scholars are not sure what this term means, there are only five other *miḵtām* psalms in the Psalter (Pss 56–60). Remarkably, in almost every other *miḵtām* the verb *šḥṯ* appears (the superscription of Pss 57–59), the meaning of which is clearly "destruction" (the root of which is related to the masculine noun, "decay"). Another common theme in the *miḵtām* psalms is death (Ps 56:13; superscription of Ps 59). Several of the *miḵtām* psalms also include references to life (Pss 16:11; 56:13; 58:9). This association with death and life makes "decay" much more suited to Psalm 16 as a *miḵtām* than the Hebrew word "pit."

Third, and finally, Bruce Waltke has offered a persuasive grammatical-syntactical argument in favor of "decay" (masculine noun) rather than "pit" (feminine noun).[27] According to Waltke, because *šāḥaṯ* is an object of the verb "to see," the noun must refer to a nominative of state, "decay," rather than a nominative of place, "pit." "To see" with a nominative of state expresses the idea of "experiencing." For instance, "to see death" in Ps 89:48 means "to experience death." "To see adversity" in Ps 90:15 means to "experience adversity" (see also Jer 5:12; 20:18; 44:17; Lam 3:1). Had the author intended "pit" (i.e., a nominative of place), he would have used a verb of motion: e.g., to descend (Job 21:13), to fall (Pss 7:15-16; 57:6).

Support for Waltke's interpretation comes from the poetic parallelism in which *šaḥaṯ* is found. Psalm 16:9-10 appears in a ABA`B` pattern, where A and A` and B and B` represent parallel ideas:

(A) Therefore my heart is glad and my spirit [soul][28] rejoices	(B) my body [flesh] also rests securely
(A`) For You will not abandon me [my soul] to Sheol;	(B`) You will not allow Your Faithful One to see decay.

David speaks confidently of the soul in A and A`, and confidently of the flesh in B and B`. It makes more sense to speak of the flesh not seeing decay than the flesh not seeing the pit.

Morever, Job 17:14 offers a very clear and unambiguous interpretation of the noun used in Psalm 16:10 (*šḥṯ*) as "decay." It's worth citing this verse in its larger context since its language is so similar to Ps 16:10.

> If I await Sheol as my home, spread out my bed in darkness, and say to corruption (*šḥṯ*): You are my father, and to the maggot: My mother or my sister, where then is my hope? Who can see any hope for me? Will it go down to the gates of Sheol, or will we descend together to the dust? (Job 17:13-16)

The reason one can know with certainty this noun is masculine and comes from the verbal root "destruction" is because Job calls it "my father" (masculine), in contrast to the Hebrew word "maggot," which is feminine and which he calls "my mother or my sister."[29] It is worth noting that Job, like David, also refers to Sheol in the context of the decay of death.

Although there are examples of the feminine noun *šḥṯ* as a reference to "pit" elsewhere in the Psalms (see Pss 7:15; 9:15; 35:7), there are also examples in the psalms of the masculine noun, "decay" (Pss 44:10; 55:24). Thus, the reader must rely on the context to determine its meaning. As noted above, several factors (contextual, categorical [*miḵtām*], syntactical) favor the interpretation "decay" in Ps 16:10.

The king described in Ps 16:10, according to the larger context, is an ideal king who walks blamelessly and has clean hands (Pss 15:2; 24:4), a king who has been viciously assaulted and put to death (Pss 17:9-12; 22:12-18), who loves the Torah more than gold or silver (Ps 19:1), whom David identifies as the Messiah (Pss 18:50; 20:6). Not only is this king blameless (Pss 15:2; 18:23, 25, 32; 19:13), but one who is laid in the grave and does not experience decay. The description of this ideal king leads us to the same conclusion the apostle Peter came to in his first post-Pentecost sermon to the people of Israel: David cannot be speaking about himself!

> Brothers, I can confidently speak to you about the patriarch David: He is both dead and buried, and his tomb is with us to this day. Since he was a prophet, he knew that God had sworn an oath to him to seat one of his descendants on

his throne. Seeing this in advance, he spoke concerning the resurrection of the Messiah:

> He was not left in Hades,
> and His flesh did not experience decay.

God has resurrected this Jesus. We are all witnesses of this. (Acts 2:29-32)

CONCLUSION

This article has argued that the NT's interpretation of Psalm 16:10 as a prophecy of the Messiah's resurrection, though often rejected on the basis of the grammatical-historical interpretation, has much in favor of it. First, this interpretation acknowledges what more and more modern scholars have come to realize over the past 20 to 30 years of Psalm scholarship: The book of Psalms is really a book with a messianic message. Second, the interpretation of the individual psalms must not be done in isolation from their larger literary context. This article has explained how the royal messianic psalms function within Book I (1–41), and most particularly within this particular grouping of psalms (Pss 15–24) that envisions the ascent of the ideal king, the Messianic King, to the eternal presence of God on His holy mountain. Third, the article has described how other psalms within this grouping speak clearly of the death of the Messianic King. Finally, this discussion looked at the word *šḥṯ* in Ps 16:10 and argued in light of the other *mikṯām* psalms that this king is not simply kept from the grave, but is actually raised from the grave and preserved from the decay of death. Given other psalms of David that have been interpreted both figuratively and messianically in Book I (Pss 3–7), one can confidently say, along with Peter, that David's focus in this psalm is not on himself, but rather upon the King who is both his son (Ps 18:50) and also his Lord (Ps 110:1).

---

1. The Septuagint's translation of the verb "set, place" ("keep in mind," HCSB), as "to see in advance" in Ps 16:8 strengthened this interpretation.

2. For a fairly typical modern approach to Psalm 16, see Gerald H. Wilson, *Psalms: From Biblical Text to Contemporary Life*, vol. 1 The NIV Application Commentary (Grand Rapids: Zondervan, 2002), 313. "There is no clear belief in immortality or resurrection expressed here. Although Acts 2:25-31; 13:35-37 quotes this passage and interprets it to explain the resurrection of Jesus, the interpretation assumes that in its original context the psalm held out no hope of resurrection to David or other humans, only for the Davidic Messiah yet to come in Jesus. Thus, most likely the psalmist's immediate hope is for divine intervention to prevent death in his present circumstance."

3. Explanations include hermeneutical error, the use of Second Temple Jewish hermeneutics, *sensus plenior*, the canonical approach, typology, single meaning, and direct prophecy. See Gregory V. Trull, "Views on Peter's Use of Psalm 16:8-11 in Acts 2:25-32," *Bibliotheca Sacra* 161 (2004): 198; Walter C. Kaiser, Jr., "The Promise to David in Psalm 16 and Its Application in Acts 2:25-33 and 13:32-37," *Journal of the Evangelical Theological Society* 23 (1980).
4. Carl R. Holladay, "What David Saw: Messianic Exegesis in Acts 2," *Stone-Campbell Journal* 19, no. 1 (2016): 95–96.
5. Form criticism looks at psalms individually and groups them according to structure and genre, rejecting the canonical order and the superscriptions as significant to the meaning. Psalm 16 is identified as a psalm of confidence or thanksgiving and interpreted in light of other Thanksgiving psalms rather than its canonical or literary context.
6. Peter C. Craigie, *Psalms 1–50*, Word Biblical Commentary (Waco, TX: Word Books, 1983), 155.
7. See the article by Seth D. Postell, "The Messianic Message of the Book of Psalms" in this book.
8. Gianni Barbiero, *Das Erste Psalmenbuch Als Einheit: Eine Synchrone Analyse Von Psalm 1–41*, Österreichische Biblische Studien (Frankfurt am Main, Germany: P. Lang, 1999); Brevard S. Childs, *Introduction to the Old Testament as Scripture* (Philadelphia: Fortress Press, 1982); David C. Mitchell, *The Message of the Psalter: An Eschatological Programme in the Books of Psalms*, Journal for the Study of the Old Testament Supplement Series 252 (Sheffield, England: Sheffield Academic Press, 1997); Gerald Henry Wilson, *The Editing of the Hebrew Psalter*, Society of Biblical Literature Dissertation Series (Chico, CA: Scholars Press, 1985).
9. Barbiero, *Das Erste Psalmenbuch*.
10. Ibid., 721.
11. Ibid., 719.
12. Psalms 1–2 serve as the literary introduction to the Psalter, and Pss 3–7 function as the introduction to Book I (Pss 3–41).
13. The importance of the reference to Absalom will be demonstrated below.
14. Pierre Auffret, *La Sagesse a Bâti Sa Maison: Études De Structures Littéraires Dans l'Ancien Testament et Spécialement Dans Les Psaumes* (Fribourg, Suisse Göttingen: Editions Universitaires; Vandenhoeck & Ruprecht, 1982); William P. Brown, "'Here Comes the Sun!': The Metaphorical Theology of Psalms 15–24," in *Composition of the Book of Psalms* (Leuven, Belgium: Peeters (2010) 259–78; *Psalms: Interpreting Biblical Texts* (Nashville: Abingdon Press, 2010); A. Groenewald, "Ethics of the Psalms: Psalm 16 within the Context of Psalms 15–24," *Journal for Semitics* 18, no. 2 (2009); Patrick D. Miller, "Kingship, Torah Obedience, and Prayer: The Theology of Psalms 15–24," in *Neue Wege Der Psalmenforschung: Festschrift Für Walter Beyerlin*, eds. Klaus Seybold and Erich Zenger (Wien, Austria: Herder, 1994), 127–42; Philip Sumpter, "The Coherence of Psalms 15–24," *Biblica* 94, no. 2 (2013).
15. Robert L. Cole, "An Integrated Reading of Psalms 1 and 2," *Journal for the Study of the Old Testament* 26, no. 4 (2002): 75–88; *Psalms 1-2: Gateway to the Psalter*, Hebrew Bible Monographs (Sheffield, England: Sheffield Phoenix Press, 2012); Michael K. Snearly, *The Return of the King: Messianic Expectation in Book V of the Psalter*, The Library of Hebrew Bible/Old Testament Studies (London; New York: Bloomsbury T&T Clark, 2016).
16. Robert L. Cole, "Psalm 3: Of Whom Does David Speak, of Himself or Another?" in *Text and Canon: Essays in Honor of John H. Sailhamer*, ed. Robert L. Cole and Paul J. Kissling (Eugene, OR: Pickwick, 2017), 137–48.
17. Early on, Jewish commentators noticed the stark contrast between the ruling Messiah in Psalm 2 and the rebellion against David in the immediately ensuing psalms (see Sa'adya HaGaon; *b. Berakhoth* 10a). Robert Cole, "Psalm 3," argues the linking of the Absalomic rebellion with the rebellion against the Messiah in Ps 2 strategically identifies David's sufferings with those of the Messiah in Ps 2. In other words, by placing this opening cluster of psalms (Pss 3–7) immediately after the messianic introduction to the Psalter, the author intends us to hear the words of David as the words of the Messianic King. These observations have profound impact on our reading of the other Davidic psalms of lament.
18. Sumpter, "Coherence of Psalms 15–24," 186.
19. The phrase "my cup" only appears these two times in the entire Hebrew Bible.
20. The phrase translated "closed in on me" in the HCSB (*hiqqipû*) in Ps 22:16 is identical in Hebrew to Ps 17:9 (*yaqqipû*).
21. The verb "maul" (Ps 22:13) and "tear" (Ps 17:12) is the same in Hebrew: *ṭrp*.
22. Though the wording of these verses is different, conceptually and thematically both verses function as expressions of confidence in the midst of deadly persecution by the king's enemies.
23. The first stanza begins with an imperative: *šāmreni* ("protect me").
24. The second stanza begins with a qatal-first-clause (*'āmartᵉ*: "I said to the LORD") and ends with a yiqtol-first-clause (*'ᵃḇāreḵ*: "I will praise the LORD).

25. The third stanza begins with a qatal-first-clause (*šiwwiṯi*: "I keep the Lord") and ends with a yiqtol-first-clause (*tôḏi'eni*: "you reveal . . . to me").

26. Cole, "Psalm 3: Of Whom Does David Speak, of Himself or Another?" 145–46; John H. Sailhamer, *NIV Compact Commentary*, NIV Compact Series (Grand Rapids: Zondervan, 1994), 318.

27. Bruce K. Waltke, J. M. Houston, and Erika Moore, *The Psalms as Christian Worship: A Historical Commentary* (Grand Rapids: Eerdmans, 2010), 324, n. 76.

28. Though Waltke, *Psalms as Christian Worship*, 323, and the LXX translate *kḇḏy* as "my liver," there is no other place in the Hebrew Bible where "heart" and "liver" are used in poetic parallelism. "Heart" and "soul" (*kḇḏ*) do appear, however, in poetic parallelism (Gn 49:6; Ps 108:2).

29. Gregory V. Trull, "An Exegesis of Psalm 16:10," *Bibliotheca Sacra* 161, no. 643 (2004): 318; P. A. Vaccari, "Antica E Nuova Interpretazione Del Salmo 16 (Volg. 15)," *Biblica* 14, no. 4 (1933): 418–19.

Psalm 22

The Suffering of the Messianic King

ROBERT L. COLE

The opening words of Ps 22 are familiar to readers of the New Testament Gospels. Both Mt 27:46 and Mk 15:34 quote Christ's words, taken from Ps 22:2,[1] while in His death throes on the cross. Both writers considered Christ's sufferings as well as His glorification to have been predicted directly in the book of Psalms.[2] Although overlooked by most contemporary commentators across the board, the position of Ps 22 in the Psalter is essential to interpretation, and it supports the view of the NT gospel writers. The immediately previous psalms, as well as the entire preceding sequence from the book's introduction (Pss 1–2) onward, support a messianic reading.

The NT interpretation and reading strategy for Ps 22, and the Psalms in general, is at odds with many commentators today, including evangelicals. The latter often confess belief in the inspiration and inerrancy of the Gospels (as well as the rest of the Scriptures), while at the same time casting doubt on their method of interpreting the OT. Somehow the NT writers read the OT Psalms using a flawed hermeneutic, but surprisingly achieved a flawless and inerrant message.

The reason for this patently contradictory stance resides in the uncritical acceptance of form-critical categories in one shape or another in Psalms interpretation. For example, Ps 22 is identified by one as an "individual lament," then states that "it is tempting to treat this psalm as messianic, predicting our Lord's suffering," based on its use by the Gospels, and that Calvin, "treats this psalm first in its original context with David as the sufferer and then applies the psalm to our

Lord."[3] That Calvin felt similar angst as this commentator simply proves that the problem precedes the rise of form criticism.[4]

The reformers, all those previous and all since, are heirs to interpretive traditions that need to be tested and refined in the light of textual evidence. Psalm 22 is messianic, not simply because Mark and Matthew understood it as such, but because that was the clear intent of the Psalter's author and composer. In fact, when the literary context of the Psalter is examined carefully, the views of Matthew and Mark make perfect sense. The angst is a result of adopting a hermeneutical stance at odds with that of the Psalter's composer.

Examples of presumably conservative commentators who are caught in this dilemma are many. For example, another states that reading these words, "*only* as words about Jesus, we ignore the original and continuous word of God to *us* this psalm represents."[5] Another insists that we must "try to hear it within its earlier OT contexts."[6] Similarly, "[I]n its OT context, it represents an individual lament psalm and portrays the suffering of an individual waiting for God's deliverance."[7] Likewise, another reads Ps 22 as "the lament of a suffering believer," but that as "Christians we may go beyond the psalmists' immediate sense."[8]

Common to all such readings is the disregard of the psalm's literary and linguistic context, in line with the basic assumption of the form critical method.[9] The immediately previous psalms such as Pss 20–21 are apparently considered irrelevant for the understanding of Ps 22, despite the numerous and explicit linguistic ties between them. A chaotic and fortuitous arrangement of the Psalter is assumed *a priori*, and no alternative possibility is given proper consideration.

The context in the book is replaced by a context of the interpreter's own making and imagination. The *Sitz im Text* ("setting of the text") is replaced by the *Sitz im Leben* ("setting in life"). However, the latter is only limited by the interpreter's imagination, the former by the literary and linguistic context. Any such "hearings" or "contexts" are simply contrived speculation apart from the context and meaning given to a psalm by the book's composer.

The only way to understand its "original" and "authorial" meaning is by consideration of its literary context in the book of Psalms, which is by no means fortuitous or happenstance. Rather, the sequence and order of the Psalms reveal a planned strategy and meaning for individual psalms as well as the entire book.[10] Evidence for this exists at the linguistic and thematic levels from psalm to psalm, groups of psalms, the five books of the Psalter, the superscriptions, and the shape of the whole.[11]

Superscriptions are present in almost every case throughout Book I, and so with Ps 22.[12] From Pss 19 through 21 the identical term is repeated, which could be translated "for/of the leader, a psalm of David." The first term *lamnaṣṣêaḥ* (Piel ptc), is common in the Psalter titles, but its meaning is difficult to pinpoint, as in many cases of vocabulary in the titles. It is used as an infinitive (Piel) in Chronicles for the direction of temple service appointed by David (1Chr 23:4). Temple service included gatekeepers, officers and singers.[13] The plural of the same participle is also found in the context of temple service in 2Chr 2:2,18 and 23:13.[14] The term in Psalms is associated specifically with the service of music, as the accompanying term "song/psalm" illustrates.[15] Music performed by the Levitical figures appointed by David is specifically defined as the practice of *prophesying* under the direction of the king (1Chr 25:1,2,5). David's words themselves are portrayed as prophetic in the Psalter,[16] and defined as so explicitly in David's last words (2Sm 23:1-3).[17]

The term occurs only in the verses cited from 2 Chronicles and the Psalm headings. Common to both contexts are the topics of David, Levitical figures, prophecy, and music. The Levitical musical service under David's direction, whether composed by him or the priestly figures themselves, was considered prophecy. The implication is that Ps 22 is to be considered likewise as a prophetic utterance of David used by the priestly singers. David the king is therefore portrayed deliberately as a priestly figure. His prophetic portrayal as priest and king has been exhibited at the very beginning in the first two psalms.[18] The title of Ps 22 likewise gives him priestly trappings by his association with singing "a psalm/song of David" and a "choir director." It is also significant that the final strophe of Ps 22 (vv. 22-31) portrays the formerly persecuted and deceased speaker of the first two strophes as now praising God within a great congregation of the faithful. The final verses (27-31) locate this congregational praise in the mouth of resurrected ones and future generations from all nations (vv. 27-31).

The two elements at the beginning and end of Ps 22's superscription[19] function likewise as a link to the psalms before and after. This practice can be seen in other psalm sequences.[20] For example, the lengthy superscription of Ps 88 matches the previous Ps 87 in its first third, and the following Ps 89 in its final words. The intervening third matches the content of the psalm itself. The situation in Pss 19–23 is similar although not identical. Nonetheless, the binding function of the superscription content is explicit and functions as another signal to read them continuously. Psalm 22 opens with the phrase "for the choir director," and ends with "a Davidic psalm." These two phrases at either end of the lengthy superscription of Ps 22 match exactly the content of the titles of Pss 19–21. Psalm 23's brief title matches exactly the final two words of the previous four. The central phrase of Ps 22's superscription, "according to 'The Deer of the Dawn,'" is difficult to comprehend in light of the content of the psalm itself.[21] It is clear however that the beginning and end of this Hebrew title create linguistic linkage to the previous and following psalms.

Psalm 22 can be divided into three distinct sections. The first two narrate in detail the suffering and eventual demise of the speaker (vv. 1-11,12-21), while the third (vv. 22-31) expresses thankfulness and praise for his deliverance. Psalm 23 will solve the apparent contradiction between the actual death of the speaker followed by praise for his deliverance. Psalm 23 is in fact a description of king Messiah dwelling in paradise after being resurrected from the death of Ps 22.[22]

The opening cries of desperation in Ps 22 can be explained logically by viewing what precedes in Pss 19–21, just as the superscription implies. Psalms 18 and 19 are connected by various terms including "servant of the Lord/your servant" (18:1—the superscription, 19:12,14).[23] The love of God's Torah as expressed in Ps 19:7-14 recalls deliberately the man of Ps 1 at the introduction.[24] David, in Pss 18 and 19, is again the mouthpiece of the future anointed king portrayed in the introduction.[25]

The opening "why?" of Ps 22 is a response to the unfulfilled promise of salvation for the king in the previous two psalms. In similar fashion the opening "why?" of Pss 2 and 10 is directed to the promise found in the previous Pss 1 and 9 respectively. At the opening of Ps 2 the nations are in full rebellion against God and His Anointed One, the messianic king, a situation which seems to contradict the promise of their destruction in the immediately previous Ps 1:5-6.

Psalm 10 asks why the Lord stands afar in times of trouble. The phrase "times of trouble" takes up the identical phrase found in Ps 9:9b, in which the Lord is affirmed as a stronghold in such a predicament. For good reason the speaker asks why He hides Himself in the trouble described by the ensuing verses of Ps 10.[26] Psalm 10:1 also uses the term "distant," which is the identical adverb used in the opening question of Ps 22:1. As a result, there exists a close similarity between the opening questions of both Pss 10 and 22:

Ps 10:1 "why . . . so far away?"
Ps 22:1 "why . . . so far . . .?"

Psalm 22 opens with another complaint about God's abandonment of the speaker and his distance or separation from "my salvation." Immediately previous in Ps 21 the king (vv. 1,5) had rejoiced in "your salvation" (NASB; "victory," HCSB). The logical conclusion of this juxtaposition of psalms is that the king of Ps 21 is now complaining directly to God over the absence of the promised "salvation" in Ps 22.

Psalm 20 also assured that God would "save" His anointed messianic king (v. 6a), answering him and "saving" him (v. 6b) with His right hand. Finally, the psalm ends with God "saving" *the king*. There can be no doubt that salvation of the messianic king is the principle topic of the two previous psalms. It is a necessary salvation because of the affliction ("trouble," HCSB) mentioned at the opening v. 1 of Ps

20. It is from within that affliction or persecution as defined in its context, that the king cries out in Ps 22:11.

His opening cry to God notes that the salvation of the previous two psalms is "far" from him. Repeated references to that distance expressed by the same root term dominate Ps 22 and reveals its structure. "Far" in v. 1 and its verbal form in v. 11 mark the beginning and end of the first strophe. The second strophe stretches from vv. 12 to 21, and its reference to distance and help (v. 19) repeats the same two concepts through identical Hebrew roots at the end of the first strophe (v. 11).[27]

I. The King Complains of Divine Abandonment (vv. 1-11)
II. The King is Surrounded by Enemies (vv. 12-21)
III. The King Joins Universal and Eternal Worship (vv. 22-31)

The complaint over God's distance from the king which dominates Ps 22 provides a striking contrast to the central and dominating concept of Ps 23. At the very mathematical center of Ps 23 is the phrase, "for you are with me." It is simply inconceivable that such a contrast between two neighboring psalms is fortuitous. Psalm 23 represents the answer in full to the complaint of abandonment to torture and death in Ps 22, as will be seen.

Strophe I is dominated by the Hebrew root "trust." A triple reference to the fathers' trust in God in vv. 4-5 is followed by the king's own expressed trust in v. 9. They were rewarded for their reliance on God, and so the king expects the same. His expression of trust in this first strophe of Ps 22:9 resonates with the term of identical root in Ps 21:7. There his "trust" in God was the reason for the eternal blessings (v. 6), and the glorious salvation including eternal life promised him (vv. 4-5). For good reason, he now asks why God has forsaken him in the opening words of Ps 22.

The fathers' trust in God resulted in their not "being ashamed" (22:5), while the king is "despised" by a people (v. 6). As can be seen, the contrast is highlighted through consonance. The same verb "despise" is found in v. 24, where it turns out that despite the apparent abandonment, the king was not despised by God Himself. This reflects the general pattern of abandonment and suffering in vv. 1-21, followed by restoration in vv. 22-31. The details of how this reversal of fortune came about is not explained at all until the following Ps 23.

Similar contrast through consonance is expressed between two nouns in vv. 3 and 6. God is defined as holy and the recipient of Israel's "praises" in v. 3, while the king describes himself as a "worm" in v. 6. His identification as a worm pictures the depths of his humiliation before men and an entire nation (v. 6).

Accompanying the resonant terms "worm" and "praises" are two initial independent pronouns opening the same two verses, 3 and 6: "Yet you" . . . "but I." They also contribute to the strong contrast. The suffering king cries directly to God who is praised by Israel (v. 3), and who delivers them (vv. 4-5), but he himself is despised as a subhuman worm (v. 6). God ignores him and men despise him. Nonetheless, he will eventually join the praises of Israel in vv. 22-26, where the same verbal root *halal,* "praise" reoccurs three times. In one case, "my praise" of v. 25, is simply the singular form of the same noun in the plural in v. 3 (praises). Despite the apparent and temporary abandonment in vv. 1-21, the king will join Israel in that praise. Both vv. 3 and 23 name Israel specifically. His praise in v. 22 is joined by those who fear God, identified as the descendants of Jacob and Israel in v. 23. It will eventually extend to the entire earth and its inhabitants, as well as the dead and those yet unborn (vv. 25-31). The mystery of how he went from one despised and shamed to praising joyfully with his brothers is unexplained and delayed until the next psalm.

His threefold reference to God using the independent pronoun "you" (*'th*) in vv. 3,9,10 reveals the close and intimate relationship between the king and God Himself.[28] Further confirmation of this personal relationship comes from the repetition of "my God" at the opening and near the conclusion of the first strophe (vv. 1,10). The king refers to him as "my God" in the present predicament and then confesses that He has been "my God" since birth. These repeated terms, along with two references to "distance" in vv. 1,11, constitute examples of *inclusio* around the first strophe. In addition, the deliberately contrasted opposites of "distant (salvation)" in v. 1 and "near (affliction)" in v. 11 likewise envelope the entire division.

Repetition of "my God" in v. 1 stresses the close relationship between the king and the Deity, but is also the occasion for highlighting the incongruous silence to his cries. Thus, his cry of "my God" twice is contrasted through the identical consonants, but reversed in order, of "you do not answer . . . nor do I have rest." He has twice addressed the Deity as my God, but the double negative stresses this surprising deafness to his pleas. The initial "my God" of v. 2 followed by the two negatives provides a further example of the sound similarity: "My God . . . you do not . . . I do not." Here the consonance again highlights the puzzling contrast between the close personal relationship with God and yet lack of response from Him.

The denied response of v. 2 ("but You do not answer") is finally resolved in v. 21 ("you answered me" [HCSB, "rescued me"]). Divine silence stretching across 22 verses is finally broken. Between these two verses are strophes I and II describing first His abandonment and then persecution to the point of death. The abandonment expressed in v. 1 ("why have you forsaken me") also resonates consonantally with the final verb of the second strophe; "you answered me." Furthermore, both vv. 1 and 21 include an example of the Hebrew root meaning "salvation." The parallels are such between vv. 1-2 and 19-21 that vv. 1-21 could be considered one integrated strophe instead of two:

I. The King's Abandonment and Persecution (vv. 1-21)
II. The King Joins Universal and Eternal Worship (vv. 22-31)

The messianic king's distress and shame are public and open. His enemies look directly at him, mock him, and wag their heads mockingly (vv. 6-7). Those same foes, now portrayed as dogs and beasts in v. 20, gaze at him as well. Two verbs placed consecutively in v. 17 express their intense scrutiny and observation of him, to the point that they can count his bones (v. 17). He is on open display before all.

Verses 12 and 16 repeat the same verb, they "surround me." The enemies of the king who despised him in the first strophe (vv. 1-11) are now portrayed as wild animals whose mouths are also open in attack mode against him. From verbal opposition in the first strophe, the assault now becomes life-threatening from aggressive or predatory animals such as bulls, lions (mentioned three times, vv. 13,16,[29]21) and dogs (twice, vv. 16,20). Their identification as human evildoers is made explicit in v. 17: "a gang of evildoers" surround him as would attacking dogs.

The repeated verbs "surround me" in vv. 12 and 16 are both accompanied in parallel position by the verbs of very similar meaning. Indeed, the fourfold repetition of references to encirclement places emphasis on the pack mentality of these human enemies depicted as vicious animals. The initial metaphor of "many bulls" of v. 12 recalls the numerous and multiplying enemies seeking to kill the same individual speaking in Ps 3:1. Death was sought, and then finally accomplished by his enemies in Ps 3 as here in Ps 22.

Positioning of these two pairs of verbs at vv. 12 and 16 effectively divides the second strophe into two evenly matched halves, vv. 12-15 and vv. 16-21. Surrounding the entire strophe is the common reference to bovines; the many bulls and bullocks of v. 12, and the wild, horned oxen of v. 21. Between them are two references to dogs and lions (v. 13—lion; v. 16—dogs, v. 20—dog, v. 21—lion). The entire unit is bounded on either end by the reference to dogs, lions, and their mouths (vv. 13,20-21).

Within this same division of vv. 12-21 the king describes the state of his own tortured body in depth. The apparent loss of fluids means his bones are visible through the skin, while his internal organs are in extreme turmoil (v. 14). His strength has dried up completely, and his tongue sticks to the roof of his mouth (v. 15). The king refers again to the external visibility of his bones in v. 17.

He is encompassed by dogs at the outset of v. 16, and these are then identified as evil men in the same verse. Following is a reference apparently to a lion, that if governed by the previous clause expresses a "surrounding" of the hands by this animal ("as a lion [*ka'ariy*] are my hands and my feet"). While that rendering seems doubtful, the alternative "they pierced" *(ka'aru)* requires emendation of the text. However, the latter does have the support of several manuscripts.[30] Whatever the original form, clearly the king's feet and hands are incapacitated by his enemies.

Following references to the anatomy of the suffering monarch include his bones, heart, intestines, strength, tongue, hands and feet, and bones again (vv. 14-17). He then describes the taking and dividing of his garments by those who have surrounded and tortured him. Presumably his clothes are of no use to him, since death is inescapable and imminent. The infliction of physical torture is followed by the disgrace of theft and nakedness.

In v. 19 he cries out again for help since he is now in the very clutches of death. The lion and other beasts have opened "their mouths against" him (v. 13), but now he asks for salvation "from the mouth of the lion" (v. 21). Now he is not only surrounded by powerful bovines (v. 12), but asking for salvation from their "horns" (v. 21). Likewise, he requests deliverance from the power of canines[31] (v. 20), which previously "surrounded" him (v. 16). The repeated references to the mouths of lions and aggressive dogs would appear to anticipate the next Ps 23. Both animals are natural predators of sheep, which they grasp and drag off in their mouths before devouring. Consequently, the sheep metaphor of Ps 23 is a perfect sequel to the same of attacking dogs and lions in Ps 22. The change in prepositions would appear to suggest a sheep presumably slain before being dragged off in the jaws of a predator.

While the dying monarch pleads to God for his life (v. 20, "deliver my life from the sword"), indications are that he indeed finally expired. In fact, v. 15 ends with the complaint to God that "you put me into the dust of death."[32] His clothes are taken, God remains distant (v. 19), and so presumably his life ended. Nonetheless, v. 21 ends with the statement that God answered him. This is followed immediately with his praise and recounting of God's name.[33] At this point the reader is left wondering whether he truly died or somehow was rescued from his tormentors.

The answer to the previous question is given at the end of the psalm. Verse 29 states quite categorically, "but his life he did not keep alive" (author translation). It is the same term for life used in v. 20 in a plea for rescue from the sword. Apparently, he was not spared death, yet nonetheless appeared alive in the immediately following v. 22, praising the name of God. Translations attempt to render it as reflexive, "the one who cannot preserve his life" or "the one who could not keep himself alive."[34] However, within the context of Ps 22 it is the sufferer who from the beginning pleads to God to rescue him from his attackers. They have even stripped him of his clothes, and he has not been able to resist them. It is not a case of keeping himself alive, but rather of God allowing him to expire at their hands.[35]

Furthermore, the immediate masculine singular antecedent of "his life [he did not keep alive]" in v. 29 is the one before whom the dead bow in the previous clause. This language of v. 29 is practically identical to that of the worship before the Lord in vv. 27-28. Following in v. 30 the assertion that a seed "will serve Him," represents another masculine singular objective pronoun with identical referent. The change from turning "to the LORD" in v. 27a to worship "before You" in v. 27b resembles the same attempt to attribute deity to this king. Note how in vv. 23-24 the third person references to the Lord are continued in v. 24, but obviously the referent is the persecuted king. Likewise, the descendants will serve "Him" in v. 30a, whose antecedent is the deceased one of v. 29c. This deceased king will receive the worship of the nations and ends of the earth, as well as all the deceased in general and generations yet unborn (vv. 27-31).

Equation of the messianic king with the deity has already been made in Pss 1–2,[36] and a comparison of his description in Pss 21 and 24 confirm the same. His glory is great (21:5), as are the majesty and splendor attributed to him. As Ps 24:7-10 declares repeatedly, the king of glory is the Lord of hosts Himself (24:10).

Why has the composer of Ps 22 delayed the overt and explicit confirmation of his demise to the conclusion of the psalm? A statement of that sort at v. 21 would possibly seem to have been more appropriate. However, its deferral to the end can be understood in view of what follows. Psalm 23 contains a similar construction using the same noun "(my) life." The traditional rendering along the lines of, "he restores my soul" (HCSB "renews my life") of Ps 23:3 should be understood as a direct response to Ps 22:29 which states literally, "he brought my life back." The delay of an explicit death reference to the end of Ps 22 situates it closely to the answer in Ps 23:3, where the same messianic king is resurrected from the dead. Not only are there matching nouns between Ps 22:29 and 23:3—*nephesh* ("life"; HCSB "soul"), but also analogous verbal patterns of Piel and Polel.[37] Death in Ps 22 is defeated in Ps 23, and likewise the distance of Ps 22 is dissolved in Ps 23.

A closely parallel use of language in Ps 30:3 to Ps 22:29 convincingly confirms that it is the messianic king who was not kept alive. Psalm 30:3 states: "Lord, you brought me up from Sheol, you spared me from among those going down to the pit." There are three verbal parallels between the latter and Ps 22:29:

Ps 30:3 *my soul . . . alive . . . go down*
Ps 22:29 *go down . . . his soul . . . alive*

Immediately following the resurrection reference in Ps 30:3 is another command to make music and praise the Lord (v. 4). This resembles closely the multitudes praising in Ps 22:22-26 after God's response to the king's pleas, which turns out to be resuscitation from the dead.

The gap of information between "you answered me" (HCSB "You have rescued me") in v. 21b and praise in vv. 22ff is somewhat bridged by a wordplay between it and v. 24. There the phrase, which is expressed literally as "the affliction of the afflicted," has close sound resemblance with "you answered me" of v. 21. The common consonants and root of the latter verb also resonate phonetically with the description of abandonment and silence of vv. 1-2, as noted above. Now the sound parallel between vv. 21 and 24 indicates the divine answer did address directly his suffering and affliction as described throughout the psalm.

The final strophe of Ps 22 stretches from v. 22 to 31 and opens with the king's expressed desire[38] to rehearse the praise of God's name. Presumably this desire to extol His name is based on the answer received in the previous v. 21. Details of that answer are not given in v. 21, nor does the third strophe offer such. It emphasizes rather the resulting praise and effect of the divine response to the king's cries.

As noted above, Ps 23 will state more explicitly the details of the divine response. At this point (v. 22) in Ps 22 the reader is taken back to the rejoicing of the king described in first half of Ps 21, because of God's salvation and strength on his behalf. In the first two strophes of Ps 22 the messianic king had questioned why the salvation promised in Ps 21 was so distant. Now he is praising again and presumably enjoying the eternal life granted him in Ps 21:4,6. Psalm 23:6 will confirm that gift by the declaration that "I will dwell in the house of the Lord forever" (NASB). The reference to eternal life in Ps 21:4b is expressed in identical fashion to that of 23:6. Psalm 21:4b adds the expression "forever and ever" to confirm that everlasting life is meant.

While Ps 21 cites the king's words of rejoicing in first-person singular, the praise of Ps 22:22-26 is from within a congregation (vv. 22,25) of those who fear the Lord (vv. 23,25). Reasons for the individual rejoicing of the king in Ps 21 were given in vv. 3 and 6, both of which open with the same Hebrew particle meaning, "because." He rejoices because God has crowned him with eternal blessings (Ps 21:3-6). Now in Ps 22:24 the same particle gives the basis for the corporate praise of the king and his fellow brothers, God-fearers, and seed of Jacob/Israel (vv. 22-23). "Because" God did not despise, spurn, or hide His face from His chosen king's cries, there is now praise from within an enormous congregation (v. 25).

God's answer and deliverance on his behalf results in an explosion of praise among the faithful with worship reaching to "the ends of the earth" (v. 27), a phrase found in Ps 2:8. There it refers to the inheritance given to the Davidic king and Son of God following the assault on his life (2:1-3) and subsequent coronation. Psalm 3 also supplied further detailed information regarding that attack on him that Ps 2 had not mentioned. Likewise, Ps 23 will fill in the gap of information left by the transition between answer (Ps 22:21) and praise (Ps 22:22).

Verse 27 also has resonance and reference to the Abrahamic covenant of Gn 12:2,3 and its reiteration to Jacob in Gn 28:13,14. The identical phrase, "all the families of . . ." in Ps 22:27b is also found in the Genesis passages of promise to the patriarchs. Reference to the nations of Ps 22:28 also repeats a common term found in the repeated patriarchal covenant (Gn 18:18; 22:18; 26:4). Likewise, the seed of Ps 22:23(2x) and 30 is a dominant term in the patriarchal promises (Gn 13:15,16; 17:7,8,10,19; 22:17[2x],18; 26:4[2x]; 28:13,14; 48:4). The twice-repeated "worship" of Ps 22:27-29,30 and reference to "service" to the king of 22:30, likewise dominate the patriarchal covenantal declarations (Gn 25:23; 27:29,40; 37:9,10; 49:8). The twice-repeated use of "assembly/congregation" in Ps 22:22,25 also represents a common term in Genesis patriarchal narratives (Gn 28:3; 35:11; 48:4). These numerous linguistic parallels indicate that this third strophe of Ps 22 sees the deliverance and rescue of the messianic king out of death as fulfillment of the eternal covenant with Abraham, Isaac, Jacob, and Judah. It is through his torment and death and subsequent resurrection that the many nations receive the blessings of Abraham.

The final strophe is bounded at either end by the verb "recount." The king himself recounts the Lord's name and fame in v. 22, but in vv. 30-31 the same "seed" will proclaim this to future generations. The switch to *'Adonay* in v. 30 appears to be deliberate. It is in fact unique in the entire psalm. In Ps 2:4 (and 110:1)[39] it is a clear reference to the divine and yet anthropomorphic king and Son of God.

As a result, vv. 30-31 should be read: "A seed will serve him. It will be recounted of the Lord to a generation to come, and they will tell of his righteousness to a nation to be born, that he acted." The "Lord" here is the one of whom his righteousness will be declared and whom a seed will serve, and yet the one who also suffered death. The righteousness of v. 31 belongs to the same one who walks and is led along the paths of righteousness in the following Ps 23:3. Psalm 24:4 also ascribes righteousness to this one who is also pure of heart and hands. This is of course none other than the suffering king of Ps 22, who is the principal focus of the entire book from its beginning, and of these psalms surrounding Ps 22 as well.

The last clause of the psalm, "that he acted" (author translation), is difficult to understand. Because the verb's subject is third-person-singular masculine, there could be two possible referents. Either God acted by being faithful to His covenant with David, as the same verb in Ps 18:50 supports, or His suffering king went through the torment of death, and so did as righteousness demanded. The latter would be a summary of the faithfulness of this king throughout the psalm itself. If

God is the subject, then it refers to the fact that He finally answered the pleas of the king (22:19-21) and so was faithful to the Davidic covenant.

Psalm 22 is a psalm describing the suffering, torment, and finally death of the messianic king who has been the book's focus since Pss 1–2. The description of his cruel torment and torture is graphic and certainly was never true of David. Neither did David's suffering of whatever type ever bring about the worldwide worship and praise depicted in the final strophe of the psalm. David's words here are prophetic of a future royal descendant according to the covenant made with him. His suffering and death in Ps 22 are followed by glorious resurrection into the paradise of God in Ps 23. This is a theme and topic repeated in psalms before Ps 22 and following as well. His joy and universal worship described in vv. 22-31 following the suffering and death of vv. 1-21 demonstrate that his suffering would have worldwide and universal effect and influence. The interpretation of Psalms and the rest of the Scriptures by Christ in Lk 24:25-27 and 44-47 is borne out by the Hebrew text of Ps 22 in its context. He did indeed have to suffer these things and "enter into His glory" as the Scriptures, including the Psalms, prophesied.

---

1. Versification here according to the Hebrew Masoretic text, in which the lengthy superscription of Ps 22 constitutes v. 1, and the opening words cited by the gospel writers v. 2.
2. Contra Darrell L. Bock, "Single Meaning, Multiple Contexts, and Referents" in *Three Views on the New Testament Use of the Old Testament*, ed. Stanley N. Gundry et al. (Grand Rapids: Zondervan, 2008), 120, who identifies Ps 22 as a "righteous-sufferer" and "regal" psalm. Indeed, both ascriptions are accurate in a very limited sense, but derive ultimately from a form-critical perspective. Consequently, the specific and deliberately given literary context of Ps 22 has been ignored. On the other hand, the *specifically* identified persecuted, righteous, and royal figure present since the book's introduction is in fact the "single meaning" of this psalm.
3. Willem VanGemeren, *Psalms*, The Expositor's Bible Commentary vol. 5 (Grand Rapids: Zondervan, 1991), 198.
4. See John Sailhamer, *Introduction to Old Testament Theology* (Grand Rapids: Zondervan, 1995), 134–41.
5. Gerald H. Wilson, *Psalms*, The NIV Application Commentary (Grand Rapids: Zondervan, 2002), 413, emphasis his.
6. Craig C. Broyles, *Psalms*, New International Biblical Commentary (Peabody, MA: Hendrickson, 1999), 115.
7. John D. Barry, et al., eds., *Faithful Study Bible* (Bellingham, WA: Lexham Press, 2012, 2016). One would think that the "OT context" would include the literary context within the Psalter itself.
8. Allen P. Ross, "The 'Thou' Sections of Laments," in *The Psalms: Language for All Seasons of the Soul*, ed. Andrew J. Schmutzer and David M. Howard, Jr. (Chicago: Moody Publishers, 2013), 140–41.
9. Hermann Gunkel, founder of the method known as form criticism stated baldly that there were no internal relationships between neighboring psalms and that their context must be disregarded: *An Introduction to the Psalms*, trans. James D. Nogalski (Macon, GA: Mercer University Press, 1998), 2–3.
10. Proof of this fact can be seen in the numerous examples of *dislegomena* (twice-only found terms or phrases) found throughout the Psalter.
11. See my book *The Shape and Message of Book III (Psalms 73–89)*, Journal for Study of the Old Testament Supplement Series 307 (Sheffield: Sheffield Academic Press, 2000), for how Book III constitutes an integrated whole and coheres sensibly and cohesively with the immediately preceding Ps 72 and immediately following Ps 90. See also, the article in this *Handbook* by Seth Postell on "The Messianic Message of the Psalms."

12. There are two exceptions in Pss 10 and 33, where the lack of superscription may indicate their original unity with the previous Pss 9 and 32.

13. Cf. Ezra 3:8-9 for a similar appointment of leadership over temple building and service.

14. It is certainly not coincidence that the Writings begin and end (Psalms, Chronicles) with the only two books where this term *(menatsach)* is located.

15. From the root that means, to make music.

16. See my comments on Ps 3 in this *Handbook*.

17. "The declaration of David . . . the Spirit of the Lord spoke through me, His word was on my tongue."

18. See my book *Psalms 1-2: Gateway to the Psalter* (Sheffield: Sheffield Phoenix, 2013).

19. "Superscription" is used to differentiate the title present in the Hebrew text as opposed to "titles" given by modern editors in modern translations.

20. The use of superscriptional content to create linkage or the opposite, division or pause in the sequence, is common and was first pointed out by Gerald H. Wilson in his seminal work, *The Editing of the Hebrew Psalter* (Chico, CA: Scholars Press, 1985). His work dealt mostly with the content of superscriptions at the book seams but pointed to a phenomenon, which appears throughout the composition.

21. Two possibilities are "concerning the deer/hind (female) of the dawn" or "concerning the help of the dawn." There exists consonantal similarity between the term "deer/hind" and "my help" in v. 20, but the relationship is not clear. On the other hand, the same term refers undoubtedly to a deer in Hab 3:19 and is accompanied by the same phrase "for the . . . director," found here in Ps 22's superscription. In the previous Ps 18 the same term "deer" and its sure-footedness is used in a context of victory over enemies. Psalm 21 concludes (vv. 8-13) with victory over the enemy, so perhaps the title of Ps 22 anticipates the victory of its last strophe (vv. 22-31).

22. See comments on Ps 23 in this *Handbook*.

23. The title "servant of the Lord" or its various permutations appears in the consecutive Pss 18 and 19, 35 and 36, 89 and 90, 134, 135 and 136, and 14 times across Ps 119. It is also a title given to Job (1:8; 2:3; 42:7-8), Moses, and Joshua (Jos 1:2,7; 12:6; 24:29), and the servant of Isaiah. The distribution (and limitation) of this term across the canon is highly significant and eschatologically charged. See Frank-Lothar Hossfeld and Erich Zenger, *Die Psalmen I* (Würzburg: Echer Verlag, 1993), 122, who identify the David of Ps 18 as the speaker of Ps 19. Repetition of the terms "servant," "my rock," and "keep" between Pss 18 and 19 are further evidence of their deliberate juxtaposition. See also Gianni Barbiero, *Das erste Psalmenbuch als Einheit* (Frankfurt am Main: Peter Lang, 1999), 241, and Franz Delitzsch, *Psalms*, trans. Francis Bolton (Grand Rapids: Eerdmans, 1982), 279–80.

24. The verb "meditate" in Ps 1:2 and noun "meditation" in Ps 19:14 are from the same Hebrew root.

25. Repeated self-designations as the Lord's servant in Ps 119 indicate the same future king Messiah is speaking of His dedication to God's Torah. Numerous connections exist as well between Pss 118 and 119, indicating continuity of speaker from one to the other.

26. Note that the specific phrase in question appears only in Pss 9:9 and 10:1 in the entire Hebrew Bible. Such a *dislegomenon* refers to a twice-read term, or phrase as in this case, in the Hebrew Bible, just as *hapax legomenon* means "once read." This instance between Pss 9–10 is not fortuitous and is vital for their interpretation.

27. See below for an alternative two-part outline.

28. See my comments on Ps 3 in this *Handbook* regarding the distribution of the masculine singular independent second-person-singular pronoun *('th)* in the opening psalms.

29. The reading is disputed between a reading of "like a lion," "they dug, perforated," or "they tied." See Luis Alonso Schökel and Cecilia Carniti, *Salmos I* (Navarra, España: Editorial Verbo Divino, 2002), 376–77.

30. See the critical apparatus of *Biblica Hebraica Stuttgartensia*. Rydelnik and Vanlaningham support the reading translated "they pierced" as follows: "The culminating statement of this suffering is **they pierced my hands and my feet** (v. 16), representing one of the most specific predictive references to Messiah's crucifixion (paralleled only by Zch 12.10). Yet this is one of the most debated passages in the Bible. The debate centers on the key Hebrew word *ka'aru*, rendered **they pierced**, though in most (but not all) medieval Hebrew manuscripts this word is written *ka'ariy*, meaning 'like a lion.' The first reading, however, is to be preferred for five reasons. First, it is supported by three of the four ancient translations (the Septuagint, the Peshitta, and the Vulgate; the fourth translation, the Targum to Psalms, was translated in the second century AD by non-Christian Jews). Second, even for Hebrew poetry, the phrase 'like a lion' is far too elliptical and makes no sense without a verb—which supporters of this reading are forced to supply (e.g., 'like a lion *they bite* my hands and my feet'). Third, were the symbol of a lion intended, it would have been employed in the plural, not the singular, in order to agree with the plural subject ('evildoers') in the verse (as in Jr 50:17 and Zph 3:3). Fourth, one of the leading medieval Jewish scribal authorities (Jacob ben Chayyim) himself affirms that the older and better manuscripts read *ka'aru* ('they pierced') rather than

ka'ariy ('like a lion'). Fifth, the reading *ka'aru* ('they pierced') is attested in earliest the manuscript of this psalm (5/6 HevPs) from the Dead Sea Scrolls, which predates the medieval manuscripts by approximately one thousand years" ("Psalms" in *The Moody Bible Commentary* ed. Michael Rydelnik and Michael G. Vanlaningham (Chicago: Moody Publishers, 2014), 779–80).

31. Probably a collective singular noun in the original Hebrew.

32. Note that "dust" in v. 30 denotes death, although in this case the dead bow down to the king, who also dies in the final clause.

33. The two verbs of praising and speaking of God's name are combined again in Ps 102:21. Presumably they are part and parcel of the same ascription of glory to God.

34. Psalm 22:29 according to the HCSB and ESV, respectively.

35. The example of Ezk 18:27 is different in that the reflexive is indicated explicitly by the pleonastic independent third-person-singular pronoun, "he himself."

36. Cole, *Gateway*, 99–102.

37. Cf. Ezk 38:4, "I will return you" (HCSB, "I will turn you around"). See also comments on Ps 23 in general in the following article in this *Handbook*. Piel and Polel are two forms of the same factitive pattern of Hebrew verbs.

38. The verbal form is a singular cohortative expressing will and desire toward oneself to carry out this extolling of the divine name.

39. Not following Masoretic punctuation *('adony)* but reading *'Adonay*, as the parallel with Ps 2:4 supports. For a detailed discussion see Cole, *Gateway*, 101–102.

Psalm 23

The Lord Is Messiah's Shepherd

ROBERT L. COLE

The 23rd psalm is probably the most beloved text of the entire Bible in the English-speaking world. It is cited or heard not only as part of hymns, liturgies, and sermons, but also in movie scripts, symphonies, and popular songs.[1] It has become part of the fabric of modern English-speaking culture, and it is not difficult to imagine the reasons for it. Perhaps its mood of hope and faith in the future despite trouble and hardship, expressed succinctly in first-person singular, along with the peaceful pastoral imagery are ingredients that endear it to believers. The intimate care evoked by the metaphor of a shepherd's care for his sheep applied to God and His people is also very appealing to readers in all contexts and situations.

Funerals have become one common context for the reading of Ps 23. It is not known exactly when this practice became popular, but undoubtedly reference to "the valley of the shadow of death" followed by eternal habitation in God's house is presumed appropriate for burial services. As will be seen here, death is present in this psalm as well as eternal life, but not in the broadly applied manner as normally understood.

A CANONICAL APPROACH TO PSALM 23

The assumption that Ps 23 speaks for any individual who wishes to appropriate it to himself is widespread and practically universal. The dominant form-critical method in psalms interpretation has perpetuated this generalized individual reading.[2] Gunkel, the author of the approach, insists that genre research is nonnegotiable and then struggles to identify that of Ps 23, noting that it "deviates considerably more from the genre," the supposed "individual complaint song."[3]

However, while form criticism is incapable of explaining the content of Ps 23, a canonical approach has cogent solutions based on the immediate and larger context of the Psalter. The problem for Gunkel is that Ps 23 "incorporates a confidence motif from the beginning."[4] From a canonical perspective that confidence expressed throughout the psalm serves as a deliberate response to the opposite mood expressed in the previous Ps 22. Canonical order and arrangement explains the content of Ps 23, while form criticism is simply powerless to do so by its very nature.

Modern "genre" categories are contrived and work explicitly at cross purposes with the program evident in the Psalter's composition. What could be more explicit than the juxtaposition of a psalm in which abandonment by God is the dominant motif and another in which the central declaration is the confidence in His presence? Such a stark contrast between lonely abandonment and confident presence is not simply fortuitous, and is further supported by calculated and strategic placement of key terms and expressions in both psalms.

Not all commentators have disregarded the suggestive association between Pss 22 and 23. One fifth-century AD commentator, Arnobius, declared that Ps 22 describes the tribulation of the passion and Ps 23 the joy of the resurrection.[5] He correctly discerned the role of Ps 23 in reversing the death of Ps 22. More recently, at the end of the 19th century, Forbes examined the book's arrangement with the stated purpose of showing that "the Psalter as a whole, is shown to have been arranged by the final editor . . . with great minuteness and delicacy of finish and with one grand purpose dominating all."[6] In the case of Ps 23 he finds, "comforting assurance to the believer . . . persecuted like his Lord," whose persecution is described in the preceding trilogy of Pss 20–22.[7] Delitzsch, who links the psalms together in a more limited fashion, viewed the sequence of Pss 22 and 23 as a case where a psalm speaking of a "great feast for mankind" (Ps 22) was followed by a psalm where "Jahve is Shepherd and Host of his people" (Ps 23).[8]

Following the appearance of Gunkel's dominating work in the 20th century, there are still sporadic examples of scholars observing cohesiveness between psalms despite the dominance of form criticism. Eaton explained Ps 23 as "a perfect sequel to Ps 22, for there also the Representative who has passed through the shadow of death eats of God's table."[9] More recently Wilson traced connections between Pss 22 and 23, and between Ps 23 and those following up to Ps 30.[10] He deemed the dependence on Yahweh and praise of His name in Ps 23 a fitting response to similar expressions in Pss 22:21-22,26-28,29-30.[11] He also observes that the focus on the dwelling of Yahweh in v. 6 is continued in subsequent psalms up through Ps 30.[12]

Hakham observes the strong contrast created between the two conditions of distance and presence: "This psalm is the opposite in its subject matter to the psalm that is previous to it. Psalm 22 describes the suffering of the man who senses that the Lord is far from him, while Psalm 23 describes the blessing of the man who senses that the Lord is with him."[13] He also recognizes the thoroughgoing use of the singular in Ps 23's composition and observes that not many attain this level of faith.[14] Nonetheless he maintains, in the face of the textual evidence, that it can refer to the faithful community of Israel at large.[15]

Hossfeld and Zenger read the canonical Psalter as a meditative prayer book, but as is common, assume form-critical categories as a given.[16] Hossfeld considers that death is faced in both Pss 22:15 and 23:4, while hope for rescue is present in 22:21 and 23:2.[17] Promised praise of God's name in 22:22 is fulfilled in 23:3, while both 22:26 and 23:5 describe a feast for the poor.[18] Zenger also detects multiple connections between Pss 23 and 16.[19]

Barbiero understands Pss 22–24 to constitute a distinct series that was originally part of a small pilgrimage liturgy, and the relation between 23 and 24 to be one of "complaint" and "trust."[20] Although obviously working within the categories of form criticism, he perceives Ps 23 to be the answer to 22: "Thereby Ps. 23 answers the complaint of 22:1."[21] Psalm 22 speaks of abandonment by God while Ps 23 is characterized by His presence.[22] He also detects continuity between the second half of Ps 22 (vv. 22-31) in the common motifs of "name" (22:22 and 23:3), "pilgrimage" (22:31 and 23:6), and "meal" (22:26,29 and 23:5).[23] The enemies of 23:5 are linked with the same in Ps 22:12-13,16-18, and the common theme of death is present in 23:4 and 22:15,39.[24]

Auwers likewise follows the traditional categories and perceives a structure of lamentation followed by a hymn in the sequence of Ps 22:1-22 and Ps 23, which is comparable to the structure of Ps 22 itself.[25] Grant also takes form-critical categories as a given, but does ask the logical question: "could 'The Lord is my shepherd; I shall not want,' in Ps 23:1 be a response to 'My God, My God, why have You forsaken me?'"[26] McCann sees a possible editorial connection between the house of the Lord in Ps 23:6 and the congregation (in the house of the Lord) of Ps 22:23,25.[27]

These examples are comparatively exceptional in recent times since commentators, by and large, have followed the form-critical approach and treated each psalm atomistically. Typical of this type of analysis is the commentary by Craigie.[28] He notes that it is "particularly difficult to interpret with respect to such matters as its form and original social or cultic setting," and that, "the language of the psalm is not sufficiently explicit to establish beyond dispute its original sense and setting."[29] Despite such an admission, the designation of it as "a psalm of confidence" is made nevertheless.[30] Absent is any comment on its position in the Psalter.

Similarly, VanGemeren notes that the "original setting or situation in life is difficult to determine."[31] He does mention in passing the repetition of the root *dashan* ("anoint") and suggests it "may be a verbal link between these two psalms."[32] However, the observation is isolated and not accompanied by further comments regarding linguistic parallels such as *nephesh* ("life") in Ps 22:29 and 23:3, or *shem* ("name") in Pss 22:22 and 23:3.[33] Nor does he address the larger explicit contrast of abandonment versus presence between the two psalms.

The problem goes beyond commentaries and extends to articles[34] and hermeneutical studies. Hermeneutics is the principal issue behind discussion of the messianic interpretation of the OT, and so it merits further comments before turning to Ps 23 itself.

Grant Osborne states that "the first step in determining the theology of the psalms as a whole as well as of individual psalms is to consider genre."[35] In other words, interpreters are to apply contrived modern genre classifications, i.e., form-critical categories, to any psalm as the primary method of understanding it. Later the form-critical classification is termed "the original sense," while the "canonical/messianic" sense is secondary.[36] In fact, the canonical or literary context of a psalm is the primary context from which to understand its purpose and message, while modern generic designations are anachronistic and subjective at best. In the case of Pss 2–3 the canonical context following Pss 20–22 is overtly messianic, and not simply in a "typological sense," but rather its intended original sense.[37] Osborne mentions Ps 23 but without any consideration of its context in the book.[38]

Remarkably, Osborne otherwise critiques modern literary approaches for the "imposition of modern literary categories upon ancient genres," but then classifies Hebrew poetry according to the types devised by Gunkel at the beginning of the 20th century.[39] The latter are nothing but the same imposition of artificial categories and are contradicted explicitly by the Psalter's composer in his arrangement of the Psalter from the very beginning. Psalms 1 and 2 are integrated lexically, semantically, phonologically, and in their message, yet form critics insist on their separation according to "genre." The Psalms are arranged carefully and coherently, although not according to modern literary conventions and categories, but in a legitimate and ingenious way nonetheless.

In another work on hermeneutics, Silva struggles with Luther's Christological use of Ps 8, which follows its exposition as such in Heb 2:6.[40] He sides with Calvin, who finds it difficult to understand the messianic reading of Ps 8 in the book of Hebrews.[41] He declares that Calvin's difficulty with this interpretation was caused by "his concern with the historical meaning."[42] However, Calvin had accepted uncritically a supposedly "historical" approach designed principally to refute Christological interpretation.[43] The method had its origin centuries before with

Rashi and was known as "peshat," often designated as the "historical" or "literal" meaning. Ultimately it is neither one of the latter two.

An example of this can be found in Rashi's reading of Ps 2. He admits the rabbis read it as a reference to "king messiah," but opts instead to read it as a reference to the historical David and explicitly admits the reason is to refute its Christological interpretation.[44] Here he reveals the underlying motivation in his choice of peshat, which ignores the "literal" universal and eschatological language of the psalm that simply does not apply to David.

The peshat method was adopted later by Nicholas de Lyra and mediated to the reformers through his commentary.[45] It was probably true of Calvin, Luther, and De Lyra, as with modern proponents of the so-called grammatical-historical method of interpretation, that they are unaware of the origins, purpose, and history of the method. Luther was undoubtedly torn between the anti-Christological method mediated to him by De Lyra and the Christological reading by the writer of Hebrews, ultimately choosing the latter. Calvin treated Ps 8 differently, as Silva correctly notes, expressing doubt over its Christological reading in Hebrews.[46] Silva sympathizes with Calvin on the problem of Hebrews' exegesis because, in his own words, "his [Calvin's] concern with the historical meaning (= authorial intent!) of Psalm 8."[47] Silva, and presumably Calvin as well, have accepted uncritically Rashi's peshat (so-called historical/literal) method, and mistakenly equated it with the author's intent.

Calvin's problem with NT interpretation is not unlike that of modern conservative scholars who insist on the "inerrancy" of the Christological message of the NT, but which message is derived through a method of interpretation contrary to the one that Silva states he holds, "unrepentantly."[48] He later designates it as "sensus literalis," which is the nothing more than the Latin equivalent of peshat.[49] However, as already noted, the latter approach is neither grammatical, historical, nor literal in the case of the Psalter (or any other book of the Hebrew Bible). It fails to account for the historical fact of the canonical Psalter's sequential arrangement and integrated composition.[50] Likewise, it fails to perceive the grammar of the Psalter's discourse pointing to a unitary reading of the book. The literal and literary features of the Psalter are ignored and so the composer's or author's intent likewise.

"Authorial intent" is the purpose behind the composer's work of arrangement and editing of the book of Psalms. This can be demonstrated not only by the numerous examples of dislegomena (twice-used only Hebrew terms or entire phrases) between psalms, but also by continuity of topic from one to another. For instance, in the case of Ps 8, there are explicit unique textual links from Ps 7 through Pss 8 and 9 that point to a purposeful "authorial" integration of them all. Such is the case from Ps 1 and following throughout the entire book. These lexical parallels show that the oft-mentioned literary technique of Hebrew parallelism extends beyond the bicolon/tricolon, strophe, or individual psalm, to groups of psalms, and ultimately to the entire book. Once this fundamental characteristic of the Psalter is recognized, the NT's Christological interpretation appears quite cogent. The so-called grammatico-historical method as conceived by most today is clearly not the one practiced by NT writers, but neither is it reflected in the composition of the Hebrew Bible itself. The integrated whole Psalter constitutes the best commentary on its meaning and message, which turns out to be consistent with the NT.

Another recent work on hermeneutics by Köstenberger and Patterson reveals the same conflict in their presumed acceptance of NT exegetical conclusions and "our modern grammatical-historical exegesis."[51] Indeed, it is modern, but hardly grammatical, nor is it genuinely historical. The authors side with the view that Paul, and presumably other NT writers, adopted conventional interpretive methods in the Jewish community of that time, yet not consistent with the so-called grammatico-historical method. They apparently follow the theory espoused by Peter Enns in a work on NT exegesis of the OT, but it is hardly consistent on any account with professions of "inerrancy."[52] Enns has concluded that the apostles adopted a hermeneutic consistent with expectations of the Second Temple period, although in violation of "what is considered to be a fundamental interpretive principle: don't take things out of context."[53] This "incarnational paradigm" was justified because it was consistent with the interpretive norm of the time.[54] For Enns, a "scientific" method requires accounting for their "historical setting," a vague term at best, which in the case of Psalms involves the dubious enterprise called form criticism.[55] Quite clearly these interpreters consider their "grammatico-historical" method as inviolate, even "inerrant," despite its ignoring the grammar of discourse and the historical fact of composition.

Köstenberger/Patterson read Ps 23 following the traditional view as a description of how "the Lord relates to his people."[56] However, in contrast to this reading of a psalm in isolation from its literary and compositional context, they note otherwise that "psalms may be linked together in the canon" and take note of what they call "stitching" from Pss 134 to 136. One wonders why the explicit "stitching" linking Ps 23 and its surrounding context was ignored.

What is ultimately at stake here is the fundamental message and apologetic of the NT, which is that the OT Scriptures prophesied from beginning to end of the Messiah (cf. Luke 24:44). If the apostles practiced interpretation in a manner that violated the intent of the writers of the OT, then the NT in general is mistaken and no amount of argument can resolve the contradiction. However, the good news is that the apostolic hermeneutic is truly consistent with the original intent, method, and context of the OT text, as opposed to the modern widespread "grammatico-historical" method.

The uncritical acceptance of form criticism and its imposition of modern categories of genre against the organization in the canonical Psalter itself, is widespread among both liberal and conservative scholars alike.[57] On form critical grounds, Pss 23 and the previous 22 are considered wholly distinct, but a comparison of their content in the original Hebrew reveals deliberate cohesiveness and cohesion.

THE CONTEXT OF PSALM 23

Not only is the immediate context of Ps 23 following Ps 22 critical for understanding its meaning in the Psalter, the language and content of the previous Pss 20 and 21 provide an essential context for its interpretation as well. Psalm 20 speaks of the salvation of God's Messiah (vv. 5,6), which comes as a response from His holy heavenly abode (v. 6b). Previously that same help was sent from a holy place identified also as Zion (Ps 20:2), proving it is heavenly Zion, just as seen in Pss 2:6 and 3:4. That salvation is described again in Ps 20:9 as accomplished in answer to and on behalf of "the king," when he called to him (*ya'anenu beyom qare'enu*). The latter is an expression that clearly anticipates the call apparently without answer in Ps 22:2 (*'eqra' yomam welo' ta'aneh*).

The compositional identification of the speaker of Ps 22 is unquestionably the king of Ps 20, and of Ps 21 as well. This king can likewise be identified as the divine and divinely chosen monarch and Son of God in Ps 2. Two references to him in Ps 2; "his Anointed One," "My King" (*meshicho*, v. 2; *malki*, v. 6) match the same in Ps 20; "His Anointed," "the king" (*meshicho*, 20:6; *hamelek*, v. 9). The Psalter's composer/author expected his readers to recognize these parallels and thereby understand its continuity of reference and topic.

Psalm 21 continues immediately by describing how the same king rejoices in God's salvation, the same term or root for salvation (*ysh'*) (HCSB "victory") seen in Ps 20:5,6 (2x),9. The same root is found in Ps 21:5 describing the enormous glory in that salvation, which included the attainment of "majesty and splendor" (*hod wehadar*). The latter pair is used exclusively in the Psalter (and in the Hebrew Bible) as attributes of the divine. So this king of Ps 20 is also deity despite the fact He prays to God (21:2-4) and trusts in Him (v. 7). Psalms 1–2 had already made the divine identification of this monarch and Son of God.

For good reason the same king cries out in Ps 22:1 over the distance from him of that same salvation. The identical suffixed feminine noun for salvation (*yashu'ah*) is deliberately repeated in Pss 20:5, 21:1, and 22:1. The sufferings of Ps 22 do not appear there out of nowhere. Psalm 20:1 had already noted that God would answer him in the time of "trouble" (*tsarah*), precisely the term in 22:11 (*tsarah*), and there are references to persecution and suffering since the book's introduction. Such repetition is present because the book repeatedly states the same themes beginning with the introduction and continuing throughout toward its culmination of praise at the end.[58]

The King Messiah of Ps 20 is favored with an answer (the root *'nh*), mentioned twice (vv. 1,6), which in Ps 21:3-6 is described as blessings, a golden crown, and eternal life. Psalm 23:6 will use the identical terminology for eternal life (*le'orek yamim*—as long as I live/*'orek yamim*—length of days; HCSB "all the days of my life") as that of Ps 21:4. There the latter phrase "length of days" is defined immediately as "forever and ever" (*'olm wa'ed*), and then in v. 6 likewise (*la'ad*). It is certainly no coincidence that "length of days" appears only four times in the Psalter, and that two instances are here in Pss 21 and 23.[59] The answer to His petition was eternal life, but the situation from which He was saved eternally is expounded in the following Ps 22. He was rescued from the death made explicit in Ps 22:15,29, to the eternal life of Ps 23:6.[60]

The suffering of Ps 22 takes the reader back to that described variously in previous psalms beginning with Ps 2, where God's Messianic King suffers an attack on His life. Immediately preceding Ps 22 in 21:8-12 is a description of the destruction of His enemies, undoubtedly part and parcel of the salvation and elevation granted Him in 21:1-6. Psalm 22 is perhaps the most extensive description of that ordeal in the Psalter.

As noted above, Ps 22 opens with the glorious salvation of Ps 21 being far from this King. It is dominated by the Hebrew root meaning "far from/distant" (*rchq*) in vv. 1,11,19. Likewise the second-person masculine independent personal pronoun "you" (*'atah*) is repeated in vv. 3,9,10,19. In addition, the psalm opens with the King invoking God as "my God" twice, indicating a close relationship consistent with the use of the pronoun. The same pronoun was repeated in each of Pss 2–6 and reflects the ongoing soliloquy between the King and God His Father, while enduring suffering and death. The fourfold repetition of the identical pronoun reveals further information regarding that relationship and conversation within that ordeal.

THE CONTENT OF PSALM 23

Psalm 23 makes a declaration in its central clause that is a direct response to the repeated complaint of Ps 22. The speaker declares with confidence, "you are with me," using the same second-person masculine singular personal pronoun "you" (*'atah*) repeated in the cries of Ps 22:3,9-10,19 over his abandonment by God. The contrast in his circumstances between the two psalms could not be more explicit.

Surrounding this pronoun "you" at either end of the psalm are the only two instances of the divine name YHWH:

YHWH – v. 1
"for You (*'atah*) are with me" – v. 4b
YHWH – v. 6

The effect of this literary inclusio (enveloping around the entire psalm at either end) is to enclose the speaker about with God's presence, in explicit contrast to the abandonment of Ps 22.

Verse 2 locates the speaker in flourishing pastures (*deshe'*), a description that parallels the paradise of Gn 1, where the noun form is found twice (Gn 1:11-12), and once as a verb (Gn 1:11). Another close verbal parallel to this description in Ps 23:2 is Jl 2:22, where the root is found again in verbal form (*dashe'u*) governing an object "pastures" (*ne'ot*) identical to the pastures of Ps 23:

(b)ne'ot deshe' "(in) flourishing pastures" – Ps 23:2
dashe'u ne'ot "pastures (of the desert) flourish" – Jl 2:22

The context of Joel 2:22 portrays a restored eschatological land of Israel and Zion, flourishing with vines, fig trees, grain, new wine, oil, abundant rain, and God's presence (vv. 18-27). Likewise, the same term *deshe'* describes the eschatological Jerusalem in Isa 66:14, while the pastoral paradise of Ezk 34:14-15 repeats five terms across Ps 23. Consequently, the formerly suffering Messianic King now states at the outset of Ps 23 that He dwells in the restored eschatological paradise of Gn 1.

The central affirmation of presence ("for you are with me") effectively divides the psalm into two equal halves. Before and after are exactly 26 words, and the two halves are also bounded on either end by parallel expressions of confidence and security. In vv. 1 and 4 are found two expressions of trust that resonate phonologically as well:

ro'i lo' 'echsar "(the Lord is) my shepherd I do not have need" – v. 1
lo' 'ira' ra' "I do not fear evil" – v. 4 (author's translations)

The terms "evil" and "my shepherd" exhibit the same consonantal sequence of *resh—'ayin*. Two verbs of the yiqtol type (first-person common singulars) preceded by the negative particle contribute to the explicit contrast. It is probably not coincidence that these two clauses envelop the entire first half of the psalm ending immediately before the central affirmation of v. 4. This literary technique is known as inclusio.

Likewise, the second half of the psalm is bounded by two terms, the first of which comes immediately after the three-word middle statement of trust. Both words are parallel in sound, and likewise express confidence and security:

shivteka "your rod" – v. 4
weshivti "my dwelling" – v. 6[61]

The beginning two consonants in each case are identical, while the third (*tet* and *tav*) are of similar articulation. This evidence demonstrates that Ps 23 has been carefully and elegantly crafted by a skilled poet. Its message of presence and confidence at its heart is surrounded literally and literarily by further expressions of the same.

The suffering and apparently abandoned king in Ps 22 had repeated the second-person masculine singular pronoun "you" (*'atah*) four times in addressing God while identifying himself only once with the first-person subjective independent pronoun "I" (*'anoki*). At the same time, the use of the first-person objective pronoun "me" (*-ni*) is ubiquitous throughout the first two-thirds of Ps 22, where his suffering is detailed (vv. 1,12,15,16 [2x],21 [2x]). Similarly, the dominant middle clause of Ps 23, expressing confidence in God's presence, uses the masculine singular subjective independent pronoun *'atah* ("you"). It is however, surrounded by five examples of the objective pronoun *-ni* ("me"–three before in vv. 1-4, two after in vv. 4,6). In Ps 22 all the subjective forms except for the final one of v. 22 complained of his persecution by enemies, but the same forms in Ps 23 by contrast, express the opposite, the guidance and comfort afforded to him by God: v. 2 "He lets me lie down," v. 3 "He leads me" (2x), v. 4 His rod and staff "comfort me," "(goodness and faithful love) will pursue me." He is hounded by wild animals in Ps 22, but by contrast is led as a sheep to lie down securely, and to restful waters in Ps 23. Furthermore, he is pursued in Ps 23 by goodness and faithfulness, not the beasts of Ps 22.

Psalm 23 describes the paradise of God's presence at either end but between them are references to the death and implied resurrection depicted in Ps 22. The statement of Ps 23:3, "he made my life return" (*naphshi yeshovev*) (HCSB "renews my life"), refers to a literal resurrection from the death affirmed in Ps 22:29.[62] His death was affirmed in Ps 22:29 using the same term for life or soul, *nephesh*, as that of Ps 23:3. Furthermore, the verb "makes return" is of the same verbal pattern and voice as (lit.) "makes alive" in 22:29.[63] The same verb "make return" (*shovev*) and noun "pastures" (*nevehu*; HCSB "grazing land") appears in the eschatological context of Jer 50:19. In the latter the nation is returned to its land, and in the present case his life is returned.

As a direct response to the death of the Messiah in Ps 22:29 the subsequent Ps 23 states that his soul was made to return. Psalm 22 had him praising in v. 22-23 after the persecution and death of vv. 1-21, which left unexplained how this could have happened. Psalm 22:29 had confirmed his death after the initial declaration in v. 15, and so his appearance within a great international congregation of worshipers in vv. 22-28 required further information, which Ps 23 supplies.

A wordplay is also present between the verb of Ps 23:3—*yeshovev* (lit., "he made return") and the twice-repeated encircling of the suffering king in Ps 22:12,16 by his attackers—*sevavuni* (lit., "they surrounded me"). The use of the verb form *yeshovev* in Ps 23:3 is deliberate and expresses what another form of the same verbal root (Hiphil: *heshiv*) could not since it does not repeat the Hebrew consonant bet. The latter Hiphil form simply describes restoration from a situation of hopelessness while still living, not resurrection from death itself (Ru 4:15). Consonantal resonance between these two verbs *svv* and *shvv* supports the semantic contrast between the speaker being encircled by attacking animals (Ps 22) and being rescued out of death itself (Ps 23).

His experience of dying is also described in v. 4 by the expression "death's shadow" (*tsalmawet*, author's translation). The same term appears in Job 10:21 in an explicit reference to death in a context where he wishes to have expired before birth (vv. 18-22).[64] Likewise Job 38:17 puts in precisely parallel lines "the gates of death" (*mawet*) and "the gates of death's shadow" (*tsalmawet*), and so identifies the latter as death itself.

The use of the unique phrase "through the darkest valley" in Ps 23:4 may have to do with the punning of consonants between it and the phrase "in paths of righteousness" [HCSB footnote] *bm'gly tsdq/bgy' tslmwt* of v. 3. Consonance, a common literary phenomenon in the Hebrew Bible, contributes further nuance to the suffering of death that he endured. His journey through death of v. 4 was part of the righteous path ordained for him. This righteousness (*tsedeq*) is the same seen in Ps 22:31 (*tsideqato*), which will be proclaimed to coming nations and generations. In other words, the passage through death and resurrection will be recounted to many peoples throughout the future.

The term "rest" in 23:2 (*menuchot*; HCSB "quiet") describing the waters, likewise indicate a sanctuarial and royal setting in the eschatological future. Psalm 132:13-14 identifies "My resting place" (*menuchati*) as eternal Zion, God's resting place (cf. v. 8, *menuchatecha*), all within the context of a description of the Davidic covenant (132:11,17). Zion is further mentioned in the subsequent Ps 133 as the place of eternal life and blessing (v. 3). Psalm 133 contains numerous parallels to Ps 23, including "sitting" (HCSB "live") "good," "head," as well as the reference to eternal life in both. The brothers living together in unity of Ps 133:1 (*shevet*) links the latter with the previous Ps 132:14, where God has desired to "make My home" (*'eshev*). In both cases the eternal dwelling place is Zion (132:13; 133:3), as is the dwelling of the king of Ps 23:6 in the house of the Lord (*shivti bebet yhwh*).

Psalm 132 reaffirms the royal promise to David (v. 17) in Zion, but situates the priests (v. 16) there also. The following Ps 133 also uses priestly language of anointing in reference to Aaron. In Ps 134:1 the house of the Lord is the Zion of v. 3 and previous Pss 132:13; 133:3. Zion is the place of blessing and eternal life, as defined in Ps 133:3. Psalm 23:6 places the king in the house of the Lord (cf. Ps 134:1), or Zion, and thus also in the place of eternal life. Psalm 23's final phrase describing his dwelling with the phrase, "for length of days" (*le'orek yamim*) is likewise a reference to eternal life, as Ps 21:5 proves. There the same phrase "length of days" (*'orek yamim*) [HCSB footnote] is immediately followed by, and defined as, "forever and ever" (*'olam wa'ed*) [HCSB footnote]. Eternal life in Zion or the house of the Lord is mentioned in both Ps 132:14 and Ps 133:3.

Such abundant parallels between Ps 23 and Pss 132–134, as well as the previous Ps 20 make it clear that "the house of the Lord" (Ps 23:6) is eternal or eschatological Zion. Furthermore, the context and language prove the king of Ps 23 is also a priest, as is also true of Pss 132–134, where the "horn" of David (Ps 132:17) sprouts forth in Zion (v. 13) in the midst of priests (v. 16). Consequently, the Davidic priest king of Ps 23 has been raised from the death of Ps 22 to dwell forever in the eternal city of Zion, which is the temple and dwelling of God. The following Ps 24 will describe His worthiness to ascend and enter that holy place as the King of glory. Great glory was ascribed to Him as king previously in Ps 21:5, which designation Ps 24 will repeat four times (vv. 7,8,9,10). There can be no doubt that Ps 23 is a messianic psalm, as are the surrounding ones. He dwells eternally in the "house of the Lord" in Ps 23:6, and is the only one righteously qualified to ascend there in Ps 24:3, where is it called "the mountain of the Lord."

As noted above, the anointing oil on the head of the king of Ps 23:5 is one of several parallels with Ps 133 (cf. "head" *ro'sh*, and "oil" *shemen* in Ps 23:5; 133:2). Psalm 23:5 portrays the king's enemies humiliated before him, the same enemies seen in Pss 21 and 22. In the second half of the same v. 5 he is anointed with oil. Likewise in Ps 45:7 he is anointed with oil (*shemen*) following the destruction of his enemies in vv. 4-6. Furthermore, his anointing in Ps 45:7b is the result of his righteousness in v. 7a. That sequence would also match that of the same king's righteous walk in Ps 23:3 followed by anointing in v. 5.

The immediately following Ps 24 expands on the final verse of Ps 23, which locates the eternal dwelling of the messianic king as the house of the Lord. The latter place is designated as "the mountain of the LORD" in consonance with the verb "ascend" in Ps 24:3. His righteousness attributed to Him in Ps 23:3 is repeated in Ps 24:5 as well. Indeed, He is the pure and blameless one and qualified thereby to ascend into the holy place (24:3). The King of glory seen in Ps 21:6 is now acclaimed at his entrance through eternal gates (24:7-10).

Psalm 31:3-4 also exhibits close parallels to Ps 23. The speaker notes that God has led and guided him because of His name (Ps 31:3, *ulema'an shimka tancheni u tenahaleni*), which is identical to the leading and guiding for the same reason in 23:2-3 (*yenahaleni . . . yancheni . . . lema'an shemo*). In the following verses in each case are two quite similar expressions of confidence in God's presence or protection: "for You are with me" (Ps 23:4 *ki 'ata 'imadi*) and "for You are my refuge" (Ps 31:4 *ki 'ata ma'uzi*). Later in Ps 31:13b there is a description of a plot to kill ("[many . . .] when they conspired against me"), matching closely that of Ps 2:2 ("[rulers] conspire together against the Lord and His Anointed One"). Psalm 31:10 had already declared that his life had ended, and so the murderous plot succeeded, just as in Ps 22.

CONCLUSION

The linguistic evidence demonstrates that Ps 23 is located precisely and carefully within a larger work that is an integrated and coherent whole. Its language and message are consistent with those psalms preceding and following, as well as those across the entire Psalter. Its location following Ps 22 is deliberate and provides an answer to the suffering and death described in the former. It also reaffirms the confidence, victory, and deliverance for the king expressed in Pss 20–21, and anticipates the glorious eschatological entrance into God's eternal city in Ps 24. It may not be the message normally associated with Ps 23, but the previous Ps 22:23-31 had already intimated the same future for a great company of people (22:26). In other words, the formerly deceased king of Ps 22:22-32 was joined by a great worshiping throng. They are the ones who fear God (22:23), praise Him (Ps 22:22,26a), and who will live forever (Ps 22:26b) with Him. The formerly deceased king in fact calls them "my brothers" (Ps 22:22a), and so they will enjoy the paradise described in Ps 23 with Him as their resurrected Lord.

1. Wikipedia, "Psalm 23," http://en.wikipedia.org/wiki/Psalm_23.
2. Hermann Gunkel, *An Introduction to the Psalms*, trans. James D. Nogalski (Macon, GA: Mercer University Press, 1998), 191.
3. Gunkel, *An Introduction to the Psalms*, 191–2.
4. Ibid.
5. Craig A. Blaising and Carmen S. Hardin, *Psalms 1–50* (Downers Grove, IL: InterVarsity Press, 2008), 178.
6. John Forbes, *Studies on the Book of Psalms: The Structural Connection of the Book of Psalms, Both in Single Psalms and in the Psalter as an Organic Whole* (Edinburgh: T&T Clark, 1888), v.
7. Ibid., 265.
8. Franz Delitzsch, *Psalms*, trans. Francis Bolton (Grand Rapids: Eerdmans, 1971), 329.
9. J. H. Eaton, *Psalms* (London: SCM Press, 1967), 77.
10. Gerald H. Wilson, *Psalms* (Grand Rapids: Zondervan, 2002), 430–31.
11. Ibid., 430.
12. Ibid., 431.
13. Amos Hakham, *Sefer Tehillim* (Jerusalem: Mossad haRav Kook, 1979), 126 (author's translation).
14. Ibid., 127.
15. Ibid.
16. Frank-Lothar Hossfeld and Erich Zenger, *Die Psalmen I* (Würzburg: Echter Verlag, 1993), 25.
17. Ibid., 146.
18. Ibid.
19. Pss 23:3 with 16:10; 23:4 with 16:8; and 23:6 with 16:1,10, Hossfeld and Zenger, *Die Psalmen*, 152.
20. Gianni Barbiero, *Das erste Psalmenbuch als Einheit* (Frankfurt am Main: Peter Lang, 1999), 275–76.
21. Ibid., 276.
22. Ibid., 276.
23. Ibid., 276.
24. Ibid., 276–78.
25. Jean-Marie Auwers, *La composition littéraire du Psautier: un état de la question* (Paris: Gabalda, 2000), 43, n.131.
26. Jamie A. Grant, *The King as Exemplar: The Function of Deuteronomy's Kingship Law in the Shaping of the Book of Psalms* (Atlanta: SBL, 2004), 15.
27. Clinton McCann, *Psalms*, New Interpreter's Bible, vol. IV (Nashville: Abingdon Press, 1996), 769.
28. Peter C. Craigie, *Psalms 1–50*, Word Biblical Commentary, vol. 19 (Nashville: Thomas Nelson, 2004).
29. Ibid., 204–5.
30. Ibid., 205.
31. Willem A. VanGemeren, *Psalms*, The Expositor's Bible Commentary, vol. 5 (Grand Rapids: Zondervan, 1991), 214.
32. VanGemeren, *Psalms*, 219.
33. The attempt to delete or radically emend the text of Ps 22:29c-30a ([22:30c-31a Hb.] as in the critical apparatus of the *Biblia Hebraica Stuttgartensia*) is not convincing and probably due to scholarly reticence to accept a reading that does not conform to preconceived notions and expectations. This is a case where the text-critical principle of considering the difficult reading to be stronger should be applied. It is the life of the one worshiped in the previous line (Ps 22:29b) now referenced in Ps 22:29c. It refers to the death of the man in Ps 22, who is resurrected in Ps 23.
34. Ron Tappy, "Psalm 23: Symbolism and Structure," *Catholic Biblical Quarterly* 57 (1995): 255–80. The latter looks for parallels in Ugaritic, Akkadian, archaeology, etc., without a word about its context in the Psalter. He basically admits the impossibility of reconstructing its historical background in Israelite history, but decides nevertheless that it represents a "vertical address" by a person who "stood among a corporate body of participants," a typical form critical assessment. The attempt to impose some sort of corporate application in the face of the linguistic evidence for its unique individual reference (see Hakham above in endnote 15) is a result of the practically inviolate religious tradition of the appropriation of this psalm by any and all of the faithful.
35. Grant R. Osborne, *The Hermeneutical Spiral* (Downer Grove, IL: InterVarsity Press, 1991), 187.
36. Ibid., 190.

37. Ibid. His use of "typological" assumes it is foreign somehow to the message of the Psalms. In fact, at the outset of the book, Ps 1:2-3 overtly uses the portrayal of Joshua typologically. In addition, he warns readers to "dare not" interpret Ps 1's promise of prosperity "apart from the larger context of the Psalms as a whole" (p. 187). However, he fails to understand that Ps 1 does not describe any and every one who would like to appropriate it, but rather the impeccable, royal, and all-conquering Messianic King who is then further designated as the unique Son of God in Ps 2. The image of mostly victorious Joshua is used typologically but extended to perfection. Psalm 23 is another portrayal of the same king dwelling in the same paradise of Ps 1. Note that typology is ubiquitous and deliberate throughout the entire Hebrew Bible. The Pentateuch is explicitly composed with one figure after another cast in ways similar to those previous, and this typological compositional technique dominates throughout the Prophets and the Writings.

38. Ibid., 188.

39. Ibid., 166, 181–85. Hermann Gunkel (*An Introduction to the Psalms*, rejects the Psalter's order and arrangement of the psalms out of hand.

40. Walter C. Kaiser, Jr., and Moisés Silva, *Introduction to Biblical Hermeneutics* (Grand Rapids: Zondervan, 2007), 312–318. Hebrews 2:5 does interpret Ps 8 Christologically despite Silva's caveat (p. 316).

41. Ibid., 314–15.

42. Ibid., 316. Silva defines the latter as "authorial intent," which reveals a misunderstanding of both terms. The book's composer is its author and the one giving each psalm its meaning.

43. Rashi sought to refute traditional rabbinic and Christian readings of the Hebrew Bible through application of the *peshat* method, often designated "historical" or "literal." See Michael Rydelnik's chapter on Rashi in *The Messianic Hope: Is the Hebrew Bible Really Messianic?* (Nashville: B&H, 2010), 112–28.

44. Rashi on Ps 2 in Menachem Cohen, ed., *Mikra'ot Gedolot 'Haketer': Psalms, Part I* (Ramat Gan, Israel: Bar-Ilan University Press, 2003), 4.

45. See Deeana Copeland Klepper, *The Insight of Unbelievers: Nicholas of Lyra and Christian Reading of Jewish Text in the Later Middle Ages* (Philadelphia: University of Pennsylvania Press, 2007), 125, "Luther's dependence on Nicholas of Lyra is well known and attested." On the book cover Copeland notes that through De Lyra "Jewish commentary was, as a result, more widely read in Latin Christendom than ever before."

46. Kaiser and Silva, *Hermeneutics*, 315.

47. Ibid., 316.

48. Ibid., 312.

49. Ibid., 316.

50. The Psalter is, if anything, a literary composition, and failure to recognize this fact, as does form criticism, distorts its meaning and purpose.

51. Andreas J. Köstenberger and Richard D. Patterson, *Invitation to Biblical Interpretation: Exploring the Hermeneutical Triad of History, Literature, and Theology* (Grand Rapids: Kregel Academic, 2011), 472.

52. Peter Enns, *Inspiration and Incarnation: Evangelicals and the Problem of the Old Testament* (Grand Rapids: Baker Academic, 2005).

53. Ibid., 153.

54. Ibid., 168.

55. Ibid., 156. The historical fact and literary evidences of composition in the text constitute the only valid context in which to discern meaning.

56. Köstenberger, Patterson, *Invitation*, 665.

57. W. Randolph Tate, *Biblical Interpretation: An Integrated Approach* (Peabody, MA: Hendrickson, 2008), 279; Jeannine K. Brown, *Introducing Biblical Hermeneutics* (Grand Rapids: Baker Academic, 2007), 149; Bruce Corley, Steve W. Lemke, and Grant I. Lovejoy, *Biblical Hermeneutics* (Nashville: Broadman and Holman, 2002), 136–37. These are just a sampling of many more that could be cited. It may be coincidence or deliberate, but none of the mentioned works on hermeneutics, including Osborne and Köstenberger/Patterson, reveals any attempt to trace the historical roots of the "grammatico-historical" method they espouse.

58. The two final psalms of praise are portrayed through repeated terminology as fulfillment of Ps 2.

59. The other two instances are Pss 91:16 and 93:5, undoubtedly another deliberate distribution on the part of the composer.

60. Contra Tappy, *Psalm 23*, 262–63, who reads *'wlm* in Ps 21:4b as equivalent to "all the days of my life," conveniently leaving out the rest of the phrase (*'wlm w'd*), where eternal life is made explicit (cf. Pss 10:16; 45:6,17; Ex 15:18). Also,

he attempts to interpret *l'rk ymym* through an Akkadian phrase dating to the Old Babylonian period (generally the first half of the second millennium BC), a linguistically suspect procedure at best. It is not the "pressure of tradition" that should be followed in rendering Ps 23:6 as "forever," but rather the explicit and editorially induced intertextual parallel in Ps 21:4 that should be heeded. However, on p. 262, n. 17, he reads *bt 'wlm* as the "grave," and so apparently *'wlm* does refer to eternity.

61. Reading as infinitive construct of *yashav* ("to dwell") as in the parallel Ps 27:4b. Note how the expression "all the days of my life" in Ps 27:4 follows the previous reference to dwelling while in Ps 23:6 the identical words precede the reference to dwelling. Undoubtedly this is a deliberate parallel.

62. This verbal form is translated by Abraham Even-Shoshan, *Konkordanzia Hadashah leTorah, Nevi'im uKetuvim* (Jerusalem: Kiryat Sefer, 1982), 1118, as "to make return, bring to a former place."

63. "Make alive" is Piel while "make return" is Polel, a variant of the former.

64. Job 10 also exhibits a very explicit and unique parallel with Ps 1:1. Only in Job and Psalms is the phrase "council/counsel of the wicked" found: Ps 1:1; Job 10:3; 21:16; 22:18. Other explicit parallels exist as well between the two books, revealing that the sequence Psalms–Job is deliberate and supported by internal content. This raises the possibility that the final shape of individual books could have been accomplished by the hand of the canon's composer.

Psalm 40

A Body Prepared for Death

DANIEL D. GREEN

Book One of the Psalter begins with Ps 1 and continues through Ps 41. Its context emphasizes "expressions of worship, focusing on God's sovereign election."[1] His chosen people will ultimately prevail. Each of the five books contains a doxology, and this one concludes with the praise of the everlasting God of Israel.[2] God has chosen a particular people, Israel, and a particular person, His Messiah, to represent Him.

Psalm 2, a royal psalm, is foundational to this book as well as the Psalter as a whole.[3] The Anointed King will be helped by the Lord as will all the faithful who struggle. The rebellious nations will be humbled under the mighty hand of God. Their fate will depend on their receptivity to the messianic son. They are commanded to give homage to Him, lest He ignite His destructive anger against them.

Psalms 37–39 focus on encouragement for the righteous in the midst of their laments over the apparent prosperity of the wicked. They suffer emotionally, struggling with anger, impatience, and lack of perspective concerning the present and future. They also are concerned that the wicked will giddily use their imperfections against them. Although they struggle with their sins, their hearts long to please God. They wait expectantly for the Lord to deliver them from their enemies and give them an accurate viewpoint for their short lives. With the Lord's encouragement, they hold onto their faith.

Psalm 41 concludes the section. Like Ps 1, it emphasizes the happiness of the upright in the midst of the wicked. God's grace in their lives will ultimately prevail over the malice of their enemies. Psalm 1 sets forth the principle of prospering through obedience to the law, as opposed to being judged for rebellion. Psalm 41 is more illustrative, showing the happiness of those who apply the law in helping the poor, and also showing the plots of the wicked, which are ultimately frustrated by God.

The point of Psalm 40 is to see in it, not only some of King David's experience, but that of the Messiah, the ultimate blessed follower of the Lord. It is He who would provide the ultimate sacrifice for Israel's sins through the sacrifice of His body. Says Kidner, "The theme of waiting, expounded in Psalm 37, has had its painful application in Psalms 38 and 39, but now its triumphant outcome."[4,5]

INTEXTUAL INTERPRETATION

The superscription of the psalm directs it to the leader of musical worship. The word rendered "choir director" is a participle, indicating direction of liturgical singers. The choir director, used in the title of 55 psalms, is an overseer.[6] First Chronicles 15:21, for instance, notes six such men who led singing with lyres. Authorship is attributed to David.[7] The word "psalm" translates the Hebrew word *mizmor* and indicates a melody.[8] This psalm seems best divided into two main units of thought: vv. 1-10 and 11-17. The first section emphasizes the dedication of the faithful to the Lord because of His mighty deliverance, and the second stresses the psalmist's cry for continual help in the midst of trouble, so that the faithful may continue to praise Him.

I. The Dedication of the Faithful to the Lord because of His Mighty Deliverance (1-10).

The first movement tells of the Lord's faithfulness in delivering His people from awful circumstances.

A. *The psalmist testifies that his persistence was rewarded when God delivered him from a hopeless situation and to renewed praise of God (1-3).* The psalmist waited for the Lord to act. The Hebrew hendiadys might be translated idiomatically here, "waiting, I waited." He *really* waited. He *eagerly* waited.[9] He probably waited a long time. He may not necessarily have been patient, but he did persist in hope. The word "wait" is often used of the attitude of the righteous in great difficulty (Jer 8:15; 13:16; 14:9). Psalm 130:5-6 says, "I wait for Yahweh; I wait and put my hope in His word. I wait for the Lord more than the watchmen for the morning . . ." The object of his persistent hope is Yahweh, the covenant-keeping God of Israel. At the right time, Yahweh acted. "Turned to me" is an anthropomorphism, indicating His concern. He would now answer the prayer of David. He graciously moved to relieve his distress. God is moved by the cries of His "dear people" (Jer 8:19), and their distressed calls for mercy reach His ears (2Sm 22:7; Ps 18:6).

David acknowledged Yahweh as the one who had delivered him (v. 2). He likened his former predicament to a "desolate pit." The words *bor sha'on* mean literally "a pit of roaring (water)."

However they are rendered, they are "figurative of calamity."[10] They may be used metaphorically for Sheol, the place of death, which is sometimes represented by the raging sea (Ps 18:4,15-16).[11] "Muddy clay" is put as "miry bog" by Kidner, who says that the metaphor "puts into two words almost all that can be suggested of horror and floundering helplessness."[12] The specific circumstances from which he had been delivered are not specified, but they were of the most desperate sort. Perhaps David had been delivered from sickness (Ps 30:3-4) but more likely, given the presumed royal context of the psalm, the rescue had been from the dangers of military conflict.[13] Yahweh had brought the psalmist up from the seemingly inescapable bog and had placed him on the solid stone of a cliff. He was no longer trying to keep his head above the circumstantial quicksand. Instead, his feet firmly gripped the high and secure rock from which he could reorient himself.

Not only did the Lord deliver David from danger, but He restored his spirit. He filled him with joy so that he wanted to sing a "new song." Such were hymns of praise to God. "The new song suggests new mercies received."[14] David responded to Yahweh's new deliverance with new praise songs.

Such fresh songs are mentioned prominently in the Psalter (33:3; 96:1; 98:1; 149:1) and often led by Levites. Their content was to be in accord with the instructions given in the psalms above. They were to be accompanied by various instruments such as lyres, ten-stringed harps, trumpets, tambourines, and ram horns. They also focused attention on attributes of God such as His love, majesty, righteousness, splendor, and strength. God was to be praised as well for His works of creation and superintendence of the world. The Messianic Servant was also associated with new songs as He would one day judge His enemies and establish His kingdom (Isa 42:1).[15] "Hymn of praise" is placed in synonymous parallel with "new song." The psalmist was "celebrating not only God's deliverance, but also the impact of victory on observers. . . ."[16] As many others would witness the wonderful rescue, they would fear Yahweh and trust in Him.

B. *The psalmist extols the exhilaration of the man who follows Yahweh and not scoundrels, and praises God for His incomparable and unfathomable works (4-5).* Verse 4 starts as v. 3 ended, with the person who trusts in the Lord. Such a person is "happy" (Hb. *'ashre*). Here, it is a state of spiritual blessedness. The term is used much more prominently in the Psalms than elsewhere. Although it is sometimes used of physical prosperity that may come from following Yahweh (41:2; 127:5; 144:15), it most often comes from spiritual obedience and/or benefits: forgiven sins (32:1), trust in difficulty (34:8), an upright heart (84:5), successful discipline from the Lord (94:12), ethical behavior (112:1), and fear of God (128:1). The use of *geber,* "mighty man" or "man of valor"[17] (HCSB "man"), here in v. 4 may hearken back to a military warrior, or may be used in a general sense of any man who trusts in the Lord. This blessed trust is demonstrated by refusing to follow after the proud or after liars. "Turning toward" the proud and liars is to look to them for help, rather than to Yahweh. Perhaps David had in mind his own enemies who asserted themselves against God, and who were untrustworthy in their testimony. For the people of God to trust such persons would be idolatry. Thus, David indirectly exhorts the people to be steadfast in faithfulness, before he turns to praise.[18] The similarity of theme with Ps 1 is striking. There the man is happy who does not follow the advice of the wicked, nor join their mocking of God's ways. He delights in the Lord's instructions and prospers thereby.

His happiness spills over into praise in v. 5. The word "many" is fronted in the sentence to emphasize the abundance of good that the Lord has done for His people. David summarizes these acts into two categories: wonderful acts and benevolent plans. The former are miraculous in their nature. These wonderful acts are too difficult for humans to do or even understand (Job 42:3); Israel's Messiah King is known as the *wonderful* counselor.[19] The plans demonstrate God's watch-care over His people (Jer 29:11). The One who is unlimited in His miraculous power also cares deeply for His own and providentially plans for their welfare. God's wondrous works and beneficent care cause David to praise the Lord as incomparable. There is no one like Him among Israel's enemies or the pagan world's many gods. The king here says that were he to try, he could not possibly describe all the acts of God on behalf of Israel. Even though he opened his mouth to praise God, to do so exhaustively was beyond him.

C. *The psalmist declares that God is more interested in obedience than ritual sacrifices, and that God has opened his ears to listen to His instruction (6-8).* The connection of thoughts here is clear. God has done wonderful things for the psalmist. How will he render thanks?[20] First, he will say how not to do it. Although the text says "You do not delight in sacrifice," the statement is hyperbolic. Indeed, the book of Leviticus is given to the details of an elaborate system of sacrifices, and such are mandated and practiced throughout the OT. What the psalmist intends is that God does not desire *ritual, heartless* sacrifice. Such had been offered by King Saul and rejected. His cold heart had resulted in the loss of his kingdom. God had spoken to the priority in sacrifice: "Look: to obey is better than sacrifice, to pay attention is better than the fat of rams (1Sm 15:22b)." As Ross says of Yahweh,

> If he has the worshipper, he will also have the gift given in the right way. Psalm 51:17 says that "the sacrifices of God are a broken spirit, a broken contrite heart." God did not need the animals (Ps 50:7-14); he desired a contrite heart, which is what the sacrifice was to signify. These statements in Psalm 40 need to be understood this way. Did God want sacrifices? Yes, for he legislated them; but he wanted what the sacrifices were designed to represent.[21]

Evidently, God did not want merely ritual sacrifice but He did want a heart attuned to Himself as His people offered sacrifices. One might now expect to see the psalmist presenting himself to God as an act of worship (Rom 12:1-2). But that is not exactly what happened. Instead he says, "*You* open my ears to listen." God did a work in David's life so that his approach might be acceptable. The ears (Hb. *'zanim*) often stand for receptivity to instruction in the OT. Sometimes they are used to describe a poor response to God: "Dull the minds of these people; *deafen their ears* and blind their eyes" (Isa 6:10; Jer 6:10). They can also be used to depict willful ignorance[22] as in Prv 21:13, "the one who *shuts his ears* to the cry of the poor will himself also call out and not be answered." On the other hand, they can reveal a teachable spirit as in Prv 18:15, "the mind of the discerning acquires knowledge, and the *ear of the wise seeks it."* It is this positive response that God brings about in the psalmist. He opens his ears. The Hebrew verb used here (*karah*) means "to hollow out," "dig." It is used of the creation of wells (Gn 26:25), graves (Gn 50:5), and pits (Ex 21:33).[23] This is an allusion to the clearing of the cavity of the ear. Therefore, these words could be paraphrased, "thou hast given me the means of hearing and obeying thy will."[24] The idea is that God has affected receptivity in the psalmist so that he is spiritually oriented to the Lord's will. He is not in any way rebellious, but is prepared to serve God. The implication is that his sacrifice(s) will be acceptable because he is spiritually attentive. Verse 6 ends with a return to the idea that God does not want sacrifices that are not offered from pure motive. The author drives home his point here with a chiastic structure:

A You do not delight in sacrifice and offerings
  B You open my ears to listen
A You do not ask for a whole burnt offering or a sin offering

First and foremost in the offering of any sacrifice was that the worshiper be fully attentive to all that God wanted to do with his life. In this instance, God had seen to it Himself, having "dug his ears." The theme of the open ear is also developed in Isa 50:4b-6: "He *awakens my ear* to listen like those being instructed. The Lord God *has opened My ear* and I was not rebellious; I did not turn back. I gave My back to those who beat Me, and My cheeks to those who tore out My beard. I did not hide My face from scorn and spitting."

Isaiah's text is pointing to the Messiah, as it appears in the context of the servant songs.[25] The author of Ps 40 also seems to be doing something with the text that goes quite far beyond the life of the psalmist. He is linking ideas that are messianic. Kidner understands vv. 6-8 to be about the Messiah. He sees them as the logical response to the thankfulness of vv. 4-5, but adds, "yet David outruns it by speaking as if his self-offering will be the sacrifice to end all sacrifices. If this is the implication of his words, then he is not speaking for himself, but the Messiah. . . ."[26] Thus, he sees the Messiah in this OT text. For him, Heb 10:5-10 *confirms* what is already present in the psalm.[27] It looks past David's own situation, describing a sacrifice that only the Messiah could offer. No one could offer himself as the final solution for sin, but the Messiah. It likely fits a category of Psalms that Delitzsch labeled typico-prophetically Messianic.[28] These are

> . . . those in which David, describing his outward and inward experiences . . . is carried beyond the limits of his . . . present condition, and utters concerning himself that which, transcending human experience, is intended to become historically true only in Christ. . . . Such Psalms are typical . . . they are, however, at the same time prophetic, in as much as (they give) descriptions which point far forward beyond the present and are only fully realised in Christ.[29]

Verse 7 calls attention to the psalmist and the scroll to which he refers. "See," *hinneh*, calls for attention. "I have come" speaks of readiness to serve. The content of the "volume of the book" is debated. The text reads *ketub 'lay,* "it is written upon me." Ross renders "in the scroll of the book it is prescribed *for me*."[30] He interprets the scroll as God's law for all believers, including the psalmist and the greater figure in view, the Messiah. The New English Translation (NET) says "What is written in the scroll *pertains* to me." Its footnotes suggest that if this is a distinctly royal psalm, then the content of the scroll may refer to the duties of the psalmist/king prescribed in Dt 17:14-20.[31] The *English Standard Version* renders "it is written of me." The *Holman Christian Standard Bible* has "it is written *about Me* in the volume of the scroll." This last translation seems to suggest, or allow for, a prophetic interpretation. Kidner posits that the very coming of this figure is a prophetic fulfillment in accord with NT passages about the Messiah (Jn 5:46; Lk 24:47).[32]

In v. 9 he states his delight to do God's will. He returns to the language of intimacy—"my God"—which he used earlier (v. 6) and also repeats the word delight. Yahweh *did not* delight in heartless sacrifice, but He did delight in the opposite: offerings from a heart that beat for Him. This Hebrew word, *chaphats*, is used often of deeply felt attitude in service as in Solomon's construction of the temple (1Kg

9:1), caring for family responsibilities (Ru 3:13), and the pursuit of God's ways (Isa 58:2). The passion and authenticity God wanted manifest in the sacrifices of His people, the psalmist possessed. With all of his heart, he wanted to make pleasing offerings to the Lord. The Torah lived within him. It impacted all of his thoughts and actions.

Some commentators do not see vv. 6-8 as directly messianic. In other words, apart from the NT record of Heb 10:5-10 there would be no conclusive evidence of Him in the text. For VanGemeren, the psalm is a royal psalm, and depicts the offering of a king after a great victory. He would have offered sacrifices to the Lord before the battle, and after the deliverance from the manifold dangers of battle. He thanks God for the military success, and pledges his allegiance to the Lord.[33] "The scroll" is the Torah, which contains instructions incumbent upon the king (Dt 17:14-20).[34] "Written of me," then, really means "written for my instruction." Craigie follows this line of thought, and speaks of "the original sense of the psalm recalling the supplicatory role of the king on behalf of his kingdom."[35] Both of these scholars recognize the messianic nature of Ps 40, but only as the NT makes use of it.

A principal assumption of Craigie and VanGemeren in their interpretation is that the psalm is royal, pointing clearly to the presentation of sacrifice by a king of Israel. Ross challenges this, saying, "No doubt if a king used this Psalm to express his dedication, he would have included in mind at least the rules for kings; but the psalm shows no clue of such a limited idea."[36] If he is right, this leaves the content of the scroll open for debate. It could be prophetic, as suggested earlier in the commentary. As Ross says, "Not only did the word instruct in righteousness, but it also revealed through prophecies and types the person and work of the Messiah."[37] The approach also fails to deal with the intertextual connection from Isa 50 that has been mentioned and which will be developed later in this article.

Although it is not within the parameters of this work to deal exhaustively with the issue, something needs to be said about how Ps 40:6-8 is used in Heb 10:5-9. How, especially, can "You open my ears to listen" (Ps 40:6) come to be rendered "You prepared a body for me" (Heb 10:5b)? The writer of Hebrews is quoting the Septuagint, a Greek translation of the OT that was widely used among Hellenized Jewish people. Three renderings of the verse are compared below:

Hebrew OT (MT) – "Ears you have dug for me"
Greek OT (LXX) – "A body you have restored for me"[38]
Greek NT (Nestle-Aland) – "A body you have prepared for me."

The words translated "restored" and "prepared" are the same Greek verb, *katartizo*. The translations are essentially identical, but both differ from the Hebrew text found in Ps 40.

Bruce explains the difference as follows: "The Greek translator evidently regarded the Hebrew wording as an instance of *pars pro toto*; the 'digging' or hollowing of the ears is part of the total work of fashioning a human body."[39] This is referred to technically as a metonymy of the part for the whole. Ross concurs with this and dismisses two other proposals: (1) that there was a reading error that confused the two words as written in Greek uncials, and (2) that the Greek reading of Hebrews got into the Greek manuscripts of the Psalms.[40]

D. *The psalmist says that he proclaims God's righteousness among the Lord's assembled people with an open mouth and heart (9-10).* He speaks out for the Lord's interest in the *rahav qahal*, "the great assembly." Israel gathered for various reasons, such as dealing with civil issues (1Kg 12:3), preparation for war (Nm 22:4), and, as here, for religious instruction and encouragement (Dt 9:10). His mouth is open to speak of God's goodness to God's people.

The content of his speech is emphasized in v. 10. He has not been one to "hide in his heart" what he has learned from his experiences with Yahweh. Rather, he has spoken boldly of them in the great crowd of Israelites. He has spoken of God's attributes—righteousness, faithfulness, abiding love, and truthfulness. These perfections have been on his tongue, as he has lifted high the person of God. In the psalmist's mind, his Lord was completely upright in His person, dependable in what He did, loyal in His constant love and true to His promises. Having escaped the horrible mud and muck of trial (v.2), he has been restored to praise God. He could not help but tell others about the greatness of Yahweh. Wilson comments here, "The Psalmist's determination to proclaim Yahweh's righteousness to the congregation of the faithful is the practical equivalent to the NT proclamation of the gospel. . . . The Psalmist does not keep the 'good news' of God's righteous and faithful saving love under wraps, but publishes it abroad."[41]

II. The Appeal to the Lord for Further Help (11-17).

A. *The psalmist prays for God to continue to show mercy to him during his troubles that have overtaken him due to sin (11-13).* Here the psalm begins a descent from the focus on the divine Messiah to an ardent, entirely human being. Delitzsch says, "We are not . . . compelled to understand the whole Psalm as typically predictive. It again descends from the typically prophetic height to which it has risen even from ver. 10."[42] "The plea of these verses began with an appeal for God to continue to show His compassion. The word used here is *rachamim*, a plural intensive form that originally meant "a brotherly feeling of those born of the same womb."[43] It is used of a father's deep concern for his children (Ps 103:4), is often associated with forgiveness (Ps 51:1), and is a long-enduring attribute of God (Ps 51:1). It appeals to God's deepest feelings for His own children. The next line in v. 11 contains a parallel term, *chesed,* translated as "loyal love" or "constant love" (HCSB). David is depending on God to continue to manifest these characteristics for his benefit. They will surpass the difficulties of his circumstances.

In v. 12, the psalmist explains his need for assistance. His troubles have multiplied so as to defy counting. The reason seems to be his past sins. They have overtaken (Hb. *nashag*) him, pursuing like an avenger of blood (Dt 19:6). "He is disconcerted, dejected as it were, driven to despair."[44]

His plea to God reaches its peak in v. 13, where he begs to be delivered and says, essentially, "hurry up!" Wilson calls attention to a major shift in the passage that occurs here: "Now, without previous mention, these final verses focus on his enemies, whom the psalmist wants Yahweh to recompense for their attacks."[45]

B. *The psalmist prays for his enemies to be emotionally shaken and destroyed (14-15).* David prays an imprecatory prayer here, asking God to destroy his oppressors. Such prayers are common in the OT, and extend to the NT as well (Pss 69:19-28; 109:1-20; Rev 6:9-11).[46] They are a cry for relief from the unjustifiable assaults of the wicked. He wants them to be "disgraced and confounded." Both Hebrew verbs have to do with being ashamed. He wants them to lose face and be embarrassed.

His wish is for the mockers to be shocked themselves. The ones who so freely filled their mouths with taunts, he wished to be "horrified" in their shame. The word (Hb. *shameem)* has the sense of being appalled by judgment that has come for rebellion (1Kg 9:8) and mockery of God's people (Ezk 35:15).[47]

C. *The psalmist wishes for the faithful to rejoice in their salvation and to proclaim the greatness of the Lord (16).* Perhaps the verbs in the verse should be rendered as jussives and, thus, "May all who seek you," and "May all who love you" (so ESV). It is his desire that these things be true. The psalmist wants those who seek the Lord to rejoice. Seeking Yahweh is a prominent theme in the OT. Believers search Him out in His temple (Ps 27:4), for intimate fellowship (Ps 27:8) in order to tap His strength (Ps 105:4), with humble repentance (Zph 2:3) for the healing of their land (2Chr 7:14) and when they are afraid (Ps 34:4). Such seekers are to rejoice and be glad for all that the Lord is and does. Their mood should be celebratory. Likewise, those who "love your salvation." Probably the sense of this phrase is "those who *love all the benefits related to* your salvation." They are to make a *continuing* proclamation: "Yahweh is great!" should be on their lips as a habit of life. The contrast with the mockers' words recorded in v. 15 should be evident.

D. *The psalmist appeals to Yahweh for swift deliverance in his time of need (17).*[48] As the psalm nears its end, he returns to his previous concern for the circumstances at hand. He describes himself first as "needy." The term (Hb. *'aney*) refers to those who are variously humble, poor, or afflicted.[49] It is often used of God's people who are materially poor (Dt 15:11), and the righteous poor who are being tormented by foes more powerful than they (Isa 3:15; 10:2; 32:7; 58:7). Those who are hunted down by the wicked (Ps 10:2) are protected by the Lord (Ps 12:5).

The second term is a virtual synonym[50] (Hb. *'abyon)*, and stands for those tormented by the rich. This is demonstrated in Ps 109:16: "For he did not think to show kindness, but pursued the afflicted, poor and brokenhearted in order to put them to death." The financial status of the psalmist is not stated, but David was certainly not needy in that sense. It is best to interpret this as a situation where he was at just as much of a disadvantage, in terms of power, as the poor of the land. In this needy state, he is still confident that God cares. The name of God now switches from Yahweh to Adonai. The force of this name is to portray might. Adonai is "Sovereign Lord." This name is associated with kings (Dan 1:10,19,24), mighty angels (Zch 4:4), and the Messiah (Ps 2:2; 110:1). It is also used of God who is able to deliver from difficulty (Ps 35:23) and save from death (Ps 68:21). David, in his weakness, calls on the Mighty One. Adonai thinks of him in his time of difficulty. The psalmist is never out of His mind. God is his help (Ps 22:20) and deliverer. Returning to the most common name for God, the psalmist entreats Him not to delay.

INNERTEXTUAL INTERPRETATION

There are a number of links between Ps 40 and other parts of the Psalter. Probably the most basic connection appears in Ps 22, which has long been viewed as messianic in Christian tradition. It may be that portions of Ps 40 can be viewed as intertextual references back to Ps 22. The Messiah's proclamations in this psalm are mirrored in Ps 40.

The first such link is that both psalms refer to the proclamation of God's character in the great assembly of Israel. This is found in Ps 22:22-25, and Ps 40:9-11. Psalm 22:22 says "I will proclaim your name to my brothers. . . . in the congregation." Psalm 40:9 says "I proclaim righteousness in the great assembly . . . I did not hide Your righteousness in my heart." Psalm 22:25 references the "great congregation" whereas Ps 40 notes the "great assembly" (vv. 9,10). The acknowledgment of God that is called for in 22:23 is given in 40:10. The compassion of God noted in 22:24 is petitioned in 40:11. In 22:25 praise is given to Yahweh, as is the case in 40:9-10.

Another link between the psalms is the struggle with mockers. In Ps 22:7-8 they sneer, shake their heads and make fun of the psalmist's predicament. He asks for deliverance in 22:21. In Ps 40:15,17 the enemies laugh contemptuously and a request for deliverance is made.

Psalm 40 may also be linked to Ps 35:16-21. In the latter, there is godless mockery from which the psalmist asks relief. The words, "Aha, aha," in 35:21 are identical to 40:15. In the context there is, as in Pss 22 and 40, a determination to praise God "in the great congregation."

Yet another link to Ps 40 appears in Ps 69, one of the psalms most frequently quoted in the NT. In both contexts there is an appeal for rescue from the "muddy clay" (Hb. *tet,* 40:2; 69:2,14). The petitions of 40:11 and 69:17 are both urgent. In 40:17 the psalmist describes his state as "afflicted and needy," and in 69:29 as "poor and in pain."

INTERTEXTUAL INTERPRETATION

There are some connections with Ps 40 in the larger context of the OT—most notably, Isaiah. Chief among these is Isa 50:5-6.

This passage has been considered messianic for hundreds of years, and is the subject of part of Handel's Messiah. Verses 4c-5 read, "He *awakens* My ear to listen like those being instructed. The Lord God has *opened* My ear, and I was not rebellious; I did not turn back." The Hebrew verb translated "awakens" in the HCSB is *'wr* and has the sense of "to awaken or arouse."[51] It is figurative for attuning the ear to listen. The Hebrew verb translated "opened" by HCSB is *patach.* Its meaning is plain when it comes to the ear—it means simply "to open."[52] Although *karah,* "to dig" in Ps 40:6, is also figurative, the meanings of the three verbs are synonymous. God has opened the ear of the messianic figure in both contexts. Ross sees the Messiah in both passages: "The psalmist's point is that God made him in such a way that he would hear and do what the LORD wanted (similarly Isaiah 50:4 says morning by morning the LORD opens the prophet's ear)."[53] The footnote to this quote continues: "This passage in Isaiah is one of the servant songs, which Christian expositors recognize to be prophetic of Christ in the same typological way that Psalm 40 is.... Thus, the emphasis on obedience using the detail of ears, occurs in both messianic passages."[54] That yielded ears mean a yielded body, is evident from what follows. The obedient servant gives his back to be whipped, his beard to be plucked, and his face to be spat upon.[55] He is completely obedient, in contrast to Israel, whose ears are not open (42:20; 48:8).

The theme of a messianic figure yielding his body to God continues in Isa 52:13–53:12. Messiah surrenders Himself to profound disfigurement in 52:14. In

53:5-7 He is pierced, crushed, wounded, oppressed, and afflicted without protest. His suffering was vicarious for the sins of the people (53:11-12).

Another connection is Zch 12:10, where it is evident that Messiah gave His body in service of Yahweh. His body was "pierced." When Israel sees Messiah Jesus coming again they will realize that the crucifixion was unjustified, and they will be brought to national repentance. The vicarious sacrifice first rejected, will then be embraced with fervor.

CONCLUSION

This article has defended the thesis that Ps 40, particularly vv. 6 through 10, is messianic. It depicts the Messiah who gratefully offered His body in the service of Yahweh.

Intextual exegesis demonstrated the unique and divine character of the Messiah, rising out of the context of a Davidic psalm. Innertextual analysis of connected psalms strengthened the thesis by discussing connections within the Psalter.

Finally, intertextual analysis traced common messianic themes to other passages in the OT. Together the three lines of evidence point to the Messiah, whose body was made ready for sacrificial service to the Lord God.

1. "Psalms," in *The Moody Bible Commentary*, ed. M. Rydelnik and M. Vanlaningham (Chicago: Moody, 2014), 743.

2. P. Craigie, "Psalms 1–50," in *The Word Bible Commentary*, ed. D. Hubbard and G. Barker (Waco: Word, 1983), 19:30.

3. A. Ross, *Psalms* vol. 1:55 (Grand Rapids: Kregel, 2011).

4. D. Kidner, *Psalms 1–72* (Downers Grove, IL: InterVarsity, 1973), 158.

5. A number of form-critical scholars have questioned the unity of this psalm, contending that it is actually two psalms tied together. This concern has been adequately addressed by Willem A. VanGemeren who demonstrates its structural unity via a chiastic structure in "Psalms" in *The Expositor's Bible Commentary* (Grand Rapids: Zondervan, 1991), 5:317.

6. Francis Brown, Samuel Rolles Driver, and Charles Augustus Briggs, *Hebrew and English Lexicon of the Old Testament* (repr., Oxford: Oxford University Press, 1977), 664.

7. The Hebrew letter, "lamed," attached to the word "David," has traditionally been understood to indicate Davidic authorship. Since there is no compelling evidence to reject this understanding, it is best to accept it. Discussing such credits to David in the Psalter, Ross says, "I am not bound to simply say a psalm is David's because a traditional note credited him with the psalm; but neither am I ready to dismiss the tradition without good reason" (Ross, *Psalms*, 1:47).

8. Brown, Driver, and Briggs, 274.

9. Hope and eager waiting are in the spectrum of meaning of the word "qawah" that is used here (Brown, Driver and Briggs, 875) and are probably intended in the context.

10. Brown, Driver, and Briggs, 92.

11. *The Net Bible* (Dallas: Biblical Studies Press, 2001), 945, tn 16.

12. Kidner, *Psalms 1–72*, 158.

13. Craigie, "Psalms 1–50," 315.

14. Ross, *Psalms*, 1:863.

15. See innertextual comments.

16. Craigie, "Psalms 1–50," 315.

17. Brown, Driver, and Briggs, 149–150.

18. VanGemeren, "Psalms," 319.

19. Brown, Driver, and Briggs, 810. A study of both noun and verb usage is profitable here.

20. F. Delitzsch, "Psalms," in vol. 5 of *Commentary on the Old Testament* (Grand Rapids: Eerdmans, Reprint, 1976), V:III:37.

21. Ross, *Psalms*, 1:862.

22. Brown, Driver, and Briggs, 24.

23. Ibid., 500.

24. Ibid. Some, however, have seen something else here, piercing, as in a slave's ear (the practice of piercing the slave's ear is described in Ex 21:5-6, but the word "open" is not used. This idea has not gotten much support, and is rejected outright by J. Perowne, *Psalms* (Grand Rapids: Zondervan, 1966), I:33.

25. This line of thought will be developed more in the intertextual section of this article.

26. Kidner, *Psalms 1–72*, 158.

27. Ibid., 159.

28. F. Delitzsch, "Psalms," V:I:69.

29. Ibid.

30. Ross, *Psalms*, 1:854.

31. Ross, *Psalms*, 946, tn6.

32. Kidner, *Psalms 1–72*, 156.

33. VanGemeren, "Psalms," 320. I am summarizing his work that is given in more detail in his commentary.

34. Ibid.

35. Craigie, "Psalms 1–50," 317.

36. Ross, *Psalms*, 865, fn. 22.

37. Ibid., 866.

38. The translation in the Lexham English Septuagint (LES), Logos Bible Software, www.logos.com.

39. F. F. Bruce, *The Epistle to the Hebrews* (Grand Rapids: Eerdmans, 1967), 240.

40. Ross, *Psalms*, 854, fn 5.

41. G. Wilson, *Psalms: From Biblical Text to Contemporary Life*, The NIV Application Commentary (Grand Rapids: Zondervan, 2002), 641–42.

42. Delitzsch, "Psalms," V:I:35.

43. Brown, Driver, and Briggs, 933.

44. Delitzsch, "Psalms," V:I:42.

45. Wilson, *Psalms*, 644.

46. For a theology of imprecatory prayers, see Chalmers Martin, "Imprecations in the Psalms" in *Classical Evangelical Essays in Old Testament Interpretation*, ed. Walter C. Kaiser, Jr. (Grand Rapids: Baker, 1972), 113–32.

47. Brown, Driver, and Briggs, 1030.

48. For a helpful summary of the similarities and differences of this verse and Ps 70:5, see Wilson, *Psalms*, 643.

49. Brown, Driver, and Briggs, 776.

50. Ibid., 2.

51. Ibid., 734.

52. Ibid., 835.

53. Ross, *Psalms*, 864.

54. Ibid.

55. So Kidner, *Psalms 1–72*, 159.

Psalm 45[1]

The Messiah as Bridegroom

SETH D. POSTELL

Context is king. Psalm 45 is typically identified as a wedding song originally penned in honor of the wedding of one of Israel's ancient kings, or a scripted wedding song in honor of every Israelite king.[2] Biblical scholars agree that messianic significance has been attached to the psalm, but many believe it to be accrued meaning, beyond the author's original intent.[3]

However, little scholarly attention has been paid to the placement of the chapter within the Psalter as a whole. Reading the book of Psalms as a single body of work causes a narrative to emerge. Along with careful study of textual indicators within this specific psalm, the attempt will be made to brush away years of failure to appreciate the wider story, to reveal a psalm that is no mere relic of royal weddings gone by, but a song about the Messiah to come.

This article will maintain that Ps 45 was specifically and directly written as a celebration of the glories of the future Divine-Davidic Messiah. The first part will outline and summarize the content of Ps 45. It will also look at the identity of both the king and the bride, since her presence in the psalm has been one of the primary reasons for denying the direct messianic interpretation. The second part will examine the literary-canonical context of Ps 45, as well as its literary relationship to other well-known references to the coming Messianic King in the Hebrew Bible.

SUMMARY OF PSALM 45

Psalm 45 is notoriously difficult to outline, and numerous suggestions have been offered.[4] Gerald Wilson and Adam Copenhaver divide the psalm into a preamble

(v. 1), praises for the king (vv. 2-9), instructions to the princess-bride (vv. 10-15), and dynastic blessings for the king (vv. 16-17).[5] Christoph Schroeder takes a different approach by dividing the main body of the psalm (excluding the superscription and the opening verse) as follows: successful warrior (vv. 2-6), marriage of the king (vv. 7-15).[6] Peter C. Craigie divides the psalm into the poet's introduction (v. 1), the praise of the royal groom (vv. 2-8), the praise of the bride (vv. 9-15), and final words to the king (vv. 16-17).[7] Amos Hakham proposes yet another structure: opening (v. 1), praises of the king (vv. 2-7), the wedding and praises of the bride (vv. 8-16), and the conclusion (v. 17).[8] Of the proposals offered, Andy Dvoracek's structural analysis (which follows) appears most persuasive because of its careful attention to the grammatical and syntactical features of the psalm, and therefore it undergirds the approach taken in this article.[9]

1. A *Maskil* Song about the King by the Sons of Korah (Superscription)[10]
2. A First-Person Introductory Dedication: A Good Word and Verses about the King (v. 1)[11]
3. A Good Word about the King's Eternal[12] Victories on the Battlefield (vv. 2-5)
    a. A Description of the King's Eternal Blessings (v. 2)[13]
    b. A Call for the King's Victory on the Battlefield (vv. 3-5)[14]
4. A Good Word about the King's Eternal Glories in the Palace (vv. 6-16)
    a. A Description of the King's Eternal Glories on the Throne (vv. 6-9)
    b. A Call for the King's Bride to Come and Celebrate Her King in the Palace (vv. 10-16)
5. A First-Person Doxological Conclusion: A Passion to Praise the King Forever (v. 17)

The psalm's two primary stanzas are divided by two different yet equally important locations: the battlefield (vv. 3-5) and the palace (vv. 6-16).[15] In the first primary stanza (vv. 3-5), the psalmist describes the king's handsome appearance (*yop yāp it o*), a notable physical feature of two key figures in the Hebrew Bible. Joseph, clearly a royal figure in the Joseph narrative (Gn 37:8), is "well-built and handsome" (Gn 39:6).[16] Likewise, when the prophet Samuel came to anoint David as the new king, the text states that David had "beautiful eyes and a healthy, handsome appearance" (1Sm 16:12).[17] Similarly, as David meets Goliath on the battlefield, the giant despised the young man because he was "just a youth, healthy and handsome" (1Sm 17:42).[18] Also, Absalom, one of David's sons who tried to usurp the throne, was the most beautiful man in all of Israel (2Sm 14:25).[19] Just as King David's handsome appearance was acknowledged at his anointing (1Sm 16:12) and also on the battlefield with Goliath, the king of Ps 45 is more handsome than the sons of

The reason for denying a direct messianic interpretation has to do with references in this psalm that appear to be rooted in the realities of Israel's historical past (e.g., the bride, the daughter of Tyre). Critics claim that the direct messianic interpretation seemingly rejects the grammatical-historical interpretation of these historical details,[32] and so allegedly resort to allegorical or figurative interpretations to make the psalm speak of Messiah directly.

However, attempts to identify the historical king to which this psalm originally referred have been particularly challenging, given the lack of specific historical details. According to Amos Hakham, three kings from Israel's history have been suggested, each of whom Hakham admits are not without their problems: King David, who did not marry a daughter of Tyre or live in an ivory palace; King Solomon, who is known as a man of peace rather than of war; and King Ahab, who did marry a daughter of Tyre (HCSB "the Sidonians" 1Kg 16:31), but falls far short of the description of this divinely righteous king.[33] Given the lack of historical specificity, Hakham suggests that Ps 45 may have been written as a wedding song template for many kings.[34]

Another challenging factor in tying this psalm to a king (every king) in Israel's past is the remarkable superlatives of divinity heaped upon this king.[35] In v. 6, the psalmist addresses the king as God (*Elohim*),[36] and in v. 17 the king is praised forever. As James M. Trotter correctly notes, "Ultimately, this psalm is a hymn of praise to the king unparalleled in the Hebrew Bible for its unrestrained exultation of a human being."[37] The scholars who deny the direct messianic interpretation of this psalm explain this "deification" of Israel's king as hyperbole, even though such hyperbolic descriptions of Israel's kings are lacking anywhere else in the Hebrew Bible. Andy Dvoracek, for example, acknowledging the king's identification as God, finds it necessary to clarify what is the rather obvious reading of the Hebrew text when he writes, "We should not, however, see this elevation as an indication that the king himself is divine."[38] But then again, perhaps we should.

The Identification of the Bride

Since the identity of the bride and her bridesmaids has been one of the primary reasons for denying the direct messianic interpretation of Ps 45, and since a figurative interpretation of the bride as the historical-grammatical meaning of this passage will most likely be met with objections,[39] we will now look at the bride in the immediate and larger literary context.

Several textual clues suggest the author of the book of Psalms presents the daughter in Ps 45:10-14 as a figurative depiction of the speakers of the three previous Sons of Korah psalms (Pss 42–44) who long to come into God's presence. First, there are only two verses in the entire Hebrew Bible that refer to "coming" (*bw'*) into someone's presence with "joy" and "rejoicing" (Pss 43:4; 45:15). In Ps 43:4, the psalmist describes his desire to come to the altar of God's presence as his "greatest joy" (*śimḥaṯ bgili*). In Ps 45:15 (see vv. 13-15), the daughter ("bride") is led into the King's palace along with her companions with "gladness and rejoicing" (*biśmāḥōṯ wāgil*).

A second reason for interpreting the king's bride figuratively is the identification of one of the bride's companions as the "daughter of Tyre," clearly used as a metaphor to represent an entire people, as the second half of v. 12 makes clear: "The daughter of Tyre, the wealthy people, will seek your favor with gifts" (Ps 45:12). As the *Hebrew and Aramaic Lexicon of the Old Testament* well notes, daughter is frequently used as a "personification of a town" or "country."[40] Thus, Scripture speaks of Israel and Jerusalem as the daughter of Zion (Isa 62:11; Zch 9:9; Ps 9:14), the "daughter of my people" (Isa 22:4; Jer 4:11 endnotes, HCSB), and the "daughter of Judah" (Lam 2:2). Other foreign nations are addressed as the "daughter of Edom" (Lam 4:21) and the "daughter of Egypt" (Jer 46:24) [all author's translations].

In fact, this metaphorical use of "daughter of Tyre" suggests its similar usage for the people of Jerusalem/Israel in 45:10 and 12. So the presence of foreign nations at the wedding banquet of God's people is quite consistent with the immediately following psalms where nations are rejoicing together with the sons of Abraham (Ps 47:9).

A third reason for regarding the bride as a metaphor for God's people is the larger context, in which the distance between the people of Israel from their God and His Temple (Pss 42–44) is clearly overcome in Pss 46-49 with the joyful celebration of God's presence with His people in the Temple (cf. Pss 45:15; 48:9), the case for which will be extensively developed later in this article.

A fourth and final reason has to do with the many other passages in the prophetic literature that depict the redemption of God's people as a wedding banquet. As noted in the *Dictionary of Biblical Imagery*, "Throughout the Bible, God's relationship to his people is pictured as a marriage."[41] With respect to this depiction, the OT prophets portray the making of God's covenant with Israel at Mount Sinai as a marriage (Jer 2:1-2; 31:32; Isa 54:5), Israel's idolatry as adultery against her Divine Husband (Jer 3:1-2, 6; Ezk 16:15-25; Hos 1:2; 2:2), her exile as a divorcée (Isa 50:1; Jer 3:8), and her end-of-days redemption as a wife once again (Isa 54:6-7; Hos 2:16-20). In one of the better-known extended metaphors, Hosea the prophet's experiences with his unfaithful wife Gomer are not only compared with God's experiences with His unfaithful wife Israel. Hosea's call to take his adulterous wife back is compared to God's redemption of the people of Israel through the Messiah in the Last Days:

> Then the Lord said to me, "Go again; show love to a woman who is loved by another man and is an adulteress, just as the Lord loves the Israelites though they

> turn to other gods and love raisin cakes."
>
> So I bought her for 15 shekels of silver and five bushels of barley. I said to her, "You must live with me many days. Don't be promiscuous or belong to any man, and I will act the same way toward you."
>
> For the Israelites must live many days without king or prince, without sacrifice or sacred pillar, and without ephod or household idols. Afterwards, the people of Israel will return and seek the LORD their God and David their king. They will come with awe to the LORD and to His goodness in the last days. (Hos 3:1-5)

Ezekiel the prophet speaks extensively of Israel's broken relationship with God in terms of a failed marriage, and her future renewal as an eschatological marriage renewal (Ezk 16; 23). Several references in Ezekiel lend further credence to a figurative interpretation of the bride in Ps 45. First, God's bride in Ezk 16 (Jerusalem = the people of Israel) is said to have an Amorite father and a Hittite mother (Ezk 16:3,45). This suggests that the call to the bride in Ps 45:10 to "forget your people and your father's house" does not necessarily mean that the bride in Ps 45 is a Gentile, but that Israel as a people continues to be called out from the idolatrous practices of the Gentile nations.

Second, God is said to dress His bride in embroidered cloth, *riqma* (Ezk 16:10,13), which is the same material worn by the bride as she is led to the king in Ps 45:14 (translated "colorful garment" in the HCSB). Moreover, the bride is adorned with gold jewelry (Ezk 16:13; Ps 45:13), and is well noted for her beauty (Ezk 16:14-15,25; Ps 45:11). And though God's bride commits adultery (Ezk 16:15-26), God will renew His marriage covenant with His people (Ezk 16:59-63).

All these factors suggest that the wedding in Ps 45 is intended to be a figurative depiction of the eschatological wedding banquet described by several of Israel's prophets. This interpretation is bolstered, not only by the relationship of Ps 45 with the psalms preceding and following it, but also by the eschatological nature of the book of Psalms, as recognized by an ever-growing body of final-form Psalms scholarship.[42]

LITERARY CONTEXT OF PSALM 45[43]: LOCATION, LOCATION, LOCATION!

Psalm 45 is located in the introductory section of psalms in Book II (Pss 42–72), a collection of psalms of the Sons of Korah (Pss 42–49).[44] The transition from Book I (Pss 1–41)[45] to Book II (Pss 42–72) marks a shift in the authorship of the individual psalms,[46] from psalms predominantly written by David in Book I (Pss 1–41), to the second book. Book II is comprised of the psalms of the Sons of Korah (Pss 42, 44–49), a psalm of Asaph (Ps 50), psalms of David (Pss 51–65, 68–70), psalms without attribution of authorship (Pss 66–67, 71), and a psalm of Solomon (Ps 72). The psalms of Korah have clearly been grouped together according to their superscriptions, and as a cohesive group, these psalms contain numerous lexical and thematic links one with another.[47]

Problems Preceding Psalm 45

As will be seen, the psalms leading up to Ps 45 deal with two urgently felt problems. So Ps 45 provides the answers to these specific problems introduced in Pss 42–44, namely, failure on the battlefield and distance from God's presence (i.e., separation from the house and mountain of the Lord). As such, Ps 45 serves as the hinge psalm that transitions the group from lament (Pss 42–44) to celebration (Pss 46–49), when both problems have been addressed and resolved.

Psalm 42 begins with what might be described as separation anxiety. There is an expression of yearning for God's presence and a question: "*When can I come* and appear before God?"[48] The pain of distance from God and desire to come/be brought into[49] God's presence (sanctuary) is repeated several times, particularly in Pss 42–43:[50]

> Send Your light and Your truth; let them lead me. *Let them bring me* [*yᵉḇi'ûni*] *to Your holy mountain*, to Your dwelling place. Then *I will come* [*'āḇô'ô*] *to the altar of God*, to God, my greatest joy. I will praise You with the lyre, God, my God. (Ps 43:3-4)[51]

The psalmist's primary motivation for returning to God's presence is to praise (*yḏh*) God, as evident by a refrain repeated five times in Pss 42–43: "Why am I so depressed? Why this turmoil[52] within me? Put your hope in God, for *I will still praise Him* [*yḏh*], my Savior and my God" (Ps 42:5; see 42:11; 43:5).

The second major problem in Pss 42–44 is that of military defeat and oppression, and a sense of God's absence when His presence and help are most needed on the battlefield. First, the psalmist questions why God has forgotten (*šḵḥ*) His people (Pss 42:9; 44:17,20,24). Second, the psalmist asks why God has rejected (*znḥ*) His people, a question found in the introduction and conclusion to Books II and III and also repeated numerous times in Books II and III of the Psalter (Pss 43:2; 44:9,23; 60:1,10; 74:1; 77:7; 88:14; 89:38).[53]

> I will say to God, my rock, "Why have You *forgotten* [*šḵḥ*] me? Why must I go about in sorrow *because of the enemy's oppression*?" (Ps 42:9)
> For You are the God of my refuge. Why have You *rejected* [*znḥ*] me? Why must I go about in sorrow *because of the enemy's oppression*? (Ps 43:2)[54]

This theme of military defeat is particularly clear in Ps 44:9-10:

> But You have *rejected* [*znḥ*] and humiliated us; *You do not march out with our armies*. You make us retreat from the foe, and those who hate us have taken plunder for themselves.[55]

Not only have the people of Israel suffered military defeat, they are also subjected to the jeers of their enemies who constantly remind them of their separation from the divine presence (i.e., the first problem). On two occasions, the adversaries mock the people of Israel by highlighting the divine absence: "Where is your God?" (Ps 42:3,10). The jeering of the victorious enemy is particularly clear in Ps 44:13-16:

> You make us an object of reproach to our neighbors, a source of mockery and ridicule to those around us. You make us a joke among the nations, a laughingstock among the peoples. My disgrace is before me all day long, and shame has covered my face, because of the voice of the scorner and reviler, because of the enemy and avenger.

This military defeat reminds the psalmist that Israel's hope is not in their own sword (Pss 44:3,6).

Psalm 44 concludes with a number of questions and requests that demand answers and resolutions:

> Wake up, LORD! Why are You sleeping? Get up! Don't reject us forever! Why do You hide Yourself and forget our affliction and oppression? For we have sunk down to the dust; our bodies cling to the ground. Rise up! Help us! Redeem us because of Your faithful love. (Ps 44:23-26)

Answers Following Psalm 45

In light of these two problems (separation from the divine presence and military defeat on the battlefield), the tone of Pss 46-49 rings of a remarkable reversal. The plea for the "distant" God to rise up and help in the last verse of Ps 44 (v. 26) becomes a celebration of God's help, a God who is "always found" (Ps. 44:1, lit., "exceedingly found": *nimṣāʾ mᵉʾōḏ*) and a God who will help "the city of God, the holy dwelling place of the Most High" (Ps 46:4-5):

Rise up! *Help* us! Redeem us because of Your faithful love. (Ps 44:26)	God is our refuge and strength, a *helper* who is always found in times of trouble. (Ps 46:1) God is within her; she will not be toppled. God will *help* her when the morning dawns. (Ps 46:5)[56]

The raging[57] nations are toppled (Ps 46:6), and the distant Lord who did not "march out with our armies" (Ps 44:9) is twice identified as the Lord of "armies" (hosts) who is "with us" (Ps 46:7,11):

But You have rejected and humiliated us; You do not march out with our *armies* [*bᵉṣiḇʾôṯenû*]. (Ps 44:9)	The LORD of *Hosts* ["armies": *ṣᵉḇāʾôṯ*] is with us; the God of Jacob is our stronghold. (Ps 46:7,11)[58]

The Lord makes wars cease, shatters bows and spears, and burns up chariots (Ps 46:9). Both problems in Pss 42–44 clearly have been resolved: the God of Hosts (Armies) has defeated the enemy armies, and now He is no longer distant, but very near indeed, present in His Temple and the city of His dwelling place (Ps 46:4-5).

This jubilant tone continues in Ps 47 as the Gentiles are invited to join in praising Israel's Great King (Ps 47:1,6,7) who rules over all the earth and who has subdued peoples and nations under His feet (Ps 47:1-3).[59] God now reigns over the nations and sits upon His holy throne (Ps 47:8; see Ps 45:6), and the nobles are assembled with the people of the God of Abraham (Ps 47:9). The joyful praise of God continues into the next psalm with the Great King dwelling in His city and holy mountain (Ps 48:1-3). God has successfully defended the city against the advance of the hostile kings (Ps 48:4-8). The psalm's jubilant praise continues because God is in His palace,[60] located on Mount Zion (Ps 48:9-14).

The final psalm of this cluster of psalms of the Sons of Korah is a call for the peoples[61] to consider contemplatively (Ps 49:1-4), in light of the previous psalms, why the psalmist has no reason to fear the threats of Israel's enemies who will one day perish with all their wealth (Ps 49:5-20).

PSALM 45 AS THE TURNING POINT FROM MOURNING TO REJOICING

This stark reversal from God's distance from His people and their defeat on the battlefield in Pss 42–44 to His glorious presence with His people and the total defeat of Israel's enemies in Pss 46–49 demands an explanation. What happened?! This reversal is best explained by the details of Ps 45, where both problems (distance and defeat) are solved in reverse order, a solution that makes most sense when considering the interpretive significance of the relationship of juxtaposed psalms throughout the Psalter.[62]

Psalm 45 begins by celebrating Israel's king, a figure who throughout the psalm is clearly distinguished from God (Ps 45:2,7) and yet mysteriously identified with God (Ps 45:6,11,17).[63] The identification of the king as a figure distinguished from God in Ps 45 is all the more startling when considering the exclusively divine identity of the king in the immediately surrounding psalms of the Sons of Korah (*'anwâ* [Ps 45:4]; *'āni* [Zch 9:9]) and *righteousness/justice* (*ṣedeq* [Gn 45:4]; *ṣaddiq* [Zch 9:9]).[70]

Other likely allusions to well-known messianic prophecies include the reference to the king's eternal throne and kingdom (Ps 45:6; see 1Ch 17:14; 22:10).[71] The reference to this king's eternal throne ties the eternal reign of this king to God's promises to the house of David (2Sm 7:13,16; Isa 9:7; Pss 89:4,36; 1Ch 17:12,14). Moreover, the divine identification of this mighty warrior (*gibbwōr*) who sits upon an eternal throne (Ps 45:3,6) is remarkably similar to Isaiah's prophecy of a future king who will reign on David's throne forever (Isa 9:7), a king whose name shall be called "Mighty God" (*'el gibbôr*; Isa 9:6).[72]

All of these above-named allusions to messianic prophecies in the Hebrew strongly favor the direct messianic prophecy view of Ps 45. Psalm 45 did not accrue a messianic meaning over time: rather, this king of superlative beauty and divine attributes is the same king of whom the Law and the Prophets spoke.

CONCLUSION

As the king in Ps 45 is more beautiful than the sons of men, we have seen that this psalm also qualifies as one of the most beautiful psalms in the Psalter. This article has argued for the direct messianic interpretation of this psalm, particularly because of its unequaled and sustained praise of the king of Israel who is mysteriously human and divine.

Additionally, this article looked at the identity of the bride in Ps 45, and argued that the author of the Book of Psalms has presented the bride as a figurative representative of the people of Israel. This is supported by the metaphorical use of the word "daughter" elsewhere in the psalm, as well as by the relationship of this psalm to the other psalms in the group. The bride's entrance into the palace is presented as the resolution to Israel's distance to God's palace. Moreover, it was shown that wedding metaphors are used in the prophetic literature to depict God's redemption of his people in the last days.

Furthermore, it was demonstrated that the Psalm's primary structure is divided between the battlefield and the palace, the settings of which provide answers to thc problems posed in the preceding psalms (42–44). The psalmist is far away from God's palace (His Temple) and His presence, and the people of Israel have suffered devastating defeat on the battlefield. Psalm 45 provides the solution to these problems. First, the Divine-Messiah King rides out to totally vanquish Israel's enemies on the battlefield. Next, the Divine-Messiah King sits upon His eternal throne and a call is given to bring the bride along with other nations into His presence (His

Temple). With the divine distance overcome and Israel's enemies vanquished, the celebrations now begin in the Sons of Korah psalms that follow after (46–49).

Finally, it was maintained that there is an intertextual relationship between Ps 45 and other well-known messianic prophecies, most notably, Gn 49, 2Sm 7, and Zch 9. The strong allusions to these passages strongly support the direct messianic interpretation of this psalm.

It is fitting to conclude this article with a citation from the last book of the Bible, which (being the prototype for a good story) ends with a climactic wedding. As in much of the book of Revelation, the following verses draw on the OT, not least the picture of the Messiah-King and His beautiful bride in Ps 45.

> Then I saw heaven opened, and there was a white horse. Its rider is called Faithful and True, and He judges and makes war in righteousness. . . . A sharp sword came from His mouth, so that He might strike the nations with it. He will shepherd them with an iron scepter. He will also trample the winepress of the fierce anger of God, the Almighty. . . . I also saw the Holy City, new Jerusalem, coming down out of heaven from God, prepared like a bride adorned for her husband. Then I heard a loud voice from the throne: Look! God's dwelling is with humanity, and He will live with them. They will be His people, and God Himself will be with them and be their God. (Rev 19:11,15; 21:2-3)

---

1. A special word of thanks to Jo Blower, esteemed colleague and lover of the Bible who provided helpful editorial feedback.
2. Amos Hakham, *The Book of Psalms*, ed. Eliezer Elinor, Aaron Mirsky, and Yehuda Kil, 7th ed. *Da'at Miqra* (Jerusalem: Mosad HaRav Kook, 1989), 1:263. This is called an ephthalamium, a poem or song composed in honor of a wedding.
3. Allen P. Ross, *A Commentary on the Psalms* (Grand Rapids: Kregel Academic, 2011), 2:69; Gerald H. Wilson, *Psalms: From Biblical Text to Contemporary Life*, The NIV Application Commentary Series (Grand Rapids: Zondervan, 2002), 708; Peter C. Craigie and Marvin E. Tate, *Psalms 1–50*, rev. ed., Word Biblical Commentary (Nashville: Thomas Nelson, 2004), 340.
4. Dvoracek notes, "There is great consensus concerning the overall shape of the Ps. 45. Nearly all interpreters recognize a threefold division: introduction, body, and conclusion" (Dvoracek, Andrew Thomas. *A King in Context: Reading Psalm 45 in Light of Psalms 42, 43, 44, and 46* [Portland, OR: Western Seminary, 2012], 280. E-book.).
5. Adam K. Copenhaver, "The Royal Bride as Historical Eggshells?: Bruce Waltke's Canonical-Process Approach Applied to Psalm 45" (Philadelphia: Westminster Theological Seminary, 2009), 18; Wilson, *Psalms*, 700.
6. Christoph Schroeder, "A Love Song: Psalm 45 in the Light of Ancient Near Eastern Marriage Texts," *Catholic Biblical Quarterly* 58, no. 3 (1996): 417.
7. Craigie and Tate, *Psalms 1–50*, 338.
8. Hakham, *Book of Psalms*, 1:258.
9. Dvoracek, "A King in Context," 87–88.
10. All quotations as well as versification are taken from the HCSB unless noted otherwise. Unlike in the English versions, the superscription is considered the first verse in Ps 45.
11. As Dvoracek astutely notes, vv. 1 and 17 are set apart as the only first-person references in the psalm.

12. The word "eternal" appears strategically three times in the psalm's two stanzas and the conclusion.

13. The two stanzas in the body of the psalm are set apart by *qatal* (perfect verbs) and nominal clauses describing the king's virtues. The good word about the king's victories on the battlefield begins with v. 2: "You are the most handsome" (second person *qatal*-first clause that ends with a "therefore" (*'al-ken*) statement in which God blesses (*qatal* clause) the king forever (*lᵉ'ôlām*). The good word about the king's glories in the palace begins with vv. 6-7: a nominal clause about the Divine King's eternal throne (*'ôlām*) (v. 6) and a *qatal*-first clause with a "therefore" (*'al-ken*) statement in which God anoints (*qatal* clause) the king with unsurpassable joy (v. 7). Verses 8-9 also continue the accolades of the king using nominal clauses and *qatal* verbs ("all your garments," "bring you joy," "stands at your right hand").

14. The call for the king's victory and the bride's celebration in both stanzas begin with imperatives (vv. 3-4: "strap your sword," "ride triumphantly"; vv. 10-11: "listen," "pay attention," "consider," "forget," "bow down") and continue with *yiqtol*-clauses (v. 4: "may your right hand show"; vv. 12-16: "will seek," "she is led," "they are led," "they enter"). Both stanzas end with a final *yiqtol*-clause in which the preposition *ṯaḥaṯ* appears (v. 5: "the peoples fall under you"; v. 16: "in your place your fathers will be"; author's translation).

15. The word "palace" appears twice in the second stanza (vv. 8,15). The palace setting is most obviously noted by the throne (v. 6), the queen standing at the king's right hand (v. 9), and the bride being led into the king's palace (vv. 14-15). As will be seen, these two locations provide the necessary context for resolving the conflict in the opening psalms of Book II (Pss 42–44): a need to defeat the enemies, and a need for the divine presence with His people.

16. Author's translation.

17. Author's translation.

18. Author's translation.

19. So also, Adonijah (1Kg 1:5-6). See James M. Trotter, "The Genre and Setting of Psalm 45," *Australian Biblical Review* 57 (2009): 39.

20. 2Sm 7:13,16; 1Kg 2:33,45; 9:5; 10:9; Isa 9:7; Jer 17:25; Pss 89:4,36; 1Ch 17:12,14; 22:10; 2Ch 9:8.

21. See G. Lloyd Carr, "The Old Testament Love Songs and Their Use in the New Testament," *Journal of the Evangelical Theological Society* 24, no. 2 (1981); Schroeder, "A Love Song."

22. Pss 45:2,11; Sg 1:8,15-16; 2:10,13; 4:1,7,10; 5:9; 6:1,4,10; 7:1,6.

23. Pss 5:7; 22:27,29; 29:2; 45:11; 66:4; 72:11; 81:9; 86:9; 95:6; 96:9; 97:7; 99:5,9; 132:7; 138:2. In Ps 106:19, the word "bow down" is used negatively with reference to the golden calf.

24. According to Murray J. Harris, "The Translation of Elohim Psalm 45:7-8," *Tyndale Bulletin* 35 (1984): 69, Ps 45:6 is "[o]ne of the most celebrated *cruces iterpretum* in the OT . . ."

25. The word "vocative" comes from the Latin word *vocare* ("to call") and is the case used for addressing someone. For instance, in the sentence, "Bob, you are a great guy," the speaker is obviously addressing Bob directly, thus "Bob" is in the vocative case.

26. Ross, *A Commentary on the Psalms*, 78.

27. Hakham, *The Book of Psalms*, 258 (translation of the Hebrew is author's).

28. Harris, "The Translation of Elohim Psalm 45:7-8," 87. Harris is working with the versification of the Hebrew Bible (verse references in parenthesis are provided for clarity; transliteration provided).

29. There is more to say about this when looking at Ps 45 in the context of the Sons of Korah psalms (Pss 45–49).

30. Ps 6:5; 7:17; 9:1; 18:49; 28:7; 30:4,9,12; 32:5; 33:2; 35:18; 42:5,11; 43:4-5; 44:8; 52:9; 54:6; 57:9; 67:3,5; 71:22; 75:1; 76:10; 79:13; 86:12; 88:10; 89:5; 92:1; 97:12; 99:3; 100:4; 105:1; 106:1,47; 107:1,8,15,21,31; 108:3; 109:30; 111:1; 118:1,19,21,28-29; 119:7,62; 122:4; 136:1-3,26; 138:1-2,4; 139:14; 140:13; 142:7; 145:10. It is used only in a negative sense to refer to the sinful boasting of a rich man when he dies (Ps 49:18).

31. Wilson, *Psalms*, 707.

32. Bruce Waltke, whose interpretative approach to the psalms involves an appreciation for the accrued meaning of a psalm from its original historical context to its final place in the Christian canon, calls these details the historical eggshells; see Copenhaver, "The Royal Bride as Historical Eggshells?"

33. Hakham, *The Book of Psalms*, 263.

34. Ibid.

35. These unparalleled ascriptions of deity led the well-known Baptist preacher Charles Spurgeon to write more than a century ago, C. H. Spurgeon and David Otis Fuller, *C. H. Spurgeon's Treasury of David* (Grand Rapids: Zondervan, 1940), 1:213, "Some here see Solomon and Pharaoh's daughter only—they are short sighted; others see both Solomon and Christ—they are cross eyed; well-focused spiritual eyes see here Jesus only . . ."

36. The various attempts to avoid the plain reading of this Hebrew text will be discussed in the next section.

37. Trotter, "Genre and Setting of Psalm 45," 45. See also Christoph Schroeder, "A Love Song," 417, who writes, "Psalm 45 is unique. Whereas hymns of praise in the psalter are normally addressed to Yhwh, this psalm is a song of praise and promise to the *human* king who is seen in godlike features."

38. Dvoracek, "A King in Context," 214; Ross, *A Commentary on the Psalms*, 69.

39. Does it make sense for the psalmist to tell Israel to "forget your people and your father's house" (Ps 45:10)?

40. Ludwig Köhler et al., *The Hebrew and Aramaic Lexicon of the Old Testament* (Leiden, Netherlands: New York: E. J. Brill, 1994).

41. Leland Ryken et al., eds., *Dictionary of Biblical Imagery* (Downers Grove, IL: InterVarsity Press, 1998), 538.

42. Brevard S. Childs, *Introduction to the Old Testament as Scripture* (Philadelphia: Fortress Press, 1982); Cole, *Psalms 1-2: Gateway to the Psalter*; David C. Mitchell, *The Message of the Psalter: An Eschatological Programme in the Books of Psalms*, Journal for the Study of the Old Testament Supplement Series 252 (Sheffield, England: Sheffield Academic Press, 1997); Michael K. Snearly, *The Return of the King: Messianic Expectation in Book V of the Psalter*, The Library of Hebrew Bible/Old Testament Studies (London and New York: Bloomsbury T&T Clark, 2016); Gerald Henry Wilson, "The Use of Royal Psalms at the 'Seams' of the Hebrew Psalter," *Journal for the Study of the Old Testament* 11, no. 35 (1986).

43. In the introductory article to the Messiah in the book of Psalms in this *Handbook*, "Messianism in the Psalms," extensive evidence was provided in support of reading and interpreting the book of Psalms as a book. Readers are encouraged to read this article before reading this section. For a helpful literary analysis of the Sons of Korah psalms (42–49), see Christine M. Vetne, "The Function of 'Hope' as a Lexical and Theological Keyword in the Psalter: A Structural-Theological Study of Five Psalms (Pss 42–43, 52, 62, 69, 71) within Their Final Shape Context (Pss 42–72)," *Andrews University Seminary Studies*. 53, no. 2 (2015): 169. Also see the article by Robert Cole, "Compositional Unity in the Five Books of the Psalms: A Canonical Approach" in this *Handbook*.

44. Although Ps 43 is lacking a superscription, its unity with Ps 42 has been well-noted. Dvoracek, *A King in Context* 4, n. 3, writes, "Although Pss. 42 and 43 have come down to us as two psalms, they almost certainly reflect a single literary unit. This finds support not only in the strong lexical and thematic links that bind them, but also in their nearly identical refrains."

45. To be more specific, Book I begins with Ps 3. Pss 1–2 function as the introduction to the book of Psalms, and Pss 146–150 function as the conclusion to the book of Psalms. See Postell, "Messianism in the Psalms" in this *Handbook*; Robert L. Cole, *Psalms 1-2: Gateway to the Psalter*, Hebrew Bible Monographs (Sheffield: Sheffield Phoenix Press, 2012).

46. This shift in authorship at the seams between Book I and Book II is somewhat eased by the relationship between the final psalm of Book I and the first psalm of Book II. In Ps 41:1, David pronounces blessings on one who "considers" (NASB; Hebrew *maśkil*) the helpless. Book II opens with several *maśkil* psalms of the sons of Korah (Pss 42; 44; 45; 47), and includes most of the *maśkil* psalms in the Book of Psalms (eight of the 14 *maśkil* psalms are in Book II).

47. See Dvoracek, "A King in Context."

48. Emphasis provided. Questions (requests) and answers (also vice versa) in adjacent psalms are a key feature in the compositional unity of the book of Psalms. For instance, Book IV ends with a request that the Lord "gather us from the nations, so that we may give thanks to Your holy name . . ." (Ps 106:47). Book IV begins with the giving of thanks to the Lord (Ps 107:1) because he "has gathered them from the lands—from the east and the west, from the north and the south" (Ps 107:3). The pervasiveness of the "question and answer" dynamic adjoining juxtaposed psalms in the Psalter strongly suggests this is one of the guiding principles behind the location of the psalms in the final form of the book of Psalms.

49. In Hebrew, the verbs "come" and "bring" derive from the same root: *ḇw'* (Pss 42:2; 43:3-4; 44:17).

50. The psalmist is clearly physically separated from the temple in Ps 42:6.

51. Hebrew transliteration and emphasis provided.

52. The root for the noun "procession" and the verb for "to rage/be in turmoil" (*hmh*) is repeated six times in Pss 42–46, and clearly functions as a key word binding these psalms together into a coherent group: process (Ps 42:4); turmoil (Pss 42:5,11; 43:5); roar (Ps 46:3); rage (Ps 46:6).

53. The verb "*znḥ*" (reject) is used only one other time in the Psalms outside of Books II–III (Ps 108:11).

54. Hebrew transliteration and emphasis provided.

55. Hebrew transliteration and emphasis provided.

56. Emphasis in Scripture quotes is added.

57. The word for "rage" (*hmh*) serves as a key word linking these psalms together: Pss 42:5,11 and 43:5 "turmoil"; 46:3 "roar," 46:6 "rage.

58. Words in brackets and emphasis provided.

59. This phrase "peoples under us" (*'ammim taḥtenû*) in 47:3 is a near identical repetition of the phrase "peoples under you" (*'ammim taḥteḵā*) in Ps 45:5 (see also v. 16, lit., "under your fathers"; 2Sm 22:48; Ps 18:47), with the sole exception of the pronominal suffix ("us" and "you").

60. See Pss 45:8,15; 48:9.

61. The "peoples" have been a constant theme since their first appearance in Psalm 45 (Pss 45:5,17; 47:1,3,9; 49:1).

62. See author's article, "Messianism in the Psalms" in this *Handbook*.

63. Trotter, ("Genre and Setting of Psalm 45") perceptively captures this dual identity when he writes, "The closest literary parallels to this psalm are the coronation psalms (2; 72; 110) and the enthronement of Yahweh in hymns (47; 93; 95–99)."

64. See Robert L. Cole, "An Integrated Reading of Psalms 1 and 2," *Journal for the Study of the Old Testament* 26, no. 4 (2002).

65. The Messiah is also known as a divine-warrior in Isa 9:6 ("Mighty God"; compare Ps 45:3).

66. What the people of Israel were unable to do with the might of their own sword in the previous psalm, God does through the sword of the divine Messiah (Pss 44:3,6; 45:3).

67. An additional lexical link is the reference to the robes/clothing [*lᵉḇûš*] of the king and the bride (Gn 49:11; Ps 45:13).

68. All emphasis and words in brackets provided.

69. Mitchell, *The Message of the Psalter*, 249–50.

70. In Mitchell's words, ibid., 250, "Such similarities seem more than fortuitous, and suggest some kind of link between the ideas of the psalm and Zech. 9.9." Note that Ps 72 and Zch 9 also share a virtually identical reference to the reign of the Messiah which "will extend from sea to sea, from the Euphrates River to the ends of the earth" (Ps 72:8; Zch 9:10).

71. These are the only three verses in the Hebrew Bible that include the words "throne" (*ḵise'*), "forever" (*'ôlām*), and "kingdom" (*malḵûṯ*).

72. The words "mighty warrior" in Ps 45:3 and "mighty" in Isa 9:6 are the same in Hebrew (*gibbôr*).

Psalm 69

The Lament of the Messiah

RANDALL L. MCKINION

Discussing Ps 69 within the context of the messianic passages of the Old Testament presents an interesting dilemma in how to read a text that made such an impact on the authors of the New Testament. Like Ps 22, Ps 69 is quoted multiple times with respect to the life and work of Christ. As a result, one temptation when considering the messianic implications of Ps 69 is to move directly into the NT to show that the psalm was being read in reference to Jesus. As such, the apostolic witness to the prophetic character of the psalm might be considered beyond dispute. However, when trying to deal faithfully with the OT text, the reader should first allow the context of the psalm to dictate the intention of the psalmist,[1] allowing the text to speak to its significance.

The goal of this article is to read carefully the textual clues that the author has left within the structure of the psalm itself, within the context of the Psalter, and within the Hebrew Bible to determine what made Ps 69 attractive to the NT writers. Such a reading intends to show that the psalm is not just messianic via analogy and/or type but rather that the context of the Psalter invites a careful reading through the lens of the covenant made with David. In this sense, it is prophetic and messianic. But this messianic meaning can become difficult to recognize if the psalm is considered to be exclusively about the historical David. The psalm must be considered within the context of the Psalter's interpretation of David's words in the Psalter's final form. As Rydelnik states, "[I]f . . . we read the Old Testament in its final form for its plain meaning, the messianic hope shines out like a clear beam of light."[2] At the same time, the use of the psalm in the NT, particularly the Gospel of John, confirms its messianic character.

THE COMPOSITION OF PSALM 69 WITHIN THE DAVIDIC PSALTER

English versions translate the first verse of the Hebrew text as the heading of Ps 69. This title attributes the psalm (or at least relates it) to David, which is an important designation in that it invites a reading from a Davidic (perhaps therefore messianic?) perspective.

Davidic psalms make up the vast majority of Books 1 and 2 (Pss 1–72) of the Psalter, broken into two sections: 3–41 and 51–71. There remain valid reasons to affirm Davidic authorship of these psalms, even though throughout David seems to speak both on behalf of himself and another (e.g., Ps 40:6-8, see below). These two groups of psalms form what has been called the "Davidic Psalter," which the author of the book indicates in Ps 72:20: "The prayers of David, the son of Jesse, are finished." Although some titles with Pss 1–72 attribute their psalms to other authors (e.g., Pss 42–49 to the sons of Korah and Ps 50 to Asaph), the conclusion in Ps 72:20 reminds the reader that the focus of these first two books is on David, the one to whom God has promised a seed to sit on an eternal throne (2Sm 7). The colophon of 72:20 "marks a division *within* a larger textual complex,"[3] and the author seems to have used this compositional strategy to invite a reading of the first two books of the Psalter that understands David as speaking. His words are spoken as one to whom the covenant was made but also as a prophet, on behalf of the King of Ps 2, who is called Son. Recognizing the strong connections between Pss 2 and 72 makes this strategy even more apparent.[4] The map leading to Ps 72 has already been given in Pss 1 and 2—namely, the path of the blessed one, the Son, who will be exalted as King on Yahweh's throne. Ps 72 echoes this with its prayer for the King who will reign with righteousness and justice over a universal kingdom. Childs states this well:

> The perspective of Israel's worship in the Psalter is eschatologically oriented. As a result, the Psalter in its canonical form, far from being different in kind from the prophetic message, *joins with the prophets in announcing God's coming kingship* [emphasis added]. When the NT authors heard in the psalms eschatological notes, its writers were standing in the context of the Jewish canon in which the community of faith worshipped and waited.[5]

This anticipated kingdom, ruled by a son of David in fulfillment of the Davidic covenant, is described in the words of and about David throughout Pss 1–72. As a result, the trajectory of the King is set by Ps 2, and the resultant kingdom toward which the first two books of the Psalter lead is clearly described in Ps 72. Yet, much like the messianic picture portrayed in Isaiah, this part of the Psalter also uses lament psalms to present the suffering David as a portrait of the righteous sufferer.

The role of Ps 69, an individual lament psalm, should be understood from this perspective, yet the question that must be raised is how the psalm serves within its near context in light of the larger royal theme. In this, relationships among Pss 69–71 shed helpful light. These psalms are connected through the use of vocabulary for shame and dishonor, as highlighted below:

Psalm 69	Psalm 70
[6] Do not let those who put their hope in You be *disgraced* because of me, Lord God of hosts; let not those who seek you be *humiliated* because of me, God of Israel. [7] For I have endured insults because of You, and *shame* has covered my face. [19] You know the insults I endure—*my shame* and *disgrace*. You are aware of all my adversaries.	[2] Let those who seek my life be *disgraced* and confounded. Let those who wish me harm be driven back and *humiliated*. **Psalm 71** [1] Lord, I seek refuge in You; let me never be *disgraced*. [13] May my adversaries be *disgraced* and destroyed; may those who seek my harm be covered with disgrace and humiliation.

"Together with Psalms 70–71, Psalm 69 prepares the way for the exalted hopes for the enduring and righteous rule of the king in Psalm 72—a rule that will last as long as the moon and will reach to the ends of the earth (72:5–8)."[6] These psalms lay the hopes of those who suffer shame and dishonor at the feet of the king who rules with righteousness and justice, despite that he himself becomes the object of shame and dishonor from his own people. The proximity of Ps 69 to and its use at the end of Book 2 mirrors that of Ps 40 near the end of Book 1. The distinction between the two psalms seems to be that David clearly acknowledged his iniquities in 40:12, whereas in Ps 69, the suffering one is proclaimed as innocent (see below on vv. 1-6). Yet, David specifically speaks for the coming deliverer about whom Moses wrote:

> Then I said, "See, I have come;
> it is written about me in the volume of the scroll.
> I delight to do Your will, my God;
> Your instruction lives within me." (Ps 40:7-8)

With this contextual foundation laid, the rest of this article will discuss the content of the psalm, with particular attention given to those areas that demonstrate its prophetic, messianic character. Allen provides a reasonable structure based on observations of repetition within the psalm.[7] For simplicity, this structure will be adopted as a framework for commentary.

Psalm 69:1-13a

Psalm 69, an individual lament psalm, opens with a personal call for salvation (v. 1a). The psalmist expresses desperation using powerful metaphors of waters, the deep, and the muddy mire that threaten imminent death (vv. 1b-2). Incessant crying out has resulted in a parched throat and weary eyes (v. 3). "That voice and eyes, the best 'gates' to life, are dying underscores the dramatic situation out of which this psalm of lament arises."[8] Yet, even in this tumultuous situation, the speaker is expressing hope and recognizing the close relationship that he has with God ("looking for my God" v. 3b).

The metaphorical becomes concrete in v. 4. The speaker has been forced by those who hate and would destroy him to return what he has not stolen. In other words, his lying enemies are slandering him and falsely accusing him, the paradigm of injustice experienced by the innocent sufferer.[9] Yet, in the next verse, there seems to be the implication that the supplicant is petitioning God for salvation from a situation that came because of his folly and wrongdoing. However, according to v. 4, the one praying is hated "without cause." As such, v. 5 does not necessarily imply culpability on behalf of the speaker; rather, it should "be considered solely as a declaration of the supplicant's cognizance of folly and guilt-liability, and therefore is not to be interpreted as a penitence as such."[10] In humility, the petitioner opens himself to God's judgment as to whether his suffering is just.[11] Although there may not be room to be dogmatic on this issue, the point of the psalm seems to be that the situation is indeed not merited, and v. 5 "is really a brief form of the speaker's protestation of innocence."[12] David was certainly a sinner, as is evident in psalms where he clearly recognizes his sin and God's forgiveness (e.g., Pss 32 and 51); and he certainly suffered as a result of his sin. By contrast, the suffering in this psalm will be described as reproach experienced by the lamenter on God's account, not his own. The reproach borne by the speaker is not of his own making but is a result of his relationship to God (v. 7) and his fervor for God's house (v. 9).

In v. 6, the speaker prays that those who are waiting for and seeking Yahweh, the God of Israel, would not be ashamed or humiliated as a result of the treatment of the one suffering. The supplicant knows that what is happening to him has possible ramifications for the community, particularly those who are faithful to the Lord. In the end, the orientation of the psalm will indeed expand to the people of

God (see vv. 32-33). Moreover, the hope of the psalmist is later expressed by a desire for a turning of events in which his enemies might experience the same types of suffering he has endured. Here David's prayer is that the faithful will not be *disgraced* or *humiliated*; in the next psalm he prays that those who seek his life may be *disgraced* and *confounded* (70:2). The way the speaker responds to his suffering is a pattern for the community of faith. For example, by directing his appeal in 69:6 to "Adonai Yahweh [Lord GOD] of hosts" and "the God of Israel," the supplicant expresses his confidence in his God and the character of the God for whom he is willing to suffer. Those who wait for and seek the Lord (v. 6) follow his example.

Whereas in v. 6 the psalmist prays that those who seek their God would not be brought to "disgrace" or "humiliation," according to v. 7, the face of the petitioner is covered with that same "dishonor" or "humiliation" (HCSB "insults" and "shame"). The potential plight of the people becomes the tangible experience of the individual, which includes alienation even from his own family (v. 8; cf. Jn 1:11). In fact, at least in the words of the supplicant, the suffering seems to be in place of those upon whom the reproach might be waged. The psalmist prays that they would avoid what he was to experience.

In v. 7, the basis for the speaker's suffering is given as "because of You" (i.e., God Himself). In vv. 9-12, the reason for his persecutors' hatred becomes more specific and is described in three ways. First, ill treatment comes in response to his zeal for the house of God (v. 9a). In other words, the supplicant expresses great joy in and concern for true worship of Yahweh in a house built for his name. In a psalm latent with messianic overtones about the house of David, the text of Ps 132:1-5 expresses how David had this hope and vowed to provide a place for God to dwell among His people. This correlation between the house of God and the son of David is an integral part of the Davidic covenant (e.g., see 2Sm 7:13; 1Chr 17:12; Hag 2:1-9). Beginning with Solomon (1Kg 8), faithful Davidic kings will model this zeal for the house of God, as will the future son of David, the Messiah (Jn 2:17, see below). Ironically enough, this zeal results in persecution from God's people, just as it did for Jeremiah (see Jer 7,26,38). For David, as for the psalmist, anticipation of this house remains a future realization, an anticipated hope that is woven into the fabric of the Psalter.

Second, the psalmist's suffering comes because "the insults of those who insult You have fallen upon me" (v. 9b). Attackers who otherwise were seeking to dethrone or attack Yahweh (as in Ps 2) instead direct their hostility toward the next best option—the Davidic king who had a passion for the house of the Lord.

Third, the supplicant's act of lament—namely, weeping with fasting and sackcloth—results in reproach (vv. 10-11). Whatever he does in humility before God means greater humiliation before his detractors. He is the object of scorn as they make up proverbs or jokes about him (v. 11b), speak of him at the gates, and sing of him in their drinking songs (v. 12). They hate him and his commitment to Yahweh, and they deride him because he has a passion for God's honor and worship. Yet, his faith never seems to waver. In contrast to those who are his enemies, he prays, "But as for me, LORD, my prayer to You is for a time of favor" (v. 13a). The content of his prayer appears in the next section.

Psalm 69:13b-29

Just as the first part of the psalm began with a call for God to "save," so the second section begins with a call for God to answer in the firmness of His "salvation" (v. 13b). This section heaps up words of petition that are common to individual laments in the Psalter, such as the following: "answer me" (vv. 13,16,17), "rescue me" (v. 14), "turn to me" (v. 16), "don't hide your face" (v. 17), "draw near," "redeem," and "ransom" (v. 18). The text returns in vv. 14-15 to the water and mire imagery used in vv. 1-2. By mentioning the "pit" (v. 15), the threat of death and the grave seems ever the more imminent. Despite the gravity of the situation, the petitioner comes boldly with these great requests because of the character of the One to whom he prays. Twice he asks his God to answer because of the Lord's "faithful love." In v. 13b, he says, "In Your abundant *faithful love*, God, answer me with Your sure salvation"; and in v. 16a, "Answer me, LORD, for your *faithful love* is good." The term otherwise translated "lovingkindness" or "steadfast love" (*ḥesed*) expresses God's faithfulness to His promises, His covenantal fidelity.

The psalmist's cry for salvation is at a favorable time because of Yahweh's commitment to the covenant He has made with David. The first line of the petition begins with a reflection on God's self-revelation to Moses in Ex 34:6: "Yahweh—Yahweh is a compassionate and gracious God, slow to anger and rich in *faithful love* and truth." The author not only hopes that his situation will not escape the purview of the God who acts with such commitment, he also seems to be recognizing that the situation of the suffering one is part of Yahweh's plan for extending mercy and grace to His people.

In v. 17, the speaker calls himself God's "servant." This way of referring to himself seems to be important, for in v. 19, this "servant" suffers the same reproach, shame, and dishonor experienced in the first section of the psalm. This one suffers the reproaches of God as an innocent servant. As in Ps 22, where the petitioner asks God not to forsake him (22:1), here the servant asks that God not turn His face away from him (v. 17). Without God's intervention, there would be no hope, and in both Pss 22 and 69, the point seems to be that God does not forsake the one praying, but delivers him, even if death is experienced and/or there is a sense of being forsaken by Yahweh. Psalm 22:24 explicitly says, "He did not hide His face from him but listened when he cried to Him for help." The servant, who is described in these two psalms that were held to be so prophetic of the Messiah's passion, is not utterly forsaken. Thus, it is fitting that Jesus Himself (as well as the NT writers) connects the Messiah's work to that expressed by David in these two important laments.

However, in the midst of his despair, the psalmist would find neither pity nor comfort from those around him (v. 20b). Rather, they would give him poison for food and sour wine for drink (v. 21; cf. Jn 19:28-29). Even in the moment of great suffering, when reproach had broken his heart (v. 20a), the psalmist found no mercy from his enemies but only continued scorn. There was no satisfaction for his parched throat (v. 3). In the great irony of how those who should have come to his aid fail to help, the text highlights the great betrayal at the hand(s) of the one(s) close to him.[13] There is no surprise, then, that 69:25 was quoted in regard to Judas, the one who betrayed Jesus, in Ac 1:20.

The prayer turns, then, to a series of imprecatory requests against these enemies (vv. 22-25). The magnitude of these petitions serves not just as an encouragement for the petitioner, but also as a commentary on the righteousness of the one praying. While he has come before the Lord as an innocent sufferer, they are indeed worthy of their "just judgments."[14] The reason for these requests for judgment comes in v. 26: "For they persecute the one You struck and talk about the pain of those You wounded." The surprising element here is not so much the persecution by enemies; this has been pervasive throughout Ps 69 (as well as throughout the first two books of the Psalter). Rather, here the additional element is that the one(s) they persecute are those whom the Lord has struck, as "the petitioner is perceived as someone wounded and stricken by God."[15] It seems that this refers to more than just an act of injustice, in that the suffering of the servant comes also at the hand of the one to whom the servant prays. However, in the supplicant's view, the persecution is an act of iniquity by the enemy (v. 27). As the reproach is also experienced by a plurality, in that more than one is pierced, this points to the idea that those who are related to the servant (see vv. 34-36) will experience the same types of persecution (cf. Jn 15:18-25).

Using a literary device called inclusio, the petitioner's last request for himself returns to where he began: "Let your salvation protect me, God" (v. 29b, cf. also vv. 1,13). This bookending sets the stage for the psalm's transition to praise by the supplicant and the community of faith in vv. 30-36.

Psalm 69:30-33

As a testimony to the confidence that the speaker has in Yahweh's hearing and answering his prayer, he says in v. 30, "I will praise God's name with song and exalt Him with thanksgiving." The response to God's work of deliverance includes singing and thanksgiving, eclipsing any pleasure God would find in the offering of a bull. Within the psalm, the weeping with fasting and sackcloth has been turned into praise, as the prayer of the servant has been answered and his death overturned.

Moreover, those who see the work of God on behalf of the lamenter respond accordingly, as the suffering and deliverance of the servant becomes a pattern for the rest of the community of faith. Just as Yahweh would hear and respond to the prayers of the petitioner, so He also hears the needy and those who are in bonds (v. 33). Those whom God hears are specifically called those who "seek God" (v. 32), about whom the supplicant prayed in v. 6. These two verses (vv. 32-33) express the same hope for the afflicted as that of Ps 22: "For He has not despised or detested the torment of the afflicted. He did not hide His face from him but listened when he cried to Him for help. . . . The humble will eat and be satisfied; those who seek the LORD will praise Him. May your hearts live forever!" (22:24,26). The last phrase in v. 26 ("May your hearts live") parallels exactly 69:32b. In both psalms, the affliction of the suffering one provides a pattern of hope for the community of faith who also suffer the same afflictions.

Psalm 69:34-36

The psalm concludes with the cosmic response to God's work on behalf of His servant: the heavens, the earth, the seas, and all that moves in them should praise God (v. 34). The reason is given in vv. 35-36: "for God will save Zion and build up the cities of Judah. They will live there and possess it. The descendants of His servants will inherit it, and those who love His name will live in it." In v. 35, the term for salvation occurs for the fourth time in the psalm, forming an inclusio with v. 1. The salvation requested by the supplicant has now been guaranteed for those who love Him, as the sufferer reflects the reality of a suffering community. If Yahweh saves His servant, He will also save Zion and the community of faith. Or perhaps, because of the work of God through and on behalf of the *servant*, there is an expectation of a work of God for the *servants*. The reproach borne by the servant means rescue and security for His servants, upon whom the reproach could have landed. Ultimately, the hope expressed through the Psalter rests on the work of another—the Anointed One, the Son, the Suffering Servant.

PSALM 69 AFTER THE DAVIDIC PSALTER

Within the Psalter, the message of Ps 69 also extends beyond Books 1 and 2. Three psalms in particular help the reader understand the themes set by the author, as supported by similarity in language and composition. Psalm 69 has a reprise in each of the following three books: Ps 86 in Book 3, Ps 102 in Book 4, and Pss 130–131 in Book 5.

In Ps 86, which is also a psalm of David, the supplicant appeals to the faithful love of Yahweh (vv. 13,15; cf. Ex 34:6) and calls upon Him to answer his prayer. As in Ps 69, the one praying appeals in the situation to his own innocence, as one who is godly and trusts in the Lord (86:2).

Psalm 102, which according to its title is "a prayer of an afflicted person," resonates with the prayer of Ps 69. As in Ps 69:35, the hope of Ps 102 centers on God's faithfulness to build up Zion (102:13,16,21). Also, Ps 102:25-27 is quoted in Heb 1:10-12 in relationship to the Son. The NT writers understood its message to be prophetic and messianic, as they did for Ps 69.

Psalms 130–131, which are connected via the repetition of "Israel, put your hope in the Lord" (130:7; 131:3), present a united message regarding waiting on the Lord. On the one hand, the supplicant of Ps 130 appeals to Yahweh's faithful love (v. 7) as the basis for an audience to his pleas. On the other hand, in Ps 131, David again appeals to his innocence (v. 1) as the pattern for those who might hope in Yahweh "both now and forever" (v. 3). This eschatological hope finds its fulfillment in God's faithfulness to the Davidic covenant, which Ps 132 makes clear. As the description of the innocent sufferer of Ps 69 who waited for God to save Zion set the stage for the triumphant reign of the son of David of Ps 72, so the patient waiting of an innocent David of Ps 131 sets the stage for the Anointed One of Ps 132 who would sit on David's throne at Zion.

Relating Ps 69 to these psalms shows that the hope of the composer of the Psalter rests (1) in the fulfillment of the Davidic covenant at Zion and (2) in the deliverance God provides for and through the innocent sufferer. Regarding the latter, the pattern of David is consistently used in each of the five books of the Psalter. He is not only the pattern of how God's people might suffer, but also—important for the psalmist—is the prototypical innocent sufferer. In this regard, the Psalter prophesies of the Messiah as the righteous King and as the Suffering Servant.

PROPHETIC RESONANCE WITH PSALM 69

With the repetition within the Psalter of the individual lament in which there seems to be an innocent sufferer, might there be a relationship with Isa 52–53 and the Suffering Servant? There is already a connection between Ps 69:13 and an earlier Servant Song in Isa 49:8-9 where the restoration of Israel "in a time of favor" is connected to the work of salvation (49:6) wrought by the Servant of the Lord. In the development of the book of Isaiah, this Servant who would bring salvation to the ends of the earth (49:6) would (surprisingly) also be afflicted and suffer on behalf of His people (Isa 50 and 53).

Consider the following example of textual overlap:

Psalm 69:26	Isaiah 53:3-5
26 For they persecute the one [the servant] You struck and talk about the pain of those You wounded.	3 He was despised and rejected by men, a man of suffering who knew what sickness was. He was like someone people turned away from; He was despised, and we didn't value Him. 4 Yet He Himself bore our sicknesses, and He carried our pains; but we in turn regarded Him stricken, struck down by God, and afflicted. 5 But He was pierced because of our transgressions, crushed because of our iniquities; punishment for our peace was on Him, and we are healed by His wounds.

As Tate says, "The description of a servant of Yahweh who undergoes such great distress because of faithful service easily recalls the striking passages in Isa 50:4-9 and 52:13; 53:12."[16] As with Job and the Suffering Servant of Isa 53, "the psalm . . . assumes that there are times when we have to discern that God's bringing suffering does not imply the guilt of those to whom it comes."[17] Although it is not Goldingay's point to show this as a messianic psalm, his point demonstrates that a faithful reading of Ps 69 recognizes that the suffering occurs by one who did not deserve it. As such, the messianic import of Ps 69 resonates with that of Isa 52–53 in laying out the inevitability of the suffering of the innocent son of David.

PSALM 69 AND THE NEW TESTAMENT

With the exception of Ps 22, Ps 69 is quoted in the NT more than any other portion of the Hebrew Bible. Eight verses from Ps 69 are quoted or alluded to in the NT: 69:4 → Jn 15:25; 69:9 → Jn 2:17; Rom 15:3; Heb 11:26; 69:21 → Mk 15:23,36; Jn 19:29; 69:22-23 → Rom 11:9-10; 69:24 → Rev 16:1; 69:25 → Ac 1:20; 69:28 → Phl 4:3; Rev 3:5; 13:8; 17:8; 20:12,15; 21:27. Not all of these are used to refer to Jesus as the Messiah or within a messianic context. However, if Ps 69 contributed to the theology of a messianic Psalter, the NT appropriation of that theology should naturally appear. As an example of this, the Gospel of John makes this textual, messianic reading explicit.

John 2:17

As a commentary to the pericope in which Jesus drives out the moneychangers from the Temple (2:13-16), John writes, "His disciples remembered that it is written: 'Zeal for Your house will consume Me'" (2:17), which is a quotation of Ps 69:9a.[18] When the disciples were considering the work of Jesus in light of the Scriptures, they understood the significance of these actions related to the Temple. Furthermore, the story of the cleansing of the Temple leads to a request by the Jewish leaders for a sign (2:18), which Jesus reorients toward His death and resurrection (vv. 19-21). The author then adds, "When He was raised from the dead, His disciples remembered that He had said this. And they believed the Scripture and the statement Jesus had made" (2:22). Their faith was prompted by Jesus' words, because these words were from the Scriptures—namely, Ps 69—which interpreted for them the sign and Jesus' words. Just as zeal for the Lord's house led to reproach for the suffering servant of Ps 69, so the quotation here points proleptically in John to the hatred of Jesus by the Jewish leaders. This reproach ultimately led to the cross.

John 15:25

In Jn 15, Jesus makes the point to His disciples that they should expect the world to hate and to persecute them. This is not a surprise, given that "it hated Me before it hated you" (15:18). Those who had seen the works that Jesus had done and rejected Him demonstrated their hatred of both the Son and the Father (15:24). His explanation for this was based on the text of the Scriptures: "But this happened so that the statement written in their scripture might be fulfilled: They hated me for no reason" (15:25). According to Jesus, Ps 69:4 was indeed pointing toward the One who would suffer, not as a result of sin, but because of the rejection of His own people. This is a central theme of Ps 69. Also, in Ps 69:26, the individual sufferer is connected with a plurality who are identified with his suffering. The psalm, as well as the text of John, show that there is an inclusiveness to the suffering. It is not just the Suffering Servant who experiences reproach, but His servants as well.

The point to be made here is that Jesus understood the written text to be about Himself (and His people), and its fulfillment depended upon these things happening in His life. Moreover, the author, John, is recording these things to convince the reader that the acts of Jesus testified to Him as the Messiah and that the texts about Him were fulfilled in His life and work.

John 19:29

Within the crucifixion narrative, which has multiple quotations of and/or allusions to the Hebrew Bible, John alludes to Ps 69:21 in Jn 19:28-29: "After this, when Jesus knew that everything was now accomplished that the Scripture might be fulfilled, He said, 'I'm thirsty!' A jar full of sour wine was sitting there, so they fixed a sponge full of sour wine on hyssop and held it up to His mouth." The significance of Ps 69 to the text of John is not just the isolated quotation of v. 21, but rather "the entire psalm as the fundamental interpretive key . . . for Jesus' suffering, death, *and* resurrection."[19] These things were happening to fulfill the Scriptures.

The way John has dealt with the text of Ps 69 certainly indicates how it was interpreted by the disciples and within the early church. The importance of the text in the preaching of Christ "according to the Scriptures" (1Co 15:3-4) cannot be understated. John's presentation of the Christ demonstrates this textual interpretation. As a summary, consider again the following:

"His disciples remembered *that it is written . . .*" (Jn 2:17)
"so that the statement *written in their scripture* might be fulfilled . . ." (Jn 15:25)
"Jesus knew . . . that *the Scripture* might be fulfilled . . ." (Jn 19:28)

All three of these passages refer to written Scripture that was used to interpret Jesus' person and work. The witnesses to this are Jesus Himself, the group of disciples when they looked back over the life and works of Jesus, and the author of John. All three confirm that the written texts of the Hebrew Bible focused on the Messiah. The point to be made in this article is that this interpretation was inherent to the text, not simply one made by analogy.

CONCLUSION

Many years ago, Delitzsch wrote of Ps 69:

> The whole Psalm is typically prophetic, in as far as it is a declaration of a history of life and suffering molded by God into a factual prediction concerning Jesus the Christ, whether it be the story of a king or a prophet; and in as far as the Spirit of prophecy has even molded the declaration itself into the language of prophecy concerning the future One.[20]

Psalm 69 portrays the words of the innocent Suffering Servant, bearing from the hands of God the reproach of those who reject Him. The lament of this psalm ultimately finds its eschatological answer in the work of the king of Ps 72, the hope toward which the first two books of the Psalter lead. This prophetic and messianic message was not lost on the writers of the NT, as the text is quoted consistently as pointing to the life and work of Jesus, the Messiah.

---

1. And when referring to the psalmist here, I am referring to the one who placed Ps 69 within the final collection of the Psalter. Strategic placing of psalms within the Psalter is an important element of the final composition and should be seen as elucidating the meaning of the text.
2. Michael Rydelnik, *The Messianic Hope: Is the Hebrew Bible Really Messianic?* (Nashville: B&H Academic, 2010), 190.
3. Frank-Lothar Hossfeld and Erich Zenger, *Psalms 2: A Commentary on Psalms 51–100*, trans. Linda M. Maloney (Minneapolis: Fortress Press, 2005), 209.
4. See the articles in this *Handbook* on Psalm 2, Psalm 72, Compositional Unity of the Psalms, and the Messianic Message of the Psalms.
5. Brevard S. Childs, *Introduction to the Old Testament as Scripture* (Philadelphia: Fortress Press, 1979), 518, emphasis added.
6. Gerald H. Wilson, *The NIV Application Commentary: Psalms–Volume 1* (Grand Rapids: Zondervan, 2002), 950.
7. See Leslie C. Allen, "The Value of Rhetorical Criticism in Psalm 69," *Journal of Biblical Literature* 105/4 (1986): 577–98.
8. Hossfeld & Zenger, *Psalms 2*, 177.
9. See Hossfeld & Zenger, *Psalms 2*, 178.
10. Alphonso Groenewald, *Psalm 69: Its Structure, Redaction and Composition*, Altes Testament und Moderne 18 (Münster: LIT Verlag, 2003), 52.
11. Consider the following from Hossfeld & Zenger, *Psalms 2*, 180: "With the reference in v. 6 to his 'folly' . . . and to his 'faults' . . . the petitioner does not contradict the guilt he has emphasized in v. 5 in view of the reproaches directed at him; instead, he subjects himself to the judgment of his God and relinquishes every kind of superiority or self-righteousness."
12. Marvin E. Tate, *Psalms 51–100* (Dallas: Word Books, 1990), 196.
13. See Tate, *Psalms 51–100*, 199: "The poison and vinegar which the suppliant receives represents a radical form of betrayal by those who should have been comforters."
14. E. W. Hengstenberg, *Commentary on the Psalms* (Edinburgh: T&T Clark, 1846), 2:365.
15. Hossfeld and Zenger, *Psalms 2*, 172.
16. Tate, *Psalms 51–100*, 197.
17. John Goldingay, *Psalms: Volume 2: Psalms 42–89*, Baker Commentary on the Old Testament Wisdom and Psalms (Grand Rapids: Baker Academic, 2007), 351.
18. 69:9b is quoted in Rom 15:3 and Heb 11:26.
19. Hossfeld & Zenger, *Psalms 2*, 185 (emphasis in original).
20. C. F. Keil and F. Delitzsch, *A Commentary on the Old Testament in Ten Volumes: Volume 5: Psalms*, trans. James Martin (Grand Rapids: Eerdmans, 1973 repr.), 278.

Psalm 72

The Messiah as Ideal King

JAMES SPENCER

In his *Exposition of the Psalms*, Augustine begins his discussion of Psalm 72 with a brief reflection of the psalm's superscription, "'For Salomon' indeed this Psalm's title is forenoted: but things are spoken of therein which could not apply to that Salomon king of Israel after the flesh, according to those things which holy Scripture speaketh concerning him: but they can most pertinently apply to the Lord Christ."[1] Augustine's words demonstrate well the messianic nature of Ps 72. Psalm 72 offers a vision of the future, depicted in connection to the past, thereby preserving the continuity with Israel's history. The psalm reinforces God's universal rule transcending time and location through the coronation of Israel's king.

Based on the superscription and the psalm's final line, "the prayers of David the son of Jesse are concluded" (v. 20), the psalm appears to signal the transition from one Israelite king to the next. The psalm is structured as a prayer for the coming ruler with the hope that he will reign with justice and righteousness (vv. 1-4), that his reign will bc long and peaceful (vv. 5-7), and that his kingdom will extend beyond the borders of Israel so that "all kings bow down to him, all nations serve him" (vv. 8-11). The psalmist does not know whether the next king will fulfill the desires of his heart. He is not clear that the monarch who follows David will rule with justice and righteousness, establish peace in Israel, or have the kings of the earth bow down at his feet. The psalmist does know, however, that the hopes of Israel rest on the God of Israel "who alone does wonders" (v. 18).

EARLY MESSIANIC INTERPRETATIONS OF PSALM 72

In the OT, Ps 72 is not written as a messianic prophecy, but as a prayer for the future king of Israel. The psalm's placement, as noted in the previous section, informs its meaning through the provision of a rich theological context describing the dynamics of the Davidic covenant. Psalm 72 is most certainly royal, exhibiting characteristics similar to other royal psalms (Ps 2,18,20,21,45,89,101,110,132,144) and seems to look forward to a day when the Davidic covenant will be realized. In reading this psalm now and knowing that Jesus is the expected Messiah, it seems clear that Ps 72 recognizes the need for the Messiah.

This aspect of Ps 72 is clear not only to those who recognize Jesus as the Messiah. Jewish interpreters also saw in Ps 72 a messianic expectation. The Targums, for instance, are interpretive renderings of various OT books written in Aramaic and offer insight into the manner in which certain Jewish communities understood the OT. The Targum's rendering of Ps 72 makes clear the interpreter's understanding of the psalm as expressing the hope of a coming Messiah. The Targum's rendering of Ps 72:1 is particularly interesting in this regard.

The Targum renders Ps 72:1 as follows: "By Solomon, uttered in prophecy. O God, give your just rulings to the King Messiah, and your righteousness to the son of King David." This rendering includes words and phrases that were not in the original Hebrew text through the addition of: "uttered in prophecy," "Messiah," and "David." The inclusion of "uttered in prophecy" suggests that the writer of the Targum understood the psalm to be forward looking and not confined to the passing of Israel's throne from David to Solomon. In suggesting that the psalm is a prophecy of Solomon, it would appear that the Targum is looking beyond Solomon to a time when a king will sit on the throne of Israel and realize the desires expressed in the prayer. The addition of "Messiah" and "David" in the Targum offers a more explicit connection to the Davidic covenant, specifying not only that the king will be from the house of David, but also that the king will be the anticipated Messiah. The prayer for the king has become a prayer for the coming Messiah who will establish the kingdom of Israel.

In addition to the Targum's rendering of Ps 72:1, v. 17 has been identified as messianic by early Jewish and Christian interpreters. The Targum translates 72:17 as, "May his name be remembered forever, his name which was made ready even before the sun came into being." This rendering is different from that found in the OT, which reads "May his name endure forever; as long as the sun shines." The difference in the final phrase prompted early Jewish and Christian commentators to underscore the significance of the Messiah. Heine offers an overview of several of these sources within his discussion of the prophetic texts used to prove the preexistence of Christ.[2] Sources including the Babylonian Talmud, Justin's *Dialogue with Trypho*, Irenaeus's *Proof of the Apostolic Preaching*, and Tertullian's *Against Marcion*, identify Ps 72:17 as messianic.[3]

Although it is not often cited explicitly in the NT, Ps 72 clearly contributes to the Bible's portrayal of the anticipated Messiah. Broyles analyzes several potential allusions to Ps 72 in the NT and concludes, "Although Psalm 72 was not a major source for literary citations and allusions in the New Testament, we have seen enough evidence to regard it as a source for messianic expectations."[4] He goes on to note, "The New Testament's notion of Messiah is based largely on the Davidic model of an 'anointed one,' and Psalm 72 is a constituent text for that model."[5] While its direct influence on the NT may be limited, Ps 72, as Broyles observes, contributes to the broader messianic vision of the Scriptures as a whole.

These early messianic uses of Ps 72 demonstrate both the messianic nature of the psalm and the interpretive strategies of interpreters through the ages who did not shy away from such messianic readings. While Ps 72 does not feature prominently in the NT and is not used as an explicit messianic prophecy in Scripture, the witness of interpreters from early Jewish and Christian circles to the messianic character of the psalm reinforce the theological themes that provide the literary context for Ps 72.

BOOK II OF THE PSALMS AND PSALM 72

Psalm 72 is situated at the conclusion of Book II of the psalms. There are 150 psalms in total, organized into five books, each with a slightly different theological emphasis and message from the others. Books I (1–41) and II (42–72) are strongly connected thematically, with both focusing on God's provision for David and the nation of Israel. The Davidic covenant is first introduced in Ps 2, the first royal psalm in the psalter. According to Wilson, Ps 2 assists "in the shaping of the first three books of the Psalter" and "has the effect of introducing the covenant relationship between Yahweh and the Davidic kings who ruled from Jerusalem."[6] Wilson also notes a stream of consciousness within Books I and II. Waltke, following Wilson, summarizes this perspective well: "Psalm 2 introduces the idea of the Davidic covenant, Psalms 3 and 41 speak of the king's assurance of *I AM's* protection and security in the face of his enemies, and Psalm 72 contains multiple petitions from the king's son."[7] Standing as it does at the end of Book II, Ps 72 serves to pass the Davidic covenant on to the next generation, entreating God to bless the new king's rule.

As the final psalm in Book II, Ps 72 transitions from a focus on David to a focus on his descendants. Book III of the psalms is less concerned with David than with those in his line. The prayers of Ps 72 are not realized in Book III. Rather than a wise and faithful ruler to whom the nations bow down, Book III offers a bleak picture of the nation of Israel as God brings other nations to discipline His people. Book III ends with Ps 89, which recalls the Davidic covenant and in which "the psalmist expresses a concern for the future as he looks back to the covenant—he hopes for the restoration of the Davidic king in accordance with the promise of God."[8]

Both Books I and II have a high number of lament psalms with many of the psalms in Book II being tied to specific events in David's life in the superscription (51, 52, 54, 56, 57, 59, 60, and 63). The intermingling of lament and royal psalms reflects the ebbs and flows of David's life and kingship. His road to the throne after his anointing (1Sm 16) was thwarted at every turn by Saul. After his installation on the throne of Israel, David's own sin with Bathsheba brought about turmoil in the kingdom. Regardless, God made a covenant with David promising that one of David's descendants would be established on the throne forever and that "my faithful love will never leave him, as I removed it from Saul; I removed him from your way" (2Sm 7:13-15).

Looking at the overall composition of the psalms in Book II provides an important context for understanding Ps 72. Whereas 39 of the 41 psalms in Book I are psalms of David, Book II contains a mix of psalms of Korah (42–49), Asaph (50), David (51–65; 68–70), Solomon (72), and three anonymous psalms (66–67, 71). House suggests that the mix of voices within Book II exhibits a particular design: "The passages ascribed to Korah and Asaph stress the establishment of worship, while those ascribed to David and Solomon focus on divine protection and the continuity of the Davidic covenant. The three anonymous texts emphasize the work of God in Israel's history from creation to David's time."[9] The mixture of voices demonstrates that the sons of Korah and Asaph join with Israel's kings in lamenting Israel's troubles, proclaiming God's acts of deliverance, confessing sin, and entreating God to act on behalf of the nation.

Book II begins with psalms attributed to the sons of Korah. Psalms 42 and 43 form an introductory unit combining the lament of Ps 42 with a call for vindication in Ps 43. Psalm 44 builds on Pss 42 and 43, calling God to help the current generation as He did the covenant community of the past. Psalm 45 marks something of a transition and may serve as an answer to the cry for help in Ps 44. Celebrating God's kingship, as well as the anointing of Israel's king, demonstrates God's ongoing faithfulness to Israel, which is fleshed out further in Pss 46–49.

While God's steadfast love for Israel is certainly cause for celebration, God will also judge His people. In Pss 50–53, the people of God are called to be wise (Ps 49), to worship God truly (Ps 50), and to confess and seek forgiveness for sin (Ps 51).

Psalms 52–53 continue the call to wise living by contrasting the wise and the fool and the fate of those who do evil. Psalm 53 concludes with the psalmist's desire for the salvation of Zion and for the restoration of God's people (53:6). This final expression of desire gives way to a series of psalms calling for the restoration of God's people (54–59), which in turn gives way to God's rejection in Ps 60. Despite this rejection, the psalmist recognizes that God is the only source of salvation that matters, "for human help is worthless" (Ps 60:11).

Psalms 61–68 highlight God as the solution to the ills of the nations and humanity more generally. This group of psalms is focused on the coming universal reign of God. Collectively these psalms underscore God's acts of salvation and look forward to the day when God will establish His kingdom and rule the nations. Following the previous group of psalms and their pleas for restoration and the lament over God's rejection, Pss 61–68 revive the hope of God's ultimate deliverance.

Having identified God as the solution to the nation's difficulties, Pss 69–71 move on to proclaim humanity's need for God's deliverance, while recognizing and praising God for His care and salvation. The timing and continuation of God's deliverance is the subject of Pss 70 and 71. In Ps 70, the psalmist calls for God to "hurry" (70:1) and not to delay in bringing His salvation. Psalm 71 addresses the issue of time in a slightly different matter, praying that God will remain with the psalmist till the end.

The progression in thought of Book II (Pss 42–72) begins with the Davidic covenant and ends with the passing of the throne to the next generation. Life in covenant is not a simple matter. As Israel and its leaders stray from their covenantal obligations, God calls His people to repent. God's people feel acutely the need for restoration and seek God's deliverance and salvation through confession of sin and renewed faithfulness. They praise Him for His acts of deliverance. Yet even in the midst of their praise, there is a recognition that Israel's future, while secure because of God's faithfulness, requires a ruler who will follow the Lord. Psalm 72 looks forward, entreating God to send a ruler capable of leading the nation so that they may enjoy the blessings of justice, dominion over the nations, peace, and prosperity. The psalm recognizes that, despite the deliverance celebrated in Pss 69–71, disobedience represents an ongoing threat to the nation. What is needed is a ruler who can sustain peace perpetually.

PSALM 71 AND THE MESSIANIC MESSAGE OF PSALM 72

In addition to the broader context of Book II, Ps 71 serves an important contextual element for understanding the messianic vision of Ps 72. As one of only a handful of psalms in Book II that are not explicitly ascribed to an author via superscription, Ps 71 has generally been understood as a plea from David for God's continued faithfulness and presence. Whether or not this psalm should be attributed to David, its content suggests that it is less lamentation than reminiscence. As Beth Tanner rightly states, "Ps. 71 takes its time arriving at the descriptions of distress (vv. 9-13) and contains more lines that praise God than those of petition to God. The mood, then, is not one of urgency but is reflective of a lifetime lived trusting in God's faithfulness."[10]

The various references to old age or end of life (71:9,17-18) and confidence expressed in God's continued faithfulness (71:19-21) offer a framework for reading Ps 72 that looks back across a life lived with God. More than many of the other psalms within Book II, Ps 71 provides an overview of life with God. While toil and trouble are part of the human experience even for those in covenant with the Lord, God's overwhelming might and lovingkindness overcome the difficulties of life. Psalms 71 and 72 close Book II with a sense of uneasy hope and expectation. The psalmist knows that God will remain faithful to the Davidic covenant. God has proven His commitment to His people over and over again. They are incapable of sustaining the sort of faithfulness required to be in covenant with God. Wilson makes a similar observation concerning Ps 72 noting that, "these petitions for God's blessings are not simply predicated on the basis of YHWH's covenant obligations. Rather the motivation behind the divine blessing is found in the king's proper action in behalf of his people."[11]

Psalm 72 is not simply a prayer that God would bless the next king, but also an articulation of the ideal king who is yet to come. As Clifford notes regarding the king, "He is a sign, a kind of sacrament of God from whom all authority on heaven and earth is derived. In this reading, a poem that seems to be a conventional praise of the king turns out to be something much more."[12] The utterance of the prayer hints at a sense of expectation that the Davidic covenant will somehow be fulfilled. The prayerful anticipation of Ps 72 provides a sense of hope that the relationship between God, king, and land will finally be restored.[13] The prayer is that the coming king "will so rule that the reign of God will be extended to the earth, and the earth will respond with abundant produce. . . . This king, then, will provide the resolution to the age-old division that has separated nation from nation and humanity from God. This king will usher in the blessing of Israel and of all the families of the earth that was promised to Abraham in Genesis 12:1-3."[14]

AN EXPOSITION OF PSALM 72

First Petition

Psalm 72 begins with a petition for the king. The psalmist appeals to God, calling Him to "give" the king the capacity to rule with justice and righteousness. It is important to recognize God's role in the king's reign. It is God who will empower the king to administer the sort of justice and righteousness that he is incapable of producing on his own. This initial entreaty highlights the futility of kingship in and of itself, pointing toward the necessity of divine intervention. Calvin expresses this well in his commentary on Ps 72 noting, "If kings possessed in themselves resources sufficiently ample, it would have been to no purpose for David to have sought by prayer from another, that with which they were of themselves already provided. But in requesting that the righteousness and judgment of God may be given to kings, he reminds them that none are fit for occupying that exalted station, except in so far as they are formed for it by the hand of God."[15]

As God gives the king his justice and righteousness and the king acts accordingly, there are certain expected results that are described in vv. 2-4. It seems clear that the kings who submit to the empowering work of the Lord will shepherd God's people, care for the poor, and enjoy the prosperity of the land. Theologically, we find here a God who does not know limitation or scarcity. Because God is willing and able to provide for His people, there is no need to withhold sustenance from the poor and the needy, no need to subvert justice or to practice greed. God empowers His king to administer justice, not simply by instilling the king with wisdom, but by blessing the nation so that acts of injustice and unrighteousness become unnecessary.

The focus on the needy in vv. 2-4 gives way to the endurance and scope of the king's reign in vv. 5-7 and 8-11 respectively. Verse 5 begins with a call that they may fear [God]. The NIV and NRSV follow a textual variant from the Septuagint and translate "may he endure" and "may he live" respectively, whereas the ESV and NASB follow the Masoretic, or Hebrew, text (MT). The variant in the Septuagint maintains a stronger focus on the eternality of the king and the endurance of his reign, whereas the Hebrew text refocuses the discourse on the Lord.

Verse 5 (NASB) shifts to the third person plural "them" as opposed to the third person singular "he" or "him" that has been the norm throughout much of the rest of Ps 72. While translators often leave the referent of "them" ambiguous in translation, some English versions identify the people as the referent. Note, for instance, the New English Translation, which reads "People will fear you as long as the sun and moon remain in the sky." While it is possible that the psalmist has the people of Israel in view, it seems more likely that v. 5 is referring to those within the royal line of David and that the "them" of v. 5 points to the kings who will rule over Israel after David and Solomon. The psalmist is highlighting the crucial link between the king's fear of the Lord and the petition that the king judge fairly (72:2) and defend the oppressed (72:4). If the Davidic kings are to rule the nation well, they must have a fear of the Lord throughout their generations.

Read in light of the history of David's house after Solomon and the division of the kingdom, v. 5 reflects far more than a passing comment regarding dynastic succession. Instead, it is an expression of deep longing for a dynasty of God-fearers who will rule the nation as God's agents, so that Israel may receive the blessing of God and realize the nation's destiny. The verse also has implications for understanding the messianic message of the psalm. Verses 1-4 present themselves as a prayer for an individual king and may have been used in rituals associated with the installation of a new king.[16] Verse 5 broadens the scope of the petition in vv. 1-4 beyond just the next king in line for the throne to include the whole of the Davidic line. The psalm, in v. 5, becomes a prayer for the perpetuation of the Davidic dynasty faithfully following God and leading the nation into His blessing.

Having petitioned the Lord for a wise king who will fear the Lord and uphold justice, the psalmist breaks into new petitions in vv. 6-11. Each of the petitions, like those related to the care of the needy in vv. 1-4, reflects themes associated with the Messiah elsewhere in the Scriptures. The psalmist prays that the king will make the righteous flourish and will bring about an extended period of peace in the land (v. 7). The psalmist calls for this peace to extend beyond Israel with a reign that spans "from the Euphrates to the ends of the earth" and encompasses all the kings of the earth (vv. 8-11). Longman rightly points to the connection between Ps 72 and the Abrahamic covenant, noting that the psalm "paints a hopeful picture that this king's influence might extend beyond the borders of Israel to include all the nations of the world, thus bringing to fruition the blessing to the nations promised to Abraham."[17] The psalmist looks prayerfully ahead to a time when a king will sit upon the throne and be the agent through whom God fulfills His promises to Israel.

The psalmist returns to the king's care for the poor and needy in vv. 12-14. Unlike the petition concerning the king's defense of the oppressed in v. 4, v. 12 is not a request. Instead, the verse proclaims transitions away from prayers and petitions to affirm the king's future acts on behalf of the needy.[18] The psalmist continues to look ahead to a day when the king of Israel, the king for whom he prays, will come to deliver the oppressed and shepherd the nation's poor. The delivery of the poor is often associated with the Messiah, thus further underscoring the messianic message of Ps 72.

The psalmist transitions back to petition in vv. 15-17, asking God to make the king's reign long and prosperous. The king's reign is not for his own benefit, but for the benefit of the nation of Israel and "all nations." The psalmist is expressing a desire for a ruler who will lead the nation of Israel into the blessing of God outlined in the Abrahamic covenant. The final line of v. 17 ("May people be blessed in him, all nations call him blessed!" ESV) serves to remind "the king and the audience . . . that this has been God's plan all along."[19] This additional connection back to the covenant underscores Israel's ideology regarding the king. It is the anointed ruler of Israel who will bring to fruition the peace and prosperity promised by God through Abraham. The king does not accomplish this reign of his own power or volition, but totally depends on the Lord. The psalmist prays that God will raise up a king willing to lean fully on the Lord and to live a life of obedience and submission to God.

Psalm 72 and the Messiah

Through the prayers and petitions of the psalmist, Ps 72 expresses the hope for the king who was to come. The psalmist entreats the Lord for a king who will reign with justice and righteousness, be prosperous and bring abundance to Israel and the nations, rule over and bless the nations, and endure on the throne so that Israel may continually experience the blessing of the Lord. Praying for the king in this manner was not novel, but part and parcel of the broader Israelite understanding of the Messiah and the Messiah's significance in God's plans for the nation of Israel. Through his prayer, the psalmist looks forward to the installation of the ideal king. As Futato comments, "The psalm drove the people to look into the future, when the justice and righteousness of God would be embodied in a human king. But only a king who was fully divine as well as fully human could live up to the ideal. Jesus came as this king."[20]

Unfortunately, even Solomon, who brought unprecedented prosperity to Israel and constructed the temple of the Lord in Jerusalem, could not live up to this ideal. The kings of Israel, whether faithful or unfaithful in the eyes of the Lord, were flawed. As Longman comments,

> No human king ever achieved the ideal of justice and righteousness described in the psalm. Even Solomon, with his promising start, ended up as an oppressor of his people (1Kg 12:4). In addition, no king ever succeeded in being a conduit of blessing on all the kingdoms of the world. In fact, the Old Testament story ends with exile in Babylon and restoration as a Persian province.[21]

Psalm 72's petitions seek God's action to install a king who could meet the expectations of the nation. This hoped-for ideal king was central to the broader messianic hopes of God's people.[22]

In reading Ps 72 today, it becomes clear that this King has come. The psalmist and the Israelites looked forward to the installation of the ideal king who would depend fully on God and usher in the blessings of the covenant. Now it is evident in the text of Scripture that the ideal King has taken His throne and will come again to establish the kingdom of God. In Ps 72, the psalmist's petitions remind us of God's faithfulness and of the nation's utter dependence on Him to provide the King capable of living up to Israel's expectations and God's standards. Jesus of Nazareth is the hoped-for King. He is the answer to the prayers of the psalmist.

Psalm 72, then, offers a crucial messianic message and is not simply a royal psalm used in the installation of Israel's kings. Instead, Ps 72 is the prayerful expression of the psalmist and of the rest of God's people for deliverance from the world's order in which oppression, scarcity, injustice, and death are far too common. The psalmist yearns for the Anointed King who will rule according to God's will to demonstrate to the nations the benefits of glorifying the Lord. The psalmist prays for the day when the Messiah will come.

---

1. Augustine, *Exposition of the Psalms*, 72:1.
2. Ronald E. Heine, *Reading the Old Testament with the Ancient Church: Exploring the Formation of Early Christian Thought* (Grand Rapids: Baker, 2007), 103.
3. Ibid., 103–4.
4. Craig C. Broyles, "The Redeeming King: Psalm 72's Contribution to the Messianic Ideal" in *Eschatology, Messianism, and the Dead Sea Scrolls*, ed. Craig A. Evans and Peter W. Flint (Grand Rapids: Eerdmans, 1997), 34.
5. Ibid., 35.
6. Gerald H. Wilson, *Psalms*, vol. 1 of NIV Application Commentary (Grand Rapids: Zondervan, 2002), 108.
7. Bruce K. Waltke, *An Old Testament Theology* (Grand Rapids: Zondervan, 2007), 886.
8. Allen P. Ross, *A Commentary on the Psalms: 42–89*, Kregel Exegetical Library (Grand Rapids: Kregel, 2013), 57.
9. Paul R. House, *Old Testament Theology* (Downers Grove, IL: InterVarsity, 1998), 412.
10. Beth Tanner, "Psalm 71," in Nancy L. deClaisse-Walford, Rolf A. Jacobson, and Beth LaNeel Tanner, *The Book of Psalms*, New International Commentary on the Old Testament (Grand Rapids: Eerdmans, 2014), 566.
11. Gerald H. Wilson, "The Use of Royal Psalms at the 'Seams' of the Hebrew Psalter," *Journal for the Study of the Old Testament* 35 (1986): 89.
12. Richard J. Clifford, *Psalms 1–72*, Abingdon OT Commentaries (Nashville: Abingdon, 2002), 335.
13. Block offers a helpful discussion of the relationship between people, land, and deity in Daniel I. Block, *The Gods of the Nations: A Study in Ancient Near Eastern National Theology* (Grand Rapids: Baker, 2000).
14. Wilson, *Psalms*, 992.
15. John Calvin on Psalm 72:1, Christian Classics Ethereal Library, trans. James Anderson from the Latin and collated with the French, n.d., https://www.ccel.org/ccel/calvin/calcom10.vii.i.html accessed July 7, 2019.
16. John Eaton, *The Psalms: A Historical and Spiritual Commentary with an Introduction and New Translation* (New York: T&T Clark, 2003), 262.
17. Tremper Longman III, *Psalms: An Introduction and Commentary* (Downers Grove, IL: InterVarsity, 2014), 270.
18. The Hebrew syntax in this verse allows for at least two possible translations. The first renders the verb in the future tense "because he will rescue . . ." as in the HCSB, NASB, NET, and NIV. The second possibility found in the ESV and NRSV renders the verb in the present tense. The future tense seems to fit best with the anticipatory nature of the psalm.

19. Tanner, "Psalm 71," 579.

20. Mark D. Futato and George M. Schwab, *Psalms, Proverbs* (Carol Stream, IL: Tyndale, 2007), 240.

21. Longman III, *Psalms*, 273.

22. For a comprehensive treatment of messianic hope see Michael Rydelnik, *The Messianic Hope: Is the Hebrew Bible Really Messianic?* (Nashville: B&H, 2010).

Psalms 86–88

The Suffering, Death, and Resurrection of the Messianic King

ROBERT L. COLE

The book of Psalms is a cohesive and coherent composition from beginning to end.[1] It is composed of five divisions or "books," as demonstrated by concluding doxologies (Pss 41:13; 72:18-19; 89:52; 106:48) and by discontinuity of language in the titles or superscriptions at their literary seams.[2] Distinctive themes characterize each division through use of parallel language expressions and themes. The entire composition develops somewhat like progressive movements in a symphony, raising previously introduced topics and language and reworking them in detail. The final stretch of Pss 146–150, while repeating and reaffirming themes from the introductory Pss 1–2,[3] brings the book to a unique and resounding conclusion. Psalms 86–88 near the end of Book III likewise constitute a harmonious and interrelated sequence within this particular division and will be examined as such in this study.

The Psalter's first two psalms function together as its introduction. They both speak of a future impeccable and divine King Messiah, who is granted absolute rule of the entire world, as well as those who submit to Him—and against the wicked who resist Him.[4] What follows in the subsequent psalms are the prophetic words uttered by a very human David, or various Levites and unnamed authors, describing mostly the sufferings, death, and resurrection of the Messianic King portrayed in the introduction.

Book III, stretching from Ps 73 to Ps 89 is distinct in its message from the previous and following Books II and IV, expressing repeated temporal questions such as "How long?" (Pss 74:9-10; 77:8; 79:5; 82:2; 85:5; 89:46) or "Why?" (Pss 74:1,11; 79:10), followed by various types of answers given in subsequent psalms.[5] Its opening Ps 73 reacts to the nonappearance of promises made in the previous Ps 72.[6] Psalms 74, 75, and 76 provide answers to Ps 73's complaint and contain reaffirmations of Ps 72's vision. Psalm 77 returns to the complaint mode with typical temporal questions (vv. 7-9), to which the lengthy Ps 78 provides surprising answers. This style of questions and answers continues through Pss 86–88 under consideration here and Ps 89 as well. Book IV's opening Ps 90 provides pointed and appropriate answers to the queries and complaints at the conclusion of Ps 89 regarding the unfulfilled promises given to David. It also represents a change from the questioning tone of Book III to confident assertion and praise of God's eternal Davidic rule.[7]

Interpretation of any one psalm requires consideration of its immediate and larger context within the book. In this respect, it is no different from any other book or passage of the Hebrew Bible. For instance, between Pss 73 and 74 the dislegomenon[8] "ruins" (*mashu'ot*)[9] is a case of explicit verbal cohesiveness that also points to coherence of meaning between them. The phrase "straightens up those bowed over" (*zoqeph kephuphim*) in Pss 145:14 and 146:8 is another example of a dislegomenon and is hardly accidental.[10] Neither dislegomena are simple literary adornments without significance for interpretation.

Gunkel, the father of form criticism, labeled these three psalms as individual lament (Ps 86), Zion psalm (Ps 87), and individual lament (Ps 88),[11] and so the Psalter's arrangement does not follow his particular conception of literary genre. The sequence is patently contrary to such categorization, and this is not a matter of coincidence. The arrangement is deliberate and purposeful, no different from any other book of the Hebrew Bible. Form critical or genre classifications actually thwart and distort recognition of the book's message and purpose in its canonical form.[12] Interpretation of this and all other psalm sequences requires a sympathetic analysis of the ancient composition on its own basis without later contrived categories.

Psalm 86 is attributed to David ("a Davidic prayer"), and yet Ps 72:20 apparently declares the prayers of David are ended. Books IV and V also contain further psalms of David (Pss 101, 103, 108, 109, 110, 133, etc.). Does Ps 72's doxology then represent an earlier stage in the evolution of the Psalter, which was retained by subsequent editors who simply ignored the apparent contradiction? Carelessness on the part of the book's composer is highly unlikely. Following Ps 72 there are repeated examples of pointed questions to its promises as well as their reaffirmation, as here in Ps 86:9. Therefore Book III and those following were not simply added haphazardly to Book II.

A better solution to this question may be found in analysis of the verb *kallu*[13] of 72:20, meaning apparently "they are completed." It is found only here and in Gn 2:1, where the heavens and earth are presumably "completed" followed by the statement that God had "completed" His work. The same pair of "heavens and earth" appear in Gn 1:1, described as created by God. It appears that the verb in Gn 2:1 would be better understood as the "perfecting" through the divine activity in the intervening verses. The latter represent the reversal of the condition of the earth in Gn 1:2.

From a literary standpoint, God's works still continue in Gn 2 and in an actual sense He continues working subsequently as well. "Perfected" may thus be a better rendering of this verb both in Gn 2:1 and Ps 72:20. The universe in its first state of Gn 1 has been brought into a perfected or completed state without any lack or deficiency as was true in Gn 1:2. Likewise the prophecies/prayers of David have reached their culmination in the description of the universal peaceful and just kingdom of Ps 72. In fact, the scene painted in Ps 72 is a reestablishment of the original paradise of Gn 1 and 2 (cf. Ps 72:16—crops [lit., fruit] . . . grass, language used in Gn 1:11,12,29). Just as the divine activity of Gn 2 represents a further exposition of the creative events of the sixth day in Gn 1:26-31, so the contents of Pss 73–89 (Book III) represent further clarification of the promises of Ps 72. God's creative work in Gn 2 does not represent a contradiction of 2:1 any more than do psalms of David subsequent to Ps 72:20.

Psalm 86 does not represent a complaint over the absence of Ps 72's conditions, as in many previous psalms of Book III, but rather a reaffirmation and further exposition of one of its particular promises. The assertion that "all the nations . . . will come and bow down before you" in Ps 86:9, repeats the same promise of universal worship in Ps 72:11, "all kings bow down to him, all nations serve him." In Ps 72:11 the nations' worship of the Davidic king is described in language identical to that of the Lord in Ps 86:9. Consequently, worship of the Lord in 86:9 is identical to the worship of the Messianic King of 72:11. This implies the deity of the messianic king of Ps 86, a notion suggested as well by the sequence of Pss 87–89, as will be explained below. Universal and international worship of Ps 86:9 is surrounded deliberately by the suffering (86:1-7,13-17), death, and resurrection (86:13) of the Davidic monarch. Indeed, the universal rule of Ps 72 will not come about without the ordeal of its king, even as the bulk of the previous Books I and II implied.

Psalm 85 likewise reconfirms the prophetic vision of Ps 72. Righteousness, peace, and salvation permeate the land in the eschatological promises of Ps 72 (vv. 1,2,3,7,8,16) as they do in Ps 85:4,7,9-13. The same eschatological description of Ps 85:9-13 includes the word pair *chesed w'emet* ("faithful love and truth," Ps 85:10-11), which is reiterated in Ps 86:15 ("love and truth"). The same two terms permeate the psalm in further single occurrences (vv. 5,13,11), indicating that Ps 86 constitutes a further commentary on the previous Ps 85. It indicates through these linguistic parallels that the nation's salvation of Ps 85:8-13 is accomplished through the individual messianic king of Ps 86.

Both Pss 85 and 86 also recall God's mercy following the idolatrous rebellion of Israel in Ex 32. Psalm 85:2-3 recalls directly the mercy shown at Sinai by referring to God's forgiveness of their iniquity and sin, and repenting of His anger ("You took away Your people's guilt; You covered all their sin")—in language identical to that of Ex 32:12 ("turn from Your great anger and relent concerning this disaster planned for Your people"). Psalm 86:15 is likewise a quote from Ex 34:6 ("a compassionate and gracious God, slow to anger and rich in faithful love and truth"). It is not coincidental that the juxtaposed Pss 85 and 86 appeal to the Exodus passage in their appeals to God for restoration.

The specific quote of Ex 34:6 in Ps 86:15 has the effect of casting the speaker as another Moses. Jonah, another prophet like Moses, also quotes the entirety of Ex 34:6 (Jon 4:2) after deliverance through the sea, and after seeing Gentiles repent.[14] In parallel fashion, Ps 86 also prophesies that nations will worship God in v. 9, followed by the quote of Ex 34:6 in v. 15. Psalm 78 recalls repeatedly that same wilderness rebellion, but also references in 78:38 God's great compassion ("He was compassionate . . . He often turned His anger aside") of Ex 32:12 (turn from Your great anger) and of Ex 34:6 ("a compassionate . . . God"). Psalm 78 also portrays God's eventual restoration of Israel after their continual rebellion and subsequent suffering (78:40-64) by His choice of David (78:66-72). Here in Ps 86 the words of David give voice to the future suffering and resurrected King Messiah who is the means of Israel's salvation in Ps 85:9-13, as described above.

According to Ps 86:13 the speaker has been resurrected from Sheol, as was Jonah (Jon 2:2). Jonah's words are designated as "my prayer" (Jon 2:8), identical to the Ps 86:6—"my prayer," and "a Davidic prayer" (in the chapter's superscription). Psalm 86's many parallels with Jon 2 indicate a purposeful casting of the individual sufferer here as a prophet like Jonah, and therefore Moses as well.

Parallels to Jonah continue in Ps 88, which itself is a detailed exposition of the death mentioned in Ps 86. Repetition of "Sheol" in 88:3 and 86:13, and "lowest" in 88:6 and "depths" in 86:13, confirms the continuity of topic between Pss 86 and 88. Psalm 88 also uses terms such as "Your waves" in 88:7, matching Jon 2:3; or "sweeps over me" in 88:16 matching Jon 2:3 "swept over me"; or "depths" in 88:6 matching Jon 2:4 "depths." Such gratuitous watery terminology in the otherwise dry Ps 88 (cf. "grave" of v. 5) apparently has as its primary purpose the casting of the speaker and his rescue from death according to the pattern of Jonah, and also of Moses.

Psalm 85 is expressed in the first-person plural on behalf of the nation. Psalm 86 following then reverts to the singular seen in Ps 84, as the term "my prayer" in 84:8 and 86:6 indicates. The latter term dominates Pss 84–88 (84:9; 86:1,6; 88:2,13), pointing to a common individual voice throughout. Psalm 86 is superscripted as "a Davidic prayer," while the speaker of Ps 84:9 is identified as "Your anointed one" or Messiah. It is the same voice of the Davidic King Messiah heard in the book's introduction (Ps 2:7, cf. the same king speaking in Ps 89:26) and following. Another parallel between these two psalms (84, 86) indicates His trust in God in Ps 86:2, and identifies Him as the prime example of the blessed man who trusts in God in Ps 84:12, "Happy is the person who trusts in You."

The change of voice from plural in Ps 85 to singular in Ps 86:1-7, accompanied by the linking language cited above such as mercy, faithfulness, and salvation, is significant. The "faithful love" (*chesed*) that His people and land will enjoy in Ps 85:7,10 is now "great" upon the individual king of Ps 86:13. The great miracle working God of Ps 86:10 explains why all the nations now worship Him (Ps 86:9). The adjective "great" of 86:13 is specified for Him individually as the miracle of resurrection from the dead ("You deliver my life from the depths of Sheol"). The deliberate repetition of the adjective (in vv. 10 and 13) implies His resurrection brings about international worship of the God of Israel.

A further lexical and phonological parallel connects the One who "performs wonders" in 86:10 with the deed requested by the King in 86:17 for Himself, perform or "show . . . a sign," within a detailed further description (vv. 14-17) of the sufferings He endured. Verse 17 is within this description of sufferings that explain the mention of resurrection in v. 13. In other words, the great God who performs deeds in v. 10 is linked verbally to the great deed of resurrection in v. 13 and to the miraculous sign of v. 17.

His suffering in the first and third strophes of Ps 86 (I—vv. 1-7, III—vv. 14-17) surrounds the assurance of worldwide worship in the middle section (II—vv. 8-13). However, v. 7 concluding the first strophe of His affliction had already assured an answer, as does v. 13 at the end of the second. His suffering (vv. 1-7), leading to His death and resurrection (v. 13), is integrated closely with the eventual worldwide worship of God (v. 9) in the same strophe of vv. 8-13.

The resurrection of this King not only ushers in international worship of the God of Israel, it also is connected with Israel's restoration. As noted above, the pairing of the words "faithful love and truth" promised for the nation in Ps 85:10 is repeated in 86:15 in the request by this individual King, which vv. 7 and 13 indicate was answered. He also requests goodness in v. 17 (cf. v. 5), which was assured to Israel in 85:12. His request for salvation in 86:16 reiterates the same promised for Israel in 85:9. These are further vocabulary links between the two psalms that imply that deliverance for the individual king is joined to that of God's people, who include every nation in Ps 86.

His self-identification as "Your servant" in Ps 86:2,4,16, found 50 times in the Psalter, has broad canonical resonance, recalling Moses (Dt 34:5), Joshua (Jos 24:29), David (2Sm 7:19,29), the sufferer of Isaiah (Isa 52:13–53:12), Jeremiah (33:21), Ezekiel (34:23; 37:24, 25), Haggai (2:23), Zechariah (3:8), and Job (1:8; 2:3; 42:8—3x!). These past figures portrayed as servants of the Lord, as well as unnamed ones, all point to a future eschatological figure along the lines of Moses or David.

His suffering in the first and third strophes of Ps 86 (vv. 1-7, vv. 14-17), portrayed as death and resurrection in Ps 86:13, surrounds the promise of worldwide worship in the middle strophe of vv. 8-13. The second strophe (vv. 8-13) is an answer to the affliction of the first (vv. 1-7) and shows, surprisingly, that the response to His cries of v. 7 was rescue out of the realm of death (v. 13). His suffering was unto death, and His rescue was resurrection from the dead, resulting in worldwide worship of the God of Israel. The third strophe concludes promising the shame and fear His enemies and haters will experience. A contrast is apparent between an international multitude of those who honor God (v. 9), and those who hate His resurrected servant (v. 17). The Psalter's introduction had already implied the same. Psalm 2:11-12 presented the kings of this world a choice between service and homage to God and His Son or rebellion leading to God's anger and the rulers of the earth perishing. Presumably the community of the righteous in Ps 1:5-6 and the blessed faithful of Ps 2:12 chose service to God and His divine Davidic Son.

Strophe III opens (v. 14) with information regarding the previously mentioned death and resurrection at the end of strophe II (v. 13). A council of arrogant and ruthless evildoers has sought his life, which he mentions with the same term ("my life") in the resurrection of v. 13.[15] Presumably they took it seeing as He was rescued from "lowest Sheol" (HCSB "the depths of Sheol"). Note as well that strict chronology is not present here between 86:13-14, nor across the psalm generally. Strophes I and III rehearse His suffering, while the answer to that suffering and its universal results appear in strophe II.

Note how all three assurances of an answer to His cries for help are linked by the identical particle *ky* (literally "for" or "because," vv. 7,13,17). In the middle strophe, His desire to honor God's name eternally (v. 12) is because of (*ky*) His resurrection from death (v. 13). The same particle *ky* ("for") in v. 10 of strophe II followed also by the same adjective "great," implies His resurrection of v. 13 is part and parcel of the great miracles of v. 10. Consequently, the content of strophe II (vv. 7-13) affirming eventual worldwide worship of the Lord is directly linked to the suffering and deliverance of this king in the surrounding strophes I and II. The international worship and honor given to God's name in Ps 86:9 is affirmed by the following Ps 87, along with its accompanying benefits.

Psalm 87 is attributed to the sons of Korah, so four psalms of Korah (Pss 84,85,87,88) surround the lone Davidic Ps 86 of Book III. David is also prominent at the end of Ps 78 (v. 70), and beginning of Ps 89 (vv. 3,20), and in both cases he is identified as God's "servant," as here in Ps 86:2,16. Thus the Davidic character of the Psalter is maintained here in Book III in spite of its relative absence. This is consistent with the focus on the Davidic covenant in the introductory Pss 1–2. Obviously, David never experienced resurrection from the dead accompanied by worldwide worship, and so his words in Ps 86 and indeed previous psalms following Pss 1–2 are prophetic of a yet future descendant. Close conceptual parallels between this Davidic Ps 86 with the previous Korahite Pss 84–85 and following Pss 87–88 (as well as Ps 89), demonstrate that the words of these various Levitical individuals are likewise to be understood as prophetic of the future Messianic King in view since the book's introduction.

Psalm 87 functions principally as further comment on the promised international worship in 86:9. Psalm 88 will narrate in detail the death mentioned in Ps 86:13. This is proven by the abundance of vocabulary parallels between Pss 86 and 88. Psalm 89 opens (vv. 1-4) with answers to the pointed rhetorical questions of Ps 88:10-12, expressed from the depths of death. The use of lexical parallels to Ps 88's questions in Ps 89's opening four verses imply the speaker escaped from death's realm. The speaker of course is the same divine messianic figure seen since Pss 1–2. In fact, His divinity can be shown by parallels between Ps 87:2, where the Lord loves the gates of Zion, and Ps 88:18, where He is separated in death from the ones He loves.

Psalm 87 opens with reference to "his foundation" without any antecedent reference to the identity of "his." Psalm 78:69 refers to the founding of Zion—"lit. He founded" or "He established"—and to God's love for her in the previous Ps 78:68. Presumably the pronoun of Ps 87:1 is proleptic, referring to the Lord in the subsequent v. 2. Verse 5 describes how He "Himself" founded Zion, but again without a clear identification of its antecedent. Who is "He"? The answer is found in v. 6 where the Lord is named directly (YHWH) just as in the case of v. 2. Indeed, Zion is called "the city of God" in v. 3 and so "His foundation" means the foundation of God's city.

While the pronoun "he" in v. 5 (literally, "and he establishes her as the highest") is probably proleptic to YHWH in v. 6, it also has an antecedent in the subject of the opening verb of v. 4, literally, "I will record"[16] (HCSB "mention"), who is also YHWH. The pronouncement of this act is then verbalized as "this one was born there" (NASB) at the end of v. 4, which is then repeated twice more in vv. 5,6. This is a further reference to enrollment, as the numerous verbal parallels with Nm 1 imply.[17] Thus all three phrases across vv. 4-6: "I will record," "this one was born there," and "when He registers the peoples, the Lord will record" refer to the same act of official enrollment of people of different nations in this eschatological Zion, city of God.

At the heart of these references to registration is the phrase, "and he will establish her as the highest" [author's translation]. God is building His city of Zion, which He loves (v. 2) by officially enrolling people from every nation (vv. 4-6). Presumably they are the "assembly/council of the holy ones" in Ps 89:5,7. Note that the language of building is also repeated in Ps 89:2 ("is built . . . You establish") and v. 4 ("I will establish" . . . "and build"). In Ps 89 the subject is the throne and seed of David, which of course are part of the city of Zion in Ps 87. The pilgrimage of all nations in Ps 86:9 to worship the Lord and honor His name includes their adoption as beloved citizens of His metropolis.

As noted above, the term "born" (Ps 87:4,5,6) refers to their adoption as citizens. In Ps 2:7 the same verb root *yeladtika* is used to describe the official establishment of the King of the same heavenly Zion as is the verb *'asapera* ("I will recount"), from the root *spr* of Ps 87:6. Zion's foreign inhabitants here in Ps 87 appear then to have been granted status similar to its King in Ps 2.

Reference to inanimate objects such as foundations (vv. 1,5), gates and dwellings (v. 2), in this psalm are figurative. "Holiness" in v. 1 is not a quality of mountains, nor of city foundations, nor is God's love for Zion's city gates a reference to doors and bars. Rather, as vv. 4-7 indicate, this city consists of peoples of international origin, including Egypt, Babylon, Philistia, Tyre, and Cush. Undoubtedly, as noted above, they are the nations of Ps 86:9 streaming to worship the God of Israel. Likewise, the glorious things spoken within the city of God (Ps 87:3) resonate with the glorification of God's name in 86:9. The city of God is also the subject of Pss 46:4 and 47:1,8, where the same figurative language is used in 48:11—"let the mountain of Zion rejoice" [author's translation]. Within that city, He is praised (Ps 48:1), equivalent to His glorification in 86:9 and 87:3. Note as well that Ps 128 equates the blessed man with sons, and descendants with the blessed Jerusalem and Israel. The man blessed from Zion (v. 5) sees the good of Jerusalem all the days of his life, and sees sons and descendants under the peace of Israel (v. 6).

Psalm 133:3 defines Zion, "there" (cf. identical adverb in Ps 132:17) as the place of blessing and eternal life, and compares it to dew on "the mountains of Zion," language comparable to Ps 87:1, "mountains of holiness." Psalm 2 has already described Jerusalem as an eschatological city (cf. Ps 2:4,6), as does Ps 48:1-2, calling it the "city of our God" and "the city of the great King." The holy mountains of this city of God in Ps 87 are its inhabitants, as are its gates (vv. 1-2), and so even its Gentile inhabitants are holy and beloved of God (vv. 1-2). They are holy by virtue of their description in v. 4 as "those who know me." Then by use of a pun on the former term, they are designated as having "been born" in Zion.

The implication of common construction language between Pss 87 and 89 is that Zion is the place where David's throne will be eternally established, and this is confirmed explicitly in Ps 132:17. Zion (v. 13) is the place ("there"—v. 17) where David's horn springs up. It is also the locale of the blessing of eternal life as indicated by Ps 133:3. Eternal life is in fact the subject of Ps 89:1-4 (note repeated use of "forever" in vv. 1,2,4), which functions as a direct answer to the death of Ps 88.

Psalm 88 expresses a direct contrast to the conditions of Ps 87 and further details on the affliction and death of Ps 86. Support for Ps 88's function as a response to 87 appears in the lengthy superscription, while its content parallels closely that of Ps 86. Consequently, Ps 88 matches the language and message of 86 in many ways, but their superscriptions are unrelated. The content of Ps 87 presents a direct contrast to 88, but their superscriptions resemble each other closely. This compositional evidence indicates that the sequence of Pss 86–88 was meant to be read coherently and cohesively.

Psalm 88's superscription is quite lengthy and includes three separate noun phrases. The first part mirrors Ps 87's superscription. In other words, Ps 87 opens with "A Psalm of the sons of Korah. A song," which is reversed in, "A song. A psalm of the sons of Korah," of Ps 88. The middle phrase contains what appears to be a verbal form "to afflict or overwhelm," infinitive construct of *'anah*, from a verbal root repeated three times across the psalm (vv. 7,9 ["crying"],15). The latter refers to affliction or suffering and represents the principal theme of the psalm. The final third of the superscription of Ps 88 reads, "A Maskil of Heman the Ezrahite," is similar to that of the following Ps 89, "A Maskil of Ethan the Ezrahite." There is little doubt that the lengthy superscription of Ps 88 functions to link it with the previous Ps 87, and to the following Ps 89. Such superscriptional evidence of linkage is accompanied by lexical parallels confirming they are to be read as an integrated and coherent sequence.

The abundant parallels on the level of vocabulary between Pss 86 and 88 indicate that the latter is a further commentary on the former as well. Both are labeled as individual laments by form critics, a method that lacks the power to explain the presence of the intervening Ps 87 and its lexical linkage to them. Psalm 86 is dominated by descriptions of suffering in its first and third strophes, while the second strophe ends (v. 13) with a single referencc to death and resurrection. Psalm 88 provides further details on what is the same suffering and death of this Messianic King, but ends without mention of rescue or resurrection. That will be implied by the juxtaposition and vocabulary parallels between Pss 88 and 89.

Parallels between Pss 88 and 86 begin at the opening verses of both psalms. Psalm 86 begins as "a prayer" of David followed by the words, "incline (O Lord) your ear," while 88:2 states, "my prayer, incline your ear"[18] [author's translations]. The noun "prayer" is mentioned twice in each psalm (86:1,6, and 88:2,13), and each, except the example in the superscription of Ps 86, are literally, "my prayer." Such close parallels at the outset of each psalm indicate the same speaker is in view, despite one of them being attributed to David (Ps 86) and the other to Heman (Ps 88). In fact, the parallels uniting the three Pss 86 through 88, each attributed to different authors, are to be understood as ultimately the words of the future King Messiah introduced in Pss 1–2.

Psalm 88:3 states, "my life/soul . . . near Sheol" has arrived, which recalls Ps 86:13 where he declares that God had rescued "my life from the depths of Sheol." Sheol, the domain of the dead, is then described as "the Pit" (Ps 88:4), and later as the "lowest part of the Pit" (88:6). Psalm 88's words are spoken in the realm of death, from where Ps 86 previously informs that He was resurrected. A similar anachronism occurs in the sequence of Pss 2–3. Psalm 2 described the same King Messiah's coronation (v. 6), preceding details of His death in the following Ps 3:5.[19]

The reality of death is undeniable in Ps 88. He has arrived in Sheol (v. 3) and multiple references to death follow in v. 5: "among the dead . . . grave," v. 6 in a pit, v. 10 "for the dead," v. 11 "in the grave." "Darkness" is another metaphor for death, repeated in various forms in vv. 6,12, and the final v. 18, where the speaker finds himself consigned without deliverance.

Psalm 86 also opens with reference to His affliction, "for I am afflicted" (NASB), which matches Ps 88:15, "I have been afflicted." Affliction is ever present in Ps 88 (vv. 7,9 [crying],15), and appears as well in the central part of the superscription about the song, as described several paragraphs above. Indeed, Ps 86:1 could fit seamlessly into Ps 88 or serve as its opening verse as well. The similarities are deliberate and unmistakable, and point to an integrated reading of both psalms, along with the intervening Ps 87.

Psalm 88 also speaks repeatedly of separation. Verses 8 and 18 declare by identical vocabulary, "you have separated me from my friends/acquaintances" [author's translation], with v. 18 adding "loved one." Both verses are positioned at important seams in the psalm's literary structure. Verse 8 is near the end of strophe I, and v. 18 concludes the psalm. More important, the terms "loved one/one who loves" and "my friends/neighbor" appear in Ps 87:2,4 identifying those in Zion whom the Lord has enrolled as His beloved citizens. Abandonment or distance from friends in this psalm, expressed by the verbal root *rchq*, is used repeatedly in Ps 22 to complain about abandonment and distance from God himself ("far" Ps 22:1,11,19). That distance from God in Ps 22 was resolved in Ps 23, as will Ps 89 resolve the abandonment of Ps 88.

These relatively rare terms shared by both psalms point to a remarkable contrast and identification. The Lord's beloved citizens in Zion of Ps 87 are now separated from Him as the speaker of Ps 88, where apparently He has suffered affliction to death. In other words, the Lord speaking of communion and friendship in Zion in Ps 87 has been consigned to death in Ps 88. Furthermore, while being the voice of the Lord in Ps 88 from 87, He cries out to the Lord in this affliction and death. So again, as in Pss 1–2, deity is attributed to the suffering Messianic King. Such an interpretation is rooted in a serious grappling with the deliberate linguistic parallels between these two psalms.

Psalm 88 is composed of three strophes. The first two, as noted above, conclude with identical complaints of abandonment. At its heart are three verses (vv. 10,11,12) expressing rhetorical questions from the depths of death. Each of these three verses includes at least two verbal parallels with the first five verses of Ps 89. Thus Ps 89 functions as a pointed response to the previous questions posed in Ps 88 by the Messianic King from the realm of death. In the first and third queries, He asks whether God will do "wonders," or whether it will be known among the dead (Ps 88:10,12). Parallel to this in v. 10b is the question whether the dead will arise and praise Him. That answer is given in Ps 89:5 where the heavens "praise Your wonders" (*pil'akha*), words both found in the question of Ps 88:10. Apparently the dead, now defined as the congregation ("assembly") of holy ones in heaven (89:5), will arise to praise God's wonder.

The second question of Ps 88:11 asks if God's kindness and faithfulness[20] are recounted in the grave, and Ps 89 opens with pointed answers to it. Psalm 89:1 states that those two qualities of kindness and faithfulness (*chasdei yhwh . . . 'emunatekha*) of God are in fact being sung and made known by the individual speaker. By means of explicit repetition of two terms from Ps 88 at the beginning of Ps 89, the composer of the Psalter has identified the voice as one. Presumably the Messianic King of Ps 88 is not now in the grave but rather singing eternally and from generation to generation the praises of God's faithfulness. His eternal praise in Ps 89:1 is linked quite deliberately to the eternal covenant with David by repetition of "eternity" (HCSB "forever") and "generation to generation" (HCSB "all generations") in Ps 89:4.

The verb "I will make known" (NASB) of Ps 89:1 represents another direct verbal link to the previous psalm. Psalm 88:12 had asked if God's "wonders" would be "known" in the realm of death, and so Ps 89:1 has answered that question in the affirmative. He is making it known with His mouth, implying a bodily and physical resurrection. His death in Ps 88 has been reversed, and as seen in Ps 89:1-5, that resurrection fulfills the Davidic covenant that has been in view since Ps 2.[21]

Psalm 89:2 praises the "forever" nature of God's faithfulness (*chesed* again) and the "establishment" of His faithful kindness (*'emunatekha*). Verse 4 quotes God's decision to "establish" David's descendant forever, thereby linking the covenant with the eternal praise of the resurrected speaker in v. 1 from the death of Ps 88. The Davidic covenant of Ps 89:3-4 is enveloped before and after by linking terms such as "forever," "establish," and "all generations to generation" in vv. 1-2,4. As just described above, the entire sequence of Ps 89:1-5 is linked verbally to the threefold series of questions of Ps 88:10-12. The Davidic Messianic King has somehow been rescued out of death to sit eternally on His throne in fulfillment of the Davidic covenant. Psalm 86:13 simply informed the reader that He was delivered from the presence of death because of God's great "faithful love" (*chasdekha*). Now it is understood He has come out of the clutches of death to reign forever on the Davidic throne (Ps 89:3-4).

Psalm 89 opens as an answer to Ps 88's desperate queries from the realm of death, but ends with further questions in a manner consistent with the entirety of Book III and with Ps 89 itself. God's covenant with David is recalled again (89:49), and the question of v. 46 resembles closely those previously across Book III. "How long LORD? Will you hide Yourself forever?"—compare Ps 74:10-11; 79:5; 88:14. In other words, Book III ends on much the same note with which it began and continued throughout. This constitutes substantial evidence of compositional intent to create a coherent and cohesive composition from Pss 73 to 89.

The complaint over the non-appearance of the Davidic restoration at the end of Ps 89 contrasts with its confident quotation and interpretation at the beginning. Its quotation in Ps 89:3-4 affirms its eternal nature in contrast to the temporary death of the Davidic king in Ps 88. Apparently that king has not appeared because the psalm's conclusion asks who the man might be who will live forever (vv. 36,48a) after escaping the clutches of death (v. 48b). Verse 50 makes it clear that these questions refer to the delayed fulfillment of the Davidic covenant. Psalm 90 will provide a direct answer to the temporal question, and so both ends of Ps 89 are entirely fitting to the previous Ps 88 and following Ps 90. This is evidence of a purposeful composition of individual psalms into the composition of the whole sequence.

The string of questions, "How long . . .?", "What man . . .?", and "Where is your faithful love . . . to David?" brings Book III and Ps 89 to an end without an answer. Repeated temporal questions across Book III of like nature indicate they are inspired by the hope of a return of the Davidic kingdom. That kingdom was portrayed in the prayer for Solomon of Ps 72 and was nowhere to be seen, which inspired the ensuing questions, complaints, and answers across Book III. As Ps 89 ends without an answer, so did Ps 88. However, in both cases the ensuing Pss 89 and 90 offer positive responses to each of the previous questions through verbal repetition and thematic parallels.

By way of summary, the three Pss 86–88 under examination here constitute a deliberate sequence that exhibits coherence and unity. Psalm 86 narrated prophetically the suffering, death, and resurrection of the Messianic King, resulting in many Gentile nations coming to worship the Lord. Psalm 87 identified holy and eschatological Zion, the city of God, as their goal, of which they became official and beloved citizens. Psalm 88 narrated the death of the Messianic King, separating Him from those beloved dwellers of Zion. His resurrection from that realm, already stated in Ps 86, is implied directly by abundant parallel language in the first verses of Ps 89. There He appears singing and making known the faithfulness of God, followed by a quotation of the Davidic covenant, which promised Him a seed seated forever on an eternal throne. That promise is fulfilled in Him by His resurrection from the death of Ps 88 and His rule in the eschatological Zion of Ps 87.

---

1. Contra Tremper Longman III and Raymond B. Dillard, *An Introduction to the Old Testament* (Grand Rapids: Zondervan, 2006), 244–55; Norman Whybray, *Reading the Psalms as a Book* (Sheffield, England: Sheffield Academic Press, 1996), 118–24; Hermann Gunkel, *An Introduction to the Psalms*, completed by Joachim Begrich, trans. James D. Nogalski (Macon, GA: Mercer University Press, 1998), 2–3, 334–35; David Willgren, *Like a Garden of Flowers: A Study of the Formation of the "Book" of Psalms* (Lund, Sweden: Lund University Press City, 2016), 397–400; Craig C. Broyles, *Psalms*, New International Biblical Commentary (Peabody, MA: Hendrickson, 1999), 8–22, et al. Examples are ubiquitous since the method still dominates scholarship across the board.
2. Gerald H. Wilson, *The Editing of the Hebrew Psalter*, Society for Biblical Literature, Dissertation Series 76 (Chico, CA: Scholars Press, 1985), 139–90.
3. Cf. Pss 146:8-9; 147:6 and Pss 1:5-6; 2:12; Ps 148:11 and Ps 2:1,8; Ps 149:7-9 and Ps 2:1,3,9; Ps 149:2 and Ps 2:11.
4. Robert L. Cole, *Psalms 1 & 2: Gateway to the Psalter* (Sheffield, England: Sheffield Phoenix Press, 2013).
5. Robert L. Cole, *The Shape and Message of Book III (Psalms 73–89)*, Journal for the Study of the Old Testament Supplement Series 307 (Sheffield, England: Sheffield Academic Press, 2000).
6. Psalm 73 responds to Ps 72's picture of a future kingdom dominated by peace (*shalom*), no oppression (*'osheq*), nor violence (*chamas*) (cf. Ps 72:3,4,7,14,16b). Psalm 73 decries the present opposite conditions of violence (*chamas*, v. 6), oppression (*'osheq*, v. 8), and peace (*shalom*, v. 3)—but by and of the wicked. These parallel and linking terms are appropriately found in the first strophe of Ps 73 (vv. 1-12) immediately following the promised paradise of Ps 72.
7. Language characterizing the eternal Davidic throne in Ps 89:36-37 is repeated in Pss 93:2 and 97:2 in reference to the divine throne. Within Ps 89 itself there is an equation of the divine and Davidic thrones (cf. 89:13-14 with 89:4, 24-25, 36-37).
8. Occurring only twice in the entire Hebrew Bible.
9. Transliterations of the Hebrew in this study are rough and without phonetic precision. Also, verse numbers follow English Bible numbers, which do not include the superscriptions.
10. Another example is Pss 3:2 and 4:6—*rabim 'omerim* ("many are saying").
11. Gunkel, *Introduction to the Psalms*, 22, 121,
12. Contra Grant R. Osborne, *The Hermeneutical Spiral: A Comprehensive Introduction to Biblical Interpretation* (Downers Grove, IL: IVP Academic, 2006), 181–83.
13. Pual qatal of verb *kalah*
14. Note the use of *suph* ("seaweed") in Jon 2:5, the term used in Ex 2:3 for the reeds of the Nile where Moses' basket was trapped, and for the sea through which Moses led Israel. This is simply one of many parallels between Moses and Jonah, two recalcitrant prophets.
15. This death and resurrection is narrated as well from the beginning of the Psalter in 3:2, where "my life" (HCSB "me" *naphshy*) is the object of attack by many, without hope of rescue. Nonetheless, He does rise from the dead in Ps 3:5.
16. A Hifil verb form which in its participial form in 2Kg 18:18 refers to a royal recorder under Hezekiah.
17. The process of enrollment of the tribes in Nm 1 includes the sequence, "a man" of v. 4, as in Ps 87:5, and the root in v. 18 as the threefold Pual (or Qal passive) in Ps 87:4-7 (*yulad*), and the numbering of v. 18 matching the same root of Ps 87:6 "will record." The parallels are too numerous to be fortuitous. It is quite likely that the contrast of

Sinai and Mt. Zion/eschatological Jerusalem and enrollment of citizenry in the letter of Heb 12:18-24 comes from recognition of these parallels.

18. The lengthy superscription/title of Ps 88 is numbered as v. 1, in contrast to English translations. The result is that English verses 1-18 correspond to the Hebrew verses 2-19. Here the English versification is used in citation, but the Hebrew transliteration refers of course to their form in verses numbered differently.
19. Psalm 2:2 does imply His death (cf. Ps 31:13b) preceding His coronation. See Cole, *Gateway*, 142–62.
20. Perhaps the word pair expresses a hendiadys, meaning "faithful kindness" or the like.
21. Psalm 3 immediately following expresses the resurrection of the Messianic King of Ps 3, as do many psalms such as Pss 16,23, etc.

Psalm 89

God's Faithful Promise of Messiah

EUGENE H. MERRILL

This, the last psalm of Book III of the Psalter, is described in its title as a "Maskil of Ethan the Ezrahite." The term '*maskil*[1] refers to a literary product of the wisdom genre, in the case of Ps 89 a "Communal Complaint."[2] He is identified further in 1Kg 4:31 as a wise man, a peer to whom Solomon is favorably compared, and in the genealogies of Chronicles as a descendant of Judah through Zerah (1Chr 2:6), a Levite in the ark procession to David's sanctuary (1Chr 15:17), and as a singer along with Heman and Asaph (1Chr 15:19).[3] As for 'Ezrahite,' the ethnic title probably refers to the clan or family of Zerah, certainly not the well-known Ezra of the postexilic period.[4]

The poet, Ethan the Ezrahite, in the opening verses extolls Yahweh for His covenant reliability, the covenant in this case being the one He made with David (v. 3).[5] He describes the promises of God as heavenly in origin but subsequently put into effect on earth and in history. He pledges to praise Yahweh as long as he lives and, though certainly unaware of the impact of the written word in this composition, he continues through his hymn to praise Yahweh till this day.

Covenant with David (vv. 3-4)

> 3 I have made[6] a covenant[7] with my Chosen One[8],
> I have sworn[9] by an oath to my servant[10] David,
> 4 "I will establish your seed[11] forever,
> And I will build up your throne forever." (author's translation)

The "Davidic Covenant" is a logical and theological continuation of the stream of redemption that commenced hard on the heels of mankind's sin in the garden of Eden (Gn 3:15), then broadened in scope from the "seed of the singular woman" to the seed of a man, namely, Abraham, who would become the father of a servant nation through which all the peoples of the earth will be blessed (Gn 12:1-3; 22:17b-18). This unilateral pledge was sealed to Abraham by a covenant. The ceremony of that Abrahamic covenant involved the staggering idea of the slaughter of animals as a sign of the judgment Yahweh would bring upon Himself should He fail to keep His promise (Gn 15:12-21; cf. 17:1-8,15-21). Isaac, son of Abraham, was heir to him of the grace of transmitting the covenant further (Gn 26:3-4), as was his son Jacob, who, renamed "Israel," was the father of 12 sons (tribes), one of which, Judah, was selected to be the covenant bearer (Gn 27:27-29). Moreover, from Judah someday would come the ruler of the chosen nation, a promise fulfilled eight centuries later with the coronation of King David (Gn 49:10; Ru 4:12; 1Sm 16:6-13; 2Sm 2:4,7-11; 5:3-5).

Praise and Glory to Yahweh (vv. 5-7)

5 The heavens praise your wondrous deeds, O Yahweh,
And the Assembly of Holy Ones[12] your faithfulness[13];
6 For who in the clouds above can compare to Yahweh?
Who among all the sons of the mighty ones[14] is like Yahweh,
7 A Mighty One feared in the Assembly of Holy Ones,[15]
One greatly revered by those who surround him? (author's translation)

Jesus reminds us that the character and true nature of a man can be seen in his works, a maxim true with regard to Yahweh as well. What kind of a god can receive the adulations of all the heavenly host? Who can He be that is incomparable among all that are called gods? The poet launches his homage with thoughts like these.

The setting described here is the heavens, the realm of God and those who attend Him. The language about "mighty ones" and "holy ones" can by no means be understood as endorsing polytheism; rather, it is poetic imagery, commonly employed in the ancient Near East to refer to the minor deities, but in Scripture to the angels of heaven of which the sacred texts speak voluminously.[16] The angels are described with a metonymy of location, called variously here "heavens," "assembly,"[17] "the mighty ones," and "those who surround him." Though they are powerful in their own right, in comparison to the Incomparable One, they are weak and subservient, nothing more (or less) than the servants of Almighty God. One of their principal responsibilities is to render constant praise to God for His majesty and works (Rev 5:11-12; 15:3-4). In the present context, the poet is celebrating what God has done in fulfilling His promise to David that he would be enthroned as king over his people.

The major point to be made is that Yahweh, the God of covenant, is sovereign, omnipotent, and reliable. As He is praised in this psalm, the point to be stressed is that the promises of Yahweh to David of an everlasting dynasty cannot be frustrated by time or circumstances. David may fail (as indeed he did and on more than one occasion), but the unilateral nature of this covenant,[18] while not overlooking David's sins, demands that the pledges made must come to pass.

The Person and Deeds of Yahweh in Creation and Nature (vv. 8-12)

8 O Yahweh, God of Armies,[19] who is like you, a Mighty One, O Yah[20]?
And your steadfast reliability encircles you.
9 You are the ruler over the presumptuous uprising of the sea;[21]
When its waves rear up, you make them still.
10 You have utterly crushed Rahab[22] like a corpse;
With Your strong arm you have scattered your enemies.
11 The heavens belong to you; indeed, the earth as well;
The world[23] and everything in it—You founded it all.
12 North and South—You created[24] them;
Tabor and Hermon rejoice in Your Name.
13 You have a mighty arm;
Strong is your hand and high your right hand. (author's translation)

Ethan continues his expostulations of praise and declarations of the uniqueness of the Almighty by lowering His gaze to earth as well as heaven. He commands the beings of the heavenly realms as a general issuing His orders to His troops (vv. 8-9). With allusions to pagan mythology, a polemic against which, among others, he speaks frequently in the psalm, the writer contrasts Yahweh to the awesome deities of the nations including the gods of the waters, as in Babylonian and Canaanite cosmogony (v. 10), and concludes that Yahweh, not these make-believe gods, is the creator of all things (vv. 11-13).

The Special Relationship of Yahweh with Israel (vv. 14-18)

14 Righteousness and justice are the foundation
of Your throne; faithfulness and truth go before your face.
15 Blessed is the people that know the joyful sound:
They walk, O Yahweh, in the light of your countenance.
16 In your name they rejoice all day;
In your righteousness are they exalted.

17 For you make their strength glorious;
And in your favor our horn[25] shall be raised up.
18 For our shield[26] belongs to Yahweh;
And our king to the Holy One of Israel. (author's translation)

Most astounding, perhaps, is Yahweh's righteous and merciful nature, a sharp contrast to the epical characterizations of the gods of the nations. His justice[27] flows from His righteousness,[28] and His righteousness demands justice. These attributes of Yahweh are the basis for His own disposition of them to His people (Israel). They are raised up from their sin and misery by His righteousness (v. 16) and are made strong by his favor[29] (v. 17).

Yahweh's Election and Protection of David (vv. 19-29)

19 When you spoke by vision[30] to your pious ones,[31]
And said, I have put in place[32] an assistant[33] who is mighty,
One lifted up,[34] chosen[35] from among His own people.
20 I found one, my servant David,
Whom I have anointed[36] with my holy oil,[37]
21 Through whom[38] my own hand will be established,
(And) my arm will strengthen him as well.
22 Enemies will not (be able to) visit him with destruction,
Nor will the unjust reduce him to humiliation.
23 I will crush to pieces his enemies in his presence,
And strike down those who hate him.[39]
24 Indeed, my steadfastness and covenant loyalty[40] will be with him;
And through my name his horn will be exalted.
25 I will set his hand upon the sea,[41]
His right hand upon the rivers.
26 He will say to me, "You are my Father[42]
My God, the foundation of my salvation."
27 Moreover, I will appoint him to be (my) firstborn,
Highly elevated over all earthly kings.[43]
28 Forever I will guarantee my fidelity[44] to him,
And my covenant with him will remain without fail.
29 I will set up his offspring for all the future,
And his throne like the (eternal) days of heaven. (author's translation)

The poet now speaks clearly of the fact that David's appointment to kingship was a matter long predicted by the ancients as a *fait accompli.* Thus, Moses and the prophets not only knew that such a redemptive figure would arise, but they also were informed of the particulars about his origin, national and tribal connections, and individual identity.[45] He would be "a mighty helper" to God, one on whom Yahweh could depend. This astounding statement occurs only here, and in its boldness suggests that though David was chosen by Yahweh, it was so he could help Yahweh! Clearly, none of God's independence and total self-reliance is lost here, but the role of a king on earth would be to exercise on earth the authority and power of God in heaven.

The origin of the concept lies in the very beginning of human history. In fact, mankind was created in the first place to reign on earth as a surrogate for God, his very image endowed with regal authority (Gn 1:26-28). Moreover, even after the Fall, the mandate remained unchanged as its repetition to Noah in the post-deluge world puts beyond doubt (Gn 9:8-17). All through the Old Testament and into the New the anticipation never faded from view that a line of kings would weave its way through the metanarrative until it found at last its reinstatement in the God-Man who would be after the line of David and who would resume the all-encompassing authority of Almighty God forever.[46]

The covenant in view here is, of course, the one initiated by Yahweh when He was seeking out a suitable king for Israel. The people had preempted Yahweh, as it were, by selecting Saul to be their king (1Sm 8:4-5, 19-22), a choice that proved to be most unwise, as Samuel himself had anticipated (1Sm 8:10-18; cf. 1Sm 15:17-31). The prophet then announced that Yahweh had stripped Saul of the kingship and would give it to "your neighbor who is better than you" [Saul]. That man was David, a man "after God's own heart" (1Sm 13:14)."

Yahweh's Judgment on Faithless Israel but Continuing Faithfulness to the Covenant (vv. 30-37)

30 If, on the other hand, His people desert Torah
And no longer walk according to my laws;
31 If they break my statutes;
And refuse to observe my commandments,
32 I will apply (lit., visit them) to them my rod for their trespasses,
And whippings for their transgressions.
33 But I will never, ever completely remove my merciful grace;
Nor withdraw [from them] my unfailing faithfulness.
34 I will not break my covenant,
Nor change anything that has come from my mouth.
35 I once swore by [my own] holiness[47]
That I would never lie to David.

36 His seed shall exist forever,
And his throne like the sun before me;
37 Like the moon it will be established forever;
That reliable heavenly witness. (author's translation)

The poet arranges this section as follows:

- Four hypotheticals (vv. 30-31)
- Two kinds of punishment (v. 32)
- Four statements of divine mercy (vv. 33-34)
- Three reinforcing promises (vv. 35-37)

The four verbs of hypotheticals have to do with four kinds of covenant infraction: desertion from Torah (*'azav*), failure to walk (*l'o yelechun)* by its laws, secularizing (*yechalelu* [*piel*]) its statutes, and refusing to guard (*l'o yishmaru*) its commandments. Then follow the two punishments: The application of God's rod (of punishment) and of His whipping. Next are the four expressions of Yahweh's covenant dependability: He will not remove His covenant loyalty; He will not break faith with His covenant partner; He will not change anything[48] He has said; and He will never lie to David. Last, He utters four reinforcing words of comfort: David's seed will live forever; his throne (= kingdom) will endure always; his dynasty will be established evermore; and his offspring will be an everlasting witness to the world of God's loving grace.

The Present Effect of the Judgment of Yahweh on His Rebel Nation (vv. 38-48)

38 You, however, have rejected[49] (Me)[50];
(And you have become infuriated with your anointed one.[51]
39 You have repudiated your servant's[52] covenant;
You have polluted his throne (by casting it) to the ground.
40 You have penetrated all his fence-lines[53];
His fortifications you have demolished (and) wiped clean.
41 All who come near him rob him;
He has become a reproach to his neighbors.
42 You have strengthened the hand of his antagonists;
You have caused all his enemies to rejoice.
43 Indeed, you even turn his sword aside,
So that he can no longer stand firm in battle.
44 You have made his (cultic) purification[54] to cease;
You have dashed his throne to the ground.

45 You have cut short his life;
You have wrapped him up in shame.[55] Selah
46 O Yahweh, how long will you conceal yourself—forever?
(How long) will your anger burn like fire?
47 As for me (for example), remember concerning (my) length of days,
For what meaningless[56] purpose did you create humanity?
48 What human being can live and never die?
(Who) can escape the power of the grave? Selah (author's translation)

The language of this section of the poem expresses some of the most harsh and bitter indictments of Yahweh by His people to be found anywhere in the Scriptures. At the same time, most of the complaint is against Yahweh through David as the verbiage of royalty suggests.[57] The hubris of the author is astounding and even fearsome to read in light of the awesomeness of God and His perfections. One must remember, however, that Ethan is viewing the nation as the speaker, recounting thereby its egregious sins, its refusal to repent, and the inevitable judgment that must ensue. However, despair is nullified as the poet proclaims in most glorious terms the eternal and infallible covenant Yahweh had made with the nation as a whole and with David, the messianic king, in particular. Sin must, indeed, be judged and punished, but the punishment is intended as a means of discipline for His covenant son (in this case Israel) to be purified and brought back into unbroken fellowship. The ameliorating end result has been seen already in the psalm in the many places where God's gracious hand has been seen at work in restoration (vv. 1-6,15-18,20-29,33-37) and will be seen clearly at the end of this magnificent declaration of praise in v. 52, short, but oh so sweet.

The psalmist, writing on the behalf of his nation as well as himself, asks a series of questions that seem natural, given the circumstances already described. The question "Where are you, God?" is commonly voiced by God's people in times of calamity. The appeal here is to the promises of God, those enunciated especially in the covenant with David.[58] The major concern is deliverance from the enemies who are oppressing the servants of God, God Himself, and, notably, His anointed one. In the context of this stanza, that anointed one can only be David, whose name occurs four times in the Psalm (vv. 3,20,35,49).

The Appeal to Yahweh's Covenant Faithfulness (vv. 49-51)

49 O Lord, where is your ancient covenant faithfulness?
(That which) you swore to David in your utter reliability?
50 Remember, O Adonai, the reproach (against) your servants;
(How can I) bear within myself all this for so many people?

51 (Remember) those, your enemies, who have reproached you;
Who have reproached the very footprint of your Messiah (as well).
(author's translation)

In terms of name choice in describing God, the poet has followed the expected pattern of naming Him Yahweh 10 times, but at the end he has switched twice to Lord (*Adonai*). The reason, perhaps, is that the covenant name Yahweh is the one by which He identifies Himself as the God of the chosen people Israel. Of the 10 times the name Yahweh occurs in the psalm, six of them are embedded in a context of technical covenant terms (vv. 1-2,5,6,8,15,18), four of which also mention David, as noted above. The contexts of the two occurrences of *Adonai* seem heavy with fear and almost exasperation that Yahweh their God has become one in which only His lordship seems appropriate. This observation abets the theological truth that lament, peppered with doubt and theodicy, is not only appropriate but at times, and ironically, is at the end most honoring of God.

Benediction (v. 52)

52 May you, O Yahweh, be blessed forever.[59]
Amen and amen![60] (author's translation)

The verb "to bless" (here as Qal passive participle), with God as object (also here), is declarative, not objective; that is, God cannot be blessed by a human being in any other sense than to praise and exalt Him, for He needs nothing that anyone or anything can bestow.[61] For God to bless man is for Him to do some good thing for him or her.

Messianic Implications

Psalm 89 is universally recognized as one of the most apparent and beloved of the messianic psalms. Among other features, it includes the noun *mashiach* ("anointed [one or thing]") twice (vv. 39,52) and the verb *mashach* ("anoint, set apart") once (v. 20), with David as recipient. The name of the "proto-messiah" David occurs four times (vv. 3,20,35,49) plus several allusions to him: "horn" (vv. 17,24), "king" (vv. 18,27), "chosen one" (v. 19), "firstborn" (v. 27). Among other messianic terms associated with him are; "servant" (vv. 3,20,39,50); "seed" (or "offspring," vv. 4,29,36); "throne" (vv. 4,29,36,44); and "shield" (v. 18). The NT affirmation of the messianic character of the psalm is abundant. Apart from their clear textual correspondences, as noted in the following table, less obvious connections also are evident and will be cited below.

Additional Allusions to the Davidic Messiah as Fulfilled in the New Testament in Jesus Christ

Psalm 89	NT references	Psalm 89 wording	NT wording
3-4	Jn 7:42	David	David
89:4	Jn 12:24	"I will establish your line"	"it produces many seeds"
89:10	Lk 1:51	"you scattered your enemies"	"he has scattered the most proud"
89:11	1Co 10:26	"the heavens are yours, and yours also the earth"	"the earth is the Lord's and everything in it"
89:26	1Pt 1:17	"You are my Father"	"you call on a Father who judges impartially"
89:27	Rev 1:5	"most exalted of all the kings of the earth"	"the Ruler of the kings of the earth"
89:36	Jn 12:34	"his line will continue forever"	"the Messiah will remain forever"
89:50-51	1Pt 4:14	"Lord, remember how you servant was mocked"	"if you are insulted for the name of Christ, you are blessed"

The words of Hans-Joachim Kraus provide a suitable resolution of the tension between the indisputable covenant promises of God and the too real appearance of its seeming brokenness. The issue will be resolved in the coming of the Davidic Messiah: "Does [God] break the covenant? Indeed, He has dissolved it [in v. 39]! He has hidden Himself and placed His servant in the midst of his enemies as one scorned and despised. Here the OT comes upon an inconceivable situation. But the NT proclaims that Jesus is the offspring of David in whom all the promises of God are fulfilled. . . . The prophets looked, as it were, through the provisional primal image of David—to the exalted Christ."[62]

---

1. The Hiphil participial form (as here) derives from the verb שָׂכַל, "have success (Qal)," or "have insight" or "make wise." See *Hebrew and Aramaic Lexicon of the Old Testament*, 1128–29. The *maschil*, then, is form-critically or generically a wisdom piece whose purpose is to inform or instruct the reader/hearer.

2. Thus Erhard S. Gerstenberger, *Psalms, Part 2, and Lamentations* Vol XV, The Forms of the Old Testament Literature (Grand Rapids: Eerdmans, 2001), 147. C. Hassell Bullock, however, labels it a Royal Psalm (pp. 178–179), heavily messianic (pp. 182–183), and steeped in Torah teachings (pp. 218, 252); C. Hassell Bullock, *Encountering the Book of Psalms* (Grand Rapids: Baker, 2001). For other examples of the *maschil*, see Pss 32, 42, 44, 45, 52, 53, 54, 55, 74, 78, 88, and 142.

3. For Heman as a sage and musician, along with Ethan, see 1Kg 4:31; 1Ch 2:6; and for Asaph also as an associate of Ethan, see 1Ch 15:19.

4. Hebrew *'Ezrachi'* is explained by a prosthetic 'aleph' with *'Zerach'*. On the identification of the 'Ezra' in view here, see C. F. Keil, *The Books of the Kings*, Biblical Commentary on the Old Testament (Edinburgh: T&T Clark, 1883; repr. Grand Rapids: Eerdmans, 1950), 55.

5. More ancient and foundational covenants were the so-called Abrahamic (Gn 12:1-3; 15–18; 17:1-8) and Mosaic (Ex 19:3-6; Dt 5:1-27).

6. The technical term used here and commonly elsewhere (*krt*) is to "cut a covenant," that is, to make it valid at the cost of an animal cut up when offered in sacrifice (*Hebrew and Aramaic Lexicon of the Old Testament*, 500; cf. Gn 15:9-11, 17-18; Jer 34:18-19).

7. By far, the most common Hebrew term for covenant is *beriyt*, the etymology for which is disputed. The most likely derivation is found in the cognate Akkadian terms *bīrtu*, "clasp" or "manacle," or the preposition *beritu*, "between." See Gordon J. McConville, בְּרִית, *New International Dictionary of Old Testament Theology and Exegesis* 1:747.

8. The elliptical manner in which the poet makes his point is worth noting: The fact of David's "chosen-ness" takes precedence over David himself. That is, the purposes of God do not depend on man; the choice of a particular man (in this case David) is a gracious condescension by the Almighty. For David as the chosen one, see 1Sm 13:14: "Yahweh has sought for a man according to his own choice (lit., "according to his [Yahweh's] heart") and has appointed him to be prince over his people" (cf. 1Kg 8:16). See also David's selection instead of his brothers on the occasion of his anointing (1Sm 16:6-13). The manifold juxtaposition of "David" and "covenant" attests overwhelmingly to the importance of this arrangement to both OT and NT biblical theology. See 1Sm 20:8; 2Sm 23:5; 2Chr 7:18; Jer 33:21; Pss 18:50; 122:4-9; 132:10,12; Isa 55:3; Jer 33:15,20,21,22; Ezk 34:24-25.

9. This anthropomorphic way of speaking of God's promises binds even Him to a course of action when He speaks of Himself. See T. W. Cartledge, שׁבע, *New International Dictionary of Old Testament Theology and Exegesis* 4, p. 33.

10. The epithet "servant" is a common covenant term beginning with Abraham (Gn 26:24; Ps 105:6,42) and continuing through Moses (Ex 14:29; Nm 12:7; Jos 1:2), Jacob (Isa 44:1; 45:4; 48:20), Israel (1Chr 16:13; Ps 136:22; Isa 41:8), and David (2Sm 3:18; 8:26; Pss 78:70; 144:10; Jer 33:21,22,26; Ezk 34:23; 37:24). Most striking are the references to the unnamed, messianic Servant of Isaiah (42:1; 43:10; 52:13).

11. "Seed," whether in the singular (as here) or the plural, refers in general to familial offspring. The seed of David will be all his offspring for countless generations to come. See Paul's discussion of "seed" singular and/or plural (Gal 3:16). The parallel "throne" adds the information that David's descendants will be of royal stock.

12. For allusions to this body elsewhere, see Jb 1:6; 2:1; 15:8; Jer 23:18,22. Rashi defines as the assembly as angels.

13. "Faithfulness" or *'emuna* (as in v. 8 "steadfast reliability") translates, a technical term associated with covenants or covenant-making in order to emphasize its durability or irrefragability, especially when God is the initiator, as here. Cf. Dt 32:4; Isa 25:1; Pss 33:4; 36:6; 40:11; 88:12; 92:2; 96:13; 98:3; 100:5; 119:90, 138; 143:1.

14. The reference again is to angels. For other occurrences of the term (בְּנֵי אֵלִים) with this meaning, see Job 38:7; Ps 29:1.

15. The term for "assembly" refers to, "circle of confidants" (*Hebrew and Aramaic Lexicon of the Old Testament*, 745); cf. Job 15:8; Jer 23:18-22.

16. Stephen F. Noll, מַלְאָךְ, *New International Dictionary of Old Testament Theology and Exegesis*, 2:941–42.

17. The "assembly" (*kahal*) is in this case the gathering of the angelic host to praise, serve, or otherwise attend to their assigned missions. Clearly, these are angels and not human beings; the terms "assembly" and "heavens" are used in a parallel usage.

18. By "unilateral" is meant a covenant initiated by a greater power with a lesser one, here Yahweh with David. It is modeled after the so-called "Sovereign-Vassal" treaties associated with the Hittites at the height of their imperial power (ca. 1500–1200 BC). See Kenneth A. Kitchen, *On the Reliability of the Old Testament*, (Grand Rapids: Eerdmans, 2003), 283–307.

19. The combination of this name and epithet is rare. The usual form is "Yahweh of Hosts" as opposed to "Yahweh, Elohim of Hosts"; see elsewhere 2Sm 5:10; 1 Kg 19:10,14; Pss 50:1; 59:5; 80:4,19; 84:8; Jer 5:14; 15:16; 35:17; 38:17; 44:7; Am 4:13; 5:14,15,16; 6:8,14. "Hosts" is an outmoded translation reflecting the Elizabethan period of English terminology. The idea is that the angelic armies of heaven are at God's bidding to wreak havoc and destruction on all wicked and rebellious people (cf. Gn 19:13; 2Sm 24:15-17; 2Kg 19:35-37; 1Chr 21:12-30).

20. This abbreviated form of Yahweh occurs only here and in Ex 15:2; Isa 12:2; 26:4; 38:11; Pss 68:19; 115:17,18; 122:4; 130:3; 135:3; 150:6. However, it is common as a theophoric device found in names such as Yehoahaz, Yehoash, Yehoiakin, and even in the Hebrew name for Jesus, Yehoshua.

21. Reference to the sea and waves anthropomorphically provides clear connection to pagan mythologies in which the

raging sea is an enemy to gods and men that must be controlled. The Babylonian Creation epic Enuma Elish is illustrative of this motif as are the Ba'al epics of Ugarit. In both instances the Great Deep (Tiamat) in the Babylonian tale had to be slain by Marduk (Baal in the Canaanite tradition), Babylon's head of the pantheon, and from her body the earth and heavens were made. In Ugaritic thought, the Sea (Yammu) contended with Ba'al for lordship over the realm and thus similarly was dispatched. See *The Context of Scripture*, ed. William W. Hallo and K. Lawson Younger, vol. 1 (Leiden, Netherlands: Brill, 1997), 390–402 and 243–273, respectively.

22. "Rahab" ("Rager" or "Stormer"; cf. *Rahav*, "to storm, assault" (*Hebrew and Aramaic Lexicon of the Old Testament*, 1192) is a mythical monster unique by this name to the OT (cf. Job 9:13; 26:12; Ps 87:4; Isa 30:7; 51:9). He (it) is similar to Tiamat of Sumero-Babylonian myth, who was crushed by Marduk to secure the latter's dominance, and to Yammu and Naharu of Ugaritic lore, who were slain by Baal for the same reason. Egypt is especially in mind in this *nomen* (Ps 87:4; Isa 30:7). Rashi and other early Jewish interpreters equate, in fact, Rahab and Egypt. Ps 89 is celebrating the dominion of Yahweh over all claimants and pretenders to kingship.

23. The poetic parallel to "earth" (*'erets*) is "world" (*tevel*), attested very few times comparatively (36x, all in poetry) but in a few cases parallel to or in collocation with "earth" (2Sm 22:16; Isa 14:21; Jer 10:11; Job 37:12; Ezr 5:11).

24. The verb is *bara '*, the verb most commonly used (53x) to communicate the concept of creation from nothing (cf. Gn 1:1,21,27; 2:4; 5:1; etc). This is in sharp contradiction to the gods of the nations, none of which is said to have created *ex nihilo*.

25. "Horn" (*keren*), and its association with a bull or other powerful horned animal, is a common metaphor in the Old Testament to describe strength or power (*Hebrew and Aramaic Lexicon of the Old Testament*, 1145–1146). For its use in other eschatological/messianic contexts, see 1Sm 2:1,10; Pss 92:10; 148:14; 132:17; Lk 1:69.

26. Its parallel with "king" (David) cements the idea that "shield" (*magen*) is in a few cases also metaphorical for the Davidic king (Ps 84:9), though usually Yahweh Himself is called a shield (Gn 15:1; 2Sm 22:3,31; Pss 3:3; 7:10; 18:2,30,35; 33:20; 59:11; 84:11; 119:114; Zch 9:15; 12:8).

27. The legal or judicial language used here portrays Yahweh as fair, impartial, and thorough in His judgment—He is both just and righteous. "Just" (*tsedek*) occurs 119 times in the Hebrew Bible and "righteous" (*mishpat*) 424. As a paired cliché (as here), they occur 8 times and in reverse order 7 times.

28. The righteousness noted here does not denote Yahweh's moral perfection, for that is unique to Him and inherent in His God-ness. Rather, the idea is that when God's people reflect righteousness, they testify thereby to the righteousness of their God as well.

29. "Favor" here (*ratson*) is a mild form of election or divine choice. It is employed in the sense of satisfying His pleasure (*Hebrew and Aramaic Lexicon of the Old Testament*, 1282–1283).

30. The reference to visions (*chazon*; literally, "a vision") presupposes prophets or a prophet, the first and perhaps the only one in this context being Moses (Dt 18:15,18; 34:10; Lk 16:29,31).

31. The term here (*chasiyd*) connotes one who is uncommonly godly and observant of Torah (*Hebrew and Aramaic Lexicon of the Old Testament*, 337). The plural (*chasiydiym*) refers in modern times to a Jewish sect that is considered "ultra" orthodox. Here the reference is to all the pious ancestors who preceded David.

32. Thus the rare (Piel only) *shawah*, "to place with" (*Hebrew and Aramaic Lexicon of the Old Testament*, 1438).

33. The word for "helper" (*ezer*) is, of course, used most commonly with God as subject. It is He who helps humankind and not frail flesh that helps Him (Ex 4:12,15; 18:4; Dt 33:26,29; Jos 24:7; Jdg 4:3; 1Sm 12:8; 2Kg 6:27; 1Ch 12:18; Neh 6:16; Pss 5:2; 10:14; 18:6,29; 27:9; 30:10; 33:20; 37:40; 40:13,17; 54:4; 59:4; 70:1,5; 71:12; 77:1; 94:17; 109:26; 115:10; 118:7; 119:86; 121:2; 146:5; Isa 31:1; 41:10,13; 50:7,9; Dan 6:11; Hos 13:9; Jon 2:2). If God is a helper who maintains his sovereignty and dignity, Eve's having been created as a "helper" to Adam should not be viewed as a servile subordination to him (Gn 2:19-20).

34. Hiphil of *rum*; Yahweh not only chose David, but elevated him to a position of predominance, a ruler as suggested already by the imagery of scepter in Gn 49:10 and Nm 24:17.

35. This very important theological expression suggests divine selection to service, not one left to human chance. See Neh 9:7 (Abram); Ps 135:4 (Jacob); Ps 78:68 (Judah); Ps 105:26 (Aaron); Ps 78:70 (David); 1Ch 29:1 (Solomon); Hag 2:23 (Zerubbabel).

36. The verb "to anoint" (*mashach*) means, in its passive participial form (and then its nominal), "anointed (one)," hence "Messiah."

37. "Holy oil" refers to olive oil used in anointing persons or things to set them apart for service (Ex 29:7; 40:9; Lv 8:10,30; Nm 35:25; Pss 23:5; 45:7; Ecc 9:8).

38. Thus the relative pronoun; the idea is in line with the concept of helper (v. 19 above). Yahweh will remain king, indeed, but He will rule through His "assistant." The preposition *'iym*, lit., "with him," plus the 3ms suffix suggests agency. Yahweh will show strength through His Chosen One, who in turn will serve Yahweh.

39. The victories of David over his many enemies testified to the full realization of God's promises; cf. 1Sm 17:38-57; 30:1-19; 2Sm 8:1-15; 21:22.

40. The important covenant term *chesed* (merciful grace) occurs throughout this psalm (vv. 1,2,5,14,24,28,33,49) and others (c. 125 attestations). When especially referring to David as the forebear of the Messianic King *chesed* speaks powerfully to covenant certainty (Pss 18:50; 25:10; 61:7; for explicit use with *berit* ["covenant"] see Neh 1:5; Dt 7:9,12; 1Kg 8:23; Dan 9:4; Neh 9:32; 2Chr 6:14.

41. Quite possibly Canaanite mythology is in mind, particularly the Ugaritic Ba'al Epic in which Ba'al, the young contender for the heavenly throne, must eliminate Yammu, god of the sea, and Naharu, god of the rivers, in order to show his supremacy as the god of clouds, thunder, lightning, and rain, the fertility deity who enriches the soil, makes plants and animals reproduce, and thus becomes a god *non pareil*. The poet here argues that it is Yahweh, not Ba'al, who possesses all these powers and who alone is god. See "Ba'al Cycle," in *Readings from the Ancient Near East*, ed. Bill T. Arnold and Brian E. Beyer (Grand Rapids: Baker, 2002), 50–52.

42. For its ultimate fulfillment in Jesus Christ, see his assertions and the apostolic witness in Mt 7:21; 11:27; Jn 3:35; 5:19,20; 6:44; 8:54; 10:17,30; Rm 15:6; 2Co 1:3; Eph 1:3; 1Pt 1:3; 1Jn 2:22-24.

43. Although the immediate reference is to David, and deservedly (2Sm 3:18; 5:12; 8:13-14; 1Chr 14:2; 18:6), the ultimate Ruler in view is the Messiah (Jn 12:13; 1Tm 1:17; 6:15; Rev 15:3; 17:14).

44. The term here *chesed* is one of the key terms of biblical theology to describe the basis and durability of the various covenants of God. Its difficulty of translation may be seen in the numerous works devoted to the matter. Thus, D. A Baer and R. P. Gordon, חֶסֶד, *New International Dictionary of Old Testament Theology and Exegesis*, vol. 2 (Grand Rapids: Zondervan, 1997), 211–18: "loyalty, faithfulness, goodness"; "the essence of the covenantal relationship" (Glueck); "deliverance or protection as a responsible keeping of faith with another with whom one is in a relationship" (Sakenfeld); "when used of God, [it] will by definition, involve relationships of superior (God) and inferiors (individual or nation) " (Baer and Gordon).

45. Gn 17:6,16; 35:11; Dt 17:15; 28:36; 1Sm 2:10; 16:1; 23:17; 2Sm 2:4; 5:3,12; 1Kg 1:13; 8:23; Ps 2:6; Isa 16:5; 32:1; Jer 23:5; 30:9; 33:17; 36:30; Ezk 34:23; 37:22,24,25; Hos 3:5; Zch 12:8,10,12; 14:9.

46. Eugene H. Merrill, *Everlasting Dominion: A Theology of the Old Testament* (Nashville: B&H, 2006).

47. This startling statement bears witness to the fact that since no higher power exists by which Yahweh can swear, He must swear by Himself, by His own fundamental essence, His holiness. See Gn 22:16; Ex 32:13; Jer 22:5; 44:26; 49:13; Heb 6:13; Rev 10:6.

48. The verb *shachaq* and its cognate noun are of uncertain etymology; cf. *Hebrew and Aramaic Lexicon of the Old Testament*, 1464-65.

49. The verb *zanach* is employed elsewhere with overtones of covenant rupture or at least excommunication. It clearly has covenant in mind here, as v. 39 makes clear. Cf. Hos 8:3,5; Zch 10:6; Pss 43:2; 44:9,23. Helmer Ringgren, *Theological Dictionary of the Old Testament*, 4:105–106; E. H. Merrill, *New International Dictionary of Old Testament Theology*, 1:1126–1127

50. Since the addressee is Yahweh, the "me" here is, in context, a reference to collective Israel and its king. There is a hint here of Yahweh's having broken covenant with Israel. See previous note.

51. Heb. Mashiach (Messiah). The immediate reference is to King David. Examples of the abuse of David and his dynasty by the nation abound in the record. See, e.g., 2Sm 3:9; 15:1-6; 16:5-6; 20:1-2; 1Kg 1:5-10; 11:26.

52. "Servant" has a wide range of application in the OT. It seems here to have double reference, first to Israel and the Mosaic covenant and then to David and the messianic covenant made with him and his dynasty, as "crown" presupposes. For Israel as a servant, see Isa 41:8,9; 42:19; 44:1,21; 48:20; 49:3; Jer 30:10; 46:27,28; Ezk 28:25; for David, see Isa 37:35; Jer 33:21,22,26; Ezk 34:23,24. David records in his many psalms his own persecution at the hands of his subjects, for example, Pss 41:9; 55:12-14; 63:9; 69:7-9.

53. The defensive structure here is not one designed for utmost security. The "wall" (גָּדֵר) viewed here is an easily penetrated wall made of un-mortared stone, the same kind of which Ezra spoke derisively as barely strong enough to merit the term "wall" (Ezr 9:9).

54. This difficult phrase has been reconstructed in various ways by scholars (cf. BHS *sub* 45[ab]). However, it reads well as it is if one understands "purification" as a metonymy of effect in which the cultic impurity occurred as a result of the person himself becoming impure. This would often happen in times of war through contact with blood and other effluents of the body.

55. The preceding acts of violence (vv. 43-45) appear to refer to Yahweh's "whipping" of his own servants, the kings who followed David. The *hiphil* imperfects of שׁוּב and רוּם ("turn aside" and "stand firm") in v. 43 and the *hiphil* perfect of שָׁבַת ("cease") and *piel* perfect of מָגַר ("cease" and "hurl down") can in each case convey present or perfect

tense action. However, they can also function as so-called "prophetic perfect," suggesting that what is to come is as good as already done from Yahweh's omniscient standpoint. See GKC.

56. Heb. *shave'* "purposeless, meaningless." The sentiment is much at home in the poetic and wisdom literature (22 times out of 53 in all). It seems to the poet that life at times is not worth living because there seems to be no sensible reason to exist.

57. Terms such as "anointed one" (v. 38); "servant" (v. 39); and "throne" (vv. 39,44) are applicable here only to David and his dynasty.

58. The technical terms *chesed* and *'emuna* (or *'emet*; "merciful grace" and "utter reliability") are by themselves sufficient to establish the context as one of covenant and covenant promises (cf. Gn 24:12; 47:29; Ex 34:6,7; Josh 2:14; Isa 57:1; Jer 32:18; Hos 4:1; Pss 25:10; 61:8; 92:3). It is to these the poet appeals. See NIDOTTE 1:428-429.

59. The verb "to bless" (here as Qal passive participle), with God as object (also here), is declarative, not objective; that is, God cannot be blessed by a human being in any other sense than to praise and exalt Him, for He needs nothing that anyone or anything can bestow. For God to bless man is for Him to do some good thing for him or her. See Josef Scharbert, ברך, TDOT 2:279-308; and especially Ernst Jenni, *Das Hebraishe Pi'el.* Zurich:EVZ, 1968.

60. The double 'Amen' occurs 5 times, also and only in Nm 4:22; Neh 8:6; Pss 41:14; 72:19; 89:52. Interestingly, it marks off the various 'books' of the Psalter as follows: the last psalm in Book I, the last in Book II, and the last in Book III. Its absence at the end of Book IV is compensated by the powerful combination אָמֵן הַלְלוּ–יָהּ: "Amen! Halleluyah!" This affirming word derives from the root אמן, "be firm, trustworthy, safe" (*Hebrew and Aramaic Lexicon of the Old Testament*, 53).

61. Other examples of *brk* with Yahweh as object are Gn 9:26; 14:20; 24:27; 1Sm 25:32,39; 2Sm 18:28; 1Kg 1:48; 5:7; 8:15,56; Zch 11:5; Pss 28:6; 31:21; 41:13; 66:20; 68:35; 72:18; 89:52; 106:48; 124:6; 135:21; 144:1; Ru 4:14; Ezr 7:27; 1Ch 16:36; 2Ch 2:12; 6:4. The only other time where God is blessed is the blessing by the name of El Elyon (HCSB "God Most High"; Gn 14:20). Of a total of 27 occurrences where God is object of the blessing, 11 are in Psalms.

62. H. J. Kraus, *Psalms 60–150* (Minneapolis: Fortress, 1993), 211.

Psalm 90

The Fulfillment of the Davidic Covenant

ROBERT L. COLE

In studying Psalm 90, it is necessary first to understand how Ps 89 prepares the reader for Ps 90, the first psalm of Book IV (just as Malachi prepares for Psalms in the Hebrew canonical order[1]). That is because the Psalter is an integrated whole and shows compositional unity, both from psalm to psalm and throughout the whole book.

The final questions of Ps 89, which conclude Book III, concern God's enduring anger and rejection in light of the promises of the Davidic covenant enumerated at length from vv. 19 to 39. That covenant is the principal topic of Ps 89, as seen by explicit references to David himself at the beginning (v. 3), middle (vv. 20,36), and end (v. 49). Book II also ended with an implicit reiteration of the Davidic covenant by reference to worldwide worship of the king's son (cf. Ps 72:8-11, which resonates verbally with the same pact in Ps 2:1,2,8,10,11).

Subsequent psalms of Book III lament the delayed appearance of that promised kingdom and its attendant conditions of peace, justice, and worldwide worship of the Davidic son. Thus, both Books II and III end with a portrayal of the Davidic covenant, either in its paradisiacal future fulfillment (Ps 72), or by contrasting its promises with the sad, present conditions (Ps 89). The immediately subsequent psalms in either case lament the absence of that kingdom in a lengthy description of either violence and oppression (Ps 73), the very opposite of *shalom* (Ps 72), or the brevity and suffering of life lived under God's anger (Ps 90), which is the opposite of existence in an eternal Davidic kingdom (Ps 89). In other words, the transitions from Book II to III and from Book III to IV exhibit the same pattern of Davidic covenant reiterated (Pss 72, 89), followed by complaint over its absence (Pss 73, 90).

Psalm 89 expresses at its outset the determination to praise to God eternally and from generation to generation (*'olam . . . ledor vador . . . 'olam*—Ps 89:1-2), for the eternal or the enduring generation-to-generation Davidic covenant (*'olam . . . ledor vador*—v. 4). It is not by accident that the first verse of Ps 90 also declares God has been His people's dwelling place from generation to generation (*bedor vador*) and from everlasting to everlasting (*ume'olam 'ad 'olam*). The same confidence is expressed in both psalms at the outset, and furthermore, they conclude with identical questions, also of a temporal nature, "How long?" (*'ad mah, 'ad matay*, Pss 89:46; 90:13). So both Pss 89 and 90 begin and end on an identical note, and include, as will be seen below, multiple parallels of both content and language.

Psalm 89	Psalm 90
"all generations" vv.1,4	"every generation" v. 1
"forever" (3x) vv. 1,2,4	"from eternity to eternity" v. 2
"How long?" v. 46	". . . how long?" v. 13

Juxtaposition of psalms and their common language and content are signposts to their interpretation. Similar opening references to "eternity" in Pss 89–90 indicate that the God who made the eternal promise to David (89:3,4) has been Israel's protector and guide throughout all generations since, despite its delay (90:1). That eternal divine nature assures the eventual fulfillment of the promise, however long it is delayed. Indeed, Ps 89 concludes with a litany of complaints and questions over its nonfulfillment. As just noted, the "How long?" of Ps 89:46 parallels the same in Ps 90:13. This suggests, along with further evidence to be shown, that questions regarding the unfulfilled Davidic covenant conclude both psalms. It is God's eternal nature emphasized at the outset of Ps 90 that leaves open the possibility of a long and extended delay of the promise. The psalmist therefore rightly asks at its conclusion how long before its conditions are finally seen.

As noted in the article in this *Handbook* on Pss 86–88, the death described in Ps 88 and its three rhetorical questions in the central vv. 10-12 are resolved in these first five verses of Ps 89, as the linguistic evidence demonstrates. The messianic king's death in Ps 88 is implicitly reversed at the outset of Ps 89. Numerous verbal parallels to Ps 88 at the very outset of Ps 89 support such a reading, and the accompanying reference to the Davidic covenant (Ps 89:3-4) indicates that resurrection was part of the fulfillment of that particular promise.

However, as just noted, Ps 89 concludes with protests that the promise has not been fulfilled. How long will God hide Himself from His people (89:46), and where is the man who lives forever after escaping from the realm of death (89:48)? This resurrected Davidide sings in Ps 89:1, and yet 89:48 asks for his identity ("What man can live and not see death? Who can save himself from the power of Sheol?"). Indeed, the question as to the fidelity to David in the immediately following Ps 89:49 assumes that covenant promised a rescue from the realm of death.

Following the opening confidence in the eternal kingdom promised to David in 89:1-4, the speaker begins to praise the matchlessness of God's power and kingdom in vv. 5-18. This then transitions to another longer rehearsal of the Davidic covenant in vv. 19-37, which contains numerous parallels of a verbal nature to the divine kingdom described immediately previous. Their thrones (*kis'e*) are eternal and "established" (the verbal root *kun* appears in conjunction with *kis'e* in three out of four occurrences—89:4,14,36-37) in identical manner. So, in 89:4 David's throne (and "offspring") are established (*'akhin . . . kis'akha*), as they are in 89:36-37 (*vekis'o . . . yikon*), while the same language describes the divine throne (*mekhon kise'kha*, Ps 89:14). Furthermore, the Davidic throne and covenant in 89:28-29 are eternal (*le'olam . . . la'ad . . . vekis'o*) and sustained through God's fidelity and kindness (*lo chasdi . . . beriti ne'emenet lo*, 89:28). Likewise, the same Davidic covenant and throne in vv. 2-4 are sustained by the same divine faithfulness (*chasdei . . . 'emunatekha . . . chesed . . . 'emunatekha . . . berit . . . kis'akha*). Between these three references to David's throne (vv. 4,29,36) is God's throne (v. 14), also sustained by the identical characteristics of fidelity and kindness (*kis'ekha chesed ve'emet*). Undoubtedly the writer of Ps 89 envisions the messianic son of David occupying that very throne, and ruling over the kingdom of God. The same idea of the Davidic son as divine ruler is present in Ps 2:1-6.[2]

The foregoing evidence within Ps 89 linking God's throne with the Davidic has repercussions for the next book. It refutes the idea that the divine kingdom as described repeatedly in Book IV ("the Lord reigns," Pss 93,97,99) replaces the Davidic kingdom.[3] Thus, Ps 89, as with Ps 2 at the book's introduction, has already equated the future Davidic throne as divine.[4] There is in fact, no divine abandonment of His covenant in Book IV (Pss 90–106), one which Ps 89 has insistently described as eternal. Furthermore, explicit references to the Davidic covenant continue later in the Psalter, as in Pss 110,132.[5] God will restore His rule and plan for the world through the divine reign of the son of David and Son of God (Ps 2:7-8).

Further parallels in the Hebrew text support the equating of divine and Davidic kingdoms in Ps 89. God rules over the seas (*hayam*) in v. 9, while He puts the hand of His messianic king on the seas (*bayam*) in v. 25. God's arm of strength (*zeroa'*, 89:13) raises His own hand (*yadekha*, 89:13), and His right hand (*yeminekha*, 89:13), as His [My] hand (*yadi*, 89:21) establishes (*tikhon*, 89:21) His messianic king through His

[My] strength (*zero'i*, 89:21). In other words, that king's hand and right hand (*yado . . . yemino*, 89:25) are placed by God Himself on the sea and the rivers.

Another explicit parallel involves God raising Israel's [our] horn (*tarum qarnenu*), defined subsequently as their shield (*maginenu*) and king (*malkenu*), all in the description of God's kingdom of 89:17-18. Then in the context of the Davidic covenant (v. 24), God raises the horn of His messianic king (*tarum qarno*). Again, language describing the establishment and dominion given to the messianic kingdom of David is identical to that of God's own rule, and the effect is to equate the two. His kingdom is realized on earth through the messianic king.

Psalm 89:1-4, 19-43 DAVID'S THRONE	Psalm 89:5-18, 52 GOD'S THRONE
"I will establish . . . your throne" v. 4 "his throne . . . his throne . . . he will establish" vv. 29,36-37	"foundation of Your throne" v. 14
"forever" vv. 1,2,4,29,36,37	"forever" v. 52
"(like the days of-*kimei*) heaven . . . clouds" (HCSB "sky") vv. 29,37	"heaven . . . (for who-*ki mi*) in clouds" (HCSB "skies") vv. 5-6
"fidelity and faithfulness" vv. 1-2, 24,28,33,49	"fidelity and faithfulness" v. 14
"(his hand over the) sea" v. 25	"(You rule) the sea" v. 9
"his hand . . . his right hand" v. 25	"Your hand . . . Your right hand" v. 13
"my hand . . . my (God's) arm/strength (empowers him)" v. 21	"(Yours is) arm/strength . . . Your hand (You raise)" v. 13
"through My name his horn will be exalted" v. 24	"in Your name . . . by Your favor our horn is exalted" vv. 16,17

Likewise, verbal parallels exist between the divine kingdom of Pss 92ff in Book IV, and of the Davidic kingdom of Ps 89. So, the eternally "established" throne of God in Pss 93:2 (*nakhon kis'akha*) and 97:2 (*mekhon kis'o*), matches not only the divine throne of 89:14 (*mekhon kis'ekha*), but also the Davidic of 89:4,36-37 (*'akhin . . . kis'akha, vekis'o . . . yikon*) in both the verbal root ("to establish") and noun ("throne"). The lamented absence of David's throne and covenant in Ps 89 is answered by continued assurance of divine rule and control in spite of the delay in its restoration.

The merging and identification of the presumably *heavenly* divine throne of Book IV also matches the Davidic throne. Psalm 2 affirmed emphatically the coronation of the messiah on the universal divine throne (vv. 4-12).[6] That throne was on the heavenly Mount Zion, as a comparison of vv. 4 and 6 reveals, along with other texts such as Pss 3:4, 45:6, 46:4, 48:1-3. Note that the holy mountain of Zion in Ps 3:4 is the place from which prayer is answered, and links explicitly to the same mountain of Ps 2:6, upon which the messianic king is crowned. As a result, Book IV's declaration that "the Lord rules" (*yhwh malakh*) functions to reaffirm the presence of the Davidic son of God on the heavenly throne of Ps 2, despite its apparent absence on earth. In this sense, the declarations that the Lord rules across Book IV are another affirmation of God's faithfulness to the Davidic covenant, all the while admitting that as of yet it was not implemented on earth.

Calls across Book IV for the nations and peoples to sing praises to God (cf. Pss 96:1-13; 98:1-2; 99:1; 100:1-5) offer an escape from the judgment they will surely suffer in the future if they fail to obey this command. He reigns in heaven but will eventually come to the earth and judge it, as Ps 96:10-13 declares. Psalm 96:13 reads, "before the Lord for he is coming—for He is coming to judge the earth." The same command was given in Ps 2:11, "Serve (masc. pl. impv.) the Lord with reverential awe, and rejoice with trembling. Pay homage to the son," accompanied by a warning of destruction, "you will perish in your rebellion," if they did not. Reaffirmation of the warning of Ps 2 is proven by Ps 100:2—"serve the Lord" (*'ivdu 'et yhwh*), which repeats the command of 2:11. This coronation of the Davidic son in heaven, as declared in Ps 2:4-12, but delayed in its implementation on earth, is supported by Ps 110:1—"The Lord (*yhwh*) declared to the Lord (*la'donay*); Sit (*shev*) at My right hand *until* I make your enemies Your footstool" (italics mine). All three of these Hebrew terms are found, or implied, in Ps 2:4 and constitute a deliberate parallel. His reign in heaven, previously declared in Ps 2, awaits a time when in His anger (Pss 2:5,12; 110:5) He will judge enemy nations (Pss 2:1-2,10; 110:6). These are nations who have not rejoiced in the Lord, as repeated across Book IV (Pss 96:1-2; 100:1-2; 105:1-2) and the concluding Book V, dominated by the plural imperative, "praise (plural imperative) the Lord" (*halelu-yah*).

The superscription of Ps 90, "a prayer of Moses, the man of God," is an abrupt change from the Qorahite and Asaphite psalms dominating Book III, and has little in common with the superscription of Ps 89 ascribing it to Ethan the Ezrahite. The same divergence in content marks the transition between Books II and III of Pss 72 ("Solomonic") to 73 ("a psalm of Asaph"). As Wilson observed, there appears to be a concerted effort by the editor of the Psalter to include linking elements from psalm to psalms within books, as against disparate content at book borders.[7] This evidence does not imply that Books III and IV are to be read separately, rather that a new triumphant and confident emphasis dominates the latter, as opposed to the repeated complaints and questions of the former.

Moses, "the man of God," is a title identical to the one given to him in Dt 33:1 and Jos 14:6. It is also found repeatedly in the book of Kings in reference to prophets, including Elijah and Elisha. Thus, Moses' prophetic role is the focus of this superscription. Deuteronomy 33 also concludes (v. 27) with reference to God as Israel's dwelling (*me'onah*), essentially identical to the opening term "dwelling," of Ps 90:1 (*ma'on*). Psalm 90 serves in the Psalter as confirmation of the delay in bringing about the Eden-like conditions under the ultimate Davidic king of Pss 1–2, 23, 72, 89:25, etc. Nonetheless, it is a delay, not a cancellation, of the promise to David. Deuteronomy 33 likewise reaffirms the restoration of the blessing of Eden (cf. vv. 27-29), which as Pss 1–2 reveal, is to be accomplished by the son of David and Son of God.

Note that Ps 90 is attributed to Moses as an answer to complaints over a fallen Davidic monarchy centuries later. According to the "historical-grammatical" approach or hermeneutic propounded by many, one should presumably attempt to reconstruct the background or context of Moses' words as a means to understanding the message of the psalm.[8] However, such a procedure would inevitably distort and misinterpret the purpose and message of Ps 90 intended by the book's composer in the Psalter, as evinced by its canonical location. The Psalter's composer clearly read Moses' words in the psalm as prophetic, being a fitting answer to the complaints over the yet future Davidic monarchy's demise. The "historical-grammatical" method turns out to be neither historical nor grammatical. It ignores the historical fact of literary composition as it does the grammar of literary discourse. The arrangement of the Psalter represents a compositional moment in history and likewise exhibits literary patterns and parallelism, i.e., the grammar of discourse. Language binding together Pss 89–91 is typical of the arrangement throughout the Psalter.

Psalm 90 can be divided into three strophes of vv. 1-2, 3-12, and 13-17. The first focuses on the eternal and timeless God's role as perpetual abode for His people. Twice in its two verses the speaker in the first strophe addresses God by the independent masculine second person pronoun "you" (*'atah*). This pronoun is not necessary in most cases because of the use of masculine singular verbal endings and noun suffixes. Its presence indicates a strong emphasis on the addressee—"you yourself." The psalm continues in direct address to Him throughout, but by means of the suffixed pronouns and masculine singular imperatives. Psalm 89 is punctuated by numerous examples of the same second person masculine pronoun *'atah*

(vv. 9 [2 times], 10,11,12,17,38), especially at its beginning. Consequently, its twofold use in the first two verses of Ps 90 indicates explicit continuity and coherence with the previous Ps 89.

Psalm 89	**Psalm 90**
"all generations" vv. 1,4	"in every generation" v. 1
"forever" (3x) vv. 1,2,4	"from eternity to eternity" v. 2
"You" (ms) vv. 9-12,17,38	**"You" (ms) vv. 1,2**
"How long?" v. 46	"... how long?" v. 13

The second strophe (vv. 3-12) is dominated by temporal terms such as "day/days" (vv. 4,9,10,12), "years" (vv. 4,9,10—3x), "anger" (vv. 7,9,11—2x). It highlights the ephemeral nature of man compared with the eternal divine nature expressed in strophe I. Brevity of life, along with toil and vanity (v. 10b), characterizes human existence. However, the human lives at issue here are those of "Your servants" (Ps 90:13,16). They are also the lives of "Your servants" in Ps 89:50.

The previous Ps 89, which also complains about the transience of human (*beney 'adam*, v. 47) life, a term Ps 90:3 (*beney 'adam*) reiterates, (thus constituting another deliberate verbal parallel between the two psalms). This is expressed within the context of the promised eternal Davidic covenant (89:49). Divine wrath perpetually continues against God's chosen Davidic Messiah and servant (89:38-45). His life is cut off in his youth (89:45). According to Ps 90, man lives seventy or eighty years (Ps 90:10), while from God's perspective a millennium is comparable to a night watch. This is equivalent to the brevity of life portrayed in Ps 89:47, as the comparison above between 90:3 and 89:46 confirms.

Psalm 89	**Psalm 90**
"all generations" vv. 1,4	"in every generation" v. 1
"forever" (3x) vv. 1,2,4	"from eternity to eternity" v. 2
"You" (ms) vv. 9-12,17,38	"You" (ms) vv. 1,2
"How long?" v. 46	"... how long?" v. 13
"sons of men" v. 47 NASB	**"sons of men" v. 3** (author's translation)

Ephemeral life in general, within the context of the unfulfilled Davidic covenant, which promised an eternal throne for his descendant, also raises the question as to the identity of the man who lives forever. According to Ps 89:48, which is followed by an explicit reference to the Davidic covenant in v. 49, there will be a

Davidic descendant who will rise from the dead ("What man can live and never see death? Who can save himself from the power of Sheol?"). According to the composer of this psalm, the Davidic covenant must be fulfilled through a descendant who will conquer death and rule on an eternal throne. Psalm 90 is an extended description of how death strikes down all men after brief years of life, and so that particular question of Ps 89:48 remains unanswered until Ps 91.

Further parallels link Pss 89 and 90. Both conclude with temporal questions (as noted above) and requests on behalf of "your servants" (*'avadikha*). They are the ones requesting God's intervention at the end of Ps 89 (v. 50) and at the end of Ps 90 (vv. 13,16). They represent in each case faithful ones longing for the appearance of the eternal throne of the Davidic Messiah. The particular divine name *'Adonay* is the opening word of Ps 90 and once again at its end (v. 17). Likewise, it is repeated twice in Ps 89:49,50 at the psalm's conclusion in the queries asking the whereabouts of God's fidelity (*'ayeh chasdeikha . . . 'adonay*), and for Him to remember His servants' reproach (*zekhor 'adonay cherpat 'avadeikha*). The more typical Tetragrammaton *YHWH* appears in Ps 89:51-52 and throughout the body of that psalm. The twofold use of *'Adonay* in the question and request of Ps 89:49,50 again creates continuity across the divide from Book III to Book IV.

The repeated term "faithfulness" (*chesed*) across Ps 89 concerns divine fidelity to the Davidic covenant, and likewise in Ps 90:14 (*chasdekha*). Psalm 90 is pleading for the fulfillment of that promise and the attendant conditions of eternal joy and delight it brings.

Psalm 89	Psalm 90
"all generations" vv. 1,4	"in every generation" v. 1
"forever" (3x) vv. 1,2,4	"from eternity to eternity" v. 2
"You" (ms) vv. 9-12,17,38	"You" (ms) vv. 1,2
"Your faithfulness" vv.1-2,24,28,33,49	"Your faithfulness" v. 14
"How long?" v. 46	". . . how long?" v. 13
"sons of men" v. 47 NASB	"sons of men" v. 3 (author translation)
"Adonai" (Lord) v. 50	**"Adonai" (Lord) vv. 1,17**
"Your servants" v. 50	**"Your servants" vv. 13,16**

The opening address to *'Adonay* of Ps 90 and its counterpart at the end of the psalm (v. 17) exhibit a remarkable example of calculated and deliberate word play. Note that only in these two verses at the beginning and end of Ps 90 (vv. 1,17) does the term *'Adonay* appear, forming thereby an inclusio around the poem. In v. 1 it is followed by the Hebrew term *ma'on*, meaning "dwelling," while in v. 17 it is preceded by the consonantally resonant Hebrew term *no'am*, meaning in this context, "kindness" or "delight" (HCSB "favor"). The consonantal sequence of—*mem*, *'ayin*, *nun*, in the term "dwelling" of v. 1 (HCSB "refuge"), is reversed in the term "delight" to *nun*, *'ayin*, *mem*, with each term accompanied by the identical divine name *'Adonay*:

'adonay ma'on Ps 90:1
no'am 'adonay Ps 90:17

This exact correspondence of consonants functions to envelope the psalm within an initial confession of faith (v. 1) and a final request for divine favor on His servants (v. 17). The first recognizes God's presence throughout the long periods of suffering implied by the repeated temporal questions of the previous Book III. The second is found in a series of requests at the end of Ps 90 (vv. 13-17) for full restoration of God's favor or delight upon them. These requests include the aforementioned plea for God's faithfulness (*chasdekha*) in Ps 90:14 upon "your servants" (Ps 90:13,16; cf. Ps 89:50) and, as said previously, it is actually a request for the fulfillment of the covenant with David in Ps 89:49 (*chasdeikha*).

Psalm 91 describes a faithful man rescued from trouble and danger. Parallels between Pss 91 and 89 support his identification as the messianic son of David. His escape in Ps 91 resembles that of the expected son of David from Sheol in Ps 89 (cf. "I will deliver him" *va'phaletehu* of 91:14, and "who can save himself" *yemalet* of 89:48). His reward is to be satisfied with eternal days, i.e. eternal life (cf. *'orekh yamim* of 91:16 with 21:4 where the meaning is "eternal life").[9]

According to Ps 91:15 he will call to God (*yiqra'eni*), just as Ps 89:26 predicted (*yiqra'eni*), of the promised eternal Davidic king of kings and firstborn of God (Ps 89:26-28). That messianic king would confess God as the rock of his "salvation" in 89:26 (*yeshua'ti*), which "salvation" (*bishu'ati*) is revealed in 91:16 to the rescued, exalted, delivered, and glorified man of Ps 91:14-16. These two latter explicit parallels between Pss 89:26 and 91:15-16 suggest that the "rock" (*tsur*) of 89:26, and the "(I will be with him in) trouble" (*betsarah*) of 91:15, add further resonance on both phonological and semantic levels.[10] Again, Ps 90 answers the time question posed by Ps 89, while Ps 91 continues seamlessly by responding to the questions regarding the yet absent messianic king, also posed by Ps 89.

Strophe II of Ps 90 also refers to "a watch/keep (in the night)" (*'ashmurah*, v. 4), which contrasts divine and human perspectives on time. A three-hour span in the night is considered short by human standards, while a thousand years is equally brief from the divine perspective. Use of the Hebrew term for "watch/keep" in this particular analogy of Ps 90:4 matches the same root in verbal form of Ps 89:28 (*'esh-mor*, HCSB "preserve"), meaning "I will keep."

Psalm 89	Psalm 90
"all generations" vv. 1,4	"in every generation" v. 1
"forever" (3x) vv. 1,2,4	"from eternity to eternity" v. 2
"You" (ms) vv. 9-12,17,38	"You" (ms) Ps 90:1,2
"Your faithfulness" vv.1-2,24,28,33,49	"Your faithfulness" v. 14
"I will watch/keep" v. 28 (author translation)	**"a night watch/keep" v. 4** (author translation)
"How long?" v. 46	". . . how long?" v. 13
"sons of men" v. 47 NASB	"sons of men" v. 3 (author translation)
"Adonai" (Lord) v. 50	"Adonai" (Lord) vv. 1,17
"Your servants" v. 50	"Your servants" vv. 13,16

Psalm 89:28 quotes God's promise to eternally watch or keep His faithfulness to the covenant with David by means of this *yiqtol* verb form. Its unusual *ketiv* or "written" form in 89:28 using a *matres lectionis* (use of a consonant as a vowel) *holem vav* (*'eshmôr*) may be deliberate so as to highlight its resonance with the noun "watch/keep" (*'ashmûrah*) of 90:4.[11] From a human standpoint the millennia-long delay in implementation of the promises to David seems unending. From the divine perspective, the promise was made recently and certainly has not been forgotten. The promise that God would keep His covenant with David forever (Ps 89:28) has not been forgotten by any means, and is in no danger of being jettisoned or replaced.

The analogy of a night of watching in Ps 90:4 (NASB) is followed by two references to "morning" in vv. 5-6, which refer to generation after generation coming and going, like the daily blooming and withering of flowers of the field. There may also be deliberate resonance with the Davidic covenant as cited in 2Sm 7:14, which mentions judgment on David's descendants for their wrongdoing (*beha'avoto*). The divine wrath expressed as the judgment of death mentioned repeatedly across Ps 90:7,9,11-2x, was due to sins (*'avonotenu*, v. 8a), as "sons of men" (HCSB "descendents of Adam," *benei 'adam*, v. 3). Psalm 89 also refers specifically to the unfaithful descendants of David. Their lack of obedience, or failure to "keep" (*yishmoru*) the commandments (Ps 89:31), contrasts with the divine promise to always "keep" (HCSB "preserve"*'eshmor*) His covenant (Ps 89:28).

Another reference in strophe III to "morning" (Ps 90:14) is part of a request that God satisfy (*sabe'enu*) the speaker representing God's people with "Your faithful love" (*chasdekha*). As noted above, the latter term is identical to the recalled divine promise of fidelity of Ps 89:28 (*chasdi*) to the Davidic covenant. Consequently, Ps 90 represents a request that the long night of "watching" over the Davidic covenant implied by the parallel between Pss 89:28 and 90:4 be dispelled in the morning *(boqer)* light of fulfillment. This recalls the last prophetic words of David in 2Sm 23:4-5 referring to the fulfillment of the "everlasting" (*'olam*, cf. Ps 90:2) and "secured" (*ushemurah*, cf. Ps 90:4) covenant, as the sunrise of "morning' (*boqer*-2x, cf. Ps 90:5,6,14).

The request to "satisfy us" in Ps 90:14 (*sabe'enu*) parallels the same verbal root at the conclusion of Ps 91:16, "I will satisfy him" (*'asbi'ehu*). Similarly, the request of 90:16 that God "let Your work be seen" (*yera'eh*) matches the same verbal root of 91:16, "I will . . . show him" (*ve'ar'ehu*). In other words, the two final verbs of Ps 91 expressing God's salvific and beneficial intentions towards this favored messianic king, match two verbs of request in the final verses of Ps 90. Apparently, the request from God's faithful servants at the end of Ps 90 is answered by divine favor upon the single individual figure of Ps 91, the messianic king.

Strophe II of Ps 90 opens in v. 3 with two verbs of the same Hebrew root *shuv*, meaning "return." In the first case God causes man to return (*tashev*) to the dust and in the second he commands them to do likewise (*shuvu*). A contrast is thus created between the eternal existence of the deity in vv. 1-2 and the ephemeral life of the "descendants of Adam" (*benei 'adam*). "Sons of men" (*benei 'adam*) are mentioned in Ps 89:47 NASB in a question concerning the futility of created human life. Brevity of human life is inconsistent for the psalmist in light of divine promises to David of an eternal throne occupied by a resurrected king.

Strophe III then opens as well (v. 13) with the same Hebrew root in imperatival form requesting of God to "return" (*shuvah*) and have compassion on "Your servants" (*'avadeikha*), who are again mentioned in v. 16, forming an *inclusio* around strophe III (vv. 13-17). Repetition of this Hebrew verbal root *shuv* indicates Ps 90 is apparently requesting a reversal of the divine death sentence dominating His people in vv. 3-12. Instead of living "all our days" (*kol yameinu*) under divine wrath (v. 9), they ask in v. 14 for the reversal of such conditions, enjoying joy and gladness "all our days" (*bekol yameinu*). That would be achieved through enjoyment of God's "faithful love" (*chasdekha*), meaning fidelity to the Davidic covenant of Ps 89:28 (*chasdi*). Consistent with this attribution to God's people of the benefits of the Davidic covenant is the answer of eternal life in Ps 91:16 ("I will satisfy him with a long life;"*'orekh yamim 'asbi'ehu*) given to one man to the request for satisfaction (*sabe'enu*) for all their days in 90:14 expressed by His servants.

Consequently, the ultimate destiny of the messianic Davidic king and that of God's servants is one and the same, as was true from Pss 1–2.[12] "Blessings" (*'ashrei ha'ish*) attributed to the impeccable messianic king of Ps 1:1, who is identified in Ps 2 as the enthroned, messianic, Son of God (and of David), are identical to the blessings available to those who trust in Him in Ps 2:12 (*'ashrei kol chosei vo*).

Psalm 89 also concludes, as does Ps 90 (vv. 13,16), with a request for "Your servants" (89:50, *'avadeikha*), who are exposed to shame (*cherpat 'avadeikha*), as is the anointed messianic king of the following v. 51 (*cherphu . . . meshichekha*). They are also condemned to the death and brevity of life portrayed and lamented in Ps 89:47-48, as noted above. Again, the messianic king and His faithful people are united in troubles as in rescue.

Both Pss 89 and 90 contain multiple references to days and time inspired by God's eternal and timeless promise to David. Without that type of covenant there would be no requests such as those found in these two psalms. There would be no hope to escape the brevity and suffering of life, along with its toil and trouble, if that promise had not been made. So Psalm 90:13-17 is hoping and asking for a new day, a reversal of present conditions, in which gladness, rejoicing, and happiness never end.

These servants of God in Ps 89:50, so closely linked to the Davidic covenant in v. 49, are presumably to be identified as well with the blessed people of 89:15.[13] They will rejoice with God (89:16), through the raising up of their horn, shield, and king, who is the "Holy One of Israel" (89:17-18), immediately identified thereafter in 89:19-37 as the promised descendant of David (v. 20), and Son of God (v. 26). Their desire to rejoice in Ps 90:13-15 through fulfillment of the promise to David, is cited at length and in detail by Ps 89. In fact, they desire to rejoice and be glad all their days (*venismechah bekol yameinu*) in Ps 90:14, as was promised in Ps 89:16—"They rejoice in Your name all day long" (*yegilun kol hayom*).

Psalm 89	Psalm 90
"all generations" vv. 1,4	"in every generation" v. 1
"forever" (3x) vv. 1,2,4	"from eternity to eternity" v. 2
"You" (ms) vv. 9-12,17,38	"You" (ms) vv. 1,2
"Your faithfulness" vv.1-2,24,28,33,49	"Your faithfulness" v. 14
"(they rejoice) . . . all day long" v. 16	**"(be glad) all our days" v. 14**
"I will watch/keep" v. 28 (author translation)	"a night watch/keep" v. 3 (author translation)
"How long?" v. 46	". . . how long?" v. 13
"sons of men" v. 47 NASB	"sons of men" v. 3 (author translation)
"Adonai" **(Lord)** v. 50	"Adonai" **(Lord)** vv. 1,17
"Your servants" v. 50	"Your servants" vv. 13,16

Their perpetual joy will be realized under the reign of the eternal—"as long as heaven lasts" (*kimei shamayim*), throne of David (Ps 89:29). The days of Ps 89:29 are eternal and so are those of Ps 90:14. Days of life can be cut short, as those of the people in Ps 90:9 (*kol yameinu panu*), and of the promised messianic king in 89:45 (*hiqtsarta yemei 'alumayv*), but the promise of eternal days to David's seed has not been broken. Those are the new morning, days, and years requested in Ps 90:14-15 (*boqer... yameinu... kimot... shenot*), by God's servants.

The use of "morning," in Ps 90 (vv. 5-6), another temporal reference along with "days" and "years," is repeated in v. 14 as an endless dawn without mention of evening or night. In vv. 5-6 we read the analogy of human life as grass of the field, which blooms in the morning, but withers in the evening. It is the fleeting morning of the cycle of day and evening, to which humanity is limited. The final reference in v. 14 is a request calling for the eternal morning of God's *chesed* (faithfulness, fidelity), a term characterizing the covenant with David (Ps 89:1,2,14,24,28,33,49—seven times total). The plea is for nothing less than the reversal through the Davidic covenant of the endless human cycle of a brief life of toil and trouble, followed by death.

Psalm 90 concludes with a combination of requests, first for God's direct action and favor toward His servants and then His active intervention for the enduring success of their deeds (vv. 16-17). Divine involvement is recognized as the requisite and ultimate agent for realization of any endeavor. This idea is underscored by repeated sequences of the Hebrew consonant *nun* across v. 17, mostly in the company of a long u/o vowel: ***no****'am 'ad****o****nai 'elohei****nu**** 'alei****nu****... yadei****nu**** ****kon****e****n****ah 'alei****nu**** ... yadei****nu**** ****kon****e****n****ehu* "(Let the) *favor of the Lord our God be upon us; establish for us* (the work) *of our hands—establish* (the work) *of our hands.*" The initial sequence of consonant and vowel describes God's favor, and its repetition thereafter links the establishment and perpetuity of His servants' work solely to His grace. His direct involvement and mediation in their works will assure their perpetuity. Again, that intervention requested is seen as the fulfillment of the Davidic covenant.

Repetition of the combination of *nun* and the "o" vowel likewise began and ended Ps 90, as already noted above (v. 1—*'adonai maon*, "Lord ... dwelling," HCSB "refuge," v. 17—*noam 'adonai*, "favor of the Lord"). The first verse declared the eternal nature of God as a dwelling for His people, and now they call for Him to favor them with the perpetual establishment of their works as well, not the futility of vv. 3-12. Ephemerality characterizes their present life and labors (strophe II), but based on previous reiterations of the Davidic covenant and its attendant conditions, they plead for an end to transience. Instead of years and days of "toil and vain" (*'amal va'aven*, HCSB "struggle and sorrow" v. 10), they plead for the paradise portrayed repeatedly since the Psalter's beginning in Ps 1:3.[14] Ecclesiastes 1:3

uses the same term "toil" (*'amal*, HCSB "efforts") when pondering its profit in life. The answer of course is that everything is "fleeting" (*hebel*, Ecc 1:14, HCSB "futile"), including the entirety of man's deeds (*hama'asim*), the same term used in Ps 90:17 (*uma'aseh*). The psalmist expects a fundamental change in human existence so that terror (Ps 90:7) and transient toil (v. 10), are replaced by satisfaction (v. 14), joy (vv. 14-15), honor (v. 16), and permanence (v. 17).

The overflowing divine anger of 89:38 (*'vr*) against God's messianic king matches the anger of 90:9,11 (*'evratekha*), directed against His people, which results in brevity of life and the curse of death. Both psalms plead for a cessation of that anger and ushering in of the Davidic pact. Divine wrath in Ps 89:46 (*chamatekha*) also matches verbally the same in 90:7 (*ubachamatekha*).

Psalm 89	Psalm 90
"all generations" vv. 1,4	"in every generation" v. 1
"forever" (3x) vv. 1,2,4	"from eternity to eternity" v. 2
"You" (ms) vv. 9-12,17,38	"You" (ms) vv. 1, 2
"You became enraged" v. 38	**"Your wrath/anger" vv. 9,11**
"Your [burning] anger" v. 46	**"(by) Your anger" v. 7**
"Your faithfulness" vv. 1-2,24,28,33,49	"Your faithful love" v. 14
"(they rejoice) . . . all day long" v. 16	"(be glad) all our days" v. 14
"I will watch/keep" v. 28 (author translation)	"a night watch/keep" v. 4 (author translation)
"How long?" v. 46	". . . how long?" v. 13
"sons of men" v. 47 NASB	"sons of men" v. 3 (author translation)
"Adonai" (Lord) v. 50	"Adonai" (Lord) vv. 1,17
"Your servants" v. 50	"Your servants" vv. 13,16

Psalm 90 also prescribes the manner in which God's people should carry on while awaiting their Davidic king, and while under the curse of transience and death. Verses 11a and 12a repeat the verb "to know," first asking "who can know (*yodea'*) the power of your wrath?" (author translation) and then requesting that God "make us/cause us to know" (*hodea'* HCSB "teach") how to number our days. Between them is the statement that the fear of God corresponds to the wrath of God. Essentially the request is for wisdom to understand the reality of God's anger and power and to live the limited days allotted to us accordingly. In spite of that somber assessment of life in the present age, the following strophe of vv. 13-17, as demonstrated above, looks to life without ephemerality, toil, trouble, and presumably the sin (v. 8) that is the cause of such an existence. Such an existence will actually bring about divine honor and splendor (*hadarkha*) for His people (v. 16), quite opposite the present sorrowful conditions of life. It will also involve the pure delightfulness or blessedness or "favor" of the Lord (*no'am 'adonai*) upon His people (v. 17), again quite the reverse of conditions described in vv. 3-12. That is the hope and confidence of the reader who holds to the fulfillment of God's promise to David, reiterated repeatedly since the Psalter's introduction in Pss 1–2.

At the heart of Ps 91 (v. 9), following, is the coincidence of both the independent pronoun "you" (*'atah*), and the term "dwelling" (*me'onekha*, HCSB "refuge"), both of which are found in the first verse of Ps 90. It is most probable then that Ps 91:9 represents another deliberate parallel to the previous Ps 90. Indeed, Ps 91:1 speaks of "inhabiting" (*yoshev*, HCSB "lives") in the secret place of the Most High, a similar assertion to the "dwelling" of Ps 90:1. Use of "Most High" (*'eliyon*) in both Ps 91:1 and 9 links these two verses directly, the latter of which, as just shown, is parallel to Ps 90:1. In other words, the idea of habitation under divine care links Pss 90:1; 91:1,9.

However, the subject of Ps 91 is singular as opposed apparently to the plural speakers of Ps 90. Why is the request in the plural of Ps 90:13-17 expressed in the singular of 91:14-16? In other words, a request in 90:14 for satiety, "satisfy (*sabe'einu*) us in the morning with Your faithful life," is answered directly by a verb of the same root, "I will satisfy him (*'asbi'ehu*) with a long [eternal] life."[15] Likewise Ps 90:15 notes the years "we have seen (*ra'inu*) adversity," and v. 16 asks that his servants be shown (*yera'eh*) a divine "work,"[16] which will bring great joy. Then Ps 91:16, as if in direct response declares, "I will . . . show him (*'ar'ehu*) My salvation." There can be no doubt that the parallels are deliberate and designed to present Ps 91 as an answer to Ps 90. Presumably the deliverance promised to the individual of Ps 91:14-16 constitutes an answer to the community of Ps 90:13-17. His deliverance is their deliverance.

This interplay between the individual Davidic king and his people at large was already expressed in Ps 89:46-51. The poet moves from mankind's subjection to death (89:47), to the individual man who escapes death (89:48), and who constitutes the fulfillment of the Davidic covenant (89:49). The universal death sentence detailed across the central core of Ps 90 is because of God's anger (*ubechamatekha*—90:7), under which the speaker of Ps 89 also suffers (*chamatekha*—89:46). The latter complaint assumes an eventual end to that divine wrath and its deadly effects, which comes in Ps 91:14-16 through the deliverance of the individual righteous man. Verbal parallels cited above between the end of Pss 90 and 91 demonstrate this deliverance of the individual as answer to the community.

In conclusion, Ps 90 through its position and numerous links of a verbal and structural nature to Ps 89, constitutes an answer to the latter's protest, which is consistent with the patterns evident through verbal parallels from psalm to psalm across Book III. The answer to Ps 89's questions regarding the fulfillment of the Davidic covenant are answered in the affirmative, but with a caveat. God's perspective on time is wholly different from that of His people, and humanity in general. He will bring it to pass in His own good time, and with it will come an entirely new order of existence, without death, toil, and trouble, through His promised, death-conquering, son of David.

---

1. Masoretic Hebrew canonical traditions include those with Ruth at the head as well as Chronicles, which are unmistakable later attempts within the rabbinic tradition to impose chronology on the third division of the Hebrew Bible, as against its explicitly anachronistic and "genre"-violating position ("genre" as understood in Hellenistic culture, not as conceived by the composer of the Hebrew canon) between Proverbs and Canticles, contra Stephen G. Dempster, *Dominion and Dynasty* (Downers Grove, IL: InterVarsity, 2003), 191. The continuing effects of Hellenistic literary influence on the reading of the Hebrew Bible were felt in the Middle Ages, as they are today. In fact, the medieval rabbinic *peshaṭ* hermeneutic has its ultimate origin in Hellenistic literary canons and conceptions as well. The Greek tradition places Ruth between Judges and Samuel, consistent with chronological and "generic" concerns, but quite contrary to its pre-Hellenistic position in the Writings following Proverbs. The transition between Judges and Samuel is practically seamless and represents an original order consistent with their content and message, contra Michael Stone, *The Compilational History of the Megilloth* (Tübingen: Mohr Siebeck, 2013), 209–10.
2. Robert L. Cole, *Psalms 1–2: Gateway to the Psalter* (Sheffield: Sheffield Phoenix Press, 2013), 99–105.
3. Contra Gerald H. Wilson, *The Editing of the Hebrew Psalter* (Chico, CA: Scholars Press, 1985), 215; Hossfeld and Zenger, *Psalms 2*, p. 424, following Thomas Krüger, 'Psalm 90 und die 'Vergänglichkeit des Menschen,' *Biblica* 75 (1994), 191–219; J. Clinton McCann Jr., *A Theological Introduction to the Book of Psalms: The Psalms as Torah* (Nashville: Abingdon Press, 1993), 156; Nancy L. DeClaissé-Walford, *Reading from the Beginning: The Shaping of the Hebrew Psalter* (Macon, GA: Mercer University, 1997), 81–88, et al.
4. John Forbes, *Studies on the Book of Psalms* (Edinburgh: T&T Clark, 1888), p. 98, notes the title *'eliyon* "Most High (of kings of the earth)" applied to the Davidic king in Ps 89:27, and then to the deity in Pss 91:1,9; 92:1; 97:8 implies them to be "almost one and the same."
5. Psalm 2, with its clear reference to Davidic covenant in vv. 7-8 and Ps 110 are parallel on multiple levels, with the latter being a reiteration of the former.
6. Cole, *Psalms 1–2*, 79–141.
7. Wilson, *Editing*, 145–90.
8. Andreas Köstenberger, *Invitation to Biblical Interpretation* (Grand Rapids: Kregel, 2011); Grant Osborne, *The Hermeneutical* Spiral (Downers Grove, IL: IVP Academic, 2001); Gordon D. Fee and Douglas Stuart, *How to Read the Bible for All Its Worth* (Grand Rapids: Zondervan, 2003), *et al.* These and many others adopt perhaps unwittingly, and certainly uncritically, an approach that has its ultimate roots in the *peshat* of rabbinic medieval commentators. Rashi, the well-known medieval interpreter, as well as Qimhi and others, saw the approach as a way to refute Christianity and its Christological claims; cf. Erwin I. J. Rosenthal, "Medieval Jewish Exegesis: Its Character and Significance," *Journal of Semitic Studies* (9.2) 1964, 265–81, see especially pp. 270–72. "*Peshaṭ* " for the medieval rabbis was "the historical interpretation" and developed specifically to refute Christian interpretations (Rosenthal, 272). Ironically, this hermeneutic, mediated through Christians such as De Lyra and later the reformers, has been adopted uncritically by much of "conservative" scholarship today under the rubric, "historical grammatical." Indeed, the entire problem of the NT's use of the OT, discussed repeatedly and unconvincingly, is bound up in the unbending commitment to *peshaṭ*. The latter is in fact at odds with the compositional purpose of the Hebrew Bible, whether in individual books or the canon at large.
9. Contra Ron Tappy, "Psalm 23: Symbolism and Structure," *Catholic Biblical Quarterly* 57 (1995), 255–80.

10. Direct verbal parallels between psalms two removed from each other (Pss 89 and 91) occur otherwise in the Psalter, as is the case between Pss 73:3 and 75:4-5, where the word pair, "arrogant/wicked" (*holelim . . . resha'im*), is repeated. Only in these two verses in the entire Psalter is this pair repeated and indicates how Ps 75 provides further answers to the questions of Ps 73 beyond what is provided in Ps 74 immediately following. The same principle is operating between Pss 89, 90 and 91, or between Pss 1 and 3, and throughout the Psalter, cf. Robert L. Cole, *The Shape and Message of Book III* (Sheffield, UK: Sheffield Academic Press, 2001), 39.

11. The editor of *Biblia Hebraica Stuttgartensia* labels "a watch in the night" as a possible secondary gloss to be deleted, undoubtedly for metrical reasons. Verse 4 is unusually long in comparison with most other lines of the poem. However, in light of its resonance with Ps 89, it makes perfect sense, and could be the work of the canonical book's composer/editor.

12. Cole, *Psalms 1–2*.

13. The term "blessed" (HCSB "happy") used in Ps 89:15 (*'ashrei*) is identical to Ps 1:1, 2:12 and supports their identification above as one and the same.

14. Psalm 1 portrays a restored Eden, its conditions being part of the restored Davidic kingdom of Ps 2. Psalm 72:16-17 also foresees an Edenic restoration under the Davidic king.

15. Psalm 21:4[5] defines the phrase also found here in Ps 91:16 (*'orekh yamim*) as eternal life.

16. "Your exploit" (*po'olekha*, HCSB "Your work") of 90:15 matches Ps 92:4 (*bepo'olekha*), showing that Ps 92 continues presenting answers to Ps 90.

Psalm 109

The Betrayal of the Messiah

RYAN J. COOK

After the ascension of Jesus, the disciples returned to the upper room and devoted themselves to prayer (Ac 1:13-14). Following this, their first recorded act was to replace Judas. Peter gave the following rationale for filling Judas's position, "Brothers, the Scripture had to be fulfilled that the Holy Spirit through the mouth of David spoke in advance about Judas . . ." (Ac 1:16a). Peter went on to quote a line from two different Psalms, "'Let his dwelling become desolate; let no one live in it' and 'Let someone else take his position'" (Ac 1:20; cf. Pss 69:25; 109:8). A straightforward reading of this passage indicates Peter's believed that Judas's betrayal and subsequent death fulfilled Ps 69:25, while Ps 109:8 gave guidance for what to do next (i.e., select another apostle to replace Judas).[1] This quotation raises two questions: (1) is Peter using Ps 109:8 appropriately? That is, does his use of this verse line up with its original meaning? (2) In what way does the act of replacing Judas fulfill Ps 109:8? Is this a direct, typological, or applicational fulfillment?[2]

Regarding the first question, many Psalms scholars have maintained that Peter's use of Ps 109:8 is not in line with its original meaning.[3] Their main argument has to do with the identity of the speaker in vv. 6-20. Traditionally these verses have been understood as David's imprecation against his enemy.[4] However, others have understood these verses as the psalmist quoting his enemies' curses against himself. That is, these imprecations are not directed at David's enemy, but rather are David's quotation of his enemies against him. This perspective has been so persuasive that several Bible translations insert a nonexistent "they say" before v. 6.[5] The main arguments for this view are clearly outlined by Erich Zenger:[6] (1)

The judicial scene implied by the psalm, which Zenger envisions as portraying a court scene. The psalmist is making his case against his enemies. As a part of his case, he quotes his enemies demonstrating their hostility toward him. (2) Verses 1-5 describe the psalmist as in mortal danger because of the false testimony of his accusers. Verses 6-19, then, describe the sentence the accusers want to see carried out against the psalmist as a result of their false testimony. (3) In v. 20, the psalmist reverts back to his own voice and picks up the thread of thought from vv. 1-5. In this way, vv. 6-19 are syntactically bracketed off from the rest of the psalm, which has the enemies (plural) vs. the enemy (singular). (4) Psalms of lament often have the speaker quoting his opponents. (5) The psalmists "reference to being cursed by enemies fits best with the dramaturgy of the psalm if the hostile curse has been previously mentioned."[7]

Despite these arguments, there are good reasons to take David as the speaker in this section: (1) the switch in enemies from the plural to the singular, while important for the interpretation of the psalm (see below), does not necessitate a change in speaker. There are several examples of this in the Psalms (e.g., Pss 5:4-5; 7:1-4; 12:1-3). (2) Enemy quotations in the Psalms are normally clearly identified (e.g., Pss 2:2-3; 3:2; 10:4,6,11,13; 12:4; 22:7-8; 35:21, 25; 41:5-8).[8] (3) It would be highly unusual, even unprecedented, to quote the curse of an enemy at this length. Erhard Gerstenberger comments, "It is almost unimaginable that ancient writers or redactors would extensively quote their hateful opponents, copying meticulously all their—presumably false—accusations against the righteous suppliant."[9] Additionally, rather than enacting a judicial scene, as Zenger avers, the psalm can be understood as a complaint to God using judicial language. The judicial metaphor need not color our interpretation of the entire poem. For these reasons, it is best to understand vv. 6-19 as the imprecation of David against his enemy.[10]

PSALM 109 IN CONTEXT

Psalm 109 needs to be understood within the context of the Psalter as a whole. We do not know for certain who compiled and ordered the book of Psalms. This process likely began in the preexilic era and ended in the postexilic era. These inspired editors structured the Psalter in such a way that the book communicates an eschatological hope in a Davidic Messiah.[11] This Messianic hope can also be seen in the structure of Book 5 of the Psalter.

Book 5 takes as its theme the ingathering of the nation of Israel to the land, and so has many resonances in the prophets.[12] Psalm 107 introduces the book with a celebration of the ingathering of Israel utilizing the language of the exodus

(107:1-2,3-5,33-43). Psalms 108–110 form the first Davidic collection of Book 5 followed two acrostic hymns of praise (Pss 111–112). Psalms 113-118 are hymns related to Passover, paralleled by Pss 120–137 as hymns associated with Succoth/Zion.[13] These festival hymns bracket the central Ps 119, which celebrates Torah. Psalms 138–145 form the second Davidic collection, which ends in a resounding acrostic praise psalm. The whole Psalter is then concluded with five hymns of praise (146–150). Book 5 can be pictured in this way:

Royal / Acrostic[14]		Acrostic		Royal / Acrostic
107, 108–110 / 111–112	113–118	119	120–137	138–145
David Eschatological/ Messianic	Exodus	Torah	Zion	David Eschatological/ Messianic

This chart clarifies the overall eschatological/messianic thrust of Book 5. In the first panel, Ps 110 describes the hope of a future Davidic priest-king who will reign over all the earth. In the final panel, Ps 145 celebrates God's kingdom as an "everlasting kingdom" (145:13) and declares that He will destroy the wicked (145:20). This messianic hope carries forward the message of Ps 2. Indeed, there are a number of connections between Ps 110 and Ps 2, including the theme of a Davidic king subduing enemy nations and establishing an everlasting kingdom.

The first Davidic collection of Book 5 begins with Ps 108. In this psalm, David celebrates God's ownership of Israel *and* the nations (vv. 7-10). However, the psalm also has a note of a lament. It seems that God has rejected Israel and is not helping them, but David realizes this is only temporary. When God acts, the threatening nations will be defeated (v. 13). Psalm 109 takes the lament in a deeper and more personal direction. David has been betrayed and slandered. The threat is real and could result in the end of his life. He prays for God's intervention and for his accusers and enemy to be defeated. Psalm 110 serves as an answer to the cries for help in Pss 108–109. Here the Messiah is presented as the answer to the laments. The Messiah will reign over the nations.[15] Psalms 111–112 then celebrate this answer through acrostic hymns. These psalms emphasize God's faithfulness to His covenant (111:5) and His compassionate and gracious nature (111:4; 112:4). Thus, the Messianic answer of Psalm 110 is not simply an answer to prayer, but also a demonstration of God's faithfulness to His covenant.

EXPOSITION OF PSALM 109

David opens with a plea that God not be silent. He does not direct God in what to say, but assumes that if God were to speak, surely He would be on David's side. The address "God of my praise" is significant.[16] While some have seen David expressing confidence in God in the midst of his suffering,[17] it is more in line with the psalm to see this as a part of David's argument for God to act. He is saying, in effect, "I have not been silent about You. I have praised You. Do not be silent with me in my hour of need!" In addition to David not being silent, his enemies have not been silent either, which serves as another reason for God to act.

Verses 2-5 vividly describe David's plight. Many enemies have surrounded him with mouths gaping open (vv. 2-3). However, these mouths attack not with their teeth, but with their tongues. They breathe out hateful words and false accusations.[18] False accusations are especially dangerous and could lead to one's death (e.g., 1Kg 21:1-14). This attack is particularly painful because these are people whom David has loved and treated well (vv. 4-5). The picture here is of former close associates slandering David and thus damaging his reputation and possibly threatening his life. Verse 4 ends with a halting phrase, "But I—prayer"[19] (HCSB footnote). This stuttered speech reflects the agitated state of David's mind. The overall point is clear. He has prayed for them, yet they have repaid him with opposition and hatred.

After describing the plight he is in, David then petitions God to act in a specific way toward his enemy (vv. 6-19). The shift from the plural (enemies) to singular (enemy) in these verses is significant. Some have understood David as using the singular in a generic way so as to single out each individual enemy.[20] However, it is more natural to understand this as David directing his imprecation at the ringleader, or the one primarily responsible for his situation.[21]

This is often a difficult section for Christians to read. However, two points are worth noting; (1) David prays that God would act in this way toward his enemy. That is, he is not acting out the judgment on his own authority, but rather begging God to act. This is one way of being faithful to God's declaration that vengeance is His (Dt 32:35). (2) David's imprecation is grounded in the *Torah*. Deuteronomy 19:18-19 clarifies that if someone falsely accuses another, their punishment should be to "do to him as he intended to do to his brother" (Dt 19:19). This is precisely what David asks for (vv. 18-19).

The enemies of David are frequently referred to as "accusers" (*satan*, 109:4,20,29).[22] This root was not used as a title, but describes an "opponent" or "adversary." The fact that Satan regularly filled this role led to the word being used as a proper name (cf. Zch 3:1).

In his long imprecation, David specifically asks: (1) that an opponent and accuser would rise up against him (v. 6); (2) that he be found guilty and his prayers not answered (v. 7); (3) that his life be cut short and that another would take over his position;[23] (4) that his children be fatherless and his wife a widow (v. 9); (5) that his children would have to beg for their food (v. 10); (6) that his possessions would be seized (v. 11); (7) that no one would show loyalty to him or his offspring (v. 12); (8) that his descendants would be cut off within one generation (v. 13); (9) that the guilt of his forebears would be remembered (v. 14); (10) that his own sin would be remembered by God (v. 15); (11) that the memory of him would perish from the earth (v. 15).

This is quite a startling list. What he is asking for is that every trace of this man's work be wiped out from the earth. The reason for this harsh treatment is that this is how this man has treated others, especially the poor and afflicted (v. 16). This is an example of David asking that the actions of the wicked rebound back upon them.[24] The wicked did not show them kindness/loyalty (*chesed*), but instead hounded them to death. Thus, it is fitting that he be treated in like manner. Similarly, the enemy should also be cursed, because cursing was such an important part of his life. He "wore cursing like his coat—let it enter his body like water and go into his bones like oil" (v. 18). In praying that the life and work of this enemy be halted and judged, David is essentially asking for justice to be done.

In vv. 21-25, David again appeals to God for help. He gives two reasons for God to intervene. (1) Because God's own reputation is at stake (v. 21). As the anointed king, David has a unique relationship with God, therefore God should be concerned with what happens to him. (2) Because David is in such a lamentable state. He describes the physical toll this ordeal has taken upon him. His heart is wounded, his knees are weak, and his body is emaciated (vv. 22-24). That David's body is "weak from fasting" gives an indication of how fervently he has been praying for God's action (v. 24).

David's final plea is that God act in such a way that his enemy will know that the Lord is with him (v. 27). David asks that God counter the actions of his enemies. They curse, so God should bless (v. 28); When they rise up to shame him, they should be shamed (v. 28).

In typical lament fashion, David ends his prayer with praise. He will give thanks to the Lord because God saves the needy (v. 31).

PSALM 109, MESSIANIC?

While many have argued that Psalm 109 is a postexilic composition, there are good reasons to trust the Psalm title, which indicates Davidic authorship.[25] Still, it is not easy to place when in David's life this psalm was written. Commentators have suggested Doeg, Ahithophel, or Shimei as the "enemy" of the psalm.[26] While certainty in this matter is not possible, the overall situation seems fairly clear: a group of enemies, headed by a ringleader, have slandered David with false accusations and threats. David prays that these enemies will be stopped and judged. Based on this exposition, the psalm does not directly speak to the betrayal of Judas.

However, when the psalm was included in the Psalter, it was housed in the first Davidic collection of Book 5. These psalms culminate in the directly prophetic and messianic Ps 110. Thus, at the stage of its inclusion in the Psalter by an inspired editor, Psalm 109 functioned typologically in relation to Psalm 110. That is, just as David was slandered and betrayed by a close associate, so would the future Messiah. There is a biblical theme of enemies opposing the messianic line (e.g., Gn 3:15), finding its culmination in Judas's betrayal of the Messiah.[27] The Messiah's victory over His enemies is then prophesied and celebrated in Psalm 110. Understanding the enemy in Psalm 109 as a type fulfilled in Judas is not an arbitrary or haphazard connection. Rather, this psalm was intended to serve as a messianic type by the compiler of the Psalter, as demonstrated in its arrangement and connection with Psalm 110. Thus, Peter's use of this psalm as a warrant to fill Judas's position is in line with its original intent in the Psalter.

INNERTEXTUAL STUDY OF PSALM 109

The closest parallel to Ps 109 in the Psalter is Ps 69. There are many verbal connections between the two imprecatory psalms, including: "without cause" (*hinom*, 109:3; 69:4); "for your faithful love is good" (109:21; 69:16); "prayer" (*tephilah*, 109:4; 69:13); "guilt" (of enemy) (*'awon*, 109:14; 69:27); "poor" (of psalmist) (*'ani*, 109:22; 69:29); "I will praise" (*hll*, 109:30; 69:30); "needy" (*'evyon*, 109:31; 69:33). In addition to these verbal connections, the two psalms are thematically parallel. In both psalms, David is surrounded by enemies who hate and falsely accuse him without cause (69:4). He is socially isolated, shunned and mocked (69:7,12; 109:25). In both, David prays an imprecation against his enemy (69:22-28; 109:6-15). In both, David promises to praise God with thanksgiving for his salvation (69:29-30; 109:30). This psalm also predicts the betrayal of the Messiah in a typological fashion. This typology is again seen in the placement of the psalm. Psalm 69 comes in the closing section of Book 2 of the Psalter, which ends with three prayers followed by a royal/eschatological psalm (Ps 72). The three prayer psalms (Ps 69–71) were originally prayers of a king to be delivered from an enemy. These are followed by a picture of the reign of the ideal Messiah (Ps 72). As Kaiser states, "if the psalm comes out of the experience of David, who, as the holder of the office and the benefits that are to come from the Messiah, experiences in miniature form the identical malice that his namesake will experience, then it becomes evident that the suffering is both literal and predictive of the Messiah, or at least is true in a typical sense and therefore predictive."[28]

Psalm 109 also has resonances with Ps 35. In this Psalm, David is also surrounded by enemies who seek to shame him through false accusations (35:11). This is done "without cause" (35:7). As in Ps 109, David laments that he was their close friend, but they have repaid him evil for his good (35:12). David likewise promises to give thanks to God in the congregation for his deliverance (35:18). While there are some imprecations in Ps 35, they lack both the depth and specificity of Ps 109.

INTERTEXTUAL STUDY OF PSALM 109

Genesis 12:1-3 describes God's promise to Abraham. In this foundational text, the dynamic between blessing and cursing is clarified. God declares that He will bless those who bless Abraham and curse those who curse him. This dynamic is also seen in the Mosaic covenant, where God promises blessing to the obedient and curses upon those who break His covenant (Lv 26; Dt 28). In a sense, David prays this God will act in a way that demonstrates covenant faithfulness by cursing his enemies. This theology also undergirds the oracles against the nations in the prophets (Isa 13–23; Jer 46:1–51:64; Ezk 24–32; Am 1:2–2:3; Ob; Nah; Zch 9). The idea of cursing the enemies of God's people is also present in the NT. Paul declares, "If anyone does not love the Lord, a curse be on him" (1Co 16:22a). To the Galatians he proclaims, "But even if we or an angel from heaven should preach to you a gospel other than what we have preached to you, a curse be on him" (Gal 1:8). Thus, it is appropriate that the Messiah should call down a curse upon the enemies who betray, slander, and shame Him. The typology of a messianic king being betrayed and cursing his enemies is rooted in the Psalter itself and applied in an appropriate way by Peter and the church.

CONCLUSION

Psalm 109 serves as a stark reminder of how deeply fallen humanity has become and the kind of pain and anguish that can cause. In this psalm, David is on the receiving end of unjust accusations. This situation leads him to cry out for justice. He believes God cares about injustice and pleads with Him to act on his behalf out of His covenant faithfulness. This psalm was paired with Pss 108 and 110 to form a Davidic collection. This collection has a movement from lament because of enemies, including foreign nations, to the victory of the Messianic king (Ps 110). As such, Ps 109 functions typologically to represent the betrayal and suffering of the Messiah within the Psalter itself. Peter recognizes this use and appropriately uses one of its imprecations to call for Judas's replacement. This is one of several passages that grounds Jesus' statement, "Didn't the Messiah have to suffer these things and enter into His glory?" (Lk 24:26).

---

1. For a discussion of Ps 69:25, see the relevant article in this book.
2. See article by Michael Rydelnik, "The Old Testament in the New" in this book.
3. E.g., Frank-Lothar Hossfeld and Erich Zenger, *Psalms 3: A Commentary on Psalms 101–150*, trans. Linda Maloney, Hermeneia (Minneapolis: Fortress, 2011), 137; Hans-Joachim Kraus, *Psalms 60–150*, trans. Hilton C. Oswald (Minneapolis: Fortress, 1993), 342;
4. This option is still held by many commentators, e.g., Erhard Gerstenberger, *Psalms: Part 2 and Lamentations*, Forms of Old Testament Literature Series 15 (Grand Rapids: Eerdmans, 2001), 257; Derek Kidner, *Psalms 73–150*, Tyndale Old Testament Commentaries 16 (Downers Grove, IL: InterVarsity, 1975), 423.
5. NRSV; NLT; NCV; the NJB does not include "they say," but puts vv. 6-19 in quotation marks.
6. Hossfeld and Zenger, *Psalms 3*, 129–130. Cf. Erich Zenger, *God of Vengeance? Understanding the Psalms of Divine Wrath* (Louisville: John Knox, 1994), 55–62.
7. Hossfeld and Zenger, *Psalms 3*, 130.
8. Gerstenberger, *Psalms: Part 2 and Lamentations*, 259.
9. Gerstenberger, *Psalms: Part 2 and Lamentations*, 259. For a robust defense of vv. 6-19 as the speech of the psalmist against his enemies, see, Amy Cottrill, *Language, Power, and Identity in the Lament Psalms of the Individual*, Library of Hebrew Bible/Old Testament Studies 493 (New York: T&T Clark, 2008), 138–56.
10. One other perspective is that vv. 6-19 represent God speaking an imprecation against David's enemy. However, this interpretation has some of the same difficulties. The change in speaker is not clearly marked. Additionally, in vv. 13-14 the imprecation speaks about God in the third person, a bit unusual if God is the speaker. For this interpretation, see Walter Kaiser, *The Messiah in the Old Testament* (Grand Rapids: Zondervan, 1995), 109.
11. For a detailed and persuasive exposition of this, especially with regard to Books 4 and 5 of the Psalter, see David C. Mitchell, *The Message of the Psalter: An Eschatological Programme in the Book of Psalms, Journal for the Study of the Old Testament, Supplement Series* 252 (Sheffield: Sheffield, 1997). For a more concise presentation of his argument, see, David C. Mitchell, "Lord, Remember David: G. H. Wilson and the Message of the Psalter," *Vetus Testmentum* 56 (2006), 526–48.
12. Mitchell, *The Message of the Psalter*, 351–58.
13. Psalms 120–34 are each labeled as *shir hamma'aloth* ("the song of ascents"). These psalms were a collection of pilgrim psalms for worshipers on their way to Zion. In an exilic context, they began rightly to be understood as songs of hope for the restoration of Israel and "as a precursor of the time of the Messiah (cf. Is 40)," see, "Psalms," in *The Moody Bible Commentary* (Chicago: Moody, 2014), 859. Thus, it is natural to append this collection with Pss 135–136, two hymns of praise followed by an exilic lament in which the author longs for Zion.
14. Chart adapted from Erich Zenger, "The Composition and Theology of the Fifth Book of Psalms, Psalms 107–145," *Journal for the Study of the Old Testament* 80 (1998), 98.
15. See the article on Ps 110 in this *Handbook*.
16. The LXX reflects a slightly different reading, Ὁ θεός, τὴν αἴνεσίν μου ("God, my praise, do not be silent."). Not much is at stake with either reading, and the MT makes good sense as it stands.
17. E.g., Kraus, *Psalms 60–150*, 339.

18. The language here literally reads, "for a mouth of wickedness (*phi rasha'*) and a mouth of deception (*phi mirmah*), they have opened against me / they have spoken against (for this reading of the preposition, see DCH, I.450) me with a deceptive tongue (*lishon sheqer*)."

19. The LXX has smoothed this out by making it a verb, "I prayed."

20. Kidner, *Psalms 73–150*, 423.

21. See, Tremper Longman, III, *Psalms*, Tyndale Old Testament Commentaries (Downers Grove, IL: InterVarsity, 2014), 379.

22. In v. 4, the verb is used, while in vv. 20 and 29 the participle is functioning as a substantive.

23. Some have understood the word "position" (*pequdah*) as referring primarily to possessions (e.g., John Goldingay, *Psalms: Psalms 90–150*, Baker Commentary on the Old Testament Wisdom and Psalms [Grand Rapids: Baker Academic, 2008], 281). However, this is a marginal meaning of the word used only in one context (Isa 15:7). Far more common is the understanding of the word as an office or position (Nm 3:36; 4:16; 1 Chr 23:11; 24:3,19; 2 Chr 17:14; 26:11), see *Hebrew and Aramaic Lexicon of the Old Testament*, 958. This understanding is supported by the LXX translation of the term as "overseer," "supervisor" (ἐπισκοπή).

24. On the actions of the wicked rebounding back upon them, see, J. Kenneth Kuntz, "The Retribution Motif in Psalmic Wisdom," *Zeitschrift für die alttestamentliche Wissenschaft* 89 (1977), 223–33.

25. See, Wilhelm VanGemeren and Jason Stanghelle, "A Critical-Realistic Reading of the Psalms Titles, "in *Do Historical Matters Matter to Faith? A Critical Appraisal of Modern and Post-Modern Approaches to Scripture*, ed. James Hoffmeier et al. (Wheaton, IL: Crossway, 2012), 281–301.

26. A. F. Kirkpatrick, *The Book of Psalms* (Cambridge: Cambridge University Press, 1902), 652.

27. See, Kaiser, *The Messiah in the Old Testament*, 107.

28. Kaiser, *The Messiah in the Old Testament*, 104.

Psalm 110[1]

The Messiah as Eternal King Priest

MICHAEL A. RYDELNIK

Psalm 110 has long been understood as a direct prediction of the Messiah. Even Franz Delitzsch, who generally viewed the messianic character of the psalms to be merely typical, recognized Ps 110 as a direct messianic prophecy. In his commentary on Psalms, he wrote that in Ps 110 David "looks forth into the future of his seed and has the Messiah definitely before his mind."[2] Also, according to Delitzsch, "the Messiah stands objectively before the mind of David."[3] For reasons derived from the text of the psalm itself, even among interpreters who, like Delitzsch, did not interpret any other psalm messianically, Ps 110 has been consistently interpreted as directly prophetic of the Messiah.

But this is no longer the case. For example, Tremper Longman III states of the psalms in general, "Some people believe that a few psalms are messianic in the narrow sense. That is, some psalms are prophetic and have no direct message of significance for the Old Testament period. They only predict the coming Messiah." Longman rejects this possibility, writing, "no psalm is messianic in the narrow sense."[4]

Speaking specifically of Ps 110, evangelical scholar Herbert W. Bateman IV rejects the messianic interpretation and instead affirms that Ps 110 is directed to David's son Solomon, stating, "Thus it seems reasonable that Psalm 110 refers to Solomon's second coronation in 971 B.C. when David abdicated his throne to his son Solomon" and "that David did not speak the psalm to the Messiah, the divine Lord."[5] Eugene Merrill is another evangelical scholar who rejects reading Ps 110 as speaking directly of the Messiah. While affirming that David is indeed the author of the psalm, Merrill maintains that in Ps 110:1, David is calling himself "my lord." According to him, David is merely establishing a motif of royal priesthood for all Davidic kings and only generally fulfilled by the Messiah Jesus.[6]

Is it possible to view Ps 110 as a direct messianic prediction while still practicing sound exegesis? In this article, I will attempt to demonstrate that the most reasonable interpretation of Ps 110 is to view it as a direct messianic prediction. To do so, I will begin by examining the presuppositions that should guide the interpretation of Ps 110. Having done that, I will present a careful exegesis of the psalm, examining its location in the Psalter, analyzing the exegesis of the text itself, and then noting the psalm's innertextual and intertextual relationship with other passages in the Hebrew Scriptures. The conclusion will emphasize the messianic significance of the psalm.

INTERPRETIVE PRESUPPOSITIONS

Much of the interpretation of Ps 110 depends on the interpreter's presuppositions. If one presupposes that there are no direct messianic predictions or any concept of a Messiah in the Hebrew Bible, then certainly it would be necessary to look for alternative interpretations of Ps 110. However, if there is good support to presuppose that the Psalms are indeed messianic, then this will yield a messianic explanation of the psalm. Hence, these preliminary considerations will attempt to establish the presuppositions that provide a foundation for interpreting Ps 110 as a direct prediction of the Messiah.

Davidic Authorship of Ps 110

The first of the interpretive presuppositions pertains to the authorship of the psalm. If David is not the author of the psalm, it is more likely that the subject of the psalm is David himself or the Davidic king. If he did write the psalm, it allows for the likelihood that the Messiah is the subject of the psalm. With regard to the suggestions for authorship of Ps 110, H. H. Rowley suggested that it was David and Zadok together[7] while others have proposed that it was some unnamed author.[8] Yet some interpreters still take the superscription *ledavid* (of David) at face value, ascribing authorship to David.[9]

The first reason for accepting Davidic authorship is that this is the plain meaning of the superscription. The Hebrew preposition can indeed mean "for David," indicating a psalm written for or about David. Alternatively, it can mean "of David," showing that David was the author. Of course, critical scholars frequently reject Davidic authorship of any of the psalms. Yet evangelicals tend to accept that David was the author of many of them.[10] As such, most of the Davidic psalms have the identical superscription *ledavid.* It would be inconsistent to accept other psalms as written by David but to reject Davidic authorship of Ps 110 merely to avoid taking a messianic interpretation. David L. Cooper makes the case well, noting that the many usages of this superscription generally indicate David as the author of a given psalm. "Hence, the remaining possibility, unless there is unmistakable proof to the contrary, must be accepted as the only plausible one, namely, that this preposition indicates authorship. Since in this case negative proof is lacking, we must accept David as the inspired writer."[11]

A second reason to maintain Davidic authorship of Ps 110 is that Jesus Himself asserted it.[12] In a controversy with the Pharisees, Jesus quoted Ps 110 and asked them, "How is it then that David, inspired by the Spirit, calls Him (i.e., the son of David) 'Lord' . . . If David calls Him 'Lord,' how then can the Messiah be his Son" (Mt 22:41-46; cf. also Mk 12:35-37; Lk 20:41-44)? Delitzsch correctly asserts that if David were not the author of this psalm, then Jesus' question to the Pharisees concerning this psalm "would lack . . . cogency as an argument."[13] Some might object that Jesus, in His humanity or self-limitation, failed to know that David was not actually the author of the psalm. Others might suggest that perhaps He was merely repeating, not actually affirming, the common contemporary Jewish understanding of the psalm's authorship. But both these possibilities are unlikely because the point of Jesus' argument entirely rests on the Davidic authorship of Ps 110. Therefore, based on the superscription of Ps 110 and Jesus' identification of the author, it can be assumed that David wrote Ps 110.

Even if David were the author, it may not be automatic that his subject was the future royal Messiah. For example, Merrill maintains Davidic authorship but argues that David was writing of himself. In his view, the word *ʾadoni* (my lord) "became so formulaic that a king could use it even of himself. That is, 'my lord' came to mean nothing more than 'I' or 'me' when employed by the royal speaker." Yet, Merrill also demonstrates the grave weakness of his own assertion when he states, "There is no other clear reference in the Old Testament to an individual addressing himself in this manner."[14]

Similarly, Bateman maintains Davidic authorship but identifies Solomon as the subject of the psalm. In his view, David wrote Ps 110 after he had abdicated kingship and given the crown to Solomon. Bateman bases his view on the word *ʾadoni* as pointed in the Masoretic Text, (as opposed to the term *ʾadonay,* so often used of God) asserting that 94% of its 168 usages refer to a human king.[15] Barry C. Davis responds that in two cases (Jos 5:14 and Jdg 6:13), the word *ʾadoni* is used of "the Lord God." Thus, he concludes, "there is nothing to preclude the possibility that the referent of David's use of *ʾadoni* is the Messiah."[16] Hence, Davidic authorship seems to indicate that David was writing of one far more eminent than himself or his son Solomon. Rather, he wrote of his greater Son, the Davidic royal Messiah. Further evidence for this will be seen in David's last words, which provide David's own authorial explanation of his psalms.

Authorial Intent of Psalm 110

A second interpretive presupposition for understanding Ps 110 as messianic is that David himself in his last words (2Sm 23:1-5) identified the Messiah as his favorite subject in the psalms. In this paragraph, much like an author interview in the *Paris Review*,[17] David reveals his own authorial intent, that his psalms refer to the Messiah. This interpretation of David's last words is not as evident in the Masoretic Text of 2Sm 23:1 as it is in the Septuagint. The Masoretic Text contains a seeming self-description of David, when it reads:

> These are the last words of David:
> The proclamation of David, son of Jesse,
> The proclamation of the man rose *on high*,
> The one anointed by the God of Jacob,
> The favorite singer of Israel.[18]

According to the Masoretic Text reading, the passage contains four synonymous parallelisms, with each one describing David so that David himself is the one "anointed by the God of Jacob." This translation and interpretation hinge on the MT reading *'āl*, which means "on high." However, the Septuagint reads *epi* ("concerning"), apparently reading the same Hebrew consonants with a different Hebrew vowel: *pathah* (yielding *'al*) rather than a *qamets* (yielding *'āl*). This is significant in that the vocalization of the consonantal text did not occur until the ninth through tenth centuries AD and the original LXX reading would have been based on an unpointed text. Thus, the LXX reading, based on a slight difference in understanding the vowel pointing, results in a substantial difference in translation (for a more detailed defense in support of taking the variant reading as the correct one, see my article in this *Handbook*, "Textual Criticism and Messianic Prophecy"):

> These are the last words of David:
> the declaration of David son of Jesse,
> and the declaration of the man raised up *concerning*
> the Messiah [Anointed One] of the God of Jacob,
> and the Delightful One of the songs of Israel.

Sailhamer aptly explains the significance of the different readings when he writes, "The effect of the difference in the length of the vowel is such that the title 'anointed one' in the Masoretic Text refers to King David, whereas in other, non-Masoretic versions of the text, David's words are taken as a reference to the Messiah (cf. 2 Sa 22:51)."[19] In his last words, David has said that the future Messiah was his favorite subject in the psalms. This passage gives a crucial interpretive clue to reading Davidic psalms in general and Ps 110 in particular. David, by his own assertion, claims he frequently wrote about the Messiah, the Delightful One of the songs of Israel, indicating that Psalms has a messianic focus and that Ps 110 has the Messiah as its subject.

Postexilic Redaction of the Psalms

Yet a third interpretive presupposition for interpreting Ps 110 as a messianic prediction is to view the entire book of Psalms as a postexilic redaction. Although it is normal for contemporary interpreters to view the psalms as individual texts gathered with little regard for structure or theme, in recent years this trend has begun to shift. There is considerable movement to understanding the book of Psalms as the product of a purposeful redaction in the postexilic period with an identifiable theme.[20]

By recognizing the Psalms as a coherent collection of the postexilic period, the message of the entire book becomes clearer. That is not to say that the later redaction altered the original meaning of the book of Psalms.[21] Rather, as Bruce Waltke maintains, the postexilic redaction of the psalms did not change the "original authorial intention" but rather "deepened and clarified" it.[22] The clarification of the message of Psalms came about because there no longer was a "son of David sitting on Yahweh's throne."[23] In light of this reality, Brevard Childs insightfully asks, "Indeed, at the time of the final redaction, when the institution of kingship had long since been destroyed, what earthly king would have come to mind other than God's Messiah?"[24]

In fact, as Mitchell states, the very inclusion of the royal psalms in the Psalter suggests that the redactor understood them to refer to a future *mashiah*-king. For otherwise, their presence in a collection for use in Second Temple times, when the house of David was in eclipse, would have made little sense.[25] Since the book of Psalms was a postexilic redaction, then its message looks forward to the restoration of the Davidic dynasty in fulfillment of the Davidic covenant. Thus, Mitchell accurately states, "the messianic theme is central to the purpose of the collection."[26] In the context of the whole book and not just individual songs, Psalms should be read as referring to the future king, namely, the Messiah. And in Ps 110, the king described as seated at the right hand of God is not David, Solomon, or any other historical king—it is the royal Messiah. Having established that the psalms in general and Ps 110 in particular should be read messianically, the issue arises as to whether the details of the psalm allow for this approach. Therefore, it is necessary to evaluate the details of the psalm itself.

EXEGETICAL CONSIDERATIONS

A careful reading of Ps 110 will show that the most natural interpretation is that it describes the future Messiah, the eschatological son of David. This will become evident by an examination of the literary context of Ps 110, a close intextual reading of the psalm (an examination of the literary coherence and strategy of Psalm 110), and evaluation of the innertextual (relation of other psalms to Psalm 110) and intertextual references (found in other books of the Bible), all serving to confirm the messianic interpretation of Ps 110.

Contextual Analysis

Book Five of the Psalter begins with Ps 107 and continues to 150. The first seven psalms of Book Five contain a discernible unit of thought, with Ps 110 forming their focal point. As Davis says, Ps 110 is the "thematic unifier of Pss 107–13."[27] In this section of the psalms, Pss 107–109 each contain a plea for deliverance, while Pss 111–113 each express praise for deliverance. Psalm 110 is central to the thoughts of these psalms since it reveals the Messiah as King, Priest, and Warrior, who, as the answer to God's people's supplications for rescue (Pss 107–109), is the reason for their praises to God (Pss 111–113). The point of Ps 110's location in the Psalter is that Israel is to find the answer to their pleas for deliverance from oppression in the future Messiah and is to offer praise to God for the messianic redemption He provides.

Psalm 110 as a Thematic Unifier of Psalms 107–113

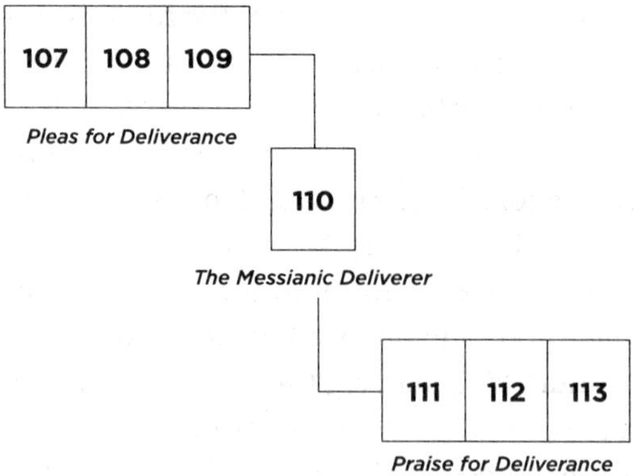

Adapted from Barry C. Davis "Is Psalm 110 a Messianic Psalm?"

Intextual Interpretation

At the outset, the superscription begins by ascribing authorship to David.[28] To those who have denied Davidic authorship and argued that this is merely a royal psalm describing David, Kidner has responded, "Therefore those who deny David's authorship of the psalm on the ground that the psalm reads like an enthronement oracle curiously miss the point. It is just such an oracle. What is unique is the royal speaker, addressing this more-than-royal person."[29]

The psalm can be divided into three units of thought, each describing the messianic son of David. The first three verses show Him to be the Divine King (110:1-3), the central verse identifies Him as an eternal priest (110:4), and the final three verses reveal Him as a victorious warrior (110:5-7).[30] The central verse, in its brevity, forms the literary focal point of the psalm. The theme of the psalm is that the Lord has granted universal dominion to the Messianic Priest-King.

I. Messiah, the Divine King (110:1-3). The first stanza of the psalm emphasizes the royalty of the Messiah, describing Him in a variety of His kingly roles.

A. The Messiah is Lord (110:1a). The psalm opens with the phrase "The Lord declared," using the Hebrew word *ne'um yhwh,* (lit., "declaration/proclamation/oracle of the Lord), an oracular term frequently used in the Prophets and translated "declares the Lord." Hence, at the outset of the psalm, the use of prophetic imagery casts the sense that this psalm is a prophetic oracle.

This oracle is addressed to "my lord" (*'adoni*), using a word that is generally used of a human superior, not a deity. Yet as explained above, the word is used of the angel of the Lord in Jos 5:14 and Jdg 6:13, where He is then identified with the Lord Himself. Furthermore, the psalm was originally written with consonants alone, with the Masoretic vowels added much later (between the eighth and tenth centuries AD). As Robert Alden observes, "The vowels in the Hebrew expression for 'my lord,' which the Jewish scribes put in, indicate a human title, but the inspired consonantal text would allow either human or divine."[31] It would be mistaken, therefore, to base the entire interpretation of the psalm (i.e. where the addressee is human or divine) solely on a single Hebrew vowel. There are in fact strong reasons to conclude that the original author of the psalm intended to speak of a divine Lord. David, Israel's most exalted king, was looking forward to the coming of a future ruler even more exalted than himself.

B. Messiah Is at God's Right Hand (110:1b). The exalted king is directed by "the Lord" to sit at His right hand. This appears to be a special place of honor (see Ps 45:9), as indicated by Solomon setting up a throne for his mother Bathsheba so that she could sit at his right hand (1Kg 2:19). Leupold states that the location of the throne at the right hand of God indicated "that the Lord God of Israel Himself ('Yahweh') had designated for the Messiah a position at his own right hand, making

Him coequal in rank and authority with Himself, and so virtually declaring His divine character."[32] This may very well overstate the significance of the right hand, as Solomon merely exalted Bathsheba but did not necessarily present her as an equal to himself. It seems safer to surmise that the right hand is more likely a place of exaltation and honor. However, it still does not disallow viewing the exalted one seated at the right hand as being divine.

Some have speculated that the right hand of God refers to the placement of the royal palace in close proximity to the ark[33] or the king's enthronement on the side of the Holy of Holies at the outset of the fall festival.[34] More likely, being seated at the right hand of God refers to reception of authority and dominion in God's own heavenly throne room.[35]

C. The Messiah Awaits Victory (110:1c). The royal Messiah is seated at the right hand of God, awaiting the day that God makes the King's enemies a footstool for His feet. The phrase "your enemies" (*'oyebeykā*), used in Ps 110 (both vv. 1 and 2) is commonly used of God's enemies in the book of Psalms (8:2; 21:8; 66:3; 74:23; 89:10,51; 92:9).[36] The only exception might be Ps 21:8, but Dahood maintains that even in this verse, the opponents are the enemies of the divine King, not the human ruler.[37] The image of the footstool is that of triumph. Just as the victor subdues the defeated underfoot (cf. Ps 47:3; Jos 10:24, Isa 49:23), so this divine Ruler awaits the day when His feet will rest on His enemies. Moreover, the word "footstool" (*hadom*) is used as belonging to God (1Chr 28: 2; Pss 99:5; 132:7; Isa 66:1; Lam 2:1).[38] To summarize, Ps 110:1 describes an exalted Ruler, in a supreme place of honor in the throne room of God, awaiting victory over the enemies of God, who will become a divine footstool. This could not describe anyone other than an exalted, eschatological messianic figure.

D. The Messiah Will Rule (110:2-3). Although the King initially awaits victory in God's heavenly throne room, vv. 2-3 indicate a descent from heaven to the earth, where He receives dominion over His enemies and leads His servants into battle. Thus, Messiah will rule over His enemies (v. 2) and His willing servants (v. 3).

The Messiah's rule is described as "the LORD" extending the King's scepter from Zion (v. 2), a figure for His reign from earthly Jerusalem.[39] The implication of the King's dominion issuing forth from Zion and the King's role in the final earthly battle (v. 5) shows that He will descend from the heavenly heights to the earth. Thus, the King will descend upon His enemies[40] and rule over them.

Not only will the future King have dominion over His enemies. According to v. 3, the King will also lead His faithful servants in war. His people are described as voluntary warriors on the day of battle (see also Jdg 5:2). This depiction of an eschatological army, volunteering to fight for the Messiah, makes good sense with either Hebrew reading. According to the more well-attested reading, the warriors are dressed "in holy splendor" (*behadrey qodesh*). In a significant variant reading,[41] (*beharrey qodesh*), their battlefield is "on holy mountains." In the former reading, the soldiers of the Messianic Priest-King are wearing priestly garments for the "sacrificial feast" of slaughter on the mountains of Israel during the great eschatological war (Ezk 39:17). The latter reading describes the battlefield as the "holy hills" of the great eschatological war that will take place on the mountains of Israel (Ezk 38:21). Either reading fits the messianic presentation of the eschatological Warrior-King in Ps 110.[42]

David M. Hay correctly notes that the last phrase of 110:3 is "virtually unintelligible."[43] The MT reads "from the womb of the dawn, your youth (*yalduteykā*) are to you as dew," leading to a variety of strained and unlikely interpretations since these words make virtually no sense. Booj describes the phrase as "especially problematic and indeed . . . meaningless." He concludes that "some deformation must have crept in."[44] Although a canon of textual criticism is that the harder reading is to be preferred, there is a difference between a harder reading and an incoherent, impossible one. For this reason, Sigmund Mowinckel and other scholars prefer the LXX, which reads, "from the womb of the dawn, I have begotten you," a translation based on the same Hebrew consonants but with different vowel pointings (*yelidtikā*).[45] Additionally, Bentzen has suggested that the corruption of the Masoretic Text resulted from deliberate scribal efforts to obfuscate the meaning and its plain allusion to Ps 2:7.[46]

Since the LXX reading is preferable, it leads to a strongly messianic interpretation, describing in Hay's words "the birth of a divine child" as King. The King is said to be begotten "from the womb of the dawn," a phrase Kraus links to the coming of the Messianic King described in Nm 24:17 as a star that comes forth from Jacob. Furthermore, Kraus sees "the place and procedure of the begetting" as belonging "to the heavenly sphere. The 'divine king' comes from the superworldly heights, from God's world." Linking the phrase "from the womb of the dawn I have begotten you" to Ps 2:7, Kraus rightly concludes that it is "a reference to the heavenly divine origin of the king."[47] McCaul adds that it not only indicates origin from heaven but One begotten "before conception of the morning light" or "before creation."[48]

Thus, the first stanza of Ps 110 presents a divine King, seated at the right hand of God and awaiting future victory. On that eschatological day of triumph, He will descend from God's heavenly throne room as the begotten one and establish His dominion from Zion over the whole world. In that great last battle, the King will establish his rule, destroying His enemies while leading His willing servants to victory.

II. Messiah, The Priest-King (110:4). A major break occurs at this juncture in the psalm. The shorter but more surprising description of the King in v. 4 draws attention to this verse as the focal point of the psalm.

A. The Promise of God (110:4a). Providing a second oracle in the psalm, the writer focuses on the certainty of God's promise to His chosen King. Since the Lord swore it, He will cause it to happen and He will not be sorry.[49] This "assures us that Yahweh's statement is guaranteed by a declaration that is irrevocable and sworn."[50] Yahweh's promise to the Messiah is absolute and certain to occur because of His strong oath.

B. The Office of Messiah (110:4). God's strong oath was required because of the unusual promise that the Messiah would be a priest. There are three unique features of the Messiah's priesthood, the first of which is that God would unite the offices of priest and king in the Messiah. This is special in that these offices were always separate in Israel. Some interpreters who see David or an Israelite king as the subject of the psalm maintain that the office of priest-king was common in Israel.[51] Merrill supports this by citing several biblical passages. For example, in 2Sm 8:18 David's sons are called "priests" (*kohanim*), although in the parallel passage (1Chr 18:17) they are called "chief officials" (*rishonim*). Merrill writes, "Despite various efforts to explain *kohanim* as something other than priests, it seems best to view these sons as priests in the same sense in which David was."[52] In direct contradiction to this statement, Merrill writes in another work, "The Hebrew word, usually rendered 'priests,' is explained in 1 Chronicles 18:17 as "chief officials" (cf. 2Sm. 20:26). This no doubt is the better meaning since David's sons, as Judeans, were ineligible to serve as priests."[53, 54]

Merrill also argues that in 2Sm 6, David is described as wearing priestly attire (v. 14, "a linen ephod"), offering sacrifice (vv. 17-18), and issuing priestly benedictions (v. 18). The linen ephod was indeed priestly attire, but as Keil and Delitzsch point out, it was not the clothing required to be worn when performing priestly duties. Rather, it denoted the character of the wearer.[55] Furthermore, David did not offer the sacrifices himself but rather *through* the Levitical priests present.[56] He also blessed the people as their king and leader, not as their priest. In ancient Israel, David was not, nor were any of his royal descendants, priest-kings. The Law made it clear that there was "a clear distinction between Israel's three theocratic officers, king, prophet, and priest."[57]

The point is that the Lord's oath to the Messianic King promises Him a unique office—not merely as royalty but as a Priest-King, who would both rule and represent His people before God. Yet a second aspect of the King's unique priesthood is that He would not serve as a Levitical priest but as a "priest like Melchizedek."[58] Melchizedek, described in Gn 14, served as a priest-king of God Most High. From him, Abram received bread and wine for a meal of sacral worship (Gn 14:18) and a blessing from God Most High (Gn 14:19-20). To him Abram also offered a tenth of all the spoils he had just taken in his war with the four kings (Gn 14:20). Just as

Melchizedek shared the office of priest and king, so the messianic figure of Ps 110 will likewise be a Priest-King, in the manner of Melchizedek.

Yet a third unique facet of the Messiah's royal priesthood is that it is "forever." Kidner remarks that "this is the most significant clause of all" in that it shows the eternal work of this Priest-King "in contrast to the ephemeral priests whose labours were manifestly inconclusive."[59]

The point of v. 4, in the center of the psalm, is to emphasize the priesthood of the coming King. This is significant in that both the verses before and those after v. 4 describe the King at war. Thus, the priesthood of the Messianic King is one in which He offers up God's enemies in a great "sacrificial feast" (Ezk 39:17-20) to the Lord in the end of days.

III. Messiah, the Victorious King (110:5-7). The final stanza of the psalm emphasizes Messiah's victory over the nations in the great eschatological battle He will fight. In this description of Messiah's triumph at war, vv. 5-6 identify those whom He will defeat, while v. 7 reveals the refreshment He will experience after the battle.

A. The Defeated Nations (110:5-6). This stanza begins with the statement: "The Lord (*'adonay*) is at your right hand." Unlike in v. 1, where the vowels used generally (although not exclusively) indicate a human master (*'adoni*) rather than God, in v. 5 the vowels (*'adonay*) indicate that it is certainly a Divine Master being described. This has led many commentators to assume that this is not the King at Yahweh's right hand but instead Yahweh at the King's right hand.[60]

Yet it is better to view this as the King at the right hand of God. First, grammatically, all the third-person singular pronouns in vv. 5-7 modify the Lord (*'adonay*).

The Lord [*'adonay*, the messianic king] is at Your right hand;
He will crush kings on the day of *His* anger.
He will judge the nations, heaping up corpses;
He will crush leaders over the entire world.
He will drink from the brook by the road;
Therefore, *He* will lift up His head.

Plainly, it is the King who battles and drinks. Since there is no change in subject, it is the King who is called the Divine Lord (*'adonay*) in v. 5. Edward J. Kissane notes the error of understanding *'adonay* as Yahweh while taking the third-person singular pronouns that follow as referring to the King: "This introduces a change of subject of which there is no indication in the text. If the Messiah is the subject of verse 7, he must also be the subject of the preceding verses."[61]

Second, just as it is the Lord (*'adoni*) who is seated at the right hand of God in v. 1, so He is once again described in v. 5 as the One who is on the right hand of God.

As Perowne says, "It is hardly probable that in so short a Psalm the King should first be said (ver. 1) to be at the right hand of Jehovah, and then that in ver. 5 Jehovah, on the contrary, should be said to be at the right hand of the King."[62] The logical conclusion is that the King is called "the Lord" (*ʾadonay*), a title reserved for God alone. While it is possible to object that the King would not have been granted a divine title, there are implications of the King's deity throughout the psalm. In light of Ps 45:6 saying to the King "Your throne, God, is forever and ever," therein calling Him "God" (*ʾelohim*),[63] why is it so objectionable, apart from dogmatic presupposition, for Him to be called "Lord" (*ʾadonay*) in this one?

Thus, in 110:5-6 the victorious divine Messiah is graphically depicted defeating all those who have rebelled against God. He crushes kings and rulers, judges the people (nations), and heaps up corpses, indicating that no rebels will escape. The violence of the imagery recalls Isa 63:1-6, where the Messianic King tramples through the winepress of the nations, staining His garments with blood and crushing nations in His anger.[64] The psalmist says all this will occur on "the day of His anger," with the pronoun "His" referring to the King. Since the phrase "day of anger" (*yom ʾap*) occurs in only six verses in Scripture[65] and in each case, it refers to God's wrath, this would imply that the triumphant King is indeed a divine King.[66]

B. The Refreshed King (110:7). The last verse of the psalm "forms an anticlimax to the gore of the preceding lines."[67] Using a refreshment metaphor, the Messianic King is pictured drinking from the brook after His last battle. In contrast to 110:1, where He sits, awaiting the day when His enemies become a footstool, in 110:7, having vanquished the rebels, "He will lift up His head." Psalm 110 as a whole paints a picture of the divine Priest-King of Israel who will rule over all from Zion when He crushes all rebellion against Himself and then brings peace to the world.

INNERTEXTUAL INTERPRETATION

Much could be said about the links between Ps 110 and other parts of the Psalter. Yet, it seems that the most basic interaction is with Ps 2, which describes the King as "the Anointed One" (*mashiach*) and has been viewed as a messianic psalm in both Jewish and Christian tradition. Based on its location in the Psalter, in a sense, Ps 110 can be viewed as an innertextual reference back to Ps 2, using a variety of verbal and thematic associations.

The first link from Ps 110 to Ps 2 is that in both psalms God promises the King dominion over rebellious enemy nations. In Ps 110, God tells the King to sit at His right hand until He makes all enemy nations His "footstool" and tells Him to "rule over" the surrounding enemy nations (110:1-2). Psalm 2 describes the nations as rebellious, whose leaders "take their stand . . . against the LORD and His Anointed

One" (2:2). God then promises the King that He will give Him "the nations" as an "inheritance" and the "ends of the earth" as a "possession" (2:8).

A second link between Ps 110 and Ps 2 shows that the King acts with righteous wrath. In Ps 110:5 the King "crushes kings on the day of His anger [*beyom appo*]," while in Ps 2:5 God speaks "to them in His anger [*be'appo*]." Moreover, the nations are warned that if they fail to "pay homage" to the King, "He will be angry" (ʾnp) and they "will perish" (2:12). Not only does Ps 2:5 use the same word for anger as 110:5, but it also uses two synonyms, "burning anger" (*charon*) and the verb "be angry" (*ʾanp*), heightening the thematic links between the two psalms.

A third innertextual link between Ps 110 and Ps 2 is in the description of the King's victorious battle. In Ps 110:2 God promises to extend the King's "mighty scepter (*matteh*) from Zion" over all the nations. Similarly, in Ps 2:9 the King is promised the nations as an inheritance, noting that He "will break them with a rod (*shevet*) of iron," using the synonyms *matteh* and *shevet*. Both psalms depict the King's victory in graphic terms: Ps 110:5-6 describes Him as crushing kings, piling corpses, and crushing leaders; similarly, Ps 2:9 portrays Him as shattering earthly kings and nations into pottery shards.

Yet another link between the two psalms is that the King is to reign from Zion. In Ps 110:2, "the Lord" stretches forth the King's scepter "from Zion." Accordingly, Ps 2:6 presents the King as enthroned on "Zion," God's "holy mountain."

A final but significant innertextual link between the two psalms is derived from the variant reading for 110:3.[68] There, God declares to the King, "from the womb of the dawn, *I have begotten You* (*yelidtikā*), the exact same word used in God's oracle to the King in 2:7, "You are my Son, today *I have begotten you* (*yelidtikā*)." Although Pss 2 and 110 are clearly linked in the NT (Heb 1:3-5,13; 5:5-6), the phrases about the Begotten One were not associated until Justin Martyr did so in the second century. Hay proposes that the NT authors neglected to do so "because they knew that its meaning (and form) were disputed and because they could find other scriptural texts to support ideas of Jesus' divine sonship."[69] Another possible explanation for the NT omission of this link is that perhaps the association of this word was so obvious that it was unnecessary for the NT authors even to cite it. With or without the association of the phrase "I have begotten you," plainly Pss 2 and 110 use verbal and thematic links to present a fully orbed picture of the eschatological Messianic King.

Intertextual Interpretation

A number of later biblical authors refer to Ps 110 and interpret it in an eschatological, messianic way. Three of these intertextual associations are especially significant. The first, Dan 7, with its glorious vision of the Ancient of Days and the

Son of Man, appears to be a reference to the seating of the Messianic King at the right hand of God (Ps 110:1). Daniel 7:9 states, "Thrones were set in place, and the Ancient of Days took His seat." Further on in the passage, "One like a son of man" approaches "the Ancient of Days" and receives "authority to rule, and glory, and a kingdom." The Son of Man is also given "an everlasting dominion that will not pass away" and a kingdom "that will not be destroyed" (Dan 7:13-14). In light of the plural use of "thrones," it seems that this Son of Man will take His seat next to the Ancient of Days, a vivid reminder of Ps 110:1, where the Lord takes His seat at the right hand of God.[70] A possible link between the two passages is Ps 80:17:[71] "Let Your hand be with the man at Your right hand, with the son of man You have made strong for Yourself."[72] Rabbi Akiba made the connection between Dan 7 and Ps 110: when explaining the plural "thrones" used in Dan 7:9, he said, "One [throne] was for Himself and one for David," that is, for the Messiah.[73] As Hay points out, "It seems distinctly possible that both Akiba and the writer of Dan 7 were thinking of Ps 110:1."[74]

Yet a second important intertextual reference to Ps 110:4 is Zch 6:9-15. There it describes the eschatological unification of the royal and priestly offices with a role-play by Joshua the high priest. A composite crown, representing kingship and priesthood, is placed on Joshua's head and he is called by the messianic title, "Branch." This Priest-King will build the eschatological Temple and "sit and rule on His throne . . . He will be a priest on His throne, and the counsel of peace will be between the two offices" (Zch 6:12-13 NASB). Clearly this refers to the King described in Ps 110:4, who is a priest like Melchizedek, uniting the offices of king and priest. Delitzsch aptly writes of the relationship between Zch 6 and Ps 110:4:

> Zechariah removes the fulfillment of the Psalm out of the Old Testament present, with its blunt separation between the monarchial and hierarchical dignity, into the domain of the future, and refers it to Jahve's Branch. . . . [*tzemakh*] that is to come. He who will build the true temple of God, satisfactorily unites in his one person the priestly with the kingly office. . . . Thus, this Psalm was understood by the later prophecy.[75]

Delitzsch concludes by rhetorically asking how Ps 110:4 could have been understood in light of Zechariah's reference to it other "than in the eschatological Messianic sense?"[76]

The third crucial intertextual link is also with Zch 14. There "the LORD" is said to "go out to fight against those nations as He fights on a day of battle" so that "His feet will stand on the Mount of Olives" which "will be split in half from east to west" (Zch 14:3-5). This certainly refers to the coming of the messianic deliverer as representative of "the LORD." Mitchell points out that "it would be a high degree of anthropomorphism indeed to regard Yhwh as physically touching the earth with his feet so that it split."[77]

The imagery of Zch 14 relies on Ps 110 in several ways. Both passages depict a descent from heaven—Ps 110 from the right hand of God to the battlefield (110:1,5-6) and Zch 14:3-5 from the heights of heaven to Jerusalem in defense of God's people. Both passages describe a deliverer coming to the battle accompanied by a holy army. Psalm 110:3 states, "Your people will volunteer on Your day of battle. In holy splendor . . . ," while Zch 14:5 proclaims, "Then the LORD my God will come and all the holy ones with Him." Finally, Ps 110:5-6 graphically portrays the King destroying the rebellious nations, crushing them and "heaping up corpses." Similarly, Zch 14:12-14 graphically displays the plague and panic that will seize enemy armies in their defeat.

The point of what has been discussed in this section is this: in the postexilic era, the books of Daniel and Zechariah provide a clear messianic hope by relying on the words and images contained in Ps 110. Plainly, these later writers understood Ps 110 to refer to the Messiah of Israel.

It is not the intertextual references alone that point to a messianic interpretation. By placing the psalm in context of the whole Psalter and performing careful intextual and innertextual readings, it appears that Ps 110 presents the glorious Messiah Priest-King, seated at the right hand of God and returning in power to establish His dominion over all the earth.

CONCLUSION

This article began by asking if Ps 110 should be read as a messianic text. The case has been made that Ps 110 does indeed picture the divine Priest-King, now seated at the right hand of God, but who will descend from heaven at the end of days to save Israel and extend His rule over all the earth. This is none other than the Messiah.

Likely that is why both Jewish and Christian sources have long held that Ps 110 is about the Messiah.[78] It is not necessary to blame their messianic interpretations on their historical circumstances or exegetical predispositions. It seems better to say that they derived their views from the text of Scripture. That is why Jesus, speaking to some of His Jewish contemporaries about Ps 110, pointedly asked how David could call the son of David, Lord (Mt 22:41-46). Their failure to answer Jesus' question demonstrated that they must certainly have agreed with the messianic interpretation of Ps 110[79] but could not explain how the psalm could present the Messiah as deity (Lord). Although Jesus does not add any further commentary to this text, it is obvious that He too interpreted Ps 110 as about a divine Messiah.

What Alexander McCaul wrote of Ps 110 in the middle of the 19th century, in response to the growing critical denial of messianic prediction in his day, is as valid today: "The words of the psalm, taken in their ordinary sense, admit of no other interpretation. The subject of the psalm is the king in Zion, exalted to heaven, as Dan. vii. 13; in verse 5 is called . . . [*'Adonay*], THE LORD, and is described as judge of kings and nations. The description can apply only to him who is David's son and David's Lord."[80]

---

1. This article is adapted from a chapter in Michael Rydelnik, *The Messianic Hope: Is the Hebrew Bible Really Messianic?* NAC Studies in Bible and Theology, ed. E. Ray Clendenen (Nashville: B&H Publishers, 2010), 164–84. Used with permission.
2. F. Delitzsch, "Psalms," in *Commentary on the Old Testament*, by C. F. Keil and F. Delitzsch, trans. J. Martin (Grand Rapids: Eerdmans, 1980), V:I:66.
3. Ibid., V:III:184.
4. T. Longman III, *How to Read the Psalms* (Downers Grove, IL: InterVarsity, 1988), 67–68. Longman does say the Psalms ultimately speak of Messiah Jesus, but only in a secondary sense, not in a directly predictive way. His argument is that direct messianic psalms remove the significance of a psalm from its Old Testament context. According to him, the psalmist's intended meaning must not be eschatological and future oriented but rather must refer to events in the writer's own day.
5. H. W. Bateman IV, "Psalm 110:1 and the New Testament," *Bibliotheca Sacra* 149 (1992): 452–53.
6. E. H. Merrill, "Royal Priesthood: An Old Testament Messianic Motif" *Bibliotheca Sacra* 150 (1993): 50–61
7. H. H. Rowley, "Melchizedek and Zadok (Ge 14 and Ps 110)," in *Festschrift: Alfred Bertholet zum 80. Geburtstag*, ed. W. Baumgartner (Tubingen: J. C. B. Mohr, 1950), 461–72.
8. C. A. Briggs and E. G. Briggs, *A Critical and Exegetical Commentary on the Book of Psalms*, ICC (Edinburgh: T&T Clark, 1986), 2:375; M. Dahood, *Psalms*, AB (Garden City, NY: Doubleday, 1970), 3:113; J. Goldingay, *Psalms*, Baker Commentary on the Old Testament (Grand Rapids: Baker, 2008), 3:291.
9. Bateman, "Psalm 110:1 and the New Testament," 444–45; Merrill, "Royal Priesthood: An Old Testament Messianic Motif," 54–55; J. J. S. Perowne, *The Book of Psalms* (Grand Rapids: Zondervan, 1966), 2:295–98. H. C. Leupold, *Exposition of the Psalms* (Grand Rapids: Baker, 1969), 770–75.
10. Although the term *l'david* is capable of several interpretations, it has generally been understood as referring to authorship. W. A. VanGemeren explains, "The Bible clearly teaches that David was a poet of extraordinary abilities (2Sm 23:1) and a musician (Am 6:5; cf. 1Sm 16:15-23; 18:10; 2Sm 1:17-27; 3:33-34; 23:1-7) and that he created the temple guilds of singers and musicians (1Ch 6:31-32; 15:16,27; 25:1-31; 2Ch 29:25-26; cf. Neh 12:45-47). The NT writers likewise assumed that David was the author of many psalms (cf. Mt 22:43-45; Ac 2:25-28; 4:25-26; Heb 4:7) and even spoke of the Book of Psalms as being David's (Lk 20:42)." See Expositors Bible Commentary 5:34.
11. D. L. Cooper, *Messiah: His Redemptive Career* (Los Angeles: Biblical Research Society, 1963), 64.
12. D. Kidner has remarked that most contemporary scholarship views the author of the psalm as "an anonymous cultic official" writing for "either David or one of his successors." He bitingly comments, "Our Lord and the apostles, it is understood, were denied this insight." *Psalms 73–150* (Downers Grove, IL: InterVarsity, 1975), 392.
13. F. Delitzsch, *Psalms* in *Commentary on the Old Testament* vol. V (Three Volumes in One), V:III:184.
14. Merrill, "Royal Priesthood: An Old Testament Messianic Motif," 55.
15. Bateman, "Psalm 110:1 and the New Testament," 448–49.
16. B. C. Davis, "Is Psalm 110 a Messianic Psalm?" *Bibliotheca Sacra* 157 (2000): 162–63.
17. The *Paris Review* is an English language literary magazine most known for its interviews of authors in which they explain their work.

18. A slightly more literal translation would be: "These are the last words of David: / David son of Jesse declares, / And the man raised *on high* declares, / The anointed of the God of Jacob, / And the delightful one of the songs of Israel."

19. J. H. Sailhamer, *Introduction to Old Testament Theology* (Grand Rapids: Zondervan, 1995), 221.

20. G. H. Wilson has effectively made the case for viewing the Psalms as having a purposeful postexilic redaction with an identifiable theme (*The Editing of the Hebrew Psalter* [Chico, CA: Scholars Press, 1985], 9–10, 182–99. However, according to Wilson, that theme looks backward historically, focusing on the failure of the Davidic dynasty. In his view, the Psalms do not look forward to a restored Davidic dynasty under the Messiah but a return to the premonarchic days when the Lord alone was Israel's king (pp. 214–15). Treating the Psalms as a postexilic redaction is not merely a current approach. J. Forbes, in the late nineteenth century, made the case that the Psalms were a coherent postexilic collection with a messianic intent (*Studies on the Book of Psalms* [Edinburgh: T&T Clark, 1888]).

21. B. K. Waltke's article, "A Canonical Process Approach to the Psalms," in *Tradition and Testament*, ed. J. Feinberg and P. Feinberg (Chicago: Moody, 1981), 3–18, is a masterful explanation of the nature of the book of Psalms and the way the Psalms should be read as a messianic text.

22. Ibid., 8.

23. Ibid., 15.

24. B. S. Childs, *Introduction to the Old Testament as Scripture* (Philadelphia: Fortress, 1979), 516.

25. D. C. Mitchell, *The Message of the Psalter: An Eschatological Programme in the Book of Psalms* (Sheffield, England: Sheffield Academic Press, 1997), 86. Mitchell, much like Forbes a century before, has persuasively argued for interpreting the Psalms as a coherent postexilic redaction with an eschatological/messianic theme throughout the Psalter. D. M. Howard has recognized the importance of Mitchell's thesis, writing, "The overall force and logic of his argument is impressive, however, and his work will surely occupy a pivotal position in future discussions of the Psalter's composition and message" ("Recent Trends in Psalm Study," *The Face of Old Testament Studies*, ed. D. W. Baker and B. T. Arnold [Grand Rapids: Baker, 1999], 338).

26. Ibid., 87.

27. Davis, "Is Psalm 110 a Messianic Psalm?" 168.

28. See pages 220–23 for support for maintaining Davidic authorship of Psalm 110.

29. Kidner, *Psalms 73–150*, 392.

30. This structure is adapted from Kidner, *Psalm 73–150*, 393–96.

31. R. L. Alden, *Psalms: Songs of Discipleship* (Chicago: Moody, 1976), 3:31–32.

32. Leupold, *Exposition of the Psalms*, 771.

33. A. F. Kirkpatrick, *The Book of Psalms* (Cambridge: Cambridge Univ. Press, 1902), 666.

34. H.-J. Kraus, *Psalms 60–150*, trans. H. C. Oswald (Minneapolis: Fortress, 1993), 348.

35. D. C. Mitchell argues for this interpretation based on this understanding in Dan 7:13-14, 11QMelch, the New Testament, and the *Testament of Job* (*The Message of the Psalter: An Eschatological Programme in the Book of Psalms*, 259–60).

36. Davis, "Is Psalm 110 a Messianic Psalm?" 164.

37. M. Dahood, *Psalms*, AB (Garden City, NY: Doubleday, 1970), 1:131.

38. Davis, "Is Psalm 110 a Messianic Psalm?" 164.

39. Mitchell suggests that there may be further evidence for the King's descent from the heavenly heights. He notes that the word often translated "rule" may, in fact, be a further reference to a descent from the heavenly throne room. D. C. Mitchell, *The Message of the Psalter*, 260.

40. Note the comment on v. 1 that the word for enemies is generally used in the psalm of God's enemies, once again hinting that this King is more than royal, even divine.

41. So in 83 Masoretic manuscripts, Symmachus, and Jerome; see Th. Booj, "Psalm 110: Rule in the Midst of Your Foes," *Vetus Testamentum* 41 (1991): 398.

42. Mitchell, *The Message of the Psalter*, 261.

43. D. M. Hay, *Glory at the Right Hand: Psalm 110 in Early Christianity* (Nashville: Abingdon, 1973), 21.

44. Booj, "Psalm 110: Rule in the Midst of Your Foes," 398.

45. S. Mowinckel, *He That Cometh*, trans. G. W. Anderson (Nashville: Abingdon, 1956), 67; A. McCaul, *The Messiahship of Jesus* (London: Parker, 1852), 172, 174.

46. A. Bentzen, *Introduction to the Old Testament* (Copenhagen: Gad, 1952), 100.

47. Kraus, *Psalms 60–150*, 350.

48. McCaul, *The Messiahship of Jesus*, 172, 174.

49. BDB identifies the verb *yinachem* ("He will not take it back") as a Niphal imperfect, third-person singular with a negative particle, with the translation, "he will not be sorry."

50. Kraus, *Psalms 60–150*, 350.

51. John G. Gammie, "A New Setting for Psalm 110," *Anglican Theological Review* 51 (1969): 4–17; J. L. Mays, *Psalms*, IBC (Louisville: John Knox, 1994), 350–55; Merrill, "Royal Priesthood: An Old Testament Messianic Motif," 59–61.

52. Merrill, "Royal Priesthood: An Old Testament Messianic Motif," 60.

53. Eugene H. Merrill, "2 Samuel," *The Bible Knowledge Commentary: Old Testament*, ed. J. F. Walvoord and R. B. Zuck (Wheaton, IL: Victor Books, 1985), 464.

54. Keil and Delitzsch make a good case for translating *kohanim* as royal officials in 2Sm 8:18 and not "priests," demonstrating that the word is explained as "the king's friend" in 1Kg 4:5 (*Biblical Commentary on the Books of Samuel* [Grand Rapids: Eerdmans, n.d.], 368–69). Note also that the LXX translates "priests" as *aularchai* ("court rulers") and not priests.

55. Keil and Delitzsch, *Biblical Commentary on the Books of Samuel* (Grand Rapids: Eerdmans, n.d.), 336.

56. A. McCaul notes various scriptural references where people are said to offer sacrifice without themselves being priests (cf. Jos 8:31; Jdg 20:26). His point is that "There were, according to the traditions of the Jews, certain operations in the act of sacrifice performed by the laity, and others peculiar to the priest. The owner of the victim laid his hands on it, killed, flayed, cut it up, and washed the inwards. The priest received the blood and sprinkled it, put fire on the altar, arranged the wood on the fire, and the sacrifice on the wood. The expressions referred to do not prove that either David or Solomon was a priest." *The Messiahship of Jesus*, 174.

57. W. A. VanGemeren, "Psalms," *The Expositor's Bible Commentary*, ed. F. E. Gaebelein, (Grand Rapids: Zondervan, 1991), 5:699.

58. Mitchell suggests the strained interpretation that this passage should view the name Melchizedek as a vocative. Then it would be translated, "You are priest forever according to my promise, Melchizedek." He speculates that 11QMelch derives its understanding of Melchizedek as an eschatological figure from this passage. See D. C. Mitchell, *The Message of the Psalter*, 259–60.

59. Kidner, *Psalms 73–150*, 395.

60. VanGemeren, "Psalms," in *Expositor's Bible Commentary*, 5:699; Kidner, *Psalms 73–150*, 396; Klaus, *Psalms 60–150*, 351–52; Mitchell, *The Message of the Psalter*, 262.

61. E. J. Kissane, *The Book of Psalms* (Dublin: Browne and Nolan, 1954), 2:194.

62. Perowne, *The Book of Psalms*, 2:309.

63. The words addressed to the King are: "Your throne, God, is forever and ever."

64. Perowne has objected to the messianic interpretation of this section, wondering how it can describe the Messiah as "literally reigning in Zion" and engaging "in fierce and bloody war with his enemies." (*The Book of Psalms*, 2:296). This sort of objection stems from a false image of Jesus as the meek and mild one. Although at present "He will not break a bruised reed" (Isa 42:3), in the Hebrew Bible there are many wrathful images of the Messiah executing justice against the nations, such as Ps 2 and Isa 63. There will one day be a literal last battle in which the Messiah will crush all rebellion against the true God. D. Sayers's observation is helpful: "We have very efficiently pared the claws of the Lion of Judah, certified Him 'meek and mild,' and recommended Him as a fitting household pet for pale curates and pious old ladies" (*The Whimsical Christian: Eighteen Essays* [New York: Macmillan, 1978], 14).

65. Job 20:28; Lam 2:1,21-22; Zph 2:2-3.

66. Davis, "Is Psalm 110 a Messianic Psalm?" 166.

67. J. P. Sterk, "An Attempt at Translating a Psalm," *The Bible Translator* 42 (1991): 441.

68. See exegesis of Ps 110:3 above.

69. Hay, *Glory at the Right Hand*, 22.

70. Ibid., 26; Mowinckel, *He That Cometh*, 352.

71. Ps 80:17 in the English versions.

72. Hay cites this verse as a link and credits N. A. Dahl with the suggestion (*Glory at the Right Hand*, 26).

73. *b. Sanh.* 38b.

74. Hay, *Glory at the Right Hand*, 26.

75. Delitzsch, "Psalms" in *Commentary on the Old Testament*, V:III:194.

76. Ibid.

77. Mitchell, *The Message of the Psalter*, 264.

78. For a discussion of the messianic interpretation of Psalm 110 in Jewish and Christian sources, see Hay, *Glory at the Right Hand*, 19–51. Although some Jewish sources identify Abraham as the subject of Ps 110, *Midr. Tehillim* 18:29 provides the clearest messianic interpretation: "R. Yudan said in the name of R. Hama: In the time to come when the Holy One, blessed be He, seats the Lord Messiah at His right hand, as is said *The Lord saith unto my lord: 'Sit thou at My right hand'* and seats Abraham at His left, Abraham's face will pale, and he will say to the Lord: 'My son's son sits at the right, and I at the left!'" According to these sages, Abraham will be shocked at his descendant's greater glory.

79. According to Hay, "Having reviewed the evidence, Billerbeck concluded that the messianic interpretation was the norm for rabbis of the first century." *Glory at the Right Hand*, 29.

80. McCaul, *The Messiahship of Jesus*, 175.

Psalm 118

The Rejected Stone

MICHAEL K. SNEARLY

Psalm 118 is framed by an inclusio—the repetition of the same entreaty: "Give thanks to the Lord, for He is good; His faithful love endures forever" (Ps 118:1,29).[1] What lies in the middle of the psalm can be characterized as the recounting of a salvation experience, with v. 5 functioning as a proper heading, "I called to the Lord in distress; the Lord answered me and put me in a spacious place." Psalm 118, then, incorporates the common Psalter themes of salvation and the celebration of that salvation.

EXPOSITION

In narrowing the scope of analysis to view the psalm in more detail, three main sections emerge. The introduction and conclusion, consisting of vv. 1-4,29, form a singular frame around the body of the psalm. These five verses follow the same pattern: a volative verb (imperative and jussive) followed by a common confessional statement. The frame draws the reader in to the salvation recounted in the body of the psalm.

The body of the psalm (vv. 5-28) can be divided into two distinct sections—vv. 5-18 and vv. 19-28. The section consisting of vv. 5-18 speaks of the psalmist's personal deliverance from enemies and salvation from death. It is interspersed with personal confessions of trust (vv. 6-9) and contains multiple examples of "step parallelism" (e.g., vv. 10-12). The setting seems to be a military camp or even a battlefield, based on the repetition of being surrounded by the nations (vv. 10-12) and the reference to "shouts of joy and victory in the tents of the righteous" (v. 15). Also, the threat of death indicates a martial theme.

The second section, on the other hand, is characterized by a festal celebration that culminates in worship of the highest order. Opening gates for the righteous (vv. 19-20), blessing from the house of the Lord (vv. 25-26), and making a pilgrimage to the horns of the altar (v. 27) evoke temple imagery. There seems to be a progression into the temple that starts at the gates (vv. 19-21), followed by entrance into the outer court and a reflection on the construction of the temple (vv. 22-26), ultimately leading to the conclusion of the pilgrimage at the horns of the altar (vv. 27-28). Based on the structure of Ps 118, the Lord's eternal covenant faithfulness is demonstrated in the salvation experienced by the psalmist (section 1) and the festal procession to the temple (section 2).

PSALM 118 IN CONTEXT: THE BOOK OF PSALMS

As is the case with most psalms, the "I" of the psalm and the historical circumstances are generic enough that readers feel warranted in reading themselves and their life experience into the psalm. But contextual clues in the book of Psalms point to a more specific "I." Assuming editorial intentionality in the arrangement of the Psalter, the book of Psalms can be read like any other book in the Bible—as a complete book with a storyline and literary context.

Starting with Pss 1–2, which together form a unified introduction to the Psalter, the book proceeds along a royal trajectory. Psalms 1–2 portray a royal figure, but not just any royal figure—an *ideal* royal figure. In fact, Ps 2 goes so far as to identify this figure as the Messiah (Ps 2:2). David then dominates Pss 3–72 (Books I–II) with essentially all the psalms being linked to him via the superscription. David was considered the ideal kingly ruler in the historical books of 1–2 Chronicles. Messianic promises are made to him in 2Sm 7, and the prophets aligned their messianic hope with the Davidic line (Jer 23:5; Ezk 34:23-24; Hos 3:5; Am 9:11).

Book III (Pss 73–89), then, wrestles with loss, and the figure of David fades from focus. The conclusion to Book III, Ps 89, poignantly addresses this loss as it relates to David by calling into question the Lord's "eternal covenant faithfulness" to David. Book IV (Pss 90–106) highlights the Lord Himself as king and royal figure, with glimmers of hope that the Lord's covenant faithfulness to David is still operative (Pss 104–106).

Book V begins with an emphasis on this theme of the Lord's eternal covenant faithfulness. Read in the context of the book of Psalms as a whole, Book IV and the beginning of Book V seem to be addressing the question raised in Ps 89 of whether the Lord had abandoned His covenant with David. The answer given in these psalms is, no, the Lord has not abandoned His covenant with David because His covenant faithfulness is eternal.

In its more immediate context, Ps 118 is the final psalm of the first section of Book V (Pss 107–118). The theme that links these psalms together is the Lord's eternal covenant faithfulness. Both Pss 107 and 118 begin the same way: by calling attention to the Lord's eternal covenant faithfulness (Pss 107:1; 118:1). And Ps 118 concludes the section with the same sentiment, forming an *inclusio* around the entire section (Pss 107:1; 118:29).

Furthermore, there are many similarities between Pss 107 and 118. Not only do the psalms share the same opening verse, but they also share essentially the same beginning of the second verse—"Let [them] say. . . ." Psalm 118 repeats this same grammatical construction in the next three verses as well (Ps 118:2-4). The topic or theme of both psalms is similar: both celebrate the Lord's deliverance from "distress" or "trouble" (Hb. *tsar*, Pss 107:2,6,13,19,28; 118:5), and share multiple instances of that salvation. Finally, both psalms entreat the reader to celebrate this salvation and to recognize that it is evidence of the Lord's covenant faithfulness (Pss 107:8,15,21,31; 118:19,21,28,29).

It is not just at the beginning and end of the section, however, that the emphasis on the Lord's eternal covenant faithfulness is found. In Ps 108, the Lord's covenant faithfulness is manifest in His sovereignty over the nations. Psalm 109 maintains the theme by highlighting how the Lord's covenant faithfulness is demonstrated when He saves David from his enemies (vv. 25-27). Psalm 110 speaks of the eternal priesthood promised to the ideal ruler who has been delivered from his enemies (a sign of the Lord's covenant faithfulness in Ps 109:26-27).

Psalm 111 is a meditation on the eternal—especially how that which is associated with the Lord is eternal. Most significantly, the Lord's covenant is eternal (vv. 5,9). The man of the Lord is the subject of Ps 112, and he is described similarly to the way the Lord is described in Ps 111. Just as the Lord's covenant is eternal in Ps 111, so the man of the Lord's righteousness is eternal in Ps 112 (vv. 3,9). Psalm 113 calls for the Lord to be praised eternally. Psalm 114 does not specifically mention either of these two themes, but there is evidence that suggests that Pss 114 and 115 were originally one unit and were separated for liturgical purposes. In Ps 115, the Lord is praised for His covenant faithfulness (v. 1), and He will be praised eternally (v. 18). Psalm 116 speaks of those who are covenantally faithful to the Lord (v. 15). Psalm 117 brings these two themes together again and makes the Lord's eternal covenant faithfulness the grounds for worship and praise (v. 2).

The purpose of this summary has been to place Ps 118 in its broader literary context. Assuming the outline sketched above, Ps 118 appears in a section of the

Psalter that highlights the Lord's eternal covenant faithfulness because of the implications that it has for the ideal royal figure who functions as His co-regent—His Messiah. Psalm 89 can be read as a lament about the sorry state of the Davidic dynasty in exile, but the beginning of Book V (Pss 107–118), along with Pss 104–106, regularly repeats the refrain of the Lord's eternal covenant faithfulness.

PSALM 118 IN CONTEXT: THE OLD TESTAMENT

Themes and motifs in Ps 118 can be found elsewhere in the Hebrew Bible, and their appearance in various sections of the OT help illuminate their significance in the individual texts. Because there are numerous motifs in Ps 118 that have significant OT parallels,[2] the focus of this section will examine two specific themes found in Ps 118—two themes that also show up in the NT—and how they are used elsewhere in the OT.

Psalm 118:22 says, "The stone that the builders rejected has become the cornerstone." This same sentiment can be found in Isa 28:14-19 and Zch 10:3-5 (cf. also Dan 2:44-45), and all three passages have analogous interpretations and applications. Isaiah 28:14-19 is the most expansive treatment of this topic in the OT. There, the proud and unjust rulers of God's people are rejected by the Lord and replaced by His chosen leader—v. 16 reads, "I have laid a stone in Zion, a tested stone, a precious cornerstone, a sure foundation; the one who believes will be unshakable." The leadership of this ruler will be characterized by justice and righteousness.

The reference in Zch 10:3-5 follows the same trajectory—the Lord rejects the current leaders of His people and promises a future leader from the tribe of Judah who will deliver His people from their enemies. Taken together, the prophetic passages teach that the "cornerstone" is a ruler from Judah who will establish the Lord's ideal kingdom of justice, righteousness, and peace (deliverance from enemies). Psalm 118's contribution to this theological metaphor is that the cornerstone will be a stone rejected by the builders, that is, the arrogant leaders who are themselves rejected by the Lord.

Second, the theme of "coming in the name of the Lord" appears in key NT passages, but it also has significance in the larger OT framework. Psalm 118:26 reads, "He who comes in the name of the LORD is blessed." The only other instance in the OT in which someone "comes in the name of the LORD" is 1Sm 17:45, a verse found in the David and Goliath narrative. There, the young shepherd David responds to the taunts of the Philistine hero by boldly relating, "You come against me with a dagger, spear, and sword, but I come against you in the name of [the LORD] of Hosts."

The phrasing "to *call on* the name of the Lord" is quite common throughout the OT, but "to *come in* the name of the Lord" is unique to these two instances. As with the example related above, both passages help illuminate each other. First Samuel 17:45 provides color to what it means "to come in the name of the Lord." David comes in the name of the Lord to deliver God's oppressed people from their distress and to fight an enemy they are powerless against. David, as has already been stated, becomes the ideal kingly figure par excellence. There is, then, a link between the ideal royal figure who defeats the enemies of God's people and "coming in the name of the Lord." Psalm 118:26 draws upon this link by giving voice to the festive throng who—in the second section of Ps 118—have just cried out "[Hosanna]—Lord, save us!" in the previous verse. They recognize that their plea for salvation will be answered by the one who "comes in the name of the Lord," that is, the ideal royal figure who delivers them from their enemies.

PSALM 118 IN CONTEXT: THE NEW TESTAMENT

Psalm 118 is integral to the story about Jesus in the NT. The apostles, in various genres of the NT, understood Ps 118 to be about Jesus of Nazareth. It shed light on His work and ministry, and its themes took on messianic significance when applied to His life. In fact, Erich Zenger goes so far as to say, "Psalm 118 is the psalm most often cited or evoked in the New Testament. The number of the intertextually relevant passages varies from twenty to sixty, depending on the judgment of individual exegetes."[3]

Before looking at the NT texts themselves, one question that arises is: how can the apostles be so sure that Ps 118 is about Jesus, since the subject of Ps 118 seems to be so vague? The clues are found in the psalm itself and in understanding the psalm in its various contexts—within Book V of Psalms, within the book of Psalms as a whole, and within the OT.

Earlier in this article it was concluded that Ps 118 is a celebration of the Lord's eternal covenant faithfulness, which is demonstrated in a victory experienced by the psalmist and the festal procession to the temple that follows that victory. Then it was posited that Ps 118 concludes a section of psalms in Book V of the Psalter that function to highlight the Lord's eternal covenant faithfulness in their own ways. This is significant in the unfolding storyline of the Psalter because the Lord's faithfulness to His covenant with David had been called in to question most poignantly in Ps 89. This section of psalms affirms the Lord's eternal covenant faithfulness, thus signaling that it would not be consistent with the Lord's nature to abandon the messianically significant covenant He had made with David. Finally, certain themes from Ps 118 appear in other portions of the OT, and those passages maintain a consistent trajectory: The Lord's chosen leader, though rejected by those in positions of power, will be the primary building block for establishing His eternal kingdom on earth. He will also "come in the name of the Lord" to win a victory over the "Goliath" enemies of God's people. In summary, the psalm itself, its immediate context in Psalms, and the broader OT context all consistently point to the Messiah. And since the apostles understood Jesus of Nazareth to be that Messiah, they consequently understood Ps 118 to be about Him.

The most extensive treatment of Ps 118 in the NT is found in Mt 21–23, which recounts Jesus' triumphal entry into Jerusalem and ultimately into the temple. This passage opens with the triumphal entry into Jerusalem.*and* the temple (21:1–11), which draws upon imagery from Ps 118. The crowds that surround Jesus have Ps 118 in their mouths as they acclaim, "Hosanna" and "Blessed is he who comes in the name of the Lord" (Mt 21:9; cf. Ps 118:25-26). The people, and even the children (21:15), confess their understanding that Jesus is the Lord's appointed leader and that He is entering Jerusalem and the Temple as a victor. They recognize that He is the royal figure who can deliver them from their most powerful enemies, functioning as David did against Goliath when he is said to "come in the name of the Lord." They are looking to Jesus for salvation, thus they cry "Hosanna." The chief priests and teachers of the law acknowledge the significance of the crowd's acclamations because Matthew says that they became "indignant" when they heard these words applied to Jesus (21:15).

Once in the temple, Jesus begins teaching and engages in a lengthy contest, over the course of multiple days, with a group of people who are at times referred to as chief priests (21:23), elders (21:23), teachers of the law (23:13), Pharisees (21:45), and Sadducees (22:23)—in other words, the leaders of God's people. It is in this context that the next reference to Ps 118 occurs. After relating two parables that cast these leaders in a negative light, Jesus refers to Ps 118:22-23, the section of the psalm that celebrates how God will unseat the arrogant and unjust leaders from their positions of power and replace them with His chosen leader (Mt 21:42-43). Jesus does not assertively say that they are being rejected and that He will replace them as leader of God's people, but His quotation of the psalm says as much. Those who are attuned to the meaning and significance of Ps 118:25,26 can "hear" clearly the statement that Jesus is making (cf. Mt 11:15; 13:9,43).

Jesus continues teaching and highlighting how the leaders He is engaging are corrupt. He even goes so far as to pronounce judgment over them (23:13-32) and to castigate them as "snakes" and a "brood of vipers" (23:33). Matthew concludes this section with one last reference to Ps 118. In Mt 23:39, Jesus makes reference to a future return to Jerusalem, at which time they will celebrate His arrival in the same way that they had just celebrated His arrival to Jerusalem: by proclaiming "blessed is he who comes in the name of the Lord." Jesus sees the full breadth of His ministry as Messiah—both His first and second coming—in the light of Ps 118. It is as if Jesus is signaling that the final fulfillment of Ps 118—the total deliverance of God's people and the consummate victory over all their enemies—will have to wait until a future time.

From a chronological perspective, shortly after Jesus delivers this denunciation of the leaders of the Jewish people, Peter follows in his master's footsteps by preaching the same sermon and using the same text. Peter, however, makes explicit who "the builders" are in Ps 118:22. He begins by denominating his audience as "rulers of the people and elders" (Ac 4:8). He then goes on to say, "This [Jesus] is the stone rejected by *you* builders, who has become the cornerstone" (emphasis added—Ac 4:11). Peter explicitly links the builders who rejected the cornerstone as the rulers and elders of the people, and he also explicitly links Jesus with the cornerstone. He understands Ps 118 as teaching that the rejected Messiah would be vindicated by the Lord.

The apostles Paul and Peter specify the purpose of this cornerstone—to be the principal stone in the building of a new temple, the Lord's church. Accompanying the cornerstone as the foundation are the apostles and the prophets, and upon that foundation believers are joined together to become a temple in which God dwells by His Spirit (Eph 2:19-22). Peter corroborates this interpretation by echoing Paul's line of reasoning: Jesus is the cornerstone of a new Temple, the Church, and believers also constitute part of the construction. Peter describes Jesus as a rejected "living stone" that believers can be built upon as "living stones" themselves. This new edifice is a spiritual house where the acceptable worship of the Lord takes place (1Pt 2:1-8).

READING PSALM 118 MESSIANICALLY

The apostles understood Ps 118 to be about the Messiah and that Jesus of Nazareth matched the description of the Messiah portrayed in it. Consequently, Ps 118 provided evidence that Jesus was the Messiah, which explains why this psalm appears so often in the NT. And there was good reason for them to see that the subject of Ps 118 was the Messiah. Evidence suggests—from the psalm itself, the surrounding context in the Psalms, and from the larger OT context—that the subject of the psalm was the ideal royal figure who would fulfill the Lord's covenant with David.

When read in the light of the full context of the Christian canon, Ps 118 celebrates the Lord's eternal covenant faithfulness to David. It is a reminder that the

Lord would save and protect His Anointed one, not allowing Him to see death (Ps 118:17-18), and that the Lord's anointed—Jesus—will lead a festal procession to the Temple and inaugurate a new work: the building of a new temple. All of this is a demonstration of the Lord's eternal covenant faithfulness. God's people can, therefore, have confidence that the Lord is a faithful promise keeper and that Jesus is His Messiah, sent to conquer all the enemies of His people.

---

1. The HCSB translates the significant Hebrew noun *chesed* as "faithful love," which is a defensible translation. I believe, however, there is an important covenantal nuance to the noun, so I prefer to translate it as "covenant faithfulness." Consequently, when quoting the HCSB, I will retain their translation, but when referring to this word in the body of this article, I will highlight its covenantal nature.
2. Note the numerous similarities between Psalm 118 and the Song of Moses (Ex 15). For example, Ps 118:14 is a verbatim quotation of Ex 15:2. Both recount salvation from distress, and both begin with a cohortative/jussive appeal to praise the Lord as a result of His salvation, just to name a few.
3. Erich Zenger, "Psalm 118," in Frank Lothar Hossfeld and Erich Zenger, *Psalms 3: A Commentary on Psalms 101–150*, trans. Linda M. Maloney, Hermeneia: A Critical & Historical Commentary on the Bible (Minneapolis: Augsburg Fortress Press, 2011), 245.

Psalm 132

The Messianic Restoration of the Davidic Throne

MICHAEL VOWELL

Why does Psalm 132 borrow so much from other parts of the Hebrew Bible? In every stanza of Ps 132 there is a referent or direct quote from a much older part of the Scriptures. There is priestly language from Nm 10, kingship promises from 2Sm 7, parts of a prayer offered by Solomon in 2Chr 6, references to the story of the retrieval of the ark by David, the building of the Temple, the high priest's crown, and a host of vocabulary words that appear in other key psalms like Ps 110 and Ps 89. Twice it directly refers to the Anointed One, Messiah. In light of these features, Hans-Joachim Kraus asks, "Into which situation should this psalm, with all its changing citations, explanations, and exclamations, be placed?"[1]

The same question has been raised by a multitude of scholars over the last 100 years. But the main question is, Why does Ps 132 borrow most of its language from other places in the Hebrew Bible? Does Ps 132 repeat itself just for the sake of repetition? Or, does all this repetition encourage the reader to understand something new and fascinating about Israel's Messiah? If we fail to take seriously the author's use of repetition in Ps 132, along with its strategic placement in book of Psalms, then we risk leaving the intended goal of this elaborate song lost in the sands of time.

Someone might say the author of Ps 132 is using repetition as a modern-day preacher does. A well-worn homiletical axiom says, "Tell them what you are going to tell them; tell them what you are telling them; then tell them what you have told them."[2] This axiom does make good homiletical sense. However, the Scriptures do not repeat themselves in the way a preacher does trying to deliver a point to an audience. The Scriptures repeat themselves to advance promises, build upon promises, expand promises, refocus promises, and redirect promises. And Ps 132 does not just repeat other passages of Scripture to drive an old point home; rather, it adds something new of significant value to Israel's messianic hope. The strategic placement of Ps 132 in Book V and its use of repetition to answer the issue raised in Ps 89, is designed to give hope to worshiping pilgrims that there will be a restoration of God's exiled presence by the same Messiah who will come and bring salvation to Zion.

THE STRATEGIC PLACEMENT OF PSALM 132 IN THE BOOK OF PSALMS

It is important to consider Ps 132's strategic placement in Book V of the Psalter. It is possible to think that, without the exact historical context of the psalm, its original meaning and intent would be lost. James Boice takes this position in his commentary when he boldly says, "Psalm 132 is about the ascent of the ark of God to Jerusalem in the days of David . . . and probably dates from Solomon's reign."[3] Yet, the writer of Ps 132 writes from a time beyond the life of David. This is because David is memorialized as a past noble king in v. 1, "Lord, remember David and all the hardships he endured" (Ps 132:1–2).[4] David's actions are memorialized and are in the past, and the last two verses of Ps 132 indicate a period of time that is not peaceful like Solomon's reign, but one where great threats exist against the nation.

Thus, Erhard Gerstenberger states that "a pre-exilic 'royal ideology' hardly plays a role in this psalm. Its setting is not really recognized unless we abandon the pre-exilic use and origin of the psalm."[5] Without an author title or historical referent in the title, Ps 132 defies all the best attempts to put it into an exact historical setting. So the question of historical inquiry should be set aside and a different question—in my opinion a better question—should be asked. What about the purposeful and strategic placement of Psalm 132 in Book V of the Psalter?

Interpreting the Psalms as a purposefully arranged and edited book has led to some of the richest discoveries in the history of Psalms studies. G. H. Wilson dedicated his academic talents to systematically and cogently demonstrating that the Psalter in its final form is a single, purposefully edited and arranged work.[6] Although Wilson was unable to connect the royal psalms of Books I–III to Books IV–V of the Psalter, his call to uncover the purposeful arrangement of these last two books has not gone unheeded by many others.[7]

There are three observations to consider about the strategic placement of Ps 132: *First, Ps 132 is the only royal psalm placed within the Songs of Ascent (Pss 120–134).* The Songs of Ascent intentionally give worshipers, as families or individuals, hope that the God of Israel has not broken covenant with His people. "Indeed, the Protector of Israel does not slumber or sleep" (Ps 121:4); and "If the LORD had not been on our side—let Israel say" (Ps 124:1); and again, "Jerusalem—the mountains surround her. And the LORD surrounds His people, both now and forever" (Ps 125:2). Yet, Ps 132 is a royal psalm amid a collection of pilgrim songs assuring faithful pilgrims that God's exiled presence will return to Israel and that Zion will again have its Anointed One, a Davidic Messiah (vv. 1,17-18). As in other royal psalms (cf. Pss 2, 110), Ps 132 is the only one in the Songs of Ascents offering both prayers to God and divine responses from God.

Further, Ps 132 provides the guarantee that the lament from a faithful exile oppressed in foreign lands (Ps 120) can end with a blessing from the Lord out of Zion to all exiles (134:3). How is it that the guarantee of this change in circumstances functions like bookends in the Songs of Ascents? Psalm 132 alone promises a restoration of God's exiled presence by the same Messiah who will come and bring salvation to Zion.

What is more, Ps 132 is strategically placed as a royal psalm in the Songs of Ascent. Since Herman Gunkel, scholars have agreed that Ps 132 is one of the many royal psalms. Though the song does contain elements that also make it appear as a "Song of Zion,"[8] it is best to see this whole song as a royal psalm that involves the Messiah's saving action on behalf of Zion. All this to say, among the Songs of Ascent, Ps 132 stands out like a bright red shirt in a sea of people wearing white. It calls attention to itself because it is a royal psalm in the midst of a song group designed for faithful pilgrims on their way to Zion.

Second, Psalm 132 is strategically placed in the middle position of three royal psalm groupings in Book V. This placement can be seen here:[9]

PSALMS GROUP	ROYAL PSALM	ENDING DOXOLOGY	ADDITIONAL DOXOLOGIES
Pss 107–118	Ps 110	Ps 111	Pss 112–118
Pss 119–134	Ps 132	Ps 133	Ps 134
Pss 135–150	Ps 144	Ps 145	Pss 146–150

G. H. Wilson said of Pss 2, 72, 89 that, "The appearance of 'royal' psalms at . . . significant junctures cannot be accidental and demands some explanation in our quest for understanding of the Psalter arrangement."[10] While Wilson's statement is to be commended, his call to action must expand to these three royal psalms in Book V. Just a cursory glance reveals that there is a purposeful arrangement of these three royal psalms, and this also demands an explanation.

It seems that Ps 132 is strategically located in the middle position of these three royal psalms to be the center of gravity for the whole of Book V. First, it follows the pattern established by the introduction the Psalter in Pss 1–2. These two psalms introduce the twin themes of God's people being faithful to the Torah while waiting for God to establish His messianic kingdom. Book V contains the largest acrostic poem in Ps 119. This psalm calls Israel to be faithful to the Torah just as Ps 1 does. And, if the Songs of Ascent are one large group of songs instead of 15 individual songs, then it is easy to see how this grouping of songs also is calling worshipers to receive a blessing from the God of Israel while waiting for the establishment of the messianic kingdom—just as Ps 2 does. Moreover, its final blessing "May the LORD, Maker of heaven and earth, bless you from Zion" (Ps 134:3) closely matches the blessing formula found at the other major seams of the Psalter (Pss 41:13; 72:18-19; 89:52; 106:48). Last, its middle position means it must be read in light of the grouping around Ps 110 and that the grouping around Ps 144 must be read in light of Ps 132 and its grouping, thereby making it the gravitational center of Book V.

Third, Ps 132 is strategically placed in Book V to resolve the issue begun in Ps 89. Ps 132 offers a response to the accusation that God has abandoned the line of Davidic Kings (Ps 89:38-45). This will be discussed in more detail below.

THE USE OF VERBAL ANALOGY IN PSALM 132

Now that the strategic placement of Ps 132 has been explored as the gravitational center of Book V, it is necessary to examine the use of verbal analogy, reading it canonically and seeing how it resolves the issue begun in Ps 89.

To begin, Ps 132 is easily divided into four major stanzas composed of two strophes within each of the four stanzas.[11] The eight strophes contained within the four stanzas provide the rich language of repetition that gives new life to the old promises. The following table shows this layout:

	STROPHE 1	STROPHE 2
Stanza 1 (vv. 1b-5)	1b-2—Plea based on **David's merit.**	3-5—David's **Oath** to God
Stanza 2 (vv. 6-10)	6-7—**Oath** Fulfilled	8-10—Invocation based on **David's merit.**
Stanza 3 (vv. 11-12)	11a—Divine Response: David's line is **Chosen** by God for Kingship in Zion.	11b-12—God's **Promise** to David
Stanza 4 (vv. 13-18)	13-16—Divine Response: Zion is **Chosen** by God for His Presence.	17-18—God's **Promise** to Zion about future Davidic Messiah's rule and victory.

The first stanza reflects on David's affliction and resolve in founding God's residence. The first strophe stresses David's affliction for God's dwelling. John Goldingay suggests David's afflictions are related to the vast expenditure he provided for Solomon to build the temple: "And the psalm's point is that David indeed imposed expenditure or weakening or trouble or affliction on himself in making it possible for Yhwh to settle in Jerusalem."[12] The second strophe relates David's personal resolve to locate the exact place for God's dwelling. Hence, the first stanza relates that David personally paid a great price for God's dwelling place and that his personal resolve would not waver until it was accomplished. This is more than just mere historical reflection; indeed, it is a looking forward to the future Davidic Messiah—a future Davidic Messiah willing to pay a great price to establish God's dwelling and an unrelenting personal devotion in seeing it through.

The second stanza confirms that David dedicated his entire life to retrieving the ark and leading the throngs to establish God's presence in Zion. The first strophe references Ephrathah and the fields of Jaar (identified with Kiriath-jearim). Ephrathah is usually attached with Bethlehem, David's hometown (1Sm 17:12; Ru 4:11; Mic 5:2), and Kiriath-jearim is where the ark rested for at least two decades (1Sm 6:21; 7:1-2). Commentators and authors are divided on what v. 6 is referring to. Likely this is just a simple poetic merism stating that from David's early years in Bethlehem until his adult years as king when his men retrieved the ark (1Sm 6–7), David was dedicated to the cause of God's Temple, as noted in stanza 1. Verse 7 is most probably a historical reflection of David leading the throng of people in bringing the ark back from exile in joyful procession to Zion. The second strophe uses a merism to call all Israel, from priests to faithful worshipers, to restore right judgments and proper worship of the Lord. It also introduces a plea on behalf of an unnamed Messiah (who is not David), "Because of Your servant David, do not reject Your Anointed [Messiah]" (v. 10). This plea in v. 10, read canonically, looks forward to a Messiah as described in Ps 110, a Priest-King in the order of Melchizedek. Stanza 2 adds to stanza 1 that the future Messiah will also return the exiled presence of God and lead the throngs to worship in His presence.

The first two stanzas present an often-neglected messianic idea that should not be overlooked, since this is the only psalm to explicitly mention the ark box. The idea is that the Messiah is the founder of the sanctuary and returns the exiled presence of God to it. This is the confirmation of His rule and part and parcel of the full restoration and salvation of Israel and God's kingdom on planet Earth. In Ps 132, the real presence of God comes back to Zion by means of the Anointed One, the Messiah, the King of Israel. While Ps 110 creates the figure of the Melchizedekian King, Ps 132 connects the return of the exiled presence of God to Israel with this Messiah. Further, Ps 110 and Ps 132 would not have mentioned the need for a

Priest-King from the line of Melchizedek if the priesthood and Davidic line as it stood could perfect its mission. Neither the priests nor kings brought about perfection or full restoration. The first two stanzas of Ps 132 could be summed up well this way, "a better hope is introduced, through which we draw near to God" (Heb 7:19, cf. 7:11,28).

The third stanza in two strophes reiterates the promises given to David by Nathan in 2Sm 7:14-15 and ends the dispute created in Ps 89. In Psalm 89, the psalmist charges God with infidelity to His promises to David, declaring, "But You have spurned and rejected him; You have become enraged with Your anointed. You have repudiated the covenant with Your servant; You have completely dishonored his crown" (Ps 89:38-39). Psalm 89 leaves the impression that the monarchy has reached its end. Psalm 110 establishes the Melchizedekian King, but Psalm 132 assures the reader that this King is still going to be from the line of David. Psalm132 turns the accusation of Ps 89 upside down and says the Messiah will not be dishonored but that He will be honored. The conditional statement of v. 12 is meant to teach faithful pilgrims that they are to look to a future Messiah from David's throne who will delight in the Torah of God in His heart. Hence, it reiterates the continual validity of the promises to David in 2Sm 7:14-15 but also reflects back on the opening of the Psalter and ideal Messianic King (Pss 1, 2). Psalm 132 is not just repeating the promises given to David, it answers the accusations of Ps 89 posed about the future of Israel's salvation and restoration by a Davidic Messiah.

The last stanza is the Lord's response to the Messianic King's work of restoring His presence to Zion. In the first strophe, He responds positively to blessing Zion with material goods and restoring righteousness and worship from the priesthood to the laity with an assurance that He will restore a Davidic Messiah and His presence to Zion in the future. The second strophe contains some of the richest messianic imagery in the Psalter. First, in v. 17a the psalmist looks forward to a day when a new, powerful Davidic king will come to Zion: "there I will make a horn sprout up for David" (*sham atsmiach qeren ledawid*). The word(s) "to sprout up" [author's translation] (*atsmiach*) refers to a plant just sprouting up out of the ground.[13] This is a common way of referring to the new beginning of a messianic king (cf. Isa 11:1; Zch 3:8; 6:12; Lk 1:69). When this word gets attached to the symbol of the horn (*qeren*), it refers to a powerful new king coming to the earth (Pss 75:5-6; 89:18,25; 112:9; Dan 7:8,20; 8:3,9,22,23). What is more, he is going to sprout up there (*sham*) in Zion. This does not refer to his birth but indicates that His kingship will be from Zion.

Second, in v. 17b the Lord says, "I have prepared a lamp for My Messiah" [author's translation] (*arakhti ner limshihi*, HCSB "anointed one"). Barbiero is right that the Hebrew word for lamp (*ner*) is "typical of priestly language" and is synonymous with the word *nir* "lamp," which is used in reference to the Davidic dynasty (cf. 1Kg

11:36; 15:4, 2Kg 8:19).[14] But he fails to see the connection of this word to the Messiah being a Priest-King. This becomes even more evident as the crown on His head is imagined as a floral crown in v. 18: "the crown he wears will be glorious" (literally, upon Him a crown will *blossom, wealayw yatsits nizro*). This floral crown refers to the high priest's crown (Ex 28:36; 29:6; 39:30; Lv 8:9) and is also the crown that Ps 89:39 says had been cast down (HCSB footnote: "dishonored his crown to the ground"). So v. 17 reverses the speech of Ps 89:39. It establishes the dynasty of this Messiah who is a Priest-King like a "lamp" that will be kept burning and will light everything that is in darkness.

Last, when the psalmist says in v.18 "I will clothe his enemies with shame," he is confirming the Messiah's future universal reign predicted in Ps 110:5-7. This is the great universal reign of God's kingdom on planet Earth. It is not just speaking of the establishment of the nation as a state in the Middle East but as the world superpower under the direction and leadership of this Messiah.

So, from the start of the Psalm to its end, there is a repetition of key promises and motifs that are meant to assure faithful pilgrims that despite the charges of Ps 89, a Davidic Messiah would return the exiled presence of God to Zion and bring total salvation to Zion. And the Lord does all of this by an oath in v. 11: "the LORD swore an oath to David, a promise He will not abandon." This word of God's oath appoints a Messiah greater than David who will be a Priest-King over Israel and all the world (Heb 7).

There is good reason to think that the use of repetition was meant to point to someone greater than David or one of his immediate heirs. The interpreter of the Hebrew Bible who penned the letter to the Hebrews believed repetition served a key function in advancing the messianic hope. For instance, he argues for a greater Sabbath rest based on verbal repetition of the word "rest." He said, "For if Joshua had given them rest, God would not have spoken later about another day" (Heb 4:8). He concludes that the repetition of the need for rest points to the Messiah Jesus who gave ultimate rest to all who trust in Him. This interpretative device is known as *gezera shawa* ("verbal analogy"). Clearly, the author of Hebrews was familiar with this Jewish mode of interpretation, indicating that he saw repetition as something important in the development of key biblical concepts (cf. Heb 4:14 16; 7:11,19,27; 8:11).

Admittedly, there is no one author of Scripture who applies *gezera shawa* to Ps 132. However, a canonical reading of this psalm and application of *gezera shawa* shows that this psalm speaks boldly about a specific Messiah and not just an expected heir of David in the preexilic or postexilic community. Seemingly, the editors of the Psalter purposefully placed Ps 132 so that faithful pilgrims would understand that the line of David had not been cut off. Yet, if David or one of his descendants had truly brought back God's exiled presence and accomplished the full salvation of Zion, then there would be no need to talk about it here again. Yet, it had not happened for the postexilic community.

Psalm 132 could be fulfilled only by one monadic referent, one unique Davidite, the exclusive one-and-only Messiah Jesus. Some researchers argue this is too strong a claim and argue for multiple fulfillments and then one ultimate fulfillment in the Messiah Jesus. Their arguments are cogent and make good historical sense of this psalm. However, they often neglect to read the psalm canonically or address why the author would use so much repetition. By reading Ps 132 canonically and paying attention to the use of repetition, one can easily see how no king in Israel has ever emerged as Priest-King from the line of Melchizedek. Never has there been a king who perfectly or permanently restored God's exiled presence and brought about the full restoration and salvation of Zion. Yet, reading Psalm 132 canonically demonstrates that it is a prophecy like a well-trained arrow aimed at a specific target, not an arrow meant to be shot through 20 paper targets along the way to the one target. The strategic placement of Ps 132 in the Psalter and its use of repetition indicate that it is a specific arrow aimed at a specific person—Jesus the son of Joseph from Nazareth (Lk 1:69).

Erhard Gerstenberger speculates that this psalm emerged because of "a precarious outside circumstance and growing hope inside a religious group for a total change to the better."[15] This may in fact be true, but it is also too limited. It must be asked, what did the editors of the Psalter want Ps 132 to do in the hearts of faithful pilgrims and worshipers throughout all ages? When the question is asked this way, it becomes evident that this psalm inspired hope that the Davidic Messiah would one day restore God's exiled presence and bring about the full salvation and restoration of Zion. This song had value when times were stable or unstable because the worshiper knew circumstances could get even better in the days of King Messiah. This song had value in the face of precarious outside circumstances because the worshiper could trust that the world would one day get better in the days of King Messiah. So, when the nation faced internal corruption, they could hope for a day when a Messiah who was both King and Priest would clothe His own priests with righteousness and cause joy among all the people. There was hope that one day, when King Messiah comes, He will bring the real presence of God back from exile into His sanctuary and accomplish the total restoration and salvation of Zion.

An oft-quoted maxim says, "the past can remind of you of many things, but it does not have to define you." Psalm 89 says that the past failures of David's sons did define the future—a future where the hopes for the Messiah of Israel seemed dismal, if not completely destroyed. Yet, the editors of the Psalter knew they were crafting not only liturgy but also a story, a story told through songs that would predict the future. This future would not be defined by the failures of the past but by God's enduring promises to David regarding a coming Messiah. That Messiah has come once to Zion, and he will come again to Zion as it says, "And in this way all Israel will be saved, as it is written: The Liberator will come from Zion; He will turn away godlessness from Jacob. And this will be My covenant with them when I take away their sins" (Rom 11:26-27).

Psalm 132 gave hope to all the faithful pilgrims going to Jerusalem from all over the world, as it should give hope to all people as well. No matter how dark the past history of humankind nor how dark the future may become, God's promises have not changed. There is still hope for tomorrow that Messiah Jesus will come and bring with Him God's exiled presence and then all of Israel shall be saved.

---

1. Hans-Joachim Kraus, *A Continental Commentary: Psalms 60–150* (Minneapolis: Fortress Press, 1993), 474.
2. Haddon W. Robinson, *Biblical Preaching: The Development and Delivery of Expository Messages*, 3rd ed. (Grand Rapids: Baker Academic, 2014), 80.
3. James Montgomery Boice, *Psalms 107–150: An Expositional Commentary* (Grand Rapids: Baker Books, 2005), 1151. See also Hans-Joachim Kraus, *A Continental Commentary: Psalms 60–150*, 478.
4. Mark Lanier (author and lawyer) in a private email correspondence to me observed astutely that David is "not a distant memory . . . one might think God had forgotten and needed reminding of." Rather, David is being remembered as one might remember General George Washington.
5. Erhard Gerstenberger, *Psalms Part 2, and Lamentations*, vol. 15, The Forms of the Old Testament Literature (Grand Rapids: Eerdmans, 2001), 369.
6. G. H. Wilson, "Evidence of Editorial Divisions in the Hebrew Psalter," VT 34 (1984), 337–52; *The Editing of the Hebrew Bible*, Society for Biblical Literature, Dissertation Series (Chico, CA: Scholars Press, 1985), 76; "The Use of Royal Psalms at the 'Seams' of the Hebrew Psalter," *Journal for the Study of the Old Testament* 35 (1986): 85–94; "The Shape of the Book of Psalms," *Interpretation* 46 (1992): 129–42.
7. Wilson, "Understanding the Purposeful Arrangement of the Psalms," 50. See also, Robert Cole, "The Shape and Message of Book III," *Journal for the Study of the Old Testament* 307 (2000); Norman Whybray, "Reading the Book of Psalms as a Book," *Journal for the Study of the Old Testament* 222 (1996). See also, Jinkyu Kim, "The Strategic Arrangement of Royal Psalms in Books IV–V," *Westminster Theological Journal* 70 (2008): 143
8. Hans-Joachim Kraus, *A Continental Commentary: Psalms 60–150*, 474.
9. Jinkyu Kim first proposed this strategic arrangement in his article "The Strategic Arrangement of the Royal Psalms in Books IV–V." This current chart represents this author's own understanding and adjustments to the layout of the psalms, especially in the section on Ps 132.
10. See G. H. Wilson, "The Use of Royal Psalms at the 'Seams' of the Hebrew Psalter," *Journal for the Study of the Old Testament* 35 (1986): 85–94.
11. For this layout, I am indebted to Gianni Barbiero's work in G. Barbiero, "Psalm 132: A Prayer of Solomon," CBQ 75 (2013), 241–255, though I see differences in the strophe structure and application of this psalm in Solomon's day.
12. John Goldingay, *Psalms 90–150*, ed. Tremper Longman III, vol. 3, Baker Commentary on the Old Testament (Grand Rapids: Baker Academic, 2006), 545.
13. Ludwig Koehler, Walter Baumgartner, M. E. J. Richardson, and Johann Jakob Stamm, *The Hebrew and Aramaic Lexicon of the Old Testament* (Leiden, Netherlands: E. J. Brill, 1994–2000), 1033.
14. Barbiero, "A Prayer of Solomon," 256.
15. Erhard Gerstenberger, *Psalms Part 2, and Lamentations*, 369.

Messianism in the Psalms of Ascent

RANDALL L. MCKINION

The Psalms of Ascent (Pss 120–134) make up a discrete collection woven into an intelligently-designed Psalter. As such, the teaching of these pilgrimage psalms resonates with the theology of the book of Psalms, particularly with respect to its theological reflection about the future work of the son of David enthroned at Zion. This article will discuss the messianic hope of the Psalms of Ascent by demonstrating the ways in which these psalms relate to each other (i.e., the compositional strategy of the collection), to Book 5 of the book of Psalms, and to the Psalter as a whole. These observations will show that the theology of the Psalms of Ascent is the same as the messianic hope of the Torah (the Pentateuch) and the Prophets.[1] In the same way as the Torah and the Prophets, the eschatological fulfillment of the Davidic covenant provides the basis for understanding the journey to Zion painted in these psalms not as a simple, historical pilgrimage theme, but as a journey toward a new Zion in the eschaton.

COMPOSITIONAL STRATEGY WITHIN THE PSALMS OF ASCENT

Several characteristics demonstrate the unity of the Psalms of Ascent. First, all 15 come together under a common title, "Song of Ascents" (*šîr hammaʿălôt*).[2] No unanimity has been reached on the intention of the term "ascents," but whether it refers historically to annual pilgrimages or to going up the steps of the temple, the title certainly brings the psalms together around the purpose of "going up." Second, with the exception of Ps 132, these psalms are characterized by their brevity. Third, common literary devices are used, such as an abundance of imagery and metaphor, as well as anadiplosis (or stepped parallelism).[3] Fourth, the psalms speak often of Israel, Jerusalem, and Zion. Finally, the Psalms include a series of common phrases:[4]

- "maker of heaven and earth" (121:2; 124:8; 134:3)
- "both now and forever" (121:8; 125:2; 131:3)
- "let Israel now say" (124:1; 129:1)
- "peace upon Israel" (125:5; 128:6; and possibly 133:3 according to 11QPsA)
- "the Lord bless you from Zion" (128:5; 134:3)

As will be shown below, the first two of these phrases is quite important in the compositional strategy of the collection.

Zenger has proposed that the Psalms of Ascent are intentionally grouped into three sets of five psalms, in which the middle psalms (122, 127, and 132) have a common theme, though there is no scholarly consensus on the structure of the collection.[5] Although a strict structure may strain the evidence, a careful reading shows evidence of strategy within the collection, particularly around psalms that have been clustered together. Moreover, the overall composition has been set with a consistent (messianic) perspective, showing an intentional strategy manifest in all the collection's manifold relationships. Given that a detailed analysis of each of the psalms is beyond the scope of this article, the focus here will be on two clusters, the first of which consists of the first six psalms.

Cluster #1: Psalms 120–125

Careful consideration of Pss 120–125 will show that these psalms have been brought together under the program set out by Ps 121 and under the influence of the priestly blessing of Nm 6. Yet, the Psalms of Ascent begin with Ps 120.

Psalm 120

Psalm 120 has a twofold function as the first psalm in the Psalms of Ascent. First, it transitions from Ps 119, a grand reflection upon the Lord's words (torah). The strategy for placing Pss 119 and 120 together will be discussed below, as it has important implications for the place of the Psalms of Ascent in the Psalter. Second, the psalm acts as an introduction to the collection by presenting an unresolved situation where the one praying calls upon Yahweh from a place of distress where no peace is found.[6] The rest of the collection provides perspective and hope about how the reader should respond when war and peace collide. The answer begins in the next psalm.

Psalm 121

In Ps 121, the (unnamed) speaker looks to the hills in expectation of Yahweh's help, a help needed by the speaker of Ps 120, in which his situation goes unresolved. Several literary features of Ps 121 show its role within the collection as well as its relationship to the psalms in the immediate vicinity. Compositionally, the psalm uses repetition to highlight its purposes. On the one hand, step parallelism is used in which v. 1 ends with "my help" and v. 2 begins with "my help." His help is found in Yahweh, the "Maker of heaven and earth." On the other hand, vv. 3-8 repeat that Yahweh is the "Protector" (vv. 3,4,5; literally, "Keeper") who "will protect" (vv. 7,8; literally, "keep") those who are His. These six occurrences of this root (*šmr*) obviously focus on Yahweh's protection, which is eternal: "both now and forever."

Together with Ps 120, Ps 121 is programmatic for the rest of the collection, as these two psalms are strategically connected to Pss 123–125. The following points show how Ps 121 unites this first cluster of psalms (see also Figure 1).

- A unique title. Whereas each psalm in the rest of the collection has the title "Song of Ascents,"[7] the title of Ps 121 is literally "A Song *for* the Ascents." The next psalm shows that Jerusalem is the destination, as the tribes "go up" (122:4) there.[8]

- Lifting the eyes. In 121:1, the psalmist says, "*I raise my eyes* to the mountains," and he is reminded of the "Maker of heaven and earth" (v. 2); in 123:1, the writer says, "*I lift my eyes* to You, the One enthroned in heaven."

- Help from the maker of heaven and earth. Just as the writer of Ps 121 expresses confidence in help that comes from the creator God (v. 2), so David in Ps 124 expresses the corporate hope found "in the name of the LORD, *the Maker of heaven and earth*" (v. 8).

- Eternal peace and protection. Ps 125 brings the reader back around to the eternal hope of Ps 121 by use of the phrase "both now and forever" (literally, "from now until forever," 125:2; 121:8). At the same time, it envelopes this first set of psalms by bringing the reader back to the prospect for (or at least hope for) peace (125:5; 122:6-7; 120:6-7).

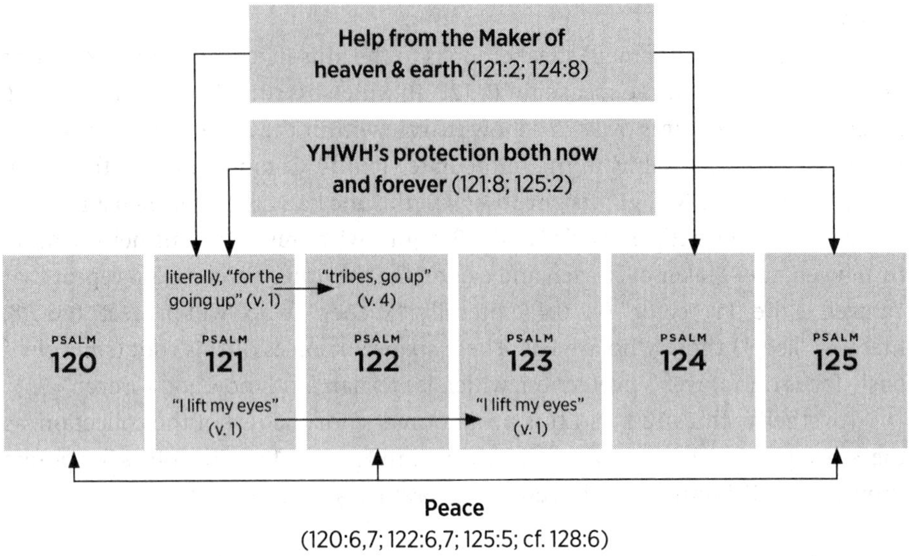

Figure 1: Relationship of Psalms 120–125

All of these observations show that Ps 121 has a type of valence that draws together these six psalms. What is intriguing about this is how each of these psalms resonates with a key concept or term from the priestly blessing.[9]

> The LORD spoke to Moses, saying, "Speak to Aaron and his sons, saying, Thus you shall *bless* the people of Israel: you shall say to them, The LORD *bless* you and *keep* you; The LORD make his face to shine upon you and *be gracious* to you; The LORD lift up his countenance upon you and give you *peace*. So shall they put *my name* upon the people of Israel, and I will *bless* them." (Nm 6:22-27 ESV, emphasis added)

Psalms 120, 122, and 125 carefully highlight the need for "peace" in Jerusalem. Psalm 121 finds hope that Yahweh will "protect" the suppliant unto eternity. Psalm 123 repeats "favor" three times. Psalm 124 links the "help" of Ps 121 to "the name of the LORD" (124:8).[10] Although not appearing in this cluster of psalms, the theme of blessing appears multiple times in the Psalms of Ascent (128:5; 134:3; 133). The priestly blessing does not seem to guide the entire collection, but these first six psalms seem to resonate around this benediction. As in the discussion below, the purpose of taking up these themes of the priestly benediction may be to link this blessing from Nm 6 back to the creation blessing of Gn 1 and forward to eternity. This conclusion rests upon a proper appreciation of the role of the first two phrases listed below that appear three times in the Psalms of Ascent.

The two phrases are "the Maker of heaven and earth" (121:2) and "both now and forever" (121:8). The use of these phrases in Ps 121 and then at strategic places in the Psalms of Ascent to relate other psalms to one another highlights their importance. In 121:2, the psalmist's help comes not from the mountains but from the God who formed the mountains, namely the "Maker of heaven and earth." The "help" that comes from the "Maker of heaven and earth" (121:1-2) links Pss 121 and 124, as Ps 124:8 states: "Our *help* is in the name of the LORD, the *maker of heaven and earth*." This phrase not only highlights the powerful Creator who is Israel's helper and keeper; it also directs the reader back to the text of Gn 1–2. By doing so, the focus of hope—through the lens of the priestly blessing—relates to the original purposes for which God created and blessed humanity. This is highlighted within the Psalms of Ascent in 134:3, where blessing from the LORD comes from Zion, where Yahweh has taken up residence as the "Maker of heaven and earth." Just as God created humanity and blessed them on the land (Gn 1:28), so Israel's hope was that Yahweh would bless them on the land (Ps 134:3). However, the nature of this blessing within the Psalms of Ascent has an eternal perspective, as highlighted by the second phrase, "both now and forever."

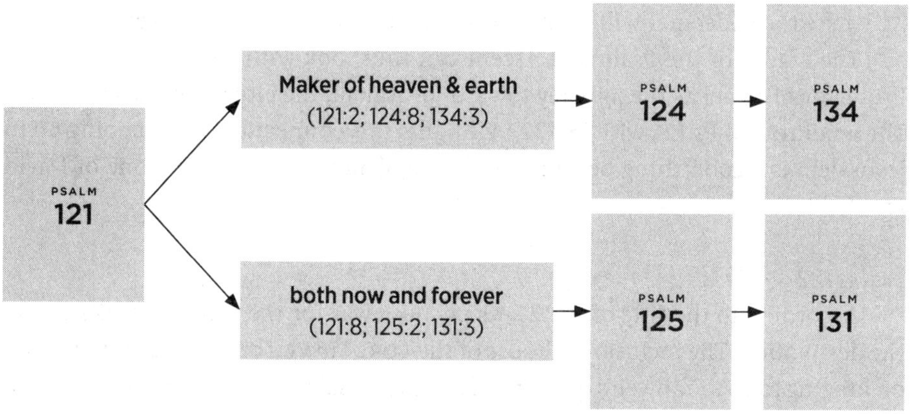

Figure 2: Key Phrases of Psalm 121

According to Ps 121, Yahweh's sixfold keeping would extend "both now and forever," a phrase that plays a key role in the composition of Ps 121 as well as the larger collection (see Figure 2). Alter states, "This concluding reference to the eternality of God's protection completes an arc begun with the reference to creation at the beginning of the poem in the designation of God as 'Maker of heaven and earth.'"[11] According to 125:1, "Those who trust in the LORD are like Mt. Zion," which does not totter and remains forever. Just as in v. 2 mountains surround Jerusalem, so Yahweh surrounds His people "both now and forever." Thus, Pss 121 and 125 are related by means of the mountain imagery and this phrase. Furthermore, the combination of these two phrases at the end of Ps 124 (v. 8: "Maker of heaven and earth") and beginning of Ps 125 (v. 2: "both now and forever") serves to unite those two psalms. In a similar way, these phrases are used to unite psalms near the end of the collection in Ps 131:3, where David calls upon Israel to hope in the LORD "both now and forever." As Pss 130–134 form a tight-knit group (see discussion below), the strategic use of these phrases shows that the teaching of these psalms extends from creation to the eschatological future. In other words, whatever the hope of the Psalms of Ascent turns out to be, it is an eternal hope.

The end-time nature of this phrase comes from seeing its use in the Prophets in Isa 9:6; 59:20-21; and Mic 4:7, each of which relates to the Psalms of Ascent. Interestingly, in Mic 4:7, the context of which also includes the eschatologically latent phrase "in the last days" (v. 1), it is Yahweh reigning on Mount Zion "both now and forever" (see Ps 132). Mic 4:7 follows the clear eschatological hope of a return to a restored Zion where Yahweh dwells. The context of Isa 9:6 also complements the Songs of Ascents in that it speaks of the king who sits on the throne of David "from now on and forever." The phrase is latent with prophetic hope for the son of David reigning over Yahweh's kingdom at Zion. This is the same hope of Isa 59:20-21, where the Redeemer will return to Zion and implement a new covenant.

The reader of the Psalms of Ascent can thus look with certainty toward the Protector of Israel as the journey toward Jerusalem, the city of David, continues. The adjoining of Ps 121 with Ps 122 highlights this connection in that going up to Jerusalem is a good thing because the house of Yahweh and the throne of David are there.

Psalm 122

According to the title of Ps 121, its purpose was for the ascents; Ps 122 shows the destination. The inclusio of "house of the LORD" in vv. 1 and 9 focuses the psalm on longing to go to Yahweh's dwelling place, in Jerusalem, the importance of which is highlighted poetically in two ways. First, step parallelism brings attention to Jerusalem in v. 2b (last word Jerusalem) and v. 3a (first word Jerusalem). It is to Jerusalem that the tribes of Yah "go up." Second, vv. 6 and 7 (and by extension 8) play off of the name Jerusalem with phonetic repetition in the words for "pray," "peace," and "prosperity," which all have similar sounds.[12]

The significance of Jerusalem stems from the presence of the house of Yahweh in its midst. During David's lifetime, only the kingdom was residing at Jerusalem, as the house of Yahweh had not yet been built. As a result, the psalm takes on a note of anticipation and hope for the fulfillment of what Yahweh had promised to David. In other words, David could only hope to go to the house of Yahweh in Jerusalem as an anticipation of a future fulfillment of the Davidic covenant (see 2Sm 7). This accentuates the larger scheme within the Psalms of Ascent in which, after the exile, the psalms interpret eschatologically the promises made to David.

Subsequent readers then join David's hope for God's faithfulness to these promises, specifically in His establishing a kingdom for David's Son in a peaceful, worshiping Jerusalem. In essence, then, Ps 122 gives a clearer picture of the expectations of the Davidic kings and of the son of David to come. There existed (and would exist) a close relationship between the king and the worship of Yahweh at Jerusalem in the house of Yahweh. Both the king and the congregation would work toward that end (see Ps 132). The former would administer justice as part of a reign that promoted peace and goodness (see Ps 72); the latter would pray for the peace of the city within which they would give thanks to the name of their God (Ps 122). Thus, the hope that David had in the establishment of the central sanctuary of worship and justice becomes the hope of all who read this psalm. As Sailhamer writes, "To pray for the peace of Jerusalem (v. 6) is to pray for the coming of the Promised Seed of David, the Messiah."[13] Such is the hope of the Psalter, as it reflects the theology of the Prophets.

Psalms 123–125

Reminiscent of Ps 121, the speaker in Ps 123 lifts his eyes to the one enthroned in the heavens, for it is He who has mercy/grace to give. Here the psalmist directs an address to Yahweh as the One who sits in the heavens. Elsewhere, the Psalter describes Yahweh as the One dwelling in the heavens (among other places, such as 11:4) in Ps 2:4, where the One sitting in the heavens cannot but laugh at those who would dare try to usurp Him and His king. But much in the same way that Pss 1 and 2 laid out a definite relationship between Yahweh and the righteous versus Yahweh and the wicked, so here the speaker does not find a God who scoffs at him; rather, he looks with hopeful expectation to Yahweh. According to v. 2, the eyes of God's people look to Him "until He shows us favor." In anticipation, the prayer—repeated twice—of v. 3 is the imperative, "Show us favor, LORD, show us favor." As with Ps 120, repetition is a strategic part of the composition. Since no specific situation is identified, it seems that the psalm is intended to fit any situation in which the people of God are the object of contempt.

Summarizing, in Ps 121, Yahweh is their Protector both now and forever. In Ps 122, peace is anticipated in Jerusalem, where both the house of God and the house of David would be found. In Ps 123, there is a hope-filled look to the heavens in anticipation of Yahweh's grace and favor. This cluster of psalms wraps this eschatological expectation in the mantle of the priestly blessing. Pss 124 and 125 contribute to this theme as they connect "our help" to "the LORD" as the Maker (124:8), and by linking eternal preservation and peace to those who trust in "the LORD"

(125:1-2). Peace and grace will be experienced in a secure Jerusalem over which the son of David reigns and in which Yahweh, their Protector, dwells. This messianic purpose is even clearer in the last five psalms.

CLUSTER #2: PSALMS 130–134

Enveloping Ps 132, which is *about* David, are 131 and 133, which are attributed *to* David (see Figure 3). In turn, enveloping this Davidic triad are two psalms that essentially cannot be removed from these three. In other words, the compositional work of the author in bringing the five psalms together is on full display. The Davidic triad of 131–133 is important in that it places the hope of the fulfillment of the Davidic covenant in a future, idealized Zion.

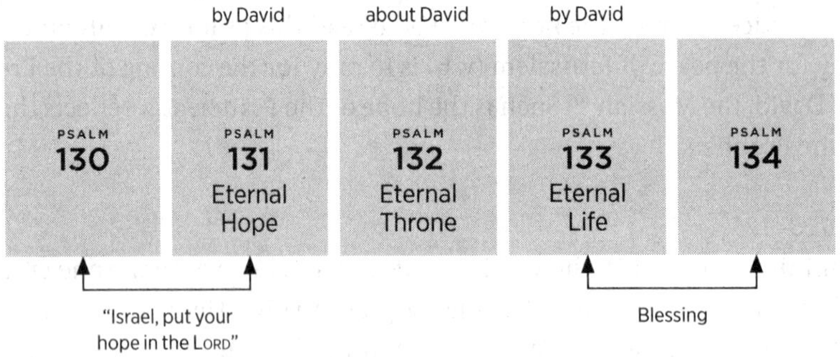

Figure 3: Composition of Psalms 130–134

Psalms 130–131

Whereas Ps 131 begins with a first-person confession of truth and dependence upon Yahweh (vv. 1-2), an appeal is made to the congregation in v. 3: "Israel, put your hope in the LORD." This same phrase appears in Ps 130:7. So Pss 130 and 131 might be considered twins. Yet, David's call in 131:3 reflects back to that important phrase in 121:8: "both now and forever." Ps 121 continues to set the framework. The hope of Israel ought to persist perpetually, i.e., it is eternal. In Ps 130, Israel's hope in her future redemption was predicated upon Yahweh's loyal love and His bountiful redemption, for which the psalmist was willing to wait and hope. Psalm 131:3 echoes this eschatological hope for the one whose heart mirrors the humility and dependence of David. The basis for the eternal hope that Israel should have is the subject of Ps 132.

Psalm 132

Within the collection, Ps 132 becomes the high point, for in many ways it is the end or "liturgical climax"[14] toward which the Psalms of Ascent lead. According to this Song, Zion is the place (1) where the son of David sits (vv. 11-12) and (2) where Yahweh Himself dwells (vv. 13-14). Both of these are said to be "forever." For this reason, the messianic hope in the Psalms of Ascent finds its greatest declaration in Ps 132. Psalm 132 opens with a prayer that Yahweh might remember David (v. 1), who swore to build a house for Yahweh. As such, the psalm is following the giving of the Davidic covenant in 2Sm 7 closely. But at the hinge of the poem, v. 11 turns to the oath that Yahweh swore to David, specifically regarding his lineage that would dwell on his throne "forever" (v. 12). In the same context, beginning with v. 13, attention turns to Yahweh's choice of Zion, His resting place "forever" (v. 14). "The psalm represents a further theological development, inextricably linking Davidic rule with Zion as Yahweh's resting place (cf. Ps 78:68; 2Sm 5:7)."[15] As such, within the collection, the trend has been to develop the importance of Jerusalem, Zion, and Israel within Yahweh's eschatological program. This psalm sets this program clearly within the context of the messianic hope as established in the promises made to David.

At several key points Ps 132 relates to earlier portions of the Psalter. First, this psalm relates Yahweh's presence and the presence of the king to the blessing of provisions and food for the poor in a way similar to Ps 72: "For he [i.e., the king's son] delivers the needy when he calls, the poor and him who has no helper" (v. 12) and "May there be an abundance of grain in the land . . . may its fruit be like Lebanon" (v. 16). As a result of placing the Psalms of Ascent as a collection within the Psalter, the theology of the psalms has been made to serve the larger emphases of the book, namely, the role of the Davidic king in Yahweh's future kingdom inaugurated and led from Jerusalem/Zion. This eschatological understanding of the future Davidic ruler remains a part of the "hopeful anticipation of the Davidic descendant."[16]

Second, within the context of the Psalter, there seems to be a relationship created with Ps 89 in theme and keywords. According to Ps 89:3-4, "The LORD said, 'I have made a covenant with My chosen one; I have sworn an oath to David My servant: "I will establish your offspring forever, and build up your throne for all generations."'" Likewise, Ps 132:11-12 states, "The LORD swore an oath to David, a promise He will not abandon: 'I will set one of your descendants on your throne. If your sons keep My covenant and My decrees that I will teach them, their sons will also sit on your throne forever.'" However, as more than one commentator has noted, Ps 89 makes a dramatic shift that seems to transition the Psalter at the end of Book 3 with Yahweh's seeming rejection of the Davidic line, which He has "spurned and rejected" (89:38). According to Ps 89:39, Ethan declares, "You have renounced the covenant with your servant; you have defiled his crown in the dust" (ESV). Yet, Ps 132:18 seems to answer the hope that Ethan had that Yahweh remember the covenant He had made with David, and the solution to the dilemma seems to rest on the one whose horn will sprout up and upon whom his crown "will be glorious." The postexilic perspective of the Psalms of Ascent remains the eschatological hope that the son of David would reign in Zion. Yet, what sticks out in this declaration of the Davidic covenant is the king's keeping of the covenant by learning Yahweh's testimonies. This might point to the significance of Ps 119 within the composition of Book 5 and the Psalter (see below). The blessed man of Ps 1, namely the Son/King of Ps 2 (see the article on Psalms 1–2 "The Divine Son of God" by Robert Cole in this *Handbook*), is characterized by his delight in Yahweh's Torah.

Much more could be said of Ps 132. What is significant here is that this psalm echoes the expectation of the Prophets in an eschatological reign of the son of David in Zion. Blessing in Zion continues in the next psalm, as well.

Psalm 133

Psalm 133 breaks into two sections: vv. 1-2, which speak metaphorically of the goodness of brotherly unity,[17] and v. 3, which turns to speak of eternal blessing emanating from Mount Zion.[18] During the reign of the descendant of David (Ps 132), there will be a return to the blessing of worship at Mount Zion. The goal of the psalm seems to be to idealize the future reign of the son of David in light of images of the past: kingdom unity, Aaron, and worship at Zion. This worship will climax in the call of Ps 134, as well. But an important element of such worship appears in v. 3, where blessing is given an eternal aspect—"life forevermore." As Allen states: "Like Ps 122, this psalm indicates the high place assigned in OT theology to Zion as focus of the divine presence. It also provides a background for the later conception of a heavenly counterpart, 'Mount Zion, . . . city of the living God . . . the assembly of the firstborn whose names have been written in heaven,' to which a new pilgrim people are making their way and whose benefits they already enjoy in part (Heb 12:22-24; 13:14-16; cf. Gal 4:26; Rev 14:1)."

The Davidic triad of Pss 131–133 focuses the reader on the following themes: eternal hope (Ps 131), eternal throne (Ps 132), and eternal life (Ps 133). And all three of these stem from the presence of Yahweh, which, in the context of the Psalms of Ascent, is in Zion, the place of David's throne. The eschatological hope found in the Davidic covenant is then brought together with the interpretation of the priestly blessing seen in Pss 120–125. On the one hand, Ps 133 explicitly mentions Aaron, who has become a symbol of community unity and holiness (see the quote by Berlin in endnote 17). On the other hand, the conclusion to the Songs of Ascents is a priestly blessing from Zion in Ps 134:3: "May the LORD, Maker of heaven and earth, bless you from Zion." Zenger describes this teaching of the Songs of Ascents as a new Zion theology, which he describes specifically in comparison to Pss 42–48:

> Zion is no longer the mythic mountain of God on which stands YHWH's throne stretching to the heavens. Now YHWH is enthroned in heaven and has a dwelling on Zion—not from of old, but since and because he has chosen it for this purpose. From there he works as the creator God, but not as a spectacular battler against chaos; rather, he is the giver of blessing—as in the Priestly theology of Gn 1 and according to the Priestly theology of blessing in the Aaronic blessing in Nm 6:24-26.[19]

The Psalms of Ascent within the Psalter

Some observations on the role of the composition in the larger context have already been discussed, particularly as psalms reflect hope in the Davidic Son. The goal was to show that the purpose of the Psalms of Ascent reflects the biblical-theological teachings of the Psalter as a whole. Thus, to consider their messianic teaching, one must consider how the collection relates to its context, both in Book 5 of Psalms and to the Psalter as a whole.[20]

Psalms that were perhaps originally used during pilgrimages or worship have been consolidated into the Psalter so that the collection of these psalms might reflect the theology of the whole. Therefore, the reading of the Psalms of Ascent is less an *historical* venture and more of a *textual* one. For example, Pss 135–136 serve as a commentary on the collection, both by taking up its language and by bringing Book 5 back around to Pss 113–118. In other words, the author of Psalms seems to encourage the reader to relate Pss 113–118 to Pss 120–134 by welding them to 135–136. This is done by virtue of important repeated phrases and obvious intertextuality.

Psalms 135–136, which are tightly bound together,[21] are stitched together with the Psalms of Ascent by means of strategic connections to Ps 134. For example, having just read in 134:1 about "the servants of the Lord," namely, "the ones who stand in the house of the Lord," Ps 135:1 encourages praise of the Lord by "the servants of the Lord," specifically as those who "stand in the house of the Lord" (135:2).[22] In addition, just as Ps 134:3 ends the collection with the blessing, "May the Lord, Maker of heaven and earth, bless you from Zion," so Ps 135:21 ends the psalm with the command, "May the Lord be praised from Zion: He dwells in Jerusalem." Blessings *from* Yahweh and *to* Yahweh relate to His presence in Zion. Compositionally, Ps 135 has taken the central themes of blessing and Zion from the Psalms of Ascent and tied them together with various texts from the Torah, the Prophets, and earlier psalms. Examples of this include: (1) 135:1 and 113:1 are essentially the same, (2) 135:7 is identical to Jer 10:13; 51:16, (3) 135:14 quotes Dt 32:36, and (4) 135:15-20 are virtually the same as much of 115:4-11. In the same way, the phrase "for His steadfast love endures forever" (ESV), which is repeated in every verse of Ps 136, appears at the beginning (vv. 1-4) and end (v. 29) of Ps 118 as "His faithful love endures forever."

The psalmist seems to be organizing this part of the Psalter strategically in order to merge the Psalms of Ascent into the larger collection (see Figure 4). Thus, this collection is related to the larger themes of Book 5, which include praise for deliverance (Pss 111–113) wrought by the messianic deliverer of Ps 110.[23] The hope for the reader of the Psalter rests on this King-Priest, who sits on the throne at the right hand of Yahweh.

The phrases discussed above—"Maker of heaven and earth" and "both now and forever"—that are so important to the unity and theology of the Psalms of Ascent also appear in the psalms that precede the collection. In fact, both appear in Ps 115. The phrase "Maker of heaven and earth" (121:2; 124:8; 134:3) is used in 115:15, "May you be blessed by the LORD, *the Maker of heaven and earth.*" Also, Ps 115:18 says, "But we will praise the LORD, *both now and forever.*" Within a few short verses, two phrases appear together that are integral to the Psalms of Ascent and especially Ps 121. Just as Ps 121 longs for the "help" that comes from Yahweh, so Ps 115:9-11 calls upon Israel, the house of Aaron, and those who fear Yahweh to trust in Him, as He is their "help" and shield. Those who "trust" in Yahweh are promised this "help," just as in 125:1-2, those who "trust" in Yahweh are given the hope that Yahweh surrounds them "both now and forever" (125:1-2). The future hope encouraged in the Psalms of Ascent mirrors that already presented in Book 5. Furthermore, the eschatologically latent phrase "both now and forever" also appears in 113:2, "Let the name of the LORD be praised *both now and forever.*"

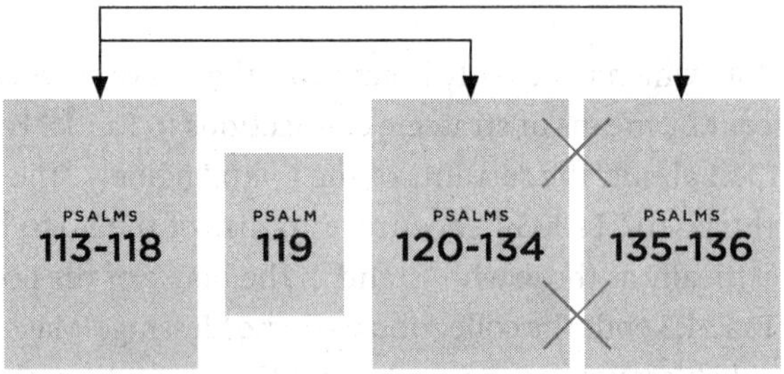

Figure 4: Intertextual Connections within Book 5

However, if this is the case, then the extensive reflection on Torah in Ps 119 might seem to interrupt this compositional strategy. Yet, Ps 119 actually seems to be used by the psalmist to connect this collection to the larger messianic focus of the Psalter (see Figure 5). There are three major "Torah" psalms, namely, Pss 1, 19, and 119. Ps 1, which shows that the great blessing that comes from meditation upon the Lord's Torah is clearly connected to Ps 2, which encourages the proper recognition and worship of the King, that is, the Son, who is set upon Yahweh's throne.[24]

Ps 1 (a Torah psalm) and Ps 2 (a messianic psalm) set the trajectory for the rest of the Psalter around these two themes. Similarly, after Ps 19, which also declares the primacy of Yahweh's Torah, the author has set a series of psalms concerning the King (Pss 20–24). These psalms resonate both with Pss 1–2 as well as the Psalms of Ascent. Consider the following specific connections:

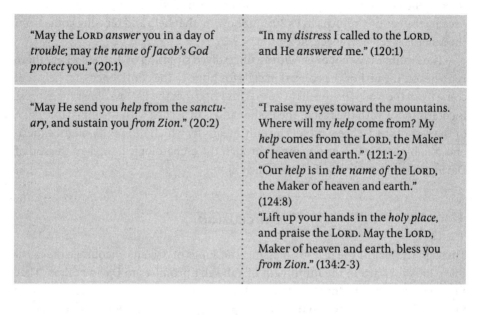

"May the Lord *answer* you in a day of *trouble*; may *the name of Jacob's God protect* you." (20:1)	"In my *distress* I called to the Lord, and He *answered* me." (120:1)
"May He send you *help* from the *sanctuary*, and sustain you *from Zion*." (20:2)	"I raise my eyes toward the mountains. Where will my *help* come from? My *help* comes from the Lord, the Maker of heaven and earth." (121:1-2) "Our *help* is in *the name of* the Lord, the Maker of heaven and earth." (124:8) "Lift up your hands in the *holy place*, and praise the Lord. May the Lord, Maker of heaven and earth, bless you *from Zion*." (134:2-3)

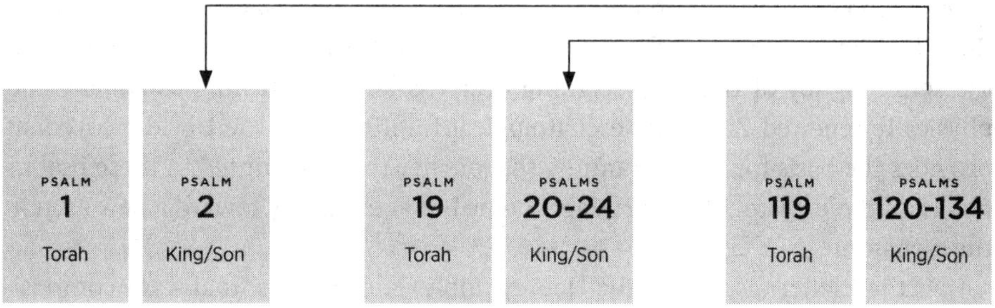

Figure 5: Intertextual Connections among Pss 1, 2, 19, 20-24 and Psalms of Ascent

The first of these is particularly significant, as the transition is made from Torah to a request for Yahweh to answer in a time of distress. Psalm 120 acknowledges that a love for God's Word (or Torah) does not mean immunity from times of distress. Rather, reading and meditating upon that Word leads the reader to seek help in the One who answers by sending help from the sanctuary in Zion, which is the hope of the Psalms of Ascent. Psalm 120 transitions the reader from a reflection on God's word (Ps 119) during times of distress to Ps 121, which truly sets the stage compositionally for the rest of the collection (see above). Psalm 20:2 relates to the Psalms of Ascents in significant ways, as well, as it is echoed in Pss 121:1-2; 124:8; 134:2-3 (see above). With the programmatic function of Ps 121, the connections to Ps 20 seem significant. Moreover, as corroboration of this, the end of the Psalms of Ascent strategically returns to Ps 20:2 in showing that help and blessing come from the sanctuary (or holy place) at Zion (134:2-3).[25]

The Psalms of Ascent open with an unresolved situation of distress where there is no peace; the rest of the collection calls for hope in the confidence that help will come from the God who dwells at Zion. This hope that the Psalms of Ascent express is coterminous with the rest of the Psalter and is in accord with the messianic hope of the rest of the Hebrew Bible. The only means by which humanity might experience the blessing of creation comes through the eschatological work of the son of David, who reigns over God's kingdom at Zion.

CONCLUSION

Through the lens of the priestly blessing, the Songs of Ascents encourage the faithful to look forward to the fulfillment of Yahweh's promises to David at Zion. They fill out what it means for the Lord to bless, to keep, to be gracious to, and to give peace to His people. They do this by interpreting their past, present, and future in light of God's intention to bless them through the son of David at Zion. As such, they also join the chorus of the larger canon, especially the Prophets, as they repeat the sounding joy of the King reigning over His kingdom from a spiritually and physically renewed Zion. The eschatological fulfillment of the Davidic covenant provides the basis for understanding the journey to Zion painted in these psalms not as a simple, historical pilgrimage theme but as a journey toward a new Zion in the eschaton.

As the Psalter (as well as the Hebrew Bible) comes to its final stage compositionally and therefore theologically, the author uses the collection of the Songs of Ascents with perspectives coterminous with those of the rest of the Hebrew Bible. In particular, the collection makes an important contribution in showing how the covenants were understood at the time the text was coming to a place of stability. Specifically, the Songs of Ascents show that, within the administration of the Mosaic covenant, hope for blessing remained a manifestation of the Abrahamic covenant, specifically as it was to be fulfilled via the promises of the Davidic covenant. This relates to a restoration of God's original creation purposes to bless humanity on the land (Gn 1–2). As such, the Songs of Ascents testify to a hope that was beyond the expectations of the Mosaic covenant, and in speaking of this hope, the Songs simply echo the hope of the Torah and the Prophets. Blessing would come from the hand of and in the reign of the son of David, whose kingdom would be a manifestation of the kingdom of Yahweh from a particular place—Zion. Therefore, the Songs of Ascents encourage and perhaps model the path for the reader with the same hope as the Chronicler: "Let him go up!" (2Chr 36:23 NASB).

1. To speak of composition of the Psalms of Ascent and its subsequent theology differs from an approach that tries to find the purpose of the collection outside of its place within the Psalter. The approach of this article remains that of carefully reading these psalms as a unit within the context of a book that has signs of being strategically brought together. To search for a historical purpose is at times a futile exercise, which even Gunkel observed when speaking about the Songs of Ascents: "The small collection's goal is not clearly recognizable because the meaning of the expression *ma'ălôt* is not certain" (Hermann Gunkel, *Introduction to Psalms: The Genres of the Religious Lyric of Israel*, trans. James D. Nogalski [Macon: Mercer University Press: 1998], 347.) His hesitant acceptance of the meaning of "pilgrimage" means that "the purpose of the collection would fall between a devotional and prayer book on the one hand and a cultic psalter on the other" (347). The point is that Gunkel was looking for a purpose of the collection outside of its place within the Psalter.

2. The only exception to this is Ps 121, where the title is *šîr lamma'ălôt*, or "a song for the ascents." Although there are various explanations for this, this change probably at the very least signals the importance of this psalm for the rest of the collection. Most important, Ps 121 uses two of the most significant phrases that provide unity both among the Psalms of Ascent and to the surrounding psalms in Book 5. See discussion on Ps 121 below.

3. Bullinger defines anadiplosis as "the repetition of the same word or words at the end of one sentence and the beginning of another" (E. W. Bullinger, *Figures of Speech in the Bible: Explained and Illustrated* [New York: Young and Co., 1898], 251). In fact, this pattern of repetition has been taken by some as the meaning of the titles, as in going up the steps, literarily (see e.g., Ps 121:1-2).

4. The other four phrases occur only twice. They are "let Israel say" (124:1; 129:1), "peace be with Israel" (125:5; 128:6; and possibly 133:3 according to 11QPsA), and "the Lord bless you from Zion" (128:5; 134:3). For a discussion of these phrases see Loren D. Crow, *The Songs of Ascents (Psalms 120–134): Their Place in Israelite History and Religion* (Atlanta: Scholars Press, 1996), 130 ff.

5. Erich Zenger, "The Composition and Theology of the Fifth Book of Psalms, 107–145," *Journal for the Study of the Old Testament* 80 (1998): 92. "The Psalms of Ascents . . . are also an artistic construction consisting of three parts of five psalms each, 120–24, 125–29, and 130–34. In the middle of each of the three subgroups of five psalms there is a psalm that has been influenced by royal theology and the theology of Zion: 122, 127, 132. With their different emphases (122: Jerusalem; 127: the temple; and 132: David), these three psalms produce a coherent theological view which acclaims Zion as the place of blessing and salvation to which Israel should go in 'ascents' or a 'pilgrimage' (executed as a second Exodus from exile or foreign lands)."

6. Delitzsch (Keil & Delitzsch, III: 268-69) states that Ps 120 "attaches itself to Ps. cxix. 176 [119:176]. The writer of Ps. Cxix., surrounded on all sides by apostasy and persecution, compares himself to a sheep that is easily lost, which the shepherd has to seek and bring home if it is not to perish; and the writer of Ps. Cxx. is also 'as a sheep in the midst of wolves.'"

7. In addition, some psalms combine this title with an attribution to David (Pss 122, 124, 131, 133) or to Solomon (Ps 127).

8. Verse 8 uses the same root as appears in the titles of the Psalms of Ascent.

9. See Leon J. Liebreich, "The Songs of Ascents and the Priestly Blessing," *Journal of Biblical Literature* 74 (1955): 33–36. His conclusion: "Furthermore, regarded as a unit, this collection of Psalms affords us an insight into how at least four of the basic words of the Priestly Blessing were actually understood or applied by the gifted and inspired authors of the Songs of Ascents. In this group of Psalms is preserved the earliest interpretation of the priestly blessing, an interpretation that may be considered to be the precursor of the homilies on the Priestly Blessing found in Midrashic literature" (36).

10. The "name of the LORD" also appears in 122:4. Also, blessing is linked with the "name of the LORD" in 129:8.

11. Robert Alter, *The Book of Psalms: A Translation with Commentary* (New York: Norton & Company, 2007), 438.

12. The alliteration is obvious in the Hebrew of v. 6: שַׁאֲלוּ שְׁלוֹם יְרוּשָׁלָ͏ִם יִשְׁלָיוּ אֹהֲבָיִךְ (*šaʾalû šəlôm yərûšālāim yišlāyû ʾohəbāyik*).

13. John Sailhamer, *NIV Compact Bible Commentary* (Grand Rapids: Zondervan, 1994), 218.

14. See Frank-Lothar Hossfeld and Erich Zenger, *Psalms 3: A Commentary on Psalms 101–150*, trans. Linda M. Maloney (Minneapolis: Fortress Press, 2011), 457.

15. Sheri Klouda, "Zion," in *Dictionary of the Old Testament: Wisdom, Poetry & Writings* (Downers Grove, IL: IVP Academic, 2008), 939–40.

16. Gerald H. Wilson, "Psalms and Psalter: Paradigm for Biblical Theology," in *Biblical Theology: Retrospect and Prospect*, ed. Scott J. Hafemann (Downers Grove, IL: InterVarsity Press, 2002), 109. He states (108–109): "The final form of the Psalter would ultimately affect the way the royal psalms and earlier references to Davidic kingship were interpreted. In light of the distancing that takes place in the later books, these references would have been increasingly understood eschatologically as hopeful anticipation of the Davidic descendant who would—as YHWH's anointed servant—establish God's direct rule over all humanity in the kingdom of God." This does not necessarily mean that the earlier writings were not also viewed eschatologically. This eschatological understanding of the future Davidic ruler includes a view of Zion.

17. There is much uncertainty about the meaning of v. 1b. Some possibilities are literal brothers dwelling together (see context of Dt 25:5 where the phrase is used), celebrating at feasts together, brotherly harmony, and national unity. For the last, consider the statement of Berlin, 142, 145–46: "It seems likely that Ps 133.1 is using the phrase שבת אחים גם יחד in the same sense as Gn 13.6, 36.7, and Dt 25.5. The image is not one of a quarrel-free family snuggling around the hearth, but of undivided land holdings. This is a metaphor for an undivided kingdom. The psalm expresses hope for the reunification of the north and south, with Jerusalem as the capital of a united kingdom. . . . The main theme is the unification of the country. This is achieved through the central image of flowing together. The picture is one of continuous flow: from head to beard, from beard to collar, from Hermon to Zion. . . . The entire country is pictured as a priestly visage: from Hermon to Zion—from head to body. And . . . the land is anointed with dew as Aaron is anointed with the consecrating oil. The country is thus not only united, it is also holy; and not only is it holy, it is also blessed. . . . Ps 133 is an ode to Zion with a religious and nationalistic message." Adele Berlin, "On the Interpretation of Ps 133," in Elaine R. Follis, ed., *Directions in Biblical Hebrew Poetry*, Journal for the Study of the Old Testament, Supplement Series 40 (Sheffield: JSOT Press, 1987), 141–48, quoted in Zenger, 476.

18. Leslie C. Allen, *Psalms* (Waco: Word Books, 1983), 215.

19. Hossfeld and Zenger, *Psalms 3*, 297.

20. This article assumes that the individual psalms that make up the book have been strategically put together into a book that has structure and purpose.

21. Psalms 135 and 136 are connected in multiple ways, but significantly 135:10-12 are essentially quoted in 136:17-22.

22. Note that the phrase in 135:2 includes the proclitic particle שֶׁ, which is used multiple times in the Psalms of Ascent. Moreover, just as Ps 134 uses the name of God, Yahweh (HCSB, the LORD), five times in three short verses, so Ps 135:1 opens with the call to praise "the name of the LORD."

23. See Michael Rydelnik's article on Ps 110 in this *Handbook*.

24. These connections include an inclusio (1:1 and 2:12) as well as the use of related words (meditate and plot) and themes (way of wicked perishing).

25. These connections between 20:1-2 and the first and last Psalms of Ascent tend to show that the entire collection serves this purpose. In a similar way, it is the beginning and end of Ps 135 that will show the connections to Ps 134 and, thus, the Psalms of Ascent.

Messianism in Proverbs

BARRY R. LEVENTHAL

As Israel's Messiah, Jesus Christ (Heb. *Yeshua HaMashiach*) is prophetically and historically sovereign, not only as Israel's Messianic King, Prophet, and Priest, but also as Israel's Messianic Sage. His messianic place in the Hebrew Bible is so prominent that some scholars have called the OT "A Messianic Primer."[1] Another scholar, in referring to David's dual offices of king and prophet, said, "Here, then, was the messianic prototype."[2]

In developing the messianic setting of the book of Proverbs, one must be sure to discern the progressive nature of God's self-disclosure concerning His Davidic Messianic *King* as well as His Davidic Messianic *Son*. This messianic self-revelation is both historic and progressive (i.e., progressive revelation). In other words, the messianic nature of the book of Proverbs was not revealed in isolation.[3] It had, and still does have, both a historic and prophetic backdrop, and therefore a messianic setting.[4]

To begin with, Prv 1:1-7 forms the preamble to the book. Bruce Waltke introduces the preamble by saying, "Syntactically connected with the book's main title (1:1), the preamble states its aims for its addressees (1:2-6) and its epistemology (1:7)."[5]

The final editors of the book of Proverbs introduced the original readers to *the historic setting of the book* in Prv 1:1.[6] The seven historic persons named in the book of Proverbs firmly anchored the book in biblical history. Along with Solomon's name, which appears three times in the book (1:1; 10:1; 25:1), six other historic names also appear in the book: David (1:1), Hezekiah (25:1), and four other names: Agur, Jakeh, Ithiel, and Ucal (30:1).[7] In addition, one historic group is mentioned: "the men of Hezekiah," that is, Hezekiah's "court officials"[8] (25:1). Most scholars agree that in a certain sense Solomon was the original benefactor of the wisdom literature, the so-called "Patron of Wisdom"[9] (cf. 1Kg 3:5-28; 4:29-34; 5:12; 10:1-13,23-25; 11:41; etc.).

But it is David and Solomon specifically, who are both mentioned in the preamble (Prv 1:1), who set the book in *its historic and messianic settings*: "The proverbs[10] of *Solomon* son of *David*, king of Israel" (Prv 1:1, italics added; cf. 10:1; 25:1).

Since David and Solomon are both anchored to *the historic setting of the book of Proverbs*, one can assume, from an intertextual perspective, first, that the book of Proverbs was already linked to several messianic prophecies (all prior to and including the reign of Hezekiah); and second, that they were already linked to the Davidic covenant as well.

The historic setting of the book of Proverbs also laid the groundwork for *the messianic setting of the book of Proverbs*. By determining the historic dating of these proverbial collections, the messianic setting will become apparent.[11]

First, by dating Solomon's reign from 971–931 BC and Hezekiah's reign from 715–686 BC, Israel's prophets had approximately 285 years to continue building up Israel's messianic prophetic library, which also laid the historic and messianic foundations for the book of Proverbs. In addition, the dating of the reigns of Solomon and Hezekiah means that the editorial process for the book of Proverbs also ran for approximately 285 years. So, it is not surprising that the final editors of the book of Proverbs, working from an intertextual framework, greatly anticipated Israel's final Messianic Hope, which included such messianic prophecies as God's Messianic Warrior King who would be a descendant of (among others) Adam and Eve, Seth, Noah, Shem, Abraham, Isaac, Jacob, Judah, David, and Solomon.[12]

Second, since David was obviously connected to the book of Proverbs (Prv 1:1), then the Davidic covenant must also be linked to the book of Proverbs. The biblical authors laid out the Davidic covenant in three different passages and in three different settings: (1) the original institution of the Davidic covenant around 1000 BC (2Sm 7); (2) the final application of the Davidic covenant around 450 BC (1Chr 17); and (3) the confrontation of the Davidic covenant around 650 BC (Ps 89;[13] cf. Pss 72; 132; etc.).

Walter Kaiser, in remarking on the majestic Davidic covenant in 2Sm 7 and its relationship to the other two Davidic covenant passages, said:

> God's promise to David in 2 Samuel 7 has to be among the most brilliant moments in the history of salvation. It is matched in importance and prestige only by the promise made to Abraham in Genesis 12 and later to all Israel and Judah in Jeremiah's New Covenant (Jer. 31:31-34). . . .
>
> Next to the promise given to Abraham[14] must rank the word of blessing poured out on David. The classical OT passage dealing with this new [royal] addition to the ever-expanding promise and plan of God was 2 Samuel 7 with its duplicate in 1 Chronicles 17 and commentary in Psalm 89.[15]

Martin Selman, in commenting on Nathan's oracle to David in 2Sm 7:11b-16, said, "This passage is often rightly regarded as the foundation of Israel's messianic hope."[16]

One of the significant aspects of the Davidic covenant that has a unique relationship to the messianic nature of the book of Proverbs is the father-son relationship between God and David's royal descendants. The Lord, speaking through the prophet Nathan concerning David's son Solomon, said (2Sm 7:14-15; cf. Ps 89:30-32):

> (14) "I will be a father to him, and he will be a son to Me. When he does wrong, I will discipline him with a human rod and with blows from others. (15) But My faithful love will never leave him as I removed it from Saul; I removed him from your way."[17]

Down through the centuries, as the people of Israel reflected on the father-son relationship in the Davidic covenant, they rested the Messianic Hope on the one, final Davidic King, the One who would never need to come under the discipline of the rod of men.[18] John Sailhamer made this messianic stipulation clear:

> As a reward for David's faithfulness to the Lord, God made a special covenant with the dynasty of David, in which he promised that a "descendant" of the house of David would establish an eternal kingdom in Jerusalem. That Davidic descendant would be a faithful king like David himself. Solomon apparently understood his own reign to be a fulfillment of God's covenant promise. The biblical writers are clear, however, that neither Solomon nor any of the subsequent Davidic kings could be reckoned as the true fulfillment (1 Kings 11:9-13). Thus, the promise made to David went beyond any of the Davidic kings. It pointed to a future messianic king who would establish God's kingdom in Jerusalem forever. That promise finds its fulfillment in the reign of Jesus, the Son of David.
>
> Though David's reign prefigured the reign of the future Messiah, David's own life had many shortcomings and ultimately ended in disgrace.... In the end, however, David's trust in God's promises remained firm, and he died in the hope of a future glorious kingdom.... God's promise to David remained linked to David's future Son.[19]

In another place, in reaffirming the same Davidic covenant stipulation, Sailhamer said, "After Solomon's reign, the kingdom built by David all but fell to ruin, and no descendant could rightly claim to be the fulfillment of God's promise to David. There were revivals in which godly kings did their best to lead the people in obedience to God's Word, but they all ended in failure. The reader's hope is directed to the fulfillment of a promise not yet realized."[20]

Kaiser also explained the tenuous nature of the father-son relationship: "In a totally unique way David could now call Him 'my Father' [Ps 89:26], for each

Davidite stood in this relation of son to his God. Yet it is not said that any single Davidite would ever realize purely or perfectly this lofty concept of divine sonship. But should any person qualify for this relationship, he would also need to be a son of David."[21]

So then, this unique father-son relationship plays out in the book of Proverbs in the following messianic ways: the Wise King and the Wise Son, the One who would always live *wisely* in the fear of the Lord.[22]

The people Israel needed the ability to discern the *specific* skill-sets of her ultimate (1) Wise King and (2) Wise Son, (3) the One who would always live in the fear of the Lord. That would enable Israel to look forward to, and live in, her God-given Messianic Hope. Derek Kidner was certainly correct when he said, "[T]here are details of character small enough to escape the mesh of the law and the broadsides of the prophets, and yet decisive in personal dealings. Proverbs moves in this realm, asking what a person is like to live with, or to employ; how he manages his affairs, his time and himself."[23]

God had already given Israel the broad mesh of the law to help discern the *general* stipulations for Israel's kings (Dt 17:14-20). Moses left Israel seven *general* prerequisites for determining all true and righteous future kings: (1) the king must be an Israelite (14-15); (2) the king must not build up his army on horses (and thus on chariots) that he would obtain from Egypt (16); (3) the king must not multiply wives to himself that would turn his heart away from God (17a); (4) the king must not build up his treasury to the degree that he would trust it rather than God (17b); (5) the king must always live under the authority of God's law and His authoritative leaders, the Levitical priests (18-19a); (6) the king must learn to fear the Lord his God by carefully observing all the words of God's law and statutes (19b); and (7) the king must not turn aside from the commandment of God (17:14-20) and thus lift up his heart in hubris against his fellow countrymen; in other words, the kings of Israel were to live as servants under the One and only true King of Israel, the Covenant Lord Himself (20).

Even measured by the broad mesh of the law, each king of Israel failed, some in the most gruesome ways. The father-son stipulation of the Davidic covenant brought each king of Israel under the rod of God. In addition, the broad mesh of the law continued to keep the Royal Messianic Hope aflame. When an Israelite king failed, Israelite citizens looked upward and forward to the Royal, Messianic King, the One who would never fail. But Israel still needed a more judicious evaluative tool to search out the finer details of character of Israel's Davidic kings and especially for appraising that One Davidic King who would never need God's discipline. He alone would be qualified to sit on the throne of David forever. So God gave the book of Proverbs to Israel (and the other wisdom books as well) as just that judicious evaluative tool needed to search out the *specific* details of character of Israel's Davidic kings and especially for assessing the ultimate Davidic King who would qualify to sit on the throne of David forever.

First, then, God gave the book of Proverbs to Israel as just such an evaluative tool needed for the line of Davidic kings and, even more important, for God's final Davidic King.[24] So it is not surprising that the Sages of Israel laid out such an elevated number of *specific* royal characteristics. If Moses set out the *general* behavioral parameters for Israel's kings, and for Israel's coming Messianic King as well (recorded in Dt 17:14-20), then the Sages of Israel laid down the *specific* behavioral qualities of Israel's kings, and *specifically* of Israel's coming Messianic King (recorded in Proverbs).

The *specific* proverbial, messianic behavioral qualities for Israel's kings in the book of Proverbs, and for Israel's Great and Marvelous King as well, the so-called royal proverbs, include:[25] living "in the fear of the Lord" (14:26-28), reliable kindness [lovingkindness, NKJV] (20:28), just (16:10-11; 29:4,14; cf. 8:15), righteousness (16:12,13; cf. 25:5; 28:15-16; 29:2,12), righteous favor (14:35), righteous judgment (16:10-16; 31:9; cf. 19:12; 25:5 [i.e., keeping covenant fidelity]; 28:2,15-16; 29:4,12,26), wise judgment (8:12-16), just [fair] judgment (20:8; cf. 20:2; 29:4,12,14), righteous judgment (20:28; cf. 16:12-13; 20:26; 29:12), compassionate judgment (31:8-9), truthfulness (16:13), purity and graciousness (22:11), discernment and perseverance (25:2; cf. 22:11,29; 23:1-3; 24:21-22; 25:2,6-7), separation from the wicked (20:8,26; 25:5; cf. 14:35; 16:10-15), alcoholic abstinence (31:4-7), moral purity (31:3), moral sensibility (16:12-13), loyalty and faithfulness (20:28; cf. 29:4,14), and inscrutability: "As the heaven is high and the earth is deep, so the hearts of kings cannot be investigated" (25:3; cf. 25:1-6; 16:2; 21:1-2; 24:12; also Dt 29:29).

After reviewing these proverbs concerning Israel's ideal king, it becomes immediately obvious that no king in Israel's history ever came close to meeting these specific high standards (including the more general Mosaic standards in Dt 17:14-20). So, as Thomas Schreiner has said, Israel's messianic vision must have been directed toward another King:

> It seems that no ordinary king is in view [in Proverbs]. The proverbs in the book are mainly ascribed to King Solomon (1:1; 10:1; 25:1). No human king fulfills the ideal king described here, for all kings, to one extent or another, practice injustice. If Proverbs is viewed from a canonical perspective, the ideal picture of the king points to a future king—a king who fulfills the promise of the covenant with David. The righteousness, wisdom, and godlike stature of the king point to Jesus of Nazareth. The righteousness and wisdom and godly rule described in Proverbs are fulfilled in Jesus Christ.[26]

Second, then, God not only gave the book of Proverbs to Israel for evaluating her Davidic kings, especially God's final Davidic King, but He also gave Proverbs to Israel as an evaluative tool needed for assessing God's final Davidic Son. The term "son" is used 46 times in the book of Proverbs, being framed[27] by Prv 1:1 and 30:4.[28] Of course, since the Davidic covenant firmly anticipates that one of David's sons would ultimately sit on the Davidic throne forever (2Sm 7:14; 1Chr 17:13; cf. Pss 2:7,12; 89:30), it is not surprising to see Israel's Sages building this sonship truth into the book of Proverbs.

The opening reference to "son" for this theological motif (i.e., the opening frame or bracket) is in the title of the book of Proverbs: "The proverbs of Solomon son of David, king of Israel" (Prv 1:1). So, from the beginning, the final editors included this historical title in the book of Proverbs (Prv 1:1; cf. 10:1; 25:1; etc.). The book of Proverbs, like the other books recorded after God's initial establishment of the Davidic covenant (2Sm 7),[29] is also grounded on the Davidic covenant (cf. 2Sm 7; 1Chr 17; Ps 89; etc.).

The closing reference to "son" for this theological motif (i.e., the closing frame or bracket), not counting the references to "son" in 30:1 and 31:2 (all referring to just the identity of a particular "son"), is at the end of the book of Proverbs (30:1-4, esp. 4):

> 1 The words of Agur son of Jakeh. The oracle.
>
> The man's oration to Ithiel, to Ithiel and Ucal:
>
> 2 I am more stupid than any other man,
> and I lack man's ability to understand.
> 3 I have not gained wisdom,
> and I have no knowledge of the Holy One.
> 4 Who has gone up to heaven and come down?
> Who has gathered the wind in His hands?
> Who has bound up the waters in a cloak?
> Who has established all the ends of the earth?
> What is His name, *and what is the name of His Son*—
> if you know? (italics added).

Arnold Fruchtenbaum makes these pertinent observations concerning Prv 30:4:

> Then comes the sixth—the trick—question. *What is His son's name*? At that point in history when Agur wrote this passage, it was not yet revealed what the name of the Messiah was going to be. Later, Isaiah gives us a number of names and says that He will be called Immanuel. The book of Daniel calls Him the Anointed One, *Mashiach*, Messiah. It is only in the revelation of the New Testament where the answer to this question is to be found, His personal name is *Yeshua*. However, the point of Proverbs 30:4 is that God does have a Son whose name had not yet been revealed.[30]

The older biblical commentary by John Peter Lange says, concerning Prv 30:4, quoting, with agreement, J. Pye Smith, "The concluding clauses of this energetic passage [30:1-4] are rationally and easily interpreted, if we admit that the ancient Jews had some obscure ideas of a plurality in the divine nature."[31] Lange goes on to say, "But the Messianic Psalms [e.g., Pss 2; 110; etc.] had already spoken of 'the Son,' mysteriously, perhaps, and yet enough to supply germs of knowledge as well as of faith."[32]

Sailhamer summarized this final messianic "Son" reference in Prv 30:4, "Through the words of Agur . . . the compiler of the book of Proverbs turns the reader's attention to Israel's future messianic hopes. The wisdom portrayed here and embodied in the sayings of Solomon thus becomes emblematic of the Wisdom of the divine Son of God known in other biblical texts."[33]

With Agur's personal and intimate confession (vv. 1-3) and God's mysterious and majestic revelation (v. 4), the Sage is now able to embrace the fear of the Lord, which both begins and ends the book of Proverbs (1:7 and 31:30, another *inclusio*).[34]

Of the royal, messianic behavioral qualities laid out for Israel's kings in the book of Proverbs, "the fear of the LORD" stands out as the most significant of all, especially in light of this major theme in the Wisdom Literature. Concerning "the fear of the LORD" in the Wisdom Literature, Kaiser says by way of introduction:

> When we come to wisdom books and wisdom psalms, the fear of the Lord has become the essence of the knowledge and wisdom of God. Even though this phrase occurred just over two dozen times apart from the suffixial forms such as "thy fear" or the verbal statements, its locations are all extremely strategic and often served the whole purpose for writing some of these books. In Proverbs 1:7 it functioned as the motto for the whole book.[35]

C. Bridges aptly summarized the fear of the Lord: "[The fear of the Lord is] that affectionate reverence, by which the child of God bends himself humbly and carefully to his Father's law."[36]

Of all of Israel's kings and her so-called sons, not one ever lived up to the divine calling to live in the fear of God. Therefore, God pointed Israel ever forward to His Messianic King and Son, the only One who would always live in the fear of the Lord (meaning, living in reverential obedience to His Father). In fact, Moses had already confirmed this fear of the Lord truth in his Deuteronomic stipulations for all Israel (cf. Dt 4:10; 5:29; 6:1-2,13,24; 8:6; 10:12,20; 13:4; 14:22-23; 21:21; [25:17-18]; 28:58; 31:12-13), and especially for Israel's kings (Dt 17:18-19). As Schreiner says, "Indeed, the heart and soul of wisdom is the fear of the Lord, which is a major theme in Deuteronomy."[37]

Further, this truth was also confirmed by the prophet Isaiah, a contemporary of King Hezekiah and the Sages of his time, when he prophesied of the Messiah and His commitment to a Spirit-inspired fear of the Lord (Isa 11:1-3a, italics added): "Then a shoot will grow from the stump of Jesse, and a branch from his roots will bear fruit. The Spirit of the LORD will rest on Him—a Spirit of wisdom and understanding, a Spirit of counsel and strength, *a Spirit* of knowledge and *of the fear of the LORD. His delight will be in the fear of the LORD*" (Isa 11:3b-16 lays out the results of 11:1-3a).[38]

Again, Schreiner correctly observes, "If Psalms emphasizes praising the Lord, Proverbs focuses on fearing him. These are two different perspectives on the same reality. Only those who fear the Lord will praise him, and those who praise him will fear him. Proverbs points to Jesus Christ, who is wiser than Solomon and rules the world with a wisdom greater than his."[39]

It is for this reason that, in the long run, Ortlund was correct when he said, "But the wisdom of Proverbs comes from 'Solomon, the son of David, king of Israel.' Right up front, the book tells us it stands in the flow of Biblical history, which leads us to Jesus. Here is the point: The fear of the Lord Jesus Christ is the beginning of *this* wisdom."[40]

So, in sum, it is not so surprising that the Lord Yeshua could, by His own prophetic claim, be that Messianic Sage greater than Solomon himself (Mt 12:42; Lk 11:31). The Lord Yeshua is the only One who actually lived, and continues to live, in the fear of God as the Messianic Son and the Messianic King, always without ever missing a beat.

---

1. On the OT as "A Messianic Primer," see Walter C. Kaiser Jr., *Toward Rediscovering the Old Testament*, Academie Books (Grand Rapids: Zondervan, 1987), 101–120; and Michael Rydelnik, *The Messianic Hope: Is the Hebrew Bible Really Messianic?* New American Commentary Studies in Bible and Theology (Nashville: B&H Publishing Group, 2010), 66.

2. Walter C. Kaiser Jr., *The Messiah in the Old Testament*, Studies in Old Testament Theology (Grand Rapids: Zondervan, 1995), 17.

3. For details concerning the progressive nature of biblical theology, especially as it relates to the OT, see Eugene H. Merrill, "Introduction," in *A Biblical Theology of the Old Testament*, ed. Roy B. Zuck (Chicago: Moody Press, 1991), 1–6.

4. For more on the book of Proverbs' "wise sage, the Messiah," as well as the "Woman Wisdom as a symbol of the future Messiah" (Prv 1:20; 4:6; 7:4; 8:1,11-12,22-36; 9:1,11; 14:33; cf. 3:19; 8:30), see Rydelnik, *The Messianic Hope*, 77–78, and Daniel J. Treier, *Proverbs and Ecclesiastes: Brazos Theological Commentary on the Bible* (Grand Rapids: Brazos Press, 2011), 44–57.

5. Bruce K. Waltke, *The Book of Proverbs: Chapters 1–15* (Grand Rapids: Eerdmans, 2004), 173. For more on the Preamble, see Raymond C. Ortlund Jr., *Proverbs: Wisdom That Works*, Preaching the Word Series (Wheaton, IL: Crossway, 2012), 19–20.

6. Concerning the specific details behind the final editing of the book of Proverbs, see Derek Kidner, *Proverbs: An Introduction and Commentary*, Tyndale Old Testament Commentaries (1964; repr. Chicago: InterVarsity Press, 1968), 26; also see William J. Dumbrell, *The Faith of Israel: Its Expression in the Books of the Old Testament* (Grand

Rapids: Baker, 1988), 224; plus John H. Sailhamer, *Introduction to Old Testament Theology: A Canonical Approach* (Grand Rapids: Zondervan, 1995), 257–58; and Waltke, *The Book of Proverbs: Chapters 1-15*, 36–37.

7. Although 1Kg 4:30-31 names some of Solomon's fellow-sages (both within Israel and without), these four names (Agur, Jakeh, Ithiel, and Ucal) are unknown in biblical history.

8. See John H. Sailhamer, *The Books of the Bible*, The Zondervan Quick Reference Library (Grand Rapids: Zondervan Publishing House, 1998), 37. For more on the setting of the book of Proverbs, see Waltke, *The Book of Proverbs: Chapters 1-15*, 58, 62–63.

9. The source of the Solomonic title "Patron of Wisdom" comes from Walter A. Brueggemann, "The Social Significance of Solomon as a Patron of Wisdom," in *The Sage in Israel and the Ancient Near East*, ed. John G. Gammie and Leo G. Perdue (Winona Lake, IN: Eisenbrauns, 1990), 117–32, cited by William P. Brown, *Character in Crisis: A Fresh Approach to the Wisdom Literature of the Old Testament* (Grand Rapids: Eerdmans, 1996), 24n8, 166.

10. The Hebrew noun for "a proverb" means "a likeness" (*māšāl*, used 40 times in the OT); it is from a verb meaning "to be like" (*māšal*, used 17 times in the OT). The Hebrew title of the book of Proverbs is *Mishlë* [a mas. pl. construct/genitive noun] Š*ᵉlōmōh* [a proper noun]: "The Proverbs of Solomon." Kidner, also commenting on Prv 1:1, the title, explains the various biblical uses of the term "proverb": *The proverbs*: the opening noun (*mišlê*) gives the book its name in the Hebrew Bible as in ours. The Heb. term (in the singular, *māšāl*) basically means "a comparison" (e.g. the sharp simile such as—at random—11:22; 12:4; or the full-grown allegory of Ezk 17:2; cf. Jdg 9:8), but it came to stand for any kind of sage pronouncement, from a maxim or observation (see the middle chapters, *passim*) to a sermon (e.g., chap. 5), and from a wisecrack (Ezk 18:2) to a doctrinal revelation (Ps 49:4). See also the companion terms in v. 6 (Kidner, *Proverbs: An Introduction and Commentary*, 58).

11. For dating the persons connected with the book of Proverbs, plus all other dating matters, see Merrill, *Kingdom of Priests: A History of Old Testament Israel*, 2nd ed. (Grand Rapids: Baker Academic, 2008), 210, 260, 265, 430, etc.

12. By the inclusion of the collection of proverbs attributed to "the men of Hezekiah, king of Judah" (Prv 25:1), the latest date of the final editorialized book of Proverbs must have been within the time framework of the reign of Hezekiah (from 715 to 686 BC). Waltke says, "Since no tendentious purpose can be suspected in the mentioning of the otherwise unknown 'men of Hezekiah,' this is first-rate historical evidence that as early as 700 BC, Israel associated Solomon with proverbs. . . . The care to preserve and transmit Solomon's spiritual heritage is entirely consistent with this reforming king" (Bruce K. Waltke, *The Book of Proverbs: Chapters 15-31* [Grand Rapids: Eerdmans, 2005], 301n8). For the dating of Hezekiah's reign and his events, see Merrill, *Kingdom of Priests: A History of Old Testament Israel*, 422–446. This historical reference to "the men of Hezekiah, king of Judah" means that, from an intertextual biblical theology perspective, the messianic prophecies that preceded and included Hezekiah must also have served as the messianic backdrop to the book of Proverbs. These messianic prophecies would have included: Isa 7:14; 9:6-7; 11:1-16; 52:13–53:12; 61:1-11 (remembering that Isaiah and Hezekiah sustained a close personal relationship: Isa 1:1; 36–39; 2Kg 18–19; 2Chr 32:1-23); Mic 5:2 (also remembering that Micah was a contemporary of Isaiah and Hezekiah; cf. Isa 1:1; Mic 1:1).

13. Concerning the messianic nature of the Davidic covenant referred to in Ps 89, see Allen P. Ross, "Psalms," in *The Bible Knowledge Commentary: Old Testament Edition*, ed. John F. Walvoord and Roy B. Zuck (Wheaton, IL: Victor Books, 1985), 857–858; also idem, *A Commentary on the Psalms: Volume 2 (42–89)*, Kregel Exegetical Library (Grand Rapids: Kregel Academic, 2013), 823. Kaiser calls "Psalm 89, a commentary on 2 Sam 7" (Kaiser, *Toward Rediscovering the Old Testament*, 117n40).

14. On the unilateral, unconditional, and eternal patriarchal promises given to Abraham, Isaac, and Jacob, commonly called the Abrahamic covenant (concerning land, seed, and blessings), see Gn 12:1-3; 13:14-18; 15:1-21; 17:1-27; 22:15-18; 26:2-5; 28:13-15; 32:24-32; 35:9-15; 48:3-4; etc. More specifically, on the eternal patriarchal kingship promises, see Gn 17:1-8,15-16; 35:9-12; (36:31); cf. Gn 49:10; Nm 24:17; etc. It is the Davidic covenant that narrows these general patriarchal kingship promises to one specific man, from one specific family, and from one specific tribe: the Davidic Messiah, David's Greater Son, who will sit on the Davidic throne, reigning over the universal Davidic kingdom forever (cf. Pss 2; 72; 89; 110; etc.).

15. Walter C. Kaiser Jr., *Toward an Old Testament Theology* (Grand Rapids: Zondervan, 1978), 143, 149. In addition, for more details on the Davidic covenant, see ibid., 149–64. Plus, see id., "The Blessing of David: A Charter for Humanity," in *The Law and the Prophets*, ed. John Skilton (Philadelphia: Presbyterian and Reformed, 1974), 298–318. Another intertextual connection between the Davidic covenant, the messianic promises, and the book of Proverbs is the Hebrew term *nāgîd*, used 44 times in the OT, translated "prince," "leader," "ruler," etc. In the Davidic covenant it is used by the Lord for David himself (2Sm 7:8; 1Chr 17:7). The Chronicler refers to the *nāgîd* as the Messiah from the tribe of Judah (1Chr 5:2; "a ruler"). *Nāgîd* is used in two unrelated ways in the book of Proverbs (8:6; 28:16).

16. Martin J. Selman, "Messianic Mysteries," in *The Lord's Anointed: Interpretation of Old Testament Messianic Texts*, ed. Philip E. Satterthwaite, Richard S. Hess, and Gordon J. Wenham (Grand Rapids: Baker Books, 1995), 286.

17. In the similar verses on the Davidic covenant recorded in 1Chr 17:10b-14, the temporal discipline of the father-son relationship in 2Sm 7:14b is omitted, but still retained in Ps 89:30-32. The reason for this omission is that the books of 1–2Chr are addressed to the final period of Israel's history. The covenant threat of exile under the rod of men is no longer a viable option (2Sm 7:14b; Ps 89:30-32; cf. Lv 26:40-46; Dt 30:1-20; 2Chr 36:19-23; etc.). The last kings of Israel and Judah (20 each) have come and gone, each under the rod of men, each failing to meet the high calling of God in the Davidic covenant. This divine approach to Israel's history has been called "The Deuteronomic History" (Deuteronomy–Kings) [also called "The Deuteronomistic History"]. For more on this, see Bruce K. Waltke, with Charles Yu, *An Old Testament Theology: An Exegetical, Canonical, and Thematic Approach* (Grand Rapids: Zondervan, 2007), 21; cf. 57–58, 93, 155–56, 373–74, 479–80, 544–46, 624n2, 689–692. Plus, Sailhamer, *Introduction to Old Testament Theology: A Canonical Approach*, 308n52. Sailhamer also applied the Deuteronomic History to Solomon, "The deuteronomic lesson that if the king is not faithful his kingdom would fall into the hands of his enemies is applied to Solomon in 1 Kings" [cf. Dt 17:14-20; 28:36ff.; etc.] (Ibid., 306). For a more detailed explanation of the Deuteronomic History, see John H. Sailhamer, *The NIV Compact Bible Commentary* (Grand Rapids: Zondervan, 1994), 175–78, 227–28.

18. The phrase "the rod of men," whereby Israel came under the severe temporal discipline of other nations (both in national invasion and national exile), was applied to three groups: the Midianites (Isa 9:4); Assyria (Isa 10:5,24); and Babylon (Lam 3:1; Ezk 7:10-11; Mic 5:1).

19. John H. Sailhamer, *Old Testament History*, The Zondervan Quick Reference Library (Grand Rapids: Zondervan, 1998), 58, 64.

20. Sailhamer, *The Books of the Bible*, 31. Also see id., *The NIV Compact Bible Commentary*, 241.

21. Kaiser, *Toward an Old Testament Theology*, 152.

22. The Hebrew term for the noun "wisdom" is *ḥokmâ* and the Hebrew term for the adjective "wise" is *ḥākām*. Both of these terms carry the idea of "a skill" which ultimately produces a thing of beauty and harmony, a lasting legacy. Dumbrell says about the book of Proverbs, "Proverbs is a book about wisdom and its application to human life. The Hebrew word *ḥokmâ*, 'wisdom,' refers broadly to some skill or expertise, a natural endowment that one may possess, intelligence of most general kind" (Dumbrell, *The Faith of Israel: Its Expression in the Books of the Old Testament*, 223). For the non-ethical/moral uses of "wisdom" in the sense of "a skill," see Ex 28:1-3ff.; 35:25-26,30-35; 36:1-8; etc. For the ethical uses of the noun "wisdom" in the sense of a moral "skill," see the book of Proverbs where the term "wisdom" is used 42 times and in the OT a total of 149 times. And for the ethical uses of the adjective "wise," also in the sense of a moral "skill," see the book of Proverbs where the term "wise" is used 47 times and in the OT a total of 138 times. Also see Waltke, *The Book of Proverbs: Chapters 15–31*, 76–78, 93–100; plus Kaiser, *Toward an Old Testament Theology*, 175–78.

23. Kidner, *Proverbs: An Introduction and Commentary*, 13.

24. The noun "king" (Hb. *melek*) in the book of Proverbs appears 32 times, both in the singular (22 times) and the plural (10 times), and a total of 2,523 times in the OT. The related verb "to reign" (Hb. *mālak*) is used two more times in Proverbs (Prv 8:15; 30:22), plus a total of 347 times in the OT.

25. Quoted, as well as adapted, from Waltke, *The Book of Proverbs: Chapters 1–15, passim*; also *The Book of Proverbs: Chapters 15–31, passim*.

26. Thomas R. Schreiner, *The King in His Beauty: A Biblical Theology of the Old and New Testaments* (Grand Rapids: Baker Academic, 2013), 294.

27. The verb "framed" functions as a literary marker used of the same term or phrase at the beginning and the conclusion of a major section, like the use of bookends, bracketing, or framing (as the use of "son" in Prv. 1:1 and 30:4). Another literary device used in the same way in biblical studies is the Latin term *inclusio*.

28. The Hebrew term *bēn*, translated "son," is used a total of 46 times in the book of Proverbs. It is used in the singular 41 times and in the plural five times. In addition, it is used in the Hebrew with the first person common singular pronominal suffix, translated "my," for another 22 times in the singular ("my son") and another four times in the plural ("my sons").

29. The OT books (or sections) that were recorded after the initial granting of the Davidic covenant (in 2Sm 7) are: 2Sm 8–24, 1–2 Kings, 1–2 Chronicles, Ezra, Nehemiah, Esther, select Psalms, Proverbs, Ecclesiastes, Song of Songs, the Major and Minor Prophets; and additionally, of course, the NT.

30. Arnold G. Fruchtenbaum, *Messiah Yeshua, Divine Redeemer: Christology from a Messianic Perspective*, Ariel's Come and See Series, vol. 3 (San Antonio: Ariel Ministries, 2015), 44–45.

31. J. Pye Smith, *Scripture Testimony, etc.*, I. 469 (n.p., n.d.), quoted in John Peter Lange, *Lange's Commentary on the Holy Scriptures: Critical, Doctrinal, and Homiletical: Proverbs, Ecclesiastes, Song of Solomon*, vol. 5, trans. Philip Schaff (Grand Rapids: Zondervan, 1974), I. 248.

32. Lange, *Lange's Commentary on the Holy Scriptures*, 248.

33. Sailhamer, *The NIV Compact Bible Commentary*, 354–355.

34. Proverbs 1:7 and 31:30 form another *inclusio* (see note #27 above).

35. Kaiser, *Toward an Old Testament Theology*, 169. Kaiser then went on to say, "In addition to its appearance as the motto for the book of Proverbs, the 'fear of the Lord' occurs thirteen more times in that book: 1:29; 2:5; 8:13; 9:10; 10:27; 14:26-27; 15:16,33; 16:6; 22:4; and 23:17. In addition to this, one should consider the verbal forms in 3:7; 14:2; 24:21; and 31:30" (ibid., 170).

36. C. Bridges, *An Exposition of Proverbs* (Evansville: Sovereign Grace Book Club, 1959), 3–4, quoted in Waltke, *The Book of Proverbs: Chapters 1–15*, 101. For a detailed discussion of "the fear of the Lord," see Bruce K. Waltke, "The Fear of the Lord: The Foundation for a Relationship with God," in *Alive to God: Studies in Spirituality Presented to James Houston*, ed. J. I. Packer and Loren Wilkinson (Downers Grove, IL: InterVarsity, 1992), 17–33.

37. Schreiner, *The King in His Beauty: A Biblical Theology of the Old and New Testaments*, 299.

38. Baylis says concerning Isa 11:1-3, "The name of Solomon became known not only for royal splendor and proverbs but also stood for the idea of the wise king—in spite of his failures in old age. . . . Yet Isaiah predicts a future king in David's line who would be perfect in his wise rule [cf. Isa 11:2-3]. . . . The King with these qualities will provide Israel with a ruler who will do what no king has managed to date—bring perfect justice and peace (Isa 11:3-9)" [Albert H. Baylis, *From Creation to the Cross: Understanding the First Half of the Bible* (Grand Rapids: Zondervan, 1996), 266–267].

39. Ibid.

40. Ortlund, *Proverbs: Wisdom That Works*, 26–27.

Proverbs 8

The Messiah: Personification of Divine Wisdom

SETH D. POSTELL

Proverbs 8:22-31 has long been regarded as an important passage for the Christology of the Church. For many throughout Church history, this passage referred to the preincarnate Son of God, Divine Wisdom, who is the Father's eternal delight and through whom all things were created. In modern times, however, the majority of Christian commentators have rejected the Christological interpretation. Bruce Waltke, in his recent commentary on Proverbs, states emphatically, "The notion that Wisdom is eternally being begotten is based on Christian dogma, not exegesis. . . . Augustine, Calvin, et al. erred in that they wrongly interpreted Wisdom as a hypostasis of God that they equated with Jesus Christ and not as a personification of the sage's wisdom."[1]

The thesis of this article is that Prv 8:22-31 does in fact refer to God's eternal Son, through whom the universe was created. The goal of this exposition is to invite God's people to emulate the Father by joining Him in the delight of His Son. The first section of this article will examine how Prv 8 was interpreted in early Jewish and Christian sources. The second section will look at the place of Proverbs within the Hebrew canon and also set the context of chap. 8 within the book itself. There it will be argued that the messianic interpretation is substantiated by the innertextual testimony of Prv 30:4-6. The third section will offer an exposition of the passage.

THE PROMINENCE OF PROVERBS 8:22-31 IN THE HISTORY OF INTERPRETATION

The prominence of Prv 8 in the effective history of interpretation, both Jewish and Christian, is amazing. Before looking at how this passage influenced the Targums and Rashi in their interpretation of Gn 1:1, it is crucial to recognize that Prv 8 has not only *been* interpreted, it *is* an interpretation. There is an obvious correlation between this portion of Scripture and the early chapters of Genesis. Most striking of all is the appearance of "beginning" (v. 22; *reshit*) in the opening colon of this poem. In Prv 8:22, the "beginning" chronologically precedes "the beginning" of Gn 1:1. In other words, if Gn 1:1 is understood temporally ("In the beginning") then Prv 8:22 personifies this as One who was with God before the beginning.[2] The "beginning" One is with God before the works of old (8:22b), before the depths (8:24), before the heavens were fashioned (8:27-28), before creation.

Proverbs 8:22-31 has many other words besides "beginning" (*reshit*) in common with the early chapters of Genesis.[3] These lexical similarities indicate that Prv 8:22-31 should be understood as a poetic (and theological) interpretation of Gn 1:1. It is clear from the Aramaic Targums and Rashi that this interpretation was taken seriously. In fact, Prv 8:22-31 proved to be an interpretation so powerful that subsequent interpreters did not read Gn 1:1 apart from the interpretation offered in Prv 8.

The Fragmentary Targum (FT) likely preserves a pre-Christian interpretation of Gn 1:1, and reflects an understanding of the creation account informed by Prv 8. The FT uses the single word *reshit* in Gn 1:1 twice, once temporally and the second nominally. Thus, the word *reshit* is first included to mean "in the beginning." Then, with its intertextual connotation connecting it to Prv 8, it is identified as the personification of wisdom. Therefore, the FT reads, "In the beginning (*reshit*) with wisdom (*reshit* = *chochmah*) God created the heavens and the earth."[4] This interpretation of the creation account has been noticeably influenced by the wisdom literature in the OT.[5] There are many clues within the opening and closing chapters of the Pentateuch to suggest that such a reading is also consistent with the final composition of the Pentateuch itself.[6]

More remarkable than the FT is the famous Targum Neophyti (TN). This Targum, even more expansive than the FT, includes yet a third interpretation of *reshit*: "In the *beginning*, with *wisdom*, the *Son* of the LORD[7] created the heavens and the earth."[8] To many modern readers, this extraordinary pre-Christian interpretation appears fanciful. Several lines of evidence, however, suggest that this Targum offers an interpretation that is attentive to the details of Gn 1:1 within the final composition of the Pentateuch and also identical to the interpretation of the creation account provided by the book of Proverbs.

There are at least four textual factors that support TN interpretation of Gn 1:1: (1) the poetic and literary qualities of Gn 1:1 lend themselves to a poetic interpretation;[9] (2) *rishonah*, ("at first") rather than *reshit* ("beginning") is the proper Hebrew word for initiating temporal sequence in Hebrew;[10] (3) the appearance of *reshit* in the poetic-eschatological seams of the Pentateuch (Gn 49:3; Nm 24:20; Dt 33:21); and finally, (4) the interpretation of Gn 1:1 offered by the book of Proverbs. Rashi, following in the tradition of the Targums, refers to Prv 8:22 in his interpretation of Gn 1:1. He writes, "For the sake of the Torah [by the Torah] God created the heavens and the earth."[11] Proverbs 8:22 left an indelible mark on the Jewish interpretation of the creation account.

Proverbs 8 also proved to be an important passage for the Christology of the early Church fathers. Among the Church fathers who understood Prv 8:22-31 as a reference to the Son of God are Justin Martyr, Athenagoras, Tertullian, Origen, Eusebius of Caesarea, Athanasius, Hilary of Poitiers, and Augustine.[12] Proverbs 8, however, was also wielded as a textual weapon by the Arian heretics, largely because of the Septuagint's rendering of the Hebrew *kanah* ("possess," "create," or "beget") as *ktizo* ("create"). The Arians used this verse to argue that the Son of God was created (see below for the response to this exegetical claim).[13]

PLACE OF PROVERBS IN THE CANON AND CHAPTER 8 IN THE BOOK

The book of Proverbs appears in the final portion of the tripartite division of the Hebrew canon, the Writings. Proverbs follows Job and precedes the book of Ruth. Several textual factors suggest that the "Canonicler"[14] intentionally placed Proverbs between these two books based on his interpretation of the individual books. The book of Job introduces Job as an upright man who departs from evil (1:1,8; 2:3; 28:28), a phrase that appears just shy of center in the book of Proverbs, according to the Masoretic number of verses (16:17).[15]

A key theme in the book of Job is mediation. Job not only appears as a mediator in the opening and closing chapters of the book, Satan's accusation of Job is rich with courtroom imagery. Furthermore, in key places in the book he calls for a mediator who will stand between himself and God (9:2-3,15,32-33; 16:19-21). The infinite divide separating Job (and all humanity) from God is divine wisdom (see 28:12-28; 38:36-37).

On the other side of Proverbs is the book of Ruth. Appended to the book of Proverbs is an acrostic dedicated to a virtuous woman (Prv 31:10-31). John Sailhamer calls attention to several key terms in this poem that have strategic import in the book of Ruth. Most noticeable is the "virtuous woman" (Prv 31:10; Ru 3:11) who is praised at the gate (Prv 31:31; Ru 3:11).[16] Ruth's virtue is tied not only to her decision to leave her people and their gods (like the patriarch Abraham), but also to her personal participation in God's covenant purposes for and through David (Ru 4:17-22; Gn 49:8-12).

The position of these three books in the Hebrew canon, though not inspired, does offer valuable insight for interpreting Proverbs. The book of Proverbs, throughout, praises wisdom and its importance in the horizontal and vertical directions (toward man and God). In the canon, Proverbs anchors Job's pursuit of a mediator into God's promises to the house of David. Furthermore, a great place of prominence must be attributed to Prv 8:22-31 within the Wisdom literature of the Hebrew Bible. It offers the answer to Job's pursuit: God's firstborn Son, God's eternal wisdom, is the mediator between God and men.

The book of Proverbs displays certain compositional features essential for interpretation. Sailhamer divides the book into four major sections: Title (1:1), Prologue (chaps. 1–9), Body of the Book (chaps. 10–24; 25–29), and Conclusion (chaps. 30:1-33; 31:1-9; 31:10-31).[17] Brevard Childs calls attention to two important passages in the final composition of the book: Prv 8:22-31 and 30:5-6. Childs calls chap. 8 "the most striking development of the 'self-revelation' of wisdom (cf. Job 28; Sir 24). . . . [I]ts hermeneutical effect for interpreting the whole book is worth exploring."[18] Childs further suggests that Prv 30:5-6, a passage rich with intertextual references, many of which are directly related to the coming Messiah,[19] serves to ground wisdom theology into Israel's Sacred Scripture.[20] If Childs has correctly identified Prv 8:22-31 and 30:5-6 as holding a place of prominence in the book, then 30:4 is all the more striking, for this verse binds Prv 8:22-31 and 30:5-6 together. Here, the hypostasis of Wisdom (chap. 8) is firmly rooted within the framework of God's promises contained in the Sacred Scripture. "Who has ascended into heaven and descended? Who has gathered the wind in His fists? Who has wrapped the waters in His garment? Who has established all the ends of the earth? What is His name or His [S]on's name? Surely you know!"[21] This verse, according to Sailhamer, is an intentional allusion to Prv 8:27-30, for the purpose of "raising the question of the identity of the One who is with God and who brings wisdom from God to the human race."[22] The answer is provided by the author: it is God's Son, the promised Messiah.

AN EXPOSITION OF PROVERBS 8:22-31

Proverbs 8:22-31 may be divided into two stanzas. Verses 22-26 emphasize the supernatural nature of Wisdom and vv. 27-31 highlight the participation of Wisdom in the creation of the world. Several features of the Hebrew text suggest that *reshit* should be translated, not temporally ("the beginning"), but as a reference to the firstborn Son. First, several words are used in the Hebrew text, all of which suggest "birth" or "begetting" language.[23] For instance, though *kanah* is used synonymously with the verb "create" in certain places (see Gn 14:19,22), it first occurs in Gn 4:1, referring to birth. The abundance of lexical connections linking Prv 8:22-31 with the early chapters of Genesis likely forms the backdrop for interpreting *kanah* in v. 22. Genesis 4:1 reads: "I have begotten (*kanah*) a man with the LORD" (author translation). This verse appears to mirror Prv 8:22.[24]

In addition to the use of *kanah*, several other "begetting" words are also used in this passage. In vv. 24-25, the author uses the word *cholal*, "to bring forth, to travail [in childbirth]" (see Isa 51:2; Job 39:1; Dt 32:18). Another word that resonates with "child" imagery is *sha'ashuim* ("delight;" vv. 30,31). This word is used seven times in the Hebrew Bible, not counting the two references in Prv 8:30-31; five times for the Torah (see Pss 119:24,77,92,143,174), and twice for Israel as God's delight (Isa 5:7; Jer 31:20). Particularly helpful is the reference in Jer 31:20: "Isn't Ephraim a precious son to Me, a *delightful* child?" This reference to a "delightful child" in Jeremiah may shed light on the enigmatic *'amon* in v. 30. Though this is translated as "master workman" or "craftsman" in the HCSB, NASB, ESV, NIV, and NKJV, Harmut Gese convincingly argues for another translation: "a child sitting on the lap." He writes:

> The frequently discussed question of the meaning of *'mon* in v. 30 seems to me to be answered best with the basic signification of the root *'mn* (qal): "to hold on one's lap." God is imaged here as sitting on a throne in the act of creation while wisdom seated on his lap, as his child, shares the royal position (cf. wisdom as companion, Sap. 9:4), even the masculine form is explained in this explanation because it avoids an otherwise obscene idea.[25]

Gese's explanation is consistent with the other "begetting" words in the passage. For the reasons mentioned above, and considering the innertextual connection to Prv 30:4, a likely translation of Prv 8:22 is: "The Lord has begotten me, the firstborn [Son] of his ways." It is also worth noting that the word *nisachti* ("I was established" NASB) in v. 23 is used in only one other place in the Hebrew Bible, Ps 2:6: "I have installed *(nisach)* my king upon Zion, my holy mountain." The JPS retains this royal imagery: "From the distant past I was enthroned."[26]

An important question any exposition of Prv 8 must tackle is whether or not Wisdom is created or eternal. To answer this question, it is important to keep the following in mind: (1) the LXX wrongly rendered *kanah* as "create," rather than "beget," causing the Church fathers a terrible, but unnecessary, headache; (2) this passage is a poetic interpretation of the creation account; poetic imagery must never be pressed too far; and (3) Wisdom exists, here, before creation. With respect to this third point, Franz Delitzsch writes, "[S]ince to her (wisdom) the poet attributes an existence preceding the creation of the world, he thereby declares her to be eternal, for to be before the world is to be before time."[27] Finally, as Athanasius pointed out, it is inconceivable to think of a time when God was without His *Logos* or Wisdom.[28] For these reasons, Prv 8:22-26 must not be understood as the creation of Wisdom at a point in time. Rather, because Wisdom precedes creation, it must be regarded as uncreated, and, as a consequence, eternal.[29]

The second stanza (vv. 27-31) emphasizes Wisdom's unique relationship with God. Although these verses do not clearly spell out Wisdom's active participation with God in creation, information provided in Prv 3:19 by implication informs this conclusion. The primary point of this passage, however, is not Wisdom's instrumental role in creation. Rather the emphasis lies in the joyous exchange between Father and Son in the process of creation. In v. 30, Wisdom is portrayed as a child sitting in His Father's lap, laughing, playing, and bringing rapturous delight to his Father's heart throughout the creation event. One cannot but think of v. 18 in John's Prologue ("in the bosom of the Father" HCSB footnote) where, as Gese writes, "there appears the description of wisdom on God's lap, the *'mun*, known from Prov. 8:30."[30]

The conclusion of this passage (v. 30) holds profound implications for those willing to heed Wisdom's invitation (Prv 8:1-4). Not only does Wisdom bring joy to the Father's heart, but for those who heed the call, Wisdom can bring divine delight to the sons of men (v. 31). The good news is staggering: by virtue of God's Wisdom, the sons of men may participate in the delight of God!

CONCLUSION

Proverbs 8 provides a glimpse of the Father and His Son behind the veil of man's finite experience. It celebrates the Father and the Son prior to, and throughout, the creation jubilee. This passage has played a formative role in both Jewish and Christian theology. It was foundational to a reading of the creation narrative as something much more than a solo sung by a lonely, apathetic God. Rather, God sang the creation song in Triune harmony, His Son laughing, dancing, and playing in His lap as each day unfolded. Although a Christological reading of Prv 8:22-31 has fallen on hard times of late, Targum Neophyti and the Church fathers correctly understood Prv 8 as a reference to the Son of God, the promised Messiah. Treier rightly says that the Christological reading "does not finally complicate the interpretation of Prov. 8 but presents instead the resolution of a mystery latent in the text."[31] This key passage points the way to participation in the Father's delight for any genuine seeker of God. Those who desire to enter into this joy are invited, provided they can each answer just one simple question: "What is the name of His Son? Surely you know" (Prv 30:4).[32]

1. Bruce Waltke, *The Book of Proverbs: Chapters 1–15*, New International Commentary on the Old Testament, vol. 1 (Grand Rapids: Eerdmans, 2004), n. 104, 409.

2. "Beginning" being understood as a reference to the undefined length of time in which God created the universe. See John Sailhamer, *Genesis Unbound* (Sisters, OR: Multnomah, 1999).

3. See *reshit* (v. 22; Gn 1:1); *shamayim* (v. 27; Gn 1:1); *'aretz* (vv. 23,26,29,31; Gn 1:1,2,11,12,15,17,20,24,25,26,28,29,30); *'al pney tehom* (v. 27; Gn 1:2a); *tehom* (vv. 24,27; Gn 1:2); *mayim* (vv. 24,29; Gn 1:2); *yom* (v. 30; Gn 1:5); *`asah* (v. 26; Gn 1:7); *yam* (v. 29; Gn 1:10); *'adam* (v. 31; Gn 1:26); *terem* (v. 25; Gn 2:5); `afar (v. 26; Gn 2:7; 3:14, 19); *kedem* (v. 22; Gn 2:8). See also *ma`yan* (v. 24; Gn 7:11; 8:2); *kanah* (v. 22; Gn 4:1; 14:19, 22; Dt 32:6; Ps 139:13).

4. *Miqraoth Gedoloth*, vol. 1 (Tel Aviv: Pardes, 1957).

5. See, for example, Ps 33:6, Prv 3:19, and Job 28.

6. John Sailhamer cogently argues that the Pentateuch is a wisdom composition. See "A Wisdom Composition of the Pentateuch?" in *The Way of Wisdom: Essays in Honor of Bruce K. Waltke*, ed. J. I. Packer and Sven K. Soderlund, 15–35 (Grand Rapids: Zondervan, 2000).

7. Some have suggested that "the Son of God" was a Christian gloss, but a careful look at the actual manuscript of TN proves this to be untenable. The spacing in the verse reveals (1) the ד ("of") is original; (2) the ו ("and") was obviously a gloss that was later erased because it was not original.

8. Alejandro Díez Macho, *Neophyti 1: Targum Palestinense MS de la Biblioteca Vaticana, Tomo I, Génesis* (Madrid: Consejo Superior de Investigaciones Cientícas, 1968), 3 (emphasis added).

9. On the literary qualities of Gn 1:1 see Gordon Wenham, *Genesis 1–15*, Word Biblical Commentary, vol. 1 (Waco, TX: Word Books, 1987), 6; Shimon Bar-Efrat, *Narrative Art in the Bible* (Sheffield, England: Sheffield Academic Press, 1984), 203; and John Sailhamer, *Genesis*, Expositor's Bible Commentary, vol. 2 (Grand Rapids: Zondervan, 1990), 35.

10. See Rashi's comments in *Miqraoth Gedoloth*.

11. *Miqraoth Gedoloth* (words in brackets provided).

12. See J. Robert Wright, ed., *Proverbs, Ecclesiastes, Song of Solomon*, Ancient Christian Commentary on Scripture: Old Testament, vol. 9 (Downers Grove, IL: InterVarsity, 2005), 59–71.

13. Michael V. Fox, *Proverbs 1–9*, Anchor Yale Bible Commentaries, vol. 18a (Doubleday: New York, 2000), 279.

14. This term was coined by John Sailhamer to refer to the individual or group of scribes that gave the final form to the Hebrew Bible.

15. The author is indebted to Robert Cole for this observation.

16. John Sailhamer, *The NIV Compact Bible Commentary* (Grand Rapids: Zondervan, 1994), 355.

17. Ibid., 350.

18. Brevard Childs, *Introduction to the Old Testament as Scripture* (Philadelphia: Fortress, 1979), 554.

19. Several key messianic passages are quoted and/or alluded to in vv. 1-6, including Dt 30:12-13; Nm 24:3-9; 2Sm 23:1-7; and Ps 18:50. See Bruce K. Waltke, *The Book of Proverbs: Chapters 16–31*, New International Commentary on the Old Testament, vol. 2 (Grand Rapids: Eerdmans, 2005), 474.

20. Childs, 556–57.

21. Prv 30:4 NASB (capitalization provided).

22. Sailhamer, *NIV Compact Commentary, 354.*

23. See Richard J. Clifford, *Proverbs: A Commentary* (Louisville: Westminster John Knox Press, 1999), 96.

24. "I have begotten a man, the Lord" mirrors Prv 8:22: "The Lord has begotten me" (author translation).

25. Hartmut Gese, "Wisdom, Son of Man, and the Origins of Christology: The Consistent Development of Biblical Theology," *Horizons in Biblical Theology* 3 (1981): 31.

26. *Complete Tanach with Rashi* software (Brooklyn: Judaica Press, Davka Corporation, 1999).

27. C. F. Keil and F. Delitzsch, *Pentateuch*, Commentary on the Old Testament, vol. 1 (Peabody, MA: Hendrickson, 1996), 133. The phrase "before time," is considered by some to be philosophically problematic. Perhaps a better expression might be, "before the existence of any created thing."

28. Athanasius, "Four Discourses Against the Arians," Discourse 1.24, *Athanasius: Selected Works and Letters*, Nicene and Post-Nicene Fathers, vol. 4, ed. Philip Schaff and Henry Wace (Peabody, MA: Hendrickson, 2004), 320.

29. See the exposition and theological evaluation by Daniel J. Treier, *Proverbs and Ecclesiastes* Brazos Theological Commentary on the Bible (Grand Rapids: Baker, 2011), 44–57. Treier notes that those who argue for the language of creation see wisdom as created. This is also problematic since wisdom is part of the attributes of God and must necessarily be part of His eternal being (p. 49).

30. Gese, "Wisdom, Son of Man, and the Origins of Christology," 54.

31. Daniel J. Treier, *Proverbs and Ecclesiastes*, 51.

32. Author's translation.

Proverbs 30:4

The Riddle of the Son

EVA RYDELNIK

The identity of the Messiah revealed by the Old Testament prophets is central to faith in the Lord Jesus. Questions that often arise include: Where is His identity revealed in the Hebrew Scriptures? and What is His relationship with the Lord God Almighty? Clues to the identity of the promised Messiah appear throughout the Tanakh, but perhaps one of the most intriguing passages is the riddle of the Son's identity in Prv 30:1-6.

This article will decipher that riddle by looking first at the context of Prv 30, then at the author and message of the saying, 30:1-3. Next, it will examine the questions of Prv 30:4 involving both the description and the identity of the figures in this verse. Finally, it will look at the solution to the riddle as found in Prv 30:5-6.

THE CONTEXT OF PROVERBS 30

The book of Proverbs is a handbook for wise, godly living—the heart of the wisdom literature of the Bible. The collected sayings were primarily from King Solomon, but the book also included other sources. Applying the principles of Proverbs will supply skill for life and a deeper knowledge of the Lord, as well as insight regarding the Messiah.[1]

The book of Proverbs is not merely a random collection of wise sayings, but rather it has structure and indicates a specific purpose. The book opens with a prologue and an appeal to wisdom with a series of 12 exhortations (chaps. 1–9). The central teaching of the book (chaps. 10–29) comprises wise sayings for study and meditation. These include 375 proverbs of Solomon (10–22:16), and a smaller group of sayings of the wise (22:17–24:34), along with proverbs collected by King Hezekiah (25–29). The book concludes with words from Agur and King Lemuel presenting application of wisdom in specific situations (30–31).[2]

The last two chapters of Proverbs, the sayings of Agur and Lemuel, serve as an appendix to the book. The theme of Proverbs is: "The fear of the LORD is the beginning of wisdom and the knowledge of the Holy One is understanding" (9:10). The riddle of the son, found in 30:1-6, speaks to this core issue as Agur expresses his "knowledge of the Holy One" (30:3) before presenting the riddle of the Son (30:4-5).

THE WRITER OF PROVERBS 30

The identity of Agur is often debated. His name means "to gather," and it has been suggested that this is a pseudonym for Solomon, who wrote the majority of the book of Proverbs.[3] Just as Solomon identified himself as Qoheleth, the "teacher/caller/preacher," in Ecclesiastes (Ecc 1:1,12), here it is suggested Solomon is using Agur to identify his work of gathering wise sayings. Seeing Agur as a pseudonym for Solomon is one of the ancient Jewish understandings from the Midrash, which sees an allusion to Solomon; he was called *Agur* because he stored up knowledge of the Torah.[4] This tradition of authorship was followed by the early Christian traditions from Jerome, but the majority of modern Christian and Jewish commentators reject this idea and take the name Agur to be a proper name of an individual, the son of Jakeh, meaning "obedient or pious." Neither of these names is used elsewhere in Scripture, but they are found as proper names in cognate Semitic languages.[5] Perhaps Agur was a wise man and a contemporary of King Solomon, similar to Ethan or Heman (1Kg 4:31; Ps 89). Anything beyond this is mere speculation regarding his identity. However, far more important than his identity is the content of his message.

THE MESSAGE OF PROVERBS 30

The opening words of Prv 30 give a preview of the significance of the message to follow. First, Agur identifies his words as "the oracle" (*ha-massa, "the burden"*) at the start of the verse (30:1a). This term is frequently used of the message of a prophet given by God (e.g., Prv 31:1; Isa 13:1; 14:28; Jer 23:33; Nah 1:1; Hab 1:1; Zch 12:1). However, the translation of this word has caused some speculation. Rather than translating this as "the oracle," a few commentators have suggested Agur was a Massaite because one of Ishmael's sons was named Massa (Gn 25:14). Ascribing this passage to a non-Jewish writer was an attempt to show that the plain truth of Scripture is evident to the pious of any nation, or perhaps suggesting that Agur was a proselyte. However, this is highly conjectural and not based on the clearest meaning of the Hebrew.[6] It is best to identify Agur as a Jewish sage presenting these truths.

Agur further identifies his words as a prophetic message. They are an "oracle" (*ne'um, "utterance, declaration, revelation"*). The genitive which follows is usually the name of the Lord, Yahweh ("the declaration or oracle of Yahweh") or occasionally, a synonym for God's name (cf. Isa 1:24; 19:4). Therefore this phrase describes direct words from the Lord.[7] This word is used with a human in only four places in the OT. The first two refer to an oracle of Balaam (Nm 24:3,15), the third identifies an oracle of David (2Sm 23:1), and the fourth is here in Prv 30:1 where it says of Agur, "the man's *oration*." The Hebrew word *ne'um* should be translated "oracle" and indicates a prophetic oracle. Therefore, these words of Agur are not a simple collection of wise sayings, but rather in his opening words, he declares that what follows is a prophetic message. This is evident by his use of these two specific Hebrew words for a divine utterance. Moreover, the other three similar usages of *ne'um* introduced a messianic prediction, as does Agur's oracle here. This obviously becomes important in light of the riddle regarding the Son in Prv 30:4b.

As the passage begins, two individuals are specifically addressed. First is "Ithiel," a name meaning "with me is God." Nothing is known about this individual, but Ithiel is the name of a Benjamite who returned from the exile with Nehemiah (Neh 11:7). Next "Ucal," a name meaning "I am strong" or "I am consumed," is likewise unknown beyond this passage. Their names suggest they were seriously seeking to know the Lord. Their exact relationship to Agur is not given, but perhaps they were his sons, disciples, or students. His message was directed to them, but also it was universal in scope, as is all Scripture. However, if the words ithiel and ucal are not considered names, but are combined with a different word division in the MT, with different vowel points, the verse is translated as: "I am weary, God, but I can prevail" or "I am weary, O God, and worn out" (NIV, NLT, ESV). This reading is primarily an attempt to deal with a difficult phrase and make it an introduction to Agur's description of himself, "I'm the least intelligent of men" (v. 2). This "weary" phrase does not seem as likely a translation of the Hebrew as simply Agur's address to the men Ithiel and Ucal (as it is translated in HCSB, NASB, KJV, NKJV).[8]

Agur not only describes himself as "least intelligent of men," he also goes on to describe himself as a man who lacks "ability to understand" (v. 2). He is thus pointing out the need for divine revelation. Most translations continue this negative description as: "I have not gained wisdom, and I have no knowledge of the Holy One" (v. 3). This, however, is not the literal reading of the Hebrew text, which should be translated, "but I do possess knowledge of the Holy One."[9] Although Agur has not gained wisdom, the last half of verse indicates he does have knowledge of the Holy One as demonstrated by the questions he raises.

Agur may lack wisdom, but he is committed to know "the Holy One," a name for the Lord used here as well as in Prv 9:10. This phrase "the Holy One" is a shortened form of the divine title of the "Holy One of Israel" frequently found in the OT, with 25 of those uses in Isaiah. Isaiah 40:25 presents a similar question regarding the work of the Holy One (cf. Ps 71:22; Isa 1:4; 12:6; 41:14; 43:3; 60:9). This name for God highlights His unique character, since He alone is "glorious in holiness" (Ex 15:11; Rev 15:4). He is supreme in wisdom, power, authority, purity, and perfection. Agur refers to his knowledge of the Holy One (cf. Prv 2:5) and displays its significance by raising the profound questions which follow in v. 4. By using two sets of rhetorical questions, he will draw out a strong conclusion.

THE "WHO?" QUESTIONS (PROVERBS 30:4A)

After Agur declares his knowledge of the Holy One, he asks four questions or riddles to provoke the reader to greater understanding. Riddles are a type of word puzzle often used in Scripture as a test of wisdom or to disclose important truth in a thought-provoking manner (Prv 1:6; 30:18-23; Jdg 14:12-14). The first four questions are in an anaphoric style, each one beginning with the same word, "Who," and draw the reader to reach a clear conclusion at the end. All of the questions are answered directly elsewhere in Scripture. These questions are reminiscent of the lessons the Lord taught Job from the whirlwind (Job 38–41), asking questions such as: "Who fixed [the] dimensions [of the earth]?"; "Who enclosed the sea behind doors?"; "Who cuts a channel for the flooding rain?" (Job 38:5,8,25). The implied answer to all these questions to Job is, "God alone." Agur's questions are likewise parallel to a poetic declaration of God's greatness posed in the form of a series of questions and statements, for example: "Who has measured the waters in the hollow of his hand . . . Who has gathered the dust of the earth in a measure" (Isa 40:12). Then the prophet Isaiah supplies the answer to his series of questions: "God is enthroned above . . ." (Isa 40:22).

The first "who?" question, "Who has gone up to heaven and come down?" is an allusion to Dt 30:12. The question is not just who has gone up, or perhaps the answer might be Elijah (2Kg 2:1-18). However, the prophet did not go up and come down with divine wisdom. The Lord God alone is the One who has done this, as He is portrayed in Ps 68, descending from heaven and ascending to His throne in Zion (esp. vv. 17-21; see also Ps 47 and Jn 3:13).

The second "who?" question, "Who has gathered the wind in His hands?" is answered in Amos, "He is here: the One who forms the mountains, creates the wind" (Am 4:13). The psalmist also says, "He . . . brings the wind from His storehouses" (135:7; cf. Jer 10:13). No one but God has this power.

The third "who?" question, "Who has bound up the waters in a cloak?" is similar to the Lord's query of Job: "Who enclosed the sea behind doors . . . when I made the clouds its garment and thick darkness its blanket?" (Job 38:8-9, see also Job 26:8; 37:11). It is also parallel to Isaiah's inquiry: "Who has measured the waters in the hollow of His hand?" (40:12). Only God has the power to collect water into rain clouds, as a cloak. Grisanti observes that "God's sovereignty is often emphasized by means of his control over water [cf. Gn 1:9-10; chaps 6-9; Ps 104:6-7,10-13; Am 5:8]."[10]

The fourth "who?" question, "Who has established all the ends of the earth?" is also parallel to the Lord's question of Job: "Where were you when I established the earth?" (Job 38:4-5). Here the idea is establishing a fixed boundary of the earth by separating the land from the waters and setting a boundary for the sea (Job 38:10-11; Prv 8:29; Ps 104:9; Jer 5:22). This work is unique to the Lord, and found throughout the Scriptures, beginning in the Genesis creation account (Gn 1:1; Ps 104:5; Isa 45:18). God alone "established the earth, and it stands firm" (Ps 119:90).

The phrase "ends of the earth" is frequently used as a synecdoche indicating He has created, and has dominion over, everything in the world (Dt 30:4; 1Sm 2:10; Job 28:24; 37:3; Ps 2:8). The Lord's dominion as Creator is further indicated by the chiastic pattern of these four "who?" questions. The first and the fourth questions compose a merism of "heaven" ("Who has gone up to heaven?") and "earth" ("Who has established the earth?"). The center two questions concerning "wind" and "water" reflect the Lord's daily sustaining care of all of His creation.[11] Thus the four "Who?" questions encompass the idea of the Lord being the powerful creator and sustainer of everything between heaven and earth.

THE "NAME" QUESTIONS (PROVERBS 30:4B)

The "What-is-His-name?" questions at the end of v. 4 are a further request for an answer to the "Who?" questions earlier in the verse. It is necessary to understand that the request for the name in this instance is more than a demand for identification. The divine name is an expression of the character of God by which He reveals Himself (Ex 3:13-15; 34:5-7). Throughout the Bible, He has presented Himself with many identifying names (e.g., God Most High/El Elyon, Ps 7:17; God who Sees/El Roi, Gn 16:14; God Almighty/El Shaddai, Ps 91:1; Lord/Yahweh, Ex 3:13-14). Taken as a whole, the collected names of God in the Scriptures bring to light His attributes and nature. Often the Lord's character and His work are identified by His "name" (e.g., Ex 20:7; Lv 19:12; Ps 30:4; Prv 18:10; Isa 26:13; Mic 4:5; Zch 10:12). The essence of the Lord's character is focused in His name, and reveals His power, authority, and holiness. God is identified as "Holy One" (30:3), and His attributes described in 30:4a are extensive.

The answer to the first "What-is-His-name?" question is straightforward. A close look at the characteristics of the four "who" questions reveals a clear answer: the Lord alone.[12] The question echoes the foundational question of Scripture asked by Moses—"What is His name?" (Ex 3:13)—and "can produce but one answer—'Yahweh.'"[13] The early rabbinic writings also understood this to be God, and they respond to these questions, "His name is the Lord."[14] The answer is found intertextually in the Scriptures and is particularly clear in the parallel ideas of Job, where the Lord asks him questions that demand the answer: not you, Job, or any man, but God alone is the all-powerful creator and sustainer of life. This pattern of "who" with an implied answer of "the Lord" has a remarkable parallel to the hymnic refrain, "The Lord of Hosts is His name" (cf. Ex 15:3; Isa 48:2; Jer 10:16; 31:35; 32:18; 33:2; Am 4:13; 5:8,27; 9:6).[15]

The second question ("what is the name of His Son?") is a more challenging inquiry. It is linked with the first name request, and "since 'God' is the only possible answer to that question, it is striking that the text speaks of his 'son.'"[16] Although this question is frequently glossed over by commentators, it is essential to understanding the passage. The answer lies at the heart of solving the riddle: What is the name of His Son in this passage? Several identities have been suggested as the answer to this puzzling question.[17]

First, perhaps the weakest possibility is that it refers to Agur's sons, Ithiel and Ucal. This is based on the lexical presupposition that in Proverbs "son" refers to the son being taught by his father (Prv 1:8; 2:1; 3:1; 5:1; 6:20). There are two problems with this view. First, although Agur identifies Ithiel and Ucal, they are not identified as his sons. Furthermore, the question of the son's identity is not linked to Agur, but to the Lord, the One who is described in the four "Who?" questions.

Second, the people of Israel have been suggested as the name of the son. This links the name of the son with that of the Lord, as Israel is related to Him. At the time of the exodus, Israel is called God's firstborn son (Ex 4:22). Israel is often called the son of God throughout the OT (e.g., Dt 14:1; 32:5-6,19; Isa 43:6; 45:11; Jer 3:19). The problem with seeing the people of Israel as the answer to the riddle of the name of the Son is that the people of Israel are a group, whereas the question of the name of the Son seems to be demanding an individual person. Jewish interpreters wrestled with this verse by understanding the noun as plural, rather than singular, identifying son as "the children of Israel" or "the name of his sons." This is the LXX translation, as well as Midrash Yalkut Shimoni,[18] but does not seem true to the question of the name of the son as an individual.

Third, the son has been identified as the demiurge, based on the description of God in Prv 30:4. Understood thus, the son is not God, but is somehow involved in the creation, having been created by God. A similar idea is to identify the son as the LXX concept of logos (Ps 33:6) but not fully God.[19]

Fourth, it has been suggested that this individual is an ideal son. He is a son who gains wisdom from his father who teaches him the Scriptures as the source of divine knowledge and understanding. This is a good general description of any individual who has a right relationship with the Lord and applies the Word of God to his (or her) life, as Prv 9:10-11 teaches; however, it seems to fall far short of the urgent question regarding the name of the son.

A clearer understanding of the identity of the Son is found by considering his relationship to the One identified as the answer to the first "name" question, the Lord. His name and the name of His Son suggest a unique relationship between the two, and a hint at the divine quality of the Son.[20]

The book of Proverbs provides a helpful insight into the identity of the Son in the personification of wisdom passage (Prv 8:22-31). In the wisdom passage, God's creative activity is described, similar to Prv 30:4a, and wisdom is present with Him "from the beginning" (8:22-23), at His side as a "skilled craftsman." This innertextual connection further suggests the relationship between the Lord and this Son. Thus, there is a tradition of understanding His name and His Son's name as alluding to a Trinitarian understanding of God.[21]

The implied answer to the first question is the Lord, the Creator of all. As such, there is an implied dynamic relationship between that One and the Son in the second "name" question. Linking the Lord as Creator with the Son raises the implication of the role of the Son in creation. The personification of wisdom is linked with creation in Prv 8. A close textual study of Prv 8 suggests that Wisdom should be understood as eternal, not created.[22] Thus, clues are being revealed to solve the riddle of the Son. Delitzsch points out that the writer of Proverbs "attributes an existence preceding the creation of the world, he thereby declares her to be eternal, for to be before the world is to be before time."[23]

Targum Neofiti (TN), a pre-Christian rabbinic Aramaic paraphrase of the Bible, provides an insight into the role of Wisdom in creation. Linking Prv 30:4 with Gn 1:1, TN reads "In the beginning, with wisdom, the Son of Yahweh created the heavens and the earth." The prophet Jeremiah also says God established the world by His wisdom (Jer 10:12; 51:15), as does Psalms (Ps 104:24). Shepherd refers to the linkage of Prv 30:4 and Gn 1:1 and says, "The Targum also finds support within the book of Proverbs for its understanding of the Son's role in creation."[24]

There is a remarkable comment at the end of 30:4. After asking for "His name" and "the name of His Son," the verse poses an interesting inquiry—"if you know?" (HCSB). This phrase, however, is more likely translated as a positive statement based on the asseverative use of *ki*, indicating certainty.[25] A better translation would read: "surely you know" (ESV, NIV, NASV, YLT), as the same phrase is found in Job 38:5 as "Certainly you know." As in the questions raised in Job, the identity of God is implied as an answer to this question regarding the Son. Based on the reference to the Son, the link to the Creator and the parallelism for His name "Christian interpreters have understood this to be a reference to the Son of God (a subtle anticipation of the full revelation of the NT)."[26]

THE PURITY OF SCRIPTURE AND THE RIDDLE OF THE SON (30:5-6)

The passage concludes by pointing to Scripture as the source of the answer to all these questions. It is from the understanding of Scripture that the answer is surely known (30:5a). The verse affirms that "Every word of God is pure" (*tserupah*), meaning "flawless," a term used to describe the purifying of metal by the smelting process (cf. Isa 1:25; 48:10; Jer 9:7). Thus, every word of Scripture is trustworthy, and has stood the test, and is the source of knowledge by which God, the Holy One, is known (cf. Pss. 119:89,142,160). The source of this truth is God, who is linked here with His Son. Ecclesiastes, another of the wisdom books, identifies the words of wisdom as being given by "one Shepherd," a messianic title used by Ezekiel (Ecc 12:11; Ezk 34:23; 37:24).

The passage then illustrates the reliability of Scripture. First, it points to God and His word as "a shield," a defender who protects His faithful ones; this is a familiar description (e.g., Ps 3:3; Prv 2:7). Proverbs 30:5 makes an intertextual reference that is almost a direct quote of David's affirmation of the reliability of the Lord's word (2Sm 22:31).

Next, God's word is a "refuge," an image used earlier as "the name of [the Lord] is a strong tower" to which the righteous run and are safe (Prv 18:10). Taking refuge in the Lord means to trust in Him by obedience to His word in every circumstance of life.

More significant, in light of the riddle of the name of the Son, is the connection of "refuge" in Prv 30:5 to Ps 2, a key messianic text. That Psalm speaks of "the Lord and His Anointed (Messiah)" and identifies Him, the Anointed One (2:2), as "You are My Son" (2:7), an important correlation to the "name" questions of Prv 30:4b. Psalm 2 concludes with the demand that homage be given to the Son, resulting in blessing to "all those who take refuge in Him" (Ps 2:12). Thus, Prv 30:4-5 is illustrated and the identity of the Son brought into focus by Ps 2.

This section ends with a warning not to "add to His words" or "you will be proved a liar" (30:6). This echoes the words of Moses (Dt 4:2; 12:32), as well as the closing words of the NT (Rev 22:18-19). So the passage concludes with a stern emphasis on the importance of the lesson regarding the identity of the Son.

Thus, taking all the evidence together, the name of the Son is the Messiah. As Gill remarks, "This Scripture is a proof of Christ's being the eternal Son of God; of his equality with his divine Father as such, their name and nature being alike ineffable; of his co-existence with his Father as such; and of his omnipresence and omnipotence, expressed by the phrases here used of ascending and of his distinct personality from the Father; the same question being distinctly put of him as of the Father."[27]

CONCLUSION

Considering the question of the "name of His Son" in the context of Prv 30:1-6, it is best to see this as a reference to the Messiah. The identity of the Son is not a matter of human biological relationships, speaking of father as older and the begetter of the young son. Instead it should be understood as the Son of God as one of the divine persons, coexistent with the Father from eternity (Mic 5:2). This, as Cooper points out, is the view of the inspired writer of Prv 30:4.[28] This text does not give a full-orbed description of the Lord Jesus revealed in the NT as drawn from a broad base of Messianic prediction and profile throughout the whole Tanakh (OT). However, a careful reading of the passage does provide a cogent answer to the riddle of His Son's identity. He is the Messiah, whose personal name is revealed in the NT as Jesus (Mt 1:21).

1. See B. Leventhal's article in this *Handbook*, "Messianism in Proverbs."

2. J. Sailhamer, *NIV Compact Bible Commentary* (Grand Rapids: Zondervan, 1994), 350.

3. For a thorough discussion of the identity of Agur, see Bruce Waltke, *The Book of Proverbs: Chapters 15–31.* (Grand Rapids: Zondervan, 2005), 465.

4. A. Cohen, *Proverbs*, The Soncino Books of the Bible (London: Soncino Press, 1980), 200.

5. Waltke, *Book of Proverbs*, 465, fn 89.

6. A. Cohen, *Proverbs*, 200.

7. S. R. Driver, *Notes on the Hebrew Text of Samuel* (Winona Lake, IN: Alpha Publications, repr. 1984; Oxford 1889), 356.

8. Waltke, *Book of Proverbs*, 455, 467–68. For a more detailed discussion of this issue see Waltke's comments in his footnotes 9, 100, and 101.

9. Sailhamer, *NIV Compact Bible Commentary*, 354. See also *The Jewish Study Bible* (Oxford: JPS, 2004), note on Prv 30:3.

10. M. A. Grisanti, *New International Dictionary of Old Testament Theology*, 2:929, s.v. *mayim*.

11. Waltke, *Book of Proverbs*, 471–72.

12. R. K. Harrison, "Proverbs" in *Baker Commentary on the Bible*, ed. W. A. Elwell, (Grand Rapids: Baker, 1989), 429.

13. J. Pauls, "*Proverbs 30:1–6*, 'The Words of Agur' as Epistemological Statement" (ThM thesis, Regents College, 1998), 117; quoted from Waltke, *The Book of Proverbs*, 473.

14. B. L. Visotzky, *Midrash on Proverbs* (Yale University Press, 1992), 118.

15. J. L. Crenshaw, *Hymnic Affirmation of Divine Justice* (Society for Biblical Literature, Dissertation Series 24: Missoula: Scholars, 1975), 75–92.

16. D. A. Garrett, "Proverbs" in *Proverbs, Ecclesiastes, Song of Songs*, The New American Commentary, (Nashville: Broadman Press, 1993) 237.

17. C. F. Keil and F. Delitzsch, "Proverbs" in *Commentary on the Old Testament, vol.* 6 (Grand Rapids: Eerdmans, 1980), 279.

18. Visotzky, *Midrash on Proverbs*, 118.

19. NET Bible 30:4. fn 2, 1144.

20. Keil and Delitzsch "Proverbs" in *Commentary on Old Testament*, 277.

21. D. J. Treier, *Proverbs & Ecclesiastes*, Brazos Theological Commentary on the Bible (Grand Rapids: Brazos Press, 2011), 106–107.

22. One essential translation issue is that the Hebrew verb *kanah* should be translated "begotten" not "made" in Prv 8:22. See Seth Postell's article in this *Handbook*—"The Messiah: Personification of Divine Wisdom."

23. C. F. Keil and F. Delitzsch, *The Pentateuch*, Commentary on the Old Testament, vol. 1 (Peabody: Hendrickson, 1966, 133.

24. M. A. Shepherd "Targums, the New Testament, and Biblical Theology of the Messiah," *Journal of the Evangelical Theological Society* (51:1, March 2008), 51.

25. The absolute certainty with which a result is to be expected is frequently emphasized by the insertion of *kiy*. Gesenius, Kautzsch, Cowley, Advanced Hebrew Grammar, Title, Gesenius Hebrew Grammar. W. Gesenius, *Gesenius' Hebrew Grammar*, ed. E. Kautzsch and A. E. Cowley, 2nd English ed. (Oxford: Clarendon Press, 1982), 498.

26. A. P. Ross, "Proverbs," *Expositor's Bible Commentary*, vol. 5, ed. F. E. Gaebelein (Grand Rapids: Zondervan, 1991), 1119–20.

27. J. Gill "Proverbs" in *Exposition of the Whole Bible*, www.biblestudytools.com/commentaries/gills-exposition-of-the-bible/proverbs-30-4.html (accessed February 9, 2019).

28. D. L. Cooper, *The God of Israel, Messianic Series Number One* (Los Angeles: Biblical Research Society, 1945), 63–64.

Messianism in Ecclesiastes

NICHOLAS PERRIN

While the book of Ecclesiastes is not typically associated with messianism, evidence suggests that its so-called narrative frame, comprised of an incipit (Ecc 1:1) and postscript (12:9-14), is stamped with a messianic significance that in turn is meant to shape our understanding of the book as a whole.

The opening verse's "son of David" (Ecc 1:1) has generally been interpreted either as the literal person of Solomon or as someone who was, as it were, channeling Solomon pseudonymously; in the postscript, the "one Shepherd" (12:11) has been variously identified with any one of a number of figures, including Solomon (again), Moses, or God.[1] As I have argued elsewhere, however, both phrases are best understood along eschatological lines, more exactly, as circumlocutions for the Davidic Messiah.[2]

The case for this argument rests on the following considerations: (1) that if Ecc 1:1 and 12:11 were in fact appended to the book (as an incipit and part of a postscript, respectively), they nevertheless seem to have derived from the same editorial hand; (2) that Ecc 1:1 shares substantive connections with other messianic texts of the period, not least the first-century BC *Psalms of Solomon* and the second-century BC Ben Sira; (3) that the "one Shepherd" of Ecc 12:11 constitutes a striking allusion to the Davidic messianic figure of Ezk 34 and 37; and (4) that, once the messianic figures of Ecc 1:1 and 12:9 14 arc understood in tandem, they arguably bear a literary and theological function analogous to Woman Wisdom, the idealized sage figure of Prv 8. These assertions, if true, entail important implications for our understanding of the relationship between Ecclesiastes and ancient Jewish messianic belief.

ECCLESIASTES AND ITS NARRATIVE FRAME (ECC 1:1; 12:9-14)

Any discussion of potential messianism in Ecclesiastes must be properly oriented to the issue of dating. Despite the book's ascription to the son of David (1:1) and its Solomon-*esque* quality, it is far from certain that Ecclesiastes was actually written by the traditionally ascribed author, namely, *the* "son of David," the early first-millennium (BC) ruler Solomon. For various reasons, scholars are more inclined to tie the text to the later part of the third century BC, i.e. (250–200 BC).[3] If this is accurate, then Ecclesiastes was composed at a time when sapiential (wisdom) and apocalyptic categories were beginning to converge. Riding the wave of a messianic fervor, much Second-Temple Jewish literature begins to point to a Messiah who is at once an eschatological figure, making his entrance at the watershed of history, and a sage, uttering the very wisdom of God.[4] Therefore, one should not be surprised if Ecclesiastes, given its historical setting within this milieu, likewise yields hints of a Messiah figure that was at once eschatological and sapiential.

Such hints are no less likely to occur in the narrative frame of Ecclesiastes than in the book as a whole. In this connection, it is important to note scholarship's virtual consensus that the incipit/title (1:1) and the postscript (12:9-14) comprising the narrative frame were most likely attached by one and the same editor who intended to commend the book or otherwise qualify its contents.[5] This scholarly judgment rests quite simply on ancient Near Eastern literary precedent. A conventional compositional technique, the narrative frame was regularly set around larger texts (a narrative or sayings collection) with a view to imposing or reinforcing an overarching logic controlling the text as a whole (body and narrative frame). For this reason, narrative frames are generally assumed to have been put in place by a single author, whether or not identical with the author/compiler of the main text. In either case, unless there is compelling evidence to the contrary, one must naturally assume that Ecc 1:1 + 12:9-14 was added as a piece to 1:2–12:8 (close to the time of the latter's final composition), and as a kind of lens for interpreting the larger book.

ECCLESIASTES 1:1 AND THE DAVIDIC MESSIAH IN MIDDLE JUDAISM

Ecclesiastes begins with an ascription of the book's ensuing contents to a notable figure: "The words of the Teacher, son of David, king in Jerusalem" (Ecc 1:1). The introduction finds comparison not only with the incipits of self-contained books (Am 1:1; Neh 1:1; Bar 1:1 [Apoc.]), but also with the sub-collections within Proverbs (e.g. Prv 22:17; 24:23; 30:1; 31:1),[6] which like Ecc 1:1 use "words of . . ." to introduce a string of sayings. Among these comparisons, Ecc 1:1 and Prv 1:1 stand out for their similar language and structure:

> "The words of the Teacher, son of David, king in Jerusalem" (Ecc 1:1)
> "The proverbs of Solomon son of David, king of Israel" (Prv 1:1)

In both verses, the phrase "son of David" is straddled by, on the one side, a construct phrase focusing on his wisdom discourse ("words of," "proverbs of"), and, on the other side, another phrase focusing on his royal office ("king in Jerusalem," "king of Israel"). Such similarities have led some scholars to conclude either that the author of Ecc 1:1 specifically had Prv 1:1 in mind, or that the two texts were written by one and the same author.[7]

As instructive as similarities between Ecc 1:1 and Prv 1:1 may be, an important point of difference lies in the former's retention of the epithet "son of David" rather than "Solomon" (as in Proverbs). The introduction of a wisdom text with the phrase "son of David" is not only unusual (we have no instance in Scripture in which the epithet "son of David" functions as a stand-in for Solomon), but also introduces a dilemma. On the one hand, it is possible that when the author of Ecc 1:1 composed his text, he meant "Solomon" but for whatever reason chose to write "son of David." On the other hand, it is also possible that the author's use of the epithet instead of the name was meant to convey not so much the historical personage of Solomon but the eschatological role to which he pointed, that is, the Davidic messiah (2Sm 7).

The second possibility gains strength on considering another expression in v. 1: "king in Jerusalem." Again, one must appreciate the oddity of expression. If the epithet "son of David" was specifically and strictly meant to designate David's immediate successor, then one might ordinarily expect not "king in Jerusalem" but "king of Israel" (so the Septuagint [LXX] which emends the Masoretic text exactly along these lines). Instead the text reads: "king *in* Jerusalem" (a phrase without parallel in the Scriptures), implying either that Jerusalem itself was a kingdom or, perhaps, that there might have been other locations from which this son of David could have ruled. Neither implication sits well with the historical reality as we know it.[8]

In my view, the best explanation for this strange phrase comes first by way of the second-century BC text, the *Psalms of Solomon*, more specifically, its 17th chapter:

> See, Lord, and raise up for them their king, the son of David, to rule over our servant Israel in the time known to you, O God. Undergird him with the strength to destroy the unrighteous rulers, to purge Jerusalem from the gentiles, who trample her to destruction; in wisdom and in righteousness to drive out the sinners from the inheritance; to smash the arrogance of sinners like a potter's jar;

> to shatter all their substance with an iron rod; to destroy the unlawful nations with the word of his mouth. . . .
>
> And he will have gentile nations serving him under his yoke, and he will glorify the Lord in (a place) prominent (above) the whole earth. And he will purge Jerusalem (and make it) holy as it was even from the beginning. . . . And he will be a righteous king over them, taught by God. There will be no unrighteousness among them in his days, for all shall be holy, and their king shall be Lord Messiah. (*Pss Sol* 17.21-24, 30, 32)

However *Psalms of Solomon* 17 may illuminate our study of pre-Christian messianism, its chief relevance here consists of its attributing to the Messiah (1) the title "son of David" precisely as a stand-alone messianic title; (2) traits characteristic of figures who embody wisdom; and (3) activity *in* Jerusalem. Partially because the *Psalms of Solomon* was written within the general period of Ecclesiastes, the parallel between the key terms of Ecc 1:1 ("son of David," "*the* Teacher," and "king *in* Jerusalem") and the leading features of the Messiah, as described in the *Psalms*, deserve exploration.

As far as we know, the use of "son of David" (*Pss Sol* 17:21) in this passage is the first unambiguous instance in which the term is used of the Messiah not simply in His healing or exorcistic capacity (as some have argued) but precisely as a title for the Messiah in the full scope of His expected activities. This "son of David" ideology is of course part and parcel of a long-standing expectation fueled by prophetic texts such as Isa 11:10; Jer 23:5; 33:15; Zch 3:8; 6:12. Again, given the vital expectation for a future Davidic Messiah in this period, together with the instantiation of a distinctively messianic "son of David" in the *Psalms of Solomon*, it is not unreasonable to suppose that the author of Ecc 1:1 strategically utilized the phrase "son of David" as an in-house cipher for the eschatological son of David. This is not to theorize that the final editor of Ecclesiastes was claiming that the messianic son of David literally authored the contents of Ecclesiastes, but rather more likely that he saw the future-coming Messiah as the intermediary source of his inspiration.

In Ecc 1:1 the son of David is depicted as a wise teacher; the connection between the messianic son of David and wisdom was certainly not lost on the author of the *Psalms of Solomon*. As seen from the above text, the Messiah's most powerful weapons are the "word of his mouth" (*Pss Sol* 17.24) used "in wisdom" (or "with wisdom"). He removes the wicked from the land (17.23) (cf. *Pss Sol* 17.36-37). Further on in the chapter, the Messiah blesses "the Lord's people with wisdom" (*Pss Sol* 17.35) with "words purer than the finest gold, the best . . . as the words of the holy ones among the sanctified peoples" (*Pss Sol* 17.43). The Messiah characterized here is not only sage-like, but virtually the quintessence of wisdom—very much like the first and immediately direct son of David.

Finally, the phrase "king in Jerusalem" in Ecc 1:1 corresponds to the vision of the Psalms with its focus on Jerusalem as the seat of the Messiah's rule. In the Psalms, the Messiah's goal is to "purge Jerusalem from Gentiles" (*Pss Sol* 17.22), restoring Zion to its pristine glory (*Pss Sol* 17.30). The obvious links here with the messianic Ps 2 (*Pss Sol* 17.23//Ps 2:9; *Pss Sol* 17.30//Ps 2:3-6), which focuses on the Anointed One established on Zion (Ps 2:2,6), reveal that the author of the Psalms takes seriously the Messiah's role as king *in* Jerusalem. To summarize: if Ecc 1:1 speaks to a "son of David" who functions as a sage and rules in Jerusalem, the very same predicates are attached to the Messiah in the near contemporaneous *Psalms of Solomon*.

To fill out the background further, one may also consider another text, this one composed slightly closer to the time of Ecclesiastes: Ben Sira (Sirach). In Sirach 24, the sage adopts the persona of Wisdom:

> Before in the ages, in the beginning, he created me.
> and for all the ages I shall not cease to be.
> In the holy tent I ministered before him,
> and so I was established in Zion.
> Thus in the beloved city he gave me a resting place,
> and in Jerusalem was my domain.
> I took root in an honored people
> in the portion of the Lord, his heritage. (Sir 24:9-12) (cf. Sir 36:13)

Wisdom and Jerusalem are strongly associated here; so too, though more subtly, is the Davidic Messiah. The specter of the Davidic Messiah emanates not least from the recognizable parallels between the "holy tent" of Wisdom (Sir 24:10) and the Davidic throne on which "will sit in faithfulness in the tent of David one who judges and seeks justice and is swift to do righteousness" (Isa 16:5 ESV). Three times in this passage Wisdom takes pains to identify her location: "in Zion" (Sir 24:10), "in the beloved city" (v. 11) and "in Jerusalem" (v. 11), a point not unrelated to David taking his "glorious throne over Jerusalem" (47:11). If, as is often noted, Ben Sira tends to collapse the concepts of Wisdom and Torah, he also merges Wisdom with the Davidic figure. According to Ben Sira and the *Psalms of Solomon* alike, then, the messianic "son of David" distinguishes himself by embodying Wisdom and ruling in Jerusalem. (In the real estate business, they say that there are three cardinal principles to keep in mind: location, location, and location. Perhaps something similar can be said of Jewish messianic expectation, though in this case: in Jerusalem, in Jerusalem, and in Jerusalem.) Strikingly, these very motifs are succinctly crystalized in the opening verse of Ecclesiastes, written not long before either text.

On balance, given the close association between the son of David, Wisdom, and Jerusalem in postexilic messianic speculation, as we have it in the *Psalms of Solomon* and Ben Sira, a messianic reading of the same verse commends itself as eminently plausible. In this case, then, Ecc 1:1 is pseudonymous neither in the sense either that the writer was hoping to pass himself off as Solomon, nor, alternatively, in the sense that he was simply writing as one who stood in the trajectory of wisdom. Instead, the incipit then would serve to identify the wisdom contained within Ecclesiastes with the very words of Wisdom, who in the frame-writer's mind bears close association with the messianic son of David.

ECCLESIASTES 12:11 AND THE MEANING OF "ONE SHEPHERD"

Another line of evidence comes out of the epilogue of Ecclesiastes, a passage that has attracted considerable scholarly attention. The text reads as follows:

> [9]Besides being wise, the Teacher also taught the people knowledge, weighing and studying and arranging many proverbs. [10]The Teacher sought to find pleasing words, and he wrote [*wktûb*] words of truth plainly [*yšr*]. [11]The sayings of the wise are like goads, and like nails firmly fixed are the collected sayings that are given by one shepherd. [12]Of anything beyond these, my child, beware. Of making many books there is no end, and much study is a weariness of the flesh. [13]The end of the matter; all has been heard. Fear God, and keep his commandments; for that is the whole duty of everyone. [14]For God will bring every deed into judgment, including every secret thing, whether good or evil. (Ecc 12:9-14 NRSV)

On the one hand, there is much about this text that would serve to characterize Qoheleth as an entirely typical sage. On the other hand, his role is distinctive. This begins to become clear on close consideration of the Hebrew standing behind the NRSV translation: "and he wrote words of truth *plainly* (*yšr*)" (v. 10). Although a few exegetes translate *yšr* adjectivally (i.e. "honest words"), for most it is more natural to understand the word adverbially.[9] Even so, this does not completely clarify issues of translation. The proffered NRSV reading stresses the clarity or honesty with which the author communicates; other translations want to focus on Qoheleth's technical ability ("correctly" [e.g. NASB]) or sensibility ("appropriately").[10] But marshalling Ugaritic and Phoenician parallels, C. L. Seow convincingly argues that *yšr* underscores the legitimacy of the Preacher's words, offering "an endorsement of Qoheleth's aptitude as a sage."[11] This certainly makes sense, if one chooses to read *wĕ-kātûb* actively. But in adhering to the Masoretic pointing, one could just as easily translate the verse as follows: "and what was written was legitimately [considered] words of truth," that is, as divinely inspired verities (2Sm 7:28; Ps 119:160).[12] Accordingly, this interpretative option is more likely, given the close biblical association between "what is written" (*wĕ-kātûb*) and Scripture itself (see Jos 8:31; 2Kg 14:6; 23:21; 2Chr 25:4; Ezk 2:10; etc.); in fact, in postexilic writings the same form becomes a shorthand way of referring to Scripture (e.g., Ezr 3:4). On this line of interpretation, we end up with the following: "Qoheleth sought to find pleasing words, and what was written [i.e., the 'inscripturated' text] can legitimately be said to be words of [authoritative] truth." In other words, Ecc 12:10 functions as a plea for the scriptural status of the preceding text of Ecclesiastes.

The plea is backed up by v. 11: "The sayings of the wise are like goads, and those from masters of collections are like firmly embedded nails. The sayings are given by one Shepherd." But just who is this "one Shepherd"? As mentioned above, most commentators have suggested that God is in view. Others see an allusion to Moses here; another option presents itself in Solomon. Still others have treated "one" as an indefinite article, thus: "These words of the wise are given by *a* shepherd," that is, any shepherd. Given this array of options along with their concomitant weaknesses, Whybray understandably laments "no plausible alternative interpretation of the sentence has been offered."[13]

But here we must keep in mind that the epilogue is concerned not only with right praxis (12:13), but also with a right source of authority (12:11-12). Cutting across the din arising out of the marketplace of competing Hellenistic ideas, Qoheleth's voice becomes the final authoritative voice. It is the voice that cautions against the incautious study of "many books" and commends the "words of the wise" given by "one Shepherd." Whereas vv. 13-14 exhort the readers of Ecclesiastes to live life according to the reality of eschatological judgment, vv. 11-12, with their reference to "one Shepherd," appeal to a transcendental authority typically associated with such judgment—the wisdom-filled Messiah.

Toward showing that the phrase "one Shepherd" was intended to refer to the Messiah, it is necessary to clarify the connection of the phrase with earlier prophetic material. Two passages are germane, both proclamations of Yahweh:

> I will set up over them *one shepherd*, my servant David, and he shall feed them: he shall feed them and be their shepherd. And I, the LORD, will be their God, and my servant David will be a prince among them. I, [the LORD], have spoken. (Ezk 34:23-24)

> My servant David will be king over them, and there will be *one shepherd* for all of them. They will follow My ordinances and keep My statutes and obey them. (Ezk 37:24)

Importantly, the very same phrase used in Ecc 12:11 also occurs here in these two verses in Ezekiel—and nowhere else in the Hebrew Scriptures. In both cases, "one shepherd" is the symbol for a Davidic Messiah who will fulfill the role of restoring Israel and reestablishing the kingdom. In that eschatological scenario, while Yahweh will judge between the sheep (Ezk 34:22), "My servant David" will shepherd the sheep (34:23) as "king over them" (37:24). This is consistent with the Davidic ideology detected in the *Psalms of Solomon* and Ben Sira.

In the early Hellenistic period, closer to the time of Ecclesiastes, there is recurring reference not only to the Davidic shepherd motif, but also, more narrowly, to the texts of Ezk 34 and 37 which gave it rise. Here, for example, we may think of the *Animal Apocalypse* (*1 En* 83–90) which offers a symbolical account of the Maccabean crisis while drawing on the imagery of Ezk 34 and 37. By implicitly situating the events of the second-century BC Maccabean revolt in the framework of Ezk 34 and 37, the author interprets the same events as preparing for the advent of the Davidic shepherd. For the author of the *Animal Apocalypse*, in other words, David is the *one* shepherd who will unify the once-scattered tribes into *one* people, so that they might serve the *one* God.

Returning to the *Psalms of Solomon*, we likewise find evidence of this text's dependence on the specifically Ezekielian expectation of an eschatological David ruling over his sheep. To be sure, though the *Psalms of Solomon* make repeated reference to the kingship of Yahweh (*Pss Sol* 2:30,32; 5:19; 17:1,3,34,45; cf. Ezk 34:24), this in no way precludes the notion of a messianic rule: "See, Lord, and raise up for them their king, the son of David, to rule over your servant Israel in the time known to you O God" (*Pss Sol* 17:21; cf. Ezk 37:24). Like Ezekiel, the author of the *Psalms of Solomon* looks forward to a theocratic kingdom in which Yahweh and David exert their rules collaboratively (*Pss Sol* 17:28; cf. Ezk 45:8). Likewise, both texts envision the eschatological ingathering of the remnant (*Pss Sol* 17:26; Ezk 37:21) as well as God's judging of oppressors (*Pss Sol* 17:3,10; Ezk 34:22). In the *Psalms of Solomon*, the messianic figure and his subjects are portrayed as being completely righteous (*Pss Sol* 17:36,41); this lines up with the description of the Ezekielian servant-shepherd (Ezk 37:23-24). The close conceptual correspondence between the *Psalms of Solomon* and Ezekiel hardly needs more evidence. Ezekiel may not necessarily have been *the* most important source for the author of the *Psalms of Solomon*, but it certainly was *an* important source.

The same Ezekielian passages figure prominently in the Gospel of John. Part of a text written in the late first-century AD, Jn 10:16 also alludes to Ezk 34 and 37 to advance certain Christological claims: "I have other sheep that are not of this fold; I must bring them also, and they will listen to My voice. Then there will be one flock, *one shepherd*." Here now we come to the last of the four biblical instances of "one shepherd." The connection here between Jesus' self-reference as the "one shepherd" and the Ezekielian shepherd has not been entirely lost on modern commentators.[14] That the motif occurs as late as the writing of John attests to the robust nature of this tradition throughout the course of the postexilic period into the first century.

If the Ezekielian phrase "one shepherd" had its own semantic trajectory, retaining an enduring messianic significance across the centuries of the postexilic period, then it virtually follows that the instantiation of the same phrase in Ecc 12:11 also belongs to this trajectory. Along these lines, the words of Ecc 12:11 ("The sayings are given by one Shepherd") were meant to show that in some fashion the Messiah Himself, likely a preexistent Messiah at that, was the true source of Qoheleth's wisdom. This role was appropriate to the Messiah because the Messiah embodied wisdom; He was, as one of the Gospels would later put it, one "greater than Solomon" (Mt 12:42).

THE MESSIAH IN ECCLESIASTES

Having demonstrated that the messianic ideal has left its traces within the narrative framework of Ecclesiastes, it remains to be asked how this might impact our understanding of Ecclesiastes as a "messianic text." In order to answer that question, we return to the book whose incipit provides the closest comparison to Ecc 1:1, where I would propose that the Wisdom/Messiah figure of Qoheleth's narrative frame takes on a role that is in some ways analogous to that of Woman Wisdom in Prv 8–9, who also bears messianic qualities. Simultaneously a literary construct and theological assertion, Woman Wisdom is employed to introduce the material of Prv 10–30, but her authority to do so is grounded on certain transcendental attributes that approach divinity (Prv 8:22-26,33-36). However one might explain Woman Wisdom, it is beyond doubt that she is described with the most exalted terms possible without explicitly identifying her with Yahweh. The same of course could be said for the eschatological David, at least as He is presented by Ezk 34 and 37, not to mention a number of subsequent texts. At the same time, insofar as both figures offer wisdom with life-and-death consequences hanging in the balance (Prv 1:20-33; Ecc 12:9-10), they both claim the right to be identified with Wisdom itself. We also notice that the two figures carry out similar functions within their respective narratives. Both Woman Wisdom and the Messiah figure of Ecclesiastes are used to introduce (Prv 1:20-33; 8:1–9:12; Ecc 1:1) and wrap up (Prv 31:10-31; Ecc 12:9-14) their respective collections of wisdom material.[15] The rhetorical strategy behind this compositional move is clear: as idealized sage figures, both serve to legitimize the content of the intervening material, a content that may otherwise be called into question by competing pagan "wisdoms" (Prv 9:13-18; Ecc 12:12).[16]

Perhaps, too, in both texts here we have—from the perspective of the ancient Jewish author—a notion of concurrent dual authorship. Although the verses following Prv 10:1 are ascribed to Solomon, Woman Wisdom is the one who stands behind Solomon with her beckoning call: "And now, my sons, listen to me . . . For the one who finds me finds life" (Prv 8:32,35). While Solomon is the personage who gives historic and human expression to the proverbs, it is Woman Wisdom who introduces and thereby authorizes the Solomonic text as inspired text. Likewise, in Ecclesiastes the words of Qoheleth are introduced in a narrative voice who speaks in the guise of a Solomonic figure. Qoheleth's words are not just human or even Solomonic words: they are ultimately "given by one shepherd," the Wisdom-embodying Messiah. Again, for the author of Ecclesiastes, it is the book's roots in messianic wisdom that vouches for its final authority. In this sense, the whole of Ecclesiastes can be deemed "messianic."

CONCLUSION

It is commonly maintained that the incipit and postscript of Ecclesiastes were appended to the body text with a view to underwriting the book's authority. This is only partly right. True, the narrative frame of Ecclesiastes was indeed added as a bid for legitimacy, but its final appeal is not to any historical figure of the past, but to the spirit of Wisdom dwelling within the Messiah who is still to come. Even prior to His coming, the Messiah—the "son of David," "king in Jerusalem," and "one shepherd"—could and would speak through the sayings of Qoheleth. In this respect, Ecclesiastes is not primarily a set of observations on life in past or present experience. Rather it is about living life wisely in the present, in light of the messianic future.

---

1. On Ecc 1:1 see, e.g., Timothy J. Sandoval, "Reconfiguring Solomon in the Royal Fiction of Ecclesiastes," in *On Prophets, Warriors, and Kings: Former Prophets through the Eyes of Their Interpreters*, ed. George J. Brooke and Ariel Feldman; Beihefte Zur Zeitschrift Fur die Alttestamentliche Wissenschaft, 470 (Berlin/Boston: de Gruyter, 2016), 13–40; Stuart Weeks, *Ecclesiastes and Scepticism*, Library of Hebrew Bible/Old Testament Studies (New York: T&T Clark, 2012), 541; Craig G. Bartholomew, *Ecclesiastes* (Grand Rapids: Baker Academic, 2009), 43, 103–4; A. Schoors, *Ecclesiastes* (Walpole, MA: Peeters, 2013), 29, 36.

   While most commentators understand "one shepherd" (12:11) as a circumlocution for God (e.g., Daniel J. Treier, *Proverbs & Ecclesiastes* [Grand Rapids: Brazos, 2011], 230; Daniel C. Fredericks and Daniel J. Estes, *Ecclesiastes & the Song of Songs* [Apollos Old Testament Commentary, 16; Nottingham: Apollos, 2010], 248; Bartholomew, *Ecclesiastes*, 43, 367–9), Michael Fox (*Ecclesiastes: The Traditional Hebrew Text with the New JPS Translation* [Philadelphia: Jewish Publication Society, 2004], 84) argues that this interpretation fails to show relevance to the context.

2. Nicholas Perrin, "Messianism in the Narrative Frame of Ecclesiastes?" *Revue Biblique* 108 (2001), 37–60. For critique of my position on the grounds that such alleged messianism goes unsupported in the body of Ecclesiastes, see Schoors (*Ecclesiastes*, 37, 840) and Sneed, *The Politics of Pessimism in Ecclesiastes: A Social-science Perspective*, Ancient Israel and Its Literature, 12 (Atlanta: Society of Biblical Literature, 2012), 142 n72 and 226 n67.

3. See Bartholomew, *Ecclesiastes*, 46; Schoors, *Ecclesiastes*, 2–4.

4. See J. J. Collins, "Wisdom, Apocalypticism, and Generic Compatibility," in *In Search of Wisdom: Essays in Memory of John G. Gammie*, ed. L. G. Perdue et al. (Louisville, KY: Westminster/John Knox, 1993), 173.

5. So e.g., Michael V. Fox, "Frame Narrative and the Composition of the Book of Qoheleth," *Hebrew Union College Annual* 48 (1997): 83–106; Martin A. Shields, *The End of Wisdom: A Reappraisal of the Historical and Canonical Function of Ecclesiastes* (Winona Lake, IN: Eisenbrauns, 2006), 47, 49–52; Weeks, *Ecclesiastes and Scepticism*, 12–13, 17; with some qualifications, C. Seow, "Beyond Them, My Son, Be Warned: The Epilogue of Qoheleth Revisited," in *Wisdom, You Are My Sister: Studies in Honor of Roland E. Murphy, O. Carm., on the Occasion of His Eightieth Birthday*, Catholic Biblical Quarterly Monograph Series, 29 (Washington: Catholic Biblical Association, 1997), 125–41.

6. On the similarities between Ecc 1:1 and the introduction of Proverbs, see Milton P. Horne, "Intertextuality and Economics: Reading Ecclesiastes with Proverbs," in *Reading Ecclesiastes Intertextually*, ed. Katherine J. Dell and Will Kynes, Library of Hebrew Bible/Old Testament Studies, 587 (London: Bloomsbury, 2014), 107; Schoors, *Ecclesiastes*, 30.

7. As argued, e.g., by G. H. Wilson, "'The Words of the Wise': The Intent and Significance of Qoheleth 12:9–14," *Journal of Biblical Literature* 103 (1984): 175–92.

8. H. L. Ginsberg (*Studies in Koheleth* [New York: Maurice Jacobs, 1950], 12) considers each of the possibilities, respectively, "astonishing" and "amazing"; similarly, R. N. Whybray (*Ecclesiastes*, [Old Testament Guides; Sheffield: Sheffield Academic Press, 1997], 34) and Tremper Longman (*The Book of Ecclesiastes* [New International Commentary on the Old Testament; Grand Rapids: Eerdmans, 1998], 58).

9. Contra, e.g., Fox, *Qoheleth and His Contradictions*, 324.

10. For the former sense, see Whybray, *Ecclesiastes*, 171.

11. Seow, "The Epilogue of Qoheleth Revisited," 132.

12. Schoors, *Ecclesiastes*, 835.

13. Whybray, *Ecclesiastes*, 172.

14. Most notably, see R. Bultmann, *The Gospel of John* (Göttingen: Vandenhoeck and Ruprecht, 1964; ET: Philadelphia: Westminster Press, 1971), 384 n2. See also Andreas Köstenberger, "John," in *Commentary on the New Testament Use of the Old Testament*, ed. G. K. Beale and D. A. Carson (Grand Rapids: Baker Academic, 2007), 463.

15. Estes ("Seeking and Finding in Ecclesiastes and Proverbs," in *Reading Ecclesiastes Intertextually*, ed. Katherine J. Dell and Will Kynes, Library of Hebrew Bible/Old Testament Studies, 587 [London: Bloomsbury, 2014], 107) argues that Qoheleth's stated inability to find a wise woman in Ecc 7:28 echoes the words of Woman Folly in Proverbs.

16. See Bernhard Lang, *Wisdom and the Book of Proverbs: An Israelite Goddess Redefined* (New York: Pilgrim, 1986); Claudia V. Camp, *Wisdom and the Feminine in the Book of Proverbs* (Decatur, GA: Almond, 1985), 186–91.

Messianism in Song of Songs[1]

JAMES M. HAMILTON JR.

In academic discussions of the Song of Songs, the nearest thing to a discussion of the Messiah in the Song is a nod to the Christian, allegorical reading of the Song, which interprets the poetry with reference to Christ and the church.[2] I have yet to find a discussion of the Song of Songs that highlights the interlocking messianic themes of the Song's music: the Song is about Israel's shepherd king, a descendent of David, who is treated as an ideal Israelite enjoying an ideal bride in a lush garden[3] where the effects of the fall are reversed.[4] The thesis of this article is that when the Song is heard in the context of the three-movement symphony of Torah (Law), Nevi'im (Prophets), and Ketuvim (Writings), this lyrical theme, the sublime Song, proves to be an exposition of the messianic motif of the OT.[5] I am suggesting that the Song of Songs (or Canticles), read in the context of the OT, is messianic music that we do not need allegorically imaginative ears to hear.[6]

An allegorical approach to the Song would be characterized by the abstraction of the text from its historical meaning, followed by the pursuit of an edifying, and perhaps fanciful, interpretation. As Tremper Longman notes, the two errors of the allegorists were the suppression of the emphasis on human love in the Song and the imposition of arbitrary meanings.[7] While an interpretation of the Song that reads into it either the relationship between Yahweh and Israel or the relationship between Christ and the church may indeed have its rightful place, it is not sought here.[8]

Rather this study pursues an interpretation that sees the Song in the light of the messianic expectations evident in the OT canon. A recent article by W. H. Rose provides a helpful working definition: "The phrase 'messianic expectations' will be used to refer to expectations focusing on a future royal figure sent by God who will bring salvation to God's people and the world and establish a kingdom characterized by features such as peace and justice."[9] In this vein, John Sailhamer has written, "In the Pentateuch . . . the Messiah is a prophetic priest-king like Moses, who will reign over God's kingdom, bring salvation to Israel and the nations, and fulfill God's covenants. . . . In the Prophets and Writings, we find a full and detailed *exposition* of the Pentateuch's messianism."[10] To use Sailhamer's phrasing, this seeks the Song's *exposition of pentateuchal messianism*. Sailhamer goes on to write,

> I believe the messianic thrust of the OT was the *whole* reason the books of the Hebrew Bible were written. In other words, the Hebrew Bible was not written as the national literature of Israel. It probably also was not written to the nation of Israel as such. It was rather written, in my opinion, as the expression of the deep-seated messianic hope of a small group of faithful prophets and their followers.[11]

If this view is correct, it opens the door to a more satisfactory explanation of how the Song got into the canon than is generally given. On the one hand there are some who see the Song as basically secular, with only an "incidental" connection to Israel's faith.[12] On the other hand are those who would see the Song as a celebration of God's good creation, with a particular focus on human love.[13] Nevertheless, I maintain that Roland Murphy is right to conclude that "the eventual canonization of the work . . . can best be explained if the poetry originated as religious rather than secular literature."[14] In other words, combining the insights of Murphy and Sailhamer, the Song of Songs is in the canon because it was written from a messianic perspective in order to nourish a messianic hope.[15] This messianic hope is rooted in the soil of the promise that the seed of the woman will crush the head of the seed of the serpent,[16] watered by the expectation of a king from the seed of Abraham via Judah, and fertilized by anticipations of an eschatological return to the garden of Eden.[17]

In order to validate this reading of the Song of Songs, the messianic elements of the Song will be discussed under the two broad rubrics of The Royal Son of David and The Conquered Curses of Genesis 3. As these topics are considered, the broader canonical context will be briefly sketched before considering the Song's interpretation of these themes.[18]

THE ROYAL SON OF DAVID

The Hebrew Bible is much concerned with kingship. Genesis readies readers of the OT for a monarch. It would seem that even Adam is presented in royal terms: having stated that man and woman are to be in His own image and likeness, God's first statement about them is that they are to rule (Gn 1:26; cf. 1:28).[19] Walter Wifall finds the early narratives of Genesis so harmonious with the messianic kingship of Jesse's son that he gives the following explanation: "Apparently, Gen 3:15 owes its present form to the Yahwist's adaptation of both the David story (2 Sam–1 Kgs 2) and ancient Near Eastern royal mythology to Israel's covenant faith and history."[20] Whatever view one takes of the relationship between the narratives concerning David and the statements in Gn 3, Wifall's presentation of Gn 2–11 and Gn 3:15 as "messianic" is stimulating evidence that these texts testify to a common hope.[21]

Wifall also argues for a "Davidic background of Gen 3:15" from the correspondences between it and the "royal Psalms." He writes,

> David is addressed as God's "anointed" or "messiah" (Ps 89:21,39; 2 Sam 22:51) whose "seed" will endure forever under God's favor (Ps 89:5,30,37). As Yahweh has crushed the ancient serpent "Rahab" (Ps 89:11), so now David and his sons will crush their enemies in the dust beneath their feet (Ps 89:24; 2 Sam 22:37-43). Other "royal" Psalms tend further to establish the Davidic background of the Yahwist's portrait in Gen 3:15. In Ps 72:9, the foes of the Davidic king are described as "bowing down before him" and "licking the dust." In the familiar "messianic" Psalms, God is described as having placed "all things under his feet" (Ps 8:6) and will make "your enemies your footstool" (Ps 110:1).[22]

It seems more likely that these statements in the royal Psalms and in the David narratives are scattered echoes of the compact, primal narrative of Gn 3 than that Gn 3 was shaped after the Psalms and narratives were in place. But whether the chicken or the egg came first is not the issue. The issue is that these texts are testifying to a common messianic expectation.

The kingship expectation is organically related to the promises to Abraham that through his seed would come blessing for all the nations (Gn 12:3; 18:18; 22:18). T. Desmond Alexander notes that "although he is nowhere designated a king, Abraham is presented in various episodes as enjoying a status similar to that of contemporary monarchs (Gn. 14:1-24; 21:22-34; 23:6)."[23] Abraham is promised that he will sire kings (17:6,16), and Jacob is told that "kings will descend from you" (35:11). Then Judah is blessed with the "scepter" and the "ruler's staff" (49:10). Sailhamer observes that "Balaam's words about a future king in Num 24:9a . . . are virtually identical to Jacob's words about the king of Judah in Gen 49:9b."[24]

Sailhamer writes of Genesis 49:1-28,

> The central compositional theme of this poem is found in the segment about Judah (Gn 49:8-12). It presents a vision of the victorious reign of a future Davidic monarch whose authority extends even to the Gentile nations. The imagery of 49:11-12 suggests that the days of this monarch will be accompanied by a restoration of the abundance of the Garden of Eden.[25]

Then of Numbers 24:1-24 Sailhamer states,

> In Num 24:5, Balaam begins his oracle with a vision of the restoration of the garden planted by Yahweh (24:5-7a) and the rise of a future king in Israel (24:7b-9). The poem thus begins with allusions both to the Garden of Eden, Genesis 2, and the king in Genesis 49. According to Balaam, the king, who is consciously identified with the king in Genesis 49, will be victorious over 'Agag' . . . Most if not all commentaries see the specific mention of the historical king, Agag, as an obvious attempt to identify the Davidic monarchy (which ruled over the Amalekites) as the fulfillment of Balaam's prophecy.[26]

Alexander concludes from these kinds of observations and more that "when . . . Genesis is viewed as a literary unity, there can be little doubt that it is especially interested in pointing towards the coming of a unique king."[27] Observing that "special care is taken to establish the identity of the one through whom this line of seed is traced," Alexander adds to this the claim that "it becomes evident that the book of Genesis in its final form anticipates the coming of a king through whom God's blessing will be mediated to all the nations of the earth."[28]

But this is not limited to Genesis, for Alexander concludes, "By giving due attention to the existence of a unique line of 'seed' in Genesis, it becomes apparent that the entire Genesis-Kings narrative is especially interested in the coming of a divinely promised king."[29] Some confirmation of Sailhamer's claim that the rest of the OT develops the hope engendered by the Pentateuch is provided by Rose's conclusion regarding the predictions of the coming of a Davidic king in Amos, Isaiah, and Micah, "This future king was in many ways an ideal figure who would meet the expectations of peace and justice, which many of the actual kings failed to meet."[30]

This is but a brief summary of the messianic expectations seen in the Song's canonical context. The Song is in harmony with this expectation, for it names Solomon in its opening verse (Sg 1:1). The only Solomon in the OT is the son of David, third king over Israel. Whatever view one takes of the "lamed" prefixed to the name "Solomon" in Sg 1:1 (*leshlomo*),[31] the person who is the immediate referent of the promises to David concerning his "descendant" (2Sm 7) is invoked. It is generally agreed that "Beginning with the time when the oracle of Nathan fixed the hope of Israel on the dynasty of David (2Sm 7:12-16), each king issuing from him became the actual 'Messiah' by whom God wished to fulfill His plan with regard to His people."[32]

The male in the Song is repeatedly referred to as "king" (1:4,12; 7:5), and in 6:12 he is referred to as a prince (HCSB "noble people"; footnote "prince"). The name "Solomon" also recurs in the Song (1:5; 3:7; 8:11,12), and there are a pair of references to "King Solomon" (3:9,11).[33] It has been suggested that when the lover is called a king, for instance in 1:4, what we have is "probably an expression of endearment and esteem."[34] Pope writes, "For the allegorists the king is either YHWH or Christ; for proponents of dramatic theories, it is Solomon; in the Syrian wedding festival the bridegroom is 'king'; and 'king' is a common title of the male deity in fertility liturgies throughout the ancient Near East."[35] The option that Pope does not name is the interpretation taken here: the king is the son of David, presented as Solomon. But the Solomonic king here represents the ultimate expression of David's royal seed.[36] To establish that the designation "king" is used as a "term of endearment," examples of this use in the OT would be necessary. This does not appear, however, to be a meaning of *melech* (king) attested in the OT.[37] Thus, the door is open to the possibility that the male in the Song is presented as the Davidic king, with all the messianic connotations that status carries.

Pope's observation that the title "king" is used in Syrian wedding festivals[38] and in ANE fertility liturgies does not support the conjecture that the Song only uses the term as one of endearment, for these settings are hardly representative of the OT canon.[39] Fox observes, "Nor does the statement in Pirquey [*sic*] de R. Eliezer §16, 'a bridegroom resembles a king,' show that it was customary to *call* a bridegroom 'king.'"[40] Nevertheless, Fox thinks that "'king' is simply a term of affection," and compares this to Egyptian love songs where "The lovers are called kings, princes, and queens because of the way love makes them feel about each other and about themselves."[41] But with so much attention given to the genealogies in the OT, the main purpose of which appears to be the record of the male line of descent of the expected king (cf. e.g., Ru 4:18-22),[42] such a casual use of the appellative in a canonical document seems unlikely.[43] This highlights what seems to be the decisive issue with regard to the Song's interpretation: the Song must be interpreted not only in its ancient Near Eastern context, but also in the context of the OT canon.[44]

Other factors would seem to point to interpreting the references to the king in the Song as messianic. For instance, though Carr argues against the possibility of the interpretation being advanced here, he nevertheless observes, "It is worth noting here that the name David (Hb. *dawid*) is derived from the same Hebrew root as *dôdî* ["my beloved"], and in the old consonantal text the two words would be written in identical form *dwd*. Might it be worth suggesting here that, if the Song is to be understood as a royal wedding song, the king in question ought to be David rather than Solomon? King David, *mlk dwd*, would be the 'beloved king', and the lover of the Song."[45] In the context of the OT canon, the royal imagery in the Song, the invocation of the name Solomon, the similarity of *Dawid* to *dodiy*, and the garden setting all point us to the possibility of a messianic understanding of the Song of Songs.

The Song is messianic in the sense that it is leading readers to combine the images of Israel's wisest king with the hints at her king after God's own heart. As the Song progresses, readers hear of a king accompanied not by 30 mighty men but by 60 (Sg 3:7), while the din of battle (3:8)[46] and the uproar of the harem are a distant memory (6:8)[47] replaced by this idealized relationship (6:9). Here the recent emphasis on the Song as confirmation of "earlier teachings about marriage while adding its own unique contribution about pre- and postmarital passions"[48] is complemented by the fact that the model lover in the Song is also the model Israelite, the messianic king.

This messianic understanding of Canticles is not allegorical, nor need it even be typological; it is strictly historical and canonical. It assumes that the Song of Songs was written from the hope for an anointed king reflected in the rest of the OT,[49] but it neither imposes foreign concepts nor imports the NT into the interpretation of the poetry.[50] The garden imagery and the Edenic quality of the Song call for a consideration of the points of contact between the lyrical beauty of the Song, the pristine bliss of Eden, and the one who would bring restoration.

THE CONQUERED CURSES OF GENESIS 3

Alan Jon Hauser has carefully treated the themes of intimacy and alienation in Gn 2–3,[51] but he focuses on the loss of intimacy and the onset of alienation, neglecting the hints at a return to intimacy seen in Gn 3. These pointers toward reconciliation are developed in chap. 4 and through the rest of the book. That God initiates contact with the transgressing couple at all moves in that direction. When Adam names his wife Eve because she was "the mother of all living" (3:20), he appears to be convinced that they will be allowed to continue in life because God has shown them mercy, and therefore they are not going to die (cf. 2:17). Eve's responses to the births of Cain and then Seth (4:1,25) indicate that she is expecting a fulfillment of the promise of a "seed" who will triumph over the serpent (3:15), and the same can be said of other uses of "seed" in Genesis.[52]

This movement back toward intimacy in spite of alienation would appear to be the rhythm of the Song of Songs.[53] I have argued above that the Song's male character, the king, the son of David, should be understood in light of Israel's hope for the promised anointed one. In this section I wish to explore the Song's gravitation toward intimacy and the implications of the resonations with Eden that can be heard in the Song. One of the arguments against a messianic understanding of the Song might be that it would fail to deal with the details of the Song apart from allegorization.[54] Dumbrell, however, gets at the nature of poetry when he writes, "Since the Song of Songs is a symbolic representation of ideal love, characters or figures cannot be pressed for literal correspondence to historical persons (e.g., to

Solomon or to the daughters of Jerusalem)."[55] It does not seem wise to press the details, but a major theme of the Song seems to be the recovery of intimacy after alienation, and this appears to match the hope engendered by Gn 3:15 for a seed of the woman, who would come as the royal messiah to restore the gladness of Eden.[56] Here I will trace the theme of the abolition of alienation and the restoration of intimacy through the Song, hoping to highlight the messianic meter of the music.

Overcoming Alienation: The Rhythm of the Music

This theme is introduced in the first words of the Song, where the woman longs for the kisses of the king (1:2-4). She yearns for the intimacy she is not presently experiencing. Somehow the love depicted here is love in which it is "right" (*meysariym*) for others to indulge (1:3c,4c). I would suggest that it is upright for all the righteous to admire the Davidic king and to benefit from the depicted glories of the idealized relationship between the hoped-for Messiah and his splendid bride.[57]

The theme of intimacy overcoming alienation continues when the woman appears to doubt her appearance (1:5-7). This attitude is the opposite of the unabashed nakedness of Adam and Eve in the garden (Gn 2:25).[58] Israel's king, depicted here as a good[59] shepherd, overcomes the fears and shame of his beloved with reassuring compliments (Sg 1:8-11). By her confident response and exultation in the king (1:12-14), and through their mutual affirmation and enjoyment of the health of their relationship, the Song's audience experiences their "edenesque" enjoyment (1:15-2:6). The Song then seems to go from verse to refrain, as the daughters of Jerusalem are urged not to stir up love until it pleases (2:7).[60]

Alienation resurfaces in 2:8-15. As the bride observes the king coming for her, they are separated by a wall, windows, and lattice (2:8-9). Seeking to overcome the separation, the king pleads for intimacy. Urging the bride to rise and flee with him to springtime hills (2:10-13), that he might see her face and hear her voice (2:14), he calls for spoiling elements to be removed (2:15). From the bride's response in 2:16-17, the separation appears to have been successfully overcome.

The longing of the bride's dream in 3:1-2 renews the motif of separation, so central to all love stories. The bride passes by watchmen (3:3) before finding the king (3:4) and voicing again the refrain (3:5), whose point seems to be that, when the time is right, love will awaken.

The king comes to his wedding in glory in 3:6-11,[61] and upon his arrival he sings a song of praise to his beloved (4:1-5),[62] followed by a declaration of both her beauty and his desire (4:6-16). She invites him to put an end to separation and alienation (4:16b), and when he announces that he has done so (5:1a), the return to intimacy is celebrated (5:1b).

Estrangement has not been banished for good, however, and the struggle for intimacy continues in 5:2-6. Interestingly, the bride repulses her king, only to be roughly handled by the watchmen, whose presumed responsibility is to protect her (5:7). Then the refrain returns like a chorus between the verses of the Song (5:8).

The question posed in 5:9 provides the bride with an opportunity to extol her king, and the first characteristic named is that he is "ruddy" (5:10 footnote), bringing David to mind (1Sm 16:12; 17:42). After the virtues of the king are sung (5:10-16), another question is posed as to the location of the king (6:1). It is remarkable here that the king with Davidic characteristics has gone to his garden (6:2), where he enjoys the intimacy of his bride (6:3). If the music is in a messianic key, it has an Edenic pitch.[63]

This section is followed by another song of praise (6:4-10), the bride's account of how she came to be with the king (6:11-12), and delight in the gracefulness of the bride (7:1). The king and his bride then exchange the pleasantries of their renewed intimacy (7:1-13), before the slightest hint of lingering alienation is alluded to in 8:1-2. But this alienation appears to be finally overcome in 8:3. The refrain-chorus is sung again (8:4), with a recapitulation on the coming of the one born of a woman, who comes from the wilderness (8:5). Then the song swells and rolls to its conclusion with reflections on the worth of love and the cultivation of faithfulness (8:6-12), punctuated by final calls for the end of alienation (8:13-14).

Details and Impressions: The Melody of the Music

How does the reading of the Song being advanced here deal with the specific details of the text? For instance, if, as I am suggesting, the male in the Song is to be understood as Israel's hoped-for Messiah, who is the woman? This question can be met on two levels: first, with observations on poetic language; and second, with an observation on the nature of messianic expectation. Gordis offers helpful comments on interpreting the language of the Song. He writes,

> It is of the essence of poetry that it employs *symbolism* to express nuances beyond the power of exact definition. . . . Symbolism is much more profound than allegory. In allegory, the imaginary figures that are chosen as equivalents for the real characters and objects involved have no independent reality of their own. The language of symbolism, on the other hand, is superior to literal speech as well, because its elements possess both existential reality and a representational character.[64]

Read this way, the Song symbolizes an ideal relationship in which the lovers are succeeding in overcoming the obstacles presented to love in life outside Eden. To explain every figure of speech moves one closer to understanding, but it also uncoils the poetry's spring.

So if we ask who the female *symbolizes* if the male is the Messiah, the simplest answer is that she is the Messiah's beloved. If it is true that the sons of David who were anointed king over Israel were in a sense Israel's Messiah, then it would seem plausible to suppose that the developing messianic expectation could have extended to the Messiah's most intimate relationship. The Song sings that the Messiah will attain intimacy, and that overcoming the obstacles to it is as triumphant as the subjugation of the nations. Why would Israel's expected messianic king not have a queen? And why would their relationship not be worthy of the most majestic Song?

CONCLUSION

In this article, I have sought to interpret the Song as it might have been understood by a member of the messianic remnant within Israel in the years prior to the coming of Jesus of Nazareth. I am thus trying to read the Song as it might have been understood prior to the allegorizations introduced by both the Rabbis and the early Christians. It seems to me that this non-allegorical messianic interpretation of the Song is simultaneously the most plausible interpretation of the Song given its canonical context,[65] and the most "Christian" understanding of the Song, for the early Christians read similar texts messianically (cf. the use of Ps 45 in Heb 1).

The hermeneutical implications of this study are far reaching. Roland Murphy writes: "Recent critics have been unable to establish an objective exegetical basis for decoding the Song along the lines of patristic and medieval Christian exposition. While this does not negate the value of the expository tradition in its own right, it leaves us without empirical criteria by which to assess the possible connection between 'original' authorial intent and subsequent creations of hermeneutical imagination."[66] If the non-allegorical messianic interpretation of the Song proposed here is correct, it would appear to explain the allegorizations produced by both Jewish and Christian interpreters after the life, ministry, death, and resurrection of Jesus of Nazareth. The Christians ascribed deity to Jesus, and quickly conceptualized Him in ways that corresponded with His divine status.[67] In their view, the Messiah described by the OT would have His people as His bride rather than a particular human female. It is conceivable that the Rabbis developed their understanding of the Song in response to and in dialogue with the way the early Christians treated it. Adjusting their interpretation in light of the claims of the Christians, they might have shifted their interpretation away from messianic expectation toward the allegorization of the Song as the story of Yahweh's love for His people Israel.[68]

To understand the Song messianically, it is necessary to listen to the words, which derived from deep emotions recollected and written afterward, while calmly considering those deep emotions.[69] And perhaps the strongest impression one gets from reading the Song as a unified poem in its canonical context is of a shepherd king rejoicing with his bride in a garden. The Song is certainly ripe with garden imagery, evoking scenes from Eden.[70] Interestingly, what might be the Song's climactic expression of the restoration of the intimacy lost in Gn 3 is expressed in language that echoes the onset of alienation. The end of the curse on the woman in Gn 3:16 reads, "Your desire (*teshukatcha)* will be for your husband, yet he will dominate you." This is reversed in Song 7:10 which reads, "I belong to my love, and his desire (*teshukato)* is for me."[71] Even Duane Garrett, who doubts that this is a "deliberate allusion to Genesis," states when commenting on this verse, "In the Song, the ideal of love and marriage is represented almost as though the fall had never happened."[72]

The Song sings of the son of David,[73] who is king,[74] in ideal terms.[75] In spite of the alienation that must be overcome, this king—seed of the woman, seed of Abraham, seed of Judah, seed of David—enjoys uninhibited, unashamed intimacy with his beloved,[76] in a garden that belongs to him.[77] It would seem that the burden of proof would be on those who would argue that this, the OT canon's sublime Song, is anything other than messianic. This messianic interpretation of the Song not only explains the Song's presence in the canon and sheds light on how it exposits the Pentateuch's messianism, it also connects the Song to the rest of OT theology.

In the music of the Song of Songs, the messianic remnant of Israel got a glimpse of the one they hoped would arise to restore them to Eden. In the fragmentation and ruin the nation experienced outside Eden, though the hearts of her kings were led away from Yahweh by foreign women, the Song sang the beauty of the king who would piece them back together. It is fitting that the Song is poetry, for as Percy Bysshe Shelley wrote, "Poetry is a mirror which makes beautiful that which is distorted."[78]

---

1. This article is adapted from James M. Hamilton, "The Messianic Music of the Song of Songs: A Non-Allegorical Interpretation," *Westminster Theological Journal* 68 (2006) 331–45. Used with permission.
2. This is not to deny the openness of some to what might be termed a "Christian appropriation" of the Song, but that is not what I have in mind when I speak of a *messianic reading* of the Song. In the modern discussion, I have found no one who argues that the Song was intended as a messianic document. See, e.g., Michael V. Fox, *The Song of Songs and the Ancient Egyptian Love Songs* (Madison, WI: University of Wisconsin Press, 1985), 236–39; Marvin H. Pope, *Song of Songs*, Anchor Bible 7C (New York: Doubleday, 1977); Tom Gledhill, *The Message of the Song of Songs* (Downers Grove, IL: InterVarsity, 1994); Roland E. Murphy, *The Song of Songs*, Hermeneia (Minneapolis: Fortress, 1990), 91–94; Barry G. Webb, *Five Festal Garments*, New Studies in Biblical Theology (Downers Grove, IL:

InterVarsity, 2000), 17–35; Renita J. Weems, "The Song of Songs," in *The New Interpreter's Bible* (Nashville: Abingdon, 1997) 5:361–434; F. Delitzsch, *The Song of Songs*, in *Commentary on the Old Testament* by C. F. Keil and F. Delitzsch, 10 vols., trans. M. G. Easton (Edinburgh: T&T Clark, 1866–91; repr., Peabody: Hendrickson, 2001), 6:493–626; G. Lloyd Carr, *The Song of Solomon*, Tyndale Old Testament Commentaries (Downers Grove, IL: InterVarsity, 1984), 31; Duane Garrett and Paul R. House, *Song of Songs/Lamentations*, Word Biblical Commentary 23B (Nashville: Thomas Nelson, 2004); Robert Gordis, *The Song of Songs and Lamentations*, rev. ed. (New York: Ktav, 1974), 3–4; T. Longman III, *Song of Songs*, New International Commentary on the Old Testament (Grand Rapids: Eerdmans, 2001); H. G. Reventlow, "Hoheslied I," *TRE Theologische Realenzyklopädie* [Theological Encyclopedia] 15:501–502; P. Kuhn, "Hoheslied II," *TRE* 15:503–508; U. Köpf, "Hoheslied III/1," *TRE* 15:508–13; J. M. Vincent, "Hoheslied III/2," *TRE* 15:513–14; cf. also W. Brueggemann, *An Introduction to the Old Testament* (Louisville: Westminster John Knox, 2003), 323–28; B. S. Childs, *Introduction to the Old Testament as Scripture* (Philadelphia: Fortress, 1979), 569–79; W. J. Dumbrell, *The Faith of Israel*, 2nd ed. (Grand Rapids: Baker, 2002), 278–83; Paul House, *Old Testament Theology* (Downers Grove, IL: InterVarsity, 1998), 463–69.

3. Though I do not explore it, I should note that the Song is in part set in a city (e.g., 3:2-4; 5:7), and the most natural interpretation is that the city is Jerusalem (cf. the reference to "young women of Zion" in 3:11). Zion is, of course, also associated with messianism (cf., e.g., Ps 2:6; *Pss Sol* 17:22,30; *Sir.* 24:9–12).

4. None of the studies catalogued in Peter Enns, *Poetry & Wisdom*, IBR Bibliographies 3 (Grand Rapids: Baker, 1997), 148–58 (§700–58) are described as (non-allegorical) messianic interpretations. Nor do we find discussions of what the Song adds to messianic expectation in discussions of OT messianism. See, e.g., T. N. D. Mettinger, *King and Messiah: The Civil and Sacral Legitimation of the Israelite Kings*, Coniectanea Biblica, OT Series 8 (Lund: CWK Gleerup, 1976); Antti Laato, *A Star Is Rising: The Historical Development of the Old Testament Royal Ideology and the Rise of the Jewish Messianic Expectations*, University of South Florida International Studies in Formative Christianity and Judaism (Atlanta: Scholars Press, 1997); John Day, ed., *King and Messiah in Israel and the Ancient Near East*, Journal for the Study of the Old Testament Supplement Series 270 (Sheffield: Sheffield Academic, 1998); Philip E. Satterthwaite, Richard S. Hess, and Gordon J. Wenham, eds., *The Lord's Anointed: Interpretation of Old Testament Messianic Texts*, Tyndale House Studies (Grand Rapids: Baker, 1995); Gerard Van Groningen, *Messianic Revelation in the Old Testament* (Grand Rapids: Baker, 1990), 407.

5. Cf. Nicholas Perrin, "Messianism in the Narrative Frame of Ecclesiastes?" *Revue Biblique* 108 (2001), 38: "It is my view that both phrases ['Son of David' in Ecc 1:1 and 'one shepherd' in 12:11] are in fact denominations for the Davidic messiah who functions within Ecclesiastes (in its final form) as sage *par excellence*." I owe this reference to conversation with Tremper Longman, who alerted me to Perrin's excellent study after I had completed this essay. The degree to which the OT is messianic is, of course, disputed in scholarship. For a thoughtful discussion of the issue, see J. Gordon McConville, "Messianic Interpretation of the Old Testament in Modern Context," in *The Lord's Anointed*, 1–17.

6. A messianic reading of the Song might have motivated the translator of the Song into Greek to stay close to the Hebrew. Pope notes, "One would expect to find in the earliest translation of the Song of Songs, in the Septuagint (LXX), some intimations of the mystical or allegorical interpretation. The evidence, however, is surprisingly meager" (Pope, *Song of Songs*, 90).

7. Longman, *Song of Songs*, 70. See also Gerald Bray, *Biblical Interpretation* (Downers Grove, IL: InterVarsity, 1996), 103. Bray and Longman both note that allegorical interpretation can be used positively.

8. See L. Cantwell, "The Allegory of the Canticle of Canticles," *Scripture* 16 (1964): 76–93.

9. W. H. Rose, "Messiah," in *Dictionary of the Old Testament Pentateuch*, ed. T. Desmond Alexander and David W. Baker (Downers Grove, IL: InterVarsity, 2003), 566; similarly, Perrin, "Messianism in the Narrative Frame of Ecclesiastes," 38 n. 3. See also John Barton's narrow and broad definitions of "the Messiah" in "The Messiah in Old Testament Theology," in *King and Messiah in Israel and the Ancient Near East*, 373. Barton helpfully cites Neusner's definition of "A Messiah." These definitions orbit around concepts of Davidic kingship and eschatological salvation.

10. John H. Sailhamer, "The Messiah and the Hebrew Bible," *JETS* 44 (2001), 13–14 (emphasis his).

11. Sailhamer, "The Messiah and the Hebrew Bible," 23. Cf. Isa 8:16–20.

12. Cf. Fox, *The Song of Songs and the Ancient Egyptian Love Songs*, 250: "How then did a song of this sort become holy scripture? We do not know." Fox goes on to suggest, "It may be enough to postulate that the Song, though not intrinsically religious, was sung as part of the entertainment and merrymaking at feasts and celebrations, which would naturally take place for the most part on holidays in the religious calendar. . . . When (according to this hypothesis) the Song had worked its way into the people's religious life and had thus acquired a certain aura of sanctity, the religious leadership legitimized that association by means of allegorical interpretation." I find this suggestion implausible at best.

13. Cf. Duane A. Garrett, *Proverbs, Ecclesiastes, Song of Songs*, New American Commentary (Nashville: Broadman, 1993), 365: "The best interpretation of Song of Songs is that it is what it appears to be: a love song." I would stress

that the instructions for human love are to be derived from the Song's picture of the messianic king. The picture of the ideal messianic king who overcomes the curses does have a secondary effect of inspiring others to pursue the kind of relationship depicted in the Song, but in my view the Song's primary purpose is to celebrate the glory of the Davidic king. This focus will naturally also benefit those who are blessed to behold this picture of the beauty of the consummation of God's promises.

14. Murphy, *Song of Songs*, 94–95.

15. For a history of the discussion of the Messianism of the OT, see R. E. Clements, "The Messianic Hope in the Old Testament," *Journal for the Study of the Old Testament* 43 (1989): 3–19. I am increasingly convinced that the OT is a messianic document, written from a messianic perspective, to sustain a messianic hope. I am advocating this as a historical perspective, not an allegorical one. Not all early Christian interpretation of the OT was allegorical. For a beautiful treatment of the desire to be the mother of the hoped-for seed of Abraham, the Messiah, see Jacob of Serugh's "Verse Homily on Tamar." For translation and commentary of this lovely piece of early Christian literature/interpretation, see Sebastian Brock, "Jacob of Serugh's Verse Homily on Tamar (*Gen.* 38)," *Le Museon* 115 (2002): 279–315. I wish to express my gratitude to Tim Edwards for alerting me to this piece.

16. Jack Collins has persuasively argued that when the term "seed" is accompanied by singular verb inflections, independent pronouns, object pronouns, suffixes, and adjectives, it can be read as singular rather than as collective. See Jack Collins, "A Syntactical Note (Genesis 3:15): Is the Woman's Seed Singular or Plural?" *Tyndale Bulletin* 48 (1997), 139–48.

17. Commenting on Gn 3:15, Stephen G. Dempster writes, "In the light of the immediate context, the triumph of the woman's seed would suggest a return to the Edenic state, before the serpent had wrought its damage, and a wresting of the dominion of the world from the serpent" (Stephen G. Dempster, *Dominion and Dynasty: A Theology of the Hebrew Bible*, New Studies in Biblical Theology 15 [Downers Grove, IL: InterVarsity, 2003], 68). Incidentally, the proposal I am setting forth regarding the interpretation of the Song fits so well with Dempster's exploration of the theology of the OT through the lens of "dominion and dynasty, genealogy and geography" that I was honestly surprised to find that he did not argue for this view in his book. Perhaps he inadvertently moved me to this view, though no one, of course, should blame him for my position.

18. Another argument that the Song was written from a messianic perspective is that the NT interprets the *whole* of the OT messianically (cf. Lk 24:27,44). Particularly relevant here is the messianic interpretation of the wedding song of Ps 45 found in Heb 1:8-9. Pope notes that before moving on to an allegorical interpretation, "Origen conceded that the Song might be an epithalamium for Solomon's marriage with Pharaoh's daughter" (Pope, *Song of Songs*, 89). If Ps 45 can be read messianically, why not read the Song in the same typological way? Though Carr argues against this view of the use of the OT in the New (Carr, *Song of Solomon*, 26–32), I do not think that he has accounted for the arguments presented in G. K. Beale, "Did Jesus and His Followers Preach the Right Doctrine from the Wrong Texts?" *Themelios* 14 (1989), 89–96, and Bruce K. Waltke, "A Canonical Process Approach to the Psalms," in *Tradition and Testament* (Chicago: Moody, 1981), 3–18. Waltke presents a way to understand all the Psalms as messianic, and Beale argues that the NT uses legitimate historical and contextual methods to interpret the OT. Perhaps the common assumption that the NT does not interpret the OT according to its own intended meaning results from a failure to understand the messianism of the OT.

19. Cf. Dumbrell, *The Faith of Israel*, 16–17. Commenting on Gn 1:26, the "image" of God, Dumbrell writes: "Mesopotamian analogies to which we could appeal indicate that the king as an image of the deity was conceived of as a servant of the gods. 'Image' referred to his royal function, as one having a mandate from the gods to rule. . . . humankind is depicted in royal terms."

20. Walter Wifall, "Gen 3:15—A Protoevangelium?" *Catholic Biblical Quarterly* 36 (1974): 365.

21. Ibid., 361–64.

22. Ibid., 363.

23. T. Desmond Alexander, "Royal Expectations in Genesis to Kings," *Tyndale Bulletin* 49 (1998), 205.

24. John H. Sailhamer, "Creation, Genesis 1–11, and the Canon," *Bulletin for Biblical Research* 10 (2000), 93.

25. Ibid., 96.

26. Ibid., 97; cf. also Dempster, *Dominion and Dynasty*, 115–16.

27. Alexander, "Royal Expectations in Genesis to Kings," 199.

28. Ibid., 204; cf. also Rose, "Messiah," 567: "The expectation of a future royal figure is from the beginning focused on one particular family line."

29. Alexander, "Royal Expectations in Genesis to Kings," 211.

30. Rose, "Messiah," 567.

31. For the options, see Pope, *Song of Songs*, 295–96, who concludes, "It is, nevertheless, most likely that the intent of the superscription was to attribute authorship to Solomon."

32. Pierre-Emile Bonnard and Pierre Grelot, "Messiah," in *Dictionary of Biblical Theology*, ed. Xavier Léon-Dufour, trans. P. Joseph Cahill (London: Geoffrey Chapman, 1967), 312.

33. I take the view that the Song has three speakers: the male, the female, and the witnesses of the relationship. I do not think that there is a lover in addition to Solomon. The Song is presented as a unified poem, for as Fox observes, "The title of Canticles identifies the book as a 'song' in the singular. . . . the singular is unambiguous in Hebrew. Whoever added the title to Canticles saw it as a single song" (Fox, *The Song of Songs and the Ancient Egyptian Love Songs*, 95); cf. also Garrett, *Proverbs, Ecclesiastes, Song of Songs*, 366: "Song of Songs is a single, unified work, as its chiastic structure demonstrates" (now also Garrett, *Song of Songs/Lamentations*, 25–35). For a possible (among the many proposed) chiastic structure of the Song, see Williams H. Shea, "The Chiastic Structure of the Song of Songs," *Zeitschrift für die alttestamentliche Wissenschaft* 92 (1980), 378–96; similarly Webb, *Five Festal Garments*, 22; *Pace* Pope, *Song of Songs*, 54. Murphy's comments are also relevant, *Song of Songs*, 97.

34. Weems, "The Song of Songs," 5:380; similarly Longman, *Song of Songs*, 92; Garrett, *Proverbs, Ecclesiastes, Song of Songs*, 385: "this is not to be understood literally; rather it is the language of love."

35. Pope, *Song of Songs*, 303.

36. Perrin refers to Solomon as "a kind of prototypical messiah," ("Messianism in the Narrative Frame of Ecclesiastes," 44), and N. T. Wright, commenting on Mt 12:42/Lk 11:31, writes, "Solomon, the Temple-builder, is an obvious messianic model. . . . for Jesus to compare himself with Solomon . . . was to stake a definite messianic claim" (*Jesus and the Victory of God* [Minneapolis: Fortress, 1996], 535).

37. Cf. Brown-Driver-Briggs, 572–73; *Hebrew and Aramaic Lexicon of the Old Testament*, 591–92; Philip J. Nel, "*melech*" in *New International Dictionary of Old Testament Theology and Exegesis*, 2:956–65.

38. Fox calls this parallel "rather shaky" (Fox, *The Song of Songs and the Ancient Egyptian Love Songs*, 98).

39. Cf. Dempster, *Dominion and Dynasty*, 42: "The celebration of human sexuality in the Song of Songs should not be understood apart from the general context of human sexuality in the canon."

40. Fox, *The Song of Songs and the Ancient Egyptian Love Songs*, 98 (emphasis his).

41. Ibid., 98.

42. Eusebius appears to confirm this assessment, for he recounts the tradition that though Herod burned the records of the Israelites "because he was goaded by his own consciousness of his base birth, thinking to appear noble if no one else was able by public documents to trace his family . . . a few who were careful, having private records for themselves, either remembering the names or otherwise deriving them from copies, gloried in the preservation of the memory of their good birth; among these were those mentioned above, called *desposyni*, because of their relation to the family of the Saviour, and from the Jewish villages of Nazareth and Cochaba they traversed the rest of the land and expounded the preceding genealogy of their descent" (Eusebius, *The Ecclesiastical History*, I. VII.13–14, translation from Kirsopp Lake, LCL 153 [Cambridge, MA: Harvard University Press, 1926], 63). Cf. also Abraham Malamat, "King Lists of the Old Babylonian Period and Biblical Genealogies," in *I Studied Inscriptions from before the Flood*, ed. Richard S. Hess and David Toshio Tsumura, Sources for Biblical and Theological Study 4 (Winona Lake, IN: Eisenbrauns, 1994), 183–99.

43. Cf. Philip J. Nel, *New International Dictionary of Old Testament Theology and Exegesis*, 2:958–60; Alexander, "Royal Expectations in Genesis to Kings."

44. Paul House and Stephen Dempster stress this point, but they do not draw out its messianic implications (cf. House, *Old Testament Theology*, 464; Dempster, *Dominion and Dynasty*, 207–208).

45. Carr, *The Song of Solomon*, 65.

46. Cf. David's bloody hands that kept him from building the temple (2Chr 22:8; 28:3).

47. Cf. the many women of Solomon, who turned his heart away (1Kg 11:3).

48. House, *Old Testament Theology*, 469.

49. The hope for an anointed king is not limited to the OT. It is also reflected in the Targum on the Song at 1:8, where the reference to the "shepherds' tents" apparently prompts admonishment to "present prayers by the mouth of the pastors and leaders . . . of her generation" and "to go to the Assembly House and to the House of Learning; then by that merit, they will be sustained in the Exile until the time when I send the King, the Messiah, who will lead . . . them to rest in their Dwelling, the Sanctuary which David and Solomon, the shepherds of Israel, will build for them" (as cited by Pope, *Song of Songs*, 335, bracketed notes mine). So it seems that the tents of the shepherds in Sg 1:8 are interpreted in the Targum as the Assembly House, the House of Learning, their Dwelling, and the Sanctuary. The reference to "shepherds" in 1:8 appears to be interpreted as contemporary leaders, the Messianic King who will lead them when the exile is over, and this Messianic King will lead them to a Sanctuary built by David and

Solomon. The Messiah is also a shepherd in *Pss. Sol.* 17:40. My references to the original language of the Targum are taken from the text provided by *BibleWorks6*, whose Targum material is derived from the Hebrew Union College CAL (Comprehensive Aramaic Lexicon) project. See further the Targum's messianic statements at Sg 1:17; 4:5,9; 7:4,5(?),14; 8:1,2,4. Sigmund Mowinckel states, "The bridegroom in the Song of Songs was interpreted in the Targums as the Messiah" (*He that Cometh*, trans. G. W. Anderson [Nashville: Abingdon, 1954], 283). Unfortunately, he cites no text(s). His statement seems to oversimplify the issue, for the Targum on the Song does not interpret the Song so much as it takes different words and statements made in the Song as points of departure for wider discussions of Israel's past, present, and future. The Messiah comes up in these discussions, as noted above, but the Targum on the Song does not even attempt to present a consistent interpretation of the male in the Song.

50. That the Song is a canonical document persuades me that it should be read in light of the rest of the OT. Contra Garrett, *Song of Songs/Lamentations*, 99.

51. Alan Jon Hauser, "Genesis 2–3: The Theme of Intimacy and Alienation," in *I Studied Inscriptions from before the Flood*, 383–98.

52. See Dempster, *Dominion and Dynasty*, 68–72; and T. Desmond Alexander, "Further Observations on the Term 'Seed' in Genesis," *Tyndale Bulletin* 48 (1997), 363–67.

53. See Longman's discussion of "The Story of Sexuality Redeemed," in his *Song of Songs*, 63–67.

54. Cf. Dumbrell, *The Faith of Israel*, 283: "While the interpretation of the book as an analogy of Christ and the church fails to deal adequately with its contents, the Song of Songs as an idyll of perfect love clearly points in this direction."

55. Dumbrell, *The Faith of Israel*, 283.

56. Cf. Webb, *Five Festal Garments*, 31: "The love experienced by the lovers becomes a kind of return to Eden." So also R. M. Davidson, "Theology of Sexuality in the Song of Songs: Return to Eden," *Andrews University Seminary Studies* 27 (1989): 1–19.

57. I find this explanation of the MT as it stands, taking in its usual sense of "rightly/correctly," more plausible than the suggested re-pointing and re-division of the text argued by Fox, *The Song of Songs and the Ancient Egyptian Love Songs*, 98–100. Cf. Pope, *Song of Songs*, 305: "There is no warrant for assuming a sense for *mêšārîm* other than the well-attested meaning 'equity,' or the like."

58. Commenting on Gn 2:25, Barry G. Webb writes, "With some justification the Song of Songs may be seen as a kind of extended commentary or poetic meditation on this verse" (*Five Festal Garments*, 30). Similarly, Carr, *The Song of Solomon*, 35. Francis Landy refers to this as "inversion," *Paradoxes of Paradise* (Sheffield: Almond, 1983), 183. Garrett demurs concerning this view (*Song of Songs/Lamentations*, 99).

59. He appears unsoiled by the veiled women of 1:7 (contrast Judah's failure, Gn 38).

60. Murphy rightly observes that these "touches" argue against a "free love" interpretation of the Song (Murphy, *Song of Songs*, 97).

61. I find Fox's arguments that Canticles is not a wedding song, and that "the couple that speak in it are not a bride and groom," altogether unconvincing. The Song's place in the OT canon ensures a more "moral" hearing of the Song than Fox prefers (cf. Fox, *The Song of Songs and the Ancient Egyptian Love Songs*, 231–32). Rightly, Gordis, *The Song of Songs and Lamentations*, 19–20, 43. Similarly, Garrett, *Song of Songs/Lamentations*, 102–104.

62. A *wasf* is "a song in which one lover praises the other's body part by part" (Fox, *The Song of Songs and the Ancient Egyptian Love Songs*, 128). Cf. M. Falk, *Love Lyrics from the Bible* (Sheffield: Almond, 1982), 80–87.

63. *Pace* Garrett, who contends, "Relating the Song to Gen 2–3 is . . . extraneous" (*Song of Songs/Lamentations*, 99).

64. Gordis, *The Song of Songs and Lamentations*, 37–38 (italics his).

65. It is the Song's canonical context that invalidates readings of the Song such as Pope's. Cf. Murphy, *Song of Songs*, 97; and for a broader discussion, see Dempster, *Dominion and Dynasty*, 41–43.

66. Murphy, *Song of Songs*, 94. Pope notes that the development of the "normative Jewish interpretation" of the Song as an allegory of the love of Yahweh for Israel "apparently" took place "between the destruction of the Temple, A.D. 70, and the revolt of Bar Kokhba, A.D. 132" (Pope, *Song of Songs*, 92). Cf. also his discussion of the interplay between church and synagogue regarding the Song's interpretation (Pope, *Song of Songs*, 96–101).

67. Cf. R. E. Murphy, "The Song of Songs: Critical Biblical Scholarship vis-à-vis Exegetical Traditions," in *Understanding the Word*, ed. J. T. Butler, E. W. Conrad, and B. C. Ollenburger, Journal for the Study of the Old Testament Supp 37 (Sheffield: JSOT, 1985), 68: "The traditional understanding of the Song complements the literal historical sense by extending it along certain paths which, as we have seen, can themselves be illumined by means of modern scholarship."

68. See Ephraim E. Urbach, "The Homiletical Interpretations of the Sages and the Expositions of Origin on Canticles, and the Jewish-Christian Disputation," *Scripta Hierosolymitana* 22 (1971), 257: "By comparing the homilies of the Sages with Origen's interpretation we can recover, in this instance, a Judeo-Christian dialogue that began in the third century and continued in the fourth." I wish to thank Tim Edwards for this reference. Further, in his presentation on "The Targum of the Psalms" at the meeting of the Tyndale Fellowship on Wednesday, June 30, 2004, Edwards noted that the only place in Rabbinic literature where Ps 45 is treated as messianic is in the Targum on the Psalter. For discussion of Jewish interpretations, cf. also Murphy, *Song of Songs*, 12–14.

69. I am here paraphrasing the comments of William Wordsworth in his "Preface to *Lyrical Ballads, with Pastoral and Other Poems*" (1802), in *Norton Anthology of English Literature*, 6th ed., vol. 2, ed. M. H. Abrams (New York: Norton, 1993), 151.

70. See Francis Landy, "The Song of Songs and the Garden of Eden," *Journal of Biblical Literature* 98 (1979), 513–28. Gledhill notes, "There are a number of literary and thematic parallels between the Song and the garden of Eden story in Genesis 2. Both contain imagery of luscious vegetation and of beautiful and mouth-wateringly sweet fruit. Both refer to a garden watered by springs or wells. There is joyful complementarity and union between the man and his wife. There is nakedness and no sense of shame. The Song seems to look back on and recapture these scenes of primal innocence, and reaffirms the doctrine of the goodness of God's creation" (T. D. Gledhill, "Song of Songs," in *New Dictionary of Biblical Theology*, 217). Similarly, Webb, *Five Festal Garments*, 30–31.

71. I owe this observation to Dumbrell, *The Faith of Israel*, 282. Dumbrell, however, does not connect this to OT messianism. Gordis (*The Song of Songs and Lamentations*, 98) refers to this as the lovers desiring one another, but the text speaks only of the male's desire for the female, which makes this the true opposite of Gn 3:16. Similarly Phyllis Trible, *God and the Rhetoric of Sexuality*, Overtures to Biblical Theology 2 (Philadelphia: Fortress, 1978), 160.

72. Garrett, *Song of Songs/Lamentations*, 99, 246.

73. Sg 1:1,5; 3:9,11; 8:11,12.

74. Sg 1:4,12; 3:9,11; 7:5.

75. Sg 3:6-11; 5:10-16.

76. Sg 2:16-17; 4:16b–5:1; 6:2-3; 7:11-13; 8:3,13-14.

77. Sg 6:2.

78. Percy Bysshe Shelley, "A Defence of Poetry," (1821) in *Norton Anthology of English Literature*, 757. An earlier draft of this essay was presented to the Christian Theology and the Bible group at the national meeting of the Society of Biblical Literature in November, 2004.

Isaiah 2:2-4/Micah 4:1-5

The Restoration of Israel in the Messianic Age

J. RANDALL PRICE

Isaiah 2:2-4/Micah 4:1-5 are texts giving nearly parallel explanations of the way God will restore national Israel and the Gentile nations under the new covenant in the Messianic Era.[1] Leading rabbinic commentators such as Rambam, Radak, Ibn Ezra, and Rashi interpreted these passages as occurring in messianic times with a focus on King Messiah, who will teach the nations Torah, arbitrate national disputes, and thereby secure world peace.[2] Modern Orthodox Judaism follows these Sages in explaining these texts as the basis for the arrival of Messiah and the establishment of His rule in the rebuilt Temple in Jerusalem that will be exalted to serve as the center of world government for both Jews and Gentiles.[3] This is reflected in the daily prayers of the Jewish people around the world: "Restore the most holy service of Your house and accept in love the offerings and prayers of Israel. May it please You always to accept the service of Your people Israel. May our eyes see You return to Zion in mercy. Blessed are You, O LORD, Who restores His Presence to Zion" (Benediction 17, *Avodah*, Amidah).

MESSIANIC INTERPRETATION

Most Christian interpreters have also recognized these two passages as messianic texts, even though they make no mention of the Messiah and are not explicitly quoted in the NT. However, it is worthy of note that "Isaiah" (Heb. *Yeshiyahu*) means "the LORD saves" and Micah (Heb. *Micah*) means "who is like the LORD?" both expressions of Messiah's divine nature and redemptive work elsewhere presented by these prophets (Isa 9:6-7; 53:4-12; Mic 7:18). Likewise, the restoration context of the "last days" and the central figure personally deciding justice for the nations, ending war, and guaranteeing international peace can be none other than King Messiah, the Prince of Peace (Isa 9:6-7; cf. Isa 52:7; 66:12; Ezk 37:26; Hag 2:9; Zch 9:10). Thus, restoration texts are messianic texts, since the agent of restoration is the Messiah. Differences in Christian interpretation of these texts are based on the understanding of *when* and *how* eschatological events will take place. While all Christian interpreters adopt a messianic interpretation, historicists have traditionally understood the events to take place within the Church age (Spiritual Kingdom),[4] while futurists understand the events to occur in the messianic kingdom on earth (see below for further discussion).

Interpretive issues involve which prophet authored the prophecy and whether the eschatological-messianic fulfillment is in the present age or the end time. As to the first question, the texts as they are appear to represent edited texts that differ minimally from each other in style and substance. Some have thought this to indicate dependence on an earlier original text, but it seems more likely the differences reflect individual attempts to fit the text into their respective contextual arguments.[5] An analysis of the language of the Hebrew text of Isaiah here reveals it to be uniquely Isaianic. While it has been argued that the appearance of a restoration passage at this point in the book seems abrupt, the immediately preceding verses of the first chapter (1:26-30) are a prediction of redemption and restoration upon which the prophet naturally expands in 2:2-4. This pattern of alternating condemnation with the promise of restoration is typical Isaianic style. In this context, the judgment announced in 2:5–3:26 is followed by details of restoration in 4:2-6, and the condemnation in chaps. 5–10 is followed by the restoration of chaps. 11–12. However, within the condemnation section of chaps. 5–10 appear the messianic texts of 7:14 and 9:6-7 that are built upon in the messianic eschatological/restoration texts of 11:1-5, 10-12, and 12:2-6. Micah, on the other hand, elaborates immediately in 4:5 (Hb. v. 4) concerning the conditions that will accompany the fulfillment of the prophecy (something Isaiah does not do), implying that the less elaborate passage may have been the original.

With respect to vocabulary, Isaiah 2:2-4 and Micah 4:1-3 differ in the inversion of the word-pair "peoples/nations." Isaiah uses nations/peoples and Micah prefers peoples/nations. While this is a clear indication of borrowing, it does not indicate which text is the original. However, Micah in his discussion of the peoples/nations has the addition of two adjectives "mighty, distant," which are missing from Isaiah's text. This may signal an intentional expansion of the spatial focus of the original prophecy, indicating that Micah borrowed from Isaiah and disrupted the rhythm of the text to make a theological point.[6]

Micah also tends to personalize the period of God's reign in Zion: "each man will sit under his grapevine and under his fig tree" (Mic 4:4), while Isaiah maintains a universal reference. This, too, may indicate that Micah was the borrower since he theologically wanted to show the fulfillment of the restoration embodied in this expected hope (1Kg 4:25; Isa 36:16-17; Zch 3:10). Finally, in this verse, Micah concludes with the prophetic declaration "the mouth of the LORD of Hosts has promised this," a literary device that seems to mark the use of a verbal parallel (cf. Isa 1:20, 40:5, 58:14). If this is the case, Micah's intertextual development shows the universal prosperity and permanent peace predicted by Isaiah as illustrated by an individual agricultural ideal.

However, the case of dependency is hard to decide. Both texts were equally inspired, for as John Oswalt has pointed out, "inspiration can involve guidance in the utilization of existing materials."[7] With respect to messianic interpretation, both appear to employ intertextuality in their use of previously revealed messianic and eschatological terminology and concepts.

As to the second interpretive question, critical scholars have suggested various past historical settings for the fulfillment, taking the prophetic language as exaggerated (hyperbolic) style. Some find past fulfillment taking place literally in Jerusalem in the NT where there is a gathering of worshipers from the nations at Shavuot (Weeks)/Pentecost (Ac 2:8-11).[8] However, Isaiah and Micah clearly distinguish the Gentile nations from national Israel in their use of the exclusive terms "all the nations" and "many peoples," as does the text in Ac 2, stating that these were Diaspora *Jews* and proselytes to Judaism living in Judea (Ac 2:5, 14; cf. 3:12), rather than Gentiles from the foreign nations.

In light of Luke's frequent use of OT citations to explain the events at Shavuot, it would be remarkable that he would not include an allusion to these famous texts that would clearly show fulfillment. This may have been because the result of Shavuot as well as the preaching of Messiah resulted in division and disorder within the Jewish community (Ac 4:1-2; 5:17; 7:54–8:3; 9:1-2; 11:19; 12:1-5,23; 13:44-46; 14:2-6, 19-20; 15:37-39; 16:19-24; 17:32; 19:28-34; 20:3; 21:30-36; 24:5-6; 28:25-27), and the Second Temple period ended with war and the Gentile destruction of Jerusalem, not universal peace as these prophets predicted. In fact, Peter cites from the OT (Ps 2:1-2) as evidence that "the Gentiles" and "the kings of the earth" continue to rage against Messiah (Ac 4:25-26). This does not sound like the new covenant Messianic Era in which there will be universal spiritual and physical harmony (Jer 31:31-34; cf. Isa 11:6-13).

Another way Christian interpreters have handled these texts is by viewing them as symbols of spiritual realities, assuming Jesus' statement in Jn 4:21-24 as a guide. By this method, terms such as "Mount Zion" are understood in light of the NT reference to "the heavenly Jerusalem" (Heb 12:22). Following this approach, Leslie Allen concludes on the Micah text, "the Christian will set little value on the geography of the piece and regard it as a cultural adornment to a deeper and universal truth."[9] However, this method is based on a reverse interpretation, using the NT as a theological (Christological) lens through which to understand the OT's land-based new covenant promises as spiritual trajectories fulfilled in universal terms. It is difficult to imagine the Jewish audience, which had suffered desolation and exile from their land, understanding the restoration to the land promises as strictly spiritual. To do so requires a reinterpretation rather than an interpretation of the OT. However, messianic prophetic interpretation does not require a new (deeper spiritual) understanding of the biblical covenants, but a realization that the predicted spiritual fulfillment would have a literal and land-based context.

The issue here is whether to adopt a theological interpretation that prioritizes the revelation of the NT (reading the OT in light of the NT) or to take the OT text as primary (reading the NT in light of the OT). All interpreters understand exegetically that the Messianic Era of redemption is in view, but their respective hermeneutical method takes them in different directions. From the standpoint of a grammatical-historical exegesis alone, these texts argue that the literal intent of the prophets in relation to the historic terms they use ("the mountain of the house of the Lord," "house of the God of Jacob," "Zion," "Jerusalem"), and the corpus of prophetic revelation that defines the restoration they describe, have in view the final fulfillment of the covenant promises to national Israel in the end time.

These texts, then, predict the international harmony among Israel and the nations resulting from Messiah's reign from the Temple Mount in Jerusalem. However, based on a theological reading of the OT from a Christocentric perspective, others argue that Jesus is the ultimate "house" or dwelling place of God's glory (Jn 1:14; 2:19-21), that through Him the believing community becomes a [spiritual] temple (1Co 3:16; Eph 2:20-22), and therefore fulfills the promised new covenant expectation presented by Isaiah and Micah and other OT prophets. In this interpretation, the promised restoration came with Jesus' exaltation and was demonstrated by the advent of the Holy Spirit in Jerusalem bringing the gospel to people from many nations at Pentecost (Lk 24:47; Ac 1:8; 2:8-11). According to this view, the promised restoration has its fulfillment with the Church in the present age, rather than with national Israel in a future age. Again, while this does not affect the messianic interpretation of these texts, the different methods of approaching the text affect how an interpreter arrives at and understands messianic prophecy.

CONTEXTUAL INTERPRETATION

With respect to these texts in Isaiah and Micah, there are no quotations or allusions to these texts in the NT that would justify interpreting them in a way other than that given by the prophets in their original context. The absence of discussion on such restoration passages in the NT does not mean that they were not considered messianic or had already found fulfillment. The OT was the Scripture of Jesus and the early Church, and they considered it to be a living and valid testimony as they wrote and transmitted the NT. They did not need to repeat what was already known, and most of the NT is directed toward the concern of Gentile inclusion, not Israel's future. It is therefore unwarranted to hold that the OT promises have no validity unless they are repeated in the NT or explicitly restate what was previously taught.

However, where appropriate to the contextual argument, the NT does *reaffirm* the OT expectations concerning a restoration of Israel (e.g., Mt 8:11; 19:28/Lk 22:30; Lk 13:28; Ac 1:6-7; 3:19-21; 26:7; Rom 11:12,15, 23-29). When this is coupled with the fact that there are no clear texts in the NT that identify the church as Israel,[10] or that the promises to Israel are fulfilled in the church, or that teach the permanent rejection of Israel, the case for a literal understanding of national Israel's restoration as given by the OT prophets is validated. As S. Lewis Johnson has stated, "Their principles [use of the OT in NT exegesis], probably taught them by the Lord in His pre-resurrection ministry, are not obtuse and difficult."

STRUCTURE AND CONTEXT OF ISAIAH 2:2-4/MICAH 4:1-3

Micah from Moreseth (1:1, 14) was a contemporary of Isaiah from Jerusalem. As Judean prophets, they denounced the spiritual and social decline in Israel (see 2Ch 32:20; Jer 26:18). Isaiah 2:1 designates Judah and Jerusalem as the subject of the vision, as does Mic 3:1. The placement of Isaiah's and Micah's texts have been given a prominent position in the books as a whole, finding their place early in Isaiah and late in Micah. However, in each case, the positioning is set to show a reversal for Israel and the nations; the former as a rejected people suffering divine judgment and the latter as a foreign people used as instruments of judgment (as well as judged).

The role of Isa 2:2-4 within the compositional structure of the first major literary unit of the whole book is to introduce the plan for messianic restoration. Isaiah 1 presents an overview of the entire book. The subheading at 2:1 marks the first main section that extends through chap. 12. Isaiah 1 introduces the theme of condemnation, with the prophet himself serving as prosecutor arguing the divine indictment of chaps. 1–39 (chaps. 1–12 to Judah, chaps. 13–23 to the nations, chaps.

24–35 to all the earth—with chaps. 36–39 as a transition focusing on Assyrian and Babylon). In Isaiah, Judah was rebellious and sinful (1:2,4), an "adulteress" practicing injustice (1:21-23), and a spiritual adulterer subject to destruction (1:28-31). The sections of condemnation (1:23; 2:5–4:1; 5:1-30; 7:1–8:22; 9:8–10:34) alternate with sections of restoration (1:24-27; 2:1-4; 4:2-6; 7:14; 9:1-7; 11:1–12:6).

The basic message to national Israel is that restoration will follow judgment—with the prediction of divine punishment for the immediate future and the promise of divine restoration for the far future (the last days in which Israel and the nations are under the rule of King Messiah). Andrew Bartelt has argued that the prospect for this restoration is introduced in 1:24-27 and its plan presented in 2:2-4. While 1:26-27 presents Jerusalem as a righteous and faithful city and its people redeemed with justice, 2:2-4 explains this status comes from the presence of King Messiah in His Temple and His just rule over Israel and the nations.[11] Bartelt has elsewhere observed that Isa 6 introduces the central section of a tripartite structure within chaps. 2–12 (the three major sections are 2:1–5:30; 6:1–8:18; 8:19–12:6). These pieces form an intentionally structured unity with an A-B-A chiasm, and the focus of the central unit is the sign of Immanuel in chap. 7.[12] The final literary unit (chaps. 40–66) builds upon the previous revelation concerning restoration and the advent of the Messiah to focus on the theme of comfort. This is introduced by words of comfort in 40:1, which itself is part of the messianic mission (40:3-5).

In Micah, Judah (and Israel) are sinful rebels, bringing idolatry to Jerusalem (1:5,9,13), and spreading injustice and corruption in the land (2:1-2, 8-9,11), and therefore subject to discipline and destruction, especially the false rulers, prophets (3:6-11), and the city of Jerusalem (3:12). Micah 4:1-3 is positioned to draw a textual and theological contrast between the sinful status of Jerusalem in the prophet's day, which led to desecration of the Temple, and its future status in the Messianic Era, which climaxes with the restoration of the Temple. Micah 3:10-12 predicts a near fulfillment when Zion with its Temple Mount, filled with bloodshed and injustice, will be plowed as a field (cf. Jer 26:18) and desolated (cf. Lam 5:18), whereas Mic 4:1-3 predicts a far fulfillment when this same Zion, now crowned by a rebuilt Temple and filled with peace and justice, will be exalted. The former text declares that Zion will become a "forested hill," whereas the latter that Zion will be elevated above the surrounding hills and serve as the world's worship center. Both pericopes use the terms "house of Jacob," "Zion," "Jerusalem," and "the mountain of the Temple/house of the LORD." In the day of the prophet, "the word of the LORD" was set against "the house of Jacob" (3:9) and "Zion and Jerusalem" (3:10), and the "hill of the Temple" (3:12c), but in the future the nations will be drawn to the "mountain of the LORD's house" (4:1) and to "the house of Jacob" (4:2b) to receive "the word of the LORD" from Zion and Jerusalem (4:2c). It is interesting that later rabbinical opinion based on Mic 3:12 states that this verse indicates that no building will ever be established on the site of the Temple until the end of days (Ari'zal, *Emek HaMelech*, preface #9, the Maharasha on Tractate *Makot*—end).

Isaiah prepares for the subsequent explanation of the restoration with an announcement of it (1:26-27) as Micah follows the explanation with the announcement of the coming of the Messiah, the agent of restoration (4:7b-8; 5:2-5a). The following outlines are suggested for each passage:

Isaiah 2:2-4		Micah 4:1-4 [5]	
2:2-3a	Celebration of Jerusalem's exaltation	4:1-2a	Celebration of Jerusalem's exaltation
2:3b-4	Expansion and results of the messianic instruction	4:2b-4	Expansion and results of the messianic instruction
2:5	Call for change	4:4b [4:5	Call for change Condition of change]

In addition, Isaiah presents a scene of divine punishment of Israel and the nations resulting in a united worship at the Temple in Jerusalem and universal peace. Micah, by contrast, reveals that peace among the nations and the universal worship at the Temple follow the installation of the new house. These different perspectives of the order of the restoration complement each other, presenting the same information from distinct vantage points. Both underscore the universality of worship and peace that are part and parcel to the messianic restoration.

LITERARY ANALYSIS OF ISAIAH 2:2-4/MICAH 4:1-3

In dealing with Isaiah 2:1-5 and Micah 4:1-5, it is important to view them from a text-centered approach that respects the intention of the historical and canonical authors, while interpreting their individual literary contexts within the larger literary (messianic) context of the Bible.[13] John Sailhamer has demonstrated that the theological purpose of the Pentateuch is to reveal the inherent relationship between the past and the future.[14] The narrative-typology of the Pentateuch is designed so that earlier events foreshadow and anticipate later events. Therefore, later narratives in the OT remind the reader of past narratives and their proleptic and messianic content. Thus, the Israel that finds its origin and formation in the Pentateuch is destined to be at the center of the messianic program throughout time and will serve as the nexus of its culmination in the "last days."

The hermeneutical basis for the above conclusion is found in literary use of the phrase "the days to come" or "in the future" in three blocks of poetry from three key figures (Jacob in Gn 49:1; Balaam in Nm 24:14; Moses in Dt 31:29) intentionally inserted into structurally strategic locations in the compositional structure of the Pentateuch. This sets the framework for understanding the use of "the last days" in Isa 2 and Mic 4, especially when viewing both as setting the stage for the messianic restoration under the messianic King and His kingdom as presented respectively in The Book of Immanuel (Isa 7–12) and Mic 5. Understanding that the messianic interpretation is not found in the historical events that form the historical setting, but in the words of the text. The text itself functions as the divine interpretation of God's activity in history, and not vice versa. This enables the words of Scripture themselves to reveal their intended messianic goal. If the text is viewed only historically, the interpretation will involve only the people and events of the immediate historical context and not the future figures and events envisioned by the author.[15]

INTERTEXTUAL ANALYSIS

While Isa 2:2-4 and Mic 4:1-4, in these contexts, do not identify the figure who rules in Jerusalem maintaining spiritual and political order, these prophets expected their readers to know the identity of this One based on the intertextual revelation of the conquering seed of the woman (Gn 3:15), the ruler from Israel (Nm 24:17), the Mosaic prophet (Dt 18:15-19), the One like a Son of Man who will receive the imperishable kingdom in which the nations will serve (worship) Him (Dn 7:13-14), and the messianic psalms portraying a king who rules from the "holy mountain" and "Zion" over the nations (Pss 2,110).

However, from an innertextual perspective, these prophets do identify this figure. Both prophets predict this ruler's birth (Isa 7:14; 9:6-7; Mic 5:2-4). Isaiah 11 provides details of His Davidic origin (Isa 11:1), His spiritual character (11:2-3), His dominion over the nations (11:4-5), His reign in universal peace (11:6-8), His global dissemination of Torah from the Temple (11:9), His worship by the nations (11:10), and His global regathering of the Jewish people (11:11-12) in a miraculous manner comparable to the exodus (11:15-16). Similarly, Micah says this ruler in his actions toward Israel will show miracles like the exodus (Mic 7:14-15), cause the nations to come to the Lord in fearful submission (Mic 7:16-17), and redeem Israel (Mic 7:18-20).

Isaiah also presents this theme of redemption through a Savior (Isa 12:2-5) who is described as "the Holy One of Israel . . . among you" (12:6). While this might be interpreted as the Divine Presence dwelling in the Temple in Jerusalem, Isa 2 has already personified the One dwelling on Zion in more concrete terms as a teacher and arbiter, which is why the Sages rightly identified this figure here as King Messiah. Isaiah later explains, in language similar to the theophany of Ex 24:9-11, that the Lord of hosts would reign on Mount Zion and that His glory would be before His elders (Isa 24:23). It is this One who at the conclusion of His victorious advent will prepare a messianic banquet on Mount Zion for all peoples and remove the earthly grief suffered by the nations, resulting in peace (Isa 25:6-8). He will also personally bring justice and redemption to the earth (Isa 59:16-20a), turning Israel to repentance (Isa 59:20b). This latter text Paul used to support his statement of the national repentance and redemption of the remnant of Israel ("all Israel") in Rom 11:26.

Micah opens his prophetic message with the statement that "the Lord is leaving His place and coming down to trample the heights of the earth" (Mic 1:3), leveling the mountains and valley under Him (v. 4). The same is announced by Isaiah in 40:3-5. Hosea, a contemporary of both prophets, offers this same perspective in his presentation of the "last days" return of Israel to "the Lord their God and David their King" (Hos 3:5). Who can this Davidic King be in the last days but the Branch of the Lord/David introduced by Isaiah (Isa 4:2; 11:1), a figure recognized and carried forward by Jeremiah (23:5; 33:15) and Zechariah (3:8; 6:12). This innertextual perspective in both prophets also reveals their intertextual relationship, not simply in the use of the same material in Isa 2:2-4 and Mic 4:1-4, but also in their affinity in the use of the supporting concepts of the Messianic Era.

There is something more here. In Exodus, Moses, at the beginning of national Israel's promise, gave the Torah from Mt. Sinai (Ex 3:12; Dt 4:35-40), and commanded Israel to be a witness to it to the nations (Ex 34:10; cf. Dt 32:43). Further, Moses pointed to the future mountain of divine revelation from where the Lord will reign forever (Ex 15:17-18) and announced the coming of the Messiah, one like himself who saw God face-to-face, who would fulfill this future hope (Dt 18:15-19). In Isaiah 2:2-4, this prophecy finds fulfillment as Messiah, at the culmination of national Israel's promise, gives the law from Mt. Zion through national Israel to the nations, and reigns forever.

Isaiah's and Micah's contextual presentation of judgment on Israel prior to redemption and restoration may also have messianic significance. Isaiah 6:9-13 ("like the terebinth or the oak which leaves a stump when felled, the holy seed is the stump") and 10:21-22 explain that the remnant will find redemption only after the judgment of the nation ("destruction has been decreed; justice overflows"). Micah's words immediately preceding those of his restoration of Jerusalem/Zion (4:1-4) are of Zion/Jerusalem's destruction and ruin, focusing on the Temple (3:12). Such typological intent was declared in Isaiah 8:17-18, where Israel is to look eagerly for the Lord, who has hidden His face from the house of Jacob (v. 17), but may be found by understanding God's purpose revealed in the prophet and his family: "Here I am with the children the LORD has given me to be signs and wonders in Israel from the LORD of hosts who dwells on Mount Zion" (cf. Isa 25:9-10a). In like manner, Isaiah 22:22-23 gives typological significance to Eliakim, describing his Davidic authority in messianic terminology (cf. Isa 9:6b-7), a fact not missed by the NT in its portrayal of the glorified Messiah (Rev 3:7; cf. Rev 1:18; Mt 16:19).

If the intention of these prophets here is to show that the divine agent of both judgment and redemption is the Messiah, then this arrangement of events may typify the messianic advent(s). Jerusalem, the city beloved of God (Isa 14:32; 31:5; 33:5; 35:10; 37:32; 44:26,28; 46:13; 49:14,15; 51:3,11,16; 52:1,7,9; 60:14; 61:3; 62:7,11; 65:18, 19; and 66:10,13,20) and the place where He dwells (Isa 8:18; 12:6; 18:7; 24:23; 40:9; 52:8; 59:20) had to be judged before the promised redemption of the remnant in Judah could take place (Isa 1:26-27; 40:2; 53:3; 62:1; cf. Rom 3:21-26; Eph 1:7,8; Col 1:13,14; Heb 9:11-15). In the NT, Messiah must suffer divine judgment before the redemption of Israel (and the nations) can occur (Rom 3:21-26; Eph 1:7-8; Col 1:13-14; Heb 9:11-15). There may also be a typical significance to the gifts of worship brought to Messiah in Jerusalem by the nations (Isa 18:7; 23:18; 66:20; cf. 60:5) in the NT's presentation of the gifts of the Gentile Magi (representing the nations) to the young Messiah (Mt 2:11).[16]

IDENTIFYING MESSIAH IN ISAIAH 2:2-4/MICAH 4:1-3

The temporal setting for the parallel context of our passages is defined in Isa 2:2/Mic 4:1 by the Hebrew phrase *b^e'aharit hayyamim* ("the latter days"). This expression appears as a fixed form of speech (always in the same construct state with the same preposition— *b^e* "in").[17] Literally, the words translate as "the days that follow or come after, the backside of days" ("latter days"), but many translations translate this as "the last days." Jewish translations all understand this as referring to the "messianic times," though variously translate it as "the days to come"[18] or "the end of days,"[19] "the time of the end,"[20] or "in future days."[21] Each has understood this as an eschatological time indicator. The reference to the future is debated on textual grounds because it is thought that this is not a technical term for the "end time," but only conveys the meaning "after an indefinite, indeterminate, rather long time."[22]

Depending on how one interprets the context (as discussed previously), this may be either the near future (the time of restoration following the exile) or the far or distant future (the time of restoration in the Messianic Age). Franz Delitzsch contended that the term is "always used in the eschatological sense"[23] and C. F.

Keil noted that "it always denotes the Messianic Era when used by the prophets."[24] Classical Dispensationalists suggest a distinction in the chronological application of the term. They argue that the term "last days" or "end time" does not always refer to the same time period. The contextual referent enables the reader to know whether the Bible is speaking of the latter/last days of Israel or the latter/last days of the Church.

It is true that prophetic terms for the restoration, as well as temporal expressions that govern them, may have both an indefinite and definite sense of futurity. The idiomatic nature of prophetic speech allows for an immediate application or a more remote or ultimate application to a future event. While the cognate languages appear to favor a general future, recognize that eschatology in Israel was an inner-Israelite development[25] and that ancient Near Eastern parallels simply represent concepts common to their unique concept of prediction and fulfillment.

In its OT use, *bᵉ'aharit hayyamim* ("the latter days") may refer to the eschatological period (e.g., Jer 23:20; 34:20; 48:47; 49:39; Ezk 38:8, 16; Hos 3:5; Dn 2:28; 8:19,23; 10:14; cf. 12:8).[26] In particular its use in Dan 8:19 paralleled by the expression *qetz hayyamin* ("final or end period") strengthens the eschatological meaning of "latter days," since the substitution of *qetz* ("end"), the proper Hebrew expression for a completion of time, coming from the root *qutz* ("cut off"), for *'aharit* ("last") makes the meaning decisive of the ultimate end.[27]

The restoration context of the Isaiah/Micah passage requires that it be interpreted eschatologically. However, the intertextual use of the phrase understands it as a reference to the Messiah and the Messianic Era. Sailhamer argues that the phrase occurs in poetic seams of the Pentateuch where a central figure assembles a group to announce what will occur in the "last days" (Gn 49:1, Nm 24:14; Dt 31:28-29). It is this understanding of how Israel's eschatology informs and directs Israel's history that forms the narrative typology behind the Pentateuch's compositional strategy.[28] In other words, the prediction of the coming Messiah and the Messianic Age conveyed in the use of "the last days" intentionally provides the interpretive framework and the goal for Israel's history (the eschaton) for the whole of the Pentateuch. That, in turn, provides the foundation for interpreting the prophets in their revelation of Israel's restoration under Messiah (e.g., Isa 11:1 16; Mic 5:1-5).

An example of this eschatological perspective is evident in Hosea, who follows Isaiah's and Micah's use of the phrase in his prediction of the post-Diaspora return of Israel to the Lord in national repentance (Hos 3:5). These contemporary prophets were aware of each other's technical use of this phrase in their day and time. Since all were alike inspired by the Lord in their prophetic writing, the divine intention would have been to link their statements of the Messianic Era to those previously revealed. This, as Sailhamer and others have shown, has been preserved in the final edited form of the OT.

Some commentators have tried to argue that the reference to Mount Zion is not a geographical location, but merely a symbol of government. However, the concern here is for the geographical areas of "Judah and Jerusalem" (Isa 2:1) and "Jerusalem/ Zion" (Mic 3:12). Moreover, the 154 uses of the term "Zion" throughout the OT are of a geographical site that came to be synonymous with the city of Jerusalem and therefore inclusive of the Temple Mount. Isaiah and Micah through literary parallelism make this point here when they write: "For instruction [Torah] will go out of *Zion* and the *word* of the Lord from *Jerusalem*" (Isa 2:3c; Mic 4:2c, emphasis added). "Zion" and "Jerusalem" are in synonymous parallelism 40 times in Hebrew poetry (including here),[29] and recognized in these contexts as geographic locations.

The "mountain of the house of the Lord" indicates the *place* of Messiah's rule. Kissane states that "Sion (*sic*) will be a place of pilgrimage because it will be the abode of the Messiah."[30] The word "established" (*nakôn*) occurs at the beginning of Isa 2:2a, but at the end of Mic 4:1a. This different position in Micah seems to emphasize this exalted "establishment" will "remain" and is therefore permanent. This agrees with the messianic prediction made at the time of the establishment of the Davidic Covenant that one of David's descendants would be installed in the Temple and in His kingdom "forever" (1Ch 17:14).

Just as "Zion" must refer to the literal "City of Jerusalem" and the "mountain of the house of the LORD" must refer to the literal "Temple Mount," being "raised above the other mountains" must be understood in concert. This elevation of "the mountain of the house of the LORD" might be regarded as only an increased esteem and preeminence were it not for the qualification in Zechariah that "all the land [around the Temple Mount] will be changed into a plain" (Zch 14:10), thereby increasing the physical height of the mount, and Ezekiel's depiction of the Sanctuary City (which includes the Temple) on a "very high mountain" (Ezk 40:2). In the ancient Near East, local gods were often associated with the high places or hills, and going to high places to worship was associated with idolatry (Isa 36:7; Jer 19:5; Ezk 6:3; Hos 10:8; Am 7:9; Mic 1:3; Hab 3:19) and compromise (1Kg 3:3). The Jewish temples of the past were not built on the highest point of Mt. Moriah, but somewhat below, in contrast to this pagan practice.[31] However, with Israel's national repentance the land will come under the new covenant, and this prohibition will no longer be necessary. Instead, establishing the mountain of the house of the Lord high "above" all the other hills demonstrates that Messiah's house (see 1Ch 17:14; cf. Mt 21:13; Mk 11:17; Lk 19:46; Jn 2:16) and Israel's worship of Messiah are preeminent.

Isaiah later states that the messianic government is to be centered in Jerusalem

(Isa 9:7), a fact repeated at the time of the announcement of Jesus' birth by the angel Gabriel (Lk 1:32-33). Just as the throne (government) of King David was in Jerusalem, so the throne of Messiah Jesus would be established there, and as previously mentioned from 1Ch 17:14, situated in the Temple. Therefore, there is no reason to argue against the literal restoration of Mount Zion as the center of messianic rule, especially since in both texts the preceding verses spoke of the literal desolation of "Zion" (Isa 1:27; Mic 3:12).

Indeed, other prophets make a point of using geographical locations and physical measurements to mark the extent of the elevation of the Temple Mount in the Messianic Age (Ezk 40:2; 48:8–15,35; Zch 14:10). Since the Temple was the place of the Divine Presence (1Kg 8:13, 29; Ps 132:7-8,13-14), only the Temple Mount could be exalted as the "chief" (*rosh*, "head") of the mountains, a term that expresses rank and priority. It is there that God "will make a horn grow for David . . . a lamp for My anointed one" (Ps 132:17). This is a prediction that Messiah as the son of David will have His rule on David's throne in Jerusalem, the City of David (2Sm 5:9), and appropriately, as NT exegesis reveals (implicit use of Ex 13:21 in Jn 1:14), in the Temple, God's dwelling place.

Complementing this exaltation of the Temple Mount is the event that "all the nations will stream to it." Micah has "peoples" instead of "nations" and lacks the "all"; however, these terms seem to be interchangeable and make no difference in the interpretation. The verb *nah^{a}ru,* "flow, stream," usually applies to the water of a river (*nahar*) that flows downhill, but this is a movement *up* the mountain and so seems to defy gravity. However, that may be the point: a supernatural flow of the nations to Jerusalem for worship defies past Gentile nature and performance when they were drawn to Jerusalem only for war (Zch 12:2-3; 14:2). If one event (restoration) follows the other (warfare) in the temporal context, then the allusion is even more fitting. In the past (especially the Tribulation) the nations went against Messiah; now at its conclusion (at the time of the second advent) they will go to Him (see Isa 11:12, where Messiah is the rallying point for the nations as well as for the regathered remnant). Some have seen unified Gentile pilgrimage to the Temple Mount as a reversal of the Tower of Babel (Gn 11), where God divided the nations and they streamed out into the world (a place of conflict), but now come to Jerusalem (a place of peace).

This language and event also bring the mission of the Church full circle, as that flow of the gospel to the nations beginning at Jerusalem (Ac 1:8) now flows back to its source with a company of Gentile believers. This was the intention of Messiah in His commission to "go . . . and make disciples of all nations. . . . to the end of the age" (Mt 28:19-20) and in His revelation to John that those "redeemed people for God . .

. from every tribe and language and people and nation" would become a "kingdom and priests . . . and they will reign on the earth" (Rev 5:9-10).

Isaiah 2 and Mic 4 depict the ingathering of the Gentile remnant joining the Jewish remnant in the messianic kingdom, fulfilling the restoration goal of the new covenant for Israel (Jer 31:33-34) and the nations (Jer 33:7-9). Indeed, the Messianic Era was predicted as the time under the new covenant when the Messiah ("a righteous Branch of David") would restore the Davidic rule and dispense justice on earth. At that time, the Levitical priests would return to their duties within the Temple (Jer 33:15-18) and, as Messiah stated during His first advent, the nations will be brought to the Temple Mount to offer sacrifices in the Temple. Thus, "My house will be called a house of prayer for all nations" (Isa 56:7).

The nations refer to the "the house of the God of Jacob" (Isa 2:3). It may be simply that here is a familiar parallelism where "Jacob" = "Israel" (cf. Isa 9:8; 48:1) as numerous passages have this term in synonymous parallelism with "Israel" (cf. Nm 23:7; 24:17; 1Ch 16:17; Pss 17:14; 22:23; 53:6; 81:4; 105:10; 135:4, et. al.). The term "house of Jacob" (2:5,6; 8:17; 10:20; 14:1; 29:22; 46:3; 48:1; 58:1) is favored by Isaiah, who specifically predicts that a "remnant will return, the remnant of Jacob, to the mighty God" (Isa 10:21). It is possible that the use of "Jacob" in Isaiah may reflect an implied messianic connection. Jacob had a unique and personal encounter with God in theophanic form (Gn 32:20). He later prophesied Messiah's rule: ("the obedience of the peoples belongs to Him" [Gn 49:10]), and that from "Jacob" would come the "Shepherd, the Rock of Israel" (Gn 49:24). Later, the prophecy of Messiah's rule is given as a "star" that shall come "from Jacob" and "rule" (Nm 24:17, 19). King David, a type of messiah, referred to himself as "the one anointed (*mashiach*) by the God of Jacob" (2Sm 23:1) and said, "Oh, that Israel's deliverance (*yeshuah*) would come from Zion! When the LORD restores the fortunes of His people, Jacob will rejoice" (Pss 14:7; 53:6; cf. 85:1). Also, David says concerning the nations, following their divine judgment, "then they will know to the ends of the earth that God rules over Jacob" (Ps 59:13).

These passages tie together through the name "Jacob" the messianic prophecies concerning Messiah's restoration of the Jewish remnant in their land, His rule over the nations, and their submission to Him as their Judge and King. Additionally, this restoration follows the time known as the "time of trouble for Jacob" (Jer 30:7a). These concepts are all expressed in Isa 2:2-4/Mic 4:1-4 and suggest that these prophets had this in mind as they penned these words. For this reason, there has been little doubt among interpreters that King Messiah is the central figure of these texts.

The God of Jacob, the future Savior of Jacob (Jer 30:7b), is the Messiah who will rally the nations to Himself (Isa 11:10, 12), bringing them the knowledge of His Torah and ways, terms that taken together encompass the entirety of God's revelation of Himself and its requirements for mankind. The result of this divine education, the nation's submission to Messiah and respect for national Israel (Isa 60:3,14; 62:2; 66:18; Zch 8:21-23), and the subsequent divine arbitration between the nations, will eliminate war and result in universal peace (Isa 2:4/Mic 4:4; cf. Zch 9,10c). With Messiah ruling from Jerusalem and having dominion over the nations, who have joined national Israel in its worship and work (Isa 56:6-7; 61:4-5; 66:20-21; Hag 2:7; Zch 6:15), the land of Israel will be secure and prosperous (Mic 4:4a). There no longer will be anyone to cause fear (Mic 4:4b), as in times past when the nations invaded the land (Zch 12:3) and divided Jerusalem (Zch 14:2; cf. Rev 11:2). These arguments in Isaiah 2:2-4/Micah 4:1-3 for the literal interpretation of these locations, structures, and peoples within an eschatological context argue also for the identification of the Messiah and His actions fulfilling the promises of the new covenant.

NEW TESTAMENT USAGE

As stated in the introduction, there is no explicit citation of these prophecies in the NT. Likely, this is because the NT authors did not see a complete fulfillment of their prophecies in the Church Age. However, there are frequent allusions to these texts and similar OT texts defining the Jewish apostolic outreach to the Gentiles. These allusions relate to the prediction that Messiah would have a ministry that included Gentiles (Ac 15:17 citing Am 9:12) as a light of revelation to the nations. Moreover, Messiah will bring justice and peace to both Israel and the nations. Paul understood this mission (Ac 13:46) citing from Isa 51:4: "for instruction will come from Me, and My justice for a light to the [Gentile] nations." This wording parallels in thought the ministry of the Messiah in Isa 2:3/Mic 4:2 with respect to giving the law and dispensing justice for the nations. It was first heard in the righteous Simeon's citation of Isa 52:10 recorded at the time of Jesus' ritual dedication (Lk 2:30-32).

Based on the restoration prophecies, which involve the redemption of national Israel and the Gentile nations in the messianic kingdom, Matthew cites Isa 42:1, 4: "Behold, My Servant whom I have chosen; My Beloved in whom My soul is well-pleased; I will put My Spirit upon Him, and He shall proclaim justice to the Gentiles . . . until He leads justice to victory. And in His name the Gentiles will hope" (NASB), connecting the Messiah ("My Servant") with Gentile salvation (Mt 12:18,20,21). Paul, likewise, in Rom 15:12, cites Isa 11:10: "The root of Jesse will come, even he who arises to rule the Gentiles; in him will the Gentiles hope" (ESV), but with a future expectation of the messianic rule, the same event announced by Isa 2 and Mic 4.

While it is proper to view these NT uses of the OT as finding an explanation for Gentile inclusion in the Church Age, historicists make an illegitimate totality transfer, ignoring the prophecies' respective contexts, which contain other new covenant prophecies that can only be fulfilled with a regenerate national Israel in its own land. The Church, comprised of a remnant of national Israel and a remnant of the Gentile nations, serves as a proleptic microcosm that reveals the new covenant is in effect, but experienced only in part and on a limited scale—whereas complete fulfillment on a universal scale awaits the time of the messianic kingdom on earth (the millennium). The coming of the Holy Spirit has produced and preserves this partial and limited experience (Eph 2:11-22), but it is the coming of Messiah that will finalize the new covenant promises (Rom 11:25-27). Therefore, the NT rightly utilizes these prophecies to show a present fulfillment, but only in the understanding that the present fulfillment is in harmony with the complete fulfillment that includes national Israel in the period of restoration following the second advent of Messiah (see the use of Am 9:12 and intertextual allusions in Ac 15:15-18).

---

1. Micah's statement in 4:4 of the conditions that follow the restoration is not present in Isa 2, but the same concept is presented later by the prophet (Isa 27:6).
2. See Rabbi Nosson Scherman, *Isaiah: The Later Prophets with a Commentary Anthologized from the Rabbinic Writings*, Milstein Edition (New York: Mesorah Publications, Ltd., 2013), 17–19.
3. See "Mashiach" at *Judaism 101* accessed at http://www.jewfaq.org/mashiach.htm.
4. Oswalt states that this passage cannot be said to refer only to the millennial age, noting that "in a proximate sense it can relate to the Church age when the nations stream to Zion to learn the ways of her God through his incarnation in Christ." However, he immediately adds the caveat: "To be sure, we await Christ's second coming for the complete fulfillment of this promise, but the partial fulfillment began at Pentecost." John Oswalt, *The Book of Isaiah 1–39*, New International Commentary on the Old Testament (Grand Rapids: Eerdmans, 1986), 116–17.
5. The decision on authorship cannot be made on the basis of the textual variations or based on form alone because as Hillers has observed, "the transmission of the texts may have been kinder to the borrower's book than to the original author's, or vice versa." D. R. Hillers, *Micah: A Commentary on the Book of the Prophet Micah* (Philadelphia: Fortress Press, 1984), 52.
6. Rick Byargeon, "The Relationship of Micah 4:1-3 and Isaiah 2:2-4: Implications for Understanding the Prophetic Message," *Southwestern Journal of Theology* 46:1 (2003), 17–18.
7. Oswalt, *Isaiah 1–39*, 115.
8. James E. Smith, *What the Bible Teaches about the Promised Messiah* (Nashville: Thomas Nelson, 1993), 244.
9. Leslie C. Allen, *The Books of Joel, Obadiah, Jonah, and Micah*, New International Commentary on the Old Testament (Grand Rapids: 1976), 327.
10. This includes Gal 6:16, where the argument for identifying "the Israel of God" with the church depends on the grammatical understanding of the Greek conjunction *kai*. If a rare sense is imported to this term it may have the sense of "even," denoting identity. However, there appears to be no sound grammatical reason to take it other than in its usual sense of "and," denoting distinction. For the argument on this issue, see S. Lewis Johnson, "Paul and the 'Israel of God': An Exegetical and Eschatological Case-Study," in *Essays in Honor of J. Dwight Pentecost*, ed. Stanley D. Toussaint and Charles H. Dyer (Chicago: Moody, 1986).
11. See A. H. Bartelt, *The Book Around Immanuel: Style and Structure in Isaiah 2–12*, Biblical and Judaic Studies, vol. 4 (Winona Lake, IN: Eisenbrauns, 1996).

12. Andrew H. Bartelt, "The Centrality of Isaiah 6 (–8) Within Isaiah 2–12," *Concordia Journal* (October 2004), 316–17.

13. The text-centered approach considers the final (canonical, i.e., situating individual texts within a historical continuum of other texts) form of the text as inspired and authoritative (respecting the intention of the Divine Author). At the same time, it also considers the worldview and intention of the original author respect to the historical place and events that motivated and shaped the literary composition. The goal is to discern the intention of the author's strategy in composing his text as a part of the whole corpus of Scripture. For more details on this methodology, see Seth D. Postell, *Adam as Israel* (Eugene, OR: Pickwick Publications, 2011), 55–74.

14. John Sailhamer, *The Pentateuch as Narrative* (Grand Rapids: Zondervan, 2000), 36–41.

15. See John Sailhamer's discussion of the primacy of the text of Scripture as opposed to the events behind the text in "Text or Event," *Introduction to Old Testament Theology* (Grand Rapids: Zondervan, 1995), 36–85.

16. See Nathan Patrick Love, "The Mountain of The Lord in the Book of Isaiah: Prominent Themes in Contexts Mentioning the Mountain of The Lord and Related Terminology" (PhD dissertation: Trinity Evangelical Divinity School, 1996), 526–27.

17. In the OT, the phrase appears in this fixed form 14 times (Gn 49:1; Nm 24:14; Dt 4:30; 31:29; Isa 2:2; Jer 23:20; 30:24; 48:47; 49:39; Ezk 38:16; Hos 3:5; Mic 4:1; Dan 2:28 [Aramaic]; 10:14).

18. Ya'akov Elman, "Isaiah," *The Living Nach: Latter Prophets.* A New Translation Based on Traditional Jewish Sources (New York/Jerusalem: Moznaim, 1995), 5. This translation argues against the translation "end of days" because, as it states, "time will not end with Messiah's coming."

19. "Isaiah," *Tanach* (Jewish Publication Society, 1917) followed by Fred and Robin Sussman, Keith Chilson, and Dianne H. Smith, "Yeshayahu," *The Israel Bible* (Ramat Beit Shemesh: Israel 365, 2015), 10:19. While the *Complete Jewish Bible* follows the Jewish Publication Society 1917 in their translation of the Tanach, author David Stern preferred to leave the phrase untranslated in Isa 2:2 and simply rendered "In the *acharit-hayamim*"; Stern, "Yesha'yahu (Isaiah)," *Complete Jewish Bible* (Jerusalem: Jewish New Testament Publications, 1998), 438.

20. Rabbi Nosson Scherman, *Isaiah,* The Later Prophets with a Commentary Anthologized from the Rabbinic Writings. Milstein Edition (New York: Mesorah, 2013), 17.

21. Oswalt, *Isaiah 1–39*, 116.

22. J. P. M. van der Ploeg, O. P., "Eschatology in the Old Testament," *The Witness of Tradition. Oudtestamentische Studien* 17 (1972): 89–99; John T. Willis, "The Expression *be' acharith hayyamin* in the Old Testament," *Restoration Quarterly* 22 (1979): 54–71.

23. F. Delitzsch (Grand Rapids: Eerdmans, Repr. 1965), 74.

24. C. F. Keil, "Micah" in *The Minor Prophets,* Biblical Commentary on the Old Testament by C. F. Keil and F. Delitzsch (Grand Rapids: Eerdmans, Reprint 1965), 309.

25. Orthodox Jewish interpreters share the belief of evangelical Christians that eschatology can be traced for the explication of the development of later motifs to the pre-prophetic period. Hartman, as a representative of this view, contends that "in the age of the Patriarchs, of Moses and Joshua, and of the Judges, and in the first few centuries of the monarchy there is little evidence of true eschatology. Yet the basis of later Israelite eschatology was really laid down in that early age," Louis F. Hartman, "Eschatology: In the Bible," *Encyclopedia Judaica* 6 (1972), 862.

26. The future sense may indicate an end of time as contrasted with its beginning (cf. Isa 46:10), while at other times a time of change or a historical turning point is in view (cf. Hos 3:5; Ezk 38:8,16). This definite future sense encompasses both near (historical) and far (eschatological) points of reference, some being of an immediate future, and others spanning a comprehensive period from the author's vantage point until the Messianic Age. In some cases, a specific turning point in future Israelite history is eschatological (Dt 4:30; Isa 2:2; Jer 23:20; 30:24; Mic 4:1), while in others it is not (Dt 31:29; Jer 48:47; 49:39). In other cases of eschatological reference, the "latter days" are either comprehensive of a time stretching from the period of the conquest and monarchy until the Messianic Age (Gn 49:1; Nm 24:14), from the viewpoint of the prophet down to the Millennium (Dan 2:28; 10:14), specific to the Messianic Age itself (Isa 2:2; Mic 4:1; Hos 3:5), or to the time preceding the Messianic Age whenever the battle of Gog and Magog occurs (Ezk 38:16).

27. In a similar manner, both the expression *'acharit* ("last") and *qetz* ("end") are used with *hayamim* ("the days") in the Dead Sea Scrolls; with *'acharit hayamim* ("the last days") having the sense of the "messianic time," which comes, in distinction to *qetz* ("end [time]"), comes after the "end" (*qetz*) of wickedness. Examples of usage are: *be'acharit hayamim* (D IV. 4, 10)/*le'acharit hayamim* (pHab II. 5; V. 3-6; IX. 6), and *qetz* (D VI. 10, 14; XII. 23; XV. 7, 10; pHab VII. 7, 12)/*qetz 'acharon* (S IV. 16; pHab VII. 7, 12).

28. John H. Sailhamer, *The Pentateuch as Narrative* (Grand Rapids: Zondervan, 1992), 34–44, and "Creation, Genesis 1-11, and the Canon," *Bulletin of Biblical Research* 10 (2000): 86–106.

29. These uses are Pss 51:18; 76:2; 102:21; 128:5; 135:21; 147:12; Jl 2:32, 3:16,17; Isa 2:3; 4:3,4; 10:12,32; 24:23; 30:19; 31:4; 33:20; 37:22,32; 40:9; 41:27; 52:1,2; 62:1; 64:10; Am 1:2; Mic 3:10,12; 4:2, 8; Jer 26:18; Zph 3:14,16; Lam 2:10, 13; Zch 1:14,17; 8:3; 9:9.

30. Edward J. Kissane, *The Book of Isaiah* (Dublin: Browne and Nolan Ltd., 1941), 1:26.

31. Harry K. Moskoff, "Were the Temples Built on the Summit of Mount Moriah?" *Jerusalem Post*, accessed at http://www.jpost.com/Opinion/Were-the-Temples-built-on-the-summit-of-Mount-Moriah-385804.

Isaiah 4:2

The Branch of the Lord in the Messianic Age

J. RANDALL PRICE

Isaiah 4:26 introduces the first technical use of the messianic term *ṣemaḥ YHWH* ("the Branch of the LORD") in the OT. Although several of the versions have a different reading, the interpretation may still be messianic.[1] There are, as would be expected, nonmessianic and messianic interpretations of this text.

Among the medieval Jewish sages who hold a nonmessianic view, Rashi takes the lead (with Ibn Ezra following), interpreting the term "branch" as God's commendation of the "beauty of the people [of Israel]," in contrast to the preceding verse where the people's false beauty was condemned. He correctly saw this term as parallel to the following phrase "fruit of the earth," and therefore takes it also as a reference to the people. Isaiah 60:21 does refer to the people of Israel as a "branch," but there it is the term *neṣer* and not *ṣemaḥ*. It is also difficult to see how the "Branch" (v. 2) can be Israel and at the same time be "the adornment" of Israel (v. 2b). Abarbanel (on 2Chr 29) takes a historical interpretation, finding the reference to righteous King Hezekiah, who in contrast to his evil father Ahaz (whose reign Abarbanel believes is being described in the previous chapter) brought about a glorious religious revival.

However, another medieval Jewish sage, David Kimchi (Radak) took the messianic interpretation, following the most ancient sources, such as Targum Jonathan (see below), saying the day described is when "the Messiah, son of David, will arrive." Additionally, the sages employed the messianic term *ṣemaḥ* to the concept of resurrection and salvation (acts envisioned for the Messiah in the end of days) in the daily prayer: "You are a king who causes death and resurrects, and you make salvation sprout forth (*ṣemaḥ*). Blessed are you LORD, who resurrects the dead" (*Amidah* 2). Modern Jewish interpretation has followed both rabbinic paths as has modern Christian interpretation, with earlier scholarship (both critical and conservative) generally adopting the messianic interpretation and later scholarship (primarily critical, but recently also some conservative) adopting a nonmessianic interpretation.

Factors that determine the interpretation of *ṣemaḥ* are intertextuality in early traditions and later interpretations and context and structure. These factors will be found to argue for the messianic character of the passage.

EARLY TRADITIONS

Although the nominal use of the term *ṣemaḥ* is the first usage in the biblical text, the use of the noun appears in a third-century BC Phoenician document from Cyprus with reference to a legitimate royal heir. While this foreign usage may not have influenced Isaiah's terminology, it demonstrates, as Smith observes, "that this imagery was an appropriate term to represent the appearance of a new king in the ancient Near Eastern world."[2] The verbal use, in a messianic context, occurred some 300 years earlier. However, the verbal use of the root *ṣmḥ* appears in the record of King David's last words in 2Sm 23:5: "Will He [God] not make *spring forth* (Hb. *yaṣmîaḥ*) my salvation?" (author's translation). This statement is like that concerning David (probably written by Solomon)[3] in Ps 132:17 (NASB): "There I will cause the horn of David to *spring forth* (*'aṣmîaḥ*); I have prepared a lamp for Mine *anointed* (*mᵉšîḥî*)." It seems that the psalmist understood David having connected the concept of "springing forth" with the coming of the Messiah from the line of David. This is the meaning given this phrase in Ezk 29:21 where the future Messianic King will bring about the restoration of the Davidic rule as promised in the Davidic covenant (cf. Jer 33:20-26).

Sailhamer[4] has argued for an original messianic interpretation of 2Sm 23:5 since the LXX 2Sm 23:1c used a preposition (*epi*) "concerning" in place of the MT's use of a noun (*'āl*) "on high."[5] Thus, while the title "anointed one" in the MT refers only to King David (a nonmessianic interpretation), the earlier witness of the LXX refers to the Messiah ("the Anointed One"), a messianic interpretation. This would apply also to the next term in this verse "the Delightful One of the songs of Israel" (Messiah), rather than the MT: "the sweet psalmist of Israel" (David). Following this understanding, 2Sm 23:1-3 declares that David spoke prophetically about the Messiah.

The apostle Peter makes this point in Ac 2:29-31, observing that David's reference to God's "anointed" ["Your Faithful One" HCSB] in Ps 16:8-11 was not about himself, but about the Messiah. This observation may be strengthened in 2Sm 23:5 if the Hebrew phrase *kî lō kēn bêtî 'im 'ēl* is translated as a negative statement: "for not so is my house with God" rather than made an interrogative statement: "Is not my house so with God?" Most English translations assume a nonmessianic interpretation and that David is speaking about himself, and therefore the natural reading of this phrase would be a denial of that fact and would present an internal contradiction. But, the required interrogative particle is absent, and there is no contradiction if David was *not* speaking about himself, but about the Messiah.[6] There should be no doubt that the prophet Isaiah knew these passages employing the root *ṣmḥ* and that his use of *ṣemaḥ* in Isa 4:2 reflects this intertextuality as he builds upon prior messianic revelation in his description of the messianic restoration.

LATER INTERPRETATIONS

The book of Isaiah provides its own commentary on the concept of *ṣemaḥ*. In Isa 11:1,10 the prophet uses the botanical terms "stump" (*gezar*), "shoot" (*choter*), "root" (*shoresh*), and "branch" (*neṣer*) for the Davidic lineage. While this verse does not use the term *ṣemaḥ*, the term unfolds the Davidic dynasty from its beginning (Jesse) and reveals that from the seemingly dead stump of David's dynasty will come the Messiah. The "stem/stump," Jesse, produces a "shoot," his son David, from whose "root" will come a "Branch" (Messiah), who as the "root (*shoresh*) of Jesse" will gather the remnant who were preserved through the tribulation from among the nations (verses 10,12) and Israel (verses 11-12).

Therefore, as Rashi and others have argued, the *ṣemaḥ* cannot refer to the people of Israel. Rather, it is the people (Israel and the Gentiles) who come to the "root of Jesse" thereby equating the "root" innertextually with the *ṣemaḥ*. In fact, Isaiah uses all the terms in Isaiah 11:1,10 innertextually to develop the previously mentioned *ṣemaḥ* of Isa 4:2 to reveal the Messiah as the One who effects the messianic restoration. This innertextuality follows the same pattern of progressive revelation concerning Isaiah's messianic advent (Isa 7:14), followed by the description of the nature of the One "born/given" (Isa 9:6-7), the description of Messiah's ministry (Isa 11:1-5), and the messianic regathering and restoration (11:6-16; 12:1-6).

It seems that Isaiah coined the terms *neṣer* and *ṣemaḥ* as titles for Messiah, and following him, other prophets (Jeremiah and Zechariah) used the terms to refer to the Messiah. Jeremiah provides an example of such intertextual usage with reference to the "Righteous Branch" (*ṣemaḥ ṣadiq*) raised up for David (Jer 23:5). He will reign and save Judah and Israel as the "Righteous Branch . . . for David" who will "spring forth" (NASB) to execute justice and righteousness on earth (Jer 33:15). In both of these texts with restoration contexts, the messianic figure is identified as *YHWH ṣidᵉkenu*, "[the LORD] Our Righteousness" (Jer 23:6; 33:16). Zechariah also demonstrates intertextually when he speaks of "My Servant, the Branch" (*'avdi ṣemaḥ*) and the "man whose name is Branch" (*'ish ṣemaḥ*) in Zch 3:8; 6:12. Here the crowning of Joshua the high priest to "bear royal honor and shall sit and rule on his throne" (ESV) foreshadowed the crowning of Messiah, who at His second advent will build the final (Millennial) Temple and unite the offices of king and priest in one person.

However, the primary argument against a messianic interpretation of Isa 4:2-6 is the parallelism between "Branch of the LORD" (v. 2a) and "fruit of the land" (v. 2b). This is a contextual matter and therefore needs to be addressed by a careful examination of the immediate and wider context of the passage.

THE CONTEXT OF ISAIAH 4:2-6

The NET Bible (produced by evangelical scholars) adopts a nonmessianic interpretation based on the context and translates v. 2: "At that time the crops given by the LORD will bring admiration and honor; the produce of the land will be a source of pride and delight"—with a footnote stating, "Hebrew: 'and the vegetation of the LORD will become beauty and honor.'" This follows the interpretation of scholars, such as R. E. Clements, who says the verse only means the survivors in Jerusalem would live in a very fertile land that would produce plentiful crops.[7] He argues further that while later prophets do use the term *ṣemaḥ* of a human ruler and metaphorically of human offspring, those texts have contextual indicators that allow for this interpretation. In contrast, Isa 4 does not have these contextual indicators and the parallelism with "produce of the land" argues for taking *ṣemaḥ* in its usual sense of literal vegetation or crops.

W. H. Rose makes the argument that *ṣemaḥ* in Isa 4:2 cannot be messianic, since by nature a *ṣemaḥ* grows directly from the ground and not from another tree or plant, and therefore would not fit the messianic concept of Davidic progeny.[8] H. G. M. Williamson thinks his position is unassailable and remarks "the common translation 'branch' is certainly mistaken, as has been most recently demonstrated by the full and thorough analysis of Rose."[9]

However, the term here, as in the later uses of the term, is a *compound* title. Therefore, the identity of *ṣemaḥ* cannot be determined by an understanding of the term in isolation, as Gary V. Smith explains:

When the verbal form of *ṣemaḥ* is used, it is normally connected to a noun (hair, herbs, trouble, truth, health, vine, east wind, horn, tree) so that it is clear what is "springing forth/growing." The nominal form of "branch" (*ṣemaḥ*) is used seven times of a literal plant growth or a "shoot from the ground" (Isa 61:11; cf. Gn 19:25), but the phrase "Branch of the LORD" or "Righteous Branch" never refers to the literal growth of plants elsewhere in the OT. The Aramaic Targum translates Isa 4:2 as "Messiah of the Lord," showing that early Jewish interpreters thought this was a messianic reference.[10]

In a similar manner, Isa 1:8 and 3:14 refer to a vineyard in the literal botanical sense. However, in Isa 5, the prophet employed a vine/vineyard as imagery for the people of Judah and Jerusalem (5:1-6), while also retaining the strictly literal sense (5:10). The prophetic author makes his identification clear by use of a compound term "the vineyard of the LORD of Hosts" and then states the obvious: "[It] is the house of Israel and the men of Judah, the plant He delighted in" (5:7). This same idea was previously expressed with possessive pronouns "[His] vineyard" (5:1) and "My vineyard" (5:3). There is no ambiguity here—later prophets use the same terminology with the same reference (Jer 2:21; 12:10; Ezk 19:10; Hos 10:1), and Jesus employs the term "his vineyard" in a parable with the same intent (Mt 20:1). However, when Isaiah and other prophets refer to the Messianic Age, they use a literal sense of "vine/vineyard" to picture the renewed abundant produce as a sign of the restoration blessings for Israel (Isa 27:2; 65:21; Jer 31:5; Ezk 28:26; Hos 2:15; 14:7; Jl 2:22-26; Am 9:14; Mic 4:4; Zch 3:10; 8:12).

Therefore, while the restoration of crops may be in the context, this does not require *ṣemaḥ* to be reduced to merely a botanical reference. The parallelism of "Branch of the LORD" and "fruit of the earth" may be identical (A=B) or complementary (A+B), with the result that the Branch may be another description of the Messiah or the increase of the remnant population as a result of the messianic restoration.[11]

If the former, some commentators suggest the first term refers to the deity of the Messiah (i.e., a shoot of the LORD Himself) and the second to His humanity ("of the earth").[12] Steveson, accepting "the Branch of the LORD" as a messianic title, argues that the term in parallelism, "fruit of the earth," must also be a messianic title. He cites as an example Ps 132:11: "The LORD has sworn to David a truth from which He will not turn back: 'Of the fruit of your body I will set upon your throne'" (NASB). Here, "fruit" refers to the Davidic descendants ("seed of David"), which is ultimately fulfilled in Messiah as the "son of David" (Ps 89:4,35-36; 1Chr 17:14; cf. Mt 22:42).

However, this may also imply that the term *ṣemaḥ*, even in isolation, may have messianic significance, since it refers to a "sprout" that comes from the ground (i.e., "the land of Israel") and is connected to the Davidic dynasty (Jer 33:15), here identified with YHWH Himself ("the Branch of the Lord"). Isaiah explains this messianic significance in 11:1 (though not using this term), where in parallel language he speaks of a "shoot" (*ḥoter*) that comes from the stump of Jesse (David's father) and a "branch" (*neṣer*) that grows from his roots. Jeremiah 23:5-6 then describes this "Branch" (*ṣemaḥ*) as a righteous judge and triumphant ruler (with obvious messianic overtones, cf. Isa 61:1).

Steveson also argues that the stress in vv. 2-3 is not upon the multiplication of the population, but upon the "survivors of Israel" left in the land, and those who are "left in Zion" and remain in Jerusalem.[13] This would move the focus away from that of material prosperity, required if "branch" and "fruit" are taken as botanical metaphors of God's national blessing. While this may be the case for vv. 2-3, the following vv. 4-6 describe the future era of Israel's restoration and reveal the context (in harmony with 2:2-4 upon which this text builds, see below) is eschatological and messianic.

Therefore, a better solution is to take the clauses in v. 2 to refer to parallel *acts of God* that will restore and transform Zion/Jerusalem: God brings forth His Messiah (to bring about the deliverance of Zion/Jerusalem and serve as the agent of the restoration), and God brings forth renewed fertility in the land (the new life that Messiah brings, which suggests a mental association with "branch") as a witness to the advent of the Messianic Age/restoration to "the survivors of Israel" (those who escaped the great tribulation and now have entered the millennial reign of Messiah).[14]

Oswalt supports this interpretation, noting that "if the branch is the Messiah, then the point would seem to be that the real and lasting produce of Israel is God's gift, not the result of her own fruitfulness and power."[15] These two acts of God best fit the wider context of what will be done to move Israel from a state of judgment to that of restoration and reverse the condition of both the people and the land.

Isaiah condemned the ritualistic worship of national Israel (1:1-15), but promised future ritual cleansing (1:16-20) and restoration (1:21-31) for Israel and the nations in the messianic kingdom (2:1-5). In 2:6–4:1 the prophet resumes the theme of condemnation to add a present warning of divine judgment concerning idolatry (2:6-21), evil rulers in the land (2:22–3:15), and the attitude of pride in prosperity, as typified in the nation's materialistic women (3:15–4:1).

Having issued this promise of punishment, Isaiah now returns to the promise of restoration and kingdom rule from chap. 2. The prophet's argument is that Israel's pride and consequent punishment will not prevent God's plan and His coming glorious kingdom. This will be accomplished as God brings a future glory (Messiah) that will beautify Zion/Jerusalem (4:2), a cleansing that will purify and thus create a holy people in Zion/Jerusalem (4:3-4), and a glorious protection for Zion/Jerusalem that will uniquely set it apart to God (4:5-6).

Therefore, while the context (3:1–4:1) may refer to the problem of the inglorious nature of rulers, priests, and people, and 4:2-4 may be the solution, reversing this condition of the people, this restoration occurs through divine agency (redemption/deliverance and purification/ sanctification). Isaiah 4:2, as well as the parallel uses of the term *ṣemaḥ* in the prophets, reveal the agent of this restoration to be the Messiah. This connection is established in this context from the previous description of this restoration in Isa 2:2-4, and this innertextual development forms a structural pattern that argues for the messianic interpretation.

THE STRUCTURE OF ISAIAH 4:2-6

How Isa 2:2-4 is interpreted affects how Isa 4:2-6 will be understood in the larger context. The reason for this, as shown above, is that the prophet interrupted his description of the Messianic Age in 2:2-4 to explain how the coming judgment of the nation would not cancel this hope, now continued in 4:2-6. The structure of these two texts argues for their being understood in continuity. As Isa 2:2 began with the glory of the future Temple, so 4:6 ends with a description of its glory. Both Isa 2:3 and 4:3 center on Zion and Jerusalem and the sanctification of its people. As Isa 2:4 ended a restoration section with Messiah's rule, so 4:2 begins the renewed restoration focus with this theme. This A:B:A:A:B:A arrangement indicates that the prophet joined these two sections in his thought as complementary descriptions of the Messianic Age. Because most commentators view Isa 2:2-4 as being messianic and as having its setting in the Messianic Age, textual consistency argues for 4:2-6 being messianic as well.

There is an intertextual parallel to this dual act of God in restoration in Ezk 34:20-31. In this text both aspects of messianic rule and botanical fertility are present in the context of the future glorious kingdom with "one shepherd, my Servant David" (NASB) (= Messiah) who will tend (rule) God's sheep (national Israel) in Ezk 34:23 (cf. Ezk 36:29-30) and "the trees of the field will give their fruit and the land will yield its produce" in Ezk 34:27 (cf. Ezk 37:24-25). Here, there is clearly a person and a plant. Even though Ezekiel was aware of Isaiah's text and may have constructed his text with it in mind, he did not equate the fruit or crops with the "Branch of the LORD," indicating he understood this same distinction in Isaiah made in 4:2. Moreover, the context of Isaiah reveals an eschatological/messianic setting. Isaiah 4:2 opens with the temporal marker *bayôm hahu'* ("in that day"). While the term refers to any time of divine intervention in history,[16] in this context it must be understood as eschatological, since in Isa 2:2 a future restoration setting was established with the term *b^e'arḥarit hayamim* ("the last days" or "the end time").

THE MESSIANIC SIGNIFICANCE OF THE TERM *ṢEMAḤ YHWH*

The term "Branch of the LORD" has a royal-messianic significance based on the concept that it "sprouts" or "branches out" from the tribe of Judah and the royal line of David, and other prophets provide the details concerning this figure (Jer 23:5; 33:15; Zch 3:8; 6:12). In the Dead Sea text of Isa (*1QIsa^a*) there is the addition of the word "Judah" to that of "Israel" in v. 2b to remind the reader of the messianic prediction made concerning this tribe (Gn 49:10).

While David is not mentioned in the immediate context, Isaiah will soon make this identification when he describes the "Branch" as coming from the root of "Jesse," David's father (Isa 11:1). Jeremiah builds on this Davidic/messianic connection, writing, "I will raise up a righteous Branch of David. He will reign wisely as king" (Jer 23:5). It has been recognized that in Jer 23:6, where the name of this king is called "the LORD our righteousness" (NASB) (*ṣemaḥ ṣedikenu*), that the full Tetragrammaton (YHWH) is included in the name given to "the Branch." Compound names containing the divine name are common in the Hebrew Bible, but they always appear in an apocopated (shortened) form (*-yah*). Only here are all four letters of the Tetragrammaton found together to designate a human ruler of the Davidic line. Given this usage, it is easy to understand why in the postexilic prophets, *ṣemaḥ* became a technical term for the ideal king (King Messiah) who would be God's servant and rebuild the Temple (Zch 3:8; 6:12).[17]

This messianic significance was not lost to Tannaitic Judaism as seen in Targum Jonathan Ben Uziel's paraphrase of the opening words of Isa 4:2: "In that time the Messiah of the LORD shall be for joy and for glory." From this it becomes plain that the meturgeman ("translator"), who produced the Targums at the oral and written level, realized the exegetical significance of the verbal trigger "branch" and developed a messianic transformation of the Hebrew text through the targumic laws of addition and substitution. In particular, he read this text innertextually with that of Isa 2:3-4 in which the "law" or "instruction" (Torah) emanates from Zion and the "word of the LORD" from Jerusalem (the place of the Temple and the messianic throne, 1Chr 17:14), and Messiah arbitrates for the nations (based on the word/law of the Lord). These further additions are explained by Paul Flesher and Bruce Chilton:

> The dominance of the association between "branch" and "Messiah" is such that further transformations of the Hebrew text occur. "Fruit of the land" in Isaiah 4:2b of the Masoretic Text becomes "those who perform the law" in the Targum

> because the Messiah will inspire that fruitful performance of Torah . . . That is, the Targum is better understood if one knows that "branch" is now Messiah and that "fruit" is now Torah. Those promises are still present, and vivified by the eschatological dimension of messianic meaning.[18]

The remaining context (vv. 4-6) unfolds the messianic nature of "the Branch of the LORD." "The LORD" ritually cleanses[19] the sin ("filth") of the "daughters of Zion" (typifying the defiled people of Jerusalem from Isa 3:16–4:1, but by extension all the inhabitants of the land, although the focus of the sanctifying work is Jerusalem). At the same time the Lord also "purged" (a ritual term for removing impurity, Ezk 40:38) the guilt of Jerusalem's bloodshed (including ritual violations for making contact with blood), constituting this remnant ("whoever remains") as "holy" (v. 3b). This fulfills the divine ideal to constitute Israel a "holy people/nation" (Ex 19:6), a necessary condition for entering the millennial kingdom (Zch 14:20; cf. Rev 21:27; 22:14-15) and dwelling with the Messiah (the "Holy One of Israel," Isa 12:6; 60:9,14) in holy Jerusalem (Zch 2:12; 8:3) on His "holy mountain" (Isa 2:2; 11:9; 65:11,25; 66:20; Ezk 20:40; Jl 3:17; Zph 3:11).

This purgation (*dûaḥ*) is performed by the Spirit (*rûaḥ*), an intentional wordplay that connects intertextually with the action of the cleansing Spirit in Ezk 36:25-27 (cf. Jn 3:5), emphasizing the removal of ritual defilement incurred by corpse impurity (the consequence of exile). This is followed in context by restoration to the land, fertility, and prosperity (vv. 28-31) and the later prophecy of Jerusalem's spiritual cleansing in Zch 12:10–13:2 in relation to Messiah's death and Israel's national repentance for restoration (cf. Rom 11:26-27). Therefore, Isaiah identifies the Spirit with the acts of "judgment" and "burning" (Isa 4:4c) because both terms (in this context) describe the purification/sanctification (by removal of those that sin/defile) of the Jewish (Rom 11:27) and Gentile remnant (Mt 25:31-40) that will occur in Jerusalem at the end of the tribulation period prior to the commencement of the millennial reign of Messiah.

As a result of the separation and ritual purification of the "holy" remnant, Isaiah describes in 4:5-6 how the Divine Presence (Shekinah), explained here in terms of its original appearance from Mount Sinai (Ex 19:16; 20:21; 24:15) through the wilderness (Ex 13:21; 16:10; 19:9) to the Tabernacle (Ex 40:34) and First Temple (1Kg 8:10-13) as "a cloud of smoke by day . . . a glowing flame of fire by night," (v. 5) will return to the restored Jerusalem. The city is referred to here as "glory" (*kābôd*), and Isaiah later connects this "glory" with that of the Messiah as He reigns on Mount Zion (Isa 24:23; 25:6-10a).

This term is also connected in the history of Israel with the Shekinah ("glory cloud"), and although Isaiah is the first among the prophets to announce the return of the Shekinah, Ezekiel also revealed the way this return would take place, reversing the direction of its departure before the destruction of the First Temple (Ezk 9–11) and filling the Millennial Temple as a sign of the messianic restoration (Ezk 43:1-7). Isaiah states that the Shekinah will return to overshadow the sacred area containing the Millennial Temple (an elevated Mount Zion, Isa 2:2; Ezk 40:2; Zch 14:10), providing physical protection from harsh conditions (heat, storm, rain).[20]

The term Isaiah uses for this supernatural shelter provided by the Shekinah is "canopy," an expression well-known in the Jewish wedding ceremony as a *ḥuppāh*, which may reflect the idea of Israel as the bride of YHWH (Hos 2:19-20), although, here divine protection seems to be the focus (cf. Ps 105:39). This protection is referred to in v. 6 as a "shelter" (*sukkāh*), a term used for the erection of temporary dwellings during the wilderness wandering and to the practice of their Jewish descendants to commemorate this "protection" during the Feast of Sukkot (or Festival of Booths or "Tabernacles"), Lv 23:33-43, by building and living in a *sukkāh* ("booth"), Neh 8:13-18.

It was during Sukkot that the water-drawing ceremony took place at the Pool of Siloam, transporting its water to the altar in the Temple in promise of the latter rains that would complete the agricultural cycle and bring forth the harvest. This place, the Pool of Siloam, (*Šiloaḥ*, "sent"), had messianic significance. The water taken from it and poured on the altar symbolized the outpouring of the Holy Spirit in the days of the Messiah (the time of the final harvest). It was also in this area that Isaiah had issued a challenge of faith to Ahaz (Isa 7:3), which is part of the book of Immanuel containing the prophecy of the virgin birth (Isa 7:14) and the divine nature and Davidic rule of the Messiah (Isa 9:6-7). At that time, the flowing waters of the *Šiloaḥ* were rejected (Isa 8:6), revealing the spiritual defection of the nation's leadership from YHWH.

In Jn 7:37-38, with this background in view, Jesus as Messiah offered the nation of Israel the opportunity to reverse its spiritual condition as those who believed in Him [as Messiah] would have "living deep within," symbolizing the promise of the gift of the Holy Spirit that characterized the new covenant (Jl 2:29; Ezk 36:27), to be fulfilled with national Israel in the millennial kingdom. The Feast of Sukkot is also part of the millennial obligation of Gentile believers from among the nations that went to war against Messiah at Armageddon and will now have to demonstrate their fidelity to King Messiah in Jerusalem (Zch 14:16-19). Egypt is singled out, probably because of the long history of animosity toward Israel, especially in the exodus. This may connect with Isa 2:3-4, which depicts the nations coming to Jerusalem to learn Torah and find arbitration from Messiah.

Isaiah continues these verbal and theological associations in vv. 5-6 with the concept of a "new exodus," a theme in Isaiah that has a distinct messianic connotation. For example, Ex 15:2 uses the term *Yah* ("LORD") in the song of salvation (from the sea) and Isa 12:2 uses this term *Yah* paired with YHWH in its song of salvation (from the tribulation). Isaiah again uses *Yah* YHWH in 26:4 for yet another song of salvation (in the kingdom). Isaiah by using this dual term in the context of deliverance not only connects with the exodus, but may be expressing his belief in the Lord (YHWH) and the Messiah (*Yah*) who together brought about the exodus.

This link to the exodus seen in Isa 4:5-6 with the return of the Shekinah to Jerusalem may have an intertextual use in the NT when it describes the advent of the "Logos" ("Word" = God, Jn. 1:1) as taking on flesh and dwelling with man (Jn 1:14) with the Greek verb *eskēnosēn*. The nominative form of this word is *skēnē* ("Tabernacle"), which simply transliterates the Hebrew *šekînāh* (the nominative form being *miškān*). What John is saying here is that just as YHWH temporarily manifested His Divine Presence (Shekinah) in a visible form in the exodus and at the sanctuary, so YHWH has now permanently manifested ("tabernacled") with His people in the form of human flesh, i.e., the Messiah (Yeshua). At His return for the messianic restoration, the perspective of Isaiah in 4:5-6, the Messiah will occupy the throne of David within the Millennial Temple in fulfillment of the Davidic covenant (Isa 16:5; 2Sm 7:10-13,16; 1Chr 17:9-13, especially v. 14).

The messianic and divine connection between YHWH in the first exodus and Messiah in the new exodus has been explained by Hendren: "The divine nature of the 'Son' is confirmed by the prediction of His everlasting rule in the kingdom and in the very house of God. The latter parallels Ezekiel's description of the returning 'glory of the LORD' personified, establishing the throne of His kingdom in the restored temple (Ezk 43:4-7)."[21] These connections ("Branch," "Shekinah") made by Isaiah and affirmed by other prophets and the NT, argue decisively for the messianic character of Isa 4:2-6.

---

1. Several of the versions understand this differently: The LXX (Greek translation of the OT) translated this key term as ἐπιλάμψει ὁ θεός ("God will shine forth"), possibly misreading צחח for צמח with the sense of the Aramaic צמחא ("brightness"). Aquila Symmachus and Theodocian (translators of a pre-Masoretic Hebrew Bible to Greek, ca. AD 200) read ανατολη κυριος ("Lord [will be] rising"). The Syriac Peshitta (version translated from the Hebrew in the 2nd century AD) is similar with *denḥeh dᵉmārja*ˆ("appearance or glory of the Lord"). While these do not use the term "branch," they promote a messianic interpretation as the term "brightness" is used in Isa 4:5 (NASB). The phrase "brightness of your (Messiah's) rising" appears in Isa 60:3 (NASB), with a similar reference to Zion/Jerusalem's restoration in Isa 62:1 (NASB). The Latin Vulgate (produced by Jerome in Bethlehem in AD 382) has *germen Domini* ("sprout of the Lord"), which has the messianic connection with a Davidic messiah as in Isa 11:1 and Jer 23:5. The MT reading is supported by the Dead Sea scroll Isaiah (1QIsa[a]), our oldest known example of the Hebrew biblical text (ca. 125 BC).
2. Gary V. Smith, *Isaiah 1–39*, New American Commentary 15A (Nashville: B&H, 2007), 155.
3. The words of this psalm were cited in part at the dedication of Solomon's Temple (2Chr 6:41f), demonstrating that the psalm was preexilic (as its archaic grammar attests) and existed early enough in the reign of Solomon to be available to use at this event. Some ascribe it to David at the occasion of the bringing of the ark to Jerusalem or

one of the Zion festivals. For discussion on the date, see Leslie C. Allen, *Psalms 101–150*, Word Biblical Commentary (Waco, TX: Word, 1983), 206–208.

4. John H. Sailhamer, *Introduction to Old Testament Theology: A Canonical Approach* (Grand Rapids: Zondervan, 1995), 221.

5. The difference in the Hebrew text is in the understanding of vowels: *'āl* with a long vowel (*qamaṣ*) is the noun "on high," whereas *'ăl* with a short vowel (*pataḥ*) is the preposition "on, about, concerning." Since the original Hebrew text was written without vowels, the Jewish translators of the LXX must have been familiar with an oral reading of the text that had the short vowel (= preposition). This implies that the Masoretic scribes discerned this messianic emphasis and downplayed it by adding the long vowel (= noun).

6. See Michael Rydelnik, *The Messianic Hope: Is the Hebrew Bible Really Messianic?* (Nashville: B&H Publishers, 2010), 39–41.

7. R. E. Clements, *Isaiah 1–39*, New Century Bible Commentary (Grand Rapids: Eerdmans, 1980), 54.

8. See the discussion in W. H. Rose, *Ṣemaḥ and Zerubbabel: Messianic Expectations in the Early Postexilic Period*, Journal for the Study of the Old Testament Supplement 304 (Sheffield, JSOT Press, 2000): 91–106.

9. H. G. M. Williamson, *A Critical Commentary on Isaiah 1–27* (London: T&T Clark, 2006), 1:301.

10. Gary V. Smith, *Isaiah 1–39*, New American Commentary 15A (Nashville: B&H, 2007), 155–56.

11. J. J. M. Roberts, "The Meaning of 'יה חמצ' in Isaiah 4:2," *Jewish Bible Quarterly* 28:20–27.

12. Peter A. Steveson, *A Commentary on Isaiah* (Greenville, SC: BJU Press, 2003), 39. See also Arnold Fructenbaum, "Isaiah," *The Popular Bible Prophecy Commentary*, ed. Tim LaHaye and Edward Hindson (Eugene, OR: Harvest House, 2006), 126.

13. Steveson, *Commentary on Isaiah*, 39, n1.

14. Kissane notes that "the marvelous fertility of the soil in the Messianic Age is a favorite theme of the prophets (cf. Isa 30:23; Jer 31:12; Ezk 34:26-30; 36:34f; Am 9:13; Hos 2:21f; Zch. 10:1; Mal 3:12)." Edward J. Kissane, *The Book of Isaiah* (Dublin: Browne and Nolan, Ltd., 1941), 1:48-49.

15. John N. Oswalt, *The Book of Isaiah 1–39*, New International Commentary on the Old Testament (Grand Rapids: Eerdmans, 1998), 146.

16. Isaiah uses this phrase frequently (2:2,17,20; 3:7,18; 4:1; 5:30; 7:18,20-23; 10:20,27; 11:10; 12:4; 17:4,7; 17:9; 19:16,18-19,21,23-34; 20:6; 22:8,12,20,25; 23:15; 24:21; 25:9; 26:1; 27:1-2,12; 28:5; 31:7; 52:6). The specific time in view must be derived from the context, but also from innertextual use, as argued above.

17. Joyce G. Baldwin, "*ṣemaḥ* as a Technical Term in the Prophets," *Vetus Testamentum* 14:93-97

18. Paul V. M. Flesher and Bruce Chilton, *The Targums: A Critical Introduction* (Waco, TX: Baylor University Press, 2011), 184–85.

19. While this term may refer to general washing (Gn 18:4; 19:2; Jdg 19:21; Ru 3:3; Ezk 16:4,9; 23:40) as well as ritual and sacrificial washing, especially for the removal of sin for purification (Ex 30:18,20; 40:30,32; Lv 14:8-9; 15:5,9,13,16; 17:15-16; 22:6; Nm 19:19; Dt 23:11; cf. Ezk 16:9), the context here demands the ritual understanding. This is well supported by its use in the Dead Sea sectarian texts for ritual purification (*1QS* 3:5; *4QRitPurB* 1.12:5; 42.2:5).

20. The need for protection from the heat and storm and rain may refer to the Exodus plagues where God protected Israel in the land of Goshen from the specific plague involving these elements (Ex 9:22-26). This thought may have influenced the Qumran scribe in *1QIsa*[a] who substituted the word *sa 'ēr* ("storm") for *ba 'ēr* ("burning"), perhaps to allow the problem of v. 5 ("storm" of judgment) to be clearly resolved by the protection provided from "storm" in v. 6.

21. Noam Hendren, "The Divine Unity and the Deity of Messiah." Unpublished paper (Netanya: Israel College of the Bible), 8.

Isaiah 7:1-16

The Virgin Birth in Prophecy[1]

MICHAEL A. RYDELNIK

In his book *Velvet Elvis*,[2] Rob Bell asked,

> What if tomorrow someone digs up definitive proof that Jesus had a real, earthly, biological father named Larry, and archaeologists find Larry's tomb and DNA samples and prove beyond a shadow of a doubt that the virgin birth was really just a bit of mythologizing the Gospel writers threw in to appeal to the followers of the Mithra and Dionysian religious cults that were hugely popular the time of Jesus, whose gods had virgin births? But what if as you study the origin of the word *virgin*, you discover that the word *virgin* in the Gospel of Matthew actually comes from the book of Isaiah, and then you find out that in the Hebrew language at that time, the word *virgin* could mean several things. And what if you discover that in the first century being "born of a virgin" also referred to a child whose mother became pregnant the first time she had intercourse?[3]

After raising these questions, Bell does affirm the historic Christian faith, including the virgin birth.[4] Nevertheless, Bell's conjecture regarding "Larry, the human father of Jesus" is troublesome, not because he believes it but rather because evangelicals have accepted some of the presuppositions presented here.

For centuries Christians understood Isaiah 7 to be a prediction of the virgin birth. Now it is not uncommon for evangelicals to assert that the Hebrew word Isaiah used does not mean "virgin" but rather "young woman." Moreover, the passage is not viewed as a prediction of Messiah's birth but rather of a child born in Isaiah's day. Bell's popular-style book reflects the trend in contemporary evangelical OT scholarship that denies that Isaiah was predicting the virgin birth of the

Messiah. For example, John Walton understands Isaiah predicting the natural birth of a child to a young woman in the court of King Ahaz.[5] He writes, "Exegesis gives us no clue that Isaiah had been aware that he was speaking of the Messiah. The child's name merely expressed the hope that accompanied God's deliverance."[6] Walton and other evangelical scholars who agree with his view take this position not to deny a biblical essential but rather to affirm biblical scholarship and sound exegesis. But is their approach to interpreting Isa 7 as accurate and safe as they suppose?

For now, the evangelical commitment to faith in Jesus and His virgin birth is secure. But, will not the questioning of the predictive value of Isa 7 or, as Bell does, the questioning of even whether belief in the virgin birth of Jesus is essential for evangelical faith lead to a slippery slope culminating in a spiritual disaster? It seems that to maintain faith in the virgin birth over the long term, it will be necessary to address the seemingly troublesome Isa 7 passage. Is it possible to view Isaiah's prophecy as a direct messianic prediction while still practicing sound exegesis? In this article, that is precisely what I propose to do.

THE VIRGIN BIRTH IN PROPHECY

In my experience, Isa 7:14 is the most controversial of messianic prophecies. Disputes revolve around a variety of issues, chiefly, the meaning of the word *'almah*, the relationship of Isaiah's "sign" to the context, the way the original readers of the prophecy would have understood it, and Matthew's citation of this verse in support of the virgin birth.

As a result, interpreters have divided into three primary views of the passage, and even among these views, expositors present their own unique perspectives. The first view, held by many traditional Christian interpreters, is to see the prophecy as a *direct prediction* of the virgin birth of the Messiah. Taking different approaches as to how the prophecy relates to the original context, they each conclude that the word *'almah* means "virgin" and refers to the mother of Jesus.

A second position, frequently held by critics and Jewish interpreters, is that of a purely *historical interpretation*. It views Isaiah's promise to be that a young woman in the eighth century BC would have sexual relations and then give birth to a child that would serve as a sort of hourglass for Judah—before that child reached a certain age, the two kings threatening Judah would be removed.

Third, a common approach taken by contemporary Christian scholars is to view the prophecy as having some sort of *dual* or *multiple fulfillment*. Isaiah is understood to refer to the natural birth of a child in his own day to function as a sign to Judah. Nevertheless, they contend that this does not exhaust the meaning.

Rather, by double fulfillment, *sensus plenior*, type, a later rereading, progressive fulfillment, or even by the use of first-century Jewish hermeneutics, the prophecy also refers to the virgin birth of Jesus.

I believe that by placing the prophecy in context, through a careful reading of the text of Isa 7 and relating it to innerbiblical interpretations of the passage, a view that supports a direct prediction of the virgin birth makes the most sense. That would explain Matthew's reason for citing Isa 7:14 as a prediction of the virgin birth.

THE CONTEXT OF THE PROPHECY

The historical setting of the prophecy was a threat against Judah around the year 734 BC. At that time, Rezin, king of Syria (Aram) and Pekah, king of the northern kingdom of Israel, formed an anti-Assyrian alliance. They in turn wanted Ahaz, king of Judah, to join their alliance, and when he refused, they decided to make war against Ahaz to force the issue (7:1). The northern alliance against Ahaz caused great fear in the royal family of David (7:2) because the goal was not just to conquer Judah but also to "install Tabeel's son as king" in the place of Ahaz (7:6). Their plan would place a more pliable king on the throne and also put an end to the Davidic house. This threat provides a significant detail in understanding the passage. While some have contended that there would be no reason to foretell the coming of the Messiah, the danger to the house of David explains the messianic concerns of the passage. It was the Davidic covenant (2Sm 7:12-16; 1Ch 17:11-14) that led to the expectation of a future Messiah who would be a descendant of David. Therefore, if Ahaz and the entire royal house were to be destroyed, it would bring an end to the messianic hope. A long-term prophecy of the birth of Messiah would assure the Davidic house and the readers of the scroll of Isaiah that the messianic hope was indeed secure.

With this threat looming, the Lord sends Isaiah to give assurance to Ahaz, telling him to meet Ahaz at "the conduit of the upper pool, by the road to the Fuller's Field" and specifically to bring his son, Shear-jashub (7:3). Frequently, commentators overlook this command to bring the boy as if it were an unnecessary detail. Nevertheless, it seems strange to think that Isaiah would include this precise requirement without it having any significance. As will be seen, this seemingly minor detail will play a significant role in understanding the passage.

At the conduit of the upper pool, Isaiah gave Ahaz his God-directed message: "It will not happen; it will not occur" (7:7). The Lord, through Isaiah, promised that the attack would not succeed and the alliance would be broken. In fact, Isaiah predicted that within 65 years, the northern kingdom of Israel would no longer be recognized as a people (7:8, "Ephraim will be too shattered to be a people"). This prediction came true in three phases. First, Tiglath-pileser, king of Assyria, conquered Israel in 732 BC, sending many captives back to Assyria (2Kg 15:29). Second, Assyria destroyed the northern kingdom in 721 BC, deporting much of the Israelite population to Assyria and settling the land of Israel with other peoples (2Kg 17:24). It was completely fulfilled in 669 BC when Ashurbanipal enacted the final population transfers between Israel and Assyria (Ezr 4:2,10). Thus in 669 BC, 65 years from the date of the events described in Isaiah's prophecy, the northern kingdom was indeed "too shattered to be a people" (7:8) and the land was inhabited by Samaritans, a people of mixed ethnicity (Ezr 4:2).[7]

To confirm the promise that the attack on Judah would not succeed, the Lord offered a sign to Ahaz of his own choosing.[8] The king was told that the sign could come "from the depths of Sheol to the heights of heaven" (7:12). This is an obvious merism,[9] calling Ahaz to ask God to provide a sign that would be stupendous enough to elicit faith. Although the Hebrew word for "sign" (*'ot*) does not necessarily require a miracle, it does include the supernatural within its range of meaning (cf. Ex 4:8-9,17,28,30; 7:3; 10:1-2; Nm 14:11,22; Dt 4:34; 6:22; 7:19, etc.). In light of the nature of the offer, it appears that Ahaz was to ask for a miraculous sign.

Nevertheless, Ahaz, with false piety, refuses to test God. The disingenuous nature of his response is plain in that this is a king who had so little regard for the Lord that he practiced idolatry, even offering his own son as a child sacrifice to Molech (2Kg 16:3; 2Ch 28:3). While he might claim biblical justification (Dt 6:16) for his refusal to ask or test the Lord (7:12), this seems ridiculous because the Lord Himself has just called upon him to do so. So, when Ahaz was under his greatest threat, he refused the Lord's comfort and rejected the offer of a sign. In response, Isaiah declared that, nonetheless, the Lord would give a sign—one that would become a source of controversy for generations.

THE CONTENTS OF THE PROPHECY

The most significant difficulty in interpreting the prophecy is that from a cursory reading it appears that the sign would be fulfilled within just a couple of years of Isaiah's meeting with the king and not more than 700 years later with the birth of Jesus. The reason for this difficulty is the failure to read the prophecy carefully and pick up the clues the author has left. A close reading of the text will disclose that there is not one prophecy here but two—a long-term prediction addressed to the house of David (7:13-15) and a short-term prediction addressed to Ahaz (7:16-23).

The Long-Term Prophecy to the House of David: The Birth of Messiah (Isaiah 7:13-15)

Since the northern alliance was threatening to replace Ahaz with the son of Tabeel, the entire house of David was endangered. Were Syria and Israel to succeed, the messianic promise of a future son of David who would have an eternal house, kingdom, and throne (2Sm 7:16) would be demolished. This provides the need for a long-term sign of hope that, despite the menace to the house of David, the Messiah would be born, with the sign of His coming being His virgin birth. The details of this prophecy are as follows:

"Listen, house of David." Isaiah's declaration of the Lord's sign shifted the direction of the prophecy away from Ahaz to the whole house of David (7:13). This is evident not only from the vocative "house of David" but also from the change of singular pronouns and verbs of command (7:4,11) to plural. When addressing Ahaz alone, the *singular* was used. However, in 7:13-14, Isaiah used the second-person *plural*. This is not an obvious change in the English Bible, but in v. 13 the imperative verb "listen" is plural, the expression "Is it not enough for *you*" is plural, and "Will *you* also try" is plural. Then in v. 14 "you" is plural.[10] The reason for the shift is that God was clearly fed up with this wicked and sanctimonious king, so he addressed the royal house he represented. Moreover, it was not only Ahaz who was being threatened but also the entire house of David.[11]

"Therefore, the Lord Himself will give you a sign." Although Ahaz, as the head of the house of David, had tried God's patience, Isaiah promised that the Lord Himself would still grant a sign—but one that would now be of God's own choosing. As mentioned above, the Hebrew word for "sign" can refer to the miraculous or the non-miraculous. However, in light of the previous offer of a sign "from the depths of Sheol to the heights of heaven," it would appear that the sign to follow would be of a miraculous nature. Moreover, this is how Isaiah uses the same word in the parallel situation with Hezekiah (Isa 38:1-8). There, as a "sign" that Hezekiah's life would be extended, the shadow on the stairway would miraculously retreat ten steps (38:7-8).[12]

"[Behold] the virgin will conceive [lit., the virgin is pregnant], have a son, and name him Immanuel." The Lord called special attention to the ensuing sign with the word *hinnê*, traditionally rendered "behold!" When used in similar constructions in the Hebrew Bible (Gn 16:11; 17:19; Jdg 13:5-7), the word *hinnê* serves to bring attention to a birth of special importance.[13] The sign that the Lord promised the house of David is that of a pregnant *almah* who would bear a son. The use of the article (frequently untranslated in modern English versions) with the word *almah* indicates that the Lord has a specific woman in mind. It is not some generic woman in the court of Ahaz but one whom the prophet sees in particular.

Controversy has surrounded the word *almah* since the second century when Aquila substituted "young woman" (Gk. *neanis*) in his Greek translation of the Hebrew Bible for the LXX translation of "virgin" (*parthenos*). Was Isaiah speaking of a virgin or merely a young woman?[14] Various arguments have been put forward to make the case for translating the word as virgin.

Etymologically, *almah* is derived from a word that means "to be sexually strong, sexually mature, sexually ripe or ready."[15] This would seem to emphasize the age of the woman (pubescent) rather than indicating whether she was sexually active. Cyrus Gordon has argued that ancient (pre-Mosaic) Ugaritic, which is cognate to Hebrew, used the word parallel to *almah* of a virgin goddess. Since the Ugaritic annunciation formula used a similar construction to Isa 7:14, Gordon concluded that *almah* should rightly be translated "virgin."[16] Furthermore, many have maintained that the Septuagint translation of *almah* with the Greek word *parthenos* ("virgin") is evidence that in the pre-Christian era, the word was understood as referring to virginity.[17]

The best way to determine the meaning of the *almah* is by examining its usage throughout the Hebrew Bible. If there were a place in Scripture where it clearly refers to a non-virgin, it would widen the range of meaning to make it possible that it might refer to a non-virgin in Isa 7:14. However, in every situation the word is used either of a virgin or in an indeterminate, neutral sense.

Genesis 24:43. Here Rebekah, the soon-to-be wife of Isaac, is called an *almah*. This chapter of Genesis describes Rebekah as a "girl" (*na'arah*, 24:14), a virgin (*bethulah*, 24:16), and a maiden (*almah*, 24:43). These three synonyms are used to describe a virginal young woman.

Exodus 2:8. In this passage, Miriam, the sister of Moses, is called an *almah*. As a young girl, still in the home of her parents, it is legitimate to infer that the word includes the idea that she was a virgin.

Psalm 46:1. In this verse, the superscription uses the word as a musical direction. So it is indeterminate, not supporting or contradicting the meaning virgin.

Psalm 68:25. This verse refers to a musical worship procession in which *alamot* (plural of *almah)* play the tambourines. Perhaps this verse is indeterminate, not speaking to the virginity of the maidens. But possibly it hints at virginity because it calls to mind Jephthah's daughter who lamented her being offered as a sacrifice to the Lord (Jdg 11:34-40). While some commentators believe that Jephthah's daughter was an actual human sacrifice, others maintain that she was given by Jephthah to lifelong service in the tabernacle. Thus, she was never to marry and went with her friends to mourn her virginity. If this is the case, then perhaps it indicates that serving in the Temple was restricted to virgins. Therefore, the young women in the Temple worship procession, spoken of in Ps 68:25, would be virgins.

First Chronicles 15:20. Once again, the word is used as a musical direction. So it is neutral, not supporting or contradicting the meaning "virgin."

Song of Solomon 1:3. This verse refers to the love of the *alamot* for Solomon. These are not married women but maidens who wanted husbands but have not yet been married. Therefore, the word would imply the concept of virginity.

Song of Solomon 6:8. This description of the king's harem includes three categories: 60 queens, 80 concubines, and *alamot* without number. The queens are those whom the king has married, the concubines are those with whom he has had sexual relations, and the *alamot* are the virgins who will one day be elevated to either concubine or queenly status. If these *alamot* were not virgins, they would be in the concubine category. Hence, the use of the word here describes virgins.

Proverbs 30:19. This verse is the most controversial of the usages since it describes "the way of a man with an *almah*." The entire proverb is found in 30:18-19 and refers to four wonderful and incomprehensible things: an eagle in the sky, a serpent on a rock, a ship in the sea, and a man with an *almah*. Some have maintained that what unites these four is in each one something disappears. A soaring eagle is easily lost from sight. A serpent quickly slithers off the rock, disappearing from sight. A ship can be lost in a fraction of time. And a virgin can lose her virginity to a young man very quickly. Even if this were the correct interpretation of the proverb, the word *almah* would indeed be virgin. But since there is no moral evil in the first three examples, it seems unlikely that the fourth would call extramarital sex "wonderful." Moreover, the contrast with the adulterous woman in 30:20 would imply that the *almah* in the previous verse was not engaged in illicit sex. Probably the best way to understand this proverb is as referring to the mysterious and wonderful qualities of youthful attraction.[18] Thus, it once again would refer to a virgin.

In its every use in the Hebrew Bible, the word *almah* either refers to a virgin or has a neutral sense.[19] Based on this study, it appears that Isaiah chose his words based on precision. While the Hebrew *bethulah*[20] could refer to a virgin of any age, *almah* would refer to a virgin that has just arrived at puberty. She is a maiden in the truest and purest sense. So, there does not seem to be cause to abandon the traditional interpretation of *almah* as a "virgin" except for an antisupernatural or antimessianic bias.[21]

This virgin, according to the translation, will be with child. However, the Hebrew in the verse is even more emphatic. It uses the feminine singular adjective *harah* ("pregnant"), which in context would more accurately be translated "the virgin is pregnant" or "the pregnant virgin." Were it not for the context calling for a sign as deep as Sheol or high as heaven, such a translation would seem impossible. However, the prophet, by means of a vision, sees a specific pregnant virgin before him who would be the sign of hope for the house of David.[22] This indeed would meet the qualification of being "deep as Sheol or high as heaven."

"And she will call his name Immanuel" (NASB). The virgin mother of the child will recognize His special nature. Therefore, she will give Him the title "Immanuel," which means "God with us."[23] The message to Judah was that God would be with them in a special way through this child. The title hints at the divine nature of the boy. Even clearer is Isa 8:8, which describes the Assyrian conquest of Judah, saying that the Assyrians will sweep over Judah "and its spreading streams will fill your entire land, Immanuel!" If the child Immanuel were not divine, Isaiah would not identify the land as belonging to Him.[24] Moreover, in the next great vision of the coming Davidic king (Isa 9:6), the child receives other divine throne titles including "Mighty God" and "Father of Eternity" (my translation). Isaiah was not merely promising a future Davidic king that would secure the line of David. He was not only promising that He would have a supernatural birth. Ultimately, the prophet has revealed that the Messiah would be God in the flesh, Immanuel.[25]

"By the time he learns to reject what is bad and choose what is good, he will be eating butter [or curds] and honey." The Lord continues His description of the virgin-born Davidic Messiah, giving a clue to the situation into which He would be born (7:15). Many mistake the butter and honey He would eat as the food of royalty, ignoring the context in Isa 7 itself. Later in the chapter, Isaiah writes of the coming Assyrian oppression, when Assyria would shave the land (7:20). At that time, fields will not be cultivated and will become pastures for oxen and sheep (7:23-25). The effect of this will be an overabundance of dairy (or butter/curds) because of the pasturing of livestock and an excess of honey because bees will be able to pollinate the wild flowers. Therefore, because of "the abundant milk they give," a man "will eat butter, for every survivor in the land will eat butter and honey" (7:21-22). So, in this passage, butter and honey do not represent the food of royalty but rather the food of oppression. The point then of the description of the future virgin-born, Davidic king eating butter and honey is to accentuate that he would be born during a time of political oppression. In other words, the prophecy of Messiah concludes with a hint that He will be born and grow up ("learn[ing] to reject what is bad and choose what is good") at a time when Judah is oppressed by a foreign power.[26]

With this, Isaiah has completed his first prophetic message. With the northern confederation of Syria and Israel threatening to replace Ahaz with a substitute king, the entire house of David was imperiled and with it, the messianic hope. Isaiah has come with a message of hope—the future son of David would indeed be born someday. The supernatural sign that will reveal His identity is that He will be born of a young virgin and have a miraculous divine nature. Moreover, He will grow up during a time of oppression over the Jewish people and their land. With the assurance that the house of David and the messianic hope are both secure, the prophet turns his attention to the immediate threat and gives a near prophecy to wicked King Ahaz.

The Short-Term Prophecy to Ahaz: The Sign of Shear-jashub (Isaiah 7:16-17)

While many have considered v. 16 to be a continuation of the prophecy in 7:13-15, the grammar of the passage suggests otherwise. The opening phrase in Hebrew can reflect an adversative nuance, allowing for a disjunction between the child described in 7:13-15 and the one described in v. 16. There is a different child in view in this verse.[27]

The Identity of the Child. So, who is the child in 7:16? In light of Isaiah being directed to bring his own son to the confrontation with the king at the conduit of the upper pool (cf. 7:3), it makes most sense to identify the lad as Shear-jashub. Otherwise there would be no purpose for God directing Isaiah to bring the boy. Thus, having promised the virgin birth of the Messiah (7:13-15), the prophet then points to the small boy that he has brought along and says, "But before *this* boy (using the article with a demonstrative force) knows to reject what is bad and choose what is good, the land of the two kings you dread will be abandoned."[28] In this way, Shear-jashub functioned as a sign to the king. Appropriately, Isaiah could tell Judah in the very next chapter, "Here I am with the children the Lord has given me to be signs and wonders in Israel from the Lord of Hosts who dwells on Mount Zion" (8:18).

The Identity of the Addressee. To whom does Isaiah make this prediction? What is not evident in the English text is plain in the Hebrew. The prophet returns to using the second-person singular pronoun in 7:16 ("the land of the two kings *you* (sg.) dread" [emphasis added]). In 7:10-11 he used the singular to address King Ahaz. Then, when addressing the house of David with the prophecy of Messiah, he shifted to the plural. But in 7:16, he addressed King Ahaz, using the singular pronoun once again and giving him a near prophecy: before Shear-jashub would be able to discern good from evil, the northern confederacy attacking Judah would fail. Within two years, Tiglath Pileser defeated both Israel and Syria, just as the prophet had predicted.

Having completed his long-term prophecy, Isaiah gave a short-term prophecy. In doing so, he followed a frequent pattern in his book. He consistently did this so his readership could have confidence in the distant prediction by observing the fulfillment of the near one.[29]

THE CONFIRMATION OF THE PROPHECY

The messianic interpretation of Isaiah 7:13-15 does not only stand strongly through a careful reading of the text itself but it is also confirmed by innerbiblical allusions to the prophecy. While some have argued that only Mt 1:23 reads Isa 7:14 as a messianic prophecy, that is really not the case. To begin with, Isaiah himself substantiates the messianic reading with two passages that follow. Isaiah's contemporary Micah does the same.

Isaiah 9:6-7. After giving hope to the house of David that the promise of the Davidic covenant was secure, as would be seen in the birth of Immanuel (7:13-15), Isaiah proceeded to identify when the son of David would come. He described the time of judgment to fall on Judah (Isa 8) when Judah would be "dejected and hungry" and would "see only distress, darkness, and the gloom of affliction" (8:21-22). At that time, it will be said "the people walking in darkness have seen a great light; a light has dawned on those living in the land of darkness" (9:2). This light was the son of David described in Isa 7:13-15.[30] He was the child that would be born and given four glorious, twofold titles, "Wonderful Counselor, Mighty God, Eternal Father [Father of Eternity], Prince of Peace" (9:6). He would sit "on the throne of David and over his kingdom to establish and sustain it with justice and righteousness from now on and forever" (9:7). Just as this future king would be called Immanuel, indicating His deity, so also would the other throne titles reflect His divine nature.[31] The point of Isa 9:1-7 was to alert the house of David that the virgin-born King for whom they were to look would only come after a long period of darkness. Nevertheless, He would indeed come, possessing a divine nature, to establish a righteous and eternal kingdom.

Isaiah 11:1-10. Although Isa 9 clarifies that the son of David would come after a time of darkness, Isa 11 elucidates even further that Immanuel, the virgin-born Child, on whom the hopes of the entire house of David rests, will come in the distant future. Only after the mighty tree of David was cut down with "terrifying power" (10:33) and the Davidic dynasty had become a mere stump would a shoot "grow from the stump of Jesse" (11:1). This King from David's line would be empowered by the Spirit of God and establish a righteous reign (11:2-5). His kingdom would be so peaceful that it would even alter the nature of predatory animals (11:6-9). He would not just be the King of Israel, but when He comes, all the nations will seek "the root of Jesse" (11:10). This description is an innertextual clarification of the King as described in Isa 9, giving further details of His peaceful and righteous reign.

Robert Culver has conceded that perhaps Isa 7:13-15 is a difficult passage and hard to identify as messianic without careful reading. However, it becomes clearly messianic "when one continues to the final verses of the prophecy,"[32] referring to Isa 9 and 11. He adds that reading Isa 7:13-15 within the context of these other passages would cause a reader to "understand that a virgin was someday to bear a very human baby whose very character would be divine."[33] Certainly, the prophet has included these passages in the book of Immanuel, as Isaiah 7-12 is frequently called, to clarify on whom it is that the house of David should pin their hopes. It was the child written about in Isa 7:13-15, namely, the future Davidic Messiah who would be "God with Us."[34]

Micah 5:3. The prophet Micah, a contemporary of Isaiah, provides an intertextual confirmation of the messianic reading of Isa 7:13-15. Located in the well-known prophecy of the Messiah's birth in Bethlehem (Mic 5:2-5), this prophecy is clearly related to Messiah's birth. It identifies His human origin ("Bethlehem Ephrathah . . . One will come from you to be ruler over Israel for Me"), His eternal source ("from antiquity, from eternity"), and the time of His coming ("when she who is in labor has given birth"). This last phrase has long been recognized as an intertextual reference to the virgin birth in Isa 7:13-15.[35]

The passage indicates that Israel will be abandoned (referring to the captivity and exile) until "she who is in labor has given birth" to the son of David. Only after this birth will the remnant of Messiah's brethren reunite as a nation (they will "return to the people of Israel"). The reason they will be able to return is the glorious reign of the Messiah, of whom it says, "He [this One] will be their peace" (5:5).

Micah 5:2-5 has multiple allusions and references to the Book of Immanuel. Both Micah 5 and Isaiah 7 refer to the Messiah's birth; both refer to the pregnant woman giving birth; both allude to His divine nature (Micah saying He comes from long ago and the days of eternity, and Isaiah calling Him Immanuel, Mighty God, and Father of Eternity); both Micah ("He will stand and shepherd them in the strength of Yahweh," 5:4) and Isaiah (9:7; 11:1-10) refer to the glorious reign of the Messiah; both point out that Messiah will be the source of peace for Israel ("He will be their peace," Mic 5:5; "He will be named . . . the Prince of Peace," Isa 9:6).

These many intertextual references are significant. If a plainly messianic passage like Mic 5:2-5[36] cites Isa 7:13-15, it shows that the earliest interpretation of Isa 7:14 (and, no less, an inspired interpretation) recognizes the messianic prophecy of the virgin birth.

Matthew 1:23. Matthew's use of Isa 7:14 in his narrative of the virgin birth has been regarded in a variety of ways: a double fulfillment or *sensus plenior*; an example of typical fulfillment; a pesher interpretation;[37] or even a misuse of Isaiah who, they allege, was not referring to the virgin birth in any way at all. However, it appears to me that Matthew was following a careful and close reading of Isaiah[38] and recognized that the prediction given to the house of David had found its fulfillment in the virgin birth of Jesus of Nazareth. Immanuel had come just as prophesied eight centuries earlier. God was with Israel. The inspired words of the apostle Matthew in 1:22 (lit., "Now all this happened *in order that* what was spoken by the Lord through the prophet might be fulfilled") make it clear that God's words to Isaiah in 7:14 had made the particular nature of the Messiah's birth to the virgin as inevitable as thunder that follows the lightening. Furthermore, to remove the intentionality of this connection is to deny the truthfulness of Matthew's words.

THE VIRGIN BIRTH IN PROCLAMATION

We end where we began. What if Jesus did indeed have a human father named Larry? What if the gospel writers were merely mythologizing to make their message more palatable to pagans? What if Isaiah's prediction referred to a young woman giving birth to a child via natural means in eighth-century BC Judah? According to some, these are insignificant questions. This approach says that faith in Jesus is still the truth even if the virgin birth is questioned or if Isaiah's prediction of it is explained away as exegetically untenable. But truth is foundational to faith. According to Bell and others, we must believe in Jesus because "it works," not because it is true. In fact, Jesus' claim is just the opposite. According to Him, faith in Him only works because it is a true faith. Moreover, He is the truth.

It appears that according to prophecy, the Messiah's virgin birth was an essential to be believed for two reasons. First, the virgin birth was to be a major sign to confirm Messiah Jesus' position as the messianic son of David. If Jesus of Nazareth had a human father named Larry or Joseph, it would prove that He really was not the Messiah. No matter how good a life one could lead by believing in Jesus, it would be a sham. Following Jesus changes our lives because He truly is the Messiah.

Second, the virgin birth is in some way related to the deity of Jesus. The prediction foretells that the Messiah would be Immanuel or "God with us." Luke, when recording the virgin birth, records the angel's message to Mary: "The Holy Spirit will come upon you and the power of the Most High will overshadow you. Therefore, the holy One to be born will be called the Son of God" (Lk 1:35). Just as Isaiah related the virgin birth to Messiah being God with us, so Luke regards the virgin birth as the basis for Jesus' being the Son of God, that is, Deity. Foundational to our faith is that God became a man in order to redeem us. Without the virgin birth, we deny the doctrine of Messiah's deity and lose the truth of His atonement.

Philip Roth's short story, *The Conversion of the Jews,* relates the tale of a young Jewish boy, Ozzie, who asked his rabbi about the virgin birth. Retelling his question to his friend, young Ozzie says,

> I asked the question about God, how if He could create the heaven and earth in six days, and make all the animals, and the fish and the light in six days . . . if he could make all that in six days, and He could *pick* the six days he wanted right out of nowhere, why couldn't He let a woman have a baby without having intercourse?[39]

Ozzie's point about the possibility of a supernatural birth makes perfect sense. I would go one step further to affirm supernatural revelation. If God could create the world and miraculously enable a young Jewish virgin to have a baby, certainly He could have allowed an eighth-century BC Jewish prophet to predict the first-century virgin birth of the Jewish Messiah.

---

1. This article is adapted from Michael Rydelnik, "Proclaiming Jesus from the Hebrew Bible: The Virgin Birth as Predicted in the Hebrew Scriptures," in *Proclaiming Jesus: Essays on the Centrality of Christ in the Church in Honor of Joseph M. Stowell*, ed. Thomas H. L. Cornman (Chicago: Moody Publishers, 2007). Used with permission. A version of it later appeared as Michael Rydelnik, "An Example from the Prophets: Interpreting Isaiah 7:14 as Messianic Prophecy" in *The Messianic Hope: Is the Hebrew Bible Really Messianic?* NAC Studies in Bible and Theology, ed. E. Ray Clendenen (Nashville: B&H Publishers, 2010), 65–82.
2. R. Bell, *Velvet Elvis* (Grand Rapids: Zondervan, 2005).
3. Ibid., 26–27.
4. Ibid., 27.
5. J. H. Walton, "Isa 7:14: What's in a Name?" *Journal of the Evangelical Theological Society* 30 (1987): 289–306.
6. Ibid., 300.
7. J. J. Davis and J. C. Whitcomb, *A History of Israel* (Grand Rapids: Baker, 1980), 429–34.
8. J. Walton has speculated that Isa 7:10 ("Then the Lord spoke again to Ahaz . . .") begins a new setting for the prophecy at a later time and that Isaiah and his son Shear-jashub were no longer present at the conduit of the upper pool. He also cites a number of sources both supporting and rejecting this conjecture ("Isa 7:14: What's in A Name?" 289). J. Oswalt correctly affirms that 7:10 is a continuation of Isaiah's meeting at the upper pool. He writes that the word "*again* may merely indicate a second part of a single conversation, vv. 3-9 being the promise and vv. 10, 11 the challenge (cf. Gen. 18:29; etc.). There being no evidence of a change in time or location, it seems best to see the paragraph as a direct continuation of vv. 1-9" (*The Book of Isaiah: Chapters 1-39*, New International Commentary on the Old Testament [Grand Rapids: Eerdmans, 1986], 204).
9. A merism is a figure of speech in which "the totality or whole is substituted by two contrasting or opposite parts." See R. B. Zuck, *Basic Bible Interpretation* (Wheaton, IL: Victor Books, 1991), 151.
10. English cries out with the need for a second-person plural. Hence, the southern colloquialism "Y'all" or the Brooklynese "Youse."
11. An implication is that the sign offered in vv. 13-15 was no longer intended to encourage Ahaz to have faith since he was now under judgment. Note the prophet's change from "*your* God" in v. 11 to "*my* God" in v. 13. See J. A, Motyer, *The Prophecy of Isaiah: An Introduction and Commentary* (Downers Grove, IL: InterVarsity, 1993), 84.
12. See the discussion of the word "sign" or "*'ot*" in D. L. Cooper. *Messiah: His Nature and Person* (Los Angeles: Biblical Research Society, 1933), 36–37. R. L. Reymond maintains that since "the referent of the word 'sign' in verse 11 clearly is of that order lends strong credence to the presumption that, when God declared in verse 14 that He Himself would give a 'sign' since Ahaz had refused to ask for one, the words that then followed upon His declaration that He would give a 'sign' also entailed the miraculous" (*Jesus, Divine Messiah: The Old Testament Witness* [Ross-Shire, Scotland: Christian Focus, 1990], 24).

13. E. J. Young not only cites these verses but also shows that the Ras Shamra literature does the same (*Studies in Isaiah* [Grand Rapids: Eerdmans, 1954], 159–60). The word "hinnê" is a deicitic particle whose function is generally to call attention to what follows. It occurs first in Gn 1:29 calling attention to God's announcement of His abundant provision of food for Adam and Eve and thus serving as an important part of the context for the temptation narrative in Gn 3.

14. Walton "alumim" (entry 6596), in *New International Dictionary of Old Testament Theology and Exegesis*, vol. 3, ed. Willem VanGemeren (Grand Rapids: Zondervan, 1997), 417, has made the case for translating *almah* as "young woman." His strongest argument is that when used as an abstract noun in Isa 54:4, *alumim* ("youth") is used with "a metaphorical attribution of this term to Israel, she is also described as having a husband (v. 5) and of being barren (v. 1). In parallel phrases the 'shame' of her [*'alumim*] is paired with the shame of her widowhood." He maintains that this "would suggest a close connection with childbearing," thus concluding that the word does not indicate virginity. However, a closer look at Isa 54:4 will demonstrate that while Israel is indeed being spoken of figuratively as a woman, the promise the Lord is making is that "you will forget the shame of your *virginity ('alumim)* and the reproach of your widowhood you will remember no more." The contrast is between Israel's youth (before she married, hence a virgin) and when she was a widow (again with no husband, after she married). Isaiah's usage of the abstract noun *'alumim* would seem to indicate virginity.

15. See Francis Brown, S. R. Driver, and C. A. Briggs, *Hebrew and English Lexicon of the Old Testament* (Oxford: Oxford University Press, 1906), 761.

16. C. H. Gordon, "Almah in Isaiah 7:14," *Journal of Bible and Religion* 21 (1953): 106.

17. For example, see E. E. Hindson, *Isaiah's Immanuel (*Phillipsburg, NJ: Presbyterian and Reformed, 1978), 67–68. G. Delling (παρθενος *TDNT* 5:826-37) maintained that the word *parthenos* did not yet mean "virgin" when the LXX was translated. While this is questionable, the Isaiah translator clearly understood *almah* as virgin and so rendered the feminine singular adjective *harah* ("pregnant") as a feminine singular verb ("will conceive"). Surprisingly, most interpreters miss what has long been seen as an attempt by the translator to come to terms with the "difficulty" of a "pregnant virgin" in Isa 7:14.

18. This is the view of Hindson, *Isaiah's Immanuel*, 38–39, and also D. Hubbard, who describes it as "the positive picture of romance." *Proverbs* (Waco, TX: Word Books, 1989), 465–66. W. McKane, while denying that *almah* means "virgin," interprets the proverb as referring to the "irresistible and inexplicable attraction which draws together the man and the woman." *Proverbs: A New Approach* (Philadelphia: Westminster, 1970), 658.

19. For a more thorough discussion of the meaning of *almah*, see R. Niessen, "The Virginity of the עלמה in Isaiah 7:14," *Bibliotheca Sacra* 546 (1980): 133–50.

20. In response to the proposal that if Isaiah had wanted to stress the girl's virginity, he would have used the word *bethulah*, see G. J. Wenham, "*Bethulah* A Girl of Marriageable Age," *Vetus Testamentum* 22 (1972): 325–48, who points out that virginity was not a necessary element of the semantic content of *bethulah* any more than it is with the English word "girl." He also argues, "It is not until the Christian era that there is clear evidence that *bethulah* had become a technical term for 'virgin.'" Motyer concludes that *almah* suited the task of expressing virginity better than *bethulah* (The Prophecy of Isaiah, 84).

21. The antimessianic bias is readily apparent in the great Jewish biblical commentator Rashi, who interprets *almah* as "virgin" in Song 1:3 and 6:8 but argues for "young woman" in Isa 7:14. This same bias motivated Aquila in his second-century Greek translation of the Hebrew Bible, changing the LXX *parthenos* to *neanis* (young girl).

22. This vision explains why Isaiah speaks of a future event in the present tense.

23. Some have objected to Matthew's use of this passage in the birth narrative (Mt 1:23) because Mary did not name the child "Immanuel." However, "Immanuel" is not the given name of the Messiah. Rather, it was to be seen as a symbolic, descriptive throne title. Similarly, David's son was given the name Solomon, but his descriptive royal title was "Jedidiah" or "Beloved of the Lord" (2Sm 12:24–25).

24. See Motyer, *The Prophecy of Isaiah*, 86.

25. Reymond, *Jesus, Divine Messiah: The Old Testament Witness*, 31–34.

26. "The 'butter and honey' serve as figures for an oppressed land: natural rather than cultivated products; cf. vv. 22-23 . . . Fulfillment: the moral growth of Jesus, learning to distinguish between good and evil (cf. Luke 2:40, 52), yet in a land that was afflicted—as it worked out historically, by the Romans—and no longer ruled by the dynasty of David." J. Barton Payne, *The Encyclopedia of Biblical Prophecy* (Grand Rapids: Baker, 1973), 293.

27. The two Hebrew words, *kiy beterem*, are only used twice in the Hebrew Bible, and the other use, in Isa 8:4, may indeed be causal. However, the causal nuance does not make sense here. Both the NIV and NLT (first edition) recognize the contrast with the translation "but before." Calvin and more recently R. Vasholz ("Isaiah and Ahaz: A Brief History of Crisis in Isaiah 7 and 8," *Presbyterion: Covenant Seminary Review* 13 [1987]: 82–83) recognized the adversative phrase *kiy beterem* as signaling a new and different boy under discussion. Oswalt argues to the

contrary, "It is not necessary to separate v. 16 from v. 15; in fact, the opening *ki* of verse 16 can be taken as causal, indicating why the child will eat curds and honey: Judah will be delivered from her neighbors' threat" (*The Book of Isaiah: Chapters 1–39*, 213). However, the causal nuance makes no sense if the butter and honey represent the food of oppression, as it plainly does in the next paragraph. How would Judah's deliverance explain why the child would eat butter and honey, the food of oppression?

28. Calvin and R. Vasholz, "Isaiah and Ahaz: A Brief History of Crisis in Isaiah 7 and 8," 83, maintain that 7:16 begins a second prophecy but that it is not a particular boy but a generic child, leading to the idea "but before a boy grows old enough to refuse evil and choose good." To come to this view they must claim a generic use of the article, which is not supported by the context. D. L. Cooper (*Messiah: His Nature and Person*, 150–51) and A. Fruchtenbaum (*Messianic Christology* [Tustin, CA: Ariel Press, 1998], 37) have recognized that the boy is Shear-jashub, but they mistakenly, and without syntactical warrant, begin his description in 7:15, seeing only 7:13-14 as referring to the Messiah. To my knowledge, only W. Kelly, *An Exposition of the Book of Isaiah* (London: Paternoster, 1897), 144–45; and H. Bultema, *Commentary on Isaiah*, trans. D. Bultema, (Grand Rapids: Kregel, 1981), 108, have written that 7:16 begins a second, distinct near prophecy *and* identified the lad as Shear-jashub. Kelly states that others hold this view, but he does not give attribution to anyone.

29. Vasholz, "Isaiah and Ahaz: A Brief History of Crisis in Isaiah 7 and 8," 82.

30. Even C. L. Blomberg, who advocates a "double fulfillment" hermeneutic, recognizes that "the larger, eschatological context, especially of Isa. 9:1-7, depicted a son, never clearly distinguished from Isaiah's [Maher-Shalel-Hash-Baz according to Blomberg], who would be a divine, messianic king." That is, the canonical book of Isaiah itself clearly linked, in some way at least, the divine Messiah of Isa 9:1-7, 11:1-10, etc., with the prophecy of a virgin-born son in 7:14. "Matthew could indeed speak of Isaiah's prophecy as fulfilled in Christ. The canonical form of Isaiah was already pointing in this twofold direction" ("Matthew" in *Commentary of the New Testament Use of the Old Testament*, ed. G. K. Beale and D. A. Carson [Grand Rapids: Baker, 2007], 5).

31. While some have objected finding the deity of the Messiah in the Hebrew Bible, it appears that this is purely circular reasoning. It begins with the presumption that the Hebrew Scriptures do not reveal a divine Messiah. Then every passage that appears to indicate the deity of the future Messiah is dismissed because "the Hebrew Scriptures do not reveal a divine Messiah." The classic defense of taking Isa 9:6 as referring to Messiah as God is J. D. Davis. "The Child Whose Name is Wonderful," in *Biblical and Theological Studies* (New York: Scribner, 1912). For authoritative defense of the Messiah's deity in the Hebrew Scriptures, see B. B. Warfield, "The Divine Messiah in the Old Testament," in *Christology and Criticism* (New York: Oxford, 1921).

32. R. D. Culver, "Were the Old Testament Prophecies Really Prophetic?" in *Can I Trust My Bible?* ed. Howard Vos (Chicago: Moody, 1963), 104.

33. Ibid.

34. Moreover, the author also provides an innertextual reference between the Messiah of Isaiah 11 and the Suffering Servant of Isa 52:13–53:12. Just as the Messiah "the *root* of Jesse will stand as a banner for the peoples" (Isa 11:10), He would also be compared to a "*root* out of dry ground" (Isa 53:2). When all the innerbiblical dots are connected in Isaiah, it serves to inform the reader that (a) the future son of David would be the virgin-born Immanuel (Isa 7:13-15); (b) He would be God in the flesh (Isa 9:6); (c) He would reign over a righteous and peaceful, eternal Kingdom (Isa 9:7; 11:1-10); and (d) He would only accomplish this after His substitutionary death and resurrection (Isa 52:13–53:12).

35. N. Snaith, while denying the messianic interpretation of both Isa 7:13-15 and Mic 5:2-5, has recognized that Micah is indeed referring to the Isaiah passage (*Amos, Hosea, and Micah* [London: Epworth, 1960], 95). Snaith admits that Mic 5 is referring to the birth of a great king who, as heir to the Davidic throne, would be endowed with remarkable qualities.

36. Certainly some have disputed that Mic 5:2-5 is messianic and have regarded it as nothing more than hope for the restoration of a Davidic king. Nevertheless, the messianic interpretation is ancient and well established. It is only those interpreters with a presumption that the OT has no messianic hope at all who seem to reject the messianic interpretation of Mic 5:2-5; cf. K. L. Barker, "Micah" in *Micah, Nahum, Habakkuk, Zephaniah*, NAC 20 (Nashville: B&H, 1998), 95–103.

37. Evangelicals who hold this view would consider this rabbinic-style, creative exegesis under the inspiration of the Holy Spirit.

38. Some might object that the careful reading available to Matthew was not understandable to Ahaz, who might be considered "the original audience" of this prophecy. This objection fails to understand the nature of the Bible as a text. While Ahaz did receive this prophecy in a particular time and place, all we have is a textual record of that event in the composition known as the book of Isaiah. Thus, Ahaz is not the original audience of the book of Isaiah but a character in the inspired narrative written in the book. The audience of the book is eighth-century BC Judah, to whom a careful reading of the visible compositional strategies was available. They could read it in context with Isa

9 and 11 just as any reader of the book of Isaiah can after them. In other words, what was available and understandable to Matthew was also available and understandable to the original readers.

39. P. Roth, "The Conversion of the Jews," in *Goodbye Columbus and Five Short Stories* (New York: Vintage Books, 1987), 140–41.

Isaiah 9:1-7

The Deity of Messiah

EDWARD E. HINDSON

The messianic trajectory of the prophet Isaiah extends from the prediction of the birth of Immanuel (7:14) to the divine child (9:6) and culminates in the future Davidic King (11:1-6). Taken as a unit, the Immanuel prophecies (7–12) paint a picture of the coming messianic king. His birth is unique (7:14); His character is majestic (9:6); His land is threatened (8:8); and His triumph is assured (11:4).

The Assyrian invasion described in chap. 8 of Isaiah serves as a connection between the prediction of the birth of the virgin's son in chap. 7 and his royal description in chap. 9. Robert Culver warns, "Too many expositors have sought to explain one portion of the prophecy without the other."[1] In Isa 7:14 there is a glimpse of a forthcoming miraculous conception that will guarantee the perpetuity of the Davidic and messianic line. Now in 9:1-6 there is a further clarification that provides a more definite picture of the nature of the one who is coming.[2]

The opening verse of chap. 9 promises a future blessing to the people of "Galilee of the Gentiles" among the tribes of Zebulun and Naphtali. These were the most remote regions of Israel and were the most subject to heathen influences and attack (because of their location on a major road/trade route). This often-despised district and its mixed population would be the first to see the light of the good news of God's grace. Importantly, the NT clearly affirms this as occurring during Jesus' Galilean ministry, which He launched in Capernaum (Mt 4:13-16). While the NT does not directly quote Isa 9:6-7, Matthew's quotation of 9:1-2, in relation to Jesus indicates that he viewed the entire passage as referring to Jesus. J. A. Alexander responded to this matter by pointing out that the essential aspects of Isa 9:6-7 are quoted in Gabriel's announcement of the child's birth to Mary (Lk 1:32-34).[3]

HISTORICAL SETTING

Commentators disagree over the exact dating of the prophecies in Isa 9–11. The immediate context would seem to place this section in the time of the Syro-Ephraimite War (734–732 BC) in which Israel and Syria were threatening to attack Judah (chap. 7). However, the reference (10:9) to the route the Assyrian army is pictured as traveling (Calno, Charchemish, Hamath, Arpad, Samaria, Damascus) suggests the invasion by Tiglath-Pileser III around 734 BC.[4]

The overall literary unity is structured around the birth of the promised child in light of the gloom of potential invasion from the north. Gary Smith writes, "The first paragraph in this section introduces a future righteous Davidic king who will bring a period of light and peace to God's people."[5] The peace and justice of his reign contrast to the pride and oppression of Judah's enemies.

Critical scholars generally limit the historical influence of Isa 9–11 to either the birth or the ascension of Hezekiah as the potential deliverer.[6] By contrast, many conservative scholars prefer viewing the child king as an exclusive prophecy of the birth of the Messiah.[7] In between, Gordon Johnston prefers both options, suggesting that Isaiah initially spoke of Hezekiah but left his prophecy "open" to refer ultimately to a future Davidic Messiah.[8]

INTERPRETIVE PRESUPPOSITIONS

Johnston views the "messianic trajectories" in Isaiah as three dynastic oracles (9:1-7; 11:1-9; 11:10-16), followed by the Ideal Servant passages (42:1-9; 49:1-13; 50:4-11; 52:13–53:12).[9] He bypasses 7:14 altogether and says little about 61:1-3 having any direct messianic significance.[10] His general approach to the "messianic trajectories" accommodates nonmessianic interpretations of these passages, while suggesting a supposed "linguistic openness" that allows for a final fulfillment in the Messiah. He views this interpretive approach as "both/and," rather than "either/or." He clearly implies that Isaiah expected to see an imminent deliverance of the northern tribes "in his own day." When this failed to materialize, Johnston assumes that Isaiah's initial promise simply became what he calls a "broader generic prediction" that can be applied to the future Messiah as its final fulfillment.[11]

Unlike the double fulfillment view which some take on 7:14, Johnston prefers an interpretive concept of no immediate fulfillment/later fulfillment view of the prophecies of chaps. 9–11. In other words, he clearly admits Isaiah was mistaken in his supposed assumption that these prophecies were about Hezekiah. When the king failed to live up to the prophet's expectations, Isaiah simply left his prophecy "open" to other possibilities, leading to what Johnston calls a "typological escalation."[12] While some interpreters may appreciate Johnston's ultimate aim, his view should be rejected because the attempt to fix the prophet's miscalculation of an imminent fulfillment actually weakens, rather than strengthens, the messianic view of these passages. Moreover, it makes unnecessary concessions to the nonmessianic approach to these prophecies.[13] Since Jesus said Abraham rejoiced to "see [His] day" (Jn 8:56), how much more so Isaiah (Lk 4:17-21)!

More critical interpretations of Isa 9:1-6 typically view the passage as the king's accession rather than his actual birth. They place the historical context in the time of the Assyrian threat and focus the promised hope on a Davidic ruler, preferably Hezekiah.[14] This approach views the redaction of this section in a hagiographic manner in which Hezekiah is viewed as having the ultimate qualities described in the fourfold title of the child king following the pattern of Egyptian royal tutelaries.[15] In the Egyptian pattern the fourfold names describe the king as the embodiment of deity, contain his throne name, and then add his personal name (e.g., Thutmose, Ramesses). However, in the fourfold title in Isa 9:6, no personal name is given, indicating that Isaiah was not basing his prediction on Egyptian throne announcements nor limiting his expectation to Hezekiah.

Although Johnston assumes that Isaiah's oracle most likely was given at the time of Hezekiah's enthronement, he goes on to suggest that the prophecy finds its fullest expression in the eschatological Messiah.[16] This approach is not unlike Brevard Childs's opinion, which also recognizes the "predominantly eschatological movement of the oracle."[17] However, Childs warns against "historicizing assumptions," which overlook the larger literary context of the passage. In his opinion, "it is a major misunderstanding of this passage to politicize its message and derive the oracle from an enthusiasm over the accession of one of Judah's kings."[18] In this regard, Oswalt observes that 9:6 is not a coronation hymn but a birth announcement of the final, eschatological King, the Messiah. As such, he sees what he calls "a remarkable congruence with the Immanuel prophecy," adding "surely this child (also described in 11:1-5) is presented as the ultimate fulfillment of the Immanuel sign."[19]

EXEGETICAL CONSIDERATIONS

The "gift child" of chap. 9 further elucidates the description of the promised royal child. His miraculous birth (chap. 7) and magnificent land (chap. 8) will survive the coming threat because "God is with us" (8:10). That Isaiah identifies the land of Judah with the promise of Immanuel indicates His royal authority over the land. The failure of Judah's human kings typifies the failure of the nation as a whole. As a result, God will bring both judgment to the faithless and hope to the faithful. The source of this hope is God's gracious intention to bring a ruler to the throne who will perpetuate David's dynasty forever. Leupold observes, "This leads to the conclusion that the Immanuel of 7:14 and the child of 9:6 are identical.[20]

PROCLAMATION OF DELIVERANCE (9:1)

The first verse of chap. 9 introduces a promise of deliverance for the northern tribes of Zebulun and Naphtali in Galilee. The verse serves as a transitional bridge from the end of chap. 8 to the promise in chap. 9.[21] Johnston notes, "Whereas he (Isaiah) portrayed judgment on the northern kingdom in 8:16-22 as a time of gloom, the coming deliverance in 9:1-2 would be seen as a light shining over a dark land."[22] Thus, a time of gloom and darkness (punishment) would be followed by a time of joy and light (deliverance).

Galilee was threatened by Tiglath-Pileser III who ruled Assyria from 745 to 727 BC. His troops invaded Galilee in 734–732 BC and later destroyed Samaria, the northern capital, in 722 BC, thus bringing an end to the northern kingdom. Despite this, Isaiah foresaw a time of restoration coming for Galilee in the distant future. Johnston assumes that Isaiah "expected to see an aspect of deliverance in his own day." However, such a deliverance never came in the prophet's own time, leaving Johnston to suggest a "broader generic prediction" because of the "linguistic openness" in which the original promise was written.[23] While this may appear to some to provide a solution to the prophet's miscalculation (presumably basing his hopes for the future on Hezekiah), it leaves in doubt the matter of Isaiah's original intent.

It is clear that 9:2-5 predicts a glorious future victory for the people of Galilee. Nevertheless, the prophet gives no time indicator as to when this will be fulfilled. Oswalt notes, "all these events are manifestly in the future from the prophet's point of view, yet the verbs are all in the perfect tense."[24] These verbs are viewed as prophetic perfects by which the prophet sees and speaks of future events as though they have already occurred.[25] Such grammatical usage indicates the prophet's certainty in the fulfillment of his predictions. Therefore, it seems best to leave the matter of what Isaiah really foresaw to be determined in light of its actual fulfillment.[26]

Concerning the location of the fulfillment, Ray Ortlund writes, "God came to his people first where they had suffered the most, and from that place he launched salvation for the world."[27] A careful reading of Isa 7–12 reveals the prophet's focus on the significant role of the child who is coming. He is the Davidic son called Immanuel (7:14), the promised king (9:6), and the anointed Branch from the line of Jesse (11:1-5). The progressive nature of this revelation paints an unfolding portrait of the king who is coming in the distant future. Brevard Childs adds, "The description of his reign makes it absolutely clear that his role is messianic."[28]

Provision of Victory **(9:2-5)**

The royal birth announcement begins at v. 2 and builds anticipation that culminates in the arrival of the royal son (v. 6). The darkness of the northern area was spiritual, moral, social, and political. It affected every aspect of life in the northern kingdom and would soon result in its utter collapse. Yet, Isaiah boldly proclaimed a future triumph as the light of God would begin to shine in this dark land (v. 2).[29]

With the coming of the light of God's presence, there immediately follows the joy of God's provision. The people will rejoice as they would at the sight of a harvest of plenty or the spoils of victory (v. 3). Triumph over Israel's enemies is assured as in the days of Gideon's victory over the Midianites (Jdg 6–7). Also illustrative of this victory would be Israel's ultimate triumph over the enemy's yoke, staff, and rod (v. 4).[30] Even the boots and cloaks of warfare will be burned as peace prevails in a new kingdom of righteousness (v. 5). Thus, Oswalt asks, "Who is this person through whom God intends to bring war to an end and establish true freedom upon the earth?"[31] He points out that the text clearly identifies him as a royal ruler, who is both human and divine.

Promise of the Child **(9:6-7)**

Michael Rydelnik and James Spencer note, "The joys described in vv. 1-5 are grounded in the birth of a child within the Davidic line."[32] This passage provides a further identification of both Immanuel's human birth and divine origin. Again, the emphasis in the passage, as in 7:14, falls on the Child whom the prophet speaks of as if He were already born.[33]

The perfect tense of the verbs emphasizes the actual historicity of this birth. It is an actual event in a definite time and place. The promise of eternal sovereignty had already been connected to David's throne since the divine declaration in 2Sm 7:8-17. Also, the messianic concept of the One who is both the son of David and the Son of God (Ps 2:7; 110:1) was not new at this time. Victor Buksbazen observes that Jewish commentators did not dispute the messianic nature of this prophecy until recent times. He states, "The ancient (first century BC) Aramaic *Targum Jonathan* paraphrases this passage:

> And there was called His name from of old, Wonderful, Counsellor, Mighty God, He who lives forever, the Messiah in whose days peace shall increase.[34]

The four titles of the child's name are obviously significant. Oswalt notes, "The titles underscore the ultimate deity of this child-deliverer."[35] Others have attempted to view this as one lengthy name, but normal Hebrew accentuation does not support this.[36] Such a lengthy personal name is unparalleled in Scripture. Also the use of the disjunctive accent *telisha* at the head of the name would not give the type of separation required for this.[37] Young supports the concept of four names by which "a remarkable symmetry is obtained."[38] He affirms that each doublet emphasizes the child's humanity and His deity. Thus:

Pele Yoetz, El Gibbor, Avi AD, Sar Shalom

Others see the four titles based upon a formal Egyptian tutelary, expressing four theophoric royal titles as part of the royal enthronement ritual in typical Near Eastern practice.[39] However, there is no clear indication that a Hebrew king ever used such a title. Rather, Hebrew titles form a series of descriptive epithets which are stylistically closer to Ugaritic literature than to specialized tutelary of the pharaohs.[40] Isaiah gives no personal name to his ideal king. Rather, his four titles are actually descriptions of his person. Thus, it is obvious that he does not have Hezekiah in mind but a greater king who is yet to come in the future.

Wonderful Counselor (pele' yoetz)

The initial description of the child is that He is a wonder, meaning "extraordinary." Motyer notes that *pele'* is used 15 times of extraordinary acts of God.[41] He suggests, "to designate the child as *pele'* makes him out of the ordinary, one who is something of a 'miracle.'"[42] Young adds, "Isaiah begins by using the abstract for the concrete, 'wonder' for 'wonderful' . . . Not merely is the Messiah wonderful but He is Himself a wonder through and through . . . To designate the Child with the word *pele'* is to make the clearest attestation to His deity."[43]

Second, the Child is called "counselor" (*yoetz*) because of the spirit of counsel that He possesses (11:2). With this amazing quality He will provide wisdom, counsel, and guidance for the people of God. He will not depend on human counselors, as did Hezekiah and the other kings of Judah. Delitzsch suggests that to apply this designation to Hezekiah is a disgrace in light of his eventual shortcomings.[44] These two words are also used together of the Lord of Hosts Himself, who is "wonderful in counsel" (Isa 28:29 ESV).

Mighty God ('el gibbor)

The deity of the coming king is accentuated by the designation *el*, the common Hebrew term for God. Delitzsch insists, "There is no reason why we should take *El* in this name of the Messiah in any other sense than *Immanu-El*; not to mention the fact that *El* in Isa is always a name of God."[45] Motyer adds, "when we find a construction identical with Isa 9:6 (*el* with a following adjective or noun), *el* is never adjectival but is always the ruling noun . . . There is no evidence supporting an adjectival use of *el* in Isa 9:6."[46]

The term *gibbor* ("mighty") is often used of God (Dt 10:17; Ps 24:8; Jer 20:11; Zph 3:17). Although it can also refer to "warriors" or "heroes" (Ezk 32:21), linking *gibbor* with *el* clearly indicates that Isaiah intended to describe this wondrous child as deity. Isaiah uses the same exact title of the Lord Himself in 10:20-21 (cf. also Dt 10:17; Jer 32:18). Goldingay observes that "the recurrence of the phrase rendered 'Mighty God' *('el gibbor)* in 10:21 with definite reference to Yahweh makes it harder to accept that here the phrase means 'God-like warrior.'"[47] Thus, attempts to limit this title to a mere human "hero" seem to betray the expositor's proclivity to reject the deity of the Messiah in general or that it was specifically revealed in the OT. Taken in the normal grammatical sense, *'el gibbor* means "God, the mighty One." It is similar to *'el shaddai* ("God almighty") or *'el olam* ("God the eternal").[48]

Everlasting Father (abi ad)

Kings were often depicted in the ancient world as "fathers" to their people. However, this person's fatherhood is described as being "eternal." The word *'ad* signifies perpetuity or duration and is used by Isaiah to describe the "high and lofty one" (57:15 NLT). Delitzsch notes, "The word 'Father' [*abi*] designates a quality of the Messiah with respect to His people. He acts toward them like a father."[49] This describes His relationship to His children as a "fatherly king." As such, "father" does not eliminate the possibility that this describes the one who is also called "son" in this prediction. Thus, the newborn son will be the eternal One who is eternally a father to His people.

Notwithstanding the above, there is an alternative way of translating these two words. Gary Smith correctly notes that the expression may also be translated as a genitive phrase ("father of eternity").[50] This translation indicates that the newborn son is actually the author or creator of time, clearly an attribute of deity. Hence, Rydelnik and Spencer state, "The child born here is not to be confused with the Father in the Triune Godhead. Rather, the Son of God is the creator of time, the author of eternity."[51] In either case, "everlasting" is a term that refers to God or God's promises (2Sm 7:16), not to mere human beings. Kaiser comments, "Thus the one who will arrive later is one who has been here from the beginning of time and more!"[52]

Prince of Peace (sar shalom)

The promised child will be both a peaceful prince and one who reigns in peace.[53] Oswalt emphasizes, "It is appropriate that this title should come as the last in the series, for it is the climactic one (cf. 32:17)."[54] The messianic goal of world peace is clearly emphasized throughout Isaiah's prophecies (53:5; 57:19; 66:12). The Messiah is the only one who will come as the triumphant warrior and ensure lasting peace (63:1-6).

The divine child is the only one who can bring the reality of world peace. No human leader of any kind has ever been able to give such assurance. Delitzsch said this promised One will prove "Himself to be what He is not only called, but actually is."[55] Young adds, "Inasmuch as the peace to be established is eternal, it is clear that this peace includes more than a temporary cessation of hostilities among the nations."[56] The NT amplifies the messianic rule to include a literal earthly millennial kingdom in which Jesus the Messiah rules the entire world (Rev 20:4).

Having described the coming King by His titles, Isaiah concludes with the triumphal observations of v. 7, which describe the quality and extent of His reign. Smith notes four characteristics of the messianic rule: (1) peace will increase, (2) the ruler will sit on David's throne, (3) He will rule based on principles of justice and righteousness, and (4) He will reign forever. Thus, he concludes, "These descriptive parameters, titles, time frame, and interlocking references to the Davidic promise rule out any attempt to identify this son with Ahaz, Hezekiah, or Josiah."[57]

Collectively, vv. 6-7 promised hope to the Davidic dynasty, rather than to any contemporary king. Despite the constant threats of war, God would preserve the Davidic and messianic lines. Kaiser observes, "The throne he occupies will be '[David's] throne' (2Sa 7:16), and he will rule over David's 'kingdom' (v. 7c; 2Sa 7:13, 16). Thus, everything promised to David will be fulfilled in this coming scion of David."[58] This is the prophet's message of hope to the people of Judah during the dark days of the reign of Ahaz. God will protect the Davidic line in spite of the failure of the current Davidic king. Thus, the prophetic revelation connects the promise of Immanuel (7:14) to the Divine Child (9:6-7). Rydelnik and Spencer affirm that this promised kingdom will not be the "outworking of a king with human wisdom and power. The child will rule with the wisdom, power, and peace of God."[59] No longer is the identity of Immanuel obscure as in 7:14; now in 9:6-7 we know His human birth, divine nature, Davidic throne, the extent of His reign, and the peaceful character of His rule.

INNERTEXTUAL INTERPRETATION

The prophecy of the Divine Child is set within the context of Isaiah's predictions of a coming king. Expositors of all types (both critical and conservative) have connected the child in chap. 7 with the one in chap. 9. Christopher Seitz states, "there are good grounds for interpreting the closing royal oracle as an integral part of the much wider tradition complex, now located in 7:1–9:7. It is fitting that the final oracle speaks of the birth of the child who was only promised in 7:14, yet whose maturation and reign were to figure in such important ways in days to come."[60]

Within the book of Isa are several allusions that connect with the prophecy in 9:1-7. For instance, the entire book emphasizes the significance of names: "Mighty One of Israel" (1:24), "Lord of Hosts" (6:5), Shear-jashub (7:3), Immanuel (7:14), Maher-shalal-hash-baz (8:3), "Holy One of Israel" (10:20), "stump of Jesse" (11:1), Ariel (29:1), "Redeemer" (44:6), Cyrus (44:28), Zion (52:1), "My Servant" (52:13), Hephzibah (62:4), and Beulah (62:4).

"Mighty God" (*'el gibbor*) is the title given to the Lord Himself in 10:21-22. Motyer suggests, "Isaiah means us to take seriously the *el* component of this name as of Immanuel."[61] "Everlasting Father" is reflected in God's care for His people (Isa 63:16; 64:8). Isaiah uses "eternity" (*ad*) more than any of the prophets (26:4; 30:8; 57:15; 64:9; 65:18). "Prince of Peace" forecasts the future reign of the Messiah where all creation is at peace (65:17-25).

Isaiah's prophecies shine as a beacon of hope both in his time and throughout the ages. The promises the Lord made to the Davidic dynasty would indeed be fulfilled by the birth of a child who would be both the son of David and the son of God. Rydelnik claims, "The point of Isa 9:1-7 was to alert the house of David that the virgin-born King for whom they were to look would only come after a long period of darkness. Nevertheless, He would indeed come possessing a divine nature, to establish a righteous and eternal kingdom."[62] God's promise of peace and justice would be fulfilled in the coming of a future messianic king for the "zeal of the Lord of Hosts will accomplish this" (9:7).

INTERTEXTUAL INTERPRETATION[63]

Gary Yates defines intertextuality as: "how biblical texts echo, allude to, quote, reapply, or even reconfigure other canonical passages for various rhetorical and theological purposes."[64] In this regard, Isaiah's picture of the coming messianic king is painted against the backdrop of various passages in the Hebrew Bible. The "enlarging" or "multiplying" of the nation (9:3) is a Solomonic motif that pictures the true Davidic successor as the new Solomon (1Kg 4:20) with resultant shouts of joy and rejoicing. Motyer suggests "in your presence" speaks of "entrance and acceptance in the Lord's presence (cf. Ex 23:15, 17; Dt 12:7; 14:26), the fulfillment of all that the old feasts anticipated."[65] The contrasting experiences of harvest and plunder express joy. Motyer adds, "Harvest belongs to the sphere of nature, plunder to the sphere of history."[66]

There are two historical biblical references in 9:4-5. First, is the exodus motif that recalls their deliverance from Egypt (Ex 3:7-8) wherein the "yoke" (Lv 26:13) and burdens of "forced labor" (Ex 2:11) were lifted by divine intervention. Second, is the reference to Gideon's victory over Midian (Jdg 6–8), which involved the miraculous deliverance of Zebulun and Asher (Jdg 6:35). Every "trampling boot" of the invading warriors will be burned with fire (v. 5), a concept picked up in Ezekiel's prophecy of the defeat of Gog and Magog and the burning of the military hardware (Ezk 39:9).

The theme of the kingdom of God runs throughout the Hebrew Scriptures (Ps 72:4; 103:13; Prv 3:12; 2Kg 23:2; 1Chr 23–27; 28:5; Jer 33:15).[67] Thus, Eugene Merrill writes, "only David could adequately serve as a prototype of the messianic King."[68] Moses had clearly predicted and sanctioned the idea of kingship generations earlier (Dt 17:14-20; 33:1-5) and the Hebrew Scriptures depict God as a righteous king, protector, and divine warrior who rules with wisdom and justice (Ps 145:11-13). Eventually the figure of the Messiah ("anointed one") came to refer to an ideal son of David (2Sm 22:51) who was central to Israel's eschatological hope for the future (Dan 9:25-26).[69]

The child born destined to become God's ideal king is far more than a human ruler. He is in fact the "mighty God" who will come to rule the kingdom of God on earth. He is Immanuel ("God with us"), and Isaiah can say to the cities of Judah, "Behold your God!" (40:9 ESV). Thus, Jesus would begin His earthly ministry announcing, "the kingdom of God has come near" (Mk 1:15). When Pilate later asked, "So you are a king?" Jesus responded, "For this purpose I was born and for this purpose I have come into the world" (Jn 18:37 ESV). At His return to earth, the Scripture declares Him to be "King of kings and Lord of lords" (Rev 19:16).

---

1. Robert Culver, "Were the Old Testament Prophecies Really Prophetic?" in *Can I Trust My Bible?* (Chicago: Moody Press, 1963), 104. He states that, "In context it is most difficult to prove that the virgin's son has any connection at all with Mary's babe unless one continues to the final verses of the prophecy."

2. E. W. Hengstenberg, *Christology of the Old Testament* (Grand Rapids: Kregel, 1970), 172. He both discusses and rejects the idea that 9:6 could possibly refer to Hezekiah with "such senseless flattery" (182) since he never in any way ruled over the northern tribes of Galilee (9:1-2). He also clearly rejects the suggestion of Gesenius that the prophecy could refer to both Hezekiah immediately and to the Messiah ultimately. He states unequivocally "that no analogous example can be produced, where a prophet had connected his hopes of the Messiah with a definite person, by whom they were not realized" (183).

3. J. A. Alexander, *Commentary on the Prophecies of Isaiah* (Grand Rapids: Zondervan, 1970), 207. Gabriel promised the child born to Mary would be "great . . . Son of the Most High . . . (rule on) the throne of his father David" and "reign over the house of Jacob forever" (Lk 1:32-34).

4. See J. A. Irvine, *Isaiah, Ahaz, and the Assyrian Crisis* (Atlanta: Scholar Press, 1990), 274–79.

5. Gary V. Smith, *Isaiah 1–39*, New American Commentary (Nashville: B&H, 2007), 235.

6. Cf. Joseph Blenkinsop, *Isaiah: A New Translation with Introduction and Commentary*, Anchor Yale Bible Commentaries (New York: Doubleday, 2000), 245–251; G. von Rad, "The Royal Ritual in Judah," in *The Problem of the Hexateuch and Other Essays* (New York: Macmillan, 1966), 222–31.

7. Cf. J. Alec Motyer, *Isaiah: An Introduction and Commentary* (Downers Grove, IL: InterVarsity, 1999), 88–105; John Oswalt, *Isaiah 1–39*, New International Commentary on the Old Testament (Grand Rapids: Eerdmans, 1986), 242–48.

8. Herbert Bateman, Darrell Bock, and Gordon Johnston, *Jesus the Messiah* (Grand Rapids: Kregel, 2012), 133–47. The material on Isaiah is attributed to Johnston, *Jesus the Messiah*, 7.

9. Ibid. Johnston's treatment of Isaiah attempts to defend a final messianic application of these selective passages while suggesting they had no original messianic intent. Rather, he sees the three dynastic oracles as initially applying to Hezekiah and rejects them as "exclusive direct prophecies" about the Messiah (133).

10. Johnston clearly rejects the direct prophetic fulfillment view of these passages as expressed by Motyer, *Isaiah*, 98–105; Walter C. Kaiser Jr., *The Messiah in the Old Testament* (Grand Rapids: Zondervan, 1995) 162–164; Oswalt, *Isaiah*, 242–48; Edward J. Young, *The Book of Isaiah* (Grand Rapids: Eerdmans, 1965), 322–346, all of whom he references.

11. Johnston, *Jesus the Messiah*, 136.; cf. also John Goldingay, *Isaiah*, New International Biblical Commentary (Peabody, MA: Hendrickson, 2001), 70. He acknowledges that the promises "picture what any king should be . . . yet . . . go far beyond what any king ever achieved." Therefore, "they are messianic."

12. Ibid., 145.

13. See J. Lindblom, *A Study of the Immanuel Section in Isaiah* (Lund: Gleerup, 1958), 4. His comments are typical of critical scholars. He argues that the original collections of Isaiah's prophetic utterances were orally transmitted with little interest in their actual historical situation and were not preserved in chronological order in their original form. Thus, the Immanuel prophecy (Isa 7–11) is viewed as an interregnum, which Lindblom refers to as "a period of happiness" under a series of "ideal Davids," falling between Judah's initial deliverance and the coming Assyrian catastrophe (39). Therefore, he viewed Hezekiah as the royal prince of Isa 9:6, despite the chronological problem in 2Kg 18. He concludes that the ideal king of the entire section (7–11) is not at all the Messiah in a proper sense but only an idealized figure in a "relative sense" (57).

14. R. E. Clements, *Isaiah 1-39*, New Century Bible Commentary (Grand Rapids: Eerdmans, 1980), 104–105; cf. also C. R. Seitz, *Isaiah 1–39*, Interpretation (Louisville: John Knox Press, 1993), 86–87. Seitz connects the promise of Immanuel in 7:14 to the royal child in 9:6 but views both passages as speaking of Hezekiah; cf. also, von Rad, "Royal Ritual," 206–225. Calvin, by contrast, repudiates the idea that 9:6 could refer to Hezekiah because he had already been born years earlier. See John Calvin, *Isaiah* (Grand Rapids: Associated Publishers & Authors, nd), 138.

15. See Johnston, *Jesus the Messiah*, 141; and K. A. Kitchen, *Ancient Orient and Old Testament* (Downers Grove, IL: InterVarsity, 1966), 109.

16. Johnston, *Jesus the Messiah*, 138.

17. Brevard Childs, *Isaiah*, Old Testament Library (Louisville: Westminster John Knox Press, 2001), 80.

18. Ibid.

19. Oswalt, *Isaiah*, 247. He also believes that Isaiah has an eschatological figure in mind who will not just be a king among kings in Israel but will be the final king (248).

20. H. C. Leupold, *Exposition of Isaiah*, (Grand Rapids: Baker, 1968), 1:80.

21. Isaiah 9:1 appears in most English translations, whereas the same verse is 8:23 in the Masoretic Text. In the one case it serves to introduce the promise in chap. 9. In the other case, it serves to conclude the prediction of chap. 8. In either case, it serves as a bridge between the two chapters. See Oswalt, *Isaiah*, 242.

22. Johnston, *Jesus the Messiah*, 134; cf. Oswalt, 240, who observes that Isaiah's concern for the fate of northern Israel indicates that he was concerned for the future of all Israel, not just Judah. Oswalt writes, "All Israel was involved in rebellion against God (8:14), and all Israel would participate in the redemption and restoration."

23. Johnston, *Jesus the Messiah*, 136; cf. also P. Wegner, *An Examination of Expectations in Isaiah 1-35* (Lewiston, NY: Mellen Biblical Press, 1992), 425.

24. Oswalt, *Isaiah*, 242.

25. E. Kautzsch, ed., *Gesenius' Hebrew Grammar* (Oxford: Clarendon Press, 1963), 312–313. The perfect tense (*perfectum propheticum*) was used by the prophets to describe future events as though they had already occurred, indicating the certainty of their fulfillment.

26. While many have pointed out possible Assyrian loan words in vv. 3-5 (e.g., "yoke" and "boot"), this does not in itself mean that Isaiah limited his prediction of deliverance to the time of the Assyrian invasion. Virtually all similar prophecies are written within the culture of the time in which they were given (cf. Mic 5:2). Matthew (4:12-16) clearly views the reference to the light shining in Galilee as being fulfilled in Jesus' Galilean ministry and not before.

27. Ray Ortlund, *God Saves Sinners* (Wheaton, IL: Crossway, 2005), 97. For more detailed comments see Grant Osborne, *Matthew*, Zondervan Exegetical Commentary on the New Testament (Grand Rapids: Zondervan, 2010), 141–145.

28. Childs, *Isaiah*, 81.

29. Light is used throughout Scripture to illustrate the illumination of truth that comes from God Himself (cf. Isa 42:16; 60:1-3; Job 29:3; Pss 43:3; 119:30).

30. These were the instruments of Assyria's oppression in 10:24-27. Oswalt, *Isaiah*, 244, suggests, "Here Isaiah looks off to a day when One mightier than the Assyrians of this world will break those yokes to pieces."

31. Oswalt, *Isaiah*, 244.

32. Michael Rydelnik and James Spencer, "Isaiah" in *The Moody Bible Commentary*, ed. Michael Rydelnik and Michael Vanlaningham (Chicago: Moody Press, 2014), 1024.

33. See Edward J. Young, *Book of Isaiah*, 1:329, for a lengthy discussion of the grammatical structure of this passage and its significance in regard to interpreting the child's identity.

34. Victor Buksbazen, *The Prophet Isaiah: A Commentary* (Bellmawr, NJ: Friends of Israel, 2008), 163–164. Cf. also J. Stenning, *The Targum of Isaiah* (London: Oxford University Press, 1949), 62.

35. Oswalt, *Isaiah*, 246.

36. J. Klausner, *Messianic Ideal in Israel* (New York: Macmillan, 1955), 64. He reads the name as "wonderful in counsel is God the Mighty, the Everlasting Father, the Ruler of peace." Dillmann earlier remarked that this would be an "unparalleled monstrosity." August Dillmann, *Das Prophet Jesaja* (Leipzig: Hirzel, 1890), 251. Nevertheless, most contemporary Jewish scholars view this as the name of the royal child. A. Berlin and M. Z. Brettler state, "the name given to the child in this verse does not describe that child or attribute divinity to him, contrary to classical Christian readings of this messianic text." *The Jewish Study Bible* (New York: Oxford University Press, 2004), 802.

37. The *telisha* in *pele* is the smallest of all disjunctive accents. For the best discussion of the use of accents in this passage see Franz Delitzsch, *Biblical Commentary on the Prophecies of Isaiah* (1877; repr., Grand Rapids: Eerdmans, 1965), 1:250.

38. Young, *Book of Isaiah*, 1:333. Cf. also Michael Rydelnik, *The Messianic Hope* (Nashville: B&H, 2010), 43–44. He notes the accentuation in the Masoretic Text may deliberately disconnect the two doublets to negate the idea of the deity of the child which is clearly affirmed by the Greek translation in Lk 1:32-33.

39. Johnston, *Jesus the Messiah*, 140. He notes that the Egyptian tutelary bestowed on their kings at their coronation involved four titles given to the king on the day of his enthronement, plus a fifth title (personal name) having been previously given at his birth. G. von Rad, "Das judaische königsritual," in *Theologische Literaturzeitung*, 72 (1942), 215–216 argued that such a dependence on the Egyptian tutelary reflects an Egyptian influence on the Israelite concept of kingship.

40. For a scholarly criticism on the idea that Hebrew kingship was based upon the Egyptian model, see Kitchen, *Ancient Orient and Old Testament*, 106–111.

41. Motyer, *Isaiah*, 104. He suggests the term is also used of the Angel of the Lord in Jdg 13:18, regarding His name and Manoah's recognition of the incident as a theophany (Jdg 13:22).

42. Ibid.

43. Young, *Book of Isaiah*, 1:334. He explains that the root is used to describe the miracles God performed in Egypt (Ps 78:12).

44. Delitzsch, *Prophecies of Isaiah*, 1:251. He argues that 7:14 and 9:6 are deliberately connected to paint the prophet's picture of the coming king. He points out that both the designation "Immanuel" and the four titles in 9:6 were descriptions of the Coming One and not His personal names.

45. Ibid., 1:252. He points out that *El gibbor* was a traditional name of God appearing in Dt 10:17; Jer 32:18; Neh 9:32; Ps 24:8.

46. Motyer, *Isaiah*, 105. He adds, "Nothing justifies 'god like' . . . in the modern sense of 'remarkable.'"

47. Goldingay, 73. He acknowledges that in isolation the four terms might appear to be descriptors of a hoped-for king but that the parallel reference in 10:21 clearly indicates a divine king.

48. See W. Baker and E. Carpenter, *Complete Word Study Dictionary: Old Testament* (Chattanooga, TN: AMG Publishers,

2003), 2045; and R. Laird Harris, ed. *Theological Wordbook of the Old Testament* (Chicago: Moody Press, 1980), 2:907.

49. Delitzsch, *Prophecies of Isaiah,* 1:338. He adds, "The quality of fatherhood is defined by the word eternity. The Messiah is an eternal Father."

50. Smith, *Isaiah 1–39,* 1:241.

51. Rydelnik and Spencer, 1024.

52. Walter C. Kaiser Jr., *The Messiah in the Old Testament* (Grand Rapids: Zondervan, 1995), 164.

53. Johnston, *Jesus the Messiah,* 145–146, to the contrary, suggests this ruler will bring peace "by defeating the foreign army occupying the land" as the "human coregent of God's rule on earth." Since this did not actually occur, Johnston jumps ahead to suggest "these four titles should be seen as climactically prophetic of the Messiah." He indicates the initial historical contextualization was "conventional royal hyperbole," which was originally true of the human Davidic King (presumably Hezekiah) and only literally true of the eschatological Messiah as a result of "escalated realization."

54. Oswalt, *Isaiah,* 248.

55. Delitzsch, *Prophecies of Isaiah,* 1:253.

56. Young, *Book of Isaiah,* 1:339.

57. Smith, *Isaiah 1–39,* 1:242.

58. Kaiser, *Messiah in the Old Testament,* 164.

59. Rydelnik and Spencer, "Isaiah," 1025.

60. Seitz, *Isaiah 1–39,* 87. He admits whether Immanuel is the prophet's son or a royal son, his birth is a hopeful sign of deliverance both from the Syro-Ephraimite threat and the Assyrian assault. Nevertheless, he definitely connects the prediction in chap. 7 with chap. 9.

61. Motyer, *Isaiah,* 102. He also notes that David called his son Solomon (Heb., *Shlomoh,* "man of peace").

62. Rydelnik, *The Messianic Hope,* 159.

63. The term "intertextuality" was coined by Julia Kristeva, *Desire in Language: A Semiotic Approach to Literature and Art* (Oxford: Blackwell, 1980), 66. Her approach to intertextuality suggests that the meaning of the text is both "inside" and "outside" the text itself. Secular approaches combine Saussurean linguistics, Bakhtinian dialogism and the sociology of knowledge suggesting that literary texts are the product of the wider culture in which they are produced. Intertextuality within biblical studies has come to express a complex network of references to other texts, both biblical and nonbiblical. Cf. G. Aichele and G. A. Phillips, "Introduction: Exegesis, Eisegesis, Intergesis," *Semeia* 69/70 (1996), 7–18; T. K. Beal, "Ideology and Intertextuality," in D. N. Flewell, *Reading Between Texts: Intertextuality and the Hebrew Bible* (Louisville: Westminster John Knox Press, 1992), 27–39.

64. Gary Yates, "'The Weeping Prophet' and 'Pouting Prophet' in Dialogue: Intertextual Connections Between Jeremiah and Jonah," *Journal of the Evangelical Theological Society* 59 (June 2016): 223.

65. Motyer, *Isaiah,* 101.

66. Ibid. Motyer points out that the gathering of plunder pictures the fruits of victory.

67. On the Israelite concept of kingship cf. J. D. Douglas, ed., *New Bible Dictionary* (Grand Rapids: Eerdmans, 1962), 692–693; W. A. Elwell, ed., *Baker Encyclopedia of the Bible* (Grand Rapids: Baker, 1988), 2:1264–1269.

68. Eugene Merrill, *Kingdom of Priests* (Grand Rapids: Baker, 1987), 209. He develops the theme of the kingdom throughout his survey of the history of Israel in the OT.

69. See the discussion of kingdom oracles by Andreas Köstenberger and Richard Patterson, *Invitation to Biblical Interpretation* (Grand Rapids: Kregel, 2011), 327–328.

Isaiah 11:1-16

The Reign of the Righteous Messianic King

EDWARD E. HINDSON

The prophet Isaiah looked down the tunnel of time into the distant future to foresee the coming Messianic King emerging from the Davidic line. His prophecies in chaps. 7 through 9 indicate that Immanuel, the virgin-born divine child, could possibly come soon. However, chap. 11 makes it clear that His coming has definitely moved into the distant future. That is because in Isa 11:1, the tree that symbolizes David's kingdom has been cut down, and a shoot (Hb. *chộtêr*) must grow out of its stump before the tree can flourish again. The Branch (Hb. *nêtser*) will spring from the roots of the Davidic dynasty and bring hope to Israel again in the future.[1] John Oswalt states, "In 11:1-16 the messianic hope which began to be expressed in 7:14 and which was amplified in 9:1-6 comes full flower. The Messiah is not merely promised or announced but is depicted as ruling."[2]

John Calvin believed the prediction applied "solely to the person of Christ; for till he came no such *branch* arose."[3] Thus, in the midst of the threatened invasion and potential destruction of Assyria and within that same metaphorical content, Isaiah also predicted the revitalization of the Davidic line by the "springing" forth of a new Branch from the "stump of Jesse" (11:1). This hope, as Calvin notes, was "held in suspense" until Christ appeared.

The prophecy of the Branch follows Isaiah's prediction of the eventual destruction of Assyria. The cutting down of the tree of the Davidic dynasty is contrasted with God cutting down the "trees of (the) forest" of Assyria in 10:15-34. God used Assyria as His instrument of judgment against northern Israel, culminating in the destruction of Samaria in 722 BC (Isa 9:8–10:4). But next God promised judgment on Assyria, the "rod of My anger" (10:5). They too, like Israel, failed to understand God's sovereign purposes. They were like an ax in God's hand, boasting against the One who wielded it in judgment.

HISTORICAL SETTING

Assyria lay in the region of the upper Tigris River in northern Iraq, north of Babylon and east of Syria.[4] Assyria began as the tiny city-state of Asshur on the western bank of the Tigris. It was the seat of the worship of the sun god Asshur. As time progressed, Assyria grew stronger and was considered the ultimate "symbol of terror and tyranny" in the Near East.[5] The Assyrian King, Shalmanesar V, besieged Samaria in northern Israel and deported its people in 722 BC. For Isaiah, a Judean prophet, the fall of Samaria certainly appeared to be God's judgment on Israel because of their abandonment of the worship of Yahweh, their rejection of the temple at Jerusalem, and their rebellion against the "house of David."[6]

Strikingly, the prophet predicted an equally disastrous fall of the mighty Assyrian empire that also failed to acknowledge God (Isa 10:5-19, 27-34). The Assyrian King Sennacherib's invasion of Judah in 701 BC was halted by God, and the Assyrian army was turned back (Isa 36–37). By 612 BC, the Assyrian empire would fall to Cyaxares of Media and Nabopolassar of Babylon. A final attempt to resist the Babylonians would be crushed by Nebuchadnezzar at Carchemish in 605 BC. The once-feared Assyrians would thereafter be reduced to a province within the later empires of Babylon, Persia, and Greece.

Gary Smith outlines Isaiah 10:5-34 in three sections: (1) God will judge Assyria's pride (10:5-19). (2) God will save a remnant of Judah (10:20-27). (3) Assyria will be cut off (10:28-34).[7] In these verses, Assyria is described as the "rod" of God's anger, the "staff" of His wrath (v. 5), and the "ax" in His hand (v. 15). While God used Assyria to destroy Samaria and ravage Judah, He would yet judge Assyria for its arrogant pride by cutting down and burning the "trees of its forests" (v. 19). Alec Motyer comments, "The Assyrians marching on Jerusalem are in reality jumping into a fire."[8] The light of God (9:1-2 [Heb. 8:23-9:1]) that represents His glory will extinguish the darkness of the Assyrians (8:20-22). The Lord Yahweh is the "light" of Israel who will become a "flame" of fire to consume the splendor of Assyria (10:17).

In contrast to the immediate Assyrian threat (Isa 7–10), the prophet Isaiah again extends the hope of a royal messiah (11:1-16). Since the final cutting down of the Davidic royal line was yet to come in 586 BC, it rightly can be concluded that the shoot arising from the stump of that line is coming in the future as well. Thus,

Isaiah provides his readers with a confident hope of a coming king who will rule on David's throne.

EXEGETICAL PRESUPPOSITIONS

Just as God promised to cut down the power of Assyria, He also promised to spare the stump of the Davidic line, which would also be cut down by His divine judgment. Gordon Johnston is certainly correct that Isa 11:1-9 may be classified as an "oracle of restoration" that foresees an ideal Davidic King. However, his suggestion that Isaiah initially believed this King to be Hezekiah is not supported by the biblical text.[9] First, the Davidic line was not "cut down" or reduced to a "stump" in Hezekiah's time. In response to Isaiah's later warning about the coming disastrous Babylonian invasion, Hezekiah remarked, "For there will be peace and security during my lifetime" (Isa 39:8). Second, the Babylonians, not the Assyrians, removed the last Davidic king from the throne in Jerusalem (2Kg 25:5-7). Third, the context of Isa 11:1-16 is clearly eschatological ("on that day") and is in no way limited to Hezekiah's time.[10]

Isaiah predicted that the kingdom of Judah would sink so low that the very Davidic line, whose perpetuity was such a matter of Ahaz's concern (Isa 7:1-14), would actually be cut down in the future and have to begin anew. In Isa 11:2, this "shoot" is personalized as an individual ruler. The Spirit of the Lord will be upon Him and give Him wisdom, understanding, counsel, strength, knowledge, and the fear of the Lord. Michael Rydelnik and James Spencer note, "Isaiah is not simply looking forward to the installation of the next Davidic monarch, but to the installation of *the* Davidic monarch, the *supreme* son of David, who will live in full obedience to God and rule with God's wisdom, strength, and justice (vv. 2-3)."[11]

The entire context of the Immanuel passage (Isa 7–12) assures that Judah need not fear the extinction of the throne of David for "God is with us" in the birth of the virgin's son (7:14). Then, it indicates that this son is to be identified with the land because it is His land (8:8). Next, He is described as a gift-child who will assume the government (9:6). Further, the readers are told He is the Mighty God whose rule will bring peace through His wonderful counsel (9:7). Finally, the readers learn that before He comes, the tree of David's royal line will be reduced to a stump (11:1). Yet Judah need not fear because God's king definitely will come in the future when the Branch sprouts from the stock of Jesse (11:1-5).

Seen collectively, the various predictions of the Immanuel prophecy clearly point to the divine Messiah ("anointed" King) who is coming in the future. This is no ordinary human king because the One Isaiah foresees has such attributes as will bring in world peace, global prosperity, and divine blessing. There is no realistic manner in which these promises ever were fulfilled by Hezekiah, Josiah, or any other Judean king. Brevard Childs suggests chap. 11 has been "editorially positioned to form the culmination of a theological direction that commenced at chap. 6, moved through the promise of a coming messianic ruler in chap. 7, and emerged in chap. 9 with the portrayal of a righteous messianic king upon the throne of David."[12] Childs astutely observes chap. 11 combines the "various themes" of the previous chapters in order to provide a "holistic reading of the entire Isaianic message."[13]

EXEGETICAL CONSIDERATIONS

The prophet Isaiah introduces the Prince of Peace and the place of His rule in 11:1-16. His message in this section emphasizes the future restoration of the Davidic monarchy and the return of the people to the promised land.

Prince of Peace[14]

The messianic figure is pictured as a "shoot" (Hb. *chọtêr*) springing from the "stump" (Hb. *geza'*) of Jesse (v. 1). This is variously translated as "stem" (KJV; NASB), "stump" (NIV; ESV), or "stock" (Tanakh). Jesse was the father of David (1Sm 17:12) and thus the progenitor of the Davidic line. Many, including Calvin, believe the reference to Jesse points to the humble origin of the dynasty, in contrast to the haughty Assyrian kings who will themselves be cut down (Isa 10:33-34).[15]

That the dynastic line of David will itself be cut down (Isa 6:13) clearly indicates that the promised heir will come in the distant future. The prophet predicts that the "tree" of the line of David will be cut down to the "stump" and that a "shoot" must grow out of the root stock of Jesse before the tree can flourish again. Isaiah's point is to show that the kingdom has sunk so low that the Davidic line will appear to be cut down, and yet somehow will spring forth again in the person of the Messiah.[16]

The prophet predicts that a "shoot" (rod or sprout) will spring up from the "stem" (root stock) of Jesse. The imagery of the prophet is that of a felled tree out of whose "roots" a "branch" (Hb. *nêtser*) would flourish again. This process is typical of olive trees, which can be cut down to their roots and yet spring up again with new branches.[17]

Alec Motyer states, "One of the most striking features of this remarkable passage is the dual title of the coming King as both the *shoot* (v. 1) and the *root* (v. 10) of Jesse."[18] No other king of Judah is called the "Son of Jesse," except David himself (1Sm 20:27-33). Thus, Isaiah is not predicting the rise of Hezekiah or any other ancient Davidic king. By referring to this coming one as both a "root" and "branch" of Jesse, the prophet means that He is both the source ("root") and the fulfillment ("branch") of the entire Davidic line from which He Himself sprang (Mt 1:1).[19]

The coming king is described as being anointed by the "Spirit of the LORD" (Hb. *Ruach Yahweh*). Throughout the OT, the Spirit of God endowed selected people with unique gifts and abilities, including craftsmen (Ex 31:3; 35:31), warriors (Jdg 6:34; 11:29; 13:25; 14:6), prophets (Nm 11:25), and leaders (Moses, Nm 11:17; Joshua, Nm 27:18; David, 1Sm 16:13). Here in 11:2, Isaiah declares that the future Davidic Messiah will be endowed with the Spirit of wisdom (*chokmâh*), understanding (*bîyn*), counsel (*'etzah*), strength (*geburah*), knowledge (*da 'ath*), and fear (*yir'âh*) of the Lord.[20] Thus, Oswalt concludes, "Everything about his leadership will testify to a supernatural endowment for his calling."[21]

The gifts of the Spirit are listed in three pairs. Walter Kaiser identifies these as *intellectual* gifts of wisdom and understanding; *administrative* gifts of counsel and might; and *spiritual* gifts of knowledge and fear of the Lord.[22] Motyer adds, "The sevenfold elaboration of the Spirit and his work here begins with his divine person as *the Spirit of the LORD* and continues with three pairs of characteristics."[23] I. W. Slotki states, "The qualities which will distinguish the ideal ruler are enumerated under three headings, each of which consists of two terms relating to his intellectual, administrative, and spiritual attributes respectively."[24]

Franz Delitzsch notes that the words for "counsel" and "might" are the same as those used in Isa 9:6 to describe the divine child.[25] Isaiah 61:1 also emphasizes the idea of the anointing of the Spirit on the messianic figure in order to rule with godly qualities. It is no mistake that Jesus saw this anointing applying to Himself (Lk 4:18-21). Gary Smith points out that the idea of kings ruling by the power of God to establish a just society was an ideal goal of ancient Near Eastern kings in general.[26] John Goldingay observes the emphasis on the Spirit suggests "a link to the origin of the monarchy."[27]

In Isa 11:3-5, the ideal ruler will not judge with his eyes and ears alone, but will do so with righteousness and justice. While many kings in the Davidic line had failed, this future King will succeed. Motyer suggests that the character and rule of this King are in "total harmony" because whatever the Lord gives to enable Him is met by "glad responsiveness."[28] Inwardly the Spirit-empowered King delights (v. 3), and outwardly He executes righteous judgment (v. 4). "He will delight" is an infinitive construct from the verb "to smell" (Hb. *heriach*), indicating His sensitivity to the fear of God. Delitzsch comments, "Thus the second David scents the fear of God, and only the fear of God, as a pleasant fragrance."[29] Young suggests that His power of perception is "graphically expressed as His sense of smelling."[30] The picture is that of the Messianic King rejoicing in the fear of the Lord just as if an offering had been brought to Him. Thus, He will not judge with His eyes and ears alone

(v. 3), but with divine perception for both the "poor" and the "oppressed" (v. 4).[31] Gary Smith refers to this anointing as "a source of moral direction derived from a divine perspective on judicial affairs."[32]

The Branch will judge with righteousness (Hb. *tsedeq*) and will condemn the wicked of the earth with the rod (Hb. *shêbeṭ*) of His mouth and the breath (Hb. *rûach*) of his lips (v. 4), meaning His royal decrees. This indicates the Messiah will rule by the power of His spoken word, which expresses His divine will. The picture of slaying the wicked with His breath is expressed clearly in the NT as well (cf. 2Th 2:8; Rev 19:15).[33] The annotation in the *Jewish Study Bible* notes: "The messianic age will not be perfect; some people will still be poor, others ruthless or wicked. The difference from the current age will lie, rather, in the king's response to these problems."[34] The Branch (Davidic Messiah) is clearly pictured in this context as ruling a literal kingdom. It is His "righteousness" and "faithfulness" that will be the belt (Hb. *'êzôr*) that holds His kingdom together in peace, justice, and spiritual greatness (v. 5).

The future messianic kingdom is described as an idyllic paradise of peace, safety, and security (vv. 6-9). Nature is transformed, hostilities fade, and many of the effects of the curse are removed; even predators (wolf, leopard, and lion) and prey (lamb, goat, and calf) are reconciled. The prophet Isaiah paints a picture of Eden restored (cf. Gn 1:29-30). Motyer states, "So secure is this peace that a youngster can exercise the dominion originally given to humankind."[35] Commentators vary on whether to interpret the drastic change of animal behavior literally (e.g., Delitzsch), or metaphorically (e.g., Goldingay), but either way the ultimate point of this passage is that the Messiah's reign will result in world peace for both the human and natural world (cf. Rom 8:19-21).[36]

This future time of unparalleled spiritual and natural peace will be "full of the knowledge of the LORD" (v. 9). Isaiah now introduces his readers to a new and universal emphasis on the salvation of the Lord. Not only will there be a remnant spared in Judah, but the day is coming when the Messiah will rule the entire world. The prophet foresees a dramatic return of the former exiles to the land of Israel with worldwide consequences. Rydelnik and Spencer comment, "This prophecy, the future that it reveals, and the past in which it is rooted, solidifies Israel's identity and offers assurance of the nation's continued existence and prosperity as God's covenant people."[37]

PROMISED RETURN (11:10-16)

These verses predict and presuppose a scattering and regathering of Israel in the future. Again, the prophet refers to the "root (Hb. *shoresh*) of Jesse" in reference to the Davidic, hence a messianic line.[38] Goldingay comments, "As Yahweh raised a banner to summon the nations to punish (5:26), so now the Davidic shoot draws the remnant back, standing as a banner to summon the nations to help their victims go home."[39] Oswalt adds, "the primary focus of the passage seems to be upon the historical nation of Israel, so that one is led to believe it points to some great final ingathering of the Jewish people such as that referred to by Paul in Rom. 11."[40]

The prediction of this regathering ("on that day," 11:10-11) clearly indicates a future fulfillment.[41] In light of this return to the land, all people (Jews and Gentiles) will come there seeking the Lord. Motyer notes that as the light (9:1-6) dispelled the darkness and reached the Gentile nations, so those nations will come to Zion seeking the Messiah. He states, "what begins one poem (the outshining of his light) ends the other (the gathering of the people)."[42] The Messiah is pictured as "standing" (continually) as a "banner" (ensign or signal) to call the nations to seek Him. He is pictured as extending His hand a "second time" to recall His people (Hb. *'ami*) from the regions of the earth where they have been scattered among the nations (Hb. *goyim*): Assyria, Cush, Elam, Shinar, Egypt, Pathros, Hamath, and the "islands of the west" (11:11).[43] This promise indicates a national restoration of the remnant of "dispersed" and "scattered" of Israel and Judah (11:12).[44] Oswalt says of v. 12, "This verse seems to say in poetic form what the preceding verses say in prose." It pictures the returnees as coming from the entire earth in a final eschatological regathering to the land of Israel.

Amillennial commentators attempt to interpret this passage as referring to the abolishment of national distinctions in Christ. They view the Philistines as the "enemies of the Church."[45] This seems highly unlikely in view of the historical setting of Isaiah's prophecies. He clearly foresees the future Davidic King ruling in Jerusalem and extending His sovereignty over the nations. He is speaking throughout this section about these specific people and places. Therefore, the passage should be taken literally. In this light, Gleason Archer viewed this passage from a premillennial position suggesting that the unconverted enemies of Israel (Philistia, Edom, Moab, and Ammon) would be converted to the Messiah at the beginning of the millennial kingdom.[46] Even the natural barriers of the River (either the Nile or Euphrates) and the Red Sea will be removed miraculously at that time, and communication between these formerly hostile nations will be unimpeded during the reign of the Prince of Peace (v. 15).

Isaiah's prophecy indicates that nothing will stand in the way of Israel's future return to the promised land. God will create a "highway" (Hb. *m^{e}sillâh*) from Assyria for the remnant (Hb. *sh^{e}'âr*) of His people (Hb. *'ami*) as in the time of the exodus from the "land of Egypt" (v. 16). The prophet's reference to the exodus anchors his predicted events in Israel's past experiences with God. "The LORD of hosts" (Isa 10:26) will accomplish this deliverance for Israel as He did in the time of the exodus. Just as God used a strong east wind (Ex 14:21) to dry up the Red Sea, so He will send a "mighty wind" (v. 15) to bring about this future deliverance of His people (cf. Ezk 20:34).

Oswalt comments, "Unless there were genuinely predictive prophecies pointing to the salvation and restoration of the Jewish nation, it is hard to understand how that nation retained its identity and its traditions when others did not."[47] Historians, such as Barbara Tuchman and Paul Johnston, have pointed to the unique purpose and historical significance of Israel in relation to human destiny, which is only explainable by divine intervention.[48] God's promises of deliverance had both immediate implications for Judah in the time of Ahaz and ultimate prophetic significance for Israel's final return to the promised land. Gary Smith observes, "These prophecies of hope show how the old world will pass away and a new one will be established . . . promising that one day the ideal will become reality."[49]

The Immanuel prophecy (Isa 7–11) is followed by a hymn of promise in 12:1-6. The annotation in *The Jewish Study Bible* refers to it as "a song of thanksgiving to be recited in the ideal age," combining phrases associated with the exodus (cf. Ex 15:2; Pss 105:1; 118:14; 148:13).[50] Motyer indicates, "The words *On that day* (1,4) link the song to the day when the old exodus will be superseded by the new (11:10-11)."[51] Thus, this chapter serves as a dramatic climax to the Immanuel prophecy. In this future day, God's anger will no longer be directed toward Judah, who will continually "praise" the Lord because He has done "glorious things" (12:5). These things are to be proclaimed, sung, and shouted for "the Holy One of Israel is . . . in His greatness" (v. 6). In the beautiful language of this triumphant doxology, Isaiah brings this section of his prophecy to a close.[52]

INNERTEXTUAL INTERPRETATION

The prophetic symbolism of the Branch (11:1) is used by Isaiah to indicate the blessing of God on the Davidic Messiah. The roots of the prophet's understanding of this concept may well go back to the promised blessing of the patriarch Joseph whom Jacob called a "fruitful bough" (Hb. *pourot*), thereby indicating his depth of character and breath of influence.[53] Since agricultural images were used to illustrate the blessings of prosperity in the Messianic Age (Lv 26), Grant Osborne suggests that a term like "branch" became a technical designation for the Messiah.[54]

Isaiah first refers to the Branch (*tsemach*) in 4:2 where it is described as "beautiful and glorious" in an eschatological messianic context in which Zion is covered by a cloud in the day and flaming fire by night (4:5). Gary Smith points out that the root idea of *semah* ("to spring forth") is used in David's last words about his descendants (2Sm 23:4 "sprouting").[55] It also appears in Ps 132:17 as a horn that will "spring forth" from (HCSB "grow for") David. The figure of the Branch in Isa 4:2 provides the harvest, establishes holiness, and executes judgment in a manner that reflects the "beauty" and "splendor" of God Himself (Isa 28:5).

Osborne notes that Isa 11:1 adds a "Davidic element" to the messianic prophecy by noting that the "shoot" grew out of the "stump" of David's father, Jesse (cf. 1Sm 16:1-13; Ps 72:20).[56] By contrast, Isaiah depicts the king of Babylon as a "rejected branch" (14:19 NASB; HCSB "worthless branch") "brought down to Sheol" (14:15). Thus, it is clear from the Isaianic context that he is using the "branch" as a symbol of kings whose reigns represent their dynastic line. While the tree of the Davidic dynasty appears to have been cut down, there is life in the stump, from which the fruitful shoot will spring forth and reign in the power of the Spirit. This same anointing of the Spirit is described in Isa 61:1-3, which connects the messianic figure to the "righteous trees," which are described as "planted by the Lord." The very conditions of peace in both the human and natural world that Isa 11:6 predicts, Isa 65:25 promises will be fulfilled. In Isa 32:15, the Spirit "from heaven is poured out," resulting in both temporal ("orchard") and spiritual/social ("justice . . . righteousness . . . peace") blessings.

The imagery of the "shoot" (*yônêq*, HCSB "young plant") and "root" (*shoresh*) is picked up again in Isa 53:2 in the description of the Suffering Servant. Oswalt describes the "root" here as "the normally unwanted shoot that springs up from an exposed root of a tree."[57] Thus, again, Isaiah connects the origin of the Messiah to the humble roots of His humanity, acknowledging that He is not one who naturally attracts people to Him. Rather, it is because He has been anointed by the Spirit of God that He is recognized as the Promised One. The empowerment of the Spirit will enable Him to fulfill His task, even as Bezalel was so endowed (Ex 31:2-3). Walter Kaiser notes that the covenant promises of God given to King David (2Sm 7:16) included a throne, a dynasty, and a kingdom, which Isaiah described as God's "promises assured" (55:3) to the Davidic line.[58]

INTERTEXTUAL INTERPRETATION

The prophet Jeremiah (23:5; 33:15) also used the symbol of the Branch to depict the righteous King coming from the line of David. Jeremiah clearly saw this king in the future, declaring "the days are coming" when He would appear (23:5). Osborne states, "In both passages a remnant is pictured under the metaphor of a flock gathered . . . under caring shepherds," who are, in turn, ruled by the Branch. He is given the title "Yahweh our Righteousness" (23:6; 33:16) as a "deliberate word-play" on the name Zedekiah (Judah's last king), who was "righteous in name but not in his reign."[59] In both passages, Jeremiah reiterated the very same themes of wisdom, justice, and righteousness as are formed throughout the book of Isaiah (11:2; 33:6; 9:6; 11:4; 32:1; 45:8; 61:3; 62:2).

The "spirit of wisdom" that will rest upon the shoot of Jesse embodies the emphasis of the wisdom literature where *chokmâh* is described as the key to understanding God's will (Prv 1:2; 2:2-6; 3:13; 4:7). Alan Fuhr comments that "the greatest potential for success in an uncertain world lies in wisdom . . . [which] nevertheless provides greater opportunity for the present and the capacity to enhance the potential for success in the future."[60] Isaiah 11:3 connects true wisdom with the "fear of the LORD" as do the Proverbs (Prv 1:7,29; 2:5; 9:10; 15:33).

In the postexilic era, Zch 3:8 and 6:12 apply the symbol of the Branch to Joshua (Hb. *Yeshuah*) the high priest as a symbol of the servant-Branch, who is pictured performing a priestly function by restoring righteousness and true worship to the land. Thus, Osborne concludes that both the royal line and the priestly line would be "reconstituted in the Branch."[61] While the term "branch" is not used in the NT specifically of Jesus, there are what Osborne calls "hints" of the influence of this concept in the "vine and branches" metaphor (Jn 15:1-8) and in the use of palm branches to welcome Jesus at the triumphal entry (Jn 12:13).

Visualizing kings as trees and their fallen dynasties as "stumps" can be clearly seen in reference to Nebuchadnezzar of Babylon (Dan 4:15,23,26). He too is pictured as a tree cut down, whose stump remains and will be secured for a time. The "stump" (Aram. *'iqqar*) with its "roots" (Aram. *shôresh*) would be banded with iron and bronze (symbols of the third and fourth kingdoms of Dan 2:32-33) until Nebuchadnezzar would acknowledge that the Most High (Aram.*'illay*) alone was ruler over the realm of mankind (Dan 2:47).

The references to the "rod of His mouth" and the "breath of His lips" indicate the power of the king's word. His royal decrees enforce his moral nature on the society that he governs. Oswalt notes, "The word itself becomes his weapon."[62] New Testament writers certainly allude to this concept in numerous passages. Hebrews 4:12 pictures the word of God as being "sharper than any double-edged sword." In 2Th 2:8, Christ is pictured as slaying the lawless one (antichrist) with the "breath of His mouth." Revelation 1:16 describes the glorified Christ with a "sharp double-edged sword" in His mouth, and Rev 19:15 repeats this imagery adding that He will strike the nations and rule them with an (Gk. *rhabdos*) iron scepter at the time of His triumphal return.

The prophets Isaiah, Jeremiah, and Zechariah foresaw what the NT writers identified in Jesus. Richard Gaffin Jr. indicates that the OT reveals a "multiple set of paths" that lead to the Messiah. He specifically notes "Isaiah said this because he saw Jesus' glory and spoke about Him" (Jn 12:41). Gaffin comments, "In fact, with an eye to the syntax of verse 41, he spoke 'because he saw,' he said it because he saw it."[63] The manner in which the NT writers viewed the OT indicates their confidence in their understanding of the fulfillment of its predictions as pointing to the Messiah alone.

The apostle Paul (Rom 15:12) was certainly convinced that Isa 11:10 applied to Jesus since he quoted it in the context of His ministry to both the Jews and Gentiles. John Stott comments, "Thus the Messiah would be simultaneously the root of Jesse and the hope of the nations."[64] Robert Mounce writes, "Paul cited the well-known messianic promise from Isaiah 11. The Messiah will come as a shoot springing up from the stump of David's line."[65] If Paul, under the inspiration of the Holy Spirit, viewed Isaiah 11 as applying to Jesus, how much more should we?

This section of Isaiah (chaps. 7–12), known frequently as "The Book of Immanuel," contains three significant Messianic predictions: the virgin birth, the birth of the divine King, and the reign of the righteous messianic King. In the first, the Messiah's birth is predicted (7:13-15); in the second, His deity is revealed (9:6-7); and here in this last prediction (discussed in this article), the Messiah's ultimate destiny is unveiled (11:1-16). He will be the glorious King of the line of David, whose belt is "righteousness" and "faithfulness" (11:5) and whose role will be to make the land to "will be filled with the knowledge of the Lord's glory, as the waters cover the sea" (Hab 2:14). This is the one true hope of Israel and the world, to "seek Him" and the glorious peace that He alone will give.

---

1. See "Olives" under "Plants and Herbs," in J. I. Packer, M. Tenney, and W. White, eds., *The Bible Almanac* (Nashville: Thomas Nelson, 1980), 260–61. Olive trees have the capability of regenerating new shoots or branches. *Chộtêr* ("shoot") occurs only here and in Prv 14:3 (HCSB "rod"). *Nêtser* typically refers to the new "branches" that spring up from the old stump. Isaiah 60:21 uses *nêtser* to refer to Israel in the messianic kingdom as "the branch I planted."

2. John Oswalt, *The Book of Isaiah, Chapters 1–39*, New International Commentary on the Old Testament (Grand Rapids: Eerdmans, 1986), 277. Cf. the same emphasis in Walter Kaiser, *The Messiah in the Old Testament* (Grand Rapids: Eerdmans, 1995), 164–67.

3. John Calvin, *Isaiah* (Grand Rapids: Associated Publishers & Authors, nd.), 170.

4. See "Assyria," in A. C. Meyers, ed., *Eerdmans Bible Dictionary* (Grand Rapids: Eerdmans, 1987), 99–102; W. C. Gwaltney, "Assyrians," in *Peoples of the Old Testament World*, ed. A. J. Hoerth, G. L. Mattingly, and E. Yamauchi (Grand Rapids: Baker, 1994), 77–106; G. Roux, *Ancient Iraq* (New York: Penguin Books, 1979), 256–317; H. W. F. Saggs, "The Assyrians," in D. J. Wiseman, *Peoples of Old Testament Times* (Oxford: Oxford University Press, 1973), 156–78.

5. Walter Elwell, ed., *Baker Encyclopedia of the Bible* (Grand Rapids: Baker, 1988), 219.

6. The term "House of David" has been verified in an Aramaic inscription found at Tel Dan in northern Israel. The inscription, contained on the Tel Dan Stele unearthed in 1993–1994, was most likely originally created by King Hazael of Aram-Damascus circa 825 BC. It specifically mentions Hazael's father, Hadad II, defeating the Judean King Jehosaphat by citing Hadad II's defeat of "foot soldiers, charioteers, and horsemen of the King of the House

of David." See Richard A. Freund, *Digging Through the Bible: Modern Archaeology and the Ancient Bible* (New York: Rowman & Littlefield, 2009), 36.

7. Gary V. Smith, *Isaiah 1–39*, The New American Commentary (Nashville: B&H, 2007), 254. Smith notes that the entire oracle "demonstrates the foolishness of Ahaz's dependence on Assyria for protection" (254).

8. Alec Motyer, *The Prophecy of Isaiah: An Introduction and Commentary* (Downers Grove, IL: InterVarsity, 1999), 116. Motyer points out the contrast of *forests* (uninhibited natural growth) and *fertile fields* (ordered cultivation) as expressing the totality of destruction.

9. Gordon Johnston, "Messianic Trajectories in Isaiah," Herbert Bateman, Darrell Bock, and Gordon Johnston, *Jesus the Messiah* (Grand Rapids: Kregel, 2012), 147–52. Johnston suggests the resurgence of the Davidic dynasty under Hezekiah was the "initial realization of the promise" (150). Rather than an "openness" to a potential future eschatological fulfillment, as he suggests, Isaiah's prophecy is a deliberate prediction of an eschatological fulfillment that goes beyond any historical ruler and finds its fulfillment only in Jesus. John 12:41 declares Isaiah foresaw Jesus and spoke of Him, not someone else!

10. Hb. *Byom hahu* ("in that day" [HCSB "on that day"]) generally points to a future day, not "this day," as in the present (cf. Zch 12:3,6,8-9; 13:1-2,20).

11. Michael Rydelnik and James Spencer, "Isaiah," in *The Moody Bible Commentary*, ed. Michael Rydelnik and Michael G. Vanlaningham (Chicago: Moody, 2014), 1027.

12. Brevard Childs, *Isaiah*, Old Testament Library (Louisville: Westminster John Knox Press, 2001), 102. He also points out the evidence for chap. 65 reflecting a holistic reading of chap. 11.

13. Ibid.

14. The points of this outline are from Oswalt, *Isaiah 1–39*, 276, 284.

15. Calvin, *Isaiah*, 170.

16. The annotation in *The Jewish Study Bible* (Oxford: Oxford University Press, 2004), 807, reads: "The poem's final section is a messianic and eschatological prophecy comparable to 2:1-4 and 9:1-6."

17. See note 1. Cf. also Smith, *Isaiah 1–39*, 271. Smith points out that the later Assyrian King Essarhaddon was called a "precious branch . . . an enduring shoot," indicating a similar use of the same imagery. He also observes that Isa 4:2 uses *tsemah* for the "branch of the Lord," but in 11:1 *hoter* and *netzer* are used "because they describe the growth coming from the roots of a tree." Motyer, *Prophecy of Isaiah*, 65, suggests that the "branch of the Lord" refers to the Messiah's divine origin, whereas the branch from Jesse's roots refers to His human origin.

18. Motyer, *Prophecy of Isaiah*, 121. Motyer notes that the prophetic expectation is not merely for "another king in David's line, but rather another David."

19. Franz Delitzsch, *Biblical Commentary on the Prophecies of Isaiah* (Grand Rapids: Eerdmans, 1965), 1:282, observes, "Consequently the state of humiliation will be followed by one of exaltation and perfection." Motyer, *Prophecy of Isaiah*,121, connects the idea of the "root" to Gn 3:15.

20. E. J. Young, *The Book of Isaiah* (Grand Rapids: Eerdmans, 1965), 1:381, interprets "rest upon" as a genitive of causality, thus the activity of the Spirit gives, or produces, the gifts.

21. Oswalt, *Isaiah 1–39*, 279. Rydelnik, "Isaiah," *Moody Bible Commentary*, 1026, adds, "The presence of the Lord's Spirit denotes the human ruler's access to supernatural resources that will give Him a more-than-human capacity to rule."

22. Walter Kaiser, *The Messiah in the Old Testament* (Grand Rapids: Zondervan, 1995), 165.

23. Motyer, *Prophecy of Isaiah*, 122. Young, *Book of Isaiah*, 381, follows J. A. Alexander, *Commentary on the Prophecies of Isaiah* (Grand Rapids: Zondervan, 1970), 249–50, emphasizing the reference is to the six effects of the one Spirit, not to seven spirits. Alexander points out that the genitives do not denote the qualities of the Spirit, rather they express the effects of the Spirit. He states, "This is evident from the last clause where the fear of Jehovah cannot be an attribute of his Spirit, but must be a fruit of his influence."

24. I. W. Slotki, *Isaiah* (Jerusalem: Socino Press, 1976), 56. He provides the Hebrew text and an English translation and commentary.

25. Delitzsch, *Prophecies of Isaiah*, 1:282–283. He also parallels the sevenfold description to the seven-lighted candlestick (menorah) and the reference to the seven spirits in Rev 4:5.

26. Smith, *Isaiah 1–39*, 272. He notes similar objectives in the Lipit Ishta Laws and the Ugaritic Keret Epic.

27. John Goldingay, *Isaiah*, New International Biblical Commentary (Peabody, MA: Hendrickson, 2001), 84. He points to the coming of God's Spirit on the prophets, judges, and kings of Israel as a prelude to this promise in 11:1–2.

28. Motyer, *Prophecy of Isaiah*, 123.

29. Delitzsch, *Prophecies of Isaiah,* 1:283. He adds, "For the fear of God is a sacrifice of adoration continually ascending to God."

30. Young, *Book of Isaiah,* 1:383. He suggests the Messiah will have "infallible knowledge and so will find delight in the presence of true piety in others."

31. The Talmud uses colorful imagery, saying "The Messiah sniffs and He judges (Sanhedrin 93b)." He does not need to have facts presented to Him because He does not use His eyes or ears. Rather, He will use His sense of smell when judging.

32. Smith, *Isaiah 1–39,* 272.

33. Second Thessalonians 2:8 states that the Lord will slay the lawless one with the "breath of His mouth" and by the "brightness of His coming." Revelation 19:15 describes Christ as having a sharp sword in His mouth "so that He might strike the nations with it. He will shepherd them with an iron scepter."

34. *The Jewish Study Bible,* 807. This annotation clearly indicates the Jewish anticipation of a literal, earthly, messianic kingdom, not a merely spiritual one.

35. Motyer, *Prophecy of Isaiah,* 124. He notes the infant (Hb. *yônēq,* suckling child) and young child (Hb. *gāmûl,* toddler) indicate that the risk of danger is removed even for the most vulnerable.

36. Delitzsch, *Prophecies of Isaiah,* 1:285, and Goldingay, *Isaiah,* 85. The transformation of the animals' carnivorous natures seems to point to a pre-Noahic herbervial world.

37. M. Rydelnik and J. Spencer, "Isaiah," *The Moody Bible Commentary,* 1027.

38. *Shoresh* is the word for the literal root of a plant but is also often used as a term for ancestors or descendants (cf. Isa 53:2).

39. Goldingay, *Isaiah,* 85. He interprets the fact that the nations (Gentiles) will resort or rally to Him as "seeking" Him, thus they will be "drawn to the branch as they will be drawn to Zion."

40. Oswalt, *Isaiah 1–39,* 286. He deals at length with the critical view that suggests this passage is actually postexilic, pointing out that its focus is on Assyria, not Babylon.

41. Goldingay, *Isaiah,* 86, admits that no such regathering has ever yet occurred at any one particular moment in history. However, his comment that "most of the Jewish people do not live there" (today), overlooks the fact that almost half of the world's Jewish population has returned to Israel in the past hundred years. See Pew Research Center, "Jews," http://www.pewforum.org/2015/04/02/jews/.

42. Motyer, *Prophecy of Isaiah,* 125. The nations are attracted to the *shoot* and the *root* of Jesse (vv. 1,10) and then drawn by the Lord's own *hand* (vv. 11,15), which Motyer calls "the symbol of personal action."

43. The participle "standing" indicates continuous action. The verb "extend" is missing (though assumed) in the Masoretic Text and "second" is missing from the Septuagint, though present in 1QIS[a] and the Targum.

44. The masculine form indicates the *men* of Judah and the feminine form indicates the *women* of Israel as an idiomatic construction indicating the exiled men and scattered women both of Israel and Judah.

45. Cf. Young, *Book of Isaiah,* 1:398. He suggests that Israel and Judah can only be reunited in Christ and rejects a literal future fulfillment for the Jewish people. Rather, he views the work of conquering the enemy world as the church sending missionaries to proclaim the gospel to the nations. In light of this approach, he views the return to the land of promise, not as Israel, but the heavenly city of God (401). J. A. Alexander, *Commentary on the Prophecies of Isaiah* (Grand Rapids: Zondervan, 1970), 256, views the "place of rest" as the Church where Christ's glorious presence is on display for all the nations to see. This "spiritualized" approach totally overlooks the original intent of the author on the assumption that Isaiah leaves his prophecy "open" to a non-literal fulfillment.

46. Gleason Archer, "Isaiah," *Wycliffe Bible Commentary* (Chicago: Moody Press, 1962), 621.

47. Oswalt, *Isaiah 1–39,* 289. He quotes G. E. Wright saying, "It is because of the prophecies such as this that the Hebrews as a people survived the destruction of their nation."

48. Barbara Tuchman, *Bible and Sword* (New York: Ballentine Books, 1956), ix–x; Paul Johnson, *A History of the Jews* (New York: Harper & Row, 1987), 2–3; cf. also David Larsen, *Jews, Gentiles and the Church* (Grand Rapids: Discovery House, 1995).

49. Smith, *Isaiah 1–39,* 1:279.

50. *The Jewish Study Bible,* 808.

51. Motyer, *Prophecy of Isaiah,* 127. He views the song in chap. 12 as reaching back to chap. 6, so that "together they are prologue and epilogue to this whole section."

52. See comments in Edward Hindson, "Isaiah," *King James Bible Commentary* (Nashville: Thomas Nelson, 2005), 786–88.

53. Stephen Schrader, "Genesis," in *King James Bible Commentary*, 74, notes that the root *parah* ("fruitful") may reflect the name of Joseph's son Ephraim. Therefore, Isaiah may intend the reference to the Davidic branch as the one to reconnect the divided tribes of Judah and Ephraim.

54. Grant Osborne, "Branch," in W. A. Elwell, *Baker Encyclopedia of the Bible* (Grand Rapids: Baker, 1988), 376–77.

55. Smith, *Isaiah 1–39*, 1:155. He discusses at length the issue of whether the reference to the Branch in Isa 4:2 refers to the Davidic Messiah or to the simple blessing of nature. He points out that vegetation is never called the "branch of the Lord." Isaiah 4:2-6 refers to the One who will rule God's kingdom on earth in a manner attributed only to God (Isa 2:19-21; 4:5). Cf. also J. G. Baldwin, "*Semah* as a Technical Term in the Prophets," *Vetus Testamentum* Vol. 14, Fasc. 1 (Jan., 1964): 93–97. She supports the messianic interpretation based on the use of the term by Jeremiah and Zechariah.

56. Osborne, "Branch," 377.

57. John Oswalt, *The Book of Isaiah, Chapters 40–66*, New International Commentary on the Old Testament (Grand Rapids: Eerdmans, 1998), 382. Cf. also Darrell Bock and Mitch Glaser, eds., *The Gospel According to Isaiah 53* (Grand Rapids: Kregel, 2012), 33–83.

58. Walter Kaiser, *The Messiah in the Old Testament* (Grand Rapids: Zondervan, 1995), 182. He notes that the "sure mercies" of God are applied to Christ in Acts 13:34.

59. Osborne, "Branch," 377.

60. Richard A. Fuhr Jr., *An Analysis of the Interdependency of the Prominent Motifs in the Book of Qohelet* (New York: Peter Lang, 2012), 185.

61. Osborne, "Branch," 377.

62. Oswalt, *Isaiah 1–39*, 281.

63. Richard Gaffin Jr., "Biblical Theology," in *Seeing Christ in All of Scripture*, ed. P. A. Lillback (Philadelphia: Westminster Theological Press, 2016), 86.

64. John Stott, *Romans: God's Good News for the World* (Downers Grove, IL: InterVarsity, 1994), 373.

65. Robert Mounce, *Romans*, New American Commentary (Nashville: B&H, 1995), 261–62. He notes that Paul quotes four OT Scriptures that come from all three divisions of the Hebrew canon: Law (Dt 32:43), Prophets (Isa 11:10), and Writings (Ps 18:49; 117:1).

Isaiah 16:5

The Context of the Promise

KEVIN D. ZUBER

The promise of a throne to be established "in the tent of David" in Isaiah 16:5 occurs in a surprising context." Isaiah 13–23 has a series of burdens or oracles (*massa'*) in which the prophet preaches the Lord's judgment against "the nations" (cf. Isa 13:1; 15:1; 19:1, 21:1; 22:1; 23:1; see Jer 46–51 and Ezk 25–32). These oracles come immediately after the great prophecies of the coming and future (national) reign of the Messiah in Isaiah chaps. 7–12. Among other things, those prophecies announce His coming reign over the nations (Isa 9:6-9; 11:1-10) and the restoration of the remnant (10:20-22; 11:11-16) from among "the nations." Those prophecies reveal that the purpose of the Lord—in the Person of and through the ministry of the Messiah—is to demonstrate His glory among and authority over "the nations" (Ps 96:3; 1Chr 16:24). Specifically, these oracles against "the nations" in Isa 13–23 reveal the absolute supremacy and righteous justice of the Lord in two complementary ways. First, they establish His sovereign right to bring judgment upon "the nations" (mostly for their ill-treatment of His chosen nation) and His right to rule over "the nations." Second, they reveal His sovereign intention for His people Israel. That intention is to bring justice and peace to them, and then through blessing them, to bring justice and peace to all "the nations."

The promise in Isa 16:5 is found in the oracle against Moab, comprising all of chaps. 15 and 16. Moab was located east of the Dead Sea and south of the Arnon River. The Moabites were the descendants of Lot (Gn 19:37). The history of relations between Israel (Judah) and Moab were mixed. At times the relationship was amicable (see the story of Ruth) and other times it was enmity (see Nm 25,31; Jdg 3:12-30).

In his day, David subdued Moab and made it a vassal state (2Sm 8:12). At a later time an apparently reinvigorated Moab, in alliance with Ammon, invaded Judah (2Chr 20). That alliance failed, and Moab and Ammon were defeated for the most part because of the prayers of Jehoshaphat.

The historical setting of Isaiah's oracle against Moab is the invasion of Assyria around 715–711 BC.[1] The northern kingdom of Israel was defeated by Assyria and taken into captivity in 722 BC, and the southern kingdom of Judah was attacked in 701 BC. That Assyrian attack on Judah was unsuccessful (see the accounts in Isa 36–39; 2Kg 18:13–20:19; 2Chr 32:1-23). Isaiah gives a general description of the Assyrian invasion of Moab in Isa 15; here the prophet lists the cities that were attacked ("Ar in Moab," "Kir in Moab, "Dibon . . . Nebo and Medeba," "Heshbon and Elealah . . . Jahaz" "Zoar to Eglath-shelishiyah . . . Luhith . . . Horonaim," "Nimrim," "Arabim" [NASB], "Eglaim . . . Beer-elim," "Dibon," Isa 15:1,2,4,5,6,7,8,9), and he describes the distress the invasion caused ("devastated and ruined," "the waters . . . are desolate," "the grass is withered," "the waters . . . are full of blood," 15:1,6,9). In particular, the prophet highlights the futility the Moabites experienced when they appealed to the Moabite gods (15:2) and their plaintive but futile cries ("wails," "weeping," "cry out, "raise a cry," "wailing," 15:2,3,4,5,8).

In Isa 16 (with genuine and deep concern— "I join . . . to weep," "I moan like the sound of a lyre," 16:9,11) the prophet seems to be offering some counsel to Moab; he seems to be advising them (from the relative security of Jerusalem) on what they must do to be delivered form the scourge of Assyria.[2] He instructed Moab to appeal to Judah (16:1); which was, in fact, the one nation the Assyrians were not able to completely conquer (10:24-34; chaps. 36, 37). The prophet directed the "daughters of Moab" (16:2) on what they needed to do if they wanted to escape the scourge of Assyria. First, they needed to "send the tribute lamb to the ruler of the land" (16:1a). The act of sending a lamb in tribute was an act of submission. Moab had been a vassal state of the northern kingdom since the days of Omri (c. 880 BC) and had sent tribute in the form of sheep and wool to the king of Israel (cf. 2Kg 3:4). Isaiah was telling Moab to "send the lamb" to the "ruler of the land" (*moshel aretz*). The phrase "the ruler of the land" is somewhat ambiguous, and Motyer suggests that the "vague description of *the ruler of the land* is intentional."[3] On the one hand, the identification of "the land" is made clear by the mention of "the mountain of Daughter Zion" (16:1b).[4] This is an obvious reference to Jerusalem, and so it seems obvious that the refugees from Moab were being instructed to appeal to the king who is ("ruler of the land") of Judah. Still, the precise identity of "the ruler" is indefinite in v. 1, possibly intended to foster the question "Just who is *the ruler*?" In other words, the indefiniteness of *the ruler* prepares the reader for the fuller disclosure to come in v. 5. As the prophet continued his advice to Moab, he even instructed the refugees on how they needed to run, "like fleeing birds" (16:2). They were told what they needed to say, "Give us counsel . . . hide the refugees . . . be a refuge . . ." (16:3-4a). This appears to be a petition that the prophet essentially "puts in the mouth of some of the Moabites,"[5] which they were to make should they follow the prophet's instructions and make the suggested appeal to *the ruler* in Jerusalem.

In short, the prophet assures Moab that if the people (the "remnant"—see 15:9, 16:14 NASB) of that nation would submit to, and seek refuge from, Judah and her "ruler" they would find relief from the coming oppression and distress (16:4b).

At this point (16:5) the prophet adds a promise of blessing to the offer of refuge. In the messianic promise of a throne "in the tent of David," the prophet looks to the ultimate promise of safety and security for those who submit and seek the refuge of Jerusalem and its ruler. Here Isaiah is telling Moab that if she were to submit to and seek the assistance of Judah, Jerusalem, and her ruler (king) she would not only find relief from her distress, but she also would find a nation whose Ruler governs, not in the terror and destruction of the Assyrians, but in lovingkindness, faithfulness, justice, and righteousness.

This offer made to the refugees of Moab was not an idle one, or an ethereal offer of a distant future salvation—that is, it was not a theoretical, mystical, or merely spiritual offer—it was not a promise of future salvation (in a soteriological sense). Had Moab allied herself with Judah, had she sought the protection of the only nation whose God was "the LORD" (cf. Isa 37:20), and had she submitted to the Davidic king ruling there at the time, at least the remnant of Moab (16:14) would have been preserved. While the qualities of the ruler described in Isa 16:5 will be fully realized only in the Messiah (see below), each Davidic king was to be a practical example of that messianic ideal, and Moab had the chance (in a literal, actual historical sense) to experience a foretaste of a practical (if not perfect, messianic) deliverance.

However, Moab did not heed the counsel and appeal of the prophet, but in rebellious pride (16:6) and persistent, futile idolatry (16:12) suffered destruction and bitter loss (16:7-10,13-14). Moab "could only enjoy Zion's security at the price of owning Zion's king," but she tragically "refused what was offered."[6]

THE CONTENT OF THE PROMISE

Moab had been offered the hope of deliverance and the promise of an essentially messianic blessing[7] by submitting to the Davidic king in Jerusalem; but this was rejected. The promise would nevertheless have been a reminder to the nation and people of Israel and Judah that this was still their hope, and it was assured.

Because Isaiah has already established the fact of the Messiah's future reign

(Isa 9:6-9; 11:1-10), the reader who comes upon this prophecy of "the throne" (in 16:5) may be permitted to assume several points. *First*, the temporal existence and assured futurity of this throne (as such, as a reign on the earth) may be taken for granted—it "will even be established." *Second*, it may be presupposed that the One who "shall sit" on this throne is the Messiah[8], the son of David. The expression in the NASB "a judge will sit on it in faithfulness in the tent of David" is literally "he shall sit on it in faithfulness (truth), in the tent of David, judging . . ." The "tent of David" (as with the expression "house of David," 2Sm 20:16; "booth of David," Am 9:11; cf. Ac 15:16-18) is a reference to the dynastic line of David.[9] *Third*, since the offer to Moab was a genuine offer, made in the course of actual, temporal history, so the fulfillment is to be understood as taking place in an actual, temporal, genuinely historical (yet future) reign of the Messiah. In sum, in this brief reference to the "throne" the prophet is not attempting to *argue* for the fact, futurity, or the genuine (literal) historical fulfillment of the messianic promise—here all that is assumed. The emphasis of the prophetic word in Isa 16:5 is on the quality of that reign.

The prophet mentions four qualities of the Messiah's reign: (1) It is "established in lovingkindness" (NASB) or "faithful love" (HCSB) (*hesed*). (2) It will be accomplished in "faithfulness" (*'emet*). (3) Its objective is "justice" (*mishpat*). (4) Its principle is "righteousness" (*sedeq*).

"Lovingkindness" (*hesed*) "is the Lord's covenanted love for His people."[10] This term, "one of the richest, most theologically insightful terms in the OT,"[11] may be best translated "loyal-love" and is meant to emphasize the steadfast love of God for the nation and His covenant people, Israel. The note of *hesed* as a quality of the Messiah's throne (linked here with "justice and righteousness") recalls the description of the throne of the "Lord God of Hosts" in Ps 89:8 (cf. 89:14). The throne in view here in Isa 16:5 is "established" on the "loyal-love" of the Lord and is therefore utterly secure and sound. The Moabites could have known that security. All who submit to that throne will find lasting security.

"Faithfulness" (*'emet*) "means reliability or steadfastness and is the opposite of fickleness and capriciousness."[12] This king will be the true Davidic king who "will sit in the tent of David" not as "a usurper but one with a true lineage, an undoubted [rightful] claim" to this throne.[13] And in his judgment, and in the execution and exercise of his ruling prerogative, this king will be "true and sure." As a "faithful" king, he will exhibit the utmost integrity and demonstrate absolute reliability. He will rule with the highest degrees of "fidelity, and trustworthiness, honesty and moral rectitude."[14] The Moabites could have enjoyed that faithfulness. All who will live under that throne will enjoy His faithfulness.

"Justice" (*mishpat*) and "righteousness" (*sedeq*) "are a frequent pair in Isaiah" . . . and "they are equally rooted in divine holiness (5:16): righteousness embodies holiness in sound principles, and justice is the expression of righteousness in sound precepts (see 32:1)."[15] "Justice" (*mishpat*) is "often found in prophetic literature" and "is tied to God's execution of world affairs."[16] "Justice" is the object of God's actions in the world—that is, it is the actualization of God's holiness in world and human affairs. "Justice," impartial judgments, evenhanded pronouncements, fairness, and equity are the characteristics of the One who rules, and "righteousness" is the underlying principle of all His actions and decisions that are undertaken or made from this throne. In short, righteousness, defined by the standard of the holiness of God, is the basis for all He does. The throne of the Messiah will be founded on that holiness, and every decision made on it will display God's holiness. The Moabites could have experienced that justice and learned of that righteousness. All who come to that throne will know and live that under that justice and experience that righteousness.

The Moabites were offered a deliverance based in "the Messianic best that Zion [could] offer"[17] but in their overweening pride, arrogance, and self-sufficiency ("empty boasting" 16:6) they refused it. This prophecy serves as a literal, historical lesson that those who are offered that "Messianic best," both now and in the future, should not make the same, tragic mistake. The oracle ends with a sad (narrative form) postscript (16:13-14); indeed, "in three years" of the prophet's words thc nation of Moab was destroyed.

---

1. John N. Oswalt, *The Book of Isaiah Chapters 1–39*, New International Commentary on the Old Testament (Grand Rapids: Eerdmans, 1986), 335. The reference to the three years in 16:14 may be the time from the beginning of Assyria's invasion of Moab to its devastating end. It is not possible to correlate the specifics of the destruction mentioned by Isaiah with known historical records of Assyrian destruction; cf. *Ancient Near Eastern Texts Relating to the Old Testament* (Princeton, NJ: Princeton University Press), 286-87.

2. It is unlikely that any of the leaders or citizens of Moab actually heard this prophetic advice at the time, nor does it seem that the prophet is giving a summary of an actual Moabite delegation to Jerusalem. The prophet is using the rhetorical device of advising Moab (this is what Moab should have done, v. 1) and of putting words into the mouths of the Moabite refugees (this what the Moabites should have said, vv. 3-4) to make the point that the nations should cease their stubborn nationalistic pride and devotion to false deities and direct their loyalty to, and place their trust in, the Lord and His chosen sovereign—the One who will sit on the throne "in the tent of David" (v. 5).

3. J. Alec Motyer, *The Prophecy of Isaiah* (Downers Grove, IL: IVP Academic, 1993), 151.

4. The expression "from Sela . . . to the mountain . . ." is literally "*from the rock . . . to the mountain* [and] seems to be a play on words" (J. N. Oswalt, *The Book of Isaiah, Chapters 1–39*, 341). If a specific place is the meaning of "Sela" it may be a spot in Edom, near the famous city of Petra (cf. 2Kg 14:7) and so indicate that the Moabite refugees had fled their homeland and were seeking refuge in the hills and caves of their neighbor.

5. Oswalt, *The Book of Isaiah*, 341.

6. Motyer, *The Prophecy of Isaiah*, 153.

7. The blessing for Moab would have been "essentially messianic" because the Davidic king, the current "ruler of the land," would have occupied the throne on the basis of the promise the Lord made to David in 2Sm7 (cf. 1Chr 17:1-15; Ps 89). Each Davidic king was in a sense a partial fulfillment of the Davidic covenant and an anticipation of

ultimate fulfillment of the Lord's promise to David, "I will raise up your descendant after you, who will come forth from you, and I will establish his kingdom . . . and I will establish the throne of his kingdom forever" (2Sm 7:12-13 NASB). The greater son of David, the One who fulfills this promise completely, is the Messiah (see Mt 1:1; Lk 1:32); but each legitimate Davidic king (however imperfectly) ruled on the basis of that promise, and hence that rule was "essentially messianic."

8. See Oswalt, *The Book of Isaiah*, 343; the reference is "clearly Messianic, as a comparison with 9:1-6 (Eng. 2-7) and 11:1-9 must show."

9. "In the light of the promise to Amos regarding the tent of David (Amos 9:11-12) and Isaiah's words concerning the Ruler and refuge to come (7:14; 9:6-7; 14:32), verse 5 must be seen as messianic." Homer Hailey, *A Commentary on Isaiah: With Emphasis on the Messianic Hope* (Grand Rapids: Baker, 1985), 149. (See note 7.)

10. Motyer, *The Prophecy of Isaiah*, 152.

11. William D. Mounce, "Love," *Mounce's Complete Expository Dictionary of Old & New Testament Words* (Grand Rapids: Zondervan, 2006), 426.

12. Motyer, *The Prophecy of Isaiah*, 152.

13. Ibid, 152–53.

14. W. D. Mounce, "Faithfulness," *Complete Expository Dictionary*, 234.

15. Motyer, *The Prophecy of Isaiah*, 49.

16. W. D. Mounce, "Justice," *Complete Expository Dictionary*, 373.

17. Motyer, *The Prophecy of Isaiah*, 153.

Isaiah 24:21-23

The Victory and Rule of the Messianic King

MICHAEL J. VLACH

One great theme of Scripture is that God will judge a rebellious world *en route* to establishing His righteous kingdom on the earth. Accomplishing this will involve the defeat of God's enemies through the coming of the Messiah and His kingdom reign from Jerusalem. Passages such as Ps 2, Ps 110, and Zch 14 explicitly teach this. This truth also is found in Isa 24, including its climactic section of 24:21-23. With Isa 24:21-23 we have a messianic text that speaks of the reign of the Messiah from Jerusalem after a period of global tribulation.

ISAIAH 13–23 AND 24–27

A proper understanding of Isa 24:21-23 involves noting its broader context. Isaiah 13–23 is devoted to God's message for various Gentile cities, nations, and peoples, including Babylon, the Philistines, Moab, Damascus, Cush, Egypt, Edom, Arabia, and Tyre. *Yahweh* is sovereign over these entities both for judgment and blessing. Isaiah 13–23 reveals that while the nations currently rebel, God will bring victory over them on behalf of His people. And yet, the nations eventually will experience blessings in the kingdom of God (see Isa 19:24-25).

Next comes Isa 24–27, a section that predicts global judgment and tribulation that will be followed by the kingdom of God on earth. While God has been patient in the years since the fall of Adam, a Day of the Lord is coming when God will judge a sinful world and establish His kingdom on the earth. Such a scenario is described in other Isaiah sections including chaps. 13–14 and 34–35. Yet, Isa 24–27 could be the greatest OT section explaining tribulation followed by God's kingdom. This section is often called "Isaiah's Little Apocalypse" since it describes a coming tribulation period and subsequent kingdom that parallels much of what is found in Rev 6–20.

ISAIAH 24:1-20

Isaiah 24:1-6: Divine Global Judgment for Sin

Isaiah 24 focuses on the coming Day of the Lord. Verses 1-6 describe a coming devastating judgment upon the entire world and its inhabitants.[1] Verse 1 declares: "Look, the Lord is stripping the earth bare and making it desolate. He will twist its surface and scatter its inhabitants." Verses 3-4 state that both the earth and the "exalted people of the earth" will "waste away." Thus, earth itself and its people will face God's judgment. Verse 2 reveals that this devastation will include everyone regardless of status, occupation, or wealth. Isaiah 24:5 then reveals the reason this will happen—man's sinfulness:

"The earth is polluted by its inhabitants, for they have transgressed teachings, overstepped decrees, and broken the everlasting covenant."

Thus, "the earth's inhabitants"[2] (24:6b) are viewed as law transgressors, violators of statutes, and breakers of "the everlasting covenant." The breaking of the "everlasting covenant" could refer to man's obligation to obey the Creator, beginning with Adam (see Gn 2:15-17), or to man's breaking of the Noahic covenant (see Gn 9).[3] Either way, the result of these grave violations is that "a curse has consumed the earth, and its inhabitants have become guilty" (24:6a).

The Hebrew term translated as "earth" is *erets*, which occurs seven times in 24:1-6. This word can be translated as "earth" or "land," yet the context points to the broader sense of "earth" and not just the land of Israel. As mentioned, the section immediately prior, Isa 13–23, detailed God's predictions concerning the Gentile nations. So, both the context involving Gentile nations and the extensive judgment of Isa 24 point to a global judgment. The realm of this judgment also is significant since the earth that is consumed will also be the realm of Messiah's reign as discussed in Isa 24:23b. What is described in Isa 24 is not just a spiritual judgment or kingdom. God's judgments will occur on earth, and so too will His kingdom reign.

Isaiah 24:7-20

Isaiah 24:7-20 describes in poetic form the wideness and extent of the divine judgments from the Lord. In sum, everyday life and its activities will be dramatically interrupted by devastating calamity. Prosperity and celebrations will cease, including music and drink (vv. 7-9). We are told, "The city of chaos is shattered" (v. 10).[4]

The earth itself is shaken violently and totters back and forth like a drunkard (Isa 24:19-20). No one will escape! The only exception to the gloomy tone of this chapter is 24:14-16a and the mention of some who "sing out" concerning "the majesty of the LORD" (Isa 24:14). So even in the midst of judgment God graciously has His people. But 24:16b-20 quickly returns to the severe judgment theme that dominates Isa 24.

ISAIAH 24:21-23

Isaiah 24:21-23 is strategic since it brings together not only the message of Isa 24, but also Isaiah 13–23. As Wilson de A. Cunha observes: "Isa 24:21-23 will have to be viewed as not only the climax of Isa 24:1-20 but also as the climax of Isa 13–23."[5] This is because the promised Day of the Lord judgment of the nations now comes to fruition.[6] Judgment is coming to the nations, and the Messiah will reign upon the earth.

Isaiah 24:21-23 reveals three specific realities. First, v. 21 foretells a coming period of judgment when both evil spiritual and human forces will be punished. Second, v. 22 speaks of a future two-stage judgment of the wicked, consistent with the message of Rev 19–20. And third, v. 23 is a messianic passage that reveals a coming kingdom reign of the Messiah in Jerusalem. Isaiah 24:21-23 reads:

> On that day, the LORD will punish
> the host of heaven above and kings of the earth below.
> They will be gathered together like prisoners in a pit.
> They will be confined to a dungeon;
> after many days they will be punished.
> The moon will be put to shame and the sun disgraced,
> Because the LORD of hosts will reign as king
> on Mount Zion in Jerusalem,
> and He will display His glory in the presence of His elders.

THE JUDGMENT OF GOD'S ENEMIES (V. 21)

Isaiah's mention of "on that day" in v. 21 points to the future period of judgment consistent with the "day of the LORD" as explained in passages such as Isa 13.[7] The "day" is primarily about judgment, but also includes the kingdom of God that is ushered in as a result of divine judgment.

Verse 21 also tells of the punishment of both evil spiritual and human forces. The "host of heaven above" destined to be punished in this context must be evil spirits, involving Satan and demons.[8] Thus, wicked spiritual forces are in view here. The "kings of the earth below" refer to human governmental leaders who represent the nations in their opposition to God (see Ps 2). The parallels with Rev 19–20 here are striking. Concerning the second coming of Jesus in Rev 19:11-15 we are then told in v. 19, "the kings of the earth, and their armies gathered together to wage war against the rider on the horse [Jesus]." This is human opposition. Revelation 20:1-3 then speaks of the binding of Satan in the abyss for 1,000 years. As with Isa 24, the global tribulation of Rev 6–19 results in a judgment upon wicked human rulers and spiritual forces. The connections between Isa 24:21-23 and Rev 19–20 are too many and obvious to be coincidental. Concerning Isaiah 24:21-23, Harry Bultema rightly notes that Revelation 19:19-20 and 20:1-3 "provide an infallible commentary on these verses."[9]

Isaiah 24:21-23	Revelation 19–20
"Punish the host of heaven above" (21b)	"He seized the dragon, that ancient serpent, who is the Devil and Satan" (20:2a)
"kings of the earth below" (21c)	"the kings of the earth, and their armies" (19:19a)
"confined to a dungeon" (22c)	"threw him into the abyss, closed it, and put a seal on it . . .
"after many days" (22d)	until the 1,000 years were completed" (20:3a)
"after many days they will be punished" (22d)	"When the 1,000 years are completed, Satan will be released from his prison. . . . The Devil who deceived them was thrown into the lake of fire and sulfur" (20:7,10)

Two-Stage Judgment (v. 22)

Verse 22 then foretells a two-stage judgment of God's enemies. First, an initial confinement occurs: "They [God's enemies] will be gathered together like prisoners in a pit. They will be confined to a dungeon" (22a). This speaks of the imprisonment of nefarious spiritual and human forces. But this act is not the end. Second, Isaiah states, "after many days they will be punished." Thus, a gathering of evil forces for prison is followed by a *punishment* that occurs *after many days.* A two-stage judgment, with a gap between these judgments, happens. We are not told how long "many days" is, but the similarity with Rev 20 leads many to believe that the "many days" indicates an intermediate period[10] of a thousand years mentioned in Rev 20. Grogan notes that Isa 24:22 "harmonizes with a premillennial interpretation of Revelation."[11] Blaising agrees:

> The many days of imprisonment between the coming of God in the Day of the Lord and the punishment after which the Lord reigns in glory greater than sun or moon bear a correspondence to the millennial period in Revelation 20, which also follows the coming of the Lord in the Day of the Lord.[12]

The imprisonment of evil forces will last for "many days" or a thousand years until a final punishment takes place after that. To put it another way:

Evil forces are imprisoned and confined in prison
↓
Many days (thousand years)
↓
Evil forces punished.

THE MESSIAH'S RETURN AND KINGDOM (V. 23)

Verse 23 is a messianic verse. It starts by mentioning cosmic signs in connection with the Day of the Lord—"The moon will be put to shame and the sun disgraced" (23a). This detail is consistent with the cosmic signs of the book of Revelation (see Rev 6:12-14). It also parallels Jesus' predictions concerning cosmic signs in Mt 24:29: "Immediately after the tribulation of those days the sun will be darkened, and the moon will not shed its light; the stars will fall from the sky, and the celestial powers will be shaken." Verse 23b then mentions the reign of the Lord on earth:

> the LORD of hosts will reign as king on Mount Zion in Jerusalem, and He will display His glory in the presence of His elders.

The global judgments, confining of evil spiritual and human forces, and cosmic signs will culminate in a reign of "the LORD of hosts . . . on Mount Zion in Jerusalem."[13] This shows that the sphere of this kingdom reign is earth and is related to a real city—Jerusalem. Opposition to God took place on earth, and the Lord's reign will be on earth as well.

The One who will reign on Mount Zion in Jerusalem is the "LORD of hosts" or *Yahweh Tsaba* (or *Sabaoth*), which means "LORD of the armies of heaven" or the "LORD Almighty." This designation refers to God as King and Ruler over Israel and the universe.[14] So this One destined to rule is divine. Yet this reign of the Lord is also the reign of the Messiah. Other Isaiah passages link the coming earthly reign of God with the Messiah. In the messianic passage of Isa 9:6-7, the "child" and "son" "given to us" is the One about whom it says, "the government will rest on His shoulders" as He reigns from "the throne of David" in Jerusalem.

According to Isa 11 a "shoot" "from the stump of Jesse," a reference to the

Messiah, will reign over the earth, bringing righteous judgment to the earth (Isa 11:1,4). The thrust of Isaiah concerns a Messiah who will rule the world from Jerusalem (see Isa 2:2-4), and it is this King, the Messiah, who will reign as described in Isaiah 24:23.[15] Concerning the King described in Isaiah 24:23, Kaiser states, "The person can be no one else but the Messiah, for he is described elsewhere as ruling and reigning on Mount Zion in Jerusalem (see 2:1-4; Mic 4:1-4)."[16] Also commenting on this verse, Bultema notes, "Christ with His ancients will reign in Mount Zion."[17]

Some might object to this messianic understanding of Isa 24:23 by claiming that the Messiah is not explicitly mentioned.[18] But this argument is not convincing. As Edward. J. Young observes, "It is true that the Messiah is not mentioned in this verse, but that is not sufficient reason for the assumption that no room is here found for the Messiah."[19] Among the nations of the earth it must be known that Yahweh is King over all the earth, and it will be the Messiah who accomplishes this. Thus, lack of explicit mention of the Messiah does not mean the Messiah is absent from this context. Concerning Isa 24:23, John Oswalt notes, "In this context, it is not surprising that the figure of the Messiah does not appear, for the Messiah's kingship is God's and vice versa."[20]

The reign of the Lord in Isa 24:23 is not the invisible universal reign of God from heaven, but the tangible mediatorial, earthly, kingdom rule of the Messiah from Jerusalem. The next chapter (Isa 25) will explain the details of this reign. It will involve a lavish banquet for all peoples and the removal of death (25:6-8).

What is described in Isa 24 is not unique. With Zch 14, a time of tribulation is associated with cosmic signs and the return of the Lord to Jerusalem to establish an earthly kingdom with implications for the nations of the earth. Zechariah 14:4 speaks of the return of the Messiah to the Mount of Olives: "On that day His feet will stand on the Mount of Olives, which faces Jerusalem on the east." His return culminates in an earthly kingdom: "And the Lord will be king over all the earth; in that day the Lord will be the only one, and His name the only one" (NASB). This pattern of global tribulation with cosmic signs, followed by the return of the Lord to Jerusalem to establish His kingdom, is also described in Mt 24–25 and Rev 6–20.

CONCLUSION

Isaiah 24 is a major eschatological passage. It predicts global tribulation, cosmic signs, the defeat of God's enemies, the coming of the Lord to earth, and the establishment of His kingdom. It is also a messianic passage since the One who defeats God's enemies and establishes God's kingdom upon the earth is the Messiah—the One we now know as Jesus.

1. The scope goes beyond the land of Israel or even immediate nations surrounding Israel. While the center of the kingdom will be in Jerusalem (Isa 24:23), what is described here involves the entire planet, including "the islands of the west" (24:15).
2. Isaiah's mention of "inhabitants" of the earth most probably parallels John's mention of "those who live on the earth" tested by God in Rev 3:10.
3. In addition to these two views, Robert Chisholm adds the Mosaic covenant as a third option. Chisholm views the "everlasting covenant" of Isa 24:5 as ambiguous and could include the nations breaking the Noahic covenant and Israel breaking the Mosaic covenant. See Robert B. Chisholm, Jr., "'The Everlasting Covenant' and the 'City of Chaos': Intentional Ambiguity and Irony in Isaiah 24," *Criswell Theological Review* (January 1993): 249.
4. Debate exists concerning what this "city of chaos" is. This could refer generally to mankind's disobedience to God or the eschatological Babylon discussed in passages such as Isa 13–14 and Rev 17–18.
5. Wilson de A. Cunha, "'Kingship,' and 'Kingdom,': A Discussion of Isaiah 24:21-23; 27:12-13," in *Formation and Intertextuality in Isaiah 24–27*, ed. J. Todd Hibbard and Hyun Chul Paul Kim (Society of Biblical Literature, 2013), 66.
6. "Whereas the oracles against the nations begin with a proclamation of Yahweh's coming day, Isa 24:23 declares that that day has now arrived." Ibid.
7. "This 'day' is probably the same as the 'day of the Lord,' referred to so frequently in the Old Testament." Walter C. Kaiser Jr., Peter H. Davids, F. F. Bruce, Manfred T. Brauch, *Hard Sayings of the Bible* (Downers Grove, IL: InterVarsity Press, 1996), 304.
8. Kaiser believes the reference here "is probably an allusion to Satan and all his supernatural hordes." Walter C. Kaiser, Jr., *The Messiah in the Old Testament* (Grand Rapids: Zondervan, 1995), 168. Bultema refers to these as "wicked angels" and links these with Paul's words in Eph 6:10-19. Bultema, *Commentary on Isaiah* (Grand Rapids: Kregel, 1981), 240. See also, Kaiser, Davids, Bruce, Brauch, *Hard Sayings of the Bible*, 304.
9. Bultema, *Commentary on Isaiah*, 240.
10. As Blaising states, "The structure of the oracle in Isaiah 24–25 indicates some kind of intermediate situation between the coming of God in the Day of the Lord and the everlasting reign in which sin and death are done away completely." Craig A. Blaising, "Premillennialism," in *Three Views on the Millennium and Beyond* (Grand Rapids: Zondervan, 1999), 203.
11. Geoffrey W. Grogan, "Isaiah," *Expositor's Bible Commentary* (Grand Rapids: Zondervan, 2008) 6:155.
12. Blaising, 203. Kaiser, Davids, Bruce, Brauch identify the "after many days" with "the millennium." *Hard Sayings of the Bible*, 304.
13. Micah 4:7 states: "Then the LORD will rule over them in Mount Zion from this time on and forever."
14. See Brad Creed, "Names of God," in *Holman Illustrated Bible Dictionary* (Nashville: Holman Bible Publishers, 2003), 1172.
15. In Psalm 110:1-2, the Messiah (i.e., David's "Lord"), is pictured as One who is seated at the Father's right hand in heaven for a time ("until") this Messiah begins His reign from Jerusalem ("Mount Zion").
16. Kaiser, *The Messiah in the Old Testament*, 168.
17. Bultema, *Commentary on Isaiah*, 240.
18. See George Buchanan, *A Critical and Exegetical Commentary on the Book of Isaiah I-XXXXIX*, The International Critical Commentary (Edinburgh: T&T Clark, 1956), 424.
19. Edward J. Young, *The Book of Isaiah*, vol. 2 (Grand Rapids: Eerdmans, 1993), 183.
20. John N. Oswalt, *The Book of Isaiah, Chapters 1–39*, The New International Commentary on the Old Testament (Grand Rapids: Eerdmans, 1986), 456.

Isaiah 28:16

The Messianic Cornerstone

J. RANDALL PRICE

The identity of the cornerstone/foundation is a key issue for understanding the messianic interpretation of Isaiah 28:16 and for the Church's justification for trust in Jesus as the promised Messiah-Savior for Israel and the whole world. Despite the ancient history of interpretation of this text as referring to Messiah, modern scholarship has offered multiple explanations as to the imagery used in this text as well as its referent. Nevertheless, from a careful examination of the text, the referent is clearly Messiah.

CONTEXT OF ISAIAH 28:16

The fifth division of the book of Isaiah (chaps. 28–33) has been called the "Book of Woes," and its six woes reveal the ungodly depths to which the national leadership (prophets, priests, and kings) have sunk. This will lead finally to the Servant Oracles (49–53), climaxed by chapter 53 and national rejection of the Servant (Messiah). If Israel refuses salvation and rejects the Savior (depicted here as the cornerstone, foundation stone), then there is nothing left to the covenant nation but to receive the covenantal curses (Dt 28–30) in the form of foreign attack and exile. Therefore, in Isa 28:1-4, after briefly addressing Samaria (Ephraim), the prophet moves to accusing Judah of following the example of Samaria, specifically drunkenness and mockery of God's prophetic revelation (vv. 7-10). As a result, in the future, God would speak through a foreign power rather than through His prophets (vv. 11-13). The purpose of the foundation stone section (vv. 14-22) is to assure the leaders in Judah (especially those in Jerusalem) that the only means to achieve national security is through the divinely provided foundation stone, the source of national stability. The section's purpose is also to warn of the dreadful consequences of rejection of God's covenant and foolish reliance upon worldly powers.

Isaiah 28:14 and 22 form an *inclusio* specifically addressing the self-assured "scoffers" in Jerusalem who are trusting in their covenant with "Death" and falsehood (28:15). The Lord warns them against this false covenant (28:18) that will not deliver them from judgment. The covenant with "Death" (Sheol) may refer to an alliance with Egypt (cf. 30:2-7; 31:1). This would prove to be a refuge that would one day fail, since a foreign invasion still came, revealing the certainty of divine judgment (vv. 15,17-18). The central verse in the pericope, v. 16, explains that the divine solution to the nation's problem revolves around its acceptance or rejection of the cornerstone, given to the nation to secure it as promised in the covenant with God, as opposed to the covenant with "Death" in 17b-22. In summary, Isa 28:16 is situated in a section characterized by judgment. However, in the middle of this crisis, v. 16 offers a word of hope and salvation. The one who believes in the stone will remain secure despite the judgment.

HISTORICAL BACKGROUND OF ISAIAH 28:16

Specific references to Assyria and Egypt are absent in the immediate context but occur in the larger context (chaps. 30–31). History of the mid-to-late seventh century BC reveals that Egypt was ascending in power and influence, while from 652 to 640 BC Assyria was declining and would suffer defeat at the gates of Babylon in 626 BC. Egypt had traditionally had a position of power in the region, including over Israel, and recent conquests along Israel's coast made it appear it would resume this position. For this reason, the leaders in Jerusalem wanted to make alliances with Egypt to secure their future—especially ca. 642–633 BC with internal problems (assassination and violence) occurring within the Judean royal house and kingdom (2Kg 21:23-24; 23:26-27). It is clear from King Josiah's death at the hands of Pharaoh Neco in 609 BC (2Kg 23:29), his son and successor's imprisonment and death by the same (2Kg 23:33,34), and Neco's appointment of Eliakim (Jehoiakim) to the Judean throne that Egypt later exercised hegemony over Judah.[1] Some in Jerusalem saw this extension of Egyptian power as a safeguard against Assyrian authority and as an opportunity for Judah to assert itself in the region. But this foreign policy decision was being made without regard to the national covenant with God and His promise of divine protection. How does this background fit with a messianic interpretation?

Messianic prophecies may sometimes appear to be "out of context," a point that may lead interpreters to isolate the interpretation to the historical event. However, while the historical audience may have been seeking an immediate solution to a historical crisis, the prophets are pointing to the ultimate solution, the Messiah. The diatribe in Isa 28 fits the pattern seen earlier in the book (Isa 7–9) where, in a threatened Syro-Ephraimite crisis, the Judean king Ahaz rejected a similar offer from the prophet in order to pursue an Assyrian alliance. In that case, the Immanuel prophecy offered signs to Judah of the future supernatural (virgin-born) Messianic King (7:14), of the Lord Himself as a stumbling stone (8:14-15), of a human born but divinely sent Child (9:6), and further in 11:1-5 of the Davidic Branch who would come to judge the earth and rule in righteousness (v. 4). In this prophecy, Isaiah warned Ahaz that if he did not have faith in God as required by the covenant, he would not remain (7:9b). Therefore, the sign was given to Judah of a deliverer who would identify with the Lord (Immanuel) and fulfill the promise to Judah of Davidic rule (9:6-7).

The consequence of national rejection of the Cornerstone by the leadership is a disaster. The impending Assyrian conquest was certain, with even more dire events in Israel's future, because of the rejection by Israel's leaders of the divine stone (8:6-15; cf. 6:9-10; Jn 12:37-40). The present section (28:14-22) connects to these passages of judgement with the national crisis with Jerusalem as its center (vv. 14,16). This stone is a combination of divinity and humanity (v. 16), which fits the character of the Messiah, and the messianic concept of the stone as the foundation of the nation's trust and security as well as the object that, if rejected, results in its judgment (28:17-18). This accords with the warning concerning rejection of the Messiah as the prophet like Moses in Dt 18:18. God uses historical situations like these as a context for providing messianic revelation, forming intertextual links to reveal the ultimate divine purpose, regardless of the king or crisis in the immediate context.

EARLY MESSIANIC INTERPRETATIONS OF ISAIAH 28:16

The identity of the "stone" (*'even*) in the immediate context and the larger context of the OT, along with the use of this imagery in the NT, is the central issue of Isa 28. Identifying the "stone" has been a cause for stumbling for exegetes, who continue to add to the list of hypothetical interpretations. Thus, the "stone" has been identified with (1) God Himself, faith in God, the prophetic message, Zion-David theology; (2) an ideal leader: archetypal Davidic monarchy, the Messiah, King Hezekiah (and his rehabilitation of the Temple), or even Nebuchadnezzar; (3) an ideal place: the Temple, Jerusalem, Zion, the sacred rock on Mount Zion, the law of God to be revealed in Zion, God's saving activity on Zion, His future building project in Zion; (4) or ideal people: the remnant, the community of believers, and the relationship between God and His people. Others, due to the multiplying views, have abandoned a literal interpretation and simply reduced the figure to a metaphor unifying several central themes of the book.[2]

Despite the plethora of interpretations, the messianic interpretation receives support from the LXX, the Targums (ancient rabbinic paraphrases and interpretations of the Hebrew Bible), rabbinic sources, the NT (see below), and the church fathers, who unanimously accept the apostolic interpretation.[3] The LXX reading ("the one who believes in him") clearly sees a personal figure. The LXX's addition of *ep autō* shows that early Judaism interpreted this text messianically, along with Ps 118:22; Dan 2:34,44; Ex 17:6; and Nm 20:7-8. As Jeremias declares, "The oldest example of Messianic interpretation of an OT stone statement is to be found in the LXX addition *ep autō* to Isa 28:16."[4]

This concept is seen in Peter's reference to Messiah as a "living stone" (1Pt 2:4), and reveals how it was appropriate to represent by extension the Temple founded on this stone as an assembly of human beings (1Pt 2:5, Eph 2:20-22). This idea was already expressed by the sectarian community at Qumran, which took Isa 28:16 as eschatological, with its community's council as the foundation (1 *QS* 8.4-8).[5] Targum Jonathan ben Uziel seems to also have Messiah in view with its paraphrase, replacing "stone" with "king": "I appoint a King in Zion, a King mighty, powerful, and terrible."[6] This figure must be read separate from God, since the Targum goes on to say "I (God) will make Him powerful, and I will strengthen Him," so the King would be King Messiah. The final clause in the Targum Jonathan reads, "But the righteous, who believe these things shall not be moved, when distress shall come." This implies that the object of trust is in what God says He will do, but as the previous line identifies this work with making King Messiah as God's foundation of security, the perspective is of faith in Messiah Himself.

Following the Targum, Rashi (**RA**bbi **SH**lomo **I**tzhaki, 1040–1105, the most influential Jewish commentator) says all of the references to the stone refer to the future Davidic King, Messiah, in Zion, "who will be strong and secure and his advent will be preceded by the events of the Messianic Era mentioned in the following verses as eradicating sinners and establishing justice in society." The final phrase in v. 16, "the one who believes will not hasten" (author's translation; HCSB footnote "will not hurry"), is taken by Rashi as "let the believer not expect it soon," meaning that the messianic prophecy will be fulfilled but one should not try to hasten it to be fulfilled quickly. Abarbanel (Rabbi Isaac ben Judah Abarbanel 1437–1508, Spanish Bible scholar-commentator) took the phrase as meaning "the one who believes should not be silent," teaching that people who believe in the Messiah should proclaim their faith in His coming.[7] While other Jewish sources do not specifically refer to the stone in Isaiah 28:16 as the Messiah, their general messianic interpretation of OT stone texts is well noted. For example, the stone receives a messianic interpretation in Gn 28:18 (Tanchumah *Toledoth* 20, *Aggadat Bereshit* 33a,6); Isa 8:14 (b *Sanhedrin* 38a); Zch 4:7 (*Tg* Zech 4:7; *Aggadat Bereshit* 33a,5) and Zch 4:10 (Tanch *Toledoth* 20; *Aggadat Bereshit* 33a,3); Dn 2:34-35,44-45 (*Nm Rabbah* 13:14; Tanch, *Trumah* 6; *Tanch Toledoth* 20 = *Aggadat Bereshit* 33a,7); Tanch *Ya'acov* 10; and Josephus, *Ant.* 10.210.[8]

The context best argues for the cornerstone being a personal figure of a divinely installed leader who stands in contrast to the unrighteous, scornful officials. But who is this ideal leader? In v. 16, the stone is laid as a "foundation" for the lives of God's people. This figure has implications of deity based on previous metaphorical uses of the figure in relation to God. Moses referred to the "Mighty One of Jacob" (God) as "the stone (*'even*) of Israel" (Gn 49:24) and to the Lord as *ha-Tzur* "the Rock" (Dt 32:4,15,18,31; cf. Isa 26:4).[9] Both of these terms for the Lord, a stone as well as an obstacle over which Israel stumbles in unbelief, are used in Isa 8:14-15. But this is the same context in which the sign to Israel is Immanuel (7:14), who must be identified with Messiah.

Similarly, in Isa 28:16 the stone is the Lord, but since He lays the stone in Zion, it is also distinct from Him. "For this reason," observes James Smith, "the Stone was identified by the apostles [in their citations of these passages] as being the Messiah (1Pt 2:6)."[10] Previously in Isa 9:6 the concept of a divine Messiah is present, so the reader is prepared for this implication of the divine-human character of the stone.

The rejected "cornerstone" in Ps 118:22 is universally interpreted as representing the Messiah, and a majority of interpreters understand the divinely cut "stone" that pulverizes and replaces the last earthly kingdom in Nebuchadnezzar's statue to refer to the Messiah and the establishment of the messianic kingdom (Dn 2:34). The stone of Zch 3:9 (cf. 4:7) in association with "My servant, the Branch" in 3:8, likewise supports a messianic identity. Zechariah 3:8-10 also has intertextual connections with Isa 28:16. In both texts the Lord is the One laying/setting the stone (Isa 28:16b/Zch 3:9a) for the purpose of removing iniquity (Isa 28:16c/Zch 3:9b) and bringing stability/peace and prosperity (Isa 28:16c/Zch 3:10). Other prophetic texts that couple removal of sin with bringing peace and prosperity are seen as the act of the Messiah (Isa 11:1-5; 53:1-12; Jer 23:6; Ezk 36:29-30; 37:24-28; Am 9:13-14; Mic 4:3-4) and further argue for the "stone" in Isa 28:16 being a messianic title. In addition, *pinnâ* ("corner"), one of the adjectives modifying "stone," is used to foreshadow the Messiah in Ps 118:22 and Zch 10:4. Also, the association in Isa 28:17 of "righteousness" and "justice" with the stone relates to characteristics elsewhere mentioned by Isaiah in connection with the Messiah (9:7; 11:4-5; 16:5; 32:1,16; 42:1-6).

TEXTUAL WORD STUDIES OF ISAIAH 28:16

A careful look at several key words in this verse will provide understanding of the meaning of the text. The first word of 28:16 (Hb. *kî*) is a word of assurance ("therefore, surely"). God has already provided the nation with a means of security (the previous revelation of Messiah), so it is not only an act of distrust but also a violation of covenant (Dt 18:15-19) to reject this provision. Like the messianic prophecy of Isa 7:14, this prophecy is introduced with the word "behold" (*hin*^{e}*nî*). The first-person pronominal suffix ("I") on this word puts the focus on this being a divine act, like the giving of Immanuel (cf. 9:6).

The next words "I am laying" (Hb. *ysd*) have been the source of grammatical debate. The MT points the verb as a Pi'el perfect, *yissad* ("lay a foundation"). Some rabbinic sages (Rashi, Rabbi Joseph ben Simeon Kara, 1065–1135) see it as a past tense ("I have laid"), as does HCSB, while Targum Jonathan, Rabbi Ibn Ezra (1089–1167 Jewish scholar philosopher), and Radak (**RA**bbi **DA**vid **K**imkhi, 1160–1235, Jewish commentator and Hebrew grammarian) read a present-progressive ("I am laying"). These constructions are syntactically rare, as the *hinneh* particle usually requires a participle. This is the way the Qumran Isaiah texts read with 1QIsa^{a} as a Pi'el participle and 1QIsa^{b} as a Qal prophetic perfect ("See, I will establish for the foundation"). The LXX has also interpreted this as a Qal participle with its translation in the future tense (*embalō*). *Biblia Hebraica Stuttgartensia* suggests an original Qal perfect participle *yosed* ("I lay"), which is found in most of the versions. The use of the perfect implies, as Smith observes, that "the stone already had been laid at the time the prophet is writing. The plan of God for the salvation of his people was formulated before the foundation of the earth. What God decreed then was as good as accomplished."[11]

The "stone" is described as having three characteristics: "tested, tried" (Hb. *bochan*), "costly, precious corner[stone]" (Hb. *pinat yiqrat*), and "sure, firm or fixed foundation" (Hb. *musar musar*, lit. "a founded foundation"). These two-word combinations ("tested stone," "costly stone," "sure foundation") are unique to Isaiah and exclusive to this text.

The first term *bochan* occurs only two times in the OT, both in Isa (23:13; 32:14). It may mean a "touchstone," "testing stone," "tested stone," or "fortress." The Hebrew root, used elsewhere, looks at divine "testing" of the heart (1Ch 29:17; Jer 11:20; 12:3; 17:10), the "righteous" (Jer 20:12), and the refining of men (Job 23:10; 34:36; Zch 13:9). These uses imply a spiritual evaluation to determine its quality to gain divine approval. Therefore, its use in 28:16 appears to denote the "quality" of the stone for use. In the attributive genitive construction, *bochan* as an adjective emphasizes the qualitative nature of the "stone" that makes it fit for the foundation. G. Smith notes,

"This is a *tested* stone that has proven its worth as a safe and solid piece of rock . . . one that could function as a valuable cornerstone of a wall. Because it had all the right characteristics, it would serve as a 'sure foundation' for a building."[12] Valuable stones were used for foundations in antiquity (1Kg 5:17; 7:9-11). This usage for any Israelite would draw his thoughts to the Temple and its foundation (see below).

The second term *pinat*, a feminine construct of *pinna* ("corner"), has both literal (architectural) and metaphorical connotations. Literally, it may refer to the corner of the altar (Ex 27:2), houses (Job 1:19), city walls (Neh 3:24), or the city itself (2Ch 28:24). Metaphorically, it may also refer to human leaders (Jdg 20:2; 1Sm 14:38; Ps 118:22; Isa 19:13; Zch 10:4; Isa 19:13). The word in construct with *pinat*, *yiqrat* means "precious" in the sense of value or cost (cf. 1Kg 7:9). *Yiqarâ* also can denote human leaders (Jer 15:19; Lam 4:2). The term is used with respect to God's goal to make His people more "precious" (HCSB "scarce") than gold (Isa 13:12), a quality Judah already holds in God's sight (Isa 43:4). The stone is specifically called *pinat yiqrat* ("costly corner[stone]"). The LXX translates *pinat* as *akrogōniaiov*, which indicates a stone "situated at an extreme angle," usually interpreted as a cornerstone.[13] However, the use of this word in 1Pt 2:6 in the immediate context of Temple imagery argues that the Temple's foundation stone was in view. This better fits a messianic interpretation since Jesus depicted His body as a temple (HCSB "sanctuary"; Jn 2:19-21) and both Paul and Peter explain that the body of Messiah is a spiritual Temple with Messiah as its cornerstone, also symbolized as a building's foundation in 1Co 3:11.

Since the "stone" (*'even*) is used for God Himself, this combination of the elements of both divinity and humanity indicates no mere stone is in view; this is a supernatural imagery best fitting the character of the Messiah (cf. Ps 118:22 and Zch 10:4). Israel's rejection of the *rōš pinnâ* ("head of corner") in Ps 118:22 clearly refers to a person rather than to a piece of building material. Both Jesus and the Jewish crowd, which heard His teaching on this verse, identified this verse with Messiah (Mt 21:42; 23:39; Mk 12:10), the divine source of salvation (Ps 118:25-26). Likewise, the cornerstone in Zch 10:4 is from the human house of Judah (v. 3), yet is the object of divine deliverance, redemption, and restoration (vv. 5-8).

The third term *musar musar* is a superlative adjective, made evident by the repetition of the word, and indicates an object "absolutely unshakable." Even the Temple's Herodian retaining wall required such foundation stones, and one visible in the Western Wall tunnel measures 45'x15'x15', weighing an estimated 600 tons. It was needed to keep the structure built upon it stable and secure during earthquakes that frequent the region. Nevertheless, while there may be an analogy to the Jerusalem Temple, the point made here is that the physical Temple cannot save. The people of God are called upon to make the Lord their sanctuary. The only One who can save is the Messiah, who will restore Israel and reign in the Millennial Temple in the eschatological age. As Cullmann has said: "Acc. to the custom of his age the prophet gave an inscr. for the foundation stone of the temple: 'He that believeth shall not be put to shame,' 28:16. But this is the inscr. of the cornerstone of the new temple which God will build, not of the old temple."[14] To maintain the adjectival force of *yiqrat* and the function of *musar*, it is best to render this combination as "a precious corner(stone) of a founded foundation." Thus, *'even* and its synonyms (*even bochan, pinat, yiqrat*) designate the unparalleled quality of the Lord's saving "foundation" in the Messiah.

Although Isa 28:16 would inform its historical audience that reliance on YHWH is the only source of security in the impending calamity, this security is promised to those who believe. Isaiah has previously emphasized the importance of faith to handle similar crises (7:4-9) as well as the present one (30:15; 36:4-15; cf. Hab 2:4). The context of Isa 28:14-22 declares that faith in the symbolic "stone" leads to salvation, a concept further developed in 33:5-6 where in the context of crisis, YHWH is said to be "the sure foundation for your times, a rich store of salvation and wisdom and knowledge" who will "fill Zion with his justice and righteousness" (NIV) in the eschatological age. Therefore, the imagery used here transcends the immediate situation and encompasses the future, pointing ultimately to the coming of the Messiah in whom eternal salvation is grounded. "In this regard, 'stone' and its synonyms, designate the unparalleled quality of the Messiah as the true foundation of human salvation."[15]

To "believe" in this context means to accept the stone (Messiah) as truly laid by God. We have already noted that the LXX added the words *ep autō* ("in him"), probably to make a connection to Isa 8:14,17, which use the personal pronoun for the object of faith, the divine stone. The scorn and mocking seen in this context (28:22) as a result of misplaced trust in a deceptive object (vv. 15,18) is related intertextually to Isa 53:3-4, where the leaders of Judah were ashamed of the Servant of the Lord and concluded that He had not come from God but was being punished by Him. The LXX, followed by the NT, renders the final word of 28:16c as "ashamed." Those who are ashamed of an object make haste to distance themselves from it when difficulty arises. Like Isa 8:14; 28:16 offers mercy in judgment by the provision of the cornerstone foundation imagery. Thus, Messiah is God's mercy to Israel (Rm 11:12,15,23-24,31) if Israel will receive Him as God's means of deliverance from sin and as His sure foundation for the future promises of the covenants (Rm 11:27).

NEW TESTAMENT USE OF ISAIAH 28:16

The NT interprets several OT references to "stone" as referring to Isa 28:16 and a combination of several other OT references to "stone" (Ex 17:6; Nm 20:7-10; Ps 118:22; Isa 8:14; Dan 2:34-35,44-45; Zch 4:7-10) as referring to Jesus the Messiah. It explicitly makes this messianic interpretation in Rm 9:33; 10:11; Eph 2:19-22 and 1Pt 2:4-8. According to Becliako, the messianic interpretation of "stone" in the NT can be classified into three categories: (a) the keystone and foundation stone of the true Temple of God (Mk 12:10; Lk 20:18; Ac 4:11; Rm 9:33; 10:11; Eph 2:20-22; 1Pt 2:4-6); (b) the stone that crushes and is the stumbling stone (Mt 21:44; Lk 20:18; Rm 9:32; 1Pt 2:8); and (c) the living Rock that dispenses water of life (Jn 7:37-38; 1Co 10:4).[16]

The NT does not always quote the OT passages directly but uses combination quotations concerning a stone in Rom 9:32-33 (cf. 10:11) from Isa 8:14 and 28:16, showing Messiah Jesus as the cornerstone of believers' salvation; but to unbelievers, He is a stumbling stone. Sullivan says of the Pauline usage in Romans:

> Paul has taken the judgment section of Isaiah 8:14 and placed it literally in the middle of the comforting portion of Isaiah 28:16 . . . and thereby makes a clear and more concise statement of judgment . . . Paul combines the quotation from Isaiah 28:16 in Romans 9:33 and 10:11 with another from Deuteronomy 30:12–14 in Romans 10:6–8 . . . Paul appears to bring the context of Deuteronomy 30:11–14 into Romans 10:6–8 because Deuteronomy fits the theological framework of the new exodus salvation reflected in the new covenant language of the law written on the heart and the circumcision of the heart. This new heart gives people the ability to love and obey God . . . Romans 10:9–13 is used by Paul to further the explanation of 10:8. The central theme of Romans 10:8–10 is that whoever believes and confesses the resurrected Lord will be saved. To substantiate this central theme, Paul quotes part of Isaiah 28:16 in Romans 10:11 . . . Romans 10:12–13 focuses on the word "all" . . . and stresses the universality of the gospel to both Jews and Gentiles. The word "all" with Isaiah 28:16 includes "Jews and Greeks" (10:12) . . . Since anyone can believe, anyone can partake of the Isaianic promises.[17]

Paul therefore anticipates the promise of salvation through the Messiah at the time of the new covenant's inauguration (Jer 31:31-34; Lk 22:20; 1Cor 11:25). He understood the new covenant to include the current Church age as well as that of the age to come. In the age to come, all national Israel will turn to Jesus the Messiah (Rom 11:25), and the Gentile nations will also come under all the new covenant provisions (Am 9:11-12; cf. Ac 15:15-18).

An analogy from the physical Temple to explain the function of the spiritual Temple is what Paul uses in Eph 2:20-22 (cf. 1Co 3:16-17; 2Co 6:16-17). In the spiritual Temple (the Church), Messiah Jesus is the chief cornerstone, with the apostles serving as the foundational level of this spiritual building, and believers as its building stones. The Temple's foundation stone mentioned previously is surely in view, because it secured and safeguarded the entire Temple's structure, as does the Messiah, promising salvation individually and corporately in the Messianic Age to Israel.

Paul cites Isa 28:16 in Rom 9:31-33, saying the leadership of Israel pursued righteousness by works rather than by faith, causing them to stumble over the stumbling stone, Jesus the Messiah, in fulfillment of Isa 28:16. Like Paul, Peter uses the OT texts as an aspect of fulfillment in Messiah. Similarly, Peter quotes Isa 28:16 and Isa 8:14 from a version that is more similar to the MT than to the LXX. However, for Peter (1Pt 2:6-8) the ones rejecting the stone are those who mock believers, whereas for Paul it was the leaders in Israel who stumbled over the stone. First Peter identifies its readers' situation with that depicted in Isaiah to comfort and encourage believers in Asia Minor facing hostility and suffering from mockery. The texts containing the citations (not direct quotations) are preceded by vv. 4-5 that connect Messiah as the One rejected, but now the living (resurrected) stone. Believers, by virtue of their relationship with the Living Stone, are also living stones of a spiritual Temple (similar to Paul's analogy in Eph 2:20-22). This statement requires explanation, and that is found in the stone (Isa 28:16) and cornerstone passages (Isa 8:14 and Ps 118:22). Peter's use of Ps 118, whose context mentions the Temple and sacrifice (vv. 26-27), also alludes to Jesus' prediction in Mt 23:38-39 that Israel's "house" will be restored after its leaders ultimately recognize Jesus as Messiah. Therefore, Beale identifies Peter's use of the OT texts as "direct fulfillment."[18]

CONCLUSIONS CONCERNING ISAIAH 28:16

From the context, exegesis, and intertextual use of "stone" and "cornerstone" in Isa 28:16, this is clearly a passage referring to the Messiah. The history of interpretation from the church fathers, to ancient and medieval Judaism, indicates that this is a messianic text. Most important, the NT writers applied the cornerstone images to Jesus the Messiah. All the evidence argues for a messianic interpretation: Isaiah 28:16 prophesied Messiah as the cornerstone. As Walter C. Kaiser observes, "this Stone is the 'cornerstone' or 'foundation stone' that ties the building together. That is why it makes such a 'sure foundation' (v. 16c). It cannot be wiggled back and forth; it is immoveable and secure." All who believe in this stone by accepting Him as their Messiah "will be unshakeable" (v. 16d). As Walter Kaiser says, the Messiah "will prove Himself dependable, reliable, trustworthy, and foundational for everything else in life!"[19]

1. See Page H. Kelly, "Isaiah," *Proverbs–Isaiah*, Broadman Bible Commentary, vol. 5 (Nashville: Broadman, 1971), 271.

2. Summary of the list discussed in Daniel K. Becliako, "The Identity of the Stone in Isaiah 28:16," *Journal of AIIAS African Theological Association 1, no. 1* (2010): 64–65.

3. Justin Martyr, "Dialogue with Trypho" 34.2; 36.1; 70.1; 76.1; 86.2–3; 90.5; 100.4; 113.6; 114.2,4; 126.1; Cyprian, "Treatises of Cyprian," "Treatise 12: Testimonies 2.16–17"; Tertullian, "Against Marcion," 3.7; 5.5,7; idem "An Answer to the Jews," 10,14; Irenaeus, "Against Heresies," 3.21.7; Origen, "Commentary on John 1.36 and 265"; Methodius, "Fragments: Oration Concerning Simeon and Anna 6"; "Acts of Philip: Of the Journeyings of Philip the Apostle"; Augustine, "Letters," 159.5.16; idem "On the Gospel of John," 7.23; idem "On the Psalms," 74.8; idem "On the Catechising of the Uninstructed," 23.43; Gregory of Nyssa, "On the Baptism of Christ"; Jerome, "Letters," 108.13; Gregory of Nazianzen, "On the Great Athanasius: Oration," 21.7; Ambrose, "Duties of the Clergy," 1.29.141; idem "Of the Christian Faith," 4.5.53; Aphrahat, "Demonstrations I: Of Faith," 1.6–8.

4. J. Jeremias: "λίθος," in *Theological Dictionary of the New Testament* 4:272.

5. For additional references and discussion see D. A. Carson, "I Peter," in *Commentary on the New Testament Use of the Old Testament*, ed. G. K. Beale and D. A. Carson (Grand Rapids: Baker Academic, 2007), 1025.

6. Similarly, the Targum of Zechariah 4:7 replaces the MT's "stone" with "anointed one" (Tg Zch 3:8) as do other targumim (Tgs Jer 23:5; 33:15; Isa 4:2; Zch 6:12 and Lam Rab 1:51).

7. See Rabbi Nosson Scherman, "Isaiah" in *The Latter Prophets with Commentary Anthologized from the Rabbinic Writing*, Artscroll Series (Brooklyn, NY: Mesorah, 2013), 215. Note that Metzudos, Radak, Abarbanel take a nonmessianic view and believed the stone referred to Hezekiah who would be strong and remove Sennacherib from the land of Judah. Mahari Kara thought it referred to Nebuchadnezzar who would banish the wicked from Zion.

8. References from J. Jeremias, "lithos," in *The Theological Dictionary of the New Testament*, ed. Gerhard Kittel, trans. Geoffrey W. Bromiley (Grand Rapids: Eerdmans, 1967), 4:273.

9. An examination of the use of *tzur* shows that (1) the term is associated with God as a "rock" in about 31 verses in the Hebrew Bible (Dt 32:4,15,18,30,31 [bis]; 1Sm 2:2; 2Sm 22:3,32,47 [bis]; 23:3; Ps 18:2,31,46 [LXX 17:3,32,47]; 19:14 [LXX 18:15]; 28:1 [LXX 27:1]; 62:2,6,7 [LXX 61:3,7,8]; 71:3 [LXX 70:3]; 78:35 [LXX 77:35]; 89:26 [LXX 88:27]; 92:15 [LXX 91:16]; 94:22 [LXX 93:22]; 95:1 [LXX 94:1]; 144:1 [LXX 143:1]; Isa 8:14; 17:10; 26:4; 30:29; 44:8; Hab 1:12). The translators of the LXX seem to translate the reference of the word צוּר instead of literally translating the word into Greek. Almost every one of the verses has some Greek word that references God.

10. James E. Smith, *What the Bible Teaches about the Promised Messiah* (Nashville: Thomas Nelson Publishers, 1993), 277.

11. Ibid.

12. Gary V. Smith, *Isaiah 1–39*, The New American Commentary 15A (Nashville: B&H, 2007), 488.

13. T. Muraoka, *A Greek-English Lexicon of the Septuagint* (Leuven, Belgium: Peeters Publishers, 2009), 23.

14. Oscar Cullmann, "Πέτρα" in *The Theological Dictionary of the New Testament* (Grand Rapids: Eerdmans, 1968), 6:96–97.

15. Beckliako, "Identity of the Stone," 81.

16. Ibid., 79.

17. Stephen P. Sullivan, *The Isaianic New Exodus in Romans 9-11: A Biblical and Theological Study of Paul's Use of Isaiah in Romans* (Silverton, OR: Lampion Press, LLC, 2017), 248–54, esp. 255–78.

18. G. K. Beale, *Handbook on the New Testament Use of the Old Testament: Exegesis and Interpretation* (Grand Rapids: Baker Academic, 2012), 56.

19. Walter C. Kaiser Jr., *The Messiah in the Old Testament* (Grand Rapids: Zondervan, 1995), 171.

Isaiah 30:19-26

The Messianic Teacher King

MICHAEL GABIZON

> And the Lord will give to you bread, *which is* distress,
> and water, *which is* oppression.
> But your Teacher will no longer be hidden,
> and your eyes will see your Teacher.[1]

The book of Isaiah plays a central role in the study of messianic prophecy. Indeed, earning the sobriquet "the fifth gospel," Isaiah's prophecies provide stunning details pertaining to the Messiah's birth, life, death, and resurrection. Among these, Isa 30:20 presents insight into the messianic era and further delineates the mission of the Messiah, portraying Him as a Divine Teacher and Instructor of God's Law.

Within biblical scholarship, this passage has not received the same level of attention as other Isaianic oracles due to certain syntactical and contextual ambiguities embedded in the text. The passage includes a peculiar grammatical structure where the subject of the phrase is plural, yet the corresponding verb is singular. In contrast, conventional Hebrew grammar necessitates that the subject and verb agree in both number and gender. In Isa 30:20, the phrase, "your Teacher will no longer," uses a plural form for the subject "your teacher/teachers" (*mworeyka*), yet is preceded by the singular verb "[he] will no longer be hidden" (*yikkaneph*), causing much debate regarding the proper interpretation and identity of the teacher/teachers.

Three interpretations are often proposed to determine the referent. First, some claim that the verb "[he] will no longer be hidden" (*kkanaph*) should be translated as a plural, thereby underscoring a plural inference of the subject (*mworeyka*). As a result, the referent of "teachers" is "your prophets."[2] A second position views the subject as an *apparent* plural, meaning that the Hebrew spelling is plural, yet the referent is a single individual (i.e., a king or Isaiah). The third option, the one supported in this paper, is that *mworeyka* is a plural of majesty, referring to God. Hans Wildberger correctly notes that grammar and syntax alone are not enough to dictate "whether *[mworeyka]* is singular or plural."[3] Therefore, it is necessary to analyze the broader context of Isa 30:20 as well as grammatical tendencies in Isaianic literature to make an informed decision concerning the messianic nature of this passage.

It is important to interpret and identify the referent of the teacher/teachers appropriately. This study will provide: (1) a better understanding of this Isaianic pericope, and (2) a greater comprehension of the eschatological figure anticipated in the book of Isaiah, who is expected to precipitate the spiritual and physical restoration for Judah.

This article will begin by summarizing the context of Isa 30 and will then provide an exegetical examination of Isa 30:18-26. Next, each referent proposed for the teacher/teachers will be discussed and analyzed in light of the syntax and context of the passage. Finally, the messianic implications of this pericope will be discussed. In this article, I propose that the referent of the Teacher in Isa 30:20 is God, not a plurality of teachers or a human individual. In light of Jn 12:41, where John identifies Jesus as the One whom Isaiah saw in his vision (Isa 6:1), it becomes apparent that the Teacher in Isa 30:20 is the divine Messiah, Jesus.

HISTORICAL CONTEXT

Context of Isaiah 30

The book of Isaiah presents itself as the work of the eighth-century Judean prophet, Isaiah the son of Amoz, and contains both judgments and promises of restoration for Israel and Judah. In the context of chap. 30, God rebukes Judah for her national alliance with Egypt, which denotes her own refusal to trust in the Lord for protection against the Assyrian Empire.[4] Isaiah 30 begins with God's condemnation of Judah, identifying her as spiritually bankrupt and negligent toward His law (Isa 30:1-17). However, in vv. 18-26, the tone of the passage changes as God promises spiritual and physical restoration for Judah once the teacher/teachers arrive(s) (Isa 30:18-26).

The contrast between Isa 30:9-11 and Isa 30:18-26 is quite striking, illustrating the positive influence of Judah's teacher/teachers. For example, Isaiah initially recorded Judah's refusal "to obey (*shema'*) the LORD's instruction" (Isa 30:9b), yet later proclaimed that "your ears will hear (*shema'*) this command" once the teacher/teachers arrive (Isa 30:21). Also, the leaders of Judah commanded the seers to neglect God's revelation: "Do not see (*ra'ah*)" (Isa 30:10). However, once the teacher/teachers reveal(s) himself/themselves, Isaiah predicted "your eyes will see (*ra'ah*) your Teacher/teachers" (Isa 30:20).[5] Lastly, although Judah initially instructed her prophets to "leave the pathway (*derek*)" of God (Isa 30:11), the presence of the teacher/teachers will guide the nation in "the way (*derek*)" of God whenever they stray (Isa 30:21). Therefore, Isa 30:18-26 clearly depicts an eschatological era where the teacher/teachers operate as the catalyst for Judah's spiritual and physical revival, culminating in the coming rain and agricultural blessing.

A Close Reading of Isaiah 30:18-26

Verses 18 and 19 begin the eschatological pericope and establish an optimistic platform for Isa 30:20. Verse 18 immediately highlights God's strong desire and love for Judah, stating that "the Lord is waiting (*yechakkeh*) to show you mercy."[6] Significantly, prior to Isa 30:20, the verb "wait" (*chakkah*) is found only once in this book, when Isaiah expresses his longing (*wechikiytiy*) for God "who is hiding His face from the house of Jacob" (Isa 8:17). The context of Isa 30 uses similar imagery, noting how the teacher/teachers will no longer be hidden from Judah.

Verse 19 promises the dwellers of Jerusalem that the Lord will faithfully respond to the remnant once Judah repents. Yet in the midst of a positive future proclamation, *Adonai* pronounces "water," *which is* adversity, and "bread," *which is* affliction upon Judah, signifying a pending judgment on the nation (Isa 30:20). Following this period of turmoil, however, the teacher/teachers will be revealed to the Judeans and will provide spiritual and physical restoration. The last clause of v. 20 begins with a verbal form *wehaywu* that "expresses the durative aspect of future action."[7]

The remainder of the pericope is divided into two sections. The first depicts the spiritual restoration of Judah (vv. 21-22), whereas the second focuses on the agricultural blessing of God (vv. 23-26). In vv. 21-22, Isaiah changes the metaphor from Judah *seeing* her teacher/teachers to being *guided* by him/them (Isa 30:21).[8] Although the text does not explain the reason for this shift, the word "from behind you" (*me'achareyka*) in Isa 30:21 may emphasize the teacher/teachers' role of shepherding the people of Israel. In the ancient Near East, it was "quite common for a shepherd to guide and lead his flock from behind."[9] The Hebrew conjunction *waw* beginning v. 22 signifies that, as a result of the teacher/teachers, Judah will defile (*tame'*) their images and idols.[10] The only other time the Hebrew verb "defile" (*tame'*) is applied to the destruction of idols is during Josiah's exemplary national reform (2Kg 23:8-16). The second section records the agricultural blessings as God promises rain and bread, which is language that typically represents blessings and restoration from the book of Deuteronomy (Dt 11:23-26).[11] Moreover, this language intentionally reverses the negative imagery of Isa 30:20a. The primary thrust of this section is that Israel will prosper spiritually and physically after a time of judgment, once they are led by their teacher/teachers.

IDENTITY OF TEACHER

The Hebrew subject "teacher/teachers" (*mworeyka*) in Isa 30:20 is a form of the verb *yarah* which means "to teach."[12] This verb appears 46 times in the Hebrew Bible and four times in Isa (Isa 2:3; 9:14 [9:15 English]; 28:9; 28:26). In light of this, let us analyze which interpretation of "teacher/teachers" best fits the context of Isaianic literature.

The first view argues that the plural form "teachers" refers to a plurality of individuals, namely, the priests and prophets. In defense of this view, proponents typically interpret the verb "to hide oneself" as a plural form, referring to the prophets who were hiding during the time of Isaiah because their lives were in danger (cf. 1Kg 18:4; Jer 36:26).[13] In the *eschaton,* they will reveal themselves once again to proclaim God's Word to Judah.

There are several issues with this approach. First, there is no textual justification for translating the singular verb "to hide oneself" as a plural. Although both the LXX and the Qumran scroll of Isa (1QIsa[a]) attempt to rectify this syntactical issue by making this verb plural, neither text should be adopted as an authoritative witness of the original version of Isa 30:20.[14] Second, the plural form of the subject "teacher" does not necessarily require a plural referent. According to W. Gesenius, "the plural is by no means used in Hebrew solely to express a number of individuals."[15] Lastly, J. Alec Motyer appropriately notes that the problem with Israel "was not the concealment of teachers but the unwillingness of hearers."[16] It is apparent from Isa 30:8-10 that the prophets of Israel were not hidden at all, but remiss in guiding Judah spiritually.

A second argument in defense of translating "teacher/teachers" to mean a plurality of individuals is the reference to multiple prophets and teachers in the broader context of Isa 30. Since the preceding pericope deals with a plurality of false teachers (Isa 30:8-11), it may be assumed that the form *mworeyka* "is a plural, according to the context."[17] However, the broader context does not favor this reading. Instead, Isaiah includes a string of plural imperatives when addressing the false prophets in the first pericope, creating grammatical symmetry between the subjects and verbs.[18] In contrast, Isa 30:20 uses the singular verbal form *kkanaph*, signifying a change of referent. Also, neither *mworeh* nor *yarah* are used to identify the teachers or prophets in Isa 30:8-11. For these reasons, it does not appear that the plural form "teachers" is an appropriate translation.

A second interpretation proposes that the referent of "teacher/teachers" is a single individual. Hayes and Irvine, for example, claim that the referent "teacher" may be a king, or even Isaiah.[19] In defense of this view, advocates argue that the Hebrew form *mworeyka* is only an "apparent" plural since the letter *yod*, which identifies the verb as plural, was inserted only due to the suffix at the end of the participle.[20] Although this is a viable explanation, this suggestion does not advance our understanding of the passage. Indeed, if this approach were embraced, the identity of the teacher would remain completely ambiguous, since no other description is provided. For example, Alexander supports the interpretation that teacher (*mworeyka*) is an apparent plural, yet he concludes that it "must of course be applied to God himself," not a human individual.[21] Therefore, although the syntax of Isa 30:20 may *support* a singular reading, there is no compelling evidence in the text that the teacher (*mworeyka*) has a human referent.

A third proposal is that the plural form for "teacher" is a *pluralis majestaticus* (plural of majesty), and therefore refers to God as the Teacher. This interpretation should be adopted for numerous reasons. First, in light of the singular verb "[he] will no longer be hidden" (*kkanaph*), the plural subject should be understood as a plural of majesty.[22] The plural of majesty is prominent in Isaianic literature, with various examples of a singular verb followed by a plural noun, referring to God as the subject.[23] Furthermore, Isa 30:20 begins with the subject *'adonay,* which is a plural form of *'adwon*, and is preceded by the singular verb *natan*, thereby providing another example of the *pluralis majestaticus* and potentially creating a parallel between *'adonay* and *mworeyka*.

A second argument is the predominant understanding of the passive form *yikkqneph*, which is typically rendered "to hide oneself."[24] In the book of Isaiah, God is often portrayed as hiding Himself from His people as a result of their sin. For example, in Isa 8:17, it states: "I will wait for the Lord, who is hiding his face from the house of Jacob."[25] In contrast, the presence of God "is a gracious and deliberate gift" that results in the eschatological redemption found in Isa 30:20-26.[26] Therefore, the description of the Teacher hiding Himself draws a strong parallel with God's actions in Isaiah.

Third, the verbal form *haray* in Isa 30:20 is translated as "teacher" four other times in the book of Isaiah, three of which refer to God's teaching role.[27] The act of teaching is frequently attributed to God as He often instructs His people, which is also evident in the broader context of Isa 28–30 (see Isa 28:9-13; 29:11-12; 30:15).[28]

In contrast to the prophets who were rejected (Isa 30:8-10), God is depicted as the Teacher *par excellence*.

Fourth, the portrayal of the Teacher shepherding Judah also draws a strong parallel with the depiction of God in the Hebrew Bible, who is often described as Israel's Shepherd (Ezk 34:11-16; Ps 80:1; Isa 40:11). Wildberger claims that the term "behind you" (*me'achareyka*) in Isaiah 30:21 illustrates how "God is depicted as a shepherd that watches over his flock from behind it."[29] The close relationship between the Shepherd and His people is further supported by the noun "way" (*derek*), which represents the sanctified lifestyle of Isaiah.[30]

Finally, the interpretation of "Teacher" as God has been understood in some early Jewish translations of Isaiah. For example, in the Targum of Isaiah, the author translated "Teacher" as *Shekinah*.[31] While the Aramaic Targums only present a theological perspective, the term *Shekinah* is often employed to "deliberately emphasize some aspect of God's activity."[32] Therefore, this third interpretation appears to be the strongest based on the syntax of the passage, the connotations of the verb "[he] will be hidden," the imagery of God as Teacher and Shepherd, and the Targum of Isaiah.

NEW TESTAMENT IMAGERY

One difficulty with this interpretation, however, is God's statement that "no one can see Me and live" (Ex 33:20). Indeed, after Manoah's interaction with the Angel of the Lord in the book of Judges, he proclaimed to his wife "We're going to die . . . because we have seen God!" (Jdg 13:22).[33] How is it, then, that Judah will see their Teacher? This predicament is only rectified once it is understood that Isa 30:20 is referring to the divine manifestation of God: the second Person of the Godhead, the Messiah. The correlation between Jn 12:37-43 and Isa 6:1-13 sheds further light on this explanation.

In Jn 12:37-43, the author appeals to two passages from Isaiah in order to explain the reason Israel has rejected her Messiah: Isa 53:1 and Isa 6:10. Following the quotation of Isa 6:10, John writes, "Isaiah said these things because he saw His glory and spoke about Him," alluding to Jesus (Jn 12:41). John is referring to the vision in Isa 6:1-4, where Isaiah wrote, "My eyes have seen the King, the Lord of Hosts" (Isa 6:5). In turn, John directly associates the glory of God from Isa 6:1-4 with the preincarnate Son, meaning that the Son is the manifestation of God in that vision. This understanding is consistent with Johannine literature (Jn 1:18; 5:37; 6:46).[34] Therefore, just as the theophany in Isa 6:1 was the glory of Messiah, so the appearance of the Teacher in Isa 30:20 may refer to the divine Messiah, the Son.

THREE APPROACHES TO THE IDENTITY OF "THE TEACHER"

THREE VIEWS	ARGUMENTS	TRANSLATION
Plural of Individuals	1. The verb "to hide" (*kkanaph*) should be translated as a plural (cf. LXX and 1QIsa[a]) 2. The context makes reference to a plurality of teachers (Isa 30:8-11)	"And your prophets will no longer be hidden, and your eyes will see your prophets."
A Single Individual	1. The singular verb "to hide oneself" (*kkanaph*) 2. The *apparent* plural form of "teacher" *(mworeyka)*	"And your teacher will no longer be hidden, and your eyes will see your teacher."
A Plural of Majesty	1. The prominence of the plural of majesty in Isaiah. 2. Isaiah's portrayal of God as a Teacher who hides Himself because of Israel's sin. 3. The verbal form of *yarah* refers to God elsewhere in Isaiah. 4. The imagery of the Teacher as Shepherd. 5. The Targum on Isaiah translated the referent as God.	"And your Teacher will no longer be hidden, and your eyes will see your Teacher."

The Gospel of John also includes imagery from the Isa 30:18-26 pericope, which further augments the importance of this prophecy. John 12:36, for example, records how Jesus "went away and hid" from the crowds as a result of their unbelief (Jn 12:36b). Although Jesus is depicted as hiding elsewhere in the book of John (Jn 8:59), this act in Jn 12:36 represents the end of His public ministry because of Israel's rejection. This is similar to the rationale provided in Isaiah when explaining the reason for God hiding His face from Judah.

Furthermore, Jn 10:1-18 highlights Jesus' role as the Good Shepherd, which is the same imagery used in Isa 30:21. The Hebrew Bible often identifies God as the ultimate Good Shepherd. While Israel's shepherds are often condemned for their negligence toward God's law and people (Isa 56:11; Zch 11), their denunciation is typically followed by a promise that God will shepherd His people. For example, in Ezk 34:1-6, God's condemnation of Israel's leaders precedes His promise to be their Shepherd. The passage ultimately culminates in the guarantee of a messianic ruler: "I will appoint over them a single shepherd, My servant David, and he will shepherd them" (Ezk 34:23). Jeremiah 23:1-2 also includes the promise of God shepherding His people, culminating in the prophecy of the Righteous Branch who will reign (Jer 23:5-6). Therefore, the shepherding imagery in Jn 10:1-18 may bring to mind the depiction of God as the ultimate Shepherd, as well as the coming of a messianic figure. Both of these concepts appear in Isa 30:20-21.

THE MESSIANIC AGE

Isaiah 30:20 depicts an eschatological era when Judah's Teacher will be revealed after a time of distress. Based on the context and wider Isaianic literature, the referent of the Teacher should be understood as the divine figure of the Godhead, the Messiah Jesus, who will guide His people and instruct them in obedience to God's Word. Isaiah 30:20 is referring to the second coming of Jesus, when Messiah will return and reign on earth after a period of tribulation. This view is supported by the correlation between Isa 30:20 and Isa 2:3, which is another eschatological passage portraying God's universal reign in the Messianic Age. Isaiah writes, "Come, let us go up to the mountain of the Lord, to the house of the God of Jacob. He will teach us about His ways so that we may walk in His paths" (Isa 2:3). Not only do both passages use the verbal form *yarah* for God as the subject, but the Lord is depicted as instructing Judah in the way (*derek*) they should walk (Isa 2:3; 30:21).[35]

Jesus' return following the tribulation is clearly defined by the prophet Zechariah, who also notes how Judah will *see* their Messiah. In Zch 10–12, Zechariah remarks how God will have compassion on Judah (Zch 10:6; cf. Isa 30:18) and will shepherd His people (Zch 11; cf. Isa 30:21). After a time when "all the nations of the earth gather against [Jerusalem]" (Zch 12:3), God will pour His spirit on the inhabitants of Jerusalem so that "they will look at Me whom they pierced" (Zch 12:10). Indeed, when the Lord returns for the second time, He will establish His Messianic Kingdom on earth and teach His followers how to walk in His law. Isaiah 30:20, therefore, further describes the time when the Messiah, our ultimate Teacher, will instruct, guide, and shepherd His people into holiness and obedience during the Messianic Age. Today, we still wait for the glorious day when our Messiah will return, and when the Jewish people in unison proclaim, "He who comes in the name of the Lord is the blessed One" (Mt 23:39).

---

1. Translation is author's.

2. Various authors, such as Delitzsch, Alexander, and Goldingay, view the referent of *mworeyka* to be priests and prophets. The LXX translation of Isaiah also interprets the noun as plural, although it translates the Hebrew form *mworeyka* as *planao*, implying that the referents are "deceptive teachers" who will be judged.

3. Hans Wildberger, *Isaiah 28–39: A Continental Commentary*, trans. Thomas H. Trapp (Minneapolis: Fortress Press, 2002), 167. Beuken also states that, "from a grammatical point of view the word can have both a singular and a plural significance." See Willem A. M. Beuken, "What Does the Vision Hold: Teachers or One Teacher? Punning Repetition in Isaiah 30:20," *Heythrop Journal* 36 (1995): 451–66.

4. Israel's trust in foreign powers rather than in God is a reoccurring theme in Isaiah (Isa 20:6; 31:1; 36:6).

5. Both *shema'* and *ra'ah* have spiritual implications in the book of Isaiah since they are used to depict Israel's calloused hearts and disobedient lifestyle. See Isa 6:9 and 33:15.

6. This verb is used 14 times in the Hebrew Bible and only four times in Isaiah. Isaiah uses this verb to depict a "desire with anticipation," typically referring to those who yearn for the Lord (Isa 8:17; 30:18; 64:3; see also Ps 33:20; Dan 12:12).

7. Beuken, "Teachers or One Teacher?," 459. The use of the verb *wehaywu* signifies a future time. Joüon agrees, claiming that "to emphasize the durative aspect in the future, a form of the verb *hayah* with a future meaning is added to the participle." See Paul Joüon and T. Muraoka, *A Grammar of Biblical Hebrew* (Rome: Pontificio Instituto Biblico, 2006), 381. The construction of *waw* with the perfect form of *hayah* followed by a Qal participle is found eight times in Isaiah and is used in a future sense (10:18; 14:2; 22:21; 49:23), a comparative sense (16:2; 28:4), and as a hypothetical future (24:18). In this context, however, the future sense should be adopted.

8. According to Beuken, this "is an expression from the genre of torah-preaching in the broadest sense of the word" (Beuken, "Teachers or One Teacher?," 461). Although the phrase "to the right or to the left" is used in various contexts (Gn 13:9; 1Chr 12:2), it often refers to turning from the commandments of God (Dt 5:32; 17:20; 28:14; Jos 1:7; 2Kg 22:2; 1 Macc 2:22). The notion that God leads and instructs His people is a common sentiment in the book of Isaiah (42:16; 48:17) as well as other biblical writings (Jer 42:3; Ps 25:9,12; 32:8; 101:6; 139:24; Prv 1:15).

9. Ibid., 462. The construction translated "from after/behind" is used 59 times in the Hebrew Bible. It is sometimes used of God or the angel of the Lord guiding Israel from behind (Ex 14:19). However, it is also employed in a negative context, depicting Israel abandoning the Lord (Nm 14:43; 32:15; Dt 7:4; Jos 22:16,18,29; 1Sm 15:11), and of God turning away from mankind (Dt 23:14).

10. Although there is a syntactical difficulty since the suffix on *tame'* is plural whereas the possessive suffix on the noun *keseph* is singular, Young claims that "the plural presents the picture of entirety; the people as such will remove the idols . . . [and that] the singular points to the action as that of individuals." See E. J. Young, *The Book of Isaiah*, The New International Commentary on the Old Testament, vol. II (19–39) (Grand Rapids: Eerdmans, 1972), 358.

11. Rain often represents God's blessing or curse. At times, the Lord withheld rain as a judgment (Dt 11:17; Isa 5:6; 1Kg 8:35; Am 4:7) and at other times, provided it as a sign of blessing (Dt 11:13-14; 28:12). See also Dt 11:11,17; 28:12,24; 32:2. In addition, this eschatological pericope also focuses on the presence of cattle, which further illustrates their agricultural prosperity. According to Kaiser, "in an agrarian society it is necessary for a prosperous life that the animals too have plenty to eat and are so able to provide wool and meat in abundance." See Otto Kaiser, *Isaiah 13–39*, trans. R. A. Wilson (Philadelphia: Westminster Press, 1974), 303. Agricultural prosperity was a main focus in the book of Deuteronomy (3:19; 14:22,28; 16:15; 22:9; 26:12; 33:14).

12. One may argue that *mworeyka* derives from the noun *mworeh* though this seems unlikely since the noun *mworeh* is never used in Isaianic literature. This noun is found 14 times in the Hebrew Bible and is translated as "teacher" in only three passages (Job 36:22; Prv 5:13). It is used for the geographical location of Moreh (Gn 12:6; Dt 11:30; Jdg 7:1), a razor (Jdg 13:5; 16:17; 1Sm 1:11), archers (1Sm 31:3; 2Sm 11:24), rain (Jl 2:23b; Ps 84:6) and fear (Ps 9:20).

13. The noun, *kkanaph*, which is used 85 times in the Hebrew Bible, is typically translated as "wing." However, it has also been rendered as tassels (Nm 15:38), nakedness (Dt 23:1; 27:20), a corner (1Sm 15:27; 24:4,11; Ezk 16:8), corners

of the world (Isa 11:12; Ezk 7:2; Job 37:3), ends of the world (Isa 24:16), a skirt (Ezk 5:3), and a garment (Hag 2:12; Zch 8:23; Job 38:13). In certain contexts, the noun is used to denote protection (Dt 32:11; Isa 6:2; 8:8; Ezk 1:11; Pss 17:8; 36:8; 57:2). According to Alexander, "it is now commonly agreed . . . that the primary sense [in Isa 30:20] is that of covering, and that the *niphal* means to hide one's self." See Joseph Addison Alexander, *Commentary on the Prophecies of Isaiah* (Grand Rapids: Zondervan, 1976), 481.

14. See Emanuel Tov, "Theologically Motivated Exegesis Embedded in the Septuagint," in *The Greek & Hebrew Bible: Collected Essays on the Septuagint,* ed. Emanuel Tov (Leiden, Netherlands: Brill, 1999): 257-69. In Isa 30:20, there are various differences between the LXX and MT. For example, the translator supplemented the denominal verb *kkanaph,* which implies "hiding" (*Hebrew and Aramaic Lexicon of the Old Testament,* 486) with *engizo,* meaning "to bring near, to approach" (Liddell Scott Jones, *Greek-English Lexicon,* 467). The Greek word *engizo* is often used as a translation for *qarav* (to come near) and *nagash* (to approach). Also, the translation of *planao* for *mworeyka,* as well as the additional pronominal suffix, changes the text, stating "your oppressors will no longer come near *to you*" (Isa 30:20 LXX). Due to these changes, Troxel notes that the author of the LXX "seems to have gone beyond simply offering a translation," and may be better characterized as an interpreter. See Ronald L. Troxel, *LXX-Isaiah as Translation and Interpretation: The Strategies of the Translator of the Septuagint of Isaiah* (Leiden, Netherlands: Brill, 2008), 2. The Qumran scroll of Isaiah also has some issues, as Tov notes. He writes that "the ancient versions and extra-Masoretic Hebrew variants often agree in elements which remove certain irregularities of MT on the grammatical level, such as the interchange of singular and plural forms." Emanuel Tov, *The Text-Critical Use of the Septuagint in Biblical Research.* Jerusalem Biblical Studies 8 (Jerusalem: Simor, 1997), 80. Tov defines "harmonization" as the "various types of textual intervention which bring differing elements into harmony with each other." See Emanuel Tov, "The Nature and Background of Harmonizations in Biblical Manuscripts," *Journal for the Study of the Old Testament* 31 (1985): 6. He uses Isa 30:20 as a prime example.

15. W. Gesenius, *Gesenius' Hebrew Grammar,* ed. E. Kautzsch and A. E. Cowley, 2nd English ed. (Oxford: Clarendon Press, 1982), 396. Instead, Gesenius proposes different ways to understand the plural form of a verb or noun. First, the plural may refer to a "combination of various external constituent parts" (i.e., *shamayim;* Ex 26:12; Isa 33:16; Job 16:19). Second, it may refer to the *pluralis excellentiae* (Ps 7:10). Third, the plural may be used as an intensifier for "the characteristics inherent in the idea of the stem" (Isa 27:11; 30:18; 40:14,26). Ibid.

16. J. Alec Motyer, *Isaiah: An Introduction and Commentary* (Downers Grove, IL: InterVarsity Press, 1999), 198. See Isa 28:9-10; 30:10-11.

17. See C. F. Keil and F. Delitzsch, *Commentary on the Old Testament,* vol. 7 (repr., Peabody, MA: Hendrickson Publishers, 1989), 322. See also Alexander, *Commentary on the Prophecies of Isaiah,* 481, and John Goldingay, *Isaiah,* New International Biblical Commentary (Peabody, MA: Hendrickson Publishers, 2011), 171.

18. See Isa 30:10-11. Furthermore, the subject changes to a singular referent in Isa 30:12 and is preceded by a singular verb.

19. Hayes and Irvine state that it "is uncertain whether the 'teacher' . . . refers to God, to the king, or to Isaiah." See John H. Hayes and Stuart A. Irvine, *Isaiah: The Eighth-Century Prophet* (Nashville: Abingdon Press, 1987), 343. Unfortunately, they do not provide any validation for the latter two referents. Also, Irwin claims that *mworeyka* may also be Ba'al. See William Henry Irwin, *Isaiah 28–33: Translation with Philological Notes* (Rome: Biblical Institute Press, 1977), 90-91.

20. According to Gesenius, "in a few instances, before a suffix beginning with a consonant, the original ăy of the termination has been contracted to ê, and thus there arise forms which have apparently plural suffixes" (Gesenius, *Gesenius' Hebrew Grammar,* 273). For other examples of apparent plural forms, see Dt 23:15; Isa 5:12; 30:23; Dan 1:10,16.

21. Alexander, *Commentary on the Prophecies of Isaiah,* 481.

22. Kissane, for example, writes that "as the verb is singular, the plural may be taken as the plural of majesty, and the teacher being Jahweh Himself, whose teaching they have now rejected." See Edward J. Kissane, *The Book of Isaiah,* vol. I (Dublin: The Richview Press, 1941), 346. According to Gesenius' *Grammar* §145.h, "plurals which have a singular meaning (§124 a) are frequently construed with the singular, especially the *pluralis excellentiae.*" See Gen 1:1,3; Ex 21:4; Job 16:16; Prv 12:10; Ecc 12:9. See Gesenius, *Gesenius' Hebrew Grammar,* §124 for various uses of the plural form.

23. This construction is found 64 times in Isaiah. Although a singular verb with a plural subject is used in contexts not addressing God (Isa 13:22; 17:6; 34:13), it typically refers to Him (Isa 3:17-18; 4:4; 5:16; 7:7,14,20; 9:7,16; 10:12,16,24,26; 11:11; 17:10; 19:12,25; 21:6,16; 22:12,14-15; 24:23; 25:6-8; 28:5,16,26; 29:13; 30:15,20; 31:4-5; 35:4; 37:4,10,21; 38:5; 40:1; 41:17; 45:13; 49:22; 51:22; 52:4,7; 54:6; 57:21; 62:5; 65:13,15-16; 66:9). According to Jensen, "the Hebrew has the plural, but this is regularly taken as a plural of majesty to refer to the Lord." See Joseph Jensen, *Isaiah 1–39* (Wilmington, DE: Michael Glazier, Inc, 1984), 240. The idea of *pluralis excellentiae* focuses on the characteristics inherent in the idea of the noun and may be portraying God as the Teacher *par excellence.*

24. Alexander, *Commentary on the Prophecies of Isaiah,* 481.

25. For other examples of God hiding Himself, see Isa 1:15; 45:15; 54:8; 57:17; 59:2; 64:7. For examples outside of Isaiah, see Dt 31:17-18; 32:20; Pss 10:11; 27:9; 44:24; 51:9; 102:2; 143:7; Jer 33:5; Ezk 39:23; Mic 3:4. Throughout the Scriptures, beginning in Deuteronomy, God warned Israel that He would hide His face as a result of their sin. Therefore, Israel associated calamity with God's absence (Isa 64:7; Mic 3:4; Pss 10:11; 51:9).

26. John D. W. Watts, *Isaiah 1–33,* Word Biblical Commentary, vol. 24 (Nashville: Thomas Nelson, 2005), 470.

27. For example, see Isa 2:3, 28:9,26. The verb *yarah* is used once to depict prophets who teach lies (Isa 9:15).

28. Watts, *Isaiah 1–33,* 469. Isaiah often depicts God as Israel's Teacher. See Isa 1:10; 2:3; 26:9-13; 28:26; 30:2,9; 31:1; 48:17; 54:13. Isaiah 2:3 uses the *hiphil* form of *yarah* in order to represent God's teaching role in the Messianic Kingdom (Isa 28:26; see also Ex 4:15; Dt 4:36; Ps 25:12; 32:8; 71:17; Jer 32:33; Mic 4:2). See John N. Oswalt, *The Book of Isaiah: Chapters 1–39,* The New International Commentary on the Old Testament (Grand Rapids: Eerdmans, 1986), 560.

29. Wildberger, *Isaiah 28–39,* 175.

30. The emphasis is on *derek,* which is "manner, custom, behavior" (*Hebrew and Aramaic Lexicon of the Old Testament,* 231) and is often found in Deuteronomic language for conducting oneself appropriately (Dt 2:27; 5:32; 17:11,20; 28:14; see Jos 23:6; 1Sm 6:12; 2Kg 22:2).

31. J. F. Stenning, *The Targum of Isaiah,* ed. and trans. J. F. Stenning (Oxford: Clarendon Press, 1949), 98–99.

32. Bruce D. Chilton, *The Isaiah Targum: Introduction, Translation, Apparatus and Notes,* The Aramaic Bible, vol. 11 (Wilmington, DE: Michael Glazier, Inc., 1987), xvi.

33. One may appeal to Ex 33:20-23 where God explicitly states that "no man can see Me and live." See also Ex 19:21; 20:21-22; 23:20-23. Stacey acknowledges this tension, claiming that the referent "may be Yahweh himself, despite the tradition that Yahweh must never be seen." See David Stacey, *Isaiah: Chapters 1–39* (London: Epworth Press, 1993), 188-89. The notion of seeing God is a prevalent theme throughout Isaiah, however (Isa 6:5; 17:7; 30:20; 33:17; 52:8,10; 64:4).

34. The NT appeals to the presence of the preincarnate Messiah in the Hebrew Bible (1Co 10:4). Furthermore, the NT elsewhere applies language reserved for God to the Messiah (see Heb 1:10-12 and Ps 102:12,25-27). As Carson appropriately notes, "in those Old Testament passages where God is said to reveal himself rather spectacularly to someone, it must have been through the agency of his Son." D. A. Carson, *The Gospel According to John* (Grand Rapids: Eerdmans, 1991), 450.

35. Isaiah also explains God's desire for *mishpat,* which is sometimes employed as a characteristic for the Messiah's reign (Isa 9:6; 42:1,3-4; 49:4; 51:4; 53:8).

Isaiah 32:1-8; 33:17-24

The Righteous and Majestic King

EVA RYDELNIK

Isaiah has been called the premier messianic prophet, for many of the most familiar predictions of the coming Messiah are found in his writings.[1] This article will focus on two of the perhaps lesser considered messianic predictions. In these texts, Isaiah presents the coming Messiah as the Righteous King (32:1-8) and the Majestic King (33:17-24).

In this article, first, the context of the prophecy will be appraised. Next, the prophecy of the future Righteous King (32:1-8) will be examined, followed by a brief view of the messianic kingdom (32:15-20). After briefly reviewing a refrain of woes and prayers of the righteous remnant (33:1-16), the article will focus on the Lord's response to those prayers with another messianic prophecy about sending the Majestic King Messiah (33:17-24).

THE CONTEXT OF THE PROPHECY

The book of Isaiah has a distinct outline that is helpful in understanding the placement of these prophecies concerning the King. Following the prologue (chaps. 1–6), the book is divided into two major sections: Judgment of Israel and the Nations (chaps. 7–35) and Blessings of Israel and the Nations (chaps. 36–66). The first major section, the Judgment of Israel and the Nations, has five divisions: The Narrative of a sign rejected (chaps. 7–12); the Oracles against the Nations (chaps. 13–23); the Little Apocalypse (chaps. 24–27); the Book of Woes on Israel and Judah (chaps. 28–33); and Summary of Judgments (chaps. 34–35). It is in the Book of

Woes that Isaiah unexpectedly gives a glimmer of hope and presents his messianic prophecies of the Righteous King and Majestic King, as well as a quick snapshot of the messianic kingdom.[2]

The immediate context of the prophecy is the Book of Woes, a message of coming judgment, for Judah's failure to trust the Lord to defend them. At the time of Isaiah's ministry, Assyria was on the brink of invading the northern kingdom, and even threatening to invade Jerusalem. To prevent this invasion, Judah was seeking a military allegiance with Egypt (31:1-3) instead of trusting the Holy One of Israel for His help (31:1). Although the northern kingdom of Israel would fall to Assyria, Jerusalem would be rescued by the Lord of Hosts (31:5). At this point, Judah is called to return to the Lord, and not behave like rebellious Israel (31:6-9). Ultimately the Assyrian Empire would fall by the judgment of God (31:8-9). Despite the threats against her, the Lord would protect Jerusalem because His "fire is in Zion" (31:9b).

THE MESSIAH, THE RIGHTEOUS KING (32:1-8)

After calling Judah to return to the Lord, the prophecy of the Righteous King, a king who "will reign righteously" (32:1), is given. To draw attention to the importance of the message, the prophet introduces it with "Indeed" (v. 1, *hen* lit. "behold"), an exclamation of certainty. A central question in this passage is whether this is speaking of a human king or giving a messianic prophecy. The difficulty is that the word "anointed one" is not supplied in the text, leading some to doubt the messianic nature of the passage. Therefore, some have suggested this king refers to Hezekiah, but as Bultema points out, "during his reign there was hardly a shadow of all the glory promised here."[3] This righteous ruler, as described in the following verses, is not merely a good king. The Hebrew wording places righteousness in the foreground of the announcement: "Behold in righteousness will reign a king . . ." He is the Messianic King, as is understood from the several characteristics describing Him.

The chapter begins by showing this is a righteous king (v. 1). Isaiah frequently identified the Messiah as the King who is righteous or rules righteously (Isa 9:1-7; 11:1-16; 16:4-5; 24:21-25; 32:1-8; 33:17-24). Furthermore, the Messiah is described by the prophets as a ruler (Isa 9:6-7; Mic 5:2) who will rule in righteousness or is righteous (Jer 23:5; 33:15; Zch 9:9). The Messiah is identified elsewhere as acting in righteousness (Isa 11:4-5; 16:5; Ps 45:6-7; 72:2). Significantly, one of the names of God is the "the LORD our righteousness" (*YHWH Tsidkenu*, Jer 23:6 NASB). As Oswalt points out, "it does not seem possible to say ordinary human beings are being discussed."[4]

This Righteous King will govern with "rulers" who "will rule justly" (v. 1). Under

His leadership, "each" (v. 2) one of the leaders will care for the people with justice (Ps 72:1-4; Isa 9:6-7; 11:4-5; Jer 23:5; Zch 9:9,14). They will truly protect the people under their care, and not be like the selfish, wicked rulers who oppressed the people in the past (Isa 3:13-15). Righteousness is thus the key characteristic of this King and His reign (see Isa 33:5; Jer 23:5). From these descriptions, these events will take place under the rule of Messiah during the messianic kingdom (cf. Isa 9:7; 11:4; 16:5).[5] Not only is He identified as righteous, there are also several other characteristics of this King identified.

The word "each" (v. 2) indicates those rulers who will rule justly under the King's oversight (cf. Jer 3:15; 23:4). They provide care for the people "like a shelter from the wind" and "a refuge from the rain" (Isa 32:2). This is not simply describing security in times of bad weather, but is a more expansive image of protection against all adversity. Not only will the Righteous King provide protection and security, He also will supply the needs of the people "like streams of water in a dry land" and "shade of a massive rock in an arid land" (32:2). Water and shade, especially in the Negev areas of Israel, are essential for life. Under His kingship, the people will not simply be supplied with the minimum of water, but "streams of water." Nor just a little shade; under His leadership, there will be the shadow of "a massive rock" casting cooling shade and providing shelter in an arid land. This is an interesting parallel to being protected in the shadow of the Almighty (Ps 91:1). These are images of refreshing relief, comfort, and protection.[6] These are terms of generous supply that are applied to the Lord elsewhere and indicate the supernatural nature of this Righteous King (cf. Isa 25:4-6; 35:6-7; 41:18; 49:10).

The Righteous King's reign will not only bring about a time of physical protection, but also spiritual transformation (32:3-4, cf. 35:5; 42:7). The parallel passage speaks of a time of transformation of the needy and afflicted when they "will rejoice in the Holy One of Israel" (29:19), another indication of the identity of the Righteous King with the Holy One of Israel. Under His rule, people will change the way they think and behave. The "reckless mind (literally 'the heart of rashness') will gain knowledge" (32:4), most likely the "knowledge of the Holy One" (Isa 29:23-24; Prv 9:10). Those who once acted without restraint will gain discernment and live obediently to the Lord.

Earlier in his message to Israel, Isaiah had condemned the wicked who "call evil good and good evil " (Isa 5:20; cf. Ps 11:3). Now under the rule of the Righteous King, people will be transformed, so that the fool (*nabal*, "morally bankrupt and ethically corrupt") and the scoundrel (*kelay*, "fraudulent, deceivers") will no longer be called noble or important (v. 5). In the past, the wicked leaders of Judah had set aside God's standards and corrupted the people, yet were honored (cf. 8:14; 29:14-16). Their wicked behavior is evident because they plotted iniquity, mistreated the poor and needy, and spoke falsely about the Lord (vv. 6-7). Under the Righteous King all people will be seen for their true character, and the wicked will no longer be honored for bad behavior or abusive power.

Under the rule of the Righteous King, the "noble person," who "plans noble things" and "stands up for noble causes" (v. 8), will be honored. The thrice repetition of "noble" (*nadib*, "generous, willing, princely") emphasizes the character of these worthy individuals (Isa 32:8). Nobility, in this context, is not a social class rank; rather it is a designation of character quality that demonstrates God's values and character. This noble person is an individual of integrity who relies on the all-wise God to supply his needs and to be generous to all.[7] He is concerned, not just for his own well-being, but for the well-being of others for the sake of the Lord. In contrast to the fools and scoundrels (v. 5-7), this noble person lives with uprightness, as is appropriate in the reign of the Righteous King.

A CALL TO REPENTANCE BEFORE THE OUTPOURING OF THE SPIRIT (32:9-14)

After the prophecy of the Righteous King Messiah, Isaiah returns to his cycle of calling for repentance (cf. 31:6). Here he addresses the "complacent women" (*sa'nannot*, "those who feel secure, at ease" vv. 9,11) of Judah, calling them to repent. He reminds them that all their plans for success and protection will fail (32:10). The book of Isaiah contains some short-term prophecies (e.g., 7:8,16); here the prophet foretells that "in a little more than a year" judgment and disaster will fall. This prophecy was likely given shortly prior to the invasion of Judah by Sennacherib, king of Assyria (701 BC).[8] Or it may possibly refer to the one of the 46 cities destroyed by Sennacherib as recorded in his annals. More likely from the mention of "hill" (*ophel*, v. 14; the southern extremity of Mount Moriah, the most ancient area of David's Jerusalem), this is a reference to the siege of Jerusalem.[9] Although Assyria did not succeed in capturing Jerusalem, his warfare against the city created hardship on the land and people. The devastation of field and vineyards, and the abandonment of the busy city to wild asses (vv. 12-14) might also be a sign that Sennacherib's threat would portend Jerusalem's destruction by Nebuchadnezzar 115 years later in 586 BC.[10]

When the Jewish people were ready to enter the land of promise, Moses warned them not to "forget the Lord," but rather trust in Him for abundant blessings (Dt 6:11). The danger was that the people would forget the Lord and depend on themselves for security. In Isaiah's day, this came to pass; the complacent people neglected their God and sought military security from foreign alliances, resulting in grief and mourning (Isa 32:10-14).

Although the effects of this coming judgment and devastation are described as lasting forever (v. 14), the Hebrew phrase *'ad olam* does not always refer to eternity, but can mean "for a limited period of time." In fact, in the immediate next verses Isaiah predicted a time when the devastation would end, so it is best to understand *'ad olam* to mean "for a very long time" (cf. Ex 21:6; 1Sm 1:22; Neh 2:3).[11]

THE SPIRIT POURED OUT IN THE MESSIANIC KINGDOM (32:15-20)

After describing Messiah the Righteous King (32:1-8), and a call to repentance prior to Messiah's coming (32:9-14), Isaiah presents a brief prophecy of the outpouring of the Spirit in the messianic kingdom (32:15-20). The devastation described in vv. 9-14 will only last until "the Spirit from heaven is poured out on us" (32:15).

This outpouring of the Spirit is one aspect of the initiating of the millennial kingdom. Often prophets connect the establishment of the messianic kingdom with the coming of the Spirit upon His people (Ezk 36:27; Jl 2:28-32; Zch 12:10). At that time, it is God's Spirit that brings about transformation of the land and its inhabitants. The transformation from "desert" to "orchard" to "forest" (vv. 15-16) is similar to other prophetic descriptions of eschatological transformations (Isa 29:17-24; 44:3-5). This is a time of messianic plenty seen in the desert becoming an orchard, and the orchard like a forest, and more important, the bringing of peace to the land.[12]

When the Spirit is poured out upon the people, justice and righteousness will fill the land with peace (32:16-18). The combination of these ideas is a common theme in Isaiah, frequently linked to the Messiah and His kingdom (cf. 1:27; 5:7,16; 9:7; 11:4-9; 16:5; 28:16-17; 32:1; 33:5; 51:4-8; 56:1; 58:2; 60:17). F. Delitzsch points out "'justice and righteousness' (*mishpat* and *tsedauah*) are throughout Isaiah the stamp of the last and perfect time."[13] This righteousness will come about when Israel will turn in faith to the Lord at the end of days (cf. Dt 4:29-31; Ezk 36:24-38; Hos 3:4-5; Zch 12:10). This blessing and restoration will come from the Lord, as a result of being in proper relationship with the Righteous King. As Motyer says, it "is more than moral integrity; it is the righteousness of being right with God."[14] This pouring out of the Sprit brings about regeneration in the hearts of the people and a transformation of the land during the messianic kingdom (cf. Ezk 36:33-38). When injustice is banished from the land, the people will experience the Lord's abundance, peace, security, and rest in the Messianic Era. This rest represents the fulfillment of God's promise to establish His people in the messianic kingdom.

This picture of the messianic kingdom ends with two closing statements. First, there is a short-term prophecy of the coming destruction of Assyria, declaring that "the hail will level the forest and the city will sink into the depths" (32:19). The "hail" represents God's judgment (Isa 28:2,17; 30:31) and the "forest" refers to Assyria, a term Isaiah previously used of Assyria (cf. 10:18,33-34). The identity of the "the city" is likely the capital of Assyria.[15]

The second statement concludes the section with a message of future blessing (32:20). The images of fruitful crops, abundant water, and secure livestock mirror the messianic blessings presented in an extended description by Isaiah of when Israel would see their Teacher, the Messiah (30:19-25). In these days to come, the people will be "happy" (*asher*, "blessed") a frequent biblical description of those who are in right relationship with the Lord (e.g., Dt 33:29; Job 5:17; Ps 1:1; 2:12; 32:1).[16]

THE CONTEXT OF THE PROPHECY OF THE MAJESTIC KING (33:1-16)

Following the promise of the Righteous King, the national call to repentance, and the snapshot of the promise of messianic blessing with outpouring of the Spirit (chap. 32), chap. 33 begins another "woe." This message of judgment is against the "destroyer" (33:1-16), the foes of Israel. This judgment, in the "woe" section, has a long-range view looking to the end of days when Israel will be under assault, surrounded by her enemies. It is the context for the prophecy of the Messiah the Majestic King.[17]

Even during those difficult days there will be a faithful remnant who "lives righteously and speaks rightly" (vv. 2,5-6,15-16). This righteous remnant will call out to the Lord, recognizing His strength, and the Lord will care for them (cf. Ps 15:1-5; 24:2-6). This is an interlude prior to the prophecy of the Majestic Messianic King (33:17-24).

THE PROPHECY OF THE MAJESTIC KING MESSIAH (33:17-24)

In response to the prayer of the remnant (vv. 13-16) the Lord will send the Majestic King Messiah. At that time, the people of Israel will "see the King" (33:17). The phrase "your eyes will see" indicates a personal experience of seeing clearly for oneself (cf. Dt 3:21; 4:3). Although many expositors suggest this refers to King Hezekiah, as Young points out, the attributes of this individual go beyond a mere man. Therefore, he concludes, "the king is not Hezekiah, nor any mere human king. . . . He is and can only be the Messiah."[18]

The identification of this King as Messiah does not contradict the identification in v. 22 that "the LORD is our King." That is because, first, the rule of Messiah is the expression of the rule of the Lord God on earth, and second, more significantly, because the Messiah is divine. He is God (Isa 7:14; 9:6; Mic 5:2; Dan 7:13-14, etc.), so it does not conflict with the identity of the Messianic King as the Lord.

This King is described as beautiful (*yofi*). The same root is used as a verb in describing the Messianic King in Ps 45:3. The use of this descriptive word here is another evidence that the King Messiah is intended. As Bultema points out, "the context irrefutably points to Christ who in verse ten announced His coming and exaltation above the nations."[19]

Furthermore, the word "king" has no definite article; this idiom of indeterminateness for the sake of emphasis indicates: "a king—you know who!"[20] This King is quickly identified as the Lord in the text (33:22).

There is a connection between seeing the Messianic King and the "vast land" (v. 17, lit., "a land of far distances"). This describes a land with unrestricted movement, without enemy threat as far as the eye can see. It is a land, under the reign of King Messiah (cf. Isa 9:3; 26:11-15), characterized by peace and stability. Although the people were once oppressed, those difficult days of "past terror" under the rule of "barbarians" (lit., "people of unintelligible speech," Isa 28:11; 36:11; Jer 5:15; Ezk 3:5-6) will be a distant memory.

Attention is now directed toward "Zion" (v. 20) of which Isaiah had earlier said: "the LORD of Hosts will reign as king on Mount Zion in Jerusalem, and He will display His glory in the presence of His elders" (24:23). Focus is directed toward Zion and Jerusalem because Messiah is the Righteous King (Isa 32:1-8) who has "filled Zion with justice and righteousness" (Is 33:5-6). This city is significant because the Lord has "installed My king on Zion, My holy mountain" (Ps 2:6; Isa 2:2-4), and it is "the city of the great King" (Ps 48:1-3). Jerusalem is the center of spiritual activity, "the city of our festival times" a reminder of the joy found in celebrating the festivals of the Lord (v. 20; e.g., Ps 84:1-2; 95; 100:1-2). As the Spirit of God is poured out on His people, He will make justice, righteousness, and peace the hallmarks of the messianic kingdom.[21]

When the Messiah reigns as King, Jerusalem will be filled with peace (v. 20). Her inhabitants will "not wander," as demonstrated by the illustration of a "tent" whose pegs are "not pulled up," nor its "cords . . . loosened." This is a permanent, secure residence, and it is not packed up and ready to move. This same analogy of a tent for the messianic kingdom is used in Isa 54:2-3, with the picture of the enlarged tent and far reaching land (cf. 33:17). Although some have suggested the tent refers to the Tabernacle, "tent" here is a general word and does not necessarily denote the Tent of Meeting. More likely it is a poetic image of permanent stability (cf. 4:5; 32:17-18).[22]

The messianic understanding of the text is further supported by the declaration "the majestic (*adir*) One, our LORD, will be there" (v. 21). This adjective was used by Isaiah to describe the Lord (10:34; "Lebanon will fall by the Mighty One," NASB), and it is frequently applied as a description of the Lord (Ps 8:1,9; 76:4; 93:4). He will be for His people, a familiar word of comfort for the Lord to His people (cf. Ps 56:9; 118:6-7). Although geographically Jerusalem had no important rivers, here the city of the Majestic King is poetically pictured as "a place of rivers and wide canals," a place amply supplied and protected by water; her position is safe from attack from boats "with oars" as well as any "mighty ship" (v. 21 NASB).

The Lord, the divine Messiah, is described with three significant titles (v. 22). A causal relation between the divine character and the effects cited in the previous verse is introduced with the opening "For" (*ki*).[23] These titles are frequently associated with the work of the Lord on behalf of His people Israel. First, He is "our Judge" who will be the nation's defender, champion, and adjudicator (Isa 2:4; 11:4; 16:5). Second, He is "our lawgiver" who is the source of all righteous standards and decrees (Isa 2:3; 51:4; Mic 4:2). Third, He is "our King," who reigns in power, justice, and righteousness (Isa 32:1; 33:17; Ps 84:3; 89:18; Zch 9:9). Because He has all of these qualities, "He will save us." The Lord is the only source of salvation, a key theme in the book of Isaiah (12:2; 25:9; 35:4; 51:6; 60:16).

The messianic understanding of this text is made clear by the declaration "the LORD is our King" (v. 22). Since Isaiah previously described the Messiah as deity (cf. 7:14, 9:6), it seems logical to recognize the Messiah as the King in view in this text (33:17,22). His kingdom will be empowered by His rule on His throne.

Isaiah closes this prophecy of the Majestic King Messiah with an illustration of His abundant provision. Those nations, "ships" (cf. 33:21,23), that attempt to attack God's people will not succeed. They will be like a drifting wreck whose "ropes are slack," having a broken "mast" and no hoisted "flag" (v. 23). "Then" after the shipwreck, "the abundant spoil" will be so easily taken that even the "lame" will have time and strength to "plunder it" (v. 23).

In those days of the victorious King Messiah, He will provide healing to the people so that "none there will say 'I am sick'" (v. 24a; Ps 103:3; Isa 57:18-19; 58:8-12; Jer 33:6). More important, in that day the people will be "forgiven for their iniquity" (v. 24b; Isa 52:13–53:12; Jer 31:34; 33:8). Only the Lord is able to forgive sins; only the Messiah is the source of forgiveness and atonement.

CONCLUSION

At a time when Israel was on the brink of invasion by Assyria, and Judah was foolishly seeking a military alliance with Egypt for protection, Isaiah delivers a message of hope—not expectation of political defense or deliverance, but two glorious prophecies of the Messianic King. First, the Righteous King will rule justly and transform the nation during His millennial reign (32:1-8). Then Isaiah gives the promise of the outpouring of the Spirit to usher in a time of justice, righteousness, and peace under the reign of Messiah (32:15-20). Finally, the prophet declares there will be a day when their eyes will see the Majestic King in all His beauty, and they will dwell in peace in Zion because the majestic King Messiah will rule as Judge, lawgiver, and King who forgives all sin (33:17-24).

1. W. C. Kaiser, Jr., *The Messiah in the Old Testament* (Grand Rapids: Zondervan, 1995), 155.
2. See Michael Rydelnik and James Spencer, "Isaiah," in *The Moody Bible Commentary* (Chicago: Moody Publishers, 2014), 1006–07.
3. Harry Bultema, *Commentary on Isaiah* (Grand Rapids: Kregel, 1981), 296.
4. J. N. Oswalt, *The Book of Isaiah, Chapters 1–39*, The New International Commentary on the Old Testament (Grand Rapids: Eerdmans, 1986), 579.
5. E. J. Young, *The Book of Isaiah, Volume 2 Chapters 19–39* (Grand Rapids: Eerdmans, 1969), 385.
6. Bultema, *Commentary on Isaiah*, 297.
7. Oswalt, *The Book of Isaiah*, 582.
8. G. W. Grogan, "Isaiah," in The Expositor's Bible Commentary, vol. 6., ed. F. E. Gaebelein (Grand Rapids: Zondervan, 1986), 206.
9. J. A. Alexander, *Commentary on the Prophecies of Isaiah,* 2 volumes complete and unabridged in 1 (Grand Rapids: Zondervan, 1953), II: 4.
10. H. M. Wolf, *Interpreting Isaiah: The Suffering and Glory of the Messiah* (Grand Rapids: Zondervan, 1985).
11. Young, *The Book of Isaiah*, 399.
12. Grogan, "Isaiah," 207.
13. F. Delitzsch, *Isaiah,* vol. 7, Biblical Commentary on the Old Testament, ed. C. F. Keil and F. Deilitzsch, trans. James Martin (Grand Rapids: Eerdmans, 1980), II: 53.
14. J. A. Motyer, *The Prophecy of Isaiah: An Introduction and Commentary* (Downers Grove, IL: InterVarsity, 1993) 260–61.
15. Oswalt, *The Book of Isaiah*, 588–89.
16. Motyer, *The Prophecy of Isaiah*, 261.
17. W. E. Vine, *Isaiah: Prophecies, Promises, Warnings* (Grand Rapids: Zondervan, 1969), 82–83.
18. Young, *The Book of Isaiah*, 421.
19. Bultema, *Commentary on Isaiah*, 307.
20. Motyer, *The Prophecy of Isaiah*, 267.
21. J. H. Sailhamer, *NIV Compact Bible Commentary* (Grand Rapids: Zondervan, 1994), 366.
22. Wolf, *Interpreting Isaiah*, 164.
23. Oswalt, *The Book of Isaiah*, 604.

Isaiah 35:1-10

The Messianic Era

JAMES F. COAKLEY

Isaiah 35 has been understood to be describing the future blessings of the millennium, but it has not always been depicted as containing messianic prophecy. This article aims to make the case that this passage is not just millennial, but messianic as well. The goal is to demonstrate how Isa 35, and the section of Isaiah in which this passage is embedded (chaps. 32–35), and the wider context of the entire book demonstrate that Isa 35 is indeed messianic prophecy.

INITIAL QUESTIONS AND CHALLENGES

Even a cursory review of this text and the secondary literature written about it reveal some obstacles about taking Isa 35 as a messianic prophecy.

First glance reading: How is it that anyone doing a straightforward reading of this text would conclude that it is messianic? Certainly, readers can ascertain the general predictive nature of this text as depicting future millennial-type blessings being visited on the physical land of Israel at some future date. Yet to argue that it is messianic prophecy and not just a millennial one seems to be a bit of a stretch. In this regard, it may be similar to Hos 11:1, "and out of Egypt I called My son," which at first glance does not appear to be making a prediction about Jesus' sojourn in Egypt after His birth. Is Isa 35 similar to Hos 11:1 in that it makes a seemingly veiled prediction that the Messiah would be a healer at His first appearance?

Gap in fulfillment: If, for sake of the argument, one grants that Isa 35 is in fact a messianic prophecy, is it more along the lines of Lk 4:17-21? In that passage,

Jesus, in the synagogue at Nazareth, reads the first part of Isa 61:1-2, which talks of proclaiming liberty to the captives and the year of the Lord's favor. But He stops short of reading the Isaiah text that goes on to mention a day of God's vengeance. Therefore, it might be contended that that scenario is similar to the fulfillment of Isa 35, with the prediction that the Messiah is to be a healer at the first coming and a judge executing vengeance at His second coming.

Messiah as healer: Scholars debate about where the OT clearly predicts that the Messiah will physically heal the blind, deaf, and lame. If the OT does predict that the Messiah will be a healer, is Isa 35 the strongest text to support that understanding? Alternatively, is it a conclusion that can be discovered only after reading Isa 35 in conjunction with other prophetic texts?

Physical or spiritual fulfillment? Another challenge regards how this messianic text is fulfilled. Even if one grants that Isa 35 is messianic, is the prophesied healing physical, spiritual, or both?

Relationship of future blessings to judgment: In this Isa 35 passage, the predictions of future blessings to the land (vv. 1-3) and physical acts of healing (vv. 5-6) are intertwined with the notion that these great acts of physical transformation will be accompanied by God's coming with vengeance and deliverance from enemies (v. 4). What is to be made of their juxtaposition, since it appears that when Messiah does come there will be a gap between the time of blessings and the time of judgment? This same juxtaposition of blessings and vengeance in a messianic passage is present as well in Isa 61:1-2.[1] How were the original readers of the text supposed to separate the messianic time of blessing from the time of Messiah's vengeance?[2]

Role of Mt 11:2-6/Lk 7:18-23: In answering John the Baptist's question, "Are You the One who is to come, or should we expect someone else?" (Mt 11:3), if Jesus did not tie His performing of healing miracles to Isa 35, would someone actually conclude that Isa 35 is messianic or only see a prediction of future millennial blessings for God's covenant people in the land of Israel?

In spite of these challenges and questions, it is legitimate to view this chapter as messianic prophecy and not just because Mt 11:2-6/Lk 7:18-23 do so. That thesis derives from the book of Isaiah specifically and from the broader context of the OT generally. The following presuppositions undergird this study.

PRESUPPOSITIONS

Authorship: For the sake of this study, a single author/editor of the book of Isaiah is presumed. Further, it is presumed to have been written as a single composition. This does not mean that Isaiah himself had to be the one who put the book together in its present form, even though he was the source of the content of the book. Even those who argue for multiple authorship of the book of Isaiah recognize that the themes and vocabulary used in Isa 35 are the same as those in Isa 40–55. Some[3] even argue that these texts were written by the same author, even though they reside in different sections (Isa 1–39 and Isa 40–55) allegedly written by different authors (Isaiah of Jerusalem versus Deutero-Isaiah).

Here is one reason to argue for a single composition and the possible implications it has for this particular study. One of the repeated themes in the book of Isaiah is blindness. That concept of Israel's spiritual blindness surfaces in multiple texts throughout the book (5:12; 6:10; 29:9; 42:18). God's judgment against this condition is stated in Isa 1; 6:9-10; 29:9-10; and 44:18. The future prospect and hope of reversing this malady is communicated in 29:18; 32:3; 35:5; 42:7; and 43:8. Isaiah 35 is just one of many texts that touches upon the theme of blindness—an idea that runs through all the major sections of the books. One argument in this study is that the notion of Messiah as healer is developed not just in a single text but in the entire composition of Isaiah. The view that the book was written by multiple authors and compiled by many editors would seem to argue against such a unified intentional thematic composition that was in the mind of the author/compiler right from the start.

Authorial intent: Also presumed for this study is that the messianic interpretation of this chapter conforms with the author's intent. The author's intent becomes evident through a holistic reading of the wider context of this chapter and the whole book. The messianic interpretation of Isa 35 is not based on taking a few verses from this text and simply making a beeline to Christ to prove that He was the Messiah. The original readers of this text did not have the benefit of chapter and verse markings, nor did they typically resort to the proof-texting model that many systematic theology works follow today where one looks to find a definitive verse to muster an argument for a position. The messianic interpretation of this chapter will be subtle, but nonetheless definitive, when this text is seen through the broader authorial intent of the wider context of Isaiah.

EXEGETICAL CONSIDERATIONS

A careful contextual study of Isa 35 will reveal that it not only foretells a messianic age but also gives details about the Messiah's characteristics and identity.

As to genre, Isa 35 is poetic and prophetic, combining both hortatory and expository text. The hortatory nature of this passage is seen in the use of imperative verbs in vv. 3-4, but the bulk of this passage is expository, detailing the characteristics of the future messianic age. That this particular text is poetic in genre does make it line up with other messianic texts such as Gn 49, Nm 22–24 and Dt 31–32 where a poetic/prophetic text is positioned in a strategic location as part of a larger discourse.[4]

STRUCTURAL AND CONTEXTUAL ANALYSIS

The structure of the overall book of Isaiah and the placement of Isa 35 within that structure play a pivotal role in this study. Even though the book of Isaiah is a single composition, there are clear and distinguishable units within the book. The most obvious units are Isa 1–39 and 40–66. Within Isa 1–39 there seem to be four distinct sections: 1–12; 13–27; 28–35; and 36–39.

Isaiah 35 concludes one of those sections and serves to bring a sense of closure before the next section, which is a historical narrative section regarding Hezekiah and the Assyrians. Isaiah 35 links back to the first major section to recall Isa 6:10, reversing that passage's threat of blindness and deafness for Israel. Additionally, it looks forward by introducing major themes that will be developed in Isa 40–66. For example, the themes of a holy road (35:8) and of strengthening weak hands (35:3) are greatly expanded upon in 40:3-5,29-31. The prediction of streams in the desert (35:6-7) shows up again in 41:18. In addition, the final verse (35:10) is repeated verbatim in 51:11.

INTEXTUAL INTERPRETATION

It is my contention that Isa 35 is a discourse peak within the book of Isaiah. This is evident not only in the important role it plays within the structure of the book, but also by several linguistic and literary features present in the passage. These characteristics create what Longacre has called a "zone of turbulence"[5] as a way of showing the prominence of a text within the wider discourse. The discourse peaks of a larger discourse are not as easily detected linguistically in poetic expository texts (like Isa 35) as they are in narrative texts. Nevertheless, there are a number of literary devices used and embedded in this relatively short discourse that are not found proportionally in other parts of Isaiah or other Scripture passages as they are in this text. The author of Isaiah uses a number of devices to make this discourse "pop" to make this text more prominent. Here are a number of those features demonstrating that Isa 35 is a discourse peak:

1. It does not start with a standard introductory discourse marker, so it begins with a more jolting approach.[6] This has the tendency to grab the reader's attention for what follows.
2. Structurally this passage functions as a hinge. It looks backward and uses some of the same lexical terms from previous passages to link them together. But it also looks forward and introduces words and themes that will be prominent in Isa 40–66. So it helps to prepare the reader for what is coming next after the historical interlude of Hezekiah (Isa 36–39).
3. The passage uses ambiguity. Normally ambiguity is not recommended in communication but when used either intentionally or by accident it does cause the reader/listener to slow down and spend more time processing the discourse. Scholars debate about who or what is the referent for the pronoun "they" in v. 2 ("They will see the glory of the LORD"), as the context is not entirely clear as to whether it means people or if it refers to the combination of "wilderness" and "desert" in v. 1. If it is an intentional use of ambiguity by the author, it is another example of a rhetorical device being used in this passage.
4. It uses word repetition. Verses 1 and 10 contain words with the same Hebrew root *sws* (glad and gladness), forming a lexical bracket for the passage. Internally there are three instances of the Hebrew root *rnn* "to sing or shout" (vv. 2,6,10). Word repetition like this heightens the rhetorical effect of the passage.
5. Alliteration is also used in the main verbs of v. 5, a key verse in this passage: *tippaqachnah* "opened" and *tippathachnah* "unstopped." Sound rhythm like this makes the text more memorable and musical for the reader/listener.
6. There is a cluster of key salvific terms in this passage: "save" (*ysh'* v. 4), "redeemed" (*g'l* v. 9), and "ransomed" (*pdh* v. 10). This collocation of terms within the semantic domain of salvation serves to highlight this passage's thematic focus on salvation and deliverance.

Any one of the above features is not significant by itself but, used together, they demonstrate that this passage is located in a "zone of turbulence" signaling to the reader that this passage is a discourse peak. The prominence of this passage within the surrounding context is helpful to be aware of, as it may be one of the ancillary reasons that a number of rhetorical devices are employed in the first place—to bolster the argument of the author of Isaiah in embedding messianic prophecy within this text.

OVERALL CONTEXT

Isaiah 34–35 are to be taken as a unit because this discourse draws the first part of Isaiah to a close by summarizing the broad themes of blessing and judgment that have dominated the book until now.[7] Isaiah 35 contrasts with the previous chapter and includes several lexical connections and thematic contrasts.

One of the major questions the book of Isaiah continually asks is "whom should you trust?" When Isaiah responded positively to the call to serve, he trusted the Lord despite being told he would not be successful in turning the hearts of the people (Isa 6). The historical section following that call (Isa 7–9) is really about whom Ahaz will trust. Will he trust in the Lord or in military allies? The next section contains oracles against the other nations that surround Judah (Isa 10–33), communicating the danger of trusting in foreign nations rather than in the Lord alone, because those nations will be judged. Isaiah 34 gives a graphic picture of what will happen to one of those nations (in this case Edom) whom Judah might be tempted to trust instead of the Lord. That nation with all its arrogance (i.e., described in great detail in the book of Obadiah) will be reduced to a desert wasteland. In contrast, Isa 35 reverses that image.

For those who trust in the Lord, even if they are blind, deaf, mute, and lame, they will experience healing and live in a veritable garden of Eden! Those who trust in Edom, along with Edom itself, will live in a desolate wilderness, haunted by the screeching of owls and howling of hyenas (34:11,14). Those who trust in the Lord can hear melodious songs (35:10) and see His glory manifested as they walk the Holy Way (35:8) to Zion without any threat of wild animals (35:9). The thrust of this chapter is for Israel to trust the Lord, though they be weary and disabled, since the Lord will deliver them, judge their enemies, and put joy and gladness into their hearts (35:10). This is clearly a foretaste of the Messianic Age when it is under the sovereign guidance of a compassionate, healing Messiah.

1. *The glory of the Lord manifested in nature (vv. 1-2)*

The Lord will transform the dry land and desert into a luxurious garden environment. Although the text does not designate where this wilderness area is located within the borders of Israel, it is probably the area in the south of Israel near the Negev and the Dead Sea. The Hebrew word translated "desert" (HCSB) is *arabah*, which is the current name given for the lower Jordan Rift valley. For this location and for others mentioned in Isa 35, see the map titled "The Geographical Regions of Israel."

The Geographical Regions of Israel

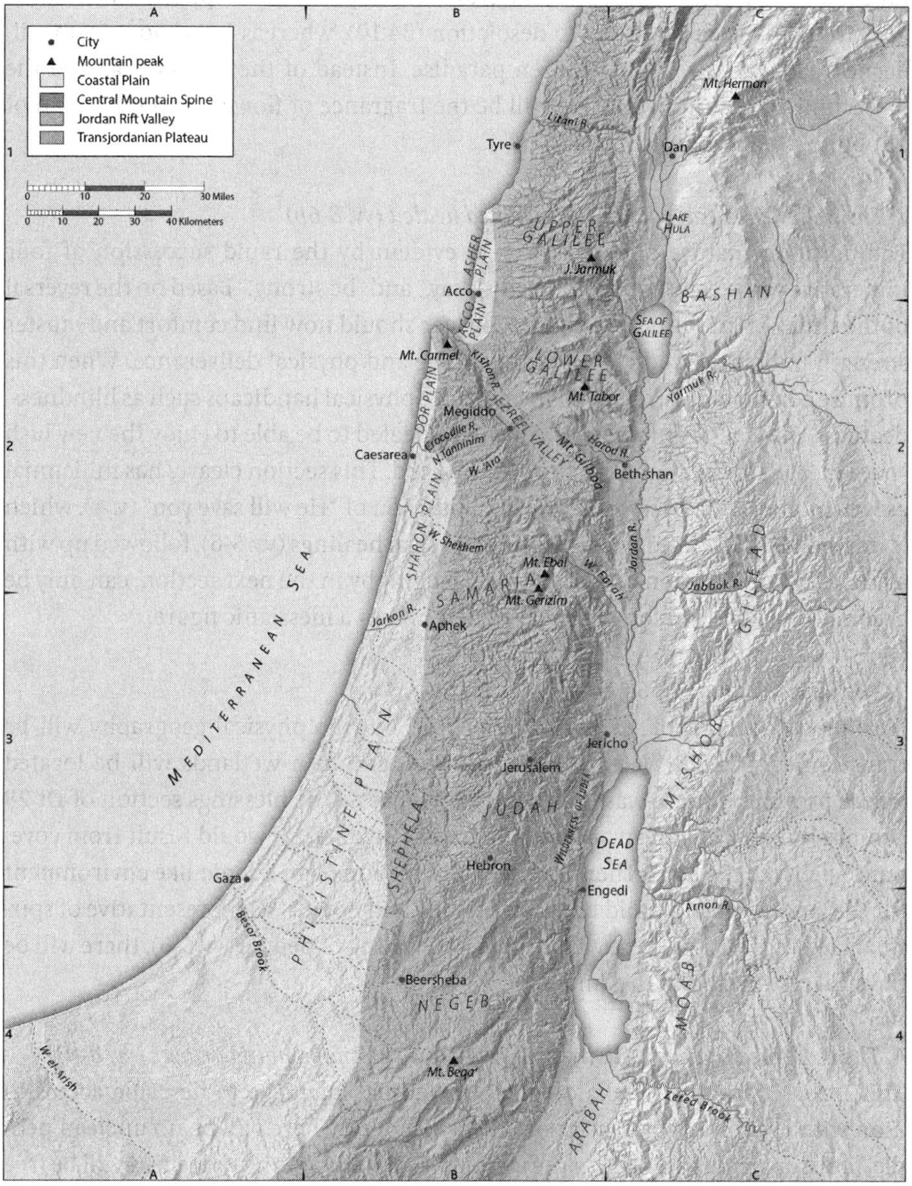

The three most productive and fertile areas of the Levant (Lebanon, Carmel and Sharon), known for their stately cedars, sturdy oaks, lush vineyards, and fragrant wildflowers, will pale in comparison to this desert wasteland when it is transformed. This renovation is a fulfillment of the verse from the Song of the Lord's vineyard: "In days to come, Jacob will take root. Israel will blossom and bloom and fill the whole world with fruit" (Isa 27:6). In the previous chapter, wicked Edom goes from a land of fat (34:6) to desolation (34:10), whereas Israel goes from wilderness (35:1) to a veritable garden paradise. Instead of the smell of tar and the screeching of desert owls, there will be the fragrance of flowers and the sound of bubbling streams of water.

2. *The weary encouraged and the disabled healed (vv. 3-6b)*
The hortatory nature of this section is evident by the rapid succession of four imperative verbs: "strengthen," "steady," "say," and "be strong." Based on the reversal of the situation in the desert, those who fear should now find comfort and muster strength in light of God's coming vengeance and physical deliverance. When this promise comes to pass, there will be no more physical handicaps such as blindness, deafness, muteness, or lameness. All will be healed to be able to enjoy the new lush space created to highlight the glory of the Lord. This section clearly has millennial as well as messianic overtones. The juxtaposition of "He will save you" (v. 4), which is immediately followed by miraculous physical healings (vv. 5-6), followed up with a marvelous description of transformed geography in the next section, can only be accomplished by a personally engaged deity, if not a messianic figure.

3. *The land restored (vv. 6c-7)*
Healing will occur not just with the people, but the physical geography will be transformed as well. Water will be plentiful, and lush wetlands will be located where previously there was only desert wilderness. The blessings section of Dt 28 promised that rain and an abundant harvest (Dt 28:11-12) would result from covenant fidelity to the Lord. Therefore, this description of an Edenic-like environment for the land of Israel should be taken literally and not just as representative of spiritual blessings. Just as there will be physical healing of people (vv. 5-6), there will be physical restoration of the land.

4. *The redeemed as they walk the Holy Way toward Zion singing praises (vv. 8-10)*
This next section uses eschatological, millennial language to describe access to Zion with every form of barrier or threat removed. There will be no unclean people, fools, or vicious animals in the vicinity—so that all of the redeemed will be free to travel on this roadway and be able to rejoice along the way. This "Holy Way" or "Highway of Holiness" is similar to other eschatological passages in Isaiah (like Isa 11:16; 19:23; 40:3; 62:10) that use the pilgrimage metaphor as a picture of unfettered access to the presence of God. When the Messiah reigns, all of His people will have access to use this roadway as they attend annual feasts in Zion.

INNERTEXTUAL INTERPRETATION

This passage taps into many of Isaiah's themes, many of which carry messianic overtones.

Blindness: One main argument for the messianic, prophetic nature of Isa 35 is in the development of the theme of blindness. Throughout the book, Isaiah stresses that recovery from blindness and the cure of deafness are aspects of God's salvation and deliverance (29:18; 32:3; 35:5; 42:7; 43:8). Therefore, the removal of such maladies can be argued to be part of Messiah's mission. This is to what the Gospel writers are referring when they depict Jesus' miraculous healing of the deaf, blind, and lame. They are tapping into the broader Isaianic theme of restoring sight to the blind as a divine act. Then they identify those miraculous healings as a proof of the identity of the Messiah because the healings are viewed as acts of salvation/deliverance within the broader frame of the book of Isaiah, not just Isa 35.

Regarding whether the healing in Isa 35 is spiritual or physical, there is no question that the spiritual deafness and blindness of the people of Israel is a theme used earlier in the book (i.e. Isa 6:10), but the context of Isa 35 is more physical overall in nature. The literal physical transformation of the desert and wilderness places into a blossoming garden does not lend itself to be just a figurative fulfillment, even though these verses are cast in poetic form and personification is used. In addition, while Isaiah does use blindness and deafness as spiritual metaphors for the people's unresponsiveness to spiritual matters (Isa 6:10), Isa 35:6, which immediately follows the mention of blindness and deafness, describes healings like the lame leaping and the mute being able to shout for joy. Lameness and muteness are not associated with spiritual dullness. This helps make the argument that because the healings in v. 6 refer to physical healing, the same would be true for the healings of blindness and deafness mentioned in the previous verse (v. 5).

Kingship: Another theme embedded throughout Isaiah is Messiah as king. Even though Isa 35 does not use the lexeme "king," it is clear that there are royal overtones to this chapter. It employs the notion of pilgrims proceeding along a "Holy Way" (v. 8) to return to a restored and glorified Zion to behold their God in all of His glory. Abernethy makes a strong argument that through "coordination with chapter 35, along with 60–62, in addition to their strategic placement within the structure of Isaiah, Isaiah 40:1–11 and 52:7–10 emboss the hope of God's coming as king and the need to prepare for it at the core of Isaiah's message."[8] This argument drives home the point that Isa 35 anticipates the Lord's coming to Zion as the saving king—and that the coming of God as depicted in Isa 35 is the anchor of these chapters.[9]

Thus, there are two messianic themes embedded in Isa 35 that are further developed and expanded upon elsewhere in Isaiah that begin to lay the foundation for Isa 35 indeed being a messianic prophecy. Specifically, this chapter articulates two major roles for the Messiah: The Messiah will be a king, and the Messiah will be a healer (one who restores the senses of hearing and sight). So, in addition to this passage describing the return of God's people to Zion with accompanying blessings, it also begins to make the case that the Messiah will perform physical healings.

INTERTEXTUAL INTERPRETATION

There are a number of intertextual connections to this passage as well, especially Mt 11:2-5. In that passage John the Baptist, who was imprisoned, sent word to Jesus to inquire if He is "the One who is to come, or should we expect someone else?" (Mt 11:3). John the Baptist's doubts about the messiahship of Jesus are understandable. He had preached about the one who was to come who would bring forth both judgment and blessing. Now he was only hearing of Jesus bringing blessing with no hint of judgment.[10] Moreover, the Messiah was to set the captives free, and instead John found himself a captive in the prison of Herod Antipas.

Jesus responded to John's question by pointing to the miraculous healings that He was performing (Mt 11:4-5), by conflating Isa 35:5 and 61:1. Isaiah 35 describes the return of the redeemed to Zion with accompanying signs like the restoration of sight and hearing. Jesus clearly tied these physical miracles to the messianic mission being fulfilled. Perhaps the strongest argument for taking Isa 35 as messianic is that the Messiah Jesus Himself did so.

Manifestation of Glory: Another intertextual clue that bolsters the messianic quality of this text is that Isa 35:2 states that the "glory of the LORD" will be manifested and will be cause for great joy. Israel had previously encountered God's glory during the exodus from Egypt (Ex 16:7) and at Mt. Sinai (Ex 24:16-17). The glory of God was also present in the tabernacle (Ex 40:34-35) and Solomon's temple (1Kg 8:11). The "glory of the LORD" in these instances represented a theophany—a physical manifestation of God's presence. This physical manifestation was often accompanied by supernatural and miraculous signs. So, although this argument is perhaps subtle, the juxtaposition of "the glory of the LORD" (35:2) with miraculous physical healings may imply a defense of the messianic notion of Isa 35. The Messiah could well be physically manifested in glory, which is then accompanied by miraculous healings as the order and pattern displayed here.

Water: Isaiah 35 uses water as a physical and tangible outward display of God's restorative physical transformation of the land. In the previous chapter, Edom's streams were being turned to pitch as judgment for their hostility against Zion (Isa

34:8-9). In contrast, water is assumed to be present in 35:1 in order to make the wilderness and desert bloom. Moreover, it is explicitly mentioned in vv. 6-7. During the desert wandering period after the exodus, God Himself supplied water a number of times in the wilderness (Ex 17:6; Nm 20). The connection with God being the source of water and refreshment and restoration could also play a minor support role in the messianic overtones of this chapter.[11]

There is also a possible intertextual tie between Isa 35, 2Sm 5 and John's Gospel. In 2Sm 5 after David became king, he marched to Jerusalem to capture it from the Jebusites. The Jebusites taunted David and his men saying, "You will never get in here. Even the blind and the lame can repel you" (2Sm 5:6). So there is a clear connection with the blind and the lame of Jerusalem or Zion.[12] Isaiah 35 predicts the healing ministry of the Messiah and specifically mentions sight being restored to the blind (35:5) and the lame being able to leap like a deer (35:6). These miracles would help identify the Messiah when He came. In the Gospels, only two healing miracles are recorded as taking place in Jerusalem. The healing of the paralytic (lame man) at the pools of Bethesda (Jn 5) and the healing of the man born blind at the pool of Siloam (Jn 9). It would be a strange coincidence for those elements to intersect like that without Isa 35 being the link that ties them together.[13] In addition, not only is there the common element of Jerusalem/Zion and blind/lame present in each text, but each passage also references water (2Sm 5:7; Isa 35:6-7; Jn 5:7; 9:11).

Second Temple Judaism: A Dead Sea Scroll fragment (4Q521)[14] may lend support to the messianic expectation that the Messiah, who is mentioned at the beginning of this fragment (line 1), would be a healer. Moreover, it specifically mentions that the Messiah will "make the blind see" in line 8.[15] Important to the argument here is that, according to Wise, the Messiah of this Dead Sea text "controls heaven and earth, heals the wounded, and raises the dead. He rules over nature."[16] These characteristics, excluding the power of resurrection, are the core ideas of Isa 35.

CONCLUSION

Although Isa 35 may at first glance not appear to be a messianic prophecy, once the entire structural, contextual, and linguistic evidence is examined, the case for this passage being messianic is much stronger than it first appears. This passage clearly establishes that one of the marks of the Messiah will be that He will heal all sorts of physical handicaps such as blindness and deafness (v. 5). Similar to Isa 61:1-2, where there is a gap between the first and second coming of the Messiah Jesus, this passage also portrays the Messiah as healer, followed by a gap in which the

Messiah will return to fulfill the millennial kingdom blessings on the people and on the land. Although there may be some aspect of spiritual fulfillment in this text at some future time (healing from spiritual blindness and deafness), the passage emphasizes physical healing for both people and the land.

In conclusion, this study has made the case that Isa 35 is located in a zone of turbulence in the book, to demonstrate that Isa 35 is indeed a messianic passage. Poetic exuberance in this text gives way to a glorious description of the new Zion where miracles will take place. The Messianic Age will be established only under the glorious royal reign of the compassionate, miracle-working Messiah!

---

1. This seems to be the point that Jesus was trying to make while reading that passage at the synagogue in Nazareth as recorded in Lk 4:18-20, when He stopped reading the Isaiah text before the part about a coming day of vengeance.
2. It is this very tension that presumably led John the Baptist in Mt 11 to question whether Jesus was the coming One—Messiah or not. John had been preaching repentance and getting ready for the day of judgment. But Jesus was not stressing the day of vengeance element in His teaching. That perplexed John because he saw repentance and judgment, perhaps from texts like Isa 35 and 61, as commingled, not separate. It appears that John expected that judgment and salvation would come simultaneously.
3. R. B. Y. Scott, "The Relation of Isaiah, Chapter 35, to Deutero-Isaiah," *The American Journal of Semitic Languages and Literatures* 52, no. 3 (1936).
4. John Sailhamer, *The Pentateuch as Narrative: A Biblical-Theological Commentary* (Grand Rapids: Zondervan, 1995), 36.
5. Robert E. Longacre, "Discourse Peak as Zone of Turbulence," in *Beyond the Sentence: Discourse and Sentential Form*, ed. Jessica Wirth (Ann Arbor: Karoma, 1985).
6. For instance, several of the previous chapters begin with an interjection such as "woe" (chaps. 31, 33), "indeed" (chap. 32), or an imperative verb (chap. 34), all of which are typical introductory discourse devices for this section of Isaiah. The technical terms for these devices in discourse are asyndeton and parataxis. When employed in composition, they help to speed up the rhythm of words, which helps readers stay focused on what the author is trying to convey.
7. The themes of judgment and blessing are introduced early on in the book in 1:25-26 and are prominent at the conclusion of this section of Isaiah.
8. Andrew Abernethy, *The Book of Isaiah and God's Kingdom: A Thematic-Theological Approach* (Downers Grove, IL: InterVarsity Press, 2016), 95.
9. Ibid., 54.
10. Jeannine Brown makes the case that the John the Baptist passage in Mt 11 begins a major section in the Gospel of Matthew, concluding at Mt 16:20, which deals with Jesus' emerging identity. The section begins with John's questioning of Jesus' messianic identity and concludes with Peter's dramatic confession of Jesus as Messiah (Mt 16:16). She observes that at key "hearing junctures" in this section appear Matthew's placement of Isaianic quotations. Jeannine K. Brown, "The Rhetoric of Hearing: The Use of Isaianic Hearing Motif in Matthew 11:2–16:20," in *Built Upon the Rock: Studies in the Gospel of Matthew*, ed. D. M. Gurtner (Grand Rapids: Eerdmans, 2008), 249–51.
11. Certainly John's Gospel makes a connection about the Messiah Jesus being a source of everlasting refreshing water (Jn 4:14), but it is not entirely clear that the water motif as used in Isa 35 is intended to be messianic.
12. This is made even more obvious in 2Sm 5:8 when it becomes a maxim, "The blind and the lame will never enter the house."
13. Cousland goes further in his assessment and argues that Matthew in his Gospel has inverted the entire episode from 2Sm 5 to stress the humility and compassion of the son of David—in that Matthew's son of David is not a military conqueror like the first David, but rather a humble, compassionate healer (J. R. C. Cousland, *The Crowds in the Gospel of Matthew* [Leiden, Netherlands: Brill, 2002]).

14. 4Q521, which was found at Cave 4 in Qumran, is also called 4QMessianic Apocalypse. The wording of this DSS fragment is similar to that of Ps 146, but the term Messiah is not used in that psalm.

15. For a complete discussion of this fragment and a full translation, see Michael O. Wise and James D. Tabor, "The Messiah at Qumran," *Biblical Archaeology Review* 18, no. 6 (1992). Wise's assessment is that this "Dead Sea Scroll text is virtually identical to that in Matthew and Luke. The Christian signs of the Messiah were, as it were, foreshadowed in the Jewish literature from Qumran" (65).

16. Ibid., 61.

The Message of the Servant Songs

ELLIOTT E. JOHNSON

The prophecy of Isaiah[1] features two historic kings, Ahaz and Hezekiah, who reigned after the death of Uzziah, the patriarch (1:1 and 6:1-13). The father, Ahaz, was unwilling to accept the Lord's promise to protect the house of David and so was disqualified from his role in the line of David (7:14; 9:6,7; 11:1-9). The son, Hezekiah, inherited the consequences of his father's choice to be protected by Assyria, but by faith he experienced the Lord's deliverance from Assyria (chaps. 36, 37). At the same time, he was unwilling to serve a limited role because of an announced premature sickness and death. This failure to serve according to God's Word would result in the Babylonian captivity (chaps. 38–39). And that raised a question: Is Israel willing to *serve* the Lord according to His Word?

The focus of the remaining prophecy (chaps. 40–66) features Israel's responsibility to *serve* while the "cities lie in ruins without inhabitants, houses are without people, and the land is ruined and desolate" (6:11). The remaining prophecy features two subsequent historic figures. One of them initially addresses the physical captivity: Cyrus the Persian is to rebuild Jerusalem and the Temple (44:28). The other addresses the spiritual captivity: the *Servant* of the Lord[2] is to bring the Lord's salvation to the ends of the earth (49:1-13).

The message of the Servant Songs will be addressed in the answers to three questions:

1. What is the nature of the prophecy?

2. What are the Servant Songs saying within the symphonic literary structure of the prophecies: Isaiah 40–55?
3. To what do the Servant Songs refer within the historic realm to which the prophecy has reference: Isaiah 40–55?

NATURE OF THE PROPHECY

While there are some who contend that prophecy cannot be understood until what is prophesied happens, Isa 48:5-7 challenges that notion. Rather, E. J. Young writes, "The revelation was made by God long before the fulfillment of the prophecy, that Israel might not attribute the fulfillment to its idols. Furthermore, the revelation was made specifically *to thee*, that Israel might have no excuse for not obeying."[3] Oswalt adds, "The verb here *hāzā*, see, is not the common verb for seeing. This is the verb for looking intently, the verb used to describe Isaiah's activity as he considered the vision of God (1:1, 2:1)."[4] Moses had prophesied about the day of national judgment (Ex 32:34) and now Isaiah prophesies about national judgment and dispersion (6:11-12) in the captivity by Babylon (39:5-7). Israel was to look intently into what had been said and what was being said. Thus, the nature and purpose of prophecy is to provide a word from God to be understood as written in that historical context. Israel was responsible to respond to the prophecy. Further the nation was expected to recognize the events that were prophesied. Thus, we should expect to be able to understand the message of the Servant Songs based on the texts.

THE SYMPHONIC LITERARY STRUCTURE: ISAIAH 40–55

Oswalt captures the literary structure of Isaiah's whole prophecy well. "Precisely what is taught in chapters 1–39 requires chapters 40–66. Had the theology of chapters 1–39 been less pretentious, it would not need to be extended into the new conditions. But precisely because it claimed so much, it must be either extended or abandoned."[5] Later he adds, the final section of the book (40–66) "serves as a reprise of the opening themes of the Isaian symphony, showing how later movements have affected those themes without fundamentally altering them"[6]

"The fundamental point that chapters 40–55 address is the possibility of restoration. That possibility is called into question by two factors. First, *ability*: can God restore? Second, *intention*: does he *want* to restore?"[7] The first question was answered in the Lord's deliverance from Assyria under Hezekiah (chaps. 36–37). Further, assurance of God's ability to deliver from Babylon is featured in the contrast between the Lord and Babylonian idols, and the Lord's capacity to raise up Cyrus (chaps. 41–48) while the idols are impotent. But the answer to the second question of God's intent demands a more complete consideration (chaps. 42, 49–55).

Isaiah had been called to bring divine hardening on the historic people before captivity: to "deafen their ears and blind their eyes" (6:9-10a). Otherwise these people may "turn back, and be healed" (6:10b). Israel was about to be sent into captivity by the Lord as the hardening precipitated the judgment. Yet the Lord will call His Servant "to be a covenant for the people[8] and a light to the nations, in order to open blind eyes, to bring out . . . those sitting in darkness from the prison house" (42:6-7).

The service of the Servant, found in the Servant Songs, is necessary because Isaiah continues to address the people in dispersion: "Listen, you deaf! Look, you blind, so that you may see. Who is blind but My servant . . . blind like the servant of the LORD?" (42:18-19 and 42:16). Isaiah's messages continue: "Bring out (of captivity) a people who are blind, yet have eyes, and are deaf, yet have ears" (43:8). In conclusion, the Lord declares, "You (Israel) are My witnesses . . . and My servant whom I have chosen so that you may know and believe Me and understand that I am He" (43:10). If Israel is to be restored, God must raise up a Servant to represent Israel in service under the law and to restore Israel by His service. And thus God's intention to restore is expressed in the service of the Servant.

These themes in the prophecy of Isaiah have been developed but not altered in the progress of revelation. It began when Israel had been chosen to be a servant in the reception of the law: "We will do everything that the Lord has commanded" (Ex 19:7; 24:3,7). As servants, they were responsible to see and hear what God had said about Himself and about themselves as servants with responsibilities. By Isaiah's time, as represented by Ahaz and Hezekiah, Israel was deaf and blind. They remained the Lord's servant, who would become increasingly blind and deaf as the day of judgment by Babylon neared. To fulfill Jeremiah's prophecy (Jer 25:11-,12), God raised up Cyrus to address captivity, and would introduce His Servant to the returned remnant to deal with Israel's sin. The Lord would use His arm (Isa 53:1) to be His Servant to assume Israel's responsibility and to restore the Lord's mediated reign on earth (53:2-12).

Thus, the theme of the Servant Songs will be examined and traced intermingled with themes addressing Israel's failure to serve. In spite of all nations facing an ultimate trial before the Lord (41:1-7), Israel, the Lord's servant, need not fear because they are chosen (41:8-14). The Holy One of Israel will redeem her (41:15-29) as His people.

The First Servant Theme

The first Song declares that the individual *Servant* of the Lord will bring justice to all nations (42:1-4). That reality is confirmed because the Servant will be a *covenant* with the people, i.e., the means through whom the people will come into covenant partnership with the Lord (42:6a). "The *covenant* was Israel's distinctive privilege."[9] In addition, the Servant's mission is to bring light to the nations (42:6b).

Since Israel, God's chosen servant, is blind and deaf, God poured out on Jacob His furious anger in the dispersion (42:18-25). Yet the blind servant will be redeemed to be God's witness (43:1–44:23). In the near future, Cyrus will fulfill the Lord's pleasure to rebuild Jerusalem and lay the foundation for the Temple (44:24–46:13). Babylon will fall as prophesied (47:1-15). The house of Jacob must hear the Lord's word—both what was said in the past and what is being said about the future (48:1-28).

The Second Servant Theme

The second Servant Song announces the Lord's salvation (49:1-13). The Servant announces this to a worldwide audience (49:1). His testimony witnesses to the Lord's preparation that His speech would say what is appropriate (49:1-2). The Lord's call came: "You are My Servant, Israel; I will be glorified in him" (49:3). In what sense is the Servant identified with Israel? The identity is not as a replacement for national Israel but as a representative to reconcile Jacob with the Lord (49:5). Yet that reconciliation would include a struggle in bringing Jacob back (49:4). That devolved into a worldwide provision of salvation with light shining to the ends of the earth (49:6). As Israel experienced rejection by the nations, so the Servant will similarly be rejected by Israel. In this shared rejection between the two, both in the end will have their destiny reversed (49:7). Both Israel and the Servant eventually will be accepted.

Despite God's assurances that Zion will not be abandoned, there was a lingering fear that, in dispersion, the people have been forgotten. God's faithfulness in spite of their mother's divorce certification will then be compared to God's faithfulness to His Servant under attack from those of Israel who returned to Zion (49:14–50:3). It is from him that Israel had to learn (50:10-11).

The Third Servant Theme

The third Servant Song (50:4-11) does not name the Servant, yet the voice of One suffering is heard. That suffering, which began to cast a shadow in the earlier song (49:4,7), now forms the heart of the third song (50:6). And this Sufferer's response becomes a model to be accepted by the people in fear of the Lord (50:10-11). Such sufferings and stress prepared the Servant (50:4-6) to trust the Lord who stands ready to help in adversity (50:7-9).

Then Isaiah makes an appeal to listen, to wake up as though the climax of restoration was about to happen at any moment—"Look, I have removed the cup of staggering from your hand; that goblet, the cup of My fury. You will never drink it again" (51:22). Jerusalem exists, it only awaits festive garments (52:1-2). The final appeal is to "not leave in a hurry . . . the LORD is going before you" (51:1–52:12). This anticipates the climax with which Isaiah began (40:1-2).

THE FOURTH SERVANT THEME

The fourth and climatic Servant Song heralds both suffering and triumph (52:13–53:12). Three speakers sing in the song. In the beginning, *the Lord* speaks of the Servant—with humanity appalled at Him, yet serving wisely so He will be greatly exalted (52:13-15). At the climax, *the Lord* crushed Him so that the Servant will justify many. As a result, He will be given many as His portion (53:10-12).

The prophet questions whether the Lord's arm has been revealed to Israel—as One who is God yet distinct in action from God. As a member of Israel, the people didn't value Him since He was unimpressive (53:1-3). The *prophet* declares that the Servant acted as a sacrificial lamb yet no one realized that His fate was their fate (53:7-9).

The irony of *the people's* confession was that they saw the Servant's death as God's judgment on Him, yet that judgment was for their own transgressions. As a result, His wounds healed them since they alone had gone astray in rejecting Him (53:4-6).

The final two poems speak to the consequences of the ministry of the Servant's suffering and exaltation. The first poem anticipates the future glory of Israel (54:1-17). At the outset, distinct generations of Israel are compared as two wives: a future barren wife who has never borne children but will bear them abundantly as partners in a new covenant of peace (54:10) and a past-married partner in the Mosaic covenant who saw only a few children. Israel is called to bask in the reality of a covenant of peace concerning which the Servant is their covenant (42:6 and 49:8). The Servant would provide the mediating sacrifice, and the covenant would be cut (ratified) to unite God's partner Israel with the Lord in peace.

The second sermon is a call for Israel to accept individually all the consequences of the Servant's wonderful ministry (55:1-13). The individuals addressed are not addressed as covenant partners but are addressed with the promise of the covenant, "I will make an everlasting covenant with you" (v. 3) so that each one can share the benefits of "the promises assured to David."[10] These mercies are available to both Israelites and Gentiles and involve the gift of eternal life (Ps 2:7 quoted by Paul in Ac 13:30-34). And these promises are available in the sacrifice of the Servant.

HISTORICAL REFERENCES IN ISAIAH 40–55

Peter spoke of the historic prophets' uncertainty regarding the future time about which they prophesied. "Concerning this salvation, the prophets who prophesied about the grace that would come to you searched and carefully investigated. They inquired into what time or what circumstances the Spirit of Christ within them was indicated when He testified in advance to the messianic sufferings and the glories that would follow" (1Pt 1:10-11).[11]

That seems to be the case with the related themes in the symphonic structure in Isa 40–55. We now live following the messianic sufferings but have not yet seen all of the glories that follow. Thus, from our historic perspective we will attempt to recognize what has passed and to anticipate what yet lies ahead. Oswalt proposes that Isa 40:1-11 sets the stage for the climax. And yet that stage fits as the climax within the overall framework of Isaiah's ministry (6:9-13).

THE FRAMEWORK OF ISAIAH'S MINISTRY

In Isaiah's ministry to his generation, he was commissioned to dull, to deafen, and to blind them (6:9-10). As a result, this effect would continue until the cities lie in ruins because of dispersion (6:11-12). In spite of this dispersion, a surviving stump holds out a ray of hope (6:13).

That ray of hope appeared periodically in the first portion of the prophecy (chaps. 7–39, and most notably in 7:1-19; 9:1-7; 11:1-9) but now bursts into a bright gleaming light in the Servant Songs (40–55). This is introduced by featuring three turning points in history (40:1-11). That is followed by a stunning review of God's surpassing greatness (40:12-26). Yet only those who trust Him will renew their strength (40:27-31). The framework of Isaiah's ministry seems to be focused on the three turning points in Israel's future. Each turning point below is followed by the related prophecies listed.

1. The termination of Israel's forced labor (40:1-2)—Israel will be going into dispersion, which will continue but not indefinitely. It will come to an end when Israel has received double for all her sins.

   The nations are called to court with the challenge concerning who else could control history. Can anyone meet the challenge of the Lord? (41:1-7,21-29).

   A new song celebrates the restoration of the blind by a way they did not know (42:10-17).

   The Lord's blind servant failed to listen to the Lord and was judged (42:18-25).

Israel will be brought out in blindness yet having eyes (43:1-13).

The Lord will send them to Babylon but Jacob didn't call on Him, having become weary of Him (43:14-28).

The Lord will bless His Servant yet the call remains unanswered (44:1-23).

Cyrus will fulfill the Lord's pleasure rebuilding Jerusalem and laying the foundation of the Temple (44:24–54:13).

God alone is the Savior and Lord (45:14–46:13).

Babylon will fall as prophesied (47:1-15).

Jacob called to flee from Babylon (48:1-22).

This theme will converge with the final theme and be fulfilled together.

2. The advent of the Lord's glory (40:3-8)—the glory of the Lord will appear in the wilderness for all humanity to see, yet the people are called to prepare the way to see His glory. Still humanity is weak, fading at the very breath of the Lord.

   While Zion wonders whether she had been forgotten, yet the Lord assures herthat He will certainly not forget her (49:8–50:3).

   The Servant Songs explain that the Servant of the Lord comes:

      to quietly pursue His mission to establish justice (42:2-4);

      to be the Lord's salvation to the ends of the earth in spite of being despised by His own people (49:1-13);

      to endure suffering with the help of the Lord, providing a model for Isaiah's audience (50:4-11), and

      to be rejected by His people and to die as a substitution for the nation and all mankind, yet to be raised and greatly exalted (52:13–53:12).

3. The advent of the Lord's rule in Zion (40:9-11)—Zion will announce that the Sovereign Lord will establish the rule of His arm (HCSB "power") and will shepherd His flock.

   Israel, the Lord's servant, will be brought from the ends of the earth back to the land (41:8-20).

   The descendants of Abraham lingering in captivity are called to awaken for Zion and told they will be comforted (51:1–52:12).

   The flock is formed as partners in the covenant of peace (54:1-10; 59:21).

Everyone is offered the drink of eternal life—anyone who is thirsty and willing to come (55:1-13).

The Servant of the Lord will establish justice on earth to the nations (42:1,4).

Jerusalem will be founded in righteousness (54:11-17).

The Lord's own arm will come to Zion (59:15-20).

The glory of the Lord shines over Zion (60:1-22).

Zion will be restored in righteousness (62:1-12).

While the Servant Songs address the service of the Davidic King, the royalty of the King will be evident in the righteous mediated rule in Jerusalem. Then His people will be the Lord's servants (56–66).

THE MESSAGE OF THE SERVANT SONGS

The Anointed-Servant Songs celebrate the service necessary to accomplish the Lord's plan for Israel and the nations. That service was necessary because Israel was unwilling to serve. As a result, Isaiah's ministry focused on God's glory, which hardened the heart of an unwilling people. As a further result, the people were dispersed into Babylon. Cyrus was raised up to restore Jerusalem, yet in time, the people who had returned would again be blinded by God's glory at the appearance of the Servant (Jn 12:37-61). That generation would abandon the holy Servant (Ac 4:23-31 and 13:26-48).

Two consequences followed: First, the Servant would be put to death as a substitute for mankind's sin, yet would overcome death in exultation to bring salvation to the end of the earth.

Second, the people would continue in dispersion until Zion would announce that the Servant would complete His mission to establish justice for the nations. Israel would then fulfill her role as servants partnered in the covenant of peace with the Lord.

The four Messiah-Servant Songs are interwoven with related themes concerning Israel-servant. In spite of the nation-servant's chosen status, the people are blinded and hardened in view of Isaiah's ministry. As a result, the people are dispersed from the land.

This dispersion is interrupted by a return under Cyrus to rebuild Jerusalem and lay a foundation for the Temple. The Messiah-Servant has a mission to bring both justice for the nations and salvation to the ends of the earth.

The Servant achieves this mission through personal suffering at the hands of His own people, yet in dependence on the Lord. And in suffering, He dies, only to overcome death and be triumphant in the Lord. As a result, Israel realizes her role in serving as His covenant people and as individuals in the nation who share eternal life.

1. The prophecy of the book of Isaiah is accepted as it appears in the canon—a single unified prophecy, authored by the historic Isaiah, son of Amoz.
2. The interpretation of the identity of the Servant as a directly messianic prophecy is contended for by J. Ridderbos, *Isaiah*, trans. J. Vriend (Grand Rapids: Zondervan, 1984), 366–70.
3. E. J. Young, *The Book of Isaiah*, vol. 111 chap. XL–LXVI (Grand Rapids: Eerdmans, 1972), 248.
4. John N. Oswalt, *The Book of Isaiah, Chapters 40–66,* New International Commentary on the Old Testament (Grand Rapids: Eerdmans, 1998), 266–67.
5. Ibid., 8.
6. Ibid., 11.
7. Ibid., 8.
8. Or "a covenant-people," as in xlii.6. Israel W. Slotki, *Isaiah* (London: The Soncino Press LTD, 1961), 241. Many commentators object to any distinction between *'am* people and *gôyim* nations. Israel will be formed by the Servant into a covenant partner, and nations are only enlightened by the Servant's ministry. In addition, Israel is commonly referred to by the term "people" in Isa 40–55. There is a marked contrast between "these people" (6:9 and 6:10) and "My people" (40:1-2). My people are a covenant people. Further, there is a plurality of nations but a singular, chosen people (41:8; 43:10; 44:1, etc.), descendants of Abraham, God's friend.
9. J. Alec Motyer, *The Prophecy of Isaiah* (Downers Grove, IL: InterVarsity, 1993), 322.
10. Ibid., 433.
11. These verses do not mean, as is commonly claimed, that the ancient prophets did not know they were writing about the Messiah. Rather, it indicates they did not know when the Messiah would come, or if the alternate reading is correct ("what person or time" NASB), they did not know the identity of the referent or when He would come. See Michael Rydelnik, *The Messianic Hope: Is the Hebrew Bible Really Messianic?* (Nashville: B&H, 2010), 88–90.

Isaiah 42:1-9

The Commission of the Servant of the Lord

ROBERT B. CHISHOLM JR.

Isaiah 42:1-9 is the first of Isaiah's so-called Servant Songs (Isa 42:1-9; 49:1-13; 50:4-9; 52:13–53:12). These Songs describe the ministry of an individual Servant, pictured as an ideal Israel, who leads sinful, exiled Israel out of bondage and back to its land. This Servant also establishes worldwide justice as he brings the Lord's deliverance to the nations. The Lord ultimately exalts the Servant, but the Servant must first suffer humiliation on behalf of Israel and "the many" so that they may be reconciled to the Lord. In the progress of biblical revelation, we discover that Jesus the Messiah is the Servant depicted in this Song.

STRUCTURE

This first Servant Song contains three literary movements, outlined as follows:

1. The Lord describes the Servant's ministry (Isa 42:1-4).
   - A. The Lord has chosen the Servant (v. 1a).
   - B. The Lord has empowered the Servant with His Spirit so he may bring justice to the nations (v. 1b).
   - C. The Servant will not promote himself (v. 2).
   - D. The Servant will not beat down the hurting and oppressed (v. 3a).
   - E. The Servant will persevere until he establishes justice (vv. 3b-4).

2. The Lord speaks directly to the Servant about his ministry (Isa 42:5-7).
   A. The Lord, the creator of the world, has chosen the Servant (vv. 5-6a).
   B. The Lord commissions the Servant to be a covenant mediator and His agent of salvation (vv. 6b-7).
3. The Lord, who will not share His glory, affirms that His announcement about the Servant will come to pass (Isa 42:8-9).

THE SONG IN ITS CONTEXT

The first Servant Song is part of a larger speech that extends from Isa 41:1 through 42:12. This speech may be outlined as follows:

Trial Speech against the Nations (Isa 41:1-7). The incomparable Lord challenges the nations to meet Him in court. As proof of His sovereign control of history, He announces He will raise up a powerful warrior-king (later identified as Cyrus the Persian, see Isa 44:28–45:1), who will conquer nations on behalf of the Lord. In panic, the nations will attempt to thwart this king by manufacturing more idol gods, but their efforts will be to no avail. No one will be able to resist the Lord and His chosen conqueror.

Salvation Oracle and Announcement (Isa 41:8-20). The Lord turns to His chosen people Israel, reminding them of His commitment to their ancestor Abraham. He exhorts His people not to fear, for He is with them and will empower them against their enemies. He knows His needy people are hungry and thirsty for divine blessing, and He will restore His favor as He produces water in the desert and causes trees to grow there. When His people see His miraculous intervention on their behalf, they will know that their powerful God is still active among them.

Trial Speech against the Nations (Isa 41:21–42:9). The incomparable Lord challenges the idol gods of the nations to confront Him in court and to demonstrate their power by announcing what will happen. He then denounces them as worthless. In contrast to these powerless so-called gods, the Lord will demonstrate His sovereignty by empowering a conquering king (Cyrus) to defeat the nations as a prelude to restoring Jerusalem. The Lord then draws attention to His Servant, whom He will empower with His Spirit to establish worldwide justice. Speaking as the sovereign creator of the heavens, earth, and humankind, He commissions the Servant, who will be a covenant mediator for people and a light to nations as he brings forth justice and delivers the downtrodden from captivity. The fulfillment of the Lord's announced plan will demonstrate His sovereign majesty, which He refuses to share with other gods.

Call to Praise (Isa 42:10-12). The prophet urges everyone to praise the Lord with a new song. This is appropriate since the whole earth will benefit from the Servant's mission. In short, the incomparable and sovereign Lord deserves worldwide praise.

As one can readily see, the Lord's overriding concern in this speech is to demonstrate His superiority to the idol gods (Isa 41:5-7,24,29; 42:8) and to reveal His glory to the nations (Isa 41:20; 42:8,10-12). His work through the Servant, which establishes justice on a global scale, is the culminating proof of His sovereignty.

THE IDENTITY OF THE SERVANT

Since the Servant, who is not specifically identified in this first Song, establishes justice, he appears to be a royal figure. In the ancient Near Eastern world kings were responsible for promoting and maintaining justice within their jurisdiction. So, one could conceivably identify the Servant with the conqueror of nations described just before this (see Isa 41:2-3,25). This individual is later identified as Cyrus, the Persian conqueror of Babylon, who decreed that the Lord's exiled people could return to their homeland (Isa 44:28–45:5). However, in contrast to the description of Cyrus the conqueror, the Servant is not depicted as warlike (see especially Isa 42:2-3). As Oswalt observes, "whereas all the other royal figures who have claimed to set up justice on the earth have done so through a gleeful use of their power to smash and rebuild, this one will be radically different."[1]

More important, intertextual connections with the immediate context make it clear that the Servant must be associated with Israel in some sense. Several times in these chapters the Lord refers to exiled Israel as His servant (Isa 41:8-9; 43:10; 44:1-2; 45:4; 48:20). Verbal links between the first Servant Song and Isa 41:8-9 suggest that the Servant might be exiled Israel. The Lord refers to Israel as "My servant" (*'avdi*), just as He does the Servant in the first song (Isa 41:8; 42:1). The Lord chooses (*bachar*, Isa 41:8-9; 42:1), supports (*tamak*, Isa 41:10; 42:1), calls (*qara'*, Isa 41:9; 42:6), and holds (*chazaq*, Isa 41:13; 42:6) both his servant Israel and the Servant of the first Song. It is no surprise that the Septuagint identifies the Servant of the first Song specifically as Jacob and Israel (cf. Isa 42:1 LXX).[2]

In addition to these intertextual connections with Isa 41:8-13, the first Servant Song is closely linked with the second Servant Song (Isa 49:1-13). Both Songs speak of the Servant as a covenant mediator and a light to the nations (cf. Isa 42:6 with 49:6,8) who releases prisoners (cf. Isa 42:7 with 49:9). It is clear that the same individual is in view in both the first and second Songs. Unlike the first Song, the second Song specifically identifies the Servant as Israel (Isa 49:3). This means that Cyrus, the conquering king described in Isa 41:25, cannot be the Servant of the Songs.

But the Servant in the second Song cannot be identified as exiled Israel either, for the Song depicts this Servant "Israel" as delivering exiled Israel (Isa 49:5-6). (For a fuller discussion of this, see the article on Isa 49:1-13, the second Servant Song.) Furthermore, exiled Israel is described as blind and deaf and fails to understand the Lord's purposes (Isa 42:19). In contrast to exiled Israel, the Servant of the Songs opens blind eyes (Isa 42:7) and is eager to carry out the Lord's commission (Isa 50:4-9).

So, the Servant is Israel in some sense, while at the same time being distinct from exiled Israel. He is best identified as an ideal Israel who is all that God intended the nation to be, in contrast to exiled Israel, which failed to fulfill God's purposes. This ideal Israel will deliver exiled Israel from bondage (Isa 49:5,8-13) and will carry out God's ideal for Israel by bringing God's salvation to the nations (Isa 42:6; 49:6). He will mediate a covenant on behalf of both Israel (cf. Isa 49:8) and the nations (Isa 42:1-7). He will do this by bearing the sins of "the many," including both Israel and the nations (Isa 52:13–53:12). Though the Servant will suffer the judgment of God on behalf of "the many" (Isa 53:4-6,10-12; cf. 49:7), the Lord will eventually reward him by elevating him to kingship over the nations (Isa 52:13-15; 53:11-12; cf. 49:7).

THE MINISTRY OF THE SERVANT

The Servant as Champion of Justice. The Servant's primary mission is to establish justice on the earth (Isa 42:1,4). As noted above, this is a royal task when viewed in its ancient Near Eastern context. The statement "he has established justice on earth" (Isa 42:4) also appears in Mesopotamian royal edicts of liberation.[3] This royal portrait of one who promotes justice coincides with the ideal expressed in royal psalms (Pss 45:4,6-7; 72:1-4,12-14) and with the description of David's reign (2Sm 8:15).[4] Perhaps most important, it corresponds to the image of the ideal Davidic king depicted in Isa 11:1-9.[5] The ideal Davidic king (cf. Isa 11:1), like the Servant, is endowed by the divine Spirit (Isa 11:2; cf. 42:1) to establish justice (Isa 11:3-5).[6] He intervenes on behalf of the poor and afflicted, assuring them of fair treatment. It is likely that the bruised reed and smoldering wick of 42:3 are metaphors for these oppressed ones.[7] The thematic link between the first Servant Song and Isa 11:1-9 strongly suggests the Servant is a king, more specifically, the ideal Davidic king.

The Servant as Covenant Mediator. According to 42:6, the Servant is also "a covenant of people" (literal Hebrew translation), the meaning of which is not immediately transparent. Some understand the phrase in the sense of "covenant people," apparently taking "people" as appositional or as an attributed genitive.[8] In this case, the Servant is equated with the people. However, this proposal is unlikely for several reasons:

1. The parallel phrase in Isa 42:6 refers to the Servant as one who is "a light to the nations." He is one who mediates light (symbolic of salvation, cf. Isa 49:6) to nations as God's agent of deliverance. They are the beneficiaries of the Servant's work. This suggests that the people mentioned in the parallel line are also beneficiaries of the Servant's ministry and are not to be equated with the Servant.

2. The singular noun "people," when following a singular noun elsewhere, is only rarely appositional (cf. Dt 20:1, "literally "*people* more numerous than you" as opposed to the HCSB, "an army larger than yours"), where it appears to be appositional to the preceding "horses, chariots"). When following a singular construct form, it is never used in a sense that would yield the meaning "covenant people" as in Isa 42:6 (cf. 49:8).

3. When a modifying (genitival) noun follows "covenant" elsewhere, it can indicate: (a) an attribute or characteristic of the covenant (as in the phrases "perpetual covenant," "covenant of priesthood," "covenant of salt," "covenant of peace," "covenant of brotherhood," and "holy covenant"); (b) the initiator of a covenant (e.g., "covenant of the Lord," "covenant of God"); or (c) the one with whom a covenant is made (e.g., "covenant with Abram," "covenant with our fathers," "covenant with the Levites," "covenant with your servant").

4. Furthermore, "covenant" does not appear to be followed by an appositional noun or attributed genitive elsewhere.[9]

In light of the evidence, it is best to understand "covenant" in Isa 42:6 as referring to one who mediates a covenant with people on the Lord's behalf. In this case, the phrase "covenant of people" is most naturally understood as meaning "covenant with people" or "covenant-mediator for the people." He is a covenant, as it were, in the sense that he is the Lord's agent in establishing a covenant with people. This fits the parallelism of the verse well. As the Servant mediates a covenant with people, he also serves as a light to the nations, in the sense that he is the Lord's agent in bringing light (salvation) to the nations.

Goldingay supports the reading "covenant with people." He states: "The metonymy may be compared with being turned into a light for nations, and it parallels the idea that Abraham will become a blessing. . . . In each case the idea is that the person not only mediates but embodies the thing, as Jesus will *be* resurrection and life rather than merely bringing it. Genesis 12:1-3 suggests that Abraham will be the embodiment of Yhwh's blessing, demonstrating in a life what it means to experience that blessing, and arousing in other people a desire for it. As a covenant with people, the addressee here will embody and express Yhwh's commitment to people."[10]

The identity of "people" in Isa 42:6 is uncertain. In the second Song "people" appears to refer to exiled Israel, whom the Servant releases from bondage and leads home (Isa 49:8-13; cf. 49:6a). Furthermore, this section of Isaiah speaks of the Lord making a covenant with Israel (Isa 55:3; 59:20-21; 61:2-8), but not with nations. Additionally, Oswalt opts for Israel being the "people" on the basis of the parallel with 49:5-8.[11] However, the immediate context of the first Servant Song may suggest a broader scope for this covenant. As noted above, the parallel line focuses on the Servant's ministry to the nations. Furthermore, v. 5 uses the word "people" in a generic sense for human beings, who have received their life's breath from the Lord. It is most natural to understand "people" in v. 6 in the same way, especially when it corresponds to "nations" in the poetic structure of the verse.[12]

The Servant as a Light to Nations. As the Servant establishes justice on earth and mediates a covenant between the Lord and humankind, he proves to be a "light of [that is, for] nations." The meaning of the imagery is clarified in Isa 42:7, where the Servant delivers those in bondage from prison. This interpretation is confirmed in Isa 49:6, where the statement "I will also make you a light of nations" is immediately followed by "to be my salvation to the ends of the earth." In Isa 51:4-5 the light of salvation to the nations is all but equated with establishing justice. Elsewhere the imagery of opening blind eyes is associated with the just treatment of the afflicted (see Ps 146:8-9; Isa 29:18-21; 35:4-5). The motif of freeing prisoners is used in a similar manner (Pss 69:33; 79:11; 102:20; 107:10; 146:7; Isa 49:9; 61:1). This picture of the Servant being a light to the nations and delivering prisoners from bondage casts the Servant in a royal role, for the imagery finds parallels in Mesopotamian texts where kings liberate the oppressed.[13] Assyrian kings applied similar titles to themselves. Tiglath-pileser III was called "the light of all humankind," while one of Esarhaddon's titles was "the light of the world."[14]

The broader context gives fuller insight into how the Servant brings deliverance to the nations. Elsewhere in this section of Isaiah, the prophet depicts the nations as idol worshipers (cf. Isa 44:9-20). Though the Lord God has created all people (Isa 42:5), they fail to give Him the honor He deserves and demands (Isa 42:8). All nations are in a covenant relationship with the Lord, whether they know it or not. God established a covenant with Noah and his sons. He commissioned them to be fruitful and fill the earth, warned them to respect the image of God residing in their fellow human beings, and promised that He would not again destroy all life as He had done through the flood (Gn 9:1-17). But the nations of the earth have broken this "everlasting covenant" with God by polluting the earth with human bloodshed (Isa 24:5; 26:21; cf. Gn 9:4-6). For this reason, the nations are destined for destruction (Isa 24:1-23; 26:20-21), but God warns them to turn to Him for deliverance (Isa 45:22) before the day of judgment, when all of God's enemies will bow before Him in defeat (Isa 45:23-24). Those who humbly accept God's mercy will participate in God's kingdom of peace and justice (Isa 2:2-4; 19:23-25). As the first Servant Song makes clear, it is the Servant who is God's agent in mediating a renewed covenantal relationship between God and humankind and in bringing the light of salvation to the repentant among the nations (Isa 42:6-7). As the fourth Song explains, his suffering is foundational to this redemptive program, for his sin-bearing on behalf of "many" (Isa 53:12) enables him to make "the many" righteous (Isa 53:11).[15]

THE MESSIANIC FULFILLMENT OF THE FIRST SERVANT SONG

The NT identifies Jesus as the Servant depicted in Isaiah's first Servant Song, as seen in the following examples:

Simeon's testimony (Lk 2:28-32). When the aged prophet Simeon held the infant Jesus in his arms, he declared that he had seen the Lord's "salvation," the One who would be "a light for revelation to the Gentiles" (Lk 2:30,32). The reference to "light," which is associated with "salvation," is an allusion to Isa 42:6-7 (as well as Isa 49:6) that casts Jesus, even from infancy, in the role of God's servant.

Jesus' baptism (Mt 3:17; Mk 1:9). As Jesus launched His public ministry, He did not present Himself as a conquering king. He instead got in line to be baptized (Mt 3:13; Mk 1:9), as if He were a repentant sinner in need of cleansing. When John protested (Mt 3:14), Jesus insisted that John baptize Him (Mt 3:15). Though Jesus was sinless, He identified with sinners. As the Suffering Servant, He came to bear the effects of human sin (Mt 8:17), offer Himself as a sacrifice for sinners (Mt 20:28), and lay the foundation for a new covenant (Mt 26:28). He was compelled to "fulfill all righteousness." In Matthew "righteousness" is "moral conduct in accord with God's will."[16] It was God's will for Jesus to identify with sinners, so Jesus inaugurated His public ministry by doing just that. Jesus' baptism was the first step in His ministry, which He later summarized in this way: "the Son of Man did not come to be served, but to serve, and to give His life—a ransom for many" (Mt 20:28).

Jesus' commitment to carry out God's will was pleasing to God. As Jesus came out of the water, the Spirit descended on Him (Mt 3:16), recalling the Lord's words in Isa 42:1: "I have placed my Spirit upon him." God then identified Jesus as follows: "This is My beloved Son. I take delight in Him!" (Mt 3:17). God alluded here to Ps 2:7, where He declares the Davidic king His son, and to Isa 42:1, where He declares His delight in His Spirit-endowed Servant. With this single statement God identified Jesus as the messianic king (cf. Mt 16:16 and 26:63, where Messiah is identified as God's Son) and as His special Servant who would carry out His will and suffer to save sinners.

Jesus' early healing ministry (Mt 4:23-25). According to Mt 4:23-25, Jesus' proclamation that the kingdom was at hand was accompanied by a demonstration of His messianic power. He exhibited power over nature by healing every kind of disease and illness. He continued His victorious spiritual battle against the Devil by curing the demon-possessed. While showing His messianic power and authority, however, He did not abandon His role as Suffering Servant. Through His healing ministry He continued to identify with sinners in their awful plight, for physical disease is ultimately an effect of sin. By erasing the effects of sin in the lives of those He healed, Jesus foreshadowed the day when He would go beyond this approach and deal once and for all with the root of the problem, humankind's alienation from God.

The news of His ministry spread far and wide, even into regions where Gentiles lived, such as Syria and the Decapolis (Mt 4:24-25). Already the ministry of the Servant as a "light to the nations" (Isa 42:6; cf. 49:6) was underway, foreshadowing His final commission to His disciples to "make disciples of all nations" (Mt 28:19).

Jesus' proclamation in the synagogue at Nazareth (Lk 4:16-21). At the beginning of His ministry, Jesus stood up in the synagogue at Nazareth and read Isa 61:1-2a: "The Spirit of the Lord is on Me, because He has anointed Me to preach good news to the poor. He has sent Me to proclaim freedom to the captives and recovery of sight to the blind, to set free the oppressed, to proclaim the year of the Lord's favor" (Lk 4:18-19). He then boldly announced, "Today as you listen, this Scripture has been fulfilled" (Lk 4:21).[17]

By identifying Himself as the speaker of the words recorded in Isa 61:1-2a, Jesus was identifying Himself as the Servant of the Lord, the same one spoken of in Isaiah's first Servant Song.[18] Like the Servant, the speaker in Isa 61:1-2a is clearly a royal figure. He states that the Lord has anointed him. The appearance of the verb "anoint" suggests a royal anointing, especially following a statement that the Lord's Spirit is upon him.[19] This anointed one proclaims freedom and the release of captives as he declares the year of the Lord's favor (a Jubilee of sorts, cf. Lv 25:10). Proclaiming freedom is a royal prerogative (see Jer 34:8,15, where Zedekiah proclaims freedom for slaves). More specifically, there are several intertextual links between the anointed one's words in Isa 61:1-2a, the description of the royal Servant in Isaiah's first two Servant Songs, and Isaiah's depiction of the ideal Davidic king in Isa 11. Like the Servant/messianic king, the speaker in Isa 61:1-3 is empowered by the divine Spirit (cf. Isa 11:2; 42:1) to encourage the oppressed (Isa 11:4), to proclaim the deliverance of prisoners (cf. Isa 42:7; 49:9), and to console the afflicted (Isa 49:13; cf. 50:4). The good news is that God will restore the exiles to the land, where they will rebuild their ruined cities (Isa 61:4; cf. Isa 49:8). He will make a new covenant with them and richly bless them (Isa 61:8-9; cf. Isa 49:8).[20]

Based on these intertextual links, we can safely conclude that Isa 61:1-3 is a fifth Servant Song. Because critics typically view chapters 40–55 and 56–66 of Isaiah as distinct literary units, it is easy to overlook the presence of this fifth Servant Song, but the linguistic evidence is compelling.[21] The fifth Song corresponds thematically with the first two Servant Songs. The first two Songs focus on the Servant's commission to bring justice to Israel and the nations, only hinting at his suffering (Isa 49:4). Songs three and four develop fully the theme of the Servant's suffering, while this fifth Song returns to the theme of justice, the ultimate goal of the Servant's mission. So, while Lk 4:16-21 does not directly quote from the first Servant Song, the intertextual linking of Isa 61:1-2a with the first two Servant Songs provides further evidence that Jesus is indeed the Servant depicted in the first two Songs.

Jesus' retreat from public ministry (Mt 12:15-21). Knowing that His time had not yet come and that He still had a great deal to accomplish, Jesus retreated in the face of persecution, just as He had instructed His disciples to do (see Mt 10:11-15). He continued to heal those who followed Him, but He warned them not to broadcast the fact. According to Matthew, Jesus' behavior fulfilled Isaiah's prophecy in the first Servant Song (Isa 42:1-4). The Servant would not come as a self-promoting conquering king. Instead, he would be careful not to crush and oppress the weak and hurting, for his ultimate task was to bring salvation to the world and establish a just society.

Jesus' transfiguration (Mt 17:1-9; Lk 9:28-36). Shortly after Jesus announced that some of His disciples would witness His second coming before they died, He took Peter, James, and John with Him up a high mountain, where He was transformed before them. God came in a cloud and declared, as He did at Jesus' baptism (Mt 3:17), that Jesus is His Son in whom He is well pleased (Mt 17:5). The declaration recalls Psalm 2:7, where God declares the Davidic king His son, and Isa 42:1, where He declares His delight in his Spirit-endowed Servant. As at Jesus' baptism, with this single statement God again identified Jesus as the messianic king and as His special Servant who would carry out His will and suffer to save sinners.

Luke's version differs slightly. In Luke's account God says: "This is My Son, the Chosen One" (Lk 9:35). (Some Lukan manuscripts agree with Mt 17:5 in reading, "with whom I am well pleased." But this reading is most likely secondary in Luke and has been assimilated to Matthew's version.) This version of God's statement also alludes to Isa 42:1, where the Lord calls the Servant "My Chosen One."

SUMMARY

In the first of Isaiah's Servant Songs, the Lord speaks first about, and then to, His chosen Servant. He commissions the Servant to establish justice in the earth. The Servant will not draw attention to himself or beat down those who are suffering. Instead he will mediate a renewed covenant between God and humankind and bring the light of God's salvation to the nations as he releases prisoners from bondage.

The Servant is not specifically identified in the first Song. His task of establishing justice is a royal function, but he is not to be identified with the conquering king (Cyrus) of the earlier verses (Isa 41:2-3,25), for the Servant is not depicted as warlike. More important, the Servant is associated with exiled Israel through intertextual links with Isa 41:8-9 and the second Servant Song, which identifies the Servant specifically as Israel (Isa 49:3). Yet the Servant cannot simply be equated with blind, exiled Israel, for the Servant opens blind eyes (Isa 42:7) and, in the second Servant Song, delivers exiled Israel. So while the Servant is related to exiled Israel, he is distinct. He is best identified as ideal Israel, who fulfills God's purpose for the nation by extending God's salvation to the nations. Since the Servant's primary mission of establishing justice is royal, it makes sense to identify him with the ideal Davidic king described in Isa 11:1-9. Indeed, intertextual links between the first Servant Song and this earlier passage support the proposed identification. This being the case, one can legitimately argue that the Servant is a messianic figure.

The NT identifies Jesus as the Servant of Isaiah's first Servant Song. Simeon identified the infant Jesus as the "light" of God's revelation who would bring salvation to the nations (Lk 2:30,32; cf. Isa 42:6-7). From the very beginning of His ministry, Jesus began to take this light to the Gentiles (Mt 4:23-25). At His baptism the divine Spirit came upon Jesus and God identified Him as His Son, in whom He delighted (Mt 3:17; Mk 1:11; cf. Isa 42:1). At the transfiguration, God identified Jesus as the one whom He had chosen (Lk 9:35; cf. Isa 42:1) and again declared that He was well pleased with Him (Mt 17:5; cf. Isa 42:1). Very early in His ministry, Jesus read from Isa 61:1-2 and identified Himself as the Spirit-empowered anointed one described there (Lk 4:16-21). Intertextual connections between this passage, which is Isaiah's fifth Servant Song, and the first Servant Song make it clear that Jesus was identifying Himself as the Servant of the Lord described in Isaiah's Servant Songs. When Jesus later retreated from the public eye, Matthew saw in this the fulfillment of Isa 42:2-3, which says the Servant would not promote himself (Mt 12:15-21).

---

1. John N. Oswalt, *The Book of Isaiah, Chapters 40–66*, New International Commentary on the Old Testament (Grand Rapids: William B. Eerdmans, 1998), 111.

2. Joseph Ziegler, *Septuaginta* (Göttingen: Vandenhoeck & Ruprecht, 1983), 276.

3. Moshe Weinfeld, *Social Justice in Ancient Israel and in the Ancient Near East* (Jerusalem: Magnes, 1995), 141. For excerpts from such edicts, see Weinfeld, 47-52, 60-61.

4. On parallels between these royal psalms and Mesopotamian royal edicts, see Weinfeld, *Social Justice*, 48-49, 62-64. On 2Sm 8:15 see Weinfeld, 46-47. In addition to the justice theme, both the first and second Servant Songs contain several details that "fit well with the royal ideal" depicted in the psalms. See J. H. Eaton, *Festal Drama in Deutero-Isaiah* (London: SPCK, 1979), 48, 62-63.

5. Several commentators have recognized the connection between the two figures. See, for example, J. Alec Motyer, *The Prophecy of Isaiah* (Downers Grove, IL: InterVarsity, 1993), 13-14; and Oswalt, *Isaiah, Chapters 40–66*, 109–10.

6. Once more, parallels with Mesopotamian royal edicts are apparent. See Weinfeld, *Social Justice*, 62-63.

7. In Isa 43:17 the extinguished wick symbolizes those who are dead, so the image of a dim wick pictures one on the verge of extinction.

8. See the *Tanakh Translation* and Shalom M. Paul, *Isaiah 40–66*, Eerdmans Critical Commentary (Grand Rapids: Eerdmans, 2012), 189.

9. Robert B. Chisholm Jr., "The Christological Fulfillment of Isaiah's Servant Songs," *Bibliotheca Sacra* 163 (2006): 394.

10. John Goldingay, *The Message of Isaiah 40–55* (London: T&T Clark, 2005), 164.

11. See Oswalt, *Isaiah, Chapters 40–66*, 118.

12. See Motyer, *Isaiah*, 322.

13. Shalom Paul, "Deutero-Isaiah and the Cuneiform Royal Inscriptions," *Journal of the American Oriental Society* 88 (1968): 182, and *Isaiah 40-66*, 190. See as well Weinfeld, *Social Justice*, 141.

14. Paul, *Isaiah 40–66*, 189.

15. See Robert B. Chisholm Jr., "Forgiveness and Salvation in Isaiah 53," in *The Gospel According to Isaiah 53*, ed. Darrell L. Bock and Mitch Glaser (Grand Rapids: Kregel, 2012), 207-08.

16. W. D. Davies and D. C. Allison, *Matthew Matthew 1–7*, International Critical Commentary, vol. 1 (London: T & T Clark, 2004), 327.

17. The text form from which Jesus reads differs in some details from the Hebrew text of Isa 61:1-2a. He also omits vv. 2b-3, apparently for theological reasons. See Darrell L. Bock, *Luke, Volume 1: 1:1—9:50*, Baker Exegetical Commentary on the New Testament (Grand Rapids: Baker, 1994), 404-05, 411.

18. R. N. Whybray acknowledges the close connection between Isa 61:1-3 and the Servant Songs, but he identifies the servant as Deutero-Isaiah and the speaker in 61:1-3 as Trito-Isaiah. See *Isaiah 40-66*, New Century Bible Commentary (Grand Rapids: Eerdmans, 1975), 239-40. John Goldingay acknowledges that the imagery of Isa 61:1-3 is royal, but he sees the Davidic promises as democratized in Isa 55:3-5 and regards the speaker in Isa 61:1-3 as the prophet. See *Isaiah*, New International Biblical Commentary (Peabody, MA: Hendrickson, 2001), 346.

19. In three passages in 1-2 Samuel, royal anointing is accompanied by the gift of the divine Spirit (cf. 1Sm 10:1,6; 16:13; 2Sm 23:1-2).

20. On the parallels between Isa 61:1-3 and the Servant Songs, see Franz Delitzsch, *Biblical Commentary on the Prophecies of Isaiah*, 2 vols., trans. James Martin (Grand Rapids: Eerdmans, 1949; repr.), 2:425. Having surveyed the linguistic links, Delitzsch states: "For these reasons we have no doubt that we have here the words of the Servant of Jehovah." See as well the chart in John H. Walton, "The Imagery of the Substitute King Ritual in Isaiah's Fourth Servant Song," *Journal of Biblical Literature* 122 (2003): 742.

21. Oswalt, *Isaiah, Chapters 40–66*, 562–65. Brevard S. Childs is sympathetic to this position; he states that in "the final shape of the Isaianic corpus" there is a "resonance between the eschatological Messiah and the suffering servant." However, he considers a messianic figure foreign to the message of Isaiah 56-66. See *Isaiah*, Old Testament Library (Louisville: Westminster John Knox, 2001), 504–05.

Isaiah 49:1-13

The Ministry of the Servant of the Lord

ROBERT B. CHISHOLM JR.

Isaiah 49:1-13 is the second of Isaiah's so-called Servant Songs (Isa 42:1-9; 49:1-13; 50:4-9; 52:13–53:12). These Songs describe the ministry of an ideal Israel, an individual who leads sinful, exiled Israel out of bondage and back to its land. This Servant also establishes worldwide justice as he brings the Lord's deliverance to the nations. The Lord ultimately exalts the Servant, but the Servant must first suffer humiliation on behalf of Israel and "the many" so that they may be reconciled to the Lord. In the progress of biblical revelation, we discover that Jesus the Messiah is the Servant depicted in this Song.

STRUCTURE

The second Servant Song is a companion to the first Song (Isa 42:1-9). Both Songs depict the Servant as a covenant mediator who is an agent of divine salvation. However, the formats of the Songs differ. In the first Song, the Lord speaks—both about and directly to the Servant. In the second Song, the Servant speaks. He addresses the distant coastlands and those who reside there (Isa 49:1) and then concludes with a call to praise addressed to the heavens, earth, and mountains (Isa 49:13). Though the Servant is the speaker, within the Song he quotes what the Lord has said (Isa 49:3, 6-12). Within this quoted material, the Lord directly addresses the Servant (Isa 49:3, 6-8).

The structure of the second Song is clearly marked. The Song opens with a call to attention (Isa 49:1) followed by a series of third-person verbs with the Lord as subject (49:2-3). The last of these ("He said to me," v. 3) introduces a quote from the Lord. The next major unit within the Song contains the Servant's response to the Lord, introduced with "But I myself said" (49:4). The next three units, all of which contain quotations of what the Lord has said, begin with "And now, says the Lord" (49:5) or "this is what the Lord says" (49:7,8). The Song concludes with a call to praise, probably spoken by the Servant, who refers to the Lord in the third person (49:13).

THE SONG IN ITS CONTEXT

The second Servant Song is strategically placed in the prophet's argument. Immediately prior to this the Lord urged the exiles to leave Babylon and promised to provide for their needs on their trip home (Isa 48:20-21). But He also warned them that the wicked would not prosper (Isa 48:22). The warning is consistent with the Lord's words to the exiles earlier in the chapter. He accused them of dishonesty (Isa 48:1,8), stubbornness (Isa 48:4), and idolatry (Isa 48:5). He reminded them that they could have experienced the blessings promised to Abraham (Isa 48:18-19), but instead they were in exile. Yet the Lord also announced His plan to rescue His people through a conquering warrior (Isa 48:14), earlier identified as Cyrus the Persian (see Isa 44:28–45:1). As the Lord's plan unfolds, the people should be prepared to leave the place of bondage.

Like the first Servant Song (Isa 42:1-9), which comes on the heels of an announcement of the Lord's intention to intervene through a warrior king (Isa 41:25), this second Song speaks of the Lord's ultimate purpose. The Servant will complete what the conquering king begins. He will mediate a covenant on behalf of the Lord's people and then fully restore them to their land. But the Lord's plan extends beyond His covenant people. The Servant will be a light to the nations, even those who live on the edges of the world. He will bring God's deliverance to all nations and receive the honor he deserves as the Lord's faithful agent of salvation.

THE IDENTITY OF THE SERVANT

Unlike the first Servant Song, which does not specifically identify the Servant, this second Song leaves no doubt about the Servant's identity. The Servant is called Israel (Isa 49:3). Several times in these chapters the Lord refers to exiled Israel as His servant (Isa 41:8-9; 43:10; 44:1-2; 45:4; 48:20). But the Servant in this second

Song cannot be identified as exiled Israel, which has failed miserably (Isa 48:1-5). Exiled Israel is described elsewhere as blind and deaf and fails to understand the Lord's purposes (Isa 42:18-19; 43:10), in contrast to the Servant of the Songs, who opens blind eyes (Isa 42:7) as he delivers people from prison (Isa 42:7; 49:9). The second Song depicts the Servant "Israel" delivering exiled Israel (Isa 49:5-6), so he must be distinct in some way from the exiles.

In this regard, the meaning of the key text, Isa 49:5-6, has been the focus of much debate. It appears that both verses describe the Servant restoring exiled Israel to the Lord. In v. 5, the phrase "to bring Jacob back to Him" appears to indicate the Lord's purpose in forming the Servant. The closest grammatical parallel is in 1Sm 2:28, where the Lord declares regarding Eli: "I chose him from all the tribes of Israel for myself for a priest [i.e., to be my priest] in order to [i.e., in order that he may] go up on my altar, to offer incense, (and) to lift up an ephod before me" (author's translation). The words "to go up," "to offer," and "to lift up" (all three are infinitives construct with the prefixed preposition *le-*, "to") modify "I chose him" and explain the purpose for the Lord choosing Eli as His priest. All three phrases describe what the priest will do. In the same way, in Isa 49:5 the phrase "to restore Jacob" modifies "who formed me" and explains the Lord's purpose in forming the Servant. It describes what the Servant will do: he will restore Jacob to the Lord. If this is correct, then the Servant, who accomplishes the restoring, must be distinct from exiled Jacob, who is the recipient and beneficiary of the Servant's restorative work.

Some think that the idea of Servant Israel (cf. Isa 49:3) restoring exiled Israel is illogical. They prefer a different interpretation of the grammar. For example, the *Tanakh* translation translates v. 5a, "And now the Lord has resolved—He who formed me in the womb to be His servant—to bring back Jacob to Himself, that Israel may be restored to Him."[1] The verb *'amar*, "says," is given the nuance "resolved," the second line is treated as parenthetical, and the phrase "to bring back" is viewed as an objective complement of "resolved." In this case Servant Israel affirms that the Lord has resolved to save him. But it seems odd, in light of what precedes and follows, where the Servant refers to himself in the first person (note "who formed me" and "I am honored" in 49:5), that he would refer to himself here in the third person.[2]

In Isa 49:6 the phrases "to reestablish" and "to restore" appear to give the purpose for the Servant being given that role. As the Lord's Servant, his job is to reestablish the exiled tribes of Jacob and to restore the remnant (HCSB, "protected ones") of Israel. In this case, it is obvious that the Servant is distinct from Jacob/Israel, who is the beneficiary of his ministry.

But again some see the notion of Servant Israel saving exiled Israel as illogical. For example, in v. 6 the *Tanakh* translation reads, "It is too little that you should be My servant In that I raise up the tribes of Jacob And restore the survivors of Israel: I will also make you a light to the nations." Mettinger, citing several earlier commentators, also understands God, not the servant, as the subject of the three infinitives in Isa 49:5-6a.[3] He translates v. 6 as follows (p. 37): "And he said: 'It is too light a thing, considering that you are my Servant, that I should only raise up the tribes of Israel: but I shall also (or: I hereby also) make you a light to the nations, so that my salvation may reach to the end of the earth.'" He appeals to Isa 51:16 as a syntactical parallel, where, he argues, God is the subject of the three infinitives (pp. 35-36). According to this understanding of the syntax, the servant Israel is the one raised up through the restoration of the exiles. But it seems odd that the Lord would address Israel directly and also refer to him in the third person. Granted in v. 3 He addresses the Servant directly and also calls him Israel, but the syntax is entirely different there. In v. 3 "Israel" is either vocative or in apposition to "my servant." As for the alleged parallel in Isa 51:16, the syntactical structure differs there, for the infinitives are dependent on a first-person verb form with no intervening prepositional phrase, whereas in Isa 49:6 a prepositional phrase immediately precedes "to restore" (note "to me [for] a servant"). The prepositional phrase is dependent on an infinitive, not a first-person verb form. The proposed reading of v. 6 is awkward. It is far more likely that "to reestablish" and "to restore" identify the Servant's purpose in being chosen.

So the Servant is Israel in some sense, while at the same time being distinct from exiled Israel. He is best identified as an ideal Israel who is all that God intended the nation to be, in contrast to exiled Israel, which failed to fulfill God's purposes. This ideal Israel will deliver exiled Israel from bondage (Isa 49:5,8-13) and will carry out God's ideal for Israel by bringing God's salvation to the nations (Isa 42:6; 49:6). He will mediate a covenant on behalf of both Israel (cf. Isa 49:8) and the nations (Isa 42:1-7). He will do this by bearing the sins of "the many," including both Israel and the nations (Isa 52:13–53:12). Though the Servant will suffer the judgment of God on behalf of "the many" (Isa 53:4-6,10-12; cf. 49:7; 50:10), the Lord will eventually reward him by elevating him to kingship over the nations (Isa 52:13-15; 53:11-12; cf. 49:7).

In defense of the position articulated above, Oswalt points out that "it is the function, not the identity, of Israel that is emphasized" here. He explains: "This Servant is going to function as Israel." In what way will he do this? Oswalt continues: "He will be for Israel, and the world, what Israel could not be. Faced with Israel's failure, God does not wipe out the nation; he simply devises another way in which Israel's servanthood could be worked out: through the ideal Israel."[4]

THE MINISTRY OF THE SERVANT

As in the first Servant Song, the Servant is chosen to be a covenant mediator for people. In the first Song the Servant mediates a covenant with people in a general sense (on the syntax and meaning of the phrase "covenant for the people" in Isa 42:6, see the article on Isa 42:1-9, the first Servant Song). But in this second Song, his mediatorial work is focused more on exiled Israel. Isaiah 49:5-6 describes the Servant's work on behalf of Israel/Jacob and the tribes of Jacob/remnant of Israel. In his mediatorial role he rebuilds a land and reassigns desolate property after he releases prisoners and leads them home (49:8b-12). The subsequent context makes it clear that the release, return, and restoration of exiled Israel are in view (see Isa 49:17-22; 51:11-14; 52:9-12; 54:3). In this role he is, as it were, a new Moses, who leads the exiles from bondage, and a new Joshua, who leads them into their promised home.

The promise of a renewed covenant coincides with other references to covenant renewal with Israel in Isa 40–66. In Isa 55:3 the Lord calls Israel to repentance, promising them He will make an everlasting covenant with them. In Isa 59:20-21 the Lord promises the repentant in Zion He will inaugurate a covenant with them in conjunction with imparting His Spirit to them. In Isa 61:2-8 the Lord, after proclaiming release from bondage and restoration of the desolate land, promises the people that they will be His priests and that He will make an everlasting covenant with them.

Hugenberger has shown that both the first and second Servant Songs contain exodus imagery, as the prophet anticipates a release of the exiles from bondage. He points out that the context of the first Song alludes to the exodus (cf. Isa 41:17-20; 42:13-16). The Song itself depicts the Servant delivering prisoners from bondage (Isa 42:7; cf. Ex 13:3,14; 20:2). Exodus imagery also appears in the immediate context of the second Servant Song (Isa 48:20-21), as well as in the Song itself (Isa 49:9-10; cf. Ex 15:27; 17:6).[5]

Within the framework of this anticipated second exodus, the Servant functions as a new Moses. Consequently, it is no surprise that the Servant is a covenant mediator for Israel in the second Song. Moses, who is called the Lord's servant several times (see, for example, Nm 12:7; Dt 34:5; Jos 1:1-2), is depicted as Israel's covenant mediator.[6] In Exodus 34:27 the Lord says to him: "Write down these words, for in accordance with these words I have made a covenant with you and with Israel." Hugenberger observes: "Moses is so thoroughly identified with the people that in Exodus 34:27 the covenant was deemed to have been made with Moses, whether in addition to Israel or, more likely, as their representative."[7] The close association of Moses with the people makes sense if he is their covenant mediator. The covenant is made with him and then extended through him to the entire covenant community.

The Servant's task is not limited to delivering and restoring exiled Israel. As in the first Song, he is a light to nations, extending God's deliverance to the remote corners of the earth (Isa 49:6b). As the first Song makes clear, this entails establishing justice on the earth (see Isa 42:1-4) and releasing the oppressed from bondage (Isa 42:6-7). As one who executes justice, the Servant assumes a royal role. (For more on this, see the article on 42:1-9, the first Servant Song.)

The language of Isa 49:2 may point to this royal role of establishing justice. Here the Servant declares that the Lord has made his words to be "like a sharp sword" and has made him into a sharp arrow that He hides in His quiver. The language sounds militaristic, making it tempting to associate the Servant with the military figure (Cyrus) alluded to in Isa 48:14. But this cannot be the case, for Isa 49:3 specifically identifies the Servant as Israel (see above). The imagery of Isa 49:2 suggests the Servant will be an effective instrument in the Lord's hand, much like a sword or an arrow is to a warrior. The mention of the Servant's "words" points to his being an effective spokesman, perhaps as a prophet in his role of a new Moses (see above). Even if this is the case, it may also reflect his royal role. In establishing justice, the Servant will make just decrees and, of necessity in a world filled with unjust would-be oppressors, he will destroy the wicked. The description of the ideal king in Isa 11:4 speaks of this: "He will judge the poor righteously and execute justice for the oppressed of the land. He will strike the land with discipline from His mouth, and He will kill the wicked with a command from His lips." When one correlates this passage with the first Servant Song (Isa 42:4) and in turn the second, it is likely that Isa 49:2 points to the Servant's commission to establish justice on the earth. When the time comes for the Lord to inaugurate His kingdom of justice and peace, He will accomplish the task effectively through the Servant—His sword and arrow, as it were.

In this second Song a new dimension to the Servant's ministry emerges: opposition. This may have been hinted at in Isa 42:4, which says the Servant will not grow weak or be crushed until he completes his mission. But in this second Song it is clear the Servant will have reason for discouragement (Isa 49:4a) and will actually be despised by a nation[8] (49:7). This notion of rejection gets expanded more fully in the third and fourth Songs, which depict the Servant's suffering in vivid detail and reveal its redemptive purpose. In the fourth Song we discover that the Servant is despised by Israel, the very nation he comes to restore (Isa. 53:1-8).

Another theme emerges in this second Song—the Servant's exaltation. This is hinted at in the first Song (42:4), but it is more fully developed here. In Isa 49:4-5 he speaks of being vindicated, rewarded, and honored by God. According to Isa 49:7, kings will rise in respect before him while princes bow down. This response from royalty is consistent with the royal status of the Servant as the one who brings justice to the earth (see Isa 42:1-4). The Servant's exaltation becomes a central theme in the fourth Servant Song, where the Lord announces He will give the Servant special status, much to the surprise of nations and their kings (Isa 52:13-15). Because of his willingness to suffer for the sins of "the many," the Lord will reward him (Isa 53:11-12).

THE MESSIANIC FULFILLMENT OF THE SECOND SERVANT SONG

The NT identifies Jesus as the Servant depicted in Isaiah's second Servant Song.

The testimony of Simeon and Paul (Lk 2:28-32; Ac 13:47; 26:23). As in the case of the first Servant Song, the NT views Jesus as the Servant of the second Song by identifying Him as the light to the nations. The prophet Simeon, while holding the infant Jesus in his arms, declared that he had seen the Lord's "salvation," the one who would be "a light for revelation to the Gentiles" (Lk 2:30,32). The allusion to the first two Servant Songs (see Isa 42:6-7; 49:6) casts Jesus, even from infancy, in the role of God's agent of salvation to the nations. When Paul was speaking with Agrippa, he explained that the Messiah, in fulfillment of the OT Scriptures, would suffer and then proclaim "light" to both Jews and the nations (Ac 26:23). Indeed, Paul and Barnabas understood they were Jesus' agents in taking this "light" to the nations (Ac 13:47).

Jesus' proclamation in the synagogue at Nazareth (Lk 4:16-21). At the beginning of His ministry, Jesus stood up in the synagogue at Nazareth and read Isa 61:1-2a: "The Spirit of the Lord is on Me, because He has anointed Me to preach good news to the poor. He has sent Me to proclaim freedom to the captives, and recovery of sight to the blind, to set free the oppressed, to proclaim the year of the Lord's favor" (Lk 4:18-19). He then boldly announced, "Today as you listen, this Scripture has been fulfilled" (Lk 4:21).[9]

As pointed out in the article on the first Servant Song, there are several intertextual links between the anointed one's words in Isa 61:1-2a, the description of the royal Servant in Isaiah's first two Servant Songs, and Isaiah's depiction of the ideal Davidic king in Isa 11. Like the Servant/messianic king, the speaker in Isa 61:1-3 is empowered by God's Spirit (cf. Isa 11:2; 42:1) to encourage the needy (Isa 11:4), to proclaim the deliverance of prisoners (cf. Isa 42:7; 49:9), and to console those who mourn (Isa 49:13; cf. 50:4). God will restore the exiles to the land, where they will rebuild their ruined cities (Isa 61:4: cf. Isa 49:8). He will make a new covenant with them and richly bless them (Isa 61:8-9; cf. Isa 49:8).[10] When He identified Himself with the speaker in Isa 61:1-2a, Jesus claimed to be the Servant of the Lord spoken of in Isaiah's first and second Servant Songs.[11]

John's vision of springs of water (Rev 7:16-17). In the book of Revelation, John sees a vision of a multitude from all nations dressed in white robes. They praise God for the salvation He has provided them (Rev 7:9-10). We are then told that those who have been redeemed by the Lamb will never hunger or thirst again. They will be protected from the scorching sun and will drink from springs of water (Rev 7:16-17). The imagery comes from Isa 49:10, which in its literary context describes the return of the exiles after being delivered by the Servant (see 49:8b-9). Yet the same context also depicts God's salvation being extended to the nations, as in the first Servant Song (Isa 49:6; cf. Isa 42:6-7). This facilitates John's transfer of imagery used for the return from exile to the salvation of the nations. The Servant's deliverance of Israel is merely the first stage in his work of salvation, which will culminate in the deliverance of nations (Isa 42:6-7).

SUMMARY

In the second of Isaiah's Servant Songs, the Servant speaks to the people of the earth. He tells them of his commission as the Lord's Servant. He is to mediate a covenant on behalf of the Lord's exiled people, rescue them from their foreign imprisonment, and lead them home. But the Servant's mission is not limited to Israel. He will also take the light of God's salvation to the nations, prompting their kings to honor him.

This second Servant Song identifies the Servant specifically as Israel (Isa 49:3). Yet the Servant cannot simply be equated with exiled Israel. Because he delivers exiled Israel from bondage, he must be distinct. He is best identified as an ideal Israel, who restores sinful, exiled Israel to a covenant relationship with the Lord and carries out the Lord's original design for Israel by extending His salvation to the nations.

The NT identifies Jesus as the Servant of Isaiah's second Servant Song. Simeon identified the infant Jesus as the "light" of God's revelation who would bring salvation to the nations (Lk 2:30,32; cf. Isa 49:6). Paul later identified Jesus as this light and viewed his own ministry as taking this light to the nations. Very early in His ministry Jesus read from Isa 61:1-2 and identified Himself as the one who speaks in that passage (cf. Lk 4:16-21). Like the Servant of the Second Song, He will release prisoners (cf. Isa 49:8-13 with Isa 61:1). The apostle John later applied the language of the second Servant Song to the salvation of a multitude from many nations (Rev 7:16-17).

1. See also Shalom M. Paul, *Isaiah 40-66*, Eerdmans Critical Commentary (Grand Rapids: Eerdmans, 2012), 326.

2. Robert B. Chisholm, Jr., "The Christological Fulfillment of Isaiah's Servant Songs," *Bibliotheca Sacra* 163 (2006): 397-98. Christopher R. North says translations that try to make Yahweh the subject here are "grammatically possible, but they are awkward and involved" (*The Second Isaiah* [Oxford: Clarendon, 1964], 189). R. N. Whybray says making Yahweh the subject here is "syntactically clumsy" (*Isaiah 40-66*, New Century Bible Commentary [Grand Rapids: William B. Eerdmans, 1975], 138). John Goldingay and David Payne argue that the "order of clauses" suggests that "to restore" refers "to the role that Yhwh seeks to fulfill to Jacob-Israel through the servant Israel" (*Isaiah 40-55, Volume II*, International Critical Commentary [London: T&T Clark, 2006], 162).

3. See Tryggve N. D. Mettinger, *A Farewell to the Servant Songs*, trans. F. Cryer (Lund: CWK Gleerup, 1983), 34-37.

4. John N. Oswalt, *The Book of Isaiah, Chapters 40–66*, New International Commentary on the Old Testament (Grand Rapids: William B. Eerdmans, 1998), 291. See also Gordon P. Hugenberger, "The Servant of the Lord in the 'Servant Songs' of Isaiah: A Second Moses Figure," in *The Lord's Anointed: Interpretation of Old Testament Messianic Texts*, eds. Philip E. Satterthwaite, Richard S. Hess, and Gordon J. Wenham (Grand Rapids: Baker Books, 1995), 106-11; and J. Alec Motyer, *The Prophecy of Isaiah* (Downers Grove, IL: InterVarsity, 1993), 386.

5. Hugenberger, "The Servant of the Lord," 126–27.

6. See D. H. Odendahl, *The Eschatological Expectation of Isaiah 40-66 with Special Reference to Israel and the Nations* (Nutley, NJ: Presbyterian and Reformed, 1970), 132-33.

7. Hugenberger, "The Servant of the Lord," 134.

8. The Jewish Publication Society *Tanakh* translates this as "to the abhorred nations," seemingly to support the view that the Servant is collective Israel. However, the noun "nation" (*goy*) is singular, suggesting that the Servant is abhorred or despised by a nation, namely, the nation of Israel.

9. The text form from which Jesus reads differs in some details from the Hebrew text of Isa 61:1-2a. He also omits 61:2b-3, apparently for theological reasons. See Darrell L. Bock, *Luke, Volume 1:1–9:50*, Baker Exegetical Commentary on the New Testament (Grand Rapids: Baker, 1994), 404-05, 411.

10. On the parallels between Isa 61:1-3 and the Servant Songs, see Franz Delitzsch, *Biblical Commentary on the Prophecies of Isaiah* (reprint; trans. James Martin, 2 vols., Grand Rapids: Eerdmans, 1949), 2:425. Having surveyed the linguistic links, Delitzsch states: "For these reasons we have no doubt that we have here the words of the Servant of Jehovah." See as well the chart in John H. Walton, "The Imagery of the Substitute King Ritual in Isaiah's Fourth Servant Song," *Journal of Biblical Literature* 122 (2003): 742.

11. R. N. Whybray acknowledges the close connection between Isa 61:1-3 and the Servant Songs, but he identifies the Servant as Deutero-Isaiah and the speaker in 61:1-3 as Trito-Isaiah. See *Isaiah 40-66*, New Century Bible Commentary (Grand Rapids: William B. Eerdmans, 1975), 239-40. John Goldingay acknowledges that the imagery of Isa 61:1-3 is royal, but he sees the Davidic promises as democratized in Isa 55:3-5 and regards the speaker in Isa 61:1-3 as the prophet. See *Isaiah*, New International Bible Commentary (Peabody, MA: Hendrickson, 2001), 346.

Isaiah 50:4-11

The Mission of the Servant in a Darkened World

ELLIOTT E. JOHNSON

The third Servant song features the Servant's personal testimony. The first song speaks of the Servant's mission bringing justice, which extends to all nations (Isa 42:1-9). The second song is a testimony of His mission to restore Israel (49:5), as salvation extends to the nations (49:1-13). In the third song, the Servant again speaks personally about how He accomplishes that mission in a darkened world (42:7; 49:6; 50:10,11). One of the mysteries in the history of creation is God's permission of a darkened world for humanity. Although Israel was chosen to serve as a light to the nations in darkness (Gn 12:3; Ex 19:4-6), Isa 6 indicates that Israel too was blinded and deepened in the same darkness. Only the Servant will avoid sin, and this testimony discloses how that would happen (50:4-9). That testimony is followed by a word of caution from the prophet for those who fear the Lord in a dark world and those who choose to make their own light (apart from the Lord) in the darkness (50:10-11). The prophet clarifies the two options for them—to listen to the testimony of the Servant or to attempt to enlighten a direction for themselves.

Now this third song, unlike the earlier ones, does not identify the speaker as the Servant directly. In the prophet's conclusion (50:10-11), he speaks of the voice of the Servant who has spoken (50:4-9), and he needs to be heard by all other servants. This unique Servant is also identified by His uncompromised obedience (50:5b-6) and by His unqualified faith, without any doubt (50:7-9). In this fallen world, the prophecy has confronted Israel with their disobedience and their absence of faith, as the prophecy of Isaiah indicates. Thus, this song gives adequate evidence that this is the third in a series of four Servant songs.

The exposition that follows will feature three themes: The Servant Hearing God's Instruction (50:4-6); The Servant Trusting the Lord God (50:7-9); and The Prophet's Encouragement and Warning (50:10-11).

Since NT authors and many evangelical interpreters acknowledge that the Servant Songs prophesy about Jesus, the Messiah,[1] this article will include in the exposition the full meaning in the progress of revelation—*senus plenus* (full sense) but not *sensus plenior* (fuller sense). This sense acknowledges that NT authors, in their accounts of Jesus in the Gospels and Epistles, fill in meanings alluded to in a song but not directly expressed in the text. Nonetheless, the author intended the full meaning in what was expressed but not a fuller, expanded, or transformed meaning. So, the prophecy of the OT is true; it simply does not state the truth in its entirety. The NT authors specified truths implied in the original prophecy but clarified when the prophecy was fulfilled. An interpretation of a fuller meaning is not an interpretation but a revelation of meanings in addition to the original prophecy.

THE SERVANT HEARING GOD'S INSTRUCTION (50:4-6)

"The Servant here (but nowhere else) uses the designation *The Lord God* (*'donay YHWH*), which occurs four times in this passage and always at the beginning of a verse (vv. 4,5,7,9)."[2] The name highlights the majesty of God in spite of the fallen human race and the darkened creation. All else seems to have been affected by evil, but God. He remains sovereign over all creation and covenant partner with Israel. His word is *true*. His power is *sufficient* to be *trustworthy* in spite of the evil world. "All this meant nothing to Zion; it means everything to the Servant (5,7,9)."[3] The prominence of the Lord in the mind of the Servant indicates His recognition that He needs to be given what is essential to accomplish His mission.

That essential is an instructed tongue, or the *instructed tongue* of those who are taught—the disciples (*limmûdîm*, Isa 8:16). The Servant "was not endowed with an instant gift, an *instructed tongue*, but was subjected to the training procedures appropriate to all discipleship—concentration on the word of the Lord (as in 8:9-20)."[4] This gift accentuates the humanity of the Servant who needs to come to know, to be taught, what God's instruction means in the course of life in a darkened world. Childs seems to qualify this: "What the servant learned was not information but to accept the experience of suffering and change."[5] While information is not an end, it is an important aspect of scriptural revelation. And that information seems to be included in what the Servant was instructed about as the basis for His life and ministry, even though Isaiah does not specify the subject matter.

Scriptural revelation seems to be confirmed in the NT account of Jesus' life and ministry. In His earliest appearance, at 12 years of age, His parents "found Him in the temple complex sitting among the teachers, listening to them and asking them questions" (Lk 2:46). These were teachers of the law with whom He was conversing. "And all those who heard Him were astounded at His understanding and His answers" (2:47). He was learning as a disciple. Yet later in the same temple, they "were amazed [at His teaching] and said, 'How does he know the Scriptures, since he hasn't been trained?' Jesus answered them, 'My teaching isn't Mine but is from the One who sent Me'" (Jn 7:14-16). Thus, it was His Father in heaven who instructed Him about the meaning of the Scriptures.

Further, Hebrews specifies that Jesus, the Son of God, is able "to sympathize with our weaknesses" as "One who has been tested in every way as we are, yet without sin" (Heb 4:15). Overcoming temptation comes through the use of Scripture, as Jesus was tested by Satan (Mt 4:1-11 and Lk 4:1-13, quoting Dt 6:16,13).

To sustain the weary with a word—"The Word comes to all those who are weary of their own efforts to justify their living, those whose labors seem pointless to find rest in Him who comes to get into the harness with them (53:4-5; 61:1-3; Mt 11:28-29)."[6] Matthew's account alludes to this very word, "weary," for one burdened down in a dark world, who can only receive rest from the Servant's finished work and for one who finds rest in a partnership with Jesus, as a disciple is instructed by Him (11:28,29). As Jesus was sustained by the Father's Word, so Jesus sustains His own followers with the Father's Word.

Awakens Me each morning—"*He wakens* [v. 4] is a continuous tense. As in the case of the conqueror (41:2, 25; 45:13), the primary impulse comes from the Lord"; the instructed tongue "[was the product] of prolonged attention, defined here as the discipleship of the *morning-by-morning* appointment with God. Not that the Servant imposed this discipline on himself, but he showed his discipleship by responding to the Lord's disciplined and regular approach to him."[7] Delitzsch emphasizes it comes *each morning* in the full light of rationality and personal interaction.[8]

Awakens My ear to listen—The primary focus of awakening is to receive instruction. As demonstrated by the young Jesus visiting the Temple, He had learned the Scriptures. He had raised questions concerning their meaning. It may be assumed that Jesus had read or heard the Scriptures read at the local synagogue at Nazareth. Having the mind of a sinless human, He remembered flawlessly the words of the text. But the interpretation of those texts on which the Servant meditated became the focus of this daily instruction. And that became the substance of

His understanding that so amazed the Temple teachers. Nevertheless, the Servant learned from God just as any disciple would be instructed by a teacher.

Has opened My ear—It may seem surprising that God needed to open the Servant's ear (50:5), but that contrasts with His treatment of Israel (6:9-10). So, there must be something in the atmosphere of a darkened generation that compelled blindness (Jn 12:37-50) "to fulfill the word of Isaiah the prophet" (12:38). Moses had earlier revealed the need for this gift for his generation: "To this day the LORD has not given you a mind to understand, eyes to see, or ears to hear" (Dt 29:4).

Now, in judgment on the generations of Israel, both in Isaiah's day and in Jesus' day, the Lord commanded: "Dull the minds of these people; deafen their ears and blind their eyes; otherwise they might see with their eyes and hear with their ears, understand with their minds, turn back, be healed" (Isa 6:10). In distinction to his generation, the Servant had His ears opened to the Lord's instruction from His Word. The prophet Isaiah portrayed the need for this gift as a generational issue, one that had a personal application by the Servant.

An open ear that hears implies certain characteristics that can be enumerated. To hear implies that one is open, willing to be persuaded, and willing to obey God's commands in any way. Now these responses are delineated:

> I was not rebellious, or defiant (1:20; 3:8; 30:9), and
>
> I did not turn back or take evasive action (59:13).

In saying that He was not rebellious, the Servant was clearly distinguishing Himself from the nation of Israel. As Rydelnik and Spencer state, "There is only one place where the expression is used of Israel as not being rebellious (Ps 105:28) and that describes Israel before the exodus. Every time afterward the Scripture describes Israel as rebellious."[9]

This submissive response is clearly reflected in Jesus' prayer in Gethsemane. "My soul is swallowed up in sorrow—to the point of death . . . My Father, if this cannot pass unless I drink it, Your will be done" (Mt 26:38,42). Or "Father, if You are willing, take this cup away from Me—nevertheless, not My will, but Yours, be done" (Lk 22:42).

As Smart says, "From verse [50:]6 it becomes difficult to maintain that . . . the Servant . . . is no more than a personification (of Israel/the remnant). The impression is conveyed strongly that there is some one man who actually felt the blows."[10] In the retrospective perspective of the NT, what is implied in the OT is specified completely in the Gospel accounts:

> "I gave My back to those who beat Me, and My cheeks to those who tore out My beard. I did not hide My face from scorn and spitting" (Isa 50:6; see Mt 26:67; Lk 22:63-65; Jn 19:1-5).

> "The fact . . . is of a revelation of suffering to come, bravely faced and endured in obedience to the Lord God. Not a suffering because of wrongdoing (as 42:24; 50:1) but through costly obedience; a suffering not merited but accepted, described in terms of the judicial act of flogging, gratuitous torture, and personal humiliation."[11]

THE SERVANT TRUSTING "THE LORD GOD" (50:7-9)

The instruction of 50:4-5a led to the determination of will in 50:5b-7, and that instruction provides the reason for a confidence in God for the future (50:7-9).

Motyer summarizes: "If verse 6 reviews the past then 'helps' [v. 7] must be 'was helping me' (throughout). Out of this confidence of help comes certainty of outcome . . . and resolute determination to carry things through to success . . ."[12] Therefore, I have not been ashamed—"The presence of the waw conjunction on the first [Hebrew] word of v. 7 [this conjunction is left untranslated in the HCSB] makes plain that there is a sequential connection between the verses. The repetition of shame in the two verses further confirms the connection . . . This is the particular Hebrew use of 'shame' in the sense of being shown to have taken a foolish course of action. Yes, the Servant may have been set up for public ridicule, but in the end it will be amply proved that his decision to trust God, be obedient to him, and leave the outcome in his hands was the right decision."[13]

Therefore I have set My face like flint—This resolute determination to complete His mission is featured in the three synoptic accounts (Mt 16:21-23; Mk 8:31-33; and Lk 9:51). In Matthew's account, the phrase "From then on Jesus began . . ." highlights the decision. It follows the same use of the phrase to introduce His ministry: "From then on Jesus began to preach, 'Repent, because the kingdom of heaven has come near.'" Jesus had just resisted Satan in the wilderness, which was followed by these miraculous invasions into Satan's domain as a token of the coming near of the kingdom. At the climax of His ministry, Jesus began to go to Jerusalem to submit to Satan's power in death on the cross (16:21). Rather than an invasion of Satan's domain, the change represented a submission to the power of death. Peter resisted, but Jesus rebuked him because he had expressed Satan's interests (16:23). Satan preferred any alternative besides facing the Seed of the woman in direct conflict (Gn 3:15). As Luke's account recorded it, "When the days were coming to a close for Him to be taken up, He determined to journey to Jerusalem" (Lk 9:51).

And I know I will not be put to shame—"For He knows in the end it is not He but His adversaries who will be put to shame."[14] He would be taken up.

The *One who vindicates Me is near*—This verse anticipates a coming contest with opponents as a trial at law. "'Vindicates' is a forensic term meaning 'brings a verdict of innocent: He who vindicates me is the one who accounts me righteous.' 'Near' is parallel in meaning to *gō'ēl* (cf. Lv 21:2f; 25:25; Nm 27:11; Ru 2:20; 3:12). It means . . .'the Lord is on my side.'"[15] This picture is clearly consistent with the Gospel portrayal. Some six months before His trial, Jesus challenged the descendants of Abraham: "Who among you can convict Me of sin? If I tell the truth, why don't you believe Me? The one who is from God listens to God's words. This is why you don't listen, because you are not from God" (Jn 8:46-47). The active presence of God is described as in those *from God*, as those who are given ears to hear, who listen and believe. Those who contend with Me, who have a case against Me "don't listen, because [they] are not from God" (8:47).

This happened in the trial before Annas. In response to the question about His teaching, Jesus responded, "Why do you question Me? Question those who heard what I told them. Look, they know what I said" (Jn 18:19-23). After they brought Him "to the governor's headquarters," the Jewish leaders responded to Pilate's demand for evidence to support their charge, "If this man weren't a criminal, we wouldn't have handed Him over to you" (Jn 18:28-30). So, these religious leaders reached a verdict, not on the basis of what they heard from Jesus, nor on the basis of what they saw that Jesus did, but because they "want to carry out [their] father's desires. He was a murderer from the beginning and has not stood in the truth, because there is no truth in him" (Jn 8:44). While Israel's contention with Jesus seemed to succeed, yet Jesus awaited the Father's vindication.

Who will condemn Me? (50:9). The One who *vindicates* and the one who *condemns* "are formal antitheses of each other, much like a 'defense attorney' and a 'prosecuting attorney.' The Servant is confident that, with the help of his defense attorney, no prosecuting attorney would even have a case."[16] That case in reality consisted not merely in the trials, not merely on the cross, but also in the grave that had to enforce their verdict and condemnation. The ultimate *help* from God was expressed in Peter's words on the day of Pentecost: "You [Jews] used lawless people [Romans] to nail Him to a cross and kill Him. God raised Him up, ending the pains of death, because it was not possible for Him to be held by it" (Ac 2:23b-24). Because in truth He would not be condemned for personal sin but as a representative Servant, bearing the sin of all humanity (Isa 52:13–53:12). And the resurrection would loose Him from the case in which He was condemned.

THE PROPHET'S ENCOURAGEMENT AND WARNING (50:10-11)

The speaker now changes from the Servant to the prophet who challenges the audience based on the testimony of the Servant. The prophet addresses those who fear God (50:10) and those who reject Him (50:11). The common feature of both is that they walk in darkness, having no ability to see on their own to navigate their journey through the darkness of the world. The prophet's encouragement to those who fear God is to listen to the voice of the Servant (50:10a). Therefore, it is not surprising that Jesus would claim: "I am the light of the world. Anyone who follows Me will never walk in darkness but will have the light of life" (Jn 8:12). Then as Jesus and His disciples met a man born blind, Jesus would explain: "This came about so that God's works might be displayed in him. We must do the works of Him who sent Me while it is day. Night is coming when no one can work. As long as I am in the world, I am the light of the world" (Jn 9:3b-5).

This is compatible with the prophet's prophetic word in Isaiah. But for those believers living after Christ's first advent, a question remains about the coming night. What does Jesus have reference to? Carson correctly comments: "The focus here, however, is not what prevails after Jesus is glorified and has poured out his Spirit (7:37-39), but the darkness of the period when Jesus is first taken from his disciples. The association of the disciples with Jesus' work ('we must do . . .') refers to the period before Jesus is taken away by the cross, not to the period when, empowered by the Spirit, they will work until he returns."[17] So, the words of the prophet in Isa 50:10-11 apply to followers of the Servant, whose world is filled with darkness in the absence of Jesus Christ. Yet His voice still enlightens the way for those who fear God.

Motyer clarifies the significance of walking in darkness (50:10). He writes, "To walk in darkness and have no light is part of the description of the one who fears and hears. Those who commit themselves to the Servant-way will have a Servant experience, normative for them because true of him. It is not an indication that they have missed the will of God but is, as for the Servant, intrinsic to the life of obedience."[18] This call to listen to the Servant anticipates a natural transition to "listen to Me" (51:1,7). Zion is the Lord's people (51:16), and the message to Zion is "Your God reigns!" (52:7).

By contrast, a warning is addressed to those who disregard the voice of the Servant (50:11). The image is vivid, speaking of fire and firebrands lit and perhaps attached to themselves. However, the point of lighting the fires is interpreted differently. Ridderbos posits that "in their hostility to the Servant of the Lord they light a fire, as it were, to destroy Him."[19] More likely, since walking in darkness is common to both verses (50:10-11), they who reject the voice and light of the Servant

(50:10) must kindle a fire and walk in the light of their own fire. Ironically, "the thought is reminiscent of the closing verses of chap. 8, where the persons who have refused the light of God are plunged into a deep darkness in which they turn to the occult to light the way for them. Those flames may well eat their bearer alive."[20] Ahaz calling to Assyria was such an instance on behalf of Israel.

CONCLUSION

The third Servant Song is a testimony. In that testimony, the Servant appreciated the Lord God's instruction that He did not resist. As a result, the Servant will rest in help coming from the Lord God, in spite of the enemy contending with him (50:4-9). To bring justice (42:1-9), the Servant will face legal judgment from the enemy and overcome (50:6-11). To bring salvation (49:1-13), the Servant will provide a substitutionary sacrifice from which He will be saved along with those who are His own. The prophet finally cautions Israel to heed the voice of the Servant (50:10) or suffer the consequences (50:11).

1. J. Ridderbos, *Isaiah*, Bible Student's Commentary (Grand Rapids: Zondervan, 1985), 365–70.
2. E. J. Young, *The Book of Isaiah III,* chaps. XL–LXVI (Grand Rapids: Eerdmans, 1972), 298.
3. J. Alec Motyer, *The Prophecy of Isaiah* (Downers Grove, IL: InterVarsity, 1993), 399.
4. Ibid.
5. Breward S. Childs, *Isaiah* (Louisville, KY: Westminster John Knox, 2001), 394.
6. John N. Oswalt, *The Book of Isaiah, Chapters 40–66* (Grand Rapids: Eerdmans, 1998), 324.
7. Motyer, *Prophecy of Isaiah,* 399.
8. Franz Delitzsch, *Commentary on Isaiah*, vol. 2 (Grand Rapids: Eerdmans, 1973).
9. Michael Rydelnik and James Spencer, "Isaiah" in *The Moody Bible Commentary*, ed. Michael Rydelnik and Michael Vanlaningham (Chicago: Moody Publishers, 2014), 1083–84.
10. J. D. Smart, *History and Theology in Second Isaiah* (Philadelphia: Epworth, 1965), 165.
11. Motyer, *Prophecy of Isaiah,* 400.
12. Ibid.
13. Oswalt, *Book of Isaiah,* 325.
14. Ridderbos, *Isaiah*, 451.
15. Motyer, *Prophecy of Isaiah,* 400.
16. Oswalt, *Book of Isaiah,* 326.
17. D. A. Carson, *The Gospel According to John* (Grand Rapids: Eerdmans, 1991), 363.
18. Motyer, *Prophecy of Isaiah,* 401.
19. Ridderbos, *Isaiah,* 452.
20. Oswalt, *Book of Isaiah,* 330.

Isaiah 52:13–53:12

The Substitution of the Servant of the Lord

MICHAEL L. BROWN

At the center of the gospel message is the atoning, substitutionary death of Jesus the Messiah, and nowhere in the Bible is this theme of vicarious suffering laid out more clearly than in Isa 53. Accordingly, among those who affirm Jesus as the Messiah of Israel, this chapter (or, more precisely, Isa 52:13–53:12) is widely considered to be the most specific messianic prophecy in the Tanakh. While it is not quoted in the New Testament as frequently as Ps 110,[1] it has been pointed to through the centuries as a central messianic prophecy because of its clearly expressed theology of vicarious atonement, its vivid description of the Servant of the Lord being rejected by His own people, and its glorious portrayal of the Servant's exaltation.

Of this passage, Franz Delitzsch exclaimed, "How many are there whose eyes have been opened when reading this 'golden passional of the Old Testament evangelist,' as Polycarp the Lysian calls it! In how many an Israelite has it melted the crust of his heart! It looks as if it had been written beneath the cross upon Golgotha, and was illuminated by the heavenly brightness of the full *shēb lîmînî* ('sit at my right hand')."[2]

Nonetheless, this passage has numerous interpretative issues that must be addressed, including: (1) How does this prophecy relate to the larger context of Isa 40–55, which focuses on Judah's return from Babylonian exile? (2) Who is the Servant of the Lord in Isaiah 52:13–53:12? Is it the nation of Israel, the righteous remnant within Israel, the prophet, an unidentified individual, or the Messiah Himself? (3) What is the history of interpretation of Isa 53, especially in traditional

Jewish sources? (4) What is the passage actually saying, and who are the principal speakers? (5) What were the biblical antecedents to the theology of vicarious atonement expressed so clearly in this pericope? (6) How can this chapter be applied to the Messiah?

THE LARGER CONTEXT OF ISAIAH 53

Judah's exile was predicted in chaps. 1–39 (see, e.g., 6:9-13, and then note 39:3-7, which is especially significant, given its placement immediately before chap. 40), and the return of the Jewish people from exile is a central theme of chaps. 40–55. More central still is the theme of the supremacy of Yahweh the God of Israel over the gods of the nations, who are not really gods at all. He alone predicted the exile and the return, and He alone orders history, raising up Cyrus to restore the exiles and rebuild Jerusalem (see 44:24–45:7). These chapters, then, portray the return from exile as the backdrop for God's salvific actions in the earth.

In keeping with other prophetic voices (see, e.g., Jer 3:14-18; 23:8; Ezk 34:1-31; 36:16-38), Isaiah saw the future glory of Israel and the work of the Messiah in the context of the end of the exile, speaking of a new beginning for Israel, a new creation, a new exodus, and a time when all the world will see the glory of the Lord (see 40:3-5; 41:17-20; 42:14-16; 43:1-3,14-21; 48:20-21; 49:8-12; 51:9-10; 52:11-12; 55:12-13). The events predicted here are thus far greater than the return of about 45,000 Jews from Babylon in the sixth century BC. Rather, in these passages in Isaiah, the exile also serves as a symbol of the spiritual bondage of the Jewish people, while the return from exile serves as a figure of their redemption. These prophecies of redemption culminate in Isa 52:13–53:12, which leads to the exuberant cries that open up chap. 54, and some have suggested that, with the new exodus, there is a new Moses, namely the Servant of Isa 53 (see, e.g., Klaus Baltzer; G. P. Hugenberger).[3]

THE IDENTITY OF THE SERVANT

Christian interpreters have identified four Servant songs in Isa 40–55, based on what appears to be the individual identity of the Servant in 42:1-4 (some include 5-7); 49:1-6 (some include 7-11); 50:4-10; and 52:13–53:12. While this is attractive, given the apparent thematic harmony of these four passages, it is best to examine every reference to the word servant (Hebrew *'ebed*) in chaps. 40–55 before isolating any of the texts from their larger context. This will bring 52:13–53:12 into clearer focus.

The noun *'ebed* (in the singular) appears a total of 17 times in Isa 40–51, sometimes with reference to the nation of Israel as a whole (41:8-9; 42:19 [2x]; 43:10;

44:21 [2x]; 45:4; 48:20), and sometimes with reference to a righteous individual within the nation (49:1-2,4-7; 50:10). In several verses, it is not clear whether an individual or the nation (or, perhaps the righteous remnant within the nation) is referred to, although a good case can be made for the individual interpretation (42:1; 44:1-2).[4] The noun occurs again in 52:13 and 53:11, with an individual interpretation appearing to be the most likely, which would mean that the references to the servant *as a people* actually end with Isa 48:20, while the references to the servant *as an individual* come into clearest focus beginning with Isa 49 and continuing through the end of chap. 53. Accordingly, in chaps. 40–48, "Israel" occurs 34x and "Jacob" 19x, whereas in chaps. 49–53, "Israel" occurs 6x (5 in chap. 49) and "Jacob" 3x (all in chap. 49). Thus, by the time Isa 52:13 is reached, the spotlight is on a person, not a people, although the person is certainly connected to his people. ("Servant" in the singular does not occur again in Isaiah after 53:11; in the plural, see 54:17; 56:6; 63:17; 65:9,13 [3x],14-15; 66:14.)

Rabbinic exegesis also recognizes an individual servant in several passages; cf., e.g., Targum to 42:1; 52:13 (the Messiah; this is expressed even more clearly in Midrash Tanchuma to 52:13; see below); Rashi and Ibn Ezra to 49:1 (the prophet); Radak to 42:1 (the Messiah), 49:1 and 50:10 (the prophet); Abravanel to 42:1 (the Messiah), 49:1, and 50:10 (the prophet); note also that Rashi interprets 50:10 with reference to the prophets. It is therefore inaccurate to state that traditional Jewish exegesis always recognizes Israel as the servant of the Lord in Isa 40–55, since an individual servant (either the Messiah or the prophet) is identified by the rabbis in several passages outside of Isa 53. Significantly, in 49:1-6, the Servant, who is clearly an individual, is called "Israel" in v. 3 but has the mission of restoring Jacob and regathering Israel in vv. 5-6.

As stated in Metzudat David, "Behold, before Me, you [meaning the prophet] are like the multitude of Israel [*hāmôn yiśrā'ēl*], and I will be glorified in you as in all of them" (cf. Ibn Ezra, who explains that God views the servant, who is the prophet, as if he were all Israel). Thus, the servant of the Lord, as an individual within Israel, fulfills the mission of Israel, which includes being a light to the nations (49:6-7; see also 42:3-7; remember that Israel was first a personal name before being a corporate name, just as was the case with Jacob, so a personal use of the name in 49:3 is hardly inappropriate).

Note also that while the Servant of the Lord in Isa 53 is a righteous, guiltless sufferer (see further below), Israel as the servant is often anything but righteous. Thus, in 42:24-25, it is stated that the servant Israel was exiled because of sin, incurring God's wrath; in 43:8, servant Israel is blind and deaf (see also 42:18-19); in 43:22-28, Israel fails to call on the Lord; in 47:6, God is angry with Israel; in 48:1-6, Israel is guilty again, with the exile and return foretold (see also 48:8b-11,17-19);

and in 50:1, God's indictment is forthright: "for your iniquities you were sold, and for your transgressions your mother was sent away" (Isa 50:1 ESV; being "sold" and "sent away" is synonymous with being exiled). As noted by Hugenberger, "Deutero-Isaiah repeatedly stresses that contemporary Israel is a sinful people who suffer on account of their own transgressions (40:2; 42:18-25; 43:22-28; 47:7; 48:18f.; 50:1; 54:7; 57:17; 59:2ff.). This point is made specifically with reference to the remnant in 43:22; 46:3,12; 48:1,8; 53:6,8; 55:7; 58:1ff.; 63:17; 64:5-7."[5]

This is in harmony with prophetic voices like Amos (e.g., 4:4-12) and Hosea (e.g., 5:7-15), along with the explicit testimony of 2Kg 17 (see esp. vv. 7-23), stating emphatically that the Assyrian exile of the 10 northern tribes of Israel was because of Israel's persistent, unrepentant rebellion and sin. Correspondingly, prophets like Jeremiah (e.g., 32:28-36) and Ezekiel (e.g., 5:5-17), along with the explicit testimony of 2Chr 36 (see esp. vv. 15-16), state emphatically that the Babylonian exile of the southern tribes of Judah was because of Judah's persistent, unrepentant rebellion and sin. This is confirmed by the retrospective testimony of Lamentations (1:5,8,14,18,20,22; 2:14; 3:40-42; 4:12-13; 5:7,16), along with Ezra (9:6-7), Nehemiah (9:26-36), Daniel (9:4-13), and Zechariah (1:1-6).

Traditional Jewish exegesis primarily sees Israel (or, the righteous remnant of Israel) as the servant of Isa 53, understanding 52:14–53:8 to reflect the astonishment of kings of the nations, who, upon Israel's future exaltation (52:13) are shocked to realize that the people of Israel, who were exiled in their midst, were not suffering for their own sins but rather for the sins of these foreign countries. And, these kings realize, it was Israel's suffering that brought them forgiveness and healing.

Thus, Rashi and a number of other Jewish interpreters understood Isa 53 to be speaking of vicarious sufferings—indeed, even vicarious atonement—despite the difficulty of explaining how this applied to the effects of Israel's suffering in exile. Rashi commented (to 53:4) that the servant "was chastised with pains so that all the nations be atoned for with Israel's suffering. . . . he was chastised so that there be peace for the entire world." Similarly, the 11th century rabbi Yoseph Kara wrote that, "the Holy One created for Himself one just nation in the world, which carried on itself all iniquities in order that the whole world might be preserved; *and by his stripes* there was healing for us." In keeping with this, the 13th century, anti-Christian apologist rabbi Yoseph ben Nathan explained, "*But he carried our sickness*: now we [meaning, the Gentile kings] see that that was not the cause: the sickness which ought to have come upon us, came upon him, and through them atonement was made for us: his chastenings were for our transgressions, and they resulted in our peace; the Holy One did not, as he would otherwise have done, destroy the world for our iniquities."[6]

Rabbi Yehudah HaLevi in the Kuzari also understood Isa 53 to speak of vicarious suffering, with reference again to Israel's sufferings in exile: "Now we are burdened by them [viz., the infirmities and diseases of Isa. 53:4], whilst the whole enjoys rest and prosperity. The trials which meet us are meant to prove our faith, to cleanse us completely, and to remove all taint from us. If we are good the Divine Influence is with us in this world" [2:44, Hirschfeld tr.].[7] And then, the heart of the matter from the Kuzari is as reproduced almost verbatim by Isaac Troki, the Karaite polemicist and author in his work *Hizzuk Emunah*, "Faith Strengthened": "The reason for this is that Israel is the choicest of human kind, just as the heart is the choicest organ in the body; when, therefore, they are in exile in the midst of the nations, like the heart in the midst of the other organs, they bear all the calamities which fall upon the Gentiles in whose midst they are exactly as the heart bears the bitterness and anguish of all the body in the centre of which it resides."[8]

All this, however, is completely untenable in the larger biblical context (see above, with reference to the unanimous testimony of the prophets, priests, and leaders that Israel and Judah were justly exiled because of their many sins). Ezekiel tells us what the verdict of the nations will be regarding the cause of Israel's exile: "And the nations shall know that the House of Israel were exiled only for their iniquity, because they trespassed against Me, so that I hid My face from them and delivered them into the hands of their adversaries, and they all fell by the sword. When I hid My face from them, I dealt with them according to their uncleanness and their transgressions" (Ezk 39:23-24 NJPS).

So, far from the nations discovering that the people Israel were not suffering for their own sins but rather for those of the nations, these nations learn that "the House of Israel were exiled only for their iniquity." Moreover, Israel's sufferings in exile did not bring healing to the nations but rather judgment. As stated in Jer 50:17-18 (ESV), "Israel is a hunted sheep driven away by lions. First the king of Assyria devoured him, and now at last Nebuchadnezzar king of Babylon has gnawed his bones. Therefore, thus says the Lord of hosts, the God of Israel: Behold, I am bringing punishment on the king of Babylon and his land, as I punished the king of Assyria" (for the general principle of God destroying the nations to which He exiled His people, see Jer 30:11; Zch 2:6-9).

In sum, the national servant, Israel, is loved by God but guilty, blind, and deaf, suffering for its own sins. The individual Servant is righteous, suffering vicariously for the sins of others. This agrees with the Sinai theology of blessings for national obedience and curses for national disobedience (Lv 26; Dt 28). In light of this, righteous, national Israel would be established in the land, triumphing over her enemies; unrighteous Israel would be exiled to the nations, vanquished by her enemies. In the words of Daniel, uttered while in Babylonian captivity, "All Israel has transgressed your law and turned aside, refusing to obey your voice. And the curse and oath that are written in the Law of Moses the servant of God have been poured out upon us, because we have sinned against him" (Dn 9:11 ESV). Under no circumstances, then, would the Lord exile Israel if they were righteous as a people. Thus Isa 53 cannot apply to the nation of Israel, regardless of longstanding Jewish tradition.

Could Isa 53 instead apply to the righteous remnant, as posited by some rabbinic commentators? The voice of that remnant appears to be heard in passages like Ps 44, where the author protests that terrible calamities have come upon his people "though we have not forgotten you, and we have not been false to your covenant" (Ps 44:17 ESV).

Certainly, there were righteous individuals like Daniel and Ezekiel who suffered in exile because of the guilt of the nation as a whole. Yet once again, this interpretation breaks down since: (1) The suffering of the righteous remnant did not bring healing to the nations which, instead, were severely judged by the Lord for their excessive treatment of Israel (see above, with reference to Jer 50:17-18; see also Mic 5:5-6, where God's deliverance of His people means judgments for the oppressor nations); (2) In contrast to Ibn Ezra's view, that the "healing" of the nations came through exiled Israel's prayers for their wellbeing (in keeping with Jer 29:7), not only were those nations not healed, but it appears that the righteous remnant interceded for judgment (rather than healing) to come upon their enemies. See, e.g., Lam 1:22 and 3:61-66, and note that this righteous remnant identified with the sin and guilt of the rest of the nation of Israel, thereby recognizing that their suffering was just; (3) Since the servant is clearly an individual elsewhere in Isa 40–55 (see again above), and since Isa 53 reads most naturally as personal rather than collective, there is no good reason to apply it to the righteous remnant, unless that remnant is reduced to one, namely, the Messiah, the truly righteous One whose vicarious suffering brings healing to repentant Israel and the nations.

HISTORY OF INTERPRETATION

In keeping with ancient rabbinic interpretation of biblical texts, there was no systematic, exegetical treatment of the passage as a whole in the talmudic and midrashic writings, with the most comprehensive (and surprising) interpretation found in the Targum. To summarize traditional Jewish interpretation of Isa 53 up through the 16th century of this era: Targum Jonathan interprets Isa 53 with reference to the Messiah, but with a fairly radical reworking of the text, emphasizing the Messiah's victory rather than His suffering, and with some application of the text to the nation of Israel as a whole, which does suffer. In the Palestinian Talmud, 53:12 is applied to Rabbi Akiva (y. Shekalim 5:1); in the Babylonian Talmud, 53:4 is explained with reference to the Messiah (the "leper scholar") in Sanhedrin 98b; 53:10 is applied to those whom God disciplines (b. Berakhot 5a); 53:10 is cited as a word of encouragement for the recovering sick person (b. Berakhot 57b); 53:12 is explained with reference to Moses (b. Sotah 14a).

In the major midrashim, which make homiletical, atomistic application of the texts, Numbers Rabbah 13:2 refers 53:12 to Israel in exile and Ruth Rabbah 5:6 interprets 53:5 with reference to the Messiah. Midrash Tanchuma applies both 52:13, speaking of the servant's exaltation, as well as 53:3, "a man of suffering who knew what sickness was," to the Messiah. Yalkut Shimoni (a 13th compilation of earlier midrashic writings) applies 52:13 to the Messiah, stating that the Messiah, called the great mountain according to the Yalkut's interpretation of Zch 4:7, is "greater than the patriarchs . . . higher than Abraham . . . lifted up above Moses . . . and loftier than the ministering angels" (2:571; see also 2:621; this follows Midrash Tanchuma). Isaiah 53:5 is applied to the sufferings of "King Messiah" (2:620). In Sifrei, Parashat Pinchas, Paragraph 131, 53:12 is applied to Phinehas (Pinchas) son of Eleazar (Nm 25:1-13). Midrash Tehillim (Psalms) to Ps 2:7 applies 53:12 to the Messiah. Later (and more minor) midrashic works continue to make varied application of the text, including references to Israel, individuals, and the Messiah.

The 10th century philosopher Sa'adia Gaon interprets the entire passage with reference to Jeremiah, while in the next two centuries, Rashi, Ibn Ezra, and Radak, the influential "big three" interpreters, all understand the passage to apply to Israel or the righteous remnant. Rambam (Maimonides) refers Isa 53:2 (along with the "Branch" prophecy in Zch 6:12) to the Messiah in his Letter to Yemen (Iggeret Teman). Ramban (Nachmanides), while stating that the text in reality referred to Israel, followed the Messianic interpretation of the text found in the Midrash (see Tanchuma and Yalkut, just cited), beginning with the Messiah's highly exalted state based on 52:13. Noteworthy also is the oft-quoted comment of Rabbi Moshe Alshech, writing in the 16th century, that, "Our rabbis with one voice accept and affirm the opinion that the prophet is speaking of the Messiah, and we shall ourselves also adhere to the same view," although this statement seems to be pointing primarily to 52:13–53:1 as opposed to the entire chapter.[9] In the Zohar, Isa 53 is applied to the vicarious suffering of the righteous, to Israel, to individuals, and to the Messiah, who also suffers vicariously.

There is also Christian testimony that the corporate interpretation was attested as far back as Origen, who wrote in the early third century work *Contra Celsum*: "Now I remember that, on one occasion, at a disputation held with certain Jews, who were reckoned wise men, I quoted these prophecies; to which my Jewish opponent replied, that these predictions bore reference to the whole people, regarded as one individual, and as being in a state of dispersion and suffering, in order that many proselytes might be gained, on account of the dispersion of the Jews among numerous heathen nations. And in this way, he explained the words, 'Thy form shall be of no reputation among men;' and then, 'They to whom no message was sent respecting him shall see;' and the expression, 'A man under suffering.'"[10]

This passage appears to confirm the rabbinic response to the Christian/ Messianic Jewish argument that the messianic interpretation, rather than the corporate interpretation, was prevalent before the time of the 11th century commentator Rashi. To the contrary, rabbinic apologists answer, it was the corporate interpretation that was prevalent.[11] A more nuanced answer would be that: (1) other than in the Targum, which consistently deviates from the plain sense of the text, Isa 53 was not treated systematically before the time of Sa'adiah Gaon, followed by Rashi, Ibn Ezra, and Radak, as was the case for most of the Tanakh prior to the 11th century; (2) Isa 53 is variously applied to Israel, the righteous remnant, the Messiah, and other individuals, but primarily in homiletical, non-contextual citations; (3) prior to the medieval exegetical works, 52:13 was commonly applied to the Messiah in His exaltation.[12]

As expected, the patristic literature follows the example of the NT and sees Isa 53 as a direct prophecy of Jesus the Messiah. As summarized by Laato, the text "played a central role in catechumenical teaching. It provided a suitable starting-point to present the Christian kerygma as indicated in the account in Acts 8. . . . With its aid the Christian theologians have refuted different Christological heresies."[13]

THE MESSAGE OF ISAIAH 52:13–53:12

As Lot urged his family to flee Sodom (Gn 19:14) and as Pharaoh urged Moses and Aaron to flee Egypt with the people of Israel (Ex 12:31), so the Lord urges the Judean exiles to flee Babylon in Isa 52:11 (see also 48:20; Jer 51:45, all with *tsĕ'û*, get out). But this time, in contrast with the exodus from Egypt, where the Passover lamb was sacrificed and eaten in haste and the departure itself was conducted in haste (*hipāzôn*; see Ex 12:11; Dt 16:3), the exodus from Babylon will not be in haste or by flight, since the Lord will march before them and behind them (see Isa 52:12). As noted by Seth Postell, "This blatant reference to the Exodus and the Feast of Passover appears to establish the literary context for understanding the ministry of the Suffering Servant: he is to die as a lamb for the redemption of his people (see Jn 1:29; Isa 53:7 LXX)."[14]

Against this clear backdrop, as the nation marches out of Babylon, a singular figure emerges, a new leader of the nation, even a new Moses, the Servant of the Lord who will be highly exalted (52:13; elsewhere in Isaiah, the verb couplet of being "high" and "lifted up" (*r-w-m* and *n-ś-'*) is used only for the Lord, see 6:1; here, it is joined with *g-b-h*, be exalted). As a famous midrash states, this Servant of the Lord, identified with the Messiah, will be "greater than the patriarchs . . . higher than Abraham . . . lifted up above Moses . . . and loftier than the ministering angels" (Yalqut Shimoni 2:571, following Midrash Tanchuma). First, however, the Servant will suffer extreme disfigurement to the point of being almost unrecognizable as a man (52:14). But just as surely as He was disfigured, so will he ritually sprinkle (or, startle; cf. LXX) many nations to the point that the kings of these nations will be astonished and dumbstruck by what they see and hear.[15]

Isaiah 53:1 then asks, "Who has believed what he has heard from us? And to whom has the arm of the LORD been revealed?" Traditional Jewish exegesis from Rashi on (see above, #3) has put these words on the lips of the just-mentioned kings of the nations (52:15). Having been startled by what they heard (from š-m-'), they now ask, "Who believes us when we declare what we heard [again, from š-m-'], namely, what we have discovered about Israel, the servant of the Lord?" But there are serious problems with this interpretation, most pointedly the issue of vocabulary and style. As Hugenberger observed, "throughout Isaiah whenever the pronouns 'we,' 'our,' or 'us' are introduced abruptly, as in 53:1ff. (that is, without an explicit identification of the speakers, as in 2:3; 3:6; 4:1; etc.), it is always the prophet speaking on behalf of the people of Israel with whom he identifies (1:9f.; 16:6; 24:26; 33:2,20; 42:24; 59:9-12; 63:15-19; 64:3-11; etc.). Accordingly, if the 'we' or 'us' in 53:1ff. is the prophet speaking on behalf of Israel, then the 'he' or 'him' of these same verses cannot also be a reference to Israel,"[16] and the "we" cannot be the kings of the nations. This also means that the prophet cannot be speaking of himself in the verses that follow.

Speaking, then, for his people, the prophet asks, who has believed this startling news and to whom has God's salvific action ("the arm of the LORD"; see 51:9) been revealed? He observes that this Servant, one day to be highly exalted, had inauspicious beginnings, with nothing special about His outward appearance (53:2). In fact, He was a Man shunned and despised, a man intimate with pain and suffering, and we did not esteem Him (53:3). Yet the suffering He endured was for us—He suffered for our sins and was carrying our pain—but we, for our part, judged Him to be smitten by God. He was paying the price for our guilt, yet we judged Him to be a guilty sinner (53:4). The reality is that everything He endured—being pierced and crushed and punished—was in payment for our transgressions, and our healing and well-being came at the price of His wounds (53:5). Indeed, every single one of us—all but Him—have strayed far from God's path and gone our own way, yet the LORD laid the guilt and iniquity of all of us on Him (53:6).

Strikingly, as this Servant is being afflicted and attacked, He neither defends Himself nor protests, just as a lamb goes to slaughter (53:7; perhaps this is an allusion to the imagery of the Passover lamb). He is taken away through violent injustice and put to death (lit. cut off from the land of the living), suffering the stroke that was due to the prophet's (or God's) people (53:8).[17] Both His death[18] and burial were ignominious, even though He Himself was guiltless, committing no violence and speaking no deceit (53:9). But all this happened by the explicit will of God, who crushed Him in order that the Servant would make His own life a guilt offering (*'āšām*)[19] so that He would see future generations (lit. seed, offspring), His life would be extended (= resurrection; cf. also 4QIsa[a]), and He would succeed in doing God's work (53:10), ultimately seeing the light (of life).[20] As a result of this, the Lord Himself declares, His righteous Servant will make many righteous, having also carried their iniquities (53:11). Accordingly, God will apportion His reward with the mighty and strong, since He suffered vicariously for sinners, among whom He was counted, and for whom He died (53:12).

The comment of Delitzsch, quoted at the beginning of this article, seems even more justified now, stating that this chapter "looks as if it had been written beneath the cross upon Golgotha." But it would be wrong to argue, as some critics and counter-missionaries[21] have, that the NT writers constructed the narrative of Jesus' suffering and death based on this passage so as to give the impression that prophecy was being fulfilled. First, scholars recognize the historicity of the crucifixion of Jesus, so the events at His ignominious suffering are not in dispute, being confirmed in the Talmud (b. Sanh. 43a; t. Sanh. 10:11; y. Sanh. 7:16,67a) and Mishneh Torah as well (*Hilkhot Melakhim*, 11). Second, although the NT does point back to Isa 53 on several occasions (see note 1), it is not the most quoted passage from the Tanakh (see Ps 110), and had the Gospel authors wanted to draw more attention to the striking fulfillment of Isa 53 in their writing, they would have quoted it far more often.[22]

BIBLICAL ANTECEDENTS TO VICARIOUS SUFFERING AND ATONEMENT

According to Hermann Spieckermann, "Five criteria seem central to the idea of vicarious suffering in Isaiah 53: a. One person intercedes for the sins of others. . . . b. The one who intercedes for the sins of others is himself sinless and righteous. . . . c. The vicarious act of the one occurs once for all. . . . d. One intercedes for the sins of others of his own will. . . . e. God brings about the vicarious action of the one for the sins of the others intentionally."[23] Or, as expressed by Bernd Janowski: "The bottomless depth of this text is reflected in the vicarious event: an innocent one bears the guilt of others, perishes by it, and will nevertheless have 'success.'"[24] But are there biblical antecedents to this concept of vicarious suffering and atonement?

Shalom Paul, while rejecting a messianic interpretation of Isa 53, writes, "What makes this servant song sui generis is the idea of suffering for another. The servant bears the sins of the many, and because of his afflictions the multitude is forgiven—an idea that became axiomatic to Christianity, which interpreted these verses as referring to the death and resurrection of Jesus.

The roots of this belief that one can be held culpable for the sin of another, however, appear in a number of places throughout the Hebrew Bible." In support of this, he cites: (1) texts that speak of the guilt of one generation being visited on the next (cf. Ex 20:5; 34:7; Nm 14:18; Dt 5:9; see also Nm 14:33; Lam 5:7); (2) texts that speak of the punishment of guilty leaders satisfying judgment for the nation (Nm 25:4); (3) texts that speak of intercessory acts (Ezk 4:4-6); and (4) texts that speak of an animal being sacrificed in place of a person (Gn 22:13; Ex 13:13; 34:20; Lv 4:13-21; and see especially Lv 16:22). He also notes, "For further examples of this 'bearing of the cross' for another's sake, note the case of accidental manslaughter, in which the murderer must reside in a chosen city of refuge until the death of the high priest, and only 'after the death of the high priest may the manslayer return to his landholding' (Num 35:28), as well as the annulment of a wife's vows *post facto* by her husband: 'But if he annuls them some time after he has heard them, he shall bear her guilt' (Num 30:16). The prophet confronts the issue of theodicy and offers his interpretation of the people's suffering."[25]

Similarly, Orthodox rabbi and historian Berel Wein, speaking of the Jewish people's ability to endure terrible suffering and martyrdom, wrote,

> Another consideration tinged the Jewish response to the slaughter of its people. It was an old Jewish tradition dating back to Biblical times that the death of the righteous and innocent served as an expiation for the sins of the nation or the world. The stories of Isaac and of Nadav and Avihu, the prophetic description of Israel as the longsuffering servant of the Lord, the sacrificial service in the Temple—all served to reinforce this basic concept of the death of the righteous as an atonement for the sins of other men. . . . This spirit of the Jews is truly reflected in the historical chronicle of the time [meaning, the 17th century]: "Would the Holy One, Blessed is He, dispense judgment without justice? But we may say that he whom God loves will be chastised. For since the day the Holy Temple was destroyed, the righteous are seized by death for the iniquities of the generation." (*Yeven Metzulah*, end of chap. 15).[26]

That Jewish theology developed the concept of the atoning power of the death of the righteous, despite its centrality in Christian theology, indicates just how deep the biblical roots of vicarious suffering can be found, even if they are brought to a distinct climax in Isa 53.

ISAIAH 53 AS A MESSIANIC PROPHECY

While we have no way of knowing if there was any figure contemporary with the author of Isa 53 who served as an inspiration for the theme of the chapter, the chapter finds striking and specific fulfillment in the life, death, and resurrection of Jesus. But since there is no reference here to "David" (see, e.g., Ezk 34:23-24; 37:24-25) or to the "stump of Jesse" (see Isa 11:1), one might question on what basis this passage can be identified as messianic. First, Isa 53 connects to the priestly ministry of the Messiah, an essential and important part of his work (see Zch 6:9-13), and the chapter is filled with priestly language (cf. Paul). Second, the promised exaltation of the Servant (Isa 52:13; 53:12) is in messianic proportions. Third, the Servant of the Lord fulfills the mission of failing Israel, becoming a light to the nations while being rejected by His own people before ultimately regathering and restoring the tribes of Jacob (see Isa 42:1-7; 49:1-7). No one other than the Messiah is tasked with this mission, and it is Isa 53 that opens up the dimensions of just how this will happen, as the people of Israel realize that the One they thought was dying a criminal's death was actually paying the price for their sins. It is through His wounds that Israel will be healed.

F. B. Meyer was correct in saying, "There is only one brow upon which this crown of thorns will fit."[27] It is Jesus of Nazareth, who suffered innocently, died vicariously, was raised gloriously, and will return triumphantly, just as Isaiah foretold.

---

1. See Ps 110; for the use of Isa 53 in the NT, see the following chapters in Darrell Bock and Mitch Glaser, eds., *The Gospel According to Isaiah 53: Encountering the Suffering Servant in Jewish and Christian Theology* (Grand Rapids: Kregel, 2012): Michael J. Wilkins, "Isaiah 53 and the Message of Salvation in the Four Gospels," 109–132; Darrell Bock, "Isaiah 53 in Acts 8," 133–144; and Craig A. Evans, "Isaiah 53 in the Letter of Peter, Paul, Hebrews, and John," 145–170. See also William H. Bellinger and William R. Farmer, eds., *Jesus and the Suffering Servant: Isaiah 53 and Christian Origins* (Harrisburg: Trinity Press International, 1998). See also the relevant articles in Bernd Janowski and Peter Stuhlmacher, eds., *The Suffering Servant: Isaiah 53 in Jewish and Christian Sources*, Eng. trans. Daniel Bailey (Grand Rapids: Eerdmans, 2004).

2. *Keil and Delitzsch Commentary on the Old Testament* (New Updated Ed., Electronic Database; Peabody, MA: Hendrickson Publishers, 1996), to Isaiah 52:13.

3. Klaus Baltzer, *Deutero-Isaiah: A Commentary on Isaiah 40–55*, Hermeneia, Eng. trans. Margaret Kohl (Philadelphia: Fortress, 2001); G. P. Hugenberger, "The Servant of the Lord in the 'Servant Songs' of Isaiah: A Second Moses Figure," in P. E. Satterthwaite, R. S. Hess, and G. J. Wenham, eds., *The Lord's Anointed: Interpretation of Old Testament Messianic Texts* (Grand Rapids: Baker, 1995), 105–40.

4. Regarding Isa 42:1-7, note that the servant is given as a covenant *to/for the people* (meaning the people of Israel) and a light *for the nations* (meaning the Gentiles). This would clearly point to the servant *as an individual*. A further "servant" reference is found in Isa 44:26, which seems to refer to God's prophetic servants in general, not to one particular servant or to the nation of Israel as a whole.

5. "The Servant of the Lord in the 'Servant Songs' of Isaiah: A Second Moses Figure," 108.

6. S. R. Driver and Ad. Neubauer, ed. and trans., *The Fifty-Third Chapter of Isaiah according to the Jewish Interpreters* (repr., New York: Ktav, 1969), 2:72–73; cf. 1:69–70.

7. Cited in Stefan Schreiner, "Isaiah 53 in the *Sefer Hizzuk Emunah*," Janowski and Stuhlmacher, *The Suffering Servant*, 446 (full article 418–461).

8. Driver and Neubauer, *The Fifty-Third Chapter of Isaiah*, 2:246.

9. Rabbi Moshe Shulman, "Rabbi Moseh Al Sheich and Isaiah 53," http://judaismsanswer.com/AlSheich.htm.

10. *Contra Celsum*, Book I, Chapter 55. His reply was: "Many arguments were employed on that occasion during the discussion to prove that these predictions regarding one particular person were not rightly applied by them to the whole nation. And I asked to what character the expression would be appropriate, 'This man bears our sins, and suffers pain on our behalf;' and this, 'But He was wounded for our sins, and bruised for our iniquities;' and to whom the expression properly belonged, 'By His stripes were we healed.' For it is manifest that it is they who had been sinners, and had been healed by the Savior's sufferings (whether belonging to the Jewish nation or converts from the Gentiles), who use such language in the writings of the prophet who foresaw these events, and who, under the influence of the Holy Spirit, applied these words to a person. But we seemed to press them hardest with the expression, 'Because of the iniquities of My people was He led away unto death.' For if the people, according to them, are the subject of the prophecy, how is the man said to be led away to death because of the iniquities of the people of God, unless he be a different person from that people of God? And who is this person save Jesus Christ, by whose stripes they who believe on Him are healed, when 'He had spoiled the principalities and powers (that were over us), and had made a show of them openly on His cross?'" The suggested dates for his interaction with these Jewish interlocutors are either 215–17 or 230–31; see Christoph Marskschies, "Jesus Christ as a Man before God," in Janowski and Stuhlmacher, *The Suffering Servant*, 225–323, esp. 284–92.

11. See Rabbi Moshe Shulman, "Isaiah 53 in the Talmud and Major Midrashim," http://judaismsanswer.com/Isaiah53TalmudMidrash.htm

12. See further Michael L. Brown, "Jewish Interpretations of Isaiah 53," in Bock and Glaser, *The Gospel According to Isaiah 53*, 61–81.

13. Antti Laato, *Who Is the Servant of the Lord? Jewish and Christian Interpretations on Isaiah 53 from Antiquity to the Middle Ages* (Studies in Rewritten Bible 4; Turku, Finland: Abo Akademi University; Winona Lake, IN: Eisenbrauns; 2012), 257–58.

14. Seth Postell, "A Christological Interpretation of the Feasts of Israel: Warrant and Significance for Biblical Theology," 22, privately distributed.

15. Rydelnik and Spencer explain the issue about "sprinkle" vs. "startle" as follows: "There is a dispute about the meaning of the word translated here as 'sprinkle' *(yazzeh)*, with some translations indicating that the word should be 'startle.' The basis for the alternate translation 'startle' is that this fits the parallelism with appalled or amazed in the previous verse as well as the parallelism with the line that follows: Kings will shut their mouths [in astonishment]. Furthermore, while it is agreed that the Hebrew word used here consistently means 'sprinkle' throughout the Hebrew Bible (e.g., Ex 29:16; Lv 17:6; Nm 18:17; Ezk 36:25), it always has a preposition following it ('to sprinkle something *on* . . .'), indicating what object is being sprinkled. However, there is no preposition in this passage. Perhaps this is why the Septuagint translated this word 'astonish.' Some have conjectured an Arabic cognate word to support this.

"The argument for the traditional translation 'sprinkle' is: (1) It is the plain definition of the word. (2) Taking it as 'startle' requires identifying it with a root completely unattested in the Hebrew language. (3) This need not be parallel to 'appalled' but could rather mean that the Servant's disfiguring death would be the way He would 'sprinkle' the nations. (4) As a causative verb, it could be an exception to the general rule of needing a preposition, with the idea 'He besprinkles many nations.' This verb is unattested in Hebrew for the concept of being 'astonished' or 'startled.' It seems best, therefore, to translate *yazzeh* as sprinkle. This is the same word used in Leviticus for sprinkling sacrificial blood (Lv 4:6; 16:14,19), indicating that the Servant's disfiguring death would function as a sacrifice for many nations. As a result, when Gentile kings understand the sacrificial reason for the Servant's death, they will shut their mouths in reverence and submission" (Michael Rydelnik and James Spencer, "Isaiah," *The Moody Bible Commentary* [Chicago: Moody Publishers, 2014], 1087–88).

16. Hugenberger, "The Servant of the Lord," 110.

17. Throughout Isaiah *'ammî*, my people, always refers to Israel, either as God's people or as the prophet's people. Some traditional Jewish interpreters (e.g., Radak) along with contemporary counter-missionaries, have argued that the final word *lāmô*, normally, "to them, for them" points to a plural subject, as if the text was saying, "the stroke that was due to my people fell *on them*," namely, the people of Israel. But this interpretation is untenable, since the servant is explicitly singular throughout, and it is more likely that the text is saying, "the servant received a stroke *for them*," namely, for the people (cf. also the potentially passive form of the verb *n-g-'* in the 4QIsa[a]). Note that *lāmô*

can also mean "to it/him, for it/him," as in Isa 44:15. For an extended, typical counter-missionary exposition, see Gerald Sigal, *Isaiah 53: Who Is the Servant?* (n.p.: Xlibris, 2007).

18. Again, some traditional Jewish interpreters (most forcefully, again, Radak) along with contemporary counter-missionaries (see endnote 20), have argued that *bĕmōtāyw*, lit., "in his deaths," points to the many different ways that the people of Israel died over the centuries. But this not only contradicts the language of the rest of the chapter, it is also an unnecessary deduction, since the plural form for death is used elsewhere to depict the violent death of an individual (see, e.g., Ezk 28:8), as is the case here. Note further that the 4QIsa[a] reads *bwmtw*, suggesting the meaning "burial mound" (as if *bāmâ*), which would be quite fitting; cf. W. Boyd Barrick, "The Rich Man from Arimathea (Matt 27:57-60) and 1QIsa[a]," *JBL* 96 (1977), 235–39; idem, *BMH as Body Language: A Lexical and Iconographical Study of the Word BMH When Not a Reference to Cultic Phenomena in Biblical and Post-Biblical Hebrew* (Edinburgh: T&T Clark International, 2008).

19. A reference to the restitution offering (cf. Lv 5:14–6:7), which provided both atonement before God and restitution to the human who was wronged.

20. The Masoretic Text (MT) does not have an object for the word "see" but the Septuagint (LXX) and Qumran do have the word "light." Likely, this refers to the Servant, after the anguish of His experience, will be resurrected to see the light of life.

21. "Counter-missionaries" refers to Jewish rabbis and teachers who actively work to turn Jewish people away from Jesus. They see Messianic Jews and Christians as missionaries, and therefore they view themselves as counter-missionaries. They seek to prevent Jewish people from believing in Jesus and to convince Jewish followers of Jesus to abandon that faith.

22. For a comparison of the Masoretic Text, Septuagint, and Dead Sea Scrolls texts of Isaiah, see David A. Sapp, "The LXX, 1QIsa, and MT Versions of Isaiah 53 and the Christian Doctrine of Atonement," in Bellinger and Farmer, *Jesus and the Suffering Servant: Isaiah 53 and Christian Origins*, 170–92.

23. Hermann Spieckermann, "The Conception and Prehistory of the Idea of Vicarious Suffering in the Old Testament," in Janowski and Stulmacher, *The Suffering Servant*, 5–7.

24. Bernd Janowski, "He Bore Our Sins: Isaiah 53 and the Drama of Taking Another's Place," in ibid., 71.

25. Shalom M. Paul, *Isaiah 40–66: Translation and Commentary* (Grand Rapids: Eerdmans, 2012), 398–99.

26. Berel Wein, *The Triumph of Survival: The Story of the Jews in the Modern Era 1650–1990* (Brooklyn: Shaar, 1990), 14.

27. F. B. Meyer, *Christ in Isaiah: Expositions of Isaiah XL–LV* (New York: Revell, 1895), 158.

Isaiah 55:3-5

The Fulfillment of the Davidic Promise

ROBERT B. CHISHOLM JR.

In Isa 40–55 the Lord promises to deliver His exiled people from Babylon, as He delivered them from Egyptian bondage in the time of Moses. Through His Servant, an individual who functions as an ideal Israel (49:3), He will lead them back to the promised land and rebuild downtrodden Jerusalem.

The section begins with a promise of restoration that sounds unconditional. The Lord's word of promise is reliable, unlike frail, mortal human beings and their promises (40:6-8). The Lord assures His people that He remains committed to them and that nothing can stand in the way of the realization of His goal for His people. But as the message of Isa 40–55 unfolds, the Lord confronts the exiled nation with their sin, which is the reason they have been removed from their homeland. Yet there is good news. The Lord will make provision for His sinful people through the atoning work of His Suffering Servant. In Isa 55 the Lord calls His people to repentance and promises to renew His covenant relationship with them. Once again, He emphasizes the reliability of His purposes and promise. His thoughts and ways are vastly different from those of humankind. The Lord's plans are realized, and His promises arc fulfilled.

Isaiah 55 is important to a study of the OT's messianic vision for at least two reasons: (1) It anticipates the positive outcome of the ministry of the Suffering Servant, who comes in the person of Jesus the Messiah. His atoning work opens the door to repentance and covenant renewal. (2) The Servant, as described in the first two Servant Songs (42:1-9; 49:1-13), brings justice to the nations, as does the ideal Davidic king depicted in Isa 11:1-9.

Consequently, it is reasonable to equate the Servant with the messianic king of Isa 11 and regard the Servant Songs as messianic. However, some argue that the Davidic promises are democratized in Isa 55:3-5, meaning that Israel replaces an individual Davidic king as God's instrument of salvation. If so, this affects our understanding of the Servant Songs. That is one of the reasons so many scholars are hesitant to view the Songs as messianic. This essay will attempt to show that the promise is not democratized in Isa 55:3-5, at least not in the way some scholars argue. Rather, the passage envisions the national benefits that result from the realization of the Davidic promises, just as 2Sm 7, the classic text on the Davidic covenant, anticipates.

STRUCTURE AND SUMMARY

Isaiah 55 is a call to repentance and covenant renewal. It consists of two sets of exhortations with supporting motivating arguments. In the first (55:1-5) the Lord speaks to His people directly. In the second (55:6-13) the prophet follows up and urges the nation to respond positively to the Lord's appeal. He includes words of assurance from the Lord (vv. 8-11).

The passage begins with an invitation to the exiles to quench their thirst and satisfy their hunger. The Lord uses an oxymoron as He urges them to "buy" what they need free of charge. The image shifts slightly in v. 2. Now the people have money, but they should not waste it on what will not meet their needs or satisfy their appetite. The blessings of a renewed covenant relationship are the reality behind the imagery of bread, water, and wine. These blessings are readily available to the people, if they respond. The reality behind the invitation to come and eat is repentance, as vv. 6-7 make clear. The people must turn from their evil ways and plans and seek the Lord, while He makes Himself available. If they respond appropriately, the Lord will forgive them and they will live (v. 3).

The syntax of v. 3 bears out the logic. Three imperatives (pay attention, come, listen) are followed by a jussive with a *waw* conjunctive, indicating purpose ("so that you may live") or result ("so that you will live"). The life in view here includes material blessing and national security (see Dt 30:6,15,19-20). The cohortative that follows in v. 3 expresses an additional purpose ("in order that you may live *and I will make an everlasting covenant with you*") or result ("and consequently you will live *and I will make an everlasting covenant with you*").

This covenant is connected in some way with the Lord's promises to David.

(For discussion, see below.) The Lord recalls how He made David His witness to the nations that He enabled David to conquer and rule (v. 4). The Lord recalls how He promised to give David jurisdiction over nations that previously did not recognize ("know") his authority. Verse 5 is best understood as addressed to David because second-person-singular forms are used, in contrast to the second-person-plural forms used in vv. 1-3, 6-9, and 12.

After the call to repentance (vv. 6-7), the Lord assures the exiles of the reliability of His promise (vv. 8-11). The Lord's plans and ways differ significantly from those of the people (v. 8). They are vastly superior to human plans and ways, which He compares to the earth, over which the sky (representing the Lord in the comparison) towers (v. 9). According to vv. 10-11, the Lord's plans and ways are accomplished. His promise, which reveals His plan and commits Him to a certain course of action, will be fulfilled. He compares His plan to the rain and snow. Once they begin to fall from the sky, they do not suddenly reverse their course. They fall to the earth and contribute to agricultural growth. Likewise, the Lord's promise does not return to Him empty. It accomplishes the purpose for which it is sent. In contrast, Israel's plans and ways, if not abandoned (v. 7), will lead to death (implied in v. 3). Human plans are like a mere breath (Ps 94:11). Humans may form many plans, but only the Lord's plans are certain of fulfillment (Prv 19:21). Humankind's way, when accompanied by wickedness (see Isa 55:7), leads to destruction (Prv 1:15; 3:31; 4:19). In short, human plans and ways are doomed to failure, in contrast to the Lord's plans and ways, which are accomplished. This means that the Lord will deliver His people, who will experience His renewed blessing (vv. 12-13).

THE PROMISED COVENANT AND ITS RELATIONSHIP TO THE DAVIDIC COVENANT

The Lord promises to make a perpetual covenant with the people. This covenant is associated with the Davidic promise in some way, but the precise connection is uncertain. Two difficult questions arise in relation to the final line of v. 3: (1) How is "David" functioning in relation to the preceding word (*chasde*)? It could be taken as subjective, in which case it refers to the faithful deeds *performed by* David. Or it could be interpreted as objective, in which case it refers to the faithful promises *given to* David.[1] (2) How is the final line of v. 3 related to the preceding line? It would appear that "perpetual covenant" is in apposition to "faithful deeds" (or "promises"), suggesting they are equated in some way. Some extrapolate from this that the Davidic promises are "democratized" and transferred to the whole nation. But it is also possible that "faithful deeds" (or "promises") could be adverbial, in the sense of "according to" or "like," in which case the promised covenant is an extension of or analogous to the Davidic promises.

An examination of the evidence suggests that the phrase *chasde david* refers to the Lord's faithful promises to David. The plural construct form *chasde* is followed by a modifying genitive in only six passages, including Isa 55:3. Four times the divine name Yahweh follows as a subjective genitive describing the loyal deeds performed by the Lord (Pss 89:1 [Hb. v. 2]; 107:43; Isa 63:7; Lam 3:22). In 2Chr 6:42 the name David follows, as in Isa 55:3. A subjective sense is possible, referring to the faithful deeds performed by David. But an objective sense, referring to the faithful promises made to David, is more likely in light of the context.

In 2Chr 6:15-17, Solomon praises the Lord: "You have kept what you promised [lit. "word"] to Your servant, my father David. You spoke directly to him, and You fulfilled Your promise by Your power, as it is today" (6:15). He then prays: "keep what You promised to Your servant, my father David [lit. 'that which you spoke to him']" (6:16). He adds, "please confirm what you promised" [lit. "spoke"] (6:17). The focus in these verses is God's faithful promise to David, not David's faithful deeds. Furthermore, the noun *chesed* is used one other time in Solomon's prayer. In v. 14, it refers to the Lord's promise: "LORD God of Israel, there is no God like you in heaven or on earth, keeping His gracious covenant [lit. 'the covenant and the faithfulness'] with your servants who walk before You with their whole heart."

The contextual evidence strongly suggests that *chasde david* in v. 42 refers to the faithful promises made to David. This is likely the case as well in Isa 55:3, where the phrase is followed by the attributive plural participle *hanne'emanim*, "the reliable" (HCSB "assured"), which modifies the plural noun *chasde*. In light of Ps 89:28 [Hb. v. 29], it is probable that the reliable promises made to David are in view. There the Lord says, "I will always preserve [lit. "keep"] My faithful love [*chasdi*] for him, and My covenant with him will endure [*ne'emenet*, lit. 'my covenant is reliable for him']." The niphal participle of *'aman* affirms the reliability of the Lord's covenantal love. Finally, Ac 13:34 supports this interpretation; it quotes Isa 55:3 as follows: "I will grant you the faithful covenant blessings made to David."

As noted above, "the faithful covenant blessings made to David" and "the covenant" mentioned in the preceding poetic line appear to be appositional. Some scholars equate the two by seeing a "democratization" of the Davidic promises, whereby they are transferred to the nation, which replaces David.[2] However, numerous prophets, including Isaiah (11:1-10), envision a Davidic ruler serving as the Lord's vice-regent in the future. Particularly important is the testimony of the postexilic prophets. Haggai attached great hope to David's descendant Zerubbabel (2:20-23), while Zechariah viewed him as fulfilling Jeremiah's prophecies concerning David's "branch" (3:8; 6:12-13; cf. Jer 23:5; 33:15). Proponents of democratization in Isa 55:3 are forced to see conflicting viewpoints in the prophetic literature.[3]

But why create such a scenario when there is a better explanation that harmonizes Isa 55:3 with the messianic vision? Furthermore, if the promise to David could be transferred to others, what does this imply about the covenant with Israel that is patterned after it? What guarantee is there that Israel will not be replaced? Such a notion is antithetical to the message of Isa 40–55, which emphasizes Yahweh's continuing commitment to Israel, despite their failure and exile. Responding to the democratization view, Eaton states:

> "But there is nothing in the text to express such a drastic change; it seems that these scholars are making it fit their own misreading of royal elements in earlier chapters. For it is entirely natural that the text should mention blessings accruing to the nation from the Davidic covenant, without thereby implying a break with the central point of the covenant, a covenant expressly described here as eternal. God's work with the king always had implications for the people. . . . The nation is to be blessed within the radius of the Davidic covenant, but the destiny of the royal house remains. . . . It would be a poor sort of eternity that the covenant would have, if its heart were taken out."[4]

Because of the problems created by the democratization view, it is better to understand "the faithful promises to David" as adverbial and specifying: "with respect to the faithful promises to David." But what is the precise nature of the specification? One option is to understand the covenant as analogous to the Davidic promises: "And I will make a perpetual covenant with you, *like* the faithful promises I made to David." In this case, the covenant will entail Israel ruling over nations as David did (Isa 55:4-5). But such a covenant would overlap with the Davidic promises and, if merely analogous to them, would all but usurp them. In other words, this interpretation is plagued by the same problems as the democratization view outlined above.

A better option is to see the covenant as being established in accordance with the Davidic promises: "And I will make a perpetual covenant with you, *according to* the faithful promises I made to David." In this case, the covenant is rooted in and brings to fulfillment the Davidic promises. Israel becomes the beneficiary of the ideal Davidic king's rule.[5] Second Samuel 7 envisions this. After telling David how He will bless his rule, the Lord then said, "And I will provide a place for my people Israel and will plant them so that they can have a home of their own and no longer be disturbed. Wicked people will not oppress them anymore, as they did at the beginning and have done ever since the time I appointed leaders over my people Israel" (author's translation, vv. 10-11a). When David responded to the Lord's promise, he understood its implications for Israel: "And who is like your people Israel—the one nation on earth that God went out to redeem as a people for Himself, and to make a name for Himself, and to perform great and awesome wonders by driving out nations and their gods from before your people, whom you redeemed from Egypt? You have established your people Israel as your very own forever, and you, LORD, have become their God" (author's translation, vv. 23-24). Likewise, in Ps 144, David prayed for the Lord's saving intervention (vv. 1-11) and understood that the Lord's intervention on his behalf meant security and blessing for Israel (vv. 12-15).

To summarize, Isa 55:3-5 anticipates the national blessings that will result when the Davidic promise is fulfilled through an ideal king.[6] This interpretation, which is consistent with the corporate dimension of the Davidic promise, nicely harmonizes Isa 55:3 and the messianic vision of Isa 11. Both the Davidic king of Isa 11 and the Servant of the Servant Songs bring justice to the earth and deliverance to Israel. The Servant's relationship to Israel is stressed in the Songs. He is actually called Israel (Isa 49:3) because he fulfills the Lord's ideal for the nation while delivering the exiled, sinful nation from bondage (see articles on Isa 42 and Isa 49). This royal Servant restores the Lord's servant Israel by creating a new covenant community (55:3-5; 59:21; 61:8) consisting of loyal followers, called the Lord's "servants" (see Isa 54:17; 56:6; 63:17; 65:8-9,13-15; 66:14). According to Isa 55:3, He will mediate a new, perpetual covenant with Israel that will bring about the fulfillment of the Lord's ancient promise to David. As Odendaal states with regard to the Servant: "As covenant representative he can therefore also be called 'Israel' (49:3), because in himself he comprehends all the hopes, privileges, and responsibilities of Israel, and as Messianic King he leads Israel to the consummation of its calling in the history of salvation."[7]

SUMMING UP

In Isa 55, the Lord calls Israel to covenant renewal, assuring them that repentance will bring forgiveness of sins and restoration of divine blessing. He promises He will make a new, perpetual covenant with them. This covenant is not democratized in the sense that the Lord's promises to David are now transferred to the nation Israel. On the contrary, this covenant, which will be mediated through the Suffering Servant of the Lord (see Isa 49:8), is rooted in and will bring to fulfillment the Lord's ancient promises to David that He will exalt His people Israel through His chosen king. This should come as no surprise, since the Suffering Servant and the ideal Davidic king, the Messiah, are one and the same. Isaiah 55 is an important messianic text, for it describes the goal of the Servant's ministry. Through Him the new covenant is inaugurated and the Davidic promise is realized.

1. For a survey of opinion, see Gary V. Smith, *Isaiah 40–66*, New American Commentary (Nashville: Broadman & Holman, 2009), 498–99.

2. See, for example, Otto Eissfeldt, "The Promises of Grace to David in Isaiah 55:1-5," in *Israel's Prophetic Heritage*, ed. Bernhard W. Anderson and Walter Harrelson (New York: Harper & Brothers, 1962), 196–207; Christopher R. North, *The Second Isaiah* (Oxford: Clarendon, 1964), 257–58; Claus Westermann, *Isaiah 40–66*, Old Testament Library Commentary Series (trans. David Stalker; Philadelphia: Fortress, 1969), 283–84; R. N. Whybray, *Isaiah 40–66*, New Century Bible Commentary (Grand Rapids, William B. Eerdmans, 1975), 192; W. J. Dumbrell, *Covenant and Creation: A Theology of Old Testament Covenants* (Nashville: Thomas Nelson, 1984), 196; Benjamin D. Sommer, *A Prophet Reads Scripture: Allusion in Isaiah 40–66* (Stanford, CA: Stanford University Press, 1998), 112–19; and Klaus Baltzer, *Deutero-Isaiah*, Hermeneia: A Critical & Historical Commentary on the Bible (trans. Margaret Kohl; Minneapolis: Fortress, 2001), 470–71; John Goldingay, *The Message of Isaiah 40–55* (London: T&T Clark, 2005), 547; John Goldingay and David Payne, *Isaiah 40–55*, vol. 2 of International Critical Commentary (London: T&T Clark, 2006), 372; Shalom M. Paul, *Isaiah 40–66*, Eerdman's Critical Commentary (Grand Rapids: William B. Eerdmans, 2012), 434–35.

3. See, for example, Katherine Doob Sakenfeld, *The Meaning of Hesed in the Hebrew Bible: A New Inquiry* (Missoula, MT: Scholars Press, 1978), 203–04.

4. J. H. Eaton, *Festal Drama in Deutero-Isaiah* (London: SPCK, 1979), 87–88. Blenkinsopp observes that the democratization view of Isa 55:3-5 "goes some way beyond what the author says." He adds, "Furthermore, it is difficult to understand why this analogy [nation to David] would be used if the author was not persuaded of the permanence of Yahveh's commitment to David and the dynasty." See Joseph Blenkinsopp, *Isaiah 40–55*, Anchor Yale Bible Commentaries (New York: Doubleday, 2002), 370.

5. See John N. Oswalt, *The Book of Isaiah, Chapters 40–66* (Grand Rapids: William B. Eerdmans, 1998) 438–39; J. Alec Motyer, *The Prophecy of Isaiah* (Downers Grove, IL: InterVarsity, 1993), 453–55; and Walter C. Kaiser, Jr., "The Unfailing Kindnesses Promised to David: Isaiah 55:3," *Journal for the Study of the Old Testament* 45 (1989): 96–97.

6. See Robert B. Chisholm, Jr., "The Christological Fulfillment of Isaiah's Servant Songs," *Bibliotheca Sacra* 163 (2006): 399–400.

7. See Dirk H. Odendaal, *The Eschatological Expectation of Isaiah 40–66 with Special Reference to Israel and the Nations* (Nutley, NJ: Presbyterian and Reformed, 1970), 134.

Isaiah 61:1-6

The Spirit-Anointed Messiah and His Promise of Restoration

EDWARD E. HINDSON

The announcement of the messianic anointing (Hb. *mašiah*) in Isa 61:1-3 introduces the voice of the Messiah who will proclaim the "good news" (Hb. *basser*; LXX *euangelizomai*). That Jesus quoted this passage in the synagogue in Nazareth and applied it to Himself clearly indicates that He understood its messianic implications (Lk 4:16-22). To deny this or to simply limit the voice of the speaker to the role of some other prophet flies in the face of Jesus' own declaration.[1] Noting the continuity of the Servant's anointing with the Spirit (Isa 42:1) and that of the Messiah (Isa 11:2), John Oswalt identifies the speaker as the servant/Messiah.[2] Walter Kaiser suggests that the act of anointing is the central factor in the installation of the Anointed One, stating, "Yahweh appoints the Servant and the Spirit anoints him, thereby making one of the earliest constructs of the doctrine of the Trinity."[3]

The Anointed One is "sent" with what Joseph Blenkinsopp calls "five charges that coalesce into one undertaking."[4] A series of infinitives follows dependent on the verb "sent": "bind . . . proclaim . . . proclaim . . . comfort . . . grant" (NASB). Thus, the speaker not only acknowledges His anointing but also describes His evangelistic calling to proclaim "good news" to those who desperately need it most: "afflicted . . . brokenhearted . . . captives . . . prisoners . . . mourners" (NASB). The message of proclamation in vv. 1-2 is then followed by a description of salvation in v. 3 through a use of what Claus Westermann calls "paronomasia" (a series of contrasts emphasized by a list of "insteads").[5] Thus, the sent one will grant a garland instead of ashes; gladness instead of mourning; praise instead of fainting (v. 3).

The rest of Isa 61 describes the "double portion" (v. 7) of God's blessing on Israel as a result of the ministry of the Anointed One. Rydelnik and Spencer comment: "The Servant Messiah's ministry will also include the rebuilding of the ancient ruins of Israel, the elevation of Israel above the nations, and the renewal of Israel to her proper place as a nation of priests (cf. Ex 19:6), mediating the knowledge of God to the nations."[6] Alec Motyer notes: "Through the Anointed One, all this long-standing and inherited brokenness will be restored."[7] Thus, the anointed Servant Messiah will both repossess and restore Israel with a greater recovery than they could ever imagine. The coming future prosperity predicted in vv. 4-7 confirms the promises of vv. 1-3. These promises and affirmations are made with such obvious application to literal Israel it is difficult to imagine how these can be referring to the church.[8]

The references to Israel's future blessings include her renewal as a "kingdom of priests" (cf. Ex 19:5-6; Zch 8:23), and the "double portion" of blessing as the firstborn of the Lord (cf. Ex 4:22; Dt 21:17). God also promises to make an "everlasting covenant" with Israel, which Michael Rydelnik and James Spencer understand as the new covenant (Jer 31:31-34).[9] The major theme of Isa 61:4-11 is that God will use the Anointed One to accomplish His purposes for both Israel and the nations (v. 9). That Isaiah himself foresaw this promise applying to literal Israel through whom righteousness would "spring up" before the nations is clearly indicated in the text of 61:11, and he emphasizes its relation to its eventual fulfillment.

HISTORICAL SETTING

There is extensive disagreement among scholars regarding the historical context of Isa 61:1-11. Virtually all scholars agree that Isa 61:1-3 is a proclamation made by a man who believed God had anointed him to proclaim a message of salvation. Some view the speaker as Trito-Isaiah who has taken up the task of Deutero-Isaiah. Some critical scholars place the setting in the postexilic era at the time of Nehemiah, emphasizing the need to resume the rebuilding efforts of the returnees. Others emphasize the liberating work of the Lord through the prophet. Still others view the speaker as the collective voice of the Levitical community.[10]

The text itself provides no immediate historical context. Attempts to identify a context based on literary analyses change with every generation of commentators. Critics of the unity of Isaiah generally view chaps. 40–55 as exilic (written in Babylon) and chaps. 56–66 as postexilic (written in Judah). In contradiction of this, Motyer points out, "There is, however, no external, manuscriptal, authority for the separate existence at any time of the three supposed divisions of Isaiah."[11] He suggests that the material in chaps. 40–66 was written and edited by Isaiah himself. To support his cause, he looks at the usage of "the Anointed One." He points out that the Anointed One appears for the second time (49:1-6) speaking in His own person about Himself. As in 59:21, He is endowed with the Spirit and the Word (as in 59:21), proclaiming favor and vengeance. Motyer comments, "This is the passage the Lord Jesus deliberately sought out as the starting point of his public ministry. His action validates authoritatively . . . that Isaiah displays here a messianic figure."[12]

Jesus' own interpretation of the passage in Lk 4:17-21 clearly indicates the messianic significance of Isa 61:1-2. The Lucan version of the account includes several important factors that leave no doubt that Jesus saw Himself as the fulfillment of Isaiah's prophecy. If this is indeed the case, the setting is prophetic and points to the message of the coming Messiah as envisioned to Isaiah by divine revelation.

INTERPRETIVE PRESUPPOSITIONS

Since Jesus Himself commented on the meaning and fulfillment of Isaiah's prophecy in Lk 4:16-30, His views of fulfillment and application of the passage must be taken seriously.

Jesus' Interpretation

Jesus read and applied Isa 61:1-2 to Himself as the One anointed to preach the "good news." The passage in Lk 4:16-30 provides the longest account of the occasion of Jesus' teaching in the synagogue in Nazareth. While the parallel accounts in Mk 6:1-4 and Mt 13:54-58 are shorter, all three clearly refer to the same incident. In each account, Jesus quotes the proverb that a prophet is not honored in his hometown (Mt 13:57; Mk 6:4; Lk 4:24). Also the reaction of the audience is the same in each passage: amazement, criticism, and rejection. In regard to the placement of the account in Luke's Gospel, William Hendriksen suggests that the Nazareth visit occurred sometime after Jesus' initial miracle in Capernaum.[13] Darrell Bock notes that "Luke has moved this event forward in the sequence of his Gospel to highlight it . . . (as) an event (that) typifies Jesus' preaching and people's reaction to it."[14]

The setting of Lk 4:14-30 is at Nazareth in Galilee sometime after Jesus "returned to Galilee in the power of the Spirit" (v. 14). Capernaum was the main headquarters of Jesus' initial ministry. From there, news of His messages and miracles spread throughout the region (4:37). Thus, His arrival back in the town where He had been raised by Mary and Joseph created a great deal of anticipation. Jesus went to the synagogue as was His custom (4:16), indicating that He was functioning within Jewish religious practices. Bock notes: "Jesus does not attempt to separate himself from Judaism. Rather, he presents his mission as the natural extension and realization of Israel's hope."[15]

Hendriksen suggests the following sequence for a typical synagogue service of that time:[16]

1. Blessings spoken in relation to the dedication of the *Shema* (Dt 6:4-5).
2. Prayer with "Amen" response from congregation.
3. Reading from the Torah (Pentateuch).
4. Reading from the Prophets.
5. Sermon or Exhortation.
6. Benediction followed by "Amen."

Some suggest the Isa 61 passage may have been the *haftarah* (prescribed reading). However, the phrase that Jesus "found the place" (literally "unrolled" the scroll, Lk 4:17) indicates that it is more likely that He deliberately selected the reading and even possibly translated it from Hebrew into Aramaic, as was customary. Others suggest He may have read from the Greek Septuagint (LXX) version because of the phrase "recovery of sight to the blind," which reads "the opening of the prison" in the MT.[17] However, Jesus may have provided this explanation in light of Isa 42:7, which clearly indicates the Servant Messiah will both "open blind eyes" and "bring out prisoners" from the "darkness [of] the prison house."[18] It is certainly most likely that the reading came from the Hebrew as is indicated by the presence of Hebrew scrolls of Isaiah among the Dead Sea Scrolls and Luke's general use of Isaiah throughout Luke–Acts.[19]

Jesus' assertion that Isa 61:1-2 was fulfilled "today" (as in His time) shows that He did not view it as having been fulfilled previously (as in the time of the prophet or any succeeding time, e.g., Nehemiah's time). In the context of Lk 4:14-30, Jesus certainly understood that His ministry of proclaiming the Gospel (*euangelion*, "good news") was designed to fulfill Isaiah's prophecy. The perfect tense (Gk. *peplērōtai*), "has been fulfilled," indicates that He believed Isaiah's prophecy was being fulfilled in His own life and ministry.[20] The emphatic "today" (Gk. *sēmeron*) primarily refers to the very day of Jesus' declaration, signifying the launching of His messianic ministry.[21] Kevin Zuber states: "Jesus was making an unmistakable claim to be the Messiah."[22]

Hendriksen provides the following helpful chart comparing Isa 61:1-2 in Hebrew (MT), Greek (LXX), and the question in Lk 4:18-19, each translated into English.[23]

A Comparison of Isaiah 61:1-2a with Luke 4:18-19

(Author's Translations)

Hebrew Isa 61:1-2a Translated into English	LXX (Greek Version) of Isa 61:1-2a Translated into English	Greek Luke 4:18-19 Translated into English
1. The Spirit of the Lord God (is) upon me,	The Spirit of the Lord (is) upon me,	The Spirit of the Lord (is) upon me,
2. Because the Lord has anointed me to announce good news to the poor	Because he has anointed me; He has sent me to proclaim good news to the poor,	Because he has anointed me to proclaim good news to the poor,
3. He has sent me to bind up the brokenhearted;	To heal the broken-hearted,	
4. To proclaim to the captives liberty;	To proclaim to the captives release;	He has sent me to proclaim to the captives release:
5. And to those bound opening of eyes;	And to the blind recovery of sight;	And to the blind recovery of sight:
6.		To set free the oppressed;
7. To proclaim the year of the Lord's favor.	To announce the year of the Lord's favor.	To proclaim the year of the Lord's favor.

The passage in Luke goes on to include the Jewish audience's initial curious anticipation, pleasant surprise, and indignant transition when Jesus communicated that Gentiles (widow in Sidon and Naaman the Syrian) are often more responsive to God than are the Jewish people to whom He came (vv. 24-27). Bock notes: "The price of rejecting God's message is severe: mercy moves on to other locals."[24] Jesus' very use of the two illustrations of Gentiles responding to God anticipates what will eventually follow in the future as the Gospel spreads rapidly among the Gentiles in Luke's account in the book of Acts. For the immediate context within Luke's Gospel, the incident in Nazareth serves to introduce what will happen in Jesus' forthcoming ministry. Often the most unlikely people will respond to the

Savior's offer of grace: fishermen, prostitutes, tax collectors, the thief on the cross, and yes—the blind and the lame.[25]

Messianic Expectation at Qumran

The significance of the book of Isaiah among the Dead Sea Scrolls found at Qumran has long been recognized. J. J. M. Roberts states: "It now appears there were at least twenty separate scrolls of Isaiah in use in the Qumran community."[26] These included the large, basically complete scroll of Isaiah, 1QIsa[a]. The similarity of this text to the MT has been recognized even by some critical scholars as a "single channel of transmission of this book" since c. 300 BC.[27] Also, the extensive list of citations from Isaiah in extrabiblical texts from Qumran demonstrate the importance of Isaiah at Qumran.[28] Significant citations among these are "the shoot from the stock of Jesse" (Isa 11:1-16) and "the Spirit of the Lord God is upon me" (Isa 61:1-2). The Dead Sea Scrolls also include several commentaries (Hb. *pesharim*) on biblical books or texts, including Isaiah.

The method of interpretation of the *pesharim* have been analyzed, discussed, and revised since F. F. Bruce's work in 1959, which focused on the eschatological expectation of the Qumran exegetes.[29] By 1979, Hervé Gabrion's extensive analysis indicated that virtually every scroll reflected a serious attempt to interpret the Hebrew Bible in light of messianic and eschatological concerns.[30] He states: "The eschatological sensitivities of [the time] were especially significant in motivating a particular reading of Scripture."[31]

What has now become clear to most scholars is that a common, although diverse, Jewish hope for the future rested on the expectation of a royal messiah, priestly messiah, and an eschatological prophet. J. J. Collins states, "The Dead Sea scrolls shed much light on the messianic expectations of early Christianity by clarifying the expectations that were current at the time."[32] Collins points out that early Christianity shared the same expectations as the Jews but modified them in light of the experience of Jesus as both a prophet and the Davidic Messiah, with "the militant role of the Messiah" transferred to the second coming.[33]

In regard to Isa 61:1-3, the Qumran *Messianic Apocalypse* (4Q521), also known as *On Resurrection*, supplies what Emile Puech calls "very important evidence" concerning the Essene eschatological hope of an anointed prophet/king who will bless the pious, the faithful, the just, and the poor in light of the promises of Isa 61.[34] The Dead Sea scroll text 4Q521 contains a thematic *pesher* on Ps 146 that draws connections to Isa 61:1-2. God's Spirit is pictured as hovering over the poor, freeing the captives, opening the eyes of the blind, healing the wounded, resurrecting the dead, and proclaiming "glad tidings" to the poor. Joseph Fitzmyer suggests the Qumran community expected a coming "anointed herald" based on Isa 61:1.[35]

While this is clearly the one who will free prisoners, give sight to the blind, heal the wounded, and revive the dead, Fitzmyer views this as deeds of the Lord, whereas Collins views them as the deeds of an "eschatological prophet."[36]

Hannah Harrington notes that "the messianic usage of Isa 61:1 was apparently a popular Jewish interpretation in Second Temple times (cf. Lk 4:18). The author of 4Q521 makes a further connection between the Spirit and the Messiah by alluding to Gn 1:2 as well."[37] George Brooke observes that Jewish adaptation of Isa 61 is certainly reflected in Lk 7:18-35, where Jesus answers the inquiry of the disciples of John the Baptist with the reassurance that "the blind receive their sight, the lame walk, the lepers are cleansed, the deaf hear, the dead are raised up, and the poor have the gospel preached to them." He argues that this quote preserves elements of a contemporary Jewish understanding of Isa 61.[38]

Fitzmyer notes that Lk 7:18-23 "conflates phrases that allude to Isa 35:5; 26:19; 61:1, without exact quotation."[39] Darrell Bock suggests the list of miracles in Jesus' response is based on the same passages, plus Isa 29:18-19. He comments, "These OT texts look for God's deliverance and the events in them point to such a decisive time."[40] He indicates that Jesus' reply to John's disciples both explicitly and implicitly assures them that He is indeed the Messiah. In regard to this, M. Daniel Carroll suggests that Isa 61:1-3 combines both kingly and prophetic elements with links to the Servant Songs in a "composite figure who incorporates royal, prophetic, and servant features."[41]

In commenting on Isaiah 61:1-3, Randall Price observes that Luke's quotation of Jesus' words in Lk 4 reveals that He believed He had come to proclaim the "good news" through the redemptive acts that Isaiah had predicted.[42] If indeed Jesus believed that He was the prophetic voice that Isa 61:1-3 envisioned, to suggest any less is to impugn Jesus' integrity and credibility. Either He clearly understood His calling and mission in light of Isaiah's prophetic trajectory, or else He was mistaken in claiming its fulfillment.

EXEGETICAL CONSIDERATIONS

The Call (61:1a)

Isaiah 61:1 begins with the declaration that the "Spirit of the Lord God" (Hb. *Ruach Adonay Yahweh*) has anointed (Hb. *Mashiach*) the speaker to proclaim "good news." The divine title is used throughout Isaiah to attribute sovereignty to Yahweh![43] Motyer notes, "it is the Spirit of this God—Sovereign, Savior, Judge—which rests on the Anointed One so that he can work the works of God."[44]

While many commentators identify the speaker as a prophet, Oswalt notes, "the only places in the OT where Spirit-filling and anointing are mentioned together are in connection with Kingships."[45] Daniel Block points to the relation of anointing to the kingly role of Isa 11:1-5, emphasizing that he has "the authority to inaugurate a reign of justice and peace that no prophet could claim."[46] However, M. Daniel Carroll shows that the person is described as a prophetic figure as well (cf. Mic 3:8) because "the commission in Isa 61 has to do preeminently with speaking (seven infinitives that clearly pick up terminology of several announcement passages in chaps. 40–50)."[47] Thus, in light of these considerations, many prefer to view the speaker as a "composite figure" who incorporates royal, prophetic, and servant features.[48] Connecting the Anointed One to the Servant, Delitzsch comments, "We can hardly expect that, after the prophet has described the Servant of Jehovah . . . he will now ascribe . . . to himself those very same official attributes which he has already set forth as characteristic features in his portrait of the predicted One."[49]

Oswalt and Rydelnik and Spencer view the context of chaps. 56–66 as eschatological with the Davidic Messiah/Servant as the primary means by which God's righteousness will be extended to the nations.[50] Oswalt writes, "Jesus' appropriation of these words in Luke 4:16-21 plainly indicates that he understood himself to be the realization of the synthesis that Isaiah was describing in the Servant/Messiah."[51] The empowerment of the anointing by the Spirit is often coupled with the spoken word throughout Isaiah's prophecies (11:2; 32:15-16; 42:1; 44:3; 48:16; 59:21) and, thus, is aptly applied to Jesus as the messianic Prophet/Messiah.

The Commission (61:1b)

The Anointed One is empowered and commissioned to preach "good news" (Hb. *basser*) to the poor (Hb. *anawim*, "afflicted" or "downtrodden"). His message will "bind up" (bandage) those who need hope and healing. Westermann observes that the series of infinitives are dependent on the verb "to send" by which the Anointed One is to "bind up . . . proclaim . . . proclaim . . . comfort . . . grant."[52] Slotki adds that to "bind up" indicates "to cure."[53] Thus, the messenger's task is not to merely announce "good news" but to bring about radical transformation. That Jesus viewed Himself as doing exactly that is clear from His response to the disciples of John the Baptist (Mt 11:1-5). Edward Young notes, "the speaker not merely announces but also dispenses the great gifts of God."[54]

The Anointed One will "proclaim liberty . . . and freedom" (Hb. *deror*) to the "captives" and "prisoners." Slotki notes that *deror* is the term used in connection with the Year of Jubilee (Lv 25:10).[55] John D. W. Watts observes that "it calls for a general emancipation of slaves on every fiftieth year."[56] It is a technical term for the *semitta* (Jer 34:17). Just as prisoners and debtors were to be released at that time, so the prophet Isaiah foresees a time when spiritual prisoners will be released from the bondage of sin by the work of the Anointed One.

The phrase "freedom to prisoners" (NASB) is also translated "opening of the eyes" (Hb. *peqah-qoah*) of those that the LXX refers to as the "blind" (Lk 4:18). Motyer translates it as "release from darkness" or "wide-opening," which is only used here as a reduplicated noun.[57] He further notes that *paqah* ordinarily means "opening of the eyes," which in Isa 42:7 is associated with bringing people out of the darkness of prison.[58] Thus, the full usage of the term can refer to "opening the eyes" of those who are blinded either spiritually, literally, or temporarily.

The Comfort (61:2)

Verse 2 combines the proclamation of the "year of the Lord's favor" and the coming "day of our God's vengeance" to comfort (Hb. *lanachem*) all who mourn. Motyer observes, "The repetition of the verb *to proclaim* signals that what follows recapitulates what has preceded from a new point of view."[59] Both a "year of favor" (Hb. *shenat-rason*) and a "day of vengeance" (Hb. *yom naqam*) are forthcoming. That Jesus stopped reading after the words "favorable year" and did not go on to read "day of vengeance" indicates a clear distinction between His first and second comings. Rydelnik and Spencer state, "This passage will be fulfilled by Jesus in His two advents . . . Jesus inaugurated this messianic ministry, but it will not be fulfilled in its entirety until His return."[60] Similarly, Motyer suggests, "what Isaiah sees is a double-faceted ministry the Lord Jesus apportions respectively to His first and second comings, the work of the Servant and the Anointed Conqueror."[61]

At His first coming, Jesus came to proclaim "good news" (LXX, *euangelion*) to the poor (Gk. *ptokos*). The Year of Jubilee, Darrell Bock notes, "was interpreted in Judaism as a reference to the dawn of God's new age."[62] Thus, Jesus came to inaugurate that new age through a process of spiritual deliverance and transformation that He viewed as having been predicted in Isa 61:1-3. His mission at His first coming was to bring comfort and hope, not condemnation and vengeance. The latter would result at His second coming (cf. 1Th 5:2-3; 2Th 1:7-9; Rev 20:11-15).

The promise of "comfort" (Hb. *nacham*) will be given to "all who mourn" (Hb. *ebolim*).[63] This comfort will be provided for "those who mourn" (Hb. *abelim mit'abbelim*). Blenkinsopp notes, "At this point the reversal is from mourning to comfort . . . and will reappear in the Matthean Beatitudes."[64] Thus, Jesus will also announce: "those who mourn are blessed, for they will be comforted" (Mt 5:4). It is this promise of comfort that Isaiah first raised in 40:1 ("comfort, comfort My people") and now finds its fulfillment in the ministry of the Anointed One.

THE CONTRASTS (61:3A)

This prophesied reversal of conditions is next exemplified in a series of contrasts related to the traditions associated with fasting, which often accompanied times of mourning. Instead of sprinkling ashes on one's uncovered head, there will be a festive "garland"; instead of disheveled "mourning," there will be "oil of gladness"; instead of a "spirit of fainting" (bowing down), there will be a "mantle of praise" (v. 3 NASB).

Slotki observes these are the symbols of honor and joy. He states, "There is a notable play on words in the Hebrew: *peer* for *epher*, the first two letters being transposed.[65] Thus, Blenkinsopp writes, "The point is also made by the reversal of consonants and sound in the first of the three images: *pe'er tahat 'eper*, 'a turban instead of ashes.'"[66] Thus, the Anointed One will not only proclaim "good news" but He will also bring its results to fruition for those who mourn with fasting.

THE CONSEQUENCE (61:3B)

Those who respond to the message of the Anointed One will receive a new name: "they will be called oaks of righteousness" (v. 3 NASB). Motyer observes, "the construction changes from the infinitives which express the aims of the Anointed One to a statement of what He has achieved."[67] The promise of this new name describes the condition that fulfills the prediction of 60:21, where Zion is promised the days of her mourning will be over and she will be the "branch I planted."

The oak tree is a symbol of strength, stability, and prominence. These "oaks of righteousness" are the opposite of the withered oaks of 1:29-31, which symbolized unrepentant Israel. At the beginning of his prophecies, Isaiah promised salvation and redemption to the "repentant ones" of Israel (1:27). Now, the prophet foresees that promise fulfilled in the ministry of the Anointed One. He alone can reverse Israel's fortunes and restore her beauty as a "planting of the LORD" (61:3, Hb. *mata yahweh*).

THE COMPLETION (61:4-11)

In addition to Israel's new name and new status, she receives a new commission: they will rebuild . . . restore . . . renew (v. 4). Oswalt notes that v. 4 "closely agrees with v. 3 in its continuation of the theme of restoration."[68] This verse serves as a transitional passage from vv. 1-3 to 5-11, where the people of Israel are designated as "priests" of the Lord and "ministers of our God" (v. 6). In vv. 7-10, the prophet continues his series of contrasts from humiliation to joy. They will wear the "garments of salvation" . . . "a robe of righteousness" as a bridegroom wears a "garland" (NASB Hb. *pe'er*) or "turban." Isaiah mixes the same terms, illustrations, and images as he did earlier, connecting them to the work of the Anointed One.

The promise of rebuilding, which critical scholars tend to apply to the work of Nehemiah, actually looks further ahead to the work of the Anointed One. He alone will bring Jerusalem to its ultimate glory as the city God intended her to be—the recipient of His "eternal joy" (v. 7). Just as He will spring forth from the line of David (Isa 11:1), so righteousness and praise will spring up before all nations (Hb. *ha goyim*, "Gentiles"). In all of Israel's history, there has never been anyone who has come close to fulfilling these promises except the One who claimed they were fulfilled in Him (Lk 4:21).

---

1. Jewish commentators almost unanimously interpret the speaker as the prophet himself. Cf. I. W. Slotki, *Isaiah*, SBB (Jerusalem: Socino Press, 1976), 298; A. Berlin and M. Z. Bretter, eds., *The Jewish Study Bible* (Oxford: Oxford University Press, 2004), 905. Most critical scholars do the same with little or no reference to Jesus. Some view the speaker as Trito-Isaiah, the presumed author of chaps. 56–66. See Claus Westermann, *Isaiah 40–66*, Old Testament Library (Philadelphia: Westminster Press, 1969), 366. He claims, "Trito-Isaiah knows that his task takes up that of Deutero-Isaiah."

2. John Oswalt, *The Book of Isaiah 40–66* (Grand Rapids: Eerdmans, 1998), 562–563. He argues that the book of Isaiah presents a unified synthesis of the servant/messiah throughout, noting that "Christians in all ages since have agreed." Even Joseph Blenkinsopp, *Isaiah 56-66* (New York: Doubleday, 2003), 220, admits, "We may accept this in a general sense." However, he proceeds to identify the speaker in Isa 61:1-3 as an individual prophet (disciple) whose ministry represents the "seed" (Hb. *zera'*) of the Servant in Isa 53:10.

3. Walter Kaiser, *The Messiah in the Old Testament* (Grand Rapids: Zondervan, 1995), 183. Franz Delitzsch, *Biblical Commentary on the Prophecies of Isaiah* (Grand Rapids: Eerdmans, 1965), 2:425-426, states, "the Servant of Jehovah and the Messiah are one and the same person." Thus, Jesus viewed Himself as both the "herald of the gifts of God" and the "dispenser of them." Edward Young, *The Book of Isaiah* (Grand Rapids: Eerdmans, 1972), 3:459, also sees a "trinitarian shade" in the contrast between *spirit* at the beginning of the first clause and *me* at the close of the second.

4. Blenkinsopp, *Isaiah 56-66*, 223. While he limits the speaker to the prophet, his observations of the Hebrew text are helpful and insightful.

5. Westermann, *Isaiah 40-66*, 367. He views this method as being unique to Trito-Isaiah whom he dates in the postexilic period. Interestingly, he admits that God could just as easily be the speaker here as well as the prophet, which is certainly the case if the speaker is in fact the divine Messiah. Delitzsch, *Prophecies of Isaiah*, 424–425, insists that it is highly unlikely that a true prophet of God would ascribe to himself such lofty attributes that he had already set forth as "characteristic features in his portrait of the predicted one."

6. Michael Rydelnik and James Spencer, "Isaiah," in *The Moody Bible Commentary*, ed. Michael Rydelnik and Michael Vanlaningham (Chicago: Moody Publishers, 2014), 1097. By contrast, critical scholars tend to view vv. 4-7 as a late insertion in light of the rebuilding under Nehemiah and vv. 8-11 as a covenant promise followed by a hymn of thanksgiving (cf. Blenkinsopp, *Isaiah 56-66*, 224).

7. Alec Motyer, *The Prophecy of Isaiah: An Introduction & Commentary* (Downers Grove, IL: InterVarsity, 1993), 502. He acknowledges that vv. 5-7 may be a deliberate insertion to make the divine confirmation clear, calling the insertion an "Isaianic mosaic of originally disparate pieces."

8. Young, however, does exactly that (3:462). Nevertheless, he rightly observes, "The reference is not merely to the rebuilding of Jerusalem after the exile, for the language is hardly applicable to that." But then he suggests that it refers to the "building up of the church from the ravages sin has made throughout the ages."

9. Rydelnik and Spencer, "Isaiah," 1097.

10. See the list of options in Blenkinsopp, *Isaiah 56-66*, 220–221, and Westermann, *Isaiah 40-66*, 366–367. Cf. also Paul Hanson, *Isaiah 40-66*, Interpretation: A Bible Commentary for Teaching and Preaching (Louisville: John Knox Press, 1995), 223–225.

11. Motyer, *Prophecy of Isaiah,* 27. See also Richard Schultz, *Do Historical Matters Matter?* (Wheaton, IL: Crossway, 2012).

12. Ibid. 499.

13. William Hendriksen, *Exposition of the Gospel According to Luke,* New Testament Commentary (Grand Rapids: Baker, 1978), 249–250. He provides one of the best and most thorough treatments of Luke 4:14-30, 247–262.

14. Darrell Bock, *Luke,* The IVP New Testament Commentary Series (Downers Grove, IL: InterVarsity, 1994), 86–87. He suggests that Luke's account is thematic and not intended to be a strictly chronological account, thus posing no historical problem. See also David Pow and Eckhard Schnabel, "Luke," in *Commentary on the New Testament Use of the Old Testament,* eds. G. K. Beale and D. A. Carson (Grand Rapids: Baker, 2007), 251–414.

15. Ibid., 88. Bock notes the original synagogue audience initially would have understood Jesus' claim to a divinely anointed prophetic ministry but not necessarily His messianic claim, which the readers of Luke's Gospel have already encountered in 3:21-22.

16. Hendriksen, *Gospel According to Luke,* 251. I. Howard Marshall, *The Gospel of Luke,* The New International Greek Testament Commentary (Grand Rapids: Eerdmans, 1978), 181, suggests a similar pattern based on Emil Schürer, *The History of the Jewish People in the Age of Jesus Christ* (New York: Shocken Books, 1973), 52–89.

17. Hendriksen, *Gospel According to Luke,* 253, suggests two possible options for the different translations: 1. Dungeons are dark and those set free finally see the "light of day"; 2. An alternate reading, "and to those bound opening of eyes." He also notes that neither the Masoretic Text nor Septuagint (LXX) has any reference to "set free those who are oppressed" (v. 18). He then suggests this phrase is an insertion (*midrash* or comment) indicating the implication of setting captives free from spiritual as well as physical blindness. Compare Lk 7:22 where Jesus assures the disciples of John the Baptist that "the blind receive their sight" as proof of His messianic claims.

18. Marshall, *Gospel of Luke,* 188.

19. Compare Oswalt, *Isaiah 40–66,* 2:30. Also, F. M. Cross and S. Talmon, *Qumran and the History of the Biblical Text* (Cambridge, MA: Harvard University Press, 1975).

20. Arndt and Gingrich, *A Greek-English Lexicon of the New Testament,* 677, indicate *plērothē* means "the same fulfillment of divine prediction or promise."

21. See comments by Marshall, *Gospel of Luke,* 185. He suggests that the initial day of declaration was an announcement that the messianic era had already begun and would continue.

22. Kevin Zuber, "Luke," in *The Moody Bible Commentary,* ed. Michael Rydelnik and Michael Vanlaningham (Chicago: Moody Publishers, 2014), 1561.

23. Hendriksen, *Gospel According to Luke,* 252.

24. Bock, *Luke,* 92.

25. Compare 2Sm 5:6 where the Jebusites taunt David with the words: "the blind and the lame can repel you" prior to his conquest of Jerusalem. Interestingly, Jesus performed only two significant miracles in Jerusalem proper prior to His resurrection. He healed the blind man at the pool of Siloam (Jn 9:1-12) and the lame man at the pool of Bethesda (Jn 5:1-17), indicating that the true son of David had arrived.

26. J. J. M. Roberts, "The Importance of Isaiah at Qumran," in *The Bible and the Dead Sea Scrolls,* ed. James H. Charlesworth (Waco, TX: Baylor University Press, 2006), 1:273.

27. Patrick Skehan, "IV. Litterature de Qumran: A. Textes biblique," *DB Sup,* 813.

28. Many of these are listed by F. J. Morrow, Jr., *The Text of Isaiah at Qumran* (Washington, DC: The Catholic University of America, 1973), 205–213.

29. F. F. Bruce, *Biblical Exegesis in the Qumran Texts* (Den Haag: Van Keulen, 1959).

30. Hervé Gabrion, "L 'interpretation de l' Ecriture dans al literature de Qumrân," ANRW 19:1779-848.

31. George Brooke, "Biblical Interpretation at Qumran," in *The Bible and the Dead Sea Scrolls,* ed. James H. Charlesworth (Waco, TX: Baylor University Press, 2006), 1:298.

32. This is discussed at length by J. J. Collins, "Messianic Expectation at Qumran," in *The Bible and the Dead Sea Scrolls,* ed. James H. Charlesworth (Waco, TX: Baylor University Press, 2006), 2:71–92.

33. Ibid., 92.

34. Emile Puech, *La Croyance des Esséniens* (Paris: Gabalda, 1993), 426–440; cf. also his "Resurrection: The Bible and Qumran," in *The Bible and the Dead Sea Scrolls,* 2:268–271.

35. Joseph Fitzmyer, SJ, *The Dead Sea Scrolls and Christian Origins* (Grand Rapids: Eerdmans, 2000), 93. He provides the full text in Hebrew; cf. also E. Puech, "Une apocalypse messianique (4Q521)," *Rev Q* (1991-92): 475–522.

36. J. J. Collins, "The Works of the Messiah," *Dead Sea Discoveries* 1 (1994), 98.

37. Hannah Harrington, "Purification in the Fourth Gospel," in *John, Qumran, and the Dead Sea Scrolls*, ed. Mary Coloe and T. Thatcher (Atlanta: Society of Biblical Literature, 2011), 135.

38. George Brooke, "Luke, John, and the Dead Sea Scrolls," in Coloe and Thatcher, *John, Qumran*, 86–87.

39. Fitzmyer, *Dead Sea Scrolls*, 109. He believes the 4Q521 text of Isa 61 and conflated phrases from Ps 146 are "characteristics of the time and coming of the Messiah as a prophetic figure."

40. Darrell Bock, *Luke 1:1–9:50*, Baker Exegetical Commentary on the New Testament (Grand Rapids: Baker, 1994), 668–669.

41. M. Daniel Carroll, "New Lenses to Establish Messiah's Identity?" in R. Hess and M. D. Carroll, eds., *Israel's Messiah in the Bible and the Dead Sea Scrolls* (Grand Rapids: Baker, 2003), 78.

42. Randall Price, *Secrets of the Dead Sea Scrolls* (Eugene, OR: Harvest House, 1996), 325.

43. Compare Isa 7:7; 25:8; 28:16; 40:10; 48:16; 50:4-9; 52:4; 56:8; 61:1,11; 65:13-15. Adonay Yahweh is also used 207 times in Ezekiel and 20 times in Amos.

44. Motyer, *Prophecy of Isaiah*, 500.

45. Oswalt, *Isaiah 40–66*, 564. Cf. 1Sam 10:1-7; 16:13; 2Sam 23:1-7. Oswalt argues that viewing the speaker as an unknown prophet (Deutero or Trito Isaiah) is "asking too much" in light of the fact that the Anointed One does the work of the Servant as previously pictured by Isaiah.

46. Daniel Block, quoted by M. Daniel Carroll, "New Lenses," 78.

47. Carroll, "New Lenses," 78. By contrast, Oswalt, *Isaiah 40–66*, 563, points out that the most potent instrument of the Anointed One in 11:2 is the "word of his mouth" (11:4).

48. Cf. various approaches by Grace Emmerson, *Isaiah 56–66*, Old Testament Guides (Sheffield: Sheffield Academic Press, 1992), 75-76; Paul Hanson, *Isaiah 40-66*; Hugh Williamson, *Variations on a Theme: King, Messiah and Servant in the Book of Isaiah* (Carlisle: Paternoster, 1998), 176–178; Westermann, *Isaiah 40-66*, 364–367; Elizabeth Achtemeier, *The Community and Message of Isaiah 56-66* (Minneapolis: Augsburg, 1982), 86–94.

49. Franz Delitzsch, *Biblical Commentary on the Prophecies of Isaiah* (Grand Rapids: Eerdmans, 1965), 2:425

50. Oswalt, *Isaiah 40–66*, 563; Rydelnik and Spencer, "Isaiah," 1096.

51. Oswalt, *Isaiah 40–66*, 563.

52. Westermann, *Isaiah 40-66*, 366. While he views the speaker as Trito Isaiah, he admits that "to proclaim salvation is almost as much to summon it into existence or bring it about."

53. I. W. Slotki, *Isaiah* (Jerusalem: Socino Press, 1976), 298.

54. Edward J. Young, *The Book of Isaiah*, New International Commentary on the Old Testament (Grand Rapids: Eerdmans, 1972), 3:459. He states, "It is the Messianic work, which no prophet in himself could carry out."

55. Slotki, *Isaiah*, 298. He notes that what that year signified to the individual, the coming redemption would mean for the nation.

56. John D. W. Watts, *Isaiah 34-66*, Word Biblical Commentary (Nashville: Thomas Nelson, 1987), 303. He notes that the prophets use it as a metaphor for release and freedom (cf. Jer 34:8,15,17).

57. Motyer, *Prophecy of Isaiah*, 500.

58. Slotki, *Isaiah*, 298, states, "it signifies the ability to see clearly as contrasted to the gloom of a prison."

59. Motyer, *Prophecy of Isaiah*, 500. He connects this passage to 49:8, where the "time of favor" referred to the coming of the Servant.

60. Rydelnik and Spencer, "Isaiah," 1097.

61. Motyer, *Prophecy of Isaiah*, 500.

62. Bock, *Luke 1:1-9:50*, 410.

63. Critical commentators tend to view this as the mourning of the returned Israelites to Jerusalem after their release from the Babylonian captivity. However, this is based on their view that this promise was written by Trito-Isaiah in the Persian era. See Watts, *Isaiah 34-66*, 303–304. Blenkinsopp, *Isaiah 56-66*, 226, goes to great lengths to defend this while admitting most critical explanations do not work well.

64. Blenkinsopp, *Isaiah 56-66*, 225.

65. Slotki, *Isaiah*, 298. The word *pe'er* also appears in the catalog of finery in chap 3.

66. Blenkinsopp, *Isaiah 56-66*, 226. Motyer, *Prophecy of Isaiah*, 501, adds, "The preposition *instead of* (*tahat*), expresses 'exact equivalence, substitution' (eg. Gn 22:13)."

67. Motyer, *Prophecy of Isaiah*, 501. He comments, "The passive (lit.) 'It will be called to them' stresses the objective reality, the achievement." Oswalt, *Isaiah 40–66*, 567, views the *waw* apodosis as expressing result (cf. NIV, "so").

68. Oswalt, *Isaiah 40–66*, 570.

Isaiah 63:1-6

The Messianic Warrior-Judge

MIKE STALLARD

At the outset of any study of the book of Isaiah, certain presuppositions must be asserted. First, one must approach the book with the understanding that the prophet's words are inspired by God (2Tm 3:16-17). As a result, the entire book is inerrant or true. This means that there are credible harmonizations for any alleged contradictions in the book. In fact, when the book is understood as true, it makes enormous sense for any reader in every respect.

Second, the use of grammatical-historical interpretation, sometimes called literal interpretation, is required. The goal is to understand the words as they were given and meant to be understood in their original language and historical setting. This means that there is autonomy for the text of Isaiah regarding its own interpretation. Consequently, the New Testament will not be read into Isaiah, although confirmation about fulfillment cited in NT texts will be briefly explored.

Third, an evangelical understanding of Isaiah believes in the unity of the 66 chapters. There is one author, not two or three, who has handed down a large and complete work. Such an approach is contrary to modern historical-critical views of the history of the text of Isaiah. The evidence for the unity of Isaiah is accepted as reasonable and correct; Isaiah's authorship will be assumed throughout the discussion to follow.[1]

VIEWS OF ISAIAH 63:1-6 AND CONTEXTUAL CONSIDERATIONS

Several different views have been offered as explanations of the judgment imagery of Isa 63:1-6. These interpretations attempt to identify Edom and Bozrah (v. 1), the bloody wrath described (vv. 2-6), and the time of the day of vengeance and year of redemption (v. 3). Several minor views have been put forward, which few have embraced. One such view is that Edom refers to Rome or to the Roman Catholic Church. There is nothing contextual to justify such speculation, although later rabbinical writings used Edom as a symbol of Rome[2] and Josephus speaks of Rome's conquering of the territory in AD 69.[3] Others have suggested that Michael the Archangel mentioned in Dan 10:13 during the Persian period is the intended referent. Yet the insertion of an angel into the storyline of the prophecy of Isa 63 seems to be far-fetched. Another view of limited acceptance is that the prophecy portrays the victorious Nebuchadnezzar of Babylon when he established sovereignty over Edom in the late seventh century BC. This new situation for Edom, however, was one of great taxation or tribute and not absolute destruction as Isaiah seems to depict.[4] The Edomites united with Babylon in 587 BC to support the destruction of Jerusalem (Ps 137:7; Lam 4:21-22) and thus continued as a nation, even if subservient.

One opinion that fortunately has had limited support is the view of Martin Luther, the great German Reformer. In his commentary on this section of Isaiah, Luther, blinded as he was by his anti-Semitism, identified Edom as the "ungodly synagogue," meaning the Jews. The Edomites were "red Jews" who are "bloodthirsty and murderous."[5] Tragically, Luther went on to comment on the sprinkled blood of v. 3 with these words: "every calamity of the Jews is for the sake of Christ." He apparently saw the second coming of Christ as the final destruction of the Jewish people.[6] In this way, he viewed the passage as Messianic. Nonetheless, it is such statements about Jewish people (particularly from a biblical passage that actually promises the blessing of national salvation for Israel; cf. Isa 63:7-9) that support the charge that Luther was anti-Semitic. He saw only cursing and not blessing for Israel.

Four significant views emerge for Isa 63:1-6 that are more widely held. First, a view popularized by John Calvin in the 16th century is identification of the victor who has judged Edom as God or Jehovah and not the Messiah in any technical sense. Calvin reacted to the idea that Christ in His passion is the picture being portrayed, something to be addressed below. He appeared to take Edom literally, but the timing of the punishment is indefinite. It was future to Isaiah's time when Edom would be appropriately judged as, indeed, Yahweh judges all peoples in the goings and comings of history.[7] This approach fails to address the elements in the context that point to ultimate eschatological events.

A second major position held by many interpreters is that the prophet Isaiah predicts the subjugation of Edom during the Maccabean period. The victor in v. 1 would be either Judas Maccabeus who had a major victory over Edom in 164 BC (1 Macc 5) or John Hyrcanus who led Judah to occupy Idumaea in 120 BC, a victory that was well known for forcing the conversion of the Edomites to Judaism.[8] One modern commentator suggests that this was the end of the Edomite kingdom.[9] Nonetheless, the Maccabean view has points of weakness. First of all, the language describing the victor in these verses goes beyond the accomplishments of Judas Maccabeus and John Hyrcanus.[10] The possible retort that Isaiah is using hyperbolic language falls to the ground when the context of Isa 63:1-6 suggests that the victory over Edom is also the time of ultimate kingdom restoration for Israel. Consequently, it is unlikely that Isaiah is prophesying a Maccabean event.

A third major view sees Isa 63:1-6 as a reference to the victory of Jesus the Messiah on the cross. Often, the resurrection and the ascension constitute part of the victory as well. The blood-stained garments and the judgment imagery in this view describe the shedding of Messiah's blood, in behalf of sinners, that took place in the first century. Usually Edom is taken as representative of all those who have opposed God and over whom Jesus has been victorious in His first advent. Thus, this interpretation takes Isa 63:1-6 as messianic. The thinking of the early church fathers was dominated by reading the passage as a prediction of the passion. Tertullian in the third century, for example, noted, "The prophetic Spirit contemplates the Lord as if he were already on his way to his passion, clad in his fleshly nature; and as he was to suffer therein, he represents the bleeding condition of his flesh under the metaphor of garments dyed in red, as if reddened in the treading and crushing process of the winepress."[11] Recent commentaries have also endorsed the conclusion that the work of Christ on the cross is in view. Oswalt, for example, acknowledges that at the second coming, Jesus will destroy all enemies, but this is only possible because Jesus went to the cross to die for our sins, thereby focusing on the passion.[12]

Although the great work of Christ in His death and resurrection is central and crucial to faith, the attempt to see this accomplishment particularly outlined in Isa 63 falls short. The immediate observation surfaces that the blood on the clothes of the Victor in Isa 63:1-2 is not His blood; it is the blood of His enemies. The imagery of the winepress demonstrates clearly that the staining of the clothes does not come from the treader of the grapes Himself but from the grapes that He is trampling. The scene is not the judgment of the cross but a different judgment where God pours out the blood of His and of Israel's enemies. As Leupold notes, nothing redemptive can be found in this particular scene.[13] "The year of my redemption" mentioned in v. 4 points to Israel's redemption at the point of the destruction of her enemies and not to the redemption bought by Christ on the cross. This redemption of Israel in context involves the glorious national as well as spiritual restoration. The various views highlighted thus far often miss this significant context.

Consequently, the best interpretation is eschatological because it takes into account the context in which Isa 63:1-6 is embedded. The last section of the book, chaps. 58–66, describes the final completion of God's intended restoration of His people Israel. The Victor in 63:1-6 has already been introduced in other messianic images throughout the text of Isaiah: Son (7:14), Child and Son (9:6-7), Branch (4:2; 11:1), and Servant in the so-called "Servant Songs" (42:1; 49:3; 50:10; 52:13; 53:11). This individual Messiah brings about the divine restoration of Israel. Chapter 61 announces His coming. He is the One upon whom the Spirit rests and is anointed by the Lord to bring good news to the poor (v. 1) and to "proclaim the year of the LORD's favor, and the day of our God's vengeance" (v. 2).[14] In chap. 62, the Messiah describes His intention to save and restore Jerusalem and Israel. They will be called "the Holy People, the LORD's Redeemed" (v. 12). Taking the passage at face value, one should not miss the context of Israel in the land and in her capital city Jerusalem. Allegorical understandings of this section should be abandoned.

Next under consideration is the judgment section of Isa 63:1-6. Israel's final restoration is accompanied by the judgment brought by the coming of Messiah, the Victor in the passage whose garments are stained with blood. The following section (Isa 63:7–64:12) constitutes a prayer of the nation asking for deliverance and forgiveness for themselves but punishment for their enemies, the last part a request that the imagery of 63:1-6 would indeed be carried out in history.[15] Chapter 65 gives God's answer to the prayer, the chief part being the promise of a new heaven and a new earth (vv. 17-25) where the "wolf and the lamb will feed together" (v. 25; cp. 11:6-9).[16] Isaiah's final chapter, 66, confirms God's promise of ultimate restoration and appropriate judgment. In light of this overwhelming focus on the coming of God's ultimate kingdom for Israel in this section of Isaiah, it is impossible to suggest any other referent for Isa 63:1-6 than judgment associated with the end-time days.

Note that the hope of Israel for a final and ultimate national and spiritual restoration of its kingdom on earth springs from OT expectation and does not depend on any later explanations from the NT, although books like Revelation confirm and elaborate on OT revelation. In particular, the understanding expressed here relies on the text of Isaiah alone.

One other view that must be addressed is double fulfillment. Some interpreters believe that the prophecy of Isa 63:1-6 uses the same language to predict two or more different events in future history. Delitzsch, for example, proposes that in Isa 63:1-6, the prophet saw events fulfilled in the time of the Maccabeans and in the time of the destruction of Jerusalem by Rome. This is a "both/and" approach that comes close to seeing the passage as fulfilled anytime in history when God judges the enemies of Israel. Both the evil ones in Israel as well as the enemies of Israel are thus covered in the judgments that are predicted. Presumably, Delitzsch's position also encompasses the second coming in Rev 19 as "formed upon the basis of that of Isaiah." This could be a borrowing of imagery, Isa 63 prefiguring the second coming, or such an elastic approach to the prophecy that it denotes any time on the stage of world history when God breaks through to judge those in and outside of Israel in a significant way.[17] As in other views critiqued above, this position fails to recognize Isaiah's surrounding emphasis on end-time events, including Israel's restoration.

EXEGESIS OF ISAIAH 63:1-6

These verses constitute the negative middle between 61:1 and the end of the book. Easily characterized as a gory passage, this section depicts the encounter of an apparent watchman, perhaps in Jerusalem, with a victorious warrior traveling from the south. The unit consists of two simple parts (63:1 and 63:2-6), both giving a question and an answer. The two questions are roughly the same; the second elaborates more fully on the first. Similarly, the two answers are equivalent in substance, although the second answer enlarges the content of the first. In context, the victorious warrior is the Messiah who has come to judge the enemies of Israel so that the nation will no longer experience trouble.

I. First Question and Answer (63:1): The Victor from the South. The previous chapter speaks of Zion's or Jerusalem's restoration. The city's designation at that time is "A City Not Deserted" (62:12). This is the perspective of the unnamed watchman in the next verse (63:1) who sees the figure coming from the south.

A. Question # 1: Who is this coming from Edom? (63:1a). Positioned probably in Jerusalem, a watchman—maybe even Isaiah is in view—spied an unnamed personage coming from Edom.

THE TERRITORY OF THE EDOMITES

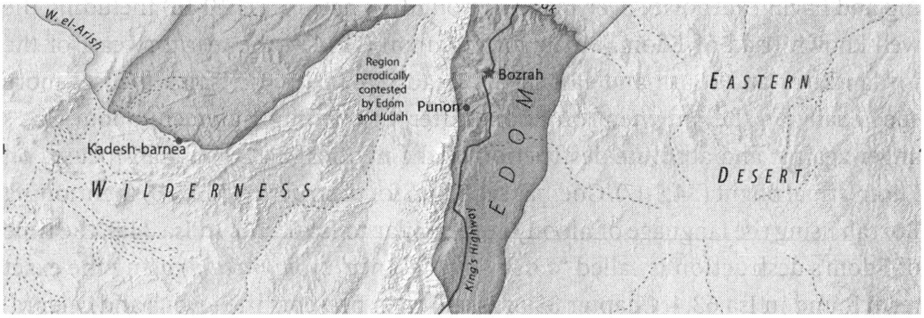

Adapted from Barry J. Beitzel, *The New Moody Atlas of the Bible* (Chicago: Moody, 2009), 169.

Edom is located south of Moab and of the Dead Sea. The word "Edom" means "red" and goes back to Esau, the older twin brother of Jacob, who was born "red-looking" (Gn 25:25) and who sold his birthright to Jacob to eat some reddish stew (Gn 25:31-33). The red color appropriately helps to explicate the judgment imagery that is expressed throughout the passage as the shedding of blood. Esau's descendants became a nation in their own right. Their posture, however, was one of hostility to Israel from the beginning of the relationship of Esau and Jacob and continuing throughout history. According to this passage, their judgment is inevitable.

The first verse also refers to Bozrah, a leading city and sometime capital of Edom that stood on the road between Petra and the Dead Sea. Scholars debate the meaning of the word "Bozrah." Some see it as referring to a stronghold or fortress, which fits its location surrounded on three sides by deep valleys, or a sheepfold, which fits its use in Isa 34:6. Another intriguing possibility is that it is related to the word "Bazir" which means "a vintage."[18] This reference to the fruit from a vineyard certainly fits the context of the passage under consideration in light of the winepress imagery throughout vv. 2-6. Today a city exists near the location as modern Buseirah. The inclusion of Bozrah intensifies the prophet's identification of the location from which the Messianic Victor is coming.[19]

Edom naturally references the people from Esau's lineage. History, however, records that the Edomites disappeared as a people following the destruction of Jerusalem by the Romans in AD 70.[20] Therefore, if the eschatological view is correct, as this article proposes, then the word "Edom" in the prophecy refers to the general geographical area that had been occupied by the Edomites.

Other prophecies in Isaiah help to confirm this end-time perspective on the judgment on Edom. In Isa 11, the prophet sees the coming kingdom in three portraits. First, the righteous presence of the Branch or Messiah from the house of David dispenses justice (11:1-4). Second, the natural world experiences radical transformation—"the wolf will live with the lamb" (11:6-9). Third, Israel experiences national restoration in its land. Part of this last picture finds Israel plundering and having authority over many surrounding nations (11:10-16) including the well-known triad of Edom, Moab, and Ammon (11:14)—the territory east of the Jordan River and south and east of the Dead Sea. In Isa 34, Isaiah focuses more specifically on the judgment on Edom. After an opening statement about God's anger against and absolute destruction of the nations (34:1-4), Isaiah focuses on Edom's final plight (34:5-17). God has set Edom for destruction (34:5-6) mentioning Bozrah using the language of bloody gore similar to Isa 63:1-6. In Isa 34:8, the time of Edom's destruction is called "a day of vengeance" (*yom nakam*) using the exact term found in Isa 63:4. Chapter 35 of Isaiah then presents the joyous and celebratory restoration of Zion.

One additional consideration about the identification of Edom in Isa 63:1 involves whether the reference is only to Edom itself or is emblematic of all the enemies of Israel. The plurality of nations that are judged at the time of the restoration of Israel appears multiple times in Isaiah (11:14; 17:12-14; 24:21; 33:3; 34:1-4; 61:6; 66:24). In one example, Moab appears as the exemplar of nations to be judged (25:7-10). Most often the prophecy is generally against the nations. Edom, however, is the exemplar of the nations in Isa 34:5-17 and 63:1-6. Edom should not be viewed as a *type* of the nations to be judged in any formal sense. Rather, Isaiah describes what judgment upon a nation looks like using Edom as an example. In this scheme, the people of the territory of Edom will literally receive judgment in the end-time days as will all nations for how they have treated Israel and for rebellion against the God of heaven (Jl 3:1-15; Mt 25:31-46). Isaiah 63:1-6 certainly goes beyond the judgment on Edom when the text twice mentions God's anger toward the nations (63:3,6).

Isaiah describes the Messianic Victor of Isa 63:1 in three ways. First, the wording "crimson-stained" depicts the garments of Messiah in parallel with the red clothes of 63:2. The word for "crimson-stained" designates more than the mere color red. The meaning includes the idea of sharpness or brightness. What Isaiah saw in his vision was something that could not be missed. The stained garments stood out with the brilliance of red colors. Second, Isaiah describes the Messiah as "one who is splendid in his apparel." The wording implies that He has been made splendid by the apparel He is wearing. It is a term that can imply honor. Isaiah voiced his sense of something special in what he saw. The mention of the apparel takes the reader back to the crimson-stained garments. The bright red color is what made the picture in front of Isaiah splendid. The first two depictions thus reinforce one another. Third, Isaiah notes that the Messianic Victor is "rising up proudly in His great might." In general terms, the image is one of a warrior. With the blood of His enemies on His garments, the warrior has conquered. The verb *rising up* has been debated. It means to incline, bend, or tilt and is used of tipping a container to empty its contents (Jer 48:12). In this context, it could refer to the tilting of the head backwards or upright in a demonstration of pride and victory. It could also be rendered *marching* or *striding*. At any rate, the Messianic Victor is moving in great strength or power, by "His great might." This is the confidence of one who procured absolute victory over His enemies. The entire portrait is one that attracts attention and helps to engender the beginning question, "Who is this?"

B. Answer # 1: It is I, proclaiming vindication, powerful to save (63:1b). The unintroduced answer given by the Victor is simply "It is I." The use of the first-person singular is common in the section of Isaiah that begins in chap. 40, usually referring to God speaking. Here it is the voice of the divine, messianic figure coming from Edom. This personage gives two qualifiers for His identity. The first one involves action: "proclaiming vindication." The word "vindication" (*sedaqah*) can also be translated *righteousness*. The concept of vindication fits the context. The Victor by destroying the enemies of Israel vindicates that nation as being chosen by God. The translation *righteousness* also fits the context since the righteous standards of God are upheld through the judgment described in the passage. Isaiah uses this word more than 30 times in the book. The HCSB translates it as vindication only in this one passage but with a note offering the alternative meaning of righteousness. The idea of righteousness is the best view.

The second qualifier for the identity of the Victor in this first answer is that He is "powerful to save." The word "powerful" expresses the idea of great or mighty. The idea of salvation in this context is the deliverance or rescue that the Victor has given Israel as He destroyed its enemies. This points to the final and ultimate deliverance for the nation that is the overall context of the surrounding sections of Isaiah. Also, the presence of the element of salvation reminds readers that judgment and deliverance often coincide. In the midst of judgment there is salvation, something that will again be asserted in v. 4. In this case, the judgment of Edom is part of the rescue of Israel.

II. Second Question and Answer (63:2-6): The Fury of Messiah's Wrath. The second round of question and answer gives greater detail about the judging work of the Victor from Edom. In particular, Isaiah's vision graphically fleshes out, in sometimes disturbing language, the wrathful judgment wrought by the Messiah.

A. Question # 2: Why are Your clothes red? (63:2). The onlooker's first question asked in v. 1 is "who." Here he asks "why?" Nonetheless, repetition exists. In v. 1, the stranger he wanted to identify had crimson-stained garments. In v. 2, making a play on the word "Edom," he asks directly, "Why are Your clothes red?" The question is then expanded: "and Your garments like one who treads a winepress?" The garments refer to the outer cloak of the Messiah, the part of His clothing that would be stained red. The staining of His garments looks as if He has been treading grapes in a winepress. The winepress in biblical times was a large container or trough holding grapes that were then stomped on by foot by a person standing in the winepress. Naturally, any garments would be stained by the juice being squeezed out. The image of treading grapes can be used as an analogy for slaughter, as the passage goes on to express.

B. Answer # 2: The wrath of Messiah (63:3-6). Each of the four verses in this section contains a reference to the Victor's anger or wrath. The entire section gives the elongated answer to the question of v. 2. In short, the Messiah's garments are red with the blood of the nations because of deserved judgment.

1. Trampling the nations in anger (63:3). From this point to the end of 63:6, the messianic Victor speaks without interruption. In response to the question about looking like a treader in the winepress, He embraces the image: "I trampled the winepress alone, and no one from the nations was with Me" (cf. Isa 59:16). The Messiah does His judgment work alone without help, an idea reiterated in 63:5. He takes full responsibility for the verdict that was carried out. That there was no one from the nations implies that no nation escaped this particular judgment. All who rebelled against God and persecuted Israel are the subjects of such wrathful disposition.

The Victor summarizes the thought of the winepress in the next statement: "I trampled them in My anger." The truth that people are being judged under the figure of one crushing grapes now becomes explicit. Using Hebrew parallelism, the messianic figure highlights the depth of this anger when He adds that He "ground them underfoot in [His] fury." The word for "fury" is a strong one meaning rage, venom, or a fierce wrath. Such unremitting anger is a necessary condition for the end-time judgment in view.

The next two statements are also parallel as Messiah directly answers the second question from v. 2—"why are Your clothes red?" Simply put, the blood of the rebellious nations "spattered my garments." The picture comes from the squirting of grape juice into the air as the treader tramples the grapes with his feet in the winepress. Tragically, what is being seen is not juice but real blood, the blood of those under actual judgment. As a result of this spattering, the Victor notes, "all my clothes were stained." His garments became unclean or stained with the blood of His enemies. Isaiah cites a similar notion in Isa 59:3 where the text says, "For your hands are *defiled* with blood," referring to judgment upon Israel (emphasis added). However, in 63:3, the Lord is not defiled in any sinful way. The idea of stain is merely a visual picture of what has happened in carrying out true judgment.

2. The day of vengeance and the year of My redemption (63:4). The Victor vocalizes a reason for the bloody judgment just described. His words give two aspects: the planning of the day of vengeance and the coming of the year of my redemption. The term "day of vengeance" occurs also in Isa 34:8 where it is described as "a time of paying back Edom for its hostility against Zion." Although such vengeance is not valid for men, God can appropriately and morally carry out such vengeance as Moses taught (Dt 32:35). In Isa 61:2, thc phrase "the day of our God's vengeance" occurs in the context of renewal for Israel. In Isa 63:4, the translation "I planned" is the rendering of the Hebrew phrase for "in my heart." The idea of planning is a good way of describing a time of vengeful judgment in the heart of Messiah. Anger does not automatically imply haste or a lack of thoughtfulness. Judgment is a divine prerogative.

The term "year of My redemption" ties blessing to the judgment by acknowledging that there is a morally good side to the day of vengeance. The phrase carries the notion of "blood revenge" within the general idea of release or redemption. The wording of the text demonstrates that the timing of the year of redemption is the same as the day of vengeance. Israel receives restoration, gaining what was lost and even more, partly because of the destruction of her enemies by the Messiah on the day of vengeance. Isaiah 63:4 serves as a kind of caption for the entire passage.

3. Victory for Messiah (63:5). This verse describes the "accomplished victory" of the Messiah on the day of vengeance just mentioned. The use of the past tense throughout the prophecy should not be taken as a reference to past events but to future accomplishment from God's perspective. From a human perspective, this coming of Messiah to judge is future to Isaiah's time as well as to the present time.

Isaiah 63:5 echoes what 63:3a depicts and also reproduces the wording of Isa 59:16. The Victor looks and finds "there was no one to help," which corresponds to "no one from the nations was with me" as He trampled the nations in the winepress in 63:3a. The messianic figure repeats this observation: "I was amazed that no one assisted." The statement of amazement points to the lack of human intercession in the needed vengeance and redemption (cf. Isa 59:16). No mere human was qualified to accomplish such an important task. Messiah stands alone as the destroyer of the enemies of Israel. He performs the bloody business of judgment by His own "arm," that is, His own power. The Victor is assisted only by His own wrath. The unwavering purpose and power of the Lord accomplishes such a great victory in behalf of Israel. Modern culture does not like judgment, but from God's point of view, it is a victory.

4. The nations crushed by Messiah's angry judgment (63:6). This verse repeats the concepts from the latter portion of 63:3. The language, however, is intensified in making three statements. First, the Victor says, "I crushed nations in my anger." The term "crushed" goes beyond the action of treading to the result of the trampling. In this context, the word refers to the absolute destruction of enemies in battle. Second, the Messiah comments, "I made them drunk with my wrath." The metaphor of drunkenness implies that the Victor's work of treading down the nations completely overpowered the nations in the same way an inebriated person is totally controlled by wine. The wrathful actions of the Victor accomplished this state of affairs. Third, the warrior from Edom states that he "poured out their blood on the ground." There is no reason not to take such language literally. When Messiah comes, He will pour out the lifeblood of the enemies of God. The spilling of blood means death, not just injury. Perhaps it is to this bloody judgment that Rev 14:19-20 is referring when it speaks of blood flowing "to the horses' bridles."

JEWISH RABBINICAL SOURCES

One interesting area of complementary support for the messianic nature of the prophecy in Isa 63:1-6 comes from the Jewish Targums. Jacob's last words to Judah in Gn 49:11 include "He ties his donkey to a vine, and the colt of his donkey to the choice vine. He washes his clothes in wine and his robes in the blood of grapes." Pseudo-Jonathan on Genesis, dated by some scholars in the time of the Crusades,[21] gives an expanded interpretation: "How noble is the king, Messiah, who is going to rise from the house of Judah. He has girded his loins and come down, setting in order the order of battle with his enemies and killing kings with their rulers . . . reddening the mountains with the blood of their slain. With his garments dipped in blood, he is like one who treads grapes in the press."[22] The language mimics Isa 63:1-3, although the picture of the winepress appears elsewhere in Scripture as a metaphor for judgment (Jl 3:13). This particular statement appears to embrace an eschatological view of the Messiah's judgment.

NEW TESTAMENT CONFIRMATION

In Rev 19:11-21, the description of the second coming of Christ lends its support to the end-time understanding of the judgment language of Isa 63:1-6. Although Revelation adds information not found in the Isaiah passage, it does not explain the wording of the OT text beyond what is already available in Isaiah on its own. According to the Apocalypse, when Jesus returns to establish the millennial kingdom, He comes as a warrior and judge (Rev 19:11-12). He wears a robe dipped in blood (Rev 19:13; Isa 63:1-3), an image borrowed from the Victor from Edom. Christ strikes the nations by His spoken word (Rev 19:15). Then, with wording right out of Isa 63, the Apocalypse notes, "He will also trample the winepress of the fierce anger of God, the Almighty" (Rev 19:15). A description of the "great supper of God" follows, in which the flesh of the enemies of God is eaten by birds (Rev 19:17-18). The beast (Antichrist) and false prophet are "thrown alive into the lake of fire" (v. 20). Jesus the Messiah then kills the remaining enemies of God as their lifeblood is spilled on the ground and their flesh eaten (Rev 19:21; Isa 63:6). When the two passages are put side by side, the influence of Isaiah on the Apocalypse becomes obvious. In this way, the book of Revelation reinforces the conclusion that the language of Isa 63:1-6 points to the eschaton, when Messiah will make all things right in judging the enemies of God and establishing His earthly kingdom.

CONCLUSION

The negative language of Isa 63:1-6 and Rev 19:11-21 provides an obstacle for some readers who struggle with the harshness of judgment imagery. However, as the case is for many of the prophets, hope is coupled with deserved judgment. The songwriter Julia Ward Howe wrote an American Civil War song entitled "Battle Hymn of the Republic" (1861), whose language borrows heavily from Isaiah and Revelation: "Mine eyes have seen the glory of the coming of the Lord; He is trampling out the vintage where the grapes of wrath are stored." The horror of war and notions of judgment often go together. But the judgment of God is a reality that all people must face. The warning of Isa 63:1-6 is that people should put their trust in Jesus the Messiah and have confidence in God's plan for history, both the judgment and the blessing.

---

1. Mike Stallard, "Answering the Higher Critics," *Israel My Glory* (March/April 2012): 26–29; Oswald T. Allis, *The Unity of Isaiah: A Study in Prophecy* (Philadelphia: Presbyterian and Reformed Publishing Company, 1950), 20–21.
2. Victor Buksbazen, *The Prophet Isaiah: A Commentary* (repr., Bellmawr, NJ: Friends of Israel Gospel Ministry, 2008), 471.
3. Josephus, *The Wars of the Jews*, 4.9.7.
4. R. K. Harrison, "Edom" in *The Zondervan Pictorial Encyclopedia of the Bible* (Grand Rapids: Zondervan, 1976), 2:204.
5. Here Luther extravagantly uses the familial relationship of Jacob (Israel) and Esau (Edom) to apply statements about the latter to the former.
6. Brooks Schramm and Kirsi I. Stjerna, eds., *Martin Luther, the Bible, and the Jewish People: A Reader* (Minneapolis, MN: Fortress Press, 2012), 117–21.
7. John Calvin, *Commentary on the Book of the Prophet Isaiah*, trans. William Pringle (Bellingham, WA: Logos Bible Software, 2010), 4:337–343.
8. Harrison, "Edom," 204.
9. Buksbazen, *The Prophet Isaiah: A Commentary*, 472.
10. Albert Barnes, *Notes on the Old Testament Explanatory and Practical: Isaiah Vol. II*, ed. Robert Frew (repr., Grand Rapids: Baker Book House, 1977), 386.
11. Tertullian, *Against Marcion*, 4.40. See Mark W. Elliott, ed., *Isaiah 40–66*, Ancient Christian Commentary on Scripture, Old Testament, ed. Thomas C. Oden (Downers Grove, IL: InterVarsity Press, 2007), 11:251. For another example from the church fathers of first advent interpretations of Isa 63:1-6, see Gregory of Nazianzus, *Oration: The Second Oration on Easter* 45.25.
12. John N. Oswalt, *The Book of Isaiah, Chapters 40–66*, The New International Commentary on the Old Testament (Grand Rapids: William B. Eerdmans, 1998), 591.
13. H. C. Leupold, *Exposition of Isaiah* (Grand Rapids: Baker Book House, 1971), 2:337.
14. Isaiah looks down the corridor of time and sees the Messiah doing all these things without distinguishing between a first advent and a second advent concerning Jesus Christ. The point being made here is that Isa 63 looks into the future to find the eschaton, the end of days, when all things will be made right with proper judgments and blessings.
15. John A. Martin, "Isaiah" in *The Bible Knowledge Commentary: An Exposition of the Scriptures* ed. John F. Walvoord and Roy B. Zuck (Wheaton, IL: Victor Books, 1985), 1:1118–19.

16. This section gives elements that suggest that the millennial kingdom is in view. Isaiah looks forward in history and telescopically writes down what he sees without any time distinctions made. It remained for John in Revelation to help nail down the distinction between the millennium and the new heaven and earth as the eternal state.

17. F. Delitzsch, *Isaiah*, vol. 2 of Commentary on the Old Testament in Ten Volumes by C. F. Keil and F. Delitzsch, trans. James Martin (repr., Grand Rapids: William B. Eerdmans, 1978), 2:448–49.

18. Buksbazen, *The Prophet Isaiah: A Commentary*, 471.

19. For the view that Bozrah means "sheepfold" and refers to the city of Petra, see Larry Feldman's article on Micah 2:12-13 in this *Handbook*.

20. Harrison, "Edom," 2:204.

21. Michael L. Klein, "A New Edition of Pseudo-Jonathan," *Journal of Biblical Literature* 94:2 (June 1975): 277–79.

22. John Bowker, *The Targums and Rabbinic Literature: An Introduction to Jewish Interpretations of Scripture* (New York: Cambridge University Press, 1969), 278.

Jeremiah 23:5-6

The Divine Branch of the Lord

MICHAEL L. BROWN

Jeremiah 23:5-6 is an important messianic prophecy because: (1) it envisions the coming of the Messianic King on the heels of the return from Babylonian exile, which is in keeping with a larger prophetic pattern that expected the establishment of God's glorious kingdom in the aftermath of this return; (2) it explicitly connects the title Branch (*ṣemaḥ*)[1] with this Davidic King (see further Jer 33:15; cf. also Isa 4:2; Zch 3:8; 6:12; see Zch 6:9-15); (3) it hints at the Messiah's divine nature in the name *yhwh ṣidqēnû*.[2]

CONTEXTUAL BACKGROUND

It is significant that this section of Jeremiah (20:1–23:8) focuses on the sinning leaders of Judah, specifically, the four descendants of Josiah who reigned as kings (three sons and one grandson, namely, Jehoahaz, Jehoiakim, his son Jehoiachin, and Zedekiah). They were as wicked as Josiah had been righteous, which underscores the great responsibility of the leadership for the exile of the nation. The failure of the current Davidic dynasty caused God to promise to raise up another, superior Davidide (Davidic king) to restore the nation.[3] Verses 1-6 of this chapter bring this polemic against the kings (here, called shepherds) to a close.[4] As noted by S. Amsler, "Jeremiah employs the expression *ṣemaḥ ṣaddîq* 'righteous sprout' to designate the expected king who will perform the royal office, so poorly administered at the moment by the Davidides, namely by Zedekiah, in the fullest sense (Jer 23:5)."[5] This is heightened by the play on words of *ṣemaḥ ṣaddîq* vs. *ṣidqiyāhû* (Zedekiah),[6] and is in keeping with the rendering of *ṣemaḥ ṣaddîq* by some scholars as "legitimate scion."[7]

This King would do everything the recent kings had not, ruling wisely and practicing justice (contrast Jer 21:12; 22:1-4; and see Isa 11:1-5). During His reign, both Israel and Judah will be saved (Jer 23:6), not primarily in the New Testament sense of *sōzō*, as in, e.g., Ac 2:47, but rather in the sense of being delivered from their enemies and restored to their land. Right relationship with God, however, is presupposed, meaning that natural restoration will accompany spiritual restoration. Of importance here is the promise to Israel and Judah together, which always has major implications—often of messianic proportions—in the prophetic literature (cf., e.g., Jer 3:18; Zch 8:13; 10:6; Ezk 37:15-28). Clearly, this King will do more than any of His predecessors, including even His forefather David.

When was the reign of this Righteous Branch expected? The Lord had just indicted the sinning leaders for banishing and scattering His flock (Jer 23:1-2) before giving this word of promise: "'I will gather the remnant of My flock from all the lands where I have banished them, and I will return them to their grazing land. They will become fruitful and numerous. I will raise up shepherds over them who will shepherd them. They will no longer be afraid or dismayed, nor will any be missing.' This is the LORD's declaration" (Jer 23:3-4). This oracle, then, presupposes that some (or much) of God's flock is in exile (including the scattering of the northern tribes, along with at least the first exile of the southern kingdom in 605 BC, if not the final exile in 586 BC), hence the promise to regather the sheep "from all the lands where I have banished them." But note that this promised regathering, which surely had as its first referent the return from Babylonian captivity under Cyrus, is depicted in glorious terms: "I will return them to their grazing land. They will become fruitful and numerous. I will raise up shepherds over them who will shepherd them. They will no longer be afraid or dismayed, nor will any be missing." Not only so, but it is in this context that the Righteous Branch is promised. "'The days are coming'—this is the LORD's declaration—'when I will raise up a Righteous Branch of David. He will reign wisely as king and administer justice and righteousness in the land. In His days Judah will be saved, and Israel will dwell securely. This is what He will be named: Yahweh Our Righteousness'" (Jer 23:5-6).

These glorious expectations are in keeping with other oracles in Jeremiah (e.g., 24:5-7; 30:8-9; 31:38-40; 32:37-42; 50:4-5) along with oracles in Isaiah and Ezekiel (see, e.g., Isa 40:1-11; 52:1–54:17; Ezk 36:1-38) which promise: (1) the wondrous, physical return of the exiles to the land; (2) their blessed resettlement there; (3) their spiritual renewal and restoration; and (4) the glorious reign of the Messianic King.

Each of these promises has a *historic, partial fulfillment*, beginning in the 530s BC, when the first wave of Babylonian exiles returned home and when Jerusalem was initially rebuilt, culminating in the Messiah's first coming before the Second Temple was destroyed, and each of these promises has a *future, ultimate fulfillment* that awaits the end of the age. At that time—at the eschaton—there will be a final, supernatural regathering of Israel's remaining exiles, a Jewish return to God of national proportions, the Messiah's second coming, the establishing of God's kingdom on the earth, and the final, glorious rebuilding of Jerusalem. The promises in the late sixth century BC would have the quality of "already/not yet"—to borrow George Eldon Ladd's terminology—signifying that the time of redemption had begun, but its final consummation was still to come.[8]

So then, just as the return from exile *did* take place after 70 years, as prophesied, although not with the expected glory, so also the Messianic Era began and the new covenant was established—only not with the expected glory and not in the immediate aftermath of the return from Babylon and the rebuilding of the Temple, but rather during the Second Temple period, before its destruction in AD 70. But the historic events of the return from exile and the first coming of the Messiah serve as the deposit and down payment of the future events, namely, the final, eschatological ingathering of the Jewish exiles and the return of the Messiah to complete His mission. The former events thus guarantee the latter, with the return from Babylon in the late sixth century BC serving as the "first coming home," while the final ingathering of the exiles will serve as the "second coming home," parallel to the Messiah's first and second comings. So also with the establishing of the new covenant: It *did* begin, as promised, in the Second Temple period—the "days are coming" oracles cannot be pushed into the eschaton in their entirety—but touching a much smaller group of people than expected and still not in its full force. When the Messiah returns, the promise will reach its ultimate fulfillment (see Zch 12:10–13:2). Thus, the realization of the new covenant will follow the same pattern outlined in Zch 9:9-10, growing from humble beginnings (the Messianic King begins his reign "humble and riding on a donkey") until in the end, it encompasses the entire world ("His dominion will extend from sea to sea and from the Euphrates River to the ends of the earth").

When was this glorious King expected to be raised up? Certainly, in context, sandwiched as it is between Jer 23:3-4 and 7-8, the reader would naturally associate the return from the exile with the raising up of this Righteous Branch, as, presumably, Jeremiah himself had done (see 1Pt 1:10-12; cf. also Jer 33:10-17). This is confirmed by other prophecies as well; see, e.g., Isa 11:1, which follows on the heels of Isa 10:33-34, and note that Isa 52:1-12 and 54:1-17 provide the immediate context for 52:13–53:12; see further texts such as Ezk 40–48, which clearly associated the ushering in of a glorious age with the return from exile (cf. further Isa 40:1-11; and note Zch 6:12-13, stating that the Branch will build the "LORD's temple"—spoken at the very time in which the Second Temple was being constructed).

This was certainly central to Jeremiah's hopes as well, expressed throughout Jer 30–33; see also Jer 3:14-18; 4:1-2, leaving three main lines of possible interpretation: (1) The prophecies were the exaggerated creations of excited human minds, and, not surprisingly, they failed.[9] Against this is not only the belief in the inspiration of the Scriptures but the unlikelihood that all these allegedly failed prophecies would then be preserved as sacred writ by subsequent generations of believers. (2) The prophecies are yet to be fulfilled, which is why observant Jews still pray thrice daily for the coming of the Messiah. Yet this is still an admission that the predictions did, in fact, fail, and it does not address key messianic prophecies that declared that God would act in a glorious and redemptive way during the days of the Second Temple (see Dn 9:24-27; Mal 3:1-5; Hag 2:20-23).[10] (3) Although things did not unfold exactly as the prophets foresaw, and although there is yet future fulfillment to some of their words, the Righteous Branch did, in fact, come during the days of the Second Temple, bringing salvation to the world, and laying the foundation for the fulfillment of all the other promises spoken by the Lord through the prophets. He is the divine deposit, guaranteeing that God will surely bring to pass the rest of what He has promised.[11]

IS "BRANCH" (*ṢEMAḤ*) A MESSIANIC TITLE?

Martin Abegg refers to *ṣemaḥ* (branch) in Jeremiah and Zechariah as a "clearly messianic figure."[12] *The Hebrew and Aramaic Lexicon of the Old Testament* defines *ṣemaḥ* in Jer 23:5 and 33:15 as "a particular shoot, referring to an individual person, a descendant of David and of the king in the Messianic era of salvation," while the Clines *Dictionary of Classical Hebrew* defines *ṣemaḥ* in these verses, along with Isa 4:2 and Zch 6:12, as speaking "of a future messianic ruler." Amsler notes that, "A specialized usage [of *ṣ-m-ḥ*] occurs in the context of royal ideology. The 'last words of David' (2 Sam 23:1-7) . . . depict the political success granted David with *ṣmḥ* hi. (v. 5). Psa 132:17 uses it to express the expectation of a renewal of the Davidic dynasty."[13] Furthermore, "At Qumran, 4QPBless 1:3f. and 4QFlor 1:11 use the title 'sprout of David' to designate the legitimate ruler who will reestablish the Davidic dynasty in the place of the Herodian and who will restore them to their appropriate place among the people."[14]

The Targum also recognizes the messianic significance of *ṣemaḥ*, rendering it with *m*ᵉšîḥā', Messiah, at Isa 4:2; Jer 23:5; 33:15; Zch 3:8; 6:12. The messianic use of this title continues in the traditional Jewish prayer known as the Amidah or the Shemoneh Esrei (Eighteen Benedictions), with the Fifteenth Benediction containing both nominal *ṣemaḥ* and verbal *ṣ-m-ḥ* (in the Hiphil, as in Ps 132:17, which is clearly alluded to in this benediction as well; cf. also 2Sm 23:5) in the space of just six Hebrew words ("The Branch of Your servant David, cause to spring forth speedily"). Verbal *ṣ-m-ḥ* (again in the Hiphil) is also found in the closing clause of the prayer ("Blessed are You, O Lord, who causes the horn of salvation to sprout forth"). So from the Hebrew Scriptures to Qumran to some of the oldest preserved prayers of Judaism, prayers that are still recited to this day, the Messianic King has been identified as the "Branch of David."[15] As for NT usage, G. H. Parke-Taylor notes that the LXX renders *ṣemaḥ* in Jer 23:5 (not 33:14) and in Zch 3:8; 6:12 with *anatolē* (rise, rising of the sun), citing Raymond E. Brown's comments on Lk 1:78 in *The Birth of the Messiah* (New York: Doubleday, 1977), 390: "... *anatole* was a term used among Greek-speaking Jews to describe the expected king of the house of David."[16]

G. H. Johnston, however, argues that Jeremiah used the term "righteous branch" as a collective title for the future, renewed Davidic dynasty, pointing to the virtual repetition of the oracle in Jer 33:14-16, which is followed by 33:17-26, verses that guarantee an unbroken chain of Davidic kings and Levitical priests. Thus,

> The use of plural forms throughout the passage makes clear that Jeremiah understood the singular branch in a collective sense.... By alluding to God's promise of innumerable descendants (Gn 13:6; 15:5; 22:17; 26:4), it is clear that Jeremiah envisages, not a single eternal Davidic king, nor a single Levitical priest, but a multiplicity of Davidides on the throne and Levites before the altar. Rather than identifying the 'righteous branch' as the single eschatological Messiah of Second Temple period literature, Jeremiah has in mind a dynasty of godly Davidides ruling in succession one generation after another.[17]

Johnston cites S. Mowinckel, M. Fishbane, W. J. Wessels, J. J. Collins, G. Gakuru, and J. J. M. Roberts in support of this position, also arguing that Jer 33:17-26 is to be dated later than 33:14-16 (and 23:5-6), hence providing a clear explication of the author's understanding of these earlier Branch oracles.[18] Is it correct, then, to view Jer 23:5-6 (and 33:14-16) as messianic, or should these passages be seen first and foremost as predicting an ongoing Davidic dynasty, and therefore only messianic in a secondary (*sensus plenior*?) manner? Wolter H. Rose describes the messianic hope as "expectations focusing on a future royal figure sent by God who will bring salvation to God's people and the world and establish a kingdom characterized by features like peace and justice."[19] Is this what Jeremiah spoke of, or did he envision here a succession of godly, Davidic kings? It seems clear that it is a singular king—the Messiah—whom Jeremiah predicted.

Note first that an eschatological David was already spoken of by Hosea in the eighth century BC: "Afterward, the people of Israel will return and seek the Lord their God and David their king. They will come with awe to the LORD and to His goodness in the last days" (Hos 3:5). This points to a final, glorious ruler rather than a succession of godly Davidic kings, and Hosea's influence on Jeremiah is widely recognized.[20] The oracles in Ezekiel, which overlap with those of Jeremiah and then postdate his oracles, confirm this interpretation as well. See Ezk 34:23-34 and 37:24-25, both of which focus on an individual ruler, beginning with 34:23a: "I will appoint over them a single shepherd, My servant David." It is this new and greater David, a singular future king, who will be even greater than His eponymous ancestor, a ruler who will be the legitimate scion, the Righteous Branch indeed.

As for Jer 33:17-26, there is no contradiction, since Jeremiah only guaranteed that "David will never fail to have a man sitting on the throne of the house of Israel" (Jer 33:17). This could be fulfilled through a succession of Davidic kings leading up to the final, greater David, or it could be fulfilled through the ongoing reign of that greater David. Either way, given that the Babylonian exile, the first years of which were witnessed by Jeremiah (as he saw Jerusalem fall), did bring a temporary end to Davidic rule over the nation, the prophet fully realized that there would be a hiatus in Davidic rulers sitting on his throne in Jerusalem. What he promised, by the superintending of the Spirit, was that this would not be permanent, not that there would be an endless succession of future Davidic kings. Johnston is thus partly correct in stating that, "It was, in fact, the non-restoration of the Davidic throne in the Second Temple period that caused a theological crisis in Israel, which ultimately led to the hermeneutical soil in which an eschatological Messianic hope was planted."[21] It would be more accurate to state that it was this crisis that ultimately led to a clearer understanding of the eschatological messianic hope of the prophets.

DOES THE NAME *YHWH ṢIDQĒNÛ* POINT TO THE MESSIAH'S DIVINE NATURE?

While there appear to be definite references to the Messiah's deity in the Hebrew Scriptures (see Isa 9:6 [5]; Ps 45:6 [7]),[22] or, at the least, indications that He would be highly exalted (see Isa 52:13) and greater than David (see Ps 110:1), there are always clear distinctions between Yahweh and His Messiah (e.g., in Ps 110:1, it is the Lord who invites the Davidic Messiah to sit at His right hand while in Ps 45:6-7 [7-8] it is God who anoints the Davidic king). It would therefore seem improbable that the Messiah would actually be called Yahweh, making it unlikely that *yhwh ṣidqēnû*, the name of the Righteous Branch, should be rendered, "Yahweh our righteousness" (cf., e.g., KJV; NKJV; NASB; HCSB) as if the Messiah was Yahweh Himself. Instead, it would appear that the name should be translated, "Yahweh is our righteousness" (cf. NRSV; ESV; NLT), meaning, "Yahweh is the source of our righteousness and vindication" (cf. Rashi's, "The Lord will vindicate us during this one's days").[23] Further confirmation for this view comes from Jer 33:16, where *it is the city of Jerusalem*, rather than the Messiah, who bears this name, and surely the city was not being addressed as Yahweh. (Note that all versions cited here render *yhwh ṣidqēnû* identically at 23:6 and 33:16.)

It would be wrong, however, to dismiss this name as merely another theophoric onomasticon (referring to a name which bears a divine element), in the class of names like Elijah and Jeremiah, which bear the shortened divine name *yah*, or names like Ezekiel or Daniel, which bear the noun *'ēl*, God/god, or names like Adonijah, which combines the noun *'ādôn*, Lord/lord, with the shortened divine element *yah*, since names that contain the tetragrammaton (*yhwh*) always use it in abbreviated form, either at the beginning (represented by names such as Jehoram or Josiah) or at the end (represented by names ending in *iah* or *jah*).

Only when speaking of the Messianic King is the Lord's name written in full, suggesting that, in a unique way, He bears that divine name, similar to the Angel of the Lord in certain key contexts (see, e.g., Ex 3:1-6; Jdg 13:1-23). This becomes even more significant when we realize that the Lord's full name, the tetragrammaton, was used in place names, such as "Yahweh Is There" (Ezk 48:35), since it was not possible to mistake a place for a person, and His presence could be especially associated with a particular locale. It was therefore of great significance when His name was on/in one of His messengers. Note Ex 23:20-21: "I am going to send an angel before you to protect you on the way and bring you to the place I have prepared. Be attentive to him and listen to his voice. Do not defy him, because he will not forgive your acts of rebellion, for My name is in him." As explained in the Chizkuni commentary (13th century), "seeing that My name is within him, he has the right to speak of himself by proclaiming: 'I am the Lord,' meaning I am His general manager of the universe, known in kabbalistic parlance as Mattatron [or, Metatron, the highest-ranking angel]. That name [viz., Metatron] can be understood as 'chief of the angels,' or 'G-d in miniature.'"[24]

Even more distinctly, God's name is in/on His Messiah, as reflected in His own name being "Yahweh Is Our Righteousness."[25] The Talmud recognizes the significance of this as well, without, of course, deducing from the text that the Messiah is divine. As found in b. Bava Bathra 75b,

> Rabbah in the name of R. Johanan further stated: The righteous will in time to come be called by the name of the Holy One, blessed be He; for it is said: Every one that is called by My name, and whom I have created for My glory, I have formed him, yea, I have made him [Isa 43:7]. R. Samuel b. Nahmani said in the name of R. Johanan: Three were called by the name of the Holy One; blessed be He, and they are the following: The righteous, the Messiah and Jerusalem. [This may be

> inferred as regards] the righteous [from] what has just been said. [As regards] the Messiah—it is written: And this is the name whereby he shall be called, The Lord is our righteousness [Jer 23:6]. [As regards] Jerusalem—it is written: It shall be eighteen thousand reeds round about; and the name of the city from that day shall be "the Lord is there." [Ezk 48:35] Do not read, "there" [*šammâ*] but "its name" [*šᵉmah*].[26]

In sum, then, while it is best to render with "Yahweh Is Our Righteousness" rather than "Yahweh Our Righteousness," the name speaks of the intimate connection between the Messiah and Yahweh, who in a unique and unprecedented way is thereby identified with the Lord, presumably carrying His presence and authority.

---

1. For an extensive discussion of *ṣemaḥ* with a somewhat different emphasis, see Wolter H. Rose, *Zemah and Zerubbabel: Messianic Expectation in the Early Postexilic Period* (Journal for the Study of the Old Testament Supplement 304; Sheffield: Sheffield Academic Press, 2000), 91–120.

2. Some of the material that follows has been adapted from Michael L. Brown, "Jeremiah," in Tremper Longman III and David Garland, eds., *The Expositor's Bible Commentary, Revised Edition* [Grand Rapids: Zondervan, 2010], 7:309–12, with permission. See there for further discussion and annotation.

3. Parallel to this is the need for a new covenant (Jer 31:31-34) because of the failure of the people to observe the Sinaitic covenant, seen clearly in the aftermath of Josiah's futile attempt to renew the nation in Torah obedience followed by the collapse of the monarchy, the destruction of the Temple, and the exile into Babylon; see Brown, "Jeremiah," 7:398–403.

4. For the use of the term "shepherd" in prophetic oracles, cf. Gerhard Wallis, "*râ'â*," in *Theological Dictionary of the Old Testament* 13:551–52 (full article 13:544–53).

5. S. Amsler, "*ṣmḥ* to sprout," in *Theological Dictionary of the Old Testament* 3:1086 (full article 3:1085–87).

6. For the proposed chiastic structure highlighting this from 21:1–23:8, see Gordon H. Johnston, "What Did the Hebrew Prophets Know About the Messiah and When Did They Know It?" A Paper Presented to the Jeremiah and Ezekiel Section, 2010 Meeting of the Evangelical Theological Society, 3. This is an expanded version of his discussion in Herb Bateman III, Darrell Bock, and Gordon Johnston, eds., *Jesus the Messiah: Promises, Expectations, and the Coming of Israel's King* (Grand Rapids: Kregel, 2010).

7. See, e.g., the Jeremiah commentaries of William L. Holladay (Hermeneia) and Jack R. Lundbom (Anchor). Cognate evidence in Phoenician and Ugaritic suggests the meaning "rightful, legitimate," rather than "righteous," but in the context of Jer 20–23, "righteous" makes excellent sense.

8. See in particular Ladd's work *The Presence of the Future: The Eschatology of Biblical Realism* (repr. Grand Rapids: Eerdmans, 1996).

9. In the words of S. R. Driver, "It must be evident that many of these promises have not been fulfilled, and that now circumstances have so changed that they never can be fulfilled; but, like the similar pictures drawn by other prophets, they remain as inspiring ideals of the future which God would fain see realized by or for His people, and of the goal which man, with God's help, should ever strive to attain." See S. R. Driver, *The Book of the Prophet Jeremiah* (London: Hodder and Stoughton, 1906), xli; for further discussion, cf. Brown, "Jeremiah," 7:560–65.

10. See Michael L. Brown, *Answering Jewish Objections to Jesus, Vol. 1: General and Historical Objections* (Grand Rapids: Baker, 2000), 69–88.

11. It is true, as William McKane pointed out, that "most commentators have rightly supposed (cf. Duhm) that *hnh ymym b'ym* [behold, days are coming] is indicative of a distant rather than an immediate future" (see William McKane, *A Critical and Exegetical Commentary on Jeremiah: Vol. I* International Critical Commentary [Edinburgh: T&T Clark, 1986], 560), but, from the prophet's perspective, as he observed, "the portrayal is not that of a Messianic kingdom beyond the present age" (ibid., 561). In this case, that "present age" cannot be severed completely from the return from exile.

12. M. G. Abegg, Jr., "*ṣmḥ*," in *New International Dictionary of Old Testament Theology and Exegesis* 3:816 (full article 3:815–17).

13. Amsler, "*ṣmḥ* to sprout," in *Theological Lexicon of the Old Testament* 3:1086. See also Joyce G. Baldwin, "*Semach* as a Technical Term in the Prophets," *Vetus Testamentum* 14 (1964), 93–97.

14. Ibid., *Theological Lexicon of the Old Testament* 3:1087.

15. Cf. also Numbers Rabbah 18:21; Lamentations Rabbah 1:51; Midrash Mishlei (Proverbs) 19:3.

16. Geoffrey H. Parke-Taylor, *The Formation of the Book of Jeremiah: Doublets and Recurring Phrases* (Atlanta: Society of Biblical Literature, 2000), 56–57.

17. Johnston, "What Did the Hebrew Prophets Know About the Messiah and When Did They Know It?," 6.

18. Ibid., 6–7. Johnston does affirm Jer 23:5-6; 33:14-16 in terms of *sensus plenior* to be Messianic prophecies, finding their ultimate fulfillment in Jesus, but not understood as Messianic by Jeremiah or his contemporaries. For the larger question of the development of the Messianic hope in Israel, cf. Rydelnik; Brown.

19. Wolter H. Rose, *Zemah and Zerubbabel: Messianic Expectations in the Early Postexilic Period* (Sheffield, UK: Sheffield Academic Press), 249.

20. See, e.g., Jeremiah Untermann, *From Repentance to Redemption: Jeremiah's Thought in Transition* (*Journal for the Study of the Old Testament Supplement* 54; Sheffield: JSOT Press, 1987), 165–66, with reference to K. Gros, *Die literarische Verwandtschaft Jeremias mit Hosea* (Borna-Leipzig: Universitätsverlag von Robert Noske, 1930); H. L. Ginsberg, "Studies in Hosea 1–3," in Menahem Haran, ed., *Yehezkel Kaufmann Jubilee Volume* (Jerusalem: Magnes Press, 1960), 50–69. See further Martin Schulz-Rauch, *Hosea und Jeremia: zur Wirkungsgeschichte des Hoseabuches* (Calwer theologische Monographien. Reihe A, Bibelwissenschaft; Bd. 16; Stuttgart: Calwer Verlag, 1996).

21. Johnston, "What Did the Hebrew Prophets Know About the Messiah and When Did They Know It?," 10.

22. Ps 45:7[8], rendered by H. J. Kraus "O divine one," *Psalms 1–59* (English translation, H. C. Oswald; Minneapolis: Augsburg, 1988), 455; see further Michael L Brown, *Answering Jewish Objections, Vol. 2: Theological Objections* (Grand Rapids: Baker, 2000), 14–48, for extensive discussion of the Messiah's divinity.

23. Cf. NJV's, "The LORD is our Vindicator"; NIV's "The LORD Our Righteous Savior"; and NET's "The LORD has provided us with justice."

24. As translated on Sefaria.com. Cf. also Rashi on Exodus 23:21 on the meaning of "My name is in him," with reference to the Talmudic discussion on this passage in b. Sanh 38b, identifying this angel with Metatron, whose name has the same numerical value as Shaddai. Ramban explains that the call to heed the angel's voice in 23:21a is based on the fact that the Lord's name is in him (23:21b), thus, "his voice is the voice of God Most High." Similarly, the commentary of Bekhor Shor notes, "if you are listening to him, behold, you are listening to Me."

25. See further Edward Lipinski, "Etudes sur des texts messianiques de l'Ancien Testament," *Semitica* 20 (1970), 41–57; Bernard Gosse, "La nouvelle alliance et les promesses d'avenir se referent a David dans les livres de Jeremie, Ezechiel, et Isaie," *Vetus Testamentum* 41 (1991), 419–28.

26. Note, however, that in Lam Rab 1:51, it is stated that the Messiah's name will be YHWH, based on Jer 23:6.

Jeremiah 30:1-24

The Messiah: Israel's Deliverer and King

ANDREW M. WOODS

Jeremiah 30 predicts the coming Messiah and His subsequent kingdom. Although some hints of Israel's restoration have been disclosed earlier (Jer 3:14-18; 16:14-15; 23:1-8; 24:4-7), Jeremiah's prophecies primarily focused upon imminent deportation. However, Jer 30 begins the "Book of Consolation"[1] (Jer 30–33), which furnishes prophecies of future restoration. Arnold G. Fruchtenbaum notes, "Through most of his book, Jeremiah has been majoring on judgment and minoring on blessing. In these four chapters, he majors on blessing and minors on judgment."[2]

God initially commissioned Jeremiah to "uproot and tear down" and to "build and plant" (Jer 1:10). His earlier chapters focused on the first part of this assignment while chap. 30 inaugurates the second aspect.[3] Commentators have observed that these chapters focus on a second day. Earlier Jeremiah predicted a day of destruction (Jer 5:17; 7:32; 9:25; 19:6), which transpired when Judah was taken into Babylonian captivity in 586 BC. However, in Jeremiah's later chapters, a second day of future restoration is in view (Jer 30:3,8,24; 31:1,27,29,31,33,38; 33:14-16).[4]

ISRAEL'S PROMISED RESTORATION (JER 30:1-4)

God instructed Jeremiah to record all God's words of restoration in a book (30:1-2). The emphasis upon "all the words" indicates that Jeremiah was not to omit any detail. Such an emphasis reaffirms that the very words of God are inspired (Mt 4:4; 5:18; 24:35), and it also emphasizes the necessity of the divine spokesman to convey all that God has communicated (Ezk 3:17-19; 33:7-9; Ac 20:26-27; 2Tm 3:16). The book's purpose was to encourage Judah. "The Lord, the God of Israel told Jeremiah to write his promises of comfort in a book so they would be available to the exiles after Jerusalem fell."[5]

Jeremiah predicted that the restoration promises would ultimately be accomplished in "the land" that God had given to the nation's ancestors (30:3). Some interpret the prediction of "the land" as mere heavenly blessing or as finding its fulfillment in the church.[6] However, when this expression is read in its normal sense, it is a reference to the land that God unconditionally promised to the physical descendants of Abraham (Gn 13:17; 15:18-21). Such a prediction will find its fulfillment in the earthly reign of Christ.

The emphasis upon the return of both houses, Israel and Judah (30:3-4), makes it difficult to argue that these prophecies were fulfilled in the historic return of the southern kingdom from Babylon since the southern kingdom alone returned from the captivity. Except for those northern residents who migrated to the south before or after the Assyrian invasion in 722 BC, the dispersion of the northern kingdom left only tiny Judah and Benjamin to return following the exile. Simply put, Jeremiah's prediction of the return of both the northern and southern kingdoms does not fit the historical details concerning the return from Babylon and therefore awaits a future fulfillment.[7]

The unfulfilled details of Jer 30–33 has led Charles L. Feinberg to conclude, "Jeremiah is contemplating the distant, not near, future of the nation."[8] Those who place these prophecies of future restoration in the same period as the prophecies regarding the nation's historical destruction neglect the principle of prophetic "telescoping" or "foreshortening,"[9] which acknowledges that a series of predictions does not always mention the time gaps between the events (Isa 9:6-7; 61:1-2; Lk 4:16-21).[10] Thus, Jeremiah predicted Israel's ancient fall and ultimate restoration without mentioning the intervening time.[11]

ISRAEL'S TRIBULATION (JER 30:5-7)

Verses 5-7 provide a description of the coming time of tribulation, a time God will use to restore the nation. Jeremiah notes the "terror, dread," and lack of "peace" associated with this time (30:5). Consequently, Jeremiah analogizes it to men acting as women do when they place their hands on their loins to suppress the pains of childbirth (30:6).[12] Here, Jeremiah asks, if a man cannot give birth, then why do I see men acting like women in labor? The answer relates to the arrival of the terrible Day of the Lord. This birth pangs motif is used elsewhere in Scripture to depict the same time of distress preceding the coming of Messiah. Isaiah 66:7-9 uses birth pangs to describe Israel's sudden millennial birth after the tribulation.[13] Matthew 24:8 employs the identical imagery to describe the time of upheaval leading to Christ's return (Mt 24:27,30) and the subsequent birth of His kingdom (Mt 25:31-46). First Thessalonians 5:3 also uses labor pains imagery to describe the same period that will catch the unexpecting world off guard.

Verse 7 continues the description of this time through the phrase, "There will be none like it!," which draws attention to the uniqueness of the period. Jesus called attention to the uniqueness of the same period when He said, "For at that time there will be great tribulation, the kind that hasn't taken place from the beginning of the world until now and never will again!" (Mt 24:21). Daniel also emphasized the tribulation's uniqueness when he predicted, "There will be a time of distress such as never has occurred since nations came into being until that time" (Dan 12:1). Both Jer 30:7 and Dan 12:1 (NASB) use the same Hebrew word for "trouble" or "distress" (*tsarah*) that is also used in Dan 12:1 to describe the coming tribulation. Joel 2:2 similarly predicted, "A day of darkness and gloom . . . such as never existed in ages past and never will again in all the generations to come." Such descriptions of unprecedented terror only harmonize with the future time of unparalleled distress depicted in Rev 6–19, rather than to a past event. Attempts to tie these prophecies in with the adversity that the nation suffered at the hands of the Babylonians in 586 BC or the Romans in AD 70 are unconvincing.[14] "The period includes a unique time of judgment on the nation for their sin . . . including events more extreme than the fall of Jerusalem to Babylon (586 BC) or Rome (AD 70)."[15] Although these events brought distress of some magnitude, they are not unique enough to satisfy the language of Jer 30:7.

Verse 7 continues its description of the coming tribulation by labeling it the time of "trouble for Jacob." This reference to the patriarch Jacob, whose name was later changed to "Israel" (Gn 32:28; 35:10), indicates that this time is specifically focused upon Israel. "The use of Jacob represents the whole nation."[16] The equation of "Jacob" with "Israel" is made expressly in the same context where the prophet uses both names synonymously (30:10a). "Israel" is a technical term in both Testaments[17] always referring to the physical descendants of Abraham, Isaac, and Jacob. Although global in scope, the primary purpose of this time is to bring distress upon the nation to accomplish a foreordained result.

The last phrase in 30:7 enumerates this result when it says, "but he will be delivered out of it" (cf. also v. 10). Thus, both spiritual salvation (Rom 11:25-27) and physical rescue of the nation (Mt 24:31) will result from the tribulation. The tribulation will accomplish God's purpose of purging Israel, producing a believing remnant, and then purifying this remnant in preparation for the second advent and the kingdom (Zch 13:7-9). Thus, the disciplinary purposes of God through the tribulation will provide the mechanism that results in the salvation of His elect nation.

ISRAEL'S LIBERATION (JER 30:8-11)

Jeremiah describes the freedom that the nation will experience after her Messiah rescues her (Jer 30:8-11). These verses elaborate upon the salvation that Israel is promised at the end of v. 7. In v. 8, Jeremiah describes this liberation in terms of the breaking off a yoke from the neck, the tearing off of bonds, and no longer being slaves to strangers. Here, Jeremiah describes the termination of the curses associated with the Mosaic covenant. Part of this covenant involved blessings for obedience (Lv 26:1-13; Dt 28:1-14) and curses for disobedience (Lv 26:14-46; Dt 28:15-68). The curses are depicted as escalating in intensity as Israel's disobedience persisted. These curses would climax in the form of oppression by a foreign power (Dt 28:49). Thus, Israel has routinely experienced foreign oppression throughout her history. However, Jeremiah predicts a time following the nation's spiritual transformation when she will obey God, which will consequently terminate the foreign oppression and usher in covenant blessings. The final phase of this "yoke [will be] the Antichrist in that end-time period. His yoke over the Jews will be broken, and Israel will be freed."[18]

Jeremiah 30:8 also depicts the conclusion of the "times of the Gentiles" (Lk 21:24). This expression refers to the era between the Babylonian captivity beginning in 586 BC and the second advent, when the nation would have no king reigning on David's throne and thus will experience oppression at the hands of various Gentile powers.[19] Charles H. Dyer and Eva Rydelnik describe this period as follows: "From the Babylonian captivity until the coming of the Messiah there was no king in Israel, just as the prophets foretold. Today we await the return of the King, the second coming of Jesus the Messiah to rule in His kingdom on earth (Hos 3:4-5)."[20] Daniel 2–7 describes this period. From these chapters, it can be surmised that the various nations that would oppress Israel during the times of the Gentiles would be Babylon, Medo-Persia, Greece, Rome, and revived Rome.[21] However, according to Jer 30:8, when Jesus the Messiah returns, He will break this yoke of Gentile oppression and formally terminate the times of the Gentiles. Yet, as noted by Fruchtenbaum, such a prediction was never fulfilled in the past: "'Foreigners will no more enslave them'... This prophecy is not referring to the return from the Babylonian captivity, for since that time, strangers have in fact made the Jews their bondmen (servants). After the tribulation will come the final restoration, which is when this promise will be fulfilled."[22]

According to v. 9, the nation would no longer serve foreign oppressors, but rather would serve God. Instead of enslavement, they will be devoted solely to the service of the Lord and David, whom the Lord will enthrone. It is common for interpreters to understand this reference to "David" as referring to David's greater Son, Jesus Christ (Lk 1:32,69; Ac 2:29-30; 13:22-23,34).[23] Based on the Davidic covenant (2Sm 7:12-16), other passages depict a future king from "the fallen booth of David" (Am 9:11). Even Jeremiah predicted that God would "raise up a Righteous Branch for David" (Jer 23:5), and Isaiah spoke of a child reigning on "the throne of David" (Isa 9:7). The close association of the Messiah with the house of David thus caused some prophets even to associate the Messiah with the name "David," the head of the dynasty from which He would descend (cf. Hos 3:5; Ezk 34:23; 37:24). Thus, Daniel I. Block concludes, "There is no thought in these prophecies of the resurrection of the historic king, as some kind of David *redivivus*."[24] As a result, "Jesus is frequently identified as the son of David in the NT" (2Tm 2:8; Rev 5:5).[25]

However, it is also possible to interpret this reference to David as referring to literal David. Fruchtenbaum explains:

> Nothing in the text indicates that *David* is to be taken symbolically. If the prophets wanted to refer to the messiah in connection with David, they used terms such as "Root of Jesse," "Branch of David," "Son of David," or "Seed of David." None of these expressions are used here. The text simply states, *David*. In keeping with literal interpretation, it is best to take the text as it reads, meaning the literal David, who, in his resurrected form, will function as the king over Israel and as a prince in subjection to the King of the world.[26]

Thus, David will be resurrected at the same time as all the other Old Testament saints (Dan 12:2; Jn 5:28-29; Ac 24:15; Rev 20:4) and rule in submission to Christ during the millennium in a co-regency form of government. Jesus will reign over the entire earth, and the resurrected David will reign with Christ as vice regent over national Israel. Regarding these predictions concerning David, John F. Walvoord similarly observes, "Though some have attempted to take this prophecy in less than its literal meaning, the clear statement is that David, who is now dead and whose body is in his tomb in Jerusalem (Ac 2:29), will be resurrected."[27] Thus, v. 9 is messianic in tone regardless of whether it is interpreted to refer to Christ or to the resurrected David.

In vv. 8-9, Jeremiah indicates that the establishment of the Davidic monarchy will follow Israel's spiritual transformation and rescue by the Messiah. The reestablishment of the monarchy also renders implausible the notion that these events have already taken place. According to Kaiser, "These passages cannot refer to the destruction of Jerusalem in A.D. 70, for the Davidic monarchy was not restored after that date and the Jews were not saved out of it, but were killed by the thousands and many were carried away."[28]

Thus, v. 10 exhorts Jacob not to be afraid. The verse then provides more promises of Israel's salvation and pictures her dwelling at ease in her own land. Feinberg explains, "The picture of quiet ease is that of sheep lying undisturbed in their pastures . . ."[29] Ezekiel 34:25 similarly predicts, "I will make a covenant of peace with them and eliminate dangerous animals in the land, so that they may live securely in the wilderness and sleep in the forest."

In v. 11, God vows to destroy those nations that oppressed Israel. This prediction has its roots in Gn 12:3, where God promised to bless those who blessed Abraham's descendants and curse those who cursed them. Interestingly, every world power that has persecuted Israel is now on the ash heap of history. Scripture records how Egypt, Assyria, Babylon, Persia, Greece, and Rome all came against the Jewish nation. Despite once dominating the known world, they no longer exist as world powers.

Jeremiah also draws a contrast "between the fate of God's people and that of their oppressors" (Jer 30:11).[30] Although God will eradicate Israel's enemies, He will only chasten Israel with the intent of humbling her. God's goal is Israel's restoration rather than her affliction. The affliction is simply the divine means of achieving this goal. He will remember His unconditional covenant (Gn 15) and not destroy Israel completely. Although Israel will be purged, God will use the tribulation to preserve and purify a believing remnant (Zch 13:8).

Jer 30:11 also describes Israel as scattered among all the nations. While some connect these verses to the events surrounding the Babylonian captivity, during this captivity Israel was exiled to one geographic locale rather than dispersed throughout the earth, as v. 11 indicates. Similarly, when Israel is ultimately regathered, she will be collected from all the nations (Isa 11:11) rather than from one region, as was the case in the historical return from Babylon. Because the details of v. 11 do not fit the known facts of history, they await a future fulfillment.

ISRAEL'S HEALED WOUNDS (JER 30:12-17)

These verses describe this restoration as the nation being restored to health. However, she first must comprehend the seriousness of her sickness. Thus, Jeremiah describes the present incurable sickness of the nation. Verse 12 describes Israel's present wounds as incurable absent God's intervention. In v. 13, the prophet uses lawsuit imagery by portraying the nation as a helpless defendant with no one to plead her case. Jeremiah then transitions to the imagery of medicine by speaking of

Israel's incurable sores.[31] Israel's lovers had forgotten her (v. 14). The nation's lovers refer to the false gods and alliances in which she had put her trust.

Scripture frequently uses the imagery of adultery and harlotry to convey the idolatry among God's people (Ezk 16; 23; Jms 4:4). "The lovers, her allies, in whom the nation had placed such great hope, had forgotten her."[32] Such was the nation's predicament. "Jeremiah uses the language of an unfaithful wife (Judah) who has deserted her husband (the Lord) and now because she has lived the difficult life of prostitution, is all battered and bruised and has lost her beauty. In this condition, none of those with whom she has been having relations are interested in her."[33] Israel's sins had actually made God act as her enemy. Israel's rebellion had forced God to pour out upon her the covenant curses. Thus, in v. 15, God asks, "Why do you cry out about your injury?" The nation had no right to complain since it was her rebellion that had created her predicament. What is sown is also reaped (Gal 6:7-8); hence, the nation had sown to the wind and was now reaping the whirlwind (Hos 8:7).

However, in vv. 16 and 17, the prophet's tone alters as he describes Israel's healing. Verse 16 reiterates that Israel's enemies will be destroyed. As previously discussed, such a prediction is the outworking of God's protection of the Jewish people against anti-Semitism (Gn 12:3). This protection works out literally in history. For example, God killed the firstborn throughout Egypt because Egypt (Ex 11) had similarly persecuted Israel, God's firstborn son (Ex 4:22). Moreover, God drowned the pursuing Egyptians in the Red Sea (Ex 14:23-31) because the Egyptians had similarly drowned the Hebrew children in the Nile (Ex 1:22). The end times will be no different, as those who persecuted Israel will be recompensed by God. After all, he who touches Israel touches the very apple of His eye (Zch 2:8, HCSB note).

The nation's healing is finally described in v. 17, "very soon God will be the physician of the people of the land of Israel!"[34] Prior to these events, Zion was considered an outcast. In fact, Jerusalem will be considered a burdensome stone (Zch 12:3) that all the nations will eventually come against (Zch 14:2). Yet, God in Ps 137:5-6 says, "If I forget you, O Jerusalem, may my right hand forget *its skill*. May my tongue stick to the roof of my mouth if I do not remember you, if I do not exalt Jerusalem as my greatest joy!" (emphasis added). Once this restoration is complete, Israel will no longer be called an outcast, but rather, she will receive a place of preeminence in the millennium. Once the nation is brought back into fellowship with God, she will be the head and not the tail (Dt 28:13). The law of the Lord will go forth from Zion. The nations of that time will stream to Jerusalem to worship (Isa 2:2-3). Those who refuse to do so will receive no rain (Zch 14:17). According to the end of v. 17, Israel's restoration is related to the charge of the nations that God had forsaken His people. Therefore, God responds to this taunt by miraculously restoring His people.

ISRAEL'S MILLENNIAL PROSPERITY (JER 30:18-20)

Once the nation turns in faith to the Lord's pierced Messiah at the end of the Tribulation (Zch 12:10), the curses will be removed and the covenant blessings will be introduced. Verses 18-20 describe the prosperity that Israel will then enjoy as the nation's fortunes are restored (18a). Amos 9:13-14 predicts that "the plowman will overtake the reaper and the one who treads grapes, the sower of seed. The mountains will drip with sweet wine. . . . They will . . . plant vineyards and drink their wine, make gardens and eat their produce."

According to the rest of v. 18, the permanent fixture of the city of Jerusalem will replace the impermanent dwellings of the tents that characterized the Jews throughout the wilderness wanderings, exile, Diaspora, and persecution under the Antichrist (Mt 24:15-20; Rev 12:6-17).[35] This contrast emphasizes the permanency of Israel's national existence after the tribulation. Amos 9:15 similarly predicts this permanence when it says, "I will plant them on their land, and they will never again be uprooted from the land I have given them. Yahweh your God has spoken." Although they were oppressed during the times of the Gentiles and the tribulation, God guarantees the eternal perpetuity of the nation of Israel because of the Abrahamic covenant (Gn 15).

In contrast to the fear that the Jewish people lived under during the times of the Gentiles (Dt 28:66), the sounds of thanksgiving and merrymaking will emanate from the millennial Jerusalem (v. 19). Zechariah 8:3-5 likewise predicts, "The LORD says this, 'I will return to Zion and live in Jerusalem. . . . The streets of the city will be filled with boys and girls playing in them.'"

Verse 19 also predicts the multiplication of the Jewish people during the kingdom age. Historically, Satan saw the multiplication of the Jews as a threat and consequently thwarted it. Satan was no doubt behind the efforts by Egypt to enslave the burgeoning Jewish population (Ex 1) as well as Haman's attempt to eradicate the Jews, as recorded in the book of Esther. Satan will pursue a similar pattern in the future tribulation. Revelation 12 speaks of the dragon's, or Satan's (Rev 12:9), perpetual hostility against the woman, or Israel (Rev 12:1; Gn 37:9-10). By contrast, because Satan will be bound throughout the millennium (Rev 20:1-3), he will be unable to pursue his historic hostility against the nation, thereby allowing the nation to enjoy unhindered multiplication throughout the kingdom era.

Jeremiah further speaks of honor being bestowed to the Hebrew nation (Jer 30:19). No longer will she be deemed insignificant, but rather will be given a place of honor befitting God's covenant people. Even the Gentile nations that lorded authority over Israel throughout times of the Gentiles will serve Israel during the kingdom age (Dt 15:6; Isa 49:22-23; 61:6-7).[36]

The prophet also promises "His children will be as in past days" (Jer 30:20). Thus, Israel's children will become just as prosperous during the millennial age as they had been under the reigns of David and Solomon.[37] In other words, "As it was with the exodus, as it was with the monarchy, so it will be again."[38] The Davidic and Solomonic eras are not fulfillments of the millennial promises but rather serve as a pattern for these future blessings. Thus, "events described in this section go beyond the return from Babylon and detail a set of events that will take place at the end of days."[39]

The security of the nation during this time is also reemphasized when v. 20 speaks of Israel's congregation being established before the Lord. Unlike modern Israel that has rejected God's ruling authority through its refusal to acknowledge Jesus as their Messiah and Redeemer, millennial Israel will be the beneficiary of God's direct rule. Verse 20 further elaborates upon Israel's millennial prosperity by reiterating the demise of Israel's oppressors because of the protection against anti-Semitism of Gn 12:3.

ISRAEL'S LEADER (JER 30:21-22)

To demonstrate who will be responsible for ushering in these millennial blessings, Jeremiah's prophecies focus upon the specific identification of Israel's future ruler. For four reasons, the future ruler is the Messiah, Jesus Christ.[40] First, v. 21 describes the leader as being "one of them" indicating that this leader will be Jewish. "Nevertheless, this coming glorious ruler will come forth from their midst, be from the Jewish people, as predicted of the Messiah (Gn 49:10; Dt 18:15)."[41] Such a prediction would encourage the nation during the times of the Gentiles as Israel was being subjugated under perpetual Gentile powers. Yet, during the millennium Israel will be ruled by one of its own. "Their leader will be one of them . . . from their midst instead of some foreign despot."[42] Fruchtenbaum also observes, "From here onward their rulers will be Jews, not Gentiles."[43] Jesus certainly fulfills this initial criterion since He was not only Jewish (Rom 9:5) but also the rightful heir to David's throne (Mt 1:1).

Second, the leader will have the privilege of approaching God. The Lord asks the question, "who would otherwise risk his life to approach me?" There is great significance of this privilege. "This ruler will come close to God as the Lord brings Him near into His service and will approach the Lord. Since unauthorized approaches to God were punishable by death (Ex 19:21; Nm 8:19) this leader's proximity to God indicated spiritual qualifications for leadership."[44] In OT times, mere humans could not approach God. The only exception was the high priest on the

Day of Atonement after an animal sacrifice had been administered for his sins (Lv 16). The unapproachability of God related to the sin barrier separating sinful man from a holy God (Mt 27:50-51; Heb 10:20). Yet, Israel's future leader is portrayed as having unlimited access to God. Only Jesus the Messiah, Israel's sinless High Priest could qualify for such a privilege.

Third, the future leader will enjoy a dual role. He will be both ruler and priest. He is referred to as a ruler in v. 21. This verse also infers he is a priest because the privilege of approaching God was a priestly function. No mere mortal could fulfill both roles. If a king attempted to usurp a priestly function, he was penalized. When King Saul attempted to usurp priestly prerogatives, Samuel predicted his kingdom would not endure (1Sm 13). When King Uzziah attempted the same, he was permanently smitten with leprosy (2Chr 26). Because Jeremiah predicts that the ruler will be both king and priest, he is speaking of the Messiah rather than a mere man (cf. Ps 110:4). Only Jesus the Messiah is qualified to fulfill both roles. He alone will be eligible to serve as the branch that Zechariah predicted who can simultaneously fulfill both roles of king and priest (Zch 6:12-13). Therefore:

> The phrase "I will bring him near and he shall approach me" indicates a priestly office of this ruler. To come near or to approach (Ex 24:2; Nm 16:5) means "to engage in the work of a priest." The privilege of drawing near to God in this technical sense belongs only to those persons whom God had set apart for the task. The closing challenge, who would dare risk his life to approach Me? implies that only the Messiah would be qualified for the task of the Glorious Ruler-Priest.[45]

Fourth, v. 22 describes the result of the leader's ministry through the phrase "You will be My people, and I will be your God." This phrase is used consistently to depict the ideal relationship between Israel and God (Lv 26:12; Dt 7:6; 26:16-19; Jer 7:23; 11:4; 24:7; 31:1,33; Ezk. 11:20; 14:11; 34:30; 36:28; 37:23,27; Hos 2:23; Zch 8:8; 13:9).[46] No mere human has the capacity to bring about this ideal condition. Only Christ can do so. Consequently, "Israel will finally experience the relationship with God that He always had intended under the leadership of King Messiah."[47]

In sum, the leader's Jewish heritage, unhindered access to God, dual role, and ability to bring about ideal conditions all argue for a messianic interpretation of vv. 21-22. Feinberg observes that even the extrabiblical material has embraced this messianic interpretation: "The Targum, though interpretive, is correct in its rendering 'Messiah shall be revealed to them out of their own midst.'"[48] Fruchtenbaum similarly observes, "The Hebrew word used here is *adder*, meaning 'a noble one,' and this was taken by the rabbis to be a messianic term . . . These verses may very well speak of the messianic Person. In fact, the rabbis took these verses to be exactly that."[49] Furthermore, "The Hebrew word translated leader ('*addir*') can be translated 'glorious one' and indicates divine origin; it is used four times of either the Lord or God."[50]

ISRAEL'S PURPOSES TO BE ACCOMPLISHED (JER 30:23-24)

Jeremiah 30 reveals God's future purposes, including the spiritual transformation and purification of the Jewish remnant in preparation for the second coming, the earthly messianic kingdom, and the destruction of Israel's enemies. Verses 23-24 reveal the means that God will use to bring about these purposes. As alluded to earlier (30:7), divine anger to be poured out upon the world during the future tribulation period will be the means that God will use to accomplish His purposes. Consequently, the tribulation is described as a storm that will suddenly come upon the wicked (v. 23). God's anger will not be appeased until the intent of His heart is accomplished (v. 24). Thus, Fruchtenbaum summarizes, "God used judgment not as an end in itself, but as a means of bringing Israel back to Himself."[51]

Jeremiah concludes this chapter with a prediction that Israel would not understand these prophecies until "the latter days" (NASB). This expression is used elsewhere to speak of tribulation and millennial events (Dt 4:30; Dan 2:28; 10:14; Jer 48:47). Jeremiah's use of the expression further confirms that the details of this chapter await a future fulfillment. Although Jeremiah's generation would not understand his predictions, Jewish people living in the future would understand them. Thus, "The full meaning of this message will be understood only in the latter days (an eschatological expression pointing to the day of the Lord; 23:20; Gn 49:1), and points to a time after the judgment has passed."[52] Biblical prophecy becomes more understandable as the fulfillment of the prophesied events draws nearer (1Pt 1:10-11).

Similarly, Daniel was told to seal up his prophecies because they were meant to be understood by a future generation. Daniel 12:4,9 says, "But you, Daniel, keep these words secret and seal the book until the time of the end. Many will roam about, and knowledge will increase. . . . Go on your way, Daniel, for the words are secret and sealed until the time of the end." According to Am 8:12, the "roaming about" and "knowledge" increasing relates to God's prophetic word becoming progressively understandable among Israel as the allotted events begin to transpire. Thus, the rebellious Hebrew nation will one day acknowledge that divine discipline manifested through the tribulation was necessary for Israel to be restored to God.

CONCLUSION

Jeremiah 30 predicts Israel's restoration through the coming tribulation. This chapter's details call for a futuristic interpretation of these events. They reveal how and when the times of the Gentiles as well as the covenant curses will end, thus paving the way for Israel's kingdom blessings. Jeremiah 30 also emphasizes the outworking of God's protection of the Jewish people from anti-Semitism (Gn 12:3). Most significantly, this chapter focuses upon Jesus the Messiah, the rightful heir to David's throne (30:9) and Israel's prophesied leader (30:21-22), the One who will bring Israel into her glorious inheritance.

---

1. Charles L. Feinberg, "Jeremiah," in *Isaiah–Jeremiah*, ed. Frank E. Gaebelein and Richard P. Polcyn, The Expositor's Bible Commentary (Grand Rapids: Zondervan, 1986), 6:558; Merrill F. Unger, *Unger's Commentary on the Old Testament* (Chicago: Moody, 1981; repr. Chattanooga, TN: AMG, 2002), 1416.
2. Arnold G. Fruchtenbaum, "Jeremiah," in *The Popular Bible Prophecy Commentary: Understanding the Meaning of Every Prophetic Passage*, ed. Tim LaHaye and Ed Hindson (Eugene, OR: Harvest, 2006), 153.
3. Irving L. Jensen, *Jeremiah and Lamentations*, Everyman's Bible Commentary Series (Chicago: Moody, 1966), 85.
4. Charles H. Dyer, "Jeremiah," in *Bible Knowledge Commentary*, ed. John F. Walvoord and Roy B. Zuck (Colorado Springs, CO: Chariot Victor, 1985), 1167; Charles H. Dyer and Eugene H. Merrill, *Nelson's Old Testament Survey: Discover the Background, Theology and Meaning of Every Book in the Old Testament*, ed. Charles R. Swindoll and Roy B. Zuck (Nashville: Word, 2001), 617.
5. Charles H. Dyer and Eva Rydelnik, "Jeremiah," in *The Moody Bible Commentary: A One-Volume Commentary on the Whole Bible by the Faculty of Moody Bible Institute*, ed. Michael Rydlenik and Michael Vanlaningham (Chicago: Moody, 2014). Kindle version. See also Dyer, "Jeremiah," 1167.
6. Derek Kidner, *The Message of Jeremiah*, The Bible Speaks Today Series (Downers Grove, IL: InterVarsity Press, 1987), 103, 105.
7. Dyer, "Jeremiah," 1168.
8. Feinberg, 559.
9. Dyer and Rydelnik, "Jeremiah."
10. Roy B. Zuck, *Basic Bible Interpretation: A Practical Guide to Discovering Biblical Truth* (Colorado Springs, CO: Victor, 1991), 246–47.
11. Dyer, "Jeremiah," 1167–68.
12. Unger, *Unger's Commentary on the Old Testament*, 1417.
13. Ibid.
14. Feinberg, "Jeremiah," 560.
15. Dyer and Rydelnik, "Jeremiah."
16. Ibid.
17. Arnold G. Fruchtenbaum, *Israelology: The Missing Link in Systematic Theology*, rev. ed. (Tustin, CA: Ariel, 1994), 684–90.
18. Fruchtenbaum, "Jeremiah," 154.
19. J. Dwight Pentecost, *Things to Come: A Study in Biblical Eschatology* (Findlay, OH: Dunham, 1958; repr. Grand Rapids, Zondervan, 1964), 315.
20. Dyer and Rydelnik, "Jeremiah."

21. See the article on Daniel 2 in this *Handbook*.

22. Fruchtenbaum, "Jeremiah," 154.

23. Robert B. Chisholm, *Handbook on the Prophets* (Grand Rapids: Baker, 2002), 192 n. 74; 348.

24. Daniel I. Block, "Bringing Back David: Ezekiel's Messianic Hope" in *The Lord's Anointed*, ed. P. E. Satterthwaite, R. S. Hess, and G. J. Wenham (Grand Rapids: Baker, 1995), 173–74.

25. Dyer and Rydelnik, "Jeremiah."

26. Arnold G. Fruchtenbaum, *Footsteps of the Messiah: A Study of the Sequence of Prophetic Events*, rev. ed. (Tustin, CA: Ariel, 2003), 403.

27. John F. Walvoord, *Every Prophecy of the Bible* (Colorado Springs, CO: Victor, 1999), 187.

28. Walter Kaiser, "Evidence from Jeremiah," in *A Case for Premillennialism: A New Consensus*, ed. Donald Campbell and Jeffrey Townsend (Chicago: Moody, 1992), 112.

29. Feinberg, "Jeremiah," 561.

30. Ibid.

31. Ibid., 562.

32. Dyer and Rydelnik, "Jeremiah."

33. Tim LaHaye, ed. *Tim Lahaye Prophecy Study Bible* (Chattanooga, TN: AMG Publishers, 2001), 876.

34. Mal Couch, "Jeremiah 30—A Warning to the Palestinians and the Gentiles!" *Conservative Theological Journal* 7, no. 21 (August 2003): 138.

35. Unger, *Unger's Commentary on the Old Testament*, 1418; Fruchtenbaum, "Jeremiah," 155.

36. Fruchtenbaum, *Footsteps of the Messiah: A Study of the Sequence of Prophetic Events*, 406–07.

37. Feinberg, "Jeremiah," 564; Unger, *Unger's Commentary on the Old Testament*, 1419.

38. Fruchtenbaum, "Jeremiah," 155.

39. Dyer and Rydelnik, "Jeremiah."

40. Feinberg, "Jeremiah," 564; Unger, *Unger's Commentary on the Old Testament*, 1419.

41. Dyer and Rydelnik, "Jeremiah."

42. Ibid.

43. Fruchtenbaum, "Jeremiah," 156.

44. Dyer and Rydelnik, "Jeremiah."

45. Ibid.

46. Dyer, "Jeremiah," 1169.

47. Dyer and Rydelnik, "Jeremiah."

48. Feinberg, "Jeremiah," 564.

49. Fruchtenbaum, "Jeremiah," 155–56.

50. Dyer and Rydelnik, "Jeremiah."

51. Fruchtenbaum, "Jeremiah," 156.

52. Dyer and Rydelnik, "Jeremiah."

Jeremiah 31:31-34

The New Covenant

JOSH MATHEWS

Jeremiah 31:31-34 is a theologically significant passage for the message of the book of Jeremiah and for the whole Old Testament and New Testament as well. The passage is familiar for its presentation of the new covenant. These four verses include a grouping of features associated with the anticipated new covenant. In Jeremiah, they are intended to instill hope in a future time of restoration from the dismal circumstances God's people are experiencing. The cluster of features also continues a trajectory of eschatological anticipation that has been advancing in the Tanakh from its earliest chapters, which find their realization in the NT.

In the NT, the fulfillment of new covenant expectations is clearly associated with the coming of the Messiah Jesus and with His messianic life and ministry. In Lk 22 Jesus breaks bread and distributes the cup of the new covenant, established by His blood shed for His followers (Lk 22:20; 1Co 11:25). In 2Co 3 Paul assures his readers that, as ministers of the new covenant, they have confidence toward God through the Messiah Jesus. In the Messiah, and only in the Messiah, the veil over the old covenant is set aside, bringing about the Spirit-empowered freedom and transformation of the new covenant (2Co 3:4-18). The most extensive expression of the new covenant in the NT is in Hebrews, which quotes Jer 31 repeatedly. The great high priestly sacrifice and ministry of Jesus and the new covenant He established and continues to mediate are presented as profoundly superior to the old covenant and its priesthood (Heb 7:22–10:18).

In each of these passages the life, death, and work of Jesus provide the context within which the new covenant comes to fruition. Yet, in Jer 31:31-34, the foundational new covenant text from the OT, there is no explicit mention of an individual, messianic figure. Nevertheless, the passage does depict the new covenant using themes and language elsewhere associated with OT messianic hope. Indeed, the passage assumes a close correlation between messianic hope and new covenant hope, and the author intends it to be understood in this way. The aim of this article is to outline the ways in which Jer 31:31-34 envisions an eschatological situation that includes a cluster of recognizable realities associated with a new covenant, all of which correspond to the coming and life of the Messiah.

To begin, this article will consider the Pentateuch's presentation of covenant language and themes. Jeremiah envisions a coming new covenant that will be different from the covenant Yahweh made with Israel at Mt. Sinai when they came out of Egypt (Jer 31:31-32). This contrast is not novel to Jeremiah, however. A few key texts in the Pentateuch will be considered, especially in Deuteronomy, that already anticipate a new covenant distinct from the Sinai covenant.

The second and longer portion of this article will move to the text of Jeremiah itself. Jeremiah 31:31-34 is properly understood only within the context of chaps. 30–33 and the book as a whole. What emerges as chap. 31 is examined against the backdrop of Deuteronomy, and within the context of Jeremiah's overall message, is the hope for an eschatological future brought about by Yahweh's own gracious work through His messianic king.

COVENANTS OLD AND NEW IN THE PENTATEUCH

In Jeremiah's prophetic statement the coming new covenant is juxtaposed over against a different, previous covenant. The newness of the new covenant is incoherent without this element of contrast with the old covenant. The foundation for covenant and covenant-making is found in the early chapters of Genesis (e.g. Gn 6:18; 9:8-17; 15:18-21; 17:1-21).[1] Covenant (*berit*) language is prevalent in these passages, but Jeremiah identifies the old covenant as that which Yahweh made with the Israelites when He took them by the hand to bring them out of the land of Egypt (Jer 31:32). He is not referring to the covenants God made with Abram/Abraham and Noah in Genesis, but rather to the covenant between the Lord and the Israelites given at Mt. Sinai.

In Ex 19 the Israelites arrived at Mt. Sinai, led by Moses. Moses ascended the mountain, and God instructed him to say to the people, "If you will listen to Me and carefully keep My covenant, you will be My own possession out of all the peoples, although all the earth is Mine, and you will be My kingdom of priests and My holy nation" (Ex 19:5-6). The people were afraid at God's presence on the mountain, and so Moses went up to receive the commandments from Yahweh. Moses wrote down the words of the Lord and took this scroll, the covenant (*berit*) scroll, and read it aloud to the people (Ex 24:7-8).

Near the end of the Pentateuch, in Dt 29, Moses contrasted this covenant of Sinai with a future covenant (Dt 29:1).[2] He reminded them that they had not been given a heart to understand (Dt 29:4), while also encouraging them to keep the words of the covenant and do them (Dt 29:9). The conditionality of the covenant is then highlighted as Moses warned the people that they will be punished for their sin and their stubborn hearts "according to all the curses of the covenant written in this book of the law" (Dt 29:19-21; cf. Lv 26:14-17). The covenant identified in Dt 29:25 is expressed in nearly identical language to the expression of the old covenant in Jer 31:32, which is there contrasted with the promised new covenant.

Chapter 30 of Deuteronomy continues these covenant themes. Moses looks into Israel's distant future, after the curses of the exile and broken covenant come upon them (30:1). This will be a time in which they will obey the Lord with a whole heart and He will restore their fortunes (vv. 2-3). The Lord Himself will circumcise their hearts, and they will keep the commands of the Torah faithfully (vv. 6-10). Not only does this move the hope of a new covenant into the more distant future, but it also anticipates the new covenant passage in Jer 31:31-34. As will be seen below, these texts in Deuteronomy contain many of the concepts and much of the language that coalesces as a cluster of new covenant hope in Jeremiah.

This eschatological outlook is clarified further in Dt 31, where the prospect of keeping the covenant appears quite bleak. At the twilight of Moses' life, as the people are about to enter the promised land, the Lord makes this disconsolate prediction to Moses: "You are about to rest with your fathers, and these people will soon commit adultery with the foreign gods of the land they are entering. They will abandon Me and break the covenant I have made with them" (Dt 31:16; cf. v. 20). The result of the broken covenant will be God's wrath, abandonment, and the punishment of troubles and afflictions (vv. 17-18,21).

There are many ways in which these predictions of Deuteronomy offer a clarifying perspective on the covenant at Sinai. Even within the Pentateuch, the Sinai covenant is viewed as provisional.[3] Because of the stubborn, sinful heart of God's people, they have not been and will not be able to keep His law and His covenant. Something else, a work of God in the future, is needed for God's people to be able to follow Him with a whole heart. This is the backdrop for understanding Jeremiah's prophetic message from the perspective of the later stages of Israel's history.

COVENANTS OLD AND NEW IN JEREMIAH

The anticipation of a new covenant is not something new to Jeremiah, but it does take on more nuanced implications in light of the prophetic context and Israelite history. The time period of Jeremiah spans from the reigns of the last few kings in Judah and into the time of exile in Babylon. Much of the punishment predicted in Deuteronomy has come to fruition because of the idolatrous infidelity of Israel and Judah. God's people have failed incessantly to keep the covenant of Sinai.

In this context, Jeremiah declares a prophetic message of truth telling, mourning, and calling for repentance. His oracles unfold in a series of complex layers that together communicate a profound prophetic message. The logic of Jeremiah's message can be summarized quite simply: The Lord remains faithful to His covenant with His people, and He is just. God's people continue in their sinful ways, breaking covenant relationship with Him and committing idolatry. This rebellion deserves and results in God's judgment and punishment. Yet hope for restoration remains.

The last statement appears to disrupt the logic of the message, for how can there be restoration if God's people are only ever sinful and deserving of the judgment they are experiencing? The implication that becomes increasingly obvious throughout the book is that, for the circumstances to change, there must be a fundamental change of their cause; namely, the sin Israel and Judah have relentlessly committed. God has not neglected His people. He has been faithful to His covenant, and the punishment will change, and fortunes will be restored, but only if His people succeed in keeping covenant relationship with Him. However, given recent and distant history, the possibility for sustained repentance and faithfulness looks bleak as well. Hope is all but lost.

Nevertheless, somehow, in spite of this apparently hopeless cycle of sin and punishment, a thread of hope remains, and the basis for this hope is the work of God Himself. Jeremiah 10:17-25 contains perhaps the clearest and most succinct explanation of Israel and Judah's situation and expression of the book's logical progression, and in v. 23 Jeremiah acknowledges the inability of humankind to direct their steps. A work of God is needed. It must be the Lord Himself who accomplishes the change of heart that is necessary for His people to be restored and for the blessings of the covenant to be renewed again.

This is why a new covenant is necessary, and this new covenant hope builds subtly throughout the book. It culminates in what is referred to as the Book of Consolation in chaps. 30–33.[4] At the heart of this Book of Consolation lies Jer 31:31-34, which functions as a succinct summary statement of new covenant hope. It is the culmination of a cluster of ideas and language that builds throughout the book.

What follows will trace the ideas from the beginning of the book through the Book of Consolation.

Jeremiah begins with the Lord's calling Jeremiah to prophetic ministry, appointing him a "prophet to the nations" (1:5). The message he is to proclaim is a message of disaster coming from Babylon to attack Jerusalem and the other cities of Judah (1:14-15). This coming judgment is a result of sin and idolatry (1:16). Chapter 2 uses a marriage metaphor to describe Israel's relationship with Yahweh (2:2-3), rebuking them for unfaithful idolatry (2:5). The Lord's rebuke emphasizes the apparent irreversibility of their sin and idolatry. The stain of their sin will remain even if they wash with lye and a great amount of soap, and yet they stubbornly protest that they have not followed the Baals (2:22-23).

The marriage metaphor continues in chap. 3.[5] Israel has acted as an adulterous wife, and "her treacherous sister Judah" observed Israel's unfaithfulness and still intransigently acted as a prostitute as well. They feigned returning to the Lord, but never did so with a whole heart (3:6-10). Verses 14-18 include a thread of hope as God, through Jeremiah, calls His faithless children to repent and turn back to Yahweh their master (3:14).[6] This includes visions of a future in which God's people will multiply and increase, and all nations will gather to Jerusalem (3:16-17).[7] The Lord will give to them shepherds that are loyal to Him, whose shepherding will be according to knowledge (*de'ah*) and skill (or wisdom/understanding, *haskel*). This reference to knowledgeable shepherds hints at the kind of future envisioned in the new covenant passage, characterized by widespread knowledge (*yed'u*) of God (31:34).

It also provides a contrast with Jeremiah's critical stance toward Israel's corrupt, stupid shepherds elsewhere in the book (e.g. 10:21).[8] This contrast returns to focus in chap. 23, where a future is envisioned in which the evil shepherds are condemned and replaced with new shepherds (23:1-4). The Lord promises to raise up, in the coming days, a Righteous Branch of David who will reign wisely (*hiskil*) as king (23:5). This passage will be discussed further below, but the point here is that, in spite of the predominantly dark tone of the book, shades of future hope are present early in Jeremiah, and the language and themes associated with that hope prepare the way for later expressions of the new covenant and particularly the messianic expectations associated with it.

The optimism of this passage in chap. 3 does not defy the logic of the book, however, as seen in the statement in v. 17, "They will cease to follow the stubbornness of their evil hearts." This motif of a changed heart continues in the next chapter when Israel is instructed to circumcise their hearts (4:4). This recalls the new covenant language of Deuteronomy (Dt 30:6) and anticipates the passage in Jer 31, where the Lord says He will put His Torah within them and write it on their hearts (31:33).

Another important text for understanding the new covenant is Jer 7:21-26. This passage looks back to the old covenant as it considers the new covenant as well. Jeremiah reminds his readers that, from their beginning as a nation, when God first brought them out of Egypt, His command was to obey Him, not merely to offer sacrifices and burnt offerings. If they could have achieved simple, faithful obedience, Yahweh would be their God and they would be His people (7:23). This kind of relationship is depicted in the virtually identical statement in 31:33[9] and was at the heart of the Lord's covenant desires for His people all along. Yet God's people have displayed stubborn, evil hearts of disobedience since that time when they came out of Egypt, up to the day of Jeremiah's prophetic ministry and even beyond (7:24-25), continuing until the new covenant comes.

Chapter 9 also includes several elements related to the new covenant passage. Like much of Jeremiah, the chapter's outlook is quite pessimistic. The exile is looming. God is about to judge Israel and Judah for abandoning His Torah and for following their stubborn hearts and the Baals as their fathers did before them (9:13-14). Those who are uncircumcised, both in flesh and in heart, will face God's punishment (9:25-26).

In spite of these negative circumstances, however, there are several hints of new covenant hope as well. The only appropriate posture for God's people in response to His judgment will be one of mourning and humility, recognizing their only boast will be that they understand and know (*haskel weyadoa'*) Yahweh and His faithful love, justice, and righteousness (9:24). This is a subtle reminder of the skilled and knowledgeable shepherds of 3:15, and it also links to the coming righteous Branch of David, whose reign as king will be characterized by understanding, justice, and righteousness (23:5-6). Although the immediate future will include God's just judgment, even within this prediction there are reminders of hope for a more distant future to come.[10]

Several instances of language and motifs associated with the new covenant in chap. 31 have been identified, but chap. 11 is where "covenant" (*berit*) terminology explicitly enters Jeremiah's vocabulary.[11] By the word of the Lord, Jeremiah instructs the people of Judah to heed the words of the covenant (11:1-3). This is the covenant God gave their ancestors when He brought them out of Egypt, emphasizing once again that if they simply obeyed, Yahweh would be their God, and they would be His people (11:4,6-7).

Nevertheless, they have not obeyed the covenant, instead following their stubborn, evil hearts, and continuing in the idolatrous ways of their predecessors (11:8a,9-10). This has resulted in the punishment of covenant curses and disaster from which they cannot escape (11:8b,11). These details bring to mind 7:21-26 but with addition of explicit "covenant" terminology, thereby continuing to highlight the covenant failures of the past in order to set the stage for a contrasting anticipation of the future and the new covenant.

Jeremiah 17 and 18 describe further the depths of Judah's sin and the correlation between sin and God's punishment. Sin is said to be engraved on the tablet of the people's hearts (17:1), an emphatically different situation from the one envisioned in 31:33 where the Lord says He will put His Torah within them and write it on their hearts. Here it says their hearts are incurably deceitful and deserving of the Lord's righteous punishment (17:9-10).

There is a cause-and-effect relationship between a nation's actions and the Lord's response, whether for good or for ill. Jeremiah 18:1-11 outlines this reasoning. If a nation previously destined for destruction repents, God would relent from the disaster He had planned (18:8). Likewise, if a nation, like Israel, had been destined to be built up, it is also God's just prerogative to tear it down if it does evil in His sight, turning from the good He had planned. This is presented as a warning to the people of Judah (18:11), to which they respond by continuing in hopeless stubbornness of their evil hearts (18:12). Yet again the emphasis is on the sin of the heart and the helplessness and hopelessness of the situation. Something different, a work of God Himself, is needed for the hearts of God's people to change.

This cause-effect motif resurfaces in chap. 22, which also sets up a contrast with the future-oriented, messianic chapter that follows. The Lord addresses the royal house of David and instructs the king to administer justice and righteousness (22:1-3; cf. 23:5).[12] If the Davidic king obeys, they will experience God's blessing, but if they disobey, the Davidic house will come to ruin (22:4-5). Then the Lord predicts coming destruction, which the nations will recognize as an effect caused by idolatry and abandonment of the covenant of Yahweh their God (22:8-19). Jerusalem's destruction is a result of the sin of their kings, those who sit on David's throne. The chapter ends on a particularly melancholic note with the Lord's promise to tear the king, Coniah (Jehoiachin, cf. 2Kg 24:6) from His right hand and hand him over to the Babylonians where he will die (22:24-27). No descendant, or seed (*zera'*), of his will ever rule as the rightful heir on the Davidic throne (22:30).

Thus, the promise of the capture, exile, and extinguishing of a Davidic heir sets the stage for the hopeful prediction of another Davidic heir in chap. 23. This is the clearest messianic expression of eschatological hope in the entire book of Jeremiah up to this point. The opening woe, spoken to the corrupt shepherds of God's people (23:1-2), flows out of the predicted punishment of Shallum, Jehoiakim, and Coniah in chap. 22. Then Jeremiah transitions to a vision of a future in which Yahweh will return His people to the land from which He has banished them. As it said in 3:15-16, they will again be fruitful and multiply (cf. Gn 1:28) and they will be cared for by good shepherds (23:3-4).

The shift from a dismal view of the past to a cheerful, hopeful view of the future is signaled more clearly in v. 5, with the statement, "'The days are coming'—this is the LORD's declaration." This introduces the promise of a future where the Lord will raise up a Righteous Branch of David, whose name will be "Yahweh our Righteousness" and in whose time Judah will be saved and Israel will be secure (23:6).

Messianic language pervades this declaration. The expectation of a Branch from David is familiar from other prophetic passages such as Isa 4:2; and 11:1 (also cf. Zch 3:8; 6:12).[13] By referring to David and a Branch from his lineage, Jeremiah evokes God's promise to David in 2Sm 7. This connection will become even more explicit in chap. 33, where more details are added to the anticipation of the new covenant.

The reign of this future Davidic King brings to mind the previously traced themes associated with future hope and a new covenant relationship between God and His people. This King will rule wisely, with justice and righteousness. This recalls Jer 3:15 and the knowledgeable and skillful leadership of the shepherds the Lord promises to give, as well as 9:24 where, in the context of a prediction of the coming days (v. 25), God's people are encouraged to boast only in knowledge of Yahweh and His faithful love, justice, and righteousness. Here in chap. 23 this trajectory surfaces with a clear promise of a coming Messiah. In these anticipated future days, the Lord's wisdom, justice, and righteousness will be displayed fully in a Righteous Branch from David's line.

As the prophetic message develops throughout Jeremiah, what is clear after arriving at chap. 23 is that future hope of restoration centers on the coming of a Davidic Messiah. This framework provides context for and understanding of the Book of Consolation, and specifically the new covenant passage of 31:31-34. Moreover, this new covenant trajectory continues in the intervening chapters. For example, in 24:4-7 the Lord promises to bring back the exiles from Judah and plant them in the land, giving them a heart to know Yahweh. He repeats the hopeful declaration, "They will be My people, and I will be their God," and the reason is that they will return to God with all their heart.

A major transition occurs in Jeremiah at the beginning of chap. 30. Chap. 29 concluded the previous section and leaves the book, to this point, on a disheartening note marked by themes of exile, destruction, and judgment. In 29:16-19 the Lord promised to punish severely "the king sitting on David's throne" because of wickedness and failure to listen to the words of the prophets. Thus, the context preparing the way for the Book of Consolation is a context of hopelessness and God's just punishment of His people, particularly focusing on the Davidic king.

Jeremiah 30–33 looks ahead to a time in the distant future, after the exile and the consequences of Israel and Judah's unfaithfulness to the Lord and His covenant. The change to an emphasis on an eschatological perspective is signaled in

30:3, where, like in 23:5 and later in 31:31, it says, "'The days are coming'—the Lord's declaration." In these future days, God promises to "restore the fortunes" of His people, a phrase familiar from Dt 30:3 and common throughout this Book of Consolation (30:18; 31:23; 32:44; 33:7,11,26). In this way, these opening verses resume the optimistic tone that has been present as a subtle undertone throughout Jeremiah. This hopeful, eschatological perspective is rooted in Deuteronomy's new covenant expectation, and it governs the whole of the next four chapters, which coalesce around the summary statement of the new covenant in 31:31-34.

In 30:8-9 the characteristically eschatological language "On that day" introduces the Lord's declaration that His people will be freed from slavery to serve Yahweh their God and David His king. This clearly does not refer to the historic King David from Israel's past, but rather to a future, Messianic King from David's lineage. The eschatological expectation of a Davidic ruler links back to 23:5-6 and will return to focus again in chap. 33.

Chapter 31 begins with the Lord's statement "At that time." He declares, "I will be the God of all the families of Israel, and they will be My people." This is a slight modification of the proclamation we have encountered throughout Jeremiah in association with covenant themes (7:23; 11:4; 24:7). In addition to the occurrence here and in 31:33, it is repeated twice more in the Book of Consolation as well (30:22; 32:38). As chap. 31 continues, leading up to the new covenant summary passage starting in v. 31, the hopeful prophetic vision is of rebuilding and regathering to Yahweh at Mt. Zion. Past mourning will be turned to a future of repentance and joy. It is in this context that Jeremiah presents the summary statement of the new covenant in 31:31-34.

The summary of the new covenant in Jer 31:31-34 identifies several of its distinctive features. First, the new covenant will be eschatological. This is evident from the phrase "Look, the days are coming" (v. 31), a phrase used 16 times in Jeremiah. Seven times it is used of the coming judgment, including the destruction of Judah and other nations (cf. 7:32; 9:25; 19:6; 48:12; 51:47,52), with these also having eschatological implications. Nine times it points to God's eschatological blessing of Israel (Jer 16:14-15; 23:7-8; 30:3; 31:27-28; 31:38-40; 33:14,16) including the time when the messianic Branch of the line of David will rule over the united kingdom of Israel (23:5-6; 33:14-15).

Second, the new covenant will be established with Israel and Judah, indicating that in the end of days, the nation will be reunited. Third, the new covenant will be distinct from the covenant God gave Israel after the exodus from Egypt, the Sinai covenant, "a covenant they broke" (31:32). A fourth feature of the new covenant is that it will internalize God's instructions. The Lord declares that He "will put [His] teaching within them and write it on their hearts" (v. 33). This is the circumcised heart God promised to give Israel when they turn to Him in faith in the end of days, as prophesied by Moses (Dt 30:6; cf. Dt 4:25-31).

A fifth aspect of the new covenant is that it will establish a new spiritual relationship between God and Israel. Not only is Israel God's elect nation, but also the new covenant will establish a different kind of vital spiritual bond between Israel and their God, He "will be their God and they will be [His] people" (v. 33). Finally, the entire nation will experience God's forgiveness, and all will know the Lord (v. 34). Similarly, Zechariah refers to a day when Israel will repent of their failure to believe in the Messiah and recognize Him as the pierced One (Zch 12:10). This is when "a fountain will be opened for the house of David and for the residents of Jerusalem, to wash away sin and impurity" (Zch 13:1).

After this article's central passage (Jer 31:31-34), the focus on eschatological hope continues in Jeremiah's book, with an increasingly pronounced messianic emphasis. Immediately following the new covenant summary is the mention of Israel's descendants, or seed (*zera'*), in 31:36,37. The Lord ensures His people that the seed will most certainly continue forever (cf. 33:26), a reminder that is likely meant to recall messianic hope going all the way back to Gn 3:15.[14]

In chap. 32 Jeremiah recalls the great miraculous deeds of the Lord in delivering His people from Egypt, and also their failure to keep His commandments and the subsequent punishment for their sin (32:20-24). However, Jeremiah also envisions a future time when God will return His people to the land where they will be His people, and He will be their God (vv. 37-38). He will give them one heart to fear Him always (v. 39), and He will make an everlasting covenant with them (v. 40). Just as the Lord has punished them according to His just character, so too will He bless them with the good He is promising, returning them to the land once desolate and restoring their fortunes (vv. 42-44).

Although the Book of Consolation does not entirely neglect themes of God's righteous judgment, an optimistic outlook pervades the chapters, arriving at its climactic expression in chap. 33. The chapter begins with another reminder of judgment (33:3-5) but quickly moves to the promise of future healing and the restoration of the fortunes of Judah and Israel (vv. 6-7). Verse 8 echoes 31:34, including the forgiveness of sin and purification from wrongdoing in the hope of restoration.

The messianic anticipation of a Davidic Branch was first expressed explicitly in 23:5-6. Those verses are repeated almost identically in 33:14-16. The Lord declares again that "the days are coming." He will fulfill His good promises to the house of Israel and the house of Judah (cf. 31:31), and they will be fulfilled with the coming of a Righteous Branch for David. He will be named "Yahweh our Righteousness" and will reign with justice and righteousness. His days will bring salvation and security for God's people.

Then the Lord issues a reminder of His promise from 2Sm 7, expressed in the formal way it occurs throughout Kings and Chronicles: "David will never fail to have a man sitting on the throne of the house of Israel" (cf. 1Kg 2:4; 8:24; 9:4; 2Chr 6:16).[15] Jeremiah builds on this repeated promise of the Righteous Branch and the reiterated promise for David's house as the Book of Consolation draws to a close. The promise of a messianic ruler on David's throne is secure as an unfailing covenant promise of God (33:19-26).[16] This recalls the Lord's promise to David in 2Sm 7 as well as the themes traced through Jeremiah. The covenant promises of 31:31-34 are thus closely linked with the covenant promises for a descendant, or seed, of David to reign on the throne forever.[17]

After the conclusion of the Book of Consolation, Jer 34 moves back to a historical perspective, resuming the pessimistic outlook of most of the rest of the book. The Davidic king Zedekiah attempts to institute a new covenant with the people. However, this short-lived attempt fails, thus confirming eschatological nature of hope anticipated in chaps. 30–33. The true new covenant must be a work of the Lord in the distant future, which God Himself establishes under the rule of His Messianic King.

THE MESSIANIC FULFILLMENT OF THE NEW COVENANT

The NT reveals that all followers of the Lord Jesus experience the benefits of the new covenant. For example, Paul tells the Corinthians that they are "ministers of the new covenant" (2Co 3:6). Furthermore, in Hebrews, Jer 31:31-34 is quoted repeatedly (cf. Heb 8:7-12) because "Jesus has also become the guarantee of a better covenant" (7:22). The redemptive work of Messiah Jesus shows Him as "the mediator of a better covenant" (8:6) than the Mosaic covenant. The great high priestly sacrifice and ministry of Jesus and the new covenant He established and continues to mediate are presented as profoundly superior to the old covenant and its priesthood, where Jer 31:31-34 is quoted extensively (Heb 7:22–10:18).

At issue is how the new covenant, promised to Israel and Judah in the last days, is applied to both Jewish and Gentile followers of Jesus, meaning, to the Church at the present time. One explanation is that the Lord Jesus announced the new covenant at His final Passover meal with His disciples. The Gospels record that Jesus broke bread and distributed the cup, saying "This cup is the new covenant established by My blood" (Lk 22:20; 1Co 11:25). Afterward, the death of the Messiah Jesus inaugurated the new covenant with His Jewish disciples. Thus, Jewish followers of Jesus are the remnant of Israel (Rom 11:1-5). They represent the first stage in the new covenant, anticipating the day in the future when all of Israel will believe and the new covenant will be established in its entirety (Rom 11:25-26). Gentile followers of Jesus also experience the spiritual benefits of the new covenant, having been grafted "against nature" (Rom 11:24) into the spiritual promises God made to Israel (Rom 11:17-24).

CONCLUSION

This survey of several key texts, a few from the Pentateuch and several from Jeremiah, inform the understanding of Jer 31:31-34 as a messianic text. Various terms and themes occur throughout these passages, and together they form a cluster related to the anticipation of a new covenant. Leading up to the Book of Consolation and its central new covenant text, there is a thread of eschatological hope running through Jeremiah's prophetic message of judgment. Already by the beginning of chap. 30 there has appeared a great deal of content influencing this understanding of what new covenant expectation entails.

Then in chaps. 30–33 these future-oriented expectations burst forth with God's own eschatological resolution to the sin problem. Until the new covenant came, this problem remained without any solution, and the history of God's relationship with His people was riddled with failed attempts to obey God's law and keep the stipulations of the covenant. The solution, which must be a work of the Lord Himself, will be found in a new covenant in the distant future from Jeremiah's perspective.

Jeremiah 31:31-34 summarizes this new covenant hope of a work of God that is fundamentally different from the old covenant. The Scripture context leading up to and surrounding this passage makes clear an integral element of this new covenant work of God: the coming of His Messianic King. In this new covenant situation, instead of law written on tablets of stone, or sin written on uncircumcised hearts of stone, God's Torah will be within His people and written on their hearts. They will no longer need to mediate the knowledge of Yahweh for each other, because by the coming and mediation of the Righteous Branch of David, all will know Him. This new covenant will resolve the problem of sin, which has been insurmountable through the entire life of God's people. Wrongdoing will be forgiven, and sin will be forgotten forever. The new covenant has come, the Messianic King is seated at the right hand of His Father, and He will return to take up His eternal throne.

1. A great deal of theological debate exists related to the various covenants or expressions of the covenant throughout Scripture. But this article attempts to avoid that complex debate to focus on the question of messianism associated with the new covenant and Jer 31:31-34.

2. Sailhamer points out that this is not technically a renewal of the covenant, as is sometimes thought. Rather, the covenant in view here is a different, additional covenant meant to be seen in contrast to the Sinai covenant. John H. Sailhamer, *The Pentateuch as Narrative: A Biblical-Theological Commentary* (Grand Rapids: Zondervan, 1992), 471.

3. Kaiser refers to "planned obsolescence" of the old covenant. Walter C. Kaiser Jr., "The Old Promise and the New Covenant: Jeremiah 31:31-34," *Journal of the Evangelical Theological Society* 15.1 (1972): 19, 21. Also see Sailhamer's extended discussion of the composition of the Sinai corpus within the Pentateuch and its implication for understanding the purpose of the law and covenant given at Sinai. John H. Sailhamer, *The Meaning of the Pentateuch: Revelation, Composition, and Interpretation* (Downers Grove, IL: IVP Academic, 2009), 360–415.

4. See R. K. Harrison, *Jeremiah and Lamentations: An Introduction and Commentary*, Tyndale Old Testament Commentaries, vol. 21 (Downers Grove, IL: IVP Academic, 1973), 136; Christopher J. H. Wright, *The Message of Jeremiah: Grace in the End*, ed. Alec Motyer and Derek Tidball, The Bible Speaks Today (IVP, 2014), 300.

5. There are several similarities to the early chapters of Hosea. See John Bright, "An Exercise in Hermeneutics: Jeremiah 31:31-34," *Interpretation* 20.2 (1966): 196.

6. The term here for "I am your master" is *ba'alti*. This appears to be an intentional play on the themes of Baal (*ba'al*) idolatry in 2:8,23. This interplay and the marriage metaphor here early in the book are also likely the background for the somewhat mysterious language at the end of 31:32: "even though I had married them" *we'aniki ba'alti bam*.

7. This language not only recalls Gen 1:28, but it also reflects the eschatological language of Isa 2:2-4; Mic 4:1-4, which look ahead to "the last days."

8. These shepherds are described as stupid and not prospering (*lo' hiskilu*).

9. The only difference is that 7:23 addresses the people in second person (". . . your God, and you will be . . .") while 31:33 uses the third person (". . . their God, and they will be . . .").

10. The prophetic phrase, "'The days are coming'—the LORD's declaration" is identical here in 9:25; 23:5; and 31:31. It also occurs elsewhere in the book.

11. The first use of *berit* in Jeremiah was in reference to the ark of the covenant in 3:16.

12. Whereas the following passage (22:10-12) addresses Shallum, son of Josiah specifically, vv. 1-9 address the Davidic dynasty more generally. See F. B. Huey, *Jeremiah, Lamentations*, The New American Commentary, vol. 16 (Nashville: B&H, 1993), 203.

13. The terms translated "shoot" (*choter*) and "branch" (*netser*) in Isa 11:1 are different from "branch" (*tsemach*) in Isa 4:2; Jer 23:5; Zch 3:8; 6:12. Nevertheless, the semantic overlap, prophetic and literary context, eschatological perspective, and other factors suggest strongly that they are meant to be understood as referring to the same coming Messiah. Note also Isa 11:2-9, where, as in Jer 23:5-6, the Branch's reign will be characterized by wisdom and understanding, justice and righteousness, and the knowledge of Yahweh.

14. See James Hamilton, "The Seed of the Woman and the Blessing of Abraham," *Tyndale Bulletin* 58.2 (2007): 253–73.

15. Johanna Erzberger, "Jeremiah 33:14-26: The Question of Text Stability and the Devaluation of Kingship," *Old Testament Essays* 26.3 (2013): 666.

16. The MT and LXX versions of Jeremiah differ significantly, and this is one significant instance of that divergence. In the LXX, Jer 33:14-26 is missing. On this complex issue see Gleason Leonard Archer Jr., "The Relationship between the Septuagint Translation and the Massoretic Text in Jeremiah," *Trinity Journal* 12.2 (1991): 139–50; Erzberger, "Jeremiah 33:14-26"; Johan Lust, "Messianism and the Greek Version of Jeremiah: Jer 23,5-6 and 33,14-26," in *Messianism and the Septuagint: Collected Essays*, Bibliotheca Ephemeridum Theologicarum Lovaniensium 178 (Leuven: University Press, 2004), 41–67.

17. The passage in Jer 33 also includes promises related to Levitical priests. Messianic hope associated with both royal and priestly offices is also reflected in Zch 3:8 and 6:9-15, which refers to the royal and priestly figure Joshua, son of Jehozadak (*yehotsadaq*), which means "Yahweh is righteous." Cf. *YHWH tsidqenu*, "Yahweh our Righteousness" in Jer 23:6 and 33:16). As in Jer 23 and 33, this messianic figure is referred to as "Branch" (*tsemach*). For more on this and the thread of priest-king themes throughout the Tanakh going back to Gen 14, see Joshua G. Mathews, *Melchizedek's Alternative Priestly Order: A Compositional Analysis of Genesis 14:18-20 and Its Echoes throughout the Tanak* (Winona Lake, IN: Eisenbrauns, 2013), 122–29.

Jeremiah 33:14-26

The Branch and the Abrahamic Promises

RANDALL L. MCKINION

The message of the book of Jeremiah is that the messianic hope encapsulates the fulfillment of all the promises Yahweh has made to Israel and the nations, as these promises are seen through and framed by the biblical covenants. Ultimately, the book points to a last-days restoration of the fortunes of God's people—namely, the house of Israel and the house of Judah—in a sanctified Jerusalem ruled over by the righteous son of David. Those over whom this righteous Branch rules will have been made righteous as part of their entrance into the new covenant. Restoration entails hope in multiple facets of God's promises from creation to new creation, from Abraham to the seed of Abraham, from David to the son of David, and from Levitical priest to last-days priest(s).

Despite the fact that Jer 33:14-26 is neither quoted in the New Testament nor witnessed to in the Septuagint, there is little doubt that this is a messianic passage. In fact, Thompson straightforwardly begins his commentary on this section with these words: "A small collection of messianic prophecies is gathered in these verses."[1] This article will attempt to show that Jer 33:14-26 speaks of this messianic hope within the context of the following: the just and righteous rule of the seed of David, the ministry of the priests, the Levites, the fulfillment of the Abrahamic covenant, particularly the promises of land, seed, and nation, the purposes of creation, the restoration of Jerusalem, the relationships among the covenants throughout the OT, and the demonstration of Yahweh's mercy as expressed through the new covenant.

OVERVIEW OF THE PASSAGE

According to Jer 33:1-13, the Lord would not utterly abandon His people despite the judgment that came as a result of their sin. Rather, the "great and wondrous things" (v. 3) that Yahweh has planned for His people include their healing, cleansing from their sin, the restoration of Judah and Israel, and the return of true worship. On the heels of this message, the author adds five short messages that accentuate and expand upon the first half of the chapter.

In the first message (vv. 14-16), the text speaks of coming days in which the righteous Branch will rule with justice and righteousness over a Judah that has been redeemed and a Jerusalem that dwells secure. The "branch" imagery refers to an individual, and based on the context of Jeremiah and the rest of the Hebrew Bible, to the ideal Davidic king (see below). That He is righteous speaks to His character and to His legitimacy, as opposed to Zedekiah ("Yahweh is righteous"), the last king of Judah, who continued a long line of kings who failed to maintain this righteous standard.[2]

The work of Yahweh in raising up the Branch will bring a new identity to the city of Jerusalem, which will be known as "Yahweh Our Righteousness." All of this is seen as the fulfillment of Yahweh's "good word" (v. 14, HCSB "good promises"). Although this "good word" may be referring to the promise made to David in 2Sm 7—and certainly the Davidic covenant is implied here and in the rest of the passage—there is good reason to believe that this refers to the promise of Jer 23:5-6, which is virtually quoted in the next two verses.[3] Yet, as the author elaborates upon earlier passages in the book, he does not just quote, but rather expands (see below). The "good word" of 23:5-6 is filtered through the promises of the new covenant (Jer 31:31-34), which is also made with the houses of Israel and Judah (cf. 31:31 and 33:14).

The second message (vv. 17-18) ensures that the reader of Jeremiah understands that the judgment of God upon Israel, Judah, and Jerusalem will not mean the cutting off of Yahweh's promises to David and to the Levitical priests. These verses assuage any fear on behalf of the reader regarding the future of king and priest. "These fears and cares the Lord now meets by declaring that, in both respects, the perishing would be an arising, that life should arise from death."[4] Within the context of these messianic prophecies, Jeremiah brings together royalty and priesthood. A righteous kingdom demands legitimate worship. The basis for this assurance appears in the next oracle.

According to the third message (vv. 19-22), the covenants with David and with the Levites are as certain as the covenant made with day and night (Gn 1:5; 8:22). Not only does the passage refer to the creation narrative of Gn 1 and to the Noahic covenant of Gn 8–9, it also links these promises to the Abrahamic covenant by means of v. 22. Just as Abraham's seed would be innumerable (cf. Gn 13:16; 15:5; 22:17), so would the seed of David and the Levites. Specifically, this correlates the promises made to Abraham as finding their fulfillment through the covenants made with David and the priests. That is, to speak of the seed of David (and the Levites) in this section is paramount to speaking of the seed of Abraham. Yahweh will multiply the seed of David and the seed of Levi, as promised in the Abrahamic covenant. Yet, as will be discussed below, the author does not seem to view these two covenants as one, at least in their fulfillment. The text maintains the independence of the covenants made with David and the priests.

Furthermore, according to the fourth (vv. 23-24) and fifth (vv. 25-26) messages, the implications of these promises are confirmed in that they are related not only to the king and priest but also to the whole nation. Verses 23-24 raise the question of claims that were made regarding Yahweh's seeming abandonment of His people. Some in Israel may have thought that judgment on the two families of Israel and Judah meant Yahweh's choice of them was made void. However, according to vv. 25-26, this idea was ill-founded. On the one hand, Yahweh's election of them was as certain as the statute He had made for the day and night (v. 25). Only when this order was broken would God break His promises to the seed of Judah and the sons of David. On the other hand, Yahweh's election was not based on the Mosaic covenant, which they had broken, but upon the promises made to "Abraham, Isaac, and Jacob" (v. 26). The presence of these three names together is rare in the Prophets; its significance is to point the reader back to the patriarchs, ensuring the reader that the hope of a messianic kingdom in the future relies on the promises made to the fathers in the past. Finally, as a fitting conclusion to this section, as well as to the Book of Consolation (see below), the prophecy of v. 26b promises restoration and mercy.

In summary, these five prophecies bring together in a comprehensive way promises that have been made throughout the OT. Far from being curtailed by judgment, hope for the Messiah—the son of David—was all the more sure because of God's promises that stretched from creation, to Noah, to Abraham, to the priesthood, to David, and ultimately to the new covenant. The righteous Branch will rule over a kingdom made up of the seed of Abraham, Isaac, and Jacob, who have received mercy from Yahweh.

SHOULD THERE EVEN BE A JEREMIAH 33:14-26?

This question may seem strange, but Jer 33:14-26 presents an interesting problem in that the passage is not found in the Greek translation (the Septuagint) of the

Hebrew Bible. The Greek text of Jeremiah tends to be shorter and arranged differently, but this passage is the longest of those passages that do not have a Greek translation. This presents a unique challenge. Without becoming too mired down in the deep waters of textual criticism, it appears that there are two witnesses to the book of Jeremiah. The first is the Masoretic Text (from which our English versions are translated), representing a longer reception of the prophecies of Jeremiah. The other is the Greek translation, a version confirmed by Hebrew passages found at Qumran. It witnesses to a Hebrew collection that differs somewhat from that retained in the Hebrew Bible and the OT of English translations.[5]

What bearing does this have on the study of the passage being examined? First, how the passage coheres with the rest of the book should be discussed. The relationship of the text within the present form of Jeremiah would help discern whether the passage is a late insertion—perhaps unoriginal—or whether it is an important part of the author's textual strategy. Second, given the way that this passage interacts with earlier passages of Jeremiah, the interpretation given by the author may give a slightly nuanced interpretation of earlier oracles in the text. How this passage is related to other sections of the book shows intentionality of the author. Discussion of both of these points contributes to the interpretation of the text and ultimately to its messianic teaching.

JEREMIAH 33:14-26 WITHIN THE BOOK OF CONSOLATION

Jeremiah 30–33 brings together texts from other portions of Jeremiah to "offer a sustained development of the theme of hope."[6] Thus, these chapters make up what is often called the "Book of Consolation" or the "Book of Comfort." Though composed of both poetry and prose, Jer 30–33 seems to be a discrete collection knit intelligently into the book, and 33:14-26 plays an important role in this regard.

Two aspects of the composition show that the oracles of Jer 33:14-26 appear to be integrally woven into the context of Jer 30–33 as a fitting conclusion. First, the author returns to words that began these chapters with what is called an inclusio. According to the oracle of 30:3, "'days are certainly coming'—this is the LORD's declaration—'when . . .'" Yahweh would "restore the fortunes of [His] people," namely both Israel and Judah. Likewise, 33:14 begins with the introductory phrase, "'Look, the days are coming'—this is the LORD's declaration." Those days would include God's bringing about "the good promises" that He spoke concerning the houses of Israel and Judah (v. 14). The section concludes, "I will restore their [namely, the seed of Abraham, Isaac, and Jacob] fortunes" (33:26).[7] "In 30:3 and 33:26, the phrase serves as a kind of inclusio, or envelope, around these chapters, identifying their theme at the very beginning and at the end."[8] Not only does this text echo and enhance these themes, its position also shows intentionality in its composition. Although this observation does not rule out the possibility that the words were added at a later point, the presence of the inclusio does show the strategic placement of the oracles. Thus, these verses are closing off this important section before the book transitions back to more material concerned specifically with Zedekiah. Its message of hope proves to be important as the city, which is promised security in 33:16 at the hands of the righteous Branch, is promised a fiery destruction in 34:2 at the end of Zedekiah's ("Yahweh is righteous") reign. The irony should not be missed.

Second, this passage takes up a significant number of terms and themes that have already appeared in Jer 30–33. "This passage . . . is well integrated into MT. Like the rest of chap. 33, these verses restate and extend promises found elsewhere in the book."[9] For example, consider the following:

- The introductory phrase discussed above—"'Look, the days are coming'—this is the Lord's declaration"—also appears in 30:3; 31:27,31,38. What is intended by "days" will be discussed below.
- These verses concern *the house of Israel* and *the house of Judah* (v. 14). In fact, the phrase, "the days are coming—this is the Lord's declaration" introduces oracles concerning the houses of Israel and Judah in two other places. The first is Jer 31:27: "'The days are coming'—this is the Lord's declaration—'when I will sow *the house of Israel* and *the house of Judah* with the seed of man and the seed of beast" (emphasis added). The second is as an introduction to the new covenant, which Yahweh would make "with the house of Israel and with the house of Judah" (31:31). As such, the good word of 33:14 was made "to the house of Israel and the house of Judah" and is set within the context of the restoration of the nation and the establishment of the new covenant.
- The restoration formula "restore their fortunes" (33:26) appears in 30:3, 18; 31:23; 32:44; 33:7,11 (cf. also 29:14). Repetition marks this as a prevalent theme of the Book of Consolation, a theme that is pictured by the buying of land in Jer 32. It is also connected to the purpose of the book by linking this restoration with Jeremiah's prophetic word that Yahweh would build and plant (see 31:27-28 and 1:9-10).
- The author connects the phrase "restore the fortunes" with the compassion (or mercy) of God in 30:18 and 33:26. They also occur in close proximity in 31:20,23. Whatever the restoration of Israel might include—e.g., political, geographical—the promises here "have to do with the extended future of

> this people which will marked [*sic*] by an ongoing experience of the mercy of God."[10]

In summary, the message of 33:14-26 accentuates and encapsulates the message of 30–33, a message that the fortunes of the house of Israel and the house of Judah will be restored in the days to come. This begs the question of when exactly these days would come.

Phrases that refer to "days" are replete throughout these chapters, as they are in much of the Prophetic Books. The question to be asked is, What days? Should the reader assume a temporal context for the oracles being made? More specifically, are these the days that followed the exile? There is no doubt that Jeremiah (especially the version of the Hebrew text in which this passage occurs) has much to say about the exile and its 70-year limit (see Jer 25:11-12). However, within Jer 30–33, the context for those "days" during which these great promises would occur is specifically described as "the latter days" (NASB) in 30:24. This phrase is latent with an eschatological (end-times), messianic focus. Although it is not an extremely common phrase, it is used strategically in several important messianic passages throughout the OT. As M. B. Shepherd notes,

> Its sparse and strategic use always occurs in passages that speak of the messianic kingdom: in the poems of the Pentateuch that interpret the preceding narratives (Gen. 49:1, 8-12; Num. 24:7-9, 14, 17; Deut. 4:30; 31:29; 33:5, 7), in the programmatic and restoration passages of the Prophets (Isa. 2:1–5; Jer. 23:20; 30:24; 48:47; 49:39; Ezek. 38:14–17; Hos. 3:5; Mic. 4:1–5), and in the visions of Daniel (Dan. 2:28; 10:14).[11]

As such, the text places the fulfillment of the oracles in Jer 30, and by inference those throughout these chapters, within the eschatological kingdom of the son of David. Thus, the promises of Jer 33:14-26 refer to the last-days work of God through the Messiah. This is an important observation in that these prophecies point beyond the return from Babylonian exile.

So far, this section has shown (1) that these verses seem to be an intentional conclusion to the Book of Consolation and (2) that the message of this passage coincides (via repetition of significant phrases) with that of the rest of chaps. 30–33. One further point of comparison is the close relationship between 31:35-37 and 33:19-22, 25-26, as seen below.

31:35 This is what the LORD says: The One who gives the sun for light by day, the fixed order of moon and stars for light by night, who stirs up the sea and makes its waves roar—Yahweh of Hosts is His name: 36 If this fixed order departs from My presence—this is the LORD's declaration—then also Israel's descendants will cease to be a nation before Me forever. 37 This is what the LORD says: If the heavens above can be measured and the foundations of the earth below explored, I will reject all of Israel's descendants because of all they have done—this is the LORD's declaration.	31:19 The word of the LORD came to Jeremiah: 20 "This is what the LORD says: If you can break My covenant with the day and My covenant with the night so that day and night cease to come at their regular time, 21 then also My covenant with My servant David may be broken so that he will not have a son reigning on his throne, and the Levitical priests will not be My ministers. 22 The hosts of heaven cannot be counted; the sand of the sea cannot be measured. So, too, I will make the descendants of My servant David and the Levites who minister to Me innumerable." 25 This is what the LORD says: If I do not keep My covenant with the day and with the night and fail to establish the fixed order of heaven and earth, 26 then I might also reject the seed of Jacob and of My servant David—not taking from his descendants rulers over the descendants of Abraham, Isaac, and Jacob. Instead, I will restore their fortunes and have compassion on them."

The highlighted words and phrases show that these two texts are making similar points, particularly in regard to Yahweh's commitment to the nation, despite judgment. At the same time, the text of Jer 33 applies these promises to the seed of David and the seed of the Levites. The hope is not just that they will be maintained as a nation (31:36) but that their leadership and their worship will be maintained. The message of judgment does not mean the annulment of the king and the priest.

The way 33:14-26 resonates with the rest of 30–33 shows that the author rehearses the same promises made throughout the section, but in a way that is not redundant. So these verses repeat prophecies from the rest of the Book of Consolation, but in a way that extends their words. These textual connections (along with the inclusio discussed above) also show that the passage is intelligently designed to provide a fitting conclusion to the Book of Comfort. But this is done not just by reminding the reader of former words, rather by interlacing the earlier promises regarding the new covenant with those concerning David and the Levites.

As such, this text also relates closely to other messianic prophecies of Jeremiah and the rest of the Hebrew Bible.

33:14-26 WITHIN THE BOOK OF JEREMIAH AND THE HEBREW BIBLE

As shown above, 33:14-26 takes up earlier words and phrases that are important within Jer 30–33. Moreover, these verses also interact with earlier texts in Jeremiah, the most significant of which is 23:5-6. Yet, as mentioned above, the author does not simply quote the passage verbatim. Consider the similarities and differences highlighted below:

23:5 "The days are coming"—this is the LORD's declaration—"when I will raise up a Righteous Branch of David. He will reign wisely as king and administer justice and righteous- ness in the land. 6 In His days Judah will be saved, and Israel will dwell securely. This is what He will be named: Yahweh Our Righteousness.	33:14 "Look, the days are coming"— this is the LORD's declaration— "when I will fulfill the good promises that I have spoken concerning the house of Israel and the house of Judah. 15 In those days and at that time I will cause a Righteous Branch to sprout up for David, and He will administer justice and righteousness in the land. 16 In those days Judah will be saved, and Jerusalem will dwell securely, and this is what she will be named: Yahweh Our Righteousness.

The messianic teaching of these two passages seems to be obvious, as they reflect the hope of an end-of-days son of David who will (1) reign with justice and righteousness and (2) bring salvation and security to the nation at Jerusalem.

> The promise of a new and eternal covenant with Israel (31:31-34; 32:36-41) raises the question of the status of the other covenanted institutions in the nation's life, the Davidic monarchy and the priesthood. The promise of a 'righteous [צדקה] sprout' who will do 'righteousness' (צדקה) provides a hopeful stance for the reader of the following chapters about the decline and fall of Zedekiah's (צדקיהו) monarchy.[12]

These two passages also resonate with the messianic hope of Isaiah and Zechariah.

Isaiah 4:2-6. Having already spoken in Isa 2 about the end-of-days raising of Zion/Jerusalem as the place of peace to which the nations stream to learn Yahweh's instruction (torah), Isaiah prophesies that in that day there would be a beautiful and glorious "branch of the LORD" (4:2). The effect on the people would be that they are "called holy" (4:3). Using the imagery of God's presence among the people in the wilderness during the exodus, the writer shows that the effect on the city would be security. These are the same results of which Jer 33:14-16 speaks.

Isaiah 11. Although it does not use the same term for "branch," Isa 11 speaks of the Spirit-filled branch (or shoot) from the line of David (11:1) that would judge (same root as "justice") the people with righteousness (11:3-4). In this, Isa 11 extends the same promises made in Isa 9:6-7 regarding the Son who would sit on the throne of David and rule "with justice and righteousness."

Zechariah 3 and 6. The prophecy of Zch 3 relates to Jer 33:14-26 in at least three ways. First, the text uses Joshua and his friends as a sign for the Branch, saying, "Listen . . . I am about to bring My servant, the Branch" (3:8). Second, the coming of the Branch would be accompanied by the removal of guilt of the land (3:9). Third, the use of Joshua is significant in that he was the high priest (3:8). As such, there is the bringing together of the priesthood with the Branch, which is similar to Jer 33 where promises to David and the Levitical priests are discussed together. The prophecy regarding Joshua is elaborated upon in Zch 6, where a crown is made and set upon the head of Joshua, the high priest (6:11). The prophecy states,

> This is what the LORD of Hosts says: "Here is a man whose name is Branch; He will branch out from His place and build the Lord's temple. [13] Yes, He will build the LORD's temple; He will be clothed in splendor and will sit on His throne and rule. There will also be a priest on His throne, and there will be peaceful counsel between the two of them." (6:12-13)

The relationship between the Davidic Son and the priesthood that Jeremiah makes in relationship to the covenants is made even more explicit in Zechariah. At the same time, Jeremiah specifically talks about the future of the Levites as a group who will serve Yahweh.

The point of showing these connections is to demonstrate that the reference to the Branch of David in Jer 23 and 33 relates intertextually with other important messianic passages within the prophets. Moreover, as in Zechariah, the bringing together of royal and priestly aspects of the messianic hope is not unique to Jeremiah.[13] However, an important contribution of Jeremiah is to speak to the ongoing validity of the covenant that was made with the Levitical priests. Jeremiah does not show the Davidic king negating the role of these servants in the future.

To summarize, the messianic promises of 33:14-16 are not breaking new ground, in that they are already made in essence earlier in Jeremiah, and they resonate with other messianic passages throughout the Prophets. However, since these verses do not simply quote Jer 23:5-6, additional attention should be given to where and why the two passages are different.

Israel → Jerusalem. There seems to be a turn in chap. 33 to a focus on Judah along with Jerusalem (cf. v. 7 to vv. 10,12,16).[14] Since these prophecies focus on Yahweh's commitment to king and priest, which are both related closely in their work to Jerusalem, this seems reasonable, especially in view of Jerusalem's imminent destruction. This is consistent with the Psalter's hope in the messianic kingdom at Zion (e.g., Ps 132). This also focuses attention on the literal aspect of the messianic kingdom in the land. The future of king, priest, and worship in the land is guaranteed by God's commitment to His promises within the context of the new covenant and its application to Israel.

Yahweh our Righteousness. Jeremiah 33:16 makes a significant extension in that the name "Yahweh our righteousness" is given to the city of Jerusalem rather than to the King (23:6); yet, the name of the city is connected to the prophecy regarding the individual called Branch. In both cases, the connection of righteousness to Yahweh stands in stark contrast to the person of Zedekiah, the last king of Judah, whose name means "Yahweh our righteousness."[15] The author here is not correcting the earlier oracle but extending it in order to show that the righteousness of the Branch of 23:6 extends to the city. This is most likely a reference to the people who have thus been saved and transformed by the work of the Branch. "The inference is that Jerusalem would so manifest the qualities of justice and righteousness (in contrast to her past bad record) that she would be worthy of such a name and exemplify the divine order for all the cities and all the people of Israel."[16]

This is consistent with other portions of the Book of Comfort, such as Jer 31:23, which states, "This is what the LORD of Hosts, the God of Israel, says: 'When I restore their fortunes, they will once again speak this word in the land of Judah and in its cities, "May the LORD bless you, righteous settlement, holy mountain."'" This may also be insinuated by 31:38-40, when the city is rebuilt and, as a result, the whole valley and all the fields "will be holy to the LORD" (31:40). In other words, the righteousness of the coming Branch of David will mean the presence of righteousness in the nation and the city, given that "Jerusalem reflects the righteousness which is bestowed on her by the Messiah."[17] The transition of righteousness from the individual to the community seems to be the point. Hope consists in the future display of righteousness by the Branch that is shared with a restored people. Within the context of 30–33, the hope that stems from the work of the Davidic Son is thus in concert with the new covenant promises. In fact, one of the key contributions of Jer 33:14-26 is the way the text relates the various covenants of the OT.

JEREMIAH 33:14-26 AND THE COVENANTS

Given that Jer 33:14-26 alludes to all of the major covenants of the OT—except the Mosaic—this text goes a long way in helping explain how the prophets related the promises made to David backward to creation and to the Abrahamic covenant and forward to the promise of the new covenant. It would not be exaggerating to say that these verses portray the Messiah through the lens of the biblical covenants.

The focus on the covenants helps answer a difficult question that the text raises, specifically, How is the promise to the priests to be understood in light of the Davidic covenant and the new covenant, both of which are related to the house of Israel and the house of Judah in the Book of Comfort?

First, within the context of Jer 30–33, the new covenant has already been expressed as a replacement of the old Mosaic covenant (cf. 31:31-34). In fact, the new is explicitly described as distinct from the one made with the ancestors (31:32). Moreover, according to 31:32, the Mosaic had already been broken anyway. Fretheim states it this way:

> Just how these perpetual covenants to David and the Levites are to be related to the new covenant of 31:31-34 or the everlasting covenant of 32:40 is not altogether clear. But, at the least, the covenants with Abraham (see ch. 30), David, and the Levites are statements that affirm the continuity in the divine commitment to Israel through the fall of Jerusalem and the exile. *And so the new, everlasting covenant does not set these other covenants aside; that shift pertains only to the Sinai covenant. This text thus signals a new way that the people of the new covenant are to understand themselves within the framework of these continuing, promissory covenants.*[18]

The prophet points to the superiority of the new in relationship to the old, not just as a mere replacement but "from the shadow to the substance!"[19] As Hengstenberg points out, this is consistent with the message of Jer 3:16 that days would come when there would no longer be a need for the ark, as the presence of Yahweh would reside in Jerusalem. The shadow would pass away.

Therefore, second, any future work of the priests must be understood in conjunction with the Abrahamic, Davidic, and new covenants, especially as they are understood in the book of Jeremiah. As discussed above, the bringing together of royal and priestly promises is not unique to Jeremiah. But the new covenant of Jeremiah displaces neither the Davidic nor priestly. Within this context, the author strategically sets both the Davidic and priestly within the context of Yahweh's creation purposes and the Abrahamic promises. Jeremiah 33:25 refers to Yahweh's covenant with day and night as well as "the fixed order of heaven and earth." The first of these refers to a promise made in the Noahic covenant that "day and night will not cease" (Gn 8:22). The second alludes to the creation narrative and labels God's superintending as a statute (Gn 1:5). These narratives are related in Genesis as the text depicts the flood as a de-creation and re-creation. After the promises of Gn 8–9, Gn 10–11 traces the seed of Noah—which had earlier been linked to Adam—forward to Abraham. As a result, the creation purposes for land, seed, and blessing are traced through these early chapters of Genesis and culminate in the promises made to Abraham in such passages as Gn 12, 15, and 17.

The Pentateuch's depiction of the priests also does not originate first with the giving of the Mosaic covenant. Not only is humanity seen as serving a priestly role in the garden,[20] but also there are priestly activities attributed to the patriarchs. All of this takes place before the giving of the law as part of the covenant at Sinai. In fact, the initial giving of the covenant at Sinai in Ex 19:5-6, which the people reject and break, includes their being a "kingdom of priests," which should probably be understood as distinct from and more comprehensive than being a nation *with* priests.[21] What is more, priests already appear (see Ex 19:24) before the covenant is ultimately given. All of this is to say that the role of priesthood and its relationship to the Abrahamic promises precedes that of the covenant at Sinai. Priests already had a role, even though the text does not elaborate. As such, it is not surprising that the prophets recognize the correlation between the king (prophesied already by Moses in such passages as Gn 17 and 49) and the priest(s) (pictured already in Abraham (Gn 12:8; 13:4,18), Melchizedek (Gn 14:18-20), and perhaps even Moses (Dt 33:4-5).

The frame of reference for Jeremiah, however, is the Levitical priesthood and their sacrifices and offerings. Jeremiah's prophecies warned of the ceasing of the theocracy, with both its king and temple (and, therefore, priesthood) cut off. The cutting off of service by the Levites certainly occurred with the destruction of the temple and the exile. By referring to the future of both the Davidic kingship and the Levitical priesthood, the text assures the reader that "the Lord, in order to keep His people from despair, declares that these two institutions, in accordance with His promise, shall not fall to the ground, but shall stand for ever."[22] Thus, the focus of Jeremiah seems to be the identification of the seed of the Levites as continuing to perform a priestly role, which is consistent with the pervasive knowledge of God by all of those who will be in the new covenant (31:33-34).

Furthermore, the author links the hosts of heaven and the sand of the sea to the multiplication of the seed of David. This seems to associate David with Abraham, and the seed of David with the seed of Abraham. Specifically, this correlates the promises made to Abraham as finding their fulfillment through the covenant made with David. That is, to speak of the seed of David in this section is paramount to speaking of the seed of Abraham. The text could be read in such a way that the seed of the Levites is also referred to this way. If this is the case, the text would push forward the ideas that (1) the work of the righteous Branch has both kingly and priestly aspects and (2) those who enjoy the salvation that the Branch brings have a priestly role similar to but greater than that which existed before the Mosaic law restricted the priesthood to the house of Levi. This would be consistent with the message of Isa 56:6-7, where foreigners are made to be ministers to Yahweh.[23]

Nevertheless, to read the text as referring to a group of spiritual priests who supersede the promises made to the Levites neglects that these promises were confirmed not as part of the Mosaic covenant but as an extension of the priesthood already in place before it was made. That is, the text of Jeremiah looks to the fulfillment of these promises even from within a new covenant that abrogates the Mosaic. As such, the author seems to recognize the perpetual nature of the promises made to Phinehas and his seed in Nm 25:11-13. Moreover, by specifying Jerusalem as the place of security and righteousness and by intentionally keeping the Davidic and priestly covenants separated, the literalness of the future kingdom at Zion should be maintained. To say that the promises to the Levites are simply spiritualized may be a flattening of the hope the Hebrew Bible instills in its reader by maintaining the hope of the kingdom at Zion ruled over by the seed of David and led in worship by the Levites.

A fitting interpretation of this passage is probably best understood from the view of a literal millennial kingdom in which the Levitical priesthood continues to serve.[24] This is in keeping with the vision of Ezk 40–48, where "the Levitical priests, descended from Zadok . . . approach me to serve me" (44:15; cf. also 43:19).

Thus, by referencing each of these covenants and ultimately pointing the reader back to creation, Jer 33:14-26 links the messianic hope of the new covenant back through the lens of the Davidic covenant, reiterating the promise made to Judah in Gn 49 and showing the means God would use to bring about the "seed" promised through Abraham. Moreover, by its focus on the land and the multiplication of lineage, Jeremiah shows that the Branch would bring these Abrahamic promises to fulfillment, as the Lord would bless them once again on the land.

---

1. J. A. Thompson, *The Book of Jeremiah*, New International Commentary on the Old Testament (Grand Rapids: Eerdmans, 1980), 600.

2. Thompson, *Book of Jeremiah*, 489: "There was much in the representatives of the Davidic dynasty during Jeremiah's day which suggested that they were a sham, for they failed to demonstrate the true qualities of kingship (21:11-14; 22:1-3)."

3. In fact, both of these verses have an obvious tie to the Davidic covenant of 2Sm 7.

4. E. W. Hengstenberg, *Christology of the Old Testament: Commentary on the Messianic Predictions*, 2nd. ed., trans. Theod. Meyer (London: T&T Clark, 1861), 2:460.

5. For a discussion of this, see John H. Sailhamer, "Biblical Theology and the Composition of the Hebrew Bible," in *Biblical Theology: Retrospect and Prospect*, ed. Scott J. Hafemann (Downers Grove, IL: InterVarsity Press, 2002), 26–32. Compare also Emanuel Tov, *Textual Criticism of the Hebrew Bible* (Minneapolis: Fortress Press, 1992), 320–21.

6. Patrick D. Miller, "The Book of Jeremiah: Introduction, Commentary, and Reflections," *The New Interpreter's Bible* (Nashville: Abingdon Press, 2001), 6:797.

7. The importance of this connection is heightened by the addition of "I will have compassion on them." There is not just redundancy but also escalation and interpretation.

8. Miller, "The Book of Jeremiah," 6:797.

9. Gerald L. Keown, Pamela J. Scalise, and Thomas G. Smothers, *Jeremiah 26–52*, Word Biblical Commentary (Nashville: Thomas Nelson, 1995), 173.

10. Terence E. Fretheim, *Jeremiah*, Smyth & Helwys Bible Commentary (Macon, Georgia: Smyth & Helwys, 2002), 480.

11. Michael B. Shepherd, *A Commentary on the Book of the Twelve: The Minor Prophets* (Grand Rapids: Kregel Academic, 2018), 53–54.

12. Keown, Scalise, and Smothers, *Jeremiah 26–52*, 173.

13. Note, as well, that the passages in Isa 2–12 that discuss the coming of the Branch/Emmanuel/son of David also include the vision that Isaiah had of the Lord being high and lifted up within the temple (Isa 6). As such, the *King* was exalted within the *temple*.

14. Despite the clear movement to focus on Judah and Jerusalem in chap. 33, Israel is mentioned in vv. 14 and 17. This is not to take the spotlight off Judah and Jerusalem, merely a recognition that Judah and Israel were divided when Jeremiah wrote and that vv. 14 and 17 anticipate the eschatological reunification of the nation with Jerusalem as its capital.

15. Consider, e.g., Dane Ortlund, "Is Jeremiah 33:14-26 a 'centre' to the Bible? A Test Case in Inter-Canonical Hermeneutics," *Evangelical Quarterly* 84.2 (2012), 126: "It is probably not coincidence, in light of Jer. 33:16, that the name of the last king of Judah, Zedekiah, means 'Yahweh is righteous/Yahweh is my righteousness'—the supreme irony at the end of a long line of kings who consistently failed to embody such a truth (cf. 52:1-3)."

16. Thompson, *Book of Jeremiah*, 601.

17. C. F. Keil, *The Prophecies of Jeremiah*, in *Biblical Commentary on the Old Testament* by C. F. Keil and F. Delitzsch (Grand Rapids: Eerdmans, 1991), 8:2:72.

18. Fretheim, *Jeremiah*, 478, emphasis added.

19. Hengstenberg, *Christology of the Old Testament*, 2:465.

20. For example, see T. Desmond Alexander, *From Paradise to the Promised Land: An Introduction to the Pentateuch*, 3rd ed. (Grand Rapids: Baker Academic, 2012), 123–25.

21. Cf. John H. Sailhamer, *Introduction to Old Testament Theology: A Canonical Approach* (Grand Rapids: Zondervan, 1995), 277–89.

22. Keil, *Prophecies of Jeremiah*, 8:2:73. They go on to say that the text is silent about the nature of the reestablishment of both of these institutions, "but in the emphatic confirmation of the prophecy which follows, we find brief indications which clearly show that the restoration spoken of will not be a reinstitution of the old form which is now perishing, but a renovation of it, in the essential features, to a permanent existence" (74).

23. E.g., see Hengstenberg, *Christology of the Old Testament*, 2:465.

24. See Irvin A. Busenitz, "Introduction to the Biblical Covenants; The Noahic Covenant and the Priestly Covenant," *The Master's Seminary Journal* 10/2 (Fall 1999), 186–89.

Ezekiel 17:22-24

Ezekiel's Tender Sprig and the Messiah

DANIEL I. BLOCK

Although more than one fourth of Ezekiel's preserved prophecies look forward to Israel's glorious tomorrow, overt references to the Messiah in the book are remarkably few.[1] Ezekiel 29:21 may allude to the Messiah. In an oracle against a foreign nation (Egypt) and supportive of a foreign king (Nebuchadnezzar), Ezekiel concludes his pronouncement with an enigmatic reference to "a horn" (*qeren*) that YHWH will cause to sprout for the house of Israel. Literally, the noun denotes an animal's horn, and is often used synonymously with *šôpār*, though the latter usually refers more specifically to a ram's horn.

Since horns are the focus of many creatures' power, *qeren* naturally functions figuratively for "strength." With this statement, YHWH offers hope to the exiles. That the fulfillment of Ezekiel's prophecy against Tyre was delayed for more than a decade does not mean YHWH has forgotten His promises to Israel or His debt to Nebuchadnezzar. When the prophet and his people see him settling this outstanding account, they may take heart that YHWH's long-standing account with Israel (albeit of a different nature) will also be settled.

But the issue has another side. The mixed metaphor involving a "horn" that will "sprout" also occurs in Ps 132:17, where YHWH promises to "cause a horn to sprout for David" (author translation). This link provides the basis for the long-standing messianic interpretation of 29:21. However, most scholars reject the messianic assessment—on the grounds that the idea of a royal messianic deliverance was not important in Ezekiel, and that the notion would in any case be intrusive in this context. However, elsewhere Ezekiel makes pronouncements that have obvious messianic implications, especially in 34:22-23 and 37:22-25. While Ezk 17:22-24 may not refer explicitly to the Messiah, the topmost crown of the cedar, identified as *rak* ("sprig, shoot," v. 22), serves as a harbinger of the figure to be developed later. This text demands a closer look.

THE HISTORICAL AND LITERARY CONTEXT OF EZEKIEL 17:22-24

Cast as an imaginative fable, involving cedar trees, vines, and eagles, Ezk 17 declares the end of the Davidic dynasty, specifically the judgment and demise of Zedekiah, the last member to occupy the throne in Jerusalem. Although the text exhibits structural and thematic links with Ezekiel's sign act in 12:1-16, in terms of genre, chap. 17 is explicitly characterized as a "riddle" and a "parable" (17:2). We may well imagine Ezekiel's exilic audience trying to figure out its significance for them (cf. 24:19). This chapter has a curious structure, involving a two-part riddle followed by a two-part interpretation. Based on the subject matter, the four parts exhibit the following chiastic arrangement:

A The Riddle of the Cedar Sprig (vv. 3-4)
  B The Riddle of the Vine (vv. 5-10)
  B' The Interpretation of the Riddle of the Vine (vv. 11-21)
A' The Interpretation of the Riddle of the Cedar Sprig (vv. 22-24)

The chapter actually involves two riddles that appear together. However, as we would expect, the interpretation of the second riddle follows immediately after the riddle itself, but the interpretation of the first is oddly delayed until the end. The first riddle concerns Jehoiachin, who ruled in Jerusalem only three months (2Kg 24:8), while the second riddle focuses on the character and fate of Zedekiah (cf. 2Kg 24:17–25:21). Technically, in the interpretation of the first riddle (vv. 22-24), only v. 22 pertains to Jehoiachin. The remainder (vv. 23-24) concerns a future far beyond this man.

If Ezekiel's main concern in vv. 5-10 is Jehoiachin, the primary character in this complex metaphor is a great eagle (v. 3). Throughout the ancient world eagles served both as positive symbols of strength (Isa 40:31) and royal splendor,[2] but also as fearful symbols of terror. Esarhaddon's boast, "Like a furious eagle I spread my pinions to destroy my enemies,"[3] illuminates the meaning of Hosea's reference to the Assyrian hordes as "an eagle com[ing] against the house of the Lord" (Hos 8:1; cf. Dt 28:49). But this eagle is different; he is cast as a genuinely benevolent figure, plucking off a sprig of a cedar (that is about to be cut down?), taking it away to Babylon, and planting it there, apparently in favorable circumstances.

While the prophet obviously spoke of a particular and special bird, it may not have been so obvious to Ezekiel's audience whom this eagle represented. Could this be YHWH, who both narrative and hymnic tradition says had carried Israel on His eagles' wings and brought them to Himself (Ex 19:4; cf. Dt 32:11)?[4] Or was this some human monarch? After all, the eagle was a common military and royal symbol, and kings were often portrayed as cherub-like figures with eagles' wings.[5]

In an act quite uncharacteristic of eagles, this magnificent bird snipped off essentially the crown of a cedar and carried the top shoot of fresh growth off to a "land of merchants" and a "city of traders," veiled references to Babylon, identified in 16:29 as Chaldea. Since a city is by definition a dwelling or group of buildings surrounded by defensive walls for the protection of the residents, in contrast to the fields outside it where crops and vineyards are planted, the purpose of bringing the sprig to this city presumably was to protect it—just as merchants protect their goods in warehouses within the walls of the city. Ezekiel has painted the bird and its actions in positive and noble strokes, in stark contrast to the images of the second eagle (Egypt) and the vine (Zedekiah) in vv. 5-21.

As already observed, unlike the central core of this chapter, which consists of a second metaphor (vv. 5-10) and then follows immediately with an interpretation (vv. 11-21), the opening scene lacks an interpretation, leaving the reader to ponder its significance—until the coda in vv. 22-24. While many delete the coda as a postexilic insertion,[6] without it the riddle of vv. 3-4 remains unresolved. Like the interpretation of the riddle concerning the vine, vv. 22-24 declare that behind the actions of the magnificent eagle we need to see the hand of YHWH. Ultimately He is the one who plucks a shoot from the top of the cedar, and sets it (in a secure place), until the time is right to retrieve it and plant it on a high and lofty mountain.

THE IDENTITY AND CHARACTER OF THE TENDER SPRIG

But whom does this sprig represent—this foremost of the fresh young twigs of the cedar? Actually, we must distinguish between two tender twigs. Assuming the cedar of vv. 3 and 22a symbolizes the Davidic dynasty, the freshness of the sprig suggests either a youthful king or one whose tenure was cut off prematurely.[7] This could apply either to Jehoahaz, the 23-year-old son of Josiah who reigned only three months before he was taken away to Egypt (2Kg 23:31-34), or Jehoiachin, the 18-year-old son of Jehoiakim, who also reigned only three months before he was taken away to Babylon (2Kg 24:8-16). However, because the interpretation of the riddle of the vine expressly identifies the magnificent eagle with the king of Babylon, who came to Jerusalem and took its king (and the princes) back to Babylon (v. 12), the sprig is obviously Jehoiachin.

The rest of the coda (vv. 22b-24) concerns the long-range implications of this action. Even so, the eagle's motivation is not immediately clear. In contrast to 2Kg 24:9 and 2Ch 36:9,[8] which suggest Jehoiachin's exile was punishment for "doing *the* evil in the eyes of YHWH" (which involves unfaithfulness to YHWH and going after other gods), to the extent that this riddle speaks to the issue it appears positive. Although v. 22a attributes the sprig's transplant to YHWH rather than to the king of Babylon, the statement is silent on any punitive motivation. Indeed, the earlier reference to "the land of merchants" and the "city of traders" (v. 4) opens the door for a beneficent purpose.[9]

So far, the sprigs that the eagle and YHWH transplant are obviously one and the same; this is Jehoiachin. However, the referent changes in the second half of v. 22. The sprig that YHWH had transplanted took root and grew into a tall cedar itself. From this new tree, YHWH "plucked" its topmost branch (cf. v. 4) and planted it on a towering high mountain. In this statement and the remainder of the coda, Ezekiel highlights the special quality of the sprig.

First, its link to the cedar confirms its Davidic roots, and its origin as the topmost sprig of the tall cedar confirms its significance within the history of the dynasty.

Second, the shoot is fresh and tender. The expression *yōnĕqôtāyw*, "its new shoot," derives from the root, *yānaq*, "to suckle," and is often used of fresh shoots on a plant.[10] Its freshness is reinforced with the addition of the modifier, *rak*, "tender.[11] Etymologically the word derives from *rākak*, "to be tender, soft,"[12] but Ezekiel's usage is unparalleled. Inasmuch as YHWH says of Josiah, "Your heart was tender" (2Kg 22:19), the word invites us to associate this figure with the last positive representative of the Davidic house. These expressions suggest a person who is both responsive to YHWH and offers promise for a new beginning for the dynasty.[13] Ezekiel's horticultural imagery links this passage with other texts that use related language for the revived scion of David, but are more explicit in their messianic thrust: "shoot" and "branch" in Isa 11:1; "branch" in Jer 23:5; 33:15; Zch 3:8; 6:12. In this context its tender shoot sets the stage for the messianic figure who will be presented in greater detail in later salvation oracles (34:23-24; 37:24-25).[14]

Third, this shoot will have cosmic significance. The referent's exalted status is reflected in the physical size of the tree (a towering tree), its splendor ("a majestic cedar"), and its location "on a high towering mountain" (v. 22b ESV). This is truly a *Weltenbaum*, a cosmic tree towering over the forest and over the landscape more generally.

Fourth, the mission of this tree was universal; the purpose of its planting was that its branches might bear fruit, offer secure places for birds to nest, and for all to find relief from the sun in its shade (v. 23). The reference to birds "of every kind" (lit. "every bird, every wing") obviously speaks to the tree's expansiveness and universal appeal.[15] However, since Ezekiel's fable has used birds—albeit of a particular kind ("eagle")—to represent Babylon and Egypt respectively, it is possible that these birds represent the nations of the earth.[16] The problem with this interpretation is that v. 24 portrays the nations as trees, rather than birds. However, since this is a fable, the imagery does not need to be consistent or conform to reality. This may be another intentional dimension of the "riddle" that this chapter represents. The prophet leaves it to his hearers either to scratch their heads over the double allusions, or at least to be entertained by them. This image is unreal in other respects as well. Cedar trees do not bear fruit, but this one offers its fruit to all the birds.[17] Even so, the present passage may have been inspired by Isa 11:1-10, where the elements of a newly sprouted messianic shoot, the mountain of YHWH, and peaceful co-existence with wild animals are all conjoined.

Fifth, the tree is located on "the high mountain of Israel" (v. 23 NASB). This plant, whose story had begun in "Lebanon" (v. 3), presumably an allusion to the royal places in Jerusalem (cf. 1Kg 7:2), after spending some time in Babylon, has returned home. Here "the mountain of Israel" obviously alludes to Mount Zion. Although this mountain will become increasingly significant in later oracles, only here in Ezekiel are the motifs of Davidic line and Zion brought together.[18] Both elements are truly remarkable, reminding the exiles that YHWH had not forgotten His covenant with David (2Sm 7; Ps 132:10-18). The dynasty would survive the deportation; it would be revived within the context of its original founding, and its protective influence would be felt all around the world.

The last verse highlights the tree's universal impact in the form of a complex recognition formula: when all the trees of the field see this tree flourishing and offering its benefits to the world, they will know "that I am YHWH." When YHWH finally exalts the tree, the tree will exalt YHWH. One might have anticipated that when all the trees, that is, the nations of the earth, observe the splendor, the productivity, and the protection offered by the tree, they would fall down before it in homage and submission. But this prophecy is not about Davidic imperialism; it is about the cosmic sovereignty and fidelity of YHWH in the interest of His creation. The former is highlighted by four sensitively constructed parallel lines:

> I bring down the tall tree,
>   and make the low tree tall.
> I cause the green tree to wither
>   and make the withered tree thrive.

Ezekiel's utterance is reminiscent of Hannah's, a half millennium earlier. In anticipation of what YHWH would do with her son Samuel, and ultimately the appearance of YHWH's king and His Messiah, she declared:

> The LORD brings death and gives life;
> He sends *some* to Sheol, and He raises *others* up.
> The LORD brings poverty and gives wealth;
> He humbles and He exalts.
> He raises the poor from the dust
> and lifts the needy from the garbage pile.
> He seats them with noblemen
> and gives them a throne of honor.
> For the foundations of the earth are the LORD's;
> He has set the world on them.
> He guards the steps of His faithful ones,
> but the wicked perish in darkness,
> for a man does not prevail by *his own* strength.
> Those who oppose the LORD will be shattered;
> He will thunder in the heavens against them.
> The LORD will judge the ends of the earth.
> He will give power to His king;
> He will lift up the horn of His anointed. (1Sm 2:6-10, italics added)

For a concrete illustration of bringing down the high, readers need look no further than Zedekiah, whose fate had been described in vv. 19-21. As for the low being lifted up, this must be Jehoiachin. He may have been languishing in captivity in Babylon at the time of this oracle, but before long he would be elevated above the other kings in the Babylonian court (2Kg 25:27-30). But this is not about Jehoiachin; this is about his scion, who will be restored to the throne of Israel and elevated to the status of universal king!

This probably seemed like an impossible dream to the exiles who heard Ezekiel's riddle, but it is guaranteed in the final three lines. YHWH has spoken; He will act! The roots of this oracle are found in His covenant with David, communicated four centuries earlier by Nathan the prophet. Not only had YHWH promised him eternal title to the throne of Israel; David had recognized in it the "revelation" or "instruction" (ESV) for humanity (2Sm 7:19). YHWH had not forgotten His ancient word. Nor would He betray this new word, issued through Ezekiel, in the interests of Jehoiachin. The dynasty would survive the exile. Its best years were still in the future.

How focused Ezekiel's vision of the Messiah was at this point is unclear. What is clear is that the divine purpose in taking Jehoiachin into exile in Babylon was positive—to preserve a branch of the house of David to which He had irrevocably and eternally committed Himself. Just as the exiles as a group represented the key to Israel's future as a nation (Ezk 11:14-21), so the hopes of the Davidic house were pinned on Jehoiachin. This man, who had gone into exile as an eighteen-year-old stripped of all honor, would be rehabilitated. As it turned out, his grandson, Zerubbabel (522–486 BC; 1Chr 3:19; Hag 1:1), would serve as the governor of the new commonwealth of returned exiles established under Persian administration. But this "seed of Babylon"[19] would never fulfill the vision of this cosmic tree. That must await the arrival of a greater son of David, the Messiah (*hammāššîah*), who would claim the world as His kingdom (Jn 12:32; cf. Rev 22:18).

CONCLUSION

The two Gospels that recount the birth of the Messiah in the New Testament both begin on a remarkable note. In his opening genealogy of Jesus the Messiah, Matthew acknowledged the significance of Jehoiachin (Jeconiah) in the history of God's great redemptive plan. The history of the royal line divides into three parts, each consisting of 14 generations (the numerical value of the consonantal name of David (d + v + d = 4 + 6 + 4). But note the anchors of this lineage: Abraham, David, Jehoiachin, and Jesus the Messiah. Jehoiachin represented that phase in the history of the line where the messianic hope was almost extinguished; but he also represented the key to its continuation. The messianic hope of Ezk 17:22-24 is fulfilled in Jesus the Messiah.

Luke's allusion to the Ezekiel prophecy is of an entirely different order. Reminiscent of Hannah's oracle in 1Sm 2:6-10,[20] upon hearing Gabriel's announcement that she would give birth to "the holy One," "the Son of God" (Lk 1:35), Mary declared:

> He [the Mighty One] has done a mighty deed with His arm;
> He has scattered the proud because of the thoughts of their hearts;
> He has toppled the mighty from their thrones
> and exalted the lowly.
> He has satisfied the hungry with good things
> and sent the rich away empty.
> He has helped His servant Israel,
> mindful of His mercy,
> just as He spoke to our ancestors,
> to Abraham and his descendants forever (Lk 1:51-55).

1. The messianic interpretation of specific texts like Ezk 34:23-24 is implicit in LXX and Peshitta, and overt in the Vulgate and the Rabbinic *Gen. Rab.* 97.

2. With Sennacherib's reference to the eagle as "the prince of the birds" (D. D. Luckenbill, *The Annals of Sennacherib*, [Chicago: University of Chicago Press, 1924], 36), compare Pindar's "king of the birds" (*Olympian Odes*, 13.21).

3. R. Borger, *Die Inschriften Asarhaddons Königs von Assyrien* (AfO Beih. 9; Graz: 1956), §44. Cf. also §65.

4. These texts are reminiscent of the Etana Legend in which the shepherd Etana is carried to heaven on the wings of an eagle. Cf. *Ancient Near Eastern Texts*, 114–18, esp. 118; Stephanie Dalley, *Myths from Mesopotamia: Creation, the Flood, Gilgamesh, and Others*, rev. ed. (Oxford: Oxford University Press, 2009), 189–202.

5. Compare the description of the King of Tyre as a cherub in 28:14.

6. For a defense of its inclusion see Daniel I. Block, *The Book of Ezekiel Chapters 1–24*, New International Commentary on the Old Testament (Grand Rapids: Eerdmans, 1997), 549–50.

7. The characterization of the sprig as *rak*, "tender," in v. 22 recalls Prv 4:3-4, "When I was a son with my father, tender (*rak*), and my mother's favorite, he taught me and said to me, 'Let your heart hold fast my words; keep my commands, and live.'"

8. Both texts declare that Jehoiachin "committed the evil in the eyes of YHWH." This dim view of Jehoiachin is also shared by Jeremiah (Jer 22:24-30). On the other hand, if our identification of the first branch of 19:10-13 with Jehoiachin is correct, then even in Ezekiel's mind Jehoiachin is implicated in the pervasive hubris of the Davidic house and punished for this arrogance with destruction by fire.

9. According to 2Kg 25:27-30, Nebuchadnezzar's successor Evil-Merodach also had a favorable view of Jehoaichin.

10. Hos 14:7; Ps 80:11 [Hb 12]; Job 8:16; 14:7; 15:30.

11. LXX omits the word, probably because the notion is assumed in thought in *yōnĕqôtāyw*, "its new [tender] shoot."

12. *Hebrew and Aramaic Lexicon of the Old Testament*, 1230.

13. So also, Matthew H. Patton, *Hope for a Tender Sprig: Jehoiachin in Biblical Theology* (PhD dissertation, Wheaton College, 2014), 185.

14. Compare the Aramaic Targum, which offers a subdued paraphrase:

> I myself will bring near *a child from the kingdom of the house of David which is likened to* the lofty cedar, *and I will establish him from among his children's children; I will anoint (nd) and establish him by my Memra [Word]* on a high and exalted mountain. On the *holy* mountain of Israel will I *establish him, and he shall gather together armies and build fortresses and become a mighty king;* and *all the righteous shall rely upon him, and all the humble* shall dwell in the shade *of his kingdom.* And all *the kings of the nations* shall know that I the Lord *have humbled the kingdom which was mighty and have made mighty the kingdom that was weak. I have humbled the kingdom of the nations which was mighty* as a green tree, and *have made mighty the kingdom of the House of Israel, which had been as weak as* a dried-up tree. I the Lord, *have decreed it by My Memra and I* will fulfill it.

As translated by Samson H. Levey, *The Targum to Ezekiel: Translated, with a Critical Introduction, Apparatus, and Notes,* The Aramaic Bible 13 (Wilmington, DE: Michael Glazier, 1987), 56–57. Despite the Targumic reading, Jewish interpreters have generally rejected an eschatological messianic interpretation of this passage. Kimchi identified the person as Zerubbabel, son of Shealtiel, son of Jehoiachin (cf. Zch 4:7). However, Zerubbabel scarcely fits the picture painted here. He never actually sat on the throne of David, and he certainly did not fulfill the cosmic role envisioned here. On the nonmessianic eschatology of the Targum to Ezekiel see Samson H. Levey, "The Targum to Ezekiel," *Hebrew Union College Annual* 46 (1975): 144–45. For recent responses to Levey's interpretation, and defenses of messianic readings, see Alinda Damsma, "The Merkabah as a Substitute for Messianism in Targum Ezekiel?" *Vetus Testamentum* 62 (2012): 51533; William R. Osborne, "The Early Messianic 'Afterlife' of the Tree Metaphor in Ezekiel 17:22–24," *Tyndale Bulletin* 64 (2013): 171–88. See also Antti A. Laato, *Josiah and David Redivivus: The Historical Josiah and the Messianic Expectations of Exilic and Postexilic Times, Coniectanea Biblica: Old Testament Series* 33 (Lund: Almqvist & Wiksell, 1992), 154–64.

15. Thus Block, *Ezekiel 1–24*.

16. Thus Patton, *Hope for a Tender Sprig*, 187.

17. Ezekiel's image of a huge tree offering nourishment and protection for all creatures represents a Hebrew version of a widespread ancient mythological motif, known as "the cosmic tree." Typically, this tree is not to be associated with the "Tree of Life" in a paradisic garden (cf. H. N. Wallace, "Tree of Knowledge and Tree of Life," *Anchor Bible Dictionary* 6.658). For studies on the tree as a symbol of an ordered world in the face of the threat of death in ancient Near Eastern written and visual sources, see Uwe Winter, "Der Lebensbaum in der altorientalischen Bildsymbolik," in "*. . . Baume braucht man doch!" Das Symbol des Baumes zwischen Hoffnung und Zerstourung*, ed. H. Schweizer (Sigmaringen, Thorbecke, 1986), 57–88; Donald E. Gowan, *When Man Becomes God: Humanism and*

Hybris in the Old Testament, Pittsburgh Theological Monograph Series 6 (Pittsburgh, 1975), 102–106. Cf. also P. R. Frese and S. J. M. Gray, "Trees," *Encyclopedia of Religion*, ed. M. Eliade (New York: Macmillan, 1987) 15.27–28. In 31:1-18 Ezekiel develops the motif as a symbol of Egypt in much greater detail. In Dan 4 the world tree represents Nebuchadnezzar.

18. While absent from 34:23-24 and 37:24-25, the present association of mountain and king recalls Pss 78:68-73 and 132:10-18, which juxtapose the election of David and the establishment of his dynasty with the choice of Mount Zion as YHWH's dwelling place. Ezekiel studiously avoids the name Zion, probably because it had been so badly misused in official theology and because of the shame priests and kings had brought to the place. On the concept of Zion as a world mountain see Richard J. Clifford, *The Cosmic Mountain in Canaan and the Old Testament*, HSM 4 (Missoula, 1972), 131–60; R. L. Cohn, *The Sacred Mountain in Ancient Israel* (1975), 187–207.

19. On this etymology of Zerubbabel see J. J. Stamm, *Akkadische Namengebung* (Darmstadt: Wissenchaftliche Buchgesellschaft, 1968), 269–70.

20. While not in the Hebrew text, the Targum rightfully understands Hannah's oracle as prophetic utterance; "And Hannah prayed *in a spirit of prophecy* . . ."

Ezekiel 21:25-27

The Hope of Israel

ABNER CHOU

Traditionally, scholars understood Ezekiel 21:25-27 as a significant messianic prophecy.[1] Commentators note that this passage alludes to and develops the messianic prophecy of Gn 49:10. It also speaks of the convergence of the priestly (turban) and royal (crown) offices mentioned in Ps 110:1-4. In context, this establishes how God will reverse Israel's exile and the fall of the Davidic dynasty. This passage also sets up readers for other depictions of the Messiah as priest and king (cf. Jer 23:5-6; Zch 3:1-10; 6:12-15). These observations show that this passage contains immense theology.

However, in recent years, some have questioned the traditional interpretation of this text. They argue that the referent of the coming one in Ezk 21:25-27 is not the Messiah but Nebuchadnezzar.[2] Proponents of this view still acknowledge the connection of Gn 49:10 and even a messianic undertone to the passage. At the same time, they see that Ezekiel uses messianic language to show the ironic reversal Israel will have in Nebuchadnezzar. Instead of their desired savior, Israel will have a destroyer. Thus, to these scholars, the passage is indirectly messianic as opposed to a direct messianic description.

The argument for this is threefold. The first deals with context. The issue surrounding the passage is judgment as God directs Ezekiel to point Nebuchadnezzar to attack Jerusalem (Ezk 21:19-23). Since that is God's main agenda, it makes sense that the coming one in Ezk 21:26-27 deals with judgment and not hope.

The second argument deals with the "this" in the phrase "yet *this* will not happen until He comes" (v. 27, emphasis added). Proponents of the nonmessianic view argue that, in light of the context, the word refers to God's judgment. Consistently, the phrase means God's wrath against Jerusalem will not happen until a certain individual comes. Nebuchadnezzar certainly fits this description, especially since he is explicitly mentioned in context (cf. Ezk 21:21).

Third, scholars also point to the word "the judgment" in the phrase "I have given *the judgment* to him" (emphasis added) in v. 27. Some translations render the word "judgment" (Hb. *mishpat*) as "right" (KJV, NASB, NIV). That would support the messianic interpretation. However, some commentators point out the word most likely means "judgment," given parallel passages in Ezekiel (23:24b) and that Ezekiel never uses *mishpat* to denote "right."[3] This means God does not give the coming one the "right" to rule (messianic interpretation). Rather He ordains that individual to judge Jerusalem. That idea also fits well with Nebuchadnezzar. Overall, those who hold a nonmessianic view have based their interpretation upon the context and wording of the passage.

Messianic interpretations should not be assumed but shown. This article aims to do just that. Closer examination of the exegetical evidence will show the accuracy of the directly messianic view—that Ezekiel wrote clearly and consciously about the Messiah. Further exposition of the passage will demonstrate how this text makes a profound contribution to messianic theology. In sum, this text brings past revelation to show how the Messiah will be the culmination of Israel's entire leadership. He alone has the right to unite all authority in Himself.

RESOLVING INTERPRETATIVE ISSUES

As just noted, the main arguments revolve around the context of the passage and the wording in Ezk 21:27. The traditional interpretation can address this point for point.

Concerning the first point of context, while the broader context discusses judgment, the immediate context deals with the overturning of the Davidic dynasty. This is explicitly stated in the opening verse of this passage (Ezk 21:25). It addresses the "wicked prince of Israel," and the grammar of vv. 25-27 indicates that royalty remains the topic throughout those verses.[4] Hence, the context does not merely regard judgment (as nonmessianic proponents imply) but particularly regards God's agenda for the Davidic king. That factor supports a messianic interpretation.

Second, the pronoun "this" most likely does not refer to God's judgment, contra what the nonmessianic reading proposes. The reading of "judgment" is grammatically problematic. The pronoun "this" is part of a series of feminine pronouns throughout vv. 26-27. Syntactically, there is no indication of a change of referent, so they should all refer to the same noun or idea. The referent cannot be judgment, for it makes little sense in certain places (does God make "judgment" a ruin in v. 27a?). Instead, the nouns "turban" and "crown" are the only feminine nouns that can act as the referent for the entire chain of pronouns. Hence, the phrase "this will not happen" does not deal with how judgment will not come until an individual arrives. Rather it deals with how the turban and crown will be no more until a particular person comes. Such an idea does not fit at all with Nebuchadnezzar but fits perfectly with the Messiah.

Finally, the term "judgment" (*mishpat*) in context does denote something akin to "right," again contra to what the nonmessianic reading proposes. The nonmessianic reading neglects that the term "judgment" has an article in Ezk 21:27. It is "*the* judgment" (emphasis added). The article on the noun is significant. Throughout the Hebrew Bible, "the judgment" refers to a legal verdict (Dt 17:9,11; 1Kg 3:28; 7:7; Hos 5:1). Thus, "I have given the judgment to him" does not refer to the act of punishing but rather God giving a certain legal ruling or pronouncement. That fits with a messianic interpretation where God decides that Messiah will uphold both offices of king and priest.

Thus, each of the points raised against the traditional view in the end support a messianic interpretation. The phrase, "Yet this will not happen until He comes; I have given the judgment to Him," does not refer to judgment not happening till Nebuchadnezzar comes. Rather, it denotes that the turban and crown will not exist in Israel until the one comes whom God decrees will have them. This reading accounts for the exegetical details of the text. It also makes sense of the context that not only deals with judgment but particularly with how that will affect the Davidic dynasty.

Additional evidences exist for the messianic reading. For one, this interpretation is consistent with the exact message of Gn 49:10, a text scholars agree underlies this passage.[5] It is also consistent with how later passages, like Jer 23:5, Zch 3:1-10, and 6:12-15, read this text. In fact, Jauhiainen argues that Ezk 21:25-27 is the "interpretative key" for Zch 3:1-10 and 6:12-15.[6] The prophets seem to have read Ezk 21:25-27 as messianic. Moreover, the LXX, the Greek translation of the OT, indicates that the Jews read these verses the same way. As Pasinya points out, the LXX omits the term "judgment" to make it clear that this is about a worthy individual, not Nebuchadnezzar, but the Messiah.[7]

Thus, a close examination of the evidence points to the traditional, messianic interpretation. The messianic understanding of the verse can factor in the exact immediate context, the grammar of the text (referent of pronoun and the article on *mishpat*), as well as the precise meaning of words (*mishpat*). Even more, the reading remains consistent with past revelation, is the way the OT prophets read it, and is the way even the earliest audience read it as reflected in the Greek translations.

With that, the messianic reading is traditional because no other reading for centuries has existed.[8] Such consistency reflects the clarity of the text in the first place. Ezekiel intended to speak of Messiah.

EXEGETICAL CONSIDERATIONS

Since Ezk 21:25-27 describes the Messiah, we should proceed to know what it says of Him. This begins by understanding the text's literary and intertextual context. A close reading of the text will then provide further information showing how indeed Messiah is the climactic ruler who reverses exile.

LITERARY CONTEXT

The book of Ezekiel was written in Babylon (1:1-3) to those who wondered if God was still with Israel, especially those in exile.[9] The main issue of Ezekiel therefore is God's presence and relationship. This is accentuated via Ezekiel's visions, which show God's presence goes anywhere (Ezk 1:1-28), has an agenda to fill the earth (Ezk 43:2), will depart to judge Israel for their sin (Ezk 11:11-25), and will return to a Spirit-filled Israel to fulfill His relationship with them exhibited by a physical millennial temple (Ezk 43:1-4). As the visions punctuate and structure the book, they give the specific purpose of the respective section within Ezekiel's prophecy.[10]

In light of this, Ezk 21 falls into the section dealing with how God's glory will depart Israel in judgment. This will lead Israel into exile and yet anticipates that God will still be with His people to ultimately bring them back to Himself (Ezk 11:16). Nevertheless, God's departure in judgment triggers the collapse of all Israel's infrastructure that facilitates a relationship with God. In Ezk 14–19, God refuses to listen to the prophets (Ezk 13:1-23), He rejects the intercessory work of a priest (Ezk 14:1-3), and He also puts aside the king (Ezk 19:1-14), who often stands between Israel and God (1Chr 21:16-18). The exile brings a temporary end to prophet, priest, and king.

Ezekiel 21 will expound upon this focus of leadership in context. Ezekiel 20 provides the timing surrounding Ezk 21, approximately five years before the fall of Jerusalem.[11] Since the fall of Jerusalem is so close, Israel might wonder whether God will relent at the last minute as He has done at other times (cf. 2Kg 19:35-37). However, that will not be. Israel's sin is so advanced that there is no turning back (Ezk 20:1-49). God's sword is polished for wrath (Ezk 21:1-17). God even commands Ezekiel to direct the king of Babylon to attack Jerusalem (Ezk 21:18-20) and ensures the king's false divination will point him in that direction (Ezk 21:21-23). Judgment is inevitable, not only because of Israel's sin as a whole (Ezk 21:24), but specifically because of the wicked prince of Israel (Ezk 21:25). Reviewing these verses brings the discussion to the passage at hand.

The mention of the prince continues the subject rehearsed earlier: the collapse of the prophet, priest, and king. Ezekiel 21:25-27 will clarify and expound upon that issue. Thus, contextually, the point of Ezk 21:25-27 concerns God's agenda for the royal dynasty in light of exile and His relationship with His people. Since Israel's leadership is headed to inevitable judgment, what will become of them? Can and will God save Israel? If so, how will He do that? These are the issues surrounding Ezk 21:25-27.

Intertextual Context

Although Ezk 21:25-27 may have many connections, two passages stand out particularly for this discussion. First, Gn 49:10 is a vital text. As noted, most scholars recognize the allusion.[12] Both passages have the unique phrase "until he comes" (HCSB footnote). In addition, the phrase "the one to whom judgment belongs" (ESV; Hb. *'asher lo*) in Ezk 21:27 is actually a play on words with the title "Shiloh" in Gn 49:10.[13] Ezekiel uses these allusions to Gn 49:10 to import theology from that text into his writing. In context, Gn 49:10 speaks of the eschatological advent of the One who perfects Judah's rule.[14] In the context of the rightful downfall of leadership (see above), Ezekiel invokes the language of Gn 49:10 to show the One who will perfect this very imperfect rule in Israel.

Second, Ps 110 is in view. Like Gn 49:10, Ps 110 is messianic.[15] David declares that the Messiah must be in the order of Melchizedek (Gn 14:18), and thereby a king and priest (Ps 110:1,4). He will be the one who is the culmination of Israel's government. Ezekiel 21:25-27 refers to this idea with its mention of turban and crown, in addition to the earlier context of the collapse of prophet, priest, and king. Ezekiel brings out the theology of Ps 110 to show the only way for the collapse Davidic dynasty to be repaired. Another Davidic monarch cannot fix this. Only the individual of Ps 110, the culmination of king and a new priestly order, can make both leadership and Israel right.

Both literary and intertextual context help to frame the purpose and ideas within Ezk 21:25-27. The literary context raises the need to discuss the Messiah, given the question of the collapse of leadership in light of God's wrath. The allusions to previous messianic text anchor this text as messianic. They also help bring to light critical theological elements taking place in the text (i.e., ultimate ruler, king, and priest). Moreover, the context of the book provides the full significance of this discussion. Ezekiel's point is that the convergence of king and priest in Messiah is the only way leadership is restored, exile ends, and God's relationship with His people is fulfilled. He shows the reason that the theology of Gn 49:10 and

Ps 110 is not merely helpful, but absolutely essential. Hence, context clarifies what is happening in Ezk 21:25-27, as well as its full depth and impact.

INTERPRETATION OF TEXT

With this in mind, Ezk 21:25-27 addresses these issues in two main parts. The first is the pronouncement of the prince's guilt (Ezk 21:25), and the second deals with the nature of punishment (Ezk 21:26-27).

I. Pronouncement of Guilt (21:25). With the opening phrase "And you," God shifts from discussing the wickedness of the people to specifically that of Israel's king, Zedekiah. He is called the "prince" because he is not truly in the kingly line (2Kg 24:17),[16] which already implies the Davidic house is destabilizing.

The description of the prince confirms this. He is "profane" in that he is defiled (cf. Ezk 11:6; 20:9) and unable to be in God's presence (Ezk 6:4-7; 7:21-24). The prince is unfit to be the mediator he should be. Furthermore, he is "wicked." In Ezekiel, the "wicked" refer to a category of people opposite of the "righteous" (cf. Ezk 3:18-19; 18:20-27; 21:3). As opposed to being righteous and resisting or reforming the wicked, Zedekiah is the leader of the wicked. He not only cannot mediate between God and the people, he also steers them in the opposite direction. The Davidic house has utterly failed in its duties.

For this reason, God declares His verdict. He states that "the day has come for your punishment." The "day has come" shows the inevitability of wrath. The past tense verb implies it is as if the time for wrath has already arrived. There is no escaping this now. Furthermore, the idea of "your punishment" in Hebrew is "the time of the punishment of the end" (NASB). The idea is that the prince's guilt and penalty will result in a complete end. This is the end of Zedekiah himself, his iniquitous behavior, and even the Davidic house.[17]

In context, Israel wondered whether God might relent at the last minute. The verdict is clear. Not only is Israel guilty, but also the royal dynasty is guilty. This demands judgment, one that will bring the royal house to an end. In declaring this, God begins to reveal His plan for the entire leadership structure of Israel.

II. Nature of Punishment (21:26-27). With the opening words, "this is what the Lord God says," God announces the exact punishment that will ensue. The next two verses will discuss the extremity and duration of this judgment.

A. Extreme of God's Punishment (21:26). The Lord will remove the turban and take off the crown. The latter term, crown (Hb. *'atarah*), refers to the royal diadem symbolizing the ruler's authority (2Sm 12:30). Taking off the crown will end the office of king.

What, though, is the significance of the turban? Some argue this refers to the king's own turban.[18] That makes sense in context. However, the term turban (Hb. *mitsenephet*) exclusively refers to the turban worn by the high priest (Ex 28:4,37,39; 29:6; 39:28; Lv 8:9; 16:4). It is not used in any other way in the entire Hebrew Bible. Consistently, the removal of the turban then refers to the collapse of the priesthood triggered by the fall of the Davidic dynasty.[19] The collapse of this hierarchy is already established in context (see above). This passage picks up on that idea.

The next phrases in the verse confirm this. God states that, "Things will not remain as they are." The idea in Hebrew is that "this will not be this," where "this" refers to the turban and the crown. The symbols of leadership are negated as Israel's leadership will cease to exist. Subsequently, God pronounces "exalt the lowly and bring down the exalted." The entire societal order will be overturned.

With that, God shows His punishment will be extreme. It will be extreme in that not just the Davidic house but the entire governmental system will be destroyed. It will be extreme in that this will plunge all of society into chaos.

B. Duration of God's Punishment (21:27). The oracle does not end there, though. God reiterates the extremity of punishment. He will make the turban and crown a ruin. The use of ruin shows the fairness of this punishment. The word (Hb. *'avah*) sounds like the word for "guilt" used earlier (Hb. *'avon*). It is used three times corresponding to how "guilt" was used three times in vv. 23-25. This word play shows how Israel's punishment fits their crime.[20] At the same time, ruin denotes making something desolate (cf. Jos 8:28). The leadership of Israel is made nothing.

The next line interjects a surprising turn. God states that "Things (the turban and crown) will not remain as they are." Indeed, as stated, Israel's government is made to utter naught. However, this will only occur "until." The preposition denotes a time will come to reverse this collapse. That moment is when "He comes." As noted, the language comes from Gen 49:10 and the arrival of Messiah who will complete Judah's rule. God has not forgotten His promise of the ultimate ruler. That One will end the chaos.

Even more, God states that "I have given the judgment to Him."[21] As discussed, "the judgment" refers to God's verdict or decision to give the Messiah the crown and turban. This is the reality prophesied in Ps 110. The Messiah will bear all the government upon His shoulders and thereby have an order superior to that of His predecessors. In context, that will be why God's relationship can be restored with His people and the exile ended. The Messiah will fulfill the role other mediators and leaders could not do.

INTERTEXTUAL INTERPRETATION

Later revelation picks up on these very realities. In Zechariah's night visions, God reveals that there still will be One who is king and priest (3:1-10).[22] Zechariah 6:12-15 acts out the moment when the king/priest comes, ends exile, and restores Israel's relationship with God just as Ezekiel foretold.[23] These passages reiterate exactly what Ezk 21:25-27 states in context. They also bring out the importance of Ezekiel's prophecy. The convergence of the turban and crown of Messiah is critical for God's plan (Zch 3:1-10), and the hope of Israel (Zch 6:12-15). Ezekiel's prophecy is a vital piece of messianic theology.

CONCLUSION

Ezekiel 21:25-27 is a crucial text about the Messiah. Its details not only show that Ezekiel intentionally spoke of Him but also proclaim the immense way the prophet describes Him. In the midst of judgment and exile, the Messiah is the only hope for the nation. From the ashes of Israel's fallen leadership, the Messiah will arise to singlehandedly take the turban and the crown. In the midst of separation from God, the Messiah will mediate and restore His people. The prophet shows that all of Israel's hope and functions converge in Him. He is central and climactic. As later revelation will show, this truth drives redemptive history (Zch 3:1-10) and will be the eternal honor of the Messiah (Zch 6:12-15).

---

1. Lamar E. Cooper, *Ezekiel*, New American Commentary (Nashville: Broadman & Holman, 1994), 214; Marko Jauhiainen, "Turban and Crown Lost and Regained: Ezekiel 21:29-32 and Zechariah's Zemah," *Journal of Biblical Literature* 127, no. 3 (October 1, 2008): 501.
2. Leslie C. Allen, *Ezekiel 20–48*, vol. 29 Word Biblical Commentary (Dallas: Word, 1998), 28; Daniel I. Block, *The Book of Ezekiel 1–24*, New International Commentary on the Old Testament (Grand Rapids: Eerdmans, 1997), 689.
3. Allen, *Ezekiel 20–48*, 28; Walther Zimmerli, *Ezekiel: A Commentary on the Book of the Prophet Ezekiel*, Hermeneia (Philadelphia: Fortress Press, 1979), 447.
4. Verse 25 begins with a disjunctive clause slightly separating it from the discussion. The disjunctive clause in v. 28 marks the beginning of the next subunit, making vv. 25-27 one unit. See Bruce K. Waltke and M. O'Connor, *An Introduction to Biblical Hebrew Syntax* (Winona Lake, IN: Eisenbrauns, 1990), 39.2.3c, 651–52. See also Harvey H. Guthrie, "Ezekiel 21," *Zeitschrift für die alttestamentliche Wissenschaft* 74, no. 3 (1962): 278.
5. Cooper, *Ezekiel*, 214; Block, *Ezekiel 1–24*, 692; Allen, *Ezekiel 20–48*, 28; Ralph Alexander, "Ezekiel," Vol. 6 *Expositor's Bible Commentary*, ed. F. Gaebelein, (Grand Rapids: Zondervan, 1979), 758.
6. Ibid., 501.
7. Laurent Monsengwo Pasinya, "Deux Textes Messianiques de La Septante: Gn 49,10 et Ez 21,32," *Biblica* 61, no. 3 (1980): 376.
8. Zimmerli, *Ezekiel*, 447.

9. Block, *Ezekiel 1–24*, 14–15.
10. Abner Chou, *I Saw the Lord: A Biblical Theology of Vision* (Eugene, OR: Wipf & Stock, 2013), 85–87.
11. Block, *Ezekiel 1–24*, 618.
12. Ibid.
13. William L. Moran, "Gen 49:10 and Its Use in Ezk 21:32," *Biblica* 39, no. 4 (1958): 409–17. Moran cogently argues that Shiloh is a title.
14. Ibid., 409–19; K. A. Matthews, *Genesis 11:27–50:26*, New American Commentary (Nashville: Broadman and Holman, 2005), 896.
15. This view has controversy as well. However, see Rydelnik, "Psalm 110," in this *Handbook* for further discussion of the matter.
16. Block, *Ezekiel 1–24*, 373.
17. Ibid., 697; Allen, *Ezekiel 20–48*, 29:27.
18. Block, *Ezekiel 1–24*, 697; Allen, *Ezekiel 20–48*, 29:27.
19. Carl F. Keil and Franz Delitzsch, *Commentary on the Old Testament* (Peabody, MA: Hendrickson, 2002), 9:175; Alexander, "Ezekiel," 884.
20. Allen, *Ezekiel 20–48*, 28.
21. See above for wordplay between Shiloh (Gn 49:10) and this phrase.
22. George L. Klein, *Zechariah*, New American Commentary (Nashville: B&H, 2008), 144.
23. Jauhiainen, "Turban and Crown Lost and Regained," 510–11; Klein, *Zechariah*, 201.

Ezekiel 34:20-31

The Shepherd of Israel

DANIEL I. BLOCK

As is widely recognized, the book of Ezekiel divides into two halves, the first being devoted principally to oracles of judgment against Judah and Jerusalem, and the second to oracles of restoration for all Israel.[1] Although an earlier oracle predicting the demise of the Davidic monarchy had ended with a metaphorical but enigmatic hint of a future Davidic Messiah (17:22-24), for rhetorical purposes in 21:27 [Hb 32] Ezekiel had actually removed from the conversation one of the rare messianic texts in the Pentateuch (Gn 49:10). Within the oracles against the foreign nations (chaps. 25–32), the only utterance that we could by any stretch interpret messianically is YHWH's promise in 29:21: "In that day I will cause a horn to sprout for the house of Israel." Ezekiel 34:23-24 and 37:22-25 contain the most overtly messianic language in the book. While I will occasionally allude to the latter of these two passages, the purpose of this essay is to analyze the former.

THE LITERARY CONTEXT OF EZEKIEL 34:23-24

We will not grasp the significance of this prophecy if we fail to consider its context. In the judgment oracles of chaps. 1–24, Ezekiel's rhetorical strategy had involved demolishing the four covenantal pillars on which the people of Judah had staked their security (Fig. 1):

1. YHWH, the divine patron of Israel, has entered into an eternal covenant with His people.
2. YHWH, the divine patron of Israel, has given the nation the land of Canaan as their eternal territorial possession.
3. YHWH, the divine patron of Israel, has chosen Jerusalem as His eternal residence, from which He exercises sovereignty over His people.
4. YHWH, the divine patron of Israel, has promised the Davidic house eternal title to and occupancy of the throne of Israel.

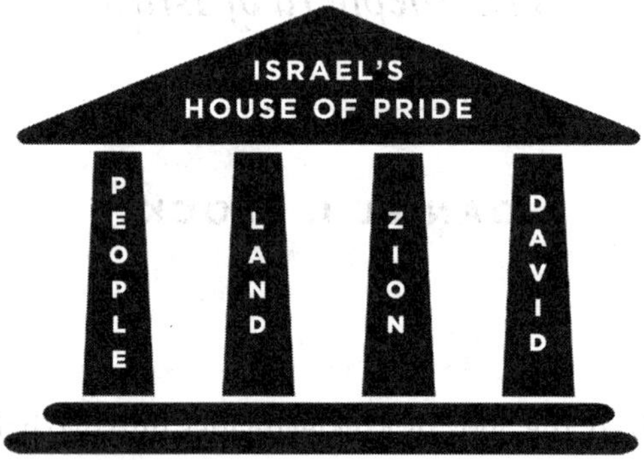

FIG. 1

However, with these privileges had come the responsibilities of exclusive allegiance to YHWH and being a light of YHWH's glory and grace to the world. In His pronouncements of judgment upon Judah and Jerusalem, Ezekiel systematically attacked the pillars listed above, and when the disaster struck (Ezk 33:21) the entire theological structure, and with it the tripartite covenantal relationship involving YHWH, Israel, and the land God had given them (Fig. 2), was in ruins—in precise fulfillment of the covenant curses in Lv 26 and Dt 28.

But within the foundational covenant documents YHWH had declared at the outset that Israel's story could not and would not end with the curse (Lv 26:40-46; Dt 4:30-32; 30:1-10; 32:34-43). The covenant promises were indeed eternal and irrevocable. Accordingly, once Ezekiel had received word that Jerusalem had fallen, his tune changed completely. The prophet's rhetorical strategy in his restoration oracles involved systematically reconstructing these structures. Building on the contemporary prophecy of Jeremiah in Jer 23:1-6,[2] Ezk 34 plays a vital

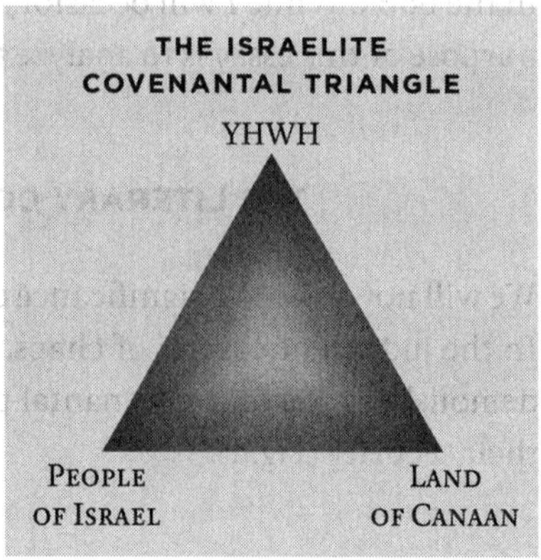

FIG. 2

role in that agenda, announcing at the outset that the triangular relationship involving deity, nation, and land would be completely restored.

Ezekiel's first explicit reference to the Messiah (34:23-24) occurs near the end of an extended restoration oracle in which YHWH poses as a benevolent divine shepherd, rescuing His beleaguered human flock from the tyranny of exploitative rulers and bullying members within the flock (34:1-31).[3] The abuse they had experienced at the hands of the shepherds (Davidic kings) had contributed significantly to the disintegration of the covenantal triangle.[4] The chapter commences with a "woe" oracle pronounced upon the Davidic house (vv. 1-10) that climaxes in YHWH's declaration of hostility to the same royal line to whom He had promised eternal title to the throne of Israel and whom He had commissioned to shepherd His flock (v. 10; cf. 2Sm 7:8-16; Ps 78:68-72).[5] Indeed, they are cast as wild animals and His rescue (*hiṣṣîl*) of the sheep from the mouths of their rulers (cf. 1Sm 17:34-35) is described with vocabulary often associated with Israel's deliverance from the slavery of Egypt (e.g., Ex 5:23).

YHWH's promise in v. 10 to rescue his sheep from those who had abused them and caused them to be scattered "over the whole face of the earth" (v. 6) is brief, compared to the description of their restoration in vv. 11-22. Posing as the Chief Shepherd (cf. 1Pt 5:4), YHWH promised to resolve all the problems the people's own sin and the sins of their Davidic leaders had created. The agenda would be fulfilled in stages:

1. YHWH will personally seek the welfare of His flock by examining their physical condition, and rescuing them from the clutches of the enemy (vv. 11-12).
2. YHWH will bring them out of their places of exile, gather them, and bring them to their own land (v. 13a).
3. YHWH will tend them on their own soil, by leading them to lush pasture and providing rest (vv. 13b-15; cf. Ps 23:1-3).
4. YHWH will bind up the bruised and broken and heal the sick.

With these four actions, the covenantal triangle has been restored: YHWH is reconciled with His people, the people have been brought back home to the land, and the land is yielding its abundance for them. But everything is not yet as it should be, so YHWH's direct involvement in the restorative actions will continue.

5. YHWH will rescue (v. 22) victimized sheep from the bullying rams and bucks among them (vv. 17-22). Now, it becomes apparent the Davidic rulers were not the only problem the flock faced. Among their own were individuals (presumably elders in local communities) who ran roughshod over other sheep and goats as they sought their own interest.

These actions by YHWH provide the background for the appointment of the Davidic Messiah in vv. 23-24. Note that the Messiah is not portrayed as the agent of restoration; rather, having restored the Israelites to Himself, to the land, and to each other, the time has now arrived to install the new David. This sequence of events not only corresponds with ancient Near Eastern paradigms of state renewal and restoration,[6] but also parallels the events leading up to the installation of the first King David. In Moses' "charter for kingship" (Dt 17:14-20), the earliest reference to "the king [YHWH] your God chooses," he set the context as "When you enter the land that [YHWH] your God is giving you, take possession of it, live in it" (v. 14). This image is reinforced by the anticipation of YHWH's choice of a place to establish his name (Dt 12:10): "when you cross the Jordan and live in the land [YHWH] your God is giving you to inherit, and He gives you rest from all the enemies around you and you live in security." It is confirmed in 2Sm 7:1, which describes the context for David's initiative in preparing to build a temple for YHWH: "When the king had settled into his palace and [YHWH] had given him rest on every side from all his enemies."

To be sure, YHWH had already declared David to be the one He had had in mind from the beginning (cf. 1Sm 13:14). However, David's request to Nathan the prophet for permission to build a house for YHWH became the occasion for YHWH to declare that He would build the Davidic "house" (*bayit*) and would grant them eternal and irrevocable title to the throne of Israel (2Sm 7:11-16; Ps 89:19-29 [Hb 20-20]; 132:10-12).[7] David had neither delivered the Israelites from their bondage in Egypt nor delivered the land into the hands of the Israelites so that they had rest (Jos 21:43-45; 23:1). As he himself recognized, YHWH's granting him the kingship was significant because it represented YHWH's signature act on His redemption of Israel from Egypt and His claim of Israel as His covenant people (2Sm 7:23-24).[8] This is precisely the function of the Davidic Messiah in Ezk 34; he would be the "kingpin," the symbol of YHWH's commitment to Israel and the guarantor of the smooth operation of the tripartite covenant triangle (Fig. 3).

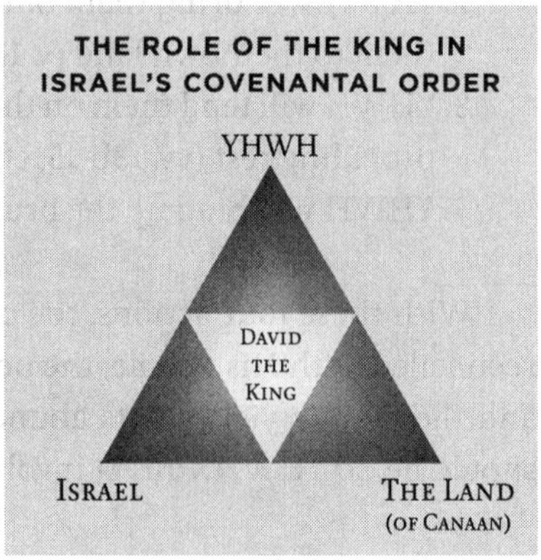

FIG. 3

THE IDENTITY AND ROLE OF THE MESSIAH IN EZEKIEL 34:23-24

Although vv. 25-31 also represent context for vv. 23-24, for a brief moment YHWH's focus shifts from the status and fortunes of His flock to the appointment of David as His (under)shepherd. Without warning the attention moves from YHWH's negative activity, viz., resolving problems within the flock, to exciting new positive actions on Israel's behalf, culminating in the appointment of a human shepherd over them and the restoration of peace and security (vv. 23-31).[9] The covenant formula, which summarizes the goal of YHWH's salvific actions, appears at the beginning (v. 24) and at the end (vv. 30-31), providing a framework for interpreting the intervening material. The two principal motifs dealt with here, the appointment of David as (under)shepherd of YHWH's flock, and the covenant of peace, are fundamental to the Jewish messianism that would flourish in the intertestamental period.[10] The repetitious and staccato style of vv. 23-24 reflects Ezekiel's increasing excitement as he approaches the climax of the oracle. These verses are packed with vital information on the new shepherd's status and role within Israel.

First, this ruler will be neither self-appointed nor elected by the people, but chosen by YHWH Himself.[11] Like his contemporary Jeremiah, Ezekiel perceived Israel as a theocracy.

Second, the shepherd will be singular. The reference to "one shepherd" goes beyond Jer 23:4, which has YHWH installing responsible shepherds (plural) to replace the present exploitative and irresponsible rulers. In announcing a single ruler, YHWH will reverse the division of Israel into northern and southern kingdoms that occurred after the death of Solomon (1Kg 11–12). Like the rest of the prophets, Ezekiel perceived the nation as one and recognized as legitimate only the dynasty reigning from Jerusalem.[12]

Third, the shepherd will be David. Ezekiel's identification of the divinely installed king as David is based on a long-standing prophetic tradition, although this ruler is explicitly identified as David only twice outside this book.[13] On the one hand, the eighth-century prophet Hosea had looked forward to the day when the sons of Israel would "return and seek [YHWH] their God and David their king" (Hos 3:5). On the other hand, however, Ezekiel's diction is closer to Jer 30:8-10, which also combines the appointment of David with the anticipated restoration of the nation. There is no thought in these prophecies of the resurrection of the historic king as some kind of David *redivivus*. Ezekiel's use of the singular "shepherd" and his emphasis on "one" (*eḥād*) also preclude the restoration of the dynasty in the abstract, that is, simply a series of kings. He envisions a single person, who may perhaps embody the dynasty, but who occupies the throne himself.

Although Ezekiel's hope of a divinely appointed shepherd king in the context of national restoration agrees with common Near Eastern thinking, his specific prediction of a revival of the nation's original royal house[14] contrasts with the general nature of extra-Israelite expectations.[15] Having earlier foretold and witnessed the fall of the Davidic house (chap. 17), Ezekiel now declared its restoration. His pronouncement was based upon YHWH's covenant with David, announced by Nathan the prophet in 2Sm 7:8 [1Chr 17:7].

Significantly for this discussion, David's divine election had earlier been described as a call "from the pasture, from following the flock, to be ruler of YHWH's people Israel."[16] YHWH's affirmation of the eternality of the Davidic covenant[17] had provided the basis for all the prophetic hopes.[18] However, the capture of Zedekiah and the collapse of the Davidic house in 586 BC raised doubts about YHWH's ability and/or will to keep His word. Ezekiel hereby announced that the ancient promise had not been forgotten. YHWH would fulfill His irrevocable promise and His unfailing covenant to the house of David as the sole legitimate dynasty in Israel.

Fourth, the shepherd will be the servant of YHWH. Ezekiel's repetition of *ʿabdî*, ("my servant") simultaneously presents an intentional contrast with the self-seeking shepherds of vv. 1-10 and recalls the traditional view of David's willing subordination to YHWH.[19] Moreover, in the Hebrew Bible, "servant of YHWH" (*ʿebed YHWH*) also functioned as an honorific title for others who functioned in an official capacity for God, often with the implication of a special election to a task.[20] David's own standing was expressed most clearly by YHWH Himself, who identified him as "David my servant, whom I have chosen" (1Kg 11:34).

Fifth, the shepherd will be a "prince" (*nāśîʾ*) in the midst of his people. Ezekiel's use of the archaic title *nāśîʾ* contrasts with Hosea and Jeremiah, who had both spoken explicitly of "David their king." However, it is consistent with his efforts elsewhere to downplay the roles of Israel's monarchs,[21] and harkens back to 1Kg 11:34, where YHWH said of Solomon, "I will make him 'prince' (*nāśîʾ*) all the days of his life for the sake of David my servant" (author translation). In chaps. 40–48 Ezekiel will apply the title to the official sponsor and patron of the cult, but usually the term functions primarily as a political designation. Ezekiel's preference for *nāśîʾ* over *melek* ("king"), the normal designation for Israel's rulers, did not deny this new David's true kingship, but highlighted the qualitative distinction between him and the recent occupants of the office. The prophet emphasized the ruler's identification with the people by noting that he will not only be prince over Israel (v. 24),[22] but also prince in their midst. Officially the "prince" may be the promoted one,[23] but in view of his presence in the midst of (*bětôk*) Israel, some view him simply as *primus inter pares*, the first among equals.[24] One may perhaps recognize here an ironic allusion to Dt 17:19-20, which had prescribed for Israel's kings the reading of the Torah to prevent their hearts from being exalted "above [their] countrymen." However, both his status as shepherd among sheep and the expression "prince among them" suggest authority as well as identification.[25] In this arrangement, YHWH was the divine patron of the people; David was His representative and deputy.

Ezekiel's announcement of the appointment of a new David for Israel was intended to instill new hope in the hearts of the exiles. Contrary to appearance, the demise of the Davidic house in 586 BC did not reflect divine impotence or indifference to previous commitments. These events had both fulfilled previous prophetic utterances[26] and set the stage for a dramatic and new act of YHWH. The decadence of the old order had been removed; now Ezekiel challenged the people to look forward to a new day when YHWH's Davidic servant would be reinstated in accordance with His eternal and irrevocable covenant.

Second Samuel 7:23-24 and the texts from Hosea and Jeremiah cited above have hinted at an inseparable link between the election of David and the status of Israel as the people of YHWH.[27] A similar development is evident in Ezk 34:24, which ties YHWH's national covenant with Israel to the dynastic covenant with David. Indeed, a comparison of the national covenant formula and Ezekiel's statement suggests that the prophet perceives the appointment of David as "prince" as an aspect of the fulfillment of the national pledge, "I will be your God and you will be my people." The echo of the first line of this covenant is obvious in the first statement of v. 24,[28] and will be heard again in v. 30. But how is Ezekiel's assertion that "My servant David will be prince among them" related to this formula? The answer is found in the prepositional expression, "in their midst" (*bĕtôkām*), which recalls an auxiliary affirmation often viewed as a part of the covenant formula, "I will dwell in your midst."[29] For Ezekiel, the prince would be more than a political or military functionary, effecting the restoration; his role would begin after the restoration has been achieved by God, at His initiative, and in His time.[30] In short, he symbolizes the renewed presence of YHWH in the midst of His people.

The messianic promise of David the prince taking his place among the people of Israel is sealed in v. 24 with an expanded version of the divine self-introductory formula. The statement is inserted deliberately to reinforce confidence in the present prophetic pronouncement and YHWH's irrevocable commitment to David, the promise celebrated in Ps 89:34-38 [33-37]. Accordingly, YHWH's restoration of His flock and the appointment of David is not motivated primarily by pity for the bruised and battered sheep of Israel, but from His covenant with His people (cf. Dt 4:31). The goal of the restoration is the reestablishment of that covenant in its full force and scope. The Messiah, who will function as a servant of YHWH and symbolize the new unified national reality, must come from the house of David, a theme to be developed more fully in 37:15-28.

THE SIGNIFICANCE OF THE APPOINTMENT OF THE DAVIDIC MESSIAH (EZEKIEL 34:25-31)

A consideration of the Messiah in Ezk 34 may not end with a discussion of vv. 23-24, for, like vv. 1-22, vv. 25-31 provide context for the subject. Indeed, they link the covenant of peace that YHWH will make with "them" (v. 25), the antecedent being "My flock," that is the nation of Israel in v. 22. Some interpret the idiom *kārat bĕrît šālôm* in the statement, "I will make [lit. 'cut'] a covenant of peace with them" (and in 37:26) as signaling a brand-new covenant.[31] However, this view may be challenged on three grounds. First, Dt 29:1 [Hb 28:69] speaks of the renewal on the Plains of Moab of the covenant that YHWH made with Israel at Sinai as "cutting the covenant" (*kārat bĕrît*).[32] Second, in Ezk 16:60,62 the prophet uses the idiom, *hēqîm bĕrît*, "to establish a covenant," in reference to the same covenant that is in view in 34:25. Third, the clear echoes of Lv 26:4-13 in Ezk 34:25-30 confirm that the present covenant involves the realization of the ideals of the ancient Israelite covenant (Table 1).[33]

Ezekiel's description of the effects of YHWH's covenant of peace is intentionally repetitious, highlighting security as the central issue; the key word *lābeṭah* , "in safety, securely," occurs three times (vv. 25c,27c,28c). This expression is ambiguous and may denote both freedom from fear and casual smugness.[34] Ezekiel casts his vision of the flock's security with six specific actions by YHWH, citied in the following order:

A peace with the animals (vv. 25b-d)
  B the blessing of the vegetation (vv. 26-27c)
    C deliverance from oppression (vv. 27d-28a)
A' peace with the animals (vv. 28b-d)
  B' the blessing of the vegetation (vv. 29a-b)
    C' deliverance from oppression (v. 29c)

Three types of divine activity are involved in YHWH's restoration of Israel's security: eliminating predatory animals from the land (vv. 25b-d,28b-d), blessing the land with great fruitfulness (vv. 26-27c,29a-b); removing the oppression of foreign enemies (vv. 27d-28a,29c).[35]

These external demonstrations of messianic *shalom* are welcome enough, but Ezekiel's portrayal of the new day climaxes with his announcement of the new covenant (v. 30). Casting this promise in a modified form of the recognition formula, Ezekiel declares YHWH's true goal in His salvific activity: that the family of Israel might realize the presence of God among them, and the reestablishment of the covenant relationship between them and their God. The tragedy of 586 BC will

Table 1

A Synopsis of Leviticus 26:4-13 and Ezekiel 34:25-30

	Leviticus 26:4-13		Ezekiel 34:25-30
4	***Then I will give you rains in their season,***	25	***I will make a covenant of peace for them.***
	and the land will yield her produce,		***I will remove dangerous animals from the land.***
	and the trees of the field will yield their fruit.		***They will dwell securely in the desert;***
5	Your threshing will last until the vintage,		and sleep in the forest.
	and your vintage will last until sowing time.	26	I will make them a blessing
	You will eat your fruit to the full,		round about my hill.
	and you will live securely in the land.		***I will send down the rain in its season;***
6	***And I will grant peace in the land***		They will be showers of blessing.
	So you may lie down	27	***The trees of the field will yield their fruit;***
	with none to frighten you.		***And the land will yield her produce.***
	I will remove dangerous animals from the land;		***They will live securely on their own land.***
7	Nor will the sword pass through your land.		And they will know ***that I am YHWH,***
	But you will pursue your enemies,		***when I break the bars of their yoke,***
8	And they will fall before you to the sword.		and rescue them from the hand
	Five of you will chase a hundred,		of those ***who enslave them.***
	And a hundred of you will chase ten thousand,	28	They will no longer be booty for the nations;
9	And your enemies will fall before the sword.		Nor will the wild animals devour them.
	Thus I will turn toward you;		***They will dwell securely,***
	I will make you fruitful;		***with none to frighten them.***
	I will multiply you;	29	***I will establish for them a peaceful plantation.***
10	***I will confirm my covenant with you.***		No more will there be victims
	You will eat the old supply,		of famine in the land;
11	And clear out the old because of the new.		Nor will they suffer the derision of the nations.
	I will make my dwelling among you,	30	They will know
12	And my person will not reject you.		***that I am YHWH their God with them,***
	I will walk about in your midst;		***and that they, the house of Israel, are my***
	I will be your God;		***people.*** The declaration of the Lord YHWH.
13	***And you will be my people.***		
	I am Yahweh your God,		(author's translations)
	Who brought you out of the land of Egypt,		
	to end *your slavery.*		
	I broke the bars of your yoke,		
	And I made you walk erect.		

finally be reversed. The signatory formula seals Ezekiel's glorious promise with the divine imprimatur.

Ezekiel's idyllic picture of the messianic age as a time of universal peace, involving even the animal world, recalls Isa 11:6-9. But his association of covenant renewal with the taming of the wild animals and the rejuvenation of the vegetation bears even closer resemblance to Hos 2:18-23, which portrays YHWH not as a principal to the covenant but as a covenant mediator, establishing peace between feuding parties. Some such covenant also underlies Job 5:19-23, which describes divine deliverance from a series of disasters:

> He will rescue you from six calamities;
> no harm will touch you in seven.
> In famine He will redeem you from death,
> and in battle, from the power of the sword.
> You will be safe from slander
> and not fear destruction when it comes.
> You will laugh at destruction and hunger
> and not fear the animals of the earth.
> For you will have a covenant with the stones of the field,
> and the wild animals will be at peace with you.

Remarkably this list is framed by the two elements found in Ezekiel's picture of peace, suggesting famine and dangerous animals function as a kind of shorthand for the full range of divinely commissioned calamities.

Ezekiel's vision of the messianic age (vv. 25-30) has temporarily suspended the shepherd-flock imagery that has dominated the oracle to this point. He does not attempt to relate the wild animals to creatures that prey upon the flock, nor is the rejuvenation of vegetation connected with the renewal of pasture land. Even the evil shepherds have disappeared. Therefore, it is fitting that he wraps up the prophecy by returning to the central issue. Verse 31 reaffirms that the flock of which the prophet had spoken earlier represents the nation of Israel by reversing the order of the bipartite form of the covenant formula. In place of "You are My people," the prophet declared, "You are My flock." YHWH clarifies the issue by reiterating that Israel is the flock of His pasture,[36] and affirming that the flock of which He spoke was indeed a human (*'ādām*) flock. The obverse of YHWH's taking Israel as His flock is represented in YHWH's renewed commitment of Himself to be their God. Once again, the signatory formula guarantees the veracity of the divine word.

CONCLUSION

The theological implications of Ezk 34 are both profound and exhilarating. First, when YHWH extends His grace to Israel again, the disintegrated deity-nation-land triangle will be restored. Ezekiel's vision of the messianic age recognizes a measure of truth in his contemporaries' theological formulations: YHWH had indeed entered into an eternal marriage covenant with them; YHWH had an enduring interest in His land; YHWH's promise to David of eternal title to the throne of Jerusalem still stands. These covenant hopes will all be fulfilled in the messianic age. At that time, when YHWH's people live securely in their land, are ruled by a divinely appointed David, and enjoy the *shalom* of God's presence and grace, they will finally acknowledge Him as their Savior and covenant Lord.

Second, the true shepherd of God's people is the Lord Himself. Where human leaders capitalize on positions of power and privilege for personal gain, YHWH has the interests of His people at heart (cf. Ps 23). He gathers the strays, nurtures the sick, feeds the flock from the finest of pastures, offers them His personal presence, and protects them from enemies, whether inside or out. Looking back on this text from the perspective of the NT, the reaction of the Jewish leaders to Jesus' characterization of them as "thieves and robbers" (Jn 10:8) and His own assumption of the title "The Good Shepherd" becomes understandable. This was not only an attack on them, nor simply the statement of a lunatic (Jn 10:19-21); it was a blasphemous identification with deity, worthy of death (vv. 31-33).

However, there is another dimension to the NT's portrayal of Jesus relating to this text. He is not only the divine Shepherd of Ezk 34:11-22 and 25-31; He is also the Messianic son of David, that is "the Christ" (*ho Christos*) of vv. 23-24. Indeed, since "Son of God" functions as a messianic title for the Davidides (Davidic kings) (2Sm 7:14; Ps 2:7; 89:26-29), when the NT identifies Jesus as "Son of God" the reference is primarily to Jesus as the Davidic Messiah, rather than to His divinity. This conclusion is reinforced by the association of this title with "Messiah" / "Christ" (Mt 16:16; 26:63; Mk 1:1; Lk 4:41; Jn 11:27; Ac 8:37; 2Co 1:19; Gal 2:20; 2Jn 1:3), by its association with the title "King of Israel" (Jn 1:49), and by divine references to Jesus as "My beloved Son" (Mt 3:16; 17:5; Mk 1:11; 9:7; Lk 3:22; 2Pt 1:17). Luke 1:32 is especially significant in this regard: "He will be great and will be called the Son of the Most High, and the Lord God will give Him the throne of His father David." However, this is not to declare that Jesus' identity is limited to His descent from David (or Adam, for that matter; Lk 3:38). First John 5:20 explicitly declares the true divinity of the Messiah: "And we know that the Son of God has come and has given us understanding so that we may know the true One. We are in the true One—that is, in His Son Jesus Christ. He is the true God and eternal life."[37] Ezekiel 34 provides First Testament textual background for this extraordinary NT truth.

---

1. The second part also divides into two sections. The first involves oracles against foreign nations who have been problematic for Israel in the past but whom YHWH will "take care of" in Israel's interest (28:24-26) by punishing them for past crimes (what I call "the good bad news"; chaps. 25–32). After the transitional chap. 33, the second part ("the good good news"; chaps. 34–48) concerns primarily the restoration of Israel in all conceivable dimensions. For discussion of the structure of the two divisions of the restoration oracles, see Daniel I. Block, *The Book of Ezekiel Chapters 25–48*, New International Commentary on the Old Testament (Grand Rapids: Eerdmans, 1998), 3–6, 268–72, respectively.
2. For discussion of the relationship between Jer 23:1-16 and Ezk 34, see Block, *Ezekiel Chapters 25–48*, 274–77.
3. For ancient Near Eastern parallels to YHWH's identification of Himself as the [divine] shepherd of His people, see Block, *Ezekiel Chapters 25–48*, 284–85.
4. For defense of the view that the shepherds in 34:1-10 are the Davidic rulers, see ibid., 182; Iain M. Duguid, *Ezekiel and the Leaders of Israel*, Vetus Testamentum Supplements 56 (Leiden, Netherlands: Brill, 1994), 39–40. Margaret S. Odell (*Ezekiel*, Smyth & Helwys Bible Commentary [Macon, GA: Smyth & Helwys, 2005], 424–26), argues unconvincingly that the shepherds are foreign rulers who function as YHWH's appointed agents.
5. Ancient Near Easterners often referred to rulers as "shepherds of the people." In the prologue to his law code, Hammurabi of Babylon identified himself as follows:

   Hammurabi, the shepherd, called by Enlil, am I;
   the one who makes affluence and plenty abound;
   who provides in abundance all sorts of things for Nippur-Duranki;
   the devout patron of Ekur;
   the efficient king, who restored Eridu to its place (*Ancient Near Eastern Texts*, 281).

   For additional examples and references, see Block, *Ezekiel Chapters 25–48*, 280–81.
6. For discussion and bibliography, see Daniel I. Block, "Divine Abandonment: Ezekiel's Adaptation of an Ancient Near Eastern Motif," in *Perspectives on Ezekiel: Theology and Anthropology*, ed. M. S. Odell and J. T. Strong; Society of Biblical Literature Symposium Series 9 (Atlanta: Scholars, 2000), 15–42 (republished in idem, *By the River Chebar: Historical, Literary, and Theological Studies in the Book of Ezekiel* [Eugene, OR: Cascade, 2013], 73–99); idem, *The Gods of the Nations: Studies in Ancient Near Eastern National Theology*, ETS Monograph, rev. ed. with added appendix (Eugene, OR: 2013); Grand Rapids: Baker, 2000), 113–47; idem, *Ezekiel Chapters 25–48*, 290–91.
7. Although in David's response to the heady offer of eternal title to the throne of Israel his primary concern was the significance of this promise for the nation (2Sm 7:23-24), his remarkable prior declaration in v. 19 laid the groundwork for the universalization of the Davidic covenant and with it the messianic hope: "You have also spoken about your servant's house in the distant future. And this is a revelation for mankind, Lord GOD."
8. Cf. the designation of the Davidide Zerubbabel as his "signet" (*ḥôtām*) in Hag 2:23.
9. For the conjunction of these motifs, see also Jer 23:1-8; 30:8-11; 33:12-26.
10. On these two features as fundamental elements of Jewish messianism in the intertestamental period, see Samson H. Levey, *The Messiah: An Aramaic Interpretation. The Messianic Exegesis of the Targum* (Cincinnati: Hebrew Union College Press, 1974), XIX. Levey defines the messianic age as

    ... the predication of a future Golden Age in which the central figure is a king primarily of Davidic lineage appointed by God. . . . It was believed that during the time of the Messiah the Hebrew people will be vindicated, its wrongs righted, the wicked purged from its midst, and its rightful place in the world secured. The Messiah will pronounce doom upon the enemies of Israel, will mete out reward and punishment in truth and in justice, and will serve as an ideal king ruling the entire world. The Messiah may not always be the active agent in these future events, but his personality must always be present, at least as the symbol of the glorious age which will be ushered in.
11. A principle established already in the "Mosaic Charter for Kingship," Dt 17:14-20. *hēqîm* ("to raise up"), in the sense of "install in office," with YHWH as the subject, is applied in the First Testament to the appointment of prophets

(Dt 18:15,18; Jer 29:15; Am 2:11), judges (Jdg 2:16,18), priests (1Sm 2:35), kings (1Kg 14:14; Jer 30:9), watchmen (Jer 6:17), deliverers (Jdg 3:9,15), shepherds (Jer 23:4,5; Zch 11:16), and even adversaries (1Kg 11:14).

12. He will expand on this notion in 37:15-24, where the term *ehād*, "one," occurs no fewer than 11 times.

13. Jeremiah 23:5 speaks of raising up *for* David "a Righteous Branch," cf. 33:15); Am 9:11, of restoring "the fallen hut of David." Compare Isa 9:5-7 [5-6], which speaks of the child upon the throne of David, Isa 11:1, referring to "a shoot from the stump of Jesse"; cf. "the root of Jesse" in v. 10).

14. Excluding the failed Saulide experiment.

15. The *ex eventu* reference to Cyrus with the archaic title "King of Elam" in the "Dynastic Prophecy" provides the nearest analogue; cf. A. K. Grayson, *Babylonian Historical-Literary Texts* (Toronto: University of Toronto Press, 1975), 24–37. The "Prophetic Speech of Marduk" (II:19–34) refers to the promised king simply as "a king of Babylon." For the text see Block, Appendix: The Prophetic Speech of Marduk," in *Gods of the Nations*, 155–62; Tremper Longman III, *Fictional Akkadian Autobiography* (Winona Lake, IN: Eisenbrauns, 1991), 234. Other "Akkadian Prophecies" define the tenures of a series of kings, but refer to them generically as *šarru*; cf. A. K. Grayson and W. G. Lambert, "Akkadian Prophecies," *Journal of Cuneiform Studies* 18 (1964): 12–14.

16. Note the popular awareness of David's divine election reflected in 2Sm 5:2: "YHWH also said to you, 'You will shepherd (*tir'eh*) My people Israel, and be ruler (*nāgîd*) over Israel.'" Compare the psalmist's celebration of the same notion in Ps 78:70-72:

> He chose David, his servant
> and took him from the sheepfolds;
> He brought him from tending ewes
> to be shepherd over (*lir'ôt*) his people Jacob—
> over Israel His inheritance.
> He shepherded (*ra'â*) them with a pure heart;
> and guided them with his skillful hands.

17. The word *'ôlām*, "forever," occurs eight times in 2Sm 7:13,16,24-29. See especially v. 13 ("I will establish the throne of his kingdom forever") and v. 16 ("Your dynasty and your kingdom will endure before me forever; your kingdom will be established forever").

18. A fact reflected most clearly in Jer 33:17,20-21,25-26, but enthusiastically celebrated by the psalmist in Ps 89:28-29,33-36 [29-30,34-37].

19. *'abdî* is used of David 31 times in the Hebrew Bible. See 2Sm 3:18; 7:5,8,26; etc. (see F. Brown, S. R. Driver, and C. A. Briggs, *Hebrew and English Lexicon of the Old Testament* [Oxford: Oxford University Press, 1906], 714). The title is also applied to Hezekiah (2Chr 32:16), Zerubbabel (Hag 2:23), and "my servant the Branch" (Zch 3:8; cf. 6:12).

20. Accordingly, the patriarchs served as the bearers of the divine revelation, promise and blessing (Abraham, Gn 26:24 and Ps 105:6,42; Isaac, Gn 24:14 and 1Chr 16:13; Jacob, Ex 32:13 and Dt 9:27); Moses served as YHWH's agent of deliverance and the mediator of the divine covenant (so designated 40 times: Ex 14:31; Jos 1:2,3,13,15; Nm 12:7-8, etc.); the Levitical singers performed as official blessing proclaimers for YHWH (Ps 113:1; 134:1; 135:1), and the prophets functioned as YHWH's officially commissioned spokespersons (Ezk 38:17; 2Kg 17:13; Dan 9:6, etc.). For references see BDB, 714. Even the non-Israelite Job was a servant of YHWH, modeling the divine ideals of piety and (unwittingly) functioning as a vehicle through whom the pattern of divine-human relationships was vindicated before Satan (Job 1:8; 2:3; 42:7-8).

21. Compare the use of the term in 7:27; 12:10,12; 19:1; 21:17,30 [12,25]; 22:6; 26:16; 27:21; 30:13; 32:29; 37:25; 38:2,3; 39:1,18. Except for the reference to Jehoiachin as *melek* in 17:12, and David in 37:22-24, Ezekiel reserves this title for foreign kings of Egypt, Babylon, and Tyre.

22. Cf. "princes of Israel" in 19:1; etc.

23. *nāśî'* derives from *nāśā'*, "to lift up." Except for 7:27, when Ezekiel juxtaposes *nāśî'* with the people of the land, the term refers to the king (45:16,22; 46:2-3,8-9). For a helpful study of the word, see Duguid, *Ezekiel and the Leaders*, 10–18.

24. So Frank Lothar Hossfeld, *Untersuchungn zu Komposition und Theologie des Ezechielbuches*, FB 20 (Würzburg: Echter, 1977), 272.

25. So also Duguid, *Ezekiel and the Leaders*, 49.

26. Ezk 12:1-16; 17; 19.

27. Both Hos 3:5 and Jer 30:9-10 speak of "YHWH their God and David their king."

28. Variations of the formula, "I, YHWH, will be their God" occur elsewhere in Ezk 11:20; 14:11; 36:28; 37:23,27.

29. Cf. Ex 29:45-46; Lev 26:12-13; etc.

30. André Caquot, "le messianisme d'Ezékiel," *Semitica* 14 (1964): 18–19.

31. See Peter J. Gentry and Steven Wellum, *Kingdom through Covenant: A Biblical-Theological Understanding of the Covenants* (Wheaton, IL: Crossway, 2012), 475.

32. For further discussion, see Daniel I. Block, *Deuteronomy*, NIV Application Commentary (Grand Rapids: Zondervan, 2012), 646–47, 662–63.

33. To facilitate closer comparison, the translations given are the author's own. For further discussion, see Block, *Ezekiel Chapters 25–48*, 303–307.

34. Judges 18:7,27. The word occurs elsewhere in Ezekiel in 28:26; 38:8,11,14; 39:26.

35. For fuller discussion, see Block, *Ezekiel Chapters 25–48*, 305–306.

36. *mar'îtî*, "my pasture," occurs elsewhere only in Jer 23:1 and Ps 74:1; 79:13; 95:7; 100:3.

37. Cf. the comment of Robert W. Jensen (*Ezekiel*, Brazos Theological Commentary on the Bible [Grand Rapids: Brazos, 2009], 267), "In the traditional formulation: the hypostasis of God the Son is the hypostasis also of the human Davidic Messiah, Jesus." The recently discovered extrabiblical reference to Jesus Christ as God: "The God-loving Akeptous has donated the table to God Jesus Christ as a memorial." For discussion, see Vassilios Tzaferis, "Inscribed 'To God Jesus Christ': Early Christian Prayer Hall Found in Megiddo Prison," *Biblical Archaeology Review* 33/2 (March–April, 2007): 38–49; Edward Adams, "The Ancient Church at Megiddo: The Discovery and an Assessment of its Significance," *Expository Times* 120/2 (2008): 62–69.

Ezekiel 37:15-28

The Restoration of Israel under the One Shepherd

J. RANDALL PRICE

In this text of Ezekiel 37, God promises Israel that the unjust rule suffered by the divided nation would end, national repentance and regeneration would occur, divine rule in the land under King David would be restored, and the Temple with the Divine Presence would return. Only a restoration that could reunite the two kingdoms spiritually, end the possibility of further idolatry and covenant violation, and secure a common allegiance to the Davidic King and access to the Jerusalem Temple would fulfill the divine ideal.

The repetition of the word "forever" in this text informs the reader that once this condition exists it will remain uninterrupted. The word "forever" (Hb. *'olam*) denotes "an indefinite period of time," the duration often defined by the context.[1] However, David Friedman in his doctoral dissertation examined the use of more than 80 biblical uses of *'olam* and concluded that it expresses the time element of "as long as the present heaven and earth exists."[2] This understanding of the term also takes into account duration for a period of time but reveals that the time is "until this present world has run its course." On this basis, the land promise is extended to Israel for "all time," which in context would mean only until the end of the millennial kingdom, at which time the present earth will be destroyed and a new earth created (Isa 65:17; 66:22; 2Pt 3:10-13).

Even so, the Hebrew grammatical construction here favors an extension of the duration of the term to an infinite degree: v. 25b prefixes the separable preposition *'ad* to *'olam* while vv. 25c-26, 28 add the inseparable preposition *le*. The first of these constructions is the stronger and appears elsewhere with *'olam* in the phrase *min 'olam v'ad 'olam* ("from everlasting to everlasting" or "forever and ever"). This expression refers exclusively to God's eternal nature or rule, except in two cases where it describes Israel's possession of the land of Israel (Jer 7:7; 25:5).

The second construction seems to stress the future state, which given in the context of the millennial kingdom would mean the eternal state. Indeed, God has promised that Israel's "offspring and . . . name will endure" in the eternal state (Isa 66:22). However the outworking of God's government is to be understood in this future period, it is evident from Ezekiel's portrayal of it by the fivefold "forever" that it is meant to assure Israel that its new relationship with God will never be changed. A similar affirmation with these same elements is made concerning the Church in the New Jerusalem (Rev 22:3-5).

In verses 22, 24 (cf. 34:23) Ezekiel appears to define this rule as solitary: "*one* king . . . *one* shepherd." This raises the question of *who* will assume this rule: King Messiah or King David. Aiding the resolution to this question will be the answer to other questions, namely, *how* and *when* will the covenant be fulfilled. The answer has been given in opposing schools of interpretation. According to some, Christ alone fulfills the promise as the Good Shepherd and son of David by His present session at the right hand of the Father in heaven. This interpretation would see the Davidic covenant as spiritually fulfilled in the new covenant with the Church and David as a type of Christ. Support for this depends primarily on a reading back into the OT of NT passages, in this case, the "Good Shepherd" statements of Jesus (Jn 10).[3]

By contrast, the Futurist school of interpretation sees Messiah fulfilling the promise by His return and righteous reign on earth during the future messianic (or millennial) kingdom. They would see the Davidic covenant as continuing and literally fulfilled in a new covenant *with Israel* in the land during the millennial kingdom. How this fulfillment occurs with David as servant, king, and prince and whether it is fulfilled only by King Messiah or also with King David is a matter of debate; however, the adoption of a consistent literal hermeneutic aids in the final decision. First, let us look at an overview of the various interpretations that have been offered for this text.

THE VARIOUS INTERPRETATIONS

The interpretation of the critical school (both Jewish and non-Jewish) is that the exilic period mention of a royal shepherd called "my servant David," first mentioned in Ezk 34:22-24 as a "prince" and as "king over them" (Israel) in Ezk 37:24-25, is a literary device to connect past promise with future fulfillment in the return from the exile in 538 BC. For them it indicates a human ruler, a David *redivivus* (the image of the historical David serving as a type of Israel's ideal ruler), who will reestablish monarchical rule over a united Israel. This school adopts a historical interpretation in the Prophets and so views the use of "David" here as an anointed agent of the Lord's rule that finds fulfillment with a ruler (variously identified) during the postexilic period, in which some of the Jewish people from Judah and Israel were reunited in a return to the land.[4]

This view has problems with a historical fulfillment on any scale, since the return from the exile to the land of Israel was significantly incomplete (Ezr 2:64-68; Neh 6:6-7), occurred under foreign domination (2Chr 36:22–Ezr 1:4), had a reduced (materially and spiritually) Temple (Ezr 3:12-13), and the spiritual life of the Jewish community was insufficient (Ezr 9:1-2; Neh 13:10-11,15-17,23-24; Mal 3:7-9). All of these factors indicate a lack of a historical restoration as envisioned by the prophets. While these scholars contend that prophetic language was hyperbolic and not intended for literal fulfillment, the historical and territorial elements in these prophecies (as tied to the original covenants) argue otherwise.

The interpretation of Orthodox (traditional) Judaism takes the figure of David literally, but as a Davidic descendant, King Messiah. This view was espoused by Rashi and other interpreters (Radak, Metzudos) with Rambam viewing the time described in the text as "the messianic times" since it contained a unified Israel, Edenic splendor, and ritual purity with the return of the Temple. Abarbanel reported a similar view given in the Kabbalah, but there the soul of David would be reincarnated as the King Messiah.[5] On the basis that Yeshua was referred to as the "son of David" from the outset of the NT (Mt 1:1) and promised David's throne (Lk 1:32), Messianic (Jewish-Christian) interpretation has usually followed the traditional Jewish view.

Evangelical Christian interpretation has primarily adopted a figurative interpretation of David to mean David's greater son, the Messiah (the old David versus the new David). As John MacArthur states in his note on Ezk 37:24-25: "This is to be understood as Jesus Christ the messiah, descendant of David."[6] Reform interpretation would further see "King David's" reign as the universal reign of Christ over the Church (i.e., kingdom), interpreting the "two sticks" in Ezk 37:15-21 as a prophecy of the "one new man" (Eph 2:15), the union of Jews and Gentiles in the Church (Jn 10:16).[7] By contrast, some dispensationalists have interpreted the figure of David literally *in distinction to* the Messiah, seeing the "servant David" as an under-shepherd appointed by God to serve as a messianic vice-regent (co-regent) over national Israel. Even so, they consider their view a messianic interpretation since the "one king" is Messiah with David acting in concert with Him and for Him on behalf of Israel. Before looking at the arguments for the messianic interpretations, it is necessary to consider the context and how it affects the understanding of these figures.

THE PROPHECY'S RESTORATION CONTEXT

The first step in deciding an interpretation that honors the original authorial intent is to understand the context of the prophecy. The broader context is the restoration section of Ezekiel (chaps. 33–48), which in contrast to the first division (chaps. 4–32) that contains near-fulfillment prophecies (necessary to confirm Ezekiel's prophetic status), contains far-fulfillment prophecies that deal with the full realization of Israel's unconditional covenants in the land of Israel. These are exclusively eschatological in nature, and therefore their content regarding the future Davidic ruler must be understood in this final restoration context. The focus of the immediate context is the Davidic covenant (2Sm 7), where David is called by the Lord "my servant" (vv. 5,8) and he refers to himself by this title no fewer than 10 times (vv. 19,20,21,25,26,27,28,29). In addition, this covenant with David is described as "forever" (eternal) eight times (vv. 13,16,24,25,26), a fact David considered foundational (1Chr 28:4,7,8,9) as did later biblical writers (Ps 89:3-4,34-37). The restoration promise comes to a climax in Ezk 37, which addresses the nation's doubts concerning reviving the corporate people of Israel after the devastation and exile they have suffered. Verses 1-14 depict the community as desiccated corpses that the Lord will resurrect to continue the national life. The remaining verses (15-28) promise a reconstitution and reunification of the Israelite tribes (vv. 15-23), as well as a leadership role for a future Davidic ruler (vv. 24-28).

The nearer context of Ezk 37:24-28 is the preceding section of 15-22 that focuses on the restoration through the imagery of "two sticks" (Judah and Ephraim/Joseph) that will become in the future, unlike the past, an indivisible unified nation. The recipients and nature of this "union" have been variously interpreted, with one modern version mistakenly identifying Judah with messianic Judaism and Ephraim with the Gentile Christianity coming together in the Church. However, the names to be written on these sticks (vv. 16-19) must be read in context.

Verse 21 clearly identifies these two sticks with "the Israelites" that had been dispersed among "the nations" and will be regathered "into their own land." Verse 22 again mentions the historic division of the southern and northern Jewish tribes into "two kingdoms," while v. 25 speaks of these *same* tribes and their land in continuity with "Jacob" (Israel) and "[their] fathers." These references could apply only to the historic Jewish people descended from the patriarchs to whom the land of Israel was given—that is, those of the southern kingdom having David as its dynastic ruler ("the house of David)" and its name (1Kg 12:20-24), and the northern kingdom, called by its most prominent tribe from the house of Joseph, Ephraim (cf. Hos 5:3,5,11-14). Thus, the only "messianic" fulfillment for the two sticks will be in the millennium, not the Church Age.

In this nearer and immediate context, the restoration is conveyed by terms of a permanent condition—"no longer" (vv. 22,23) and "forever" (vv. 25,26,28), the covenant formula following restoration: "They will be My people and I will be their God" (vv. 23,27), as well as the nature of the covenant ("covenant of peace," "everlasting covenant," v. 26), the spiritually/ritually purified condition of the nation (v. 23) and the return and permanent dwelling of the Shekinah in the final Temple (vv. 27-28; cf. 43:1-7). In chapter 37, the basis for restoration is the fulfillment of the promises to "My servant David" (v. 24) and to "My servant Jacob" (v. 25). Respectively, these are the Davidic covenant (2Sm 7), with its focus on an eternal rule and the land covenant with its promise of unlimited possession given specifically to Jacob in Gn 28:13-14. In chap. 37, restoration is presented as both physical return to the land (vv. 1-13, esp. v. 12), and spiritual (v. 14), a return to the Lord (cf. Ezk 36:22-28). The restoration theme continues in vv. 15-28 with a restoration of national unity (vv. 15-20), ethnicity (v. 21a), territorial possession (v. 21b), political theocracy (vv. 22-25), and covenant relationship (vv. 26-28). The specific promise of a Davidic descendant's forever rule is confirmed in Ps 89:3-4,34-37. As Walvoord notes, "In this and other Old Testament references there is no allusion anywhere to the idea that these promises are to be understood in a spiritualized sense as referring to the church or to a reign of God in heaven. Rather, it is linked to the earth and to the seed of Israel, and to the land."[8] Therefore, the proper interpretation of Ezk 37:15-28, and the identification of its central figures, will be in harmony with this eschatological land-based context.

THE PROPHECY'S MESSIANIC CONTEXT

Given this eschatological restoration context, it is further necessary to see Ezk 37:15-28 in its messianic context, which was introduced in chap. 34. The land covenant required Israel to seek and return to the Lord in national repentance toward Messiah (Ps 118:22-26; Mt 23:39) before restoration to the land could occur (Dt 4:29-31; 30:2-6). Ezekiel reveals that the Lord Himself will secure the necessary spiritual obedience of His sheep to fulfill this condition (34:11; 36:24-28; 37:5-6, 11-14). This act of the Shepherd delivering His sheep (from the nations) and bringing them into their own land demonstrates the work of a Savior, a characteristic of Messiah as the True Shepherd who came for the lost sheep of the house of Israel (Mt 15:24) to seek and return them to the fold (Lk 15:4-6).

Moreover, the national regathering predicted in Ezk 37:25 is unconditional in the context. It is therefore based on the Abrahamic covenant that promised Israel permanent possession of the land (Gn 13:15; 17:8; cf. 2Chr 20:7) and a "seed" from the Davidic dynasty (Gn 22:17; Ps 89:4) in order to be a spiritual blessing to the nations (Gn 12:3; Isa 2:3-4; 9:1-2; 11:12; 42:6-7; Am 9:11-12; Ac 15:16-18; Mt 12:21; Rm 15:12). The fulfillment of these promises is ultimately in the Messiah (Gal 3:19-22; Ac 1:6-7). This unilateral divine action is in keeping with the declaration in Ezk 36:21-24 that the Lord would act for the sake of His "holy name" (reputation) to vindicate (Hb. *qidashti*, Piel perfect) His profaned holiness (as the result of exile) as Israel's national Savior in the sight of the nations (Ac 13:23).

Left to itself, Israel could never fulfill the prophecies of return and restoration. The event that secures Israel's national repentance and establishes it in its promised land is Messiah's advent and the establishment of the millennial kingdom. The setting, according to Ezk 37:26-28, is when Israel comes under the new covenant, called here "covenant of peace" (v. 26) and has the Lord dwelling in their midst in a rebuilt Temple (vv. 27-28). These aspects of the new covenant with national Israel in the land are clearly set forth in Jeremiah as a new (spiritual) nature (31:31-34), a new (messianic) rule (Righteous Branch/Davidic King) and renewed priestly (Levitical) service (33:14-22).

THE PROPHECY'S DESCRIPTION OF MESSIANIC RULE

The subject of restoration to the land as an undivided nation under a single Davidic ruler is first introduced in chap. 34 in the prophecy of Israel's shepherds. The placement of this theme at the commencement of the restoration prophecies serves to reprove Israel's concept of a human king (shepherd) who had been false to Israel's needs while feeding his own, just as God had previously warned through the prophet Samuel (1Sm 8:11-18). The promise here in 34:1-16 is that the Lord Himself will replace the human king as the nation's True Shepherd ("My flock," i.e., the remnant), by regathering them under the rule of King Messiah (vv. 17-31). This act will correct the abuses of human leadership that previously led Israel into exile and provide a divine leadership capable of sustaining the nation in restoration through the millennial kingdom. Such restoration can only come once theocratic rule is restored. This rule will accompany the advent of the Messianic King. Chapter 34, in concert with chap. 37, establishes that the whole of the restoration prophecy in this last division of the book is intended for the eschatological period and forms the foundation upon which the rest of the prophecy (including chap. 37) is built.

In the ancient Near East, the term "shepherd" (Hb. *ro'eh*) was employed for rulers of nations appointed by a deity; these rulers were primarily kings.[9] The Bible employs the term as part of a shepherd motif, in which the king is depicted as a shepherd (e.g., Gn 48:15; 49:24; Ps 23:1) and the nation as a flock of sheep (e.g., 2Sm 24:17; Isa 53:6).

In Israelite preexilic history, "shepherd" is used of the man appointed to lead Israel (Nm 27:17), of David as a "ruler over Israel" (2Sm 5:2; 7:8) and as "king" of Israel (Ps 78:70-72), and of evil kings whose unjust rule made the nation like sheep without a shepherd (1Kg 22:17; 2Chr 18:16). Closer to Ezekiel's time (exilic period), the term was used of the Persian ruler Cyrus (Isa 44:28). In the exilic period, Jeremiah condemned "false shepherds" (Jer 23:1), distinguishing them from "false prophets and priests" (Jer 23:9-40; cf. 2:8), indicating that they must have been political leaders or kings.

While the term "shepherd" indicates the kind of rule as national/political, Ezekiel envisions replacing corrupt rule with "caring" rule (Ezk 34:12; 37:24; cf. Jer 3:15; 23:4), indicating that human rule (political king) will be replaced by divine rule (theocratic king). Even David, who had been the prototype of the ideal shepherd, violated the command for social justice in the Mosaic law (Lv 25:25,35,47; Dt 15:7; 24:14-15), as pointed out by the prophet Nathan in his indictment of the king (2Sm 12:1-9). By contrast, the righteous ruler (Messiah) will care for the weakest and neediest members of the community (Ezk 34:16; Mk 6:34).

The eschatological context here suggests, especially in light of the new covenant revelation, that the ultimate "false shepherd" (political leader) of the people will be the Antichrist (Rev 13:5-8,18) and the "True Shepherd" (theocratic ruler) will be Christ (Mt 2:6; Jn 10:11,14; Heb 13:20). The final fulfillment of this will be Christ's rescue of national Israel from the armies of the Antichrist in the campaigns of Armageddon, whose mission is to devour God's people (Zch 14:2-5; Rev 19:11-16). In both these texts the divine deliverance is demonstrated by a declaration of the Lord's sovereign rule replacing that of the wicked rulers (Zch 14:9; Rev 19:15-16).

Israel's promised political renewal was envisioned as the fulfillment of the Davidic covenant, in which David would have an eternal dynasty and eternal rule (2Sm 7:13,16). This would require an equally eternal descendant of David to fulfill it—the Messiah. However, the Ezekiel text does not say "son [descendant] of David," but refers to the historical person of David, which taken literally must be a person distinct from Messiah. Let us consider the arguments for these major messianic interpretations.

THE DAVIDIC MESSIAH

It has been previously noted that the prominent medieval rabbis identified the Davidic shepherd with King Messiah. This may have been the view of late Second Temple Judaism, as seen in the commentary preserved from the Qumran Community.

Patriarchical Blessings (*4QPBless* 3) states: "until the coming of the Righteous Messiah, the sprout of David" (cf. *4QFlor* 1-2. 2:11; *4QpIsa*^{a} 8-10:17). In the *War Scroll*, "your servant David" is invoked, as well as the "Star from Jacob," the "Scepter from Israel," and "your anointed ones" (*1QM* 11:1-7). These all seem to be established "messianic" terms in the Qumran literature, but this text based on Nm 24 is also cited in other Qumran Scrolls (cf. *CD* 7:19; *1QM* 11:6-7) and in the *Testament of Judah* 24:1-6 (although no fragment with this text has yet been found at Qumran). The passage concerns a militant messiah who conquers the borderland of Moab and destroys the Shethites. According to other traditions, this figure is the royal or Davidic Messiah. Rabbi Akiba saw it referring to the "King Messiah" (cf. TJ *Ta'anit* 68d), Philo to a great "warrior" (cf. *De Praemiis et Poenis*, 95), and the Testament of Judah to a "savior-judge."[10] Likewise in the Genesis *Florileguim* (4Q252), a thematic pesher (commentary) on the blessing of Judah in Gn 49:10, reads: "Whenever Israel rules there shall [not] fail to be a descendant of David upon the throne. For the [ruler's] 'Staff' is the Covenant of the Kingdom (or kingship), [and the leaders/clans] of Israel, they are 'the feet' (referred to in Gn 49:10), until the Messiah of Righteousness, the Branch of David comes. For to him and his seed was given the Covenant of the Kingdom (or kingship) of (or over) His people for everlasting generations . . ." (4Q252 5.1-4). Here, the terminology is borrowed from Jer 23:5-6; 33:15 to equate the messianic figure in Gn 49 ("Shiloh") as the Davidic King Messiah. This view also finds support from the Mishnah, *Sanhedrin* 98b, *Targum Onkelos* on Gn 49:10, and *Midrash Rabbah* (*Bereshit* 99) where "Shiloh" is understood as a proper noun referring to the name of the Messiah. These messianic titles are connected with Davidic descent and the "Staff" or object of rule. The eschatological picture here is of a coming Messiah, of the tribe of Judah, of the lineage of David, who will rule over Israel for "everlasting generations."[11]

Other intertestamental Jewish literature, such as the *Animal Apocalypse* (*1 En* 83-90), a text possibly based on Ezk 34:23-24, identified Judas Maccabeus as the fulfillment of the king like David who would serve as God's shepherd over Israel. His depiction of Judas as a ram indicates that he saw the Maccabees as kingly, since the only previous figures so identified with rams were Saul, David, and Solomon (*1 En* 89:42-49). The author may have understood "David" simply as a literal ruler destined to restore Israel to the kind of independent and united kingdom that existed in the time of the Davidic monarchy. However, according to Gary T. Manning Jr., "the author may have seen Judas as more than just 'kingly.' The description of Judas as the ram with a strong horn that could not be overcome by any of the birds of prey invites a 'messianic' interpretation. That God's deliverance comes to this horned ram, and final judgment comes after his conquest of the Gentiles, gives further evidence that the author of the *Animal Apocalypse* saw Judas as the anointed king."[12] This sampling[13] provides a glimpse of the messianic interpretation of some of the sects during the late Second Temple period, affirming an understanding of the promise to David as being fulfilled by the Davidic Messiah.

Biblical support for the idea that only one King, King Messiah, would reign as the Davidic King, may be found in Jer 23:5-6: "The days are coming"—this is the Lord's declaration—"when I will raise up a Righteous Branch of David. He will reign wisely as king and administer justice and righteousness in the land. In His days Judah will be saved, and Israel will dwell securely. This is what He will be named: Yahweh Our Righteousness."

The time of fulfillment in this passage (with Judah and Israel both restored under a divine ruler identified with David) is the same as that in Ezk 37. Based on the use of Jeremiah's divine epitaph, who could the single shepherd and king be but the Messiah?

In his dissertation "Ezekiel's Use of the Term *nasi'* with Reference to the Davidic Figure in His Restoration Oracles" Hwi Cho concluded: "The prophet Ezekiel uses this pre-monarchic term (*nasi'*) for the coming messianic figure from the Davidic dynasty (Ezk 34 and 37)."[14] David's greatest descendant was to be the Messiah, and he would be born in David's tribe of Judah and his city of Bethlehem (Mic 5:2-3). The ideal Shepherd-King in Ezk 34 is the background for the statement in Ezk 37:24 that all of Israel will have "My servant David" as "one shepherd." In Ezk 34 the Shepherd is God (v. 16), but in vv. 23-24 he is "my servant David." This idea is repeated in Ezk 37:23-24, where it is stated "I will be their God. My servant David will be king over them." The text then goes on to say "and there will be one shepherd."

According to Kutsko, "The connection between the divine kingship and the earthly is vivid as in Ezekiel 34. Kingship and shepherd are juxtaposed . . . the 'Prophetic Speech of Marduk' and Esarhaddon's account of the reconstruction of Babylon reveal the divine election of the earthly king and the shepherd motif as in Ezekiel 34. Thus, the promise of a Davidic shepherd (Ezk 34:23-24) would be a surprise to us . . . but not to the exiles who were familiar with such kingship ideology in Babylon. In addition, both the metaphors of Yahweh as shepherd (Ps 23:1; Mic 2:12, 4:6-8) and David as shepherd (Ps 78:70-72) may apply in Ezekiel 34. In the mind of the exiles, Yahweh as divine shepherd and a Davidic figure as his shepherd over Israel may not be separable."[15] Thus, the pairing of "God" with "My servant David" in rule over Israel in these texts implies the theological pairing of "God and Christ" in the rule over the people of God in the New Jerusalem (Rev 21:22-23; 22:1,3). Messiah is clearly stated to be of "the house and family line of David" (Mt 1:1-17; cf. Lk 2:4) and is related to David in the prophetic promises of establishing "the everlasting covenant" (Isa 55:3) and ruling as the Davidic King in the millennial kingdom (Isa 9:7; Jer 23:5; Lk 1:31-33,69; cf. Mt 1:1; 19:28).

Moreover, Messiah is promised as the One who will be given the "throne of

His father David" (Lk 1:32). Also, the rule is singular, "one shepherd/one king" (Ezk 34:23; 37:24). According to Zch 14:9, in the millennial kingdom, "Yahweh will become king over all the earth; Yahweh alone, and His name alone." This exclusivity of rule and recognition implies that no other one will be "king" except God Himself. Such divine rule would be appropriate for King Messiah, but not for a resurrected David, since he is still only a man. John 10:16, clearly with the new covenant in view in its inclusion of Gentiles with national Israel as "one flock," states that Messiah will be this singular ruler ("one shepherd").

John 10:30 (cf. Rm 9:5) affirms the equality of God and Messiah so they may be understood as Israel's divine and royal Ruler. God was understood as the King of Israel during Messiah's days in the flesh (Mt 5:35 = Ps 48:1-2), but Jesus also confessed that He was Israel's King (Mt 27:11/Mk 15:2/Lk 23:2/Jn 18:37), a messianic title continued in the NT (1Tm 6:15; Rev 15:3; 17:14; 19:16).

That Messiah was also understood by the Jewish people in Jesus' time as Israel's king is recorded in the Gospels (Mt 2:1; 21:5; 27:37,42; Lk 19:38; Jn 1:49; 12:13; 19:14,19). The final observation is from Jer 23:5-6 (see my article in this *Handbook* on Isa 4), in which God declares He will "raise up a Righteous Branch of David" who will "reign . . . as king" with wisdom, justice, and righteousness (v. 5) during the time of reunited Israel's restoration (v. 6). Here the king is identified as being raised up "for David" (NASB), implying that he will be both a descendant of David and the one who will fulfill the promises made to David in the Davidic covenant. Since this entails a separate entity, also identified by name at the end of v. 6 as "the Lord . . . Our Righteousness," this figure must be King Messiah.

A MESSIANIC VICE-REGENT

Many futurists, especially dispensational premillennialists, interpret Ezk 37:25 as the historical David literally resurrected at the time of resurrection of the OT saints (Dan 12:2) at the beginning of the millennial kingdom (Rev 20:4-5). As John Walvoord states, "There is no good reason for not taking this exactly as it is written, namely, that David will be raised from the dead and will with Christ reign over the people of Israel in the millennium."[16]

Therefore, the One raised up "for David" in Jer 23:5-6 (NASB) is a distinct entity from David himself. Most who adopt this view see the resurrected David assuming a role in the millennial government as vice-regent under King Messiah over a united Israel. Arnold Fruchtenbaum explains this arrangement in the organizational hierarchy of the millennial kingdom: "In the governmental system of the Messianic or Millennial Kingdom, Jesus will rule as King over the whole world.

Under Him, there will be two branches of government: the Gentile branch and the Jewish branch. The Gentile branch of government will be comprised of the Church saints and Tribulation saints, who are destined to co-reign with the Messiah over the Gentile nations. The resurrected David is destined to co-reign with Jesus over the Jewish branch."[17]

In v. 25, David is referred to by the political title "prince" or "leader" (Hb. *nasi'*). This is also the standard term Ezekiel uses in chaps. 44–48 for the vice-regent subordinate to God. As Lister has observed, "The Davidic leader that will be installed (*melek* in Ezk 37:22 and 24; *nasi'* in v. 25) is also a recipient of God's restoration."[18] This, then, is not Messiah, but a human representative of the Messiah in the millennial kingdom, since the *nasi'* later described in Ezekiel with reference to his ruling and Temple duties offers a sin offering for himself and the people (45:22), bears sons (46:16-17), is warned against oppression (46:18), and is allotted a territorial inheritance with Israel (48:22). In addition, he has a ritual function in the Millennial Temple "to make atonement on behalf of the house of Israel" (45:17; 46:1-15). Therefore, it could be argued that same identification belongs to the *nasi'* in Ezk 37:25 since the very next verses (vv. 26-28) are in the context of "the sanctuary" (Hb. *miqdash*) and lead (after the excursive section of chaps. 38–39) to the discussion of the Millennial Temple (Ezk 40–48). In Ezk 34:24, "prince" is also used in distinction to the divine ruler: "I, the LORD, will be their God and My servant David will be prince among them." Ezekiel 34:23 states that David himself would *shepherd* them, which is explained in the next verse as "My servant David will be *a prince*" (Hb. *nasi'*).

This distinction is seen in Hos 3:5: "Afterwards the people of Israel will return and seek the LORD their God and David their king. They will come with awe to the LORD and to his goodness in the last days," and Jer 30:9: "They will serve the LORD their God, and I will raise up David their king for them." Israel's obedient service is to the Lord (King Messiah) and King David; however, since David is Messiah's representative (prince), Messiah alone is the High King over all the earth (Zch 14:10). The distinction is also seen in the Davidic covenant in 1Chr 17, where God declared that after Israel was irreversibly settled in their land (v. 9) He would permanently settle a Davidic descendant in "My house" (the Temple) and in "My kingdom," and this rule would be "forever" (v. 14). This describes the messianic rule in the millennium (cf. Isa 2:2-4). This is the same language and distinction given in the birth announcement of Jesus (Lk 1:32-33).

Even though there is an emphasis on singleness of leadership in this section and elsewhere (Jer 23:5-6; Zch 14:9), David could still be considered a vice-regent ruling over Israel for the Messiah after He has established the messianic kingdom and secured Israel within it. David's rule is Messiah's rule because he communicates and enforces Messiah's will with Israel. "David My servant" is called "prince" (Hb. *nasi'*) in Ezk 37:25, a term that usually designates a "head of state" or a regent under God. Allen notes concerning this term: "Ezekiel revived this archaic title for an elected tribal chieftain or intertribal president and used it often, although not to the exclusion of *melek*, to differentiate minor kings in the ancient Near East from imperial kings (cf. 1Kg 11:34,37)."[19] This term was used frequently by Ezekiel of princes from the Davidic line that were denounced and put under divine judgment (7:27; 12:10,12; 19:1; 21:25; 22:6,25). Terry Clark notes the significance of the use of this lesser office for the interpretation of the Davidic figure: "referred to as *melek* 'king,' in v. 24 and *nagid* 'prince,' in v. 25. The use of a lower title in v. 25 clarifies that this king, unlike many former ones, will play his proper role as the representative servant of the divine king Yahweh. In a very subtle way, this reminds the reader that Yahweh alone will be acknowledged as the true sovereign of Israel in the ideal future, even as the monarchy is upheld as a legitimate human institution."[20]

The close association of David with the Messiah as *nasi'* and *nagid* may relate specifically to David ruling for Messiah over Israel. In this case, as other texts reveal, Messiah as "king over all the earth" (Zch 14:9) would exercise the supreme position of universal rule (Ps 2:6-9; Rev 12:5; 19:15), and would receive global worship at the Millennial Temple in Jerusalem from both Israel and the nations (Isa 2:2-3; Zch 14:16), while David would represent Him to Israel alone. It was, in fact, David who was king over a united Israel and such a fact fits the context in Ezk 37:16-22 of a united Israel in a millennial restoration setting (v. 23).

When the tribes divided after David's death, they continued to voice their identification with his successors under the name "David" (1Kg 12:16, see also the mention of "house of David" on the ninth century BC Tel Dan stele). Since Ezk 37:19-22 predicts the re-uniting of the two kingdoms as one nation under one king (v. 22), it would be appropriate for David to assume this role as part of the promise of the Davidic covenant that his "house and kingdom would endure before Me forever" (2Sm 7:16; Ps 89:35-36). In fact, David is mentioned by name in other eschatological texts that focus on national Israel's restoration (Jer 30:9; Hos 3:5). Note that Jer 23:4 states: "And I will raise up *shepherds* (plural) over them who will shepherd them." What Jeremiah may have in view are royal officials (of which David is the head) who serve in the political echelon of the millennial kingdom.

As Lord, the King Messiah may confer these offices on a political representative. In this context of the political rule of the shepherd, it fits King David, chosen by God because he was a man after God's own heart (1Sm 13:14) who had the responsibility as king to uphold God's commandments (cf. 1Sm 13:14c; 15:28). Furthermore, as David's psalms reveal, he was instrumental in Israel's worship of the Lord. At David's coronation, it was stated that the Lord said to him: "You will shepherd My people Israel and be ruler (or "prince"; Hb. *nagid*) over Israel" (2Sm 5:2). This same term is used in Dan 9:25 for "Messiah the Prince" (Hb. *mashiach nagid*) as the expected ruler who will deliver Israel (Isa 59:20; cf. Rm 11:26-27), in contrast to the coming ruler (*nagid haba'*) who will destroy Israel (Dan 9:26-27; cf. Mt 24:15-22; 2Th 2:3b-4; Rev 13:7).

Furthermore, David will be a "servant" (of Messiah and the nation). Some have noted that the term "My servant," while used of Messiah in His humiliation, is never used of Him after His exaltation. This, again, would require "My servant David" to be distinct from the Messiah, who is Lord. We have seen that David, though a servant, is also a king, prince, and shepherd—all royal offices with the function of a shepherd. Fruchtenbaum explains this relationship: "From the viewpoint of the Messiah, David is His *servant*; but from the viewpoint of Israel, David will be their *king*. . . . From the viewpoint of Israel, he will be their king; but from the viewpoint of the Messiah, he will be a *prince*, because He will be under authority of King Messiah."[21]

As a true shepherd and ideal king, David will lead and feed Israel so it will observe the divine ordinances and statutes in the kingdom. As a prince, he will serve Messiah as he governs Israel for Messiah and by His laws. Because David is ruling under and for King Messiah (exclusively for Israel) and in concert with all of His laws, it is proper to recognize a solitary Sovereign (v. 23; Zch 14:9). For Israel, this fits their new united status as a nation in contrast to the two (rival) kings that existed in the days of national division. For the Gentile nations, the Lord Jesus the Messiah will be understood as the only king (Phl 2:10-11). Therefore, those who view David as a ruler distinct from King Messiah still retain a messianic interpretation of this text.

THE PROPHECY'S MESSIANIC COVENANT

In v. 26 Ezekiel speaks of the "covenant of peace" (*b^{e}rit shalôm*) that will be established by Messiah and enforced by King David over Israel. This term is appropriate to describe the restored conditions of the millennial age, because the Hebrew word *shalom* ("peace") denotes a comprehensive peace ("security, welfare, health, prosperity, harmony"). It is also called here an "everlasting covenant" (Ezk 16:60-63; cf. Isa 55:3; 61:8; Jer 32:40).

As in Ezk 34:25-30 where the list of millennial blessings under the new covenant is based on the terms of the Mosaic covenant (Lv 26:4-13), here the promise of peace for the land and the perpetuity of provision is drawn from Lv 26:4,6. The term "everlasting covenant" (v. 26b) describes the nature of God's enduring promise and the inviolability of His commitment to Israel demonstrated by the historic covenants of the past that have now been fulfilled. The term "everlasting covenant" was used of the Noahic covenant (Gn 9:12-16), the Abrahamic covenant (Gn 17:7,13,19; 1Chr 16:17; Ps 105:10), and the Davidic covenant (2Sm 23:5; cf. Ps 89:34-37; Jer 33:21,26), and the Sabbath and priestly service (Ex 31:16; Lv 24:8; Nm 18:19; cf. Jer 33:17-26). In keeping with the focus on David, Isa 55:3 speaks of the "everlasting covenant" made with Israel on the basis of God's "promises assured to David" (Hb. *hasdei David hane'emanim*), that is, the unconditional Davidic covenant (Ps 89:24,28,49).

The "covenant of peace" is a synonym for the new covenant and describes its function of making and maintaining universal peace for Israel and also for the nations (Zch 9:10), as the Noahic covenant had demonstrated God's universal commitment to never again destroy the earth by flooding (Isa 54:9). The advent of the Messianic King was predicted to bring an unending reign of peace, for He is the "Prince of Peace" (Isa 9:6-7; cf. Mic 5:5; Nah 1:15; Lk 1:79), and peace characterizes His government (Jer 33:9; Isa 52:7; 55:12; 60:17; 66:12; cf. Rm 14:17). Elsewhere the covenant of peace is described in terms of the cessation of war and of military disarmament (Isa 2:4), of exceptional agricultural prosperity of the land (Zch 8:12), and of the building of the Messianic Temple (Hag 2:9; Zch 6:13).

By contrast, the first messianic advent was not to be a time of peace (Mt 10:34; Lk 12:51), and especially not for Jerusalem (Lk 19:42), which will be the center of peace in the millennial kingdom (Isa 2:2-4; Jer 3:17). The promise of the Divine Presence among His people (vv. 27-28) is often associated with the covenant formula (Ex 29:45-46), and its use here expresses final fulfillment in which Yahweh will never again abandon His people (cf. Jesus' parting promise to His disciples, Mt 28:20).

Exodus 25:8 had declared that the original purpose of the sanctuary was to make possible the presence of the holy God in the midst of unholy Israel. Through the ceremonial service, Israel was kept in a state of ritual purification sufficient to enable it to serve the Lord as a "holy nation" and a "kingdom of priests" (Ex 19:6). The return of the Lord to the Tabernacle at the foot of Mount Sinai reversed the long absence of the Creator from His creation that had resulted from the intrusion of human sin in the garden of Eden (Gn 3:8-19). As a result, God had exiled man from His presence and prevented his return to the garden by stationing cherubim at the entrance of Eden (Gn 3:22-24). Once constructed, the earthly sanctuary with its ark of the covenant topped by cherubim allowed God's presence to return to Israel and to make possible its establishment as a nation governed by a theocracy.

Since the desecration of the First Temple and the departure of God's presence, Israel has experienced exile either in part or in whole. The capstone of the millennial kingdom and of its new covenant is the promise of the erection of the

Restoration Temple in which God's presence returns to never depart. Verses 26-28 provide the template upon which the grand design of the Millennial Temple are detailed in chaps. 40–48. Here God takes the initiative in building the Temple: "*I will set* My sanctuary among them" (v. 26d), which is one of the expected tasks of King Messiah (Zch 6:12-15). Verse 27 explains that the specific place of God's dwelling will be *over* His people (the Hebrew preposition *'al* is "over," "upon," rather than "with" as in some translations). In the past, the Shekinah Glory appeared over Israel in the wilderness as a cloud by day (to provide shelter from the sun) and a pillar of fire by night (to provide illumination) and to communicate divine revelation (Ex 13:21-22; 16:10; 40:34-38). Isaiah 4:5-6 reveals that in the future the Shekinah Glory will exist as a canopy over the millennial Jerusalem, and Rev 21:10 describes the descent of the New Jerusalem (apparently to remain suspended over the millennial Jerusalem), in which God's glory is manifest (vv. 22-23), illuminating the earthly sanctuary into which the nations will bring their tribute (vv. 24-26; cf. Isa 66:18-20; Zch 14:16-19).

The conclusion of this section of restoration (Ezk 37:28) reminds us again of God's purpose to sanctify His Name among the nations. However, here the fulfillment of this purpose is connected to the sanctification of Israel that is accomplished through the establishment of the Millennial Temple. Once Israel is finally functioning as a priestly nation at the Temple, the nations will come to Jerusalem to learn God's Word and ways from the Jewish people (Isa 2:2-3).

As a result of this messianic covenant the Gentile nations will recognize that Israel's God is the only true God (because He has restored and reunified the nation, revived Davidic rule under the Messiah, and has returned His Presence to the midst of Israel at the Messianic Temple (v. 28). The millennial kingdom's "covenant of peace" stands in bold relief to the conditions of the tribulation that precede it, for it is a time in which peace is taken from the earth (Rev 6:4), and only a pseudo-peace appears for Israel during the first half of this period (1Th 5:3). For Ezekiel's exilic audience it also marks a dramatic contrast to the conditions of deceptive peace of false prophets (Jer 6:14; 8:11) and siege by the foreign nations (Jer 8:15; 12:12; 14:19; 16:5; 30:5; Lam 3:17).

CONCLUSION

Ezekiel 37:15-28 is a messianic prophecy that reveals that the unconditional covenant promises will find fulfillment through the theocratic kingdom of Messiah, either with Messiah as King in final fulfillment of the Davidic covenant or in concert with a resurrected David who will rule under and for Messiah specifically over a reunited Israel. The messianic government will restore the ideal conditions of spiritual/ritual purity for the nation with the Temple and the Divine Presence in its midst under a perpetual covenant of peace that seals the covenant relationship of the Messiah with His people.

---

1. For example, in Ex 21:6 it is used of an Israelite slave who has his ear pierced in token of his pledge to serve his master "forever." In this case, the duration of "forever" is until his service is terminated by his or his master's death or by the year of Jubilee.
2. David Friedman, "Israel from the Eyes of a Messianic Jew Living in the Land," *Kesher* 13 (Summer 2001): 17.
3. See endnote 7 below for Jesus' application of the shepherd/sheep motif.
4. This schism was never healed even though representatives of both kingdoms returned in 538 BC because during the Second Temple period Israel never regained its former status with a Davidic monarchy and Zadokite priesthood. The problem of division was not physical geography, since the tribes had always been separated by territorial allotments, but spiritual unity.
5. Sefer Yechezkel in chaps. 1–39 by Rabbi Nosson Scherman (Brooklyn, NY: Artscroll/Me'sorah Publications, Ltd., 2015), 272.
6. John MacArthur, "Note on Ezekiel 37:24-25," *John MacArthur Study Bible* (Nashville: Thomas Nelson, 2006), 1180.
7. Note, however, that Jesus' application of the shepherd/sheep motif to His relationship with believers in the Gospels does not appear to have been intended to fulfill the Davidic covenant nor to replace Israel as the covenant people. Jesus' statement in Jn 10:14-16 that the Jewish remnant ("My own sheep") and the Gentile remnant ("other sheep") would become "one flock" is certainly proleptic of the Church (Eph 2:11-22), but this stands apart from the divine covenant with national Israel. The use of the term "flock" for local church congregations in the epistles (Ac 20:28-29; cf. 1Cor 9:7; 1Pt 5:2-3) is therefore appropriate in light of this having become a reality (Ac 14:27; 15:8-11). One of the concerns of the Jerusalem Council had been how the Gentiles coming into the Church would affect God's program for Israel. James, the head of the Jerusalem church, assured Jews at the Council (based on the prophecy of Am 9:11-12) that Gentile inclusion was predicted to take place prior to the second advent and God's restoration of national Israel in the millennial kingdom, which would result in the rest of the Gentiles being called by His Name (Ac 15:14-18). Comments excerpted from Randall Price, "Ezekiel," The Popular Bible Prophecy Commentary, ed. Tim LaHaye and Ed Hindson (Eugene, OR: Harvest House, 2006), 188.
8. John F. Walvoord, "Millennial Series: Part 17: The Kingdom Promises to David," Walvoord.com, https://walvoord.com/article/55.
9. J. J. Gleuck, "Nagid-Shepherd," *Vetus Testamentum* 13 (1963): 144–50; Valentine Muller, "The Prehistory of the Good Shepherd," *Journal of Near Eastern Studies* 3 (1944): 87–90.
10. Randall Price, *Secrets of the Dead Sea Scrolls* (Eugene, OR: Harvest House, 1996), 304.
11. Ibid., 307–308.
12. Gary T. Manning Jr., "Echoes of a Prophet: The Use of Ezekiel in the Gospel of John and in Literature of the Second Temple Period" (PhD dissertation, Fuller Theological Seminary, 2003), 121.
13. For additional references from the Qumran and other Second Temple literature on messianic epithets and a Davidic/prince connection see Herbert W. Bateman IV, Part II: "Expectations of a King" in Bateman, Bock, and Johnston, *Jesus the Messiah: Tracing the Promises, Expectations, and the Coming of Israel's King* (Grand Rapids: Kregel Academic, 2012): 256–329.
14. Hwi Cho, "Ezekiel's Use of the Term *nasi'* with Reference to the Davidic Figure in His Restoration Oracles" (PhD dissertation, Trinity Evangelical Divinity School, 2002), iii.
15. John Francis Kutsko, "The Presence and Absence of God in the Book of Ezekiel" (PhD dissertation, Department of Near Eastern Languages and Cultures, Harvard University, 1997), 215–16.
16. John F. Walvoord, "Chapter V The Kingdom Promised To David," Walvoord.com, https://walvoord.com/article/286.
17. "Ezekiel 37:24," Ariel Ministries, http://arielb.org/archives/789.

18. John Ryan Lister, "The Lord Your God Is in Your Midst: The Presence of God and the Means and End of Redemptive History" (PhD dissertation, Southern Baptist Theological Seminary, 2010), 128.

19. Leslie C. Allen, "Ezekiel 20–48," Word Biblical Commentary 29 (Nashville: Thomas Nelson, 1990), 194. See also E. A. Speiser, "Background and Function of the Biblical Nāśī'," *Catholic Biblical Quarterly* 25 (1963): 111–17; Jon D. Levenson, *Theology of the Program of Restoration of Ezekiel 40–48*, Harvard Semitic Monograph Series 10 (Missoula, MT: Scholars Press, 1976), 57–107; and Iain M. Duguid, *Ezekiel and the Leaders of Israel* (Leiden, Netherlands: E. J. Brill, 1994), 10–57.

20. Terry Ray Clark, "I Will Be King over You: The Rhetoric of Divine Kingship in the Book of Ezekiel" (PhD Dissertation, University of Denver/Colorado Seminary and the Iliff School of Theology, 2008), 44.

21. "Ezekiel 37:15-28," Ariel Ministries, http://arielb.org/archives/789.

Daniel 2:29-45

The Times of the Gentiles and the Messianic Kingdom

ANDREW M. WOODS

Daniel was a prophet whom God used in a strategic way to bless His chosen people, the nation of Israel, during a difficult period in her history known as the Babylonian captivity. During that era, the nation had been removed from her homeland and instead found herself captive roughly 350 miles to the east of Jerusalem. Because the nation of Israel had only limited prophetic information governing this era, God raised up Daniel to prophetically reveal and explain it. Chapter 1 relates how Daniel and his three friends had been taken into captivity by the Neo-Babylonian king Nebuchadnezzar. Chapters 2–7 form an independent literary unit. Not only does the language shift from Hebrew to Aramaic, but also this section is organized as a chiasm.

Thus, the information in chap. 2 lines up with information in chap. 7. Similarly, the theme of chap. 3 is recapitulated in chap. 6 just as chap. 4 lines up with chap. 5. Chapters 2 and 7 give a revelation concerning the course of Gentile history.

Daniel 2 begins with a dream that Nebuchadnezzar had in the second year of his reign, or 603 BC (2:1). (This date becomes important because it means that many of the things Daniel predicts as a result of this dream he saw far in advance of his time.) In trying to understand his dream, Nebuchadnezzar created an impossible standard for his own wise men by demanding not only the interpretation of the dream but also the content of dream the itself. Of course, the revelation of the dream's content in addition to its interpretation is something that only the God of heaven can disclose.

Consequently, the wise men of Babylon failed to meet Nebuchadnezzar's demand (2:3-12). This failure led to Nebuchadnezzar's decree to eradicate all of the wise men of Babylon, which included Daniel and his three friends who were among the exiles of Judah. With their lives on the line, Daniel and his friends prayed to the Lord, who graciously answered by providing Daniel both the revelation and interpretation of Nebuchadnezzar's dream (2:14-19). Such insight caused Daniel to praise God (2:20-23). Having those prayers answered, Daniel reported the dream and its interpretation to Nebuchadnezzar, noting that he was only able to do so because of "a God in heaven who reveals mysteries" (2:24-28).

In so doing, Daniel used the words "mystery" (2:27) and "mysteries" (2:28-29). A biblical mystery is a disclosure of God that could be known no other way than by a revelation from God. As is made clear later, God, through both this dream and its interpretation had pulled back the veil and revealed to His chosen people the destiny of the nation of Israel—not only during the days of the captivity but also beyond and into the distant future. The prophetic period that the dream reveals would begin with Nebuchadnezzar and stretch until Christ Himself physically returns to the earth and rule the world from David's throne in Jerusalem.

THE PURPOSE OF THE DREAM (2:29-30)

Verse 30 says, "in order that the interpretation might be made known to the king, and that you may understand the thoughts of your mind." The God of heaven purposefully targeted Nebuchadnezzar in giving the dream. Through the dream, God disclosed a period called the "times of the Gentiles." Although this identical term is not found in Dan 2, the phrase is employed by Jesus Christ Himself in Lk 21:24. The "times of the Gentiles" has a specific, concrete meaning in Scripture. It represents an era when the Gentile nations will have the upper hand over the nation of Israel. It is also an era when the nation of Israel will have no king reigning on David's throne and will be oppressed by various Gentile powers. It is a period that began in 586 BC when Nebuchadnezzar deposed Zedekiah, the last king of Judah to reign on David's throne. That time period continues on today and will not terminate until the second advent of Jesus the Messiah, when He will reoccupy the Davidic throne at the conclusion of the tribulation period (Mt 25:31). The dream of Dan 2 reveals the specific nations that would trample Israel during this time period, and it is strategically disclosed specifically to Nebuchadnezzar because he was the first Gentile king to oppress Israel during the times of the Gentiles.

Whereas Dan 2 presents the various empires during the times of the Gentiles in the form of an attractive, dazzling statue, Dan 7 presents them as four grotesque and disgusting beasts. In Dan 2 the vision was first given to Nebuchadnezzar, the first king during the times of the Gentiles, and who trampled the nation of Israel. From the king's point of view the times of the Gentiles seemed like an attractive, wonderful, and glorious time. When Daniel saw that same period in Dan 7, it was not glorious to him at all since he and the Hebrew people were being trampled. This change of perspective explains why Dan 7 reveals this era as beastly while Dan 2 reveals it as an attractive statue.

THE CONTENTS OF THE DREAM (2:31-35)

Verse 31 says, "You, O king, were looking and behold, there was a single great statue; that statue, which was large and of extraordinary splendor, was standing in front of you, and its appearance was awesome." Nebuchadnezzar saw something that appeared in human form, like a giant statue, which was great, large, awesome, and of extraordinary splendor. Verses 32-35 describe the statue's body:

> The head of the statue was pure gold, its chest and arms were silver, its stomach and thighs were bronze, its legs were iron, and its feet were partly iron and partly fired clay. As you were watching, a stone broke off without a hand touching it, struck the statue on its feet of iron and fired clay, and crushed them. Then the iron, the fired clay, the bronze, the silver, and the gold were shattered and became like chaff from the summer threshing floors. The wind carried them away, and not a trace of them could be found. But the stone that struck the statue became a great mountain and filled the whole earth.

First, some general observations about the statue. From top to bottom not only does the metallic value of the various metals represented disintegrate, but so also does each metallic weight. The hardness of each metal increases, or intensifies, moving downward.

All of this reveals an important pattern of history. The increasing deterioration of the metal indicates that God is revealing the gradual degeneration of the human race. Human history began at a very high level, but as man fell in the garden of Eden and moved away from God humanity has been gradually deteriorating ever since. This historical pattern is the exact opposite of secular anthropology's perspective.[1] The world of people, in many respects, is declining rather than improving. Such decline seems apparent through the decreasing value of the metals, descending from head to toe, in this statue described in Nebuchadnezzar's dream.

THE INTERPRETATION OF THE DREAM (2:36-45)

The interpretation of the dream is provided in vv. 36-45. Verse 36 says, "This was the dream; now we will tell the king its interpretation"—demonstrating how the Bible interprets itself. So, not only do the Scriptures reveal a vision (2:31-35), they also give an interpretation (2:36-45). In visionary material such as the kind encountered here, the Bible typically is its own interpreter. In this sense, the Bible is a self-interpreting document. For example, John Walvoord identifies 26 instances in the book of Revelation when the Apocalypse itself defines the symbols that it employs.[2]

Here, Daniel saw a total of six empires that would trample Israel during the times of the Gentiles. Each empire is represented by a different body part on the statue.

Babylon

Verses 37-38 show Daniel speaking to Nebuchadnezzar, "Your Majesty, you are king of kings. The God of heaven has given you sovereignty, power, strength, and glory. Wherever people live—or wild animals, or birds of the air—He has handed them over to you and made you ruler over them all. You are the head of gold." Therefore, "the head of gold" represents the first empire during the times of the Gentiles, which is Neo-Babylonia. This empire began to oppress Israel around 605 BC and it would last about 70 years, terminating in 539 BC when Babylon would be overthrown by the Persians. By stating that the head of gold would eventually be replaced by the chest and arms of silver, Daniel was predicting that the Babylonian empire would eventually come to an end. Such a predicted termination became a reality just a few decades later in Daniel's own lifetime, described in Dan 5, depicting the Persian overthrow of the Babylonians.

Babylon was the empire in place when Daniel was first taken into captivity and was ruling over Israel at the time that the dream was given. This helps explain why Nebuchadnezzar was given the dream from God; it was because his was the first empire during the times of the Gentiles. Interestingly, Daniel said to Nebuchadnezzar, "the God of heaven has given sovereignty" (2:37) and "He has handed them over to you and made you rule them all" (2:38). God wanted Nebuchadnezzar (and, more important, the original Israelite readers of the book) to understand that Nebuchadnezzar was king of this great empire only because of the sovereignty of God. Although the different nations during the times of the Gentiles would run their course, God still retained sovereignty. He had actually appointed the times when these pagan powers would exist and when these empires would terminate.

information of Dan 7 must be included. Daniel 7:23 states, "This is what he said: 'The fourth beast will be a fourth kingdom on the earth, different from all the other kingdoms. It will devour the whole earth, trample it down, and crush it.'" Rome Phase II, therefore, must be much bigger than ancient Rome. Although the culture of ancient Rome might represent some kind of origination point, Rome Phase II is an empire that will dominate the world. What is being described here in vv. 41-43 is the coming worldwide kingdom of a future world ruler to whom Scripture gives various titles (the beast, the man of sin, the coming prince, and the antichrist). The ten toes are interpreted in Dan 7:24 as ten horns or ten kingdoms. Daniel 7:24, says "The 10 horns are 10 kings who will rise from this kingdom." Revelation 17:12 similarly clarifies, "The 10 horns you saw are 10 kings who have not yet received a kingdom, but they will receive authority as kings with the beast . . ." Therefore, the ten toes represent a ten-king or ten-nation global confederacy. This ten-king confederacy will be immediately and instantaneously destroyed by the stone cut without human hands (Dan 2:34-35).

The depiction of the feet of clay is inconsistent with the known facts of history because ancient Rome never consisted of a worldwide ten-king confederacy nor did it ever experience a sudden and instantaneous termination as described in the vision. In fact, Rome deteriorated gradually, over many centuries, as the morals and values of the Roman people progressively weakened. Thus, while the image from the head to the ankles is historical, the feet of iron and clay along with their immediate destruction are yet future. In between the ankles and the feet there appears to be an indefinite period of time.

In biblical prophecy, it is common for Scripture to present prophetic events without mentioning the vast expanse of time in between the prophesied events. For example, Isa 9:6a says, "For unto us a child is born, a son will be given," which is a prophecy about Christ's first coming. However, the rest of the verse (Isa 9:6b) speaks of Christ's second coming when it goes on to say "and the government will rest upon His shoulders." Thus, Isa 9:6 conflates two prophecies, one about the first advent and another about the second advent, without revealing the vast expanse of time in between them. There is a similar pattern in Dan 2, with a seemingly indefinite period of time in between the ankles and feet in the statue.

By way of analogy, it is like looking at two mountains in the distance. There is the first mountain and the other behind it, but what is not seen is the valley separating the two mountains. Similarly, the prophets of old could not see what was happening in the prophetic valley in between two prophesied events. With a completed canon and the vantage point of history, the valley becomes evident. The valley is the period of time between the two advents of Christ.

However, at some point the valley will end, and the feet comprised of iron mixed with clay, or the ten-king confederacy, will come into existence and cover the entire earth. This will be the kingdom of the Antichrist. However, this kingdom will be short lived. It will last a mere 42 months (Dan 7:25; Rev 13:5). And even when this empire comes into existence, Daniel indicates that it will not consist of a cohesive structure. This is what Daniel means about the iron and the clay not mixing together. Walvoord, of these verses, says:

> The final form of the kingdom will include diverse elements, whether this refers to race, political idealism, or sectional interests, and this will prevent the final form of the kingdom from having any real unity. This, of course, is borne out by the fact that the world empire at the end of the age breaks up into a gigantic civil war in which forces from the south and the east and the north contend with the ruler of the Mediterranean force supremacy as Daniel himself will explain in Daniel 11:36-45.[5]

The future kingdom of the Antichrist will represent only a superficial unity at best. Its deep divisions will ultimately come to the surface as that empire will go to war against itself in the second half of the tribulation period.

The Kingdom of God

Rome Phase 2 will be instantaneously overthrown. Dan 2:44-45 says:

> "In the days of those kings, the God of heaven will set up a kingdom that will never be destroyed, and this kingdom will not be left to another people. It will crush all these kingdoms and bring them to an end, but will itself endure forever. You saw a stone break off from the mountain without a hand touching it, and it crushed the iron, bronze, fired clay, silver, and gold. The great God has told the king what will happen in the future. The dream is true, and its interpretation certain."

The vision depicts a smiting stone striking the feet of the statue, which brought to an end not just the empire of the Antichrist but also all of Gentile dominion over Israel that began in the days of Nebuchadnezzar. This stone refers to the future and final kingdom of God. It is the very kingdom Jesus taught His followers to pray for in Mt 6:10 when He said, "Thy kingdom come." The stone represents an unshakeable kingdom that every child of God will inherit (Heb 12:28). Verse 34 indicates that this stone is "cut out by no human hand" (ESV) indicating that this coming kingdom will not be of human origin. Rather, it will be the work of God, and it will immediately overthrow the Antichrist's kingdom.

Verse 44 indicates that this kingdom will be established "in the days of those kings." "Those kings" refers to the ten-king confederacy of the Antichrist. There is an important chronology here. First, will come the ten-king confederacy. Then, after it reigns for a season, God will overthrow it instantaneously, miraculously, and cataclysmically. Then and only then will God's kingdom be established upon the earth. Thus, Merrill Unger writes:

> Hence, the iron kingdom with its feet of iron and clay (cf. 3:33-35, 40, 44) and the nondescript beast of 7:7-8 envision . . . the form in which it will exist *after the church period*, when God will resume His dealing with the *nation* Israel. How futile for conservative scholars to ignore that fact and to seek to find literal fulfillment of those prophecies in history or in the church, when those predictions refer to events yet future and have no application whatever to the church.[6]

In v. 44, there is the expression "the God of heaven," indicating that although the content of the final kingdom will be physical and earthly, it will originate from heaven itself. This also helps explain why it is characterized as a stone cut without human hands. The stone's exponential growth indicates that God's coming kingdom will be both universal and eternal.

It is significant that all of the kingdoms comprising the different body parts of the statue surveyed thus far (Babylon, Persia, Greece, historical Rome, Rome Phase II) are all literal kingdoms that existed for a literal time, occupied specific lands with identifiable borders, and had a capital city. This demands the question, why would not the last kingdom, represented by the stone cut without human hands, also not be a literal kingdom that will reign for a literal time (Rev 20:1-10), that will occupy a specific land with identifiable borders (Gn 15:18-21), and have a capital (Isa 2:2-3)? Such a presentation represents a premillennial view of history. The expression "millennium" simply means a thousand years. Premillennialism is the belief that the thousand-year kingdom will not come into existence until Jesus comes back first (or "pre") and then sets up His earthly kingdom (cf. Rev 20:4-6).

However, the premillennial view is not the majority view of church history. The majority view instead is amillennialism, which argues that Jesus set up His kingdom spiritually in the first century. However, to arrive at this conclusion one must interpret everything in the statue literally except the smiting stone and then interpret it non-literally. Such interpretive vacillation is tantamount to switching hermeneutical horses in midstream. A consistent interpretation of the statue demands premillennialism. Dwight Pentecost explains why the presentation of the smiting stone found in Dan 2 is inconsistent with the belief that Christ established His kingdom at His first advent:

> Amillennialists hold that this kingdom was established by Christ at His *First* Advent and that now the church is that kingdom. They argue that: (a) Christianity, like the growing mountain, began to grow and spread geographically and is still doing so; (b) Christ came in the days of the Roman Empire; (c) the Roman Empire

fell into the hands of 10 kingdoms (10 toes); (d) Christ is the chief Cornerstone (Eph. 2:20). Premillenarians, however, hold that the kingdom to be established by Christ on earth is yet future. At least six points favor that view: (1) The stone will become a mountain suddenly, not gradually. Christianity did not suddenly fill "the whole earth" (Dan. 2:35) at Christ's First Advent. (2) Though Christ came in the days of the Roman Empire, He did not destroy it. (3) During Christ's time on earth the Roman Empire did not have 10 kings at once. Yet Nebuchadnezzar's statue suggests that when Christ comes to establish His kingdom, 10 rulers will be in existence and will be destroyed by Him. (4) Though Christ is now the chief Cornerstone to the church (Eph. 2:20) and "a stone that causes [unbelievers] to stumble" (1 Peter 2:8), He is not yet a smiting Stone as He will be when He comes again. (5) The Stone (Messiah) will crush and end all the kingdoms of the world. But the church has not and will not conquer the world's kingdoms. (6) The church is not a kingdom with a political realm, but the future Millennium will be. Thus Nebuchadnezzar's dream clearly teaches premillennialism, that Christ will return to earth to establish His rule on the earth, thereby subduing all nations. The church is not that kingdom.[7]

CONCLUDING EXHORTATION

This prophecy constitutes a tremendous source of encouragement for the nation of Israel throughout the millennia comprising the times of the Gentiles. Although the nation would be oppressed by various political powers, God intends to preserve Israel as a distinct nation and eventually establish His kingdom through them. God will ultimately fulfill His Word according to His own timetable. On the horizon is a coming kingdom which cannot be shaken that God's people will inherit. While the message to the Jewish people would be one of comfort, the message to the Gentile nations would be one of warning. Although they may now have the upper hand in history, their day in the sun will one day come to an end. How important, therefore, it is for us to heed this warning and not live for the fleeting values of this world but, rather, for the values of God's coming and eternal kingdom.

1. For more information on this, see John F. Walvoord, *Daniel: The Key to Prophetic Revelation* (Chicago: Moody, 1971), 66.
2. John F. Walvoord, *The Revelation of Jesus Christ: A Commentary* (Chicago: Moody, 1966), 29–30. For a more complete listing, see J. B. Smith, *A Revelation of Jesus Christ: A Commentary on the Book of Revelation*, trans., J. Otis Yoder (Scottsdale, PA: Herald, 1961), 18–19.
3. Walvoord, *Daniel: The Key to Prophetic Revelation*, 66.
4. Ibid., 68.

5. Ibid., 71.
6. Merrill F. Unger, *Unger's Commentary on the Old Testament* (Chicago: Moody, 1981; repr. Chattanooga, TN: AMG, 2002), 1643.
7. J. Dwight Pentecost, "Daniel," in *Bible Knowledge Commentary*, ed. John F. Walvoord and Roy B. Zuck (Colorado Springs, CO: Victor, 1985), 1336.

Daniel 7:13-27

The Glorious Son of Man

J. PAUL TANNER

One of the most profound messianic prophecies of the Old Testament appears in Daniel 7:13-14. In this passage, an individual referred to as "One like a son of man" is presented before the "Ancient of Days" and given an everlasting kingdom over all nations who will "serve" Him. In this passage, Daniel records what he saw in a night vision,

> I continued watching in the night visions, and I saw One like a son of man coming with the clouds of heaven. He approached the Ancient of Days and was escorted before Him. He was given authority to rule, and glory, and a kingdom; so that those of every people, nation, and language should serve Him. His dominion is an everlasting dominion that will not pass away, and His kingdom is one that will not be destroyed.

Although the phrase "one like a son of man" is strikingly similar to Jesus' favorite self-designation, the Son of Man, there is great debate in scholarly circles as to the identity of the one mentioned in Dan 7:13, as well as to how and when the fulfillment takes place. The traditional Christian opinion has been to identify Daniel's "one like a son of man" (*kᵊbar ʾĕnāš*) with Jesus Christ, and even Jewish expositors—although they reject the identification with Jesus—have historically understood this as a reference to the Messiah. Critical scholars, on the other hand, have rejected the messianic view and have offered several alternative interpretations in its place. Nevertheless, the traditional Christian interpretation that sees the ultimate fulfillment in Messiah Jesus is the most defensible position and is the view expounded in this article.

USE OF THE EXPRESSION "SON OF MAN" ELSEWHERE IN THE OT

Since chapters 2:4–7:28 of Daniel were written in Aramaic, the expression "son of man" appears in the Aramaic text of Dan 7:13 as *bar 'ĕnāš*, and is comparable to the Hebrew phrase "son of man," *ben 'āḏām*.[1] The latter occurs close to 200 times in the Hebrew Bible, and simply means "a mortal human being." For example, Jer 49:18 states, "'As when Sodom and Gomorrah were overthrown along with their neighbors,' says the Lord, 'no one will live there; no *human being* (*ben 'āḏām*) will even stay in it as a temporary resident.'" Quite legitimately, in this case it is translated "human being" in the HCSB. Again, the same use appears in Ps 8:4, where "son of man" appears in parallelism with "man": "What is *man* that You remember him, the *son of man* (*ben 'āḏām*) that You look after him?" Several times *ben 'āḏām* is used in the book of Ezekiel for the prophet himself (e.g., Ezk 2:1). So in the OT the phrase itself is commonly used to indicate a human being (or a specific human being such as Ezekiel), and is not particularly messianic. Yet as will be discussed later, if Jesus entered our humanity by His incarnation, the generic sense of "son of man" would appropriately describe Him [all emphasis added].

THE CONTEXTUAL SETTING FOR "ONE LIKE A SON OF MAN" IN DANIEL 7

According to Dan 7:1, the vision given to Daniel occurred in the first year of the Babylonian king Belshazzar, about 553 BC, during the time the nation lived in exile in Babylon. Daniel 7 is also the concluding chapter of that part of the book written in Aramaic, namely, chaps. 2–7. These chapters depict the role, character, and succession of the Gentile nations of the world under whom Israel was being disciplined prior to Messiah's kingdom. The opening chapter of this unit (Dan 2) depicts a succession of Gentile kingdoms (normally interpreted by evangelical scholars as Babylon, Medo-Persia, Greece, and Rome) that is ultimately superseded by the kingdom of God (note Dan 2:44-45). This is paralleled by a similar succession of Gentile kingdoms in Dan 7. Again, a kingdom set up by God ultimately replaces the preceding Gentile kingdoms. This kingdom of heaven in both chapters is what gives emphasis to a kingdom theology in the book of Daniel, and because of which one would expect to find revealed a king suitable for such an important rule. Furthermore, this king is not alone, but also "the holy ones of the Most High will receive the kingdom and possess it forever" (Dan 7:18), i.e., they have an important part to play in the life of this kingdom that replaces all earthly Gentile kingdoms (Dan 7:27).

The kingdom theology introduced in Dan 2 is not merely paralleled by Dan 7, for the latter makes two important contributions not found in that earlier chapter.

First, out of the final Gentile kingdom of Dan 7, one emerges who is identified symbolically as a "little horn" (see Dan 7:7-8 and compare 7:23-25). To appreciate his role, one should first understand something about the literary structure of the chapter. Hill has observed the literary aspects that underscore the structure and that reveal the importance that the presentation of "One like a son of man" has to the kingdom theology:

> The introductory formula ("in my vision at night I looked," v. 13a) echoes the formula introducing the vision (v. 2a) and forms an envelope for the literary unit (vv. 2-14). The construction serves to underscore the importance of the final scene as the climax of Daniel's vision.[2]

Yet within this larger unit of Dan 7:2-14, there are two primary subsections: (1) the general revelation of the four Gentile kingdoms that culminates in the appearance of the "little horn" (Dan 7:2-8) and (2) the throne scene of judgment before the Ancient of Days (Dan 7:9-14). Significantly, the "little horn" that is introduced in the first subsection appears also in the subsequent throne scene of judgment: "I watched, then, because of the sound of the arrogant words the horn was speaking. As I continued watching, the beast was killed and its body destroyed and given over to the burning fire" (Dan 7:11). Critical scholars typically interpret the "little horn" as Antiochus IV Epiphanes, the famous Syrian king who ruled from 175–164 BC and who initiated a persecution of Israel that resulted in the Maccabean revolt. Evangelical scholars, however, have rejected that interpretation. First, the statement in Dan 7:11 ("given over to the burning fire") does not accurately describe the demise of Antiochus. Second, with his defeat and judgment, the kingdom of heaven did not come about as described in Dan 7:26-27. For this and other reasons, evangelical scholars have rightly concluded that this "little horn" is one and the same as the Antichrist described elsewhere in Scripture (also known as "the beast" in Rev 13–19). That the beast of Revelation is "thrown alive into the lake of fire that burns with sulfur" (Rev 19:20) corresponds precisely with Dan 7:11.

The kingdom theology of Dan 2–7 reaches its climax in Dan 7:13-14 when "One like a son of man" is presented before the Ancient of Days (God the Father) and is "given authority to rule, and glory, and a kingdom." He is the ultimate victor, not the Antichrist. (The remainder of Dan 7 is simply an elaboration of some of the details that lead up to this event). His kingdom is the kingdom of God, and it comes about following the destruction of the "little horn" (the Antichrist) when all Gentile kingdoms and peoples are made subject to Him. This theological development in Daniel harmonizes perfectly with the NT's portrayal of Jesus as "the Son of Man" who ultimately returns to defeat the Antichrist and establish His kingdom rule on earth.

ALTERNATIVE VIEWS OF "ONE LIKE A SON OF MAN"

As mentioned earlier, despite the historic position of the Christian church that this figure is the Messiah and fulfilled by the Lord Jesus Christ, other suggestions have been made.[3] These include the historic Jewish view and several views set forth by critical scholars:

Historic Jewish interpretation. In Jewish rabbinical tradition (which, though later than NT documents, could preserve earlier traditions), there is evidence that "one like a son of man" in Dan 7:13 was regarded as the Messiah (though not Jesus). Casey has found ten references to Dan 7:13-14 in this literature, at least four of which interpret this figure as Messiah: b. Sanh. 98a; *Num. Rab.* 13.14; *ʾAggadat Bĕrʾēšît* 14:3; 23:1; and *Midr. Haggadol Gen.* 49.10.[4]

Rabbi Akiba, prominent in the early second-century AD, took him to be the Messiah (as did thc later Talmud), and this view was embraced by most rabbinical exegetes. Montgomery writes,

> Joshua b. Levi, c. 250, taught that, if Israel deserved it, the Messiah would come with the clouds of heaven, after Dan. 7, or, if otherwise, riding upon an ass, after Zech. 9[9] (*Sanh.* 98*a*). This interpretation was followed by all the Jewish comm., with the exception of AEz., as noted above, including the Karaite Jepheth, *e.g.*, Rashi, 'This is King Messiah.'[5]

The "human being" view. According to this view, the Aramaic phrase *bar ʾĕnāš* ("son of man") simply means a "human being" in general, without reference to any particular individual. In a similar vein, Driver suggested that this represents "a figure in human form."[6] The main defense for this view is the use elsewhere in the OT for this phrase and its Hebrew equivalent (*ben ʾāḏām*). Related to this view is the suggestion that the promise is to a particular human, namely, Judas Maccabeus.[7] This view depends on a dating of the book to the second century BC (common with critical scholars). Not only is this theory questionable, but also Judas Maccabeus obviously did not receive an everlasting kingdom in which all people and nations served him.

The collective or personification view. This view interprets the reference to "one like a son of man" not as an individual at all, but rather as a collective representation or personification for a group of people.[8] The group is then understood as the Jewish people, the saints of the Most High, who stand to gain the kingdom. Those who take the second century BC view of Antiochus IV would understand them to be the "faithful Jews" who opposed Antiochus.[9] One rationale offered for this view is the statement in Dan 7:27 that "The kingdom, dominion, and greatness of the kingdoms under all of heaven will be given to the people, the holy ones of the Most High" (cf. Dan 7:18). Nevertheless, this view suffers from a fatal problem, namely, the statement in Dan 7:14 that all the peoples, nations, and languages should serve (i.e., worship) him.[10]

The angelic view. Other scholars have taken the collective view and modified it to interpret the group as angels. Defenders of this view have pointed out that it is customary in visions to have an angel(s) appearing in human semblance. Some proponents of the angelic interpretation hold that a specific angel is in view, such as Gabriel or Michael. Collins, for instance, views the "one like a son of man" as Michael and the "holy ones" as his angelic followers on whose behalf he receives the kingdom.[11] This view depends on understanding "the holy ones of the Most High" (*qadîšê ʿdîšê*) in Dan 7:18 as angels, not human "saints" (the NASB renders this as "saints"). It is true that the equivalent Hebrew term (*qᵊdôšîm*) commonly refers to angels in the Hebrew Bible and in deuterocanonical books associated with the OT (but in some places, to "men"). The major weakness to this view, however, is that the suffering and defeat of the "holy ones" is implied in vv. 21 and 25. Furthermore, that all nations will serve (i.e., worship) "one like a son of man" is hardly fitting of an angelic figure.[12]

A DEFENSE OF THE MESSIANIC VIEW

Christian interpreters quite naturally have seen the fulfillment of Dan 7:13-14 in the Lord Jesus Christ, especially because of Jesus' frequent reference to Himself as "the Son of Man" (e.g., Mt 16:28; 19:28; 24:27,30,39,44; 25:31, etc.).[13] Of particular importance is the reference in Mk 14:62. When asked at His trial by the Jewish high priest whether or not He was the Messiah, Jesus replied, "I am, and all of you will see the Son of Man seated at the right hand of the Power and coming with the clouds of heaven." His response was a direct allusion to Dan 7:13-14, especially considering the reference to the "clouds" (cf. Mt 24:30 and Lk 21:27-31, which associate this scene with the second coming). Of further interest is the repeated connection in *1 Enoch* between the Son of Man and the Messiah (see *1 En.* 37–71, esp. 46:1-6; 48:1-7), a topic that will be further explored later in this article.

There is also a striking intertextual feature of Daniel that argues for the messianic interpretation, namely the Hebraism "at the end of the days" (*bᵊʾaḥărîṯ yômayyāʾ*, author's translation) mentioned in Dan 2:28 (and in the Hebrew text of Dan 10:14). The nation's hope is on a future king, the son of man, who appears at the end of days (Isa 2:2; Jer 23:20; 30:24; 48:47; 49:39; Ezk 38:16; Hos 3:5; Mic 4:1). Shepherd explains the connection between the end of days and the son of man:

> The use of "at the end of the days" in Daniel links the eschatology of the book to that of the rest of the canon. Therefore, the coming king from Judah is the most likely candidate for the head of the everlasting kingdom in Daniel (Dan 2:44; 3:33; 4:31; 6:27; 7:14, 18, 27). God is the ruler of the kingdom, and he gives it to whomever he pleases (Dan 4:14, 22, 29). His choice is the coming king from Judah—the one "like a son of man" in Dan 7:13.[14]

All things considered, the messianic view has the most to commend it. After a lengthy discussion of the development of messianic theology in the OT, including such themes as dominion given to man (Gn 1:26), kingship (particularly in the Psalms), and even kingly suffering, Rowe posits three arguments that favor "one like a son of man" being a reference to Messiah rather than collectively the saints or some angelic figure:[15]

> 1. The enthronement of God (v. 9) followed by the granting of kingship to 'one like a son of man' (v. 13) is reminiscent of the coronation of the Davidic king in Psalm 2. . . . the structure of the dream reflects the celebration of Yahweh's kingship, which we have seen in the Psalms is associated with the Davidic (messianic) king. . . .
> 2. It is difficult to conceive of the 'saints of the Most High' without a leader. . . . Having received the kingship, he shares it with the saints, by virtue of his close identification with them.
> 3. If, as we have seen, 'one like a son of man' who comes 'with the clouds of heaven' is a heavenly being, although he may represent the saints he cannot be merely a symbol for them. . . . it is the heavenly origin of the 'one like a son of man' which finally proves his individuality and thus (taken with other indications in the chapter) his messianic role.

Hence, "One like a son of man" refers to and finds its fulfillment in Jesus the Messiah. When properly understood, "son of man" does have reference to a human being (as it customarily does elsewhere in the OT). This One, however, who receives a kingdom is "like" a son of man, i.e., He Himself partakes of humanity. If anything, Dan 7:13-14 should have prompted the reader to look for a Messiah who would be both human on the one hand, and yet able to receive worship on the other hand, i.e., He would need to be both human and divine. That is exactly what the virgin birth of Jesus of Nazareth provides: He was born of a woman (virgin!) and yet conceived by the Holy Spirit. In the consciousness of Jesus, it was an easy transition from "one like a son of man" to "the Son of Man," and the connection Jesus understood of this phrase to Dan 7:13-14—though deliberately vague in the initial stages of His ministry—became very evident by the time of His trial before the Sanhedrin.[16]

Daniel's anticipation of "One like a son of man," that is, One who had a unique connection with mankind, would find its fulfillment in Jesus of Nazareth. As such, He (and He alone) would be the representative of all mankind who would bear the punishment for the sins of each human being. Grassmick explains the appropriateness of the phrase for the Lord Jesus:

> This title especially suited Jesus' total mission. It was free of political connotations, thus preventing false expectations. Yet it was sufficiently ambiguous (like a parable) to preserve the balance between concealment and disclosure in Jesus' life and mission (cf. [Mark] 4:11–12). It combined the elements of suffering and glory in a way no other designation could. It served to define His unique role as Messiah.[17]

DANIEL'S "ONE LIKE A SON OF MAN" IN INTERTESTAMENTAL LITERATURE

Related to this discussion of the phrase "One like a son of man" is the question of whether or not there was a stable and generally accepted set of beliefs regarding messianism at the beginning of the Christian era and, if so, to what extent "the son of man" might be associated with this hope. While it is difficult to set forth such views with certainty, what we can say is that there is some evidence that the expression "son of man" was used in a messianic sense prior to Jesus' ministry. It is found, after all, in the fragmentary *Aramaic Apocalypse* (4Q246), in the *Parables of Enoch*, i.e., chaps. 37–71 of *1 Enoch* (also known as the *Similitudes*), and at least the concept in *4 Ezra* 13.[18] In the case of *4 Ezra* 13, the vision begins with "something like the figure of a man" (13.3) arising from the sea. Later, God calls him "my son" (13.32), and in the latter days he takes his stand on Mt. Zion, destroying an army that attacks it, and regathering the ten tribes of Israel. Though he is clearly a messiah figure, both Collins and Burkett point out differences with the "son of man" in *1 Enoch*.[19]

Aramaic Apocalypse (4Q246), published by É. Puech in 1992, has been dated to the first century BC.[20] There, a "son of man" figure has been given the title "Son of God" and becomes a great king over the whole earth. K. A. Kuhn has concluded,

> The *Aramaic Apocalypse* not only borrows from Daniel 7 but also offers an interpretation of that text by designating the Danielic "one like a son of man" as the "Son of the Most High" and "Son of God." These titles, I claim, cast Daniel's eschatological redeemer against the royal background of the Davidic monarchy, and yet also mark a development in the transcendent character of this heavenly figure by attributing to him divine sonship.[21]

Of perhaps greater interest is the material found in the *Parables of Enoch*, i.e., chaps. 37–71 of *1 Enoch* (also known as the *Similitudes*). It is here that we find the earliest Jewish evidence for the interpretation and re-use of Dan 7:13-14. Although some scholars date the *Parable of Enoch* after Jesus' public ministry (e.g., Collins), more recently D. L. Bock has argued for the "strong likelihood that the *Parables of Enoch* are Jewish and most likely were composed prior to the work of Jesus of Nazareth or contemporaneous with his Galilean ministry."[22] If this more recent dating of the *Parables of Enoch* proves true, the relationship between the *Parables of Enoch* and Jesus' use of "son of man" (as well as what this might have meant to first-century hearers) will have to be carefully reconsidered. Several passages from this section of *1 Enoch* (e.g., *1 En.* 46:1-4; 47:3) clearly allude to Dan 7:9-10, 13-14, and reflect a messianic understanding of "one like a son of man."

Although no mention is made in *1 Enoch* of "the son of man" coming with the clouds of heaven (Dan 7:13), Enoch's vision goes beyond that of Daniel by referring to the throne on which the son of man will sit (*1 En.* 51:3). Of further interest is the fact that *1 En.* 48:3 portrays the son of man's preexistence, for he existed before the sun, stars, and heavens were made. Burkett summarizes how the "son of man" is presented in *1 Enoch*:

> The main part of the Similitudes of Enoch (1 Enoch 37–70) presents a pre-existent Messiah. This figure combines the attributes and functions of the one like a son of man in Daniel 7.13, the Davidic Messiah of Isaiah 11 and Psalm 2, the servant of the Lord in Second Isaiah, and Yahweh as eschatological judge. The Similitudes explicitly identify the figure as the Messiah (1 Enoch 48.10; 52.4). From a servant passage, his primary title is 'the Chosen One' (Isa. 42.1). God chose him and hid him in heaven before the world was created (1 Enoch 48.3, 6; 62.7). At the final judgment, he will sit on God's throne of glory and execute judgment for the righteous against the rebellious angels and sinners, especially the kings and rulers of earth.[23]

CONCLUSION

Daniel 7:13-14 predicts that "One like a son of man" will come with the clouds of heaven, and He will be given "authority to rule, and glory, and a kingdom; so that those of every people, nation, and language should serve Him." This passage most certainly finds its fulfillment in Messiah Jesus, despite the skepticism of critical scholars. Their skepticism stems from a presupposition that the book of Daniel was not authored by the prophet Daniel in the sixth century BC, but rather was composed about 165 BC during the Jewish persecution of Antiochus IV Epiphanes. This theory colors all other interpretations of the book, including Dan 7. Hence, they interpret the "little horn" of Dan 7 as Antiochus IV and propose various nonmessianic identifications for "one like a son of man" that they consider commensurate with this era. Yet their dating of the book is entirely wrong, and Daniel did write the book bearing his name, much of which contains authentic prophecies.[24]

As this article has pointed out, there were some early indications that "One like a son of man" from Dan 7:13-14 was already being viewed as messianic (especially in that portion of *1 Enoch* known as the *Parables of Enoch* or *Similitudes*). Even if this was not a widely understood messianic designation at the time of Jesus' public ministry, it is easy in retrospect to see why He would have chosen the phrase "the Son of Man" as His favorite self-designation. It was sufficiently ambiguous in the initial stages of His ministry to allow for His identification with humanity, and yet it was perfectly suited at the climactic time of His trial before the Jewish Sanhedrin when, in answer to the question if He were indeed the Messiah, He could declare, "I am, and all of you will see the Son of Man seated at the right hand of the Power and coming with the clouds of heaven." By adding the comment about "coming with the clouds of heaven"—an obvious allusion to Dan 7:13—Jesus clearly indicated that He understood Himself to be the fulfillment of Dan 7:13-14.[25] The Jewish leaders at the time of His trial might have rejected His messianic claim, but He would be vindicated by His resurrection from the grave and subsequently be given rule over all peoples in fulfillment not only of Dan 7:13-14 but also of the Davidic covenant promise of reigning over the eternal kingdom of God.

Finally, this cloud motif associated Dan 7:13–14 with (1) Jesus' ascension to the Father's right hand, and (2) His return in glory to claim His victory and impose His kingly rule upon the world He created and for which He went to the cross. With His ascension to the Father's right hand, the "Son of Man" has been proclaimed "Lord" (Ac 2:36) and possesses "all authority" (which He uses for building His church, Mt 28:18). With His second coming, He will use His authority to bring the entire world into submission in preparation for fulfilling the Abrahamic promise of worldwide blessing (Gn 12:3).

---

1. An alternative form for "son of man" in Hebrew is *ben 'ěnôš*. The form is rare, but see Ps 144:3.

2. A. E. Hill, "Daniel," in *Expositor's Bible Commentary*, rev. ed., 10 vols., ed. T. Longman III and D. E. Garland, 8:19–212 (Grand Rapids: Zondervan, 2008), 139.

3. For a more detailed study of the history of interpretation of Dan 7:13-14, see M. Müller, *The Expression 'Son of Man' and the Development of Christology: A History of Interpretation* (London and New York: Routledge, 2008).

4. P. M. Casey, *Son of Man: The Interpretation and Influence of Daniel 7* (London: SPCK, 1979), 80–83. *Num. Rab.* 13.14, for instance, states: "How do we know that he [the Messiah] will hold sway on land? Because it is written . . . Behold,

there came with the clouds of heaven one like unto a son of man . . . and there was given unto him dominion . . . that all the peoples should serve him" (cited in D. Burkett, "Son of Man in Apocalyptic and Rabbinic Texts," in *The Son of Man Debate: A History and Evaluation*, ed. D. Burkett, SNTSMS 107 [Cambridge: Cambridge Univ. Press, 2004], 115). Secondary references include *Midr. Ps.* 21.5; *Tanchuma Toledoth* 20; *Midr. Ps.* 2.9; *'Ag. Ber.* 14.3; and *Gen. Rab.* 13.11 and 13.12.

5. J. A. Montgomery, *A Critical and Exegetical Commentary on the Book of Daniel,* ICC (Edinburgh: T&T Clark, 1927), 321.

6. S. R. Driver, "Son of Man," in *Dictionary of the Bible,* 4 vols., ed. J. Hastings, 4:579–89 (Edinburgh: T&T Clark, 1902), 579. Yet Driver (579) did go on to acknowledge that, in its context, this human figure denoted "the glorified and ideal people of Israel."

7. The identification of Judas Maccabeus was espoused by the anti-Christian philosopher Porphyry (ca. AD 232/4–ca. AD 305), and more recently by G. W. Buchanan (*The Book of Daniel,* Mellen Biblical Commentary, Old Testament Series 25 [Lewiston, NY: Edwin Mellen Press, 1999]) and H. Sahlin ("Antiochus IV Epiphanes und Judas Mackabäus," *Studia Theologica* 23 [1969]: 41–68).

8. P. M. Casey, "The Corporate Interpretation of 'One Like a Son of Man' (Dan. Vii 13) at the Time of Jesus," *Novum Testamentum* 18 (1976): 167–80 attempted to defend the corporate interpretation based on midrashic interpretations found in *Midr. Ps.* 21, 5 and *Tanch. Tol.* 20.

9. This view is taken by Hartman (L. F. Hartman and A. A. Di Lella, *The Book of Daniel,* AB [Garden City, NY: Doubleday & Co., Inc., 1978], 87) and J. A. Montgomery (*A Critical and Exegetical Commentary on the Book of Daniel,* 317–24).

10. The translation "should serve" (*yiḇlᵉḥûn*) means more than "waiting upon" his needs. Of the ten times that *pᵉlaḥ* is used in Aramaic Daniel, it is always used with the idea of service or worship of a deity. It is more than "to give honor" or "wait upon," because (for Hebrews) to render *pᵉlaḥ* to anyone other than Yahweh would be tantamount to idolatry (note the use in Dan 3:12).

11. J. J. Collins, *Daniel,* Hermeneia (Minneapolis: Fortress Press, 1993), 304–10.

12. For further refutation of the angelic view, see V. S. Poythress, "The Holy Ones of the Most High in Daniel VII," *Vetus Testamentum* 26 (1976): 208–13.

13. The phrase "Son of Man" occurs about 84 times in the Gospels (cf. Stephen's reference in Acts 7:56).

14. M. B. Shepherd, "Daniel 7:13 and the New Testament Son of Man," *Westminster Theological Journal* 68 (2006): 104.

15. R. D. Rowe, "Is Daniel's 'Son of Man' Messianic?" in *Christ the Lord: Studies in Christology Presented to Donald Guthrie,* ed. H. H. Rowdon (Leicester/Downers Grove, IL: InterVarsity Press, 1982), 94–96. Rowe's insights regarding the concept of "son of man" in relationship to messianic kingship are particularly insightful (82): "To summarize our consideration of messianic kingship in Israel, we have seen that in the context of worship the Davidic king was closely associated with the kingship of Yahweh, was sometimes represented as suffering and also played the role of 'representative man' (analogous to the first man) in relation to God; here he acted out, in his person and on behalf of his people Israel, on the one hand the frailty and humiliation of mankind and on the other the kingly authority and exaltation of mankind. In that role, he was known as *ben 'āḏām.*"

16. Regarding Jesus' understanding and use of "son of man," see D. L. Bock, "The Son of Man in Luke 5:24," *Bulletin for Biblical Research* 1 (1991): 109–21; and "The Use of Daniel 7 in Jesus' Trial, with Implications for His Self-Understanding," in *Who Is This Son of Man? The Latest Scholarship on a Puzzling Expression of the Historical Jesus,* ed. L. Hurtado, and P. L. Owen, 78–100 (London and New York: Bloomsbury T&T Clark, 2012). In both articles, Bock clarifies how Jesus played upon the ambiguity of the phrase for His own purposes, first (in Lk 5:24) concerning His ability to forgive sins, and then late in His earthly ministry (in Mk 14:62—where He obviously draws upon Dan 7:13)—to signify His ultimate authority over the religious leaders. Bock's explanation of the shift from ambiguity in using the phrase (for most of His ministry) to intentional application with explicit connection to Dan 7 (near the end of his ministry) is insightful ("The Use of Daniel 7 in Jesus' Trial," 89):

> Numerous issues surround the discussion, including an intense debate over whether the expression is representative of a title (like the form of its consistent NT use) or is an idiom. If it is an idiom, then it has been argued that the meaning is either a circumlocution for "I" (Vermes) or an indirect expression with the force of 'some person' (Fitzmyer). It seems that, for most students of the problem today, a formal title, or at least a unified Son of Man concept, did not yet exist in the early first century and that Fitzmyer has more evidence available for his view on the idiom. It is the idiomatic element in the Aramaic expression and the lack of a fixed concept in Judaism that allow any 'son of man' remark to be ambiguous unless it is tied to a specific passage or context. This means the term could be an effective vehicle as a cipher for Jesus that he could fill with content, defining it as he used it. One can argue, looking at the flow of Jesus' ministry as it appears in the Synoptics, that Jesus used the term ambiguously initially and drew out its force as he continued to use it, eventually associating it with Daniel 7.

Bock goes on to conclude (99): "So Jesus' evocation of Son of Man before the Jewish leadership raises the issue of kingdom authority. Who speaks for God, Jesus or the leadership? The reaction of the Jewish leadership to Jesus in this scene shows that they got Jesus' point. What Jesus saw as vindication pointing to the support of his mission from God, they viewed as blasphemous, giving them a reason to take a political charge to Pilate."

17. J. Grassmick, "Mark," in *The Bible Knowledge Commentary: New Testament*, ed. J. F. Walvoord and R. B. Zuck, 95–197 (Wheaton, IL: SP Publications, Inc., 1983), 140. F. F. Bruce came to similar conclusions ("The Background to the Son of Man Sayings," in *Christ the Lord: Studies in Christology Presented to Donald Guthrie*, ed. H. H. Rowdon [Leicester/ Downers Grove, IL: InterVarsity, 1982]: 70):

> Jesus' special use of the expression (as distinct from its general Aramaic use in the sense of 'man', 'the man', or a possible use to replace the pronoun 'I') was derived from the 'one like a son of man' who is divinely vested with authority in Daniel 7:13f. Because it was a current title, it was not liable to be misunderstood, as current titles were, and Jesus was free to take up the expression and give it what meaning he chose.

18. One other pseudepigraphal work of possible relevance is the *Testament of Abraham*, which shows obvious reliance on Dan 7, and in which Abel (the son of Adam) is given authority to judge creation. The date of this work, however, is uncertain. Some would date it to the first half of the first century AD, but others after AD 70.

19. For a description and analysis of *4 Ezra* 13 (probably to be dated to the end of the first century AD), see J. J. Collins, "The Son of Man in First-Century Judaism," *New Testament Studies* 38 (1992): 459–66; and D. Burkett, "Son of Man in Apocalyptic and Rabbinic Texts," 102–8.

20. É. Puech, "Fragment d'une Apocalypse en Arameén (4Q246 = pseudo-Dan[d]) et le 'Royaume de Dieu,'" *Revue Biblique* 99 (1992): 98–131.

21. K. A. Kuhn, "The 'One like a Son of Man' Becomes the 'Son of God,'" *Catholic Biblical Quarterly* 69 (2007): 24. Kuhn brings forth ample evidence demonstrating that the *Aramaic Apocalypse* is dependent upon Dan 7. He states (28), for instance, "The most striking verbal parallels between Daniel 7 and the *Apocalypse* consist of the two phrases הנטלש וןטלש עלמ('whose dominion is an everlasting dominion' [Dan 7:14; cf. 4Q246 2:9]) and מלכותה מלכות עלם ('his/its kingdom will be an everlasting kingdom' [Dan 7:27; cf. 4Q246 2:5])." He goes on to conclude (30), "The nature and extent of the correspondences between these two texts indicate that the writer of the *Aramaic Apocalypse* intended to recast the Danielic 'one like a son of man' as a figure to be known by the titles 'Son of the Most High' and 'Son of God.' . . . these titles present him in the royal tradition of the Davidic kingship."

22. D. L. Bock, "Dating the *Parables of Enoch*: A *Forschungsbericht*," in *Parables of Enoch: A Paradigm Shift*, ed. D. L. Bock and J. H. Charlesworth, 58–113 (London and New York: Bloomsbury T&T Clark, 2013), 112. Bock adds, "The current state of research makes a turn of the era date for this material (from c. 40 BCE to the first half of the first century CE) the most likely setting with the period earlier in this range more likely than the later. . . . One factor that is not disputed is that there is no reference to the fall of Jerusalem in the *Parables of Enoch*. This is yet another key fact that favors an earlier date over one in the latter part of the first century CE. In summation, the likelihood is that the *Parables of Enoch* and ideas like them were in circulation at the time of the rise of the movement Jesus started." Charlesworth, in the same volume (xiii), further pointed out that many leading scholars now "judge the *Parables of Enoch* to be Jewish. They concur that the work, most likely, was composed just before, or roughly contemporaneous with, Jesus from Nazareth." For J. J. Collins, see *The Apocalyptic Imagination; An Introduction to Jewish Apocalyptic Literature*, 2nd ed. (Grand Rapids: Eerdmans, 1998), 178.

23. D. Burkett, "Son of Man in Apocalyptic and Rabbinic Texts," 98.

24. It is beyond the scope of this article to defend the early sixth-century BC dating of the book of Daniel. A recommended starting point is the excellent evangelical commentary by Stephen R. Miller (*Daniel*, The New American Commentary series [Broadman & Holman, 1994]). See the section on "Authorship and Date," 22–45. I will also have an extensive discussion on this in my forthcoming commentary on Daniel in the Evangelical Exegetical Commentary series (Bellingham, WA: Lexham Press). I would make one point in passing. Since critical scholars reject the notion of authentic prophecy, they work from the presupposition that everything written in Daniel pertains to events prior to 165 BC. A fundamental problem for their system, however, is Dan 9:26. Although they attempt to interpret this verse in light of Antiochus IV's assault on Jerusalem during the years 168–164 BC, the fact remains that Antiochus did not *destroy* Jerusalem and the temple as this verse specifically states. (The verb *šāḥaṯ* in this context certainly means "destroy," and virtually every Bible translation has rendered it this way).

25. Daniel 7:13 indicated that "one like a son of man" would come with the *clouds* (*ʿănānê*) of heaven (or the sky). There is some evidence that the element of "clouds" (*ʿănānê*) was associated with the Messiah in rabbinic tradition (*Tanḥuma Toledoth* 20 and Tg. 1Chr 3:24). Considering the cloud motif in the OT, it is not without significance that Messiah Jesus is said to appear this way. Clouds are frequently connected with theophanies in the OT (Ex 16:10; 19:9; Lv 16:2; Dt 1:33; 1Kg 8:10; Ps 104:3; Isa 19:1). The OT depicts the Lord (Yahweh) riding upon the clouds (as though His chariot), and this also hints toward the deity of the Messiah in Dan 7:13.

The NT takes up the imagery of a divine figure coming with clouds, envisioning a literal fulfillment at the time of Christ's second coming (Mt 24:30; Mk 13:26). The Matthaean passage reads, "Then the sign of the Son of Man will appear in the sky, and then all the peoples of the earth will mourn; and they will see the Son of Man coming on the clouds of heaven with power and great glory." This is something of a counterpart to His ascension, when "He was taken up as they were watching, and a cloud took Him out of their sight" (Acts 1:9).

Daniel 9:24-27

When Will Messiah Come?

KEVIN D. ZUBER

It would be difficult to exaggerate the significance of this prophecy. Many would argue that this is the key text, both for understanding the person and work of the Messiah and also for comprehending the Lord's whole unfolding program for His chosen nation, Israel. "The study of Daniel, and especially this chapter, is the key to understanding the prophetic Scriptures," wrote John F. Walvoord. He added, "the third vision of Daniel . . . provides one of the most important keys to understanding the Scriptures as a whole. In many respects, this is the high point of the book of Daniel."[1]

The book of Daniel is, roughly speaking, an alternating series of histories and prophetic dreams and visions. The histories concern the experiences of Daniel and his fellow captives in Babylon (e.g., chaps. 1, 3, 6, et. al.). The dreams (Dan 2) and visions (Dan 7, 8, 10, et. al.) have to do with the unfolding program of God for *the nations* (the pagan nations and empires that are the main concern of "world history") and *the Nation*—Israel, the people of Daniel (9:24; 12:1), "Your people [who] are called by Your name" (9:19).

After a particularly detailed and dramatic vision of a ram (Media and Persia) and a goat (Greece and the four kingdoms that arose after the death of Alexander the Great), Daniel was "exhausted" and "astounded" (8:27 NASB).[2] He was concerned to know what it all meant for his people, leading Daniel to search the Scriptures.[3] Apparently, in his search for solace and guidance Daniel discovered in the book of Jeremiah (cf. Jer. 25:11-12; 29:10-14) that the desolations (the result of the Babylonian captivity) now being inflicted on Jerusalem were to last 70 years; he further realized that those 70 years were about to be completed (9:2). This in turn led Daniel to seek the Lord in a prayer of contrition and confession to discover what was next for His people, Israel, and His city, Jerusalem (9:3,19).

In response to this prayer a divine agent[4] arrived to give Daniel "instruction" and "insight with understanding" (9:22 NASB) about the future of the nation of Israel. This is the prophecy of the 70 weeks in Dan 9:24-27.

THE INTRODUCTION TO THE PROPHECY OF THE 70 WEEKS (9:24A)

A proper understanding of this prophecy must begin with four questions or issues that arise from the very first line "Seventy weeks are decreed about your people and your holy city . . ." (9:24a). Those issues are: (1) What is the meaning of a "week?"; (2) What is the meaning of "have been decreed?"; (3) What is the significance of "seventy"; (4) Who is being referred to by the designation "your people and your holy city?"

(1) What is the meaning of a "week?" The term translated "weeks" here is *shabu'im* (lit. "sevens") and means "a unit of seven."[5] For that reason it frequently means "a week"—as in "a unit of seven days."[6] Indeed, it seems this is what it means in Dan 10:2-3. However, as Leon Wood notes, the term here is a participle, thus "be-seven-ed," or "made up of sevens"[7] which could still mean either "seven days" (i.e. a week of days) but more likely means "seven years." John C. Whitcomb, argues for the meaning "seventy weeks of years"[8] by proposing an instance "of analogous Hebrew usage." Whitcomb observes that the Hebrew word *asor* can mean "ten days"[9] but "on three occasions it does not mean 'ten days' at all, but rather 'ten strings' or 'an instrument of ten strings'" (see Pss 33:2; 92:3 [Hb. 92:4]; 144:9).[10] "Therefore, the word *asor* must mean 'decad' or 'unit of ten,' and whether it means 'ten days' or 'ten strings' must be determined entirely by the context, not by the word itself."[11] Therefore, Whitcomb suggests, just as *asor* should be taken to mean "decad" or "unit of ten," so the word *shabu'* should be understood as having "the basic meaning of 'heptad' or 'unit of seven.'"[12] The question of whether *shabu'* indicates seven days or seven years must be determined by the context. As Wood writes "it cannot mean [week of days] here, because a total of only 490 days (seventy such weeks [of days]) would be meaningless in the context."[13] In this context, "Daniel was concerned with years not days (9:2)."[14]

Furthermore, Wood points out that the "Hebrew people were familiar with the idea of weeks of years" from the sabbatical laws of Lv 25 and Dt 15.[15]

(2) What is meaning of "have been decreed?" The Hebrew term is *chatak* ("are determined" in some versions) and is found only here in the whole of the OT.[16] It has

the basic notion of "'to cut off' and from this "to decide, to determine," "to demarcate." The thought is that God had "cut off" [demarcated] "these 490 years from the rest of history through which to accomplish the deliverances needed for Israel."[17] *Decreed* thus "means divided or severed off from the whole period of world-empire in the hands of the Gentiles, as to which Daniel was already well informed. It points to a fixed and limited period, of definite duration, forming part of a longer period, the duration of which is not fixed, or at least not declared."[18]

(3) What is the significance of "seventy?" It is significant that Gabriel's message of the 70 weeks came just at the time that Daniel had discovered that Judah's captivity, which had lasted 70 years, was coming to an end. Michael Rydelnik notes that "Judah's captivity lasted 70 years because the nation had failed to keep the Sabbatical rest of the land seventy times (cf. Lv 26:34-35,43). Thus, 70 years of captivity provided the land with the 70 Sabbatical rests it had missed (2Ch 36:21)."[19] Daniel's prayer was essentially a request to know what "Your people [who] are called by You name" could expect next. (See the chart "Daniel's Vision of the 70 Weeks.")

Daniel's Vision of the 70 Weeks

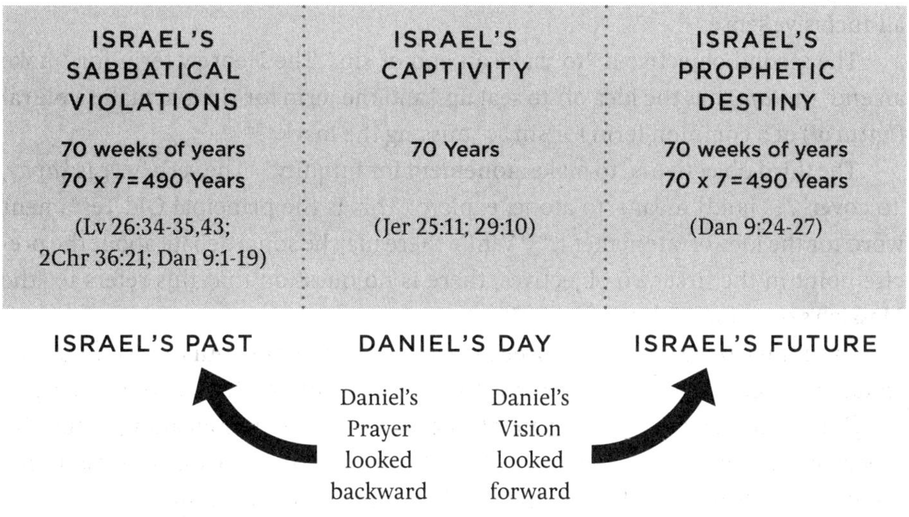

In other words, just as one 490-year period of time for Israel was ending, another 490-year period of time for the nation was prophetically revealed.[20] (4) Who is being referred to by the designation "your people and your holy city?" While some interpreters attempt to include a wider reference (including the Church)[21] it seems clear that this is a reference to Daniel's people—the Jewish people—and to the city of Jerusalem. Lang argues "The endeavor to apply this prophecy, in general or in detail, to others than Daniel's people, Israel, and Daniel's city, Jerusalem, is an outrage upon exegesis, being forbidden in advance by the express terms used."[22]

THE OVERALL SUMMARY OF THE SEVENTY WEEKS (9:24B)

Following the introductory issues is a summary of the entire period of the 70 weeks. In six infinitival phrases, Gabriel reveals that six objectives would be accomplished over the course of these 70 weeks. These six objectives are listed in two groups of three; the main concern of group one is the matter of sin ("to finish the transgression, to make an end of sin, to make atonement for iniquity" NASB) and the main concern of group two is the matter of righteousness ("to bring in everlasting righteousness, to seal up vision and prophecy, to anoint the most holy place").[23]

The first objective is "to finish the transgression." The term "to finish" is the term *kalah* "to bring to an end, to finish."[24] In the form found here (Piel) it has an intensive nuance—"to finish completely." Some take the meaning "to restrain"[25] but "it is better to understand it as the removal of sin from God's sight."[26] The term "transgression" is *h*^{e}*pesha*[27] (with the article) and "it probably refers to sin in an all-inclusive sense."[28]

The second objective is "to make an end of sin." The Hebrew term for "make an end" (*hatam*) has the idea of "to seal up," and the term for sin is actually a plural (*hatta'ot*) of a common term for sin as "missing the mark."[29]

The third objective is "to make atonement for iniquity." "The verb here is *kapar*, 'to cover' . . . [and] means 'to atone, expiate.' This is the principal Old Testament word for the idea of 'atonement.'"[30] While there may be some debate about the precise point in the first two objectives, there is no question that this refers to "the Messiah's once for all death for sin."[31]

In summarizing these first three objectives, Wood notes, "All three refer to the riddance of sin—that which brought the Israelites into their state of captivity in Babylon." "Though Christ is not mentioned in the verse, the meaning is certain, especially in view of verse twenty-six, that He would be the One making this atonement . . . It is clear that reference in these first three items is mainly to Christ's first coming, when sin was brought to an end in principle." However, "Since Gabriel was speaking primarily in reference to Jews, rather than Gentiles . . . this fact requires the interpretation to include also Christ's second coming, because only then does Israel as a nation turn to Christ (cf. Jer. 31:33, 34; Ezk. 37:23; Zch. 13:1; Rm. 11:25-27)."[32]

The fourth objective is "to bring in everlasting righteousness." The key term here is "everlasting" (*'olamim*) and has the core meaning of "long duration [in the direction of] antiquity, [or] futurity."[33] The term can have the nuance of "continuous existence" (cf. Ps 78:69 as of the earth; 148:3-6 as of the heavens). The term "righteousness" (*sedeq*)[34] denotes "a state or quality of that which accords with some recognized standard"[35] and in Scripture that standard is God Himself (cf. Isa 45:24; Jer 23:6; 33:16). The concepts "righteousness and justice" are often paired together (Isa 5:16), and both are grounded in God's holiness (*qodes*), that is, His absolute moral purity (cf. Lv 18-20) and total separation from evil (cf. Hab 1:13). Thus, the righteousness expected will be the manifestation of the very holiness of God brought to fruition on the earth in judgment on all His enemies (cf. Isa 13-23; Jer 46-51; Ezk 25-32) and blessing for God's people (cf. Isa 6–62, 66); and it will not be temporary or sporadic (as had been the case for the nation in its history of good and bad kings) but it "will be permanent."[36]

The fifth objective is "to seal up vision and prophecy." The idea of "seal up" (*hatam*) is "to affix a seal"[37] as on an official document to indicate a completed transaction (as on a deed, cf. Jer 32:10,11). Here the idea is that there will be a "seal on a book of prophecy"[38] (cf. Dan 12:4; cf. Isa 8:16) to indicate "that the prophecy was complete."[39] In other words, when these (prophetic) objectives have been fulfilled there will be a "seal affixed" to officially mark that fact.

The sixth objective is "to anoint the most holy place." The "most holy place" refers to the "holy of holies" in the Tabernacle and Temple (cf. Ex 26:33 NASB). "The phrase 'holy of holies' (*qodesh qadashim*) occurs . . . thirty-nine times in the Old Testament, always with reference to the Tabernacle or Temple or to the holy articles in them."[40] The idea of anointing would have been well known from the rituals and services of the Tabernacle (Ex 40:9; Lv 8:10). The single clear implication of this objective is that there will be (as Ezekiel certainly indicates, Ezk 38–40) a temple and a "holy of holies" to anoint—"a yet future literal, millennial temple."[41]

In sum, it seems best to understand that the first three objectives were fulfilled in principle at Christ's first coming and that all six will be fulfilled "completely for Israel by the time of the return of the Messiah and the establishment of the messianic kingdom."[42] These six objectives are in effect a summary of the entire period of the 70 weeks, and they are a survey of some (but certainly not all) of the significant details of this period.

THE SIXTY-NINE WEEKS: (9:25)

Gabriel began this portion of the revelation with an admonition to Daniel—"you are to know and discern" (NASB). This is a telling admonition for, as John Walvoord says, "The history of the interpretation of these verses is confirmation of the fact that this prophecy is difficult and requires spiritual discernment."[43] Even Daniel was encouraged to pay close attention.

Somewhat surprisingly, Gabriel revealed that the 70 weeks would be divided into three unequal portions. To begin, the divine agent noted the division of the "seven weeks and 62 weeks"; that is, there would be an initial 69 weeks which are divided into two parts. The first question to deal with is: "What is the significance of the first seven weeks (49 years)?" Most likely this span of time concerns the matter of restoring and rebuilding the city, "to restore and rebuild Jerusalem." If that is so, then the (semi-parenthetical) phrase "it will be built again, with plaza and moat" probably refers to completion of that rebuilding, and the final phrase "even in times of distress" describes the circumstances that prevailed during that entire process. If the rebuilding process is in mind here, the one recorded in the book of Nehemiah (cf. Neh 4:1–6:14; see the discussion below), then that description is an apt one.

This initial seven weeks (49 years from the "decree to restore and rebuild" to the completion of a public square and moat) is followed by another 62 weeks (434 years) that end with "Messiah the Prince." All told then, the seven weeks plus the 62 weeks yields a period of 69 weeks; taking the term "weeks" as "weeks of years" (as noted above) yields a period of years 49 years plus 434 years for a total of 483 years.

The second issue to deal with here is the meaning and significance of "Messiah the Prince." "The Hebrew term *mashiach* (Messiah) is commonly and accurately translated 'anointed.' It is used 39 times in the Hebrew Bible and often has a technical meaning commonly translated as 'the Messiah.'"[44] The term "prince" is *nagid* and literally means "leader, lead one" or "one who goes before."[45] "Both terms are applied to various leaders in the Old Testament, but here they clearly refer to Jesus the Messiah. He is the supreme Ruler and Prince [and] no one else fits the chronology in this text."[46]

The third concern to address is the timing, that is, to determine the beginning (*terminus ad quo*) and the end (*terminus ad quem*) of the 69 weeks. The 69 weeks begin with "the issuing of a decree to restore and rebuild Jerusalem" and end the time of "Messiah the Prince." Walvoord writes, "The key to the interpretation of the entire passage is found in the phrase 'from the going forth of the commandment to restore and build Jerusalem.'"[47] Determining the *terminus ad quo* "the date on which the seventy sevens begin, is obviously most important both in interpreting the prophecy and in finding suitable fulfillment."[48] Some have suggested that since the term for "decree" might also be translated "word," then this "refers to Jeremiah's prophetic word (Jer 30:18-22; 32:38-40) issued in 587 BC about Jerusalem's restoration."[49] Thus the fulfillment would most likely be Joshua the high priest in the days of Zerubbabel (c. 538). However, this is untenable because "the passages cited from Jeremiah" are better understood as referring not "to the return from captivity" but are "eschatological, looking forward to the end time restoration of Israel."[50] Also, the dates proposed simply do not add up; that is, the time between 587 BC and 538 BC cannot be calculated so as to add up to 69 (or 70) years. Some interpreters posit the starting point (*terminus ad quo*) as the decree of Cyrus the Great to rebuild the Temple, given in 538 BC.[51] But the decree Daniel has in mind is a decree to rebuild the city, Jerusalem, not the temple.[52] Another decree was issued by Artaxerxes Longimanus in 458/7 BC (cf. Ezr 7:11-26), but this decree had to do with "the restoration of the temple's utensils and permission to appoint civil leaders,"[53] and was, again, not a decree to rebuild the city, Jerusalem. Yet another decree was also issued by Artaxerxes Longimanus, this one on March 5/4, 444 BC, and that decree is referenced in Neh 2:1-8. Hoehner makes the following arguments in support of this decree as the *terminus a quo* as recorded in Neh 2:1-8:

> First, there is a direct reference to the restoration of the city (2:3, 5) and of the city gates and walls (2:3, 8). Second, Artaxerxes wrote a letter to Asaph to give materials to be used specifically for the walls (2:8). Third, the books of Nehemiah and Ezra 4:7-23 indicate that certainly the restoration of the walls was done in the most distressing circumstances, as predicted by Daniel (Dan. 9:25). Fourth, no later decrees were given by the Persian kings pertaining to the rebuilding of Jerusalem.[54]

Thus, the decree of March 5/4, 444 BC is the decree in view in Dan 9:25 and is the starting point of the first 69 weeks.

The end point (*terminus ad quem*) of the first 69 weeks is identified in the phrase "until Messiah the Prince."[55] The 69 weeks of years (483 years) if calculated by "biblical/prophetic years of 360 days each"[56] would yield 173,880 days. Starting with the decree of March 5/4, (Nisan 1) 444 BC and calculating the 173,880 days, the 69-week period ends on March 29/30, (Nisan 10), AD 33. This best fits with "the date of Jesus the Messiah's triumphal entry (Lk 19:28-40)."[57] That Dan 9:26 mentions the death of the Messiah (see below) supports this chronology, as Walvoord notes, "the best explanation of the time when the sixty-nine sevens ended is that it occurred shortly before the death of Christ anticipated in Daniel 9:26."[58]

THE TIME *AFTER* THE 69 WEEKS (9:26)

Having established the timing of the 69 weeks, the angel Gabriel revealed the climactic events that will follow. Note that the very term "after" ("*After* those 62 weeks") suggests a termination of the period (that is, *after* the 69th week) and points to a "chronologically distinct" event to follow. That is, if the end point (*terminus ad quem*) is the triumphal entry (Lk 19:28-40), then the event indicated by the words "the Messiah will be cut off and will have nothing" takes place at an indistinct time *after*, that is beyond, the 69th week. That, plus there being no mention of the 70th week at this point, indicates that there is a pause (or gap) in the strict chronology of the prophecy to this point. As Robert Culver states, "There can be no honest difference of opinion about that: the cutting off of Messiah is 'after' the sixty-two weeks. It is not the concluding event of the series of sixty-two weeks. Neither is it said to be the opening event of the 70th. It is simply after the seven plus 62 weeks."[59]

Daniel 9:26 reveals that "the Messiah will be cut off." The term here is *karat* "to cut"[60] and "is the regular OT term for the idea of 'cutting off.' It is used sometimes to express the thought of execution of a person deserving the death penalty (e.g., Lv 7:20; Ps 37:9; Prv 2:22 NASB)."[61] The expression "and will have nothing" can be rendered "and have no one," that is, the Messiah will be deserted and alone at the time of the "cutting off." There can be no question that this refers to the crucifixion of Jesus; "He was despised and forsaken of men" (Isa 53:3; cf. Mk 14:50 NASB). It may also indicate "He did not receive the Messianic kingdom at that time."[62]

The next event in this period *after* the 69th week concerns the city of Jerusalem and the Temple. The phrase "the people of the prince to come" (lit. "people of the coming prince") requires careful analysis. First, the "prince" here is not the same person as "Messiah the Prince" (Dan 9:25). This prince is yet to come, and Messiah the Prince has already come (and been cut off). The designation here indicates a prince (lit. "the prince") or leader already familiar to Daniel (and the reader), someone "who has been noted in the book earlier."[63] And, "indeed this is the case" for this one is "identified with the 'little horn' of [Dan] 7:8"[64] "also known as the beast or the antichrist."[65]

But it is not this prince who comes; rather it is "the people of the prince." Since the prince was identified (in the prophecy of Dan 7:7-8) as coming from the fourth great empire "the people of the prince" are also to be associated with this empire. This empire is none other than Rome.[66] It is "the people of the prince" who will come to "destroy the city" and not the prince himself (as Wood notes, "the subject of the verb 'will destroy' is the 'people' not the 'prince.'"[67]) The destruction is "the city and the sanctuary," referring to Jerusalem and the Temple. Viewed historically—after the triumphal entry ("until Messiah the Prince" v. 25) and after the crucifixion ("the Messiah will be cut off" v. 26)—this can refer to nothing other than the destruction of Jerusalem and the Temple in AD 70 by the Romans (the fourth empire). Since this event happened more than 40 years after the death of Jesus there can likewise be little question that there is a gap of time between the end of the 69th week (even beyond the gap noted already by the term "after" in v. 26a) and the beginning of the 70th week. Actually, there is nothing remarkable about this—those interpreters who "insert" this gap do so with contextual justification.[68] As noted, Daniel's own words require a "gap" between the end of the 69th week and the crucifixion; Daniel's description of events requires a "gap" between the crucifixion and the destruction of Jerusalem in AD 70; and Daniel's chronology from chap. 7 seen in the light Dan 9:26 requires a "gap" between the destruction of the city "by people of the coming prince" and the appearance of that "prince" in history.[69]

The final descriptive points in v. 26 indicate a swift execution of the destruction: "The end will come with a flood," referring to Jerusalem. "'Flood' or 'overflowing' can refer only to the degree of destruction meted out. History records that the destruction of Jerusalem was devastatingly extensive. [The Roman general] Titus, with four legions, brought an overflowing ruin on the city, including the Temple."[70] The angel Gabriel concluded with the note that the effects and consequences of the destruction ("desolations are determined") will extend far into the future ("even to the end there will be war"). Charles Feinberg accurately states, "The final words of verse 26 sum up the history of Israel since AD 70 . . . Surely the determined wars and desolations have come upon them (cf. Lk 21:24). Such has been the lot of Israel and the city of Jerusalem, and such will be the portion, until the 'time of the Gentiles' have been fulfilled."[71]

THE 70TH WEEK (9:27)

God's messenger Gabriel then turned Daniel's attention to the final, 70th week. Although not specifically identified as such, the "week" mentioned here must be the 70th week. As Wood notes, "The special significance of the seventieth week . . . is treated separately from the first sixty-nine and its content is examined in a manner different from them."[72] The prophecy reveals that the events in view will take place during "one week." Although nothing is revealed about the first half of the week, something significant will happen in the "middle of the week" that is, after the first three and a half years of this last week. As far as matters of timing are concerned, this corresponds to the timing Daniel noted in respect to the actions of the "little horn" of the fourth empire in Dan 7:25. This unique and boastful leader ("different from the previous ones," Dan 7:24) will "speak out against the Most High and wear down the saints of the Highest One" for "time, times and half a time," (Dan 7:25). In another text, Daniel writes that the distress of Daniel's people will be for "a time, times and half a time," according to the man dressed in linen (Dan 12:7; cf. Rev 12:14). The expression "time, times, and half a time" refers to period of three and a half years[73] which, as noted, corresponds to one half of the final seven-year "seventieth week." Other eschatological texts refer to this chronology; for example, the two witnesses will prophesy for 1,260 days, which is three and a half years (Rev 11:3; cf. 12:6), and the nations will tread underfoot the holy city for 42 months, also a period of three and a half years (Rev 11:2), and the beast will have authority for 42 months (Rev 13:5). Clearly, a great deal will happen in this 70th week.

The key to understanding Gabriel's prophecy is the identity of "he" in Dan 9:27. There are only two possible antecedents for this pronoun: Messiah the Prince (v. 25) or the "prince who is to come" (v. 26). Rydelnik notes, "Although some consider this prince to be Christ, establishing a new covenant and [therefore] ending the OT sacrificial system, it is inconceivable that Messiah would be the one who would commit the abomination of desolation."[74] Nor did Jesus the Messiah make a "firm covenant" as such with the people.[75] Nothing in Jesus' earthly life corresponds to the timing of "one week," however, (as noted above) this chronology fits quite well with that of the "little horn" of chap. 7. And finally, applying the rule of grammar that says the nearest antecedent (proper noun) of a personal pronoun is to be preferred, the "he" of v. 27 should be understood as referring to "the prince who is to come."[76,77] Furthermore, "the firm covenant" to be made is yet future ("he will make"), and so is the revelation of the personal identity of the "he" who makes this covenant. Thus the "he" of v. 27 should be understood as the same individual identified as the "little horn" of Dan 7, and it is this "he" who will break that covenant in the middle of the week. In short, the "he" of (9:27) is the "prince who is to come," and he is the Antichrist.[78]

Apparently, the "prince who is to come," makes "a firm covenant" during the first half of the 70th week. The nature of this covenant is not directly indicated, but it may be inferred that it granted "the many" the safety and privileges that made the practice and ritual of the "sacrifices" and offerings possible. This is likely not a "renewed" covenant but a new one "made at this time for the first time . . . and probably will concern some type of nonaggression treaty."[79] The identity of "the many" is not made explicit and may mean "the leadership of Israel"[80] or simply "the Jewish people."[81] Since the entire revelation concerns "your people and your holy city" (Dan 9:24) and since leaders make treaties for the nation and its population, it seems better to affirm that "the many" refers to the nation as a whole. Regardless, the making of this covenant marks the beginning of this final seven-year period (the 70th week).

The significant event that happens in the middle (*ḥᵉsi* "half") of the week is twofold: (a) the Antichrist will "put a stop to sacrifice and grain offering," and (b) he will commit an act known as the "abomination of desolation," that is, there will be an "abomination" set up by "one who makes desolate" (NASB). Fairly obvious is that if the Temple was destroyed in AD 70 (v. 26) but then at a future time "sacrifice and grain offering" are halted by the Antichrist and such an "abomination" is possible, then at some future point the Temple must be rebuilt. Of course, this is exactly what other Scriptures such as Ezk 40–43 reveal. As Wood says, "The words for will 'sacrifice' (*zebah*) and 'offering' (*minhah*) are the regular Old Testament words for these concepts."[82] Thus, in some sense completely commensurate with the Old Testament practice, these words indicate that Temple worship will be revived.[83]

Accompanying this action of causing the sacrifices to cease is "the overspreading of abominations of desolation."[84] The term for "overspreading" (NASB "wing") is *kᵉnap*, from the root *kanap* "to cover over." In Isa 8:8, it definitely has the idea of "overspreading" in a destructive sense.[85] The term "abominations" (*shiqqutsim*) refers to "things detestable," especially with respect to false worship. The term for "desolation" (*shamen*) has the idea of "deserted, lay waste."[86] Taken as a whole, the phrase pictures an act or actions by the Antichrist that spread a scene of destruction and waste over the Temple, probably by some act of idolatrous worship.

The end will come when the appointed judgment ("decreed destruction") is "poured out on the desolator." This is a general description of the events that will take place in the second half of the 70th week.

CONCLUSION

The sweep of this prophecy is staggering, and the implications are considerable. For those who deny the possibility of predictive prophecy or of literal fulfillment of the same, this passage presents an insurmountable problem. The timing and details of this prophecy concerning the first 69 weeks and the events that were to take place immediately after those weeks—namely the earthly (physical) advent and atoning death of Messiah the Prince, and the Roman destruction of the city of Jerusalem and its Temple in AD 70—have been so clearly and utterly fulfilled in Jesus Christ and in the historical record of the first century AD. So to deny a literal and complete fulfillment of the prophecy of the 70th week (v. 27) is to abandon all pretense to "literal interpretation" of the Scriptures. But if taken in a literal way, this prophecy makes it clear that what the Lord intends "for His city and His people"—for Jerusalem and the Jewish people—while ultimately glorious, will include a time of serious adversity and suffering, a time of "Jacob's trouble" (Jer 30:7 KJV).

---

1. J. F. Walvoord, *Daniel: Key to Prophetic Revelation* (Chicago: Moody Press, 1989), 201; A. J. McClain adds, "Probably no single prophetic utterance is more crucial in the fields of Biblical Interpretation, Apologetics, and Eschatology" (*Daniel's Prophecy of the 70 Weeks* [Grand Rapids: Zondervan, 1969], 9).

2. Of particular interest in that vision is the king ("insolent and skilled in intrigue") mentioned in 8:23-25. This is a prophecy with a literal "near" fulfillment and a deliberate typological meaning that will be fulfilled in the distant

future. The "near" was Antiochus Epiphanes IV (see 8:9, "little horn") and the antetype will be the Antichrist (see 9:27). See M. Rydelnik, "Daniel," *The Moody Bible Commentary* (Chicago: Moody Publishers, 2014), 1302.

3. "Although the book of Jeremiah the prophet was completed only a generation before the events described in Dan 9, Daniel already recognized it as Scripture or 'the word of the LORD.'" Rydelnik, "Daniel," 1303.
4. Daniel notes that it was "Gabriel, the man" who brought this prophecy (9:21). Gabriel is the divine agent who was sent with the interpretation of Daniel's vision of the Ram and Goat in chap. 8 (8:16). There he was identified as "someone who appeared to be a man" (8:15), and here the term for "man" is "mighty man." Gabriel is clearly identified as an angel in Lk 1:19,26.
5. See F. Brown, S. R. Driver, and C. A. Briggs, *Hebrew and English Lexicon of the Old Testament* (Oxford: Oxford University Press, 1906), 797, 988–89; W. L. Holladay, *A Concise Hebrew and Aramaic Lexicon of the Old Testament* (Grand Rapids: Eerdmans, 1971), 358; Koehler-Baumgartner, *Lexicon in Veteris Testament Libros*, 940.
6. L. Wood, *A Commentary on Daniel*, (Grand Rapids: Zondervan, 1973), 247.
7. Ibid.
8. J. C. Whitcomb, "Daniel's Great Seventy-Weeks Prophecy: An Exegetical Insight," *Grace Theological Journal* 2:2: Fall 1981: 259–63.
9. Indeed, "that is its correct translation in thirteen out of the sixteen times it appears in the Old Testament" (See Gn 24:55; Ex 12:3; Lv 16:29; 23:27; 25:9; Nm 29:7; Jos 4:19; 2Kg 25:1; Jer 52:4,12; Ezk 20:1; 24:1; 40:1).
10. Ibid., 260.
11. Ibid., cf. Brown, Driver, Briggs, *Hebrew and English Lexicon*, 797; W. L. Holladay, *Hebrew and Aramaic Lexicon*, 285.
12. Ibid., 261.
13. Wood, *Commentary on Daniel*, 247. Whitcomb also observes that the use of *shabu'* is found in three instances (Ezk 45:21; Dn 10:2,3) with the term *yamim* ("days") as though to imply that *shabu'* by itself was not sufficient to show that a period of seven days was intended. The most interesting point, however, is that two of these three combinations . . . appear in the second and third verses of Dan 10 immediately following the 70 weeks prophecy of the preceding chapter, as though to warn the reader that *shabu'* is now being used in a different sense! (Whitcomb, "Daniel's Great Seventy-Weeks Prophecy," 261).
14. Rydelnik, "Daniel," 1305.
15. Wood, *Commentary on Daniel*, 247.
16. Ibid., 248.
17. Ibid.
18. G. H. Lang, *The Histories and Prophecies of Daniel*, (Miami Springs, FL: Conley and Schoettle Publishing, 1985), 127.
19. Rydelnik, "Daniel," 1305.
20. There is no reason to suggest, as some have (cf. E. J. Young, *The Prophecy of Daniel* [Grand Rapids: Eerdmans, 1949], 196; C. F. Keil, trans. M. G. Easton, *Biblical Commentary on the Book of Daniel* [Grand Rapids: Eerdmans, repr. 1975], 339) that the numbers here refer to "an intentionally indefinite designation of a period of time." Wood asks simply, "Why would definite numbers be applied to indefinite periods of lengths [of time]? Wood, *Commentary on Daniel*, 247. The consideration of the significance of the number 70 should be enough to conclude that "it is more likely that the 70 weeks also refer to a literal number" (Rydelnik, "Daniel," 1305).
21. It seems Young obliquely tries to include the church by use of the phrase "the true people of God" (*The Prophecy of Daniel* [Grand Rapids: Eerdmans, 1949], 197).
22. Lang, *The Histories and Prophecies of Daniel*, 130.
23. "The six items divide themselves into two groups. The first three are negative in force, speaking of undesirable factors to be removed; and the last three are positive, giving desirable factors to be effected." Wood, *Commentary on Daniel*, 248.
24. Brown, Driver, Briggs, *Hebrew and English Lexicon*, 478.
25. So Wood, *Commentary on Daniel*, 248.
26. C. L. Feinberg, *A Commentary on Daniel* (Winona Lake, IN: BMH Books, 1981), 127.
27. Brown, Driver, Briggs, *Hebrew and English Lexicon*, 833.
28. Wood, *Commentary on Daniel*, 248. Some take the "definiteness" of the transgression ("*the* transgression"; "The article in Hebrew, as in Greek, is very definite and points clearly to some outstanding thing or object." [David L. Cooper, *Messiah: His First Coming Scheduled*, (Los Angeles: Biblical Research Society, 1939), 371]) The specific transgression refers to "Israel's history of rebellion against God" (Rydelnik, "Daniel," 1305).

29. Wood, *Commentary on Daniel*, 249.

30. Ibid.

31. Rydelnik, "Daniel," 1305. "In the parallel section to follow, Christ is described as being 'cut off' (v. 26), a clear reference to His crucifixion, when atonement for sin was made." Wood, *Commentary on Daniel*, 249.

32. Wood, *Commentary on Daniel*, 249.

33. Brown, Driver, Briggs, *Hebrew and English Lexicon*, 761–62. Daniel 9:24 is noted as a plural intensive with the specific sense of "everlastingness, or eternity."

34. Ibid., 841.

35. W. D. Mounce, "Righteous, Righteousness," *Mounce's Complete Expository Dictionary* (Grand Rapids: Zondervan, 2006), 593.

36. Wood, *Commentary on Daniel*, 249.

37. Brown, Driver, Briggs, *Hebrew and English Lexicon*, 367.

38. Ibid., 367.

39. Feinberg, *A Commentary on Daniel*, 128.

40. Wood, *Commentary on Daniel*, 250. "In view of these matters, it is highly likely that the phrase refers to the Temple also here, which, in view of the context, must be a future Temple; and, since the phrase is used without the article, reference must be to a complex of that Temple, rather than its most holy place."

41. Rydelnik, "Daniel," 1305.

42. Ibid.

43. Walvoord, *Daniel: Key to Prophetic Revelation*, 224.

44. Rydelnik, "Daniel," 1305; "Throughout the history of interpretation [of this verse], overwhelmingly, the Church has understood '*maschiach nagid*' to refer to the Messiah the Prince."

45. Wood, *Commentary on Daniel*, 251.

46. Ibid.

47. Walvoord, *Daniel: Key to Prophetic Revelation*, 224.

48. Ibid.

49. Rydelnik, "Daniel," 1306. See Marvin C. Pate and Calvin B. Haines, Jr., *Doomsday Delusions: What's Wrong with Predictions About the End of the World* (Downers Grove, IL: InterVarsity, 1995), 72–73.

50. Ibid.

51. See K. Riddlebarger, *A Case for Amillennialism* (Grand Rapids: Baker Books, 2003), 152–53; cf. Wood, *Commentary on Daniel*, 253; cf. Walvoord, *Daniel: Key to Prophetic Revelation*, 225.

52. "Cyrus's edict refers to the rebuilding of the temple and not to the city." H. W. Hoehner, *Chronological Aspects of the Life of Christ* (Grand Rapids: Zondervan, 1977), Kindle edition; print edition, 115–39.

53. Rydelnik, "Daniel," 1306.

54. Hoehner, *Chronological Aspects of the Life of Christ*, 126.

55. In determining the *terminus ad quem* of Dan 9:25 many scholars rely on the work of Hoehner cited above and Sir Robert Anderson, *The Coming Prince*, 10th ed. (Grand Rapids: Kregel, 1957).

56. Rydelnik, "Daniel," 1306.

57. Ibid.

58. Walvoord, *Daniel: Key to Prophetic Revelation*, 228, 229 "the Messiah will be living at the end of the sixty-ninth seven and will be cut off, or die, soon after the end of it."

59. R. D. Culver, *Daniel and the Latter Days* (Chicago: Moody Press, 1977), 157.

60. This term is often found in the phrase *karat berith*, "to cut a covenant" (see for instance Gn 15 where the making of a covenant involved some physical cutting). Its use here may be a subtle reference to the death of Jesus as covenant sacrifice (see Lk 22:20).

61. Wood, *Commentary on Daniel*, 255.

62. C. L. Feinberg, *Daniel: The Man and His Visions* (Chappaqua, NY: Christian Herald Books, 1981), 132.

63. Ibid., 256.

64. Ibid.

65. Rydelnik, "Daniel," 1307.

66. Ibid., 1298, 1307.

67. Wood, *Commentary on Daniel*, 255.

68. Contra Riddlebarger, who argues that there is no contextual justification for seeing a gap here in *A Case for Amillennialism*, 153.

69. Other OT prophecies require a "gap" in time; see Zch 9:9-10 and Isa 61:1-2 with Lk 4:18-19.

70. Wood, *Commentary on Daniel*, 256.

71. Feinberg, *Daniel: The Man and His Visions*, 133. For an excellent history of the wars and devastation of Jerusalem, see Simon Sebag Montefiore, *Jerusalem: The Biography* (New York: Vintage Books, 2012).

72. Wood, *Commentary on Daniel*, 260.

73. Rydelnik, "Daniel," 1300.

74. Ibid., 1307.

75. Wood, *Commentary on Daniel*, 257.

76. See Feinberg, *A Commentary on Daniel*, 134. "Logically and grammatically the 'he' of v. 27 must refer to 'the prince who is to come' of v. 26."

77. Culver explains that "If the pronoun "he" were present in the Hebrew, a case might possibly be made for the introduction of an entirely new personality into the story at this point. However, there is no pronoun; only the third masculine singular form of the verb indicates that an antecedent is to be sought, and that of necessity in the preceding context. Usually, the last preceding noun that agrees in gender and number and agrees with the sense is the antecedent. This is unquestionably . . . "the coming prince" of v. 26. He is a "coming" prince, that is, one whom the reader would already know as a prince to come, because he is the same as the "little horn" on the fourth beast of chap. 7 (Culver, *Daniel and the Latter Days*, 161–62).

78. Some have identified this "he" with Antiochus Epiphanes, who committed a heinous act of sacrilege in the temple (cf. 1 Macc 1:45-54) identified as an "abomination of desolation" (cf. Dan 11:31; 12:9). But the chronology will not allow that act as fulfillment of this prophecy. Furthermore, Jesus mentioned the "abomination that causes desolation, spoken of by the prophet Daniel" as something yet future from His day (Mt 24:15). See Rydelnik, "Daniel," 1307–08.

79. Wood, *Commentary on Daniel*, 259.

80. Rydelnik, "Daniel," 1307.

81. Wood, *Commentary on Daniel*, 261.

82. Wood, *Commentary on Daniel*, 261.

83. See John C. Whitcomb, "Christ's Atonement and Animal Sacrifices in Israel," Grace Theological Journal 6.2 (1985), 201–217.

84. Rendering of Wood, *Commentary on Daniel*, 261.

85. Ibid.

86. Mounce, "Desolate, (Be) Desolate," *Expository Dictionary*, 174.

Hosea 3:4-5

Israel's Present Estrangement and Future Restoration

DAVID FINKBEINER

The book of Hosea is best known for the gut-wrenching account of the prophet's relationship with his wife, Gomer. The account itself actually takes up only the first three of Hosea's 14 chapters. Yet it introduces themes that figure prominently throughout the whole book. In particular, Hosea's relationship with Gomer presents a powerful picture of the painful relationship between the Lord and His people Israel. While Israel (like Gomer) proves to be unfaithful to the Lord, God unfailingly demonstrates His longsuffering love toward her. The account ends in Hos 3:4-5 with the prediction of a temporary period of national suspension followed by a glorious restitution of the relationship when Israel returns to the Lord and to "David their King." This text is a messianic prediction yet to be fulfilled by the Messiah Jesus.

BACKGROUND

Hosea 1:1 provides important historical background for the book. It indicates that Hosea prophesied when the Jewish people were divided into two nations, the northern kingdom of Israel and the southern kingdom of Judah. In particular, Hosea prophesied during the reigns of Uzziah, Jotham, Ahaz, and Hezekiah in Judah, who together reigned from about 792–686 BC. The verse also says that he prophesied during the reign of Jeroboam II in Israel, who reigned from about

793–753 BC.[1] This information suggests that Hosea's ministry lasted from late in the reign of Israel's Jeroboam II until early in the reign of Judah's Hezekiah, or roughly 755–715 BC.

Although Hosea addresses Judah as well, his message focuses on Israel, whose national life displayed dramatic decline during Hosea's ministry. Jeroboam II was a successful king militarily and economically, and Israel prospered during his reign; but this success was short-lived. In the 30 years after Jeroboam II's death (753–723 BC), Israel experienced political, military, and economic upheaval during the unsuccessful reigns of the next (and last) six kings of Israel, culminating in Israel's destruction by Assyria in 722 BC. Hosea's message throughout his career reflects these changing times in Israel, as the "complacency of the early days (2:7, 10, 15 [2:5, 8, 13]) gives way to a desperation in foreign (7:8–12; 12:1) and domestic (7:3–7; 13:10–11) affairs, evidenced in the latter chapters."[2]

There is a startling omission in the list of kings mentioned in Hos 1:1 that might suggest the importance of the Davidic line for Israel's future. While Hosea includes all of the kings of Judah who reigned during his prophetic ministry, he fails to mention any of Jeroboam II's six hapless successors in the northern kingdom. This is surprising because Hosea prophesied primarily to Israel during the 30 years after Jeroboam II's death. This puzzling omission might be explained in part by the possibility that Hosea considered Jeroboam the last legitimate king of Israel. But more significantly in light of Hos 3:5, this omission may well suggest that Hosea saw Israel's future hope as being tied directly to the Davidic dynasty in Judah,[3] particularly David's greater Son, the Messiah.

THE BROADER CONTEXT

Since Hos 3 concludes the narrative that begins in chap. 1, there are several features of chaps. 1–3 to consider in order to understand the context of Hos 3:4-5. First, some have argued that the Hosea-Gomer narrative is simply an allegory, but this is unlikely. The details of the account (e.g., the price paid for Gomer in 3:2) and Hosea's first-person account of his actions in 3:1-3 suggest rather that these events really did happen in Hosea's life. They are an "enacted prophecy" in which Hosea, at God's command, lives out what the Lord is experiencing with Israel.[4]

Second, regarding the structure of chaps. 1–3, they can be divided into three sections roughly corresponding to the chapter divisions. The first section (1:2–2:1) focuses primarily on the children, whose names symbolize Israel's coming judgment. The second section (2:2-23) focuses primarily on the unfaithful wife (Israel in particular). The third section (3:1-5) primarily focuses on the faithful husband

(Hosea/God). Whereas the second section is made up of a judgment oracle (almost in the form of a legal divorce proceeding) followed by a prophecy of future restoration, the first and third sections are primarily narrative in form, as they draw a direct parallel between Hosea's family and God's relationship to Israel.[5] Although the first section account is related in third person, and the third section in first person, they are parallel in terms of structure. In both sections, God gives a command to Hosea, he obeys, and the Lord then explains the significance of the action for His relationship with Israel. All three sections share the themes of coming judgment on Israel followed by a promise of future restoration, a pattern that is exhibited throughout the whole book.[6]

Third, the relationship between the third section and the first two must be clarified. Some have argued that the account in 3:1-2 simply restates the account in the first section. Others claim that the woman Hosea is commanded to love in 3:1 is not Gomer but another woman whom he takes into his home subsequent to his relationship with Gomer. Neither view is convincing from the text.[7] Most likely, the third section continues the account of Hosea's relationship with Gomer and chronologically follows the material in sections 1–2.

The First Section (Hosea 1:2–2:1)

The Hosea-Gomer narrative could therefore best be summarized as follows:[8] God commanded Hosea to take "a promiscuous wife" and to "have children of promiscuity" (1:2). In obedience, he took Gomer as his wife (1:3). Most likely, she was already promiscuous before they married.[9] Hosea thus took on a marriage that parallels God's marriage (covenant) to unfaithful Israel (1:2).

After their marriage, Gomer had three children who are characterized as "children of promiscuity" (1:2). They are probably given this designation because they bear the stigma of their mother's promiscuity.[10] After each child is born, God gives each of them names that signify judgment on Israel. The first child's name is "Jezreel" (God sows)—the name of a valley and a town within that valley. It marks the place where Jeroboam II's ancestor Jehu came to power after he overthrew and destroyed Ahab's dynasty, as well as other violent events in Israel's history. Thus, it refers to a place where God has sown judgment. In a similar way, Jeroboam's dynasty and Israel's military power will be judged/destroyed in the same valley.[11]

The name of the second child, "No Compassion," indicates that God will not show mercy to Israel, which will be destroyed at the hands of the Assyrians, unlike Judah, whom He will mercifully preserve from Assyrian destruction. The third child's name, "Not My People," is particularly striking. The term "my people" is often an expression of endearment and relationship, appearing almost 20 times in the book of Exodus alone. This is not an abrogation of God's faithfulness of His covenant (Ex 6:7; Ps 89:30-37), but an expression of a broken relationship based on the unfaithfulness of His people. God's covenant with Israel has been estranged—but not forever.

In a pattern typical of Hosea, a word of judgment is followed by a word of hope. In 1:10–2:1, God makes clear that there will be a restoration of Israel. Indeed, Israel will be reconciled to God, will grow in population and prosperity, and will be united with Judah. Of particular interest is the claim that Israel/Judah "will appoint for themselves a single ruler." The identity of this one leader is given greater clarity in 3:5: He is the great Davidic King, the Messiah. It is noteworthy that the restored people themselves "appoint" Him, suggesting that the Messiah receives their full support.[12] All this demonstrates a dramatic reversal of the judgment predicted in the names of Hosea's three children (1:11-2:1).

The Second Section (Hosea 2:2-23)

The judgment-hope pattern is repeated in the two major oracles of Hos 2:2-23. The first oracle (2:2-13) presents God's indictment against His wayward wife Israel. Because of her repeated idolatries, God will bring judgment on the nation as a whole (the wife) and her children (individual Israelites). Hosea and Gomer are not explicitly mentioned in this whole section; the Hosea-Gomer narrative does not explicitly resume until 3:1-3. There is, therefore, some question about how closely Israel's adultery parallels Gomer's. Given Gomer's situation in chap. 3, it is likely Gomer's behavior is roughly similar to Israel's in chap. 2. That is, she likely left her husband to pursue adulterous relationships with other lovers, who left her in dire straits.

The second oracle in chap. 2 (2:14-23) expresses hope for future Israel. The Lord will renew His love for Israel and restore His marriage with Israel, and they will return to Him and be restored to prosperity and peace in the land. It is this promise of a renewed marriage that sets the stage for the resumption of the Hosea-Gomer narrative in the third section, chap. 3.

The Immediate Context (Hosea 3:1-3)

Since the messianic text in 3:4-5 is directly tied to the Hosea-Gomer narrative in 3:1-3, it is essential to consider carefully these verses in the immediate context. In 3:1a, God issues another command to Hosea. He tells him to renew his love for Gomer. It is true that Gomer is not named specifically here, and some think that Hosea is commanded to love another woman after Gomer has passed off the scene.[13] But it is far more likely that this woman is Gomer and that this text continues the Hosea-Gomer narrative. After all, Hosea is told to love this unnamed woman "again,"[14] and she is described as a woman who is loved by another man[15] and who is an adulteress. In the context of the larger narrative, such descriptions can only fit Gomer. Perhaps the text omits the use of her name to indicate that she has lost her status as Hosea's wife because of her infidelity, just as Israel has lost her status as "My people" because of her infidelity (cf. 1:8).[16] In any case, her wayward ways have clearly left her in a degrading position, as v. 2 makes clear.

The Lord explains the significance of His command in 3:1b, "just as the Lord loves the Israelites" though they were unfaithful to Him. Hosea's love to Gomer parallels God's loving covenant faithfulness to Israel, and like Gomer, Israel does not deserve such love. Instead, the faithless Israelites "turn to other gods and love raisin cakes." While there was nothing inherently immoral about eating raisin cakes (cf. 2Sm 6:19), they were often associated with pagan worship (Jer 7:18; 44:19). Clearly in this context, their love of raisin cakes indicates more broadly their love of pagan worship and the false gods who are the objects of that worship.

Hosea obeys God's command. In a terse account in 3:2, Hosea specifies what it meant for him to love her again: he had to buy her for himself. This clearly indicates that she had sunk to new lows, but what exactly was her situation? It is possible that her waywardness had left her in significant debt and that Hosea had to pay it to free her of the resulting legal entanglements; but the account details suggest a situation that was far worse. The price for her was "15 shekels of silver and five bushels of barley," the equivalent of the price of a slave in Israel (30 silver shekels according to Ex 21:32). This implies that she may well have been enslaved, quite likely as a prostitute.[17] Buying her out of her dire circumstances was costly for Hosea, and paying half the price in food might indicate that collecting the funds for the purchase stretched his resources.

Whatever the exact nature of her situation, Hosea returned her to his home and issued a set of parameters for her in 3:3. These parameters are important as they parallel the prediction for Israel in 3:4-5, but their exact sense is disputed. There are several significant features of these parameters, the first being that they pertain for "many days." This suggests a long, unspecified period of time but not a permanent situation; eventually, these strictures will end. Second, the first clause is captured best by the ESV: "you must dwell as mine." This indicates that she will be brought back to live in his home, segregated from her former way of life and from further opportunities to wander. In addition, it suggests that she belongs to him. "She was his not only by right of marriage but also by right of purchase."[18] Third, she must become completely celibate. He tells her, "Do not be promiscuous or belong to any man." This obviously involves all illicit sexual relations (a stricture that will, of course, never end) but likely also includes sexual relations with Hosea himself.

The fourth feature of v. 3, the last clause of the verse, is difficult. Translated more literally, the clause says, "and I also to you." Many would argue that the clause makes explicit what was implied in the previous clause, that Hosea would not have sexual relations with her for a time (as in the HCSB). While this understanding certainly has much to commend it, the context would slightly favor an alternate translation, such as, "Then indeed I will be yours."[19] That is, Hosea anticipates the end of the time of celibacy for both of them, when they will resume normal sexual relations and experience a full restoration of their marriage covenant. This would anticipate the future restoration of Israel described in 3:5 and a reversal of 1:9.

A final feature of this verse has to do with the rationale for these strictures. Why does Hosea love Gomer again, buy her out of slavery and prostitution, and bring her home, but then not restore her fully in their marriage relationship for "many days?" In part, wisdom would dictate that Gomer would need time to transition from her former lifestyle into a faithful wife, and these restrictions would protect her from sinful patterns, turn her heart to Hosea, and fully restore the marriage.[20] But even more significantly, these strictures picture God's plan for Israel in preparation for the coming of Messiah, as seen in the next two verses, the key messianic aspect of this section.

THE MESSIANIC TEXT: HOSEA 3:4-5

Picking up on the immediate context, 3:4 begins with "For" (*ki*), signaling the symbolic significance of Hosea's stipulations for Gomer. Like Gomer, Israel also "must live many days without" (ESV) several privileges and taboos. And as with Gomer, such disciplinary limitations are intended to purge Israel of idolatry and prepare her for full reconciliation with the Lord. Just how long these restrictions will pertain is unspecified, but it will be for an indefinitely long period of time, not removed until "the last days"—an eschatological term frequently used by the prophets (3:5).

What are these limitations and to whom do they apply? The passage lists six items that "the Israelites" will go without. It should be understood that "Israelites" here is a broader term than the northern kingdom, but includes both Israel and Judah as the term was used prior to the division of the kingdom (930 BC). These are broad and specific restrictions, some related to government and civil functions, others to worship and institutional religious life. As regards government, Israel will dwell "without king or prince." The monarchy, for a time, will be discontinued, as will the officials associated with the monarchy. The term *sar*, translated "princes," is likely not restricted to royal sons but could include government officials and military leaders working for the king.[21] While the right kind of king could be a blessing to his people, all too often in Israel's history Israel was tempted to put her hopes in her kings rather than in the Lord, or worse still, follow her kings into idolatry. This is why, with the exception of the coming Davidic King, Hosea tended to view Israel's kings and their administrations as generally corrupt[22] and therefore predicted their removal by God (cf. 7:16; 10:3,7; 13:10-11). For most of Israel's subsequent history, this loss of the monarchy was accompanied by military defeat and loss of national sovereignty.

Key features of Israel's religious life will also be removed. Some of these features are clearly associated with pagan worship, others more ambiguously could include worship of Yahweh. Like Gomer, who would abstain from sexual relations both with her lovers and her husband, Israelites also would experience the cessation of key institutions in their religious life, both pagan and Yahwistic. A "sacrifice" could be made to pagan deities, like Baal, or legitimately to Yahweh, although even in the latter case it could be corrupted when offered away from the Temple or with a rebellious heart (Hos 6:6; 8:11-13;1Sm 15:22). Although Jacob legitimately made use of a stone "sacred pillar" to honor the Lord, they were later banned in the law (Lv 26:1; Dt 16:22), since they were associated with Canaanite worship and, later still, with Baal worship (2Kg 10:26-27; 17:10; cf. Hos 10:1). The "ephod" was part of the priest's garments (Ex 28), often used in connection with discerning God's will. But its use could also be corrupted into false worship and pagan divination (Jdg 8:24-28; 17:5; 18:14-20), especially when paired as it is here with "household idols,"[23] which are unequivocally idolatrous.

Taken together, these elements in v. 4 picture a time when Israel will no longer have a monarchy or temple service and priesthood, but she will also no longer worship idols. "Today the people of Israel have no king, they do not practice idolatry, and they no longer observe the Levitical institution of sacrifices. The prophet had no basis on which to prognosticate these things in the day in which he lived. It is a remarkable prediction"[24]—a prediction that has been in the process of fulfillment since idolatry ceased in Israel with the Babylonian captivity in 586 BC, and temple sacrifice ended with the Roman destruction of Jerusalem in AD 70.

But as with Gomer, v. 5 indicates these restrictions are not permanent for Israel. The term "afterwards" suggests that the time of deprivation for the people of Israel is only temporary, even if quite prolonged. Indeed, Israel's deprivation will continue until "the last days." Hosea uses this phrase, as do other contemporary prophets (cf. Isa 2:2; Mic 4:1), to point to a future time when Israel is restored, as predicted in Dt 4:30. Given the nature of this restoration, it is something that has yet to happen, awaiting the eschaton, "the last days."[25]

When the time is complete, what will this restoration of Israel look like? It has three features. First, "the people of Israel will return and seek the LORD their God." Working together, these two verbs here indicate genuine, heartfelt repentance and renewed commitment to the Lord (cf. 7:10). Too often Israel has turned *from* the Lord to seek false gods (7:16; 2:7; 11:2) and refused to turn back to seek Him with genuine commitment (5:5-7; 7:10).[26] This results in exile away from their land (8:13-14; cf. 9:3; 11:5). The "return," therefore, involves both spiritual and physical restoration from exile (cf. 11:10-11) so that the Lord will receive them (11:1-11). The language here directly parallels what is predicted in Dt 4:27-31.

Second, Israel will also return and seek "David their king." This is a direct messianic prediction. By referring to him as David, the text is not predicting a literal resurrection of David himself to rule Israel.[27] It is instead affirming that He is of the royal line of David (as in 1Kg 12:16), the legitimate heir to the Davidic throne and rightful king of all Israel. He is the "single ruler" (Hos 1:11) who will unite all "the people of Israel" (Hos 3:5), both northern and southern kingdoms. "Hosea connected Yahweh's future victory to the renascence of Davidic rule. For Hosea, the return to Yahweh carried with it the reversal of all that Jeroboam's splitting of the kingdom had wrought. The spiritual return and the national reunion were connected—a reminder that the OT sees Israel as a flesh-and-blood entity whose loyalty to Yahweh is lived not in an otherworldly realm but in the real economics, politics, and geography of history."[28]

Perhaps even more striking, the Messiah is closely tied to "the Lord their God." The close connection between the rule of the Lord and of His anointed is seen elsewhere in the OT (e.g., Ps 2:2; Jer 30:9),[29] but what is noteworthy here is that Israel will actually commit themselves to full loyalty *both* to the Lord *and* to this new David.[30] This suggests that he is more than a mere scion of David, but David's greater Son the Messiah,[31] one deserving of a loyalty similar to that of the Lord Himself! When seen in light of Hosea's message calling for Israel's exclusive covenant loyalty to the Lord *alone* (as in a marriage relationship), this statement is indeed striking as well as significant.

Third, in returning to the Lord, Israel "will come with awe to the LORD and to His goodness" (v. 5). Israel's attitude of arrogance and disrespect toward the Lord is gone (cf. Israel's attitude in 5:5-6) and replaced with a proper reverential awe, displayed by their trembling. Yet their trepidation does not cause them to withdraw from Him, but to seek Him nonetheless. What they will find is not rejection or wrath but rather Him and "His goodness." The Lord's goodness here is His kindness to them expressed concretely in bringing them covenant blessings, such as those displayed so vividly in 2:14-23. Israel therefore experiences "not only a recovery of fellowship with Yahweh but the restoration of all his generosity in the produce of the land which Israel's foolishness credited to the Baals," as in 2:5.[32]

Israel's final restoration, then, will involve a complete national and spiritual renewal, resulting in great blessing. All of this will happen only in connection with the coming Messiah in the "last days."

HOSEA 3:4-5 IN THE THEOLOGY OF HOSEA

In context, Hos 3:4-5 reinforces Hosea's theology in his book as a whole. The pattern of Israel's spiritual unfaithfulness, God's judgment, and Israel's ultimate repentance and restoration, depicted so vividly in chaps. 1-3, is repeated in the book. Of note is 11:1-11. Here Israel is presented not as a wayward wife but as a rebellious child. But the same themes are present: God's staggering love and graciousness, Israel's stunning ingratitude and unfaithfulness, God's fierce judgment, and God's merciful restoration. In particular, Israel's judgment in exile is seen in 11:5, as elsewhere in Hosea (8:13; 9:3,6), as an undoing of the exodus—a return to Egypt (ironic since they seek Egypt's help in 7:11,16).

So similarly, the restoration described in 11:10-11 is depicted as a new exodus (as implied in 2:15). As in 3:4-5, in the restoration Israel will "come trembling" in awe to the Lord from their places of exile and will "follow" Him (v. 10). They will experience God's goodness when He "settle[s] them in their homes" (v. 11). The Lord is depicted elsewhere in Hosea as a fierce, roaring lion who attacks Israel for her sin so she would repent (5:14-15; 13:7-8); here in v. 10 He is depicted as a roaring lion summoning His repentant people back to Himself.

It is possible but probably too subtle to consider that Hosea is connecting this image directly to the ruling lion of Judah (Gn 49:9-10; cf. Rev 5:5) and therefore to the messianic figure in 3:5. Hosea may be hinting that the Messiah should be considered a prophet like Moses who leads his people out of exile (cf. 12:13). But what is clear in Hosea is that the Messiah is the one Davidic ruler who unites Israel (1:11), and as the agent of restoration is owed their allegiance (3:5).

HOSEA 3:4-5 IN THE BIBLICAL CANON

Hosea 3:4-5 picks up on earlier biblical texts, reinforces other contemporary prophets, and is used by later biblical texts. In terms of *antecedent biblical texts*, two are particularly important. The first background text is Dt 4:23-31, where Moses calls Israel not to forget the Lord's covenant and not to worship other gods because God is jealous (vv. 23-34). Moses then predicts that, when settled in the land, they will eventually become unfaithful to Him, calling God's judgment on them and bringing them to exile where they will "worship man-made gods" (vv. 25-28). But then Moses predicts that in exile Israel will "search for the LORD," and if they do so with all their "heart" and "soul" they will "find" Him (v. 29). Indeed, Moses promises that in the midst of all these distressful judgments, "you will return to the Lord your God in later days and obey Him" (v. 30). All of this is because of God's covenant loyalty and compassion toward His people Israel (v. 31). In picking up on this text—even using some of the same language—Hosea is similarly affirming that the Lord is both just and unfailing in His covenant love to His people.

The second important background text is the Davidic covenant of 2Sm 7:4-17. In this text, the Lord promises that David's house, throne, and kingdom would endure forever. It is this text that is the basis for Hosea's conviction that Israel would be united again under the Davidic dynasty and which contributes to his messianic expectation.

Hosea's contemporaries pick up on similar themes of a coming Davidic king who will restore His people. In Am 9:11-15, Amos predicts a time in the future when the Lord will "restore" and rebuild "the fallen booth of David" (v. 11). David's dynasty had already fallen on hard times with the division of Israel, and it would only get worse when Judah fell to Babylon. But seen in light of Hos 3:5, the nation would be restored by the coming son of David who "in that day" will restore its glory "as in the days of old." His blessed rule will extend beyond the borders of Israel to the nations (Am 9:12), while also bringing restoration and prosperity to Israel in their land (vv. 13-15).

Micah 5:2-5a also speaks of this coming ruler over all of Israel in ways similar to Hosea. Although the promised one hails from insignificant Bethlehem, it is also true that "His origin is from antiquity, from eternity" (v. 2). Scholars debate whether this text speaks of His pedigree in the ancient line of David or of His eternal nature. Either view is consistent with Hos 3:5, indicating that this ruler is another David who is also closely associated with the Lord Himself. He will unite scattered Israelites (v. 3) and shepherd them in the power of the Lord so that His rule extends over the earth while Israel dwells in security and peace (vv. 4-5a).

Isaiah was another prophet generally contemporary to Hosea. Though Isaiah says much about the coming Davidic ruler, consider just two passages that relate to themes in Hosea 3:4-5. First, in Isa 9:1-7, Isaiah predicts that "in the future" those who dwell in "Galilee of the nations" will have "seen a great light" (vv. 1-2), resulting in the joy and flourishing of the nation as her enemies are defeated (vv. 3-5). This joy and deliverance are because of a "son" who will rule Israel (v. 6a). He is described in remarkable, supernatural terms (vv. 5b-6). Not only is He a ruler, He is called "wonderful," a term meaning extraordinary to the point of miraculous, and generally applied only to God Himself; He guides his people ("counselor") and brings peace to them ("prince of peace"). He is also described remarkably in divine terms as "Mighty God" and "Eternal Father," more accurately "father of eternity." Yet, at the same time He is also the son of David, seated on the Davidic throne as he rules eternally over a greatly expanded kingdom (v. 7).

The other passage is Isa 11, which describes the kingdom of the Messiah in all its incredible glory. Without summarizing the whole chapter, consider two critical elements related to Hos 3:5. First, the Messiah here is described as being of the

Davidic line. He is the "branch" from Jesse's "roots" (v. 1) while also being called the "root of Jesse" (v. 10). This suggests that the Messiah is the Davidic Son who eclipses His ancestors, just as He is the ultimate "David" in Hos 3:5. Second, as He does in Hosea, here too the Messiah summons scattered Israel back to Himself (vv. 11-12) and unites the nation once more (vv. 13-14) in a second exodus (vv. 15-16).

The themes that Hosea and his contemporaries introduce are reiterated in *later prophetic texts.* Two prophets in particular use language similar to Hosea. Jeremiah predicts in 23:5-8 that in the coming days, "a Righteous Branch of David. . . . will reign wisely as king" and justly rule over a unified Israel, restored in a second exodus. He speaks of this righteous Branch of David again in 33:14-26, declaring that in the coming days God will show His goodness to Israel and Judah through the Messiah, rooted in His covenant faithfulness to David. Moreover, Jer 30 closely parallels the language of Hosea. "On that day" when Israel cries out in agony from her distress, the Lord will free Israel from foreign oppression (vv. 5-8) and "they shall serve the LORD their God and David their king, whom I will raise up for them" (v. 9 NASB[33]). This is not because of their worthiness; their pursuit of "lovers [who] have forgotten" them causes God to discipline them faithfully, leaving them with an incurable, grievous wound only He can cure (vv. 10-15). And He does, restoring both their national and spiritual health (vv. 16-20). This restoration is led by their Messiah, their "leader" who is one of them but is able to approach God on their behalf and thus "performs political and priestly duties" (v. 21).[34] The nature of this spiritual restoration is further unpacked in the new covenant text of Jer 31:27-37.

Ezekiel similarly echoes the prediction of Hosea. In chap. 34, Ezekiel predicts that, in contrast to Israel's human leaders who fail to rightly shepherd the flock of Israel (vv. 1-10), the Lord Himself will shepherd them well and justly (vv. 11-22). Yet even though the Lord will be Israel's shepherd, He will also "appoint over them a single shepherd, My servant David"[35] who will be a good shepherd who will rule Israel (vv. 23-24) and lead them to prosperity and worship of God (vv. 25-31). Ezekiel reveals more about this coming David in 37:15-28. Using an enacted parable (vv. 15-18), he predicts that Israel will one day be regathered in their own land and united as "one nation in the land" under "one king" (vv. 19-22). The Lord will also remove their idolatrous hearts, "cleanse them," and renew genuine fellowship with them (v. 23). Furthermore, He will appoint "My servant David" as their king, "one shepherd," and ruler "forever," and He will lead them in faithful worship of the Lord in their own land (vv. 24-25). They will prosper in fellowship with the Lord (vv. 26-27) and will be an example to the nations (v. 28). Both passages here clearly reflect Hosea's prediction.

Although the NT writers do not quote or allude to Hos 3:4-5 specifically, they do address and develop Hosea's predictions. Fundamentally, the NT as a whole insists that Jesus is the Messiah, the "David" to whom Hosea testifies. He is David's Son and rightful heir, Israel's true king (Mt 1:1-17; 2:1-2; Rom 1:3). Moreover, He is greater than even David himself (Mt 22:41-46) because He is also the Son of God (Mt 16:16-17; Rom 1:4; Jn 5). Indeed, He Himself is fully divine (Jn 1:1-18; 8:58-59; 20:28). Little wonder, then, that Hosea connects the Lord and Messiah so closely.

Although "David" came in the person of Jesus the Messiah, the "last days" of Hos 3:5 have yet to be fulfilled.[36] Although Israel had learned to no longer worship idols, the majority failed to recognize Jesus as their Messiah (Jn 1:11) and rejected Him (Rom 9:1-5; 11:1-10), demonstrating that they still needed to "return and seek the LORD their God and David their king" (Hos 3:5). Furthermore, although dwelling in the land (albeit under foreign domination) and engaging in temple service in the time of Jesus, Israel did not yet experience the triumphal reign of the Davidic king with all its attendant blessings. Messiah's first coming therefore did not fulfill this prophecy. Indeed, after the time of Messiah Jesus' earthly ministry, the nation lost even its temple life and (until recently) its land.

But Israel's plight is not permanent. The NT teaches that when the Messiah Jesus returns, "all Israel will be saved" when they genuinely seek the Lord and His Messiah (Rom 11:25-27). The fulfilling of this prophecy of Hosea thus awaits Messiah's second coming, when He establishes His millennial kingdom on the earth and thereby restores Israel spiritually, nationally, and materially in accord with the word of the prophet Hosea.

---

1. The dates used here come from E. R. Thiele, *The Mysterious Numbers of the Hebrew Kings* (Grand Rapids: Zondervan, 1983), 10.
2. D. Stuart, *Hosea-Jonah*, Word Biblical Commentary, Vol. 31, ed. B. M. Metzger, D. A. Hubbard, and G. W. Barker (Dallas, TX: Word, 1987), 9.
3. D. A. Garrett, *Hosea, Joel*, Vol. 19A, New American Commentary (Nashville: Broadman & Holman, 1997), 42.
4. D. A. Hubbard, *Hosea: An Introduction and Commentary*, Tyndale Old Testament Commentaries (Downers Grove, IL: InterVarsity, 1989), 52–53.
5. C. H. Silva, "The Literary Structure of Hosea 1–3," *Bibliotheca Sacra* 164 (2007): 181–97.
6. Ibid., 182–83.
7. See the helpful arguments in favor of the view presented above in Hubbard, *Hosea*, 52–53; F. I. Andersen and D. N. Freedman, *Hosea: A New Translation with Introduction and Commentary*, Anchor Bible (New York, NY: Doubleday, 1980), 293; Garrett, *Hosea, Joel*, 98–99. These are some of the reasons supporting this view: (1) The word "again" suggests that the narrative continues from chap. 1. (2) Although Gomer is not mentioned specifically, she is called an adulteress, suggesting she is married to Hosea. (3) He is commanded to "love" her rather than take her as a wife (as in ch. 1), suggesting they are already married and this is an attempt at restoration.
8. For a nice summary of the dizzying varieties of interpretation of the Hosea-Gomer story, see Garrett, *Hosea, Joel*, 43–50. The view presented above is in accord with the view Garrett defends.
9. Hubbard, *Hosea*, 54–55, and Andersen and Freedman, *Hosea*, 293, maintain that Gomer at her marriage to Hosea was not yet promiscuous. They consider the description of Gomer as a "promiscuous wife" to be an anticipation

of what she will become later after she violates her marriage covenant. This is less likely because God commands Hosea to take a wife of whoredom without specifying Gomer. So Hosea must have chosen Gomer because she already displayed her promiscuous character.

10. Garrett, *Hosea, Joel*, 53–54. It is also possible that some of Gomer's children were "children of promiscuity" because Hosea was not their physical father. While the text is explicit that Hosea was Jezreel's father (1:3), it does not specifically say that Hosea was the father of "No Compassion" (1:6) and "Not my People" (1:8). Still, the text does not clearly state that Hosea was not their father either, so this view is speculative.

11. For a helpful discussion of the meaning and fulfillment of this prediction, see Garrett, *Hosea, Joel*, 55–59.

12. Ibid., 72.

13. For example, G. I. Davies, *Hosea*, New Century Bible Commentary (Grand Rapids: 1992), 97–98.

14. There is widespread dispute about whether the adverb "again" modifies the verb "said" or the verb "love." It is a difficult exegetical question, and good arguments can be marshalled for both sides, but the argument in favor of the latter is slightly more persuasive. See T. E. McComiskey, "Hosea," in *The Minor Prophets: An Exegetical and Expository Commentary, Volume 1: Hosea, Joel, Amos*, ed. T. E. McComiskey (Grand Rapids: Zondervan, 1992), 50–51. Davies, *Hosea*, 97–98, rightly points out that either view eliminates the possibility that the narrative in chap. 3 is merely a repetition of chap. 1.

15. The Hebrew noun *re'a* is best translated as "another" man or even a lover; the NASB's translation of this term as "*her* husband" makes little sense in the context. Some commentators, following the Septuagint, re-vocalize the term to make the text say that she loves evil. But this is unlikely, especially since the text specifies this love for another as adultery.

16. Garrett, *Hosea*, 99.

17. Given the parallel between Gomer and Israel, it is possible that she had been given over to cultic prostitution in the context of pagan worship.

18. McComiskey, *Hosea*, 53. He rightly points out that the preposition *le* signifies possession; thus, it is better to read "dwell as mine" rather than "dwell with me."

19. Andersen and Freedman, *Hosea*, 291. They seem to support their translation based on their understanding of the structure of the verse as well as the immediate context; cf. Hubbard, *Hosea*, 93. The *Lexham English Bible*'s translation of this clause appears to be similar. See also Garrett, *Hosea*, 101–03, who translates it, "and then I shall be yours." He too bases his interpretation on the immediate context, and appeals to Ex 19:9 as an example where *wegam* implies sequence.

20. See Andersen and Freedman, *Hosea*, 304; J. A. Dearman, *The Book of Hosea*, New International Commentary on the Old Testament (Grand Rapids: Eerdmans, 2010), 136; G. V. Smith, *Hosea/Amos/Micah*, NIV Application Commentary (Grand Rapids: Zondervan, 2001), 74–75; and Hubbard, *Hosea*, 93, who draws a parallel with the time of purification in Lv 12:4-5.

21. Anderson and Freedman, *Hosea*, 306, rightly point out that these two terms "are frequent parallels in Hosea." It therefore makes sense to consider a *sar* to be some kind of leader in the king's administration, whether civil or military.

22. Dearman, *Hosea*, 137.

23. Unlike the other four elements mentioned in this verse, each of which is preceded by *eyn* ("without"), "ephod" and "household idols" are together preceded by *eyn*, literally "without ephod and household items."

24. McComiskey, "Hosea," 54.

25. It is debated whether the phrase itself is eschatological here, or merely just a nonspecific reference to some time in the future. See the helpful discussion in Dearman, *Hosea*, 139, n. 22. See also Andersen and Freedman, *Hosea*, 308–9. Whether the phrase itself is a technical expression for the eschaton, the description of the restoration best fits the eschatological return of the Messiah Jesus.

26. Hubbard, *Hosea*, 94.

27. The resurrection of David and his becoming king again is argued by A. G. Fruchtenbaum, *The Footsteps of the Messiah: A Study of the Sequence of Prophetic Events* (Tustin, CA: Ariel Ministries Press, 1983), 283.

28. Hubbard, *Hosea*, 95.

29. A helpful discussion of the convergence of the rule of Yahweh and His Messiah can be found in C. A. Blaising and D. L. Bock, *Progressive Dispensationalism* (Grand Rapids: Baker, 1993), 218–231.

30. In Hebrew, the Lord and David are both marked as the direct object of the verb "seek."

31. Garrett, *Hosea*, 104.

32. Hubbard, *Hosea*, 95.

33. The HCSB obscures the Hebrew text here by not making clear that Israel also "serves" David their king.

34. Walter Kaiser, Jr., *The Messiah in the Old Testament* (Grand Rapids: Zondervan, 1995), 191. Kaiser argues (190) that the term *adder*, translated "leader," is better translated as "Glorious One." This strongly suggests His "divine origin, since it is used four times of either Yahweh or God" and never refers to a man when in the singular, as it is here.

35. Here again there is a close connection between the Lord and the coming Davidic ruler.

36. It is true that in one sense, with Christ's first coming, the last days have already begun (Acts 2:16-17), but as argued above, not yet in the sense Hosea predicts.

is "seemingly appropriate to the context" but says of the "teacher of righteousness" translation, "it is difficult to see what this would mean in context."[6] However, Jl 2:23 is located in the section of the book that describes the eschatological restoration and blessing of Israel in the Messianic Age. Therefore, how appropriate it is to the context to describe the end-of-days messianic "Teacher of Righteousness" who will usher in the prosperity of the messianic kingdom.

THE INTEXTUAL INTERPRETATION OF JOEL 2:23

Interpretative History

The King James Version translates the key phrase *hamoreh litsdaqah* in Jl 2:23 as "the former rain moderately." This translation understands *moreh* with the unusual sense of "early rain" (the normal word for rain would actually be *yoreh*) and *litsdaqah* not with its normal sense of "righteousness" or "justice" but with the unusual sense of "moderately," meaning not too much or too little rain but just the right amount. The reason for this translation is the second half of the verse, which describes the "rain" that God pours as both "early and latter rain" (HCSB "autumn and spring rain") using the word *moreh* with that unusual sense of "early rain." Thus, translators concluded that both uses of *moreh*, in the first and second parts of the verse, should be translated with the unusual meaning of "early rain."

Most English versions maintain this translation but vary it slightly. For example, the HCSB translates Jl 2:23 "the autumn rain for your vindication" and the NASV and ESV do so similarly as "early rain for your vindication." The NIV adopts "the autumn rains because he is faithful." The difficulties these translations face are twofold: taking *moreh* with the unusual sense of "early rain" and *litsdaqah* without its normal sense of "righteousness."

The LXX, the earliest translation of Joel from Hebrew, shows that even in ancient times this text was problematic. Translating 2:23 as "food for righteousness" perhaps indicates a variant textual tradition altogether. On the other hand, other ancient versions such as Symmachus, the Vulgate, and the Targums (rabbinic paraphrases in Aramaic) translated the phrase with its plain sense of "Teacher of Righteousness." Rashi, the most influential medieval Jewish interpreter sees it as "teacher of righteousness" and understood it to refer to the prophets collectively. The medieval Jewish Karaite interpreter Yefet ben Ali understood it as referring to the messianic Teacher of Righteousness as did the Jewish medieval interpreter Abarbanel who translated the phrase as "the Teacher of Righteousness" saying "this is the King Messiah.[7]

Among modern translations, there are a few that adopt the translation "teacher" for the word *moreh*. The Roman Catholic translations Douay and the first edition of the New American Bible follow the Vulgate and translate the phrase "teacher of justice." Additionally, *God's Word Translation*, translated by members of the Lutheran Church–Missouri Synod, translates it "the Teacher of Righteousness," and *Young's Literal Translation* renders it "the Teacher for righteousness."

One significant interpreter who took the phrase to speak of a person and not rain was C. F. Keil, who understood it collectively of all the priests and prophets of Israel culminating in the Messiah "as the final fulfillment of this promise."[8] G. W. Ahlstrom interpreted Jl 2:23 as a royal figure, a Davidic leader and teacher, but not the Messiah.[9] Other interpreters who translate the phrase as "Teacher of Righteousness" and understand it as referring exclusively to the Messiah include E. B. Pusey,[10] T. Laetsch,[11] and W. C. Kaiser, Jr.[12]

Exegetical Issues

The central exegetical issue is whether to translate the Hebrew phrase *hamoreh litsdaqah* as "early rain for your vindication" or as "the Teacher of Righteousness." Although "The Teacher of Righteousness" is the less common translation, it is the more likely one for several reasons. First, the general definition of the word *moreh* is "teacher." The singular form of *moreh* is used in seven other places in Scripture (2Kg 17:28; 2Ch 15:3; Jb 36:22; Isa 30:20 [twice]; Hab 2:18, 2:19), and it means "teacher" in each case. Admittedly, there are two possible exceptions to this simple definition, one in Ps 84:6 and the other in the second half of Jl 2:23.

As to the reference in Ps 84:6, Keil rightly notes that this passage is not useful as evidence for "early rain" since the meaning of *moreh* there is disputed.[13] In fact, translating *moreh* as "early rain" in that verse requires emending the Masoretic Text, changing the word "blessings" to "pools" as in the *NET Bible*.[14] With regard to the reference in the second half of Jl 2:23, it is possible that *moreh* means "autumn rain," but this is an extremely unusual form (it would normally be *yoreh*). Possibly, this was an intentional bit of word play, revealing that when the Teacher (*hamoreh*) arrives, He would bring the blessing of rain (*moreh*). Another possibility is that the original reading of this second usage in Jl 2:23 was in actuality "*yoreh*," the normal word for "autumn rain." According to the critical apparatus of the Hebrew Bible (*Biblia Hebraica Stuttgartensia*), multiple manuscripts have the word "*yoreh*."[15] Therefore, these two exceptions do not mitigate against understanding the first use of *hamoreh* in Jl 2:23 as "the Teacher."

Second, in addition to the normal meaning of the word *moreh*, the use of the article (*hamoreh*) supports the translation "teacher." Keil notes that the words for rain, both former (*yoreh*) and latter (*malqosh*), never use the article, and as he states "no reason can be discovered why *moreh* should be defined by the article here if it signified early rain."[16]

Third, understanding the *hamoreh* as "Teacher" avoids the redundancy of the passage saying that God will give autumn rain followed by the promise that He will give rain, the autumn and spring rain. Pusey notes that according to Hebrew grammar[17] the phrase "He sends showers for you" must relate "to a separate action, later, in order of time or of thought than the former action. But if the former word *moreh* signified *early rain*, both would mean one and the same thing."[18]

Fourth, the use of the linked word *litsdaqah* ("of righteousness") is appropriate only if describing "the Teacher" rather than precipitation. Translating the word *litsdaqah* as "vindication" or "just measure" is far-fetched from the meaning of the Hebrew. The plain meaning of *litsdaqah* is "righteousness" because it consistently has a moral/ethical sense.[19] It is utterly inapplicable to the word "rain."

Finally, as mentioned previously, "*moreh*" was translated as "teacher" in several ancient texts (the Vulgate, the Targum, the Gk Symmachus, and the Dead Sea Scrolls). These ancient versions demonstrate that "the Teacher of Righteousness" was an old and accepted interpretation of Jl 2:23.

So who is this Teacher of Righteousness? Joel's use of the definite article with "the Teacher" (*hamoreh*) indicates that he is speaking of a particular person. Moreover, the linking of "the Teacher" with the word "for righteousness" indicates that this Teacher acts with righteousness and grants it to others. He fully personifies righteousness.[20] Thus, Jl 2:23 is saying that the blessings described will occur when God the Father gives the Messiah, "the Teacher of Righteousness," to the people of Zion[21] who should "rejoice and be glad." At the same time, God will send blessing to Israel in the form of the autumn and spring rains so that the land will have great productivity, an idea introduced and promised in the Torah (Dt 11:10-15; 28:12).

The next verse (Jl 2:24) states there will be agricultural abundance ("the threshing floors will be full of grain") and great prosperity ("the vats will overflow with new wine and olive oil"). Along with the physical restoration, God promises to repay Israel for their losses and take away their shame (2:25-26). Ultimately, Israel will understand that God is present with them and that He alone is God. Kaiser notes that in the latter part of this chapter (2:28-32), in addition to sending literal rain in the eschaton, God will also send a metaphorical downpour of the Holy Spirit (2:28-29). According to him, Pentecost was merely the down payment of this downpour "but the mighty force of it still awaits a final enactment by God."[22]

THE INTERTEXTUAL EXAMINATION OF JOEL 2:23

As confirmation of the messianic meaning of Jl 2:23, Isa 30:19-26 provides an intertextual reference to it. There Isaiah predicts an eschatological Teacher who will guide Israel upon His arrival and God will send rain and prosperity.

Isaiah begins this passage (30:19-26) with a word of comfort to Zion, a term encompassing Jerusalem, and the Jewish people. Despite their past failures, the Lord mercifully calls on Israel to cry to Him for help. Then God will respond to their voices when the people long for Him, and He will answer them (30:19). The Lord disciplines His people for just cause, to instruct them for a specific purpose. His discipline of limiting their food to the bread of privation and water of oppression was designed to direct them back to Him. It is through their starvation rations and difficult circumstances that they will turn to the Lord. At this difficult time, they will be receptive to their great Messianic Teacher and His message. Then, Israel's "Teacher will not hide Himself any longer" (Isa 30:20).

The word "Teacher" is key to the text, but somewhat of a puzzle. The problem is that the word "teacher" (*moreykha*) is a plural form but the Hebrew verb "hide Himself" (*yikanef*) is a third-person masculine singular form. Therefore, some translations understand the word "teacher" as a plural, referring to many teachers (NIV, NET, KJV, ISV). Thus, the translation would be "your teachers will no longer be hidden" indicating that the verse promises true teachers (but not the Messiah) who will be revealed to Israel when the nation repents. On the other hand, others translate it as a singular, "Teacher" (HCSB, ESV, NASV, CEV, JPS1917, GW, RSV), thus focusing on the singular verb corresponding to it and interpret it as the Messiah. The resulting translation is "Your Teacher will no longer be hidden."

Yet, the problem of the singular verb not agreeing with the plural noun remains. A few possible solutions have been employed to interpret the noun "Teacher" as a singular. First, there is the possibility that the noun is a plural of majesty; being plural only in form, but not in meaning. It would indicate an individual, highly important "Teacher." This solves the problem of verb/noun agreement and reveals a glorious teacher. As Kaiser says, "In that case, the 'Teacher' is God's Messiah . . ."[23]

A second possible solution to the difficulty is to note that the Hebrew pronominal suffix ("your") on the noun "Teacher" (*moreykha*) begins with a consonant. In Biblical Hebrew, as Gesenius, Kautzsch, and Cowley point out, when a suffix begins with a consonant, it can yield a form change so that a true singular is formed as a plural yet remains singular.[24] This yields the translation, "your Teacher will not hide Himself any longer. Your eyes will see your Teacher" (30:20). Understanding the Hebrew suffix in this way seems to be the appropriate solution of the grammatical issue of agreement, identifying the Teacher as an individual who will reveal Himself to Israel. At the time, the Teacher (Messiah) will no longer hide Himself from His people. When Israel turns to the Lord, the Teacher will guide them in obedience to the ways of the Lord, whispering in their ears, "This is the way. Walk in it" (30:21).

In addition to the revelation of the Messianic Teacher to the people of Israel, here in Isa 30:23-26, similar to Jl 2:23, God also promises prosperity to the land by sending rain. Rain is an evidence of God's blessing for obedience (Lv 26:4; Dt 11:13-15) and will water the ground to such an extent as to bring forth crops enough to feed even the livestock plentifully (30:23). The blessing of rain in conjunction with the revelation of the Teacher supports the messianic interpretation of Jl 2:23. Both here in Isaiah and in Joel, when the great Messianic Teacher comes to Israel, God will provide both the former and the latter rains and will bring them rich and abundant harvests.

God will bless Israel with such a great quantity of grain that they will give their oxen and donkeys salted fodder (30:24) that has had the chaff removed, a particularly extravagant animal feed. Furthermore, Isa 30:25 notes the abundance of rain will produce great flows of streams and watercourses in the mountains and hills so there will be no fear of drought in any area.

The coming of the Teacher Messiah will be attended by extraordinary light. His appearance will usher in a time of brightness that will drive away darkness. First, the moon will be as bright as the sun, and the sevenfold increase in the sun's brightness indicates the power of the light. Second, the combination of healing and light is a brilliant contrast to that of disease and darkness. Next, God is presented as a physician who will heal the brokenness and injuries of His people (30:26). In the Messianic Age, God will not only heal His people physically but also emotionally and spiritually. The future characterized by the Lord's healing of His people and illumination of His world is a glimpse of the coming restoration. Isaiah's description of God's actions, taking place after the arrival of the Teacher, are very like the restoration of Israel described in Jl 2:25-27, when not only will God grant prosperity but also heal the nation of their shame.

The association of Isa 30:19-26 with Jl 2:23 should not be overlooked.[25] In both passages the Messiah comes as a Teacher to guide Israel to God's truth. In so doing, the Messiah ushers in the Messianic Age, bringing the blessing of rain, and thus, He provides great agricultural abundance and prosperity.[26]

CONCLUSION

Joel 2:23 reveals the great eschatological Teacher of Righteousness, the Messiah, who will usher in the Messianic Age, bringing rain and prosperity. This passage clearly indicates that the fulfillment of these words will take place at the end of days, when Israel turns to the Messiah to save the nation (Zch 12:10; Rom 11:26). Nevertheless, Jesus of Nazareth clearly accepted the title of teacher, frequently being called that by His own disciples (Mk 9:38; 10:35), by scribes and Pharisees (Mt 8:19; 12:38); by Herodians and Sadducees (Mt 22:16; 23-24), and also by the people in general (Mt 19:16). James Smith has noted that "of the sixty instances of the use of the word *didaskolos* (teacher) in the New Testament, more than thirty are in reference to Jesus, mostly in direct address."[27]

Not only did Jesus accept the title of teacher, He also practiced teaching with authority (Mt 7:29), with great skill at interpretation, such as in the Sermon on the Mount (Mt 5-7), and captured the interest of His listeners with true-to-life and intriguing stories (Mt 13:11-13). These observations lead to the conclusion that Jesus saw Himself as the One who was the promised Teacher of Righteousness, who would also fulfill Jl 2:23 upon His return. Therefore, Jesus reminded all His disciples, "You have one Teacher and . . . you have one Master, the Messiah" (Mt 23:8,10).

---

1. J. Neusner and W. S. Green, eds., "The Teacher of Righteousness," in *Dictionary of Judaism in the Biblical Period* (Peabody, MA: Hendrickson Publishers, 1999), 619–20.
2. Ibid.
3. M. O. Wise, "Dead Sea Scrolls," in *Dictionary of Jesus and the Gospels*, ed. J. Green, S. McKnight, and I. H. Marshall (Downers Grove, IL: InterVarsity Press, 1992), 146.
4. J. C. Reeves, "The Meaning of 'Moreh Ṣedeq' in the Light of 11QTorah" *Revue De Qumrân* 13, no. 1/4 (49/52) (1988): 289.
5. The Qumran sect used the title *"Moreh Tsaddiq"* and not *"hamoreh litsdaqah"* as found in Jl 2:23, causing some to object to seeing Joel as the source of the name. However, since there is no biblical text that uses their title verbatim, it makes sense that they merely derived the title from Jl 2:23 and did not quote it directly.
6. M. B. Shepherd, *The Book of the Twelve: The Minor Prophets* (Grand Rapids: Kregel Academic, 2018), 127. Note that Shepherd does recognize that the "early rain" translation "is not without its problems," which he proceeds to list.
7. E. B. Pusey, *The Minor Prophets: A Commentary*, 2 vols. (Grand Rapids: Baker, 1967), I:190.
8. C. F. Keil, *Minor Prophets,* Commentary on the Old Testament, vol. 10, ed. C. F. Keil and F. Delitzsch (Grand Rapids: Eerdmans, 1980), 207.
9. G. W. Ahlstrom, *Joel and the Temple Cult of Jerusalem* (Leiden, Netherlands: Brill, 1971), 107–09.
10. E. B. Pusey, *The Minor Prophets: A Commentary*, I:190–92.
11. T. Laetsch, *The Minor Prophets* (St. Louis: Concordia, 1956), 125–27.
12. W. C. Kaiser, Jr. *The Messiah in the Old Testament* (Grand Rapids: Zondervan, 1995), 139–42.
13. C. F. Keil, *Minor Prophets*, 205.
14. The HCSB translation "the autumn rain will cover it with blessings" does not make much sense. However, the *NET Bible* emends the word *be**ra**khot* (blessings) to *be**re**khot* (pools) to make it read "the rain even covers it with pools of water." Alternatively, the teacher could be a source of blessing. Thus, the translation "autumn rain" is not certain. See the discussion in Laetsch, *The Minor Prophets*, 125–26.
15. Laetsch states there are 34 manuscripts with *"yoreh"* (*The Minor Prophets*, 126). One reason to adopt the unusual reading *"moreh"* for rain is because it certainly is the harder reading. The variant reading *yoreh* could just be an early attempt to eliminate the difficulty of the strange rendering of *moreh* for rain. On the other hand, *"moreh"* could just as well be the result of a kind of dittography error, where the scribe inadvertently wrote a second *mem,* having just used it for the word "teacher" (*moreh*) in the previous phrase. Thus, where the scribe should have written *yoreh* (the normal word for rain), he wrote *moreh* in the last phrase of Jl 2:23.
16. C. F. Keil, *Minor Prophets*, 206.
17. This refers to what Pusey called the *vav* conversive.
18. E. B. Pusey, *The Minor Prophets: A Commentary*, I:190.

19. W. C. Kaiser, *The Messiah in the Old Testament*, 141.

20. Ibid.

21. To the objection of the use of the idea of "giving" the Messiah to Israel, note that Isaiah said, "a son will be given to us" (Isa 9:6).

22. W. C. Kaiser, *The Messiah in the Old Testament*, 141–42.

23. Ibid, 172.

24. W. Gesenius, *Gesenius' Hebrew Grammar*, ed. E. Kautzsch and A. E. Cowley, 2nd English ed. (Oxford: Clarendon Press, 1982), 273–74.

25. W. C. Kaiser, *The Messiah in the Old Testament*, 172.

26. In similar fashion, Ps 72:5-7 depicts the Messiah as one who would bring great abundance. He will be "like rain that falls on the cut grass, like spring showers that water the earth." The coming of the Messiah begins the Messianic Age, when both abundant rain and spiritual blessing will shower the earth.

27. James Smith, *What the Bible Teaches about the Promised Messiah* (Nashville: Thomas Nelson, 1993), 228.

Joel 2:28-32

The Messianic Outpouring of the Spirit

EDWIN A. BLUM

The book of Joel was written by a prophet named Joel whose name means "Yah is God." Fourteen individuals in the Bible have the same name. He identifies himself only as the "son of Pethuel." No other information about kings or nations is given that would help in the dating of his prophecy. From the mention of priests (1:9; 2:17), the temple ("house of the LORD/God") 1:9,13), Judah (3:1), Zion, and Jerusalem (2:32), scholars have given various guesses from 900 BC to 300 BC for the date of composition.

There is agreement that the central theme of the book is "the Day of Yahweh [the LORD]." Joel uses this phrase five times: 1:15, 2:1, 2:11, 2:31, and 3:14. The full phrase occurs about 19 times in the OT with some minor variations, cf. Zch 14:1. There is also agreement that the phrase is about the future and Yahweh's breaking into human history. A related expression "in/on that day" occurs almost 200 times in the Prophets. Zechariah 14:1 speaks of a day coming for Yahweh and then goes on to give details of what happens "on that day" seven times. The phrase "the Day of the Lord" does not always mean that the day/period reaches down to the end of history.

THE SUMMARY OF JOEL

The first chapter of Joel tells about a horrific plague of locusts that shows that the Day of the Lord is near (1:15). Ezekiel (13:1-9) in v. 5 uses the "day of the LORD" for the judgment on Judah and Jerusalem that took place in 586 BC.

The desert locust (arba) occurs 24 times in the Hebrew Bible and is used by the Lord in judgments. The eighth plague on Egypt was of locusts that ate everything green in the land (Ex 10:1-15). Amos 7 relates five judgment visions shown to Amos that were to come to the northern kingdom. The first was of locusts that the Lord was preparing. Amos asked for forgiveness and God relented. In the case of the book of Joel, the locust devastation (1:6,7; 2:7-10) had destroyed the grapevine, the wheat, the barley, the fig, and all the trees of the orchard. Joel asked, "Has anything like this ever happened in your days or in the days of your ancestors?" (Jl 1:2-3). Why has this occurred? Although the book of Joel does not reveal the reason, clearly for such a judgment there must have been covenant violations.

The prophetic cure is a sacred fast by the entire community (1:14); repentance from the heart (2:12); and a return to the Lord (2:12). Joel laments over the Day of the Lord (1:15-20).

It is difficult to be dogmatic as to what the next section (2:1-11) is referring. Some see the passage as an invading army (perhaps Assyria) that comes from the North (2:20), comparing it to a locust invasion. It is "the Day of the LORD . . . terrible and dreadful—who can endure it?" The use of locusts as a metaphor for an invading army is also used in Rev 9:3-11. The locusts have mixed features: armor, stingers like scorpions, and wings that sound like battle horses and chariots, darkening the sun. They are not allowed on this occasion to harm the grass, green plants, and trees (Rev 9:4).

The next section (2:17-27) calls the nation to return to the Lord. The prophet conjectures, "Who knows? He may turn and relent and leave a blessing behind Him (2:14)." Joel reminds his people about the attributes of Yahweh from Ex 34:6: "a compassionate and gracious God, slow to anger and rich in faithful love and truth." The Lord "became jealous for His land and spared His people" (2:18). He will repay them for the great army of devouring locusts that He sent against them (2:25). He will renew their land, and they will "have plenty to eat and be satisfied" (2:16).

God promises that the Day of the Lord will bring to His repentant people a pouring out of His Spirit (2:28-32):

> After this, I will pour out My Spirit on all humanity, then your sons and your daughters will prophesy, your old men will have dreams, and your young men will see visions. I will even pour out My Spirit on the male and the female slaves in those days. I will display wonders in the heavens and on the earth: blood, fire, and columns of smoke. The sun will be turned to darkness and the moon to blood before the great and awe-inspiring Day of the LORD comes. Then everyone who calls on the name of Yahweh will be saved, for there will be an escape for those on Mount Zion and in Jerusalem, as the Lord promised, among the survivors the Lord calls.

In the Hebrew text the verses are 3:1-5 and make a separate chapter. The next chapter (3 in English and 4 in Hebrew) continues with the prophecy about the gathering of all nations for judgment. This judgment is about how the surrounding nations have treated Yahweh's people, Israel (Eng. 3:2,12).

THE MEANING OF JOEL 2:28-32

The Spirit of God

What is the pouring out of God's "Spirit" or "spirit"? The OT has about one hundred instances of God's Spirit, the Spirit of God, or the Spirit of the Lord. Jewish translations in Gn 1:2 normally have a "wind from God" or something similar to the mistaken "vital force" of James Crenshaw in the Anchor Bible on Joel (rather than the more literal "the Spirit of God").[1] The OT word (ruakh) occurs 387 times in the OT. It has a wide range: breath, wind, mind, spirits (good) i.e. angels, evil spirits, and the Holy Spirit. The context determines the meaning of the word "ruakh." The NT context and analogy supports a Trinitarian understanding of God's Spirit. Isaiah perhaps has the fullest revelation of the Spirit among the prophets. In Isa 11:1-9, a "shoot will grow from the stump of Jesse . . . the Spirit of the Lord will rest on Him." In Isa 42:1, God puts His Spirit on the chosen Servant. In Isa 48:16, the Lord says "and now the Lord God has sent me and His Spirit." In Isa 59:21, the Lord says, "My Spirit who is on you, and My words that I have put in your mouth."

Ezekiel records the word of the Lord (36:26-27) as He restores His people, saying "I will place My Spirit within you" (cf. 11:19). In Ezk 39:29 He says: "I will no longer hide My face from them, for I will pour out My Spirit on the house of Israel." Zechariah predicted a day when God would "pour out a spirit of grace and prayer [from the Spirit] on the house of David and the residents of Jerusalem, and they will look at Me whom they pierced" (Zch 12:10). The result is deep sorrow and "a fountain will be opened . . . to wash away sin and impurity" (13:1; cf. Rev 1:7).

Prophetic Revelation

The pouring out of the Spirit on "all humanity" (literally, "flesh") in Jl 2:28 would fulfill the ancient longing of Moses that all of God's people would prophesy. At the time of Moses, 70 men had God's Spirit placed on them, and they prophesied. When Joshua heard that two men were prophesying in the camp, he wanted Moses to stop them. But Moses said: "If only all the Lord's people were prophets and the Lord would place His Spirit on them!" (Nm 11:29). Joel prophesied that the result of the Spirit's working would be widespread revelation to the people of God. Prophesying is the telling and revealing of God's will in both the near and far time.

Dream revelation is common in both the OT and the NT. Abram had the word of God in a vision (Gn 15:1), but also during a "deep sleep" when God spoke to him (15:12-16). Jacob in his dream saw a stairway, and God spoke to him (Gn 28:12-15). Joseph and Daniel both had numerous dreams of revelation. Joseph had two dreams as a young man of 17 years (37:5-7,9-11), and telling his brothers caused him pain. Many years later, when he met with his brothers, unbeknownst to them, he was reminded of the meaning of those dreams (Gn 42:9). While Joseph was in prison, he interpreted dreams (40:5-23). Later the Pharaoh of Egypt had two dreams, and Joseph was able to explain their significance (Gn 41:16-36). God used all six of these dreams to preserve Jacob's family, to bring Jacob's family out of Canaan for 400 years (Gn 15:13), and to save Egypt during a famine. The book of Daniel in chapters 2, 4, 7, 8, 10, 11 contains both dream and vision revelation.

In Isa 6, the prophet "saw" a vision of the Lord that marked His call and mission. His book is entitled "The vision concerning . . ." (1:1). The book of Zechariah begins (1:8) with "I looked out in the night and saw . . ." This starts a series of eight night visions. In the NT, visions are most common in the book of Revelation. Dream revelation occurs in the books of Matthew and Acts. Joseph, the adoptive father of Jesus, had a visit from an angel in a dream (Mt 1:20-21) Also, an angel warned Joseph to take Mary and Jesus to Egypt and also later to go to Galilee (Mt 2:19-23). The magi were also warned in a dream (Mt 2:12), and years later Pilate's wife had a troubling dream about Jesus (Mt 27:19).

Joel 2:29 predicts that the gift of God's Spirit would extend even to male and female slaves. This revelation is radical for that period of time. Female prophets did exist, but they were rare. The lot of a slave was difficult, although the Mosaic laws limited abuse of slaves and provided for freedom. Nevertheless, a slave receiving prophetic revelation was still remarkable.

Cosmic Signs and Wonders

Joel 2:30-31 predicts "wonders" in the heavens and on the earth at the end of days. These unusual events portend a warning to people that God is doing something special. During the Egyptian plagues, the locust invasion was followed by three days of darkness. The Egyptians had a number of gods and goddesses, but their major deities were Ra (or Re) and Amun/Aten. These sun-gods were "blacked out" for three days, followed by Death taking their firstborn. At the crucifixion (Mt 27:45; Mk 15:33; Lk 23:44), from noon to three in the afternoon, "darkness came over the whole land" (Mt 27:45). Jesus also predicted heavenly "signs" before His return (Mt 24:29-30). Additionally, Revelation predicts a series of cosmic events before the return of the Lord (6:12-14; 11:19; 16:17-21). Similarly, Joel 2:31b predicts cosmic signs "before the great and awe-inspiring Day of the Lord comes," linking Joel's prediction to the end-times signs predicted by Jesus and the book of Revelation. Joel also promises that anyone who calls on Yahweh (2:32) will be delivered.

The expression "as the LORD promised" (2:32) is obscure. Some have connected this to the promise of deliverance in Ob 17, but this was possibly written too late to influence Joel. The book of Zechariah promises deliverance to a remnant of the people of Jerusalem during the Day of the LORD (Zch 14:2), but this was certainly written after Joel. Perhaps it is best to say that Joel was specifying the general promise of deliverance given to Israel if the nation would call on the name of the Lord (cf. Isa 58:9).

The doctrine of "calling" is two sided in Jl 2:32. The individual has the responsibility to call out to the Lord. The Lord says "I called and you did not answer" (Isa 65:12b), but later He says "Even before they call, I will answer (65:24). Ps 145:18 says, "The Lord is near who call out to Him, all who call out to Him with integrity." Joel 2:32b closes with the phrase "among the survivors the LORD calls." This is close to the "effectual" calling commonly found in Paul's writings, that is, the sovereign call of God to faith that will result in trust by those who are called. As Paul writes, "And those He predestined, He also called" (Rm 8:30; cf. 1Co 1:9; Gal 1:15; 2Tm 1:9, and 1Jn 3:1).

THE NEW TESTAMENT AND JOEL 2:28-32

The NT ministry of John the Baptist started with his powerful call to the people to repent. His prophetic call and dress made his hearers wonder if he might even be the promised Messiah. He answered that he baptized with water but the One to come after him would baptize with the Holy Spirit and with fire. This dual ministry of the coming One was described in terms of the eschatological harvest: "His winnowing shovel is in His hand to clear His threshing floor and gather the wheat into His barn, but the chaff He will burn up with a fire that never goes out" (Lk 3:17; cf. Rev 14:14-20). The Messiah's dual ministry of grace and judgment is seen in Isa 61:1-2: "The Spirit of the Lord GOD is on Me, because the Lord has anointed Me to bring good news to the poor. He has sent Me to heal the brokenhearted, to proclaim liberty to the captives and freedom to the prisoners; to proclaim the year of the LORD's favor, and the day of our God's vengeance."

Jesus chose this passage in His Nazareth sermon (Lk 4:18-19) to announce His gracious ministry (Lk 4:20-22). Many have noted that Jesus omitted the words "the day of our God's vengeance" from His reading. Even John the Baptist was confused by the messianic sufferings and the rejection of Jesus (Cf. 1Pt 1:10-12; Lk 7:20). All four Gospel writers (Mt 3:11; Mk 1:8; Lk 3:16; Jn 1:33) report John's prediction of the Holy Spirit baptism, but no detail of what that meant or when that would happen was given. Jesus in His ministry was the servant of the Lord endued with the Holy Spirit (Mt 12:18), and He cast out Satan's demons by the power of the Holy Spirit (Mt 12:28). Jesus chose to reveal more about the Holy Spirit to His disciples in the upper room discourse (Jn 14–16). Jesus promised that the Father would send another Counselor (paracletos) to be with His disciples, who will teach and remind them of Jesus' ministry (Jn 14:16-18,25-26; 16:5-15). The Holy Spirit would guide them into "all the truth" and glorify Jesus (16:13; cf. 15:26,27).

Even though Jesus had told His disciples about His coming death and burial and His resurrection (Mt 16:21; 20:17-19), they were not able to grasp what He was predicting. The beheading of John the Baptist, the betrayal by Judas, the total denial by their leader Peter, and then the grisly, horrible crucifixion by the Romans and the Jewish leaders caused great disorientation to them. Jesus said to them "Tonight all of you will run away because of Me, for it is written: I will strike the shepherd, and the sheep of the flock will be scattered" (Mt 26:31; cf. Zch 13:7). The resurrection of Jesus was almost unbelievable (Lk 24:11; Jn 20:24,25), and it took a number of appearances of Jesus to convince them. The book of Acts begins with Jesus teaching His disciples for 40 days about the kingdom. His final earthly instruction concerned the Holy Spirit. He reminded them about the "Father's promise," His instruction, and the words of John the Baptist about the Spirit baptism (Ac 1:4-8). The Holy Spirit would give them the spiritual power to carry out the mission.

After this instruction, Jesus ascended to heaven, and the disciples were to wait for the coming of the Holy Spirit's empowerment. Ten days later, during the feast of Pentecost, the city of Jerusalem was filled with thousands of pilgrims, and the disciples were all together, when suddenly a visual and auditory phenomenon occurred. A violent wind blew, and tongues appeared on each one of the disciples. Then, "They were all filled with the Holy Spirit and began to speak in different languages, as the Spirit gave them the ability for speech" (Ac 2:4).

A crowd gathered, amazed that they could all understand the Galilean disciples' speech as they proclaimed God's magnificent acts in their own native languages. Luke records, "They were all astounded and perplexed, saying to one another, What could this be?" (Ac 2:12). By this time, the disciples had moved to the temple courtyards, and Peter with the Eleven stood up to explain the significance. It was not drunkenness as some thought, but rather he associated these events with what Joel the prophet said: "And it will be in the last days, says God, that I will pour out My Spirit on all humanity [lit. "all flesh]; then your sons and your daughters will prophesy, your young men will see visions, and your old men will dream dreams. I will even pour out My Spirit on My male and female slaves in those days, and they will prophesy. I will display wonders in the heaven above and signs on the earth below: blood and fire and a cloud of smoke. The sun will be turned to darkness and the moon to blood, before the great and remarkable Day of the Lord comes. Then everyone who calls on the name of the Lord will be saved" (Ac 2:17-21).

Peter's sermon has two main ideas: (1) an apologetic and explanation of what the Pentecostal events mean and (2) a proclamation of God's plan and its fulfillment in Jesus of Nazareth. The major part is the proclamation that "God has made this Jesus, whom you crucified,[2] both Lord and Messiah!" (Ac 2:36). Peter in the first part explains that the pouring out of the Spirit means that they are in the "last days" (2:17). The Spirit is at work with the restoration of the gift of prophecy. The speaking in foreign languages by the 120 disciples was a sign of prophecy. He did not say this, but he could have said that this is a sign that the curse of Babel is being lifted (Gn 11:1-9). How long will the last days last? No one knows, and perhaps the Day of the Lord is close.

Peter made some changes in his quotation from Joel. The most interesting is the phrase "in the last days" rather than Joel's "after this" or "then afterward." Peter, as an apostle, was also one of those at Pentecost who had been filled by the Holy Spirit and therefore was prophesying by the Spirit. The Spirit's advent brought numerous ministries: the baptism of the Spirit, which forms the Church—the body of Christ (1Co 12:13), the distribution of spiritual gifts, the filling by the Spirit, and the conviction of sin (Jn 16:8-9). The crowd hearing the Word of God through the prophetic and apostolic preacher were convicted ("under deep conviction" Ac 2:37). They were in the "last days," and they heard the promise "everyone who calls on the name of the Lord will be saved." Peter directed them to come to Jesus the Messiah for the forgiveness of sins, to be baptized, and to receive the gift of the Spirit.

Joel has "call on Yahweh" in the Hebrew text. The LXX has *kurios* (Lord), and Peter quotes from the LXX. What is striking is that Peter directs his audience to call on Jesus for the forgiveness of sins. Early in Jesus' ministry, He forgave sins (Mk 2:5). The scribes objected "Who can forgive sins but God alone" (Mk 2:7). The apostolic faith is that there is only one God; as Thomas said to Jesus: "My Lord and My God!" (Jn 20:28).

The NT has a number of passages that teach the last days are present. In 1Pt 1:20, Jesus was "revealed at the end of the times." We are those "on whom the ends of the ages have come" (1Co 10:11). "In these last days, He has spoken to us" (Heb 1:2). "But now He has appeared one time, at the end of the ages" (Heb 9:26). Peter once asked "So what will there be for us?" (Mt 19:27-28), and Jesus responded by telling about the coming Messianic Age. But in Mt 24, as one of the disciples present for this discourse, Peter was told that the last days were longer and not predictable (Mt 24:3,14,36).

The other changes to Joel's prophecy are minor. Acts 2:18 says that the slaves belong to the Lord—"My male and female slaves." In the new age, even the slaves will be able to prophesy. This is an addition or a clarification. The cosmic signs in 2:19 and 20 have not occurred yet. Jesus, in the Olivet Discourse, places the great cosmic signs immediately after the tribulation (Mt 24:29).

The Day of the Lord is called "remarkable" and "great" in the LXX. But in the Hebrew text it is "great and terrible." The expression does not occur often in the NT. Paul wrote to the church of the Thessalonians saying that the Day of the Lord had not come (1Th 5:1-9). He wrote again to clarify about the Day of the Lord (2Th 2:2-4) that certain things must occur first. The book of Revelation does not use the exact phrase nor does the phrase occur in the nonbiblical Dead Sea Scrolls. Peter's citation of Joel's prophecy reminded his hearers that the Day of the Lord may be near and that they need to call on the Lord.

So, should Peter's sermon be considered the fulfillment of Joel's prophecy? According to some, Peter's citation is taken as a direct fulfillment. Therefore, the predictions, while originally given to Israel, are seen as referring to the Church. A second approach is to view the use of Jl 2:28-32 in Ac 2 as a partial or progressive fulfillment. Thus, what has been inaugurated for the Church will ultimately be fulfilled for Israel. Both of these views are problematic for two reasons. First, the fulfillment language in Acts varies (*pleroo*: "fulfill" or "fill up" in 1:16, 3:18, 13:27; *teleo*: "fulfill" or "complete" in 13:29; *expleroo*: "fulfill" or "carry out" 13:33), and none of these terms is used in Ac 2. Second, there were no cosmic signs, no visions, and no prophecies in Ac 2. The events at Pentecost do not seem to match the words of Joel.

More probably, Peter was citing Joel in an applicational sense, meaning Peter found a principle in Joel's prophecy and applied it to the events at Pentecost.[3] When the disciples began to speak in other languages supernaturally, they were thought to be drunk (Ac 2:13). So Peter cited this principle from Jl 2:28-32 to indicate that these remarkable signs they were seeing were not the work of alcohol but of God's Spirit. Moreover, Peter revealed that the pouring out of the Spirit signifies that a new age has begun. The Messianic Age that brings salvation has been inaugurated, and it will also bring judgment as the Day of the Lord. Nevertheless, the prophet's predictions have not been abrogated or changed. At the end of days, God's Spirit will indeed come upon Israel, and they will call upon the Lord (Zch 12:10). There will be prophets who will testify to God's Messiah (Rev 11:1-6), and there will also be cosmic signs (6:12-14; 11:19; 16:17-21) revealing God's end-time wrath. And then heaven will declare, "The salvation and the power and the kingdom of our God and the authority of His Messiah have now come" (Rev 12:10).

1. James L. Crenshaw, *Joel: A New Translation with Introduction and Commentary*, vol. 24C of The Anchor Bible (New York: Doubleday, 1995), 52, 164–65.

2. It is inappropriate to use this phrase to support the false "Christ Killer" charge against the Jewish people. This untrue accusation has been the basis for the terrible history of the Christian hatred of the Jewish people. Also known as the deicide charge, the Christ killer "accusation is that only Jews and all Jews for all time are guilty of killing Jesus, and in doing so, murdering God." (Michael Rydelnik, *They Called Me Christ Killer*, Discovery Series [Grand Rapids: RBC Ministries, 2005], 8.) In Acts 4:27-28, those humanly responsible for the death of Jesus are identified as a conspiracy of a Gentile leader, a Jewish leader, some Jewish people, and some Gentiles (4:27). Moreover, God is also identified as planning and predestining the death of the Messiah Jesus (Ac 4:28). Beyond this, the Lord Jesus Himself stated "No man takes it [My life] from Me, but I lay it down on My own" (Jn 10:18). Likely, in Acts 2:36, Peter is addressing many who were present in the crowd some seven weeks previous, shouting "Crucify! Crucify Him!" (Lk 23:21), and not all Jewish people generally. Moreover, in Ac 3, when Peter once again addresses many of the people who had called for the Lord's death, he says, "brothers, I know that you did it in ignorance, just as your leaders also did" (Ac 3:17).

3. See the article by Michael A. Rydelnik, "The Old Testament in the New Testament" in this *Handbook*.

Amos 9:11-15

The Messiah and the Restoration of the House of David

JOHN A. JELINEK

The prophet Amos, like other Old Testament prophets, called Israel to account for her continual sin and covenantal infidelity. He delivered his message to the northern kingdom (between 810 and 785 BC) when the nation was deep in rebellion against God. His warnings were stern, with no words of comfort until the final verses of his book. In his words of comfort, he used an interesting and somewhat enigmatic reference to "the fallen booth of David" (Am 9:11), an interesting image of the long-delayed fulfillment of the Davidic covenant.

The Davidic covenant is one of the most important covenants in Scripture. It comprises God's unconditional promises to David in 2Sm 7:10-16 (cf. 1Chr 17:11-14 and 2Chr 6:16). The Davidic covenant is unconditional because God does not place any requirements of obedience for it to be fulfilled; its fulfillment depends completely on the Lord. The aspects of the covenant are summarized in 2Sm 7:16: "Your house and kingdom will endure before Me forever, and your throne will be established forever." David is promised a "house"—a dynasty; a "kingdom"—a nation/land; a "throne"—given the right to rule forever. These promises were not fulfilled in David's lifetime or even in the lifetimes of the kings of Judah, but find their fulfillment in Messiah Jesus, the son of David (Isa 11:1-5; Mt 1:1; Lk 1:32-33). It is from the Davidic covenant that Amos offers comfort in his prophecy.[1]

Amos gives a word of hope to Israel by saying "In that day I will restore the fallen booth of David" (9:11). The phrase "in that day" indicates an eschatological event, but to what does the "tent (*sukka, booth, shanty*) of David" refer? How would the original readers of Amos's text have understood his meaning? There were surely elements of Amos's message in these verses that were to be understood and applied, even if their fulfillment was pending an uncertain number of years ahead. Secondarily, how does James's citation of Amos in the Jerusalem Council (Ac 15:16-18) relate to the prophet in its context? To what does this promise refer as James ties it to the concerns of Gentile inclusion in Ac 15? Can Amos's original text be messianic in its intent, or is James importing a messianic implication into Amos's message? This article will address these questions.

AMOS 9 IN ITS BIBLICAL CONTEXT

Amos, like other OT prophets,[2] called Israel to account for her covenantal infidelity. So stern is his overall remonstrance against Israel that no words of comfort appear until the final verses of the book. Even in those verses, Amos used the image of the *sukka,* or booth, of David in describing a reversal that would accompany the fulfillment of the promised blessing. In the divine design, the booth in the Feast of Booths was a yearly commemorative reminder of the Lord's loving care for His people during their 40-year wilderness wanderings, when they dwelt in tents (Ex 23:16; Lv 23:34; Dt 16:13). Prophets sometimes used the term *sukka*, however, to depict a harsher perspective, casting it as an image that portrayed the ruin experienced by Israel as a result of God's judgment.[3] In Am 3:11-15, the prophet described the coming devastation of exile upon the whole nation, the "entire clan [the LORD] brought from the land of Egypt" (v. 1). He portrayed it as destroying both summer and winter houses together with the palaces of ivory—clear references to the wealthy and even kingly houses when Israel was living "at ease" but forgetting the Lord (e.g., Am 6:1-7) prior to the Assyrian captivity. To say that the house of David is reduced to a *sukka* in need of restoration shows how far Amos portended that the monarchy would sink under God's discipline!

"In that day" Amos related that the Lord would miraculously intervene and also restore that booth (dynasty) of David that had suffered destruction (9:11; cf. Lv 23:33-42; 2Sm 11:11). David's royal "tent" had suffered major damage because of the division of the kingdom, though it had not yet collapsed. In the future God would rebuild it as "in the days of old," with a descendant of David ruling over a united kingdom (Jer 30:3-10; Ezk 37:15-28; Hos 3:4-5). This restoration will follow the tribulation period,[4] when Messiah will return to rescue Israel and rule in the messianic kingdom, during the millennium.

At that time, other nations will participate in and reap the benefit of the blessing on the house of David (Am 9:12; cf. Ac 15:11) as Israel becomes a source of blessing to them. The Edomites, who had formerly been implacable enemies (cf. Ob 19; Ps 83), here represent all Israel's enemies. All nations associated with the name of the Lord will enjoy His lordship as He accomplishes this restoration. Here, Amos brings the element of Gentile inclusion to the forefront, and the nations' role serves James's purposes in his reference to the Amos text (see further below).

The blessings accompanying the restored Davidic tent will include the restoration of the land's fertility and fruitfulness. Farmers planting seed for the next harvest will push reapers of the same fields to finish their work so they will be able to plant the next crop: "the plowman will overtake the reaper" (9:13). The mountains will be full of fruitful grapevines that will "drip with sweet [the best] wine" (9:13). All the hills will "flow with it"; that is, the whole area will be filled with abundant produce. Israel will "rebuild and occupy ruined cities" (9:14) in a return to the land, marked by security, joy, abundant food, and blessing only possible in peacetime (cf. Lv 26:5-6; Dt 28:6)—an important contrast to her former desolate condition. Israel will put down roots in the promised land when the Lord will "plant them on their land, and they will never again be uprooted from the land" the Lord has "given them" (v. 15; Gn 15:18-21; Mic 4:4-7; Zch 14:11). Nothing in Israel's restoration to the land after exile (539 BC) fulfilled the promises given here.

AMOS 9 AND ACTS 15

Looking at James's use of Am 9 in Ac 15 at the Jerusalem Council raises critical issues and implications. Though James referred to "the words of the prophets" (plural in Ac 15:15) and not Amos's particular "word" in his conciliar speech,[5] it is clear that the main substance of the reference is from Am 9 with some adaptation of the LXX to his argument.[6] Excellent discussions of the textual details and alternatives pertaining to James's speech abound,[7] with the following critical points emerging. According to James, God's aim is to restore David's fallen dynasty together with all that relates to it. The MT of Am 9:12 indicates the rebuilding of the Davidic dynasty would lead Israel to "possess the remnant of Edom"; in the LXX the Lord restores David's tent "so that the remnant of men may seek" (no object of seeking is given). However, from the MT, "all the nations that are called by my Name" indicates that when the fallen booth of David is restored, it will coincide with the remainder of mankind, the nations, seeking the Lord (cf. Is 56:7-8).

James compressed several prophetic statements in his selected use of Scripture for his declaration in Acts.[8] "After these things" is common in prophetic speech (e.g., Jl 2:28; Hos 3:5) and could refer to Amos's earlier prophetic judgments (e.g., 3:1–4:13). James also may have been compressing Jer 12:15 into Am 9:11-12 in his introduction by using the words, "I will return" (omitting: "and have mercy on them, and I will make them dwell in their own inheritance and each in his own land" from Jeremiah; author's translation).

James's argument in Ac 15 brings together two significant prophetic promises. First, the covenantal promise to David personally as to his "dynasty" (tent) is not denied. A son of David will sit on his throne and will be fulfilled in Messiah Jesus the son of David, yet in the future (Mt 1:1; Mk 12:35; Rm 1:3; Rev 5:5). Second, that restored throne will also fulfill God's purpose of bringing Gentiles into His salvation (Am 9:12; Isa 56:5-6). The fulfillment of either of these promises is not a denial of the national elements that attend to the covenantal promises to David and Israel in 2Sm 7.

God's discipline and devastation of Israel through exile did not overturn Israel's status as recipient of God's national promises to and through David. The response James gives is in keeping with Luke's presentation of Jesus' ministry in Nazareth, where Jesus pointed out that God worked outside the boundaries of Israel in healing Namaan and in providing for the widow of Zarephath (Lk 4:24-27). While Jesus' teaching enraged the Nazareth synagogue with its focus on Gentile inclusion, both there and in Ac 15, there is no indication that Davidic promises to Israel are abandoned (cf. Rom 9:1-5; 11:29). God often does *more* than He promises when keeping His word, but He does not do *less* than He has promised He will do. The covenant with David illustrates this principle.

James contends that Gentile inclusion was part of what God promised. He supports this truth with texts like Am 9—and with the corroboration of the apostolic witness of Peter (the salvation of Cornelius's household) and of Paul and Barnabas (the salvation of Gentiles on the first missionary journey) as confirmation. The restoration of the kingdom to Israel, rebuilding it as in the days of old (Am 9:11), is not a blessing that *excluded* Gentiles in fulfilling promises to Israel. It is, instead, a restoration that God foretold would enable Gentiles to seek the Lord and to worship Him. The Gentiles will be blessed as Gentiles, and the Jewish people as Jewish people, but the unifying element is faith in the atoning work found in the person of Messiah Yeshua. There is no need for Gentiles to become Jews; God has had this in mind all along.

WHAT IS DAVID'S TENT?

At the heart of the issue in Ac 15 is the identity of the referent intended by James in invoking David's tent.[9] Strauss, among others, sees this as referring to a restored Israel comprised of "Jews who have accepted Jesus as their messiah."[10] Proponents

distinct ethnic identities of Jew and Gentile. The effect of the decision of the Jerusalem Council allowed Gentiles to retain their ethnic identities while being in Christ, not the eradication of the covenant with David.

9. The reference to a "tent" is a figurative way in which Amos describes the restored royal line of David. At issue is the reason for James's quotation. Is he saying the tent of David has already been restored or will it be yet in the future? As J. Paul Tanner has observed, "Covenant theologians have understood this as indicative of the church replacing Israel in God's program (replacement theology), whereas dispensational theologians have traditionally argued that the fulfillment of Amos 9:11-12 is not for the present age, but rather in the millennium when Israel is restored." See Tanner, "James's Quotation," 65-66.

10. Strauss, *Davidic Messiah*, 187.

11. Ibid, 188.

12. Glenny, "The Septuagint," 17.

13. Also found in many commentaries, the view is fleshed out in Richard Bauckham, "James and the Gentiles (Acts 15:13-21)" in *History, Literature and Society in the Book of Acts*, ed. Ben Witherington (Cambridge: Cambridge University Press, 1996), 158–59, 181.

14. These interpreters generally propose that James's argument is not aimed at present fulfillment, but at pointing out that if Gentiles are in the millennium *as Gentiles*, then this must imply that they can be part of the Church in the present without becoming Jews. One wonders whether this position, based as it is in a future millennium, would have had any influence on some of the Jewish audience at the Jerusalem Council, who were stressing the need for Gentile observance of the Law. Pressing James's intent in the wording of Ac 15 into this understanding makes it difficult to see what bearing this has on the central question James addresses: Do Gentile believers need to be circumcised? It seems that James has some sequencing in mind with the phrase "after these things I will return." Does this mean, "After the conversion of the Gentiles, I will return"? If that is the case, one sees in v. 17, there will be Gentiles "who are called by my name." If Gentiles are present at the time of Christ's second advent upon whom the name of the Lord is called, then Gentiles do not need to be circumcised (become Jews). This is an alternative line of argumentation.

15. Strauss, *Davidic Messiah*, 190; Glenny, "The Septuagint," 18–19.

16. By "fullness" I have in view the seemingly physical elements of the promises to national Israel that accompany the Davidic restoration: a fruitful presence, restored in her own land. Once again, I emphasize that fulfillment of prophecy never amounts to God doing less than He says He wills/intends to do!

17. E.g., Strauss and Glenny.

18. See Tanner, "James's Quotation," 82.

Micah 2:12-13

Messiah, the Breaker and the Deliverance of Israel

LARRY FELDMAN

The small book of Micah proportionately has more prophecies about the advent and kingdom of Messiah and Israel's future than any other prophetic book. His prophecy of Israel's future and her Deliverer King are valuable and intriguing. However, the prophecy of Mic 2:12-13 is often overlooked as a messianic prophecy and misunderstood.

Micah the prophet prophesied to the southern kingdom of Judah during the reigns of Jothan, Ahaz, and Hezekiah. He was a contemporary of Hosea and Isaiah, as well as Habakkuk, Zephaniah, and possibly Joel. His ministry as a prophet took place from 749–697 BC.

It was a time of intense social injustice in Judah, with false prophets preaching for riches, not for righteousness. Princes were cruel, violent, and corrupt. Priests ministered for greed, not for God. Landlords stole from the poor and evicted widows. Judges took bribes, businessmen were dishonest, and sin had infiltrated every segment of society.[1] Micah spoke out against all of these sins, foretelling the judgment that was to come, and the future restoration of the Jewish people.

Micah himself came from the town of Moresheth-Gath about 25 miles southwest of Jerusalem on the border of Judah and Philistia. He had a clear prophetic calling: "But as for me, I am filled with power by the Spirit of the Lord, with justice and courage, to proclaim to Jacob his rebellion and to Israel his sin" (3:8), and boldly proclaimed the Lord's message.

During Micah's time, the northern kingdom of Israel reached its pinnacle for disobedience to the Lord and fell to the Assyrian conquest in 722 BC (2Kg 17:6). A few years later, Judah was threatened to be overrun by the Assyrian armies (701 BC). Through a sudden, miraculous intervention by God, Judah was spared capture by the Assyrians (2Kg 19:35-36; 2Chr 32:21; Isa 37:36-37).

THE MESSAGE OF THE PROPHET MICAH

Throughout his book, Micah exposes the injustice of Judah, the righteousness and justice of God, and the coming of the messianic deliverer. About one-third of the book consists of the prophet exposing Judah's specific sins of oppression, bribery, exploitation, covetousness, cheating, violence, and pride. Another third is spent on the coming judgment for sin, and a final third on hope and consolation from the Lord. God's justice will triumph, and the divine deliverer will come bringing true peace and justice under the Messiah's reign.[2]

The book of Micah consists of three messages (chaps. 1–2; 3–5; 6–7). The three sections are identified by the call to "listen" 1:2; 3:1; 6:1 (Hb. *shema'*; cf. Dt 6:4). Each of the divisions of the book begins with a rebuke for sin, an announcement of judgment, and a promise of blessing in the Messiah[3] (2:12; 4:7; 5:7-8; 7:18).

The book begins with the first and most of the second chapters as an indictment for sin by the Lord as judge. Then suddenly Micah gives a message of hope and salvation, the first messianic prophecy in the book, in Mic 2:12-13.

EXPOSITION OF MICAH'S PROPHECY

Micah 2:12

The prophecy of Mic 2:12 raises several issues. These are (1) the time of the gathering of Israel; (2) the identity of the remnant of Israel; and (3) the location of the sheep pen, to which Israel will be gathered. Each of these will be addressed in order.

(1) *The time when God will "gather" His people together (Mic 2:12a)*

There are many suggestions as to when these events took place or will take place. To begin, consider the phrase "gather all of you" (v. 12), which speaks of God gathering together the Jewish people. This indicates that they had been scattered in some kind of dispersion or captivity.

If this text is read in isolation, then it may seem possible that this speaks of the Jewish people being brought back to Israel from Babylon after 70 years of captivity. (This event was yet in the future at the time of Micah's ministry.) Nebuchadnezzar took them captive to Babylon in phases (605, 597, and 586 BC). The Babylonian captivity and restoration were foretold by Micah's contemporary, Jeremiah (Jer 29:10).

As predicted, the exile occurred (2Kg 24–25), as did the return from captivity (as found in the books of Ezra and Nehemiah). Although the return from Babylon has been suggested as being the time of this gathering, the passage actually points to an eschatological fulfillment.[4] First, the return from Babylon was partial, yet in Mic 2:12 God promises to gather "all of you" (i.e., the whole remnant of Israel). Second, Mic 2:13 promises that the people would literally be led back to the land of Israel by "their King . . . the LORD," but the return from Babylon was led by a mortal prince, Zerubbabel.

Others suggest the gathering involved God's protection of Jerusalem from the siege of Jerusalem by Sennacherib, King of Assyria, in 701 BC.[5] The northern kingdom of Israel had been taken captive in 722 BC. After 20 years, Assyria once more invaded the land and came up to Jerusalem to conquer it. The Jewish people were gathered from across Judea into Jerusalem to avoid the siege of Sennacherib. If Mic 2:12 refers to a gathering during the siege of Sennacherib, there are two possible meanings: Perhaps, it refers to God's gathering of His people into Jerusalem to avoid the attacking Assyrian enemy. Alternatively, it might refer to God gathering His people, who had been forced to take refuge in Jerusalem, back into the rural areas and villages of their land after He miraculously destroyed the Assyrians (2Kg 19:35-36; also in Isa 37:36-37).

Still others say that the gathering spoken of in Mic 2:12 cannot be a promise of deliverance but must rather be a prediction of punishment because of the prophets' denunciations of their sins in the previous chapters.[6] Still others identify this as a prophecy of the return from Babylon but written by an exilic or postexilic prophet.[7]

The answers to these objections seem clear when the nature of Scripture, the concept of predictive prophecy, and the idea of hope and restoration in the prophets and throughout the Bible are understood. For instance, when God speaks of dispersion of His people, He speaks of them being dispersed by Assyria and Babylon and a future dispersion to the ends of the earth and to all nations (Dt 4:26-31; 28:36,49-50,64-65; Ezk 20:1-44; Hos 3:3-5; Zph 1:2-18). He does the same regarding their return from Babylon and Assyria at the end of the age from all lands to Israel to establish His kingdom (Isa 1:2–2:4; 10; 11; Jer 16:10-15; 23:1-8; 29–31; Ezk 36:16-38; 37; Hos 1:1-11; 2:8-23; Am 9:1-15; Zch 2:1-13). There is often a telescoping view of the first and second comings of the Messiah (Isa 61:1-3; Mic 5:2-5a; Zch 13:7-9; 9:9-10; Rev 12:5-6). Scripture also speaks of the destruction of nations and the end-time destruction in the tribulation (Isa 13:1-16; 23–24; 33–34; Dan 2, 7, 11:1-45). All of these can be seen in short- and long-term fulfillments within a few verses.

Walter Kaiser points out that the prophets refer to God's regathering the nation of Israel so frequently that, to be faithful to the prophetic message, the topic of regathering is unavoidable. Furthermore, he states that regatherings may have a number of fulfillments (such as Jerusalem's deliverance from Sennacherib's siege or Judah's restoration from captivity). These are only earnests or down payments on what God is going to do in the final day on a much larger and grander scale. There is a "now-and-not-yet" aspect to God's work of fulfillment. Even more convincing of a future gathering is that after the nation did return from Babylon under Zerubbabel in 536 BC, the same promise about Israel's restoration from many distant lands is repeated by Zechariah in 518 BC (Zch 8:2-8; 10:6-12). Thus, none of the previous returns can be what the prophets ultimately had in mind, since a return is anticipated by the postexilic prophets speaking of future regathering of the Jewish people back to the land after the return from Babylon under Cyrus.[8] Feinberg also states that the restoration from Babylon through Cyrus cannot exhaust the promise because it was only a partial return to the land, since many Jewish people chose to stay in Babylon, and the prophet says "all of you."[9]

As for the idea that seeing this as a promise of regathering is too sudden a change from the punishment sections, it is simply not so. Abrupt changes in the prophets are entirely keeping with the method of the messages of the prophets (see Hos 2:2; 6:1; 11:9).[10] T. Miles Bennett points out that it is common, after severe denunciation and threat without introduction or transition, to go into a gracious promise (Am 9:8-15; Isa 29:1-8; Ezk 11:5-21). If this is admitted, the objection of "appended by a later hand" need not be explained. If one allows the predictive element in Hebrew prophecy, many of the difficulties associated with this and similar passages are removed. It should not be surprising therefore to find Micah predicting the future restoration of a remnant in the very midst of his words of a more immediate judgment.[11]

With these objections aside, it is evident that Micah was prophesying of the Jewish people being gathered again at the end of days. This raises the question of why would the Jewish people need to be "gathered" again near the end of time. The answer is found in Rev 12 where Satan is depicted to be at war with God, His plans, and His Jewish people (Rev 12:13,17). The future tribulation period begins when Satan's man, the false messiah, or as many people call him the Antichrist, signs a covenant with God's Jewish people (Dan 9:27) for one prophetic week, that is, for seven years. In the middle of the week, or after 3 ½ years, the false messiah breaks the covenant with Israel and begins major warfare against the Jewish people. He is indwelt by Satan, who has just been removed from heaven after waging war with Michael the archangel, the chief prince over the affairs of Israel (see Rev 12:7-9,13; Dan 10:13; 12:1). At that time, Satan will attack the Jewish people with great rage and wrath (Rev 12:17).

The false messiah will then gather his troops to wage war in the Middle East with aid from the many countries surrounding Israel (Dan 11:36-44). He will then move his campaign headquarters to the ancient city of Megiddo (*Har Megiddo* or Armageddon) where he will begin his military assault (Dan 11:45; Rev 16:16). There really is no single battle called Armageddon, only a campaign that begins there for about 3 ½ years and is probably better called the campaign of or the war of "the great day of God, the Almighty" (Rev 16:14).[12] At this point he begins a major offensive war with the Jewish people and attacks Jerusalem from the north (Zch 12:2-3 and 14:2-3.)[13] So the Jewish people will be under great persecution. In order to escape this persecution, the Jewish people will flee as predicted by the prophet Daniel and restated by the Messiah Jesus in His Olivet Discourse (Mt 24:15-22).

So, the time of Israel's flight seems to come at some time after the false messiah gathers his troops at Megiddo (the gathering place of the Campaign of Armageddon), puts an end to the sacrifices in a future Jewish Temple, and wages war on the Jewish people in Israel, specifically Jerusalem. The Jewish people will be forced to flee, as they were warned to do so by their Messiah as recorded in the book of Matthew. These events occur in the second half of the great tribulation period. It is only after this flight that the Lord will once again "gather" the Jewish people back to their land (Mic 2:12a).

(2) *The identity of the remnant of Israel (Micah 2:12b)*

Micah 2:12 identifies those who will be gathered as "Jacob" and "the remnant of Israel." This is a common Hebrew poetic form called parallelism, when synonymous terms are used for emphasis. Using both terms identifies the group as the Jewish people, often called Jacob, but a specific part of the Jewish people, the "remnant." The remnant implies a small amount of the whole and is often used in the OT to identify the faithful of the Jewish people. For example, after the exodus, when Moses sent the 12 spies into Canaan to evaluate the land, 10 of the men were fearful, not trusting God, and gave a bad report on the land; only 2 men, Joshua and Caleb, believed the Lord and said, "We must go up and take possession of the land because we can certainly conquer it" (Nm 13:30). Also, when Elijah felt he was the only man in Israel still trusting God after the defeat of the prophets of Baal, the Lord said there were yet 7,000 in Israel who remained faithful to Him (1Kg 19:18). Likewise, after his final siege of Jerusalem, Nebuchadnezzar carried into captivity the majority of the Jewish people, but "left some of the poorest," a remnant of the Jewish people in Israel (2Kg 25:12). It is this remnant idea in Micah's prophecy that McComisky observes:

> Micah's doctrine of the remnant is unique among the Prophets and is perhaps his most significant contribution to the prophetic theology of hope. The remnant is a force in the world, not simply a residue of people, as the word "remnant" (*she'erit*) may seem to imply. It is a force that will ultimately conquer the world

> (4:11-13). This triumph, while presented in apparently militaristic terminology (4:13; 5:5-6), is actually accomplished by other than physical force [cf. Matt. 5:3-12]. By removing everything that robs his people of complete trust in him (5:10-15), the Ruler from Bethlehem will effect the deliverance of his people. The source of power for God's people in the world is their absolute trust in him and his resources.[14]

During the tribulation period God will gather the remnant of Jewish people who have escaped Jerusalem and bring them back to their land, probably to keep them from harm or destruction from their enemies. He will bring them to and from a specific location, namely Bozrah.

(3) *The location of the gathering (Micah 2:12c)*

In the prophecy, God tells where He will gather the remnant of Israel. They will be gathered in a specific location called a "pen" or a sheep "fold." The imagery is one of a shepherd gathering his sheep for protection from those who would destroy them. In the figure, the danger could be thieves, the elements, or wild animals like wolves, lions, or bears.

In this scenario, the Lord is frequently identified as the Shepherd of Israel (Gn 48:15; 49:23-24; Pss 23; 80:1; Isa 40:11; Ezk 34:11-16; Jn 10). The familiar image of the shepherd in Ps 23 demonstrates that the Lord our Shepherd provides, comforts, protects, and leads the sheep. The Gospels use this image of the Good and Great Shepherd being Jesus the Messiah. Here the Messiah, the Good Shepherd, is willing to lay down His life for His own, giving them eternal life, and is also at the door of the gate to protect them (Jn 10).

Micah reveals that God will gather the Jewish people like sheep in a fold. The Hebrew word "sheepfold" is *bozrah*. Parallel passages in Isa 34 and 63 seem to indicate that the word sheepfold is not merely a descriptive term but a reference to a specific city named Bozrah in the mountain range of Mount Seir, southeast of the Dead Sea in Edom. Two sites have been suggested for its location. One is the Arab village of Buseira, which is similar in sound to Bozrah. The alternative suggestion is the city of Petra. Both cities could fit, as both are in the Mount Seir range in Southern Jordan, or ancient Edom. But Petra seems preferable for a number of reasons. First, the name Bozrah means sheepfold, and Petra is shaped exactly like a natural sheepfold. It is located in a basin within Mount Seir and is totally surrounded by cliffs and mountains. The only way in or out is via a slot canyon, a narrow passageway like the gate of a sheepfold. Once inside, Petra is more spacious. Thus, Petra is shaped like a giant sheepfold with a narrow passage and a spacious circle surrounded by cliffs. This is not true for the other proposed site of Buseira.

Also, a site near Petra is called Butzeira, which is more like the Hebrew word for Bozrah.[15]

Fruchtenbaum gives three other clues for Petra being the location of Bozrah. First, he cites Mt 24:16, indicating that the place of refuge is to be the mountains. Second, he refers to Rev 12:6,14, that the refuge is to be in the wilderness. Third, he mentions Isa 33:16, which identifies the place of refuge as a rocky fortress. Then Fruchtenbaum writes that Petra

> was located in the region of Mount Seir. Mount Seir is a very rocky range of mountains, and its name means the "hairy mountains." This fulfills the requirement of the Matthew passage. It is located in the wilderness section of ancient Edom and so fulfills the requirement of the Revelation passage. The very nature of the chain of mountains of Mount Seir makes it quite defensible, fulfilling the requirements of the Isaiah passage.[16]

To summarize, Micah reveals that God will bring the Jewish people to the "sheep pen" or Bozrah. It appears that this will occur in the second half of the tribulation when the false messiah attacks the Jewish people and they flee out of Jerusalem. God will gather them together for safety, protection, and preservation in Petra, the ancient city of Bozrah located in the western side of ancient Edom, today in Southern Jordan.[17]

Again using Hebrew poetic parallelism, Micah's images of "sheep in a pen" and "a flock in the middle of its fold" refer to the people of Israel, not actual sheep. They will be gathered during the tribulation period to the sheepfold of Bozrah. Details continue by telling it will be "noisy with people" in the area where the people are gathered together. The noise is probably coming from all the people as they are anticipating salvation and deliverance from their enemies by the One who has gathered them. It is as if the pen and the people, who are so many, would be like a huge herd of sheep causing a great noise.[18] The image is clearly one of the Jewish people being gathered in a safe place in preparation for a coming event foretold in the next verse.

Micah 2:13

The next verse continues the prophecy and raises three other issues: (1) the identity of the breaker; (2) the meaning of "breaks open the way"; and (3) the identity of "their King" and "Lord as their leader."

(1) *The identity of the One who breaks open the way (Micah 2:13a)*

After the remnant of Israel has been gathered to Bozrah and they wait eagerly for the Lord to act, the prophet begins to identify their deliverer. He is the One who "breaks open the way" and advances before them. He will break out of the sheep pen, pass through the gate, and lead the remnant of Israel.

This "One who breaks open the way," (often called "the Breaker") is parallel to "their King" and "the LORD" at the end of the verse, and is a reference to the Messiah. He is called "the Breaker" because of His work of breaking down and overcoming all the obstacles to Israel's safety and blessing.

As with the discussion of the time of the gathering, some have suggested this refers to events after God destroyed the Assyrian army surrounding Jerusalem in 701 BC.[19] The argument is that God leads the people out of Jerusalem back to their homes in the countryside of the land. They leave by the gate, and their God leads them as He did out of Egypt in a pillar of fire at night and with a cloud by day. However, the tone of this passage and the events described seem to go well beyond the Assyrian suggestion, for two reasons. First, it is alleged that these verses describe Israel being saved from Assyria by fleeing into Jerusalem. But, that would not be a captivity into Jerusalem. The passage suggests a gathering from danger and then a freeing or deliverance from the enemy. The noise the people make is joyful, not fearful. Second, this passage does not describe the destruction of the Assyrian army but rather God's release of the Jewish people by their Breaker, King, and Lord Himself to lead them in their return to the land of Israel. The Assyrian suggestion makes Jerusalem the gate and Zion the sheepfold or pen. This makes the whole passage too symbolic because the passage clearly states it is in Bozrah, located in Edom or modern-day Jordan. The people are leaving Bozrah to return to Jerusalem to be part of the kingdom with their Messiah, as seen in chaps. 4 and 5.

Another explanation of the time of breaking out of the gate is the return to Zion out of Babylon under Cyrus in 536 BC.[20] Strangely, these interpreters refer to the release from captivity for both ideas for the breaking out: the gathering together in Israel for captivity in Babylon and also the release from Babylon. Either way, such an interpretation removes the normal understanding of the passage. Also, it seems clear, as in the discussion about v. 2:12, this is a time that looks for its fulfillment in the future restoration in the kingdom.

(2) *The meaning of "breaks open the way" through "the gate" (Micah 2:13b)*

Some interpreters suggest an opening is made to pass through a gate to Jerusalem,[21] but this interpretation seems to stretch the Scripture more than should be allowed. Too much symbolism is involved to make Jerusalem the gate and Judah the land. A better understanding is to place these events in the end times. It is the Lord who breaks open the way through the gate in a great final battle. When the Lord returns, He will deliver His people at Bozrah (Petra). Then, He will take them through the narrow passageway or gate and lead them from there to the Mount of Olives (Zch

14:4). He will then judge the Gentile nations in the Kidron Valley (Jl 3:2,12-13; Mt 25:31-46) and finally establish the promised messianic, millennial kingdom with His people.

The scene is now set for the final battles and the return of the Lord who "breaks open the way" and "will advance before them." This will take place at the glorious return of the Messiah. Both Zch 14:4 and Ac 1:11 indicate that the Lord will return and set His feet on the Mount of Olives. However, His arrival at the Mount of Olives will take place only after He first returns to Petra/Bozrah, to fight for and deliver the Jewish people who have fled there for safety.

In the prophecy of Mic 2:12-13, there appears to be a gap between vv. 12 and 13. In v. 12, God gathered His people together at Bozrah to protect and preserve the remnant of Israel during the second half of the tribulation period. After the false messiah and his cohorts descend to this area to annihilate the Jewish people, the Jewish people will recognize their sin, make a national confession, receive/welcome Jesus as their long-awaited Messiah, and call on Him to save them. Then He will return, and when they see Him they will weep, mourn, and repent for their many years of rejecting Him (Zch 12:10-14). Although many biblical passages deal with Messiah's return, the following are the most germane to the prophecy of Mic 2:12-13.

The return of the Lord is described in Rev 14:14-20 as the reaping of God's harvest. The picture is one of God saving His people and destroying His enemies. The earth's vineyard and grape harvest is the visible picture of the defeat of the enemy and the flow of blood that will be shed at that time.

The judgment of God's (and Israel's) enemies is described as the great winepress of God's wrath where the "blood flowed out of the press up to the horses' bridles for about 180 miles." This is approximately the distance from Jerusalem to the Gulf of Eilat or the round-trip distance from Jerusalem to Bozrah (Rev 14:14-20). The image in Revelation is a culmination of Isaiah's prophetic description of a future bloody battle and the vengeance God will bring on His and the Jewish people's enemies (Isa 34:1-3,5-8). Isaiah specifically states that God will go to war against these enemies in Bozrah (Isa 34:5-6).

Another passage that further describes this awful scene appears in Isa 63:1-6. Here it actually describes the blood on the Messiah at His return and is in perfect harmony with Isa 34 and Rev 14. It also explains that He alone fights in these battles. He is advancing before His people in victory. Messiah is the Breaker, the One who breaks open the way, the One coming from Bozrah "in crimson stained garments" (Isa 63:1) to fight for His people. Isaiah, speaking in the name of the Lord, declares, "For I planned the day of vengeance, and the year of My redemption came. I looked, but there was no one to help . . . so My arm accomplished victory for Me, and My wrath assisted Me. I crushed nations in My anger; I made them drunk with My wrath and poured out their blood on the ground" (Isa 63:4-6). The Lord will return to Bozrah to make war in defense of His people and then lead the people, as the Breaker, to the Mount of Olives in Jerusalem, to deliver those Jewish people still besieged in Jerusalem (Zch 14:3).

(3) *The Messiah King and Lord their leader (Micah 2:13c)*
The One who is the Breaker is further identified as "their King" and "the LORD as their leader." He is their "King," a frequent title for the Lord (Dt 33:5; Pss 24:9-10; 47:6; 48:2; 95:3). This messianic title is alluded to in Gn 49:9-10; Nm 24:17; 2Sm 7:16. This King is none other than the Lion of Judah (He whose right it is), the Star from Jacob, and the future son of David, the King-Messiah Himself, Jesus the Messiah.

Finally, the verse goes on to say who their Breaker and their King is by saying He is "the LORD as their leader," none other than God Himself, their leader and the Messiah of Israel.

God Himself will gather them together and then lead them to victory and freedom from all their enemies.

SUMMARY OF MICAH'S PROPHECY

This important messianic prophecy speaks about future hope and restoration promised to the remnant of the Jewish people. God Himself will emphatically gather together all the Jewish people, Jacob, the remnant of Israel. In the Scriptures and history God has done this many times, such as out of Egypt, back from Babylon, the establishment of the modern state of Israel. He will once again gather them in the end-time tribulation period to bring about the future messianic kingdom on earth with the Messiah reigning from Jerusalem. The people will rejoice at the coming of the Breaker, who will go before them and lead them to safety and victory. The prophecy in Mic 2:12-13 concludes by making clear that their leader who leads them to victory is none other than God Himself. This is their King-Messiah who is God in the flesh (cf. Hab 3:3-4).

---

1. Bruce Wilkinson and Kenneth Boa, *Talk Thru the Old Testament*; *Talk Thru the Bible*, vol. I (Nashville: Thomas Nelson, 1983), 261.
2. Ibid., 263.
3. Charles Lee Feinberg, *Jonah, Micah and Nahum* (New York: ABMJ, 1951), 54.

4. T. E. McComiskey, "Micah," in *Daniel–Minor Prophets*, vol. 7 of The Expositor's Bible Commentary, ed. Frank Gabelein (Grand Rapids: Zondervan, 1985), 415; Feinberg, *Jonah, Micah and Nahum*, 70; Daniel Green, "Micah," in *The Moody Bible Commentary*, ed. Michael Rydelnik and Michael Vanlaningham (Chicago: Moody Publishers, 2014), 1373.

5. Walter C. Kaiser, *The Messiah in the Old Testament* (Grand Rapids: Zondervan, 1995), 150; Bruce K. Waltke, *A Commentary on Micah* (Grand Rapids: Eerdmans, 2008), 140.

6. Feinberg, *Jonah, Micah, and Nahum*, 69.

7. Waltke, *A Commentary on Micah*, 139.

Leslie C. Allen, *The Books of Joel, Jonah, and Micah* (Grand Rapids: Eerdmans, 1976), 242, 244, 301.

8. Kaiser, *The Messiah in the Old Testament*, 150.

9. Feinberg, *Jonah, Micah, and Nahum*, 70.

10. Ibid., 69.

11. T. Miles Bennett, *The Study of Micah, a Study Manual* (Grand Rapids: Baker Book House, 1968), 31.

12. Arnold G. Fruchtenbaum, *The Footsteps of the Messiah* (San Antonio: Ariel Ministries, 2003), 294–317.

13. Ibid., 334–35.

14. T. E. McComiskey, "Micah," in *Daniel–Minor Prophets*, vol. 7 of The Expositor's Bible Commentary, ed. Frank Gabelein (Grand Rapids: Zondervan, 1985), 396–97.

15. Fruchtenbaum, *Footsteps of the Messiah*, 294–97.

16. Ibid., 296.

17. Ibid.

18. Daniel Green, "Micah," in *The Moody Bible Commentary*, ed. Michael Rydelnik and Michael Vanlaningham (Chicago: Moody Publishers, 2014), 1371.

19. Waltke, *A Commentary on Micah*, 140.

20. See Kaiser, *Messiah in the Old Testament*, 150.

21. Waltke, *A Commentary on Micah*, 139

Micah 5:2-5a

Bethlehem: Birthplace of the Messianic King

LEON ENGMAN

Micah 5:2-5a stands out in the book of Micah like a diamond on a ring. The ring is lovely and well-wrought but designed to direct attention to the diamond. Contrasted against the darkening time of Israel's kings, this passage directs attention to the hope of Israel. The New Testament employs this passage as a resounding, unambiguous announcement: the promised Lion of Judah has arrived.

Scholarship in the West has assaulted Micah's straightforwardness and clarity for the last several centuries. Critical scholars have assumed the human mind as reference point of all reality, the Bible as merely ancient literature, and predictive prophecy as impossible. Under those assumptions, this passage is squeezed into a small, pathetic space. Being curious, critical, even skeptical have their place but must be brought into a frame of respect for the book of Micah as the Word of God.

The perpetual conundrum is that God chose human authors and editors with their language skills and styles. The humanity of it helps people relate to Scriptures on one hand, but can leave others looking askance at the same time. Reading as a believer is not simply a leap of faith; it demands coherence and cogency. When reading Scripture, it is essential to pay attention, always on razor's edge.

Micah's message creates difficulties for those who assume that predictive prophecy is not possible or likely. For them, Micah is necessarily reduced to a patchwork of texts amended by disciples and redactors to some previously written core bits produced by Micah long ago. There is undoubtedly an editing process in play, but it should not be forced to carry the burden of accommodating the reader's unbelief in the possibility of prophecy.

In 1979, Brevard Childs bemoaned the state of scholarship on Micah: "In sum, few books illustrate as well as does Micah the present crisis in exegetical method . . . the growing confusion over conflicting theories of composition has increasingly buried the book in academic debris. Needless to say, no general consensus of the book's form or function appears in sight."[1]

Fortunately, Childs's efforts in canonical, literary reading as well as biblical theology have reintroduced some clarity to the current understanding of Micah. Critical scholarship's peculiar obsession with reductionism in biblical studies has been tempered in some quarters by these efforts.

John Sailhamer shouldered this movement in the evangelical world. The fruit of his labor is a new generation of scholars reading the biblical text as it has come to us. As the text is released from bondage to modern theological and academic schema, it is possible to hear more clearly the ancient voices from which it comes.

One of the arguments for dissecting the text into separate sources is the rapid change of topics and occasionally mismatched grammar. The first step in evaluating this should be to consider the possibility that disjointedness is intentional. Perhaps the author gathered his own material and chose to communicate with roughness, knowing how it would sound because it would most likely be read aloud. Contemporary authors write children's stories, plays, and poetry in a peculiar way knowing they will be read aloud (consider Dr. Seuss). That is an important and underappreciated dynamic in Micah.

The advent of vowel markings on the Hebrew text came many centuries later, in part because it was no longer exclusively read aloud. The sound of the text being read out loud faded from corporate memory. Micah's roughness read aloud is rather like a movie scene where the camera is carried into a battle by hand instead of on a smooth track. The bouncing and confusion in the picture is part of the message. It is reminiscent of soldiers under attack trying to shout to one another. The lack of correct grammar heightens the desperation of the message.

Stark fear is a strong element in the original audience's hearing. The dreadful prospect of the Assyrians is real and happening during Micah's ministry. Judah is watching Israel get raided, taken apart, and eventually overwhelmed. Nothing obvious is keeping them from the same fate. The rumors and reports are terrifying. That is the human backdrop of the book of Micah.

Judah's economic and geopolitical success is their comfort. They have the palace, Temple, and ark of the covenant. This poses a theological difficulty. Is God obligated to them on that account? "God chose us because we are special and He has to help us." That assumption demands that God take care of them because they are the chosen people, fulfilling their religious duties at the Temple. Or is the truth quite opposite? "We are special because God graciously chose us and we have presumed on His gift." That assumption demands something from the hearer on account of God's great generosity. The prophets preach the latter. God is not pleased with outward perfections overlaying their inner corruption. That message is strongly reinforced by the presence of foreign troops in their land.

Micah is well situated, nestled into the history of Israel. Verse 1 names him as author and gives a range of dates when he prophesied. His ministry spans the reigns of Jotham, Ahaz, and Hezekiah, which are covered by other narrative passages (2Kg 15:32–20:21, Isa 36–39, Jer 26:16-19 and 2Chr 27–33). The only narrative in the book of Micah is the first verse; the rest is his message.

INTEXTUAL AND INNERTEXTUAL EXEGESIS: ARGUMENT OF THE EMBEDDED SECTION AND THE WHOLE BOOK OF MICAH

Verse 2

The text of Mic 5:2-5a falls in the midst of the three large cycles of judgment and salvation that comprise Micah (1:2–2:13; 3:1–5:15; 6:1–7:20). The prophet contrasts what seems great to his readers against what is, in fact, great. Jerusalem seems great; it is the City of David. David conquered Jerusalem and consolidated political and religious power there with a palace and a Temple (built by his son). In Micah, Jerusalem is now under siege. Just as David forgot his own humble beginnings, Israel has forgotten theirs. As David's line has failed in its mission, so Israel has failed. Following 1Sm 16 where David, the youngest brother and humble shepherd, is anointed king, the Lord again will choose a seeming no-one from a now-familiar nowhere to be the ruler who will walk in His ways.

The Lord directly addresses Bethlehem with good news. The "and you" ("but you" in many versions) that begins 5:2 matches the beginning "and you" of 4:8, where Jerusalem is addressed. (HCSB breaks the pattern in 5:2 by putting "you" after "Ephrathah.") The intentional contrast is that in 4:8, Jerusalem is assured of its eventual salvation despite its terrifying present, and ironically in 5:2, that salvation will come again from little, unremarkable Bethlehem.

There is a series of three mini-cycles of judgment and salvation between the "and you" markers at 4:8 and 5:2. The mini-cycles all begin with "now" (4:9, 5:1), or "nations have now" (4:11). "You" and "now" in Hebrew are spelled differently but sound alike.[2] "Now" (*'atah*) sounds like "you" (*'atah*). Sounds are important in documents read aloud. The assonance is part of the design to catch the hearer's ear. The pattern has five sound-alike words that start vv. 4:8-9,11; 5:1-2. The "now" mini-cycles, like the larger three cycles that comprise the whole book, all start at the difficult present situation and move to the Lord's future salvation.

The first cycle (4:9) is weighted toward the present trouble, the second (4:11) more toward salvation, and the final (5:1) is resolved in a clear expression of messianic hope in the present passage. Bethlehem is the biggest and best expression of salvation of those three small "now" cycles. All the cycles are literary devices that serve to emphasize and point out the present passage.

The place names of this future hope are full of what is lacking in their present distress: Bethlehem means "house of bread" and Ephrathah means "fruitfulness." The feminine expression of hope in 4:8, "Daughter Jerusalem," and 5:1's bracing "daughter who is under attack" is now focused and girded in the masculine language of 5:2 toward a very specific salvation.

The humility of the Lord's ruler is emphasized first in the contrast between Jerusalem and Bethlehem and then within the clans or thousands of Judah. It is a reminder that the Lord chose Jesse's youngest, unthought-of son ("do you have no more sons?"). The Lord is not impressed with the misplaced pride Israel has in their institutions, including the impregnable city of David and the corrupted monarchy and priesthood. Those gifts given by God have been abused and used by Judah's leaders as weapons against their own countrymen.

The Lord's direct address to Bethlehem continues to this One who comes out from there. The grammar here is not smooth, inviting many proposed emendations to the MT; however, none of the proposed changes answers the difficulty.[3] As Bruce K. Waltke writes, "The rough text is more likely due to the process of compilation . . . Micah builds up his prophecies . . . by employing earlier, probably written, sources."[4]

It reads literally "from you (Bethlehem) to Me (the Lord) He will come out." The same verb here, *yetse* ("coming out"), is used to describe the shoot coming from the stump of Jesse in Isa 11:1, and the descendants coming out from David's body in 2Sm 7:12. The identity of the one spoken of as "He" is not yet clear, but Micah continues drawing the curtain back. He will be ruler in Israel; Micah is careful to not call this One "king." To name another king might demand a response from a sitting king, rather like Jesus' refusal to call Himself Messiah until His trial. That notion is important in the way this passage is used in Matthew centuries later.

Further identifying this One, Micah moves from His future coming forth back to His beginnings long ago. The prophet reuses *yetse* in another form in the next phrase indicating the "place from which one comes or to which one goes."[5] HCSB's translation "origin" is thin for what is being said here. NASB's "goings forth" or NIV's "origins" better captures the essence. His origins are described from two angles: "antiquity" *qedem*, and "eternity" *olam*. Those terms fill up whatever capacity the hearer of Micah has to take in the greatness of this ruler, from the time of David himself and certainly beyond into the heavenly realm. Whether the grandeur of tradition or of infinity, whatever distance in time one can imagine, this One comes before.

VERSE 3

In response to the question "when?" left hanging by v. 2, the hearer pivots on v. 3's beginning "therefore." Having moved from the present horror of 5:1 to the amazing statement of 5:2, the reader unavoidably wants that greatness applied to the present difficulty. The future fulfillment is ahead in time, but how far? Is the fulfillment as far forward in time as the origins (of v. 2) go back? That there is a point marked in future time can only be a tremendous relief.

The text and context for the hearer is that Israel (5:2) is given up to the enemy they can see in front of them. In v. 3 "abandon them" (plural) works with the singular Israel as the antecedent because it is collective. Either the Lord is doing the giving up or they are given up without a personal reference.[6]

The period of how long they are given over lasts until the child is born to the woman in labor. This picture of a woman in labor has been used in 4:9-10 as a reference to how weak, vulnerable and in trouble Israel is in its present situation, but in 5:3 this picture is a pathway to the salvation of the Lord. The birth will be a sign that this ruler from Bethlehem is on the scene.

The first woman giving birth in 4:9-10 is called the daughter of Zion. Her agony will result in exile from which there will be eventual rescue. The next woman in 5:3 gives birth to the ruler from Bethlehem, and this increases specificity about the Lord's salvation. That Israel is given over until that time is a hard message from a human point of view. In other words, the Lord is saying, "you may not see it but your descendants eventually will." The HCSB captures this with the word "abandon," a huge letdown for the recipient of the message. It is both good news and bad: "There is a victorious future, but you are not going to be part of it."

They have hope in the sense that the abandonment is not permanent, and their people will not be dissolved. These words will, later on, be more hopeful to those already in exile and later to those who have returned.

What will they see? After the people are given up, the arrival of the ruler, Messiah, will reunite the rest of His brothers with Israel. What will Messiah do by way of reuniting? In this context, a reuniting looks back to David's accomplishment of bringing all the tribes together in a united kingdom. The Messiah will do this in a way that will not fall apart as David's kingdom did. The original audience is witnessing the ongoing deportations from the northern tribes, a further dividing of brothers. The ranks of allies are getting thinner, whomever one may regard as a brother in this difficult time. Judah and Israel were enemies and allies at different times, but seeing Israel destroyed is no comfort to Judah. This is a signal for further development of the remnant concept.[7] The rest, or remnant, will be critical in the dividing now and reuniting later.

Israel will be united because of this ruler, the Messiah. The difference between Messiah and David will show in the everlasting nature of His kingdom. There will be an end of exile and a return before the Messiah, but His eternal reuniting will expand beyond tribal concerns. The return after the exile, with no Messiah yet, will be divisive again on tribal issues; for example, breaking marriages in Ezra–Nehemiah and hostility toward Samaritans even in Jesus' day. The theme of a united people of God is central to the NT, but where does the reuniting of Israel proper fit into that? This verse raises an issue that is still in conversation to this day. Most likely it looks to the future day that Paul anticipated, when the nation of Israel would turn in faith to their Messiah Jesus (Zch 12:10) and "all Israel will be saved" (Rom 11:26).

VERSE 4

When this ruler brings about reunification of Israel, He will do it as a shepherd over His flock for the sake of the Lord. All along, this ruler distinguishes Himself from the others in the line of David by being wholeheartedly in the service of Israel's God. That is why His reign will be far beyond David's or Solomon's.

The notion of a ruler as shepherd was common in the ANE. It reflected the best that a ruler could be. What contemporary society would consider a dictatorship, in Micah's perspective is a truly benevolent master, a king committed to His God and the security of His people. The security promised was addressed earlier in 4:4, but when and how? Here the shepherd is bringing the answer into focus. Security is what shepherds provide, and this one provides it like none other.

Uniquely, this shepherd is not only committed to the Lord but also draws all His strength from Him.[8] David was portrayed this way (2Sm 5:2, 7:8), and this ruler would be much more so, not giving way to the temptations of power. To rule in the Lord's name is to rule in His authority.[9] The universal reign is the fulfillment of all hope vested in the Davidic line that had been so disappointing. Waltke rightly takes this promise of the Shepherd's rule as a continuation of the thought started in 5:2, making 5:3 a parenthetical, albeit important, note.[10]

Curiously, the last phrase of v. 4 uses "now" again but not as a section marker as it was in 4:9,11; 5:1. Here it indicates the future, rather than the present situation. The *ki-'tah* is well caught by the HCSB as "for then," even though literally it is "for now." The "now" is in the sequence of future things.[11] The extension of the kingdom has no limits but the earth itself.

Verse 5a

The phrase, "He will be their peace," captures what the Messiah will do for His people by way of reigning and providing security everywhere. This is reflected in Isa 9:6 and pointedly specified in Jesus at Eph 2:14 as the catalyst for the reuniting unity: "For He is our peace, who made both groups one and tore down the dividing wall of hostility."

In Sum

This passage is the central piece, the jewel of the book of Micah. From a literary design prospect, 5:2-5a is in the second of the three judgment and salvation cycles that comprise the whole book. The cycles are set so that the second, or middle, cycle is the focus of the book. The reader walks into the center of the book through the first cycle, stands in the climax of the message in the second cycle, and exits through the third. Inside the second judgment and salvation cycle, this passage is in the third and penultimate of three smaller "now" statements mentioned earlier (4:9-10, 11-13, 4:14–5:5a).

From a thematic perspective, Micah's themes are all given hope by the ruler described in 5:2-5a. The judgment carried out by the Assyrians will be brought back on them by the ruler in the following verses of chap. 5. The remnant of Israel will be the representative of Israel until the fulfillment of this ruler. The security they lack will be brought about by the Shepherd who will not compromise in His relationship with God. The division they see happening as Israel is carved up will be brought together in this One. Knowing about this ruler is a lifeline carrying the hearers through the present terror.

From an identification point of view, this passage is critical to recognizing this ruler when He appears. That is why Jesus' birth in Bethlehem is highlighted in the argument of three of the Gospels.

INTERTEXTUAL EXEGESIS: HOW MIC 5:2-5A FITS IN THE CONTEXT OF THE OLD TESTAMENT BOOKS

By bringing together Bethlehem, Ephrathah, and Judah, Micah echoes 1Sm 17:12, where Jesse and David are named in association with them. The richness of the David story in relation to hometown Bethlehem Ephrathah is fleshed out in the book of Ruth. The reader will not miss that in this ruler (Mic 5:2), the line of David is being restarted as in Isa 11:1, with a shoot growing from the stump of Jesse.

Parts of Mic 4 are virtually identical to corresponding parts of Isa 2. Micah and Isaiah were contemporaries. They were later portrayed in intertestamental literature as living together along with other prophets (*Martyrdom and Ascension of Isaiah* 2:7-11; 6:1-8).[12] Their close association relates Micah's picture of the woman in labor to the virgin of Isa 7:14. Isaiah writes, "Therefore, the Lord Himself will give you a sign: The virgin will conceive, have a son, and name him Immanuel." And Micah, "Therefore, He will abandon them until the time when she who is in labor has given birth." Micah begins verse 5:3 with the same words for "therefore," *lakeyn yiteyn,* as Isa 7:14. Micah takes the verse in a different direction to the same goal but is making a clear allusion to Isaiah with the same elements.[13]

All the amazing characteristics of this ruler's coming in Mic 5:2-5a are also brought out in Isaiah chapters 7, 9, and 11. Michael Rydelnik brings them side-by-side: pregnant virgin giving birth, divine nature, glorious reign, and source of Israel's peace. All of these stand out in both Isaiah and Micah. Further, "If a plainly messianic passage like Mic 5:2-5 cites Isa 7:13-15, it shows that the earliest interpretation of Isa 7:14 (and no less, an inspired interpretation) recognizes the messianic prophecy of the virgin birth."[14] In other words, Micah's reading of Isaiah is an inspired reading set out in his own writing, just as the NT writers interpreted the prophets.

HOW THE NEW TESTAMENT REFLECTS MICAH'S INTENTION

In the NT, this prophecy shows up most prominently in Matthew's gospel, as a quote in a pattern of other quotes, and as an element in the developing narrative. The pattern in Mt 2 is of four quotes all concerning geographic references: Bethlehem, Egypt, Ramah, and Nazareth. Each also represents one of the four major types of prophecy interpretation in the NT, with Micah as a prophecy of direct fulfillment.[15]

Matthew's birth narrative is set by many scholars into the category of a midrash. A midrash is sometimes considered a storytelling not necessarily based in fact; here it would characterize who the Messiah will be. Matthew's account is not fiction, but fact and narrative shaping are not necessarily mutually exclusive. The Scripture quotes in Matthew do lend shape to the narrative, but not at the expense of historical reality. This happens in other parts of the Gospels, where characters (e.g., John, Jesus) are cast in the familiar terms of characters whose roles they are filling. Jesus is cast in the role of Moses in the Sermon on the Mount. John is cast as Elijah in his mode of dress (2Kg 1:7-8; Mt 3:4; Mk 1:6). Jesus clearly connects John with Elijah (Mt 11:14), despite John's protests to the contrary (Jn 1:21). These are simply literary ways of emphasizing certain elements of the story, connecting the dots with the ongoing story of God's salvation, setting the present story into its larger framework.

In Matthew's birth story, Herod is cast in the role of Pharaoh killing baby boys. The magi are cast in the role of the Queen of Sheba seeking the King of the Jews. The Christmas star is an echo of Balaam's prophecy predicting a star rising out of Jacob to rule the nations.[16]

None of these intentional connections mean that the event in question did not take place. They simply shape the story into a familiar form. The birth in Bethlehem is casting God's choice in the same humble, unexpected terms as when He anointed David.

Why wouldn't Matthew use those factors in the telling of the story? Those events got his attention in the first place. Also, since Jesus grew up in Nazareth, the place of His birth was still an issue in the Jewish community at the time Matthew was writing. Matthew was apparently in the middle of that discussion, as he had been for years, and wanted to be clear that Jesus the Nazarene was born in Bethlehem. Certainly, Matthew was concerned with the facts, not just the telling of the story. This writing is close enough in time to get eyewitness testimony, most pointedly from Mary, the mother of Jesus (Ac 1:14). Conversely, Matthew, along with the rest of the biblical authors, was not simply recording facts. The OT connections are both theologically and historically important.[17]

The baby Jesus' connection with David as ancestor, king, and anointed one (messiah) is crucial, as well as dangerous. To mention someone as king, while there is a sitting king, was as hazardous in Jesus' day as it had been for David. Herod brooked no potential usurpers. Matthew has the quote of Mic 5 in the collective mouth of the chief priests and scribes Herod has summoned to inquire about the King of the Jews that the magi were seeking.

The topic "King of the Jews" comes up again in the passion narratives, as testimony again of how dangerous it is to take this title. The magi inquired after the King of the Jews, and Herod knew enough to ask where the Christ (Messiah) was to be born. The birth in Bethlehem is heavy with spiritual/theological significance, but at its base, it is a physical reality with which to identify the Messiah. It is not possible to know exactly how much messianic speculation was afoot at that time. But based on Daniel's timetable (Dan 9:24-27) that started from Cyrus's decree, left dangling like a question mark at the close of the Hebrew Bible (2Chr 36:22-23), it must have been considerable.

Matthew's quote drops Micah's reference to Ephrathah but keeps the focus on the house of David by substituting "land of Judah." "*Ge* (land) is a favorite word and betrays Matthew's typically Jewish land-consciousness."[18] This pushes back against Waltke's notion that the land is not a factor in the NT.[19]

The disciples assumed that the people of Israel would be restored to the land of Israel. Witness their question to the risen Jesus in Acts 1, "Lord, will you now restore the kingdom to Israel?" Jesus does not say this will *not* happen but that only the Father knows when. Several of His disciples are zealots, committed to the restoration of the kingdom to Israel, and they cannot see it any other way.

Matthew's quote finishes by skipping to Mic 5:4 and steering closer to 2Sm 5:2 (and later 1Chr 11:2), which in their contexts were clearly spoken to David: "You will shepherd My people Israel and be ruler over Israel." For Matthew, it is a clear reference to Davidic fulfillment by Jesus.

As an element in Matthew's narrative, Messiah's birth in Bethlehem precipitates Herod's attack and the flight of Joseph and Mary with the baby Jesus. Messiah's birth in Bethlehem is featured in Luke and John to clarify the identity of Jesus as Messiah. Israelites, especially those schooled in the Scriptures, were looking for the Messiah to be born in Bethlehem and to be from the house of David. That expectation clearly expressed in the Gospels leaves no doubt that they were interpreting that part of Micah quite literally and geographically.

One of the large, historical influences of Christian interpretation shows up in the reading of Mic 4 but carries over into the present passage. That reading takes the worldwide reign, the mountain of the Lord, and this ruler as being the Church, to the exclusion of the nation Israel. Waltke pushes aside any notion of an ethnic Israel in "that day," noting that there is no reference in the NT to any relation of the kingdom and the land so prominent in the OT.[20] That line of interpretation has been dominant since the early Church fathers.

What is at play here has been a faulty foundation-piece of Christendom for its two millennia, its 100 generations. This interpretation strips away all things Jewish from the interpretation of the Bible. It is clearly a post-NT movement because the NT, a Jewish document, opens the door of salvation to all, but from a Jewish framework and context. That became troublesome to the early church because of its conflict with early Rabbinic Judaism. It affected how the Bible was and is read, even to this day. Christendom, outside its ongoing remnant of believers, has historically been a largely political force in the form of a religion.

This line of interpretation became the camel nose under the tent (where the camel enters and takes down the whole tent). It started small and ended up affecting everything. This recycles back into the message of Micah. There is clearly more than Israel in view in the worldwide scope of the vision, but the replacement/elimination of Israel from the meaning is incoherent and untenable.

The first and insurmountable problem in sweeping aside Israel with a replacement theology is that it renders God a promise-breaker, One who deals from the bottom of the deck. The wishful thinking of that logic comes out of human nature, "I'm the favorite now," but it flies in the face of God's character and His promises. God was so insistent that His promise was unconditional that in Gn 15, He put Abraham to sleep while He sealed the covenant. Nothing was required, or possible, for Abraham to do by way of agreement. Micah's prophecy of a Ruler from Bethlehem stands as a true foundation stone in identifying Jesus of Nazareth as the Jewish Messiah of Israel and also of all who believe in Him.

---

1. Brevard S. Childs, *Introduction to the Old Testament as Scripture* (Philadelphia: Fortress, 1979), 431.
2. Bruce K. Waltke, *A Commentary on Micah* (Grand Rapids: Eerdmans, 2007), 294.
3. Ibid., 270.
4. Ibid., 271.
5. R. Laird Harris, Gleason L. Archer Jr., and Bruce K. Waltke, *Theological Wordbook of the Old Testament* (Chicago: Moody, 2003), 893.
6. Waltke, *Commentary on Micah*, 278.
7. James Luther Mays, *Micah* (Philadelphia: Westminster, 1976), 117.
8. A. Cohen, *The Twelve Prophets* (London: Soncino, 1985), 175.
9. Leslie Allen, *The Books of Joel, Obadiah, Jonah, and Micah* (Grand Rapids: Eerdmans, 1976), 346.
10. Waltke, *Commentary on Micah*, 282.
11. Ibid., 285.
12. James H. Charlesworth, ed., *The Old Testament Pseudepigrapha Volume Two* (Peabody, MA: Hendrickson, 1983).
13. Hans Walter Wolff, *Micah* (Minneapolis: Augsburg, 1990), 145.
14. Michael Rydelnik, *The Messianic Hope: Is the Hebrew Bible Really Messianic?* (Nashville: B&H, 2010), 161.
15. Ibid., 97.
16. Donald A. Hagner, "Matthew 1–13," in *Word Biblical Commentary*, vol. 33a, ed. Bruce M. Metzger, Ralph P. Martin, and Lynn Allan Losie (Dallas: Word, 1993), 25.
17. D. A. Carson, "Matthew," in *The Expositor's Bible Commentary*, vol. 8, ed. Frank Ely Gaebelein (Grand Rapids: Zondervan, 1984), 83.
18. Robert Horton Gundry, *Matthew: A Commentary on His Literary and Theological Art* (Grand Rapids: Eerdmans, 1982), 29.
19. Waltke, *Commentary on Micah*, 206–207.
20. Ibid., 305.

Haggai 2:6-9, 21-23

The Messiah: The Chosen Signet Ring of God

DAVID FINKBEINER

Written in the period soon after Israel first returned from exile, the message of the Lord through Haggai was given to spur Israel to rebuild the Second Temple and to encourage them during the process. In so doing, the Lord promised great things for the future of this Temple and for the people of Israel. Included in this great future is the promise of the coming Messiah. Although he does not speak extensively about the Messiah, Haggai does refer to Him in 2:23 and in a qualified sense, in 2:7 as well. This article will explore both of these texts in both their immediate contexts as well as the larger biblical context.

BACKGROUND AND STRUCTURE OF HAGGAI

We know little about the prophet Haggai, except that he prophesied in Jerusalem to the postexilic community. His name derives from the Hebrew word for "feast," possibly reinforcing his message—delivered in several oracles on feast days—to rebuild the Temple where feast days would again be celebrated.[1]

The need to rebuild the Temple was great. The Babylonians had destroyed the Temple, along with Jerusalem and the kingdom of Judah, in 586 BC, and exiled the people of Judah to Babylon. But the Babylonian empire was short-lived. In 539 BC, Cyrus the Great of Persia defeated Babylon and established his Persian empire. Reversing the Babylonian policy of exiling conquered peoples, he decreed in 538 BC that the Jews could return to Jerusalem and rebuild the city and the Temple.

These efforts started out well. Some 50,000 Judeans returned to the land (Ezr

2), and after about seven months they were able to rebuild the altar and begin sacrificing again (Ezr 3). The next year, they laid the foundation of the new Temple (Ezr 3). But even as they began building the new Temple, many of the older, returned exiles wept when they remembered how much greater the first Temple had been, no doubt demoralizing those trying to rebuild it. The situation worsened when non-Israelites living in the land began to oppose the building of the new Temple, and the Persian authorities apparently sided with them. As a result, the construction process ceased entirely in 536.

This lack of a temple was no small matter. As B. Waltke writes, "The need to rebuild is urgent, because temples in their world are the center for administering the political, economic, judicial, social, and religious life of the nation. In other words, rebuilding *I AM*'s [the Lord's] Temple would symbolize his rule over the life of his people and his prophesied rule of the world (cf. Zch 1:14-17)."[2] If Israel was to fully serve the Lord in the land, and if they wanted to affirm the importance of God's presence among them, they needed to rebuild.

But for the next 16 years the construction project remained dormant. This fostered only spiritual apathy, as their interest in building the Temple took second place to their own personal interests (1:2-4), particularly building their own homes (perhaps even using building materials collected for the Temple). Yet instead of prospering, their material prospects only waned (1:5-11). They therefore became an apathetic and demoralized people who, lacking a temple, had not yet fully returned to the land, despite living there for 16 years. It is to these people that Haggai addressed his message.

This message came in four addresses over the space of about four months in 520 BC (the second year of Darius I, King of Persia; cf. 1:1; 1:15; 2:10). The first address and its aftermath take up all of chap. 1. First delivered on August 29, 520 BC, it actually involved three phases. In the first phase (1:1-2), the Lord addressed Zerubbabel (the Governor) and Joshua (the High Priest), who as civic and religious leaders bore responsibility for what was happening. They were told that the people kept delaying the rebuilding project with excuses, probably implying that they would need to rally the people to action. The second phase (1:3-11) was addressed directly to the people themselves. The Lord called the people to reverse their misplaced priorities and reconsider their ways—that is, to begin rebuilding the Temple and glorifying Him (1:4-8). He then motivated them to action by showing them that their lack of prosperity was caused by His judgment (1:9-11). The third phase involved a series of responses to the first address. Zerubbabel and Joshua led the people to fear the Lord and obey (v. 12). God responded to their change of heart with staggering encouragement, declaring "I am with you" and stirring their hearts to action (1:13-14). Twenty-three days later the work began.

The remaining three addresses, recorded in chap. 2 and spread over the next few months, were given to encourage the leaders and people as they continued the work of rebuilding. The second address, delivered on October 17, 520 BC, to the leaders and people, was given to strengthen their hand as they compared the humble beginnings of the Second Temple with the glory of the first (2:1-9). On December 18, 520 BC, Haggai delivered the Lord's third address to the people (2:10-19). Using a case study pertaining to ritual defilement (2:11-13), Haggai declared that Israel's sacrificial worship had been defiled by their past failure to obey and rebuild the Temple, prompting God to judge them with loss of prosperity (2:14-17). But not anymore; now He would bless them for dutifully continuing the work (2:18-19). The final address (2:20-23) was delivered on the same day as the third address. It was directed specifically to Zerubbabel, who may have needed encouragement as well. Here the Lord predicted that He will overthrow the nations who oppose Him (2:21-22) and restore the Davidic line in Zerubbabel (2:23). The remainder of this essay will focus specifically on the second and fourth messages in chap. 2, since these contain the two messianic texts in Haggai.

HAGGAI 2:7

The Context of Haggai 2:7

As indicated above, this message was given about a month after the people began to rebuild the Temple and was designed to encourage them in the task. Such encouragement was needed, both for the leaders and the people (2:2). The oracle was delivered on the last day of the Feast of Booths (2:1; cf. Lv 23:33-44), a time meant to celebrate the harvest. But given the poor harvest from the famine (1:10-11), the mammoth task still ahead of them, the unimpressive nature of the new building (2:3), the relative lack of resources to build even that, and the meager progress after a month,[3] the people were already in sore need of encouragement.[4] The reminder that Solomon dedicated his glorious First Temple in this same month (1Kg 8:2) would only make the discouragement worse.[5] The Lord Himself acknowledges the obvious: anyone who saw the Temple "in its former glory" (the First Temple) knew that the current version (the Second Temple now under construction) seemed "like nothing" in comparison (2:3).

To a people so discouraged, the sovereign "Lord of Hosts" delivered a solemn "declaration" (repeated three times in 2:4) consisting of three commands: "be strong" (repeated three times, once each to Zerubbabel, to Joshua, and to the people), "work," and "don't be afraid" (2:4-5). David issued the same three commands to Solomon in commissioning him to build the First Temple (1Chr 28:10,20).

The Lord then gave two reasons for Israel to obey these exhortations. The first reason is His promised presence (2:4-5). Israel's rebellion had caused God to remove the glory of His presence from the First Temple before its destruction (Ezk 10). Even so, despite their past, He was now with them once again in the person of His Spirit. His renewed presence for this task was rooted in His covenant faithfulness.[6]

The second reason is the promised future of the Temple (2:6-9). The words "Once more, in a little while" indicate that the Lord is making a prediction about the future (2:6). In light of God's plan, the people's present labors matter, for God will bring greatness to this place in the future. To be sure, this promised future is not necessarily near in time; "in a little while" only indicates that the prediction is imminent—it could happen at any time.[7] But it will be a dramatic future (2:6-7a). The Lord is going to "shake" the cosmos ("the heavens and the earth, the sea and the dry land"), including "the nations." Reminiscent of an earthquake, the idea of shaking is traditional language in which God reveals Himself powerfully in actions that make the world itself tremble in response to His awesome power. He has acted in similarly dramatic fashion in the past ("once more," 2:6),[8] and He declares that He will do so again in the future, in His time.[9] The prophets use this imagery to speak of the coming Day of the Lord, a time of God's judgment on His enemies and blessing to His people, particularly in connection with the coming Messiah (Isa 24:17-23; Ezk 38:17-23; Jl 3:14-21; cf. Heb 12:26-28).

What will be the result of His powerful shaking? "The treasures of all the nations will come" to the Temple, filling it with "glory" (2:7). After all, all the world's wealth belongs to the Lord (2:8). Furthermore, the future glory of the Temple will exceed any past glory, and He "will provide peace in this place" (2:9). Such a bright future would indeed encourage the people in this task.

THE TEXT OF HAGGAI 2:7

There is widespread disagreement among scholars today whether this text is messianic at all. The clause "the treasures of all nations will come" is the heart of the controversy. One's interpretation of this text—including whether it is messianic at all—depends on a web of exegetical questions in vv. 7-9. This section will briefly survey those exegetical questions and the major interpretations of the text before presenting a case for a qualified messianic interpretation.

Four exegetical issues need consideration. First, the meaning of *chemdat* ("treasures") is central. This noun can refer either to a desirable/precious *object* or to a desirable/precious *person*.[10] The former option results a translation like "the wealth of all nations" (NASB), a translation with no evident messianic implications.

The latter option is the basis for a messianic understanding of the text, as reflected in the NKJV's "the Desire of All Nations."[11]

Further complicating the meaning of *chemdat* is a second exegetical issue. Scholars dispute whether the noun is singular or plural. To be sure, *chemdat* is singular in the MT,[12] but this is not decisive, for two reasons. First of all, the original Hebrew text included only the consonants; vowels were added much later. The consonants of the singular and plural forms of this noun are identical. It is thus possible that the original text intended the plural form (*chemudot*), the view that the LXX translators clearly took. Second, the verb *ba'u* ("will come") in this clause is third-person plural, which expects a plural subject. Although there are several possible explanations for this grammatical anomaly in the MT,[13] the most natural explanation is either that the term is to be understood as a collective singular or that the plural reading of the noun, *chemudot*, is preferable to the MT reading. Whether interpreting the noun as plural in form or as a collective noun, translations like the HCSB[14] render the term as plural, as in the "treasures of all the nations." Even so, a plural form does not preclude a personal referent; "the same plural Hebrew word is used in this way of other individuals like Daniel (Dan 9:23; 10:11,19)," rendering it a "plural of majesty."[15]

A third exegetical issue relates to what exactly God will do to "shake all the nations." This shakeup of the world order could be positive or negative. A positive interpretation would suggest that God changes their hearts toward Him (e.g., Isa 2:2-4). If *chemdat* refers to wealth or treasures, the nations' positive response would result in freewill gifts and offerings given to the Lord in worship (as in Isa 60:1-7).[16] If *chemdat* is a reference to the Messiah, it would mean that the nations turn to the Messiah as the one to be highly prized (as in Isa 11:10; 42:6; 49:6). A negative interpretation would suggest that the Lord defeats the nations utterly, destroying them or at least forcing them to acknowledge, however begrudgingly, His lordship (as in Zch 14). In this case *chemdat* would refer to wealth taken from a defeated enemy as tribute or even spoils of war. Verse 8 indicates that, whether treasure is given voluntarily or taken by force, God is just in receiving it because all the world's "silver and gold belong to" the Lord.[17]

The nature of the terms "glory" (*kabod* in 7,9) and "peace" (*shalom* in 9) is the fourth exegetical issue. The Lord predicts that in the future, the Temple will be filled with even greater glory than in the past.[18] What is the nature of this glory? Some argue that it is primarily material glory, due to the riches of the nations that flow into its development.[19] Others maintain that beyond any material splendor, the ultimate glory of the Temple is the presence of the Lord Himself.[20] Closely tied to the glory of the Temple is the peace (*shalom*) that the Lord will provide there.[21] Perhaps *shalom*, like glory, should be limited primarily to the material prosperity from the nations that God brings to the Temple or to Israel because of their obedience in building the Temple (cf. chaps. 1; 2:15-19).[22] But *shalom* can be also be understood more comprehensively as a "many-sided reality—peace with God, harmonious society, personal fulfilment—and all as a divine gift."[23] This sense of abundant life can hardly be separated from the Lord's saving work and the glory of His very presence (cf. Nm 6:22-27),[24] or even more specifically, the glorious presence of the Messiah.[25]

This web of exegetical issues yields three basic interpretations of the messianic import of v. 7. The first is the nonmessianic view.[26] It takes *chemdat*, whether singular or plural, as a reference to the wealth (singular) or material treasures (plural) of the nations. Advocates of this view debate whether God takes this wealth by force or changes the hearts of the nations to give it voluntarily. But they all agree that *chemdat* refers only to material wealth in light of the immediate context in v. 8, which speaks of "the silver and gold" belonging to the Lord. In addition, advocates will appeal to parallel passages such as Isa 60:1-7 and Zch 14:14, which speak of wealth from the nations coming into Jerusalem in the future.[27] Surprisingly, rather than taking a strictly material view of *kabod* and *shalom* in v. 9, many advocates of this view do associate *kabod* with God's presence and take a comprehensive view of *shalom*, often finding its fulfillment in Jesus the Messiah. Even so, all advocates of this view agree that v. 7 is definitely not messianic.

The second view, the messianic view, disagrees. It maintains that *chemdat*, whether singular or plural, should be understood in a personal sense as a reference to the Messiah. A translation like "the Desire of All Nations" is therefore appropriate. The glory of the Lord in the Temple refers to the presence of the Messiah Himself. His glorious presence and the peace He provides are fulfilled at least in His first coming and likely also in His second coming. Advocates point to the close connection between God's glory and His presence, to passages like Mal 3:1 and Zch 6:11-15, which predict that the Messiah will indeed come to His Temple, and to strong support of the messianic interpretation in both Jewish and Christian tradition.[28] Beyond these supports, advocates can point to the messianic prediction later in the chapter (v. 23) as proof of messianic expectations in Haggai's theology.

The third and most likely view, the qualified messianic view, blends the first two views.[29] In this view, the ambiguity of *chemdat* is purposeful, allowing for both a personal (Messiah) and material (wealth) referent.[30] Several factors support this view. First, it builds on the strengths of the first two views. Second, it superbly accounts for the context of vv. 8-9.[31] Verse 8 justifies a material interpretation of *chemdat*, but wealth alone is insufficient to endow the future Temple with the greater glory and comprehensive peace envisioned in v. 9. Only the presence of the Messiah Himself could make that happen. Indeed, the glory of the future Temple will not consist merely in its impressive wealth, but also in the presence of the Lord Himself in the person of Immanuel—the one whom Simeon identified when meeting the baby Jesus in the Temple as "a light for revelation to the Gentiles and glory to Your people Israel" (Lk 2:32).

Third, the qualified messianic view also allows room for ambiguity in the meaning of the Lord's declaration that He "will shake all the nations." The future relationship between the nations and the Lord is complex in the OT. On the one hand, those nations that oppose the Lord will be crushed by Messiah at His return (Zch 14), but on the other hand many Gentiles will turn toward the Lord and His Messiah (Isa 60:1-7; 11:10; 42:6; 49:6). True, the shaking of the nations described later in vv. 20-21 stresses the former. But the latter is suggested in v. 9 by the glory of God and the *shalom* He brings after the kingdom rule of the victorious Messiah is fully established. In accord with the qualified messianic view, then, the Messiah will both defeat those Gentiles who oppose Him and delight those who seek Him. As Kaiser says, "Just as he is the epitome and center of all that is valuable, so in his train will flow all the treasures of the nations,"[32] whether given voluntarily or taken by force as rightfully belonging to Him.

When are the predictions in Hag 2:7-9 fulfilled? One could cite several possibilities for fulfillment or at least partial fulfillment. In the short term, Darius decreed financial support for the rebuilding project (Ezr 6:8). Later on, this Second Temple would be renovated in material grandeur by the Idumean king, Herod I (Mk 13:1-2; Lk 21:5). This was the Temple graced by the presence of Jesus the Messiah during His first coming. As Immanuel (Mt 1:23), the Prince of Peace (Isa 9:6-7; Zch 9:9-10), and the glory of Israel who brings salvation to all peoples (Lk 2:27-32), He endowed Herod's Temple with a glory greater than that of Solomon's Temple. If the qualified messianic view is correct, all of these items pertain to the fulfillment of Haggai's prediction, but only partially and in anticipation of the final fulfillment at the return of the Messiah (Rev 19–20). Only then will the Lord Jesus destroy His enemies, deliver Israel, fully establish His kingdom, adorn the millennial messianic Temple with His glorious presence, and reign over Israel and the nations, whose hearts have been fully turned to Him—an earth-shaking event indeed. This remarkable promise does not exhaust the messianic expectation in Haggai. The prophet, in Hag 2:23, also provides the prediction of the fulfillment of the Davidic covenant in the person of the ultimate son of David.

HAGGAI 2:23

THE CONTEXT OF HAGGAI 2:23

About two months after the second message, on December 18, 520 BC, Haggai issued both his third and fourth messages. Each message is a word of encouragement. The third (2:10-19) is directed to the people as a whole, declaring that the time of material scarcity caused by their disobedience is over and that they could look forward to material prosperity "from this day on" (v. 19). The fourth message (2:20-23) is an apt companion because it too looks toward the future optimistically. But it is directed specifically to Zerubbabel, and its fulfillment awaits a more distant future.

As in the second message, here too God declares that He is "going to shake the heavens and the earth" (v. 21). Unlike the second message, however, the nature of this shaking is not ambiguous. Verse 22 is clear that the Lord is going to destroy all the power of the nations raised up in opposition to His rule.[33] The description of this future judgment is reminiscent of God's past acts of judgments against nations opposing Him. As the Lord overthrew Sodom and Gomorrah (Gn 19:25; Dt 29:23; Isa 13:19; cf. Jer 20:16; Am 4:11), so He will "overturn royal thrones." As the Lord destroyed the Canaanite nations so Israel could inherit the land (Dt 9:1-6; Am 2:9),[34] so He will "destroy the power of Gentile kingdoms." As the Lord threw Pharaoh's army, with its horses, riders, and chariots, into the sea (Ex 15:1,4,19,21),[35] so He will "overturn chariots and their riders," and "horses and their riders will fall." As the Lord turned the swords of the Midianites against one another in Gideon's day (Jdg 7:22), so He will bring down his enemies, "each his brother's sword." Why will the Lord do this? His primary purpose in "annihilating the power bases of world empires" is, as v. 23 will make clear, "to establish the universal and absolute rule of his own representative, Zerubabbel."[36]

THE TEXT OF HAGGAI 2:23

In this verse, the Lord makes a firm and exalted promise to Zerubbabel. It is firm because three times in this one verse the Lord insists that this is His own declaration.[37] It is exalted because it speaks of Zerubabbel using expressions connecting him both with David and the Messiah. First, the Lord says to Zerubbabel, "I will take you." This expression indicates that Zerubbabel has been selected by God. It is used of Israel (Ex 6:7; Dt 4:20,34), Abraham (Jos 24:3), and David (2Sm 7:8; cf. Ps 78:70). The Davidic reference is notable because, coming in the context of the Davidic covenant, it establishes the basis for God's declaration that He will not fail from "taking from [David's] descendants rulers over the descendants of Abraham, Isaac, and Jacob" (Jer 33:26). This promise underlies the messianic hope.

A second expression reinforces the idea that God has specially selected Zerubbabel. The Lord tells him, "I have chosen you." Zerubbabel's ancestor David was similarly chosen (Ps 78:70). But even more significantly, the Lord designates David's greater Son, the Servant of the Lord in Isaiah's Servant Songs, as "My Chosen One" in Isa 42:1. Later, the Father directly applies this title to Jesus at His transfiguration (Lk 9:35).

God also addresses Zerubbabel with a third exalted designation: "My servant."[38] This term is often applied to people, even Gentiles, "whom the Lord has appointed to a particular task."[39] Motyer points out that, while Moses is most frequently called "servant" in the OT, David is most frequently designated as "My servant" (e.g., 2Sm 3:18; 1Kg 11:34).[40] The Davidic title naturally leads to the same title being applied to the Messiah. It is a dominant title for the Messiah in Isaiah (e.g., Isa 42:1-9; 49:1-13; 50:4-11; 52:13–53:12), and Ezekiel calls the Messiah "my servant David" (Ezk 34:23-24; 37:24-25).

Given these exalted designations, God promised to make Zerubbabel "like My signet ring."[41] Comparing Zerubbabel to the Lord's seal was significant. Motyer notes, "Whether the signet was worn as a neck pendant (Gn 38:18,25), a finger ring (Jer 22:24), or a bracelet (Sg of Sol 8:6), it bore the owner's name or mark so that it could be used as personal identification (Gn 38:18; 1Kg 21:8)."[42] Zerubbabel is thus pictured as the signet ring on the hand of the Lord Himself, the Sovereign over the universe. As the Lord's seal, Zerubbabel is precious to Him because he will bear the royal authority of the great King Himself. More broadly, the signet ring is an apt picture of the Davidic kingship.[43] For the king of Israel was never meant to be more than a vassal who served under the Lord and whose authority derived from the Lord (Isa 33:22; Dt 17:14-20).

More specifically, the image likely comes from Jer 22:24-25. Here the Lord compares Zerubbabel's grandfather, King "Coniah" (i.e., Jehoiachin) of Judah, to his signet ring as well. But in this case, the Lord promised in judgment to tear Coniah from his right hand and cast him away into exile in Babylon. The exile seemed to bring the Davidic kingship to an ignominious end. The promise in Hag 2 to take up Zerubbabel as the Lord's signet ring thus represents "a sovereign reversal of fortunes for Israel's monarchy and a renewal of the Lord's blessing upon a people that he previously disciplined through the trauma of the exile."[44] Zerubbabel marks the restoration of the Davidic line to rule as God's valued representative.[45]

Zerubbabel as a historical person does, however, raise a problem for this prediction. In his day, the Lord neither crushed the power of the nations nor raised up Zerubbabel as the messianic king to rule over a restored Israel and the world. Instead, shortly after this time, this governor of Judah fades into obscurity in the historical record.[46] Some critical scholars therefore argue that Haggai mistakenly thought that Zerubbabel was the Messiah, perhaps even calling for a rebellion against Judah's Persian overlords under Zerubbabel's leadership.[47] But there is a much better way to understand Haggai's prophecy.

For Haggai, Zerubbabel personifies continuity in the Davidic kingship running from David to the yet future Messiah. Zerubbabel is the link between them, signifying "God's renewed blessing upon the Davidic royal line"[48]—a line that had seemed to end with the exile but still has a glorious future. The promise therefore is not finally about Zerubbabel himself but about the future Messiah he represents. Two factors support this contention. First, the text indicates that the fulfillment will take place "on that day." Frequently this phrase in the OT is eschatological (e.g., Isa 2:11-21; Am 8:3,9; Hos 2:18,21), pointing to future decisive action of the Lord. Given the upheaval of this day described in vv. 21-22, this must be nothing less than the Day of the Lord at the end of days, when God defeats His enemies and redeems His people through His Messiah.

Second, it is not unprecedented in OT prophecies to speak about eschatological figures using people from history. For example, the future prophet preceding the Day of the Lord is called "Elijah the prophet" (Mal 4:5-6; cf. Lk 1:17; Mt 17:11). More significantly, the Messiah is called "David" in several places (Hos 3:5; Jer 30:9; Ezk 34:23-24). To be sure, this text refers to the Messiah by using a contemporary figure rather than one from Haggai's distant past. But this is appropriate here, for Zerubbabel uniquely instills hope for Haggai's audience as the link between past and future. They have no need to take action to establish the kingdom and presently crown Zerubbabel as king. In accordance with His timing, God Himself will act powerfully through the Messiah some day in the future. In the meantime, the figure of Zerubbabel reminds them that "they are to wait with hope and anticipation because God has already begun to act to restore his people and to fulfil his ancient promises."[49]

If Zerubbabel himself does not fulfill the predictions of Hag 2:21-23, when are they fulfilled? Clearly the Lord Jesus the Messiah, the descendant of David and the offspring of Zerubbabel (Mt 1:12; Lk 3:27), is the final Zerubbabel of which the text speaks. He is the ultimate Servant of the Lord and Chosen One (Lk 22:27; 4:16-21; 9:35; Ac 8:32-35). And as the "King of kings" (Rev 19:16 ESV). He is the signet ring on the Lord's right hand. But while Messiah Jesus' first coming established His messianic identity and inaugurated His reign (Mt 21:5; Jn 1:49-51; Ac 2:29-36), it did not bring about the kind of cataclysmic political and military upheaval described in vv. 21-22. That reality awaits His second coming, when He defeats all His enemies arrayed against Him (Rev 19:11-21), fully establishes His reign, and sets up His millennial kingdom on the earth (Rev 20).

THE MESSIAH IN THE THEOLOGY OF HAGGAI

When the two messianic texts in Hag 2 are taken together, what picture of the Messiah emerges in Haggai's theology? The Messiah will rise in the context of God's dramatic action in the world of the nations. Positively, this action will create a change of heart in some. But it will also produce staggering political and military upheaval in the world order, resulting in the destruction of God's enemies and the unmitigated rule of His Messiah. The Messiah, specially chosen by the Lord as His servant, will bear the full authority of the Lord Himself over all the world, as His signet ring. Like Zerubbabel His ancestor, He represents the Davidic kingship renewed, in fulfillment of the Davidic covenant. His reign will enrich the Temple with the wealth of the nations, brought voluntarily as offerings by those who value Him and taken forcefully from others who do not. It will bring the glorious presence of God Himself to the Temple. And His rule will bring peace, comprehensive well-being inextricably connected to the presence of the Lord Himself with all its attendant blessings.

HAGGAI'S MESSIAH IN THE REST OF THE BIBLICAL CANON

The discussion above showed that Haggai's prophecies about the Messiah referred to texts and themes from earlier biblical revelation. But Haggai's picture of the Messiah also is consistent with the picture of Messiah presented in the other two postexilic prophets, Zechariah and Malachi.

Zechariah was a contemporary of Haggai, although most of His messages come either right after Haggai's messages or much later. His oracles include a number of messianic predictions. Five are noteworthy for their similarity with Haggai's picture of the Messiah. A good place to start is Zch 4:1-14, since this is the only passage in the book where Zerubbabel is addressed. Given shortly after Haggai's last message, this passage also seeks to encourage Zerubbabel in his efforts to rebuild the Temple. Although Zerubbabel is not directly addressed in messianic terms here as he is in Haggai, he likely is one of "the two anointed ones" (the other being Joshua the High Priest) "who stand by the Lord of the whole earth" (v. 14). The point is that the Messiah unifies the anointed roles of Davidic King (as represented by Zerubbabel) and High Priest (as represented by Joshua).

Earlier in Zch 3:8-10, the Lord declares that Joshua and his fellow priests "are a sign that I am about to bring My servant, the Branch"—clear messianic designations. The Servant-Messiah will remove the guilt of the land and, as in Hag 2, will bring peace to the land (vividly described in v. 10). The nature of the Messiah's kingdom of peace is further described in Zch 9:9-10 in ways similar to Haggai. The righteous and humble King is also victorious (v. 9), having a kingdom that extends "to the ends of the earth." His rule will abolish weapons of warfare—including horse and chariot—and "will proclaim peace to the nations" (v. 10).

Joshua the High Priest once again becomes a picture of the Messiah in 6:9-15. Joshua here is crowned as a picture of the "Branch" whose rule will unite the offices of Priest and Davidic King (v. 13). He will build the Temple, which will be graced with his splendor (v. 13). And as in Haggai 2, Gentiles ("People who are far off") will also be involved in building the Lord's Temple (v. 15).

Finally, Zch 14 describes God's dramatic intervention in the eschatological day of the Lord. It vividly expands on the shaking of the nations mentioned in Hag 2, with the same ambiguity seen there. On the one hand, God will act decisively to destroy all the nations who attack His people at Jerusalem. They will turn on one another (14:13), and their wealth will be plundered for the benefit of God's people (14:14). And those who fail to pay homage to the King will be punished (14:17-19). On the other hand, those Gentiles that remain will worship Him at His Temple in Jerusalem.

Malachi came many decades after Haggai, likely during the ministries of Ezra and Nehemiah. His messianic prediction in Mal 3:1-4 picks up on elements of Haggai's messianic picture. The Lord declared that He will send "My messenger" who will, Elijah-like (cf. 4:5), prepare the way for the Messiah, described as a second messenger: "Then the Lord you seek will suddenly come to His Temple, the Messenger of the covenant you desire." Similar to Haggai's picture, here too the Messiah is desired, and He comes to grace His future Temple with His presence. In the larger context (vv. 2:17–3:6), Israel desires Him because they want the Messiah to deal justly with evil. But His return will bring more than expected blessings for themselves. His coming will be a refiner's fire which no one can endure. The focus of His refining work in this text is not the nations, but Israel and her priests, for He will purge Israel of her wickedness and create a people who are righteous and fear Him (vv. 3:2-5). Yet God is gracious and faithful. Although Israel, as all the nations, deserves complete destruction, she will not be consumed. The Lord will purify and preserve her, as He has promised in His covenant with her (v. 6).

What does the NT teach about Haggai's Messiah? As seen above in the discussion of the fulfillment of both messianic texts in Haggai, the NT makes it abundantly clear that the Messiah of whom Haggai speaks is Jesus of Nazareth, who fulfills both texts primarily in connection with His second coming. But in addition to the NT texts mentioned there, two other NT texts are noteworthy in light of their connection with Hag 2.

The first of these is Heb 12:26, which quotes from Hag 2:6 and the promise "yet once more" to "shake not only the earth but also heaven." In this context, the reference to Hag 2:6 "points to the cataclysmic judgment coming on the earth at the end of the age, when Christ returns. In light of that coming event, believers should reverently serve God."[50]

The second noteworthy NT text is Rev 21:22-27. In this description of the New Jerusalem in the new heaven and earth, the existence of the Temple itself is replaced by "the Lord God the Almighty and the Lamb" (v. 22). Their glory makes the need for any other light superfluous (v. 23). "The nations will walk in its light," and their kings "will bring the glory and honor of the nations into" the New Jerusalem (vv. 24-26). In light of this passage, Haggai's picture of the glorious Messiah reigning over His worldwide millennial kingdom from His spectacular Temple anticipates the greatest manifestation of His glorious presence in the New Jerusalem, dwelling with His people forever.

---

1. M. J. Boda, *The NIV Application Commentary: Haggai, Zechariah* (Grand Rapids: Zondervan, 2004), 32–33. The significance of Haggai's name is admittedly speculative; for a brief survey of other theories, see P. A. Verhoef, *The Books of Haggai and Malachi*, New International Commentary on the Old Testament (Grand Rapids: Eerdmans, 1987), 4–5.

2. B. K. Waltke, with C. Yu, *An Old Testament Theology: An Exegetical, Canonical, and Thematic Approach* (Grand Rapids: Zondervan, 2007), 846. This is why it is appropriate to date the ending of Jeremiah's prediction of 70 years of captivity to the completion of the Temple in 515 BC (i.e., from the destruction of the Temple in 586 to the completion of its rebuilding in 515). Some date those 70 years from 605 BC when Nebuchadnezzar took the first captives until 536 BC when the Judeans first returned to the land. But in light of the importance of the Temple, the first set of dates is more likely.

3. Verhoef, *Books of Haggai and Malachi*, 32, points out that the lack of progress was understandable, given the need to clear the construction site of debris from the First Temple's destruction and to organize the construction. Add to that the reality that the seventh month had a number of major holidays that would have halted work. "In addition to Sabbath rest days, the first day of the month was the Feast of Trumpets, and the tenth the Day of Atonement (Lev. 23:3-32). Then on the fifteenth day the Feast of Tabernacles began (Lev. 23:33-36, 39-42; Deut. 16:13-15), which lasted for seven days. It would be understandable if the enthusiasm was frustrated by a lack of progress due to the compulsory holidays."

4. Rydelnik aptly compares their discouragement during the Feast of Tabernacles to trying to celebrate Thanksgiving without the turkey! See M. Rydelnik, "Haggai," *The Moody Bible Commentary*, ed. Michael Rydelnik and Michael Vanlaningham (Chicago: Moody Publishers, 2014), 1408.

5. A. Motyer, "Haggai," in *The Minor Prophets: An Exegetical and Expository Commentary*, ed. Thomas McComiskey (Grand Rapids: Baker, 1998), 986.

6. Boda, *Haggai, Zechariah*, 122–23, provides helpful background here. He suggests that Haggai's oracle is alluding to the golden calf incident in Ex 32–34, particularly as it is understood by Nehemiah (9:16-18,30) and Isaiah (63:10,11) in connection with the Spirit's presence with Israel. "The allusion to the covenant in Haggai 2:5 coupled with a reference to the Spirit remaining indicates that Haggai intends to remind the people of God's presence after the golden calf rebellion. It is important to remember that the golden calf narrative interrupts the account of the tabernacle construction (Ex. 25-40). Now in the rebuilding of the place of God's manifest presence, Haggai comforts the people by reminding them of God's promised presence after rebellion in the desert, a presence that enabled that community to build the tabernacle." See also Anthony Petterson, *Haggai, Zechariah, and Malachi*, Apollos Old Testament Commentary (Downers Grove, IL: InterVarsity, 2015), 69. Petterson helpfully lists various ways the Spirit had empowered His people in the OT times (e.g., empowering judges, kings, and prophets).

7. See the discussion in Motyer, "Haggai," 989–90. He notes that in biblical eschatology, the imminence of God's eschatological plans is compatible with the reality that those plans may be temporally distant. The day of the Lord's

judgment may be imminent (e.g., Ps 96:13; 98:9), but that does not mean it is not delayed in time (cf. 2Pt 3:1-15). Motyer's illustration is helpful. "Hikers often see the summit of a mountain looming over the immediate crest and are kept toiling on by the sense of being almost there—only to find, on mounting the crest, that a valley and intermediate crests come between them and the summit. The Lord's promise of "a little while" was not false, for it was related to his plan, not our timetable; neither was it purposeless, for the prospect of attainment (as in the case of the hiker) is the stimulus we need."

8. The idea is used in connection with the exodus events: Ex 19:16-19; Pss 68:8; 77:16-20.

9. See I. Duguid, *A Study Commentary on Haggai, Zechariah, Malachi* (Carlisle, PA: EP Books, 2010), 42–43, who points out that the shaking language had become standard for describing the Lord's deliverance of His people as a warrior (e.g., Ps 18:7-15). But here it is used for the "ultimate theophany" in which the Lord comes "to transform the present world order into the final eschatological state," thereby introducing "a new world order" through the presence of the Lord Himself.

10. Tim Meadowcroft, *Haggai*, Readings: A New Biblical Commentary, ed. J. Jarick (Sheffield, England: Sheffield Phoenix Press, 2006) 166–67; H. Wolf, "Desire of All Nations in Haggai 2:7: Messianic or Not?" *Journal of the Evangelical Theological Society* 19 (1976): 98–99. W. Kaiser, Jr., *The Messiah in the Old Testament* (Grand Rapids: Zondervan, 1995), 207, nicely summarizes the use of the term, pointing out that it "occurs twenty-five times in the OT. In the singular it depicts the land God will give Israel (Ps 106:24; Jer 3:19; 12:10; Zech 7:14), their houses (Ezk 26:12), and their valuables (2Ch 32:27; 36:10; Isa 2:16; Jer 15:34; Dan 11:8; Hos 13:15; Na 2:9). But it is also used of persons. Saul was the 'desire of Israel' (1Sa 9:20). Three times the word is used of Daniel, though interestingly enough in the plural (Heb. Chamudot, Da 9:23; 10:11, 19, rendered in the NIV as 'highly esteemed')."

11. See also the KJV, NIV (1984), and LB. The Latin Vulgate is similar.

12. The singular form of the noun is *chemdah*, but because it is in construct state with "all nations," its form in the MT is *chemdat*.

13. Other possible grammatical explanations include the following: (1) Classical Hebrew grammar sometimes just ignores grammatical agreement between subject and verb (Meadowcroft, *Haggai*, 167); (2) Abstract (Boda, *Haggai, Zechariah*, 124, n. 22) or collective (Verhoef, *Books of Haggai and Malachi*, 103) nouns can take the plural verb; (3) the singular noun is treated as plural by being in construct with "all nations" (Motyer, "Haggai," 991); (4) the clause is better rendered as in the NASB, "they will come with the wealth of all nations," treating "they" (i.e., the nations) as the subject of the clause and the "wealth" as what the nations bring.

14. The ESV, NET Bible, NLT, and NASB are similar.

15. Rydelnik, *Moody Bible Commentary*, 1409.

16. It is possible that the change of heart falls short of conversion toward the Lord, but rather would involve a change of disposition toward Israel, as when Cyrus earlier returned the Temple treasures stolen by Nebuchadnezzar in his conquest of Jerusalem (Ezr 1:7-11). See David Petersen, *Haggai and Zechariah 1-8: A Commentary*, The Old Testament Library (Philadelphia: Westminster Press, 1984), 68.

17. Petersen, *Haggai and Zechariah 1-8*, 69, takes a different approach to v. 8. He argues that God here is declaring that these treasures belong to Him, not to the Israelites, lest they think the wealth is theirs "by right." While this could be an implication, it is unlikely in the context of trying to encourage a demoralized people that the Lord here is rebuking a potentially arrogant attitude in the future.

18. The grammar of v. 9 is ambiguous. The HCSB translates it as, "The final glory of this house will be greater than the first." The NASB, NLT, and RSV are similar. The NIV (1984) presents the other option: "The glory of this present house will be greater than the glory of the former house." The KJV and NKJV are similar. The first option considers the Temple in its various iterations as one "house," while the second option considers the First and Second Temples different "houses." If the second option is correct, then this prediction only applies to the Second Temple. The first option sees continuity between all iterations of the Temple, even a future Third Temple. In light of v. 3 as well as grammatical considerations, the first option is the stronger one. See R. A. Taylor and E. R. Clendenen, *Haggai and Zechariah*, The New American Commentary (Nashville: Broadman and Holman, 2004), 167, for a very helpful discussion and case for the first option.

19. For example, Verhoef, *Books of Haggai and Malachi*, 104; Petersen, *Haggai and Zechariah 1-8*, 68.

20. While Boda, *Haggai, Zechariah*, 125, sees the focus of "glory" in v. 7 as material glory, he rightly points out that the "combination of the verb 'fill,' the concept of God's dwelling place ('this house'), and the word 'glory' is only found elsewhere in the Hebrew Bible in connection with God's glory filling the Tabernacle/Temple (Ex. 40:34, 35; 1 Kings 8:11; 2 Chron. 5:14; 7:1, 2; Ezek. 10:3, 4; 43:5)."

21. The text says that the Lord will give peace "in this place." It is possible that the "place" refers to the whole city of Jerusalem (including the Temple, of course) because there could be a word play between Jerusalem and *shalom* and because sometimes "this place" is used to designate Jerusalem (2Kg 22:16; Jer 7:3; 19:3). But more likely "this

place" refers to the Temple, since the context focuses on the Temple and the term "place" in the OT "often has the technical meaning of holy place or temple; see but to; 14:13; 1Kg 8:29; 2Ch 6:20; Gen 22:3" (Petersen, *Haggai and Zechariah 1-8*, 69). See also Taylor and Clendenen, *Haggai and Zechariah*, 168, who primarily favor the Temple as the referent of "this place" but also think that Jerusalem as a whole should not be excluded "since both city and sanctuary will be blessed objects in the fulfillment of the promise."

22. See Petersen, *Haggai and Zechariah 1-8*, 69–70.

23. Motyer, "Haggai," 991; cf. Meadowcroft, *Haggai*, 172.

24. See Duguid, *A Study Commentary*, 43–44; Boda, *Haggai, Zechariah*, 126.

25. J. Baldwin, *Haggai, Zechariah, Malachi: An Introduction and Commentary*, Tyndale Old Testament Commentaries (Downers Grove, IL: InterVarsity, 1972), 49, says that *shalom* "sums up all the blessings of the Messianic age, when reconciliation with God and His righteous rule will ensure a just and lasting peace. The temple was the source from which all blessings would flow (Ezk. 47:1) to make Jerusalem the centre of the world's well-being, the 'city of peace.'"

26. For example, Boda, *Haggai, Zechariah*, 124–126; Taylor and Clendenen, *Haggai and Zechariah*, 161–165; Peterson, *Haggai and Zechariah 1-8*, 67–70. This view is more typical among modern commentators.

27. Two observations should be kept in mind. First, the nations' wealth in Isa 60 is given voluntarily, but it does not appear to be a voluntary in Zch 14. Second, the term for wealth in these two passages is *chayil*, not *chemdat*.

28. Rydelnik, *Moody Bible Commentary*, 1409.

29. Wolf, "Desire of All Nations in Haggai 2:7," 97–102. Kaiser, *Messiah in the Old Testament*, 206–9 takes a similar view.

30. A paraphrase like "and that which is desired by all the nations will come" might capture the ambiguity in English.

31. Wolf, "Desire of All Nations in Haggai 2:7," 101, says that v. 8 "leans toward a material explanation, but verse 9 favors the personal aspect."

32. Kaiser, *Messiah in the Old Testament*, 208.

33. Eugene Merrill, *Haggai, Zechariah, and Malachi: An Exegetical Commentary* (Chicago: Moody Publishers, 1994), 56.

34. Verhoef, *Books of Haggai and Malachi*, 144, makes this helpful connection.

35. Ibid., where Verhoef points out that similar language is also used of the defeat of Sisera's army in Jdg 4:15.

36. Ibid., 143.

37. Motyer, "Haggai," 1002, points out that the threefold repetition that this promise is the Lord's declaration indicates that "each element of the promise—the certainty of the coming day and the divine election and status of Zerubbabel—is thus signed, sealed, and settled."

38. Interestingly, Ps 78:70 actually uses all three of these messianic expressions in reference to David. And Isa 42:1 uses both "My Servant" and "My Chosen One" in reference to the Messiah.

39. Taylor and Clendenen, *Haggai and Zechariah*, 196. See n. 22, which gives a helpful list of those so designated.

40. Motyer, "Haggai," 1002. He says that David is so designated 21 times.

41. The MT does not have the personal possessive pronoun "my," but the HCSB reasonably infers this from the context.

42. Motyer, "Haggai," 1002.

43. Kaiser, *Messiah in the Old Testament*, 209, calls it the "God-ordained emblem of the office and authority of the Davidic kingship."

44. Taylor and Clendenen, *Haggai and Zechariah*, 198.

45. It is beyond the scope of this article to deal with the complex issue of the genealogies of Jesus (Mt 1:1-12; Lk 3:23-38) and the curse on Coniah in Jer 22:28-30, where God declares that "None of his descendants will succeed in sitting on the throne of David or ruling again in Judah." Matthew's genealogy of Jesus includes Coniah (Jechoniah), but Luke's genealogy does not include Jechoniah because the line Luke presents goes through David's son Nathan rather than Solomon. The problem, however, is that Zerubbabel son of Shealtiel appears in both genealogies, although Luke lists Neri as Shealtiel's father rather than Jechoniah (as in Matthew's list). For a helpful discussion of these issues, see D. Bock, *Luke 1:1–9:50*, Baker Exegetical Commentary on the New Testament (Grand Rapids: Baker, 1994), 348–62.

46. Taylor and Clendenen, *Haggai and Zechariah*, 199, point out that various theories have been proposed about what happened to Zerubbabel, including that he died in office, or that he continued in this office for quite a while, or that he even was removed by the Persians due to fears of an insurrection, in part due to the prophecies of Haggai

and Zechariah. The last view is highly speculative, but in any case, the historical record is silent about what happened to Zerubbabel the governor.

47. See the discussion in Petersen, *Haggai and Zechariah 1-8*, 104, esp. n 25. See also the discussion in Taylor and Clendenen, *Haggai and Zechariah*, 198–200.

48. Taylor and Clendenen, *Haggai and Zechariah*, 197.

49. Duguid, *A Study Commentary*, 61.

50. George H. Guthrie, "Hebrews," in Commentary on the New Testament Use of the Old Testament, ed. G. K. Beale and D. A. Carson (Grand Rapids: Baker, 2007), 990.

Zechariah 3:1-10

The Messiah and His Restoration of Israel

MIKE STALLARD

The book of Zechariah contains mostly prophecy with some apocalyptic elements. Virtually the entire book predicts the future from Zechariah's perspective, with some scattered references to ethical commands interspersed. More important, scholars describe the work as the most messianic and eschatological of all the books in the OT. On that account, Zechariah appears to be a favorite of NT authors when they refer to the OT.[1]

The perspective of this article accepts the unity of the book of Zechariah. Some higher critics divide the book into two parts, each with its own author. Usually in this scheme, chaps. 9–14 are divided from the earlier part of the prophecy based upon alleged differences.[2] However, the interpreter should not overlook the similarities. The references to Messiah begin in the eight night visions in the first six chapters. The messianic figure of 3:1-10 under the symbols of servant, branch, and stone, for example, points to the ultimate national and spiritual restoration of Israel in the land, the major subject of Israel's deliverance in chaps. 12–14. In light of such similarities, the reader of the prophecy must accept the singular authorship of Zechariah the prophet for the entire text.[3]

The approach of this article also admits the clarity of the details of prophetic and apocalyptic language, something doubted by various interpreters.[4] While the hard work of study must increase in light of the large amounts of symbols and poetic language, one must still propose the understandability of the details of such prophetic texts. The prophecy of Zechariah also demonstrates traits of apocalyptic literature that complicate the issue: symbols and visions, composition during oppressive conditions, exact recording of visions, use of an interpreting angel, and theological content with eschatological overtones.[5] Yet such elements observed in the text do not change the overall use of grammatical-historical interpretation. Apocalyptic genre does not demand a highly subjective interpreter given to flights of fancy. The approach taken in this article assumes that God is trying to communicate a message in Zch 3:1-10 and that He has succeeded.

CONTEXTUAL CONSIDERATIONS

Zechariah 3:1-10 constitutes the fourth of eight visions that span Zch 1:7 to 6:8. At the time of the prophecies of the book, the rebuilding of the Temple in Jerusalem is incomplete and the land of Israel unsettled in spirit. Consequently, the prophecies center on the sin of Israel and the world, as well as on the need for forgiveness and deliverance. After the prophet addresses issues within the first generation of postexilic Israel, the book progresses to the kingdom age when a messianic figure will establish righteous rule and final, absolute forgiveness (Zch 12–14).

The fourth vision is unlike the other seven revelations in a few ways. In the other visions, an interpreting angel explains the details of the vision to Zechariah. Usually, the text states the words "the angel who was speaking with me" (see 1:9,14; 2:3; 4:1; 5:5; 6:4). The only exception is the sixth vision of the flying scroll in which the speaking of the interpreting angel is understood from the context. In Zch 3:1-10, this angel shows the high priest Joshua to Zechariah but does not speak throughout the vision. God, in the person of the Angel of the Lord, acts and speaks more directly to Joshua and others rather than to the prophet Zechariah. Additionally, there are no questions voiced by the prophet that require answers, although the question-and-answer format fits the other visions.

EXEGETICAL CONSIDERATIONS

The third chapter of Zechariah easily breaks down into a two-part outline: the symbolic act (3:1-5) and the interpretation of that symbolic act (3:6-10). In this respect, the chapter follows a common feature in other parts of the Bible that have apocalyptic elements (for example, the vision of the four beasts in Dn 7:1-14 followed by the interpretation of the vision in Dn 7:15-28). Several figures appear in this vision: Joshua the high priest of Israel, the Angel of the Lord, the Lord or the Lord of Hosts, Satan, "those who are standing here," Joshua's "colleagues," "My servant, the Branch," and the stone.

I. The Symbolic Act (3:1-5). Joshua the high priest stands before the Angel of the

Lord with filthy clothes as a symbol of sin, for himself and all Israel. In a ceremonial way, the Angel of the Lord has new clothes placed on Joshua to picture future forgiveness and pardon for the sin of the nation.

A. Joshua's Predicament (3:1-2). The words "then he showed me the high priest Joshua" (3:1) mark the simple transition from the third night vision of chap. 2 (the surveyor) to the fourth night vision of chap. 3. The interpreting angel from the previous three visions shows Joshua to Zechariah. This angel, however, does nothing more in the fourth vision, remaining silent and inactive through the end of the vision.

1. Standing before the Angel of the Lord (3:1). Zechariah sees Joshua "standing before the Angel of the LORD." Two issues emerge at this point. First, the text does not reveal the circumstance of Joshua's position. Does he stand in a heavenly Temple, the earthly Temple, or a courtroom of some sort? If the described situation speaks of the high priest's regular temple service, then the seer describes a scene from the earthly Temple. The rebuilding of the Temple in Jerusalem remains an issue at the time of Zechariah's prophecy. Furthermore, the vision ends with an earthly promise for the removal of guilt (v. 9) from the land and the image of sitting under the vine and fig tree (v. 10). These reasons push toward the conclusion that the location in the vision is the earthly Temple, even though the Temple is not yet finished in Zechariah's day.

Nonetheless, the courtroom idea looms over the passage as an option as well. Satan's accusatory position (v. 1), and the Angel of the Lord's defense of Joshua (v. 2) portray a judicial tone in the passage. Charles L. Feinberg correctly brings both the temple service and the judicial aspects of the passage together: "The best solution of the matter seems to be that the priestly scene is changed into a judicial one."[6] What starts as a priestly service before the Lord in the Temple in the vision turns into a judicial confrontation when Satan brings his indictment against Joshua.

A second issue to resolve is the identification of the Angel of the Lord. One view sees the Angel of the Lord as being the same as the interpreting angel who shows Joshua to Zechariah. Against this view, the Angel of the Lord and the interpreting angel appear to be two distinct persons in chap. 1. Another view notes the evidence of the deity of the Angel of the Lord in the context.

The official scene shows Joshua before the Angel of the Lord while Satan is standing to Joshua's side (v. 1). Immediately in 3:2, the text says, "The LORD said to Satan." God could possibly be uttering a voice from heaven in the vision with the three characters listening. However, in the flow of the passage, the better interpretation sees Joshua standing before God and God talking to Satan. Another support for the divine nature of this Angel arises in 3:4. The Angel removes guilt, thereby forgiving sins against the Lord, a prerogative that the Scriptures clearly limit to God. This proof of deity gains strength in the consideration that the Lord of Hosts

(God) forgives the sin of the land of Israel (its people) in 3:9. Zechariah easily moves from the Angel to God in this divine prerogative. A final thought stems from earlier revelation in the book of Job, assuming that Job was written before Zechariah. The scene of three persons showing Satan accusing and opposing a holy man before God may have formed the backdrop of Zechariah's vision here. If so, the case is strengthened that Zechariah is presenting the Angel of the Lord as deity.[7]

2. *Satan's accusation (3:1).* The text states that Satan was "standing at his right side to accuse him." The word "Satan" refers to "the accuser," an adversary who opposes someone, in this case verbally. Although the designation can refer to any opposing enemy, by the time of Zechariah "Satan" was a proper name for the supreme fallen angel who appeared as a serpent in Gn 3 and accused Job before God (Job 1–2). He is the enemy of both God and men. Satan stands to the right side of Joshua, not the Angel of the Lord. Some interpreters suggest that such a position to the right constitutes the customary place for a prosecutor. Studies have shown that extrabiblical Jewish sources do not emphasize this idea.[8] Nonetheless, Ps 109:6 speaks of the accuser at the right hand. Zechariah 3:1 does not directly record the content of Satan's accusation against Joshua. However, the Lord's rebuke in v. 2 suggests that the accuser has opposed God's people Israel, whom Joshua represents as the high priest.

3. God's rebuke of Satan (3:2). God, as the Angel of the Lord, speaks to Satan directly and by name: "The LORD rebuke you, Satan!" The term "rebuke" carries with it the idea of an insulting or mocking tone that Satan deserves. God defends Joshua and the people he represents in two ways. First, the Lord reminds Satan that his accusations cannot be appropriate because He, the Lord Himself, has chosen Jerusalem. The mention of the city coincides with Joshua's Temple service, which is located within the city. Second, the Lord notes His own special choice of Joshua as a "burning stick snatched from the fire." The image of snatching a stick from a fire predates the exile (Am 4:11). The word "snatched" (*nasal*) means to pull out, remove, or take away. Applied to a person, the concept of being "saved" is a fitting idea. Joshua had been removed from the Babylonian captivity. Both the choosing of Jerusalem and the saving of Joshua from captivity point to more than Joshua, even to the nation he represents. In rather strong language, God's rebuke of Satan shows God's love and purpose for the nation of Israel. His judgment upon the people in the captivity was not permanent destruction.

B. Joshua's Acquittal (3:3-5). In the vision at this point, the Angel of the Lord orders a ceremony to announce Joshua's innocence. The starting point, however, shows Joshua dressed in "filthy clothes" (3:3). The word "filthy" (*soir*) refers to the filth of excrement, one of the strongest Hebrew terms to show uncleanness. At first glimpse, Satan's accusation seemingly holds true. Some interpreters suggest that the symbolism of dirty garments refers to the customary garments of defendants at trial, but this was Roman custom, not Jewish convention. Among the Jews, the accused often wore black clothes for mourning.[9] As the passage continues, the indication is that the filthy clothes represent sin and guilt.

The next two verses change the scene entirely. The Angel of the Lord commands "those standing before Him," people now being mentioned for the first time (3:4). These special ones could be human priests who stand with Joshua the high priest. Other possible priests appear to be mentioned later in 3:7. The best interpretation, however, identifies these as subordinate good angels "standing before Him."

As the section unfolds, such a view helps to demonstrate that men cannot purify themselves. Thus, good angels help to answer the rebuke of the chief fallen angel. God orders the angels to remove the dirty clothes Joshua wears. The ceremonial significance of this action becomes clear in two parts. First, the removal of the clothes pictures the elimination of sin: "I have removed your guilt from you" (3:4). The Hebrew word for "guilt" is often translated iniquity, an aspect that speaks of sin's crooked trajectory in life. However, it can also refer to the "liability" or "consequence of iniquity," that is, "guilt" as in HCSB. The removal of both iniquity and guilt apparently takes place in God's action cited in the ceremony. According to the statement, God is the One who removes the guilt of Joshua and Israel. They cannot remove their own sin. Divine action carries out the deliverance. The second note of significance in this action highlights a positive addition: "I will clothe you with splendid robes" (3:4). The excrement-like clothes give way to the gift of "splendid robes," the translation of one Hebrew word that refers to expensive outer garments usually worn on special festival occasions. These would be appropriate for a high priest.

Up to this point, Zechariah has been a silent observer in the vision. In 3:5, however, he blurts out rather abruptly, "Then I said." Apparently, he wants the new clothing for Joshua to be complete by adding a "clean turban." The pure nature of the turban is perhaps a reminder of God's design for the turban for Aaron and his sons in Ex 28:36-38, which had fastened to it a "pure gold medallion" engraved with the words "Holy to the Lord." Zechariah's wish is carried out by the angels as they obey the Angel of the Lord who is standing nearby giving directions. The ceremonial picture portrays Joshua's acquittal and restoration as a pure high priest. Both subtraction (removal of filthy clothes) and addition (clothing with splendid garments) join to make this happen. Since Joshua represents the nation, Israel also receives acquittal and restoration. The implications of these actions will be fleshed out in the second section of the vision.

II. Interpretation and Application of the Symbolic Act (3:6-10). Not every feature of 3:1-5 is explained in this section. The significance of the earlier vision, however, yields both rewards and responsibilities for Joshua. At the same time, elements of that vision act as a sign to point to the future Messiah and the ultimate restoration of Israel.

A. God's Charge to Joshua (3:6-7). The content of the charge of the Angel of the Lord to Joshua covers 3:7-10 except for the last portion of v. 10. The word "charged" (3:6) means that all of these statements constitute an admonition, warning, or instruction. The entire section is characterized as "what the LORD of Armies says" (3:7). The phrase "LORD of Armies" (in most translations "LORD of Hosts") occurs well over 200 times in the Bible, with 53 of those in Zechariah alone. The meaning of "Armies" probably refers to God as Commander in Chief of all creatures or powers in the universe, including the angelic hosts.

1. Two Responsibilities (3:7). As part of the charge, God lays out two similar responsibilities for Joshua. These serve as conditions for the blessings to follow. The phrase "walk in My ways" constitutes the first responsibility. The metaphorical expression uses a common biblical means to speak about obedience to all of God's commands for daily living. Zechariah's vision replicates God's statement to the young Solomon, "If you walk in My ways and keep My statutes and commandments just as your father David did, I will give you a long life" (1Kg 3:14). The focus takes on a personal and moral character for all followers of God.

God words the second responsibility in the imperative, "Keep My instructions." The phrase, however, carries a more specific connotation than the first condition. The wording of the responsibility or requirement here speaks of ritual or official duties that can be applied to a priest properly executing the required ceremonies. God points out that Joshua must perform his duties of high priest as he ministers to the nation.

2. Three Rewards (3:7). If Joshua meets the two conditions, God promises three rewards. The first two are coupled together, since they both deal with the Temple. God tells Joshua he will "rule My house." The word "house" refers to the Temple in Jerusalem. The term "rule" (*dyn*) refers to the function of governing, defending, or judging, that is, handling all matters of dispute and organization. God's second promise is that Joshua will "take care of My courts." One view is that this promise refers to Joshua's rule of the courtyard around the Temple and not the Temple proper as in the first promise.[10] Under this view, no aspect of Temple life escapes Joshua's authority. Another view sees this phrase meaning to "guard the temple from idolatry and other religious defilement."[11] In either case, God assures Joshua that his obedience means he will keep his leadership role relative to the activities of the Temple precincts.

The third reward promised to Joshua presents more difficulties. The Lord tells Joshua, "I will grant you access among these who are standing here" (3:7). The ones standing appear before the Lord. One wonders if they are the same as the colleagues of Joshua from 3:8, in which case they would be human. If so, they should be identified as other subordinate priests. But this view presents the problem of why Joshua would need a promise of similar access to God with other priests. More likely, however, the ones standing before the Lord of Hosts are the same angels who stand before God earlier in the passage and perform the cleansing ceremony for Joshua (3:4). Because angels have special access to God, the promise of access "among these" becomes an exceptional pledge. The obedient high priest as he represents Israel will receive the hoped-for extraordinary communion with the Lord of Hosts.

B. Things to Come (3:8-10). In this section, the message of Zechariah demonstrates that the prophecies about a postexilic Joshua go beyond that time in history. These verses give the culmination of the vision by pointing to the coming of Messiah and the end-time spiritual and national restoration of Israel. As a result, the passage is clearly messianic and eschatological.

1. Servant Branch (3:8). To begin the discussion of future things, God speaks directly to Joshua the high priest and "[his] colleagues sitting before [him]" (3:8). The imperative term "listen," which introduces the statement, shows the importance of what God is about to say. These colleagues of Joshua cannot be angelic beings since the word "colleagues" would be too strong for such a relationship to a human being. They must be subordinate priests under Joshua's direction. These priests (presumably including Joshua) are a "sign" (*mopet*), the only time this Hebrew word appears in Zechariah. The OT, however, uses the word frequently, often designating the signs and wonders associated with Moses and the Exodus (e.g., Ex 4:21; 7:3,9; 11:9-10; Dt 6:22; 7:19). In Zch 3:8, the word carries the idea of a token of future events that an omnipotent God will bring to pass. Throughout the prophets, God sometimes declares individuals to be signs pointing to other truths or demonstrating His power (Isa 8:18; Ezk 12:6,11).

God states what the sign points to: "I am about to bring My servant, the Branch." The text gives no time frame for the fulfillment of the sign, although some help comes from the identification of the terms "servant" and "Branch." The term "servant" occurs also in Zch 13:5, although its usage there is unrelated to this discussion. The idea of servant in Zch 3:8 comes from the messianic use of the terminology in Isaiah. In particular, the four "Servant Songs" (Isa 42:1-4; 49:1-6; 50:4-9; 52:13–53:12) present an individual who will judge the nations, atone for sin, and restore Israel. In these passages, God calls this individual "My servant," as Zechariah does two centuries later affirming the messianic nature of this person.

The title "Branch" also carries messianic overtones. Both Isaiah (Isa 4:2; 11:1) and Jeremiah (23:5; 33:15) use the term in a formal way of the coming Messiah. The portrait of Messiah as the Branch in Isa 11:1-5 describes the setting of the eschatological kingdom over which He rules with massive changes in the natural world (11:6-9) and the permanent, end-time restoration of Israel as leader among the nations (11:10-16). The Branch is from the house of David in Jer 23:5 and 33:15. In both of these verses, Jeremiah gives the title "Righteous Branch" to the one who will come to "administer justice and righteousness in the land." Thus, the prophet looks forward to the time when Messiah from the house of David will come to make all things right. The term "servant" in Isaiah highlights both the suffering and the ruling of Messiah. The term "Branch" only refers to the future rule of the Messiah in the context of both Isaiah and Jeremiah. Zechariah appeals to this end-time making of all things right as he appeals to the future coming of the Branch.

An unusual twist on the term "Branch" occurs in Zch 6:12 where it is applied to Joshua the high priest. God tells Zechariah to make a crown of gold to place on the head of Joshua "whose name is Branch." Not only will Joshua lead the completion of the Temple, he will "sit on His throne and rule" (6:13). The rule may be limited to priestly rule of the temple complex mentioned in 3:7. However, the people of Israel may have thought Joshua a potential candidate for Messiah. Zechariah 6:12 may indicate a larger leadership role for Joshua than the Temple Mount. Thus, Joshua appears to be pictured as playing a role, pointing to the future Messianic King-Priest who is the ultimate and actual Branch. The NT then identifies Jesus of Nazareth as the fulfillment of this prediction.

2. Stone (3:9). Perhaps the most complicated interpretive issue in this chapter is the mention of a stone that God sets before Joshua. Several views exist on the identity of this stone. One view equates the stone to the foundation stone of the Temple that is still under construction. In the next chapter, the capstone of the Temple is mentioned, although it is in conjunction with Zerubbabel, not Joshua. Another opinion classifies the stone as a precious jewel like those in the clothing of the high priest.[12] A third view recognizes the stone as a reference to the personal Messiah, the view that is accepted here.[13] Such a designation should not be surprising since the idea of a rock or stone is used in other messianic contexts (Isa 28:16; Ps 118:22). Zechariah gives two descriptions concerning the stone. First, the stone has seven eyes. In the fifth vision, Zch 4:10 describes the "seven eyes of the LORD, which scan throughout the whole earth." Such language emphasizes the full knowledge and intelligence of the Lord as He exercises His ways in the world. The Holy Spirit could be in mind since the Spirit is mentioned in the context of chap. 4, although the identification is not explicit.

The second description of the stone comes about as God engraves an inscription on the stone: "And I will take away the guilt of this land in a single day." While the first depiction of seven eyes portrays the omniscience of God through Messiah, this second characterization highlights the purpose of Messiah's coming. Messiah will remove guilt in the same way the ceremony of removing Joshua's filthy clothes took place in 3:4. The guilt of "the land" refers to the guilt of the people of the land—all Israel. This establishes spiritual forgiveness of the nation in its land. Messiah accomplishes such removal of guilt from the nation "in a single day." Only a sudden and swift coming of Messiah into the world can accomplish such a feat. This event has not yet occurred and so remains to be fulfilled in the end time. This cleansing of Israel is the event foretold later in the book, when, after the nation turns in faith to the Messiah Jesus (Zch 12:10), He returns and "a fountain will be opened for the house of David and for the residents of Jerusalem, to wash away sin and impurity" (Zch 13:1).

3. Restoration of Israel (3:9-10). The vision finishes by reinforcing the spiritual restoration of Israel just mentioned. On the day when Messiah comes, the situation will be altered to the point that "each of you will invite his neighbor to sit under his vine and fig tree" (3:10). To sit under your own vine and fig tree means generally to enjoy a time of rest and peace (2Kg 18:31; Isa 36:16). A parallel passage to Zch 3:10 appears in Mic 4:4—"Each man will sit under his grapevine and under his fig tree with no one to frighten him." Both passages then add that the Lord of Hosts has declared or promised these words. The book of Micah predates Zechariah by two centuries, making it quite possible that Zechariah was well aware of his wording. The statements of Mic 4 concern "the last days" (4:1) when Zion becomes the center of the world with nations coming up to it for instruction from the Lord (4:1-2). This is a time of peace and safety in the land (4:3). Zechariah's end-time focus matches that found in Micah. Consequently, Zechariah's fourth vision ends with Israel in the land in its kingdom and Messiah leading the way.

ZECHARIAH IN THE NEW TESTAMENT

Although the scope of this article cannot do justice to the information in the NT about the use of language and themes from the book of Zechariah, a brief survey will assist in placing the prophet Zechariah in proper perspective. The sketch below will address several significant quotes and allusions from Zechariah by NT authors.

The NT quotes Zechariah in seven passages: three in Matthew (Mt 21:5; 26:31; 27:9-10), two in John (Jn 12:15; 19:37), one in Mark (Mk 14:27), and one in Paul (Eph 4:25). None of these come from Zch 3. NT authors allude to the language of Zechariah in 64 verses, three of which borrow from Zch 3.[14] In Rev 12:10, the text refers to Zch 3:1 and the celebration in the words "because the accuser of our brothers and sisters who accuses them before our God day and night has been thrown down" (author's translation). Behind this statement may also be the accusation of Job by Satan in Job 1–2. The two other allusions to Zch 3 are found in Jd 9 and 23. In disputing with Satan about the body of Moses (Jd 9), Michael the Archangel forcefully asserts, "The Lord rebuke you!" This statement is identical to the one uttered by the Lord Himself in Zch 3:2 when God rebukes Satan as he accuses Joshua. That the Jude passage carries an allusion to the extrabiblical work entitled *Assumption of Moses* is also a distinct possibility.[15] However, the statement about rebuke in this work is most likely taken directly from Zch 3:2.

The final allusion to Zch 3 contains two parts. In Jd 23, the biblical author encourages believers to point other people to God, describing the work as "snatching them from the fire." This wording echoes the picture of Joshua the high priest as a "burning stick snatched from the fire" by God as given in Zch 3:2. In addition, Jd 23 notes that this snatching out of the fire should be done with the attitude of "hating even the garment defiled by the flesh." Such language recalls the next verse (Zch 3:3) in which Joshua's filthy clothes are changed in the vision. In these references, Jude shows abundant understanding of this vision in Zechariah and applies its phrasing to evangelistic responsibility.

THEOLOGICAL CONSIDERATIONS

In addition to quotes and allusions, several intersecting threads require consideration of the relationship between Zechariah and the NT without reading the latter into the former. The discussion here is not exhaustive and constitutes a sampling of available connections.

First, Rev 5:6 links the Holy Spirit to Messiah in the use of the term "seven eyes." The Apocalypse makes explicit what is only implicit in Zechariah. There is no mention of the Holy Spirit in conjunction with the seven eyes in Zch 3:9, although Zch 4:10 refers to the seven eyes of the Lord in a context containing symbolism involving the Spirit of God (4:1-6).

In a second example, the apostle John calls Jesus an "advocate" (1Jn 2:1) to defend Christian believers if they sin. This courtroom terminology presumes an accuser. Revelation 12:10 calls Satan the accuser who is thrown down to earth. In Zch 3:2, the Angel of the Lord who is the Lord rebukes Satan for his unwarranted denunciations. In the NT, Jesus is the One who rebukes Satan and defends believers. This correlation provides partial evidence that leads some theologians to speak of the Angel of the Lord as a preincarnate appearance of Jesus the Messiah in some OT passages.[16]

Third, the apostle Paul in Rom 9–11 teaches that Israel is not cast aside forever.

God promises "all Israel will be saved" (Rom 11:26). This deliverance takes place when a deliverer comes from Zion and takes away the nation's sin (Rom 11:26-27). The eschaton is in view. The second coming of Jesus sets up His kingdom on earth for the saved in both Israel and among the nations (Rev 19–22). Similarly, Zechariah clearly sees the end times when Messiah removes the sin of Israel in one day (Zch 3:9; 12:10; 13:1). Such teaching from both the OT and NT rejects any supersessionist theology in which Israel no longer receives such a future promise.

The work of Jesus the Messiah on the cross and in the resurrection provides a final example. Jesus took away our sins as He died as the substitute for our sins and was raised from the dead. However, He not only removed our sins, He also imputed righteousness to us. In the great swap, He gets our sins while believers get His goodness so they can stand before God. This twofold aspect of His work is precisely what Zch 3:3-5 teaches. Joshua the high priest needed his filthy clothes (sin and guilt) removed, but he also required new "splendid robes" in their place. A subtraction and an addition were required. In the analogy between Zechariah and the NT on this matter, the work of God is perhaps best summed up in 2Co 5:21—"He made the One who did not know sin to be sin for us, so that we might become the righteousness of God in Him."

CONCLUSION

Zechariah 3:1-10 gives a significant messianic prophecy using the postexilic circumstance of Joshua the high priest. Joshua, together with other priests, serves as a sign that Messiah is about to come. The overall prediction points to the future end times. That future contains for Israel the hope of final forgiveness of sin in the land, national restoration, and the hoped-for peace of the kingdom.

---

1. F. Duane Lindsey, "Zechariah," in *The Bible Knowledge Commentary* (Victor Books, 1983), 1:1545.
2. Joseph Klausner, *The Messianic Idea in Israel* (New York: Macmillan Company, 1955), 197.
3. For a list of 14 elements of congruity between chaps. 1–8 and 9–14, see Michael Rydelnik, "Zechariah" in *The Moody Bible Commentary*, ed. Michael Rydelnik and Michael Vanlaningham (Chicago: Moody Publishers, 2014), 1413–14.
4. D. Brent Sandy, *Plowshares and Pruning Hooks: Rethinking the Language of Biblical Prophecy and Apocalyptic* (Downers Grove, IL: InterVarsity Press, 2002).
5. David E. Aune, *Prophecy in Early Christianity and the Ancient Mediterranean World* (Grand Rapids: Eerdmans, 1983), 107–21.
6. Charles Lee Feinberg, *God Remembers*, 3rd ed. (Portland, OR: Multnomah Press, 1977), 54.
7. Ibid.
8. David Baron, *The Visions & Prophecies of Zechariah* (repr., Fincastle, VA: Scripture Truth Book Co., 1962), 89.

9. Feinberg, *God Remembers*, 59.

10. David J. Clark and Howard A. Hatton, *A Handbook on Haggai, Zechariah, and Malachi* (New York: United Bible Societies, 2002), 125.

11. Lindsey, "Zechariah," 1554; see also Feinberg, *God Remembers*, 61.

12. Both of these views fit the duties of Joshua. See Clark and Hatton, *Handbook on Haggai, Zechariah, and Malachi*, 129.

13. Baron, *Zechariah*, 114–15; David Levy, *Zechariah: Israel's Prophetic Future and the Coming Apocalypse* (Bellmawr, NJ: Friends of Israel, 2011), 39.

14. The information here about the use of Zechariah in the NT is taken from the list in Kurt Aland et al., eds., *The Greek NT*, 4th ed. (New York: United Bible Societies, 1998), 888, 900.

15. For a discussion of this possibility and the implications, see Thomas R. Schreiner, *The New American Commentary: 1, 2 Peter & Jude* (Nashville: Broadman & Holman, 2003).

16. James A. Borland, *Christ in the OT* (Chicago: Moody Press, 1978), 65–72.

(Zech. 6:9-15), typified by the crowning of Joshua the high priest. . . . The crowning of King-Priest Messiah is thus set forth symbolically by the coronation of Joshua, which is not a vision, but an actual historical act, which evidently took place the day following the night of visions."[5]

TEXTUAL ISSUES

The pivotal question in the text is the number of crowns involved. Are the exiles instructed to make *crowns* (presumably two, one gold and one silver), one for Zerubbabel and one for Joshua (the gold for Zerubbabel and/or the Messiah, the silver for Joshua, according to rabbinic interpretation), or are they instructed to make *one single crown*, which is then put on the head of Joshua?[6]

The MT has *crowns* in 6:11 and 14, but written *plene* in 6:11 (with the pl. ending -ô) and defectively in 6:14 (with the pl. ending -ō). Note also that the only verb associated with the crowns in MT is *tihᵉyeh*, it will be, in 6:14, but that verb is feminine singular, suggesting that MT may have originally read the singular *'aṭeret* (crown) here.[7] The LXX reads the plural in 6:11 (*stephanous*) but singular in 6:14 (*stephanos*). Conversely, the Vulgate translates with the singular in 6:11 (*coronas*) and the plural in 6:14 (*coronae*), while the Peshitta has the singular for both verses. Targum Jonathan renders 6:11 with *ᵉlîl ra* (great crown)[8] and 6:14 with *ûš ᵉḥā* (glory or splendor; the accompanying verb is singular).

Among English versions, the KJV, NJPSV, and CJB render with "crowns" in both verses; NKJV renders with "elaborate crown" in both verses (understanding the plural form as conveying majesty); HCSB has "crowns" in 6:11 and "crown" in 6:14; NIV, NRSV, ESV, NET, and NLT have "crown" in both verses. In resolving these textual difficulties, scholars have taken three primary approaches: (1) There was only one crown, but it was elaborately made, hence the plural form (according to Barker, the plural form refers "to an ornate crown with many diadems—a plural of extension [cf. Rev 19:12])"; (2) Two crowns were spoken of in 6:11, but the function of only one of them is described in 6:14; (3) Only one crown was involved, and a plural form incorrectly crept into the MT, as reflected by some of the versions.

Also difficult is the exact significance of 6:11, if plural "crowns" is understood, since the Heb. simply says in v. 11b, "and place them on the head of Joshua son of Jehozadak, the high priest." If singular "crown" is read, then there is no difficulty, with "it" being understood as the object of the verb "place, set," thus, "Make a crown and place *it* on the high priest's head." If, however, the plural form is retained, it would have to mean: "Make [two] crowns and place [one of them] on the high priest's head," which would be quite forced. Otherwise, one would have to envision placing both (or, all of the) crowns on Joshua's head, which, again, is unlikely.

In light of the cumulative evidence, it seems best either to retain the singular reading of "crown" throughout or, if a plural form was original in the Hebrew, to take it to refer to a single ornate and elaborate crown.

INTERPRETIVE AND TRANSLATION ISSUES

Although some rabbinic interpreters identify Zerubbabel with the Branch (see below, **Traditional Jewish Interpretation**), most commentators recognize that neither Joshua nor Zerubbabel are being called the Branch themselves,[9] although there is a debate as to which of these two men represent Him. In Zch 3:8, the Lord said, "Listen, Joshua the high priest, you and your colleagues sitting before you; indeed these men are a sign [*'anšê môpēṯ*] that I am about to bring my servant the Branch." While this does associate Joshua with the Branch on some level, it hardly states that Joshua himself will be the forerunner or representative of the Branch.

Zechariah 6 is more explicit, with the NIV rendering vv. 11-13 (the key words and phrases are set here in italic): "Take the silver and gold and make *a crown*, and *set it* on the head of the high priest, Joshua son of Jozadak. Tell him this is what the LORD Almighty says: 'Here is the man whose name is the Branch, and he will branch out from his place and build the temple of the LORD. It is he who will build the temple of the LORD, and he will be clothed with majesty and will sit and rule on his throne. *And he will be a priest on his throne.* And there will be harmony between the two'" (Zch 6:11-13). So, the crown is put on the head of Joshua the high priest, of whom it is then said, "Here is the man whose name is the Branch." Accordingly, Joshua as a royal priest serves as a direct type of the Messiah, the Branch. This reading of the text mirrors that of the Targum (see immediately below). As for the closing phrase, "there will be harmony between the two," that would imply between the priesthood and the kingship; the problem with this, however, is that there is no explicit mention of the king, especially as someone other than Joshua, in the passage (see below, **Christological Interpretation**). Compare the rendering of R. L. Smith in the Word Biblical Commentary: "And he shall build the temple of Yahweh, and he shall bear honor. And he shall sit and rule on his throne, and he shall be a priest upon his throne. And a counsel of peace shall be between the two of them."[10]

In contrast, the NJPSV renders, "Take silver and gold and make **crowns**. Place ***one*** on the head of High Priest Joshua son of Jehozadak, and say to him, 'Thus said the LORD of Hosts: Behold, a man called the Branch shall branch out from the place where he is, and he shall build the Temple of the LORD. He shall build the

Temple of the LORD and shall assume majesty, and he shall sit on his throne and rule. **And there shall also be a priest seated on his throne**, and harmonious understanding shall prevail between them'" (Zch 6:11-13, emphasis added). The Stone version, reflecting Orthodox Jewish thought, translates v. 13 with, "He will build the Sanctuary of HASHEM [the LORD], he will bear majesty, and he will sit and rule upon his throne. The Kohen [priest] will sit upon his own throne, and there will be a disposition of peace between the two of them."[11]

In all these translations, there are two distinct figures: the future Messiah (= the Branch) and the future high priest, both apparently typified by Joshua the high priest wearing a crown (unless the one typifying the Branch is Zerubbabel, who is not mentioned, however, in the chapter; see further below, **Traditional Jewish Interpretation**). And there will be "harmonious understanding" between the Branch and the future high priest. This is also a valid way of reading the text (specifically, 6:13b, "And there shall also be a priest seated on his throne"),[12] since it speaks of two distinct figures between whom there would be harmony. But it fails to explain why Joshua the high priest is crowned and why he alone typifies the Branch, as opposed to crowns being put on the heads of both Zerubbabel and Joshua. Indeed, why not simply crown Zerubbabel, who was of Davidic descent and whose grandfather was Jehoiachin, one of the last kings of Judah before the Babylonian exile?[13] Zerubbabel is not mentioned at all in chap. 6 (in fact, outside of Zch 4:6-7,9-10, he is not mentioned anywhere else in the book), and while some critical scholars have argued that it was Zerubbabel, rather than Joshua, who was the original subject of 6:11-15, there is not a stitch of evidence to support this contention.

As Ehud Ben Zvi observes in the *Jewish Study Bible*, "One would expect that the king would be crowned, but only the high priest Joshua is. Ibn Ezra, Radak, Rashi, and others consider Zerubbabel to be the Branch, and the person for whom the other crown was meant. The Targum, however, reflects a different understanding [referencing one large crown, and referring to the Branch as the Anointed = Messiah].... Significantly, it is likely that the text reads 'crown' in vv. 11 and 14 (see NRSV) rather than *crowns*. If this is the case, then there was only one crown in the world of the book, and it was Joshua's."[14]

Smith notes that "Beuken, Ackroyd, and D. R. Jones believe that Zechariah was speaking to Zerubbabel and Joshua alternatively in v. 13:

> And he (Zerubbabel) shall build the temple,
> And he (Joshua) shall put on splendor,
> And he (Zerubbabel) shall sit and rule upon his throne;
> And he (Joshua) shall be priest upon his throne;
> And a counsel of peace shall be between them.[15]

As Zerubbabel does not appear anywhere in this chapter, his introduction here would be therefore quite gratuitous. Besides, the proposed alternating of subjects presumes too much and disqualifies itself by what it demands. In contrast, Baldwin defends the older Christian, messianic interpretation, explaining, "The symbolic coronation and the enigmatic term 'Branch' referred to a future leader, who would fulfill to perfection the offices of priest and king, and build the future Temple with all appropriate splendour (Hag 2:6–9). In this way, the priestly and royal offices will be unified." And, Baldwin adds, "Nowhere else in the OT is it made so plain that the coming Davidic king will also be a priest. It is for this reason that the passage has occasioned so much questioning."[16] See also Wolter Rose, *Zemah and Zerubbabel*, for a detailed defense of the messianic interpretation of Zch 3 and 6.[17]

TRADITIONAL JEWISH INTERPRETATION

Rashi, Ibn Ezra, and Radak all understand Zerubbabel himself to be the Branch (in Zch 3:8 as well), interpreting the entire prophecy in Zch 6 with reference to building of the Second Temple, although Ibn Ezra and Radak recognize a possible reference to both Zerubbabel and the Messiah.[18] At 3:8b ("I am about to bring my servant the Branch"), Rashi explains, "For now Zerubbabel, the governor of Judah, is insignificant in the king's court, but I will make his greatness burgeon. I will also give him favor in the eyes of the king, so that he will grant [Zerubbabel's] request for the building of the Temple and the city."[19] At 6:12, Rashi points back to his comments at 3:8, adding, "Some interpret this as referring to the King Messiah, but the entire context deals with the [time of the] Second Temple." Rashi then understands 6:13 to speak first of Zerubbabel, who will bear the glory of the kingship, being of Davidic descent, then of the High Priest, who will sit "on the throne of the priesthood," and, "The king and the Priest shall love one another."

In favor of Rashi's interpretation is the Second Temple context, since Zerubbabel and Joshua were directly involved with the building of that Temple, and it would seem odd to point to a man who was involved in building that structure 2,500 years ago, only to prophesy of another figure who would build a Third Temple in the distant future. The problems with Rashi's interpretation, however, outweigh its merits. First, he fails to explain why there is no actual mention in the text of Zerubbabel; second, he downplays the messianic significance of the term Branch; third, he fails to explain why it is only Joshua, the High Priest, who is mentioned by name in the text and explicitly crowned (although both Rashi and Ibn Ezra understand 6:13 to say that the High Priest will sit on his own throne); fourth, there seems little reason for the crowns to be placed as a memorial in the temple (Zch 6:14) if they had no future significance; fifth, there is no indication that Zerubbabel ever "ruled" over his people in any royal way, let alone with royal splendor (as emphasized by Abravanel). This would have been anathema to the Persian government, to whom Judah was accountable, and again, nowhere is such a role for Zerubbabel hinted at in any other biblical book dealing with this period of time (in particular, Ezra and Nehemiah).

The other, major rabbinic interpretation also recognizes two figures, Zerubbabel and Joshua, but sees the former as typifying the future Messiah and the latter as typifying the future High Priest, with the Targum explicitly identifying the Branch in 3:8 and 6:12 with the Messiah. As summarized by Stavsky (citing Abravanel, with reference also to Metzudot and Malbim):

> Others see the verse as alluding both to Zerubbabel and to the Messiah. Although Zerubbabel was the leader of the Jewish people at that time, he was given the golden crown designated for the monarchy because he was yet only a shoot in the process of growing. He was merely a satrap under Persian rule. However, from among his descendants an individual will rise and sprout who will attain the full glory of the Kingdom of Israel and upon his head will [lie] the golden crown. Nevertheless, since this greatness will come through Zerubbabel he shall merit building the sanctuary of Hashem at this time.[20]

Accordingly, 6:13 is interpreted with reference to the Messiah, a descendant of Zerubbabel who will build the Third Temple, and the future High Priest, who "shall come before the king to advise him and guide him in carrying out the will of G-d."[21]

While this interpretation has the merit of recognizing the messianic significance of the passage, it again fails to appreciate the significance of singling out Joshua the High Priest. Why crown the High Priest and then say to him, "Behold, there is a man, his name is Zemah, and he will flourish in his place; he will build the Sanctuary of HASHEM," and why leave out all reference to Zerubbabel?

CHRISTOLOGICAL INTERPRETATION

According to the Lange commentary to Zch 6:13, "Nearly all interpreters, ancient and modern, render as in the text, and understand the clause to mean, that the Branch would be both king and high priest on one and the same throne."[22] Reflecting this Christological reading, the *Pulpit Commentary* states, "The Authorized Version is doubtless correct, as the clause is intended to declare that Messiah should, like Melchizedek, combine the offices of Priest and King (Ps. 110:4; Heb. 5:6, 10)."[23] Similarly, Keil explains,

> The crowning of Joshua the high priest with a royal crown. . . . pointed to a man who would sit upon his throne as both ruler and priest, that is to say, would combine both royalty and priesthood in his own person and rank. The expression "Speak thou to him" shows that the words of Jehovah are addressed to Joshua, and to him alone (אֵלָיו [*'elāyv*] is singular), and therefore that Zerubbabel must not be interpolated into v. 11 along with Joshua. The man whom Joshua is to represent or typify, by having a crown placed upon his head, is designated as the Messiah.[24]

More recently, the Christological interpretation has been defended by Baldwin (see above) and also by Barker, who writes,

> In the fourth vision (ch. 3), Joshua was priest; here (6:13) the Branch is to officiate as priest. In the fifth vision (ch. 4), Zerubbabel was the governing civil official; here (6:13) the Branch is to rule the government. In 4:9 Zerubbabel was to complete the rebuilding of the temple; here (6:12) the Branch will build the temple. In 4:14 Zerubbabel and Joshua represented two separate offices; here the Branch is to hold both offices (6:13). Thus, restored Israel is seen in the future under the glorious reign of the messianic King-Priest. The passage is typical-prophetical. Joshua serves as a type of the Messiah, but at certain points the language transcends the experience of the type and becomes more directly prophetic of the antitype.[25]

And so, as the city of Jerusalem and the temple are being restored under the leadership of Zerubbabel and Joshua, the latter is singled out as a type of the coming Messiah who would combine kingship and priesthood in himself, building the future holy temple.

Some interpreters (most notably Wellhausen) found it so odd that Joshua, the high priest, would serve as the type of the Branch, rather than Zerubbabel, the governor of Davidic descent (spoken of also in Hag 2:20-23 in a significant prophetic passage), that they posited an original Hebrew text in which Zerubbabel's name replaced Joshua's.[26] But there is not a stitch of evidence to support this, nor is there a reason to reject the universal reading of all the ancient texts and versions, since Zch 3:8 already connected Joshua to the Branch (albeit not as directly) while Ps 110 specifically connected a priestly role to David (and/or the Messiah), hence a priestly king. Here, that image is further drilled home: The Branch, clearly identified as the Davidic Messiah in Jer 23:5 and 33:15 (see also Isa 4:2) will combine the offices of high priest and king as one.

The key question, again, revolves around the interpretation of 6:13. The ESV has, "And there shall be a priest on his throne [meaning, the Branch's throne], and the counsel of peace shall be between them both"[27] (cf. NET's "Moreover, there will be a priest with him on his throne and they will see eye to eye on everything.").[28] In contrast, the NKJV renders, "So He shall be a priest on His throne, and the counsel of peace shall be between them both" (cf. the NLT's, "He will also serve as priest from his throne, and there will be perfect harmony between his two roles.").[29] In favor of the ESV's rendering, which would be in harmony with the traditional Jewish view, is the final clause, which most likely (but not definitively)[30] speaks of two people rather than two offices. In favor of the NKJV's rendering is that one man, Joshua, is singled out as a type of the Branch, which would point to both roles (royal and priestly) being fulfilled in one person.

From the viewpoint of Christological fulfillment, however, either reading is acceptable. If one person alone is envisaged, then that one person, Joshua, serves as the type of the Messiah, here pictured as a royal priest, which complements the more common picture of the Messiah as a king who engages in some priestly functions. If two persons are envisaged, the Branch and the priest, both of them crowned and both ruling on their thrones, that these two personages are typified by one man, Joshua, a crowned high priest, points again to the Messiah combining both roles in himself.

After detailing the significance of the term *ṣemaḥ* and the verbal form *ṣ-m-ḥ* in key OT passages, Boda (*Zechariah*, 398–99) notes in particular the similarities between Jer 33, a restoration passage that includes a Branch prophecy, and Zch 6:9-15. He adds: "It is important, however, not to miss that the promise is expanded beyond the Davidic line in Jeremiah 33, proceeding to intertwine the future destinies of both the royal Davidic line and the priestly Levitical line (33:17-18), linking both to the enduring covenant with day and night (33:20) and promising not only continual service for both lines, but also a multitude of descendants (33:21-22)."[31]

In sum, although a strong argument can be made to read 6:13 with reference to one figure only, the Branch, typified by Joshua, and combining the offices of priest and king in one, it is also possible to see a reference to two future figures, one royal and one priestly, ultimately fulfilled in Jesus the Messiah. But even if two different individuals are spoken of, it is significant that: (1) it is the high priest Joshua who is crowned and who represents the Branch (thereby merging priesthood and the Davidic Messiah); and (2) it is Joshua, more commonly known as Yeshua, who represents the Branch, since that is the very name borne by the Messiah Himself when He took on human flesh (Mt 1:21).

THE PRIESTLY MESSIAH IN ANCIENT JEWISH HISTORY AND THOUGHT

The Jewish uprising against Antiochus IV beginning in 166 BC was led by the priestly family of Mattathias (the father of the Maccabees), and so it is not surprising that during the subsequent Hasmonean Dynasty (163–142 BC), some of the national leaders combined the priesthood with the monarchy (beginning with Aristobulus I). Thus, it was a descendant of Aaron rather than a descendant of David who ruled the nation as king. Although this was a political phenomenon rather than a theological one (in other words, the hope of a Davidic king was not displaced, nor does it appear that theological justification for a priestly ruler was sought for based on Scripture),[32] the fact that the national leader was a priest must have helped prepare the way for the concept of two messianic figures, one from David and one from Aaron. Thus, the Dead Sea Scrolls speak of "the Messiahs of Aaron and Israel" (along with the Prophet),[33] while the Testament of the Twelve Patriarchs (c. 100 BC–AD 100; see further, below) speaks of messianic figures from Judah and Levi, both of them highly exalted. While there is no connection made in these texts to Zch 6, it is highly probable that biblical texts such as this (along with Ps 110) played a role in shaping the thinking of these religious Jews whose teachings overlap chronologically, if not intersect theologically, with the ministry of Jesus.

Interestingly, at Qumran, Melchizedek took on an eschatological, semi-divine status in the Melchizedek Scroll (cited as either 11QMelch or 11Q13), being closely identified with YHWH in some texts (especially Isa 61:1-2, which was quoted by Jesus in Lk 4:18-19) and apparently associated with the "anointed one" in Dan 9:25.[34] The Testaments of the Twelve Patriarchs also speak of two messianic figures, one from Judah (the royal Messiah, descended from David) and one from Levi (the priestly Messiah, descended from Aaron). This writing, however, must be used with caution since the work in its final form is certainly Christian, although it just as certainly utilized earlier Jewish sources. As Collins notes, "We must tread carefully here, however, since many of the Levi-Judah passages in the *Testaments* actually speak of only one figure, who must be identified as Christ."[35] In some of the key messianic passages, in particular T. Levi 18 and T. Judah 24, Collins suggests that "we should think in terms of a Jewish core, expanded by a Christian redactor," summarizing with this: "it would seem that *T. Levi* 18 builds on a Jewish text that envisaged an eschatological priest, and *T. Judah 24* incorporated a Jewish prediction of an eschatological king."[36]

It is significant that in rabbinic thought, the priestly work of the Messiah has all but disappeared, let alone any concept of a future, priestly Messiah.[37] It is impossible to determine whether this was in reaction to the Christian emphasis on the priestly ministry of Jesus (see especially Hebrews for NT foundations) or whether it was simply the result of the Messiah being envisioned more and more in the image of the rabbi-teacher. Either way, it is the lack of recognition of the Messiah's priestly work that has made it more difficult for traditional Jewish people to recognize Jesus as the Messiah.

Even so, Zch 6:9-15 does anticipate a messianic figure, a royal-priest, just as

Ps 110:4 looks forward to an eternal king priest. Thus the author of Hebrews recognizes Jesus as that royal high priest, writing, "It is evident that our Lord came from Judah, and about that tribe Moses said nothing concerning priests" (Heb 7:14). Therefore, he concludes that Jesus is indeed a priest after a different order, not of Levi, but of Melchizedek (Heb 7:15-17). The author of Hebrews also identifies Jesus, the son of David, as the referent of both Zch 6 and Ps 110, concluding that Jesus "is the kind of high priest we need: holy, innocent, undefiled, separated from sinners, and exalted above the heavens" (Heb 7:26), in fact, a high priest, "who has been perfected forever" (Heb 7:28).

---

1. Unless those prophecies are interpreted with reference to the Messiah son of Joseph, a figure of secondary importance in rabbinic literature. See the article "Messiah in Rabbinic Literature" in this book.
2. Note the parallel passage in 1Chr 18:17 which reads "the chief officials at the king's side."
3. See Psalm 110.
4. Mark J. Boda, *The Book of Zechariah* (New International Commentary on the Old Testament; Grand Rapids: Eerdmans, 2016), 383. Rabbinic interpretation of Zch 6:1-8 is varied and tends not to make a direct connection with what follows. Kenneth Taylor, however, finds the placement significant, based on the earlier visions of chaps. 3 and 4, writing here, "Thus restored Israel is seen in the future under the glorious reign of the messianic King-Priest" ("Zechariah," in Tremper Longman III and David Garland, eds., *The Expositor's Bible Commentary, Revised Edition* [Grand Rapids: Zondervan, 2008], 8:779). He also notes (ibid.) that, "The passage is typical-prophetical. Joshua serves as a type of the Messiah, but at certain points the language transcends the experience of the type and becomes more directly prophetic of the antitype."
5. Merrill F. Unger, *Zechariah* (Grand Rapids: Zondervan, 1962), 109–10.
6. According to V. H. Matthews, M. W. Chavalas, and J. H. Walton, *The IVP Bible Background Commentary: Old Testament* (Downers Grove, IL: InterVarsity Press, 2000), in Zch 6:11, "The crown referred to here is a circlet, and, though it is occasionally worn by royalty, it more often adorns a person who is being honored or celebrated. It can be made of precious metals, as it is here, but can also be made of flowers or greenery." But since the context speaks of the High Priest sitting on a throne and ruling, it is clear that the crown was also of royal significance. According to Boda, *Zechariah*, 393, "The term for *crown* here (*ᵃṭārâ)* is one regularly associated with royalty in the OT, described on the head of a king in 2 Sam. 12:30//1 Chr. 20:2; Ps. 21:3; Jer. 13:18; Ezek. 21:31(26); Song 3:11. Other passages, however, show that such a crown is not restricted to the king in a royal court."
7. Compare, however, Boda, *Zechariah*, 387, who notes that "it is possible that a singular verb can be used with a plural noun (see GKC §464k; Davidson §113)." Conversely, he adds, "The plural form of the noun may also be used for a singular entity, either to indicate a 'plural of excellence' (see [Zch 6:11] NASB, 'ornate crown') or a composite headpiece (see Rev. 19:12, *diadēmata polla*)."
8. See Kevin J. Cathcart and Robert P. Gordon, *The Targum of the Minor Prophets* (Aramaic Bible 14; Wilmington: Glazier, 1989), 199.
9. According to the *Jewish Study Bible*, reflecting both traditional and contemporary Jewish scholarship, "it is unlikely that the readership of the book as a whole . . . would have understood references to a messianic king (cf. Jer 23:5-6; 33:15-16) as being actually fulfilled in the person of Zerubbabel by the time he built the Temple" (1253, to Zch 3:8). This is contrary to Rashi's view, cited below.
10. Ralph L. Smith, *Micah–Malachi*, Word Biblical Commentary (Dallas: Word, 1998), 216.
11. Yaakov Elman, ed. and trans., *The Living Nach: The Later Prophets* (Brooklyn, NY: Moznaim, 1996), 776, also reflecting Orthodox Jewish thought, renders v. 13b with, "And there will be a priest before his throne," meaning the throne of the Branch, understanding Heb. *'al* to mean "before" rather than "on."
12. Boda, *Zechariah*, 395, renders v. 13: *He himself will build the temple of Yahweh. He himself will bear majesty. He will sit and rule on his throne. A priest will be on his throne . . .*"

13. See also the significant prophetic word to Zerubbabel in Hag 2:20-24.

14. *Jewish Study Bible*, 1256.

15. Smith, *Micah–Malachi*, 218.

16. Joyce G. Baldwin, *Haggai, Zechariah, and Malachi*, Tyndale Old Testament Commentary (Downers Grove, IL: InterVarsity Press, 1981), 136–37.

17. Wolter H. Rose, *Zemah and Zerubbabel: Messianic Expectation in the Early Postexilic Period* (Journal for the Study of the Old Testament Supplement 304; Sheffield: Sheffield Academic Press, 2000). Rose also views the oracle to Zerubbabel in Hag. 2:20–23 as messianic.

18. Ibn Ezra also notes that some interpreters believe the Messiah will be called Zerubbabel in the future, just as some passages (e.g., Ezk 34:23-24; 37:24-25) speak of the Messiah being a future David.

19. The end of Rashi's comment, following b. Sanh. 38a, equates Zerubbabel with Nehemiah.

20. Rabbi Yitzchok Stavsky, *Trei Asar: The Twelve Prophets, Vol. II: Micah, Nahum, Habakkuk, Zephaniah, Haggai, Zechariah, Malachi* (ArtScroll Tanach Series; Brooklyn: Mesorah Publications, 2009), 239.

21. Ibid.

22. J. P. Lange, P. Schaff, and T. W. Chambers, *A Commentary on the Holy Scriptures: Zechariah* (Electronic edition; Bellingham, WA: Logos Bible Software, 2008), 53.

23. H. D. M. Spence-Jones, ed., *The Pulpit Commentary: Zechariah* (London; New York: Funk & Wagnalls Company, 1909), 59.

24. C. F. Keil and F. Delitzsch, *Commentary on the Old Testament*, electronic ed. (Pcabody, MA: Hendrickson, 1996), 10:554.

25. Barker, "Zechariah," 770. At v. 12, Barker points to Jn 19:5 (spoken of Jesus), "Here is the man!" noting that this verse "may well be intended by John as an allusion to the statement, "Here is the man whose name is the Branch" (ibid., 771–72).

26. According to Boda, *Zechariah*, 384–85, "For the majority of interpreters, the Sprout figure was from the outset linked to Zerubbabel. Many of these see in the interpretive difficulties and textual variances associated with 6:9–15 evidence of later revisions that shifted this original hope onto other figures, whether that is an anonymous future royal figure from the Davidic line or the present priestly figure of Joshua and the priestly Zadokite line he reestablished."

27. LXX renders v. 13 with, "And he will receive distinction, and he will sit and rule upon his throne, and the priest will be on his right hand, and there will be a peaceful plan [between] both" (as translated in the *Lexham English Septuagint*).

28. Cf. also RSV; NRSV; TEV; REC; CEV; CJB.

29. Cf. also KJV; RV; NASB; NIV.

30. Cf., however, D. J. Clark and H. A. Hatton, *A Handbook on Zechariah* (New York: United Bible Societies, 2002), 175, who states that the final clause "definitely speaks of two people."

31. Boda, *Zechariah*, 400.

32. Note, however, that Abravanel believes that both crowns in Zch 6 symbolized the monarchy, one for the high priest and one for the king, in anticipation of the Hasmonean dynasty, although because Joshua was the high priest and not a descendant of David, only the silver crown was placed on his head.

33. 1QS 9:11; see also 4Q175 (Testimonia); for discussion, see Collins, *Scepter and Star*, 79–109, where other relevant texts are also analyzed. Collins notes that there is "impressive evidence that the Dead Sea sect expected two messiahs, one royal and one priestly" (ibid. 83).

34. See Sam Shamoun, "The Dead Sea Scrolls and God's Uniplurality: Some Observations on Melchizedek," Answering Islam, http://www.answering-islam.org/Shamoun/melchizedek-scroll.htm. He claims that in this text, Melchizedek is associated directly with the God of Israel, indicating that devout Jews at that time did not have a problem with such a concept.

35. Collins, *Scepter and Star*, 102, with reference to M. de Jonge, "Two Messiahs in the Testaments of the Twelve Patriarchs," in Jan W. van Henten, et al., eds. *Tradition and Re-Interpretation in Jewish and Early Christian Literature: Essays in Honour of Jurgen C. H. Lebram (Studia Post Biblica; Supplements to the Journal for the Study of Judaism*, 36; Leiden, Netherlands: E. J. Brill, 1997), 191–203. See also T. Judah 21:1–4, where it is asserted that the kingship is subservient to the priesthood.

36. Ibid., 105. See ibid., 105–08, for further discussion of the "Levi tradition," including the Levi Apocryphon from Qumran (4Q541).

37. Note that the Messiah son of Joseph, a secondary messianic figure in rabbinic thought, does not correspond to the priestly messianic figure of the Dead Sea Scrolls or the Testament of Levi, and his function is martial rather than priestly, dying in war rather than serving as a priest. Even although Al-Sheikh's homiletical comment to Zch 12:10 speaks of the atoning power of the death of Messiah son of Joseph, this appears to be linked to the rabbinic concept that the death of the righteous atones (see Michael L. Brown, *Answering Jewish Objections to Jesus: Vol. 2: Theological Objections* [Grand Rapids: Baker, 2003], 153–167), as opposed to the idea that the Messiah would function as a priest.

Zechariah 9:9-10

Rejoice, Your King Is Coming

KEVIN D. ZUBER

The prophecy of Zechariah 9:9-10 has the distinction of being one of the most recognizable messianic prophecies in the Old Testament. This is because one portion of this prophecy is quoted in the Gospels in the account of Jesus' triumphal entry into Jerusalem (Mt 21:5; Jn 12:15).[1] However, this prophecy may be one of the least understood in its own OT context.

PRE-CONTEXT OF ZECHARIAH 9:9

The prophet Zechariah was a prophet (1:1) and a priest (cf. Neh 12:12-16). His father, Berechiah, probably died young, so Zechariah is identified as the "son of Iddo," his grandfather. He was born in captivity but returned to Jerusalem with his grandfather when Zerubbabel and Joshua the high priest led the captives back (cf. Neh 12:1). His contemporary was Haggai, and both began their prophetic ministries in 520 BC, "the second year of Darius" (cf. Hag 1:1, Zch 1:1).

The book of Zechariah may be divided into three main sections: The first section contains the eight night visions, chaps. 1–6. The second section deals with the question of the men of Bethel (about fasting) and the answer of the Lord of Hosts, chaps. 7–8. The third section is made up of two extended messages or burdens of the prophet concerning the coming of the Messiah, chaps. 9–14. The term "burden" (*massa*) literally means a heavy load, a substantial weight to be borne. But it is also used to introduce "an oracle" of a prophet (cf. Isa 13:1; 14.28; Jer 23:33,34,36,38).[2] The idea seems to be that these messages are an oracle or word from the Lord that is a burden for the prophet—a weighty, loaded, message that must be borne and delivered.

The first of these burdens is in two parts: chaps. 9–10 and then chap. 11; and the first part of this first burden may itself be divided into two (very imbalanced) parts: 9:1-8 and 9:9–10:12. Part one (9:1-8) concerns the Lord's judgment that will come (through the instrument of Alexander the Great) upon the northern and coastal nations of the Levant. This prophetic word of conquest and destruction contrasts with part two (9:9–10:12), the coming of the Lord's Messiah.

The list of places and peoples named in 9:1-8 follows the very path Alexander took in his conquests (c. 333 BC). Understand that this is a prophecy, not a history, of the conquests of Alexander the Great in this region. Alexander defeated Persia (modern Iran) c. 333 BC and turned his attention west and then south to the regions and cities listed here. As noted, Zechariah prophesied in 520 BC, and the conquests foretold here took place in 333/332 BC.

The list begins with Hadrach (a region) and Damascus and Hamath (cities) in the far north of the so-called "fertile crescent" (9:1-2). The prophet notes this conquest will attract the attention of the surrounding nations ("for the eyes of men") but that "all the tribes of Israel" will view these events with their attention "on the Lord" (9:1b). That is, the faithful in Israel will see these world events not just as the conquests of Alexander, but they also will "recognize [the Lord's] action" of judgment on these nations.[3]

The list continues with the Phoenician cities of Tyre and Sidon (9:2-4). Tyre receives specific and extended attention, probably because of its prominence and wealth (9:3) and the spectacular manner of its defeat by Alexander's forces (9:4).[4]

The list next identifies the Philistine cities along the Mediterranean coast (9:5-7). At the time these Philistine cites were under the influence of Egypt, which was Alexander's main target. Of the five cities of Philistia (Jos 13:3; 1Sm 6:17), only Gath is omitted. The prophet indicates that the coming destruction by Alexander is a judgment for their idolatry (their "detestable things" 9:7a). However, this will cause many of them to turn to the Lord and be integrated into the nation ("like a clan in Judah" v. 7b), as were the Jebusites (the original inhabitants of Jerusalem, 9:7c).

Finally, the conqueror will arrive at Jerusalem. Here Alexander's juggernaut will be halted. The prophet recalls a promise of the Lord to "camp at My house" (9:8a). This "house" may be the Temple, Jerusalem itself, or the entire land of Israel; in any case the prophet is "indicating He [the Lord] would protect Jerusalem and its temple from Alexander."[5] The promise that "no oppressor will march against them again" (9:8b) was literally kept, and Jerusalem itself was spared by Alexander (Josephus tells an interesting tale about how this happened).[6]

However, this historical preservation was merely the foreshadowing of a future final deliverance, when the city and the nation would be delivered "from every oppressor" and would be "protected against its final enemies."[7] "The prophet turn[ed] his gaze from contemplating the movements of the ruthless conqueror, Alexander, to view the Person and work, in humiliation and then exaltation, of the coming King of Israel."[8]

CONTENT OF ZECHARIAH 9:9

The main point of this entire section (9:9–10:12) is the simple but glorious truth that the Lord's Messiah (the King) is coming: "Your King is coming to you" (9:9c). "Here is a direct prediction of the future Messiah."[9] This is a note Zechariah has already sounded in Zch 2:10 [MT14] where the "Daughter Zion" is called to rejoice because the Messiah is coming and will "dwell among you." Laetsch notes, "your king" is "the Messiah," "Zion's king, the King of the Jews; a descendant of Israel, of the tribe of Judah, of the royal house of David, who had established Zion, Jerusalem, the royal city. The long-expected, eagerly desired (Gn 49:10; Ps 14:7) King is coming."[10] "The Hebrew tense . . . vividly describes Him as He is on the way."[11] The phrase translated "your King is coming *to* you" (9:9a) can also be translated, "your King is coming *for* you," that is, He is coming "for your benefit."[12] On this salient note, Zechariah proceeds to reveal aspects of His Person and to explain the benefits to be brought by this coming King, this Messiah.

The prophet begins with a most significant aspect of His Person, namely "He is righteous" (*saddiq*) or just. "The Messiah is described as 'righteous' (i.e., 'in the right'). His nature and character will set the norms for what is lawful, just, and correct. This characteristic also implies a quality of impartiality in judgment as he exercises his kingly office."[13] The term "righteous" (*sedeq*)[14] denotes "a state or quality of that which accords with some recognized standard"[15] and in Scripture that standard is God Himself (cf. Isa 45:24; Jer 23:6; 33:16). To say that the Messiah is just or righteous means He is, in His person, the One who embodies the holiness of the Lord God, but even more it means that He will actively reign in righteousness (cf. Isa 9:7; 11:4-5; 32:1). Baldwin notes, "This is no static quality. In each passage [in Isaiah just noted] righteousness is seen in the activity of the King, governing, administering justice, encouraging right."[16] Furthermore, the affirmation that "He is just" (Zch 9:9 NASB), that He is "righteous," is a reminder of other prophetic affirmations: He is "that righteous Servant (Isa 53:9,11), that righteous Branch (Jer 23:5f.) . . . whose judgments are always right (Isa 11:3f). This righteous King is the Lord Our Righteousness (Jer 23:5f.)."[17]

The first benefit the coming of the King will bring is great joy: "Rejoice greatly,

Daughter Zion! Shout in triumph, Daughter Jerusalem!" (9:9a,b). The phrase "Daughter Zion" (hereafter DZ) (and the equivalent "daughter(s) of Judah/Jerusalem) occurs over 30 times in the OT; it is a personification of Jerusalem and is "used as a synecdoche, the capital city representing the entire Jewish nation."[18]

A survey of the use of this title reveals three main themes: (1) The DZ had been blessed by being delivered from her enemies (e.g., the Assyrians in Hezekiah's day; Isa 10:32; 37:22). But (2) the sins (mainly idolatry and indifference to the Lord) of the DZ caused them to experience chastisement, judgment, devastation, even desolation. This came first with the Babylonian captivity (Jer 4:31; Lam 2:1,2; Mic 4:10); (it would come again in the destruction of AD 70; and it will come once more with the devastation caused by the Antichrist; cf. Dn 9:27). But (3) afterward the DZ could expect the coming of her King/Messiah when He will bring salvation, retribution on her enemies, restoration (of the remnant), (re-)inauguration of the kingdom (Zph 3:20; Zch 2:10). The note here in Zch 9:9 is about the latter theme; this is the cause of the rejoicing.

The term "rejoice" (*gili*) has the notion of "excitement,"[19] and "literally means 'to twirl.'"[20] The term "shout" is "used of war cries (Jos 6:10) or loud shouting (Mic 4:9)."[21] "Both verbs emphasize the intensity of irrepressible joy, that manifests itself not only in leaping, but also in loud proclamation."[22]

The coming King will also bring the benefit of "salvation": He "has salvation" (9:9d, HCSB footnote). "The form of the word 'salvation' is either a passive one or a reflexive one. If it is passive, the Messiah will 'be saved'—that is he will be delivered form the power of death. If it is reflexive . . . then the Messiah will show himself to be the Savior. Both ideas may be intended."[23] This whole phrase has the notion that in His coming He is empowered and authorized to deliver a victory.

But the question is: "What sort of victory?" Is it a victory over unrighteousness and sin (a salvation in a soteriological sense)? Or is it a victory over the nation's enemies and establishment of the promised earthly kingdom (a salvation in a geo-political sense)? The short answer is: it is both (see Ps 85:1-13). To understand why this is so requires an awareness and appreciation about the prophecy that is not immediately evident from this prophecy on its own, as it stands here, presented by the prophet. Simply by looking at the text and taking vv. 9 and 10 together, it is not evident that the fulfillment of this prophecy is to be accomplished in two phases. Nothing in the text itself actually indicates that the fulfillment will not come all at once, that indeed there will be two comings of the Messiah. Nevertheless, when comparing other OT prophecies and clear NT fulfillments it becomes quite clear that "verse 9 covers the first coming of the Messiah; verse 10 indicates His purpose and accomplishments in the second coming."[24] "This is a classic example of a telescoped prophecy"[25] where in one OT text there are several features of Messiah's ministry, revealed together, and revealed without any indication or clues that the fulfillment of some of the features of Messiah's ministry would happen at a time separated by centuries from the fulfillment of other features. This type of prophecy is not unusual (see Isa 61:1-3; cf. Lk 4:16-22).

This helps answer the question of the meaning of "salvation" here in 9:9d. The one sense of salvation (soteriological sense) was accomplished at the first coming (Mt 1:21; Lk 19:10), and the other salvation (geopolitical) will be accomplished at the second coming.[26]

The distinction of the two comings of the Messiah is made evident by observing the manner and purpose of Messiah's coming in these verses. At the first He will come "humble and riding on a donkey, on a colt, the foal of a donkey" (9:9e,f). This describes a somewhat surprising aspect of His Person: He is humble and lowly. There is something incongruous and unexpected about this. It might have been expected that Messiah the King would enter in grand fashion, "riding in chariots and on horses" (cf. Jer 17:25); "in New Testament times, a great leader would have ridden on a horse or in a chariot."[27] But here He makes His appearance in humility, on a donkey. Actually, Kaiser notes, in "the ancient Near East the donkey was not thought of as a beast of burden . . . instead, the donkey was the preferred mount of princes (Judges 5:10; 10:4; 12:1), kings (2 Samuel 16:1-2), and leaders who mingled with the people in a peaceful manner (Genesis 49:11; 2 Samuel 19:26; 1 Kings 1:33)."[28] Thus, it was quite appropriate for a king to come in such a manner.

It is not just His transport that surprises but also His manner—He is "humble." The term "humble" (*'ani*) "is often used with the sense of 'poor' (cf. Zch 7:10; 11:7, 11 RV) or 'afflicted' (Isa 14:32; 51:21; 54:11), and though when the Servant is described as 'afflicted' (Isa 53:7) another word is used, there is a correspondence of idea here also between the Servant and the King."[29] The Messiah will not come in "pomp and circumstance" but in humility and lowliness. In contrast to the juggernaut of the war machine of Alexander the Great, this King rides in humility and conquers with humility, and a self-giving sacrifice.

This was, of course, "literally fulfilled on Palm Sunday when Jesus of Nazareth entered Jerusalem on a foal of a donkey"[30] (Mt 21:1-11; Mk 11:1-10; Lk 19:29-39; Jn 12:12-19). Through the years, ancient rabbis[31] and modern rationalists[32] have interpreted this verse in such a way as to deny that this is a direct prophecy of the Messiah, Jesus of Nazareth. However, the Gospel writers clearly and unequivocally affirm that Zch 9:9 was fulfilled by Jesus at the so-called triumphal entry and, as Baldwin notes, even the "Passover crowds recognized the fulfillment of prophecy in a man's journey into Jerusalem on a donkey."[33] Thus, beyond question, v. 9 refers to Messiah's first coming.

But it is just as obvious that the rest of the prophecy (9:10) was clearly *not fulfilled* at the first coming! "Even though the Evangelists (gospel writers) saw fulfillment of verse 9, they did not go on to quote verse 10, which may indicate that they were conscious of having witnessed only a partial fulfillment." It was "only too evident that the disarmament of Jerusalem and peace among the nations [were] features yet to be fulfilled."[34] This can refer only to the second coming.

The prophet proceeds to describe the other benefits the Messiah will bring (at His second coming). In v. 10 the key words are "peace" and "dominion."

The "peace" (9:10d) will be accomplished by a dramatic program of disarmament (9:10a,b,c). The expression "cut off" (*hicarathi*)[35] indicates a breaking, destroying, or disabling. "Three weapons will be abolished when the Messiah returns a second time: the 'chariots,' 'the war-horses,' and the 'battle bow.' These, or their modern equivalents, will be banished from his kingdom and his realm."[36] The manner or means of this disarmament is not specified, but likely is made possible by the defeat of the nation's enemies (cf. Jl 3:2; Rev 19:15). It is because their enemies are completcly vanquished that the nation no longer needs to maintain these weapons. "Once these weapons are done away with, the Messiah speaks peace authoritatively to the nations. He commands it and it is brought to pass. His word of authority accomplishes what man could never bring about by his own schemes."[37]

The Messiah's "peace" ushers in the Messiah's "dominion" (9:10e). This peace is not merely the cessation of hostilities among "the nations" (9:10d) but also a time of prosperity for the nation, that is, for both Ephraim (the northern kingdom) and Judah (the southern kingdom)[38] (cf. 9:10a and 9:13). The extent of this "dominion" is "from sea to sea" (9:10e) and "from the Euphrates River to the ends of the earth" (9:10f). These descriptions cannot be restricted to the Holy Land.[39] "The terminology is similar to Psalm 72:8."[40] Thus, "from the general force of the prophetic Scriptures, we are driven to the conclusion that the reign of Messiah will be centered in the Holy Land and will extend to the ends of the earth. His will be a universal reign."[41]

POST-CONTEXT OF ZECHARIAH 9:9

In the rest of this first part of this first burden (9:11–10:12) the prophet extends and expands his prophecy to describe more specific benefits for the nation, benefits that will accrue to "Judah" and "Ephraim" as the result of the establishment of Messiah's peace and dominion. There will be a restoration (9:11-12) and a victory (9:13-15) along with prosperity (9:16–10:1). The primary referent here is to the era and the wars of the Maccabees against the Seleucids (i.e., Greeks, 9:13). "Verses 13 and 17 refer to the conflicts and victories of the Maccabean age when they were successful against Antiochus Epiphanes in the second century BC (Dan 11:32; also Dan 8:9-14)."[42]

These victories usher in a time of prosperity and flourishing. The nation will be "as the flock of His people" (9:16), and the produce ("grain," and "new wine") will make the "young men" and "young women" "flourish" (9:17). There is more than physical blessing here: "The ultimate benefit to Israel will be spiritual deliverance after physical victory; she will be the flock of the Lord and as a glittering crown."[43]

Zechariah further reveals what the Lord's Messiah (the King) will do when He comes: He will judge all false teachers and corrupt leaders (10:2-3a); He will reign in power and compassion (10:3b-6a); He will restore and regather the nation (10:6b-12).

In the description of the Messiah's reign in power (10:3b-6a) the prophet describes the Messiah with a series of four unique metaphorical titles (10:4).[44] In contrast to the false leaders (bad "shepherds" 10:3), the prophet announces a "new stable leadership that will be granted directly 'from the Lord.'"[45] "The ancient rabbinic Targum correctly understood these to be figures for the King Messiah coming from Judah."[46]

The *first title* is "cornerstone" (10:4). In the construction of ancient buildings, the cornerstone was not a decorative afterthought but was "the principle stone" and "the focal point of a building."[47] On this stone depended both the structural integrity and the design arrangement of the entire structure. The layout of the entire structure, the measurements for, and the placement of, every other component of the building would be made in reference to this stone. It was literally the stone on which the building rested (the foundation), and the stone that gave integrity to every other part of the building. As the "cornerstone" the King Messiah will provide stability, a solid "foundation" for the nation to build on (cf. Isa 28:16). He will be the focal point of the nation, the One to whom all will look for guidance and direction. Hence, He is the One who assures that the nation as a whole will enjoy unanimity of purpose and a constancy of integrity. Unfortunately, as Ps 118:22a predicts, the builders will reject this "cornerstone." This is exactly what happened when the nation rejected the Lord Jesus (cf. Mt 21:42; Mk 12:10; Lk 20:17; Ac 4:11). However, the psalmist also promises this rejected stone will "become the chief cornerstone" (NKJV) as He indeed is and will be (Eph 2:20; 1Pt 2:7).

The *second title* is "tent peg" or "nail." (10:4). This unusual title may refer to something like a "tent pole" that keeps a tent suspended and holds it upright and secure. In this case, the idea is a pole or hook on a pole "in the center of a tent where frequently used items are kept (Isa 22:22-23; Ezk 15:3)."[48] Or it may refer to the "tent peg" that secures a tent to the ground (Ex 27:19; 35:18; Jdg 4:21-22).[49] Either referent has the notion of security and preservation. "It depicts endurance under the strains implicit in leadership."[50] "On the Messiah will rest the hope and trust of His people. He will be worthy of support of the nation, the altogether dependable One, the true Eliakim (note: Isa 22:23-24)."[51]

The *third title* is "battle bow" (10:4). This is "a symbol of strength for military conquests (2Kg 13:17). It describes the same character of the Messiah given in Ps 110:5-6 and Isa 63 (cf. Rev 19)."[52]

The *fourth title* is simply "ruler" (10:4). The term here (*noges*) may have the sense of "oppressor" (as in 9:8; cf. Ex 3:7), "taskmaster," or "exacter." But in this case it seems best to take it as "ruler" in a "good sense."[53] "In Isaiah 3:12; 14:2, and 60:17 it is used in the sense of someone who rules."[54] "Accordingly, [the Messiah is] a *noges* . . . an absolute Ruler, on whom all sovereignty rests."[55] He will, indeed, be an "exacting" Ruler, One who rules "with a rod of iron" (Ps 2:9; cf. Rev 19:15). "In Messiah's reign on the earth God's sovereignty will be fully manifested . . . His absolute autocratic rule, therefore, though a terror to the ungodly, is a thought full of comfort to the righteous."[56]

These four titles are precious promises that the reign of the Messiah will be everything the leadership of the "bad shepherds" (10:2-3) is not.

The hope of Israel is found here in Zechariah. It was the anticipation of the coming King, bringing salvation from sin and deliverance from oppression. Moreover, Jesus the Messiah, who fulfilled these predictions, remains not only the hope of Israel but also the hope of the world. He is the only One who can provide forgiveness of sin, and He is the Ruler who will return to deliver Israel and reign over the world in righteousness.

---

1. James Montgomery Boice, *The Minor Prophets: Micah–Malachi* (Grand Rapids: Kregel, 1983, 1996), 194. "Few Messianic prophecies are better known than this."
2. F. Brown, S. R. Driver, and C. A. Briggs, *Hebrew and English Lexicon of the Old Testament* (Oxford: Oxford University Press, 1906), 672 (hereafter BDB); BDB has the word listed twice—once as "load, burden," et al. and once as "utterance, oracle."
3. See M. Rydelnik, "Zechariah," *The Moody Bible Commentary*, ed. Michael Rydelnik and Michael Vanlaningham (Chicago: Moody Publishers, 2014), 1427.
4. Tyre was thought to be impregnable. Indeed, the Assyrians had besieged it for five years and failed to conquer it. Nebuchadnezzar (Babylon) besieged it for 13 years and also failed to conquer it. Alexander defeated it in seven months. Ezekiel described this in greater detail (Ezk 26:3-14; 28:20-24). Tyre was a two-part city, one part on the mainland and one part on an island. On the island a 150-foot wall was constructed to prevent any attack by boat. (There is a pun in 9:3a; in the original Hebrew, the term for Tyre is *tsor* and the term "fortress" is *matsor*; thus "Tyre *tsor* built a tower *matsor*.") The previous conquests had sacked the mainland city, which resulted in a great deal of rubble and ruins. Alexander took the leftover rubble, and also reduced the rest of the mainland city to rubble, and dumped all the rubble into the sea to create a causeway out to the island (he literally "cast her wealth into the sea" v. 4b) from which he attacked the island part of the city and defeated it.
5. Rydelnik, "Zechariah," 1428.

6. See ibid., 1428; cf. Josephus, *Ant.* 11.8, 304–5; 313–39.

7. C. L. Feinberg, *The Minor Prophets* (Chicago: Moody Press, 1952, 1978), 317.

8. Ibid. Feinberg adds, "That the reference is to Messiah is abundantly attested in Matthew 21:5 and all the early Jewish writers. Both Jews and Christians have recognized this to be Messianic prophecy of great importance."

9. Rydelnik, "Zechariah," 1428.

10. T. Laetsch, *Commentary on the Minor Prophets* (St. Louis: Concordia, 1956), 455.

11. Ibid. The Hebrew tense is an imperfect.

12. K. Barker, "Zechariah," *Expositor's Bible Commentary*, vol. 7 (Grand Rapids: Zondervan, 1985), 662.

13. W. C. Kaiser, *The Messiah in the Old Testament* (Grand Rapids: Zondervan, 1995), 216.

14. BDB, 841.

15. W. D. Mounce, "Righteous, Righteousness," *Mounce's Complete Expository Dictionary* (Grand Rapids: Zondervan, 2006), 593.

16. J. C. Baldwin, *Haggai, Zechariah, Malachi*, Tyndale Old Testament Commentaries (Downers Grove, IL: InterVarsity Press, 1972), 165.

17. Laetsch, *Commentary on the Minor Prophets*, 455.

18. Rydelnik, "Zechariah," 1428. Zechariah's use of the two parallel titles (DZ and D Jerusalem) strongly suggests he had read Jeremiah (e.g., Lamentations 2:1ff).

19. BDB, 162, "go around, be excited."

20. Rydelnik, "Zechariah," 1428.

21. Ibid.

22. Laetsch, *Commentary on the Minor Prophets*, 455.

23. Kaiser, *The Messiah in the Old Testament*, 216; Kaiser mentions that "the ancient versions such as the Septuagint, the Vulgate, the Syriac and the Targum took it" as a reflexive." Ibid. However, Feinberg suggests that it is passive, not in the sense that He is the One delivered (saved) from death, but that He is the One "entrusted with salvation" (Feinberg, *The Minor Prophets*, 317).

24. Ibid., 318.

25. Rydelnik, "Zechariah," 1428.

26. In many ways, the failure to see two comings that will accomplish both senses of "salvation" is the biggest mistake made by many who try to understand the mission and ministry of the Messiah. The Jewish scholars and the Jewish leadership of Jesus' generation (even the disciples) were anticipating salvation in a geopolitical sense. They were expecting the Messiah to defeat the Romans and reestablish the kingdom of David. They missed (almost) completely the Messiah's mission "to seek and to save the lost" (Lk 19:10; i.e., in the salvation-soteriological sense; cf. Mt 1:21). Yet today many students of Scripture make the opposite mistake when they characterize Messiah's mission exclusively in salvation in soteriological terms. They fail to appreciate that the Messiah's mission in the second coming will be salvation (deliverance) in a geopolitical sense (cf. Ps 14:7; Isa 17:10; 61:10; 62:11—the context in these references is to national restoration). The prophet Zechariah (as with Isaiah) foretold that the Messiah will bring both a salvation in a soteriological sense *and* a salvation in a geopolitical sense, but that the two would be accomplished in two comings; in the first coming Messiah accomplishes a salvation in a soteriological sense (for all who put their personal faith in Him; Jn 3:16-17), and at the second coming He will accomplish a salvation in a geopolitical sense for the nation of Israel (Isa 62:10-12).

27. Homer Heater Jr., *Zechariah: Bible Study Commentary* (Grand Rapids: Zondervan, 1987), 80.

28. Kaiser, *The Messiah in the Old Testament*, 216; see also Gn 49:10-11.

29. Baldwin, *Haggai, Zechariah, Malachi*, 165.

30. Rydelnik, "Zechariah," 1428; cf. Kaiser, *The Messiah in the Old Testament*, 216–17.

31. See Rydelnik, "Zechariah," 1428.

32. See David Baron, *The Visions and Prophecies of Zechariah* (Grand Rapids: Kregel, 1918, 1975), 303.

33. Baldwin, *Haggai, Zechariah, Malachi*, 164.

34. Ibid.

35. BDB, 504.

36. Kaiser, *The Messiah in the Old Testament*, 217.

37. Feinberg, *The Minor Prophets*, 318.

38. Cf. Heater, *Zechariah: Bible Study Commentary*, 80–81; cf. Kaiser, *The Messiah in the Old Testament*, 217.

39. Feinberg, *The Minor Prophets*, 318.

40. Kaiser, *The Messiah in the Old Testament*, 217; cf. Feinberg, *The Minor Prophets*, 318.

41. Ibid.

42. Ibid., 319.

43. Ibid.

44. One of the best expositions of these titles can be found in David Baron, *Rays of Messiah's Glory: Christ in the Old Testament* (Grand Rapids: reprint n.d.), 151–78.

45. Kaiser, *The Messiah in the Old Testament*, 217. The first words of v. 4 are literally "from him." The NASB renders this "from them," and the NIV has "from Judah." However, the most likely antecedent of this personal pronoun is the Lord in v. 3 ("For the LORD of Hosts"). Thus, this new leader, the Messiah, will be sent "from the LORD." (See Isa 61:1 where the phrase "because the LORD has anointed me" is spoken by the Messiah. See also Jn 3:17,34; 5:36,38; 6:29,38,57; 7:29; 8:42; 10:36; 11:42; 17:3, 8,18,21,23,25; 20:21; 1 Jn 4:14.)

46. Rydelnik, "Zechariah," 1429.

47. See s.v. "Cornerstone," *Dictionary of Biblical Imagery*, ed. L. Ryken, J. C. Wilhoit, T. Longman III (Downers Grove, IL: InterVarsity Press, 1998), 166.

48. Kaiser, *The Messiah in the Old Testament*, 219; cf. Baldwin, *Haggi, Zechariah, Malachi*, 174.

49. Kaiser, *The Messiah in the Old Testament*, 219.

50. Baldwin, *Haggi, Zechariah, Malachi*, 174.

51. Feinberg, *The Minor Prophets*, 321.

52. Kaiser, *The Messiah in the Old Testament*, 219.

53. BDB, 620; "*ruler* (good sense) Zc 10^4."

54. Kaiser, *The Messiah in the Old Testament*, 220. Feinberg (among others) does not agree that this is a fourth title to be applied to the Messiah. He maintains the meaning "oppressor" or "exacter" for *noges* and argues that the point of this fourth description is that the Messiah will expel every oppressor from the nation. "Because He is the cornerstone, the nail, and battle bow, every oppressor and exactor will go forth from the midst of God's people . . . the work of the Messiah will bring about the removal of every exactor from Israel." Feinberg, *The Minor Prophets*, 321; cf. Rydelnik, "Zechariah," 1429. However, if the positive sense of *noges* is allowed then "the context and obvious sense" of the verse, moving from title-to-title in 10:4a, b, c, argues for yet another title (not a descriptive action) in 10:4d. In the words of Baron: "It seems to me that, as the first terms in this verse undoubtedly refer to the Messiah . . . so must this last clause also." Baron, *The Visions and Prophecies of Zechariah*, 355–56.

55. Kaiser, *The Messiah in the Old Testament*, 220.

56. Baron, *The Visions and Prophecies of Zechariah*, 356.

Zechariah 11:4-14

The Rejected Shepherd

ABNER CHOU

For Old Testament scholars, Zch 11:4-14 poses one of the greatest interpretive challenges of the Hebrew Bible. At least 40 different interpretations exist, and scholars cannot even agree on the basic ideas of the passage.[1] For instance, some argue the point of the passage is that the shepherd is good, whereas others contend the point is that he is evil.[2] The fact that scholars interpret the passage in polar opposite ways illustrates why they describe Zch 11:4-14 as "the most enigmatic prophecy" and a passage with impenetrable logic.[3] These difficulties in turn complicate the NT's use of this passage. If this text is not about the Messiah, then how do the Gospels apply it to Jesus?[4]

So what is happening in this text? This article intends to further examine Zch 11:4-14 and argue that although the passage is complex, in the end, the traditional, messianic interpretation best handles all the factors. In studying these issues, we can also discover the theological depth of this text. Hence, the goal of this article is to defend the messianic interpretation of this text and grasp its impact on messianic theology. Indeed, this passage describes the full theological dynamics of a pivotal moment in redemptive history realized in Jesus.

RESOLVING INTERPRETATIVE ISSUES

Various factors, such as exegetical issues, textual emendation, and higher criticism, make this passage difficult for commentators and produce a multiplicity of views.

Nevertheless, at risk of oversimplification, the approximately 40 different views can be placed into three major categories:[5]

First, this passage has long been viewed as a messianic prophecy. Supporters cite the many allusions of this passage to earlier messianic texts (e.g., Branch in Jer 23:5, Zch 3:8 and Shepherd in Ezk 34:15, Zch 11:4). They also note this view's consistency with the NT and that it poses the least exegetical problems.[6] However, problems do still exist. Scholars wonder who the three shepherds are (Zch 11:8), how Jesus deserted the flock of His people (Zch 11:9), and how He annulled the unity between Judah and Israel (Zch 11:14).[7]

Hence, the second view arises, maintaining that Zch 11:4-14 depicts the present situation of the prophet himself. This predominantly comes from higher critical methodology that rejects the possibility of prophecy and assumes Zechariah must be describing the political situation of his own time. Based upon this, critical scholars disagree about whether the main shepherd is good or bad.[8] They also variously identify the main shepherd as well as the three additional shepherds. These identifications range from foreign nations/leaders to particular governors in Judah to the offices of prophet, priest, and king.[9] In sum, the "present" view of the text stems from higher criticism's desire to reconcile Zechariah's words with his time, its politics, and with the varying (and even contradictory) thrusts within the book. This is done with varying degrees of success (as reflected in the number of proposals).

The third type of reading tries a different tack. Instead of seeing this text as future or present, it views the passage as a discussion of the past. After all, certain prophetic acts describe Israel's history (cf. Ezk 4:5). This may follow in suit. The frequent allusions to Jeremiah seem to anchor Zechariah to Jeremiah's description of the past exile.[10] Based upon this, the view contends the main shepherd in the passage is actually Yahweh who will judge the nation into exile.[11] The three shepherds He judges in one month are either three specific rulers deposed or the destruction of the three offices of king, prophet, and priest.[12] Either way, it refers to the events taking place in 586 BC. The strength, then, of this view is that it is rooted in previous revelation and can account for numerous details of the text.

How does one deal with these issues? We can proceed by thinking through each view.

A major disqualifier for the "present" view is its reliance upon higher criticism. The main reason scholars continue to try to collate the text with Zechariah's situation to no avail is because higher criticism presumes this must be the case. Conversely, without such an assumption, the impetus of the entire view disappears. Likewise, higher critics acknowledge that if one read the text cohesively in context and not via source critical method, then the "present" view has no grounds.[13] Since higher criticism is incompatible with a high view of Scripture and a cohesive reading of the passage within the context of the book, the "present" interpretation can be ruled out.

Likewise, the "past" view has serious problems. It has difficulty identifying the "potter" in Zch 11:13 to the point where it advocates changing the text to "storehouse."[14] However, such textual emendation is without any evidence. The need to change the text to make a view work is a substantial problem. Other problems arise as well. The view also has difficulty exactly identifying the "three shepherds." More fundamentally, this view has contextual and exegetical objections. To be sure, as proponents of this view allege, dramatic acts in prophecy can refer to the past (cf. Ezk 4:5). But in those cases, the text provides some indication of this.[15] Zechariah has none of these indications; in fact, it has the opposite. The other dramatic acts in the book are unmistakably future in nature (cf. 3:1-8; 6:9-15), which would suggest that this passage does not refer to the "past" but to the future. The imperfect tense of the verbs in the text also implies this. Thus, the "past" view has contextual and exegetical problems to the point that it might need to change the text to work. These are substantial issues that indicate the view is not tenable.

So far, we have observed problems in the non-messianic views. While these arguments can help exclude those interpretations, a case still must be made for the traditional messianic view. Three major lines of reasoning support the traditional interpretation.

First, the context overwhelming directs the reader to a messianic interpretation. This begins with the intertextuality of the book with other messianic passages. Zechariah is replete with messianic titles and descriptions like the "Branch" (Zch 3:8), "riding on a donkey" (Zch 9:9), king/priest (Zch 6:11), and "pierced" (Zch 12:10). Scholars recognize that such language alludes to messianic texts in Isa (11:1), Jer (23:5), Gn (49:10), Ezk (34:15), and Dan (9:26).[16] Scholars also note the interplay of messianic discussion in the minor prophets, which culminates in Zch.[17] Indeed, key texts in Zch expound the Minor Prophets' picture of how the rise of Messiah would establish the nations' judgment and Israel's restoration (6:9-15; 9:9; 14:1-21; cf. Hos 3:5; Am 9:11; Mic 5:1; Hab 3:13; Hag 2:21-23). Zechariah's rich intertextuality with prior revelation anchors it as a book that discusses Messiah. In fact, Kline observes that the book is structured to emphasize the Messiah.[18] This broad context already guides the reader to think of Zechariah as a book about messianic theology.

The argument within the book shows that Zch 11:4-11 is critically part of that discussion. For one, Zechariah speaks of Messiah in the immediate context. In Zch 9:9, the prophet describes the Messiah riding humbled on a donkey.[19] This text not only introduces the notion of Messiah but also that He suffers as He is "humbled" or "afflicted." These ideas certainly fit with what is described in Zch 11:4-11. The immediate context sets up for a messianic viewpoint of what happens in that text.

Furthermore, the passage connects with earlier messianic discussions in the book. Scholars observe that this text is part of a series of passages where God calls on the prophet to dramatically act out His message (Zch 3:1-8; 6:9-15).[20] Since those earlier passages are about Messiah, one would expect that Zch 11:4-11 follows suit. The content of this passage confirms it. Kline notes how the texts uniquely share the language and ideas of royalty/shepherd (6:9-15; 11:4), "silver" (6:11; 11:13), and "temple" (6:14; 11:13). Accordingly, Zch 11:4-11 is interwoven into the development of Messiah in the book. Consistently, later passages maintain a messianic interpretation of this text. Zechariah 12:10 discusses the One who was pierced, and Zch 13:7 refers to the Shepherd that was struck down. Those texts, in discussing the Messiah,[21] refer to Him in the way Zch 11 describes. Their descriptions assume a messianic interpretation and confirm it thereby.

With that, all the layers of context, from the book as a whole to the immediate context of the passage itself, situate the text in a messianic train of thought. That tremendously supports the traditional view.

Second, the content of the passage also favors a messianic reading. As noted, the language of Zch 11:4-11 is connected with messianic texts earlier in the book (cf. Zch 3:1-8; 6:9-15). On top of this, the passage employs the motif of a shepherd with the staffs of Union and Favor. Such language explicitly refers to Ezk 34:1-15 and 37:16, both of which speak of Messiah.[22] Hence, Zch 11:4-11 not only embeds itself in prior messianic discussion in the book but also is based upon a messianic text outside of the book. This is messianic claim upon messianic claim.

Third, one can deal with the challenges to the traditional reading. As discussed, there are three major objections to the messianic reading: Who are the three shepherds (Zch 11:8), how did Jesus desert His people (Zch 11:9), and how did He annul the unity between Judah and Israel (Zch 11:14)?[23] These problems must be resolved.

Concerning the first issue of the shepherds, the context of Zechariah begins to answer this. The book emphasizes the offices of prophet (Zch 7:3), priest (Zch 6:11), and king (Zch 6:11). In fact, the only other usages of "shepherd" occur in the immediate context and refer to the prophet (Zch 10:2-3) and the royal house (Zch 11:3, "young lions" and "shepherds" refer to the royal house). Thus, the three shepherds best refer to the governing offices of Israel.[24] The use of shepherd elsewhere in Scripture supports this (cf. 2Sm 5:2). The grammar of the text also confirms this. Zechariah uses the article with the phrase "three shepherds," a sign that Zechariah speaks not of individual shepherds (cf. Zch 11:5) but governmental offices (cf. Zch 10:2). Hence, language and context show Zechariah speaks of prophet, priest, and king. This idea is easily harmonized with the work of Messiah. Jesus certainly confronted Israel's leadership (Lk 13:32; 22:66-71), and they even acknowledged the loss of power they would face as a result (Jn 11:48). The objection is resolved.

What about the other issues of Jesus deserting His people and annulling unity? These matters can be resolved through the detail of "the potter" (Zch 11:13). As noted, other views struggled to make sense of this phrase. A key observation is that the Hebrew word, in its particular form *(hayotzer)*, occurs only in Jer 18–19, out of the entire Hebrew Bible. Others have already recognized the numerous allusions to Jeremiah in this passage.[25] "The potter" is another one of those. In that book, "the potter" signifies God's right to judge Israel in exile.[26] His appearance again in Zechariah signifies a repetition of the same event: Israel's rejection of Messiah will cause the nation to enter deeper into the exile. This interpretation accounts for the reason scholars often do not harmonize these details with Israel's history (because they are not the same event), but yet why it connects with Jeremiah. This interpretation also is easy to harmonize with Jesus' life. Israel's rejection of their Messiah plunged them deeper into exile; hence, Messiah left their house desolate (Mt 23:38) and destroyed any immediate opportunity for Israel's reunification in the kingdom (cf. Ezk 37:17).[27] Again, the objections are resolved.

With the objections resolved, the evidence thoroughly supports the messianic reading. In fact, given the immensely messianic progression of context and content, the reader would have no other expectation. That is confirmed by later revelation that, as will be seen, reads the text exactly this way. The Scripture is completely consistent in how it builds up for this passage and how it subsequently interprets it. The messianic interpretation is the reading of Scripture in every regard.

This discussion has sought to defend the messianic interpretation of Zch 11, which helps readers better see the significance of this passage. Israel's rejection of their King will only lead them deeper into exile. This is a defining moment of redemptive history and thereby of great importance for understanding the Messiah in God's plan.

A brief exposition of this text can help bring out this theological significance, providing further proof that it is messianic. This discussion will review the context and exposition of the text to show the prophet's intent in discussing the Messiah's rejection.

LITERARY CONTEXT

The name "Zechariah" means "YHWH remembers." This is fitting for a book that refers to so much prior revelation. Zechariah wrote to Israelites who had returned from Babylon (Zch 1:1-3) and were rebuilding the temple. His task was to demonstrate that God remembers His promises, and to assure the nation and exhort them to faithfulness.[28]

Within this, Zechariah reveals a series of night visions. These proclaim that God remembers His promises about His readiness to act (1:7-17; 6:1-8), and about the nations (1:18-21; 5:5-11), and Israel (2:1-13; 5:1-4). Technically, these visions are arranged chiastically, centering on God's promises of His Messiah, who is King and Priest (3:1–4:14).[29] In light of this, the prophet's theology is clear: God is faithful, and His Anointed One is central to His guarantees.

For this reason, after the night visions, Zechariah uses various people to depict the future moment when the Messiah resolves Israel's exile (Zch 6:9-15). Because God still will accomplish this reality, Zechariah exhorts the people to truly worship God and repent (Zch 7–8). Again, Zechariah establishes that the Messiah is critical.

In the latter half of the book the prophet presents God's plan, from the present to its culmination. Zechariah reveals redemptive history that will revolve around God's purposes for the nations (9–11) and His purposes for Israel (12–14). Within this, Zechariah continues his emphasis on the Messiah. The issues with the nations will resolve via a conquering Messiah riding on a donkey (Zch 9:9). Israel's restoration will come about when they mourn over the One they pierced (Zch 12:10) and via the Shepherd who was stricken (Zch 13:7). In the end, the Messiah will reign over Israel and the world in victory forever (Zch 14:1-21).

At this point, some questions should arise. While it makes sense in context for the Messiah to be a conquering hero (cf. Zch 9:9), it may surprise some to hear that He is also pierced and a stricken Shepherd. One cannot disregard these details, for the prophet links them with Israel's repentance (Zch 12:10-12) and the forgiveness of their sins (cf. Zch 13:1). So how did the Messiah become stricken, and how does this set up for Israel's restoration? Although such suffering was hinted at earlier in the book (cf. Zch 9:9 and the term "humbled"), more information is needed to answer these questions.

That is precisely where Zch 11:4-11 comes into play. In fact, M. G. Kline rightly notes that Zch 9–11 is a chiasm and that this passage is its center. It is the pivot that explains how the King victorious riding on His donkey (cf. Zch 9:9) becomes afflicted and how that ultimately leads to the redemption of His people (Zch 12–13). This is what the content of the passage will expound upon.

INTERTEXTUAL CONTEXT

Although Zechariah is replete with allusions, this discussion will focus on the allusions that bring out the "hinge" nature of the text.

The immediate context alludes to some key texts along this line. In Zch 9:9, God unveils the Messiah *humbly* riding on a donkey. Krause observes that the word "humble" alludes to Isa 53 and Dan 9.[30] These texts help interpret the Shepherd's suffering in Zch 11. They show that the Messiah's betrayal deals with His sacrificial death (Isa 53:3-5) that accomplishes atonement (Dan 9:24,26).

Within the passage itself, two other allusions help to express the pivotal nature of the passage. Zechariah alludes to Ezk 34 with the shepherd motif (Zch 11:4) and staffs (Zch 11:7; cf. Ezk 37:16). He also alludes to Jeremiah with the reference to the "potter," among others (Zch 11:13; cf. Jer 18:6). On the one hand, the allusions to Ezk 34 demonstrate that the shepherd of the text is the Messiah who will fulfill the promise to restore His people (see Zch 11:7). On the other hand, the Shepherd breaks the staffs of unity and harmony unlike in the prophecies of Ezk 34. Israel's restoration is not yet. For this reason, Zechariah also alludes to Jeremiah to show that Israel goes deeper into exile as discussed in that book (cf. Zch 11:13; Jer 18–19). Thus, Zechariah's allusions establish a tension of judgment along with future hope. The rest of the book bears out this tension. The verses immediately after this passage speak of the climax of Israel's judgment in the tribulation (Zch 11:15-17). Yet, the very next chapters speak of Israel's restoration as described in Ezk 34. That is because of the Shepherd's suffering in this passage (Zch 12:10; 13:7).

Therefore, the intertextual context helps to bring out that Zch 11:4-11 is a pivotal text. It shows that this moment leads Israel to the low point of their judgment in redemptive history. It also hints that this very same moment is the hinge that turns their immense judgment into total restoration and forgiveness. Such intertextuality helps to show the significance of Israel's rejection of the One who is responsible for ending their exile.

EXPOSITION

The text has three parts, dealing with God's summons for the prophet to shepherd (11:4-6), the shepherding of Israel (11:7-12), and the significance of God's judgment (11:13-14).

I. God's Summons (11:4-6). With the opening words, "Yahweh my God says this," the prophet introduces divine revelation. It includes God's instruction to the prophet and His agenda.

A. God's Instructions (11:4). God calls Zechariah to take on the role as shepherd. This continues the dramatic presentations of the Messiah throughout the book (Zch 3:1-8; 6:9-15). The specific role of shepherd not only alludes to earlier messianic prophecy (cf. Ezk 34) but also is important in context. Having just decried Israel's wicked shepherds (cf. Zch 10:2; 11:1-3), the prophet now presents the true Shepherd.

However, the overall agenda is not positive. Zechariah must shepherd "the flock intended for slaughter." Although sheep are often slaughtered, the Hebrew word *(harag)* is not used for sacrificial slaughter but for killing.[31] This indicates that this flock is destined for God's judgment.

B. God's Agenda (11:5-6). Accordingly, the next two verses will discuss the nature of this judgment. The fifth verse walks through the parties involved in the flock's destruction and shows, at every turn, there is no relief from judgment. The buyers (likely the nations, cf. v. 10) can slaughter without any harm coming to them. People (probably non-governmental leaders in Israel, see next verse) will sell Israelites seemingly with God's blessing and great profit. Most shocking, Israel's shepherds (prophet, priest, and king, see above and next verse) have no compassion on the sheep. This is jarring not only because shepherds were to protect their flock but also because the Messiah is supposed to be the shepherd. Why are these shepherds involved? What happened to the good Shepherd? Already the text hints that the good Shepherd was rejected in favor of destructive shepherds, who facilitate the entire chain of events. With that, Israel is betrayed from the start by their leaders and inevitably ends up in judgment.

Verse 6 provides the reason for this. Yahweh has no compassion on His people. He drives this entire process of judgment. Within this process, He ensures that every Israelite will face punishment as He forces them to be turned over to "his neighbor and his king." That refers to how the sellers and shepherds of the previous verse will take over and sell their countrymen in judgment to the nations. God not only ensures that the judgment is comprehensive but also extensive. The leaders "will devastate the land." They will cause the land and nation to be in complete ruin. On top of this, God ensures this judgment will be unrelenting. He states, "I will not deliver it from them." With that, the flock of Israel is indeed intended for the most destructive slaughter.

Overall, these opening verses introduce what is about to take place. Zechariah dramatizes his prediction—that true leader of Israel will come to His people, but somehow He will end up moving the nation to judgment at the hands of their own leaders.

II. Messiah's Shepherding (11:7-12). Zechariah's dramatization will demonstrate how what was just described will precisely work out.

A. Positive Shepherding (11:7-9). At first, Zechariah depicts the Messiah's ministry as positive. The Messiah specifically shepherds "the afflicted of the flock." He cares about those afflicted.[32] Along that line, He takes two staffs, Favor and Union, and shepherds the sheep, which alludes to Ezk 34 and 37:16. The Messiah's actions show He is the One who will fulfill the promises to bring favor between Israel and God, as well as unity between Israel and Judah.

However, v. 8 shows that this is not what happens. The good Shepherd ultimately destroys three shepherds. As discussed, this action refers to the future overturning of the offices of prophet, priest, and king in "one month," a short period of time alluding to the rapid turnover in the exile (cf. Jer 52:6-27). The collapse of Jerusalem and its government in 586 BC will happen again. The outcome of the Messiah's positive work is far different from what was expected.

Why does this happen? As the rest of the verse explains, the good Shepherd is exasperated with the false shepherds and they "detested" Him. Thus, in v. 9, the Messiah declares He will judge His people. He is unwilling to shepherd them any longer and relinquishes the flock to their doom. He states, "let the rest devour each other's flesh." This imagery describes how sellers and shepherds (Israel's leaders) would cannibalistically profit from the destruction of their own people—exactly what was stated in v. 6. Thus, the leaders' rejection of Messiah pushes the nation in the very direction of judgment that God stated. It also moves the leaders (shepherds) to their own demise (see v. 8).

B. Negative Shepherding (11:10-12). In light of this rejection, the Messiah transitions from shepherding Israel positively to doing so negatively. In verse 10, He takes the staff of Favor and breaks it. As a result, the covenant or agreement God had instituted with the nations is gone. This agreement refers to how God would ensure the nations in the end would support Israel (cf. Gn 12:1-3; Isa 2:2-4). Because God's favor is gone, so Israel's peace with the nations is removed. God prepares the nations to judge His people.

Accordingly, v. 11 states "It was annulled on that day." The language of "on that day" points to a definitive future moment.[33] It not only confirms a "future" interpretation of the passage but also that indeed, a pivotal moment has occurred when Israel shifts into the trajectory of judgment.

What happens next solidifies this course. Verse 11 shows that the leaders were not the only cause of Israel's demise. The entire nation—"the afflicted of the flock"—is also responsible. Zechariah describes the nation as "watching me." The word "watching" (Hb. *shamar*) describes guarding someone or watching someone in an unfriendly way (Pss 56:6; 71:10).[34] Why would the sheep watch the shepherd in this manner? The implication is the nation itself was hostile to the Messiah, definitively rejecting Him. After all, as noted, Zechariah states that those who did so were particularly "the afflicted of the flock," the very people the Messiah was shepherding. Even more, these people understood that the judgment that was happening "was the word of the LORD." Thus, the entire nation joins with their leaders to reject their Savior consciously and without excuse.

Verse 12 confirms this rejection. In seeing the distrust of the oppressed of the flock, the shepherd states "If it seems right to you, give me my wages, but if not, keep them." The animosity is so clear that the Shepherd does not even require payment to quit His position. In response, the "flock" weighs out "thirty pieces of silver" as His wage. Is this a lot of money? From a financial perspective, this is a hefty sum (cf. Neh 5:15).[35] From a social perspective, the amount is designed to be insulting for it is the value of one's sum profit from a debtor slave (Ex 21:32).[36] A shepherd would have produced greater financial gain than that of a slave. The wage then was meant to demean what He had accomplished.[37] It demonstrates His spiteful rejection by the people.

At this point, the following picture emerges. The Messiah begins his ministry full of hope and promise (v. 7). However, Israel's leaders (v. 8b) and the nation itself (v. 11) reject him. Hence, He ceases His work as shepherd (vv. 9,12), and subsequently Israel's false shepherds take control. This will bring not only their own downfall (v. 8a) but the entire nation's demise (v. 10), turning Israel into a "flock intended for slaughter" (vv. 4-6).

III. The Significance of Judgment (11:13-14). So far, God has shown how the Messiah's rejection would plunge the nation into judgment (vv. 7-12). He has also shown its destructive nature (vv. 5-6). With the words "the LORD said to me," God now comments on the theological significance of this judgment.

A. Deeper into Exile (11:13). God commands Zechariah to throw the silver away. Casting the silver aside shows rejection. Such rejection is further seen in sarcastically describing the money as "this magnificent price." Israel scorned their Messiah and so the Messiah scorns them. Specifically, God rejects the temple as the silver is thrown into "the house of the LORD." In context, Israel has been rebuilding the temple (cf. Ezr 5:1-2) with the hope that it would conclude exile (cf. Isa 2:2-4; Ezk 40–48). With this act, God rejects such efforts at least for this time. For this reason, the silver is not cast merely to the temple, but also to the potter. As noted, the potter was a figure in Jeremiah denoting exile. This figure helps Israel understand the full significance and severity of their situation. They are not merely going to lack peace (see vv. 5-6,10) but actually are thrust deeper into the era of exile. That is the complete picture of what was happening.

B. Hope Deferred (11:14). The next verse expounds upon the nature of this exile. The shepherd cut the "second staff, Union, annulling the brotherhood between Judah and Israel." The reunification of the nation is a hallmark for the end of exile (cf. Ezk 37:17; Zch 11:7). However, such hopes are now put away. Israel is not in the era of resolution but rather deeper into a time when Israel will have no nation, promises will be unfulfilled, and the nation will be under the most austere discipline (cf. Dt 28:48). These consequences are confirmed in the next verses that show Israel on a collision course with the peak of exile, the tribulation (11:15-17). God impresses upon Israel that this single moment will shape the duration of their history.

While the end of this passage is dire, the context establishes the Messiah's rejection as necessary to atone for Israel's sin per Isa 53 and Dan 9:24-26. Furthermore, the passage earlier asserts that the shepherd's original job is to bring Israel's exile to an end. So, while Israel's judgment looms immediately, God still remembers His promise of salvation and will use this moment to that end as well (Zch 12:10; 13:1-9). Thus, Zch 11:4-11 is pivotal for all redemptive history in judgment and salvation.

INTERTEXTUAL USAGE

The Gospels show how Jesus' life fulfills Zch 11:4-11 with remarkable precision. Just as Zechariah prophesied that the Messiah would shepherd the people with Favor and Union (Zch 11:7), so the Gospels describe Jesus as a shepherd (Jn 10:11), who mediates God's goodness to the people (Jn 10:13-15) and ministers to the whole of Israel (Mt 3:5; Jn 4:1-5). Just as Zechariah described the conflict between the leaders and the Messiah (Zch 11:8), so Jesus confronts hostile leadership (Mt 23:1-6; Lk 23:1-12). Just as Zechariah announced that the Messiah will bring down the leadership in "one month" (Zch 11:8), so Jesus' rejection leads to AD 70 (cf. Lk 21:20), which repeats the scenario of the fall of Jerusalem and its government that took place in Jeremiah's day.[38] On top of all this, just as Zechariah proclaims, Jesus is betrayed for 30 pieces of silver (Mt 26:15), which is then thrown into the temple (Mt 27:5) and given to the potter (Mt 27:7). With that, Jesus' life bears out every detail of this text. This not only shows that Jesus fulfills this prophecy but also thoroughly confirms the interpretation given above.

Along that line, the Gospels not only confirm the details of the text but even its intertextuality as outlined above. For instance, Nolland notes that Matthew most likely read Zch 11:4-14 in light of the messianic shepherd imagery of the OT (cf. Mic 5:2; Ezk 34:5; Ps 78:1-72).[39] Likewise, Crowe acknowledges that in Mt 27:9, Matthew's use of Zechariah likely mixes Zechariah with portions of Jer 19.[40] This accounts for Matthew's statement that the prophecy comes from Jeremiah, even though the quotation is mainly from Zechariah (Mt 27:9),[41] demonstrating that this article is not alone in making the above connections. Matthew saw the same links, attesting that they were always intended by Zechariah.

All of this not only confirms the above analysis, but even more, shows that the gospel writers were employing the full theology of Zechariah in their own writings. After all, the intertextuality of Zechariah is what grounds the notions of Messiah, exile, judgment, atonement, and restoration in the passage. By seeing the text in this way, the gospel writers declare that the Messiah's betrayal will lead Israel into judgment (cf. Mt 27:1-9) and also secure their redemption by His atoning sacrifice (cf. Mt 27:38-54). Seeing the theology of OT prophecy allows one to see the deep theology of the Gospels.

CONCLUSION

Zechariah 11:4-14 is a complex passage. In the end, wading through its challenges allows one to have greater confidence in a messianic interpretation and even more in the theological depth it carries. This text is not merely about the fact of Messiah's betrayal, but also its importance in redemptive history. It is the pivot point that leads Israel to the height of its judgment in exile and also to fullness of its restoration via the shepherd stricken for them. Accordingly, Zechariah shows that this moment makes history. The immensity of a single event reflects the power and impact of the central figure of that moment: the Messiah, the rejected Shepherd of Israel.

1. R. L. Foster, "Shepherds, Sticks, and Social Destabilization: A Fresh Look at Zechariah 11:4-17," *Journal of Biblical Literature* 126 (2007): 737.

2. George L. Klein, *Zechariah*, New American Commentary (Nashville: B&H Publishing, 2008), 323–25; Paul L. Redditt, "Israel's Shepherds: Hope and Pessimism in Zechariah 9–14," *Catholic Biblical Quarterly* 51, no. 4 (1989): 640–42.

3. Foster, "Fresh Look at Zechariah 11:4-17," 737.

4. Redditt, "Israel's Shepherds," 683; Stephen L. Cook, "The Metamorphosis of a Shepherd: The Tradition History of Zechariah 11:17 + 13:7-9," *Catholic Biblical Quarterly* 55 (1993): 453.

5. Anthony R. Petterson, "The Shape of the Davidic Hope across the Book of the Twelve," *Journal for the Study of the New Testament* 35, no. 2 (December 2010): 229.

6. Klein, *Zechariah*, 322.

7. Petterson, "Shape of Davidic Hope," 229.

8. L. Redditt, "The Two Shepherds in Zechariah 11:4-14," *Catholic Biblical Quarterly* 55, no. 4 (1993): 687; Cook, "The Metamorphosis of a Shepherd," 453. If Zch 11:4-11 came from a different source than the rest of the more optimistic book, the shepherd is evil and dashes the hopes of the rest of the book.

9. Redditt, "Israel's Shepherds," 634; Douglas R Jones, "Fresh Interpretation of Zechariah 9-11," *Vetus Testamentum* 12, no. 3 (July 1962): 252; Samuel I. Feigin, "Some Notes on Zechariah 11:4-17," *Journal of Biblical Literature* 44, nos. 3–4 (1925): 205.

10. Michael R. Stead, "The Three Shepherds: Reading Zechariah 11 in the Light of Jeremiah." In *A God of Faithfulness: Essays in Honour of J. Gordon McConville on His 60th Birthday*, ed. J. G. McConville, Jamie Grant, Allison Lo, and Gordon J Wenham (New York: T&T Clark, 2011), 154. See also Jones, "Fresh Interpretation of Zechariah 9-11," 253.

11. Stead, "The Three Shepherds," 154.

12. Petterson, "Shape of Davidic Hope," 233; Eugene H. Merrill, *Haggai, Zechariah, Malachi: An Exegetical Commentary* (Chicago: Moody, 1994), 258.

13. Petterson, "Shape of Davidic Hope," 246.

14. Merrill, *Haggai, Zechariah, Malachi*, 259.

15. Daniel I. Block, *The Book of Ezekiel 1–24*, New International Commentary on the Old Testament (Grand Rapids: Eerdmans, 1997), 178.

16. Deborah Krause, "The One Who Comes Unbinding the Blessing of Judah: Mark 11:1-10 as a Midrash on Genesis 49:11, Zechariah 9:9, and Psalm 118:25-26," in *Early Christian Interpretation of the Scriptures of Israel: Investigations & Proposals*, ed. Craig A. Evans and James A. Sanders (Sheffield: Sheffield Academic Press, 1997), 141–53; Roy A. Rosenberg, "The Slain Messiah in the Old Testament," *Zeitschrift für die alttestamentliche Wissenschaft* 99 (1987): 259–61.

17. Petterson, "Shape of Davidic Hope," 225–46.

18. See M. G. Kline, "The Structure of the Book of Zechariah," *Journal of Evangelical Theology* 34 (1991): 179–83.

19. Klein, *Zechariah*, 207.

20. Kline, "The Structure of the Book of Zechariah," 186–93.

21. Klein, *Zechariah*, 201.

22. Foster, "Fresh Look at Zechariah 11:4-17," 740.

23. Petterson, "Shape of Davidic Hope," 229.

24. Dean R Ulrich, "Two Offices, Four Officers, or One Sordid Event in Zechariah 12:10-14?" *Westminister Theological Journal* 72, no. 2 (2010): 260–62.

25. Stead, "The Three Shepherds," 155.

26. F. B. Huey, *Jeremiah, Lamentations*, New American Commentary (Nashville: Broadman & Holman, 1993), 181.

27. This also further affirms the notion of the three shepherds as prophet, priest, and king. Just as those offices were undone in the original exile, so they are again in the Messiah's first advent. See below for the significance of "one month."

28. Eugene H Merrill, "The Book of Zechariah," in *The World and the Word: An Introduction to the Old Testament*, ed. E. H. Merrill, M. F. Rooker, and M. A. Grisanti (Nashville: Broadman and Holman, 2011), 488–89.

29. Kline, "The Structure of the Book of Zechariah," 179–82.

30. Krause, "The One Who Comes Unbinding," 149–51.

31. Mark J. Boda, *The Book of Zechariah*, New International Commentary on the Old Testament (Grand Rapids: Eerdmans, 2016), 660.

32. Ibid., 663.

33. Klein, *Zechariah*, 336.

34. Boda, *The Book of Zechariah*, 668.

35. Joyce G. Baldwin, *Haggai, Zechariah*, Tyndale Old Testament Commentaries (Downers Grove, IL: InterVarsity, 1972), 184–85.

36. Klein, *Zechariah*, 337.

37. Merrill, *Haggai, Zechariah, Malachi*, 261.

38. See above for an explanation of "one month."

39. John Nolland, "The King as Shepherd: The Role of Deutero-Zechariah in Matthew," in *Biblical Interpretation in Early Christian Gospels*, 2008, 133–36.

40. Brandon D. Crowe, "Fulfillment in Matthew as Eschatological Reversal," *Westminister Theological Journal* 75, no. 1 (2013): 117.

41. Abner Chou, *The Hermeneutics of the Biblical Writers: Learning Interpretation from the Prophets and Apostles* (Grand Rapids: Kregel, 2018), 140.

Zechariah 12:10-13:1

The Pierced Messiah

DANIEL E. STUART

The early rabbis and Christian expositors interpreted Zechariah 12:10 as a messianic prophecy.[1] Today, many Bible scholars reject the "messianic interpretation" by choosing to identify the one(s) pierced in Zch 12:10 with slain Israelites or any number of Jewish martyrs instead. The Koren Jerusalem Bible (JBK) reflects this trend with, "and they shall look towards me, regarding those whom the nations have thrust through. And they shall mourn for him (that is slain) as one mourns for an only son." In other words, the verse describes the mourning over Jews who die in a battle while defending their home country. On the other hand, the HCSB reads, "And they will look at Me whom they pierced. They will mourn for Him as one mourns for an only child." This translation is more conducive to a messianic interpretation since the Lord is the one pierced (cf. Jn 1:1; Jn 19:37). With that in mind, it becomes clear how the identity of the "pierced one" depends on the translation of the Hebrew text. So the way to discover the identity of the "pierced one" and thereby the messianic potential of Zch 12:10 is through proper grammatical analysis and translation.

This article will defend the "messianic interpretation" by carefully investigating the passage's grammar and providing an interpretation congruent with the findings. Then it will be suggested that the verse refers to a future time when Israel will somehow pierce the Lord—thus, opening up a door for the NT's claim that Jesus is God in the flesh, who was pierced at His death.

HISTORY OF INTERPRETATION

The early rabbis saw a reference to Messiah ben Joseph who suffers and dies in Zch 12:10.[2] Although Jewish scholars such as Isaac of Troki and Kimchi argued for a reference to slain Israelites rather than a slain Messiah,[3] some of the greatest rabbis like Rashi, Ibn Ezra, Abarvanel, and Alshech preferred a reference to Messiah ben Joseph.[4] Clearly, this is an argument from oral tradition and extrabiblical sources; Zch 12:10 says nothing about a Messiah ben Joseph.[5] These Jewish scholars, however, reveal the antiquity of the "messianic interpretation."

Zch 12:10 has a long history of interpretation, and Rex Mason summarizes the lack of consensus among its commentators over the identity of the one pierced:

> Many have found it difficult to understand how the people [of Israel] could have been said to "pierce" Yahweh, and so they have emended the text to read "they shall look to him whom they have pierced" (the version found in John 19:37). Others have taken it to mean that they have pierced Yahweh by their treatment of his representative. Some have rendered the verse, "They shall look to me. (As for) him whom they have pierced, they will mourn for him. . . ." Some have linked the "pierced one" with the good shepherd of ch. 11. Some have found a messianic reference here. Others have thought that there is an allusion to the Suffering Servant of Second Isaiah, or to a supposed feature of the earlier enthronement festival in which the king was ritually humiliated. Several have attempted to identify the "pierced one" with some historical figure, e.g., Onias III, the high priest, while still others have taken the "him" in a collective sense to represent the godly community which has been persecuted.[6]

The total number of theories is particularly indicative of how enigmatic the prophecy is. Nevertheless, the case has been made for Zch 12:10 as a messianic prophecy for a long time with proponents and detractors based on how they access the evidence for the revelation of a suffering Messiah in the book of Zechariah and whether they interpret the verse as predictive prophecy. The aim of this article is to bring some clarity into the scholarly discussion by discovering the author's intent when he wrote, "and they will look at Me whom they pierced."

CONTEXTUAL ANALYSIS

This article rejects the methods of higher criticism and assumes that the prophet Zechariah authored his entire book, which places the time of writing in the postexilic period. There is enough evidence to warrant interpreting the book in this way, and discussions can be found elsewhere.[7]

If Israel only had chaps. 1–8 they might have believed postexilic Judah was a poor fulfillment of God's promises, but chaps. 9–14 reveal that Zechariah's day was one of "small things" (4:10) and that the promises of old were still awaiting future fulfillment.[8] So Israel's initial return to the promised land was a preview of their ultimate restoration in the future—chaps. 9–14 helped them to see what that would look like.

In chaps. 12–13, the prophet Zechariah envisions a future day when Jerusalem is besieged by its enemies (12:2) and delivered by the Lord, who achieves victory on the battlefield (12:3-9) and in the spiritual lives of His covenant people (13:1-6). By a special work of His Spirit, the Lord stimulates an attitude of penitence within His people over the one whom they rejected. The entire land, especially David's ruling house, grieves over the act as one grieves the death of an only child (12:10-14).

INTEXTUAL ANALYSIS

Textual Integrity of "To Me"

The Hebrew text (specifically the Masoretic Text hereby referred to as the MT) reads "to me," but some ancient medieval manuscripts have "to him." The latter reading can significantly alter the meaning of the text and, therefore, necessitates a close investigation of the evidence for both options.[9]

H. G. Mitchell, among other Bible scholars, doubts the reliability of the MT because it makes God the object of the fatal piercing: "And they will look at Me (God) whom they pierced." Mitchell believes if the author intended the Lord to be the object of the piercing, then he would not have switched from first person ("me") to third person ("him") in the second part of Zch 12:10 to describe the mourning; he would have used "me" throughout and made the idea obvious.[10]

There are two problems with these common objections to the "to me" translation. First, although the concept of piercing God is difficult theologically, lower criticism (the study of surviving manuscripts in order to establish the original text) has nothing to do with one's theological orientation. Second, Zechariah's switch from first person to third person almost certainly represents a change in perspective, a not uncommon feature in the Hebrew OT (e.g., Zch 7:13; 9:10).[11] Thus, it is likely that there is a switch from the Lord speaking of Himself to Zechariah speaking of the Lord in this text. This view is reflected in the HCSB through capitalization: "And they will look at Me whom they pierced. They will mourn for *Him* . . . and weep bitterly for *Him*" (emphasis added).

The reading of all the old versions such as the Septuagint (LXX), the Greek versions of Aquila, Symmachus, and Theodotion, the Aramaic Targums, Syriac Peshitta, Old Latin Bible, and the Latin Vulgate all support the integrity of "to me."[12] Generally, if the versions agree on a reading, then that reading is most likely original (i.e., what Zechariah wrote). In fairness, "to him" is found in a number of manuscripts—but merely as a marginal note or a marginal note that eventually invaded the actual text itself.[13]

Even the principles of lower criticism support the MT here. When confronted with this type of textual issue, the first question is, Which reading is more likely to have caused the other? Did "to me" originate from "to him" or conversely did "to him" originate from "to me"? David Baron has suggested a reasonable solution for the existence of "to him" based on this principle: "'To him' originated in the very natural difficulty, from the Jewish point of view, of conceiving how God, who is undoubtedly the speaker in the first part of the verse [. . .] can be 'pierced.'"[14] One certainly has more difficulty explaining how "to him" would have given rise to "to me" since the tendency was for scribes to soften theological problems in the text, not the other way around.

Ultimately, those who reject "to me" use the NT to support "to him." The apostle John quotes a singular phrase from Zch 12:10 in Jn 19:37: "They shall look on *Him* whom they pierced" (NASB, emphasis added). The NASB was chosen here because it uses "Him" and suggests John specified the true reading of Zch 12:10 as God led him, but "Him" is not required by the Greek text (cf. the New English Translation [NET]).[15] Regardless, John could have used "Him" because he believes Jesus is God. So Jn 19:37 refers to "Him" who is the "Me" of Zch 12:10. Jesus is the object of the looking and is not the speaker in the NT, whereas the Lord is the object of the looking *and* speaker in the OT.

In view of the foregoing evidence, "to me" should be considered as original because there is no substantial evidence to the contrary.[16] Those who accept "to him" or other revisions[17] do so out of theological concern because the ancient versions and principles of lower criticism support "to me." Thus, the Lord is the "Me" of Zch 12:10.

Interpretation of "Whom"

The HCSB's "whom" translates the Hebrew *'et 'asher*. The table below categorizes the different ways this two-word phrase been translated (cf. italicized text).

Table I.

Zechariah 12:10 in the English Versions *(all emphases added)*

LXX, Brenton	And I will pour upon the house of David, and upon the inhabitants of Jerusalem, the spirit of grace and compassion: and they shall look upon me, *because* they have mocked me, and they shall make lamentation for him, as for a beloved friend, and they shall grieve intensely, as for a first-born son.

JPS, 1917	And I will pour upon the house of David, And upon the inhabitants of Jerusalem, The spirit of grace and of supplication; And they shall look unto Me *because* they have thrust him through; And they shall mourn for him, as one mourneth for his only son, And shall be in bitterness for him, as one that is in bitterness for his first-born.
NJPS, 1985	But I will fill the House of David and the inhabitants of Jerusalem with a spirit of pity and compassion; and they shall lament to Me *about* those slain, wailing over them as over a favorite son and showing bitter grief as over a firstborn.
JBK	But I will pour upon the house of David, and upon the inhabitants of Yerushalayim the spirit of grace and of supplication: and they shall look towards me, *regarding those whom* the nations have thrust through. And they shall mourn for him (that is slain) as one mourns for an only son, and shall be in bitterness over him, as one that is in bitterness for a firstborn.
HCSB	Then I will pour out a spirit of grace and prayer on the house of David and the residents of Jerusalem, and they will look at Me *whom* they pierced. They will mourn for Him as one mourns for an only child and weep bitterly for Him as one weeps for a firstborn.
KJV	And I will pour upon the house of David, and upon the inhabitants of Jerusalem, the spirit of grace and of supplications: and they shall look upon me *whom* they have pierced, and they shall mourn for him, as one mourneth for his only son, and shall be in bitterness for him, as one that is in bitterness for his firstborn.
RSV	And I will pour out on the house of David and the inhabitants of Jerusalem a spirit of compassion and supplication, so that, when they look on him *whom* they have pierced, they shall mourn for him, as one mourns for an only child, and weep bitterly over him, as one weeps over a first-born.
ESV	And I will pour out on the house of David and the inhabitants of Jerusalem a spirit of grace and pleas for mercy, so that, when they look on me, *on him whom* they have pierced, they shall mourn for him, as one mourns for an only child, and weep bitterly over him, as one weeps over a firstborn.
NIV	And I will pour out on the house of David and the inhabitants of Jerusalem a spirit of grace and supplication. They will look on me, *the one* they have pierced, and they will mourn for him as one mourns for an only child, and grieve bitterly for him as one grieves for a firstborn son.

The LXX (Greek translation of the Hebrew OT) has "because" (*anth hon*)[18] instead of "whom." Randolph Bynum suspects, however, that the LXX translator might have forced himself to use "because" based on his mistranslation of a key word and his attempt to harmonize the surrounding words to fit the sense of that one mistranslated word. This key Hebrew word is the verb *daqar* (pierce).[19] Oddly, the LXX has instead "danced in mockery" (*katorcheomai*)—a word that occurs only once in the LXX.[20] The variance probably arose because the LXX translator confused the consonants of the Hebrew verb *daqar* and accidently read *raqad* (dance).[21] These two Hebrew words look and sound the same, so it is possible that the translator had mistakenly switched the d (ד) and the r (ר) in *daqar* and *read* "dance" (*raqad*) instead of "pierce."[22] This explains why he *wrote katorcheomai* (dance in mockery).

Table II.

LXX Translation Scenario

1. Hebrew text has *daqar* (pierce).
2. While reading, the LXX translator mistakenly confuses the d and the r in *daqar* (pierce).
3. This results in the translator *reading raqad* (dance) instead of *daqar*.
4. After mistakenly reading *raqad* the translator *writes katorcheomai* (dance in mockery).

If this translation scenario is true, then, according to Bynum, it would make better sense for the translator to use "whom" producing the difficult "they will look on me *whom* they danced in mockery" (emphasis added).[23] Rather, in view of the mistranslated word "danced in mockery," the translator was forced to use "because" in order to make sense of everything and wrote the more intelligible "they will look on me *because* they danced in mockery."[24] To this end, the reading "because" in the LXX should be rejected as this is not a careful translation of the Hebrew text.

The apostle John quoted Zch 12:10 in Jn 19:37 and alluded to it in Rev 1:7. Rev 1:7 reads, "Look! He is returning with the clouds, and every eye will see him, even those who pierced [*hoitines*] him, and all the tribes on the earth [or "on the land"] will mourn because of him. This will certainly come to pass! Amen" (NET, Greek added), contrasting strongly with the LXX. The Gospel passage quotes part of Zch 12:10 and also disagrees with the LXX: "And again another Scripture says, 'They will look on the one whom [*hon*] they have pierced'" (NET, Greek added).[25]

The Jewish Publication Society Bible (JPS) has, "And they shall look unto me *because* they have thrust him through" (emphasis added). Of course, *'asher* may sometimes mean "because." However, when the definite direct object marker (*'et* in Hebrew but usually untranslatable) appears before *'asher*, which is the case in Zch

12:10, then the word means "who, that, which."[26] In our context *'et 'asher* simply means "whom" and refers to the Lord ("Me").[27]

Table III.

JPS Compared with Hebrew and HCSB

Hebrew	*wehibiytu*	*'elay*	*'et 'asher*	*daqaru*	?
JPS	And they shall look	unto me	because	They have thrust through	him
HCSB	and they will look	at Me	whom	they pierced	

The Koren Jerusalem Bible (JBK) has "And they shall look towards me, *regarding those whom* the nations have thrust through" (emphasis added). In a similar way, the New Jewish Publication Society Tanakh (NJPS) reads, "And they shall lament to me *about those who* are slain" (emphasis added).[28] So, according to these translations, Israel is looking to Yahweh with deep sorrow concerning their fellow Israelites whom the nations slayed by the sword.

Table IV.

JBK Compared with Hebrew and HCSB

Hebrew	*wehibiytu*	*'elay*	*'et 'asher*	?	*daqaru*
JBK	and they shall look	towards me	regarding those whom	the nations	have thrust through
HCSB	and they will look	at Me	whom		they pierced

Table V.

NJPS Compared with Hebrew and HCSB

Hebrew	*wehibiytu*	*'elay*	*'et 'asher*	*daqaru*
NJPS	and they shall lament	to me	about those who	are slain
HCSB	and they will look	at Me	whom	they pierced

The problems with the JBK and NJPS are several. First, the NJPS renders "they pierced" (*daqaru*) improperly with "are slain," as if it were in a passive voice (as if it were in the Hebrew Niphal stem); but, it is in the Hebrew Qal stem, so the verb should be translated in the active voice as "they pierced." This mistranslation allows them to retain "about those who" and avoid using "whom," which would make God the one pierced.

Second, according to the JBK the "nations" are the ones doing the piercing: "regarding those whom the nations have thrust through." "Nations" is not in the Hebrew text, and the most natural reading requires that Israel be the one doing the act, not the nations, since there is no indication of the subjects changing whatsoever for the verbs of "looking," "piercing," and "mourning." A. McCaul agrees:

> Now, in the first place, this interpretation introduces a new subject to the verb "pierce," for which there is no authority. No one who reads the words, "They shall look upon me on account of him whom they have pierced," would ever suppose that those who pierced are different from those who shall look; and still less that the one are the Gentiles, and the other the Jews. There is not the slightest intimation of a change of subject.[29]

It is possible that the "they" in "they pierced" is vague (indefinite person). If this is true then its subject could be the nations, theoretically speaking. But, as David Mitchell states, "To assume the indefinite person for 'they pierced' is hardly warranted when 'they will look' only four words before is definite. And to assume a new definite subject ('the nations') when none intervenes amounts to rewriting the biblical text."[30] Regardless of what appears to place the full blame on the nations, careful analysis of this text and its context affirms that Israel pierces the Lord—which is why a fountain of cleansing for sin is opened specifically for them in Zch 13:1!

The reason for the sensitivity of Jewish translations to the idea that Israel would be guilty of piercing the Messiah is the church's history of anti-Semitism based on the Christ-killer accusation against the Jewish people. Therefore, with regard to the human responsibility for piercing the Messiah, Walter C. Kaiser Jr. wisely warns, "This is not to add fuel to the fires of those who have castigated our Jewish neighbors by the stigma of being 'Christ killers.' That slur is as unfair as it is untrue! In fact, the Messiah was put to death by the Jews *and the Romans* [italics his]. It is also true that He was put to death for the sins of all the world. So caution must be exercised in this area when describing the roles that were carried out by the first-century participants in the death of Christ."[31] Michael Rydelnik adds, "These verses do indicate that at their end-time repentance, Jewish people will recognize that their ancestors were participants in the conspiracy against the Messiah, not that they acted alone or were perpetually guilty (see Ac 4:27-28)."[32]

Another problem with these versions is the insertion of "those" (standing for Israelites) before "who/whom." (See Tables IV and V above.) What follows the relative pronoun is mourning over the death of a pierced individual ("Him/him"), not Israelites plural ("they"). It was already suggested that the switch from first person ("Me") to third person ("Him") in this text represents a change in perspective from the Lord speaking of Himself to Zechariah speaking of the Lord. However, it is possible for "him" to stand for Israelites in the collective sense as "them," which Hebrew occasionally allows.[33]

This is the interpretation of the NJPS: "And they shall lament to Me about those who are slain, wailing over *them* as over a favorite son and showing grief as over a first-born" (emphasis added). While this translation is grammatically possible, the immediate context does not say anything about Israelites dying in this battle; rather, Zechariah explains how the weakest Israelites in that day experienced a metamorphosis of sorts, becoming like Israel's greatest warrior, David, and like God himself (v. 8). Israel will utterly consume its enemies as fire devours a woodpile (v. 6). The eyes of the Lord will be on the house of Judah while He strikes the enemy's cavalry with blindness and madness (v. 4). Zechariah consistently emphasizes Judah and Jerusalem as safe and defended on that great Day of the Lord.

The collective "them" also fails to appreciate how Zch 13 impinges upon the meaning of 12:10. That the cleansing and repentance of Israel in 13:1-6 is a response to the sin in 12:10 is likely for four reasons. (1) The prophet uses his key temporal expression "on that day" from chap. 12 to continue his discourse through into chap. 13. (2) The author's second reference to "the house of David," "the residents of Jerusalem," and a "fountain" (similar to "pour") in 13:1 indicates that 13:1 continues the language and thought begun in 12:10.[34] (3) The cleansing fountain for sin and impurity in 13:1 is specifically opened for "the house of David" and "the inhabitants of Jerusalem." (4) Zechariah uses "pierce" for a second time in 13:3 (a pun) and thereby associates the piercing in 13:3 with the one in 12:10. The logical conclusion is that Israel is participating in an illegal piercing in 12:10 as opposed to a lawful piercing in 13:3 and is now in need of cleansing for "sin" (*chata't*) and "impurity" (*niddah*). These two terms appear in contexts where purification is needed once someone became ritually unclean through contact with a corpse, which correlates with the stabbing and death recorded in 12:10-14 (cf. Nm 19:13). Therefore, the Israelites are not mourning over what the nations have done to their fellow brothers (the collective "them"); Israel is mourning for their participation in the piercing of the Lord.

Closer to the true meaning of the text are those who suggest that "Him" does not refer to the Lord per se but introduces a new subject into the verse, presumably a divine and/or suffering Messiah.[35] In my judgment, that the author would introduce here a new subject who becomes the recipient of the mourning even though the Lord is pierced is overly complicated. Since the Lord is the one who is pierced, it logically follows that He is the one who is mourned over.[36] Thus, the most natural and faithful way to render the verse is, "And they [Israel] will look at Me [God] whom they [Israel] pierced. They [Israel] will mourn for Him [God] as one mourns for an only child."[37]

Interpretation of "Pierce"

Now that the subject (Israel) and object (God) of the verb "pierce" are clarified, the meaning of the verb may be studied. One issue this word study attempts to solve is whether a metaphorical interpretation of the verb is justifiable. The "metaphorical view" does not require viewing the verse as having a direct fulfillment at Jesus' crucifixion and second coming. In its original context, the verse speaks metaphorically of Israel's rejection of the Lord. John Calvin said, "The Jews had pierced His heart" and that the piercing prefigured Israel's ultimate rejection of God in the person of Jesus.[38] But this interpretation is inconsistent with how OT authors used the verb, as this study will show.

Word Study of "Pierce"

"Pierce" translates the Hebrew word *daqar*, which appears 13 times in the OT—11 times as a verb and twice as a noun.[39] The verb is always used in reference to the human body (with the possible exception of Zch 12:10). On one occasion the weapon of choice is a spear (Nm 25:8), but usually the action involves a sword (sometimes the weapon is not specified). The weapon causes a fatal wound (except in Jer 37:10), often hastening a violent and almost always shameful death of one or more people (e.g., the shameful deaths of Abimelech and Saul). The basic idea behind the verb is "to pierce."[40]

Scholars debate the verb's meaning in two passages. The first is Lam 4:9: "Those slain (*chalal*) by the sword are better off than those slain (*chalal*) by hunger, who waste away, pierced (*daqar*) with pain because the fields lack produce" (HCSB, Hebrew author's). According to the HCSB, "pierced" and the second use of "slain" speak metaphorically of the pain and death caused by starvation. This might suggest that the piercing in Zch 12:10 could have a metaphorical meaning as well, but there are other translations of this text that do not require one to interpret these verbs figuratively.[41] Besides, Lam 4:9 contains parallelism and poetry conducive for a figurative meaning—and these elements are not found in Zch 12:10. The second is Prv 12:18: "There is one who speaks rashly, like a piercing sword (*daqar*); but the tongue of the wise brings healing" (HCSB, Hebrew author's). W. H. Lowe rightly notes how "the gnomic nature of the composition, and the use of the comparative preposition 'like' with 'pierce', prepare one for the figurative use of the word. Such is not the case [in Zch 12:10]."[42]

Despite usage and the overwhelming evidence of contexts, some scholars insist that the verb in Zch 12:10 must be understood metaphorically. For example, H. C. Leupold argues,

> But if God is pierced, it is very obvious that the verb "they pierced" must be used in a figurative sense and not literally, for God cannot be literally pierced. A good parallel is Lev. 24:11, 16, where also a verb pierced is used (not daqar as here but naqab), and its object is the "name of God." But "to pierce God's name" must mean something like "profane his name." The same meaning may, therefore, be assumed for the expression under consideration. At one time they insulted and blasphemed the Holy One.[43]

There are three problems with Leupold's reasoning. First, stating that the metaphorical meaning of the verb is obvious begs the question. Merrill Unger raises a second problem: the words for "pierce" are different, and Zechariah does not employ the idiom in Lv 24:11,16 ("to pierce God's name").[44] Third, *chalal* (pierce, fatally wound) is surely a better synonym than *naqav*, as *chalal* occurs in parallelism with *daqar* on two occasions (Jer 51:4 and Lam 4:9), unlike *naqav*.

Although the metaphorical view appears to be a genuine way of dealing with the theological tension "pierce" creates in Zch 12:10, it does not provide answers to the following two questions. First, if Zechariah meant the verb to be understood metaphorically, then why did he not use *naqav*, which clearly has a wider range of meaning than *daqar*?[45] Second, does Zechariah's use of the verb again in 13:3 not illustrate what is going on in 12:10? This can hardly be accidental. The juxtaposition of the two events by means of "pierced" implies that "the pierced one in 12:10 deserved honor but received the ultimate expression of disrespect—execution. The malefactor in 13:3 also suffered piercing, but he deserved his punishment."[46] In light of the parallelism, Zechariah meant both words to be read in the same way.

The context of Zechariah 12:10, specifically the excessive mourning in 12:11-14 as over one dead, combined with the verb's consistent usage throughout the OT, suggest that Zechariah foresees the literal piercing of the Lord at the hands of His covenant people. The NT makes clear how this happens through the incarnate Son.

Timing of the Piercing

Mitchell believes many who identify the Messiah as the verb's object "overlook a point of great importance, namely . . . the act of piercing the nameless victim belongs to the past. This means that the pierced one is not Messiah, whose advent, all will agree, was still future when these words were written."[47] He assumes the verb portrays a past event from Zechariah's perspective. However, "pierced" is in the Hebrew perfect form. This form portrays an action as a simple fact, whether in the past, present, or future. Thus, the verb being in the perfect form does not require the piercing to have occurred prior to Zechariah's writing because the verb's form is temporally undefined. In biblical Hebrew, the time factor is determined from context.

George Klein agrees and suggests that the verb is better understood as a Hebrew prophetic perfect in view of the future time *context*. With the prophetic perfect, the verb describes the certainty of a future event as if it were done because the seer has seen it. The action is not yet a reality, but described as if it is. So, Zechariah chose to express his confidence in the prophecy's fulfillment through past expression.[48] Another option is to categorize the verb as a Hebrew future perfect. With the future perfect form two actions are envisioned, and one of the actions must take place before the other.[49] Here, the verbs "look" and "pierced" both portray future actions, but the piercing takes place before the looking. So, Zechariah is describing how Israel will at some point in the future "pierce" the Lord and, in retrospect, mourn over what they had done to Him.

The futuristic context of Zch 9–14 strongly implies a futuristic orientation for "pierced." Meyers and Meyers observe how the prophet uses "on that day" a total of 17 times in Zch 12–14. "Nowhere else in Hebrew prophecy is there such an oft-repeated invocation of stereotyped terminology heralding God's final judgment of all the world."[50] Al Wolters adds that what ties "these chapters together is the repeated use of the phrase 'on that day,' which sounds like a drum-beat on the average of every two or three verses."[51] It is certainly possible that Zechariah conceived of the piercing and the verse in its entirety as occurring in the future with a direct fulfillment at the crucifixion and second coming of Jesus.

INNERBIBLICAL INTERPRETATION OF ZECHARIAH 12:10

Much has been said about the influence of Isaiah's Servant Songs (Isa 42, 49–50, 52–53) on Zch 12:10, and the connection is strengthened if the Servant is linked with the King of Zch 9 and the Shepherd of Zch 13:7.[52] A full investigation would exceed the limits of this article, but something should be said for the purpose of completeness.

In Isa 53:5, the prophet Isaiah says the Servant (understood as Messiah) will suffer unjustly and be "pierced" (*chalal*), a verb already established as synonymous with *daqar*. The Shepherd of Zch 13:7 is also "struck" (*nakah*), and the exact same word (*nakah*) is applied to the Servant in Isa 50:6 and 53:4. Additionally, the

Servant is stylized as a shepherd (Isa 53:6-7); and, since it was common practice in antiquity for royalty to stylize themselves as shepherds (e.g., 2Sm 5:2), the Servant and Shepherd compare with the "pierced one" on account of the kingly overtones in Zch 12:10-14.[53]

Strikingly, the Servant and Shepherd are both closely associated with the Lord. Based on its use in Leviticus, McCaul believes "fellow" (*'amiytiy*)[54] in Zch 13:7 (KJV) is synonymous with "brother" and "expresses the relation of fellow-Israelite, or fellow-man, and points out an identity of nature."[55] So when the Lord calls the Shepherd his "fellow," "it necessarily implies that that being stands in the same relation to God as one Israelite or man does another; that is, that he is of the same nature or substance, that is, he is very God"—the same God pierced in Zch 12:10.[56] Many doubt the divinity of Isaiah's Servant, "the arm of the Lord," but there are reasons to conceive of Him as Israel's divine Messiah. For example, in Isa 6:1 and 57:15, the prophet Isaiah sees the Lord "high and exalted." Then, in 52:13, the prophet sees the Servant "raised and lifted up and greatly exalted," applying the prerogatives of the Lord, who is the "pierced one" of Zch 12:10, to the Servant.

There is also a striking resemblance between the King in Zch 9 and Isaiah's Servant. Anthony Petterson has observed how both are described as "humble" (Zch 9:9; see Isa 42:2), bringing hope and justice to the nations (Zch 9:10; Isa 42:1,4,6; 49:6), releasing captives from a pit or prison (Zch 9:11-12; Isa 42:7), and gathering exiled Israelites (Zch 9:12; Isa 49:5-6).[57]

By association with the Servant, one can deduce that all three share a likeness with the Lord. Perhaps Isaiah and Zechariah, in typical Hebrew fashion, present us with a multifaceted picture of the ideal King whose distinction with the Lord is intentionally blurred. The NT, by drawing these images together and applying them to one individual (Jesus), clarifies the prophets' intentions and supports the innerbiblical associations suggested here (cf. Jn 12:15; 19:37; Mt 26:31).

CONCLUSION

Zechariah foresees how Israel will one day pierce the Lord. But the Lord is gracious and faithful to His covenant. After defending the homeland of His people from their enemies, the Lord will pour out His Spirit upon the inhabitants of the land, stimulating their repentance over the sinful act. Ultimately, the Lord will forgive them and provide a way of cleansing. Although Zechariah simply makes this assertion without commenting on how it will happen, the NT clarifies how this messianic prophecy finds direct fulfillment in the incarnation, crucifixion, and second coming of Jesus (cf. Jn 1:1; 19:37; Lk 23:48; Rev 1:7). Surely God has already provided the Israelites with the theological framework necessary to understand the incarnation and crucifixion through Isa 53 and Zch 9–14 so that when He would come to suffer in the person of Jesus He would come to a people theologically prepared for the idea.[58]

1. For a summary of the ancient interpretations see Talbot W. Chambers, "The Book of Zechariah," in *Lange's Commentary on the Holy Scriptures*, vol. 13 (Grand Rapids: Zondervan, 1976), 96–97.
2. For example, the Babylonian Talmud (Succah 52a). The Targumic Tosefta on Zch 12:10 differs from the Messiah ben Joseph tradition in that it features a Messiah bar Ephraim, but any son of Ephraim is also a son of Joseph. See also the comment on p. 469 in the Artscroll Stone Edition of the Teri Asar.
3. On Troki see David Baron, *The Visions and Prophecies of Zechariah* (Eugene, OR: Wipf and Stock Publishers, 2002), 438–39; on Kimchi see A. M'Caul, *Rabbi David Kimchi's Commentary Upon the Prophecies of Zechariah: Translated from the Hebrew with Notes, and Observations on the Passages Relating to the Messiah* (London: James Duncan, 1837), 155.
4. Rashi said, "The words, 'The land shall mourn,' are found in the prophecy of Zechariah, and he prophesies of the future, that they shall mourn on account of Messiah, the son of Joseph, who shall be slain in the war of Gog and Magog" (A. M'Caul, *Rabbi David Kimchi's Commentary upon the Prophecies of Zechariah*, 161). Ibn Ezra said, "All the heathen shall look to me to see what I shall do to those who pierced Messiah, son of Joseph" (Ibn Ezra, quoted in ibid., 158). Abarvanel said, "It is more correct to interpret this passage of Messiah, the son of Joseph, as our rabbis of blessed memory have interpreted in the treatise Succah, for he shall be a mighty man of valour, of the tribe of Joseph, and shall, at first, be captain of the Lord's host in that war, but in that war shall die" (Abarvanel, quoted in ibid., 158–59). Alshech said, "I will yet do a third thing, and that is, that 'they shall look unto me,' for they shall lift up their eyes unto me in perfect repentance, when they see him whom they pierced, that is, Messiah, the Son of Joseph; for our Rabbis, of blessed memory, have said that he will take upon himself all the guilt of Israel, and shall then be slain in the war to make atonement in such manner that it shall be accounted as if Israel had pierced him, for on account of their sin he has died; and, therefore, in order that it may be reckoned to them as perfect atonement, they will repent and look to the blessed One, saying that there is none beside him to forgive those that mourn on account of him who died for their sin: this is the meaning of 'They shall look upon me" (Alshech quoted in Baron, *The Visions and Prophecies of Zechariah*, 442).
5. David Mitchell explains why the early rabbis saw Messiah ben Joseph in this verse: (1) Like the "pierced one" Joseph was "pierced" (Gn 49:23). (2) He, Joseph, was mourned (Gn 37:35) as a firstborn son (Gn 37:3). (3) If there is a connection between Zch 12:10 and 11:12-13, then the "pierced one" is priced for silver like Joseph (Gn 37:28). According to Mitchell, the rabbis were probably just making explicit what they felt was implicit (David C. Mitchell, "Messiah bar Ephraim in the Targums," *Aramaic Studies* 4, no. 2 [2006]: 227).
6. Rex Mason, *The Books of Haggai, Zechariah, and Malachi* (Cambridge: University Press, 1977), 118–19.
7. See B. S. Childs, *Introduction to the Old Testament as Scripture* (Philadelphia: Fortress Press, 1979), 475–76. H. G. Mitchell provides good evidence for the unity of the book. Helpful are the numerous examples of unity cataloged in George L. Klein, *Zechariah*, New American Commentary (Nashville: B&H, 2008), 51–58. See especially R. D. Moseman, "Reading the Two Zechariah's as One," *Review and Expositor* 97 (2000): 487–98.
8. Barry G. Webb, *The Message of Zechariah*, The Bible Speaks Today (Downers Grove, IL: InterVarsity, 2003), 35; e.g., foreign (Ezr 4) and domestic oppression (Neh 5) plagued the postexilic community, and the new Temple lacked the glory of the former Temple (Ezr 3:11-13).
9. Significant to my comprehension and treatment of this problem is Larry R. Overstreet's fine exegesis in his "Israel Responds to Grace: A Study of Zechariah 12:10," *Calvary Baptist Theological Journal* 13 (Spring 1977): 23–30.
10. H. G. Mitchell, *A Critical and Exegetical Commentary on Haggai and Zechariah*, International Critical Commentary (Edinburgh: T&T Clark, 1912), 334.
11. Wilhelm Gesenius, E. Kautzsch, and A. E. Cowley, *Gesenius' Hebrew Grammar*, 2nd English ed. rev. in accordance with the 28th German ed. (1909) by A. E. Cowley, with a facsimile of the Siloam inscription by J. Euting, and a table of alphabets by M. Lidzbarski (Oxford: Clarendon Press, 1982), §144p.

12. Baron, *The Visions and Prophecies of Zechariah*, 438; Mitchell, "A Critical and Exegetical Commentary on Haggai and Zechariah," 334.

13. T. Jansma, "Inquiry into the Hebrew Text and the Ancient Versions of Zechariah ix-xiv," *Oudtestamentishe Studiën* 7 (1950): 118; E. B. Pusey, *The Minor Prophets*, vol. 2 (New York: Funk & Wagnalls, 1886), 438; Baron, *The Visions and Prophecies of Zechariah*, 442.

14. Ibid., 443.

15. Raymond E. Brown, *The Gospel according to John*, vol. 2, Anchor Bible 29A (New York: Doubleday, 1970), 938. The appeal to the NT in support of "to him" is further complicated in that we do not know exactly from which version John quoted. Brown says, "John's citation of Zech xii 10 does not follow verbatim either the MT or the most common LXX reading" (Ibid.).

16. Eventually, Mitchell admits that the evidence favors the reading in the MT: "['to me'] is the easier reading; hence it is more probable that it is an error for ['to him'] than vice versa. There is great force to this objection. Indeed, it so weakens the case for ['to him'] that those who feel the incongruity of the Masoretic text will have to resort to emendation" (Mitchell, *A Critical and Exegetical Commentary on Haggai and Zechariah*, 335).

17. For other emendations see the note in the textual apparatus of Biblia Hebraica Stuttgartnesia (an edition of the Masoretic text); see also Julius Wellhausen, *Die kleinen Propheten* übersetzt *and erklärt* (Berlin: de Gruyter, 1963), 50 and Gesenius et al., *Gesenius' Hebrew Grammar* §138e, n. 1.

18. Liddell-Scott-Jones, 153.

19. Assuming the manuscript the LXX translator was working from read *daqar*.

20. Henry Liddell, Robert Scott, Henry Stuart Jones, eds., *A Greek-English Lexicon* (Oxford: Oxford University Press, 1996), 508.

21. Assuming the manuscript the LXX translator was working from read *daqar*.

22. This is a common mistake during translation known as metathesis (rearranging of letters).

23. Randolph Bynum, "The Fourth Gospel and the Scriptures: Illuminating the Form and Meaning of Scriptural Citation in John 19:37," *Supplements to Novum Testamentum* 144 (Leiden, Netherlands: Brill, 2012), 96.

24. Ibid., 95–96.

25. Raymond Brown notes, "John's citation of Zech xii 10 does not follow verbatim either the MT or the most common LXX reading" (Brown, *The Gospel according to John*, 938). He postulates that the apostle quoted an early recession of the LXX.

26. *Dictionary of Classical Hebrew* by David Clines 8 vols. 1:441; *Introduction to Biblical Hebrew Syntax* by Waltke and O'Connor §10.3.1, a12–15.

27. Keil, *The Minor Prophets*, vol. 2 (Edinburgh: T&T Clark, 1871), 387–88. That the JPS translators added the object "him" to "they have thrust through" is odd, as "him" is not in the Hebrew text at this point. Perhaps this is their attempt to retain "because."

28. The New Jewish Publication Society version uses "lament" instead of "look." They may simply be giving a more metonymical translation.

29. M'Caul, *Rabbi David Kimchi's Commentary upon the Prophecies of Zechariah*, 158.

30. Mitchell, "Messiah bar Ephraim in the Targums," *Aramaic Studies* 4, no. 2 (2006): 229.

31. Walter C. Kaiser Jr., *The Messiah in the Old Testament* (Grand Rapids: Zondervan, 1994), 223.

32. Michael Rydelnik, "Zechariah," *The Moody Bible Commentary*, ed. Michael Rydelnik and Michael Vanlaningham (Chicago: Moody Publishers, 2014), 1433.

33. *Introduction to Biblical Hebrew Syntax* §16.4b 3. Rabbi A. J. Rosenberg's translation is very different with, "And they shall look to me because of those who have been thrust through [with swords], and they shall mourn over *it* as one mourns over an only son" (emphasis added). So Israel is mourning over the *act* of the nations ("it"). While grammatically possible (*Introduction to Biblical Hebrew Syntax* §16.4f 30–33), E. W. Hengstenberg notes, "When *'al* (over) follows the verb *saphad* (mourn) [as in Zch 12:10], though it may denote the cause ["it"] generally, it is universally connected with the *person* for whom lamentation is made" (emphasis added).

34. Al Wolters, *Zechariah: Historical Commentary on the Old Testament* (Leuven, Belgium: Peeters, 2014), 424.

35. See Charles L. Feinberg, *God Remembers: A Study in the Book of Zechariah* (Wheaton, IL: Van Kampen, 1950), 177–83, Gerald van Croningen, *Messianic Revelation in the Old Testament* (Grand Rapids: Baker, 1990), 907; E. W. Hengstenberg, *Christology of the Old Testament*, vol. 2 (McLean, VA: MacDonald, n.d.), 1109–40.

36. The HCSB, KJV, ASV, ESV, and NIV allow for both interpretations (see Table I).

37. As stated above, this is not to advance the "Christ-Killer" accusation or the deicide charge; rather, to state that the leadership of Israel, along with the Gentiles, did indeed pierce the Messiah. This is the reason Paul, when speaking of the rulers of this age, both Jewish and Gentile, identifies them as ignorant of Jesus' deity for "if they had known it, they would not have crucified the Lord of glory" (1Co 2:8; cf. Ac 3:17; Lk 23:34).

38. John Calvin, *John*, The Crossway Classics Commentary, ed. Alister McGrath (Wheaton, IL: Crossway Books, 1994), 437.

39. Nm 25:8; Jdg 9:54; 1Sm 31:4; 1Kg 4:9; 1 Chr 10:4; Isa 13:15; Jer 37:10; 51:4; Lam 4:9; Zch 12:10; 13:3; Prv 12:18.

40. See Herbert Wolf, "daqar," in *Theological Wordbook of the Old Testament* (Chicago: Moody Publishers, 1980), 449a.

41. A. Cohen, "Critical Notes: Lamentations 4:9," in *Journal of Near Eastern Studies* 27 (October 1910–July 1911): 191.

42. W. H. Lowe, *The Hebrew Student's Commentary on Zechariah* (London: Macmillan, 1882), 111.

43. H. C. Leupold, *Exposition of Zechariah* (Grand Rapids: Baker, 1956), 237.

44. Merrill F. Unger, *Zechariah: Prophet of Messiah's Glory* (Grand Rapids: Zondervan, 1976), 216.

45. Milton Fisher observes, "naqav can mean 'pierce'" but "the other senses attributed to this verb in passages which themselves indicate different usage constitute a striking demonstration of the semantic flexibility of Semitic languages" (Milton C. Fisher, "naqav," *Theological Word Book of the Old Testament*, 1409d). On *chalal*, see Donald J. Wiseman, "*chalal*," *Theological Word Book of the Old Testament*, 660.

46. George L. Klein, *Zechariah*, New American Commentary (Nashville: B&H, 2008), 379.

47. Mitchell, *A Critical and Exegetical Commentary on Haggai and Zechariah*, 330.

48. See George L. Klein, "The Prophetic Perfect," *Journal of Northwest Semitic Languages* 16 (1990): 45–60.

49. Ronald J. Williams, *Hebrew Syntax*, 3rd ed. (Toronto: University of Toronto Press, 2007), §163.4.

50. C. L. Meyers and E. M. Meyers, *Zechariah 9–14*, Anchor Bible (New York: Doubleday, 1992), 316–17.

51. Wolters, *Zechariah*, 401.

52. Many assume the Shepherd is a bad shepherd because God strikes him with the sword (presumably in judgment) and, therefore, should not be associated with the Servant. However, the flock was scattered after the Shepherd was smitten, which necessarily means he kept the flock intact or unified. This is a characteristic of good shepherds (Jer 23:1), not bad shepherds (M'Caul, *Rabbi David Kimchi's Commentary upon the Prophecies of Zechariah*, 172).

53. E.g., the place of Hadad-rimmon in the plain of Megiddo is where King Josiah died. For more on the kingly overtones see Dean Ulrich, "Two Offices, Four Officers, or One Sordid Event in Zechariah 12:10-14?" *Westminster Theological Journal* 72 (2010): 251–65.

54. On *'amiytiy*, *Hebrew and Aramaic Lexicon of the Old Testament* has "literally, the man of my society; more freely, the man who is friendly to me; one of the same community, fellow citizen" (HALOT, 845).

55. M'Caul, *Rabbi David Kimchi's Commentary upon the Prophecies of Zechariah*, 175.

56. Ibid.

57. Anthony Robert Petterson, *Behold Your King: The Hope for the House of David in the Book of Zechariah* (New York: T&T Clark, 2009), 240.

58. I am indebted to the work of Thomas McComiskey in his "Zechariah," in *The Minor Prophets*, vol. 3 (Grand Rapids: Baker, 1992) for directing my attention to the likelihood of the Lord being the one pierced in this text.

Zechariah 13:7-9

The Striking of the Shepherd King

J. RANDALL PRICE

The prophet Zechariah addressed the Jewish people who had returned to Judah from exile in Babylon. The goal of his ministry was to motivate the community to complete the rebuilding of the Temple and re-consecrate themselves to the Lord. For motivation, he gave them his prophetic message of the coming of Messiah. When Messiah comes, He will end the dominion of the nations and establish the millennial kingdom on earth. Zechariah 13:7-9 is a direct messianic prophecy that encompasses the first and second advents of the Messiah. It is a pivotal passage cited in the NT as explaining both the nature of Messiah's death as well as the ultimate (eschatological) result for Israel in the divine program.

THE CONTEXT OF ZECHARIAH 13:7-9

While there is eschatological content in Zch 1–8, the sharpest eschatological focus is found in chaps. 9–14. Within that section, there is an even greater end-time emphasis in chaps. 12–14, where the prophetic eschatological phrase *ba-yom ha-hu'* ("in that day") occurs 17 times (vs. four times in the rest of Zechariah). In this last section, there are initial judgments on Israel with ultimate deliverance, restoration, and blessing. Chapters 12–13 concern the national repentance and spiritual restoration (cleansing) of Israel, and chap. 14 presents the national restoration of Israel with the coming of the Messianic King. The relationship between 12:10-14 and 13:1 is not only logical but also chronological. As Feinberg has noted, "Once

Israel is brought to a penitent condition and is brought face to face with her crucified Messiah, then the provision of God for cleansing will be appropriate."[1]

Predictive prophecy about national cleansing and the problem of ritual defilement in the land appears in the opening of chap. 13. The focus is on the purification of the "house of David" and the people of Jerusalem,[2] a phrase that refers to the entire covenant-nation. Mason sees this as a response to a political crisis, stating that "Zch 12:10 and 13:1 describe a millennial purification and cleansing of the house of David, again holding out a positive Davidic expectation in the face of present corruption within the civil government of Yehud."[3] Whether or not a historical situation is in the background, the focus of the text is plainly eschatological.

This nature of this cleansing is a ritual purification with water as per the Levitical system (Ex 30:17-21; Nm 8:5-7; cf. Nm 19:9; Ezk 36:25). The cleansing is from a fountain, a spring of water that gushes from the side of a hill (probably Mt. Zion) and provides a never-ending supply of living water to keep the inhabitants of Jerusalem in a perpetual state of ritual purification (Zch 13:1; 14:8). Part of the need for purification arose from the problem of false prophets who in a day of national cleansing seek to disguise their identity in order to avoid punishment by saying, "I am not a prophet" (v. 4-6).

Most commentators interpret this passage in light of 1Kg 18:28 at Elijah's confrontation with the prophets of Baal. Those false prophets used self-inflicted wounds as part of an ecstatic religious practice. In Zechariah, the false prophet tried to evade identification by claiming the wounds between his arms were received in the house of his friends as parental wounding as a discipline or domestic infighting (Zch 13:3). However, one author has recently argued that a messianic interpretation of v. 6 should not be ruled out because of linguistic ambiguities, structural parallels, and subtle ties between vv. 6 and 7.[4] Nevertheless, the isolation of v. 7 from v. 6 in the Gospel citations and the absence of any reference to v. 6 in the NT where such would be appropriate (cf. Mt 26:23; Lk 22:21; Jn 13:18 where Ps 41:9 is cited) argues against this view.

The significance of these false teachers does have relevance to the end times as well. Some might contend that Judaism dealt with the problem of idolatry and false prophets in the postexilic period. However, modern Judaism is rife with spiritual compromise, and this problem will worsen in the tribulation period when false prophets and false messiahs appear (Mt 24:24; Rev 13:11-14); with the coming of the Antichrist, the future false messiah who will claim deity will make an idol of himself to be worshiped (2Th 2:4; Rev 13:14-15).

THE CRITICAL EVALUATION OF ZECHARIAH 13:7-9

In summary, Zch 13:7-9 indicates that the Messiah will be struck down, the children of Israel will be scattered and, when back in their land, two-thirds will perish, but a remnant will be purified and return to God. It has been said that no other book in the OT is as messianic as Zechariah and that it has more to say about Messiah than all the other Minor Prophets combined.[5]

Critical scholars, however, noting the reuse of the shepherd/sheep imagery from chaps. 1–8 in chaps. 9–14 have questioned the literary unity of Zechariah and divided the book into a Proto-Zechariah (1–8) and Deutero-Zechariah (9–14).[6] Some further see the present text (13:7-9) as a Trito–Zecharian section.[7] The unity of the book has been defended based on similarities in language and style[8] and congruent aspects between chaps. 1–8 and 9–14.[9] Another problem is that the critical perspective interferes with the consistent literal interpretation of the book, as well as the messianic interpretation supported by intertextual usage.

With this in mind, it is best to view Zechariah as a whole text written by the prophet as a literary unity. This is how the book has been preserved in the canon, and this appears to have been the way it was understood by the Second Temple period Qumran Community. The Qumran manuscripts contain a Greek fragment of Zechariah that includes the end of chap. 8 and the beginning of chap. 9 with no break in the text, implying a single author.

Another critical, nonmessianic interpretation, argues that the smitten figure (13:7) is one of the Judaic kings of the Davidic line whose rule ended violently in the sixth century BC, with the Babylonian exile. Then the Jewish remnant was purified in Babylon and restored to their land and national life after the exile.[10] In response to this, however, Zechariah is capable of identifying important historical figures by name (cf. Zch 1:7; 3:6-10; 6:9-14; 7:1-2), Furthermore, the postexilic period did not see a purging of the Jewish people that led to ongoing national purity (Ezra and Nehemiah as well as the postexilic prophets complain of national sins). Following the return from exile, and into the intertestamental and NT periods, the land was primarily under Gentile dominion (despite a temporary period of indigenous Jewish rule during the Hasmonean period). The subsequent history was one of continued domination and nothing like what Zechariah depicts as a victorious war against the nations. Therefore, since this did not occur, Zechariah cannot be referring to the immediate postexilic situation.

THE RABBINIC INTERPRETATION OF ZECHARIAH 13:7-9

Neither the Mishnah nor the Talmud cite Zch 13:7, and it is completely ignored in the other rabbinic writings of the Tannaitic and Amoraic periods. One exception appears at the end of the Babylonian Talmud in the legendary account of the martyrdoms of R. Ishmael and R. Simeon ben Gamaliel. As a tribute to R. Simeon at his death, R. Ishmael cites part of Zch 13:7 eulogistically: "Concerning you was it stated, Awake, O sword, against My shepherd, and against the man that is near unto Me" (Abot R. Nathan §38). However, this is so isolated from its context that it offers no insight into early rabbinic interpretation of our text. Modern Orthodox Jewish interpretation sees the context set in the messianic era and describes the punishment of (a sword turned against) the enemies of Israel. The leaders of the (Gentile) nations were the shepherds (God's colleagues), to whom He entrusted the fate of His people Israel (the flock). However, when these shepherds oppress "the flock," the sword is unleashed against them, and the flock escapes while God's vengeance is turned against subordinates who helped oppress Israel. Based on their understanding that v. 6 refers to a false prophet, they see the one smitten in v. 7 as a false shepherd and therefore reject a messianic interpretation of this figure.[11]

THE SUPPORT FOR A MESSIANIC INTERPRETATION OF ZECHARIAH 13:7-9

Seeing this text within an eschatological context provides a better understanding of the events in Zch 13:7. An end-of-days interpretation is the basis for this future repentance and the final covenant restoration it depicts (v. 9) under the Divine King (Zch 14:9). The context requires a greater interpretation in harmony with related passages in other prophets, and therefore the argument for this passage as a direct messianic prediction is made on several grounds.

First, there is the innertextual relationship between the rejected shepherd of chap. 11, the pierced one of chap. 12, and the smitten shepherd of chap. 13. The good shepherd of 11:4 who is detested (11:8) and rejected (11:12-13) is like the formerly rejected and pierced one of 12:10, who is equated with the Lord ("look at Me whom they pierced"), as is the smitten shepherd of 13:7 ("the one who is My associate"). The LXX has "smite" (aorist imperative v. 13:7), but Mk 14:27 changes it to "I (YHWH) will strike" (future indicative), as does Mt 26:31. On this basis, Jeremias argues that this change connects the shepherd motif with the suffering servant motif in Isa 53:6b: "The smitten Shepherd is the Servant of the Lord. God vicariously lays on him the judgment which should have smitten the whole flock."[12]

The original audience was expected to understand these intended connections as establishing the identity of the Divine Shepherd; One who was rejected by the Nation and consequently put to death. Likewise, Zch 13:7 is intertextually related to Ezk 34 where the good Shepherd (who is said to be the Lord, v. 11) will rescue and restore His sheep to the land of Israel (vv. 13-14). In like manner, the sheep, who have experienced worthless shepherds (leaders) in a time of national discipline (Zch 13:8) will be refined and restored (v. 9). Ultimately, this will be "a single shepherd, My servant David" (Ezk 34:23-24). Here, through Ezk 34, is an intertextual connection to Jer 23:1-6 which extends the metaphor of the shepherd to the righteous Branch of David (v. 5) who will reign as king, save Judah, and secure Israel in its land (v. 6). Judah is also the object of Zch 12, with chap. 13 focusing specifically on the "house of David" in its prediction of its repentance and restoration. Jeremiah 23:6 concludes by linking the Davidic shepherd with the Lord ("This is what He will be named: Yahweh Our Righteousness"), similar to Zch 12:10 and 13:7, where the Lord is also the figure upon whom He acts.

All of these passages are set in eschatological restoration contexts. The events described are defined in their respective contexts (Ezk 34–37; Zch 12–14) and by comparison with other prophets who give details of the end time, specifically the 70th week of Daniel (Dan 9:27) and the "time of trouble for Jacob (Israel)" (Jer 30:7). There is also an intertextual connection between Zch 13:7 and Isa 53:10, where the Lord is the One responsible for the action against the Shepherd/Servant. A sword oracle is also found in Jer 50:35-38 in connection with the shepherd/sheep imagery. A careful reader should have understood the greater authorial intent and identified the messianic connection implicit in these texts.

One text found at Qumran cited Zch 13:7-9 and may reflect an early Jewish messianic understanding. The Qumran text CD 19:6-11 reads:

> When God visits the earth, when there comes the word which is written by the hand of the prophet Zechariah [Zch 13:7] "Wake up, sword, against my shepherd, and against the male who is my companion—oracle of God—strike the shepherd, and the flock may scatter, and I shall turn my hand against the little ones." Those who revere him are the poor ones of the flock. These shall escape in the age of the visitation; but those that remain shall be delivered up to the sword when there comes the Messiah of Aaron and Israel.

The text may be interpreted as referring to God visiting the land to repay the evil ones who despise the law (CD 19:5-7). Some scholars see this text reflecting the Qumran community's view of the illegitimate Jewish authority in Jerusalem, employing the biblical royal Davidic tradition, which was referred to as the "Branch of David" and "prince" and also associated with the shepherd metaphor, to establish the eschatological hope for their community.[13] However, the interpretation also speaks of "the afflicted of the flock" (Zch 11:11) as "those who guard him/it" (God's precept?) and who will "be rescued at the time of the visitation" (CD 19:9-10). The shepherd figure mentioned in the Qumran quotation may connect with the messianic figure (a priestly/Davidic messiah?), however, it is clear that they relegate this event to the time of the end.[14]

Some others see this as a reference to a plural messiah, but the tradition of Jer 23:5 and Ezk 34:23-34 (36:24-25) stands behind the Qumran community hope for one shepherd. The Qumran text 4Q266, fragment 4:11-13 (Parallels: CD XX 33-34), says: "God will set up one shepherd who will feed them in the pasture and will be [. . .] and will choose unto himself mercy." Geza Vermes notes that while lines 11-12 are badly preserved, he considered them to be an allusion to the Messiah and translates: "God [will set up] a shep[herd for His people] and he will feed [them] in [pasture] . . ."[15] Therefore, the Qumran interpretation may lend support to a messianic interpretation.

Another source of early Jewish messianic interpretation is found in the apocryphal Psalms of Solomon (mid-first century BC). In *Pss Sol* 17:21-22,32,40-42 the psalmist explicitly connects the Davidic Messiah and the shepherd metaphor:

> Behold, O Lord, and raise up unto them their king, the son of David, at the time known to you, O God, in order that he may reign over Israel your servant. And gird him with strength, that he may shatter unrighteous rulers, and that he may purge Jerusalem from Gentiles who trample (her) down to destruction . . . And he will be a righteous king over them, taught of God. And there shall be no unrighteousness in his days in their midst, for all shall be holy and their king the Lord Messiah . . . faithfully and righteously shepherding the Lord's flock, he will not let any of them stumble in their pasture. He will lead them in holiness and there will be no arrogance among them, that any should be oppressed. This is the beauty of the king of Israel which God knew, to raise him over the house of Israel to discipline it.

This text, and its greater context (17:21-45), apparently reflects a crisis when Israel will be ruled by Gentile powers, a problem said to have been caused by the people's sins. Nevertheless, God did not abandon Israel, for this divine discipline will end one day, and He will again have mercy on Israel (cf. *Pss Sol* 7:3-10; 9:9-11). This eschatological hope is expressed in the prophecy of the Davidic Messiah, who like David will be God's shepherd for His people. The psalmist looks forward to the day when the Messiah, the son of David, will come and rid the nations of its enemies and restore Jerusalem and the people to their proper place (17:21-25,45).

Second, as mentioned above, the smitten shepherd is identified as "My associate" (v. 7). He is associated with YHWH ("the Lord"). The Hebrew term *geber 'amiti* ("the man close to me") implies one united to another by possession of common nature, rights, and privileges. The only other use of this term is in the priestly context of Leviticus (Lv 18:20; 19:11,15,17; 24:19; 25:14-15,17) where it has the idea of neighbor, fellow, associate, or companion, and is closely related to the word *'ah* ("brother"), such as in Lv 19:17; 25:14. J. Baldwin defines this as one "who stands next to me," indicating essentially an equal.[16] In all of the early Christian discussions of this passage, the shepherd has a positive function as the one who is on God's side.[17]

The Targum translates Zch 13:7 as: "O sword, be revealed against the king and against the prince his companion who is his equal, who is like him . . ." indicating the two figures share a royal connection. The shepherd is often used as a figure of the ruling king, as in 1Kg 22:17 where the prophet Micaiah predicts that the absence of the king would result in the sheep (Israel) being scattered on the mountains. The historical interpretation therefore understands this "associate" as a member of the failing Davidic dynasty (Zerubbabel or Elnathan). However, James Smith contends, "It is not likely that God would apply this epithet even to the most godly among men whom He might appoint as shepherd over the nation. Only one man could be denominated God's equal, and that is the Messiah."[18] Since this equates the Lord who struck the shepherd with the shepherd himself, the only shepherd that would qualify would be a divine Messiah. This identification is appropriate biblically (cf. Isa 9:6-7; Jer 23:6; Dan 7:13; Pss 45:6-7; 110:1). In theological terms, the shepherd is a man, but he is also deity, and such a person could only be the God-man, the Lord Jesus (cf. Jn 1:1; 8:58; 14:9-10; 17:24; Rm 10:13; Col 2:9; Ti 2:13; Rev 1:8; 22:12-13 with Isa 44:6).

Third, the NT interprets Zch 13 as a messianic text and applies it as a direct prediction to a specific historical event in the passion of Messiah Jesus, a treatment that requires further discussion.

THE MESSIANIC INTERPRETATION OF ZECHARIAH 13:7-9 IN THE NEW TESTAMENT

The NT quotes and alludes to Zechariah some 41 times. The Gospels cite Zch 9–14 (especially in the Passion Narratives) more than any other portion of the OT. It is the second most cited OT book in Revelation, second only to the book of Ezekiel. Therefore, the messianic interpretation of Zch 13:7 should not be unexpected. The point of the possible intertextuality between the two passages points out connections to the shepherd/sheep metaphor. Jeremiah, Ezekiel, and Zechariah are in harmony in the use of this sheep/shepherd metaphor in messianic terms. Thus, through this prophetic tradition, despite the presence of evil shepherds, God will raise up good shepherds and particularly send a Shepherd-Messiah to care for His people.

Matthew appears to adjust the text in Mark to be closer to the Alexandrinus text of the LXX, which emphasizes the relationship between the flock and the shepherd. The citation begins with the first singular future active indicative ("I will strike") for the MT's second singular imperative ("Strike"). This change may be required grammatically, since the citation includes only a section from the middle of Zch 13:7. It does not mention the "sword." probably because the sword only personifies the one who commands it, revealing that the action against the shepherd and the sheep is initiated by the Lord.[19]

Jesus cites Zch 13:7 as a direct prediction of His disciples abandoning Him at the time of His arrest (Mt 26:31/Mk 14:27). This was the beginning of being "struck" by the "sword" (judicial punishment by the Jewish and Roman authorities). That prophetic prediction is intended is clearly indicated by the introductory statement "it is written . . ." (Mt 26:31/Mk 14:27; cf. Jn 16:32) and the summary statements: "How then would the Scriptures be fulfilled that say it must happen this way?. . . But all this has happened that the prophetic Scriptures would be fulfilled" (Mt 26:54, 56; Mk 14:49). The use of the prophets (plural) by Matthew is obvious in intertextual analysis: Mt 9:36 alludes to Ezk 34:4-8; Mt 15:24 to Jer 50:6 and Ezk 24:23-25 (cf. also Ps 119:176; Isa 53:6). Matthew 25:32 draws upon Ezk 34:17,20-24, and Mt 26:31-32 cites Zch 13:7 and is intertextually related to Ezk 34:11-13. In addition, the metaphor of Israel as "scattered" sheep in Zch 13:7, which implies the loss or lack of a shepherd, is alluded to or implied elsewhere in the OT (Nm 27:17; 1Kg 22:17 and 2Chr 18:16; and especially in Isa 53:5-6 and Ezk 34:5).

The Lord Jesus self-identifies with the smitten shepherd of Zch 13:7 and views the scattered sheep as His disciples. This understanding justifies reusing the shepherd/sheep metaphor from Zch 11 in chap. 13. Jesus will make two predictions: first, the defection of all the disciples (Mt 26:31), which He notes is "because of [Him]" (i.e., they will be scandalized/shocked by His arrest); and second, the prediction of His subsequent death and resurrection and further meeting with the disciples in the Galilee (Mt 26:32; Mk 14:28). Thus, His predicted "falling away" of the disciples (Mt. 26:31; Mk 14:27) is the fulfillment of the "scattering" of the sheep (Zch 13:7). This "falling away" is further defined as defection from or betrayal of Messiah when Jesus answers Peter's objection by declaring that he would be guilty of denying Him that very night (Mt 26:33-35; Mk 14:30-31). The historic reality of the fulfillment came when the disciples "left Him and fled" (Mt 26:56; Mk 14:50). The nation's rejection of the Messiah will result in dispersion for Israel ("snared and captured," Isa 8:13-15), a national suffering the Jewish disciples will also experience.

Some commentators see the Gospel's quotation from Zch 13:7 as including vv. 8-9, although it is not present in the NT text. They then interpret Jesus' death as the birth pangs that initiate the eschatological tribulation (the disciples' scattering) and ultimately create the (spiritually refined) people of God in the new age (the new covenant Church).[20] But there is nothing that implies that a reference to these verses was intended since the Gospel writers do not cite or even allude to the remainder of the Zechariah passage (Zch 13:8-9). While the Gospels (Mk 13, like Mt 24), include a discussion of the eschatological tribulation and the second coming of the Messiah, this was given as an explanation to the disciples' question with response to the announced destruction of the Temple (Mk 13:2; Mt 24:1-2; Lk 21:6). Their question was "when will these things happen? And what will be the sign when all these things are about to be fulfilled/about to take place?" (Mk 13:4; Lk 21:7).

Matthew expands the question to include three distinct elements: "When will these things happen. And what is the sign of Your coming and of the end of the age?" (Mt 24:3). Jesus' answers in these chapters treat the near fulfillment of the Temple's destruction in AD 70 ("when will these things happen?") and the far (eschatological) fulfillment in the end time ("what is the sign of Your coming and of the end of the age?"), which includes the tribulation and the messianic advent in the judgment of the nations and the restoration of Israel. The subsequent chapters that include reference to Zch 13 are in a different context of the sufferings of the Messiah, and the messianic interpretation in the Gospels is restricted to v. 7.

Historicist and preterist interpreters are eager to read the entire prophecy (vv. 7-9) as being fulfilled by the citation of v. 7, a practice they employ in other such references, interpreting Zch 9:9-10 in Mt 21:5 and Jn 12:15 where only v. 9 is cited. However, Jesus, and thereafter His disciples, understood how to distinguish what OT texts applied to His first and second comings and were careful to cite only the text that applied to the point of immediate fulfillment. Consequently, in the synagogue in Nazareth, Yeshua stopped in the middle of His reading of Isa 61:1-2a and did not include the rest of the passage (2b-3) in His declaration that "today, as you listen, this Scripture has been fulfilled" (Lk 4:21).

Likewise, Matthew and John were aware that only Zch 9:9 was appropriate for fulfillment in the historical context and did not include v. 10 which has an eschatological reference. This can be argued from the greater context of Zch 9–14: This section concerns Israel's future and presents the purpose of the messianic advent as being to save the people spiritually. This becomes the basis for their final restoration nationally. This context also includes the conflicting elements of a humble Messiah and a conquering Messiah (Zch 9:9-10; 12:10; 14:3-4), along with a rejected and repentant Israel and a redeemed and restored Israel (Zch 10:6-12; 12:8-13:1; 14:9,20-21).

These elements appear in tension until He is recognized in the initial fulfillment with the first coming as the Suffering Messiah and Israel's national rejection, and in the final fulfillment with His second coming as Conquering Messiah.[21] Therefore, while Zch 13:7-9 is a direct messianic prophecy, the NT authors telescope it with a near fulfillment at Messiah's first advent (v. 7) and then a far fulfillment in the second advent (vv. 8-9). Peter seems to understand the far eschatological reference of vv. 8-9 when he alludes to the "testing by fire" (Zch 13:9 in 1Pt 1:7) as being fulfilled before the revelation of Messiah (i.e., in the trials of the tribulation).

THE IDENTIFICATION OF THE SHEPHERD IN ZECHARIAH 13:7-9

Another major theme of Zch 13:7 is its focus on the means of national cleansing. This comes first through the shepherd and affects the sheep. Thus, the identification of the Shepherd is essential in understanding this passage. In Scripture, the Lord alone is the ultimate Shepherd of Israel (e.g., Gn 48:15; 49:24; Pss 28:9; 80:1; Isa 40:11) and by extension of the metaphor, the people (Israel) are the sheep of His pasture (Ps 100:3). The Patriarchs were shepherds (Gn 13,26,30) and the Lord's provision to Abraham of a ram for the covenant son (Isaac) is a preview of God's provision for a substitutionary sacrifice in the future (Gn 22). Springing from this background in Genesis are two other traditions that inform the shepherd/sheep metaphor throughout Scripture: the exodus tradition, where Moses is the prototype shepherd of Israel (Isa 63:11) and the royal Davidic tradition where a shepherd becomes a king to "shepherd My people Israel" (2Sm 5:2). This same phrase is used in Mic 5:2 of the hope of an eschatological David who will be God's Messiah-Shepherd.[22] The shepherd, as a representative of God, is to exemplify godly virtues.

A third tradition of the evil shepherd emerged as the one who rejected these godly qualities and standards, leading Israel astray. Such shepherds were subjects of divine wrath (Ezk 34). Although some suggest this is the case for the shepherd judged by God in Zch 13:7, this is not supported by the text. The shepherd is identified as "My (the Lord's) associate" (see above). This is not an evil shepherd that has arisen, it is still the good shepherd, though misunderstood, since the divine judgment was not caused by His failure, but because of His rejection by the nation. This shepherd cannot be an evil figure since He cooperates with God's purpose of scattering the sheep so that they may be purified by suffering.[23] There is a contrast with the shepherd here and the "worthless shepherd" in Zch 11:17 where the sword does not inflict a fatal injury, but only strikes the arm and right eye. In chap. 11, the good shepherd (prophet) was unable to turn the people to the Lord, and so judgment fell on the evil shepherds and the people.

In Zch 13:7 the judgment does not stop with the evil shepherds (10:2-3; 11:15-17) but falls also on God's good shepherd, providing purification/refining of the nation. As Hedrick notes, "The shepherd is willing to pay the ultimate price in providing the salvation and deliverance of the sheep. In these opening verses of Zechariah 13:1-9, the promise is that God will provide cleansing for 'the house of David.'"[24] The language here, as discussed above, sends the reader back to Isa 53 for the explanation, which is that the Servant/Shepherd was being judged for Israel's sins and in their place. This is a second mention of the death of the Messiah (Zch 12:10; 13:7). The good shepherd was first pierced (12:10) and now is struck with the sword (13:7). This, as S. Lewis Johnson, Jr. observes, "is recorded from the standpoint of God."[25] Moreover, it is God Himself who executes the shepherd, since the term "strike" is masculine and agrees with "the LORD of Hosts." The two imperatives "awake" and "strike" are parallel, and both are addressed to the sword, the symbol of judicial authority (see Rom 13:4) by the Lord. Therefore, Zechariah is consistent with other prophets in presenting Messiah's death as God's divine activity (cf. Isa 53:10; Ac 2:23) as well as part of Israel's purification (12:10-14; Ac 2:36; 4:10; 5:30).

The results of the striking of the shepherd are described (13:7b-9), both for the immediate period surrounding His death (v. 7b) and the future period in which a remnant, brought through a time of testing, will be restored to covenant relationship identified as "My people" who will say "The LORD is our God" (vv. 8-9). The prophecy moves to the end times (v. 8), after the people of Israel have returned to the land (in unbelief), when they will face great affliction designed to both purge and prepare a remnant. The intertextual reference is Ezk 5:12-13, where two-thirds of Israel are destroyed and one-third is scattered as a remnant with the sword behind them, indicating continued discipline. This is clearly a prediction of devastation as the two-thirds "perish" (Hb. *gawa*, which always refers to the act of dying). Ezekiel's reference is to the Babylonian destruction and exile, but the pattern is set for the preserved, yet disciplined remnant, by this text.

Zechariah explains that the judgment of Israel in the eschatological future tribulation will follow this precedent, and the preserved remnant will be brought to repentance and restored in the end time at the coming of Messiah (v. 9; cf. Isa 10:22-23). The final remnant will call on the Messiah for salvation (Zch 12:10; cf. Rom 11:25-27). The term *qara* ("call") alongside *'ana* ("answer") denotes both a human cry for help in the form of a prayer and God calling a human being in v. 9. Here are the national repentance of Israel toward Messiah and the divine response in His return to revive the nation and restore it in the millennial kingdom. For this reason, the covenantal formula of loyalty "they are My people . . . the LORD is my God" is employed to show that Israel is in a restored relationship with God. This passage as a messianic text predicted the whole program of God for Israel from ruin to restoration. The passage fits well within Zechariah's presentation of the

Messiah's initial humble role as a suffering king (Zch 9:9) and His final victorious reign as the sovereign king (Zch 14:9).

1. Charles L. Feinberg, *God Remembers: A Study of Zechariah* (Multnomah, OR: Multnomah Press, 1977), 233.
2. For a comparison of the priestly purification of this passage with that of Joshua the high priest in Zch 3 see Daniel F. O'Kennedy, "Purification of Priest," *Old Testament Essays* 27/1 (2014): 231–46.
3. R. Mason, *The Books of Haggai, Zechariah and Malachi*, Cambridge Bible Commentary (Cambridge: Cambridge University, 1977), 117.
4. Ingram London, "Messianic Allusions of Zechariah 13:6 Revisited" (Research paper for course OTST 555 Prophets, Andrews University 2011). Merrill F. Unger also championed the messianic interpretation of Zch 13:6 in *Zechariah: Prophet of Messiah's Glory* (Grand Rapids: Zondervan, 1963), 228–30.
5. George L. Robinson described Zechariah as "the most Messianic, the most truly apocalyptic and eschatological, of all the writings of the OT." "The Book of Zechariah" *International Standard Bible Encyclopedia*, ed. James Orr, John L. Nuelson, and Edgar Young Mullins (Chicago: Howard-Severance Company, 1915), V:3136.
6. See James A. Hartle, "The Literary Unity of Zechariah" *Journal of the Evangelical Theological Society* 35/2 (June 1992): 145–157. Some evangelical scholars have also accepted this view. See Bruce K. Waltke, *An Old Testament Theology* (Grand Rapids: Zondervan, 2011), 846–47 and Kenneth L. Barker, "Zechariah," in *Daniel and the Minor Prophets*, The Expositor's Bible Commentary, ed. Frank E. Gaebelein (Grand Rapids, Zondervan, 1985), 7:597, who proposed that Nehemiah wrote chaps. 9–14 later in his life.
7. Stephen Cook, "The Metamorphosis of a Shepherd: The Tradition History of Zechariah 11:17 + 13:7-9," *Catholic Biblical Quarterly* 55:3 (July, 1993), 453–466.
8. Barker, "Zechariah," 7:596.
9. See B. C. Childs, *Introduction to the Old Testament as Scripture* (Philadelphia: Fortress Press), 482–83, and Michael Rydelnik, "Zechariah," in *The Moody Bible Commentary*, ed. Michael Rydelnik and Michael Vanlaningham (Chicago: Moody Publishers, 2014), 1413–14.
10. See E. M. and C. L. Meyers, *Zechariah 9–14*, Anchor Bible 25C (New York: Doubleday, 1993), 385–87.
11. Oddly, the popular anti-missionary and founder of Outreach Judaism, R. Tovia Singer, does not include a discussion on Zch 13:7 in either of volume of his expanded work *Let's Get Biblical: Why Doesn't Judaism Accept the Christian Messiah?* although he does treat Zch 13:1-6 and 8–9.
12. Joachim Jeremias, *Theological Dictionary of the New Testament* (Grand Rapids: Eerdmans, 1966) 6:493, n. 78.
13. For a discussion of this document with some parallel texts in CD A VII, 7-XIII, 21 and CD B XIX, 1-XX, 34, see Joseph M. Baumgarten and Daniel R. Schwartz, "Damascus Document (CD)," in James H. Charlesworth, ed., *The Dead Sea Scrolls: Hebrew, Aramaic, and Greek Texts with English Translations*, vol. 2, Damascus Document, War Scrolls, and Related Documents, The Princeton Theological Seminary Dead Sea Scrolls Project, ed. James H. Charlesworth (Louisville: Westminster/John Knox, 1995), 25.
14. J. de Waard, *A Comparative Study of the Old Testament Text in the Dead Sea Scrolls and in the New Testament*, Studies on the Texts of the Desert of Judah 4 (Leiden, Netherlands: Brill, 1965), 196.
15. Geza Vermes, *An Introduction to the Complete Dead Sea Scrolls* (Minneapolis: Fortress Press, 1998), 136 n. 9.
16. Joyce Baldwin, *Haggai, Zechariah, Malachi: An Introduction and Commentary*, Tyndale Old Testament Commentaries, ed. D. J. Wiseman (Downers Grove, IL: Tyndale, IVP), 197–98.
17. Maarten J. J. Menken, "Striking the Shepherd. Early Christian Versions and Interpretations of Zechariah 13,7," *Biblica* 92:1 (2011), 45.
18. James E. Smith, *What the Bible Teaches About the Promised Messiah* (Nashville: Thomas Nelson Publishers, 1993), 458.
19. Clay Alan Ham, "Zechariah in Matthew's Gospel: Jesus as Coming King and Rejected Shepherd" (PhD dissertation, Southwestern Baptist Theological Seminary, 2003), 112.
20. See Paul Sloan, "The Return of the Shepherd: Zechariah 13:7–14:6 as the Interpretive Framework for Mark 13," in *Ancient Readers and their Scriptures: Engaging the Hebrew Bible in Early Judaism and Christianity*, Ancient Judaism and Early Christianity, Volume: 107 (Brill 2016), 128–58.

21. See Won Jin Jeon, "The Chronology of the Events in Zechariah 12–14" (Honors Thesis, Andrews University, 2016). The author found that the literary structures, key terms, Hebrew grammar, and general theological motifs aided in the holistic understanding of the timeliness of the events in Zch 12–14 and separated the timing of the events in chaps. 12–13 from those in chap. 14. The weakness in the interpretive approach is the failure to distinguish that national Israel has a future in these texts and has not been superseded by the Church. This approach applies the texts spiritually to all believers and thereby loses the significance of the timing argument it proposes.

22. Terry J. Hedrick, "Jesus as Shepherd in the Gospel of Matthew" (Durham e-theses, Durham University, 2007), 179.

23. See C. Stuhlmueller, *Rebuilding with Hope: A Commentary on the Books of Haggai and Zechariah* (Grand Rapids: Eerdmans, 1988), 152–53.

24. Terry J. Hedrick, "Jesus as Shepherd in the Gospel of Matthew," 177.

25. S. Lewis Johnson, Jr., "Israel's National Cleansing" - Zechariah 13:1-9 (Transcript, Dallas TX: Believer's Chapel, 2008): 11.

Zechariah 14:1-11

The Return of the Messiah

EUGENE H. MERRILL

The disruptive and destructive conquest of Jerusalem in 586 BC at the hands of Nebuchadnezzar's Babylonian armies seemed to many who survived to mark the end of God's covenant promise to Abraham, Moses, and David. They determined that God's promise to establish the messianic and eternal kingdom of God over everything in heaven and on earth had come to an end.[1] However, God's plan was contrary to this pessimism and hopelessness. He had promised recovery and re-establishment, and after the prophesied 70 years of exile, a state called Yehud was brought into being, albeit merely a client state under the Babylonian and then Persian empires. There still lacked a clear word from Yahweh that the mighty kingdom dreamed of and expected by the patriarchs and prophets would still come in all its triumphant glory.

That word was the burden of the three prophets of God who rose up in the postexilic era to herald the message of the coming Messiah and the kingdom over which He would reign. Haggai focused on the Temple to be built (Hag 2:1-9), Zechariah on the Davidic scion who would occupy the throne of his celebrated ancestor (Zch 12:8-12). Malachi focused on the danger of the people missing out on all this because of social and religious corruption on every hand. At the same time, he also highlighted the patient and loving call of God that they should return to fellowship with Him as the Father (Mal 1:6-14; 2:10-17; 3:16-18).[2]

STRUCTURAL ANALYSIS OF ZECHARIAH 14:1-11

A holistic view of the passage with attention to scene and subjects yields the following palindrome:

Conquest of Jerusalem (1)
  Violation of Jerusalem (2)
    Yahweh the Warrior (3)
      Yahweh the De-creator (4)
        The flight of God's people (5)
          The curse of total darkness (6)
        The light for God's people (7)
      Yahweh the Re-creator (8)
    Yahweh the King (9)
  Resettlement of Jerusalem (10)
Contentment of Jerusalem (11)

The central pole of the structure is surprising at first glance, perhaps, but it describes well the human condition of antiquity and of all ages, including the current one. Humanity's propensity since the Edenic fall has always been the tendency—like the Second Law of Thermodynamics—to become increasingly random, oblivious of God and His standards, and trapped in the inevitable slide to anarchy and depravity. The final end is extreme darkness, the obliteration of reason, the shedding of moral restraints, and the denial of God, who said at the beginning, "Let there be light." But redemption reverses that slide. God ignites the light of truth, and those who believe become "new creations" (2Co 5:17) who celebrate Him as the "King of kings and Lord of lords" (1Tm 6:15). Those driven from their own "Jerusalems" will rebuild and re-occupy them in God's good time, and there they will find everlasting Shalom.

EXEGESIS AND EXPOSITION

The Attack on Jerusalem 14:1-2

Zechariah draws attention first of all to "a day of Yahweh," a figure employed by the prophets of God in dozens of contexts, almost always with the ominous overtone of judgment.[3] Some "days of the Lord" refer to historical events on the immediate horizon, but more often, especially with the definite article "the," to an eschatological time when the entire series of events can be encapsulated within the single term "day."[4] Zechariah uses adjectives of many kinds just within this passage to speak of this: "a day" (14:1); "that day" (vv. 4,6,8,9); and "one day" (v. 7 NKJV). This aggregation of six uses in 11 verses is a density designed to draw attention to last days judgment.

In a remarkable example of Yahweh's sovereignty over all nations and His power to use even their hostility as an instrument of discipline and judgment against His rebel people—and in the end against themselves!—the prophet declares in Yahweh's own words, "I will gather all the nations against Jerusalem for battle" (v. 2) [lit. "that they may make war with [it]," i.e. Jerusalem].[5] The ominous aspect of "that day" is affirmed by the prophet's reference to "plunder . . . divided" in Jerusalem's midst (v. 1). These are not spoils of war brought back to the city by foreign campaigns of a Davidic Age,[6] but rather the loot stolen by Jerusalem's conquerors in the immediate past (2 Kgs 24:13; 25:13-16) as well as in the eschatological age. Not only that, but much of the population will be deported, the dwellings robbed, and the women raped. The phrase "all the nations," though hyperbolic, lends support to the last days nature of the prophet's message, since in no time in Israel's (or Judah's) history had masses of nations combined to attack the Holy City.[7]

The Defense of Jerusalem 14:3-5

14:3 Anti-God nations will not have the last word, in any case. Israel's history antecedent to the prophet provides numerous examples of God's intervention on behalf of His beleaguered people no matter how deserving they were of His wrath. The attack of Amalek in the days of the desert migration was blunted by Moses and reversed as he held the "rod of God" in his hand, the same rod with which he "slew" the Nile and ironically the rod that smote the rock which gushed with life-giving water (Ex 7:20; 17:6,8-16). The same was true of the foray of Canaanite Arad against the tribes in the north Sinai (Nm 21:1-3) and of the Amorite kings Sihon of Heshbon (Nm 21:21-30) and Og of Bashan (Nm 21:33-35), both in the Trans-Jordan.

Instances too numerous to mention exist in the narratives of Joshua and Judges where Yahweh's involvement is explicitly stated. The following can be listed only by references: Jos 8:1-2; 10:14,42; 11:6-8; Jdg 3:9,10,15; 4:15,23; 5:11; 7:9,14.[8] Zechariah makes clear that Yahweh's salvific work for Israel is not all in the past. The same God who once delivered (and delivers) will come as a Warrior "on that day" (v. 4) and *He* will fight for His chosen ones. Though He had brought the nations to "spank" his children, in a most ironical way He had also brought them to the holy city so that He might defeat them there. He had called them *to* battle, a wonderfully ambiguous way of using the preposition ל to mean either so they could make war with Jerusalem or so that Yahweh could make war with them. There is double purpose in this display of the mysteries of God's dealings with men: He can employ evil to do good, but thus employed, evil must then be cast aside, all without doing damage to His own sense of justice and to His righteousness.

14:4a The Warrior alluded to in v. 3, Yahweh Himself, is clearly the referent here as well, the One whose feet will stand on the Mount of Olives *"on that Day."* The standing in this context connotes lordship, ownership, and the like. Of the 14 times the Mount of Olives is mentioned in the Bible, all but two, here and in 2Sm 15:30, occur in the NT and in all instances with reference to Jesus.[9] Its messianic associations and message come through loud and clear. Adding to this is the unnamed mountain of Ezk 11:23 ("the mountain east of the city"). After having filled the Temple with His Glory,[10] that Glory departed from it and lighted upon the mountain, all of which portrayed to the exilic community then with Ezekiel (and to his later readers) that Yahweh had been "dispossessed" from His house, as it were, and pagan deities had filled its every room (see Ezk 8:3-6,9-10,14,16).

The terms describing God's departure from His house and His apostate people are most compelling: (1) He will go far away (lit., "to a far [place]") from His sanctuary (Ezk 8:6); (2) He went up from the Ark of the Covenant to the threshold (Ezk 9:3); (3) He rose up from the threshold (Ezk 10:4); (4) He went forth from the threshold (Ezk 10:18); (5) He went up from the midst of the city (Ezk 11:23); and (6) set foot on the Mount of Olives (Ezk 11:23). Michael Rydelnik, for several reasons, maintains that the phrase "His feet will stand on the Mount of Olives" is not to be understood figuratively but literally. He states, "The term 'feet' seems to indicate the Lord will be literally present in Jerusalem, so much so that the Mount of Olives is literally split in two. Other prophetic passages seem to indicate the Lord's literal presence with Israel at the end of days, leading the people in battle (cf. Isa 63:1-6 with Rev 14:14-19 and 19:11-16; Mic 2:12-13). Also, the apostles were promised that the Lord Jesus Himself would descend upon the Mount of Olives when He returns to restore the kingdom to Israel (Ac 1:11)."[11]

This verse's parallels with the experiences of Jesus in the passion week are perceptible and clearly intentional. All four Gospels share at least some elements of Jesus' resort to this favorite place. The chart helps to visualize its role in His experiences, especially at the very end.

Chart One: The Messianic Setting of the Mount of Olives

References	Event	Time	Pertinence	Relevance to Zch 14:1-11
Matthew 21:1-11	Triumphal Entry	Five days before the crucifixion	Announcing Davidic King	Proclamation of Yahweh as King (v. 9)
Mark 11:1-10	Triumphal Entry	Five days before the crucifixion	Announcing Davidic King	Proclamation of Yahweh as King (v. 9)
Luke 19:29-40	Triumphal Entry	Five days before the crucifixion	Announcing un-named King	Proclamation of Yahweh as King (v. 9)
Matthew 24:3-14	Instruction	Four days before the crucifixion	Announcing the second coming of the King (25:31)	Yahweh shall be King (v. 9)
Mark 13:26,35	Instruction	Four days before the crucifixion	Announcing the second coming of the Son of Man	"The LORD my God will come and all the holy ones with Him." (v. 5)
Luke 21:37-38	Instruction	unclear	Silent	None
Matthew 26:36-38	Prayer	Day before Crucifixion	Agony's crushing[12]	None
Mark 14:33-34	Prayer	Day before Crucifixion	Agony's crushing	None
Luke 22:44-45	Prayer	Day before Crucifixion	Agony's crushing	None
Acts 1:9-12	Jesus' Ascension	Ascension Day	Departure of the King (v. 9)	Return of the King (v. 4)

14:4b-5 The foot that stands on the Mount of Olives in the last days is that of "One" who comes to destroy in order to reconstruct. The imagery here is striking in that it depicts violent upheavals in the heavens and on earth that will reduce all things material and immaterial to a chaotic state in which nature itself reverts back to a near pre-creation state. A kind of "de-creation" will take apart the constitutive elements that make up the world of familiarity, but with those same "building blocks" will emerge a re-creation by the hands of God, almost in imitation of primal creation. A list of alterations and renewals of which the prophet speaks may help more easily to evoke comparisons between what God did and what the prophet says He will do when He returns, this time not as Elohim, the God of remote and transcendent power, but as Yahweh, the covenant God and Savior. This new creation is by the King and for His subjects, the chosen ones of Israel and the nations.

The Genesis Creation Account
1. The heavens and the earth (Gn 1:1)
2. The emptiness of the earth (1:2)
3. Darkness covered all (v. 2)
4. Light appeared (vv. 3-4)

The Zechariah De-creation Account
1. The splitting of Olivet (Zch 14:4b)
2. The creation of a great valley (v. 4b)
3. Humanity will scatter (v. 5)
4. No need for a light source (v. 6)

The Zechariah 14 Re-creation Account
1. Light shall appear at evening (v. 7)
2. Spring waters shall flow year round (v. 8)
3. Yahweh will be King over all (v. 9)
4. Jerusalem will be rebuilt and with security (vv. 10-11)

Granted, the comparisons are not obvious or consistent in detail, but the prophet's intention to portray a new creation order upon the arrival of the King to Olivet is well-founded and in line with other prophetic voices that describe millennial and everlasting bliss.[13]

The splitting of Olivet from east to west is designed accomplish two objectives: (1) to provide a way of escape for the imperiled citizens of Jerusalem and (2) to permit water to flow from the rebuilt Temple toward the eastern deserts. The best but most difficult way this could be done is by the creation of a valley, a pathway unavailable, it seems, in the days of Amos, 200 years earlier when a great earthquake drove the people out of the city (Am 1:1-2).[14] One is reminded of David's flight from Absalom that forced him to scale the mountain to reach safety in the Trans-Jordan (2Sm 15:30); or the frantic attempt by Zedekiah, Judah's last king, to flee in the same direction, a route surely impeded by the Mount of Olives (2Kg 25:4-5).

The Renovation of Jerusalem 14:6-11

14:6-7 The prophet proposes that this flight will be replicated in the future, and beyond all that, a time of 24-hour light will be fueled by the sun; one rather like that in the beginning when there was no day or night (vv. 6-7; cf. Gn 1:3-5,14-18).

The sun, moon, and stars will find their "work" at an end (6b), for Yahweh Himself will be the Light.[15]

14:8 As for the flowing water, its clearest source and destination are best described by Ezekiel who, in vision, saw a river issuing from the Temple eastward to the Arabah and on to "the sea" (Ezk 47:1-8). What is clearly in view is the Dead Sea (or Salt Sea), the waters of which are so laden in mineral content that no life can flourish there. The waters, says the prophet, will become pure enough that fish will abound there and, in fact, the streams will inject into it life-giving properties. The most logical path will, of course, be through the Mount of Olives, as Zechariah describes it, and not around it. The solution is the creation of a watercourse straight through the middle of the mountain. Zechariah, unlike Ezekiel, sees the waters flowing not only to the Dead Sea, but to the Mediterranean[16] as well, the objective of which was to replenish all the earth.

The significance of the vision is not to display the mighty power of God alone—though that is worthy of praise—but to describe metaphorically the gracious gift of Israel's renewed national existence and renewed, regenerated individual personal life. The perennial stream that energizes is akin to the one that bisected the garden of Eden, leaving the garden as one stream and then dividing into four, suggesting that all four quarters of the earth would thereby have access to life.[17] More to the point, however, is that the water does not come *to* Jerusalem but flows *from* there to the whole world. Thus, Israel will fulfill, in part at least, its "Great Commission" of being a light to the nations, a witness to direct them to the one and only God (Pss 22:27-28; 72:11; 86:9; Isa 2:2; 49:6; Jer 4:2; 27:7; Mic 4:2; Zph 3:8; Hab 2:5; Zch 2:11; 8:22; Mal 3:12; Gal 3:8). Yet, historical Israel still failed to accomplish perfectly what God intended for her as His servant (2Kg 17:7-23). Therefore, He Himself, in the Person of the God-Man Jesus, undertook to draw and redeem the nations through His atoning work (Isa 52:13–53:12).

14:9 The following description of the sovereignty of God can hardly be equaled in Scripture. The prophet piles up names and epithets in such an inordinate manner that one is left speechless with awe and reverence. He declares literally that "Yahweh shall be as a king[18] over all the earth" (v. 9a). The point is that though Yahweh has been *de facto* king over all that exists since before the beginning of time, His lordship has in practice seldom been acknowledged even by His own chosen people. In Zechariah's vision, Yahweh will be confessed *as* King "on that day," that is, in the day of His coming. The epithet "king" brings to mind also the historical kingship of David whose scion will be known as "the son of David" and who will sit on David's throne forever. Psalm 2:2 expresses this well: "The kings of the earth . . . conspire together against the LORD and His Anointed One (*Messiah*)."

More striking perhaps is the allusion in v. 9b to the Great Shema of Dt 6:4:

"On that day [Yahweh] will be one and his name one[19]" (ESV). The nuances of the lexeme *'echad* (one) range all the way from the literal numeral to an unwarranted incipient Trinitarianism.[20] Context here (as well as in Dt 6) leads to the concept of Yahweh's sole existence in general or, at the least, as the only God for Israel among all the other so-called gods. Eschatologically (as here), there will be no lingering doubt as to the solitary existence of the everlasting Creator of the universe, the Yahweh of Israel and the Christ of the Church. Ontologically He is the only God and by His name,[21] that is, His renown, He will be confessed as the only God by all the nations (see Ex 15:3; 20:24; Dt 12:5,11-12; 16:11; 1Kg 5:5; Neh 1:9; Pss 54:6; 68:4; Isa 42:8; Rev 16:9).[22] To confess His name is to confess Him as God; to make light of His name is to dishonor Him as God (Ex 20:7; Dt 5:11).

14:10 Another cosmic change will be the transformation[23] of desert lands to fertile acreage for pasturing and agricultural pursuits. One of the principal terms in the OT for desert is "Arabah," the word employed ironically here to denote a place of agricultural bounty (cf. *Hebrew and Aramaic Lexicon of the Old Testament*, 880). Though *'arāvāh* in general denotes desert, it also refers to the wide plains of the Great Rift Valley that include the verdant Jordan River, whose banks still produce a wide variety of fruits and vegetables. Zechariah, though no doubt with an eye toward the immediate future, is primarily concerned throughout his writings with the eschatological world that will be so radically altered that what was useless for farming then, will in the future be as a second Eden.[24]

Part of its alteration will be the leveling of the Hill Country between Geba of Benjamin and Rimmon of the Upper Negev southern border of Judah.[25] Beyond this, Jerusalem, the Holy City, will also be elevated, but not in geographical terms. She will be lifted back into her David-Solomon splendor with all her circumventing walls rebuilt, and, most important, she will be repopulated, no longer under Yahweh's curse and in perfect safety. A historical preview of this eschatological picture is the return of the Babylonian diaspora to Jerusalem and environs following the gracious decree of Cyrus the Great in 538 BC. This return came in stages, one reflected in Haggai and Zechariah ca. 520–516 BC and the others in the immigrations of Ezra in 458 BC and of Nehemiah in 445 BC. Ezra's census of returnees numbered about 50,000 (Ezr 2:64-67; cf. Neh 7:66-67), but the number of the retinue accompanying Nehemiah is not recorded (Neh 2:11-12).

Both of these men were confronted with a number of problems, among which was rebuilding Jerusalem and persuading the returnees to live there as opposed to the surrounding villages and agricultural areas. Ezra recounts the sorrow of the old men who had seen the glorious temple of Solomon and who had compared it to the meagre facsimile that would become the Second Temple and had judged it to be "as nothing" (Hag 2:3; cf. Ezr 3:9-13). Strong defensive walls were lacking, however, so

Jerusalem continued to remain a place of sparse population until Nehemiah came to undertake their reconstruction to make them adequate for providing the citizens' safety (Ezr 4:12-13,16; 5:8; Neh 6:15). But the mere assurance of safety was not enough to persuade enough people to make their home in the city, so Nehemiah mandated that one out of ten must relocate there, thus making the city a proper capital for the New Jerusalem (Neh 11:1-2). This, it seems, is what Zechariah meant when he spoke of future Jerusalem being "raised up" (v. 10)[26] and its citizens "will live there" or literally, "will be settled in their [rightful] place" (v. 11). Isaiah also speaks of the Temple mount being "established at the top of the mountains and . . . raised[27] above the hills" (2:2), a vision captured by Amos as well (9:11).

14:11 Unlike the resettlement of Jerusalem that took place under Sheshbazzar, Ezra, and Nehemiah, which, like many to follow, was of but brief duration, the inhabitants of the city to come will live in security and peace, no longer under the curse of God's judgment. Nothing in Scripture suggests that will occur in a world like the present one, but only when the rightful King comes with His mighty entourage, the hosts of heaven. Then there will be blessed rest and peace for His long-suffering people.

The catalog of destructions, abandonments, and rebuildings of the Holy City in history seems almost beyond reckoning. Such a rhythm took place under Antiochus Epiphanes, after the death of the beneficent Alexander and only 200 years following Nehemiah (ca. 170 BC). Josephus recounts that the Seleucid army under Antiochus "came upon the Jews with a great army, and took their city by force, and slew a great multitude of those that favoured [*sic*] Ptolemy, and sent out his soldiers to plunder them without mercy. He also spoiled the temple and put a stop . . . to offering a daily sacrifice . . . for three years and six months." The succeeding Maccabees, under their leader Judas Maccabeus, rebounded to a degree, "rebuilt the walls round about the city, and reared towers of great height against the incursions of enemies" (*Antiquities* Book XII, Chapter VII 7). This "Band-Aid" lasted but briefly, and a few years after Judas's death the city fell once again, this time to Rome under Pompey (*Ant.* Book XIV, Chapter IV 4).

CONCLUSION

Recent history attests to the ongoing faithfulness of Yahweh to His chosen nation, even in their present unbelief.[28] They suffered through the terrible opposition of neighboring peoples in their UN-granted establishment of a Jewish state in 1948; the so-called Suez War of 1956; the struggle against what seemed apparent to most observers to be overwhelming odds in the attack by a coalition of nations in 1967, the miracle of which gave rise to its description as "The Six-Day War;" and then on the most holy day of the Jewish calendar, Yom Kippur of 1973, after a nearly devastating defeat, they once more prevailed and so decisively that "he who has eyes to see and ears to hear" can interpret the outcome as nothing short of divine intervention.

But still, true and lasting *shalom* will be a reality only when the Sar Shalom, "the Prince of Peace," comes in clouds and great glory. Then He shall bear His kingly scepter, wear His Davidic crown, and sit at the right hand of the Father on His royal throne. It is to all this that Zechariah directed his attention and upon which we too are invited to gaze with longing, and also with great assurance.

---

1. See, among others, Gn 12:1-2; 18:18; 46:3; Ex 19:6; 32:13; 2Sm 7:16; 1Ch 17:11-14.

2. For a more extensive treatment on background and introduction to these books, see Eugene H. Merrill, *Haggai, Zechariah, Malachi. An Exegetical Commentary.* Chicago: Moody Press, 1994, 3–18, 71–85, 371–386.

3. The formula here is *yom bā layhwh* with the preposition indicating that the action is always underway. The *lamed* (לְ) likely suggests that the Day of Yahweh either issues from him or is attached to him as the eschatological Judge; cf. Wilhelm Gesenius, E. Kautzsch, and A. E. Cowley, *Gesenius' Hebrew Grammar*, ed. E. Kautzsch, 2nd English Edition, Revised in Accordance with the 28th German Edition (1909) by A. E. Cowley (Oxford: Clarendon Press, 1910, 16th impression, 1982), 129 1(a). The formula as found here occurs in 13 other places in the OT: Isa 13:6,9; Jl 1:15; 2:1,11; 3:1,13-14; Am 5:18,20; Ob 15; Zph 1:7,14; Mal 3:1-3, only one of which (Isaiah) is preexilic.

4. See Konrad R. Schaefer, "Zechariah 14: A Study in Allusion," *Catholic Biblical Quarterly* 57 (1995): 66–91.

5. The idea that the nations are mere puppets in the hands of the master "puppeteer" is a common motif in the prophetic literature. See Isa 10:5-6; Jer 5:15-18; Am 6:14; Hab 1:5-11.

6. See 1Sm 30:20; 2Sm 5:21; 8:7,8.

7. Eschatology is replete with extravagant language as part of its special repertoire. Isaiah 29, for example, in its discourse on the war against Ariel (Jerusalem). The enemies will be like "fine dust" and chaff in number (v. 5), they will be accompanied by thunder, earthquake, clamor, whirlwind, storm, and fire (v. 6), and they shall consist of "the multitude of all the nations" (v. 7; cf. Jer 1:15-16; 25:8-11; Ezk 5:5-12; Hos 10:10; Jl 2:1-11; Am 2:5; Lk 21:20,24; Rev 20:9).

8. Not included here are the many instances of the so-called "Holy" or "Yahweh" War, most of which are related in Joshua and Judges, since these technically were not defensive actions, but offensive. For the ethics of this kind of engagement, see M. Daniel Carroll, R. and J. Blair Wilgus, eds., *Wrestling with the Violence of God: Soundings in the Old Testament* (Winona Lake, IN: Eisenbrauns, 2015). Paul Copan and Matthew Flannagan. *Did God Really Command Genocide? Coming to Terms with the Justice of God.* (Grand Rapids: Baker, 2014).

9. Four times the texts refer to the triumphal entry of Jesus (Mt 21:1; Mk 11:1; Lk 19:29,39); four times as a place for instruction and repose (Mt 24:3; Mk 13:3; Lk 21:37; Jn 8:1); four times as a place of prayer prior to Jesus' crucifixion (Mt 26:30; Mk 14:26; Lk 22:39); and once as the location of His ascent to heaven (Ac 1:12).

10. Sometimes referred to as "Shekinah" (Heb שְׁכֵנָה, Qal fs ptcp. שָׁכַן/שָׁכֵן, "dwell") Glory, the radiance of God in His dwelling-place in all His unapproachable glory. *Theological Dictionary of the Old Testament* 14:696.

11. Michael Rydelnik, "Zechariah," in *The Moody Bible Commentary*, ed. Michael Rydelnik and Michael Vanlaningham (Chicago: Moody Publishers, 2014), 1435.

12. The place of prayer, Gethsemane, derives from Heb גַּת + שֶׁמֶן, "oil press," of which many existed in and around the Mount of Olives, as one would expect. The term serves to emphasize the intense suffering of Jesus both in prayer (He sweat, as it were, great drops of blood; Lk 22:44) and on the cross, crushed until His life expired (cf. Isa 53:10).

13. The following are well-known representative messianic passages in support of this point. See Isa 4:2-6; 9:6-7; 11:1-9; 33:17-24; 41:8-16; Jer 23:5-8; 31:1-9,23-26,31-40; Ezk 34:11-31; Hos 1:10-11; Jl 3:14-21; Am 9:11-15; Ob 17-21; Mic 4:1-8; Zph 3:8-20; Hag 2:20-23.

14. Evidence for such a quake c. 760 has come to light, establishing the veracity of both Amos and Zechariah; cf. S. A. Austin, G. W. Franz, and E. G. Frost, "Amos's Earthquake: An Extraordinary Middle East Seismic of 750 BC," International Geology Review 42/7 (2000): 657–671.

15. This is reminiscent of the words of John in Rev 21:23-24: "The city [of Jerusalem] does not need the sun or the moon to shine on it, for the glory of God gives it light, and the Lamb is its lamp" (NIV).

16. For the Mediterranean as the "Western Sea," cf. Dt 11:24, NASB; 34:2, HCSB footnote; Jos 1:4; Jl 2:20, NASB. The more common name is "Great Sea" (Nm 34:6,7; Jos 1:4; 9:1; 15:12,47; Ezk 47:10,15,19, all NASB).

17. For water as metonymy for life, see Pss 36:9; 114:8; Prv 10:11; 13:14; 14:27; 16:22; Sg 4:15; Jer 2:13; Jl 3:18; Rev 21:6; 22:1,2,17.

18. The construction *lemelech* is identical to the very common psalms heading *leDavid* that is usually translated either "by David," "for David," or "to David."

19. Deuteronomy 6:4 states: "Hear, O Israel! The Lord is our God, the Lord is one" (NASB). See an early but still helpful study on this concept by Cyrus H. Gordon, "His Name Is 'One'," *Journal of Near Eastern Studies* 29 (1970): 198–99.

20. See *Theological Dictionary of the Old Testament* 1:193-201; *New International Dictionary of Old Testament Theology and Exegesis* 1:349–51.

21. In biblical usage, the name of a person was, as much as possible, suited to the circumstances of his birth or to developing character traits. It became nearly synonymous with the individual himself or herself.

22. Paul develops the "name theology" when, referring to Jesus, he says: "[God] gifted him with *the* name, the 'above-all-things name' that in the name of Jesus every knee in heaven, earth, and the netherworld will bend and everyone will acknowledge that Jesus Christ is Lord to the Father's glory" (Phl 2:9-11, author's translation). For a full development of the theme of divine name, see Walther Eichrodt, *Theology of the Old Testament*, Vol. II, (Philadelphia: Westminster, 1975), 40–45.

23. For the difficult MT *yissov* "he (masc.) will turn into," read *tissov* "it (fem) will turn into," that is, the land (eretz) (fem. noun) will do so by God's gracious intervention.

24. Precursors of this already exist in parts of Israel (including the Arabah Valley) where only a century ago lands that were totally unfit for farming have, thanks to modern techniques of irrigation, fertilizers, and construction of pipelines and other conveyors of water, become miraculously transformed into lush fields and orchards, all in fulfillment to the last detail of everything of which the ancient prophet speaks. For a personal tour of ancient Negev agricultural enterprises, see Eugene H. Merrill, "Agriculture in the Negev: An Exercise in Possibilitism," *Near East Archaeological Society Bulletin* (NS) 9 (1977): 25–35.

25. Geba and Rimmon, respectively, represent the northern- and southernmost extent of Judah. The land between the two is part of the Hill Country, not densely populated. It will become arable land.

26. The verb *r'm* is an Aramaic loan word akin to Heb *rwm*, "be exalted" (*Hebrew and Aramaic Lexicon of the Old Testament*, 1202). The associated verb *yshv*, here in the Qal impf, denotes settling down, generally with the notion of permanence.

27. Here the Hi impf of *rwm*, "will be raised up."

28. Many accounts have been published of the perilous state of the nation Israel in the past 75 years especially, to say nothing of the two millennia preceding that date. The following provide excellent overviews from both secular and biblical viewpoints: From a journalistic point of view, *Lightning Out of Israel. The Six-Day War in the Middle East* (The Associated Press, 1967); For the Second Temple and First Christian Century, see Flavius Josephus, "Wars of the Jews," Books I–VII, 429–605, *Complete Works of Josephus* (Grand Rapids: Kregel, 1995); repr. of William Whiston (Edinburgh: William P. Nimmo, n.d.); Max I. Dimont, *The Indestructible Jews* (New York: Signet, 1973); S. Ettinger, "The Modern Period," *A History of the Jewish People*, ed. H. H. Ben-Sasson (Cambridge, MA: Harvard University Press, 1976), 1040–1096; Edward Flannery, *The Anguish of the Jews: Twenty-Three Centuries of Antisemitism* (New York: Paulist Press, 1985); Irving Howe and Carl Gershman, *Israel, the Arabs and the Middle East* (New York: Bantam, 1972); Benjamin Netanyahu, *A Durable Peace: Israel and Its Place among the Nations* (New York: Warner, 2000). Helpful articles and essays may now be found in *War and Religion: An Encyclopedia of Faith and Conflict*, ed. Jeffrey M. Shaw and Timothy J. Demy, 3 vols. (Santa Barbara, CA: ABC-CLIO), 2017. For the Six-Day War, see vol. 3, 751–754; for the Yom Kippur War, vol. 3, 870–873; Abraham Rabinovich. *The Yom Kippur War: The Epic Encounter That Transformed the Middle East* (Prague: Schocken, 2005).

Malachi 3:1; 4:1-5

The Messiah as Messenger of the Lord

E. RAY CLENDENEN

The TV show "Alfred Hitchcock Presents" aired from 1955 to 1965. It always began with a line drawing of a man in profile, into which the rotund Alfred Hitchcock walked. The drawing fit him perfectly. The New Testament writers and (according to them) even Jesus Himself declared that Jesus is found in the Old Testament (cf. Lk 24:27; Jn 1:45; 5:39,46; Ac 3:24; 10:43; 26:22). Christians disagree over how to describe the nature of that discovery and how certain "messianic passages" in the OT are to be interpreted. But Jesus' statement that Moses "wrote about me" (Jn 5:46) implies a high degree of intentionality and understanding on Moses' part. No NT writer would be shocked or disappointed to find that a book had been written that laid out the OT teaching about Jesus the Messiah.

Paul wrote that "the sacred Scriptures [in the OT] . . . are able to give you wisdom for salvation through faith in Christ Jesus" (2Tm 3:15). Like the line drawing, the OT leaves out a great deal that the NT fills in. Nevertheless, the NT revelation of Jesus fits perfectly the OT composite "line drawing" of Him that is found in so many places. One of those places is Mal 3:1, which reads, "'See, I am going to send [m]y messenger, and he will clear the way before [m]e. Then the Lord you seek will suddenly come to [h]is temple, the [m]essenger of the covenant you desire—see, he is coming,' says the LORD of Hosts" (the pronouns have been lowercased for the sake of our study). The primary challenge in interpreting this verse is to identify the various agents involved. They are as follows:

"I/my/me"
"my messenger/he"
"the Lord (*ha'adon*)/his [temple]"
"the messenger of the covenant/he"
"the LORD of Hosts"

The concluding phrase, "says the LORD of Hosts," apparently identifies the initial "I/my/me" as God, the one being quoted by the prophet. Identifying the other three agents is more difficult. The tradition of identifying "my messenger/he" with John the Baptist and the other two phrases with the Messiah Jesus has a very long history. According to John Calvin, for example, by "the Lord" the prophet "speaks distinctly of Christ, who is afterwards called the Angel or Messenger of the covenant."[1] We must consider here whether the textual evidence supports this tradition, especially since some contemporary scholars reject it. Rikk E. Watts, for example, concludes, "The key point is that Mal. 3 makes no mention of a messianic figure."[2]

But first, we must put the passage in context. After defeating Babylon, the Persians had allowed the exiled Jewish people to return to Judah. But the population was under the control of a Persian governor (Mal 1:8). The temple had been rebuilt (515 BC) and worship established (Mal 1:6-11; 2:1-3; 3:1,10), but the initial excitement and enthusiasm of the returnees had waned. The social and religious problems Malachi addressed reflect the situation portrayed in Ezr 9 and 10 and Neh 5 and 13, suggesting dates not long before Ezra's return (c. 460 BC) or Nehemiah's second term as governor (Neh 13:6-7; c. 435 BC). Linguistic data favors the earlier date.[3]

Malachi presents Judah's sins largely on their own lips, quoting their words, thoughts, and attitudes (1:2,6,7,12-13; 2:14,17; 3:7-8,13-15). He was faced with a failure of leadership. The priests were failing to fear God and to serve the people conscientiously during times of financial insecurity, religious skepticism, and personal disappointments (perhaps including locusts and drought, 3:11). This failure had contributed to Judah's indifference to God. Blaming their economic and social troubles on the Lord's supposed unfaithfulness, the people were treating one another faithlessly (especially their wives) and were profaning the temple by marrying pagan women. Since they surmised that the Lord had not been faithful to His promises to care for His people (the wicked were prospering while the righteous were suffering), they were selfishly taking care of themselves with no sense of responsibility or regard for one another. This included their self-protective sense of ownership of their personal property, causing them not only to bring God their worst animals as "sacrifices," but also to refuse to pay the tithes on which the temple personnel, the Levites and priests, depended for their livelihood.

Most scholars analyze the book of Malachi as consisting of six oracles or disputations. The fourth spans 2:17–3:5 (or 3:6 or 3:7). Andrew Hill, for example, titles this oracle "Judgment and Purification,"[4] and Marvin Sweeney titles it "Argument that YHWH's Messenger will Come to Establish Justice."[5] The position taken here, however, is that Malachi's message is communicated in three interrelated addresses:

I. Priests Exhorted to Honor Yahweh (1:1–2:9)
  A. Positive motivation: the Lord's love (1:2-5)
    B. Situation: failure to honor the Lord (1:6-9)
      C. Command: stop the vain offerings (1:10)
    B'. Situation: priests profane the Lord's name (1:11-14)
  A'. Negative motivation: results of disobedience (2:1-9)
II. Judah Exhorted to Faithfulness (2:10–3:6)
  A. Positive motivation: spiritual kinship (2:10a)
    B. Situation: faithlessness (2:10b-15a)
      C. Command: stop acting faithlessly (2:15b-16)
    B'. Situation: complaints of the Lord's injustice (2:17)
  A'. Negative motivation: coming messenger of judgment (3:1-6)
III. Judah Exhorted to Return to the Lord (3:7–4:6)
  A. Command: return to the Lord with tithes (3:7-10a)
    B. Positive motivation: future blessing (3:10b-12)
      C. Situation: complacency in serving the Lord (3:13-15)
    B'. Negative Motivation: the coming day of the Lord (3:16–4:3)
  A'. Command: remember the law (4:4-6)

Each address contains five sections arranged in a mirror-like repetitive structure surrounding a central section (a b c b a). The first two addresses begin with *positive motivation* or *hope* (1:2-5; 2:10a) and end with *negative motivation* or *judgment* (2:1-9; 3:1-6). In between is God's *indictment* (1:6-9; 1:11-14; 2:10b-15a; 2:17), with His *commands* being in the center (1:10; 2:15b-16). The final (climactic) address begins and ends with *commands* to repent (3:7-10a; 4:4-6). In between are sections of *motivation* (3:10b-12; 3:16–4:3), with the *indictment* being in the center (3:13-15).[6]

Malachi 3:1-6 concludes the second address that focuses on the issue of unfaithfulness. The logical connection between 2:10-16 and 2:17–3:6, however, is not immediately apparent. The key is v. 16, where Malachi says that the unfaithful man who "hates and divorces" his wife will find his garment covered with "injustice" (*chamas*), that is, "cold-blooded and unscrupulous infringement of the personal rights of others, motivated by greed and hate and often making use of physical violence and brutality."[7] Such a traitor to his marital responsibilities, who would deny his wife the very things he had pledged to provide—devotion, care, companionship, protection, intimacy, peace, justice (Gn 2:24; Ex 21:10; Dt 22:13-19; Prv 5:15-20)—stood condemned by God, and he wore the stain of his crime like a garment for all to see (Ps 73:6).[8] According to 2:17, the people were claiming that the Lord was guilty of the same thing as the treacherous husbands: injustice and, therefore, unfaithfulness. He was failing to punish the wicked. In effect, they complained, "Where is this God of justice [*mishpat*] we have heard about? We don't see any sign of Him. Maybe He really delights in wickedness, or maybe He just doesn't care." The people's words betrayed a basic attitude of unbelief and amounted to a blasphemous refusal to believe what the Lord had said in Scripture, that those who do evil are "detestable" (Dt 18:12). Consequently, God says that Israel's words had metaphorically "wearied" Him, meaning that God's patience was running out (cf. Isa 43:24).

Amazingly, God condescends to answer them in 3:1-6 (the chapter division after 2:17 is unfortunate), but His answer announces a coming day of *mishpat* that will be different from what they expect or desire. These verses consist of four main predictions and their accompanying results (notice the change from first person to third, then back to first):

1. See, I am going to send [m]y messenger (v. 1).
2. Then the Lord you seek will suddenly come to [h]is temple (v. 1).
3. He will purify the sons of Levi (v. 3).
4. I will come to you in judgment [*mishpat*] (v. 5).[9]

The speaker throughout is God, the "Lord of Hosts"/Armies (see 3:1,5). He refers to Himself in the first person in predictions one and four, but in the third person in predictions two and three. There he is "the Lord" (*ha'adon*). The Hebrew word *'adon*, "lord," plus the definite article prefix *ha* occurs seven times elsewhere in Scripture and always refers to Yahweh (Ex 23:17; 34:23; Isa 1:24; 3:1; 10:16,33; 19:4). It is God Himself who will "suddenly come to [h]is temple." This is confirmed by the clause (lit.) "whom you are seeking," which is logically connected to the question in 2:17, "Where is the God of justice?" It is also confirmed by the place of His coming as "[h]is temple" (cf. 2Sm 22:7; Ps 18:6; 27:4; 29:9; Jer 50:28; 51:11).

Who is "[m]y messenger" in v. 1? Almost all scholars identify him as a prophet (cf. 2Chr 36:15-16) and see this passage as parallel to 4:5, where God says, "Look, I am going to send you Elijah the prophet before the great and awesome Day of the Lord comes." Although some consider 4:4-6 (Hb. 3:22-24) to be a later editorial addition to the book, a strong case can be made for its being original.[10] But regardless, Jesus identified both passages (3:1; 4:5) as predicting John the Baptist (Mt 11:10-14; cf.

Mt 17:10-13; Lk 1:17). Verbal and semantic parallels between Mal 3:1 and Isa 40:3 suggest an identification between "[m]y messenger" and the "voice" that cries out, "Prepare the way of the LORD in the wilderness." The phrase "prepare the way" uses the same Hebrew words as "clear the way" in Mal 3:1 (it is also found in Isa 57:14 and 62:10, but there God's people are the ones coming from exile). The identification is also made in Mk 1:2-3. The NT also quotes Mal 3:1 in Mt 11:10 and Lk 7:27. All three passages interpret "[m]y messenger" as referring to John the Baptist and Jesus as the One whose way [h]e prepared (cf. Mt 3:3; Lk 3:4; Jn 1:23, which connect Isa 40:3 to John the Baptist). Each quotation changes Malachi's "I am going to send My messenger" to "I am sending My messenger ahead of You" (alluding to Ex 23:20 where God says to [h]is people, "I am going to send an angel [*mal'ak* can refer either to an "angel," that is, a supernatural messenger from the heavenly court, or to a human "messenger"[11]] before you to protect you on the way and bring you to the place I have prepared") and changes "clear the way before *Me*" to "prepare your way ahead of *You*." Jesus and the Gospel writers interpret the One whose way is preceded and prepared for by a messenger as Jesus Himself, who is therefore identified with Yahweh of Armies, whose temple He would enter and whose priests He would cleanse (Mal 3:2-4).[12]

But who is "the [m]essenger of the covenant"? Since the term *mal'ak* is used twice, both in "my messenger" and in "the [m]essenger of the covenant," it would be natural to assume the identity of the two is the same.[13] Nevertheless, the structure of 3:1b seems to dictate that the second "[m]essenger" is not the prophetic forerunner but rather "the Lord." The parallel between the two is clearer in a more literal translation:

And suddenly he will *come* to his temple—
  the Lord
    whom you are seeking ['asher 'attem mebaqshim]
  even/and the messenger of the covenant
    in whom you delight ['asher 'attem chaphetsim]—
see, He is *coming*.

The context makes clear that "whom you are seeking" and "in whom you delight" are ironic, and the sense could be captured by translating, "whom you claim to seek" and "in whom you claim to delight." The root *chaphats* occurs four times in Malachi (1:10; 2:17; 3:1,12) and refers to delighting in, being pleased with, or wanting/desiring something (or someone). It occurs several times elsewhere as well in parallel with either *biqesh* (Ps 40:14[15]; 70:2[3]; Ecc 12:10) or *darash* (1Chr 28:9; Ps 111:2; Isa 58:2), synonyms meaning to "seek." This, in addition to the other lexical (*bo'*, "come") and structural parallels in the verse, supports the contention that "the Lord" and "the [m]essenger of the covenant" both refer to the same person.[14]

This raises a problem, however. If "the Lord" refers to God, how could He also be "the [m]essenger of the covenant"? To be a messenger implies being sent. Who could send God? R. T. France recognizes the parallel between "the Lord" and "the [m]essenger of the covenant" but argues that "the Lord" does not refer to God but to "my messenger," since *'adon* can refer to man as "master, lord."[15] He claims that although *ha'adon* always refers to Yahweh, it is only a title whose meaning is determined by context. But aside from the problem of usage, why would a human prophetic messenger be referred to as "the Lord," who is coming to "[h]is temple"? "The Lord" must refer to God.[16]

Others reject the parallel identification of "the Lord" and "the [m]essenger of the covenant," and argue that the latter must refer to "my messenger." So the second half of the verse simply repeats the first half, using a different designation for the messenger. This might be a reasonable solution if the parallel construction were not so clear. Furthermore, if the second messenger is simply a prophet, then the following relative clause *'asher 'attem chaphetsim* would probably mean "in *which* you delight," referring to "the covenant." Nothing in the context suggests they were *wanting* a messenger. Although it is true that their "delight" is ironic,[17] this does not eliminate the fact that 2:17 says nothing about their looking for a "messenger." But delight in a covenant is almost equally foreign to the context. Elsewhere, Malachi refers to the "covenant with Levi" that the priests were violating (2:4-5,8), the "covenant of our fathers" that the people were "profaning" (2:10), and the marital covenant that the men of Judah were violating (2:14). Which covenant was Judah delighting in, pleased with, or wanting? According to 2:17, it was God for whom they were calling. So if "the [m]essenger of the covenant" refers to a prophet, the following relative clause makes no sense. Merrill's interpretation on the basis of John's message being "attractive to those who came to hear him"[18] would have no application to Malachi's audience. Finally, vv. 2-4 describe the work of cleansing and judgment by the one who is "coming." That coming one fits better the God of judgment in vv. 5-6 than the prophetic messenger who prepares His way in 3:1a.[19]

So we are left with the identification of "the Messenger of the covenant" with God. To quote Sherlock Holmes, "When you have eliminated the impossible, whatever remains, however improbable, must be the truth."[20] But what is the significance of God referring to Himself as "the Messenger of the covenant" (*mal'ak habberit*)? The phrase occurs nowhere else in the OT. Some have argued that God speaking of Himself in the third person ("the Lord you seek," "His temple," "the Messenger of the covenant," "He is coming") requires a messianic interpretation.[21] Andrew Malone points out that this is not necessarily the case.[22] In Zch 3:2, for example, we find, "The LORD said to Satan: 'The LORD rebuke you, Satan! May the LORD who has chosen Jerusalem rebuke you!'"[23] Malone argues further that by changing "Me" to "You," it is the Gospels that introduce a distinction between Yahweh and the one whose way would be prepared by "my messenger."[24] He points out that "New Testament commentators [citing D. A. Carson, R. H. Gundry, M. D. Hooker, R. T. France, I. H. Marshall, and D. L. Bock] regularly refuse to see messianic intention in Malachi's original words."[25] He seems to think this trumps the OT scholars he cites who find in Malachi a reference to the Messiah (D. Stuart, J. A. Motyer, O. P. Robertson, W. Kaiser, D. I. Block, J. B. Payne). But the issue will not be decided by measuring scholars.

Malone also rejects the identification of *mal'ak habberit* with *mal'ak yhwh/ ha'elohim*, "the angel/messenger of Yahweh/God." *Mal'ak yhwh* occurs 59 times and *mal'ak ha'elohim* nine times. Though sometimes referring to human messengers (Hag 1:13; Mal 2:7), the "angel" is often treated as if he were Yahweh (Gn 16:7-14; 22:11-18; 31:11-13; Ex 3:2-6; 14:19-25; Nm 22:20-38; Jdg 2:1-5; 6:11-24; 13:8-22; cf. Gn 18:1–19:1; 31:11-13; 32:24-30 [with Hos 12:4]; 48:15-16; Zch 12:8). As P. A. Verhoef explains, "The relationship between 'the Angel' and 'the Lord' is clearly the same as elsewhere in the OT where 'the angel of the Lord' is both identified with and distinguished from God."[26] Malone charges this view with being "obviously inconsistent,"[27] as if it is based simply on the similar use of the word *mal'ak* (which we have determined refers to two different individuals in Mal 3:1). Rather, the identification is based primarily on the similarity of function between *mal'ak habberit* and *mal'ak yhwh/ha'elohim*. Both are "identified with and distinguished from God." Both are "messengers" sent by God who can at the same time speak and be addressed and even *described* as God. Since they were representatives, messengers in the biblical world could at times be addressed as if they were the person who sent them (cf. 2Sm 3:12-13; 1Kg 20:2-6). But the *mal'ak yhwh/ha'elohim* passages listed above seem to go beyond that.

Before we say that the "angel of the Lord" must be the Messiah or the "preincarnate Christ," however, we must take Bruce Waltke's objections seriously.[28] Nowhere does the NT make such an identification. As Waltke says, "The New Testament never lowers the identity of the Son of God to an angel of any sort." Also, the one who announced the birth of the Messiah to Joseph (Mt 1:20) and the one who rolled away the stone from Jesus' tomb (Mt 28:2) are identified as "an angel of the Lord." The Greek is *angelos kuriou*, without the article. The absence of the article, however, does not necessarily mean that the phrase is indefinite. As Dan Wallace notes, "It is not necessary for a noun to have the article in order for it to be definite."[29] In Lk 11:13 the phrase *pneuma hagion*, without the article, is correctly rendered "the Holy Spirit," and in Lk 1:35 *huios theou* is correctly rendered "the Son of God."[30] Regarding *angelos kuriou* he says, "Although most scholars treat *angelos kuriou* in the NT as 'an angel of the Lord,' there is no linguistic basis for doing so."[31] The Septuagint often renders *mal'ak yhwh* as *angelos kuriou* (e.g., Gn 16:7-11; 22:11,15; Ex 3:2; Jdg 2:1; 6:11-12,22; 13:3).

So did Christ announce His own birth and move His own stone? Besides, "angels" are created beings. According to Neh 9:6, "You alone are Yahweh. You created the heavens, the highest heavens with all their host" (cf. Ps 148:2,5). The apostle Paul declared, "For everything was created by Him, in heaven and on earth, the visible and the invisible, whether thrones or dominions or rulers or authorities—all things have been created through Him and for Him" (Col 1:16). Thus, if *mal'ak yhwh* is to be identified in certain passages as a divine manifestation of some sort—whether the preincarnate Christ or otherwise—it would be better rendered "the Messenger of Yahweh."

What may be derived from the *mal'ak yhwh* passages listed above is that the OT can speak of one who is "God" and at the same time the messenger of God. This is also what is happening in Mal 3:1. Regardless of how we understand *mal'ak yhwh,* in Mal 3:1, there is one who is both God and His messenger—one who is sent from God with a message. In Malachi, that message has to do with "the covenant."[32] God's covenant with Israel underlies the entire book, which has sometimes been categorized as a "covenant lawsuit."[33] In fact, as I have argued elsewhere, "The primary mark of the prophetic genre is its apparent intention to preserve the covenant by calling for behavioral changes on the part of the covenant people" (cf. 2Kg 17:13).[34]

Malachi begins with God's declaration of covenant love for Israel, which may be defined as His sovereignly determined attitude of affection and compassion that motivates Him to establish and zealously maintain a relationship with sinful people and to seek their highest good in spite of their rebelliousness. It is that God who was coming as "the Messenger of the covenant" to purify (3:2-4), to judge (3:5-6), to renew His covenant with those who feared Him (3:16-17), to heal them (4:2), and to eliminate the wicked (4:1,3), thus producing a people who would recognize His greatness (Mal 1:5) and worship Him in righteousness (3:3-4) in a "delightful land" (3:12). In the NT, "Jesus takes on the role of the 'messenger of the covenant' in Mal. 3:1."[35]

Like Alfred Hitchcock, Jesus walked into that OT outline of a God/Man sent as the Messenger of the covenant, and He declared the Father's love and became His "righteous Servant" to carry away iniquity (Isa 53:11). Jesus' role as the Messenger of the covenant may be seen in the multiple times He is described as "sent" by the Father (Mt 10:40; 15:24; 21:37; Mk 9:37; Lk 4:18,43; 10:16; Jn 3:17,34; 4:34; 5:23-24,30,36-38; 6:29,38-39,44,57; 7:16,18,28-29,33; 8:16,18,26,29,42; 9:4; 10:36; 11:42; 12:44-45,49; 13:20; 14:24; 15:21; 16:5; 17:3,8,18,21,23,25; 20:21; Ac 3:20,26; 10:36; Rm

8:3; Gal 4:4; 1Jn 4:9-10,14). As Doug Stuart explains, the conundrum of Mal 3:1 is the conundrum of the NT: "How can God both send and be sent? . . . How can [Christ] be sent by God and also be God in the flesh?" The answer, he says, "to the partial extent that humans can comprehend it, is found in the doctrine of the Trinity."[36]

Another clue that Malachi may have had the Messiah in mind is the context of justice and the purification of the Levites. Wolter Rose defines the OT Messiah as "a future royal figure sent by God who will bring salvation to God's people and the world and establish a kingdom characterized by features like peace and justice."[37] The first reference to God's anointed king is in 1Sm 2:10: "The LORD will judge the ends of the earth. He will give power to His king; He will lift up the horn of His anointed." Yahweh's chosen king turned out to be his servant David (cf. 1Sm 13:14; 2Sm 5:2; 19:21; 23:1), among whose descendants would be the eschatological Messiah (2Sm 7:9-20; Jer 30:9) who would "reign on the throne of David and over his kingdom, to establish and sustain it with justice and righteousness from now on and forever" (Isa 9:7).[38] This Davidic King would be "a judge who seeks what is right and is quick to execute justice" (Isa 16:5). He would be "a Righteous Branch of David. He will reign wisely as king and administer justice and righteousness in the land" and would be named "Yahweh Our Righteousness" (Jer 23:5-6; cf. 33:15). Through Ezekiel, the Lord declared, "I will judge between one sheep and another. I will appoint over them a single shepherd, My servant David, and he will shepherd them. He will tend them himself and will be their shepherd. I, Yahweh, will be their God, and My servant David will be a prince among them." (Ezk 34:22-24; cf. 37:24-25).

Several passages also associate this righteous Davidic King with cleansing the temple personnel. The man of God who brought God's message of judgment on Eli also promised, "I will raise up a faithful priest for Myself. He will do whatever is in My heart and mind. I will establish a lasting dynasty for him, and he will walk before My anointed one for all time" (1Sm 2:35). Then after announcing again the "Righteous Branch," who would "administer justice and righteousness in the land," and that "David will never fail to have a man sitting on the throne of the house of Israel," God promised, "The Levitical priests will never fail to have a man always before Me to offer burnt offerings, to burn grain offerings, and to make sacrifices" (Jer 33:15-18). The Lord then underlines His promise in vv. 20-22:

> If you can break My covenant with the day and My covenant with the night so that day and night cease to come at their regular time, then also My covenant with My servant David may be broken so that he will not have a son reigning on his throne, and the Levitical priests will not be My ministers. The hosts of heaven cannot be counted; the sand of the sea cannot be measured. So, too, I will make the descendants of My servant David and the Levites who minister to Me innumerable.

Finally, in Zch 3:8, in the context of the purification of the priesthood, the *mal'ak yhwh* declares to Joshua the high priest and his "colleagues" assisting him at the temple, "These men are a sign that I am about to bring My servant, the Branch." The passage alludes not only to Jer 23:5-6 and 33:15 but also to Isa 4:2 ("On that day the Branch of the LORD will be beautiful and glorious, and the fruit of the land will be the pride and glory of Israel's survivors"), all of which use the same word for "Branch," *tsemach*. The glorious "day" in Isa 4:2 is said to follow the time "when the Lord has washed away the filth [a Hb. word related to "filthy" in Zch 3:4] of the daughters of Zion and cleansed the bloodguilt from the heart of Jerusalem by a spirit of judgment and a spirit of burning" (4:4). As Mark Boda explains, "The reemergence of priestly service in this fourth vision report [Zch 3:1-10] is a sign foreshadowing the reemergence of the royal line through the Sprout [Branch] figure."[39] The link between "Branch" and priest is also present in Zch 6:12-13. The appearance of the Messiah in Mal 3:1, therefore, would be fitting in the context of a prediction of divine justice and of God's cleansing of His Levitical priests.

Thus, the explanation of the use of the phrase *mal'ak habberit* in Mal 3:1 that best accounts for all the data is that, as Stuart proposes, "The verse is overtly messianic in outlook."[40] As Block asserts, "In the Malachi passages, the messenger/prophet announces the coming of the messiah."[41] The view of Malone that the NT has simply "appropriated" the verse ("whereby the attributes and activities of YHWH himself are recognized in and ascribed to Jesus"[42]) is inadequate.

Malachi's message in 3:1, then, was that the God of justice whom the self-righteous Judahites claimed to be seeking in 2:17 was surely coming on a day that He was preparing (3:17; 4:3). But as the Lord told Israel through the prophet Amos (5:18-20), His coming would bring the darkness of judgment on them rather than the light of deliverance because of their sins. Painful refining and purification were required (3:2-3) as the Lord separated the righteous and the wicked (3:18). Before the Lord's coming, He would mercifully send another prophetic messenger to warn the people again.

Then the Lord Himself would come in the person of the divine Messianic King, who would bring the full weight of the covenant curses against all who had refused to fear the Lord. At that time, "all the arrogant and everyone who commits wickedness will become stubble" (4:1). Malachi goes on to explain that judgment was not the end, but the Lord would pour out His compassion on those who feared Him and make them His special possession (3:16-17), healing them with His righteousness (4:2). The Lord came in Jesus the Messiah, but His work of judgment and compassion continues until He comes again. Then, as Peter explained, the "various trials" of those who fear the Lord will be over, and "the genuineness of your faith—more valuable than gold, which perishes though refined by fire—[will] result in praise, glory, and honor at the revelation of Jesus Christ" (1Pt 1:6-7).

1. John Calvin, *Calvin's Commentaries: Complete*, Christian Classics Ethereal Library, https://www.ccel.org/ccel/calvin/commentaries.html (accessed June 30, 2016).
2. Rikk E. Watts, "Mark," in *Commentary on the New Testament Use of the Old Testament*, ed. G. K. Beale and D. A. Carson (Grand Rapids: Baker, 2007), 119.
3. Cf. E. Ray Clendenen, "Malachi," in Richard A. Taylor and E. Ray Clendenen, *Haggai, Malachi: An Exegetical and Theological Exposition of Holy Scripture*, vol. 21A, The New American Commentary (Nashville: B&H, 2004), 205-7.
4. Andrew E. Hill, *Malachi*, vol. 25D, Anchor Bible (New York: Doubleday, 1998), 259.
5. Marvin A. Sweeney, *Berit Olam: The Twelve Prophets* (Collegeville, MN: The Liturgical Press, 2000), 739.
6. See E. Ray Clendenen, "The Structure of Malachi: A Textlinguistic Study," *Criswell Theological Review* 2 (1987): 3-17; idem, "Malachi," 227-31.
7. H. Haag, "*chāmās*," in *Theological Dictionary of the Old Testament*, eds. G. J. Botterweck and H. Ringgren (Grand Rapids: Eerdmans, 1980), 4:482.
8. Clendenen, "Malachi," 369.
9. Ibid., 383.
10. Ibid., 455.
11. R. E. Watts argues that Mal 3:1 itself alludes to Ex 23:20: "In both cases the sending of the messenger prior to Yahweh's personal intervention is the consequence of Israel's faithlessness" (*Isaiah's New Exodus in Mark* [Grand Rapids: Baker, 2000], 72). Cf. G. K. Beale, *A New Testament Biblical Theology: The Unfolding of the Old Testament in the New* (Grand Rapids: Baker, 2011), 392, who sees Mal 3:1 as alluding to Ex 23:20 and interpreting Isa 40:3. He says, "The Exodus text speaks of God's sovereign guidance of Israel's way to the land at the first exodus, and Malachi, utilizing the Exodus language, foresees another exodus, when God's way will be prepared to come in judgment upon Israel" (p. 695).
12. W. D. Davies and D. C. Allison, *Matthew 8-18*, International Critical Commentary, vol. 2 (London: T&T Clark, 1991), 250: "So Jesus has replaced Yahweh." On the use of Mal in Mt 11:10 see J. B. DeYoung, "The Function of Malachi 3.1 in Matthew 11.10," in *The Gospels and the Scriptures of Israel*, ed. C. A. Evans and W. R. Stegner (Sheffield: Sheffield Academic, 1994), 66-91; also the work of Craig Blomberg (on Mt 11:10), Rikk E. Watts (on Mk 1:2-3), and David W. Pao and Eckhard J. Schnabel (on Lk 7:27) in Beale and Carson, *Commentary on the New Testament Use of the Old Testament*, 38-40, 113-20, 300-3.
13. E. H. Merrill, *An Exegetical Commentary: Haggai, Zechariah, Malachi* (Chicago: Moody Publishers, 1994), 429.
14. Cf. A. S. Malone, "Is the Messiah Announced in Malachi 3:1?" *Tyndale Bulletin* 57.2 (2006), 219.
15. R. T. France, *Jesus and the Old Testament* (London: Tyndale, 1971), 91.
16. Cf. Watts, *Isaiah's New Exodus in Mark*, 69; Hill, *Malachi*, Anchor Bible 25D (New York: Doubleday, 1998), 268, 287; Malone, "Is the Messiah Announced in Malachi 3:1?" 218-19.
17. Merrill, *An Exegetical Commentary: Haggai, Zechariah, Malachi*, 433; A. R. Petterson, *Haggai, Zechariah, and Malachi*, Apollos Old Testament Commentary (Nottingham, England; Downers Grove, IL: Apollos/IVP, 2015), 362.
18. Merrill, *An Exegetical Commentary: Haggai, Zechariah, Malachi*, 433.
19. Cf. Watts, *Isaiah's New Exodus in Mark*, 70 (although he seems to have changed his view in Beale and Carson, *Commentary on the New Testament Use of the Old Testament*, 117); Petterson, *Haggai, Zechariah, and Malachi*, 363. Mark Boda identifies the two messengers of 3:1 and sees the agent who refines the Levites in 3:2-4 as "YHWH with this messenger at his side" ("Figuring the Future: The Prophets and Messiah," in *The Messiah in the Old and New Testaments*, ed. S. E. Porter [Grand Rapids: Eerdmans, 2007], 71).
20. Arthur Conan Doyle, *The Sign of the Four* (1890; repr., New York: Oxford University Press, 1993), 41.
21. Cf. W. A. Grudem, *Systematic Theology* (Downers Grove, IL: InterVarsity, 1994), 228; J. S. Feinberg, *No One Like Him* (Wheaton, IL: Crossway, 2001), 454.

22. Malone, "Is the Messiah Announced in Malachi 3:1?," 222–24.

23. Note, however, Mark Boda's comment: "Even when Yahweh spoke in v. 2, the speech refers to him in the third person, suggesting that it was actually spoken by the messenger of Yahweh" (*The Book of Zechariah,* New International Commentary on the Old Testament [Grand Rapids: Eerdmans, 2016], 227; see also p. 232).

24. Ibid., 224.

25. Ibid.

26. P. A. Verhoef, *The Books of Haggai and Malachi,* New International Commentary on the Old Testament (Grand Rapids: Eerdmans, 1987), 289. Cf. J. G. Baldwin, *Haggai, Zechariah, Malachi,* Tyndale Old Testament Commentaries (Downers Grove, IL: InterVarsity, 1972); R. L. Smith, *Micah-Malachi,* Word Biblical Commentary (Waco, TX: Word, 1984), 327; B. Glazier-McDonald, *Malachi: The Divine Messenger* (Atlanta: Scholars Press, 1987), 131.

27. Malone, "Is the Messiah Announced in Malachi 3:1?," 225.

28. B. K. Waltke, *An Old Testament Theology* (Grand Rapids: Zondervan, 2007), 363.

29. Dan Wallace, *Greek Grammar Beyond the Basics* (Grand Rapids: Zondervan, 1996), 243.

30. Cf. ibid., 248–52.

31. Ibid., 252.

32. Cf. S. L. McKenzie and H. N. Wallace, "Covenant Themes in Malachi," *Catholic Biblical Quarterly* 45 (1983): 549–63.

33. J. O'Brien, *Priest and Levite in Malachi,* Society of Biblical Literature Dissertation Series 121 (Atlanta: Scholars Press, 1990), 63. But see the critique in Hill, *Malachi,* 31–33.

34. E. R. Clendenen, "Interpreting the Minor Prophets for Preaching," *Faith and Mission* 13 (1995): 57.

35. Pao and Schnabel, "Luke," in Beale and Carson, *Commentary on the New Testament Use of the Old Testament,* 303.

36. Douglas Stuart, "Malachi," *The Minor Prophets: An Exegetical and Expository Commentary,* ed. T. E. McComiskey (Grand Rapids: Baker, 1998), 3:1353.

37. Wolter H. Rose, *Zemah and Zerubbabel: Messianic Expectations in the Early Postexilic Period* (Sheffield: Sheffield Academic Press, 2000), 23.

38. Cf. Daniel I. Block, "My Servant David: Ancient Israel's Vision of the Messiah," in *Israel's Messiah in the Bible and the Dead Sea Scrolls,* ed. R. S. Hess and M. Daniel Carroll (Eugene, OR: Wipf & Stock, 2003), 36–49.

39. Boda, *The Book of Zechariah,* 255.

40. Stuart, "Malachi," 1351.

41. Block, "My Servant David: Ancient Israel's Vision of the Messiah," 32.

42. Malone, "Is the Messiah Announced in Malachi 3:1?," 228.

Scripture Index

Old Testament

Genesis

1 172, 619, 714, 721
1-2 715, 724–725
1-3 504
1-11 241–242, 245, 249
1-48 123
1:1 218–219, 223, 619, 740–741, 751, 753, 1320
1:1-2:3 170
1:2 163, 170, 208, 619, 1179, 1320
1:3 208
1:3-4 1320
1:3-5, 14-18 1320
1:4 209
1:4, 7 171
1:5 1050, 1060
1:5, 8, 13, 19, 23, 31 170, 1168
1:6-8 171
1:9-10 751
1:11 551
1:11, 12 551
1:11, 12, 29 619
1:11, 29 482
1:14 171
1:14-16 171
1:22 138
1:22, 28 171
1:24 454
1:26 352, 771, 1132
1:26, 28 304, 345, 505, 508
1:26, 28-30 165
1:26-28 151, 187, 635
1:26-31 619
1:27 137
1:28 162, 163, 164, 241, 287, 304, 509, 715, 771, 1041
1:28-2:2 163
1:28-31 246
1:28a 137
1:28b 137
1:29-30 850
1:31a 171
2 172, 619
2-3 253, 774
2-11 771
2:1 618–619
2:1-3 170
2:1-4 171
2:1-6 138
2:2 165, 171
2:2-3 165
2:3 165, 171
2:4 171
2:4-4:26 170
2:7 454
2:7-16 242
2:8 172, 242, 253
2:8-9 163, 246
2:9 171
2:10-15 164
2:11, 13 241
2:12 165, 171
2:15 138, 164, 171
2:15-17 866
2:16-17 242
2:17 149, 151, 242, 243, 774
2:18-20 163
2:18-24 349–350
2:19 138, 165
2:22-3:1, 6 165
2:24 350, 351, 352, 353–354, 1330
2:25 253, 775
3 52, 53, 130, 149, 245, 509, 770, 771, 774–777, 778, 1238
3:1, 14 164
3:1-6 345
3:4 149
3:6 163, 164, 243, 246
3:7 253
3:7, 21 163
3:7a 246
3:7b 247
3:8 151, 164, 170, 171, 172
3:8-9, 13a 244
3:8-19 1110
3:14 163, 244, 247
3:14, 17 163, 242
3:14-15 150, 260
3:14-19 220
3:15 52, 58, 124, 130, 131, 149, 150, 151, 163, 164, 166, 177, 179, 202, 219–220, 239–249, 242, 244, 247, 248, 255, 282, 304, 305, 345, 510, 632, 668, 771, 774, 775, 792, 957, 1044
3:15b 249
3:16 130, 150, 163, 243, 778
3:17 150
3:17-19 245, 509
3:19 138, 150, 163, 242
3:20 774
3:21 151, 171, 254
3:22 151, 165
3:22-24 1110
3:23-24 163, 164, 242, 244
3:24 165, 171
4 245
4:1 743
4:1, 25 774
4:3-5 177
4:7 130
4:7a 243
4:7b 243
4:8 163, 243

4:9-10 244
4:10-11 244
4:11 163, 242
4:14, 16 244
4:16 172, 241, 242
4:17, 25 244
4:17-24 261
4:25 207, 242, 245, 248, 261
4:25-26 221
4:26 261
5 260, 346
5:1 207
5:1-2 137
5:5 151
5:5, 8, 11, 14, 17, 20, 27, 31 242
5:22 151
5:22, 24 454
5:29 163, 242, 245, 261
6-9 751
6:1-2 163
6:7 163, 251
6:9 151, 252, 454
6:11-21 261
6:18 1036
7:6-9 163
7:22 242
8-9 1051, 1060
8:1 163
8:20 177
8:20-22 251
8:22 1050, 1060
9 253, 454, 866
9:1 253
9:1-7 251
9:1-9 163, 246
9:1-17 936
9:2 163
9:4-6 936
9:8-17 261, 635, 1036
9:9 251
9:12-16 1110
9:12-17 251
9:20 246, 253
9:20-21 252
9:20-27 251–252
9:21 163
9:21-22, 24 253
9:21a 246
9:21b-22 246
9:22 252
9:23 163, 247, 252
9:24 252
9:25 163, 242, 253
9:25-27 247, 251–258
9:26 248, 254, 255
9:26-27 163, 242, 247, 255
9:27 256, 257
9:27b 256
9:29 242
10 254
10-11 1060
10:2-5 256
10:5 256
10:6 254
10:6-20 254
10:7-14 254
10:21 255
10:21-31 255
11 254, 260, 261, 454, 797
11:1-9 164, 242, 1183
11:10 242, 255
11:10-26 254, 255
11:10-32 282, 346
11:27 231, 255
11:27-22:19 260
11:27-25:11 261
11:27-32 231
11:28, 32 242
11:30 231, 265
12 397, 454
12, 15, 17 1060
12-15 266
12-22 260
12:1-3 163, 164, 255, 259–268, 272, 385, 610, 632, 669, 935, 1279
12:1-4 414
12:1-7 219
12:2 388
12:2-3 286, 397, 468, 539
12:3 52, 156, 164, 241, 242, 248, 257, 286, 349, 771, 953, 1026, 1027, 1029, 1032, 1102, 1135
12:5-7 254
12:7 266, 389
12:7-8 177
12:8 1060
12:10-20 351
13:4, 18 177, 1060
13:6 1015
13:15 394, 1101
13:15, 16 539
13:16 1051
13:17 1022
14 139, 207
14:1-24 771
14:8-12 139
14:14 216
14:17-24 1248
14:18 137, 139, 682, 1077
14:18-20 1060
14:19, 22 743
14:19-20 139, 266, 682
14:20 454, 682
15 267, 397, 1026, 1028, 1217
15:1 454, 1180
15:1-6 395
15:2 216
15:2, 8 392
15:5 95, 151, 1015, 1051
15:12-16 1180
15:12-21 632
15:13 454, 1180
15:16 253, 406
15:17-21 272
15:18 242
15:18-21 254, 266, 1022, 1036, 1189
16 151
16:1-16 267
16:2 152
16:3-4 152
16:6 152, 454
16:7 152
16:7-11 1334
16:7-14 1333
16:8-10 152
16:11 819
16:11-12 152
16:13 152
16:14 152, 751
16:15-16 152
17, 49 1060
17:1 454
17:1-8, 15-21 632
17:1-21 1036
17:1-27 267
17:2, 6 241
17:6 124, 151, 281

17:6, 15-16 272
17:6, 16 262, 310, 362, 771
17:7, 8, 10, 19 539
17:7, 13 ,19 1110
17:7-8 394
17:8 1101
17:10, 11, 13, 14 396
17:19 819
18 151
18:1-19:1 1333
18:18 539, 771
19 315
19:14 968
19:25 807, 1226
19:30-38 343
19:37 859
20:7 136
21 152
21:12 256
21:17 152
21:18 152
21:22-34 771
21:33 396
22 265, 1310
22:9 177
22:11, 15 1334
22:11-18 1333
22:13 971
22:15 265
22:16-18 259–268
22:17 242, 248, 266, 304, 1015, 1051, 1102
22:17-18 126, 539
22:17b 266
22:17b-18 632
22:17b-19 124, 151
22:18 266, 468, 539, 771
22:20-25:11 260
22:23 260
23:1-20 260
23:6 771
24:1-67 260
24:14 820
24:16 820
24:43 820
24:60 242, 248, 304
25:1-11 260
25:11 231
25:12 231
25:12-18 261
25:14 748
25:19-23:18 346
25:19-35:29 261, 262
25:21-34 348
25:23 539
25:25 1002
25:29-34 262
25:31-33 1002
25:34 262
26:3-4 632
26:4 539, 1015
26:5 56
26:25 177, 563
27:27-29 262, 632
27:29 219, 248, 286
27:29, 40 539
28:3 539
28:3-4 163
28:10-12 152
28:12-15 1180
28:13 152
28:13-14 346, 539, 1101
28:13-15 256
28:18 877
29:35 280
30:1 442
31 152
31:11-13 1333
31:13 30, 152, 231
31:54 177
32:20 179, 798
32:24-30 1333
32:28 1023
33:20 177
35:1, 3, 7 177
35:10 1023
35:11 281, 310, 539, 771
35:21 179
36:1-37:1 261
37 264
37-50 262, 263–264
37:2-50:26 261
37:5-7, 9-11 1180
37:5-10 263
37:8 263, 574
37:9-10 539, 1028
37:25-28 280
37:26-27 281
38 263, 280, 351
38:1-11 280
38:11 281
38:12-26 280
38:18 1227
38:18, 25 1227
38:27-30 346
39:6 574
40:5-23 1180
41:16-36 1180
42:9 1180
42:37-38 281
43:8-11 281
44:14 281
44:18-34 264
44:24-28 281
44:33 264
46:1 177
48 263
48:4 539
48:15 1103, 1200, 1310
49 52, 55, 64, 123, 194, 221, 248, 297, 298, 370, 584, 586, 772, 792, 910, 1061
49:1 31, 99, 124f2, 220, 248, 297, 298, 301, 303, 583, 795, 1031
49:1, 8 304
49:1, 8-12 95, 220–221, 288, 298, 305, 1054
49:1, 10-12 201
49:1-27 271
49:1-28 771
49:3 741
49:8 219, 242, 298, 539
49:8, 10 346
49:8-11 124
49:8-12 124, 151, 165, 166, 248, 271–283 287, 294, 298, 302, 583, 742, 771
49:8a 583
49:8b 584
49:9 64, 96, 221, 282, 287, 294, 295, 296, 298, 302, 303
49:9-10 297, 298, 1161, 1204
49:9b 771
49:10 30, 31, 139, 209, 220, 233, 256, 257, 271–279, 274, 287, 288, 303,

	310, 362, 369, 377, 632, 771, 798, 810, 1029, 1073, 1077–1078, 1079, 1083, 1104, 1263, 1273
49:10-12	202
49:10a	584
49:10b	584
49:11	221, 275, 584, 1007, 1265
49:11-12	771
49:12	274, 584
49:17	240
49:23-24	1200
49:24	798, 877, 1103, 1310
49:28	287
50	123
50:5	563
50:20	263

Exodus

1	1028
1-2	95
1:7	164
1:10, 16	335
1:12	287
1:15-16	348
1:22	1027
2	287
2:1-10	169
2:1ff	95
2:6	380
2:8	820
2:11	840
2:14	169, 333
2:15	169
3	328
3:1-6	37, 1017
3:2	169, 1334
3:2-6	1333
3:5	167
3:7	1268
3:7-8	840
3:12	793
3:13	752
3:13-14	751
3:13-15	751
3:20	36
4	161, 331
4:1	333
4:3	331
4:6	331
4:8-9, 17, 28, 30	818
4:19-20a	166
4:20	161, 162
4:21	1241
4:22	752, 984, 1027
4:22-23	107
5:23	1085
6:7	1155, 1226
6:16-20	140
7	136
7:1	140
7:1-2	136
7:3	818
7:3, 9	1241
7:20	1317
10:1-2	818
10:1-15	1178
11	1027
11:9-10	1241
12:7	167
12:11	968
12:31	968
12:42	201
13:3, 14	947
13:13	971
13:21	797, 811
13:21-22	1111
14:5	169
14:16, 21, 29	167
14:19-25	1333
14:21	852
14:23-31	1027
15	123, 124, 362, 368, 370
15, 17	336
15:1, 4, 19, 21	1226
15:1-4	368
15:1-18, 21	362
15:2	812–813, 852
15:3	752, 1322
15:4	169
15:8	167
15:11	36, 750
15:17-18	793
15:18	368
15:24	333
15:27	947
16:2-3	333
16:4	161
16:7	916
16:8	333
16:10	811, 1111
17:2-3	333
17:4	333
17:6	876, 881, 917, 947
17:6, 8-16	1317
17:11-13	168
17:16	201, 299
18	169
18:17-23	140
18:26	140
19	1036
19:1	169
19:4	1065
19:4-6	279, 953
19:5-6	984, 1036, 1060
19:6	35, 164, 811, 984, 1110
19:7	923
19:9	811
19:16	811
19:21	1029
19:24	1060
20:1-17	242
20:2	947
20:5	971
20:7	752, 1322
20:12	252
20:18-19	169
20:19	140
20:21	811
20:24	576, 1322
20:26	171
21:4, 22	454
21:6	901
21:10	1330
21:32	114, 1157, 1280
21:33	563
22:5-6	215
23:15	839
23:16	1188
23:17	1330
23:20	1331
23:20-21	1017
24:1, 9-11	172
24:2	1030
24:3	172
24:3, 7	923
24:7-8	1037
24:8	179
24:9-11	793
24:14-18	172
24:15	811
24:16-17	916
24:18	336
25:1	170
25:6	171

25:7 171
25:8 1110
25:18-22 171
25:22 171
25:32-36 171
26:31 171
26:33 171, 1143
27:2 879
27:19 1267
27:20 171
28 1159
28:3, 41 171
28:4, 37, 39 1079
28:9-14, 20 171
28:36 707
28:36-38 1239
29 180
29:5, 8 171
29:6 707, 1079
29:45-46 1110
30:11, 17, 22, 34 170
30:17-21 1302
30:26 30
30:30 191
31:1, 12 170
31:2-3 853
31:3 170, 849
31:12-18 171
31:16 396, 1110
32 56, 171, 180, 620
32-34 141, 468
32:11-13 141
32:12 620
32:30-32 334
32:34 922
33:7-11 140, 332
33:20 890
34:5-7 751
34:6 469, 596, 599, 620, 1178
34:7 971
34:10 36, 793
34:20 971
34:23 1330
34:27 947
34:28 167, 336
35:8 171
35:18 1267
35:31 170, 849
39:3 171
39:28 1079
39:30 707
39:32 171
39:43a 171
39:43b 171
40:9 1143
40:9, 11 30
40:9-11 201
40:14 171
40:33b 171
40:34 811
40:34-38 1111
49:1 124
49:7 114
50:6 114
53:2 114
53:3 114

Leviticus

1 181
1-7 177, 181
1:1-6:13 181
1:4 179
1:5 178
2 181
3:2, 8, 13 178
4:1-5:13 182
4:1-21 183
4:3 30
4:3, 5, 16 370
4:3-12 179
4:6, 17 179
4:7, 18 179
4:13 183
4:13-21 971
4:16, 17 178
4:22-35 183
4:25 179
5 180, 184
5:1-4 183
5:2 184
5:3-4 184
5:5-13 183
5:14-6:7 32, 184
5:14-19 184
6-7 181
6:2-5 184
6:8-13 181
6:14-7:38 181
6:14-18 181
6:22 370
6:24-30 182
7:1-10 184
7:2, 14 179
7:20 1146
8-9 180
8:7, 13 171
8:9 707, 1079
8:10 1143
8:14-15 169
10-16 178
11-15 183
12 178, 184
13:2 178
13:9 326
14:7 178
14:10-20 184
15:1-18 184
16 177, 183, 185, 1030
16:4 171, 1079
16:16, 30 185
16:21-22 181
16:22 971
17:11 329
18 98, 252, 253
18-20 1143
18:5 98
18:6-18 252
18:20 1307
19:9-10 354
19:11, 15, 17 1307
19:12 752
19:17 1307
21:2f 958
22:18-25 181
23:22 354
23:33-42 1188
23:33-43 812
23:33-44 1221
23:34 1188
24:8 396, 1110
24:11, 16 1295
24:19 1307
25 1140
25:10 938, 990
25:13 199
25:14-15, 17 1307
25:25 442, 958
25:25, 35, 47 1103
26 669, 852, 965, 1084
26:1 1159
26:1-13 1024
26:4 1173
26:4, 6 1109
26:4-13 1090, 1091t, 1109
26:5-6 1189
26:12 170, 171, 1030
26:13 840
26:14-17 1037
26:14-46 1024
26:33 242

26:34-35, 43 1141
26:40-46 1084

Numbers

1 623
3:7-8 171
6 714
6:12 184
6:22-27 1224
6:24-26 721
8:5-7 1302
8:19 1029
8:26 171
10 701
11 332
11-12 331
11-17 333
11:7 171
11:17 849
11:25 849
11:26 201
11:29 1179
12 331
12:6-8 35, 124, 143, 329, 333, 465
12:7 947
12:10 331
12:11, 17 286
13:2-3 167
13:30 1199
14:11 56
14:11, 12 818
14:18 971
14:33 169, 971
15:30 183
16:1-2 169
16:5 1030
18:5-6 171
18:19 1110
19:9 1302
19:13 1293
19:13, 18-21 178
19:19-20 183
19:20 178
20 917
20-21 336
20:7-8 876
20:7-10 881
20:12 56, 470
21 331
21:1-3 1317
21:6-9 331
21:18 336
21:21-30 1317
21:33-35 1317
22 96
22-24 95, 343, 910
22:2-14 288, 289
22:2-24:25 285
22:2-35 288, 289
22:3 287
22:4 566
22:6 285, 286
22:6, 12 286
22:15-21 288, 289
22:18 285, 290
22:20-38 1333
22:22-23 289
22:22-23, 24-25, 26-35 289
22:22-35 289, 290
22:24-25 289
22:26-23:12 289
22:26-35 289
22:28 291
22:28, 31 289
22:28, 32-33 96, 291
22:28-29 291
22:31 96, 291, 296
22:31a 291
22:31b 292
22:32-33 292
22:36-24:25 289
22:41 292
22:41-23:12 290
23 53, 107
23-24 95, 123, 287, 370
23:4, 16 302
23:5, 16 291
23:7 286, 798
23:7, 18 285
23:7-10 303
23:8, 11, 13, 25, 27 286
23:9 303
23:11, 20, 25 286
23:13-26 289, 290, 292
23:18-24 96, 108, 294
23:19 506
23:20 253
23:21 107, 201, 294
23:21-22 295, 470
23:22 95, 96, 107, 293, 294, 295
23:22-24 107
23:22a 107
23:22b 107
23:24 107, 287, 294, 295, 296
23:27-24:9 290
23:27-24:13 289, 302
23:27-24:25 289–290
23:27-29 296
24 53, 55, 107, 248, 297, 298, 1104
24:1 292
24:1, 9-10 286
24:1-9 95
24:1-24 772
24:2 292
24:2-4 296
24:3 302
24:3, 14, 20-21, 23 289
24:3, 15 220, 749
24:3, 15, 20-21, 23 285
24:3-4 96, 302
24:3-4, 15-16 302, 401
24:3-9 282, 287
24:4 291, 292, 302
24:5 772
24:5, 7 294
24:5-6 107
24:5-7a 772
24:5-9 107, 285–305, 289, 290, 294
24:7 57, 64–65, 107, 124, 201, 293, 298, 299
24:7, 17 287
24:7, 19 303
24:7-8 295, 470
24:7-8a 293
24:7-9 96, 107, 108, 124, 151, 288, 299
24:7-9, 14 ,17 1054
24:7-9, 17-19 287, 288, 291
24:7-9, 17-24 95
24:7b-9 772
24:7b-9a 292
24:8 95, 96, 109, 293, 294, 298, 302
24:8, 17 302, 303
24:8-9 108
24:9 64, 96, 219, 282, 285, 286, 287, 290, 294, 295, 296, 297, 298, 302, 303, 305

24:9, 14 221
24:9a 771
24:10 96, 286, 291, 292
24:13 285, 290
24:14 31, 53, 64, 99, 124, 124f2, 248, 282, 297, 298, 300, 301, 303, 304, 792, 795
24:14, 17-24 95
24:14, 17ff 95
24:14-19 289, 297, 298
24:15 302
24:15-16 302
24:15-17 221
24:15-24 278
24:16 291, 302
24:17 209, 215, 220, 221, 233, 285, 288, 300, 302, 303, 304, 310, 369, 377, 681, 792, 798, 1204
24:17, 19 798
24:17-18 231
24:17-19 31, 166, 233, 242, 285, 288, 300, 301, 362
24:17-24 201, 202
24:17b 221
24:18 304
24:19 304
24:20 289, 741
24:21-22 289
24:23-25 289
24:24 57
25, 31 859
25:1-13 967
25:1-18 343
25:4 971
25:8 1294
25:11-13 1061
27:11 958
27:16-17 169
27:17 193, 1103, 1308
27:18 849
28-29 185
29:12-38 185
30:16 971
31:1-16 343
31:6 285
31:8 290
31:8, 16 290
31:16 285
32:22, 29 164, 241
32:32 326
33:20 221
35:28 971

Deuteronomy

1:5 52
1:6-4:40 312
1:21 379
1:31 314
3:21 902
4:2 755
4:3 902
4:10 733
4:20, 34 1226
4:23-31 1161
4:23-34 1161
4:25-28 1161
4:25-31 297, 298, 1044
4:26-28 242
4:26-31 1197
4:27 297
4:27-31 1160
4:29 98, 417, 1161
4:29-31 901, 1101
4:30 99, 297, 298, 301, 1031, 1054, 1159, 1161
4:30-32 1084
4:31 1089, 1161
4:34 818
4:35-40 793
4:37 310
5-11 312
5:7 316
5:9 314, 971
5:11 1322
5:28-29 221
5:29 733
5:31-32 313
6:1-2, 13, 24 733
6:4 1196, 1321
6:4-5 986
6:4-9 351
6:5 312, 313, 417
6:11 900
6:12-13 417
6:13 316
6:13, 16 955
6:16 818
6:20-25 313
6:22 818, 1241
7:1-4 242
7:3-4 311–312
7:6 1030
7:6, 7 310
7:14 310
7:19 818, 1241
8:6 733
8:25 417
9:1-6 1226
9:4, 6-7 417
9:9 336
9:10 566
10:8 137
10:12, 20 733
10:12-11:1 322
10:12-13 322
10:14-11:1 322
10:15 310
10:17 36, 837
10:17-20 351
10:20 316
11:1-10 319
11:6 316
11:8-9 113
11:10-15 1171
11:13-15 1173
11:23-26 888
11:34, 38 316
12-26 312
12-26, 28 309
12:5, 11-12 1322
12:5, 14 310
12:7 839
12:10 1086
12:15, 21 178
12:20 310
12:32 755
13:4 733
13:5 316
14:1 314, 351, 752
14:2 310
14:8 316
14:22-23 733
14:26 839
15 1140
15:3 316
15:5 316
15:6 1028
15:7 1103
15:11 568
16-18 331
16:2 316
16:3 202, 968
16:11 1322
16:13 1188

16:18 309
16:18-17:20 331
16:18-18:22 309
16:18-20 311
16:20 309, 320
16:22 1159
17 482
17:8-13 309
17:9 311
17:9, 11 1075
17:14 315, 1086
17:14-15 730
17:14-20 309–322, 564, 565, 730, 731, 840, 1086, 1227
17:14-29 320
17:15 310–311, 321, 362
17:16 317, 730
17:16-17 311–312, 315, 317
17:16-20 311–314
17:17a 317, 730
17:17b 730
17:18 321
17:18-19 733
17:18-19a 730
17:18-20 311, 312–314, 482
17:19-20 1088–1089
17:19a 312
17:19b 313, 730
17:20 318, 320, 321, 730
18 54, 136, 140
18:1-5 139
18:1-8 309, 311, 331
18:5 310
18:9-14 330
18:9-22 309, 311, 330–331
18:12 1330
18:14ff 333
18:15 167, 168, 309, 329, 330, 470, 1029
18:15-19 12, 35, 124, 142, 325–338, 330, 792, 793, 878
18:18 136, 140, 309, 875
18:18-19 221
18:19 329
18:19-20 140
18:20 330
18:20-22 309, 330
19:6 567
19:8-9 231
19:18-19 666
19:19 666
20:1 311, 935
21:5 310
21:17 984
21:21 733
22:13-19 1330
23:3-6 343
23:4-7 285
23:5-6 290
23:14 171
23:21-23 354
24:14-15 1103
25:5-10 349, 351, 353
25:17-18 733
26:16 417
26:16-19 1030
28 312, 669, 965, 1084
28-30 873
28:1-14 137, 1024
28:6 1189
28:11-12 914
28:13 1027
28:15-68 1024
28:16-19 242
28:21 1171
28:36, 49-50, 64-65 1197
28:48 1280
28:49 1024, 1064
28:58 733
28:66 1028
29 1037
29:1 1037, 1090
29:1-4 334
29:2-30:20 312
29:4 956, 1037
29:9 1037
29:10-14 98
29:19-21 1037
29:23 1226
29:25 1037
29:29 731
30 55, 97, 98, 1037
30:1 1037
30:1-10 298, 1084
30:2, 6 417
30:2-3 1037
30:2-6 1101
30:3 98
30:3-5 231
30:4 751
30:4-6 127
30:4-9 201
30:6 1039, 1044
30:6, 15, 19-20 976
30:6-10 1037
30:11-14 881
30:12 750
30:12-14 98, 242, 881
31 248, 297, 1037
31-32 910
31:8 379
31:9-13 312
31:12-13 733
31:16 1037
31:16-21 168
31:17-18, 21 1037
31:20 1037
31:28 248, 297
31:28-29 95, 795
31:29 56, 99, 124, 124f2, 248, 297, 298, 792, 1054
31:30 368
31:33 1039
32 55, 298, 368
32-33 123, 368
32-34 370
32:1-43 207, 298, 312, 362
32:3 368
32:4 368
32:4, 15, 18, 31 877
32:4, 15, 31 365, 369
32:5-6, 19 752
32:6, 18 314
32:10 368
32:11 1065
32:18 743
32:26, 39 365, 370
32:34-43 1084
32:35 666, 1005
32:36 721
32:43 793
33 221, 242
33:1 164, 287, 650
33:1-5 840
33:2-29 312
33:4-5 1060
33:5 169, 287, 1204
33:5, 7 95, 1054

33:7	288
33:8-11	221
33:15	105
33:17	368
33:20	287
33:21	272, 288, 741
33:26-29	368
33:27	105, 396, 650
33:27-29	650
33:29	902
34	48, 121f1, 124, 481
34:5	622, 947
34:9	167, 332
34:9-10	168, 327
34:9-12	12, 120, 121
34:10	12, 35, 326, 368, 465, 470
34:10-12	124
34:10ff	333

Joshua

1	48, 121f1, 481, 482
1:1-2	947
1:1-9	12, 120, 121, 164
1:3	481
1:7-8	121, 482
1:7-9	481
1:8	315, 321, 482
1:8-9	485
1:17	167
2:1	167
2:18	167
3:5	36
3:16-17	167
4:18, 22	167
5:14	675, 679
6:10	1264
6:26	221, 419
8:1-2	1317
8:18-19, 25	168
8:28	1079
8:31	762
9:4, 23	164
9:23	254
10:14, 42	1317
10:24	509, 680
11:6-8	1317
13:3	1262
13:22	290
14:6	650
17:16-18	311
18:1	164, 241
20:3-9	442
21:43-45	1086
23:1	1086
24:3	1226
24:9-10	285, 290
24:14-20	168
24:29	622

Judges

1:19	311
2:1	1334
2:1-5	1333
3:9, 10, 15	1317
3:12-30	343, 859
3:15	181
4:15, 23	1317
4:21, 22	1267
5	362
5:2	680
5:10	1265
5:11	1317
5:15	272
5:26	220
6-7	835
6-8	840
6:11-12, 22	1334
6:11-24	1333
6:13	675, 679
6:34	849
6:35	840
7:9, 14	1317
7:22	1226
8:24-28	1159
10:4	1265
11:29	849
11:34-40	820
12:1	1265
13:1-23	37, 1017
13:3	1334
13:5-7	819
13:7	113
13:8-22	1333
13:15-21	36
13:18	36, 153
13:19	36
13:22	890
13:25	849
14:6	849
14:12-14	750
17:5	1159
17:6	125, 354
18:14-20	1159
18:30	63–64, 125
19-21	315
20:2	879
21:25	125, 354, 369

Ruth

1:1	202
1:6	344, 353
1:9	353
1:11-13	353
1:14, 16	354
1:15	353
1:16-17	354
2:1	347
2:3	347, 354
2:5	380
2:7	506
2:20	347, 958
3:2	347
3:9	347
3:11	742
3:12	347, 958
3:13	565
3:15	202
4:2-4	442
4:3	347
4:5-6	442
4:9-10	347
4:11	223, 705
4:12	632
4:17-22	223, 742
4:18-22	263, 773

1 Samuel

1	369
1:6-7	364
1:10-12	361
1:11	369
1:19-20	361
1:20	369
1:22	380, 901
1:24	380
1:24-25	369
1:28	362
2	377
2:1	364–365, 368
2:1, 10	368
2:1-10	191–192, 202, 366–368
2:1-10, 35	361–370
2:2	365, 368–369
2:2-8	365
2:3	363, 369
2:5	363–364, 365
2:6	364, 365, 370
2:6-10	1068, 1069
2:7	364
2:7, 10	369

2:7-10, 35 201
2:8 365, 369
2:9-10 365–366
2:10 364, 365, 368, 369, 370, 377, 751, 1335
2:10, 35 30, 137
2:10b 192
2:11 362
2:20 369
2:21 363
2:21, 26 369
2:28 945
2:34 366
2:34-35 366
2:35 142, 202, 366, 370, 377, 378, 1335
4:4 272
4:11, 18 366
5:7 917
6-7 705
6:17 1262
6:21 705
7:1-2 386, 705
7:10 364
8 369
8:4-5, 19-22 635
8:10-18 635
8:11-17 315
8:11-18 316, 1102
8:19-20 315
8:20 374
9:1 299
9:16 191
10:1 137, 191, 368
10:5 466
10:27 374, 378
11:1-4 348
11:13 374
12:16-18 364
13 374, 1030
13:14 13, 315, 321, 635, 1086, 1108, 1335
13:14c 1108
13:19-22 379
14:29, 43 506
14:38 879
15 374
15:1, 17 377
15:8-9 64
15:8-9, 20, 32-33 293, 299
15:17-31 635
15:22 186, 1159
15:22b 562
15:23 299
15:28 1108
16:1, 13 368
16:1-13 853
16:6-13 632
16:7 363
16:12 574, 776
16:13 13, 193, 849
16:18 575
16:18, 23 466
16:23 466
17 373–383
17:1-3 378
17:1-11 378–379
17:10, 25 381
17:12 379, 381, 705, 848, 1213
17:12-27 379
17:13 380
17:14 380
17:15 380
17:22 379
17:23 379
17:26 380
17:26, 36, 45 381
17:28 378, 381
17:28-30 379–380
17:31-39 380–381
17:33 380
17:34-37 380
17:37 381
17:39 575
17:40-51a 381
17:41 380
17:42 574, 776
17:43 381
17:43-44 363
17:45 696, 697
17:45, 46 381–382
17:50-51 382
18:10-11, 12-19, 20-29 374
19 374
20 375
20:27-33 848
21:1-6 1247
23:1-14, 19-28 374
24 374
24:4-6 377
24:6, 10 13
25:28 366
26 374
26:9, 11, 16, 23 13
28 364, 375
30 375
30-31 375

2 Samuel

1:14, 16 13
2:4 13, 30, 283
2:4, 7-11 632
2:28-32 202
3:12-13 1333
3:18 1227
5 917
5:2 223, 1103, 1109, 1212, 1216, 1274, 1297, 1310, 1335
5:3 13, 30, 283
5:3-5 632
5:6 917
5:7 719
5:9 797
6 386, 682
6-7 414
6:2 141
6:7 141
6:14 682, 1247
6:17-18 682
6:18 142, 682
6:19 1157
7 81, 141, 154, 195, 385–397, 414, 492, 586, 592, 701, 716, 719, 728, 732, 759, 772, 976, 979, 1042, 1045, 1050, 1067, 1101, 1190
7:1 386, 1086
7:1-3 386
7:1-11 980
7:2 386
7:4-11 386–389, 388
7:4-17 256, 1162
7:5 388, 426
7:5, 8 1100
7:5, 11c 386
7:5-16 425
7:6 426
7:7 272, 426
7:8 426, 1088, 1103, 1212, 1226

7:8-16 1085
7:8-17 272, 835
7:9 388, 426
7:9-20 1335
7:10 388, 426
7:10-11a 979
7:10-13, 16 813
7:10-16 1187
7:10a 388
7:10c-11a 388
7:11 126, 194, 388, 426
7:11-14 164
7:11-16 377, 389, 470, 1086
7:11b 388
7:11b-16 729
7:11c 386, 390
7:11d 389
7:11d-16 389
7:12 34, 499, 1210
7:12-13 389, 514
7:12-14a, 16 192
7:12-15 980
7:12-16 30, 125–126, 139, 142, 156, 393, 403, 405, 407, 772, 817, 1025
7:12a 389, 426
7:12b 426
7:12c 389, 426
7:13 391, 492, 595
7:13, 16 585, 838, 1103
7:13, 16, 24, 25, 26 1100
7:13, 16, 29 319
7:13-15 608
7:13-16 394
7:13a 426
7:13b 389, 426, 430
7:14 654, 732, 1093
7:14-15 389, 706, 729
7:14a 389, 432
7:14a-b 426
7:14b 432
7:14b-c 389
7:14c 426
7:15 389, 426
7:15-16 428, 429, 432
7:16 126, 137, 346, 355, 366, 385, 389, 391, 397, 426, 470, 819, 837, 838, 853, 1108, 1187, 1204
7:18 392
7:18-26 320
7:19 1068
7:19, 20, 21, 25, 26, 27, 28, 29 1100
7:19, 20, 22, 28, 29 392
7:19, 29 622
7:19b 385, 392–394
7:23-24 980, 1086, 1089
7:28 762
8:2 301
8:12 860
8:15 934
8:18 682, 1247
11:1 375
11:11 1188
12 405
12:1-9 1103
12:24 321
12:30 1078
14:24 496
14:25 574
15:9 496
15:30 1318, 1320
16:1 506
16:1-2 1265
16:11-12 417
17:17b 385
18:5, 31-33 496
18:5, 32 493
18:31-32 517
19:21 1335
19:26 1265
20:16 862
20:26 682
21 364
21:1c 804
21:3 179
21:17 390
22 366–368, 369
22-23 377
22:1, 47-51 368
22:2, 47 368
22:2-4, 32 369
22:6 514
22:7 561, 1330
22:14 364
22:31 754
22:37-43 771
22:39 509
22:51 30, 65, 368, 377, 401, 677, 771, 840
23:1 30, 65–66, 377, 401, 402, 404, 405, 406, 408, 676, 749, 798, 1335
23:1-2 466, 494
23:1-3 531, 804
23:1-5 202, 676
23:1-7 399–408, 1014
23:1a 400–401
23:1b 401–402
23:2 66, 402
23:2-3a 402–403, 406, 408
23:3 403, 405, 407
23:3-4 65, 66, 402
23:3a 402
23:3b 403
23:3b-4 403–404, 406
23:4 403, 407, 853
23:4-5 655
23:5 37, 65–66, 396, 402, 404–406, 407, 408, 804, 805, 1014, 1015, 1110
23:6 406
23:6-7 406
23:7 406
24 405
24:1 142
24:10 142
24:13 142
24:14 142
24:15 142
24:17 1103
24:18-19 142
24:25 142
24:26 1247

1 Kings

1-10 412
1-11 412, 414
1:7-8 416
1:8 416
1:21 499
1:33 1265
1:35 416
2:2-4 395, 415
2:3 315, 321, 417
2:3-4 416
2:4 417, 1045

2:9 417
2:10 499
2:19 679
2:23 418
2:24 418
2:31 417
2:32 417
2:33, 45 319
2:35 366
2:36-37 417
2:44 418
2:45 417
3:3 317, 796
3:3-9 317
3:4-28 317
3:5-28 727
3:6 316
3:9 165
3:10-15 317
3:14 316, 1240
3:28 1075
4:20 839
4:21, 24 165
4:24 304
4:25 787
4:26-28 315
4:29-34 317, 727
4:31 631, 748
4:33 165
5:3 509
5:5 1322
5:12 727
5:13 202
5:13-18 315
5:17 879
6:12 126, 395
6:22 165
6:23-28 165
6:38 165
7:2 1067
7:7 1075
7:9 165, 879
7:9-11 879
7:14 165
7:40 165
8 317, 595
8:2 1221
8:10-13 811
8:11 916
8:12-13 165
8:13, 29 797
8:14, 55 165
8:24 1045
8:25 395
8:46-53 420
8:49-50 420
8:56 165
8:64 165
9:1 564–565
9:2-9 316
9:3 414
9:4 316, 317, 1045
9:4-9 395
9:5 319
9:8 567
9:15, 20-22 317
9:15-16 311
9:17-29, 24 317
9:20-21 254
9:26-28 317
10:1-13, 23-25 727
10:1-25 317
10:9 314, 319
10:11-23 317
10:23 315
10:26, 28-29 317
10:26-29 315
11 412
11-12 1087
11-16 412
11:1 311
11:1-4 126
11:1-6 165
11:1-8 317, 344, 414
11:1-10 348
11:1-13 315
11:4 316
11:7 416
11:9-13 729
11:9-13:33 315
11:9-43 317
11:11-13 414
11:11-43 317
11:12-13 414
11:13 413
11:30-39 317, 414
11:32-33 317
11:34 1088, 1227
11:34, 37 1108
11:36 707
11:41 727
12-2 Kings 17 412
12-17 315
12:3 566
12:4 613
12:16 1108, 1160
12:20-24 1100
15:3 316
15:4 707
15:5 316
15:11 317
16:21-2 Kings 12 418
16:23-2 Kings 12 412
16:30 419
16:31 311, 577
16:32-33 419
16:33 419
17:1 419
17:1-2 Kings 8:15 412
18:4 420, 888
18:28 1302
19:16 30
19:18 1199
20:2-6 1333
20:14-19 380
21:1-14 666
21:8 1227
22:17 1103, 1307, 1308
25 242

2 Kings

1:7-8 1214
2:1-14 328
2:1-18 750
2:12-16 419
3:4 860
3:4-27 301
3:15 466
4:1-7 415
4:18-37 415
4:31 522
8:16-17:41 412
8:19 707
8:25-27 419
10:26-27 1159
11:1 419
11:2 419
13:17 1268
14:6 762
15:29 818
15:32-20:21 1209
16:3 818
17:6 1195
17:7-18 319
17:7-23 428, 964, 1321
17:10 1159
17:13 1334
17:22-24 1064
17:24 818
17:28 1170
18-25 412, 413
18:3 317
18:13-20:19 860
18:31 1243

19:35-36 1196, 1197
19:35-37 1076
21:11, 16, 17 319
21:23-24 874
22:1-8 318
22:1-23:30 318
22:2 317, 411
22:8-16 321
22:12-13 318
22:15-17 318
22:19 1066
23:1-3 318
23:2 840
23:4-20 318
23:8-16 887
23:21 762
23:21-23 318
23:24-25 318
23:25 318, 321
23:26-27 420, 874
23:28-30 318
23:29 874
23:31-34 1065
23:33, 34 874
24-25 1197
24:1-7 427
24:3-4 315, 319
24:6 1041
24:8 1064
24:8-16 1065
24:8-17 427–428
24:9 1066
24:13 1317
24:17 1078
24:17-25:21 1064
25 164
25:1-22 428
25:4-5 1320
25:5-7 847
25:12 1199
25:13-16 1317
25:27-30 319, 412, 427, 428, 1068
25:28 421

1 Chronicles

2:6 631
2:11-12 355
3:19 1069
3:24 202
5:1-2 263
9:8 314
11:2 223, 1216
12:2 326
15:17 631
15:19 631
15:20 821
15:21 560
16:12 36
16:17 396, 798, 1110
16:24 859
16:24-29 507
17 131, 385, 425–433, 728, 732
17:1 386
17:1-2 386
17:1b 386
17:3-9 386–389
17:4 426
17:4-14 425, 428, 429, 432
17:4b 388
17:4b, 10c 386
17:5 426
17:6 426
17:7 426, 1088
17:8 426
17:9 426, 1107
17:9-13 813
17:10 426
17:10-14 389
17:10-15 405
17:10c 388, 389, 390
17:11-12 385
17:11-14 817, 1187
17:11a-b 389
17:11b 426
17:11c 389, 426
17:12 389, 595
17:12, 14 319, 585
17:12a 426
17:12b 426
17:13 389, 732
17:13a 426
17:13b 426
17:14 389, 426, 585, 796, 797, 807, 810, 813, 1107
17:14b-c 389
17:16 392
17:17b 392–394
18:17 682
21:16-18 1076
21:28 142
22:10 319, 585
23-27 840
23:4 531
25:1, 2, 5 531
25:1-4 465
28:2 680
28:4 319
28:4, 7, 8, 9 1100
28:5 840
28:9 1331
28:10, 20 1221
29:17 878
29:23 321, 576

2 Chronicles

2:2, 18 531
6 701
6:14 978
6:15 978
6:15-17 978
6:16 978, 1045, 1187
6:17 978
6:42 978
7:14 567
7:17 316, 317
9:31 499
15:3 1170
17:3 316, 317
18:16 1103, 1308
20 860
20:7 1101
23:13 531
25:4 762
26 1030
27-33 1209
28:1 316
28:3 818
28:24 879
29 803
29:2 316
29:30 465
30:18 179
32:1-23 860
32:20 789
32:21 1196
34:2 316
35:20-27 318
36:9 1066
36:15-16 964, 1330
36:21 1141
36:22-23 428, 1215
36:22-Ezra 1:4 1099
36:23 50, 131, 725

Ezra

1:1-4 131
2:2 1248
2:64-67 1322
2:64-68 1099

3 1220
3:4 763
3:9-13 1322
3:12-13 1099
4:2 818
4:2, 10 818
4:7-23 1145
4:12-13, 16 1323
5:1-2 1280
5:8 1323
6:8 1225
6:14 1248
7:6 321
7:11-26 1145
9 1328
9:1-2 1099
9:6-7 964
9:10-12 113
10 1328

Nehemiah

1:1 758
1:9 1322
2:1-8 1145
2:3 901
2:3, 5 1145
2:3, 8 1145
2:8 1145
2:11-12 1322
3:24 879
4:1-6:14 1144
5 1328
5:15 1280
6:6-7 1099
6:15 1323
7:66-67 1322
8:1-18 321
8:8 216, 218
8:13-18 812
9:5-37 218
9:6 1334
9:17 36
9:26-36 964
9:32 36
9:32-37 218
11:1-2 1323
11:7 749
12:1 1261
12:12-16 1261
12:26 1248
13 1328
13:2 285, 290
13:6-7 1328
13:10-11, 15-17, 23-24 1099

13:26 321

Esther

1:1 202
2:5 299
2:12 575
3:1, 10 299
8:3, 5 299
9:24 299
9:30 431

Job

1-2 437, 1238, 1244
1:1, 8 741
1:3 437
1:6 437
1:8 437, 480, 622
1:9-10 438
1:12 443
1:19 879
1:20-21 439
2:3 480, 622, 741
2:7 438
2:7, 12 438
2:8 438
2:9 438
3:24 438
3:24-25 439
3:26 439
4:7 439
4:19 443
5:1 442
5:2, 3 439
5:17 902
5:19-23 1092
6:4 439
7:3 438
7:4 438
7:4, 13-14 439
7:5 438
7:17-19 439
7:21 443, 499
8:2 439
9:2, 28 442
9:2-3, 15, 32-33 741
9:17 220
9:20 439
9:21 439
9:25 439
9:33 129
9:33-34 442
10:3 480
10:9 443
10:13 442

10:18-22 553
10:20 506
10:21 553
11:4 439
11:12 439
11:13, 14 439
11:18 499
12:4 439
13:18 442
14:7-12 441
14:8, 19 443
14:10 442
14:10-14 443
14:12 499, 522
14:13-17 441
14:13ff 442
14:14 444
15:2 439
15:8-9 439
15:11-16 439
15:20 439
16:8 438, 443
16:10 439
16:15 443
16:16 438
16:19 442
16:19-21 129, 741
16:20 442
16:21 505
17:2, 6 439
17:6 439
17:7 438
17:13-16 524
17:14 524
17:16 443
18:3 439
18:5-22 439
18:17 441
19 443
19:2 443
19:13-19 439
19:17 438
19:17-20 439
19:18 439
19:20 438, 443
19:22 439
19:23-24 441
19:23-27 437–446, 439
19:25 128, 441–442
19:25-27 441
19:25b 443
19:26 442, 443
19:26-27 443
19:27 440
19:28-29 443

20:11 443, 499
20:19 439
21:6 438
21:16 454, 480
21:26 443, 499
22:5-11 439
22:9 439
22:18 454, 480
23:8-9, 15 439
23:10 878
24:24 506
26:8 751
27:19 499
28 742
28:12-28 741
28:24 751
28:28 741
29:2 438
30:9 439
30:17 438
30:27 438
30:28, 30 438
30:30 438
30:31 439
31:4 443
33:23-28 129
34:36 878
35:8 506
36:22 1170
37:3 751
37:11 751
38-41 750
38:4-5 751
38:5 754
38:5, 8, 25 750
38:8-9 751
38:10-11 751
38:17 553
38:36-37 741
39:1 743
40:12 751
42 445
42:3 562
42:5 443
42:7, 8 480
42:8 622

Psalms

1 12, 48, 120, 121, 121f1, 463, 477–489, 521, 547, 562, 720, 722
1, 2 706
1, 19, 119 722
1-2 462, 477–489, 493, 537, 617, 623, 626, 627, 650, 655, 659, 694, 704, 717, 723
1:1 454, 479, 480, 488, 489, 516, 656, 902
1:1, 5, 6 494, 500
1:1, 6 479
1:1, 8 486
1:1-2 484
1:2 315, 321, 463, 479, 516
1:2, 8 486
1:2-3 121, 481, 482
1:3 479, 482, 483, 484, 485, 657
1:3, 4 479
1:3ab 482, 488
1:3c 485, 488
1:4 483, 484, 486, 516
1:5 479, 483, 494
1:5, 6 486
1:5-6 468, 484, 485, 500, 532
1:6 463, 479, 480, 484, 486, 500
1:6b-2:1a 479
2 33, 156, 233, 453, 458, 459, 467, 470, 477–489, 485, 521, 547, 550, 559, 592, 595, 607, 627, 649, 665, 684, 685, 703, 720, 722, 733, 754–755, 761, 865, 867, 1132, 1134
2, 8, 18, 20-21 514
2, 72, 89 703
2, 110 510, 792
2-3 546, 626
2-6 550
2:1 192, 209, 452, 463, 479, 484, 485, 486, 493, 516
2:1, 2 485
2:1, 2, 8, 10, 11 645
2:1, 3, 9-10 464
2:1-2 468, 517, 787
2:1-2, 10 649
2:1-3 487, 498, 500, 538–539
2:1-6 647
2:2 30, 137, 480, 486, 493, 497, 499, 507, 549, 555, 568, 684–685, 694, 1160, 1321
2:2-3 492, 496
2:3 487, 496
2:3-6 761
2:4 156, 479, 480, 481, 485, 488, 516, 539, 649, 717
2:4, 6 624
2:4-6 487, 496, 500, 507
2:4-9 487
2:4-12 649
2:5 485, 685
2:5, 12 649
2:6 462, 468, 471, 479, 482, 485, 492, 493, 497, 498, 500, 549, 626, 649, 685, 743, 903
2:6-7 497
2:6-8 321
2:6-9 1108
2:7 33, 479, 485, 488, 492, 493, 494, 497, 507, 514, 621, 624, 681, 685, 835, 925, 937, 939, 967, 1093
2:7, 8 485
2:7, 12 732
2:7-8 192, 647
2:7-9 487
2:8 156, 207, 462, 467, 479, 481, 483, 487, 488, 538, 685, 751
2:8-9 221, 485, 517
2:9 156, 479, 486, 487, 488, 685, 761, 1268
2:9, 12 500
2:10 479, 483, 487

2:10-12 487, 507
2:11 486, 487, 494, 649
2:11-12 156, 622
2:11a 485
2:12 33, 463, 479, 480, 484, 485, 486, 488, 489, 500, 516, 622, 656, 685, 755, 902
2:12d 488
3 453, 459, 480, 488, 517, 535, 539, 607
3-7 468, 517, 518
3:1 492, 494, 516, 517, 535
3:2 463, 493, 496, 497, 499, 664
3:2, 7 493
3:2, 8 494
3:2-3 491, 498
3:2-5 498
3:3 493, 496, 497, 498, 499, 754
3:4 493, 497, 498, 549, 649
3:4, 6 497
3:4-6 491, 497, 498
3:5 463, 493, 497, 498, 517, 626
3:6 493, 494, 497, 498, 499–500
3:7 494, 496
3:7-9 491, 498
3:8 493, 494, 496–497, 499, 500
3:9 500
4 459
4:2 498
4:4 516, 517
4:4, 8 517
4:6 463
4:7 498
4:8 463
4:9 498
5:1 516
5:4-5 664
7 510, 517, 547
7:1 517
7:1-4 664
7:4-6 510
7:6 498
7:7-8 199
7:15 524
7:17 463, 504, 518, 751
8 503–511, 546, 547
8-9 518
8:1 463, 504, 505
8:1, 9 504, 904
8:1, 13 507
8:2 507, 509
8:3 505, 508
8:3, 6 508
8:4 503, 505, 506, 510, 1128
8:4-6 518
8:5 506, 507, 508
8:5-6 505, 507, 511
8:5-8 505
8:6 508, 509, 771
8:7-8 508
8:8-12 507
8:9 505
9 510, 547
9:1-2 504
9:3-6 510
9:9b 532
9:14 578
9:15 524
9:19-20 510
10 479
10-14 518
10:1 452, 532
10:1-11 510
10:2 568
10:4, 6, 11, 13 664
11-13 566
11-14 518
11:3 899
11:4 717
12 510
12:1 510
12:1-3 664
12:4 664
12:5 568
13 499
13:3 499
13:5 499
13:6 499
14:1-3 510
14:7 798, 1263
15 521
15, 24 519
15-24 514, 516, 518–521
15:1 521
15:1-5 519, 902
15:1-5a 521
15:2 524
15:5b 521
15:8 513
16 80, 407, 458, 460, 513–525, 521, 545
16, 23 520
16:1 521
16:2 520
16:2-7 521
16:5 520
16:8 521
16:8-11 407, 521, 805
16:9-10 523
16:10 408, 514, 522, 523, 524, 525
16:10-11 521
16:11 520, 521, 522, 523
17 522
17, 22 520
17:5 521
17:9 520, 522
17:9-12 524
17:11 520, 522
17:12 520, 522
17:13 520
17:14 798
17:15 520, 522
18 46, 463, 494, 521
18, 20-21 520
18:1 532
18:2 520
18:4, 15-16 561
18:4-5 523
18:6 514, 561, 1330
18:23, 25, 32 524
18:28-32 202
18:35 520, 521
18:38 509
18:50 521, 522, 524, 525, 539, 583
18:51 207
19 463, 521, 723
19-21 531
19-23 531
19:1 524
19:7-14 532
19:11, 13 463
19:12, 14 532
19:13 480, 524

20 521, 532, 549, 550, 554
20-21 530, 555
20-22 544, 546
20-24 723
20:1 532–533, 550, 723
20:1, 6 550
20:2 520, 549, 723, 724
20:5 549
20:5, 6 549
20:5, 6, 7, 9 549
20:6 30, 137, 521, 522, 524, 549
20:6, 9 521
20:6a 532
20:6b 532, 549
20:7 112, 549, 576
20:9 549
20:13 554
20:16 554
21 508, 521, 532, 537, 538, 549, 550, 554
21:1 549
21:1, 5 532
21:1-3 508
21:1-6 550
21:1-8 202
21:2-4 549
21:3, 6 538
21:3-6 538, 550
21:4 550
21:4, 6 538
21:4-5 206
21:4b 538
21:5 507, 537, 549, 554, 583
21:6 555
21:7 533
21:8 521, 680
21:8-12 550
22 114, 229, 458, 471, 521, 522, 529–540, 544, 549, 550, 553, 554, 555, 568, 626
22-24 545
22:1 452, 532, 533, 534, 545, 549, 596
22:1, 10 534
22:1, 11 534
22:1, 11, 19 550, 626
22:1, 12, 15, 16, 21 552
22:1-2 535, 538
22:1-11 533, 535
22:1-11,12-21 532
22:1-21 533, 534, 535, 540, 553
22:1-22 545
22:2 529, 549
22:3 533, 534
22:3, 9, 10 534
22:3, 9, 10, 19 550, 551
22:3, 23 534
22:4 520
22:4-5 533, 534
22:5 533
22:6 533
22:6-7 535
22:7-8 568, 664
22:8 520
22:9 533
22:11 533, 550
22:12 520, 535, 536
22:12, 16 535
22:12-13, 16-18 545
22:12-15 535
22:12-18 524
22:12-21 533, 535
22:12,16 553
22:13 520, 535, 536
22:13, 16, 21 535
22:13, 17 522
22:13, 21 522
22:14 535
22:14-17 536
22:15 522–523, 535, 536, 545, 553
22:15, 29 550
22:15, 39 545
22:16 68–69, 520, 522, 523, 535, 536
22:16, 20 535
22:16-21 535
22:17 535
22:18 523
22:19 533, 536
22:19-21 535, 540
22:20 535, 536, 568
22:21 520, 534, 535, 536, 537, 538, 539, 545, 569
22:21, 22, 26-28, 29-30 544
22:21, 24 538
22:21b 538
22:22 520, 534, 536, 538, 539, 545, 546, 552, 568
22:22, 25 538, 539
22:22, 26a 555
22:22-23 538, 553
22:22-25 568
22:22-26 534, 538
22:22-28 553
22:22-31 531, 532, 533, 535, 538, 540, 545
22:22-32 555
22:22a 555
22:22ff 538
22:23 539, 555, 568, 798
22:23, 25 538, 545
22:23-24 537
22:23-31 555
22:24 537, 538, 596–597
22:24, 26 598
22:25 534, 538, 568
22:25-31 534
22:26 545, 555, 598
22:26, 29 545
22:26b 555
22:27 538, 539
22:27-28 537, 1321
22:27-29, 30 539
22:27-31 537
22:27a 537
22:27b 537, 539
22:28 539
22:29 443, 523, 536, 537, 546, 552, 553
22:29c 537
22:30 539
22:30-31 539
22:30a 537
22:31 539, 545, 553
23 532, 533, 535–553, 626, 1093, 1200
23:1 545, 551, 1103, 1105
23:1, 4 551
23:1-3 1085
23:1-4 552
23:2 545, 551, 552, 553

23:2-3	555
23:3	537, 539, 545, 546, 552, 553, 554, 555
23:4	545, 552, 553, 555
23:4, 6	523, 552
23:4-6	554
23:4b	551
23:5	520, 521, 545, 554
23:6	520, 538, 545, 550, 551, 552, 554
23:7a	554
23:8	553
24	521, 537, 554, 555
24:2-6	902
24:3	518, 554, 555
24:3-5	519
24:4	524, 539
24:5	555
24:7	105
24:7, 8, 9, 10	554
24:7-10	537, 555
24:8	36, 837
24:9-10	1204
24:10	537
25-34	516
25:6	105
25:22	516
27:4	567, 1330
27:8	567
27:9	480
27:10	378
28:8	30, 137
28:9	1310
29:9	1330
30:3	537, 538
30:3-4	561
30:4	538, 752
31:3	555
31:3-4	555
31:4	555
31:10	555
31:13	486
31:13b	555
31:16	480
32	470, 594
32:1	562, 902
32:3	516
33	479, 650
33:2	1140
33:3	561
33:6	753
34:4	567
34:8	562
35:4	517
35:5	516
35:7	524, 669
35:10	517, 669
35:11	669
35:12	517, 669
35:12, 20, 27	517
35:16-21	569
35:18	669
35:19	517
35:21	517, 569
35:21, 25	664
35:23	568
35:26	517
35:28	516
36:4	516, 517
37	560
37-39	559
37:9	1146
37:11, 21, 37	517
37:13	516
37:14	517
37:30	516
38	560
38:12	516
38:19	517
38:20	517
39	465, 560, 608
40	186, 559–570
40:1-3	560
40:1-10	560
40:2	566, 569
40:3	561
40:4-5	561, 564
40:4c-5	569
40:5	36, 562
40:6	563, 564, 569, 570
40:6-8	186, 187, 564, 565, 592
40:7	564
40:7-8	593
40:9	564, 568
40:9-10	566, 568
40:9-11	568
40:10	566, 568, 570
40:11	568, 569
40:11-17	560, 566–567, 568
40:12	470, 567, 593
40:13	567
40:14	1331
40:14-15	567
40:15	517, 567, 569
40:15, 17	569
40:16	567
40:17	567–568, 569
40:18	517
41	479, 607, 608
41:1	463, 467, 516
41:2	562
41:3	517
41:3, 8	517
41:5-8	664
41:7	517
41:8	499
41:9	516, 517, 1302
41:10	517
41:10-11	517
41:11	517
41:13	452, 461, 617, 704
42	608
42, 44-49	579
42-44	577, 578, 580, 582
42-48	720–721
42-49	579, 608
42:3, 10	581
42:5	580
42:9	580
42:11	580
42:20	569, 583
43	608
43:2	452, 580
43:3	233
43:3-4	580, 583
43:4	578
43:5	580
44	608
44:1	581
44:3, 6	581
44:4	583
44:8	576
44:9	582
44:9, 23	580
44:9-10	580–581
44:10	524
44:13-16	581
44:17	966
44:17, 20, 24	580
44:23	452
44:23-26	581
44:26	581
45	156, 573–586, 608, 777
45:1	574

45:1-5	156
45:1-7	319
45:2	574, 584
45:2, 7	582
45:2-5	574
45:2-6	574
45:2-7	574
45:2-8	574
45:2-9	574
45:3	575, 903
45:3, 6	585
45:3, 7, 17	583
45:3-4	507
45:3-5	574
45:4	584
45:4, 6-7	934
45:4-5	575
45:5	583, 584
45:6	156, 272, 575, 577, 582, 583, 585, 649, 684, 1016
45:6, 11, 17	582
45:6-7	575, 898, 1016, 1307
45:6-9	574
45:6-16	574, 575
45:6a	584
45:7	156, 554, 575
45:7-15	574
45:7-18	202
45:7b	554
45:8	202, 575
45:8-16	574
45:9	575, 679
45:9-15	574
45:10	578, 579
45:10-11	575
45:10-14	577
45:10-15	574, 583
45:10-16	574
45:11	575, 576, 579
45:11, 17b	584
45:12	578
45:13	579
45:13-15	575, 578
45:14	579
45:15	578
45:16	575
45:16-17	574
45:17	574, 575, 576, 577, 583, 584
46-49	578, 580, 581, 582, 583, 608
46:1	581, 820
46:4	482, 624, 649
46:4-5	581, 582
46:5	326, 581
46:6	582
46:7, 11	582
46:9	582, 583
47	750
47:1, 6, 7	582
47:1, 8	624
47:1-3	582, 583
47:2, 6-7	583
47:3	509, 680
47:6	1204
47:6-7	583
47:8	582
47:9	578, 582
48:1	624
48:1-2	624, 1106
48:1-3	582, 649, 903
48:2	1204
48:2, 4	583
48:4, 20	517
48:4-8	582
48:8	569
48:9	578
48:9-14	582
48:11	624
49	608
49:1-4	582
49:5	452
49:5-9	185
49:5-20	582
49:8	188
50	465, 579, 608
50-53	608
50:7-14	563
50:8-14	186
50:16-21	180
51	468, 470, 594, 608
51-65	579
51-65, 68-70	608
51:1	567
51:16-17	186
51:16-19	186
51:17	563
52	608
52-53	609
53	609
53:6	609, 798
54	608
54-59	609
54:6	1322
55:19	105
55:24	524
56	523, 608
56:6	1279
56:9	904
56:13	523
57	523, 608
58	523
58:7	568
58:9	523
59	523, 608
59:13	798
60	523, 608
60:1, 10	580
60:7	272
60:11	609
61-68	609
61:7-9	202
62	465
63	608
66-67, 71	579, 608
68	750
68-70	579
68:4	1322
68:16	386
68:17-21	750
68:21	568
68:22	220
68:29	207
68:33	105
69	114, 458, 471, 569, 591–602, 668
69-71	593, 609, 668
69:1	598
69:1, 13	597
69:1-2	596
69:1-6	593
69:1-13a	594–596
69:1a	594
69:1b-2	594
69:2, 14	569
69:3	594, 597
69:3b	594
69:4	594, 600, 601, 668
69:5	594
69:6	594–595, 598
69:7	594, 595
69:7, 12	668
69:8	595
69:9	594, 600
69:9-12	595
69:9a	595, 601
69:9b	595
69:10-11	595
69:11b	596

69:12	596
69:13	599, 668
69:13, 16, 17	596
69:13a	596
69:13b	596
69:13b-29	596–597
69:14	596
69:14-15	596
69:15	596
69:16	596, 668
69:16a	596
69:17	569, 596
69:18	596
69:19	596
69:19-28	567
69:20a	597
69:20b	597
69:21	597, 600, 601
69:22-23	600
69:22-25	597
69:22-28	668
69:24	600
69:25	597, 600, 663
69:26	597, 600, 601
69:27	597
69:28	600
69:29	569, 668
69:29-30	668
69:29b	597
69:30	597, 668
69:30-31	186
69:30-33	597–598
69:30-36	597
69:32	598
69:32-33	595, 598
69:32b	598
69:33	598, 668, 936
69:34	598
69:34-36	597, 598
69:35	598, 599
69:35-36	598
70	593, 609
70:1	609
70:2	595, 1331
70:3	517
71	593, 609–610
71:9, 17-18	610
71:9-13	610
71:10	1279
71:19-21	610
71:21	326
71:22	750
72	52, 298, 452, 467, 470, 484, 579, 583, 592, 599, 602, 605–614, 645, 649, 650, 668, 717, 719, 728
72, 89	646
72:1	202, 606
72:1, 2, 3, 7, 8, 16	619
72:1-4	605, 612, 899
72:1-4, 12-14	934
72:1-20	202
72:2	32, 612, 898
72:2-4	611
72:3	32
72:4	32, 612, 840
72:5	66–67, 611–612
72:5, 11, 13	619
72:5-7	605, 611
72:5-8	593
72:6	404
72:6-11	612
72:8	32, 207, 304, 467, 1266
72:8-11	605, 611, 645
72:9	771
72:9b	53
72:11	575, 619, 1321
72:12	612
72:12-14	612
72:15-17	612–613
72:16	161, 619
72:17	464, 468, 606, 607, 613
72:17, 19	583
72:18	605
72:18-19	452, 461, 617, 704
72:20	464, 592, 605, 618, 853
72:70	619
73	465, 484, 618, 645, 649
73, 90	646
73-89	619
73:6	1330
74	465, 618
74:1	452, 580
74:1, 10	451
74:1, 11	452, 617
74:2	272
74:9-10	617
74:10-11	628
75	465, 618
75:5-6	706
76	465, 618
76:1-2	272
76:4	904
77	465, 618
77:7	580
77:7-9	618
77:8	431, 451, 617
77:20	464
78	465, 618
78:1-72	1281
78:12	326
78:38	620
78:40-64	620
78:66-72	620
78:67-72	264
78:68	623, 719
78:68-70	272
78:68-72	1085
78:69	623, 1143
78:70	623, 1226, 1227
78:70-72	1103, 1105
79	465
79:5	617, 628
79:5, 10	451
79:10	452, 617
79:11	936
80	465
80:1	37, 272, 890, 1200, 1310
80:12	452
80:15-18	202
80:17	686
81	465
81:4	798
82	465, 467
82:1	199
82:2	617
83	465, 1189
83:1-12	1168
84	621
84-85	623
84-88	620
84:1-2	903
84:3	904
84:5	562
84:6	1170
84:8	620
84:9	30, 137, 620, 621
84:10	256
84:12	621
85:1	798
85:1-13	1264
85:2-3	620
85:4, 7, 9-13	619

85:5 617
85:7, 10 621
85:8-13 620
85:9 621
85:9-13 619, 620
85:10 621
85:10-11 619
85:12 621
86 599, 621
86-88 617–629, 646
86:1 626
86:1, 6 620, 625
86:1-7 621, 622
86:1-7, 13-17 619
86:2 599, 621
86:2, 4, 16 480, 621
86:2, 16 623
86:5 621
86:6 620
86:7 621, 622
86:7, 13 621
86:7, 13, 17 622
86:7-13 622
86:8-13 621, 622
86:9 618, 619, 621, 622, 623, 624, 1321
86:10 621, 622
86:10, 13 621
86:12 622
86:13 619, 620, 621, 622, 623, 625, 626, 628
86:13, 15 599
86:14 496, 622
86:14-17 621, 622
86:15 619, 620, 621
86:17 621, 622
87 531, 622
87-88 623
87:1 623, 624
87:1, 5 624
87:1-2 624
87:2 623, 624
87:2, 4 626
87:3 623, 624
87:4 623, 624
87:4, 5, 6 624
87:4-6 623, 624
87:4-7 624
87:5 623, 624
87:5, 6 623
87:6 623, 624
87:13 625
88 465, 531, 623, 626, 646
88:2 625
88:2, 13 620, 625
88:3 620, 626
88:4 626
88:5 499, 620, 626
88:6 620, 626
88:6, 12 626
88:7 620
88:7, 9 ,15 625, 626
88:8, 18 626
88:10 626, 627
88:10, 11, 12 627
88:10, 12 627
88:10-12 623, 628, 646
88:10b 627
88:11 626, 627
88:12 627
88:14 451, 452, 580, 628
88:15 626
88:16 620
88:18 626
88:36, 48a 628
88:48b 628
89 128, 141, 154, 389–392, 451, 453, 484, 531, 618, 623, 631–639, 646, 653, 659, 660, 696, 697, 701, 702, 704, 706, 707, 708, 728, 732, 748
89-90 646
89-91 650
89:1 627, 647, 978
89:1, 2, 4 625, 646, 651, 652, 654, 656, 658
89:1, 2, 4, 29, 36, 37 648
89:1, 2, 14, 24, 28, 33, 49 657
89:1, 4 646, 651, 652, 654, 656, 658
89:1-2 646
89:1-2, 4 628
89:1-2, 24, 28, 33, 49 648, 652, 654, 656, 658
89:1-4 623, 625, 647
89:1-4, 19-43 648
89:1-5 627
89:1-6, 15-18, 20-29, 33-37 637
89:1-37 128
89:2 627
89:2-3, 5, 29, 36-37, 52 583
89:2-4 647
89:3 631, 645
89:3, 4 646
89:3, 20, 35, 49 637
89:3-4 627–628, 631–632, 639, 646, 719
89:3-4, 19-37 267
89:3-4, 34-37 1100, 1101
89:4 627, 639, 646, 647, 648, 1102
89:4, 14, 36-37 647
89:4, 29, 35 468
89:4, 29, 36 647
89:4, 35-36 807
89:4, 36 585
89:4, 36-37 648
89:4-5 514
89:5 627
89:5, 7 624
89:5, 29, 34 470
89:5, 30, 37 771
89:5-6 648
89:5-7 632–633
89:5-18 647
89:5-18, 52 648
89:8 862
89:8-9 633
89:8-12 633
89:9 647, 648
89:9-12, 17, 38 651, 652, 654, 656, 658
89:10 633, 639
89:10, 51 680
89:11 639, 771
89:11-13 633
89:13 647, 648
89:14 647, 648, 862
89:14-18 633–634
89:15 656
89:16 634, 656, 658
89:16, 17 648
89:17 634
89:17-18 648, 656
89:18 904
89:18, 25 706
89:19-29 634–635, 1086
89:19-37 647, 656

89:19-39 645
89:20 656
89:20, 36 645
89:21 647, 648
89:21, 39 771
89:24 648, 771
89:24, 28, 49 1110
89:25 647, 648, 650
89:26 192, 621, 639, 653, 656, 729
89:26-28 653
89:26-29 1093
89:27 452, 639
89:27-29 192
89:28 207, 647, 654, 655, 656, 658, 978
89:28-29 647
89:28-37 394, 395
89:29 657
89:29, 36 319
89:29, 36-37 648
89:29, 37 648
89:30 623, 732
89:30-31 636
89:30-32 729
89:30-37 319, 635–636, 1155
89:31 654
89:32 636
89:33 395
89:33-34 636
89:33-45 460
89:34-37 1110
89:34-38 1089
89:35-36 1108
89:35-37 391, 636
89:36 639
89:36-37 647
89:38 580, 658, 719
89:38-39 706
89:38-45 651, 704
89:38-48 636–637
89:39 390, 469, 480, 639, 707, 719
89:39-52 468
89:40 128
89:44 128, 468
89:45 651, 657
89:46 451, 460, 463, 470, 617, 628, 646, 647, 651, 652, 654, 656, 658
89:46-51 319, 659
89:47 651, 652, 654, 655, 656, 658, 659
89:47-48 656
89:48 523, 647, 651, 652, 653, 659
89:49 451, 628, 645, 647, 651, 653, 656, 659
89:49, 50 652
89:49-51 128, 637–638
89:50 452, 651, 652, 653, 654, 656, 658
89:50-51 639
89:51 30, 128
89:51-52 652
89:52 452, 461, 617, 637, 648, 704
90 451, 453, 468, 484, 485, 618, 645–660
90:1 464, 646, 650, 651, 652, 653, 654, 656, 658, 659
90:1, 2 651, 652, 654, 656, 658
90:1, 17 652, 654, 656, 658
90:1-2 655
90:1-2, 3-12, 13-17 650
90:2 105, 646, 651, 652, 654, 655, 656, 658
90:3 651, 652, 654, 655, 656, 658
90:3-12 452, 651, 655, 657, 659
90:4 460, 463, 653, 654, 655
90:4, 9, 10 651
90:4, 9, 10, 12 651
90:5, 6, 14 655
90:5-6 654, 657
90:7 658, 659
90:7, 9, 11 452, 654
90:7, 9 ,11 651
90:8 658–659
90:8a 654
90:9 655, 657
90:9, 10, 11, 12, 17, 38 650–651
90:9, 11 658
90:10 651, 657, 658
90:10b 651
90:11a, 12a 658
90:13 451, 464, 646, 651, 652, 654, 655, 656, 658
90:13, 14 451–452
90:13, 16 651, 652, 653, 654, 656, 658
90:13-15 656
90:13-17 452, 653, 655, 656, 658, 659
90:14 451, 452, 652, 654, 655, 656, 657, 658
90:14-15 658
90:15 523, 659
90:16 655, 658, 659
90:16-17 657
90:17 652, 653, 657, 658, 659
91 453, 652, 653, 659
91:1 659, 751, 899
91:1, 9 452, 659
91:9 659
91:14 653
91:14-16 653, 659
91:15-16 653
91:16 653, 655, 659
92:1 452
92:3 1140
92:9 680
92:12 482
92:13 482
92ff 648
93, 97, 99 647
93:1 452, 469
93:2 648
93:4 904
94:3 452
94:11 977
94:12 562
95 903
95:3 469, 1204
95:7 205
96:1 561
96:1-2 649
96:1-13 649
96:3 859
96:3-8 507
96:10 469
96:10-13 649
96:13 649
97:1 452, 469

97:2 648
97:9 452
98:1 561
98:1-2 649
98:6 469
99:1 272, 452, 649
99:1, 4 469
99:5 680
99:6 140, 464
100:1-2 649, 903
100:1-5 649
100:2 649
100:3 1310
101 464
101:1 468
102 599
102:13, 16, 21 599
102:20 936
102:25-27 599
103 464, 468
103:1 468
103:1-5 471
103:3 904
103:4 566
103:7 464
103:7-8 469
103:13 840
104-106 694, 696
104:1, 31 507
104:5 751
104:6-7, 10-13 751
104:9 751
104:24 218, 753
104:35 464
105:1 852
105:1-2 649
105:4 567
105:10 396, 798, 1110
105:26 464
105:28 956
105:39 812
105:45-106:1 464
106 451
106:16, 23, 32 464
106:45 469
106:47 463, 469
106:48 452, 461, 464, 617, 704
107 664, 695
107-109 678
107-113 678
107-118 703
107:1 469, 695
107:1-2, 3-5, 33-43 665
107:1-3 463
107:2, 6, 13, 19, 28 695
107:3 469
107:8, 15, 21, 31 795
107:10 936
107:43 978
108 665, 669–670, 695
108-109 665
108-110 665
108:7-10 665
108:8 272
108:13 665
109 663–670, 695
109:1-5 664
109:1-20 567
109:2-3 666
109:2-5 666
109:3 668
109:4 668
109:4, 20, 29 666
109:4-5 666
109:6 663, 666–667, 1238
109:6-15 668
109:6-19 664, 666
109:6-20 663
109:7 667
109:8 663
109:9 667
109:10 667
109:11 667
109:12 667
109:13 667
109:14 667
109:15 667
109:16 514, 568, 667
109:18 667
109:18-19 666
109:20 664
109:21 667, 668
109:21-25 667
109:22 668
109:22-24 667
109:24 667
109:25 668
109:25-27 695
109:26-27 695
109:27 667
109:28 667
109:30 668
109:31 667, 668
110 139, 141, 233, 458, 460, 469, 471, 668, 669–670, 673–688, 695, 701, 703, 705, 706, 722, 733, 865, 961, 970, 1077–1078, 1079, 1247–1248, 1254, 1256, 1257
110, 132 647
110:1 139, 141, 156, 471, 481, 514, 525, 539, 568, 649, 674, 683, 684, 686, 771, 835, 1016, 1307
110:1, 4 1077
110:1, 5-6 687
110:1-2 680, 684
110:1-3 679–681
110:1-4 1073
110:1a 679
110:1b 679–680
110:1c 680
110:2 207, 304, 680, 685
110:2-3 680–681
110:3 680, 681, 685, 687
110:4 139, 156, 583, 679, 681–683, 686, 1030, 1248, 1253, 1256–1257
110:4a 682
110:5 649, 680, 683, 685
110:5-6 683, 684, 685, 687, 1268
110:5-7 679, 683, 707
110:6 220, 649, 1168
110:7 683, 684
111 695, 703
111-112 665
111-113 678, 722
111:1 464
111:2 1331
111:4 665
111:5 665
111:5, 9 695
112 695

112-118 703
112:1 464, 562
112:3, 9 695
112:4 665
112:9 706
113 695
113-118 665, 721
113:1 721
113:1, 9 464
113:2 722
114 695
114:2 272
115 695
115:1 695
115:2 452
115:4-11 721
115:9-11 722
115:15 722
115:18 464, 695, 722
116:15 695
116:16 480
117:2 464, 695
118 693–700, 721, 882
118:1 695
118:1, 29 693
118:2-4 695
118:5 693, 695
118:5-18 693
118:5-28 693
118:6-7 904
118:6-9 693
118:10-12 693
118:14 852
118:15 694
118:17-18 700
118:19, 21, 28, 29 695
118:19-20 694
118:19-21 694
118:19-28 693
118:22 696, 699, 876, 877, 879, 881, 882, 1242
118:22-23 698
118:22-26 694, 1101
118:22a 1267
118:25, 26 698
118:25-26 694, 698, 879
118:26 696, 697
118:26-27 882
118:27 694
118:27-28 694
118:29 695
119 665, 704, 722, 724
119-134 703
119:24, 77, 92, 143, 174 743
119:38, 84, 176 480
119:89, 142, 160 754
119:90 751
119:116 500
119:160 762
119:176 1308
120 703, 712, 714, 723
120-125 712–718, 720
120-134 702, 711, 721
120-137 665
120:1 723
120:6-7 713, 714
121 713–716, 717, 718, 722, 724
121:1 713
121:1-2 715, 723, 724
121:2 712, 713, 714, 715, 722
121:3, 4, 5 713
121:3-8 713
121:4 703
121:7, 8 713
121:8 712, 713, 714, 715, 718
122 712, 714, 716–717, 720
122:1, 9 716
122:2b 716
122:3a 716
122:4 713
122:6 717
122:6, 7, 8 716
122:6-7 713, 714
123 717
123-125 713, 717–718
123:1 713
123:2 717
123:3 717
124 714, 717
124:1 703, 712
124:8 712, 713, 714, 715, 716, 717, 722, 723, 724
125 713, 714, 717
125:1 715
125:1-2 717–718, 722
125:2 703, 712, 713, 714, 715, 716
125:5 712, 713, 714
126 469
126:1 469
127 712
127:5 562
128 624
128:1 562
128:5 712, 714
128:6 712, 714
129:1 712
130 718
130-131 599, 718
130-134 716, 718–721
130:5-6 560
130:7 599, 718
131 718, 720
131-133 720
131:1 599
131:1-2 718
131:3 599, 712, 715, 716, 718
132 389–392, 471, 701–709, 711, 712, 716, 717, 718–720, 728, 1058
132-134 554
132:1 702, 719
132:1, 17-18 703
132:1-2 702
132:1-5 390, 595
132:1b-2 704
132:1b-5 704
132:3-5 704
132:6 705
132:6-7 390, 704
132:6-10 704
132:7 680, 705
132:8-10 390, 704
132:10 480, 705
132:10-12 1086
132:10-18 202, 1067
132:11 514, 719, 807
132:11, 13-14, 17-18 390
132:11, 17 553–554
132:11-12 395, 704, 719
132:11-18 469, 471
132:11a 704
132:11b-12 704
132:12 319, 706, 719
132:13 554, 719
132:13-14 553, 719
132:13-16 704
132:13-18 704
132:14 554, 719
132:16 554, 719
132:17 554, 624, 625,

	707, 797, 804, 853, 1014, 1015, 1063
132:17-18	390, 704
132:17a	706
132:17b	706
132:18	390, 469, 707, 719
133	554, 703, 714, 720–721
133:1	554
133:1-2	720
133:2	554
133:3	554, 624, 625, 712, 720
133:7-8, 13-14	797
134	548, 703, 720
134:1	554, 721
134:2-3	723, 724
134:3	703, 704, 712, 714, 715, 720, 721, 722
135-136	721
135-150	703
135:1	721
135:1, 21	464
135:2	721
135:4	798
135:7	721, 751
135:14	721
135:15-20	721
135:21	721
136	548
136:1-4	721
136:29	721
137:5-6	1027
138-145	665
139:11	220
140:2	517
140:4, 6, 9	464
141:2	186
143:2, 12	480
144	703, 704, 980
144:9	1140
144:15	562
145	703
145:4, 9-10, 17	508
145:5, 11-12	507, 508
145:11-13	840
145:13	431, 508, 665
145:14	500, 618
145:18	1181
145:20	665
145:21	461
146	988
146-150	469, 617, 665, 703
146:1, 10	464
146:3	505
146:6	198
146:6-8	198
146:7	936
146:7-8	198
146:8	618
146:8-9	936
147:1	464
147:20-148:1	464
148:2, 5	1334
148:3-6	1143
148:13	852
148:14-149:1	464
149	477–489
149:1	561
149:5	516, 517
149:6-9	471
149:7-9	464
149:9-150:1	464
150:6	464, 471
498:4-8	583

Proverbs

1-9	742, 747
1:1	727, 728, 731, 732, 742, 759
1:1-7	727
1:2	854
1:2-6	727
1:6	750
1:7	727, 733
1:7, 29	854
1:8	752
1:15	977
1:20-33	765
2:1	752
2:2	754
2:2-6	854
2:4	750
2:5	750, 854
2:7	754
2:22	1146
3:1	752
3:1-9	313
3:12	840
3:13	854
3:19	744
3:31	977
4:7	854
4:19	977
5:1	752
5:15-20	1330
6:20	752
7:17	326, 575
8	739–745
8-9	765
8:1-4	744
8:1-9:12	765
8:15	731
8:22	219, 740, 741, 743
8:22-23	105, 753
8:22-26	742, 744
8:22-26, 33-36	765
8:22-31	218, 219, 739, 740–741, 742–744, 753
8:22-36	129
8:22b	740
8:23	743
8:24	740
8:24-25	743
8:27-28	740
8:27-30	742
8:27-31	742–743, 744
8:29	751
8:30	744
8:30-31	743
8:31	744
8:32, 35	766
8:33, 35	129
9:10	748, 750, 854, 899
9:10-11	753
9:13-18	765
10-22:16	748
10-24	742
10-29	747–748
10-30	765
10:1	129, 727, 728, 731, 732, 765
12:18	1294
14:26-28	731
14:35	731
15:33	854
16:2	731
16:10-11	731
16:10-15	731
16:10-16	731
16:12-13	731
16:13	731
16:17	741
18:10	752, 754
18:15	563
19:12	731
19:21	977
20:1	252

20:8, 26 731
20:26 731
20:27 326
20:28 731
21:1-2 731
21:13 563
22:11 731
22:11, 29 731
22:17 758
22:17-24:34 748
23:1-3 731
24:12 731
24:21-22 731
24:23 758
25-29 742, 748
25:1 727, 728, 731, 732
25:1-6 731
25:2 731
25:2, 6-7 731
25:3 731
25:5 731
28:2, 15-16 731
28:15-16 731
29:2, 12 731
29:4 731
29:4, 14 731
29:12 731
30 748–750
30-31 748
30:1 401, 727, 732, 749, 758
30:1-3 733, 747
30:1-4 732, 733
30:1-6 747, 748, 755
30:1-33 742
30:1a 748
30:2 749
30:3 748, 749, 752
30:4 218, 732, 733, 745, 747–755, 751, 755
30:4-5 748, 755
30:4-6 739
30:4a 750–751
30:4b 749, 751–754
30:5 754
30:5-6 742, 747, 754–755
30:5a 754
30:6 755
30:18-23 750
30:19 821–822
31:1 748, 758
31:1-9 742
31:2 485, 732
31:3 485, 731
31:3-9 312
31:4-7 731
31:8-9 731
31:9 731
31:10 742
31:10-31 741, 742, 765
31:30 733
31:31 742

Ecclesiastes

1:1 129, 757, 758–762, 765
1:1, 12 748
1:2-12:8 758
1:3 657–658
1:11 202
7:24 202
12:9-10 765
12:9-14 757, 758, 762, 765
12:10 762, 763, 1331
12:11 129, 754, 757, 762–765
12:11-12 763
12:12 765
12:13 763
12:13-14 763

Song of Solomon

1:1 772
1:2-4 775
1:3 821
1:3c, 4c 775
1:4 772–773
1:4, 12 772
1:5 772
1:5-7 775
1:8, 17 202
1:8-11 775
1:12-14 775
1:13 575
1:15-2:6 775
2:7 775
2:8-9 775
2:8-15 775
2:10-13 775
2:14 775
2:15 775
2:16-17 775
3:1-2 775
3:3 775
3:4 775
3:5 775
3:6 575
3:6-11 775
3:7 772, 774
3:8 774
3:9, 11 772
4:1-5 775
4:5 202
4:6 575
4:6-16 775
4:11 326
4:14 575
4:16b 775
5:1, 13 575
5:1a 775
5:1b 775
5:2-6 776
5:7 776
5:8 776
5:9 776
5:10 776
5:10-16 776
5:11 575
6:1 776
6:2 776
6:3 776
6:4-10 776
6:8 774, 821
6:9 774
6:11-12 776
6:12 772
7:1 776
7:1-13 776
7:4 202
7:5 772
7:10 130, 778
8:1-2 776
8:1-4 202
8:3 776
8:4 776
8:5 776
8:5b 130
8:6 1227
8:6-12 776
8:11, 12 772
8:13-14 776

Isaiah

1 789, 909
1-6 897
1-12 910
1-39 909, 910, 922, 962
1:1 921, 922, 1180
1:1-15 808
1:2, 4 790

1:2-2:4 1197
1:4 750
1:8 807
1:9f 969
1:11-17 186
1:16-20 808
1:19 113
1:20 787, 956
1:21-23 790
1:21-31 808
1:23 790
1:24 749, 839, 1330
1:24-27 790
1:25 754
1:26-27 790, 791, 794
1:26-30 786
1:27 797, 901, 992
1:28-31 790
1:29-31 992
2 792–793, 1057
2:1 789, 796, 922
2:1-4 338, 790, 870, 1247
2:1-5 808, 1054
2:1-5:30 790
2:2 99, 297, 808, 809, 810, 811, 812, 1132, 1159, 1321, 1323
2:2-3 808, 1027, 1108, 1111, 1123
2:2-3a 791
2:2-4 785–800, 786, 790, 808, 809, 870, 903, 936, 1107, 1110, 1223, 1279, 1280
2:2a 796
2:3 798, 799, 809, 888, 892, 904, 969
2:3-4 810, 812, 1102
2:3b 811
2:3b-4 791
2:3c 796
2:4 36, 809, 904, 1110
2:4-6 808, 811
2:5 791
2:5, 6 798
2:5-3:26 786
2:5-4:1 790
2:6-4:1 808
2:6-21 808
2:11-21 1228
2:22-3:15 808
2:44 965
3:1 1330
3:1-4:1 809
3:6 969
3:8 956
3:12 1268
3:13-15 899
3:14 36, 807
3:15 568
3:15-4:1 808
3:16-4:1 811
4 1106
4:1 969
4:1-6 202
4:2 36, 37, 793, 803–813, 852, 853, 1000, 1011, 1014, 1042, 1057, 1241, 1247, 1254, 1336
4:2-4 809
4:2-6 786, 790, 806, 1057
4:2b 803, 806, 810
4:3 809, 1057
4:3-4 809
4:4c 811
4:5 811, 852, 903
4:5-6 809, 811, 812, 813, 1111
4:6 809, 812
4:26 803
5-10 786
5:1 807
5:1-6 807
5:1-30 790
5:3 807
5:7 743, 807
5:7, 16 901
5:10 807
5:12 909
5:16 862, 1143
5:20 899
5:26 851
6 790, 848, 912, 1180
6-62, 66 1143
6:1 218, 488, 890, 969, 1297
6:1-4 890
6:1-8:18 790
6:1-13 890, 921
6:5 839, 890
6:9 454
6:9-10 334, 875, 909, 926, 956
6:9-10a 923
6:9-13 793, 926, 962
6:10 563, 890, 909, 910, 915, 956
6:10b 923
6:11 921
6:11-12 922, 926
6:13 848, 926
7 153, 790, 825, 831, 832, 833, 848
7, 9, 11 1214
7-9 845, 875, 912
7-10 846
7-11 852
7-12 31, 792, 825, 831, 834–835, 847, 855, 897
7-35 897
7-39 926
7:1 817
7:1-8:22 790
7:1-9:7 838
7:1-14 847
7:1-16 815–827
7:1-19 926
7:2 817
7:3 817, 823, 839
7:4, 11 819
7:4-9 880
7:6 817
7:7 817
7:8 153, 154, 817–818
7:8, 16 900
7:9b 875
7:10-11 823
7:11 153
7:12 818
7:13 454, 819
7:13-14 819
7:13-15 818, 819–823, 824, 825, 855, 1214
7:14 35, 53, 126, 154, 786, 790, 792, 805, 816, 819, 824, 825, 831, 832, 834,

	835, 838, 839, 845, 847, 875, 877, 878, 903, 904, 921, 1000, 1214
7:14-15	54
7:14-17	154
7:15	53
7:15-16	154
7:16	53, 823
7:16-17	823
7:16-23	818
7:17	53, 154
7:17-25	53
7:20	822
7:21-22	822
7:23-25	822
8	831, 833
8:3	839
8:6-15	875
8:8	35, 822, 831, 847, 1149
8:9-20	954
8:10	834
8:13-15	1308
8:14	877, 880, 881, 882, 899
8:14, 17	880
8:14-15	875, 877
8:16	954, 1143
8:16-22	834
8:17	794, 798, 887, 889
8:17-18	793
8:18	794, 823, 1241
8:19-12:6	790
8:20-22	846
8:21-22	824
8:22-9:2	404
9	154, 824, 831, 833, 848
9-11	832
9:1	834–838
9:1-2	831, 834, 846, 1102, 1162
9:1-6	154, 831, 833, 845, 851
9:1-7	192–193, 790, 824,831–840, 898, 926, 1162
9:2	404, 407, 824, 835
9:2-5	834, 835
9:3	835, 839, 903
9:3-5	1162
9:4	835
9:4-5	839–840
9:5	835
9:5-6	67–68, 202, 233
9:5b-6	1162
9:6	35, 36, 126, 153, 154, 223, 585, 716, 822, 824, 825, 831, 833, 834, 835, 837, 838, 847, 849, 854, 875, 877, 878, 903, 904, 1016, 1121, 1213
9:6-7	30, 192–193, 319, 786, 792, 805, 824, 831, 832, 835–838, 855, 869, 875, 898, 899, 921, 1000, 1022, 1057, 1110, 1225, 1247, 1307
9:6-9	859, 862
9:6a	1121
9:6b	1121
9:6b-7	794
9:7	31, 32, 154, 403, 585, 797, 824, 825, 839, 847, 877, 899, 901, 1025, 1105, 1162, 1263, 1335
9:7c	838
9:8	798
9:8-10:4	846
9:8-10:34	790
9:14	888
10	1197
10-16	1002
10-33	912
10:2	568
10:5	846
10:5-19	846
10:5-34	846
10:9	832
10:15	846
10:15-34	845
10:16, 33	1330
10:17	846
10:18, 33-34	902
10:19	846
10:20	798, 839
10:20-21	837
10:20-22	859
10:20-27	846
10:21	36, 68, 837
10:21-22	793, 839
10:22-23	1311
10:24-27	202
10:24-34	860
10:26	851
10:27-34	846
10:28-34	846
10:32	1264
10:33	824
10:33-34	848, 1013
10:34	904
11	195, 209, 824, 848, 938, 980, 1057, 1134, 1162–1163, 1197
11-12	786
11:1	34, 113, 205, 233, 706, 792, 793, 808, 810, 824, 839, 845, 847, 848, 852, 853, 934, 972, 993, 1000, 1013, 1042, 1057, 1066, 1163, 1210, 1214, 1241, 1247, 1273
11:1, 4	870
11:1, 10	221, 805
11:1-2	155, 193
11:1-3a	734
11:1-4	1002
11:1-5	805, 833, 835, 847, 875, 877, 990, 1012, 1187, 1242
11:1-5, 10-12	786
11:1-6	831
11:1-9	172, 832, 847, 921, 926, 934, 940, 976, 1179
11:1-10	126, 824–825, 859, 862, 978, 1067
11:1-12:6	790
11:1-16	202, 795,

	845–855, 898, 988, 1247
11:1ff	233
11:2	31, 403, 407, 836, 847, 849, 854, 934, 938, 949, 983, 990
11:2-3	792, 847
11:2-5	824
11:3	203, 849, 854
11:3-4	1057
11:3-5	849, 934
11:3b-16	734
11:3f	1263
11:4	31, 32, 403, 831, 849, 850, 854, 875, 899, 904, 938, 948
11:4-5	792, 877, 898, 899, 1263
11:4-9	901
11:5	31, 407, 850
11:5-9	165–166
11:6	853
11:6-7	232
11:6-8	792
11:6-9	36, 824, 850, 1000, 1002, 1092, 1242
11:6-13	787
11:6-16	805
11:7	208
11:9	32, 232, 792, 811, 850
11:10	326, 760, 792, 799, 824, 848, 855, 1163, 1223, 1225
11:10, 12	798, 805
11:10-11	851, 852
11:10-16	832, 850–852, 1242
11:11	851, 1026
11:11-12	792, 805, 1163
11:11-16	859
11:12	797, 851, 1102
11:13	233
11:13-14	1163
11:14	1002, 1003
11:15	851
11:15-16	792, 1163
11:16	914
12:1, 4	852
12:1-6	805, 852
12:2	813, 904
12:2-5	792
12:2-6	786
12:4	576
12:5	852
12:6	750, 792, 794, 811, 852
13-14	865
13-23	669, 859, 865–866, 897
13-27	910
13:1	748, 859, 1261
13:1-16	1197
13:12	879
13:19	1226
14:1	798
14:2	1268
14:15	853
14:19	853
14:28	748, 1261
14:29-30	202
14:32	794, 1265
15:1	859
15:1, 2, 4, 5, 6, 7, 8, 9	860
15:1, 6, 9	860
15:2, 3, 4, 5, 8	860
15:9	861
16:1	860
16:1-5	202
16:1a	860
16:1b	860
16:2	860, 861
16:3-4a	861
16:4-5	898
16:4b	861
16:5	30, 761, 813, 859–863, 877, 898, 899, 901, 904, 1335
16:6	861, 863, 969
16:7-10, 13-14	861
16:9, 11	860
16:12	861
16:13-14	863
16:14	861
17:12-14	1003
18:7	794
19:1	859
19:4	749, 1330
19:13	879
19:23	914
19:23-25	936
19:24-25	865
21:1	859
21:5	30
22:1	859
22:22-23	794, 1267
22:23-24	1268
23-24	1197
23:1	859
23:13	878
23:18	794
24	866
24-27	865–866, 897
24:1-6	866
24:1-20	866–870
24:1-23	936
24:2	866
24:3-4	866
24:5	866, 936
24:6a	866
24:6b	866
24:7-9	866
24:7-20	866–870
24:10	866
24:14	867
24:14-16a	867
24:16b-20	867
24:17-23	1222
24:18	233
24:19-20	867
24:21	867–868, 1003
24:21-23	865–870, 867
24:21-25	898
24:21b	868
24:21c	868
24:22	867, 868–869
24:22a	868
24:22c	868
24:22d	868
24:23	793, 794, 811, 867, 869–870, 903
24:23a	869
24:23b	866, 869
24:26	969
25	870
25:1	36
25:4-6	899
25:6-8	793, 870
25:6-10a	811
25:9	208, 904
25:9-10a	794
26:4	431, 813, 839, 877
26:11-15	903
26:13	576, 752
26:19	198, 443, 499, 522, 989

26:20-21 936
26:21 936
27:2 807
27:6 914
28-30 889
28-33 873, 897
28-34 846
28-35 910
28:1-4 873
28:2, 17 902
28:5 853
28:5-6 202
28:7-10 873
28:9 888
28:9-13 889
28:11 903
28:11-13 873
28:14 874
28:14, 16 875
28:14-19 696
28:14-22 873, 875, 880
28:15 874
28:15, 17-18 874
28:15, 18 880
28:16 696, 873–882, 1242, 1267
28:16-17 901
28:16b 877
28:16c 877, 880, 882
28:16d 882
28:17 877
28:17-18 875
28:17b-22 874
28:18 874
28:22 874, 880
28:26 888
28:29 36, 836
29:1 839
29:1-8 1198
29:9 909
29:9-10 334, 909
29:11-12 889
29:14 36, 899
29:17-24 901
29:18 909, 915
29:18-19 989
29:18-21 936
29:19 899
29:22 798
29:23-24 899
29:31 910
30 886
30-31 874
30:1-17 886
30:2-7 874
30:8 839
30:8-10 888, 890
30:8-11 888, 889, 891
30:9 956
30:9-11 886
30:9b 886
30:10 887
30:11 887
30:15 880, 889
30:18-19 887
30:18-26 886, 887–888, 891
30:19-23 404
30:19-25 902
30:19-26 885–893, 1171, 1172, 1173
30:20 885, 887, 888, 889, 890, 892, 1170, 1172
30:20-21 34, 892
30:20-26 889
30:20a 888
30:21 887, 890, 892, 1172
30:21-22 887
30:22 887
30:23 34, 1173
30:23-26 887, 1172
30:24 1173
30:25 1173
30:26 208, 1173
30:31 902
31:1 874, 898
31:1-3 898
31:5 794, 898
31:6 900
31:6-9 898
31:8-9 898
31:9b 898
32 902
32:1 193, 854, 863, 898, 901, 904, 1263
32:1, 16 877
32:1-8 897–905
32:2 898–899
32:3 909, 915
32:3-4 899
32:4 899
32:5 899
32:5-7 900
32:6-7 899–900
32:7 568
32:8 900
32:9, 11 900
32:9-14 900–901
32:10 900
32:10-14 901
32:11 169
32:12-14 900
32:14 878, 900, 901
32:15 853, 901
32:15-16 901, 990
32:15-20 901–902, 905
32:16-18 901
32:17 837
32:17-18 903
32:19 902
32:20 902
33 902
33-34 1197
33:1-16 897, 902
33:2, 5-6, 15-16 902
33:2, 20 969
33:3 1003
33:5 794, 899, 901
33:5-6 880, 903
33:6 854
33:13-16 902
33:15 1014
33:16 1201
33:17 902, 903, 904
33:17, 22 904
33:17-24 897–905
33:20 903
33:21 904
33:21, 33 904
33:22 903, 904, 1227
33:23 904
33:24a 904
33:24b 904
34 912, 1200, 1203
34-35 865, 897, 912
34:1-3, 5-8 1203
34:1-4 1002, 1003
34:5-6 1002, 1203
34:5-17 1002, 1003
34:6 914, 1002
34:8 1002, 1005
34:8-9 916–917
34:10 914
34:11, 14 912
35 907–918, 1002
35:1 911, 914, 917
35:1, 10 911
35:1-2 912–914
35:1-3 908
35:1-10 907–918
35:2 911, 916

35:2, 6, 10	911
35:3	910
35:3-4	909–910
35:3-6b	914
35:4	904, 908, 911, 914
35:4-5	936
35:5	899, 909, 911, 915, 916, 917, 989
35:5-6	198, 908, 914
35:6	915, 917
35:6-7	899, 910, 917
35:6c-7	914
35:8	910, 912, 915
35:8-10	914
35:9	911, 912
35:10	208, 794, 910, 911, 912
35:15-29	897
36-37	846, 860, 921, 922
36-39	860, 910, 911, 1209
36-66	897
36:4-15	880
36:7	796
36:11	903
36:16	1243
36:16-17	787
37:16	272
37:20	861
37:22	1264
37:32	794
37:36-37	1196, 1197
38, 39	921
38:1-8	819
38:7-8	819
39	53
39:3-7	962
39:5-7	922
39:8	847
40-48	963
40-50	990
40-55	168, 333, 470, 909, 922, 926, 938, 962, 963, 975, 979, 984
40-66	790, 910, 911, 921, 922, 947, 985
40:1	790, 991
40:1-2	925, 926
40:1-11	915, 926, 1012, 1014
40:2	964
40:3	914, 1331
40:3-5	790, 793, 910, 962
40:3-5, 29-31	910
40:3-8	927
40:5	787
40:6-8	975
40:9	840
40:9-11	927
40:11	890, 1200, 1310
40:12	750
40:12-26	926
40:13	36
40:22	750, 794
40:25	750
40:27-31	926
40:31	1064
41-48	923
41-66	53
41:1	932
41:1-7	923, 932
41:1-7, 21-29	926
41:2, 25	955
41:2-3, 25	933, 940
41:5-7, 24, 29	933
41:8	933
41:8-9	933, 940, 944, 962
41:8-13	933
41:8-14	923
41:8-20	927, 932
41:9	933
41:10	933
41:13	933
41:14	750
41:15-29	923
41:17-20	376, 947, 962
41:18	899, 910
41:20	933
41:21-42:9	932
41:25	207, 933, 944
42, 49, 50, 52-53	1296
42, 49-55	923
42:1	30, 31, 155, 334, 561, 933, 934, 937, 938, 939, 940, 949, 963, 983, 990, 1000, 1134, 1179, 1227
42:1, 4	799, 928, 934
42:1, 4, 6	1297
42:1-4	168, 470, 923, 931, 939, 948, 949, 962, 1241
42:1-6	877
42:1-7	934, 946, 972
42:1-9	126, 202, 319, 832, 931–940, 943, 944, 953, 960, 976, 1227
42:1-13	30
42:1a	931
42:1b	931
42:1ff	233
42:2	931, 1297
42:2-3	933, 940
42:2-4	927
42:3	31, 934
42:3-7	963
42:3a	931
42:3b-4	931
42:4	38, 333, 934, 948
42:5	936
42:5-6a	932
42:5-7	932
42:6	31, 320, 925, 933, 934, 935, 938, 946, 947, 1223, 1225
42:6-7	923, 937, 940, 948, 949, 950, 1102
42:6a	924
42:6b	924
42:6b-7	932
42:6c	334
42:7	169, 899, 909, 915, 933, 934, 936, 938, 940, 945, 947, 949, 953, 986, 991, 1297
42:8	508, 933, 936, 1322
42:8, 10-12	933
42:8-9	932
42:9	208
42:10-12	932–933
42:10-17	926
42:13-16	947
42:13-53:12	202
42:14-16	376, 962
42:16	923
42:18	909
42:18-19	923, 963

42:18-20 334
42:18-25 924, 926, 964
42:18-29 945
42:19 34, 934, 962
42:24 957, 969
42:24-25 963
43:1-3, 14-21 962
43:1-4 376
43:1-13 927
43:1-44:23 924
43:3 750
43:4 879
43:6 752
43:7 1017
43:8 334, 909, 915, 923, 963
43:10 34, 202, 923, 933, 944, 945, 962
43:14-28 927
43:16-19 168–169
43:16-21 376
43:22 964
43:22-28 963, 964
43:24 1330
44 154
44:1 34
44:1-2 933, 944, 963
44:1-23 927
44:3 990
44:3-5 901
44:6 154, 839, 1307
44:6-8 154
44:9-20 936
44:18 334, 909
44:21 34, 963
44:24-45:7 428, 962
44:24-46:13 924
44:24-54:13 927
44:26, 28 794
44:28 839, 921, 1103
44:28-45:1 932, 944, 1119
44:28-45:5 933
45:1 30, 42, 127
45:4 933, 944, 963
45:8 854
45:11 752
45:13 955
45:14-46:13 927
45:17 431
45:18 751
45:22 936
45:23-24 936
45:24 1143, 1263
46:3 798
46:3, 12 964
46:10 26
46:13 794
47:1-15 924, 927
47:6 963
47:7 964
48:1 798
48:1, 8 944, 964
48:1-5 945
48:1-6 963
48:1-22 927
48:1-28 924
48:2 752
48:4 944
48:5 944
48:5-7 922
48:8b-11, 17-19 963
48:10 754
48:11 204
48:14 944, 948
48:15 155
48:16 155, 990, 1179
48:18-19 944
48:18f 964
48:20 933, 944, 963, 968
48:20-21 944, 947, 962
48:22 944
49 963
49-53 873, 963
49:1 169, 924, 943, 944, 963
49:1-2 924
49:1-2, 4-7 963
49:1-6 168, 319, 470, 962, 963, 985, 1241
49:1-7 30, 972
49:1-13 126, 832, 921, 924, 927, 931, 933, 934, 943–950, 953, 960, 976, 1227
49:2 169, 948
49:2-3 944
49:3 924, 933, 940, 944, 945, 948, 950, 963, 975, 980, 1000
49:3, 6-8 943
49:3, 6-12 943
49:4 169, 938–939, 944
49:4, 7 924
49:4-5 948
49:4a 948
49:5 35, 924, 936, 944, 945, 953
49:5, 8-13 934, 946
49:5-6 30–31, 169, 934, 945, 947, 1297
49:5-6a 946
49:5-8 936
49:5a 945
49:6 35, 38, 599–600, 924, 934, 935, 936, 938, 945–946, 949, 950, 953, 1223, 1225, 1297, 1321
49:6, 8 933
49:6-7 963
49:6a 935
49:6b 948
49:7 924, 934, 946, 948
49:7, 8 944
49:8 31, 925, 934, 935, 938, 949, 980
49:8-9 599
49:8-12 962
49:8-13 935, 950
49:8-50:3 927
49:8b-9 950
49:8b-12 947
49:9 933, 936, 938, 945, 949
49:9-10 947
49:10 899, 950
49:13 938, 943, 944, 949
49:14, 15 794
49:14-50:3 924
49:17-22 947
49:22-23 1028
49:23 680
50 565, 600
50:1 578, 957, 964
50:4 569, 938, 949, 955
50:4, 5, 7, 9 954
50:4, 9 1241
50:4-5a 957
50:4-6 924, 954–957
50:4-9 168, 319, 470, 600, 931, 934, 943, 953, 960

50:4-10 962
50:4-11 30, 126, 334, 832, 924, 927, 953–960, 1227
50:4b-6 563–564
50:5 956
50:5, 7, 9 954
50:5-6 569
50:5b-6 953
50:5b-7 957
50:6 333, 924, 956, 957, 1296
50:6-7 31
50:6-11 960
50:7 957
50:7, 9 924
50:7-9 953, 954, 957–958
50:9 958
50:10 946, 959, 963, 1000
50:10-11 924, 953, 954, 959–960
50:10a 959
50:11 959, 960
51:1, 7 959
51:1-52:12 925, 927
51:2 743
51:3 946
51:3, 11, 16 794
51:4 799, 904
51:4-5 936
51:4-8 901
51:6 904
51:9 969
51:9-10 169, 962
51:11 910
51:11-14 947
51:16 946, 959
51:21 1265
51:22 925
52-53 599, 600
52:1 839
52:1, 7, 9 794
52:1-2 925
52:1-12 1013
52:1-54:17 1012
52:7 199, 786, 959, 1110
52:7-10 915
52:9-12 947
52:10 799
52:11 968
52:11-12 962
52:12 968
52:12-13 168
52:13 35, 168, 169, 202, 222, 600, 839, 963, 964, 967, 968, 972, 1000, 1297
52:13-15 925, 934, 946, 949
52:13-53:1 967
52:13-53:12 30, 31, 126, 186,202, 221–223, 319, 470, 569, 622, 832, 904, 925, 927, 931, 934, 943, 946, 958, 961–972, 1013, 1227, 1241, 1321
52:14 222, 569, 969
52:14-53:1-8 964
52:15 969
53 168, 233, 235, 321, 600, 873, 1247, 1277, 1281, 1298, 1311
53:1 334, 890, 923, 969
53:1-3 925
53:1-8 948
53:1-12 877
53:1ff 969
53:2 222, 853, 969
53:2-12 923
53:3 169, 333, 794, 967, 969, 1146
53:3, 7 222
53:3, 7, 8 333
53:3-4 880
53:3-5 600, 1277
53:4 964, 965, 966–967, 969, 1296
53:4-5 955
53:4-5, 10 169
53:4-5:11 222
53:4-6 31, 925
53:4-6, 10-12 934, 946
53:4-12 786
53:5 36, 223, 333, 837, 967, 969, 1296
53:5-6 32, 963, 1308
53:5-7 570
53:6 223, 334, 969, 1103, 1308
53:6, 8 964
53:6-7 1297
53:6b 1304
53:7 334, 968, 969, 1265
53:7-8 222
53:7-9 925
53:8 32, 35, 970
53:9 223, 970
53:9, 11 1263
53:10 32, 185, 334, 967, 970, 1305, 1311
53:10-12 925
53:11 31, 32, 320, 937, 963, 970, 1000, 1334
53:11-12 570, 934, 946, 949
53:12 169, 222, 334, 600, 937, 966, 967, 970, 972
54:1-10 927
54:1-17 925, 1013
54:2-3 903
54:3 947
54:5 578
54:6-7 578
54:7 964
54:9 1110
54:10 925
54:11-12 208, 1265
54:11-17 928
54:17 963, 980
55 975–976, 980, 1192
55:1-3, 6-9, 12 977
55:1-5 976
55:1-13 925, 928
55:2 976
55:3 31, 396, 853, 925, 936, 947, 976, 977, 978, 1105, 1109, 1110
55:3-5 975–981, 976, 980
55:4 977
55:4-5 979
55:5 195, 977
55:6-7 976, 977
55:6-13 976
55:7 964, 977

55:8	977
55:8-11	976, 977
55:9	977
55:12	1110
55:12-13	962, 977
56-66	928, 938, 984, 990
56:2	506
56:5-6	1190
56:6	963, 980
56:6-7	195, 799, 1061
56:7	798
56:7-8	1189
56:11	892
57:5	837
57:14	1331
57:15	839, 1297
57:17	964
57:18-19	904
57:19	837
58-66	1000
58:1	798
58:1ff	964
58:2	901, 1331
58:6	218
58:8-12	904
58:9	1181
58:14	787
59:2ff	964
59:3	1005
59:9-12	969
59:15-20	928
59:16	204, 1005, 1006
59:20	31, 233, 1109
59:20-21	716, 936, 947
59:20b	793
59:21	927, 980, 985, 990, 1179
60-62	915
60:1	208
60:1-7	1223, 1224, 1225
60:1-22	928
60:3, 14	799
60:5	794
60:9	208, 750
60:9, 14	811
60:14	794
60:16	904
60:17	901, 1110, 1268
60:21	204, 803, 992
60:22	204
61:1	808, 849, 916, 936, 950, 988 989, 1000, 1001
61:1-2	198, 199, 908, 917–918, 940, 950, 983, 985, 986, 988, 1022, 1181, 1256
61:1-2a	938, 939, 949, 987, 1309
61:1-3	155, 832, 853, 938, 949, 955, 983, 984, 988, 989, 991, 992, 1197, 1265
61:1-4	127
61:1-6	983–993
61:1a	989–990
61:1b	990–991
61:2	199, 991, 1000, 1005
61:2-8	936, 947
61:2b-3	1309
61:3	794, 854, 983, 984, 992
61:3a	992
61:3b	992
61:4	938, 949, 992
61:4-5	799
61:4-11	984, 992–993
61:5-11	992
61:6	992, 1003
61:6-7	984, 1028
61:7	984, 993
61:7-10	992
61:8	396, 980, 1109
61:8-9	938, 949
61:9	984
61:11	807, 984
62:1	794
62:1-12	928
62:2	799, 854
62:4	839
62:7, 11	794
62:10	914, 1331
62:11	578
62:12	1000, 1001
63	1200, 1268
63:1	998, 999, 1001, 1003, 1004, 1203
63:1-2	999
63:1-3	1007
63:1-6	52, 684, 837–838, 997–1008, 1203, 1318
63:1a	1001–1003
63:1b	1003–1004
63:2	221, 1003, 1004, 1005
63:2-6	998, 1001, 1002, 1004
63:3	998, 1004, 1005, 1006
63:3, 6	1003
63:3-6	1004
63:3a	1006
63:4	999, 1002, 1004, 1005, 1006
63:4-6	1204
63:5	1005, 1006
63:6	1004–1005, 1006, 1007
63:7	978
63:7-9	998
63:7-64:12	1000
63:11	1310
63:15-19	969
63:16	839
63:17	963, 964, 980
64:3	206
64:3-11	969
64:5-7	964
64:7-8	839
64:9	839
65:8-9, 13-15	980
65:9	272
65:9, 13, 14-15	963
65:11, 25	811
65:12b	1181
65:17	1097
65:17-25	839, 1000
65:18	839
65:18, 19	794
65:19	208
65:21	807
65:24	1181
65:25	853, 1000
66	1000
66:1	680
66:7-9	1022–1023
66:10, 13, 20	794
66:12	786, 837, 1110
66:14	551, 963, 980
66:18	799, 1168
66:18-20	1111
66:20	794, 811

66:20-21 799
66:22 1097, 1098
66:24 1003
67:17 334

Jeremiah

1 328
1-28 97
1:5 1039
1:9-10 1053
1:10 1021
1:14-15 1039
1:16 1039
2:1-2 578
2:2-3 1039
2:5 1039
2:8 1103
2:21 807
2:22-23 1039
3:1-2, 6 578
3:6-10 1039
3:8 578
3:14 1039
3:14-18 962, 1014, 1021, 1039
3:15 899, 1042, 1103
3:15-16 1041
3:16 1059
3:16-17 1039
3:17 1039, 1110
3:18 1012
3:19 752
4:1-2 1014
4:2 1321
4:3 1264
4:4 1039
5:12 523
5:15 903
5:17 1021
5:22 751
6:10 563
6:14 1111
7, 26, 38 595
7:7 1098
7:18 1157
7:21-22 186
7:21-26 1040–1041
7:23 1030, 1040, 1043
7:24-25 1040
7:32 1021, 1043
8:8 312, 321
8:11 1111
8:15 560, 1111
8:19 561
9:7 754
9:13-14 1040
9:24 1040, 1042
9:25 1021, 1042, 1043
9:25-26 1040
10:10 396
10:12 218, 753
10:13 721, 751
10:16 752
10:17-25 1038
10:21 1039
10:23 1038
11:1-3 1040
11:4 1030, 1043
11:4, 6-7 1040
11:8a, 9-10 1040
11:8b, 11 1040
11:20 878
12:3 878
12:10 807
12:12 1111
12:15 1189
13:16 560
14:19 560, 1111
15:19 879
16:5 1111
16:10-15 1197
16:14 31
16:14-15 376, 1021, 1043
16:19 326
17-18 1041
17:1 1041
17:9-10 1041
17:10 878
17:25 1265
18-19 1275, 1277
18:1-11 1041
18:6 1277
18:8 1041
18:11 1041
18:12 1041
19 1281
19:5 796
19:6 1021, 1043
20-22 1335
20:1-23:8 1011
20:11 837
20:12 878
20:16 1226
20:18 523
21:12 1012
22 1041
22:1-3 1041
22:1-4 1012
22:4-5 1041
22:8-19 1041
22:14 30
22:24 1227
22:24-25 1227
22:24-27 1041
22:30 1041
23 155, 1041, 1057
23:1 1103
23:1-2 320, 892, 1012, 1041
23:1-4 1039
23:1-6 320, 1011, 1084, 1247, 1305
23:1-8 202, 1021
23:1-8, 29-31 1197
23:3-4 320, 1012, 1013, 1041
23:4 899, 1087, 1103, 1108
23:5 32, 34, 36, 37, 155, 195, 202, 390, 403, 406, 407, 694, 760, 793, 805, 810, 853, 898, 899, 979, 1012, 1014, 1015, 1025, 1039, 1041, 1042, 1043, 1066, 1075, 1105, 1106, 1241, 1242, 1247, 1254, 1272, 1273, 1305, 1306
23:5-6 31, 37, 127, 233, 320, 808, 892, 1011–1018, 1040, 1043, 1044, 1050, 1056, 1058, 1073, 1104, 1105, 1106, 1107, 1335, 1336
23:5-8 1163
23:5f 1263
23:6 37, 155, 207, 806, 810, 853,

877, 898, 1017, 1018, 1042, 1058, 1106, 1143, 1263, 1305, 1307
23:7-8 376, 1013, 1043
23:08 962
23:9-40 1103
23:16-22 309
23:20 99, 297, 795, 1031, 1054, 1132
23:33 748
23:33, 34, 36, 38 1261
24:4-7 1021, 1042
24:5-7 1012
24:7 1030, 1043
25:5 1098
25:11 1141
25:11-12 923, 1054, 1139–1149
25:32 1168
26:16-19 1209
26:18 789, 790
27:7 1321
29 98, 99, 1042
29-33 97
29:1-3 98
29:7 966
29:10 1141, 1196
29:10-11 98
29:10-14 1139–1149
29:11 562
29:13-14 98
29:14 1053
29:16-19 1042
30 1031, 1032, 1042, 1054, 1059
30-33 99, 1014, 1021, 1036, 1038, 1042–1043, 1045, 1052, 1054, 1059
30:1-2 1021
30:1-4 1021–1022
30:1-9 127
30:1-24 1021–1032
30:3 31, 1022, 1042–1043, 1052, 1053
30:3, 8, 24 1021
30:3, 18 1053
30:3-4 1022
30:3-10 1188
30:5 1022, 1111
30:5-7 1022–1024
30:5-8 1163
30:6 1022
30:7 1023, 1024, 1031, 1149, 1305
30:7a 798, 1023–1024
30:7b 798
30:8 1024
30:8-9 193, 1012, 1025–1026, 1043
30:8-10 1087
30:8-11 1024–1026
30:8-11, 21 202
30:9 34, 97, 1025, 1032, 1107, 1108, 1160, 1163, 1228, 1335
30:10 1023, 1026
30:10-15 1163
30:10a 1023
30:11 965, 1026
30:12 1026
30:12-17 1026–1027
30:13 1026
30:14 1026–1027
30:15 1027
30:16, 17 1027
30:16-20 1163
30:18 1028, 1043, 1053
30:18-20 1028–1029
30:18-22 1144
30:18a 1028
30:19 1028
30:20 1029
30:21 1029, 1030, 1163
30:21-22 1030, 1032
30:22 1030, 1043
30:23 1031
30:23-24 1031
30:24 97, 99, 297, 1031, 1054, 1132
31 56, 1036, 1043
31:1, 27, 29, 31, 33, 38 1021
31:1, 33 1030
31:5 807
31:15 109–112
31:20 743
31:20, 23 1053
31:23 1043, 1053, 1058
31:27 1053
31:27, 31, 38 1053
31:27-28 1043, 1053
31:27-37 1163
31:31 31, 99, 1043, 1044, 1050, 1053
31:31-32 1036
31:31-34 97, 98, 127, 334, 728, 787, 881, 984, 1035–1046, 1056, 1059
31:32 578, 1036, 1037, 1043, 1059
31:33 1040, 1041, 1043, 1044
31:33-34 798, 1060, 1142
31:34 99, 904, 1039, 1044
31:35 752
31:35-37 396, 1054
31:36 1055
31:36, 37 1044
31:38-40 1012, 1058
31:40 1058
32 1053
32:10, 11 1143
32:18 36, 752, 837
32:20-24 1044
32:28-36 964
32:36-41 1056
32:37-38 1044
32:37-42 1012
32:38 1043
32:38-40 1144
32:39 1044
32:40 396, 1059, 1109
32:42-44 1044
32:44 1043, 1053
33 1042, 1053, 1055, 1057, 1058
33:1-13 1050
33:2 752
33:2-26 431
33:3 1050

33:3-5 1044
33:6-7 1044
33:7, 11 1053
33:7, 11, 26 1043
33:7-9 798
33:7-9, 15, 17 431
33:7-10, 12, 16 1058
33:8 904, 1044
33:9 431, 1110
33:10-17 1013
33:12-26 202
33:14 1050, 1052, 1053
33:14-15 1043
33:14-16 1015, 1021, 1044, 1050
33:14-26 1049–1061, 1163
33:14,16 1043
33:15 31, 32, 34, 36, 155, 202, 390, 403, 406, 407, 760, 793, 806, 808, 810, 840, 853, 898, 979, 1011, 1014, 1066, 1104, 1241, 1242, 1247, 1254, 1335, 1336
33:15-16 37
33:15-17 272
33:15-18 798, 1335
33:16 37, 155, 806, 853, 1017, 1053, 1058, 1143, 1263
33:17 1016
33:17-18 1050, 1255
33:17-26 1015, 1016, 1110
33:19-22 1050
33:19-22, 25-26 1054
33:19-26 37, 1045
33:20 1255
33:20-26 804
33:21 622
33:21, 26 1110
33:21-22 1255
33:22 1051
33:23-24 1051
33:25 1051, 1060
33:25-26 1051
33:26 1044, 1051, 1052, 1053, 1226
33:26b 1051
34 1045
34:2 1053
34:8, 15 938
34:17 990
34:20 795
36:26 888
37:4 406
37:10 1294
40:1-2 110
44:17 523
44:19 1157
46-51 859, 1143
46:1-51:64 669
46:24 578
48:12 1003, 1043
48:47 99, 297, 795, 1031, 1054, 1132
49:18 1128
49:39 99, 297, 795, 1054
50:4-5 1012
50:5 396
50:6 1308
50:8 326
50:17-18 965, 966
50:19 553
50:28 1330
50:35-38 1305
51:4 1295
51:5 271
51:11 1330
51:15 218, 753
51:16 721
51:33 506
51:39 499
51:39, 57 522
51:41 216
51:45 968
51:47, 52 1043
51:57 499
52:6-27 1279

Lamentations

1:5, 8, 14, 18, 20, 22 964
1:22 966
2:1 680
2:1, 2 1264
2:14 964
2:22 202, 578
3:1 523
3:17 1111
3:22 978
3:34 509
3:40-42 964
3:61-66 966
4:2 879
4:9 1294, 1295
4:12-13 964
4:21 578
4:21-22 998
4:22 202
5:7 971
5:7, 16 964
5:18 790
5:21 131

Ezekiel

1-24 1083
1:1-3 1076
1:1-28 1076
2:1 506, 1128
2:10 762
3:5-6 903
3:17-19 1021
3:18-19 1078
4-32 1100
4:4-6 971
4:5 1272, 1273
4:14 437
5:5-17 964
5:12-13 1311
6:3 796
6:4-7 1078
7:21-24 1078
7:27 1108
8:3-6, 9-10, 14, 16 1318
8:6 1318
9-11 812
9:3 1318
10 1222
10:4 1318
10:18 1318
11:5-21 1198
11:6 1078
11:11-25 1076
11:14-21 1069
11:16 1076
11:19 1179
11:20 1030
11:23 1318
12:1-16 1064
12:6, 11 1241
12:10, 12 1108
13:1-9 1177

13:1-23	1076
13:5	1177
14-19	1076
14:1-3	1076
14:11	1030
15:3	1267
16	579
16:3, 45	579
16:10, 13	579
16:13	579
16:14-15, 25	579
16:15-25	578
16:15-26	579
16:23	1027
16:29	1065
16:55	208
16:59-63	579
16:60	396
16:60, 62	1090
16:60-63	1109
17	1064, 1088
17:2	1064
17:3	1064, 1065, 1067
17:3-4	1064, 1065
17:4	1066
17:5-10	1064, 1065
17:5-21	1065
17:11-21	1064, 1065
17:19-21	1068
17:22	1064
17:22-24	202, 1063–1069, 1083
17:22a	1065, 1066
17:22b	1066
17:22b-24	1066
17:23	1067
17:24	1067
18:20-27	1078
19:1	1108
19:1-14	1076
19:10	807
20	1076
20:1-44	1197
20:1-49	1076
20:9	1078
20:34	852
20:40	811
21	1076
21:1-17	1076
21:3	1078
21:18-20	1076
21:19-23	1073
21:21	1074
21:21-23	1076
21:23-25	1079
21:24	1076
21:24-27	282
21:25	1074, 1077, 1078, 1108
21:25-27	1073–1080
21:26	1078
21:26-27	1073, 1074, 1078
21:27	272, 278, 282, 1073, 1074, 1075, 1077, 1079, 1083
21:27a	1074–1075
22:6, 25	1108
23	579
23:24b	1074
24-32	669
24:19	1064
24:23-25	1308
25-32	859, 1083, 1143
28:26	807
29:21	804, 1063, 1083
31:31-34	1102
32:21	837
33-48	1100
33:7-9	1021
33:14-22	1102
33:21	1084
34	37, 757, 764, 1086, 1090, 1093, 1105, 1277, 1278, 1305, 1310
34-37	1305
34:1-6	892
34:1-10	320, 1085, 1088, 1163
34:1-15	1274
34:1-16	1102
34:1-22	1090
34:1-31	962, 1085
34:4-8	1308
34:5	1281, 1308
34:6	183, 1085
34:10	1085
34:11	1101, 1305
34:11-12	1085
34:11-13	1308
34:11-16	890, 1200
34:11-22	320, 1085, 1093, 1163
34:12	1103
34:13	37
34:13-14	1305
34:13a	1085
34:13b-15	1085
34:14-15	551
34:15	1272, 1273
34:16	1103, 1105
34:17, 20-24	1308
34:17-22	1085
34:17-31	1102
34:20-31	202, 809, 1083–1094
34:22	764, 1085, 1090
34:22-23	1064
34:22-24	1098, 1335
34:23	37, 622, 754, 764, 809, 892, 1025, 1098, 1106
34:23-24	34, 127, 129, 320, 694, 763, 972, 1016, 1083–1086, 1087–1090, 1093, 1104, 1105, 1163, 1227, 1228, 1305, 1306
34:23-24a	193
34:23-31	1087
34:23a	1016
34:24	37, 764, 1087, 1088, 1089, 1107
34:24a, 31	320
34:25	194, 1026, 1090
34:25-30	1090, 1091t, 1092, 1109
34:25-31	1087, 1090, 1093, 1163
34:25b-d	1090
34:25b-d, 28b-d	1090
34:25c, 27c, 28c	1090
34:26-27c	1090
34:26-27c, 29a-b	1090
34:26b	1109–1110
34:27	809
34:27d-28a	1090
34:27d-28a, 29c	1090
34:28b-d	1090
34:29a-b	1090

34:29c 1090
34:30 1030, 1089, 1092
34:30-31 1087
34:31 1092
34:31-33 1093
35:13 517
35:15 567
36 56, 127
36:1-38 127, 1012
36:16-38 962, 1197
36:21-24 1102
36:22-28 1101
36:24-25 1306
36:24-28 1101
36:24-38 901
36:25 1302
36:25-27 811
36:26-27 1179
36:27 812, 901
36:28 1030
36:28-31 811
36:29-30 809, 877
36:33-38 901
37 443, 757, 764, 1100, 1105, 1197
37:1-13 1101
37:1-14 1100
37:5-6, 11-14 1101
37:12 1101
37:14 1101
37:15-18 1163
37:15-20 1101
37:15-21 1099
37:15-22 1100
37:15-23 1100
37:15-28 1012, 1090, 1097–1112, 1163, 1188
37:16 1274, 1277,
1278
37:16-19 1100
37:16-22 1108
37:17 1275, 1280
37:19-22 1108, 1163
37:21 764, 1100
37:21-28 202
37:21a 1101
37:21b 1101
37:22 1108
37:22, 24 1098, 1107
37:22-23 1101, 1111
37:22-25 1064, 1083, 1100, 1101
37:23 1101, 1108, 1109, 1142, 1163
37:23, 27 1030, 1101
37:23-24 764, 1105
37:24 37, 754, 763, 764, 1025, 1101, 1103, 1105, 1106, 1108
37:24-25 129, 193, 622, 809, 972, 1016, 1098, 1099, 1163, 1227, 1335
37:24-26 1111
37:24-28 877, 1100
37:25 113, 1100, 1101, 1106, 1107, 1108
37:25, 26, 28 1101
37:25b 1097
37:25c-26, 28 1097
37:26 396, 786, 1090, 1101, 1102
37:26-27 1163
37:26-28 1101, 1102, 1107, 1111
37:26d 1111
37:27 1111
37:27-28 1101, 1102, 1110
37:28 1111, 1163
38 57
38-39 124, 299
38-40 1143
38:2-3, 14, 16, 18 299
38:3 64, 299
38:8, 16 299, 795
38:14-17 1054
38:16 99, 298, 300, 1132
38:17 57, 64, 299
38:17-23 1222
38:21 681
39:1, 11, 15 299
39:5 840
39:9 840
39:17 681
39:17-20 683
39:21 1168
39:23-24 965
39:29 1179
40-43 1149
40-48 1013–1014, 1061, 1107, 1111, 1280
40:2 796, 797, 812
40:38 811
43:1-4 1076
43:1-7 812, 1101
43:2 1076
43:4-7 813
43:19 1061
44-48 1107
44:15 1061
45:8 764
45:17 1107
45:22 1107
46:1-15 1107
46:16-17 1107
46:18 1107
47-48 172
47:1-8 1321
47:9 208
47:12 208, 482
48:8-15, 35 797
48:22 1107
48:35 1017, 1018

Daniel

1 1115
1, 3, 6 1139–1149
1:1 99
1:1-6 98
1:3-4 311
1:10, 19, 24 568
2 1123–1124, 1139–1149
2, 4, 7, 8, 10, 11 1180
2, 7 1197
2-7 1024, 1115, 1120–1121, 1128, 1129
2:3-12 1116
2:4-7:28 1128
2:9 1132
2:13 1132
2:14-19 1116
2:20-23 1116
2:24-28 1116
2:27 1116
2:28 99, 795, 1031, 1054, 1131
2:28-29 1116
2:29-30 1116–1117
2:29-45 1115–1124
2:30 1116

2:31 1117
2:31-35 156, 1117, 1118
2:32-33 854
2:32-35 1117
2:34 876, 877, 1122
2:34-35 1121
2:34-35, 44-45 877, 881
2:35 1124
2:36 1118
2:36-45 1118–1124
2:37 1118
2:37-38 1118
2:38 156, 1118
2:39 1119
2:40 1120
2:41-43 1120
2:44 156, 233, 876, 1122–1123, 1132
2:44-45 696, 1122, 1128
2:47 854
3 1115
3:33 1132
3:33-35, 40, 44 1123
4 1115
4:14, 22, 29 1132
4:15, 23, 26 854
4:31 1132
5 1115, 1119
5:28 1119
6 1115
6:6, 11, 15 486
6:27 1132
7 50, 131, 197, 685–686, 1116–1117, 1128–1129
7, 8, 10 1139–1149
7:1 1128
7:1-8 157
7:1-14 1236
7:2-8 1129
7:2-14 1129
7:2a 1129
7:7-8 1123, 1129, 1146
7:7-8, 24 390
7:8 1146
7:8, 20 706
7:9 33, 157, 686
7:9-10 1134
7:9-14 1129
7:11 1129
7:13 33, 157, 204, 205, 1127, 1128, 1130, 1132, 1134, 1135, 1307
7:13-14 33, 34, 131, 686, 792, 903, 1127, 1129, 1130, 1131, 1132, 1134–1135
7:13-27 1127–1135
7:13a 1129
7:14 34, 157, 1131
7:14, 18, 27 1132
7:14, 27 221
7:15-28 1236
7:18 157, 1128, 1131
7:21, 25 1131
7:23 1121
7:23-25 1129
7:24 1121, 1147
7:25 1122, 1147
7:26-27 1129
7:27 1128, 1131
7:41-43 1121
8 1119
8:3, 9, 22, 23 706
8:5-7 1120
8:9-14 1267
8:17 506
8:19 795
8:19, 23 795
8:20 1119
8:21 1119
8:27 1139–1149
9 98, 99, 131, 1277
9:1 99
9:1-19 1141
9:2 99, 1140
9:3, 19 1140
9:4-13 964
9:11 966
9:11, 13 321
9:19 1139–1149
9:20-23, 25 99
9:22 1140
9:23 1223
9:24 431, 1139–1149
9:24, 26 1277
9:24-26 1281
9:24-27 32, 99, 131, 1014, 1139–1149, 1215
9:24a 1140–1142
9:24b 1142–1143
9:25 1109, 1143–1145, 1146, 1148, 1256
9:25-26 30, 137, 840
9:26 99, 1145–1147, 1148, 1273
9:26-27 1109
9:26a 1146
9:27 1147–1149, 1198, 1264, 1305
10 1119
10:2-3 1140
10:11, 19 1223
10:13 998, 1198
10:14 99, 298, 795, 1031, 1054, 1131
10:20 1119
10:33 1119
11:1-2 1119
11:1-45 1197
11:14 231
11:32 1267
11:36-44 1198
11:36-45 1122
11:45 1199
12 194
12:1 1023, 1139–1149, 1198
12:2 499, 522, 1025, 1106
12:4 1143
12:4, 9 1031
12:7 1147
12:8 795

Hosea

1-3 1154
1:1 1153, 1154
1:1-11 1197
1:2 578, 1155
1:2-2:1 1154, 1155–1156
1:3 1155
1:4 506
1:6-7 155
1:7 155
1:8 1157
1:9 1158
1:10-2:1 1156
1:11 1160, 1161

1:11-2:1 1156
2:2 202, 578, 1198
2:2-13 1156
2:2-23 1154, 1156
2:5 1160
2:5, 8, 13 1154
2:7 1159
2:7, 10, 15 1154
2:8-23 1197
2:14-23 1156, 1160
2:15 807, 1161
2:16-20 578
2:18, 21 1228
2:18-23 1092
2:19-20 812
2:20 208
2:23 1030
3:1-2 1155
3:1-3 1154, 1156–1158
3:1-5 578–579, 1154–1155
3:1a 1156
3:1b 1157
3:2 1154, 1157
3:3 1157
3:3-5 202, 1197
3:4 1158
3:4-5 34, 127, 192, 223, 901, 1024, 1153–1164, 1188
3:5 53, 99, 233, 298, 694, 793, 795, 1016, 1025, 1054, 1087, 1107, 1108, 1132, 1154, 1156, 1158, 1159, 1160, 1161, 1164, 1189, 1228, 1273
5:1 1075
5:3, 5, 11-14 1100
5:5-6 1160
5:7-15 964
5:14-15 1161
6:1 1198
6:6 186, 1159
7:3-7 1154
7:8-12 1154
7:10 1159
7:11, 16 1161
7:16 1158, 1159
8:1 1064
8:7 1027
8:11-13 1159
8:13 1161
8:13-14 1159
9:3 1159
9:3, 6 1161
10:1 807, 1159
10:3, 7 1158
10:8 796
10:12 1167
11:1 106–109, 907
11:1-11 1160, 1161
11:2 1159
11:5 1159
11:9 1198
11:10 1161
11:10-11 1160, 1161
11:11 1161
12:1 1154
12:4 1333
12:13 1161
13:7-8 1161
13:10-11 1154, 1158
14:5-8 202
14:7 807
48:15-16 1333

Joel

1:1-20 1168
1:2-3 1178
1:6, 7 1178
1:9 1177
1:9, 13 1177
1:14 1178
1:15 1177
1:15-20 1178
2 1168
2:1 1177
2:1-11 1178
2:1-17 1168
2:2 105, 1023, 1168
2:7-10 1178
2:10-11 1168
2:11 1177
2:12 1178
2:14 1178
2:16 1178
2:17 1177
2:17-27 1178
2:18 1178
2:18-27 551
2:18-32 1168
2:19, 20 1184
2:20 1178
2:22 551
2:22-26 807
2:23 1167–1174
2:23a 34, 404
2:23b 34
2:24 1171
2:25 1178
2:25-26 1171
2:25-27 1173
2:28 1179, 1189
2:28-32 901, 1171, 1177–1184
2:29 812, 1180
2:30-31 1180
2:31 1177
2:31b 1180–1181
2:32 1177, 1181
2:32b 1181
3:1 1177
3:1-15 1003
3:1-16 1168
3:2 1266
3:2, 12-13 1203
3:4 1168
3:13 1007
3:14 1177
3:14-21 1222
3:16 454
3:16-21 1168
3:17 811
3:19 1168
3:20-21 272
4:18 161

Amos

1:1 758
1:1-2 1320
1:2 454
1:2-2:3 669
2:9 1226
3:1-4:13 1189
3:11-15 1188
4:4-12 964
4:11 1226, 1238
4:13 751, 752
5:8 751
5:8, 27 752
5:18-20 1336
5:21-24 186
6:1-7 1188
6:10 576
7 1178
7:9 796

8:3, 9 1228
8:12 1031
9:1 1188
9:1-15 1197
9:6 752
9:8-15 1198
9:11 694, 862, 1025, 1162, 1187, 1188, 1190, 1273, 1323
9:11-12 30, 127, 881, 1102, 1189–1190
9:11-14 125
9:11-15 1162, 1187–1192
9:12 799, 800, 1162, 1188, 1189, 1190
9:13 1189
9:13-14 877, 1028
9:13-15 1162, 1191
9:14 807, 1189
9:15 1028, 1189

Obadiah
1:21 231
17 1181
19 1189

Jonah
2 620
2:2 620
2:3 620
2:4 620
2:8 620
4:2 620

Micah
1-2 1196
1:1 1209
1:1, 14 789
1:2 1196
1:2-2:13 1209
1:3 793, 796
1:4 793
1:5, 9, 13 790
2:1-2, 8-9, 11 790
2:5a 1213
2:12 1105, 1196–1201, 1202, 1203
2:12-13 223, 1195–1204, 1196, 1203, 1204, 1318
2:12a 1196–1199
2:12b 1199–1200
2:12c 1200–1201
2:13 1197, 1201–1204
2:13a 1201–1202
2:13b 1202–1204
2:13c 1204
3-5 1196
3:1 789, 1196
3:1-5:15 1209
3:6-11 790
3:8 990, 1195
3:9 790
3:10 790
3:10-12 790
3:12 790, 791, 793, 796, 797
3:12c 790
4 1216
4:1 99, 298, 716, 790, 1132, 1159, 1243
4:1, 3 233
4:1-2 1243
4:1-2a 791
4:1-3 790
4:1-4 793, 870
4:1-5 785–800, 1054
4:1a 796
4:2 799, 904, 1321
4:2b 790
4:2b-4 791
4:2c 790, 796
4:3 1243
4:3-4 877
4:4 787, 807, 1212, 1243
4:4-7 1189
4:4a 799
4:4b 791, 799
4:5 752, 786
4:6-8 1105
4:7 716, 1196
4:7b-8 791
4:8 202, 205, 1209
4:8, 9, 11 1210
4:9 1209, 1210, 1264
4:9, 11 1212
4:9-5:1 105
4:9-10 1211
4:9-10, 11-13 1213
4:10 1264
4:11 1209, 1210
4:11-12 1168
4:11-13 1200
4:13 1200
4:14-5:5a 1213
5 792, 825
5:1 155, 202, 233, 1209, 1210, 1211, 1212, 1273
5:1, 2 1210
5:1-3 202
5:1-4 127
5:1-5 795
5:2 104–106, 155, 192, 215, 223–224, 273, 391, 403, 407, 705, 755, 898, 903, 1162, 1209–1211, 1212, 1214, 1281, 1310
5:2-3 1105
5:2-4 792
5:2-5 825
5:2-5a 224, 320, 791, 1162, 1197, 1207–1210
5:2b 223
5:3 825, 1162, 1211–1212
5:3-5a 223
5:4 223, 825, 1212–1213, 1216
5:4-5a 1162
5:4b 223
5:5 1110
5:5-6 966, 1200
5:5a 223
5:7-8 1196
5:24 105
6-7 1196
6:1 1196
6:1-7:20 1209
6:3-5 285
6:5 290
7:6 203
7:14-15 792
7:16-17 792
7:18 786, 1196
7:18-20 792

Nahum
1:1 748
1:15 1110

Habakkuk
1:1 748
1:12 105
1:13 1143
2:2 52
2:4 880
2:5 1321
2:18 1170
2:19 522, 1170
3:3-4 1204
3:13 30, 137, 220, 1273
3:17-18 202
3:19 796

Zephaniah
1:2-18 1197
2:3 567
3:8 1321
3:11 811
3:17 837

Haggai
1 1224
1:1 1069, 1220, 1261
1:1-2 1220
1:1-14 1248
1:2-4 1220
1:3-11 1220
1:4-8 1220
1:5-11 1220
1:9-11 1220
1:10-11 1221
1:12 1220
1:12-14 194
1:13 1333
1:13-14 1220
1:15 1220
2:1 1221
2:1-9 595, 1221, 1315
2:2 1221
2:2-4, 20-23 194
2:3 1221, 1322
2:4 1221
2:4-5 1221, 1222
2:6 1222, 1230, 1231
2:6-7a 1222
2:6-9 1222, 1252
2:6-9, 21-23 1219–1231
2:7 799, 1219, 1221–1225
2:7, 9 1223
2:7-9 1222, 1225
2:8 1222, 1223, 1224
2:8-9 1224
2:9 786, 1110, 1222, 1223, 1224, 1225
2:10 1220
2:10-19 1221, 1226
2:11-13 1221
2:14-17 1221
2:15-19 1224
2:17-3:6 1230
2:18-19 1221
2:19 1226
2:20-21 1225
2:20-23 978, 1014, 1221, 1226, 1254
2:21 1226
2:21-22 1221, 1228
2:21-23 1228, 1273
2:22 1226
2:23 622, 1219, 1221, 1224, 1225, 1226–1228
3:2-5 1230
3:6 1230
6:9-15 1230
6:13 1230
6:15 1230

Zechariah
1-6 1261
1-8 1286–1287, 1301, 1303
1:1 1261
1:1-3 1275
1:1-6 964
1:7 1236, 1303
1:7-17 1276
1:8 1180
1:9, 14 1236
1:14-17 1220
1:18-21 1276
2:1-13 1197, 1276
2:3 206, 208, 1236
2:6-9 965
2:8 1027
2:10 155, 1263, 1264
2:10-13 1248
2:11 156, 1321
2:12 273, 811
3 1254
3, 6 1057
3:1 666, 1237, 1238, 1243
3:1, 3, 6, 8, 9 1248
3:1-2 1237
3:1-4:14 1276
3:1-5 1236–1237, 1239
3:1-8 1273, 1274, 1277
3:1-10 1073, 1075, 1080, 1235–1245, 1336
3:2 1237, 1238, 1244, 1332–1333
3:3 1238
3:3-5 1238–1239, 1245
3:4 1237, 1239, 1241, 1336
3:5 1239
3:6 1240
3:6-7 1240
3:6-10 194, 1236, 1239–1240, 1303
3:7 1239, 1240, 1242
3:7-10 1240
3:8 36, 202, 390, 622, 706, 760, 793, 806, 810, 854, 877, 979, 1011, 1014, 1015, 1042, 1057, 1066, 1241, 1247, 1248, 1250, 1252, 1253, 1254, 1272, 1273, 1336
3:8-10 37, 1229, 1241
3:8b 1252
3:9 877, 1057, 1237, 1238,

	1242–1243, 1244, 1245
3:9-10	1243
3:9a	877
3:9b	877
3:10	787, 807, 877, 1229, 1237, 1240, 1243
3:20	1264
4	1254
4:1	1236
4:1-6	1244
4:1-14	1229
4:2-5, 11-14	194
4:3	208
4:4	568, 1336
4:6-7, 9-10	1248, 1251
4:7	202, 877, 967
4:7-10	881
4:9	1254
4:10	877, 1242, 1244, 1287
4:11-12	1248
4:14	194, 1248, 1254
5:1-4	1276
5:5	1236
5:5-11	1276
6	686, 1057, 1257
6:1-8	1248, 1276
6:4	1236
6:5	1248
6:8	1236
6:9-13	972
6:9-14	1303
6:9-15	686, 1011, 1247–1257, 1273, 1274, 1276, 1277
6:11	1057, 1249, 1254, 1273, 1274
6:11, 14	1251
6:11-13	1250
6:11-15	1224, 1251
6:11b	1249
6:12	36, 37, 390, 706, 760, 793, 806, 810, 854, 967, 1011, 1014, 1015, 1042, 1066, 1242, 1247, 1252, 1253, 1254
6:12-13	202, 686, 979, 1014,1030, 1057, 1336
6:12-15	233, 1073, 1075, 1080, 1111
6:13	1110, 1242, 1251, 1252, 1253, 1254, 1255
6:14	1249, 1253
6:15	799
7-8	1261, 1276
7:1-2	1303
7:3	1274
7:10	1265
7:13	1287
8:2-8	1198
8:3	811
8:3-5	1028
8:8	1030
8:12	807, 1012, 1110
8:13	273
8:15	273
8:21-23	799
8:22	1321
8:23	984
9	586, 669, 1296
9-10	1262
9-11	1276
9-14	1235, 1261, 1287, 1296, 1298, 1301, 1303, 1307
9:1-2	1262
9:1-8	1262
9:2-4	1262
9:3	1262
9:4	1262
9:5-7	1262
9:7	204, 205, 273
9:7a	1262
9:7b	1262
9:7c	1262
9:8	1268
9:8a	1262
9:8b	1262
9:9	161, 233, 235, 273, 275, 403, 407, 578, 584, 898, 904, 1230, 1263–1268, 1273, 1276, 1297, 1309, 1312
9:9, 10	1264
9:9, 14	899
9:9-10	467, 1013, 1197, 1225, 1229, 1261–1268, 1309
9:9-10:12	1262, 1263
9:9a	1263
9:9a, b	1264
9:9d	1264, 1265
9:9e, f	1265
9:10	231, 467, 786, 1110, 1230, 1265, 1287, 1297, 1309
9:10a	223, 1266
9:10a, b, c	1266
9:10b	223
9:10c	799
9:10d	1266
9:10e	1266
9:10f	1266
9:11-10:12	1266
9:11-12	1266, 1297
9:12	1297
9:13	1266
9:13, 17	1266–1267
9:13-15	1266
9:16	1267
9:16-10:1	1266
9:17	1267
10-12	892
10:2	1274, 1277
10:2-3	1268, 1274, 1310
10:2-3a	1267
10:3	879, 1267
10:3-5	696
10:3b-6a	1267
10:4	202, 877, 879, 1267, 1268
10:4-6	273
10:5-8	879
10:6	1012
10:6-12	1198, 1309
10:6b-12	1267
10:12	752
11	892, 1262, 1304, 1308
11:1-3	1277
11:3	1274

11:4 1272, 1274, 1277–1278, 1304
11:4-6 1277, 1280
11:4-14 114, 1271–1282
11:5 1274
11:5-6 1278, 1280
11:5-6, 10 1280
11:6 1278, 1279
11:7 1277, 1280, 1281
11:7, 11 1265
11:7-9 1278–1279
11:7-12 1277, 1278–1279, 1280
11:8 1272, 1274, 1278–1279, 1281, 1304
11:8b 1280
11:9 1272, 1274, 1279
11:9, 12 1280
11:10 1278, 1279, 1280
11:10-12 1279–1280
11:11 1279, 1280, 1306
11:12 1279–1280
11:12-13 1304
11:13 1273, 1274, 1275, 1277, 1280
11:13-14 1277, 1280–1281
11:14 1272, 1274, 1280–1281
11:15-17 1277, 1280, 1310
11:17 1310
12 1304, 1305
12-13 1276, 1287, 1301
12-14 1235, 1236, 1276, 1296, 1301, 1305
12:2 1287
12:2-3 797, 1199
12:3 799, 892, 1027
12:3-9 1287
12:4 1293
12:6 1293
12:7-13:1 428
12:8 153, 1293, 1333
12:8-12 1315
12:8-13:1 1309
12:10 127, 153, 202, 206, 233, 570, 748, 892, 901, 1028, 1044, 1173, 1179, 1184, 1212, 1243, 1245, 1273, 1274, 1277, 1281, 1285–1298, 1288–1289t1, 1302, 1304, 1309, 1311
12:10-12 1276
12:10-13:1 1285–1298
12:10-13:2 811, 1013
12:10-14 1203, 1287, 1311
12:11-14 1295
12:12 206
13 1304, 1305
13:1 127, 1044, 1142, 1179, 1243, 1245, 1276, 1292, 1293, 1301, 1302
13:1-6 1287, 1293
13:1-9 1281, 1311
13:3 1293, 1295, 1302
13:4-6 1302
13:5 1241
13:7 37–38, 233, 1182, 1274, 1276, 1277, 1296, 1297, 1303, 1304, 1305, 1306, 1307, 1308, 1309, 1310, 1311
13:7-9 1024, 1197, 1301–1312
13:7b 1311
13:7b-9 1311
13:8 1026, 1305, 1311
13:8-9 1308, 1309, 1310, 1311
13:9 878, 1030, 1310, 1311
14 686, 687, 865, 870, 1223, 1225, 1301
14:1 1177, 1317
14:1-2 1316–1317
14:1-11 1315–1324
14:1-21 1273, 1276
14:2 797, 799, 1027, 1181, 1317
14:2-3 1199
14:2-5 1103
14:3 1204, 1317–1318
14:3-4 1309
14:3-5 686, 687, 1317–1320
14:4 870, 1202–1203, 1317, 1319
14:4, 6, 8, 9 1317
14:4a 1318
14:4b 1320
14:4b-5 1319–1320
14:5 687, 1320
14:6 1320
14:6-7 1320
14:6-11 1320–1323
14:6b 1320
14:7 1317, 1320
14:8 1302, 1320, 1321
14:8-21 172
14:9 1103, 1106, 1107, 1108, 1109, 1304, 1312, 1319, 1320, 1321–1322
14:9, 20-21 1309
14:9a 1321
14:9b 1321
14:10 796, 797, 812, 1107, 1322–1323
14:10-11 1320
14:11 1189, 1323
14:12-14 687
14:13 1230
14:14 1224, 1230
14:16 1108
14:16-19 812, 1111
14:17 1027
14:17-19 1230
14:20 811

Malachi
1:1-2:9 1329
1:2, 6, 7, 12-13 1328
1:2-5 1329
1:5 1334
1:6-9 1329
1:6-11 1328
1:6-13 181, 186
1:6-14 1315
1:8 1328
1:10 1329, 1331
1:11-14 1329
2:1-3 1328
2:1-9 1329
2:4, 5, 8 1332
2:7 1333
2:10 1332
2:10-3:6 1329
2:10-16 1329
2:10-17 1315
2:10a 1329
2:10b-15a 1329
2:14 1332
2:14, 17 1328
2:15b-16 1329
2:16 1329
2:17 1329, 1330, 1331, 1332, 1336
2:17-3:5 1329
2:17-3:6 1329
3 48, 481
3:1 233, 1224, 1327–1337
3:1, 5 1330
3:1, 10 1328
3:1, 12 1331
3:1-4 1230
3:1-5 1014
3:1-6 1329
3:1a 1332
3:1b 1331
3:2-3 1336
3:2-4 1331, 1332, 1334
3:3 1330
3:3-4 1334
3:5 1330
3:5-6 1332, 1334
3:6 1329
3:7 1329
3:7, 8, 13-15 1328
3:7-4:6 1329
3:7-9 1099
3:7-10a 1329
3:10b-12 1329
3:11 1328
3:12 1321, 1334
3:13-15 1329
3:16-4:3 1329
3:16-17 1334, 1336
3:16-18 1315
3:17 1336
3:18 1336
3:22 232
3:22-24 12, 328
4 121f1
4:1 1336
4:1, 3 1334
4:1-5 1327–1337
4:2 403, 407, 1334, 1336
4:3 509, 1336
4:4 454
4:4-5 127
4:4-6 120, 121, 1329, 1330
4:5 121, 232, 1230, 1330, 1331
4:5-6 1228

APOCRYPHA

1 Maccabees
1:1-2 431
2:9 431
2:49-70 431
2:50 431
2:57 431
5 999
2 Esdras
12:31-32 431
Baruch
1:1 758
Wisdom of Sirach
24 742
24:9-12 761
24:10 761
24:11 761
36:13 761
47:3-7 431
47:9 431
47:9-11 431
47:11 761
47:15, 22 431
48:15-16 431
49:4 431–432

PSEUDEPIGRAPHA

1 Enoch
37-70 1134
37-71 1131, 1133, 1134
46:1-4 1134
46:1-6 197, 1131
47:3 1134
48:1-7 1131
48:3 1134
48:6 197
48.3, 6 1134
48.10 1134
51:3 1134
52:4 1134
62.7 1134
83-90 764, 1104
89:42-49 1104
4 Ezra 194
7:27-30 196
12:32-34 196–197
13 1133
13:32, 37, 52 196
13.3 1133
13.32 1133
Martyrdom of Isaiah
2:7-11 1214
6:1-8 1214
Psalms of Solomon
2:30, 32 764
5:19 764
7:3-10 1306
9:9-11 1306
17 759–760
17-18 195
17:1, 3, 34, 45 764
17:3, 10 764
17:4 195
17:21 195, 764
17:21-22, 32, 40-42 1306
17:21-25, 45 1306
17:21-45 1306
17:24, 29, 36-37 193
17:26 195, 764
17:28 195, 764
17:30b 195
17:31 195
17:32 195
17:36-37 195
17:36-41 764
17:40b 195
17:42 195
17.21 760

17.21-24, 30, 32 760
17.22 761
17.23 760, 761
17.24 760
17.30 761
17.35 760
17.36-37 760
17.43 760
Similitudes of Enoch
48:10 197
52:4 197
Testament of Judah
24:1-6 1104
Testaments of the Twelve Patriarchs
T. Issachar 5:7-8 196
T. Judah 24 1256
T. Levi 18 1256
T. Naphtali 8:2 196
T. Simeon 7:1-2 196

Dead Sea Scrolls

1QIsa 810, 878, 888, 891, 988
1QM 199, 431
5:1 199
11:1-7 1104
1QS
2:3-4:22 431
8.4-8 876
9:11 194, 199, 200
1QSa
2:11-15, 20-21 199
1QSb
5:20 199
5:22, 25, 26 193
4Q161
2-6 ii 19 199
7-10 iii 22 199
4Q174 430
1-3 i 11 199
4Q175 221
4Q246 198, 199, 1133
4Q252
1 v 3-4 199
5.1-4 1104
4Q252-254a
Col 5 273
4Q254 194
4Q266
3 iv 9 199
4:11-13 1306
18 iii 12 199
4Q285
4 2, 4, 6 199
5 3-4 199
5 4 199
5 i 3 193
6 2 199
4Q376 1 iii 1 199
4Q504 frg. 4.5-8 431
4Q521 197–198, 199, 989
line 1 917
line 8 917
4Q1617 iii 15-19 193
4QFlor
1-2.2:11 1104
1:11 1014
4QIsa 970
4QPBless
1:3f 1014
3 1104
4QpIsa[a] 8-10:17 1104
11Q13 199, 1256
11Q13 2:9 199
11QMelch 1256
CD
7:19 1104
7:19-20 199
12:23-13:1 199
14:19 199
19:5-7 1305
19:6-11 1305
19:9-10 1306
CD XX 33-34 1306

Rabbinic Works

Mishnah
Laws of Kings and Their Wars
12:2 230
m. Berakhot
1:5 201
m. Sotah
9:15 201, 202, 204
Tosefta
t. Berakhot
1:12 202
t. Sanhedrin
10:11 970
Talmud
b. Avodah Zarah
9a-b 205
b. Bava Batra
75b 205, 207, 1017
b. Berakhot
1:5 202
5a 967
7b 233
34b 26, 123, 205
57b 967
b. Chul
63a 205
b. Hagigah
12a 209
b. Ketubbot
112b 205
b. Nedarim
39a 205
b. Pesahim
54a 205
68b 205
b. Rosh HaShanah
11b 205
b. Sanhedrin
38a 877
41a 275
43a 970
91b 205
93 203
93b 205, 209
96b-99a 200, 204
97a 202
97a-b 204
97b 204
98a 1130, 1132
98b 205, 209, 229, 275, 969, 1106
99a 206
b. Shabbat
30b 205
63a 205
118b 205
151b 205
b. Sotah
14a 967
49b 202
b. Sukkah
52a 206, 227, 233
52a-b 206, 208
52b 206
b. Ta'anit
14b-15a 205
Berach
7 b 209
Dt Rabbah
1:20 209
Ecc Rabbah
1:12 207
Ex Rabbah
15:21 207–208
19:7 207
35:5 207
Gn Rabbah
1:4 207

2:5 208
23:5 207
42:4 207
44:8 207
51:8 207
75:6 208
85:9 209
98:8 209
99:2 208
Hilkhot Melakhim
11 970
Lam Rabbah
1:51 207
2:4 203
Lv Rabbah
14:1 208
15:1 207
Numbers Rabbah
13:2 207, 967
13:14 207, 877, 1130
14:1 208
18:23 207
Pesitka d'Rav Kahane
5:9 230
Ruth Rabbah
5:6 967
S. of S. Rabbah
2:33 206
Sg Rabbah
2:33 208
y. Berakhot
2:4 205
5a 209
y. Hagigah
2:2 205–206
y. Ketubbot
12:3 205
y. Kil'ayim
9:3 205
y. Sanhedrin
7:16, 67a 970
y. Shekalim
5:1 966
y. Sotah
9:16 202
y. Sukkah
5:2 206
y. Ta'anit
4:5 203
4:8 209
64a 205
Yalkut Shimoni
§ 570 208
2:571 967, 969
2:620 967
2:621 967
Yeven Metzulah
15 971

Talmuds

Abhodah Zarah
3 b 209

Targums

Fragmentary Targum 274
Jonathan or Yerushalmi 273–274
Onkelos (or Aquila) 273
TJ Ta'anit
68d 1104
Zech
4:7 877

Midrash

Aggadat Bereshit
14:3 1130
23:1 1130
33a,3 877
33a,5 877
33a,6 877
33a,7 877
Hagadol Gen
49:10 1130
Pesikta Rabbati
33-37 229–230
Pesitka d'Rav Kahane
5:9 230
Josephus
Ant.
10.210 877
Mekhilta
2:120 207
Midrash Rabbah Bereshit
99 1104
Sifrei Parashat Pinchas
Paragraph 131 967
Tanchumah
11:3 208
Toledoth
20 877
Trumah
6 877
Ya'acov
10 877
Yalkut Shimoni
§ 570 208
2:571 967, 969
2:620 967
2:621 967

New Testament

Matthew

1 50
1:1 274, 849, 1029, 1099, 1105, 1187, 1190
1:1-17 391, 1105, 1164
1:5 355
1:12 1228
1:12-16 392
1:18-25 104
1:20 1333
1:20-21 1180
1:21 166, 755, 1255, 1265
1:22 826
1:23 143, 824, 825–826, 1225
2 45, 104, 166, 1214
2:1 1106
2:1-2 1164
2:1-7 155
2:2 104, 221
2:4-6 223
2:5-6 104–106
2:6 1103
2:10-11 202
2:11 794
2:13 166
2:14 166
2:15 95, 96, 106–109
2:16-18 109–112, 111, 335
2:19-23 112–114, 1180
2:20-21 166
2:23 112, 113
2:56 106
3:3 1331
3:4 1214
3:5 1281
3:11 1181
3:13 166, 937
3:14 937
3:15 321, 937
3:16 937, 1093
3:17 937, 939, 940
4:1-11 166, 955
4:4 1021
4:13-16 831

4:18-22 167
4:23-25 937–938, 940
4:24-25 938
5-7 1174
5:3-12 1200
5:4 991
5:10-15 1200
5:17 321
5:18 1021
5:20 322
5:35 1106
5:44-47 351
5:46-47 352
6:10 1122
7:29 1174
8:11 789
8:17 937
8:19 1173
9:36 1308
10:11-15 939
10:34 1110
10:34-36 203
10:40 1334
11:1-5 990
11:2-5 916
11:2-6 908
11:3 908, 916
11:4-5 916
11:5 198
11:9 327
11:10-14 1331
11:14 1214
11:15 698
11:28-29 955
12;18, 20, 21 799
12:15-21 939, 940
12:18 1182
12:21 1102
12:28 1182
12:38 1173
12:42 195, 734, 765
13:9, 43 698
13:11-13 1174
13:17 220
13:54-58 985
13:57 985
15:21-28 258
15:24 1101, 1308, 1334
16:16 937, 1093
16:16-17 1164
16:18 369
16:19 794
16:21 957, 1182
16:21-23 957
16:23 957
16:28 1131
17:1-8 336
17:1-9 939
17:3 444
17:5 939, 940, 1093
17:10-13 1331
17:11 1228
19:16 1174
19:27-28 1183
19:28 789, 1105, 1131
20:17-19 1182
20:28 188, 937
21-23 698
21:1-7 162
21:1-11 698, 1265, 1319
21:5 1106, 1228, 1243, 1261, 1309
21:9 274, 698
21:13 796
21:15 698
21:23 698
21:37 1334
21:42 879, 1267
21:42-43 698
21:44 881
21:45 698
22:16, 23-24 1173
22:23 698
22:32 444
22:41-45 141, 460
22:41-46 675, 687, 1164
22:42 807
22:42-45 274, 1248
23:1-6 1281
23:8, 10 1174
23:13 698
23:13-32 698
23:29 893
23:33 698
23:35 455
23:37-39 322
23:38 1275
23:38-39 882
23:39 698–699, 879, 1101
24 1309
24-25 870
24:1-2 1309
24:3 1309
24:3, 14, 36 1183
24:3-14 1319
24:4-13 203
24:8 1023
24:15-20 1028
24:15-22 1109, 1199
24:16 1201
24:21 1023
24:24 1302
24:27, 30 1023
24:27, 30, 39, 44 1131
24:29 869, 1184
24:29-30 1180
24:30 1131
24:31 1023
24:35 1021
25:31 1116, 1131
25:31-40 811
25:31-46 1003, 1168, 1023, 1203
25:32 1308
25:40 1168
26:15 1281
26:17-30 336
26:23 1302
26:28 937
26:31 1182, 1243, 1297, 1304, 1308
26:31-32 1308
26:32 1308
26:33-35 1308
26:36-38 1319
26:38, 42 956
26:54, 56 1308
26:56 1308
26:63 937, 1093
26:64 34
26:65 34
26:67 957
26:71 114
27:1-9 1282
27:5 1281
27:7 1281
27:9 1281
27:9-10 1243
27:11 1106
27:19 1180
27:34, 38 470
27:37, 42 1106
27:38-54 1282
27:45 1180
27:46 529
27:50-51 1030
28:2 1333
28:18 1135
28:19 257, 349, 938
28:19-20 797

28:20 1110
40:6 36

Mark
1:1 1093
1:2-3 1331
1:6 1214
1:8 1181
1:9 937
1:11 940, 1093
1:14 840
2:5 1183
2:7 1183
4:11-12 1133
4:35-41 198
6:1-4 985
6:4 985
6:34 1103
6:47-52 198
8:31-33 957
9:2-8 336
9:7 1093
9:37 1334
9:38 1173
10:2 350
10:7-9 350
10:35 1173
10:45 177, 446
11:1-10 1265, 1319
11:12-14, 20-21 198
11:17 796
12:10 879, 881, 1267
12:35 1190
12:35-37 200, 675
13 1309
13:1-2 1225
13:2 1309
13:4 1309
13:26, 35 1319
14:12-25 336
14:27 1243, 1304, 1308
14:28 1308
14:30-31 1308
14:33-34 1319
14:49 1308
14:50 1146, 1308
15:2 1106
15:23, 36 600
15:33 1180
15:34 529
15:36 470

Luke
1:1 337
1:17 1228, 1331
1:19 156
1:31, 60 369
1:31-33, 69 1105
1:31-35 198
1:32 1093, 1099, 1106
1:32, 69 1025
1:32-33 68, 143, 797, 1107, 1187
1:32-33, 69 370
1:32-34 832
1:35 826, 1069, 1333–1334
1:46-55 369
1:48 369
1:51 639
1:51-55 1227
1:69 706, 708
1:78 1015
1:79 1110
2:4 1105
2:11 196
2:22-35 369
2:27-32 1225
2:28-32 937, 949
2:30, 32 937, 940, 949, 950
2:30-32 799
2:32 1225
2:40, 52 369
2:46 955
2:47 955
3:4 1331
3:16 1181
3:17 1181
3:22 1093
3:23, 36 256
3:27 1228
3:32 355
3:38 1094
4 989
4:1-2 335
4:1-13 955
4:14 985
4:14-30 985, 986
4:16 217, 985
4:16-21 938, 939, 940, 949, 950, 990, 1022, 1228
4:16-22 983, 1265
4:16-30 217, 985
4:17 217, 218, 986
4:17-21 833, 907
4:18 218, 989, 991
4:18, 19 987
4:18, 43 1334
4:18-19 155, 938, 949, 986, 1181, 1256
4:18-21 849
4:20 218
4:20-22 1181
4:21 218, 938, 949, 993, 1309
4:24 218, 985
4:24-27 987, 1190
4:29 218
4:37 985
4:41 1093
5:1-11 198
5:8 198
5:17-21 985
6:32-34 352
6:35 351
7:18-23 908, 989
7:18-35 989
7:20 1181
7:22 198
7:27 1331
9:28-36 336, 939
9:35 939, 940, 1227, 1228
9:51 957
10:16 1334
10:24 220
11:13 1333
11:31 195, 734
12:51 1110
13:28 789
13:32 1274
15:4-6 1101
15:23, 27, 30 178
16:22-23 444
19:10 1265
19:28-40 1145, 1146
19:29-39 1265
19:29-40 1319
19:38 1106
19:42 1110
19:46 796
20:17 1267
20:18 881
20:41-42 274
20:41-44 675
21:5 1225
21:6 1309
21:7 1309
21:20 1281
21:24 1024, 1116, 1147

21:27-31 1131
21:37-38 1319
22 1035
22:7-23 336
22:20 99, 881, 1035, 1045
22:21 1302
22:27 1228
22:30 789
22:37 222
22:42 322, 956
22:44-45 1319
22:63-65 957
22:66-71 1274
23:1-12 1281
23:2 1106
23:34 141
23:36 470
23:43 444
23:44 1180
23:48 1297
24:11 1182
24:16 335
24:25 335
24:25-26 149
24:25-27 540
24:26 670
24:26, 27, 44 488
24:27 25, 149, 1327
24:44 26, 38, 48, 94, 399, 455, 548
24:44-45 149
24:44-47 540
24:45 21
24:47 564, 788

John

1:1 219, 813, 1285, 1297, 1307
1:1, 14 153
1:1-3 219
1:1-18 147, 1164
1:2 219
1:11 595, 1164
1:14 219, 788, 797, 813
1:18 890
1:21 335, 1214
1:23 1331
1:29 151, 968
1:33 1181
1:45 94, 173, 1327
1:49 1106
1:49-51 1228
2 336
2:13-16 601
2:16 796
2:17 470, 595, 600, 601, 602
2:18 601
2:19-21 601, 788, 879
2:21 602
2:22 601
3:5 811
3:16 219
3:17, 34 1334
3:35-36 356
4:1-5 1281
4:10 162, 336
4:34 1334
4:41-24 787
5 148, 149, 917, 1164
5:5 148
5:7 917
5:10 148
5:17 148
5:18 148
5:21-29 148
5:23-24, 30, 36-38 1334
5:28-29 1025
5:31-37 148
5:37 890
5:37-39 148
5:39, 46 1327
5:45-47 26–27
5:45b-46 12
5:46 95, 564, 1327
5:46-47 148
6:14 336
6:29, 38-39, 44, 57 1334
6:46 890
6:51-58 162
7:14-16 955
7:16, 18, 28-29, 33 1334
7:37-38 162, 812, 881
7:37-39 959
7:40 336
7:41-42, 52 114
7:42 639
8:12 959
8:16, 18, 26, 29, 42 1334
8:44 249, 958
8:46-47 958
8:47 958
8:56 833
8:58 1307
8:58-59 1164
8:59 891
9 917
9:3b-5 959
9:4 1334
9:11 917
10 1098, 1200
10:1-18 891–892
10:8 1093
10:11 1281
10:11, 14 1103
10:13-15 1281
10:15 320
10:16 764, 1099, 1106
10:19-21 1093
10:30 1106
10:35 147
10:36 1334
11:27 1093
11:42 1334
11:48 1274
12:12-19 1265
12:13 854, 1106
12:15 1243, 1261, 1297, 1309
12:24 639
12:32 1069
12:34 639
12:36 891
12:36b 891
12:37 890
12:37-40 875
12:37-43 890
12:37-50 956
12:37-61 928
12:38 334, 956
12:41 855, 886, 890
12:44-45, 49 1334
12:49-50 140
13 336
13:18 1302
13:20 153, 1334
14-16 1182
14:9-10 1307
14:16-18, 25-26 1182
14:24 1334
15:1-8 854
15:18 601
15:18-25 597
15:21 1334
15:24 601
15:25 470, 600, 601, 602

15:26, 27 1182
16:5 1334
16:5-15 1182
16:8-9 1183
16:13 1182
16:32 1308
17:3, 8, 18, 21, 23, 25 1334
17:18 153
17:24 1307
18:19-23 958
18:28-30 958
18:37 840, 1106
19:1-5 957
19:14, 19 1106
19:15 322
19:28 470, 602
19:28-29 597, 601
19:29 600, 601–602
19:37 1243, 1285, 1288, 1290, 1297
20:21 153, 1334
20:24, 25 1182
20:28 147, 1164, 1183
20:31 467
50:10 959

Acts

1 1216
1:4-8 1182
1:6-7 789, 1102
1:8 257, 788, 797
1:9-12 1319
1:11 1203, 1318
1:13-14 663
1:14 1215
1:16 466, 1184
1:16a 663
1:20 470, 597, 600, 663
2 458, 1184
2:4 1182
2:5, 14 787
2:8-11 787, 788
2:12 1182
2:13 1184
2:17 1183
2:17-21 1183
2:18 1183–1184
2:23 1311
2:23b-24 958
2:24 514
2:25-31 460
2:29 1025
2:29-30 1025
2:29-31 407, 804–805
2:29-32 525
2:29-36 1228
2:30 396, 408, 514
2:30-31 466
2:31 396, 407, 408, 513
2:33-35 514
2:36 1135, 1183, 1311
2:37 514, 1183
2:42 224
2:47 1012
3:12 787
3:14-26 309
3:18 1184
3:19-21 789
3:20, 26 1334
3:21 309
3:22-23 337
3:24 13, 26, 123, 1327
3:25-26 267
3:26 309
4:1-2 787
4:8 699
4:10 1311
4:11 699, 881, 1267
4:23-31 928
4:24-26 156
4:25-26 787
4:27-28 1292
5:17 787
5:30 1311
7:2-53 218
7:35-39, 51-53 309
7:37 337
7:51-53 218
7:52 309
7:54-8:3 787
7:55-56, 59 444
8 257, 968
8-10 257
8:27-39 222
8:32-35 1228
8:35 168, 222
8:37 1093
9:1-2 787
10 257
10:36 1334
10:43 1327
11:19 787
12:1-5, 23 787
13:13-41 218
13:14 218
13:15 218
13:22-23, 34 1025
13:23 1102
13:26-48 928
13:27 1184
13:29 1184
13:30-33 1191
13:30-34 925
13:33 514, 1184
13:34 978
13:36 514
13:36-37 513
13:38-41 218
13:44-46 787
13:46 799
13:47 949
14:2-6, 19-20 787
15 1189–1190
15:11 1188, 1192
15:15-18 800, 881, 1189
15:16 1191
15:16-18 862, 1102, 1188
15:17 799, 1191
15:37-39 787
16:19-24 787
17:11 27, 95
17:32 787
19:28-34 787
20:3 787
20:26-27 1021
20:28 446
21:30-36 787
24:5-6 787
24:15 1025
26:7 789
26:22 1327
26:23 949
28:25-27 787

Romans

1:3 137, 141, 274, 1164, 1190
1:4 1164
3:21-26 794
3:25 188
5:12-21 138, 162
5:14 162
8:3 1334–1335
8:19-21 850
8:30 1181
9-11 1191, 1244–1245
9:1-5 1164, 1190

9:5 1029, 1106
9:31-33 882
9:32 881
9:32-33 881
9:33 881
10 98
10:6-8 98, 881
10:8-10 881
10:9-13 881
10:11 881
10:12 881
10:12-13 881
10:13 1307
10:16 334
11:1-5 1045
11:1-10 1164
11:9-10 600
11:12, 14, 23-24, 31 880
11:12, 15, 23-29 789
11:17-24 1046
11:24 1046
11:25 881
11:25-26 1045–1046
11:25-27 800, 1023, 1142, 1164, 1311
11:26 793, 1173, 1212, 1245
11:26-27 709, 811, 1109, 1245
11:27 811, 880
11:29 1190
12:1-2 563
13:4 1311
14:17 1110
15:3 470, 600
15:12 799, 855, 1102
15:16 257
16:20 151, 220

1 Corinthians

1:9 1181
1:30 219
2:11-16 149
3:11 879
3:16 788
3:16-17 881
5:21-22, 45-49 138
8:6 219
10:4 369, 881
10:11 1183
10:26 639
11:25 881, 1035, 1045
12:13 1183
15:3, 4 602
15:20-22, 44-49 162
15:27 503
15:45 162
15:55-57 249
16:22a 669

2 Corinthians

1:19 1093
3 1035
3:4-18 1035
3:6 1045
5:1-8 444
5:17 1316
5:21 188
6:16-17 881
6:18 432

Galatians

1:8 669
1:15 1181
2:8 257
2:20 1093
3 267
3:8 156
3:16 267, 305
3:18 1321
3:19-22 1102
3:28 258
4:4 248, 1335
4:4-5 338
4:26 720
6:7-8 1027

Ephesians

1:3 489
1:3, 5, 10, 11, 14, 19-22 488
1:7 446
1:7, 8 794
1:22 503
2:6 488, 489
2:11-22 800
2:13 446
2:14 1213
2:15 1099
2:19-22 699, 881
2:20 1124, 1267
2:20-22 788, 876, 881, 882
4:17-19 352
4:25 1243
5:25-30 352
5:31-32 162

Philippians

2 506
2:10-11 1109
4:3 600

Colossians

1:11-20 141
1:13, 14 794
1:15 151, 219
1:18 219
1:20 446
2:3 129
2:9 1307
2:13 188
3:11 258

1 Thessalonians

5:1-9 1184
5:2-3 991
5:3 1023, 1111
5:23 444

2 Thessalonians

1:7-9 991
2:2-4 1184
2:3b-4 1109
2:4 1302
2:8 850, 854

1 Timothy

2:5 140, 446
2:7 257
4:13 216
6:15 1106, 1316

2 Timothy

1:9 1181
2:8 1025
3:15 1327
3:16 26, 1021
3:16-17 997

Titus

2:13 1307
2:14 188

Hebrews

1 777
1:1-2 143
1:2 219, 1183
1:3 143, 151
1:3-5, 13 685
1:5 430, 432
1:5-14 143

1:10-12 599
2:5-8 518
2:6 546
2:6-8 503
2:6-9 506
2:9 506
2:17 188, 366
3:1-6 327, 337
3:6 143
4:8 707
4:12 854
4:14-16 707
4:15 143, 955
5:5 143
5:5-6 685
5:6, 10 1253
5:9-10 143
7 707
7:1-22 143
7:3 139
7:7 140
7:8-10 140
7:11, 19, 27 707
7:11, 28 706
7:14 1257
7:15-17 1257
7:19 706
7:22 143, 1045
7:22-10:18 1035, 1045
7:23-8:12 143
7:26 1257
7:28 1257
8:1-10:18 337
8:6 1045
8:7-12 1045
8:11 707
9:1-10 187
9:1-10:18 187
9:6-9 187
9:9 187
9:10 187
9:11-15 794
9:12 188
9:12-13 187
9:22 183
9:26 1183
9:26-28 188
10:1 143, 187
10:3 187
10:5-7 187
10:5-9 565
10:5-10 564, 565
10:5b 565
10:9 187
10:10-12 143
10:13 144
10:20 1030
10:22 188
11:23-27 337
11:26 600
12:2 144
12:22-24 720, 788
12:23 444
12:26 1230
12:26-28 1222
12:28 144, 1122
13:14-16 720
13:20 1103
13:20-21 144
13:22 218
41:3 463

James

1:21 373
4:4 1027
5:11 437

1 Peter

1:1-12 397
1:6-7 1337
1:7 1310
1:10-11 94, 220, 926, 1031
1:10-12 1013, 1181
1:11 383
1:17 639
1:18 188
1:18-19 446
1:20 1183
2:1-8 699
2:4 876
2:4-6 881
2:4-8 881
2:5 876
2:6 877, 879
2:6-8 882
2:7 1267
2:8 1124
2:22 223
2:24 223
2:25 223
4:14 639
5:4 1085

2 Peter

1:17 1093
1:21 26
2:15 290
2:15-16 285
3:4, 8-9 460
3:10-13 1097

1 John

2:1 1244
2:2 188
3:1 1181
4:9-10, 14 1335
4:10 188
5:20 1094

2 John

1:3 1093

Jude

9 1244
11 285, 290
23 1244

Revelation

1:5 446, 639
1:7 1179, 1290, 1297
1:8 1307
1:16 854
1:18 794
2:14 285, 290
2:26-28 221
3:5 600
3:7 794
5:5 274, 1025, 1161, 1190
5:6 1244
5:9 258, 446
5:9-10 798
5:10 221
5:11-12 632
6-19 868, 1023
6-20 870
6:4 1111
6:9-11 444, 567
6:12-14 869, 1180, 1184
7:9-10 950
7:16-17 950
9:3-11 1178
9:4 1178
11:1-6 1184
11:2 799, 1148
11:3 1148
11:19 1180, 1184
12 249, 1028, 1198
12:1 1028
12:5 1108
12:5-6 1197

12:6	1148
12:6, 14	1201
12:6-17	1028
12:7-9	249
12:7-9, 13	1198
12:9	1028
12:10	1184, 1243, 1244
12:13, 17	1198
12:14	1147
12:17	1198
13-19	1129
13:5	1122, 1148
13:5-8, 18	1103
13:7	1109
13:8	177, 600
13:11-14	1302
13:14-15	1302
14	1203
14:1	720
14:14-19	1318
14:14-20	1181, 1203
14:19-20	1006
15:3	1106
15:3-4	632
15:4	750
16:1	600
16:9	1322
16:14	1199
16:16	1199
16:17-21	1180, 1184
17:8	600
17:12	1121
17:14	1106
19	52, 1001, 1268
19-20	867
19-22	1245
19:11, 15	586
19:11-12	1007
19:11-15	867–868
19:11-16	1103, 1318
19:11-21	1007, 1008, 1228
19:12	1249
19:13	221, 1007
19:13, 15	221
19:15	850, 854, 1007, 1108, 1266, 1268
19:15-16	1103
19:16	221, 840, 1106, 1228
19:17-18	1007
19:19	868–869
19:19-20	868
19:19a	868
19:20	1007, 1129, 1225
19:21	1007
20	868, 1228
20:1-3	868, 1028
20:1-10	1123
20:1-22:5	344
20:2a	868
20:3a	868
20:4	838, 1025
20:4-5	1106
20:4-6	1123
20:7, 10	868
20:7-10	249
20:10	348
20:11-15	991
20:12, 15	600
21:2-3	586
21:7	432
21:10	1111
21:22	1231
21:22-23	1105
21:22-27	1231
21:23	1231
21:24-26	1231
21:25	389
21:27	600, 811
22:1, 3	1105
22:3-5	1098
22:12-13	1307
22:14-15	811
22:16	221, 274
22:18	1069
22:18-19	755

Early Christian Writings

Augustine of Hippo
City of God
Book XVIII 276
Chrysostom, John
The Gospel of St. Matthew 276
Jerome
Letter to Eustochium
cviii.10 276
Maimonides
11:4 231
Philo of Alexandria
De Praemiis et Poenis
95 1104

assembly/congregation, 539, 566, 568
Assis, Ellie, 328
Assumption of Moses, 1244
Assyria
 conquest of, 1195
 decline of, 874
 destruction of, 902
 as enemy of Israel, 1026, 1168
 historical setting of, 846–847
 invasion of, 860
 judgment of, 845–846
 recall of people from, 851
 victory of, 818
Athaliah, 419
Athanasius of Alexandria, 276, 741, 744
Athenagoras, 741
atonement, 179, 904, 970–971
attorney, imagery of, 958
Augustine, 276, 440, 605, 741
Author of Eternity, 36, 837
Auwers, Jean-Marie, 545
Avihu, 971
Azulai, Rabbi Chaim David, 326

B

Baal cult, establishment of, 419
Babylon
 Abram as called from, 242
 book of Ezekiel written in, 1076
 defeat of, 1328
 in dream of Daniel, 1118
 as enemy of Israel, 1024, 1026, 1168
 as Gentile kingdom, 1128
 God's message for, 865
 Judean exiles to flee from, 968
 as land of merchants, 1065, 1066
 people from, 624
 seed of, 1069
Babylonian exile, stages of, 427–428
Babylonians, 110, 420–421
Balaam
 blessing of, 287–288
 discourses of, 95–96, 291–298, 300, 301–305
 donkey of, 288–291
 last days proclamation by, 248
 literary context of, 286–288
 literary structure of, 288–293
 oracles of, 31, 107–109, 282, 749, 771
 prophecy of, 64, 96–100, 310, 1215
 story of, 285
 third oracle of, 298–300
 use of the last days phrase by, 792
 vision of, 53, 220
 wickedness of, 290
Balak, 95, 286, 287, 289, 290–291, 343
Baldwin, J., 1252, 1254, 1263, 1307
Balentine, Samuel E., 437
Baltzer, Klaus, 962
baptism, 167, 321, 937, 1181
Bar Kochba, Simon, 203, 231
Barbiero, Gianni, 515–516, 545, 706
Barker, Kenneth L., 1254
Barnabas, 218, 949, 1190
Baron, David, 1288
Barr, James, 216
Bartelt, Andrew, 790
Barth, Christoph, 478
Bateman IV, Herbert W., 673, 675
Bathsheba, 348, 405, 416, 470, 608, 679–680
battle bow, 1268
"Battle Hymn of the Republic" (song), 1008
Baxter, Wayne, 336
Beale, Gregory K., 882
beast, 1007, 1146
Beatitudes, 991
Becker, Joachim, 79
Beckwith, R. T., 120
Becliako, Daniel K., 881
Beecher, Willis J., 76–77, 85f4
beginning, as theme in Proverbs, 740–741, 743
begotten, coronation as, 33
Belial. *See* Satan
Bell, Rob, 815
Belshazzar, 1128
Benaiah, 416–418
Benjamin, tribe of, 125
Bennett, T. Miles, 1198
Bentzen, Aage, 78, 85f3, 681
Berechiah, 1261
Berekiah, Rabbi, 162
Berkhof, Louis, 138, 151–152
Bethesda, pools of, 917
Bethlehem
 bringing together of, 1213
 as home of David, 392, 705, 1105, 1213–1214
 Matthew's reference to, 1214
 meaning of, 1210
 Messiah as coming from, 105, 192, 223, 272–273, 321, 407, 825, 1162, 1207–1217
 salvation from, 1209
betrayal, of the Messiah, 663–670, 1281–1282
Beuken, William A. M., 1251
Beulah, 839
Bezalel, 853
Biblical commentaries, Messiah in, 233–234
Bildad, 441
bird, imagery in Ezekiel, 1067
The Birth of the Messiah (Brown), 1015
birth pangs, imagery of, 1022–1023, 1211, 1214, 1308–1309

birthright, connection with blessing, 262
Black, Matthew, 215
Blaikie, W. G., 402–403
Blaising, Craig A., 868–869
Blenkinsopp, Joseph, 983, 991, 992
blessing(s)
  of Adam and Abram, 163–164
  agricultural, 887–888
  connection with birthright, 262
  creation purposes for, 1060
  double portion of, 984
  enjoyment of, 489
  eschatological, 1043
  future, 907
  to the Gentiles, 1192
  from God, 392, 488, 721
  of Israel, 242, 902, 1301
  of man, 545
  millennial under new covenant, 1109–1110
  national, 980
  for obedience, 1024
  to people of Galilee, 831
  priestly, 714, 715, 724
  promise of, 861
  of provisions, 719
  in Psalms, 483
  purpose of, 187, 241
  of rain, 1170, 1171, 1173
  relationship to judgment, 908
  of renewed covenant relationship, 976
  of restored Davidic tent, 1189
  Sinai theology of, 965
  of successful man, 485
  as theme in Isaiah, 912
  as theme of Balaam narrative, 286–288, 304
  of those who take refuge in Him, 755
  of wisdom, 760
blindness, 909, 915, 923–924, 953, 963, 987–988
Block, Daniel I., 327, 990, 1025, 1333, 1336
Blomberg, Craig, 106, 107
blood, 178, 180, 183, 336, 1005
Boaz, 347, 349, 354–355
Bock, Darrell L., 985–986, 987, 989, 991, 1134, 1333
Boda, Mark J., 327, 1248, 1255, 1336
Boice, James, 702
Booij, Th., 681
Book of Comfort (Jeremiah), 1052–1056
Book of Consolation (Jeremiah), 1021, 1038–1039, 1042, 1044, 1045, 1052–1056
Book of Woes (Isaiah), 873, 897–898
Boorer, Suzanne, 442
booth, of David, 1188, 1189
"both now and forever," as phrase in Psalms, 714–715, 716, 718, 722
Boyd, James Oscar, 391
Bozrah, 998, 1002, 1200
Branch
  Joshua as, 1242, 1247
  as judging with righteousness, 850
  justice from, 1002
  Messiah as, 13, 113, 155, 319, 390, 406, 686, 793, 810, 835, 877, 1014–1016, 1229, 1235, 1254, 1273
  prophecy of, 845–846
  symbolism of, 852–853
  Zerubbabel as, 233, 1251, 1252
Branch of David
  Messiah as, 197, 199, 273, 1015, 1163, 1305
  reign of, 1040
  righteousness of, 1058
Branch of the Lord, Messiah as, 36–37, 803–813, 1011–1018, 1057
Breaker, Messiah as, 1202
"breaks open the way," 1202–1204
bride, 577–579
Bridegroom, Messiah as, 573–586
Bridges, C., 733
Briggs, Charles A., 76
Brooke, George, 989
Brown, Raymond E., 1015
Broyles, Craig C., 607
Bruce, F. F., 566, 988
Buksbazen, Victor, 835–836
Bultema, Harry, 868, 870, 898, 903
burden, 1261–1262
Burkett, D., 1133, 1134
burnt offering, 178, 180, 181, 188
Buseira, 1200
Butzeira, 1201
Bynum, Randolph, 1289–1290

C

Cain, 243–245, 261, 348, 774
Cairo Genzia, dating of, 214–215
Caleb, 1199
the call, doctrine of, 1181
call to repentance, 900–901, 976, 977
Calvin, John
  method of, 546–547
  quote of, 239, 277–278, 301, 444, 529–530, 611, 1294
  viewpoint of, 135, 504, 845, 848, 998
Canaan, 247, 251, 253–254
Canaanites, 247, 254
Canon, 119–123, 454, 741–742
canonical seams, 12, 120
"canopy," as term used by Isaiah, 812
Canticles. *See* Song of Solomon
Capernaum, 985

Carmel (Israel), 913
Carr, G. Lloyd, 773
Carroll, M. Daniel, 989, 990
Carson, D. A., 107, 959, 1333
Casey, P. M., 1130
cedar, imagery of, 1064–1065, 1066
celebration, sacrifices and offerings for, 180, 181–182
Chafer, L. S., 154
chaff, as term used in Psalms, 483
Chakham, Amos, 457
Chaldea, 1065
Champion of Justice, Messiah as, 934
Channa bar bar, Rabba, 63
Cherubim, 171
chesed, as the character of God, 351–352
Chief Shepherd, God as, 1085
child, as theme in Proverbs, 743
childbearing, 184
Childs, Brevard
  quote of, 128, 278, 469, 592, 677, 742, 833, 835, 848, 1208
  works of, 478
Chilion, 344
Chilton, Bruce, 810–811
Cho, Hwi, 1105
Chosen One, Messiah as, 1228
Christ, Messiah as, 1093
Christianity, advent of, 1124
Chrysostom, John, 276, 440, 441
Church, 394, 881–882
circumcision, 267
city of God, 624
Clark, Leslie, 1108
cleansing ceremonies, 178
Clement of Rome, 440
Clements, R. E., 79, 86f5, 806
Cleopas, 25
Clifford, Richard J., 610
Clines, David, 332, 1014
Cole, Robert, 517, 720
Collins, Anthony, 11–12, 73–74, 83f1, 1131, 1133, 1134, 1256
Collins, J. J., 988, 1015
comfort, 790, 991, 1172, 1187
"coming in the name of the Lord," as theme of Psalms, 696–697, 698
commandments, 242
commands, as theme in Malachi, 1329
compassion, of God, 1336
compositional/canonical approach of prophecy, 88–89, 88f7
confessional/dogmatic approach of prophecy, 88, 88f7
Coniah, 1041
Conqueror, Messiah as, 488
Consecrated Person, Messiah as, 29–30
consecration, 30
Contra Celsum (Origen), 967–968
The Conversion of the Jews (Roth), 826–827
Cooper, David L., 112, 334, 406, 675, 755
Copenhaver, Adam, 573–574
Cornelius, 257, 258, 1190
cornerstone
  characteristics of, 878–879
  concept of, 696
  description of, 1242–1243
  identity of, 875–876
  Messiah as, 699, 873–882, 1235, 1242–1243, 1267
  purpose of, 699, 1267
  rejection of, 874, 875
  in the Temple, 879
  in the Western Wall, 879
coronation, 33, 1252
corruption, as theme in Psalms, 522, 523–524
cosmic signs and wonders, 870, 1066, 1180–1181, 1322
counselor, meaning of, 836
covenant
  blessing of renewed, 976, 1028
  curses of, 1027
  disobedience of, 1040–1041
  formula in Ezekiel, 1087, 1101, 1110
  God's faithfulness to, 1038
  infractions, 636
  Jeremiah 33:14-26 and, 1059–1061
  land, 1101
  to Levi, 1332
  Levitical, 1050
  marital, 1332
  meaning of, 935
  messianic, 1109–1111
  to Noah, 251
  old, 1036–1037, 1038–1045, 1046, 1090
  of peace, 1026, 1087, 1090, 1102, 1110
  people, 935
  perpetual, 977, 980
  priest violation of, 1332
  promise as irrevocable and eternal, 1084
  promise of, 947
  promised *versus* Davidic covenant, 977–980
  relationship, 1092, 1101
  renewal, 980
  as theme in Deuteronomy, 1037
  as theme of First Servant Song, 923–924
  triangle of the Israelites, 1084f2
a covenant for the people, Messiah as, 320
covenant mediator, Messiah as, 934–936, 947

Covenant of Sinai, 328
Cowley, A. E., 1172
Craigie, Peter C., 69, 509, 545, 565, 574
creation
  blessing, seed, and land as theme of, 304, 1060
  as conveyed in heaven and earth, 504
  Father and Son in process of, 744
  God in, 633
  God's promises to, 1051
  as in Jeremiah, 1050–1051
  meaning of, 172
  praise to God within, 598
  response to global judgments, 869–870
  restoration of, 724
  role of Son in, 753
  Song of Solomon as celebration of, 770
  story of, 137–138, 170–171, 1320
  as theme in Psalms, 503
Creator, God as, 503, 751, 753
Creator of time, God as, 36, 837
Crenshaw, James, 1179
Crowe, Brandon D., 1281
crown, 390, 707, 1077, 1078–1079, 1080, 1253
crucifixion, 249, 601–602, 1120, 1146, 1180, 1182, 1245
Cullmann, Oskar, 880
Culver, Robert, 824–825, 831, 1146
Cunha, Wilson de A., 867
curses
  of Canaan, 254
  as conquered, 774
  from disobedience, 242, 1024
  of Israel, 242
  with Mosaic covenant, 1024
  over enemies, 669
  removal of, 1028
  Sinai theology of, 965
  as theme of Balaam narrative, 286–288
Cush, 254, 517, 624, 851, 865
Cyaxares of Media, 846
Cyrus
  addressing of captivity by, 923
  appointment of Zerubbabel by, 1248
  as conqueror of Babylon, 933, 1198, 1219
  as king, 30, 42, 131, 333, 428
  as military figure, 948
  rebuilding of Jerusalem by, 921, 962, 1145
  significance of, 839
  as warrior-king, 932

D

Dalman, Gustaf, 214
Damascus, 865, 1262
Daniel (book)
  cloud motif in, 1135
  dream in, 1115–1124, 1180
  kingdom theology in, 1128–1129
  little horn imagery in, 1129, 1135, 1146
  messianic view of, 1131–1133
  mystery as theme in, 1116
  "One like a son of man" in, 1128–1131, 1133–1134, 1135
  prediction of, 1023
  presentation of Messiah in, 131
  prince as theme in, 1146
  prophecies sealed by, 1031
  role of, 1115
  69 weeks prophecy, 1143–1147
  70 weeks prophecy, 1140, 1141, 1142–1143, 1305
  the 70th week, 1147–1149
  statue, description of, 1117
  structure of, 1139
  vision of, 1127, 1128, 1139
  "week" definition of, 1140
Daniel (man), 98, 1017, 1115
Darius I, 1220, 1225
darkness, walking in, 959–960
daughter of Zion, 578, 1211, 1263–1264
daughters of Moab, 860
David
  Amalekite victory by, 375
  as the anointed one, 46, 771, 804
  anointing of, 13
  appearance of, 574–575
  as author of Psalms, 33, 465, 608
  in Balaam's fourth discourse, 301–305
  betrayal of, 665
  booth of, 1188
  confessions by, 471
  conquering of Agag by, 57
  coronation of, 1108–1109
  covenant of (*See* Davidic covenant)
  death of, 499
  descendants of, 34, 396–397, 607–608, 807, 1069, 1101, 1105, 1107
  dynasty of (*See* Davidic dynasty)
  election of and status of Israel, 1089
  enemies of, 567, 663–664, 666–667, 668
  failure of, 348, 405, 470, 594, 608, 633
  faithfulness to God by, 729
  genealogy of, 355
  God's deliverance for, 561
  God's protection for, 634–635
  and Goliath, 378–382, 696–697, 698
  as a good shepherd, 1163
  horn of, 554, 853
  house of, 1187–1192, 1293, 1302, 1305

installation of, 608
as Israel's ideal ruler, 1098–1099
Jonathan and, 375
as king, 13, 125, 137, 191, 200, 316, 577, 632, 1086, 1187
laments of, 468
last words of, 37, 399–408
as leader, 1107
life of, 608
long-term prophecy to house of, 819–823
as mediator, 141
Messiah and, 202, 256, 404–406, 728, 1057, 1108
as messianic vice-regent, 1106–1109
mighty men of, 416–418
as my servant, 1100, 1227
obligations on the house of, 411
as One Shepherd, 764, 809
oracle of, 401, 494, 749
prayer of, 494, 618, 620, 621, 625–626, 666, 980
prediction of, 64
as priest, 141, 531
as priestly king, 1247
as prince, 1089, 1107
promises assured to, 31, 126, 385, 414, 554, 706, 724, 976–977, 1051
prophecy from Nathan to, 386
as prophet, priest, and king, 141–142
prophetic role of, 402–403
in Proverbs, 727, 728
relationship with God by, 594
request from Nathan, 1086
restoration of house of, 1187–1192, 1189
resurrection of, 1025
retrieval of ark by, 701, 705
Royal Son of, 770–774
royal tent of, 1188
as ruler over Israel, 1103
as ruling for Messiah, 1108
Saul as rival of, 125
seed of, 1051, 1060–1061, 1101–1102
as selected by God, 1226
self-description of, 65–66, 401
as servant of the Lord, 463, 621–622, 1109
serving of, 377
as shepherd, 1087, 1212
Solomon as son of, 772
sons of as priests, 682
soul of as King Messiah, 1099
suffering of, 540, 593, 595, 597, 705
as taunted by the Jebusites, 917
tent of, 1189, 1190–1192
throne of, 32, 468, 606, 624–625, 647–649, 720, 1187
and the Torah, 565
ultimate warning of, 406
as under-shepherd, 1099–1100
as witness to the nations, 977
David, Dale, 389
Davidic covenant
in 1 and 2 Kings, 414–415
as in 2 Samuel, 1050
Adonai Yahweh as used in, 392
in the Apocrypha, 431–432
compositional and thematic comparisons of, 426
context of, 1226
core of, 389
expectation of, 817
faithfulness in, 452
father-son stipulation of, 730
final fulfillment of, 1111–1112
fulfillment of, 31, 592, 645–660, 718, 724, 813
God's faithfulness to, 599, 635–636, 637–638
historical settings of, 427–429
idealization of, 192
ideological and theological comparisons, 429
Messiah as coming through, 34, 125–126, 1025, 1061
in the Midrash, 432
new covenant and, 1055
in the New Testament, 432
overview of, 385–397
priests and, 1059–1060
promise made in, 406, 1088, 1107, 1162, 1187
promised covenant and, 977–980
promises made in, 976–977, 1051
in Proverbs, 728
in the Psalms, 451, 467, 607, 627–628, 631–632, 719
reference to, 155
as of royal house, 488
servants of God as linked to, 656
significant aspects of, 729
stipulation of, 729
tenets of, 272
terms of, 1101
as unconditional, 394–396, 411
Davidic dynasty
as cedar in Ezekiel, 1065, 1066
end of, 30, 1064, 1083
establishment of, 386–389
history of, 131
lamp as reference to, 706–707
lost hope in, 319
Messiah as coming from, 105, 805, 807–808
offspring of the woman to, 264
overturning, 1074

perpetuation of, 612
promised hope to, 838, 1187
restoration of, 282, 1191
seed from, 1101–1102
selection of, 280
as stump, 847
tree of, 845
Davidic King, 235, 538–539, 1016, 1102
Davidic kingship, signet ring as symbol of, 1227
Davidic Messiah, 1103–1106
Davidic promises, 978–979
Davidic Son, priesthood and, 1057
Davis, Barry C., 675
Davis, Ralph, 391
"day has come," wrath in, 1078
Day of Atonement, 183, 185, 1029–1030
Day of the Lord
coming of, 866, 1022
description of, 1184
Elijah as coming before, 121
God's intervention in, 1230
imagery of, 1222
judgment at, 867
as used in Ezekiel, 1177
as used in Joel, 1168
day of vengeance, 998, 1005–1006
"the Day of Yahweh," 1177, 1316
de Lyra, Nicholas, 277, 495, 547
de Solms, E., 478
de Vaux, Roland, 380
deafness, healing of, 915
death
as a curse, 242
of Israel, 242
of male babies, 335
of the Messiah, 536–537, 553, 555, 617–629, 646, 928–929, 958
metaphors for, 499
seeing the Lord through, 444, 445
as theme in Psalms, 524, 545, 552, 626, 627
Deborah, 362
decay, as theme in Psalms, 522, 523–524
de-creation, event of, 1319–1320
deep, as metaphor in Psalms, 594
defiant sin, 183
Deism, heretical view of, 11
deity, of the Messiah, 148–157, 505–510, 831–840
delightful child, as theme in Jeremiah, 743
Delightful One, Messiah as, 66, 677, 804
Delitzsch, Frank
quote of, 278, 403, 404, 564, 566, 602, 673, 682, 686, 744, 753, 794–795, 836, 837, 838, 849, 901, 955, 961, 970, 990
viewpoint of, 63, 68, 478, 850, 1000–1001
works of, 75–76
deliverance
aspects of, 915
from enemies, 908
God's promise of, 560–561, 852, 1044
for Israel, 1301
of prisoners, 936
response to, 597–598
as theme in Psalms, 567–568, 678, 693
Deliverer, Messiah as, 30, 155, 593–594
demons, 248–249
denouement, 344–345, 355–356
Deuteronomy, book of, 97, 1037, 1038
development view of prophecy, 76
diarchic messianism, 194
Dictionary of Biblical Imagery, 578
Dictionary of Classical Hebrew (Clines), 1014
direct fulfillment of prophecy, 88–89, 88f7, 104–106
disciples, 663, 959, 1308
discipleship, 954, 955
disease, 184–185, 438–439
disobedience, 242, 252, 1040–1041
Distant Star, Messiah as, 285–305
Divine King, Messiah as, 679–681
Divine Lord, Messiah as, 683
Divine Presence, 792, 811–812, 813, 1110
Divine Shepherd, 1305
Divine Teacher, Messiah as, 885
Divine Wisdom, Messiah as, 739–745
Documentary Hypothesis, 55
Doeg, 668
dogmatic/confessional approach of prophecy, 88, 88f7
donkey, 584, 1265
donkey, stories of, 288–291
Douglas, J. D., 178
doxologies, in the Psalms, 461–462, 559, 618
dream revelation, 1180
Driver, Samuel Rolles, 404–405, 1130
drunkenness, 252
dual fulfillment of prophecy, 74, 84, 84f2
Duhm, Bernahrd, 53, 67
Dumbrell, William, 774
Duncan, John, 11
dust, 443, 523, 655
Dvoracek, Andy, 574, 577
Dyer, Charles H., 1024

E

eagles, imagery of, 1064–1065, 1066, 1067
early church, synagogue tradition of, 216–218
early Rabbinic Literature, Messiah in, 208–209
ears, opening of, 563, 569, 956
earth, 504, 598, 867
Eaton, John H., 544, 979

Ecclesiastes, 758–766
Ecclesiastes Rabbah, 161
Eden. *See* Garden of Eden
Edersheim, Alfred, 11, 75, 208–209
Edom
    conversion of, 851
    as enemy of Israel, 1168
    God's message for, 865
    identification of, 998
    judgment for, 916–917
    trusting in, 912
    watchman from, 1001–1003
Edomites, 1001m, 1002, 1189
Egypt
    as eagle, 1065
    God's message for, 865
    gods of, 1180
    Israel and, 106, 293, 812, 874, 886, 898, 968, 1026, 1028, 1168
    Joseph (patriarch) sold in slavery to, 264
    Joseph (father of Jesus) told to flee to, 106
    Matthew's reference to, 1214
    Messiah out of, 96, 293
    naming pattern of, 833
    oracles against, 1063
    people from, 624, 851
    plague on, 1178
    position of power of, 874
    return of Moses to, 162
    as son of Ham, 254
Ehud Ben Zvi, 1251
Eichhorn, J. G., 74
Eichrodt, Walther, 278–279
El Elyon, God as, 751
El Roi, God as, 152, 751
El Shaddi, God as, 751
Elam, 851
Eleazar, R., 207
Eli, as priest, 366, 945
Eliab, 380
Eliakim, 874
Eliezer, 216
Eliezer, Rabbi, 204, 207
Elihu, 129
Elijah
    appearance of, 205
    arrival of, 232
    clothing of, 1214
    as coming before the Day of the Lord, 121
    as compared to Moses, 327–328
    miracles of, 419–420
    name meaning of, 37, 1017
    as prophet, 415
    prophets of Baal and, 1302
    question of, 750
    trust of, 1199
Elimelech, 344, 347
Elisha, 415, 419, 466
Elkanah, 364
Ellison, H. L., 439
Elnathan, 1307
Elohim, God as, 464–465, 506
"end of days," 203, 282, 297–298, 1132, 1198, 1200–1201
enemies
    crushing of, 305
    cursing, 669
    of David, 567, 663, 666–667, 668
    deliverance from, 908
    of God, 865–868, 869, 1203
    of Israel, 583, 851, 1026, 1168, 1189, 1304
    of the Messiah, 494, 522, 535–536, 668, 680
    victory over, 582
Engnell, Ivan, 78
Enns, Peter, 548
Enoch, 151, 261, 1134
enthronement oracle, Psalm 110 as, 679
ephemeral life, Davidic covenant and, 651–652
Ephrathah, 705, 1213
Ephriam, 154, 228–229, 263, 1266
Er, 263, 280, 351
Esarhaddon, 936, 1064
Esau, 262, 348, 1002
Eschatological Deliverer, Messiah as, 31
eschatological time indicator, 794–795
Eschatological/Messianic Psalms, 665
Esther, 131, 299, 1028
eternal covenant faithfulness, 694–695, 697, 699
Eternal Father, Messiah as, 154, 824, 1162
eternal hope, 718, 720
Eternal King Priest, Messiah as, 673–688
eternal life, 538, 550, 655, 720
eternal thrones, 720
eternity, 646, 839
Ethan the Ezrahite, 625, 631, 633, 637, 649, 719, 748
Ethiopia, 254
Ethiopian eunuch, 257
ethnicity, restoration of, 1101
Euphrates River, 851
Eusebius of Caesarea, 741
Evans, C., 201–202
Eve. *See also* woman
    birth of Seth by, 207
    command to, 241
    creation of, 350
    disobedience of, 242, 345
    Genesis 3:15 and, 58
    Messiah as descendant of, 728
    nakedness of, 775

name meaning of, 774
role in the Fall by, 150–151
seed from, 124, 163, 255
everlasting, meaning of, 837
everlasting covenant, 1109–1110. *See also* new covenant
Everlasting Father, Messiah as, 837
evil, 316, 551–552
exile(s), 242, 297–298, 420–421, 433, 1089, 1249
Exodus, imagery of, 947
the Exodus, 968
Exodus Psalms, 665
expiation/propitiation, 188
Ezekiel (book)
17:22-24, overview of, 1064–1065
21:25-27, overview of, 1073–1079
34:23-24, overview of, 1083–1090
37:15-28, overview of, 1100–1106, 1109–1111
bird imagery in, 1067
covenant formula in, 1087
Day of the Lord imagery in, 1177, 1222
eagle imagery in, 1064–1065, 1066, 1067
forever as theme in, 1097–1098
hope of shepherd king by, 1087–1088
horticultural imagery in, 1066
judgment as theme in, 1074
oracles in, 1012–1013, 1016, 1084, 1085, 1100
presence of God as theme in, 1076
prince as theme in, 1108
pronouncement of guilt in, 1078
prophecy of, 1163
relationship as theme in, 1076
restoration as theme in, 1101
riddles in, 1064
ruin as theme in, 1079
shepherd imagery in, 1085, 1092, 1307
structure of, 1083
themes in, 1076
two sticks imagery in, 1100
vision of, 1093, 1321
woe oracles in, 1085
Ezekiel (man), 126, 622, 1017
Ezra, 1322
Ezra-Nehemiah, 99, 131

F

faith, 186
faithful love, 862
faithful priest, Messiah as, 366
faithfulness
of David, 729
in the Davidic covenant, 452
of God, 560, 599, 627–628, 635–636, 654, 717, 1038, 1297, 1323
as quality of Messiah's reign, 862
as theme in Psalms, 621, 652
The Fall
as compared to Jacob's blessings, 248
as compared to story of Cain, 245
as compared to story of Noah, 245–247
story of, 138, 150–151, 162–163, 242, 345, 632, 1117
false prophet, 1007
false teachers, 1302
fasting, 992, 1178
Father, in Triune Godhead, 837
Father of Eternity, Messiah as, 36, 822, 824, 825
favor, 659, 714, 717, 991, 1278–1279, 1281
fear of God, 403
"the fear of the Lord," 733–734
Feast of Booths, 185, 1188, 1221
Feast of Firstfruits, 185
Feast of Passover, 968
Feast of Sukkot, 812
Feast of Trumpets, 185
Feast of Unleavened Bread, 185
Feast of Weeks, 185
Feiler, Paul Frede, 337
Feinberg, Charles, 97, 1022, 1026, 1147, 1198, 1237, 1301–1302
festival hymns, in Psalms, 665
Festival of Booths, 812
Festival of Tabernacles, 812
Fiddler on the Roof (play), 94
First Adam, 163
First Temple, 812, 1110
Fishbane, M., 1015
Fitzmyer, Joseph, 988–989
Flesher, Paul, 810–811
Flood, story of, 163, 251–258, 261
footstool, as theme in Psalms, 680
Forbes, John, 478, 544
forever, as theme in Ezekiel, 1097–1098
forgiveness, 179, 620, 904, 1276
former prophets, 125–126
foundation, Messiah as, 1267
Fox, Michael V., 773
France, R. T., 106, 110, 1332, 1333
Fretheim, Terence E., 1059
Friedman, David, 1097
Fruchtenbaum, Arnold, quotes of, 732, 1021, 1025, 1029, 1030–1031, 1106–1107, 1109, 1201
Fuhr, Alan, 854
full consecration, sacrifices for, 181
Futato, Mark D., 613

G

Gablan, 203

Gabriel
    announcement to Mary by, 142–143, 198, 1069
    Daniel's vision and, 99, 1131, 1142, 1143–1145, 1148
Gabrion, Hervé, 988
Gad, 466
Gaffin, Jr., Richard, 854–855
Gakuru, G., 1015
Galilee, 203, 831, 834, 985
Gaon, Hai, 228
Gaon, Sa'adiah, 207, 227, 228, 967
Garden of Eden
    exile from, 242
    Fall in, 632, 1117
    God as walking in, 151
    meaning of, 172
    perennial stream in, 1321
    reconciliation in, 282
    restoration of, 771–772, 778, 850
    in Song of Solomon, 776, 778
    story of, 171
garments of salvation, 992
Garrett, Duane, 778
"the gate," 1202–1204
Gedaliah, 466
Genesis, 255, 260–261, 279–280, 772, 774, 1320
Gentiles
    blessings promised to, 1192
    branch of millennial government for, 1107
    destruction of Jerusalem by, 787
    God's blessing to, 267
    Jewish apostolic outreach to, 799
    judgment on, 1168
    kingdoms of, 1128–1129
    lands of, 256
    Messiah as light to, 940
    messianic covenant to, 1111
    oppression from, 1024
    pilgrimage to Temple Mount by, 797
    promise to, 394, 1190
    responsiveness to Jesus by, 987
    as ruling Israel, 1306
    salvation of, 799, 1190, 1225
    seed of Abraham and, 290
    as serving Israel, 1028
    times of, 1115–1124
    vision for, 257
Gerstenberger, Erhard, 702, 708
Gese, Hartmut, 129
Gesenius, W., 1172
Gesenius' Hebrew Grammar (Gesenius), 404
Gethsemane, 956
Gideon, 835, 840
gifts, spiritual, 849
Gill, John, 329, 755
Glenny, W. Edward, 1191
Gloag, Paton J., 74
global judgment, 866, 869–870
glory, 507–508, 912–914, 916, 927, 928, 1223–1224, 1318
glory of Israel, Messiah as, 1225
God. *See also* Yahweh
    actions of, 1090
    acts in history by, 42–43, 45, 376
    Adonay as name of, 539, 683–684
    'adoni as name of, 675
    as Ancient of Days, 1129
    as Angel of the Lord, 1236
    anger of, 452, 645, 846, 963
    attributes of, 561, 566, 633
    as author of eternity, 837
    blessings from, 488, 721
    care for humans by, 503, 505, 506, 567
    character of, 351–352, 752
    as Chief Shepherd, 1085
    compassion of, 1336
    covenant with David by, 1088
    creation and, 633, 744, 1051
    creative work of, 619
    as Creator, 503, 751, 753
    as creator of time, 36, 837
    David and, 594
    as defender, 497
    delight of, 745
    deliverance of, 560–561, 977, 1044
    departure of presence of, 1110–1111, 1318
    discipline of, 1172
    as El Elyon, 751
    as El Roi, 751
    as El Shaddi, 751
    as Elohim, 506
    enemies of, 865–868, 869, 1203
    eternal covenant faithfulness of, 694–695, 697, 699
    faithfulness of, 560, 599, 627–628, 635–636, 637–638, 654, 717, 1038, 1297, 1323
    favor of, 659
    forgiveness from, 620
    gathering of people by, 1196–1199
    glory of, 916, 927, 928
    as God Almighty, 751
    as God Most High, 751
    as God who Sees, 751
    as The Good Shepherd, 1093
    grace of, 559–560
    "great and wondrous things" from, 1050
    great supper of, 1007
    help from, 566–568
    as the Holy One, 750

inspiration of, 122
instructions of, 954–957, 1043
intervention of, 1230
Israel and, 107, 164–165, 452, 608–609, 633–634, 752, 963, 980, 1044, 1055, 1092, 1097, 1155–1156, 1157, 1160, 1334
Jacob and, 152
Job and, 439–440
Joshua and, 1240
Judah and, 887
judgment from, 635–637, 865–867, 1168, 1278
justice of, 634
kingdom of, 665, 764, 1122–1124
as light of Israel, 846
as Lord, 751
as Lord of Armies, 1240
as Lord of Hosts, 1330
as the Lord our Righteousness, 898
love of, 532
as magnificent, 504–505, 507–508
majesty of, 954
mercy of, 880
Messiah and, 498, 534
as mighty, 837
as the Mighty One of Jacob, 877
as my glory, 498
as name of God, 751
names of, 255
pattern of, 376
people and, 548
as people's dwelling place, 646
as performing wonders, 621
as physician, 1173
plan of in Zechariah, 1276
power of, 954
praise and glory to, 632–633
praises to, 632–633, 649
prediction of destruction by, 1041
presence of, 577–578, 580, 835, 1076, 1110–1111
promises of, 251, 682, 977, 1051
protection for David by, 634–635
as Protector of Israel, 703, 713, 717
provision of, 835
punishment from, 636
rebuke of Satan by, 1238, 1244
reign in Zion by, 787, 927–928
rejection of, 580, 609, 1279–1280
as rescuer, 497
restoration from, 808, 809
as the Rock, 877
role in king's reign, 611
sacrifices and, 177, 179–180
salvation from, 596, 609, 834–835
as Shepherd of the Messiah, 535–553
as shield, 498
sign from, 1241
signet ring as seal of, 1227
as solution to nation's difficulties, 609
sovereignty of, 1317
as the stone of Israel, 877
as Teacher, 889
three commands from, 1221
throne of, 647–649
as true shepherd, 1093
vindication from, 958
warning of, 944
as Warrior, 1317–1318
wonders of, 627
Word of, 955
as working outside boundaries of Israel, 1190
worship of, 624, 717
as Yahweh, 152, 255, 751
God Almighty, God as, 751
God Most High, God as, 751
God of Jacob, Messiah as, 798
God who Sees, God as, 751
The God Who Sees, Messiah as, 152
Godet, Frederic, 336
goel, theme of, 354–355, 440, 441–442
Gog, 57, 64, 209, 232, 299
Goldberg, Louis, 152–153
golden calf, 141
Goldingay, John
observation of, 837
quote of, 420, 705, 849, 850–851, 935
viewpoint of, 600, 850
Goliath, 363, 378–382, 574, 696–697, 698
Gomer, 256, 578–579, 1153, 1155–1156, 1157–1158
Gomorrah, 208, 1128, 1226
"good news," 990
Good Shepherd
David as, 1163
God as, 1093
Messiah as, 1098, 1200
Goodspeed, G. S., 75
Gordis, Robert, 776
Gordon, Cyrus, 820
governing rod, Judah as, 272
government, 1079, 1107, 1112
Gowan, Donald, 222
grace, 559–560, 1181
grain, as used for sacrifices, 180–182
Grassmick, J., 1133
Great Commission, 1321
Great Flood. *See* Flood
Great Rift Valley, 1322
"great supper of God," 1007

Greece, 1024, 1026, 1119–1120, 1128
Gressmann, H., 77
Grisanti, Michael S., 751
Grogan, Geoffrey W., 868
Grudem, Wayne, 138–139
guilt, 1078, 1239, 1243, 1245
guilt offering, 179, 180, 181, 184–185
Gundersen, David Alexander, 468
Gundry, R. H., 1333
Gunkel, Hermann, 278, 459–460, 477, 478, 543–544, 546, 618, 703

H

Hadrach, 1262
Hagar, 152
Haggai (book), 1219–1228, 1229–1231
Haggai (man), 622, 1219, 1248, 1315
Hakham, Amos, 544–545, 574, 576, 577
HaLevi, Rabbi Yehudah, 227, 964–965
Ham, 251, 252, 253–254, 257
Hama b. R. Hanina, Rabbi, 274
Haman, 299, 1028
Hamath, 851, 1262
Hamilton, James, 123, 130–131
Handel, George Frederick, 12, 440, 569
Hannah, 191–192, 361–370, 1068, 1069
harlotry, imagery of, 1027
Harrington, Hannah, 989
Harris, Murray J., 576
Hartley, John, 439, 445–446
Hashabiah, 466
Hasmonean Dynasty, 431, 1255
Hauser, Alan Jon, 774
Hay, David M., 681
healer, Messiah as, 908, 916
healing
- of Israel, 1026–1027
- by Jesus, 937–938
- of lame man, 148
- from the Messiah, 904, 917, 1173
- of Namaan, 1190
- of the nations, 966
- as theme in Isaiah, 914, 915

Heaven, 487, 504, 632–633, 717
Hebrew and Aramaic Lexicon of the Old Testament, 578, 1014
Hebrew canon. *See* Canon
Hedrick, Terry J., 1311
Heim, Knut, 67
Heine, Ronald E., 606–607
help, as theme in Psalms, 714, 715, 722, 723–724
Heman, 465, 466, 748
Hendren, Noam, 813
Hendriksen, William, 985, 986–987
Hengstenberg, Ernst Wilhelm, 42–44, 47, 48, 478, 1059
Hens-Piazza, Gina, 419–420
Hephzibah, 839
Herman the Ezrahite, 625
hero, Messiah as, 1276
Herod, 104, 112, 335, 1215
Herod Agrippa, 196
Herod Antipas, 916
Herod the Great, 196
Heschel, Abraham Joshua, 52
Hever, Nahal, 69
Hezekiah
- Davidic promise and, 838
- failure of, 836
- as king, 317, 466, 921, 1153, 1154, 1195
- as potential deliverer, 832, 833, 898
- proverbs of, 727, 748
- quote of, 847
- as righteous, 803
- sign for, 819

Hiattusilis III, 394–395
High Priest, Messiah as, 200
high priest(s), 191, 1057, 1257
Highway of Holiness, 914
Hilary of Poitiers, 741
Hill, Andrew, 1329
His anointed, Messiah as, 365, 754
historical fulfillment of prophecy, 83f1, 84
Hitchcock, Alfred, 1327, 1334
Hittite Suzerainty Treaty, 394–395
Hitzig, Ferdinand, 478
Hiyya bar Abba, Rabbi, 206
Hizzuk Emunah (Troki), 965
Hodge, Charles, 150
Hoehner, Harold W., 1145
holiness, 863
Holladay, Carl R., 514
Holladay, William, 328
Holmes, Sherlock, 1332
Holy City, 1323
Holy of Holies, 172, 1143
Holy One (of Israel), Messiah as, 13, 208, 750, 792, 839, 899, 1069
Holy Place, of the Tabernacle, 172
Holy Spirit
- advent of, 788
- coming of, 800
- final installment of, 1192
- forms of, 1179
- Messiah's anointing by, 983
- outpouring of the, 812, 900–902, 1171, 1177–1184
- power from, 1182–1183
- promise of, 812

purgation by, 811
Holy Way, 914, 915
honor, 507–508, 992, 1003
Hooker, M. D., 1333
hope
for anointed king, 774
eschatological, 1044, 1306
of the exiles, 1089
of Israel, 1073–1080
of the new covenant, 1040
of the remnant, 1204
of restoration, 1038, 1042
of shepherd king, 1087–1088
as theme in Psalms, 720
Hophni, 366
Horbury, William, 82, 88f7, 127–128
horn
Antichrist as little, 1146
of David, 554, 853
from house of Israel, 1063
imagery in Daniel, 1129, 1135
of Israel, 648
Messiah as, 390
as theme in Psalms, 706
as theme of Song of Hannah, 368
Hosea (book), 578–579, 793, 1153–1160, 1161–1164
Hosea (man), 53, 578–579, 1156, 1157
Hossfeld, Frank-Lothar, 545
House, Paul R., 414, 608
House of David, 1187–1192, 1293, 1302, 1305
house of God, 595
house of Israel, 1053
house of Judah, 1053
house/dynasty, as gift in covenant, 394
Howard, Jr., David, 462
Howe, Julia Ward, 1008
Hugenberger, G. P., 168, 169, 333, 947, 962, 969
humanity, 503, 505, 506, 511, 651, 655, 1316
humility, of the Messiah, 1265, 1276–1277, 1297
hymns of praise, 665
Hyrcanus, John, 999

I

Ibn Ezra, Rabbi, viewpoints of, 233, 785, 803, 878, 963, 966, 967, 1251, 1252–1253, 1286
Iddo, 1261
ideal Israel, Messiah as, 934, 946
Ideal King, Messiah as, 605–614
ideal ruler, Messiah as, 849
Ideal Servant passages, in Isaiah, 832
Idel, M., 234
idolatry
of Ahaz, 818
imagery of, 1027
of Israel, 620, 790, 1038, 1158
of Judah, 790, 1038
judgment for, 808
of the king, 311–312
of the nations, 932, 936
Iggeret Teman, 967
Ignatius of Antioch, 275
Immanuel
Isaiah's book of, 31
Messiah as, 35, 50, 53, 126, 143, 732, 822, 824, 825, 833–834, 835, 839, 840, 845, 1225
prophecy of, 875
significance of, 839
immediate fulfillment of prophecy, 84, 84f2
immersion, of Jesus, 167
inadvertent sin, 183
incarnation, 42
indictment, as theme in Malachi, 1329
inheritance, given to Davidic king, 538–539
inspiration, divine, 122
Instone-Brewer, David, 111
instructed tongue, of the Messiah, 954
Instructor of God's Law, Messiah as, 885
instruments, 561, 948
intellectual gifts of the Spirit, 849
intertestamental literature, messianism in, 194–200
intertextuality, 839
intimacy, in Song of Solomon, 775–776
Introduction to Old Testament Theology (Sailhamer), 81
Irenaeus of Lyons, 150, 607
Isaac
Abraham and, 260
blessing from, 262, 286
covenant with, 539, 632
descendants of, 282–283, 1023, 1226
marriage of, 260
Messiah as coming from, 255–256, 728
Rebekah as wife of, 820
sacrifice of, 971
as sheep, 1310
Isaac, Rabbi, 162
Isaac of Troki, 1286
Isaiah (book)
2:2-4, overview of, 785–800
4:2-6, overview of, 806–810
28:16, overview of, 873–874, 875–877, 878–880, 881–882
30, content of, 886–887
35, overview of, 907–909, 910
40-55, historical references in, 926
42:1-9, overview of, 931–933
49:1-13, overview of, 943–946, 949–950
50:4-11, overview of, 953–960

52:13-53:12, overview of, 961–962, 968–970
53, overview of, 962, 964, 966–968, 972
55, structure and summary of, 976–977
61:1-6, overview of, 984–989
63:1-6, overview of, 998–1006, 1007
Apocalypse and, 1007
"the arm of the Lord" in, 969
blessing as theme in, 897, 912
blindness as theme in, 909, 915
blood as theme in, 1005
Book of Woes in, 873, 897–898
the call in, 989–990
"canopy" term as used by, 812
comfort as theme in, 790, 991, 1172
the commission in, 990–991
the completion in, 992–993
connection to Micah by, 1214
the consequence in, 992
the contrasts in, 992
"corner" as stone characteristic, 879
Day of the Lord imagery in, 1222
day of vengeance in, 998, 1005–1006
Deutero-Isaiah, 984
divine hardening to Israel by, 923
dream revelation of, 1180
dynastic oracles of, 832
eternity as theme in, 839
Exodus imagery in, 947
the Exodus in, 968
Feast of Passover in, 968
foundation stone section, 873–874
healing as theme in, 914, 915
historical setting of, 832, 846–847
holy road as theme in, 910
hymn of promise in, 852
Ideal Servant passages, 832
Immanuel passage in, 31, 847, 852
Jacob as term use in, 798
judgment as theme in, 897, 912, 998, 1003
justice as theme of, 901
kingship as theme in, 915–916
labor pains imagery in, 1214
as latter prophet, 126
Little Apocalypse passages in, 866, 897
Messianic Era in, 907–918
messianic hope of, 1057
Narrative of a sign rejected in, 897
New Exodus of, 470
New Testament imagery in, 890–892
oracles in, 847, 859, 860, 873, 897, 1012–1013
"people/nation" as used by, 786
"pierced" as used by, 1296
presuppositions for, 997
proclamation of deliverance in, 834–838
prologue in, 897
promise of the child in, 835–838
promised return in, 850–851
prophecy of, 1162
provision of victory in, 835
redemption as theme in, 792
return from exile as theme of, 962
righteousness as theme of, 901, 1004
Servant hymns of, 195
as servant of the Lord, 622
Servant Songs of, 30–31, 319–320, 333, 564, 599, 922–925, 931–940, 943–950, 953–960, 1000, 1296 (*Seealso* Servant Songs)
streams in the desert as theme in, 910
strengthening of weak hands as theme in, 910
structure of, 897–898, 910–911
Suffering Servant passages in, 185
Summary of Judgments in, 897
supremacy of Yahweh as theme of, 962
"tested" as stone characteristic, 878–879
Trito-Isaiah, 984
trust as theme in, 912
vindication as theme of, 1004
water as theme in, 916–917
wine press imagery in, 999, 1002, 1004, 1005
year of redemption in, 998, 1005–1006
Isaiah (man), 785–786, 897, 926–928, 1055
Ishmael, 152, 267
Ishmael, Rabbi, 1304
Islam, 325–326
Israel
abandonment of, 825
authority of, 1002
Babylonians and, 420–421
blessing of, 242, 902, 1043, 1301
blindness of, 909, 915, 923–924, 953, 963
breaking of Sinai covenant by, 297
captivity of, 30, 1141, 1196
Carmel, 913
celebrating king of, 582–583
cleansing of, 1293, 1301
covenant and, 935–936, 980, 1026, 1027
covenant with, 980
covenantal infidelity of, 1188
as daughter of Zion, 578
deafness and blindness of, 923, 924, 934
deliverance for, 851–852, 1244–1245, 1301
departure from Egypt by, 106
departure of God's glory in, 1076
deportations of, 420
discipline of, 1172
disobedience of, 1040–1041, 1195
division of, 1087, 1212
double portion blessing on, 984

Egypt and, 106, 293, 812, 874, 886, 898, 968, 1026, 1028, 1168
enemies of, 583, 851, 1026, 1168, 1189, 1304
evil shepherds in, 1039
exile of, 297–298
exodus of, 96
final restoration of, 1160
forgiveness to, 1276
as fulfilling the Great Commission, 1321
future of, 926–928
gathering of, 1297
Gentiles as serving, 1028
geographic regions of, 913m
God and, 107, 164–165, 452, 608–609, 633–634, 752, 963, 980, 1044, 1092, 1097, 1155–1156, 1157, 1160, 1334
great assembly of, 568
healing of, 1026–1027
hope for, 1000, 1073–1080
horn of, 648, 1063
house of pride, 1084f1
identity of remnant of, 1199–1200
idolatry of, 343, 790, 1038, 1158
Jesus as truest representative of, 169
judgment upon, 635–636, 636–637, 845–846, 926–928, 1281–1282, 1301, 1311
king for, 125, 165, 635
as king in Song of Solomon, 775
king stipulations in, 730–731
kings of, 78
land promise for, 1097
leadership of, 882
Lebanon, 913
Levant, 913
liberation of, 1024–1026
as light to the nations, 953
marriage imagery for, 1039
Messiah and, 204, 727, 846, 880, 890, 1029–1031, 1280, 1297
military defeat of, 581
millennial prosperity of, 1028–1029
as ministers, 992
mosaic paradigm of kingship in, 310–322
as My People, 1156–1157
as My servant, 933
nations oppressing, 1024
new covenant with, 1043, 1102
new David for, 1089
pagan priesthood within, 63
partial fulfillment of promises for, 1012–1013
peace in, 835
political territory of, 315
prayer for future king of, 605, 606
present estrangement of, 1153–1164
as priests, 992
prophetic destiny of, 1141
prophetic message given to, 11
purification of, 1230
purposes to be accomplished, 1031
rebellion of, 141, 620, 873, 898, 956, 964, 1027, 1161, 1222
rebuilding of Second Temple, 1219
redeemers of, 287
redemption for, 578–579, 999–1000
regathering of, 851
remnant of, 1045–1046
removal of guilt from, 1239
removal of religious life, 1159
repayment to, 1171
repentance of, 1276, 1293
rescue of, 1023
responsibility to serve by, 921
restoration of, 599, 763, 800, 808, 945, 1021–1022, 1049, 1050, 1053–1054, 1085, 1153–1164, 1159–1160, 1164, 1196, 1198, 1242, 1243, 1301
restored land of, 551
return from exile by, 1012, 1013
return to promised land by, 851
reunification of, 1211–1212
ritual purification of, 1110
royal warrior of, 291–292
as ruled by Gentile powers, 1306
Sabbath day and, 207
sabbatical violations of, 1141
salvation of, 620, 1026
Satan's work against, 1028
Saul as king of, 13, 125, 137, 140, 293, 315, 635, 1030
security of, 874, 1090
as selected by God, 1226
as servant, 944, 964
Sharon, 913
as sheep, 320, 1103, 1308
Shekinah Glory in, 1111
Shepherd of, 890, 1083–1094
shepherds of, 1278
as source of blessing, 1188–1189
status of and election of David, 1089
sufferings of, 229, 789, 965, 1208
themes of story of, 242
as theocracy, 1087
threats to prosperity of, 287
tribulation of, 1022–1024
typological interpretations of, 167–170
ultimate fulfillment of promises for, 1013
as unfaithful wife, 578–579
unfaithfulness of, 1153, 1161

unrepentance of, 992
unrighteousness of, 963
victory of, 835
wars of, 1317, 1323
Israelites. *See also* people of God
covenant triangle of, 1084f2
disobedience of, 1040–1041
gathering of, 1297
historical recordings of, 279
items to go without, 1158–1159
metamorphosis of, 1293
at Mount Sinai, 1036–1037
mourning by, 1293
threats against Moses by, 332
Ithiel, 727, 749, 752
Itzhaki, Rabbi Shlomo. *See* Rashi (Rabbi Shlomo Itzhaki)

J

Jaar, fields of, 705
Jacob
birthright of, 348, 1002
blessing to, 241, 248, 264, 286, 287–288
covenant with, 539, 632
descendants of, 260, 280, 282–283, 346, 1023, 1226
dream of, 152, 1180
king arising from, 64
last days proclamation by, 248
Messiah as coming from, 256, 728, 771
oracles of, 31, 282
prophecy of, 96–100, 296–298, 302, 304, 310
seed of, 107
story of, 262–263
use of the last days phrase by, 792
as used in book of Isaiah, 798
"Jacob's trouble," tribulation as, 1023, 1149, 1305
Jael, 362
Jakeh, 727, 748
James, 939, 1188, 1189
Janowski, Bernd, 970
Janzen, J. Gerald, 441
Japheth, 252, 256–258
Japheth ben Eli, Karaite, 478
Javan, 256
Jebusites, 917
Jeconiah, 1069
Jeduthun, 465, 466
Jehoahaz, 1011, 1065
Jehoiachin
exile of, 1065–1066, 1068–1069
imprisonment of, 420–421
as king, 1011
punishment of, 1041
release of, 319, 427
riddle of, 1064
significance of, 1069, 1227
Jehoiakim, 874, 1011, 1041, 1065
Jehoshaphat, 466
Jehovah, 255
Jehozadak, 1247
Jehu, 419, 1155
Jephthah, 820
Jeremiah (book)
23:5-6, overview of, 1011–1014
33:14-26, overview of, 1050–1061
birth pangs imagery in, 1022–1023
Book of Comfort in, 1052–1056
Book of Consolation in, 1021, 1038–1039, 1042, 1044, 1045, 1052–1056
branch references in, 1066
condemnation of false shepherds, 1103
creation reference in, 1050–1051
delightful child as theme in, 743
dependency on Deuteronomy by, 97
eschatological perspective in, 1042–1043, 1044
the house of Israel in, 1053
the house of Judah in, 1053
Jacob's trouble in, 1149
labor pains imagery in, 1023
as latter prophet, 126
lawsuit imagery in, 1026
major themes in, 1042
marriage imagery in, 1039
medicine imagery in, 1026–1027
message of, 1049
Noahic covenant in, 1050–1051
old and new covenants in, 1038–1045
oracles in, 1012–1013, 1052, 1054, 1305
potter reference in, 1275, 1280
prophecies of future restoration in, 1021
prophecy of, 31, 923
prostitute imagery in, 1039
sheep analogy of, 320
shepherd imagery in, 1305, 1307
sword oracle in, 1305
terms in, 1053
themes in, 1053
"times of the Gentiles" in, 1024
tribulation description in, 1022–1024
vision of the future by, 1041
warnings from, 1060
Jeremiah (man), 37, 328, 622, 1017, 1021, 1039, 1041
Jeremias, J., 876, 1304
Jeroboam II, 1153–1154
Jerome, 276, 440, 748
Jerusalem
attack on, 1316–1317

conquest of, 1315
as daughter of Zion, 578
defense of, 1317–1320
destruction of, 787, 998, 1076, 1147, 1199, 1279
God's choosing of, 1238
God's presence in, 1059
God's protection of, 898, 1197
Holy Spirit outpouring at, 1182–1183
idolatry brought to, 790
Jesus' entrance to, 698
as The Lord Is Our Righteousness, 1050
Messiah's kingdom in, 796–797, 869
as the mountain of Daughter Zion, 860
past fulfillment in, 787
peace in, 797, 903, 1057
people of, 807
rebuilding of, 1248, 1320–1323, 1322
resettlement of, 1323
restoration of, 808–809, 993, 1254
69 weeks prophecy and, 1146
salvation of, 333
sanctification of people of, 809
siege of, 900, 1209
significance of, 716
spiritual activity in, 903
suffering in, 1149
Wisdom and, 761
as Yahweh our Righteousness, 1058
Jerusalem Council, 1188, 1189
Jervell, Jacob, 337
Jeshaiah, 466
Jesse, 13, 848
Jesus. *See* Messiah (Jesus)
Jewish mysticism, Messiah in, 234–235
Jews
branch of millennial government for, 1107
deaths of, 203, 1120
division of, 1153
ethnicity of, 255
hope of, 988
messianic writings of, 208
need for repentance from, 228
piercing of Messiah by, 1292, 1297
prayers of, 785, 1015
Satan and, 1028, 1198–1199
suffering for, 1149
weeping mothers of, 110, 112
Jezebel, 419–420
Jezreel, 1155
Joab, 375, 416–418
Job (book)
19:23-27, overview of, 440–445
mediation as theme in, 741, 742
Redeemer in book of, 128
Job (man)
attitude toward God by, 439–440
background of, 438–440
God as teaching, 750
Satan and, 437–438, 741, 1238
as servant of the Lord, 480, 622
suffering of, 438–439, 480, 600
vindication of, 444, 445
Joel, 1168–1173, 1177–1178, 1179–1184, 1222
Johanan, Rabbi, 26, 123, 1017
John, 892, 939, 950, 1288
John the Baptist
beheading of, 1182
clothing of, 1214
doubts of, 916
imprisonment of, 198
ministry of, 1181
as my messenger, 1331
as a prophet, 327
testifying of, 148
Johnson, Jr., S. Lewis, 114, 444, 789, 1311
Johnston, Gordon, 832–833, 834, 847, 1015, 1016
Johnston, Paul, 852
Jonah, 620
Jonathan, as son of Saul, 375
Jonathan, pagan priesthood and, 63, 125
Jones, D. R., 1251
Jones, Hywel R., 443
Joram, 419
Joseph (father of Jesus), 106, 143, 1180
Joseph (patriarch), 112, 260, 262–264, 466, 574, 852
Joseph ben Simeon Kara, Rabbi, 878
Josephus, 203, 1323
Joshua
acquittal of, 1238–1239
as before the Angel of the Lord, 1236–1238
as anointed one, 1248
as Branch, 1242
as compared to Moses, 332
coronation of, 1249
crown of, 1250, 1254
as descendant of Aaron, 1248
filthy clothing of, 1244, 1245
God's charge to, 1240
as high priest, 686, 854, 1057, 1144, 1220, 1229, 1230, 1236
as land spy, 1199
leadership of, 120–121, 314–315, 1254
life of, 167–168
Messiah and, 1247
military success of, 254, 481, 482
predicament of, 1237–1238
removal of guilt from, 1239
responsibilities of, 1240

rewards for, 1240–1241
saving of, 1238
as servant of the Lord, 622
as type of Messiah, 1255
Joshua ben Levi, Rabbi, 204, 205
Josiah, 285–287, 317–319, 838, 874, 1011, 1065
Jotham, 1153
Jothan, 1195
joy, symbols of, 992
Judah
affliction on, 887
attack on, 818
Babylonian captivity of, 1021
behavior of, 281
benefits for, 1266
blessing on, 264
covenant with, 539, 632
descendants of, 263, 282–283, 346
Egypt and, 898
exile of, 420, 962
fleeing Babylon by, 968
four covenantal pillars of, 1083–1084, 1084f1
gathering of, 30, 1213
God and, 886, 887, 1328
idolatry in, 790, 1038
invasion of, 860
judgment on, 824, 887
marriage of, 280
Messiah and, 256, 271–283, 728
new covenant with, 1043
people of, 807
prophecies for, 272–273
rebellion of, 790
restoration of, 887, 1049, 1050
role of teachers in, 887
as scepter, 272
scepter from, 771
social injustice in, 1195
status of during time of Micah, 1208–1209
Tamar and, 280, 351
wicked leaders of, 899–900
Judah, Rabbi, 275
Judaism, 325–326, 1302
Judas, 597, 663, 668, 1182
Judas Maccabeus, 999, 1104, 1130, 1323
Judge, Messiah as, 798, 904, 997–1008, 1007
judges, leadership of, 309–310
judgment
blessings and, 908
blood from, 1005
on the Day of the Lord, 867
on enemies of God, 1203
eschatological, 1168
of evil shepherds, 1310–1311
of Gentile nations, 1168
God and, 635–636, 865–868, 869, 1000, 1076, 1079, 1168, 1278
imagery of, 998
Israel and, 635–637, 845–846, 926–928, 1281–1282, 1301, 1311
Judah and, 824, 887
meaning of, 1074–1075
Messiah and, 1006, 1181
nations and, 859
oracles, 1083–1084, 1155
restoration following, 790
significance of, 1280–1281
for sin, 866
as theme in Ezekiel, 1074
as theme in Hosea, 1155
as theme in Isaiah, 912, 1000, 1003
through Alexander the Great, 1262–1263
two-stage, 868–869
for the wicked, 406
Juel, Donald H., 79, 87f6, 430–431
justice
coming day of, 1330
David's prayer for, 667
of God, 634
of the Levites, 1335
of the Messiah, 862–863, 934, 939, 948, 1040, 1050, 1056, 1297
as theme of Isaiah, 901
as theme of Servant Songs, 939

K

1 Kings and 2 Kings
God in, 415
Messianic message in, 416–418
Omride dynasty and, 418–420
role of prophets in, 415
Solomon and, 416–418
structure of, 411–413
theology of, 414–415
Kabbalah, Lurianic, 235
Kahle, Paul, 213, 214
Kaiser, Jr., Walter C.
quote of, 25, 41, 59, 80, 105–106, 443, 668–669, 728, 729–730, 733, 837, 838, 853, 870, 882, 983, 1025–1026, 1225, 1292, 1333
viewpoint of, 30, 85f4, 103, 366, 849, 1170, 1197–1198
Kara, Rabbi Yoseph, 964
Karo, Yoseph, 227
Kaufman, Stephen, 216
Kautzsch, E., 1172
Keil, C. F., quotes of, 46, 63, 278, 403, 404, 682, 794–795, 1170, 1253 1254
Ketuvim. *See* Writings

Kidner, Derek, 561, 564, 679, 683, 730
Kim, Yoon-Hee, 331–332
Kimchi, David (Radak). *See* Radak (David Kimchi)
King from the Line of David, Messiah as, 30
"king in Jerusalem," 759–770, 761
King of Israel, Messiah as, 705
King of Kings, Messiah as, 1228
King of the Jews, 1215
kingdom
  of David, 1187
  of God, 665, 840, 1122–1124
  of the Messiah, 850
  unity, 720
king(s). *See also specific kings*
  actions of, 1012
  anointing of, 30, 554
  appearance of, 574–575
  association with women by the, 311–312
  care for poor and needy by, 612
  celebrating, 582–583
  collapse of, 1077
  coming of, 1263–1264
  conduct of, 311–314
  defined, 147
  as described in Psalm 23, 554
  description of, 524, 903
  dominion of, 304
  eternal throne of, 585
  failure of, 1050
  God's role in reign of, 611
  historical significance of mosaic paradigm of, 314–315
  identification of, 575–579
  Israel and, 78, 309–310, 730, 1086f3
  of Jacob's prophecy, 298
  Messiah as, 137, 142–144, 207, 488, 576, 592, 599, 678, 682–683, 727, 798, 904, 916, 1204, 1253, 1273, 1296, 1321
  messianic significance of mosaic paradigm of, 315–322
  overturning office of, 1278–1279
  petition for, 611
  prayer for, 605, 606, 610
  as priest, 554
  as prophesied by Moses, 1060
  proverbial behavioral qualities for, 731
  qualifications of, 310–311
  reign of, 612–613
  request for, 310
  royal characteristics for, 731
  in Song of Solomon, 772–774, 775, 778
  throne of, 575
  treatment of Torah by, 312–314
  tree imagery of, 854
  types of, 137–142
  victory of, 565, 687, 1264
  worship of God and, 717
kingship, 262–263, 369, 915–916
Kiriath-jearim, 705
Kirkpatrick, A. F., 77
Kissane, Edward J., 683, 796
Klein, George, 1296
Kline, M. G., 1273, 1276
Konkel, August H., 437
Köstenberger, Andreas, 548
Kraus, Hans-Joachim, 503, 639, 681, 701
Krause, Deborah, 1276–1277
Kuhn, K. A., 1133
Kutscher, E. Y., 214
Kutsko, John Francis, 1105

L

Laato, Antti, 80–83, 968
Laban, 280
labor pains, imagery of, 1023, 1211, 1214
Ladd, George Eldon, 1013
Laetsch, T., 1170, 1263
lamb, Messiah as, 334
Lamb of God, Messiah as, 151
lame man, healing of, 148, 987–988
Lamech, 261
lament Psalm, 593, 594–596, 608, 618, 645, 664, 665, 667, 696
lamp, Messiah as, 390, 706–707
land
  Abraham and, 1022
  Adam and Abraham and, 163–164
  buying of in Jeremiah, 1053
  covenant of, 1101
  creation purposes for, 1060
  desert transformation of, 1322
  as gift in covenant, 394
  God's promise of, 392
  Israel and, 242, 1097
  prosperity to, 1172–1173
  purpose of, 241
  restoration of, 914, 1102, 1189
  as theme of Balaam narrative, 304
Lang, Peter, 1141–1142
Lange, John Peter, 402, 732–733
LaSor, W. S., 107
Last Adam, Messiah as, 166
the last days
  as in Balaam's fourth discourse, 297
  coming Messiah in, 1160
  in Daniel, 99
  events at, 203
  Jacob's prophecy and, 304
  Pentateuch role in, 301, 791

as phrase in the Prophets, 716
in poem, 124f2
restoration in, 786
translation of, 794–795
use of phrase, 791, 793
last redeemer, Messiah as, 162
Last Supper, 336–337, 1035, 1045
latter prophets, 126–128
The Law, 119, 120, 121f1, 149–153, 769. *See also* Torah
Law of Moses, 26
lawgiver, Messiah as, 904
lawsuit, imagery of, 1026
Leah, 280
Lebanon (Israel), 913
Leithart, Peter J., 413, 418
Lemuel, 748
leprosy, 184
Leupold, H. C., 679–680, 834, 999
Levant (Israel), 913, 1262
Levi, 140, 1332
Levi ben Gershon, Rabbi, 326
levirate marriage, 349–351
Levites, 216, 466, 561, 1051, 1335
Levitical covenant, 1050–1051, 1055
Levitical priesthood
establishment of, 137, 139
leadership in Israelite community by, 309–310
music performed by, 531
promise to, 1335
purification ritual of, 1302
renewal of, 1102
role of, 171, 1060
Lewis, C. S., 440
libations, sacrifices for, 180
Libya, 254
light
Messiah as, 403–404, 407, 824, 846, 950, 1173
as symbol of salvation, 935, 937
Light to the Nations
Messiah as, 38, 320
Light to the Nations, Messiah as, 933, 936–937, 944
lighthouse, analogy of, 58
Lindsey, F. Duane, 334
Lion of Judah, Messiah as, 125, 271–283, 1204
Lister, John Ryan, 1107
living stone(s), 699, 876, 882
locust, imagery of, 1177–1178
London Baptist Confession, 135
Longacre, Robert E., 910
Longenecker, Richard, 79, 87f6, 104, 110, 111
Longman III, Tremper, 327, 612, 673, 769
Lord, 679, 751, 859, 975, 1333
The Lord Is Our Righteousness, 127, 1050
Lord of Armies, God as, 1240
Lord of Hosts, God as, 839, 1330
Lord (Yahweh) our Righteousness, Messiah as, 37, 898
"the Lord their God," Messiah as, 1160
Lot, 139, 968
love of God, 532, 621
lovingkindness, 862
Lowe, W. H., 1294–1295
Luke, 1069
Lunde, Jonathan, 93
Luria of Safed, Isaac, 234
Luther, Martin, 277, 495, 546–547, 998

M

MacArthur, John, 1099
Maccabees, wars of, 1266–1267
Machen, J. Gresham, 148
Macho, Alejandro Diez, 213
magi, 104, 1180, 1215
Maginot Line, 428
magnificent, God as, 507–508
Magog, 209, 232, 256
Maher-shalal-hash-baz, 839
Mahlon, 344
Maimonides, 227, 230–233, 967
Majestic King, Messiah as, 897–905
majesty, as term of praise, 507–508
make atonement, 179
"Maker of heaven and earth," as phrase in Psalms, 714–715, 716, 722
Malachi, 1315, 1328–1330
Malbim, Rabbi, 1253
Malone, Andrew, 1332–1333
man, 504–505, 545
man of valor, 562
Manasseh, 63
Manatti, M., 478
Manesseh, 263
Manning, Jr., Gary T., 1104–1105
Manoah, 36, 890
marriage, 352, 1039, 1160, 1329–1330, 1332
Marshall, I. H., 1333
Martyr, Justin, 153, 275, 607, 685, 741
Mary (mother of Jesus), 142–143, 826, 832, 1069, 1215
Mary's Magnificat, 369
Mashiach, 30, 231
Mason, Rex, 1286, 1302
Masoretes, 62
Masoretic Text
messianic prophecy in, 63–69

Masoretic Text, structure and consideration of, 57, 61–69, 81
Massa, 748
material prophecy, 44
Mathews, Kenneth A., 279
Mattathias, 1255
Matthean Beatitudes, 991
Matthew (book of), 937, 1214–1215
Mattithiah, 466
McCaul, Alexander, 681, 688, 1292, 1297
McComiskey, T. E., 1199–1200
McConville, Gordon, 41, 59
McConville, J. G., 97–98
McNamara, Martin, 213, 215, 219, 220
mediate/mediation/mediator, 129, 136, 141, 481, 742, 933, 946
medicine, imagery of, 1026–1027
Medieval Jewish Literature, Messiah in, 227–235
Medo-Persia, 1024, 1119, 1128
Meek, T. J., 440
Melchizedek, 137, 139–140, 199, 682–683, 1060, 1077, 1248
menorah, 171
mercy, 621
mercy seat, Messiah as, 188
Merrill, Eugene, 138, 142, 673–674, 675, 682, 840, 1332
Meschch, 256
Messenger of the covenant, Messiah as, 1331, 1334
Messenger of the Lord, Messiah as, 1327–1337
Messiah (Handel), 569
Messiah (Jesus). *See also specific titles*
  Adam and, 165–166
  anger against, 658
  animals and, 536
  anointing of, 853
  as answer to laments, 665
  appearance of, 1173
  appointment of, 1090–1093
  ascension of, 1191
  atonement through, 904, 975
  authority of, 272, 1229
  as awaiting victory, 680
  in Balaam's fourth discourse, 301–305
  baptism of, 167, 321, 937
  behavioral qualities of, 733
  beloved of, 777
  betrayal of, 663–670, 1281–1282
  birth of (*See* virgin birth)
  body of, 879
  as breaking old covenant, 1035
  as breaking open the way, 1201–1202
  call of, 989–990
  as calling nations to seek Him, 851
  challenge from, 958
  characteristics of from the Targum, 274
  characteristics of rule of, 838
  claim of, 959
  coming of (*See* Second Coming)
  commission of, 990–991
  confrontation by, 1281
  as a covenant for the people, 320
  crown of, 707, 1080
  crucifixion of, 249, 601–602, 999, 1120, 1146, 1182, 1245
  curse upon enemies of, 669
  David and, 1108, 1215
  David as vice-regent under, 1106
  death of, 536–537, 553, 555, 601, 617–629, 646, 928–929, 958, 968, 970, 1292, 1311
  death plot of, 496, 499
  deity of, 148–157, 505–510, 831–840
  in the details, 57
  disciples of, 959
  discipleship of, 955
  distress preceding coming of, 1022–1023
  dominion of, 304, 1266
  donkey of, 1265
  dual ministry of, 1181
  in the early midrashim, 206–208
  in early Rabbinic Literature, 234–235
  ears of as opened, 956
  enemies of, 494, 522, 535–536, 668, 680
  evangelical views of, 42–47
  exaltation of, 925, 948–949, 972
  faithfulness of, 850, 862
  fasting of, 335–336
  favor as staff of, 1278–1279, 1281
  fidelity to Torah by, 195
  as final resolution, 422
  first coming of (*See* virgin birth)
  forgiveness from, 904
  foundations of kingship of, 309–322
  four titles of, 836
  garments of, 1003, 1004
  at God's right hand, 679–680
  government on shoulders of, 1079
  grace of, 1181
  as greatest descendant of David, 1105
  hatred for, 601
  as healer, 148, 904, 908, 916, 917, 937–938, 1173
  as in Heaven, 496
  holiness of, 863
  as the holy One, 1069
  as a horn, 390
  humility of, 1265, 1276–1277, 1297
  instructed tongue of, 954

Israel and, 204, 287, 727, 846, 880, 890, 1024–1026, 1029–1031, 1280, 1297
in Jewish mysticism, 208–209
as judging with righteousness, 850
judgment from, 1006, 1181
justice of, 934, 939, 948, 1002, 1056, 1297
lament of, 591–602
as a lamp, 390
Last Supper and, 336–337, 1035, 1045
learning of, 955–956
as like morning light of the sun, 403–404
line of, 396–397
Lord as Shepherd of, 535–553
in the Maimonides, 230–233
meaning of, 29–33
in Medieval Jewish Literature, 227–235
meeting of Cleopas by, 25
metaphorical titles of, 1267–1268
millennial kingdom of, 1231
ministry of, 799, 805, 985, 986, 1030, 1182
miracles of, 336
in the Mishnah, 202–203
mission of, 991
Moses and, 1214
nations against, 797
as a Nazarene, 125–126
new covenant and, 1045–1046
as new Joshua, 947
as new Moses, 947
offices of, 136–137, 682–683
opposition to, 948
oracle of David about, 401
as in the order of Melchizedek, 1077, 1248
as out of Egypt, 96, 293
peace from, 1213, 1266
Pharisees and, 675
as pierced, 1273, 1285–1298
power of, 1004
prayer in Gethsemane by, 956
presence of, 1224
priestly ministry of, 972
prisoners and, 936, 1297
promise of, 631–639
in the Prophets, 125–128
protection from, 899
provision from, 904
in the Psalms, 457–471, 583–585, 613–614
purpose of life of, 840
rage against, 787
as reading from Isaiah, 217–218
rebellion against, 518
as rebuilder of the Temple, 202
reign of, 720, 845–855, 862, 1012
rejection of, 693–700, 873, 1281
relationship with God by, 498, 534
removal of guilt by, 1243
renewals by, 208
restoration by, 763, 786, 808, 983–993
resurrection of, 249, 488, 513–525, 617–629, 646, 652, 803–804, 958, 1182, 1191, 1245
retreat from public ministry by, 939
return of (*See* Second Coming)
reunification of, 1211–1212
riddle of, 747–755
righteousness of, 849, 850, 898–899, 1056
role of, 1087–1090
as royal, 64–65, 202, 505–510, 1247–1248
as royal-priest, 1256–1257
rule of, 403, 680–681, 865–870, 1030, 1268
sacrifice of, 564
salvation from, 258, 880, 946, 949, 950, 1003–1004, 1056, 1225, 1311
Satan and, 955, 957
as seated on heavenly throne, 487
second coming of (*See* Second Coming)
security from, 899, 1056
shame of, 609
as source of wisdom, 765
Spirit of the Lord on, 193, 983–993, 1057
Spirit of wisdom of, 849
staffs of, 1278–1279, 1281
suffering of, 222, 228–230, 235, 333–334, 529–540, 550, 600, 601, 617–629, 925, 929, 957, 1273, 1277
surrender of, 569–570
as sustained by the Father's Word, 955
in the synagogue, 908, 938–939, 949
in the Talmuds, 204–206
in the Targums, 201–202, 273–274
teaching of, 698–699, 1173–1174
in the temple, 955
term origin, 13
theological definition of, 32–33
throne of, promise of, 859–863
as tied to "the Lord their God," 1160
time of, 220–221
titles for, 13, 33–38, 904
titles in Zechariah for, 1273
and the Torah, 321–322
in the Torah, 123–124, 124f2
transfiguration of, 939
triumphal entry and, 698, 1265
turban of, 1080
understanding within Hebrew Bible, 49–57
union as staff of, 1278–1279, 1281
victory of, 491–502, 518, 668, 684, 687, 865–870, 999, 1006
views about Hebrew Bible's revelation of, 26–27
vindication from, 1003–1004

virgin birth of (*See* virgin birth)
war against, 812
"word of his mouth" as weapon, 760
wrath of, 1004
in the Writings, 128–131
in Zion, 709
Messianic Age, 788, 892–893, 907–918, 1013, 1092, 1093, 1184
Messianic Apocalypse (Qumran), 988
messianic covenant, 1111
messianic government, 1112
messianic hope, in the Tanak, 121f1
Messianic Sage, Messiah as, 727
Mettinger, Tryggve N. D., 946
Metzudat, David Altschuler, 963, 1253
Metzudos, 1099
Meyer, F. B., 972
Meyers, C. L., 1296
Meyers, E. M., 1296
Micah (book)
2:2-5a, overview of, 1213–1214
4:1-3, overview of, 791–800
4:1-5, overview of, 785–791, 1202–1204
"breaks open the way" in, 1202–1204
connection to Isaiah by, 1214
daughter of Zion reference in, 1211
"the gate" in, 1202–1204
giving birth imagery in, 1211
human backdrop of book of, 1208
judgment and salvation cycles in, 1209–1210, 1213
"people/nation" as used by, 786
prophecy exposition of, 1196–1204
prophecy time period of, 1195
shepherd imagery in, 1200–1201
themes in, 1213
Micah (man), 785–786, 1195, 1196, 1214–1217
Micaiah, 1307
Michael (angel), 998, 1131, 1244
Michelangelo, 43
midrash fulfillment of prophecy, 87, 87f6
Midrash Tanchuma, 963
Midrashim, Messiah in the early, 206–208
Mighty God, Messiah as, 36, 68, 154, 585, 822, 824, 825, 836–837, 839, 840, 847, 1162
mighty helper, Messiah as, 635
Mighty One of Israel, Messiah as, 839
Mighty One of Jacob, God as, 877
military defeat, 580–581
millennial kingdom, 1231
Millennial Temple, 812, 813
Millgram, Jacob, 419
Miriam, 329, 362, 820
Mishnah, 202–203
Mitchell, David, 128, 677, 686–687, 1292, 1295–1296
Mitchell, H. G., 1287
Moab, 851, 859–861, 863, 865, 1002
Moabites, 343, 859–861
mockers, as theme in Psalms, 568–569
Mohammed, 326
monarchy, combined with priesthood, 1255–1256
Montgomery, J. A., 1130
Moore, G. F., 103
Moresheth-Gath, 1195
morning, as theme in Psalms, 654–655, 657
Mosaic covenant, 669, 1024, 1051, 1059, 1109–1110
Mosaic Pentateuch, 97
Moses
allegiance to, 26
as author of Psalms, 465
blessing of, 287–288
call of, 328
charter for kingship by, 1086
as compared to Elijah, 327–328
as compared to Jeremiah, 328
as compared to Joshua, 332
descendants of, 63, 125
fasting of, 335–336
fear of the Lord and, 733
fleeing Egypt by, 968
instructions from, 309–310
and Jesus, 1214
last days proclamation by, 248
life of, 167–170
longing of, 1179
as the Lord's servant, 947
as the man of God, 650
mediation of, 468
Miriam as sister of, 820
at Mount Sinai, 793, 1036–1037
negative commands of, 311–312
as One Shepherd, 763
opposition to, 333–334
poetic discourses by, 95
positive commands of, 312–314
prayer of, 649
prediction of, 1161
as priest, 1060
as priest-king, 50, 770
as prophet, 136, 309, 332, 620, 650, 922, 1060
as prophet, priest, and king, 140–141
questions asked by, 752
as redeemer of Israel, 287
return to Egypt by, 162
rod of God and, 1317

role in sacrifices by, 179
as servant of the Lord, 622, 1227
as shepherd, 1310
stipulations given by, 730
typological interpretations of, 167–170
use of the last days phrase by, 792
warning from, 900, 1161
writings of, 279
Most High, 659
motivation, 1329
Motyer, Alec
quote of, 836–837, 839, 846, 848, 849,850, 851, 852, 860, 888, 901, 957, 959, 984–985, 989, 991, 992, 1227
viewpoint of, 31, 1333
Mounce, Robert, 855
Mount of Olives, 1202, 1318, 1319t
Mount Sinai, 172, 793, 1036–1037, 1060, 1110
Mount Zion, 793, 796, 1067, 1302
the mountain of Daughter Zion, Jerusalem as, 860
mourning, 992
Mowinckel, Sigmund, 78, 459, 681, 1015
muddy mire, as metaphor in Psalms, 594
Murphy, Roland, 130, 770, 777
music, 466, 531, 538, 560
My Beloved Son, Messiah as, 1093
My Chosen One, Messiah as, 939
my glory, God as, 498
My King, Messiah as, 549
my messenger, 1230, 1330–1331
My People, Israel as, 1156–1157
My Servant, as title, 839, 877, 933, 1100, 1227, 1229, 1241
My Son, Messiah as, 485–486, 497, 754
mystery, as theme in Daniel, 1116

N

Naaman, 987, 1190
Nabopolassar of Babylon, 846
Nachmanides (Ramban), 233, 785, 967, 1099
Nadav, 971
nail, Messiah as, 1267–1268
nakedness, 246–247, 253, 775
"the name of the Lord," as phrase in Psalms, 714
Naomi, 344, 353
Naphtali, 831, 834
Nathan
announcement by, 414, 706, 1088
oracle of, 126, 192, 729, 772
as prophet, 386, 416–418, 466, 1086
Nathanael, 113–114
national cleansing, 1302, 1310
national unity, 1101
nations
David as witness to, 977
deliverance for, 936
destruction of, 1004–1005, 1006, 1026
as flock of sheep, 1103
healing of, 966
idolatry of, 932, 936
as instruments of judgment, 789
Messiah and, 797, 1292
prayer of, 1000
shaking of, 1222, 1223, 1225, 1226, 1230
in Zion, 624
natural restoration, 1012, 1171
nature/natural world
glory of the Lord in, 912–914
God in, 633
praise to God within, 598
transformation of, 850, 1002, 1242
Nazarene, Messiah as, 125–126
Nazareth, 938–939, 949, 985, 1214, 1215
Nazirite vow, 184
Nebuchadnezzar
coming of, 1073, 1075
death of, 427
destruction of Jerusalem by, 900, 1199, 1315
dream of, 156
fallen dynasty of, 854
Judea's exiling by, 98
as king, 965, 1063, 1115, 1116, 1196
victory of, 846, 998
Nehemiah, 749, 993, 1322–1323
Nehemiah, Rabbi, 275
Nelson, Richard D., 412, 413
Neofiti, 201
Nethaniah, 466
Neusner, Jacob, 207, 230
Nevi'im. *See* Prophets
New Adam, 162–166, 345
new covenant
as covenant of peace, 1110
David and Levites and, 1055
establishment of, 1013
finalizing of, 800
God's promises to, 1051
hope of, 1040
in Jeremiah, 1038–1045
messianic fulfillment of, 1035, 1045–1046, 1061
millennial blessings under, 1109–1110
overview of, 1035–1046
in the Pentateuch, 1036–1037
priests and, 1059–1060
summary of, 1043–1044, 1046
New Exodus, 470
New Jerusalem, 1111, 1231
New Moon, sacrifices for, 185

New Testament
application of sacrifice to Jesus, 187–188
Davidic covenant in, 432
goal of, 47–48
imagery in Isaiah, 881–882, 890–892
Psalm 118 in context of, 697–699
understanding through prophets, 97–98
understanding through the Writings, 98–100
unity as theme in, 1212
Nile River, 851
"No Compassion," as child of Gomer, 1155
Noah
descendants of, 260, 261, 346, 728, 1060
fall of, 252, 253
God and, 151, 1051
promise through, 251–258
prophecy of, 252–253
story of, 163, 245–247
Noahic covenant, 866, 1050–1051, 1060, 1110
Noahide Laws, 251
nobility, 900
Nolland, John, 1281
North Africa, 254
Norwood, W. Berry, 153
"Not My People," as child of Gomer, 1155

O

oak tree, symbolism of, 992
oaks of righteousness, 992
Obed, 355
Obed-Edom, 386
obedience, 562–563
Oden, Thomas, 142
Oesterley, W. O. E., 77
offerings, 180, 181–185
offices, functions of, 136–137
Og of Bashan, 1317
oil, anointing, 554
old covenant, 1036–1037, 1038–1045, 1046, 1090
Old Testament
Adam typology in, 162–166
Anointed term within, 13
antecedents, 191–194
canonical seams within, 12
geographical element of, 104
Messianic vision within, 51–52
Psalm 118 in context of, 696–697
structure of, 119
Tanakh within, 48–49
typological interpretations of Moses and Israel, 167–170
use of Old Testament in, 94–95
use of prophets, 97–98
use of Writings in, 98–100
Omride dynasty, 413, 418–420
On Resurrection (Qumran), 988
"on that day," phrase use of, 1296, 1318
Onan, 280, 351
one flesh, theme of, 349–351, 352, 353–354
"One like a son of man," 1127, 1130–1131, 1132, 1133–1134, 1135
One Shepherd
David as, 764, 809
Messiah as, 37–38, 129–130, 754, 757, 762–765
Moses as, 763
Solomon as, 763
opponent, as theme in Psalms, 666
oracles
of Balaam, 31, 107–109, 282, 749, 771
against Egypt, 1063
of Ezekiel, 1012–1013, 1016, 1084, 1085, 1100
against foreign nations, 1083
of Haggai, 1219, 1221, 1229
of Hosea, 1156
of Isaiah, 847, 859, 860, 873, 897, 1012–1013
of Jeremiah, 1012–1013, 1052, 1054, 1305
judgment, 1083–1084, 1155
of Malachi, 1328–1329
against Moab, 859–861
restoration, 1084
salvation, 932
sword, 1305
woe, 1085
of Zechariah, 1261–1262
ordination, animals used for, 180
Origen, 276, 440, 741, 967–968
Orpah, 344
Ortlund, Ray, 734, 834–835
Osborne, Grant, 546, 852, 853
Oswalt, John
quote of, 787, 808, 833, 834, 835, 836, 837–838, 845, 849, 851, 852, 853, 854, 870, 898, 922, 933, 946, 989–990, 992
viewpoint of, 983, 999
outer court, Tabernacle, 172

P

pagan mythology, 633
Pao, David, 333
Paris Review, 400–401, 676
Parke-Taylor, G. H., 1015
Pasinya, Laurent Monsengwo, 1075
Passover, 180, 185, 665, 1035, 1045
Passover lamb, 969–970
pastures, as theme in Psalms, 551
Patai, R., 229
Pathros, 851
Patron of Wisdom, Solomon as, 727

Patterson, Richard, 548
Paul, 218, 257, 513–514, 881, 949, 1190
Payne, J. Barton, 79–80, 1333
peace
animals and, 1092
covenant of, 1087, 1090, 1102, 1110
Holy Spirit bringing, 901
of Israel, 835
Jerusalem as place of, 797
Messiah and, 223, 583, 850, 1213
promise of, 619
prophecy of, 837–838
in the Temple, 1223–1224
as theme in Psalms, 714
universal, 1092
peace offering, 178
Pekah, King, 817
Peninnah, 364
Pentateuch, structure and theological purpose of, 123, 791
Pentecost, 787, 788, 958, 1171, 1182–1183
Pentecost, Dwight, 1123–1124
people of God. *See also* Israel; Israelites
as bride, 578
confession by, 925
as covenant people, 935
delight by God in, 745
deliverance of, 977
dwelling place of, 646
as forgetting the Lord, 900–901
gathering of, 1196–1199, 1200–1201
as living stones, 699
Lord as sanctuary of, 879
restoration of, 535
salvation for, 1044
security for, 1044
as sheep, 1310
signing of covenant with Antichrist, 1198
as warriors, 680–681
Perez, 263, 280, 346, 355–356
Perfect Ruler, Messiah as, 32
Perowne, J., 684
perpetual covenant, 977, 980
Perrin, Nicholas, 129
Persia, 846, 1119–1120, 1123, 1139, 1262
Persians, 1328
pesher, 79
pesher fulfillment of prophecy, 87, 87f6
Peter
argument for replacing Judas, 663
denial of, 1182
resistance of, 957
sermon of, 13, 26, 513–514, 524–525, 699, 882, 958, 1182–1183
at transfiguration of Jesus, 939
viewpoint of, 94–95, 222–223
vision of, 257
witness of, 1190
Peterson, David, 139
Petra, 1002, 1200–1203
Petterson, Anthony, 1297
Pharaoh, 95, 287, 333, 335, 968, 1180, 1215, 1226
Pharaoh Neco, 874
Pharisees, 675
Philip, 222
Philistia, 624, 851, 1168
Philistines, 379, 865, 1262
Phinehas, 366, 967, 1061
pierce(d), 1273, 1294–1296
Pilate, 840, 1180
pilgrim psalms, 390, 711
the Pit, as theme in Psalms, 626
plagues, 1177–1178
Plains of Moab, 1090
political theocracy, 1101
Polycarp, 961
Pool of Siloam, 812, 917
Pope, Marvin H., 773
Postell, Seth, 968
potter, theme of, 1273, 1280
power of God, 954, 1004
praise
call to, 932–933
command to, 538
as response to deliverance, 597–598
as response to lament, 667
terms of, 507–508
as theme in Psalms, 533–534, 561–562, 598, 649
in Zion, 914
prayer
of David, 620, 621, 625–626
of the disciples, 663
for future king, 605, 606, 610
of Jewish people, 785
of the nations, 1000
for Solomon, 628
as theme in Psalms, 599
prayer psalms, 668
Preacher, Messiah as, 129
pregnant, meaning of, 821–822
Premillennialism, 1123–1124
presence of God, 577–578, 580, 835, 1076, 1110–1111
Price, Randall, 989
priesthood, 180, 1051, 1057, 1255–1256
priest-king, 482, 681–683, 705, 770
priest(s)
Aaron as, 180
Abrahamic covenant and, 1059–1060

actions of, 1195
anointing of, 30, 191
blessing of, 714, 715, 724
collapse of, 1077
covenant violation by, 1332
David as, 141–142, 531
Davidic covenant and, 1059–1060
David's sons as, 682
failure of, 1328
Joshua as, 686, 1057
king as, 554
kingdom of, 1060
Melchizedek as, 139–140
Messiah as, 136–137, 142–144, 678, 682–683, 727, 1030, 1252, 1253, 1255–1257, 1273
Moses as, 140
new covenant and, 1059–1060
overturning office of, 1278–1279
Pentateuch's depiction of, 1060
purpose of, 945
role in burnt offering by, 181
role in Tabernacle, 171
types of, 137–142
Zechariah as, 1261
prince
actions of, 1195
David as, 1089, 1107
guilt of, 1078
Messiah as, 197, 199, 200, 1109, 1144, 1305
purpose of, 193
as shepherd, 1088–1089
as theme in Daniel, 1146
as theme in Ezekiel, 1108
Prince of Peace, Messiah as, 36, 154, 786, 824, 837–838, 839, 848–850, 1110, 1162, 1225, 1324
prisoners, 936, 988, 991, 1297
Pritchard, Ray, 151
progressive (epigenetic) fulfillment of prophecy, 85f4, 86
prominence, oak tree as symbol of, 992
promised covenant, 977–980
the promised king, Messiah as, 835
Promised Messiah, 93–94
Promised One, Messiah as, 853
prophecy
applicational fulfillment of, 109–112
comparison of Jacob and Balaam, 96–100
defined, 1179
development view of, 76
direct fulfillment of, 88–89, 88f7, 104–106
dual fulfillment of, 74, 84, 84f2
gift of, 1183
historical fulfillment of, 83f1, 84
as history for the future, 47
immediate fulfillment of, 84, 84f2
judgment against the nations, 859
messianic, 1247
midrash fulfillment of, 87, 87f6
music as partner to, 466, 531
pesher fulfillment of, 87, 87f6
as prediction and identification, 49–51
progressive (epigenetic) fulfillment of, 85f4, 86
between promise and prediction, 76–77
relecture fulfillment of, 86, 86f5
royal, 1247
sealing up of, 1143
Sensus Plenior, 84, 84f2
suffering, 1247
summary fulfillment of, 112–114
telescoped, 1264–1265
of the throne, 862
typical fulfillment of, 85, 85f3, 106–109
ultimate fulfillment of, 84, 84f2
virgin birth in, 815–827
Prophet like Moses
Messiah as, 35, 162, 166–170, 329–332, 333–334
in the New Testament, 335–337
nonmessianic view, 327–329
prophecy in Islam, 325–326
prophecy in Judaism, 325–326
prophecy in sectarian interpretations, 334–335
prophetic history, interpretation of, 46
prophet(s)
anointing of, 30
of Baal, 1302
collapse of, 1077
Daniel as, 1115
David as, 402–403
Elijah as, 415
Elisha as, 415, 466
encouragement and warning by, 959–960
end-time use of, 716
false, 1007
female, 1180
former, 125–126
historic terms used by, 788
latter, 126–128
leadership in Israelite community by, 309–310
Melchizedek as, 139
Messiah as, 136, 142–144, 325–338, 727
Moses as, 140, 650
office of, 331
original meaning of, 329–330
overturning office of, 1278–1279
and the Pentateuch, 57

prophetic valley of, 1121–1122
role of, 136, 415
types of, 137–142
use of Old Testament by, 97–98
visions of, 43, 52
Zechariah as, 1261
The Prophets (books)
canonization of, 120, 121f1
deity of the Messiah in, 153–156
as division of the Hebrew Bible, 481
Messiah in, 125–128
Song of Solomon in, 769
structure of, 119, 120
visions within, 52
prostitutes, 987–988, 1039
protection, 714, 812, 899
Protector of Israel, God as, 703, 713, 717
protevangelium, 149–151, 260–261
Proverbs
30, overview of, 747–750
beginning as theme in, 740–741, 743
child as theme in, 743
Davidic covenant in, 728
"the fear of the Lord" as theme in, 733–734
historical setting of, 728
history of interpretation of, 740–741
identity of the Son in, 753
Messianism in, 727–734
the "name" questions in, 751–754
place in Canon, 741–742
purpose of, 747–748
"son" use in, 732–733
structure of, 742, 747–748
virtuous woman in, 741–742
the "who" questions in, 750–751
Wisdom as character in, 743–744
Woman Wisdom in, 757, 765–766
provision, 835, 904
Psalms
1-2, overview of, 462, 478
3, overview of, 491–502
15-24, chiastic structure of, 519–521
16, overview of, 515–525
23, overview of, 543–555
40, overview of, 560–570
45, overview of, 573–575, 579–585
69, overview of, 592–602
72, overview of, 606–614
86, as Davidic prayer, 618
88, structure of, 627
89, Davidic covenant in, 631–632
90, overview of, 650–655, 657–658
107-113, thematic unifer of, 678
109, overview of, 667–669
110, overview of, 674–677, 678, 679–687
118, overview of, 693–694, 696–700
120-125, overview of, 712–718, 714f1
130-134, overview of, 718–721, 718f3
132, overview of, 702–709
abandonment as theme in, 626
acrostic praise psalm, 665
anointing as theme in, 546
Asaph, 592, 608
Asaphite psalms, 649
assembly/congregation as theme in, 539, 566
blessing compared to wicked, 483
Book 1, 515–518, 559
Book 2, 579–580, 607–609
Book 5, 664–665, 722f4
"both now and forever" as phrase in, 714–715, 716, 718, 722
chaff analogy used in, 483
city of God as theme in, 624
"coming in the name of the Lord" as theme in, 696–697, 698
common phrases in, 712, 715f2
composition time of, 469
compositional unity of books of, 451–455
concatenation of, 463
corruption as theme in, 522, 523
creation as theme in, 503
Davidic covenant in, 451, 607, 627–628
Davidic Psalter, 592
death as theme in, 499, 545, 552, 626, 627
decay as theme in, 522, 523
deep as theme in, 594
deliverance as theme in, 567–568, 678, 693
doxologies in, 461–462, 559, 618, 703
dust as theme in, 523, 655
ears as theme in, 563, 569
encouragement for righteous in, 559
entrance liturgy, 519
Eschatological/Messianic, 665
eternal hope as theme in, 718, 720
eternal life theme in, 538, 550, 655, 720
eternal thrones as theme in, 720
eternity as theme in, 646
evil as theme in, 551–552
Exodus, 665
faithfulness as theme in, 621, 652
favor as theme in, 714, 717
festival hymns, 665
footstool as theme in, 680
"for His steadfast love endures forever" as phrase in, 721
fulfillment of, 26
happiness meaning in, 484
help as theme in, 714, 715, 722, 723–724
hope as theme in, 720
horn as theme in, 706

hymnbook approach to, 460
hymns of praise, 665
individual lament, 618
instruments in, 561
introduction to, 491
key words in, 464–465
king description in, 524
kingdom unity as theme in, 720
lament, 593, 594–596, 608, 645, 664, 665, 696
lamp as theme in, 706–707
literary inclusios in, 463–464
"Maker of heaven and earth" as phrase in, 714–715, 716, 722
mercy as theme in, 621
Messianism in, 457–471, 504
military defeat as theme of, 580–581
mockers as theme in, 568–569
modern assumptions about, 458–459
morning as theme in, 654–655, 657
Most High in, 659
muddy mire as theme in, 594
music as theme in, 560
music reference in, 538
"my God" as theme in, 534
"my help" as phrase in, 713
"the name of the Lord" as phrase in, 714
obedience as theme in, 562–563
Passover hymns, 665
pastures as theme in, 551
peace as theme in, 714
pilgrimage psalms in, 711
the Pit as theme in, 626
postexilic redaction of, 677–678
praise as theme in, 533–534, 538, 561–562, 598, 649
prayer as theme in, 599
prayer for help, 520
as prayer of David, 620, 621, 625–626
prayer psalms, 668
priest king in, 482
prophetic nature of, 465–467
protection as theme in, 714
Psalms of Ascent, 390, 711–725
puns in, 486
Qorahite psalms, 649
redemption as theme in, 718
rest as theme in, 553–554, 707
resurrection as theme in, 491–492, 499–500, 521–525, 552
righteous meaning in, 484
royal, 515, 520, 606, 665, 702, 703, 771
sacrifice as theme in, 562–563
salvation as theme in, 499, 532–533, 549–550, 567, 594, 596, 598, 621, 653, 694, 695, 708
sanctuary language of, 482
security as theme in, 552
sequence and order of, 530
servant of the Lord as theme in, 532
Sheol in, 620, 626
shepherd as theme in, 551–552
song of trust, 520
Song of Zion, 703
songs in, 561
Songs of Ascent, 702–703, 711
Sons of Korah and, 156, 465, 592, 608
to sprout up as theme in, 706
story of, 467–471
structure of, 459–465, 694–696, 702–704
Succoth/Zion hymns, 665
superscriptions in, 462, 530–531
time as theme in, 653–654, 656, 657
times of trouble as theme in, 532
Torah, 665, 722
tree metaphor in, 483
trust as theme in, 533, 562, 722
verbal links of, 493–494
vocabulary parallels in, 454
waiting as theme in, 560–561
warning in, 487
waters as theme in, 594
weeping as theme in, 598
wicked in, 494
works of your hands phrase used in, 508–509
worm as theme in, 533–534
worship as theme in, 560, 694
Zion in, 618, 623–625, 629
Psalms of Ascent, 390, 711–725
Psalms of Solomon, shepherd imagery in, 1306
Pseudo-Jonathan, 201
Ptolemy, 1323
Puech, Emile, 988, 1133
punishment, 1078–1079
purification, 1230, 1302, 1335
purification offering, 182–184
pursuit of righteousness, 319
Pusey, E. B., 1170, 1171
Put, 254

Q

Qimhi, David, 453
Qoheleth, 748, 762, 765
Qorahite psalms, 649
Queen of Sheba, 1215
Quran, 326

R

Ra, as Egyptian god, 1180
rabbinic midrashic method, 103
Rabin, C., 216–217

Rachel, 110, 112, 264
Radak (David Kimchi), viewpoints of, 233, 478, 785, 803, 878, 963, 967, 1099, 1251, 1252, 1286
rain, 1169, 1170, 1171, 1173
Ramah, 110, 1214
Ramban (Nachmanides), 233, 785, 967, 1099
Rashi (Rabbi Shlomo Itzhaki)
  method of, 495, 546–547, 785, 803
  quote of, 876
  viewpoint of, 170, 233, 240, 276–277, 481, 740, 963, 964, 967, 1099, 1251, 1252, 1286
Rebekah, 260, 264, 820
rebellion, 141, 485–487, 620, 964, 1027, 1161
rebuilding, 993
rebuke, 1238
reconciliation, 282
re-creation, event of, 1320
Red Sea, 851
Redeemer, Messiah as, 128, 131, 150, 154–155, 177, 716, 839
Redeemer from Sin, Messiah as, 31–32
redemption, 718, 788, 998, 1005–1006
refiner's fire, Messiah's coming as, 1230
Refreshed King, Messiah as, 684
refuge, Word of God as, 754
Rei, 416–418
rejected stone, Messiah as, 693–700
rejection, 580, 609
rejoicing, 1264
relationship, as theme in Ezekiel, 1076
relecture fulfillment of prophecy, 86, 86f5
Rembrandt, 43
remnant
  as followers of Jesus, 1045–1046
  identity of, 1199–1200
  purification of, 1031
  relief for, 861
  restoration of, 851, 945, 1204
  salvation of, 1311
  spiritual transformation of, 1031
repentance, 1276, 1293, 1301, 1305
Representative, Messiah as, 544
rest, as theme in Psalms, 553–554, 707
restitution offering, 32, 185
restoration
  of Davidic dynasty, 1187–1192, 1191, 1305
  following judgment, 790
  following tribulation, 1188
  formula of, 1053, 1101
  future, 1021, 1049, 1305
  goal of, 1089–1090
  historical, 1099
  hope of, 1038, 1042
  Isaiah as oracle of, 847
  of Israel, 800, 1026–1027, 1049, 1050, 1196, 1198, 1301
  of Jerusalem, 1254
  of Judah, 887, 1049, 1050
  of land, 914, 1189
  Messiah and, 763, 786, 808, 983–993
  Millennial Temple and, 812
  national, 1235
  natural, 1012
  oracles, 1084
  physical, 1171
  promise of, 975, 1000
  prophetic terms for, 795
  providing a means for, 180
  of the remnant, 851
  of security, 1090
  spiritual, 1012, 1235, 1301
  stages of, 1085
  of the temple, 790, 1254
  as theme in Ezekiel, 1101
  as theme in Hosea, 1155
  of Zion, 790, 1002
Restoration Temple, 1111
"restore their fortunes," as phrase in Jeremiah, 1053
resurrection
  of the dead, 205, 988
  hope of, 521–525
  of the Messiah, 249, 488, 513–525, 617–629, 646, 652, 803–804, 958, 1182, 1191, 1245
  as theme in Psalms, 491–492, 499–500, 552
Reuben, 263
Reymond, Robert L., 156, 157
Rezin, King, 817
Ridderbos, J., 959
riddles, as used in Scripture, 747–755, 750, 754–755, 1064
"riding on a donkey," Messiah as, 1273
Riehm, Edward, 75
the righteous
  encouragement for, 559
  happiness of, 559–560
  Messiah as, 403, 1263
  suffering of, 559
Righteous Branch
  justice/righteousness/security from, 1050, 1053
  Messiah as, 31, 155, 272, 320, 403, 407, 805–806, 1012, 1016, 1102, 1163, 1242, 1263
  prophecy of, 892
  raising up of, 1013–1014
  through Davidic covenant, 1025
Righteous Branch of David, Messiah as, 798, 1042, 1046, 1105

Righteous King, Messiah as, 403–404, 407, 492, 897–905
Righteous Messiah, 1104
Righteous One, Messiah as, 309
righteous Servant, Messiah as, 1334
righteousness
 of the Branch of David, 1058
 of the Messiah, 849, 862–863, 1040, 1050, 1056
 promise of, 619
 robe of, 992
 as theme of Isaiah, 901, 1004
 as theme of Matthew, 937
Righteousness, Messiah as, 282
Ringgren, Helmer, 78
ritual issue, as part of sacrifice, 178
robe of righteousness, 992
Roberts, J. J. M, 988, 1015
Robertson, A. T., 25
Robertson, O. Palmer, 391–392, 1333
rock, theme of, 368–369
the Rock, God as, 877
Rock of Israel, Messiah as, 798
rod, 197, 272
Romans, 1292
Rome, 203, 1024, 1026, 1120–1121, 1128
root, imagery of, 853
root and progeny of David, Messiah as, 221
root of Jesse, Messiah as, 799, 805, 824, 855, 1025, 1163
Rose, Wolter, 769–770, 806, 1015, 1252, 1335
Ross, Allen, 33, 141, 178, 562–563, 564, 565, 610
Roth, Philip, 826–827
Routledge, Robin, 411
Rowe, R. D., 1132
Rowley, H. H., 443, 674
royal figure, Messiah as, 30, 64–65
royal priesthood, of the Messiah, 1247–1248
Royal Psalms, 467, 606, 665, 702, 703, 771
royal-priest, Messiah as, 1256–1257
ruin, as theme in Ezekiel, 1079
ruler
 as from Bethlehem, 223
 identity of, 860–861
 Messiah as, 403, 680–681, 1030, 1268
 seeking refuge from, 861
Ruler of Peace, Messiah as, 36
Russia, 256
Ruth (book), 343–356, 1213–1214
Ruth (woman), 344, 742
Rydelnik, Michael, quotes of, 147, 150–151, 249, 329, 330–331, 421, 591–592, 835, 837, 838, 847, 850, 956, 990, 991, 1024, 1141, 1148, 1214, 1292, 1318
Ryle, Herbert Edward, 119

S

69 weeks prophecy of Daniel, 1143–1147
70 weeks prophecy of Daniel, 1140, 1141, 1142–1143, 1305
the 70th week, in Daniel, 1147–1149
Sabbath day, 171, 185, 207
sacred history, 45
sacrifice(s), 177–182, 184–188, 328–329, 562–563, 564
sacrificial system, 328–329
safety, 850
sages, 232
Sailhamer, John
 quote of, 62, 65, 95, 108, 123, 131, 241, 248, 297, 334, 401, 405, 676–677, 717, 729, 733, 770, 771–772
 viewpoint of, 12, 81–82, 88f7, 120, 130, 331, 365, 741–742, 791, 795, 796, 804, 1208
salvation
 from Bethlehem, 1209
 garments of, 992
 of the Gentiles, 799, 1190, 1225
 geopolitical sense of, 1265
 from God, 609, 834–835, 904
 healing through, 915
 of Israel, 620, 1026
 light as symbol of, 935, 937
 meaning of, 1265
 Messiah and, 258, 803–804, 880, 946, 949, 950, 1003–1004, 1044, 1056, 1225
 in the Messianic Age, 1184
 oracles, 932
 promise of, 619, 881
 of the remnant, 1311
 song of, 813
 soteriological sense of, 1265
 spiritual, 1023
 as theme in Psalms, 499, 532–533, 549–550, 567, 594, 596, 598, 621, 653, 694, 695, 708
 as theme of coming of the King, 1264
 as theme of Second Servant Song, 924
 through descendant of Abraham, 263
Samaria, 846
Samaritan Pentateuch, 61, 64
Samuel, 13, 26, 191, 315, 316, 369, 376–378, 574
Samuel ben Nahmani, Rabbi, 1017–1018
sanctuary, 482, 1110
Sanctuary City, 796
Sarachek, J., 227–228
Sarah, 151, 260, 264, 265
Satan. *See also* serpent
 as accuser, 1237–1238, 1244
 binding of, 868
 defeat of, 199, 1243–1244

God and, 1198, 1238, 1244
Israel and, 1028
Jews and, 1198
Job and, 437–438, 741, 1238
Messiah and, 955, 957
as proper name for serpent, 1238
Saul
anointing of, 191
conversion of, 258
David and, 141, 608
death of, 1294
as greater than Agag, 298–300
as king, 13, 125, 137, 140, 293, 315, 635, 1030
leadership taken away from, 389
rejection of, 64
role in David and Goliath story, 378–382
story of, 374–375
victory of, 378
Savior, Messiah as, 792
Savior of Jacob, Messiah as, 798
Savran, G., 412, 413
scepter, 272, 273, 304, 680
Scepter from Israel, Messiah as, 1104
Schmitt, Hans-Christoph, 299
Scholem, G., 228, 234
Schreiner, Thomas, 731, 733, 734
Schroeder, Christoph, 574
Schürer, E., 203
Scripture, purity of, 754–755
Second Adam, Messiah as, 504
Second Coming
of the Messiah, 396–397, 681, 800, 867–868, 892–893, 991, 999, 1007, 1013, 1121, 1135, 1228, 1263–1264, 1301, 1309
salvation at, 1265
second exodus, 151
Second Temple
building of, 1014, 1252
destruction of, 205
Judaism, 917
meager facsimile of, 1322
messianic figures in, 197
overview of, 430–431
period of, 787, 1013
prophecies of, 193–194
Psalms as composed during, 469
security
Israel's, 874
from the Messiah, 850, 899, 1044, 1053, 1056
restoration of, 1090
tent peg as symbol of, 1267–1268
as theme in Psalms, 552
seed
of Abraham, 126, 163–164, 241, 257, 305, 310, 632, 1051, 1060–1061
of Adam, 163–164, 242, 1060
attack on, 353–354
of Babylon, 1069
creation purposes for, 1060
of David, 1051, 1060–1061, 1101–1102
future of, 539
in Genesis, 772
of Israel, 242
of Jacob, 107
of the Levites, 1051
of Noah, 1060
promise of, 774
as promised by God, 392
purpose of, 241
of the serpent, 150, 163, 241, 244, 245, 247, 248–249, 770
as theme of Balaam narrative, 304
of the woman, 124, 150, 157, 163, 244, 245, 247, 260, 345–346, 632, 770
Seitz, Christopher, 838
Seleucids, wars of, 1266–1267
Selman, Martin, 729
ṣemaḥ yhwh, Messianic significance of, 810–813
Sennacherib, King, 846, 900, 1197
Sensus Plenior, 84, 84f2, 107
Seow, C. L., 762
Sepher HaBrit, 233
Septuagint, 61, 62–63, 455
Sermon on the Mount, 336, 1174, 1214
serpent. *See also* Satan
Canaanites and, 247
deception of, 345, 347–348
defeat of, 240, 249, 305, 348
man's abhorrence to, 239
role in The Fall by, 150–151
seed of, 150, 163, 241, 244, 245, 247, 248–249, 770
servant
affliction of, 969–970
anointing of by the Spirit, 983
as Champion of Justice, 934
as Covenant Mediator, 934–936, 947
David as, 621–622, 1109
death of, 928–929, 958
deliverance of prisoners by, 936
ear of, 956
as effective spokesman, 948
exaltation of, 925, 948–949
as hearing God's instruction, 954–957
as ideal Israel, 934, 946
identity of, 933–934, 944–946, 962–966
as instrument in the Lord's hand, 948
Israel as, 944, 964
judging of, 1311
justice establishment by, 932

as light to the nations, 933, 936–937, 944
as mediator, 933
Messiah as, 13, 333–334, 561, 1235, 1296
ministry of, 934–937, 947–949
mission of, 934, 953–960
as My Chosen One, 939
opposition to, 948
personal testimony of, 953
Psalmist as, 596
purpose of, 944
resolute determination of, 957
restoration from, 923
as restoring the remnant, 945
resurrection of, 958
as shepherd, 1297
suffering of, 925
trusting the Lord by, 957–958
use of "The Lord God" by, 954
Servant Branch, Messiah as, 1241–1242
Servant of God, Messiah as, 309
servant of the Lord
commission of, 931
David as, 463
Job as, 480
Messiah as, 30–31, 34–35, 599–600, 938, 1228
ministry of, 943–950
people who were, 622
substitution of, 961–972
as theme in Psalms, 532
Servant of YHWH, Messiah as, 319
Servant Songs
call to praise, 932–933
Exodus imagery in, 947
Fifth, 938–939
First, 923–924, 931–933, 937–939
Fourth, 925, 939
influence of Zechariah by, 1296
of Isaiah, 30–31, 168, 195, 319–320, 333, 564, 599
Israel covenant in, 935–936
message of, 921–929
overview of, 939–940
prophecy of, 922
prophet of, 925
salvation oracle, 932
Second, 924, 943–946, 949–950
servant in, 1000
structure of, 922–925, 938–939
Third, 924–925, 939, 953–960
trial speech against the nations, 932
Servant-King, Messiah as, 126
servants of God, 656
Seth, 207, 245, 261, 774
Sforno, Obadiah ben Jacob, 233
shaking, as theme in Haggai, 1222, 1223, 1225, 1226, 1230
Shallum, 1041
Shalmanesar V, 846
shalom, 32, 412
Shalom Paul, 971
Sharon (Israel), 913
Shavout (Weeks)/Pentecost, 787
Shear-jashub, 817, 823, 839
sheep, 320, 1308, 1310
Shekinah, 811–812, 813, 890, 1111
Shelah, 280, 281, 351
Shelley, Percy Bysshe, 778
Shem, 247, 252, 254–256, 282, 346, 728
Shemoneh Esrei, 1015
Sheol, 524, 561, 620, 626
shepherd
Abraham as, 1310
act of, 1101
Antichrist as false, 1103
David as, 1087, 1212
defined, 1102–1103
evil, 1039, 1310
false, 1103
gathering of sheep by, 1200–1201
God as, 535–553, 1093
imagery in Ezekiel, 1085, 1092, 1307
imagery in Jeremiah, 1305, 1307
imagery in Zechariah, 1277, 1281, 1303, 1304, 1307, 1310–1312
of Israel, 890, 1083–1094, 1278
judging of, 1311
Messiah as, 320, 798, 891–892, 1212, 1276, 1281, 1296
Moses as, 1310
as prince, 1088–1089
purpose of, 193
as rejected, 1271–1282
as ruling king, 1307
as servant, 1088
striking of, 1311
suffering of, 1277
teacher as, 887
as theme in Psalms, 551–552
theological terms of, 1307
Zechariah as, 1277–1278
Shepherd, M. B., 1054, 1132, 1168–1169
Shepherd King, Messiah as, 1105, 1301–1312
Shepherd of Israel, Messiah as, 127
Sherlock, Thomas, 73–74, 79, 84f2
Sheshak, 216
Sheshbazzar, 1323
shield, 498, 754
Shila, Rabbi, 275
Shiloh, 273, 275, 276–279, 1077, 1104

Shimei, 416–418, 466, 668
Shinar, 851
Shlomo Itzhaki, Rabbi, 876
shoot from the line of David, Messiah as, 1057, 1066
shoot of Jesse, Messiah as, 854
Sidon, 1168, 1262
sign from God, 1241
signet ring, imagery of, 1227
signs and wonders, cosmic, 870, 1066, 1180–1181, 1322
Sihon of Heshbon, 1317
Silva, Moisés, 104, 546–547
Simeon, 50, 937, 940, 949, 950, 1225
Simeon ben Gamaliel, Rabbi, 1304
Simeon ben Yohai, Rabbi, 205
sin, 172, 182–185, 187, 328, 566–567, 637, 866, 1245
sin offering, 178, 180, 182–184
Sinai covenant, 1043
Sinai theology, 965
singing, 597–598
The Six-Day War, 1324
Skinner, John, 278
Slaughter of the Innocents, 109–110
slaves, 1180
Slotki, I. W., 849, 990, 992
Smart, J. D., 956–957
Smith, Gary V.
  outline of, 846
  quote of, 806–807, 832, 837, 838, 849, 850, 878–879
  viewpoint of, 852–853
Smith, J. Pye, 733
Smith, James E., 80, 877, 878, 1174, 1307
Smith, R. L., 1250, 1251
Smith, W. Robertson, 77
snakes, 331. *See also* serpent
snatched, 1238
Snodgrass, Klyne, 111
Sodom, 208, 968, 1128, 1226
Solomon
  as author of Psalms, 465, 608, 649
  breaking of shalom by, 412
  character flaws of, 317
  death of, 1087
  dominion of, 304
  exile and, 420
  as king, 165, 315, 317, 321, 414, 492, 577, 595
  Messiah as descendant of, 728
  as One Shepherd, 763
  as Patron of Wisdom, 727
  praise of, 978
  prayer for, 628
  prayer of, 701, 978
  promise fulfilled through, 126
  proverbs of, 728, 748
  reign of, 702
  slavery of Canaanites by, 254
  as son of David, 772
  temple and, 395, 564–565, 613, 705, 1322
  throne for Bathsheba by, 679–680
  throne of, 576, 606
  Zadok and, 366
son
  creation and, 744
  identity of in Proverbs, 753
  Messiah as, 485–486, 598
  riddle of, 747–755, 754–755
  role in creation by, 753
  as used in Proverbs, 732–733
Son of David, Messiah as, 34, 85, 127, 129, 141, 205, 228–230, 407, 720, 758, 759, 760, 824, 1051, 1056, 1098, 1204, 1257
Son of God, Messiah as, 33, 219, 477–489, 1069, 1093
Son of Joseph, Messiah as, 206, 228–230
Son of Man
  as connected with end of days, 1132
  Jesus as, 1131
  Messiah as, 33–34, 157, 505–510, 685–686, 1127–1135
  Old Testament use of, 1128
Song of David, 366–368
Song of Deborah, 362
Song of Hannah, 361–370
Song of Miriam, 368
Song of Moses, 362, 368–369
Song of Solomon, 769, 770, 772–777, 778
Song of the Sea, 362, 368
Song of Zion, 703
songs, in Psalms, 561
Songs of Ascent, 702–703, 711, 725
Sons of Korah, 156, 465, 592, 608, 622–623
sons of men, humans as, 655
spear, 1294
Spencer, James
  quote of, 835, 837, 838, 847, 850, 956, 991
  viewpoint of, 990
Spieckermann, Hermann, 970
Spirit of God
  gifts and abilities from, 849
  as hovering over disadvantaged, 988
  Messiah and, 193, 849, 853, 937
  pouring out of, 1179
  role of in construction of Tabernacle, 170
Spirit of wisdom, 849, 854
spiritual blindness, 909
spiritual gifts, 849
spiritual restoration, 1012, 1235

spiritual transformation, 899
sprig of a cedar, imagery of, 1064–1069
springs of water, John's vision of, 950
sprinkle, process of, 178–179
sprout of David, 1014, 1104
to sprout up, as theme in Psalms, 706
staff, 197, 272
star, Messiah as, 221
Star from Jacob, Messiah as, 1104, 1204
statute, God's superintending as, 1060
Stavsky, Rabbi Yitzchok, 1253
Steinmann, Andrew E., 414
Stephen, 218, 337
Steveson, Peter A., 807, 808
stone. *See* cornerstone
the stone of Israel, God as, 877
story, patterning in, 373–376
Stott, John, 855
Strauss, Mark, 141, 1190, 1191
strength, symbols of, 992, 1063, 1268
Stuart, Doug, 1333, 1335, 1336
stump of Jesse
  Davidic dynasty as, 847
  Messiah as, 34, 193, 734, 808, 824, 839, 845, 848, 853, 869–870, 972, 1210, 1214
  significance of, 839
  Spirit of God on, 1179
stumps, fallen dynasties as, 854
subdue, 137
Succoth/Zion, 665
Suez War, 1323
suffering
  Biblical antecedents to vicarious, 970–971
  cause of, 595
  of David, 593, 595, 597, 705
  of Israel, 229, 789, 965, 1208
  of Jerusalem, 1149
  of the Jews, 1149
  of Job, 438–439, 480, 600
  of man, 545
  of the Messiah, 222, 228–230, 235, 333–334, 529–540, 550, 600, 601, 617–629, 925, 929, 957, 1273, 1277
  obedience through, 957
  of the righteous, 559
  within the Targums, 222
  as theme of Fourth Servant Song, 925, 939
  as theme of Isaiah 53, 964
  as theme of Third Servant Song, 924–925
Suffering Servant
  atoning work of, 975
  covenant mediated by, 980
  description of, 853
  in Isaiah, 185, 1304
  Messiah as, 598, 599, 601, 937
  ministry of, 968
  words of, 602
Sullivan, Stephen P., 881
summary fulfillment, of prophecy, 112–114
Sumpter, Philip, 519
Supreme Command, violation of, 316
surrender, 569–570
sustain, as theme in Psalms, 499–500
Sweeney, Marvin, 1329
sword, 1294, 1311
synagogue, 193, 216–218, 224, 986
Syriac Peshitta, 217
Syro-Ephraimite War, 832

T

The Tabernacle, 170–172, 1110, 1143
Table of Nations, 254, 255, 256
Talmuds, Messiah in, 204–206
Tamar, 280, 351
Tanakh, 48–49, 81, 119, 120, 121f1, 122, 504
Tanchum, R., 63
Targums, 201–202, 213–216, 217, 219, 222, 273–274
Tate, Marvin, 600
tax collectors, 987–988
teacher
  God as, 889
  identity of, 888–890, 891
  Messiah as, 34, 793, 885–893
  role as shepherd, 887
  as shepherding Judah, 887, 890
  translation of, 1169, 1170
Teacher of Righteousness, Messiah as, 1167–1174
telescoped prophecy, 1264–1265
temple
  building of, 613, 701, 705
  cleansing of, 601
  cornerstone in, 879
  dedication of, 395
  destruction of, 203
  glory of, 809–810, 1223–1224
  glory of God in, 1318
  Haggai and, 1315
  holy of holies in, 1143
  loss of, 428
  Messiah and, 202, 792
  peace of, 1223–1224
  personnel cleansing, 1335
  physical, 881–882
  purpose of, 1220
  rebuilding of, 1219–1220, 1248, 1328
  restoration of, 790, 1254
  69 weeks prophecy and, 1146
  spiritual, 881–882
Temple Mount, 796, 797

temple service, 531
temptations, 242
tender sprig, 1065–1069
tent of David, 1190–1192
tent peg, Messiah as, 1267–1268
territorial possession, 1101
Tertullian, 607, 741, 999
Testaments of the Twelve Patriarchs, 194, 196
Tetragrammaton, 810
textual criticism, 61
thanksgiving, 597–598
theophoric onomasticon, 1017
thief on the cross, 987–988
Thielman, Frank, 136
Thompson, J. A., 328, 1049
throne, 647–649, 720, 859–863, 1187
thunder of the Lord, 364
Thutmose III, Pharaoh, 387
Tiglath-Pileser, 818, 823, 832, 834, 936
time, as theme in Psalms, 653–654, 656, 657
"times of the Gentiles," 1024, 1115–1124
times of trouble, as theme in Psalms, 532
Torah
  allegiance to, 26
  canonization of, 120, 121f1
  David and, 565
  Genesis 1-11 as introduction to, 241–242
  Jesus and, 321–322
  the king and the, 312–314
  love of God in, 532
  Messiah and, 123–124, 124f2, 195
  poems of, 287–288
  poetic seams of, 95
  prophet like Moses theme in, 331–332
  Psalms, 665, 722
  structure of, 119, 124f2
  use of Torah in, 95–96
Tov, Emmanuel, 62, 63
Tower of Babel, 254, 797
transfiguration, 939
treasures, as theme in Haggai, 1222–1223, 1224
tree, imagery of, 483, 1066–1067, 1248
tribulation, 797, 870, 1022–1024, 1023, 1028, 1198, 1200, 1280, 1302, 1308–1309
triumph, as theme of Fourth Servant Song, 925
triumphal entry, 1265
Troki, Isaak, 965
Trotter, James M., 577
True Shepherd, Messiah as, 1101, 1102, 1103
Truest Israelite, Messiah as, 166–170
trust, 533, 562, 722, 912
Tsemach Tsedek, 37
Tuchman, Barbara, 852
Tudhaliyas, 394–395
turban, significance of, 1077, 1078–1079, 1080, 1239
Turner, David, 332
two sons of oil, 194
"two sticks," imagery of, 1100
Tyndale, William, 255
typical fulfillment of prophecy, 85, 85f3, 106–109
typology, 375–376
Tyre, 624, 865, 1063, 1168, 1262

U

Ucal, 727, 749, 752
Ulmi-Teshup of Datasa, 394–395
ultimate David, Messiah as, 1163
ultimate fulfillment of prophecy, 84, 84f2
ultimate victor, Messiah as, 1129
unclean, 178
unfaithfulness, 1329–1330
Unger, Merrill, 1123, 1248–1249
union, as Messiah's staff, 1278–1279, 1281
unity, 1212
Uziel, Jonathan Ben, 810
Uzzah, 141
Uzziah, 921, 1030, 1153

V

Van Groningen, Gerard, 79, 80
VanGemeren, Willem, 363, 545–546, 565
Velvet Elvis (Bell), 815
vengeance of God, 991
Verhoef, P. A., 1333
Vermes, Geza, 1306
Victor, Messiah as, 1000
Victorious King, Messiah as, 683–684
Victorious Warrior, Messiah as, 1001
victory, 491–502, 518, 565, 582, 865–870, 1006, 1267
vindication, 958, 1003–1004, 1171
vineyard, imagery of, 807
virgin, meaning of, 820–821
virgin birth
  announcement of, 198, 826–827
  event of, 142–143, 154, 681, 1069, 1132
  fulfillment view of, 816–817, 832–833
  in Matthew, 1214–1215
  of Messiah, 35
  prophecy of, 53, 812, 815–827
visions, 43, 51–52, 1143. *See also specific prophets*
von Hengstenberg, E. W., 74, 88f7
von Herder, J. G., 74
von Hofmann, Johann Christian Konrad, 42, 44–47, 48
von Rad, Gerhard, 412

W

waiting, as theme in Psalms, 560–561
walking in darkness, 959–960
Wallace, D. H., 147
Wallace, Dan, 1333
Walsh, Jerome T., 417
Waltke, Bruce K.
    quote of, 414, 415, 607, 727, 739, 1210, 1220
    viewpoint of, 399–400, 523, 677, 1212, 1216, 1333
Walton, John, 239–240, 816
Walvoord, John F., 1025, 1101, 1106, 1118, 1122, 1139, 1143–1144
Warburton Lectures, 75
Warfield, B. B., 77
Warrior King, Messiah as, 728
warrior(s)
    God as, 1317–1318
    meaning of, 837
    Messiah as, 678, 997–1008, 1003, 1007
    people of God as, 680–681
watchman, imagery of, 1001
water(s), 336, 594, 887, 916–917, 1321
Watts, John D. W., 990
Watts, Rikk E., 1328
weary, meaning of, 955
wedding song, 573, 579
weeping, as theme in Psalms, 598
Weeping Prophets, letter by, 98
Wegner, Paul D., 79, 86f5
Wein, Berel, 971
Wellhausen, Julius, 55, 1254
Wenham, Gordon, 171, 178, 279
Wessels, W. J., 1015
Westermann, Claus, 278, 983–984, 990
Western Wall, 879
Whitcomb, John C., 1140
Whybray, Norman, 763
wicked, 406, 483, 484, 485, 494, 559, 667, 1078
widow in Sidon, 987
widow of Zarephath, 1190
Wiersbe, Warren, 439
Wifall, Walter, 771
Williamson, H. G. M., 806
Wilson, Gerald
    Psalms research from, 460–462, 478, 544, 573–574, 649–650, 702
    quote from, 567, 576, 607, 703
wine, symbolism of, 336
wine press, imagery of, 999, 1002, 1004, 1005, 1203
wisdom, 477, 658, 743–744, 760, 761
Wisdom literature, 733–734, 742
Wise, M. O., 1167
Wise Men, 104, 1180, 1215
woe oracles, in Ezekiel, 1085
Wolters, Al, 1296
woman
    association with the king by, 311–312
    descendents in opposition with serpent's descendants, 219
    in Proverbs, 741–742
    role in The Fall by, 150–151
    seed of, 124, 150, 157, 163, 241, 244, 245, 247, 260, 345–346, 632, 770
    in Song of Solomon, 776
Woman Wisdom, 129, 757, 765–766
Wonderful, Angel of the Lord as, 153
Wonderful Counselor, Messiah as, 35–36, 68, 154, 824, 836, 1162
Wood, Leon, 1140, 1142, 1146, 1147, 1149
the Word, Messiah as, 219
word of exhortation, 218
Word of God, 26, 143, 754, 955
"word of his mouth," as Messiah's weapon, 760
"works of your hands," as used in Psalms, 508–509
worm, as theme in Psalms, 533–534
worship, 180, 181–182, 560, 694, 720, 1050
wrath, 1004, 1078
Wray-Beal, Lissa, 417, 418
Wright, Chris, 80
Writings
    canonization of, 120, 121f1, 481
    Messiah in, 128–131, 156–157
    Song of Solomon in, 769
    structure of, 119, 120
    use of Old Testament for, 98–100
    visions within, 52
Wurthwein, Ernst, 62

Y

Yahweh. *See* God
Yahweh is our Righteousness, Messiah as, 37, 1016–1018
Yahweh Our Righteousness, 155, 1012, 1042, 1044, 1058, 1305
Yates, Gary, 839
Year of Jubilee, 990, 991
year of redemption, 998, 1005–1006
Yehud, 425, 433, 1315
Yeshua, Messiah as, 732
YHWH Ṣidqēnû, as Messiah's divine nature, 1016–1018
Yohanan ben Toreta, Rabbi, 203, 204, 206, 275
Yom Kippur, 1324
York, A. D., 215
Yoseph ben Nathan, Rabbi, 964
Young, Edward J., 836, 838, 849, 870, 922, 990

Z

Zaccur, 466
Zadok, 200, 366, 416–418, 674, 1061
Zebulun, 831, 834, 840
Zechariah (book)
3:1-10, overview of, 1236–1245
6:9-15, overview of, 1248–1255
9:9, overview of, 1263–1268
11:4-14, overview of, 1274, 1275–1282
12:10, overview of, 1288–1289t1, 1290t2, 1291t3, 1291t4, 1291t5, 1296–1297
12:10-13:1, overview of, 1287–1296
13:7-9, overview of, 1303, 1304–1312
14:1-11, overview of, 1316–1317
coronation symbolism in, 1252
Davidic scion and, 1315
"a day of Yahweh" in, 1316
de-creation in, 1319–1320
Deutero-Zechariah section, 1303
dominion as theme in, 1266
dream revelation of, 1180
eschatological content in, 1301
fifth vision of, 1254
four chariot vision in, 1248
fourth vision of, 1254
God's plan in, 1276
"house of David" reference in, 1293
interpretative issues with, 1271–1275
Messiah in, 1057, 1235, 1266, 1267–1268, 1273
in the New Testament, 1243–1244
olive tree imagery in, 1248
"on that day" use in, 1296
oracles of, 1261–1262
peace as theme in, 1266
"pierce" overview in, 1294–1295
potter in, 1273, 1275, 1277
Proto-Zechariah section, 1303
as quoted by John, 1288
re-creation in, 1320
shepherd imagery in, 1277, 1281, 1303, 1307
shepherd innertexual relationship, 1304–1307
shepherd translation in, 1274
sin and guilt symbolism in, 1244, 1245
situation of, 1272
stone descriptions in, 1242–1243
structure of, 1235, 1261–1262, 1286–1287, 1301–1302, 1303
temple rebuilding and, 1248
themes of, 1236, 1264
three shepherds in, 1273, 1278–1279
traditional reading challenges of, 1274
Trito-Zecharian section, 1303
use of term Shepherd by, 37–38
visions of, 1080, 1276
water in, 1321
Zechariah (man), 622, 1261, 1275, 1277–1278
Zedekiah
capture of, 1088
freedom proclaimed by, 938
judgment of, 853–854, 1012, 1064, 1068, 1116
as king, 1011
name meaning of, 1058
new covenant by, 1045
unrighteousness of, 1050, 1053, 1078
as vine, 1065
Zenger, Erich, 545, 663–664, 697, 712, 720–721
Zerah, 280
Zeri, 466
Zerubbabel
as anointed one, 1229, 1248
as the Branch, 233, 978, 1251, 1252
crown of, 1250, 1253
as governor, 1069, 1198, 1220
Haggai's message to, 1221
leadership of, 1254
as member of Davidic dynasty, 1307
as my servant, 1227
as prince, 1197
prophecy directed at, 1226
role in temple building by, 1248
Ziegler, Bernard, 277
Zimmerli, Walther, 478
Zion
as cornerstone identity, 875–876
as dwelling place, 719
as fulfillment of Davidic covenant, 718
God and, 599, 706, 787
help sent from, 549
hostility against, 916–917
hymns related to, 665
justice and righteousness in, 903
literal term of, 796
as location of Wisdom, 761
Lord's rule in, 927–928
Messiah and, 709, 720, 1058
Old Testament term use of, 796
peace to, 1057
as place of eternal life and blessing, 554
presence of God in, 720, 721
in the Psalms, 623–625, 629
Psalms of, 618, 665
redeemed in, 914, 915
relationships in, 626–627
restoration of, 708, 716, 790, 808–809, 1002
restored land of, 551
sanctification of people of, 809
scepter from, 680
significance of, 839

word of comfort to, 1172
worship at, 720
Zion psalm, 618, 665
Zohar, 229
Zuber, Kevin, 986

the Christian understanding of the divine identity of the Messiah. Thus, Amos Hakham interprets "God" as genitival: "Your throne is the throne *of God* and will be established forever."[27] Hakham derives his interpretation from 1Ch 29:23, which states that Solomon sat on the "LORD's throne," the obvious implication being that the Davidic kings sat on a borrowed throne. Though a "borrowed throne" theology is most certainly correct, there is no good reason for choosing a more complex reading of the Hebrew syntax in preference for the far more straightforward interpretation of God as a vocative. Thus, Harris's thorough syntactical analysis leads him to the following conclusion:

> We conclude that the objections to taking [God] אֱלֹהִים [*'ᵉlōhim*] as a vocative in Psalm 45:7 [6], whether they are drawn from grammar, the structure of the poem, the context of v. 7 [6], or from general theological considerations, are by no means insuperable. The traditional rendering, 'Your throne, O God, is for ever and ever,' is not simply readily defensible but remains the most satisfactory solution to the exegetical problems posed by the verse.[28]

Moreover, the larger context supports the divine identity of the king.[29] This is seen most notably in the call to the bride to bow down to her lord (v. 11) and the call to praise or give thanks (*yhôḏuḵā*) to this king forever in the final verse (v. 17), an action that is only fittingly offered to God in the book of Psalms.[30] In fact, the praise being offered to the king in Ps 45:17 is remarkably similar to the praise being offered to God in Ps 44:8, the psalm just preceding Ps 45: Ps 44:8: "We boast in God all day long; we will praise Your name forever. Selah."

Gerald Wilson, furthermore, points out the implications of causing the name of the king to be remembered for all generations in Ps 45:17. According to Wilson, the Hiphil of the verb *zkr* ("to cause remember") with the noun "name" in a positive sense refers exclusively to the name of the Lord (Ex 20:24; Ps 20:7; Isa 12:4; 26:13; Am 6:10). Wilson then goes on to write, "Add to this the fact that in the psalms the image of 'the peoples' (*'ammim* ['peoples'], not 'nations' as in the NIV) 'praising' someone is *always* a reference to praising Yahweh."[31]

In light of these facts that only God is praised in the psalter, and that His name is to be remembered through all generations in the Hebrew Bible, there are no syntactical and theological reasons to reject the divine identification of the king in v. 6. Moreover, the divine identification of the king makes the direct messianic interpretation most appealing. This is particularly persuasive, given that there is no other example in the Hebrew Bible of any historical king being identified as "God," whereas there are many examples of ascriptions of deity to the future Messianic King, which will be evident when examining the relationship of Ps 45 to other well-known messianic prophecies in the Hebrew Bible.

men, one who is victorious on the battlefield (Ps 45:4-5), and anointed with the oil of joy above his companions (Ps 45:7). These features preeminently qualify him for royalty far above all kings who preceded him. Like David, this king is also identified as a "mighty warrior" or mighty man of valor (*gibbôr*; 1Sm 16:18; Ps 45:3), but unlike David in his failed attempt to gird a sword for the battle against the giant, the king of Ps 45 girds his sword for battle against the enemies (1Sm 17:39; Ps 45:3).

The second primary stanza focuses upon the king's grandeur in his palace (vv. 6-16). This change in location is evident because of the reference to the king's eternal throne (v. 6), an obvious reference to the promise that one of David's descendants would sit upon the throne forever.[20]

With the king having been established upon a throne of justice (vv. 6-7), the psalmist describes the king's garments which have been perfumed with "myrrh and aloes," a phrase used elsewhere only in the Song of Songs (the exact phrase found only in Ps 45:8 and Sg 4:14; but see also Prv 7:17; Sg 1:13; 3:6; 4:6; 5:1,13; Est 2:12). Other similarities with the Song of Songs suggest that Ps 45 describes the wedding banquet of the king.[21] Gold is mentioned in Ps 45:9 and Sg 5:11. And as in the Song of Songs, the beauty (a key word in Song of Songs) of both king and bride are celebrated in Ps 45.[22] The bride is summoned to abandon all and "bow down" to her lord (vv. 10-11), a particular action which is only properly and exclusively rendered to God in the book of Psalms,[23] the sole exceptions being the exalted King who appears in the introduction and conclusion to Book II of the Psalms (Pss 45:11; 72:11). The psalm concludes with the joyous entrance of the bride into the palace with her companions and wedding guests (vv. 13-15), a reference to the king's descendants ruling over "the earth" (not "the land" as in the HCSB) (v. 16), and the psalmist and the nations praising the king forever (v. 17).

THE IDENTIFICATION OF THE KING

Particularly striking within this psalm are the divine descriptions of this king, which will be even more striking when these descriptions are seen in the context of the Sons of Korah psalms at the introduction to Book II (Pss 42–49).

As is well noted, the major interpretive crux in Ps 45 is found in v. 6.[24] According to the HCSB translation, "God" is in the vocative[25] voice: "Your throne, God, is forever and ever; the scepter of Your kingdom is a scepter of justice." Though this is the most straightforward reading of this verse, several emendations of the Hebrew text and at least four other interpretations of the Hebrew text have been offered for obviously theological reasons.[26]

For Jewish scholars, the vocative reading would most obviously lend itself to

(Pss 44:4; 47:2, 6-7; 48:2,4). The praise of this king of Ps 45:17 both ar
reverberates with the call for all peoples and nations to praise Israel's
psalms that follow (Ps 47:6-7). Moreover, the identification of the king
rounding psalms suggests that the author of Ps 45 has intentionally and
uously identified the king in Ps 45 as both divine and human.[64] The King
vanquished Israel's enemies in Pss 46–49 (Pss 46:9; 47:1-3; 48:4-8) is someh
same King and mighty warrior[65] who rides forth with his sword[66] to subdue Is
enemies under his feet (Ps 45:5).

Having defeated Israel's enemies, the divine warrior King takes his seat up his eternal throne (Ps 45:6), in order to address the second problem: divine absence The earlier longing and calls in Pss 42–43 to come into God's presence (Pss 42:2; 43:3-4) are now depicted by the means of a marital metaphor: the bride is brought joyfully into the King's palace (Ps 45:10-15).

> Listen, daughter, pay attention and consider: forget your people and your father's house, and the king will desire your beauty. Bow down to him, for he is your lord. The daughter of Tyre, the wealthy people, will seek your favor with gifts. In her chamber, the royal daughter is all glorious, her clothing embroidered with gold. In colorful garments, she is led to the king; after her, the virgins, her companions, are brought to you. They are led in with gladness and rejoicing; they enter the king's palace.

By the time the Psalter was finalized and groups of psalms placed in this particular order, the kingship of David was no longer existent, and a scripted wedding would no longer be relevant. To be positioned here, at this point in this string of Psalms, it is best to understand Ps 45 to be speaking figuratively about a wedding between the divine Messiah-King and His people.

PSALM 45 AND THE MESSIANISM OF THE HEBREW BIBLE

Before concluding this article, it is important to look at Ps 45 and its relationship to several other passages about the Messiah in the Hebrew Bible. To begin, note the way in which Book II of the Psalms begins and ends with an exalted king. In Ps 45, the Messiah-King is depicted as a man of war. In Ps 72, the Messiah-King is depicted as a man of peace. Like the other royal messianic psalms in the book of Psalms, Ps 45 speaks of the Messiah's eternal name, eternal throne, and crucial role in the redemption of God's people (Pss 18:50; 21:5; 45:3,7,17; 72:17,19; 89:2-3,5,29,36-37,52; 110:4).

Psalm 45 appears to draw also from other well-known messianic passages of the Hebrew Bible. According to Gn 49:8-12, a king who will come from the tribe of Judah in the last days (Gn 49:1) will be *praised* by his brothers (v. 8a), and the sons of his mother will *bow down* to him (v. 8b). Jacob prophesies of the king's victory over Israel's enemies (v. 8b), Judah's ruling *scepter* (v. 10a), the reverence of the king by the *peoples* (v. 10b), the king riding upon a donkey/colt (v. 11), and king's superlative eyes and teeth (v. 12).[67] Given the extreme rarity of praise (*yḏh*) being offered to a human in the Hebrew Bible, and given the overtly royal overtones in this prophecy about Judah, the numerous lexical and thematic links strongly suggest that Ps 45 intentionally alludes to Gn 49, thereby confirming the king's messianic identity and supporting the direct messianic interpretation of this psalm.

	The Messiah in Genesis 49[68]	The King in Psalm 45
The king is praised and bowed down to	Judah, your brothers *will praise you* [*yôḏûḵā*] . . . your father's sons *will bow down* [*yištaḥᵃwû*] to you. (v. 8)	and the king will desire your beauty. *Bow down* [*wᵉhištaḥᵃwi*] to him, for he is your lord . . . therefore the peoples *will praise you* [*yhôḏuḵā*] forever and ever. (vv. 11,17b)
The king's victory over Israel's enemies	Your hand will be on the necks of your enemies (v. 8b)	Your arrows pierce the hearts of the king's enemies; the peoples fall under you. (v. 5)
The king's scepter	The *scepter* [*šeḇeṭ*] will not depart from Judah (v. 10a)	the *scepter* [*šeḇeṭ*] of Your kingdom is a scepter of justice. (v. 6a)
The king's is reverenced by the peoples	and the obedience of the *peoples* [*ʿammim*] belongs to Him.	therefore the *peoples* [*ʿammim*] will praise you forever and ever. (v. 17)
The king rides upon a mount	He ties his donkey to a vine, and the colt of his donkey to the choice vine. (v. 11)	in your splendor ride triumphantly in the cause of truth, humility, and justice. (v. 4)
The king's superlative appearance	His eyes are darker than wine, and his teeth are whiter than milk. (v. 12)	You are the most handsome of men (v. 2)

The likelihood of an intentional allusion to the king of Gn 49 in Ps 45 is bolstered by its shared connection to Zch 9:9, a well-known messianic prophecy that itself alludes to Gn 49:11.[69] Genesis 49:11 and Zch 9:9 are the only two passages in the Hebrew Bible that refer to the coming of an eschatological king riding upon a colt (*ʿir* [Gn 49:11]; *ʿayîr* [Zch 9:9]) and the foal/colt of his donkey (*bᵉni ʾᵃṯōnô* [Gn 49:11]; *ben-ʾᵃṯōnôṯ* [Zch 9:9]). Likewise, Pss 45:4 and Zch 9:9 are the only two passages that speak of a king who *rides out* [*rkḇ*]with the characteristics of *humility*

Joel 2:23

The Teacher of Righteousness

MICHAEL A. RYDELNIK

The Qumran sect had a mysterious and revered leader. In the mid-to-late second century BC, they mention "The Teacher of Righteousness" some 15 times in the published Dead Sea Scrolls.[1] Although he does not appear to be considered the Messiah, "the Teacher of Righteousness" did have messianic-like characteristics attributed to him, including the idea that "fidelity to his inspired teaching [was] considered necessary for salvation."[2]

M. O. Wise notes that both the Gospel of Matthew's portrait of Jesus and the Qumran Scrolls' depiction of the Teacher of Righteousness viewed this person "as a new Moses."[3] This was part of Matthew's portrayal of Jesus as the Messiah and the Qumran sect's attribution of messianic qualities to their mysterious teacher.

Scholars recognize the Qumran community's source of the title, "The Teacher of Righteousness," as biblical, although the specific reference is disputed. Some attribute it to Hos 10:12 ("until He comes and sends righteousness on you like the rain" *'ad yavo' weyoreh tsedeq lakhem*), while others see it as derived from Jl 2:23 ("He gives you the autumn rain for your vindication" *kiy natan lakhem et hamoreh litsdaqah*), and yet others view it as coming from both verses.[4]

What is pertinent to this discussion is the phrase in Jl 2:23 translated as "autumn rain for your vindication," which could just as well be translated "the teacher for righteousness." This is the most likely source of the Qumran community's founder's name.[5] Is it possible that the Qumran sect was accurate in their understanding of this phrase in Jl 2:23, seeing it as a prophecy of a future "Teacher of Righteousness" but incorrect in identifying their founder as the referent? This article will maintain that the correct translation of Jl 2:23 is, lit., "the teacher for righteousness" and affirm it is a prediction of the Messiah coming to Israel, who will usher in the Messianic Era.

THE BIBLICAL CONTEXT OF JOEL 2:23

Since there is no specific date indicated in the book of Joel or any reference to reigning kings, the date cannot be determined categorically. However, the references to Israel's early enemies Tyre, Sidon, Philistia (Jl 3:4), Egypt, and Edom (Jl 3:19), along with the absence of any mention of the nation's later foes Assyria and Babylon, leads to the conclusion that Joel is a fairly early preexilic book.

The first chapter of Joel deals with a recent locust plague, an event viewed as God's judgment. The prophet uses this temporal devastation by God to anticipate and prefigure the eschatological Day of the Lord (Jl 1:1-20). The Day of the Lord is described in Jl 2 as a coming devastation of the land of Israel—along with its ultimate deliverance. Although some have argued that this judgment anticipates the imminent destruction by Babylon, which occurred in 586 BC, it is more likely a reference to the eschatological Day of the Lord. This is evident in the description of these events as unprecedented and unrepeated (Jl 2:2), along with massive earthly, solar, and lunar disturbances (Jl 2:10-11). Moreover, although the date of writing was preexilic, the book was compiled into the Book of the Twelve in the postexilic period. As such, the events described in Jl 2 were not considered as having yet been fulfilled and were still predicting the eschatological Day of the Lord. Just as in the biblical description of a "day," the Day of the Lord has both an evening and morning portion (cf. Gn 1:5,8,13,19,23,31). The evening portion consists of judgment (Jl 2:1-17), and the morning is composed of blessing (Jl 2:18-32).

The third and final chapter of Joel continues the description of eschatological judgment but focuses more on God's end-of-days judgment of the Gentile nations for their mistreatment of Israel (3:1-16). Gathering the nations to the last battle for Jerusalem (cf. Pss 83:1-12; 110:6; Is 66:18; Jr 25:32; Ezk 39:21; Mic 4:11-12) in the Valley of Jehoshaphat ("Yahweh Judges," 3:2,12), a title for the Kidron Valley that runs east of Jerusalem, the Lord will judge them for their oppression of Israel (cf. Mt 25:31-46, esp. v. 40). Afterwards, Jl 3:16-21 describes God's taking up residence in Jerusalem and His physical restoration of that city, along with the spiritual renewal of the people of Israel in His kingdom.

This discussion of the context of Jl 2:23 is significant because one of the arguments against the translation "teacher of righteousness" is that it does not fit the context of Joel. For example, M. B. Shepherd says that the translation "early rain"

Medo-Persia

However, eventually, according to this vision, the head of gold would give way to the chest and arms of silver. The first part of v. 39 says, "After you [Nebuchadnezzar] there will arise another kingdom inferior to yours." This is the meaning of the chest and arms of silver and the empire that would replace Babylon.

The book of Daniel itself designates this second empire as Medo-Persia. As indicated previously, Dan 5 records the overthrow of the Babylonians and in the process, furnishes the name of the next empire to follow Babylon. Dan 5:28 says, "your kingdom has been divided and given over to the Medes and Persians." Similarly, Dan 8 and Dan 10 are both visions concerning the middle two empires during the times of the Gentiles. Dan 8:20 also identifies "Media and Persia" and Dan 10:13 uses the word "Persia" twice. A similar enumeration occurs in Dan 11:1-2, which is a description of the angelic conflict concerning the second empire during the times of the Gentiles. The Persian empire would come to power over Israel around 539 BC, and her influence would last until roughly 331 BC.

It is puzzling that in v. 39, when Daniel is identifying the empire that will depose Babylon, he describes it as "inferior to yours." How can this be since Persia conquered more territory than Babylon? However, the Babylonian Empire was centralized and under the authority of Nebuchadnezzar. The Persians were characterized by more decentralized authority. This is also part of the meaning of the gradual decline of the value of the metals previously discussed.[3]

The chest and arms of silver depicted in the vision cover the human heart. The heart was the seat of affection in the ancient world. Apparently, the Persian Empire was close to God's heart. God had a special calling on Persia. Just as God used Babylon to start the captivity, Persia's job was to end the captivity: It was under the Persian Empire that the nation of Israel began to return to their own land 70 years later. Their three successive returns are recorded in the books of Ezra and Nehemiah. Such returns would begin under the Persian king Cyrus, whose role the prophet Isaiah predicted about 150 to 200 years earlier (Isa 44:28–45:1).[4]

Greece

The chest and arms of silver would eventually give way to the belly and thighs of bronze. The end of v. 39 mentions "a third kingdom, of bronze, which will rule the whole earth." The belly and thighs of bronze refer to Greece, the third empire during the times of the Gentiles. Although the specific name Greece does not appear here, the book of Daniel itself identifies Greece as the empire that would follow Persia. As indicated previously, both Dan 8 and 10 contain prophecies about the middle two empires during the times of the Gentiles, and both Dan 8:21 and 10:20 specifically use the word "Greece" in reference to the empire that would follow Persia.

Dan 8:5-7 also predicts Greece's conquest of Persia. Greece as an empire came into existence about 331 BC and retained influence over the land of Israel until 63 BC. It would be Greece that would make the Greek language the *lingua franca* of the known world. Greece was the empire of Alexander the Great and his dynastic successors, which become the focus of Daniel's prophecies in Dan 8 and 11.

Rome Phase I

The belly and thighs of bronze would then give way to the legs of iron. Daniel 2:40 states, "A fourth kingdom will be as strong as iron; for iron crushes and shatters everything, and like iron that smashes, it will crush and smash all the others."

This empire is known as "Rome Phase I" or historical Rome. Rome moved into the land of Israel around 63 BC, which is almost 600 years after Daniel made this prophecy. Rome would eventually push the nation of Israel out of her homeland in AD 70. Additionally, in the vision, Rome is represented as two different legs. Such a description fits well with what is known about ancient Rome, since there were both an eastern and a western division of the Roman Empire.

No verse in Daniel uses the word "Rome" as clearly as it uses the name "Persia" or "Greece." However, Rome is clearly in view here since the historical record shows that Greece was eventually replaced by Rome. Daniel also uses fitting imagery to describe the ancient Roman Empire, using terms like "strong, crushes, smashes, shatters." These terms accurately describe the ruthless regime of ancient Rome. It was the Romans who popularized the cruel method of capital punishment known as crucifixion and consequently crucified Christ. It was also Rome that was responsible for the death of over a million Jews in the events of AD 70.

Rome Phase II

Ultimately, the legs of iron would eventually give way to the feet of iron and clay. Verses 41-43 predict:

> You saw the feet and toes, partly of a potter's fired clay and partly of iron—it will be a divided kingdom, though some of the strength of iron will be in it. You saw the iron mixed with clay, and that the toes of the feet were part iron and part fired clay—part of the kingdom will be strong, and part will be brittle. You saw the iron mixed with clay—the peoples will mix with one another but will not hold together, just as iron does not mix with fired clay.

This passage no longer depicts ancient Rome; instead, the feet of iron and clay describe a future empire, "Rome Phase II." But even this title is inadequate. Since Dan 2–7 is structured as a chiasm, the themes begun in Dan 2 are repeated in Dan 7. Therefore, to understand this aspect of the future empire, the supplemental of this view understand Israel to retain its ethnic identity with the one people of God, the church.[11] Glenny's criticism of this view is instructive: Is it meaningful to speak of Jews becoming Christians "so that" Gentiles would seek the Lord?[12] Romans 9–11 would seem to indicate that Gentile salvation provokes Jewish jealousy, not the opposite.

Some argue that the restoration of the tent is referring to the "temple of the messianic age," the true Israel, which is the Christian community.[13] This view is difficult to sustain in light of the rebuilt "tent" in Ac 15:16 being differentiated from the tent's *effect,* which is "so that" the Gentiles would seek the Lord and thus be included in God's people. The purpose clause in 15:17 (*opos an,* "so that" plus the subjunctive *ekzetesosin,* they "may seek") indicates the goal of the action in the grammar in relation to the main verb. The view simply does not give sufficient weight to Am 9:13-15 and tips toward a figurative interpretation of the land promises and Israel's restoration, explanations that do not comport with the words and perspective of Amos.[14]

One may ask, "How much (if anything) of the promised future *national* Davidic reign is fulfilled in the current heavenly position of the Lord Jesus?" Is His current heavenly reign the only reign needed to fulfill the promise? Strauss, and then Glenny in support of Strauss, posit that the tent of David alludes to the "restoration of the Davidic dynasty accomplished through the life, death, resurrection, and exaltation of Jesus."[15] However, nothing in the immediate context indicates that the *fullness* of the promised future Davidic reign is presently in place through the effects of Jesus' resurrection and ascension.[16] Some authors make an appeal to Ac 2, which, while certainly supportive of a relationship to Jesus' future earthly kingdom, expresses the current heavenly reign of Messiah heralding a forthcoming earthly, and then eternal, fulfillment.[17] In fulfillment of the promises made to David, Messiah's resurrection and ascension secured some measure of the promises to David (cf. Ac 13:30-33). These promises relate to the nature of a Davidic descendant currently ruling from heaven, but do not preclude a more complete fulfillment in the messianic kingdom, the millennium.[18]

With issues such as these at the forefront, it is clear that the promises of Am 9:11-15 are messianic in focus and purpose. They point to a future time after God's discipline of Israel in her exile when there will be great blessing through restoration and fulfillment. In that time, God restores David's line to its earthly supremacy and brings Israel and the nations under the Davidic blessing. The covenantal aspects are realized over time and fulfilled eschatologically "in that day." Both aspects of the prophecy, however, are met in a normal/literal fashion. The lineage/dynastic element of God's promise is fulfilled in a person, Messiah Yeshua ben David. Thus, Amos's prophecy portended the fulfillment of the promise to

David in a person, in the revival of the dynasty pictured by the image of David's weakened *sukka*. The national elements of the promise are fulfilled in the kingdom that Messiah brings! Encompassed within the raising of David's booth are issues of David's dynasty and posterity as well as national reinstatement. Gentiles rejoice today in God's grace extended to them in the blessings promised as God restores this lowly image of the fallen tent of David—so that we all might be saved "through the grace of the Lord Jesus" (Ac 15:11; Isa 55). The final installment of the Spirit as possessed by Gentiles today foreshadows the future restoration of all things. Israel plays a unique role as the servant by which the gospel is brought to the nations, and national Israel continues to have significance in God's inclusion of Jewish people among the redeemed.

---

1. See the articles in this *Handbook* by Walter C. Kaiser Jr. on "2 Samuel 7" and Eugene H. Merrill on "1 Chronicles 17."
2. Later, the prophet Isaiah described the coming Babylonian invasion and the destruction that God would inflict upon the Jewish people through foreigners (e.g., Isa 45:20,22).
3. See also Isa 1:7-8, where Isaiah depicts the result of the Babylonian invasion as reducing the daughters of Zion in status to that of a *sukka* in a vineyard—like a hut guarding a field of melons. Similarly, in Zch 14:16, the prophet foretold a day when the Feast of Booths would be celebrated by a remnant of those nations who went up against Jerusalem.
4. The tribulation is the period of time known as "a time of trouble for Jacob" (Jer 30:7) and encompasses Daniel's 70th week, a period of seven years (Dn 9:24-27). It is when God will judge the world (Rev 6:16) and purge Israel (Zch 13:7-9). Ultimately, the Messiah Jesus will return at the end of the seven years, delivering Israel (Zch 14:1-21) when the nation trusts in Him (Zch 12:10; Rom 11:25-26).
5. James may have been referring to the book of the twelve Minor Prophets (cf. Ac 7:42) or to other passages that could be cited in support of his contention. Luke's wording reflects the LXX of Am 9:11-12 with some differences in wording. See G. K. Beale and D. A. Carson, *Commentary on the New Testament Use of the Old Testament* (Grand Rapids: Baker Academic, 2007), 589.
6. The Septuagint text makes it clear that Gentile inclusion/salvation aligned with the restoration of David's fallen *sukka*. Neither the Septuagint nor the Masoretic Text of Am 9 spells out the details as to how this will occur, but the Septuagint reading lends itself more naturally to James's argument that the Gentiles remain Gentiles while being brought under the promises. The Septuagint version of the text does not posit Israel as possessing the nations, but presents the nations as seeking God. Luke presents a consistent argument in Luke-Acts on this theme. Jesus' death and resurrection are part of the fulfillment, but do not preclude national fulfillment of the Davidic covenant. The hopes expressed by Zechariah, Elizabeth, and Mary in the infancy narratives in Luke all point to the national promises, and these carry forward into the apostles' expectations of the kingdom in Ac 1:6-8 (which Jesus does not rebut or correct). Further, Peter's sermon in Ac 2 and Paul's sermon in Ac 13 highlight the theme of a universal blessing afforded in the promise to David.
7. See, for example, Mark Strauss, *The Davidic Messiah in Luke-Acts: The Promise and its Fulfilment in Lukan Christology*, The Library of New Testament Studies (Sheffield, England: Sheffield Academic Press, 1995); W. Edward Glenny, "The Septuagint and Apostolic Hermeneutics: Amos 9 in Acts 15" *Bulletin for Biblical Research* 22, no. 1 (2012): 1–26; I. Howard Marshall, "Acts," in *Commentary on the New Testament Use of the Old Testament*, ed. G. K. Beale and D. A. Carson (Grand Rapids: Baker, 2007), 588–89; J. Paul Tanner, "James's Quotation of Amos 9 to Settle the Jerusalem Council Debate in Acts 15," *Journal of the Evangelical Theological Society* 55, no. 1 (2012): 65–85.
8. Luke made it clear to his readers that he had provided a compressed narrative in what he related (e.g., Ac 15:7, "after there had been much debate"). Ben Witherington calls this a "composite citation" (see *The Acts of the Apostles: A Socio-Rhetorical Commentary* [Grand Rapids: Eerdmans, 1998], 439). Luke does not present every aspect of the case for Gentiles becoming Jews, a point that should not be lost in this discussion. The issue at hand in Ac 15 was the

Subject Index

A

Aaron
  anointing of, 191
  fleeing Egypt by, 968
  golden calf made by, 141
  as image in Psalms, 720
  Joshua as descendant of, 1248
  as priest, 140, 180
  as a prophet, 136
  rebellion of, 329
  turban of, 1239
abandonment, 626
Abarbanel, Rabbi Don Isaac, viewpoints of, 233, 803, 876–877, 963, 1099, 1169, 1253, 1286
Abegg, Martin, 1014
Abel, 261, 348
Abiathar, 366, 416–418
Abimelech, 1294
Abinadab, 386
Abner, 417
Abraham
  blessing of, 935
  call of, 264, 1226
  covenant with, 255, 259–268, 539
  death of, 260
  descendants' land of, 1022
  descendants of, 124, 260, 262, 281, 282–283, 346, 1023, 1069, 1226
  dream revelation of, 1180
  faith of, 56
  God walking with, 151
  marriage of, 351
  Melchizedek and, 682–683
  Messiah as descendant of, 255–256, 728
  as priest, 1060
  promises to, 126, 385, 414, 468, 610, 669, 728, 771, 1051
  as a prophet, 136
  rejoicing by, 833
  seed of, 126, 163–164, 241, 257, 305, 310, 632, 1051, 1060–1061
  as shepherd, 1310
  story of, 139–140, 151–152, 163–164
  territory of, 266, 267
Abrahamic covenant
  Adonai Yahweh as used in, 392
  blessings of, 95
  connection of Judah-David to, 271–272
  everlasting covenant as used in, 1110
  in Ezekiel, 1101–1102
  manifestation of, 724
  priests and, 1059–1060
  promises in, 392, 539, 632, 1051
  Psalm 72 and, 612
  as theme of Balaam narrative, 286–288
  unconditional elements of, 395, 411
Abram. *See* Abraham
Absalom, 492, 496, 517–518, 574
accuser(s), 666, 1244
acrostic praise psalm, 665
Adam
  Abraham and, 163–164
  as commanded to subdue the earth, 241
  descendants of, 242, 260, 261, 346, 655
  disobedience of, 242, 866
  dominion of, 304
  earthly rule of, 509
  Eve and, 350, 774
  Israel and, 164–165
  Messiah and, 165–166, 728
  nakedness of, 775
  Noah and, 163
  as prophet, priest, and king, 137–139
  role in The Fall by, 150–151
  seed of, 163–164, 242, 1060
  as a type of Christ, 162
Adam typology, 162–166
administrative gifts, 849
Adonai Yahweh, as name for God, 392, 568
Adonay
  as name of God, 539, 652–653, 683–684, 889
  of Psalms, 481, 488
Adonijah, 416–418, 1017
adultery, 1027
adversary, 666
advocate, Messiah as, 129, 1244
affliction, 626. *See also* suffering
Agag, 57, 298–300
agriculture, abundance in, 1171
Agrippa, 949
Agur, 727, 732, 733, 748–750, 752
Ahab, 419–420, 577, 1155
Ahaz
  Davidic line and, 847

Hezekiah as compared to, 803
Isaiah's message to, 812, 817–818, 921
as king, 816, 819, 875
trust of, 912
Ahaziah, 419
Ahithophel, 668
Ahlstrom, G. W., 1170
Akiva, Rabbi, 203, 231, 686, 966, 1104, 1130
Albright, W. F., 65
Alden, Robert, 679
Alexander, J. A., 831–832
Alexander, T. Desmond, 125, 242–243, 281, 478, 771, 772
Alexander the Great, 1120, 1139, 1262–1263, 1265
Alexandri, Rabbi, 204
"Alfred Hitchcock Presents," 1327
alienation, in Song of Solomon, 775–776
Allen, David, 143, 594, 720, 1108
Allen, Leslie, 788
Allison, Dale, 167, 328, 336
Alshech, Moshe, 1286
Amalek, 1317
Amasa, 417
Ambrose of Milan, 276
Amen-hotep III, Pharaoh, 387–388
Amidah, as Jewish prayer, 1015
Ammon, 851, 860, 1002
Amon-Re (god), 387
Amos, 1162, 1187, 1188–1189, 1191–1192
Amoz, 886
Amsler, S., 1011–1012, 1014
Amun/Aten, as Egyptian god, 1180
Ancient of Days, 33, 157, 685–686, 1129
Anderson, Francis I., 442
Angel of the Lord
as called Wonderful, 153
description of, 36
God as, 1236
identity of, 1333–1334
Joshua as standing before, 1236–1238
Manoah's interaction with, 890
Messiah as, 151–153
Messiah's name compared to, 1017
rebuke of Satan by, 1244
speaking to Balaam, 288–289, 290
angel(s), 198, 632–633, 1236
Ani Ma'amin, formulation of, 230
Animal Apocalypse, 764, 1104
animals, 138, 180, 181, 536, 1092
Anna, 50
Annas, 958
Anointed, Old Testament use of, 13
Anointed King, Messiah as, 507, 559, 614, 847
anointed of Aaron and of Israel, Messiah as, 200
Anointed One
empowerment of, 990–991
Messiah as, 30, 156, 385, 507, 549, 598, 599, 621, 637, 684, 701, 703, 705, 732, 754, 804, 983–984
new names given by, 992
Anointed One, David as, 771, 804
anoint(ed)(ing)
of high priests, 191
of the king, 554
meaning of, 147, 377, 938
of the Messiah, 849, 983
as messianic term, 197
purpose of, 30
as theme in Psalms, 546
antecedents, Old Testament, 191–194
Antichrist
armies from, 1103
coming of, 1302
demise of, 1007
as false shepherd, 1103
kingdom of, 1122
as little horn, 1129, 1146
persecution under, 1028
in the 70th week, 1148–1149
signing of covenant by, 1198–1199
Antiochus IV Epiphanes, 1129, 1130, 1134, 1135, 1255, 1267, 1323
Antiquities, 1323
Apocalypse, 1007, 1118, 1244
applicational fulfillment of prophecy, 109–112
Aquila of Sinope, 64, 820
Arabia, God's message for, 865
Arabs, ethnicity of, 255
Arad, 1317
Aramaic Apocalypse (Puech), 1133
arbiter, Messiah as, 793
Archelaus, 112
Archer, Gleason, 851
Arian heretics, 741
Ariel, 839
Aristobulus I, 1256
ark of the covenant, 141–142, 386, 705, 1059
"the arm of the Lord," 969, 1297
Armageddon, 812, 1103, 1199
Arnobius, 544
Artaxerxes I, 1145
Asa, King, 317
Asaph, 272, 465, 466, 592, 608, 649
Asaphite psalms, 649
Asarelah, 466
ascension, of the Messiah, 1191
Asher, 840
Asherah, building of, 419
Ashley, Timothy, 64–65
Ashurbanipal, 818

Zechariah 6:9-15

The Royal Priesthood of Messiah

MICHAEL L. BROWN

Messianic Jewish and Christian scholars speak of two streams of messianic prophecy: the royal prophecies, which point to the worldwide reign of the son of David, and the suffering prophecies, which point to his vicarious suffering and death (see especially Isa 53). In contrast, traditional Judaism embraces the royal stream of prophecy as messianic while rejecting, for the most part, the messianic interpretation of the suffering passages[1] since these passages neither speak of a descendant of David nor describe the beatific Messianic Era prophesied elsewhere (see, e.g., Isa 2:1-4; 9:6-7 [5-6]; 11:1-16; Jer 23:1-6).

Zechariah 6:9-15, then, is highly significant, since it explicitly connects the high priest Joshua, son of Jehozadak, with "the Branch," which is an epithet of the Messiah son of David (see esp. Jer 23:5; 33:15; cf. also Isa 4:2; Zch 3:8, all with *ṣemaḥ*; cf. further Isa 11:1 with *neṣer*). Thus, the royal messianic prophecies connect here with the priestly (= suffering) messianic prophecies, since it is a high priest who is crowned and who sits on a throne, all while serving as a sign of "a man whose name is the Branch" (Zch 6:12). The Messiah, then, will be a priestly King, just as David was, doing the priestly work of making atonement for the sins of the world before doing the royal work of establishing the kingdom of God on earth.

As for David's own identity as a priestly king, note that: (1) as a king, he performed a number of priestly acts (see 1Sm 21:1-6; 2Sm 6:14; 24:26); (2) somewhat cryptically, his own sons are called "priests" in 2Sm 8:18 in some Bible versions (HCSB "chief officials")[2]; (3) according to the most natural reading of the superscription of

Ps 110, David was the author of this psalm and prophesied that his future, exalted descendant (the Messiah; see Mt 22:42-45) would be a priest forever in the order of Melchizedek, the priestly king of Salem (see Ps 110:4; Gn 14:17-24).

Alternatively, the superscription *lᵉdāwid,* could mean "for David" as opposed to "by David" (or, "of David"), thereby a psalm written for the king by a court poet who declared that his master, David, would be a priest forever in the order of Melchizedek.[3] Yet on either reading, the Messiah would function as a priestly king, like Melchizedek, since, if David was the author of the psalm, he directly prophesied the Messiah's priestly role, and if David was the subject of the psalm, it was prophesied that he would be a lasting priest in the order of Melchizedek, and it is David who serves as the prototype of the Messiah. As king, the Messiah would rule and reign and defeat the enemies of God; as priest, he would make atonement for sin, identifying with God's people in their suffering.

BACKGROUND TO ZECHARIAH 6:9-15

The prophecies of Zch 6 were delivered against the backdrop of the rebuilding of the temple in Jerusalem after the Jewish exiles returned from Babylonian exile. The prophets Haggai and Zechariah helped spur this rebuilding project (Ezr 5:1; 6:14; Hag 1:1-14), which was carried out under the civil leadership of Zerubbabel, a descendant of David appointed as governor of Judah by Cyrus, king of Persia, and Joshua, a descendant of Aaron, serving as the high priest (he is referred to as Jeshua/Yeshua in Ezra and Nehemiah, beginning in Ezr 2:2 and ending in Neh 12:26). Elsewhere in Zechariah, Joshua is mentioned in 3:1,3,6,8,9, where he is associated with "the Branch" (3:8), Zerubbabel is mentioned in Zch 4:6,7,9-10, and it seems likely that it is Zerubbabel and Joshua who are "the two anointed ones . . . who stand by the Lord of the whole earth" (4:14). This is symbolized by two olive trees and two branches of these olive trees "beside the two golden conduits from which the golden oil is poured out" (4:11-12; note that the Hebrew word for "branches" in these verses is not the same as the word for the Branch of chaps. 3 and 6).

As for Zch 6:1-8, the vision of the four chariots, which represent "the four winds of heaven, after presenting themselves before the Lord of all the earth" (6:5), the specific connection to vv. 9-15 is unclear. However, Boda argues that "the prophetic sign-act report in 6:9-15 flows out of the final vision report [in 6:1-8], presenting the role of those who would escape from Babylon in the aftermath of its punishment foreseen in 2:10-13 (6-9)."[4] According to Unger, "Immediately following the overthrow of Gentile world power by the earth judgments symbolized by the horsed chariots (Zech. 6:1-8) occurs the manifestation of Christ in His kingdom glory

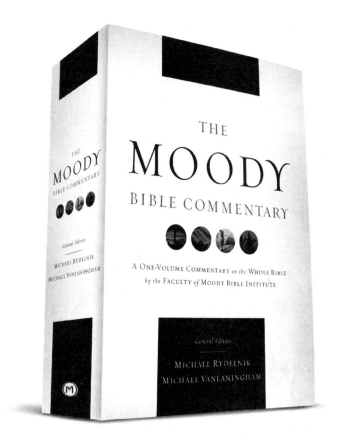